CALL AND RESPONSE

As part of Houghton Mifflin's ongoing commitment to the environment, this text has been printed on recycled paper.

CALL AND RESPONSE

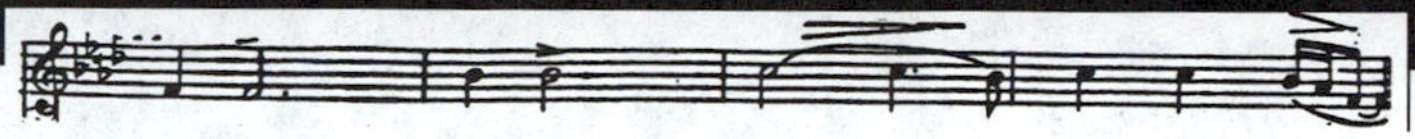

The Riverside Anthology of the African American Literary Tradition

GENERAL EDITOR

Patricia Liggins Hill
Professor of English
University of San Francisco

EDITORS

Bernard W. Bell
Professor of English
The Pennsylvania State University

Trudier Harris
J. Carlyle Sitterson Professor of English
The University of North Carolina at Chapel Hill

William J. Harris
Associate Professor of English
The Pennsylvania State University

R. Baxter Miller
Professor of English and Director of the Institute for African American Studies
University of Georgia

Sondra A. O'Neale
Dean of the College of Liberal Arts and Professor of English
Wayne State University

with Horace Porter
Associate Professor of English and Chair of African American Studies
Stanford University

HOUGHTON MIFFLIN COMPANY   BOSTON   NEW YORK

Sponsoring Editor: Jayne M. Fargnoli
Editorial Assistant: Terri Teleen
Senior Project Editor: Janet Edmonds
Associate Production/Design Coordinator: Jennifer Meyer
Senior Manufacturing Coordinator: Marie Barnes
Senior Marketing Manager: Nancy Lyman

Cover design: Diana Coe
Cover image: Aaron Douglas, *Aspects of Negro Life: From Slavery through Reconstruction.* Oil on canvas. 1934. Art and Artifacts Division, The Schomburg Center for Research in Black Culture, The New York Public Library. Astor, Lenox, and Tilden Fund.

Credits and acknowledgments for copyrighted material: See pages 2001–2013, which are to be considered an extension of the copyright page.

Printed in the U.S.A.

Library of Congress Catalog Card Number: 96-76925

Paperback ISBN: 0-395-80962-2
Hardback ISBN: 0-395-80961-4

456789-HWK-01 00 99 98

In memory of my mother,
Haroldine Lillian Cummings Liggins

Contents

CONTENTS OF AUDIO COMPACT DISC

Credits:
Use of Tracks 1–25 under license from Smithsonian/Folkways Records; Track 26 used by permission of India Navigation Records
Produced and Annotated by Robert H. Cataliotti
Mastered by Airshow Inc., Springfield, Virginia. David Glasser, Engineer; Charles Pilzer, No Noise (TM) Processing
The Producer would like to thank: Ann Cobb, Coppin State College; Djimo Kouyate, Manding Griot; Smithsonian/Folkways Records: Anthony Seeger, Director/Curator, Amy Horowitz, Assistant Director, Kevin Doran, Director of Licensing, Jeff Place, Archivist, Stephanie Smith, Assistant Archivist, Michael Maloney, Manufacturing Coordinator; Bob Cummins, India Navigation Records.
For further information:
Smithsonian/Folkways Records: 800 410-9815 or http://www.si.edu/folkways/
India Navigation Records: 177 Franklin Street, NY, NY 10013

Preface

In response to the call of many teachers, critics, and writers of African American literature, we, the editors of *Call and Response: The Riverside Anthology of the African American Literary Tradition*, are proud to present this groundbreaking textbook that joins students in centuries of conversations. It is the first comprehensive anthology of literature by African Americans presented according to the Black Aesthetic, a criteria for black art developed by Americans of African descent. As proponents of the aesthetic, we believe that African American literature is a distinct tradition, one originating in the African and African American cultural heritages and in the experience of enslavement in the United States and kept alive beyond slavery through song, sermon, and other spoken and written forms.

The uniqueness of *Call and Response* is that our aesthetic approach enables us to give equal place to the oral and written dimensions of African American literature. By broadly defining the literature, we represent in the anthology the centuries-long emergence of this aesthetic in poetry, fiction, drama, essays, speeches, letters, autobiographies, sermons, criticism, journals, and folk literature from secular songs to rap. Unlike other literature anthologies, *Call and Response* unfolds the historical development of the oral tradition simultaneously with the written literature.

In order to enhance its usefulness, clarity, and coherence, we have drawn from three motifs unique to the African American experience to give shape to the anthology. The first is the distinct African and African American antiphonal pattern of call and response. This black folk sermonic and literary technique is one of black America's major cultural art forms that fosters and reinforces a dynamic, artistic, and cultural relationship between the individual and the group. Accordingly, we use call and response in a variety of ways. Not only do we present the pattern as it is most often recognized, that is, in black sermon, song, and speech, but we also use it structurally and thematically. Structurally, we incorporate it in each section of the volume to shown the written literature answering the call of the folk culture. Thematically, we use it to feature African Americans throughout American history raising important socio-political issues and the responses to those issues either by their contemporaries or heirs in succeeding generations.

The second is the theme of the journey of African American people toward freedom, justice, and social equality. We present the culture, history, and literature of African Americans in a double structure of the literary tradition, that of the narrative of slavery through black spirituals and the poetic blues response to that experience. When the blues receives and responds to the historical call of the spirituals, the black communal voice becomes easily discernible.

The third motif overlaying the call and response pattern and black musical idioms is that of turning points. In other words, we present the oral and written literature in continual crossroads of African American experience, those crucial points throughout African American history where a decision has had to be made by Americans of African descent. We highlight this crossroads that links the African American experience from an ever-shifting past to a never-ending struggle for a more promising future.

The Organization

Arranged chronologically, *Call and Response* is divided into six historical periods that trace the journey of African American people from the arrival of the first slave ship to the North American continent to the Exodus and, then, through slavery's aftermath. Carrying through on the book's title, the first three periods, which are titled with lines from the spiritual "Go Down, Moses," trumpet the call for deliverance from slavery and oppression. They are "Go Down, Moses, Way Down in Egypt's Land" (1619–1808), "Tell Ole Pharaoh, Let My People Go" (1808–1865), and "No More Shall They in Bondage Toil" (1865–1915). As indicated in the subtitles of these chapters, these periods are constructed as a four-part slave narrative: the description of the conditions of slavery and/or oppression; the explanations of the desire for freedom; the escape to freedom; and the considerations of whether the new freedom is the ideal freedom. Shifting from the spirituals to the blues are the latter three periods: "Bound No'th Blues" (1915–1945), "Win the War Blues" (1945–1960), and "Cross Road Blues" (1960 to the present). The subtitles of these chapters take on the form of the blues idiom. Based on Langston Hughes's blues poem "Misery," they sound the responding but repetitive chords of the people's ongoing struggle for freedom and social equality, beginning with the Great Migration from the rural South to the urban North and, eventually, to the crossroads of complex social issues facing contemporary African Americans.

The Selections: An Aim of Inclusiveness

For each historical period, we have woven selections, extensive introductions, and author headnotes into a unified approach to African American literature and the culture that informs it. *Call and Response* features over 150 authors, both major and minor writers, and over 550 selections, both major and minor works. It highlights one full-length slave narrative, Frederick Douglass's *The Narrative of the Life of Frederick Douglass, An American Slave;* four full-length plays, Lorraine Hansberry's *A Raisin in the Sun*, Alice Childress's *Wedding Band*, Amiri Baraka's *Dutchman*, and August Wilson's *Joe Turner's Come and Gone;* one full-length novel, Toni Morrison's *The Bluest Eye;* and three novellas, Ann Petry's "Miss Muriel," Paule Marshall's "Barbados," and Ernest Gaines's "Three Men." Rather than reprinting lengthy novels by writers, we have chosen numerous, significant, and sometimes difficult-to-find short fictional works, selections that illuminate the relationship between these literary artists and the black culture within which they were writing. Along with several excerpts from novels that extend from William Wells Brown's *Clotelle* (1853) to Terry McMillan's *How Stella Got Her Groove Back* (1996), we have reprinted over thirty short stories, including Alice Dunbar-Nelson's "Sister Josepha," Rudolph Fisher's "Miss Cynthie," Richard Wright's "Long Black Song," Chester Himes's "Marihuana and a Pistol," James Baldwin's "Sonny's Blues," and Dorothy West's "The Richer, the Poorer." Our volume also contains several contemporary classics such as Alice Walker's "Everyday Use," James McPherson's "Solo Song: for Doc," and Albert Murray's "Train Whistle Guitar" as well as Kristin Hunter's previously unpublished tale, "Forget-Me Not," Toni Morrison's single skillfully crafted short story "Recitatif," and Randall Kenan's fascinating piece, "The Foundations of the Earth."

In addition to providing a substantial range of period and theme within the literary tradition, the anthology underscores the delicate balance of gender. In particular, *Call and Response* redresses the long neglect of African American women authors, many of whom have been critically misunderstood or summarily dismissed from existing anthologies. Over seventy women are represented and the most recent research in African American women's studies is discussed in the appropriate introductions and headnotes. Not only does *Call and Response* explore the themes of the double standard and women's rights in the works, ranging from such literary figures as Maria W. Stewart, Frances Watkins Harper, Sojourner Truth, and Anna Julia Cooper to Toni Morrison, Toni Cade Bambara, Alice Walker, Audre Lorde, and Ntozake Shange, but it also reveals the secondary positions to which black women writers had been relegated in both the Harlem Renaissance and Black Arts Movements. Of special interest are the selections and discussions on works that represent different brands of feminism embraced by black female intellectuals: black feminism, womanism, and Africana womanism. They include essays such as Barbara Smith's "Toward a Black Feminist Criticism," bell hooks's "Black Women: Shaping Feminist Theory," Alice Walker's "In Search of Our Mother's Gardens," and Clenora Hudson-Weems's "Africana Womanism: An Historical, Global Perspective for Women of African Descent." Appealing to both the beginning and the advanced student, the volume can be used in a variety of courses, whether focused on gender, genre, historical period, or theme.

The Introductions and Headnotes: Extended Scholarship

To place the generous selections within a historical and sociopolitical context, we have written thorough introductions to each section, information that appears with a refined clarity so appropriate for newcomers to the scope and breadth of African American literature. In each introduction we inquire into contested ideas and theories that will challenge even professionals in the field. The author headnotes contain a critical analysis and selected bibliography of each author's works. We trace each author's career and address the question of that writer's place in African American and American history.

We begin the volume with a chapter on the transplantation of African culture to North America and its transformation to African American orature. We give a broad survey of African cultural survivals in Colonial slave folk culture and an overview of the re-Africanization of Christianity. We provide extensive research on the unmistakably African origins of African American music and folklore such as African praise songs and oral epic narratives.

The forms of these and other black folk idioms in the anthology are explained in headnotes that were prepared by editor Patricia Liggins Hill. She, along with editors Bernard Bell and Trudier Harris, also wrote the folk culture sections in the introductions. For the research on the oral tradition, we, the editors, are greatly indebted to Hildred Roach's *Black American Music: Past and Present* (1992), Eileen Southern's *The Music of Black Americans* (1971; 1983, second edition) and the other authoritative sources that follow: Mary F. Berry and John Blassingame's *Long Black Memory: The Black Experience in America* (1982); J. Mason Brewer's *American Negro Folklore* (1968); Dena Epstein's *Sinful Tunes and Spirituals: Black Folk Music to the Civil War* (1977); LeRoi Jones's (Amiri Baraka's) *Blues People* (1963); John Lovell, Jr.'s *Black Song: The Forge and the Flame* (1972); J. H. Kwabena Nketia's *The Music of Africa* (1974); John W. Roberts's *From Trickster to Badman* (1989); Tricia Rose's *Black Noise: Rap Music and Black Culture in Contemporary America* (1994); and Ben Sidran's *Black Talk* (1971).

While *Call and Response* traces the oral literature from Africa to present-day black America, it simultaneously shows the written literature that corresponds and responds to the crossroads reflected in the oral heritage. In the introduction to Part I, editor Sondra O'Neale unveils the historical crossroad of eighteenth-century black tradition, the constant tension between overt and subtle protest against the slave condition. As evidenced in the worksongs, spirituals, and folktales of the day and in the works of such writers as Jupiter Hammon and Phillis Wheatley, the only safe form of resistance in both the written and oral literature has always been a veiled form. As O'Neale points out, the successful attempts at overt protest came after the founding of the Black Church in the northern colonies, when African American authors such as Richard Allen, Absalom Jones, and Prince Hall were free to write to and address black audiences. These forms of protest lead to the historical crossroads within the militant black abolitionist movement of the early nineteenth century covered by Part II editor Patricia Liggins Hill, namely, whether leaders of the movement should strive for the black community's emigration from the United States or integration into the mainstream of American society. Liggins Hill also delves into the origins of another crossroad that continues to the present day, the crossroad of black rights versus women's rights as seen in the literary exchanges between Frederick Douglass, Frances Watkins Harper, and Sojourner Truth. As this historical crossroad runs its course throughout the late nineteenth century, Part III editor Trudier Harris presents the decade of the 1890s as both the era of Booker T. Washington and that of the black woman. In the historical introduction Harris features the controversy between the racial accomodationist Booker T. Washington and the black radical W.E.B. Du Bois as to the solution to the black dilemma of overcoming the legacies of slavery and racism.

The latter three periods also highlight the historical crossroad between black colonization and social integration, from Marcus Garvey's Back to Africa Movement of the 1920s to the integrationist philosophy of Martin Luther King, Jr., and the separatist ideology of Malcolm X of the 1960s. These chapters also focus on the literary crossroad, namely, whether black art should be art for art's sake or art for people's sake. Part IV editors R. Baxter Miller and Patricia Liggins Hill feature the debate during the Harlem Renaissance between Alain Locke and W.E.B. Du Bois on the theory of black art. The debate as to the nature of black art continues on in Part

V as editors Bernard Bell, Patricia Liggins Hill, and Horace Porter discuss the debate in the 1950 issue of *Phylon* among several black critics, including Hugh M. Gloster and Nick Aaron Ford. With the collaborative efforts of Liggins Hill and O'Neale, Part VI editor William J. Harris presents, in the final and largest section of the anthology, the critical debate of the contemporary period between black aesthetician Joyce Ann Joyce and black post-structuralists Henry Louis Gates, Jr., and Houston Baker, Jr., on the Black Aesthetic versus Black Post-structuralism.

Ancillaries

A comprehensive instructor's manual and an audio compact disc containing recorded versions of some of the spoken and musical selections accompany the anthology. Prepared with the assistance and expertise of our colleague Johnanna Grimes of Tennessee State University, the *Instructor's Manual* weaves successful practices for generating innovative classroom discussion and ideas for linking authors and selections. Paralleling the content of *Call and Response*, the manual also includes recommendations for effectively introducing the compact disc into both lecture formats and class discussions. The audio disc, produced by our Coppin State College colleague Robert H. Cataliotti, consists of selections that reflect the development of the oral tradition. Beginning with an African griot's exciting version of the African oral epic *Sunjata* (also spelled *Sundiata* or *Sunyetta*), the disc moves forward through decade and century featuring recordings not only of black folklore, music, and speeches, but also of poets Langston Hughes, Sterling Brown, Margaret Walker, Gwendolyn Brooks, Amiri Baraka, Sonia Sanchez, and Nikki Giovanni reading their verse.

Acknowledgments

For the licensing of the audio disc, we owe much to Smithsonian/Folkways Records for their interest, financial support, and collaborative efforts. We also owe much to the University of San Francisco, University of Georgia, The Pennsylvania State University, Stanford University, The University of North Carolina at Chapel Hill, University of Wisconsin-LaCrosse, and Wayne State University for their institutional support. We thank the Modern Language Association, South Atlantic Modern Language Association, National Council for Teachers of English, the James Irvine Foundation Grant committee at the University of San Francisco, and especially the College Language Association for making available forums to refine the premises of the manuscript. We appreciate the efforts of our chief advisor Ernest Mason and our other colleagues Clenora Hudson-Weems, William H. Robinson, and Dorothy Tsuruta, who exceeded normal expectations for even enlightened consultants. We wish to thank our colleagues who reviewed drafts of this book, including: Sandra Adell, Lena Ampadu, Craig Bartholomaus, Joe Benson, Ralph Berets, Linda Blanton, Sandra Bowen, Butler Brewton, Joseph Brown, Marlene Brown, Loretta S. Burns, Rudolph Byrd, Nancy Chinn, Deborah Clark, Edwin Coleman II, L. M. Collins, Gloria Cronin, Daryl Dance, Carolyn Denard, Robert Frank, Joanne Gabbin, Gloria Gayles, Glenda Gill, Nikki Giovanni, Judith Hatchett, Helen Houston, Maude Jennings, Garnett Lloyd Mack, Doris Morton, Sandra Motz, Celeste Nichols, Erskine Peters, Donald Petesch, Ilene Rubinstein, Marilyn Saunders, Pancho Savery, Elisabeth Schultz, Robert Secor, Bede Ssellsalo, Gary Lee Stonum, Daniel Walden, Marilyn Waniek, Sarah Washington, Robyn Wegman, Gay Wilentz, and Ethel Young. The diligent work of numerous student researchers also provided excellent assistance: Cheryl Abrams, Wassel Al-Mashagbeh, Sylvia Audiger, Teresa Bavibidila, Samantha Blackman, Sheldon Chock, Michael D. Hill, Solomon P. Hill, Melanie Levinson, Mursalata Muhammad, Nancy O'Neale, Tanya Page, Afreka Reeves, Darren Rhym, Ilona Rosson, Elizabeth Sacha, Susan Searls, Nicole Vasser, Leatrice Sirls-Webb, Nikki Webb, and Kristine A. Yohe.

We give special thanks to publisher C. Steven Pensinger for seven years of guidance, support, and vision. Our gratitude also goes to Herb Nolan and Books By Design (and earlier, Sheila Gilliams) for their seemingly tireless hours of design and editorial effort.

Finally, we wish to give thanks to the entire staff at Houghton Mifflin: Chairman, President, and CEO Nader Darehshori; Executive Vice President and Director of the College Division June Smith; Publisher Alison Zetterquist; Sponsoring Editors Jayne Fargnoli and George Kane; Senior Associate Editor Linda M. Bieze; Senior Marketing Manager Nancy Lyman; Senior Project Editor Janet Edmonds; Associate Production/Design Coordinator Jennifer Meyer; Senior Manufacturing Coordinator Marie Barnes; Cover Designer Diana Coe; Permissions Editor Lyn Holian; Contracts and Permissions Supervisor Jill Dougan; Assistant Editor Jennifer Roderick; Administrative Associate Paulie LeComte; Editorial Assistant Terri Teleen; and Marketing Assistant Jennifer Good. Their commitment to publish a refreshingly new anthology of African American literature has made a difference.

The Editors

Call and Response

"Listen, Lord, My Prayer"

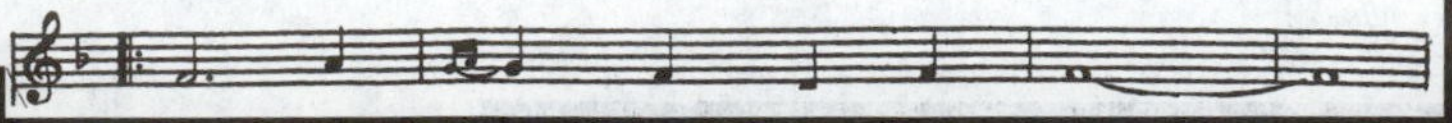

Call for Deliverance

By the end of the seventeenth century, thousands of black Africans, who had been transported on the Middle Passage, were enslaved throughout the Western Hemisphere, including what we now know as the United States.

***Portrait by Aaron Douglass from James Weldon Johnson's* God's Trombones**

I

"Go Down, Moses, Way Down in Egypt's Land"

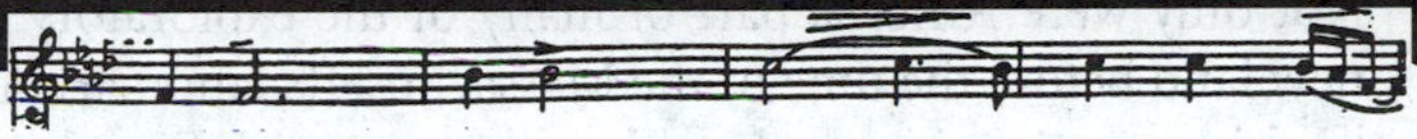

African American History and Culture, 1619–1808

The Description of the Conditions of Slavery and Oppression

Racial and Religious Oppression

When Israel was in Egypt's land,

Let my people go;

Oppress'd so hard they could not stand,

Let my people go.

(Chorus)

Go down, Moses, Way down in Egypt land,

Tell ole Pharoah, Let my people go.

Contemporary scholarship on the sixteenth to eighteenth centuries reveals that the full account of the origins of the United States has been ignored in popular history and, thus, erased from national consciousness. However, it is necessary for that obscured history to be uncovered in order to understand the beginning of the African American literary tradition and the repressive environments in which its birth took place. Crucial historical background is often deemphasized, devalued, or not mentioned in order to substantiate the popular myth that this nation began at Plymouth, Massachusetts, in 1620. Not only were Africans part of many of the exploratory expeditions of the new land before the time of the Massachusetts landmark, but, even as popular history sometimes acknowledges, twenty abducted Africans arrived in this country as indentured servants in Jamestown, Virginia, in 1619, which would, if anything, make their arrival the *first or second* colonial entity as they came to these shores with white settlers even before the New England pilgrims landed at Plymouth Rock.

The reality of black America as a *second* colonial entity has held true from 1619 to the present. African Americans constitute a separate nation within this nation, one that has survived as a social division receiving treatment different from that of European ethnic groups who voluntarily migrated to the New World. This separate nation endures as a collective identity with unique sociocultural idioms and as a value system different from that of their European captors. It also endures as a nation of singers, poets, dancers, and philosophers with innate abilities to speak, sing, and write in coded and otherwise variated language and to create its own written and oral literature from the basis of that value system. On the surface, the work songs and spirituals of the oral tradition, which started primarily in the South, and the poetry, prose, and sermons of the written tradition, which started primarily in the North, may seem weak, benign, or lacking in the rigor of antislavery protest when judged by today's standards. However, such assumptions have, heretofore, been made within the confines of scant general knowledge about the oppressive circumstances experienced by the African Americans of the period.

This significant history of the development of that literature, of those who produced the literature, and of the resulting cultural and literary traditions, embraces a rich body of oral and written genres, which have roots traceable back to Africa. Though transported from Africa to the New World in shackles and in chains, Americans of African descent retained memories of their African cultural heritage. To survive inhumane attempts to strip them of all basic dignities and fundamental human rights, they created an African-based culture in the New World, a multipurposed and unique culture that not only reaffirmed their humanness but also allowed them to construct pathways of ethereal and temporal escape. When in slavery, they sang work songs and spirituals to alleviate suffering and to mask codes of escape; they told imaginative folktales to retain African culture and to create lasting artistic forms in a ruinous world; and they wrote poetry and prose to prove their intellectual capability and to elicit antislavery support. With slavery ended, they were no longer defined as property but as inferior humans fit solely for menial labor. Thus, they often migrated to America's cities in search of work. In these urban industrial centers, which, although different, were often equally as harsh as the plantations, African Americans created the blues, jazz, and toasts to counteract new forms of discrimination, frustration, and tension they experienced. The seculars, spirituals, and folk narratives form the basis of the black poetics indigenous to the American continent and subversive to its social, political, and economic systems. Grounded primarily in its folk heritage, African American literature is, in the words of Richard Wright, "a long black song" of the black life experience in the United States from slavery to the present.

The African American literary tradition evolved from the Colonial period, specifically between 1619 and 1808, extending from the arrival of the first cargo of Africans to Jamestown, Virginia, to the prematurely declared end of the transatlantic slave trade. Given the change in their social status from indentured servants in 1619 to perpetual slaves beginning in the 1620s, it is to their credit that African Americans produced and published a body of literature by using the language and professed religious beliefs of their enslavers while often simultaneously protesting their enslavement. Some more fortunate Africans in northern slavery were taught to read and write, either at the insistence of British missionaries or so they could clerk for masters who owned shipping and merchandising interests. But for the vast majority of black people living in colonial America and later in the new republic, the exercise of any intellectual pursuits such as reading and writing was forbidden because a fundamental premise of their enslavement was that they did not have sufficient intelligence for such activities. For cultural expression, therefore, they drew essentially from their African oral heritage, in which music and poetry were inexorably linked. Using these roots as the basis for their unique folk forms and incorporating Euro-American folk elements as well as their own interpretations of biblical myth and typology, they created work songs, spirituals, and folktales.

From the early eighteenth century until the Civil War era, the fountainhead and mainstay of the antislavery movement among white colonists and Europeans was European Christianity and the structured church. Given the religious background of the age, it is not surprising that African American literature was born during the tidal wave of eighteenth-century revivalism now referred to as "the Great Awakening." To support their professed commitment to abolitionist causes, the various Christian denominations, most prominently the Quakers, provided the only opportunities that people of African descent had to publish written works or to garner support for attaining positions of leadership. Thus, a few northern black people were able to draw on the African tradition of the poet-historian, called the *griot,* along with the discipleship of preaching—which was the only acceptable form of public utterance allowed to slaves—to emerge as literate spokespersons for their people.

However, there was a price to pay. To be certified as safe, noninflammatory authorities, they were obliged to imitate European genres (neoclassical poetry and prose, sermons, and formal letters) and to incorporate biblical rhetoric and symbolism in stating their political objectives. But these restrictions also allowed them to covertly communicate (usually through masters or missionaries reading to slave audiences) with other slaves, who no doubt well understood embedded meanings, simultaneously allowing them to convict the consciences of white people. Thus, the Colonial period would produce black America's first antislavery essay and poem. Just as significantly, it would also give birth to the literary genre unique to African ex-slaves in both Colonial America and England: the slave narrative. The few narratives written by literate black people during the eighteenth century would popularize the form to such an extent that, by the following century, hundreds of slave narratives would be circulated by white people in the American and British abolitionist movements both as shocking evidence of the inhumanity of slavery and as proof that black people had the intelligence not only to read and write but to create. The theme of black self-determination, at the very core of the slave narrative, would not only become the genesis of the nineteenth-century black novel, but, subsequently, much of the focus of African American literature as a whole. In general, early Americans of African descent brought their often rough-hewn communal consciousness—a collective identity that institutional slavery intended to destroy along with any sense of the potential for individual and group achievement—to the verbal structure of the literature. In this way, they shaped the fundamental aesthetic on which the African American literary tradition is based.

On Being Brought from Africa to America: Sixteenth-, Seventeenth-, and Eighteenth-Century Slave Experience in the British Colonies

"What Ship Is This That's Landed on the Shore?"

When a Dutch ship carrying twenty Africans, including at least three women, landed on the coast of Jamestown, Virginia, in 1619, the indelible stain of slavery tarnished what has become the American landscape. Over the next few years, the position of Africans in the newly formed British colonies would be changed from temporary indentured servitude to perpetual slavery for life, a 250-year degradation systematically purposed to deny their humanity and to deprive them of basic human rights. Although the overwhelming majority of colonial Africans were reduced to this state of perpetual slavery, Africans in the North American British colonies made up only a portion of a larger black population that had been transported as slaves on the Middle Passage to destinations throughout the New World. Through the slave trade and also through subsequent procreation, by the end of the seventeenth century, Africans, numbering in the thousands, could be found throughout the entire Western Hemisphere, including what is now known as the United States, Canada, Mexico, Central America, the Caribbean, and South America.

Yet, crucial to this early history of the black presence in the Americas is the fact that not all Africans arrived in bondage or even in indentured service. Black people were among the first explorers to reach the New World in 1492. Pedro Alonzo Nin, identified as black, arrived with Columbus. Many others traveled with Balboa, Ponce de Leon, Cortez, and Menendez on their explorations, and others assisted Europeans as they appropriated lands for the Spanish crown. One black Spaniard, Estevanico, cleared a space for Spanish settlers in what is now New Mexico and Arizona. A black Frenchman, Jean-Baptiste Point du Sable, explored the Great Lakes region of North America and eventually set up a settlement trading post on the south shore of Lake Michigan, on the site of what is now the city of Chicago. Their feats merely hint at what thousands more of the nearly ten million Africans brought to the Americas could have achieved had it not been for the institution of chattel slavery.

Certainly, a form of slavery, usually resulting from the fortunes of war, existed in Africa before the continent was colonized by Europe, but it was not nearly as inhumane as "the peculiar institution" in the Americas. In Africa, among the Ibo people, the enslaved were incorporated into the tribe. Although the slaves knew the indignity of not being able to eat with free people, they performed no more daily labor than did freeborn members of the tribe. Even the slaves themselves could own slaves. Some Africans used slavery not only as a privilege of victory in battle but also as social punishment. Chiefs sold into slavery those members of the tribe found guilty of such crimes as adultery or kidnapping, which otherwise could be punishable by death. But, as the African European abolitionist Olaudah Equiano states in his classic slave narrative, *The Interesting Narrative of the Life of Olaudah Equiano, or Gustavus Vassa, the African, Written by Himself* (1789), slavery instituted by Europeans differed greatly from traditional African practice. After detailing the comparison, Equiano laments, "O, ye nominal Christians! might not an African ask you—learned you this from your God?"

In contrast, sixteenth- and seventeenth-century Europeans believed in bondage as the natural and proper condition for particular races of people. By virtue of the vast physical and cultural differences between Africans and themselves, these Europeans further assumed that the darker race was morally and mentally inferior—and, thus, best suited for slavery. They believed that black people had no souls or, if they did have souls, that they were preordained to eternal damnation. Thus, as early as the seventeenth century, one justification for slavery was to bring Africans to the New World to rescue them from this state of damnation stemming from African "heathenism" and to convert them to Christianity. Presuming that they were the sole arbiters and possessors of a higher moral authority, slave owners taught their slaves servility and submission—only a partial presentation of biblical principles, which they presented as the African's inevitable and soul-saving Christian duty. Thus, Europeans positioned themselves as indispensable saviors of a people who were supposedly unable to save themselves.

Moreover, slavery was concordant with the worldview of the Puritans—the most representative and the most dogmatic sect among the New World Calvinists. God was for them a God of force, one who overtook the human mind and will for salvation and sanctification regardless of the subject's choice. In fact, Calvinists ardently believed that all humanity was so totally depraved that no one had enough human or, in this case, divine, goodness to accept God unless God so ordered it. The concept of men and women as creatures with a fate already preordained by God without free will was, therefore, easily translatable to slavery. For those few chosen or "elect" Puritans and Anglicans of Calvinist persuasion who founded the American colonies, this prescribed fate, better known as *predestination,* was primary evidence only of their own selectivity. That selectivity became a religion within itself, one that overrode all other aspects of Christianity and effused itself into the society that America's colonizers created. Within this value system are the assumptions that God controls humans in order to control the universe and that, as faithful representatives in a Christian society, God's chosen people must likewise enforce rules of order to prevent chaos—a collapse that they feared that humankind, without that control, was uniquely capable of causing. For most Calvinists in Puritan society, the African—as black, as heathen, as savage, as ignorant, as animal—represented the ultimate extreme of the "necessary" evil within that volatile universe. These characteristics with which the New World colonists defined Africans cast Africans among the nonelect. They were also the very characteristics that made Africans ideal subjects for enslavement.

Three seventeenth-century Calvinists, two of whom are well-known historical figures, made statements about slavery that represent the full range of theological opinion governing social custom. As several eighteenth-century black authors would later state, the preeminent Puritan theologian Samuel Sewall wrote that slavery was an ungodly evil, akin to what the Bible refers to as "men-stealing"—to counter the arguments of proslavers that slaves were purchased, not stolen. To refute another proslavery argument, namely, that slavery gave Africans opportunities to hear the gospel, Sewall wrote in his most famous tract, *The Selling of Joseph* (1700), that "Evil must not be done, that good may come of it." He concluded in many of his tracts that the evil institution of slavery would eventually bring divine wrath on the nation. At the opposite end of the Calvinist spectrum, however, was the lesser-known John Saffin. In "A Brief and Candid Reply to a Late Printed Sheet, Entitled, *The Selling of Joseph*" (1701), Saffin took the political position dominating colonial thought that Calvinism and Christianity condoned slavery because the African was incapable of being anything but a brute. He wrote, moreover, that it was un-Christian for "true" churchmen to believe anything else about the slave institution. Saffin joined the slavery debate because of his vested interest as an owner of human chattel. Like Thomas Jefferson, he supported much of his argument from his ostensibly reasoned experience with and observations of his slaves. But Cotton Mather, who was probably the most influential theologian of the late seventeenth and early eighteenth centuries, approached slavery ambiguously. He believed that slavery was necessary to support a master-servant class system. Mather also said that the slave must be "saved," thus, rationalizing that God permitted African enslavement so that the captives could hear the gospel. He published several plans for evangelizing the slaves with the purpose of accomplishing the impossible task of freeing people in spiritual realms while keeping them enslaved in the world. In the first plan, a broadside titled *Rules for the Society of Negroes* (1693), he advocated the position of separate slave worship services to be held under the supervision of white people.

Cotton Mather had also published a book on the New England witchcraft trials called *The Wonders of the Invisible World* (1862 ed.), in which he expressed the widely held Calvinistic beliefs that Africans were really offspring of Satan who was himself a black man, and that black skin was the mark of certain Old Testament curses. Slavery, racism, and extreme social separation were fueled both by the hysteria about indigenous witchcraft and by deep suspicion about the purportedly mysterious powers of African "heathenism." In the book, Mather reported the claim of a "possessed" woman who said that she had seen Satan: "There exhibited himself unto her a Divel [sic] having the Figure of A Short and a Black man . . . of the same Stature, Feature, and complexion with what the Histories of the Witchcraft beyond-sea ascribe unto him." Another trial judge collaborated her testimony with a report from another witness who said that the devil was a black man. Although the woman reportedly said that the specter looked more like a Native American than an African, the damage was done to the darker race and Mather's text supported Saffin's allegation that black people were merely "imps."

The concept of Satan as a black man was compatible with nearly every scheme of causality within religious and scientific spheres in the eighteenth century. Whether the image was the Calvinists' classification of the black man as the ultimate symbol of depravity or the evolutionary Linnean-Jeffersonian theory of the African as the link between humans and nature, Africans were held to be furthest away from God, from *light*, from perceptions of absolute truth and educable genius, and closest to bestiality, ignorance, and evil. This concept of black people was also supported by the eighteenth-century Eurocentric view of the universe known as the Great Chain of Being Theory. Scientifically, the theory explored the plurality and interrelatedness of all existence based on the idea of the established order of the universe as a pyramid-shaped chain. From top to bottom, that order consisted of God, the angels, humanity, beasts, fowl, and, finally, insects. Sociologically and politically, the theory fostered the beliefs that within such a divinely sanctioned social order, the Anglo-aristocracy was second only to a ruling king and that various other white people were placed in restrictive class levels that could not be ascended. Lower-class white men and women were usually the indentured servants, most women and all nonadults were placed at the theoretical bottom of this social order, and all Africans were placed beneath the children. According to Winthrop Jordan in *White Over Black: American Attitudes Towards the Negro, 1550–1812* (1968), the Great Chain of Being Theory led to the assumption that black people were the link between animals and humans. When tied to Calvinism, the theory helped to convince even the newly emergent white middle class that Africans were God's least-chosen people. Historian Arthur Lovejoy in *The Great Chain of Being: A Study in the History of an Idea* (1936) states that these concepts "attained their widest diffusion and acceptance" in the eighteenth century. Only a few white colonists spoke out against the convoluted logic. Notable exceptions were Robert Calef, who said that it was Mather himself who was under the influence of Satan; John Woolman, who almost single-handedly began the strong abolitionist movement among the Quakers; and Benjamin Lay, an eccentric, often cave-dwelling Quaker, who said that all slave holders were "Hellish Miscreants." Nonetheless, a deep and pervasive hatred and distrust of African slaves effused throughout eighteenth-century colonial society. This thinking pervaded the colonial mind. Such was the philosophical underpinning of chattel slavery; and such was the cultural atmosphere of religion, superstition, and fear during this so-called Age of Reason in which African American literature was born.

Equiano and other black writers and spokespersons had evidently experienced a very different Christianity and certainly held to very different biblical interpretations than were held by most Euro-Americans. But to get their works published in a society in which the economic and social order rested on their assumed God-ordained inferiority, black writers appeared to have internalized the worldview of their oppressors. However, two of the earliest American poets of African descent, Jupiter Hammon and Phillis Wheatley, like Equiano and other black writers of the period, turned to biblical theology to address in one way or another the theories of the divine preselection of white Christians only, and to point out the unchristian immorality of slavery. Wheatley, in her poem "On Being Brought from Africa to America" (1773), reminded them that, according to obvious and direct biblical interpretation, the most "heathen" African was equal to any "chosen" European if he or she were united in true Christian fellowship. Likewise, in his poem "An Evening Thought: Salvation by Christ, with Penetential [sic] Cries" (1760), Hammon argued that Christ alone was the true Savior of all humankind and that authentic conversion was available to everyone on an equal basis with no preordained conditions based on race or any other factors.

Another conclusion the New World colonists wrung from their Calvinistic religious doctrine was that God had provided Africans to facilitate European economic exploitation of the New World. Beginning in the seventeenth century and continuing well into the nineteenth century, American slave holders, thus, passed strict laws, called "slave codes," designed to augment their rights as owners of human property, otherwise known as "chattel," and to more severely restrict any rights and freedoms remaining to the African slaves. Not surprisingly, with increasingly repressive legislation came greater numbers of slave escapes and revolts. While some fugitive slaves sought refuge among various Native American tribes, others formed independent communities and often harassed local white residents. In retaliation, many slave owners passed more stringent codes to ensure that their slaves would continue to be treated as property, not the least being the laws banning miscegenation (interracial marriage) and meetings for church services. Interracial relations were considered fornication and punishable by death. Slaves congregating in groups of more than two or three at a time was both a feared and illegal activity. Unreasonable laws were unevenly applied to violations ranging from the slightest infractions—such as curfew violations and petty thefts—to the more serious and potentially economically damaging actions to slave holders—such as escapes, revolts, fires, and violence against whites. The legal code provided for severe penalties for recalcitrant slaves, including beatings, torture, imprisonment, crippling, and death. The right of any Euro-American to inflict assault against any African American was upheld by the courts. For example, in 1735 in New York, Dutch Burgher John Van Zandt whipped his slave to death for having been found outside of his quarters. A coroner's jury tried Van Zandt but ruled that the slave was killed "by visitations from God." However, it was unlawful and ineffective for any black person to testify against any white person.

With the expanding agricultural economy in the southern colonies came a greater demand for slaves. By the middle of the eighteenth century, the black population had increased to about 250,000, the total number equally divided between African-born slaves and those born in the colonies. Virginia held the largest concentration of slaves, estimated at 100,000; New Hampshire had the smallest, at approximately 500. More Africans were either taken to or bred in southern colonies, such as Virginia, because of the area's greater potential agricultural profits from larger land masses and warmer climates. Strong hands and backs and compliant minds were necessary to maximize profits. Not only did the much colder North have less need for massive numbers of slaves, its economy based on shipping, mercantile, and banking generated more pressure for literacy among slaves. These demographic differences help to explain why the black oral tradition emanated primarily from the large numbers of slaves on southern plantations where literacy among slaves was suppressed. However, both the oral and the written traditions share many cultural themes, covert functions, and political purposes.

The oral tradition had been able to sustain itself in the midst of a predominantly Eurocentric culture in the United States since the seventeenth century. This tradition constituted the primary mode of artistic expression for African Americans during the Colonial era just as it had for black people for centuries. The centrality of oral expression in African society encouraged the continued vitality of such forms among African American slaves. As William Robinson points out in *Reconstructing American Literature* (1983), "The fact that whites were generally deaf to the subtle complexity of black oral expression permitted African American culture to maintain a resilience, integrity, and subversive thrust that played an important role in the spiritual survival of the slaves." Since its beginnings, the black oral tradition has been constantly evolving and functioning as a mode of black resistance to total cultural assimilation or even annihilation.

Call for Deliverance: Origins of the Oral Tradition

"Didn't My Lord Deliver Daniel"

Whether they lived and worked on a southern plantation with numerous other African slaves or in one of the New England colonies as the one slave to the family of a farmer or sea merchant, colonial blacks—most of whom were old enough to have vivid memories of their African homelands—resisted complete assimilation into Eurocentric culture by retaining the African worldview embedded in their religious beliefs, folklore, and music. As Olaudah Equiano explains in *The Interesting Narrative,* in Africa the spoken word, music, and dance were at the center of a communal and profoundly religious way of life. Most Africans believed that spirits lived in all things—in plants, in trees, in animals, and even in stones, as well as in people. All things on earth were connected by a life force that tied people to people and people to things. Most Africans also practiced ancestral worship. They believed that a person's soul survived after death and that they could reach the souls of their long-dead ancestors. People prayed to ancestors for protection against evil spirits and for help in solving problems of everyday life. They uttered the names of their ancestors frequently to make sure that they would always be connected to them. However, according to John S. Mbiti in *African Religions and Philosophy* (1990), there was also a belief in a superior God with omnipotent powers. To African people, religion was not something apart from other aspects of life; it was life itself. Hence, the African slaves brought to the New World stronger communal and religious bonds than most of their New World masters, who believed that religion was something apart from the secular world—except when the tenets of their religion could be manipulated to enhance their wealth in that secular world.

Most of these cultural retentions were strongest in the southern colonies of Virginia, North and South Carolina, and Georgia, where thousands of Africans labored on cotton, rice, and tobacco plantations and lived among themselves in segregated quarters that somewhat afforded temporary respite from the master class. There, and in otherwise secret and forbidden gatherings, they could exchange stories about African life, create new lore about their American experience, and express these reflections in dance and song. Usually, they sang two types of songs—religious and secular—although one kind of music was not necessarily exclusive of the other.

Yet, the precise origins of slave folk music are relatively unknown because folklorists did not begin to *formally document* the songs until the Civil War. Before that time, white southerners had ignored African American folk culture because they believed that it would be against their interests to give slaves credit for any kind of achievement. As a result, since nearly a century ago, literary critics, folklorists, musicologists, and theologians have had to rely heavily on explanations found in the oral traditions of Africa and black America, on historical accounts written primarily by European traders and travelers to Africa and the South, and on slave narratives in order to trace the roots of the folk culture.

Specifically, scholars have debated the methods used to ensure the survival of African culture in the New World as related in folk sayings and compositions, trying to determine which elements of the proverbs, folk cries, hollers, shouts, work songs, spirituals, and folktales derived from indigenous African cultures. The issue of which elements were borrowed from biblical and Christian symbolism, which come from European and Euro-American folk elements, and which resulted from the African Americans' own creativity remains at the heart of the debate.

Proverbs

The slaves' proverbs have both African and Euro-American origins. For example, J. Mason Brewer, in his comparative study on African and African American proverbs, *American Negro Folklore* (1968) and *Southern Workman, 1872–1900,* has shown that black people brought at least 122 proverbs directly from Africa. According to Mary F. Berry and John Blassingame in *Long Black Memory: The Black Experience in America* (1982), many of the proverbs are parallel in content and form to African proverbs, but they often reflect the New World environment. This is evident in the moral and philosophical precepts contained in slave proverbs and in their African parallels. For example, the slaves said, "The pitcher goes to the well every day; one day it will leave its handle." There is little difference between this pronouncement on the inevitable punishment of evil deeds and the Hausa proverb "If there is a continual going to the well, one day there will be a smashing of the pitcher." Approximately half of the slaves' proverbs reflected a surreptitious African critique of the plantation experience. For instance, they created proverbs that served as a form of instruction on appropriate labor to render in a slave state ("Don't fling all your power into a small job"), as a warning that masters reacted with a cruel whip when slaves used straightforward verbal resistance to protest their enslavement ("Don't say more with your mouth than your back can stand"), and as a clever way of covertly stating that slavery was primarily created because animalistic masters were too lazy to do the work themselves ("It is a poor dog [whites] that won't wag its own tail"). Black artists used their masters' own language (its imagery, rhetoric, and idiom) to house their denouncements of the masters' character and practice. The genius of African American folk tradition and prose combines African tradition with this veiled rhetoric of indictment.

Folk Cries, Hollers, and Shouts

The black folk cries, hollers, and shouts are so deeply embedded in African American folk song and culture that folklorists have insisted for over a century that they are purely African in origin and tradition. Because folklorists have been unable to identify other forerunners of these folk forms, they have accepted their African provenance. To date, no documentation exists to support these conclusions. However, folklorist Harold Courlander, in *Negro Folk Music USA* (1963), briefly describes a folk cry he heard one night while traveling through the Nigerian countryside. From the bush, one Nigerian let out an eerie cry and another Nigerian, who seemed to be quite a distance away in another part of the bush, responded in like manner. Courlander maintains that the cry he heard strikingly resembled those of slaves heard by white people traveling through the South in the nineteenth century and who reported them in their narrative accounts. The slaves' cries (sometimes called "field hollers" or "whoops") functioned as calls for help, food, or water, and as cries of loneliness, sorrow, or happiness. These cries were the means by which slaves could communicate with one another and send warnings to other slaves of an approaching master or overseer.

The slaves performed the "ring shout" as a way of communicating with God. This type of holy dance, which combined the singing of sacred songs with rhythmic shuffle dancing, took place at prayer meetings and at other types of religious services. The slaves formed a circle to sing these songs, which consisted primarily of a single stanza or "walk" and a single chorus usually with a faster and more marked rhythm. When white people first witnessed "the shout," which eventually built up to a state of ecstasy and frenzy, they described it as primitive, savage, and barbaric. Ignorant of African tradition, they did not understand that the shouters reached the pinnacle of divine essence when the Holy Spirit entered their bodies and took possession of their souls. As African American musicologist Eileen Southern explains in *The Music of Black Americans* (1971; 1983, second ed.), "Nowhere in the history of the black experience in the United States was the clash of cultures—the African versus the European—more obvious than in the differing attitudes taken toward ritual dancing and spiritual possession."

Work Songs and Other Secular Songs

In the debate on borrowings, the least controversial of the African American folk forms are the African origins of the secular songs, notably the work songs, which is one of the largest groupings of secular music among the slaves. Intended to provide some relief from the incessant doldrums of slave labor—including rowing, stevedoring, cornhusking, rice-threshing, cotton-picking, grinding, weaving, and spinning—these rhythmic accompaniments are the earliest documented segment of African American music. These work songs have received the most critical attention over the years because they incorporate many of the usual elements of secular music: satire, social criticism, praise, ridicule, gossip, and protest. Although most of the work songs were not collected until the twentieth century, most scholars readily accept their African provenance because, as with the black folk cries, hollers, and shouts, musicologists have so far been unable to find any traces of the African American work song idiom in the Eurocentric music tradition.

The earliest documentation of work songs are African and African American boat songs from the eighteenth century. In his colorful travelogue titled *A Philadelphia Surgeon [William Chancellor] on a Slaving Voyage to Africa, 1749–1751* (1968 ed.), David D. Wax gives his account of the West African boat song. Chancellor wrote in a diary entry, "Early this morning the King of the Fantees [a Ghanaian tribe] sent his canoe with 12 Negroes for me and from the Ship to the Shore I was attended with the singing of them." Several historians have made a direct connection between these boat songs and similar boat songs, particularly in seaport towns along the Atlantic coast with which African American slaves assuaged the misery of their labor. In *The History of South Carolina, from Its First Settlement in 1670 to the Year 1808* (1809), David Ramsey describes slaves and their boat songs during the 1760s: "In their voyages to the city they were wont to beguile the time and toil of rowing with songs and extravagant vociferation's [sic]." Likewise, in

Men and Times of the Revolution; or Memoirs of Elkannah Watson, Including His Journals of Travels in Europe and America, from the Year 1777 to 1842 (1856), Elkannah Watson details an extraordinary ride on a South Carolina ferry immediately after the Revolutionary War; the slaves "amused us, the whole way by singing their plaintive African songs in cadence with the oars."

Comparative studies of the structural patterns of African and African American work songs show that the latter have retained their traditional African form while adapting to the New World environment. Like their African American offspring, African work songs are multifaceted. They include boating, hunting, fishing, instructional, religious, weaving, and spinning songs, and songs of social commentary, including gossip and satire. Based on group participation, antiphonal singing (call and response), the rhythmic use of work tools, and synchronized body movements, African work songs informed and shaped the work songs of African American slaves. In both form and function, the work songs of black-Americans, like their spirituals, bespeak a folk poetry that simultaneously gives rise to individual expression and group empathy.

Spirituals

The most heated dispute surrounding the origins of African creativity has centered on the origins of the African American spirituals, the socioreligious folk songs created and sung by southern slaves. These original and beautiful expressions of human life are among the most impressive achievements of African American and American literature and culture. An amalgam of African and biblical tradition, spirituals are folk poetry, the cultural and historical record of African American people in their struggle for survival, freedom, and equality. Originally shaped for group singing, the songs reflect the slaves' daily life experiences—their sorrows, troubles, weariness, dreams, and hopes of release from bondage—and their strong, but coded, antislavery messages. They are what W.E.B. Du Bois calls "sorrow songs," such as the deeply moving pieces "I Been 'buked and I Been Scorned," "Nobody Knows de Trouble I've Had," "Motherless Child," and "Lay Dis Body Down." Yet, as can be seen in the words of the first two songs, feelings of despair are often counteracted by a deepened sense of hope or affirmation. These sorrow songs are powerful calls for deliverance from collective oppression and exile and for redemption from individual hardship.

Because most of the slaves were unlettered, they drew images for songs primarily from biblical epic narratives they had heard from itinerant preachers and missionaries. The narratives on which most of the spirituals are based are from Old Testament accounts depicting Israel and Judah's enslavement first under the pharaoh in Egypt and later in Assyria and Babylon. The vivid imagery and dramatic stories of biblical heroes and feats of faith made it easy for the African slaves to visualize and to believe in the impact of God's power. These narratives fired the imaginations of the slave-song creators to such an extent that they came to firmly believe that as God delivered the Israelites from bondage in Egypt, Assyria, and Babylon, so would He deliver them from slavery in the New World. Just as God saved "Daniel from de lion's den/Jonah from de belly of de whale/an' de Hebrew chillun from de fiery furnace," so would He save them. Their favorite scriptural heroes were the Old Testament warriors—"Brudder Moses" who "smote de Red Sea over," "Brudder Joshua" who "fit [fought] de battle of Jericho," "Brudder Samson" who "killed about a thousan' of de Philistine," and "Lil David" who "kill'd Golia [Goliath] an shouted for joy." But their favorite anti-hero was "Ole Satan" himself—as seen throughout the folklore and written literature, especially in the slave narratives (like that of Olaudah Equiano) as the archetypal slave master who's "a liar and conjurer too." These ancient exploits were performed by biblical heroes who were fighting the oppression of empires so their people could be set free. Thinking that their slaves were just engaging in their usual religious sorrow songs, slave masters allowed the hymns, usually unaware that the singing of a spiritual might well be used as a signal that a planned escape was pending. Because of sermons by white preachers and missionaries—and sometimes African American ministers, such as "Black" Harry Hoosier who accompanied Francis Asbury and other white Methodist ministers throughout the south, and other black people who accompanied Quakers in the same territories—the types of actions performed by central biblical figures, as well as the biblical accounts themselves, probably already would have been familiar to the slaves. As Prince Hall, the founder of African American Masonry, reiterated in all of his recorded charges, the African presence is depicted in thoroughly positive references throughout the Bible. He mentions, for example, the Africans—Jethro, Sheba, and Ebedmelech—who are shown as closely involved in the accomplishments and escapes of such heroes as Moses, Solomon, and Jeremiah. Recent scholarship by such Africanist scholars as Askia Toure, Anton Diop, and Asa Hilliard also discovered the close involvement and often dominating influence of Africans in the ancient biblical world.

In addition, as other recent studies have shown, African oral epics, which focus on the heroes' quests for supernatural powers, have not only been told for centuries, but had also been a vital art form throughout Africa at the time of the transatlantic slave trade. Consequently, scholars have begun to examine the African oral epic tradition as the most likely model for spiritual song creation. For instance, based on comparisons of numerous African epics and black spirituals, John W. Roberts has shown in his study *From Trickster to Badman* (1989) that spiritual song creation more closely resembles the African heroic tradition in content, form, and performance style than it does the Eurocentric religious song tradition. As he explains, "Heroic epic performances involve more than the recitation in song form of narratives chronicling in literal or linear terms the exploits of figures recognized as heroes. They are complex events that include music, dance, drama, and song and involve performers and audiences in a dynamic interaction to celebrate the deeds of heroes." The slaves transformed the biblical saga into African heroic tradition, Roberts concludes, to protect their identity and values as African people from both tangible and covert threats.

Confronted with new European interpretations of old religious patterns, the New World slaves apparently found much material in the narrated accounts of ancient history to adapt to traditional African epic treatment and dramatic statement. Collectively, the songs form a mosaic of their sacred cosmos, a mythological world in which the cultural heroes are a true mixture of both worlds. The African epic hero, for instance, is the representative man like Sunjata of the Mandingo tradition who, threatened from birth, sets out in search of mystical knowledge and power to defeat his foes and change the destiny of his people; the biblical hero is the courageous, often larger-than-life Old and New Testament hero who is empowered by a strong faith in God to overcome personal tribulations, upheavals, and evil. With their own situation in mind, the slaves recast heroes known in their Old World, such as Sunjata, Kambili, Mwindo, and Ozidi, into biblical figures known in the New World as Moses, Job, Joshua, Daniel, Samson, Jonah, David, Noah, Jesus, and Mary, who also faced moral dilemmas and adverse conditions similar to those faced by the slaves.

Moreover, the slaves' spirituals take on the structure of the African heroic epic, which is multiformed. The latter tradition includes long narrative recitations and songs interlaced with praise poems, prayers, hymns, and improvisations, which are sung episode by episode, then narrated and acted out. Similarly, the spirituals are lengthy epic narratives, praise poems, prayers, sermons, lyrical songs and poetry, and frequent improvisations.

Although leading African American musicologists and folklorists acknowledge biblical idioms in the spirituals, they also maintain that the songs are rooted in African musical structures, rhythmic patterns, and performance styles. Accordingly, in their comparative studies on African and African American folk traditions, they have proved that the spirituals embody numerous elements indigenous to African music, including the major characteristics of African poetry and song, rhythmic complexity and antiphony, and overlapping call and response (the overlapping of the leader or soloist's music phrase with the choral refrain).

Such strong African influences have led several scholars, including John Lovell, Jr., in *Black Song: The Forge and the Flame* (1986), to conclude that the origins of the spirituals are traceable not only to the eighteenth century but also possibly back to the Middle Passage. He believes that "the conditions which made the spirituals possible were already in place by the late seventeenth century at least." His theory is consistent with the findings of

Elizabeth Donnan, editor of *Documents Illustrative of the History of the Slave Trade to America* (1965), which indicate that African slaves sang melancholic lamentations about exile from their native land during the transatlantic passage. Similarly, Sir Hans Sloane, in *A Voyage to the Islands of Madera, Barbados, St. Christopher and Jamaica, with the Natural History of the Last of These Islands* (1707), establishes the Jamaican spiritual in the Colonial period and, thus, the existence of African spirituals in the New World in the early eighteenth century.

As part of the Great Awakening, which spread through the North American colonies during the eighteenth century, traveling ministers taught at least a fraction of slaves in both the North and South the hymnals that grew out of these revivals. The traveling ministers' reports give the earliest documented evidence of biblical influences on even the earliest African American spirituals. Samuel Davies, a Presbyterian missionary from Hanover, Virginia, used the colonial editions of Isaac Watts's *Psalms of David* (1717) and *Hymns and Spiritual Songs* (1707) as texts for religious instruction to Virginia's slaves in the 1740s and 1750s. In a letter dated June 28, 1751, to "Mr. Bellamy of Bethlem in New England," Davies observes "that the Negroes, above all the Human Species that I ever knew, have an ear for Musik, and a kind of exact Delight in Psalmody"; and, in a letter to "J.F." dated August 26, 1758, he describes black people "all breaking out in a torrent of sacred harmony, enough to bear away the whole congregation to heaven." In *Sinful Tunes and Spirituals: Black Folk Music to the Civil War* (1977), Dena Epstein also argues that the slaves had adapted Watts's music to their own unique rhythmic patterns of singing and performance.

Eighteen years after Davies's observation, William Bartram, an Anglo-Irishman traveling through Georgia, wrote of slaves in a chorus whom he heard singing "songs of their own composition." Then, in 1793, Bartram published more descriptions in his *Travels through North and South Carolina, Georgia, East and West Florida, and the Cherokee Country* (1793). Likewise, in a published interview with the abolitionist Lydia Maria Child, Charity Bowery, an ex-slave from Pembroke, North Carolina, recalled a number of religious and secular songs she had heard other slaves singing when she was a child around 1774. These historical accounts are supported by a 1942 article titled "Plantation Songs of Our Old Negro Slaves," by researcher Lydia Parish. Another scholar, John W. Work, in *American Negro Songs* (1940), also insists that the spirituals existed before the American Revolution.

Folktales

As with most of the work songs, African American folktales were not collected until the early twentieth century. In fact, a paradigmatic system for collecting them was not established until the late nineteenth century. The same debate over origin and background that accompanied study of the work songs was waged over various elements within the tales. Comparative studies of African, European, and Euro-American folktales revealed, however, that numerous folktales recited by American slaves had their origins in Africa. Folklorists such as Alcee Fortier, Elizabeth Pringle, and Joseph LeConte have traced many of the tales directly to Senegal, Nigeria, Ghana, and Mauritius, and the lore to such African tribes as the Ashanti, Ewe, Yoruba, Ibo, Temne, and Woloff. In addition, a significant number of African American folktales have common elements with tales from both Africa and Europe, while others have been shaped solely by Euro-American influence or are independent creations of New World origin.

Especially among the southern slaves, the most consistent element of African folklore was clearly seen in the animal tales. Most of the stories evolved from African tales about the small trickster animal who outwits those of superior strength by the use of cunning and wit. The wily African tricksters, Hare and Tortoise, found their way to the New World when black mothers used traditional folk wisdom to teach their children how to survive the oppression of slavery. There are numerous references to the trickster animal in African American literature of such women as the eighteenth-century matriarch Lucy Terry, the earliest recorded African poet in North America. Like her griot foremothers, Terry kept her small New England community of slaves and quasi-free black people spellbound with her folktales. During the 170 years of American slavery and throughout African American history, thousands of American black men and women used these African tales for several purposes: to impart moral values, to instill codes of conduct, to explain natural phenomena, and, of course, to entertain. Other categories of folktales also reflect African beginnings. A predominant number of tales attempt to answer questions about the origin of the cosmos and, more generally, how present circumstances have evolved. Similarly, religious tales embodying conjuring, voodoo, and the well-known myths about flying Africans were adapted to the New World setting while still reflecting African concepts and practices.

Whether through their spirituals, secular songs, or folktales, early African Americans expressed one recurrent theme: the weak must assert themselves against the strong because, while the latter may have controlled the slave's outer world, that power was neither permanent nor irrevocable. The belief in the possibility of transcendence and in the potential of being flying Africans, and their faith in the certainty of change serve as direct links between black Americans and their African heritage. Nevertheless, the worldview of eighteenth-century Africans in America was not African; rather, it was one that must be described as "African American"—a worldview that had been formed by over a century of social oppression on the North American continent and a worldview that was always expressed through a rich variety of song, story, and enduring folk forms.

Response: Black Literary Declarations of Independence: Poetry, Essays, Letters, Slave Narratives, and Oratory

"Oh! de Song of Salvation Is a Mighty Sweet Song"

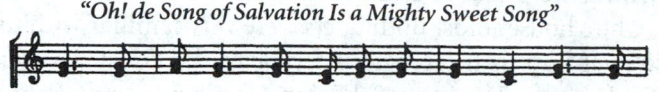

While the legacy of African culture may be more readily apparent in African American folk culture, the written literature of colonial African Americans seemed to draw primarily from Eurocentric art forms. However, the same biblical renderings and interconnectedness between ancient Africa and ancient biblical accounts, as well as the same appreciation of contemporary slavery, must be applied in order to thoroughly understand the written forms of African American literary art. Because literacy is a precondition for creative written expression, it is no wonder that the few black Americans who had been allowed to learn to read and write were encouraged by white people to do so by imitating European literary models and styles. One requirement for successful imperialism is that all permanent (i.e., written) records of defeated civilizations be destroyed. Thus, only Western European written expression—including sacred texts; grammatical readers; and books on history, poetry, and other traditional subjects—was available for any writer to build on, not only in the colonies but in all of the world. Not only was any other form of rhetoric or system of literacy not available for reduction to written texts, but to have pioneered such a form would have been unintelligible production for part of the audience that colonial Africans wished to reach—that is, sympathetic and empowered white people. A more Africanized form, even if known, would have made their works unacceptable for publication and distribution by members of that same white audience. Without the cooperation of these white Christian abolitionists, who, as missionaries, teachers, and preachers, had access to the houses and plantations where slaves lived, the African American audience could not have been reached.

Because of the nonagrarian nature of the northern economy, African Americans who did write were primarily northern blacks, who adopted a variety of conventional eighteenth-century English literary forms and techniques that enabled their works to be published. Though often conforming to these necessary restrictions, the earliest African American writers were no mere imitators of Eurocentric tradition. Instead, like the slave folksinger-poets and tale-tellers, they articulated the theme of freedom in a variety of ways. Their works or "mighty sweet song[s] . . . of salvation" ranged from those that veiled their antislavery attacks in biblical and neoclassical forms, idioms, or language to direct social protests calling for the immediate end to slavery.

Two black poets whose work embodied the technique of protest were Jupiter Hammon and Phillis Wheatley. Hammon was born in the colonies. Wheatley was kidnapped and brought to America as a child of about seven years old. Both were reared from early childhood as slaves in upper-class, northern, white households. Both poets were very familiar with the Bible and both were swept up in the religious fervor of the Great Awakening. Hammon's "An Evening Thought: Salvation by Christ, with Penetential [sic] Cries," published on Christmas day, 1760, is the first poem published by an African American. Wheatley's *Poems on Various Subjects, Religious and Moral,* published in 1773, is the first collection of poetry published by an American of African descent. With this volume of verse, several leading African American literary critics contend, Wheatley launched both the African American and the women's literary traditions.

Although Wheatley and Hammon were greatly attached to eighteenth-century revivalism, some critics point out that their writings demonstrate that they each were conscious of their black cultural identity. For instance, as William Robinson points out, Wheatley confidently uses the moral authority of her position as an "Ethiop" in her poetry to call white society to task for not living up to its own ideals. In addition, Hammon, who was apparently a minister as well, wrote several sermons addressed to "my African brethren" and "fellow servants and brothers, Africans by nation," which disturbed some white people who did not think a black man was qualified to preach. Equally important, he, along with poet Lucy Terry, began what Robinson calls the African American tradition of "orator-poets," bards whose strong sense of orality and vivid and dramatic sense of the present carried over from African culture.

Not all of Wheatley's reminiscences of her native African land are bleak. She is said to have told her white captors that she recalled that "her mother poured out water before the sun at his rising." This could explain the persuasiveness of the sun imagery and its blending with Christian symbolism in her poetry, which, according to John C. Shields in *The Collected Poems of Phillis Wheatley* (1988), demonstrates how she artfully maneuvers neoclassical idioms and techniques to create in her poems a better world, one that is devoid of slavery. As Shields concludes, her "use of poetry as a means to achieve freedom constitutes a poetics of liberation."

As Sondra O'Neale discusses in her book, *Jupiter Hammon and the Biblical Beginnings of African American Literature* (1993), some modern critics, not familiar with biblical imagery, have often stated that Hammon and Wheatley were so involved with Christian subjects that they neglected to mention their enslavement and the slave institution. She insists that, as with the spirituals, the symbols and topics they used are rooted in biblical contexts about slavery, abolition, and anti-imperialism. According to O'Neale, when Hammon and Wheatley (as well as other early black slaves and ex-slaves such as Equiano) used seemingly religious terms such as "savior," "redemption," "saved," "Ethiopian," "Ham," "Cain," they were making veiled references to such issues as slavery, escape, the money needed to purchase a slave's freedom, the hardness of slave masters, the African presence in the Bible, or the attempts by some whites to interpret sections of the Bible to support the slave institution.

Modern scholarship is needed to provide the context for correct analysis of African American literature. Like the relationship between ancient Africa and Israel and their resulting cultures, the understanding of the practice of slavery in the northern colonies is obscured for lack of research. For years, the majority of scholars of African American literature have criticized Hammon for being too conciliatory toward "the peculiar institution" and too otherworldly in his view of freedom. They have been particularly critical of his statement in *An Address to the Negroes in the State of New York* (1787) that as an old man he wished to remain in slavery, but that he wished freedom for younger black slaves. Their conclusions, however, were drawn before Higgenbotham, Hurd, E. J. McManus, and other historians had pointed out a devious antiabolition practice in the northern colonies. Slaveholders, waiting until slaves were too old to work, turned them out on the street to be cared for by the public dole and then insisted that they were simply manumitting the slaves as abolitionists wanted. This practice was especially common in Hammon's home territory of New York. Throughout the colonies, taxes had to be levied to care for these older and usually sickly ex-slaves, and sometimes slave owners were even sued to provide for them.

Other African American writers who, unlike Hammon and Wheatley, were not slaves at the time their works were published and who perhaps were not as dependent on the political machinery established by eighteenth-century abolitionists were somewhat freer to more directly attack "the peculiar institution." One thing that all black writers in the colonies, including Hammon and Wheatley, agreed on was the absolute, blatant religious and political hypocrisy of the American colonists who fought for independence during the Revolutionary War but who denied the same to African American slaves. What enraged not only the writers but all colonial black people even more was that many slaves and *free* black men had fought and died at Lexington, Concord, and Bunker Hill, and in other battles of the war that won freedom for white people only. Realizing that their fate was tied to the plight of their enslaved brothers and sisters, men such as Lemuel Haynes, Prince Hall, Richard Allen, Absalom Jones, John Marrant, and Benjamin Banneker, even in the severe discriminatory confines of their so-called free status, wrote essays, petitions, sermons, and letters demanding the same unalienable rights to equality and freedom for all African Americans that the white colonials had claimed for themselves in the Declaration of Independence.

Long regarded as another early black minister who was silent on the issue of racism, Lemuel B. Haynes, as has been recently discovered, wrote an essay titled "Liberty Further Extended." The essay, which was unearthed in

1983 at Harvard University by Ruth Bogin, is now considered to be black America's first essay overtly protesting slavery. Incorporating biblical texts and the democratic rhetoric of the American Revolution, Haynes's manuscript, according to Bogin, dates back to 1776, preceding David Walker's *Appeal* by about fifty years. Equally important, the manuscript contains an antislavery piece, "The Battle of Lexington," now recognized as perhaps the earliest poem of overt protest by an American of African descent.

In contrast to Haynes, Prince Hall has long enjoyed the critical reputation of being an outspoken opponent of racism. Around 1775, he and fourteen other free blacks formed an army lodge of Free and Accepted Masons attached to a British regiment stationed in Boston. Hall became the first person in American history to organize an African American society for social, political, and economic improvement. A year after the end of the Revolutionary War, he—along with Richard Allen and Absalom Jones—headed a group of eight black Masons who signed a petition to the General Court of Massachusetts "humbly" demanding the abolition of slavery and the restoration of the "Natural Right of all Men," so the "Inhabitants of these Stats [sic]" might no longer be "charageable [sic] with the cinonsistency [sic] of acting themselves the part which they condemn and oppose in others." Of course, slavery was not abolished in Massachusetts until long after that war, but the act of petitioning local governments to outlaw the institution represents an important beginning of the history of organized black political protest against racial injustice. Hall, Allen, and Jones provided instrumental support for other black leaders, including John Marrant, one of the earliest black ministers to receive official ordination from established white churches. Marrant's "Sermon Preached on the 24th day of June, 1789," is among the first recorded speeches by an American of African descent that spoke out against the racism of white slave holders.

Unlike Marrant and several other eighteenth-century black activists, Benjamin Banneker was not a preacher but a scientist, mathematician, and almanac publisher who has the distinction of being a surveyor on the six-man team that designed the present layout of Washington, D.C. Yet Banneker was not too involved in his scientific pursuits to be concerned about the problems that plagued his race. In 1791, he wrote an important and well-publicized letter to then–Secretary of State Thomas Jefferson in which he took the prestigious statesman to task for the racist statements in *Notes on the State of Virginia* (1787). In that text, Jefferson argued that Africans were inferior to whites in both reason and imagination and that they were incapable of producing worthwhile original art. In particular, Jefferson had focused his derogatory criticism toward Phillis Wheatley's poetry, which he insisted was actually written by one or more of her white abolitionist supporters. Using the most exquisite and formal English in contemporary America, Banneker asked Jefferson to use his position as one of the most influential men of the century to help relieve his fellow countrymen who were suffering from slavery's oppression and to extend to African Americans the same rights that he as a white man enjoyed. Banneker further reminded Jefferson that, given his historical reputation as a composer of the Declaration of Independence with its international calls for freedom and equality, it was hypocritical for the statesman to allow slavery to continue in a country that he had helped to mold on a foundation that promised freedom to all.

Alongside the letters, petitions, and other "mighty sweet songs" calling for the abolition of slavery were the first published autobiographical accounts of slaves. Because "the peculiar institution" had denied most authors of these autobiographies any formal education, many dictated their texts to cooperative white people. Some of the earliest recorded accounts by slaves are testimonials called "confessionals." This genre in African American literature is characterized by the poignant statements of African Americans whom the slave-holding state had condemned to death because they either passively or aggressively resisted their bondage. As is evident in the 1786 affidavit of Johnson Green, confessional narratives describe both the marginalized lives of African American slaves and the typical methods of questionable legality used to keep them enslaved. Two colonial blacks confessed only to repeated thievery, but both were hanged for allegedly raping white women. Only one of those executed, a slave named John Joyce, actually confessed to murder. As in the case of the main character, Bigger Thomas, in the ultimate African American slave narrative, Richard Wright's *Native Son* (1940), it is difficult to conclude whether the speakers in the confessionals were guilty criminals or helpless victims of a society that had showered them with hatred and rejection all of their lives.

In some of the lengthier confessionals, the speakers tell of months of homeless wanderings in the wild, sometimes venturing into towns to forage among garbage for food. Others tell of repeated misadventures and oppressive conditions in colonial maritime service. These testimonials are the precursors to the famous *Confessions of Nat Turner* recorded later in the nineteenth century. From the earliest recorded narratives of the eighteenth century, the confessional genre continued to be used throughout the period when black people were lynched in the early twentieth century. It is, in fact, a fundamental informant of the modern African American novel.

Additional engaging personal accounts, which usually recounted successful escape-from-slavery ventures, would later come to be known as "slave narratives." That identification of the genre was taken from the titles of the first published accounts, although it is not certain that the first two published narrators had ever been slaves. These include *A Narrative of the Uncommon Sufferings and Surprizing [sic] Deliverance of Briton Hammon,* (1760); *A Narrative of the Lord's Wonderful Dealings with J. Marrant, a Black Taken Down from His Own Relation* (1785); and the text identified by Arna Bontemps, author of *Great Slave Narratives* (1969), as "the first truly notable book in the genre," Olaudah Equiano's *The Interesting Narrative.*

First published in England, Equiano's remarkable narrative soon became a sensational hit throughout Europe and the British Isles; and, of course, it was read both by and to black and white people in the United States. With vivid memory and cogent detail, the articulate, African-born Equiano was the first known author of African descent to verify and report what we now understand as the casting of the African diaspora around the New World. Moreover, Equiano's impeccable style gave the English-speaking world its first detailed eyewitness account of slavery and the slave trade. With emotional eloquence, the author offers poignant recollections of his boyhood among the Ibo people in West Africa, of the day when he first saw white people and was kidnapped into slavery, and of the brutality he both witnessed and experienced at the hands of white people during the Middle Passage. With biblically based knowledge and a forceful, prophetic style, Equiano also tells white Christians that the God of Christianity certainly did not teach them to steal humans for bondage or to abduct children away from their parents to make them perpetual slaves. Hence, as an African writing about his own experiences as a slave, Equiano waged several crucial battles in the abolition war. He assaulted the notion that Africans had no intellectual or creative powers. He demanded that his white readers renounce their stereotypes of black people as inarticulate subhuman animals. He questioned the viability of the accepted doctrine that white people were indeed God's chosen people. He stripped the institution of slavery and the slave trade of the facade of any humanity or compassion among slavers. And, through the use of artistic, balanced, and life-enthused narrative, he garnered an abolitionist following around the world. Moreover, by fusing social protest with the tradition of spiritual autobiography that had been established by the Puritans and Quakers, Equiano cast a die not only for the literary genre of the nineteenth-century slave narrative but also for that of the African American novel. As Wilfred D. Samuels, in *Dictionary of Literary Biography* (1986), has concluded:

> Like the modern alienated hero in black fiction, Equiano remains above all in his narrative an exile. In response to life, Equiano epitomizes the black fictional character whose quest is for wholeness and meaning in a world that often does not offer aggregation or fulfillment.

There were also a few other autobiographical accounts by free blacks. But, as these narratives relate, the prevailing hostility of racism in the eighteenth century meant that free blacks actually did not fare much better than slaves. Most were ex-slaves who had had to purchase their freedom or the freedom of their spouses and children. For example, in the autobiographical narrative that he published in 1798 when he was 69 years old, Venture Smith of Stonington, Connecticut, writes about the stealthy ways in which he tried to secure or buy the freedom he never had:

> By cultivating this land with the greatest diligence and economy, at times when my master did not require my labor, in two years I laid up ten pounds. This my friend tendered my master for myself . . . I raised one year with another, ten cart loads of watermelons . . . Various other methods I pursued in order to enable me to redeem my family.

Major African American writers of the latter decades of the eighteenth century were part of a much wider movement of preachers, evangelists, and lay ministers of African descent who sincerely found in their own interpretations of Christianity hope for physical as well as spiritual emancipation. Under the leadership of David George, the first Baptist church for African Americans was founded in South Carolina in 1773. Fifteen years later, Andrew Bryan started a huge church (First Bryan Baptist) in Savannah, Georgia. In the same year, Samuel Morris, an African-born itinerant preacher, kept thousands of viewers captivated for days as he delivered his thunderous sermons from the deck of an unspecified anchored ship. By the end of the eighteenth century, George Liele had established churches in Jamaica. But the most significant early black church movement began in 1787, when two African American ministers, Richard Allen and Absalom Jones, led a congregation of thirty black parishioners out of the white St. George's Methodist Episcopal Church of Philadelphia after they had been denied integrated seating. Against strong resistance from the white church establishment, the two men, along with Peter Williams, went on to establish the first African American Methodist and Episcopal churches in the United States. As the beginning of what would become one of the largest Protestant denominations of African Americans around the world, Richard Allen's church, Bethel African Methodist Episcopal Church (the A.M.E. church) was founded in 1794. The same year, Allen and Jones wrote a defense of the efforts of black people in Philadelphia who were accused of not doing enough during the yellow fever epidemic that paralyzed the life of the city. That pamphlet was titled *A Narrative of the Proceedings of the Black People during the Late Awful Calamity in Philadelphia; and a Refutation of Some Censures Thrown Upon Them in Some Late Publications.* From the pulpit of Bethel A.M.E. Church, Allen would go on to become a Methodist Episcopal bishop and the most powerful African American religious leader of the eighteenth century. Seven years after the plague in Philadelphia. Allen published *A Collection of Spiritual Songs and Hymns Selected from Various Authors,* which included several hymns that he had written himself. This collection would, in turn, inform several black spirituals composed in the nineteenth century and would be widely used by black ministers as they rallied their congregations to wage war on slavery and on the social injustices committed against their people.

Allen and other black ministers in the Colonial age can be linked to African griots, who for centuries have served as influential court officials, advisors, and official record keepers in highly centralized African states. Skilled in oratory, music, history, and poetry, griots have functioned in a variety of capacities, not the least being the role of personal consultants to tribal rulers. Griots have recorded and recited the cultural history of their people, have guided men and women into proper societal roles, and have exhorted troops going into battle. Thus, like their African predecessors, early African American ministers such as Allen, Liele, and Jones, and, to varying degrees, other black writers and spokespersons of that era became political leaders of a society that functioned within a society. Using the inherited verbal artistry and eloquence of the griots, they crafted sermons, prayers, narratives, hymns, poems, essays, and songs to educate, uplift, and stir the African American spirit toward social action.

From their churches, these early ministers founded benevolent societies that not only aided needy African Americans but offered services to larger communities as well. More importantly, they formed and supported forceful protest groups that constantly bombarded municipal, state, and national officials on behalf of escaped or beleaguered slaves and free black people with petitions for financial justice, including the payment of slaves for unreimbursed labor, and with calls for the complete end to slavery. They were often joined in these endeavors by the hundreds of men in the various lodges organized throughout the northern colonies by Prince Hall's Masons. Moreover, Allen, Jones, Liele, and thousands of their followers worked jointly with the organized bodies of white abolitionists in churches and political action groups in England, Europe, and throughout the United States.

Thus, the black church began and has continued to the present as not only a place of worship but also as the sociopolitical center of African American life. Because the New World experience severely limited free and open public expression for black people, the church provided them a public forum and leadership opportunities denied them by white organizations. Not surprisingly, therefore, since its eighteenth-century origin, the black church has produced important, dynamic, and eloquent African American preachers such as Martin Luther King, Jr., Jesse Jackson, Adam Clayton Powell, Leon Sullivan, and Benjamin Chavez. Their leadership stemmed from a long line of African American church leaders beginning with Allen, Jones, and others who led the first civil rights movement in the United States. These New World griots called for the abolition of the transatlantic slave trade and southern slavery at the turn of the nineteenth century. The march toward freedom had begun.

Choral Refrain

The analogy of the arrival of seventeen African men and three African women to the establishment of a *second* colonial entity in North America is appropriate. For the white pilgrims of Jamestown and Plymouth, the new land meant freedom, opportunity, and escape from persecution. For the African entrants, however, the new land meant enslavement, perpetual denial of opportunity, and the beginning of unrelenting persecution. Neither group viewed the society to which it belonged, any of its institutions, or its language in the same way. These dichotomies were true in 1619 and, unfortunately, they are in too many ways just as true in this last decade of the twentieth century. Nevertheless, whether through sacred or secular voice or whether through folk art or formal expression, African Americans still respond uniquely to the call of their own history, literature, and culture—not an inheritance of ignorance and paganism as perceived by many white Americans. Some of those who came to this country as European immigrants have never agreed that Americans of African descent are the equivalent of biblical Egypt. However, conditions in which most African Americans live substantiate the undeniable fact that "Go down, Moses, way down in Egypt's land, Tell ole Pharaoh, let my people go" best describes what is still a *second colony* existence.

Call for Deliverance: The Oral Tradition
Origins: African Survivals in Slave Folk Culture

Numerous scholarly studies of African and African American folklore have documented the types of African survivals found in African American culture and the means by which they have survived. As has been previously discussed, researchers have ascertained that certain features of slave folk culture, namely, proverbs, work songs and other secular music, spirituals, and folktales, have distinct origins in Africa.

Proverbs
African Prototypes

African proverbs are used to impart a way or philosophy of life to a people by building on the experiences and wisdom of the past. These proverbs are similar to those of Europe and other world cultures. Notwithstanding, as Mary Frances Berry and John Blassingame in *Long Memory: The Black Experience in America* (1982) have observed, they "in general had greater flexibility of imagery and application, symmetrical balance, poetic structure, and rhythmic quality than European ones." Because of the flexibility of the folk form, Africans relied on proverbs more so than most people. Besides teaching modes of conduct, religious beliefs, respect for elders, and ultimate moral values, they were used in the litigation of disputes within a community and, more informally, as greetings. In addition, they were played on drums; included in songs, epics, and folktales; and applied as nicknames. In fact, in several West African cultures such as Yoruba and Ibo, a person's mental powers and literary skills were and still are measured by the fluency with which one can use this folk form. The best statement of the value of proverbs in African speech comes from Nigerian novelist Chinua Achebe who says in *Things Fall Apart* (1959), "Proverbs are the palm-oil with which words are eaten."

Slave Proverbs

Many African proverbs appeared in the language and folktales of the New World slaves. As can be seen in the following table from Berry and Blassingame's *Long Memory*, many of the slave proverbs are identical in form and content to the African ones, but they often reflect the impact of slavery and the New World environment. As the authors explain in detail, "About 50 percent of the proverbs the slaves used reflected the plantation experience. The slaves borrowed less than 20 percent of them from their white masters. These plantation proverbs contained advice about how much labor the slave should perform, how to avoid punishment, and frequently referred to such activities as plowing and harvesting cotton, corn, and wheat, religious meetings, corn shuckings, and singing."

Slave Proverbs and Their African Parallels

Slave Proverb	African Parallel	Meaning
If you play with a puppy, he will lick your face.	If you play with a dog, you must expect it to lick your mouth. (Ashanti)	Familiarity with inferiors may cause them to lose respect for you.
Distant stovewood is good stovewood.	Distant firewood is good firewood. (Ewe)	Things look better from a distance.
"Almost kill bird" don't make soup.	"I nearly killed the bird." No one can eat "nearly" in a stew. (Yoruba). "Almost" is not eaten. (Zulu)	Literal.
One rain won't make a crop.	One tree does not make a forest. (Ewe, Kpelle, Ashanti)	One part does not equal the whole.
The pitcher goes to the well every day; one day it will leave its handle.	If there is a continual going to the well, one day there will be a smashing of the pitcher. (Hausa)	One's evil deeds will one day be discovered.
A seldom visitor makes a good friend.	If you visit your fellow (friend) too often, he will not respect you. But if you make yourself scarce, he will pine for your company. (Jabo)	Literal.
A scornful dog will eat dirty pudding.	When a dog is hungry, it eats mud. (Zulu)	Adversity causes one to do things he would not do in good times.
He holds with the hare (or fox) and runs with the hounds.	They forbid ram and eat sheep. (Ibo)	A deceitful person.
The best swimmer is often drowned.	The expert swimmer is carried away by the water. (Zulu, Tonga)	There is no absolute certainty of anything.

Sources: Nyembezi, *Zulu;* Junod and Jacques, *Wisdom;* Brewer, *Negro;* Ellis, *Ewe;* Rattray, *Ashanti;* Herzog, *Jabo: Southern Workman, 1872–1900.* From Berry & Blassingame *Long Memory: The Black Experience in America.* Oxford University Press, 1982.

The Folk Cry

There are various kinds of folk cries or hollers heard during and after slavery. According to African American musicologist Willis Laurence James in one of the few studies of the folk form, "The Romance of the Negro Folk Cry in America (1950),"* the slaves' song cries, which reflect the various emotions and functions of the slaves,

---

**Phylon*, vol. 16, pp. 15–30. Used by permission.

fall into three major categories: (1) plain cries; (2) florid cries; and (3) coloratura cries. Plain cries, which are the simplest in form and structure, consist of calls, selling or street cries, and dance cries. The more ornate, or florid, cries—religious cries, field cries or whoops and hollers, and night cries—are found in the spirituals, work songs, blues, folk preaching, and some jazz songs. Coloratura cries, the most elaborate and complex of the musical vocal cries, stem from the slaves' water cries. According to James, the best example of coloratura cries can be found in the recordings of Louis Armstrong, Cab Calloway, Mahalia Jackson, the Ward singers, and some of the preaching records of the Twenties era. For clarity, James provides the following examples of the seven basic types of folk cries:

Call

Selling Cry

Religious Cry

Field Cry

Night Cry

Dance Cry

Water Cry

THE SHOUT

The shout is a folk form that played a significant role in the religious and social life of the slaves. During this holy dance, the slave singers would first stand in the middle of the floor and then begin singing a song by shuffling around, one at a time, in a ring. Although every singer would move exactly in time with the rhythm, each one participated in the singing according to how he or she felt. Some would walk in the circle using jerking motions while others would clap their hands and stamp their feet. Still others would dance silently or sing only refrains of the song.

The songs were always religious and extremely simple. They consisted primarily of a single stanza, or walk, and a single chorus usually with a faster and more marked rhythm, or shout. The lead singer would sing the single stanza, or walk, twice; then, the chorus would begin singing the shout. Often, to break the monotony of the repetition, the lead singer would repeat the walk.

Among the spirituals most closely associated with the shout were " 'Ligion So Sweet," "Walk Around de Heavens," "Oh, We'll Walk 'Round de Fountain," "Humble Yo'Self, de Bells Done Ring," "I Can't Stay Behind," and "Go Ring that Bell."

'Ligion So Sweet

(*Walk*)

Keep a rollin' down de fountain,
Keep a rollin' down de fountain,
Keep a rollin' down de fountain,
Oh, de 'ligion so sweet!

(*Shout*)

Oh, de 'ligion—oh de 'ligion
Oh, de 'ligion—so sweet!
Oh, de 'ligion—oh de 'ligion
Oh, de 'ligion—so sweet!

Walk Around de Heavens

(*Walk*)
Walk around de Heavens,
We'll walk around de heavens,
Walk around de heavens, O Lord,
De room already dressed!
(*Shout*)
Oh, de room a'ready dressed—O Lord!
De room a'ready dressed, O Lord,
De room a'ready dressed, my God,
De room a'ready dressed!

Source: Robert Winslow Gordon, "Negro 'Shouts' from Georgia," in *Mother Wit from the Laughing Barrel*, ed. Alan Dundes (1973), pp. 445–451.

Work songs and other secular music

The slaves' secular music retained traditional African elements while adapting to the New World environment. As with the spirituals, many of the work songs are built on African antiphonal, or call and response, patterns as illustrated by Harold Courlander on pages 33–34.

A typical African form of antiphony, the alternation of stanza and chorus can be seen in the earliest example of an African song text, a work song music historian Eileen Southern has unearthed in Mungo Park's *Travels in the Interior Districts of Africa, Performed Under the Direction and Patronage of the African Association in the Years of 1795, 1796, and 1797.* According to Park, the song expressed the women's views about their visitor (the author himself). Sung by a group of women spinning cotton, the song, Park relates, "was sung by one of the young women, the rest joining in a sort of chorus."

Another common form of African antiphony, the alternation of verse lines and refrain, appears in the earliest texts of African American work songs. (No. 3 in Courlander's illustration). According to Southern, the African American work songs are a roustabout song heard around the year 1800 in the Philadelphia area and a boat song heard in 1808 and transcribed by a British traveler, John Lambert, in his *Travels Through Lower Canada and the United States of North America in the Years 1806, 1807, and 1808* (1810). In the boat song, Lambert observed the lead singer, the boatman, keeping time with the tune at every stroke of the boatmen's oars. It illustrates a feature indigenous to African work songs—the lead singer's call and the workers' response in words or grunts of their own or the sound of their own tools.

African Prototype

An African Spinners' Song

The winds roared, and the rains fell
The poor white man, faint and weary,
Came and sat under our tree.
He has no mother to bring him milk,
No wife to grind his corn.

(*Chorus*) Let us pity the white man.
No mother has he to bring him milk,
No wife to grind his corn.

EARLY SLAVE WORK SONGS

An Old Boat Song

(*Lead Singer*)	(*Chorus*)
We are going down to Georgia, boys,	Aye, Aye.
To see the pretty girls, boys;	Yoe, Yoe.
We'll give 'em a pint of brandy, boys,	Aye, Aye.
And a hearty kiss, besides, boys.	Yoe, Yoe.
&c. &c. &c.	

ANTIPHONAL PATTERNS OF WORK SONGS

1. The song begins with unison singing, leader and chorus singing together note for note, except for accidental harmonies in seconds, thirds, fifths, sometimes in octaves or falsetto.
2. The leader sings his first solo line, follows with the response line, then sings his second solo line, after which the group picks up the indicated response. Each line of the solo part, except for occasional repetition, is different.

Leader	*Chorus*
a) ________	
b) ________	
c) ________	
	b) ________
d) ________	
	b) ________
e) ________	
	b) ________
f) ________	
	b) ________

3. The chorus repeats in full the solo lines, each of which is different.

Leader	*Chorus*
a) ________	
	a) ________
b) ________	
	b) ________
c) ________	
	c) ________
d) ________	
	d) ________

4. The leader sings every line twice, a fixed choral response following each solo line.

Leader *Chorus*

a) ________
b ________
a) ________
b) ________
c) ________
b) ________
c) ________
b) ________
d) ________
b) ________
d) ________
b) ________

5. The leader sings a line with one or more repetitions, with the chorus picking up the last word or several words of each line and then singing the responsive part.

Leader *Chorus*

a) ________/________
a) ________/________
a) ________/________
b) ________
c) ________/________
c) ________/________
c) ________/________
b) ________

6. The leader sings each line twice, with an alternating choral response between.

Leader *Chorus*

a) ________
b) ________
a) ________
c) ________
d) ________
b) ________
d) ________
c) ________
e) ________
b) ________
e) ________
c) ________

7. Combination of these patterns.

Source: Harold Courlander, *Negro Folk Music U.S.A.* (New York: Columbia University Press, 1963), pp. 92–94.

Spirituals

As has been previously discussed, the spirituals reflect the African heroic epic in form, content, and performance style. The African oral epic consists of long narrative recitations and songs interwoven with praise poems, chants, sermons, hymns, prayers, and improvisations. Strikingly similar, the spirituals are lengthy epic narratives, praise poems, sermons and prayers, lyrical songs and poetry, and frequent improvisations, including African antiphony, or overlapping call and response.

African Prototypes of Lengthy Epic Narratives

The oral epic has served the same purpose in Africa as it has for nearly all of the world's cultures; that is, to instruct people, while entertaining them, about great heroes and historical events significant to their culture. It is constructed around the exploits of an epic hero, a human being with certain supernatural characteristics, who has had to overcome major obstacles and eventually has triumphed, both spiritually and physically, for the sake of his people. What distinguishes the African oral epic from that of the European tradition, however, is that there is a relative absence of physical confrontations between the hero and the adversary in the former. Instead, as John W. Johnson in "Yes Virginia, There is an Epic in Africa" in *Research in African Literature* 11 (1980), has observed, the hero's "major battles against his adversary are not described in epic as great conflicts of weaponry, but rather they are battles of sorcery." According to folklore critic John W. Roberts, the source of the hero's magical power with which he confronts his adversary is the focus of the heroic quest in the epics. "The epic hero's quest," Roberts contends, "becomes one of acquiring fetishes and talismans to increase his means or to gain the magical protection that he needs to perform the acts that will change his destiny." A striking contract between the African and the European epic traditions is the degree to which the theme of the hero's quest for esoteric knowledge and mystical power that comes with its possession dominates the literature.

African heroic epics such as *Sunjata* (also spelled *Sundiata* and *Sunyetta*), *The Mwindo Epic, Kambili,* and *The Ozidi Saga* have been told for centuries by griots, whose major functions have been to preserve, record, and transmit the history of their people. Measured considerably by their skills in oral performance, the griots have sung or recited the histories in the form of epic poetry or narration. However, the genre of the oral epic should be regarded as literature rather than as history because griots' versions often differ markedly in detail. Expressing a value central to African tradition, Isidore Okpewho in *The Epic in Africa* (1975) points out that the griots are "not trained in the rigid use of memory but in the flexible technique of improvisation."

Such is the case with *Sunjata* of the Mandingo tradition, an epic retold by generations of griots since the thirteenth century and one that captures all of the power and glory of medieval African kingship. In general, the epic centers around the life of Sunjata, the extraordinary Mandingo warrior-king, who led the revolt against the declining empire of Ghana around the year A.D. 1200. His successful, legendary military campaigns have linked him permanently with the cultural identity of the Mandingo people. Born the son of the King of Manding (Mali), Fata Kung Makhang (also called Naareng Makhang Konnate), and his second wife, the hunchback princess Sukulung (or Sologon) Konte, he grew up to fulfill the prophesies of the soothsayers that he would become the king who would unite the twelve kingdoms of Mali into one of the most powerful empires ever known in Africa.

However, there are obvious discrepancies among the four published versions of the epic: There are three poems by Gambian Mandinke griots—Bamba Suso's *Sunjata,* Banna Kanute's *Sunjata,* and Dembo Kanute's *Faa Koli*—and a narrative by a Guinean Mandinke bard—Mamadou Kouyate's *Sundiata.* Times, places, nature of significant events, names of important characters, and other relevant details vary from text to text. Yet, the versions do have a common core that is likely to be based on fact; namely, that Sunjata, driven from Mali and exiled for some period of time, eventually returned home and established himself as king. The mythical framework of the epic is also consistent in the accounts; that is, that the epic hero, born crippled and threatened from birth, returned home to defeat his chief adversary, the evil sorcerer king Sumanguru (referred to as "Soumaoro Kante" in Kouyate's account) through the use of magical powers. After discovering from his sister that Sumanguru's *nya,* or protective life force, is a crowing white cock, Sunjata uses the magic of a counterforce, a cockspur in a poisoned weapon (arrow or gun), to destroy his enemy's powers.

The following excerpt from Banna Kanute's *Sunjata*[1] is a description of the bitter engagement at Kankinya between Sunjata and Sumanguru. It parallels the major confrontation between the slaves' biblical warrior-hero Moses and Ole' Pharaoh and the magical feats that Moses performed to save the Israelites. With the African epic hero as model, it is not surprising, therefore, that Moses, whose trials and tribulations resemble those of Sunjata, appears in numerous spirituals and, thus, dominates the action of the songs. Such biblical epic narratives as "Go Down, Moses" reflect the African worldview of the balancing forces of nature. Hence, these narratives functioned as cultural models of good and evil, justice and injustice, or sin and retribution for the slaves.

FROM *Sunjata*

Sunjata arose,
And went and seized a white cock that day,
And killed it.
When he had killed the white cock,
They plucked it and singed it;
They burned its feet and removed the spurs,
They put silver dust and gold dust inside,
They loaded a gun and put it in the hands of Faa Koli Kumba and
    Faa Koli Daaba.

---

[1]Along with Bamba Suso and Dembo Kanute's poems, Banna Kanute's version was heard, translated into English, and published by Gordon Innes in *Sunjata: Three Mandinke Versions* (1974). Kanute's version has been chosen because he is reputed to be one of the leading African griots; he is a highly skilled musician and entertainer, and his performance of the epic is more musically complex than that of the others. Singing more songs than the other bards and using no fewer than eight different musical accompaniments throughout the poem, he played the *balo,* an eighteen-keyed xylophone, himself and switched instrumental accompaniments swiftly as required by changes in content. The other Gambian bards, Bamba Suso, the best historian of the group, and Dembo Kanute, were accompanied by players of the *kora,* a twenty-one string harp-flute. Mamadou Kouyate's performance style and instrumental accompaniments were not mentioned. Kouyate told his narrative version of the epic to Djibril Tamsir Niane, who transcribed it and translated it into French in 1960. It has been translated into English by G.D. Pickett. The notes explaining the lines of this poem derive from Gordon Innes's *Sunjata.*

Line 1868. Faa Koli was a nephew of Sumanguru who deserted his uncle when the latter stole his wife. Faa Koli joined Sunjata and became one of his outstanding commanders against Sumanguru. The names Faa Koli Kumba and Faa Koli Daaba refer to the same man, not two men, although Banna Kanute appears to be singing about two different men.

They came and circled round Manding, the three of them,
Faa Koli Kumba and Faa Koli Daaba and Sunjata;
Seven times they went round Manding, then they stood still,
They and Bala Faasigi Kuyate.
It was that day that Bala Faasigi Kuyate sang:
Ah, Sunjata has come, Sumanguru,
Ah, Sunjata has come, Sumanguru.
The town drum sounded.
Ah, Sunjata has come, Sumanguru,
Ah, Sunjata is here, Sumanguru.
They sounded the town drum and the whole town came forth.
Sunjata, with his horse,
And his long sword,
And his iron rod,
And his double-barrelled gun with the cock's spur in it.
Susu Sumanguru Baamagana came forth,
With his long sword,
And his iron rod,
And his three-pronged spear,
And his double-barrelled gun.
All of Manding came forth;
They stood at the four wondrous gates,
And they sent forth these two men.
Sunjata said to Susu Sumanguru Baamagana, 'Go ahead.'
Susu Sumanguru Baamagana replied, 'No, you go ahead, you are the younger.'
Sunjata answered, 'No, go ahead, you are the older.'
Susu Sumanguru Baamagana took his horse back some distance, then he declared, 'This is far enough.'
He charged on horseback with his three-pronged spear;
He raised it aloft and struck Sunjata with it;
The three-pronged spear shattered and fell to the ground.
Sumanguru retired;
There was a great shout.
Faa Koli Kumba and Faa Koli Daaba and Bala Faasigi Kuyate,
Only these three were in support of Sunjata,
Whereas the whole of Manding supported Susu Sumanguru Baamagana.
After Susu Sumanguru Baamagana had struck Sunjata
He retired and went a long way off on his horse,
Then he returned.
He struck Sunjata with his long sword;
The long sword broke into three pieces and fell to the ground.
He retired again
Then returned with his iron rod.
He raised it aloft and was about to strike Sunjata with the iron rod,

Line 1872. Bala Fassigi Kuyate is the griot in the poem.

But his arm remained aloft, immovable.
He said to Sunjata, 'Go ahead.'
Sunjata came and struck Sumanguru with his three-pronged spear;
The three-pronged spear was shattered.
He retired, then came with a long sword;
The long sword too was shattered and fell to the ground.
When he set his hand to his gun
And drew it and was about to aim at him,
It was then that Susu Sumanguru Baamagana turned tail
And was about to run away.
Sunjata declared:
   Sunjata has come, Sumanguru,
   Ah, Sunjata is here, Sumanguru.
He went on:
   Thatching grass, thatching grass, thatching grass,
   Other things go underneath thatching grass,
   Thatching grass does not go underneath anything;
   Thatching grass, thatching grass, thatching grass,
   Others run away from Sunjata,
   Sunjata does not run from anyone.
   A soap-taking dog,
   A dog which does not leave soap alone
   Will not leave a bone alone.
   Sunjata *ding kasi kang,* Sumanguru,
   Death is better than disgrace, Sumanguru.
He produced the chicken spur at that point
And shot Sumanguru with it;
He fell.
It was that day that Sunjata told Bala Faasigi Kuyate,
'Every smith in Manding
Will bear the name Nkante.
I want you to sing the praises of the smiths so that I can hear.'
He declared:
   Cut and Sirimang.
   It is forging and the left hand,
   Senegalese coucal and swallow,
   Cut iron with iron,
   What makes iron valuable,
   Big *kuku* tree and big silk-cotton tree,
   Fari and Kaunju.
As the Mandinka say, the eastern people understand the language of the griots;

Line 1920. "Baamagana" is Sumanguru's surname.
Lines 1925–1936. One of the best known songs associated with *Sunjata.* The lines imply that, although others may run to Sunjata for protection, he does not seek protection from anyone.
Lines 1945–1951. Sumanguru's praise names. Most of them have some reference to blacksmithing. Banna Kanute explains their meaning in lines 1952 through 1964.

All this is meaningful.
He said, 'Sege and Sirimang',
That is Sunjata and Susu Sumanguru Baamagana.
'That is forging and the left hand'—
That is pincers and iron.
'Cut iron with iron, what makes iron valuable'—
That means that one great man gets the better of another great man by
 magical means.
'Big *kuku* tree and big silk-cotton tree'—
That means that however big a silk-cotton tree may be, it stands in an
 even bigger open space.
'Fari and Kaunju'—
That is the bellows and the small clay mound through which the
 bellows pipe leads into the fire.
He turned round and presented his back;
Sunjata was standing.
Bala said, 'Dugu and Bala,
Faabaga and Taulajo,
Supreme horseman whom none surpasses,
Wuruwarang Kaba,
Dala Kumbukamba and Dala Jiibaa Minna,
Kasawura Konte,
Sankarang Madiba Konte,
It was he who was the father of Sukulung Konte,
Sukulung Konte it was who bore you, Makhang Sunjata.'
He went on,
 It is war which devastated Manding,
 It is war which rebuilt Manding.
Sunjata entered Manding with these griots' songs.
They sang:
 Kankinya,
 Kankinya, there is a gate at Kankinya,
 Kankinya, there is a gate at Kankinya,
 War at Kankinya.
The fortified position occupied by Susu Sumanguru Baamagana
Was called Kankinya.
When Sunjata entered Manding,
He destroyed the four wondrous gates;
He rebuilt them and made them into four gatehouses,
He made them into four gatehouses;
Four little beds were put inside them.
When dawn broke,

Line 1954. "Sege" means to cut. It probably refers to the cutting and shaping of metals by smiths. "Sirimang" is a nick-name for blacksmiths.
Line 1957. The pincers are held in the left hand.
Lines 1966–1974. The griot Bala Fassigi Kuyate praises the legendary Mandingo horsemen.

Bala Faasigi Kuyate would come
And play this tune—the *Janjungo* tune.
At first cock-crow
He would come and stand at Sunjata's gate;
He would play the *Janjungo* tune and say:
   Great Janjung, it is war which shattered Janjung,
   War rebuilt great Janjung.
Janjung was the name of that Manding gatehouse.
He would say to Sunjata:
   Sukulung Kutuma
   And Sukulung Yammaru here,
   Naareng Makhang Konnate,
   Cats on the shoulder,
   Simbong and Jata are at Naarena.
   In Sunjata's day a griot did not have to fetch water,
   To say nothing of farming and gathering firewood.
   Father World has changed, changed.
Sunjata would come out of his house
And come and sit on his earthen platform
Near his own doorway.
Bala would go and stand by the head of the Sooras
And he would say to him, "Soora Musa Bankaalu,
Kiliya Musa and Nooya Musa,
Bula Wuruwuru and Bula Wanjaga,
Kutu Yokhobila and Sina Yokhobila,
And Karta Yokhobila and Bumba Yokhobila.
It was your grandfather who sounded the royal drum to summon
   assemblies,
Mighty Bagadugu and Ginate,
Mighty Hanjugu and Hamina Yanga."
The head of the Sooras would also come out
And come and sit on his earthen platform.
At that time wooden platforms for sitting on were not built;
They used to beat earth into a platform,
Which they called "*bilingo.*"
Each of the four gates had an earthen platform.
He would go to Faa Koli Kumba and to Faa Koli Daaba,
He would go to Sibi Kamara,
And the latter would also come and sit at his gatehouse.

Line 1993. "*Janjungo*" is the name of the song Banna Kanute has used for most of this performance. The word "janjungo" in Gambian Mandean means a "large gathering with much movement, singing, and dancing."
Lines 2001–2005. Sukulung Kutuma is Sunjata's mother. Sukulung Yammaru is Sunjata himself. "Naareng Makhang Konnate" is Sunjata's name. "Naareng" is the name of Sunjata's father's town. It was common practice for the name of the king's town or territory to precede the name of the king. "Simbong and Jata are at Naarena" is a common line in praise of Sunjata. "Naarena" is the name of Sunjata's town.
Lines 2013–2021. "Soora Muca Bankaalu is the praise name of Sunjata's military commander, Faa Koli. The griot Bala Kuyate is praising Faa Koli and his ancestors.
Line 2025. A "*bilingo*" is a bed or platform made of beaten earth.

Bala Faasigi Kuyate would come and sit in their midst.
Sunjata was in control of Manding for seven years,
Then he rose up and went to the East;
He declared that he was going to wage war.
His first war was at Kaaba.
It so happened that the head of the traders was there;
He left Kaaba and went to Tumutu.
Whoever is a trader,
If his name is Bayo,
If his name is Daabo,
If his name is Fofana,
If his name is Dansokho,
If his name is Singaste,
All are descended from Mamudu Bayo of Tumutu.
Sunjata marched against him at Tumutu;
He captured him, but before he returned,
He learned that the people of Manding had revolted during his absence.
They said that Sunjata was not a war leader
Because a man who waged war with only four men behind him. . . .
They led the country to revolt again in his absence;
They destroyed the wondrous gatehouse of Manding,
And they built it again soundly;
Sunjata came and burned the town.
He withdrew
And went to Tanda,
Where the leader of the traders was living,
That was Koora and Danjogo.
That Mamudu Koora of Tanda
Was the ancestor of the Koora family.
Sunjata went after him at Tanda,
And captured him,
But before he returned he learned that Manding had revolted during
  his absence.
He waged war against Manding nineteen times,
He rebuilt Manding nineteen times.
Now, white man, the account of Sunjata's career as far as I know it,
As I heard it from my parents,
And my teachers,
Ends here.

Line 2034. In Niani's* notes in his *Sundiata,* he explains that Sunjata assembled at Kaaba in Sibi, the territory of the Kamaras, after the defeat of Sumanguru and those of Sumanguru's allies who had fought on after Sumanguru had been defeated. At Kaaba, there was a victory celebration and then Sunjata appointed his leading allies as sub-kings in charge of various territories, which together comprised the Manding empire. After leaving Kaaba, Sunjata went to Niani, which he rebuit as the capital of Manding. Niani is not mentioned in the epic poems of the Gambian Mandingo griots. However, it is prominent in Mamadou Kouyate's narrative version of the epic.
*Niani is the translator-editor of *Sundiata: An Epic of Old Mali.* (London): Longmans, 1986.

Spirituals as Lengthy Epic Narratives

Go Down, Moses

1. When Israel was in Egypt's land,
   Let my people go;
   Oppress'd so hard they could not stand,
   Let my people go.
   (*Chorus*) Go down, Moses, Way down in Egypt land,
   Tell ole Pharaoh, Let my people go.

2. Thus saith the Lord, bold Moses said,
   Let my people go;
   If not I'll smite your first born dead,
   Let my people go.
   (*Chorus*)

3. No more shall they in bondage toil,
   Let my people go;
   Let them come out with Egypt's spoil,
   Let my people go
   (*Chorus*)

4. When Israel out of Egypt came,
   Let my people go;
   And left the proud oppressive land,
   Let my people go.
   (*Chorus*)

5. O, 'twas a dark and dismal night,
   Let my people go;
   When Moses led the Israelites,
   Let my people go.
   (*Chorus*)

6. 'Twas good old Moses and Aaron, too,
   Let my people go;
   'Twas they that led the armies through,
   Let my people go.
   (*Chorus*)

7. The Lord told Moses what to do,
   Let my people go;
   To lead the children of Israel through,
   Let my people go.
   (*Chorus*)

8. O come along, Moses, you'll not get lost,
   Let my people go;
   Stretch out your rod and come across,
   Let my people go.
   (*Chorus*)

9. As Israel stood by the water side,
   Let my people go;
   At the command of God it did divide,
   Let my people go.
   (*Chorus*)

10. When they had reached the other shore,
    Let my people go;
    They sang a song of triumph o'er,
    Let my people go.
    (*Chorus*)

11. Pharaoh said he would go across,
    Let my people go;
    But Pharaoh and his host were lost,
    Let my people go.
    (*Chorus*)

12. O, Moses, the cloud shall cleave the way,
    Let my people go;
    A fire by night, a shade by day,
    Let my people go.
    (*Chorus*)

13. You'll not get lost in the wilderness,
    Let my people go;
    With a lighted candle in your breast,
    Let my people go.
    (*Chorus*)

14. Jordan shall stand up like a wall,
    Let my people go;
    And the walls of Jericho shall fall,
    Let my people go.
    (*Chorus*)

15. Your foes shall not before you stand,
    Let my people go;
    And you'll possess fair Canaan's land,
    Let my people go.
    (*Chorus*)

16. 'Twas just about in harvest time,
    Let my people go;
    When Joshua led his host divine.
    Let my people go.
    (*Chorus*)

17. O let us all from bondage flee,
    Let my people go;
    And let us all in Christ be free,
    Let my people go.
    (*Chorus*)

18. We need not always weep and moan,
    Let my people go;
    And wear these slavery chains forlorn,
    Let my people go.
    (*Chorus*)
19. This world's a wilderness of woe,
    Let my people go;
    O, let us on to Canaan go,
    Let my people go.
    (*Chorus*)
20. What a beautiful morning that will be,
    Let my people go;
    When time breaks up in eternity,
    Let my people go.
    (*Chorus*)
21. O bretheren, bretheren, you'd better be engaged,
    Let my people go;
    For the devil he's out on a big rampage.
    Let my people go.
    (*Chorus*)
22. The Devil he thought he had me fast,
    Let my people go;
    But I thought I'd break his chains at last,
    Let my people go.
    (*Chorus*)
23. O take yer shoes from off yer feet,
    Let my people go;
    And walk into the golden street,
    Let my people go.
    (*Chorus*)
24. I'll tell you what I likes de best,
    Let my people go;
    It is the shouting Methodist,
    Let my people go.
    (*Chorus*)
25. I do believe without a doubt,
    Let my people go;
    That a Christian has the right to shout,
    Let my people go.
    (*Chorus*)

Praise Poems

The spirituals consist of one of the most widespread types of African poetry, the praise poem. Found virtually in all regions of Africa, it extols kings, warriors, distinguished members of society, and the gods.

Short praise poems appear throughout oral heroic epics. For instance, in one poem in Banna Kanute's *Sunjata,* the griots sing of the coming of the hero before his birth by hailing him as "Simbong." In Mandean, the word, which literally means "the hunter's whistle," denotes a great hunter—an honorific title, which Sunjata later bore. Similarly, the Mandingo people pay tribute to the hero in Mamadou Kouyate's version of the epic after he has defeated his formidable foe Sumanguru, and, thus, united the kingdom of Mali. Moreover, in a poem from the epic *Kambili* by the Mandingo griot Seydou Camara, the group of hunters raise the hero Kambili above their shoulders and salute his prowess for killing his archenemy the lion-man Cekura and, thus, resolving the communal crisis.

As *Kambili* also reveals, the Mandean people who are Islamic in faith, often pay homage to Allah. The bard Camara worships the Muslim God, for instance, in the gnomic exordium that precedes the narrative. Allah is also held in reverence in Banna Kanute's *Sunjata.* In this version of the epic, however, the griot refers to Him simply as "God." At one point in the narrative a marabout warns Sumanguru that God's omnipotence will be inherited by Sunjata after his birth.

Examples of longer praise poems can be found among the Yoruba people of Nigeria. They recite *oriki,* or praise poems, honoring their high God, Oludumare, as well as *orisha,* who represent Him on earth. These *oriki* are sung by priests performing religious functions or by professional singers at nonsacred functions.

The New World slaves sang this type of poetry to glorify their God, the God of Freedom, the Great Savior, the omnipotent, omnipresent force who would deliver them from human bondage. They also hailed numerous biblical figures, especially their favorite Old Testament heroes, such as Daniel, Jonah, Joshua, Moses, Noah, and David, who had to overcome tremendous obstacles.

African Prototypes

PRAISE POEMS OF EPIC HEROES

Griot's Praise Song from Banna Kanute's Sunjata

Ah, it is of Jata that I speak, great stock,
Simbong, it is of Jata that I speak, great stock destined for high office.

Mandingo People's Praise Song from Mamadou Kouyate's Sundiata

He has come
And happiness has come
Sundiata is here
And happiness is here.

Hunter's Praise Song from Seydou Camara's Kambili

You have taken us from under the execution sword, Kambili.
You have rescued the hunters,

And saved the farmers,
And saved the whole army.
May Allah not keep you behind.
May Allah not take the breath from you, Kambili.

PRAISE POEMS OF ALLAH

Griot's Praise Poem of Allah from Seydou Camara's Kambili

Almighty Allah may refuse to do something.
Allah is not powerless before anything
Almighty Allah may refuse to do something.
Allah is not powerless before anything

Marabout's Prophecy from Banna Kanute's Sunjata

"Allahu aharu rajaku fa mang kaana kaafa,
Ming mussi, janafang kumfai kuna."
God declares that by his grace,
Whomever he has created king,
He has made in his own likeness,
And nothing will be able to injure that person.
Those things which you must enjoy,
Enjoy them now, before this child is born,
For after he is born,
You will be powerless against him.

Spirituals as Praise Poems

God Is a God

God is a God! God don't never change!
God is a God! An' He always will be God!
He made the sun to shine by day,
He made the sun to show the way,
He made the stars to show their light,
He made the moon to shine by night,
God is a God, God don't never change!
The earth his footstool an' heav'n his throne,
The whole creation all his own,
His love an' power will prevail,
His promise will never fail, saying
God is a God! An' always will be God!

FROM *Didn't My Lord Deliver Daniel*

(*Chorus*) Didn't my Lord deliver Daniel, deliver Daniel, deliver Daniel,
Didn't my Lord deliver Daniel,
An' why not every man.

He delivered Daniel from de lion's den,
Jonah from de belly of de whale,
An' de Hebrew chillun from de fiery furnace,
An' why not every man.
(*Chorus*)

De moon run down in a purple stream,
De sun forbear to shine,
An' every star disappear,
King Jesus shall-a-be mine.
(*Chorus*)

❖❖❖

Joshua Fit de Battle of Jericho

(*Chorus*) Joshua fit de battle of Jericho,
Jericho, Jericho,
Joshua fit de battle of Jericho,
And de walls come tumbling down.

You may talk about yo' king of Gideon,
Talk about yo' man of Saul,
Dere's none like good old Joshua
At de battle of Jericho.
(*Chorus*)

Up de walls of Jericho,
He marched with spear in hand;
"Go blow dem ram horns," Joshua cried,
"Kase de battle am in my hand."
Den de lamb ram sheep horns begin to blow,
Trumpets begin to sound,
Joshua commanded de chillen to shout,
And de walls come tumbling down.

Sermons and Prayers

Other literary forms such as sermons and prayers, in which the spirituals are shaped, also stem from African culture. The genre of the African oral epic can be considered a form of sermonic poetry in that the griot uses his oratorical skills, eloquence, and literary materials, such as religious songs and proverbs, to teach moral lessons and spiritually uplift his people. Often, the bard digresses from the plot of the story, as does the griot Seydou Camara in *Kambili,* to communicate a moral message to his audience directly. At a point in the epic, for example, he reminds the Mandingo people that only through the coming of the holyman, the servant of

Allah, who is the ultimate source of pity, can the people be saved. Also, the African griot interlaces prayers and hymns throughout his epic narration. Kouyate, in *Sundiata,* for example, recites a prayer of Sologon (Sukulung), Sunjata's mother, who gives thanks to Allah for healing the legs of her son. Kouyate's version of the epic also includes the famous short Mandean hymn "Niama," which African linguist N.T. Niane explains "expresses the idea that Sologon's son was the rampart behind which everyone found refuge." According to Niane, Sunjata is compared to Alexander who, in Mandingo tradition, is called "Djoulou Kara Naini." As he further explains, the Mandingo people believe "that Alexander was the second last great conqueror of the world and Sunjata the seventh and last." (*Sundiata,* p. 90.)

Several spirituals also qualify as sermons and prayers. One of the most striking sermons is "Humble Yo'self de Bell Done Ring"; many other songs, including the well-known spiritual "Keep Me From Sinking Down," are prayers to God for guidance, moral strength, and courage.

African Prototypes

SERMONS IN EPIC NARRATIVES

Griot's Sermon from Seydou Camara's Kambili

Ah! The holyman has come. . . .
The man of the Koran has come, Kambili!
Man, the hero is only welcome on trouble days.
It is not good to put aside tradition for one's own pain.
Death may put an end to a man, it does not end his name.
There is no other source of pity beyond Allah.
Hearing the wretched out is better than mine is at home.
Ah! the holyman has come!
The holyman of the Koran has come!

SHORT PRAYERS IN EPIC NARRATIVES

Sogolon's Prayer from Mamadou Kouyate's Sundiata

Oh day, what a beautiful day,
Oh day, day of joy;
Allah Almighty, you never created a finer day,
So my son is going to walk.

SHORT HYMNS IN EPIC NARRATIVES

"Niama" *from Mamadou Kouyate's* Sundiata

Niama, Niama, Niama,
You, you serve as a shelter for all
All come to seek refuge under you,
And as for you, Niama,
Nothing serves you for shelter,
God alone protects you.

Spirituals as Sermons and Prayers

FROM ***Humble Yo'self de Bell Done Ring***

Live-a humble, humble, humble, Lord;
    Humble yo'self, de bell done ring.
Live-a humble, humble, humble Lord;
    Humble yo'self, de bell done ring.
Live-a bell done ring.

(*Chorus*) Glory an' honor! Praise King Jesus!
    Glory an' honor! Praise de Lord!
Glory an' honor! Praise King Jesus!
    Glory an' honor! Praise de Lord!

Oh, my young Christians I got lots for to tell you, Jesus Christ speakin' thro' de organs of de clay.
("One day, one day, Lord!) God's gwine-ter call dem chillun f'om a distant lan'
Tomb-stones a-crackin', graves a-bustin'-Hell an' de sea am gwine-ter give up de dead.
False pretender wears sheep clothin' on his back. In his heart he's like a ravin' wolf.
("Judge ye not, brother,") For ye shall be judged false pretender gittin' in de Christian band.
(*Chorus*)

❖❖❖

Keep Me from Sinking Down

Oh Lord, Oh my Lord!
    Keep me from sinkin' down.
Oh my Lord. Oh my good Lord.
    Keep me from sinkin' down down,
    Keep me from sinkin' down.

I tell you what I mean to do,
    Keep me from sinkin' down.
I mean to go to hebben too.
    Keep me from sinkin' down.

I bless de Lord, I'm gwine to die,
    Keep me from sinkin' down,
I'm gwine to judgement by an' by.
    Keep me from sinkin' down.

Lyrical Poetry

The spirituals embody the lyrical quality of traditional African poetry, which depends on a successful integration of words, music, and the oral performance style of the singer(s) for expression of intense personal emotions and feelings. As critic Isidore Okpewho explains in *The Epic in Africa,* the griot uses repetition of certain words and phrases and a piling up of details as a part of the lyrical act. These features become evident in the chant of the Congolese griot Shekarisi Rurede in *The Mwindo Epic,* which describes the hero Mwindo's magical resuscitation of life and property in a devastated village called Tubondo, and in the lament of the warrior Kanji (Kambili's father) in *Kambili,* which deals with the soothsayer's ill-fated prophecy about his (Kanji's) futile quest for a child. In turn, the New World slaves used extended repetitions of short melodic phrases to build up powerful emotional crescendos in song. Consequently, the spirituals abound with lyrical poetry.

African Prototypes

Griot's Chant from Shekarisi Rurede's The Mwindo Epic

each one who died in pregnancy resuscitated with her pregnancy;
each one who died in labor resuscitated being in labor;
each one who was preparing paste resuscitated stirring paste;
each one who died defecating resuscitated defecating;
each one who died setting up traps resuscitated trapping;
each one who died copulating resuscitated copulating;
each one who died forging resuscitated forging;
each one who died cultivating resuscitated cultivating;
each one who died while making pots and jars resuscitated shaping;
each one who died carving dishes resuscitated carving;
each one who died quarreling with a partner resuscitated quarreling.

Warrior Kanji's Lament from Seydou Camara's Kambili

The Jimini reason-seekers are evil, Imam!
The reason-seekers have gone through my cow herd.
They have gone through the sheep herd.
They have gone through my goat herd.
And gone through my chicken flock.
They have gone through my good gowns.
They have gone through my good hats.
They have gone through my good caps.
And gone through my good pants.

Spirituals as Lyrical Poetry

Were You There When They Crucified My Lord?

1. Were you there when they crucified my Lord?
Were you there when they crucified my Lord?
Oh!—sometimes it causes me to tremble, tremble, tremble,
Were you there when they crucified my Lord?

2. Were you there when they nailed Him to the tree?
Were you there when they nailed Him to the tree?
Oh!—sometimes it causes me to tremble, tremble, tremble,
Were you there when they nailed Him to the tree?

3. Were you there when they pierced Him in the side?
Were you there when they pierced Him in the side?
Oh!—sometimes it causes me to tremble, tremble, tremble,
Were you there when they pierced Him in the side?

4. Were you there when He bowed His head and died?
Were you there when He bowed His head and died?
Oh!—sometimes it causes me to tremble, tremble, tremble,
Were you there when He bowed His head and died?

5. Were you there when the sun refused to shine?
Were you there when the sun refused to shine?
Oh!—sometimes it causes me to tremble, tremble, tremble,
Were you there when the sun refused to shine?

6. Were you there when they laid Him in the tomb?
Were you there when they laid Him in the tomb?
Oh!—sometimes it causes me to tremble, tremble, tremble,
Were you there when they laid Him in the tomb?

Motherless Child

1. Sometimes I feel like a motherless child,
Sometimes I feel like a motherless child,
Sometimes I feel like a motherless child,
A long ways from home,
A long ways from home.

2. Sometimes I feel like I'm almost gone,
Sometimes I feel like I'm almost gone,
Sometimes I feel like I'm almost gone,
A long ways from home,
A long ways from home.

3. Sometimes I feel like a feather in the air,
Sometimes I feel like a feather in the air,
Sometimes I feel like a feather in the air,
And I spread my wings and fly,
I spread my wings and fly.

Improvisations: Theme and Variation, Call and Response, Performance Styles, Rhythms and Melodic Structures

Squarely in African music and poetic traditions, the New World slaves improvised their songs. Functioning much like the African griot, bard, or praise singer, the slave lead singer would extemporize the words of a spiritual or secular song as he or she sang. When the song was sung again, the leader might vary the words or another singer might lead it. This reflects the African musical idiom *theme and variation*, namely, that the songs become altered versions of other songs.

At times, when the slave lead singer would improvise, the chorus would supply a steady, identifying refrain. Frequently, however, slave singers would begin the singing of the choral refrain before the leader concluded his or her lines and the leader might begin his or her next verse lines before the refrain had been sung. Music experts refer to this phenomenon as African antiphony, or *overlapping call and response.*

More than two-thirds of the spirituals are built on the call and response refrain and numerous spirituals have identical formal structures to certain African songs. (See Courlander's illustration of antiphonal patterns in work songs on pages 33–34, which also applies to the spirituals.) Many spirituals reflect the form so common in African music and poetry, the alternation of leading lines and refrain.

This pattern of call and response can clearly be seen in an old African song (An Old Bornu Song) found in Denham and Clapperton's account *Narrative of Travels and Discoveries in Northern and Central Africa in the Years 1822, 1823, & 1824* (1826) and cited by Edward Krehbeil in *Afro-American Folksongs* (1914). It is a song by bards of Bornu in praise of their Sultan.

Within the oral heroic epic, however, the call and response formula appears in a different form. Generally used by the griot to create dialogue between characters, it may be contained in one line or broken up into two. Notwithstanding, in one of the songs in Banna Kanute's *Sunjata,* the bard uses the sounds of the talking drum to respond to the griot's call (see lines 1873–1878).

Also emanating from African tradition is the slaves' singing style, which music historian Eileen Southern in *The Music of Black Americans* insists is "the single most important element of slave music." In African and African American singing styles, the voice functions as a highly tuned musical instrument, stressing its percussive tonalities and placing greater emphasis on timbre and pitch than in European tradition. In performance, the slaves mirrored the style of their African ancestors, which was distinctive for its high musical intensity and use of such special effects as shouts, groans, and rhythmic body movements, such as hand clapping, foot stomping, and body swaying. Correspondingly, they would sustain the steady beat of a song's meter by hand clapping or foot tapping because drums and other percussion instruments used in Africa for this purpose were prohibited to them in America.

The unwavering sense of beat that must be maintained regardless of what else happens in the song is what musicians call *time line,* or *pulse beats.* It is an idiom that marks rhythm as the most striking feature of slave and all other African-derived music and that distinguishes it from European tradition. In its simplest terms, the time line is an African musical structure based on the organic principle of regularly punctuated rhythms of the human pulse that produces a strict and continuous rhythmic pattern or beat or metronomic pulse in song. The pulse beats may sound audibly, as in the spirituals, secular songs, and the later-developed blues, or they may be unsounded, as in jazz music of the twentieth century. "Against the fixed rhythms of the time-line," Southern explains, "the melodies moved freely, producing cross-rhythms that constantly clash with the pulse patterns." Because of this rhythmic complexity, in some of the slave songs, *syncopation* occurs; that is, the shifting of melodic accents from stronger to weaker beats. Other songs become polyrhythmic and polymetered; the melodies move in different rhythmic motions from that of the time line. Furthermore, most of the spirituals and slave music in general are built on duple rhythms as seen in Example XII from J.H. Nketia's *The Music of Africa* (1974) and on the melodic structure of pentatonic scales (musical scales of five notes). The latter structure is also a major characteristic of African music. Eileen Southern provides an example of both musical structures (duple pulse beats and pentatonic scales), which can be seen in the spiritual "Jesus on de Water-Side." The song is polymetered; that is, the melody moves in groupings of three eighth notes against a duple pulse time line. She also uses the spiritual "Nobody Knows de Trouble I've Had" to demonstrate how the slaves might have syncopated the melody against a time line of hand clapping and foot tapping.

African Antiphonal Patterns

An Old Bornu Song

Give flesh to the hyenas at daybreak,
    Oh, the broad spears!
The spear of the Sultan is the broadest,
    Oh, the broad spears!
I behold thee now—I desire to see none other,
    Oh, the broad spears!
My horse is as tall as a high wall,
    Oh, the broad spears!
He will fight against ten—he fears nothing,
    Oh, the broad spears!
He has slain ten—the guns are yet behind,
    Oh, the broad spears!
The elephant of the forest brings me what I want,
    Oh, the broad spears!
Like unto thee, so is the Sultan,
    Oh, the broad spears!
Be brave! Be brave, my friends and kinsmen,
    Oh, the broad spears!
God is great! I wax fierce as a beast of prey,
    Oh, the broad spears!
God is great! Today those I wish for are come,
    Oh, the broad spears!

Antiphonal Patterns in the Spirituals

Lay Dis Body Down

I know moonrise, I know star-rise,
    I lay dis body down.
I walk in de moonlight, I walk in de starlight,
    To lay dis body down.

walk in de graveyard, I walk troo de graveyard,
  To lay dis body down.
lie in de grave an' stretch out my arms,
  I lay dis body down.
go to de jedgment in de evenin' of de day
  When I lay dis body down,
An' my soul an' your soul will meet in de day
  When I lay dis body down.

African Melodic Structures

DUPLE AND TRIPLE RHYTHMS

African rhythmic patterns are controlled by placing them within a *fixed time span.* As J.H. Kwabena Nketia illustrates in the following tables, the time span can be broken up into an equal number of pulses of different densities. It can be divided into two or multiples of two, called *duple rhythms* (Example XII–1), or three or multiples of three, called *triple rhythms* (Example XII–2). As Nketia explains, "the greater the number of divisions, the greater the density of the pulse . . . the greater the number of divisions or pulses, the faster the rhythmic motion." Therefore, in each of the two schemes of pulse structures, the rhythmic tempo ranges from the slowest pulse (a) to the fastest pulse (d).

EXAMPLE XII–1: ***TWO AND MULTIPLES OF TWO: TWO, FOUR, EIGHT, OR SIXTEEN PULSES.***

a.	2 pulses	𝅗𝅥	𝅗𝅥
b.	4 pulses	♩♩	♩♩
c.	8 pulses	♪♪♪♪	♪♪♪♪
d.	16 pulses	𝅘𝅥𝅯𝅘𝅥𝅯𝅘𝅥𝅯𝅘𝅥𝅯𝅘𝅥𝅯𝅘𝅥𝅯𝅘𝅥𝅯𝅘𝅥𝅯	𝅘𝅥𝅯𝅘𝅥𝅯𝅘𝅥𝅯𝅘𝅥𝅯𝅘𝅥𝅯𝅘𝅥𝅯𝅘𝅥𝅯𝅘𝅥𝅯

Source: J.H. Kwabena Nketia, *The Music of Africa* (New York: W.W. Norton, 1974), p. 126.

EXAMPLE XII–2: ***THREE AND MULTIPLES OF THREE: THREE, SIX, TWELVE, OR TWENTY-FOUR PULSES.***

a.	3 pulses	𝅗𝅥	𝅗𝅥	𝅗𝅥
b.	6 pulses	♩♩♩		♩♩♩
c.	12 pulses	♪♪♪♪♪♪		♪♪♪♪♪♪
d.	24 pulses	𝅘𝅥𝅯𝅘𝅥𝅯𝅘𝅥𝅯𝅘𝅥𝅯𝅘𝅥𝅯𝅘𝅥𝅯𝅘𝅥𝅯𝅘𝅥𝅯𝅘𝅥𝅯𝅘𝅥𝅯𝅘𝅥𝅯𝅘𝅥𝅯		𝅘𝅥𝅯𝅘𝅥𝅯𝅘𝅥𝅯𝅘𝅥𝅯𝅘𝅥𝅯𝅘𝅥𝅯𝅘𝅥𝅯𝅘𝅥𝅯𝅘𝅥𝅯𝅘𝅥𝅯𝅘𝅥𝅯𝅘𝅥𝅯

Source: J.H. Kwabena Nketia, *The Music of Africa* (New York: W.W. Norton 1974), p. 126.

Melodic Structures in the Spirituals

AN EXAMPLE OF DUPLE RHYTHMS AND THE PENTATONIC SCALE

Jesus on de Water-Side,

FROM *SLAVE SONGS OF THE UNITED STATES*

Source: Eileen Southern, *The Music of Black Americans,* 2nd ed. (New York: W.W. Norton 1983), p. 193.

AN EXAMPLE OF A SYNCOPATED MELODY WITH HAND CLAPPING AND FOOT TAPPING

Nobody Knows de Trouble I've Had

FROM *SLAVE SONGS OF THE UNITED STATES*

2. I pick de berry and I suck de juice, O yes, Lord!
   Just as sweet as the honey in de comb, O yes, Lord!
3. Sometimes I'm up, sometimes I'm down,
   Sometimes I'm almost on de groun'.
4. What make ole Satan hate me so?
   Because he got me once and he let me go.

Source: Eileen Southern, *The Music of Black Americans,* 2nd ed. (New York: W.W. Norton 1983), p. 195.

A Spiritual Composed by Richard Allen

1. Good morning brother Pilgrim, what marching to Zion,
What doubts and what dangers have you met to-day,
Have you found a blessing, are your joys increasing?
Press forward my brother and make no delay;
Is your heart a-glowing, are your comforts a-flowing,
And feel you an evidence, now bright and clear;
Feel you a desire that burns like a fire,
And longs for the hour that Christ shall appear.

2. I came out this morning, and now am returning,
Perhaps little better than when I first came,
Such groaning and shouting, it sets me to doubting,
I fear such religion is only a dream:
The preachers were stamping, the people were jumping,
And screaming so loud that I neither could hear,
Either praying or preaching, such horrible screaching,
'Twas truly offensive to all that were there?

3. Perhaps my dear brother, while they pray'd together,
You sat and consider'd and prayed not at all,
Would you find a blessing, then pray without ceasing,
Obey the command that was given by Paul,
For if you should reason at any such season,
No wonder if Satan should tell in your ears,
The preachers and people they are but a rabble,
And this is no place for reflection and pray'rs.

4. No place for reflection, I'm fill'd with distraction,
I wonder that people could bear for to stay,
The men they were bawling, the women were squaling,
I know not for my part how any could pray;
Such horrid confusion, if this be religion,
Sure 'tis something new that never was seen,
For the sacred pages that speak of all ages,
Does no where declare that such ever has been.

5. Don't be so soon shaken, if I'm not mistaken,
Such things have been acted by christians of old,
When the ark was a-coming, King David came running,
And dancing before it by scripture we're told,
When the Jewish nation had laid the foundation,
And rebuilt the temple at Ezra's command,
Some wept and some prais'd, and such a noise there was rais'd,
It was heard afar off, perhaps all through the land.

6. And as for the preacher, Ezekiel the teacher,
Was taught for to stamp and to smite with his hand,
To shew the transgression of that wicked nation,

That they might repent and obey the command.
For scripture quotation in the dispensation,
The blessed Redeemer had handed them out,
If these cease from praying, we hear him declaring,
The stones to reprove him would quickly cry out.

7. The scripture is wrested, for Paul hath protested,
That order should be kept in the houses of God,
Amidst such a clatter who knows what they're after,
Or who can attend to what is declared;
To see them behaving like drunkards a-raving,
And lying and rolling prostrate on the ground,
I really felt awful and sometimes was fearful,
That I'd be the next that would come tumbling down.

8. You say you felt awful, you ought to be careful,
Least you grieve the Spirit and make it depart,
For from your expressions you felt some impressions,
The sweet melting showers has tender'd your heart;
You fear persecution, and that's the delusion,
Brought in by the devil to turn you away;
Be careful my brother, for bless'd is no other,
Than creatures who are not offended in me.

9. When Peter was preaching, and boldly was teaching,
The way of salvation in Jesus' name,
The spirit descended and some were offended,
And said of the men they were fill'd with new wine.
I never yet doubted but some of them shouted,
While others lay prostrate by power struck down,
Some weeping, some praying, while others were saying,
They are as drunk as fools, or in falsehood abound.

10. Our time is a-flying, our moments a-dying,
We are led to improve them and quickly appear,
For the bless'd hour when Jesus in power,
In glory shall come is now drawing near,
Methinks there will be shouting, and I'm not doubting,
But crying and screaming for mercy in vain:
Therefore my dear Brother, let's now pray together,
That your precious soul may be fill'd with the flame.

11. Sure praying is needful, I really feel awful,
I fear that my day of repentance is past;
But I will look to the Saviour, his mercies for ever,
These storms of temptation will not always last,
I look for the blessing and pray without ceasing,
His mercy is sure unto all that believe,
My heart is a glowing, I feel his love flowing,
Peace, comfort, and pardon, I now have received.

Folktales

The African tales most noted to be imported to the New World with only slight alterations are the animal trickster tales, those of the hare, the tortoise, and the Tar Baby story. In the slaves' world, the wily trickster African Hare became the ever popular Bre'r Rabbit, while the cunning African Tortoise became T'appin (Terrapin), the America Turtle. Based on the African archetypal pattern, the trickster would manipulate the larger animal(s) not only for obtaining food or mere survival but also for all of the other human cravings—power, status, wealth, and sexual prowess. Moreover, the Ewe story "Why the Hare Runs Away" contains the basic elements of the Tar Baby tales. In the popular version of the slaves' tale referred to simply as "Tar Baby," Rabbit suffers from the same fate as the Ewe Hare: He becomes stuck to the tar baby built by the other animals he has attempted to dupe. Thus, common also in African tradition, the trickster often proves to be as cruel and merciless as his or her stronger opponent.

Other tales believed to have circulated during slavery and in the decades that followed focused on the idea of flying Africans. Such tales recount the belief in the ability of native-born Africans brought to the United States to call on a special African-derived power, lift up from the burden of slavery, and return to Africa. Even for those who did not believe in the reality of the tale, the myth, nonetheless, served a purpose: It suggested that African Americans could be bound in body and weighed down in chains, but their spirits could never be enslaved by those unscrupulous individuals who had no respect for them or for their culture.

Another source of slave folktales and beliefs that originated during slavery and continued in the decades after the Civil War centered on conjuration. A system of belief in Dahomey and Haiti, but reduced to a system of magic when it entered the United States through New Orleans in 1809, hoodoo (changed to voodoo outside the United States) became a way for African Americans to try to equalize the imbalance of power in their world. The system depended on belief (and not many slave masters believed, which is one explanation for conjure not affecting slave masters) and it contained elaborate processes by which one could be conjured, the ways in which such conjurings could be divined, and the means by which the conjured person could be cured.

Belief in conjuration was common during slavery, for both the slaves and the masters. Indeed, for those few masters who did believe, there are stories of conjurers on the plantations with whom they were afraid to interfere and whom they refrained from punishing. One scheme involved placing coffins outside the doors of slave cabins in an effort to prevent the movement of blacks between plantations at night.

Slave masters and slaves found something that was both frightening and attractive in the conjure, ghost, and haunt tales of intrigue and mysterious forces. The tales reflect how black people could attempt to influence the forces that made them feel powerful, and they also show how these forces could be both beneficial and harmful. The fact that these tales were circulated throughout slavery and are still being circulated reveals the vibrancy of an oral form that documents to some degree the circumstances in which African Americans lived and, to some extent, still live. More important, the tales exhibit the creativity in storytelling that has been and continues to be a trademark of African American culture.

African Folktales

Animal Trickster Tales

The Elephant and the Tortoise

Two beings, Elephant and Rain, had a dispute. Elephant said, "If you say that you nourish me, in what way is it that you do so?" Rain answered, "If you say that I do not nourish you, when I go away, will you not die?" And Rain then departed.

Elephant said, "Vulture! Cast lots to make rain for me!" Vulture said, "I will not cast lots."

Then Elephant said to Crow, "Cast lots!" and Crow answered, "Give the things with which I may cast lots." Crow cast lots and rain fell. It rained at the lagoons, but then they dried up, and only one lagoon remained.

Elephant went hunting. There was, however, Tortoise, to whom Elephant said, "Tortoise, remain at the water!" Thus Tortoise was left behind when Elephant went hunting.

There came Giraffe, and said to Tortoise, "Give me water!" Tortoise answered, "The water belongs to Elephant."

There came Zebra, who said to Tortoise, "Give me water!" Tortoise answered, "The water belongs to Elephant."

There came Gemsbok, and said to Tortoise, "Give me water!" Tortoise answered, "The water belongs to Elephant."

There came Wildebeest, and said, "Give me water!" Tortoise said, "The water belongs to Elephant."

There came Roodebok, and said to Tortoise, "Give me water!" Tortoise answered, "The water belongs to Elephant."

There came Springbok, and said to Tortoise, "Give me water!" Tortoise said, "The water belongs to Elephant."

There came Jackal, and said to Tortoise, "Give me water!" Tortoise said, "The water belongs to Elephant."

There came Lion, and said, "Little Tortoise, give me water!" When little Tortoise was about to say something, Lion got hold of it and beat it. Lion drank of the water, and since then all the animals drink water.

When Elephant came back from the hunting, he said, "Little Tortoise, where is the water?" Tortoise answered, "The animals have drunk the water." Elephant asked, "Little Tortoise, shall I chew you or swallow you down?" Little Tortoise said, "Swallow me, if you please," and Elephant swallowed it whole.

After Elephant had swallowed Tortoise, and it had entered his body, it tore off his liver, heart, and kidneys. Elephant said, "Little Tortoise, you kill me."

So Elephant died. But little Tortoise came out of his dead body and went wherever it liked.

[Hottentot]

Why the Hare Runs Away

This is a story of the hare and the other animals.

The dry weather was drying up the earth into hardness. There was no dew. The creatures of the water even suffered from thirst. Soon famine came, and, the animals having nothing to eat, assembled in council.

"What shall we do," said they, "to keep ourselves from dying of thirst?" And they deliberated a long time.

At last it was decided that each animal should cut off the tips of its ears, and extract the fat from them. Then all the fat should be collected and sold, and with the money they would get for the fat, they would buy a hoe and dig a well, so as to get some water.

And all cried, "It is well. Let us cut off the tips of our ears."

They did so, but when it came to the turn of the hare to cut off the tips of his ears, he refused.

The other animals were astonished, but they said nothing. They took up the ears, extracted the fat, went and sold all, and bought a hoe with the money.

They brought back the hoe and began to dig a well in the dry bed of a lagoon. "Ha! here is water at last. At last we can slake our thirst a little."

The hare was not there, but when the sun was in the middle of the sky, he took a calabash, and went towards the well.

As he walked along, the calabash dragged on the ground and made a great noise. It said—"Chan-gañ-gañ-gañ—Chan-gañ-gañ-gañ."[1]

The animals, who were watching by the lagoon, heard this noise. They were frightened. They asked each other, "What is it?" Then as the noise kept coming nearer, they ran away.

Reaching home, they said there was something terrible at the lagoon, that had put to flight the watchers by the lagoon.

Then all the animals by the lagoon were gone. The hare drew up water without interference. Then he went down into the well and bathed, so that the water was muddied.

When the next day came, all the animals ran to take water, and they found it muddied.

"Oh," they cried, "who has spoiled our well?"

Saying this, they went and took an image. Then made bird-lime and smeared it over the image.

Then, when the sun was again in the middle of the sky, all the animals went and hid in the bush near the well.

The hare came. His calabash cried, "Chan-gañ-gañ-gañ, Chan-gañ-gañ-gañ." He approached the image. He never suspected that all the animals were hidden in the bush.

The hare saluted the image. The image said nothing. He saluted again, and still the image said nothing.

"Take care," said the hare, "or I will give you a slap."

He gave a slap, and his right hand remained fixed in the bird-lime. He slapped with his left hand, and that remained fixed also.

"Oh! oh!" cried he, "let us kick with our feet."

He kicked with his feet. The feet remained fixed, and the hare could not get away.

Then the animals ran out of the bush, and came to see the hare and his calabash.

"Shame, shame, oh! hare," they cried together. "Did you not agree with us to cut off the tips of your ears, and, when it came to your turn, did you not refuse? What! you refused, and yet you come to muddy our water?"

They took whips, they fell upon the hare, and they beat him. They beat him so that they nearly killed him.

"We ought to kill you, accursed hare," they said. "But, no—run."

They let him go, and the hare fled. Since then, he does not leave the grass.

[1]Gañ-gañ (ñ, highly nasal) is a drum.

Slave Folktales

Animal Trickster Tales

Rabbit Teaches Bear a Song

Br'er Rabbit. . . . This rabbit an' Bear goin' to see a Miss Reyford's daughter. N'Br'er Rabbit been killin' Miss Reyford's hogs. Miss Reyford didn't know he was killin' her hogs. She said to him, "If you tell me who been killin' my hogs I'll give you my daughter." N' so he said he'd go an' find out. He went to Mr. Bear an' said, "They's some ladies down here an' they're givin' a social. Y'know, you have a wonderful voice, an' they want you to sing a bass solo." So Bear he felt real proud an' he said, "All right." So Rabbit said, "I'm gonna try to train your voice. Now you just listen to me an' do everything I tell you." So Bear said, "All right." So Rabbit said, "Now I'm gonna sing a song. Listen to me. When I say these lines:

"Who killed Mr. Reyford's hogs,
Who killed Mr. Reyford's hogs?"

you just sing back:

"Nobody but me."

So Br'er Rabbit started singing:

"Who killed Mr. Reyford's hogs,
Who killed Mr. Reyford's hogs?"

Then Bear answered back:

"Nobody but me."

Rabbit said, "That's right, Br'er Bear, that's fine. My, but you got one fine voice." So ol' Bear he felt real good, 'cause Rabbit flatterin' him, tellin' him that his voice was such a wonderful one. So they went up there to Miss Reyford's party an' pretty soon Rabbit an' Bear commence to sing. Rabbit sang:

"Who killed Mr. Reyford's hogs,
Who killed Mr. Reyford's hogs?"

an' Bear sang out:

"Nobody but me."

So Mr. Reyford shot Bear. Then Rabbit said to Miss Reyford, "I told you Mr. Bear killed your hogs." Bear said to Rabbit, "All right, I'll git you." Ol' Rabbit jes' grin. So later Bear caught him n' tol' him he was gonna kill him. So Rabbit said, "Please don't kill me, please don't kill me." So Rabbit said he'd show him some honey. So Rabbit carried Bear to some honey. He said, "Here's the honey." The bees started on Bear an' Bear started hollerin', but Rabbit he yelled, "Taint nothin' but the briars, 'taint nothin' but the briars." So Bear got killed by the bees.

T'appin (Terrapin)[1]

It was famine time an' T'appin had six chillun. Eagle hide behin' cloud an' he went crossed de ocean an' go gittin' de palm oil; got de seed to feed his chillun wid it. T'appin see it, say "hol' on, it har' time. Where you git all dat to feed your t'ree chillun? I got six chillun, can't you show me wha' you git all dat food?" Eagle say, "No, I had to fly 'cross de ocean to git dat." T'appin say, "Well, gimme some o' you wings an' I'll go wid you." Eagle say, "A' right. When shall we go?" T'appin say, "Morrow mornin' by de firs' cock crow." So 'morrow came but T'appin didn' wait till mornin'. T'ree 'clock in de mornin' T'appin come in fron' Eagle's house say, "Cuckoo—cuckoo—coo." Eagle say, "Oh, you go home. Lay down. 'Taint day yit." But he kep' on, "Cuckoo—cuckoo—coo." An bless de Lor' Eagle got out, say, "Wha' you do now?" T'appin say, "You put t'ree wings on this side an' t'ree on udda side." Eagle pull out six feathers an' put t'ree on one side an' t'ree on de udda. Say, "Fly, le's see." So T'appin commence to fly. One o' de wings fall out. But T'appin said, "Da's all right, I got de udda wings. Le's go." So dey flew an' flew; but when dey got over de ocean all de eagle wings fell out. T'appin about to fall in de water. Eagle went out an' ketch him. Put him under his wings. T'appin say, "Gee it stink here." Eagle let him drop in ocean. So he went down, down, down to de underworl'. De king o' de underworl' meet him. He say, "Why you come here? Wha' you doin' here?" T'appin say, "King, we in te'bul condition on de earth. We can't git nothin' to eat. I got six chillun an' I can't git nothin' to eat for dem. Eagle he on'y got t'ree an' he go 'cross de ocean an' git all de food he need. Please gimme sumpin' so I kin feed my chillun." King say, "A' right, a' right," so he go an' give T'appin a dipper. He say to T'appin, "Take dis dipper. When you want food for your chillun say:

Bakon coleh
Bakon cawbey
Bakon cawhubo lebe lebe."

So T'appin carry it home an' go to de chillun. He say to dem, "Come here." When dey all come he say:

Bakon coleh
Bakon cawbey
Badon cawhubo lebe lebe.

Gravy, meat, biscuit, ever'ting in de dipper. Chillun got plenty now. So one time he say to de chillun, "Come here. Dis will make my fortune. I'll sell dis to de King." So he showed de dipper to de King. He say:

Bakon coleh
Bakon cawbey
Bakon cawhubo lebe lebe.

Dey got somet'ing. He feed ev'ryone. So de King went off, he call ev'ryboda. Pretty soon ev'ryboda eatin'. So dey ate an' ate, ev'ryt'ing, meats, fruits, all like dat. So he took his dipper an' went back home. He say, "Come, chillun." He try to feed his chillun; nothin' came. (You got a pencil dere, ain't you?) When it's out it's out. So T'appin say, "Aw right, I'm going back

[1]Told by Cugo Lewis, Plateau, Alabama. Brought to America from West Coast Africa, 1859.

to de King an' git him to fixa dis up." So he went down to de underworl' an' say to de King, "King, wha' de matter? I can't feeda my chillun no mora." So de King say to him, "You take dis cow hide an' when you want somepin' you say:

> Sheet n oun
> n-jacko
> nou o quaako.

So T'appin went off an' he came to cross roads. Den he said de magic:

> Sheet n oun
> n-jacko
> nou o quaako.

De cowhide commence to beat um. It beat, beat. Cowhide said, "Drop, drop." So T'appin droup an' de cowhide stop beatin'. So he went home. He called his chillun in. He gim um de cowhide an' tell dem what to say, den he went out. De chillun say:

> Sheet n oun
> n-jacko
> nou o quaako.

De cowhide beat de chillun. It say, "Drop, drop." Two chillun dead an' de others sick. So T'appin say, "I will go to de King." He calls de King, he call all de people. All de people came. So before he have de cowhide beat, he has a mortar made an' gits in dere an' gits all covered up. Den de King say:

> Sheet n-oun
> n-jacko
> nou o quaako.

So de cowhide beat, beat. It beat ev'ryboda, beat de King too. Dat cowhide beat, beat, beat right t'roo de mortar wha' was T'appin an' beat marks on his back, an' da's why you never fin' T'appin in a clean place, on'y under leaves or a log.

Tar Baby

Rabbit says to himself, "Gee, it's gittin' dry here; can't git any mo' water. Git a little in the mornin' but that ain't enough." So he goes along an' gits the gang to dig a well. So the Fox goes roun' an' calls all the animals together to dig this well. He gits Possum, Coon, Bear, an' all the animals an' they start to dig the well. So they come to Rabbit to help. Rabbit he sick. They say, "Come on, Brother Rabbit, help dig this well; we all need water." Rabbit say, "Oh the devil, I don't need no water; I kin drink dew." So he wouldn't go. So when the well was done Rabbit he was the first one to git some of the water. He went there at night an' git de water in jugs. The other animals see Rabbit's tracks from gittin' water in jugs. So all the animals git together an' see what they goin' to do about Brother Rabbit. So Bear say, "I tell you, I'll lay here an' watch for it. I'll ketch that Rabbit." So Bear watched but Rabbit was too fast for him. So Fox said, "I tell you, let's study a plan to git Brother Rabbit." So they all sit together an' study a plan. So they made a tar baby an' put it up by the well. So Brother Rabbit come along to git some water. He see the tar baby an' think it is Brother Bear. He say, "Can't git any water tonight; there's Brother Bear layin' for me." He looked some more, then he said, "No, that ain't Brother Bear, he's too little for Brother Bear." So he goes up to the tar baby an' say, "Whoo-oo-oo-oo." Tar Baby didn't move. So Rabbit got skeered. He sneaked up to it an' said, "Boo!" Tar Baby didn't move. Then Rabbit run all aroun' an' stood still to see did he move. But Tar Baby kept still. Then he moved his claw at him. Tar Baby stood still. Rabbit said, "That must be a chunk o' wood." He went up to see if it was a man. He said, "Hello, old man, hello, old man, what you doin' here?" The man didn't answer, He said again, "Hello, old man, hello, old man, what you doin' here?" The man didn't answer. Rabbit said, "Don't you hear me talkin' to you? I'll slap you in the face." The man ain't said nothin'. So Rabbit hauled off sure enough an' his paw stuck. Rabbit said, "Turn me loose, turn me loose or I'll hit you with the other paw." The man ain't said nothin'. So Rabbit hauled off with his other paw an' that one stuck too. Rabbit said, "You better turn me loose, I'll kick you if you don't turn me loose." Tar Baby didn't say anything. "Bup!" Rabbit kicked Tar

Baby an' his paw stuck. So he hit him with the other an' that one got stuck. Rabbit said, "I know the things got blowed up now; I know if I butt you I'll kill you." So all the animals were hidin' in the grass watchin' all this. They all ran out an' hollered, "Aha, we knowed we was gonna ketch you, we knowed we was gonna ketch you." So Rabbit said, "Oh, I'm so sick." So the animals said, "Whut we gonna do?" So they has a great meetin' to see what they gonna do. So someone said, "Throw him in the fire." But the others said, "No, that's too good; can't let him off that easy." So Rabbit pleaded an' pleaded, "Oh, please, please throw me into the fire." So someone said, "Hang him." They all said, "He's too light, he wouldn't break his own neck." So a resolution was drawed up to burn him up. So they all went to Brother Rabbit an' said, "Well, today you die. We gonna set you on fire." So Rabbit said, "Aw, you couldn't give me anything better." So they all say, "We better throw him in the briar patch." Rabbit cry out right away, "Oh, for God's sake, don't do dat. They tear me feet all up; they tear me behind all up; they tear me eyes out." So they pick him up an' throw him in the briar patch. Rabbit run off an' cry, "Whup-pee, my God, you couldn't throw me in a better place! There were my mammy born me, in the briar patch."

Tales of Flying Africans[1]

Two Tales

I

Prince [Sneed] proved to be an interesting talker, much of his knowledge having been gleaned from conversations by the fireside with his grandfather. The following narrative was still fresh in his memory:

"Muh gran say ole man Waldburg down on St. Catherine own some slabes wut wuzn climatize an he wuk um hahd an one day dey wuz hoein in duh fiel an duh dribuh come out an two ub um wuz unuh a tree in duh shade, an duh hoes wuz wukin by demsef. Duh dribuh say 'Wut dis?' an dey say, 'Kum buba yali kum buba tambe, Kum kunka yali kum kunka tambe,' quick like. Den dey rise off duh groun an fly away. Nobody ebuh see um no mo. Some say dey fly back tuh Africa. Muh gran see dat wid he own eye."

II

We asked the old man [Wallace Quatermain] if he remembered any slaves that were real Africans.

"Sho I membuhs lots ub um. Ain I sees plenty ub um? I membuhs one boatload uh seben aw eight wut come down frum Savannah. Dat wuz jis a lill befo duh waw. Robbie McQueen wuz African an Katie an ole man Jacob King, dey's all African. I membuhs um all. Ole man King he lib till he ole, lib till I hep bury um. But yuh caahn unduhstan much wut deze people say. Dey caahn unduhstan yo talk as you caahn unduhstan dey talk. Dey go 'quack, quack, quack,' jis as fas as a hawse kin run, an muh pa say, 'Ain no good tuh lissen tuh um.' Dey git long all right but yuh know dey wuz a lot ub um wut ain stay down yuh."

Did he mean the Ibos on St. Simons who walked into the water?

"No, ma'am, I ain mean dem. Ain yuh heah bout um? Well, at dat time Mr. Blue he wuz duh obuhseeuh an Mr. Blue put um in duh fiel, but he couldn do nuttn wid um. Dey gabble, gabble, gabble, an nobody couldn unduhstan um an dey didn know how tuh wuk right. Mr. Blue he go down one mawnin wid a long whip fuh tuh whip um good."

"Mr. Blue was a hard overseer?" we asked.

"No, ma'am, he ain hahd, he jis caahn make um unduhstan. Dey's foolish actin. He got tuh

---

[1]Source: Told by Mrs. Josie Jordan in B.A. Botkin, ed., *Lay My Burden Down: A Folk History of Slavery* (Chicago: University of Chicago Press, 1945) pp. 4–5. This volume contains excerpts from the Slave Narrative Collection of the Federal Writers' Project, collected during the 1930s.

These tales are two of more than two dozen variants recorded in *Drums and Shadows: Survival Studies among the Georgia Coastal Negroes* (Athens: University of Georgia Press, 1940), pp. 78–79, 150–151.

whip um, Mr. Blue, he ain hab no choice. Anyways, he whip um good an dey gits tuhgedduh an stick duh hoe in duh fiel an den say 'quack, quack, quack,' an dey riz up in duh sky an tun hesef intuh buzzuds an fly right back tuh Africa."

At this, we exclaimed and showed our astonishment.

"Wut, you ain heah bout um? Ebrybody know bout um. Dey sho lef duh hoe stannin in duh fiel and dey riz right up an fly right back tuh Africa."

Had Wallace actually seen this happen, we asked.

"No, ma'am, I ain seen um. I bin tuh Skidaway, but I knowd plenty wut did see um, plenty wut wuz right deah in duh fiel wid um an seen duh hoe wut dey lef stickin up attuh dey done fly way."

Conjure Tales

Two Tales from Eatonville, Florida[1]

I

Aunt Judy Cox was Old Man Massey's rival. She thought so anyway. Massey laughed at the very thought, but things finally got critical. She began to boast about being able to "throw back" his work on him. They had quit speaking.

One evening before sundown, Aunt Judy went fishing. That was something strange. She never fished. But she made her grandchildren fix her up a bait pole and a trout pole and set out to Blue Sink alone.

When it got good and dark and she did not come home, her folks got bothered about her. Then one of the village men said he had heard a woman cry out as he passed along the road near the lake. So they went to look for her.

They found her lying in the lake in shallow water having a hard time holding her old neck above the water for so long a time. She couldn't get up. So they lifted her and carried her home. A large alligator was lying beside her, but dived away when the lantern flashed in his face.

Aunt Judy said that she hadn't wanted to go fishing to begin with, but that something had commanded her to go. She couldn't help herself. She had fished until the sun got very low; she started to come home, but somehow she couldn't, even though she was afraid to be down on the lake after dark. Furthermore, she was afraid to walk home when she couldn't see well for fear of snakes. *But she couldn't leave the lake.* When it was finally dark, she said some force struck her like lightning and threw her into the water. She screamed and called for help, holding her head above the water by supporting the upper part of her body with her hands.

Then the whole surface of the lake lit up with a dull blue light with a red path across it, and Old Man Massey walked to her upon the lake and thousands upon thousands of alligators swam along on each side of him as he walked down this red path of light to where she was and spoke.

"Hush!" he commanded. "Be quiet, or I'll make an end of you right now."

She hushed. She was too scared to move her tongue. Then he asked her: "Where is all that power you make out you got? I brought you to the lake and made you stay here till I got ready for you. I throwed you in, and you can't come out till I say so. When you acknowledge to yourself that I am your top-superior, then you can come out the water. I got to go about my business, but I'm going to leave a watchman, and the first time you holler he'll tear you to pieces. The minute you change your mind—I'll send help to you."

He vanished and the big 'gator slid up beside her. She didn't know how long she had been in the water, but it seemed hours. But she made up her mind to give up root-working all together before she was rescued. The doctor from Orlando said that she had had a stroke. She recovered to the point where she crept about her

---

[1]Source: Zora Neale Hurston, "Hoodoo in America: Conjure Stories," *Journal of American Folk Lore* 44(1931), 404–405.

yard and garden, but she never did any more "work."

II

But Aunt Judy was not unsung. The people had not forgotten how she fixed Horace Carter.

Horace was a husband eternally searching for love outside his home. He spent every cent he could rake and scrape on his clothes, on hair pomades and walking sticks, and the like.

When he brutally impressed his wife with the fact that there was nothing, absolutely nothing she could do about it, she said to him one Sunday in desperation: "Horace, if you don't mind your ways I'm going to take your case to Aunt Judy."

He laughed, "Tell her, sell her; turn her up and smell her." He went on about his business.

She did tell Aunt Judy and it is said she laid a hearing on Mr. Horace. He had a new suit in the post office. (It is customary to order clothes C.O.D. from mail-order houses, and they remain in the post office until paid out.) He was bragging about how swell he would look in it. An out-of-town girl was coming over the first Sunday after he got his suit out to help him switch it around. That was the next Sunday after he had laughed at his wife and Aunt Judy.

So he got his suit out. He had a hat, shoes and everything to match.

He put the suit on and strolled over to the depot to meet the train, but before it came he took sick. He seemed to be vomiting so violently that it was running out of his nose as well as his mouth. His clothes were ruined and a great swarm of flies followed him. Before he could reach home, it was discovered that he was defecating through his mouth and nose. This kept up, off and on, for six months. He couldn't tell when it would start, nor stop. So he kept himself hidden most of the time.

Aunt Judy said, "The dirty puppy! I'll show him how to talk under *my* clothes! Turn me up and smell me, hunh? I'll turn *him* up, and they'll sho smell him."

They say he paid her to take it off him after a while.

Voodoo, Ghost, and Haunt Tales

Voodoo and Witches

"I don't believe in no hoodoo at all," declared Bongy Jackson. "One time one of my nephews got into police trouble and a woman come to my house and say if I pay her she could help me with hoodoo. I give that woman some of my money and the best ham we have in the smokehouse and she give me a paper with some writing on it and some kind of powder in it and somethin' what looked like a root dried up. She told me to send 'em to that boy and tell him to chew the root in the courtroom durin' his trial and to hold the piece of paper in his hand and to spit on it now and then when the judge wasn't lookin'. I did all that and he did all that and that boy go to jail just the same. No, I don't believe in no hoodoo."

"I never seen a witch," admitted Rebecca Fletcher, "but my Grandma knew lots of 'em and she done tol' me plenty times what they looks like. My Grandma told me about a witch that went into a good woman's house when that woman was in bed. That woman knowed she was a witch so she told her to go into the other room. Ole witch went out and lef' her skin layin' on the floor and the woman jumped out of bed and sprinkled it wit' salt and pepper. Old witch come back put on her skin. She start hollerin' and jumpin' up and down like she was crazy. She yelled and yelled. She yelled, 'I can't stand it! I can't stand it! Something's bitin' me!' Ole witch hollered, 'Skin, don't you know me?' She said this three times, but the salt and pepper keep bitin'. The woman took a broomstick and shooed that old witch right out and she disappeared in the air."

The Headless Hant

A man and his wife was going along the big road. It was cold and the road was muddy and sticky red, and their feet was mighty nigh froze off, and they was hungry, and it got pitch dark before they got where they was going.

'Twan't long before they came to a big fine house with smoke coming outen the chimley and a fire shining through the winder. It was the kin of a house rich folks lives in, so they went round to the back door and knocked on the back porch. Somebody say, "Come in!" They went in but they didn't see nobody.

They looked all up and down and all round, but still they didn't see nobody. They saw the fire on the hearth with the skillets setting in it all ready for supper to be cooked in 'em. They saw there was meat and flour and lard and salsody and a pot of beans smoking and a rabbit a-biling in a covered pot.

Still they didn't see nobody, but they saw everything was ready for somebody. The woman took off her wet shoes and stockings to warm her feet at the fire, and the man took the bucket and lit out for the springhouse to get fresh water for the coffee. They 'lowed they was going to have them brown beans and that molly cottontail and that cornbread and hot coffee in three shakes.

The woman was toasting her feet when right through the shut door in walks a man and he don't have no head. He had on his britches and his shoes and his galluses and his vest and his coat and his shirt and his collar, but he don't have no head. Jes raw neck and bloody stump.

And he started to tell the woman, without no mouth to tell her with, how come he happened to come in there that a-way. She mighty nigh jumped outen her skin, but she said, "What in the name of the Lord do you want?" So he said he's in awful misery, being dead and buried in two pieces. He said somebody kilt him for his money and took him to the cellar and buried him in two pieces, his head in one place and his corpse in 'nother. He said them robbers dug all round trying to find his money, and when they didn't find it they went off and left him in two pieces, so now he hankers to be put back together so's to get rid of his misery.

Then the hant said some other folks had been there and asked him what he wanted but they didn't say in the name of the Lord, and 'cause she did is how come he could tell her 'bout his misery.

'Bout that time the woman's husband came back from the springhouse with the bucket of water to make coffee with and set the bucket on the shelf before he saw the hant. Then he saw the hant with the bloody joint of his neck sticking up and he come nigh jumping outen his skin.

Then the wife told the hant who her husband is, and the hant begun at the start and told it all over agin 'bout how come he is the way he is. He told 'em if they'd come down into the cellar and find his head and bury him all in one grave he'd make 'em rich.

They said they would and that they'd get a torch.

The hant said, "Don't need no torch." And he went up to the fire and stuck his front finger in it and it blazed up like a lightwood knot and he led the way down to the cellar by the light.

They went a long way down steps before they came to the cellar. Then the hant say, "Here's where my head's buried and over here's where the rest of me's buried. Now yo' all dig right over yonder where I throw this spot of light and dig till you touch my barrels of gold and silver money."

So they dug and dug and sure 'nough they found the barrels of money he'd covered up with the thick cellar floor. Then they dug up the hant's head and histed the thing on the spade. The hant jes reached over and picked the head offen the spade and put it on his neck. Then he took off his burning finger and stuck it in a candlestick on a box, and still holding on his head, he crawled back into the hole that he had come out of.

And from under the ground they heard him a-saying, "Yo' all can have my land, can have my house, can have all my money and be as rich as I was, 'cause you buried me in one piece together, head and corpse."

Then they took the candlestick blazing with the hant's finger and went back upstairs and washed themselves with lye soap. Then the woman made up the cornbread with the spring water and greased the skillet with hogmeat and put in the hoecake and lifted the lid on with the tongs and put coals on fire on top of the lid and round the edges of the skillet, and cooked the hoecake done. Her man put the coffee and water in the pot and set it on the trivet to boil. Then they et that supper of them beans and that rabbit and that hoecake and hot coffee. And they lived there all their lives and had barrels of money to buy vittels and clothes with. And they never heard no more 'bout the man that came upstairs without no head where his head ought to be.

RESPONSE: BLACK LITERARY DECLARATIONS OF INDEPENDENCE

Poetry, Slave Narratives, Letters, Essays, and Oratory

VOICES OF SLAVE POETS

JUPITER HAMMON
(1711–1806?)

To celebrate the birth of Christ, a middle-aged slave by the name of Jupiter Hammon gave birth to formal African American literature with his poetic publication, "An Evening Thought: Salvation by Christ, with Penetential Cries" (1760). Unlike Wheatley, Equiano, Hall, and others among his African American contemporaries, Jupiter Hammon, the often-disregarded forefather of African American literature, was fittingly born in the *new* American colonies on October 17, 1711, at the Lloyd plantation in Oyster Bay, Long Island, New York. Hammon, who was a slave in New York all of his life, was almost fifty years old before he was able to publish his first poem, "An Evening Thought," on December 25, 1760. The life of a slave in New England in the eighteenth century was just as much an incessant crucible as the life of a slave in the South in the nineteenth century. The strict and oppressive class division in the master-slave relationships, the white colonists' peculiar disdain for African identity and especially for black skin, and the owners' complete and daily involvement in the nefarious slave trade were all equal hallmarks of slavery in both historical arenas. The fact that not one nineteenth-century slave in the American South was able to even publish his or her own writings while remaining in perpetual servitude makes Jupiter Hammon's accomplishments not only unique but laudable.

Hammon lived through four successive generations of owners in the wealthy Lloyd family, one of the important spokes in the autocratic wheel of the slave economy. As the representatives of British aristocracy on Long Island, with strong ties to England and New England, the Lloyds imported slaves for sale first to their New York neighbors and then throughout New England. They prospered greatly from an exchange of human commodities and from the living derived from their acreage in Oyster Bay, Long Island, which was originally "purchased" from Native Americans for "three hatchets, three hoes, two fathom of wampum, six knives, two pair of stocking and two pair of shoes."

Although certainty is impossible because the Lloyds kept scant records of other data pertinent to the slaves' lives, it is probable that Hammon's mother and father were abducted from the West Coast of Africa by the Lloyd's shipping conglomerate operation in England and New England, business interests that eventually evolved into the well-known Lloyds of London. The family records show that the Lloyds kept only two servants for the life spans of the slaves—one was Hammon and the other a rather militant fellow named "Opium," who, by all indications, was

Hammon's father. Little more is known of Hammon's mother who well could have been an African woman named Rose who was first mentioned in the Lloyd papers in 1687 when Henry Lloyd hired her out to his tenant Edward Higby for the sum of "a pork barrel per annum." Higby was apparently pleased enough with the bargain that he released Lloyd from a prior commitment to include oxen and brush steers in the transaction. As she was of *working* age in 1687, Rose would have been in her early twenties or early thirties when Jupiter Hammon was born. She was probably traded to slavers in the southern colonies when the boy was quite young. All other Lloyd slaves were sold or regularly hired out for annual fees.

The second Lloyd son, John Lloyd I, was born in the same year as Jupiter Hammon. Growing up with John and his older brother, Henry (two years their senior), meant that Hammon may have been exposed to some of the educational and cultural training given to the heirs of the estate. In addition, Hammon would have had formal training through the ministers and teachers of the Society for the Propagation of the Gospel (SPG), a missionary arm of the Church of England, which was founded primarily to reach America's African slaves, the Native Americans, and any unchurched white colonists. The SPG first came to New York in 1705 and to Oyster Bay in 1726 when Hammon was just fifteen years old.

In the spring of 1730, when he was about nineteen years old, Jupiter became gravely ill with a goutlike disease. Three years later, he purchased a Bible from his owner Henry Lloyd. The bout of sickness along with the purchase of the Bible were typical indications of a dramatic religious conversion in the eighteenth century. This period was probably the beginning of stirrings within the boy to become a preacher, poet, and essayist, and to do so within the limitations of slavery by using biblical language to argue against the slave system.

At the beginning of the Revolutionary War, in 1776, the Lloyd family moved their household to Hartford, Connecticut. Joseph Lloyd was an aberration in the aristocratic family, who, since their arrival in America, had been British loyalists. A supporter of the Revolution, Lloyd fled to Hartford when British troops overran Long Island. Hammon's literary career thrived in Hartford. He published his next five works there.

There is no record of Jupiter Hammon ever having married or having had a child. His slim single bed in the narrow upstairs room that still stands today in the original Lloyd estate collaborates this probability. Further, because Hammon's essays have various references about his personal circumstances, it is doubtful that he would not have mentioned a wife or children if they existed. Thus, his solitary life reflects the especially inhumane treatment that northern slavery dealt especially to black males, as the North did not import a large number of black females. Rigidly enforced slavery was the financial foundation of colonial life—in the North as well as in the South. Northern colonial slave codes, of which New York, Hammon's home state, had the most stringent, strictly controlled the slave community. Marriage was discouraged. Most black females were shipped to southern colonies or to the Caribbean because of their low utility in the northern economy and to prevent black family development. The male-to-female ratio among black people was about ten-to-one in the northern colonies. Existing families were often summarily separated to accommodate slave sales.

The only difference in slave conditions between the North and South was that northern commercial interests required some literate slaves to serve as clerks and artisans, and, therefore, a higher percentage of northern slaves were allowed to receive educational and industrial skills. Jupiter Hammon was one slave who was so privileged. The Lloyd papers show that Hammon was entrusted with the family's local savings and that he worked as a clerk in the family business. When he was more than seventy years old, Hammon told a New York audience, "I am . . . able to do almost any kind of business." Obviously, the Lloyds allowed Jupiter Hammon to pursue an education so he could serve in various business and administrative capacities.

The Lloyd family belonged to the royal Church of England, although, when no Anglican pastors were available, they attended Puritan or Congregational churches whenever possible. While the SPG did work with these denominations to give a rudimentary education to some of the black children in the colonies, there is no record of that organization ever publishing any works by African American slaves, especially if that work could be construed as antislavery protest. Thus, for Jupiter Hammon to publish any of the folk poems and sermons for which historian Jacqueline Overton says Hammon was well known on Long Island in his day, it was necessary that he have the financial support and political protection of the more radical Quakers.

While Hammon does not refer to members of this denomination directly, the imprint of their influence on his work abounds. The very first Quaker church in the colonies was established on Long Island, near Hammon's birthplace; an early, perhaps the first, antislavery pamphlet was published on Long Island by a Quaker, William Burling, in 1716; and even John Woolman, the great eighteenth-century Quaker abolitionist, twice visited Oyster Bay. It is easy to assume that Woolman no doubt met and knew Jupiter Hammon when one considers the size of a small hamlet like Oyster Bay. Moreover, Philadelphia Quakers published Hammon's last prose work posthumously with a dedication, written in language that indicated years of fond association, as well as a guarantee of authorial authenticity. Charles Vertanes, an early Hammon biographer, notes that "Oyster Bay was a hotbed of Quaker abolitionism." Thus, that first poem published by Jupiter Hammon on Christmas Day in 1760 was not only the first work published by a slave of African descent in the New World, it was also the first work with which activist abolitionists promoted black artists as examples of the intellectual potential of all black Americans.

The Lloyds would have had to approve of publication of the poetic broadside before it was printed. Printing or distribution of any statement by an African was impossible without the master's permission and without his support or at least compliance with support coming from the larger white community. Also, owners, such as the Lloyds, as well as knowledgeable neighbors had to authenticate to the printer that the slave really could read and write and that the particular slave did write the manuscript. Furthermore, colonists greatly resisted any community network among slaves, especially one that extended beyond the borders of local hamlets. Thus, Hammon and other black writers of the age had to depend on the willingness of some white slave owners to read their works or to allow others to read works written by Africans to other slaves. Yet, Hammon met the challenge of these obstacles and many other obstacles to become the first slave in the modern world to publish his works and—even though he was writing about slavery—to reach a vast audience of servants and colonists alike.

By the time he reached his eighties or nineties, Hammon had published at least three other poems—"An Address to Miss Phillis Wheatly [sic], Ethiopian Poetess," "A Poem for Children with Thoughts of Death," and "A Dialogue Entitled The Kind Master and the Dutiful Servant"—and three sermon essays—*A Winter Piece: Being a Serious Exhortation, with a Call to the Unconverted, A Short Contemplation on the Death of Jesus,* and *An Evening's Improvement, Showing the Necessity of Beholding the Lamb of God.* He had apparently written much more, which, so far, is not available to us today. In fact, Overton says that Hammon was a folk poet who was well known to Long Island citizens and that he wrote several other works, including a poem celebrating the visit of Prince William Henry to Oyster Bay. That poem and *An Essay on the Ten Virgins,* which was advertised in the *Connecticut Courant* in December of 1779, are but two of several of Hammon's writings that have not yet been found.

Hammon's first poem used the four-beats-to-a-line meter, which was so familiar to the Great Awakening and to the black spiritual a cappella hymns. The twenty-two-stanza poem continues a strain that insists that Christ offers his redemption to "everyone" of "every nation" of "all the world" rather than to just a chosen few.

Clearly in all of his writings, Hammon intends both his poetry and prose to be a coded message to American black slaves. In addition to "my brethren," Hammon calls his fellow slaves "Africans by nation" or "Ethiopians." Although born in America, Hammon was the first person of African descent to leave printed evidence that slaves recognized the treachery of cultural alienation. He refers to his brethren as "ancient" to uplift his fellow servants with a sense of inclusion in a history older than that of their British masters. Whether Hammon acquired this vision of his ethnic past through parental training or biblical exposure, that view of ancient history has been a continuing source of pride and identity for African Americans to this day. It has also been the impetus for a recurring quest for authentic African history and culture. His knowledge of an African presence in ancient times—along with his eschatological hope of ultimate and everlasting victory for Africans—provided a view of time past and time future that ameliorated somewhat his suffering. His immediate literary descendant, Phillis Wheatley, also saw the ambiguous relationship that black people had with America. In her poem "On the Death of the Rev. Mr. George Whitefield. 1760," Wheatley pens, "Take him my dear Americans" and then "Take him, ye Africans," making a distinction in both race and nationality. Apparently, the tensions between African Americans and European Americans loomed as irreconcilable in the eighteenth century as they do today.

In his prose, Hammon urged African Americans to learn to read and then to read the Bible for themselves because only then could they understand the coded messages he had written about their enslavement. His topics were not so veiled, however, that knowledgeable white people in his more biblically conscious society would have missed them. In *An Evening's Improvement* he chides white people for referring to him as "an unlearned Ethiopian" and for their beliefs that Africans could not grasp the Word of God because he believed that such assumptions had no basis in Christian fellowship. Thus, when Hammon writes "my brethren" repeatedly in his essays, he is, first, being ironic toward his white audience and, second, perhaps addressing his remarks more to his racial "brethren" than to his white Christian "brethren." And, always taking strong stances against the idea that God preordained white people to be "saved" and black people to be "damned," for three decades he continued the refrain in his writing that was begun in his first poem: "salvation is for everyone."

While a few critics, such as Sondra O'Neale, Carolyn Reese, and Sidney Kaplan, have been supportive of Hammon's efforts, most modern critics have not been kind to Hammon or appreciative of his works. Primarily, they believe that because of his emphasis on Christianity he did not speak out against slavery. He is called to task especially for a statement that he made in his last work, "An Address to the Negroes in the State of New York." In that work, based on an actual sermon delivered before a group of young black activists in New York City, Hammon said that he had been a slave all of his life and that he had no desire to be free. Indicating that he thoroughly understood the politics of the day and the sentiments of his audience, he also stated:

> That liberty is a great thing we may know from our own feelings, and we may likewise judge so from the conduct of the white people in the late war. How much money has been spent and how many lives have been lost to defend their liberty! I must say that I have hope that God would open their eyes, when they were so much engaged for liberty, to think of the state of the poor blacks and to pity us.

Background on the treatment of elderly slaves during this period is helpful for full insight about Hammon's statement that he would remain a slave. Claiming that they were conveniently following abolitionists' commands, many Northern slaveholders had begun to emancipate elderly slaves when they could no longer work. After serving their masters in forced servitude all of their lives, these senior citizens were then left homeless and without food, income, or family. Historians such as Lorenzo J. Greene and others report that thousands of these elderly Africans were flooding the streets of New England in the latter part of the eighteenth century. In this context, it would seem that Jupiter Hammon had every right to expect the Lloyds to continue to provide for him.

Credit for the discovery that Jupiter Hammon, not Phillis Wheatley, was the first African American author, goes to literary critic Oscar Wegelin, who published proof of his discovery in 1915. However, Lillian Koppel discovered Hammon's date of birth in the back of a Lloyd ledger. Before her findings, scholars tried to date Hammon's birth from his writings. In a work published in 1787, the poet says that he is about seventy years old, which would indicate that he was born around 1717 instead of 1711. But several explanations can reconcile the statement to the date in the ledger. First, although the essay was published in 1787, he may have written it sometime before then. Second, in the next line he writes, "I have passed the common bounds set for man." In biblical consciousness those "common bounds" were identified by the Psalmist David as "three-score years and ten" (Ps. 90:10), or seventy years. So when Hammon says "I am now upwards of seventy years old" and then again "I have passed the common bounds," he is indicating that he was not nearing seventy years of age but past it—or, in fact, around seventy-six years old.

That same Lloyd account book indicates that Hammon was alive in 1790. But, based on eulogistic language in the Quaker reprint of *An Address to the Negroes in the State of New York,* he had died by 1806. As yet, the exact date of his death and place of burial have not been determined. Born at the beginning of the century before the antislavery movement had gained international and well-financed momentum, Jupiter

Hammon could not have had the opportunities afforded to Phillis Wheatley or Olaudah Equiano, but he did live to see much of their momentous achievements. Moreover, he left them a legacy of survival, subtle protest, and living witness—an example that they and other African Americans have been privileged to follow.

❖❖❖

Sondra O'Neale has written the most recent full-length biography and edition of Hammon's life. Her modernized version is titled *Jupiter Hammon and the Biblical Beginnings of African-American Literature* (1993). Oscar Wegelin's first article and book are "Was Phillis Wheatley America's First Negro Poet? (1904) and *Jupiter Hammon: American Negro Poet, Selections from His Writings and a Bibliography* (1915). Stanley Ransom, Jr., issued another edition of the poet's extant writings, *America's First Negro Poet: The Complete Works of Jupiter Hammon* (1970). A review of this work by Ronald B. Miller (R. Baxter Miller) in *New York History* 55 (1974) offers the student valuable insight into Hammon and his writings.

The poet is also discussed in Carolyn Reese's "From Jupiter Hammon to LeRoi Jones" in *Changing Education,* vol. I (Fall 1966); William H. Robinson's *Early Black American Poets* (1969), Bernard W. Bell's "African American Writers" in *American Literature 1764–1789: The Revolutionary Years* (1977), Benjamin Brawley's *Early Negro American Writers* (1935), and Sidney and Emma Nogrady Kaplan's *The Black Presence in the Era of the American Revolution: 1770–1800* (1973).

An Evening Thought: Salvation by Christ, with Penetential [sic] Cries

Salvation comes by Jesus Christ alone,
  The only Son of God;
Redemption now to every one,
  That love his holy Word.
Dear Jesus we would fly to Thee,
  And leave off every Sin.
Thy tender Mercy well agree;
  Salvation from our King.
Salvation comes now from the Lord,
  Our victorious King;
His holy Name be well ador'd,
  Salvation surely bring.
Dear Jesus give thy Spirit now,
  Thy Grace to every Nation,
That han't the Lord to whom we bow,
  The Author of Salvation.
Dear Jesus unto Thee we cry,
  Give us the Preparation;
Turn not away thy tender Eye;
  We seek thy true Salvation.
Salvation comes from God we know,
  The true and only one;

It's well agreed and certain true,
    He gave his only Son.
Lord hear our penetential Cry:
    Salvation from above;
It is the Lord that doth supply,
    With his Redeeming Love.
Dear Jesus by thy precious Blood,
    The World Redemption have:
Salvation now comes from the Lord,
    He being thy captive slave.
Dear Jesus let the Nations cry,
    And all the People say,
Salvation comes from Christ on high,
    Haste on Tribunal Day.
We cry as Sinners to the Lord,
    Salvation to obtain;
It is firmly fixt his holy Word,
    Ye shall not cry in vain.
Dear Jesus unto thee we cry,
    And make our Lamentation:
O let our Prayers ascend on high;
    We felt thy Salvation.
Lord turn our dark benighted Souls;
    Give us a true Motion,
And let the Hearts of all the World,
    Make Christ their Salvation.
Ten Thousand Angels cry to Thee,
    Yea louder than the Ocean.
Thou art the Lord, we plainly see;
    Thou art the true Salvation.
Now is the Day, excepted Time;
    The Day of Salvation;
Increase your Faith, do not repine:
    Awake ye every Nation.
Lord unto whom now shall we go,
    Or seek a safe Abode;
Thou hast the Word Salvation too
    The only son of God.
Ho! every one that hunger hath,
    Or pineth after me,
Salvation be thy leading Staff,
    To set the Sinner free.
Dear Jesus unto Thee we fly;
    Depart, depart from Sin,
Salvation doth at length supply,
    The Glory of our King.

Come ye Blessed of the Lord,
Salvation greatly given;
O turn your Hearts, accept the Word,
Your Souls are fit for Heaven.
Dear Jesus we now turn to Thee,
Salvation to obtain;
Our Hearts and Souls do meet again,
To magnify thy Name.
Come holy Spirit, Heavenly Dove,
The Object of our Care;
Salvation doth increase our Love;
Our Hearts hath felt thy fear.
Now Glory be to God on High,
Salvation high and low;
And thus the Soul on Christ rely,
To Heaven surely go.
Come Blessed Jesus, Heavenly Dove,
Accept Repentance here;
Salvation give, with tender Love;
Let us with Angels share.

An Address to Miss Phillis Wheatly [sic]

I

O come you pious youth! adore
The wisdom of thy God,
In bringing thee from distant shore,
To learn His holy word.

Eccles. xii.

II

Thou mightst been left behind
Amidst a dark abode;
God's tender mercy still combin'd,
Thou hast the holy word.

Psal. cxxxv, 2,3.

III

Fair wisdom's ways are paths of peace,
And they that walk therein,
Shall reap the joys that never cease,
And Christ shall be their king.

Psal. i, 1, 2; Prov. iii, 7.

IV

God's tender mercy brought thee here;
   Tost o'er the raging main;
In Christian faith thou hast a share,
   Worth all the gold of Spain.

Psal. ciii, 1, 3, 4.

V

While thousands tossed by the sea,
   And others settled down,
God's tender mercy set thee free,
   From dangers that come down.

Death.

VI

That thou a pattern still might be,
   To youth of Boston town,
The blessed Jesus set thee free,
   From every sinful wound.

2 Cor. v. 10.

VII

The blessed Jesus, who came down,
   Unvail'd his sacred face,
To cleanse the soul of every wound,
   And give repenting grace.

Rom. v. 21.

VIII

That we poor sinners may obtain,
   The pardon of our sin;
Dear blessed Jesus now constrain,
   And bring us flocking in.

Psal. xxxiv, 6, 7, 8.

IX

Come you, Phillis, now aspire,
   And seek the living God,
So step by step thou mayst go higher,
   Till perfect in the word.

Matth. vii, 7, 8.

X

While thousands mov'd to distant shore,
   And others left behind,
The blessed Jesus still adore,
   Implant this in thy mind.

Psal. lxxxix, 1.

XI

Thou hast left the heathen shore;
   Thro' mercy of the Lord,
Among the heathen live no more,
   Come magnify thy God.

Psal. xxxiv, 1, 2, 3.

XII

I pray the living God may be,
   The shepherd of thy soul;
His tender mercies still are free,
   His mysteries to unfold.

Psal. lxxx, 1, 2, 3.

XIII

Thou, Phillis, when thou hunger hast,
   Or pantest for thy God;
Jesus Christ is thy relief,
   Thou hast the holy word.

Psal. xiii, 1, 2, 3.

XIV

The bounteous mercies of the Lord,
   Are hid beyond the sky,
And holy souls that love His word,
   Shall taste them when they die.

Psal. xvi, 10, 11.

XV

These bounteous mercies are from God,
   The merits of His Son;
The humble soul that loves His word,
   He chooses for His own.

Psal. xxxiv, 15.

XVI

Come, dear Phillis, be advis'd,
To drink Samaria's flood;
There nothing that shall suffice
But Christ's redeeming blood.

John iv, 13, 14.

XVII

While thousands muse with earthly toys;
And range about the street,
Dear Phillis, seek for heaven's joys,
Where we do hope to meet.

Matth. vi, 33.

XVIII

When God shall send his summons down,
And number saints together,
Blest angels chant, (triumphant sound),
Come live with me forever.

Psal. cxvi, 15.

XIX

The humble soul shall fly to God,
And leave the things of time,
Start forth as 'twere at the first word,
To taste things more divine.

Matth. v, 3, 8.

XX

Behold! the soul shall waft away,
Whene'er we come to die,
And leave its cottage made of clay,
In twinkling of an eye.

Cor. xv, 51, 52, 53

XXI

Now glory be to the Most High,
United praises given,
By all on earth, incessantly,
And all the host of heav'n.

Psal. cl, 6.

A Winter Piece

As I have been desired to write[1] something more than poetry, I shall endeavor to write from these words: "Come unto me, all ye that labor and are heavy-laden" (Matt. 11:28). My brethren, I shall endeavor by divine assistance to show what is meant by coming to the Lord Jesus Christ laboring and heavy-laden, and to conclude, I shall contemplate the death of Jesus Christ.

My brethren, in the first place I am to show what is meant by coming to Christ laboring and heavy-laden. We are to come with a sense of our own unworthiness to confess our sins before the Most High God, to come by prayer and meditation, and we are to confess Christ to be our Savior and Mighty Redeemer. "Whosoever therefore shall confess me before men, him will I confess also before my Father which is in heaven" (Matt. 10:32). Here, my brethren, we have great encouragement to come to the Lord and to ask for the influence of his Holy Spirit and that he would give us the water of eternal life. "But whosoever drinketh of the water [as the woman of Samaria did] that I shall give him shall never thirst; but the water that I shall give him shall be in him a well of water springing up into everlasting life" (John 4:14). Then we shall believe in the merits of Christ for our eternal salvation and come laboring and heavy-laden with a sense of our lost and undone state without an interest in the merits of Christ. It should be our greatest care to trust in the Lord, as David did, "In thee, O Lord, I put my trust" (Ps. 31:1).

My brethren, we must come to the divine fountain to turn us from sin to holiness and to give us grace to repent of our sins; this none can do but God. We must come laboring and heavy-laden, not trusting to our own righteousness, but we are to be clothed with the righteousness of Christ. Then we may apply this text: "Blessed is he whose transgression is forgiven, whose sin is covered" (Ps. 32:1). This we must seek by prayer and meditation, and we are to pray without ceasing, as set forth by David in Ps. 51:1: "Have mercy upon me, O God, according to thy loving kindness: according unto the multitude of thy tender mercies blot out my transgressions." My brethren, we are to come poor in spirit.

In the second place, in order to come to the divine fountain laboring and heavy-laden, we are to avoid all bad company and to keep ourselves pure in heart. "Blessed are the pure in heart: for they shall see God" (Matt. 5:8). Now, in order to see God, we must have a saving change wrought in our hearts, which is the work of God's Holy Spirit, which we are to ask for. "Ask, and it shall be given you; seek, and ye shall find" (Matt. 7:7). It may be asked, what shall we find? Ye will find the mercies of God to allure you, the influence of his Holy Spirit to guide you in the right way to eternal life. "For every one that asketh receiveth" (Matt. 7:8). But then my brethren, we are to ask in a right manner, with faith and repentance, for except we repent, we shall surely die.[2] That is, we must suffer the wrath of the Most High God, who will turn you away with this pronunciation: ". . . depart from me, ye that work iniquity" (Matt. 7:23). Therefore you see how dangerous a thing it is to live in any known sin, either of commission or omission, for if we commit any willful sin, we become the servants of sin. ". . . Whosoever committeth sin is the servant of sin" (John 8:34).

My dear brethren, have we not rendered ourselves too much the servants of sin by a

[1]Hammon has three extant sermon essays. While all were printed, probably *An Evening's Improvement* and *An Address to the Negroes in the State of New York* were given first as public exhortations, while *A Winter Piece* was created to be a written essay.

[2]When Hammon speaks of death, it is spiritual not physical death. His language reflects familiarity with Jesus' sermon in Luke 13:3–8 in which he told his audience, "Except ye repent, ye shall likewise perish." This issue was not that those who heard Christ would die if they did not repent, as that is the end of all mankind, but that they would suffer both here and hereafter in the quintessence of spiritual death, which is life without the Light of God. All the major colonial denominations would have reached consensus on this point, but especially from the Quakers would Hammon have received this sense of God's presence as the Light within the reborn human soul.

breach of God's holy commandments, by breaking his holy Sabbath when we should have been preparing for our great and last change? Have we not been amusing ourselves with the pleasures of this life? Or if we have attended divine service, have we been sincere? For God will not be mocked,[3] for he knows our thoughts. "God is a Spirit: and they that worship him must worship him in spirit and in truth" (John 4:24). Therefore, my brethren, we see how necessary it is that we should be sincere when we attempt to come to the Lord, whether in public service or private devotion, for it is not the outward appearance, but the sincerity of the heart. This we must manifest by a holy life. For it is "not everyone that saith unto me, Lord, Lord, shall enter into the kingdom of heaven; but he that doeth the will of my Father which is in heaven" (Matt. 7:21).

Therefore we ought to come laboring and heavy-laden to the throne of grace and pray that God may be pleased to transform us anew in Christ Jesus. But it may be objected by those who have had the advantage of studying that everyone is not calculated for teaching others. To those I answer, "Sirs I do not attempt to teach those who I know are able to teach me, but I shall endeavor by divine assistance to enlighten the minds of my brethren. For we are a poor despised nation whom God in his wise providence has permitted to be brought from their native place to a Christian land, where many thousands have been born in what are called Christian families and brought up to years of understanding."

In answer to the objectors, "Sirs, pray give me leave to inquire into the state of those children that are born in those Christian families. Have they been baptized, taught to read, and taught their catechism? Surely this is a duty incumbent on masters or heads of families. Sirs, if you had a sick child, would you not send for a doctor? If your house were on fire, would you not strive to put it out to save your interest? Surely then, you ought to use the means appointed to save the souls that God has committed to your charge and not forget the words of Joshua: 'As for me and my house we will serve the Lord' (Josh. 24:15). Children should be taught the fear of God. See what Solomon says: 'The fear of the Lord is to hate evil' (Prov. 8:13); 'The fear of the Lord is the beginning of wisdom' (Prov. 9:10); 'The fear of the Lord is a fountain of life' (Prov. 14:27). Here we see that children should fear the Lord."

But I turn to my brethren, for whom this discourse is designed. My brethren, if you are desirous of being saved by the merits of Jesus Christ, you must forsake all your sins and come to the Lord; by prayer and repentance of all your former sins, come laboring and heavy-laden. For we are invited to come and rely on the blessed Jesus for eternal salvation. "Whosoever therefore shall confess me before men, him will I confess also before my Father which is in heaven" (Matt. 10:32). Here we have our Savior's words for our encouragement. See to it, my brethren, that you live a holy life and that you walk more circumspectly, or holy, than you have done heretofore. I now assure you that "God is a Spirit: and they that worship him must worship him in spirit and in truth" (John 4:24). Therefore, if you would come unto him, come as the poor publican did and say: "God be merciful to me, a sinner." "And the publican, standing afar off, would not lift up so much as his eyes unto heaven, but smote upon his breast, saying, God be merciful to me a sinner" (Luke 18:13). For if we hope to be saved by the merits of Jesus Christ, we cast off all self-dependence as our own righteousness. "For by grace are ye saved through faith; and that not of yourselves: it is the gift of God" (Eph. 2:8).

Here we see that the imperfection of human nature is such that we cannot be saved by any other way but the name of Jesus Christ and that there must be a principle of love and fear of God implanted in our hearts if we desire to come to the divine fountain laboring and

[3]Here Hammon is referring to a quotation on judgment that was familiar to most eighteenth-century readers, Gal. 6:7: "Be not deceived; God is not mocked: for whatsoever a man soweth, that shall he also reap."

heavy-laden with our sins. But the inquirer may inquire, "How do you prove this doctrine? Are you not imposing on your brethren, as you know that many of them cannot read?" To this I answer, "Sir, I do not mean to impose on my brethren but to show them that there must be a principle of fear and love to God." And now I am to prove this doctrine that we ought to fear God. "For as the heaven is high above the earth, so great is his mercy toward them that fear him. . . . Like as a father pitieth his children, so the Lord pitieth them that fear him" (Ps. 103:11, 13). "O fear the Lord, ye his saints: for there is no want to them that fear him. . . . Come, ye children, hearken unto me: I will teach you the fear of the Lord" (Ps. 34:9, 11). This may suffice to prove the doctrine that we ought to fear the Lord. Here, my brethren, we see how much our salvation depends on our being transformed anew in Christ Jesus, for we are sinners by nature and are adding thereunto every day of our lives. For man is prone to evil, as the sparks to fly upward.[4] This thought should put us on our guard against all manner of evil, especially of bad company. This leads me to say that we should endeavor to glorify God in all our actions, whether spiritual or temporal, for the apostle hath told us that whatever we do, do all to the glory of God (1 Cor. 10:31).

Let us now labor for that food which tendeth unto eternal life. This none can give but God only. My brethren, it is your duty to strive to make your calling and election sure by a holy life, working out your salvation with fear and trembling, for we are invited to come without money and without price: "Ho, every one that thirsteth, come ye to the waters, and he that hath no money; come ye, buy, and eat; yea, come, buy wine and milk without money and without price" (Isa. 55:1). This leads me to say that if we suffer as sinners, under the light of the gospel as sinners, the fault is in us, for our Savior hath told us that if he had not come, we should not have had sin, but now we have no cloak for our sins. Let us now improve our talents by coming laboring and burdened with a sense of our sins. This certainly is a necessary duty of all mankind: to come to the divine fountain for mercy and for the influence of God's Holy Spirit to guide us through this wilderness to the mansions of eternal glory.[5]

My brethren, have we not great encouragement to come unto the Lord Jesus Christ? "Ask, and it shall be given you; seek, and ye shall find; knock, and it shall be opened unto you" (Matt. 7:7). Therefore, if you desire to be saved by the merits of Christ, you must come as the prodigal son did: "And the son said unto him, Father, I have sinned against heaven, and in thy sight, and am no more worthy to be called thy son" (Luke 15:21). This is the language of the true penitent, for he is made sensible that there is no other name given by which he can be saved but by the name of Jesus. Therefore we should put our trust in him and strive to make our calling and election sure by prayer and meditation. "Give ear to my prayer, O God; and hide not thyself from my supplication" (Ps. 55:1).

But, my brethren, are we not too apt to put off the thoughts of death till we are sick or some misfortune happens to us, forgetting the bountiful hand that gives us every good gift? Doth not the tokens of mortality call aloud to us all to prepare for death, our great and last change, not flattering ourselves with the hopes of a long life, for we know not what a day may bring forth? Therefore, my brethren, let it be your greatest care to prepare for death, that great and irresistible king of terrors. We are, many of us, advanced in years and we know not how soon God may be pleased to call us out of this life to an endless eternity. For this is the lot of all men,

[4]Hammon's metaphor is a paraphrase of Job 5:7: "Yet man is born unto trouble, as the sparks fly upward."

[5]This paragraph is filled with paraphrases and allusions to various New Testament passages. The first is a partial quote of 2 Pet. 1:10: "Wherefore the rather, brethren, give diligence to make your calling and election sure: for if you do these things, ye shall never fail." Hammon combines this with a phrase from Phil. 2:12: "Wherefore, my beloved, as ye have always obeyed, not as in my presence only, but now much more in my absence, work out your own salvation with fear and trembling." Finally Hammon puts some of his readers in the position of the Pharisees of whom Jesus said in John 15:22: "If I had not come and spoken unto them, they had not had sin: But now they have no cloke for their sin."

once to die, and after that the judgement. Let us now come to the Lord Jesus Christ with a sense of our own impotence to do any good thing of ourselves and with a thankful remembrance of the death of Christ, who died to save lost man and hath invited us to come to him laboring and heavy-laden. My ancient brethren, let us examine ourselves now to see whether we have had a saving change wrought in our hearts and have repented of our sins. Have we made it our greatest care to honor God's Holy Word and to keep his holy Sabbaths and to obey his commandments? God says that he shows "mercy unto thousands of them that love me, and keep my commandments" (Exod. 20:6). Have we been brought to bow to the divine sovereignty of the Most High God and to fly to the arms of the crucified Jesus, at whose crucifixion the mountains trembled, and the rocks rent, and the graves were opened, and many bodies of saints that slept arose?

Come, my dear fellow servants and brothers, Africans by nation, we are all invited to come: "Then Peter opened his mouth, and said, Of a truth I perceive that God is no respecter of persons: But in every nation he that feareth him, and worketh righteousness, is accepted with him" (Acts 10:34–35). My brethren, many of us are seeking a temporal freedom and I wish you may obtain it; remember that all power in heaven and on earth belongs to God. If we are slaves, it is by the permission of God; if we are free, it must be by the power of the Most High God.[6] Stand still and see the salvation of God. Cannot that same power that divided the waters from the waters for the children of Israel to pass through make way for your freedom? I pray that God would grant your desire and that he may give you grace to seek that freedom which tendeth to eternal life. "And ye shall know the truth and the truth shall make you free. . . . If the Son therefore shall make you free, ye shall be free indeed" (John 8:32, 36).[7] This we know, my brethren: ". . . that all things work together for good to them that love God . . ." (Rom. 8:28). Let us manifest this love to God by a holy life.

My dear brethren, as it hath been reported that I had petitioned to the court of Hartford against freedom, I now solemnly declare that I have never said nor done anything, neither directly nor indirectly, to promote or to prevent freedom. But my answer hath always been: "I am a stranger here and I do not care to be concerned or to meddle with public affairs." By this declaration I hope my friend will be satisfied and all prejudice removed. Let us all strive to be united together in love and to become new creatures, for ". . . if any man be in Christ, he is a new creature: old things are passed away; behold, all things are become new" (2 Cor. 5:17). Now, to be a new creature is to have our minds turned from darkness to light, from sin to holiness, and to have a desire to serve God with our whole hearts and to follow his precepts. "More to be desired are they than gold, yea, than much fine gold: sweeter also than honey and the honeycomb. Moreover by them is thy servant warned: and in keeping of them there is great reward" (Ps. 19:10–11).

Let me now, my brethren, persuade you to prepare for death by prayer and meditation. That is the way of Matt. 6:6 ". . . when thou prayest, enter into thy closet, and when thou hast shut thy door, pray to thy Father which is in secret; and thy Father which seeth in secret shall reward thee openly."

My brethren, while we continue in sin, we are enemies to Christ, ruining ourselves and harming the commonwealth. Let us now, my brethren, come laboring and heavy-laden, with a sense of our sins; and let us pray that God may in his mercy be pleased to lift up the gates of

---

[6] Hammon often wrestled with the dilemma of whether slavery was the direct or permitted will of God. This was a prevalent theological question in his day. See S. Hopkins, *Timely Articles;* Sewall, *The Selling of Joseph* (1700, 1969 ed.); and Slater, *Children in the New England Mind* (1977).

[7] This entire section, particularly following a discussion of the Apostle Peter's disavowal of racial prejudice, alludes to Moses' deliverance of the Jewish slaves from Egypt. The languge is part of Moses' speech to the Israelites when he raised his staff to part the Red Sea: "Fear ye not, stand still, and see the salvation of the Lord, which he will shew to you to day: for the Egyptians whom ye have seen to day, ye shall see them again no more for ever" (Exod. 14:13).

our hearts and open the doors of our souls, that the King of Glory may come in and set these things home on our hearts. "Lift up your heads, O ye gates; and be ye lift up ye everlasting doors; and the King of glory shall come in" (Ps. 24:7). Then may we rely on the merits of Christ and say as David did: "In the Lord put I my trust" (Ps. 11:1); and again, "whom have I in heaven but thee? and there is none upon earth that I desire beside thee" (Ps. 73:25).

And now my brethren, I shall endeavor to prove that we are not only ruining ourselves by sin, but many others. If men in general were more humble and more holy, we should not hear the little children in the street taking God's holy name in vain. Surely our conversation should be yea, yea and nay, nay or to that purpose. "But let your communication be, Yea, yea; Nay, nay: for whatsoever is more than these cometh of evil" (Matt. 5:37). Therefore, my brethren, we should endeavor to walk humbly and holy, to avoid the appearance of evil, to live a life "void of offense toward God and toward man" (Acts 24:16). Hear what David saith: "Blessed is the man that walketh not in the counsel of the ungodly, nor standeth in the way of sinners" (Ps. 1:1). Here we see how much it becomes us to live as Christians, not in rioting and drunkenness, uncleanness, Sabbath breaking, swearing, taking God's holy name in vain; but our delight should be in the law of the Lord.

The righteous man is compared to a tree that bringeth forth fruit in season: "And he shall be like a tree planted by the rivers of water, that bringeth forth his fruit in his season; his leaf also shall not wither; and whatsoever he doeth shall prosper" (Ps. 1:3). Let us not forget the words of holy David: "man is but the dust, like the flower of the field" (Ps. 103:15).

Let us remember the uncertainty of human life and that we are many of us within a step of the grave, hanging only by the single thread of life, and we know not how soon God may send the cold hand of death and cut the thread of life. Then will our souls either ascend to the eternal mansions of glory or descend to eternal misery, our bodies lodged in the cold, silent grave, numbered with the dead. Then shall the Scripture be fulfilled: "In the sweat of thy face shalt thou eat bread, till thou return unto the ground; for out of it wast thou taken: for dust thou art, and unto dust shalt thou return" (Gen. 3:19).

Now I am to call to the unconverted, my brethren. If we desire to become true converts, we must be born again; we must have a spiritual regeneration. "Verily, verily, I say unto thee, Except a man be born again, he cannot see the kingdom of God" (John 3:3). My brethren, are we not, many of us, ignorant of this spiritual regeneration? Have we seen our lost and undone condition when we have no interest in the merits of Jesus Christ? Have we come weary and heavy-laden with our sins and to say with holy David, "O Lord, rebuke me not in thine anger, neither chasten me in thy hot displeasure" (Ps. 6:1). Hath it been our great care to prepare for death, our great and last change, by prayer and meditation?

My dear brethren, though we are servants and have not so much time as we could wish for, yet we must improve the little time we have. Mr. Burkitt, a great divine of our church,[8] says that a man's hand may be on his plow and his heart in heaven, by putting forth such prayers and ejaculations as these: "Hear my cry, O God; attend unto my prayer," and "whom have I in heaven but thee? and there is none upon earth that I desire beside thee" (Ps. 61:1; 73:25).

We should pray that God would give us his Holy Spirit so that we may not be led into temptation and that we may be delivered from evil, especially the evil of sin. "But now being made free from sin, and become servants to God, ye have your fruit unto holiness, and the end everlasting life. For the wages of sin is death; but the gift of God is eternal life through Jesus Christ our Lord" (Rom. 6:22, 23).

[8]William Burkitt, a seventeenth-century evangelist and Anglican clergyman, marked his career with both charity and charismatic preaching. He took pains to aid French exiles, indigent students, and missionaries bound for the colonies. His popularity stemmed from his ability to preach extemporaneously and vehemently, and many of his exhortations and guides are published (Stephen and Lee, *The Dictionary of National Biography*, 2:3). He published a two-volume expository on the New Testament, which was among the books in the Lloyd library that Hammon used as source material.

My brethren, seeing I am desired by my friends to write something more than poetry, give me leave to speak plainly to you. Except you repent and forsake your sins, you must surely die. Now we see how much it becomes us to break our alliance with sin and Satan, to fly to a crucified Savior, and to enlist under Christ's banner so that he may give us grace to become his faithful subjects—this should be our constant prayer. We should guard against every sin, especially against bad language.

Therefore, my brethren, we should always guard against every evil word, for we are told that the tongue is an evil member because with the tongue we bless God and with the tongue we curse men.[9] "For he that will love life, and see good days, let him refrain his tongue from evil, and his lips that they speak no guile" (1 Pet. 3:10). But the thoughtless and unconverted sinner is going on in open rebellion against that divine power which can in one minute cut the thread of life and cast sinners away with this pronunciation: Depart from me, you workers of iniquity. "Then shall he say also unto them on the left hand, Depart from me, ye cursed, into everlasting fire, prepared for the devil and his angels" (Matt. 25:41).

And now my brethren, shall we abuse the divine sovereignty of a holy God, who hath created us rational creatures, capable of serving him under the light of the gospel? For he hath told us that if he had not come unto us we had not had sin but now we have no cloak for our sin.[10] Come now, my dear brethren, accept Jesus Christ on the terms of the gospel, which is by faith and repentance. Come laboring and heavy-laden with your sins and a sense of your unworthiness.

My brethren, it is not we servants only that are unworthy; but all mankind by the fall of Adam became guilty in the sight of God (Gen. 2:17). Surely then, we are sinners by nature and are daily adding thereto by evil practices, and it is only by the merits of Jesus Christ that we can be saved. We are told that he is a Jew who is a Jew in his heart, so he is a Christian who is a Christian in his heart. And not everyone who says "Lord, Lord," shall enter into the kingdom of God but he that doeth the will of God.[11] Let our superiors act as they shall think best; we must resolve to walk in the steps our Savior hath set before us, which were a holy life and a humble submission to the will of God. "And he was withdrawn from them about a stone's cast, and kneeled down, and prayed. Saying, Father, if thou be willing, remove this cup from me: nevertheless not my will, but thine, be done" (Luke 22:41–42).

Here we have the example of our Savior, who came down from heaven to save men who were lost and undone without an interest in the merits of Jesus Christ. The blessed Jesus then gave his life, a ransom for all that come unto him by faith and repentance. And shall not "he that spared not his own Son, but delivered him up for us all, how shall he not with him also freely give us all things" (Rom. 8:32)? Come, let us seek first Christ, "the kingdom of God, and his righteousness; and all these things shall be added unto you" (Matt. 6:33). Here we have great encouragement to come to the divine fountain.

---

[9]Here Hammon has James 3:8–9 in mind: "But the tongue can no man tame; it is an unruly evil, full of deadly poison. Therewith bless we God, even the Father; and therewith curse we men, which are made after the similitude of God."

[10]Just as he had indicated earlier that if his African readers had not heard the Gospel they would not have been held responsible for God's word, the same standard can be implicitly applied to his white readers—i.e., had white colonists not been challenged with the presence of African Americans and Native Americans, their Christian utopia might have succeeded. But these "heathen," untoward to them, quickly evaporated whatever penchant to Christian love most early colonists possessed. If the presence of other races was the test of that love, the colonists failed that test.

[11]Like the words in the Negro spiritual, "everyone that talks about heaven ain't going there," Hammon's use of Matt. 7:21—"Not every one that saith unto me, 'Lord, Lord,' shall enter into the kingdom of heaven; but he that doeth the will of my Father which is in heaven"—is a direct confrontation with what he considers to be white hypocrisy. Hammon's description of those who had not had this heartfelt conversion but who still call Christ "Lord," is intended to show that, although they have gone through the steps that E. S. Morgan (*Visible Saints*) (1963) describes, the slave masters, because of the slave system, are not fulfilling the requirements for good moral behavior. Therefore, their actions are not to be imitated: "Let our superiors act as they shall think best." See also Agate, in Hastings, *Encyclopedia of Religion and Ethics* (1921), 611–612; and Tipson 460–471.

Bishop Beveridge says in his third resolution that the eyes of the Lord are intent upon us; he seeth our actions. If our sins are not washed out with our tears and crossed with the blood of Christ, we cannot be saved.[12] Come, my brethren, "O taste and see that Lord is good: blessed is the man that trusteth in him" (Ps. 34:8). Let us not stand as Felix did and say, "Almost thou persuadest me to be a Christian."[13] But let us strive to be altogether so. If you desire to become converts, you must have a saving change wrought in your hearts that shall bring forth good works meet for repentance: "Repent ye therefore, and be converted" (Acts 3:19). We are not to trust in our own strength but to trust in the Lord. "Trust in the Lord with all thine heart; and lean not unto thine own understanding" (Prov. 3:5).

My brethren, are we not encircled with many temptations: the flesh, the world and the devil? These must be resisted at all times. We must see to it that we do not grieve the Holy Spirit of God. Come, let us, my dear brethren, draw near to the Lord by faith and repentance, for "faith without works is dead" (James 2:20); and "for with the heart men believeth unto righteousness; and with the mouth confession is made unto salvation" (Rom. 10:10). Here we see that there is something to be done by us as Christians. Therefore we should walk worthy of our profession, not forgetting that there is a divine power which takes a just survey of all our actions and will reward everyone according to his works. "Also unto thee, O Lord, belongeth mercy: for thou renderest to every man according to his work" (Ps. 62:12). Therefore it is our indispensable duty to improve all opportunities to serve God, who gave us his only Son to save all that come unto him by faith and repentance.

Let me, my brethren, persuade you to a serious consideration of your danger while you continue in an unconverted state. Did you feel the operations of God's Holy Spirit? You then would leave all for an interest in the merits of Christ: For ". . . the kingdom of heaven is like unto treasure hid in a field; that which when a man hath found, . . . he selleth all that he hath, and buyeth that field" (Matt. 13:44). So will every true penitent part with all for the sake of Christ. I shall not attempt to drive you to Christ by the terrors of the law, but I shall endeavor to allure you by the invitation of the gospel to come laboring and heavy-laden.

Man at his best estate is like a shadow of the field.[14] We should always be preparing for death, not having our hearts set on the things of this life. For what profit will it be to us to gain the whole world and lose our own souls? (Matt. 16:26). We should be always preparing for the will of God, working out our salvation with fear and trembling. O may we abound in the works of the Lord. Let us not stand as fruitless trees or encumberers of the ground, for by your works you shall be justified and by your works you shall be condemned: for every man shall be rewarded "according to his works" (Matt. 16:27). Let us then be pressing forward to the mark, for the prize of the high calling of God is Christ Jesus. Let our hearts be fixed where true joys are to be found. Let us lay up "treasures in heaven, where neither moth nor rust doth corrupt, and

---

[12]Hammon's quote about Beveridge's third resolution is taken from the latter's *Works* (1829) 1:222. William Beveridge was a popular seventeenth-century bishop of the Church of England and a college president. He was noted for his publications of treatises in various scholarly languges and his preaching of sermons on a range of subjects from prayer to the Great Fire of 1666. Although he held many positions of power within the Anglican church, he consistently opposed attempts to relax its requirements (Stephen and Lee, *The Dictionary of National Biography* (1900), 2:447–448).

[13]To defend his beliefs against the accusations of the Jews, the Apostle Paul had to appear before three Roman governors. Felix, governor of Judea, was one of these governors, but Hammon has the three rulers—all of whom are mentioned in the book of Acts—confused. It was King Agrippa, not Felix, who said to the Apostle Paul: "Almost thou persuadest me to be a Christian" (Acts 26:28).

[14]Here Hammon seems to be meshing two Bible verses to warn his readers about the elusiveness of earthly life: "For all flesh is as grass, and all the glory of man as the flower of grass. The grass withereth, and the flower thereof falleth away. But the word of the Lord endureth for ever" (1 Pet. 1:24–25); and "For the sun is no sooner risen with a burning heat, but it withereth the grass, and the flower thereof falleth, and the grace of the fashion of it perisheth: so also shall the rich man fade away in his ways" (James 1:11). Another analogous text is Ps. 39:5: "verily every man at his best state is altogether vanity."

where thieves do not break through nor steal" (Matt. 6:20).[15]

Contemplation on the Death of Christ

Now I am come to contemplate the death of Christ; it remains that I make a short contemplation. The death of Christ who died! Died to save lost man. "For since by man came death, by man came also the resurrection of the dead. For as in Adam all die, even so in Christ shall all be made alive" (1 Cor. 15:21–22). Let us turn to the Scriptures, and there we shall see how our Savior was denied by one and betrayed by another:

> Judas . . . went unto the chief priests, And said unto them, What will you give me . . . ? And they convenanted with him for thirty pieces of silver. And from that time he sought opportunity to betray him (Matt. 26:14–16). For this is my blood of the new testament, which is shed for many for the remission of sins (Matt. 26:28). Peter answered and said unto him, Though all men shall be offended because of thee, yet will I never be offended (Matt. 26:33). Jesus said unto him, Verily I say unto thee, That this night, before the cock crow, thou shalt deny me thrice (Matt. 26:34). Then saith he unto them, My soul is exceeding sorrowful, even unto death: tarry ye here, and watch with me (Matt. 26:38). And he went a little farther and fell on his face, and prayed, saying, O my Father, if it be possible, let this cup pass from me: nevertheless not as I will, but as thou wilt. (Matt. 26:39).

My brethren, here we see the love of God plainly set before us: that while we were yet sinners, he sent his Son to die for all those that come unto him, laboring and heavy-laden with a sense of their sins. Let us come with a thankful remembrance of his death, whose blood was shed for us guilty worms of the dust:

> But Jesus held his peace. And the high priest answered and said unto him, I adjure thee by the living God, that thou tell us whether thou be the Christ, the son of God (Matt. 26:63). Jesus saith unto him, Thou hast said: nevertheless I say unto you, Hereafter shall ye see the Son of man sitting on the right hand of power, and coming in the clouds of heaven (Matt. 26:64). Then the high priest rent his clothes, saying, He hath spoken blasphemy; what further need have we of witnesses? behold, now ye have heard his blasphemy. (Matt. 26:65)

Here the high priest charged the blessed Jesus with blasphemy. But we must believe that he is able to save all that come unto him, by faith and repentance. "And Jesus came and spake unto them, saying, All power is given unto me in heaven and in earth" (Matt. 28:18). This should excite us to love and fear God and to strive to keep his holy commandments, which are the only rule of life. But how apt are we to forget that "God spake all these words, saying, I am the Lord thy God, which have brought thee out of the land of Egypt, out of the house of bondage" (Exod. 20:1–2)? Thus we see how the children of Israel were delivered from Egyptian service.

But my brethren, we are invited to the blessed Jesus, who was betrayed by one and denied by another:

> The Son of man goeth as it is written of him: but woe unto that man by whom the Son of man is betrayed! it had been good for that man if he had not been born. Then Judas, which betrayed him, answered and said, Master, is it I? He said unto him, Thou hast said. (Matt. 20:24–25)

Thus we see, my brethren, that there is a woe pronounced against everyone who sins by omission or commission. Are we not going on in our sins and disobeying these words of God? "If ye love me, ye will keep my commandments" (John 14:15). Are we not denying the Lord Jesus, as Peter did?

---

[15]Hammon's injunction on preparation is taken from Phil. 2:12—"Wherefore, my beloved, as ye have always obeyed, not as in my presence only, but now much more in my absence, work out your own salvation with fear and trembling"—and from 1 Cor. 15:58—"always abounding in the works of the Lord." While the essayist may have had in mind here the barren fig tree which Christ cursed because of its fruitlessness in Mark 11:12–26, the intended word was "encumberers." That God can prepare the sinner for his grace was a common belief in early eighteenth-century theology. See Pettit's book, *The Heart Prepared* (1966).

> Then began he to curse and to swear, saying, I know not the man. And immediately the cock crew (Matt. 26:74). And Peter remembered the word of Jesus, which said unto him, Before the cock crow, thou shalt deny me thrice. And he went out, and wept bitterly. (Matt. 26:75)

Surely then, we ought to come to the Divine Sovereign, the blessed Jesus, who was crucified for us sinners. Oh! we ought to come on the bended knees of our souls, and say, "Lord, we believe; help thou our unbelief." Come, my brethren, let us cry to the life-giving Jesus and say, "Son of God, have mercy on us! Lamb of God, that taketh away the sins of the world, have mercy on us!" Let us cast off all self-dependence and rely on a crucified Savior. "Pilate therefore, willing to release Jesus, spake again to them" (Luke 23:20). "But they cried, saying, Crucify him, crucify him" (Luke 23:21). Here we may see the love of God, in giving his Son to save all that come unto him by faith and repentance. Let us trace the sufferings of our Savior a little further: "He went away again the second time, and prayed, saying, O my Father, if this cup may not pass away from me, except I drink it, thy will be done" (Matt. 26:42). Here we trace our Savior's example set before us so that we should not murmur at the hand of Divine Providence; for God hath a right to deal with his creatures as he pleaseth.

Come, let us contemplate the death of the blessed Jesus and the fearful judgement that the Lord passes on the guilty sinner.

> Then shall they begin to say to the mountains, Fall on us; and to the hills, Cover us (Luke 23:30). And there were also two other, malefactors, led with him to be put to death. And when they were come to the place, which is called Calvary, there they crucified him, and the malefactors, one on the right hand, and the other on the left. (Luke 23:32–33)

And thus was the Scripture fulfilled: ". . . and he was numbered with the transgressors" (Isa. 53:12).

> And when they had platted a crown of thorns, they put it upon his head, and a reed in his right hand. . . . (Matt. 27:29). Likewise also the chief priests mocking him, with the scribes and elders, said, He saved others; himself he cannot save. If he be the King of Israel, let him now come down from the cross, and we will believe him (Matt. 27:41–42). Now from the sixth hour there was darkness over all the land unto the ninth hour (Matt. 27:45). And about the ninth hour Jesus cried with a loud voice, saying, Eli, Eli, lama sabachthani? that is to say, My God, my God, why hast thou forsaken me? (Matt. 27:46)

My brethren, should not a sense of these things on our minds implant in us a spirit of love to God, who hath provided a Savior who is able to save to the uttermost all that come unto him by faith and repentance? "For godly sorrow worketh repentance to salvation not to be repented of: but the sorrow of the world worketh death" (2 Cor. 7:10). My brethren, see what sin hath done: it hath made all flesh guilty in the sight of God.[16]

May we now adopt the language of David: "O remember not against us former iniquities: Let thy tender mercies speedily prevent us" (Ps. 79:8). "Turn us again, O Lord God of hosts, cause thy face to shine; and we shall be saved" (Ps. 80:19).

Let us contemplate a little further on the death of Christ.

---

[16]In the first part of this paragraph, Hammon has in mind Heb. 7:25: "Wherefore he is able also to save them to the uttermost that come unto God by him, seeing he ever liveth to make intercession for them." The term "by faith and repentance" was used often during and even before the Great Awakening as a necessary part of personal soul-searching before salvation. White people often suspected slaves who professed conversion, thinking that the servants knew nothing of true faith and repentance but were rather only seeking freedom from their duties. Yet slaveholders seemed only to want genuine conversion, because they believed that it would result in more obedient slaves. Hammon differentiated from the slave masters' requirements and wrote instead that they themselves had never fully obeyed God in faith and repentance. The irony of slave conversion is a fascinating topic in American history. See Beveridge, "Faith and Repentence" in *Works* 7 (1824); Cherry, *The Theology of Jonathan Edwards* (1966), 100, 117, 128; Greene, *The Negro* (1942), 259–75; Jernegan, "Slavery" in *American Historical Review* (1916), 507–27; McKee, *Labor in Colonial New York, 1664–1776* (1935), 24–40; Scherer, *Slavery and the Churches in Early America, 1619–1819*, 15–18, 144–49.

> Jesus, when he had cried again with a loud voice, yielded up the ghost (Matt. 27:50). And, behold, the veil of the temple was rent in twain from the top to the bottom; and the earth did quake, and the rocks rent. (Matt. 27:51)

Here we see that the death of Christ caused all nature to tremble and the power of heaven to shake. Here we may see not only the evil of sin but also the unmerited mercy of God, in giving his only Son. Should not our hearts be filled with fear and love for God? We must believe that Jesus is the Son of God.

> Now when the centurion, and they that were with him, watching Jesus, saw the earth quake, and those things that were done, they feared greatly, saying, Truly this was the Son of God. (Matt. 27:54)

Now this was done for the remission of our sins, for "without shedding of blood [there] is no remission" (Heb. 9:22) of sin. This we have confirmed in the Holy Sacrament. "For this is my blood of the new testament, which is shed for many" (Matt. 26:28). But the unbelieving Jews still persisted in their unbelief and would have prevented the resurrection of our Savior if it had been in their power:

> . . . the chief priests and Pharisees came together unto Pilate, Saying, Sir, we remember that that deceiver said, while he was yet alive, After three days I will rise again (Matt. 27:62–63). So they went, and made the sepulchre sure, sealing the stone, and setting a watch. (Matt. 27:66)

Here we see the spirit of unbelief in Nathaniel:

> Philip findeth Nathaniel, and saith unto him, We have found him, of whom Moses in the law, and the prophets, did write, Jesus of Nazareth, the son of Joseph. And Nathaniel said unto him, Can there any good thing come out of Nazareth? Philip saith unto him, Come and see. (John 1:45–46)

Thus we are to come and see the mercy of God in sending his Son to save lost men.

Let us contemplate the manner of Christ's resurrection. "Behold, there was a great earthquake: for the angel of the Lord descended from heaven, and came and rolled back the stone from the door, and sat upon it" (Matt. 28:2). Here we see that our Savior was attended by an angel, one of those holy spirits we read of in Revelation:

> . . . they rest not day and night, saying, Holy, holy, holy, Lord God Almighty, which was, and is, and is to come (Rev. 4:8). Saying with a loud voice, Worthy is the Lamb that was slain to receive power, and riches, and wisdom, and strength, and honour, and glory, and blessing. (Rev. 5:12)

And our Savior himself tells us he hath received his power: "And Jesus came and spake unto them, saying, All power is given unto me in heaven and in earth" (Matt. 28:18). Then he gives his disciples their charge: "Go ye therefore, and teach all nations, baptizing them in the name of the Father, and of the Son, and of the Holy Ghost" (Matt. 28:19).

But I must conclude in a few words and say: my dear brethren, should we not admire the free grace of God, which he is inviting us to come and accept of Jesus Christ, on the terms of the gospel? And he is calling us to repent of all our sins. This we cannot do of ourselves, but we must be saved in the use of means, not to neglect those two great articles of the Christian religion—baptism and the Sacrament. We ought, all of us, to seek by prayers, but the Scripture hath told us that we must not depend on the use of means alone. The apostle says, "I have planted, Apollos watered; but God gave the increase" (1 Cor. 3:6). Here we see that if we are saved, it must be by the power of God's Holy Spirit. But, my dear brethren, the time is hastening when we must appear.[17]

---

[17]Apparently printing space demanded that Hammon's printer end this sentence before the thought was completed. Hammon probably had written here 2 Cor. 5:10: "For we must all appear before the judgement seat of Christ; that everyone may receive the things done in his body, according to that he hath done, whether it be good or bad."

LUCY TERRY
(1730–1821)

The first known poem written by an African American is Lucy Terry's "Bars Fight, August 28, 1746." Although Terry produced the poem sometime shortly after the 1746 battle between the white people and the Native Americans, which the poem commemorates, it was not published until 1895. Thus, while she is not the first black poet with published works in the North American colonies, Terry is the first black poet to be recognized, quoted, and otherwise honored for artistic creativity in the nation's literary history.

Bars is a colonial word for meadow. Scholars tend to read the poem as a colloquial creation of her eyewitness account of a fight on the meadow of Deerfield, Massachusetts, the frontier town where she lived, during which Native Americans defeated local white people whose names and faces were familiar to Terry. Filled with colorful visual imagery in a clear style that recounts a tragic event with rather comic irony, the poem must be recognized as the first symbolic portrayal portending race relations in the United States for the next two centuries: a battle between Native Americans and Euro-Americans as witnessed and recorded by an African American. While the Native Americans may have won that battle, they have not yet won the war; and, although the racial roles of victor, vanquished, and spectator have often been shuffled, the conflict nonetheless continues in some form even today. Terry's dramatic rendition about some Euro-Americans who died while either fighting or running and of others who escaped has the momentum of a griot historian in the oral tradition of Africa, which Terry must have known before being kidnapped into slavery.

Obviously, the poem was an outstanding phenomenon of oral literature among local colonists, both European and African, because it stayed alive by word of mouth and private record for over a century before being formally published in 1895. Josiah Gilbert Holland, a friend of Emily Dickinson's, introduced the poem in his *History of Western Massachusetts.* In that book, he wrote that Lucy Terry "was noted for her wit and shrewdness."

Like Phillis Wheatley, Terry was sold into slavery from Africa as a very young girl. Records show that at age five she was enslaved by Ebenezer Wells of Deerfield; that summer, she was baptized during a revival of the Great Awakening. When she was fourteen, she was admitted to church fellowship, and when she was sixteen, she wrote "Bars Fight."

Lucy Terry married a free black, Abijah Prince, who bought her freedom after the union. Records show that he was twice her age and a landowner paying taxes. They raised six children on a hundred-acre lot he inherited from Deacon Samuel Field. The couple's home became a regular gathering place for the enslaved and the freedmen of their community, a place where Lucy entertained her guests by telling old African folktales. "Her house," Holland wrote, "was the constant resort of the boys, to hear her talk." Some modern critics allege that Terry also joined the Great Awakening revivalist movement as a Christian speaker or preacher of sorts, again, well known in her local area.

George Sheldon, a Deerfield historian, further documents that Terry's life upstaged her extant offering. She successfully petitioned the law to protect her family against the violence being perpetrated by white people during the turbulent eighteenth century, and she pleaded her own case to win in court against a white man who tried to steal land that her husband had inherited.

Records of the now-famous Williams College show that Lucy Terry petitioned the then all-white, all-male college to admit one of her sons. Although the college denied him entrance, she succeeded in holding officials up to three hours as she pressed her claim. Through her sermons, public speeches, and storytelling, she no doubt kept the crucial question of education for African Americans alive and in debate for years afterwards.

After burying her husband in 1794, Lucy Terry went on to live until age ninety-two.

❖❖❖

There are very few sources of Terry. Notwithstanding, Josiah Holland gives a regional account of Lucy Terry in *History of Western Massachusetts* (1855) and Sidney and Emma Nogrady Kaplan offer an informative discussion of her life and work in *The Black Presence in the Era of the American Revolution,* rev. ed. (1989). A discussion of the first African American poet is also included in Erlene Stetson's *Black Sister: Poetry by Black American Women, 1746–1980* (1981) and in Frances Ford Foster's *Written by Herself: Literary Productions by African American Women, 1746–1892* (1993).

Bars Fight

August 'twas the twenty fifth
Seventeen hundred forty-six
The Indians did in ambush lay
Some very valient men to slay
The names of whom I'll not leave out
Samuel Allen like a hero fout
And though he was so brave and bold
His face no more shall we behold.
Eleazer Hawks was killed outright
Before he had time to fight
Before he did the Indians see
Was shot and killed immediately.
Oliver Amsden he was slain
Which caused his friends much grief and pain.
Samuel Amsden they found dead
Not many rods off from his head.
Adonijah Gillet we do hear
Did lose his life which was so dear.
John Saddler fled across the water
And so excaped the dreadful slaughter.
Eunice Allen see the Indians comeing
And hoped to save herself by running
And had not her petticoats stopt her

The awful creatures had not cotched her
And tommyhawked her on the head
And left her on the ground for dead.
Young Samuel Allen, Oh! lack a-day
Was taken and carried to Canada.

PHILLIS WHEATLEY
(1753?–1784)

There is probably no more astounding account of emerging artistic genius in all of American literary history than that of the eighteenth-century African American poet Phillis Wheatley. Kidnapped from Africa when she was less than a decade old and sold on a Boston auction block when she was near death, the child soon mastered both the verbal and written language of her enslavers. By the time she was sixteen, she had become the best-known African writer in the colonies. Before her tragic and untimely death at thirty years of age, she was lionized in England, Europe, and New England, and she was paraded before the new republic's political leadership and the old empire's aristocracy. As the abolitionists' illustration of the African's intellectual potential, Phillis Wheatley's name was a guilt-convicting reminder to all literate colonists; her achievements were a catalyst for the colony's fledgling antislavery movement, and her presence and writings were an inspiration to every colonial slave.

Born in West Africa around 1753, Phillis Wheatley was abducted into slavery when she was about five or six years old and put on a slave ship headed for the Boston docks with a shipment of "refugee" slaves who, because of age or physical frailty, were unsuited for rigorous labor in the West Indian or southern colonies. Purchased in 1761 by an upper-class Boston couple, John and Susannah Wheatley, the girl, at about seven years old, was of slight build and quite sickly, apparently not adjusting well to the cold New England climate. Shedding her teeth, the waif had "no other covering than a quantity of dirty carpet about her." Among the final "items" purchased, Phillis was bought for "a trifle." Believing her to be terminally ill, the captain of the slave ship wanted to gain at least a small profit before she died.

John Wheatley, a successful entrepreneur, owned several slaves. He claimed that they purchased the child because his wife "wanted a Black girl to train as a domestic." The Wheatleys' daughter, Mary, began to teach theology and literature to the child worker to whom they had given the name "Phillis." The child was soon spared the menial household chores and was not allowed to associate with the other Wheatley slaves. Instead, she became a constant companion of Susannah Wheatley who, recognizing a prodigy, taught her to read and write English and Latin as well as how to study the Bible. She was soon immersed in "astronomy, geography, history, British literature (particularly John Milton, John Dryden, and Alexander Pope), and the Greek and Latin classics of Virgil, Ovid, Terence, and Homer."

She wrote her first letter to the Mohegan leader, Reverend Samson Occom, in 1765. However, neither this letter nor her first poem, which was sent to Reverend John Sewall of Boston's Old South Church, are extant. At services at the new South Congregational Church, which she attended with the Wheatleys, she embraced the religious teachings of her day, which included the idea of God as the ultimate and final source of power.

Scholars contend that poems revealing her early religious training, such as "On Being Brought from Africa to America" and "To the University of Cambridge, in New-England," may have been written prior to 1767, but they were not published until six years later. Her first poem, "On Messrs. Hussey and Coffin," based on a true adventure of survival at sea, appeared in the *Newport Mercury* on December 21, 1767, when she was about fourteen years old. Three years later, she wrote "On the Death of the Reverend Mr. George Whitefield, 1770," the poem that was to make her famous in both England and the American colonies as the "Sable Muse." Published as a broadside and a pamphlet in Boston, Newport, and Philadelphia, the poem was published with Ebenezer Pemberton's funeral sermon for Whitefield in London in 1771.

By the time she was about eighteen years old, in 1772, Phillis had composed at least twenty-eight poems. Mrs. Wheatley advertised for subscription supporters to publish them in a collection, but her attempts were unsuccessful. American colonists refused to support a volume of poems written by a slave. Mrs. Wheatley had no choice but to turn to London for publication. In December 1772, she arranged for a London printer and a ship's master to visit the wealthy Countess of Huntingdon in London with Phillis's manuscript. Agreeing to finance the volume's publication, Lady Huntingdon liked the prospect of having the book dedicated to her and asked to have Phillis's picture in the frontispiece.

In 1773, the Wheatleys sent Phillis to London to get medical care for her chronic asthma and to finalize the publication. She was accompanied by the Wheatleys' son, Nathaniel. England had abolished slavery a year earlier; according to a technicality in the law, any enslaved person who set foot in England was declared free. This, together with British newspaper reviews chiding the Wheatleys for holding the African poet in bondage, may have figured in Phillis's being formally freed when she returned to America the next year.

Following publication of her book, much of Wheatley's contemporary recognition rested on her relationships with world leaders in the abolitionist movement in England, Europe, and the American colonies. These world leaders included John Thornton, a great philanthropist and leading financial contributor to the Society for the Propagation of the Gospel in Foreign Parts, the only worldwide organization dedicated to the education of African slaves. While few slaves were educated in the southern colonies, the overwhelming majority of slaves in the northern colonies who received any education did so through this society. Thornton's home in Clapham was headquarters for the Clapham Sect, which became the fountainhead of the abolitionist movement among evangelicals, in both Europe and the colonies. Moreover, during this trip to London, Phillis met Benjamin Franklin, received unlimited renown in the British press, and was even touted by British royalty.

Through Thornton, she established connections with abolitionists who were in the British parliament, continually pressing antislavery petitions. Thornton was also a major contributor to the Native American Samson Occom's Wheelock Indian School—a forerunner of Dartmouth College. He was instrumental in introducing Phillis to Samson, thus establishing one of the many cooperative networks between oppressed Native Americans and enslaved Africans.

Thornton also arranged for Phillis, while in London, to meet with the renowned preacher George Whitefield; with the Earl of Dartmouth, who would become the British ruling governor of the American colonies; and with other prominent and wealthy benefactors in the influential Clapman society. These meetings allowed this wellspring of leadership in the antislavery movement to further disseminate Phillis's poetry to an ever-widening audience and to use her work to decry the enslavement of such representative creative potential.

Phillis Wheatley's London-published volume included Christian elegies; political and patriotic pieces; and several poems about religion, morals, nature, imagination, and memory. It also contained a highly original English translation of Ovid from the Latin. Perhaps more important, several of her poems embodied racially self-conscious lines. For instance, in her tribute "To the Right Honorable William Legge, Earl of Dartmouth," Wheatley expresses her personal desire and struggle for freedom as an enslaved African in America. Passionately, she informs the Earl that her objection to Britain's oppression of the American colonies stems mainly from the fact that because of "seeming cruel Fate," she was once "snatch'd from Afric's fancy'd happy Seat."

In 1774, hearing that Mrs. Wheatley was ill, Phillis returned to Boston. Not long after her return, Mrs. Wheatley died. Phillis was formally freed some three months later. Shortly thereafter, when Mr. Wheatley died and the remaining members of the family either died or moved away, Phillis became a free and vulnerable unattached African in the American British colonies. That year, she wrote a final letter to Occom in which she stated, "In every human Breast, God has implanted a Principle, which we call Love of Freedom; it is impatient of Oppression, and pants for Deliverance; and by Leave of our Modern Egyptians I will assert, that the same Principle lives in us." Wheatley's forceful declaration—written only *after* she was freed from slavery—speaks for her people still held in bondage as well as for enslaved people throughout the world.

On April 1, 1778, she married the man she had been seeing for about five years, a free black named John Peters. A freelance lawyer for black people before Massachusetts tribunals, Peters appears to have been an entrepreneur before and after the Revolutionary War. Apparently quite successful before the war, he kept a grocery store and at various times exchanged trade as a baker and barber. There is a record of Peters paying taxes on a house of above-average value. Early scholars render an unflattering depiction of Peters. Others, including Sidney Kaplan and Arthur Schomberg, describe him as an assertive black man who simply did not patronize white people.

M. A. Richmond and Margaretta Matilda Odell cast Peters as ambitious, shiftless, arrogant, and proud, and Odell states that distant relatives of the Wheatleys held Peters directly responsible for Phillis's death. But in an era that only valued black male brawn, Peters's business acumen was simply unacceptable. Charles Akers argues that "Peters was a free black man of considerable ability and personal charm who appears not to have deserved his reputation as a ne'er-do-well whose irresponsibility contributed to his talented wife's untimely death."

The couple had three children between 1779 and 1783. To avoid the violence of the Revolutionary War, Phillis and Peters moved temporarily from Boston to Wilmington, Massachusetts, shortly after their marriage. Richmond points out that economic conditions in the colonies during and after the war were very harsh, not only for slaves but for free blacks as well. White people especially resisted the entrance of free black people into the job market. Thus, economic recession and racial discrimination contributed to the postwar poverty that the family suffered.

Because Peters was often away either looking for work or dodging creditors, Phillis eventually took work as a charwoman. During the first six weeks after returning to Boston, Phillis and the children stayed with one of Mrs. Wheatley's nieces in a bombed-out mansion. Peters then moved them into a run-down section of Boston where, according to Odell, other Wheatley relatives found Phillis sick and destitute. Odell reports that "two of her children were dead, and the third was sick unto death. She was herself suffering for want of attention, for many comforts and that greatest of all comforts in sickness—cleanliness. She was reduced to a condition too loathsome to describe. . . . In a filthy apartment, in an obscure part of the metropolis, lay the dying mother, and the wasting child." The woman who had stood honored and respected in the presence of international prominence was "numbering the last hours of her life in a state of the most abject misery, surrounded by all the emblems of a squalid poverty."

Throughout these lean years, Phillis continued to write and publish poetry and to maintain, on a limited scale, international correspondence with numerous dignitaries. Before her death, Phillis had attempted to publish a new collection of verse. Due to racism and to the Revolutionary War, she did not realize this final hope. Some historians believe that John Peters took the manuscript with him after her death; it has never been found. She lived with the hope that her American audience was at last ready to publish this second volume of poetry. Between October 30 and December 18, 1779, with at least the partial motive of raising funds to help feed her family, Phillis ran six advertisements soliciting subscribers for "300 pages in Octavo," a proposed volume which she intended to be "Dedicated to the Right Hon. Benjamin Franklin, Esq.: One of the Ambassadors of the United States at the Court of France." The work was to include thirty-three poems and thirteen letters; however, as was the case with Phillis's first volume, no American benefactors came forth to support publication of the second volume.

In 1784, the year of her death, the ailing poet was able to publish, under the name Phillis Peters, a masterful sixty-four line poem in a pamphlet titled *Liberty and Peace,* a euphoric celebration of America's victory over Great Britain. Wheatley, in this poem, is the first American to refer to this nation as "Columbia." Earlier that year, she published "An Elegy, Sacred to the Memory of that Great Divine, the Reverent and Learned Dr. Samuel Cooper" in honor of the pastor of the Brattle Street church. In September, she published an elegy in the Poetical Essays section of the Boston Magazine titled "To Mr. and Mrs. ______, on the Death of their Infant Son," which was probably a lament on the death of one of her own children and certainly foreshadowed her own death three months later. Phillis Wheatley died sometime during the winter of 1784, when she was about 30 years old. She probably died from complications of childbirth, with the last surviving child dying in time to be buried with his mother. Her husband was incarcerated in debtors prison.

Her detractors maintain that the poet's dedication to Christianity was so overwhelming as to make her ignore her own slave status and that of her fellow Africans. However, Sondra O'Neale ("There Was No Other Game in Town") and other Wheatley supporters point out that if the poet were to address the issue of slavery at all, the only possible institution in which she could do so was evangelical Christianity. And, even in the church, only a few "radicals" on both continents spoke out against the evils of the slave trade. In other articles, O'Neale also highlights Wheatley's use of biblical terms such as "salvation," "Cain," "light," and "Christian," to discuss eighteenth-century slavery. Again, the use of this type of biblical language was the only safe way in which a slave writer could speak against his or her enslavers. Using Christian symbolism to speak to an audience that considered America to be a Christian society not only legitimized the African American slave writer as an acceptable contemporary artist—it was the only possible vehicle for those African Americans seeking to invoke Christian conscience.

Another critic offering revisionist theories of Wheatley's work is John C. Shields. In "Phillis Wheatley's Use of Classicism," he thoroughly discusses Wheatley's unusually extensive knowledge of the Greek and Roman classics and the ways in which she uses them to authenticate her poetic gifts and to allude to her ethnic identity and to innate childhood memories of familial sun worship when "her mother poured out water before the sun at his rising." Shields convincingly argues that "Wheatley's syncretism of solar worship, Christianity and classical mythology demonstrates a substantial and even provocative use of classicism." He concludes that

> What Wheatley essentially does, then, is to decide that this world, which allows slavery to remain legitimate, is unsatisfactory to her; so she manipulates the conventions of neoclassicism to build in her poems another, acceptable world. . . . Not only was Wheatley vitally concerned for the plight of her enslaved brothers and sisters, but she fervently sought her own freedom, both in this world and in the next. So complete was her absorption in the struggle for freedom that this endeavor governed her conception of poetry, causing her to be no more imitative than any other good student and writer of literature.

Wheatley's detractors disregard these accomplishments; they count it as a light thing that she met and had correspondence with the first president of the United States, that she had private meetings with Benjamin Franklin, and that she was even scheduled to have an audience with King George III. They also discount another crucial observation: No less a personage than Thomas Jefferson believed that her authenticity as an African American female poet was such a threat to the sanctity of slavery that he denounced her work as being "beneath contempt" and dismissed it as imitative of classic eighteenth-century poetry. He also castigated her writing on the grounds that it was impossible for an African woman to have the intellectual or artistic capacity to produce creative art. The statesman concluded that "Religion, indeed, has produced a Phillis Whately [sic]; but it could not produce a poet."

Another indication of the extreme racism in the eighteenth-century North was the refusal of the colonial aristocracy to raise the money needed to publish Phillis's first book, even after its astounding success in London. The first American edition was not published until 1787, three years after her death. According to William Robinson in *Reconstructing American Literature* (1983), "While her second edition, published as *Poems,* went through at least four London printings for a run of about 1200 copies, in America the same volume fared poorly early on." Even though she was identified as a black poet during her lifetime, Boston printers, who advertised the first American publication of her book, would not credit "ye performances to be by a Negro."

Critical revaluation of Wheatley and her poetry began during the early years of the contemporary women's movement when eighteen African American women poets held the Phillis Wheatley Poetry Festival at Jackson State College, Mississippi, in 1973. Such writers as Margaret Walker, Sonia Sanchez, June Jordan, Audre Lorde, Lucille Clifton, Maya Angelou, and Alice Walker paid tribute to the poet and commemorated the two-hundredth anniversary of the publication of *Poems.* Since then, Wheatley has been regarded as the foremother of the African American and women's literary traditions. To date, Wheatley's *Poems* has been reprinted more than twenty-four times in the United States and Europe, and selections have appeared regularly in literature anthologies. This resurgence of activity around Wheatley's work will surely yield further significant revelations about the depth and complexity of her work and the missing facets of her life.

❖❖❖

A helpful, full-length biographical treatment of Wheatley is Shirley Graham's *The Story of Phillis Wheatley* (1949). See also M. A. Richmond's *Bid the Vassal Soar: Interpretive Essays on the Life and Poetry of Phillis Wheatley and George Moses Horton* (1974) as well as biographical discussions of Wheatley in the *Dictionary of Literary Biography,* vol. 31 (1986) by Sondra O'Neale and Kenny J. Williams, vol. 50. Texts that include necessary history for Wheatley's biographical background include Charles W. Akers's "'Our Modern Egyptians:' Phillis Wheatley and the Whig Campaign Against Slavery in Revolutionary Boston" in the *Journal of Negro History,* vol. 60 (July 1975); and Benjamin Brawley's *The Negro Genius: A New Appraisal of the Achievement of the American Negro in Literature and the Fine Arts* (1937). Valuable revisionists' assessments of Wheatley's poetry can be found in three critical editions of her works: *Phillis Wheatley and Her Writings* (1984), edited by William H. Robinson; *The Collected Works of Phillis Wheatley* (1988), edited by John Shields; and *The Poems of Phillis Wheatley* (1966), edited by Julian Mason; as well as in the following works: O'Neale's "A Slave's Subtle War: Phillis Wheatley's Use of Biblical Myth and Symbol" in *Early American Literature* 21 (1986); O'Neale's "A Challenge to Wheatley's Critics: There Was No Other Game In Town" in the *Journal of Negro Education,* vol. 54, no. 4 (Spring 1986); Eugene B. Redmond's *Drumvoices: The Mission of Afro-American Poetry* (1976); and Kenny J. Williams's "Phillis Wheatley" in the *Dictionary of Literary Biography,* vol. 50 (1986). More recent scholarship viewing Wheatley's life and work from a feminist perspective includes Frances Smith Foster's *Written By Herself: Literary Production by African American Women, 1746–1892* (1993) and Gloria Hull's "Black Women Poets from Wheatley to Walker" in *Sturdy Black Bridges: Visions of Black Women in Literature* (1979).

Original manuscripts, letters, and first editions are in collections at the Boston Public Library; Duke University Library; Massachusetts Historical Society; Historical Society of Pennsylvania; Library Company of Philadelphia; American Antiquarian Society; Houghton Library, Harvard University; Churchill College, Cambridge; The Scottish Record Office, Edinburgh; Dartmouth College Library; William Salt Library, Staffordshire, England; British Library, London; Cheshunt Foundation, Cambridge University; Bowdoin College; Library of Congress; Moorland-Spingarn Research Center of Howard University; and the Schomburg Library Collection of the New York Public Library.

On Being Brought from Africa to America

'Twas mercy brought me from my *Pagan* land,
Taught my benighted soul to understand
That there's a God, that there's a *Saviour* too:
Once I redemption neither sought nor knew.
Some view our sable race with scornful eye,
"Their colour is a diabolic die."
Remember, *Christians, Negros,* black as *Cain,*
May be refin'd, and join th' angelic train.

To the University of Cambridge, in New-England

While an intrinsic ardor prompts to write,
The muses promise to assist my pen;
'Twas not long since I left my native shore
The land of errors, and *Egyptian* gloom:
Father of mercy, 'twas thy gracious hand
Brought me in safety from those dark abodes.

Students, to you 'tis giv'n to scan the heights
Above, to traverse the ethereal space,
And mark the systems of revolving worlds.
Still more, ye sons of science ye receive
The blissful news by messengers from heav'n,
How *Jesus'* blood for your redemption flows.
See him with hands out-stretcht upon the cross;
Immense compassion in his bosom glows;
He hears revilers, nor resents their scorn:
What matchless mercy in the Son of God!
When the whole human race by sin had fall'n,
He deign'd to die that they might rise again,
And share with him in the sublimest skies,
Life without death, and glory without end.

Improve your privileges while they stay,
Ye pupils, and each hour redeem, that bears
Or good or bad report of you to heav'n.
Let sin, that baneful evil to the soul,
By you be shunn'd, nor once remit your guard;
Suppress the deadly serpent in its egg.
Ye blooming plants of human race devine,
An *Ethiop* tells you 'tis your greatest foe;
Its transient sweetness turns to endless pain,
And in immense perdition sinks the soul.

Philis's [sic] Reply to the Answer in our last by the Gentleman in the Navy

For one bright moment, heavenly goddness! shine,
Inspire my song and form the lays divine.

Rochford, attend. Beloved of Phœbus! hear,
A truer sentence never reach'd thine ear;
Struck with thy song, each vain conceit resign'd
A soft affection seiz'd my grateful mind,
While I each golden sentiment admire
In thee, the muse's bright celestial fire.
The generous plaudit 'tis not mine to claim,
A muse untutor'd, and unknown to fame.
　The heavenly sisters pour thy notes along
And crown their bard with every grace of song.
My pen, least favour'd by the tuneful nine,
Can never rival, never equal thine;
Then fix the humble Afric muse's seat
At British Homer's and Sir Isaac's feet.
Those bards whose fame in deathless strains arise
Creation's boast, and fav'rites of the skies.
　In fair description are thy powers display'd
In artless grottos, and the sylvan shade;
Charm'd with thy painting, how my bosom burns!
And pleasing Gambia on my soul returns,
With native grace in spring's luxuriant reign,
Smiles the gay mead, and Eden blooms again,
The various bower, the tuneful flowing stream,
The soft retreats, the lovers golden dream,
Her soil spontaneous, yields exhaustless stores;
For Phœbus revels on her verdant shores.
Whose flowery births, a fragrant train appear,
And crown the youth throughout the smiling year,
　There, as in Britain's favour'd isle, behold
The bending harvest ripen into gold!
Just are thy views of Afric's blissful plain,
On the warm limits of the land and main.

　Pleas'd with the theme, see sportive fancy play,
In realms devoted to the God of day!

　Europa's bard, who the great depth explor'd,
Of nature, and thro' boundless systems soar'd,
Thro' earth, thro' heaven, and hell's profound domain,
Where night eternal holds her awful reign.
But, lo! in him Britania's prophet dies,
And whence, ah! whence, shall other *Newton's* rise?
Muse, bid they Rochford's matchless pen display
The charms of friendship in the sprightly lay.
Queen of his song, thro' all his numbers shine,
And plausive glories, goddess! shall be thine.
With partial grace thou mak'st his verse excel,

And *his* the glory to describe so well.
Cerulean bard! to thee these strains belong,
The Muse's darling and the prince of song.

December 5th, 1774.

To the Right Honourable William, Earl of Dartmouth, His Majesty's Principal Secretary of State for North-America, &c.

Hail, happy day, when, smiling like the morn,
Fair *Freedom* rose *New-England* to adorn:
The northern clime beneath her genial ray,
Dartmouth, congratulates thy blissful sway:
Elate with hope her race no longer mourns,
Each soul expands, each grateful bosom burns,
While in thine hand with pleasure we behold
The silken reins, and *Freedom's* charms unfold.
Long lost to realms beneath the northern skies
She shines supreme, while hated *faction* dies:
Soon as appear'd the *Goddess* long desir'd,
Sick at the view, she lanquish'd and expir'd;
Thus from the splendors of the morning light
The owl in sadness seeks the caves of night.

No more, *America,* in mournful strain
Of wrongs, and grievance unredress'd complain,
No longer shalt thou dread the iron chain,
Which wanton *Tyranny* with lawless hand
Had made, and with it meant t' enslave the land.

Should you, my lord, while you peruse my song,
Wonder from whence my love of *Freedom* sprung,
Whence flow these wishes for the common good,
By feeling hearts alone best understood,
I, young in life, by seeming cruel fate
Was snatch'd from *Afric's* fancy'd happy seat:
What pangs excruciating must molest,
What sorrows labour in my parent's breast?
Steel'd was that soul and by no misery mov'd
That from a father seiz'd his babe belov'd:
Such, such my case. And can I then but pray
Others may never feel tyrannic sway?

For favours past, great Sir, our thanks are due,
And thee we ask thy favours to renew,
Since in thy pow'r, as in thy will before,
To sooth the griefs, which thou did'st once deplore.
May heav'nly grace the sacred sanction give
To all thy works, and thou for ever live
Not only on the wings of fleeting *Fame,*

Though praise immortal crowns the patriot's name,
But to conduct to heav'ns refulgent fane,
May fiery coursers sweep th' ethereal plain,
And bear thee upwards to that blest abode,
Where, like the prophet, thou shalt find thy God.

To S.M. a young African *Painter, on seeing his Works*

To show the lab'ring bosom's deep intent,
And thought in living characters to paint,
When first thy pencil did those beauties give,
And breathing figures learnt from thee to live,
How did those prospects give my soul delight,
A new creation rushing on my sight?
Still, wond'rous youth! each noble path pursue,
On deathless glories fix thine ardent view:
Still may the painter's and the poet's fire
To aid thy pencil, and thy verse conspire!
And may the charms of each seraphic theme
Conduct thy footsteps to immortal fame!
High to the blissful wonders of the skies
Elate thy soul, and raise thy wishful eyes.
Thrice happy, when exalted to survey
That splendid city, crown'd with endless day,
Whose twice fix gates on radiant hinges ring:
Celestial *Salem* blooms in endless spring.
Calm and serene thy moments glide along,
And may the muse inspire each future song!
Still, with the sweets of contemplation bless'd,
May peace with balmy wings your soul invest!
But when these shades of time are chas'd away,
And darkness ends in everlasting day,
On what seraphic pinions shall we move,
And view the landscapes in the realms above?
There shall thy tongue in heav'nly murmurs flow,
And there my muse with heav'nly transport glow:
No more to tell of *Damon's* tender sighs,
Or rising radiance of *Aurora's* eyes,
For nobler themes demand a nobler strain,
And purer languge on th' ethereal plain.
Cease, gentle muse! the solemn gloom of night
Now seals the fair creation from my sight.

On the Death of the Rev. Mr. George Whitefield. 1770

Hail, happy saint, on thine immortal throne,
Possest of glory, life, and bliss unknown;

We hear no more the music of thy tongue,
Thy wonted auditories cease to throng.
Thy sermons in unequall'd accents flow'd,
And ev'ry bosom with devotion glow'd;
Thou didst in strains of eloquence refin'd
Inflame the heart, and captivate the mind.
Unhappy we the setting sun deplore,
So glorious once, but ah! it shines no more.

Behold the prophet in his tow'ring flight!
He leaves the earth for heav'n's unmeasur'd height,
And worlds unknown receive him from our sight.
There *Whitefield* wings with rapid course his way,
And sails to *Zion* through vast seas of day.
Thy pray'rs, great saint, and thine incessant cries
Have pierc'd the bosom of thy native skies.
Thou moon hast seen, and all the stars of light,
How he has wrestled with his God by night.
He pray'd that grace in ev'ry heart might dwell,
He long'd to see *America* excel;
He charg'd its youth that ev'ry grace divine
Should with full lustre in their conduct shine;
That Saviour, which his soul did first receive,
The greatest gift that ev'n a God can give,
He freely offer'd to the num'rous throng,
That on his lips with list'ning pleasure hung.

"Take him, ye wretched, for your only good,
"Take him ye starving sinners, for your food;
"Ye thirsty, come to this life-giving stream,
"Ye preachers, take him for your joyful theme;
"Take him my dear *Americans,* he said,
"Be your complaints on his kind bosom laid:
"Take him, ye *Africans,* he longs for you,
"*Impartial Saviour* is his title due:
"Wash'd in the fountain of redeeming blood,
"You shall be sons, and kings, and priests to God."

Great *Countess,* we *Americans* revere
Thy name, and mingle in thy grief sincere;
New England deeply feels, the *Orphans* mourn,
Their more than father will no more return.

But, though arrested by the hand of death,
Whitefield no more exerts his lab'ring breath,
Yet let us view him in th' eternal skies,
Let ev'ry heart to this bright vision rise;
While the tomb safe retains its sacred trust,
Till life divine re-animates his dust.

On the Death of General Wooster

MADAM

I rec[d], your favour by Mr Dennison inclosing a paper containing the Charactcr of the truely worthy General Wooster. It was with the most sensible regret that I heard of his fall in battle, but the pain of so afflicting a dispensation of Providence must be greatly alleviated to you and all his friends in the consideration that he fell a martyr in the Cause of Freedom—

From this the Muse rich consolation draws
He nobly perish'd in his Country's cause
His Country's Cause that ever fir'd his mind
Where martial flames, and Christian virtues join'd.
How shall my pen his warlike deeds proclaim
Or paint them fairer on the list of Fame—
Enough great Cheif—now wrapt in shades around
Thy grateful Country shall thy praise resound
Tho' not with mortals' empty praise elate
That vainest vapour to th' immortal State
Inly serene the expiring hero lies
And thus (while heav'nward roll his swimming eyes)
Permit, great power while yet my fleeting breath
And Spirits wander to the verge of Death—
Permit me yet to paint fair freedom's charms
For her the Continent shines bright in arms
By thy high will, celestial prize she came—
For her we combat on the feild of fame
Without her presence vice maintains full sway
And social love and virtue wing their way
O still propitious be thy guardian care
And lead *Columbia* thro' the toils of war.
With thine own hand conduct them and defend
And bring the dreadful contest to an end—
For ever grateful let them live to thee
And keep them ever virtuous, brave, and free—
But how, presumptuous shall we hope to find
Divine acceptance with th' Almighty mind—
While yet (O deed ungenerous!) they disgrace
And hold in bondage Afric's blameless race?
Let virtue reign—And thou accord our prayers
Be victory our's, and generous freedom theirs.
The hero pray'd—and wond'ring Spirit fled
And Sought the unknown regions of the dead—
Tis thine fair partner of his life, to find
His virtuous path and follow close behind—
A little moment steals him from thy Sight
He waits thy coming to the realms of light
Freed from his labours in the ethereal Skies
Where in Succession endless pleasures rise!

You will do me a great favour by returning to me by the first oppy those books that remain unsold and remitting the money for those that are sold—I can easily dispose of them here for a 12/Lm.° each—I am greatly obliged to you for the care you show me, and your condescention in taking so much pains for my Interest—I am extremely Sorry not to have been honour'd with a personal acquaintance with you—if the foregoing lines meet with your acceptance and approbation I shall think them highly honour'd. I hope you will pardon the length of my letter, when the reason is apparent—fondness of the Subject &—the highest respect for the deceas'd—I sincerely sympathize with you in the great loss you and your family Sustain and am Sincerely

Your friend & very humble Servt
PHILLIS WHEATLEY
Queenstreet
Boston July—
15TH 1778

To Arbour Tanner in New Port

DEAR SISTER
BOSTON MAY 19TH 1772
I rec'd your favour of February 6th for which I give you my sincere thanks, I greatly rejoice with you in that realizing view, and I hope experience, of the Saving change which you so emphatically describe. Happy were it for us if we could arrive to that evangelical Repentance, and the true holiness of heart which you mention. Inexpressibly happy Should we be could we have a due Sense of the Beauties and excellence of the Crucified Saviour. In his Crucifixion may be seen marvellous displays of Grace and Love, Sufficient to draw and invite us to the rich and endless treasures of his mercy, let us rejoice in and adore the wonders of God's infinite Love in bringing us from a land Semblant of darkness itself, and where the divine light of revelation (being obscur'd) is as darkness. Here, the knowledge of the true God and eternal life are made manifest; But there, profound ignorance overshadows the Land, Your observation is true, namely, that there was nothing in us to recommend us to God. Many of our fellow creatures are pass'd by, when the bowels of divine love expanded towards us. May this goodness & long Suffering of God lead us to unfeign'd repentance

It gives me very great pleasure to hear of so many of my Nation, Seeking with eagerness the way to true felicity, O may we all meet at length in that happy mansion. I hope the correspondence between us will continue, (my being much indispos'd this winter past was the reason of my not answering yours before now) which correspondence I hope may have the happy effect of improving our mutual friendship. Till we meet in the regions of consummate blessedness, let us endeavor by the assistance of divine grace, to live the life, and we Shall die the death of the Righteous. May this be our happy case and of those who are travelling to the region of Felicity is the earnest request of your affectionate

Friend & hum. Sert.
PHILLIS WHEATLEY

To Samson Occom

The following is an extract of a Letter from Phillis, a Negro Girl of Mr. Wheatley's, in Boston, to the Rev. Samson Occom, which we are desired to insert as a Specimen of her Ingenuity.—It is dated 11th Feb., 1774.

REV'D AND HONOR'D SIR,
I have this Day received your obliging kind Epistle, and am greatly satisfied with your Reasons respecting the Negroes, and think highly reasonable what you offer in Vindication of their natural Rights: Those that invade them cannot be insensible that the divine Light is chasing away the thick Darkness which broods over the Land of Africa; and the Chaos which has reign'd so long, is converting into beautiful Order, and [r]eveals more and more clearly, the glorious Dispensation of civil and religious Liberty, which are so inseparably united, that there is little or no Enjoyment of one without the other: Otherwise, perhaps, the Israelites had been less solicitous for their Freedom from Egyptian slavery; I do not say they would have been contented without it, by no means, for in every human Breast, God has implanted a Principle, which we call Love of Freedom; it is impatient of Oppression, and pants for Deliverance; and by the Leave of our modern Egyptians I will assert, that the same Principle lives in us. God grant Deliverance in his own Way and Time, and get him honour upon all those whose Avarice impels them to countenance and help forward the Calamities of their fellow Creatures. This I desire not for their Hurt, but to convince them of the strange Absurdity of their Conduct whose Words and Actions are so diametrically opposite. How well the Cry for Liberty, and the reverse Disposition for the exercise of oppressive Power over others agree,—I humbly think it does not require the Penetration of a Philosopher to determine.—

[FEBRUARY 11, 1779]

Voices of Social Protest in Prose

The Confessional Narrative

The Life and Confession of Johnson Green,

Who Is To Be Executed this Day, August 17th, 1786, for the Atrocious Crime of Burglary

I, Johnson Green, having brought myself to a shameful and ignominious death by my wicked conduct, and, as I am a dying man, I leave to the world the following History of my Birth, Education, and vicious Practices, hoping that all people will take warning by my evil example and shun vice and follow virtue.

I was born at Bridgewater, in the County of Plymouth, in the Commonwealth of Massachusetts, was twenty-nine years of age the seventh day of February last. My father was a negro, and a servant to the Hon. Timothy Edson, Esq, late of said Bridgewater, deceased. My mother was an Irish woman named Sarah Johnson. She was a widow, and her maiden name was Green. I have been called Joseph-Johnson Green. When I was five years of age my mother bound me as an Apprentice to Mr. Seth Howard of said Bridgewater, to be instructed in Agriculture. I was used very tenderly, and instructed in the principles of the Christian Religion. Whilst I was an apprentice my mother gave me much good advice, cautioned me against keeping company with those that used bad language and other vicious practices. She advised me not to go to sea nor into the army, foretold what has come to pass since the commencement of the late war, and said it would not come to pass in her day. She died about sixteen years ago, and if I had followed her good advice I might have escaped an ignominious death.

When I was eighteen years of age (contrary to my mother's advice) I enlisted into the American service, and remained in the same for the duration of the war. I would just observe to the world, that my being addicted to drunkenness, and keeping of bad company, and a correspondence that I have had with lewd women, has been the cause of my being brought to this wretched situation.

In March, 1781, I was married at Easton, to one Sarah Phillips, a mustee, who was brought up by Mr. Olney of Providence. She has had two children since I was married to her, and I have treated her exceeding ill.

When I began to steal I was about 12 years old, at which time I stole four cakes of gingerbread and six biscuit out of a horse cart, and afterwards I stole sundry small articles, and was not detected.

When I was about fourteen, I stole one dozen of lemons and one cake of chocolate, was detected, and received reproof. Soon after I stole some hens, and my conduct was so bad that my master sold me to one of his cousins, who used me well.

I continued the practice of stealing, and just before I went into the army I took my master's key, unlocked his chest, and stole two shillings; he discovered what I had done, gave me correction, but not so severely as I deserved.

Sometime after I was engaged in the American service, at a certain tavern in Sherburne I stole fifteen shillings, one case bottle of rum, one dozen of biscuit, and a pillow case with some sugar.

In April, 1781, I stole at the Highlands, near West Point, a pair of silver shoe buckles, was detected, and received one hundred lashes.

In October, the same year, when I was at West Point, and we were extremely pinched for the want of provisions, three of us broke open a settler's markee, stole three cheeses, one small firkin of butter, and some chocolate. I only was detected, and punished by receiving one hundred stripes.

Sometime in the winter of 1783, at Easton, I broke into a grist mill belonging to Mr. Timothy Randall and stole about a bushel of corn, and at sundry times the same year I broke into a cellar belonging to Mr. Ebenezer Howard, of the same place, and stole some meat and tobacco; and I also broke into a cellar and a corn house belonging to Mr. Abiel Kinsley, of the same place, and stole some meat and corn; and at East Bridgewater, the same year, I broke open a grist mill, and stole near a bushel of meal; and at the same time I stole three or four dozen herrings out of a corn house. I also went to a corn house belonging to Mr. Nathaniel Whitman, of Bridgewater, and stole two cheeses out of it.

August 1st, 1784, I broke open a house in Providence and stole goods to the value of forty dollars. Soon after I broke open a shop near Patuxet Falls, stole one pair of cards, two cod fish, and sundry other articles.

In 1784 I also committed the following crimes, viz. I broke into a cellar about a mile from Patuxet Bridge, stole about thirty weight of salt pork, one case bottle, and several other articles. About the same time I stole out of a washing tub in Patuxet a pair of trowsers, three pair of stockings, and a shirt; and at Seaconk I stole two shirts and some stockings through an open window. I stole, at a barn between Seaconk and Attleborough, a woollen blanket, and through an open window near the same place I stole two sheets, one gown, and one shirt. At Mr. Amos Shepherdson's, in Attleborough, I stole out of a wash-tub one shirt, two shifts, one short gown, and one pair of stockings.

At Norton, I broke into a cellar belonging to Col. George Leonard, and stole a quarter of mutton. The same night I broke into another cellar near that place, and stole between twenty and thirty weight of salt pork.

About the same time, I broke into a tavern near the same place, and stole near two dollars in money, and one case bottle of rum.

Between Providence and Attleborough, I broke open two cellars and stole some meat.

I broke into a house in Johnston, and stole betwixt twenty and thirty wt. of salt pork and beef, and one broom.

Some of the things I stole this year, I sold at the market in Providence.

April 23d, 1785, I was imprisoned at Nantucket for striking a truckman and some other persons, at a time when I was intoxicated with liquor: The next day I was released upon my paying a fine and the cost of prosecution.

I broke open a house in Stoughton, stole several aprons, some handkerchiefs, and some other apparel.

I stole about two yards and an half of tow-cloth from Col. David Lathrop, of Bridgewater; and the same night I stole a shirt from a clothier, in the same town; and I also stole one apron, one pocket-handkerchief, one pair of stockings, and one shift from Thomas Howard of East Bridgewater, upon the same night.

The next week I stole a piece of tow-cloth in Halifax, and at the same time I broke into a house, and stole about twenty pounds of salt beef, and three pounds of wool.

October 15th, 1785, I broke open a shop in Walpole, and stole seven pair of shoes.

Nov. 1785, I broken open a store in Natick and stole a quantity of goods from the owner, viz. Mr. Morris.

At Capt. Bent's tavern, in Stoughtonham, I went down chimney, by a rope, opened a window and fastened it up with my jack-knife; immediately after, a man came to the house for a gallon of rum; he called to the landlord, and his daughter (as I took her to be) arose and waited upon him. She discovered the open window, with the jack-knife, and said it did not belong to the house; it was concluded that it belonged to some boys who were gone to a husking, and had called there that evening. It was my design to have made my escape out at the window, when I opened it, in case I should be discovered by any person in the house: But when the man came up to the house, I, fearing I might be discovered, drawed myself up chimney and stood on the cross-bar until he was gone and all the people were asleep; I then descended again, and stole near three dollars out of the bar; then ascended the chimney and escaped without being discovered.

The same month I hid a quantity of goods which I had stole (part of them being the goods I had stolen at Natick) in a barn belonging to Mr. Nathaniel Foster, in Middleborough, and I engaged to come and work for the said Foster: It happened that I was taken up on suspicion that I had stolen a horse (which I had taken and rode about four miles) and committed to gaol in the county of Plymouth, but as no sufficient evidence appeared, I was set at liberty. In the mean time the said Foster found the goods and advertised them. I sent my wife to him; she owned and received the goods, and I escaped undiscovered, by her telling him that I came to his house in the evening preceding the day I had promised to work for him; that as it was late in the night, and the weather rainy, I did not choose to disturb him and his family, by calling them up; that I was obliged to leave the goods and return home, and being taken up on the suspicion aforesaid, I could not take care of the goods, &c.

April 1st, 1786, I broke into a house in Medford and stole two pair of stockings, one scarf, one gown, and one pair of buckles.

The same month I broke into the house of one Mr. Blake, inn-holder, opposite the barracks in Rutland, and stole a bottle of bitters, and three or four dollars in money.

Soon after I broke into Mr. Chickery's house, in Holden, and stole about thirty dollars worth of clothing. The next day I lodged in the woods, and at evening Mr. Chickery took me up after I had got into the high-way, searched my pack, and found his things. On his attempting to seize me, I ran off, and made my escape. I left my pack, and the money I had stolen from Mr. Blake.

Not long after, I went to Mr. Jotham Howe's in Shrewsbury, and opened a window, and stole a blanket.

I then went to another house, broke in, and stole a fine apron out of a desk. The same night I went to a barn belonging to Mr. Baldwin, in said Shrewsbury, and lodged in it the next day, and at evening I broke into his house, and stole about three shillings and three pence in money, and about nine dollars worth of clothing, for which crime I am now under sentence of death.

The same night I broke open the house of Mr. Farror, in said Shrewsbury, and stole in money and goods, to the value of near six dollars.

I also broke into the house of Mr. Ross Wyman, of the same town, and upon the same night, and stole from him near two dollars.

Moreover, I stole a pair of thread stockings at a house just beyond said Wyman's, and hid myself in the woods, where I lay all the next day, and at evening I set off towards Boston, and was taken up by a guard that was placed by a bridge in the edge of Westborough. I was taken before General Ward, confessed the crimes alledged, was committed to gaol, and in April last, I received sentence of death, for the crime aforementioned.

Upon the evening of the first day of June I cleared myself of all my chains, and made an escape from the gaol. And notwithstanding all the admonitions, counsels and warnings that I had received from the good ministers and other pious persons who had visited me under my confinement, I returned again to my vicious practices, "like the dog to his vomit, and the sow that is washed, to her wallowing in the mire;" for the very same evening I stole a cheese out of a press in Holden. And the next Saturday I broke into the house of Mr. James Caldwell, in Barre, and stole near twenty five dollars worth of clothing.

I tarried in Barre about twelve days, and then set off for Natick, and on the way I broke into a cellar in Shrewsbury, and stole some bread and cheese.—Whilst I tarried in Barre, I lived in the woods all the time—when I had got to Natick, I stole two pair of stockings and two pocket handkerchiefs, that were hanging out near a house.

From Natick I went to Sherburne, and broke open a store belonging to Mr. Samuel Sanger, and stole between four and five dozen of buttons.

From thence I went to Mr. John Sanger's house, in the same town, broke it open, and stole a case bottle of rum, one bottle of cherry rum, six cakes of gingerbread, and as many biscuits: I searched for money, but found none.

At another tavern in the same town, I took out a pane of glass, and opened the window, but I was discovered by the landlord, made my escape, and went back to Natick, and tarried there two days.

From Natick I went to Stoughtonham, and at Capt. Bent's (the place where I went down the chimney), the cellar being open, I went through it, and in the bar room I stole fifteen shillings in money, one case bottle of rum, and one half dozen of biscuits.

Afterwards I went to Easton, and on the way I broke open a house and stole some cheese, and two pair of shoes, and two pair of shoe buckles. At Easton I tarried two days, and then made my escape from two men who attempted to take me up on suspicion that I had broken gaol. From thence I went to Attleborough, and through a window I stole two cheeses, and at a tavern near the same place, I stole six shillings and eight pence, one case bottle of rum, a sailor's jacket, and one pair of silver knee buckles.

I then set off for Providence, and by the way I opened a window, and stole one cotton jacket, one jack-knife; and at another house on the same way, I stole through a window, one fine apron, one pocket handkerchief, and one pillow case.

I came to Providence the 26th day of June, and not long after, I broke open a cellar, and stole one bottle of beer, some salt fish, and ten pounds of butter.

A few nights after, I went to Col. Manton's, in Johnston, and the cellar being open, I went into it, and stole twenty pounds of butter, near as much salt pork, one milk pail, one cheese cloth, and one frock.

A few nights after, I went to Justice Belknap's, in the same place, and broke into his cellar, and stole about thirty pounds of salt pork, one neat's tongue, one pair of nippers, one box of awls, and one bag.—It remarkably happened on the 13th ultimo (the day that had been appointed for my execution) that I was committed to gaol in Providence, on suspicion of having stolen the things last mentioned, and on the 18th ult. I was brought back and confined in this gaol again.—Many more thefts and other vicious practices have I been guilty of, the particulars of which might tire the patience of the reader.

Some of the things I have stolen I have used myself—some of them I have sold—some have been taken from me—some I have hid where I could not find them again—and others I have given to lewd women, who induced me to steal for their maintenance. I have lived a hard life, by being obliged to keep in the woods; have suffered much by hunger, nakedness, cold, and the fears of being detected and brought to justice—have often been accused of stealing when I was not guilty, and others have been accused of crimes when I was the offender. I never murdered any person, nor robbed anybody on the highway. I have had great dealings with women, which to their and my shame be it spoken, I often too easily obtained my will of them. I hope they will repent, as I do, of such wicked and infamous conduct. I have had a correspondence with many women, exclusive of my wife, among whom were several abandoned Whites, and a large number of Blacks; four of the whites were married women, three of the Blacks have laid children to me besides my wife, who has been much distressed by my behaviour.

Thus have I given a history of my birth, education and atrocious conduct, and as the time is very nigh in which I must suffer an ignominious death, I earnestly intreat that all people would take warning by my wicked example; that they would shun the paths of destruction by guarding against every temptation; that they would shun vice, follow virtue, and become (through the assistance of the ALMIGHTY) victorious over the enemies of immortal felicity, who are exerting themselves to delude and lead nations to destruction.

As I am sensible of the heinousness of my crimes, and am sorry for my wicked conduct, in violating the laws of the great Governour of the Universe, whose Divine Majesty I have offended; I earnestly pray that he would forgive my sins, blot out my multipled transgressions, and receive my immortal spirit into the Paradise of never ending bliss.

I ask forgiveness of my wife, and of all persons whom I have injured. I return my sincere thanks to the Ministers of the Gospel, and others, who have visited me under my confinement, for their counsels and admonitions, and for the good care they have taken of me: God reward them for their kindness, and conduct us all through this troublesome world to the regions of immortal felicity in the kingdom of Heaven. AMEN.

his
JOHNSON † GREEN.
mark.

Worcester Gaol, August 16, 1786.

The following POEM was written at the request of JOHNSON GREEN, by a prisoner in Worcester Gaol, and is at said GREEN'S special request, added to his Life and Confession, as a PART of his DYING WORDS.

Let all the people on the globe
Be on their guard, and see
That they do shun the vicious road
That's trodden been by me.
If I had shun'd the paths of vice;
Had minded to behave
According to the good advice
That my kind mother gave,
Unto my friends I might have been
A blessing in my days,
And shun'd the evils that I've seen
In my pernicious ways.
My wicked conduct has been such,
It's brought me to distress;
As often times I've suffer'd much
By my own wickedness.
My lewdness, drunkenness, and theft
Has often times—(behold)
Caus'd me to wander, and be left
To suffer with the cold.
Hid in the woods, in deep distress,
My pinching wants were such,
With hunger, and with nakedness
I oft did suffer much.
I've liv'd a thief; it's a hard life;
To drink was much inclin'd;
My conduct has distress'd my wife,
A wife both good and kind.
Though many friends which came to see
Me, in these latter times,
Did oft with candour, caution me
To leave my vicious crimes;
Yet when I had got out of gaol,
Their labour prov'd in vain;
For then, alas! I did not fail
To take to them again.
If I had not conducted so;
Had minded to refrain;
Then I shou'd not have had to go
Back to the goal again.
Thus in the Devil's service, I
Have spent my youthful days,
And now, alas! I soon must die,
For these my wicked ways.
Repent, ye thieves, whilst ye have breath,
Amongst you let be wrought
A reformation, lest to death,
You, like myself, be brought.
Let other vicious persons see
That they from vice abstain;
Lest they undo themselves, like me,
Who in it did remain.
I hope my sad and dismal fate
Will solemn warning be
To people all, both small and great,
Of high and low degree.
By breaking of the righteous laws,
I to the world relate,
That I thereby have been the cause
Of my unhappy fate.
As I repent, I humbly pray
That God would now remit
My sins, which in my vicious way
I really did commit.
May the old TEMPTER soon be bound
And shut up in his den,
And peace and honesty abound
Among the sons of men.
May the great GOD grant this request,
And bring us to that shore
Where peace and everlasting rest
Abides for ever more.

his
JOHNSON † GREEN.
mark.

Printed and Sold
at the Printing-Office
in Worcester

The Slave Narrative

BRITON HAMMON
(?–?)

Very little is known about Briton Hammon, the first African American to publish a literary work in the North American colonies. He was probably not a slave but a freeman, a sailor who, in 1747, left his "master," or former ship's captain, General Winslow of Marshfield, Massachusetts, to find a ship going to sea where he, no doubt, would assume his usual duties of ship's cook. In the next thirteen years, Briton would come near death several times, would be confined in a dungeon in Cuba for four and a half years, would be marooned on an island between Jamaica and Florida, and would be rescued and ferried to England and finally returned to the colonies after a reunion with General Winslow.

Hammon says that he wrote *A Narrative of the Uncommon Sufferings and Surprising Deliverance of Briton Hammon, A Negro Man,—Servant to General Winslow, of Marshfield in New England: Who returned to Boston, after Having Been Absent almost Thirteen Years. Boston, 1760* because of a desire to "relate matters" that befell him and how, with the "kind providence of a good God," he persevered against adversity. Reprinted several times during the decades following its publication, the hazardous experiences recounted in Hammon's *Narrative* no doubt thrilled audiences both in England and in the colonies. The writer's faith in God to deliver him in the midst of such dire circumstances would have been strong testimony for one who otherwise would have been perceived by the eighteenth-century slave-holding society as merely another slave and thus assumed to be no more than an ignorant and animalistic heathen.

When he first left Marshfield, Hammon went to Plymouth, Massachusetts, and boarded a sloop bound for Jamaica. In the Florida keys, the ship got caught on a reef and the captain made a series of bad decisions that resulted in tragedy. Hammon reports that about sixty Native Americans overtook the ship, killing all of the white people and two slaves named Moses Newmock and "Mulatto." But Hammon's life was spared. He soon escaped when a Spanish schooner came by, captained by a man he had met earlier in Jamaica. However, instead of being allowed to resume his trip home to Massachusetts, Hammon was handed over to a governor in Havana, Cuba.

He spent several years as a captive in Havana before successfully escaping on board an English ship that was going to Jamaica. From there, a series of jobs on ships took him to London. While in London, he considered work on a ship bound for Guinea, but at the last minute changed his mind when he learned of a ship going to Boston. As it happened, his old "master," General Winslow of Marshfield, was booked on that ship, and Hammon notes their reunion with joy.

Because his harrowing travels were so full of exciting ventures and because of his religious witness, Hammon was probably supported by abolitionists in England and in New England in the 1760 publication of his celebrated prose piece. That same year, another Hammon, Jupiter Hammon—of no known relation—became the first African American poet to be published. Both, coincidentally, were out of the East, Briton Hammon from Massachusetts, and Jupiter Hammon from New York. Like Jupiter, Briton is most famous for being a first and for documenting an eighteenth-century black experience than for literary excellence. It is also interesting to note that, just as Jupiter published his first poem on December 25, Briton left Winslow's Marshfield estate on Christmas Day.

Most critics say that, of the two men, Jupiter Hammon's extensive writings are evidence of more schooling in letters. In his *Early Black American Prose* (1971), William H. Robinson joins other critics who, in fact, take the position that Briton Hammon probably did not write his *Narrative* but rather merely dictated it. In contrast, in her 1979 study titled *Witnessing Slavery: The Development of Ante-bellum Slave Narratives,* Frances Smith Foster assumes that Hammon did write the text; and, in *The Slave Narrative: Its Place in American History* (1981), Dorothy Porter Sterling attributes the pious opening and closing paragraphs to a scribe, implying that Hammon dictated the body of the *Narrative.* She says that the hurried, almost legal testimonial tone of the prose work seems to support the thesis that Hammon may not have been the original writer.

The underlying premises in denying authorial recognition would, of course, be his supposed status as a slave. However, unlike records left by Jupiter Hammon, the only real evidence that Briton Hammon was a slave is his use of the term "Master" when referring to Winslow or "Servant" when referring to himself. Indentured servants used the same terms, however. Moreover, Hammon, as a sailor, merely called the captain of the ships on which he served "Master." For instance, in the opening of his *Narrative,* after he left Winslow to go to sea, Hammon refers to the captain of the first ship on which he worked: "I immediately shipped myself on board of a Sloop, Capt. John Howland, Master, bound to Jamaica. . . ." Later, he was rescued from Native Americans by a Spanish captain whom he likewise identified, "A Spanish schooner arriving there from St. Augustine, the master of which, whose Name was Romond. . . ." In all three instances, Hammon refers to ship captains as "masters."

Further, it is doubtful that if Hammon were a slave, or even an indentured servant, Winslow would have so freely allowed him to go to sea alone. Readers today may also be bewildered as to why, if he actually were a slave, when Hammon was finally free in London, he would gratuitously set sail to be reenslaved in Boston, or, why, when he had worked so hard to free himself from prison in Havana, he would so willingly return to Massachusetts only to resume his slave status. The only logical conclusion is that Hammon was not a slave, that he was probably a career sailor who, when he had returned to Massachusetts, was employed by Winslow until Hammon returned to sea. When viewed in this light, it is then conceivable that, as a world traveler and a freeman, Hammon very well could have been literate and capable of writing his own *Narrative.* Certainly, the scholarly disagreement is one example of studies that remain in order for modern understanding of eighteenth-century life to be more comprehensive.

Thus, because of his extensive travels throughout the Atlantic seaboard, the author could be perceived as a rather sophisticated freeman of his day—one who, by his own testimony, was very familiar with all of the American colonies, the West Indies, Cuba, Spain, and even England. When reading the *Narrative,* one is struck by Hammon's ability to negotiate his employment and salary from ship to ship, his cleverness in establishing citizenship and political alliances to avoid being sold into slavery and to get out of prison, and his acumen in staying alive even when dozens of sailors around him are massacred. Also, the extant autobiographical sketch places Native Americans, Africans, and Europeans in alliances that some may see as odd but which in historic retrospect establish that those Native Americans who resisted colonization had particular respect for the African presence. In fact, in the annals of American literature, Hammon's survival skills and worldwide adventures can be compared to those exploits narrated by two other African Americans—Olaudah Equiano and John Marrant—who are seldom said to have been illiterate.

With his *Narrative,* Hammon sets a literary standard for Equiano, Marrant, and other Africans in England and the colonies who would manage to publish narratives or prose testimonies. He used Christianity as the main fulcrum of authenticity and thus legitimacy to communicate in print; his treacherous life on the high seas also assured an audience of readers who, to feed their hunger for stories about the high seas, were willing to look beyond the color of his skin and or his social status; he concluded his tale with the most positive outlook, providing his readers with optimistic hope, even in the face of the most impossible odds; he wrote one of very few documented accounts of Native American attacks against white settlers and also one of the few accounts of the dangers and intrigue that filled "ordinary" endeavors in the eighteenth century; he gave one of the few prose accounts of African American experience from the colonial era; and he maintained an impersonal, detached tone that belies self-pity, sentimentality, or a pose victim-centered in an attempt to engender sympathy. Thus, as the forerunner of the African American slave narrative, Hammon set the standard for the genre, which—like his text—would offer an avenue of self-expression and documentation for hundreds to follow. His *Narrative* set the example of personal power, triumph, and escape. Perhaps few other forerunners can claim the same.

❖❖❖

Briton Hammon's complete work is included in Dorothy Porter's (Sterling's) *Early Negro Writing 1760–1837* (1971); William H. Robinson, Jr.'s *Early Black American Prose* (1971); and *The Garland Library of Narratives of North American Indian Captivities,* vol. 8, selected and arranged by Wilcomb E. Washburn (1978). For a discussion of Briton as the "first invisible man in Afro-American first-person narrative," see William Andrews's "The First Fifty Years of the Slave Narrative, 1760–1810" (1982) in *The Art of Slave Narratives: Original Essays in Criticism and Theory* (1982), edited by John Sekora and Darwin T. Turner.

FROM *Narrative of the Uncommon Sufferings, and Surprizing [sic] Deliverance of Briton Hammon*

A NEGRO MAN, SERVANT TO GENERAL WINSLOW, OF MARSHFIELD, IN NEW-ENGLAND; WHO RETURNED TO BOSTON, AFTER HAVING BEEN ABSENT ALMOST THIRTEEN YEARS

Containing

An Account of the many Hardships he underwent from the Time he left his Master's House, in the Year 1747, to the Time of his Return to Boston*—How he was Cast away in the Capes of* Florida*;—the horrid Cruelty and inhuman Barbarity of the* Indians *in murdering the whole Ship's Crew;—the Manner of his being carry'd by them into Captivity. Also, An Account of his being Confined Four Years and Seven Months in a close Dungeon,—And the remarkable Manner in which he met with his* good old Master in London; who returned to New-England, *a Passenger, in the same Ship. (1760).*

❖❖❖

To the Reader,

As my Capacities and Condition of Life are very low, it cannot be expected that I should make those Remarks on the Sufferings I have met with, or the kind of Providence of a good God for my Preservation, as one in a higher Station; but shall leave that to the Reader as he goes along, and so I shall only relate Matters of Fact as they occur to my Mind—.

After being on Shore another Twelvemonth, I endeavour'd to make my Escape the second Time, by trying to get on board of a Sloop bound to *Jamaica,* and as I was going from the City to the Sloop, was unhappily taken by the Guard, and ordered back to the Castle, and there confined.—However, in a short Time I was set at Liberty, and order'd with a Number of others to carry the* *Bishop* from the Castle, thro' the Country, to confirm the old People, baptize Children &c. for which he receives large Sums of Money.—I was employ'd in this Service about Seven Months, during which Time I lived very well, and then returned to the Castle again, where I had my Liberty to walk about the City, and do Work for my self;—The *Beaver,* an *English* Man of War then lay in the Harbour, and having been informed by some of the Ship's Crew that she was to sail in a few Days, I had nothing now to do, but to seek an Opportunity how I should make my Escape.

Accordingly one Sunday Night the Lieutenant of the Ship with a Number of the Barge Crew were in a Tavern, and Mrs. *Howard* who had before been a Friend to me, interceded with the Lieutenant to carry me on board; the Lieutenant said he would with all his Heart, and immediately I went on board in the Barge. The next Day the *Spaniards* came along side the *Beaver,* and demanded me again, with a Number of others who had made their Escape from them, and got on board the Ship, but just before I did: but the Captain, who was a true *Englishman,* refus'd them, and said he could not answer it, to deliver up any *Englishmen* under *English* Colours.—In a few Days we set Sail for *Jamaica,* where we arrived safe, after a short and pleasant Passage.

After being at *Jamaica* a short Time we sail'd for *London,* as convoy to a Fleet of Merchantmen, who all arrived safe in the *Downs,* I was turned over to another ship, the *Arcenceil,* and there remained about a Month. From this Ship I went on board the *Sandwich* of 90 Guns; on board the *Sandwich,* I tarry'd 6 Weeks, and then was order'd on board the *Hercules,* Capt. *John Porter,* a 74 Gun Ship, we sail'd on a Cruize, and met with a *French* 84 Gun Ship, and had a very smart Engagement,† in which about 70 of our Hands were Kill'd and Wounded, the Captain

---

*He is carried (by Way of Respect) in a large Two-arm Chair; the Chair is lin'd with crimson Velvet, and supported by eight Persons.

†A particular Account of this Engagement, has been Publish'd in the *Boston* News-Papers.

lost his Leg in the Engagement, and I was Wounded in the Head by a small Shot. We should have taken this Ship, if they had not cut away the most of our Rigging; however, in about three Hours after, a 64 Gun Ship, came up with and took her.—I was discharged from the *Hercules* the 12th Day of *May* 1759 (having been on board of the Ship 3 Months) on account of my being disabled in the Arm, and render'd incapable of Service, after being honourably paid the Wages due to me. I was put into the *Greenwich* Hospital where I stay'd and soon recovered.—I then ship'd myself a Cook on board Captain *Martyn,* an arm'd Ship in the King's Service. I was on board this Ship almost Two Months, and after being paid my Wages, was discharg'd in the Month of *October.*—After my discharge from Captain *Martyn,* I was taken sick in *London* of a Fever, and was confin'd about 6 Weeks, where I expended all my Money, and left in very poor Circumstances; and unhappy for me I knew nothing of my *good Master's* being in *London* at this my very difficult Time. After I got well of my sickness, I ship'd myself on board of a large Ship bound to *Guinea,* and being in a publick House one Evening, I overheard a Number of Persons talking about Rigging a Vessel bound to *New-England,* I ask'd them to what Part of *New-England* this Vessel was bound? they told me, to *Boston;* and having ask'd them who was Commander? they told me Capt. *Watt;* in a few Minutes after this the Mate of the Ship came in, and I ask'd him if Captain *Watt* did not want a Cook, who told me he did, and that the Captain would be in, in a few Minutes; and in about half an Hour the Captain came in, and then I ship'd meself at once, after begging off from the Ship bound to *Guinea;* I work'd on board Captain *Watt's* Ship almost Three Months, before she sail'd, and one Day being at Work in the Hold, I overhead some Persons on board mention the Name of *Winslow,* at the Name of which I was very inquisitive, and having ask'd what *Winslow* they were talking about? They told me it was *General Winslow;* and that he was one of the Passengers, I ask'd them what *General Winslow?* For I never knew *my good Master,* by that Title before; but after enquiring more particularly I found it must be *Master,* and in a few Days Time the Truth was joyfully verify'd by a happy Sight of his Person, which so overcome me, that I could not speak to him for some Time—*My good Master* was exceeding glad to see me, telling that I was like one arose from the Dead, for he though I had been Dead a great many years, having heard nothing of me for almost Thirteen Years.

I think I have not deviated from Truth, in any particular of this my Narrative, and tho' I have omitted a great many Things, yet what is wrote may suffice to convince the Reader, that I have been most grievously afflicted, and yet thro' the Divine Goodness, as miraculously preserved, and delivered out of many Dangers; of which I desire to retain a *grateful Remembrance,* as long as I live in the World.

And now, That in the Providence of that God, *who delivered his Servant* David out of the Paw of the Lion and out of the Paw of the Bear, *I am freed from* a long *and* dreadful Captivity, among worse Savages than they; *And am return'd to my* own Native Land, to Shew how Great Things the Lord hath done for Me; *I would call upon all Men, and Say,* O Magnifie the Lord with Me, and let us Exalt his Name together!—O that Men would Praise the Lord for His Goodness, and for his Wonderful Works to the Children of Men!

OLAUDAH EQUIANO
(1745–1797)

One of the best illustrations both of irrepressible African genius and of the thriving network between eighteenth-century black abolitionists in England and the American colonies and their simultaneous connections with the fledgling international abolition movement is Olaudah Equiano. Kidnapped from his native Africa and pressed into slavery as a boy of eleven years, Equiano—as both slave and freeman—eventually traveled throughout much of the known world, including the Arctic, North and Central America, the West Indies, Europe, and Great Britain. His autobiography, *The Interesting Narrative of the Life of Olaudah Equiano or Gustavus Vassa, the African, Written by Himself,* first published in 1789, has been in print continuously for over two hundred years.

Accepted by eighteenth-century white society as a stupendous travel saga about a sailor and explorer's adventures on the high seas and as a very forceful antislavery statement, Equiano's *Interesting Narrative* is a classic example of the great African slave narratives of the eighteenth and nineteenth centuries. It is also a watershed prototype of the now essential African American autobiographical genre. Moreover, The (et al.) *Interesting Narrative* was one of few books in the public arena authored by an African who was able to give such a clear record of cultural life on the rich African continent, which wealthy European powers were working so hard to destroy. Likewise, it is one of few extant works from the eighteenth century that relates an African's eyewitness account of slavery both in the American colonies and in the Caribbean. Equiano's outspoken political activism against slavery and the slave trade was of inestimable value in the eventual decline of the nefarious institution on both sides of the Atlantic. Today, Olaudah Equiano, who was first published under the European name of Gustavus Vassa given to him by one of his masters, is claimed as an influential, if unofficial, stateman, essayist, and prose artist on three continents—Europe, Africa, and North America.

Like Prince Hall and Benjamin Banneker, Equaino was of royal African blood. He was born in a "charming fruitful vale, named Essaka," in 1745 as the youngest son of a venerated Ibo chief of the Benin nation, who reigned in the interior of Eastern Nigeria, northeast of the Niger River. "My mother adorned me with emblems, after the manner of our greatest warriors," Equiano writes. As the youngest son of seven children, including one sister, Equiano was close to his mother and spent much time with her, during which, he says, she took "particular pains to form my mind. I was trained up from my earliest years in the art of war: my daily exercise was shooting and throwing javelins. . . ." In his twelve-chapter, two-volume The (et al.) *Interesting Narrative,* Equiano recalls a harmonious village life in which there were no beggars because everyone contributed to "the common stock" and the people were "unacquainted with idleness."

Captured along with his sister by local raiders when he was about ten or eleven years old, Olaudah was taken to the West Coast of Africa and sold to slavers headed for the West Indies. His portrayal of being sold into slavery by these strange white creatures and of the horrors of his transportation to Barbados in the filthy hold of a slave ship is poignant testimony for all kidnapped and dispersed Africans. The two children were kidnapped by a woman and two men who came over the wall of his home when his parents were away. Within a short time, the siblings were separated despite their pleas that they be allowed to stay together. Briefly reunited not long afterwards, Equiano suffered even more on their second parting. The tragic separation from his family is forever after a personal point of reference, with the sensitive man, the pain over which he grieved throughout his life, which "neither time nor fortune have been able to remove."

While in Nigeria, Equiano was sold several times before eventually being sold to white slave traders. Until then, he had been among Africans he could understand, to some extent, as the languages did not "totally differ" and the cultures were familiar. The language and the culture of the white slave traders, however, eluded the grasp of the young boy's imagination. Their atrocities, on board the slave ship making the Middle Passage, had Equiano questioning the very nature and humanity of the white Europeans. As he witnessed "white people" forcing Africans to load Africans as cargo, he marveled that he had never seen people who behaved in "so savage a manner." Below deck, they created conditions that left women and men wailing in misery, chained together in a tight lock where, without fresh air, many fell "victims to the improvident avarice, as I may call it, of their purchasers." Recalling a white man who was flogged to death and then thrown into the sea, Equiano also made the observation that European inhumanity extended to their own.

When the slave ship reached Barbados, Equiano saw horses for the first time, but he learned from other Africans that they had horses in their countries also. Now, he witnessed mass separation of friends and families, lamenting it as "a new refinement in cruelty." Realizing he was in for a "new slavery," he wept, convinced that he had done something to "displease the Lord." A precocious youth, he was nonetheless assigned work as a slave-servant. His brief time of working in the field ended when he landed in Virginia in 1757 and was sold to Michael Henry Pascal, an officer in the Royal Navy. Although the ship's crew had been calling him by various names like Jacob or Michael, Pascal insisted on renaming him Gustavus Vassa, after a late Scandinavian king. During Olaudah's first voyage with Pascal, one of the crewmen, a scholarly seaman named Richard Baker, befriended the slave and tutored him in English language and culture.

Because Pascal and others had promised that he would be freed at the war's end, Olaudah fought in the Seven Years' War between England and France. During the war, he served in the waters of the Maritime Provinces of Canada, in the Mediterranean, and along the coast of France. Instead of granting him freedom, however, Pascal confiscated Equiano's books and other belongings, and sold him without notice to the captain of a slave ship that was headed for the West Indies. Equiano was eventually sold to a Quaker merchant from Philadelphia named Robert King, who lent him to a sea captain on his staff by the name of Thomas Farmer. When purchased by King, the young African went with character references, which, he says, were "found of infinite value." Because King ran rum and sugar in the famous slave route between England and Africa, the Caribbean and the colonies, Equiano witnessed the full impact of the economic and moral evil of slavery during these three years in the West Indies with King and Farmer. Remarkably, Equiano's sense of community with enslaved field workers was never severed by a house-servant mentality, and his precocious bent was always to look for ways to bring about the destruction of slavery.

By 1759, Equiano was fully articulate in the English language. As he relates in his *Interesting Narrative,* he had purchased a Bible, joined a church, and received baptism. Through the kinder Farmer, the precocious youth learned navigation and other supervisory shipboard skills, and after several years, he had saved enough money to purchase his freedom from King on July 11, 1766. King, who had acquired Equiano in 1763, for "forty pounds sterling," sold the author his freedom for seventy pounds and admitted that he had profited three hundred pounds from Equiano's labor during his three years of ownership. King prevailed on the slave to stay in his employ for pay and, in this capacity, Equiano made his second trip to Georgia, where he was almost resold into bondage.

The first thing Equiano did after obtaining his freedom was to officially discard his Scandinavian name, but later, as a published author, he would find that shedding this identity was not as easy as he had hoped. In 1768, he returned to England, where he had first traveled with Pascal, began an apprenticeship to a hairdresser, and also started part-time employment with Dr. Charles Irving, an amateur scientist whom he eventually accompanied on an expedition to the North Pole in 1773. Some of Equiano's most descriptive travel commentary is embedded in his vivid descriptions of that dangerous North Pole experience: killer whales, defensive sea horses, shipwreck, starvation, and exposure. Although he had joined a church in England, the writer says that he had not experienced real conversion. He had rejected the Catholic, Jewish, and Quaker faiths, and had even considered moving to Turkey and taking up the Turkish religion.

Near death during the treacherous voyage with Irving and in deep despair, Equiano called on God for help and experienced a Jonah-like conversion: "I wrestled hard with God in fervent prayer. . . . Now the Ethiopian was willing to be saved by Jesus Christ, the sinner's only surety, and also to rely on none other person or thing for salvation." His life was spared. During the ordeal, the inept ship's captain ordered him to nail down the hatches so that Africans in the hold could not escape, but Equiano refused because twenty or so of his fellow Africans could have died. Weary of seeing cruelty, he left America that same year to return to London, which he believed was more liberal. However, the persistence of an African presence in America lured him to make several return trips. Fearful of being retaken into slavery, he avoided travel to Africa. During this return voyage, the erudite African also sailed to Turkey, Italy, Portugal, and Spain, and he even had smooth stops in Honduras and Nicaragua, where he lived among the Miskito Indians. Throughout his accounts of all of these travels, however, Equiano seems to have been motivated by two principal hopes: to return to Africa and to be an influential force for the abolition of slavery.

His personal account of Ibo tribal life, including especially the traditional practice of religious worship, provides rich fodder for anthropological study: the respect paid to the dead, for whom libations were made and food set aside, and the beliefs that deceased family members were watching over the living. However, Equiano remembers his African people as believing in one Creator who was the Maker of all, which was the same manner in which he worshipped the Judeo-Christian God. He cites western scholars who concur with him "that the one sprung from the other" and that continental Africans were "the original" Judeo-Christian believers. Thus, culturally informed from his youth, Equiano makes the case in his *Interesting Narrative* that he (and other Americans of African descent) did not assimilate with Eurocentric religion when they filled a spiritual void during their enslavement by practicing one of the Judeo-Christian religions.

Of particular interest to the modern reader is Equiano's account of the Ibo woman's role in battle. "Our whole district is a kind of militia," he wrote. "I was once a witness to a battle in our common. We had been all at work in it one day as usual, when our people were suddenly attacked. I climbed a tree at some distance, from which I beheld the fight. There were many women as well as men on both sides; among others my mother was there, and armed with a broad sword." He observed in other northern Nigerian communities, "both the males and the females, as with us, were brought up to it, and trained in the arts of war."

During his lifetime, Equiano learned to read and write as well as to clerk. His *Interesting Narrative* records that because of these abilities his life was "checkered" with preferential treatment. That "exceptional black" treatment put him in the role of an African trickster—in a position to outwit the wickedly powerful on behalf of his enslaved compatriots. Sometimes this meant merely exploiting his "master's" presence, enough to convey the inconsistency with humanity—not to mention Christianity—when black girls, some not even ten years old, were brutally raped by crewmen, "and these abominations . . . to scandalous excess." The *Interesting Narrative* decries that even as black female virtue was robbed, a black man got staked to the ground for having relations with a white prostitute.

Equiano can, in part, be understood by the *Interesting Narrative*'s assertion that the desired effect of consciousness raising is to "melt the pride of [white] superiority into sympathy for the wants and miseries of [blacks], and to compel them to acknowledge that understanding is not confined to feature or color." Critics who render Equiano naive point to this attempt to tap white conscience, as when he tries to engage a white man who has cut off the leg of a black man who tried to escape slavery. The narrator cautions the white man about having to answer to God, only to be told that "answering was a thing of another world, what he thought and did were policy . . . that his scheme had the desired effect—it cured that man and some others of running away." Nonetheless, Equiano's *Interesting Narrative* spoke to those in power about such treatment against slaves and especially about the ways that pregnant women were used and about the awful "lodging of the field Negroes."

Eventually, observing the similarity of cultures around the world to those of black Africa, he turned his attention to further travels. In Honduras and Nicaragua, he was introduced to Native Americans whose way of life he found more honest and trusting than anything known to white Europe. Finally settling down in England in 1777, he was beset by the desire to return to Africa in the "hope of doing good, if possible, amongst my countryman." In 1779, he appealed, unsuccessfully, to the "Right Reverend Father in God, Robert, Lord Bishop of London" to send him to Africa as a missionary. For a few years, he traveled around Wales, to New York, and, in 1789, to Philadelphia, where he was impressed with the Quaker-run free schools "erected for every denomination of black people." Back in London, Equiano appealed to Quakers there to help the situation of oppressed Africans.

By the time he was in his early forties, the former sailor had become a well-known and articulate abolitionist in British circles. He maintained friendships with famous white abolitionists like Granville Sharp, James Edward Oglethorpe, Thomas Hardy, and Peter Peckard, as well as with other former African slaves, Ottobah Cugoano, who wrote *Thoughts and Sentiments on the Evil of Slavery* (1787), and Ignatius Sancho, who, because of his well-known collected letters published in 1782, was also renowned. In 1783, Olaudah appealed to Sharp concerning the Zong case, in which more than 130 slaves were thrown from a British ship so that the ship's owner could collect the cargo insurance. As recounted in the last section of his *Inter-*

esting Narrative, he petitioned Queen Charlotte of England in the year 1788 on behalf of "millions of my African countrymen, who groan under the lash of tyranny in the West Indies."

The British government recruited Equiano to aid in an effort to send Africans to Sierra Leone in 1789. At first, he was hesitant to accept. He knew that if he should come upon slave dealers, he would oppose them, "by every means in my power." Then when he did accept and was assigned Commissary of Stores, he found himself embattled trying to protect the returning Africans from being further exploited by the negligence of white businessmen. Because of his outspoken objections, he was labeled a troublemaker and his "dismission was soon after procured." The white businessmen whose mismanagement he had reported used their power to diminish him, as *The Interesting Narrative* explains, "causing me considerable personal losses." He was amazed at their "petty contest" with him, "an obscure African." Rather than countercharge that impropriety, Equiano allowed his case to rest on its own merits. Eventually, he was cleared and reimbursed retroactively for his services. After this business, Equiano says that his life "passed in an even tenor," although he never realized his desire to return to Africa.

Also in 1789, his two-volume autobiography was published, and the following years were spent in a life of organized political activism and public speaking for the cause of abolition. Thirteen years later, the now-internationally famous author, who was around forty-seven years old, married Susanna Cullen, an English woman, at Soham Church, Cambridgeshire. Notice of his wedding in *The Gentleman's Magazine* refers to him as "Gustavus Vassa, the African, well known as the champion and advocate for procuring the suppression of the slave trade." The couple had two daughters, Ann Marie and Johanna.

Equiano died in London on March 31, 1797, after fulfilling a life of commitment to his people and of triumph to the cause of their freedom. Although he did not live to see it, Equiano—according to Thomas Digges, one of his closest friends—"was a principal instrument in bringing about the motion for a repeal of the Slave act."

Critics consider *The Interesting Narrative of the Life of Olaudah Equiano or Gustavus Vassa, the African, Written by Himself* to be one of the eighteenth century's best works. In addition to being the hallmark of black autobiography, Equiano's work has significant implications for people of African descent even at the end of the twentieth century. Not only does the "pull yourself up by your own bootstraps" ethic infuse the text, it is dominated by the author's fervent activism on behalf of enslaved Africans so much less fortunate than himself. Within the Afrocentric text, the purposeful narrator carries the story of a former free Ibo, a former Ibo slave, a former slave to whites, and eventually a freeman living quite successfully in a Eurocentric world. Equiano's bold insistence on asserting himself in a world that viewed black assertiveness as an affront to white self-confidence has been thoroughly appreciated by readers of every age. His *Interesting Narrative* advanced a literary art form that was perfected a generation later in the *Narrative of the Life of Frederick Douglass, An American Slave.* In recording their experiences, autobiographical writers of African descent have, like Equiano, always hoped that by telling their story, they could help bring an end to the massive suffering endured by those scattered among the African diaspora in the Americas, in Europe, and yes, even in Olaudah Equiano's native Africa.

❖❖❖

The most authoritative sources on Equiano are Paul Edward's introduction to his abridged edition of *The Interesting Narrative* (1967) and Arna Bontemps's introduction to his *Great Slave Narratives* (1969). Excellent reference texts include *Three Black Writers in Eighteenth-Century England* (1971), by Francis D. Adams and Barry Sanders; "African-American Writers in American Literature, 1764–1789," by Bernard Bell in *The Revolutionary Years* (1977), edited by Everett Emerson; "African Writers of the Eighteenth Century," by O. R. Dathorne in *Black Orpheus* 18 (October 1965): 51–57; and "Olaudah Equiano of the Niger Ibo," by G. I. Jones in *Africa Remembered: Narratives by West Africans from the Era of the Slave Trade* (1967), edited by Philip D. Curtin. The work is also thoroughly discussed in Stephen Butterfield's *Black Autobiography in America* (1974) and in Sidone Smith's *Where I'm Bound: Patterns of Slavery and Freedom in Black American Autobiography* (1987).

Benjamin Brawley discusses Equiano under the title "Gustavus Vassa," in his *Early Negro American Writers* (1989; rpt. 1935 ed.). Discussions of the author and his work are also covered by Charles H. Nichols in *Many Thousands Gone: The Ex-Slaves Account of Their Bondage and Freedom* (1963); Richard Barksdale and Kenneth Kinnamon in *Black Writers of America* (1972); and Marion L. Starkey in *Striving to Make it My Home: The Story of Americans from Africa* (1964).

See also Houston Baker's *The Journey Back: Issues in Black Literature and Criticism* (1980); Sidney and Emma Nogrady Kaplan's *The Black Presence in the Era of the American Revolution* (1973); and Sondra O'Neale and Wilfred D. Samuels's "Olaudah Equiano" in *Dictionary of Literary Biography*, vol. 37, pp. 153–158 and vol. 50, pp. 123–129, respectively. Robert Stepto's *From Behind the Veil: A Study of Afro-American Narrative* (1979) also provides insightful information on Equiano and his *Interesting Narrative.*

Some of Equiano's papers are housed at The Schomburg Collection of the New York Public Library; the Boston Public Library; the Library Company in Philadelphia; Ridgeway Brothers in Philadelphia; Yale University; Harvard University; the Horby Collection in the Liverpool City Library; and the Atlanta University Library in Atlanta, Georgia.

FROM *The Interesting Narrative of the Life of Olaudah Equiano or Gustavus Vassa, the African, Written by Himself*

Chapter 1

The author's account of his country, and their manners and customs—Administration of justice—Embrenche—Marriage ceremony, and public entertainments—Mode of living—Dress—Manufacturers—Buildings—Commerce—Agriculture—War and religion—Superstition of the natives—Funeral ceremonies of the priests or magicians—Curious mode of discovering poison—Some hints concerning the origin of the author's countrymen, with the opinions of different writers on that subject.

I believe it is difficult for those who publish their own memoirs to escape the imputation of vanity; nor is this the only disadvantage under which they labor: it is also their misfortune that what is uncommon is rarely, if ever, believed, and what is obvious we are apt to turn from with disgust, and to charge the writer with impertinence. People generally think those memoirs only worthy to be read or remembered which abound in great or striking events, those, in short, which in a high degree excite either admiration or pity; all others they consign to contempt and oblivion. It is therefore, I confess, not a little hazardous in a private and obscure individual, and a stranger too, thus to solicit the indulgent attention of the public, especially when I own I offer here the history of neither a saint, a hero, nor a tyrant. I believe there are few events in my life which have not happened to many; it is true the incidents of it are numerous, and, did I consider myself an European, I might say my sufferings were great; but when I compare my lot with that of most of my countrymen, I regard myself as a *particular favorite of heaven,* and acknowledge the mercies of Providence in every occurrence of my life. If, then, the following narrative does not appear sufficiently interesting to engage general attention, let my motive be some excuse for its publication. I am not so foolishly vain as to expect from it either immortality or literary reputation. If it affords any satisfaction to my numerous friends, at whose request it has been written, or in the smallest degree promotes the interest of humanity, the ends for which it was undertaken will be fully attained, and every wish of my heart gratified. Let it therefore be remembered, that, in wishing to avoid censure, I do not aspire to praise.

That part of Africa, known by the name of Guinea, to which the trade for slaves is carried on, extends along the coast above 3400 miles, from Senegal to Angola, and includes a variety of kingdoms. Of these the most considerable is the kingdom of Benin, both as to extent and wealth, the richness and cultivation of the soil, the power of its king, and the number and warlike disposition of the inhabitants. It is situated nearly under the line, and extends along the coast about 170 miles, but runs back into the interior part of Africa to a distance hitherto, I believe, unexplored by any traveller, and seems only terminated at length by the empire of Abyssinia near 1500 miles from its beginning. This kingdom is divided into many provinces or districts, in one of the most remote and fertile of which, I was born, in the year 1745, situated in a charming fruitful vale, named Essaka. The distance of this province from the capital of Benin and the sea coast must be very considerable, for I had never heard of white men or Europeans, nor the sea; and our subjection to the king of Benin was little more than nominal, for every transaction of the government, as far as my slender observation extended, was conducted by the chief or elders of the place. The manners and government of a people who have little commerce with other countries are generally very simple, and the history of what passes in one family or village may serve as a specimen of the whole nation. My father was one of those elders or chiefs I have spoken of, and was styled Embrenche, a term, as I remember, importing the highest distinction, and signifying in our language a *mark* of grandeur. This mark is conferred on the person entitled to it, by cutting the skin across at the top of the forehead, and drawing it down to the eyebrows; and while it is in this situation applying a warm hand, and rubbing it until it shrinks up into a thick *weal* across the lower part of the forehead. Most of the judges and senators were thus marked; my father had long borne it; I had seen it conferred on one of my brothers, and I also was *destined* to receive it by my parents. Those Embrenche, or chief men, decided disputes and punished crimes, for which purpose they always assembled together. The proceedings were generally short, and in most cases the law of retaliation prevailed. I remember a man was brought before my father, and the other judges, for kidnapping a boy; and, although he was the son of a chief or senator, he was condemned to make recompense by a man or woman slave. Adultery, however, was sometimes punished with slavery or death, a punishment which I believe is inflicted on it throughout most of the nations of Africa,[1] so sacred among them is the honor of the marriage bed, and so jealous are they of the fidelity of their wives. Of this I recollect an instance—a woman was convicted before the judges of adultery, and delivered over, as the

[1]See Anthony Benezet, *Some Historical Account of Guinea, Its Situation, Produce, and general disposition of its inhabitants* (London: J. Phillips, 1788).

custom was, to her husband, to be punished. Accordingly he determined to put her to death; but it being found, just before her execution, that she had an infant at her breast, and no woman being prevailed on to perform the part of a nurse, she was spared on account of the child. The men, however, do not preserve the same constancy to their wives which they expect from them; for they indulge in a plurality, though seldom in more than two. Their mode of marriage is thus—both parties are usually betrothed when young by their parents (though I have known the males to betroth themselves). On this occasion a feast is prepared, and the bride and bridegroom stand up in the midst of all their friends, who are assembled for the purpose, while he declares she is henceforth to be looked upon as his wife, and that no other person is to pay any addresses to her. This is also immediately proclaimed in the vicinity, on which the bride retires from the assembly. Some time after, she is brought home to her husband, and then another feast is made, to which the relations of both parties are invited; her parents then deliver her to the bridegroom, accompanied with a number of blessings, and at the same time they tie round her waist a cotton string of the thickness of a goosequill, which none but married women are permitted to wear; she is now considered as completely his wife; and at this time the dowry is given to the new married pair, which generally consists of portions of land, slaves, and cattle, household goods, and implements of husbandry. These are offered by the friends of both parties; besides which the parents of the bridegroom present gifts to those of the bride, whose property she is looked upon before marriage; but after it she is esteemed the sole property of her husband. The ceremony being now ended, the festival begins, which is celebrated with bonfires and loud acclamations of joy, accompanied with music and dancing.

We are almost a nation of dancers, musicians, and poets. Thus every great event, such as a triumphant return from battle or other cause of public rejoicing, is celebrated in public dances, which are accompanied with songs and music suited to the occasion. The assembly is separated into four divisions, which dance either apart or in succession, and each with a character peculiar to itself. The first division contains the married men, who in their dances frequently exhibit feats of arms and the representation of a battle. To these succeed the married women, who dance in the second division. The young men occupy the third, and the maidens the fourth. Each represents some interesting scene of real life, such as a great achievement, domestic employment, a pathetic story, or some rural sport; and as the subject is generally founded on some recent event, it is therefore ever new. This gives our dances a spirit and variety, which I have scarcely seen elsewhere.* We have musical instruments, particularly drums of different kinds, a piece of music which resembles a guitar, and another much like a stickado. These last are chiefly used by betrothed virgins, who play on them on all grand festivals.

As our manners are simple, our luxuries are few. The dress of both sexes is nearly the same. It generally consists of a long piece of calico, or muslin, wrapped loosely round the body, somewhat in the form of a highland plaid. This is usually dyed blue, which is our favorite color. It is extracted from a berry, and is brighter and richer than any I have seen in Europe. Besides this, our women of distinction wear golden ornaments, which they dispose with some profusion on their arms and legs. When our women are not employed with the men in tillage, their usual occupation is spinning and weaving cotton, which they afterwards dye, and make into garments. They also manufacture earthen vessels, of which we have many kinds. Among the rest, tobacco pipes, made after the same fashion, and used in the same manner, as those in Turkey.†

*When I was in Smyrna I have frequently seen the Greeks dance after this manner.

† The bowl is earthen, curiously figured, to which a long reed is fixed as a tube. This tube is sometimes so long as to be borne by one, and frequently out of grandeur, two boys.

Our manner of living is entirely plain; for as yet the natives are unacquainted with those refinements in cookery which debauch the taste; bullocks, goats, and poultry supply the greatest part of their food. (These constitute likewise the principal wealth of the country, and the chief articles of its commerce.) The flesh is usually stewed in a pan; to make it savory we sometimes use pepper, and other spices, and we have salt made of wood ashes. Our vegetables are mostly plantains, eadas, yams, beans, and Indian corn. The head of the family usually eats alone; his wives and slaves have also their separate tables. Before we taste food we always wash our hands; indeed, our cleanliness on all occasions is extreme, but on this it is an indispensable ceremony. After washing, libation is made, by pouring out a small portion of the drink on the floor, and tossing a small quantity of the food in a certain place, for the spirits of departed relations, which the natives suppose to preside over their conduct and guard them from evil. They are totally unacquainted with strong or spirituous liquors; and their principal beverage is palm wine. This is got from a tree of that name, by tapping it at the top and fastening a large gourd to it; and sometime one tree will yield three or four gallons in a night. When just drawn it is of a most delicious sweetness; but in a few days it acquires a tartish and more spirituous flavor, though I never saw anyone intoxicated by it. The same tree also produces nuts and oil. Our principal luxury is in perfumes: one sort of these is an odoriferous wood of delicious fragrance, the other a kind of earth, a small portion of which thrown into the fire diffuses a most powerful odor.* We beat this wood into powder, and mix it with palm oil, with which both men and women perfume themselves.

In our buildings we study convenience rather than ornament. Each master of a family has a large square piece of ground, surrounded with a moat or fence, or enclosed with a wall made of red earth tempered, which, when dry, is as hard as brick. Within this, are his houses to accommodate his family and slaves, which, if numerous, frequently present the appearance of a village. In the middle, stands the principal building, appropriated to the sole use of the master and consisting of two apartments; in one of which he sits in the day with his family, the other is left apart for the reception of his friends. He has besides these a distinct apartment in which he sleeps, together with his male children. On each side are the apartments of his wives, who have also their separate day and night houses. The habitations of the slaves and their families are distributed throughout the rest of the enclosure. These houses never exceed one story in height; they are always built of wood, or stakes driven into the ground, crossed with wattles, and neatly plastered within and without. The roof is thatched with reeds. Our day houses are left open at the sides; but those in which we sleep are always covered, and plastered in the inside, with a composition mixed with cow-dung, to keep off the different insects, which annoy us during the night. The walls and floors also of these are generally covered with mats. Our beds consists of a platform, raised three or four feet from the ground, on which are laid skins, and different parts of a spongy tree, called plantain. Our covering is calico or muslin, the same as our dress. The usual seats are a few logs of wood; but we have benches, which are generally perfumed to accommodate strangers: these compose the greater part of our household furniture. Houses so constructed and furnished require but little skill to erect them. Every man is a sufficient architect for the purpose. The whole neighborhood afford their unanimous assistance in building them, and in return receive and expect no other recompense than a feast.

As we live in a country where nature is prodigal of her favors, our wants are few and easily supplied; of course we have few manufactures. They consist for the most part of calicoes, earthen ware, ornaments, and instruments of

*When I was in Smyrna I saw the same kind of earth, and brought some of it with me to England; it resembles musk in strength, but is more delicious in scent, and is not unlike the smell of a rose.

war and husbandry. But these make no part of our commerce, the principal articles of which, as I have observed, are provisions. In such a state, money is of little use; however, we have some small pieces of coin, if I may call them such. They are made something like an anchor, but I do not remember either their value or denomination. We have also markets, at which I have been frequently with my mother. These are sometimes visited by stout mahogany-colored men from the south-west of us: we call them *Oye-Eboe,* which term signifies red men living at a distance. They generally bring us fire-arms, gun-powder, hats, beads, and dried fish. The last we esteemed a great rarity, as our waters were only brooks and springs. These articles they barter with us for odoriferous woods and earth, and our salt of wood ashes. They always carry slaves though our land; but the strictest account is exacted of the manner of procuring them before they are suffered to pass. Sometimes, indeed, we sold slaves to them, but they were only prisoners of war, or such among us as had been convicted of kidnapping, or adultery, and some other crimes, which we esteemed heinous. This practice of kidnapping induces me to think, that, notwithstanding all our strictness, their principal business among us was to trepan our people. I remember too, they carried great sacks along with them, which not long after, I had an opportunity of fatally seeing applied to that infamous purpose.

Our land is uncommonly rich and fruitful, and produces all kinds of vegetables in great abundance. We have plenty of Indian corn, and vast quantities of cotton and tobacco. Our pineapples grow without culture; they are about the size of the largest sugar-loaf, and finely flavored. We have also spices of different kinds, particularly pepper, and a variety of delicious fruits which I have never seen in Europe, together with gums of various kinds, and honey in abundance. All our industry is exerted to improve these blessings of nature. Agriculture is our chief employment; and everyone, even the children and women, are engaged in it. Thus we are all habituated to labor from our earliest years. Everyone contributes something to the common stock; and, as we are unacquainted with idleness, we have no beggars. The benefits of such a mode of living are obvious. The West India planters prefer the slaves of Benin or Eboe to those of any other part of Guinea, for their hardiness, intelligence, integrity, and zeal. Those benefits are felt by us in the general healthiness of the people, and in their vigor and activity; I might have added, too, in their comeliness. Deformity is indeed unknown amongst us, I mean that of shape. Numbers of the natives of Eboe now in London might be brought in support of this assertion: for, in regard to complexion, ideas of beauty are wholly relative. I remember while in Africa to have seen three Negro children who were tawny, and another quite white, who were universally regarded by myself, and the natives in general, as far as related to their complexions, as deformed. Our women, too, were, in my eye at least, uncommonly graceful, alert, and modest to a degree of bashfulness; nor do I remember to have heard of an instance of incontinence amongst them before marriage. They are also remarkably cheerful. Indeed, cheerfulness and affability are two of the leading characteristics of our nation.

Our tillage is exercised in a large plain or common, some hour's walk from our dwellings, and all the neighbors resort thither in a body. They use no beasts of husbandry; and their only instruments are hoes, axes, shovels, and beaks, or pointed iron, to dig with. Sometimes we are visited by locusts, which come in large clouds, so as to darken the air, and destroy our harvest. This, however, happens rarely, but when it does, a famine is produced by it. I remember an instance or two wherein this happened. This common is often the theatre of war; and therefore when our people go out to till their land, they not only go in a body, but generally take their arms with them for fear of a surprise; and when they apprehend an invasion, they guard the avenues to their dwellings, by driving sticks into the ground, which are so sharp at one end as to pierce the foot, and are generally dipt in poison. From what I can recollect of these battles, they appear to have been irruptions of one little state or district on the other, to obtain prisoners or booty. Perhaps they were incited to this by those traders who brought the European goods I mentioned, amongst us. Such a mode of obtaining slaves in Africa is common; and I believe more are procured this way, and by kidnapping, than any other.[2] When a trader wants slaves, he applies to a chief for them, and tempts him with his wares. It is not extraordinary, if on this occasion he yields to the temptation with as little firmness, and accepts the price of his fellow creature's liberty, with as little reluctance as the enlightened merchant. Accordingly he falls on his neighbors, and a desperate battle ensues. If he prevails and takes prisoners, he gratifies his avarice by selling them; but, if his party be vanquished, and he falls into the hands of the enemy, he is put to death; for, as he has been known to foment their quarrels, it is thought dangerous to let him survive, and no ransom can save him, though all other prisoners may be redeemed. We have fire-arms, bows and arrows, broad two-edged swords and javelins; we have shields also which cover a man from head to foot. All are taught the use of these weapons; even our women are warriors, and march boldly out to fight along with the men. Our whole district is a kind of militia: on a certain signal given, such as the firing of a gun at night, they all rise in arms and rush upon their enemy. It is perhaps something remarkable, that when our people march to the field a red flag or banner is borne before them. I was once a witness to a battle in our common. We had been all at work in it one day as usual, when our people were suddenly attacked. I climbed a tree at some distance, from which I beheld the fight. There were many women as well as men on both sides; among others my mother was there, and armed with a broad sword. After fighting for a considerable time with great fury, and many had been killed, our people obtained the victory, and took their enemy's Chief a prisoner. He was carried off in great triumph, and, though he offered a large ransom for his life, he was put to death. A virgin of note among our enemies had been slain in the battle, and her arm was exposed in our marketplace, where our trophies were always exhibited. The spoils were divided according to the merit of the warriors. Those prisoners which were not sold or redeemed, we kept as slaves; but how different was their condition from that of the slaves in the West Indies! With us, they do no more work than other members of the community, even their master; their food, clothing, and lodging were nearly the same as theirs (except that they were not permitted to eat with those who were free-born); and there was scarce any other difference between them, than a superior degree of importance which the head of a family possesses in our state and that authority which, as such, he exercises over every part of his household. Some of these slaves have even slaves under them as their own property, and for their own use.

As to religion, the natives believe that there is one Creator of all things, and that he lives in the sun, and is girted round with a belt; that he may never eat or drink, but, according to some, he smokes a pipe, which is our own favorite luxury. They believe he governs events, especially our deaths or captivity; but, as for the doctrine of eternity, I do not remember to have ever heard of it; some, however, believe in the transmigration of souls in a certain degree. Those spirits which were not transmigrated, such as their dear friends or relations, they believe always attend them, and guard them from the bad spirits or their foes. For this reason they always, before eating, as I have observed, put some small portion of the meat, and pour some of their drink, on the ground for them; and they often make oblations of the blood of beasts or fowls at their graves. I was very fond of my mother, and almost constantly with her. When she went to make these oblations at her mother's tomb, which was a kind of small solitary thatched house, I sometimes attended her. There she made her libations, and spent most of the night in cries and lamentations. I have

[2]See Benezet's "Account of Africa," throughout.

been often extremely terrified on these occasions. The loneliness of the place, the darkness of the night, and the ceremony of libation, naturally awful and gloomy, were heightened by my mother's lamentations; and these concurring with the doleful cries of birds, by which these places were frequented, gave an inexpressible terror to the scene.

We compute the year, from the day on which the sun crosses the line, and on its setting that evening, there is a general shout throughout the land; at least, I can speak from my own knowledge, throughout our vicinity. The people at the same time make a great noise with rattles, not unlike the basket rattles used by children here, though much larger, and hold up their hands to heaven for a blessing. It is then the greatest offerings are made; and those children whom our wise men foretell will be fortunate are then presented to different people. I remember many used to come and see me, and I was carried about to others for that purpose. They have many offerings, particularly at full moons; generally two, at harvest, before the fruits are taken out of the ground; and when any young animals are killed, sometimes they offer up part of them as a sacrifice. These offerings, when made by one of the heads of a family, serve for the whole. I remember we often had them at my father's and my uncle's, and their families have been present. Some of our offerings are eaten with bitter herbs. We had a saying among us to anyone of a cross temper, "That if they were to be eaten, they should be eaten with bitter herbs."

We practised circumcision like the Jews, and made offerings and feasts on that occasion, in the same manner as they did. Like them also, our children were named from some event, some circumstance, or fancied foreboding, at the time of their birth. I was named *Olaudah*, which in our language signifies vicissitude, or fortunate; also, one favored, and having a loud voice and well spoken. I remember we never polluted the name of the object of our adoration; on the contrary, it was always mentioned with the greatest reverence; and we were totally unacquainted with swearing, and all those terms of abuse and reproach which find their way so readily and copiously into the language of more civilized people. The only expressions of that kind I remember were, "May you rot, or may you swell, or may a beast take you."

I have before remarked that the natives of this part of Africa are extremely cleanly. This necessary habit of decency was with us a part of religion, and therefore we had many purifications and washings; indeed almost as many, and used on the same occasions, if my recollection does not fail me, as the Jews. Those that touched the dead at any time were obliged to wash and purify themselves before they could enter a dwelling-house. Every woman, too, at certain times was forbidden to come into a dwelling-house, or touch any person, or anything we eat. I was so fond of my mother I could not keep from her, or avoid touching her at some of those periods, in consequence of which I was obliged to be kept out with her, in a little house made for that purpose, till offering was made, and then we were purified.

Though we had no places of public worship, we had priests and magicians, or wise men. I do not remember whether they had different offices, or whether they were united in the same persons, but they were held in great reverence by the people. They calculated our time, and foretold events, as their name imported, for we called them *Ah-affoe-way-cah,* which signifies calculators or yearly men, our year being called *Ah-affoe.* They wore their beards, and when they died, they were succeeded by their sons. Most of their implements and things of value were interred along with them. Pipes and tobacco were also put into the grave with the corpse, which was always perfumed and ornamented, and animals were offered in sacrifice to them. None accompanied their funerals, but those of the same profession or tribe. They buried them after sunset, and always returned from the grave by a different way from that which they went.

These magicians were also our doctors or physicians. They practised bleeding by cupping, and were very successful in healing wounds and expelling poisons. They had likewise some extraordinary method of discovering jealousy, theft, poisoning, the success of which, no doubt, they derived from the unbounded influence over the credulity and superstition of the people. I do not remember what those methods were, except that as to poisoning; I recollect an instance or two, which I hope it will not be deemed impertinent here to insert, as it may serve as a kind of specimen of the rest, as is still used by the Negroes in the West Indies. A young woman had been poisoned, but it was not known by whom; the doctors ordered the corpse to be taken up by some persons, and carried to the grave. As soon as the bearers had raised it on their shoulders, they seemed seized with some[3] sudden impulse, and ran to and fro, unable to stop themselves. At last, after having passed through a number of thorns and prickly bushes unhurt, the corpse fell from them close to a house, and defaced it in the fall; and the owner being taken up, he immediately confessed the poisoning.*

The natives are extremely cautious about poison. When they buy any eatables, the seller kisses it all round before the buyer, to shew him it is not poisoned; and the same is done when any meat or drink is presented, particularly to a stranger. We have serpents of different kinds, some of which are esteemed ominous when they appear in our houses, and these we never molest. I remember two of those ominous snakes, each of which was as thick as the calf of a man's leg, and in color resembling a dolphin in the water, crept at different times into my mother's night house, where I always lay with her, and coiled themselves into folds, and each time they crowed like a cock. I was desired by some of our wise men to touch these, that I might be interested in the good omens, which I did, for they were quite harmless, and would tamely suffer themselves to be handled; and then they were put into a large earthen pan, and set on one side of the highway. Some of our snakes, however, were poisonous; one of them crossed the road one day as I was standing on it, and passed between my feet without offering to touch me, to the great surprise of many who saw it; and these incidents were accounted by the wise men, and likewise by my mother and the rest of the people, as remarkable omens in my favor.

Such is the imperfect sketch my memory has furnished me with, of the manners and customs of a people among whom I first drew my breath. And here I cannot forbear suggesting what has long struck me very forcibly, namely, the strong analogy which even by this sketch, imperfect as it is, appears to prevail in the manners and customs of my countrymen and those of the Jews, before they reached the land of promise, and particularly the patriarchs while they were yet in that pastoral state which is described in Genesis—an analogy, which alone would induce me to think that the one people had sprung from the other. Indeed, this is the opinion of Dr. Gill, who, in his commentary on Genesis, very ably deduces the pedigree of the Africans from Afer and Afra, the descendants of Abraham by Keturah his wife and concubine (for both these titles are applied to her). It is also conformable to the sentiments of Dr. John Clarke, formerly Dean of Sarum, in his truth of the Christian religion; both these authors concur in ascribing to us this original. The reasonings of those gentlemen are still further confirmed by the scripture chronology; and if any further corroboration were required, this resemblance in so many respects, is a strong evidence in support of the opinion. Like the Israelites in the primitive state, our government was conducted by our chiefs or judges, our wise men and elders; and the head of a family with us enjoyed a similar authority over his house-

[3]See also Lieutenant Matthew's Voyage, p. 123.

*An instance of this kind happened at Montserrat, in the West Indies, in the year 1763. I then belonged to the *Charming Sally*, Capt. Doran. The chief mate, Mr. Mansfield, and some of the crew being one day on shore, were present at the burying of a poisoned Negro girl. Though they had often heard of the circumstance of the running in such cases, and had even seen it, they imagined it to be a trick of the corpse bearers. The mate therefore desired two of the sailors to take up the coffin, and carry it to the grave. The sailors, who were all of the same opinion, readily obeyed, but they had scarcely raised it to their shoulders before they began to run furiously about, quite unable to direct themselves, till at last, without intention, they came to the hut of him who had poisoned the girl. The coffin then immediately fell from their shoulders against the hut, and damaged part of the wall. The owner of the hut was taken into custody on this, and confessed the poisoning. I give this story as it was related by the mate and crew on their return to the ship. The credit which is due to it, I leave with the reader.

hold, with that which is ascribed to Abraham and the other patriarchs. The law of retaliation obtained almost universally with us as with them: and even their religion appeared to have shed upon us a ray of its glory, though broken and spent in its passage, or eclipsed by the cloud with which time, tradition, and ignorance might have enveloped it; for we had our circumcision (a rule, I believe, peculiar to that people), we had also our sacrifices and burnt-offerings, our washings and purifications, and on the same occasions as they did.

As to the difference of color between the Eboan Africans and the modern Jews, I shall not presume to account for it. It is a subject which has engaged the pens of men of both genius and learning, and is far above my strength. The most able and Reverend Mr. T. Clarkson, however, in his much admired essay on the Slavery and Commerce of the Human Species, has ascertained the cause in a manner that at once solves every objection on that account, and, on my mind at least, has produced the fullest conviction. I shall therefore refer to that performance for theory,[4] contenting myself with extracting a fact as related by Dr. Mitchel.[5] "The Spaniards, who have inhabited America, under the torrid zone, for an time, are become as dark colored as our native Indians of Virginia; of which *I myself have been a witness.*" There is also another instance[6] of a Portuguese settlement at Mitomba, a river in Sierra Leone, where the inhabitants are bred from a mixture of the first Portuguese discoverers with the natives, and are now become in their complexion, and in the woolly quality of their hair, *perfect Negroes,* retaining however a smattering of the Portuguese language.

These instances, and a great many more which might be adduced, while they show how the complexions of the same persons vary in different climates, it is hoped may tend also to remove the prejudice that some conceive against the natives of Africa on account of their color. Surely the minds of the Spaniards did not change with their complexions! Are there not causes enough to which the apparent inferiority of an African may be ascribed, without limiting the goodness of God, and supposing he forebore to stamp understanding on certainly his own image, because "carved in ebony." Might it not naturally be ascribed to their situation? When they come among Europeans, they are ignorant of their language, religion, manners, and customs. Are any pains taken to teach them these? Are they treated as men? Does not slavery itself depress the mind, and extinguish all its fire and every noble sentiment? But, above all, what advantages do not a refined people possess, over those who are rude and uncultivated? Let the polished and haughty European recollect that his ancestors were once, like the Africans, uncivilized, and even barbarous. Did Nature make *them* inferior to their sons? and should *they too* have been made slaves? Every rational mind answers, No. Let such reflections as these melt the pride of their superiority into sympathy for the wants and miseries of their sable brethren, and compel them to acknowledge that understanding is not confined to feature or color. If, when they look round the world, they feel exultation, let it be tempered with benevolence to others, and gratitude to God, "who hath made of one blood all nations of men for to dwell on all the face of the earth";[7] "and whose wisdom is not our wisdom, neither are our ways his ways."

Chapter 2

The author's birth and parentage—His being kidnapped with his sister—Their separation—Surprise at meeting again—Are finally separated—Account of the different places and incidents the author met with till his arrival on the coast—The effect the sight of a slave-ship had on him—He sails for the West Indies—Horrors of a slave-ship—Arrives at Barbadoes, where the cargo is sold and dispersed.

---

[4]Pages 178 to 216 of "Essay on the Slavery and Commerce of the Human Species."

[5]Philos. Trans. No. 476, Sec. 4, cited by Mr. Clarkson, p. 205.

[6]Same page.

[7]Acts 17:26.

I hope the reader will not think I have trespassed on his patience in introducing myself to him, with some account of the manners and customs of my country. They had been implanted in me with great care, and made an impression on my mind, which time could not erase, and which all the adversity and variety of fortune I have since experienced, served only to rivet and record: for, whether the love of one's country be real or imaginary, or a lesson of reason, or an instinct of nature, I still look back with pleasure on the first scenes of my life, though that pleasure has been for the most part mingled with sorrow.

I have already acquainted the reader with the time and place of my birth. My father, besides many slaves, had a numerous family, of which seven lived to grow up, including myself and sister, who was the only daughter. As I was the youngest of the sons, I became, of course, the greatest favorite with my mother, and was always with her; and she used to take particular pains to form my mind. I was trained up from my earliest years in the art of war: my daily exercise was shooting and throwing javelins, and my mother adorned me with emblems, after the manner of our greatest warriors. In this way I grew up till I had turned the age of eleven, when an end was put to my happiness in the following manner: Generally, when the grown people in the neighborhood were gone far in the field to labor, the children assembled together in some of the neighboring premises to play; and commonly some of us used to get up a tree to look out for any assailant, or kidnapper, that might come upon us—for they sometimes took those opportunities of our parents' absence, to attack and carry off as many as they could seize. One day as I was watching at the top of a tree in our yard, I saw one of those people come into the yard of our next neighbor but one, to kidnap, there being many stout young people in it. Immediately on this I gave the alarm of the rogue, and he was surrounded by the stoutest of them, who entangled him with cords, so that he could not escape, till some of the grown people came and secured him. But, alas! ere long it was my fate to be thus attached, and to be carried off, when none of the grown people were nigh. One day, when all our people were gone out to their works as usual, and only I and my dear sister were left to mind the house, two men and a woman got over our walls, and in a moment seized us both, and, without giving us time to cry out, or make resistance, they stopped our mouths, and ran off with us into the nearest wood. Here they tied our hands, and continued to carry us as far as they could, till night came on, when we reached a small house, where the robbers halted for refreshment, and spent the night. We were then unbound, but were unable to take any food; and, being quite overpowered by fatigue and grief, our only relief was some sleep, which allayed our misfortune for a short time. The next morning we left the house, and continued travelling all the day. For a long time we had kept the woods, but at last we came into a road which I believed I knew. I had now some hopes of being delivered; for we had advanced but a little way before I discovered some people at a distance, on which I began to cry out for their assistance; but my cries had no other effect than to make them tie me faster and stop my mouth, and then they put me into a large sack. They also stopped my sister's mouth, and tied her hands; and in this manner we proceeded till we were out of sight of these people. When we went to rest the following night, they offered us some victuals, but we refused it; and the only comfort we had was in being in one another's arms all that night, and bathing each other with our tears. But alas! we were soon deprived of even the small comfort of weeping together. The next day proved a day of greater sorrow than I had yet experienced; for my sister and I were then separated, while we lay clasped in each other's arms. It was in vain that we besought them not to part us; she was torn from me, and immediately carried away, while I was left in a state of distraction not to be described. I cried and grieved continually; and for several days did not eat anything but what they forced into my mouth. At length, after many days' travelling, during which I had often changed masters, I got into the hands of a chieftain, in a very pleasant country. This man had two wives and some children, and they all used me extremely well, and did all they could do to comfort me; particularly the first wife, who was something like my mother. Although I was a great many days' journey from my father's house, yet these people spoke exactly the same language with us. This first master of mine, as I may call him, was a smith, and my principal employment was working his bellows, which were the same kind as I had seen in my vicinity. They were in some respects not unlike the stoves here in gentlemen's kitchens, and were covered over with leather; and in the middle of that leather a stick was fixed, and a person stood up, and worked it in the same manner as is done to pump water out of a cask with a hand pump. I believe it was gold he worked, for it was of a lovely bright yellow color, and was worn by the women on their wrists and ankles. I was there I suppose about a month, and they at last used to trust me some little distance from the house. This liberty I used in embracing every opportunity to inquire the way to my own home; and I also sometimes, for the same purpose, went with the maidens, in the cool of the evenings, to bring pitchers of water from the springs for the use of the house. I had also remarked where the sun rose in the morning, and set in the evening, as I had travelled along; and I had observed that my father's house was towards the rising of the sun. I therefore determined to seize the first opportunity of making my escape, and to shape my course for that quarter; for I was quite oppressed and weighed down by grief after my mother and friends; and my love of liberty, ever great, was strengthened by the mortifying circumstance of not daring to eat with the free-born children, although I was mostly their companion. While I was projecting my escape one day, an unlucky event happened, which quite disconcerted my plan, and put an end to my hopes. I used to be sometimes employed in assisting an elderly slave to cook and take care of the poultry; and one morning, while I was feeding some chickens, I happened to toss a small pebble at one of them, which hit it on the middle, and directly killed it. The old slave, having soon after missed the chicken, inquired after it; and on my relating the accident (for I told her the truth, for my mother would never suffer me to tell a lie), she flew into a violent passion, and threatened that I should suffer for it; and, my master being out, she immediately went and told her mistress what I had done. This alarmed me very much, and I expected an instant flogging, which to me was uncommonly dreadful, for I had seldom been beaten at home. I therefore resolved to fly; and accordingly I ran into a thicket that was hard by, and hid myself in the bushes. Soon afterwards my mistress and the slave returned, and, not seeing me, they searched all the house, but not finding me, and I not making answer when they called to me, they thought I had run away, and the whole neighborhood was raised in pursuit of me. In that part of the country, as in ours, the houses and villages were skirted with woods, or shrubberies, and the bushes were so thick that a man could readily conceal himself in them, so as to elude the strictest search. The neighbors continued the whole day looking for me, and several times many of them came within a few yards of the place where I lay hid. I expected every moment, when I heard a rustling among the trees, to be found out, and punished by my master; but they never discovered me, though they were often so near that I even heard their conjectures as they were looking about for me; and I now learned from them that any attempts to return home would be hopeless. Most of them supposed I had fled towards home; but the distance was so great, and the way so intricate, that they though I could never reach it, and that I should be lost in the woods. When I heard this I was seized with a violent panic, and abandoned myself to despair. Night, too, began to approach, and aggravated all my fears. I had before entertained hopes of getting home, and had determined when it should be dark to make the attempt; but I was now convinced it was fruitless, and began to consider that, if possibly I could escape all other animals,

I could not those of the human kind; and that, now knowing the way, I must perish in the woods. Thus was I like the hunted deer—

——Every leaf and every whisp'ring breath,
Convey'd a foe, and every foe a death.

I heard frequent rustlings among the leaves, and being pretty sure they were snakes, I expected every instant to be stung by them. This increased my anguish, and the horror of my situation become now quite insupportable. I at length quitted the thicket, very faint and hungry, for I had not eaten or drank anything all the day, and crept to my master's kitchen, from whence I set out at first, which was an open shed, and laid myself down in the ashes with an anxious wish for death, to relieve me from all my pains. I was scarcely awake in the morning, when the old woman slave, who was the first up, came to light the fire, and saw me in the fireplace. She was very much surprised to see me, and could scarcely believe her own eyes. She now promised to intercede for me, and went for her master, who soon after came, and, having slightly reprimanded me, ordered me to be taken care of, and not ill treated.

Soon after this, my master's only daughter, and child by his first wife, sickened and died, which affected him so much that for sometime he was almost frantic, and really would have killed himself, had he not been watched and prevented. However, in a short time afterwards he recovered, and I was again sold. I was now carried to the left of the sun's rising, though many dreary wastes and dismal woods, amidst the hideous roarings of wild beasts. The people I was sold to used to carry me very often, when I was tired, either on their shoulders or on their backs. I saw many convenient well-built sheds along the road, at proper distances, to accommodate the merchants and travellers, who lay in those buildings along with their wives, who often accompany them; and they always go well armed.

From the time I left my own nation, I always found somebody that understood me till I came to the sea coast. The languages of different nations did not totally differ, nor were they so copious as those of the Europeans, particularly the English. They were therefore, easily learned; and, while I was journeying thus through Africa, I acquired two or three different tongues. In this manner I had been travelling for a considerable time when, one evening, to my great surprise, whom should I see brought to the house where I was but my dear sister! As soon as she saw me, she gave a loud shriek, and ran into my arms—I was quite overpowered; neither of us could speak, but, for a considerable time, clung to each other in mutual embraces, unable to do anything but weep. Our meeting affected all who saw us; and, indeed, I must acknowledge, in honor of those sable destroyers of human rights, that I never met with any ill treatment, or saw any offered to their slaves, except tying them, when necessary, to keep them from running away. When these people knew we were brother and sister, they indulged us to be together; and the man, to whom I supposed we belonged, lay with us, he in the middle, while she and I held one another by the hands across his breast all night; and thus for a while we forgot our misfortunes, in the joy of being together; but even this small comfort was soon to have an end; for scarcely had the fatal morning appeared when she was again torn from me forever! I was now more miserable, if possible, than before. The small relief which her presence gave me from pain, was gone, and the wretchedness of my situation was redoubled by my anxiety after her fate, and my apprehensions lest her sufferings should be greater than mine, when I could not be with her to alleviate them. Yes, thou dear partner of all my childish sports! thou sharer of my joys and sorrows! happy should I have ever esteemed myself to encounter every misery for you and to procure your freedom by the sacrifice of my own. Though you were early forced from my arms, your image has been always riveted in my heart, from which neither time nor fortune have been able to remove it; so that, while the thoughts of your sufferings have damped my prosperity, they have mingled with adversity and increased its bitterness. To that Heaven which protects the weak from the strong, I commit the care of your innocence and virtues, if they have not already received their full reward, and if your youth and delicacy have not long since fallen victims to the violence of the African trader, the pestilential stench of a Guinea ship, the seasoning in the European colonies, or the lash and lust of a brutal and unrelenting overseer.

I did not long remain after my sister. I was again sold, and carried through a number of places, till after travelling a considerable time, I came to a town called Tinmah, in the most beautiful country I had yet seen in Africa. It was extremely rich, and there were many rivulets which flowed through it, and supplied a large pond in the centre of the town, where the people washed. Here I first saw and tasted cocoanuts, which I thought superior to any nuts I had ever tasted before; and the trees, which were loaded, were also interspersed among the houses, which had commodious shades adjoining, and were in the same manner as ours, the insides being neatly plastered and whitewashed. Here I also saw and tasted for the first time, sugar-cane. Their money consisted of little white shells, the size of the finger nail. I was sold here for one hundred and seventy-two of them, by a merchant who lived and brought me there. I had been about two or three days at his house, when a wealthy widow, a neighbor of his, came there one evening, and brought with her an only son, a young gentleman about my own age and size. Here they saw me; and, having taken a fancy to me, I was bought of the merchant, and went home with them. Her house and premises were situated close to one of those rivulets I have mentioned, and were the finest I ever saw in Africa; they were very extensive, and she had a number of slaves to attend her. The next day I was washed and perfumed, and when meal time came, I was led into the presence of my mistress, and ate and drank before her with her son. This filled me with astonishment; and I could scarce help expressing my surprise that the young gentleman should suffer me, who was bound, to eat with him who was free; and not only so, but that he would not at any time either eat or drink till I had taken first, because I was the eldest, which was agreeable to our custom. Indeed, every thing here, and all their treatment of me, made me forget that I was a slave. The language of these people resembled ours so nearly, that we understood each other perfectly. They had also the very same customs as we. There were likewise slaves daily to attend us, while my young master and I, with other boys, sported with our darts and bows and arrows, as I had been used to do at home. In this resemblance to my former happy state, I passed about two months; and I now began to think I was to be adopted into the family, and was beginning to be reconciled to my situation, and to forget by degrees my misfortunes, when all at once the delusion vanished; for, without the least previous knowledge, one morning early, while my dear master and companion was still asleep, I was awakened out of my reverie to fresh sorrow, and hurried away even amongst the uncircumcised.

Thus, at the very moment I dreamed of the greatest happiness, I found myself most miserable; and it seemed as if fortune wished to give me this taste of joy only to render the reverse more poignant. The change I now experienced was as painful as it was sudden and unexpected. It was a change indeed, from a state of bliss to a scene which is inexpressible by me, as it discovered to me an element I had never before beheld, and till then had no idea of, and wherein such instances or hardship and cruelty continually occurred, as I can never reflect on but with horror.

All the nations and people I had hitherto passed through, resembled our own in their manner, customs, and language; but I came at length to a country, the inhabitants of which differed from us in all those particulars. I was very much struck with this difference, especially when I came among a people who did not circumcise, and ate without washing their hands. The cooked also in iron pots, and had European cutlasses and cross bows, which were unknown to us, and fought with their fists among themselves. Their women were not so modest as ours, for they ate, and drank, and slept with their men. But above all, I was amazed to see no sacrifices or offerings among them. In some of those places the people ornamented themselves with scars, and likewise filed their teeth very sharp. They wanted sometimes to ornament me in the same manner, but I would not suffer them; hoping that I might some time be among a people who did not thus disfigure themselves, as I thought they did. At last I came to the banks of a large river which was covered with canoes, in which the people appeared to live with their household utensils, and provisions of all kinds. I was beyond measure astonished at this, as I had never before seen any water larger than a pond or a rivulet; and my surprise was mingled with no small fear when I was put into one of these canoes, and we began to paddle, and move along the river. We continued going on thus till night, and when we came to land, and made fires on the banks, each family by themselves; some dragged their canoes on shore, others stayed and cooked in theirs, and laid in them all night. Those on the land had mats, of which they made tents, some in the shape of little houses; in these we slept; and after the morning meal, we embarked again and proceeded as before. I was often very much astonished to see some of the women, as well as the men, jump into the water, dive to the bottom, come up again, and swim about. Thus I continued to travel, sometimes by land, sometimes by water, through different countries and various nations, till, at the end of six or seven months after I had been kidnapped, I arrived at the sea coast. It would be tedious and uninteresting to relate all the incidents which befell me during this journey, and which I have not yet forgotten; of the various hands I passed through, and the manners and customs of all the different people among whom I lived—I shall therefore only observe, that in all the places where I was, the soil was exceedingly rich; the pumpkins, eadas, plantains, yams &c. &c., were in great abundance, and of incredible size. There were also vast quantities of different gums, though not used for any purpose, and everywhere a great deal of tobacco. The cotton even grew quite wild, and there was plenty of red-wood. I saw no mechanics whatever in all the way, except such as I have mentioned. The chief employment in all these countries was agriculture, and both the males and females, as with us, were brought up to it, and trained in the arts of war.

The first object which saluted my eyes when I arrived on the coast, was the sea, and a slave ship, which was then riding at anchor, and waiting for its cargo. These filled me with astonishment, which was soon converted into terror, when I was carried on board. I was immediately handled, and tossed up to see if I were sound, by some of the crew; and I was now persuaded that I had gotten into a world of bad spirits, and that they were going to kill me. Their complexions, too, differing so much from ours, their long hair, and the language they spoke (which was very different from any I had ever heard), united to confirm me in this belief. Indeed, such were the horrors of my views and fears at the moment, that, if ten thousand worlds have been my own, I would have freely parted with them all to have exchanged my condition with that of the meanest slave in my own country. When I looked round the ship too, and saw a large furnace of copper boiling, and a multitude of black people of every description chained together, every one of their countenances expressing dejection and sorrow, I no longer doubted of my fate; and, quite overpowered with horror and anguish, I fell motionless on the deck and fainted. When I recovered a little, I found some black people about me, who I believed were some of those who had brought me on board, and had been receiving their pay; they talked to me in order to cheer me, but all in vain. I asked them if we were not to be eaten by those white men with horrible looks, red faces, and long hair. They told me I was not, and one of the crew brought me a small portion of spirituous liquor in a wine glass; but being afraid of him, I would not take it out of his hand. One of the blacks, therefore, took if from him and gave it to me, and I took a little down my palate, which, instead of reviving me, as they thought it would, threw me into the greatest consternation at the strange feeling it produced, having never tasted any such liquor before. Soon after this, the blacks who brought me on board went off, and left me abandoned to despair.

I now saw myself deprived of all chance of returning to my native country, or even the least glimpse of hope of gaining the shore, which I now considered as friendly; and I even wished for my former slavery in preference to my present situation, which was filled with horrors of every kind, still heightened by my ignorance of what I was to undergo. I was not long suffered to indulge my grief; I was soon put down under the decks, and there I received such a salutation in my nostrils as I have never experienced in my life; so that, with the loathsomeness of the stench, and crying together, I became so sick and low that I was not able to eat, nor had I the least desire to taste anything. I now wished for the last friend, death, to relieve me; but soon, to my grief, two of the white men offered me eatables; and, on my refusing to eat, one of them held me fast by the hands, and laid me across, I think, the windlass, and tied my feet, while the other flogged me severely. I had never experienced anything of this kind before, and, although not being used to the water, I naturally feared that element the first time I saw it, yet, nevertheless, could I have got over the nettings, I would have jumped over the side, but I could not; and besides, the crew used to watch us very closely who were not chained down to the decks, lest we should leap into the water; and I have seen some of these poor African prisoners most severely cut, for attempting to do so, and hourly whipped for not eating. This indeed was often the case with myself. In a little time after, amongst the poor chained men, I found some of my own nation, which in a small degree gave ease to my mind. I inquired of these what was to be done with us? They gave me to understand, we were to be carried to these white people's country to work for them. I then was a little revived, and thought, if it were no worse than working, my situation was not so desperate; but still I feared I should be put to death, the white people looked and acted, as I thought, in so savage a manner; for I had never seen among any people such instances of brutal cruelty; and this not only shown towards us blacks, but also to some of the whites themselves. One white man in particular I saw, when we were permitted to be on deck, flogged so unmercifully with a large rope near the foremast, that he died in consequence of it; and they tossed him over the side as they would have done a brute. This made me fear these people the more; and I expected nothing less than to be treated in the same manner. I could not help expressing my fears and apprehensions to some of my countrymen; I asked them if these people had no country, but lived in this hollow place (the ship)? They told me they did not, but came from a distant one. "Then," said I, "how comes it in all our country we never heard of them?" They told me because they lived so very far off. I then asked where were their women? had they any like themselves? I was told they had. "And why," said I, "do we not see them?" They answered, because they were left behind. I asked how the vessel could go? They told me they could not tell; but that there was cloth put upon the masts by the help of the ropes I saw, and then the vessel went on; and the white men had some spell or magic they put in the water when they liked, in order to stop the vessel. I was exceedingly amazed at this account, and really thought they were spirits. I therefore wished much to be from amongst them, for I expected they would sacrifice me; but my wishes were vain—for we were so quartered that it was impossible for any of us to make our escape.

While we stayed on the coast I was mostly on deck; and one day, to my great astonishment, I saw one of these vessels coming in with the sails up. As soon as the whites saw it, they gave a great shout, at which we were amazed; and the more so, as the vessel appeared larger by approaching nearer. At last, she came to an anchor in my sight, and when the anchor was let go, I and my countrymen who saw it, were lost in astonishment to observe the vessel stop—and were now convinced it was done by magic. Soon after this the other ship got her boats out, and they came on board of us, and the people of both ships seemed very glad to see each other. Several of the strangers also shook hands with us black people, and made motions with their hands, signifying I suppose, we were to go to their country, but we did not understand them.

At last, when the ship we were in, had got in all her cargo, they made ready with many fearful noises, and we were all put under deck, so that we could not see how they managed the vessel. But this disappointment was the least of my sorrow. The stench of the hold while we were on the coast was so intolerably loathsome, that it was dangerous to remain there for any time, and some of us had been permitted to stay on the deck for the fresh air; but now that the whole ship's cargo were confined together, it became absolutely pestilential. The closeness of the place, and the heat of the climate, added to the number in the ship, which was so crowded that each had scarcely room to turn himself, almost suffocated us. This produced copious perspiration, so that the air soon became unfit for respiration, from a variety of loathsome smells, and brought on a sickness among the slaves, of which many died—thus falling victims to the improvident avarice, as I may call it, of their purchasers. This wretched situation was again aggravated by the galling of the chains, now became insupportable, and the filth of the necessary tubs, into which the children often fell, and were almost suffocated. The shrieks of the women, and the groans of the dying, rendered the whole a scene of horror almost inconceivable. Happily perhaps, for myself, I was soon reduced so low here that it was thought necessary to keep me almost always on deck; and from my extreme youth I was not put in fetters. In this situation I expected every hour to share the fate of my companions, some of whom were almost daily brought upon deck at the point of death, which I began to hope would soon put an end to my miseries. Often did I think many of the inhabitants of the deep much more happy than myself. I envied them the freedom they enjoyed, and as often wished I could change my condition for theirs. Every circumstance I met with, served only to render my state more painful, and heightened my apprehensions, and my opinion of the cruelty of the whites.

One day they had taken a number of fishes; and when they had killed and satisfied themselves with as many as they thought fit, to our astonishment who were on deck, rather than give any of them to us to eat, as we expected, they tossed the remaining fish into the sea again, although we begged and prayed for some as well as we could, but in vain; and some of my countrymen, being pressed by hunger, took an opportunity, when they thought no one saw them, of trying to get a little privately; but they were discovered, and the attempt procured them some very severe floggings. One day, when we had a smooth sea and moderate wind, two of my wearied countrymen who were chained together (I was near them at the time), preferring death to such a life of misery, somehow made through the nettings and jumped into the sea; immediately, another quite dejected fellow, who, on account of his illness, was suffered to be out of irons, also followed their example; and I believe many more would very soon have done the same, if they had not been prevented by the ship's crew who were instantly alarmed. Those of us that were the most active, were in a moment put down under the deck; and there was such a noise and confusion amongst the people of the ship as I never heard before, to stop her, and get the boat out to go after the slaves. However, two of the wretches were drowned, but they got the other, and afterwards flogged him unmercifully, for thus attempting to prefer death to slavery. In this manner we continued to undergo more hardships than I can now relate, hardships which are inseparable from this accursed trade. Many a time we were near suffocation from the want of fresh air, which we were often without for whole days together. This, and the stench of the necessary tubs, carried off many.

During our passage, I first saw flying fishes, which surprised me very much; they used frequently to fly across the ship, and many of them fell on the deck. I also now first saw the use of the quadrant; I had often with astonishment seen the mariners make observations with it, and I could not think what it meant. They at last took notice of my surprise; and one of them, willing to increase it, as well as to gratify my curiosity, made me one day look though it. The clouds appeared to me to be land, which disappeared as they passed along. This heightened my wonder; and I was now more persuaded than ever, that I was in another world, and that every thing about me was magic. At last, we came in sight of the island of Barbadoes, at which the whites on board gave a great shout, and made many signs of joy to us. We did not know what to think of this; but as the vessel drew nearer, we plainly saw the harbor, and other ships of different kinds and sizes, and we soon anchored amongst them, off Bridgetown. Many merchants and planters now came on board, though it was in the evening. They put us in separate parcels, and examined us attentively. They also made us jump, and pointed to land, signifying we were to go there. We thought by this, we should be eaten by these ugly men, as they appeared to us; and, when soon after we were all put down under the deck again, there was much dread and trembling among us, and nothing but bitter cries to be heard all the night from these apprehensions, insomuch, that at last the white people got some old slaves from the land to pacify us. They told us we were not to be eaten, but to work, and were soon to go on land, where we should see many of our country people. This report eased us much. And sure enough, soon after we were landed, there came to us Africans of all languages.

We were conducted immediately to the merchant's yard, where we were all pent up together, like so many sheep in a fold, without regard to sex or age. As every object was new to me, everything I saw filled me with surprise. What struck me first, was, that the houses were built with bricks and stones, and in every other respect different from those I had seen in Africa; but I was still more astonished on seeing people on horseback. I did not know what this could mean; and, indeed, I thought these people were full of nothing but magical arts. While I was in astonishment, one of my fellow prisoners spoke to a countryman of his, about the horses, who said they were the same kind they had in their country. I understood them, though they were from a distant part of Africa; and I thought it odd I had not seen any horses there; but afterwards, when I came to converse with different Africans, I found they had many horses amongst them, and much larger than those I then saw.

We were not many days in the merchant's custody, before we were sold after their usual manner, which is this: On a signal given (as the beat of a drum), the buyers rush at once into the yard where the slaves are confined, and make choice of that parcel they like best. The noise and clamor with which this is attended, and the eagerness visible in the countenances of the buyers, serve not a little to increase the apprehension of terrified Africans, who may well be supposed to consider them as the ministers of that destruction to which they think themselves devoted. In this manner, without scruple, are relations and friends separated, most of them never to see each other again. I remember, in the vessel in which I was brought over, in the men's apartment, there were several brothers, who, in the sale, were sold in different lots; and it was very moving on this occasion, to see and hear their cries at parting. O, ye nominal Christians! might not an African ask you—Learned you this from your God, who says unto you, Do unto all men as you would men should do unto you? Is it not enough that we are torn from our country and friends, to toil for your luxury and lust of gain? Must every tender feeling be likewise sacrificed to your avarice? Are the dearest friends and relations, now rendered more dear by their separation from their kindred, still to be parted from each other, and thus prevented from cheering the gloom of slavery, with the small comfort of being together, and mingling their sufferings and sorrows? Why are parents to lose their children, brothers their sisters, or husbands their wives? Surely, this is a new refinement in cruelty, which, while it has no advantage to atone for it, thus aggravates distress, and adds fresh horrors even to the wretchedness of slavery.

Chapter 3

The author is carried to Virginia—His distress—Surprise at seeing a picture and a watch—Is bought by Captain Pascal, and sets out for England—His terror during the voyage—Arrives in England—His wonder at a fall of snow—Is sent to Guernsey, and in some time goes on board a ship of war with his master—Some account of the expedition against Louisburg under the command of Admiral Boscawen, in 1758.

I now totally lost the small remains of comfort I had enjoyed in conversing with my country-men; the women too, who used to wash and take care of me were all gone different ways, and I never saw one of them afterwards.

I stayed in this island for a few days, I believe it could not be above a fortnight, when I, and some few more slaves, that were not saleable amongst the rest, from very much fretting, were shipped off in a sloop for North America. On the passage we were better treated than when we were coming from Africa, and we had plenty of rice and fat pork. We were landed up a river a good way from the sea, about Virginia county, where we saw few or none of our native Africans, and not one soul who could talk to me. I was a few weeks weeding grass and gathering stones in a plantation; and at last all my companions were distributed different ways, and only myself was left. I was now exceedingly miserable, and thought myself worse off than any of the rest of my companions, for they could talk to each other, but I had no person to speak to that I could understand. In this state, I was constantly grieving and pining, and wishing for death rather than anything else. While I was in this plantation, the gentleman, to whom I suppose the estate belonged, being unwell, I was one day sent for to his dwelling-house to fan him; when I came into the room where he was I was very much affrighted at some things I saw, and the more so as I had seen a black woman slave as I came through the house, who was cooking the dinner, and the poor creature was cruelly loaded with various kinds of iron machines; she had one particularly on her head, which locked her mouth so fast that she could scarcely speak; and could not eat nor drink. I was much astonished and shocked at this contrivance, which I afterwards learned was called the iron muzzle. Soon after I had a fan put in my hand, to fan the gentleman while he slept: and so I did indeed with great fear. While he was fast asleep I indulged myself a great deal in looking about the room, which to me appeared very fine and curious. The first object that engaged my attention was a watch which hung on the chimney, and was going. I was quite surprised at the noise it made, and was afraid it would tell the gentleman anything I might do amiss; and when I immediately after observed a picture hanging in the room, which appeared constantly to look at me, I was still more affrighted, having never seen such things as these before. At one time I thought it was something relative to magic; and not seeing it move, I thought it might be some way the whites had to keep their great men when they died, and offer them libations as we used to do our friendly spirits. In this state of anxiety I remained till my master awoke, when I was dismissed out of the room, to my no small satisfaction and relief; for I thought that these people were all made up of wonders. In this place I was called Jacob; but on board the *African Snow,* I was called Michael. I had been some time in this miserable, forlorn, and much dejected state, without having anyone to talk to, which made my life a burden, when the kind and unknown hand of the Creator (who in very deed leads the blind in a way they know not) now began to appear, to my comfort; for one day the captain of a merchant ship, called the *Industrious Bee,* came on some business to my master's house. This gentleman, whose name was Michael Henry Pascal, was a lieutenant in the royal navy, but now commanded this trading ship, which was somewhere in the confines of the county many miles off. While he was at my master's house, it happened that he saw me, and liked me so well that he made a purchase of me. I think I have often heard him say he gave thirty or forty pounds sterling for me; but I do not remember which. However, he meant me for a present to some of his friends in England: and as I was sent accordingly from the house of my then master (one Mr. Campbell) to the place where the ship lay; I was conducted on horseback by an elderly black man (a mode of travelling which appeared very odd to me). When I arrived I was carried on board a fine large ship, loaded with tobacco, &c., and just ready to sail for England. I now thought my condition much mended; I had sails to lie on, and plenty of good victuals to eat; and everybody on board used me very kindly, quite contrary to what I had seen of any white people before; I therefore began to think that they were not all of the same disposition. A few days after I was on board we sailed for England. I was still at a loss to conjecture my destiny. By this time, however, I could smatter a little imperfect English; and I wanted to know as well as I could where we were going. Some of the people of the ship used to tell me they were going to carry me back to my own country, and this made me very happy. I was quite rejoiced at the idea of going back, and thought if I could get home what wonders I should have to tell. But I was reserved for another fate, and was soon undeceived when we came within sight of the English coast. While I was on board this ship, my captain and master named me *Gustavus Vassa.* I at that time began to understand him a little, and refused to be called so, and told him as well as I could that I would be called Jacob; but he said I should not, and still called me Gustavus: and when I refused to answer to my new name, which I at first did, it gained me many a cuff; so at length I submitted, and by which I have been known ever since. The ship had a very long passage; and on that account we had very short allowance of provisions. Towards the last, we had only one pound and a half of bread per week, and about the same quantity of meat, and one quart of water a day. We spoke with only one vessel the whole time we were at sea, and but once we caught a few fishes. In our extremities the captain and people told me in jest they would kill and eat me; but I thought them in earnest, and was depressed beyond measure, expecting every moment to be my last. While I was in this situation, one evening they caught, with a good deal of trouble, a large shark, and got it on board. This gladdened my poor heart exceedingly, as I thought it would serve the people to eat instead of their eating me; but very soon, to my astonishment, they cut off a small part of the tail, and tossed the rest over the side. This renewed my consternation; and I did not know what to think of these white people, though I very much feared they would kill and eat me. There was on board the ship a young lad who had never been at sea before, about four or five years older than myself: his name was Richard Baker. He was a native of America, had received an excellent education, and was of a most amiable temper. Soon after I went on board, he showed me a great deal of partiality and attention, and in return I grew extremely fond of him. We at length became inseparable; and, for the space of two years, he was of very great use to me, and was my constant companion and instructor. Although this dear youth had many slaves of his own, yet he and I have gone through many sufferings together on shipboard; and we have many nights lain in each other's bosoms when we were in great distress. Thus such a friendship was cemented between us as we cherished till his death, which, to my very great sorrow, happened in the year 1759, when he was up the Archipelago, on board his Majesty's ship the *Preston:* an event which I have never ceased to regret, as I lost at once a kind interpreter, an agreeable companion, and a faithful friend; who, at the age of fifteen, discovered a mind superior to prejudice; and who was not ashamed to notice, to associate with, and to be the friend and instructor of one who was ignorant, a stranger, of a different complexion, and a slave! My master had lodged in his mother's house in America; he respected him very much, and made him always eat with him in the cabin. He used often to tell him jocularly that he would kill and eat me. Sometimes he would say to me—the black people were not good to eat, and would ask me if we did not eat people in my country. I said, No; then he said he would kill Dick (as he always called him) first, and afterwards me. Though this hearing relieved my mind a little as to myself, I was alarmed for Dick, and whenever he was called I used to be very much afraid he was to be killed; and I would peep and watch to see if they were going to kill him; nor was I free from this consternation till we made the land. One night we lost a man overboard; and the cries and noise were so great and confused, in stopping the ship, that I, who did not know what was the matter, began, as usual, to be very much afraid, and to think they were going to make an offering with me, and perform some magic; which I still believed they dealt in. As the waves were very high, I thought the Ruler of the seas was angry, and I expected to be offered up to appease him. This filled my mind with agony, and I could not any more, that night, close my eyes again to rest. However, when daylight appeared, I was a little eased in my mind; but still, every time I was called, I used to think it was to be killed. Some time after this, we saw some very large fish, which I afterwards found were called grampusses. They looked to me exceedingly terrible, and made their appearance just at dusk, and were so near as to blow the water on the ship's deck. I believed them to be the rulers of the sea; and as the white people did not make any offerings at any time, I thought they were angry with them; and, at last, what confirmed my belief was, the wind just then died away, and a calm ensued, and in consequence of it the ship stopped going. I supposed that the fish had performed this, and I hid myself in the fore part of the ship, through fear of being offered up to appease them, every minute peeping and quaking; but my good friend Dick came shortly towards me, and I took an opportunity to ask him, as well as I could, what these fish were. Not being able to talk much English, I could but just make him understand my question; and not at all, when I asked him if any offerings were to be made to them; however, he told me these fish would swallow anybody which sufficiently alarmed me. Here he was called away by the captain, who was leaning over the quarter-deck railing, and looking at the fish; and most of the people were busied in getting a barrel of pitch to light for them to play with. The captain now called me to him, having learned some of my apprehensions from Dick; and having diverted himself and others for some time with my fears, which appeared ludicrous enough in my crying and trembling, he dismissed me. The barrel of pitch was now lighted and put over the side into the water. By this time it was just dark, and the fish went after it; and, to my great joy, I saw them no more.

However, all my alarms began to subside when we got sight of land; and at last the ship arrived at Falmouth, after a passage of thirteen weeks. Every heart on board seemed gladdened on our reaching the shore, and none more than mine. The captain immediately went on shore, and sent on board some fresh provisions, which we wanted very much. We made good use of them, and our famine was soon turned into feasting, almost without ending. It was about the beginning of the spring 1757, when I arrived in England, and I was near twelve years of age at that time. I was very much struck with the buildings and the pavement of the streets in Falmouth; and, indeed, every object I saw, filled me with new surprise. One morning, when I got upon deck, I saw it covered all over with the snow that fell over night. As I had never seen anything of the kind before, I thought it was salt: so I immediately ran down to the mate, and desired him, as well as I could, to come and see how somebody in the night had thrown salt all over the deck. He, knowing what it was, desired me to bring some of it down to him. Accordingly I took up a handful of it, which I found very cold indeed; and when I brought it to him he desired me to taste it. I did so, and I was surprised beyond measure. I then asked him what it was; he told me it was snow, but I could not in anywise understand him. He asked me, if we had no such thing in my country; I told him, No. I then asked him the use of it, and who made it; he told me a great man in the heavens, called God. But here again I was to all intents and purposes at a loss to understand him; and the more so, when a little after I saw the air filled with it, in a heavy shower, which fell down on the same day. After this I went to church; and having never been at such a place before, I was again amazed at seeing and hearing the service. I asked all I could about it, and they gave me to understand it was worshipping God, who made us and all things. I was still at a great loss, and soon got into an endless field of inquiries, as well as I was able to speak and ask about things. However, my little friend Dick used to be my best interpreter; for I could make free with him, and he always instructed me with pleasure. And from what I could understand by him of this God, and in seeing these white people did not sell one another as we did, I was much pleased; and in this I thought they were much happier than we Africans. I was astonished at the wisdom of the white people in all things I saw; but was amazed at their not sacrificing, or making any offerings, and eating with unwashed hands, and touching the dead. I likewise could not help remarking the particular slenderness of their women, which I did not at first like; and I thought they were not so modest and shame-faced as the African women.

I had often seen my master and Dick employed in reading; and I had a great curiosity to talk to the books as I thought they did, and so to learn how all things had a beginning. For that purpose I have often taken up a book, and have talked to it, and then put my ears to it, when alone, in hopes it would answer me; and I have been very much concerned when I found it remained silent.

My master lodged at the house of a gentleman in Falmouth, who had a fine little daughter about six or seven years of age, and she grew prodigiously fond of me, insomuch that we used to eat together, and had servants to wait on us. I was so much caressed by this family that it often reminded me of the treatment I had received from my little noble African master. After I had been here a few days, I was sent on board of the ship; but the child cried so much after me that nothing could pacify her till I was sent for again. It is ludicrous enough, that I began to fear I should be betrothed to this young lady; and when my master asked me if I would stay there with her behind him, as he was going away with the ship, which had taken in the tobacco again, I cried immediately, and said I would not leave him. At last, by stealth, one night I was sent on board the ship again; and in a little time we sailed for Guernsey, where she was in part owned by a merchant, one Nicholas Doberry. As I was now amongst a people who had not their faces scarred, like some of the African nation where I had been, I was very glad I did not let them ornament me in that manner when I was with them. When we arrived at Guernsey, my master placed me to board and lodge with one of his mates, who had a wife and family there; and some months afterwards he went to England, and left me in care of this mate, together with my friend Dick. This mate had a little daughter, aged about five or six years, with whom I used to be much delighted. I had often observed that when her mother washed her face it looked very rosy, but when she washed mine it did not look so. I therefore tried oftentimes myself if I could not by washing make my face of the same color as my little play-mate, Mary, but it was all in vain; and I now began to be mortified at the difference in our complexions. This woman behaved to me with great kindness and attention, and taught me everything in the same manner as she did her own child, and, indeed, in every respect, treated me as such. I remained here till the summer of the year 1757, when my master, being appointed first lieutenant of his Majesty's ship the *Roebuck,* sent for Dick and me, and his old mate. On this we all left Guernsey, and set out for England in a sloop, bound for London. As we were coming up towards the Nore, where the *Roebuck* lay, a man-of-war's boat came along side to press our people, on which each man ran to hide himself. I was very much frightened at this, though I did not know what it meant, or what to think or do. However I went and hid myself also under a hencoop. Immediately afterwards, the press-gang came on board with their swords drawn, and searched all about, pulled the people out by force, and put them into the boat. At last I was found out also; the man that found me held me up by the heels while they all made their sport of me, I roaring and crying out all the time most lustily; but at last the mate, who was my conductor, seeing this, came to my assistance, and did all he could to pacify me; but all to very little purpose, till I had seen the boat go off. Soon afterwards we came to the Nore, where the *Roebuck* lay; and, to our great joy, my master came on board to us, and brought us to the ship. When I went on board this large ship, I was amazed indeed to see the quantity of men and the guns. However, my surprise began to diminish as my knowledge increased; and I ceased to feel those apprehensions and alarms which had taken such strong possession of me when I first came among the Europeans, and for some time after. I began now to pass to an opposite extreme; I was so far from being afraid of anything new which I saw, that after I had been some time in this ship, I even began to long for an engagement. My griefs, too, which in young minds are not perpetual, were now wearing away; and I soon enjoyed myself pretty well, and felt tolerably easy in my present situation. There was a number of boys on board, which still made it more agreeable; for we were always together, and a great part of our time was spent in play. I remained in this ship a considerable time, during which we made several cruises, and visited a variety of places; among others we were twice in Holland, and brought over several persons of distinction from it, whose names I do not now remember. On the passage, one day, for the diversion of those gentlemen, all the boys were called on the quarter-deck, and were paired proportionably, and then made to fight; after which the gentlemen gave the combatants from five to nine shillings each. This was the first time I ever fought with a white boy; and I never knew what it was to have a bloody nose before. This made me fight most desperately, I suppose considerably more than an hour; and at last, both of us being weary, we were parted. I had a great deal of this kind of sport afterwards, in which the captain and the ship's company used very much to encourage me. Sometime afterwards, the ship went to Leith in Scotland, and from thence to the Orkneys, where I was surprised in seeing scarcely any night; and from thence we sailed with a great fleet, full of soldiers, for England. All this time we had never come to an engagement, though we were frequently cruising off the coast of France; during which we chased many vessels, and took in all seventeen prizes. I had been learning many of the manœuvres of the ship during our cruise; and I was several times made to fire the guns. One evening, off Havre de Grace, just as it was growing dark, we were standing off shore, and met with a fine large French built frigate. We got all things immediately ready for fighting; and I now expected I should be gratified in seeing an engagement, which I had so long wished for in vain. But the very moment the word of command was given to fire, we heard those on board the other ship cry, "Haul down the jib"; and in that instant she hoisted English colors. There was instantly with us an amazing cry of—"Avast!" or stop firing; and I think one or two guns had been let off, but happily they did no mischief. We had hailed them several times, but they not hearing, we received no answer, which was the cause of our firing. The boat was then sent on board of her, and she proved to be the *Ambuscade,* man-of-war, to my no small disappointment. We returned to Portsmouth, without having been in any action, just at the trial of Admiral Byng (whom I saw several times during it); and my master having left the ship, and gone to London for promotion, Dick and I were put on board the *Savage,* sloop-of-war, and we went in her to assist in bringing off the *St. George,* man-of-war, that had run ashore somewhere on the coast. After staying a few weeks on board the *Savage,* Dick and I were sent on shore at Deal, where we remained some short time, till my master sent for us to London, the place I had long desired exceedingly to see. We therefore both with great pleasure got into a wagon, and came to London, where we were received by a Mr. Guerin, a relation of my master. This gentleman had two sisters, very amiable ladies, who took much notice and great care of me. Though I had desired so much to see London, when I arrived in it I was unfortunately unable to gratify my curiosity; for I had at this time the chilblains to such a degree that I could not stand for several months, and I was obliged to be sent to St. George's hospital. There I grew so ill that the doctors wanted to cut my left leg off, at different times, apprehending a mortification; but I always said I would rather die than suffer it, and happily (I thank God) I recovered without the operation. After being there several weeks, and just as I had recovered, the smallpox broke out on me, so that I was again confined; and I thought myself now particularly unfortunate. However, I soon recovered again; and by this time, my master having been promoted to be first lieutenant of the *Preston,* man-of-war, of fifty guns, then new at Deptford, Dick and I were sent on board her, and soon after, we sent to Holland to bring over the late Duke of —— to England. While I was in the ship an incident happened, which, though trifling, I beg leave to relate, as I could not help taking particular notice of it, and considered it then as a judgment of God. One morning a young man was looking up to the foretop, and in a wicked tone, common on shipboard, d—d his eyes about something. Just at the moment some small particles of dirt fell into his left eye, and by the evening it was very much inflamed. The next day it grew worse, and within six or seven days he lost it. From this ship my master was appointed a lieutenant on board the *Royal George.* When he was going he wished me to stay on board the *Preston,* to learn the French horn; but the ship being ordered for Turkey, I could not think of leaving my master, to whom I was very warmly attached; and I told him if he left me behind, it would break my heart. This prevailed on him to take me with him; but he left Dick on board the *Preston,* whom I embraced at parting for the last time. The *Royal George* was the largest ship I had ever seen, so that when I came on board of her I was surprised at the number of people, men, women, and children, of every denomination; and the largeness of the guns, many of them also of brass, which I had never seen before. Here were also shops or stalls of every kind of goods, and people crying their different commodities about the ship as in a town. To me it appeared a little world, into which I was again cast without a friend, for I had no longer my dear companion Dick. We did not stay long here. My master was not many weeks on board before he got an appointment to the sixth lieutenant of the *Namur,* which was then at Spithead, fitting up for Vice-admiral Boscawen, who was going with a large fleet on an expedition against Louisburg. The crew of the *Royal George* were turned over to her, and the flag of that gallant admiral was hoisted on board, the blue at the maintop gallant mast head. There was a very great fleet of men-of-war of every description assembled together for this expedition, and I was in hopes soon to have an opportunity of being gratified with a sea-fight. All things being now in readiness, this mighty fleet (for there was also Admiral Cornish's fleet in company, destined for the East Indies) at last weighed anchor, and sailed. The two fleets continued in company for several days, and then parted; Admiral Cornish, in the *Lenox,* having first saluted our admiral in the Namur, which he returned. We then steered for America; but, by contrary winds, were driven to Tenerife, where I was struck with its noted peak. Its prodigious height and its form, resembling a sugar loaf, filled me with wonder. We remained in sight of this island some days, and then proceeded for America, which we soon made, and got into commodious harbour called St. George, in Halifax. Here we had fish in abundance, and all other fresh provisions. We were here joined by different men-of-war and transport ships with soldiers; after which, our fleet being increased to a prodigious number of ships of all kinds, we sailed for Cape Breton in Nova Scotia. We had the good and gallant General Wolfe on board our ship, whose affability made him highly esteemed and beloved by all the men. He often honored me, as well as other boys, with marks of his notice, and saved me once a flogging for fighting with a young gentleman. We arrived at Cape Breton in the summer of 1758; and here the soldiers were to be landed, in order to make an attack upon Louisburg. My master had some part in superintending the landing; and here I was in a small measure gratified in seeing an encounter between our men and the enemy. The French were posted on the shore to receive us, and disputed our landing for a long time; but at last they were driven from their trenches, and a complete landing was effected. Our troops pursued them as far as the town of Louisburg. In this action many were killed on both sides. One thing remarkable I saw this day. A lieutenant of the *Princess Amelia,* who, as well as my master, superintended the landing, was giving the word of command, and while his mouth was open, a musket ball went through it, and passed out at his cheek. I had that day, in my hand, the scalp of an Indian king, who was killed in the engagement; the scalp had been taken off by an Highlander. I saw the king's ornaments too, which were very curious, and made of feathers.

Our land forces laid siege to the town of Louisburg, while the French men-of-war were blocked up in the harbor by the fleet, the batteries at the same item playing upon them from the land. This they did with such effect, that one day I saw some of the ships set on fire by the shells from the batteries, and I believe two or three of them were quite burnt. At another time, about fifty boats belonging to the English men-of-war, commanded by Captain George Belfour, of the *Etna,* fire ship, and Mr. Laforey, another junior Captain, attacked and boarded the only two remaining French men-of-war in the harbor. They also set fire to a seventy-gun ship, but a sixty-four, called the *Bienfaisant,* they brought off. During my stay here, I had often an opportunity of being near Captain Belfour, who was pleased to notice me, and liked me so much that he often asked my master to let him have me, but he would not part with me; and no consideration could have induced me to leave him. At last, Louisburg was taken, and the English men-of-war came into the harbor before it, to my very great joy; for I had now more liberty of indulging myself, and I went often on shore. When the ships were in the harbor, we had the most beautiful procession on the water I ever saw. All the Admirals and Captains of the men-of-war, full dressed, and in their barges, well ornamented with pendants, came alongside of the *Namur.* The Vice-admiral then went on shore in his barge, followed by the other officers in order of seniority, to take possession, as I suppose, of the town and fort. Some time after this, the French governor and his lady, and other persons of note, came on board our ship to dine. On this occasion our ships were dressed with colors of all kinds, from the top-gallant mast head to the deck; and this, with the firing of guns, formed a most grand and magnificent spectacle.

As soon as everything here was settled, Admiral Boscawen sailed with part of the fleet for England, leaving some ships behind with Rear-admirals Sir Charles Hardy and Durell. It was now winter; and one evening, during our passage home, about dusk, when we were in the channel, or near soundings, and were beginning to look for land, we descried seven sail of large men-of-war, which stood off shore. Several people on board of our ship said, as the two fleets were (in forty minutes from the first sight) within hail of each other, that they were English men-of-war; and some of our people even began to name some of the ships. By this time both fleets began to mingle, and our Admiral ordered his flag to be hoisted. At that instant, the other fleet, which were French, hoisted their ensigns, and gave us a broadside as they passed by. Nothing could create greater surprise and confusion among us than this. The wind was high, the sea rough, and we had our lower and middle deck guns housed in, so that not a single gun on board was ready to be fired at any of the French ships. However, the *Royal William* and the *Somerset,* being our sternmost ships, became a little prepared, and each gave the French ships a broadside as they passed by. I afterwards heard this was a French squadron, commanded by Monsieur Constans; and certainly, had the Frenchmen known our condition, and had a mind to fight us, they might have done us great mischief. But we were not long before we were prepared for an engagement. Immediately many things were tossed overboard, the ships were made ready for fighting as soon as possible, and about ten at night we had bent a new main-sail, the old one being split. Being now in readiness for fighting, we wore ship, and stood after the French fleet, who were one or two ships in number more than we. However we gave them chase, and continued pursuing them all night; and at day-light we saw six of them, all large ships of the line, and an English East Indiaman, a prize they had taken. We chased them all day till between three and four o'clock in the evening, when we came up with, and passed within a musket shot of one seventy-four–gun ship, and the Indiaman also, who now hoisted her colors, but immediately hauled them down again. On this we made a signal for the other ships to take possession of her; and, supposing the man-of-war would likewise strike, we cheered, but she did not; though if we had fired into her, from being so near we must have taken her. To my utter surprise, the *Somerset*, who was the next ship astern of the *Namur*, made way likewise; and, thinking they were sure of this French ship, they cheered in the same manner, but still continued to follow us. The French Commodore was about a gunshot ahead of all, running from us with all speed; and about four o'clock he carried his foretopmast overboard. This caused another loud cheer with us; and a little after the topmast came close by us; but, to our great surprise, instead of coming up with her, we found she went as fast as ever, if not faster. The sea grew now much smoother; and the wind lulling, the seventy-four–gun ship we had passed, came again by us in the very same direction, and so near that we heard her people talk as she went by, yet not a shot was fired on either side; and about five or six o'clock, just as it grew dark, she joined her Commodore. We chased all night; but the next day we were out of sight, so that we saw no more of them; and we only had the old Indiaman (called *Carnarvon*, I think) for our trouble. After this we stood in for the channel, and soon made the land; and, about the close of the year 1758–9, we got safe to St. Helen's. Here the *Namur* ran aground, and also another large ship astern of us; but, by starting our water, and tossing many things overboard to lighten her, we got the ships off without any damage. We stayed for a short time at Spithead, and then went into Portsmouth harbor to refit. From whence the Admiral went to London; and my master and I soon followed, with a press-gang, as we wanted some hands to complete our complement.

FROM *Chapter Ten*

Miscellaneous Verses:

OR,

Reflections on the state of my mind during my first Convictions, of the necessity of believing the Truth, and experiencing the inestimable benefits of Christianity.

Well may I say my life has been
One scene of sorrow and of pain;
From early days I griefs have known,
And as I grew my griefs have grown:
Dangers were always in my path;
And fear of wrath, and sometimes death:
While pale dejection in me reign'd,
I often wept, by grief constrained.

When taken from my native land,
by an unjust and cruel band,
How did uncommon dread prevail!
My sighs no more I could conceal.

To ease my mind I often strove,
And tried my trouble to remove;
I sung, and utter'd sighs between—
Assay'd to stifle guilt with sin.

But O! not all that I could do
Would stop the current of my woe:
Conviction still my vileness shew'd;
How great my guilt—how lost to good.

"Prevented that I could not die,
Nor could to one sure refuge fly:
An orphan state I had to mourn—
Forsook by all, and left forlorn."

Those who beheld my downcast mien,
Could not guess at my woes unseen;
They by appearance could not know
The troubles that I waded through.

Lust, anger, blasphemy, and pride,
With legions of such ills beside,
"Troubled my thoughts," while doubts and fears,
Clouded and darken'd most my years.

"Sighs now no more would be confin'd—
They breath'd the trouble of my mind:"
I wish'd for death, but check the word,
And often pray'd unto the Lord.

Unhappy more than some on earth,
I thought the place that gave me birth—
Strange thoughts oppress'd—while I replied
"Why not in Ethiopia died?"

And why thus spar'd when nigh to hell?—
God only knew—I could not tell!
"A tott'ring fence a bowing wall,"
"I thought myself ere since the fall."

Oft times I mus'd, and night despair,
While birds melodious fill'd the air:
"Thrice happy songsters, ever free,"
How blest were they, compar'd to me!

Thus all things added to my pain,
While grief compell'd me to complain!
When sable clouds began to rise
My mind grew darker than the skies.

The English nation call'd to leave,
How did my breast with sorrows heave!
I long'd for rest—cried, "Help me Lord;
Some mitigation, Lord, afford!"

Yet on, dejected, still I went—
Heart-throbbing woes within me pent;
Nor land, nor sea, could comfort give,
Nor aught my anxious mind relieve.

Weary with troubles yet unknown
To all but God and self alone,
Numerous months for peace I strove,
Numerous foes I had to prove.

Inur'd to dangers, griefs, and woes,
Train'd up 'midst perils, death, and foes,
I said, "Must it thus ever be?
No quiet is permitted me."

Hard hap, and more than heavy lot!
I pray'd to God "Forget me not—
What thou ordain'st help me to bear;
But O! deliver from despair!"

Strivings and wrestling seem'd in vain;
Nothing I did could ease my pain:
Then gave I up my work and will,
Confess'd and owned my doom was hell!

Like some poor pris'ner at the bar,
Conscious of guilt, of sin and fear,
Arraign'd, and self-condemned, I stood—
"Lost in the world and in my blood!"

Yet here, 'midst blackest clouds confin'd,
A beam from Christ, the day star shin'd:
Surely, thought I, if Jesus please,
He can at once sign my release.

I, ignorant of his righteousness,
Set up my labors in its place;
"Forgot for why his blood was shed,
And pray'd and fasted in its stead."

He died for sinners—I am one!
Might not his blood for me atone?
Tho' I am nothing else but sin,
Yet surely he can make me clean!

Thus light came in, and I believed;
Myself forgot, and help receiv'd!
My Saviour then I know I found,
For, eas'd from guilt no more I groan'd.

O, happy hour, in which I ceas'd
To mourn, for then I found a rest!
My soul and Christ were now as one—
Thy light, O Jesus, in me shone!

Bless'd be thy name, for now I know
I and my works can nothing do;
"The Lord alone can ransom man—
For this the spotless Lamb was slain!"

When sacrifices, works, and pray'r,
Prov'd vain, and ineffectual were—
"Lo, then I come!" the Saviour cried,
And bleeding, bow'd his head, and died!

He died for all who ever saw
No help in them, nor by the law:
I this have seen: and gladly own
"Salvation is by Christ alone!"[8]

[8]Acts 4;12.

Chapter 12

Different transactions of the author's life, till the present time—His application to the late Bishop of London to be appointed a missionary to Africa—Some account of his share in the conduct of the late expedition to Sierra Leone—Petition to the Queen—Conclusion.

Such were the various scenes which I was a witness to, and the fortune I experienced until the year 1777. Since that period, my life has been more uniform, and the incidents of it fewer, than in any other equal number of years preceding. I therefore hasten to the conclusion of a narrative which I fear the reader may think already sufficiently tedious.

I had suffered so many impositions in my commercial transactions in different parts of the world, that I became heartily disgusted with the sea-faring life, and was determined not to return to it, at least for some time. I therefore once more engaged in service shortly after my return, and continued for the most part in this situation until 1784.

Soon after my arrival in London, I saw a remarkable circumstance relative to African complexion, which I thought so extraordinary that I beg leave just to mention it. A white Negro woman, that I had formerly seen in London and other parts, had married a white man, by whom she had three boys, and they were every one mulattoes, and yet they had fine light hair. In 1779, I served Governor Macnamara, who had been a considerable time on the coast of Africa. In the time of my service, I used to ask frequently other servants to join me in family prayer, but this only excited their mockery. However, the Governor, understanding that I was of a religious turn, wished to know what religion I was of, I told him I was a protestant of the church of England, agreeable to the thirty-nine articles of that church; and that whomsoever I found to preach according to that doctrine, those I would hear. A few days after this, we had some more discourse on the same subject; when he said he would, if I chose, as he thought I might be of service in converting my countrymen to the Gospel faith, get me sent out as missionary to Africa. I at first refused going, and told him how I had been served on a like occasion, by some white people, the last voyage I went to Jamaica, when I attempted (if it were the will of God) to be the means of converting the Indian prince; and said I supposed they would serve me worse than Alexander, the coppersmith, did St. Paul, if I should attempt to go amongst them in Africa. He told me not to fear, for he would apply to the Bishop of London to get me ordained. On these terms I consented to the Governor's proposal, to go to Africa in hope of doing good, if possible, amongst my countrymen; so, in order to have me sent out properly, we immediately wrote the following letters to the late Bishop of London:

To the Right Reverend Father in God, ROBERT, Lord Bishop of London:

THE MEMORIAL OF GUSTAVUS VASSA
SHEWETH,

That your memorialist is a native of Africa, and has a knowledge of the manners and customs of the inhabitants of that country.

That your memorialist has resided in different parts of Europe for twenty-two years last past, and embraced the Christian faith in the year 1759.

That your memorialist is desirous of returning to Africa as a missionary, if encouraged by your Lordship, in hopes of being able to prevail upon his countrymen to become Christians; and your memorialist is the more induced to undertake the same, from the success that has attended the like undertakings when encouraged by the Portuguese through their different settlements on the Coast of Africa, and also by the Dutch; both governments encouraging the blacks, who, by their education are qualified to undertake the same, and are found more proper than European clergymen, unacquainted with the language and customs of the country.

Your memorialist's only motive for soliciting the office of a missionary is that he may be a means, under God, of reforming his countrymen and persuading them to embrace the Christian religion. Therefore your memorialist humbly prays your Lordship's encouragement and support in the undertaking.

GUSTAVUS VASSA
AT MR. GUTHRIE'S TAYLOR,
NO. 17, HEDGE LANE.

MY LORD,

I have resided near seven years on the coast of Africa, for most part of the time as commanding officer. From the knowledge I have of the country and its inhabitants, I am inclined to think that the within plan will be attended with great success, if countenanced by your Lordship. I beg leave further to represent to your Lordship, that the like attempts, when encouraged by other governments, have met with uncommon success; and at this very time I know a very respectable character, a black priest, at Cape Coast Castle. I know the within named Gustavus Vassa, and believe him a moral good man.

I have the honor to be, my Lord,
Your Lordship's
Humble and obedient servant,
MATT. MACNAMARA
GROVE, 11TH MARCH, 1779.

This letter was also accompanied by the following from Doctor Wallace, who had resided in Africa for many years, and whose sentiments on the subject of an African mission were the same with Governor Macnamara's.

MARCH 14, 1779.

MY LORD,

I have resided near five years on Senegambia, on the coast of Africa, and have had the honor of filling very considerable employments in that province. I do approve of the within plan, and think the undertaking very laudable and proper, and that it deserves your Lordship's protection and encouragement, in which case it must be attended with the intended success.

I am, my Lord, your Lordship's
Humble and obedient servant,
THOMAS WALLACE

With these letters, I waited on the Bishop by the Governor's desire, and presented them to his Lordship. He received me with much condescension and politeness; but from some certain scruples of delicacy, and saying the Bishops were not of opinion of sending a new missionary to Africa, he declined to ordain me.

My sole motive for thus dwelling on this transaction, or inserting these papers, is the opinion which gentlemen of sense and education, who are acquainted with Africa, entertain of the probability of converting the inhabitants of it to the faith of Jesus Christ, if the attempt were countenanced by the Legislature.

Shortly after this I left the Governor, and served a nobleman in the Dorsetshire militia, with whom I was encamped at Coxheath for some time; but the operations there were too minute and uninteresting to make a detail of.

In the year 1783, I visited eight counties in Wales, from motives of curiosity. While I was in that part of the country, I was led to go down into a coal-pit in Shropshire, but my curiosity nearly cost me my life; for while I was in the pit the coals fell in, and buried one poor man, who was not far from me; upon this, I got out as fast as I could, thinking the surface of the earth the safest part of it.

In the spring of 1784, I thought of visiting old ocean again. In consequence of this I embarked as steward on board a fine new ship called the *London,* commanded by Martin Hopkin, and sailed for New York. I admired this city very much; it is large and well built, and abounds with provisions of all kinds. While we lay here a circumstance happened which I thought extremely singular. One day a malefactor was to be executed on a gallows; but with a condition that if any woman, having nothing on but her shift, married the man under the gallows, his life was to be saved. This extraordinary privilege was claimed: a woman presented herself, and the marriage ceremony was performed.

Our ship having got laden, we returned to London in January 1785. When she was ready again for another voyage, the captain being an agreeable man, I sailed with him from hence in the spring, March 1785, for Philadelphia. On the 5th of April, we took our departure from the lands-end, with a pleasant gale; and about nine o'clock that night the moon shone bright, and the sea was smooth, while our ship was going free by the wind, at the rate of about four or five miles an hour. At this time another ship was going nearly as fast as we on the opposite point, meeting us right in the teeth; yet none on board observed either ship until we struck each other forcibly head and head, to the astonishment and consternation of both crews. She did us much damage, but I believe we did her more; for when we passed by each other, which we did very quickly, they called to us to bring to, and hoist out our boat, but we had enough to do to mind ourselves; and in about eight minutes we saw no more of her. We refitted as well as we could the next day, and proceeded on our voyage, and in May arrived at Philadelphia.

I was very glad to see this favorite old town once more; and my pleasure was much increased in seeing the worthy Quakers freeing and easing the burdens of many of my oppressed African brethren. It rejoiced my heart when one of these friendly people took me to see a free school they had erected for every denomination of black people, whose minds are cultivated here, and forwarded to virtue; and thus they are made useful members of the community. Does not the success of this practice say loudly to the planters, in the language of scripture—"Go ye and do likewise"?

In October 1785, I was accompanied by some of the Africans, and presented this address of thanks to the gentlemen called Friends or Quakers, in Grace Church Court, Lombard street:

> GENTLEMEN,
>
> By reading your book, entitled a Caution to Great Britain and her Colonies, concerning the calamitous state of the enslaved Negroes: We, part of the poor, oppressed, needy, and much degraded Negroes, desire to approach you with this address of thanks, with our inmost love and warmest acknowledgment; and with the deepest sense of your benevolence, unwearied labor, and kind interposition, towards breaking the yoke of slavery, and to administer a little comfort and ease to thousands and tens of thousands

> of very grievously afflicted, and too heavy burthened Negroes.
>
> Gentlemen, could you, by perseverance, at last be enabled under God, to lighten in any degree the heavy burthen of the afflicted, no doubt it would in some measure, be the possible means, under God, of saving the souls of many of the oppressors; and if so, sure we are that the God, whose eyes are ever upon all his creatures, and always rewards every true act of virtue, and regards the prayers of the oppressed, will give to you and yours those blessings which it is not in our power to express or conceive, but which we, as a part of those captivated, oppressed, and afflicted people, most earnestly wish and pray for.

These gentlemen received us very kindly, with a promise to exert themselves on behalf of the oppressed Africans, and we parted.

While in town, I chanced once to be invited to a Quaker's wedding. The simple and yet expressive mode used at their solemnizations is worthy of note. The following is the true form of it:

After the company have met they have seasonable exhortations by several of the members; the bride and bridegroom stand up, and, taking each other by the hand in a solemn manner, the man audibly declares to this purpose: "Friends, in the fear of the Lord, and in the presence of this assembly, whom I desire to be my witnesses, I take this my friend, M—— N——, to be my wife; promising, through divine assistance, to be unto her a loving and faithful husband till death separate us," and the woman makes the like declaration. Then the two first sign their names to the record, and as many more witnesses as have a mind. I had the honor to subscribe mine to a register in Grace Church Court, Lombard street. My hand is ever free—if any female Debonair wishes to obtain it, this mode I recommend.

We returned to London in August; and our ship not going immediately to sea, I shipped as a steward in an American ship, called the *Harmony,* Captain John Willet, and left London in March 1786, bound to Philadelphia. Eleven days after sailing, we carried our foremast away. We had a nine weeks' passage, which caused our trip not to succeed well, the market for our goods proving bad; and to make it worse, my commander began to play me the like tricks as others too often practise on free Negroes in the West Indies. But, I thank God, I found many friends here, who in some measure prevented him.

On my return to London in August, I was very agreeably surprised to find that the benevolence of government had adopted the plan of some philanthropic individuals, to send the Africans from hence to their native quarter; and that some vessels were then engaged to carry them to Sierra Leone, an act which redounded to the honor of all concerned in its promotion, and filled me with prayers and much rejoicing. There was then in the city a select committee of gentlemen for the black poor, to some of whom I had the honor of being known; and as soon as they heard of my arrival, they sent for me to the committee. When I came there, they informed me of the intention of government; and as they seemed to think me qualified to superintend part of the undertaking, they asked me to go with the black poor to Africa. I pointed out to them many objections to my going; and particularly I expressed some difficulties on the account of the slave dealers, as I would certainly oppose their traffic in human species, by every means in my power. However, these objections were over-ruled by the gentlemen of the committee, who prevailed on me to consent to go; and recommended me to the honorable commissioners of his Majesty's Navy, as a proper person to act as commissary for government in the intended expedition; and they accordingly appointed me, in November 1786, to that office, and gave me sufficient power to act for the government, in the capacity of commissary, having received my warrant and the following order:

> BY THE PRINCIPAL OFFICERS AND COMMISSIONERS OF HIS MAJESTY'S NAVY
>
> Whereas you were directed, by our warrant, of the 4th of last month, to receive into your charge from Mr. Joseph Irwin, the surplus provisions remaining of what was provided for the voyage, as well as the provi-

sions for the support of the black poor, after the landing at Sierra Leone, with the clothing, tools, and all other articles provided at government's expense; and as the provisions were laid in at the rate of two months for the voyage, and for four months after the landing, but the number embarked being so much less than we expected, whereby there may be a considerable surplus of provisions, clothing, &c. These are in addition to former orders, to direct and require you to appropriate or dispose of such surplus to the best advantage you can for the benefit of government, keeping and rendering to us a faithful account of what you do herein. And for your guidance in preventing any white persons going, who are not intended to have the indulgence of being carried thither, we send you herewith a list of those recommended by the Committee for the black poor, as proper persons to be permitted to embark, and acquaint you that you are not to suffer any others to go who do not produce a certificate from the Committee for the black poor, of their having their permission for it. For which this shall be your warrant. Dated at the Navy Office, Jan. 16, 1787.

J. HINSLOW
GEO. MARSH
W. PALMER
TO MR. GUSTAVUS VASSA, COMMISSARY OF PROVISIONS AND STORES FOR THE BLACK POOR GOING TO SIERRA LEONE.

I proceeded immediately to the executing of my duty on board the vessels destined for the voyage, where I continued till the March following.

During my continuance in the employment of government, I was struck with the flagrant abuses committed by the agent, and endeavored to remedy them, but without effect. One instance, among many which I could produce, may serve as a specimen. Government had ordered to be provided all necessaries (slops, as they are called, included) for 750 persons; however, not being able to muster more than 426, I was ordered to send the superfluous slops, &c., to the king's stores at Portsmouth; but, when I demanded them for that purpose from the agent, it appeared they had never been bought, though paid for by government. But that was not all; government were not the only objects of peculation; these poor people suffered infinitely more; their accommodations were most wretched, many of them wanted beds, and many more clothing and other necessaries. For the truth of this, and much more, I do not seek credit from my own assertion. I appeal to the testimony of Captain Thompson, of the *Nautilus,* who conveyed us, to whom I applied in February 1787, for a remedy, when I had remonstrated to the agent in vain, and even brought him to be a witness of the injustice and oppression I complained of. I appeal also to a letter written by these wretched people, so early as the beginning of the preceding January, and published in the *Morning Herald,* on the 4th of that month, signed by twenty of their chiefs.

I could not silently suffer government to be thus cheated and my countrymen plundered and oppressed, and even left destitute of the necessaries for almost their existence. I therefore informed the Commissioners of the Navy, of the agent's proceeding, but my dismission was soon after procured, by means of a gentleman in the city, whom the agent, conscious of his peculation, had deceived by letter, and who, moreover, empowered the same agent to receive on board, at the government expense, a number of persons as passengers, contrary to the orders I received. By this I suffered a considerable loss in my property; however, the commissioners were satisfied with my conduct, and wrote to Captain Thompson, expressing their approbation of it.

Thus provided, they proceeded on their voyage; and at last, worn out by treatment, perhaps not the most mild, and wasted by sickness, brought on by want of medicine, clothes, bedding, &c., they reached Sierra Leone, just at the commencement of the rains. At that season of the year, it is impossible to cultivate the lands; their provisions therefore were exhausted before they could derive any benefit from agriculture; and it is not surprising that many, especially the Lascars, whose constitutions are very tender, and who had been cooped up in ships from October to June, and accommodated in the manner I have mentioned, should be so wasted by their confinement as not to survive it.

Thus ended my part of the long talked of expedition to Sierra Leone: an expedition which, however unfortunate in the event, was humane and politic in its design, nor was its failure owing to government; everything was done on their part; but there was evidently sufficient mismanagement attending the conduct and execution of it to defeat its success.

I should not have been so ample in my account of this transaction, had not the share I bore in it been made the subject of partial animadversion, and even my dismission from my employment thought worthy of being made by some a matter of public triumph.[9] The motives which might influence any person to descend to a petty contest with an obscure African, and to seek gratification by his depression, perhaps it is not proper here to inquire into or relate, even if its detection were necessary to my vindication, but I thank Heaven it is not. I wish to stand by my own integrity, and not to shelter myself under the impropriety of another; and I trust the behavior of the Commissioners of the Navy to me entitle me to make this assertion; for after I had been dismissed, March 24, I drew up a memorial thus:

To the Right Honorable the Lord's Commissioners of his Majesty's Treasury.

The Memorial and Petition of GUSTAVUS VASSA, a black man, late Commissary to the black poor going to Africa.

HUMBLY SHEWETH,

That your Lordship's memorialist was, by the Honorable the Commissioners of his Majesty's Navy, on the 4th of December last, appointed to the above employment by warrant from that board;

That he accordingly proceeded to the execution of his duty on board of the *Vernon,* being one of the ships appointed to proceed to Africa with the above poor;

That your memorialist, to his great grief and astonishment, received a letter of dismission from the Honorable Commissioners of the Navy, by your Lordship's orders:

That, conscious of having acted with the most perfect fidelity and the greatest assiduity in discharging the trust reposed in him, he is altogether at a loss to conceive the reasons of your Lordships having altered the favorable opinion you were pleased to conceive of him, sensible that your Lordships would not proceed to so severe a measure without some apparent good cause; he therefore has every reason to believe that his conduct has been grossly misrepresented to your Lordships, and he is the more confirmed in his opinion, because, by opposing measures of others concerned in the same expedition, which tended to defeat your Lordship's humane intentions, and to put the government to a very considerable additional expense, he created a number of enemies, whose misrepresentations, he has too much reason to believe, laid the foundation of his dismission. Unsupported by friends, and unaided by the advantages of a liberal education, he can only hope for redress from the justice of his cause, in addition to the mortification of having been removed from his employment, and the advantage which he reasonably might have expected to have derived therefrom. He has had the misfortune to have sunk a considerable part of his little property in fitting himself out, and in other expenses arising out of his situation, an account of which he here annexes. Your memorialist will not trouble your Lordships with a vindication of any part of his conduct, because he knows not of what crimes he is accused; he, however, earnestly entreats that you will be pleased to direct an enquiry into his behavior during the time he acted in the public service; and, if it be found that his dismission arose from false representations, he is confident that in your Lordship's justice he shall find redress.

9 See the *Public Advertiser,* July 14, 1787.

Your petitioner therefore humbly prays that your Lordships will take his case into consideration; and that you will be pleased to order payment of the above referred to account, amounting to 321.4s, and also the wages intended which is most humbly submitted.

LONDON, MAY 12, 1787.

The above petition was delivered into the hands of their Lordships, who were kind enough, in the space of some few months afterwards, without hearing, to order me 501. sterling—that is, 181. wages for the time (upwards of four months) I acted a faithful part in their service. Certainly the sum is more than a free Negro would have had in the western colonies!!!

From that period, to the present time, my life has passed in an even tenor, and a great part of my study and attention has been to assist in the cause of my much injured countrymen.

March the 21st, 1788, I had the honor of presenting the Queen with a petition in behalf of my African brethren, which was received most graciously by Her Majesty.*

To the Queen's most Excellent Majesty:
MADAM,

Your Majesty's well known benevolence and humanity emboldens me to approach your royal presence, trusting that the obscurity of my situation will not prevent your Majesty from attending to the sufferings for which I plead.

Yet I do not solicit your royal pity for my own distress; my sufferings, although numerous, are in a measure forgotten. I supplicate your Majesty's compassion for millions of my African countrymen, who groan under the lash of tyranny in the West Indies.

The oppression and cruelty exercised to the unhappy Negroes there, have at length reached the British Legislature, and they are now deliberating on its redress; even several persons of property in slaves in the West Indies, have petitioned Parliament against its continuance, sensible that it is as impolitic as it is unjust—and what is inhuman must ever be unwise.

Your Majesty's reign has been hitherto distinguished by private acts of benevolence and bounty; surely the more extended the misery is, the greater claim it has to your Majesty's compassion, and the greater must be your Majesty's pleasure in administering to its relief.

I presume, therefore, gracious Queen, to implore your interposition with your royal consort, in favor of the wretched Africans; that, by your Majesty's benevolent influence, a period may now be put to their misery—and that they may be raised from the condition of brutes, to which they are at present degraded, to the rights and situation of freemen, and admitted to partake of the blessings of your Majesty's happy government; so shall your Majesty enjoy the heartfelt pleasure of procuring happiness to millions, and be rewarded in the grateful prayers of themselves, and of their posterity.

And my the all-bountiful Creator shower on your Majesty, and the Royal Family, every blessing that this world can afford, and every fulness of joy which divine revelation has promised us in the next.

I am your Majesty's
Most dutiful and devoted servant to command,
GUSTAVUS VASSA
The Oppressed Ethiopian
NO. 53, BALDWIN'S GARDENS

The Negro consolidated act, made by the assembly of Jamaica last year, and the new act of amendment now in agitation there, contain a proof of the existence of those charges that have been made against the planters relative to the treatment of their slaves.

I hope to have the satisfaction of seeing the renovation of liberty and justice, resting on the British government, to vindicate the honor of our common nature. These are concerns which do not perhaps belong to any particular office;

*At the request of some of my most particular friends, I take the liberty of inserting it here.

but, to speak more seriously, to every man of sentiment, actions like these are the just and sure foundation of future fame; a reversion, though remote, is coveted by some noble minds as a substantial good. It is upon these grounds that I hope and expect the attention of gentlemen in power. These are designs consonant to the elevation of their rank and the dignity of their stations; they are ends suitable to the nature of a free and generous government, and, connected with views of empire and dominion, suited to the benevolence and solid merit of the legislature. It is a pursuit of substantial greatness. May the time come—at least the speculation to me is pleasing—when the sable people shall gratefully commemorate the auspicious era of extensive freedom: then shall those persons* particularly be named with praise and honor who generously proposed and stood forth in the cause of humanity, liberty, and good policy, and brought to the ear of the legislature designs worthy of royal patronage and adoption. May Heaven make the British senators the dispersers of light, liberty, and science, to the uttermost parts of the earth: then will be glory to God in the highest on earth peace, and good will to men. Glory, honor, peace, &c. to every soul of man that worketh good: to the Britons first (because to them the gospel is preached), and also to the nations. "Those that honor their Maker have mercy on the poor." It is "righteousness exalteth a nation, but sin is a reproach to any people; destruction shall be to the workers of iniquity, and the wicked shall fall by their own wickedness." May the blessings of the Lord be upon the heads of all those who commiserated the cases of the oppressed Negroes, and the fear of God prolong their days; and may their expectations be filled with gladness! "The liberal devise liberal things, and by liberal things shall stand" (Isaiah 32:8). They can say with pious Job, "Did not I weep for him that was in trouble? was not my soul grieved for the poor?" (Job 30:25).

*Granville Sharp, Esq., the Rev. Thomas Clarkson, the Rev. James Ramsay, our approved friends, men of virtue, are an honor to their country, ornamental to human nature, happy in themselves, and benefactors to mankind!

As the inhuman traffic of slavery is to be taken into the consideration of the British legislature, I doubt not, if a system of commerce was established in Africa, the demand for manufactures will most rapidly augment, as the native inhabitants will sensibly adopt the British fashions, manners, customs, &c. In proportion to the civilization, so will be the consumption of British manufactures.

The wear and tear of a continent, nearly twice as large as Europe and rich in vegetable and mineral production, is much easier conceived than calculated.

A case in point. It cost the Aborigines of Britain little or nothing in clothing, &c. The difference between their forefathers and the present generation, in point of consumption, is literally infinite. The supposition is most obvious. It will be equally immense in Africa—The same, viz: civilization, will ever have the same effect.

It is trading upon safe grounds. A commercial intercourse with Africa opens an inexhaustible source of wealth to the manufacturing interest of Great Britain;† and to all which the slave trade is an objection.

If I am not misinformed, the manufacturing interest is equal, if not superior, to the landed interest, as to the value, for reasons which will soon appear. The abolition of slavery, so diabolical, will give a most rapid extension of manufactures, which is totally and diametrically opposite to what some interested people assert.

The manufactures of this country must and will in the nature and reason of things, have a full and constant employ, by supplying the African markets.

†"In the ship *Trusty*, lately for the new Settlement of Sierra Leona, in Africa, were 1,300 pair of shoes (an article hitherto scarcely known to be exported to that country) with several others equally new, as articles of export. Thus will it not become the interest, as well as the duty, of every artificer, mechanic, and tradesman, publicly to enter their protest against this traffic of the human species? What a striking—what a beautiful contrast is here presented to view, when compared with the cargo of a slave ship! Every feeling heart indeed sensibly participates of the joy, and with a degree of rapture reads of barrels of *flour* instead of *gunpowder—biscuits and bread* instead of *horse beans—implements of husbandry* instead of *guns* for destruction, rapine, and murder—and various articles of *usefulness* are the pleasing substitutes for the *torturing thumbscrew,* and the *galling chain,* &c."

Population, the bowels and surface of Africa, abound in valuable and useful returns; the hidden treasures of centuries will be brought to light and into circulation. Industry, enterprise, and mining will have their full scope, proportionably as they civilize. In a word, it lays open an endless field of commerce to the British manufacturers and merchant adventurer. The manufacturing interest and the general interests are synonymous. The abolition of slavery would be in reality an universal good.

Tortures, murder, and every other imaginable barbarity and iniquity, are practised upon the poor slaves with impunity. I hope the slave trade will be abolished. I pray it may be an event at hand. The great body of manufacturers, uniting in the cause, will considerably facilitate and expedite it; and as I have already stated, it is most substantially their interest and advantage, and as such the nation's at large (except those persons concerned in the manufacturing neck yokes, collars, chains, handcuffs, leg bolts, drags, thumb screws, iron muzzles, and coffins; cats, scourges, and other instruments of torture used in the slave trade). In a short time one sentiment will alone prevail, from motives of interest as well as justice and humanity. Europe contains one hundred and twenty millions of inhabitants. Query: How many millions doth Africa contain? Supposing the Africans, collectively and individually, to expend £5 a head in raiment and furniture yearly when civilized, &c., an immensity beyond the reach of imagination!

This I conceive to be a theory founded upon facts, and therefore an infallible one. If the blacks were permitted to remain in their own country, they would double themselves every fifteen years. In proportion to such increase will be the demand for manufactures. Cotton and indigo grow spontaneously in most parts of Africa; a consideration this of no small consequence to the manufacturing towns of Great Britain. It opens a most immense, glorious, and happy prospect—the clothing, &c., of a continent ten thousand miles in circumference, and immensely rich in productions of every denomination in return for manufactures.

Since the first publication of my Narrative, I have been in a great variety of scenes in many parts of Great Britain, Ireland, and Scotland, an account of which might not improperly be added here;* but this would swell the volume too much, I shall only observe in general, that in May 1791, I sailed from Liverpool to Dublin, where I was very kindly received, and from thence to Cork, and then travelled over many counties in Ireland. I was everywhere exceedingly well treated, by persons of all ranks. I found the people extremely hospitable, particularly in Belfast, where I took my passage on board of a vessel for Clyde, on the 29th of January, and arrived at Greenock on the 30th. Soon after I returned to London, where I found persons of note from Holland and Germany, who requested me to go there; and I was glad to hear that an edition of my Narrative had been printed in both places, also in New York. I remained in London till I heard the debate in the House of Commons on the slave trade, April the 2d and 3d. I then went to Soham in Cambridgeshire, and was married on the 7th of April to Miss Cullen, daughter of James and Ann Cullen, late of Ely.†

I have only therefore to request the reader's indulgence, and conclude. I am far from the vanity of thinking there is any merit in this narrative: I hope censure will be suspended, when it is considered that it was written by one who was as unwilling as unable to adorn the plainness of truth by the coloring of imagination. My life and fortune have been extremely checkered, and my adventures various. Nay even those I have related are considerably abridged. If any incident in this little work should appear uninteresting and trifling to most readers, I can only say, as my excuse for mentioning it, that almost every event of my life made an impression on

---

*Viz. Some curious adventures beneath the earth, in a river in Manchester, and a most astonishing one under the Peak of Derbyshire—and in September 1792, I went "90" fathoms down St. Anthony's Colliery, at Newcastle, under the river Tyne, some hundreds of yards on Durham side.

†See *Gentleman's Magazine* for April 1792, *Literary and Biographical Magazine*, and *British Review* for May 1792, and the *Edinburgh Historical Register* or *Monthly Intelligencer* for April 1792.

my mind, and influenced my conduct. I early accustomed myself to look at the hand of God in the minutest occurrence, and to learn from it a lesson of morality and religion; and in this light every circumstance I have related was to me of importance. After all, what makes any event important, unless by its observation we become better and wiser, and learn "to do justly, to love mercy, and to walk humbly before God"? To those who are possessed of this spirit, there is scarcely any book or incident so trifling that does not afford some profit, while to others the experience of ages seems of no use; and even to pour out to them the treasures of wisdom is throwing the jewels of instruction away.

Letters and Essays

BENJAMIN BANNEKER
(1731–1806)

A mathematician, naturalist, astronomer, farmer, inventor, surveyor, poet, writer, almanac creator, and social critic, Benjamin Banneker singularly holds the distinction of being the quintessential Renaissance African American of the eighteenth century. Banneker is one of few American-born writers of African descent who lived and wrote in the eighteenth century; he was born a freeman on November 9th, 1731. While the precocious Banneker later attended one of the rural area Quaker schools in Baltimore, Maryland, he was actually taught to read and write by his white English grandmother, Molly Welsh, who had been deported to the colony of Maryland from her home in Wessex, England, in 1683. Although brought to the colonies as a convict whose sentence would be completed in indentured servitude, after attaining her freedom, Welsh eventually prospered. She fulfilled her indentured servitude after seven years and was freed around 1690. Six years later, she bought her own farm and two slaves to run it. She freed both slaves and married one of them—a recently arrived African slave, named "Bannaka," who claimed to be an African prince and the son of the king of his country. The couple had three daughters and a son.

Banneker's grandmother is exemplary of the often close relations between African slaves and the white servant working class in the northern and mid-Atlantic colonies. Although their bondage was legally limited to a seven-year period, most of these white servants considered their actual lifestyles, working conditions, and social status to be equal to that of African slaves; and they often joined black people and Native Americans in organized revolts against the colonial economic system, which depended so heavily on various arrangements for unpaid labor.

The rest of Molly Banneker's life was a struggle to protect her family, especially her husband and her son. During the early eighteenth century, laws were changing, making it illegal for a white woman to marry a black man. Both were subject to reinstitution to servitude and slavery. Like many Africans, Bannaka—who eventually allowed the family name to be changed to Banneker but who accepted few other aspects of Eurocentric culture—never adjusted to the winter climates and arduous slave labor in the northern colonies. He died young. The Bannekers' oldest daughter, who was named Mary, married another African, who arrived on a slave ship from Guinea. This young man assumed the Christian name of Robert and proudly accepted the family's surname of Banneker. Their first child was a son, whom they named Benjamin.

Always supplementing his meager formal education, Benjamin Banneker taught himself physics, mathematics, and astronomy. At the age of twenty-two, using the workings of a watch as a model, he carved a wooden clock that struck the hour and continued to run until his death some fifty years later. One contemporary said of the clock, "It is probable that this was the first clock of which every portion was made in America; it is certain that it was as purely his own invention as if none had ever been before. He had seen a watch but never a clock, such an article not being within fifty miles of him."

Anxious to devote all of his time to scientific pursuits, Banneker signed away his interests in his family's farm to new neighbors, a wealthy Quaker family named Ellicott, who had moved from Pennsylvania to Maryland to set up flour mills. In honor of Banneker's genius, the family made tools, books, and instruments on astronomy and mathematics available to him. They also gave him a continuous annuity of twelve pounds, which enabled him to pursue his scientific studies. A lifelong bachelor, Banneker, who was cared for by his two married sisters, zealously investigated current theories of eighteenth-century science and reason, as well as existing records on ancient history and philosophy. He would often sleep during the day so he could spend countless nights in the study of the stars.

With the help of Quakers and other abolitionists who wanted to prove the wealth of African American potential in his lifetime, Banneker was celebrated for his mathematical prowess and for his multifaceted intellectual genius. He became a prominent member of the commission which, appointed by George Washington, laid out the boundary lines for Washington, D.C. Silvio Bedini, Banneker's biographer, documents the momentous contributions that the man of African genius made to the design of the nation's capital, one of the outstanding accomplishments of urban planning in the United States.

By the time he was sixty years old, Banneker was able to compile much of a lifetime of study into his first *Almanac*, which the publishers commended as "what must be considered an extraordinary effort of genius—a complete Ephemeris astronomical calendar for the year 1792, calculated by a sable descendant of Africa." The original manuscript was completed in 1791. He issued new consecutive almanacs for the next five years; and, while a strong antiabolitionist mood in Maryland discouraged support for its continuation, Banneker prepared calculations for the almanacs until 1802.

Because the Quakers planned to publish and distribute the *Almanac* in Georgetown, Baltimore, and Philadelphia—potentially large audiences for a first book by an African American—they arranged to have a copy of the book delivered to Secretary of State Thomas Jefferson, along with a letter from Banneker written to protest the statesman's stated justifications for racism and slavery. The 1795 *Almanac* included the "Letter to Thomas Jefferson" along with Jefferson's reply. Banneker eloquently and forcefully argues against Jefferson, who had *confirmed* African inferiority in his widely published "Notes on Virginia" (1787): "Comparing them by their faculties of memory, reason, and imagination, it appears to me, that in memory they are equal to the whites; in reason much inferior, as I think one could scarcely be found capable of tracing and comprehending the investigation of Euclid; and that in imagination they are dull, tasteless, and anomalous." Banneker reminded the influential statesman that, as a strong advocate for freedom and equality in the Declaration of Independence, Jefferson was being hypocritical in allowing the institution of slavery to continue in America.

A lifelong defender of his fellow blacks, Banneker freely admitted that he was motivated into solving several of his mathematical quizzes as racial boasts. He left letters, poems, and essay-type manuscripts that castigate Euro-Americans for enslavement of the Africans and that cite his beliefs that African Americans were intellectually mature and had creative and mental capacity equal to or greater than that of whites. The bulk of his manuscript writings, however, was accidentally burned two days after Banneker's death on October 9, 1806, almost 75 years from the date of his birth.

❖❖❖

See Silvio Bedini's scholarly and extensive biographical and bibliographical account of Banneker's life in *The Life of Benjamin Banneker—The Definitive Biography of the Black Man in Science* (1971). The work includes almost all extant materials by Banneker, including essays, poems, dreams, and mathematical quizzes, as well as engravings of the author's portrait, which were printed in the 1795 *Almanac.* Another excellent, full-length biography of Banneker's life is Shirley Graham's *Your Humble Servant* (1949). Other scholarly studies are Henry E. Baker's "Benjamin Banneker, The Negro Mathematician and Astronomer," *The Journal of Negro History* III (1918), 99–118, and Winthrop D. Jordan's chapter on Banneker in *White Over Black: American Attitudes Toward the Negro, 1550–1812* (1968). See also the introduction to Banneker's works in *Black Writers of America: A Comprehensive Anthology* (1972), by Richard Barksdale and Keneth Kinnamon.

Letter to Thomas Jefferson

MARYLAND, BALTIMORE COUNTY, AUGUST 19, 1791.

SIR,

I am fully sensible of the greatness of the freedom I take with you on the present occasion; a liberty which seemed scarcely allowable, when I reflected on that distinguished and dignified station in which you stand, and the almost general prejudice which is so prevalent in the world against those of my complexion.

It is a truth too well attested, to need proof here, that we are a race of beings, who have long laboured under the abuse and censure of the world; that we have long been looked upon with an eye of contempt; and considered rather as brutish than human, and scarcely capable of mental endowments.

I hope I may safely admit, in consequence of the report which has reached me, that you are a man far less inflexible in sentiments of this nature, than many others; that you are measurably friendly, and well disposed towards us; and that you are willing to lend your aid and assistance for our relief from those many distresses, and numerous calamities, to which we are reduced.

If this is founded in truth, I apprehend you will embrace every opportunity to eradicate that train of absurd and false ideas and opinions, which so generally prevail with respect to us: and that your sentiments are concurrent with mine, which are, that one universal Father hath given being to us all; that He hath not only made us all of one flesh, but that he hath also, without partiality, afforded us all the same sensations, and endowed us all with the same faculties; and that, however variable we may be in society or religion, however diversified in situation or in colour, we are all of the same family, and stand in the same relation to Him.

If these are sentiments of which you are fully persuaded, you cannot but acknowledge, that it is the indispensable duty of those who maintain for themselves the rights of human nature, and who profess the obligations of Christianity, to extend their powers and influence to the relief of every part of the human race, from whatever burden or oppression they may unjustly labour under, and this, I apprehend, a full conviction of the truth and obligation of these principles should lead all to.

I have long been convinced, that if your love for yourselves, and for those inestimable laws which preserved to you the rights of human nature, was founded on sincerity you could not but be solicitous, that every individual, of whatever rank or distinction, might with you equally enjoy the blessings thereof; neither could you rest satisfied short of the most active effusion of your exertions, in order to their promotion from any state of degradation, to which the unjustifiable cruelty and barbarism of men may have reduced them.

I freely and cheerfully acknowledge, that I am of the African race, and in that colour which is natural to them, of the deepest dye; and it is under a sense of the most profound gratitude to the Supreme Ruler of the Universe, that I now confess to you, that I am not under that state of tyrannical thraldom, and inhuman captivity, to which many of my brethren are doomed, but that I have abundantly tasted of the fruition of those blessings, which proceed from that free and unequalled liberty with which you are favoured; and which I hope you will willingly allow you have mercifully received, from the immediate hand of that Being from whom proceedeth every good and perfect gift.

Suffer me to recall to your mind that time, in which the arms of the British crown were exerted, with every powerful effort, in order to reduce you to a state of servitude: look back, I entreat you, on the variety of dangers to which you were exposed; reflect on that period in which every human aid appeared unavailable, and in which even hope and fortitude wore the aspect of inability to the conflict, and you cannot but be led to a serious and grateful sense of your miraculous and providential preservation; you cannot but acknowledge, that the present freedom and tranquillity which you enjoy, you have mercifully received, and that it is the peculiar blessing of heaven.

This, Sir, was a time when you clearly saw into the injustice of a state of Slavery, and in which you had just apprehensions of the horrors of its condition. It was then that your abhorrence thereof was so excited, that you publicly held forth this true and invaluable doctrine, which is worthy to be recorded and remembered in all succeeding ages: "We hold these truths to be self-evident, that all men are created equal; that they are endowed by their Creator with certain inalienable rights, and that among these are life, liberty, and the pursuit of happiness."

Here was a time in which your tender feelings for yourselves had engaged you thus to declare; you were then impressed with proper ideas of the great violation of liberty, and the free possession of those blessings, to which you were entitled by nature; but, sir, how pitiable it is to reflect, that although you were so fully convinced of the benevolence of the Father of Mankind and of his equal and impartial distribution of these rights and privileges which he hath conferred upon them, that you should at the same time counteract his mercies, in detaining by fraud and violence, so numerous a part of my brethren under groaning captivity and cruel oppression, that you should at the same time be found guilty of that most criminal act, which you professedly detested in others, with respect to yourselves.

Your knowledge of the situation of my brethren is too extensive to need a recital here; neither shall I presume to prescribe methods by which they may be relieved, otherwise than by recommending to you and all others, to wean yourselves from those narrow prejudices which you have imbibed with respect to them, and as Job proposed to his friends, 'put your soul in their soul's stead'; thus shall your hearts be enlarged with kindness and benevolence towards them; and thus shall you need neither the direction of myself or others, in what manner to proceed herein.

And now, sir, although my sympathy and affection for my brethren hath caused my enlargement thus far, I ardently hope, that your candour and generosity will plead with you in my behalf, when I state that it was not originally my design; but having taken up my pen in order to present a copy of an almanac which I have calculated for the succeeding year, I was unexpectedly led thereto.

This calculation is the production of my arduous study, in my advanced stage of life; for having long had unbounded desires to become acquainted with the secrets of nature, I have had to gratify my curiosity herein through my own assiduous application to astronomical study, in which I need not recount to you the many difficulties and disadvantages which I have had to encounter.

And although I had almost declined to make my calculation for the ensuing year, in consequence of the time which I had alloted for it being taken up at the federal territory, by the request of Mr. Andrew Ellicott, yet I industriously applied myself thereto, and hope I have accomplished it with correctness and accuracy. I have taken the liberty to direct a copy to you, which I humbly request you will favourably receive; and although you may have the opportunity of perusing it after its publication, yet I desire to send it to you in manuscript previous thereto, that thereby you might not only have an earlier inspection, but that you might also view it in my own handwriting.

And now, sir, I shall conclude, and subscribe myself, with the most profound respect,

Your most obedient humble servant,
BENJAMIN BANNEKER.

PRINCE HALL
(1735 c.–1807)

One of the most famous and influential black people of the eighteenth century, whose work has had far-reaching effects from his era to the present through the hundreds of organizations worldwide that bear his name, is Prince Hall, founder of the so-called *secret* societies of African American males known as Prince Hall Masons. Hall and his followers established formal and informal networks throughout the colonies facilitating communication and activism among blacks. Collectively, they probably filed more antislavery petitions with local and national governmental bodies; wrote and published more abolitionist letters, editorials, and essays; and made more public pronouncements against the dreaded institution than most other organized groups—whether white or black—in the eighteenth century.

Many eighteenth-century, upper-class white males established covertly closed group systems—such as secret clubs, societies, or orders—to facilitate societal control and to plan for expansion of their own personal power and wealth. However,

Hall and his eighteenth-century followers devoted themselves to quasi-shrouded conferences, at first called the Masons of Africa, to devise strategies for improving the lot of blacks, both slave and free, and to provide a model for manhood and freedom that all African American men could follow. These strategies included training for political, church, and business leadership; the building of local political and economic fraternities that could operate as independently as possible from a slave-endowed economy; and, perhaps most important, the implementation of creative legal and moral responses within and from the black community about the continuing oppressions of slavery and racism—responses that would get the widest possible public exposure, thereby making both blacks and whites aware of the many racial incidents and issues of the day.

Sidney Kaplan and others contend that Hall's early life is a mystery. Kaplan says, "According to new research, Hall was born around 1735, place unknown, and first crops up in the record during the late 1740s as the slave of one William Hall of Boston." But Benjamin Brawley, William H. Robinson, Jr., G. Carter Woodson, and other African American critics, as well as authorized historians for the Prince Hall Masons, insist that Hall was born at Bridge Town, Barbados, on September 12, 1748, the son of an English father named Thomas Prince Hall and a free mulatto mother of French descent. They also insist that he was given the proper name of Thomas Prince Hall. According to these accounts, in March of 1765, when he was seventeen years old, Hall worked his way from Barbados to Boston, Massachusetts, to begin profitable work in the leather-making trade, which he had learned from his father.

However, Kaplan and those who agree with him posit that Hall was actually one William Hall, a rather well-known black man in the Boston area who was listed in a 1740 registry. Further, they claim that he fathered a son named Primus in 1756 by a fellow servant named Delila and that six years later he married another slave named Sarah Ritchie. Further, they state that Hall's master freed him in the spring of 1770, that Sarah died in the summer of the same year, and that Hall subsequently married Flora Gibbs of Gloucester. Moreover, Kaplan infers that the Masons embellished a history for Hall to deny that he was ever a slave: "Recent studies of black Freemasonry have challenged parts of this version as based on lore and legend." To prove his point, Kaplan uses an example of a well-publicized photograph of Hall, which the critic says is merely a "clumsy forgery."

Three possible explanations exist for these inconsistencies. One critic points out that several black Halls (both slave and free) who worked with leather have been discovered as living and working in the Boston area in Prince Hall's day, and thus no one can prove that Hall ever "belonged" to anyone in the colonies. Second, the controversy highlights the atmosphere of conflicting scholarship and technical difficulties involved in attempts to reconstruct truths about slavery in New England, as well as aspects of race and social commitment, which influence such scholarship. Third, the very secrecy in which the black Masons had to hold their associations undoubtedly prohibited more accessibility about their methods of maintaining historical records. After all, they were not primarily a social organization, but rather a political and—certainly for the Revolutionary War era—a military one. In this light, perhaps, more credence should be given to the accounts of men who lived and worked with Hall and who succeeded him in leadership of the nationally formed group.

Critic Benjamin Brawley states that Hall was "physically small and of refined features and bearing" and that "he would seem hardly to have been adapted to the leadership of untutored people in a dark day; but he had great moral force and the power to win the allegiance of men." In 1775, Hall orchestrated the formation of a Freemasonry society from a meeting of fourteen free black men in Boston. Having been denied membership or recognition from American Masonic bodies, Hall and his followers were initiated in a British army lodge attached to a regiment stationed near Boston. On March 2, 1784, they applied to the Grand Lodge of England for specific authorization. They were recognized as an official Masonic organization on September 29, 1784, with Hall as master, although, because of inhibitions of transatlantic mail, they did not receive notification until April 29, 1787. They held their first meeting on May 6, 1787. As Master of the first officially authorized degree granting, called "African Lodge No. 459" (later changed to No. 370), Hall began what is today a worldwide fraternal movement. According to William H. Robinson, in 1977 there were more than 500,000 members of the Prince Hall Masons.

Once Hall began his work with the Masons and with the Methodist church—with the exception of Hall's participation in the Revolutionary War—scholars seem to agree about most of the rest of Hall's history, at least about that part of the history that is preserved by a considerable number of contemporary written works about Hall and the essays, sermons, and charges that he wrote himself. Critics William H. Robinson and G. Carter Woodson insist that Hall was also a Christian minister, and the many extant sermons or "charges" that Hall delivered during public Masonic services seem to support that claim. According to Robinson, Hall became "fully involved in early black Boston life as a Methodist minister in Cambridge, a manufacturer of soap, owner of real estate, and writer of many petitions of letters and tracts in behalf of his enslaved and abused brethren." Woodson states that Hall "applied himself industriously at common labor during the day and studied privately at night." He says, moreover, that when Hall was 27 years old, "he had acquired the fundamentals of education" and "saving his earnings, he had accumulated sufficient to buy a piece of property."

For several years, beginning in 1762, Hall belonged to the white Congregational Church on School Street, pastored by Reverend Andrew Crosswell. From these premises, Hall, according to Robinson, served as an unordained minister, informally pastoring "his fellow Masons and other interested blacks." However, Woodson says forcefully that Hall "passed as an eloquent preacher." He says that Hall's first church was located in Cambridge, Massachusetts, and that "there he built up a prosperous congregation." Hall's association with other black New England leaders such as Absalom Jones, John Marrant, and Lemuel Haynes is well documented. Many of these men served as his lieutenants and leaders of the established lodges in their communities.

Scholars also disagree as to whether Hall served the colonies during the Revolutionary War. Woodson says that "he entered actively in the war and acquitted himself with credit." Some say that Hall fought at Bunker Hill with Peter Salem and Salem Poor, historically known black veterans of the Revolutionary War. But, again, another group of historians points out that military records reveal that at least six black Prince Halls of Massachusetts were in the Army and Navy during the Revolution. However, a bill sent to Colonel Crafts of the Boston Regiment of Artillery on April 24, 1777, for five leather drum heads is clear evidence that Hall at least served in the war as a skilled craftsman. Furthermore, records indicate that during the War, Hall offered to Governor Bowdoin some 700 blacks as available to serve the colonies during the Revolutionary War. Present-day historians question how Hall could have been able to recruit such a large number of blacks and how he would have been able to communicate with them, but the effect and force of Hall's secret networks is evident.

As a prominent leader and black spokesperson, Hall and his writings were well known to his contemporaries. A fighter for black freedom and equality during all of his public life, Hall made countless public addresses and wrote letters, essays, news articles, editorials, and several abolitionist petitions to state and national legislators. In 1777, he solicited the state officials for the abolition of slavery in Massachusetts. In 1789, he was also among the first to sign an early petition to the General Court of Massachusetts calling for the return of African Americans to the African continent. During the same period, he petitioned, without success, that public education be provided for children of black taxpayers. In 1790, he successfully petitioned on behalf of three blacks who were kidnapped from the Boston area and sold into slavery. Thanks to his efforts, they were quickly released. Also, between 1789 and 1790, Hall welcomed Reverend John Marrant, the first African American to receive ministerial ordination, as Marrant was enroute back to his chosen home in London after a long preaching tour of Eastern Canada. The two men established a strong friendship and Hall eventually installed Marrant as chaplain of the original black masonic lodge. By the late eighteenth century, American blacks throughout New England, New York, New Jersey, and Pennsylvania knew of and revered the notable Prince Hall.

In his messages Hall, a well-read preacher and orator, stressed the constant and central presence of Africa throughout the Bible, illustrating that such Old and New Testament patriarchs as Moses, Solomon, and Philip held black Africans in high esteem because of their shrewd wisdom and sage advice and that they treated them with full equality, thereby further implying that white American Christians should do no less. Because of his connections in the Caribbean, Hall was able to coordinate the treatment of African slaves throughout the Diaspora, often documenting that those in the North American colonies were the most ill-treated of all. Despite missing parts that remain to be completed in the historical portrait of this great African American leader of the eighteenth century, no one can, or should, attempt to erase the legacy that Hall left to the black people of America. Perhaps new scholarship will reveal just how instrumental Hall may have been in helping to bring about the abolition of slavery in New England by the close of the eighteenth century.

❖❖❖

See Benjamin Brawley's introduction to a Hall sermon in *Early Negro American Writers* (1970); George W. Crawford's *Prince Hall and His Followers* (1914); editor Philip S. Foner's *The Voice of Black America: Major Speeches by Negroes in the United States, 1797–1971* (1972); Sidney and Emma Kaplan's "Prince Hall: Organizer" in *The Black Presence in the Era of the American Revolution* (1989); William H. Robinson, Jr.'s *Early Black American Prose: Selections with Biographical Introductions* (1971); William H. Upton's *Negro Masonry* (1899); Joseph A. Walker's *Black Squares & Compass: 200 Years of Prince Hall Freemasonry* (1899); Charles H. Wesley's *Prince Hall: Life and Legacy* (1977); and G. Carter Woodson's *The Negro in Our History* (1917).

A Charge, Delivered to the African Lodge, June 24, 1797

Beloved Brethren of the African Lodge,

'Tis now five years since I deliver'd a Charge to you on some parts and points of Masonry. As one branch or superstructure on the foundation; when I endeavoured to shew you the duty of a Mason to a Mason, and charity or love to all mankind, as the mark and image of the great God, and the Father of the human race.

I shall now attempt to shew you that it is our duty to sympathise with our fellow men under their troubles, the families of our brethren who are gone: we hope to the Grand Lodge above, here to return no more. But the cheerfulness that you have ever had to relieve them, and ease their burdens, under their sorrows, will never be forgotten by them; and in this manner you will never be weary in doing good.

But my brethren, although we are to begin here, we must not end here; for only look around you and you will see and hear of numbers of our fellow men crying out with holy Job, Have pity on me, O my friends, for the hand of the Lord hath touched me. And this is not to be confined to parties or colours; not to towns or states; not to a kingdom, but to the kingdoms of the whole earth, over whom Christ the king is head and grand master.

Among these numerous sons and daughters of distress, I shall begin with our friends and brethren; and first, let us see them dragg'd from their native country by the iron hand of tyranny and oppression, from their dear friends and connections, with weeping eyes and aching hearts, to a strange land and strange people, whose tender mercies are cruel; and there to bear the iron yoke of slavery & cruelty till death as a friend shall relieve them. And must not the unhappy condition of these our fellow men draw forth our hearty prayer and wishes for their deliverance from these merchants and traders, whose characters you have in the xviii chap. of the Revelations, 11, 12, & 13 verses, and who knows but these same sort of traders may in a short time, in the like manner, bewail the loss of the African traffick, to their shame and confusion: and if I mistake not, it now begins to dawn in some of the West-India islands; which puts me in mind of a nation (that I have somewhere read of) called Ethiopeans, that cannot change their skin: But God can and will change their conditions, and their hearts too; and let Boston and the world know, that He hath no respect of persons; and that that bulwark of envy, pride, scorn and contempt, which is so visible to be seen in some and felt, shall fall, to rise no more.

When we hear of the bloody wars which are now in the world, and thousands of our fellow men slain; fathers and mothers bewailing the loss of their sons; wives for the loss of their husbands; towns and cities burnt and destroy'd; what must be the heart-felt sorrow and distress of these poor and unhappy people! Though we cannot help them, the distance being so great, yet we may sympathize with them in their troubles, and mingle a tear of sorrow with them, and do as we are exhorted to—weep with those that weep.

Thus my brethren we see what a chequered world we live in. Sometimes happy in having our wives and children like olive-branches about our tables; receiving the bounties of our great Benefactor. The next year, or month, or week we may be deprived of some of them, and we go mourning about the streets, so in societies; we are this day to celebrate this Feast of St. John's, and the next week we might be called upon to attend a funeral of some one here, as we have experienced since our last in this Lodge. So in the common affairs of life we sometimes enjoy health and prosperity; at another time sickness and adversity, crosses and disappointments.

So in states and kingdoms; sometimes in tranquility, then wars and tumults; rich today, and poor tomorrow; which shews that there is not an independent mortal on earth, but dependent one upon the other, from the king to the beggar.

The great law-giver, Moses, who instructed by his father-in-law, Jethro, an Ethiopean, how to regulate his courts of justice and what sort of men to choose for the different offices; hear now my words, said he, I will give you counsel, and God shall be with you; be thou for the people to Godward, that thou mayest bring the causes unto God, and thou shall teach them ordinances and laws, and shall shew the way wherein they must walk, and the work that they must do; moreover thou shall provide out of all the people, able men, such as fear God, men of truth, hating covetousness, and place such over them, to be rulers of thousands, of hundreds and of tens.

So Moses hearkened to the voice of his father-in-law, and did all that he said. Exodus xviii. 22–24.

This is the first and grandest lecture that Moses ever received from the mouth of man; for Jethro understood geometry as well as laws, *that* a Mason may plainly see: so a little captive servant maid by whose advice Nomen, the great general of Syria's army, was healed of his leprosy; and by a servant his proud spirit was brought down: 2 Kings v. 3–14. The feelings of this little captive for this great man, her captor, was so great, that she forgot her state of captivity, and felt for the distress of her enemy. Would to God (said she to her mistress) my lord were with the prophets in Samaria, he should be healed of his leprosy: So after he went to the prophet, his proud host was so haughty that he not only disdain'd the prophet's direction, but derided the good old prophet; and had it not been for his servant he would have gone to his grave with a double leprosy, the outward and the inward, in the heart, which is the worst of leprosies; a black heart is worse than a white leprosy.

How unlike was this great general's behaviour to that of as grand a character, and as well beloved by his prince as he was; I mean Obadiah, to a like prophet. See for this 1st Kings xviii. from 7 to the 16th.

And as Obadiah was in the way, behold Elijah met him, and he knew him, and fell on his face, and said, Art not thou, my Lord, Elijah, and he told him, Yea, go and tell thy Lord, behold Elijah is here: and so on to the 16th verse. Thus we see that great and good men have, and always will have, a respect for ministers and servants of God. Another instance of this is in Acts viii. 27 to 31, of the European Eunuch, a man of great authority, to Philip, the apostle: here is mutual love and friendship between them. This minister of Jesus Christ did not think himself too good to receive the hand, and ride in a chariot with a black man in the face of day; neither did this great monarch (for so he was) think it beneath him to take a poor servant of the Lord by the hand, and invite him into his carriage, though but with a staff, one coat, and no money in his pocket. So our Grand Master, Solomon, was not asham'd to take the Queen of Sheba by the hand, and lead her into his court, at the hour of high twelve, and there converse with her on points of masonry (for if ever there was a female mason in the world she was one) and other curious matters; and gratified her, by shewing her all his riches and curious pieces of architecture in the temple, and in his house: After some time staying with her, he loaded her with much rich presents: he gave her the right hand of affection and parted in love.

I hope that no one will dare openly (tho' in fact the behaviour of some implies as much) to say, as our Lord said on another occasion, Behold a greater than Solomon is here. But yet let them consider that our Grand Master Solomon did not divide the living child, whatever he might do with the dead one, neither did he pretend to make a law to forbid the parties from having free intercourse with one another without the fear of censure, or be turned out of the synagogue.

Now my brethren, as we see and experience that all things here are frail and changeable and nothing here to be depended upon: Let us seek those things which are above, which are sure, and stedfast, and unchangeable, and at the same time let us pray to Almighty God, while we remain in the tabernacle, that he would give us the grace of patience and strength to bear up under all our troubles, which at this day God knows we have our share. Patience I say, for were we not possess'd of a great measure of it you could not bear up under the daily insults you meet with in the streets of Boston; much more on public days of recreation, how are you shamefully abus'd, and that at such a degree that you may truly be said to carry your lives in your hands, and the arrows of death are flying about your heads; helpless old women have their clothes torn off their backs, even to the exposing of their nakedness; and by whom are these disgraceful and abusive actions committed, not by the men born and bred in Boston, for they are better bred; but by a mob or horde of shameless, low-lived, envious, spiteful persons, some of them not long since, servants in gentlemen's kitchens, scouring knives, tending horses, and driving chaise. 'Twas said by a gentleman who saw that filthy behaviour in the common, that in all the places he had been in, he never saw so cruel behaviour in all his life, and that a slave in the West-Indies, on Sunday or holidays enjoys himself and friends without any molestation. Not only this man, but many in town who hath seen their behaviour to you, and that without any provocation—twenty or thirty cowards fall upon one man—have wonder'd at the patience of the Blacks: 'tis not for want of courage in you, for they know that they dare not face you man for man, but in a mob, which we despise, and had rather suffer wrong than to do wrong, to the disturbance of the community and the disgrace of our reputation: for every good citizen doth honor to the laws of the State where he resides.

My brethren, let us not be cast down under these and many other abuses we at present labour under: for the darkest is before the break of day. My brethren, let us remember what a dark day it was with our African brethren six years ago, in the French West-Indies. Nothing but the snap of the whip was heard from morning to evening; hanging, broken on the wheel, burning, and all manner of tortures inflicted on those unhappy people for nothing else but to gratify their masters pride, wantonness, and cruelty: but blessed be God, the scene is changed; they now confess that God hath no respect of persons, and therefore receive them as their friends, and treat them as brothers. Thus doth Ethiopia begin to stretch forth her hand, from a sink of slavery to freedom and equality.

Although you are deprived of the means of education, yet you are not deprived of the means of meditation; by which I mean thinking, hearing and weighing matters, men, and things in your own mind, and making that judgment of them as you think reasonable to satisfy your minds and give an answer to those who may ask you a question. This nature hath furnished you with, without letter learning; and some have made great progress therein, some of those I have heard repeat psalms and hymns, and a great part of a sermon, only by hearing it read or preached and why not in other things in nature: how many of this class of our brethren that follow the seas can foretell a storm some days before it comes; whether it will be a heavy or light, a long or short one; foretell a hurricane, whether it will be destructive or moderate, without any other means than observation and consideration.

So, in the observation of the heavenly bodies, this same class without a telescope or other apparatus have through a smoak'd glass observed the eclipse of the sun: One being ask'd what he saw through his smoaked glass, said, Saw, saw, de clipsey, or de clipseys. And what do you think of it?—Stop, dere be two. Right, and what do they look like?—Look like, why if I tell you, they look like two ships sailing one bigger than tother; so they sail by one another, and make no noise. As simple as the answers are they have a meaning, and shew that God can out of the mouth of babes and Africans shew forth his glory; let us then love and adore him as the God who defends us and supports us and will support us under our pressures, let them be ever so heavy and pressing. Let us by the blessing of God, in whatsoever state we are, or may be in, to be content; for clouds and darkness are about him; but justice and truth is his habitation; who hath said, Vengeance is mine and I will repay it, therefore let us kiss the rod and be still, and see the works of the Lord.

Another thing I would warn you against, is the slavish fear of man, which bringest a snare, saith Solomon. This passion of fear, like pride and envy, hath slain its thousands.—What but this makes so many perjure themselves; for fear of offending them at home they are a little depending on for some trifles: A man that is under a panic of fear, is afraid to be alone; you cannot hear of a robbery or house broke open or set on fire, but he hath an accomplice with him, who must share the spoil with him; whereas if he was truly bold, and void of fear, he would keep the whole plunder to himself: so when either of them is detected and not the other, he may be call'd to oath to keep it secret, but through fear, (and that passion is so strong) he will not confess, till the fatal cord is put on his neck; then death will deliver him from the fear of man, and he will confess the truth when it will not be of any good to himself or the community: nor is this passion of fear only to be found in this class of men, but among the great.

What was the reason that our African kings and princes have plunged themselves and their peaceable kingdoms into bloody wars, to the destroying of towns and kingdoms, but the fear of the report of a great gun or the glittering of arms and swords, which struck these kings near the seaports with such a panic of fear, as not only to destroy the peace and happiness of their inland brethren, but plung'd millions of their fellow countrymen into slavery and cruel bondage.

So in other countries; see Felix trembling on his throne. How many Emperors and kings have left their kingdoms and best friends at the sight of a handful of men in arms: how many have we seen that have left their estates and their friends and ran over to the stronger side as they thought; all through the fear of men, who is but a worm, and hath no more power to hurt his fellow worm, without the permission of God, than a real worm.

Thus we see, my brethren, what a miserable condition it is to be under the slavish fear of men; it is of such a destructive nature to mankind, that the scriptures every where from Genesis to the Revelations warns us against it; and even our blessed Saviour himself forbids us from this slavish fear of man, in his sermon on the mount; and the only way to avoid it is to be in the fear of God: let a man consider the greatness of his power, as the maker and upholder of all things here below, and that in Him we live, and move, and have our being, the giver of the mercies we enjoy here from day to day, and that our lives are in his hands, and that he made the heavens, the sun, moon and stars to move in their various orders; let us thus view the greatness of God, and then turn our eyes on mortal man, a worm, a shade, a wafer, and see whether he is an object of fear or not; on the contrary, you will think him in his best estate to be but vanity, feeble and a dependent mortal, and stands in need of your help, and cannot do without your assistance, in some way or other; and yet some of these poor mortals will try to make you believe they are Gods, but worship them not. My brethren, let us pay all due respect to all whom God hath put in places of honor over us: do justly and be faithful to them that hire you, and treat them with that respect they may deserve; but worship no man. Worship God, this much is your duty as christians and as masons.

We see then how becoming and necessary it is to have a fellow feeling for our distres'd brethren of the human race, in their troubles, both spiritual and temporal—How refreshing it is to a sick man, to see his sympathising friends around his bed, ready to administer all the relief in their power; although they can't relieve his bodily pain yet they may ease his mind by good instructions and cheer his heart by their company.

How doth it cheer up the heart of a man when his house is on fire, to see a number of friends coming to his relief; he is so transported that he almost forgets his loss and his danger, and fills him with love and gratitude; and their joys and sorrows are mutual.

So a man wreck'd at sea, how must it revive his drooping heart to see a ship bearing down for his relief.

How doth it rejoice the heart of a stranger in a strange land to see the people cheerful and pleasant and are ready to help him.

How did it, think you, cheer the heart of those our poor unhappy African brethren, to see a ship commissioned from God, and from a nation that without flattery faith, that all men are free and are brethren; I say to see them in an instant deliver such a number from their cruel bolts and galling chains, and to be fed like men and treated like brethren. Where is the man that has the least spark of humanity, that will not rejoice with them; and bless a righteous God who knows how and when to relieve the oppressed, as we see he did in the deliverance of the captives among the Algerines; how sudden were they delivered by the sympathising members of the Congress of the United States, who now enjoy the free air of peace and liberty, to their great joy and surprize, to them and their friends. here we see the hand of God in various ways bringing about his own glory for the good of mankind, by the mutual help of their fellow men; which ought to teach us in all our straits, be they what they may, to put our trust in Him, firmly believing that he is able and will deliver us and defend us against all our enemies; and that no weapon form'd against us shall prosper; only let us be steady and uniform in our walks, speech and behaviour; always doing to all men as we wish and desire they would do to us in the like cases and circumstances.

Live and act as Masons, that you may die as Masons; let those despisers see, altho' many of us cannot read, yet by our searches and researches into men and things, we have supplied that defect; and if they will let us we shall call ourselves a charter'd lodge of just and lawful Masons; be always ready to give an answer to those that ask you a question; give the right hand of affection and fellowship to whom it justly belongs; let their colour and complexion be what it will, let their nation be what it may, for they are your brethren, and it is your indispensable duty so to do; let them as Masons deny this, and we & the world know what to think of them be they ever so grand: for we know this was Solomon's creed, Solomon's creed did I say, it is the decree of the Almighty, and all Masons have learnt it: tis plain market language, and plain and true facts need no apologies.

I shall now conclude with an old poem which I found among some papers:

> Let blind admirers handsome faces praise,
> And graceful features to great honor raise,
> The glories of the red and white express,
> I know no beauty but in holiness;
> If God of beauty be the uncreate
> Perfect idea, in this lower state,
> The greatest beauties of an human mould
> Who most resemble Him we justly hold:
> Whom we resemble not in flesh and blood,
> But being pure and holy, just and good:
> May such a beauty fall but to my share,
> For curious shape or face I'll never care.

LEMUEL B. HAYNES
(1753–1833)

In many ways, the life of Rev. Lemuel Haynes reflects both eighteenth-century black and white race relations in the northern colonies as well as the myriad facets of African American ethnic identity. Born on July 18, 1753, in West Hartford, Connecticut, the abandoned offspring of a fully African father and an upper-middle-class white mother, Haynes never knew his father and only saw his mother once years after he was grown. Always very concerned about protecting her identity, the unwed mother sold her five-month-old infant into a twenty-one year contract for indentured servitude to Deacon David Rose of Middle Granville, Massachusetts. Yet from such an inauspicious beginning, Haynes went on to become a renowned pastor and public orator, a leading intellectual who would eventually become one of very few blacks to be granted an honorary degree from the all-white colonial system of higher education, and a close friend to statesmen, college presidents, and other prominent leaders and intellectuals.

Fortunately for the orphaned child, the Rose family turned out to be dedicated Christians who did not seem to exploit the boy as if he were merely an African lackey but, conversely, reared him as a son and heir. Haynes ended up living with the Roses and working on the family farm until he was thirty-two years old, when he left the homestead to assume a full-time pastorate as a black minister heading an all-white congregation. His only other absence from the Roses was as a volunteer soldier during the Revolutionary War.

He joined the Continental Army as one of Ethan Allen's Green Mountain Boys in 1775 and saw a great deal of fighting, including the campaign against Fort Ticonderoga. Moreover, the Revolution provided young Lemuel the inspiration for one of his first literary works, a battlefield poem written in celebration of a war victory. That poem, now generally called "The Battle of Lexington," was titled "A Poem on the Inhuman Tragedy Perpetuated on the 19th of April 1775 by a Number of the British Troops under the Command of Thomas Gage." It was merely a forerunner of a very strong antislavery statement that Haynes would make by drawing from the political rhetoric of the Revolution and on other politicized slogans that the war effort had borrowed from the church so that he could call for the immediate emancipation of all Africans held in the colonial slave system.

Like Phillis Wheatley and Jupiter Hammon, Haynes received most of his education through Bible studies. He attended missionary educational meetings held in the Rose household. He was immersed in a study of the Bible as well as the works of Isaac Watts, Edward Young, and the famed British evangelist, George Whitefield. After the war, young Lemuel, who had become quite a proficient scholar, received an invitation to attend Dartmouth College—again, a very rare attainment for a black man. However, believing that his informal farm-based education did not well equip him to compete in such an august setting, Haynes chose instead to stay with the Roses and to take up private tutelage in biblical theology and Latin and Greek under Daniel Farrand and William Bradford—well-known teachers in New England.

While Haynes was certainly well-read, even the Roses did not know that the young student had both the aspiration and the ability to become a preacher himself—a calling which, in that era, was the most respected career possible for a man of any color, but one which was quite unseemly for a black man whose close and surrounding communities and church affiliations were in all-white settings. In 1774, during one of the family's regular household Bible- and sermon-reading sessions, Lemuel astonished everyone when, instead of reading a traditional sermon by one of the notable preachers of the day, he read a sermon he had composed himself. Five years later, in 1780, after serving now and then as a substitute preacher in Deacon Rose's Congregational Church, Haynes applied for his ordination by the New Light Association of Ministers in Litchfield County, Connecticut. After this momentous occasion—which may well have made him the first ordained black man in the Western world (with the possible exception of John Marrant, who was ordained in England)—Haynes preached, usually to all-white congregations, in Connecticut and Vermont. In 1778 he accepted a call to pastor the all-white West Parish of Rutland,

Vermont, where he stayed until 1818. In 1783, the now successful and well-established clergyman accepted a proposal of marriage from a local white schoolteacher, Elizabeth Babbitt, with whom he sired ten children.

Born a black man whose parents consigned him to a slave status virtually for life, Haynes instead became a celebrity esteemed and venerated by the same white society that was to have used him merely as a beast of burden. His very presence in the pulpit was a statement against the practice of enslaving blacks because they were supposedly heathen and animalistic. And it was a statement against prevailing assumptions that blacks could not perform tasks of intellectual leadership—especially if that leadership were over white constituents.

Perhaps even more striking, Haynes's achievements directly repudiated the elitist upper-class clergy who had controlled New England pulpits since the days of Plymouth Rock and who had used their self-styled interpretations of the Bible to justify slavery in the first place. Haynes was a part of the large numbers of lower- and middle-class men who went into the pastorate as part of the upheavals occasioned by the great revivals of the eighteenth century. He served pastorates in Torrington, Connecticut; Rutland, Vermont; and Granville, New York. He was even invited to preach at the famous Blue Church in New Haven, Connecticut, where the eminent Puritan minister Jonathan Edwards had once pastored. Yet, although Haynes preached against such clerical elitism, the elite still thronged to be associated with him: President Timothy Dwight of Yale University and President Herman Humphrey of Amherst College sought his advice, and he counted playwright and jurist Royal Tyler among his closest friends. Haynes often said that if he had not gone into the ministry, he would liked to have been a man of letters. He frequently quoted such noted literary masters as Alexander Pope, John Milton, and Edward Young in his sermons and essays.

During his stay at the Rutland church, the cleric wrote some 5,500 sermons, of which 400 were for funeral occasions—a tremendous literary record for any religious writer in the eighteenth century. At least a dozen of his sermons and patriotic speeches were published during his lifetime. An example of his impressive oratory was his sermon against Jefferson's political principles—*The Nature and Importance of True Republicanism* (1801). One of his best known sermons is "Universal Salvation" (1805), which was reprinted in some seventy editions throughout the nineteenth century and which is usually still included in collections of early American literature. In 1804, the venerable Lemuel Haynes was awarded "the honorary degree of Master of Arts" by the trustees of Middlebury College—again, an astounding achievement for one who was to have been a perpetual slave.

A bit depressed because of a bitter breach with one of the congregations he served toward the end of his career, Haynes spent his last years in Granville, New York, where he died in 1833 after an eleven-year struggle against the effects of gangrene and advancing age. He had penned an autobiographical essay before his death in which he disclosed the true identity of his mother, whom he had confronted some fifty years earlier. She had refused to acknowledge him then, and after his death, her family confiscated and destroyed all copies of that revealing manuscript.

Before Ruth Bogin's 1983 discovery of Haynes's sermon, "Liberty Further Extended" (1776?), most scholars made the familiar assumption that Haynes was so involved with his religious writings that he ignored the subject of slavery. Because he argued so forcefully against slavery in that text, critics now claim the work to be the first essay of antislavery protest in the literary canon. Actually, Haynes's New Light theology argued that physical liberty was essential for the liberty of the soul and that true Christianity mandated this liberty as a moral right. He believed that those who would not yield to this divine standard of moral righteousness could not claim the blessings of salvation through Christ and, in his sermons against the liberal doctrine of Universal Salvation, Haynes was calling for judgment against those who advocated and practiced the enslavement of their fellow human beings.

❖❖❖

A great deal has been written about Haynes. See, for instance, Ruth Bogin's, "Notes and Documents: 'Liberty Further Extended,' 1776 Antislavery Manuscript by Lemuel Haynes," in *The William and Mary Quarterly* (January 1983), 85–105; Timothy Cooley's, *Sketches of the Life and Character of the Reverend Lemuel Haynes* (1839); Richard Newman's, *Lemuel Haynes, a Bibliography* (1984); and Richard Newman's, *Black Preacher to White America: The Collected Writings of Lemuel Haynes, 1774–1833* (1990), which contains Haynes's essay, "Liberty Further Extended," and poem, "The Battle of Lexington." Also note that Richard Barksdale and Keneth Kinnamon have a good discussion of Haynes in their introduction to his sermon, "Universal Salvation—A Very Ancient Doctrine," in *Black Writers of America* (1972).

Liberty Further Extended[1]

Liberty Further Extended: Or Free thoughts on the illegality of Slavekeeping; Wherein those arguments that Are used in its vindication Are plainly confuted. Together with an humble Address to such as are Concearned in the practise.

By Lemuel Haynes

WE HOLD THESE TRUTHS TO BE SELF-EVIDENT, THAT ALL MEN ARE CREATED EQUAL, THAT THEY ARE ENDOWED BY THEIR CREATOR WITH CEARTAIN UNALIENABLE RIGHTS, THAT AMONG THESE ARE LIFE, LIBERTY, AND THE PURSUIT OF HAPPYNESS.

Congress

The Preface. As *Tyrony* had its Origin from the infernal regions: so it is the Deuty, and honner of Every son of freedom to repel her first motions. But while we are Engaged in the important struggle, it cannot Be tho't impertinent for us to turn one Eye into our own Breast, for a little moment, and See, whether thro' some inadvertency, or a self-contracted Spirit, we Do not find the monster Lurking in our own bosom; that now while we are inspir'd with so noble a Spirit and Becoming Zeal, we may Be Disposed to tear her from us. If the following would produce such an Effect the auther should rejoice.

It is Evident, by ocular demonstration, that man by his Depravety, hath procured many Courupt habits which are detrimental to society; And altho' there is a way pre[s]crib'd Whereby man may be re-instated into the favour of god, yet these courupt habits are Not Extirpated, nor can the subject of renovation Bost of perfection, 'till he Leaps into a state of immortal Existance. yet it hath pleas'd the majesty of heaven to Exhibet his will to men, and Endow them With an intulect Which is susceptible of speculation; yet, as I observ'd before, man, in consequence of the fall is Liable to digressions. But to proceed,

[1]This unpublished essay, which literary historian Ruth Bogin believes was written in 1776, contains the original misspellings and stylistic errors in the original manuscript.

Liberty, & freedom, is an innate principle, which is unmovebly placed in the human Species; and to see a man aspire after it, is not Enigmatical, seeing he acts no ways incompatible with his own Nature; consequently, he that would infring upon a mans Liberty may reasonably Expect to meet with oposision, seeing the Defendant cannot Comply to Non-resistance, unless he Counter-acts the very laws of nature.

Liberty is a Jewel which was handed Down to man from the cabinet of heaven, and is Coaeval with his Existance. And as it proceed from the Supreme Legislature of the univers, so it is he which hath a sole right to take away; therefore, he that would take away a mans Liberty assumes a prerogative that Belongs to another, and acts out of his own domain.

One man may bost a superorety above another in point of Natural previledg; yet if he can produse no convincive arguments in vindication of this preheminence his hypothesis is to Be Suspected. To affirm, that an Englishman has a right to his Liberty, is a truth which has Been so clearly Evinced, Especially of Late, that to spend time in illustrating this, would be but Superfluous tautology. But I query, whether Liberty is so contracted a principle as to be Confin'd to any nation under heaven; nay, I think it not hyperbolical to affirm, that Even an affrican, has Equally as good a right to his Liberty in common with Englishmen.

I know that those that are concerned in the Slave-trade, Do pretend to Bring arguments in vindication of their practise; yet if we give them a candid Examination, we shall find them (Even those of the most cogent kind) to be Essencially Deficient. We live in a day wherein *Liberty & freedom* is the subject of many millions Concern; and the important Struggle hath alread caused great Effusion of Blood; men seem to manifest the most sanguine resolution not to Let their natural rights go without their Lives go with them; a resolution, one would think Every one that has the Least Love to his country, or futer posterity, would fully confide in, yet while we are so zelous to maintain, and foster our own invaded rights, it cannot be tho't impertinent for us Candidly to reflect on our own conduct, and I doubt not But that we shall find that subsisting in the midst of us, that may with propriety be stiled *Opression,* nay, much greater opression, than that which Englishmen seem so much to spurn at. I mean an oppression which they, themselves, impose upon others.

It is not my Business to Enquire into Every particular practise, that is practised in this Land, that may come under this Odeus Character; But, what I have in view, is humbly to offer som free thoughts, on the practise of *Slave-keeping.* Opression, is not spoken of, nor ranked in the sacred oracles, among the Least of those sins, that are the procureing Caus of those signal Judgments, which god is pleas'd to bring upon the Children of men. Therefore let us attend. I mean to white [write] with freedom, yet with the greatest Submission.

And the main proposition, which I intend for some Breif illustration is this, Namely, That an *African,* or, in other terms, *that a Negro may Justly Chalenge, and has an undeniable right to his* ["freed(om)" is blotted out] *Liberty: Consequently, the practise of Slave-keeping, which so much abounds in this Land is illicit.*

Every privilege that mankind Enjoy have their Origen from god; and whatever acts are passed in any Earthly Court, which are Derogatory to those Edicts that are passed in the Court of Heaven, the act is *void.* If I have a perticular previledg granted to me by god, and the act is not revoked nor the power that granted the benefit vacated, (as it is imposable but that god should Ever remain immutable) then he that would infringe upon my Benifit, assumes an unreasonable, and tyrannic power.

It hath pleased god to *make of one Blood all nations of men, for to dwell upon the face of the Earth.* Acts 17, 26. And as all are of one Species, so there are the same Laws, and aspiring principles placed in all nations; and the Effect that these Laws will produce, are Similar to Each other. Consequently we may suppose, that what is precious to one man, is precious to another, and what is irksom, or intolarable to one man, is so to another, consider'd in a Law of Nature.

Therefore we may reasonably Conclude, that Liberty is Equally as pre[c]ious to a *Black man,* as it is to a *white one,* and Bondage Equally as intollarable to the one as it is to the other: Seeing it Effects the Laws of nature Equally as much in the one as it Does in the other. But, as I observed Before, those privileges that are granted to us By the Divine Being, no one has the Least right to take them from us without our consen[t]; and there is Not the Least precept, or practise, in the Sacred Scriptures, that constitutes a Black man a Slave, any more than a white one.

Shall a mans Couler Be the Decisive Criterion whereby to Judg of his natural right? or Becaus a man is not of the same couler with his Neighbour, shall he Be Deprived of those things that Distuingsheth [Distinguisheth] him from the Beasts of the field?

I would ask, whence is it that an Englishman is so far Distinguished from an Affrican in point of Natural privilege? Did he recieve it in his origenal constitution? or By Some Subsequent grant? Or Does he Bost of some hygher Descent that gives him this pre-heminance? for my part I can find no such revelation. It is a Lamantable consequence of the fall, that mankind, have an insatiable thurst after Superorety one over another: So that however common or prevalent the practise may be, it Does not amount, Even to a Surcomstance, that the practise is warrentable.

God has been pleas'd to distiungs [distinguish] some men from others, as to natural abilitys, but not as to natural *right,* as they came out of his hands.

But sometimes men by their flagitious practise forfeit their Liberty into the hands of men, By Becomeing unfit for society; But have the *affricans* Ever as a Nation, forfited their Liberty in this manner? What Ever individuals have done; yet, I Believe, no such Chaleng can be made upon them, as a Body. As there should be Some rule whereby to govern the conduct of men; so it is the Deuty, and intrest of a community, to form a system of *Law,* that is calculated to promote the commercial intrest of Each other: and so Long as it produses so Blessed an Effect, it should be maintained. But when, instead of contributing to the well Being of the community, it proves banefull to its subjects over whome it Extends, then it is hygh time to call it in question. Should any ask, where shall we find any system of Law whereby to regulate our moral Conduct? I think their is none so Explicit and indeffinite, as that which was given By the Blessed Saviour of the world. *As you would that men should do unto you, do you Even so to them.* One would think, that the mention of the precept, would strike conviction to the heart of these Slavetraders; unless an aviricious Disposision, governs the Laws of humanity.

If we strictly adhear to the rule, we shall not impose anything upon Others, But what we should Be willing should Be imposed upon us were we in their Condision.

I shall now go on to consider the manner in which the Slave-trade is carried on, By which it will plainly appear, that the practise is vile and atrocious, as well as the most inhuman. it is undoubtedly true that those that Emigrate slaves from *Africa* Do Endevour to rais mutanies among them in order to procure slaves. here I would make some Extracts from a pamphlet printed in Philadelphia, a few years ago: the varacity of which need not be scrupled, seeing it agrees with many other accounts.

N. *Brue,* Directory of the *French* factory at *Senegal,* who Lived twenty-seven years in that country says, "that the *Europeans* are far from desiring to act as peace-makers among the *Negros,* which would Be acting contrary to their intrest, since the greater the wars, the more slaves are procured." *William Boseman,* factor for the Duch at *Delmina,* where he resided sixteen years, relates, "that one of the former Comma[n]ders hired an army of the Negros, of *Jefferia,* and *Cabesteria,* for a Large Sum of money, to fight the negros of *Commanry* [?], which occasioned a Battle, which was more Bloody than the wars of the Negros usually are: And that another Commander gave at one time five *hundred* pounds, and at another time Eight hundred pounds, to two other Negro nations, to induce them to take up arms against their Country people." This is confirmed by *Barbot,* agent general of the french African company, who says, "The *Hollanders,* a people very zelous for their Commerce at the Coasts, were very studious to have the war carried on amongst the Blacks, to distract, as Long as possible, the trade of the other Europeans and to that Effect, were very ready to assist upon all occasions, the Blacks, their allies, that they mite Beat their Enemies, and so the Commerce fall into their hands." And one *William Smith,* who was sent By the *African* company, to visit their settlements in the year 1726, from the information he reciev'd from one, who had resided ten years, viz. "that the Discerning Natives accounted it their greatest unhappyness that they were Ever visited by the *Europeans:*—that we Christians introduced the traffick of Slaves, and that Before our comeing they Lived in peace; But, say they, it is observable, that Wherever Christianity comes, there comes with it a Sword, a gun, powder, and Ball." And thus it Brings ignominy upon our holy religion, and mak[e]s the Name of Christians sound Odious in the Ears of the heathen. O Christianity, how art thou Disgraced, how art thou reproached, by the vicious practises of those upon whome thou dost smile! Let us go on to consider the great hardships, and sufferings, those Slaves are put to, in order to be transported into these plantations. There are generally many hundred slaves put on board a vessel, and they are Shackkled together, two by two, wors than Crimanals going to the place of Execution; and they are Crouded together as close as posable, and almost naked; and their sufferings are so great, as I have Been Credibly informed, that it often Carries off one third of them on their passage; yea, many have put an End to their own Lives for very anguish; And as some have manifested a Disposision to rise in their Defence, they have Been put to the most Cruel torters, and Deaths as human art could inflict. And O! the Sorrows, the Greif the Distress, and anguish which attends them! and not onely them But their frinds also in their Own Country, when they must forever part with Each Other? What must be the plaintive noats that the tend[er] parents must assume for the Loss of their Exiled *Child?* Or the husband for his Departed wife? and how Do the Crys of their Departed friends Eccho from the watry Deep! Do not I really hear the fond mother Expressing her Sorrows, in accents that mite well peirce the most obdurate heart? "O! my Child, why why was thy Destiny hung on so precarious a theread! unhappy fate! O that I were a captive with thee or for thee! [About seventy-five words are crossed out and utterly illegible. The mother's words continue:] Cursed Be the Day wherein I Bare thee, and Let that inauspicious Night be remembered no more. Come, O King of terrors. Dissipate my greif, and send my woes into oblivion."

But I need Not stand painting the Dreery Sene. Let me rather appeal to tender parents, whether this is Exaggarating matters? Let me ask them what would be their Distress. Should one of their Dearest *Children* Be snach'd from them, in a Clendestine manner, and carried to *Africa,* or some othe forreign Land, to be under the most abject Slavery for Life, among a strang people? would it not imbitter all your Domestic Comforts? would he not Be Ever upon your mind? nay, doth not nature Even recoil at the reflection?

And is not their many ready to say, (unless void of natural Effections) that it would not fail to Bring them Down with sorrow to the grave? And surely, this has Been the awfull fate of some of those *Negros* that have been Brought into these plantations; which is not to be wondered at, unless we suppose them to be without natural Effections; which is to rank them Below the very Beasts of the field.

O! what an Emens Deal of Affrican-Blood hath Been Shed by the inhuman Cruelty of Englishmen! that reside in a Christian Land! Both at home, and in their own Country? they being the fomenters of those wars, that is absolutely necessary, in order to carry on this cursed trade; and in their Emigration into these colonys? and By their merciless masters, in some parts at Least? O ye that have made yourselves Drunk with human Blood! alth' you may go with impunity here in this Life, yet God will hear the Crys of that innocent Blood, which crys from the Sea, and from the ground against you, Like the Blood of Abel, more pealfull [?] than thunder, *vengence! vengence!* What will you Do in that Day when God shall make inquisision for Blood? he will make you Drink the phials of his indignation which Like a potable Stream shall Be poured out without the Least mixture of mercy; Believe it, Sirs, their shall not a Drop of Blood, which you have Spilt unjustly, Be Lost in forgetfullness. But it Shall Bleed affresh, and testify against you, in the Day when God shall Deal with Sinners.

We know that under the Levitical Oeconomy, *man-stealing* was to Be punished with Death; so [?] we Esteem those that Steal any of our Earthy Commadety gilty of a very heinous Crime:

What then must Be an adiquate punishment to Be inflicted on those that Seal [steal] men?

Men were made for more noble Ends than to be Drove to market, like Sheep and oxen. "Our being Christians, (says one) Does not give us the Least Liberty to trample on heathen, nor Does it give us the Least Superiority over them." And not only are they gilty of *man-stealing* that are the immediate actors in this trade, But those in these colonys that Buy them at their hands, as far from Being guiltless: for when they saw the theif they consented with him. if men would forbear to Buy Slaves off the hands of the Slave-merchants, then the trade would of necessaty cease; if I buy a man, whether I am told he was stole, or not, yet I have no right to Enslave him, Because he is a human Being: and the immutable Laws of God, and indefeasible Laws of nature, pronounced him free.

Is it not exceeding strang that mankind should Become such mere vassals to their own carnal avarice as Even to imbrue their hands in inocent Blood? and to Bring such intollerable opressiones upon others, that were they themselves to feel them, perhaps they would Esteem Death preferable—pray consider the miserys of a Slave, Being under the absolute controul of another, subject to continual Embarisments, fatiuges, and corections at the will of a master; it is as much impossable for us to bring a man hearteley to acquiesce in a passive obedience in this case, as it would be to stop a man's Breath, and yet have it caus no convulsion in nature. those negros amongst us that have Children, they, viz. their *Children* are brought up under a partial Disapilne: their white masters haveing but Little, or no Effection for them. So that we may suppose, that the abuses that they recieve from the hands of their masters are often very considrable; their parents Being placed in such a Situation as not being able to perform relative Deutys. Such are those restrictions they are kept under By their task-masters that they are render'd incapable of performing those morral Deutys Either to God or man that are infinitely binding on all the human race; how often are they Seperated from Each other, here in this Land at many hundred miles Distance, Children from parents, and parents from Children, Husbands from wives, and wives from Husbands? those whom God hath Joined together, and pronounced one flesh, man assumes a prerogative to put asunder. What can be more abject than their condission? in short, if I may so speak 'tis a hell upon Earth; and all this for filthy Lucres sake: Be astonished, O ye Heavens, at this! I believe it would Be much Better for these Colonys if their was never a Slave Brought into this Land; theirby our poor are put to great Extremitys, by reason of the plentifullness of Labour, which otherwise would fall into their hands.

I shall now go on to take under Consideration some of those *arguments* which those that are Concern'd in the Slave-trade Do use in vindication of their practise; which arguments, I shall Endevour to Shew, are Lame, and Defective.

The first argument that I shall take notice of is this viz. *that in all probability the Negros are of Canaans posterity, which ware Destined by the almighty to Slavery; theirfore the practise is warrantable.* To which I answer, Whethear the Negros are of Canaans posterity or not, perhaps is not known by any mortal under Heaven. But allowing they were actually of Canaans posterity, yet we have no reason to think that this Curs Lasted any Longer than the comeing of Christ: when that Sun of riteousness arose this wall of partition was Broken Down. Under the *Law,* their were many External Cerimonies that were tipecal of Spiritual things; or which Shadowed forth the purity, & perfection of the Gospel: as Corporeal *blemishes,* Spurious *Birth,* flagicious *practises,* debar'd them from the congregation of the Lord: theirby Shewing, the intrinsick purity of heart that a Conceal'd Gospel requir'd as the pre-requisite for heaven, and as *Ham* uncovered his fathers nakedness, that is, did not Endevour to Conceal it, but gaz'd perhaps with a Lascivious Eye, which was repugnant to the Law which was afterwards given to the Children of Isarel [Israel]: So it was most [?] Necessary that god Should manifest his Signal Disapprobation of this hainous Sin, By makeing him and his posterity a publick Example to the world, that theirby they mite be set apart, and Seperated from the people of God as unclean. And we find it was a previlege Granted to God's people of old, that they mite Enslave the *heathen, and the Stranger that were in the Land;* theirby to Shew the Superior previleges God's people Enjoy'd above the rest of the world: So that we, Gentiles were then Subject to Slavery, Being then heathen; [illegible] So that if they will keep Close to the Letter they must own themselves yet Subject to the yoak; unless we Suppose them *free* By Being Brought into the same place, or haveing the same previleges with the Jews; then it follows, that we may inslave all Nations, be they White or Black, that are heathens, which they themselves will not allow. We find, under that Dispensation, God Declareing that he would *visit the iniquity of the fathers upon the Children, unto the third, and fourth generation, &c.* And we find it so in the case of *Ham,* as well as many others; their posterity Being Extrinsically unclean.

But now our glorious hygh preist hath visably appear'd in the flesh, and hath Establish'd a more glorious Oeconomy. he hath not only visably Broken Down that wall of partision that interposed Between the ofended majesty of Heaven and rebellious Sinners and removed those tedeous forms under the Law, which savoured so much of servitude, and which *could never make the comers thereunto perfect,* By rendering them obselete: But he has removed those many Embarisments, and Distinctions, that they were incident to, under so contracted a Dispensation. So that whatever *Bodily imperfections,* or whatever *Birth* we sustain, it Does not in the Least Debar us from Gospel previlege's. Or whatever hainous practise any may be gilty of, yet if they manifest a gospel [?] repentance, we have no right to Debar them from our Communion. and it is plain Beyond all Doubt, that at the comeing of Christ, this curse that was upon *Canaan,* was taken off; and I think there is not the Least force in this argument than there would Be to argue that an imperfect Contexture of parts, or Base *Birth,* Should Deprive any from Gospel previleges; or Bring up any of those antiquated Ceremonies from oblivion, and reduse them into practise.

But you will say that Slave-keeping was practised Even under the Gospel, for we find *paul,* and the other apostles Exhorting *Servants to be obedient to their masters.* to which I reply, that it mite be they were Speaking to Servants in *minority* in General; But Doubtless it was practised in the Days of the Apostles from what *St. paul* Says, *1. Corin. 7 21. art thou called, being a servant? care not for it; but if thou mayest Be made free, use it rather.* So that the Apostle seems to recomend freedom if attainable, q.d. "if it is thy unhappy Lot to be a slave, yet if thou art Spiritually free Let the former appear so minute a thing when compared with the latter that it is comparitively unworthy of notice; yet Since freedom is so Exelent a Jewel, which none have a right to Extirpate, and if there is any hope of attaining it, use all Lawfull measures for that purpose." So that however Extant or preval[e]nt it mite Be in that or this age; yet it does not in the Least reverse the unchangeable Laws of God, or of nature; or make that Become Lawfull which is in itself unlawfull; neither is it Strange, if we consider the moral Depravity of mans nature, thro'out all ages of the world, that mankind should Deviate from the unering rules of Heaven. But again, another argument which some use to maintain their intollerable opression upon others is this, viz., *that those Negros that are Brought into these plantations are Generally prisoners, taken in their wars, and would otherwise fall a sacrifice to the resentment of their own people.* But this argument, I think, is plainly confuted By the forecited account which Mr. *Boasman* gives, as well as many others. Again, some say they *Came honestly By their Slaves, Becaus they Bought them of their parents,* (that is, those that Brought them from Africa) *and rewarded them well for them.* But without Doubt this is, for the most part fals; But allowing they Did actually Buy them of their parents, yet I query, whether parents have any right to sel their Children for Slaves: if parents have a right to Be free, then it follows that their Children have Equally as good a right to their freedom, Even *Hereditary.* So, (to use the words of a Learned writer) "one has no Body to Blame But himself, in case he shall find himself Deprived of a man whome he tho't By Buying for a price he had made his own; for he Dealt in a trade which was illicit, and was prohibited by the most obvious Dictates of Humanity. for these resons Every one of those unfortunate men who are pretended to be Slaves, has a right to Be Declared free, for he never Lost his Liberty; he could not Lose it; his prince had no power to Dispose of him. of cours the Sale was *ipso Jure* void."

But I shall take notice of one argument more which these Slave-traders use, and it is this, viz. *that those Negros that are Emigrated into these colonies are brought out of a Land of Darkness under the meridian Light of the Gospel; and so it is a great Blessing instead of a Curs.* But I would ask, who is this that Darkneth counsel By words with out knoledg? Let us attend to the great appostle Speaking to us in *Rom. 3.8.* where he reproves some slanderers who told it as a maxim preached By the apostles that they said *Let us Do Evil that Good may come, whose Damnation* the inspired penman pronounces with an Emphasis *to Be Just.* And again *Chap.* 6 vers 1. where By way of interagation he asks, *Shall we continue in Sin that grace may abound?* The answer is obvious, *God forbid.* But that those Slavemerchants that trade upon the coasts of Africa do not aim at the Spiritual good of their Slaves, is Evident By their Behaviour towards them; if they had their Spiritual good at heart, we should Expect that those Slave-merchants that trade upon their coasts, would, insted of Causing quarrelings, and Blood-Shed among them, which is repugnant to Christianity, and below the Character of humanity, Be Sollicitous to Demean Exampleary among them, that By their wholesom conduct, those heathen mite be Enduced to Entertain hygh, and admiring tho'ts of our holy religion. Those Slaves in these Colonies are generally kept under the greatest ignorance, and Blindness, and they are scersly Ever told by their white masters whether there is a Supreme Being that governs the univers; or wheather there is any reward, or punishments Beyond the grave. Nay such are those restrictions that they are kept under that they Scersly know that they have a right to Be free, or if they Do they are not allowed to Speak in their defence; Such is their abject condission, that that *genius* that is peculiar to the human race, cannot have that Cultivation that the polite world is favour'd with, and therefore they are stiled the ignorant part of the world; whereas were they under the Same advantages to git knoledge with them, perhaps their progress in arts would not be inferior.

But should we give ourselves the trouble to Enquire into the grand motive that indulges men to concearn themselves in a trade So vile and abandon, we Shall find it to Be this, namely, to Stimulate their Carnal avarice, and to maintain men in pride, Luxury, and idleness, and how much it hath Subserv'd to this vile purpose I Leave the Candid publick to Judge: I speak it with reverence yet I think all must give in that it hath such a tendency.

But altho god is of Long patience, yet it does not Last always, nay, he has *whet* his *glittering Sword, and his hand hath already taken hold on*

Judgement; for who knows how far that the unjust Oppression which hath abounded in this Land, may be the procuring cause of this very Judgement that now impends, which so much portends *Slavery?*

for this is God's way of working, Often he brings the Same Judgements, or Evils upon men, as they unriteously Bring upon others. As is plain from *Judges* 1 and on.

But Adoni-bezek fled, and they persued after him, and caut him, and cut off his thumbs, and his great toes.

And Adoni-besek said, threescore and ten kings haveing their thumbs and their great toes cut off gathered their meat under my table: as I have Done, So god hath requited me.

And as wicked *Ahab,* and *Jezebel* to gratify their covetousness caused *Naboth* to be put to Death, and as *Dogs* licked the Blood of *Naboth,* the word of the Lord was By the prophet *Elijah, thus Saith the Lord, in the place where Dogs Licked the Blood of Naboth, Shall dogs Lick thy Blood Even thine. See 1 Kings 21.19. And of Jezebel also Spake the Lord, Saying, The Dogs Shall Eat Jezebel By the walls of Jezreel. vers 23.*

And we find the Judgement actually accomplished upon Ahab in the 22. Chap. & 38. vers.

And upon *Jezebel* in the 9 chap. 2 of *Kings.*

Again *Rev. 16.6. for they have Shed the Blood of Saints and prophets, and thou hast given them Blood to Drink; for they are worthy.* And *chap.* 18.6. *Reward her Even as She rewarded you.* I say this is often God's way of Dealing, by retaliating Back upon men the Same Evils that they unjustly Bring upon others. I Don't Say that we have reason to think that *Oppression* is the alone caus of this Judgement that God is pleas'd to Bring upon this Land, Nay, But we have the greatest reason to think that this is not one of the Least. And whatever some may think that I am instigated By a fals zeal; and all that I have Said upon the Subject is mere Novelty: yet I am not afraid to appeal to the consience of any rational and honnest man, as to the truth of what I have just hinted at; and if any will not confide in what I have humbly offer'd, I am persuaded it must be such Short-Sited persons whose Contracted Eyes never penitrate thro' the narrow confines of Self, and are mere Vassals to filthy Lucre.

But I Cannot persuade myself to make a period to this Small *Treatise,* without humbly addressing myself, more perticularly, unto all such as are Concearn'd in the practise of *Slavekeeping.*

Sirs, Should I persue the Dictates of nature, resulting from a sense of my own inability, I should be far from attempting to form this address: Nevertheless, I think that a mere Superficial reflection upon the merits of the Cause, may Serve as an ample apology, for this humble attempt. Therefore hopeing you will take it well at my hands, I persume, (tho' with the greatest Submission) to Crave your attention, while I offer you a few words.

Perhaps you will think the preceeding pages unworthy of Speculation: well, Let that be as it will; I would Sollicit you Seriously to reflect on your conduct, wheather you are not gilty of unjust Oppression. Can you wash your hands, and say, I am Clean from this Sin? Perhaps you will Dare to Say it Before men; But Dare you Say it Before the tremendous tribunal of that God Before Whome we must all, in a few precarious moments appear? then whatever fair glosses we may have put upon our Conduct, that god whose Eyes pervade the utmost Extent of human tho't, and Surveys with one intuitive view, the affairs of men; he will Examin into the matter himself, and will set Every thing upon its own Basis; and impartiallity Shall Be Seen flourishing throughout that Sollemn assembly. Alas! Shall men hazard their precious Souls for a little of the transetory things of time. O *Sirs!* Let that pity, and compassion, which is peculiar to mankind, Especially to Englishmen, no Longer Lie Dormant in your Breast: Let it run free thro' Disinterested Benevolence. then how would these iron yoaks Spontaneously fall from the gauled Necks of the oppress'd! And that Disparity, in point of Natural previlege, which is the Bane of Society, would Be Cast upon the utmost coasts of Oblivion. If this was the impulsive Exercise that animated all your actions, your Conscience's wold Be the onely Standard unto which I need appeal. think it nor uncharitable, nor Censorious to say, that whenever we Erect our Battery, so as it is Like to prove a Detriment to the intrest of any, we Loos their attention. or, if we Don't Entirely Loos that, yet if true Christian candour is wanting we cannot Be in a Sutiable frame for Speculation: So that the good Effect that these Otherwise mite have, will prove abortive. If I could once persuade you to reflect upon the matter with a Single, and an impartial Eye, I am almost assured that no more need to be Said upon the Subject: But whether I shall Be so happy as to persuade you to Cherish such an Exercise I know not: yet I think it is very obvious from what I have humbly offer'd, that so far forth as you have Been Concerned in the *Slave-trade,* so far it is that you have assumed an oppressive, and tyrannic power. Therefore is it not hygh time to undo these heavy Burdens, and Let the Oppressed go free? And while you manifest such a noble and magnanimous Spirit, to maintain inviobly your own Natural rights, and militate so much against Despotism, as it hath respect unto yourselves, you do not assume the Same usurpations, and are no Less tyrannic. Pray let there be a congruity amidst you Conduct, Least you fall amongst that Class the inspir'd pen-man Speaks of. *Rom.* 2.21 and on. *thou therefore which teacheth another, teachest thou not thy Self? thou that preachest a man Should not Steal, Dost thou Steal? thou that sayest, a man Should not Commit adultery, Dost thou Commit adultery? thou that abhoreth idols, Dost thou Commit Sacrilege? thou that makest thy Bost of the Law, through Breaking the Law Dishonnerest thou God?* While you thus Sway your tyrant Scepter over others, you have nothing to Expect But to Share in the Bitter pill. 'Twas an Exelent note that I Lately read in a modern peice, and it was this. "O when shall America be consistantly Engaged in the Cause of Liberty!" If you have any Love to yourselves, or any Love to this Land, if you have any Love to your fellow-men, Break these intollerable yoaks, and Let their names Be remembered no more, Least they Be retorted on your own necks, and you Sink under them; for god will not hold you guiltless.

Sirs, the important Caus in which you are Engag'd in is of a[n] Exelent nature, 'tis ornamental to your Characters, and will, undoubtedly, immortalize your names thro' the Latest posterity. And it is pleasing to Behold that patriottick Zeal which fire's your Breast; But it is Strange that you Should want the Least Stimulation to further Expressions of so noble a Spirit. Some gentlemen have Determined to Contend in a Consistant manner: they have *Let the oppressed go free;* and I cannot think it is for the want of such a generous princaple in you, But thro' some inadvertancy that [end of extant manuscript].

The Battle of Lexington[1]

A Poem on the inhuman Tragedy perpetrated on the 19th of April 1775 by a Number of the Brittish Troops under the Command of Thomas Gage, which Parricides and Ravages are shocking Displays of ministerial & tyrannic Vengeance composed by Lemuel a young Mollato who obtained what little knowledge he possesses, by his own Application to Letters.

[1]This unpublished poem, which Professor Ruth Bogin unearthed in 1985, reflects Haynes's corrected manuscript in terms of punctuation, spelling, and discarded words. Professor Bogin believes that this poem was written in 1775.

1

Some Seraph now my Breast inspire
whilst my *Urania* sings
while She would try her solemn Lyre
Upon poetic Strings.

2

Some gloomy Vale or gloomy Seat
where Sable veils the sky
Become that Tongue that w^{d} repeat
The dreadfull Tragedy

3

The Nineteenth Day of April last
We ever shall retain
As monumental of the past
most bloody shocking Scene

4

Then Tyrants fill'd wth horrid Rage
A fatal Journey went
& Unmolested to engage
And slay the innocent

5

Then did we see old *Bonner* rise
And, borrowing Spite from Hell
They stride along with magic Eyes
where Sons of Freedom dwell

6

At *Lexington* they did appear
Array'd in hostile Form
And tho our Friends were peacefull there
Yet on them fell the Storm

7

Eight most unhappy Victims fell
Into the Arms of Death
unpitied by those Tribes of Hell
who curs'd them wth their Breath

8

The Savage Band still march along
For *Concord* they were bound
while Oaths & Curses from their Tongue
Accent with hellish Sound

9

To prosecute their fell Desire
At *Corcord* they unite
Two Sons of Freedom there expire
By their tyrannic Spite

10

Thus did our Friends endure their Rage
without a murm'ring Word
Till die they must or else engage
and join with one Accord

11

Such Pity did their Breath inspire
That long they bore the Rod
And with Reluctance they conspire
to shed the human Blood

12

But Pity could no longer sway
Tho' 't is a pow'rfull Band
For Liberty now bleeding lay
And calld them to withstand

13

The Awfull Conflict now begun
To rage with furious Pride
And Blood in great Effusion run
From many a wounded Side

14

For Liberty, each Freeman Strives
As its a Gift of God
And for it willing yield their Lives
And Seal it with their Blood

15

Thrice happy they who thus resign
Into the peacefull Grave
Much better there, in Death Confin'd
Than a Surviving Slave

16

This Motto may adorn their Tombs,
(Let tyrants come and view)
"*We rather seek these silent Rooms*
"*Than live as Slaves to You*

17

Now let us view our Foes awhile
who thus for blood did thirst
See: stately Buildings fall a Spoil
To their unstoick Lust

18

Many whom Sickness did compel
To seek some Safe Retreat
Were dragged from their sheltering Cell
And mangled in the Street

19

Nor were our aged Gransires free
From their vindictive Pow'r
On yonder Ground lo: there you see
Them weltering in their Gore

20

Mothers with helpless Infants strive
T' avoid the tragic Sight
All fearfull wether yet alive
Remain'd their Soul's delight

21

Such awefull Scenes have not had Vent
Since Phillip's War begun
Nay sure a Phillip would relent[?]
And such vile Deeds would shun

22

But Stop and see the Pow'r of God
Who lifts his Banner high
Jehovah now extends his Rod
And makes our Foes to fly

23

Altho our Numbers were but few
And they a Num'rous Throng
Yet we their Armies do pursue
And drive their Hosts along

24

One Son of Freedom could annoy
A Thousand Tyrant Fiends
And their despotick Tribe destroy
And chace them to their Dens

25

Thus did the Sons of Brittain's King
Receive a sore Disgrace
Whilst *Sons of Freedom* join to sing
The Vict'ry they Imbrace

26

Oh! Britain how art thou become
Infamous in our Eye
Nearly allied to antient Rome
That Seat of Popery

27

Our Fathers, tho a feeble Band
Did leave their native Place
Exiled to a desert Land
This howling Wilderness

28

A Num'rous Train of savage Brood
Did then attack them round
But still they trusted in their God
Who did their Foes confound

29

Our Fathers Blood did freely flow
To buy our Freedom here
Nor will we let our freedom go
The Price was much too dear

30

Freedom & Life, O precious Sounds
yet Freedome does excell
and we will bleed upon the ground
or keep our Freedom still

31

But oh! how can we draw the Sword
Against our native kin
Nature recoils at such a Word
And fain w^d^ quit the Scene

32

We feel compassion in our Hearts
That captivating Thing
Nor shall Compassion once depart
While Life retains her String

33

Oh England let thy Fury cease
At this convulsive Hour
Consult those Things that make for Peace
Nor foster haughty Power

34

Let Brittain's king call home his Band
of Soldiers arm'd to fight
To see a Tyrant in our Land
Is not a pleasing Sight

35

Allegiance to our King we own
And will due Homage pay
As does become his royal Throne
Yet in a *legal Way*

36

On Earth prepare for solemn Things
Behold an angry god
Beware to meet the King of Kings
Arm'd with an awefull Rod

37

Sin is the Cause of all our Woe
That sweet deluding ill
And till we let this darling go
There's greater Trouble still

Voices of Orators

The Sermon

ABSALOM JONES

(1746–1818)

Without doubt, among a handful of prominent black men in the eighteenth century, Absalom Jones was one of the best-known African American leaders of early America. Jones has been referred to "as the most salient Negro leader of his day, and generation." When writing about this first Christian bishop in North America, George Bragg states, "The little state of Delaware gave to the Colored Race, The First Negro Religious and Civic Leader; The Father of Negro Organizations; The First Negro Priest; and the first Negro Grand Master of Negro Masons, of the State of Pennsylvania."

Absalom Jones was born on November 6, 1746, in Sussex, Delaware, to a large slave family of several siblings. Apparently always precocious, as a young boy, Jones was taken from the field, as he says "to The Greathouse" to serve his master. However, in historical testimony to the fact that slave holders in the northern colonies could be just as treacherous as their counterparts in the South, in 1762, when Absalom was but 16 years old, his mother, five brothers, and a sister were sparsed out in sales to various owners; and Jones was sold to a new master from Philadelphia for whom he worked as a store clerk and delivery boy.

In Delaware, Jones had purchased a primer, a spelling book, and a New Testament from meager tips he had accumulated over the years, and, like Frederick Douglass and other slaves, he taught himself to read by seeking assistance from anyone who could or would help him. With his new master's permission, for a short while Jones attended night school. Through this venture and his clerking work in the Philadelphia store, Jones was soon able to write his own letters and he immediately began a circuit of correspondence to his mother and siblings (who no doubt had his letters read to them by whites) in efforts to find out about the family and to somehow keep them together. In his autobiography, Jones writes that during two quarters of night school in 1766 he also learned "Arithmetic, Addition, Troy weight, Subtraction, Apothecary weight, Practical Multiplication, Practical Division, and Reduction."

In 1770, Jones married a fellow slave and set about immediately to purchase her freedom first, which would guarantee the safety of any children born to their union, as the law stated that the status of the children followed that of the mother. Her mistress demanded 40 pounds for her freedom, for which Jones and his father-in-law borrowed some funds and raised more by having sympathetic whites write a letter of appeal to authenticate the need, thereby enabling them to receive donations from supportive Quakers in the city. Jones writes that he and his wife "obtained a house" in which Jones, in addition to his employment as a slave, worked "until twelve and one o'clock at night to assist my wife in obtaining a livelihood, and to pay the money that was borrowed to purchase her freedom."

Jones first applied to his master for his own freedom in 1778. It was denied. Through shrewd manipulation in the monetary exchange between "the continental" British money and the American dollar, Jones obtained funds to purchase a house and lot. "My desire for freedom increased," he writes, "as I knew that while I was a slave, my house and lot might be taken as the property of my master." On October 1, 1784, when he was 36 years old, Absalom Jones was finally set free. He continued for a while to work for his former master "at good wages"; and eventually he built two small houses on his lot and leased them out for a handsome profit.

Very much like the advent of Dr. Martin Luther King, Jr., Jones's national prominence was sprung in 1787 from a seed bed of Christian revivalism, which led to peaceful but forceful social revolution. Reverends Absalom Jones and Richard Allen led a small band of African American Christians out of a congregation of mostly white, prominent slave owners in the St. George Methodist Episcopal Church, who, in the midst of the genuine eighteenth-century Christian revivals, which were sweeping the colonies and Europe, demanded that the black converts only pray and worship in segregated balcony seating.

On April 12, 1787, a few Sundays after walking out in protest, the rejected group formally organized the Free African Society and named Jones and Allen as their "Overseers." They had formed what would eventually become the nucleus of the first black Episcopal and black Methodist denominations in the world. While still harassed by the white Methodists who were determined that they rejoin the St. George Methodist Episcopal Church as second-class citizens, within a few years, the Society converted itself into a nondenominational body known as The African Church of Philadelphia. Both Allen and Jones desired to remain Methodist and Allen would, in fact, eventually become the founder of the African Methodist Episcopal denomination; however, all those who had walked out of the St. George Methodist Episcopal Church on that fateful Sunday in 1787 elected, in 1794, to establish an independent Episcopal Church, which was eventually sanctioned and supported by the white Episcopalians of Pennsylvania. The Pennsylvania Quakers also gave financial support to Jones and his fledgling congregation. The congregation asked Jones to be their pastor and, within ten years, he was ordained a priest and then a bishop by the Pennsylvania Diocesan Convention of the American Episcopalian denomination. Named The African Church of St. Thomas, Jones's church, with a membership of 500 in the first year and hundreds more in constant attendance, was the first known attempt at the self-organization of African Americans anywhere in the free states of the North.

As with all authentic African American congregations, Jones and members of his church were heavily involved in issues of politics and social justice. In 1797, inspired by four escaped slaves who appealed to him for protection against recapture under the Fugitive Slave Law, he wrote a petition to the United States House of Representatives in defense of African American rights to the protection of government in the new republic. Based on the Declaration of Independence, Jones's petition was to have been sponsored by Representative John Swanwick of Pennsylvania, but it horrified Southern politicians, such as Senator Blout of North Carolina, who blocked the petition from ever being read. President James Madison agreed with the Southern political bloc that if the petitioners were given a hearing, other African Americans would want to follow Jones's example and the remaining slave states would be quite discomforted.

In 1799 and 1800, the African Church of St. Thomas led other black people in Philadelphia in presenting petitions before the State Legislature to demand the immediate abolition of slavery in the state; and they simultaneously petitioned the United States Congress to reject the Fugitive Slave Law and to immediately abolish the slave institution. Some of the most prominent blacks in North America belonged to The African Church of St. Thomas, including the wealthy shipbuilder James Forten.

In 1814, Jones, joined by Forten and Allen, organized blacks and other Philadelphians into a militia of 2,500 to protect the city from encroaching British warships; and, in 1817, the group drew up another well-publicized document protesting the work of the Colonization Society, which wanted to repatriate better-educated blacks back to Africa. In part, the document declared, "We never will separate ourselves voluntarily from the slave population in this country. They are our brethren by the ties of blood, of suffering, and of wrong, and we feel that there is more virtue in suffering privations with them than in gaining fancied advantages for a season."

In 1793, an epidemic of yellow fever began what was to be a seven-year sweep through Philadelphia. The plague seemed particularly injurious to the white people, and in the midst of the plague's worst horrors, white physicians asked the black people of Philadelphia to attend to the whites who were sick and dying. Again, Jones and Allen organized the black community and, through much personal sacrifice and expense, helped to stem the plague's worst effects, only later to be accused, in a pamphlet by a white opportunist named Matthew Carey, of negligence in caring for the sick and of excessive overcharges for burying the dead. To vindicate their efforts and to give a true account of volunteer efforts by African Americans during the epidemic, Jones and Allen responded to Carey in *A Narrative of the Proceedings of the Black People of Philadelphia, in the Year 1793; and a Refutation of Some Censures Thrown upon Them in Some Late Publications.*

Absalom Jones, the first African American cleric and bishop, died on February 13, 1818. During twenty-two years of faithful service in The African Church of St. Thomas, he had lived to see his friend and fellow abolitionist Richard Allen also be ordained as a bishop by penitent white Methodist leaders and to see the legal end of the African slave trade in 1808. Although he is ardently remembered for the outstanding political leadership he gave to the entire American black colonial population, Absalom Jones is remembered in church history for the humble manner and fatherly solicitude with which he led his grateful flock.

❖❖❖

Good biographical information on Absalom Jones can be found in "Celebrating the Feast of Absalom Jones" in *The Black Caucus* (1987); George F. Bragg, Jr.'s *Heroes of the Eastern Shore* (1939) and *History of the Afro-American Group of the Episcopal Church* (1922); Benjamin Brawley's *Early Negro American Writers* (1935); and Sidney and Emma Nogrady Kaplan's *The Black Presence in the Era of the American Revolution* (1973).

A Thanksgiving Sermon

Preached January 1, 1808

These words, my brethren, contain a short account of some of the circumstances which preceded the deliverance of the children of Israel from their captivity and bondage in Egypt.

They mention, in the first place, their *affliction.* This consisted in their privation of liberty: they were slaves to the kings of Egypt, in common with their other subjects; and they were slaves to their fellow slaves. They were compelled to work in the open air, in one of the hottest climates in the world; and, probably, without a covering from the burning rays of the sun. Their work was of a laborious kind: it consisted of making bricks, and travelling, perhaps to a great distance, for the straw, or stubble, that was a component part of them. Their work was dealt out to them in tasks, and performed under the eye of vigilant and rigorous masters, who constantly upbraided them with idleness. The least deficiency in the product of their labour, was punished by beating. Nor was this all. Their food was of the cheapest kind, and contained but little nourishment: it consisted only of leeks and onions, which grew almost spontaneously in the land of Egypt. Painful and distressing as these sufferings were, they constituted the smallest part of their misery. While the fields resounded with their cries in the day, their huts and hamlets were vocal at night with their lamentations over their sons; who were dragged from the arms of their mothers, and put to death by drowning, in order to prevent such an increase in their population as to endanger the safety of the state by an insurrection. In this condition, thus degraded and oppressed, they passed nearly four hundred years. Ah! who can conceive of the measure of their sufferings, during that time? What tongue, or pen, can compute the number of their sorrows? To them no morning or evening sun ever disclosed a single charm: to them, the beauties of spring, and the plenty of autumn had no attractions: even domestick endearments were scarcely known to them: all was misery; all was grief; all was despair.

Our text mentions, in the second place, that, in this situation, they were not forgotten by the God of their fathers, and the Father of the human race. Though, for wise reasons, he delayed to appear in their behalf for several hundred years, yet he was not indifferent to their sufferings. Our text tells us that he saw their affliction, and heard their cry: his eye and his ear were constantly open to their complaint: every tear they shed was preserved, and every groan they uttered was recorded, in order to testify, at a future day, against the authors of their oppressions. But our text goes further: it describes the Judge of the world to be so much moved, with what he saw and what he heard, that he rises from his throne—not to issue a command to the armies of angels that surrounded him to fly to the relief of his suffering children—but to come down from heaven in his own person, in order to deliver them out of the hands of the Egyptians. Glory to God for this precious record of his power and goodness: let all the nations of the earth praise him. *Clouds and darkness are round about him,* but *righteousness and judgment are the habitation of his throne. O sing unto the Lord a new song, for he hath done marvellous things: his right hand and his holy arm hath gotten him the victory. He hath remembered his mercy and truth toward the house of Israel, and all the ends of the earth shall see the salvation of God.*

The history of the world shows us that the deliverance of the children of Israel from their bondage is not the only instance in which it has pleased God to appear in behalf of oppressed and distressed nations, as the deliverer of the innocent, and of those who call upon his name. He is as unchangeable in his nature and character as he is in his wisdom and power. The great and blessed event, which we have this day met to celebrate, is a striking proof that the God of heaven and earth is *the same, yesterday, and today, and forever.* Yes, my brethren, the nations from which most of us have descended, and the country in which some of us were born, have been visited by the tender mercy of the Common Father of the human race. He has seen the affliction of our countrymen, with an eye of pity. He has seen the wicked arts, by which wars have been fomented among the different tribes of the Africans, in order to procure captives, for the purpose of selling them for slaves. He has seen ships fitted out from different ports in Europe and America, and freighted with trinkets to be exchanged for the bodies and souls of men. He has seen the anguish which has taken place when parents have been torn from their children, and children from their parents, and conveyed, with their hands and feet bound in fetters, on board of ships prepared to receive them. He has seen them thrust in crowds into the holds of those ships, where many of them have perished from the want of air. He has seen such of them as have escaped from that noxious place of confinement, leap into the ocean, with a faint hope of swimming back to their native shore, or a determination to seek an early retreat from their impending misery, in a watery grave. He has seen them exposed for sale, like horses and cattle, upon the wharves; or, like bales of goods, in warehouses of West India and American sea ports. He has seen the pangs of separation between members of the same family. He has seen them driven into the sugar, the rice, and the tobacco fields, and compelled to work—in spite of the habits of ease which they derived from the natural fertility of their own country—in the open air, beneath a burning sun, with scarcely as much clothing upon them as modesty required. He has seen them faint beneath the pressure of their labours. He has seen them return to their smoky huts in the evening, with nothing to satisfy their hunger but a scanty allowance of roots; and these, cultivated for themselves, on that day only, which God ordained as a day of rest for man and beast. He has seen the neglect with which their masters have treated their immortal souls; not only in withholding religious instruction from them, but, in some instances, depriving them of access to the means of obtaining it. He has seen all the different modes of torture, by means of the whip, the screw, the pincers, and the red-hot iron, which have been exercised upon their bodies, by inhuman overseers: overseers, did I say? Yes: but not by these only. Our God has seen masters and mistresses, educated in fashionable life, sometimes take the instruments of torture into their own hands, and, deaf to the cries and shrieks of their agonizing slaves, exceed even their overseers in cruelty. Inhuman wretches! though You have been deaf to their cries and shrieks, they have been heard in Heaven. The ears of Jehovah have been constantly open to them: He has heard the prayers that have ascended from the hearts of his people; and he has, as in the case of his ancient and chosen people the Jews, *come down to deliver* our suffering countrymen from the hands of their oppressors. He *came down* into the United States, when they declared, in the constitution which they framed in 1788, that the trade in our African fellowmen should cease in the year 1808: He *came down* into the British Parliament, when they passed a law to put an end to the same iniquitous trade in May, 1807: He *came down* into the Congress of the United States, the last winter, when they passed a similar law, the operation of which commences on this happy day. Dear land of our ancestors! thou shalt no more be stained with the blood of thy children, shed by British and American hands: the ocean shall no more afford a refuge to their bodies, from impending slavery: nor shall the shores of the British West India islands, and of the United States, any more witness the anguish of families, parted for ever by a publick sale. For this signal interposition of the God of mercies, in behalf of our brethren, it becomes us this day to offer up our united thanks. Let the song of angels, which was first heard in the air at the birth of our Saviour, be heard this day in our assembly: *Glory to God in the highest,* for these first fruits of *peace upon earth, and good-will to man:* O! let us *give thanks unto the Lord:* let us *call upon his name,* and *make known his deeds among the people.* Let us *sing psalms unto him and talk of all his wondrous works.*

Having enumerated the mercies of God to our nation, it becomes us to ask, What shall we render unto the Lord for them? Sacrifices and burnt offerings are no longer pleasing to him: the pomp of public worship, and the ceremonies of a festive day, will find no acceptance with him, unless they are accompanied with actions that correspond with them. The duties which are inculcated upon us, by the event we are now celebrating, divide themselves into five heads.

In the first place, Let not our expressions of gratitude to God for his late goodness and mercy to our countrymen, be confined to this day, nor to this house: let us carry grateful hearts with us to our places of abode, and to our daily occupations; and let praise and thanksgivings ascend daily to the throne of grace, in our families, and in our closets, for what God has done for our African brethren. Let us not forget to praise him for his mercies to such of our colour as are inhabitants of this country; particularly, for disposing the hearts of the rulers of many of the states to pass laws for the abolition of slavery; for the number and zeal of the friends he has raised up to plead our cause; and for the privileges we enjoy, of worshiping God agreeably to our consciences, in churches of our own. This comely building, erected chiefly by the generosity of our friends, is a monument of God's goodness to us, and calls for our gratitude with all the other blessings that have been mentioned.

Secondly, Let us unite, with our thanksgiving, prayer to Almighty God, for the completion of his begun goodness to our brethren in Africa. Let us beseech him to extend to all the nations in Europe, the same humane and just spirit towards them, which he has imparted to the British and American nations. Let us, further, implore the influence of his divine and holy Spirit, to dispose the hearts of our legislatures to pass laws, to ameliorate the condition of our brethren who are still in bondage; also, to dispose their masters to treat them with kindness and humanity; and, above all things, to favour them with the means of acquiring such parts of human knowledge, as will enable them to read the holy scriptures, and understand the doctrines of the Christian religion, whereby they may become, even while they are the slaves of men, the freemen of the Lord.

Thirdly, Let us conduct ourselves in such a manner as to furnish no cause of regret to the deliverers of our nation, for their kindness to us. Let us constantly *remember the rock whence we were hewn, and the pit whence we were digged. Pride was not made for man,* in any situation; and, still less, for persons who have recently emerged from bondage. The Jews, after they entered the promised land, were commanded, when they offered sacrifices to the Lord, never to forget their humble origin; and hence, part of the worship that accompanied their sacrifices consisted in acknowledging, *that a Syrian, ready to perish, was their father:* in like manner, it becomes us, publickly and privately, to acknowledge, that an African slave, ready to perish, was our father or our grandfather. Let our conduct be regulated by the precepts of the gospel; let us be sober-minded, humble, peaceable, temperate in our meats and drinks, frugal in our apparel and in the furniture of our houses, industrious in our occupations, just in all our dealings, and ever ready to honour all men. Let us teach our children the rudiments of the English language, in order to enable them to acquire a knowledge of useful trades; and, above all things, let us instruct them in the principles of the gospel of Jesus Christ, whereby they may become *wise unto salvation.* It has always been a mystery, why the impartial Father of the human race should have permitted the transportation of so many millions of our fellow creatures to this country, to endure all the miseries of slavery. Perhaps his design was that a knowledge of the gospel might be acquired by some of their descendants, in order that they might become qualified to be the messengers of it, to the land of their fathers. Let this thought animate us, when we are teaching our children to love and adore the name of our Redeemer. Who knows but that a Joseph may rise up among them, who shall be the instrument of feeding the African nations with the bread of life, and of saving them, not from earthly bondage, but from the more galling yoke of sin and Satan.

Fourthly, Let us be grateful to our benefactors, who, by enlightening the minds of the rulers of the earth, by means of their publications and remonstrances against the trade in our countrymen, have produced the great event we are this day celebrating. Abolition societies and individuals have equal claims to our gratitude. It would be difficult to mention the names of any of our benefactors, without offending many whom we do not know. Some of them are gone to heaven, to receive the reward of their labours of love towards us; and the kindness and benevolence of the survivors, we hope, are recorded in the book of life, to be mentioned with honour when our Lord shall come to reward his faithful servants before an assembled world.

Fifthly, and lastly, Let the first of January, the day of the abolition of the slave trade in our country, be set apart in every year, as a day of publick thanksgiving for that mercy. Let the history of the sufferings of our brethren, and of their deliverance, descend by this means to our children to the remotest generations; and when they shall ask, in time to come, saying, What mean the lessons, the psalms, the prayers and the praises in the worship of this day? let us answer them, by saying, the Lord, on the day of which this is the anniversary, abolished the trade which dragged your fathers from their native country, and sold them as bondmen in the United States of America.

Oh thou God of all the nations upon the earth! we thank thee, that thou art *no respecter of persons,* and that thou *hast made of one blood all nations of men.* We thank thee, that thou hast appeared, in the fullness of time, in behalf of the nation from which most of the worshipping people, now before thee, are descended. We thank thee, that the sun of righteousness has at last shed his morning beams upon them. *Rend* thy *heavens,* O Lord, and *come down* upon the earth; and grant that *the mountains,* which now obstruct the perfect day of thy goodness and mercy towards them, may *flow down at thy presence.* Send thy gospel, we beseech thee, among them. May the nations, which now *sit in darkness,* behold and rejoice in its *light.* May *Ethiopia soon stretch out her hands unto thee,* and lay hold of the gracious promise of thy everlasting covenant. Destroy, we beseech thee, all the false religions which now prevail among them; and grant, that they may soon *cast* their *idols, to the moles and the bats* of the wilderness. O, hasten that glorious time, when the knowledge of the gospel of Jesus Christ, shall cover the *earth, as the waters cover the sea;* when *the wolf shall dwell with the lamb, and the leopard shall lie down with the kid, and the calf and the young lion and the fatling together, and a little child shall lead them;* and, *when, instead of the thorn, shall come up the fir tree, and, instead of the brier, shall come up the myrtle tree: and it shall be to the Lord for a name and for an everlasting sign that shall not be cut off.* We pray, O God, for all our friends and benefactors in Great Britain, as well as in the United States: reward them, we beseech thee, with blessings upon earth, and prepare them to enjoy the fruits of their kindness to us, in thy everlasting kingdom in heaven; and dispose us, who are assembled in thy presence, to be always thankful for thy mercies, and to act as becomes a people who owe so much to thy goodness. We implore thy blessing, O God, upon the President, and all who are in authority in the United States. Direct them by thy wisdom, in all their deliberations, and O save thy people from the calamities of war. Give peace in our day, we beseech thee, O thou *God of peace!* and grant, that this highly favoured country may continue to afford a safe and peaceful retreat from the calamities of war and slavery, for ages yet to come. We implore all these blessings and mercies, only in the name of thy beloved Son, Jesus Christ, our Lord. And now, O Lord, we desire, with angels and arch-angels, and all the company of heaven, ever more to praise thee, saying, *Holy, holy, holy, Lord God Almighty: the whole earth is full of thy glory.* Amen.

JOHN MARRANT
(1755–1790?)

Born of free parents in New York City on June 15, 1755, John Marrant—like Briton Hammon and Olaudah Equiano—writes of exotic and exciting adventures, extensive national and international travels, boundless courage, and Christian conversion in his published *Narrative.* While several of his writings are available today, very few confirmable facts outside of his own recordings have been uncovered about Marrant's life. However, the courageous Marrant left two books and several sermons that tell of his many evangelistic trips among Native Americans in the colonies and in Canada, among colonists both black and white, and among scores of dignitaries in England and the British Isles. Many among his contemporaries in Episcopal, Methodist, and Masonic circles claim that Marrant was "one of the first, if not the first, Negro minister of the Gospel in North America" and that he was a fiery, spellbinding preacher.

From his earliest years, Marrant had a bent toward music and group leadership. After his father's death, when he was four years old, Marrant's mother took him to St. Augustine, Florida, where he was sent to school "and taught to read and spell." Eighteen months later, the family relocated to a city that he identifies in his *Narrative* as "Charleston." While William Robinson believes that the move was to a suburb of Boston, no critic as been able to ascertain if this town was located in the colonies of Massachusetts, Florida, or South Carolina—all of which had urban areas by the name of Charleston or Charlestown. However, because Marrant spent many of his adult years in the colonies in the Charleston location outside of Boston, one must assume that William Robinson was correct.

While in Charleston, the young lad learned to play the violin and the French horn. Like other African American writers, Marrant was deeply stirred to Christian conversion when he heard the Rev. George Whitefield, an extremely popular British evangelist, preach a sermon in Charleston on the biblical text, "Prepare to meet thy God, O Israel." He had gone to the camp meeting with a group of young men who planned to disrupt the service. Marrant's assignment was to play his music as loud as possible to create a distraction. Instead, Marrant fell into a trance; several hours later, he received personal counseling from Whitefield. According to his *Narrative,* the young man from that time forward became quite sensitive and compassionate toward all human beings, but he seemed to be especially drawn to the Native American populations in both Canada and the United States.

Because his family ridiculed his new beliefs, the young Marrant ran away from home and wandered about in the woods until he met a Native American who befriended him. Marrant learned a particular Native American language and, in a few months, they went to a Cherokee village. There Marrant was jailed, tortured, and prepared for execution. However, when the chief and his daughter heard Marrant pray in their native language, they were both converted to Christianity and John was set free. He lived quite well among that tribe for nearly three months. Marrant then planned his first missionary journey among the Creeks, Catawards, and Howsaws, but he was not as successful. At the end of six months, he returned to give his good-byes to the Cherokees and headed back to Charleston.

Marrant writes, "My dress was purely in the Indian stile; the skins of wild beasts composed my garments, my head was set out in the savage manner, with a long pendant down my back, a sash around my middle, without breeches, and a tomahawk by my side." Thus, when the faithful evangelist returned to his hometown no one recognized him, not even his own family. After shocking them into reality, he was welcomed home, where he stayed for several months until he was drafted into the British military.

Because of his musical abilities, in 1781, when he was twenty-five years old, Marrant was pressed into serving the Royal Navy aboard the *Scorpion* as the ship's musician. However, he was still called on to serve as a professional soldier. Participating in several battles and twice washed overboard and thrown back onto the ship's deck, Marrant was so badly wounded in action that he was deemed no longer useful for the King's service. He was sent to the hospital in Plymouth, England, where he was discharged from military service. He lived in London for four years, from 1781 to 1784, where he worked for a cotton merchant.

Eventually, as Marrant writes in his *Narrative,* he reached a capstone of his life when he was *officially* recognized as a preacher and ordained in 1785 into the ministry in the Countess of Huntingdon's Dissident Methodist Connection in England. Again, however, scholars are in dispute. It has been assumed that Absalom Jones was the first African American to be ordained to preach the gospel. However, if the dates given in Marrant's account are accurate, his ordination in 1785 would mean that he was the first American ordained to be a Christian minister in the Western world. That same year, the Countess published his *Narrative of the Lord's Wonderful Dealings With John Marrant, a Black* in London. This became a very popular publication that would be reprinted some nineteen times in the next forty years. A very wealthy woman, Huntingdon was an ardent abolitionist who worked tirelessly with William Wilberforce, John and Charles Wesley, and others who were part of a small Christian circle dedicated to ending British involvement in the slave trade. She was also the patron who supported the publication of Phillis Wheatley's volume of poetry.

The Countess convinced Marrant, following his ordination, to go to Nova Scotia as a missionary. Here and in other parts of Canada, he continued his Christian ministry of evangelization among the Native American population until he returned to the United States in 1789. His *Journal of John Marrant,* which was printed in London in 1790, relates further perilous adventures in Canada and also gives some insight into great gifts of prophetic presentation. In fact, his sermons were apparently so powerful that a group of thugs in Boston planned an attack against him: "I was preaching at the west end of town to a large concourse of people, there were more than forty that had made an agreement to put an end to my evening preaching . . . they came prepared that evening with swords and clubs. . . ." However, Marrant managed to escape.

During his return trip home, Marrant caught the eye of Prince Hall, founder of the Black Masonic Lodges. Hall asked him to accept a position as chaplain of the African Lodge of the Honorable Society of Free and Accepted Masons of Boston. Delivering a sermon in celebration of St. John the Divine before his Masonic audience, Marrant delivered his most fiery and eloquent sermon presently in print. His subject was on the evils of slaveholding racism:

> And is man such a noble creature and made to convene with his fellow men that are of his own order, to maintain mutual love and society, and to serve God in consort with each other? then what can those God-provoking wretches think, who despise their fellow men, as tho' they were not of the same species with themselves, and would if in their power deprive them of the blessings and comforts of this life, which God in his bountiful goodness, hath freely given to all his creatures to improve and enjoy? Surely such monsters never came out of the hand of God.

Like all eighteenth-century black writers, Marrant also encouraged his African American audience to take pride in their African heritage: "Ancient history will produce some of the Africans who were truly good, wise, and learned men, and as eloquent as any other nation. . . ."

A triumph in the United States, where he was well known in both black and white circles, Marrant still felt the sting of racism in this country to be so bitter that he longed to return to England, which, at that time, seemed more supportive of the cause of African freedom. Despite the pleas of Prince Hall, Absalom Jones, Richard Allen, and others, the thirty-five-year-old Marrant boarded a ship to return to England on February 5, 1790. Although he was still a young man, the years in the cold of Nova Scotia, sacrificial living in the backwoods of colonial America, and his many harrowing travels and adventures finally took their toll. He died less than a year later and received a very honorable burial cemetary on Church Street in Islington, a small town outside London. As is the case with most writers of this period, literary history awaits further details about the fascinating life and works of this remarkable African American spokesman of the eighteenth century.

❖❖❖

The full titles of Marrant's published works are *A Narrative of the Lord's Wonderful Dealing with John Marrant, a Black . . . Taken Down By His Own Relation, Arranged and Corrected, and Published by the Reverend Mr. Aldridge, London, 1785; Journal of John Marrant, London, 1789;* and *A Sermon Preached on the 24th day of June 1789, Being the Festival of St. John the Baptist, Boston, 1789.* As in the case of several of the other early African American authors, there are very few sources on Marrant and his writings. His life and works are briefly discussed in Sidney and Emma Nogrady Kaplan's *The Black Presence in the Era of the American Revolution*, rev. ed. (1989) and William H. Robinson's *Early Black American Prose* (1971). In his *Introduction to Great Slave Narratives* (1969), Arna Bontemps offers a short but insightful overview of Marrant's *Narrative.* See also Lindsay Patterson's *Introduction of Black Literature in America, 1746–Present* (1978) and the *Introduction to Black Atlantic Writers of the Eighteenth Century* by Adam Potkay and Sandra Burr (1995). Potkay and Burr's *Collection of Writings* is the source of the following sermon by Marrant.

A Sermon Preached on the 24th Day of June 1789,

Being the Festival of Saint John the Baptist, at the Request of the Right Worshipful the Grand Master Prince Hall, and the Rest of the Brethren of the African Lodge of the Honorable Society of Free and Accepted Masons in Boston

A SERMON

Romans xii. 10.

BE KINDLY AFFECTIONED ONE TO ANOTHER, WITH BROTHERLY LOVE, IN HONOUR PREFERRING ONE ANOTHER.[1]

In this chapter, from whence my text is taken, we find the Apostle Paul labouring with the Romans to press on them the great duties of Brotherly Love.

By an entire submission and conformity to the will of God, whereby are given to us exceeding great and precious promises, that by these we might be made partakers of the divine nature, having escaped the corruption that is in the world through lust—That being all members of the body of Christ with the Church, we ought to apply the gifts we have received to the advantage of our brethren, those of us especially who are called to any office in the church, by discharging it with zeal and integrity and benevolence, which is the most important duty, and comprehends all the rest, and particularly the following—which the apostle here sets down—which are to love one another sincerely, to be ready to all good offices—to sympathize in the good or evil that befals our brethren, to comfort and assist those that are in affliction, and to live together in a spirit of humility, peace and unity. Benevolence does yet further oblige christians to love and bless those who hate them and injure them, to endeavour to have peace with all men, to abstain from revenge, and to render them good for evil; these are the most essential duties of the religion we profess; and we deserve the name of christians no further than we sincerely practise them to the glory of God and the good of our own souls and bodies, and the good of all mankind.

But first, my Brethren, let us learn to pray to God through our Lord Jesus Christ for understanding, that we may know ourselves; for without this we can never be fit for the society of man, we must learn to guide ourselves before we can guide others, and when we have done this we shall understand the apostle Romans xii. 16. "Be not wise in your own conceits," for when we get

[1]Marrant's two opening paragraphs are saturated with allusions to and quotations from Romans 12.

wise in ourselves we are then too wise for God, and consequently not fit for the society of man—I mean the christian part of mankind—Let all my brethren Masons consider what they are called to—May God grant you an humble heart to fear God and love his commandments; then and only then you will in sincerity love your brethren: And you will be enabled, as in the words of my text, to be kindly affectioned one to another, with brotherly love in honour preferring one another. Therefore, with the apostle Paul, I beseech you therefore brethren, by the mercies of God, that ye present your bodies a living sacrifice, holy, acceptable unto God, which is your reasonable service—let love be without dissimulation, abhor that which is evil, cleave to that which is good. These and many other duties are required of us as christians, every one of which are like so many links of a chain, which when joined together make one complete member of Christ; this we profess to believe as Christians and as Masons.——I shall stop here with the introduction, which brings me to the points I shall endeavour to prove.——

First, the anciency of Masonry, that being done, will endeavour to prove all other titles we have a just right as Masons to claim—namely, honourable, free and accepted: To do this I must have recourse to the creation of this our world—After the Grand Architect of the Universe[2] had framed the heavens for beauty and delight for the beings he was then about to make, he then called the earth to appear out of darkness, saying, let there be light, and it was so; he also set the sun, moon and stars in the firmament of heaven, for the delight of his creatures—he then created the fishes of the sea, the fowls of the air, then the beasts of the earth after their various kinds, and God blessed them.[3]

Thus all things were in their order prepared for the most excellent accomplished piece of the visible creation, Man.—The forming of this most excellent creature Man, was the close of the creation, so it was peculiar to him to have a solemn consultation and decree about his making, and God said, let us make Man.[4]—Seneca says, that man is not a work huddled over in haste, and done without fore-thinking and great consideration, for man is the greatest and most stupendous work of God.[5]—Man hath not only a body in common with all inferior animals, but into his body was infused a soul of a far more noble nature and make—a rational principle to act according to the designs of his creation; that is, to contemplate the works of God, to admire his perfections, to worship him, to live as becomes one who received his excellent being from him, to converse with his fellow creatures that are of his own order, to maintain mutual love and society, and to serve God in consort. Man is a wonderful creature, and not unde[ser]vedly said to be a little world, a world within himself, and containing whatever is found in the Creator.[6]—In him is the spiritual and material nature of God, the reasonableness of Angels, the sensitive power of brutes, the vegetative life of plants, and the virtue of all the elements he holds converse with in both worlds.—Thus man is crowned with glory and honour, he is the most remarkable workmanship of God. And is man such a noble creature and made to converse with his fellow men that are of his own order, to maintain mutual love and society, and to serve God in consort with each other?—then what can these God-provoking wretches think, who despise their fellow men, as tho' they were not of the same species with

---

[2]In Masonic lore, the Grand Architect of the Universe is God, the creator of Freemasonry. As Grand Master Henry Price of Boston's St. John's Grand Lodge said on November 23, 1768, God "incorporate[s] our Hearts with Unity, Love, Strength, and Wisdom, to Contrive, Conduct and Support the establishing in the three Grand Principles, Brotherly Love, Relief and Truth." See *The Proceedings of the Grand Lodge of Massachusetts Free and Accepted Masons 1733–1792* (Boston: Grand Lodge of Massachusetts, 1895), p. 153.

[3]See Genesis 1:3, 16–17, 20–25.

[4]Genesis 1:26.

[5]Seneca "the Younger" or "the Philosopher" (ca. 4 B.C.–A.D. 65) wrote *Epistulae Morales,* which was approved and made use of by early Christian writers. St. Jerome and others believed that Seneca had corresponded with St. Paul.

[6]The concept of man as a world within himself, reflective of God's outer cosmos, is a philosophical commonplace. Compare the first two lines of John Donne's *Holy Sonnet 5:* "I am a little world made cunningly/Of elements, and an angelic sprite."

themselves, and would if in their power deprive them of the blessings and comforts of this life, which God in his bountiful goodness, hath freely given to all his creatures to improve and enjoy? Surely such monsters never came out of the hand of God in such a forlorn condition.— —Which brings me to consider the fall of man; and the Lord God took the man and put him into the garden of Eden, to dress it and to keep it, and freely to eat of every tree of the garden; here was his delightful employ and bountiful wages, and but one tree out of all that vast number he was forbidden to eat of. Concerning this garden, there have been different opinions about it by the learned, where it was, but the most of them agree that the four rivers parted or divided the four quarters of the world. The first was Pison, that was it which compasseth the land of Havilah;[7] this river Pison is called by some the Phasis, or Phasi Tigris, it runs (they say) by that Havilah whither the Amalekites fled, see I Sam. xv. 7. and divides it from the country of Susianna, and at last falls into the Persian Gulf, saith Galtruchius[8] and others; but from the opinions of christian writers, who hold, that Havilah is India, and Pison the river Ganges. This was first asserted by Josephus, and from him Eustubius, Jerom,[9] and most of the fathers received it, and not without good reason; for Moses here adds, as a mark to know the place by, that there is gold, and the gold of that land is good; now it is confessed by all, that India is the most noted for gold, and of the best sort. It is added again, a note whereby to discover that place, that there is bdellium and the onyx stone—and India is famous for precious stones and pearls.—The name of the second river is Gihon, the same in it which compasseth the whole land of Ethiopia (or Cush as it is in the original) there is reason to believe that this Gihon is the river of Nile, as the forenamed Josephus and most of the ancient writers of the church hold, and by the help of the river Nile, Paradise did as it were border upon Egypt, which is the principal part of the African Ethiopia, which the ancient writers hold is meant there[.] The name of the third river is Hiddekel, that is it which goeth toward the east of Assyria, ver. 14. That it was a river belonging to Babylon is clear from Dan. x. 4; this is concluded to be the river Tygris, which divides Mesopotamia from Assyria, and goeth along with Euphrates, this being the great middle channel that ran through Edom or Babylon, and may be thought to take its name from its fructifying quality.[10] These are the four grand land marks which the all-wise and gracious God was pleased to draw as the bounds and habitation of all nations which he was about to settle in this world; if so, what nation or people dare, without highly displeasing and provoking that God to pour down his judgments upon them.— I say dare to despise or tyrannize over their lives or liberties, or incroach on their lands, or to inslave their bodies? God hath and ever will visit such a nation or people as this.—Envy and pride are the leading lines to all the miseries that mankind have suffered from the beginning of the world to this present day. What was it but these that turned the devil out of heaven into a hell of misery, but envy and pride?—Was it not the same spirit that moved him to tempt our first parents to sin against so holy and just a God, who had but just (if I may use the expression) turned his back from crowning Adam

[7]Genesis 2:15–17, 10–11.

[8]Petrus Galtruchius is the Latin name of Pierre Gautruche (1602–1681), author of *The Poetical History: Being a Compleat Collection of All the Stories Necessary for a Perfect Understanding of the Greek and Latin Poets and Other Ancient Authors* (pre-1669), a book of ancient mythology first translated into English from the French in 1671. Marrant may be referring to information in this volume or, alternatively, in Gautruche's *L'Histoire Sainte, avec l'explication controversée de la religion* (pre-1668), a history of biblical events that was reprinted throughout the late seventeenth and early eighteenth centuries.

[9]Flavius Josephus was a Jewish historian (ca. A.D. 37–after A.D. 93). Eusebius was a Greek Christian writer and bishop in Palestine (ca. A.D. 260–ca. A.D. 340). Jerome was a Latin father of the Church (ca. A.D. 347–420).

[10]Marrant refers to Genesis 2:11–14. Verse 14 identifies Hiddekel (the Tigris) and the Euphrates as the third and fourth rivers originating in the Garden of Eden. "Euphrates" is, according to William Smith's *Bible Dictionary* (New York: Doubleday n.d.), "probably a word of Aryan origin, signifying 'the good and abounding river'": thus, Marrant relates the river's name to "its fructifying quality."

with honour and glory?—But envy at his prosperity hath taken the crown of glory from his head, and hath made us his posterity miserable.—What was it but this that made Cain murder his brother, whence is it but from these that our modern Cains call us Africans the sons of Cain?[11] (We admit it if you please) and we will find from him and his sons Masonry began, after the fall of his father. Altho' Adam, when placed in the garden, God would not suffer him to be idle and unemployed in that happy state of innocence, but set him to dress and to keep that choice piece of earth; here he was to employ his mind as well as exercise his body; here he was to contemplate and study God's work; here he was to enjoy God, himself and the whole world, to submit himself wholly to his divine conduct, to conform all his actions to the will of his Maker; but by his sudden fall he lost that good will that he owed to his God, and for some time lost the study of God's works; but no doubt he afterwards taught his sons the art of Masonry; for how else could Cain after so much trouble and perplexity have time to study the art of building a city, as he did on the east of Eden, Gen. iv. 17. and without doubt he teached his sons the art, ver. 20,21.—

But to return, bad as Cain was, yet God took not from him his faculty of studying architecture, arts and sciences—his sons also were endued with the same spirit, and in some convenient place no doubt they met and communed with each other for instruction. It seems that the allwise God put this into the hearts of Cain's family thus to employ themselves, to divert their minds from musing on their father's murder[12] and the woful curse God has pronounced on him, as we don't find any more of Cain's complaints after this.

Similar to this we have in the 6 Gen. 12 & 13, that God saw that all men had corrupted their way, and that their hearts were only evil continually; and 14, 15, 16 verses, the great Architect of the universe gives Noah a compleat plan of the ark and sets him to work, and his sons as assistants, like deputy and two grand wardens. One thing is well known, our enemies themselves being judges, that in whatsoever nation or kingdom in the whole world where Masonry abounds most, there hath been and still are the most peaceable subjects, cheerfully conforming to the laws of that country in which they reside, always willing to submit to their magistrates and rulers, and where Masonry most abounds, arts and sciences, whether mechanical or liberal, all of them have a mighty tendency to the delight and benefit of mankind; therefore we need not question but the allwise God by putting this into our hearts intended, as another end of our creation, that we should not only live happily ourselves, but be likewise mutually assisting to each other. Again, it is not only good and beneficial in a time of peace, in a nation or kingdom, but in a time of war, for that brotherly love that cements us together by the bonds of friendship, no wars or tumults can separate; for in the heat of war if a brother sees another in distress he will relieve him some way or other, and kindly receive him as a brother, preferring him before all others, according to the Apostle's exhortation in my text, as also a similar instance you have I Kings, x. from 31st to 38th verse,[13] where you find Benhadad in great distress, having lost a numerous army in two battles, after his great boasting, and he himself forced to hide himself in a chamber, and sends a message to Ahab king of Israel to request only his life as a captive; but behold the brotherly love of a Mason! no sooner was the message delivered, but he cries out in a rapture—is he alive—he is my brother! Every Mason knows that they were both of the craft, and also the messengers.[14] Thus far may suffice

[11]See p. 12 of The Introduction to Adam Potkay and Sandra Burr's *Black Atlantic Writers of the Eighteenth Century.* New York, St. Martin's Press, 1995.

[12]That is, their father's slaying of Abel.

[13]Either Marrant or the printer makes an error here; see instead 1 Kings 20:29–34.

[14]See 1 Kings 20:32–34. In verse 34, Benhadad, king of Syria, and Ahab, king of Israel, make a peace treaty, which Benhadad seals by saying, "thou shall make streets for thee in Damascus" (the Syrian capital); it is presumably this line that Marrant interprets in a Masonic sense.

for the anciency of this grand art; as for the honour of it—it is a society which God himself has been pleased to honour ever since he breathed into Adam the breath of life,[15] and hath from generation to generation inspired men with wisdom, and planned out and given directions how they should build, and with what materials. And first, Noah in building the ark wherein he was saved, while God in his justice was pleased to destroy the unbelieving world of mankind. The first thing Noah did upon his landing was to build an altar to offer sacrifice to that great God which had delivered him out of so great a deluge; God accepted the sacrifice and blessed him, and as they journeyed from the east towards the west, they found a plain in the land of Shinar and dwelt there, and his sons.[16]

Nimrod the son of Cush, the son of Ham, first founded the Babylonian monarchy, and kept possession of the plains, and founded the first great empire at Babylon, and became grand master of all Masons, he built many splendid cities in Shinar,[17] and under him flourished those learned Mathematicians, whose successors were styled in the book of Daniel, Magi, or wise men, for their superior knowledge. The migration from Shinar commenced fifty three years after they began to build the tower,[18] and one hundred and fifty four years after the flood, and they went off at various times and travelled east, west, north and south, with their mighty skill, and found the use of it in settling their colonies; and from Shinar the arts were carried to distant parts of the earth, notwithstanding the confusion of languages, which gave rise to Masons faculty and universal practice of conversing without speaking, and of knowing each other by signs and tokens; they settled the dispersion in case any of them should meet in distant parts of the world who had been before in Shinar. Thus the edge was again planted and replenished with Masons the second son of Ham carried into Egypt; there he built the city of Heliopolis—Thebes with an hundred gates[19]—they built also the statue of Sphynx, whose head was 120 feet round, being reckoned the first or earliest of the seven wonders of arts. Shem the second son of Noah remained at Ur of the Chaldees in Shinar, with his father and his great grandson Heber,[20] where they lived in private and died in peace: But Shem's offspring travelled into the south and east of Asia, and their offspring propagated the science and the art as far as China and Japan.

While Noah, Shem and Heber diverted themselves at Ur in mathematical studies, teaching Peleg the father of Rehu, of Sereg, Nachor, and Terah, father of Abram, a learned race of mathematicians and geometricians; thus Abram, born two years after the death of Noah, had learned well the science and the art before the God of glory called him to travel from Ur of the Chaldees, but a famine soon forced him down to Egypt;[21] the descendants of Abram sojourned in Egypt, as shepherds still lived in tents, practised very little of the art of architecture till about eighty years before their Exodus, when by the overruling hand of providence they were trained up to the building with stone and brick, in order to make them expert Masons before they possessed the promised land;[22] after Abram left Charran 430 years, Moses marched out of Egypt at the head of 600,000 Hebrews, males, for whose sakes God divided the red sea

[15]Genesis 2:7.

[16]For the entire story of Noah and the Ark, see Genesis 6:1–9:17. In Genesis 11:2 the journey to Shinar is made, not by Noah and his immediate family, but by the peoples that spring from Noah's three sons.

[17]For Nimrod, see Genesis 10:8–10.

[18]Marrant is alluding to the Tower of Babel; see Genesis 11:1–9.

[19]The second son of Ham is Mizraim (Genesis 10:6), which is also the usual name of Egypt in the Old Testament. The ancient city of Thebes in Upper Egypt became the religious and political capital of Egypt during the twelfth dynasty (ca. 2000 B.C.). Homer calls the city "hundred-gated" (*hecatompylos*) in the ninth book of the *Iliad* (verse 381). Heliopolis (the city of the sun) is the Greek name for the Egyptian city of On, located in the Nile Delta region of northern Egypt.

[20]Marrant means Eber, the great-grandson of Shem (Genesis 10:24).

[21]See Genesis 11:16–26, 31, 12:10.

[22]Here Marrant alludes to the enslavement of the Jews, whom the Egyptians forced to make bricks and to build cities. See Exodus 1:8–14, 5:4–19.

to let them pass through Arabia to Canaan. God was pleased to inspire their grand master Moses, and Joshua his deputy, with wisdom of heart,[23] so the next year they raised the curious tabernacle or tent; God having called Moses up into the mount and gave him an exact pattern of it, and charges him to make it exactly to that pattern,[24] and withal gave him the two tablets of stone; these he broke at the foot of the mount; God gave him orders to hew two more himself, after the likeness of the former. God did not only inspire Moses with wisdom to undertake the oversight of the great work, but he also inspired Bezaleel with knowledge to do all manner of cunning workmanship for it.[25]—Having entered upon the jewish dispensation, I must beg leave still to take a little notice of the Gentile nations, for we have but these two nations now to speak upon, namely, the Gentiles and the Jews, till I come to the Christian æra.

The Canaanites, Phenicians and Sidonians, were very expert in the sacred architecture of stone, who being a people of a happy genius and frame of mind, made many great discoveries and improvements of the sciences as well as in point of learning. The glass of Sidon, the purple of Tyre, and the exceeding fine linnen they wove, were the product of their own country and their own invention; and for their extraordinary skill in working of metals, in hewing of timber and stone; in a word, for their perfect knowledge of what was solid in architecture, it need but be remembered that they had in erecting and decorating of the temple at Jerusalem, than which nothing can more redound to their honour, or give a clearer idea of what this one building must have been.—Their fame was such for their just taste, design, and ingenious inventions, that whatever was elegant, great or pleasing, was distinguished by way of excellence with the epithet of Sidonian.[26]—The famous temple of Jupiter Hammon, in Libian Africa, was erected, that stood till demolished by the first Christians in those parts;[27] but I must pass over many other cities and temples built by the Gentiles.

God having inspired Solomon with wisdom and understanding, he as grand master and undertaker, under God the great architect, sends to Hiram king of Tyre, and after acquainting him of his purpose of building a house unto the name of the Lord his God, he sends to him for some of his people to go with some of his, to Mount Lebanon, to cut down and hew cedar trees, as his servants understood it better than his own, and moreover he requested him to send him a man that was cunning, to work in gold and in silver, and in brass, iron, purple, crimson and in blue, and that had skill to engrave with the cunning men, and he sent him Hiram, his name-sake; this Hiram, God was pleased to inspire with wisdom and understanding to undertake, and strength to go through the most curious piece of workmanship that was ever done on earth.[28]—Thus Solomon as grand master, and Hiram as his deputy, carried on and finished that great work of the temple of the living God, the inside work

---

[23]According to eighteenth-century Masonic ritual, Moses is "the inspired Writer of Gods Commands, and Grand Master of the Lodge of Israel"; with the prophets and the apostles, he is responsible for delivering "the Grand Archive of Masonry"—the Bible (see *Proceedings*, p. 155 as cited in footnote 2, p. 195).

[24]See Exodus 25–27. The Tabernacle itself was an oblong rectangular structure, divided into two chambers: the first, with an altar of incense at its center, served as an antechamber to the second, called the "Holy of Holies," which contained the Ark of the Covenant, a chest that held the Two Tables of Law.

[25]See Exodus 31:18, 32:19, 34:1, 35:30–35. See chapters 36–39 for the construction of the Ark.

[26]In the third edition of *Lemprière's Classical Dictionary of Proper Names mentioned in Ancient Authors, Writ Large* (1788; rpt. London: Routledge and Kegan Paul, 1987), John Lemprière indicates that the "epithet of *Sidonius*" is "used to express the excellence of anything, especially embroidery or dyed garments" (pp. 583–584).

[27]In ancient times, Jupiter was worshipped in Libya under the name Ammon, or Hammon. The temple of Jupiter Ammon, located in the deserts of Libya nine days from Alexandria, boasted a famous oracle purportedly established 1,800 years before Augustus was born. Alexander the Great numbered among the oracle's most famous visitors.

Coincidentally, "Jupiter Hammon" is also the name of the earliest established African American male poet (1711–ca. 1806). Hammon was named by his master, Henry Lloyd of Long Island, New York. Although it would become the usual American custom to name slaves after their masters, Lloyd here followed the British fashion of naming slaves after classical Greek or Roman figures.

[28]See 1 Kings 4:29–34, 5:2–6, 7:13–14.

of which, in many instances as well as the tabernacle, resembles men's bodies; but this is better explained in a well filled lodge; but this much I may venture to say, that our blessed Saviour compared his sacred body to a temple, when he said, John ii. 19. Destroy this temple and I will raise it up again in three days; and the Apostle, I Peter, i. 14 says, that shortly he should put off this tabernacle.[29] I could show also that one grand end and design of Masonry is to build up the temple that Adam destroyed in Paradise—but I forbear. Thus hath God honoured the Craft, or Masons, by inspiring men with wisdom to carry on his stupendous works.

It is worthy our notice to consider the number of Masons employed in the work of the Temple: Exclusive of the two Grand Masters, there were 300 princes, or rulers, 3300 overseers of the work, 80000 stone squarers, setters, layers or builders, being able and ingenious Crafts, and 30000 appointed to work in Lebanon, 10000 of which every month, under Adoniram, who was the Grand Warden;[30] all the free Masons employed in the work of the Temple was 119,600, besides 70,000 men who carried burdens, who were not numbered among Masons;[31] these were partitioned into certain Lodges, although they were of different nations and different colours, yet were they in perfect harmony among themselves, and strongly cemented in brotherly love and friendship, till the glorious Temple of Jehovah was finished, and the cape-stone[32] was celebrated with great joy—Having finished all that Solomon had to do, they departed unto their several homes, and carried with them the high taste of architecture to the different parts of the world, and built many other temples and cities in the Gentile nations, under the direction of many wise and learned and royal grand Masters, as Nebuchadnezzar over Bablyon—Cyrus over the Medes and Persians—Alexander over the Macedonians—Julius Cæsar over Rome,[33] and a great number more I might mention of crowned heads of the Gentile nations who were of the Craft, but this may suffice.—I must just mention Herod the Great,[34] before I come to the state of Masonry from the birth of our Saviour Jesus Christ.—This Herod was the greatest builder of his day, the patron and Grand Master of many Lodges; he being in the full enjoyment of peace and plenty, formed a design of new building the Temple of Jerusalem. The Temple built by the Jews after the captivity was greatly decayed, being 500 years standing, he proposed to the people that he would not take it down till he had all the materials ready for the new, and accordingly he did so, then he took down the old one and built a new one.—Josephus describes this temple as a most admirable and magnificent fabric of marble, and the finest building upon earth.—Tiberius having attained the im-

[29]Marrant inverts the syntax of the King James version of John 2:19 (see John 2:19–21). Moreover, I Peter 1:14 is either an author's or a printer's error; instead, see 2 Peter 1:13–14.

[30]The two Grand Masters are Hiram and Solomon. 1 Kings 5:13–16 provides each of these first statistics except for the "300 princes, or rulers," for which we have not been able to find a biblical reference.

[31]Adding together the 300 princes, 3,300 overseers, 80,000 stone masons, and 30,000 workers in Lebanon results in a sum of 113,600 "free Masons," not the 119,600 quoted in the sermon. See 1 Kings 5:15 concerning the 70,000 "men who carried burdens." In the *Official History of Freemasonry Among the Colored People in North America* (1903; rpt. New York: Negro Universities Press, 1969), William H. Grimshaw states that Solomon's Temple cost "800,000,000 shekels, or in round numbers about four hundred million dollars." He even provides a monthly pay roll of the temple workers, from "Entered Apprentices" to "Super Excellent Masons," with columns of wages expended in both dollars and shekels (p. 11).

[32]The capstone, or copestone (for which capestane is a Scottish variant), is the top stone, usually slanted, of a wall or structure. It also denotes the crowning or final stroke, as in the finishing touch of a project.

[33]Under Nebuchadnezzar II, Babylon became the ruling power of the Near East. Nebuchadnezzar is (in)famous in Biblical history for his destruction of Jerusalem and the Temple of Solomon in 587 B.C., which led to the Babylonian captivity of the Jews chronicled in 2 Kings 24:10–25, 25:11–21; 2 Chronicles 26:6–21; and Jeremiah 37:1–10, 52:1–30. Cyrus the Great of Persia seized Babylon in 539 B.C. and freed the Jews from their captivity in 538 B.C. By his death at age thirty-three, Alexander of Macedonia, also known as Alexander the Great (356–323 B.C.), had conquered an immense geographical area that covered Greece, Mesopotamia, Persia (modern-day Iran), Afghanistan, western India, Palestine, and northern Africa. Julius Caesar (100–44 B.C.), renowned warrior, orator, and statesman, ruled the Roman Empire from 49 B.C. to his assassination in 44 B.C.

[34]Herod the Great, appointed Tetrarch of Judaea in 41 B.C., began his restoration of the Temple of Jerusalem in 20 B.C.

perial throne, became an encourager of the fraternity.[35]

Which brings me to consider their freedom, and that will appear not only from their being free when accepted, but they have a free intercourse with all Lodges over the whole terrestial globe; wherever arts flourish, a man hath a free right (having a recommendation) to visit his brethren, and they are bound to accept him;[36] these are the laudable bonds that unite Free Masons together in one indissoluble fraternity—thus in every nation he finds a friend, and in every climate he may find a house—this it is to be kindly affectioned one to another, with brotherly love, in honour preferring one another.

Which brings me to answer some objections which are raised against the Masons, and the first is the irregular lives of the professors of it.—It must be admitted there are some persons who, careless of their own reputation, will consequently disregard the most instructive lessons—Some, I am sorry to say, are sometimes to be found among us; many by yielding to vice and intemperance, frequently not only disgrace themselves, but reflect dishonour on Masonry in general; but let it be known that these apostates[37] are unworthy of their trust, and that whatever name or designation they assume, they are in reality no Masons: But if the wicked lives of men were admitted as an argument against the religion which they profess, Christianity itself, with all its divine beauties, would be exposed to censure; but they say there can be no good in Masonry because we keep it a secret, and at the same time these very men themselves will not admit an apprentice into their craft whatever, without enjoying secresy on him, before they receive him as an apprentice; and yet blame us for not revealing our's—Solomon says, Prov. xi. 12, 13.[38] He that is void of wisdom despiseth his neighbour, but a man of understanding holdeth his peace; a talebearer revealeth secrets, but he that is of a faithful spirit concealeth the matter. Thus I think I have answered these objections. I shall conclude the whole by addressing the Brethren of the African Lodge.

Dear and beloved brethren, I don't know how I can address you better than in the words of Nehemiah (who had just received liberty from the king Artaxerxes, letters and a commission, or charter, to return to Jerusalem) that thro the good hand of our God upon us we are here this day to celebrate the festival of St. John[39]—as members of that honorable society of free and accepted Masons—as by charter we have a right to do[40]—remember your obligations you are under to the great God, and to the whole family of mankind in the world—do all that in you lies to relieve the needy, support the weak, mourn with your fellow men in distress, do good to all men as far as God shall give you ability, for they are all your brethren, and stand in need of your help more or less—for he that loves every body need fear nobody: But you must remember you are under a double obliga-

[35]Tiberius Claudius Nero Caesar (42 B.C.–A.D. 37) reluctantly succeeded his stepfather Augustus as emperor of the Roman Empire between A.D. 14 and A.D. 37. During his reign, he actively promoted building and restoration throughout the Empire. At his decree, masons restored crumbling or ruined works originally commissioned by Augustus and Pompey and built many new roads, linking the far-flung lands under Roman rule.

[36]The philosophical laws guiding Freemasonry are known as the Twenty-Five Ancient Landmarks, which antedate and are incorporated within the official Thirty-Nine General Regulations adopted in 1721. Key to these guidelines is the right of visitation, which declares that all freemasons can visit and sit in on the rituals of any regular Lodge in the world.

[37]Apostates are people who have abandoned their religious faith, political beliefs, or ethical principles.

[38]Solomon is traditionally regarded to be the author of the book of Proverbs.

[39]St. John the Baptist and St. John the Evangelist are the two patron saints of the Freemasons. The Festival of St. John takes place on Midsummer Day (June 24), the celebration of the nativity of John the Baptist. Theories abound concerning the origin of St. John's importance to Masonry. One theory posits that Robert I of Scotland (1247–1329)—popularly known as Robert the Bruce, who ruled as Scotland's king from 1306 to 1329—revived Masonry after his army defeated the English in the St. John's Day Battle of Bannockburn in 1314.

[40]The Ninth Landmark notes the Freemasons' right to assemble in Lodges. Since the formal institution of Freemasonry in 1717, the charter, or founding document of a Masonic Lodge, has become the primary instrument through which that body garners the authority to meet as an assemblage and freely practice the rituals and lessons of Masonry.

tion to the brethren of the craft of all nations on the face of the earth, for there is no party spirit in Masonry;[41] let them make parties who will, and despise those they would make, if they could, a species below them, and as not made of the same clay with themselves; but if you study the holy book of God, you will there find that you stand on the level not only with them, but with the greatest kings on the earth, as Men and as Masons,[42] and these truly great men are not ashamed of the meanest of their brethren. Ancient history will produce some of the Africans who were truly good, wise, and learned men, and as eloquent as any other nation whatever,[43] though at present many of them in slavery, which is not a just cause of our being despised; for if we search history, we shall not find a nation on earth but has at some period or other of their existence been in slavery, from the Jews down to the English Nation, under many Emperors, Kings and Princes; for we find in the life of Gregory, about the year 580, a man famous for his charity, that on a time when many merchants were met to sell their commodities at Rome, it happened that he passing by saw many young boys with white bodies, fair faces, beautiful countenances and lovely hair, set forth for sale; he went to the merchant their owner and asked him from what country he brought them; he answered from Britain, where the inhabitants were generally so beautiful. Gregory (sighing) said, alas! for grief, that such fair faces should be under the power of the prince of darkness, and that such bodies should have their souls void of the grace of God.[44]

I shall endeavour to draw a few inferences on this discourse by way of application.—

My dear Brethren, let us pray to God for a benevolent heart, that we may be enabled to pass through the various stages of this life with reputation, and that great and infinite Jehovah, who overrules the grand fabric of nature, will enable us to look backward with pleasure, and forward with confidence—and in the hour of death, and in the day of judgment, the well grounded hope of meeting with that mercy from our Maker which we have ever been ready to shew to others, will refresh us with the most solid comfort, and fill us with the most unspeakable joy.

And should not this learn us that new and glorious commandment of our Lord Jesus Christ to his disciples, when he urges it to them in these words—Love the Lord thy God with all thy heart, and thy neighbour as thyself.—Our Lord repeats and recommends this as the most indispensable duty and necessary qualification of his disciples, saying, hereby shall all men know that ye are my disciples, if ye have love one to another.—And we are expressly told by the Apostle, that charity, or universal love and friendship, is the end of the commandment.[45]

Shall this noble and unparalleled example fail of its due influence upon us—shall it not

---

[41]The General Regulations bid all Freemasons to refrain from expressing any partisan affiliation within the Lodge, since the factiousness of party spirit could irreparably damage the peace and harmony that the Lodge and Freemasonry are instituted to uphold.

[42]The phrase "stand on the level" refers to the Masonic creed that all Masons are equal (despite societal ranking) and must pursue at a common level the same goals: knowledge and the respect accorded to virtue. Hence the level, an instrument used in masonry and carpentry to measure the straightness of a surface, is also an important Masonic symbol.

[43]Marrant's note: "Such as Tertullian, Cyprian, Origen, Augustine, Chrysostrom, Gregory Nazianzen, Arnobius, and ma(n)y others."

Tertullian (ca. A.D. 160–ca. A.D. 225) was born in Carthage; he converted to Christianity before A.D. 197. He was the first Latin theologian and was noted for his asceticism.

Cyprian (ca. A.D. 200–258), a bishop of Carthage, was beheaded for refusing to sacrifice to Roman gods.

Origen (A.D. 185–254), the most prolific Biblical commentator, was born in Alexandria. His writings, in addition to those of Augustine, most influenced the development of Christian thought.

Augustine (A.D. 354–430) is better known today as St. Augustine, bishop of Hippo in northern Africa. He profoundly influenced Western Christian thought through both personal example and prolific writings, including *The City of God* and his autobiographical *Confessions.*

John Chrysostom (ca. A.D. 347–407), an archbishop of Constantinople renowned for his eloquent preaching, was the most famous of the Greek Fathers of the Church.

Gregory of Nazianzus "the Divine" (A.D. 329–389) was a bishop of Constantinople known for his philosophical sermons. He was one of four great Greek doctors of the Church.

Arnobius (fl. A.D. 303–313) was an erudite Christian who wrote the treatise *De Rhetorica Institutione* (not extant), in which he satirizes non-Christian religious beliefs.

[44]The life of Pope Gregory the Great (ca. A.D. 540–640), including this episode, is recounted by Bede (A.D. 673–735) in *The Ecclesiastical History of the English People,* Bk. 2, ch. 1.

[45]See Matthew 22:37–39, John 13:35, 1 Corinthians 13:13.

animate our hearts with a like disposition of benevolence and mercy, shall it not raise our emulation and provoke our ambition—to go and do likewise.

Let us then beware of such a selfishness as pursues pleasure at the expence of our neighbour's happiness, and renders us indifferent to his peace and welfare; and such a self-love is the parent of disorder and the source of all those evils that divide the world and destroy the peace of mankind; whereas christian charity—universal love and friendship—benevolent affections and social feelings, unite and knit men together, render them happy in themselves and useful to one another, and recommend them to the esteem of a gracious God, through our Lord Jesus Christ.

The few inferences that have been made on this head must be to you, my worthy brethren, of great comfort, that every one may see the propriety of a discourse on brotherly love before a society of free Masons—who knows their engagements as men and as christians, have superadded the bonds of this ancient and honourable society—a society founded upon such friendly and comprehensive principles, that men of all nations and languages, or sects of religion, are and may be admitted and received as members, being recommended as persons of a virtuous character.[46]

Religion and virtue, and the continuance and standing of this excellent society in the world—its proof of the wisdom of its plan—and the force of its principles and conduct has, on many occasions, been not a little remarkable—as well among persons of this, as among those of different countries, who go down to the sea and occupy their business in the great waters, they know how readily people of this institution can open a passage to the heart of a brother; and in the midst of war, like a universal language, is understood by men of all countries—and no wonder.—If the foundation has been thus laid in wisdom by the great God, then let us go on with united hearts and hands to build and improve upon this noble foundation—let love and sincere friendship in necessity instruct our ignorance, conceal our infirmities, reprove our errors, reclaim us from our faults—let us rejoice with them that rejoice, and weep with those that weep[47]—share with each other in our joys, and sympathize in our troubles.

And let the character of our enemies be to resent affronts—but our's to generously remit and forgive the greatest; their's to blacken the reputation and blast the credit of their brethren—but our's to be tender of their good name, and to cast a vail over all their failings; their's to blow the coals of contention and sow the seeds of strife among men—but our's to compose their differences and heal up their breaches.

In a word, let us join with the words of the Apostle John in the 19th chapter of Revelations, and after these things I heard a great voice of much people in heaven, saying, Alleluia, salvation and glory, and honour, and power, unto the Lord our God; for true and righteous are his judgments——and the four and twenty elders, and the four beasts, fell down and worshipped God that sat on the throne, saying, Amen; Alleluia; and a voice came out of the throne, saying, praise our God, all ye his servants, and ye that fear him, both small and great.[48]

To conclude the whole, let it be remembered, that all that is outward, whether opinions, rites or ceremonies, cannot be of importance in regard to eternal salvation, any further than they have a tendency to produce inward righteousness and goodness—pure, holy, spiri-

[46]Freemasons imposed strict qualifications on the admission of new members. Candidates had to be free adult males who lacked physical defect and were of virtuous character and good reputation. Historian Jeremy Belknap, friend and correspondent of Freemason St. George Tucker, inscribed a brief message about the African Lodge members' qualifications on the inside cover of Tucker's copy of Prince Hall's *A Charge Delivered to the Brethren of the African Lodge on the 25th of June, 1792:* "This Lodge consists of about thirty Brethren & great care is taken to admit none but persons of good moral Character—So saith the Grand master P. Hall—March 7, 1795."

[47]Romans 12:15.

[48]See Revelation 19:1–2, 4–5.

tual and benevolent affections can only fit us for the kingdom of heaven; and therefore the cultivation of such must needs be the essence of Christ's religion—God of his infinite mercy grant that we may make this true use of it. Unhappily, too many Christians, so called, take their religion not from the declarations of Christ and his apostles, but from the writings of those they esteem learned.——But I am to say, it is from the New-Testament only, not from any books whatsoever, however piously wrote, that we ought to seek what is the essence of Christ's religion; and it is from this fountain I have endeavoured to give my hearers the idea of Christianity in its spiritual dress, free from any human mixtures—if we have done this wisely we may expect to enjoy our God in the world that is above——in which happy place, my dear brethren, we shall all, I hope, meet at that great day, when our great Grand Master shall sit at the head of the great and glorious Lodge in heaven—where we shall all meet to part no more for ever and ever—Amen.

RICHARD ALLEN
(1760–1831)

Perhaps no eighteenth-century African American writer has had a more lasting influence on the civic, social, and religious evolution of Africans in the Americas than the Right Reverend Richard Allen, founder and first bishop of the African Methodist Episcopal Church. Although Phillis Wheatley bequeathed a poetic legacy to African American literature and Prince Hall started another social movement of great consequence, Allen's groundbreaking achievements have affected the lives of thousands and even millions of Africans around the world since the close of the eighteenth century.

Allen was born a slave in Philadelphia, Pennsylvania, on February 14, 1760, in the home of a Quaker lawyer named Benjamin Crew, who would later serve as Chief Justice of The Commonwealth of Pennsylvania. Crew's house was a center of political activity during the Revolutionary War, and as a child, Allen grew up around conversations about the doctrines and rights of freedom from such eminent Americans as George Washington, Benjamin Franklin, John Adams, and Benjamin Rush—all signers of the Declaration of Independence and authors of the Constitution and Crew's friends and frequent visitors.

Allen writes that Crew, in need of ready finances, eventually sold "my mother and father and four children of us into Delaware state, near Dover" to a Mr. Stokeley. Allen was converted to Christianity in the Stokeley household when he was seventeen years old. He joined a Methodist class that met "in the forest" and Stokeley soon permitted him to hold church meetings in the household. Stokeley was so convicted of guilt by the experience that he soon permitted Allen and his brother to purchase their freedom for sixty pounds in gold and silver.

As soon as he had attained his freedom, Allen began to preach the gospel throughout the northeastern colonies, including Delaware, New Jersey, and Pennsylvania. Biographers say that Allen was more of a leader than a preacher and was well known for great orations. Moreover, Allen's personality of leadership, coupled with his fiery dedication to the "all-inclusive" message of Methodism, well suited him to help Absalom Jones establish the first Black Episcopal Church, to help Prince Hall found the Black Masonic Lodges, and to lead scores of black pastors into the groundswell of the denomination throughout the colonies.

Although Richardson and Johnson say that evidence is not conclusive, Singleton declares that Richard Allen was one of only two black preachers who attended the historic Christmas Conference at Baltimore in 1784 when Francis Asbury and Thomas Coke began the formal organization of American Methodism. Singleton further states that the other preacher of African descent was Harry Hoosier, affectionately known in Methodist circles as "Black Harry."

Allen was traveling with the white evangelist Richard Whatcoat in the Baltimore circuit when he was approached by Bishop Asbury to travel with him, not only in the North, but in the slave-holding colonies of the South as well. To be able to travel with the leading bishop of North America should have been quite a distinguished honor. But Asbury required that during their southern treks, Allen "must not intermix with the slaves," that he would often have to sleep in their carriage—presumably because the houses of Southern whites would not be open to him—and that his only allowance would be food and clothing. Allen refused Asbury's invitation: "I told him that I would not travel with him on those conditions."

Allen left Baltimore in 1785 and returned to his native Philadelphia. The next year, he was invited to preach at the famed St. George's Methodist Episcopal Church, popularly known as St. George's. Here, Allen was struck by the needs of African Americans and the general lack of hospitality offered by the white congregation: "We viewed the forlorn state of our colored brethren, and saw that they were destitute of a place of worship." As Allen continued to minister to the black community of the city in separate places for prayer and Bible study, he would bring new converts to the white congregation for Sunday worship where "they were eventually considered a nuisance." The situation soon reached a climax. One Sunday morning, Richard Allen, Absalom Jones, and several of their followers were pulled from their knees during opening prayer at St. George's Methodist Episcopal Church and told to take seats further back in the gallery.

Those who had been so ejected left the church in joint protest. They rented a storeroom and began to conduct Sunday worship by themselves, over the repeated and strong objections of the leadership at St. George's Methodist Episcopal Church. The group soon began to raise funds to erect their own church building, telling their detractors that they would not return to St. George's, where "we were treated so scandalously in the presence of all the congregation present. And if you deny us your name, you cannot seal up the Scripture from us, and deny us a name in heaven."

However, with a lot purchased and building begun, members of the congregation, by then known as the Free African Society, disagreed with Allen and Jones about establishing a Methodist denomination and voted instead to establish an African Protestant Episcopal Church, which Jones then pastored as the first black ordained in the Protestant Episcopal Church. Those who wanted the freer style of worship in Methodist congregations eventually joined Allen in building a church on Allen's own property. Again, the elders at St. George's "opposed it with all their might, insisting that the house should be made over to the Conference," and threatened to take out advertisements that Allen and his group were not true Methodists. Allen and his followers persisted and, in 1794, they held opening services at what would be known as Bethel Church. Francis Asbury presided and dedicated the edifice, which would soon become known among American blacks as "Mother Bethel."

White Methodists in Philadelphia harassed Allen and his followers for some twenty years. Only by command of a court judgment in 1816 were whites legally prevented from their attempts to *supervise* and thus to prevent the development of a separate organization for African Americans. Black people throughout the colonies who were attempting to organize separate congregations faced the same struggles. Finally, in April of 1816, Allen called black representative clerics to a joint meeting in Philadelphia to establish more formal bonds. This was the beginning of the first African American denomination in history. In 1836, five years after Allen's death, the churches numbered 86, with four conferences, two bishops, 27 ministers, 7,594 members, and some $125,000 in property—both numbers and monetary value of considerable size at that time. Singleton writes that, by 1983, A.M.E. churches had adherents in the United States (including Alaska), Canada, Bermuda, the West Indies, South America, and West and South Africa.

But Allen's churches were more than religious platforms. They formed fulcrums of antislavery protest; provided the nucleus of charitable care for indigent Africans in the American colonies; and occasioned hundreds of political statements, legal petitions, newspaper editorials, and other forms of antislavery protest—including anticolonization campaigns against the resettlement of blacks to Africa—in the late eighteenth and early nineteenth centuries.

Allen's biography traces his life in pithy detail from his birth into slavery to his conversion to Christianity and the eventual purchase of his freedom. It gives account of his service during the Revolutionary War and of the beginnings of his ministry. His text provides us with the major written history of the beginnings of the African Methodist denomination, of its struggles to avoid domination by white church leaders, and of the antislavery pursuits of Allen and his followers. A notable account titled *A Narrative of the Proceedings of the Colored People During the Awful Calamity in Philadelphia, in the Year 1793; and a Refutation of Some Censures Thrown upon Them in Some Publications* describes the harsh attack that Allen and Jones endured after they had nursed white victims of an epidemic of yellow fever in Philadelphia. Throughout the autobiography, the reader is particularly struck by both the author's great humility and his sincerity.

Richard Allen died on March 26, 1831, at the age of 71. In addition to his autobiography, he left several extant works, including *A Narrative of the Proceedings of the Colored People During the Awful Calamity in Philadelphia, in the Year 1793; and a Refutation of Some Censures Thrown upon Them in Some Publications,* which he coauthored with Absalom Jones. Several moving addresses or sermons are also extant, including "To the People of Color," "A Short Address to the Friends of Him Who Hath No Helper," "Acts of Faith," "Acts of Hope," and "An Address To Those Who Keep Slaves and Approve the Practice." Allen's legacy to African Americans is immeasurable, and the full record of his contribution to the eventual freedom of all blacks some thirty years later has yet to be fully explored. But his denomination of African Methodist Episcopal Churches stands as an impressive and singular testimony to the awe-inspiring accomplishments of a boy who had been born a slave.

❖❖❖

The best biographical information is from Allen's autobiography titled *The Life Experience and Gospel Labors of the Rt. Rev. Richard Allen* (1793), which was republished in 1960. An updated bicentennial edition with an introduction by George A. Singleton was republished in 1983.

For further background on Allen's theological career and on the development of his denomination, see G. Carter Woodson's *History of the Negro Church* (1921); Harry Richardson's *Dark Salvation: The Story of Methodism as it Developed Among Blacks in America* (1976); Daniel A. Payne's *History of the African Methodist Episcopal Church* (1969), and Carol V.R. George's *Segregated Sabbaths: Richard Allen and the Emergence of Independent Black Churches (1760–1840)* (1973).

More on Allen's life and writings can be found in Benjamin Brawley's *Early Negro American Writers* (1970); Edgar A. Toppin's *A Biographical History of Blacks in America Since 1528* (1971); and Allen Johnson's *Dictionary of American Biography*, vol. 1 (1964).

An Address to Those Who Keep Slaves and Approve the Practice[1]

The judicious part of mankind, will think it unreasonable, that a superior good conduct is looked for from our race, by those who stigmatize us as men, whose baseness is incurable and may therefore be held in a state of servitude, that a merciful man would not doom a beast to; yet you try what you can to prevent our rising from a state of barbarism you represent us to be in; but we can tell you from a degree of experience, that a black man, although reduced to the most abject state human nature is capable of, short of real madness, can think, reflect and feel injuries, although it may not be with the same degree of keen resentment and revenge that you, who have been and are our great oppressors would manifest, if reduced to the pitiable condition of a slave. We believe if you would try the experiment of taking a few black children, and cultivate their minds with the same care and let them have the same prospect in view as to living in the world, as you would wish for your own children, you would find upon the trial, they were not inferior in mental endowments. I do not wish to make you angry, but excite your attention to consider how hateful slavery is in the sight of that God who hath destroyed kings and princes for their oppression of the poor slaves. Pharaoh and his princes, with the posterity of King Saul, were destroyed by the protector and avenger of slaves. Would you not suppose the Israelites to be utterly unfit for freedom and that it was impossible for them to obtain to any degree of excellence? Their history shows how slavery had debased their spirits. Men must be wilfully blind and extremely partial, that cannot see the contrary effects of liberty and slavery upon the mind of man: I truly confess the vile habits often acquired in a state of servitude, are not easily thrown off; the example of the Israelites shows, who with all that Moses could do to reclaim them from it, still continued in their habits more or less; and why will you look for better from us? why will you look for grapes from thorns, or figs from thistles? It is in our posterity enjoying the same privileges with your own, that you ought to look for better things.

When you are pleaded with, do not you reply as Pharaoh did, "Wherefore do ye, Moses and Aaron, let the people from their work, behold the people of the land now are many, and you make them rest from their burthens." We wish you to consider, that God himself was the first pleader of the cause of slaves.

That God, who knows the hearts of all men, and the propensity of a slave to hate his oppressor, hath strictly forbidden it to his chosen people, "Thou shalt not abhor an Egyptian, because thou wast a stranger in his land." Deut. 23, 7. The meek and humble Jesus, the great pattern

[1]This speech was published in Allen's autobiography entitled *The Life Experience and Gospel Labors of the Rt. Rev. Richard Allen* (1793).

of humanity and every other virtue that can adorn and dignify men, hath commanded to love our enemies; to do good to them that hate and despitefully use us. I feel the obligations; I wish to impress them on the minds of our colored brethren, and that we may all forgive you, as we wish to be forgiven; we think it a great mercy to have all anger and bitterness removed from our minds. I appeal to your own feelings, if it is not very disquieting to feel yourselves under the dominion of wrathful disposition.

If you love your children, if you love your country, if you love the God of love, clear your hands from slaves; burthen not your children or your country with them. My heart has been sorry for the blood shed of the oppressors, as well as the oppressed; both appear guilty of each other's blood, in the sight of him who hath said, "He that sheddeth man's blood, by man shall his blood be shed."

Will you, because you have reduced us to the unhappy condition our color is in, plead our incapacity for freedom, and our contented condition under oppression, as a sufficient cause for keeping us under the grievous yoke? I have shown the cause, I will also show why they appear contented as they can in your sight, but the dreadful insurrections they have made when opportunity has offered, is enough to convince a reasonable man that great uneasiness and not contentment is the inhabitant of their hearts. God himself hath pleaded their cause; He hath from time to time raised up instruments for that purpose, sometimes mean and contemptible in your sight, at other times He hath used such as it hath pleased him, with whom you have not thought it beneath your dignity to contend. Many have been convinced of their error, condemned their former conduct, and become zealous advocates for the cause of those whom you will not suffer to plead for themselves.

"We'll Fight for Liberty"

Call for Resistance

Throughout the antebellum period, black abolitionist women and men such as Harriet Tubman, Sojourner Truth, Frances Watkins Harper, and Frederick Douglass spoke from public platforms to mixed audiences of blacks and whites calling for the end to slavery. (Portrait by Jacob Lawrence from the Harriet Tubman Series)

II

"Tell Ole Pharaoh, Let My People Go"

African American History and Culture, 1808–1865

The Explanations of the Desire for Freedom

Repression and Racial Response

Thus saith the Lord, bold Moses said,

Let my people go;

If not I'll smite your first born dead,

Let my people go.

(Chorus)

Go down, Moses, Way down in Egypt land,

Tell ole Pharaoh, let my people go.

The response to the call of Bishop Richard Allen, Reverend Absalom Jones, and other eighteenth-century black ministers, activists, and writers for the end to chattel slavery in America came in the nineteenth century. But the abolition of "the peculiar institution" came at a very high cost to the nation. Although the antebellum period was an important era of scientific and economic progress, the age of the cotton gin, industrial revolution, railroad, and expansion westward, no issue polarized the country more than slavery. The United States became a house divided—northern industrialists versus southern plantation aristocrats, antislavery organizations versus proslavery forces. Yet, despite these great tumultuous divisions, the nation endured. The years 1808 to 1865, which spanned the declared end of the trans-Atlantic slave trade to the end of the Civil War, marked the significant moral and social victory for black and white America—the triumphant struggle of Americans of African descent from slavery to freedom. Accordingly, this would be the important period that framed much of the cultural context and artistic structure of African American literature to the present—a poetics of the affirmation of the black self and one that demands of "ole pharaoh, let my people go."

This call rang out in the literature of Americans of African descent throughout the South and the North. It was heard in the orature of the majority of African Americans who were slaves during the antebellum period and who had been prohibited from learning to read and write. Building on the cultural models of their eighteenth-century predecessors, southern slaves cried out "let my people go" and variations of this sacred shout in their unrivaled folk expressions—the spirituals, secular songs, and folktales—which matured and flourished during the era. Many of those who managed to escape to the North carried the message forth in their written slave narratives, one of the first distinctly American prose forms. In turn, they and their northern black contemporaries produced personal narratives, speeches, essays, letters, novels, poetry, and plays, which primarily protested the enslavement of their people. However, it would be the age of the autobiography, the oration, and the essay more than the poem, the play, or the novel—all swelling the chorus of voices calling for freedom. "Let my people go" then echoed down through the generations and in new literary forms. Several quasi-free northern blacks created innovations of traditional genres to express their major social concerns: race (mostly antislavery protest), religion, and reform. Their message rang out in a new genre, transcribed-oral protest poetry or verse, delivered from the platform or pulpit to denounce the institution of slavery. Functioning in the African griot tradition, the early nineteenth-century black abolitionist poets prefigured the New Black Poets of the 1960s and 1970s in that they laid the foundation on which the black aesthetic would later be formulated. The call from the abolitionists' platform would also give rise to the first protest drama written and delivered by an American of African descent. Moreover, fugitive slave narratives would help to bring forth the first African American novels, the form of which closely adhered to that of their predecessors and which set the structural pattern that black novels have since followed. With the novels would come other black literary firsts: the novella, the short story, and the women's narrative. All of these innovative and traditional forms would continue the freedom call during this turbulent period—this age of repression, revolts, and resistance; of riots, response, and rights; and of reform, reaction, and rebellion.

Southern Repression and Slave Revolts

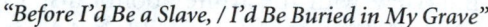

"Before I'd Be a Slave, / I'd Be Buried in My Grave"

During the first decade of the antebellum period when the transatlantic slave trade was declared to be officially abolished, quasi-free northern blacks rejoiced in their churches. However, these celebrations were short-lived. Slave trading between Africa and the United States would continue to flourish during the first decades of the nineteenth century despite the law because slave labor was essential to the southern economy and to America's westward expansion. Slave labor had built the prosperous southern cotton and sugar industries and had helped finance the War of 1812. The institution of slavery had extended the American free labor-market system as far west as Texas.

As slavery became a more vital part of the economic and social fabric of the antebellum South, southern legislators enforced the slave codes, which became even more stringent during the early nineteenth century. Under these restrictive laws, slaves could not, among other stipulations, assemble without the presence of whites, leave the plantation without authorization, strike a white person even in self-defense, possess or receive literature thought to incite revolts, or visit the homes of whites or free blacks or entertain them in their quarters. With increasingly repressive codes came more slave uprisings in the early decades of the nineteenth century. Rebellious slaves clearly communicated to the southern plantation autocracy that death was preferable to slavery or, in the words of the black spiritual, "Before I'd be a slave, / I'd be buried in my grave." Predictably, however, when rumors of or actual slave revolts occurred, southern states passed stricter laws. After the Denmark Vesey insurrection of 1822 in South Carolina, for instance, when forty-seven slaves were condemned to death and 139 of them were arrested, the state passed a law requiring the incarceration of all African American seamen during their stay in port.

Repressive legislation also followed the famous 1831 Southampton County, Virginia, slave revolt in which sixty to eighty slaves, led by Nat

Turner, killed fifty-five to sixty whites. Turner himself told his attorney, Thomas Gray, the gruesome details of the event. That year, Gray published them in his controversial *The Confessions of Nat Turner*. Shortly afterwards, Turner was hanged and his corpse skinned. Over one hundred slaves, who had not taken part in the rebellion, were brutally slaughtered as panic spread throughout Virginia and other southern states. Many slave-holding states forbade African Americans to preach, to assemble for religious purposes, and to sing songs considered insurrectionary. According to Charity Bowery, a former slave of Pembroke, North Carolina, she and other slaves on the plantation where she lived were forbidden to pray and to sing the spiritual "There's a Better Day a Coming" during the aftermath of Turner's insurrection. In an 1839 interview with the white abolitionist Lydia Maria Child, Bowery maintained that "the [whites] wouldn't let us sing that. They thought we was going to *rise* because we sung 'better days are coming.'" Despite stringent laws and regulations, many slaves continued to pray and to sing forbidden songs in clandestine meetings and worship services. As during the eighteenth century, the slaves' folk culture remained their major emotional outlet and survival mechanism against bondage.

Southern Folk Call for Resistance

"I Shall Not, I Shall Not Be Moved"

Antebellum slaves withstood the dehumanizing effects of the southern Slave Codes by maintaining the distinct Afrocentric folk culture that had originated during the Colonial era. The majority of these slaves were born in America. Yet, the significant numbers of West Africans sold to southern plantation owners during the early decades of the nineteenth century (in violation of the 1808 law prohibiting transatlantic slave trading) blended their cultural practices and religious beliefs, especially voodoo, with those of the American-born slaves. As during the eighteenth century, so too did antebellum slaves incorporate African elements into their sacred and secular songs, folktales, sermons, voodoo rites, proverbs, aphorisms, riddles, jokes, and dances. This explains how the slaves could articulate among themselves their determination to "not be moved" from their moral position of resistance to white oppression. According to historian John Blassingame in *The Slave Community* (1979), their folk forms "lightened the burden of oppression, promoted group solidarity, provided ways for verbalizing aggression, sustaining hope, building self-esteem, and often represented areas of life largely free from the control of whites." In particular, the spirituals, secular songs, and folktales illuminated the slaves' growing consciousness of their collective struggle for freedom throughout the era.

Spirituals

By the antebellum period, the spirituals had become the slaves' most flexible forms of protest. According to folklore critic Lawrence Levine in *Black Culture and Black Consciousness: Afro-American Folk Thought from Slavery to Freedom* (1977), "there was always a latent symbolic element of protest in the slaves' religious songs which frequently became overt and explicit." As suggested before, the more direct protest songs such as "There's a Better Day a Coming," "Before I'd Be a Slave," and "Many a Thousand Go" were most likely sung when the slaves were not in the company of whites. If their masters had heard such verses as "Don wid driber's dribin' [the slave driver's commands]" and "No more driver's lash for me," the singers would have certainly suffered serious repercussions.

Instead, drawing from African tradition, most of the spirituals embodied more brilliantly subtle elements of protest. As music historian and critic Ernest Borneman explains in his article "The Roots of Jazz," "the African tradition aims at circumlocution rather than at direct statement. The direct statement is considered crude and unimaginative; the veiling of all content in ever-changing paraphrase is considered the criteria of intelligence and personality." Consequently, the spirituals contained hidden meanings, with the slaves' longing for freedom couched in biblical symbols. The widespread evidence that many spirituals functioned as secret means of communication has been thoroughly documented by John Lovell, Jr., in *Black Song: The Forge and the Flame* (1972) and by Dena Epstein in *Sinful Tunes and Spirituals: Black Folk Music to the Civil War* (1977). Further, various accounts of former slaves have substantiated that the "Moses" mentioned in the sacred songs was Harriet Tubman, the courageous ex-slave and Underground Railroad conductor who repeatedly, and at great risk, returned to the South to rescue more than three hundred blacks from bondage. As African American music historian Eileen Southern points out in *The Music of Black Americans* (1988), when the slaves heard the singing of her special song, they knew that their "Black Moses" had come to deliver them:

> Dark and thorny is de pathway
> Where de pilgrim makes his ways;
> But beyond dis vale of sorrow
> Lie de fields of endless days.

In addition, former slave Frederick Douglass, a leading voice in the political and literary arenas of the period, explained that for him and for many of his fellow slaves, the spiritual "Sweet Canaan" symbolized "something more than a hope of reaching heaven. We meant to reach the North, and the North was our Canaan."

The slaves drew no clear lines of distinction between the sacred and the secular, so, on occasion, they used their religious music as work as well as social songs. A boat song such as "Michael Row the Boat Ashore" indicates that the spirituals were not purely religious songs but, instead, music that covered a wide range of emotions and functions. Above all, the songs affirmed the sense of community among the blacks in bondage and created the necessary psychological space between them and their oppressors.

Secular Songs

Along with the spirituals, the slaves continued to create secular songs, their folk poetry of love, satire, complaint, derision, and praise. Describing the nature of these songs, William Faux wrote in his *Memorable Days in America* in 1823: "Some were plaintive love songs. The verse was their own and abounding either in praise or satire intended for kind and unkind masters." The slaves' secular repertoire included dance songs, satirical songs, work songs, and field cries and hollers.

At their dances, the slaves composed and sang love songs and other merry tunes based on rhythmic rather than lyrical qualities. When they had no musical instruments, they created their own complex rhythmic patterns by *patting juba* (clapping their hands on their knees) and singing such seemingly nonsensical lyrics as "Juba dis, Juba dat, Juba skin de yaller cat." Other song lyrics were more serious in purpose. Sometimes they would satirize their white masters, as in the following popular song "Raise a Ruckus Tonight":

> My ol' missus promise me,
> When she die she set me free.
> Lived so long her haid got ball,
> Give up the notion of dyin at all.

At other times, slaves sang songs harshly critical of slavery and the master class. In his personal narrative, Frederick Douglass recalled a song he had heard on the plantation, "We Raise de Wheat," in which "a sharp hit was given to the meanness of slave holders." The enslaved used the songs to ridicule not only their oppressors but also each other publicly, as in "One Time Upon Dis Ribber." Lawrence Levine in *Black Culture and Black Consciousness* (1977) has traced the slaves' practice of exposing misconduct through song to African customs and beliefs: "The African tradition of being able to verbalize publicly in song what could not be said to a person's face not only lived on among African Americans in slavery, but continued to be a central feature of black expressive culture in freedom."

As in the eighteenth century, the majority of the secular songs were work songs. The slaves would sing them to accompany all kinds of labor, whether it consisted of rowing boats, shucking corn, picking cotton, stripping tobacco, or doing endless small jobs on the plantation. Antebellum slaves seem to have produced more corn-shucking songs than any other type of work song. Invariably, the texts of these songs included phrases referring to the work activity, such as "shuck that corn" and "round the corn." The black literary pioneer William Wells Brown recorded several corn songs sung in 1820 by slaves on the St. Louis, Missouri, plantation from which he had escaped. The seemingly endless rhythmic and verbal repetitions of these work songs helped the singers to temporarily transcend time and to make tolerable the immediate, oppressive conditions of their bondage.

Unlike the work songs, the slaves' field cries did not have a formal structure. Frances Ann Kemble, who, in 1839, resided on a Georgia plantation, described a field cry as "an extremely pretty, plaintive air: there was but one line which was repeated with a wailing chorus." Over a decade later, Frederick Law Olmsted, traveling by rail from North Carolina to South Carolina, recorded the following cry he heard among a gang of slaves picking cotton along the roadside: "Come bretheren come; let's got at it; come now, eoho! roll away! eeoho-eeoho-eeoho-weeioho-i!" Combined with work songs, spirituals, and folk ballads, cries would form the basis of the blues—the unique, black folk musical form that emerged in the latter half of the nineteenth century.

The Human Trickster Tales and Other Folktales

Throughout the antebellum period, the slaves continued to tell tales about animal tricksters and perhaps about flying Africans, conjuration, and ghosts. Several folklorists also maintain that another cycle of tales, the human trickster tales or John and Old Marster series, probably existed during slavery as well, even though they were not collected until the twentieth century.

As John Roberts contends in *From Trickster to Badman* (1989), these tales of a black slave, usually named John, who continues to outwit his master, "undoubtedly had their origins in slavery and reflected realities and situations peculiar to the black experience during this era, especially the slave-master relationship." In his article, "The John and Old Master Stories and the World of Slavery (1974)," folk critic Bruce Dickson, Jr., also concludes that, based on their realistic content, the tales could easily be conceptualized as anecdotes of slavery. These stories indicate the need of the enslaved to broaden the concept of the trickster to include human characters who reflected the reality of their situation as the dehumanized victims of the slavery system and their relationship to the master class. Through John's characteristic manipulations, Roberts insists, "the slaves were able to transmit their perceptions of wit as the most advantageous behavior in dealing with the masters' exploitation and treatment of them as animals."

The reason the tales of John the trickster were not made readily available to white folklorists is easily understood. Given their human characters, the tales more closely reflected the slaves' patterns of behavior than they functioned as entertaining folktales. The white master class might easily have assumed that slaves were forever scheming to take advantage of them and may have enforced even more repressive measures during slavery. These tales taught essential survival skills, appropriate ways for slaves to interact with their masters, who had virtually complete control over their lives. Therefore, if such tales had been discovered by whites, slaves most certainly would have been punished, sold, or even killed.

The John and Old Marster tales represent a subversive element in slave folk thought. They represent a world in which the enslaved could escape from threatening circumstances either through the facility of their verbal wit or through balancing the power differential between themselves and their masters by "appropriating" as many items that belonged to their masters as they could. The folktales, spirituals, secular songs, and other forms of the slaves' oral tradition served as a survival mechanism as valid then as now. It functioned also as the surest structure on which the African American literary tradition has continued to be built. Notwithstanding, southern slaves' folk forms did not have an impact on the written literature in the early nineteenth century for several reasons, not the least being that slaves and northern blacks existed primarily in separate, mutually hostile environments.

Northern Repression: Anti-Black Laws, Riots, and Colonization

"Now Ain't Them Hard Trials"

Similar to southern legislation, northern discrimination during the antebellum era had severely limited the social, economic, political, and literary progress of African Americans. With only half a million of four-and-one-half million African Americans classified as "free," their lives were strictly regulated throughout the era. The majority of northern states had passed laws denying free African Americans the right to vote prior to the adoption of the Fifteenth Amendment in 1870. Furthermore, Pennsylvania, New Jersey, Connecticut, Indiana, Maryland, Tennessee, and North Carolina had disfranchised African Americans who had previously been granted the ballot. Pennsylvania's assault on black civil rights, however, was met with opposition in 1837. It was then that political activist Robert Purvis drafted the *Appeal of Forty Thousand Citizens, Threatened with Disfranchisement, to the People of Pennsylvania,* in his futile but noteworthy effort to prevent the ratification of the new state constitution disfranchising black men.

During the entire period, African Americans, with the exception of a handful of successful businessmen and civil rights leaders such as James Forten, Paul Cuffe, and Solomon Humphries, had also been excluded from profitable employment. They were concentrated in the lowest-paid, least desirable jobs, including domestic occupations, common labor, maritime work, agriculture, and personal service. Moreover, throughout the North, virtually all public transportation, accommodations, and entertainment had been either segregated or placed off-limits to African Americans altogether.

Above all other hard trials for African Americans during the era was the difficulty of acquiring a quality education, the key to their ultimate freedom. With the exception of the Boston and New Bedford school systems, which were integrated in 1855, public education in the North had been segregated or inferior. Consequently, the majority of black Americans at the time were either illiterate or poorly trained. Only gradually would a small class of educated blacks develop. This lack of access to public education had prompted black churches in some states, such as Ohio, Connecticut, Maryland, and Virginia, to set up public or private institutions of instruction for adults and children. Among the teachers were Ann Plato, a poet and essayist who taught in a Zion Methodist school in Hartford, Connecticut, in 1845, and Frances Ellen Watkins Harper, a major activist in the struggle for freedom and equality. Frances Harper was an instructor in the 1850s at Union Seminary, an A.M.E. church school, near Columbus, Ohio. This institution would later be absorbed into Wilberforce University, which, along with Lincoln University in Pennsylvania during the 1850s, became the first African American institution of higher learning. Then, as now, Americans of African descent understood the vital link between education and liberation. In her essay "Education" (1841), Ann Plato expresses the collective yearnings of her people, namely, that the fight for liberation and education must be won for "the perfect day" to come.

The struggle for freedom had also been hindered by major anti-black riots in several northern cities: Cincinnati in 1829; New York City in 1834 and 1839; and Philadelphia in 1834, 1835, and 1842. In the 1834 Philadelphia riot, the reign of terror lasted for three days. A large group of whites marched into a black community, destroyed the African Presbyterian Church, burned down homes, and mercilessly attacked black residents. Twenty-nine years later, in 1863, "them hard trials" for African Americans continued when hundreds of blacks were ruthlessly slaughtered during the New York Draft Riots; white mob violence reached a climax.

An anti-black assault was also responsible for closing down the New York City drama company The African Grove. It was the first professional black theater in America. Founded during the 1820–21 season by a group of actors whose names are now unknown, the theater produced "King Shotaway," probably the first play written and performed by an African American. The actor Ira Aldridge, the earliest known black playwright, had also made his stage debut there in the role of Rolla in *Pizarro.* The New York City constable had ordered The African Grove closed after white ruffians "out for a lark brought disorder and wanton mischief." In 1824, two years after the closing of the theater, Aldridge left America to establish his permanent residence in London. There, three years later, he wrote the adaptation of *The Black Doctor* by Anicet-Bourgeois.

Perhaps as a solution to the race riots and the general problem of defining a place for Americans of African descent in the social structure of early nineteenth-century America, many whites advocated colonization. They held that black people should be deported from the United States because blacks and whites could never coexist peacefully. Slave owners had favored the plan because they saw it as an opportunity to secure the slavery system by siphoning off the free African American population. Some of the colonizationists, however, had wished to end slavery and believed African American deportation to Africa to be the best solution to the problem. Hence, in 1816, such famous humanitarians as Stephen Douglas, Henry Clay, Daniel Webster, John Randolph, James Madison, and Francis Scott Key founded and supported the American Colonization Society. This organization was responsible for establishing the Liberian colony six years later with the migration of approximately twelve thousand African Americans, most of whom were from the slave-holding states.

Black communities responded immediately in fervent opposition to colonization. Only one month after the formation of the society, Civil Rights activists Richard Allen and James Forten led three thousand Philadelphia blacks to register their complaints against the scheme, which they considered to be "an outrage, having no other object in view than the benefit of the slaveholding interests of the country." New York black church leaders James Varick, Samuel E. Cornish, Peter Williams, and Theodore S. Wright also became major spokespersons in the anticolonization movement. These northern black griots pointed out the gullibility of white abolitionists who had fallen victim to the proslavery scheme. In short, the colonization plan was condemned at every major black convention throughout the North.

Yet, there were some African Americans, mainly intellectuals, who had favored the scheme for a variety of reasons related to the quest for a better life than that in the United States. In 1815, Paul Cuffe transported thirty-eight black Americans to Africa at his own expense. A decade later, John B. Russworm, who, with Samuel E. Cornish, founded in 1827 the first black newspaper, *Freedom's Journal,* supported the American Colonization Society. Although the noted prose writer Martin Delany had denounced the society as being "anti-Christian in its character," he proposed the settlement of Americans of African descent in Central or South America in his 1852 publication titled *The Condition, Elevation, Emigration, and Destiny of the Colored People of the United States, Politically Considered.* The following year, abolitionist poet James Whitfield endorsed Delany's views and dedicated his powerful volume of verse, *America and Other Poems,* to him. Also during the 1850s, black activists Mary Ann Shadd Cary, Samuel W. Ward, and William Whipper led the emigration movement of fifteen thousand blacks to Canada. Cary, the foremost leader of the group, voiced her procolonization and antislavery agenda in her Canadian-based newspaper, *The Provincial Freedman,* which was the first newspaper published by an African American woman. Additionally, such leading black clergymen as Henry Highland Garnet, Daniel A. Payne, and Alexander Crummell (one of the finest prose writers of the period) supported the emigration plan on the grounds that it would extend Christianity to Africa. In 1861, Crummell expressed his African emigrationist sentiments eloquently in his book, *The Relations and Duties of Free Colored Men in America to Africa.* However, the following year, the increased involvement of black Americans in the Civil War pushed aside the issue of colonization as a matter of central importance for the race. Not until the twentieth century—first with Marcus Garvey in the 1920s and then with Malcolm X in the 1960s—would the issue of black separatism become a focal point of debate among African Americans again.

Northern Literary Response: Rights for Blacks, Rights for Women

"We All Got a Right to de Tree of Life"

Although African Americans varied in their opinions on colonization, they remained unanimous in their opposition to slavery. Many disagreed, however, on how to dismantle the institution. Some, such as David Walker in his *Appeal* (1829) and Robert A. Young in his *Ethiopian Manifesto, Issued in Defence of the Black Man's Rights, in the Scale of Universal Freedom* (1829), advocated an armed struggle if necessary. Even though both political tracts were published during the same year, it was Walker's powerful, fiery written assault on slavery and racism that had the most profound impact throughout the country—especially in the South—and that ushered in the militant abolitionist movement. In 1831, one year after the publication of the third edition of the *Appeal,* came the beginnings of the movement—William Lloyd Garrison's publication of the *Liberator*—and Nat Turner's slave insurrection (which the South held was directly traceable to Walker and Garrison) a few months later. Neither Garrison, a major spokesperson for nonviolent yet forceful abolition, nor the Quaker Benjamin Lundy, the cofounder of the movement, could ignore Walker's urgent, militant call to violence—one that came from within the leadership rank of the black community. As historian Charles M. Wiltse has observed in the introduction of his 1964 edition of the

Appeal, Walker's pamphlet "marked the transition from the gentle persuasion of the Quakers to the militant crusading of Garrison and Weld, the activism of James G. Birney, the martyrdom of Elizah Lovejoy and John Brown, and the ultimate political triumph of Lincoln."

Like Walker and Young, several other black abolitionists turned to the pen to advance the antislavery cause. Early in the movement, therefore, black activists used various forms of literature as primary weapons to topple slavery. In 1829, Walker's contemporary and fellow North Carolinian, the slave George Moses Horton, expressed his protest in verse in *Hope for Liberty;* and his (Walker's) intellectual and political heir, Maria W. Stewart, wrote a political manifesto titled *Religion and the Pure Principles of Morality, the Sure Foundation On Which We Must Build* two years later. As the first black woman abolitionist writer and orator, Stewart proposed physical force if necessary to achieve liberation, much in the same vein as did Walker, Young, and the black abolitionist Henry Highland Garnet a decade later. She, Walker, Young, and Garnet were the harbingers of Malcolm X and other black nationalists of the 1960s and 1970s who advocated black self-defense as a means to social justice. Horton, who was much less strident in tone than his four contemporaries, became the first black abolitionist poet in America with his volume of verse.

With Horton came the militant black abolitionist poets Frances Ellen Watkins Harper, James Whitfield, James Madison Bell, and Elymas Payson Rogers. Reciting their oral protest verse from the platform or the pulpit, they took their poetry to the people much the same way as did the black revolutionary poets of the 1960s and 1970s. Their strong, rhetorical oral style stemmed from the African American tradition of orator-poets, who ranged from the eighteenth-century bards, Lucy Terry and Jupiter Hammon, to the New Black Poets of the 1960s and 1970s: Amiri Baraka (LeRoi Jones), Etheridge Knight, Sonia Sanchez, Haki Madhubuti (Don L. Lee), and others. Like these later bards, the antebellum griot-poets embraced the aesthetic of art for people's sake rather than the Eurocentric art simply for art's sake. In her poem "Songs for the People," Frances Harper, America's best-known early nineteenth-century African American poet, articulates her sense of this collective consciousness:

Let me make the songs for the people,
Songs for the old and young;
Songs to stir like a battle-cry
Wherever they are sung.

....

Our world, so worn and weary,
Needs music, pure and strong,
To hush the jangle and discords
Of sorrow, pain, and wrong.

Harper and the other antebellum orator-poets wrote verse that was designed to be read aloud to stir and move people to action against the day-to-day harsh realities of American slavery and its aftermath. Just as the New Black Poets based their transcribed-oral protest poetry primarily on direct imagery, simple diction, and the rhythmic language of the street to reach the masses of black people, the antebellum poets relied on vivid, striking imagery, simplistic language, and the musical quality and form of the ballad to appeal to large mixed audiences for their social protest. Their "pure and strong" songs, like those of the slave folksingers, served as powerful calls to "ole pharaoh, let my people go."

These orator-poets published many of their works in black newspapers designed primarily to battle slavery. After Cornish and Russworm founded *Freedom's Journal*, Cornish published *Rights for All*, a short-lived, radical newspaper, in 1829, and the *Weekly Advocate* seven years later. Cornish also coedited with Phillip A. Bell and Charles B. Ray the *Colored American*. Other journalists in the antislavery movement were Frederick Douglass, editor of the *North Star;* William G. Allen and Henry Highland Garnet, editors of the *National Watchman;* David Ruggles, editor of the *Mirror of Liberty;* and Thomas Hamilton, editor of *The Anglo-African Magazine*, the first African American literary periodical. In addition to protesting slavery, these publications provided forums for young, aspiring black literary artists.

Black newspapers featured numerous fugitive slave narratives of various lengths. Along with the genre of women's narratives, they became the first uniquely American prose composition forms. Besides being the most popular works published in both black and white newspapers and journals, hundreds of slave narratives were published as individual books.

The slave narrators furnished white audiences and readers with information about the institution of slavery that white antislavery orators and writers could only have imagined. Writing in 1849, a white minister, Ephraim Peabody, had observed that "all the theoretical arguments for and against slavery are feeble, compared with these accounts of living men of what they personally endured when under its dominion." These storytellers answered the burning questions the northern white public wanted to know: What is it like to be a slave? How are the slaves punished? Is the institution of slavery as evil as has been reported?

The slave narrators understood their political roles well. They used vivid, specific, often graphic details, and concrete language not only to dispel any romanticized notions about slavery but, more important, to outrage the white public concerning the brutalities that existed within the institution. Usually with the aid of white sympathizers, therefore, they conscientiously shaped their narratives to adhere to the following general pattern: the description of the conditions of slavery or oppression, the explanations of their desires for freedom, the escape to freedom (usually, the white patrollers' chase after the runaway), and the considerations as to whether the new freedom in the North corresponded with the slaves' ideal of freedom. Rather than focusing on the uniqueness of their own experiences, the narrators described the conditions of their bondage as representative of the entire slave population. In other words, the narrators emphasized what it was like to be *a* black slave in America. In this way, their experiences became the prototype of the collective. Similar to the folk art forms, therefore, the slave narratives embodied a black communal consciousness, which served as a liberating force for blacks in bondage.

Classics among the nineteenth-century narratives are the *Narrative of the Life of Frederick Douglass, An American Slave* (1845), *The Fugitive Blacksmith; or, Events in the Life of James W.C. Pennington* (1849), *Running a Thousand Miles for Freedom, or, The Escape of William and Ellen Craft from Slavery* (1860), and Harriet Jacobs's *Incidents in the Life of a Slave Girl* (1861). Other noteworthy works are *A Narrative of the Adventures and Escape of Moses Roper from American Slavery* (1837), *Narrative of William Wells Brown, a Fugitive Slave* (1847), *Narrative of the Life and Adventures of Henry Bibb, Written by Himself* (1849), *The Life of Josiah Henson, Formerly a Slave, Now an Inhabitant of Canada, as Narrated by Himself* (1849), *Narrative of Henry Box Brown* (1849), and *Twelve Years a Slave: Narrative of Solomon Northup, a Citizen of New York, Kidnapped in Washington City in 1841, and Rescued in 1853, from a Cotton Plantation near the Red River in Louisiana* (1853).

Just as the political circumstances of historical struggle had been the impetus to African Americans' narrative art, so did their written works continue to complement the oratory that had been the source of their classic narratives. Oratory, one of nineteenth-century America's major literary forms, therefore, became their most useful tool to stir up antislavery sentiments throughout the northern states and abroad. As products of African-centered oral culture, several black abolitionists served as effective speakers, lecturers, and full-time agents for various antislavery societies. Among the most popular speakers with both black and white audiences were those who were former slaves: Frederick Douglass, Sojourner Truth, Harriet Tubman, William Wells Brown, Harriet Jacobs, James C. Pennington, and William and Ellen Craft. At times, Douglass, Wells Brown, and others crystallized their speeches with the published narratives of their experiences. Among others in demand on the lecture circuit were the following talented, free-born black speakers and agents: Maria W. Stewart, Frances Watkins Harper, Henry Highland Garnet, Theodore S. Wright, Robert and Harriet Purvis, Charles Lenox, Sarah Parker Remond, Alexander Crummell, Mary Shadd Cary, Henry Foster, Lunsford Lane, and Abraham Shadd.

Many of these griot-orators became the most powerful speakers in the organizations to which they belonged. For instance, Harper was hailed by her contemporaries as the "Bronze Muse" for her "captivating eloquence that held her audience in rapt attention from the beginning to the close," and Truth was described by her abolitionist peers as a "Lybian Sibyl" for her quaint speech, deep resonant voice, and passionate denouncements of slavery, which she expressed with her own brand of religious mysticism. Equally persuasive, Douglass and Garnet were known to mesmerize audiences wherever they went with the force of their rhetoric and strength of their arguments. When the two of them addressed the 1843 Colored Man's Convention in Buffalo, the audience witnessed oratory at its very best. In his "Address to the Slaves of the United States of America," Garnet held the audience spellbound with his militant rhetoric and the argument that, to destroy slavery, it was sinful not to use violence if necessary. However, it was Douglass, then a proponent of the Garrisonian philosophy of abolition, who won the debate with the thought-provoking and persuasive argument that the use of violence was opposed to Christian teaching. The highly dramatic and powerful quality of Douglass's oratory would be further evidenced in 1852 when he delivered, before the Rochester Antislavery Society, his classic address, "What to the American Slave Is the Fourth of July?" He, Garnet, and several other black abolitionists were such dynamic speakers that the societies sent them to Europe to solicit international support for their humanitarian cause as well as to link their movement with various reform movements abroad. Among others sent to England, France, Germany, and Scotland were Wells Brown, Crummell, Pennington, Ward, Paul, the Crafts, and the Remonds.

Along with being advocates of black rights, several leading black abolitionist speakers and writers—Tubman, Stewart, Truth, Douglass, Harper, the Purvises, the Remonds, Crummell, Cary, and Jacobs—were also proponents of women's rights. As Harper so eloquently stated, "If the fifteenth century discovered America to the Old World, the nineteenth century is discovering woman to herself." In fact, the women's movement in America was an outgrowth of the antislavery movement, based on the principle of the fundamental equality and rights of all human beings to "de Tree of Life" regardless of race, gender, or religion. Its close ties to abolitionism and the issue of race, more than gender, had fueled the feminism of African American women and of leading African American male abolitionists. Their race-based philosophical perspective differed greatly from that of white feminists, who saw their cause as a gender issue only, and eventually created a permanent rift between the two forces as the reform movement grew over the 1840s, 1850s, and 1860s.

As early as 1831, a decade before the feminist movement in America officially began, Maria W. Stewart had championed black women's rights by accusing American society of causing "the daughters of Africa to commit whoredoms and fornications. . . . upon thee be their curse." When she addressed a mixed audience of both men and women at Boston's Franklin Hall the following year, she became the first American-born woman who delivered public speeches that are still extant. By the time she delivered her "Farewell Address" in Boston in 1833, she had exhorted African American women to obtain a formal education not only for the purpose of developing a spirit of independence within themselves but, perhaps more important, for the purpose of furthering the social and political advancement of their people. Thus, Stewart began the line of what theorist Clenora Hudson-Weems in her book entitled *Africana Womanism* (1993) calls "Africana womanists," black feminists who are family-centered rather than female-centered, and who place race and class empowerment before gender empowerment.

More than a decade later, Douglass, Truth, Harper, the Remonds, and the Purvises became the leading black activists in the feminist movement. Together with white feminists Elizabeth Cady Stanton and Susan B. Anthony, cofounders of the movement, Douglass served as one of the major speakers at the 1848 Women's Rights Convention at Seneca Falls, New York. Historians have generally regarded this convention as the beginning of the American Women's Rights movement. Throughout his speech on women's rights, Douglass acknowledged the significant role that women played in the abolitionist movement and endorsed their struggle "for attaining the civil, social, political and religious rights" that they had been denied. Two decades later, in the fight for equal political rights for women and for African Americans, he joined the Remonds, Stanton, and Anthony on a New York State speaking tour to found the American Equal Rights Association (AERA), an organization of abolitionists and feminists whose purpose was to promote black and women's suffrage. When it became apparent, however, that only one of the groups would be franchised, Douglass urged the members of the AERA to support the passage of the Fifteenth Amendment, which would grant suffrage only to African American men.

Vehemently, Sojourner Truth opposed Douglass's views. Her strong advocacy for women's rights had expanded over two decades. She had argued for the equality of men and women in both the public and private spheres at the 1851 Women's Rights Convention in Akron, Ohio, where she delivered her now famous "Ain't I a Woman?" speech. She remained unmoved in her militant feminism at the 1867 AERA convention. Maintaining that although she would be very pleased if black men were granted the ballot, Truth insisted that denying women the same right would be repressive. It added to the oppression and powerlessness of women, she argued, particularly black women. In her "Address to the First Annual Meeting of the American Equal Rights Association," she stated: "There is a great stir about colored men getting their rights, but not the colored women theirs, you see the colored men will be masters over the women, and it will be just as bad as it was before." She continued: "I want women to have their rights. In the courts women have no rights, no voice; nobody speaks for them. If it is not a fit place for women, it is unfit for men to be there." A few black abolitionists such as Charles Remond, the Purvises, and the majority of white feminists shared

Truth's viewpoint. The previous year, at a meeting of the Pennsylvania Antislavery Society, Anthony had insisted that "black men, trained so well by their white male counterparts in the ways of tyranny and despotism, would play the role of the domineering husband with uncommon ease." Unfortunately, Stanton had added that it would be better for the black woman "to be the slave of an educated white man than that of an ignorant black man."

Stanton and Anthony's disparaging remarks about black men prompted Frances Harper to support Douglass and the passage of the Amendment. As an officer of the AERA, she declared that racism (even the racism of her white sisters), and not black men, remained the greatest obstacle to black women's progress: "The white women all go for sex, letting race occupy a minor position. Being black means that every white, including every white working-class woman, can discriminate against you." Harper's response clarified the difference between the gender-based philosophy of white feminism and the racially-based brand of feminism now known as "Africana womanism." She prioritized race before gender empowerment. According to Harper, the passage of the amendment would be the first step toward securing the future of the race. If the race had rights, then the future of black women would look brighter, and they could be victorious in their own struggle for suffrage in the near future. After the passage of the Fifteenth Amendment, Harper stood, therefore, in the forefront of the radical black and women's movement with Truth and other black women activists during the late nineteenth century. Together, they helped lay the groundwork for the Nineteenth Amendment and women's suffrage in the early twentieth century.

Another important black abolitionist writer, Harriet Jacobs, also made substantial contributions to the feminist cause. Inspired by her activities in 1849 and 1850 as a member of an antislavery feminist circle in Rochester, New York, she had composed her personal narrative *Incidents in the Life of a Slave Girl, Written by Herself* (1860) to "convince the people of the Free States what Slavery really is . . . to arouse the women of the North to a realizing sense of the condition of two millions of women at the South, still in bondage, suffering what I suffered, and most of them far worse." In accordance with the standard practice for composing slave narratives, Jacobs accepted the advice of her editor, Lydia Maria Child, to use the fictional name "Linda Brent" for her narrator. Yet, the manner in which "Linda" is sexually harassed by the southern doctor for whom she works as a house servant is based on the actual experiences of Harriet Jacobs. "Linda" suffered as a mother who is determined that her two children would not be held as slaves. In *Incidents,* Jacobs created a more fully developed characterization of the black woman than that presented in slave narratives by black men. Clearly, her feminism, like that of Stewart, Harper, and Truth, paralleled her intrinsic concern for racial equality.

Southern Resistance, Abolitionists' Reaction, and the Civil War

"Turn Back Pharaoh's Army"

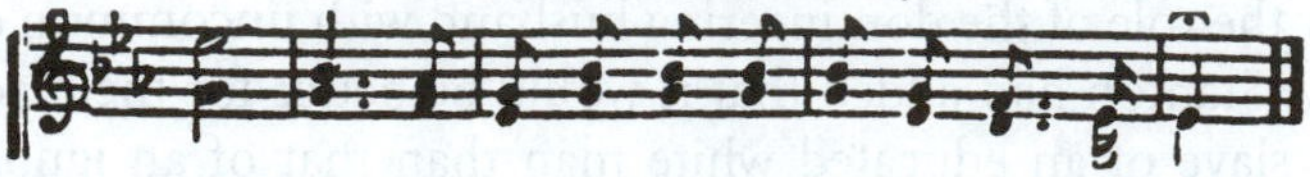

With increased activities of the abolitionists during the 1850s came mounting resistance from the proslavery forces. In the South, proslavery leaders had resolved to keep the institution inviolate by any means necessary. This included killing black or white Americans committed to the antislavery cause, censoring books and newspapers promoting abolition, and passing state and federal legislation upholding slavery. The proslavery leaders had also helped to bring about the destabilization of the Compromise of 1850 that included the passage of the stringent Fugitive Slave Act, the provisions of which required northern whites to help slave owners recover even alleged runaway slaves. Southerners had threatened to secede from the Union if strict adherence to the compromise, particularly the Fugitive Slave Act, was not maintained. With this new law against runaways, the slave holders intensified their hunting down of all fugitives, even those who had lived for years as free persons.

In resistance, militant abolitionists stepped up their political and literary activities. Whenever possible, they defied the law by returning to the free states runaways and free African Americans who had been seized by southerners. Even more effective in arousing antislavery sentiments throughout the North was the publication in 1852 of *Uncle Tom's Cabin* by the abolitionist Harriet Beecher Stowe. As historian John Hope Franklin has explained in *From Slavery to Freedom* (1956), "Its story of abject cruelty on the part of masters and overseers, its description of the privation and suffering of slaves, and its complete condemnation of Southern civilization won countless thousands over to abolition and left Southern leaders busy denying the truth of the novel. When Southerners counted their losses from this one blow, they found them staggering indeed."

The success of *Uncle Tom's Cabin* influenced black abolitionists to use the novel as a device for racial protest. Partly as a result, the first four novels by African American authors were published during the same decade: William Wells Brown's *Clotel* (1853), the first written by an American of African descent; Frank Webb's *The Garies and Their Friends* (1857); Martin Delany's *Blake* (1859), the first novel of black separatism; and Harriet Wilson's *Our Nig* (1859), the first published novel by an American black and the first written by an African American woman. Although influenced by Stowe's classic, these fictional works were not mere imitations of it. Rather, they followed the pattern of the fugitive slave narratives found also in later black novels, including such classics as Richard Wright's *Native Son* (1940), Ralph Ellison's *Invisible Man* (1952), Toni Morrison's *Beloved* (1987), and Charles Johnson's *Middle Passage* (1990)—works that several modern critics classify as "neo-slave narratives." Other noteworthy forms of the period included the first novella published by an African American, Douglass's "The Heroic Slave" (1853), and the first short story by a black writer, Harper's "The Two Offers" (1859).

Harper, Harriet Wilson, Harriet Jacobs, and other significant black women writers of the era also contributed substantially to the development of the women's narrative, a literary genre born in the first half of the nineteenth century. Influenced by the abolitionists, women's and various other social-reform movements, as well as by the white American traditions of sentimental fiction and domestic realism, the writings of both black and white women had appealed to a growing, but largely white female, reading audience. The genre contained its own perspectives and themes in a diversity of prose forms, such as novels, short stories, sketches, personal narratives, and historical tales. The need for, and hindrances to, female self-development became a major thematic focus in the writings.

Black women writers brought a unique perspective to the genre. Set apart by racism from the security and leisure of white middle-class women, they emphasized, instead, the double victimization of African American women: that of being both black and female in a predominately white and male power structure. They explored this focus in terms of the many social barriers African American women encounter in their search for self-definition, including race, social institutions, class, and conventional attitudes toward women. From the early nineteenth-century black women's narratives to the contemporary biographies and fictional works of black women, this focus would be treated from various viewpoints. For example, Jarena Lee in *Religious Experience and Journal of Mrs. Jarena Lee* (1849), one of the earliest known spiritual narratives written by an African American woman, wrote of her struggle to become the first female minister in the male-dominated hierarchy of the African Methodist Episcopal (A.M.E.) Church. Four years later, Nancy Prince in her *Narrative* (1853) would describe her difficult young girlhood as a domestic in various New England white households. Furthermore, Harper in "Two Offers" raised the issue of the severe constrictions women faced in marriage, expanding on that theme as well as on the problem of racism that confronted black women in her later novel *Iola LeRoy* (1892).

Prior to the Civil War, however, Harriet Wilson provided the fullest treatment of the double dilemma facing African American women. She portrayed her black heroine and narrator, Alfredo, an indentured servant in pre-Civil War New England, as one who had to struggle to overcome the physical and emotional abuse of her white male employer, an unfortunate marriage, single parenthood, and early widowhood. Ending her novel with her heroine pleading to the readers for help, Wilson makes a convincing argument that societal changes are desperately needed to aid one who is victimized by both racism and sexism. Fusing elements of abolitionist protest, sentimental fiction, and autobiography in the work, Wilson helped to set the stage for the further development of the genre of African American women's narrative in the second half of the nineteenth century. Such social protests as Wilson's *Our Nig* and Jacobs's *Incidents* could only have added to the already tension-filled antislavery climate of the North.

The antislavery sentiments aroused by the abolitionists during the decade before the Civil War only widened the conflict between the North and the South. In particular, the Dred Scott Decision of 1857 caused a furor when the Supreme Court denied the freedom of a black man who had lived with his master for years in the free state of Illinois. The Supreme Court held that a man once defined as property could not become free merely by residing in "free territory." The person, it said, had to return instead to the original owner. The decision, which reaffirmed the sanctity of people-as-property, was a clear victory for the South.

Basing his work on the slave-as-property theme, William Wells Brown expressed his militant abolitionist views in a five-act play, *The Escape; or, A Leap for Freedom* in 1858. *The Escape* became the first orator-protest drama written and performed by a black playwright. Brown read his abolitionist drama aloud to northern white liberal audiences to move them to take political action against slavery and the ideology of white supremacy. Even though *The Escape* is a highly melodramatic work by contemporary literary standards, whenever Brown performed it, both he and the play received critical praise.

Reacting also to new federal laws, the militant insurrectionist John Brown attacked Harper's Ferry in 1859, in what he hoped would be the beginning of a protracted guerilla warfare. He had intended to persist in his military resistance until the conscience of America could distinguish between humans and property. However, Brown was soon captured and hanged on December 2, 1859. Nevertheless, his heroic actions on the part of the slaves had certainly not been in vain. Years later, in 1881, Douglass would credit Brown's raid at Harper's Ferry as the one event that put an end to the empty "words, votes and compromises" and began the inevitable conflict of the Civil War. What Douglass had learned from Brown years before, at their meeting in Springfield, Massachusetts, in 1847, had proven to be prophetic. The institution of slavery could be destroyed only by a superior physical force. When the Republican Party won the presidency in 1860 and adopted the antislavery platform, prompting the southerners' threats to secede from the Union, the superior physical force of the Civil War became the only means of overthrowing the slave-plantation autocracy. But first the Union soldiers had to "turn back Pharaoh's army."

Literature of the Civil War

"Pharaoh's Army Drowned in the Sea" . . . "We'll Soon Be Free"

Inevitably, the Civil War influenced the literature of the period. In fact, circumstances brought about by the war promoted a northern interest in the folk literature of black Americans. In 1861, when northern teachers, school superintendents, newspaper reporters, missionaries, and soldiers went south to help the contrabands (slaves who escaped to the Union Army), they heard the singing of the slave songs for the first time. Several of these newly enlightened travellers collected the materials. That year, from Fortress Monroe, Virginia, Reverend Lewis Lockwood sent an extended text of "Go Down, Moses" to the New York City chapter of the YMCA. As a result, the *National Antislavery Standard* published the song on December 21, 1861, under the heading "The Contraband's Freedom Hymn." This version became the first publication of the complete text of a black spiritual. "Go Down, Moses," made famous under its revised title, functioned as the race's religious epic of the era. According to William Wells Brown in his *My Southern Home* (1880), blacks assembled at a December 1862 contraband camp in Washington, D.C., celebrated Lincoln's preliminary Emancipation Proclamation of Fall 1862 by singing several times their improvised version of the song's standard refrain:

Go Down, Abraham,
Way down in Dixie's land;
Tell Jeff Davis,
To let my people go.

Philadelphia-born educator Charlotte Forten Grimke, the granddaughter of black activist James Forten, also documented the slave songs. She went to the Sea Islands off the coast of South Carolina and Georgia to participate in what scholars commonly refer to as the Port Royal experiment, the teaching of slaves deserted by the rebel forces. From 1862 to 1864, Forten recorded in her diary a collection of black folk speech idioms and songs she heard on the island of St. Helena. One of her most notable contributions to African American folk literature is her account of the "shout" described in her article, "Life on the Sea Islands," published in *Atlantic Monthly* (1864):

> These "shouts" are very strange, almost indescribable. The children form a ring and move around in a kind of shuffling dance, singing all of the time. Four or five stand apart and sing very energetically, clapping their hands, stamping their feet, and rocking their bodies to and fro. These are the musicians to whose performance the shouters keep perfect time. While the grown people on this plantation did not shout, the adults might well do so on some of the other plantations.

But the most impressive collection of slave songs came from northern educators William Francis Allen, Charles Pickard Ware, and Lucy McKim Garrison, who also took part in the Port Royal experiment. In 1862, Garrison published "Roll, Jordan, Roll" and "Poor Rosy" in her *Work Songs of the Freedmen of Port Royal.* These became the first slave songs published in sheet music. Allen recorded an additional twenty-four songs in his *Diary* written from November 5, 1863, to July 10, 1865, including the now well-known spirituals, "Nobody Knows de Trouble I've Had," "Michael Row the Boat Ashore," "Wrestle Jacob," "Graveyard," and "Travel On, O Weary Soul."

The documentation of the oral tradition during and after the Civil War had certainly had a direct impact on African American life and literature. As Southern has observed, "The slaves had wisely refrained from singing their freedom songs in the presence of whites before Emancipation; now they came out into the open." Classic songs such as "No More Auction Block for Me" and "Before I'd Be a Slave" were authenticated then. After the war, when the worlds of southern ex-slaves and northern blacks merged, African American writers began to draw inspiration, content, and form from the folk tradition.

Predictably, however, situations brought about by the war severely limited the production of written works. African Americans who had dominated the social and literary scenes prior to the war became preoccupied with wartime activities. In the North, Douglass and Truth advised President Lincoln to recruit African Americans for the Union Army. Both of them and Garnet raised funds for supplies for the black soldiers. Meanwhile, Martin Delany served as one of the two majors for the One Hundred and Fourth, an all-black regiment. Harriet Tubman served as a Union spy on the eastern seaboard and Harriet Jacobs conducted relief work among the contrabands. Jacobs also used her recently acquired fame as the author of *Incidents* to raise money for the newly freed slaves. After a brief period of retirement from public life (1860 to 1864) to marry and to have a child, Frances Harper resumed her full-time activities as an agent and lecturer for the Antislavery Society of Maine to help the Union cause.

Despite their busy political and social activities, African Americans managed to record the race's involvement in, and reaction to, the war. The black journals of the period such as *Douglass' Monthly* and the A.M.E. Church's *Christian Recorder,* in particular, had been valuable resources on the wartime status of the race. These periodicals covered various issues, ranging from the announcements of social events, meetings, and speakers to more serious topics such as emancipation, colonization, and the inequities and casualties of African Americans in the war.

These topics of debate were also the focus of the oratory, which continued during the war years to be the major form of black creative expression. For instance, one of the most heated issues among abolitionists in 1863 had been the stipulation that officers of the Union Army's regiments be white.

The subject was addressed on May 28, 1863, by Douglass, William Wells Brown, and Harriet Jacobs at the Thirtieth Annual Convention of the New England Antislavery Society. In his speech, Douglass defended the federal policy by stressing the government's accomplishments rather than its failures. However, Wells Brown, Jacobs, and others focused on the inequity of allowing African Americans to fight but not to command. They based their argument on the fact that many black soldiers in the all-black regiments had fought and died in major battles and numerous engagements, including the Battle of Vicksburg and the sieges of Savannah, Fort Wagner, and Petersburg; yet, with the exception of a handful of men, they had been relegated to inferior military positions.

The epic story of African Americans' fight for freedom and social justice would, however, be told in the small body of poetry written during the period. Published in 1864 and dedicated to John Brown, James Madison Bell's volume of verse, *The Day and the War,* gave an account of the war that praised the Black Brigade and Lincoln's Emancipation Proclamation. The following year, in his collection of poems *Naked Genius,* George Moses Horton saluted war heroes in the Union army who helped to free his people; and, six years later, in *The Progress of Liberty,* Bell recorded African Americans' joyous celebration of the Fifteenth Amendment. But it was, nevertheless, Frances Harper, who, through both sacred and secular voice, gave the story its heroic epic proportions. In her forty-page blank-verse narrative poem titled *Moses: A Story of the Nile* (1869), she skillfully portrayed biblical Egyptian slavery as an allegory of the black liberation struggle; and, in her Aunt Chloe poems from *Sketches of Southern Life* (1872), Harper combined the formal and the black vernacular traditions to render a realistic, kaleidoscopic picture of southern black life during slavery, the Civil War, and early Reconstruction. This portrayal, Patricia Liggins Hill observes in her essay, "Frances W. Harper's Aunt Chloe Poems from *Sketches of Southern Life,*" is antithetical to the plantation literary tradition, the popular literary model of the period that depicted negative, stereotypical images of blacks.

Beyond these poetic records of African American life, black historical and personal narrative accounts provided perceptive insights, important details, and often firsthand experiences of the war, as well as observations of other significant events of that period. William Wells Brown published the first history of African American soldiers in the Civil War, *The Negro in the American Rebellion* (1867). George Washington Williams and Joseph T. Wilson, two writers who had served as soldiers in the all-black regiments, also produced their historical accounts of the war. Williams published his work, *History of the Negro Troops in the War of the Rebellion,* in 1888, the same year that Wilson published his *Black Phalanx.* Twenty years earlier, Elizabeth Keckley, in her fascinating autobiography, *Behind the Scenes; or Thirty Years a Slave, and Four Years in the White House* had presented a revealing picture of the Lincolns and the crisis-ridden White House where she served from

1860 to 1864 as a seamstress and personal confidante to Mary Todd Lincoln. Then, at the turn of the century, Susie King Taylor recorded in *Reminiscences Of My Life in Camp* (1902) her story as a teacher and laundress within the Union encampments on the South Carolina Sea Islands.

Choral Refrain

Whether through narrative, poetry, oratory, or song, African Americans of the period told of the exodus of four million blacks from slavery to emancipation. Even before the early days of the nineteenth century, the African American literary tradition had established a precedent in which the beauty of art was inseparable from the sacred value of freedom. Yet, the tension between those who favored the colonization of blacks and those who favored the integration of them into a highly resistant American mainstream would reappear well into the close of the twentieth century. In fact, this is still expressed today in the continuing tension between a black nationalism that sometimes implies an antagonism between races, on the one hand, and an idealistic will to live out the spirit of the Constitution, on the other. Though the oral and written shouts of African Americans would ultimately change from "Tell Ole Pharaoh, Let My People Go" to "We Shall Overcome" and, eventually, "Black Power!," the words summon the hearers to freedom. They continue to challenge new generations to keep sight of an "art for people's sake."

SOUTHERN FOLK CALL FOR RESISTANCE

FOLK POETRY: SLAVE SONGS OF REBELLION, THE UNDERGROUND RAILROAD, AND EMANCIPATION

Antebellum spirituals and secular songs played a vital role in the freedom struggle of the slaves. Through song, Underground Railroad conductors communicated secret coded messages to the enslaved to help them escape from bondage. For instance, Harriet Tubman and Nat Turner used spirituals as *alert* songs to inform slaves that an escape plot was in the air. As John Lovell, Jr., elaborates, "Harriet Tubman used 'Go Down, Moses' to call up her candidates for transportation to free land. She used 'Wade in the Water' to warn her friends how to throw bloodhounds off the scent. Nat Turner used 'Steal Away' to call his conspirators together." Lovell adds that "'The Chariot's A-Comin' ' was a clear reference, via 'singing telegraph,' to the overhanging shadow in the neighborhood of a conductor of the Underground Railroad. 'Good News, Member' reported by the same great telegraph that a runaway slave had reached freedom." Other alert songs used by conductors included "Swing Low, Sweet Chariot," "Brother Moses Gone to the Promise Land," "I Hear from Heaven Today," and "Oh, Sinner, You'd Better Get Ready." Also, spirituals such as "Follow the Drinking Gou'd" (the drinking gourd was the celestial Big Dipper) served as "musical and poetical maps" steering the fugitives to always travel northward along a particular line in the network of the Railroad.

For those who were left behind in slavery, the songs served as sources of protection and consolation. The enslaved used such songs as "Master's in the Field" to warn each other about an approaching white master or overseer and "Dere's a Meeting Here Tonight" to inform other slaves about a secret gathering. Other songs, such as "We'll Soon Be Free," gave them comfort and hope until Emancipation came.

SPIRITUALS

You Got a Right

(*Chorus*)
You got a right, I got a right,
We all got a right to de tree of life.
Yes, tree of life.
De every time I thought I was los'
De dungeon shuck an' de chain fell off.
You may hinder me here
But you cannot dere,
'Cause God in de heav'n gwinter answer prayer.
(*Chorus*)

O bretheren, O sisteren, You got a right,
You got a right, I got a right,
We all got a right to de tree of life.
Yes, tree of life.

There's a Better Day a Coming

A few more beatings of the wind and rain,
Ere the winter will be over—
    Glory, Hallelujah!
Some friends has gone before me,—
I must try to go and meet them—
    Glory, Hallelujah!
A few more risings and settings of the sun,
Ere the winter will be over—
    Glory, Hallelujah!
There's a better day a coming—
There's a better day a coming—
    Oh, Glory, Hallelujah!

Oh Mary, Don't You Weep

1. Oh Mary, don't you weep, don't you moan,
   Oh Mary, don't you weep, don't you moan,
   Pharaoh's army got drownded,
   Oh Mary, don't you weep.

2. One of dese mornings, bright and fair,
   Take my wings and cleave de air,
   Pharaoh's army got drownded,
   Oh Mary, don't you weep.

3. One of dese mornings, five o'clock,
   Dis ole world gonna reel and rock,
   Pharaoh's army got drownded,
   Oh Mary, don't you weep.

4. Oh Mary, don't you weep, don't you moan,
   Oh Mary, don't you weep, don't you moan,
   Pharaoh's army got drownded,
   Oh Mary, don't you weep.

Steal Away

(*Chorus*)
Steal away, steal away, steal away to Jesus,
Steal away, steal away home,
I ain't got long to stay here.

My Lord, He calls me,
He calls me by the thunder,
The trumpet sounds within-a my soul,
I ain't got long to stay here.

(*Chorus*)

Green trees a-bending,
Po' sinner stands a-trembling

The trumpet sounds within-a my soul,
I ain't got long to stay here.

(*Chorus*)

Swing Low, Sweet Chariot

1. Swing low, sweet chariot,
Coming for to carry me home,
Swing low, sweet chariot,
Coming for to carry me home.

2. I looked over Jordan and what did I see
Coming for to carry me home,
A band of angels, coming after me,
Coming for to carry me home.

3. If you get there before I do,
Coming for to carry me home,
Tell all my friends I'm coming too,
Coming for to carry me home.

4. Swing low, sweet chariot,
Coming for to carry me home,
Swing low, sweet chariot,
Coming for to carry me home.

Hail Mary

1. Don wid driber's dribin',
Don wid driber's dribin',
Don wid driber's dribin',
    Roll, Jordan, roll.

2. Don wid missus' scoldin',
Don wid missus' scoldin',
Don wid missus' scoldin',
    Roll, Jordan, roll.

3. Don wid massa's hollerin',
Don wid massa's hollerin',
Don wid massa's hollerin',
    Roll, Jordan, roll.

4. Sins so heaby dat I cannot get along,
Sins so heaby dat I cannot get along,
Sins so heaby dat I cannot get along,
    Roll, Jordan, roll.

5. Cast my sins to de bottom ob de sea,
Cast my sins to de bottom ob de sea,
Cast my sins to de bottom ob de sea,
    Roll, Jordan, roll.

Many Thousand Gone

(*Plaintively*)
No more auction block for me,
No more, no more,
No more auction block for me,
Many thousand gone.

No more peck of corn for me,
No more, no more,
No more peck of corn for me,
Many thousand gone.

No more pint of salt for me,
No more, no more,
No more pint of salt for me,
Many thousand gone.

Wade in nuh Watuh Childun

(*Chorus*)
Wade in nuh watuh childun
Wade in nuh watuh childun
Wade in nuh watuh
Gawd's go'nah trouble duh watuh.

If a you don't believe Ah been redeem'
Gawd's go'nah trouble duh watuh
Follow me down to Jurdun stream
Gawd's go'nah trouble duh watuh.

(*Chorus*)

Who dat yonduh drest in white
Gawd's go'nah trouble duh watuh
Mus' be the childun uv the Isralite
Gawd's go'nah trouble duh watuh.

(*Chorus*)

Follow the Drinking Gou'd

(*Chorus*)
Foller the drinkin' gou'd
Foller the drinkin' gou'd
For the ole man say,
"Foller the drinkin' gou'd."

1. When the sun come back,
   When the firs' quail call,
   Then the time is come
   Foller the drinkin' gou'd.

   (*Chorus*)

2. The riva's bank am a very good road.
The dead trees show the way,
Lef' foot, peg foot goin' on,
Foller the drinkin' gou'd.

(*Chorus*)

3. The riva ends a-tween two hills,
Foller the drinkin' gou'd;
'Nuther riva on the other side
Follers the drinkin' gou'd.

(*Chorus*)

4. Wha the little riva
Meet the grea' big un,
The ole man waits—
Foller the drinkin' gou'd.

(*Chorus*)

Sweet Canaan

(*Chorus*)
Oh, de land I am bound for, Sweet Ca-naan's happy land,
I am bound for, Sweet Ca-naan's happy land.

Pray give me your right hand, hand.
Oh, my brother, did you come for to help me?
Oh, my brother, did you come for to help me?
Pray, give me your right hand, your right hand.

(*Chorus*)

Pray, give me your right hand, hand.
Oh, my sister, did you come for to help me?
Oh, my sister did you come for to help me?
Pray, give me your right hand, your right hand.

There's a Meeting Here Tonight

(*Chorus*)
Get you ready, there's a meeting here tonight,
Come a-long, there's a meeting here tonight;

I know by your daily walk, there's a meeting here tonight,
Camp meeting down in the wilderness, there's a meeting here tonight;
I know it's among the Methodists, there's a meeting here tonight.

(*Chorus*)

Master's in the Field

Sister, carry de news on,
Master's in de field;
Sister, carry de news on,
Master's in de field.

Michael Row the Boat Ashore

1. Michael row the boat ashore, Hallelujah! (*Repeat*)
2. Michael boat a gospel boat, Hallelujah!
3. I wonder where my mudder deh [there]. Hallelujah!
4. See my mudder on de rock gwine home. Hallelujah!
5. On de rock gwine home in Jesus' name. Hallelujah!
6. Michael boat a music boat. Hallelujah!
7. Gabriel blow de trumpet horn. Hallelujah!
8. O you mind your boastin' talk. Hallelujah!
9. Boastin' talk will sink your soul. Hallelujah!
10. Brudder, lend a helpin' hand. Hallelujah!
11. Sister, help for trim dat boat. Hallelujah!
12. Jordan stream is wide and deep. Hallelujah!
13. Jesus stand on t' oder side. Hallelujah!
14. I wonder if my maussa der. Hallelujah!
15. My fader gone to unknown land. Hallelujah!
16. O de Lord he plant his garden deh. Hallelujah!
17. He raise de fruit for you to eat. Hallelujah!
18. He dat eat shall neber die. Hallelujah!
19. When de riber overflow. Hallelujah!
20. O poor sinner, how you land? Hallelujah!
21. Riber run and darkness comin'. Hallelujah!
22. Sinner row to save your soul. Hallelujah!

Before I'd Be a Slave (Oh, Freedom)

(*Chorus*)
Before I'd be a slave.
I'd be buried in my grave.

And go home to my Lord—and be saved.

1. O, what preachin'!
   O, what preachin'!
   O, what preachin' over me, over me!
2. O, what mourning, *etc.*
3. O, what singing, *etc.*
4. O, what shouting, *etc.*
5. O, weeping Mary, *etc.*
6. Doubting Thomas, *etc.*
7. O, what sighing, *etc.*
8. O, Freedom, *etc.*

Secular Songs

JUba

JUba dis and JUba dat an
JUba killed my YALlow cat, O JUba,
JUba, JUba, JUba, JUba, JUba.

Raise a Ruckus Tonight

1. My ol' missus promise me,
When she die she set me free.
Lived so long her haid got ball,
Give up the notion of dyin atall.

(*Chorus*)
Come along, little chillun, come along,
While the moon is shinin' bright.
Git on board, down the river float,
We gonna raise a ruckus tonight.

2. My ol' missus say to me,
John, Ize gonna set you free.
But when dat haid got slick an ball,
Couldn't kill her wid a big green maul.

(*Chorus*)

3. My ol' missus nevah die,
Wid her nose all hooked and skin all dry.
But when ol miss she somehow gone,
She lef po John a-hillin up de corn.

(*Chorus*)

4. Ol' massa likewise promise me,
When he die he set me free.
But ol massa go an mak his will,
For to leave me plowin ol' Beck still.

(*Chorus*)

5. Way down yonder in Chittlin Switch,
Bullfrog jump fum ditch to ditch.
Bullfrog jump fum de bottom of de well,
Swore, my Lawd, he jumped fum Hell.

(*Chorus*)

We Raise de Wheat

We raise de wheat,
Dey gib us de corn;
We bake de bread,
Dey gib us de cruss;
We sif de meal,
Dey gib us de huss;
We peal de meat,
Dey gib us de skin
And dat's de way
Dey takes us in.

One Time Upon Dis Ribber

One time upon dis ribber,
  Long time ago—
Mass Ralph 'e had a nigger,
  Long time ago—
Da nigger had no merit,
  Long time ago—
De nigger couldn't row wid sperrit,
  Long time ago—
And now dere is in dis boat, ah,
  A nigger dat I see—
Wha' is a good for nuthing shoat, ah,
  Ha, ha, ha, he—
Da nigger's weak like water,
  Ha, ha, ha, he—
'E can't row half quarter,
  Ha, ha, ha, he—
Cuss de nigger—cuss 'e libber,
  Ha, ha, ha, he—
'E nebber shall come on dis ribber,
  Ha, ha, ha, he—

Shuck Dat Corn Before You Eat

All dem puty gals will be dar,
  Shuck dat corn before you eat,
Dey will fix it fer us rare,
  Shuck dat corn before you eat,
I know dat supper will be big,
  Shuck dat corn before you eat,
I think I smell a fine roast pig,
  Shuck dat corn before you eat.
I hope dey'll have some whisky dar,
  Shuck dat corn before you eat.

Roun' de Corn, Sally

(*Chorus*)
Hooray, hooray, ho! Roun' de corn, Sally!
Hooray for all de lubly ladies! Roun' de corn, Sally!
Hooray, hooray, ho! Roun' de corn, Sally!
Hooray for all de lubly ladies! Roun' de corn, Sally!

1. Dis lub's er thing dat's sure to hab you, Roun' de corn, Sally!
   He hole you tight, when once he grab you. Roun' de corn, Sally!
   Un ole un ugly, young un pritty, Roun' de corn, Sally!
   You needen try when once he git you. Roun' de corn, Sally!

2. Dere's Mr. Travers lub Miss Jinny;
Roun' de corn, Sally!
He thinks she is us good us any.
Roun' de corn, Sally!
He comes from church wid her er Sunday,
Roun' de corn, Sally!
Un don't go back ter town till Monday.

(*Chorus*)

3. Dere's Mr. Lucas lub Miss T'reser,
Un ebery thing he does ter please her;

....

Folktales

John and Old Marster Tales

Massa and the Bear

During slavery time, you know, Old Massa had a nigger named John and he was a faithful nigger and Ole Massa lakted John a lot too.

One day Ole Massa sent for John and tole him, says: "John, somebody is stealin' my corn out de field. Every mornin' when I go out I see where they done carried off some mo' of my roastin' ears. I want you to set in de corn patch tonight and ketch whoever it is."

So John said all right and he went and hid in de field.

Pretty soon he heard somethin' breakin' corn. So John sneaked up behind him wid a short stick in his hand and hollered: "Now, break another ear of Ole Massa's corn and see what *Ah'll* do to you."

John thought it was a man all dis time, but it was a bear wid his arms full of roastin' ears. He throwed down de corn and grabbed John. And him and dat bear!

John, after while got loose and got de bear by the tail wid de bear tryin' to git to him all de time. So they run around in a circle all night long. John was so tired. But he couldn't let go of de bear's tail, do de bear would grab him in de back.

After a stretch they quit runnin' and walked. John swingin' on to de bear's tail and de bear's nose 'bout to touch him in de back.

Daybreak, Ole Massa come out to see 'bout John and he seen John and de bear walkin' 'round in de ring. So he run up and says: "Lemme take holt of 'im, John, whilst you run git help!"

John says: "All right, Massa. Now you run in quick and grab 'im just so."

Ole Massa run and grabbed holt of de bear's tail and said: "Now, John you make haste to git somebody to help us."

John staggered off and set down on de grass and went to fanning hisself wid his hat.

Ole Massa was havin' plenty trouble wid dat bear and he looked over and seen John settin' on de grass and he hollered:

"John, you better g'wan git help or else I'm gwinter turn dis bear aloose!"

John says: "Turn 'im loose, then. Dat's whut Ah tried to do all night long but Ah couldn't."

John Steals a Pig and a Sheep

Old Marster had some sheep, and a fellow named John living on the place, a tenant there, he got hungry and he stole the meat from Old Boss. Then he got tired of the sheep meat and stole him a pig. Old Marster come down night after he stole the pig, to get him to play a piece on the banjo. Old Marster knocked on the door, when John had just got through putting the pig away. So Old Marster come in and say, "Play me a piece on the banjo." John started to pick a piece on the banjo; while he's playing he looked around and sees a pig's foot sticking out, so he sings, "Push that pig's foot further back under the bed." (He was talking to his wife.)

When he got tired of that pig meat he turned around and killed him another sheep. So he went back down to the barn and told Old Marster, "Another sheep dead, can't I have him?" Old Marster give him that sheep and he took that one home and ate it up. That made two that Old Marster had given him, so Old Marster got a watch out for him. John killed another one and went and told Old Marster again that a sheep had died. Old Marster told him, "You killed that sheep. What did you kill my sheep for?" John says, "Old Marster, I'll tell you; I won't let nobody's sheep bite me."

NORTHERN LITERARY RESPONSE: RIGHTS FOR BLACKS, RIGHTS FOR WOMEN

MAJOR ABOLITIONIST VOICES

DAVID WALKER
(1785–1830)

David Walker's place in African American and American history was created with a single publication, his pamphlet titled *David Walker's Appeal, in Four Articles; Together with a Preamble, to the Coloured Citizens of the World, but in Particular, and Very Expressly, to Those of the United States of America* (1829). With his small but powerful volume came the birth of the militant abolitionist movement of the nineteenth century. As black abolitionist Henry Highland Garnet would explain two decades later when he issued the second edition of the *Appeal,* "This little book produced more commotion amongst slave holders than any volume of its size that was ever issued from an American press." Not only is Walker's pamphlet the most radical early protest work by an American of African descent, but it is also possibly the first written argument for black cultural nationalism printed in the United States. As one of the earliest black writers to argue for active resistance against slavery, David Walker advocated black pride, unity, collective action, and liberation "by any means necessary." Hailed by Sterling Stuckey as "the father of black nationalism in America," Walker heralded the militant black revolutionaries of the 1960s and 1970s.

Born in Wilmington, North Carolina, on September 28, 1785, of a slave father (who died before his birth) and a free mother, David Walker was consequently born free. Perhaps it was partly his status as a free black man and partly the powerless position in which he found himself in the slave-holding South that inspired his eloquent rage. According to Walker, he traveled extensively throughout the South, observing the brutal realities of slavery. He resolved, therefore, to "leave this part of the country. It will be a great trial for me to live on the same soil where so many men are in slavery; certainly I cannot remain where I must hear their chains continually; and where I must encounter the insults of their hypocritical enslavers. Go I must."

Appalled by the social conditions in the South and influenced by the fervent Methodism of Reverend Richard Allen, David Walker left the region for Philadelphia, the home base of the A.M.E. Church. Eventually, he settled in Boston where he became a race leader of the small community of free blacks. Described by Garnet as "emphatically a self-made man . . . [who] spent all of his leisure moments in the cultivation of his mind," he rather quickly taught himself how to read and write. In 1827, Walker opened up a new-and-used clothing store, which became a successful business. A devoutly religious man, he joined the Methodist Church, married a young woman named Eliza, and used his home as a refuge for runaway slaves. Within a short time, he became a prominent member of the Massachusetts General Colored Association, a Boston-based organization formed by leading black citizens of the city dedicated to the abolition of slavery and the betterment of local conditions. As an activist in the organization, he backed the publication of *Freedom's Journal,* the first black newspaper in America. The paper was founded when a group of leading New York blacks responded to a campaign in the white press arguing that blacks were unfit and unworthy to be citizens in New York State. When the group met in Boston in 1827, they decided to publish the periodical. The first issue of *Freedom's Journal* appeared in print on Friday, March 16, 1827, and Walker became the newspaper's Boston representative. He helped to build up its subscriptions and led a fundraising campaign in the summer of the following year so the paper might be able to purchase the freedom of his fellow North Carolinian, the slave poet George Moses Horton. When *Freedom's Journal* had ceased publication two years later and was replaced by Samuel Cornish's newspaper *Rights for All,* Walker also served as that paper's general agent.

An effective writer and speaker, David Walker attacked the institution of slavery and the colonization plan and urged blacks to unite for their common improvement. Speaking before the Massachusetts General Colored Association in 1828, he challenged the leadership of the black community to uplift the enslaved and other less fortunate blacks: "I call upon you therefore to cast your eyes upon the wretchedness of your brethren, and to do your utmost to enlighten them—go to work and enlighten your brethren!" Undoubtedly, his experience as a speaker served him well, because he used didactic and inspirational exhortation with a vengeance in his *Appeal,* which appeared in print during the fall of the following year. In 1830, he composed two other editions of the *Appeal*—each becoming increasingly inflammatory. However, on June 28, 1830, he was found dead in the street near the clothing shop that he owned. His murder has been attributed to foul play; some believe by poisoning.

Despite his death, Walker's incendiary manifesto began to take on a life of its own. Modeled after the Constitution to highlight America's democratic ideals versus its slave-holding realities, his *Appeal* consists of a Preamble and four articles. In his Preamble, Walker asserts that he intends to demonstrate (third edition) how

> the White Christians of America, who hold us in slavery, (or, more properly speaking, pretenders to Christianity,) treat us more cruel and barbarous than any Heathen Nation did any person whom it had subjected, or reduced to the same condition, that the Americans (who are notwithstanding, looking for the Millennial day) have us.

He suggests in his Preamble that writing the *Appeal* is simultaneously his civic duty and his divine calling: "I shall endeavor to penetrate, search out the sources from which our miseries are derived. If you cannot or will not profit from them, I shall have done *my* duty to you, my country and my God." Following the preamble are the four sections titled "Our Wretchedness in Consequence of Slavery," "Our Wretchedness in Consequence of Ignorance," "Our Wretchedness in Consequence of the Preachers of Jesus Christ," and "Our Wretchedness in Consequence of the Colonizing Plan." In each article, Walker aims to clarify any misconceptions that black Americans may have about the subjugating power of racism (as manifested by slavery) and its "Consequence." Although the *Appeal* is a strong condemnation of slavery and an incitement to insurrection, it is just as much a firebrand call for blacks to unite not only to fight for their liberation in this country but also for the freedom of people of African descent throughout the world. It is, therefore, not only a doctrine of black cultural nationalism but also a doctrine in which Walker plants the seeds of Pan-Africanism.

Within the structural framework of the Constitution, Walker infuses biblical and historical analogies and a variety of rhetorical devices, including various forms of intimidation—warnings, admonishments, threats of black revolt, and divine prophecies—to persuade slaveholders to loosen the yoke of black oppression. He forewarns white Americans that "every dog must have its day, the American's is coming to an end" and, like Robert A. Young in *Ethiopian Manifesto* a few months earlier, predicts that a black Messiah will come to save his people. After hurling numerous biblical and historical examples of divine retribution at white Americans, Walker concludes the work with bold words of warning:

> I speak Americans for your good. We must and shall be free I say, in spite of you. You may do your best to keep us in wretchedness and misery, to enrich you and your children; but God will deliver us from under you. And woe, woe will be to you if we have to obtain our freedom by fighting.

The fiery, moving rhetoric of Walker's *Appeal* most likely led to his untimely death. After the publication of the first edition of the work, Wanted Posters for David Walker were widespread, promising more for him if delivered dead than alive. When and wherever copies of the pamphlet were discovered, they had triggered a "white backlash," especially in the South where they had evoked enormous fear and paranoia about the probability of slave rebellion. Several states, including Georgia, North Carolina, Virginia, Mississippi, and Louisiana, held special legislative sessions to prevent the distribution of the pamphlet, and the governors of Georgia and Virginia and the mayor of Savannah sent letters to Mayor Harrison Otis of Boston protesting the publication and circulation of the pamphlet and calling for Walker's arrest. Georgia and North Carolina led the southern attack against the *Appeal* by passing laws instituting the death penalty for "the circulation of seditious publications" that incited slave insurrections and by making teaching slaves to read and write a crime. Despite these stringent legislative measures, the South feared that Walker's prophecy of a savior may have come true when Nat Turner led his slave revolt in Southampton County, Virginia, approximately one year after the publication of the third edition of the *Appeal.*

Not surprisingly, the white northern response to the pamphlet was also quite heated. The editor of the *Columbian Centennial* of Boston condemned the *Appeal* as "one of the most wicked and inflammatory productions that ever issued from the press" and supported the state of Georgia for taking measures necessary for "the immediate safety of whites." *The New England Palladium* also agreed with the southern position and the outcry for Walker's arrest. Even white abolitionists like William Lloyd Garrison and Benjamin Lundy denounced the pamphlet as "inflammatory" and "injudicious" and deprecated its circulation. While the ardent pacifist Garrison disagreed with Walker's advocacy of violence, he, nevertheless, applauded the "most impassioned and determined spirit" of the *Appeal* and considered it to be "one of the most remarkable productions of the age." Despite his earlier indictment of the work, Garrison began in January of 1831 the publication of the *Liberator,* in which he immediately reprinted most of the *Appeal* and which later became the major voice of the antislavery movement.

Perhaps more important, David Walker and his political manifesto fueled the militant activism of his own people. Black seamen bound for the South helped to distribute copies of the pamphlet, some of which were apparently planted in the clothes sold to them by Walker. In addition, several leading Boston blacks, who were pleased over the social and political upheaval the pamphlet had caused in the South, toasted Walker at an early anniversary dinner of the *Appeal.* His untimely death and his fiery manifesto also inspired his fellow Bostonian, Maria W. Stewart, to join the antislavery crusade. Like Walker, she advocated armed resistance against slavery in a militant pamphlet. Her *Religion and the Pure Principles of Morality, the Sure Ground On Which We Must Build* was published the year after his death. In like manner, the *Appeal* influenced Henry Highland Garnet, one of the most radical of the black abolitionists, who challenged Frederick Douglass and the strategy of moderation—of nonresistance, of moral persuasion, of appealing to the Christian sentiments of whites—that largely characterized the movement. In 1843, Garnet would urge the slaves to rebel in a similarly exhortative piece titled "An Address to the Slaves of the United States of America." Five years later, he would write a biographical sketch of Walker and publish one of the earliest editions of the *Appeal.* Garnet and Stewart's works are lasting tributes to David Walker, who will always be remembered as the author of the "dangerous" pamphlet—as the first African American writer who dared to speak out without fear or restraint.

❖❖❖

Considerable critical attention has been devoted to the significance of Walker's life and his *Appeal.* Henry Highland Garnet's sketch of Walker can be found in Herbert Aptheker's *One Continuous Cry: David Walker's Appeal to the Colored Citizens of the World* (1965). See also Charles M. Wiltse's discussion of Walker in his introduction to his 1964 edition of *The Appeal. The Negro Author* (1931). For scholarly treatments of Walker and the effects of the pamphlet, see Lerone Bennett's "The Fanon of the Nineteenth Century" in *Pioneers in Protest* (1968); Donald M. Jacob's "David Walker: Boston Race Leader, 1825–1830," *Essex Institute Historical Collections,* CVII (January 1971): 94–112; Sterling Stuckey's "David Walker: In Defense of African Rights and Liberty," *Slave Culture: Nationalist Theory and the Foundations of Black America* (1987). Blyden Jackson provides some acute commentary in his *History of Afro-American Literature,* Vol. I (1989).

FROM ***DAVID WALKER'S Appeal, in Four Articles***

Together with
a Preamble,
to the
Coloured Citizens of the World,
but in Particular, and Very Expressly, to Those of the United States of America

It will be recollected, that I, in the first edition of my "Appeal," promised to demonstrate in the course of which, viz. in the course of my Appeal, to the satisfaction of the most incredulous mind, that we Coloured People of these United States, are, the most wretched, degraded and abject set of beings that ever lived since the world began, down to the present day, and, that, the white Christians of America, who hold us in slavery, (or, more properly speaking, pretenders to Christianity,) treat us more cruel and barbarous than any Heathen nation did any people whom it had subjected, or reduced to the same condition, that the Americans (who are, notwithstanding, looking for the Millennial day) have us. All I ask is, for a candid and careful perusal of this the third and last edition of

---

Source: From *DAVID WALKER'S Appeal,* edited by Charles M. Wiltse. American Century Series (NY: Hill & Wang), p. 8.

my Appeal, where the world may see that we, the Blacks or Coloured People, are treated more cruel by the white Christians of America, than devils themselves ever treated a set of men, women and children on this earth.

It is expected that all coloured men, women and children,* of every nation, language and tongue under heaven, will try to procure a copy of this Appeal and read it, or get some one to read it to them, for it is designed more particularly for them. Let them remember, that though our cruel oppressors and murderers, may (if possible) treat us more cruel, as Pharaoh did the children of Israel, yet the God of the Ethiopeans, has been pleased to hear our moans in consequence of oppression; and the day of our redemption from abject wretchedness draweth near, when we shall be enabled, in the most extended sense of the word, to stretch forth our hands to the LORD our GOD, but there must be a willingness on our part, for God to do these things for us, for we may be assured that he will not take us by the hairs of our head against our will and desire, and drag us from our very, mean, low and abject condition.

PREAMBLE

My dearly beloved Brethren and Fellow Citizens.

Having travelled over a considerable portion of these United States, and having, in the course of my travels, taken the most accurate observations of things as they exist—the result of my observations has warranted the full and unshaken conviction, that we, (coloured people of these United States), are the most degraded, wretched, and abject set of beings that ever lived since the world began; and I pray God that none like us ever may live again until time shall be no more. They tell us of the Israelites in Egypt, the Helots in Sparta, and of the Roman Slaves, which last were made up from almost every nation under heaven, whose sufferings under those ancient and heathen nations, were, in comparison with ours, under this enlightened and Christian nation, no more than a cypher—or, in other words, those heathen nations of antiquity, had but little more among them than the name and form of slavery; while wretchedness and endless miseries were reserved, apparently in a phial, to be poured out upon our fathers, ourselves and our children, by *Christian* Americans!

These positions I shall endeavour, by the help of the Lord, to demonstrate in the course of this *Appeal,* to the satisfaction of the most incredulous mind—and may God Almighty, who is the Father of our Lord Jesus Christ, open your hearts to understand and believe the truth.

The *causes,* my brethren, which produce our wretchedness and miseries, are so very numerous and aggravating, that I believe the pen only of a Josephus or a Plutarch, can well enumerate and explain them. Upon subjects, then, of such incomprehensible magnitude, so impenetrable, and so notorious, I shall be obliged to omit a large class of, and content myself with giving you an exposition of a few of those, which do indeed rage to such an alarming pitch, that they cannot but be a perpetual source of terror and dismay to every reflecting mind.

I am fully aware, in making this appeal to my much afflicted and suffering brethren, that I shall not only be assailed by those whose greatest earthly desires are, to keep us in abject ignorance and wretchedness, and who are of the firm conviction that Heaven has designed us and our children to be slaves and *beasts of burden* to them and their children. I say, I do not only expect to be held up to the public as an ignorant, impudent and restless disturber of the public peace, by such avaricious creatures, as well as a mover of insubordination—and perhaps put in prison or to death, for giving a superficial exposition of our miseries, and exposing tyrants. But I am persuaded, that many of my brethren, particularly those who are ignorantly in league with slaveholders or tyrants, who acquire their daily bread by the blood and sweat of their more ignorant brethren—and not a few of those too, who are

*Who are not too deceitful, abject, and servile to resist the cruelties and murders inflicted upon us by the white slave holders, our enemies by nature.

too ignorant to see an inch beyond their noses, will rise up and call me cursed—Yea, the jealous ones among us will perhaps use more abject subtlety, by affirming that this work is not worth perusing, that we are well situated, and there is no use in trying to better our condition, for we cannot. I will ask one question here.—Can our condition be any worse?—Can it be more mean and abject? If there are any changes, will they not be for the better, though they may appear for the worst at first? Can they get us any lower? Where can they get us? They are afraid to treat us worse, for they know well, the day they do it they are gone. But against all accusations which may or can be preferred against me, I appeal to Heaven for my motive in writing—who knows that my object is, if possible, to awaken in the breasts of my afflicted, degraded and slumbering brethren, a spirit of inquiry and investigation respecting our miseries and wretchedness in this *Republican Land of Liberty!!!!!!*

The sources from which our miseries are derived, and on which I shall comment, I shall not combine in one, but shall put them under distinct heads and expose them in their turn; in doing which, keeping truth on my side, and not departing from the strictest rules of morality, I shall endeavour to penetrate, search out, and lay them open for your inspection. If you cannot or will not profit by them, I shall have done *my* duty to you, my country and my God.

And as the inhuman system of *slavery,* is the *source* from which most of our miseries proceed, I shall begin with that *curse to nations,* which has spread terror and devastation through so many nations of antiquity, and which is raging to such a pitch at the present day in Spain and in Portugal. It had one tug in England, in France, and in the United States of America; yet the inhabitants thereof, do not learn wisdom, and erase it entirely from their dwellings and from all with whom they have to do. The fact is, the labour of slaves comes so cheap to the avaricious usurpers, and is (as they think) of such great utility to the country where it exists, that those who are actuated by sordid avarice only, overlook the evils, which will as sure as the Lord lives, follow after the good. In fact, they are so happy to keep in ignorance and degradation, and to receive the homage and the labour of the slaves, they forget that God rules in the armies of heaven and among the inhabitants of the earth, having his ears continually open to the cries, tears and groans of his oppressed people; and being a just and holy Being will at one day appear fully in behalf of the oppressed, and arrest the progress of the avaricious oppressors; for although the destruction of the oppressors God may not effect by the oppressed, yet the Lord our God will bring other destructions upon them—for not infrequently will he cause them to rise up one against another, to be split and divided, and to oppress each other, and sometimes to open hostilities with sword in hand. Some may ask, what is the matter with this united and happy people?—Some say it is the cause of political usurpers, tyrants, oppressors, &c. But has not the Lord an oppressed and suffering people among them? Does the Lord condescend to hear their cries and see their tears in consequence of oppression? Will he let the oppressors rest comfortably and happy always? Will he not cause the very children of the oppressors to rise up against them, and oftimes put them to death? "God works in many ways his wonders to perform."

I will not here speak of the destructions which the Lord brought upon Egypt, in consequence of the oppression and consequent groans of the oppressed—of the hundreds and thousands of Egyptians whom God hurled into the Red Sea for afflicting his people in their land—of the Lord's suffering people in Sparta or Lacedaemon, the land of the truly famous Lycurgus—nor have I time to comment upon the cause which produced the fierceness with which Sylla usurped the title, and absolutely acted as dictator of the Roman people—the conspiracy of Cataline—the conspiracy against, and murder of Cæsar in the Senate House—the spirit with which Marc Antony made himself master of the commonwealth—his associating Octavius and Lipidus with himself in power—their dividing the provinces of Rome among themselves—their attack and defeat, on the plains of Phillippi, of the last defenders of their liberty, (Brutus and Cassius)—the tyranny of Tiberius, and from him to the final overthrow of Constantinople by the Turkish Sultan, Mahomed II. A.D. 1453. I say, I shall not take up time to speak of the *causes* which produced so much wretchedness and massacre among those heathen nations, for I am aware that you know too well, that God is just, as well as merciful!—I shall call your attention a few moments to that *Christian* nation, the Spaniards—while I shall leave almost unnoticed, that avaricious and cruel people, the Portuguese, among whom all true hearted Christians and lovers of Jesus Christ, must evidently see the judgments of God displayed. To show the judgments of God upon the Spaniards, I shall occupy but a little time, leaving a plenty of room for the candid and unprejudiced to reflect.

All persons who are acquainted with history, and particularly the Bible, who are not blinded by the God of this world, and are not actuated solely by avarice—who are able to lay aside prejudice long enough to view candidly and impartially, things as they were, are, and probably will be—who are willing to admit that God made man to serve Him *alone,* and that man should have no other Lord or Lords but Himself—that God Almighty is the *sole proprietor* or *master* of the WHOLE human family, and will not on any consideration admit of a colleague, being unwilling to divide his glory with another—and who can dispense with prejudice long enough to admit that we are *men,* notwithstanding our *improminent noses* and *woolly heads,* and believe that we feel for our fathers, mothers, wives and children, as well as the whites do for theirs.—I say, all who are permitted to see and believe these things, can easily recognize the judgments of God among the Spaniards. Though others may lay the cause of the fierceness with which they cut each other's throats, to some other circumstance, yet they who believe that God is a God of justice, will believe that SLAVERY *is the principal cause.*

While the Spaniards are running about upon the field of battle cutting each other's throats, has not the Lord an afflicted and suffering people in the midst of them, whose cries and groans in consequence of oppression are continually pouring into the ears of the God of justice? Would they not cease to cut each other's throats, if they could? But how can they? The very support which they draw from government to aid them in perpetrating such enormities, does it not arise in a great degree from the wretched victims of oppression among them? And yet they are calling for *Peace!—Peace! !* Will any peace be given unto them? Their destruction may indeed be procrastinated awhile, but can it continue long, while they are oppressing the Lord's people? Has He not the hearts of all men in His hand? Will he suffer one part of his creatures to go on oppressing another like brutes always, with impunity? And yet, those avaricious wretches are calling for *Peace! ! ! !* I declare, it does appear to me, as though some nations think God is asleep, or that he made the Africans for nothing else but to dig their mines and work their farms, or they cannot believe history, sacred or profane. I ask every man who has a heart, and is blessed with the privilege of believing—Is not God a God of justice to *all* his creatures? Do you say he is? Then if he gives peace and tranquillity to tyrants, and permits them to keep our fathers, our mothers, ourselves and our children in eternal ignorance and wretchedness, to support them and their families, would he be to us a God of *justice?* I ask, O *ye Christians! ! !* who hold us and our children in the most abject ignorance and degradation, that ever a people were afflicted with since the world began—I say, if God gives you peace and tranquillity, and suffers you thus to go on afflicting us, and our children, who have never given you the least provocation—would he be to us *a God of justice?* If you will allow that we are MEN, who feel for each other, does not the blood of our fathers and of us their children, cry aloud to the Lord of Sabaoth against you, for the cruelties and murders with which you have, and do continue to afflict us. But it is time for me to close my remarks on the suburbs, just to enter more fully into the interior of this system of cruelty and oppression.

ARTICLE I

Our Wretchedness in Consequence of Slavery

My beloved brethren:—The Indians of North and of South America—the Greeks—the Irish, subjected under the king of Great Britain—the Jews, that ancient people of the Lord—the inhabitants of the islands of the sea—in fine, all the inhabitants of the earth, (except however, the sons of Africa) are called *men*, and of course are, and ought to be free. But we, (coloured people) and our children are *brutes!* ! and of course are, and *ought to be* SLAVES to the American people and their children forever! ! to dig their mines and work their farms; and thus go on enriching them, from one generation to another with our *blood* and our *tears!* ! ! !

I promised in a preceding page to demonstrate to the satisfaction of the most incredulous, that we, (coloured people of these United States of America) are the *most wretched, degraded* and *object* set of beings that *ever lived* since the world began, and that the white Americans having reduced us to the wretched state of *slavery*, treat us in that condition *more cruel* (they being an enlightened and Christian people,) than any heathen nation did any people whom it had reduced to our condition. These affirmations are so well confirmed in the minds of all unprejudiced men, who have taken the trouble to read histories, that they need no elucidation from me. But to put them beyond all doubt, I refer you in the first place to the children of Jacob, or of Israel in Egypt, under Pharaoh and his people. Some of my brethren do not know who Pharaoh and the Egyptians were—I know it to be a fact, that some of them take the Egyptians to have been a gang of *devils*, not knowing any better, and that they (Egyptians) having got possession of the Lord's people, treated them *nearly* as cruel as *Christian Americans* do us, at the present day. For the information of such, I would only mention that the Egyptians, were Africans or coloured people, such as we are—some of them yellow and others dark—a mixture of Ethiopians and the natives of Egypt—about the same as you see the coloured people of the United States at the present day.—I say, I call your attention then, to the children of Jacob, while I point out particularly to you his son Joseph, among the rest, in Egypt.

"And Pharaoh, said unto Joseph, . . . thou shalt be over my house, and according unto thy word shall all my people be ruled: only in the throne will I be greater than thou."*

"And Pharaoh said unto Joseph, see, I have set thee over all the land of Egypt."†

"And Pharaoh said unto Joseph, I am Pharaoh, and without thee shall no man lift up his hand or foot in all the land of Egypt."‡

Now I appeal to heaven and to earth, and particularly to the American people themselves, who cease not to declare that our condition is not *hard*, and that we are comparatively satisfied to rest in wretchedness and misery, under them and their children. Not, indeed, to show me a coloured President, a Governor, a Legislator, a Senator, a Mayor, or an Attorney at the Bar.—But to show me a man of colour, who holds the low office of a Constable, or one who sits in a Juror Box, even on a case of one of his wretched brethren, throughout this great Republic! !—But let us pass Joseph the son of Israel a little farther in review, as he existed with that heathen nation.

"And Pharaoh called Joseph's name Zaphnathpaaneah; and he gave him to wife Asenath the daughter of Potipherah priest of On. And Joseph went out over all the land of Egypt."§

Compare the above, with the American institutions. Do they not institute laws to prohibit us from marrying among the whites? I would wish, candidly, however, before the Lord, to be understood, that I would not give a *pinch of snuff* to be married to any white person I ever saw in all the days of my life. And I do say it, that the black man, or man of colour, who will leave his own colour (provided he can get one, who is good for any thing) and marry a white

*See Genesis, chap. 41: 39–40.

†Genesis 41:41.

‡Genesis 41:44.

§Genesis 41:45.

woman, to be a double slave to her, just because she is *white,* ought to be treated by her as he surely will be, viz: as a NIGGER! ! ! ! It is not, indeed, what I care about inter-marriages with the whites, which induced me to pass this subject in review; for the Lord knows, that there is a day coming when they will be glad enough to get into the company of the blacks, notwithstanding, we are, in this generation, levelled by them, almost on a level with the brute creation: and some of us they treat even worse than they do the brutes that perish. I only made this extract to show how much lower we are held, and how much more cruel we are treated by the Americans, than were the children of Jacob, by the Egyptians.—We will notice the sufferings of Israel some further, under *heathen Pharaoh,* compared with ours under the *enlightened Christians of America.*

"And Pharaoh spoke unto Joseph, saying, thy father and thy brethren are come unto thee:

"The land of Egypt is before thee: in the best of the land make thy father and brethren to dwell; in the land of Goshen let them dwell: and if thou knowest any men of activity among them, then make them rulers over my cattle."*

I ask those people who treat us so *well,* Oh! I ask them, where is the most barren spot of land which they have given unto us? Israel had the most fertile land in all Egypt. Need I mention the very notorious fact, that I have known a poor man of colour, who laboured night and day, to acquire a little money, and having acquired it, he vested it in a small piece of land, and got him a house erected thereon, and having paid for the whole, he moved his family into it, where he was suffered to remain but nine months, when he was cheated out of his property by a white man, and driven out of door! And is not this the case generally? Can a man of colour buy a piece of land and keep it peaceably? Will not some white man try to get it from him, even if it is in a *mud hole?* I need not comment any farther on a subject, which all, both black and white, will readily admit. But I must, really, observe that in this very city, when a man of colour dies, if he owned any real estate it most generally falls into the hands of some white person. The wife and children of the deceased may weep and lament if they please, but the estate will be kept snug enough by its white possessor.

But to prove farther that the condition of the Israelites was better under the Egyptians than ours is under the whites. I call upon the professing Christians, I call upon the philanthropist, I call upon the very tyrant himself, to show me a page of history, either sacred or profane, on which a verse can be found, which maintains, that the Egyptians heaped the *insupportable insult* upon the children of Israel, by telling them that they were not of the *human family.* Can the whites deny this charge? Have they not, after having reduced us to the deplorable condition of slaves under their feet, held us up as descending originally from the tribes of *Monkeys* or *Orang-Outangs?* O! my God! I appeal to every man of feeling—is not this insupportable? Is it not heaping the most gross insult upon our miseries, because they have got us under their feet and we cannot help ourselves? Oh! pity us we pray thee, Lord Jesus, Master.—Has Mr. Jefferson declared to the world, that we are inferior to the whites, both in the endowments of our bodies and our minds?† It is indeed surprising, that a man of such great learning, combined with such excellent natural parts, should speak so of a set of men in chains. I do not know what to compare it to, unless, like putting one wild deer in an iron cage, where it will be secured, and hold another by the side of the same, then let it go, and expect the one in the cage to run as fast as the one at liberty. So far, my brethren, were the Egyptians from heaping these insults upon their slaves, that Pharaoh's daughter took Moses, a son of Israel for her own, as will appear by the following.

*Genesis 47:5, 6. (Wiltse, p. 9.)

†The reference is to Jefferson's *Notes on Virginia,* Query XIV. All of Walker's references to Jefferson are to this section of the *Notes.* (Wiltse, p. 10.)

"And Pharaoh's daughter said unto her, [Moses' mother] take this child away, and nurse it for me, and I will pay thee thy wages. And the woman took the child [Moses] and nursed it.

"And the child grew, and she brought him unto Pharaoh's daughter and he became her son. And she called his name Moses: and she said because I drew him out of the water."*

In all probability, Moses would have become Prince Regent to the throne, and no doubt, in process of time but he would have been seated on the throne of Egypt. But he had rather suffer shame, with the people of God, than to enjoy pleasures with that wicked people for a season. O! that the coloured people were long since of Moses' excellent disposition, instead of courting favour with, and telling news and lies to our *natural enemies,* against each other—aiding them to keep their hellish chains of slavery upon us. Would we not long before this time, have been respectable men, instead of such wretched victims of oppression as we are? Would they be able to drag our mothers, our fathers, our wives, our children and ourselves, around the world in chains and hand-cuffs as they do, to dig up gold and silver for them and theirs? This question, my brethren, I leave for you to digest; and may God Almighty force it home to your hearts. Remember that unless you are united, keeping your tongues within your teeth, you will be afraid to trust your secrets to each other, and thus perpetuate our miseries under the *Christians! ! ! !* ADDITION.—Remember, also to lay humble at the feet of our Lord and Master Jesus Christ, with prayers and fastings. Let our enemies go on with their butcheries, and at once fill up their cup. Never make an attempt to gain our freedom or *natural right,* from under our cruel oppressors and murderers, until you see your way clear[1]—when that hour arrives and you move, be not afraid or dismayed; for be you assured that Jesus Christ the King of heaven and of earth who is the God of justice and of armies, will surely go before you. And those enemies who have for hundreds of years stolen our *rights,* and kept us ignorant of Him and His divine worship, he will remove. Millions of whom, are this day, so ignorant and avaricious, that they cannot conceive how God can have an attribute of justice, and show mercy to us because it pleased Him to make us black—which colour, Mr. Jefferson calls unfortunate! ! ! ! ! ! As though we are not as thankful to our God, for having made us as it pleased himself, as they, (the whites,) are for having made them white. They think because they hold us in their infernal chains of slavery, that we wish to be white, or of their color—but they are dreadfully deceived—we wish to be just as it pleased our Creator to have made us, and no avaricious and unmerciful wretches, have any business to make slaves of, or hold us in slavery. How would they like for us to make slaves of, and hold them in cruel slavery, and murder them as they do us?—But is Mr. Jefferson's assertions true? viz. "that it is unfortunate for us that our Creator has been pleased to make us *black.*" We will not take his say so, for the fact. The world will have an opportunity to see whether it is unfortunate for us, that our Creator *has made us* darker than the *whites.*

Fear not the number and education of our *enemies,* against whom we shall have to contend for our lawful right; guaranteed to us by our Maker; for why should we be afraid, when God is, and will continue, (if we continue humble) to be on our side?

The man who would not fight under our Lord and Master Jesus Christ, in the glorious and heavenly cause of freedom and of God—to be delivered from the most wretched, abject and servile slavery, that ever a people was afflicted

*See Exodus 2:9, 10. (Wiltse, p. 11.)

[1]It is not to be understood here, that I mean for us to wait until God shall take us by the hair of our heads and drag us out of abject wretchedness and slavery, not do I mean to convey the idea for us to wait until our enemies shall make preparations, and call us to seize those preparations, take it away from them, and put every thing before us to death, in order to gain our freedom which God has given us. For you must remember that we are men as well as they. God has been pleased to give us two eyes, two hands, two feet, and some sense in our heads as well as they. They have no more right to hold us in slavery than we have to hold them, we have just as much right, in the sight of God, to hold them and their children in slavery and wretchedness, as they have to hold us, and no more.

with since the foundation of the world, to the present day—ought to be kept with all of his children or family, in slavery, or in chains, to be butchered by his *cruel enemies.*

I saw a paragraph, a few years since, in a South Carolina paper, which, speaking of the barbarity of the Turks, it said: "The Turks are the most barbarous people in the world—they treat the Greeks more like *brutes* than human beings." And in the same paper was an advertisement, which said: "Eight well built Virginia and Maryland *Negro fellows* and four *wenches* will positively be *sold* this day, *to the highest bidder!*" And what astonished me still more was, to see in this same *humane* paper! ! the cuts of three men, with clubs and budgets on their backs, and an advertisement offering a considerable sum of money for their apprehension and delivery. I declare, it is really so amusing to hear the Southerners and Westerners of this country talk about *barbarity,* that it is positively, enough to make a man *smile.*

The sufferings of the Helots among the Spartans, were somewhat severe, it is true, but to say that theirs, were as severe as ours among the Americans, I do most strenuously deny—for instance, can any man show me an article on a page of ancient history which specifies, that, the Spartans chained, and handcuffed the Helots, and dragged them from their wives and children, children from their parents, mothers from their suckling babes, wives from their husbands, driving them from one end of the country to the other? Notice the Spartans were heathens, who lived long before our Divine Master made his appearance in the flesh. Can Christian Americans deny these barbarous cruelties? Have you not, Americans, having subjected us under you, added to these miseries, by insulting us in telling us to our face, because we are helpless, that we are not of the human family? I ask you, O! Americans, I ask you, in the name of the Lord, can you deny these charges? Some perhaps may deny, by saying, that they never thought or said that we were not men. But do not actions speak louder than words?—have they not made provisions for the Greeks, and Irish? Nations who have never done the least thing for them, while *we,* who have enriched their country with our blood and tears—have dug up gold and silver for them and their children, from generation to generation, and are in more miseries than any other people under heaven, are not seen, but by comparatively, a handful of the American people? There are indeed, more ways to kill a dog, besides choking it to death with butter. Further—The Spartans or Lacedaemonians, had some frivolous pretext, for enslaving the Helots, for they (Helots) while being free inhabitants of Sparta, stirred up an intestine commotion, and were, by the Spartans subdued, and made prisoners of war. Consequently, they and their children were condemned to perpetual slavery.*

I have been for years troubling the pages of historians, to find out what our fathers have done to the *white Christians of America,* to merit such condign punishment as they have inflicted on them, and do continue to inflict on us their children. But I must aver, that my researches have hitherto been to no effect. I have therefore, come to the immoveable conclusion, that they (Americans) have, and do continue to punish us for nothing else, but for enriching them and their country. For I cannot conceive of anything else. Nor will I ever believe otherwise, until the Lord shall convince me.

The world knows, that slavery as it existed among the Romans, (which was the primary cause of their destruction) was, comparatively speaking, no more than a *cypher,* when compared with ours under the Americans. Indeed I should not have noticed the Roman slaves, had not the very learned and penetrating Mr. Jefferson said, "when a master was murdered, all his slaves in the same house, or within hearing, were condemned to death."†—Here let me ask Mr.

---

*See Dr. Goldsmith's History of Greece—page 9. See also, Plutarch's Lives. The Helots subdued by Agis, king of *Sparta.* [Walker's citation is to Oliver Goldsmith, *A History of Greece from the Earliest State to the Death of Alexander the Great.* Fifth American edition, 2 vols. in 1, Philadelphia, 1817. (Wiltse, p. 14.)]

†See Jefferson's "Notes on Virginia," page 210. (Wiltse, p. 14)

Jefferson, (but he is gone to answer at the bar of God, for the deeds done in his body while living,) I therefore ask the whole American people, had I not rather die, or be put to death, than to be a slave to any tyrant, who takes not only my own, but my wife and children's lives by the inches? Yea, would I meet death with avidity far! far! ! in preference to such *servile submission* to the murderous hands of tyrants. Mr. Jefferson's very severe remarks on us have been so extensively argued upon by men whose attainments in literature, I shall never be able to reach, that I would not have meddled with it, were it not to solicit each of my brethren, who has the spirit of a man, to buy a copy of Mr. Jefferson's "Notes on Virginia," and put it in the hand of his son. For let no one of us suppose that the refutations which have been written by our white friends are enough—they are *whites*—we are *blacks.* We, and the world wish to see the charges of Mr. Jefferson refuted by the blacks *themselves,* according to their chance; for we must remember that what the whites have written respecting this subject, is other men's labours, and did not emanate from the blacks. I know well, that there are some talents and learning among the coloured people of this country, which we have not a chance to develope, in consequence of oppression; but our oppression ought not to hinder us from acquiring all we can. For we will have a chance to develope them by and by. God will not suffer us, always to be oppressed. Our sufferings will come to an *end,* in spite of all the Americans this side of *eternity.* Then we will want all the learning and talents among ourselves, and perhaps more, to govern ourselves.—"Every dog must have its day," the American's is coming to an end.

But let us review Mr. Jefferson's remarks respecting us some further. Comparing our miserable fathers, with the learned philosophers of Greece, he says: "Yet notwithstanding these and other discouraging circumstances among the Romans, their slaves were often their rarest artists. They excelled too, in science, insomuch as to be usually employed as tutors to their master's children; Epictetus, Terence and Phædrus, were slaves,—but they were of the race of whites. It is not their *condition* then, but *nature,* which has produced the distinction."* See this, my brethren! ! Do you believe that this assertion is swallowed by millions of the whites? Do you know that Mr. Jefferson was one of as great characters as ever lived among the whites? See his writings for the world, and public labours for the United States of America. Do you believe that the assertions of such a man, will pass away into oblivion unobserved by this people and the world? If you do you are much mistaken—See how the American people treat us—have we souls in our bodies? Are we men who have any spirits at all? I know that there are many *swell-bellied* fellows among us, whose greatest object is to fill their stomachs. Such I do not mean—I am after those who know and feel, that we are MEN, as well as other people; to them, I say, that unless we try to refute Mr. Jefferson's arguments respecting us, we will only establish them.

But the slaves among the Romans. Every body who has read history, knows, that as soon as a slave among the Romans obtained his freedom, he could rise to the greatest eminence in the State, and there was no law instituted to hinder a slave from buying his freedom. Have not the Americans instituted laws to hinder us from obtaining our freedom? Do any deny this charge? Read the laws of Virginia, North Carolina, &c. Further: have not he Americans instituted laws to prohibit a man of colour from obtaining and holding any office whatever, under the government of the United States of America? Now, Mr. Jefferson tells us, that our condition is not so hard, as the slaves were under the Romans! ! ! ! ! !

It is time for me to bring this article to a close. But before I close it, I must observe to my brethren that at the close of the first Revolution in this country, with Great Britain, there were but thirteen States in the Union, now there are twenty-four, most of which are slave-holding States, and the whites are dragging us around in

*See Jefferson's "Notes on Virginia," p. 211.

chains and in handcuffs, to their new States and Territories to work their mines and farms, to enrich them and their children—and millions of them believing firmly that we being a little darker than they, were made by our Creator to be an inheritance to them and their children for ever—the same as a parcel of *brutes.*

Are we MEN! !—I ask you, O my brethren! are we MEN? Did our Creator make us to be slaves to dust and ashes like ourselves? Are they not dying worms as well as we? Have they not to make their appearance before the tribunal of Heaven, to answer for the deeds done in the body, as well as we? Have we any other Master but Jesus Christ alone? Is he not their Master as well as ours?—What right then, have we to obey and call any other Master, but Himself? How we could be so *submissive* to a gang of men, whom we cannot tell whether they are *as good* as ourselves or not, I never could conceive. However, this is shut up with the Lord, and we cannot precisely tell—but I declare, we judge men by their works.

The whites have always been an unjust, jealous, unmerciful, avaricious and blood-thirsty set of beings, always seeking after power and authority.—We view them all over the confederacy of Greece, where they were first known to be any thing, (in consequence of education) we see them there, cutting each other's throats—trying to subject each other to wretchedness and misery—to effect which, they used all kinds of deceitful, unfair, and unmerciful means. We view them next in Rome, where the spirit of tyranny and deceit raged still higher. We view them in Gaul, Spain, and in Britain.—In fine, we view them all over Europe, together with what were scattered about in Asia and Africa, as heathens, and we see them acting more like devils than accountable men. But some may ask, did not the blacks of Africa, and the mulattoes of Asia, go on in the same way as did the whites of Europe. I answer, no—they never were half so avaricious, deceitful and unmerciful as the whites, according to their knowledge.

But we will leave the whites or Europeans as heathens, and take a view of them as Christians, in which capacity we see them as cruel, if not more so than ever. In fact, take them as a body, they are ten times more cruel, avaricious and unmerciful than ever they were; for while they were heathens, they were bad enough it is true, but it is positively a fact that they were not quite so audacious as to go and take vessel loads of men, women and children, and in cold blood, and through devilishness, throw them into the sea, and murder them in all kind of ways. While they were heathens, they were too ignorant for such barbarity. But being Christians, enlightened and sensible, they are completely prepared for such hellish cruelties. Now suppose God were to give them more sense, what would they do? If it were possible, would they not *dethrone* Jehovah and seat themselves upon his throne? I therefore, in the name and fear of the Lord God of Heaven and of earth, divested of prejudice either on the side of my colour or that of the whites, advance my suspicion of them, whether they are *as good by nature* as we are or not. Their actions, since they were known as a people, have been the reverse, I do indeed suspect them, but this, as I before observed, is shut up with the Lord, we cannot exactly tell, it will be proved in succeeding generations.—The whites have had the essence of the gospel as it was preached by my master and his apostles—the Ethiopians have not, who are to have it in its meridian splendor—the Lord will give it to them to their satisfaction. I hope and pray my God, that they will make good use of it, that it may be well with them.*

---

*It is my solemn belief, that if ever the world becomes Christianized, (which must certainly take place before long) it will be through the means, under God of the *Blacks,* who are now held in wretchedness, and degradation, by the white *Chirstians* of the world, who before they learn to do justice to us before our Maker—and be reconciled to us, and reconcile us to them, and by that means have clear consciences before God and man.—Send out Missionaries to convert the Heathens, many of whom after they cease to worship gods, which neither see not hear, become ten times more the children of Hell, than ever they were, why what is the reason? Why the reason is obvious, they must learn to do justice at home, before they go into distant lands, to display their charity, Christianity, and benevolence; when they learn to do justice, God will accept their offering, (no man may think that I am against Missionaries for I am not, my object is to see justice done at home, before we go to convert the Heathens.)

SOJOURNER TRUTH

(1797-99?–1883)

A towering six-foot, black woman wearing a white turban commanded the podium at the 1851 Women's Rights Convention held in Akron, Ohio. Though not an invited speaker or a polished "lady" orator, she knew how to win over any audience with her raw, thundering voice, her down-home, folksy style, and her powerful, dramatic gestures. Drawing from her years of experience as an itinerant preacher and as an antislavery speaker, she remained confident as she spoke to the hostile crowd. To the surprise of the audience, she rolled up one sleeve to show her muscular arm: "Look at my arm! I have ploughed, and planted, and gathered into barns, and no man could head me! And a'nt I a woman?" The male hecklers drew to a hushed silence and the white feminists responded with "streaming eyes and hearts beating with gratitude." She had accomplished what none of the white women in attendance had done—she had challenged the white ministers who had denounced women's rights. With the fire and force of her rhetoric, she demanded the same social status of *womanhood* enjoyed by white women for the poor and the enslaved black women she represented. This speech changed the feminist movement in America. The speaker had brought before one of the earliest feminist conventions the issues of race and class, which would continue to haunt the predominately white middle-class women's crusade until the present. The speaker's name was Sojourner Truth, a legend in her own times—the most famous black woman antislavery feminist orator of the nineteenth century.

Many details about the life of this extraordinary woman are not known. What is known of Truth is derived primarily from the autobiography she dictated to Oliver Gilbert and her speeches, which were transcribed by Frances D. Gage. She was born in Ulster County, New York, near the turn of the nineteenth century (1797–99?) and was named Isabella Baumfree. She was one of several children of James and Elizabeth, who were the slaves of Charles Hardenbergh, a wealthy Dutch farmer. Having never been taught to read or write, she grew up speaking Dutch as her primary language. By the time she was thirteen, Isabella had been sold three times and raped by one of her slave masters. By 1810, she had become the property of her last owner, John Dumont of New Paltz, New York, where she stayed until 1826. There she married an older slave named Thomas and bore him five children.

In 1826, the year before emancipation in New York, Isabella first demonstrated a black mother's willful defiance of authority. She sued in the New York courts for the return of her youngest son, Peter, who had been illegally sold and sent to Alabama. As a result, Peter was returned unharmed. That year, she also fled slavery with Peter and her youngest child and went to work for Isaac and Maria Van Wagener, whose name she took. During this time, she experienced an ecstatic, religious conversion and contended that she often had visions and heard voices from beyond. After traveling to Kingston, New York, she joined a newly established Methodist church there. It was also in Kingston where she met a Miss Grear and by 1828 had journeyed with her to New York City.

As Isabella Van Wagener, she supported herself and her two children in the city during the early 1830s by doing domestic work. She regularly attended both black and white Methodist churches and soon began to preach at various camp meetings held near the city. After having established her reputation as a gifted evangelist and visionary, she joined a commune in 1832 and lived as a follower of the self-proclaimed prophet Matthias (Robert Matthews) until 1835. According to one account, she took the name *Sojourner Truth* in 1843, when, on June 1, she left New York City for Connecticut after hearing a summons from God directing her to go forth and preach. Hence, her name suited her chosen lifestyle: "Sojourner" means "lone traveler" or "temporary visitor" and "Truth" reflects the message she wanted to communicate to people about God, mankind, and womankind.

In the course of her itinerant preaching throughout New England in the 1840s, Sojourner Truth eventually joined a utopian organization, the Northampton Association, whose reform-minded members advocated abolition and women's rights. It was through Truth's association with this utopian community that she first met dignitaries in the forefront of the antislavery campaign—William Lloyd Garrison and Frederick Douglass, who occasionally visited the commune. Deeply influenced by the climate of social reform, Truth took to the antislavery lecture circuit as a speaker before the collapse of the commune in 1846. By 1850, she had joined the abolitionist George Thompson on a lecture tour to Indiana, Missouri, Ohio, and Kansas to sell copies of her autobiography, *The Narrative of Sojourner Truth* (1850), and to support herself and her children. Garrison, who was impressed by Truth's extraordinary talents, publicized her speeches in his monthly paper, the *Liberator,* and Douglass often appeared with her on the platform.

Soon, Truth became a black folk heroine, mainly through her speaking engagements in 1851 in Akron, during her 1852–53 tour of Andover, Massachusetts, with Harriet Beecher Stowe, and in 1858 in Indiana. She captivated her audiences to such an extent that one of her audience participants admitted that in trying to describe her one might "as well attempt to report the apocalyptic thunders." She even bared her breast before the 1858 Women's Rights Convention in Indiana when she was accused of being a man. Her dramatic flair of communication, resounding voice, and speeches, which were full of personal stories, humorous remarks, pungent wit, and biblical allusions, moved Stowe to further spread her fame by referring to her as "The Libyan Sibyl" in an 1863 *Atlantic Monthly* article. Grounding her addresses often in biblical prophecy, she functioned much like the Old Testament figure Queen Esther, who saved her Jewish people. Reminding her audience during her "Speech at New York City Convention" that King Ahasuerus granted Esther and her people half of his kingdom, Truth asks why "the king of the United States" will not grant women their rights: "The women want their rights as Esther. . . . Now women do not ask half of a kingdom, but their rights, and they don't get 'em. . . . But we'll have our rights; see if we don't."

Besides continuing her lecture series on behalf of women's rights, Truth raised funds for the Union's black regiments during the Civil War. In 1864, she was presented to President Lincoln at the White House and was appointed counselor to the freed persons of Arlington Heights, Virginia, by the National Freedmen's Relief Association. She also worked as Head Matron of Freedmen's Hospital, which was affiliated with Howard University. In 1867, she found herself siding with white feminists at the American Equal Rights Association's (AERA's) Convention in Philadelphia in the debate over the drafting of the Fifteenth Amendment (black versus women's suffrage); and, a few years later, she turned her attention to petitioning Congress concerning the need of public land for destitute slaves in the North. She envisioned a western state where African Americans could stake claims and farm rather than remain dependent on government assistance. Consequently, she first lectured on this subject in 1870, and, in 1872, she traveled widely across the country in support of this proposal. An illness prevented her from presenting petitions to Congress, and her call for a "Negro State" met with no response. A few years later, in 1883, she died at her home in Battle Creek, Michigan.

Throughout most of her life, Sojourner Truth spoke for her oppressed people with boldness, vigor, and courage. For her fight against slavery and, later, Jim Crow laws during Reconstruction, she was hailed as "the Miriam of the later Exodus." More than any other black feminist of the century, she campaigned for women's suffrage. Continuing the tradition of the antislavery-feminist speaker Maria W. Stewart, Truth challenged the nineteenth-century notion that women should be silent in public; and she rejected the idea that they should accept their social and political status of inferiority in society. Much to the contrary, Truth, like Stewart, stressed economic independence as the key to the social and political future of women; in particular, poor black women. As she tells black men, "When we get our rights we shall not have to come to you for money, for then we shall have enough money in our own pockets. . . . It is a good consolation to know that when we got this battle once fought we shall not be coming to you any more." But, unlike Stewart, Truth put her faith in the white feminist movement rather than in that of black liberation as the surest proponent for black women's rights. This stemmed from her fear of the continuation of black male domination over black females as well as from her conviction that the fate of the women of her race was better off in the hands of white women, "who are a great deal smarter, and know more than colored women." As history has proven, Truth was greatly mistaken: Black women obtained the vote approximately fifty years later, only after the National Association for the Advancement of Colored People (NAACP) and other civil rights organizations defeated the white feminist-Southern Democratic congressional bloc that attempted to exclude them from the Nineteenth Amendment. Yet, despite her error in judgment, Sojourner Truth's words and actions have lived on. More than one hundred years later, she has continued to inspire contemporary black women activists to confront injustices with courage, wisdom, and moral conviction.

❖❖❖

Truth's autobiography is titled *Narrative of Sojourner Truth,* written with Olive Gilbert and edited by Frances W. Titus. This work has gone through three editions: 1853, 1884, and 1970. The most authoritative treatment of Truth's life and works is Hertha Pauli's full-length study *Her Name Was Sojourner Truth* (1962). Other useful critical introductions to Truth's works are Bert James Loewenberg and Ruth Bogin's *Black Women in Nineteenth-Century American Life* (1976); Dorothy Sterling's *We Are Your Sisters: Black Women in the Nineteenth Century* (1984); and Nell Irving Painter's "Sojourner Truth" in Jessie C. Smith, ed., *Notable Black American Women* (1992).

Speech at Akron Convention, Akron, Ohio, May 28–29, 1851; FROM *Reminiscences by Frances D. Gage of Sojourner Truth*

The leaders of the movement trembled on seeing a tall, gaunt black woman in a gray dress and white turban, surmounted with an uncouth sun-bonnet, march deliberately into the church, walk with the air of a queen up the aisle, and take her seat upon the pulpit steps. A buzz of disapprobation was heard all over the house, and there fell on the listening ear, "An abolition affair!" "Woman's rights and niggers!" "I told you so!" "Go it, darkey!"

I chanced on that occasion to wear my first laurels in public life as president of the meeting. At my request order was restored, and the business of the Convention went on. Morning, afternoon, and evening exercises came and went. Through all these sessions old Sojourner, quiet and reticent as the "Lybian Statue," sat crouched against the wall on the corner of the pulpit stairs, her sun-bonnet shading her eyes, her elbows on her knees, her chin resting upon her broad, hard palms. At intermission she was busy selling the "Life of Sojourner Truth," a narrative of her own strange and adventurous life. Again and again, timorous and trembling ones came to me and said, with earnestness, "Don't let her speak, Mrs. Gage, it will ruin us. Every newspaper in the land will have our cause mixed up with abolition and niggers, and we shall be utterly denounced." My only answer was, "We shall see when the time comes."

The second day the work waxed warm. Methodist, Baptist, Episcopal, Presbyterian, and Universalist ministers came in to hear and discuss the resolutions presented. One claimed superior rights and privileges for man, on the ground of "superior intellect"; another, because of the "manhood of Christ; if God had desired the equality of woman, He would have given some token of His will through the birth, life, and death of the Saviour." Another gave us a theological view of the "sin of our first mother."

There were very few women in those days who dared to "speak in meeting"; and the august teachers of the people were seemingly getting the better of us, while the boys in the galleries, and the sneerers among the pews, were hugely enjoying the discomfiture, as they supposed, of the "strong-minded." Some of the tender-skinned friends were on the point of losing dignity, and the atmosphere betokened a storm. When, slowly from her seat in the corner rose Sojourner Truth, who, till now, had scarcely lifted her head. "Don't let her speak!" gasped half a dozen in my ear. She moved slowly and solemnly to the front, laid her old bonnet at her feet, and turned her great speaking eyes to me. There was a hissing sound of disapprobation above and below. I rose and announced "Sojourner Truth," and begged the audience to keep silence for a few moments.

The tumult subsided at once, and every eye was fixed on this almost Amazon form, which stood nearly six feet high, head erect, and eyes piercing the upper air like one in a dream. At her first word there was a profound hush. She spoke in deep tones, which, though not loud, reached every ear in the house, and away through the throng at the doors and windows.

"Wall, chilern, whar dar is so much racket dar must be somethin' out o' kilter. I tink dat 'twixt de niggers of de Souf and de womin at de Norf, all talkin' 'bout rights, de white men will be in a fix pretty soon. But what's all dis here talkin' 'bout?

"Dat man ober dar say dat womin needs to be helped into carriages, and lifted ober ditches, and to hab de best place everywhar. Nobody eber helps me into carriage, or ober mud-puddles, or gibs me any best place!" And raising herself to her full height, and her voice to a pitch like rolling thunder, she asked. "And a'n't I a woman? Look at me! Look at my arm! (and she bared her right arm to the shoulder, showing her tremendous muscular power). I have ploughed, and planted, and gathered into barns, and no man could head me! And a'n't I a woman? I could work as much and eat as much as a man—when I could get it—and bear de lash as well! And a'n't I a woman? I have borne thirteen chilern, and seen 'em mos' all sold off to slavery, and when I cried out with my mother's grief, none but Jesus heard me! And a'n't I a woman?

"Den dey talks 'bout dis ting in de head; what dis dey call it?" ("Intellect," whispered some one near.) "Dat's it, honey. What's dat got to do wid womin's rights or nigger's rights? If my cup won't hold but a pint, and yourn holds a quart, wouldn't ye be mean not to let me have my little half-measure full?" And she pointed her significant finger, and sent a keen glance at the minister who had made the argument. The cheering was long and loud.

"Den dat little man in black dar, he say women can't have as much rights as men, 'cause Christ wan't a woman! Whar did your Christ come from?" Rolling thunder couldn't have stilled that crowd, as did those deep, wonderful tones, as she stood there with outstretched arms and eyes of fire. Raising her voice still louder, she repeated, "Whar did your Christ come from? From God and a woman! Man had nothin' to do wid Him." Oh, what a rebuke that was to that little man.

Turning again to another objector, she took up the defense of Mother Eve. I can not follow her through it all. It was pointed, and witty, and solemn; eliciting at almost every sentence deafening applause; and she ended by asserting: "If de fust woman God ever made was strong enough to turn de world upside down all alone, dese women togedder (and she glanced her eye over the platform) ought to be able to turn it back, and get it right side up again! And now dey is asking to do it, de man better let 'em." Long-continued cheering greeted this. "'Bleeged to ye for hearin' on me, and now ole Sojourner han't got nothin' more to say."

Amid roars of applause, she returned to her corner, leaving more than one of us with streaming eyes, and hearts beating with gratitude. She had taken us up in her strong arms and carried us safely over the slough of difficulty turning the whole tide in our favor. I have never in my life seen anything like the magical influence that subdued the mobbish spirit of the day, and turned the sneers and jeers of an excited crowd into notes of respect and admiration. Hundreds rushed up to shake hands with her, and congratulate the glorious old mother, and bid her God-speed on her mission of "testifyin' agin concerning the wickedness of this 'ere people."

Speech at New York City Convention

Is it not good for me to come and draw forth a spirit, to see what kind of spirit people are of? I see that some of you have got the spirit of a goose, and some have got the spirit of a snake. I feel at home here. I come to you, citizens of New York, as I suppose you ought to be. I am a citizen of the State of New York; I was born in it, and I was a slave in the State of New York; and now I am a good citizen of this State. I was born here, and I can tell you I feel at home here. I've been lookin' round and watchin' things, and I know a little mite 'bout Woman's Rights, too. I come forth to speak 'bout Woman's Rights, and want to throw in my little mite, to keep the scales a-movin', I know that it feels a' kind o' hissin' and ticklin' like to see a colored woman get up and tell you about things, and Woman's Rights. We have all been thrown down so low that nobody thought we'd ever get up again; but we have been long enough trodden now; we will come up again, and now I am here.

I was a-thinkin', when I see women contendin' for their rights, I was a-thinkin' what a difference there is now, and what there was in old times. I have only a few minutes to speak; but in the old times the kings of the earth would hear a woman. There was a king in the Scriptures; and then it was the kings of the earth would kill a woman if she come into their presence; but Queen Esther,[1] come forth, for she was oppressed, and felt there was a great wrong.

and she said I will die or I will bring my complaint before the king. Should the king of the United States be greater, or more crueler, or more harder? But the king, he raised up his sceptre and said: "Thy request shall be granted unto thee—to the half of my kingdom will I grant it to thee." Then he said he would hang Haman on the gallows he had made up high. But that is not what women come forward to contend. The women want their rights as Esther. She only wanted to explain her rights. And he was so liberal that he said, "the half of my kingdom shall be granted to thee," and he did not wait for her to ask, he was so liberal with her.

Now, women do not ask half of a kingdom, but their rights, and they don't get 'em.—When she comes to demand 'em; don't you hear how sons hiss their mothers like snakes, because they ask for their rights; and can they ask for anything less? The king ordered Haman to be hung on the gallows which he prepared to hang others; but I do not want any man to be killed, but I am sorry to see them so short-minded. But we'll have our rights; see if we don't; and you can't stop us from them; see if you can. You may hiss as much as you like, but it is comin'. Women don't get half as much rights as they ought to; we want more, and we will have it. Jesus says: "What I say to one, I say to all—watch!" I'm a-watchin'. God says: "Honor your father and your mother." Sons and daughters ought to behave themselves before their mothers, but they do not. I can see them a-laughin' and pointin' at their mothers up here on the stage. They hiss when an aged woman comes forth. If they'd been brought up proper they'd have known better than hissing like snakes and geese. I'm 'round watchin' these things, and I wanted to come up and say these few things to you, and I'm glad of the hearin' you give me. I wanted to tell you a mite about Woman's Rights, and so I came out and said so. I am sittin' among you to watch; and every once and awhile I will come out and tell you what time of night it is.

[1]The Old Testament King Ahasuerus offered to fulfill any request made by his Jewish wife Esther, even if she asked for half of his kingdom. Esther asked for justice for her people. Prince Haman was slaughtering the Jews because he believed he had been insulted by the king's adviser, Mordecai. King Ahasuerus hanged Haman on the gallows Haman had built for Mordecai.

Address to the First Annual Meeting of the American Equal Rights Association, New York City, May 9, 1867

My friends, I am rejoiced that you are glad, but I don't know how you will feel when I get through. I come from another field—the country of the slave. They have got their liberty—so much good luck to have slavery partly destroyed; not entirely. I want it root and branch destroyed. Then we will all be free indeed. I feel that if I have to answer for the deeds done in my body just as much as a man, I have a right to have just as much as a man. There is a great stir about colored men getting their rights, but not a word about the colored women; and if colored men get their rights, and not colored women theirs, you see the colored men will be masters over the women, and it will be just as bad as it was before. So I am for keeping the thing going while things are stirring; because if we wait till it is still, it will take a great while to get it going again. White women are a great deal smarter, and know more than colored women, while colored women do not know scarcely anything. They go out washing, which is about as high as a colored woman gets, and their men go about idle, strutting up and down; and when the women come home, they ask for their money and take it all, and then scold because there is no food. I want you to consider on that, chil'n. I call you chil'n; you are somebody's chil'n, and I am old enough to be mother of all that is here. I want women to have their rights. In the courts women have no right, no voice; nobody speaks for them. I wish woman to have her voice there among the pettifoggers. If it is not a fit place for women, it is unfit for men to be there.

I am above eighty years old; it is about time for me to be going. I have been forty years a slave and forty years free, and would be here forty years more to have equal rights for all. I suppose I am kept here because something remains for me to do; I suppose I am yet to help to break the chain. I have done a great deal of work; as much as a man, but did not get so much pay. I used to work in the field and bind grain, keeping up with the cradler; but men doing no more, got twice as much pay; so with the German women. They work in the field and do as much work, but do not get the pay. We do as much, we eat as much, we want as much. I suppose I am about the only colored woman that goes about to speak for the rights of the colored women. I want to keep the thing stirring, now that the ice is cracked. What we want is a little money. You men know that you get as much again as women when you write, or for what you do. When we get our rights we shall not have to come to you for money, for then we shall have money enough in our own pockets; and may be you will ask us for money. But help us now until we get it. It is a good consolation to know that when we have got this battle once fought we shall not be coming to you any more. You have been having our rights so long, that you think, like a slave-holder, that you own us. I know that it is hard for one who has held the reins for so long to give up; it cuts like a knife. It will feel all the better when it closes up again. I have been in Washington about three years, seeing about these colored people. Now colored men have the right to vote. There ought to be equal rights now more than ever, since colored people have got their freedom. I am going to talk several times while I am here; so now I will do a little singing. I have not heard any singing since I came here.

Accordingly, suiting the action to the word, Sojourner sang, "We are going home." "There, children," said she, "in heaven we shall rest from all our labors; first do all we have to do here. There I am determined to go, not to stop short of that beautiful place, and I do not mean to stop till I get there, and meet you there, too."

HENRY HIGHLAND GARNET

(1815–1882)

Henry Highland Garnet—politician and liberator, minister, black nationalist, theorist of black independence, and rhetorical strategist of African American aesthetics—was one of the greatest orators of his era. Encouraged by the liberation and enfranchisement of former slaves in the Caribbean, he called for African American militancy in political struggle. Henry Highland Garnet supported emancipation for the human chattel in the United States, for black public suffrage as well as citizenry, and finally for the autonomous control of American black institutions. Hence, he was one of the earliest and most articulate advocates of a position that in the next century would often be maligned as "Black Power." To him, self-determination by American blacks was a logical means to secure human rights.

Early on, Garnet proposed the selective emigration of blacks from the United States to Mexico, the West Indies, and various countries in West Africa. By the time of the Civil War, he had already supported guerrilla action against the Fugitive Slave Law. As a leader, advisor, and consultant to the U.S. government, he championed education as well as temperance. Bolstered by the vision of independence in African countries, he traced the roots of slavery to what he saw as a capitalistic monopoly of land. In layered images of both time and space, he revealed in rare moments of his famous sermons a few vestiges of African philosophy for reading the cosmos of human existence. Garnet tells the story of black Americans who emerged from the world of eternity into human history (time) only to return to the world of spirit. Hence, he wrote out in sermonic language, the cultural authority of the African American artist who pays respect to the honored dead and who speaks to listeners yet unborn.

Henry Highland Garnet was born a slave on December 23, 1815, in New Market, Maryland. As the grandson of a Mandingo chieftain, he kept alive a racial pride and fervor he believed to be the destiny of African American people. His father, a shoemaker during slavery, escaped from bondage with his wife, son (Garnet), and daughter, when Garnet was nine. After the family made its way to New York City, Garnet enrolled in the African Free School No. 1. that included attendance by the young Alexander Crummell, who would become an Episcopal priest, and Ira Aldridge, who would become the founding father of the African American theater. As with the contemporary instance of Frederick Douglass and the future example of Walter White, Garnet encountered a defining moment of character during his formative years. When he returned home in 1829, following work as a cabin boy, he found that his family had scattered to avoid capture by slave catchers. At the time that he had dropped out of school to earn money, his beloved sister had been caught. For awhile, with an open knife, he walked the streets to bait the hunters and motivated his family as well as friends, who all feared for his life, to send him to Long Island. He was employed for two years as an indentured servant in New Jersey, where, in 1830, he injured his right leg, which displayed severe swelling. Nearly all his life, he struggled in severe pain of the handicap. The leg eventually would be amputated a few years later, but it seemingly never weakened his resolve to defend human rights.

Soon afterwards, Garnet returned to New York to resume his studies. In 1835, Puritans in Canaan, New Hampshire, established Noyes Academy, a high school, to expand the opportunities of African American men. During late June of that year, Garnet traveled with Crummell and two other young men by boat to New Bedford, Massachusetts, and then by horse and carriage over land. As a handicapped person who had to be strapped to the top of the coach, he endured racial abuse by passersby. After a brief time of settling at the New Hampshire site—which, false to its name, was no promised land—neighboring farmers attacked the "nigger school." As soon as the Puritans had labeled the school a public menace, three hundred bullies supported by a hundred oxen attached ropes to the edifice and dragged it to a nearby swamp. Garnet, whose painful leg was still a part of him, fired the bullets that he had molded. And it was he who, according to Richard Barksdale and Keneth Kinnamon, "directed the barricading of their quarters." Alexander Crummell would narrate years later:

> About eleven o'clock the tramp of horses was heard approaching; and as one rapid rider passed the house he fired at it. Garnet quickly replied to it by a discharge of a double barreled shotgun which blazed away through the window. At once, the hills from many a mile around reverberated with the sound. Lights were seen from scores of houses on every side of the town, and villages far and near were in a state of great excitement. But the musket shot by Garnet doubtless saved our lives. The cowardly ruffians dared not attack us.

After a few months back home, Garnet and friends entered the Oneida Institute at Whitesboro, New York. With the emotional support of his family, who had reunited in 1830, he graduated at the top of his class in 1839. Settling in Troy, New York, he taught school and studied theology for two years. While still a student, he expressed a stern indictment of slavery at the annual convention of the American Antislavery Society. Shortly after the amputation of his leg in 1841, he became a licensed pastor of Liberty Street Presbyterian Church in New York. The same year, Garnet married Julia Williams, a former classmate, who assisted him in making their home a haven for fugitive slaves.

During the 1840s, he became well known in abolitionist circles as a member of the Liberty Party and as a radical within the antislavery movement. By 1843, he began to earn the ire of the Garrisonians when he delivered his famous speech, "An Address to the Slaves of the United States of America," at the Negro National Convention held in Buffalo, New York. Garnet urged the slaves to strike, to arm themselves, and to bring slavery to an end through violent rebellion. His speech was exhortative and persuasive. Had it not been for Frederick Douglass, a staunch moral suasionist, the Convention would have passed a resolution endorsing Garnet's speech. Even after Douglass's eloquent intervention, a vote taken not to endorse the address failed by a single vote.

Garnet's address was based on the radical ideas expressed earlier in David Walker's *Appeal.* He began the speech by reminding free Negroes of the North of their good fortune, but he focused on their blood ties to their actual and figurative relatives still in bondage: "Many of you are bound to us, not only by the ties of common humanity, but we are connected by the more tender relations of parents, wives, husbands, and sisters and friends. As such we most affectionately address you." At one point during the speech, Garnet provides an honor roll of slaves who had been involved in rebellion. He praises and salutes Denmark Veazie (sic), Nathaniel Turner (Nat Turner who revolted in Southampton, Virginia, in August 1831), and Joseph Cinque (who led a mutiny on the slave ship called the *Amistad*). In his concluding paragraphs, Garnet advises the slaves that it is their Christian obligation to resist violently if necessary: "Brethren, arise, arise! Strike for your lives and liberties. . . . Let your motto be resistance! *resistance!* RESISTANCE!" His address was so militant that it went unpublished and ignored for five years. Then, in 1848, with the financial backing of John Brown, it was published, along with David Walker's *Appeal,* which had been previously published by Walker himself.

With his famous address, Garnet became the leading radical voice of abolition. His involvement in antislavery activities and his advocacy for voluntary emigration of blacks to Africa took him abroad to Germany, England, and Scotland. In 1853, the United Presbyterian Church sent him to Jamaica to pastor the Stirling Presbyterian Church. He did not return to the United States until 1855. Through his work in Jamaica, he recognized a shift in concerns from international movements for peace and liberation to those of economic relief for newly freed slaves as well as for other black Americans soon to be freed. In encouraging guerrilla actions against the Fugitive Slave Law, he conferred with John Brown about plans for the Harper's Ferry raid in 1859. As much as at any time, he disagreed with Douglass, who was skeptical about organized religion and racial nationalism. Garnet, who agitated for the abolition of slavery and for the enlistment of slaves in the Union Army, soon became a chaplain to a regiment of African American troops.

By 1865, Garnet had become the famous minister of the Shiloh Presbyterian Church in New York City, which served as a rallying place for many black organizations and causes. African Americans had met there to celebrate emancipation in 1863 and lament the dead of the New York Draft Riot in that year. As a prominent leader in New York City's black community, Garnet was invited by President Lincoln to deliver a sermon in the House of Representatives when Congress enacted the bill that became the Thirteenth Amendment in February 1865. On this occasion, he became the first African American to deliver a sermon before that congressional body. In his rhapsodic sermon, "A Memorial Discourse Delivered in the Hall of the House of Representatives, February 12, 1865," he focused on the issue of the emancipated slaves, remaining adamant and militant in his attack on the social and moral evils of "the peculiar institution." In his characteristically electrifying manner, he delivered an imperative to Congress to *"Emancipate, Enfranchise, Educate, and give the blessings of the gospel to every American citizen."* Widely and favorably received, the speech brought him into national prominence. Upon the death of Abraham Lincoln that year, Mary Todd Lincoln requested that her late husband's canes be delivered to Garnet and Douglass, whom she recognized as the two greatest black leaders.

Garnet continued for several years to lecture throughout the country on the issue of civil rights. During this time, he married Sarah J. (Smith) Thompson.* However, after having witnessed the demise of Black Reconstruction and the continuation of racial oppression in the United States, he moved to Liberia after having been appointed Minister Resident and Consul General in 1881. He died in Liberia, the land of his forefathers, on February 12, 1882. His lifelong friend, Alexander Crummell, delivered the eulogy at his funeral.

During his life, he had rendered an authentic voice for the slaves of the nineteenth century. He adopted the rhetorical strategy of speaking directly to them rather than about them. As a literary artisan who recreates his or her voice, he expressed the importance of African American political, social, and economic autonomy. In many ways, he subverted even the classical and traditional texts used by black people. His rhetorical appeal ranged from Socrates through Plato, to Cyrus in the classical period, through George Washington and Thomas Jefferson in the American Colonial era, to African American slaves and free persons of color in his time. With Frederick Douglass, Garnet also valued the Emancipation Proclamation as even more sacred than the U.S. Constitution. He believed that only verbal monuments dedicated to freedom encapsulate the deepest human morality worthy of being immortalized in poetry and narrative; he asserted that only texts with this value are worthy of either human action or human remembrance. Political action, indeed, is imperative. Although Garnet was a politician in fact, he became an African American artist who rewrote the traditional concept of American democracy.

**Editor's note:* In the existing authoritative sources on Garnet, there is no mention of the fate of Garnet's first wife, Julia Williams. In addition, there is conflicting information as to whether he had children or not.

❖❖❖

The earliest study of Garnet's life and works is James McCune Smith's *The Sketch of the Life and Labors of Rev. Henry Highland Garnet* (1865). The most recent biography is Earl J. Ofari's *Let Your Motto Be Resistance* (1972). For a literary discussion of Garnet's address and his "The Past and the Present Condition and the Destiny of the Colored Race . . ." (1848), see Blyden Jackson's *A History of Afro-American Literature,* Vol. I (1989).

An Address to the Slaves of the United States of America

Brethren and Fellow Citizens: Your brethren of the North, East, and West have been accustomed to meet together in National Conventions, to sympathize with each other, and to weep over your unhappy condition. In these meetings we have addressed all classes of the free, but we have never, until this time, sent a word of consolation and advice to you. We have been contented in sitting still and mourning over your sorrows, earnestly hoping that before this day your sacred liberties would have been restored. But, we have hoped in vain. Years have rolled on, and tens of thousands have been borne on streams of blood and tears to the shores of enternity. While you have been oppressed, we have also been partakers with you; nor can we be free while you are enslaved. We, therefore, write to you as being bound with you.

Many of you are bound to us, not only by the ties of a common humanity, but we are connected by the more tender relations of parents, wives, husbands, and sisters, and friends. As such we most affectionately address you.

Slavery has fixed a deep gulf between you and us, and while it shuts out from you the relief and consolation which your friends would willingly render, it afflicts and persecutes you with a fierceness which we might not expect to see in the fiends of hell. But still the Almighty Father of mercies has left to us a glimmering ray of hope, which shines out like a lone star in a cloudy sky. Mankind are becoming wiser, and better—the oppressor's power is fading, and you, every day, are becoming better informed, and more numerous. Your grievances, brethren, are many. We shall not attempt, in this short address, to present to the world all the dark catalogue of the nation's sins, which have been committed upon an innocent people. Nor is it indeed necessary, for you feel them from day to day, and all the civilized world looks upon them with amazement.

Two hundred and twenty-seven years ago the first of our injured race were brought to the shores of America. They came not with glad spirits to select their homes in the New World. They came not with their own consent, to find an unmolested enjoyment of the blessings of this fruitful soil. The first dealings they had with men calling themselves Christians exhibited to them the worst features of corrupt and sordid hearts: and convinced them that no cruelty is too great, no villainy and no robbery too abhorrent for even enlightened men to perform, when influenced by avarice and lust. Neither did they come flying upon the wings of Liberty to a land of freedom. But they came with broken hearts, from their beloved native land, and were doomed to unrequited toil and deep degradation. Nor did the evil of their bondage end at their emancipation by death. Succeeding generations inherited their chains, and millions have come from eternity into time, and have returned again to the world of spirits, cursed and ruined by American slavery.

The propagators of the system, or their immediate successors, very soon discovered its growing evil, and its tremendous wickedness, and secret promises were made to destroy it. The gross inconsistency of a people holding slaves, who had themselves "ferried o'er the wave" for freedom's sake, was too apparent to be entirely overlooked. The voice of Freedom cried, "Emancipate your slaves." Humanity supplicated with tears for the deliverance of the children of Africa. Wisdom urged her solemn plea. The bleeding captive plead his innocence, and pointed to Christianity who stood weeping at the cross. Jehovah frowned upon the nefarious institution, and thunderbolts, red with vengeance, struggled to leap forth to blast the guilty wretches who maintained it. But all was vain. Slavery had stretched its dark wings of death over the land, the Church stood silently by—the priests prophesied falsely, and the people loved to have it so. Its throne is established, and now it reigns triumphant.

Nearly three millions of your fellow-citizens are prohibited by law and public opinion (which in this country is stronger than law) from reading the Book of Life. Your intellect has been destroyed as much as possible, and every ray of light they have attempted to shut out from your minds. The oppressors themselves have become involved in the ruin. They have become weak, sensual, and rapacious—they have cursed you—they have cursed themselves—they have cursed the earth which they have trod.

The colonies threw the blame upon England. They said that the mother country entailed the evil upon them, and they would rid themselves of it if they could. The world thought they were sincere, and the philanthropic pitied them. But time soon tested their sincerity. In a few years the colonists grew strong, and severed themselves from the British Government. Their independence was declared, and they took their station among the sovereign powers of the earth. The declaration was a glorious document. Sages admired it, and the patriotic of every nation reverenced the God-like sentiments which it contained. When the power of Government returned to their hands, did they emancipate the slaves? No; they rather added new links to our chains. Were they ignorant of the principles of Liberty? Certainly they were not. The sentiments of their revolutionary orators fell in burning eloquence upon their hearts, and with one voice they cried, LIBERTY OR DEATH. Oh, what a sentence was that! It ran from soul to soul like electric fire, and nerved the arms of thousands to fight in the holy cause of Freedom. Among the diversity of opinions that are entertained in regard to physical resistance, there are but a few found to gainsay the stern declaration. We are among those who do not.

SLAVERY! How much misery is comprehended in that single word. What mind is there that does not shrink from its direful effects? Unless the image of God be obliterated from the soul, all men cherish the love of liberty. The nice discerning political economist does not regard the sacred right more than the untutored African who roams in the wilds of Congo. Nor has the one more right to the full enjoyment of his freedom than the other. In every man's mind the good seeds of liberty are planted, and he who brings his fellow down so low, as to make him contented with a condition of slavery, commits the highest crime against God and man. Brethren, your oppressors aim to do this. They endeavor to make you as much like brutes as possible. When they have blinded the eyes of your mind—when they have embittered the sweet waters of life—when they have shut out the light which shines from the word of God—then, and not till then, has American slavery done its perfect work.

TO SUCH DEGRADATION IT IS SINFUL IN THE EXTREME FOR YOU TO MAKE VOLUNTARY SUBMISSION. The divine commandments you are in duty bound to reverence and obey. If you do not obey them, you will surely meet with the displeasure of the Almighty. He requires you to love Him supremely, and your neighbor as yourself—to keep the Sabbath day holy—to search the Scriptures—and bring up your children with respect for His laws, and to worship no other God but Him. But slavery sets all these at nought, and hurls defiance in the face of Jehovah. The forlorn condition in which you are placed does not destroy your obligation to God. You are not certain of heaven, because you allow yourselves to remain in a state of slavery, where you cannot obey the commandments of the Sovereign of the universe. If the ignorance of slavery is a passport to heaven, then it is a blessing, and no curse, and you should rather desire its perpetuity than its abolition. God will not receive slavery, nor ignorance, nor any other state of mind, for love and obedience to Him. Your condition does not absolve you from your moral obligation. The diabolical injustice by which your liberties are cloven down, NEITHER GOD NOR ANGELS, OR JUST MEN, COMMAND YOU TO SUFFER FOR A SINGLE MOMENT. THEREFORE IT IS YOUR SOLEMN AND IMPERATIVE DUTY TO USE EVERY MEANS, BOTH MORAL, INTELLECTUAL, AND PHYSICAL, THAT PROMISES SUCCESS. If a band of heathen men should attempt to enslave a race of Christians, and to place their children under the influence of some false religion, surely Heaven would frown upon the men who would not resist such aggression, even to death. If, on the other hand, a band of Christians should attempt to enslave a race of heathen men, and to entail slavery upon them, and to keep them in heathenism in the midst of Christianity, the God of heaven would smile upon every effort which the injured might make to disenthral themselves.

Brethren, it is as wrong for your lordly oppressors to keep you in slavery as it was for the man thief to steal our ancestors from the coast of Africa. You should therefore now use the same manner of resistance as would have been just in our ancestors when the bloody footprints of the first remorseless soul-thief was placed upon the shores of our fatherland. The humblest peasant is as free in the sight of God as the proudest monarch that ever swayed a sceptre. Liberty is a spirit sent out from God, and like its great Author, is no respecter of persons.

Brethren, the time has come when you must act for yourselves. It is an old and true saying that, "if hereditary bondmen would be free, they must themselves strike the blow." You can plead your own cause, and do the work of emancipation better than any others. The nations of the Old World are moving in the great cause of universal freedom, and some of them at least will, ere long, do you justice. The combined powers of Europe have placed their broad seal of disapprobation upon the African slave-trade. But in the slaveholding parts of the United States the trade is as brisk as ever. They buy and sell you as though you were brute beasts. The North has done much—her opinion of slavery in the abstract is known. But in regard to the South, we adopt the opinion of the *New York Evangelist*—"We have advanced so far, that the cause apparently waits for a more effectual door to be thrown open than has been yet." We are about to point you to that more effectual door. Look around you, and behold the bosoms of your loving wives heaving with untold agonies! Here the cries of your poor children! Remember the stripes your fathers bore. Think of the torture and disgrace of your noble mothers. Think of your wretched sisters, loving virtue and purity, as they are driven into concubinage and are exposed to the unbridled lusts of incarnate devils. Think of the undying glory that hangs around the ancient name of Africa—and forget not that you are native-born American citizens, and as such you are justly entitled to all the rights that are granted to the freest. Think how many tears you have poured out upon the soil which you have cultivated with unrequited toil and enriched with your blood; and then go to your lordly enslavers and tell them plainly, that you *are determined to be free.* Appeal to their sense of justice, and tell them that they have no more right to oppress you than you have to enslave them. Entreat them to remove the grievous burdens which they have imposed upon you, and to remunerate you for your labor. Promise them renewed diligence in the cultivation of the soil, if they will render to you an equivalent for your services. Point them to the increase of happiness and prosperity in the British West Indies since the Act of Emancipation. Tell them in language which they cannot misunderstand of the exceeding sinfulness of slavery, and of a future judgment, and of the righteous retributions of an indignant God. Inform them that all you desire is FREEDOM, and that nothing else will suffice. Do this, and forever after cease to toil for the heartless tyrants, who give you no other reward but stripes and abuse. If they then commence work of death, they, and not you, will be responsible for the consequences. You had far better all die—*die immediately,* than live slaves, and entail your wretchedness upon your posterity. If you would be free in this generation, here is your only hope. However much you and all of us may desire it, there is not much hope of redemption without the shedding of blood. If you must bleed, let it all come at once—rather *die freemen than live to be the slaves.* It is impossible, like the children of Israel, to make a grand exodus from the land of bondage. The Pharaohs are on both sides of the blood-red waters! You cannot move *en masse* to the dominions of the British Queen—nor can you pass through Florida and overrun Texas, and at last find peace in Mexico. The propagators of American slavery are spending their blood and treasure that they may plant the black flag in the heart of Mexico and riot in the halls of the Montezumas. In language of the Reverend Robert Hall, when addressing the volunteers of Bristol, who were rushing forth to repel the invasion of Napoleon, who threatened to lay waste the fair homes of England, "Religion is too much interested in your behalf not to shed over you her most gracious influences."

You will not be compelled to spend much time in order to become inured to hardships. From the first movement that you breathed the air of heaven, you have been accustomed to nothing else but hardships. The heroes of the American Revolution were never put upon harder fare than a peck of corn and few herrings per week. You have not become enervated by the luxuries of life. Your sternest energies have been beaten out upon the anvil of severe trial. Slavery has done this to make you subservient to its own purposes; but it has done more than this, it has prepared you for any emergency. If you receive good treatment, it is what you can hardly expect; if you meet with pain, sorrow, and even death, these are the common lot of the slaves.

Fellowmen! patient sufferers! behold your dearest rights crushed to the earth! See your sons murdered, and your wives, mothers and sisters doomed to prostitution. In the name of the merciful God, and by all that life is worth, let it no longer be a debatable question, whether it is better to choose *liberty* or *death.*

In 1822, Denmark Veazie, of South Carolina, formed a plan for the liberation of his fellowmen. In the whole history of human efforts to overthrow slavery, a more complicated and tremendous plan was never formed. He was betrayed by the treachery of his own people, and died a martyr to freedom. Many a brave hero fell, but history, faithful to her high trust, will transcribe his name on the same monument with Moses, Hampden, Tell, Bruce, and Wallace, Toussaint L'Ouverture, Lafayette, and Washington. That tremendous movement shook the whole empire of slavery. The guilty soul-thieves were overwhelmed with fear. It is a matter of fact that at this time, and in consequence of the threatened revolution, the slave States talked strongly of emancipation. But they blew but one blast of the trumpet of freedom, and then laid it aside. As these men became quiet, the slaveholders ceased to talk about emancipation: and now behold your condition to-day! Angels sigh over it, and humanity has long since exhausted her tears in weeping on your account!

The patriotic Nathaniel Turner followed Denmark Veazie. He was goaded to desperation by wrong and injustice. By despotism, his name has been recorded on the list of infamy, and future generations will remember him among the noble and brave.

Next arose the immortal Joseph Cinque, the hero of the *Amistad.* He was a native African, and by the help of God he emancipated a whole ship-load of his fellowmen on the high seas. And he now sings of liberty on the sunny hills of Africa and beneath his native palm-trees, where he hears the lion roar and feels himself as free as the king of the forest.

Next arose Madison Washington, that bright star of freedom, and took his station in the constellation of true heroism. He was a slave on board the brig *Creole,* of Richmond, bound to New Orleans, that great slave mart, with a hundred and four others. Nineteen struck for liberty or death. But one life was taken, and the whole were emancipated, and the vessel was carried into Nassau, New Providence.

Noble men! Those who have fallen in freedom's conflict, their memories will be cherished by the true-hearted and the God-fearing in all future generations; those who are living, their names are surrounded by a halo of glory.

Brethren, arise, arise! Strike for your lives and liberties. Now is the day and the hour. Let every slave throughout the land do this, and the days of slavery are numbered. You cannot be more oppressed than you have been—you cannot suffer greater cruelties than you have already. *Rather die freemen than live to be slaves.* Remember that you are FOUR MILLIONS!

It is in your power so to torment the God-cursed slaveholders that they will be glad to let you go free. If the scale was turned, and black men were the masters and white men the slaves, every destructive agent and element would be employed to lay the oppressor low. Danger and death would hang over their heads day and night. Yes, the tyrants would meet with plagues more terrible than those of Pharaoh. But you are a patient people. You act as though you were made for the special use of these devils. You act as though your daughters were born to pamper the lusts of your masters and overseers. And worse than all, you tamely submit while your lords tear your wives from your embraces and defile them before your eyes. In the name of God, we ask, are you men? Where is the blood of your fathers? Has it all run out of your veins? Awake, awake; millions of voices are calling you! Your dead fathers speak to you from their graves. Heaven, as with a voice of thunder, calls on you to arise from the dust.

Let your motto be resistance! *resistance!* RESISTANCE! No oppressed people have ever secured their liberty without resistance. What kind of resistance you had better make you must decide by the circumstances that surround you, and according to the suggestion of expediency. Brethren, adieu! Trust in the living God. Labor for the peace of the human race, and remember that you are FOUR MILLIONS!

FREDERICK DOUGLASS

(1817–1895)

Frederick Douglass was one of the most gifted writers and thinkers in America during the nineteenth century. He was one of the most famous black abolitionists and one of the most talented orators. But even the best of traditional accounts neglect true appreciation for his superb gift of metaphor and symbol. Douglass was one of the first people to propose that the problem of slavery and race in America was a failure of imagination, a failure, in other words, to create new visions of humanity since the European Renaissance of the sixteenth century. He was one of the first to narrate the crisis in a captivating rhetoric exposing the irony of Christian civilization. He wrote with a precise imagery that depicts the American South as a desert of Gothic horror; and, though no real vampires inhabited his slave world, Douglass implied a symbolic connection between them and the slave masters who seemed to suck from others the life's blood of human value.

Though Douglass wrote brilliantly about the slave experience, he suggested that the power of slavery was beyond even his words. He helped restore slavery from the dispassionate recital of sociological fact to the compelling drama of story. His *Narrative* is analytical and subjectively persuasive. It is historical, religious, and political; it portrays excellent types of humans and of historical situations. It reveals patterns of history, dramatic situations, double encounters, and stunning repetitions of scenes at St. Michael's on the Eastern Shore of Maryland; and it presents one or two other scenes in England more than forty years apart. Indeed, the *Narrative* depicts classical scenes of Egypt and Avignon, France, or Genoa, Italy, against the backdrop of the memory of American slavery, and it reveals brilliantly the capacity of the human race for creativity and destruction. "There are some things and places," Douglass writes, "made sacred by their uses and by the events with which they are associated, especially those which have in any measure changed the current of human taste, thought, and life, or which have revealed new powers and triumphs of the human soul." Frederick Douglass, so aware of the historical limitations imposed on African Americans, refused stubbornly to concede that any outside obstacle could ever deter people from fulfilling their will and from assuming their rightful destiny. Although he was sometimes romantically naive, Douglass was prophetic in his understanding that racial history is cyclical. He understood that the black writer was to define and direct the flow of history.

Frederick Bailey (later Douglass) was born in 1817 of a slave mother and an unknown white father on the Eastern Shore of Maryland. As a youth, he went to Baltimore to learn ship caulking. His mistress taught him to read and write before her husband forbade continuance of the training. At twenty-one, in 1838, Bailey used his literacy to forge some papers. With some other documents provided by a free black seaman, he escaped to freedom. Shortly afterwards, he married Anna Murray, a free black woman from Baltimore. Later, and further north, he began work as an antislavery crusader in New Bedford, Massachusetts. William Lloyd Garrison, having heard him deliver a speech at an antislavery convention in Nantucket in 1841, persuaded Bailey to become a member of the antislavery society. Taking the name of Douglass, Frederick became a leader of African Americans in New England. When the publication of his *Narrative* in 1845 endangered his freedom, he fled to England for two years. There, he began to envision freedom as mental as well as physical, speaking against slavery throughout the British empire from 1845 to 1847. When British associates purchased his freedom in 1847 for 150 pounds, he returned to the United States and broke with Garrison, whose program of Northern secession from the union would have left slavery intact. Douglass avoided open quarrel; rather, he moved away peacefully to Rochester, New York, where he founded his famous newspaper, *the North Star* (1847–1863). In 1848, Douglass championed women's rights by attending the first convention of the kind. In fact, he would collapse and die after participating in a meeting for women's suffrage on February 10, 1895.

At times, Douglass became profoundly disappointed, especially with the passage in 1850 of the Fugitive Slave Law. He lectured widely, using the fees to assist fugitive slaves. Forced by lack of funds to discard his plan of an industrial college for black people, he was at first a member of the Liberty Party. Later, he would become a crucial registrant in the Republican assembly of President Abraham Lincoln. With the help of Sojourner Truth, a fellow abolitionist, he enlisted blacks in the Union army. In Massachusetts, he helped recruit the 54th and 55th regiments, both of which earned distinction in the Civil War. Afterwards, he organized blacks to oppose social restrictions based on race. Having campaigned for the Republicans, Douglass was rewarded with appointments as Assistant Secretary of the Santo Domingo Commission (1871) and the United States Marshall for the District of Columbia (1877–1881) under President Grant. Later, he would become Recorder of

Deeds (1881–1886) under President Hayes and Minister to Haiti (1889–1891) under President Arthur.

Douglass helped direct the nation away from the Garrison position on abolitionism. Douglass proposed less emphasis on moral persuasion, Northern secession, and the presumed futility of the Constitution. His considerable dialogue with John Brown, who would soon be a white abolitionist martyr, convinced him in 1847 that only a superior physical force could end slavery. Subsequent consultation with Brown early in 1858, at an "abandoned stone quarry" in Chambersburg, Pennsylvania, convinced Douglass that an attack on the Harpers Ferry federal arsenal in Virginia would be senseless. Meanwhile, he opposed colonization of African Americans as a solution to the race problem and helped to convince Abraham Lincoln to sign the Emancipation Proclamation on January 1, 1863. Finally, with the support of Frances Watkins Harper and other black abolitionists, Douglass led the fight for the passage of the Fourteenth and Fifteenth Amendments to the Constitution. Hence, he played a vital role in laying a foundation for subsequent challenges by law against what would become institutionalized segregation of the races.

The autobiographies of Frederick Douglass should be read by all Americans and all lovers of freedom worldwide. *The Narrative of the Life of Frederick Douglass: An American Slave* (1845) is factual and popular. In portraying the wonderful garden into which Colonel Lloyd forbids the slave to enter, Douglass has left to posterity the image of some men who have proclaimed themselves God over the hopes and dreams of others. Douglass vindicates his own mission as a romantic writer, who, freed from eighteenth-century conventions of a dead past, holds true to the greater promise of the human spirit. Captain Auld [the master] "was not even a good imitator; he possessed all the disposition to deceive, but wanted the power. Having no resources within himself, he was compelled to be the copyist of many, and being such, he was forever the victim of inconsistency; and of consequence he was an object of contempt, and was held as such even by his slaves." His story turns back on the presumed morality from whence it comes: "I mean, by the religion of this land, that which is revealed in the words, deeds, and actions, of those bodies, north and south, calling themselves Christian churches, and yet in union with slave holders. It is against religion, as presented by these bodies, that I have felt it my duty to testify." Although *My Bondage and My Freedom* (1855) further developed his ideas, *The Life and Times of Frederick Douglass* (1881) is the classic narrative. Here Douglass, with a precise tone and mood, restores himself from the "winter of his own mind." Telling us the story of slavery, hence reminding us that the experience was ineffable—except through lived and imagined experience—Douglass completes a dramatic reversal from man to brute and from brute back to man.

The portrait of Douglass's battle with the "Negro-breaker" Covey clarifies the artistic development in Douglass's craft from the first draft to the last one. About twenty-five percent longer in the final draft, the scene is much more specific; hence, it accentuates a more positive future. The power of change assumes a much greater value, as does the struggle for manhood. Here, his probe into the psychology of the oppressor becomes intensely more self-conscious: "Dear reader, you can hardly believe the statement, but it is true and therefore I write it down." In Douglass's analytic, the slaves themselves had to be made unthinking; the mental and moral vision had to be darkened; the master's will had to be the highest law for the system to have worked. In some way, the masters had to convey as quite reasonable their dubious right to someone else's earnings. What had been at first a plain tale about slavery shaped itself into something part story, part folk sermon: "It did not entirely satisfy me to narrate wrongs—I felt like denouncing them." Douglass uses his pen and voice to "renovate" a public mind and "build up" a public sentiment. By the effort, he would "send slavery" to the grave, hence restoring the people with whom he suffered. Never, perhaps, would be express himself more brilliantly than in the rhetorical question raised at Arlington National Cemetery on Decoration Day in 1871: "I ask, in the name of all things sacred, what shall men [and women] remember?"

To Frederick Douglass, black literary art reminds us of our own mortality and also of the imaginative freedom that we can claim even within a painful history. His story suggests a strong spirituality that keeps a dream for freedom alive and that points back to—signifies—the just person who tells the story. The narrative contributes to a communal passage from slavery to freedom, from past to future. The story is the dynamic present, passionately energetic. Douglass helps create a racial aesthetic—a fusion of beauty and communal purpose—that explains our state and explains the cycle 111 years after he wrote the following:

> In further illustration of the reactionary tendencies of public opinion against the black man [and woman] and of the increasing decline, since the war for the Union, in the power of resistance to the onward march of the rebel states to their former control and ascendancy in the councils of the nation, the decision of the United States Supreme Court, declaring the Civil Rights Law of 1875 unconstitutional, is striking and convincing. The strength and activities of the malign elements of the country against equal rights and equality before the law seem to increase in proportion to the increasing distance between that time and the time of the war.

Would the American nation, in other words, ever persist in redressing the grievances of African Americans? Frederick Douglass seemed almost to have been writing about the post–Reagan-Bush era in the twentieth century. His genius was that he was a man for all seasons.

❖❖❖

An indispensable source is Philip Foner's *The Life and Writings of Frederick Douglass,* 5 vols. (1950–1955; 1975), from which our selection of Douglass's speech titled "What to the American Slave Is Your Fourth of July?" is taken. Biographies include: Arna Bontemps's *Free at Last: The Life of Frederick Douglass* (1971), Philip Foner's *Frederick Douglass: A Biography* (1964), N.I. Huggins's *Slave and Citizen: The Life of Frederick Douglass* (1980), and William S. McFeely's *Frederick Douglass* (1991). More critical studies are David W. Blight's *Frederick Douglass' Civil War: Keeping Faith in Jubilee* (1989), and Eric Sunquist's *Critical Essays on Frederick Douglass* (1991). Of the current articles, those by Robert Stepto, James Olney, William L. Andrews, and Donald B. Gibson may prove especially informative.

Many of Douglass's papers, including his diary, are housed at the Frederick Douglass Home Museum, located in Cedar Hill, Washington, D.C. Other valuable documents can be found at the Library of Congress and Yale University.

Narrative of the Life of Frederick Douglass: An American Slave

Written by Himself

Chapter I

I was born in Tuckahoe, near Hillsborough, and about twelve miles from Easton, in Talbot county, Maryland. I have no accurate knowledge of my age, never having seen any authentic record containing it. By far the larger part of the slaves know as little of their age as horses know of theirs, and it is the wish of most masters within my knowledge to keep their slaves thus ignorant. I do not remember to have ever met a slave who could tell of his birthday. They seldom come nearer to it than planting-time, harvest-time, cherry-time, spring-time, or fall-time. A want of information concerning my own was a source of unhappiness to me even during childhood. The white children could tell their ages. I could not tell why I ought to be deprived of the same privilege. I was not allowed to make any inquiries of my master concerning it. He deemed all such inquiries on the part of a slave improper and impertinent, and evidence of a restless spirit. The nearest estimate I can give makes me now between twenty-seven and twenty-eight years of age. I come to this, from hearing my master say, some time during 1835, I was about seventeen years old.

My mother was named Harriet Bailey. She was the daughter of Isaac and Betsey Bailey, both colored, and quite dark. My mother was of a darker complexion than either my grandmother or grandfather.

My father was a white man. He was admitted to be such by all I ever heard speak of my parentage. The opinion was also whispered that my master was my father; but of the correctness of this opinion, I know nothing; the means of knowing was withheld from me. My mother and I were separated when I was but an infant—before I knew her as my mother. It is a common custom, in the part of Maryland from which I ran away, to part children from their mothers at a very early age. Frequently, before the child has reached its twelfth month, its mother is taken from it, and hired out on some farm a considerable distance off, and the child is placed under the care of an old woman, too old for field labor. For what this separation is done, I do not know, unless it be to hinder the development of the child's affection toward its mother, and to blunt and destroy the natural affection of the mother for the child. This is the inevitable result.

I never saw my mother, to know her as such, more than four or five times in my life; and each of these times was very short in duration, and at night. She was hired by a Mr. Stewart, who lived about twelve miles from my home. She made her journeys to see me in the night, travelling the whole distance on foot, after the performance of her day's work. She was a field hand, and a whipping is the penalty of not being in the field at sunrise, unless a slave has special permission from his or her master to the contrary—a permission which they seldom get, and one that gives to him that gives it the proud name of being a kind master. I do not recollect of ever seeing my mother by the light of day. She was with me in the night. She would lie down with me, and get me to sleep, but long before I waked she was gone. Very little communication ever took place between us. Death soon ended what little we could have while she lived, and with it her hardships and suffering. She died when I was about seven years old, on one of my master's farms, near Lee's Mill. I was not allowed to be present during her illness, at her death, or burial. She was gone long before I knew any thing about it. Never having enjoyed, to any considerable extent, her soothing presence, her tender and watchful care, I received the tidings of her death with much the same emotions I should have probably felt at the death of a stranger.

Called thus suddenly away, she left me without the slightest intimation of who my father was. The whisper that my master was my father, may or may not be true; and, true or false, it is of but little consequence to my purpose whilst the fact remains, in all its glaring odiousness, that slaveholders have ordained, and by law established, that the children of slave women shall in all cases follow the condition of their mothers; and this is done too obviously to administer to their own lusts, and make a gratification of their wicked desires profitable as well as pleasurable; for by this cunning arrangement, the slaveholder, in cases not a few, sustains to his slaves the double relation of master and father.

I know of such cases; and it is worthy of remark that such slaves invariably suffer greater hardships, and have more to contend with, than others. They are, in the first place, a constant offence to their mistress. She is ever disposed to find fault with them; they can seldom do any thing to please her; she is never better pleased than when she sees them under the lash, especially when she suspects her husband of showing to his mulatto children favors which he withholds from his black slaves. The master is frequently compelled to sell this class of his slaves, out of deference to the feelings of his white wife; and, cruel as the deed may strike any one to be, for a man to sell his own children to human flesh-mongers, it is often the dictate of humanity for him to do so; for, unless he does this, he must not only whip them himself, but must stand by and see one white son tie up his brother, of but few shades darker complexion than himself, and ply the gory lash to his naked back; and if he lisp one word of disapproval, it is set down to his parental partiality, and only makes a bad matter worse, both for himself and the slave whom he would protect and defend.

Every year brings with it multitudes of this class of slaves. It was doubtless in consequence of a knowledge of this fact, that one great statesman of the south predicted the downfall of slavery by the inevitable laws of population. Whether this prophecy is ever fulfilled or not, it is nevertheless plain that a very different-looking class of people are springing up at the south, and are now held in slavery, from those originally brought to this country from Africa; and if their increase will do no other good, it will do away the force of the argument, that God cursed Ham, and therefore American slavery is right. If the lineal descendants of Ham are alone to be scripturally enslaved, it is certain that slavery at the south must soon become unscriptural; for thousands are ushered into the world, annually, who, like myself, owe their existence to white fathers, and those fathers most frequently their own masters.

I have had two masters. My first master's name was Anthony. I do not remember his first name. He was generally called Captain Anthony—a title which, I presume, he acquired by sailing a craft on the Chesapeake Bay. He was not considered a rich slaveholder. He owned two or three farms, and about thirty slaves. His farms and slaves were under the care of an overseer. The overseer's name was Plummer. Mr. Plummer was a miserable drunkard, a profane swearer, and a savage monster. He always went armed with a cowskin and a heavy cudgel. I have known him to cut and slash the women's heads so horribly, that even master would be enraged at his cruelty, and would threaten to whip him if he did not mind himself. Master, however, was not a humane slaveholder. It required extraordinary barbarity on the part of an overseer to affect him. He was a cruel man, hardened by a long life of slaveholding. He would at times seem to take great pleasure in whipping a slave. I have often been awakened at the dawn of day by the most heart-rending shrieks of an own aunt of mine, whom he used to tie up to a joist, and whip upon her naked back till she was literally covered with blood. No words, no tears, no prayers, from his gory victim, seemed to move his iron heart from its bloody purpose. The louder she screamed, the harder he whipped; and where the blood ran fastest, there he whipped longest. He would whip her to make her scream, and whip her to make her hush; and not until overcome by fatigue, would he cease to swing the blood-clotted cowskin. I remember the first time I ever witnessed this horrible exhibition. I was quite a child, but I well remember it. I never shall forget it whilst I remember any thing. It was the first of a long series of such outrages, of which I was doomed to be a witness and a participant. It struck me with awful force. It was the blood-stained gate, the entrance to the hell of slavery, through which I was about to pass. It was a most terrible spectacle. I wish I could commit to paper the feelings with which I beheld it.

This occurrence took place very soon after I went to live with my old master, and under the following circumstances. Aunt Hester went out one night,—where or for what I do not know,—and happened to be absent when my master desired her presence. He had ordered her not to go out evenings, and warned her that she must never let him catch her in company with a young man, who was paying attention to her belonging to Colonel Lloyd. The young man's name was Ned Roberts, generally called Lloyd's Ned. Why master was so careful of her, may be safely left to conjecture. She was a woman of noble form, and of graceful proportions, having very few equals, and fewer superiors, in personal appearance, among the colored or white women of our neighborhood.

Aunt Hester had not only disobeyed his orders in going out, but had been found in company with Lloyd's Ned; which circumstance, I found, from what he said while whipping her, was the chief offence. Had he been a man of pure morals himself, he might have been thought interested in protecting the innocence of my aunt; but those who knew him will not suspect him of any such virtue. Before he commenced whipping Aunt Hester, he took her into the kitchen, and stripped her from neck to waist, leaving her neck, shoulders, and back, entirely naked. He then told her to cross her hands, calling her at the same time a d——d b——h. After crossing her hands, he tied them with a strong rope, and led her to a stool under a large hook in the joist, put in for the purpose. He made her get upon the stool, and tied her hands to the hook. She now stood fair for his infernal purpose. Her arms were stretched up at their full length, so that she stood upon the ends of her toes. He then said to her, "Now, you d——d b——h, I'll learn you how to disobey my orders!" and after rolling up his sleeves, he commenced to lay on the heavy cowskin, and soon the warm, red blood (amid heart-rending shrieks from her, and horrid oaths from him) came dripping to the floor. I was so terrified and horror-stricken at the sight, that I hid myself in a closet, and dared not venture out till long after the bloody transaction was over. I expected it would be my turn next. It was all new to me. I had never seen any thing like it before. I had always lived with my grandmother on the outskirts of the plantation, where she was put to raise the children of the younger women. I had therefore been, until now, out of the way of the bloody scenes that often occurred on the plantation.

Chapter II

My master's family consisted of two sons, Andrew and Richard; one daughter, Lucretia, and her husband, Captain Thomas Auld. They lived in one house, upon the home plantation of Colonel Edward Lloyd. My master was Colonel Lloyd's clerk and superintendent. He was what might be called the overseer of the overseers. I spent two years of childhood on this plantation in my old master's family. It was here that I witnessed the bloody transaction recorded in the first chapter; and as I received my first impressions of slavery on this plantation, I will give some description of it, and of slavery as it there existed. The plantation is about twelve miles north of Easton, in Talbot county, and is situated on the border of Miles River. The principal products raised upon it were tobacco, corn, and wheat. These were raised in great abundance; so that, with the products of this and the other farms belonging to him, he was able to keep in almost constant employment a large sloop, in carrying them to market at Baltimore. This sloop was named Sally Lloyd, in honor of one of the colonel's daughters. My master's son-in-law, Captain Auld, was master of the vessel; she was otherwise manned by the colonel's own slaves. Their names were Peter, Isaac, Rich, and Jake. These were esteemed very highly by the other slaves, and looked upon as the privileged ones of the plantation; for it was no small affair, in the eyes of the slaves, to be allowed to see Baltimore.

Colonel Lloyd kept from three to four hundred slaves on his home plantation, and owned a large number more on the neighboring farms belonging to him. The names of the farms nearest to the home plantation were Wye Town and New Design. "Wye Town" was under the overseership of a man named Noah Willis. New Design was under the overseership of a Mr. Townsend. The overseers of these, and all the rest of the farms, numbering over twenty, received advice and direction from the managers of the home plantation. This was the great business place. It was the seat of government for the whole twenty farms. All disputes among the overseers were settled here. If a slave was convicted of any high misdemeanor, became unmanageable, or evinced a determination to run away, he was brought immediately here, severely whipped, put on board the sloop, carried to Baltimore, and sold to Austin Woolfolk, or some other slave-trader, as a warning to the slaves remaining.

Here, too, the slaves of all the other farms received their monthly allowance of food, and their yearly clothing. The men and women slaves received, as their monthly allowance of food, eight pounds of pork, or its equivalent in fish, and one bushel of corn meal. Their yearly clothing consisted of two coarse linen shirts, one pair of linen trousers, like the shirts, one jacket, one pair of trousers for winter, made of coarse negro cloth, one pair of stockings, and one pair of shoes; the whole of which could not have cost more than seven dollars. The allowance of the slave children was given to their mothers, or the old women having the care of them. The children unable to work in the field had neither shoes, stockings, jackets, nor trousers, given to them; their clothing consisted of two coarse linen shirts per year. When these failed them, they went naked until the next allowance-day. Children from seven to ten years old, of both sexes, almost naked, might be seen at all seasons of the year.

There were no beds given the slaves, unless one coarse blanket be considered such, and none but the men and women had these. This, however, is not considered a very great privation. They find less difficulty from the want of beds, than from the want of time to sleep; for when their day's work in the field is done, the most of them having their washing, mending, and cooking to do, and having few or none of the ordinary facilities for doing either of these, very many of their sleeping hours are consumed in preparing for the field the coming day; and when this is done, old and young, male and female, married and single, drop down side by side, on one common bed,—the cold, damp floor,—each covering himself or herself with their miserable blankets; and here they sleep till they are summoned to the field by the driver's horn. At the sound of this, all must rise, and be off to the field. There must be no halting; every one must be at his or her post; and woe betides them who hear not this morning summons to the field; for if they are not awakened by the sense of hearing, they are by the sense of feeling: no age nor sex finds any favor. Mr. Severe, the overseer, used to stand by the door of the quarter, armed with a large hickory stick and heavy cowskin, ready to whip any one who was so unfortunate as not to hear, or, from any other cause, was prevented from being ready to start for the field at the sound of the horn.

Mr. Severe was rightly named: he was a cruel man. I have seen him whip a woman, causing the blood to run half an hour at the time; and this, too, in the midst of her crying children, pleading for their mother's release. He seemed to take pleasure in manifesting his fiendish barbarity. Added to his cruelty, he was a profane swearer. It was enough to chill the blood and stiffen the hair of an ordinary man to hear him talk. Scarce a sentence escaped him but that was commenced or concluded by some horrid oath. The field was the place to witness his cruelty and profanity. His presence made it both the field of blood and of blasphemy. From the rising till the going down of the sun, he was cursing, raving, cutting, and slashing among the slaves of the field, in the most frightful manner. His career was short. He died very soon after I went to Colonel Lloyd's; and he died as he lived, uttering, with his dying groans, bitter curses and horrid oaths. His death was regarded by the slaves as the result of a merciful providence.

Mr. Severe's place was filled by a Mr. Hopkins. He was a very different man. He was less cruel, less profane, and made less noise, than Mr. Severe. His course was characterized by no extraordinary demonstrations of cruelty. He whipped, but seemed to take no pleasure in it. He was called by the slaves a good overseer.

The home plantation of Colonel Lloyd wore the appearance of a country village. All the mechanical operations for all the farms were performed here. The shoemaking and mending, the blacksmithing, cartwrighting, coopering, weaving, and grain-grinding, were all performed by the slaves on the home plantation. The whole place wore a business-like aspect very unlike the neighboring farms. The number of houses, too, conspired to give it advantage over the neighboring farms. It was called by the slaves the *Great House Farm.* Few privileges were esteemed higher, by the slaves of the out-farms, than that of being selected to do errands at the Great House Farm. It was associated in their minds with greatness. A representative could not be prouder of his election to a seat in the American Congress, than a slave on one of the out-farms would be of his election to do errands at the Great House Farm. They regarded it as evidence of great confidence reposed in them by their overseers; and it was on this account, as well as a constant desire to be out of the field from under the driver's lash, that they esteemed it a high privilege, one worth careful living for. He was called the smartest and most trusty fellow, who had this honor conferred upon him the most frequently. The competitors for this office sought as diligently to please their overseers, as the office-seekers in the political parties seek to please and deceive the people. The same traits of character might be seen in Colonel Lloyd's slaves, as are seen in the slaves of the political parties.

The slaves selected to go to the Great House Farm, for the monthly allowance for themselves and their fellow-slaves, were peculiarly enthusiastic. While on their way, they would make the dense old woods, for miles around, reverberate with their wild songs, revealing at once the highest joy and the deepest sadness. They would compose and sing as they went along, consulting neither time nor tune. The thought that came up, came out—if not in the word, in the sound;—and as frequently in the one as in the other. They would sometimes sing the most pathetic sentiment in the most rapturous tone, and the most rapturous sentiment in the most pathetic tone. Into all of their songs they would manage to weave something of the Great House Farm. Especially would they do this, when leaving home. They would then sing most exultingly the following words:—

> "I am going away to the Great
> House Farm!
> Oh, yea! O, yea! O!"

This they would sing, as a chorus, to words which to many would seem unmeaning jargon, but which, nevertheless, were full of meaning to themselves. I have sometimes thought that the mere hearing of those songs would do more to impress some minds with the horrible character of slavery, than the reading of whole volumes of philosophy on the subject could do.

I did not, when a slave, understand the deep meaning of those rude and apparently incoherent songs. I was myself within the circle; so that I neither saw nor heard as those without might see and hear. They told a tale of woe which was then altogether beyond my feeble comprehension; they were tones loud, long, and deep; they breathed the prayer and complaint of souls boiling over with the bitterest anguish. Every tone was a testimony against slavery, and a prayer to God for deliverance from chains. The hearing of those wild notes always depressed my spirit, and filled me with ineffable sadness. I have frequently found myself in tears while hearing them. The mere recurrence to those songs, even now, afflicts me; and while I am writing these lines, an expression of feeling has already found its way down my cheek. To those songs I trace my first glimmering conception of the dehumanizing character of slavery. I can never get rid of that conception. Those songs still follow me, to deepen my hatred of slavery, and quicken my sympathies for my brethren in bonds. If any one wishes to be impressed with the soul-killing effects of slavery, let him go to Colonel Lloyd's plantation, and, on allowance-day, place himself in the deep pine woods, and there let him, in silence, analyze the sounds that shall pass through the chambers of his soul,—and if he is not thus impressed, it will only be because "there is no flesh in his obdurate heart."

I have often been utterly astonished, since I came to the north, to find persons who could speak of the singing, among slaves, as evidence of their contentment and happiness. It is impossible to conceive of a greater mistake. Slaves sing most when they are most unhappy. The songs of the slave represent the sorrows of his heart; and he is relieved by them, only as an aching heart is relieved by its tears. At least, such is my experience. I have often sung to drown my sorrow, but seldom to express my happiness. Crying for joy, and singing for joy, were alike uncommon to me while in the jaws of slavery. The singing of a man cast away upon a desolate island might be as appropriately considered as evidence of contentment and happiness, as the singing of a slave; the songs of the one and of the other are prompted by the same emotion.

Chapter III

Colonel Lloyd kept a large and finely cultivated garden, which afforded almost constant employment for four men, besides the chief gardener, (Mr. M'Durmond.) This garden was probably the greatest attraction of the place. During the summer months, people came from far and near—from Baltimore, Easton, and Annapolis—to see it. It abounded in fruits of almost every description, from the hardy apple of the north to the delicate orange of the south. This garden was not the least source of trouble on the plantation. Its excellent fruit was quite a temptation to the hungry swarms of boys, as well as the older slaves, belonging to the colonel, few of whom had the virtue or the vice to resist it. Scarcely a day passed, during the summer, but that some slave had to take the lash for stealing fruit. The colonel had to resort to all kinds of stratagems to keep his slaves out of the garden. The last and most successful one was that of tarring his fence all around; after which, if a slave was caught with any tar upon his person, it was deemed sufficient proof that he had either been into the garden, or had tried to get in. In either case, he was severely whipped by the chief gardener. This plan worked well; the slaves became as fearful of tar as of the lash. They seemed to realize the impossibility of touching *tar* without being defiled.

The colonel also kept a splendid riding equipage. His stable and carriage-house presented the appearance of some our large city livery establishments. His horses were of the finest form and noblest blood. His carriage-house contained three splendid coaches, three or four gigs, besides dearborns and barouches of the most fashionable style.

This establishment was under the care of two slaves—old Barney and young Barney—father and son. To attend to this establishment was their sole work. But it was by no means an easy employment; for in nothing was Colonel Lloyd more particular than in the management of his horses. The slightest inattention to these was unpardonable, and was visited upon those, under whose care they were placed, with the severest punishment; no excuse could shield them, if the colonel only suspected any want of attention to his horses—a supposition which he frequently indulged, and one which, of course, made the office of old and young Barney a very trying one. They never knew when they were safe from punishment. They were frequently whipped when least deserving, and escaped whipping when most deserving it. Every thing depended upon the looks of the horses, and the state of Colonel Lloyd's own mind when his horses were brought to him for use. If a horse did not move fast enough, or hold his head high enough, it was owing to some fault of his keepers. It was painful to stand near the stable-door and hear the various complaints against the keepers when a horse was taken out for use. "This horse has not had proper attention. He has not been sufficiently rubbed and curried, or he has not been properly fed; his food was too wet or too dry; he got it too soon or too late; he was too hot or too cold; he had too much hay, and not enough of grain; or he had too much grain, and not enough of hay; instead of old Barney's attending to the horse, he had very improperly left it to his son." To all these complaints, no matter how unjust, the slave must answer never a word. Colonel Lloyd could not brook any contradiction from a slave. When he spoke, a slave must stand, listen, and tremble; and such was literally the case. I have seen Colonel Lloyd make old Barney, a man between fifty and sixty years of age, uncover his bald head, kneel down upon the cold, damp ground, and receive upon his naked and toil-worn shoulders more than thirty lashes at the time. Colonel Lloyd had three sons—Edward, Murray, and Daniel,—and three sons-in-law, Mr. Winder, Mr. Nicholson, and Mr. Lowndes. All of these lived at the Great House Farm, and enjoyed the luxury of whipping the servants when they pleased, from old Barney down to William Wilkes, the coach-driver. I have seen Winder make one of the house-servants stand off from him a suitable distance to be touched with the end of his whip, and at every stroke raise great ridges upon his back.

To describe the wealth of Colonel Lloyd would be almost equal to describing the riches of Job. He kept from ten to fifteen house-servants. He was said to own a thousand slaves, and I think this estimate quite within the truth. Colonel Lloyd owned so many that he did not know them when he saw them; nor did all the slaves of the out-farms know him. It is reported of him, that, while riding along the road one day, he met a colored man, and addressed him in the usual manner of speaking to colored people on the public highways of the south: "Well, boy, whom do you belong to?" "To Colonel Lloyd," replied the slave. "Well, does the colonel treat you well?" "No, sir," was the ready reply. "What, does he work you too hard?" "Yes, sir." "Well, don't he give you enough to eat?" "Yes, sir, he gives me enough, such as it is."

The colonel, after ascertaining where the slave belonged, rode on; the man also went on about his business, not dreaming that he had been conversing with his master. He thought, said, and heard nothing more of the matter, until two or three weeks afterwards. The poor man was then informed by his overseer that, for having found fault with his master, he was now to be sold to a Georgia trader. He was immediately chained and handcuffed; and thus, without a moment's warning, he was snatched away, and forever sundered, from his family and friends, by a hand more unrelenting than death. This is the penalty of telling the truth, of telling the simple truth, in answer to a series of plain questions.

It is partly in consequence of such facts, that slaves, when inquired of as to their condition and the character of their masters, almost universally say they are contented, and that their masters are kind. The slaveholders have been known to send in spies among their slaves, to ascertain their views and feelings in regard to their condition. The frequency of this has had the effect to establish among the slaves the maxim, that a still tongue makes a wise head. They suppress the truth rather than take the consequences of telling it, and in so doing prove themselves a part of the human family. If they have any thing to say of their masters, it is generally in their masters' favor, especially when speaking to an untried man. I have been frequently asked, when a slave, if I had a kind master, and do not remember ever to have given a negative answer; nor did I, in pursuing this course, consider myself as uttering what was absolutely false; for I always measured the kindness of my master by the standard of kindness set up among slaveholders around us. Moreover, slaves are like other people, and imbibe prejudices quite common to others. They think their own better than that of others. Many, under the influence of this prejudice, think their own masters are better than the masters of other slaves; and this, too, in some cases, when the very reverse is true. Indeed, it is not uncommon for slaves even to fall out and quarrel among themselves about the relative goodness of their masters, each contending for the superior goodness of his own over that of the others. At the very same time, they mutually execrate their masters when viewed separately. It was so on our plantation. When Colonel Lloyd's slaves met the slaves of Jacob Jepson, they seldom parted without a quarrel about their masters; Colonel Lloyd's slaves contending that he was the richest, and Mr. Jepson's slaves that he was the smartest, and most of a man. Colonel Lloyd's slaves would boast his ability to buy and sell Jacob Jepson. Mr. Jepson's slaves would boast his ability to whip Colonel Lloyd. These quarrels would almost always end in a fight between the parties, and those that whipped were supposed to have gained the point of issue. They seemed to think that the greatness of their masters was transferable to themselves. It was considered as being bad enough to be a slave; but to be a poor man's slave was deemed a disgrace indeed!

Chapter IV

Mr. Hopkins remained but a short time in the office of overseer. Why his career was so short, I do not know, but suppose he lacked the necessary severity to suit Colonel Lloyd. Mr. Hopkins was succeeded by Mr. Austin Gore, a man possessing, in an eminent degree, all those traits of character indispensable to what is called a first-rate overseer. Mr. Gore had served Colonel Lloyd, in the capacity of overseer, upon one of the out-farms, and had shown himself worthy of the high station of overseer upon the home or Great House Farm.

Mr. Gore was proud, ambitious, and persevering. He was artful, cruel, and obdurate. He was just the man for such a place, and it was just the place for such a man. It afforded scope for the full exercise of all his powers, and he seemed to be perfectly at home in it. He was one of those who could torture the slightest look, word, or gesture, on the part of the slave, into impudence, and would treat it accordingly. There must be no answering back to him; no explanation was allowed a slave, showing himself to have been wrongfully accused. Mr. Gore acted fully up to the maxim laid down by slaveholders,—"It is better that a dozen slaves suffer under the lash, than that the overseer should be convicted, in the presence of the slaves, of having been at fault." No matter how innocent a slave might be—it availed him nothing, when accused by Mr. Gore of any misdemeanor. To be accused was to be convicted, and to be convicted was to be punished; the one always following the other with immutable certainty. To escape punishment was to escape accusation; and few slaves had the fortune to do either, under the overseership of Mr. Gore. He was just proud enough to demand the most debasing homage of the slave, and quite servile enough to crouch, himself, at the feet of the master. He was ambitious enough to be contented with nothing short of the highest rank of overseers, and perservering enough to reach the height of his ambition. He was cruel enough to inflict the severest punishment, artful enough to descend to the lowest trickery, and obdurate enough to be insensible to the voice of reproving conscience. He was, of all the overseers, the most dreaded by the slaves. His presence was painful; his eye flashed confusion; and seldom was his sharp, shrill voice heard, without producing horror and trembling in their ranks.

Mr. Gore was a grave man, and, though a young man, he indulged in no jokes, said no funny words, seldom smiled. His words were in perfect keeping with his looks, and his looks were in perfect keeping with his words. Overseers will sometimes indulge in a witty word, even with the slaves; not so with Mr. Gore. He spoke but to command, and commanded but to be obeyed; he dealt sparingly with his words, and bountifully with his whip, never using the former where the latter would answer as well. When he whipped, he seemed to do so from a sense of duty, and feared no consequences. He did nothing reluctantly, no matter how disagreeable; always at his post, never inconsistent. He never promised but to fulfil. He was, in a word, a man of the most inflexible firmness and stone-like coolness.

His savage barbarity was equalled only by the consummate coolness with which he committed the grossest and most savage deeds upon the slaves under his charge. Mr. Gore once undertook to whip one of Colonel Lloyd's slaves, by the name of Demby. He had given Demby but few stripes, when, to get rid of the scourging, he ran and plunged himself into a creek, and stood there at the depth of his shoulders, refusing to come out. Mr. Gore told him that he would give him three calls, and that, if he did not come out at the third call, he would shoot him. The first call was given. Demby made no response, but stood his ground. The second and third calls were given with the same result. Mr. Gore then, without consultation or deliberation with any one, not even giving Demby an additional call, raised his musket to his face, taking deadly aim at his standing victim, and in an instant poor Demby was no more. His mangled body sank out of sight, and blood and brains marked the water where he had stood.

A thrill of horror flashed through every soul upon the plantation, excepting Mr. Gore. He alone seemed cool and collected. He was asked by Colonel Lloyd and my old master, why he resorted to this extraordinary expedient. His reply was, (as well as I can remember,) that Demby had become unmanageable. He was setting a dangerous example to the other slaves,—one which, if suffered to pass without some such demonstration on his part, would finally lead to the total subversion of all rule and order upon the plantation. He argued that if one slave refused to be corrected, and escaped with his life, the other slaves would soon copy the example; the result of which would be, the freedom of the slaves, and the enslavement of the whites. Mr. Gore's defence was satisfactory. He was continued in his station as overseer upon the home plantation. His fame as an overseer went abroad. His horrid crime was not even submitted to judicial investigation. It was committed in the presence of slaves, and they of course could neither institute a suit, nor testify against him; and thus the guilty perpetrator of one of the bloodiest and most foul murders goes unwhipped of justice, and uncensured by the community in which he lives. Mr. Gore lived in St. Michael's, Talbot county, Maryland, when I left there; and if he is still alive, he very probably lives there now; and if so, he is now, as he was then, as highly esteemed and as much respected as though his guilty soul had not been stained with his brother's blood.

I speak advisedly when I say this,—that killing a slave, or any colored person, in Talbot county, Maryland, is not treated as a crime, either by the courts or the community. Mr. Thomas Lanman, of St. Michael's, killed two slaves, one of whom he killed with a hatchet, by knocking his brains out. He used to boast of the commission of the awful and bloody deed. I have heard him do so laughingly, saying, among other things, that he was the only benefactor of his country in the company, and that when others would do as much as he had done, we should be relieved of "the d——d niggers."

The wife of Mr. Giles Hicks, living but a short distance from where I used to live, murdered my wife's cousin, a young girl between fifteen and sixteen years of age, mangling her person in the most horrible manner, breaking her nose and breastbone with a stick, so that the poor girl expired in a few hours afterward. She was immediately buried, but had not been in her untimely grave but a few hours before she was taken up and examined by the coroner, who decided that she had come to her death by severe beating. The offence for which this girl was thus murdered was this:—She had been set that night to mind Mrs. Hicks's baby and during the night she fell asleep, and the baby cried. She, having lost her rest for several nights previous, did not hear the crying. They were both in the room with Mrs. Hicks. Mrs. Hicks, finding the girl slow to move, jumped from her bed, seized an oak stick of wood by the fireplace, and with it broke the girl's nose and breastbone, and thus ended her life. I will not say that this most horrid murder produced no sensation in the community. It did produce sensation, but not enough to bring the murderess to punishment. There was a warrant issued for her arrest, but it was never served. Thus she escaped not only punishment, but even the pain of being arraigned before a court for her horrid crime.

Whilst I am detailing bloody deeds which took place during my stay on Colonel Lloyd's plantation, I will briefly narrate another, which occurred about the same time as the murder of Demby by Mr. Gore.

Colonel Lloyd's slaves were in the habit of spending a part of their nights and Sundays in fishing for oysters, and in this way made up the deficiency of their scanty allowance. An old man belonging to Colonel Lloyd, while thus engaged, happened to get beyond the limits of Colonel Lloyd's, and on the premises of Mr. Beal Bondly. At this trespass, Mr. Bondly took offence, and with his musket came down to the shore, and blew its deadly contents into the poor old man.

Mr. Bondly came over to see Colonel Lloyd the next day, whether to pay him for his property, or to justify himself in what he had done, I know not. At any rate, this whole fiendish transaction was soon hushed up. There was very little said about it at all, and nothing done. It was a common saying, even among little white boys, that it was worth a half-cent to kill a "nigger," and a half-cent to bury one.

Chapter V

As to my own treatment while I lived on Colonel Lloyd's plantation, it was very similar to that of the other slave children. I was not old enough to work in the field, and there being little else than field work to do, I had a great deal of leisure time. The most I had to do was to drive up the cows at evening, keep the fowls out of the garden, keep the front yard clean, and run of errands for my old master's daughter, Mrs. Lucretia Auld. The most of my leisure time I spent in helping Master Daniel Lloyd in finding his birds, after he had shot them. My connection with Master Daniel was of some advantage to me. He became quite attached to me, and was a sort of protector of me. He would not allow the older boys to impose upon me, and would divide his cakes with me.

I was seldom whipped by my old master, and suffered little from any thing else than hunger and cold. I suffered much from hunger, but much more from cold. In hottest summer and coldest winter, I was kept almost naked—no shoes, no stockings, no jacket, no trousers, nothing on but a coarse tow linen shirt, reaching only to my knees. I had no bed. I must have perished with cold, but that, the coldest nights, I used to steal a bag which was used for carrying corn to the mill. I would crawl into this bag, and there sleep on the cold, damp, clay floor, with my head in and feet out. My feet have been so cracked with the frost, that the pen with which I am writing might be laid in the gashes.

We were not regularly allowanced. Our food was coarse corn meal boiled. This was called *mush.* It was put into a large wooden tray or trough, and set down upon the ground. The children were then called, like so many pigs, and like so many pigs they would come and devour the mush; some with oyster-shells, others with pieces of shingle, some with naked hands, and none with spoons. He that ate fastest got most; he that was strongest secured the best place; and few left the trough satisfied.

I was probably between seven and eight years old when I left Colonel Lloyd's plantation. I left it with joy. I shall never forget the ecstasy with which I received the intelligence that my old master (Anthony) had determined to let me go to Baltimore, to live with Mr. Hugh Auld, brother to my old master's son-in-law, Captain Thomas Auld. I received this information about three days before my departure. They were three of the happiest days I ever enjoyed. I spent the most part of all these three days in the creek, washing off the plantation scurf, and preparing myself for my departure.

The pride of appearance which this would indicate was not my own. I spent the time in washing, not so much because I wished to, but because Mrs. Lucretia had told me I must get all the dead skin off my feet and knees before I could go to Baltimore; for the people in Baltimore were very cleanly, and would laugh at me if I looked dirty. Besides, she was going to give me a pair of trousers, which I should not put on unless I got all the dirt off me. The thought of owning a pair of trousers was great indeed! It was almost a sufficient motive, not only to make me take off what would be called by pig drovers the mange, but the skin itself. I went at it in good earnest, working for the first time with the hope of reward.

The ties that ordinarily bind children to their homes were all suspended in my case. I found no severe trial in my departure. My home was charmless; it was not home to me; on parting from it, I could not feel that I was leaving any thing which I could have enjoyed by staying. My mother was dead, my grandmother lived far off, so that I seldom saw her. I had two sisters and one brother, that lived in the same house with me; but the early separation of us from our mother had well nigh blotted the fact of our relationship from our memories. I looked for home elsewhere, and was confident of finding none which I should relish less than the one which I was leaving. If, however, I found in my new home hardship, hunger, whipping, and nakedness, I had the consolation that I should not have escaped any one of them by staying. Having already had more than a taste of them in the house of my old master, and having endured them there, I very naturally inferred my ability to endure them elsewhere, and especially at Baltimore; for I had something of the feeling about Baltimore that is expressed in the proverb, that "being hanged in England is preferable to dying a natural death in Ireland." I had the strongest desire to see Baltimore. Cousin Tom, though not fluent in speech, had inspired me with that desire by his eloquent description of the place. I could never point out any thing at the Great House, no matter how beautiful or powerful, but that he had seen something at Baltimore far exceeding, both in beauty and strength, the object which I pointed out to him. Even the Great House itself, with all its pictures, was far inferior to many buildings in Baltimore. So strong was my desire, that I thought a gratification of it would fully compensate for whatever loss of comforts I should sustain by the exchange. I left without a regret, and with the highest hopes of future happiness.

We sailed out of Miles River for Baltimore on a Saturday morning. I remember only the day of the week, for at that time I had no knowledge of the days of the month, nor the months of the year. On setting sail, I walked aft, and gave to Colonel Lloyd's plantation what I hoped would be the last look. I then placed myself in the bows of the sloop, and there spent the remainder of the day in looking ahead, interesting myself in what was in the distance rather than in things near by or behind.

In the afternoon of that day, we reached Annapolis, the capital of the State. We stopped but a few moments, so that I had no time to go on shore. It was the first large town that I had ever seen, and though it would look small compared with some of our New England factory villages, I thought it a wonderful place for its size—more imposing even than the Great House Farm!

We arrived at Baltimore early on Sunday morning, landing at Smith's Wharf, not far from Bowley's Wharf. We had on board the sloop a large flock of sheep; and after aiding in driving them to the slaughter-house of Mr. Curtis on Louden Slater's Hill, I was conducted by Rich, one of the hands belonging on board of the sloop, to my new home in Alliciana Street, near Mr. Gardner's ship-yard, on Fells Point.

Mr. and Mrs. Auld were both at home, and met me at the door with their little son Thomas, to take care of whom I had been given. And here I saw what I had never seen before; it was a white face beaming with the most kindly emotions; it was the face of my new mistress, Sophia Auld. I wish I could describe the rapture that flashed through my soul as I beheld it. It was a new and strange sight to me, brightening up my pathway with the light of happiness. Little Thomas was told, there was his Freddy,—and I was told to take care of little Thomas; and thus I entered upon the duties of my new home with the most cheering prospect ahead.

I look upon my departure from Colonel Lloyd's plantation as one of the most interesting events of my life. It is possible, and even quite probable, that but for the mere circumstance of being removed from that plantation to Baltimore, I should have to-day, instead of being here seated by my own table, in the enjoyment of freedom and the happiness of home, writing this Narrative, been confined in the galling chains of slavery. Going to live at Baltimore laid the foundation, and opened the gateway, to all my subsequent prosperity. I have ever regarded it as the plain manifestation of that kind providence which has ever since attended me, and marked my life with so many favors. I regarded the selection of myself as being somewhat remarkable. There were a number of slave children that might have been sent from the plantation to Baltimore. There were those younger, those older, and those of the same age. I was chosen from among them all, and was the first, last, and only choice.

I may be deemed superstitious, and even egotistical, in regarding this event as a special interposition of divine Providence in my favor. But I should be false to the earliest sentiments of my soul, if I suppressed the opinion. I prefer to be true to myself, even at the hazard of incurring the ridicule of others, rather than to be false, and incur my own abhorrence. From my earliest recollection, I date the entertainment of a deep conviction that slavery would not always be able to hold me within its foul embrace; and in the darkest hours of my career in slavery, this living word of faith and spirit of hope departed not from me, but remained like ministering angels to cheer me through the gloom. This good spirit was from God, and to him I offer thanksgiving and praise.

Chapter VI

My new mistress proved to be all she appeared when I first met her at the door,—a woman of the kindest heart and finest feelings. She had never had a slave under her control previously to myself, and prior to her marriage she had been dependent upon her own industry for a living. She was by trade a weaver; and by constant application to her business, she had been in a good degree preserved from the blighting and dehumanizing effects of slavery. I was utterly astonished at her goodness. I scarcely knew how to behave towards her. She was entirely unlike any other white woman I had ever seen. I could not approach her as I was accustomed to approach other white ladies. My early instruction was all out of place. The crouching servility, usually so acceptable a quality in a slave, did not answer when manifested toward her. Her favor was not gained by it; she seemed to be disturbed by it. She did not deem it impudent or unmannerly for a slave to look her in the face. The meanest slave was put fully at ease in her presence, and none left without feeling better for having seen her. Her face was made of heavenly smiles, and her voice of tranquil music.

But, alas! this kind heart had but a short time to remain such. The fatal poison of irresponsible power was already in her hands, and soon commenced its infernal work. That cheerful eye, under the influence of slavery, soon became red with rage; that voice, made all of sweet accord, changed to one of harsh and horrid discord; and that angelic face gave place to that of a demon.

Very soon after I went to live with Mr. and Mrs. Auld, she very kindly commenced to teach me the A, B, C. After I had learned this, she assisted me in learning to spell words of three or four letters. Just at his point of my progress, Mr. Auld found out what was going on, and at once forbade Mrs. Auld to instruct me further, telling her, among other things, that it was unlawful, as well as unsafe, to teach a slave to read. To use his own words, further, he said, "If you give a nigger an inch, he will take an ell. A nigger should know nothing but to obey his master—to do as he is told to do. Learning would *spoil* the best nigger in the world. Now," said he, "if you teach that nigger (speaking of myself) how to read, there would be no keeping him. It would forever unfit him to be a slave. He would at once become unmanageable, and of no value to his master. As to himself, it could do him no good, but a great deal of harm. It would make him discontented and unhappy." These words sank deep into my heart, stirred up sentiments within that lay slumbering, and called into existence an entirely new train of thought. It was a new and special revelation, explaining dark and mysterious things, with which my youthful understanding had struggled, but struggled in vain. I now understood what had been to me a most perplexing difficulty—to wit, the white man's power to enslave the black man. It was a grand achievement, and I prized it highly. From that moment, I understood the pathway from slavery to freedom. It was just what I wanted, and I got it at a time when I the least expected it. Whilst I was saddened by the thought of losing the aid of my kind mistress, I was gladdened by the invaluable instruction which, by the merest accident, I had gained from my master. Though conscious of the difficulty of learning without a teacher, I set out with high hope, and a fixed purpose, at whatever cost of trouble, to learn how to read. The very decided manner with which he spoke, and strove to impress his wife with the evil consequences of giving me instruction, served to convince me that he was deeply sensible of the truths he was uttering. It gave me the best assurance that I might rely with the utmost confidence on the results which, he said, would flow from teaching me to read. What he most dreaded, that I most desired. What he most loved, that I most hated. That which to him was a great evil, to be carefully shunned, was to me a great good, to be diligently sought; and the argument which he so warmly urged, against my learning to read, only served to inspire me with a desire and determination to learn. In learning to read, I owe almost as much to the bitter opposition of my master, as to the kindly aid of my mistress. I acknowledge the benefit of both.

I had resided but a short time in Baltimore before I observed a marked difference, in the treatment of slaves, from that which I had witnessed in the country. A city slave is almost a freeman, compared with a slave on the plantation. He is much better fed and clothed, and enjoys privileges altogether unknown to the slave on the plantation. There is a vestige of decency, a sense of shame, that does much to curb and check those outbreaks of atrocious cruelty so commonly enacted upon the plantation. He is a desperate slaveholder, who will shock the humanity of his nonslaveholding neighbors with the cries of his lacerated slave. Few are willing to incur the odium attaching to the reputation of being a cruel master; and above all things, they would not be known as not giving a slave enough to eat. Every city slaveholder is anxious to have it known of him, that he feeds his slaves well; and it is due to them to say, that most of them do give their slaves enough to eat. There are, however, some painful exceptions to this rule. Directly opposite to us, on Philpot Street, lived Mr. Thomas Hamilton. He owned two slaves. Their names were Henrietta and Mary. Henrietta was about twenty-two years of age, Mary was about fourteen; and of all the mangled and emaciated creatures I ever looked upon, these two were the most so. His heart must be harder than stone, that could look upon these unmoved. The head, neck, and shoulders of Mary were literally cut to pieces. I have frequently felt her head, and found it nearly covered with festering sores, caused by the lash of her cruel mistress. I do not know that her master ever whipped her, but I have been an eyewitness to the cruelty of Mrs. Hamilton. I used to be in Mr. Hamilton's house nearly every day. Mrs. Hamilton used to sit in a large chair in the middle of the room, with a heavy cowskin always by her side, and scarce an hour passed during the day but was marked by the blood of one of these slaves. The girls seldom passed her without her saying, "Move faster, you *black gip!*" at the same time giving them a blow with the cowskin over the head or shoulders, often drawing the blood. She would then say, "Take that, you *black gip!*"—continuing, "If you don't move faster, I'll move you!" Added to the cruel lashings to which these slaves were subjected, they were kept nearly half-starved. They seldom knew what it was to eat a full meal. I have seen Mary contending with the pigs for the offal thrown into the street. So much was Mary kicked and cut to pieces, that she was oftener called "*pecked*" than by her name.

Chapter VII

I lived in Master Hugh's family about seven years. During this time, I succeeded in learning to read and write. In accomplishing this, I was compelled to resort to various stratagems. I had no regular teacher. My mistress, who had kindly commenced to instruct me, had, in compliance with the advice and direction of her husband, not only ceased to instruct, but had set her face against my being instructed by any one else. It is due, however, to my mistress to say of her, that she did not adopt this course of treatment immediately. She at first lacked the depravity indispensable to shutting me up in mental darkness. It was at least necessary for her to have some training in the exercise of irresponsible power, to make her equal to the task of treating me as though I were a brute.

My mistress was, as I have said, a kind and tender-hearted woman; and in the simplicity of her soul she commenced, when I first went to live with her, to treat me as she supposed one human being ought to treat another. In entering upon the duties of a slaveholder, she did not seem to perceive that I sustained to her the relation of a mere chattel, and that for her to treat me as a human being was not only wrong, but dangerously so. Slavery proved as injurious to her as it did to me. When I went there, she was a pious, warm, and tender-hearted woman. There was no sorrow or suffering for which she had not a tear. She had bread for the hungry, clothes for the naked, and comfort for every mourner that came within her reach. Slavery soon proved its ability to divest her of these heavenly qualities. Under its influence, the tender heart became stone, and the lamblike disposition gave way to one of tiger-like fierceness. The first step in her downward course was in her ceasing to instruct me. She now commenced to practise her husband's precepts. She finally became even more violent in her opposition than her husband himself. She was not satisfied with simply doing as well as he had commanded; she seemed anxious to do better. Nothing seemed to make her more angry than to see me with a newspaper. She seemed to think that here lay the danger. I have had her rush at me with a face made all up of fury, and snatch from me a newspaper, in a manner that fully revealed her apprehension. She was an apt woman; and a little experience soon demonstrated, to her satisfaction, that education and slavery were incompatible with each other.

From this time I was most narrowly watched. If I was in a separate room any considerable length of time, I was sure to be suspected of having a book, and was at once called to give an account of myself. All this, however, was too late. The first step had been taken. Mistress, in teaching me the alphabet, had given me the *inch,* and no precaution could prevent me from taking the *ell.*

The plan which I adopted, and the one by which I was most successful, was that of making friends of all the little white boys whom I met in the street. As many of these as I could, I converted into teachers. With their kindly aid, obtained at different times and in different places, I finally succeeded in learning to read. When I was sent of errands, I always took my book with me, and by going one part of my errand quickly, I found time to get a lesson before my return. I used also to carry bread with me, enough of which was always in the house, and to which I was always welcome; for I was much better off in this regard than many of the poor white children in our neighborhood. This bread I used to bestow upon the hungry little urchins, who, in return, would give me that more valuable bread of knowledge. I am strongly tempted to give the names of two or three of those little boys, as a testimonial of the gratitude and affection I bear them; but prudence forbids;—not that it would injure me, but it might embarrass them; for it is almost an unpardonable offence to teach slaves to read in this Christian country. It is enough to say of the dear little fellows, that they lived on Philpot Street, very near Durgin and Bailey's ship-yard. I used to talk this matter of slavery over with them. I would sometimes say to them, I wished I could be as free as they would be when they got to be men. "You will be free as soon as you are twenty-one, *but I am a slave for life!* Have not I as good a right to be free as you have?" These words used to trouble them; they would express for me the liveliest sympathy, and console me with the hope that something would occur by which I might be free.

I was now about twelve years old, and the thought of being *a slave for life* began to bear heavily upon my heart. Just about this time, I got hold of a book entitled "The Columbian Orator." Every opportunity I got, I used to read this book. Among much of other interesting matter, I found in it a dialogue between a master and his slave. The slave was represented as having run away from his master three times. The dialogue represented the conversation which took place between them, when the slave was retaken the third time. In this dialogue, the whole argument in behalf of slavery was brought forward by the master, all of which was disposed of by the slave. The slave was made to say some very smart as well as impressive things in reply to his master—things which had the desired though unexpected effect; for the conversation resulted in the voluntary emancipation of the slave on the part of the master.

In the same book, I met with one of Sheridan's mighty speeches on and in behalf of Catholic emancipation. These were choice documents to me. I read them over and over again with unabated interest. They gave tongue to interesting thoughts of my own soul, which had frequently flashed through my mind, and died away for want of utterance. The moral which I gained from the dialogue was the power of truth over the conscience of even a slaveholder. What I got from Sheridan was a bold denunciation of slavery, and a powerful vindication of human rights. The reading of these documents enabled me to utter my thoughts, and to meet the arguments brought forward to sustain slavery; but while they relieved me of one difficulty, they brought on another even more painful than the one of which I was relieved. The more I read, the more I was led to abhor and detest my enslavers. I could regard them in no other light than a band of successful robbers, who had left their homes, and gone to Africa, and stolen us from our homes, and in a strange land reduced us to slavery. I loathed them as being the meanest as well as the most wicked of men. As I read and contemplated the subject, behold! that very discontentment which Master Hugh had predicted would follow my learning to read had already come, to torment and sting my soul to unutterable anguish. As I writhed under it, I would at times feel that learning to read had been a curse rather than a blessing. It had given me a view of my wretched condition, without the remedy. It opened my eyes to the horrible pit, but to no ladder upon which to get out. In moments of agony, I envied my fellow-slaves for their stupidity. I have often wished myself a beast. I preferred the condition of the meanest reptile to my own. Any thing, no matter what, to get rid of thinking! It was this everlasting thinking of my condition that tormented me. There was no getting rid of it. It was pressed upon me by every object within sight or hearing, animate or inanimate. The silver trump of freedom had roused my soul to eternal wakefulness. Freedom now appeared, to disappear no more forever. It was heard in every sound, and seen in every thing. It was ever present to torment me with a sense of my wretched condition. I saw nothing without seeing it, I heard nothing without hearing it, and felt nothing without feeling it. It looked from every star, it smiled in every calm, breathed in every wind, and moved in every storm.

I often found myself regretting my own existence, and wishing myself dead; and but for the hope of being free, I have no doubt but that I should have killed myself, or done something for which I should have been killed. While in this state of mind, I was eager to hear any one speak of slavery. I was a ready listener. Every little while, I could hear something about the abolitionists. It was some time before I found what the word meant. It was always used in such connections as to make it an interesting word to me. If a slave ran away and succeeded in getting clear, or if a slave killed his master, set fire to a barn, or did any thing very wrong in the mind of a slaveholder, it was spoken of as the fruit of *abolition*. Hearing the word in this connection very often, I set about learning what it meant. The dictionary afforded me little or no help. I found it was "the act of abolishing;" but then I did not know what was to be abolished. Here I was perplexed. I did not dare to ask any one about its meaning, for I was satisfied that it was something they wanted me to know very little about. After a patient waiting, I got one of our city papers, containing an account of the number of petitions from the north, praying for the abolition of slavery in the District of Columbia, and of the slave trade between the States. From this time I understood the words *abolition* and *abolitionist,* and always drew near when that word was spoken, expecting to hear something of importance to myself and fellow-slaves. The light broke in upon me by degrees. I went one day down on the wharf of Mr. Waters; and seeing two Irishmen unloading a scow of stone, I went, unasked, and helped them. When we had finished, one of them came to me and asked me if I were a slave. I told him I was. He asked, "Are ye a slave for life?" I told him that I was. The good Irishman seemed to be deeply affected by the statement. He said to the other that it was a pity so fine a little fellow as myself should be a slave for life. He said it was a shame to hold me. They both advised me to run away to the north; that I should find friends there, and that I should be free. I pretended not to be interested in what they said, and treated them as if I did not understand them; for I feared they might be treacherous. White men have been known to encourage slaves to escape, and then, to get the reward, catch them and return them to their masters. I was afraid that these seemingly good men might use me so; but I nevertheless remembered their advice, and from that time I resolved to run away. I looked forward to a time at which it would be safe for me to escape. I was too young to think of doing so immediately; besides, I wished to learn how to write, as I might have occasion to write my own pass. I consoled myself with the hope that I should one day find a good chance. Meanwhile, I would learn to write.

The idea as to how I might learn to write was suggested to me by being in Durgin and Bailey's shipyard, and frequently seeing the ship carpenters, after hewing, and getting a piece of timber ready for use, write on the timber the name of that part of the ship for which it was intended. When a piece of timber was intended for the larboard side, it would be marked thus—"L." When a piece was for the starboard side, it would be marked thus—"S." A piece for the larboard side forward, would be marked thus—"L.F." When a piece was for starboard side forward, it would be marked thus—"S.F." For larboard aft, it would be marked thus—"L.A." For starboard aft, it would be marked thus—"S.A." I soon learned the names of these letters, and for what they were intended when placed upon a piece of timber in the ship-yard. I immediately commenced copying them, and in a short time was able to make the four letters named. After that, when I met with any boy who I knew could write, I would tell him I could write as well as he. The next word would be, "I don't believe you. Let me see you try it." I would then make the letters which I had been so fortunate as to learn, and ask him to beat that. In this way I got a good many lessons in writing, which it is quite possible I should never have gotten in any other way. During this time, my copy-book was the board fence, brick wall, and pavement; my pen and ink was a lump of chalk. With these, I learned mainly how to write. I then commenced and continued copying the Italics in Webster's Spelling Book, until I could make them all without looking on the book. By this time, my little Master Thomas had gone to school, and learned how to write, and had written over a number of copy-books. These had been brought home, and shown to some of our near neighbors, and then laid aside. My mistress used to go to class meeting at the Wilk Street meeting-house every Monday afternoon, and leave me to take care of the house. When left thus, I used to spend the time in writing in the spaces left in Master Thomas's copy-book, copying what he had written. I continued to do this until I could write a hand very similar to that of Master Thomas. Thus, after a long, tedious effort for years, I finally succeeded in learning how to write.

Chapter VIII

In a very short time after I went to live at Baltimore, my old master's youngest son Richard died; and in about three years and six months after his death, my old master, Captain Anthony, died, leaving only his son, Andrew, and daughter, Lucretia, to share his estate. He died while on a visit to see his daughter at Hillsborough. Cut off thus unexpectedly, he left no will as to the disposal of his property. It was therefore necessary to have a valuation of the property, that it might be equally divided between Mrs. Lucretia and Master Andrew. I was immediately sent for, to be valued with the other property. Here again my feelings rose up in detestation of slavery. I had now a new conception of my degraded condition. Prior to this, I had become, if not insensible to my lot, at least partly so. I left Baltimore with a young heart overborne with sadness, and a soul full of apprehension. I took passage with Captain Rowe, in the schooner Wild Cat, and, after a sail of about twenty-four hours, I found myself near the place of my birth. I had now been absent from it almost, if not quite, five years. I, however, remembered the place very well. I was only about five years old when I left it, to go and live with my old master on Colonel Lloyd's plantation; so that I was now between ten and eleven years old.

We were all ranked together at the valuation. Men and women, old and young, married and single, were ranked with horses, sheep, and swine. There were horses and men, cattle and women, pigs and children, all holding the same rank in the scale of being, and were all subjected to the same narrow examination. Silvery-headed age and sprightly youth, maids and matrons, had to undergo the same indelicate inspection. At this moment, I saw more clearly than ever the brutalizing effects of slavery upon both slave and slaveholder.

After the valuation, then came the division. I have no language to express the high excitement and deep anxiety which were felt among us poor slaves during this time. Our fate for life was now to be decided. We had no more voice in that decision than the brutes among whom we were ranked. A single word from the white men was enough—against all our wishes, prayers, and entreaties—to sunder forever the dearest friends, dearest kindred, and strongest ties known to human beings. In addition to the pain of separation, there was the horrid dread of falling into the hands of Master Andrew. He was known to us all as being a most cruel wretch,—a common drunkard, who had, by his reckless mismanagement and profligate dissipation, already wasted a large portion of his father's property. We all felt that we might as well be sold at once to the Georgia traders, as to pass into his hands; for we knew that that would be our inevitable condition,—a condition held by us all in the utmost horror and dread.

I suffered more anxiety than most of my fellow-slaves. I had known what it was to be kindly treated; they had known nothing of the kind. They had seen little or nothing of the world. They were in very deed men and women of sorrow, and acquainted with grief. Their backs had been made familiar with the bloody lash, so that they had become callous; mine was yet tender; for while at Baltimore I got few whippings, and few slaves could boast of a kinder master and mistress than myself; and the thought of passing out of their hands into those of Master Andrew—a man who, but a few days before, to give me a sample of his bloody disposition, took my little brother, by the throat, threw him on the ground, and with the heel of his boot stamped upon his head till the blood gushed from his nose and ears—was well calculated to make me anxious as to my fate. After he had committed this savage outrage upon my brother, he turned to me, and said that was the way he meant to serve me one of these days,—meaning, I suppose, when I came into his possession.

Thanks to a kind Providence, I fell to the portion of Mrs. Lucretia, and was sent immediately back to Baltimore, to live again in the family of Master Hugh. Their joy at my return equalled their sorrow at my departure. It was a glad day to me. I had escaped a worse than lion's jaws. I was absent from Baltimore, for the purpose of valuation and division, just about one month, and it seemed to have been six.

Very soon after my return to Baltimore, my mistress, Lucretia, died, leaving her husband and one child, Amanda; and in a very short time after her death, Master Andrew died. Now all the property of my old master, slaves included, was in the hands of strangers,—strangers who had had nothing to do with accumulating it. Not a slave was left free. All remained slaves, from the youngest to the oldest. If any one thing in my experience, more than another, served to deepen my conviction of the infernal character of slavery, and to fill me with unutterable loathing of slaveholders, it was their base ingratitude to my poor old grandmother. She had served my old master faithfully from youth to old age. She had been the source of all his wealth; she had peopled his plantation with slaves; she had become a great grandmother in his service. She had rocked him in infancy, attended him childhood, served him through life, and at his death wiped from his icy brow the cold death-sweat, and closed his eyes forever. She was nevertheless left a slave—a slave for life—a slave in the hands of strangers; and in their hands she saw her children, her grandchildren, and her great-grandchildren, divided, like so many sheep, without being gratified with the small privilege of a single word, as to their or her own destiny. And, to cap the climax of their base ingratitude and fiendish barbarity, my grandmother, who was now very old, having outlived my old master and all his children, having seen the beginning and end of all of them, and her present owners finding she was of but little value, her frame already racked with the pains of old age, and complete helplessness fast stealing over her once active limbs, they took her to the woods, built her a little hut, put up a little mud-chimney, and then made her welcome to the privilege of supporting herself there in perfect loneliness; thus virtually turning her out to die! If my poor old grandmother now lives, she lives to suffer in utter loneliness; she lives to remember and mourn over the loss of children, the loss of grandchildren, and the loss of great-grandchildren. They are, in the language of the slave's poet, Whittier,—

> "Gone, gone, sold and gone
> To the rice swamp dank and lone,
> Where the slave-whip ceaseless swings,
> Where the noisome insect stings,
> Where the fever-demon strews
> Poison with the falling dews,
> Where the sickly sunbeams glare
> Through the hot and misty air:—
>   Gone, gone, sold and gone
>   To the rise swamp dank and lone,
>   From Virginia hills and waters—
>   Woe is me, my stolen daughters!"

The hearth is desolate. The children, the unconscious children, who once sang and danced in her presence, are gone. She gropes her way, in the darkness of age, for a drink of water. Instead of the voices of her children, she hears by day the moans of the dove, and by night the screams of the hideous owl. All is gloom. The grave is at the door. And now, when weighed down by the pains and aches of old age, when the head inclines to the feet, when the beginning and ending of human existence meet, and helpless infancy and painful old age combine together—at this time, this most needful time, the time for the exercise of that tenderness and affection which children only can exercise towards a declining parent—my poor old grandmother, the devoted mother of twelve children, is left all alone, in yonder little hut, before a few dim embers. She stands—she sits—she staggers—she falls—she groans—she dies—and there are none of her children or grandchildren present, to wipe from her wrinkled brow the cold sweat of death, or to place beneath the sod her fallen remains. Will not a righteous God visit for these things?

In about two years after the death of Mrs. Lucretia, Master Thomas married his second wife. Her name was Rowena Hamilton. She was the eldest daughter of Mr. William Hamilton.

Master now lived in St. Michael's. Not long after his marriage, a misunderstanding took place between himself and Master Hugh; and as a means of punishing his brother, he took me from him to live with himself at St. Michael's. Here I underwent another most painful separation. It, however, was not so severe as the one I dreaded at the division of property; for, during this interval, a great change had taken place in Master Hugh and his once kind and affectionate wife. The influence of brandy upon him, and of slavery upon her, had effected a disastrous change in the characters of both; so that, as far as they were concerned, I thought I had little to lose by the change. But it was not to them that I was attached. It was to those little Baltimore boys that I felt the strongest attachment. I had received many good lessons from them, and was still receiving them, and the thought of leaving them was painful indeed. I was leaving, too, without the hope of ever being allowed to return. Master Thomas had said he would never let me return again. The barrier betwixt himself and brother he considered impassable.

I then had to regret that I did not at least make the attempt to carry out my resolution to run away; for the chances of success are tenfold greater from the city than from the country.

I sailed from Baltimore for St. Michael's in the sloop Amanda, Captain Edward Dodson. On my passage, I paid particular attention to the direction which the steamboats took to go to Philadelphia. I found, instead of going down, on reaching North Point they went up the bay, in a northeasterly direction. I deemed this knowledge of the utmost importance. My determination to run away was again revived. I resolved to wait only so long as the offering of a favorable opportunity. When that came, I was determined to be off.

Chapter IX

I have now reached a period of my life when I can give dates. I left Baltimore, and went to live with Master Thomas Auld, at St. Michael's, in March 1832. It was now more than seven years since I lived with him in the family of my old master, on Colonel Lloyd's plantation. We of course were now almost entire strangers to each other. He was to me a new master, and I to him a new slave. I was ignorant of his temper and disposition; he was equally so of mine. A very short time, however, brought us into full acquaintance with each other. I was made acquainted with his wife not less than with himself. They were well matched, being equally mean and cruel. I was now, for the first time during a space of more than seven years, made to feel the painful gnawings of hunger—something which I had not experienced before since I left Colonel Lloyd's plantation. It went hard enough with me then, when I could look back to no period at which I had enjoyed a sufficiency. It was tenfold harder after living in Master Hugh's family, where I had always had enough to eat, and of that which was good. I have said Master Thomas was a mean man. He was so. Not to give a slave enough to eat, is regarded as the most aggravated development of meanness even among slaveholders. The rule is, no matter how coarse the food, only let there be enough of it. This is the theory; and in the part of Maryland from which I came, it is the general practice,—though there are many exceptions. Master Thomas gave us enough of neither coarse nor fine food. There were four slaves of us in the kitchen—my sister Eliza, my aunt Priscilla, Henny, and myself; and we were allowed less than a half of a bushel of corn-meal per week, and very little else, either in the shape of meat or vegetables. It was not enough for us to subsist upon. We were therefore reduced to the wretched necessity of living at the expense of our neighbors. This we did by begging and stealing, whichever came handy in the time of need, the one being considered as legitimate as the other. A great many times have we poor creatures been nearly perishing with hunger, when food in abundance lay moldering in the safe and smokehouse, and our pious mistress was aware of the fact; and yet that mistress and her husband would kneel every morning, and pray that God would bless them in basket and store!

Bad as all slaveholders are, we seldom meet one destitute of every element of character commanding respect. My master was one of this rare sort. I do not know of one single noble act ever performed by him. The leading trait in his character was meanness; and if there were any other element in this nature, it was made subject to this. He was mean; and, like most other mean men, he lacked the ability to conceal his meanness. Captain Auld was not born a slaveholder. He had been a poor man, master only of a Bay craft. He came into possession of all his slaves by marriage; and of all men, adopted slaveholders are the worst. He was cruel, but cowardly. He commanded without firmness. In the enforcement of his rules, he was at times rigid, and at times lax. At times, he spoke to his slaves with the firmness of Napoleon and the fury of a demon; at other times, he might well be mistaken for an inquirer who had lost his way. He did nothing of himself. He might have passed for a lion, but for his ears. In all things noble which he attempted, his own meanness shone most conspicuous. His airs, words, and actions, were the airs, words, and actions of born slaveholders, and, being assumed, were awkward enough. He was not even a good imitator. He possessed all the disposition to deceive, but wanted the power. Having no resources within himself, he was compelled to be the copyist of many, and being such, he was forever the victim of inconsistency; and of consequence he was an object of contempt, and was held as such even by his slaves. The luxury of having slaves of his own to wait upon him was something new and unprepared for. He was a slaveholder without the ability to hold slaves. He found himself incapable of managing his slaves either by force, fear, or fraud. We seldom called him "master;" we generally called him "Captain Auld," and were hardly disposed to title him at all. I doubt not that our conduct had much to do with making him appear awkward, and of consequence fretful. Our want of reverence for him must have perplexed him greatly. He wished to have us call him master, but lacked the firmness necessary to command us to do so. His wife used to insist upon our calling him so, but to no purpose. In August, 1832, my master attended a Methodist camp-meeting held in the Bayside, Talbot county, and there experienced religion. I indulged a faint hope that his conversion would lead him to emancipate his slaves, and that, if he did not do this, it would, at any rate, make him more kind and humane. I was disappointed in both these respects. It neither made him to be humane to his slaves, nor to emancipate them. If it had any effect on his character, it made him more cruel and hateful in all his ways; for I believe him to have been a much worse man after his conversion than before. Prior to his conversion, he relied upon his own depravity to shield and sustain him in his savage barbarity; but after his conversion, he found religious sanction and support for his slaveholding cruelty. He made the greatest pretensions to piety. His house was the house of prayer. He prayed morning, noon, and night. He very soon distinguished himself among his brethren, and was soon made a class-leader and exhorter. His activity in revivals was great, and he proved himself an instrument in the hands of the church in converting many souls. His house was the preachers' home. They used to take great pleasure in coming there to put up; for while he starved us, he stuffed them. We have had three or four preachers there at a time. The names of those who used to come most frequently while I lived there, were Mr. Storks, Mr. Ewery, Mr. Humphry, and Mr. Hickey. I have also seen Mr. George Cookman at our house. We slaves loved Mr. Cookman. We believed him to be a good man. We thought him instrumental in getting Mr. Samuel Harrison, a very rich slaveholder, to emancipate his slaves; and by some means got the impression that he was laboring to effect the emancipation of all the slaves. When he was at our house, we were sure to be called in to prayers. When the others were there, we were sometimes called in and sometimes not. Mr. Cookman took more notice of us than either of the other ministers. He could not come among us without betraying his sympathy for us, and, stupid as we were, we had the sagacity to see it.

While I lived with my master in St. Michael's, there was a white young man, a Mr. Wilson, who proposed to keep a Sabbath school for the instruction of such slaves as might be disposed to learn to read the New Testament. We met but three times, when Mr. West and Mr. Fairbanks, both class-leaders, with many others, came upon us with sticks and other missiles, drove us off, and forbade us to meet again. Thus ended our little Sabbath school in the pious town of St. Michael's.

I have said my master found religious sanction for his cruelty. As an example, I will state one of many facts going to prove the charge. I have seen him tie up a lame young woman, and whip her with a heavy cowskin upon her naked shoulders, causing the warm red blood to drip; and, in justification of the bloody deed, he would quote this passage of Scripture—"He that knoweth his master's will, and doeth it not, shall be beaten with many stripes."

Master would keep this lacerated young woman tied up in this horrid situation four or five hours at a time. I have known him to tie her up early in the morning, and whip her before breakfast; leave her, go to his store, return at dinner, and whip her again, cutting her in the places already made raw with his cruel lash. The secret of master's cruelty toward "Henny" is found in the fact of her being almost helpless. When quite a child, she fell into the fire, and burned herself horribly. Her hands were so burnt that she never got the use of them. She could do very little but bear heavy burdens. She was to master a bill of expense; and as he was a mean man, she was a constant offence to him. He seemed desirous of getting the poor girl out of existence. He gave her away once to his sister; but, being a poor gift, she was not disposed to keep her. Finally, my benevolent master, to use his own words, "set her adrift to take care of herself." Here was a recently-converted man, holding on upon the mother, and at the same time turning out her helpless child, to starve and die! Master Thomas was one of the many pious slaveholders who hold slaves for the very charitable purpose of taking care of them.

My master and myself had quite a number of differences. He found me unsuitable to his purpose. My city life, he said, had had a very pernicious effect upon me. It had almost ruined me for every good purpose, and fitted me for every thing which was bad. One of my greatest faults was that of letting his horse run away, and go down to his father-in-law's farm, which was about five miles from St. Michael's. I would then have to go after it. My reason for this kind of carelessness, or carefulness, was, that I could always get something to eat when I went there. Master William Hamilton, my master's father-in-law, always gave his slaves enough to eat. I never left there hungry, no matter how great the need of my speedy return. Master Thomas at length said he would stand it no longer. I had lived with him nine months, during which time he had given me a number of severe whippings, all to no good purpose. He resolved to put me out, as he said, to be broken; and, for this purpose, he let me for one year to a man name Edward Covey. Mr. Covey was a poor man, a farm-renter. He rented the place upon which he lived, as also the hands with which he tilled it. Mr. Covey had acquired a very high reputation for breaking young slaves, and this reputation was of immense value to him. It enabled him to get his farm tilled with much less expense to himself than he could have had it done without such a reputation. Some slaveholders thought it not much loss to allow Mr. Covey to have their slaves one year, for the sake of the training to which they were subjected, without any other compensation. He could hire young help with great ease, in consequence of this reputation. Added to the natural good qualities of Mr. Covey, he was a professor of religion—a pious soul—a member and a class-leader in the Methodist church. All of this added weight to his reputation as a "nigger-breaker." I was aware of all the facts, having been made acquainted with them by a young man who had lived there. I nevertheless made the change gladly; for I was sure of getting enough to eat, which is not the smallest consideration to a hungry man.

Chapter X

I left Master Thomas's house, and went to live with Mr. Covey, on the 1st of January, 1833. I was now, for the first time in my life, a field hand. In my new employment, I found myself even more awkward than a country boy appeared to be in a large city. I had been at my new home but one week before Mr. Covey gave me a very severe whipping, cutting my back causing the blood to run, and raising ridges on my flesh as large as my little finger. The details of this affair are as follows: Mr. Covey sent me, very early in the morning of one of our coldest days in the month of January, to the woods, to get a load of wood. He gave me a team of unbroken oxen. He told me which was the in-hand ox, and which the off-hand one. He then tied the end of a large rope around the horns of the in-hand ox, and gave me the other end of it, and told me, if the oxen started to run, that I must hold on upon the rope. I had never driven oxen before, and of course, I was very awkward. I, however, succeeded in getting to the edge of the woods with little difficulty; but I had got a very few rods into the woods, when the oxen took fright, and started full tilt, carrying the cart against trees, and over stumps, in the most frightful manner. I expected every moment that my brains would be dashed out against the trees. After running this for a considerable distance, they finally upset the cart, dashing it with great force against a tree, and threw themselves into a dense thicket. How I escaped death, I do not know. There I was, entirely alone, in a thick wood, in a place new to me. My cart was upset and shattered, my oxen were entangled among the young trees, and there was none to help me. After a long spell of effort, I succeeded in getting my cart righted, my oxen disentangled, and again yoked to the cart. I now proceeded with my team to the place where I had, the day before, been chopping wood, and loaded my cart pretty heavily, thinking in this way to tame my oxen. I then proceeded on my way home. I had now consumed one half of the day. I got out of the woods safely, and now felt out of danger. I stopped my oxen to open the woods gate; and just as I did so, before I could get hold of my ox-rope, the oxen again started, rushed through the gate, catching it between the wheel and the body of the cart, tearing it to pieces, and coming within a few inches of crushing me against the gate-post. Thus twice, in one short day, I escaped death by the merest chance. On my return, I told Mr. Covey what had happened, and how it happened. He ordered me to return to the woods again immediately. I did so, and he followed on after me. Just as I got into the woods, he came up and told me to stop my cart, and that he would teach me how to trifle away my time, and break gates. He then went to a large gum-tree, and with his axe cut three large switches, and, after trimming them up neatly with his pocket-knife, he ordered me to take off my clothes. I made him no answer, but stood with my clothes on. He repeated his order. I still made him no answer, nor did I move to strip myself. Upon this he rushed at me with the fierceness of a tiger, tore off my clothes, and lashed me till he had worn out his switches, cutting me so savagely as to leave the marks visible for a long time after. This whipping was the first of a number just like it, and for similar offences.

I lived with Mr. Covey one year. During the first six months, of that year, scarce a week passed without his whipping me. I was seldom free from a sore back. My awkwardness was almost always his excuse for whipping me. We were worked fully up to the point of endurance. Long before day we were up, our horses fed, and by the first approach of day we were off to the field with our hoes and ploughing teams. Mr. Covey gave us enough to eat, but scarce time to eat it. We were often less than five minutes taking our meals. We were often in the field from the first approach of day till its last lingering ray had left us; and at saving-fodder time, midnight often caught us in the field binding blades.

Covey would be out with us. The way he used to stand it, was this. He would spend the most of his afternoons in bed. He would then come out fresh in the evening, ready to urge us on with his words, example, and frequently with the whip. Mr. Covey was one of the few slaveholders who could and did work with his hands. He was a hard-working man. He knew by himself just what a man or a boy could do. There was no deceiving him. His work went on in his absence almost as well as in his presence; and he had the faculty of making us feel that he was ever present with us. This he did by surprising us. He seldom approached the spot where we were at work openly, if he could do it secretly. He always aimed at taking us by surprise. Such was his cunning, that we used to call him, among ourselves, "the snake." When we were at work in the cornfield, he would sometimes crawl on his hands and knees to avoid detection, and all at once he would rise nearly in our midst, and scream out, "Ha, ha! Come, come! Dash on, dash on!" This being his mode of attack, it was never safe to stop a single minute. His comings were like a thief in the night. He appeared to us as being ever at hand. He was under every tree, behind every stump, in every bush, and at every window, on the plantation. He would sometimes mount his horse, as if bound to St. Michael's, a distance of seven miles, and in half an hour afterwards you would see him coiled up in the corner of the wood-fence, watching every motion of the slaves. He would, for this purpose, leave his horse tied up in the woods. Again, he would sometimes walk up to us, and give us orders as though he was upon the point of starting on a long journey, turn his back upon us, and make us though he was going to the house to get ready; and, before he would get half way thither, he would turn short and crawl into a fence-corner, or behind some tree, and there watch us till the going down of the sun.

Mr. Covey's *forte* consisted in his power to deceive. His life was devoted to planning and perpetrating the grossest deceptions. Every thing he possessed in the shape of learning or religion, he made conform to his disposition to deceive. He seemed to think himself equal to deceiving the Almighty. He would make a short prayer in the morning, and a long prayer at night; and, strange as it may seem, few men would at times appear more devotional than he. The exercises of his family devotions were always commenced with singing; and, as he was a very poor singer himself, the duty of raising the hymn generally came upon me. He would read his hymn, and nod at me to commence. I would at times do so; at others, I would not. My non-compliance would almost always produce much confusion. To show himself independent of me, he would start and stagger through with his hymn in the most discordant manner. In this state of mind, he prayed with more than ordinary spirit. Poor man! such was his disposition, and success at deceiving, I do verily believe that he sometimes deceived himself into the solemn belief, that he was a sincere worshipper of the most high God; and this, too, at a time when he may be said to have been guilty of compelling his woman slave to commit the sin of adultery. The facts in the case are these: Mr. Covey was a poor man; he was just commencing in life; he was only able to buy one slave; and, shocking as is the fact, he bought her, as he said, for *a breeder*. This woman was named Caroline. Mr. Covey bought her from Mr. Thomas Lowe, about six miles from St. Michael's. She was a large, able-bodied woman, about twenty years old. She had already given birth to one child, which proved her to be just what he wanted. After buying her, he hired a married man of Mr. Samuel Harrison, to live with him one year; and him he used to fasten up with her every night! The result was, that, at the end of the year, the miserable woman gave birth to twins. At this result Mr. Covey seemed to be highly pleased, both with the man and the wretched woman. Such was his joy, and that of his wife, that nothing they could do for Caroline during her confinement was too good, or too hard, to be done. The children were regarded as being quite an addition to his wealth.

If at any one time of my life more than another, I was made to drink the bitterest dregs of slavery, that time was during the first six months of my stay with Mr. Covey. We were worked in all weathers. It was never too hot or too cold; it could never rain, blow hail, or snow too hard for us to work in the field. Work, work, work, was scarcely more the order of the day than of the night. The longest days were too short for him, and the shortest nights too long for him. I was somewhat unmanageable when I first went there, but a few months of this discipline tamed me. Mr. Covey succeeded in breaking me. I was broken in body, soul, and spirit. My natural elasticity was crushed, my intellect languished, the disposition to read departed, the cheerful spark that lingered about my eye died; the dark night of slavery closed in upon me; and behold a man transformed into a brute!

Sunday was my only leisure time. I spent this in a sort of beast-like stupor, between sleep and wake, under some large tree. At times I would rise up, a flash of energetic freedom would dart through my soul, accompanied with a faint beam of hope, that flickered for a moment, and then vanished. I sank down again, mourning over my wretched condition. I was sometimes prompted to take my life, and that of Covey, but was prevented by a combination of hope and fear. My sufferings on this plantation seem now like a dream rather than a stern reality.

Our house stood within a few rods of the Chesapeake Bay, whose broad bosom was ever white with sails from every quarter of the habitable globe. Those beautiful vessels, robed in purest white, so delightful to the eye of freemen, were to me so many shrouded ghosts, to terrify and torment me with thoughts of my wretched condition. I have often, in the deep stillness of a summer's Sabbath, stood all alone upon the lofty banks of that noble bay, and traced, with saddened heart and tearful eye, the countless number of sails moving off to the mighty ocean. The sight of these always affected me powerfully. My thoughts would compel utterance; and there, with no audience but the Almighty, I would pour out my soul's complaint, in my rude way, with an apostrophe to the moving multitude of ships:—

"You are loosed from your moorings, and are free; I am fast in my chains, and am a slave! You move merrily before the gentle gale, and I sadly before the bloody whip! You are freedom's swift-winged angels, that fly round the world; I am confined in bands of iron! O that I were free! O, that I were on one of your gallant decks, and under your protecting wing! Alas! betwixt me and you, the turbid waters roll. Go on, go on. O that I could also go! Could I but swim! If I could fly! O, why was I born a man, of whom to make a brute! The glad ship is gone; she hides in the dim distance. I am left in the hottest hell of unending slavery. O God, save me! God, deliver me! Let me be free! Is there any God? Why am I a slave? I will run away. I will not stand it. Get caught, or get clear, I'll try it. I had as well die with ague as the fever. I have only one life to lose. I had as well be killed running as die standing. Only think of it; one hundred miles straight north, and I am free! Try it? Yes! God helping me, I will. It cannot be that I shall live and die a slave. I will take to the water. This very bay shall yet bear me into freedom. The steamboats steered in a northeast course from North Point. I will do the same; and when I get to the head of the bay, I will turn my canoe adrift, and walk straight through Delaware into Pennsylvania. When I get there, I shall not be required to have a pass; I can travel without being disturbed. Let but the first opportunity offer, and, come what will, I am off. Meanwhile, I will try to bear up under the yoke. I am not the only slave in the world. Why should I fret? I can bear as much as any of them. Besides, I am but a boy, and all boys are bound to some one. It may be that my misery in slavery will only increase my happiness when I get free. There is a better day coming."

Thus I used to think, and this I used to speak to myself; goaded almost to madness at one moment, and at the next reconciling myself to my wretched lot.

I have already intimated that my condition was much worse, during the first six months of my stay at Mr. Covey's, than in the last six. The circumstances leading to the change in Mr.

Covey's course toward me form an epoch in my humble history. You have seen how a man was made a slave; you shall see how a slave was made a man. On one of the hottest days of the month of August, 1833, Bill Smith, William Hughes, a slave named Eli, and myself, were engaged in fanning wheat. Hughes was clearing the fanned wheat from before the fan, Eli was turning, Smith was feeding, and I was carrying wheat to the fan. The work was simple, requiring strength rather than intellect; yet, to one entirely unused to such work, it came very hard. About three o'clock of that day, I broke down; my strength failed me; I was seized with a violent aching of the head, attended with extreme dizziness; I trembled in every limb. Finding what was coming, I nerved myself up, feeling it would never do to stop work. I stood as long as I could stagger to the hopper with grain. When I could stand no longer, I fell, and felt as if held down by an immense weight. The fan of course stopped; every one had his own work to do; and no one could do the work of the other, and have his own go on at the same time.

Mr. Covey was at the house, about one hundred yards from the treading-yard where we were fanning. On hearing the fan stop, he left immediately, and came to the spot where we were. He hastily inquired what the matter was. Bill answered that I was sick, and there was no one to bring wheat to the fan. I had by this time crawled away under the side of the post and rail-fence by which the yard was enclosed, hoping to find relief by getting out of the sun. He then asked where I was. He was told by one of the hands. He came to the spot, and, after looking at me awhile, asked me what was the matter. I told him as well as I could, for I scarce had strength to speak. He then gave me a savage kick in the side, and told me to get up. I tried to do so, but fell back in the attempt. He gave me another kick, and again told me to rise. I again tried, and succeeded in gaining my feet; but, stooping to get the tub with which I was feeding the fan, I again staggered and fell. While down in this situation, Mr. Covey took up the hickory slat with which Hughes had been striking off the half-bushel measure, and with it gave me a heavy blow upon the head, making a large wound, and the blood ran freely; and with this again told me to get up. I made no effort to comply, having now made up my mind to let him do his worst. In a short time after receiving this blow, my head grew better. Mr. Covey had now left me to my fate. At this moment I resolved, for the first time, to go to my master, enter a complaint, and ask his protection. In order to [do] this, I must that afternoon walk seven miles; and this, under the circumstances, was truly a severe undertaking. I was exceedingly feeble; made so as much by the kicks and blows which I received, as by the severe fit of sickness to which I had been subjected. I, however, watched my chance, while Covey was looking in an opposite direction, and started for St. Michael's. I succeeded in getting a considerable distance on my way to the woods, when Covey discovered me, and called after me to come back, threatening what he would do if I did not come. I disregarded both his calls and his threats, and made my way to the woods as fast as my feeble state would allow; and thinking I might be overhauled by him if I kept the road, I walked through the woods, keeping far enough from the road to avoid detection, and near enough to prevent losing my way. I had not gone far before my little strength again failed me. I could go no farther. I fell down, and lay for a considerable time. The blood was yet oozing from the wound on my head. For a time I thought I should bleed to death; and think now that I should have done so, but that the blood so matted my hair as to stop the wound. After lying there about three quarters of an hour, I nerved myself up again, and started on my way, through bogs and briers, barefooted and bareheaded, tearing my feet sometimes at nearly every step; and after a journey of about seven miles, occupying some five hours to perform it, I arrived at master's store. I then presented an appearance enough to affect any but a heart of iron. From the crown of my head to my feet, I was covered with blood. My hair was all clotted with dust and blood; my shirt was stiff with blood. My legs and feet were torn in sundry places with briers and thorns, and were also covered with blood. I suppose I looked like a man who had escaped a den of wild beasts, and barely escaped them. In this state I appeared before my master, humbly entreating him to interpose his authority for my protection. I told him all the circumstances as well as I could, and it seemed, as I spoke, at times to affect him. He would then walk the floor, and seek to justify Covey by saying he expected I deserved it. He asked me what I wanted. I told him, to let me get a new home; that as sure as I lived with Mr. Covey again, I should live with but to die with him; that Covey would surely kill me; he was in a fair way for it. Master Thomas ridiculed the idea that there was any danger of Mr. Covey's killing me, and said that he knew Mr. Covey; that he was a good man, and that he could not think of taking me from him; that, should he do so, he would lose the whole year's wages; that I belonged to Mr. Covey for one year, and that I must go back to him, come what might; and that I must not trouble him with any more stories, or that he would himself *get hold of me*. After threatening me thus, he gave me a very large dose of salts, telling me that I might remain in St. Michael's that night, (it being quite late,) but that I must be off back to Mr. Covey's early in the morning; and that if I did not, he would *get hold of me*, which meant that he would whip me. I remained all night, and, according to his orders, I started off to Covey's in the morning, (Saturday morning,) wearied in body and broken in spirit. I got no supper that night, or breakfast that morning. I reached Covey's about nine o'clock; and just as I was getting over the fence that divided Mrs. Kemp's fields from ours, out ran Covey with his cowskin, to give me another whipping. Before he could reach me, I succeeded in getting to the cornfield; and as the corn was very high, it afforded me the means of hiding. He seemed very angry, and searched for me a long time. My behavior was altogether unaccountable. He finally gave up the chase, thinking, I suppose, that I must come home for something to eat; he would give himself no further trouble in looking for me. I spend that day mostly in the woods, having the alternative before me,—to go home and be whipped to death, or stay in the woods and be starved to death. That night, I fell in with Sandy Jenkins, a slave with whom I was somewhat acquainted. Sandy had a free wife who lived about four miles from Mr. Covey's; and it being Saturday, he was on his way to see her. I told him my circumstances, and he very kindly invited me to go home with him. I went home with him, and talked this whole matter over, and got his advice as to what course it was best for me to pursue. I found Sandy an old adviser. He told me, with great solemnity, I must go back to Covey; but that before I went, I must go with him into another part of the woods, where there was a certain *root*, which, if I would take some of it with me, carrying it *always on my right side*, would render it impossible for Mr. Covey, or any other white man, to whip me. He said he had carried it for years; and since he had done so, he had never received a blow, and never expected to while he carried it. I at first rejected the idea, that the simple carrying of a root in my pocket would have any such effect as he had said, and was not disposed to take it; but Sandy impressed the necessity with much earnestness, telling me it could do no harm, if it did no good. To please him, I at length took the root, and according to his direction, carried it upon my right side. This was Sunday morning. I immediately started for home; and upon entering the yard gate, out came Mr. Covey on his way to meeting. He spoke to me very kindly, made me drive the pigs from a lot near by, and passed on towards the church. Now, this singular conduct of Mr. Covey really made me begin to think that there was something in the *root* which Sandy had given me; and had it been on any other day than Sunday, I could have attributed the conduct to no other cause than the influence of that root; and as it was, I was half inclined to think the *root* to be something more than I at first had taken it to be. All went well till Monday morning. On this morning, the virtue of the *root* was fully tested. Long before daylight, I was called to go and rub, curry, and feed the horses. I obeyed, and was glad to obey. But whilst thus engaged, whilst in the act of throwing down some blades from the loft, Mr. Covey entered the stable with a long rope; and just as I was half out of the loft, he caught hold of my legs, and was about tying me. As soon as I found what he was up to, I gave a sudden spring, and as I did so, he holding to my legs, I was brought sprawling on the stable floor. Mr. Covey seemed now to think he had me, and could do what he pleased; but at this moment—from whence came the spirit I don't know—I resolved to fight; and, suiting my action to the resolution, I seized Covey hard by the throat; and as I did so, I rose. He held on to me, and I to him. My resistance was so entirely unexpected, that Covey seemed taken all aback. He trembled like a leaf. This gave me assurance, and I held him uneasy, causing the blood to run where I touched him with the ends of my fingers. Mr. Covey soon called out to Hughes for help. Hughes came, and, while Covey held me, attempted to tie my right hand. While he was in the act of doing so, I watched my chance, and gave him a heavy kick close under the ribs. This kick fairly sickened Hughes, so that he left me in the hands of Mr. Covey. This kick had the effect of not only weakening Hughes, but Covey also. When he saw Hughes bending over with pain, his courage quailed. He asked me if I meant to persist in my resistance. I told him I did, come what might; that he had used me like a brute for six months, and that I was determined to be used so no longer. With that, he strove to drag me to a stick that was lying just out of the stable door. He meant to knock me down. But just as he was leaning over to get the stick, I seized him with both hands by his collar, and brought him by a sudden snatch to the ground. By this time, Bill came. Covey called upon him for assistance. Bill wanted to know what he could do. Covey said, "Take hold of him, take hold of him!" Bill said his master hired him out to work, and not to help to whip me; so he left Covey and myself to fight our own battle out. We were at it for nearly two hours. Covey at length let me go, puffing and blowing at a great rate, saying that if I had not resisted, he would not have whipped me half so much. The truth was, that he had not whipped me at all. I considered him as getting entirely the worst end of the bargain; for he had drawn no blood from me, but I had from him. The whole six month afterwards, that I spent with Mr. Covey, he never laid the weight of his finger upon me in anger. He would occasionally say, he didn't want to get hold of me again. "No," thought I, "you need not; for you will come off worse than you did before."

This battle with Mr. Covey was the turning-point in my career as a slave. It rekindled the few expiring embers of freedom, and revived within me a sense of my own manhood. It recalled the departed self-confidence, and inspired me again with a determination to be free. The gratification afforded by the triumph was a full compensation for whatever else might follow, even death itself. He only can understand the deep satisfaction which I experienced, who has himself repelled by force the bloody arm of slavery. I felt as I never felt before. It was a glorious resurrection, from the tomb of slavery, to the heaven of freedom. My long-crushed spirit rose, cowardice departed, bold defiance took its place; and I now resolved that, however long I might remain a slave in form, the day had passed forever when I could be a slave in fact. I did not hesitate to let it be known of me, that the white man who expected to succeed in whipping, must also succeed in killing me.

From this time I was never again what might be called fairly whipped, though I remained a slave four years afterwards. I had several fights, but was never whipped.

It was for a long time a matter of surprise to me why Mr. Covey did not immediately have me taken by the constable to the whipping-post, and there regularly whipped for the crime of raising my hand against a white man in defence of myself. And the only explanation I can now think of does not entirely satisfy me; but such as it is, I will give it. Mr. Covey enjoyed the most unbounded reputation for being a first-rate overseer and negro-breaker. It was of considerable importance to him. That reputation was at stake; and had he sent me—a boy about sixteen years old—to the public whipping post, his reputation would have been lost; so, to save his reputation, he suffered me to go unpunished.

My term of actual service to Mr. Edward Covey ended on Christmas day, 1833. The days between Christmas and New Year's day are allowed as holidays; and, accordingly, we were not required to perform any labor, more than to feed and take care of the stock. This time we regarded as our own, by the grace of our masters; and we therefore used or abused it nearly as we pleased. Those of us who had families at a distance, were generally allowed to spend the whole six days in their society. This time, however, was spent in various ways. The staid, sober, thinking and industrious ones of our number would employ themselves in making cornbrooms, mats, horse-collars, and baskets; and another class of us would spend the time in hunting opossums, hares, and coons. But by far the larger part engaged in such sports and merriments as playing ball, wrestling, running foot-races, fiddling, dancing, and drinking whisky; and this latter mode of spending the time was by far the most agreeable to the feelings of our masters. A slave who would work during the holidays was considered by our masters as scarcely deserving them. He was regarded as one who rejected the favor of his master. It was deemed a disgrace not to get drunk at Christmas; and he was regarded as lazy indeed, who had not provided himself with the necessary means, during the year, to get whisky enough to last him through Christmas.

From what I know of the effect of these holidays upon the slave, I believe them to be among the most effective means in the hands of the slaveholder in keeping down the spirit of insurrection. Were the slaveholders at once to abandon this practice, I have not the slightest doubt it would lead to an immediate insurrection among the slaves. These holidays serve as conductors, or safety-valves, to carry off the rebellious spirit of enslaved humanity. But for these, the slave would be forced up to the wildest desperation; and woe betide the slaveholder, the day he ventures to remove or hinder the operation of those conductors! I warn him that, in such an event, a spirit will go forth in their midst, more to be dreaded than the most appalling earthquake.

The holidays are part and parcel of the gross fraud, wrong, and inhumanity of slavery. They are professedly a custom established by the benevolence of the slaveholders; but I undertake to say, it is the result of selfishness, and one of the grossest frauds committed upon the downtrodden slave. They do not give the slaves this time because they would not like to have their work during its continuance, but because they know it would be unsafe to deprive them of it. This will be seen by the fact, that the slaveholders like to have their slaves spend those days just in such a manner as to make them as glad of their ending as of their beginning. Their object seems to be, to disgust their slaves with freedom, by plunging them into the lowest depths of dissipation. For instance, the slaveholders not only like to see the slave drink of his own accord, but will adopt various plans to make him drunk. One plan is, to make bets on their slaves, as to who can drink the most whisky without getting drunk; and in this way they succeed in getting whole multitudes to drink to excess. Thus, when the slave asks for virtuous freedom, the cunning slaveholder, knowing his ignorance, cheats him with a does of vicious dissipation, artfully labelled with the name of liberty. The most of us used to drink it down, and the result was just what might be supposed: many of us were led to think that there was little to choose between liberty and slavery. We felt, and very properly too, that we had almost as well be slaves to man as to rum. So, when the holidays ended, we staggered up from the filth of our wallowing, took a long breath, and marched to the field,—feeling, upon the whole, rather glad to go, from what our master had deceived us into a belief was freedom, back to the arms of slavery.

I have said that this mode of treatment is a part of the whole system of fraud and inhumanity of slavery. It is so. The mode here adopted to disgust the slave with freedom, by allowing him to see only the abuse of it, is carried out in other things. For instance, a slave loves molasses; he steals some. His master, in many cases, goes off to town, and buys a large quantity; he returns, takes his whip, and commands the slave to eat the molasses, until the poor fellow is made sick at the very mention of it. The same mode is sometimes adopted to make the slaves refrain from asking for more food than their regular allowance. A slave runs through his allowance, and applies for more. His master is enraged at him; but, not willing to send him off without food, gives him more than is necessary, and compels him to eat it within a given time. Then, if he complains that he cannot eat it, he is said to be satisfied neither full or fasting, and is whipped for being hard to please! I have an abundance of such illustrations of the same principle, drawn from my own observation, but think the cases I have cited sufficient. The practice is a very common one.

On the first of January, 1834, I left Mr. Covey, and went to live with Mr. William Freeland, who lived about three miles from St. Michael's. I soon found Mr. Freeland a very different man from Mr. Covey. Though not rich, he was what would be called an educated southern gentleman. Mr. Covey, as I have shown, was a well-trained negro-breaker and slavedriver. The former (slaveholder though he was) seemed to possess some regard for honor, some reverence for justice, and some respect for humanity. The latter seemed totally insensible to all such sentiments. Mr. Freeland had many of the faults peculiar to slaveholders, such as being very passionate and fretful; but I must do him the justice to say, that he was exceedingly free from those degrading vices to which Mr. Covey was constantly addicted. The one was open and frank, and we always knew where to find him. The other was a most artful deceiver, and could be understood only by such as were skilful enough to detect his cunningly-devised frauds. Another advantage I gained in my new master was, he made no pretensions to, or profession of, religion; and this, in my opinion, was truly a great advantage. I assert most unhesitatingly, that the religion of the south is a mere covering for the most horrid crimes,—a justifier of the most appalling barbarity,—a sanctifier of the most hateful frauds,—and a dark shelter under, which the darkest, foulest, grossest, and most infernal deeds of slaveholders find the strongest protection. Were I to be again reduced to the chains of slavery, next to that enslavement, I should regard being the slave of a religious master the greatest calamity that could befall me. For of all slaveholders with whom I have ever met, religious slaveholders are the worst. I have ever found them the meanest and basest, the most cruel and cowardly, of all others. It was my unhappy lot not only to belong to a religious slaveholder, but to live in a community of such religionists. Very near Mr. Freeland lived the Rev. Daniel Weeden, and in the same neighborhood lived the Rev. Rigby Hopkins. These were members and ministers in the Reformed Methodist Church. Mr. Weeden owned, among others, a woman slave, whose name I have forgotten. This woman's back, for weeks, was kept literally raw, made so by the lash of this merciless, *religious* wretch. He used to hire hands. His maxim was, Behave well or behave ill, it is the duty of a master occasionally to whip a slave, to remind him of his master's authority. Such was his theory, and such his practice.

Mr. Hopkins was even worse than Mr. Weeden. His chief boast was his ability to manage slaves. The peculiar feature of his government was that of whipping slaves in advance of deserving it. He always managed to have one or more of his slaves to whip every Monday morning. He did this to alarm their fears, and strike terror into those who escaped. His plan was to whip for the smallest offences, to prevent the commission of large ones. Mr. Hopkins could always find some excuse for whipping a slave. It would astonish one, unaccustomed to a slaveholding life, to see with what wonderful ease a slaveholder can find things, of which to make occasion to whip a slave. A mere look, word, or motion,—a mistake, accident, or want of power,—are all matters for which a slave may be whipped at any time. Does a slave look dissatisfied? It is said, he has the devil in him, and it must be whipped out. Does he speak loudly when spoken to by his master? Then he is getting high-minded, and should be taken down a button-hole lower. Does he forget to pull off his hat at the approach of a white person? Then he is wanting in reverence, and should be whipped for it. Does he ever venture to vindicate his conduct, when censured for it? Then he is guilty of impudence,—one of the greatest crimes of which a slave can be guilty. Does he ever venture to suggest a different mode of doing things from that pointed out by his master? He is indeed presumptuous, and getting above himself; and nothing less than a flogging will do for him. Does he, while ploughing, break a plough,—or, while hoeing, break a hoe? It is owing to his carelessness, and for it a slave must always be whipped. Mr. Hopkins could always find something of this sort to justify the use of the lash, and he seldom failed to embrace such opportunities. There was not a man in the whole country, with whom the slaves who had the getting their own home, would not prefer to live, rather than with this Rev. Mr. Hopkins. And yet there was not a man any where round, who made higher professions of religion, or was more active in revivals,—more attentive to the class, love-feast, prayer and preaching meetings, and more devotional in his family,—that prayed earlier, later, louder, and longer,—than this same reverend slave-driver, Rigby Hopkins.

But to return to Mr. Freeland, and to my experience while in his employment. He, like Mr. Covey, gave us enough to eat; but, unlike Mr. Covey, he also gave us sufficient time to take our meals. He worked us hard, but always between sunrise and sunset. He required a good deal of work to be done, but gave us good tools with which to work. His farm was large, but he employed hands enough to work it, and with ease, compared with many of his neighbors. My treatment, while in his employment, was heavenly, compared with what I experienced at the hands of Mr. Edward Covey.

Mr. Freeland was himself the owner of but two slaves. Their names were Henry Harris and John Harris. The rest of his hands he hired. These consisted of myself, Sandy Jenkins,* and Handy Caldwell. Henry and John were quite intelligent, and in a very little while after I went there, I succeeded in creating in them a strong desire to learn how to read. This desire soon sprang up in the others also. They very soon mustered up some old spelling-books, and nothing would do but that I must keep a Sabbath school. I agreed to do so, and accordingly devoted my Sundays to teaching these my loved fellow-slaves how to read. Neither of them knew his letters when I went there. Some of the slaves of the neighboring farms found what was going on, and also availed themselves of this little opportunity to learn to read. It was understood, among all who came, that there must be as little display about it as possible. It was necessary to keep our religious masters at St. Michael's unacquainted with the fact, that, instead of spending the Sabbath in wrestling, boxing, and drinking whisky, we were trying to learn how to read the will of God; for they had much rather see us engaged in those degrading sports, than to see us behaving like intellectual, moral, and accountable beings. My blood boils as I think of the bloody manner in which Messrs. Wright Fairbanks and Garrison West, both class-leaders, in connection with many others, rushed in upon us with sticks and stones, and broke up our virtuous little Sabbath school, at St. Michael's—all calling themselves Christians! humble followers of the Lord Jesus Christ! But I am again digressing.

*This is the same man who gave me the roots to prevent my being whipped by Mr. Covey. He was "a clever soul." We used frequently to talk about the fight with Covey, and as often as we did so, he would claim my success as the result of the roots which he gave me. This superstition is very common among the more ignorant slaves. A slave seldom dies but that his death is attributed to trickery.

I held my Sabbath school at the house of a free colored man, whose name I deem it imprudent to mention; for should it be known, it might embarrass him greatly, though the crime of holding the school was committed ten years ago. I had at one time over forty scholars, and those of the right sort, ardently desiring to learn. They were of all ages, though mostly men and women. I look back to those Sundays with an amount of pleasure not to be expressed. They were great days to my soul. The work of instructing my dear fellow-slaves was the sweetest engagement with which I was ever blessed. We loved each other, and to leave them at the close of the Sabbath was a severe cross indeed. When I think that these precious souls are to-day shut up in the prison-house of slavery, my feelings overcome me, and I am almost ready to ask, "Does a righteous God govern the universe? and for what does he hold the thunders in his right hand, if not to smite the oppressor, and deliver the spoiled out of the hand of the spoiler?" These dear souls came not to Sabbath school because it was popular to do so, nor did I teach them because it was reputable to be thus engaged. Every moment they spent in that school, they were liable to be taken up, and given thirty-nine lashes. They came because they wished to learn. Their minds had been starved by their cruel masters. They had been shut up in the mental darkness. I taught them, because it was the delight of my soul to be doing something that looked like bettering the condition of my race. I kept up my school nearly the whole year I lived with Mr. Freeland; and, beside my Sabbath school, I devoted three evenings in the week, during the winter, to teaching the slaves at home. And I have the happiness to know, that several of those who came to Sabbath school learned how to read; and that one, at least, is now free through my agency.

The year passed off smoothly. It seemed only about half as long as the year which preceded it. I went through it without receiving a single blow. I will give Mr. Freeland the credit of being the best master I ever had, *till I became my own master.* For the ease with which I passed the year, I was, however, somewhat indebted to the society of my fellow-slaves. They were noble souls; they not only possessed loving hearts, but brave ones. We were linked and interlinked with each other. I loved them with a love stronger than any thing I have experienced since. It is sometimes said that we slaves do not love and confide in each other. In answer to this assertion, I can say, I never loved any or confided in any people more than my fellow-slaves, and especially those with whom I lived at Mr. Freeland's. I believe we would have died for each other. We never undertook to do any thing, of any importance, without a mutual consultation. We never moved separately. We were one; and as much so by our tempers and dispositions, as by the mutual hardships to which we were necessarily subjected by our condition as slaves.

At the close of the year 1834, Mr. Freeland again hired me of my master, for the year 1835. But, by this time, I began to want to live *upon free land* as well as *with Freeland;* and I was no longer content, therefore, to live with him or any other slaveholder. I began, with the commencement of the year, to prepare myself for a final struggle, which should decide my fate one way or the other. My tendency was upward. I was fast approaching manhood, and year after year had passed, and I was still a slave. These thoughts roused me—I must do something. I therefore resolved that 1835 should not pass without witnessing an attempt, on my part, to secure my liberty. But I was not willing to cherish this determination alone. My fellow-slaves were dear to me. I was anxious to have them participate with me in this, my life-giving determination. I therefore, though with great prudence, commenced early to ascertain their views and feelings in regard to their condition, and to imbue their minds with thoughts of freedom. I bent myself to devising ways and means for our escape; and meanwhile strove, on all fitting occasions, to impress them with the gross fraud and inhumanity of slavery. I went first to

Henry, next to John, then to the others. I found, in them all, warm hearts and noble spirits. They were ready to hear, and ready to act when a feasible plan should be proposed. This was what I wanted. I talked to them of our want of manhood, if we submitted to our enslavement without at least one noble effort to be free. We met often, and consulted frequently, and told our hopes and fears, recounted the difficulties, real and imagined, which we should be called on to meet. At times we were almost disposed to give up, and try to content ourselves with our wretched lot; at others, we were firm and unbending in our determination to go. Whenever we suggested any plan, there was shrinking—the odds were fearful. Our path was beset with the greatest obstacles; and if we succeeded in gaining the end of it, our right to be free was yet questionable—we were yet liable to be returned to bondage. We could see no spot this side of the ocean, where we could be free. We knew nothing about Canada. Our knowledge of the north did not extend farther than New York; and to go there, and be forever harassed with the frightful liability of being returned to slavery—with the certainty of being treated tenfold worse than before—the thought was truly a horrible one, and one which it was not easy to overcome. The case sometimes stood thus: At every gate through which we were to pass, we saw a watchman—at every ferry a guard—on every bridge a sentinel—and in every wood a patrol. We were hemmed in upon every side. Here were the difficulties, real or imagined—the good to be sought, and the evil to be shunned. On the one hand, there stood slavery, a stern reality, glaring frightfully upon us,—its robes already crimsoned with the blood of millions, and even now feasting itself greedily upon our own flesh. On the other hand, away back in the dim distance, under the flickering light of the north star, behind some craggy hill or snow-covered mountain, stood a doubtful freedom—half frozen—beckoning us to come and share its hospitality. This in itself was sometimes enough to stagger us; but when we permitted ourselves to survey the road, we were frequently appalled. Upon either side we saw grim death, assuming the most horrid shapes. Now it was starvation, causing us to eat our own flesh;—now we were contending with the waves, and were drowned;— now we were overtaken, and torn to pieces by the fangs of the terrible bloodhound. We were stung by scorpions, chased by wild beasts, bitten by snakes, and finally, after having nearly reached the desired spot,—after swimming rivers, encountering wild beasts, sleeping in the woods, suffering hunger and nakedness,—we were overtaken by our pursuers, and, in our resistance, we were shot dead upon the spot! I say, this picture sometimes appalled us, and made us

> "rather bear those ills we had,
> Than fly to others, that we knew not of."

In coming to a fixed determination to run away, we did more than Patrick Henry, when he resolved upon liberty or death. With us it was a doubtful liberty at most, and almost certain death if we failed. For my part, I should prefer death to hopeless bondage.

Sandy, one of our number, gave up the notion, but still encouraged us. Our company then consisted of Henry Harris, John Harris, Henry Bailey, Charles Roberts, and myself. Henry Bailey was my uncle, and belonged to my master. Charles married my aunt: he belonged to my master's father-in-law, Mr. William Hamilton.

The plan we finally concluded upon was, to get a large canoe belonging to Mr. Hamilton, and upon the Saturday night previous to Easter holidays, paddle directly up the Chesapeake Bay. On our arrival at the head of the bay, a distance of seventy or eighty miles from where we lived, it was our purpose to turn our canoe adrift, and follow the guidance of the north star till we got beyond the limits of Maryland. Our reason for taking the water route was, that we were less liable to be suspected as runaways; we hoped to be regarded as fishermen; whereas, if we should take the land route, we should be subjected to interruptions of almost every kind.

Any one having a white face, and being so disposed, could stop us, and subject us to examination.

The week before our intended start, I wrote several protections, one for each of us. As well as I can remember, they were in the following words, to wit:—

"This is to certify that I, the undersigned, have given the bearer, my servant, full liberty to go to Baltimore, and spend the Easter holidays. Written with mine own hand, &c., 1835.

"WILLIAM HAMILTON,
Near St. Michael's, in Talbot county,
Maryland."

We were not going to Baltimore; but, in going up the bay, we went toward Baltimore, and these protections were only intended to protect us while on the bay.

As the time drew near for our departure, our anxiety become more and more intense. It was truly a matter of life and death with us. The strength of our determination was about to be fully tested. At this time, I was very active in explaining every difficulty, removing every doubt, dispelling every fear, and inspiring all with the firmness indispensable to success in our undertaking; assuring them that half was gained the instant we made the move; we had talked long enough; we were now ready to move; if not now, we never should be; and if we did not intend to move now, we had as well fold our arms, sit down, and acknowledge ourselves fit only to be slaves. This, none of us were prepared to acknowledge. Every man stood firm; and at our last meeting, we pledged ourselves afresh, in the most solemn manner, that, at the time appointed, we would certainly start in pursuit of freedom. This was in the middle of the week, at the end of which we were to be off. We went, as usual, to our several fields of labor, but with bosoms highly agitated with thoughts of our truly hazardous undertaking. We tried to conceal our feelings as much as possible; and I think we succeeded very well.

After a painful waiting, the Saturday morning, whose night was to witness our departure, came. I hailed it with joy, bring what of sadness it might. Friday night was a sleepless one for me. I probably felt more anxious than the rest, because I was, by common consent, at the head of the whole affair. The responsibility of success or failure lay heavily upon me. The glory of the one, and the confusion of the other, were alike mine. The first two hours of that morning were such as I never experienced before, and hope never to again. Early in the morning, we went, as usual, to the field. We were spreading manure; and all at once, while thus engaged, I was overwhelmed with an indescribable feeling, in the fullness of which I turned to Sandy, who was near by, and said, "We are betrayed!" "Well," said he, "that thought has this moment struck me." We said no more. I was never more certain of any thing.

The horn was blown as usual, and we went up from the field to the house for breakfast. I went for the form, more than for want of any thing to eat that morning. Just as I got to the house, in looking out at the lane gate, I saw four white men, with two colored men. The white men were on horseback, and the colored ones were walking behind, as if tied. I watched them a few moments till they got up to our lane gate. Here they halted, and tied the colored men to the gate-post. I was not yet certain as to what the matter was. In a few moments, in rode Mr. Hamilton, with speed betokening great excitement. He came to the door, and inquired if Master William was in. He was told he was at the barn. Mr. Hamilton, without dismounting, rode up to the barn with extraordinary speed. In a few moments, he and Mr. Freeland returned to the house. By this time, the three constables rode up, and in great haste dismounted, tied their horses, and met Master William and Mr. Hamilton returning from the barn; and after talking awhile, they all walked up to the kitchen door. There was no one in the kitchen but myself and John. Henry and Sandy were up at the barn. Mr. Freeland put his head in at the door, and called me by name, saying, there were some gentlemen at the door who wished to see me. I stepped to the door, and inquired what they wanted. They at once seized me, and, without giving me any satisfaction, tied me—lashing my hands closely together. I insisted upon knowing what the matter was. They at length said, that they had learned I had been in a "scrape," and that I was to be examined before my master; and if their information proved false, I should not be hurt.

In a few moments, they succeeded in tying John. They then turned to Henry, who had by this time returned, and commanded him to cross his hands. "I won't!" said Henry, in a firm tone, indicating his readiness to meet the consequences of his refusal. "Won't you?" said Tom Graham, the constable. "No. I won't!" said Henry, in a still stronger tone. With this, two of the constables pulled out their shining pistols, and swore, by their Creator, that they would make him cross his hands or kill him. Each cocked his pistol, and, with fingers on the trigger, walked up to Henry, saying, at the same time, if he did not cross his hands, they would blow his damned heart out. "Shoot me! shoot me!" said Henry; "you can't kill me but once. Shoot, shoot,—and be damned! *I won't be tied!*" This he said in a tone of loud defiance; and at the same time, with a motion as quick as lightning, he with one single stroke dashed the pistols from the hand of each constable. As he did this, all hands fell upon him, and after beating him some time, they finally overpowered him, and got him tied.

During the scuffle, I managed, I know not how, to get my pass out, and, without being discovered, put it into the fire. We were all now tied; and just as we were to leave for Easton jail, Betsy Freeland, mother of William Freeland, came to the door with her hands full of biscuits, and divided them between Henry and John. She then delivered herself of a speech, to the following effect:—addressing herself to me, she said, "*You devil! You yellow devil!* it was you that put it into the heads of Henry and John to run away. But for you, you long-legged mulatto devil! Henry nor John would never have thought of such a thing." I made no reply, and was immediately hurried off towards St. Michael's. Just a moment previous to the scuffle with Henry, Mr. Hamilton suggested the propriety of making a search for the protections which he had understood Frederick had written from himself and the rest. But, just at the moment he was about carrying his proposal into effect, his aid was needed in helping to tie Henry; and the excitement attending the scuffle caused them either to forget, or to deem it unsafe, under the circumstances, to search. So we were not yet convicted of the intention to run away.

When we got about half way to St. Michael's, while the constables having us in charge were looking ahead, Henry inquired of me what he should do with his pass. I told him to eat it with his biscuit, and own nothing; and we passed the word around, "*Own nothing;*" and "*Own nothing!*" said we all. Our confidence in each other was unshaken. We were resolved to succeed or fail together, after the calamity had befallen us as much as before. We were now prepared for any thing. We were to be dragged that morning fifteen miles behind horses, and then to be placed in the Easton jail. When we reached St. Michael's, we underwent a sort of examination. We all denied that we ever intended to run away. We did this more to bring out the evidence against us, than from any hope of getting clear of being sold; for, as I have said, we were ready for that. The fact was, we cared but little where we went, so we went together. Our greatest concern was about separation. We dreaded that more than any thing this side of death. We found the evidence against us to be the testimony of one person; our master would not tell who it was; but we came to a unanimous decision among ourselves as to who their informant was. We were sent off to the jail at Easton. When we got there, we were delivered up to the sheriff, Mr. Joseph Graham, and by him placed in jail. Henry, John, and myself, were placed in one room together—Charles, and Henry Bailey, in another. Their object in separating us was to hinder concert.

We had been in jail scarcely twenty minutes, when a swarm of slave traders, and agents for slave traders, flocked into jail to look at us, and to ascertain if we were for sale. Such a set of beings I never saw before! I felt myself surrounded by so many fiends from perdition. A band of pirates never looked more like their father, the devil. They laughed and grinned over us, saying, "Ah, my boys! we have got you, haven't we." And after taunting us in various ways, they one by one went into the examination of us, with intent to ascertain our value. They would impudently ask us if we would not like to have them for our masters. We would make them no answer, and leave them to find out as best they could. Then they would curse and swear at us, telling us that they could take the devil out of us in a very little while, if we were only in their hands.

While in jail, we found ourselves in much more comfortable quarters than we expected when we went there. We did not get much to eat, nor that which was very good; but we had a good clean room, from the windows of which we could see what was going on in the street, which was very much better than though we had been placed in one of the dark, damp cells. Upon the whole, we got along very well, so far as the jail and its keeper were concerned. Immediately after the holidays were over, contrary to all our expectations, Mr. Hamilton and Mr. Freeland came up to Easton, and took Charles, the two Henrys, and John, out of jail, and carried them home, leaving me alone. I regarded this separation as a final one. It caused me more pain than any thing else in the whole transaction. I was ready for any thing rather then separation. I supposed that they had consulted together, and had decided that, as I was the whole cause of the intention of the others to run away, it was hard to make the innocent suffer with the guilty; and that they had, therefore, concluded to take the others home, and sell me, as a warning to the others that remained. It is due to the noble Henry to say, he seemed almost as reluctant at leaving the prison as at leaving home to come to the prison. But we knew we should, in all probability, be separated, if we were sold; and since he was in their hands, he concluded to go peaceably home.

I was now left to my fate. I was all alone, and within the walls of a stone prison. But a few days before, and I was full of hope. I expected to have been safe in a land of freedom; but now I was covered with gloom, sunk down to the utmost despair. I thought the possibility of freedom was gone. I was kept in this way about one week, at the end of which, Captain Auld, my master, to my surprise and utter astonishment, came up, and took me out, with the intention of sending me, with a gentleman of his acquaintance, to Alabama. But, from some cause or other, he did not send me to Alabama, but concluded to send me back to Baltimore, to live again with his brother Hugh, and to learn a trade.

Thus, after an absence of three years and one month, I was once more permitted to return to my old home at Baltimore. My master sent me away, because there existed against me a very great prejudice in the community, and he feared I might be killed.

In a few weeks after I went to Baltimore, Master Hugh hired me to Mr. William Gardner, an extensive ship-builder, on Fell's Point. I was put there to learn how to calk. It, however, proved a very unfavorable place for the accomplishment of this object. Mr. Gardner was engaged that spring in building two large man-of-war brigs, professedly for the Mexican government. The vessels were to be launched in the July of that year, and in failure thereof, Mr. Gardner was to lose a considerable sum; so that when I entered, all was hurry. There was no time to learn any thing. Every man had to do that which he knew how to do. In entering the shipyard, my orders from Mr. Gardner were, to do whatever the carpenters commanded me to do. This was placing me at the beck and call of about seventy-five men. I was to regard all these as masters. Their word was to be my law. My situation was a most trying one. At times I needed a dozen pair of hands. I was called a dozen ways in the space of single minute. Three or four voices would strike my ear at the same moment. It was—"Fred., come help me to cant this timber here."—"Fred., come carry this timber yonder."—"Fred., bring that roller here."—"Fred., go get a fresh can of water."—"Fred., come help saw off the end of this timber."—"Fred., go quick, and get the crowbar."—"Fred., hold on the end of this fall."—"Fred., go to the blacksmith's shop, and get a new punch."—"Hurra, Fred! run and bring me a cold chisel."—"I say, Fred., bear a hand, and get up a fire as quick as lightning under that steambox."—"Halloo, nigger! come, turn this grindstone."—"Come, come! move, move! and *bowse* this timber forward."—"I say, darky, blast your eyes, why don't you heat up some pitch?"—"Halloo! halloo! halloo!" (Three voices at the same time.) "Come here!—Go there!—Hold on where you are! Damn you, if you move, I'll knock your brains out!"

This was my school for eight months; and I might have remained there longer, but for a most horrid fight I had with four of the white apprentices, in which my left eye was nearly knocked out, and I was horribly mangled in other respects. The facts in the case were these: Until a very little while after I went there, white and black ship-carpenters worked side by side, and no one seemed to see any impropriety in it. All hands seemed to be very well satisfied. Many of the black carpenters were freemen. Things seemed to be going on very well. All at once, the white carpenters knocked off, and said they would not work with free colored workmen. Their reason for this, as alleged, was, that if free colored carpenters were encouraged, they would soon take the trade into their own hands, and poor white men would be thrown out of employment. They therefore felt called upon at once to put a stop to it. And, taking advantage of Mr. Gardner's necessities, they broke off, swearing they would work no longer, unless he would discharge his black carpenters. Now, though this did not extend to me in form, it did reach me in fact. My fellow-apprentices very soon began to feel it degrading to them to work with me. They began to put on airs, and talk about the "niggers" taking the country, saying we all ought to be killed; and, being encouraged by the journeymen, they commenced making my condition as hard as they could, by hectoring me around, and sometimes striking me. I, of course, kept the vow I made after the fight with Mr. Covey, and struck back again, regardless of consequences; and while I kept them from combining, I succeeded very well; for I could whip the whole of them, taking them separately. They, however, at length combined, and came upon me, armed with sticks, stones, and heavy handspikes. One came in front with a half brick. There was one at each side of me, and one behind me. While I was attending to those in front, and on either side, the one behind ran up with the handspike, and struck me a heavy blow upon the head. It stunned me. I fell, and with this they all ran upon me, and fell to beating me with their fists. I let them lay on for a while, gathering strength. In an instant, I gave a sudden surge, and rose to my hands and knees. Just as I did that, one of their number gave me, with his heavy boot, a powerful kick in the left eye. My eyeball seemed to have burst. When they saw my eye closed, and badly swollen, they left me. With this I seized the handspike, and for a time pursued them. But here the carpenters interfered, and I thought I might as well give it up. It was impossible to stand my hand against so many. All this took place in sight of not less than fifty white ship-carpenters, and not one interposed a friendly word; but some cried, "Kill the damned nigger! Kill him! kill him! He struck a white person." I found my only chance for life was in flight. I succeeded in getting away without an additional blow, and barely so; for to strike a white man is death by Lynch law,—and that was the law in Mr. Gardner's ship-yard; nor is there much of any other out of Mr. Gardner's ship-yard.

I went directly home, and told the story of my wrongs to Master Hugh; and I am happy to say of him, irreligious as he was, his conduct was heavenly, compared with that of his brother Thomas under similar circumstances. He listened attentively to my narration of the circumstances leading to the savage outrage, and gave many proofs of his strong indignation at it. The heart of my once overkind mistress was again melted into pity. My puffed-out eye and blood-covered face moved her to tears. She took a chair by me, washed the blood from my face, and, with a mother's tenderness, bound up my head, covering the wounded eye with a lean piece of fresh beef. It was almost compensation for my suffering to witness, once more, a manifestation of kindness from this, my once affectionate old mistress. Master Hugh was very much enraged. He gave expression to his feelings by pouring out curses upon the heads of those who did the deed. As soon as I got a little the better of my bruises, he took me with him to Esquire Watson's, on Bond Street, to see what could be done about the matter. Mr. Watson inquired who saw the assault committed. Master Hugh told him it was done in Mr. Gardner's ship-yard, at midday, where there were a large company of men at work. "As to that," he said, "the deed was done, and there was no question as to who did it." His answer was, he could do nothing in the case, unless some white man would come forward and testify. He could issue no warrant on my word. If I had been killed in the presence of a thousand colored people, their testimony combined would have been insufficient to have arrested one of the murderers. Master Hugh, for once, was compelled to say this state of things was too bad. Of course, it was impossible to get any white man to volunteer his testimony in my behalf, and against the white young men. Even those who may have sympathized with me were not prepared to do this. It required a degree of courage unknown to them to do so; for just at that time, the slightest manifestation of humanity toward a colored person was denounced as abolitionism, and that name subjected its bearer to frightful liabilities. The watchwords of the bloody-minded in that region, and in those days, were, "Damn the abolitionists!" and "Damn the niggers!" There was nothing done, and probably nothing would have been done if I had been killed. Such was, and such remains, the state of things in the Christian city of Baltimore.

Master Hugh, finding he could get no redress, refused to let me go back again to Mr. Gardner. He kept me himself, and his wife dressed my wound till I was again restored to health. He then took me into the ship-yard of which he was foreman, in the employment of Mr. Walter Price. There I was immediately set to calking, and very soon learned the art of using my mallet and irons. In the course of one year from the time I left Mr. Gardner's, I was able to command the highest wages given to the most experienced calkers. I was now of some importance to my master. I was bringing him from six to seven dollars per week. I sometimes brought him nine dollars per week; my wages were a dollar and a half a day. After learning how to calk, I sought my own employment, made my own contracts, and collected the money which I earned. My pathway became much more smooth than before; my condition was now much more comfortable. When I could get no calking to do, I did nothing. During these leisure times, those old notions about freedom would steal over me again. When in Mr. Gardner's employment, I was kept in such a perpetual whirl of excitement, I could think of nothing, scarcely, but my life; and in thinking of my life, I almost forgot my liberty. I have observed this in my experience of slavery,—that whenever my condition was improved, instead of its increasing my contentment, it only increased my desire to be free, and set me to thinking of plans to gain my freedom. I have found that, to make a contented slave, it is necessary to make a thoughtless one. It is necessary to darken his moral and mental vision, and, as far as possible, to annihilate the power of reason. He must be able to detect no inconsistencies in slavery; he must be made to feel that slavery is right; and he can be brought to that only when he ceases to be a man.

I was now getting, as I have said, one dollar and fifty cents per day. I contracted for it; I earned it; it was paid to me; it was rightfully my own; yet, upon each returning Saturday night, I was compelled to deliver every cent of that money to Master Hugh. And why? Not because he earned it,—not because he had any hand in earning it,—not because I owed it to him,—not because he possessed the slightest shadow of a right to it; but solely because he had the power to compel me to give it up. The right of the grim-visaged pirate upon the high seas is exactly the same.

Chapter XI

I now come to that part of my life during which I planned, and finally succeeded in making, my escape from slavery. But before narrating any of the peculiar circumstances, I deem it proper to make known my intention not to state all the facts connected with the transaction. My reasons for pursuing this course may be understood from the following: First, were I to give a minute statement of all the facts, it is not only possible, but quite probable, that others would thereby be involved in the most embarrassing difficulties. Secondly, such a statement would most undoubtedly induce greater vigilance on the part of the slaveholders than has existed heretofore among them; which would, of course be the means of guarding a door whereby some dear brother bondman might escape his galling chains. I deeply regret the necessity that impels me to suppress any thing of importance connected with my experience in slavery. It would afford me great pleasure indeed, as well as materially add to the interest of my narrative, were I at liberty to gratify a curiosity, which I know exists in the minds of many, by an accurate statement of all the facts pertaining to my most fortunate escape. But I must deprive myself of this pleasure, and the curious of the gratification which such a statement would afford. I would allow myself to suffer under the greatest imputations which evil-minded men might suggest, rather than exculpate myself, and thereby run the hazard of closing the slightest avenue by which a brother slave might clear himself of the chains and fetters of slavery.

I have never approved of the very public manner in which some of our western friends have conducted what they call the *underground railroad*, but which, I think, by their open declarations, has been made most emphatically the *upperground railroad.* I honor those good men and women for their noble daring, and applaud them for willingly subjecting themselves to bloody persecution, by openly avowing their participation in the escape of slaves. I, however, can see very little good resulting from such a course, either to themselves or the slaves escaping; while, upon the other hand, I see and feel assured that those open declarations are a positive evil to the slaves remaining, who are seeking to escape. They do nothing towards enlightening the slave, whilst they do much towards enlightening the master. They stimulate him to greater watchfulness, and enhance his power to capture his slave. We owe something to the slaves south of the line as well as to those north of it; and in aiding the latter on their way to freedom, we should be careful to do nothing which would be likely to hinder the former from escaping from slavery. I would keep the merciless slaveholder profoundly ignorant of the means of flight adopted by the slave. I would leave him to imagine himself surrounded by myriads of invisible tormentors, ever ready to snatch from his infernal grasp his trembling prey. Let him be left to feel his way in the dark; let darkness commensurate with his crime hover over him; and let him feel that at every step he takes, in pursuit of the flying bondman, he is running the frightful risk of having his hot brains dashed out by an invisible agency. Let us render the tyrant no aid; let us not hold the light by which he can trace the footprints of our flying brother. But enough of this. I will now proceed to the statement of those facts, connected with my escape, for which I am alone responsible, and for which no one can be made to suffer but myself.

In the early part of the year 1838, I became quite restless. I could see no reason why I should, at the end of each week, pour the reward of my toil into the purse of my master. When I carried to him my weekly wages, he would, after counting the money, look me in the face with a robber-like fierceness, and ask, "Is this all?" He was satisfied with nothing less than the last cent. He would, however, when I made him six dollars, sometimes give me six cents, to encourage me. It had the opposite effect. I regarded it as a sort of admission of my right to the whole. The fact that he gave me any part of my wages was proof, to my mind, that he believed me entitled to the whole of them. I always felt worse for having received any thing; for I feared that the giving me a few cents would ease his conscience, and make him feel himself to be a pretty honorable sort of robber. My discontent grew upon me. I was ever on the lookout for means of escape; and, finding no direct means, I determined to try to hire my time, with a view of getting money with which to make my escape. In the spring of 1838, when Master Thomas came to Baltimore to purchase his spring goods, I got an opportunity, and applied to him to allow me to hire my time. He unhesitatingly refused my request, and told me this was another strategem by which to escape. He told me I could go nowhere but that he could get me; and that, in the event of my running away, he should spare no pains in his efforts to catch me. He exhorted me to content myself, and be obedient. He told me, if I would be happy, I must lay out no plans for the future. He said, if I behaved myself properly, he would take care of me. Indeed, he advised me to complete thoughtlessness of the future, and taught me to depend solely upon him for happiness. He seemed to see fully the pressing necessity of setting aside my intellectual nature, in order to contentment in slavery. But in spite of him, and even in spite of myself, I continued to think, and to think about the injustice of my enslavement, and the means of escape.

About two months after this, I applied to Master Hugh for the privilege of hiring my time. He was not acquainted with the fact that I had applied to Master Thomas, and had been refused. He too, at first, seemed disposed to refuse; but, after some reflection, he granted me the privilege, and proposed the following term: I was to be allowed all my time, make all contracts with those for whom I worked, and find my own employment; and, in return for this liberty, I was to pay him three dollars at the end of each week; find myself in calking tools, and in board and clothing. My board was two dollars and a half per week. This, with the wear and tear of clothing and calking tools, made my regular expenses about six dollars per week. This amount I was compelled to make up, or relinquish the privilege of hiring my time. Rain or shine, work or no work, at the end of each week the money must be forthcoming, or I must give up my privilege. This arrangement, it will be perceived, was decidedly in my master's favor. It relieved him of all need of looking after me. His money was sure. He received all the benefits of slaveholding without its evils; while I endured all the evils of a slave, and suffered all the care and anxiety of a freeman. I found it a hard bargain. But, hard as it was, I thought it better than the old mode of getting along. It was a step towards freedom to be allowed to bear the responsibilities of a freeman, and I was determined to hold on upon it. I bent myself to the work of making money. I was ready to work at night as well as day, and by the most untiring perseverance and industry, I made enough to meet my expenses, and lay up a little money every week. I went on thus from May till August. Master Hugh then refused to allow me to hire my time longer. The ground for his refusal was a failure on my part, one Saturday night, to pay him for my week's time. This failure was occasioned by my attending a camp meeting about ten miles from Baltimore. During the week, I had entered into an engagement with a number of young friends to start from Baltimore to the camp ground early Saturday evening; and being detained by my employer, I was unable to get down to Master Hugh's without disappointing the company. I knew that Master Hugh was in no special need of the money that night. I therefore decided to go to camp meeting, and upon my return pay him the three dollars. I staid at the camp meeting one day longer than I intended when I left. But as soon as I returned, I called upon him to pay him what he considered his due. I found him very angry; he could scarce restrain his wrath. He said he had a great mind to give me a severe whipping. He wished to know how I dared go out of the city without asking his permission. I told him I hired my time, and while I paid him the price which he asked for it, I did not know that I was bound to ask him when and where I should go. This reply troubled him; and, after reflecting a few moments, he turned to me, and said I should hire my time no longer; that the next thing he should know of, I would be running away. Upon the same plea, he told me to bring my tools and clothing home forthwith. I did so; but instead of seeking work, as I had been accustomed to do previously to hiring my time, I spent the whole week without the performance of a single stroke of work. I did this in retaliation. Saturday night, he called upon me as usual for my week's wages. I told him I had no wages; I had done no work that week. Here we were upon the point of coming to blows. He raved, and swore his determination to get hold of me. I did not allow myself a single word; but was resolved, if he laid the weight of his hand upon me, it should be blow for blow. He did not strike me, but told me that he would find me in constant employment in future. I thought the matter over during the next day, Sunday, and finally resolved upon the third day of September, as the day upon which I would make a second attempt to secure my freedom. I now had three weeks during which to prepare for my journey. Early on Monday morning, before Master Hugh had time to make any engagement for me, I went out and got employment of Mr. Butler, at his ship-yard near the drawbridge, upon what is called the City Block, thus making it unnecessary for him to seek employment for me. At the end of the week, I brought him between eight and nine dollars. He seemed very well pleased, and asked me why I did not do the same the week before. He little knew what my plans were. My object in working steadily was to remove any suspicion he might entertain of my intent to run away; and in this I succeeded admirably. I suppose he thought I was never better satisfied with my condition than at the very time during which I was planning my escape. The second week passed, and again I carried him my full wages; and so well pleased was he, that he gave me twenty-five cents, (quite a large sum for a slaveholder to give a slave,) and bade me to make a good use of it. I told him I would.

Things went on without very smoothly indeed, but within there was trouble. It is impossible for me to describe my feelings as the time of my contemplated start drew near. I had a number of warm-hearted friends in Baltimore,—friends that I loved almost as I did my life,—and the thought of being separated from them forever was painful beyond expression. It is my opinion that thousands would escape from slavery, who now remain, but for the strong cords of affection that bind them to their friends. The thought of leaving my friends was decidedly the most painful thought with which I had to contend. The love of them was my tender point, and shook my decision more than all things else. Besides the pain of separation, the dread and apprehension of a failure exceeded what I had experienced at my first attempt. The appalling defeat I then sustained returned to torment me. I felt assured that, if I failed in this attempt, my case would be a hopeless one—it would seal my fate as a slave forever. I could not hope to get off with any thing less than the severest punishment, and being placed beyond the means of escape. It required no very vivid imagination to depict the most frightful scenes through which I should have to pass, in case I failed. The wretchedness of slavery, and the blessedness of freedom, were perpetually before me. It was life and death with me. But I remained firm, and according to my resolution, on the third day of September, 1838, I left my chains, and succeeded in reaching New York without the slightest interruption of any kind. How I did so,—what means I adopted,—what direction I travelled, and by what mode of conveyance,—I must leave unexplained, for the reasons before mentioned.

I have been frequently asked how I felt when I found myself in a free State. I have never been able to answer the question with any satisfaction to myself. It was a moment of the highest excitement I ever experienced. I suppose I felt as one may imagine the unarmed mariner to feel when he is rescued by a friendly man-of-war from the pursuit of a pirate. In writing to a dear friend, immediately after my arrival at New York, I said I felt like one who had escaped a den of hungry lions. This state of mind, however, very soon subsided; and I was again seized with a feeling of great insecurity and loneliness. I was yet liable to be taken back, and subjected to all the tortures of slavery. This in itself was enough to damp the ardor of my enthusiasm. But the loneliness overcame me. There I was in the midst of thousands, and yet a perfect stranger; without home and without friends, in the midst of thousands of my own brethren—children of a common Father, and yet I dared not to unfold to any one of them my sad condition. I was afraid to speak to any one for fear of speaking to the wrong one, and thereby falling into the hands of money-loving kidnappers, whose business it was to lie in wait for the panting fugitive, as the ferocious beasts of the forest lie in wait for their prey. The motto which I adopted when I started from slavery was this—"Trust no man!" I saw in every white man an enemy, and in almost every colored man cause for distrust. It was a most painful situation; and, to understand it, one must needs experience it, or imagine himself in similar circumstances. Let him be a fugitive slave in a strange land—a land given up to be the hunting-ground for slaveholders—whose inhabitants are legalized kidnappers—where he is every moment subjected to the terrible liability of being seized upon by his fellowmen, as the hideous crocodile seizes upon his prey!—I say, let him place himself in my situation—without home or friends—without money or credit—wanting shelter, and no one to give it—wanting bread, and no money to buy it,—and at the same time let him feel that he is pursued by merciless men-hunters, and in total darkness as to what to do, where to go, or where to stay,—perfectly helpless both as to the means of defence and means of escape,—in the midst of plenty, yet suffering the terrible gnawings of hunger,—in the midst of houses, yet having no home,—among fellow-men, yet feeling as if in the midst of wild beasts, whose greediness to swallow up the trembling and half-famished fugitive is only equalled by that with which the monsters of the deep swallow up the helpless fish upon which they subsist,—I say, let him be placed in this most trying situation,—the situation in which I was placed,—then, and not till then, will he fully appreciate the hardships of, and know how to sympathize with, the toil-worn and whip-scarred fugitive slave.

Thank Heaven, I remained but a short time in this distressed situation. I was relieved from it by the humane hand of Mr. DAVID RUGGLES, whose vigilance, kindness, and perseverance, I shall never forget. I am glad of an opportunity to express, as far as words can, the love and gratitude I bear him. Mr. Ruggles is now afflicted with blindness, and is himself in need of the same kind offices which he was once so forward in the performance of toward others. I had been in New York but a few days, when Mr. Ruggles sought me out, and very kindly took me to his boarding-house at the corner of Church and Lespenard Streets. Mr. Ruggles was then very deeply engaged in the memorable *Darg* case, as well as attending to a number of other fugitive slaves, devising ways and means for their successful escape; and, though watched and hemmed in on almost every side, he seemed to be more than a match for his enemies.

Very soon after I went to Mr. Ruggles, he wished to know of me where I wanted to go; as he deemed it unsafe for me to remain in New York. I told him I was a calker, and should like to go where I could get work. I thought of going to Canada; but he decided against it, and in favor of my going to New Bedford, thinking I should be able to get work there at my trade. At this time, Anna,* my intended wife, came on;

*She was free.

for I wrote to her immediately after my arrival at New York, (notwithstanding my homeless, houseless, and helpless condition,) informing her of my successful flight, and wishing her to come on forthwith. In a few days after her arrival, Mr. Ruggles called in the Rev. J. W. C. Pennington, who, in the presence of Mr. Ruggles, Mrs. Michaels, and two or three others, performed the marriage ceremony, and gave us a certificate, of which the following is an exact copy:—

"THIS may certify, that I joined together in holy matrimony Frederick Johnson* and Anna Murray, as man and wife, in the presence of Mr. David Ruggles and Mrs. Michaels.

"JAMES W. C. PENNINGTON.
"*New York, Sept.* 15, 1838."

Upon receiving this certificate, and a five-dollar bill from Mr. Ruggles, I shouldered one part of our baggage, and Anna took up the other, and we set out forthwith to take passage on board of the steamboat John W. Richmond for Newport, on our way to New Bedford. Mr. Ruggles gave me a letter to a Mr. Shaw in Newport, and told me, in case my money did not serve me to New Bedford, to stop in Newport and obtain further assistance; but upon our arrival at Newport, we were so anxious to get to a place of safety, that, notwithstanding we lacked the necessary money to pay our fare, we decided to take seats in the stage, and promise to pay when we got to New Bedford. We were encouraged to do this by two excellent gentlemen, residents of New Bedford, whose names I afterward ascertained to be Joseph Ricketson and William C. Taber. They seemed at once to understand our circumstances, and give us such assurance of their friendliness as put us fully at ease in their presence. It was good indeed to meet with such friends, at such a time. Upon reaching New Bedford, we were directed to the house of Mr. Nathan Johnson, by whom we were kindly received, and hospitably provided for. Both Mr. and Mrs. Johnson took a deep and lively interest in our welfare. They proved themselves quite worthy of the name of abolitionists. When the stage-driver found us unable to pay our fare, he held on upon our baggage as security for the debt. I had but to mention the fact to Mr. Johnson, and he forthwith advanced the money.

We now began to feel a degree of safety, and to prepare ourselves for the duties and responsibilities of a life of freedom. On the morning after our arrival at New Bedford, while at the breakfast-table, the question arose as to what name I should be called by. The name given me by my mother was, "Frederick Augustus Washington Bailey." I, however, had dispensed with the two middle names long before I left Maryland so that I was generally known by the name of "Frederick Bailey." I started from Baltimore bearing the name of "Stanley." When I got to New York, I again changed my name to "Frederick Johnson," and thought that would be the last change. But when I got to New Bedford, I found it necessary again to change my name. The reason of this necessity was, that there were so many Johnsons in New Bedford, it was already quite difficult to distinguish between them. I gave Mr. Johnson the privilege of choosing me a name, but told him he must not take from me the name of "Frederick." I must hold on to that, to preserve a sense of my identity. Mr. Johnson had just been reading the "Lady of the Lake," and at once suggested that my name be "Douglass." From that time until now I have been called "Frederick Douglass;" and as I am more widely known by that name than by either of the others, I shall continue to use it as my own.

I was quite disappointed at the general appearance of things in New Bedford. The impression which I had received respecting the character and condition of the people of the north, I found to be singularly erroneous. I had very strangely supposed, while in slavery, that few of the comforts, and scarcely any of the luxuries, of life were enjoyed at the north, compared with what were enjoyed by the slaveholders of the south. I probably came to this conclusion from

*I had changed my name from Frederick *Bailey* to that of *Johnson.*

the fact that northern people owned no slaves. I supposed that they were about upon a level with the non-slaveholding population of the south. I knew *they* were exceedingly poor, and I had been accustomed to regard their poverty as the necessary consequence of their being non-slaveholders. I had somehow imbibed the opinion that, in the absence of slaves, there could be no wealth, and very little refinement. And upon coming to the north, I expected to meet with a rough, hard-handed, and uncultivated population, living in the most Spartan-like simplicity, knowing nothing of the ease, luxury, pomp, and grandeur of southern slaveholders. Such being my conjectures, any one acquainted with the appearance of New Bedford may very readily infer how palpably I must have seen my mistake.

In the afternoon of the day when I reached New Bedford, I visited the wharves, to take a view of the shipping. Here I found myself surrounded with the strongest proofs of wealth. Lying at the wharves, and riding in the stream, I saw many ships of the finest model, in the best order, and of the largest size. Upon the right and left, I was walled in by granite warehouses of the widest dimensions, stowed to their utmost capacity with the necessaries and comforts of life. Added to this, almost every body seemed to be at work, but noiselessly so, compared with what I had been accustomed to in Baltimore. There were no loud songs heard from those engaged in loading and unloading ships. I heard no deep oaths or horrid curses on the laborer. I saw no whipping of men; but all seemed to go smoothly on. Every man appeared to understand his work, and went at it with a sober, yet cheerful earnestness, which betokened the deep interest which he felt in what he was doing, as well as a sense of his own dignity as a man. To me this looked exceedingly strange. From the wharves I strolled around and over the town, gazing with wonder and admiration at the splendid churches, beautiful dwellings, and finely-cultivated gardens; evincing an amount of wealth, comfort, taste, and refinement, such as I had never seen in any part of slaveholding Maryland.

Every thing looked clean, new and beautiful. I saw few or no dilapidated houses, with poverty-stricken inmates; no half-naked children and barefooted women, such as I had been accustomed to see in Hillsborough, Easton, St. Michael's, and Baltimore. The people looked more able, stronger, healthier, and happier, than those of Maryland. I was for once made glad by a view of extreme wealth, without being saddened by seeing extreme poverty. But the most astonishing as well as the most interesting thing to me was the condition of the colored people, a great many of whom, like myself, had escaped thither as a refuge from the hunters of men. I found many, who had not been seven years out of their chains, living in finer houses, and evidently enjoying more of the comforts of life, than the average of slaveholders in Maryland. I will venture to assert that my friend Mr. Nathan Johnson (of whom I can say with a grateful heart, "I was hungry, and he gave me meat; I was thirsty, and he gave me drink; I was a stranger, and he took me in") lived in a neater house; dined at a better table; took, paid for, and read, more newspapers; better understood the moral, religious, and political character of the nation,—than nine tenths of the slaveholders in Talbot county, Maryland. Yet Mr. Johnson was a working man. His hands were hardened by toil, and not his alone, but those also of Mrs. Johnson. I found the colored people much more spirited than I had supposed they would be. I found among them a determination to protect each other from the blood-thirsty kidnapper, at all hazards. Soon after my arrival, I was told of a circumstance which illustrated their spirit. A colored man and a fugitive slave were on unfriendly terms. The former was heard to threaten the latter with informing his master of his whereabouts: Straightway a meeting was called among the colored people, under the stereotyped notice, "Business of importance!" The betrayer was invited to attend. The people came at the appointed hour, and organized the meeting by appointing a very religious old gentleman as president, who, I believe, made a prayer, after which he addressed the meeting as follows: "*Friends, we have got him here, and I would recommend that you young men just take him outside the door, and kill him!*" With this, a number of them bolted at him; but they were intercepted by some more timid than themselves, and the betrayer escaped their vengeance, and has not been seen in New Bedford since. I believe there have been no more such threats, and should there be hereafter, I doubt not that death would be the consequence.

I found employment, the third day after my arrival, in stowing a sloop with a load of oil. It was new, dirty, and hard work for me; but I went at it with a glad heart and a willing hand. I was now my own master. It was a happy moment, the rapture of which can be understood only by those who have been slaves. It was the first work, the reward of which was to be entirely my own. There was no Master Hugh standing ready, the moment I earned the money, to rob me of it. I worked that day with a pleasure I had never before experienced. I was at work for myself and newly-married wife. It was to me the starting-point of a new existence. When I got through with that job, I went in pursuit of a job of calking; but such was the strength of prejudice against color, among the white calkers, that they refused to work with me, and of course I could get no employment.* Finding my trade of no immediate benefit, I threw off my calking habiliments, and prepared myself to do any kind of work I could get to do. Mr. Johnson kindly let me have his wood-horse and saw, and I very soon found myself a plenty of work. There was no work too hard—none too dirty. I was ready to saw wood, shovel coal, carry the hod, sweep the chimney, or roll oil casks,—all of which I did for nearly three years in New Bedford, before I became known to the antislavery world.

In about four months after I went to New Bedford, there came a young man to me, and inquired if I did not wish to take the "Liberator." I told him I did; but, just having made my escape from slavery, I remarked that I was unable to pay for it then. I, however, finally became a subscriber to it. The paper came, and I read it from week to week with such feelings as it would be quite idle for me to attempt to describe. The paper became my meat and my drink. My soul was set all on fire. Its sympathy for my brethren in bonds—its scathing denunciations of slaveholders—its faithful exposures of slavery—and its powerful attacks upon the upholders of the institution—sent a thrill of joy through my soul, such as I had never felt before!

I had not long been a reader of the "Liberator," before I got a pretty correct idea of the principles, measures and spirit of the anti-slavery reform. I took right hold of the cause. I could do but little; but what I could, I did with a joyful heart, and never felt happier than when in an anti-slavery meeting. I seldom had much to say at the meetings, because what I wanted to say was said so much better by others. But, while attending an anti-slavery convention at Nantucket, on the 11th of August, 1841, I felt strongly moved to speak, and was at the same time much urged to do so by Mr. William C. Coffin, a gentleman who had heard me speak in the colored people's meeting at New Bedford. It was a severe cross, and I took it up reluctantly. The truth was, I felt myself a slave, and the idea of speaking to white people weighed me down. I spoke but a few moments, when I felt a degree of freedom, and said what I desired with considerable ease. From that time until now, I have been engaged in pleading the cause of my brethren—with what success, and with what devotion, I leave those acquainted with my labors to decide.

The Rights of Women

One of the most interesting events of the past week, was the holding of what is technically styled a Woman's Rights Convention at Seneca Falls. The speaking, addresses, and resolutions of this extraordinary meeting was almost wholly conducted by women; and although they evidently felt themselves in a novel position, it is

*I am told that colored persons can now get employment at calking in New Bedford—a result of anti-slavery effort.

but simple justice to say that their whole proceedings were characterized by marked ability and dignity. No one present, we think, however much he might be disposed to differ from the views advanced by the leading speakers on that occasion, will fail to give them credit for brilliant talents and excellent dispositions. In this meeting, as in other deliberative assemblies, there were frequent differences of opinion and animated discussion; but in no case was there the slightest absence of good feeling and decorum. Several interesting documents setting forth the rights as well as the grievances of women were read. Among these was a Declaration of Sentiments, to be regarded as the basis of a grand movement for attaining the civil, social, political, and religious rights of women. We should not do justice to our own convictions, or to the excellent persons connected with this infant movement, if we did not in this connection offer a few remarks on the general subject which the Convention met to consider and the objects they seek to attain. In doing so, we are not insensible that the bare mention of this truly important subject in any other than terms of contemptuous ridicule and scornful disfavor, is likely to excite against us the fury of bigotry and the folly of prejudice. A discussion of the rights of animals would be regarded with far more complacency by many of what are called the *wise* and the *good* of our land, than would a discussion of the rights of women. It is, in their estimation, to be guilty of evil thoughts, to think that woman is entitled to equal rights with man. Many who have at last made the discovery that the Negroes have some rights as well as other members of the human family, have yet to be convinced that women are entitled to any. Eight years ago a number of persons of this description actually abandoned the anti-slavery cause, lest by giving their influence in that direction they might possibly be giving countenance to the dangerous heresy that woman, in respect to rights, stands on an equal footing with man. In the judgment of such persons the American slave system, with all its concomitant horrors, is less to be deplored than this *wicked* idea. It is perhaps needless to say, that we cherish little sympathy for such sentiments or respect for such prejudices. Standing as we do upon the watch-tower of human freedom, we cannot be deterred from an expression of our approbation of any movement, however humble, to improve and elevate the character of any members of the human family. While it is impossible for us to go into this subject at length, and dispose of the various objections which are often urged against such a doctrine as that of female equality, we are free to say that in respect to political rights, we hold woman to be justly entitled to all we claim for man. We go farther, and express our conviction that all political rights which it is expedient for man to exercise, it is equally so for woman. All that distinguishes man as an intelligent and accountable being, is equally true of woman, and if that government only is just which governs by the free consent of the governed, there can be no reason in the world for denying to woman the exercise of the elective franchise, or a hand in making and administering the laws of the land. Our doctrine is that "right is of no sex." We therefore bid the women engaged in this movement our humble Godspeed.

The North Star, July 28, 1848

What to the Slave Is the Fourth of July?: An Address Delivered in Rochester, New York, on 5 July 1852

Mr. President, Friends and Fellow Citizens: He who could address this audience without a quailing sensation, has stronger nerves than I have. I do not remember ever to have appeared as a speaker before any assembly more shrinkingly, nor with greater distrust of my ability, than I do this day. A feeling has crept over me, quite unfavorable to the exercise of my limited powers of speech. The task before me is one which requires much previous thought and study for its proper performance. I know that apologies of this sort are generally considered flat and unmeaning. I trust, however, that mine will not be so considered. Should I seem at ease, my appearance would much misrepresent me. The little experience I have had in addressing public meetings, in country school houses, avails me nothing on the present occasion.

The papers and placards say, that I am to deliver a 4th [of] July oration. This certainly sounds large, and out of the common way, for me. It is true that I have often had the privilege to speak in this beautiful Hall, and to address many who now honor me with their presence. But neither their familiar faces, nor the perfect gage I think I have of Corinthian Hall, seems to free me from embarrassment.

The fact is, ladies and gentlemen, the distance between this platform and the slave plantation, from which I escaped, is considerable—and the difficulties to be overcome in getting from the latter to the former, are by no means slight. That I am here to-day is, to me, a matter of astonishment as well as of gratitude. You will not, therefore, be surprised, if in what I have to say, I evince no elaborate preparation, nor grace my speech with any high sounding exordium. With little experience and with less learning, I have been able to throw my thoughts hastily and imperfectly together; and trusting to your patient and generous indulgence, I will proceed to lay them before you.

This, for the purpose of this celebration, is the 4th of July. It is the birthday of your National Independence, and of your political freedom. This, to you, is what the Passover was to the emancipated people of God. It carries your minds back to the day, and to the act of your great deliverance; and to the signs, and to the wonders, associated with that act, and that day. This celebration also marks the beginning of another year of your national life; and reminds you that the Republic of America is now 76 years old. I am glad, fellow-citizens, that your nation is so young. Seventy-six years, though a good old age for a man, is but a mere speck in the life of a nation. Three score years and ten is the allotted time for individual men;* but nations number their years by thousands. According to this fact, you are, even now, only in the beginning of your national career, still lingering in the period of childhood. I repeat, I am glad this is so. There is hope in the thought, and hope is much needed, under the dark clouds which lower above the horizon. The eye of the reformer is met with angry flashes, portending disastrous times; but his heart may well beat lighter at the thought that America is young, and that she is still in the impressible stage of her existence. May he not hope that high lessons of wisdom, of justice and of truth, will yet give direction to her destiny? Were the nation older, the patriot's heart might be sadder, and the reformer's brow heavier. Its future might be shrouded in gloom, and the hope of its prophets go out in sorrow. There is consolation in the thought that America is young. Great streams are not easily turned from channels, worn deep in the course of ages. They may sometimes rise in quiet and stately majesty, and inundate the land, refreshing and fertilizing the earth with their mysterious properties. They may also rise in wrath and fury, and bear away, on their angry waves, the accumulated wealth of years of toil and hardship. They, however, gradually flow back to the same old channel, and flow on as serenely as ever. But, while the river may not be turned aside, it may dry up, and leave nothing behind but the withered branch, and the unsightly rock, to howl in the abyss-sweeping wind, the sad tale of departed glory. As with rivers so with nations.

Fellow-citizens, I shall not presume to dwell at length on the associations that cluster about this day. The simple story of it is that, 76 years ago, the people of this country were British subjects. The style and title of your "sovereign people" (in which you now glory) was not then born. You were under the British Crown. Your fathers esteemed the English Government as the home government; and England as the fatherland. This home government, you know, although a considerable distance from your home, did, in the exercise of its parental prerogatives, impose upon its colonial children, such restraints, burdens and limitations, as, in its

*Ps. 90:10.

mature judgement, it deemed wise, right and proper.

But, your fathers, who had not adopted the fashionable idea of this day, of the infallibility of government, and the absolute character of its acts, presumed to differ from the home government in respect to the wisdom and the justice of some of those burdens and restraints. They went so far in their excitement as to pronounce the measures of government unjust, unreasonable, and oppressive, and altogether such as ought not to be quietly submitted to. I scarcely need say, fellow-citizens, that my opinion of those measures fully accords with that of your fathers. Such a declaration of agreement on my part would not be worth much to anybody. It would, certainly, prove nothing, as to what part I might have taken, had I lived during the great controversy of 1776. To say *now* that America was right, and England wrong, is exceedingly easy. Everybody can say it; the dastard, not less than the noble brave, can flippantly discant on the tyranny of England towards the American Colonies. It is fashionable to do so; but there was a time when to pronounce against England, and in favor of the cause of the colonies, tried men's souls.* They who did so were accounted in their day, plotters of mischief, agitators and rebels, dangerous men. To side with the right, against the wrong, with the weak against the strong, and with the oppressed against the oppressor! *here* lies the merit, and the one which, of all others, seems unfashionable in our day. The cause of liberty may be stabbed by the men who glory in the deeds of your fathers. But, to proceed.

Feeling themselves harshly and unjustly treated by the home government, your fathers, like men of honesty, and men of spirit, earnestly sought redress. They petitioned and remonstrated; they did so in a decorous, respectful, and loyal manner. Their conduct was wholly unexceptionable. This, however, did not answer the purpose. They saw themselves treated with sovereign indifference, coldness and scorn. Yet they persevered. They were not the men to look back.

As the sheet anchor takes a firmer hold, when the ship is tossed by the storm, so did the cause of your fathers grow stronger, as it breasted the chilling blasts of kingly displeasure. The greatest and best of British statesmen admitted its justice, and the loftiest eloquence of the British Senate came to its support. But, with that blindness which seems to be the unvarying characteristic of tyrants, since Pharoah and his hosts were drowned in the Red Sea, the British Government persisted in the exactions complained of.

The madness of this course, we believe, is admitted now, even by England; but we fear the lesson is wholly lost on our present rulers.

Oppression makes a wise man mad. Your fathers were wise men, and if they did not go mad, they became restive under this treatment. They felt themselves the victims of grievous wrongs, wholly incurable in their colonial capacity. With brave men there is always a remedy for oppression. Just here, the idea of a total separation of the colonies from the crown was born! It was a startling idea, much more so, than we, at this distance of time, regard it. The timid and the prudent (as has been intimated) of that day, were, of course, shocked and alarmed by it.

Such people lived then, had lived before, and will, probably, ever have a place on this planet; and their course, in respect to any great change, (no matter how great the good to be attained, or the wrong to be redressed by it), may be calculated with as much precision as can be the course of the stars. They hate all changes, but silver, gold and copper change! Of this sort of change they are always strongly in favor.

These people were called tories in the days of your fathers; and the appellation, probably, conveyed the same idea that is meant by a more modern, though a somewhat less euphonious

*Douglass paraphrases the opening line of Thomas Paine's first *Crisis* paper, 23 December 1776. *The Political Writings of Thomas Paine*, 2 vols. (Boston, 1859), 1:75.

term, which we often find in our papers, applied to some of our old politicians.*

Their opposition to the then dangerous thought was earnest and powerful; but, amid all their terror and affrighted vociferations against it, the alarming and revolutionary idea moved on, and the country with it.

On the 2d of July, 1776, the old Continental Congress, to the dismay of the lovers of ease, and the worshippers of property, clothed that dreadful idea with all the authority of national sanction. They did so in the form of a resolution; and as we seldom hit upon resolutions, drawn up in our day, whose transparency is at all equal to this, it may refresh your minds and help my story if I read it.

> Resolved, That these united colonies *are,* and of right, ought to be free and Independent States; that they are absolved from all allegiance to the British Crown; and that all political connection between them and the State of Great Britain *is,* and ought to be, dissolved.†

Citizens, your fathers made good that resolution. They succeeded; and to-day you reap the fruits of their success. The freedom gained is yours; and you, therefore, may properly celebrate this anniversary. The 4th of July is the first great fact in your nation's history—the very ring-bolt in the chain of your yet undeveloped destiny.

Pride and patriotism, not less than gratitude, prompt you to celebrate and to hold it in perpetual remembrance. I have said that the Declaration of Independence is the RING-BOLT to the chain of your nation's destiny; so, indeed, I regard it. The principles contained in that instrument are saving principles. Stand by those principles, be true to them on all occasions, in all places, against all foes, and at whatever cost.

From the round top of your ship of state, dark and threatening clouds may be seen. Heavy billows, like mountains in the distance, disclose to the leeward huge forms of flinty rocks! That *bolt* drawn, that *chain* broken, and all is lost. *Cling to this day—cling to it,* and to its principles, with the grasp of a storm-tossed mariner to a spar at midnight.

The coming into being of a nation, in any circumstances, is an interesting event. But, besides general considerations, there were peculiar circumstances which make the advent of this republic an event of special attractiveness.

The whole scene, as I look back to it, was simple, dignified and sublime.

The population of the country, at the time, stood at the insignificant number of three millions. The country was poor in the munitions of war. The population was weak and scattered, and the country a wilderness unsubdued. There were then no means of concert and combination, such as exist now. Neither steam nor lightning had then been reduced to order and discipline. From the Potomac to the Delaware was a journey of many days. Under these, and innumerable other disadvantages, your fathers declared for liberty and independence and triumphed.

Fellow Citizens, I am not wanting in respect for the fathers of this republic. The signers of the Declaration of Independence were brave men. They were great men too—great enough to give fame to a great age. It does not often happen to a nation to raise, at one time, such a number of truly great men. The point from which I am compelled to view them is not, certainly, the most favorable; and yet I cannot con-

---

*Douglass probably refers to the term *Hunker,* which was applied to conservative Democrats in New York state politics in the late 1840s. The label originally referred to the fiscally conservative faction of the state's Democratic party, but after an 1847 split over the Wilmot Proviso the term also differentiated Unionist followers of William L. Marcy and Daniel S. Dickinson from the antislavery *Barnburners.* A study of the election of 1848 suggests that the word "was used to ridicule the conservatives' strenuous efforts to get a large 'hunk' of the spoils of office; others thought it was a corruption of the Dutch slang word *hanker,* freely translated as 'greedy.'" By the 1850s, the *Hunker* designation was commonly applied to the great conservative Unionist majority of the Democratic party throughout the North. Joseph G. Rayback, *Free Soil,* Lexington University Press of Kentucky (1971), 16n; Nichols, *Democratic Machine,* 18, 198–199.

†A text of the quoted resolution, which indicates that the word "totally" appeared before the word "dissolved," may be found in W.C. Ford et al., eds., *Journal of the Continental Congress, 1774–1789,* 34 vols., National Archives and Records, 1959; vpa. of 1904–1937 (Washington, D.C., 1904–1937), 5:507.

template their great deeds with less than admiration. They were statesmen, patriots and heroes, and for the good they did, and the principles they contended for, I will unite with you to honor their memory.

They loved their country better than their own private interests; and, though this is not the highest form of human excellence, all will concede that it is a rare virtue, and that when it is exhibited, it ought to command respect. He who will, intelligently, lay down his life for his country, is a man whom it is not in human nature to despise. Your fathers staked their lives, their fortunes, and their sacred honor, on the cause of their country. In their admiration of liberty, they lost sight of all other interests.

They were peace men; but they preferred revolution to peaceful submission to bondage. They were quiet men; but they did not shrink from agitating against oppression. They showed forbearance; but that they knew its limits. They believed in order; but not in the order of tyranny. With them, nothing was "*settled*" that was not right. With them, justice, liberty and humanity were "*final;*" not slavery and oppression. You may well cherish the memory of such men. They were great in their day and generation. Their solid manhood stands out the more as we contrast it with these degenerate times.

How circumspect, exact and proportionate were all their movements! How unlike the politicians of an hour! Their statesmanship looked beyond the passing moment, and stretched away in strength into the distant future. They seized upon eternal principles, and set a glorious example in their defence. Mark them!

Fully appreciating the hardship to be encountered, firmly believing in the right of their cause, honorably inviting the scrutiny of an onlooking world, reverently appealing to heaven to attest their sincerity, soundly comprehending the solemn responsibility they were about to assume, wisely measuring the terrible odds against them, your fathers, the fathers of this republic, did, most deliberately, under the inspiration of a glorious patriotism, and with a sublime faith in the great principles of justice and freedom, lay deep the corner-stone of the national superstructure, which has risen and still rises in grandeur around you.

Of this fundamental work, this day is the anniversary. Our eyes are met with demonstrations of joyous enthusiasm. Banners and pennants wave exultingly on the breeze. The din of business, too, is hushed. Even Mammon seems to have quitted his grasp on this day. The ear-piercing fife and the stirring drum unite their accents with the ascending peal of a thousand church bells. Prayers are made, hymns are sung, and sermons are preached in honor of this day; while the quick martial tramp of a great and multitudinous nation, echoed back by all the hills, valleys and mountains of a vast continent, bespeak the occasion one of thrilling and universal interest—a nation's jubilee.

Friends and citizens, I need not enter further into the causes which led to this anniversary. Many of you understand them better than I do. You could instruct me in regard to them. That is a branch of knowledge in which you feel, perhaps, a much deeper interest than your speaker. The causes which led to the separation of the colonies from the British crown have never lacked for a tongue. They have all been taught in your common schools, narrated at your firesides, unfolded from your pulpits, and thundered from your legislative halls, and are as familiar to you as household words. They form the staple of your national poetry and eloquence.

I remember, also, that, as a people, Americans are remarkably familiar with all facts which make in their own favor. This is esteemed by some as a national trait—perhaps a national weakness. It is a fact, that whatever makes for the wealth or for the reputation of Americans, and can be had *cheap!* will be found by Americans. I shall not be charged with slandering Americans, if I say I think the American side of any question may be safely left in American hands.

I leave, therefore, the great deeds of your fathers to other gentlemen whose claim to have been regularly descended will be less likely to be disputed than mine!

The Present

My business, if I have any here to-day, is with the present. The accepted time with God and his cause is the ever-living now.

"Trust no future, however pleasant,
 Let the dead past bury its dead;
Act, act in the living present,
 Heart within, and God overhead."*

We have to do with the past only as we can make it useful to the present and to the future. To all inspiring motives, to noble deeds which can be gained from the past, we are welcome. But now is the time, the important time. Your fathers have lived, died, and have done their work, and have done much of it well. You live and must die, and you must do your work. You have no right to enjoy a child's share in the labor of your fathers, unless your children are to be blest by your labors. You have no right to wear out and waste the hard-earned fame of your fathers to cover your indolence. Sydney Smith[†] tells us that men seldom eulogize the wisdom and virtues of their fathers, but to excuse some folly or wickedness of their own. This truth is not a doubtful one. There are illustrations of it near and remote, ancient and modern. It was fashionable, hundreds of years ago, for the children of Jacob to boast, we have "Abraham to our father," when they had long lost Abraham's faith and spirit.[‡] That people contented themselves under the shadow of Abraham's great name, while they repudiated the deeds which made his name great. Need I remind you that a similar thing is being done all over this country to-day? Need I tell you that the Jews are not the only people who built the tombs of the prophets, and garnished the sepulchres of the righteous? Washington could not die till he had broken the chains of his slaves.[§] Yet his monument is built up by the price of human blood, and the traders in the bodies and souls of men, shout—"We have Washington to *our father.*" Alas! that it should be so; yet so it is.

"The evil that men do, lives after them,
The good is oft' interred with their bones."[||]

Fellow-citizens, pardon me, allow me to ask, why am I called upon to speak here to-day? What have I, or those I represent, to do with your national independence? Are the great principles of political freedom and of natural justice, embodied in that Declaration of Independence, extended to us? and am I, therefore, called upon to bring our humble offering to the national altar, and to confess the benefits and express devout gratitude for the blessings resulting from your independence to us?

Would to God, both for your sakes and ours, that an affirmative answer could be truthfully returned to these questions! Then would my task be light, and my burden easy and delightful. For *who* is there so cold, that a nation's sympathy could not warm him? Who so obdurate and dead to the claims of gratitude, that would not thankfully acknowledge such priceless benefits? Who so stolid and selfish, that would not give his voice to swell the hallelujahs of a nation's jubilee, when the chains of servitude had been torn from his limbs? I am not that man. In a case like that, the dumb might

*The stanza quoted is from Henry Wadsworth Longellow's "A Psalm of Life." *Poems,* 22.

[†]Anglican minister Sydney Smith (1771–1845) was a master satirical essayist and lecturer. A highly partisan Whig, his barbed wit was employed to great effect in the causes of Catholic emancipation and parliamentary reform. *DNB,* 18:527–531.

[‡]Douglass appears to allude to a passage from Luke 3:8: "Bring forth therefore fruits worthy of repentance, and begin not to say within yourselves, We have Abraham to *our* father: for I say unto you, That God is able of these stones to raise up children unto Abraham."

[§]At the time of his death, George Washington owned or held claim to over three hundred slaves. His will provided that "upon the decease of my wife it is my . . . desire that all slaves whom I hold in my own right shall receive their freedom." Matthew T. Mellon, *Early American Views on Negro Slavery From the Letters and Papers of the Founders of the Republic,* Meador (Boston, 1934), 29–81; Walter H. Mazyck, *George Washington and the Negro* (Washington, D.C., 1932), 133–138; George Livermore, *An Historical Research Respecting the Opinions of the Founders of the Republic on Negroes as Slaves, as Citizens, and as Soldiers,* 4th ed., J. Wilson (Boston, 1862), 28–31; Paul F. Boller, "Washington, the Quakers, and Slavery," *JNH,* 46 (April 1961): 83–88.

[||]*Julius Caesar,* act 3, sc. 2, line 76.

eloquently speak, and the "lame man leap as an hart."

But, such is not the state of the case. I say it with a sad sense of the disparity between us. I am not included within the pale of this glorious anniversary! Your high independence only reveals the immeasurable distance between us. The blessings in which you, this day, rejoice, are not enjoyed in common. The rich inheritance of justice, liberty, prosperity and independence, bequeathed by your fathers, is shared by you, not by me. The sunlight that brought life and healing to you, has brought stripes and death to me. This Fourth [of] July is *yours,* not *mine. You* may rejoice, *I* must mourn. To drag a man in fetters into the grand illuminated temple of liberty, and call upon him to join you in joyous anthems, were inhuman mockery and sacrilegious irony. Do you mean, citizens, to mock me, by asking me to speak to-day? If so, there is a parallel to your conduct. And let me warn you that it is dangerous to copy the example of a nation whose crimes, towering up to heaven, were thrown down by the breath of the Almighty, burying that nation in irrecoverable ruin! I can to-day take up the plaintive lament of a peeled and woe-smitten people!

"By the rivers of Babylon, there we sat down. Yea! we wept when we remembered Zion. We hanged our harps upon the willows in the midst thereof. For there, they that carried us away captive, required of us a song; and they who wasted us required of us mirth, saying, Sing us one of the songs of Zion. How can we sing the Lord's song in a strange land? If I forget thee, O Jerusalem, let my right hand forget her cunning. If I do not remember thee, let my tongue cleave to the roof of my mouth."*

Fellow-citizens; above your national, tumultuous joy, I hear the mournful wail of millions! whose chains, heavy and grievous yesterday, are, to-day, rendered more intolerable by the jubilee shouts that reach them. If I do forget, if I do not faithfully remember those bleeding children of sorrow this day, "may my right hand forget her cunning, and may my tongue cleave to the roof of my mouth!" To forget them, to pass lightly over their wrongs, and to chime in with the popular theme, would be treason most scandalous and shocking, and would make me a reproach before God and the world. My subject, then fellow-citizens, is AMERICAN SLAVERY. I shall see, this day, and its popular characteristics, from the slave's point of view. Standing, there, identified with the American bondman, making his wrongs mine, I do not hesitate to declare, with all my soul, that the character and conduct of this nation never looked blacker to me than on this 4th of July! Whether we turn to the declarations of the past, or to the professions of the present, the conduct of the nation seems equally hideous and revolting. America is false to the past, false to the present, and solemnly binds herself to be false to the future. Standing with God and the crushed and bleeding slave on this occasion, I will, in the name of humanity which is outraged, in the name of liberty which is fettered, in the name of the constitution and the Bible, which are disregarded and trampled upon, dare to call in question and to denounce, with all the emphasis I can command, everything that serves to perpetuate slavery—the great sin and shame of America! "I will not equivocate; I will not excuse;"† I will use the severest language I can command; and yet not one word shall escape me that any man, whose judgement is not blinded by prejudice, or who is not at heart a slaveholder, shall not confess to be right and just.

But I fancy I hear some one of my audience say, it is just in this circumstance that you and your brother abolitionists fail to make a favorable impression on the public mind. Would you argue more, and denounce less, would you persuade more, and rebuke less, your cause would be much more likely to succeed. But, I submit, where all is plain there is nothing to be argued. What point in the antislavery creed would you

*Ps. 137:1–6.

†Douglass quotes from the first issue of the *Liberator,* in which William Lloyd Garrison promised, "I am in earnest—I will not equivocate—I will not excuse—I will not retreat a single inch—and *I will be heard." Liberator,* 1 January 1831; John L. Thomas, *The Liberator: William Lloyd Garrison,* Little Brown (Boston, 1963), 128.

have me argue? On what branch of the subject do the people of this country need light? Must I undertake to prove that the slave is a man? That point is conceded already. Nobody doubts it. The slaveholders themselves acknowledge it in the enactment of laws for their government. They acknowledge it when they punish disobedience on the part of the slave. There are seventy-two crimes in the State of Virginia, which, if committed by a black man, (no matter how ignorant he be), subject him to the punishment of death; while only two of the same crimes will subject a white man to the like punishment.* What is this but the acknowledgement that the slave is a moral, intellectual and responsible being? The manhood of the slave is conceded. It is admitted in the fact that Southern statute books are covered with enactments forbidding, under severe fines and penalties, the teaching of the slave to read or to write. When you can point to any such laws, in reference to the beasts of the field, then I may consent to argue the manhood of the slave. When the dogs in your streets, when the fowls of the air, when the cattle on your hills, when the fish of the sea, and the reptiles that crawl, shall be unable to distinguish the slave from a brute, *then* will I argue with you that the slave is a man!

For the present, it is enough to affirm the equal manhood of the negro race. Is it not astonishing that, while we are ploughing, planting and reaping, using all kinds of mechanical tools, erecting houses, constructing bridges, building ships, working in metals of brass, iron, copper, silver and gold; that, while we are reading, writing and cyphering, acting as clerks, merchants and secretaries, having among us lawyers, doctors, ministers, poets, authors, editors, orators and teachers; that, while we are engaged in all manner of enterprises common to other men, digging gold in California, capturing the whale in the Pacific, feeding sheep and cattle on the hill-side, living, moving, acting, thinking, planning, living in families as husbands, wives and children, and, above all, confessing and worshipping the Christian's God, and looking hopefully for life and immortality beyond the grave, we are called upon to prove that we are men!

Would you have me argue that man is entitled to liberty? that he is the rightful owner of his own body? You have already declared it. Must I argue the wrongfulness of slavery? Is that a question for Republicans? Is it to be settled by the rules of logic and argumentation, as a matter beset with great difficulty, involving a doubtful application of the principle of justice, hard to be understood? How should I look to-day, in the presence of Americans, dividing, and subdividing a discourse, to show that men have a natural right to freedom? speaking of it relatively, and positively, negatively, and affirmatively. To do so, would be to make myself ridiculous, and to offer an insult to your understanding. There is not a man beneath the canopy of heaven, that does not know that slavery is wrong *for him.*

What, am I to argue that it is wrong to make men brutes, to rob them of their liberty, to work them without wages, to keep them ignorant of their relations to their fellow men, to beat them with sticks, to flay their flesh with the lash, to load their limbs with irons, to hunt them with dogs, to sell them at auction, to sunder their families, to knock out their teeth, to burn their flesh, to starve them into obedience and submission to their masters? Must I argue that a system thus marked with blood, and stained with pollution, is *wrong?* No! I will not. I have better employments for my time and strength, than such arguments would imply.

What, then, remains to be argued? Is it that slavery is not divine; that God did not establish it; that our doctors of divinity are mistaken? There is blasphemy in the thought. That which is inhuman, cannot be divine! *Who* can reason on such a proposition? They that can, may; I cannot. The time for such argument is past.

At a time like this, scorching irony, not convincing argument, is needed. O! had I the ability,

*Douglass probably relies on [Weld], *American Slavery,* American Anti-slavery Society (New York, 1839), p. 149, which contrasts capital offenses in Virginia for slaves and whites.

and could I reach the nation's ear, I would, today, pour out a fiery stream of biting ridicule, blasting reproach, withering sarcasm, and stern rebuke. For it is not light that is needed, but fire; it is not the gentle shower, but thunder. We need the storm, the whirlwind, and the earthquake. The feeling of the nation must be quickened; the conscience of the nation must be roused; the propriety of the nation must be startled; the hypocrisy of the nation must be exposed; and its crimes against God and man must be proclaimed and denounced.

What, to the American slave, is your 4th of July? I answer: a day that reveals to him, more than all other days in the year, the gross injustice and cruelty to which he is the constant victim. To him, your celebration is a sham; your boasted liberty, an unholy license; your national greatness, swelling vanity; your sounds of rejoicing are empty and heartless; your denunciations of tyrants, brass fronted impudence; your shouts of liberty and equality, hollow mockery; your prayers and hymns, your sermons and thanksgivings, with all your religious parade, and solemnity, are, to him, mere bombast, fraud, deception, impiety, and hypocrisy—a thin veil to cover up crimes which would disgrace a nation of savages. There is not a nation on the earth guilty of practices, more shocking and bloody, than are the people of these United States, at this very hour.

Go where you may, search where you will, roam through all the monarchies and despotisms of the old world, travel through South America, search out every abuse, and when you have found the last, lay your facts by the side of the everyday practices of this nation, and you will say with me, that, for revolting barbarity and shameless hypocrisy, America reigns without a rival.

❖❖❖

The Internal Slave Trade

Take the American slave-trade, which, we are told by the papers, is especially prosperous just now. Ex-Senator Benton* tells us that the price of men was never higher than now. He mentions the fact to show that slavery is in no danger. This trade is one of the pecularities of American institutions. It is carried on in all the large towns and cities in one-half of this confederacy; and millions are pocketed every year, by dealers in this horrid traffic. In several states, this trade is a chief source of wealth. It is called (in contradistinction to the foreign slave-trade) "*the internal slave-trade.*" It is, probably, called so, too, in order to divert from it the horror with which the foreign slave-trade is contemplated. That trade has long since been denounced by this government, as piracy. It has been denounced with burning words, from the high places of the nation, as an execrable traffic. To arrest it, to put an end to it, this nation keeps a squadron, at immense cost, on the coast of Africa. Everywhere, in this country, it is safe to speak of this foreign slave-trade, as a most inhuman traffic, opposed alike to the laws of God and of man. The duty to extirpate and destroy it, is admitted even by our DOCTORS OF DIVIN-

*Thomas Hart Benton (1782–1858) served as a U.S. senator from Missouri from 1821 to 1851. Born near Hillsboro, North Carolina. Benton briefly studied at the University of North Carolina and at William and Mary College. Despite a promising start on a legal and political career in Tennessee, Benton migrated to Missouri after service in the War of 1812. Elected to the Senate upon Missouri's admission to the Union, he became an important Jacksonian Democrat and spokesman for western interests. When he failed to secure reelection to the Senate in 1850, Benton returned to Congress as a representative from 1853 to 1855 but lost his bid for a second term in 1854. Benton probably used his observation on slave prices to bolster his persistent denial that slaveholding interests were insecure in the Union. Although the remark does not appear in his published speeches attacking Calhoun's appeal for southern congressional unity in 1849 or in his major speeches delivered during the Senate debate on the 1850 compromise measures, Benton repeated this observation several years later when criticizing the 1850 secessionist movements in South Carolina and Mississippi: "[T]here is no danger to slavery in any slave State. Property is timid! and slave property above all: and the market is the test of safety and danger to all property. . . . Now, how is it with slave property, tried by this unerring standard? Has it been sinking in price since the year 1835? since the year of the first alarm manifesto in South Carolina, and the first of Mr. Calhoun's twenty years' alarm speeches in the Senate? On the contrary, the price has been constantly rising the whole time—and it is still rising although it has attained a height incredible to have been predicted twenty years ago." Thomas Hart Benton, *Thirty Years' View,* 2 vols., Appleton (New York, 1854–56), 2: 782; Elbert B. Smith, *Magnificent Missourian: The Life of Thomas Hart Benton,* Lippincott (Philadelphia, 1958); William N. Chambers, *Old Bullion Benton: Senator from the West* (Boston, 1956); Theodore Roosevelt, *Thomas H. Benton,* Houghton Mifflin (Boston, 1899); *ACAB,* 1:241–243; *DAB, 2:210–213.*

ITY. In order to put an end to it, some of these last have consented that their colored brethren (nominally free) should leave this country, and establish themselves on the western coast of Africa! It is, however, a notable fact that, while so much execration is poured out by Americans upon those engaged in the foreign slave-trade, the men engaged in the slave-trade between the states pass without condemnation, and their business is deemed honorable.

Behold the practical operation of this internal slave-trade, the American slave-trade, sustained by American politics and American religion. Here you will see men and women reared like swine for the market. You know what is a swine-drover? I will show you a man-drover. They inhabit all our Southern States. They perambulate the country, and crowd the highways of the nation, with droves of human stock. You will see one of these human flesh-jobbers, armed with pistol, whip and bowie-knife, driving a company of a hundred men, women, and children, from the Potomac to the slave market at New Orleans. These wretched people are to be sold singly, or in lots, to suit purchasers. They are food for the cotton-field, and the deadly sugar-mill. Mark the sad procession, as it moves wearily along, and the inhuman wretch who drives them. Hear his savage yells and his blood-chilling oaths, as he hurries on his affrighted captives! There, see the old man, with locks thinned and gray. Cast one glance, if you please, upon that young mother, whose shoulders are bare to the scorching sun, her briny tears falling on the brow of the babe in her arms. See, too, that girl of thirteen, weeping, *yes!* weeping, as she thinks of the mother from whom she has been torn! The drove moves tardily. Heat and sorrow have nearly consumed their strength; suddenly you hear a quick snap, like the discharge of a rifle; the fetters clank, and the chain rattles simultaneously; your ears are saluted with a scream, that seems to have torn its way to the centre of your soul! The crack you heard, was the sound of the slave-whip; the scream you heard, was from the woman you saw with the babe. Her speed had faltered under the weight of her child and her chains! that gash on her shoulder tells her to move on. Follow this drove to New Orleans. Attend the auction; see men examined like horses; see the forms of women rudely and brutally exposed to the shocking gaze of American slave-buyers. See this drove sold and separated forever; and never forget the deep, sad sobs that arose from that scattered multitude. Tell me citizens, WHERE, under the sun, you can witness a spectacle more fiendish and shocking. Yet this is but a glance at the American slave-trade, as it exists, at this moment, in the ruling part of the United States.

I was born amid such sights and scenes. To me the American slave-trade is a terrible reality. When a child, my soul was often pierced with a sense of its horrors. I lived on Philpot Street, Fell's Point, Baltimore, and have watched from the wharves, the slave ships in the Basin, anchored from the shore, with their cargoes of human flesh, waiting for favorable winds to waft them down the Chesapeake. There was, at that time, a grand slave mart kept at the head of Pratt Street, by Austin Woldfolk.* His agents were sent into every town and county in Maryland, announcing their arrival, through the papers, and on flaming "*hand-bills,*" headed CASH FOR NEGROES. These men were generally well dressed men, and very captivating in their manners. Ever ready to drink, to treat, and to gam-

---

*Actually Austin Woolfolk of Augusta, Georgia, who came to Baltimore in 1819 and became the best-known slave trader in the area in the 1820s and early 1930s. Attracted by the city's commercial shipping facilities, Woolfolk and his relatives made Baltimore the headquarters for their activities and annually transported between 230 and 460 slaves to New Orleans. Agents for Woolfolk were sent into counties throughout Maryland and his advertisements in local newspapers throughout the 1820s indicated that Woolfolk would pay "the highest prices and in cash" for young slaves. In his *Narrative,* Douglass noted that "if a slave was convicted of any high misdemeanor, became unmanageable, or evinced a determination to run away, he was brought immediately here [Lloyd's home plantation], severely whipped, put on board the sloop, carried to Baltimore, and sold to Austin Woolfolk, or some other slave trader, as a warning to the slaves remaining." Woolfolk's slave-trading activities declined in the early 1830s owing to increased competition from larger firms, a decrease in the number of slaves available for sale to traders as owners who left the area took the slaves into the western territories or manumitted them, and the increased opposition of Marylanders to slave trading within the state. Douglass, *Narrative,* 32; William Calderhead, "The Role of the Professional Slave Trader in a Slave Economy: Austin Woolfolk, A Case Study," *Civil War History,* 23 (September 1977):195–211.

ble. The fate of many a slave has depended upon the turn of a single card; and many a child has been snatched from the arms of its mother by bargains arranged in a state of brutal drunkenness.

The flesh-mongers gather up their victims by dozens, and drive them, chained, to the general depot at Baltimore. When a sufficient number have been collected here, a ship is chartered, for the purpose of conveying the forlorn crew to Mobile, or to New Orleans. From the slave prison to the ship, they are usually driven in the darkness of night; for since the anti-slavery agitation, a certain caution is observed.

In the deep still darkness of midnight, I have been often aroused by the dead heavy footsteps, and the piteous cries of the chained gangs that passed our door. The anguish of my boyish heart was intense; and I was often consoled, when speaking to my mistress in the morning, to hear her say that the custom was very wicked; that she hated to hear the rattle of the chains, and the heart-rending cries. I was glad to find one who sympathised with me in my horror.

Fellow-citizens, this murderous traffic is, to-day, in active operation in this boasted republic. In the solitude of my spirit, I see clouds of dust raised on the highways of the South; I see the bleeding footsteps; I hear the doleful wail of fettered humanity, on the way to the slave-markets, where the victims are to be sold like *horses, sheep,* and *swine,* knocked off to the highest bidder. There I see the tenderest ties ruthlessly broken, to gratify the lust, caprice and rapicity of the buyers and sellers of men. My soul sickens at the sight.

"Is this the land your Fathers loved,
  The freedom which they toiled to win?
Is this the earth whereon they moved?
  Are these the graves they slumber in?"*

But a still more inhuman, disgraceful, and scandalous state of things remains to be presented.

By an act of the American Congress, not yet two years old, slavery has been nationalized in its most horrible and revolting form. By that act, Mason & Dixon's line has been obliterated; New York has become as Virginia; and the power to hold, hunt, and sell men, women, and children as slaves remains no longer a mere state institution, but is now an institution of the whole United States. The power is co-extensive with the star-spangled banner and American Christianity. Where these go, may also go the merciless slave-hunter. Where these are, man is not sacred. He is a bird for the sportsman's gun. By that most foul and fiendish of all human decrees, the liberty and person of every man are put in peril. Your broad republican domain is hunting ground for *men. Not* for thieves and robbers, enemies of society, merely, but for men guilty of no crime. Your lawmakers have commanded all good citizens to engage in this hellish sport. Your President, your Secretary of State, your *lords, nobles,* and ecclesiastics, enforce, as a duty you owe to your free and glorious country, and to your God, that you do this accursed thing. Not fewer than forty Americans have, within the past two years, been hunted down and, without a moment's warning, hurried away in chains, and consigned to slavery and excruciating torture. Some of these have had wives and children, dependent on them for bread; but of this, no account was made. The right of the hunter to his prey stands superior to the right of marriage, and to *all* rights in this republic, the rights of God included! For black men there are neither law, justice, humanity, nor religion. The Fugitive Slave *Law* makes MERCY TO THEM, A CRIME; and bribes the judge who tries them. An American JUDGE GETS TEN DOLLARS FOR EVERY VICTIM HE CONSIGNS to slavery, and five, when he fails to do so. The oath of any two villains is sufficient, under this hell-black enactment, to send the most pious and exemplary black man into the remorseless jaws of slavery! His own testimony is nothing. He can bring no witnesses for himself. The minister of American justice is bound by the law to hear but *one* side; and *that* side, is the side of the

*Douglass slightly alters the first four lines of John Greenleaf Whittier's "Stanzas for the Times." Whittier, *Poetical Works,* 3:35.

oppressor.* Let this damning fact be perpetually told. Let it be thundered around the world, that, in tyrant-killing, king-hating, people-loving, democratic, Christian America, the seats of justice are filled with judges, who hold their offices under an open and palpable *bribe*, and are bound, in deciding in the case of a man's liberty, *to hear only his accusers!*

In glaring violation of justice, in shameless disregard of the forms of administering law, in cunning arrangement to entrap the defenceless, and in diabolical intent, this Fugitive Slave Law stands alone in the annals of tyrannical legislation. I doubt if there be another nation on the globe, having the brass and the baseness to put such a law on the statute-book. If any man in this assembly thinks differently from me in this matter, and feels able to disprove my statements, I will gladly confront him at any suitable time and place he may select.

Religion in England and Religion in America

One is struck with the difference between the attitude of the American church towards the anti-slavery movement, and that occupied by the churches in England towards a similar movement in that country. There, the church, true to its mission of ameliorating, elevating, and improving the condition of mankind, came forward promptly, bound up the wounds of the West Indian slave, and restored him to his liberty. There, the question of emancipation was a high[ly] religious question. It was demanded, in the name of humanity, and according to the law of the living God. The Sharps.† the Clarksons,‡ the Wilberforces,§ the Buxtons,|| and Burchells¶ and the Knibbs,** were alike famous for their piety, and for their philanthropy. The anti-slavery movement *there* was not an anti-church movement, for the reason that the church took its full share in prosecuting that movement: and the anti-slavery movement in this country will cease to be an anti-church movement, when the church of this country shall assume a favorable, instead of a hostile position towards that movement.

Americans! your republican politics, not less than your republican religion, are flagrantly inconsistent. You boast of your love of liberty, your superior civilization, and your pure Christianity, while the whole political power of the nation (as embodied in the two great political parties), is solemnly pledged to support and perpetuate the enslavement of three millions of your countrymen. You hurl your anathemas at the crowned headed tyrants of Russia and Austria, and pride yourselves on your Democratic institutions, while you yourselves consent to be the mere *tools* and *bodyguards* of the tyrants of Virginia and Carolina. You invite to your shores fugitives of oppression from abroad, honor them with banquets, greet them with ovations, cheer them, toast them, salute theme, protect them, and pour out your money to them like water; but the fugi-

*Although the 1850 Fugitive Slave Law did not specify the number of witnesses needed to establish that an individual was a fugitive slave, it did provide that "in no trial or hearing . . . shall the testimony of such alleged fugitive be admitted in evidence." No provision was made for the alleged fugitive to bring forth witnesses who might dispute the claims of the court transcript or warrant, but the commissioner or judge did have to be convinced that the person brought before him was indeed the escaped slave described in the transcript. *The Public Statutes at Large and Treaties of the United States of America, 1789–1873,* 17 vols., Little, Brown (Boston, 1845–1873), 9:462–465; Stanley W. Campbell, *Slave Catchers,* University of North Carolinia Press (Chapel Hill, NC, 1970), 110–115.

†Granville Sharp.

‡Thomas Clarkson.

§William Wilberforce.

||Thomas Fowell Buxton (1786–1845), politician, philanthropist, and successor to Wilberforce in the parliamentary struggle to end British slavery and the slave trade, was born in Essex County, England, and educated at Trinity College, Dublin. Buxton entered Parliament in 1818 and achieved prominence for his support of various reform measures, including education of the poor and equitable criminal laws. In the late 1820s, he exposed the practice of slave trading in Mauritius, Trinidad, and Jamaica, and between 1831 and 1833 led the abolition campaign in Parliament. Buxton wrote *The African Slave Trade and Its Remedy* (Philadelphia: Merrihew and Thompson, 1839) and supported several unsuccessful explorations of the Niger River. William L. Mathieson, *British Slavery and its Abolition* (London: Longmans, 1926), 115–127, 194–198, 222–224; Klingberg, *Anti-Slavery Movement in England,* 187–212; Clare Taylor, *British and American Abolitionists,* 33–34, 73–74; *DNB,* 3: 559–561.

¶Thomas Burchell.

**William Knibb.

tives from your own land you advertise, hunt, arrest, shoot and kill. You glory in your refinement and your universal education; yet you maintain a system as barbarous and dreadful as ever stained the character of a nation—a system begun in avarice, supported in pride, and perpetuated in cruelty. You shed tears over fallen Hungary, and make the sad story of her wrongs the theme of your poets, statesmen and orators, till your gallant sons are ready to fly to arms to vindicate her cause against her oppressors;* but, in regard to the ten thousand wrongs of the American slave, you would enforce the strictest silence, and would hail him as an enemy of the nation who dares to make those wrongs the subject of public discourse! You are all on fire at the mention of liberty for France or for Ireland; but are as cold as an iceberg at the thought of liberty for the enslaved of America. You discourse eloquently on the dignity of labor; yet, you sustain a system which, in its very essence, casts a stigma upon labor. You can bare your bosom to the storm of British artillery to throw off a threepenny tax on tea; and yet wring the last hard-earned farthing from the grasp of the black laborers of your country. You profess to believe "that, of one blood, God made all nations of men to dwell on the face of all the earth,"† and hath commanded all men, everywhere to love one another; yet you notoriously hate, (and glory in your hatred), all men whose skins are not colored like your own. You declare, before the world, and are understood by the world to declare, that you "*hold these truths to be self evident, that all men are created equal; and are endowed by their Creator with certain inalienable rights; and that, among these are, life, liberty, and the pursuit of happiness;*"‡ and yet, you hold securely, in a bondage which, according to your own Thomas Jefferson, "*is worse than ages of that which your fathers rose in rebellion to oppose,*"§ *a seventh part* of the inhabitants of your country.

Fellow-citizens! I will not enlarge further on your national inconsistencies. The existence of slavery in this country brands your republicanism as a sham, your humanity as a base pretence, and your Christianity as a lie. It destroys your moral power abroad; it corrupts your politicians at home. It saps the foundation of religion; it makes your name a hissing, and a byword to a mocking earth. It is the antagonistic force in your government, the only thing that seriously disturbs and endangers your *Union.* It fetters your progress; it is the enemy of improvement, the deadly foe of education; it fosters pride; it breeds insolence; it promotes vice; it shelters crime; it is a curse to the earth that supports it; and yet, you cling to it, as if it were the sheet anchor of all your hopes. Oh! be warned! be warned! a horrible reptile is coiled up in your nation's bosom; the venomous creature is nursing at the tender breast of your youthful republic; *for the love of God, tear away,* and fling from you the hideous monster, and *let*

*Douglass here refers to the turmoil in Hungary following the invasion of the country by Russian and Austrian troops in August 1849. The Magyar-dominated Hungarian Diet in the spring of 1848, after the outbreak of revolution in Austria, seized the opportunity to enact a series of internal reforms, the "April Laws," which among other things created an independent Hungarian ministry. The ministry, however, was viewed as a direct threat to Austrian control, and, in September 1848, with the support of Austrian King Ferdinand, Croatian troops invaded Hungary under the leadership of Josip Jelacic. The new ministry fled, leaving in charge Magyar nationalist Louis Kossuth, who was eventually able to rout the Croatian forces. Francis Joseph, nephew of King Ferdinand of Austria, assumed the throne of Hungary in December 1848 and revoked the "April Laws." At this point, the Hungarian Diet proclaimed its independence and Louis Kossuth became governor. The Hungarian republic was short-lived, however, and Francis Joseph, with the assistance of Russian troops, marched on Hungary and defeated the republican army in August 1849. The country was dismembered and brought under the control of Vienna. Janos Pragay, *The Hungarian Revolution: Outlines of the Prominent Circumstances Attending the Hungarian Struggle for Freedom* (New York: G. P. Putnam, 1850); B. F. Tefft, *Hungary and Kossuth: An American Exposition of the late Hungarian Revolution* (Philadelphia, 1852); Edwin L. Godkin, *The History of Hungary and the Magyars From the Earliest Period to the Close of the Late War* (London: W. Kent, 1856), 324–369.

†A paraphrase of Acts 17:26: "And [God] hath made of one blood all nations of men for to dwell on all the face of the earth."

‡Douglass quotes the American Declaration of Independence.

§Writing to Jean Nicholas Demeunier on 26 June 1786, Thomas Jefferson observed: "What a stupendous, what an incomprehensible machine is man! Who can endure toil, famine, stripes, imprisonment or death itself in vindication of his own liberty, and the next moment be deaf to all those motives whose power supported him thro' his trial, and inflict on his fellow men a bondage, one hour of which is fraught with more misery than ages of that which he rose in rebellion to oppose." Boyd, *Papers of Thomas Jefferson,* 10:63.

the weight of twenty millions crush and destroy it forever!

The Constitution

But it is answered in reply to all this, that precisely what I have now denounced is, in fact, guaranteed and sanctioned by the Constitution of the United States; that the right to hold and to hunt slaves is a part of that Constitution framed by the illustrious Fathers of this Republic.

Then, I dare to affirm, notwithstanding all I have said before, your fathers stooped, basely stooped

> "To palter with us in a double sense:
> And keep the word of promise to the ear,
> But break it to the heart."*

And instead of being the honest men I have before declared them to be, they were the veriest imposters that ever practised on mankind. *This* is the inevitable conclusion, and from it there is no escape. But I differ from those who charge this baseness on the framers of the Constitution of the United States. *It is a slander upon their memory,* at least, so I believe. There is not time now to argue the constitutional question at length; nor have I the ability to discuss it as it ought to be discussed. The subject has been handled with masterly power by Lysander Spooner, Esq.,† by William Goodell,‡ by Samuel E. Sewall, Esq.,§ and last, though not least, by Gerritt Smith, Esq.‖ These gentlemen have, as I think, fully and clearly vindicated the Constitution from any design to support slavery for an hour.

Fellow-citizens! there is no matter in respect to which, the people of the North have allowed themselves to be so ruinously imposed upon, as that of the pro-slavery character of the Constitution. In *that* instrument I hold there is neither warrant, license, nor sanction of the hateful thing; but, interpreted as it *ought* to be interpreted, the Constitution is a GLORIOUS LIBERTY DOCUMENT. Read its preamble, consider its purposes. Is slavery among them? Is it at the gateway? or is it in the temple? It is neither. While I do not intend to argue this question on the present occasion, let me ask, if it be not somewhat singular that, if the Constitution were intended to be, by its framers and adopters, a slave-holding instrument, why neither *slavery, slaveholding,* nor *slave* can anywhere be found in it. What would be thought of an instrument, drawn up, *legally* drawn up, for the purpose of entitling the city of Rochester to a track of land, in which no mention of land was made? Now, there are certain rules of interpretation, for the proper understanding of all legal instruments. These rules are well established. They are plain, common-sense rules, such as you and I, and all of us, can understand and apply, without having passed years in the study of law. I scout the idea that the question of the constitutionality or unconstitutionality of slavery is not a question for the people. I hold that every American citizen has a right to form an opinion of the constitution, and to propagate that opinion, and to use all honorable means to make his opinion the prevailing one. Without this right, the liberty of an American citizen would be as insecure as that of a French-

---

*Douglass paraphrases *Macbeth,* act 5, sc. 8, lines 20–22.

†Lysander Spooner (1808–1887), lawyer, writer, and uncompromising foe of slavery, first published his famous work. *The Unconstitutionality of Slavery,* in Boston, in 1845. An expanded version appeared in 1847, and it became one of the major sources of campaign literature used by the Liberty party in the 1840s, *ACAB,* 5:634–635; *DAB,* 17: 466–467.

‡Douglass probably refers to William Goodell, *Views of American Constitutional Law, Its Bearing upon American Slavery* (Books for Libraries 1844 Freeport, N.Y.: Books for Libraries, 1971), and idem., *Slavery and Anti-Slavery.*

§Attorney Samuel E. Sewall (1799–1888) published in 1827 his *Remarks on Slavery in the United States,* which had first appeared in the *Christian Examiner.* Although he wrote no lengthy legal analysis of American slavery, Sewall was active in the defense of fugitive slaves captured in Massachusetts and in 1843 ran for governor of the state on the Liberty party ticket. Nina Moore Tiffany, *Samuel E. Sewall: A Memoir* (Boston, Wiggin & Lunt, 1898), 33–81.

‖Among Gerrit Smith's many letters, tracts, and pamphlets denying the constitutionality of slavery are *Letter of Gerrit Smith to Henry Clay* (New York: J. A. Gray, 1839); *Letter of Gerrit Smith to S. P. Chase on the Unconstitutionality of Every Part of American Slavery* (Albany, 1847); *Abstract of the Argument on the Fugitive Slave Law, Made by Gerrit Smith in Syracuse, June, 1852 on the Trial of Henry W. Allen, U.S. Deputy Marshal, for Kidnapping* (Syracuse: John A. Gray, 1852).

man. Ex-Vice-President Dallas* tells us that the constitution is an object to which no American mind can be too attentive, and no American heart too devoted. He further says, the constitution, in its words, is plain and intelligible, and is meant for the home-bred, unsophisticated understandings of our fellow-citizens. Senator Berrien† tells us that the Constitution is the fundamental law, that which controls all others. The charter of our liberties, which every citizen has a personal interest in understanding thoroughly. The testimony of Senator Breese,‡ Lewis Cass, and many others that might be named, who are everywhere esteemed as sound lawyers, so regard the Constitution. I take it, therefore, that it is not presumption in a private citizen to form an opinion of that instrument.

Now, take the constitution according to its plain reading, and I defy the presentation of a single pro-slavery clause in it. On the other hand, it will be found to contain principles and purposes, entirely hostile to the existence of slavery.

I have detained my audience entirely too long already. At some future period I will gladly avail myself of an opportunity to give this subject a full and fair discussion.

Allow me to say, in conclusion, notwithstanding the dark picture I have this day presented of the state of the nation, I do not despair of this country. There are forces in operation, which must inevitably work the downfall of slavery. "*The arm of the Lord is not shortened,*"§ and the doom of slavery is certain. I, therefore, leave off where I began, with *hope.* While drawing encouragement from the Declaration of Independence, the great principles it contains, and the genius of American Institutions, my spirit is also cheered by the obvious tendencies of the age. Nations do not now stand in the same relation to each other that they did ages ago. No nation can now shut itself up from the surrounding world, and trot round in the same old path of its fathers without interference. The time *was* when such could be done. Long established customs of hurtful character could formerly fence themselves in, and do their evil work with social impunity. Knowledge was then confined and enjoyed by the privi-

---

*George Mifflin Dallas (1792–1864), Philadelphia-born lawyer and Democratic politician, served as U.S. vice-president (1845–1849) under James Polk. Other political offices Dallas held during his public career included U.S. attorney for the Eastern District of Pennsylvania (1829–1831), U.S. senator (1831–1833), Pennsylvania attorney general (1833–1835), and U.S. minister to Russia (1837–1839). Although retired to private law practice in 1849, he expressed his support for the Compromise of 1850 and its provisions for the return of fugitive slaves in a letter to Guy M. Bryan published in the New York *Daily Times,* 13 October 1851. Denouncing "the self-slaughter of intermeddling with the institutions and rights exclusively of state creation, state responsibility, and state control," Dallas observed that "the act for the extradition of fugitives is the pretext for protracted and persevering war upon the guarantees of the Constitution." As a candidate for the Democratic presidential nomination in 1852, Dallas was asked whether he would enforce the Fugitive Slave Law and he answered unequivocally "Yes, I would!" George Mifflin Dallas to Guy M. Bryan, 25 July 1851, in New York *Daily Times,* 13 October 1851; New York *Daily Times,* 31 May 1852; John M. Belohlavek, *George Mifflin Dallas: Jacksonian Patrician* (University Park, Pa.: Pennsylvania State University, 1977), 138–143; *NCAB,* 6:268; *BDAC,* 772; *DAB,* 5:38–39.

†Georgia senator John MacPherson Berrien (1781–1856), known as the "American Cicero" because of his magnificent oratory, was also regarded as one of the ablest constitutional lawyers in the U.S. Senate during the 1840s. Born near Princeton, New Jersey, in 1781, he grew up in Savannah, Georgia, was graduated from Princeton at age fourteen, returned to Savannah to study law, and was admitted to the bar in 1798. From 1809 until 1821 he served as solicitor and then as judge of the eastern circuit. A member of the Georgia state senate (1822–1823) and the U.S. Senate (1823–1825) and U.S. attorney general under Andrew Jackson in 1829, Berrien was returned to the Senate as a Whig in 1841 after a decade's retirement from public life. In 1849, Berrien's *Address to the People of the United States* pleaded for compromise on the slavery question. He later voted in favor of the Fugitive Slave Law and opposed the abolition of the slave trade in the District of Columbia and the admission of California as a free state. Defeated in his bid for reelection in November 1851, he spent his final years organizing the American or Know-Nothing party. Josephine Mellichamp, *Senators from Georgia* (Huntsville, Ala.: Strode Publishers, 1976), 99–103; Richard H. Shryock, *Georgia and the Union in 1850* (Philadelphia: University of Pennsylvania, 1926), 157–163, 267–269, 358; *BDAC,* 548; *DAB,* 2:225–226.

‡Sidney Breese (1800–1878), Democrat from Illinois, served in the U.S. Senate for only one term (1843–1849) and generally supported the positions of his fellow midwestern senator, Lewis Cass, of Michigan, on such issues as the constitutionality of slavery, popular sovereignty, and limited congressional authority over slavery. Born into a wealthy family in Whitesboro, New York, and a graduate of Union College, Breese headed west to study in Illinois and was admitted to the bar in 1820. In 1857, he was elected to the Illinois Supreme Court and was reelected in 1861 and 1870, from which position he gained a reputation as one of the leading American jurists of the era. Melville W. Fuller, "Biographical Memoir of Sidney Breese," in Sidney Breese, *The Early History of Illinois, From Its Discovery by the French, in 1763 . . . ,* ed. Thomas Hoyne (Chicago: E. B. Myers, 1884), 3–60; *ACAB,* 1:367; *NCAB,* 8:122; *DAB,* 3: 14–16.

§Douglass paraphrases Isa. 59:1: "Behold, the Lord's hand is not shortened, that it cannot save, neither His ear heavy, that it cannot hear."

leged few, and the multitude walked on in mental darkness. But a change has now come over the affairs of mankind. Walled cities and empires have become unfashionable. The arm of commerce has borne away the gates of the strong city. Intelligence is penetrating the darkest corners of the globe. It makes its pathway over and under the sea, as well as on the earth. Wind, steam, and lightning are its chartered agents. Oceans no longer divide, but link nations together. From Boston to London is now a holiday excursion. Space is comparatively annihilated. Thoughts expressed on one side of the Atlantic are distinctly heard on the other.

The far off and almost fabulous Pacific rolls in grandeur at our feet. The Celestial Empire, the mystery of ages, is being solved. The fiat of the Almighty, "*Let there be Light,*"* has not yet spent its force. No abuse, no outrage whether in taste, sport or avarice, can now hide itself from the all-pervading light. The iron shoe, and crippled foot of China must be seen, in contrast with nature. *Africa must rise and put on her yet unwoven garment. "Ethiopia shall stretch out her hand unto God."*† In the fervent aspirations of William Lloyd Garrison, I say, and let every heart join in saying it:

God speed the year of jubilee
  The wide world o'er!
When from their galling chains set free,
Th' oppress'd shall vilely bend the knee,
And wear the yoke of tyranny
  Like brutes no more.
That year will come, and freedom's reign,
To man his plundered rights again
  Restore.

God speed the day when human blood
  Shall cease to flow!
In every clime he understood,
The claims of human brotherhood,
And each return for evil, good,
  Not blow for blow;
That day will come all feuds to end,
And change into a faithful friend
  Each foe.

God speed the hour, the glorious hour,
  When none on earth
Shall exercise a lordly power,
Nor in a tyrant's presence cower;
But all to manhood's stature tower,
  By equal birth!
THAT HOUR WILL COME, to each, to all,
And from his prison-house, the thrall
  Go forth.

Until that year, day, hour, arrive,
With head, and heart, and hand I'll strive,
To break the rod, and rend the gyve,
The spoiler of his prey deprive—
  So witness Heaven!
And never from my chosen post,
Whate'er the peril or the cost,
  Be driven.‡

*Gen. 1:3.

†An allusion to Ps. 68:31: "Princes shall come out of Egypt; Ethiopia shall soon stretch out her hands unto God."

‡William Lloyd Garrison, "The Triumph of Freedom," in *Liberator*, 10 January 1845.

ALEXANDER CRUMMELL
(1819–1898)

With the exception of W.E.B. Du Bois, the religious leader Alexander Crummell was possibly the most impressive black scholar of the nineteenth century. Crummell documented precisely the classification or taxonomy of various kinds of minerals and natural wealth in West Africa. As a proponent of African American commerce in America, he achieved a natural balance between what would become the self-help policy of Booker T. Washington and the kind of intellectual inquiry posed by

W.E.B. Du Bois in the late nineteenth and early twentieth centuries. Sometimes, the missionary zeal of Crummell might have inadvertently declined into a license to plunder Africa to save it from "heathenism." Nevertheless, Crummell was conscious of the potential for the political abuse of Christian principles. Occasionally, his emphasis on agriculture for Africa may have looked forward to the contemporary need to facilitate a wisdom through which Africans might determine their own destiny. What Crummell's excellent training empowered him to do was to articulate the logical need for an African American enterprise to help develop the continent of Africa. Like W.E.B. Du Bois, he was at least a century ahead of his time.

Crummell was born free on March 3, 1819, in New York City of unmixed African blood. His mother was a free black woman and his father was Boston Crummell, the African immigrant son of a king in Timanee, West Africa. The young Crummell studied at Mulberry Street School and at the African Free School of Manhattan. His schoolmates included a host of notable nineteenth-century African Americans: Henry Highland Garnet, Ira Aldridge, Charles L. Reason, Patrick Reason, Samuel Ringgold, and James McCune. Along with his childhood friend, Garnet, and twelve other black classmates, Crummell attempted to improve his education by attending a new academy for black youths—the Noyes Academy in Canaan, New Hampshire. However, several white racists in the town, resenting the "nigger school, drove all the Blacks out" with ninety oxen that pulled down the school building, the remains of which were deposited in a swamp a half mile away. On May 4, 1882, Crummell would recall the scare in his eulogy for his friend Garnet:

> About eleven o'clock at night the tramp of horses was heard approaching. As one rapid raider passed the house he fired at it. [Later, Reverend Henry Highland] Garnet quickly replied to it by a discharge from a double barreled shotgun which blazed away through the window. . . . But the musket shot by Garnet doubtless saved our lives. The cowardly ruffians dared not attack us. Notice, however, was given to us to quit the State within a fortnight. When we left, the Canaan mob assembled on the outskirts of the village and fixed field-pieces charged with powder.

Consequently, Crummell and Garnet entered the respectable Oneida Theological Institute, Oneida County, New York, of which the abolitionist, Beriah Green, served as president. After graduation in 1839, Crummell became a candidate for the Holy Order under the auspices of Reverend Peter Williams, rector of the St. Phillip's Church of Whitesboro, New York.

Again, Crummell experienced racial prejudice when he decided to enter the ministry of the Episcopal Church. That same year, when he applied to the General Theology Seminary of the Protestant Episcopal Church in New York, he was refused admission because of his racial identity. In the quest to complete his training for the ministry, he had run up against the powerful proslavery forces within the New York City Episcopal diocese. After being rejected from the General Theology Seminary, he went to Boston where a Bishop Grishold ordained him an Episcopal minister and admitted him to the diocese in Massachusetts. Later, Bishop Lee of Delaware confirmed him to the Priest's Orders. Crummell continued to study independently until December of 1844, at which time he was ordained as a priest in Philadelphia. Yet, when Crummell attempted to preach in the city, the powerful Bishop Henry U.

Onderdonk refused to receive him in his diocese except on terms that Crummell could not accept. As a result, he returned to New York, where he worked for a brief period with a small, antislavery group in the old church of his family.

In 1848, Crummell went to England and earned money for three years. There, he enrolled at Queen's College at Cambridge, where he received his degree of divinity in 1853. During his years at Cambridge, he strengthened his advocacy for the antislavery and civil rights causes. Rather than return to the United States and experience further humiliation and racial prejudice, he went to Liberia apparently to establish his permanent residence. He lived there for approximately twenty years.

While in Liberia, Crummell matured into one of the leading authorities of the African Diaspora. As a professor of mental and moral science at the newly built college in Monrovia, he promoted not only African and African American self-determination and wealth but also black liberation. In an address titled "The Duty of a Rising Christian State," which he delivered before the Common Council and citizens of Monrovia on the anniversary of their independence, July 26, 1855, he emphasized the vital role that Liberia must play in the African freedom struggle. Six years later, he published his first book, *The Relations and Duties of Free Colored Men in America to Africa,* which included his 1861 letter of the same title to Charles B. Dunbar; and the following year, several essays, letters, and speeches—including "The Hope for Africa"—appeared under the title of *The Future of Africa.* In particular, his 1861 letter to Charles B. Dunbar displays the excellence of his thought. He classifies African wealth into at least twelve categories, including the valuable minerals gold and oil, along with valuable dyes, grains, and woods. Despite the transport of millions of Africans as slaves to the West since 1600, he documents that Africans are rightfully heir to perhaps the wealthiest continent on earth. He foresees "the likelihood of an early repossession of Africa, in trade, commerce, and moral power, by her now scattered children in distant lands."

When Crummell returned to America in 1873, conditions of African Americans had improved. Chattel slavery had ended and the issue of colonization of African Americans, which Crummell had advocated so passionately in previous years at home and abroad, had subsided. During this early period of Reconstruction, a few African American men at least held state as well as national legislative offices. The improved social and political climate in America convinced Crummell to remain in the country. Soon, he founded St. Luke's Church in the District of Columbia, where he served for approximately twenty years as rector.

However, as the country began to renege on its commitment to human rights for African Americans, Crummell's voice of protest became stronger. When a white Protestant minister of Jackson, Mississippi, a Reverend Tucker, made racist remarks about black people before the Church Congress of 1882, Crummell attacked him and his views in a powerful work, *A Defense of the Negro Race in America* (1883). Also in 1883, as the senior black priest in a predominately white denomination, he called for a meeting of fellow black priests to challenge the racist policy through which the church refused to confirm a black bishop. On August 15, 1883, thus, he delivered a fiery address, "The Black Woman of the South: Her Neglects and Needs," before the Freedman's Aid Society of the Methodist Church at Ocean Grove, New Jersey. Very few writings of the period could match the angry protest he expressed in this speech concerning the deplorable conditions of the southern black woman. Approximately five hundred thousand copies of this work were necessary to satisfy the public demand. Furthermore, he helped to establish the Conference of Church Workers among Colored People and spoke out continuously against the rise of racial segregation at the dawn of the Booker T. Washington era—the 1890s. Several of his later essays and speeches, which were more caustic and virulent than his earlier writings, were collected and published in 1891 under the title *Africa and America*. Crummell's other works include *The Greatness of Christ* (1882) and *Alexander Crummell, 1844–1894: The Shades and Lights of a Fifty Years' Ministry* (1894).

In March of 1897, Crummell helped to found the American Negro Academy to promote excellence among black thinkers. Among the approximate number of forty members were W.E.B. Du Bois and Paul Laurence Dunbar. Crummell continued in his efforts to help produce African American leadership for the spiritual advancement of the race until his death on September 10, 1898.

Throughout Alexander Crummell's works, he fights forcefully for black rights and he challenges almost instinctively the arbitrary separation between armed and spiritual resistance. He lends an almost unexpected authentication to the *spiritual* tradition of what nearly a century later would become the defensive violence of Malcolm X. The exemplary role of Crummell as one of the foremost progenitors of African American cultural tradition merits appreciation.

❖❖❖

Though Crummell's works, which were very polished, represent some of the best writing by an African American during the nineteenth century, significant scholarship on Crummell and his works has curiously faded and now skipped more than a generation. *Religious Leaders of America* (1991) provides a few leads. Vernon Loggins in *The Negro Author* (1931), Benjamin Brawley in *Early Negro American Writers* (1935), and Rayford Logan and Michael R. Winston in the *Dictionary of American Negro Biography* (1982) provide some information. Otey M. Scruggs offers useful biographical information in his *We the Children of Africa in This Land: Alexander Crummell* (1972) and William J. Simmons presents a lively narrative with authoritative detail in *Men of Mark* (1949; reprinted 1968).

Hope for Africa

Selection from a sermon with this title preached on behalf of the Ladies Negro Education Society at Hotwell's Church, Clifton, Bristol, England, April 21, 1852, from the text, "Ethiopia shall soon stretch out her hands unto God."

I am well aware that it is the part of a wise man not to be too sanguine. I know, too, that, looking at the untold, the unknown millions in Central Africa, upon whom the eyes of civilized man have never fallen, the work is yet but begun. But when I note the rapidity of God's work during the brief period I have mentioned, and know that God allows no obstacles to stand against Him and His cause, whether it be a pestilential shore, or a violent population, or a sanguinary king, or vindictive slave-dealers, or a slave-trading town like that of Lagos; when I see these things, I cannot but believe that we are now approaching the fulfilment of this prophecy. When I see, moreover, how this great continent is invested on every side by the zealous ardent missionary or the adventurous traveler; how, almost weekly, something is brought to our ears across the ocean, of new discovery, or of startling incident; how that now there is every probability that soon the very heart of that continent, and all its centuries of mystery, will be revealed to the gaze and scrutiny of the civilized world; and then, that by the common road, by trade, by commerce, by the flying wings of steamers, by caravans, by converted Africans, by civilized and pious Negroes, from the West Indies or America, the Bible, the Prayer-Book, and tracts, and the Church in all her functions and holy offices, will almost at once be introduced among the mighty masses of its population;—when I see these things, my heart is filled with confident assurance; I cannot but believe that the day of Africa's redemption fast draweth nigh! And vast and extensive as the work may be, it seems that it will be a most rapid one; everything gives this indication: for first, you will notice, that since the abolition of the slave trade, this race, in all its homes, has been going forward: it has had nowhere any retrograde movements. And next, you will notice, that the improvement of this race, social, civil, and religious, has been remarkably quick, and has been, almost all, included in a very brief period; and therefore I think that the work of evangelization in this race will be a rapid one. So God, at times, takes "the staff of accomplishment" into His own hand, and fulfils His ends with speed. The children of Israel were thirty-nine years performing a journey, which could have been accomplished in a few days: but in the fortieth year they marched a longer distance than all the years preceding, and entered, in a few weeks, at once, into the Promised Land. So God, now, unseen to human eyes, may be leading on His hosts to a mighty victory over Satan; and in the briefest of all the periods of the Church's warfare, may intend to accomplish the most brilliant and consummate of all His triumphs. And this is my conviction with regard to Africa. In my soul I believe that the time has come. I have the strongest impression of the nigh approach of her bright day of deliverance. The night, I am convinced—the night of forlornness, of agony and desolation—is far spent; the day is at hand! The black charter of crime and infamy and blood, which for nigh three centuries has given up my fatherland to the spoiler, is about to be erased! The malignant lie, which would deliver up an entire race, the many millions of a vast continent, to rapine and barbarism and benightedness, is now to be blotted out! And if I read the signs of the times aright, if I am not deceived in supposing that now I see God's hand graciously opened for Africa, if to my sight now appear, with undoubted clearness,

> "the baby forms
> Of giant figures yet to be,"

what a grand reversal of a dark destiny will it not be for poor bleeding Africa! What a delightful episode from the hopeless agony of her unmitigated, unalleviated suffering! For ages hath she lain beneath the incubus of the "demon of her idolatry." For ages hath she suffered the ravages of vice, corruption, iniquity, and guilt. For ages hath she been "stricken and smitten" by the deadly thrusts of murder and hate, revenge and slaughter. Fire, famine, and the sword have been her distressful ravaging visitations. War, with devastating stride, has ravaged her fair fields, and peopled her open and voracious tombs. The slave trade—that fell destroyer!—has sacked her cities, has turned the hands of her sons upon each other, and set her different communities at murderous strife, and colored their hands with fraternal blood! Yes, everything natural has been changed into the monstrous; and all things harmonious turned into discord and confusion. Earth has had her beauty marred by the bloody track of the cruel men who have robbed my fatherland of her children; and the choral voice of ocean, which should lift up naught but everlasting symphonies in the ears of angels and of God, has been made harsh and dissonant, by the shrieks and moans and agonizing cries of the poor victims, who have either chosen a watery grave in preference to slavery, or else have been cast into its depths, the sick and the emaciated, by the ruthless slave-dealer! And then, when landed on the distant strand—the home of servitude, the seat of oppression—then has commenced a system of overwork and physical endurance, incessant and unrequited—a series of painful tasks, of forced labor, of want and deprivation, and lashings, and premature deaths, continued from generation to generation, transmitted as the only inheritance of poor, helpless humanity, to children's children!

But now there is a new spirit abroad—not only in the Christian world, but likewise through the different quarters of her own broad continent. There is an uprising of her sons from intellectual sloth and spiritual inertness; a seeking and a stretching forth of her hands, for light, instruction, and spirituality, such as the world has never before seen; and which gives hopes that the days of Cyprian and Augustine shall again return to Africa; when the giant sins and the deadly evils which have ruined her, shall be effectively stayed; and when Ethiopia, from the Atlantic to the Indian Ocean, from the Mediterranean to the Cape, "shall stretch out her hands unto God!"

The Black Woman of the South: Her Neglects and Her Needs[1]

It is an age clamorous everywhere for the dignities, the grand prerogatives, and the glory of woman. There is not a country in Europe where she has not risen somewhat above the degradation of centuries, and pleaded successfully for a new position and a higher vocation. As the result of this new reformation we see her, in our day, seated in the lecture-rooms of ancient universities, rivaling her brothers in the fields of literature, the grand creators of ethereal art, the participants in noble civil franchises, the moving spirit in grand reformations, and the guide, agent, or assistant in all the noblest movements for the civilization and regeneration of man.

In these several lines of progress the American woman has run on in advance of her sisters in every other quarter of the globe. The advantage, she has received, the rights and prerogatives she has secured for herself, are unequaled by any other class of women in the world. It will not be thought amiss, then, that I come here today to present to your consideration the one grand exception to this general superiority of women, viz., *The black woman of the South.*

❖❖❖

The rural or plantation population of the South was made up almost entirely of people of pure Negro blood. And this brings out also the other disastrous fact, namely, that this large black population has been living from the time of their introduction into America, a period of more than two hundred years, in a state of unlettered rudeness. The Negro all this time has been an intellectual starveling. This has been more especially the condition of the black woman of the South. Now and then a black man has risen above the debased condition of his people. Various causes would contribute to the advantage of the *men:* the relation of servants to superior masters; attendance at courts with them; their presence at political meetings; listening to table-talk behind their chairs; traveling as valets; the privilege of books and reading in great houses, and with indulgent masters—all these served to lift up a black *man* here and there to something like superiority. But no such fortune fell to the lot of the plantation woman. The black woman of the South was left perpetually in a state of hereditary darkness and rudeness.

❖❖❖

In her girlhood all the delicate tenderness of her sex was rudely outraged. In the field, in the rude cabin, in the press-room, in the factory, she was thrown into the companionship of coarse and ignorant men. No chance was given her for delicate reserve or tender modesty. From her girlhood she was the doomed victim of the grossest passions. All the virtues of her sex were utterly ignored. If the instinct of chastity asserted itself, then she had to fight like a tigress for the ownership and possession of her own person; and, ofttimes, had to suffer pains and lacerations for her virtuous self-assertion. When she reached maturity all the tender instincts of her womanhood were ruthlessly vi-

[1]Address before the Freedman's Aid Society, Methodist Episcopal Church, Ocean Grove, N.J., August 15, 1883.

olated. At the age of marriage—always prematurely anticipated under slavery—she was mated, as the stock of the plantation were mated, *not* to be the companion of a loved and chosen husband, but to be the breeder of human cattle, for the field or the auction-block. With that mate she went out, morning after morning to toil, as a common field-hand. As it was *his,* so likewise was it her lot to wield the heavy hoe, or to follow the plow, or to gather in the crops. She was a "hewer of wood and a drawer of water." She was a common field-hand. She had to keep her place in the gang from morn till eve, under the burden of a heavy task, or under the stimulus or the fear of a cruel lash. She was a picker of cotton. She labored at the sugar-mill and in the tobacco-factory. When, through weariness or sickness, she has fallen behind her allotted task, there came, as punishment, the fearful stripes upon her shrinking, lacerated flesh.

Her home life was of the most degrading nature. She lived in the rudest huts, and partook of the coarsest food, and dressed in the scantiest garb, and slept, in multitudinous cabins, upon the hardest boards.

Thus she continued a beast of burden down to the period of those maternal anxieties which, in ordinary civilized life, give repose, quiet, and care to expectant mothers. But, under the slave system, few such relaxations were allowed. And so it came to pass that little children were ushered into this world under conditions which many cattle-raisers would not suffer for their flocks or herds. Thus she became the mother of children. But even then there was for her no suretyship of motherhood, or training, or control. Her own offspring were *not* her own. She and husband and children were all the property of others. All these sacred ties were constantly snapped and cruelly sundered. *This* year she had one husband; and next year, through some auction sale, she might be separated from him and mated to another. There was no sanctity of family, no binding tie of marriage, none of the fine felicities and the endearing affections of home. None of these things was the lot of Southern black women. Instead thereof, a gross barbarism which tended to blunt the tender sensibilities, to obliterate feminine delicacy and womanly shame, came down as her heritage from generation to generation; and it seems a miracle of providence and grace that, notwithstanding these terrible circumstances, so much struggling virtue lingered amid these rude cabins, that so much womanly worth and sweetness abided in their bosoms, as slave-holders themselves have borne witness to.

But some of you will ask: "Why bring up these sad memories of the past? Why distress us with these dead and departed cruelties?" Alas, my friends, these are not dead things. Remember that

> "The evil that men do lives after them."

The evil of gross and monstrous abominations, the evil of great organic institutions crop out long after the departure of the institutions themselves. If you go to Europe you will find not only the roots, but likewise many of the deadly fruits of the old Feudal system still surviving in several of its old states and kingdoms. So, too, with slavery. The eighteen years of freedom have not obliterated all its deadly marks from either the souls or bodies of the black woman. The conditions of life, indeed, have been modified since emancipation; but it still maintains that the black woman is the Pariah woman of this land! We have, indeed, degraded women, immigrants, from foreign lands. In their own countries some of them were so low in the social scale that they were yoked with the cattle to plow the fields. They were rude, unlettered, coarse, and benighted. But when they reach *this* land there comes an end to their degraded condition.

> "They touch our country and their shackles
> fall."

As soon as they become grafted into the stock of American life they partake at once of all its large gifts and its noble resources.

Not so with the black woman of the South. Freed, legally she has been; but the act of emancipation had no talismanic influence to reach to and alter and transform her degrading social life.

When that proclamation was issued she might have heard the whispered words in her every hut, "Open, Sesame;" but, so far as her humble domicile and her degraded person were concerned, there was no invisible but gracious Genii who, on the instant, could transmute the rudeness of her hut into instant elegance, and change the crude surroundings of her home into neatness, taste, and beauty.

The truth is, "Emancipation Day" found her a prostrate and degraded being; and, although it has brought numerous advantages to her sons, it has produced but the simplest changes in her social and domestic condition. She is still the crude, rude, ignorant mother. Remote from cities, the dweller still in the old plantation hut, neighboring to the sulky, disaffected master class, who still think her freedom was a personal robbery of themselves, none of the "fair humanities" have visited her humble home. The light of knowledge has not fallen upon her eyes. The fine domesticities which give the charm to family life, and which, by the refinement and delicacy of womanhood, preserve the civilization of nations, have not come to *her*. She has still the rude, coarse labor of men. With her rude husband she still shares the hard service of a field-hand. Her house, which shelters, perhaps, some six or eight children, embraces but two rooms. Her furniture is of the rudest kind. The clothing of the household is scant and of the coarsest material, has ofttimes the garniture of rags; and for herself and offspring is marked, not seldom, by the absence of both hats and shoes. She has rarely been taught to sew, and the field labor of slavery times has kept her ignorant of the habitudes of neatness, and the requirements of order. Indeed, coarse food, coarse clothes, coarse living, coarse manners, coarse companions, coarse surroundings, coarse neighbors, both black and white, yea, every thing coarse, down to the coarse, ignorant, senseless religion, which excites her sensibilities and starts her passions, go to make up the life of the masses of black women in the hamlets and villages of the rural South.

This is the state of black womanhood. Take the girlhood of this same region, and it presents the same aspect, save that in large districts the white man has not forgotten the olden times of slavery and with indeed the deepest sentimental abhorrence of "amalgamation," still thinks that the black girl is to be perpetually the victim of his lust! In the large towns and in cities our girls in common schools and academies are receiving superior culture. Of the 15,000 colored school teachers in the South, more than half are colored young women, educated since emancipation. But even these girls, as well as their more ignorant sisters in rude huts, are followed and tempted and insulted by the ruffianly element of Southern society, who think that black *men* have no rights which white men should regard, and black *women* no virtue which white men should respect!

And now look at the *vastness* of this degradation. If I had been speaking of the population of a city, or a town, or even a village, the tale would be a sad and melancholy one. But I have brought before you the condition of millions of women. According to the census of 1880 there were, in the Southern States, 3,327,678 females of all ages of the African race. Of these there were 674,365 girls between twelve and twenty, 1,522,696 between twenty and eighty. "These figures," remarks an observing friend of mine, "are startling!" And when you think that the masses of these women live in the rural districts; that they grow up in rudeness and ignorance; that their former masters are using few means to break up their hereditary degradation, you can easily take in the pitiful condition of this population, and forecast the inevitable future to multitudes of females unless a mighty special effort is made for the improvement of the black womanhood of the South.

I know the practical nature of the American mind, I know how the question of values intrudes itself into even the domain of philanthropy; and, hence, I shall not be astonished if the query suggests itself, whether special interest in the black woman will bring any special advantage to the American nation.

Let me dwell for a few moments upon this phase of the subject. Possibly the view I am about suggesting has never before been presented to the American mind. But, Negro as I am, I shall make no apology for venturing the claim that the Negress is one of the most interesting of all the classes of women on the globe. I am speaking of her, not as a perverted and degraded creature, but in her natural state, with her native instincts and peculiarities.

Let me repeat just here the words of a wise, observing, tender-hearted philanthropist, whose name and worth and words have attained celebrity. It is fully forty years ago since the celebrated Dr. Channing said: "We are holding in bondage one of the best races of the human family. The Negro is among the mildest, gentlest of men. He is singularly susceptible of improvement from abroad. . . . His nature is affectionate, easily touched, and hence he is more open to religious improvement than the white man. . . . The African carries with him much more than *we* the genius of a meek, long-suffering, loving virtue."

I should feel ashamed to allow these words to fall from my lips if it were not necessary to the lustration of the character of my black sisters of the South. I do not stand here to-day to plead for the black *man.* He is a man; and if he is weak he must go the wall. He is a man; he must fight his own way, and if he is strong in mind and body, he can take care of himself. But for the mothers, sisters, and daughters of my race I have a right to speak. And when I think of their sad condition down South; think, too, that since the day of emancipation hardly any one has lifted up a voice in their behalf, I feel it a duty and a privilege to set forth their praises and to extol their excellencies. For, humble and benighted as she is, the black woman of the South is one of the queens of womanhood. If there is any other woman on this earth who in native aboriginal qualities is her superior, I know not where she is to be found; for, I do say, that in tenderness of feeling, in genuine native modesty, in large disinterestedness, in sweetness of disposition and deep humility, in unselfish devotedness, and in warm, motherly assiduities, the Negro woman is unsurpassed by any other woman on this earth.

The testimony to this effect is almost universal—our enemies themselves being witnesses. You know how widely and how continuously, for generations, the Negro has been traduced, ridiculed, derided. Some of you may remember the journals and the hostile criticisms of Coleridge and Trollope and Burton, West Indian and African travelers. Very many of you may remember the philosophical disquisitions of the ethnological school of 1847, the contemptuous dissertations of Hunt and Gliddon. But it is worthy of notice in all these cases that the sneer, the contempt, the bitter gibe, have been invariably leveled against the black *man*—never against the black woman! On the contrary, *she* has almost everywhere been extolled and eulogized. The black man was called a stupid, thick-lipped, flat-nosed, long-heeled, empty-headed animal; the link between the baboon and the human being, only fit to be a slave! But everywhere, even in the domains of slavery, how tenderly has the Negress been spoken of! She has been the nurse of childhood. To her all the cares and heart-griefs of youth have been intrusted. Thousands and tens of thousands in the West Indies and in our Southern States have risen up and told the tale of her tenderness, of her gentleness, patience, and affection. No other woman in the world has ever had such tributes to a high moral nature, sweet, gentle love, and unchanged devotedness. And by the memory of my own mother and dearest sisters I can declare it to be true!

Hear the tribute of Michelet: "The Negress, of all others, is the most loving, the most generating; and this, not only because of her youthful blood, but we must also admit, for the richness of her heart. She is loving among the loving, good among the good. (Ask the travelers whom she has so often saved.) Goodness is creative; it is fruitfulness; it is the very benediction of a holy act. The fact that woman is so fruitful I attribute to her treasures of tenderness, to that ocean of goodness which permeates her heart. . . . Africa is a woman. Her races are feminine. . . . In many of the black tribes of Central Africa the women rule, and they are as intelligent as they are amiable and kind."

The reference in Michelet to the generosity of the African woman to travelers brings to mind the incident in Mungo Park's travels, where the African women fed, nourished, and saved him. The men had driven him away. They would not even allow him to feed with the cattle; and so, faint, weary, and despairing, he went to a remote hut and lay down on the earth to die. One woman, touched with compassion, came to him, brought him food and milk, and at once he revived. Then he tells us of the solace and the assiduities of these gentle creatures for his comfort. I give you his own words: "The rites of hospitality thus performed toward a stranger in distress, my worthy benefactress, pointing to the mat, and telling me that I might sleep there without apprehension, called to the female part of her family which had stood gazing on me all the while in fixed astonishment, to resume the task of spinning cotton, in which they continued to employ themselves a great part of the night. They lightened their labors by songs, one of which was composed extempore, for I was myself the subject of it. It was sung by one of the young women, the rest joining in a sort of chime. The air was sweet and plaintive, and the words, literally translated, were these: 'The winds roared and the rains fell; the poor white man, faint and weary, came and sat under our tree. He has no mother to bring him milk, no wife to grind his corn. Let us pity the white man, no mother has he,'" etc.

Perhaps I may be pardoned the intrusion, just here, on my own personal experience. During a residence of nigh twenty years in West Africa, I saw the beauty and felt the charm of the native female character. I saw the native woman in her *heathen* state, and was delighted to see, in numerous tribes, that extraordinary sweetness, gentleness, docility, modesty, and especially those maternal solicitudes which make every African boy both gallant and defender of his mother.

I saw her in her *civilized* state, in Sierra Leone; saw precisely the same characteristics, but heightened, dignified, refined, and sanctified by the training of the schools, and refinements of civilization, and the graces of Christian sentiment and feeling. Of all the memories of foreign travel there are none more delightful than those of the families and the female friends of Freetown.

A French traveler speaks with great admiration of the black ladies of Hayti, "In the towns," he says, "I met all the charms of civilized life. The graces of the ladies of Port-au-Prince will never be effaced from my recollections."

It was, without doubt, the instant discernment of these fine and tender qualities which prompted the touching Sonnet of Wordsworth, written in 1802, on the occasion of the cruel exile of Negroes from France by the French Government:

"Driven from the soil of France, a female came
From Calais with us, brilliant in array,
A Negro woman like a lady gay,
Yet downcast as a woman fearing blame;
Meek, destitute, as seemed, of hope or aim
She sat, from notice turning not away,
But on all proffered intercourse did lay
A weight of languid speech—or at the same
Was silent, motionless in eyes and face.
Meanwhile those eyes retained their tropic fire
Which burning independent of the mind,
Joined with the luster of her rich attire
To mock the outcast—O ye heavens, be kind!
And feel, thou earth, for this afflicted race!"

But I must remember that I am to speak not only of the neglects of the black woman, but also of her needs. And the consideration of her needs suggests the remedy which should be used for the uplifting of this woman from a state of brutality and degradation.

❖❖❖

Ladies and gentlemen, since the day of emancipation millions of dollars have been given by the generous Christian people of the North for the intellectual training of the black race in this land. Colleges and universities have been built in the South, and hundreds of youth have been gathered within their walls. The work of your own Church in this regard has been magnificent and unrivaled, and the results which have been attained have been grand and elevating to the entire Negro race in America. The complement to all this generous and ennobling effort is the elevation of the black woman. Up to this day and time your noble philanthropy has touched, for the most part, the male population of the South, given them superiority, and stimulated them to higher aspirations. But a true civilization can only than be attained when the life of woman is reached, her whole being permeated by noble ideas, her fine taste enriched by culture, her tendencies to the beautiful gratified and developed, her singular and delicate nature lifted up to its full capacity; and then, when all these qualities are fully matured, cultivated and sanctified, all their sacred influences shall circle around ten thousand firesides, and the cabins of the humblest freedmen shall become the homes of Christian refinement and of domestic elegance through the influence and the charm of the uplifted and cultivated black woman of the South!

FRANCES WATKINS HARPER

(1824–1911)

Just as nineteenth-century America shaped the life and works of Frances Watkins Harper, she helped to shape it as a nation. As one of the most dynamic orators and poets for various social reform causes—the abolitionist, women's suffrage, and temperance movements—she spoke to America about America—its evils, its problems, and its imperatives; and, against a background of repressive legislation throughout the country, she fueled practically every aspect of democratic reform—black rights, women's rights, and human rights. Frances Harper was the best-known nineteenth-century black poet before Paul Laurence Dunbar, the first black short-story writer, and the author of perhaps the best-selling novel written by an African American prior to the twentieth century. Moreover, her enormous quantity of verse, which emphasizes her major subject matter—race, religion, and reform—became the most valuable, single poetic record of the African American race during the turbulent antebellum period.

Born Frances Ellen Watkins in Baltimore, Maryland, September 24, 1824, she was the only child of free parents. Before she was three years old, she became an orphan when her mother died in 1828. At this time, Frances was placed in the care of her uncle and aunt, Mr. and Mrs. William Watkins. Until the age of thirteen, she attended her uncle's school for free children, the William Watkins Academy for Negro Youth. Her uncle, who was a self-educated minister, a shoemaker by trade, and a staunch abolitionist, taught her the classics, the Bible, rhetoric, and antislavery writings. When she was fourteen years old, Harper hired out as a seamstress and housekeeper to a Baltimore family, the Armstrongs. During her residence there, she published articles and poems in the local newspaper and her earliest volume of verse, *Forest Leaves,* when she was in her early twenties. However, no copies of the work are extant.

In 1850, she left Baltimore for Ohio, where she attended Union Seminary, a vocational school near Columbus, which was later absorbed into Wilberforce University. While serving there as an instructor of sewing and embroidery, Harper became the first woman faculty member connected with the institution. After a few years at Union, she left to take a teaching position in Little York, Pennsylvania.

Little York proved to be the turning point in her life. While there, she frequently saw poor, wretched, half-starved fugitive slaves traveling the Underground Railroad. Harper became deeply moved when she learned of the Fugitive Slave Act, which forbade free blacks from entering Maryland without risking capture or sale. As she told William Still, she then decided to pledge herself to the antislavery cause, "to use, time, talent, and energy in the cause of freedom." For this reason, she moved to Philadelphia in 1854 to work at the Underground Railroad Station.

Between 1854 and 1865, she launched her professional literary career by serving as a full-time lecturer and orator-poet for the Maine Antislavery Society. In 1854, Harper gave her first speech, "The Education and Elevation of the Colored Race," in New Bedford, Massachusetts, and published her best-known volume of verse, *Poems on Miscellaneous Subjects,* which was prefaced by William Lloyd Garrison and which targeted the horrors of slavery. Three years later, she delivered an address, "Liberty for Slaves," for the twenty-fourth anniversary of the American Antislavery Society. This speech is the only antislavery address of hers that is still in print. Coupled with her lectures, Harper gave dramatic readings of her abolitionist verse from *Poems* throughout eight New England states and parts of Canada. These readings were so effective that she sold over fifty thousand copies of the volume, which went through twenty editions. Despite her busy lecturing schedule, she also managed to publish in 1859 her short story "The Two Offers," which was the first written by an African American. Written within the nineteenth-century women's narrative tradition of domestic realism, the story focuses on issues popular in the feminist movement at the time—wife abuse, child neglect, wanton drunkenness, and the sexual double standard, in this case, the pressures put on women to marry.

A year later, she withdrew from public life for a short period of time to marry Fenton Harper. After the birth of their child, Mary, and the death of Fenton Harper in 1864, she resumed her work for the Society. The same year, she delivered an address, "The Mission of War," in Providence, Rhode Island, and two other lectures, "The Lesson of War" and "The Claims of the Negro," in Portland, Maine.

Until 1865, Frances Harper worked as an abolitionist in the North. With the exception of a few months in 1869, she traveled and lectured from 1867 to 1871 throughout the South at her own expense and with threats against her life. In thirteen southern states, she spoke and read her poems on plantations and in schools, churches, courthouses, and legislative halls about the physical abuse of black people, the violations of voting privileges, and the lack of education and educational facilities.

After lecturing in the South for two years, she interrupted her tour briefly to return to Philadelphia to get her volume of verse, *Moses: A Story of the Nile* (1869), published and to support Frederick Douglass and the passage of the Fifteenth Amendment at an important meeting of the American Equal Rights Association (AERA). As one of the five black women officers of the association, Harper played a major role in influencing abolitionists and feminists to back Douglass when the two forces became split over the issue of which group, black men or white women, should be franchised. Understanding that obtaining the ballot for part of the race was far better than none, she passionately pleaded for the greater urgency of black men's attainment of the vote. Without her help, Douglass would not have been able to turn back the tide of the white feminist–Sojourner Truth power bloc, which had mounted enormous support for the women's vote.

When Harper returned to the South she, therefore, encouraged many of the freedmen, as she stated in an 1870 lecture in Mobile, Alabama, to "get land, every one that can" so they would be able to act and vote independently after Congress passed the amendment. She also lectured to and assisted many black women who had been victims of physical abuse in slavery and subjugation and ignorance since emancipation. Like them, Harper had experienced both sexism and racism in this region of the country. While speaking before mixed audiences, she often heard such remarks as "She is a man" and "She is not colored, she is painted." Her eloquent speeches and poetry deliveries, nevertheless, afforded her very favorable reviews even from the most intolerant southern newspapers.

After her southern tour, she returned on February 11, 1871, to Philadelphia, where she established her permanent residence. From this year to the time of her death, Harper identified with and became actively involved in practically every moral and social reform cause and campaign she felt would transform and benefit society—Civil Rights, antilynching, women's suffrage, domestic reform, black education, and temperance. Accordingly, she became a prominent speaker for and held leadership positions in various women's organizations, which stood in the forefront of the social reform movement in the country. These organizations included the American Women Suffrage Association, National Council of Women of the United States, the National Association of Colored Women (NACW), and the Women's Christian Temperance Union. And, although Harper was a Unitarian, she became involved in many activities of the A.M.E. Church and a regular contributor to the *A.M.E. Church Review.*

The year 1871 also marked the beginning of Harper's increased literary activities, especially her poetical productions. She published nine volumes of verse, including the enlarged versions of *Poems* (1871, 1898, 1900), which contained three prose essays—"Christianity," "The Colored People in America," and "Breathing the Air of Freedom"; *Sketches of Southern Life* (1872); and a second edition of *Moses: A Story of the Nile* (1889). In addition, three smaller collections of verse, *Light Beyond Darkness, The Sparrows Fall and Other Poems,* and *The Martyr of Alabama,* appeared in a larger volume titled *Atlanta Offering Poems* in 1895; and, in 1901, Harper published her last collection of poems, *Idylls of the Bible.*

In addition to her poetry and essays, Harper wrote serial stories and one novel. Two of her serials were "Sowing and Reaping: A Temperance Story" (1876), obviously about victims of alcohol, and "Trial and Triumph" (1888–1889), concerning the struggle of a middle-class black family. But Harper was better known for her novel, *Iola LeRoy or Shadows Uplifted* (1892). Written in the tradition of the sentimental novel and centered around the popular nineteenth-century theme of the tragic mulatto, the novel reached a wide audience and was well received when it first appeared. Harper, nevertheless, renders a nontraditional, feminist treatment of the theme. In no way is her octoroon heroine Iola LeRoy the stereotypical fragile, passive, and refined tragic mulatto beauty of late nineteenth-century fiction. Rather, she is a strong, self-reliant woman who is not only determined to find her family after slavery but also to work for a living and to receive an education equal to men. A feminist much like Harper herself, Iola eventually marries a professional black man who shares both her view of marriage as a cooperative relationship and her commitment to improving conditions in the black community.

Despite the immediate success of *Iola LeRoy*, Harper is known more today for her poetry than for her prose fiction. Her popularity, however, unlike that of Phillis Wheatley of the previous generation, is not based on conventional notions of poetic excellence. In her handling of poetic forms, she is generally considered to be less a technician than her fellow abolitionist, James Whitfield. And, with the exception of her best verse, *Moses: A Story of the Nile* and the Aunt Chloe series from *Sketches of Southern Life,* her poetry varies little in form, language, and poetic technique. In general, her verse, in which she relies primarily on the ballad stanza and rhymed tetrameter, reveals the heavy influences of Henry Wadsworth Longfellow, John Greenleaf Whittier, and Felicia Dorothea Hemans.

Harper's fame, instead, rests primarily on her excellent skills in oral poetry delivery, which have been attested to by nineteenth-century and modern critics alike. A contemporary of hers, Phebe A. Hansford, for example, spoke of her "clear, plaintive, melodious voice" and "the flow of her musical speech in the logical presentation of truth," and an audience participant, Grace Greenwood, described her as a poet "with gestures few and fitting" and with a manner "marked by dignity and composure." According to Greenwood, "the woe of two hundred years sighed through her tones. Every glance of her sad eyes was a mournful remonstrance against injustice and wrong." William H. Robinson makes clear that Harper used "her disarmingly dramatic voice and gestures and sighs and tears" to move large masses of people throughout the country toward her social and political sentiments.

Her transcribed-oral poetry and other works are essentially a product of her social vision. Harper's intrinsic concern for black liberation led her to envision herself as a race-builder, a black shepherd who will provide leadership for her flock of sheep, the black masses. As she states in her February 1870 letter to William Still, "I am standing with my race on the threshold of a new era . . . and yet today, with my limited knowledge, I may help my race forward a little. Some of our people remind me of sheep without a shepherd."

In most of her poetry, therefore, Harper assumes the stance of a poet-priest whose "pure and strong" songs serve to uplift the black race in particular and humanity as a whole. This can clearly be seen in her best poem, *Moses: A Story of the Nile,* a forty-page blank-verse narrative. As the black shepherd of her people, she readily identifies with Moses, the revolutionary warrior-prophet of the Israelites who led his people to freedom. In this sense, she anticipates Amiri Baraka (Leroi Jones), Madhubuti (Don L. Lee), and other New Black Poets who viewed themselves as leaders of the black revolutionary movement of the 1960s and 1970s. Yet, at other times, Harper sees herself as merely one of the black rank and file. This becomes evident in her Aunt Chloe poems, which form a new idiom in black poetry that ripens into the dialect of Dunbar. In these poems, Harper projects her own voice—her race and gender ideology—and moral strength and courage into her witty character, Aunt Chloe, a former slave in a small, rural, southern-black community who exhorts her male counterparts to become responsible, independent voting citizens during Reconstruction. The poet's heightened sense of communal consciousness in these poems foreshadows that of another New Black Poet, Etheridge Knight, who considered himself to be simply one and the same with the black masses.

By functioning as both the poet as seer and the center of the people, as well as one of the group singers for the new black rites, Frances Harper shaped the genre of black social-protest poetry; and, by pronouncing an "art for people's sake," in her poem "Songs for the People," she articulated the precept on which the theory of the Black Aesthetic would later be based. Furthermore, by fusing the communal and the individual voice, the folk and the conventional elements, and the oral and the written forms and idioms, she ushered in a very long line of African American literary artists—beginning with Dunbar, Charles Chesnutt, and James Campbell to numerous twentieth-century poets, fiction writers, dramatists, and orators.

Hailed by her contemporary Anna Julia Cooper as "one of the most eloquent women lecturers in the country," Frances Haper spent much of the time in the final years of her life on the podium championing women's suffrage. At age 69, she delivered a speech titled "Women's Political Future" at the 1893 World Congress of Representative Women in Chicago, in which she highlighted the potential of the woman's vote.

> To-day women hold in their hands influence and opportunity, and with these have already opened doors which have been closed by others. . . . In the home she is the priestess, in society the queen, in literature the power, in legislature halls, lawmakers have responded to her appeals. . . . In the pew of the church she constitutes the majority. . . . To her is the coming of the added responsibility of political power; and what she now possesses should only be the means of preparing her to use the coming power for the glory of God and the good of mankind.

Unfortunately, however, Harper would not live long enough to see her vision of women's enfranchisement become fulfilled. Eight years before the passage of the Nineteenth Amendment, she died of heart failure on February 22, 1911. Though not the uncompromising feminist Sojourner Truth, Harper had stood in the vanguard of the radical women's movement over the last half of the nineteenth century. And, although not the black nationalist Maria Stewart, Harper had been a major militant voice of abolition and black rights during her lengthy professional career. More than any other black woman activist of the nineteenth century, Frances Harper had a rare sense of historical timing that told her when certain positions on issues had to be reassessed, negotiated, or modified. It was this mental faculty that kept her remarkably in tune with the fast-paced events and major reform movements of the tumultuous era. It was her astute readings of the subtle nuances of race, gender, and class, and her wise critical judgments that made her a significant agent in the balance of political power. With her activism and oratory, Frances Watkins Harper changed the course of American history; and, with her poetry and prose, she stood at a crucial juncture in the development of African American literature.

❖❖❖

The only full-length biography on Harper is Melba Joyce Boyd's *Discarded Legacy: Politics and Poetics in the Life of Frances E. W. Harper* (1994). Useful information on her life can also be found in William Still's *The Underground Railroad* (1871; reprinted 1970) and in Theodora William Daniels's Introduction to *The Poems of Frances E.W. Harper,* an unpublished master's thesis, Howard University (1937). Daniels's work and that of Mary Ann Graham, *Complete Poems of Frances*

E.W. Harper (1988), are collections of Harper's verse. Interest in her life and works was resurrected during the 1970s and 1980s largely as a result of the efforts of black aesthetic and feminist critics. Consequently, Harper has begun to receive the critical attention she and her works so richly deserve. See the following studies: Elizabeth Ammon's "Profile of Frances Ellen Watkins Harper," *Legacy* 2 (1985); Paula Giddings's *When and Where I Enter* (1984); Mary Ann Graham's "Frances Ellen Watkins Harper" in *Dictionary of Literary Biography,* Vol. 50 (1986); Nagueyalti Warren's "Iola LeRoy" in *Notable Black American Women* (1992); Hazel Carby's Introduction to *Iola LeRoy,* edited by Deborah E. McDowell (1987); Frances Smith Foster's Introduction to *Iola LeRoy* (1988); Patricia Liggins Hill's "'Let Me Make the Songs for the People,' A Study of Frances Watkins Harper's Poetry," *Black American Literature Forum,* Vol. 15, No. 2 (Summer 1981); "Frances Watkins Harper's Aunt Chloe Poems from *Sketches of Southern Life;* Antithesis to the Plantation Literary Tradition," *Mississippi Quarterly,* Vol. 24, No. 1 (Winter 1982–1983); and Joan R. Sherman's *Invisible Poets: Afro-Americans of the Nineteenth Century* (1974).

The largest collections of Harper's books and pamphlets are located at the Moorland-Spingarn Research Center, Howard University, Washington, D.C., and at the Schomburg Center for Research in Black Culture, the New York Public Library.

The Slave Auction

The sale began—young girls were there,
  Defenceless in their wretchedness,
Whose stifled sobs of deep despair
  Revealed their anguish and distress.

And mothers stood with streaming eyes,
  And saw their dearest children sold;
Unheeded rose their bitter cries,
  While tyrants bartered them for gold.

And woman, with her love and truth—
  For these in sable forms may dwell—
Gaz'd on the husband of her youth,
  With anguish none may paint or tell.

And men, whose sole crime was their hue,
  The impress of their Maker's hand,
And frail and shrinking children, too,
  Were gathered in that mournful band.

Ye who have laid your love to rest,
  And wept above their lifeless clay,
Know not the anguish of that breast,
  Whose lov'd are rudely torn away.

Ye may not know how desolate
  Are bosoms rudely forced to part,
And how a dull and heavy weight
  Will press the life-drops from the heart.

The Slave Mother

Heard you that shriek? It rose
  So wildly on the air,
It seemed as if a burden'd heart
  Was breaking in despair.

Saw you those hands so sadly clasped—
  The bowed and feeble head—
The shuddering of that fragile form—
  That look of grief and dread?

Saw you the sad, imploring eye?
  Its every glance was pain,
As if a storm of agony
  Were sweeping through the brain.

She is a mother, pale with fear,
  Her boy clings to her side,
And in her kirtle vainly tries
  His trembling form to hide.

He is not hers, although she bore
  For him a mother's pains;
He is not hers, although her blood
  Is coursing through his veins!

He is not hers, for cruel hands
  May rudely tear apart
The only wreath of household love
  That binds her breaking heart.

His love has been a joyous light
  That o'er her pathway smiled,
A fountain gushing ever new,
  Amid life's desert wild.

His lightest word has been a tone
  Of music round her heart,
Their lives a streamlet blent in one—
  Oh, Father! must they part?

They tear him from her circling arms,
  Her last and fond embrace.
Oh! never more may her sad eyes
  Gaze on his mournful face.

No marvel, then, these bitter shrieks
  Disturb the listening air;
She is a mother, and her heart
  Is breaking in despair.

Bury Me in a Free Land

Make me a grave where'er you will,
In a lowly plain, or a lofty hill,
Make it among earth's humblest graves,
But not in a land where men are slaves.

I could not rest if around my grave
I heard the steps of a trembling slave:
His shadow above my silent tomb
Would make it a place of fearful gloom.

I could not rest if I heard the tread
Of a coffle gang to the shambles led,
And the mother's shriek of wild despair
Rise like a curse on the trembling air.

I could not sleep if I saw the lash
Drinking her blood at each fearful gash,
And I saw her babes torn from her breast,
Like trembling doves from their parent nest.

I'd shudder and start if I heard the bay
Of blood-hounds seizing their human prey,
And I heard the captive plead in vain
As they bound afresh his galling chain.

If I saw young girls from their mother's arms
Bartered and sold for their youthful charms,
My eye would flash with a mournful flame,
My death-paled cheek grow red with shame.

I would sleep, dear friends, where bloated might
Can rob no man of his dearest right;
My rest shall be calm in any grave
Where none can call his brother a slave.

I ask no monument, proud and high
To arrest the gaze of the passers-by;
All that my yearning spirit craves,
Is bury me not in a land of slaves.

Songs for the People

Let me make the songs for the people,
  Songs for the old and young;
Songs to stir like a battle-cry
  Wherever they are sung.

Not for the clashing of sabres,
  Nor carnage nor for strife;
But songs to thrill the hearts of men
  With more abundant life.

Let me make the songs for the weary,
Amid life's fever and fret,
Till hearts shall relax their tension,
And careworn brows forget.

Let me sing for little children,
Before their footsteps stray,
Sweet anthems of love and duty,
To float o'er life's highway.

I would sing for the poor and aged,
When shadows dim their sight;
Of the bright and restful mansions,
Where there shall be no night.

Our world, so worn and weary,
Needs music, pure and strong,
To hush the jangle and discords
Of sorrow, pain, and wrong.

Music to soothe all its sorrow,
Till war and crime shall cease;
And the hearts of men grown tender
Girdle the world with peace.

A Double Standard

Do you blame me that I loved him?
If when standing all alone
I cried for bread a careless world
Pressed to my lips a stone.

Do you blame me that I loved him,
That my heart beat glad and free,
When he told me in the sweetest tones
He loved but only me?

Can you blame me that I did not see
Beneath his burning kiss
The serpent's wiles, nor even hear
The deadly adder hiss?

Can you blame me that my heart grew cold
That the tempted, tempter turned;
When he was feted and caressed
And I was coldly spurned?

Would you blame him, when you draw from me
Your dainty robes aside.
If he with gilded baits should claim
Your fairest as his bride?

Would you blame the world if it should press
On him a civic crown;
And see me struggling in the depth
Then harshly press me down?

Crime has no sex and yet to-day
I wear the brand of shame;
Whilst he amid the gay and proud
Still bears an honored name.

Can you blame me if I've learned to think
Your hate of vice a sham,
When you so coldly crushed me down
And then excused the man?

Would you blame me if to-morrow
The coroner should say,
A wretched girl, outcast, forlorn,
Has thrown her life away?

Yes, blame me for my downward course,
But oh! remember well,
Within your homes you press the hand
That led me down to hell.

I'm glad God's ways are not our ways,
He does not see as man,
Within His love I know there's room
For those whom others ban.

I think before His great white throne,
His throne of spotless light,
That whited sepulchres shall wear
The hue of endless night.

That I who fell, and he who sinned,
Shall reap as we have sown;
That each the burden of his loss
Must bear and bear alone.

No golden weights can turn the scale
Of justice in His sight;
And what is wrong in woman's life
In man's cannot be right.

FROM *Sketches of Southern Life. Learning to Read*

Very soon the Yankee teachers
Came down and set up school;
But, oh! how the Rebs did hate it,—
It was agin' their rule.

Our masters always tried to hide
Book learning from our eyes;
Knowledge didn't agree with slavery—
'Twould make us all too wise.

But some of us would try to steal
A little from the book,
And put the words together,
And learn by hook or crook.

I remember Uncle Caldwell,
Who took pot liquor fat
And greased the pages of his book,
And hid it in his hat.

Aunt Chloe's Politics

Of course, I don't know very much
About these politics,
But I think that some who run 'em,
Do mighty ugly tricks.

I've seen 'em honey-fugle round,
And talk so awful sweet,
That you'd think them full of kindness
As an egg is full of meat.

Now I don't believe in looking
Honest people in the face,
And saying when you're doing wrong,
That 'I haven't sold my race.'

When we want to school our children,
If the money isn't there,
Whether black or white have took it,
The loss we all must share.

And this buying up each other
Is something worse than mean,
Though I thinks a heap of voting,
I go for voting clean.

Liberty for Slaves

Could we trace the record of every human heart, the aspirations of every immortal soul, perhaps we would find no man so imbruted and degraded that we could not trace the word liberty either written in living characters upon the soul or hidden away in some nook or corner of the heart. The law of liberty is the law of God, and is antecedent to all human legislation. It existed in the mind of Deity when He hung the first world upon its orbit and gave it liberty to gather light from the central sun.

Some people say set the slaves free. Did you ever think, if the slaves were free, they would steal everything they could lay their hands on from now till the day of their death—that they would steal more than two thousand millions of dollars (applause)! Ask Maryland, with her tens of thousands of slaves, if she is not prepared for freedom, and hear her answer: "I help supply the coffle-gangs of the South." Ask Virginia, with her hundreds of thousands of slaves, if she is not weary with her merchandise of blood and anxious to shake the gory traffic from her hands, and hear her reply: "Though fertility has covered my soil, though a genial sky bends over my hills and vales, though I hold in my hand a wealth of waterpower, enough to turn the spindles to clothe the world, yet, with all these advantages, one of my chief staples has been the sons and daughters I send to the human market and human shambles" (applause)! Ask the farther South, and all the cotton-growing States chime in, "We have need of fresh supplies to fill the ranks of those whose lives have gone out in unrequited toil on our distant plantations."

A hundred thousand new-born babes are annually added to the victims of slavery; twenty thousand lives are annually sacrificed on the plantations of the South. Such a sight should send a thrill of horror through the nerves of civilization and impel the heart of humanity to lofty alchemy by which this blood can be transformed into gold. Instead of listening to the cry of agony, they listen to the ring of dollars and stoop down to pick up the coin (applause).

But a few months since a man escaped from bondage and found a temporary shelter almost beneath the shadow of Bunker Hill. Had that man stood upon the deck of an Austrian ship, beneath the shadow of the house of the Hapsburgs, he have found protection. Had he been wrecked upon an island or colony of Great Britain, the waves of the tempest-lashed ocean would have washed him deliverance. Had he landed upon the territory of vine-encircled France and a Frenchman had reduced him to a thing and brought him here beneath the protection of our institutions and our laws, for such a nefarious deed that Frenchman would have lost his citizenship in France. Beneath the feebler light which glimmers from the Koran, the Bey of Tunis would have granted him freedom in his own dominions. Beside the ancient pyramids of Egypt he would have found liberty, for the soil laved by the glorious Nile is now consecrated to freedom. But from Boston harbour, made memorable by the infusion of threepenny taxed tea, Boston in its proximity to the plains of Lexington and Concord, Boston almost beneath the shadow of Bunker Hill and almost in sight of Plymouth Rock, he is thrust back from liberty and manhood and reconverted into a chattel. You have heard that, down South, they keep bloodhounds to hunt slaves. Ye bloodhounds, go back to your kennels; when you fail to catch the flying fugitive, when his stealthy tread is heard in the place where the bones of the revolutionary sires repose, the ready North is base enough to do your shameful service (applause).

Slavery is mean, because it tramples on the feeble and weak. A man comes with his affidavits from the South and invites me before a commissioner; upon that evidence *ex parte* and alone he hitches me to the car of slavery and trails my womanhood in the dust. I stand at the threshold of the Supreme Court and ask for justice, simple justice. Upon my tortured heart is thrown the mocking words, "You are a negro; you have no rights which white men are bound to respect" (loud and long-continued applause)! Had it been my lot to have lived beneath the Crescent instead of the Cross, had injustice and violence been heaped upon my head as a Mohammedan woman, as a member of a common faith, I might have demanded justice and been listened to by the Pasha, the Bey or the Vizier; but when I come here to ask for justice, men tell me, "We have no higher law than the Constitution" (applause).

But I will not dwell on the dark side of the picture. God is on the side of freedom; and any cause that has God on its side, I care not how much it may be trampled upon, how much it may be trailed in the dust, is sure to triumph. The message of Jesus Christ is on the side of freedom, "I come to preach deliverance to the captives, the opening of the prison doors to them that are bound." The truest and noblest hearts in the land are on the side of freedom.

They may be hissed at by slavery's minions, their names cast out as evil, their characters branded with fanaticism, but O,

> "To side with Truth is noble when we share her
> humble crust
> Ere the cause bring fame and profit and it's
> prosperous to be just."

May I not, in conclusion, ask every honest, noble heart, every seeker after truth and justice, if they will not also be on the side of freedom. Will you not resolve that you will abate neither heart nor hope till you hear the death-knoll of human bondage sounded, and over the black ocean of slavery shall be heard a song, more exulting than the song of Miriam when it floated o'er Egypt's dark sea, the requiem of Egypt's ruined hosts and the anthem of the deliverance of Israel's captive people? (great applause)

1857

The Two Offers

"What is the matter with you, Laura, this morning? I have been watching you this hour, and in that time you have commenced a half dozen letters and torn them all up. What matter of such grave moment is puzzling your dear little head, that you do not know how to decide?"

"Well, it is an important matter: I have two offers for marriage, and I do not know which to choose."

"I should accept neither, or to say the least, not at present."

"Why not?"

"Because I think a woman who is undecided between two offers, has not love enough for either to make a choice; and in that very hesitation, indecision, she has a reason to pause and seriously reflect, lest her marriage, instead of being an affinity of souls or a union of hearts, should only be a mere matter of bargain and sale, or an affair of convenience and selfish interest."

"But I consider them both very good offers, just such as many a girl would gladly receive. But to tell you the truth, I do not think that I regard either as a woman should the man she chooses for her husband. But then if I refuse, there is the risk of being an old maid, and that is not to be thought of."

"Well, suppose there is, is that the most dreadful fate that can befall a woman? Is there not more intense wretchedness in an ill-assorted marriage—more utter loneliness in a loveless home, than in the lot of the old maid who accepts her earthly mission as a gift from God, and strives to walk the path of life with earnest and unfaltering steps?"

"Oh! what a little preacher you are. I really believe that you were cut out for an old maid; that when nature formed you, she put in a double portion of intellect to make up for a deficiency of love; and yet you are kind and affectionate. But I do not think that you know anything of the grand, over-mastering passion, or the deep necessity of woman's heart for loving."

"Do you think so?" resumed the first speaker; and bending over her work she quietly applied herself to the knitting that had lain neglected by her side, during this brief conversation; but as she did so, a shadow flitted over her pale and intellectual brow, a mist gathered in her eyes, and a slight quivering of the lips, revealed a depth of feeling to which her companion was a stranger.

But before I proceed with my story, let me give you a slight history of the speakers. They were cousins, who had met life under different auspices. Laura Lagrange, was the only daughter of rich and indulgent parents, who had spared no pains to make her an accomplished lady. Her cousin, Janette Alston, was the child of parents, rich only in goodness and affection. Her father had been unfortunate in business, and dying before he could retrieve his fortunes, left his business in an embarrassed state. His widow was unacquainted with his business affairs, and when the estate was settled, hungry creditors had brought their claims and the lawyers had received their fees, she found herself homeless and almost penniless, and she who had been sheltered in the warm clasp of loving arms, found them too powerless to shield her from the pitiless pelting storms of adversity. Year after year she struggled with poverty and wrestled with want, till her toil-worn hands became too feeble to hold the shattered chords of existence, and her tear-dimmed eyes grew heavy with the slumber of death. Her daughter had watched over her with untiring devotion, had closed her eyes in death, and gone out into the busy, restless world, missing a precious tone from the voices of earth, a beloved step from the paths of life. Too self reliant to depend on the charity of relations, she endeavored to support herself by her own exertions, and she had succeeded. Her path for a while was marked with struggle and trial, but instead of uselessly repining, she met them bravely, and her life became not a thing of ease and indulgence, but of conquest, victory, and accomplishments. At the time when this conversation took place, the deep trials of her life had passed away. The achievements of her genius had won her a position in the literary world, where she shone as one of its bright particular stars. And with her fame came a competence of worldly means, which gave her leisure for improvement, and the riper development of her rare talents. And she, that pale intellectual woman, whose genius gave life and vivacity to the social circle, and whose presence threw a halo of beauty and grace around the charmed atmosphere in which she moved, had at one period of her life, known the mystic and solemn strength of an all-absorbing love. Years faded into the misty past, had seen the kindling of her eye, the quick flushing of her cheek, and the wild throbbing of her heart, at tones of a voice long since hushed to the stillness of death. Deeply, wildly, passionately, she had loved. Her whole life seemed like the pouring out of rich, warm and gushing affections. This love quickened her talents, inspired her genius, and threw over her life a tender and spiritual earnestness. And then came a fearful shock, a mournful waking from that "dream of beauty and delight." A shadow fell around her path; it came between her and the object of her heart's worship; first a few cold words, estrangement, and then a painful separation; the old story of woman's pride—digging the sepulchre of her happiness, and then a new-made grave, and her path over it to the spirit world; and thus faded out from that young heart her bright, brief and saddened dream of life. Faint and spirit-broken, she turned from the scenes associated with the memory of the loved and lost. She tried to break the chain of sad associations that bound her to the mournful past; and so, pressing back the bitter sobs from her almost breaking heart, like the dying dolphin, whose beauty is born of its death anguish, her genius gathered strength from suffering and wonderous power and brilliancy from the agony she hid within the desolate chambers of her soul. Men hailed her as one of earth's strangely gifted children, and wreathed the garlands of fame for her brow, when it was throbbing with a wild and fearful unrest. They breathed her name with applause, when through the lonely halls of her stricken spirit, was an earnest cry for peace, a deep yearning for sympathy and heart-support.

But life, with its stern realities, met her; its solemn responsibilities confronted her, and turning, with an earnest and shattered spirit, to life's duties and trials, she found a calmness and strength that she had only imagined in her dreams of poetry and song. We will now pass over a period of ten years, and the cousins have met again. In that calm and lovely woman, in whose eyes is a depth of tenderness, tempering the flashes of her genius, whose looks and tones are full of sympathy and love, we recognize the once smitten and stricken Janette Alston. The bloom of her girlhood had given way to a higher type of spiritual beauty, as if some unseen hand had been polishing and refining the temple in which her lovely spirit found its habitation; and this had been the fact. Her inner life had grown beautiful, and it was this that was constantly developing the outer. Never, in the early flush of womanhood, when an absorbing love had lit up her eyes and glowed in her life, had she appeared so interesting as when, with a countenance which seemed overshadowed with a spiritual light, she bent over the death-bed of a young woman, just lingering at the shadowy gates of the unseen land.

"Has he come?" faintly but eagerly exclaimed the dying woman. "Oh how I have longed for his coming, and even in death he forgets me."

"Oh, do not say so, dear Laura, some accident may have detained him," said Janette to her cousin; for on that bed, from whence she will never rise, lies the once-beautiful and light-hearted Laura Lagrange, the brightness of whose eyes has long since been dimmed with tears, and whose voice had become like a harp whose every chord is turned to sadness—whose faintest thrill and loudest vibrations are but the variations of agony. A heavy hand was laid upon her once warm and bounding heart, and a voice came whispering through her soul, that she must die. But, to her, the tidings was a message of deliverance—a voice, hushing her wild sorrows to the calmness of resignation and hope. Life had grown so weary upon her head—the future looked so hopeless—she had no wish to tread again the track where thorns had pierced her feet, and clouds overcast her sky; and she hailed the coming of death's angel as the footsteps of a welcome friend. And yet, earth had one object so very dear to her weary heart. It was her absent and recreant husband; for, since that conversation, she had accepted one of her offers, and become a wife. But, before she married, she learned that great lesson of human experience and woman's life, to love the man who bowed at her shrine, a willing worshipper. He had a pleasing address, raven hair, flashing eyes, a voice of thrilling sweetness, and lips of persuasive eloquence; and being well versed in the ways of the world, he won his way to her heart, and she became his bride, and he was proud of his prize. Vain and superficial in his character, he looked upon marriage not as a divine sacrament for the soul's development and human progression, but as the title-deed that gave him possession of the woman he thought he loved. But alas for her, the laxity of his principles had rendered him unworthy of the deep and undying devotion of a pure-hearted woman; but, for awhile, he hid from her his true character, and she blindly loved him, and for a short period was happy in the consciousness of being beloved; though sometimes a vague unrest would fill her soul, when, overflowing with a sense of the good, the beautiful, and the true, she would turn to him, but find no response to the deep yearnings of her soul—no appreciation of life's highest realities—its solemn grandeur and significant importance. Their souls never met, and soon she found a void in her bosom, that his earth-born love could not fill. He did not satisfy the wants of her mental and moral nature—between him and her there was no affinity of minds, no intercommunion of souls.

Talk as you will of woman's deep capacity for loving, of the strength of her affectional nature. I do not deny it; but will the mere possession of any human love, fully satisfy all the demands of her whole being? You may paint her in poetry or fiction, as a frail vine, clinging to her brother man for support, and dying when deprived of it; and all this may sound well enough to please the imaginations of school-girls, or love-lorn maidens. But woman—the true woman—if you would render her happy, it needs more than the mere development of her affectional nature. Her conscience should be enlightened, her faith in the true and right established, scope given to her Heaven-endowed and God-given faculties. The true aim of female education should be not a development of one or two, but all the faculties of the human soul, because no perfect womanhood is developed by imperfect culture. Intense love is often akin to intense suffering, and to trust the whole wealth of a woman's nature on the frail bark of human love, may often be like trusting a cargo of gold and precious gems, to a bark that has never battled with the storm, or buffetted the waves. Is it any wonder, then, that so many life-barks go down, paving the ocean of time with precious hearts and wasted hopes? that so many float around us, shattered and dismasted wrecks? that so many are stranded on the shoals of existence, mournful beacons and solemn warnings for the thoughtless, to whom marriage is a careless and hasty rushing together of the affections? Alas that an institution so fraught with good for humanity should be so perverted, and that state of life, which should be filled with happiness, become so replete with misery. And this was the fate of Laura Lagrange. For a brief period after her marriage her life seemed like a bright and beautiful dream, full of hope and radiant with joy. And then there came a change—he found other attractions that lay beyond the pale of home influences. The gambling saloon had power to win him from her side, he had lived in an element of unhealthy and unhallowed excitements, and the society of a loving wife, the pleasures of a well-regulated home, were enjoyments too tame for one who had vitiated his tastes by the pleasures of sin. There were charmed houses of vice, built upon dead men's loves, where, amid a flow of song, laughter, wine, and careless mirth, he would spend hour after hour, forgetting the cheek that was paling through his neglect, heedless of the tear-dimmed eyes, peering anxiously into the darkness, waiting, or watching his return.

The influence of old associations was upon him. In early life, home had been to him a place of ceilings and walls, not a true home, built upon goodness, love and truth. It was a place where velvet carpets hushed its tread, where images of loveliness and beauty invoked into being by painter's art and sculptor's skill, pleased the eye and gratified the taste, where magnificence surrounded his way and costly clothing adorned his person; but it was not the place for the true culture and right development of his soul. His father had been too much engrossed in making money, and his mother in spending it, in striving to maintain a fashionable position in society, and shining in the eyes of the world, to give the proper direction to the character of their wayward and impulsive son. His mother put beautiful robes upon his body, but left ugly scars upon his soul; she pampered his appetite, but starved his spirit. Every mother should be a true artist, who knows how to weave into her child's life images of grace and beauty, the true poet capable of writing on the soul of childhood the harmony of love and truth, and teaching it how to produce the grandest of all poems—the poetry of a true and noble life. But in his home, a love for the good, the true and right, had been sacrificed at the shrine of frivolity and fashion. That parental authority which should have been preserved as a string of precious pearls, unbroken and unscattered, was simply the administration of chance. At one time obedience was enforced by authority, at another time by flattery and promises, and just as often it was not enforced at all. His early associations were formed as chance directed, and from his want of home-training, his character received a bias, his life a shade, which ran through every avenue of his existence, and darkened all his future hours. Oh, if we would trace the history of all the crimes that have o'ershadowed this sin-shrouded and sorrow-darkened world of ours, how many might be seen arising from the wrong home influences, or the weakening of the home ties. Home should always be the best school for the affections, the birthplace of high resolves, and the altar upon which lofty aspirations are kindled, from whence the soul may go forth strengthened, to act its part aright in the great drama of life, with conscience enlightened, affections cultivated, and reason and judgment dominant. But alas for the young wife. Her husband had not been blessed with such a home. When he entered the arena of life, the voices from home did not linger around his path as angels of guidance about his steps; they were not like so many messages to invite him to deeds of high and holy worth. The memory of no sainted mother arose between him and deeds of darkness; the earnest prayers of no father arrested him in his downward course: and before a year of his married life had waned, his young wife had learned to wait and mourn his frequent and uncalled-for absence. More than once had she seen him come home from his midnight haunts, the bright intelligence of his eye displaced by the drunkard's stare, and his manly gait changed to the inebriate's stagger; and she was beginning to know the bitter agony that is compressed in the mournful words, a drunkard's wife. And then there came a bright but brief episode in her experience; the angel of life gave to her existence a deeper meaning and loftier significance; she sheltered in the warm clasp of her loving arms, a dear babe, a previous child, whose love filled every chamber of her heart, and felt the fount of maternal love gushing so new within her soul. That child was hers. How overshadowing was the love with which she bent over its helplessness, how much it helped to fill the void and chasms in her soul. How many lonely hours were beguiled by its winsome ways, its answering smiles and fond caresses. How exquisite and solemn was the feeling that thrilled her heart when she clasped the tiny hands together and taught her dear child to call God "Our Father."

What a blessing was that child. The father paused in his headlong career, awed by the strange beauty and precocious intellect of his child; and the mother's life had a better expression through her ministrations of love. And then there came hours of bitter anguish, shading the sunlight of her home and hushing the music of her heart. The angel of death bent over the couch of her child and beaconed it away. Closer and closer the mother strained her child to her wildly heaving breast, and struggled with the heavy hand that lay upon its heart. Love and agony contended with death, and the language of the mother's heart was,

"Oh, Death, away! that innocent is mine.
    I cannot spare him from my arms
To lay him, Death, in thine.
    I am a mother, Death: I gave that darling birth
I could not bear his lifeless limbs
    Should moulder in the earth."

But death was stronger than love and mightier than agony and won the child for the land of crystal founts and deathless flowers, and the poor, stricken mother sat down beneath the shadow of her mighty grief, feeling as if a great light had gone out from her soul, and that the sunshine had suddenly faded around her path. She turned in her deep anguish to the father of her child, the loved and cherished dead. For awhile his words were kind and tender, his heart seemed subdued, and his tenderness fell upon her worn and weary heart like rain on perishing flowers, or cooling waters to lips all parched with thirst and scorched with fever; but the change was evanescent, the influence of unhallowed associations and evil habits had vitiated and poisoned the springs of his existence. They had bound him in their meshes, and he lacked the moral strength to break his fetters, and stand erect in all the strength and dignity of a true manhood, making life's highest excellence his ideal, and striving to gain it.

And yet moments of deep contrition would sweep over him, when he would resolve to abandon the wine-cup forever, when he was ready to forswear the handling of another card, and he would try to break away from the associations that he felt were working his ruin; but when the hour of temptation came his strength was weakness, his earnest purposes were cobwebs, his well-meant resolutions ropes of sand, and thus passed year after year of the married life of Laura Lagrange. She tried to hide her agony from the public gaze, to smile when her heart was almost breaking. But year after year her voice grew fainter and sadder, her once light and bounding step grew slower and faltering. Year after year she wrestled with agony, and strove with despair, till the quick eyes of her brother read, in the paling of her cheek and the dimming eye, the secret anguish of her worn and weary spirit. On that wan, sad face, he saw the death-tokens, and he knew the dark wing of the mystic angel swept coldly around her path. "Laura," said her brother to her one day, "you are not well, and I think you need our mother's tender care and nursing. You are daily losing strength, and if you will go I will accompany you." At first, she hesitated, she shrank almost instinctively from presenting that pale sad face to the loved ones at home. That face was such a telltale; it told of heart-sickness, of hope deferred, and the mournful story of unrequited love. But then a deep yearning for home sympathy woke within her a passionate longing for love's kind words, for tenderness and heart-support, and she resolved to seek the home of her childhood, and lay her weary head upon her mother's bosom, to be folded again in her loving arms, to lay that poor, bruised and aching heart where it might beat and throb closely to the loved ones at home. A kind welcome awaited her. All that love and tenderness could devise was done to bring the bloom to her cheek and the light to her eye; but it was all in vain; her's was a disease that no medicine could cure, no earthly balm would heal. It was a slow wasting of the vital forces, the sickness of the soul. The unkindness and neglect of her husband, lay like a leaden weight upon her heart, and slowly oozed way its life-drops. And where was he that had won her love, and then cast it aside as a useless thing, who rifled her heart of its wealth and spread bitter ashes upon its broken altars? He was lingering away from her when the death-damps were gathering on her brow, when his name was trembling on her lips! lingering away! when she was watching his coming, though the death films were gathering before her eyes, and earthly things were fading from her vision. "I think I hear him now," said the dying woman, "surely that is his step;" but the sound died away in the distance. Again she started from an uneasy slumber, "that is his voice! I am so glad he has come." Tears gathered in the eyes of the sad watchers by that dying bed, for they knew that she was deceived. He had not returned. For her sake they wished his coming. Slowly the hours waned away, and then came the sad, soul-sickening thought that she was forgotten, forgotten in the last hour of human need, forgotten when the spirit, about to be dissolved, paused for the last time on the threshold of existence, a weary watcher at the gates of death. "He has forgotten me," again she faintly murmured, and the last tears she would ever shed on earth sprung to her mournful eyes, and clasping her hands together in silent anguish, a few broken sentences issued from her pale and quivering lips. They were prayers for strength and earnest pleading for him who had desolated her young life, by turning its sunshine to shadows, its smiles to tears. "He has forgotten me," she murmured again, "but I can bear it, the bitterness of death is passed, and soon I hope to exchange the shadows of death for the brightness of eternity, the rugged paths of life for the golden streets of glory, and the care and turmoils of earth for the peace and rest of heaven." Her voice grew fainter and fainter, they saw the shadows that never deceive flit over her pale and faded face, and knew that the death angel waited to soothe their weary one to rest, to calm the throbbing of her bosom and cool the fever of her brain. And amid the silent hush of their grief the freed spirit, refined through suffering, and brought into divine harmony through the spirit of the living Christ, passed over the dark waters of death as on a bridge of light, over whose radiant arches hovering angels bent. They parted the dark locks from her marble brow, closed the waxen lids over the once bright and laughing eye, and left her to the dreamless slumber of the grave. Her cousin turned from that death-bed a sadder and wiser woman. She resolved more earnestly than over to make the world better by her example, gladder by her presence, and to kindle the fires of her genius on the altars of universal love and truth. She had a higher and better object in all her writings than the mere acquisition of gold, or acquirement of fame. She felt that she had a high and holy mission on the battle-field of existence, that life was not given her to be frittered away in nonsense, or wasted away in trifling pursuits. She would willingly espouse an unpopular cause but not an unrighteous one. In her the down-trodden slave found an earnest advocate; the flying fugitive remembered her kindness as he stopped cautiously through our Republic, to gain his freedom in a monarchial land, having broken the chains on which the rust of centuries had gathered. Little children learned to name her with affection, the poor called her blessed, as she broke her bread to the pale lips of hunger. Her life was like a beautiful story, only it was clothed with the dignity of reality and invested with the sublimity of truth. True, she was an old maid. No husband brightened her life with his love, or shaded it with his neglect. No children nestling lovingly in her arms called her mother. No one appended Mrs. to her name; she was indeed an old maid, not vainly striving to keep up an appearance of girlishness, when departed was written on her youth. Not vainly pining at her loneliness and isolation: the world was full of warm, loving hearts, and her own beat in unison with them. Neither was she always sentimentally sighing for something to love, objects of affection were all around her, and the world was not so wealthy in love that it had no use for her's; in blessing others she made a life and benediction, and as old age descended peacefully and gently upon her, she had learned one of life's most precious lessons, that true happiness consists not so much in the fruition of our wishes as in the regulation of desires and the full development and right culture of our whole statures.

Women's Political Future[1]

If before sin had cast its deepest shadows or sorrow had distilled its bitterest tears, it was true that it was not good for man to be alone, it is no less true, since the shadows have deepened and life's sorrows have increased, that the world has need of all the spiritual aid that woman can give for the social advancement and moral development of the human race. The tendency of the present age, with its restlessness, religious upheavals, failures, blunders, and crimes, is toward broader freedom, an increase of knowledge, the emancipation of thought, and a recognition of the brotherhood of man; in this movement woman, as the companion of man, must be a sharer. So close is the bond between man and woman that you can not raise one without lifting the other. The world can not move without woman's sharing in the movement, and to help give a right impetus to that movement is woman's highest privilege.

If the fifteenth century discovered America to the Old World, the nineteenth is discovering woman to herself. Little did Columbus imagine, when the New World broke upon his vision like a lovely gem in the coronet of the universe, the glorious possibilities of a land where the sun should be our engraver, the winged lightning our messenger, and steam our beast of burden. But as mind is more than matter, and the highest ideal always the true real, so to woman comes the opportunity to strive for richer and grander discoveries than ever gladdened the eye of the Genoese mariner.

Not the opportunity of discovering new worlds, but that of filling this old world with fairer and higher aims than the greed of gold and the lust of power, is hers. Through weary, wasting years men have destroyed, dashed in pieces, and overthrown, but to-day we stand on the threshold of woman's era, and woman's work is grandly constructive. In her hand are possibilities whose use or abuse must tell upon the political life of the nation, and send their influence for good or evil across the track of unborn ages.

As the saffron tints and crimson flushes of morn herald the coming day, so the social and political advancement which woman has already gained bears the promise of the rising of the full-orbed sun of emancipation. The result will be not to make home less happy, but society more holy; yet I do not think the mere extension of the ballot a panacea for all the ills of our national life. What we need to-day is not simply more voters, but better voters. To-day there are red-handed men in our republic, who walk unwhipped of justice, who richly deserve to exchange the ballot of the freeman for the wristlets of the felon; brutal and cowardly men, who torture, burn, and lynch their fellow-men, men whose defenselessness should be their best defense and their weakness an ensign of protection. More than the changing of institutions we

[1]Frances Ellen Watkins Harper, address, "Woman's Political Future," *World's Congress of Representative Women,* ed. May Wright Sewall (Chicago, 1893), pp. 433–437.

need the development of a national conscience, and the upbuilding of national character. Men may boast of the aristocracy of blood, may glory in the aristocracy of talent, and be proud of the aristocracy of wealth, but there is one aristocracy which must ever outrank them all, and that is the aristocracy of character; and it is the women of a country who help to mold its character, and to influence if not determine its destiny; and in the political future of our nation woman will not have done what she could if she does not endeavor to have our republic stand foremost among the nations of the earth, wearing sobriety as a crown and righteousness as a garment and a girdle. In coming into her political estate woman will find a mass of illiteracy to be dispelled. If knowledge is power, ignorance is also power. The power that educates wickedness may manipulate and dash against the pillars of any state when they are undermined and honeycombed by injustice.

I envy neither the heart nor the head of any legislator who has been born to an inheritance of privileges, who has behind him ages of education, dominion, civilization, and Christianity, if he stands opposed to the passage of a national education bill, whose purpose is to secure education to the children of those who were born under the shadow of institutions which made it a crime to read.

To-day women hold in their hands influence and opportunity, and with these they have already opened doors which have been closed to others. By opening doors of labor woman has become a rival claimant for at least some of the wealth monopolized by her stronger brother. In the home she is the priestess, in society the queen, in literature she is a power, in legislative halls law-makers have responded to her appeals, and for her sake have humanized and liberalized their laws. The press has felt the impress of her hand. In the pews of the church she constitutes the majority; the pulpit has welcomed her, and in the school she has the blessed privilege of teaching children and youth. To her is apparently coming the added responsibility of political power; and what she now possesses should only be the means of preparing her to use the coming power for the glory of God and the good of mankind; for power without righteousness is one of the most dangerous forces in the world.

Political life in our country has plowed in muddy channels, and needs the infusion of clearer and cleaner waters. I am not sure that women are naturally so much better than men that they will clear the stream by the virtue of their womanhood; it is not through sex but through character that the best influence of women upon the life of the nation must be exerted.

I do not believe in unrestricted and universal suffrage for either men or women. I believe in moral and educational tests. I do not believe that the most ignorant and brutal man is better prepared to add value to the strength and durability of the government than the most cultured, upright, and intelligent woman. I do not think that willful ignorance should swamp earnest intelligence at the ballot-box, nor that educated wickedness, violence, and fraud should cancel the votes of honest men. The unsteady hands of a drunkard can not cast the ballot of a freeman. The hands of lynchers are too red with blood to determine the political character of the government for even four short years. The ballot in the hands of woman means power added to influence. How well she will use that power I can not foretell. Great evils stare us in the face that need to be throttled by the combined power of an upright manhood and an enlightened womanhood; and I know that no nation can gain its full measure of enlightenment and happiness if one-half of it is free and the other half is fettered. China compressed the feet of her women and thereby retarded the steps of her men. The elements of a nation's weakness must ever be found at the hearthstone.

More than the increase of wealth, the power of armies, and the strength of fleets is the need of good homes, of good fathers, and good mothers. . . .

. . . Woman coming into her kingdom will find enthroned three great evils, for whose overthrow she should be as strong in a love of justice and humanity as the warrior is in his might. She will find intemperance sending its flood of shame, and death, and sorrow to the homes of men, a fretting leprosy in our politics, and a blighting curse in our social life; the social evil sending to our streets women whose laughter is sadder than their tears, who slide from the paths of sin and shame to the friendly shelter of the grave; and lawlessness enacting in our republic deeds over which angels might weep, if heaven knows sympathy. . . .

O women of America! into your hands God has pressed one of the sublimest opportunities that ever came into the hands of the women of any race or people. It is yours to create a healthy public sentiment; to demand justice, simple justice, as the right of every race; to brand with everlasting infamy the lawless and brutal cowardice that lynches, burns, and tortures your own countrymen.

To grapple with the evils which threaten to undermine the strength of the nation and to lay magazines of powder under the cribs of future generations is no child's play.

Let the hearts of the women of the world respond to the song of the herald angels of peace on earth and good will to men. Let them throb as one heart unified by the grand and holy purpose of uplifting the human race, and humanity will breathe freer, and the world grow brighter. With such a purpose Eden would spring up in our path, and Paradise be around our way.

FROM Iola LeRoy

Northern Experience

"Uncle Robert," said Iola, after she had been North several weeks, "I have a theory that every woman ought to know how to earn her own living. I believe that a great amount of sin and misery springs from the weakness and inefficiency of women."

"Perhaps that's so, but what are you going to do about it?"

"I am going to join the great rank of breadwinners. Mr. Waterman has advertised for a number of saleswomen, and I intend to make application."

"When he advertises for help he means white women," said Robert.

"He said nothing about color," responded Iola.

"I don't suppose he did. He doesn't expect any colored girl to apply."

"Well, I think I could fill the place. At least I should like to try. And I do not think when I apply that I am in duty bound to tell him my great-grandmother was a negro."

"Well, child, there is no necessity for you to go out to work. You are perfectly welcome here, and I hope that you feel so."

"Oh, I certainly do. But still I would rather earn my own living."

That morning Iola applied for the situation, and, being prepossessing in her appearance, she obtained it.

For awhile everything went as pleasantly as a marriage bell. But one day a young colored lady, well-dressed and well-bred in her manner, entered the store. It was an acquaintance which Iola had formed in the colored church which she attended. Iola gave her a few words of cordial greeting, and spent a few moments chatting with her. The attention of the girls who sold at the same counter was attracted, and their suspicion awakened. Iola was a stranger in that city. Who was she, and who were her people? At last it was decided that one of the girls should act as a spy, and bring what information she could concerning Iola.

The spy was successful. She found out that Iola was living in a good neighborhood, but that none of the neighbors knew her. The man of the house was very fair, but there was an old woman whom Iola called "Grandma," and she was unmistakably colored. The story was sufficient. If that were true, Iola must be colored, and she should be treated accordingly.

Without knowing the cause, Iola noticed a chill in the social atmosphere of the store, which communicated itself to the cash-boys, and they treated her so insolently that her situation became very uncomfortable. She saw the proprietor, resigned her position, and asked for and obtained a letter of recommendation to another merchant who had advertised for a saleswoman.

In applying for the place, she took the precaution to inform her employer that she was colored. It made no difference to him; but he said:—

"Don't say anything about it to the girls. They might not be willing to work with you."

Iola smiled, did not promise, and accepted the situation. She entered upon her duties, and proved quite acceptable as a saleswoman.

One day, during an interval in business, the girls began to talk of their respective churches, and the question was put to Iola:—

"Where do you go to church?"

"I go," she replied, "to Rev. River's church, corner of Eighth and L Streets."

"Oh, no; you must be mistaken. There is no church there except a colored one."

"That is where I go."

"Why do you go there?"

"Because I liked it when I came here, and joined it."

"A member of a colored church? What under heaven possessed you to do such a thing?"

"Because I wished to be with my own people."

Here the interrogator stopped, and looked surprised and pained, and almost instinctively moved a little farther from her. After the store was closed, the girls had an animated discussion, which resulted in the information being sent to Mr. Cohen that Iola was a colored girl, and that they protested against her being continued in his employ. Mr. Cohen yielded to the pressure, and informed Iola that her services were no longer needed.

When Robert came home in the evening, he found that Iola had lost her situation, and was looking somewhat discouraged.

"Well, uncle," she said, "I feel out of heart. It seems as if the prejudice pursues us through every avenue of life, and assigns us the lowest places."

"That is so," replied Robert, thoughtfully.

"And yet I am determined," said Iola, "to win for myself a place in the fields of labor. I have heard of a place in New England, and I mean to try for it, even if I only stay a few months."

"Well, if you *will* go, say nothing about your color."

"Uncle Robert, I see no necessity for proclaiming that fact on the house-top. Yet I am resolved that nothing shall tempt me to deny it. The best blood in my veins is African blood, and I am not ashamed of it."

"Hurrah for you!" exclaimed Robert, laughing heartily.

As Iola wished to try the world for herself, and so be prepared for any emergency, her uncle and grandmother were content to have her go to New England. The town to which she journeyed was only a few hours' ride from the city of P——, and Robert, knowing that there is no teacher like experience, was willing that Iola should have the benefit of her teaching.

Iola, on arriving in H——, sought the firm, and was informed that her services were needed. She found it a pleasant and lucrative position. There was only one drawback—her boarding place was too far from her work. There was an institution conducted by professed Christian women, which was for the special use of respectable young working girls. This was in such a desirable location that she called at the house to engage board.

The matron conducted her over the house, and grew so friendly in the interview that she put her arm around her, and seemed to look upon Iola as a desirable accession to the home. But, just as Iola was leaving, she said to the matron: "I must be honest with you; I am a colored woman."

Swift as light a change passed over the face of the matron. She withdrew her arm from Iola, and said: "I must see the board of managers about it."

When the board met, Iola's case was put before them, but they decided not to receive her. And these women, professors of a religion which taught, "If ye have respect to persons ye commit sin," virtually shut the door in her face because of the outcast blood in her veins.

Considerable feeling was aroused by the action of these women, who, to say the least, had not put their religion in the most favorable light.

Iola continued to work for the firm until she received letters from her mother and uncle, which informed her that her mother, having arranged her affairs in the South, was ready to come North. She then resolved to return to the city of P——, to be ready to welcome her mother on her arrival.

Iola arrived in time to see that everything was in order for her mother's reception. Her room was furnished neatly, but with those touches of beauty that womanly hands are such adepts in giving. A few charming pictures adorned the walls, and an easy chair stood waiting to receive the travel-worn mother. Robert and Iola met her at the depot; and grandma was on her feet at the first sound of the bell, opened the door, clasped Marie to her heart, and nearly fainted for joy.

"Can it be possible dat dis is my little Marie?" she exclaimed.

It did seem almost impossible to realize that this faded woman, with pale cheeks and prematurely whitened hair, was the rosy-cheeked child from whom she had been parted more than thirty years.

"Well," said Robert, after the first joyous greeting was over, "love is a very good thing, but Marie has had a long journey and needs something that will stick by the ribs. How about dinner, mother?"

"It's all ready," said Mrs. Johnson.

After Marie had gone to her room and changed her dress, she came down and partook of the delicious repast which her mother and Iola had prepared for her.

In a few days Marie was settled in the home, and was well pleased with the change. The only drawback to her happiness was the absence of her son, and she expected him to come North after the closing of his school.

"Uncle Robert," said Iola, after her mother had been with them several weeks, "I am tired of being idle."

"What's the matter now?" asked Robert. "You are surely not going East again, and leave your mother?"

"Oh, I hope not," said Marie, anxiously. "I have been so long without you."

"No, mamma, I am not going East. I can get suitable employment here in the city of P——."

"But, Iola," said Robert, "you have tried, and been defeated. Why subject yourself to the same experience again?"

"Uncle Robert, I think that every woman should have some skill or art which would insure her at least a comfortable support. I believe there would be less unhappy marriages if labor were more honored among women."

"Well, Iola," said her mother, "what is your skill?"

"Nursing. I was very young when I went into the hospital, but I succeeded so well that the doctor said I must have been a born nurse. Now, I see by the papers, that a gentleman who has an invalid daughter wants some one who can be a nurse and companion for her, and I mean to apply for the situation. I do not think, if I do my part well in that position, that the blood in my veins will be any bar to my success."

A troubled look stole over Marie's face. She sighed faintly, but made no remonstrance. And so it was decided that Iola should apply for the situation.

Iola made application, and was readily accepted. Her patient was a frail girl of fifteen summers, who was ill with a low fever. Iola nursed her carefully, and soon had the satisfaction of seeing her restored to health. During her stay, Mr. Cloten, the father of the invalid, had learned some of the particulars of Iola's Northern experience as a bread-winner, and he resolved to give her employment in his store when her services were no longer needed in the house. As soon as a vacancy occurred he gave Iola a place in his store.

The morning she entered on her work he called his employés together, and told them that

Miss Iola had colored blood in her veins, but that he was going to employ her and give her a desk. If any one objected to working with her, he or she could step to the cashier's desk and receive what was due. Not a man remonstrated, not a woman demurred; and Iola at last found a place in the great army of bread-winners, which the traditions of her blood could not affect.

"How did you succeed?" asked Mrs. Cloten of her husband, when he returned to dinner.

"Admirably! 'Everything is lovely and the goose hangs high.' I gave my employés to understand that they could leave if they did not wish to work with Miss Leroy. Not one of them left, or showed any disposition to rebel."

"I am very glad, said Mrs. Cloten. "I am ashamed of the way she has been treated in our city, when seeking to do her share in the world's work. I am glad that you were brave enough to face this cruel prejudice, and give her a situation."

"Well, my dear, do not make me a hero for a single act. I am grateful for the care Miss Leroy gave our Daisy. Money can buy services, but it cannot purchase tender, loving sympathy. I was also determined to let my employés know that I, not they, commanded my business. So, do not crown me a hero until I have won a niche in the temple of fame. In dealing with Southern prejudice against the negro, we Northerners could do it with better grace if we divested ourselves of our own. We irritate the South by our criticisms, and, while I confess that there is much that is reprehensible in their treatment of colored people, yet if our Northern civilization is higher than theirs we should 'criticise by creation.' We should stamp ourselves on the South, and not let the South stamp itself on us. When we have learned to treat men according to the complexion of their souls, and not the color of their skins, we will have given our best contribution towards the solution of the negro problem."

"I feel, my dear," said Mrs. Cloten, "that what you have done is a right step in the right direction, and I hope that other merchants will do the same. We have numbers of business men, rich enough to afford themselves the luxury of a good conscience."

Diverging Paths

On the eve of his departure from the city of P——, Dr. Gresham called on Iola, and found her alone. They talked awhile of reminiscences of the war and hospital life, when Dr. Gresham, approaching Iola, said:—

"Miss Leroy, I am glad the great object of your life is accomplished, and that you have found all your relatives. Years have passed since we parted, years in which I have vainly tried to get a trace of you and have been baffled, but I have found you at last!" Clasping her hand in his, he continued, "I would it were so that I should never lose you again! Iola, will you not grant me the privilege of holding this hand as mine all through the future of our lives? Your search for your mother is ended. She is well cared for. Are you not free at last to share with me my Northern home, free to be mine as nothing else on earth is mine." Dr. Gresham looked eagerly on Iola's face, and tried to read its varying expression. "Iola, I learned to love you in the hospital. I have tried to forget you, but it has been all in vain. Your image is just as deeply engraven on my heart as it was the day we parted."

"Doctor," she replied, sadly, but firmly, as she withdrew her hand from his, "I feel now as I felt then, that there is an insurmountable barrier between us."

"What is it, Iola?" asked Dr. Gresham, anxiously.

"It is the public opinion which assigns me a place with the colored people."

"But what right has public opinion to interfere with our marriage relations? Why should we yield to its behests?"

"Because it is stronger than we are, and we cannot run counter to it without suffering its penalties."

"And what are they, Iola? Shadows that you merely dread?"

"No! no the penalties of social ostracism North and South, except here and there some grand and noble exceptions. I do not think that you fully realize how much prejudice against colored people permeates society, lowers the tone of our religion, and reacts upon the life of the nation. After freedom came, mamma was living in the city of A——, and wanted to unite with a Christian church there. She made application for membership. She passed her examination as a candidate, and was received as a church member. When she was about to make her first communion, she unintentionally took her seat at the head of the column. The elder who was administering the communion gave her the bread in the order in which she sat, but before he gave her the wine some one touched him on the shoulder and whispered a word in his ear. He then passed mamma by, gave the cup to others, and then returned to her. From that rite connected with the holiest memories of earth, my poor mother returned humiliated and depressed."

"What a shame!" exclaimed Dr. Gresham, indignantly.

"I have seen," continued Iola, "the same spirit manifested in the North. Mamma once attempted to do missionary work in this city. One day she found an outcast colored girl, whom she wished to rescue. She took her to an asylum for fallen women and made an application for her, but was refused. Colored girls were not received there. Soon after mamma found among the colored people an outcast white girl. Mamma's sympathies, unfettered by class distinction, were aroused in her behalf, and, in company with two white ladies, she went with the girl to that same refuge. For her the door was freely opened and admittance readily granted. It was as if two women were sinking in the quicksands, and on the solid land stood other women with life-lines in their hands, seeing the deadly sands slowly creeping up around the hapless victims. To one they readily threw the lines of deliverance, but for the other there was not one strand of salvation. Some time since, to the same asylum, came a poor fallen girl who had escaped from the clutches of a wicked woman. For her the door would have been opened, had not the vile woman from whom she was escaping followed her to that place of refuge and revealed the fact that she belonged to the colored race. That fact was enough to close the door upon her, and to send her back to sin and to suffer, and perhaps to die as a wretched outcast. And yet in this city where a number of charities are advertised, I do not think there is one of them which, in appealing to the public, talks more religion than the managers of this asylum. This prejudice against the colored race environs our lives and mocks our aspirations."

"Iola, I see no use in your persisting that you are colored when your eyes are as blue and complexion as white as mine."

"Doctor, were I your wife, are there not people who would caress me as a white woman who would shrink from me in scorn if they knew I had one drop of negro blood in my veins? When mistaken for a white woman, I should hear things alleged against the race at which my blood would boil. No, Doctor, I am not willing to live under a shadow of concealment which I thoroughly hate as if the blood in my veins were an undetected crime of my soul."

"Iola, dear, surely you paint the picture too darkly."

"Doctor, I have painted it with my heart's blood. It is easier to outgrow the dishonor of crime than the disabilities of color. You have created in this country an aristocracy of color wide enough to include the South with its treason and Utah with its abominations, but too narrow to include the best and bravest colored man who bared his breast to the bullets of the enemy during your fratricidal strife. Is not the most arrant Rebel to-day more acceptable to you than the most faithful colored man?"

"No! no!" exclaimed Dr. Gresham, vehemently. "You are wrong. I belong to the Grand Army of the Republic. We have no separate State Posts for the colored people, and, were such a thing proposed, the majority of our members, I believe, would be against it. In Congress colored men have the same seats as white men, and the color line is slowly fading out in our public institutions."

"But how is it in the Church?" asked Iola.

"The Church is naturally conservative. It preserves old truths, even if it is somewhat slow in embracing new ideas. It has its social as well as its spiritual side. Society is woman's realm. The majority of church members are women, who are said to be the aristocratic element of our country. I fear that one of the last strongholds of this racial prejudice will be found beneath the shadow of some of our churches. I think, on account of this social question, that large bodies of Christian temperance women and other reformers, in trying to reach the colored people even for their own good, will be quicker to form separate associations than our National Grand Army, whose ranks are open to black and white, liberals and conservatives, saints and agnostics. But, Iola, we have drifted far away from the question. No one has a right to interfere with our marriage if we do not infringe on the rights of others."

"Doctor," she replied, gently, "I feel that our paths must diverge. My life-work is planned. I intend spending my future among the colored people of the South."

"My dear friend," he replied, anxiously," I am afraid that you are destined to sad disappointment. When the novelty wears off you will be disillusioned, and, I fear, when the time comes that you can no longer serve them they will forget your services and remember only your failings."

"But, Doctor, they need me; and I am sure when I taught among them they were very grateful for my services."

"I think," he replied, "these people are more thankful than grateful."

"I do not think so; and if I did it would not hinder me from doing all in my power to help them. I do not expect all the finest traits of character to spring from the hot-beds of slavery and caste. What matters it if they do forget the singer, so they don't forget the song? No, Doctor, I don't think that I could best serve my race by forsaking them and marrying you."

"Iola," he exclaimed, passionately, "if you love your race, as you call it, work for it, live for it, suffer for it, and, if need be, die for it; but don't marry for it. Your education has unfitted you for social life among them."

"It was," replied Iola, "through their unrequited toil that I was educated, while they were compelled to live in ignorance. I am indebted to them for the power I have to serve them. I wish other Southern women felt as I do. I think they could do so much to help the colored people at their doors if they would look at their opportunities in the light of the face of Jesus Christ. Nor am I wholly unselfish in allying myself with the colored people. All the rest of my family have done so. My dear grandmother is one of the excellent of the earth, and we all love her too much to ignore our relationship with her. I did not choose my lot in life, and the simplest thing I can do is to accept the situation and do the best I can."

"And is this your settled purpose?" he asked, sadly.

"It is, Doctor," she replied, tenderly but firmly. "I see no other. I must serve the race which needs me most."

"Perhaps you are right," he replied; "but I cannot help feeling sad that our paths, which met so pleasantly, should diverge so painfully. And yet, not only the freedmen, but the whole country, need such helpful, self-sacrificing teachers as you will prove; and if earnest prayers and holy wishes can brighten your path, your lines will fall in the pleasantest places."

As he rose to go, sympathy, love, and admiration were blended in the parting look he gave her; but he felt it was useless to attempt to divert her from her purpose. He knew that for the true reconstruction of the country something more was needed than bayonets and bullets, or the schemes of selfish politicians or plotting demagogues. He knew that the South needed the surrender of the best brain and heart of the country to build, above the wastes of war, more stately temples of thought and action.

Abolitionist Orator-Poets

GEORGE MOSES HORTON

(1797–1883)

George Moses Horton, an enslaved black man who was essentially self-taught, was born in Northampton County, North Carolina, in 1797. When George was about six years old, his master, William Horton, relocated his family and slaves to Chatham County, North Carolina. The proximity of the new farm to the University of North Carolina at Chapel Hill would provide the forge on which Horton's creative genius would be honed. After the death of his master in 1815, George became the property of William Horton's son and then grandson, first James Horton and finally Hall Horton. Despite his status as an enslaved person, the young George Horton composed verses orally long before he learned to write them down; the King James version of the Bible provided the fodder for his creative imagination.

In exchange for compensation—fifty cents a day—Hall allowed George to hire himself out at the university, where he worked as a janitor. He eventually earned enough money by composing love poems for students at either twenty-five or fifty cents per poem, depending apparently on the degree and intensity of the desired amorous effects. At a prearranged time and meeting place, students would gather around Horton to hear his compositions already paid for as well as to order new ones for the next weekend's delivery. Horton progressed from an initially skeptical student response to his poetic abilities to uniform praise for his efforts. Indeed, when he first declared that he could compose poetry, the students demanded that he create verses on the spot. He passed the imposed tests successfully enough to become a great favorite among the students.

Horton became known as the "slave poet," and that distinction earned him special privileges. It brought him to the attention of Caroline Lee Hentz, a professor's wife, author, and abolitionist from Massachusetts. She taught Horton to write and cultivated his interest in reading. The students at Chapel Hill further assisted in Horton's transformation from property to author by supplying him with volumes containing poetry popular during their school days, including works by Homer, Virgil, John Milton, James Thomason, and Edward Young. They also introduced Horton to the prose of Samuel Johnson and Plutarch. With this encouragement enhancing his own natural abilities, Horton was soon publishing poetry. His earliest efforts appeared in a newspaper, the *Lancaster Gazette,* in Hentz's hometown on April 8, 1828. His poetry also appeared in *Freedom's Journal,* the first African American newspaper, in 1828, as well as in the *Liberator* (1834) and the *Southern Literary Messenger* (1843).

The designation "slave poet" was particularly applicable to Horton's first-published and most famous collection of poems, *The Hope of Liberty* (1829), a volume of fewer than thirty pages. However, the "hope" of the book's title refers figuratively as well as literally to the plight of slaves. It was Horton's hope after publication to earn enough money to purchase his freedom and sail to Liberia. Yet, his dream of a home in Africa and of his freedom in another country, like that of another proponent of colonization, James Whitfield, never came true. However, what Horton did not reap financially, he reaped in fame. He also saw his work reprinted twice as *Poems by a Slave* (1837; 1838).

The title, *Hope of Liberty,* is somewhat deceptive. Only a few poems in Horton's volume are dedicated to themes explicitly protesting the horrors of slavery. Among them are "Slavery" and "The Slave's Complaint." His second volume of verse, *The Poetical Works of George M. Horton, the Colored Bard of North Carolina* (1845), contained ninety-six pages. The poems included in this volume, as well as most of those published in his third volume, *Naked Genius* (1865), deal with a wide range of standard poetic subjects: love, spring, nature, women, death, religion, and prominent figures in the Civil War. There is the possibility that a fourth volume, *The Museum,* and perhaps a fifth, *The Black Poet,* were also published, but no copies are extant. Horton's verse is characterized by hymnal patterns, blank verse, and heroic couplets. Excessive abstractions, the use of mythology, and a stilted diction signal styles characteristic of the era in which he wrote.

During this period, Horton kept up a letter-writing campaign to gain his freedom, addressing such notables as William Lloyd Garrison and Horace Greeley. When Sherman's army arrived in Raleigh in April of 1865, he turned his attention to more practical ways of securing his freedom. In the summer of that year, he met Captain Will H.S. Banks of the Ninth Michigan Cavalry Volunteers, who assisted Horton in publishing *Naked Genius.* Shortly after the publication of the volume, Horton accompanied Banks to Philadelphia. An ill-fated meeting to honor Horton was organized for August 31, 1866, at the Banneker Institute. Nothing came of this meeting and very little happened in Horton's poetic career after that. He died, probably in Philadelphia, in 1883.

Actual volumes of Horton's poetry are difficult to locate, although *The Hope of Liberty* was reprinted twice—in Philadelphia in 1837 as *Poems by a Slave* and with the 1838 edition of Phillis Wheatley's *Poems.* In 1997, the University of North Carolina Press will reissue all of Horton's publications in a single volume.

❖❖❖

For criticism and discussion of Horton's life and works, see Benjamin Brawley's *Early Negro American Writers* (1935), Collier and Cobb's "An American Man of Letters: George Moses Horton, the Negro Poet," *The North Carolina Review,* 3 October 1909; W. Edward Farrison's "George Moses Horton: Poet for Freedom," *CLA Journal* XIV (March 1971); Joan R. Sherman's *Invisible Poets: Afro-Americans of the Nineteenth Century* (1974); Richard Walser, *The Black Poet: The Story of George Moses Horton, A North Carolina Slave* (1967).

The Slave's Complaint

Am I sadly cast aside,
On misfortune's rugged tide?
Will the world my pains deride
Forever?

Must I dwell in Slavery's night,
And all pleasure take its flight,

Far beyond my feeble sight,
Forever?

Worst of all, must hope grow dim,
And withhold her cheering beam?
Rather let me sleep and dream
Forever!

Something still my heart surveys,
Groping through this dreary maze;
Is it Hope?—then burn and blaze
Forever!

Leave me not a wretch confined,
Altogether lame and blind—
Unto gross despair consigned,
Forever!

Heaven! in whom can I confide?
Canst thou not for all provide?
Condescend to be my guide
Forever:

And when this transient life shall end,
Oh, may some kind, eternal friend
Bid me from servitude ascend,
Forever!

On Liberty and Slavery

Alas! and am I born for this,
To wear this slavish chain?
Deprived of all created bliss,
Through hardship, toil, and pain!

How long have I in bondage lain,
And languished to be free!
Alas! and must I still complain—
Deprived of liberty.

Oh, Heaven! and is there no relief
This side the silent grave—
To soothe the pain—to quell the grief
And anguish of a slave?

Come, Liberty, thou cheerful sound,
Roll through my ravished ears,
Come, let my grief in joys be drowned,
And drive away my fears.

Say unto foul oppression, Cease:
Ye tyrants rage no more,
And let the joyful trump of peace,
Now bid the vassal soar.

Soar on the pinions of that dove
    Which long has cooed for thee,
And breathed her notes from Afric's grove,
    The sound of Liberty.

Oh, Liberty! thou golden prize,
    So often sought by blood—
We crave thy sacred sun to rise,
    The gift of nature's God!

Bid Slavery hide her haggard face,
    And barbarism fly:
I scorn to see the sad disgrace
    In which enslaved I lie.

Dear Liberty! upon thy breast,
    I languish to respire;
And like the Swan unto her nest,
    I'd to thy smiles retire.

Oh, blest asylum—heavenly balm!
    Unto thy boughs I flee—
And in thy shades the storm shall calm,
    With songs of Liberty!

On Hearing of the Intention of a Gentleman to Purchase the Poet's Freedom

When on life's ocean first I spread my sail,
I then implored a mild auspicious gale;
And from the slippery strand I took my flight,
And sought the peaceful haven of delight.

Tyrannic storms arose upon my soul,
And dreadful did their mad'ning thunders roll;
The pensive muse was shaken from her sphere,
And hope, it vanished in the clouds of fear.

At length a golden sun broke through the gloom,
And from his smiles arose a sweet perfume—
A calm ensued, and birds began to sing,
And lo! the sacred muse resumed her wing.

With frantic joy she chaunted as she flew,
And kiss'd the clement hand that bore her through;
Her envious foes did from her sight retreat,
Or prostrate fall beneath her burning feet.

'Twas like a proselyte, allied to Heaven—
Or rising spirits' boast of sins forgiven,
Whose shout dissolves the adamant away,
Whose melting voice the stubborn rocks obey.

'Twas like the salutation of the dove,
Borne on the zephyr through some lonesome grove,
When Spring returns, and Winter's chill is past,
And vegetation smiles above the blast.

'Twas like the evening of a nuptial pair,
When love pervades the hour of sad despair—
'Twas like fair Helen's sweet return to Troy,
When every Grecian bosom swell'd with joy.

The silent harp which on the osiers hung,
Was then attuned, and manumission sung;
Away by hope the clouds of fear were driven,
And music breathed my gratitude to Heaven.

Hard was the race to reach the distant goal,
The needle oft was shaken from the pole;
In such distress who could forbear to weep?
Toss'd by the headlong billows of the deep!

The tantalizing beams which shone so plain,
Which turned my former pleasures into pain—
Which falsely promised all the joys of fame,
Gave way, and to a more substantial flame.

Some philanthropic souls as from afar,
With pity strove to break the slavish bar;
To whom my floods of gratitude shall roll,
And yield with pleasure to their soft control.

And sure of Providence this work begun—
He shod my feet this rugged race to run;
And in despite of all the swelling tide,
Along the dismal path will prove my guide.

Thus on the dusky verge of deep despair,
Eternal Providence was with me there;
When pleasure seemed to fade on life's gay dawn,
And the last beam of hope was almost gone.

JAMES WHITFIELD
(1823–1871)

Technically the most skilled of the black abolitionist poets, James Whitfield voiced some of the most powerful and angry protest heard in nineteenth-century African American poetry in his volume of verse, *America and Other Poems* (1853). With force and vigor, he attacked the United States in "America," the title poem of his collection, for her blatant hypocrisy as demonstrated by her professed democratic ideals and her realities of slavery and racism. Like his contemporary, Elymas Payson Rogers, James Whitfield gave up hope of America's fair treatment of black people.

Unlike the other black abolitionist poets, however, he spent most of his life advocating black separatism as the only solution to the race problem.

Born in Exeter, New Hampshire, in 1823 to free blacks, Whitfield eventually moved to Buffalo, New York, to establish his permanent residence, after a brief stay in Boston. It was in Buffalo that he became perhaps the first black barber in American history who was a published poet. Whitfield was also a strong advocate for emigration and colonization for African Americans. In Buffalo, he published his first volume of verse, *Poems,* in 1846 and contributed poems from 1849 to 1853 to such newspapers and magazines as the *Liberator,* the *North Star,* and *Frederick Douglass's Paper.*

In 1853, he arranged with the James S. Leavitt Company in Buffalo to publish *America and Other Poems,* which he dedicated to his friend and fellow colonizationist, Martin R. Delany. This volume was so favorably received by the public that he quit barbering and took to the public platform for the abolitionist cause.

As an orator-poet, Whitfield wrote his protest verse to be read aloud. In a driving iambic pentameter metrical pattern, his poem "America," thus, begins essentially as a parody of the patriotic song of the same title:

> America, it is to thee,
> Thou boasted land of liberty,—
> It is to thee I raise my song,
> Thou land of blood, and crime, and wrong.

His anger toward America and his belief that she is incapable of redemption precede that of Amiri Baraka, Madhubuti, and other revolutionary black poets of the 1960s and 1970s. And, like these poets, he was also concerned with global oppression, which he expressed in his poem "How Long." The poem appeared in Julia Griffith's *Autographs for Freedom* in 1853.

Whitfield's bitterness and melancholy, many critics believe, stem from the influence of Byron. In particular, they point to such poems as "The Misanthropist," "Self Reliance," "Delusive Hope," and "Yes, Strike Again That Sounding String" that focus on doubt, despair, alienation, and gloom. However, as critic William H. Robinson has observed, Whitfield is "genuinely angry" and the bitterness and force of his work should not be mistaken for romantic conventions and notions. More important, his strong voice of abolitionist protest dominates his verse, including such powerful pieces as "Lines on the Death of John Quincy Adams" from *America* and "Ode for the Fourth of July," published in the *Liberator* in 1853.

Whitfield wrote fewer poems after 1854, when he became actively involved in the American Colonization Society. That year, he attended in Cleveland, Ohio, the National Emigration Convention, which was organized by Martin Delany. The purpose of the convention was to devise plans for colonizing free blacks in Central and South America and the West Indies. Frederick Douglass, who was also an associate of Whitfield's, was opposed to such efforts. A year earlier, he had written in the *North Star* that white people would consider this convention to be "a cause for rejoicing . . . and discover in this movement a division of opinion amongst us upon a vital point." Douglass's opposition had led to a lively debate on the subject between him and Whitfield. Responding to Douglass's criticism, Whitfield wrote letters that same year to the *North Star* defending the colonizationists' goals on the grounds that it was "the destiny of the Negro, to develop a higher order of civilization and Christianity than the world has yet seen" and "to possess all the tropical regions of this continent."

Further advancing his own position, Whitfield founded the quarterly newspaper *African American Repository,* which he had envisioned would serve as a procolonization propaganda instrument. The first issue of the paper was due to appear in Buffalo in July 1858. However, there is no evidence that it was ever published.

When Whitfield arrived in San Francisco three years later, he no longer advanced his separatist views. With the Civil War in full force, the issue of colonization had ceased to be of central importance to African Americans. However, Whitfield continued to be a strong advocate for the antislavery cause. Writing to the *Pacific Appeal* in August of 1862, he demanded the government to "abrogate or nullify the odious Dred Scott decision, which takes from every colored man his rights as a man and a citizen." He also expressed an antislavery message in his last two published poems: "Poem," which he read at Platt's Hall in San Francisco on January 1, 1867, in celebration of the fourth anniversary of the Emancipation Proclamation; and "Poem by J.M. Whitfield," which he read in April 1870 in Virginia City, Nevada, and which was published in the *San Francisco Elevator* on April 22, 1870.

Whitfield remained a strong believer in racial justice and black rights until he died in San Francisco on April 23, 1871, of heart disease. He was buried in the Masonic Cemetery.

❖❖❖

For selections and critical discussions of Whitfield, see Benjamin Brawley's *Early Negro American Writers* (1935) and William H. Robinson's *Early Black American Poets* (1969). Doris Lucas Laryea in "James Monroe Whitfield," *Dictionary of Literary Biography,* Vol. 50 (1986), Vernon Loggins in *The Negro Author, His Development in America to 1900* (1931), Joan R. Sherman in *Invisible Poets: Afro-Americans of the Nineteenth Century* (1974), and Eugene Redmond in *Drumvoices: The Mission of Afro-American Poetry* (1976) also discuss his life, poetry, and impact.

The largest collections of Whitfield's works—copies of *America and Other Poems* and some of his letters and speeches—are housed in the Mooreland-Spingarn Collection at Howard University, at the Library of Congress, and in the Schomburg Collection at the New York Library.

FROM *America and Other Poems. America*

America, it is to thee,
Thou boasted land of liberty,—
It is to thee I raise my song,
Thou land of blood, and crime, and wrong.
It is to thee, my native land,
From which has issued many a band
To tear the black man from his soil,
And force him here to delve and toil;
Chained on your blood-bemoistened sod,
Cringing beneath a tyrant's rod,

Stripped of those rights which Nature's God
Bequeathed to all the human race,
Bound to a petty tyrant's nod,
Because he wears a paler face.
Was it for this that freedom's fires
Were kindled by your patriot sires?
Was it for this they shed their blood,
On hill and plain, on field and flood?
Was it for this that wealth and life
Were staked upon that desperate strife,
Which drenched this land for seven long years
With blood of men, and women's tears?
When black and white fought side by side,
Upon the well-contested field,—
Turned back the fierce opposing tide,
And made the proud invader yield—
When, wounded, side by side they lay,
And heard with joy the proud hurrah
From their victorious comrades say
That they had waged successful war,
The thought ne'er entered in their brains
That they endured those toils and pains,
To forge fresh fetters, heavier chains
For their own children, in whose veins
Should flow that patriotic blood,
So freely shed on field and flood.
Oh, no; they fought, as they believed,
For the inherent rights of man;
But mark, how they have been deceived
By slavery's accursed plan.
They never thought, when thus they shed
Their heart's best blood, in freedom's cause,
That their own sons would live in dread,
Under unjust, oppressive laws:
That those who quietly enjoyed
The rights for which they fought and fell,
Could be the framers of a code,
That would disgrace the fiends of hell!
Could they have looked, with prophet's ken,
Down to the present evil time,
Seen free-born men, uncharged with crime,
Consigned unto a slaver's pen,—
Or thrust into a prison cell,
With thieves and murderers to dwell—
While that same flag whose stripes and stars
Had been their guide through freedom's wars

As proudly waved above the pen
Of dealers in the souls of men!
Or could the shades of all the dead,
  Who fell beneath that starry flag,
Visit the scenes where they once bled,
  On hill and plain, on vale and crag,
By peaceful brook, or ocean's strand,
  By inland lake, or dark green wood,
Where'er the soil of this wide land
  Was moistened by their patriot blood,—
And then survey the country o'er,
  From north to south, from east to west,
And hear the agonizing cry
Ascending up to God on high,
From western wilds to ocean's shore,
  The fervent prayer of the oppressed;
The cry of helpless infancy
  Torn from the parent's fond caress
By some base tool of tyranny,
  And doomed to woe and wretchedness;
The indignant wail of fiery youth,
  Its noble aspirations crushed,
Its generous zeal, its love of truth,
  Trampled by tyrants in the dust;
The aerial piles which fancy reared,
  And hopes too bright to be enjoyed,
Have passed and left his young heart seared,
  And all its dreams of bliss destroyed.
The shriek of virgin purity,
Doomed to some libertine's embrace,
Should rouse the strongest sympathy
  Of each one of the human race;
And weak old age, oppressed with care,
  As he reviews the scene of strife,
Puts up to God a fervent prayer,
  To close his dark and troubled life,
The cry of fathers, mothers, wives,
  Severed from all their hearts hold dear,
And doomed to spend their wretched lives
  In gloom, and doubt, and hate, and fear;
And manhood, too, with soul of fire,
And arm of strength, and smothered ire,
Stands pondering with brow of gloom,
Upon his dark unhappy doom,
Whether to plunge in battle's strife,
And buy his freedom with his life,

And with stout heart and weapon strong,
Pay back the tyrant wrong for wrong
Or wait the promised time of God,
    When his Almighty ire shall wake,
And smite the oppressor in his wrath,
And hurl red ruin in his path,
And with the terrors of his rod,
    Cause adamantine hearts to quake.
Here Christian writhes in bondage still,
    Beneath his brother Christian's rod,
And pastors trample down at will,
    The image of the living God.
While prayers go up in lofty strains,
    And pealing hymns ascend to heaven,
The captive, toiling in his chains,
    With tortured limbs and bosom riven,
Raises his fettered hand on high,
    And in the accents of despair,
To him who rules both earth and sky,
    Puts up a sad, a fervent prayer,
To free him from the awful blast
    Of slavery's bitter galling shame—
Although his portion should be cast
    With demons in eternal flame!
Almighty God! 'tis this they call
    The land of liberty and law;
Part of its sons in baser thrall
    Than Babylon or Egypt saw—
Worse scenes of rapine, lust and shame,
    Than Babylonian ever knew,
Are perpetrated in the name
    Of God, the holy, just, and true;
And darker doom than Egypt felt,
May yet repay this nation's guilt.
Almighty God! thy aid impart,
And fire anew each faltering heart,
And strengthen every patriot's hand,
Who aims to save our native land.
We do not come before thy throne,
    With carnal weapons drenched in gore,
Although our blood has freely flown,
    In adding to the tyrant's store.
Father! before thy throne we come,
    Not in the panoply of war,
With pealing trump, and rolling drum,
    And cannon booming loud and far;

Striving in blood to wash out blood,
    Through wrong to seek redress for wrong;
For while thou'rt holy, just and good,
    The battle is not to the strong;
But in the sacred name of peace,
    Of justice, virtue, love and truth,
We pray, and never mean to cease,
    Till weak old age and fiery youth
In freedom's cause their voices raise,
And burst the bonds of every slave;
Till, north and south, and east and west,
The wrongs we bear shall be redressed.

Prayer of the Oppressed

O great Jehovah! God of love,
    Thou monarch of the earth and sky,
Canst thou from thy great throne above,
    Look down with an unpitying eye?—

See Afric's sons and daughters toil,
    Day after day, year after year,
Upon this blood-bemoistened soil,
    And to their cries turn a deaf ear?

Canst thou the white oppressor bless
    With verdant hills and fruitful plains,
Regardless of the slave's distress,
    Unmindful of the black man's chains?

How long, O Lord! ere thou wilt speak
    In thy Almighty thundering voice,
To bid the oppressor's fetters break,
    And Ethiopia's sons rejoice?

How long shall Slavery's iron grip,
    And Prejudice's guilty hand,
Send forth, like bloodhounds from the slip,
    Foul persecutions o'er the land?

How long shall puny mortals dare
    To violate thy just decree,
And force their fellow-men to wear
    The galling chain on land and sea?

Hasten, O Lord! the glorious time
    When everywhere beneath the skies,
From every land and every clime,
    Paeans to Liberty shall rise!

When the bright sun of liberty
Shall shine o'er each despotic land,
And all mankind, from bondage free,
Adore the wonders of thy hand.

JAMES MADISON BELL
(1826–1902)

James Madison Bell is a relatively obscure poet who was born in Gallipolis, Ohio, in 1826. As a teenager, he moved to Cincinnati, where he learned plastering from his brother-in-law, George Knight. He attended a private school connected with Oberlin College and gained a rudimentary education. It was in Cincinnati that he met and married Louisiana Sanderlin before moving to Ontario, Canada, in 1854. His six-year stay in Canada afforded Bell the opportunity to write what would be considered his best poetry. It was also during this period in Ontario that Bell became an associate of John Brown. Bell did not go to Harpers Ferry but apparently assisted Brown in raising money and recruiting men for Brown's raid in 1859. Bell left Ontario in 1860, moving to California, where he remained until 1865 or 1866. Here he continued his skilled labor in addition to writing poetry and reading his works before primarily black audiences.

Many of Bell's poetic creations are of the occasional variety. His involvement in the A.M.E. Church and in ceremonial events in the San Francisco area provided the arenas for his poetic creations. On August 1, 1862, he delivered a poem called "A Poem" at the grand festival to commemorate the emancipation of slaves in the District of Columbia and in the British West Indies. Two years later, he published his collection of poems, *The Day and the War,* which he had composed and dedicated to John Brown; the volume chronicles the history of African Americans from slavery to freedom. On his departure from California, he penned "Valedictory on Leaving San Francisco, California," which is considered one of his best occasional poems. During his sojourn in California, Bell's poems frequently appeared in the *San Francisco Elevator* and the *Pacific Appeal.*

Bell eventually rejoined his family, whom he had left in Canada when he moved to California, and moved them to Toledo in 1866. While in California, he had become involved in politics; he was a member of the Fourth California Colored Convention held in Sacramento in October 1865. In Ohio, he renewed that interest by becoming an active Republican. In 1870, he published his volume of verse titled *The Progress of Liberty,* which is essentially Bell's praise for the efforts of black troops during the Civil War. Two years later, he was elected a delegate from Lucas County (in which Toledo is located) to the state Republican convention; he went on to the Republican National Convention as an Ohio delegate. That convention renominated Ulysses S. Grant to run for president. As late as 1888, Bell still actively combined politics and art by dedicating one of his poems to the candidacy of Benjamin Harrison, the Republican candidate.

Bell's *Poetical Works of J. M. Bell,* which included his previously published collections of verse as well as other poems, was published in 1901. Bell was reputedly a fine and dramatic reader of his own poetry, which may have enabled him to overcome the clichés and monotony of rhyme and rhythm that characterize much of his poetry on the page. Largely due to the latter and the fact that his verse was written for delivery, only a few of his poems are seriously read and discussed. "Modern Moses, or 'My Policy' Man" is a satiric portrait of President Andrew Johnson; the poem has been judged to be lively and original. Bell castigates Johnson as a modern Judas who generally sabotaged Reconstruction and specifically vetoed the Freedman's Bureau bill. By supporting southerners, Bell asserted, Johnson had "long been mortgaged to the Devil." *The Day and the War,* around 750 lines long, illustrates the fervor of Bell's convictions about the evils of slavery:

America! I thee conjure
By all that's holy, just and pure,
To cleanse thy hands from Slavery's stain,
And banish from thy soil the chain.

Other poems in the collection focus on liberty and justice by evoking the names of John Brown, William Wilberforce, and Abraham Lincoln. Racial themes are central to Bell's poetic imagination; the few deviations include poems on religious themes.

Lacking the power and anger of James Whitfield's poetry and the range and interest in subject matter of Frances Harper's verse, Bell's poems are often weighty, long, and tedious. As William H. Robinson concludes: "Not to mitigate his obvious technical flaws, it is helpful to remember that Bell is best appreciated as something of an actor, his poems regarded as scripts." Although his verse may not read as well today as it did in Bell's own time, he is generally recognized as the "Poet of Hope" for black Africans in the nineteenth century. Occasionally, he writes bitterly against racial injustices, but he mainly expresses hope concerning the outcome of the black liberation struggle. Bell's commitment to improving the freedom and rights of African Americans lends a special power to the poetry that ultimately overcomes its limitations in form.

❖❖❖

For the earliest biographical discussion of Bell, see the sketch written by Bishop B.W. Arnett in *The Poetical Works of J. M. Bell* (Lansing, Michigan 1901); for critical commentary, see William Robinson's *Early Black American Poets* (Dubuque, Iowa 1969); Eugene B. Redmond's *Drumvoices: The Mission of Afro-American Poetry* (1976); Blyden Jackson's *A History of Afro-American Literature,* Vol. I (1989); Joan R. Sherman's *Invisible Poets: Afro-Americans of the Nineteenth Century* (1974).

The Day and the War

Sacred to the Memory of the Immortal
Captain John Brown,
The Hero, Saint, and Martyr of Harper's Ferry,
The following poem is most respectfully inscribed,
by one who loved him in life, and in death
would honor his memory

Twelve score of years were long to wait
A fitting day to celebrate:

'Twere long upon one native's soil
A feeless drudge in pain to toil.
But time that fashions and destroys,
And breeds our sorrows, breeds our joys;
Hence we at length have come with cheer,
To greet the dawning of the year—
The bless'd return of that glad day,
When, through Oppression's gloom, a ray
Of joy and hope and freedom, burst,
Dispelling that insatiate thirst
Which anxious years of toil and strife
Had mingled with the bondman's life.

A fitting day for such a deed,
But far more fit when it shall lead
To the final abolition
Of the last slave's sad condition:
Then when the New Year ushers in,
A grand rejoicing shall begin;
Then shall Freedom's clarion tone
Arouse no special class alone,
But all the land its blast shall hear,
And hail with joy the jubilant year;
And maid and matron, youth and age,
Shall meet upon one common stage,
And Proclamation Day shall be
A National Day of Jubilee

No longer 'neath the weight of years—
No longer merged in hopeless fears—
Is now that good time, long delayed,
When right, not might, shall all pervade.
Drive hence despair—no longer doubt,
Since friends within and foes without
Their might and main conjointly blend
To reach the same great, glorious end—
The sweeping from this favored land
The last foul chain and slavish brand.

No longer need the bondman fear,
For lo! the good time's almost here,
And doubtless some beneath our voice
Shall live to hail it and rejoice;
For almost now the radiant sheen
Of freedom's glad hosts may be seen;
The ear can almost catch the sound,
The eye can almost see them bound,
As thirty million voices rise

In grateful paeans to the skies.

But of the present we would sing,
And of a land all bathed in blood—
A land where plumes the eagle's wing,
Whose flaming banner, stars bestud—
A land where Heaven, with bounteous hand,
Rich gifts hath strewn for mortal weal,
Till vale and plain and mountain grand
Have each a treasure to reveal:
A land with every varying clime,
From torrid heat to frigid cold—
With natural scenery more sublime
Than all the world beside unfold,
Where vine-clad France may find a peer,
And Venice an Italian sky,
With streams whereon the gondolier
His feather'd oar with joy may ply.
O heaven-blest and favored land,
Why are thy fruitful fields laid waste?
Why with thy fratricidal hand
Hast thou thy beauty half defaced?
Why do the gods disdain thy prayer?
And why in thy deep bitterness
Comes forth no heaven-clothed arm to share
A part, and help in the distress?

Hast thou gone forth to reap at noon,
And gather where thou hadst not strewn?
Hast thou kept back the hireling's fee
And mocked him in his poverty?
Hast thou, because thy God hath made
Thy brother of a different shade,
Bound fast the iron on his limb,
And made a feeless drudge of him?
Hast thou, to fill thy purse with gold,
The offsprings of his nature sold?
And in thy brutal lust, beguiled
His daughter and his couch defiled?

For all this wrong and sad abuse,
Hast thou no offering of excuse?
No plea to urge in thy defense
'Gainst helpless, outraged innocence?
Then fearful is thy doom indeed,
If guilty thou canst only plead.
Thy sin is dark, and from the law
No dint of pity canst thou draw.

If thou are charged, 'twill hear thy suit;
If guilty, swift to execute,
Eye for an eye and tooth for tooth;
Yet, Oh! forbid it, God of truth:
Let not thine arm in anger fall,
But hear a guilty nation's call;
And stay the vial of wrath at hand;
Pour not its contents on the land;
Should they the last dregs in the cup
Of bitterness be called to sup,
And all the contents of the vial
Of thy just wrath be poured the while,
With all the tortures in reserve,
'Twould scarce be more than they deserve,
For they have sinned 'gainst thee and man.
But wilt thou not, by thy own plan,
Bring them past this sea of blood,
Ere they are buried 'neath its flood?

America! I thee conjure,
By all that's holy, just and pure,
To cleanse thy hands from Slavery's stain,
And banish from thy soil the chain.
Thou canst not thrive, while with the sweat
Of unpaid toil thy hands are wet,
Nor canst thou hope for peace or joy
Till thou Oppression doth destroy.

❖❖❖

Though Tennyson, the poet king,
Has sung of Balaklava's charge,
Until his thund'ring cannons ring
From England's center to her marge,
The pleasing duty still remains
To sing a people from their chains—
To sing what none have yet assay'd,
The wonders of the Black Brigade.
The war had raged some twenty moons,
Ere they in columns or platoons,
To win them censure or applause,
Were marshal'd in the Union cause—
Prejudged of slavish cowardice,
While many a taunt and foul device
Came weekly forth with Harper's sheet,
To feed that base, infernal cheat.

But how they would themselves demean,
Has since most gloriously been seen.

'Twas seen at Milliken's dread bend,
Where e'en the Furies seemed to lend
To dark Secession all their aid,
To crush the Union Black Brigade.
The war waxed hot, and bullets flew
  Like San Francisco's summer sand,
But they were there to dare and do,
  E'en to the last, to save the land
And when the leaders of their corps
  Grew wild with fear, and quit the field,
The dark remembrance of their scars
  Before them rose, they could not yield:
And, sounding o'er the battle din,
  They heard their standard-bearer cry—
"Rally! and prove that ye are men!
  Rally! and let us do or die!
For war, nor death, shall boast a shade
  To daunt the Union Black Brigade!"

And thus he played the hero's part,
  Till on the ramparts of the foe
A score of bullets pierced his heart;
  He sank within the trench below.
His comrades saw, and fired with rage,
Each sought his man, him to engage
In single combat. Ah! 'twas then
The Black Brigade proved they were men!
For ne'er did Swiss, or Russ, or knight,
  Against such fearful odds arrayed,
With more persistent valor fight,
  Than did the Union Black Brigade!

As five to one, so stood their foes,
When that defiant shout arose,
And 'long their closing columns ran,
Commanding each to choose his man!
And ere the sound had died away,
Full many a ranting rebel lay
Gasping piteously for breath—
Struggling with the pangs of death,
From bayonet thrust or shining blade,
Plunged to the hilt by the Black Brigade.

  And thus they fought, and won a name—
None brighter on the scroll of Fame;
For out of one full corps of men,
But one remained unwounded, when
The dreadful fray had fully past—

All killed or wounded but the last!

And though they fell, as has been seen,
Each slept his lifeless foes between,
And marked the course and paved the way
To ushering in a better day.
Let Balaklava's cannons roar,
And Tennyson his hosts parade,
But ne'er was seen and never more
The equals of the Black Brigade!

❖❖❖

With one allusion, we have done
The task so joyously begun:
It is to speak, in measured lays,
Of him the Nation loves to praise.
When that inspired instrument,
The subject of this great event,
Forth from the Halls of Congress came,
With even justice as its aim,
'Twas deem'd by some a fiendish rod,
But otherwise adjudged of God,
Who, turning earthward from His throne,
Beheld great Lincoln all alone,
With earth-bent brow, in pensive mood,
Pondering o'er some unsubdued
And knotty problem, half dissolved,
And half in mystery yet involved.

The interest of a continent,
All broken up by discontent—
His own dear land, land of his love,
The fairest 'neath the realms above—
Weighed down his form and rack'd his brain,
And filled his patriot heart with pain.
But when his mind conceived the thought
To Write Four Million Captives Free!
An angel to his conscience brought
Approving smiles of Deity;
And ere he had with flesh conferr'd,
He gave the bright conception birth,
And distant nations saw and heard,
And bless'd his mission on the earth.

And we today reiterate,
With warmth of heart and depth of soul,
God bless America's Magistrate!
Long may he live to guide, control;
Long may that arching brow and high—

That spiritual and piercing eye:
That tall, majestic, manly form—
Live, our rainbow 'midst the storm;
And when the roar of battle's pass'd,
When vain Secession's breath'd his last,
When peace and order are restored,
And freedom sits at every board,
And when the Nation shall convene
In mass, as ne'er before was seen,
And render eulogistic meeds
To worthy heroes' noble deeds,
A lengthened train shall claim their boast,
But Lincoln's name shall lead the host!
His name shall grow a household word,
Where'er the human voice is heard;
And tribes and people yet unborn,
Shall hail and bless his natal morn.

Emancipation in the District of Columbia, April 16, 1862

Unfurl your banners to the breeze!
  Let Freedom's tocsin sound amain,
Until the islands of the seas
  Re-echo with the glad refrain!
Columbia's free! Columbia's free!
  Her teeming streets, her vine-clad groves,
Are sacred now to Liberty,
  And God, who every right approves.

Thank God, the Capital is free!
  The slaver's pen, the auction block,
The gory lash of cruelty,
  No more this nation's pride shall mock;
No more, within those ten miles square,
  Shall men be bought and women sold;
Nor infants, sable-haired and fair,
  Exchanged again for paltry gold.

To-day the Capital is free!
  And free those halls where Adams stood
To plead for man's humanity,
  And for a common brotherhood;
Where Sumner stood, with massive frame,
  Whose eloquent philosophy
Has clustered round his deathless name
  Bright laurels for eternity.

Where Wilson, Lovejoy, Wade, and Hale,
  And other lights of equal power,

Have stood, like warriors clad in mail,
Before the giant of the hour,—
Co-workers in a common cause,
Laboring for their country's weal,
By just enactments, righteous laws,
And burning, eloquent appeal.

To them we owe and gladly bring
The grateful tributes of our hearts;
And while we live to must and sing,
These in our songs shall claim their parts.
To-day Columbia's air doth seem
Much purer than in days agone;
And now her mighty heart, I deem,
Hath lighter grown by marching on.

Abolitionist orators

THEODORE S. WRIGHT

(1797–1847)

Though a prominent clergyman, Theodore S. Wright made his most significant contributions as an abolitionist and champion of black rights. Although writings by him are scant, he was an extraordinary race leader. With the exception of Frederick Douglass and Frances Watkins Harper, few African Americans of his generation fought harder for the freedom and equality of his people than he did. He agitated for black suffrage as early as 1838, and he petitioned the New York legislature for the suspension of property requirements for black voters in 1840. As the antislavery movement gained momentum during the 1830s and 1840s, Wright emerged as one of the most important black political, social, and religious figures in New York City.

Theodore S. Wright was born free in Providence, Rhode Island, in 1797. Like his father, R.P.G. Wright, who was an early leader in national black conventions, he dedicated himself to uplifting his people. He attended the New York African Free School and eventually enrolled (supported by Dewitt Clinton and Arthur Tappan) in Princeton Theological Seminary (1825–1828). When he graduated in 1828, he became the first African American to graduate from a theological seminary in the United States. After graduating, Wright became the pastor of the First Colored Presbyterian Church of New York City, replacing the distinguished Samuel Cornish. He served as minister until his untimely death in 1847.

Wright used his ministry as a forum from which he engaged in antislavery and Civil Rights activities. He was staunchly opposed to colonization and the colonizationists. He deeply believed that African Americans had every right to remain in the United States. Satirizing the logic of a typical advocate of colonization, Wright and Samuel Cornish coauthored "Prayer of a Colonizationist," which was published in *Early Negro Writing* 1760–1837, selected and introduced by Dorothy B. Porter (1971). He assisted in the establishment of the American Anti-Slavery Society in 1833 and became one of the four black members of the executive board. The other members were

Samuel Cornish, Peter Williams, and Christopher Rush. However, opposing the radicalism of William Lloyd Garrison, he, along with Cornish, Henry Highland Garnet, and other prominent black abolitionists, withdrew from the American Anti-Slavery Society in 1840. They formed, instead, the American and Foreign Anti-Slavery Society.

Wright was a very effective lecturer and speaker. He traveled, therefore, during the 1830s as a representative of the New England, New York, and Evangelical Union Anti-Slavery Societies. Two of his more memorable speeches, titled "The Progress of the Anti-Slavery Cause" and "Prejudice Against the Colored Man," were delivered in 1837. In them, he forcefully argues against colonization and prejudice against black Americans. In the latter address, Wright points out the racism of liberal whites in the North: "It is an easy thing to ask about the vileness of slavery in the South, but to call the dark man a brother, heartily to embrace the doctrine advanced in the second article of the constitution, to treat all men according to their moral worth, to treat the man of color in all circumstances as a man and brother—that is the test."

One of Wright's more celebrated efforts at literary expression is his "Letter to Rev. Archibald Alexander, D.D." The letter recounts for the Rev. Alexander, a former professor of Wright's at Princeton Theological Seminary, an ugly racist incident. When Wright returned as an alumnus to hear a distinguished lecturer, he was accosted and attacked by an unknown white Princetonian who kicked him, shouting "Out with the Nigger!" Wright uses this incident to illustrate two major points: the virulent nature of racial prejudice and his own profound understanding and monumental dignity in the face of it. He refused to strike back.

Wright's sober response to such a provocative incident is characteristic of his dedication to higher aims and goals. He was an active member of the New York Vigilance Committee—an organization formed in 1835 to aid fugitive slaves and to prevent the kidnapping of free Negroes. He was one of the founders of Phoenix High School—a school established by and for Negroes in 1836. In addition to his advocacy of civil rights and his antislavery efforts, he was, for a brief period, an officer of the New York Temperance Society. In 1841, he became actively involved in the Union Missionary Society, which sent missionaries to Africa. When the organization and five other groups merged into the American Missionary Association, Wright became one of its officers. During the last years of his life, he turned his attention to politics. He became a member of the nomination committee for the Liberty Party in 1844; yet, he warned blacks to be wary of affiliating themselves with political parties. Three years later, on March 25, 1847, Theodore Wright died after years of tirelessly working on behalf of black rights.

❖❖❖

Additional information on Wright's life can be found in Bella Gross's "Life and Times of Theodore S. Wright 1797–1847"; *Negro History Bulletin,* (June 1940). Charles H. Wesley's *Neglected History, Essays in Negro American History* (1965); and editor Herbert Aptheker's *A Documentary History of the Negro People in the United States* (1965–1966). Benjamin Quarles also discusses his abolitionist activities in *Black Abolitionists* (1969). Wright's speeches, "The Progress of the Anti-Slavery Cause" and "Prejudice Against the Colored Man," have been published in Dorothy B. Porter's *Early Negro Writing 1760–1837* (1971).

The Progress of the Antislavery Cause[1]

Mr. President: All who have heard the report which has been presented are satisfied it needs no eulogy. It supports itself. But, sir, I would deem it a privilege to throw out a few thoughts upon it—thoughts which arise on beholding this audience. My mind is involuntarily led back a few years to the period prior to the commencement of this great moral effort for the removal of the giant sin of oppression from our land. It is well known to every individual who is at all acquainted with the history of slavery in this land, that the convention of 1776, when the foundations of our government were laid, proclaimed to the world the inalienable rights of man; and they supposed that the great principles of liberty would work the destruction of slavery throughout this land. This remark is sustained by an examination of the document then framed, and by the fact that the term "slavery" is not even named. The opinion that slavery would be abolished—indeed, that it had already received a death-blow, was cherished by all the reformers.—This spirit actuated Woolman, Penn, Edwards, Jefferson, and Benezet, and it worked out the entire emancipation of the North.—But it is well known that about 1817 a different drift was given—a new channel was opened for the benevolence which was working so well. The principle of expatriation, like a great sponge, went around in church and state, among men of all classes, and sponged up all the benevolent feelings which were then prevalent, and which promised so much for the emancipation of the enslaved and down-trodden millions of our land. That, sir, we call the dark period.—Oh, sir! if my father who sits beside me were to rise up and tell you how he felt and how men of his age felt, and how I felt (though a boy at that time), sir, it would be seen to have been a dark period. Why, sir, the heavens gathered blackness, and there was nothing cheering in our prospects. A spirit was abroad, which said "this is not your country and home," a spirit which would take us away from our firesides, tear the freeman away from his oppressed brother.—This spirit was tearing the free father away from his children, separating husband and wife, sundering those cords of consanguinity which bind the free with the slave. This scheme was as popular as it possibly could be. The slaveholder and the pro-slavery man, the man of expanded views, the man who loved the poor and oppressed of every hue and of every clime, all united in this feeling and principle of expatriation. But, sir, there were hundreds of thousand of men in the land who never could sympathize in this feeling; I mean those who were to be removed. The people of color were broken-hearted; they knew, sir, there were physical impossibilities to their removal. They knew, sir, that nature, reason, justice and inclination forbade the idea of their removing; and hence in 1817, the people of color in Philadelphia, with James Forten at their head—(and I envy them the honor they had in the work in which they were engaged), in an assembly of three thousand, before high heaven, in the Presence of Almighty God, and in the midst of a persecuting nation, resolved that they never would leave the land. They resolved to cling to their oppressed brethren. They felt that every ennobling spirit forbade their leaving them. They resolved to remain here, come what would, persecution or death. They determined to grapple themselves to their enslaved brethren as with hooks of steel. My father, at Schenectady, under great anxiety, took a journey to Philadelphia to investigate the subject. This was the spirit which prevailed among the people of color, and it extended to every considerable place in the North and as far South as Washington and Baltimore. They lifted up their voice and said, this is my country, here I was born, here I have toiled and suffered, and here will I die. Sir, it was a dark period. Although they were unanimous, and expressed their opinions, they could not gain access to the public mind: for the press would not communicate the facts in the case—it was silent. In the

[1]Address before the Convention of the New York State Anti-Slavery Society held at Utica, September 20, 1837.

city of New York, after a large meeting, where protests were drawn up against the system of colonization, there was not a single public journal in the city, secular or religious, which would publish the views of the people of color on the subject.

Sir, despair brooded over our minds. It seemed as though everything was against us. We saw philanthropists, for instance, such men as Rev. Dr. Cox, swept away by the waves of expatriation. Other men, such as our President before us, who were engaged in schemes of benevolence in behalf of the people here, abandoning those schemes. It was a general opinion that it would do no good to elevate the people of color here. Our hearts broke. We saw that colonization never could be carried out, for the annual increase of the people of color was 70,000. We used to meet together and talk and weep and what to do we knew not. We saw indications that coercive measures would be resorted to. Immediately after the insurrection in Virginia, under Nat Turner, we saw colonization spreading all over the land; and it was popular to say the people of color must be removed. The press came out against us, and we trembled. Maryland passed laws to force out the colored people. It was deemed proper to make them go, whether they would or not. Then we despaired. Ah, Mr. President, that was a dark and gloomy period. The united views and intentions of the people of color were made known, and the nation awoke as from slumber. The *Freedom's Journal,* edited by Rev. Sam'l E. Cornish, announced the facts in the case, our entire opposition. Sir, it came like a clap of thunder! I recollect at Princeton, where I was then studying, Dr. Miller came out with his letter, disapproving of the editor's views, and all the faculty and the students gave up the paper. Benj. Lundy of Baltimore nobly lifted up his voice. But he did not feel the vileness of colonization. A young man, for making certain expositions touching slavery, was incarcerated in a dungeon, where truth took a lodgment in his heart, where he avowed eternal hatred to slavery, and where before high heaven, in the secrecy of his dungeon, with the chains upon him, he resolved to devote his life to the cause of emancipation. . . . And when the President of the American Antislavery Society stepped forward and paid the fine, we were crying for help—we were remonstrating. We had no other means but to stand up as men and protest. We declared this is our country and our home; here are the graves of our fathers. But none came to the rescue.

At that dark moment we heard a voice—it was the voice of Garrison, speaking in trumpet tones! It was like the voice of an angel of mercy! Hope, hope then cheered our path. The signs of the times began to indicate brighter days. He thundered, and next we hear of a Jocelyn of New Haven, an Arthur Tappan at his side, pleading for the rights of the Colored American. He stood up in New Haven amid commotion and persecution like a rock amid the dashing waves. Ought I not this afternoon to call upon my soul, and may I not ask you to call upon *your souls* to bless the Lord for His unspeakable goodness in bringing about the present state of things? What gratitude is called for on our part, when we contrast the state of things developed in your report with the dark period when we could number the abolitionists, when they were few and far between? Now a thousand societies exist, and there are hundreds of thousands of members. Praise God and persevere in this great work. Should we not be encouraged? We have everything to hope for, and nothing to fear. God is at the helm. The Bible is your platform—the Holy Spirit will aid you. We have everything necessary pledged, because God is with us. Hath he not said—"Break every yoke, undo the heavy burdens, and let the oppressed go free"?—"Remember them that are in bonds, as bound with them"? Why do I see so many who minister at the sacred altar—so many who have everything to lose and nothing to gain, personally, by identifying themselves with this cause? Nothing but the spirit of Almighty God brought these men here.

This cause, noble though persecuted, has a lodgment in the piety of our countrymen, and never can be expatriated. How manifest has been the progress of this cause! Why, sir, three years ago, nothing was more opprobrious than to be called an "abolitionist" or "antislavery man"!

Now you would be considered as uncharitable towards proslavery men, whether editors of newspapers, presidents of colleges or theological seminaries, if you advance the idea that they are not abolitionists or antislavery men. Three years ago, when a man professed to be an abolitionist, we knew where he was. He was an individual who recognized the identity of the human family. Now a man may call himself an abolitionist and we know not where to find him. Your tests are taken away. A rush is made into the abolition ranks. Free discussion, petition Anti-Texas, and political favor converts are multiplying. Many throw themselves in, without understanding the breadth and depth of the principles of emancipation. I fear not the annexation of Texas. I fear not all the machinations, calumny and opposition of slaveholders, when contrasted with the annexation of men whose hearts have not been deeply imbued with these high and holy principles. Why, sir, unless men come out and take their stand on the principle of recognizing man as man, I tremble for the ark, and I fear our society will become like the expatriation society; everybody an abolitionist. These points which have lain in the dark must be brought out to view. The identity of the human family, the principle of recognizing all men as brethren—that is the doctrine, that is the point which touches the quick of the community. It is an easy thing to ask about the vileness of slavery at the South, but to call the dark man a brother, heartily to embrace the doctrine advanced in the second article of the constitution, to treat all men according to their moral worth, to treat the man of color in all circumstances as a man and brother—that is the test.

Every man who comes into this society ought to be catechized. It should be ascertained whether he looks upon man as man, all of one blood and one family. A healthful atmosphere must be created, in which the slave may live when rescued from the horrors of slavery. I am sensible I am detaining you, but I feel that this is an important point. I am alarmed sometimes when I look at the constitutions of our societies. I am afraid that brethren sometimes endeavor so to form the constitutions of societies that they will be popular. I have seen constitutions of abolition societies, where nothing was said about the improvement of the man of color! They have overlooked the giant sin of prejudice. They have passed by this foul monster, which is at once the parent and offspring of slavery. Whilst you are thinking about the annexation of Texas—whilst you are discussing the great principles involved in this noble cause, remember this prejudice must be killed or slavery will never be abolished. Abolitionists must annihilate in their own bosoms the cord of caste. We must be consistent—recognize the colored man in every respect as a man and brother. In doing this we shall have to encounter scorn; we shall have to breast the storm.—This society would do well to spend a whole day in thinking about it and praying over it. Every abolitionist would do well to spend a day in fasting and prayer over it and in looking at his own heart. Far be it from me to condemn abolitionists. I rejoice and bless God for this first institution which has combined its energies for the overthrow of this heaven-daring—this soul-crushing prejudice.

The successors of Penn, Franklin and Woolman have shown themselves the friends of the colored race. They have done more in this cause than any other church and they are still doing great things both in Europe and America. I was taught in childhood to remember the man of the broad-brimmed hat and drab-colored coat and venerate him. No class have testified more to the truth on this subject. They lifted up their voices against slavery and the slave-trade. But, ah! with but here and there a noble exception, they go but halfway.—When they come to the grand doctrine, to lay the ax right down at the root of the tree, and destroy the very spirit of slavery—there they are defective. Their doctrine is to set the slave free, and let him take care of himself. Hence, we hear nothing about their being brought into the Friends' Church, or of their being viewed and treated according to their moral worth. Our hearts have recently been gladdened by an address of the Annual Meeting of the Friends' Society in the city of New York, in which they insist upon the doctrine of immediate emancipation. But that very good man who signed the document as the organ of that society within the past year, received a man of color, a Presbyterian minister, into his house, gave him his meals alone in the kitchen, and did not introduce him to his family. That shows how men can testify against slavery at the South, and not assail it at the North, where it is tangible. Here is something for abolitionists to do. What can the friends of emancipation effect while the spirit of slavery is so fearfully prevalent. Let every man take his stand, burn out this prejudice, live it down, talk it down, everywhere consider the colored man as a man, in the church, the stage, the steamboat, the public house, in all places, and the death-blow to slavery will be struck.

MARIA W. STEWART

(1803–1879)

"Many will suffer for pleading the cause of oppressed Africa and I shall glory in being one of her martyrs. . . . [God] is able to take me to himself, as he did the most noble, fearless, and undaunted David Walker." Thus wrote Maria Stewart, the black activist writer, lecturer, and educator who continued the militant legacy of David Walker in the newly organized antislavery movement. In her brief, but very productive professional career (1830 to 1834), Stewart stressed black self-determination and self-defense as well as other tenets of black cultural nationalism laid down by Walker in his *Appeal.* Infused by his uncompromising radicalism that matched her own, she went on additionally to broaden the framework of the ideology by insisting on the rights of black women and the vital moral and political leadership roles they must play in the black liberation struggle. Moreover, with her early advocacy of black and women's rights, Maria Stewart launched several important women's literary traditions. She was the first American-born woman to break the taboo against women delivering public speeches and the first American antislavery-feminist orator of African descent. Called by biographer Marilyn Richardson, "America's first black woman political writer," this remarkable woman stands as the foremother of the radical black and women's movements in the United States.

Born to free parents in Hartford, Connecticut, in 1803 and named Maria Miller, she became an orphan at the age of five. By her own account, she was then "bound out in a clergyman's family . . . but was deprived of the advantages of an education." However, the books in the family's library gave her a "thirst for knowledge," which was quenched to some extent after she left the family at the age of fifteen to work as a domestic servant. For the next five years, she attended Sabbath school classes where she studied the Bible and learned to read and write.

Sometime during her early twenties, Maria Miller moved to Boston where she met James W. Stewart, a veteran of the War of 1812 and an independent shipping agent who outfitted whaling and fishing vessels. She married him on August 10, 1826, at the Reverend Thomas Paul's African Baptist Church and, at her husband's request, added his middle initial to her name. Immediately, the couple settled in the city as members of a small, but politically active black middle class. Apparently, they became well acquainted with David Walker, who was a clothing-store proprietor and a prominent member of Boston's black community. Marilyn Richardson even suggests that James Stewart, then the only black shipping outfitter in Boston, may have helped Walker smuggle copies of his *Appeal,* which he (Walker) had planted in the pockets of black seamen sailing for southern ports. However, she also points out that if the two were in collusion, the scheme was short-lived; James Stewart died of a "severe illness" on December 17, 1829, only a few months after the publication of the first edition of the *Appeal.*

Left a widow and childless after only three years of marriage, Maria Stewart experienced the depths of emotional despair. She was also cheated of a substantial inheritance by a group of white businessmen who were the executors of James Stewart's estate. Her grief was compounded when, in 1830, the year after her husband's death, David Walker died under mysterious circumstances. In describing her life after these personal losses, Maria Stewart says that in 1830 she underwent a religious conversion, which transformed her into "a strong advocate for the cause of God and for the cause of freedom." Passionately, she intoned, "were I called upon, I would willingly sacrifice my life for the cause of God and my brethren. All the nations are crying out for liberty and equality. Away, away with tyranny and oppression."

Consequently, Maria Stewart answered, in the Fall of 1831, the call of William Lloyd Garrison and Isaac Knapp, who were recruiting black women to write for their weekly paper, the *Liberator,* the best-known antislavery newspaper in the country. She submitted to the two editors a manuscript containing several essays, including *Religion and the Pure Principles of Morality, the Sure Foundation On Which We Must Build.* Even though Garrison and Knapp disagreed with her radical antislavery views, they published her militant essay in tract form later that year. In this, the first political manifesto written by an American woman of African descent, Stewart laid down the fundamental principles of her black nationalistic ideology that she would continue to expound on in her other works. *Religion and the Pure Principles of Morality* is her special appeal to black men and women to unite, to work side by side, to raise themselves up so they can play a new role in society. With her people under siege by the white power structure, Stewart understood the importance of black women assuming leadership roles in all aspects of the black community—politics, business, education, and religion. She emphasized, therefore, the need for women to obtain a formal education and economic independence. *Religion and the Pure Principles of Morality* is, thus, the earliest written call for black women to become teachers. Stewart encourages them to pool their resources, "to raise funds for ourselves," so they "might be able to lay the cornerstone for the building of a High School, that the branches of knowledge might be enjoyed by us." Appearing in print only two months after Nat Turner's insurrection, the manifesto also supports the notion of a violent black uprising to slavery as a testament to God's retribution toward a slave-holding society. Stewart continued her program of militant black activism in another of her tracts, *Meditations from the Pen of Mrs. Maria Stewart,* which Garrison and Knapp published the following year.

Inspired by Garrison's publication of her two essays and her new personal and professional friendship with him, Stewart immediately took to the abolitionist platform in Boston. In 1832, she delivered two addresses, the first in the spring before the Afric-American Female Intelligence Society of America and the second on September 21st at Franklin Hall. The latter was the first public lecture by an American woman before an audience of both men and women. It preceded the speeches of Angelina and Sarah Grimke by five years. On February 27, 1833, Stewart commanded the podium at the African Masonic Hall and on September 12, 1833, she delivered another speech, titled *Mrs. Stewart's Farewell Address To Her Friends in the City of Boston.* Garrison published the first three of her addresses as well as an essay titled *Cause for Encouragement* (1832) and her poem, "The Negro's Complaint," in the *Liberator.*

Filled with fervent religious overtones, Stewart's impassioned speeches were characterized by a tenacious feminism expressed more than a decade before the official beginning of the women's movement at mid-century. Throughout the speeches, she exhorts black women to unite to express and further develop their full potential as women and as culture-bearers. Speaking before the Afric-American Female Intelligence Society, she charges black women with the survival and enrichment of the black community:

> O woman, woman! Upon you I call; for your exertions almost entirely depend whether the rising generation shall be any thing more than we have been or not. O woman. O woman! Your example is powerful, your influence great; it extends over your husbands and over your children, and throughout the circle of your acquaintance.

By the time she delivered her *Farewell Address,* she had expanded the historical tradition of women's activism by asserting the right of black women as well as white women to aspire to positions of authority and influence. Discouraged by both white and conservative black opposition to her speaking in public, she defends herself by vehemently exhorting,

> What if I am a woman; is not the God of ancient times the God of these modern days? Did he not raise up Deborah, to be a mother, and a judge in Israel? Did not queen Esther save the lives of the Jews? And Mary Magdalene first declare the resurrection of Christ from the dead? . . . Again; holy women ministered unto Christ and the apostles; and women of refinement in all ages, more or less, have had a voice in moral, religious and political subjects. . . . What if such women as are here described should rise among our sable race?

With her rhetorical power and polished sermonic techniques of call and response and the rhythmic cadences of her discourses, Stewart began a distinguished line of antislavery feminist speakers. These speakers included Sojourner Truth, Frances Watkins Harper, Frederick Douglass, Alexander Crummell, Mary Ann Shadd Cary, Charles and Sarah Remond, and Robert and Harriet Purvis.

With Stewart's *Farewell Address* came her last public speaking appearance. Stewart left Boston in 1833 for New York City. There, she arranged, in 1835, through her friend and publisher William Lloyd Garrison, the publication of her collected works, *Productions of Mrs. Maria Stewart.* During the late 1830s and the 1840s, Stewart continued her political activities, though on a less public scale than she had in Boston. She joined women's organizations, attended the Women's Antislavery Convention of 1837, and enhanced her reading and writing skills by participating in a black women's literacy society. Soon, Stewart embarked on a career in teaching, first in the New York public schools in the 1840s; then in the Baltimore school system in the 1850s; and, finally, in the Washington, D.C., public classrooms in the 1860s.

During the Civil War years, she befriended Elizabeth Keckley, the black seamstress and confidante to Mary Todd Lincoln and, after much difficulty, succeeded in organizing a school for black children in Washington, D.C. After Freedmen's Hospital at Howard University was founded, Stewart served in the early 1870s as its matron (head of housekeeping services) while she continued to teach school. As matron of the hospital, she succeeded Sojourner Truth, who once held that position. In 1871, Stewart opened a Sunday school for "poor and destitute children in the neighborhood of the hospital." Because the school was near Howard University, she often asked faculty members from the college to assist her.

Seven years later, while applying for a pension for widows of veterans of the War of 1812, Maria Stewart was reunited with her friend and publisher William Lloyd Garrison. Subsequently, she arranged to have published, at her own expense, a new edition of her collected works in 1879. Titled *Meditations from the Pen of Mrs. Maria W. Stewart,* this enlarged edition included supporting letters from her friends (William Lloyd Garrison and Alexander Crummell) verifying her authorship, an autobiographical essay of "her sufferings during the War," and a biographical sketch of her life written by a close friend. Shortly thereafter, she died at Freedmen's Hospital and, on December 17, 1879, she was buried at Graceland Cemetery in Washington.

Maria W. Stewart joins Frances Watkins Harper and several other nineteenth-century African American women who have been resurrected in the annals of African American history and literature, largely through the efforts of black and feminist scholars in recent years. To date, no full-length critical biographical study has been done on her. Harry A. Reed's poignant comment sums up the dilemma that Maria Stewart and other significant African American women historical and literary figures in general have faced:

> Her [Stewart's] life and her continuing obscurity illustrate the double pressures of racism and sexism on the lives of black women. Rather than being recognized as a significant advocate of Black autonomy, she has been silenced for more than four decades. Stewart's speeches and writings issue a clear challenge to our contemporary world: Black women's need for self-determination cannot be addressed if it is only an adjunct to Black men's freedom.

❖❖❖

The best source on Stewart, her writings, and her speeches is Marilyn Richardson's *Maria W. Stewart, America's First Black Woman Political Writer: Essays and Speeches* (1987). Also informative are Lisa Studier and Adrienne Lash Jones's essay "Maria W. Stewart: (1803–1879)" in Jessie Carney Smith, ed. *Notable Black American Women* (1992), and Harry A. Reed's brief, but good biographical sketch in *Black Women in America: A Historical Encyclopedia,* edited by Darlene Clark Hine II (1993). In addition, Paula Giddings in her scholarly work, *When and Where I Enter* (1984), places Stewart within the proper social context of the nineteenth-century feminist movement.

FROM *Religion and the Pure Principles of Morality, The Sure Foundation on Which We Must Build*

Introduction

Feeling a deep solemnity of soul, in view of our wretched and degraded situation, and sensible of the gross ignorance that prevails among us, I have thought proper thus publicly to express my sentiments before you. I hope my friends will not scrutinize these pages with too severe an eye, as I have not calculated to display either elegance or taste in their composition, but have merely written the meditations of my heart as far as my imagination led; and have presented them before you, in order to arouse you to exertion, and to enforce upon your minds the great necessity of turning your attention to knowledge and improvement.

I was born in Hartford, Connecticut, in 1803; was left an orphan at five years of age; was bound out in a clergyman's family; had the seeds of piety and virtue early sown in my mind; but was deprived of the advantages of education, though my soul thirsted for knowledge. Left them at 15 years of age; attended Sabbath Schools until I was 20; in 1826, was married to James W. Stewart; was left a widow in 1829; was, as I humbly hope and trust, brought to the knowledge of the truth, as it is in Jesus, in 1830; in 1831, made a public profession of my faith in Christ.

From the moment I experienced the change, I felt a strong desire, with the help and assistance of God, to devote the remainder of my days to piety and virtue, and now possess that spirit of independence, that, were I called upon, I would willingly sacrifice my life for the cause of God and my brethren.

All the nations of the earth are crying out for Liberty and Equality. Away, away with tyranny and oppression! And shall Afric's sons be silent any longer? Far be it from me to recommend to you, either to kill, burn, or destroy. But I would strongly recommend to you, to improve your talents; let not one lie buried in the earth. Show forth your powers of mind. Prove to the world, that

Though black your skins as shades of night,
Your hearts are pure, your souls are white.

This is the land of freedom. The press is at liberty. Every man has a right to express his opinion. Many think, because your skins are tinged with a sable hue, that you are an inferior race of beings; but God does not consider you as such. He hath formed and fashioned you in his own glorious image, and hath bestowed upon you reason and strong powers of intellect. He hath made you to have dominion over the beasts of the field, the fowls of the air, and the fish of the sea. He hath crowned you with glory and honor; hath made you but a little lower than the angels; and, according to the Constitution of these United States, he hath made all men free and equal. Then why should one worm say to another, "Keep you down there, while I sit up yonder; for I am better than thou?" It is not color of the skin that makes the man, but it is the principles formed within the soul.

Many will suffer for pleading the cause of oppressed Africa, and I shall glory in being one of her martyrs; for I am firmly persuaded, that the God in whom I trust is able to protect me from the rage and malice of mine enemies, and from them that will rise up against me; and if there is no other way for me to escape, he is able to take me to himself, as he did the most noble, fearless, and undaunted David Walker.

❖❖❖

Never will virtue, knowledge, and true politeness begin to flow, till the pure principles of religion and morality are put into force.

MY RESPECTED FRIENDS,

I feel almost unable to address you; almost incompetent to perform the task; and, at times, I have felt ready to exclaim, O that my head were waters, and mine eyes a fountain of tears, that I might weep day and night, for the transgressions of the daughters of my people. Truly, my heart's desire and prayer is, that Ethiopia might stretch forth her hands unto God. But we have a great work to do. Never, no, never will the chains of slavery and ignorance burst, till we become united as one, and cultivate among ourselves the pure principles of piety, morality and virtue. I am sensible of my ignorance; but such knowledge as God has given to me, I impart to you. I am sensible of former prejudices; but it is high time for prejudices and animosities to cease from among us. I am sensible of exposing myself to calumny and reproach; but shall I, for fear of feeble man who shall die, hold my peace? shall I for fear of scoffs and frowns, refrain my tongue? Ah, no! I speak as one that must give an account at the awful bar of God; I speak as a dying mortal, to dying mortals. O, ye daughters of Africa, awake! awake! arise! no longer sleep nor slumber, but distinguish yourselves. Show forth to the world that ye are endowed with noble and exalted faculties. O, ye daughters of Africa! what have ye done to immortalize your names beyond the grave? what examples have ye set before the rising generation? what foundation have ye laid for generations yet unborn? where are our union and love? and where is our sympathy, that weeps at another's woe, and hides the faults we see? And our daughters, where are they? blushing in innocence and virtue? And our sons, do they bid fair to become crowns of glory to our hoary heads? Where is the parent who is conscious of having faithfully discharged his duty, and at the last awful day of account, shall be able to say, here, Lord, is thy poor, unworthy servant, and the children thou hast given me? And where are the children that will arise, and call them blessed? Alas, O God! forgive me if I speak amiss; the minds of our tender babes are tainted as soon as they are born; they go astray, as it were, from the womb. Where is the maiden who will blush at vulgarity? and where is the youth who has written upon his manly brow a thirst for knowledge: whose ambitious mind soars above trifles, and longs for the time to come, when he shall redress the wrongs of his father, and plead the cause of his brethren? Did the daughters of our land possess a delicacy of manners, combined with gentleness and dignity; did their pure minds hold vice in abhorrence and contempt, did they frown when their ears were polluted with its vile accents, would not their influence become powerful? would not our brethren fall in love with their virtues? Their souls would become fired with a holy zeal for freedom's cause. They would become ambitious to distinguish themselves. They would become proud to display their talents. Able advocates would arise in our defence. Knowledge would begin to flow, and the chains of slavery and ignorance would melt like wax before the flames. . . .

❖❖❖

I have been taking a survey of the American people in my own mind, and I see them thriving in arts, and sciences, and in polite literature. Their highest aim is to excel in political, moral and religious improvement. They early consecrate their children to God, and their youth indeed are blushing in artless innocence; they wipe the tears from the orphan's eyes, and they cause the widow's heart to sing for joy! and their poorest ones, who have the least wish to excel, they promote! And those that have but one talent, they encourage. But how very few are there among them that bestow one thought upon the benighted sons and daughters of Africa, who have enriched the soils of America with their tears and blood: few to promote their cause, none to encourage their talents. Under these circumstances, do not let our hearts be any longer discouraged; it is no use to murmur nor to repine; but let us promote ourselves and improve our own talents. And I am rejoiced to reflect that there are many able and talented ones among us, whose names might be recorded on the bright annals of fame. But, "*I can't,*" is a great barrier in the way. I hope it will soon be removed, and "*I will,*" resume its place.

Righteousness exalteth a nation, but sin is a reproach to any people. Why is it, my friends, that our minds have been blinded by ignorance, to the present moment? 'Tis on account of sin.

Why is it that our church is involved in so much difficulty? It is on account of sin. . . .

O, ye mothers, what a responsibility rests on you! You have souls committed to your charge, and God will require a strict account of you. It is you that must create in the minds of your little girls and boys a thirst for knowledge, the love of virtue, the abhorrence of vice, and the cultivation of a pure heart. The seeds thus sown will grow with their growing years; and the love of virtue thus early formed in the soul will protect their inexperienced feet from many dangers. O, do not say, you cannot make any thing of your children; but say, with the help and assistance of God, we will try. Do not indulge them in their little stubborn ways; for a child left to himself, bringeth his mother to shame. Spare not, for their crying; thou shalt beat them with a rod, and they shall not die; and thou shalt save their souls from hell. When you correct them, do it in the fear of God, and for their own good. They will not thank you for your false and foolish indulgence; they will rise up, as it were, and curse you in this world, and, in the world to come, condemn you. It is no use to say, you can't do this, or, you can't do that; you will not tell your Maker so, when you meet him at the great day of account. And you must be careful that you set an example worthy of following, for you they will imitate. There are many instances, even among us now, where parents have discharged their duty faithfully, and their children now reflect honor upon their gray hairs.

Perhaps you will say, that many parents have set pure examples at home, and they have not followed them. True, our expectations are often blasted; but let not this dishearten you. If they have faithfully discharged their duty, even after they are dead, their works may live; their prodigal children may then return to God, and become heirs of salvation; if not, their children cannot rise and condemn them at the awful bar of God.

Perhaps you will say, that you cannot send them to high schools and academies. You can have them taught in the first rudiments of useful knowledge, and then you can have private teachers, who will instruct them in the higher branches; and their intelligence will become greater than ours, and their children will attain to higher advantages, and *their* children still higher; and then, though we are dead, our works shall live: though we are mouldering, our names shall not be forgotten. . . .

I am of a strong opinion, that the day on which we unite, heart and soul, and turn our attention to knowledge and improvement, that day the hissing and reproach among the nations of the earth against us will cease. And even those who now point at us with the finger of scorn, will aid and befriend us. It is of no use for us to sit with our hands folded, hanging our heads like bulrushes, lamenting our wretched condition; but let us make a mighty effort, and arise; and if no one will promote or respect us, let us promote and respect ourselves.

The American ladies have the honor conferred on them, that by prudence and economy in their domestic concerns, and their unwearied attention in forming the minds and manners of their children, they laid the foundation of their becoming what they now are. The good women of Wethersfield, Conn. toiled in the blazing sun, year after year, weeding onions, then sold the seed and procured money enough to erect them a house of worship; and shall we not imitate their examples, as far as they are worthy of imitation? Why cannot we do something to distinguish ourselves, and contribute some of our hard earnings that would reflect honor upon our memories, and cause our children to arise and call us blessed? Shall it any longer be said of the daughters of Africa, they have no ambition, they have no force? By no means. Let every female heart become united, and let us raise a fund ourselves; and at the end of one year and a half, we might be able to lay the corner-stone for the building of a High School, that the higher branches of knowledge might be enjoyed by us; and God would raise us up, and enough to aid us in our laudable designs. Let each one strive to excel in good housewifery, knowing that prudence and economy are the road to wealth. Let us not say, we know this, or, we know that, and practise nothing; but let us practise what we do know.

How long shall the fair daughters of Africa be compelled to bury their minds and talents beneath a load of iron pots and kettles? Until union, knowledge and love begin to flow among us. How long shall a mean set of men flatter us with their smiles, and enrich themselves with our hard earnings; their wives' fingers sparkling with rings, and they themselves laughing at our folly? Until we begin to promote and patronize each other. Shall we be a by-word among the nations any longer? Shall they laugh us to scorn forever? Do you ask, what can we do? Unite and build a store of your own, if you cannot procure a license. Fill one side with dry goods, and the other with groceries. Do you ask, where is the money? We have spent more than enough for nonsense, to do what building we should want. We have never had an opportunity of displaying our talents; therefore the world thinks we know nothing. And we have been possessed of by far too mean and cowardly a disposition, though I highly disapprove of an insolent or impertinent one. Do you ask the disposition I would have you possess? Possess the spirit of independence. The Americans do, and why should not you? Possess the spirit of men, bold and enterprising, fearless and undaunted. Sue for your rights and privileges. Know the reason that you cannot attain them. Weary them with your importunities. You can but die, if you make the attempt; and we shall certainly die if you do not. The Americans have practised nothing but head-work these 200 years, and we have done their drudgery. And is it not high time for us to imitate their examples, and practise head-work too, and keep what we have got, and get what we can? We need never to think that any body is going to feel interested for us, if we do not feel interested for ourselves. That day we, as a people, hearken unto the voice of the Lord our God, and walk in his ways and ordinances, and become distinguished for our ease, elegance and grace, combined with other virtues, that day the Lord will raise us up, and enough to aid and befriend us, and we shall begin to flourish.

Did every gentleman in America realize, as one, that they had got to become bondmen, and their wives, their sons, and their daughters, servants forever, to Great Britain, their very joints would become loosened, and tremblingly would smite one against another; their countenance would be filled with horror, every nerve and muscle would be forced into action, their souls would recoil at the very thought, their hearts would die within them, and death would be far more preferable. Then why have not Afric's sons a right to feel the same? Are not their wives, their sons, and their daughters, as dear to them as those of the white man's? Certainly, God has not deprived them of the divine influences of his Holy Spirit, which is the greatest of all blessings, if they ask him. Then why should man any longer deprive his fellow-man of equal rights and privileges? Oh, America, America, foul and indelible is thy stain! Dark and dismal is the cloud that hangs over thee, for thy cruel wrongs and injuries to the fallen sons of Africa. The blood of her murdered ones cries to heaven for vengeance against thee. Thou art almost become drunken with the blood of her slain; thou hast enriched thyself through her toils and labors; and now thou refuseth to make even a small return. And thou hast caused the daughters of Africa to commit whordoms and fornications; but upon thee be their curse.

O, ye great and mighty men of America, ye rich and powerful ones, many of you will call for the rocks and mountains to fall upon you, and to hide you from the wrath of the Lamb, and from him that sitteth upon the throne; whilst many of the sable-skinned Africans you now despise, will shine in the kingdom of heaven as the stars forever and ever. Charity begins at home, and those that provide not for their own, are worse than infidels. We know that you are raising contributions to aid the gallant Poles; we know that you have befriended

Greece and Ireland; and you have rejoiced with France, for her heroic deeds of valor. You have acknowledged all the nations of the earth, except Hayti; and you may publish, as far as the East is from the West, that you have two millions of negroes, who aspire no higher than to bow at your feet, and to court your smiles. You may kill, tyrannize, and oppress as much as you choose, until our cry shall come up before the throne of God; for I am firmly persuaded, that he will not suffer you to quell the proud, fearless and undaunted spirits of the Africans forever; for in his own time, he is able to plead our cause against you, and to pour out upon you the ten plagues of Egypt. We will not come out against you with swords and staves, as against a thief; but we will tell you that our souls are fired with the same love of liberty and independence with which your souls are fired. We will tell you that too much of your blood flows in our veins, and too much of your color in our skins, for us not to possess your spirits. We will tell you, that it is our gold that clothes you in fine linen and purple, and causes you to fare sumptuously every day; and it is the blood of our fathers, and the tears of our brethren that have enriched your soils. AND WE CLAIM OUR RIGHTS. We will tell you, that we are not afraid of them that kill the body, and after that can do no more; but we will tell you whom we do fear. We fear Him who is able, after he hath killed, to destroy both soul and body in hell forever. Then, my brethren, sheath your swords, and calm your angry passions. Stand still, and know that the Lord he is God. Vengeance is his, and he will repay. It is a long lane that has no turn. America has risen to her meridian. When you begin to thrive, she will begin to fall. God hath raised you up a Walker and a Garrison. Though Walker sleeps, yet he lives, and his name shall be had in everlasting remembrance. I, even I, who am but a child, inexperienced to many of you, am a living witness to testify unto you this day, that I have seen the wicked in great power, spreading himself like a green bay tree, and lo, he passed away; yea, I diligently sought him, but he could not be found; and it is God alone that has inspired my heart to feel for Afric's woes. Then fret not yourselves because of evil doers. Fret not yourselves because of the men who bring wicked devices to pass; for they shall be cut down as the grass, and wither as the green herb. Trust in the Lord, and do good; so shalt thou dwell in the land, and verily thou shalt be fed. Encourage the noble-hearted Garrison. Prove to the world that you are neither ourang-outangs, nor a species of mere animals, but that you possess the same powers of intellect as those of the proud-boasting American.

I am sensible, my brethren and friends, that many of you have been deprived of advantages, kept in utter ignorance, and that your minds are now darkened; and if any of you have attempted to aspire after high and noble enterprises, you have met with so much opposition that your souls have become discouraged. For this very cause, a few of us have ventured to expose our lives in your behalf, to plead your cause against the great; and it will be of no use, unless you feel for yourselves and your little ones, and exhibit the spirits of men. Oh, then, turn your attention to knowledge and improvement; for knowledge is power. And God is able to fill you with wisdom and understanding, and to dispel your fears. Arm yourselves with the weapons of prayer. Put your trust in the living God. Persevere strictly in the paths of virtue. Let nothing be lacking on your part; and, in God's own time, and his time is certainly the best, he will surely deliver you with a mighty hand and with an outstretched arm.

I have never taken one step, my friends, with a design to raise myself in your esteem, or to gain applause. But what I have done, has been done with an eye single to the glory of God, and to promote the good of souls. I have neither kindred nor friends. I stand alone in your midst, exposed to the fiery darts of the devil, and to the assaults of wicked men. But though all the powers of earth and hell were to combine against me, though all nature should sink into decay, still would I trust in the Lord, and joy in the God of my salvation. For I am fully persuaded, that he will bring me off conqueror, yea, more than conqueror, through him who hath loved me and given himself for me.

Lecture, Delivered at the Franklin Hall, Boston, September 21, 1832

Why sit ye here and die? If we say we will go to a foreign land, the famine and the pestilence are there, and there we shall die. If we sit here, we shall die. Come let us plead our cause before the whites: if they save us alive, we shall live—and if they kill us, we shall but die.

Methinks I heard a spiritual interrogation—'Who shall go forward, and take off the reproach that is cast upon the people of color? Shall it be a woman?' And my heart made this reply—'If it is thy will, be it even so, Lord Jesus!'

I have heard much respecting the horrors of slavery; but may Heaven forbid that the generality of my color throughout these United States should experience any more of its horrors than to be a servant of servants, or hewers of wood and drawers of water! Tell us no more of southern slavery; for with few exceptions, although I may be very erroneous in my opinion, yet I consider our condition but little better than that. Yet, after all, methinks there are no chains so galling as the chains of ignorance—no fetters so binding as those that bind the soul, and exclude it from the vast field of useful and scientific knowledge. O, had I received the advantages of early education, my ideas would, ere now, have expanded far and wide; but, alas! I possess nothing but moral capability—no teachings but the teachings of the Holy Spirit.

I have asked several individuals of my sex, who transact business for themselves, if providing our girls were to give them the most satisfactory references, they would not be willing to grant them an equal opportunity with others? Their reply has been—for their own part, they had no objection; but as it was not the custom, were they to take them into their employ, they would be in danger of losing the public patronage.

And such is the powerful force of prejudice. Let our girls possess what amiable qualities of soul they may; let their characters be fair and spotless as innocence itself; let their natural taste and ingenuity be what they may; it is impossible for scarce an individual of them to rise above the condition of servants. Ah! why is this cruel and unfeeling distinction? Is it merely because God has made our complexion to vary? If it be, O shame to soft, relenting humanity! "Tell it not in Gath! publish it not in the streets of Askelon!" Yet, after all, methinks were the American free people of color to turn their attention more assiduously to moral worth and intellectual improvement, this would be the result: prejudice would gradually diminish, and the whites would be compelled to say, unloose those fetters!

> Though black their skins as shades of night,
> Their hearts are pure, their souls are white.

Few white persons of either sex, who are calculated for any thing else, are willing to spend their lives and bury their talents in performing mean, servile labor. And such is the horrible idea that I entertain respecting a life of servitude, that if I conceived of there being no possibility of my rising above the condition of a servant, I would gladly hail death as a welcome messenger. O, horrible idea, indeed! to possess noble souls aspiring after high and honorable acquirements, yet confined by the chains of ignorance and poverty to lives of continual drudgery and toil. Neither do I know of any who have enriched themselves by spending their lives as house-domestics, washing windows, shaking carpets, brushing boots, or tending upon gentlemen's tables. I can but die for expressing my sentiments; and I am as willing to die by the sword as the pestilence; for I am a true born American; your blood flows in my veins, and your spirit fires my breast.

I observed a piece in the Liberator a few months since, stating that the colonizationists had published a work respecting us, asserting that we were lazy and idle. I confute them on that point. Take us generally as a people, we are neither lazy nor idle; and considering how little we have to excite or stimulate us, I am almost astonished that there are so many industrious and ambitious ones to be found; although I acknowledge, with extreme sorrow, that there are some who never were and never will be serviceable to society. And have you not a similar class among yourselves?

Again. It was asserted that we were "a ragged set, crying for liberty." I reply to it, the whites have so long and so loudly proclaimed the theme of equal rights and privileges, that our souls have caught the flame also, ragged as we are. As far as our merit deserves, we feel a common desire to rise above the condition of servants and drudges. I have learnt, by bitter experience, that continual hard labor deadens the energies of the soul, and benumbs the faculties of the mind; the ideas become confined, the mind barren, and, like the scorching sands of Arabia, produces nothing; or, like the uncultivated soil, brings forth thorns and thistles.

Again, continual hard labor irritates our tempers and sours our dispositions; the whole system becomes worn out with toil and fatigue; nature herself becomes almost exhausted, and we care but little whether we live or die. It is true, that the free people of color throughout these United States are neither bought nor sold, nor under the lash of the cruel driver; many obtain a comfortable support; but few, if any, have an opportunity of becoming rich and independent; and the employments we most pursue are as unprofitable to us as the spider's web or the floating bubbles that vanish into air. As servants, we are respected; but let us presume to aspire any higher, our employer regards us no longer. And were it not that the King eternal has declared that Ethiopia shall stretch forth her hands unto God, I should indeed despair.

I do not consider it derogatory, my friends, for persons to live out to service. There are many whose inclination leads them to aspire no higher; and I would highly commend the performance of almost any thing for an honest livelihood; but where constitutional strength is wanting, labor of this kind, in its mildest form, is painful. And doubtless many are the prayers that have ascended to Heaven from Afric's daughters for strength to perform their work. Oh, many are the tears that have been shed for the want of that strength! Most of our color have dragged out a miserable existence of servitude from the cradle to the grave. And what literary acquirements can be made, or useful knowledge derived, from either maps, books or charts, by those who continually drudge from Monday morning until Sunday noon? O, ye fairer sisters, whose hands are never soiled, whose nerves and muscles are never strained, go learn by experience! Had we had the opportunity that you have had, to improve our moral and mental faculties, what would have hindered our intellects from being as bright, and our manners from being as dignified as yours? Had it been our lot to have been nursed in the lap of affluence and ease, and to have basked beneath the smiles and sunshine of fortune, should we not have naturally supposed that we were never made to toil? And why are not our forms as delicate, and our constitutions as slender, as yours? Is not the workmanship as curious and complete? Have pity upon us, have pity upon us, O ye who have hearts to feel for other's woes; for the hand of God has touched us. Owing to the disadvantages under which we labor, there are many flowers among us that are

> "——born to bloom unseen,
> And waste their fragrance on the desert air."

My beloved brethren, as Christ has died in vain for those who will not accept of offered mercy, so will it be vain for the advocates of freedom to spend their breath in our behalf, unless with united hearts and souls you make some mighty efforts to raise your sons and daughters from the horrible state of servitude and degradation in which they are placed. It is upon you that woman depends; she can do but little besides using her influence; and it is for her sake and yours that I have come forward and made myself a hissing and a reproach among the people; for I am also one of the wretched and miserable daughters of the descendants of fallen Africa. Do you ask, why are you wretched and miserable? I reply, look at many of the most worthy and interesting of us doomed to spend our lives in gentlemen's kitchens. Look at our young men, smart, active and energetic, with souls filled with ambitious fire; if they look forward, alas! what are their prospects? They can be nothing but the humblest laborers, on account of their dark complexions; hence many of them lose their ambition, and become worthless. Look at our middle-aged men, clad in their rusty plaids and coats; in winter, every cent they earn goes to buy their wood and pay their rents; their poor wives also toil beyond their strength, to help support their families. Look at our aged sires, whose heads are whitened with the frosts of seventy winters, with their old wood-saws on their backs. Alas, what keeps us so? Prejudice, ignorance and poverty. But ah! methinks our oppression is soon to come to an end; yea, before the Majesty of heaven, our groans and cries have reached the ears of the Lord of Sabaoth. As the prayers and tears of Christians will avail the finally impenitent nothing; neither will the prayers and tears of the friends of humanity avail us any thing, unless we possess a spirit of virtuous emulation within our breasts. Did the pilgrims, when they first landed on these shores, quietly compose themselves, and say, "the Britons have all the money and all the power, and we must continue their servants forever?" Did they sluggishly sigh and say, "our lot is hard, the Indians own the soil, and we cannot cultivate it?" No; they first made powerful efforts to raise themselves, and then God raised up those illustrious patriots, WASHINGTON and LAFAYETTE, to assist and defend them. And, my brethren, have you made a powerful effort? Have you prayed the Legislature for mercy's sake to grant you all the rights and privileges of free citizens, that your daughters may rise to that degree of respectability which true merit deserves, and your sons above the servile situations which most of them fill?

An Address Delivered at the Masonic Hall in Boston on February 27, 1833

African rights and liberty is a subject that ought to fire the breast of every free man of color in these United States, and excite in his bosom a lively, deep, decided and heart-felt interest. When I cast my eyes on the long list of illustrious names that are enrolled on the bright annals of fame among the whites, I turn my eyes within, and ask my thoughts, "Where are the names of *our* illustrious ones?" It must certainly have been for the want of energy on the part of the free people of color, that they have been long willing to bear the yoke of oppression. It must have been the want of ambition and force that has given the whites occasion to say, that our natural abilities are not as good, and our capacities by nature inferior to theirs. They boldly assert, that, did we possess a natural independence of soul, and feel a love for liberty within our breasts, some one of our sable race, long before this, would have testified it, notwithstanding the disadvantages under which we labor. We have made ourselves appear altogether unqualified to speak in our own defence, and are therefore looked upon as objects of pity and commiseration. We have been imposed upon, insulted and derided on every side; and now, if we complain, it is considered as the height of impertinence. We have suffered ourselves to be considered as dastards, cowards, mean, faint-hearted wretches; and on this account, (not because of our complexion,) many despise us, and would gladly spurn us from their presence.

These things have fired my soul with a holy indignation, and compelled me thus to come forward, and endeavor to turn their attention to knowledge and improvement; for knowledge is power. I would ask, is it blindness of mind, or stupidity of soul, or the want of education, that has caused our men who are 60 or 70 years of age, never to let their voices be heard, nor their hands be raised in behalf of their color? Or has it been for the fear of offending the whites? If it has, O ye fearful ones, throw off your fearfulness, and come forth in the name of the Lord, and in the strength of the God of Justice, and make yourselves useful and active members in society; for they admire a noble and patriotic spirit in others; and should they not admire it in us? If you are men, convince them that you possess the spirit of men; and as your day, so shall your strength be. Have the sons of Africa no souls? feel they no ambitious desires? shall the chains of ignorance forever confine them? shall the insipid appellation of "clever negroes," or "good creatures," any longer content them? Where can we find among ourselves the man of science, or a philosopher, or an able statesman, or a counsellor at law? Show me our fearless and brave, our noble and gallant ones. Where are our lecturers on natural history, and our critics in useful knowledge? There may be a few such men among us, but they are rare. It is true, our fathers bled and died in the revolutionary war, and others fought bravely under the command of Jackson, in defence of liberty. But where is the man that has distinguished himself in these modern days by acting wholly in the defence of African rights and liberty? There was one, although he sleeps, his memory lives.

I am sensible that there are many highly intelligent gentlemen of color in these United States, in the force of whose arguments, doubtless, I should discover my inferiority; but if they are blest with wit and talent, friends and fortune, why have they not made themselves men of eminence, by striving to take all the reproach that is cast upon the people of color, and in endeavoring to alleviate the woes of their brethren in bondage? Talk, without effort, is nothing; you are abundantly capable, gentlemen, of making yourselves men of distinction; and this gross neglect, on your part, causes my blood to boil within me. Here is the grand cause which hinders the rise and progress of the people of color. It is their want of laudable ambition and requisite courage. . . .

I am informed that the agent of the Colonization Society has recently formed an association of young men, for the purpose of influencing those of us to go to Liberia who may feel disposed. The colonizationists are blind to their own interest, for should the nations of the earth make war with America, they would find their forces much weakened by our absence; or should we remain here, can our "brave soldiers," and "fellow-citizens," as they were termed in time of calamity, condescend to defend the rights of the whites, and be again deprived of their own, or sent to Liberia in return? Or, if the colonizationists are real friends to Africa, let them expend the money which they collect, in erecting a college to educate her injured sons in this land of gospel light and liberty; for it would be most thankfully received on our part, and convince us of the truth of their professions, and save time, expense and anxiety. Let them place before us noble objects, worthy of pursuit, and see if we prove ourselves to be those unambitious negroes they term us. But ah! methinks their hearts are so frozen towards us, they had rather their money should be sunk in the ocean than to administer it to our relief; and I fear, if they dared, like Pharaoh, king of Egypt, they would order every male child among us to be drowned. But the most high God is still as able to subdue the lofty pride of these white Americans, as He was the heart of that ancient rebel. They say, though we are looked upon as *things,* yet we sprang from a scientific people. Had our men the requisite force and energy, they would soon convince them by their efforts both in public and private, that they were men, or things in the shape of men. . . .

It is of no use for us to wait any longer for a generation of well educated men to arise. We have slumbered and slept too long already; the day is far spent; the night of death approaches; and you have sound sense and good judgment sufficient to begin with, if you feel disposed to make a right use of it. Let every man of color throughout the United States, who possesses the spirit and principles of a man, sign a petition to Congress, to abolish slavery in the District of Columbia, and grant you the rights and privileges of common free citizens; for if you had had faith as a grain of mustard seed, long before this the mountains of prejudice might have been removed. We are all sensible that the Anti-Slavery Society has taken hold of the arm of our whole population, in order to raise them out of the mire. Now all we have to do is, by a spirit of virtuous ambition to strive to raise ourselves; and I am happy to have it in my power thus publicly to say, that the colored inhabitants of this city, in some respects, are beginning to improve. Had the free people of color in these United States nobly and boldly contended for their rights, and showed a natural genius and talent, although not so brilliant as some; had they held up, encouraged and patronized each other, nothing could have hindered us from being a thriving and flourishing people. . . .

Farewell Address

Is This Vile World a Friend to Grace, To Help Me on to God?

Ah no! for it is with great tribulation that any shall enter through the gates into the holy city.

MY RESPECTED FRIENDS,

You have heard me observe that the shortness of time, the certainty of death, and the instability of all things here, induce me to turn my thoughts from earth to heaven. Borne down with a heavy load of sin and shame, my conscience filled with remorse; considering the throne of God forever guiltless, and my own eternal condemnation as just, I was at last brought to accept of salvation as a free gift, in and through the merits of a crucified Redeemer. Here I was brought to see,

" 'Tis not by works of righteousness
That our own hands have done,
But we are saved by grace alone,
Abounding through the Son."

After these convictions, in imagination I found myself sitting at the feet of Jesus, clothed in my right mind. For I before had been like a ship tossed to and fro, in a storm at sea. Then was I glad when I realized the dangers I had escaped; and then I consecrated my soul and body, and all the powers of my mind to his service, from that time, henceforth; yea, even for evermore, amen.

I found that religion was full of benevolence; I found there was joy and peace in believing, and I felt as though I was commanded to come out from the world and be separate; to go forward and be baptized. Methought I heard a spiritual interrogation, are you able to drink of that cup that I have drank of? and to be baptized with the baptism that I have been baptized with? And my heart made this reply: Yea, Lord, I am able. Yet amid these bright hopes, I was filled with apprehensive fears, lest they were false. I found that sin still lurked within; it was hard for me to renounce all for Christ, when I saw my earthly prospects blasted. O, how bitter was that cup. Yet I drank it to its very dregs. It was hard for me to say, thy will be done; yet I was made to bend and kiss the rod. I was at last made willing to be any thing or nothing, for my Redeemer's sake. Like many, I was anxious to retain the world in one hand, and religion in the other. "Ye cannot serve God and mammon," sounded in my ear, and with giant-strength, I cut off my right hand, as it were, and plucked out my right eye, and cast them from me, thinking it better to enter life halt and maimed, rather than having two hands or eyes to be cast into hell. Thus ended these mighty conflicts, and I received this heart-cheering promise, "That neither death, nor life, nor principalities, nor powers, nor things present, nor things to come, should be able to separate me from the love of Christ Jesus, our Lord."

And truly, I can say with St. Paul, that at my conversion, I came to the people in the fulness of the gospel of grace. Having spent a few months in the city of ———, previous, I saw the flourishing condition of their churches, and the progress they were making in their Sabbath Schools. I visited their Bible Classes, and heard of the union that existed in their Female Associations. On my arrival here, not finding scarce an individual who felt interested in these subjects, and but few of the whites, except Mr. Garrison, and his friend Mr. Knapp; and hearing that those gentlemen had observed that female influence was powerful, my soul became fired with a holy zeal for your cause; every nerve and muscle in me was engaged in your behalf. I felt that I had a great work to perform; and was in haste to make a profession of my faith in Christ, that I might be about my Father's business. Soon after I made this profession, the Spirit of God came before me, and I spake before many. When going home, reflecting on what I had said, I felt ashamed, and knew not where I should hide myself. A something said within my breast, "press forward, I will be with thee." And my heart made this reply, Lord, if thou wilt be with me, then will I speak for thee so long as I live. And thus far I have every reason to believe that it is the divine influence of the Holy Spirit operating upon my heart that could possibly induce me to make the feeble and unworthy efforts that I have.

But to begin my subject: "Ye have heard that it hath been said, whoso is angry with his brother without a cause, shall be in danger of the judgment; and whoso shall say to his brother, Raca, shall be in danger of the council. But whosoever shall say, thou fool, shall be in danger of hell-fire." For several years my heart was in continual sorrow. And I believe that the Almighty beheld from his holy habitation, the affliction wherewith I was afflicted, and heard the false misrepresentations wherewith I was misrepresented, and there was none to help. Then I cried unto the Lord in my troubles. And thus for wise and holy purposes, best known to himself, he has raised me in the midst of my enemies, to vindicate my wrongs before this people; and to reprove them for sin, as I have reasoned to them of righteousness and judgment to come. "For as the heavens are higher than the earth, so are his ways above our ways, and his thoughts above our thoughts." I believe, that for wise and holy purposes, best known to himself, he hath unloosed my tongue and put his word into my mouth, in order to confound and put all those to shame that have rose up against me. For he hath clothed my face with steel, and lined my forehead with brass. He hath put his testimony within me, and engraven his seal on my forhead. And with these weapons I have indeed set the fiends of earth and hell at defiance.

What if I am a woman; is not the God of ancient times the God of these modern days? Did he not raise up Deborah, to be a mother, and a judge in Israel? Did not queen Esther save the lives of the Jews? And Mary Magdalene first declare the resurrection of Christ from the dead? Come, said the woman of Samaria, and see a man that hath told me all things that ever I did, is not this the Christ? St. Paul declared that it was a shame for a woman to speak in public, yet our great High Priest and Advocate did not condemn the woman for a more notorious offence than this; neither will he condemn this worthless worm. The bruised reed he will not break, and the smoking flax he will not quench, till he send forth judgment unto victory. Did St. Paul but know of our wrongs and deprivations, I presume he would make no objections to our pleading in public for our rights. Again; holy women ministered unto Christ and the apostles; and women of refinement in all ages, more or less, have had a voice in moral, religious and political subjects. Again; why the Almighty hath imparted unto me the power of speaking thus, I cannot tell. "And Jesus lifted up his voice and said, I thank thee, O Father, Lord of heaven and earth, that thou hast hid these things from the wise and prudent, and hast revealed them unto babes: even so, Father, for so it seemed good in thy sight."

But to convince you of the high opinion that was formed of the capacity and ability of woman, by the ancients, I would refer you to "Sketches of the Fair Sex." Read to the 51st page, and you will find that several of the Northern nations imagined that women could look into futurity, and that they had about them, an inconceivable something, approaching to divinity. Perhaps that idea was only the effect of the sagacity common to the sex, and the advantages which their natural address gave them over rough and simple warriors. Perhaps, also, those barbarians, surprised at the influence which beauty has over force, were led to ascribe to the supernatural attraction, a charm which they could not comprehend. A belief, however, that the Deity more readily communicates himself to women, has at one time or other, prevailed in every quarter of the earth; not only among the Germans and the Britons, but all the people of Scandinavia were possessed of it. Among the Greeks, women delivered the Oracles; the respect the Romans paid to the Sybils, is well known. The Jews had their prophetesses. The prediction of the Egyptian women obtained much credit at Rome, even under the Emperors. And in the most barbarous nations, all things that have the appearance of being supernatural, the mysteries of religion, the secrets of physic, and the rites of magic, were in the possession of women.

If such women as are here described have once existed, be no longer astonished then, my brethren and friends, that God at this eventful period should raise up your own females to strive, by their example both in public and private, to assist those who are endeavoring to stop the strong current of prejudice that flows so profusely against us at present. No longer ridicule their efforts, it will be counted for sin. For God makes use of feeble means sometimes, to bring about his most exalted purposes.

In the 15th century, the general spirit of this period is worthy of observation. We might then have seen women preaching and mixing themselves in controversies. Women occupying the chairs of Philosophy and Justice; women harangueing in Latin before the Pope; women writing in Greek, and studying in Hebrew; Nuns were Poetesses, and women of quality Divines; and young girls who had studied Eloquence, would with the sweetest countenances, and the most plaintive voices, pathetically exhort the Pope and the Christian Princes, to declare war against the Turks. Women in those days devoted their leisure hours to contemplation and study. The religious spirit which has animated women in all ages, showed itself at this time. It has made them, by turns, martyrs, apostles, warriors, and concluded in making them divines and scholars.

Why cannot a religious spirit animate us now? Why cannot we become divines and scholars? Although learning is somewhat requisite, yet recollect that those great apostles, Peter and James, were ignorant and unlearned. They were taken from the fishing boat, and made fishers of men.

In the 13th century, a young lady of Bologne, devoted herself to the study of the Latin language, and of the Laws. At the age of twenty-three she pronounced a funeral oration in Latin, in the great church of Bologne. And to be admitted as an orator, she had neither need of indulgence on account of her youth or of her sex. At the age of twenty-six, she took the degree of Doctor of Laws, and began publicly to expound the Institutions of Justinian. At the age of thirty, her great reputation raised her to a chair, where she taught the law to a prodigious concourse of scholars from all nations. She joined the charms and accomplishments of a woman to all the knowledge of a man. And such was the power of her eloquence, that her beauty was only admired when her tongue was silent.

What if such women as are here described should rise among our sable race? And it is not impossible. For it is not the color of the skin that makes the man or the woman, but the principle formed in the soul. Brilliant wit will shine, come from whence it will; and genius and talent will not hide the brightness of its lustre.

But, to return to my subject; the mighty work of reformation has begun among this people. The dark clouds of ignorance are dispersing. The light of science is bursting forth. Knowledge is beginning to flow, nor will its moral influence be extinguished till its refulgent rays have spread over us from East to West, and from North to South. Thus far is this mighty work begun, but not as yet accomplished. Christians must awake from their slumbers. Religion must flourish among them before the church will be built up in its purity, or immorality be suppressed.

Yet, notwithstanding your prospects are thus fair and bright, I am about to leave you, perhaps, never more to return. For I find it is no use for me as an individual to try to make myself useful among my color in this city. It was contempt for my moral and religious opinions in private that drove me thus before a public. Had experience more plainly shown me that it was the nature of man to crush his fellow, I should not have thought it so hard. Wherefore, my respected friends, let us no longer talk of prejudice, till prejudice becomes extinct at home. Let us no longer talk of opposition, till we cease to oppose our own. For while these evils exist, to talk is like giving breath to the air, and labor to the wind. Though wealth is far more highly prized than humble merit, yet none of these things move me. Having God for my friend and portion, what have I to fear? Promotion cometh neither from the East or West, and as long as it is the will of God, I rejoice that I am as I am; for man in his best estate, is altogether vanity. Men of eminence have mostly risen from obscurity; nor will I, although a female of a darker hue, and far more obscure than they, bend my head or hang my harp upon willows; for though poor, I will virtuous prove. And if it is the will of my heavenly Father to reduce me to penury and want, I am ready to say, amen, even so be it. "The foxes have holes, and the birds of the air have nests, but the Son of man hath not where to lay his head."

During the short period of my Christian warfare, I have indeed had to contend against the fiery darts of the devil. And was it not that the righteous are kept by the mighty power of God through faith unto salvation, long before this I should have proved to be like the seed by the way-side. For it has actually appeared to me at different periods, as though the powers of earth and hell had combined against me, to prove my overthrow. Yet amidst their dire attempts, I have found the Almighty to be "a friend that sticketh closer than a brother." He never will forsake the soul that leans on him; though he chastens and corrects, it is for the soul's best interest. "And as a Father pitieth his children, so the Lord pitieth them that fear him."

But some of you have said, "do not talk so much about religion, the people do not wish to hear you. We know these things, tell us something we do not know." If you know these things, my dear friends, and have performed them, far happier, and more prosperous would you now have been. "He that knoweth his Lord's will and obeyeth it not, shall be beaten with many stripes." Sensible of this, I have, regardless of the frowns and scoffs of a guilty world, plead up religion, and the pure principles of morality among you. Religion is the most glorious theme that mortals can converse upon. The older it grows the more new beauties it displays. Earth, with its brilliant attractions, appears mean and sordid when compared to it. It is that fountain that has no end, and those that drink thereof shall never thirst; for it is, indeed, a well of water springing up in the soul unto everlasting life.

Again, those ideas of greatness which are held forth to us, are vain delusions, are airy visions which we shall never realize. All that man can say or do can never elevate us, it is a work that must be effected between God and ourselves. And, how? by dropping all political discussions in our behalf, for these, in my opinion, sow the seed of discord, and strengthen the cord of prejudice. A spirit of animosity is already risen, and unless it is quenched, a fire will burst forth and devour us, and our young will be slain by the sword. It is the sovereign will of God that our condition should be thus and so. "For he hath formed one vessel for honor, and another for dishonor." And shall the clay say to him that formed it, why hast thou formed me thus? It is high time for us to drop political discussions, and when our day of deliverance comes, God will provide a way for us to escape, and fight his own battles.

Finally, my brethren, let us follow after godliness, and the things which make for peace. Cultivate your own minds and morals; real merit will elevate you. Pure religion will burst your fetters. Turn your attention to industry. Strive to please your employers. Lay up what you earn. And remember, that in the grave distinction withers, and the high and low are alike renowned.

But I draw to a conclusion. Long will the kind sympathy of some much loved friend, be written on the tablet of my memory, especially those kind individuals who have stood by me like pitying angels, and befriended me when in the midst of difficulty; many blessings rest on them. Gratitude is all the tribute I can offer. A rich reward awaits them.

To my unconverted friends, one and all, I would say, shortly this frail tenement of mine will be dissolved and lie mouldering in ruins. O, solemn thought! Yet why should I revolt, for it is the glorious hope of a blessed immortality, beyond the grave, that has supported me thus far through this vale of tears. Who among you will strive to meet me at the right hand of Christ. For the great day of retribution is fast approaching, and who shall be able to abide his coming? You are forming characters for eternity. As you live so you will die; as death leaves you, so judgment will find you. Then shall we receive the glorious welcome, "Come, ye blessed of my Father, inherit the kingdom prepared for you from before the foundation of the world." Or, hear the heart-rending sentence, "Depart ye cursed into everlasting fire prepared for the devil and his angels." When thrice ten thousand years have rolled away, eternity will be but just begun. Your ideas will but just begin to expand. O, eternity, who can unfathom thine end, or comprehend thy beginning.

Dearly beloved: I have made myself contemptible in the eyes of many, that I might win some. But it has been like labor in vain. "Paul may plant, and Apollos water, but God alone giveth the increase."

To my brethren and sisters in the church, I would say, be ye clothed with the breast-plate of righteousness, having your loins girt about with truth, prepared to meet the Bridegroom at his coming; for blessed are those servants that are found watching.

Farewell. In a few short years from now, we shall meet in those upper regions where parting will be no more. There we shall sing and shout, and shout and sing, and make heaven's high arches ring. There we shall range in rich pastures, and partake of those living streams that never dry. O, blissful thought! Hatred and contention shall cease, and we shall join with redeemed millions in ascribing glory and honor, and riches, and power and blessing to the Lamb that was slain, and to Him that sitteth upon the throne. Nor eye hath seen, nor ear heard, neither hath it entered into the heart of man to conceive of the joys that are prepared for them that love God. Thus far has my life been almost a life of complete disappointment. God has tried me as by fire. Well was I aware that if I contended boldly for his cause, I must suffer. Yet, I chose rather to suffer affliction with his people, than to enjoy the pleasures of sin for a season. And I believe that the glorious declaration was about to be made applicable to me, that was made to God's ancient covenant people by the prophet, Comfort ye, comfort ye, my people: say unto her that her warfare is accomplished, and that her iniquities are pardoned. I believe that a rich reward awaits me, if not in this world, in the world to come. O, blessed reflection. The bitterness of my soul has departed from those who endeavored to discourage and hinder me in my Christian progress; and I can now forgive my enemies, bless those who have hated me, and cheerfully pray for those who have despitefully used and persecuted me.

Fare you well, farewell.

SARAH PARKER REMOND
(1826–1894)

When Sarah Parker Remond stepped before an English audience of 2,000 people to "appeal on behalf of four millions of men, women and children who are chattels in the Southern States of America," she became one of the rare, if not the first, freeborn American female abolitionist orators of African descent that the British had ever seen. Though neither a woman enslaved nor the mistress of a plantation owner, Remond closely identified specifically with her black sisters in chains when she spoke to many antislavery gatherings in England, Scotland, and Ireland in 1858 and 1859. It was her special brand of black womanhood—her sensitivity, gentility, sophistication, yet strong and firmly centered feminist consciousness—that enabled her to make a unique contribution to the American abolitionist cause abroad. Described by the British press as "a lady every inch," Sarah Remond formed a bond of sisterhood with the white Englishwomen and the black women in bondage that she represented wherever she spoke. Such strong moral alliances as this helped to solidify British support for the American antislavery cause. "Educated by Sarah Remond and her male counterparts," Ruth Bogin avers, "the laborers and middle class grew strongly Northern in their sympathies when secession polarized the issue and Lincoln heralded an end to slavery." As a prominent member of the American black abolitionist force in Europe, she helped to influence international public opinion and, ultimately, the outcome of the Civil War.

Sarah Parker Remond, a close family friend once noted, "was dedicated from birth to the cause of freedom." Born one of eight children of John and Nancy Remond on June 6, 1826, in Salem, Massachusetts, she grew up in a family of well-known activists in the antislavery movement. Sarah's father, who owned and headed the family's prosperous catering and hairdressing business, was a life member of the Massachusetts Anti-Slavery Society and her mother and sisters were members of the Salem Female Anti-Slavery Society. Her older brother, Charles, went on to distinguish himself as the first black lecturer for the Massachusetts Anti-Slavery Society and as one of the best-known abolitionist orators in the United States and in England. With so many abolitionists in the family, the Remonds' home became a regular gathering place for such leaders in the crusade for freedom as William Lloyd Garrison, William Wells Brown, and Wendell Phillips.

Sarah Remond's discussions with visiting abolitionists in the family home as well as newspapers and books she borrowed from friends or purchased from antislavery societies supplemented the limited education she received in the primary schools in Salem. It was in the city's school system that Remond first experienced racism. Although she passed the examination for Salem's high school in 1835, she was denied admission because she was black. Outraged by the school board's decision, John and Nancy Remond moved the family to Newport, Rhode Island, where Sarah and her sisters attended a private school for black youth. When the family returned to Salem six years later, Sarah Remond continued her education by reading widely and by regularly attending antislavery lectures. She joined her mother and sisters as members of the Salem Female Anti-Slavery Society.

Her second encounter with racism occurred in 1853 when she was denied a seat, for which she had purchased a ticket, in the segregated balcony of the Howard

Athenaeum in Boston. After a policeman physically forced her from the theater and caused her to fall down the stairs, Remond received much public attention when she sued and won her case for five hundred dollars in damages. As a result of her lawsuit, all Boston theaters changed their policy of segregated seating.

Her determination to fight against racism intensified in 1856 when she made a decision that shaped her adulthood. Rather than work in the family business as did her sisters, Remond decided to become a full-time lecturer for the American Anti-Slavery Society. At the age of thirty, she accompanied her brother, Charles, and other dignitaries of the Society on a lecturing tour of New York State. The group included Garrison, Phillips, Susan B. Anthony, and Stephen Foster and his wife, Abby Kelly. When and wherever Sarah Remond spoke, Garrison reported in the *Liberator,* she "commanded the respect and secured the attention of her auditors" with her "calm and dignified manner, her winning appearance, and her earnest appeals to the conscience and heart." Her successful lecturing tour led to other speaking appearances. A staunch feminist as well as a Garrisonian abolitionist, Remond also appeared on the platform in 1858 at the National Women's Rights Convention in New York City.

Later that year, she sailed for the British Isles to solicit the aid of the English people for the American antislavery movement. Under the sponsorship of the Ladies and Young Men's Anti-Slavery societies, Remond delivered more than forty-five addresses in England, Scotland, and Ireland over a period of two years. As a "colored lady" on the lecture platform, she drew large, enthusiastic crowds with her "eloquent and thrilling" speeches wherever she went. According to Remond herself, the high point of her tour came in 1859 when she addressed a ladies meeting in Warrington, England. After underscoring "the sufferings and indignities . . . perpetuated on her sisters in America," she received a watch inscribed "Presented to S.P. Remond by Englishwomen, her sisters." Deeply moved by this acknowledgment, she wrote to one of her friends back in the United States, "I have been received here as a sister by white women."

Remond's warm reception in England inspired her to press on with her abolitionist agenda in Dublin, the last part of her tour. There she urged her Irish audience to help change the minds of many of their relatives in the United States who had joined the proslavery forces. As reported in the April 1859 issue of the London newspaper, *The Antislavery Advocate,* when Remond addressed the Dublin Ladies' Society, she charged that too many Irish emigrants who knew "persecution" once in Europe "filled with aspirations of human freedom," are "holding property in their fellow men." Making an impassioned plea to Dublin women, Remond urged them to take "part in this great work" to free "the female slave . . . the most deplorably and helplessly wretched of human sufferers."

Late in 1859, she returned to London where she met with fellow abolitionists William and Ellen Craft, a couple who had fled American slavery. Together, they organized the London Emancipation Committee. That year, Remond also began her study at Bedford College for Ladies, which would eventually become absorbed into the University of London. There she studied English literature, French, Latin, history, music, and rhetoric for two years.

During the Civil War, Sarah Remond knew that Lincoln and the Union needed British diplomatic support. Hence, she delivered in 1862 an important address, *The Negro in the United States of America,* before an influential London audience, the International Congress of Charities, Correction, and Philanthropy. Eloquently she pleaded, "Let no diplomacy of statesmen, no intimidation of slaveholders, no scarcity of cotton, no fear of slave insurrections, prevent the people of Great Britain from maintaining their position as the friend of the oppressed negro." With this speech and her work in various abolitionist societies, Remond helped to sway British public opinion to support the Union blockade of the Confederacy. Between 1863 and 1865, she lectured on behalf of the freedmen and women and served as an active member of the London Emancipation Society and the Freedmen's Aid Association in London. These organizations raised funds for the newly freed slaves. Historian Dorothy Porter Wesley has, in recent years, discovered Remond's pamphlet, *The Negroes and Anglo-Africans as Freedmen and Soldiers* (1864), that Remond published in London while serving on the executive committee of the Society.

After the Civil War, Remond returned to the United States for two years. In 1866, she toured with her brother, Charles, and Frederick Douglass lecturing for the American Equal Rights Association (AERA) on behalf of suffrage for women and blacks. The following year, Remond returned to England, where she attended an affair celebrating the accomplishments of her friend, William Lloyd Garrison. A lecture titled *The Freedman or the Emancipated Negro of the Southern United States* that she gave in London was published in a local newspaper, *The Freedman,* that year.

While living in England, Remond often traveled to Rome and Florence. Eventually, she decided to make Italy her permanent home. In 1868, she enrolled in medical school at the Santa Maria Nouva Hospital in Florence and received her diploma certifying her to practice medicine three years later. This she did for more than twenty years in Florence. On April 25, 1877, she married an Italian, Lazzaro Pinto, who was a native of Sardina; and, in 1884, her friend and fellow abolitionist, Frederick Douglass, visited her in Rome. It was there that she died on December 13, 1894.

During her lifetime, Sarah Parker Remond had answered the historical call of her predecessor Maria Stewart for "women of refinement" to have "a voice in moral, religious and political subjects." As a member of the small black middle-class community in Salem, she could have easily lived a life of leisure. Instead, with compassion and dedication, she also responded to Stewart's call "for pleading the cause of oppressed Africa" from the lecture platform. With composure and dignity, she moved audiences from both sides of the Atlantic Ocean with her antislavery message. And, with gestures few and fitting, she touched the lives of thousands of women with her steadfast feminism. It is for these qualities and for her effective antislavery campaigns abroad that Sarah Parker Remond will be remembered in the annals of African American history and literature.

❖❖❖

Dorothy Porter Wesley, the leading authority on Remond, unearthed her address, *The Negro in the United States of America,* and reprinted it in the *Journal of Negro History* 27 (April 1942). See also Dorothy Porter's "Sarah Remond, Abolitionist and Physician," *Journal of Negro History* 20 (July 1935) and her updated biographical sketch on Remond in *Dictionary of American Negro Biography,* edited by Rayford W. Logan and Michael R. Winston (1982). Ruth Bogin has also done scholarly work on Remond. See her excellent article, "Sarah Parker Remond: Black Abolitionist from Salem," *Essex Institute Historical Collection C* (April 1974), which is reprinted in *Black Women in American History from Colonial Times Through the Nineteenth Century,* Vol. I, edited by Darlene Clark Hine (1990). Good introductions on Remond and her speeches can also be found in the following works: Bert James Loewenberg and Ruth Bogin's *Black Women in Nineteenth Century American Life* (1976), Dorothy Sterling's *We Are Your Sisters: Black Women in the Nineteenth Century* (1984), and Jean McMahon Humez's "Sarah Parker Remond" in *Notable Black American Women* (1992), edited by Jessie Carney Smith.

The Negroes in the United States of America[1]

Amid the din of civil war, and the various and antagonistic interests arising from the internal dissensions now going on in the United States of North America, the negroes and their descendants, whether enslaved or free, desire and need the moral support of Great Britain, in this most important but hopeful hour of their history. They, of all others, have the most at stake; not only material prosperity, but "life, liberty, and the pursuit of happiness." Almost simultaneously with the landing of the Pilgrim Fathers in 1620, a slave-ship, a Dutch vessel, with twenty negroes stolen from Africa, entered Chesapeake Bay, and sailed on to Jamestown. Here the twenty negroes were landed, and chattel slavery established in the New World; a sad, sad hour for the African race. These twenty human souls were landed most opportunely. The infant colony was then in a perilous condition; many of the colonists had died from exposure and hardships; many others from incompetency to grapple with their fate. Those who survived had become almost disheartened, when the arrival of the negroes gave new vitality to the enfeebled colony at Virginia, and revived the sinking colonists. The negroes were received as a farmer receives a useful and profitable animal; although, at that time, their services were invaluable. In return for their services, they and their posterity have been doomed to a life of slavery. Then took root chattel slavery, which has produced such physical, mental, and moral degradation upon an unprotected and unoffending race. It has always been exceedingly difficult to ascertain the exact number of slaves in the Southern states; the usual estimate is about four and a half millions. These human chattels are but property in the estimation of slaveholders, and receive by public opinion, established custom, and law, only the protection which is generally given to animals. From the son of a southern slaveholder, Mr. H.R. Helper of North Carolina, we have the number of slaves in the Southern states:—

Alabama	342,844
Arkansas	47,100
Delaware	2,290
Florida	39,310
Georgia	381,622
Kentucky	210,981
Tennessee	239,459
Texas	58,161
Carried up . . .	1,321,767
Brought up . . .	1,321,767
Louisiana	244,809
Maryland	90,368
Mississippi	309,878
Missouri	87,422
N. Carolina	288,548
S. Carolina	384,984

[1]An address delivered by Sarah P. Remond in London in 1862 before the International Congress of Charities, Correction and Philanthropy. Reprinted from the *Congrès Internationale de Bienfaisance de Londres. Session de 1862.* Tome 2. (Londrès, Bureau de L'Association National pour le Progrès des Sciences Sociales, 1863).

Virginia	472,528
Total	3,200,304
Free Coloured Population, South	228,138
Free Coloured Population, North	196,116
	424,254

These human chattels, the property of three hundred and forty-seven thousand slave-owners, constitute the basis of the working class of the entire south; in fact, they are the bone and sinew of all that makes the south prosperous, the producers of a large proportion of the material wealth, and of some of the most important articles of consumption produced by any working class in the world. The New Orleans *Delta* gives the following:—"The cotton plantations in the south are about eighty thousand, and the aggregate value of their annual product, at the present prices of cotton (before the civil war), is fully one hundred and twenty-five millions of dollars. There are over fifteen thousand tobacco plantations, and their annual products may be valued at fourteen millions of dollars. There are two thousand six hundred sugar plantations, the products of which average annually more than twelve millions of dollars." Add to this the domestic labour of the slaves as household servants, &c., and you have some conception of the material wealth produced by the men and women termed chattels. The bulk of this money goes to the support of the slaveholders and their families; therefore the dependence of slaveholders upon their chattels is complete. Slave labour was first applied to the cultivation of tobacco, and afterwards to that of rice; but rice is produced only in a very limited locality; cotton is the great staple and source of prosperity and wealth, the nucleus around which gathers immense interests. Thousands among the commercial, manufacturing, and working classes on both sides of the Atlantic, are dependent upon cotton for all material prosperity; but the slaves who have produced two-thirds of the cotton do not own themselves; their nominal wives and their children may at any moment be sold. I call them nominal *wives,* because there is no such thing as legal marriage permitted either by custom or law. The free operatives of Britain are, in reality, brought into almost personal relations with slaves during their daily toil. They manufacture the material which the slaves have produced, and although three thousand miles of ocean roll between the producer and the manufacturer and the operatives, they should call to mind the fact, that the cause of all the present internal struggle, now going on between the northern states and the south, the civil war and its attendant evils, have resulted from the attempt to perpetuate negro slavery. In a country like England, where the manufacturer pays in wages alone £11,000,000, and the return from the cotton trade is about £80,000,000 annually—where four millions of the population are almost directly interested—where starvation threatens thousands—it is well that the only remedy which can produce desirable and lasting prosperity should receive the moral support of every class—*emancipation.*

Let no diplomacy of statesmen, no intimidation of slaveholders, no scarcity of cotton, no fear of slave insurrections, prevent the people of Great Britain from maintaining their position as the friend of the oppressed negro, which they deservedly occupied previous to the disastrous civil war. The negro, and the nominally free coloured men and women, north and south, of the States, in every hour of their adversity, have ever relied upon the hope that the moral support of Britain would always be with the oppressed. The friends of the negro should recognize the fact, that the process of degradation upon this deeply injured race has been slow and constant, but effective. The real capacities of the negro race have never been thoroughly tested; and until they are placed in a position to be influenced by the civilizing influences which surround freemen, it is really unjust to apply to them the same test, or to expect them to attain the same standard of excellence, as if a fair opportunity had been given to develop their faculties. With all the demoralizing influences by which they are surrounded, they still retain far more of that which is humanizing than their masters. No such acts of cruelty have ever emanated from the victims of slavery in the Southern states as have been again and again practised by their masters.

Voices of Social Protest in Prose

The Confessional Narrative

NAT TURNER

(1800–1831)

Nat Turner directed the most deadly rebellion by black slaves in American history. Consequently, he was executed for the resistance. He was a skilled carpenter and exhorter who thought himself the agent of a punitive God, and he sought, through armed force, retribution as well as liberation for African Americans. His martyrdom came to represent the pervasive irony of Jeffersonian democracy as inherited from 1795 until the present. His armed revolt of 1831 helped complete the polarization of North and South, of industry and agriculture, as well as of free and slave states that would climax in the Civil War of 1861–1865. Nat Turner succeeded as a revolutionary by redirecting the issue of race in the United States from a polite debate about property to one about moral conscience. Indirectly, he insisted that the Union to survive him would eventually have to face the specter of slavery hidden within the national consciousness. Though many southerners saw him as a murdering demon, Turner saw racial servitude in the United States as an evil spirit that consumed the nineteenth-century South. He thought that the conflict of slavery was a holy war, and his battle was not formulated as if slaveholders existed at peace with slaves. In religious terms, Turner was a prophet and visionary, but in political terms he was a ruthless agitator. In privileging human rights over expedient laws, he looked to a higher authority than civil law. He proved that the legacy of African American spirituality would outlast Confederate power.

Nathaniel ("the gift of God") Turner was born in 1800 on the plantation of Benjamin Turner in Southampton County, Virginia, during the same year that Gabriel Prosser became a foremost freedom fighter for slaves. The slaveholder Thomas Jefferson was running for the presidency of the United States. Nat's ability to tell stories about times before he was born bolstered his claims to divine truth. From grandparents and parents, he learned to value the power of religious vision, and most predicted that he would become a prophet. Nearly everyone, even whites, suspected that he was too intelligent to be a contented slave. At least three significant influences helped shape him into a rebel: the first was the escape to the North of his father from the Turner plantation; the second was the destabilization in his young life that resulted from the loan in 1809 of his slave services, by Benjamin Turner, to Samuel, the eldest son; and the third was when Benjamin died from typhoid in 1810 and his wife Elizabeth followed soon after, and Nat, Nancy, and Old Briget became the legal property of Master Samuel.

In 1812, the boy ended his play with white youths and went to work in the cotton fields. When, by 1821, Nat realized that he was not really going to be freed as had often been suggested, he began to exhort the Turner slaves in the cabins as well as the fields. If he had been emancipated, perhaps the course of his life—and even that of American history—would have been somewhat different. By 1821, he had begun to speculate that God had spoken to him as to Ezekiel in the Old Testament. Although Nat probably ran away in 1821, after a flogging by an overseer, he was, nevertheless, available to the widowed Elizabeth Turner as listed property at her death in 1822. Nat, and his wife, Cherry, and their children Drew, Violet, Amy, Jenny, Cary, Andrew, and Pete Turner, ranked with 150 hogs, 17 cows, and 11 sheep. Nat was priced at four hundred dollars, and Cherry was marketed for forty. Both of them were allowed to remain in Southampton County rather than become part of a slave gang sold to Georgia. Nat was sold to Thomas Moore and Cherry to Giles Reese, who rented a farm across the swamps from that of the Moores. Hence, Cherry, who had two sons and a daughter by Nat, lived separate from him. With the purchase of additional slaves by 1826, Samuel Turner joined the genteel ranks of privileged planters so as to require the continued slaving of Nat throughout the week, except for Sundays. His status as slave preacher helped secure Nat considerable freedom of travel to meet with his lay congregations.

Everywhere, he seemed to read the signs of Judgment Day. As early as 1826 or 1827, he had selected some twenty loyalists among slaves and free blacks to comprise a circle of freedom fighters. During conversations with them at prayer meetings, he said, "I am commissioned by Jesus Christ and act under his direction." He had begun to prepare for a mission yet unspecified. When Thomas Moore died in 1828, the twenty-eight-year-old Nat and other slaves all became the inherited property of Putnam, the nine-year-old Moore. In October 1829, the widowed Sally Moore married a local wheelwright named Joseph Travis, who set up his carriage business and assumed supervision of seventeen slaves, including Nat.

At Richmond, Virginia, a convention had met to deliberate and draft a new state constitution. Though there had been talk among the slaves that they might be liberated, hopes had dissipated when the delegates had dismissed all considerations of emancipation. Backed by claims that some slaves had looked at a revolutionary text, *Appeal to the Colored Citizens of the World,* by David Walker, in 1829, traditionalists enacted laws in Virginia and North Carolina to forbid the teaching of literacy to slaves. In April 1831, after John Floyd had become governor, the Virginia laws were largely unenforced, despite reports of slave unrest in Wilmington, Delaware, and elsewhere. The Southampton rebellion led by Nat Turner in 1831 ended with the regrettable deaths of children, women, and men. Once and for all, however, the scene helped end the racist myth of submissive blacks who might cheerfully forfeit their pursuit of happiness. Mostly within forty-eight hours, and for four days beginning August 21, 1831, Turner responded violently to what slavery had seemed to have called for for more than two centuries. The small band of about seventy or so put to death at least fifty-seven whites. Once seized by authorities on October 30, 1831, Turner was tried and hanged on November 11.

Nat Turner helped dismiss the idea that slavery was affordable in human lives. He kept alive the public fear of the insurrection that had taken place on the Caribbean island of Santo Domingo in 1795 and of the uprising by Gabriel Prosser at Richmond in 1800. He inherited in part the same spirit or revolt that Denmark Vessey had inspired at Charleston, South Carolina, in 1822. Whatever the professions of the Christian church, Turner revealed it as a social instrument that stabilized conservatism and empowered enslavers. With his strong charisma, he disproved the myth that even forceful leadership could not unite slave masses. Nat Turner challenged the American soul.

❖❖❖

Some serious inquiry into intellectual and cultural history needs to be written. Indeed, little has been done since the 1960s, and, even so, the research methodology needs to be more rigorously focused. *The Fires of Jubilee* (1817), by Stephen B. Oates, has a wealth of historical detail written as partial biography and sentimental narrative. Herbert Aptheker's *Nat Turner's Slave Rebellion* (1966) is probably the most well-researched and thoughtful account from the white left. William Styron's prizewinning novel, *The Confessions of Nat Turner* (1967), proved to be very controversial for its distortion of historical accuracy, as apparent from *William Styron's Nat Turner: Ten Black Writers Respond* (1968), edited by John Henrik Clarke. Melvin J. Friedman added *William Styron's The Confessions of Nat Turner: A Critical Handbook* (1970). *The Southampton Slave Revolt of 1831* (1971), by Henry I. Tragle, provides historical context while the encyclopedic note by Ronald E. Lewis in *Grolier's Academic* allows for quick access via the Internet. Most recently the twenty-fifth anniversary of the Styron volume was revisited in *American Heritage* 43.6 (October 1992).

The Confessions of Nat Turner

District of Columbia, To Wit:

Be it remembered, That on this tenth day of November, Anno Domini, eighteen hundred and thirty-one, Thomas R. Gray of the said District, deposited in this office the title of a book, which is in the words as following:

"The Confessions of Nat Turner, the leader of the late insurrection in Southampton, Virginia, as fully and voluntarily made to Thomas R. Gray, in the prison where he was confined, and acknowledged by him to be such when read before the Court of Southampton; with the certificate, under seal, of the Court convened at Jerusalem, November 5, 1831, for his trial. Also, an authentic account of the whole insurrection, with lists of the whites who were murdered, and of the negroes brought before the Court of Southampton, and there sentenced, &. the right whereof he claims as proprietor, in conformity with an Act of Congress, entitled "An act to amend the several acts respecting Copy Rights."

(Seal.)

EDMUND J. LEE, Clerk of the District.

In testimony that the above is a true copy, from the record of the District Court for the District of Columbia, I, Edmund J. Lee, the Clerk thereof, have hereunto set my hand and affixed the seal of my office, this 10th day of November, 1831.

EDMUND J. LEE, C. D. C.

To the Public

The late insurrection in Southampton has greatly excited the public mind, and led to a thousand idle, exaggerated and mischievous reports. It is the first instance in our history of an open rebellion of the slaves, and attended with such atrocious circumstances of cruelty and destruction, as could not fail to leave a deep impression, not only upon the minds of the community where this fearful tragedy was wrought, but throughout every portion of our country, in which this population is to be found. Public curiosity has been on the stretch to understand the origin and progress of this dreadful conspiracy, and the motives which influence its diabolical actors. The insurgent slaves had all been destroyed, or apprehended, tried and executed, (with the exception of the leader,) without revealing any thing at all satisfactory, as to the motives which governed them, or the means by which they expected to accomplish their object. Every thing connected with the sad affair was wrapt in mystery, until Nat Turner, the leader of this ferocious band, whose name has resounded throughout our widely extended empire, was captured. This "great Bandit" was taken by a single individual, in a cave near the residence of his late owner, on Sunday, the thirtieth of October, without attempting to make the slightest resistance, and on the following day safely lodged in the jail of the County. His captor was Benjamin Phipps, armed with a shot gun well charged. Nat's only weapon was a small light sword which he immediately surrendered, and begged that his life might be spared. Since his confinement, by permission of the Jailor, I have had ready access to him, and finding that he was willing to make a full and free confession of the origin, progress and consummation of the insurrectory movements of the slaves of which he was the contriver and head; I determined for the gratification of public curiosity to commit his statements to writing, and publish them, with little or no variation, from his own words. That this is a faithful record of his confessions, the annexed certificate of the County Court of Southampton, will attest. They certainly bear one stamp of truth and sincerity. He makes no attempt (as all the other insurgents who were examined did,) to exculpate himself, but frankly acknowledges his full participation in all the guilt of the transaction. He was not only the contriver of the conspiracy, but gave the first blow towards its execution.

It will thus appear, that whilst every thing upon the surface of society wore a calm and peaceful aspect; whilst not one note of preparation was heard to warn the devoted inhabitants of woe and death, a gloomy fanatic was revolving in the recesses of his own dark, bewildered, and overwrought mind, schemes of indiscriminate massacre to the whites. Schemes too fearfully executed as far as his fiendish band proceeded in their desolating march. No cry for mercy penetrated their flinty bosoms. No acts of remembered kindness made the least impression upon these remorseless murderers. Men, women and children, from hoary age to helpless infancy were involved in the same cruel fate. Never did a band of savages do their work of death more unsparingly. Apprehension for their own personal safety seems to have been the only principle of restraint in the whole course of their bloody proceedings. And it is not the least remarkable feature in this horrid transaction, that a band actuated by such hellish purposes, should have resisted so feebly, when met by the whites in arms. Desperation alone, one would think, might have led to greater efforts. More than twenty of them attacked Dr. Blunt's house on Tuesday morning, a little before day-break, defended by two men and three boys. They fled precipitately at the first fire; and their future plans of mischief, were entirely disconcerted and broken up. Escaping thence, each individual sought his own safety either in concealment, or by returning home, with the hope that his participation might escape detection, and all were shot down in the course of a few days, or captured and brought to trial and punishment. Nat has survived all his followers, and the gallows will speedily close his career. His own account of the conspiracy is submitted to the public, without comment. It reads an awful, and it is hoped, a useful lesson, as to the operations of a mind like his, endeavoring to grapple with things beyond its reach. How it first became bewildered and confounded, and finally corrupted and led to the conception and perpetration of the most atrocious and heart-rending deeds. It is calculated also to demonstrate the policy of our laws in restraint of this class of our population, and to induce all those entrusted with their execution, as well as our citizens generally, to see that they are strictly and rigidly enforced. Each particular community should look to its own safety, whilst the general guardians of the laws, keep a watchful eye over all. If Nat's statements can be relied on, the insurrection in this county was entirely local, and his designs confided but to a few, and these in his immediate vicinity. It was not instigated by motives of revenge or sudden anger, but the results of long deliberation, and a settled purpose of mind. The offspring of gloomy fanaticism, acting upon materials but too well prepared for such impressions. It will be long remembered in the annals of our country, and many a mother as she presses her infant darling to her bosom, will shudder at the recollection of Nat Turner, and his band of ferocious miscreants.

Believing the following narrative, by removing doubts and conjectures from the public mind which otherwise must have remained, would give general satisfaction, it is respectfully submitted to the public by their ob't serv't,

T. R. GRAY

Jerusalem, Southampton, Va. Nov. 5, 1831.

We the undersigned, members of the Court convened at Jerusalem, on Saturday, the 5th day of Nov. 1831, for the trial of Nat, *alias* Nat Turner, a negro slave, late the property of Putnam Moore, deceased, do hereby certify, that the confessions of Nat, to Thomas R. Gray, was read to him in our presence, and that Nat acknowledged the same to be full, free, and voluntary; and that furthermore, when called upon by the presiding Magistrate of the Court, to state if he had any thing to say, why sentence of death should not be passed upon him, replied he had nothing further than he had communicated to Mr. Gray. Given under our hands and seals at Jerusalem, this 5th day of November, 1831.

JEREMIAH COBB, [Seal.]
THOMAS PRETLOW, [Seal.]
JAMES W. PARKER, [Seal.]
CARR BOWERS, [Seal.]
SAMUEL B. HINES, [Seal.]
ORRIS A. BROWNE, [Seal.]

State of Virginia, Southampton County, to wit:

I, James Rochelle, Clerk of the County Court of Southampton in the State of Virginia, do hereby certify, that Jeremiah Cobb, Thomas Pretlow, James W. Parker, Carr Bowers, Samuel B. Hines, and Orris A. Browne, esqr's are acting Justices of the Peace, in and for the County aforesaid, and were members of the Court which convened at Jerusalem, on Saturday the 5th day of November, 1831, for the trial of Nat *alias* Nat Turner, a negro slave, late the property of Putnam Moore, deceased, who was tried and convicted, as an insurgent in the late insurrection in the county of Southampton aforesaid, and that full faith and credit are due, and ought to be given to their acts as Justices of the peace aforesaid.

[Seal.]

In testimony whereof, I have hereunto set my hand and caused the seal of the Court aforesaid, to be affixed this 5th day of November, 1831

JAMES ROCHELLE,
C. S. C. C.

Confession

Agreeable to his own appointment, on the evening he was committed to prison, with permission of the jailer, I visited NAT on Tuesday the 1st November, when, without being questioned at all, he commenced his narrative in the following words:—

SIR,—You have asked me to give a history of the motives which induced me to undertake the late insurrection, as you call it—To do so I must go back to the days of my infancy, and even before I was born. I was thirty-one years of age the 2nd of October last, and born the property of Benj. Turner, of this county. In my childhood a circumstance occurred which made an indelible impression on my mind, and laid the ground work of that enthusiasm, which has terminated so fatally to many, both white and black, and for which I am about to atone at the gallows. It is here necessary to relate this circumstance—trifling as it may seem, it was the commencement of that belief which has grown with time, and even now, sir, in this dungeon, helpless and forsaken as I am, I cannot divest myself of. Being at play with other children, when three or four years old, I was telling them something, which my mother overhearing, said it had happened before I was born—I stuck to my story, however, and related somethings which went, in her opinion, to confirm it—others being called on were greatly astonished, knowing that these things had happened, and caused them to say in my hearing, I surely would be a prophet, as the Lord had shewn me things that had happened before my birth. And my father and mother strengthened me in this my first impression, saying in my presence, I was intended for some great purpose, which they had always thought from certain marks on my head and breast—[a parcel of excrescences which I believe are not at all uncommon, particularly among negroes, as I have seen several with the same. In this case he has either cut them off or they have nearly disappeared]—My grandmother, who was very religious, and to whom I was much attached—my master, who belonged to the church, and other religious persons who visited the house, and whom I often saw at prayers, noticing the singularity of my manners, I suppose, and my uncommon intelligence for a child, remarked I had too much sense to be raised, and if I was, I would never be of any service to any one as a slave—To a mind like mine, restless, inquisitive and observant of every thing that was passing, it is easy to suppose that religion was the subject to which it would be directed, and although this subject principally occupied my thoughts—there was nothing that I saw or heard of to which my attention was not directed—The manner in which I learned to read and write, not only had great influence on my own mind, as I acquired it with the most perfect ease, so much so, that I have no recollection whatever of learning the alphabet—but to the astonishment of the family, one day, when a book was shewn to me to keep me from crying, I began spelling the names of different objects—this was a source of wonder to all in the neighborhood, particularly the blacks—and this learning was constantly improved at all opportunities—when I got large enough to go to work, while employed, I was reflecting on many things that would present themselves to my imagination, and whenever an opportunity occurred of looking at a book, when the school children were getting their lessons, I would find many things that the fertility of my own imagination had depicted to me before; all my time, not devoted to my master's service, was spent either in prayer, or in making experiments in casting different things in moulds made of earth, in attempting to make paper, gun-powder, and many other experiments, that although I could not perfect, yet convinced me of its practicability if I had the means.[1] I was not addicted to stealing in my youth, nor have ever been—Yet such was the confidence of the negroes in the neighborhood, even at this early period of my life, in my superior judgment, that they would often carry me with them when they were going on any roguery, to plan for them. Growing up among them, with this confidence in my superior judgment, and when this, in their opinions, was perfected by Divine inspiration, from the circumstances already alluded to in my infancy, and which belief was ever afterwards zealously inculcated by the austerity of my life and manners, which became the subject of remark by white and black.—Having soon discovered to be great, I must appear so, and therefore studiously avoided mixing in society, and wrapped myself in mystery, devoting my time to fasting and prayer—By this time, having arrived to man's estate, and hearing the scriptures commented on at meetings, I was struck with that particular passage which says: "Seek ye the kingdom of Heaven and all things shall be added unto you." I reflected much on this passage, and prayed daily for light on this subject—As I was praying one day at my plough, the spirit spoke to me, saying "Seek ye the kingdom of Heaven and all things shall be added unto you." *Question*—what do you mean by the Spirit. *Ans.* The Spirit that spoke to the prophets in former days—and I was greatly astonished, and for two years prayed continually,

[1]When questioned as to the manner of manufacturing those different articles, he was found well informed on the subject.

whenever my duty would permit—and then again I had the same revelation, which fully confirmed me in the impression that I was ordained for some great purpose in the hands of the Almighty. Several years rolled round, in which many events occurred to strengthen me in this my belief. At this time I reverted in my mind to the remarks made of me in my childhood, and the things that had been shewn me—and as it had been said of me in my childhood by those by whom I had been taught to pray, both white and black, and in whom I had the greatest confidence, that I had too much sense to be raised, and if I was, I would never be of any use to any one as a slave. Now finding I had arrived to man's estate, and was a slave, and these revelations being made known to me, I began to direct my attention to this great object, to fulfil the purpose for which, by this time, I felt assured I was intended. Knowing the influence I had obtained over the minds of my fellow servants, (not by the means of conjuring and such like tricks—for to them I always spoke of such things with contempt) but by the communion of the Spirit whose revelations I often communicated to them, and they believed and said my wisdom came from God. I now began to prepare them for my purpose, by telling them something was about to happen that would terminate in fulfilling the great promise that had been made to me—About this time I was placed under an overseer, from whom I ran away—and after remaining in the woods thirty days, I returned, to the astonishment of the negroes on the plantation, who thought I had made my escape to some other part of the country, as my father had done before. But the reason of my return was, that the Spirit appeared to me and said I had my wishes directed to the things of this world, and not to the kingdom of Heaven, and that I should return to the service of my earthly master—"For he who knoweth his Master's will, and doeth it not, shall be beaten with many stripes, and thus have I chastened you." And the negroes found fault, and murmurred against me, saying that if they had my sense they would not serve any master in the world. And about this time I had a vision—and I saw white spirits and black spirits engaged in battle, and the sun was darkened—the thunder rolled in the Heavens, and blood flowed in streams—and I heard a voice saying, "Such is your luck, such you are called to see, and let it come rough or smooth, you must surely bare it. I now withdrew myself as much as my situation would permit, from the intercourse of my fellow servants, for the avowed purpose of serving the Spirit more fully—and it appeared to me, and reminded me of the things it had already shown me, and that it would then reveal to me the knowledge of the elements, the revolution of the planets, the operation of tides, and changes of the seasons. After this revelation in the year of 1825, and the knowledge of the elements being made known to me, I sought more than ever to obtain true holiness before the great day of judgment should appear, and then I began to receive the true knowledge of faith. And from the first steps of righteousness until the last, was I made perfect; and the Holy Ghost was with me, and said, "Behold me as I stand in the Heavens"—and I looked and saw the forms of men in different attitudes—and there were lights in the sky to which the children of darkness gave other names than what they really were—for they were the lights of the Savior's hands, stretched forth from east to west, even as they were extended on the cross on Calvary for the redemption of sinners. And I wondered greatly at these miracles, and prayed to be informed of a certainty of the meaning thereof—and shortly afterwards, while laboring in the field, I discovered drops of blood on the corn as though it were dew from heaven—and I communicated it to many, both white and black, in the neighborhood—and I then found on the leaves in the woods hieroglyphic characters, and numbers, with the forms of men in different attitudes, portrayed in blood, and representing the figures I had seen before in the heavens. And now the Holy Ghost had revealed itself to me, and made plain the miracles it had shown me—For as the blood of Christ had been shed on this earth, and had ascended to heaven for the salvation of sinners, and was now returning to earth again in the form of dew—and as the leaves on the trees bore the impression of the figures I had seen in the heavens, it was plain to me that the Savior was about to lay down the yoke he had borne for the sins of men, and the great day of judgment was at hand. About this time I told these things to a white man, (Etheldred T. Brantley) on whom it had a wonderful effect—and he ceased from his wickedness, and was attacked immediately with a cutaneous eruption, and blood oozed from the pores of his skin, and after praying and fasting nine days, he was healed, and the Spirit appeared to me again, and said, as the Savior had been baptised so should we be also—and when the white people would not let us be baptised by the church, we went down into the water together, in the sight of many who reviled us, and were baptised by the Spirit—After this I rejoiced greatly, and gave thanks to God. And on the 12th of May, 1828, I heard a loud noise in the heavens, and the Spirit instantly appeared to me and said the Serpent was loosened, and Christ had laid down the yoke he had borne for the sins of men, and that I should take it on and fight against the Serpent, for the time was fast approaching when the first should be last and the last should be first. *Ques.* Do you not find yourself mistaken now? *Ans.* Was not Christ crucified? And by signs in the heavens that it would make known to me when I should commence the great work—and until the first sign appeared, I should conceal it from the knowledge of men—And on the appearance of the sign, (the eclipse of the sun last February) I should arise and prepare myself, and slay my enemies with their own weapons. And immediately on the sign appearing in the heavens, the seal was removed from my lips, and I communicated the great work laid out for me to do, to four in whom I had the greatest confidence, (Henry, Hark, Nelson, and Sam)—It was intended by us to have begun the work of death on the 4th July last—Many were the plans formed and rejected by us, and it affected my mind to such a degree, that I fell sick, and the time passed without our coming to any determination how to commence—Still forming new schemes and rejecting them, when the sign appeared again, which determined me not to wait longer.

Since the commencement of 1830, I had been living with Mr. Joseph Travis, who was to me a kind master, and placed the greatest confidence in me; in fact, I had no cause to complain of his treatment to me. On Saturday evening, the 20th of August, it was agreed between Henry, Hark and myself, to prepare a dinner the next day for the men we expected, and then to concert a plan, as we had not yet determined on any. Hark, on the following morning, brought a pig, and Henry brandy, and being joined by Sam, Nelson, Will and Jack, they prepared in the woods a dinner, where, about three o'clock, I joined them.

Q. Why were you so backward in joining them.

A. The same reason that had caused me not to mix with them for years before.

I saluted them on coming up, and asked Will how came he there, he answered, his life was worth no more than others, and his liberty as dear to him. I asked him if he thought to obtain it? He said he would, or lose his life. This was enough to put him in full confidence. Jack, I knew, was only a tool in the hands of Hark, it was quickly agreed we should commence at home (Mr. J. Travis') on that night, and until we had armed and equipped ourselves, and gathered sufficient force, neither age nor sex was to be spared, (which was invariably adhered to). We remained at the feast, until about two hours in the night, when we went to the house and found Austin; they all went to the cider press and drank, except myself. On returning to the house, Hark went to the door with an axe, for the purpose of breaking it open, as we knew we were strong enough to murder the family, if they were awaked by the noise; but reflecting that it might create an alarm in the neighborhood, we determined to enter the house secretly, and murder them whilst sleeping. Hark got a ladder and set it against the chimney, on which I ascended, and hoisting a window, entered and came down stairs, unbarred the door, and removed the guns from their places. It was then observed that I must spill the first blood. On which, armed with a hatchet, and accompanied by Will, I entered my master's chamber, it being dark, I could not give a death blow, the hatchet glanced from his head, he sprang from the bed and called his wife, it was his last word, Will laid him dead, with a blow of his axe, and Mrs. Travis shared the same fate, as she lay in bed. The murder of this family, five in number, was the work of a moment, not one of them awoke; there was a little infant sleeping in a cradle, that was forgotten, until we had left the house and gone some distance, when Henry and Will returned and killed it; we got here, four guns that would shoot, and several old muskets, with a pound or two of powder. We remained some time at the barn, where we paraded; I formed them in a line as soldiers, and after carrying them through all the manoeuvres I was master of marched them off to Mr. Salathul Francis', about six hundred yards distant. Sam and Will went to the door and knocked. Mr. Francis asked who was there, Sam replied it was him, and he had a letter for him, on which he got up and came to the door; they immediately seized him, and dragging him out a little from the door, he was dispatched by repeated blows on the head; there was no other white person in the family. We started from there for Mrs. Reese's, maintaining the most perfect silence on our march, where finding the door unlocked, we entered, and murdered Mrs. Reese in her bed, while sleeping; her son awoke, but it was only to sleep the sleep of death, he had only time to say who is that, and he was no more. From Mrs. Reese's we went to Mrs. Turner's, a mile distant, which we reached about sunrise, on Monday morning. Henry, Austin, and Sam, went to the still, where, finding Mr. Peebles, Austin shot him, and the rest of us went to the house; as we approached, the family discovered us, and shut the door. Vain hope! Will, with one stroke of his axe, opened it, and we entered and found Mrs. Turner and Mrs. Newsome in the middle of a room, almost frightened to death. Will immediately killed Mrs. Turner, with one blow of his axe. I took Mrs. Newsome by the hand, and with the sword I had when I was apprehended, I struck her several blows over the head, but not being able to kill her, as the sword was dull. Will turning around and discovering it, despatched her also. A general destruction of property and search for money and ammunition, always succeeded the murders. By this time my company amounted to fifteen, and nine men mounted, who started for Mrs. Whitehead's, (the other six were to go through a by way to Mr. Bryant's, and rejoin us at Mrs. Whitehead's,) as we approached the house we discovered Mr. Richard Whitehead standing in the cotton patch, near the lane fence; we called him over into the lane, and Will, the executioner, was near at hand, with his fatal axe, to send him to an untimely grave. As we pushed on to the house, I discovered some one run round the garden, and thinking it was some of the white family, I pursued them, but finding it was a servant girl belonging to the house, I returned to commence the work of death, but they whom I left, had not been idle; all the family were already murdered, but Mrs. Whitehead and her daughter Margaret. As I came round to the door I saw Will pulling Mrs. Whitehead out of the house, and at the step he nearly severed her head from her body, with his broad axe. Miss Margaret, when I discovered her, had concealed herself in the corner, formed by the projection of cellar cap from the house; on my approach she fled, but was soon overtaken, and after repeated blows with a sword, I killed her by a blow on the head, with a fence rail. By this time, the six who had gone by Mr. Bryant's, rejoined us, and informed me they had done the work of death assigned them. We again divided, part going to Mr. Richard Porter's, and from thence to Nathaniel Francis', the others to Mr. Howell Harris', and Mr. T. Doyles. On my reaching Mr. Porter's, he had escaped with his family. I understood there, that the alarm had already spread, and I immediately returned to bring up those sent to Mr. Doyles, and Mr. Howell Harris'; the party I left going on to Mr. Francis', having told them I would join them in that neighborhood. I met these sent to Mr. Doyles' and Mr. Harris' returning, having met Mr. Doyle on the road and killed him; and learning from some who joined them, that Mr. Harris was from home, I immediately pursued the course taken by the party gone on before; but knowing they would complete the work of death and pillage, at Mr. Francis' before I could get there, I went to Mr. Peter Edwards', expecting to find them there, but they had been here also. I then went to Mr. John T. Barrow's, they had been here and murdered him. I pursued on their track to Capt. Newit Harris', where I found the greater part mounted, and ready to start; the men now amounting to about forty, shouted and hurrahed as I rode up, some were in the yard, loading their guns, others drinking. They said Captain Harris and his family had escaped, the property in the house they destroyed, robbing him of money and other valuables. I ordered them to mount and march instantly, this was about nine or ten o'clock, Monday morning. I proceeded to Mr. Levi Waller's, two or three miles distant. I took my station in the rear, and as it was my object to carry terror and devastation wherever we went, I placed fifteen or twenty of the best armed and most relied on, in front, who generally approached the houses as fast as their horses could run; this was for two purposes, to prevent escape and strike terror to the inhabitants—on this account I never got to the houses, after leaving Mrs. Whitehead's, until the murders were committed, except in one case. I sometimes got in sight in time to see the work of death completed, viewed the mangled bodies as they lay, in silent satisfaction, and immediately started in quest of other victims—Having murdered Mrs. Waller and ten children, we started for Mr. William Williams'—having killed him and two little boys that were there; while engaged in this, Mrs. Williams fled and got some distance from the house, but she was pursued, overtaken, and compelled to get up behind one of the company, who brought her back, and after showing her the mangled body of her lifeless husband, she was told to get down and lay by his side, where she was shot dead. I then started for Mr. Jacob Williams, where the family were murdered—Here he found a young man named Drury, who had come on business with Mr. Williams—he was pursued, overtaken and shot. Mrs. Vaughan was the next place we visited—and after murdering the family here, I determined on starting for Jerusalem—Our number amounted now to fifty or sixty, all mounted and armed with guns, axes, swords and clubs—On reaching Mr. James W. Parker's gate, immediately on the road leading to Jerusalem, and about three miles distant, it was proposed to me to call there, but I objected, as I knew he was gone to Jerusalem, and my object was to reach there as soon as possible; but some of the men having relations at Mr. Parker's it was agreed that they might call and get his people. I remained at the gate on the road, with seven or eight; the others going across the field to the house, about half a mile off. After waiting some time for them, I became impatient, and started to the house for them, and on our return we were met by a party of white men, who had pursued our blood-stained track, and who had fired on those at the gate, and dispersed them, which I knew nothing of, not having been at that time rejoined by any of them—Immediately on discovering the whites, I ordered my men to halt and form, as they appeared to be alarmed—The white men, eighteen in number, approached us in about one hundred yards, when one of them fired, (this was against the positive orders of Captain Alexander P. Peete, who commanded, and who had directed the men to reserve their fire until within thirty paces)—And I discovered about half of them retreating, I then ordered my men to fire and rush on them; the few remaining stood their ground until we approached within fifty yards, when they fired and retreated. We pursued and overtook some of them who we thought we left dead; (they were not killed) after pursuing them about two hundred yards, and rising a little hill, I discovered they were met by another party, and had halted, and were re-loading their guns, (this was a small party from Jerusalem who knew the negroes were in the field, and had just tied their horses to await their return to the road, knowing that Mr. Parker and family were in Jerusalem, but knew nothing of the party that had gone in with Captain Peete; on hearing the firing they immediately rushed to the spot and arrived just in time to arrest the progress of these barbarous villians, and save the lives of their friends and fellow citizens). Thinking that those who retreated first, and the party who fired on us at fifty or sixty yards distant, had all fallen back to meet others with ammunition. As I saw them reloading their guns, and more coming up than I saw at first, and several of my bravest men being wounded, the others became panick struck and squandered over the field; the white men pursued and fired on us several times. Hark had his horse shot under him, and I caught another for him as it was running by me; five or six of my men were wounded, but none left on the field; finding myself defeated here I instantly determined to go through a private way, and cross the Nottoway river at the Cypress Bridge, three miles below Jerusalem, and attack that place in the rear, as I expected they would look for me on the other road, and I had a great desire to get there to procure arms and ammunition. After going a short distance in this private way, accompanied by about twenty men, I overtook two or three who told me the others were dispersed in every direction. After trying in vain to collect a sufficient force to proceed to Jerusalem, I determined to return, as I was sure they would make back to their old neighborhood, where they would rejoin me, make new recruits, and come down again. On my way back, I called at Mrs. Thomas's, Mrs. Spencer's, and several other places, the white families having fled, we found no more victims to gratify our thirst for blood, we stopped at Majr. Ridley's quarter for the night, and being joined by four of his men, with the recruits made since my defeat, we mustered now about forty strong. After placing out sentinels, I laid down to sleep, but was quickly roused by a great racket; starting up, I found some mounted, and others in great·confusion; one of the sentinels having given the alarm that we were about to be attacked, I ordered some to ride round and reconnoitre, and on their return the others being more alarmed, not knowing who they were, fled in different ways, so that I was reduced to about twenty again; with this I determined to attempt to recruit, and proceed on to rally in the neighborhood, I had left. Dr. Blunt's was the nearest house, which we reached just before day; on riding up the yard, Hark fired a gun. We expected Dr. Blunt and his family were at Maj. Ridley's, as I knew there was a company of men there; the gun was fired to ascertain if any of the family were at home; we were immediately fired upon and retreated, leaving several of my men. I do not know what became of them, as I never saw them afterwards. Pursuing our course back and coming in sight of Captain Harris', where we had been the day before, we discovered a party of white men at the house, on which all deserted me but two, (Jacob and Nat), we concealed ourselves in the woods until near night, when I sent them in search of Henry, Sam, Nelson, and Hark, and directed them to rally all they could, at the place we had had our dinner the Sunday before, where they would find me, and I accordingly returned there as soon as it was dark and remained until Wednesday evening, when discovering white men riding around the place as though they were looking for some one, and none of my men joining me, I concluded Jacob and Nat had been taken, and compelled to betray me. On this I gave up all hope for the present; and on Thursday night after having supplied myself with provisions from Mr. Travis's, I scratched a hole under a pile of fence rails in a field, where I concealed myself for six weeks, never leaving my hiding place but for a few minutes in the dead of night to get water which was very near; thinking by this time I could venture out, I began to go about in the night and eaves drop the houses in the neighborhood; pursuing this course for about a fortnight and gathering little or no intelligence, afraid of speaking to any human being, and returning every morning to my cave before the dawn of day. I know not how long I might have led this life, if accident had not betrayed me, a dog in the neighborhood passing by my hiding place one night while I was out, was attracted by some meat I had in my cave, and crawled in and stole it, and was coming out just as I returned. A few nights after, two negroes having started to go hunting with the same dog, and passed that way, the dog came again to the place, and having just gone out to walk about, discovered me and barked, on which thinking myself discovered, I spoke to them to beg concealment. On making myself known they fled from me. Knowing then they would betray me, I immediately left my hiding place, and was pursued almost incessantly until I was taken a fortnight afterwards by Mr. Benjamin Phipps, in a little hole I had dug out with my sword, for the purpose of concealment, under the top of a fallen tree. On Mr. Phipps' discovering the place of my concealment, he cocked his gun and aimed at me. I requested him not to shoot and I would give up, upon which he demanded my sword. I delivered it to him, and he brought me to prison. During the time I was pursued, I had many hair breadth escapes, which your time will not permit you to relate. I am here loaded with chains, and willing to suffer the fate that awaits me.

I here proceeded to make some inquiries of him, after assuring him of the certain death that awaited him, and that concealment would only bring destruction on the innocent as well as guilty, of his own color, if he knew of any extensive or concerted plan. His answer was, I do not. When I questioned him as to the insurrection in North Carolina happening about the same time, he denied any knowledge of it; and when I looked him in the face as though I would search his inmost thoughts, he replied, "I see sir, you doubt my word; but can you not think the same ideas, and strange appearances about this time in the heaven's might prompt others, as well as myself, to this undertaking." I now had much conversation with and asked him many questions, having forborne to do so previously, except in the cases noted in parenthesis; but during his statement, I had, unnoticed by him, taken notes as to some particular circumstances, and having the advantage of his statement before me in writing, on the evening of the third day that I had been with him, I began a cross examination, and found his statement corroborated by every circumstance coming within my own knowledge or the confessions of others who had been either killed or executed, and whom he had not seen or had any knowledge since 22d of August last, he expressed himself fully satisfied as to the impracticability of his attempt. It has been said he was ignorant and cowardly, and that his object was to murder and rob for the purpose of obtaining money to make his escape. It is notorious, that he was never known to have a dollar in his life; to swear an oath, or drink a drop of spirits. As to his ignorance, he certainly never had the advantages of education, but he can read and write, (it was taught him by his parents,) and for natural intelligence and quickness of apprehension, is surpassed by few men I have ever seen. As to his being a coward, his reason as given for not resisting Mr. Phipps, shews the decision of his character. When he saw Mr. Phipps present his gun, he said he knew it was impossible for him to escape as the woods were full of men; he therefore thought it was better to surrender, and trust to fortune for his escape. He is a complete fanatic, or plays his part most admirably. On other subjects he possesses an uncommon share of intelligence, with a mind capable of attaining any thing; but warped and perverted by the influence of early impressions. He is below the ordinary stature, though strong and active, having the true negro face, every feature of which is strongly marked. I shall not attempt to describe the effect of his narrative, as told and commented on by himself, in the condemned hole of the prison. The calm, deliberate composure with which he spoke of his late deeds and intentions, the expression of his fiend-like face when excited by enthusiasm, still bearing the stains of the blood of helpless innocence about him; clothed with rags and covered with chains; yet daring to raise his manacled hands to heaven, with a spirit soaring above the attributes of man; I looked on him and my blood curdled in my veins.

I will not shock the feelings of humanity, nor wound afresh the bosoms of the disconsolate sufferers in this unparalleled and inhuman massacre, by detailing the deeds of their fiend-like barbarity. There were two or three who were in the power of these wretches, had they known it, and who escaped in the most providential manner. There were two whom they thought they left dead on the field at Mr. Parker's, but who were only stunned by the blows of their guns, as they did not take time to re-load when they charged on them. The escape of a little girl who went to school at Mr. Waller's, and where the children were collecting for that purpose, excited general sympathy. As their teacher had not arrived, they were at play in the yard, and seeing the negroes approach, she ran up on a dirt chimney, (such as are common to log houses,) and remained there unnoticed during the massacre of the eleven that were killed at this place. She remained on her hiding place till just before the arrival of a party, who were in pursuit of the murderers, when she came down and fled to a swamp, where, a mere child as she was, with the horrors of the late scene before her, she lay concealed until the next day, when seeing a party go up to the house, she came up, and on being asked how she escaped, replied with the utmost simplicity, "The Lord helped her." She was taken up behind a gentleman of the party, and returned to the arms of her weeping mother. Miss Whitehead concealed herself between the bed and the mat that supported it, while they murdered her sister in the same room, without discovering her. She was afterwards carried off, and concealed for protection by a slave of the family, who gave evidence against several of them on their trial. Mrs. Nathaniel Francis, while concealed in a closet heard their blows, and the shrieks of the victims of these ruthless savages; they then entered the closet, where she was concealed, and went out without discovering her. While in this hiding place, she heard two of her women in a quarrel about the division of her clothes. Mr. John T. Baron, discovering them approaching his house, told his wife to make her escape, and scorning to fly, fell fighting on his own threshold. After firing his rifle, he discharged his gun at them, and then broke it over the villain who first approached him, but he was overpowered, and slain. His bravery, however, saved from the hands of these monsters, his lovely and amiable wife, who will long lament a husband so deserving of her love. As directed by him, she attempted to escape through the garden, when she was caught and held by one of her servant girls, but another coming to her rescue, she fled to the woods, and concealed herself. Few indeed, were those who escaped their work of death. But fortunate for society, the hand of retributive justice has overtaken them; and not one that was known to be concerned has escaped.

The Commonwealth,

vs.

Nat Turner

Charged with making insurrection, and plotting to take away the lives of divers free white persons,

&c. on the 22d of August, 1831.

The court composed of ———, having met for the trial of Nat Turner, the prisoner was brought in and arraigned, and upon his arraignment pleaded *Not guilty;* saying to his counsel, that he did not feel so.

On the part of the Commonwealth, Levi Waller was introduced, who being sworn, deposed as follows: (*agreeably to Nat's own Confession.*) Col. Trezvant[2] was then introduced, who being sworn, narrated Nat's Confession to him, as follows: (*his Confession as given to Mr. Gray.*) The prisoner introduced no evidence, and the case was submitted without argument to the court, who having found him guilty, Jeremiah Cobb, Esq. Chairman, pronounced the sentence of the court, in the following words: Nat Turner! Stand up. Have you any thing to say why sentence of death should not be pronounced against you?

Ans. I have not. I have made a full confession to Mr. Gray, and I have nothing more to say.

Attend then to the sentence of the Court. You have been arraigned and tried before this court, and convicted of one of the highest

[2]The committing Magistrate.

crimes in our criminal code. You have been convicted of plotting in cold blood, the indiscriminate destruction of men, of helpless women, and of infant children. The evidence before us leaves not a shadow of doubt, but that your hands were often imbrued in the blood of the innocent; and your own confession tells us that they were stained with the blood of a master; in your own language, "too indulgent." Could I stop here, your crime would be sufficiently aggravated. But the original contriver of a plan, deep and deadly, one that never can be effected, you managed so far to put it into execution, as to deprive us of many of our most valuable citizens; and this was done when they were asleep, and defenseless; under circumstances shocking to humanity. And while upon this part of the subject, I cannot but call your attention to the poor misguided wretches who have gone before you. They are not few in number—they were your bosom associates; and the blood of all cries aloud, and calls upon you, as the author of their misfortune. Yes! You forced them unprepared, from Time to Eternity. Borne down by this load of guilt, your only justification is, that you were led away by fanaticism. If this be true, from my soul I pity you; and while you have my sympathies, I am, nevertheless called upon to pass the sentence of the court. The time between this and your execution, will necessarily be very short; and your only hope must be in another world. The judgment of the court is, that you be taken hence to the jail from whence you came, thence to the place of execution, and on Friday next, between the hours of 10 A.M. and 2 P.M. be hung by the neck until you are dead! dead! dead! and may the Lord have mercy upon your soul.

A list of persons murdered in the Insurrection, on the 21st and 22nd of August, 1831.

Joseph Travers and wife and three children, Mrs. Elizabeth Turner, Hartwell Prebles, Sarah Newsome, Mrs. P. Reese and son William, Trajan Doyle, Henry Bryant and wife and child, and wife's mother, Mrs. Catharine Whitehead, son Richard and four daughters and grandchild, Salathiel Francis, Nathaniel Francis' overseer and two children, John T. Barrow, George Vaughan, Mrs. Levi Waller and ten children, William Williams, wife and two boys, Mrs. Caswell Worrell and child, Mrs. Rebecca Vaughan, Ann Eliza Vaughan, and son Arthur, Mrs. John K. Williams and child, Mrs. Jacob Williams and three children, and Edwin Drury—amounting to fifty-five.

A list of negroes brought before the Court of Southampton, with their owners' names, and sentence.

Daniel	Richard Porter	Convicted
Moses	J. T. Barrow	Do[3]
Tom	Caty Whitehead	Discharged
Jack and Andrew	Caty Whitehead	Convicted and transported
Jacob	Geo. H. Charlton	Disch'd without trial
Isaac	Ditto	Convicted and transported
Jack	Everett Bryant	Discharged
Nathan	Benj. Blunt's estate	Convicted
Nathan, Tom, and Davy, (boys)	Nathaniel Francis	Convicted and transported
Davy	Elizabeth Turner	Convicted
Curtis	Thomas Ridley	Do
Stephen	Do	Do
Hardy and Isham	Benjamin Edwards	Convicted and transported
Sam	Nathaniel Francis	Convicted

[3]*Editor's note:* "Do" means "Ditto".

Sam	Joseph Travis' estate	Do
Hark	Do	Do and transported
Moses (a boy)	Levi Waller	Convicted
Davy	Jacob Williams	Do
Nelson	Edm'd Turner's estate	Do
Nat	Wm. Reese's estate	Do
Dred	Nathaniel Francis	Do
Arnold, Artist (free)		Discharged
Sam	J. W. Parker	Acquitted
Ferry and Archer	J. W. Parker	Disch'd without trial
Jim	William Vaughan	Acquitted
Bob	Temperance Parker	Do
Davy	Joseph Parker	
Daniel	Solomon D. Parker	Disch'd without trial
Thomas Haithcock (free)		Sent on for further trial
Joe	John C. Turner	Convicted
Lucy	John T. Barrow	Do
Matt	Thomas Ridley	Acquitted
Jim	Richard Porter	Do
Exum Artes (free)		Sent on for further trial
Joe	Richard P. Briggs	Disch'd without trial
Bury Newsome (free)		Sent on for further trial
Stephen	James Bell	Acquitted
Jim and Isaac	Samuel Champion	Convicted and transported
Preston	Hannah Williamson	Acquitted
Frank	Solomon D. Parker	Convicted and transported
Jack and Shadrach	Nathaniel Simmons	Acquitted
Nelson	Benj. Blunt's estate	Do
Sam	Peter Edwards	Convicted
Archer	Arthur G. Reese	Acquitted
Isham Turner (free)		Sent on for further trial
Nat Turner	Putnam Moore, dec'd.	Convicted

The Fugitive Slave Narrative

HARRIET A. JACOBS
(1813–1897)

If any single African American slave narrative could be said to have set the tone for critical commentary in the 1980s and 1990s, that work would be Harriet Jacobs's *Incidents in the Life of a Slave Girl, Written by Herself* (1861). The work has inspired numerous scholarly articles, several dissertations and theses, and scores of papers presented at scholarly conferences. It is required reading in many literature and women's studies courses, and it is generally recognized as *the* gendered statement on enslavement for African American women. Jacobs's focus on the peculiar plight of black women during slavery has provided the counterpoint to narratives by Frederick Douglass, William Wells Brown, Moses Roper, and other male narrators. While they usually focused on the physical battle for attaining their freedom, Jacobs focused on the sexual and the psychological. Her borrowing of the traditions of sentimental fiction in addition to the slave narrative genre enabled her to appeal to a wide range of readers, but particularly those northern white women she invited to consider her situation as typical of many young black women who were not protected by the proponents of the cult of true womanhood.

Harriet Ann Jacobs was born in Edenton, North Carolina, in 1813. As with Harriet E. Adams Wilson, many of the events of Jacobs's life are included in her narrative. They appear under the life of the fictional Linda Brent. Jacobs's mother, Delilah, was a slave who belonged to Margaret and John Horniblow, a local tavern keeper. Her father, Daniel Jacobs, was, like Brent's father, a skilled carpenter who was allowed to hire out his time. Jacobs's mother died when she was young, and she and her younger brother John went to live with Margaret Horniblow, who, over the next six years, taught Harriet to read, spell, and sew. When Margaret died in 1825, she willed Harriet to her three-year-old niece, Mary Matilda Norcom. Jacobs follows essentially the same pattern of events in *Incidents.* Jacobs and her brother went to live with the Norcoms in 1826, and their father died in 1827. Jacobs's grandmother, Molly Horniblow (freed from slavery), remained a force in her life.

At fifteen, Harriet quickly discovered the disadvantages of being an attractive black female and a slave. Dr. James Norcom, father of Mary Matilda, made repeated sexual advances to Jacobs. Her refusals led to him preventing her marriage to a free black man. Perhaps in retaliation, she became sexually involved with a local white lawyer, Samuel Tedwell Sawyer, by whom she had two children, Joseph and Louisa Matilda. This drastic measure did not allay Dr. Norcom's pursuit. He built a house for Jacobs in 1835, a short distance from his own home, and expected her to reside there, take in sewing, and provide sexual favors for him; the setting is comparable to that which William Wells Brown depicts in *Clotel; Or, The President's Daughter* (1853) and the one that Chesnutt depicts in *The House Behind the Cedars* (1900). By this point, Mrs. Norcom was also harassing Harriet in that peculiar plight of black women who found themselves hated by white mistresses for the unwarranted and unwanted attentions of their husbands.

Jacobs tried to escape from both Norcoms by moving in with her grandmother. She resorted to living in a tiny crawl space in her grandmother's attic in an effort to escape from the Norcoms. Her initial method of "escape" provides one of the most fascinating in the annals of slave narratives. Jacobs existed in the tiny space for seven years, a feat that seemed so incredible that prominent historians dismissed her narrative as fictionalized when she recounted the incident. During that time, she exercised as best she could, viewed her children from afar, read, wrote, and sewed. Eventually, she risked escape to the North and was able, with the assistance of friends, to get a boat to New York. She served as a nursemaid to Mary Stace and Nathaniel Parker Willis, who provided the friendship that she needed to begin recounting the story of her enslavement. Jacobs initially requested that Amy Post approach Harriet Beecher Stowe as a way of getting her daughter to England, but she was sorely disappointed when Stowe asserted that the English would simply "fawn" over Louisa; Stowe also wanted verification of Jacobs's story for possible incorporation into *The Key to Uncle Tom's Cabin.* Post, among others, appended certifying documents to the narrative when it was published.

Publication of the volume was not easy, however. After a portion of it appeared in Horace Greeley's *New York Tribune* (1855), Jacobs even traveled to England in an unsuccessful effort to find a publisher. She twice signed with publishers in Boston, both of whom went bankrupt before the volume could be printed, and the second of whom required a preface by Lydia Maria Child as a condition of publication. Finally, the volume appeared with a Boston publisher in 1861; in 1862, it appeared in England as *The Deeper Wrong.* Jacobs went from author to nurse as she worked during the Civil War in Alexandria, Virginia. After emancipation, she moved to Washington, D.C., where she shared a home with her daughter until her death on 7 March 1897.

Scholars interested in African American literary history owe a great debt to Jean Fagan Yellin for the diligence with which she set out to prove that the fictional Linda Brent was indeed Harriet Ann Jacobs. Her meticulous examination of records in North Carolina enabled her to identify many of the persons to whom Jacobs referred pseudonymously in her narrative. Jacobs's biography parallels *Incidents* almost exactly, thus providing several instances of the merging of fiction and history. Fagan's extensive research surely has been essential in the revival of interest in Jacobs's narrative as well as in her black and white family history.

Linda Brent, the persona Jacobs adopts in *Incidents,* illustrates the plight of slave girls. Jacobs shapes the narrative with its villains and forces for good aligned in a battle destined to keep the reader's attention. The novelistic features of the work, therefore, are just as significant in the creative process as the raw materials of Jacobs's life. Readers shudder when Linda is pursued by the notorious Dr. Flint as well as when Confederate soldiers invade and search her grandmother's house. They feel the loss of separation of brother and sister as well as mother and children. The betrayal of the white lover once again makes clear that there were few people to whom exploited black women could turn for protection. Even Brent's grandmother seems more willing to blame her for sexual indiscretion than to blame Mr. Sands for having impregnated her. With its combination of personal narrative and history adapted to the features of engaging storytelling, *Incidents* has enjoyed a new life among feminists, African Americanists, and historians interested in the slave South. It is an extraordinary text the silence of which in literary history is almost as noteworthy as the story itself.

❖❖❖

For biography and criticism, see Hazel V. Carby, *Reconstructing Womanhood: The Emergence of the Afro-American Woman Novelist* (New York: Oxford, 1987); Kelley Norman, "Harriet Ann Jacobs," in *Notable Black American Women,* edited by Jessie Carney Smith (Detroit: Gale, 1992); Valerie Smith, "'Loopholes of Retreat': Architecture and Ideology in Harriet Jacobs's *Incidents in the Life of a Slave Girl, Written by Herself*" in *Reading Black, Reading Feminist: A Critical Anthology,* edited by Henry Louis Gates, Jr. (New York: Meridian, 1990); Jean Fagan Yellin, "Introduction" to *Incidents in the Life of a Slave Girl, Written by Herself* (Cambridge: Harvard University Press, 1987); and Yellin, *Women & Sisters* (New Haven: Yale University Press, 1989).

FROM *Incidents in the Life of a Slave Girl, Written by Herself*

Preface by the Author

Reader, be assured this narrative is no fiction. I am aware that some of my adventures may seem incredible; but they are, nevertheless, strictly true. I have not exaggerated the wrongs inflicted by Slavery; on the contrary, my descriptions fall far short of the facts. I have concealed the names of places, and given persons fictitious names. I had no motive for secrecy on my own account, but I deemed it kind and considerate towards others to pursue this course.

I wish I were more competent to the task I have undertaken. But I trust my readers will excuse deficiencies in consideration of circumstances. I was born and reared in Slavery; and I remained in a Slave State twenty-seven years. Since I have been at the North, it has been necessary for me to work diligently for my own support, and the education of my children. This has not left me much leisure to make up for the loss of early opportunities to improve myself; and it has compelled me to write these pages at irregular intervals, whenever I could snatch an hour from household duties.

When I first arrived in Philadelphia, Bishop Paine advised me to publish a sketch of my life, but I told him I was altogether incompetent to such an undertaking. Though I have improved my mind somewhat since that time, I still remain of the same opinion; but I trust my motives will excuse what might otherwise seem presumptuous. I have not written my experiences in order to attract attention to myself; on the contrary, it would have been more pleasant to me to have been silent about my own history. Neither do I care to excite sympathy for my own sufferings. But I do earnestly desire to arouse the women of the North to a realizing sense of the condition of two millions of women at the South, still in bondage, suffering what I suffered, and most of them far worse. I want to add my testimony to that of abler pens to convince the people of the Free States what Slavery really is. Only by experience can any one realize how deep, and dark, and foul is that pit of abominations. May the blessing of God rest on this imperfect effort in behalf of my persecuted people!

I
Childhood

I was born a slave; but I never knew it till six years of happy childhood had passed away. My father was a carpenter, and considered so intelligent and skilful in his trade, that, when buildings out of the common line were to be erected, he was sent for from long distances, to be head workman. On condition of paying his mistress two hundred dollars a year, and supporting himself, he was allowed to work at his trade, and manage his own affairs. His strongest wish was to purchase his children; but, though he several times offered his hard earnings for that purpose, he never succeeded. In complexion my parents were a light shade of brownish yellow, and were termed mulattoes. They lived together in a comfortable home; and, though we were all slaves, I was so fondly shielded that I never dreamed I was a piece of merchandise, trusted to them for safe keeping, and liable to be demanded of them at any moment. I had one brother, William, who was two years younger than myself—a bright, affectionate child. I had also a great treasure in my maternal grandmother, who was a remarkable women in many respects. She was the daughter of a planter in South Carolina, who, at his death, left her mother and his three children free, with money to go to St. Augustine, where they had relatives. It was during the Revolutionary War; and they were captured on their passage, carried back, and sold to different purchasers. Such was the story my grandmother used to tell me; but I do not remember all the particulars. She was a little girl when she was captured and sold to the keeper of a large hotel. I have often heard her tell how hard she fared during childhood. But as she grew older she evinced so much intelligence, and was so faithful, that her master and mistress could not help seeing it was for their interest to take care of such a valuable piece of property. She became an indispensable personage in the household, officiating in all capacities, from cook and wet nurse to seamstress. She was much praised for her cooking; and her nice crackers became so famous in the neighborhood that many people were desirous of obtaining them. In consequence of numerous requests of this kind, she asked permission of her mistress to bake crackers at night, after all the household work was done; and she obtained leave to do it, provided she would clothe herself and her children from the profits. Upon these terms, after working hard all day for her mistress, she began her midnight bakings, assisted by her two oldest children. The business proved profitable; and each year she laid by a little, which was saved for a fund to purchase her children. Her master died, and the property was divided among his heirs. The widow had her dower in the hotel, which she continued to keep open. My grandmother remained in her service as a slave; but her children were divided among her master's children. As she had five, Benjamin, the youngest one, was sold, in order that each heir might have an equal portion of dollars and cents. There was so little difference in our ages that he seemed more like my brother than my uncle. He was a bright, handsome lad, nearly white; for he inherited the complexion my grandmother had derived from Anglo-Saxon ancestors. Though only ten years old, seven hundred and twenty dollars were paid for him. His sale was a terrible blow to my grandmother; but she was naturally hopeful, and she went to work with renewed energy, trusting in time to be able to purchase some of her children. She had laid up three hundred dollars, which her mistress one day begged as a loan, promising to pay her soon. The reader probably knows that no promise or writing given to a slave is legally binding; for, according to Southern laws, a slave, *being* property, can *hold* no property. When my grandmother lent her hard earnings to her mistress, she trusted solely to her honor. The honor of a slaveholder to a slave!

To this good grandmother I was indebted for many comforts. My brother Willie and I often received portions of the crackers, cakes, and preserves, she made to sell; and after we ceased to be children we were indebted to her for many more important services.

Such were the unusually fortunate circumstances of my early childhood. When I was six years old, my mother died; and then, for the first time, I learned, by the talk around me, that I was a slave. My mother's mistress was the daughter of my grandmother's mistress. She was the foster sister of my mother; they were both nourished at my grandmother's breast. In fact, my mother had been weaned at three months old, that the babe of the mistress might obtain sufficient food. They played together as children; and, when they became women, my mother was a most faithful servant to her whiter foster sister. On her death-bed her mistress promised that her children should never suffer for any thing; and during her lifetime she kept her word. They all spoke kindly of my dead mother, who had been a slave merely in name, but in nature was noble and womanly. I grieved for her, and my young mind was troubled with the thought who would now take care of me and my little brother. I was told that my home was now to be with her mistress; and I found it a happy one. No toilsome or disagreeable duties were imposed upon me. My mistress was so kind to me that I was always glad to do her bidding, and proud to labor for her as much as my young years would permit. I would sit by her side for hours, sewing diligently, with a heart as free from care as that of any freeborn white child. When she thought I was tired, she would send me out to run and jump; and away I bounded, to gather berries or flowers to decorate her room. Those were happy days—too happy to last. The slave child had no thought for the morrow; but there came that blight, which too surely waits on every human being born to be a chattel.

When I was nearly twelve years old, my kind mistress sickened and died. As I saw the cheek grow paler, and the eye more glassy, how earnestly I prayed in my heart that she might live! I loved her; for she had been almost like a mother to me. My prayers were not answered. She died, and they buried her in the little churchyard, where, day after day, my tears fell upon her grave.

I was sent to spend a week with my grandmother. I was now old enough to begin to think of the future; and again and again I asked myself what they would do with me. I felt sure I should never find another mistress so kind as the one who was gone. She had promised my dying mother that her children should never suffer for any thing; and when I remembered that, and recalled her many proofs of attachment to me, I could not help having some hopes that she had left me free. My friends were almost certain it would be so. They thought she would be sure to do it, on account of my mother's love and faithful service. But, alas! we all know that the memory of a faithful slave does not avail much to save her children from the auction block.

After a brief period of suspense, the will of my mistress was read, and we learned that she had bequeathed me to her sister's daughter, a child of five years old. So vanished our hopes. My mistress had taught me the precepts of God's Word: "Thou shalt love thy neighbor as thyself." "Whatsoever ye would that men should do unto you, do ye even so unto them." But I was her slave, and I suppose she did not recognize me as her neighbor. I would give much to blot out from my memory that one great wrong. As a child, I loved my mistress; and, looking back on the happy days I spent with her, I try to think with less bitterness of this act of injustice. While I was with her, she taught me to read and spell; and for this privilege, which so rarely falls to the lot of a slave, I bless her memory.

She possessed but few slaves; and at her death those were all distributed among her relatives. Five of them were my grandmother's children, and had shared the same milk that nourished her mother's children. Notwithstanding my grandmother's long and faithful service to her owners, not one of her children escaped the auction block. These God-breathing machines are no more, in the sight of their masters, than the cotton they plant, or the horses they tend.

II
The New Master and Mistress

Dr. Flint, a physician in the neighborhood, had married the sister of my mistress, and I was now the property of their little daughter. It was not without murmuring that I prepared for my new home; and what added to my unhappiness, was the fact that my brother William was purchased by the same family. My father, by his nature, as well as by the habit of transacting business as a skilful mechanic, had more of the feelings of a freeman than is common among slaves. My brother was a spirited boy; and being brought up under such influences, he early detested the name of master and mistress. One day, when his father and his mistress both happened to call him at the same time, he hesitated between the two; being perplexed to know which had the strongest claim upon his obedience. He finally concluded to go to his mistress. When my father reproved him for it, he said, "You both called me, and I didn't know which I ought to go to first."

"You are *my* child," replied our father, "and when I call you, you should come immediately, if you have to pass through fire and water."

Poor Willie! He was now to learn his first lesson of obedience to a master. Grandmother tried to cheer us with hopeful words, and they found an echo in the credulous hearts of youth.

When we entered our new home we encountered cold looks, cold words, and cold treatment. We were glad when the night came. On my narrow bed I moaned and wept, I felt so desolate and alone.

I had been there nearly a year, when a dear little friend of mine was buried. I heard her mother sob, as the clods fell on the coffin of her only child, and I turned away from the grave, feeling thankful that I still had something left to love. I met my grandmother, who said, "Come with me, Linda;" and from her tone I knew that something sad had happened. She led me apart from the people, and then said, "My child, your father is dead." Dead! How could I believe it? He had died so suddenly I had not even heard that he was sick. I went home with my grandmother. My heart rebelled against God, who had taken from me mother, father, mistress, and friend. The good grandmother tried to comfort me. "Who knows the ways of God?" said she. "Perhaps they have been kindly taken from the evil days to come." Years afterwards I often thought of this. She promised to be a mother to her grandchildren, so far as she might be permitted to do so; and strengthened by her love, I returned to my master's. I thought I should be allowed to go to my father's house the next morning; but I was ordered to go for flowers, that my mistress's house might be decorated for an evening party. I spent the day gathering flowers and weaving them into festoons, while the dead body of my father was lying within a mile of me. What cared my owners for that? he was merely a piece of property. Moreover, they thought he had spoiled his children, by teaching them to feel that they were human beings. This was blasphemous doctrine for a slave to teach; presumptuous in him, and dangerous to the masters.

The next day I followed his remains to a humble grave beside that of my dear mother. There were those who knew my father's worth, and respected his memory.

My home now seemed more dreary than ever. The laugh of the little slave-children sounded harsh and cruel. It was selfish to feel so about the joy of others. My brother moved about with a very grave face. I tried to comfort him, by saying, "Take courage, Willie; brighter days will come by and by."

"You don't know any thing about it, Linda," he replied. "We shall have to stay here all our days; we shall never be free."

I argued that we were growing older and stronger, and that perhaps we might, before long, be allowed to hire our own time, and then we could earn money to buy our freedom. William declared this was much easier to say than to do; moreover, he did not intend to *buy* his freedom. We held daily controversies upon this subject.

Little attention was paid to the slaves' meals in Dr. Flint's house. If they could catch a bit of food while it was going, well and good. I gave myself no trouble on that score, for on my various errands I passed my grandmother's house, where there was always something to spare for me. I was frequently threatened with punishment if I stopped there; and my grandmother, to avoid detaining me, often stood at the gate with something for my breakfast or dinner. I was indebted to *her* for all my comforts, spiritual or temporal. It was *her* labor that supplied my scanty wardrobe. I have a vivid recollection of the linsey-woolsey dress given me every winter by Mrs. Flint. How I hated it! It was one of the badges of slavery.

While my grandmother was thus helping to support me from her hard earnings, the three hundred dollars she had lent her mistress were never repaid. When her mistress died, her son-in-law, Dr. Flint, was appointed executor. When grandmother applied to him for payment, he said the estate was insolvent, and the law prohibited payment. It did not, however, prohibit him from retaining the silver candelabra, which had been purchased with that money. I presume they will be handed down in the family, from generation to generation.

My grandmother's mistress had always promised her that, at her death, she should be free; and it was said that in her will she made good the promise. But when the estate was settled, Dr. Flint told the faithful old servant that, under existing circumstances, it was necessary she should be sold.

On the appointed day, the customary advertisement was posted up, proclaiming that there would be a "public sale of negroes, horses, &c." Dr. Flint called to tell my grandmother that he was unwilling to wound her feelings by putting her up at auction, and that he would prefer to dispose of her at private sale. My grandmother saw through his hypocrisy; she understood very well that he was ashamed of the job. She was a very spirited woman, and if he was base enough to sell her, when her mistress intended she should be free, she was determined the public should know it. She had for a long time supplied many families with crackers and preserves; consequently, "Aunt Marthy," as she was called, was generally known, and every body who knew her respected her intelligence and good character. Her long and faithful service in the family was also well known, and the intention of her mistress to leave her free. When the day of sale came, she took her place among the chattels, and at the first call she sprang upon the auction-block. Many voices called out, "Shame! Shame! Who is going to sell *you,* aunt Marthy? Don't stand there! That is no place for *you.*" Without saying a word, she quietly awaited her fate. No one bid for her. At last, a feeble voice said, "Fifty dollars." It came from a maiden lady, seventy years old, the sister of my grandmother's deceased mistress. She had lived forty years under the same roof with my grandmother; she knew how faithfully she had served her owners, and how cruelly she had been defrauded of her rights; and she resolved to protect her. The auctioneer waited for a higher bid; but her wishes were respected; no one bid above her. She could neither read nor write; and when the bill of sale was made out, she signed it with a cross. But what consequence was that, when she had a big heart overflowing with human kindness? She gave the old servant her freedom.

At that time, my grandmother was just fifty years old. Laborious years had passed since then; and now my brother and I were slaves to the man who had defrauded her of her money, and tried to defraud her of her freedom. One of my mother's sisters, called Aunt Nancy, was also a slave in his family. She was a kind, good aunt to me; and supplied the place of both housekeeper and waiting maid to her mistress. She was, in fact, at the beginning and end of every thing.

Mrs. Flint, like many southern women, was totally deficient in energy. She had not strength to superintend her household affairs; but her nerves were so strong, that she could sit in her easy chair and see a woman whipped, till the blood trickled from every stroke of the lash. She was a member of the church; but partaking of the Lord's supper did not seem to put her in a Christian frame of mind. If dinner was not served at the exact time on that particular Sunday, she would station herself in the kitchen, and wait till it was dished, and then spit in all the kettles and pans that had been used for cooking. She did this to prevent the cook and her children from eking out their meagre fare with the remains of the gravy and other scrapings. The slaves could get nothing to eat except what she chose to give them. Provisions were weighed out by the pound and ounce, three times a day. I can assure you she gave them no chance to eat wheat bread from her flour barrel. She knew how many biscuits a quart of flour would make, and exactly what size they ought to be.

Dr. Flint was an epicure. The cook never sent a dinner to his table without fear and trembling; for if there happened to be a dish not to his liking, he would either order her to be whipped, or compel her to eat every mouthful of it in his presence. The poor, hungry creature might not have objected to eating it; but she did object to having her master cram it down her throat till she choked.

They had a pet dog, that was a nuisance in the house. The cook was ordered to make some Indian mush for him. He refused to eat, and when his head was held over it, the froth flowed from his mouth into the basin. He died a few minutes after. When Dr. Flint came in, he said the mush had not been well cooked, and that was the reason the animal would not eat it. He sent for the cook, and compelled her to eat it. He thought that the woman's stomach was stronger than the dog's; but her sufferings afterwards proved that he was mistaken. This poor woman endured many cruelties from her master and mistress; sometimes she was locked up, away from her nursing baby, for a whole day and night.

When I had been in the family a few weeks, one of the plantation slaves was brought to town, by order of his master. It was near night when he arrived, and Dr. Flint ordered him to be taken to the work house, and tied up to the joist, so that his feet would just escape the ground. In that situation he was to wait till the doctor had taken his tea. I shall never forget that night. Never before, in my life, had I heard hundreds of blows fall, in succession, on a human being. His piteous groans, and his "O, pray don't massa," rang in my ear for months afterwards. There were many conjectures as to the cause of this terrible punishment. Some said master accused him of stealing corn; others said the slave had quarrelled with his wife, in presence of the overseer, and had accused his master of being the father of her child. They were both black, and the child was very fair.

I went into the work house next morning, and saw the cowhide still wet with blood, and the boards all covered with gore. The poor man lived, and continued to quarrel with his wife. A few months afterwards Dr. Flint handed them both over to a slave-trader. The guilty man put their value into his pocket, and had the satisfaction of knowing that they were out of sight and hearing. When the mother was delivered into the trader's hands, she said, "You *promised* to treat me well." To which he replied, "You have let your tongue run too far; damn you!" She had forgotten that it was a crime for a slave to tell who was the father of her child.

From others than the master persecution also comes in such cases. I once saw a young slave girl dying soon after the birth of a child nearly white. In her agony she cried out, "O Lord, come and take me!" Her mistress stood by, and mocked at her like an incarnate fiend. "You suffer, do you?" she exclaimed. "I am glad of it. You deserve it all, and more too."

The girl's mother said, "The baby is dead, thank God; and I hope my poor child will soon be in heaven, too."

"Heaven!" retorted the mistress. "There is no such place for the like of her and her bastard."

The poor mother turned away, sobbing. Her dying daughter called her, feebly, and as she bent over her, I heard her say, "Don't grieve so, mother; God knows all about it; and HE will have mercy upon me."

Her sufferings, afterwards, became so intense, that her mistress felt unable to stay; but when she left the room, the scornful smile was still on her lips. Seven children called her mother. The poor black woman had but the one child, whose eyes she saw closing in death, while she thanked God for taking her away from the greater bitterness of life.

VI

The Jealous Mistress

I would ten thousand times rather that my children should be the half-starved paupers of Ireland than to be the most pampered among the slaves of America. I would rather drudge out my life on a cotton plantation, till the grave opened to give me rest, than to live with an unprincipled master and a jealous mistress. The felon's home in a penitentiary is preferable. He may repent, and turn from the error of his ways, and so find peace; but it is not so with a favorite slave. She is not allowed to have any pride of character. It is deemed a crime in her to wish to be virtuous.

Mrs. Flint possessed the key to her husband's character before I was born. She might have used this knowledge to counsel and to screen the young and the innocent among her slaves; but for them she had no sympathy. They were the objects of her constant suspicion and malevolence. She watched her husband with unceasing vigilance; but he was well practised in means to evade it. What he could not find opportunity to say in words he manifested in signs. He invented more than were ever thought of in a deaf and dumb asylum. I let them pass, as if I did not understand what he meant; and many were the curses and threats bestowed on me for my stupidity. One day he caught me teaching myself to write. He frowned, as if he was not well pleased; but I suppose he came to the conclusion that such an accomplishment might help to advance his favorite scheme. Before long, notes were often slipped into my hand. I would return them, saying, "I can't read them, sir." "Can't you?" he replied; "then I must read them to you." He always finished the reading by asking, "Do you understand?" Sometimes he would complain of the heat of the tea room, and order his supper to be placed on a small table in the piazza. He would seat himself there with a well-satisfied smile, and tell me to stand by and brush away the flies. He would eat very slowly, pausing between the mouthfuls. These intervals were employed in describing the happiness I was so foolishly throwing away, and in threatening me with the penalty that finally awaited my stubborn disobedience. He boasted much of the forbearance he had exercised towards me, and reminded me that there was a limit to his patience. When I succeeded in avoiding opportunities for him to talk to me at home, I was ordered to come to his office, to do some errand. When there, I was obliged to stand and listen to such language as he saw fit to address to me. Sometimes I so openly expressed my contempt for him that he would become violently enraged, and I wondered why he did not strike me. Circumstanced as he was, he probably thought it was better policy to be forbearing. But the state of things grew worse and worse daily. In desperation I told him that I must and would apply to my grandmother for protection. He threatened me with death, and worse than death, if I made any complaint to her. Strange to say, I did not despair. I was naturally of a buoyant disposition, and always I had a hope of somehow getting out of his clutches. Like many a poor, simple slave before me, I trusted that some threads of joy would yet be woven into my dark destiny.

I had entered my sixteenth year, and every day it became more apparent that my presence was intolerable to Mrs. Flint. Angry words frequently passed between her and her husband. He had never punished me himself, and he would not allow any body else to punish me. In that respect, she was never satisfied; but, in her angry moods, no terms were too vile for her to bestow upon me. Yet I, whom she detested so bitterly, had far more pity for her than he had, whose duty it was to make her life happy. I never wronged her, or wished to wrong her; and one word of kindness from her would have brought me to her feet.

After repeated quarrels between the doctor and his wife, he announced his intention to take his youngest daughter, then four years old, to sleep in his apartment. It was necessary that a servant should sleep in the same room, to be on hand if the child stirred. I was selected for that office, and informed for what purpose that arrangement had been made. By managing to keep within sight of people, as much as possible, during the day time, I had hitherto succeeded in eluding my master, though a razor was often held to my throat to force me to change this line of policy. At night I slept by the side of my great aunt, where I felt safe. He was too prudent to come into her room. She was an old woman, and had been in the family many years. Moreover, as a married man, and a professional man, he deemed it necessary to save appearances in some degree. But he resolved to remove the obstacle in the way of his scheme; and he thought he had planned it so that he should evade suspicion. He was well aware how much I prized my refuge by the side of my old aunt, and he determined to dispossess me of it. The first night the doctor had the little child in his room alone. The next morning, I was ordered to take my station as nurse the following night. A kind Providence interposed in my favor. During the day Mrs. Flint heard of this new arrangement, and a storm followed. I rejoiced to hear it rage.

After a while my mistress sent for me to come to her room. Her first question was, "Did you know you were to sleep in the doctor's room?"

"Yes, ma'am."

"Who told you?"

"My master."

"Will you answer truly all the questions I ask?"

"Yes, ma'am."

"Tell me, then, as you hope to be forgiven, are you innocent of what I have accused you?"

"I am."

She handed me a Bible, and said, "Lay your hand on your heart, kiss this holy book, and swear before God that you tell me the truth."

I took the oath she required, and I did it with a clear conscience.

"You have taken God's holy word to testify your innocence," said she. "If you have deceived me, beware! Now take this stool, sit down, look me directly in the face, and tell me all that has passed between your master and you."

I did as she ordered. As I went on with my account her color changed frequently, she wept, and sometimes groaned. She spoke in tones so sad, that I was touched by her grief. The tears came to my eyes; but I was soon convinced that her emotions arose from anger and wounded pride. She felt that her marriage vows were desecrated, her dignity insulted; but she had no compassion for the poor victim of her husband's perfidy. She pitied herself as a martyr; but she was incapable of feeling for the condition of shame and misery in which her unfortunate, helpless slave was placed.

Yet perhaps she had some touch of feeling for me; for when the conference was ended, she spoke kindly, and promised to protect me. I should have been much comforted by this assurance if I could have had confidence in it; but my experiences in slavery had filled me with distrust. She was not a very refined woman, and had not much control over her passions. I was an object of her jealousy, and, consequently, of her hatred; and I knew I could not expect kindness or confidence from her under the circumstances in which I was placed. I could not blame her. Slaveholders' wives feel as other women would under similar circumstances. The fire of her temper kindled from small sparks, and now the flame became so intense that the doctor was obliged to give up his intended arrangement.

I knew I had ignited the torch, and I expected to suffer for it afterwards; but I felt too thankful to my mistress for the timely aid she rendered me to care much about that. She now took me to sleep in a room adjoining her own. There I was an object of her especial care, though not of her especial comfort, for she spent many a sleepless night to watch over me. Sometimes I woke up, and found her bending over me. At other times she whispered in my ear, as though it was her husband who was speaking to me, and listened to hear what I would answer. If she startled me, on such occasions, she would glide stealthily away; and the next morning she would tell me I had been talking in my sleep, and ask who I was talking to. At last, I began to be fearful for my life. It had been often threatened; and you can imagine, better than I can describe, what an unpleasant sensation it must produce to wake up in the dead of night and find a jealous woman bending over you. Terrible as this experience was, I had fears that it would give place to one more terrible.

My mistress grew weary of her vigils; they did not prove satisfactory. She changed her tactics. She now tried the trick of accusing my master of crime, in my presence, and gave my name as the author of the accusation. To my utter astonishment, he replied, "I don't believe it; but if she did acknowledge it, you tortured her into exposing me." Tortured into exposing him! Truly, Satan had no difficulty in distinguishing the color of his soul! I understood his object in making this false representation. It was to show me that I gained nothing by seeking the protection of my mistress; that the power was still all in his own hands. I pitied Mrs. Flint. She was a second wife, many years the junior of her husband; and the hoary-headed miscreant was enough to try the patience of a wiser and better woman. She was completely foiled, and knew not how to proceed. She would gladly have had me flogged for my supposed false oath; but, as I have already stated, the doctor never allowed any one to whip me. The old sinner was politic. The application of the lash might have led to remarks that would have exposed him in the eyes of his children and grandchildren. How often did I rejoice that I lived in a town where all the inhabitants knew each other! If I had been on a remote plantation, or lost among the multitude of a crowded city, I should not be a living woman at this day.

The secrets of slavery are concealed like those of the Inquisition. My master was, to my knowledge, the father of eleven slaves. But did the mothers dare to tell who was the father of their children? Did the other slaves dare to allude to it, except in whispers among themselves? No, indeed! They knew too well the terrible consequences.

My grandmother could not avoid seeing things which excited her suspicions. She was uneasy about me, and tried various ways to buy me; but the never-changing answer was always repeated: "Linda does not belong to *me*. She is my daughter's property, and I have no legal right to sell her." The conscientious man! He was too scrupulous to *sell* me; but he had no scruples whatever about committing a much greater wrong against the helpless young girl placed under his guardianship, as his daughter's property. Sometimes my persecutor would ask me whether I would like to be sold. I told him I would rather be sold to any body than to lead such a life as I did. On such occasions he would assume the air of a very injured individual, and reproach me for my ingratitude. "Did I not take you into the house, and make you the companion of my own children?" he would say. "Have I ever treated you like a negro? I have never allowed you to be punished, not even to please your mistress. And this is the recompense I get, you ungrateful girl!" I answered that he had reasons of his own for screening me from punishment, and that the course he pursued made my mistress hate me and persecute me. If I wept, he would say, "Poor child! Don't cry! don't cry! I will make peace for you with your mistress. Only let me arrange matters in my own way. Poor, foolish girl! you don't know what is for your own good. I would cherish you. I would make a lady of you. Now go, and think of all I have promised you."

I did think of it.

Reader, I draw no imaginary pictures of southern homes. I am telling you the plain truth. Yet when victims make their escape from this wild beast of Slavery, northerners consent to act the part of bloodhounds, and hunt the poor fugitive back into his den, "full of dead men's bones, and all uncleanness." Nay, more, they are not only willing, but proud, to give their daughters in marriage to slaveholders. The poor girls have romantic notions of a sunny clime, and of the flowering vines that all the year round shade a happy home. To what disappointments are they destined! The young wife soon learns that the husband in whose hands she has placed her happiness pays no regard to his marriage vows. Children of every shade of complexion play with her own fair babies, and too well she knows that they are born unto him of his own household. Jealousy and hatred enter the flowery home, and it is ravaged of its loveliness.

Southern women often marry a man knowing that he is the father of many little slaves. They do not trouble themselves about it. They regard such children as property, as marketable as the pigs on the plantation; and it is seldom that they do not make them aware of this by passing them into the slavetrader's hands as soon as possible, and thus getting them out of their sight. I am glad to say there are some honorable exceptions.

I have myself known two southern wives who exhorted their husbands to free those slaves towards whom they stood in a "parental relation;" and their request was granted. These husbands blushed before the superior nobleness of their wives' natures. Though they had only counselled them to do that which it was their duty to do, it commanded their respect, and rendered their conduct more exemplary. Concealment was at an end, and confidence took the place of distrust.

Though this bad institution deadens the moral sense, even in white women, to a fearful extent, it is not altogether extinct. I have heard southern ladies say of Mr. Such a one, "He not only thinks it no disgrace to be the father of those little niggers, but he is not ashamed to call himself their master. I declare, such things ought not to be tolerated in any decent society!"

VII

The Lover

Why does the slave ever love? Why allow the tendrils of the heart to twine around objects which may at any moment be wrenched away by the hand of violence? When separations come by the hand of death, the pious soul can bow in resignation, and say, "Not my will, but thine be done, O Lord!" But when the ruthless hand of man strikes the blow, regardless of the misery he causes, it is hard to be submissive. I did not reason thus when I was a young girl. Youth will be youth. I loved, and I indulged the hope that the dark clouds around me would turn out a bright lining. I forgot that in the land of my birth the shadows are too dense for light to penetrate. A land

> Where laughter is not mirth; nor thought the
> mind;
> Nor words a language; nor e'en men mankind.
> Where cries reply to curses, shrieks to blows,
> And each is tortured in his separate hell.

There was in the neighborhood a young colored carpenter; a free-born man. We had been well acquainted in childhood, and frequently met together afterwards. We became mutually attached, and he proposed to marry me. I loved him with all the ardor of a young girl's first love. But when I reflected that I was a slave, and that the laws gave no sanction to the marriage of such, my heart sank within me. My lover wanted to buy me; but I knew that Dr. Flint was too wilful and arbitrary a man to consent to that arrangement. From him, I was sure of experiencing all sorts of opposition, and I had nothing to hope from my mistress. She would have been delighted to have got rid of me, but not in that way. It would have relieved her mind of a burden if she could have seen me sold to some distant state, but if I was married near home I should be just as much in her husband's power as I had previously been,—for the husband of a slave has no power to protect her. Moreover, my mistress, like many others, seemed to think that slaves had no right to any family ties of their own; that they were created merely to wait upon the family of the mistress. I once heard her abuse a young slave girl, who told her that a colored man wanted to make her his wife. "I will have you peeled and pickled, my lady," said she, "if I ever hear you mention that subject again. Do you suppose that I will have you tending *my* children with the children of that nigger?" The girl to whom she said this had a mulatto child, of course not acknowledged by its father. The poor black man who loved her would have been proud to acknowledge his helpless offspring.

Many and anxious were the thoughts I revolved in my mind. I was at a loss what to do. Above all things, I was desirous to spare my lover the insults that had cut so deeply into my own soul. I talked with my grandmother about it, and partly told her my fears. I did not dare to tell her the worst. She had long suspected all was not right, and if I confirmed her suspicions I knew a storm would rise that would prove the overthrow of all my hopes.

This love-dream had been my support through many trials; and I could not bear to run the risk of having it suddenly dissipated. There was a lady in the neighborhood, a particular friend of Dr. Flint's, who often visited the house. I had a great respect for her, and she had always manifested a friendly interest in me. Grandmother thought she would have great influence with the doctor. I went to this lady, and told her my story. I told her I was aware that my lover's being a free-born man would prove a great objection; but he wanted to buy me; and if Dr. Flint would consent to that arrangement, I felt sure he would be willing to pay any reasonable price. She knew that Mrs. Flint disliked me; therefore, I ventured to suggest that perhaps my mistress would approve of my being sold, as that would rid her of me. The lady listened with kindly sympathy, and promised to do her utmost to promote my wishes. She had an interview with the doctor, and I believe she pleaded my cause earnestly; but it was all to no purpose.

How I dreaded my master now! Every minute I expected to be summoned to his presence; but the day passed, and I heard nothing from him. The next morning, a message was brought to me: "Master wants you in his study." I found the door ajar, and I stood a moment gazing at the hateful man who claimed a right to rule me, body and soul. I entered, and tried to appear calm. I did not want him to know how my heart was bleeding. He looked fixedly at me, with an expression which seemed to say, "I have half a mind to kill you on the spot." At last he broke the silence, and that was a relief to both of us.

"So you want to be married, do you?" said he, "and to a free nigger."

"Yes, sir,"

"Well, I'll soon convince you whether I am your master, or the nigger fellow you honor so highly. If you *must* have a husband, you may take up with one of my slaves."

What a situation I should be in, as the wife of one of *his* slaves, even if my heart had been interested!

I replied, "Don't you suppose, sir, that a slave can have some preference about marrying? Do you suppose that all men are alike to her?"

"Do you love this nigger?" said he, abruptly.

"Yes, sir."

"How dare you tell me so!" he exclaimed, in great wrath. After a slight pause, he added, "I supposed you thought more of yourself; that you felt above the insults of such puppies."

I replied, "If he is a puppy I am a puppy, for we are both of the negro race. It is right and honorable for us to love each other. The man you call a puppy never insulted me, sir; and he would not love me if he did not believe me to be a virtuous woman."

He sprang upon me like a tiger, and gave me a stunning blow. It was the first time he had ever struck me; and fear did not enable me to control my anger. When I had recovered a little from the effects, I exclaimed, "You have struck me for answering you honestly. How I despise you!"

There was silence for some minutes. Perhaps he was deciding what should be my punishment; or, perhaps, he wanted to give me time to reflect on what I had said, and to whom I had said it. Finally, he asked, "Do you know what you have said?"

"Yes, sir; but your treatment drove me to it."

"Do you know that I have a right to do as I like with you,—that I can kill you, if I please?"

"You have tried to kill me, and I wish you had; but you have no right to do as you like with me."

"Silence!" he exclaimed, in a thundering voice. "By heavens, girl, you forget yourself too far! Are you mad? If you are, I will soon bring you to your senses. Do you think any other master would bear what I have borne from you this morning? Many masters would have killed you on the spot. How would you like to be sent to jail for your insolence?"

"I know I have been disrespectful, sir," I replied; "but you drove me to it; I couldn't help it. As for the jail, there would be more peace for me there than there is here."

"You deserve to go there," said he, "and to be under such treatment, that you would forget the meaning of the word *peace*. It would do you good. It would take some of your high notions out of you. But I am not ready to send you there yet, notwithstanding your ingratitude for all my kindness and forbearance. You have been the plague of my life. I have wanted to make you happy, and I have been repaid with the basest ingratitude; but though you have proved yourself incapable of appreciating my kindness, I will be lenient towards you, Linda. I will give you one more chance to redeem your character. If you behave yourself and do as I require, I will forgive you and treat you as I always have done; but if you disobey me, I will punish you as I would the meanest slave on my plantation. Never let me hear that fellow's name mentioned again. If I ever know of your speaking to him, I will cowhide you both; and if I catch him lurking about my premises, I will shoot him as soon as I would a dog. Do you hear what I say? I'll teach you a lesson about marriage and free niggers! Now go, and let this be the last time I have occasion to speak to you on this subject."

Reader, did you ever hate? I hope not. I never did but once; and I trust I never shall again. Somebody has called it "the atmosphere of hell;" and I believe it is so.

For a fortnight the doctor did not speak to me. He thought to mortify me; to make me feel that I had disgraced myself by receiving the honorable addresses of a respectable colored man, in preference to the base proposals of a white man. But though his lips disdained to address me, his eyes were very loquacious. No animal ever watched its prey more narrowly than he watched me. He knew that I could write, though he had failed to make me read his letters; and he was now troubled lest I should exchange letters with another man. After a while he became weary of silence; and I was sorry for it. One morning, as he passed through the hall, to leave the house, he contrived to thrust a note into my hand. I thought I had better read it, and spare myself the vexation of having him read it to me. It expressed regret for the blow he had given me, and reminded me that I myself was wholly to blame for it. He hoped I had become convinced of the injury I was doing myself by incurring his displeasure. He wrote that he had made up his mind to go to Louisiana; that he should take several slaves with him, and intended I should be one of the number. My mistress would remain where she was; therefore I should have nothing to fear from that quarter. If I merited kindness from him, he assured me that it would be lavishly bestowed. He begged me to think over the matter, and answer the following day.

The next morning I was called to carry a pair of scissors to his room. I laid them on the table, with the letter beside them. He thought it was my answer, and did not call me back. I went as usual to attend my young mistress to and from school. He met me in the street, and ordered me to stop at his office on my way back. When I entered, he showed me his letter, and asked me why I had not answered it. I replied, "I am your daughter's property, and it is in your power to send me, or take me, wherever you please." He said he was very glad to find me so willing to go, and that we should start early in the autumn. He had a large practice in the town, and I rather thought he had made up the story merely to frighten me. However that might be, I was determined that I would never go to Louisiana with him.

Summer passed away, and early in the autumn Dr. Flint's eldest son was sent to Louisiana to examine the country, with a view to emigrating. That news did not disturb me. I knew very well that I should not be sent with *him.* That I had not been taken to the plantation before this time, was owing to the fact that his son was there. He was jealous of his son; and jealousy of the overseer had kept him from punishing me by sending me into the fields to work. Is it strange that I was not proud of these protectors? As for the overseer, he was a man for whom I had less respect than I had for a bloodhound.

Young Mr. Flint did not bring back a favorable report of Louisiana, and I heard no more of that scheme. Soon after this, my lover met me at the corner of the street, and I stopped to speak to him. Looking up, I saw my master watching us from his window. I hurried home, trembling with fear. I was sent for, immediately, to go to his room. He met me with a blow. "When is mistress to be married?" said he, in a sneering tone. A shower of oaths and imprecations followed. How thankful I was that my lover was a free man! that my tyrant had no power to flog him for speaking to me in the street!

Again and again I revolved in my mind how all this would end. There was no hope that the doctor would consent to sell me on any terms. He had an iron will, and was determined to keep me, and to conquer me. My lover was an intelligent and religious man. Even if he could have obtained permission to marry me while I was a slave, the marriage would give him no power to protect me from my master. It would have made him miserable to witness the insults I should have been subjected to. And then, if we had children, I knew they must "follow the condition of the mother." What a terrible blight that would be on the heart of a free, intelligent father! For *his* sake, I felt that I ought not to link his fate with my own unhappy destiny. He was going to Savannah to see about a little property left him by an uncle; and hard as it was to bring my feelings to it, I earnestly entreated him not to come back. I advised him to go to the Free States, where his tongue would not be tied, and where his intelligence would be of more avail to him. He left me, still hoping the day would come when I could be bought. With me the lamp of hope had gone out. The dream of my girlhood was over. I felt lonely and desolate.

Still I was not stripped of all. I still had my good grandmother, and my affectionate brother. When he put his arms round my neck, and looked into my eyes, as if to read there the troubles I dared not tell, I felt that I still had something to love. But even that pleasant emotion was chilled by the reflection that he might be torn from me at any moment, by some sudden freak of my master. If he had known how we loved each other, I think he would have exulted in separating us. We often planned together how we could get to the north. But, as William remarked, such things are easier said than done. My movements were very closely watched, and we had no means of getting any money to defray our expenses. As for grandmother, she was strongly opposed to her children's undertaking any such project. She had not forgotten poor Benjamin's sufferings, and she was afraid that if another child tried to escape, he would have a similar or a worse fate. To me, nothing seemed more dreadful than my present life. I said to myself, "William *must* be free. He shall go to the north, and I will follow him." Many a slave sister has formed the same plans.

X

A Perilous Passage in the Slave Girl's Life

After my lover went away, Dr. Flint contrived a new plan. He seemed to have an idea that my fear of my mistress was his greatest obstacle. In the blandest tones, he told me that he was going to build a small house for me, in a secluded place, four miles away from the town. I shuddered; but I was constrained to listen, while he talked of his intention to give me a home of my own, and to make a lady of me. Hitherto, I had escaped my dreaded fate, by being in the midst of people. My grandmother had already had high words with my master about me. She had told him pretty plainly what she thought of his character, and there was considerable gossip in the neighborhood about our affairs, to which the open-mouthed jealousy of Mrs. Flint contributed not a little. When my master said he was going to build a house for me, and that he could do it with little trouble and expense, I was in hopes something would happen to frustrate his scheme; but I soon heard that the house was actually begun. I vowed before my Maker that I would never enter it. I had rather toil on the plantation from dawn till dark; I had rather live and die in jail, than drag on, from day to day, through such a living death. I was determined that the master, whom I so hated and loathed, who had blighted the prospects of my youth, and made my life a desert, should not, after my long struggle with him, succeed at last in trampling his victim under his feet. I would do any thing, every thing, for the sake of defeating him. What *could* I do? I thought and thought, till I became desperate, and made a plunge into the abyss.

And now, reader, I come to a period in my unhappy life, which I would gladly forget if I could. The remembrance fills me with sorrow and shame. It pains me to tell you of it; but I have promised to tell you the truth, and I will do it honestly, let it cost me what it may. I will not try to screen myself behind the plea of compulsion from a master; for it was not so. Neither can I plead ignorance or thoughtlessness. For years, my master had done his utmost to pollute my mind with foul images, and to destroy the pure principles inculcated by my grandmother, and the good mistress of my childhood. The influences of slavery had had the same effect on me that they had on other young girls; they had made me prematurely knowing, concerning the evil ways of the world. I knew what I did, and I did it with deliberate calculation.

But, O, ye happy women, whose purity has been sheltered from childhood, who have been free to choose the objects of your affection, whose homes are protected by law, do not judge the poor desolate slave girl too severely! If slavery had been abolished, I, also, could have married the man of my choice; I could have had a home shielded by the laws; and I should have been spared the painful task of confessing what I am now about to relate; but all my prospects had been blighted by slavery. I wanted to keep myself pure; and, under the most adverse circumstances, I tried hard to preserve my self-respect; but I was struggling alone in the powerful grasp of the demon Slavery; and the monster proved too strong for me. I felt as if I was forsaken by God and man; as if all my efforts must be frustrated; and I became reckless in my despair.

I have told you that Dr. Flint's persecutions and his wife's jealousy had given rise to some gossip in the neighborhood. Among others, it chanced that a white unmarried gentleman had obtained some knowledge of the circumstances in which I was placed. He knew my grandmother, and often spoke to me in the street. He became interested for me, and asked questions about my master, which I answered in part. He expressed a great deal of sympathy, and a wish to aid me. He constantly sought opportunities to see me, and wrote to me frequently. I was a poor slave girl, only fifteen years old.

So much attention from a superior person was, of course, flattering; for human nature is the same in all. I also felt grateful for his sympathy, and encouraged by his kind words. It seemed to me a great thing to have such a friend. By degrees, a more tender feeling crept into my heart. He was an educated and eloquent gentleman; too eloquent, alas, for the poor slave girl who trusted in him. Of course I saw whither all this was tending. I knew the impassable gulf between us; but to be an object of interest to a man who is not married, and who is not her master, is agreeable to the pride and feelings of a slave, if her miserable situation has left her any pride or sentiment. It seems less degrading to give one's self, than to submit to compulsion. There is something akin to freedom in having a lover who has no control over you, except that which he gains by kindness and attachment. A master may treat you as rudely as he pleases, and you dare not speak; moreover, the wrong does not seem so great with an unmarried man, as with one who has a wife to be made unhappy. There may be sophistry in all this; but the condition of a slave confuses all principles of morality, and, in fact, renders the practice of them impossible.

When I found that my master had actually begun to build the lonely cottage, other feelings mixed with those I have described. Revenge, and calculations of interest, were added to flattered vanity and sincere gratitude of kindness. I knew nothing would enrage Dr. Flint so much as to know that I favored another; and it was something to triumph over my tyrant even in that small way. I thought he would revenge himself by selling me, and I was sure my friend, Mr. Sands, would buy me. He was a man of more generosity and feeling than my master, and I thought my freedom could be easily obtained from him. The crisis of my fate now came so near that I was desperate. I shuddered to think of being the mother of children that should be owned by my old tyrant. I knew that as soon as a new fancy took him, his victims were sold far off to get rid of them; especially if they had children. I had seen several women sold, with his babies at the breast. He never allowed his offspring by slaves to remain long in sight of himself and his wife. Of a man who was not my master I could ask to have my children well supported; and in this case, I felt confident I should obtain the boon. I also felt quite sure that they would be made free. With all these thoughts revolving in my mind, and seeing no other way of escaping the doom I so much dreaded, I made a headlong plunge. Pity me, and pardon me, O virtuous reader! You never knew what it is to be a slave; to be entirely unprotected by law or custom; to have the laws reduce you to the condition of a chattel, entirely subject to the will of another. You never exhausted your ingenuity in avoiding the snares, and eluding the power of a hated tyrant; you never shuddered at the sound of his footsteps, and trembled within hearing of his voice. I know I did wrong. No one can feel it more sensibly than I do. The painful and humiliating memory will haunt me to my dying day. Still, in looking back, calmly, on the events of my life, I feel that the slave woman ought not to be judged by the same standard as others.

The months passed on. I had many unhappy hours. I secretly mourned over the sorrow I was bringing on my grandmother, who had so tried to shield me from harm. I knew that I was the greatest comfort of her old age, and that it was a source of pride to her that I had not degraded myself, like most of the slaves. I wanted to confess to her that I was no longer worthy of her love; but could not utter the dreaded words.

As for Dr. Flint, I had a feeling of satisfaction and triumph in the thought of telling *him.* From time to time he told me of his intended arrangements, and I was silent. At last, he came and told me the cottage was completed, and ordered me to go to it. I told him I would never enter it. He said, "I have heard enough of such talk as that. You shall go, if you are carried by force; and you shall remain there."

I replied, "I will never go there. In a few months I shall be a mother."

He stood and looked at me in dumb amazement, and left the house without a word. I thought I should be happy in my triumph over him. But now that the truth was out, and my relatives would hear of it, I felt wretched. Humble as were their circumstances, they had pride in my good character. Now, how could I look them in the face? My self-respect was gone! I had resolved that I would be virtuous, though I was a slave. I had said, "Let the storm beat! I will brave it till I die." And now, how humiliated I felt!

I went to my grandmother. My lips moved to make confession, but the words stuck in my throat. I sat down in the shade of a tree at her door and began to sew. I think she saw something unusual was the matter with me. The mother of slaves is very watchful. She knows there is no security for her children. After they have entered their teens she lives in daily expectation of trouble. This leads to many questions. If the girl is of a sensitive nature, timidity keeps her from answering truthfully, and this well-meant course has a tendency to drive her from maternal counsels. Presently, in came my mistress, like a mad woman, and accused me concerning her husband. My grandmother, whose suspicions had been previously awakened, believed what she said. She exclaimed, "O Linda! has it come to this? I had rather see you dead than to see you as you now are. You are a disgrace to your dead mother." She tore from my fingers my mother's wedding ring and her silver thimble. "Go away!" she exclaimed, "and never come to my house, again." Her reproaches fell so hot and heavy, that they left me no chance to answer. Bitter tears, such as the eyes never shed but once, were my only answer. I rose from my seat, but fell back again, sobbing. She did not speak to me; but the tears were running down her furrowed cheeks, and they scorched me like fire. She had always been so kind to me! *So* kind! How I longed to throw myself at her feet, and tell her all the truth! But she had ordered me to go, and never to come there again. After a few minutes, I mustered strength, and started to obey her. With what feelings did I now close that little gate, which I used to open with such an eager hand in my childhood! It closed upon me with a sound I never heard before.

Where could I go? I was afraid to return to my master's. I walked on recklessly, not caring where I went, or what would become of me. When I had gone four or five miles, fatigue compelled me to stop. I sat down on the stump of an old tree. The stars were shining through the boughs above me. How they mocked me, with their bright, calm light! The hours passed by, and as I sat there alone a chilliness and deadly sickness came over me. I sank on the ground. My mind was full of horrid thoughts. I prayed to die; but the prayer was not answered. At last, with great effort I roused myself, and walked some distance further, to the house of a woman who had been a friend of my mother.

When I told her why I was there, she spoke soothingly to me; but I could not be comforted. I thought I could bear my shame if I could only be reconciled to my grandmother. I longed to open my heart to her. I thought if she could know the real state of the case, and all I had been bearing for years, she would perhaps judge me less harshly. My friend advised me to send for her. I did so; but days of agonizing suspense passed before she came. Had she utterly forsaken me? No. She came at last. I knelt before her, and told her things that had poisoned my life; how long I had been persecuted; that I saw no way of escape; and in an hour of extremity I had become desperate. She listened in silence. I told her I would bear any thing and do any thing, if in time I had hopes of obtaining her forgiveness. I begged of her to pity me, for my dead mother's sake. And she did pity me. She did not say, "I forgive you;" but she looked at me lovingly, with her eyes full of tears. She laid her old hand gently on my head, and murmured, "Poor child! Poor child!"

XVII
The Flight

Dr. Flint was hard pushed for house servants, and rather than lose me he had restrained his malice. I did my work faithfully, though not, of course, with a willing mind. They were evidently afraid I should leave them. Mr. Flint wished that I should sleep in the great house instead of the servants' quarters. His wife agreed to the proposition, but said I mustn't bring my bed into the house, because it would scatter feathers on her carpet. I knew when I went there that they would never think of such a thing as furnishing a bed of any kind for me and my little one. I therefore carried my own bed, and now I was forbidden to use it. I did as I was ordered. But now that I was certain my children were to be put in their power, in order to give them a stronger hold on me, I resolved to leave them that night. I remembered the grief this step would bring upon my dear old grandmother; and nothing less than the freedom of my children would have induced me to disregard her advice. I went about my evening work with trembling steps. Dr. Flint twice called from his chamber door to inquire why the house was not locked up. I replied that I had not done my work. "You have had time enough to do it," said he. "Take care how you answer me!"

I shut all the windows, locked all the doors, and went up to the third story, to wait till midnight. How long those hours seemed, and how fervently I prayed that God would not forsake me in this hour of utmost need! I was about to risk every thing on the throw of a die; and if I failed, O what would become of me and my poor children! They would be made to suffer for my fault.

At half past twelve I stole softly down stairs. I stopped on the second floor, thinking I heard a noise. I felt my way down into the parlor, and looked out of the window. The night was so intensely dark that I could see nothing. I raised the window very softly and jumped out. Large drops of rain were falling, and the darkness bewildered me. I dropped on my knees, and breathed a short prayer to God for guidance and protection. I groped my way to the road, and rushed towards the town with almost lightning speed. I arrived at my grandmother's house, but dared not see her. She would say, "Linda, you are killing me;" and I knew that would unnerve me. I tapped softly at the window of a room, occupied by a woman, who had lived in the house several years. I knew she was a faithful friend, and could be trusted with my secret. I tapped several times before she heard me. At last she raised the window, and I whispered, "Sally, I have run away. Let me in, quick." She opened the door softly, and said in low tones, "For God's sake, don't. Your grandmother is trying to buy you and de chillern. Mr. Sands was here last week. He tole her he was going away on business, but he wanted her to go ahead about buying you and de chillern, and he would help her all he could. Don't run away, Linda. Your grandmother is all bowed down wid trouble now."

I replied, "Sally, they are going to carry my children to the plantation to-morrow; and they will never sell them to any body so long as they have me in their power. Now, would you advise me to go back?"

"No, chile, no," answered she. "When dey finds you is gone, dey won't want de plague ob de chillern; but where is you going to hide? Dey knows ebery inch ob dis house."

I told her I had a hiding-place, and that was all it was best for her to know. I asked her to go into my room as soon as it was light, and take all my clothes out of my trunk, and pack them in hers; for I knew Dr. Flint and the constable would be there early to search my room. I feared the sight of my children would be too much for my full heart; but I could not go out into the uncertain future without one last look. I bent over the bed where lay my little Benny and baby Ellen. Poor little ones! fatherless and motherless! Memories of their father came over me. He wanted to be kind to them; but they were not all to him, as they were to my womanly heart. I knelt and prayed for the innocent little sleepers. I kissed them lightly, and turned away.

As I was about to open the street door, Sally laid her hand on my shoulder, and said, "Linda, is you gwine all alone? Let me call your uncle."

"No, Sally," I replied, "I want no one to be brought into trouble on my account."

I went forth into the darkness and rain. I ran on till I came to the house of the friend who was to conceal me.

Early the next morning Dr. Flint was at my grandmother's inquiring for me. She told him she had not seen me, and supposed I was at the plantation. He watched her face narrowly, and said, "Don't you know any thing about her running off?" She assured him that she did not. He went on to say, "Last night she ran off without the least provocation. We had treated her very kindly. My wife liked her. She will soon be found and brought back. Are her children with you?" When told that they were, he said, "I am very glad to hear that. If they are here, she cannot be far off. If I find out that any of my niggers have had any thing to do with this damned business, I'll give 'em five hundred lashes." As he started to go to his father's, he turned round and added, persuasively, "Let her be brought back, and she shall have her children to live with her."

The tidings made the old doctor rave and storm at a furious rate. It was a busy day for them. My grandmother's house was searched from top to bottom. As my trunk was empty, they concluded I had taken my clothes with me. Before ten o'clock every vessel northward bound was thoroughly examined, and the law against harboring fugitives was read to all on board. At night a watch was set over the town. Knowing how distressed my grandmother would be, I wanted to send her a message; but it could not be done. Every one who went in or out of her house was closely watched. The doctor said he would take my children, unless she became responsible for them; which of course she willingly did. The next day was spent in searching. Before night, the following advertisement was posted at every corner, and in every public place for miles round:—

"$300 REWARD! Ran away from the subscriber, an intelligent, bright, mulatto girl, named Linda, 21 years of age. Five feet four inches high. Dark eyes, and black hair inclined to curl; but it can be made straight. Has a decayed spot on a front tooth. She can read and write, and in all probability will try to get to the Free States. All persons are forbidden, under penalty of the law, to harbor or employ said slave. $150 will be given to whoever takes her in the state, and $300 if taken out of the state and delivered to me, or lodged in jail.

DR. FLINT."

XXI
The Loophole of Retreat

A small shed had been added to my grandmother's house years ago. Some boards were laid across the joists at the top, and between these boards and the roof was a very small garret, never occupied by any thing but rats and mice. It was a pent roof, covered with nothing but shingles, according to the southern custom for such buildings. The garret was only nine feet long and seven wide. The highest part was three feet high, and sloped down abruptly to the loose board floor. There was no admission for either light or air. My uncle Phillip, who was a carpenter, had very skilfully made a concealed trap-door, which communicated with the storeroom. He had been doing this while I was waiting in the swamp. The storeroom opened upon a piazza. To this hole I was conveyed as soon as I entered the house. The air was stifling; the darkness total. A bed had been spread on the floor. I could sleep quite comfortably on one side; but the slope was so sudden that I could not turn on the other without hitting the roof. The rats and mice ran over my bed; but I was weary, and I slept such sleep as the wretched may, when a tempest has passed over them. Morning came. I knew it only by the noises I heard; for in my small den day and night were all the same. I suffered for air even more than for light. But I was not comfortless. I heard the voices of my children. There was joy and there was sadness in the sound. It made my tears flow. How I longed to speak to them! I was eager to look on their faces; but there was no hole, no crack, through which I could peep. This continued darkness was oppressive. It seemed horrible to sit or lie in a cramped position day after day, without one gleam of light. Yet I would have chosen this, rather than my lot as a slave, though white people considered it an easy one; and it was so compared with the fate of others. I was never cruelly overworked; I was never lacerated with the whip from head to foot; I was never so beaten and bruised that I could not turn from one side to the other; I never had my heel-strings cut to prevent my running away; I was never chained to a log and forced to drag it about, while I toiled in the fields from morning till night; I was never branded with hot iron, or torn by bloodhounds. On the contrary, I had always been kindly treated, and tenderly cared for, until I came into the hands of Dr. Flint. I had never wished for freedom till then. But though my life in slavery was comparatively devoid of hardships, God pity the woman who is compelled to lead such a life!

My food was passed up to me through the trap-door my uncle had contrived; and my grandmother, my uncle Phillip, and aunt Nancy would seize such opportunities as they could, to mount up there and chat with me at the opening. But of course this was not safe in the daytime. It must all be done in darkness. It was impossible for me to move in an erect position, but I crawled about my den for exercise. One day I hit my head against something, and found it was a gimlet. My uncle had left it sticking there when he made the trap-door. I was as rejoiced as Robinson Crusoe could have been at finding such a treasure. It put a lucky thought into my head. I said to myself, "Now I will have some light. Now I will see my children." I did not dare to begin my work during the daytime, for fear of attracting attention. But I groped round; and having found the side next the street, where I could frequently see my children, I stuck the gimlet in and waited for evening. I bored three rows of holes, one above another; then I bored out the interstices between. I thus succeeded in making one hole about an inch long and an inch broad. I sat by it till late into the night, to enjoy the little whiff of air that floated in. In the morning I watched for my children. The first person I saw in the street was Dr. Flint. I had a shuddering, superstitious feeling that it was a bad omen. Several familiar faces passed by. At last I heard the merry laugh of children, and presently two sweet little faces were looking up at me, as though they knew I was there, and were conscious of the joy they imparted. How I longed to *tell* them I was there!

My condition was now a little improved. But for weeks I was tormented by hundreds of little red insects, fine as a needle's point, that pierced through my skin, and produced an intolerable burning. The good grandmother gave me herb teas and cooling medicines, and finally I got rid of them. The heat of my den was intense, for nothing but thin shingles protected me from the scorching summer's sun. But I had my consolations. Through my peeping-hole I could watch the children, and when they were near enough, I could hear their talk. Aunt Nancy brought me all the news she could hear at Dr. Flint's. From her I learned that the doctor had written to New York to a colored woman, who had been born and raised in our neighborhood, and had breathed his contaminating atmosphere. He offered her a reward if she could find out any thing about me. I know not what was the nature of her reply; but he soon after started for New York in haste, saying to his family that he had business of importance to transact. I peeped at him as he passed on his way to the steamboat. It was a satisfaction to have miles of land and water between us, even for a little while; and it was a still greater satisfaction to know that he believed me to be in the Free States. My little den seemed less dreary than it had done. He returned, as he did from his former journey to New York, without obtaining any satisfactory information. When he passed our house next morning, Benny was standing at the gate. He had heard them say that he had gone to find me, and he called out, "Dr. Flint, did you bring my mother home? I want to see her." The doctor stamped his foot at him in a rage, and exclaimed, "Get out of the way, you little damned rascal! If you don't, I'll cut off your head."

Benny ran terrified into the house, saying, "You can't put me in jail again. I don't belong to you now." It was well that the wind carried the words away from the doctor's ear. I told my grandmother of it, when we had our next conference at the trap-door; and begged of her not to allow the children to be impertinent to the irascible old man.

Autumn came, with a pleasant abatement of heat. My eyes had become accustomed to the dim light, and by holding my book or work in a certain position near the aperture I contrived to read and sew. That was a great relief to the tedious monotony of my life. But when winter came, the cold penetrated through the thin shingle roof, and I was dreadfully chilled. The winters there are not so long, or so severe, as in northern latitudes; but the houses are not built to shelter from cold, and my little den was peculiarly comfortless. The kind grandmother brought me bed-clothes and warm drinks. Often I was obliged to lie in bed all day to keep comfortable; but with all my precautions, my shoulders and feet were frostbitten. O, those long, gloomy days, with no object for my eye to rest upon, and no thoughts to occupy my mind, except the dreary past and the uncertain future! I was thankful when there came a day sufficiently mild for me to wrap myself up and sit at the loophole to watch the passers by. Southerners have the habit of stopping and talking in the streets, and I heard many conversations not intended to meet my ears. I heard slave-hunters planning how to catch some poor fugitive. Several times I heard allusions to Dr. Flint, myself, and the history of my children, who, perhaps, were playing near the gate. One would say, "I wouldn't move my little finger to catch her, as old Flint's property," Another would say, "I'll catch *any* nigger for the reward. A man ought to have what belongs to him, if he *is* a damned brute." The opinion was often expressed that I was in the Free States. Very rarely did any one suggest that I might be in the vicinity. Had the least suspicion rested on my grandmother's house, it would have been burned to the ground. But it was the last place they thought of. Yet there was no place, where slavery existed, that could have afforded me so good a place of concealment.

Dr. Flint and his family repeatedly tried to coax and bribe my children to tell something they had heard said about me. One day the doctor took them into a shop, and offered them some bright little silver pieces and gay handkerchiefs if they would tell where their mother was. Ellen shrank away from him, and would not speak; but Benny spoke up, and said, "Dr. Flint, I don't know where my mother is. I guess she's in New York; and when you go there again, I wish you'd ask her to come home, for I want to see her; but if you put her in jail, or tell her you'll cut her head off, I'll tell her to go right back."

XXIX
Preparations for Escape

I hardly expect that the reader will credit me, when I affirm that I lived in that little dismal hole, almost deprived of light and air, and with no space to move my limbs, for nearly seven years. But it is a fact; and to me a sad one, even now; for my body still suffers from the effects of that long imprisonment, to say nothing of my soul. Members of my family, now living in New York and Boston, can testify to the truth of what I say.

Countless were the nights that I sat late at the little loophole scarcely large enough to give me a glimpse of one twinkling star. There, I heard the patrols and slave-hunters conferring together about the capture of runaways, well knowing how rejoiced they would be to catch me.

Season after season, year after year, I peeped at my children's faces, and heard their sweet voices, with a heart yearning all the while to say, "Your mother is here." Sometimes it appeared to me as if ages had rolled away since I entered upon that gloomy, monotonous existence. At times, I was stupefied and listless; at other times I became very impatient to know when these dark years would end, and I should again be allowed to feel the sunshine, and breathe the pure air.

After Ellen left us, this feeling increased. Mr. Sands had agreed that Benny might go to the north whenever his uncle Phillip could go with him; and I was anxious to be there also, to watch over my children, and protect them so far as I was able. Moreover, I was likely to be drowned out of my den, if I remained much longer; for the slight roof was getting badly out of repair, and uncle Phillip was afraid to remove the shingles, lest some one should get a glimpse of me. When storms occurred in the night, they spread mats and bits of carpet, which in the morning appeared to have been laid out to dry; but to cover the roof in the daytime might have attracted attention. Consequently, my clothes and bedding were often drenched; a process by which the pains and aches in my cramped and stiffened limbs were greatly increased. I revolved various plans of escape in my mind, which I sometimes imparted to my grandmother, when she came to whisper with me at the trap-door. The kind-hearted old woman had an intense sympathy for runaways. She had known too much of the cruelties inflicted on those who were captured. Her memory always flew back at once to the sufferings of her bright and handsome son, Benjamin, the youngest and dearest of her flock. So, whenever I alluded to the subject, she would groan out, "O, don't think of it, child. You'll break my heart." I had no good old aunt Nancy now to encourage me; but my brother William and my children were continually beckoning me to the north.

And now I must go back a few months in my story. I have stated that the first of January was the time for selling slaves, or leasing them out to new masters. If time were counted by heart-throbs, the poor slaves might reckon years of suffering during that festival so joyous to the free. On the New Year's day preceding my aunt's death, one of my friends, named Fanny, was to be sold at auction, to pay her master's debts. My thoughts were with her during all the day, and at night I anxiously inquired what had been her fate. I was told that she had been sold to one master, and her four little girls to another master, far distant; that she had escaped from her purchaser, and was not to be found. Her mother was the old Aggie I have spoken of. She lived in a small tenement belonging to my grandmother, and built on the same lot with her own house. Her dwelling was searched and watched, and that brought the patrols so near me that I was obliged to keep very close in my den. The hunters were somehow eluded; and not long afterwards Benny accidentally caught sight of Fanny in her mother's hut. He told his grandmother, who charged him never to speak of it, explaining to him the frightful consequences; and he never betrayed the trust. Aggie little dreamed that my grandmother knew where her daughter was concealed, and that the stooping form of her old neighbor was bending under a similar burden of anxiety and fear; but these dangerous secrets deepened the sympathy between the two old persecuted mothers.

My friend Fanny and I remained many weeks hidden within call of each other; but she was unconscious of the fact. I longed to have her share my den, which seemed a more secure retreat than her own; but I had brought so much trouble on my grandmother, that it seemed wrong to ask her to incur greater risks. My restlessness increased. I had lived too long in bodily pain and anguish of spirit. Always I was in dread that by some accident, or some contrivance, slavery would succeed in snatching my children from me. This thought drove me nearly frantic, and I determined to steer for the North Star[1] at all hazards. At this crisis, Providence opened an unexpected way for me to escape. My friend Peter came one evening, and asked to speak with me. "Your day has come, Linda," said he. "I have found a chance for you to go to the Free States. You have a fortnight to decide." The news seemed too good to be true; but Peter explained his arrangements, and told me all that was necessary was for me to say I would go. I was going to answer him with a joyful yes, when the thought of Benny came to my mind. I told him the temptation was exceedingly strong, but I was terribly afraid of Dr. Flint's alleged power over my child, and that I could not go and leave him behind. Peter remonstrated earnestly. He said such a good chance might never occur again; that Benny was free, and could be sent to me; and that for the sake of my children's welfare I ought not to hesitate a moment. I told him I would consult with uncle Phillip. My uncle rejoiced in the plan, and bade me go by all means. He promised, if his life was spared, that he would either bring or send my son to me as soon as I reached a place of safety. I resolved to go, but thought nothing had better be said to my grandmother till very near the time of departure. But my uncle thought she would feel it more keenly if I left her so suddenly. "I will reason with her," said he, "and convince her how necessary it is, not only for your sake, but for hers also. You cannot be blind to the fact that she is sinking under her burdens." I was not blind to it. I knew that my concealment was an ever-present source of anxiety, and that the older she grew the more nervously fearful she was of discovery. My uncle talked with her, and finally succeeded in persuading her that it was absolutely necessary for me to seize the chance so unexpectedly offered.

The anticipation of being a free woman proved almost too much for my weak frame. The excitement stimulated me, and at the same time bewildered me. I made busy preparations for my journey, and for my son to follow me. I resolved to have an interview with him before I went, that I might give him cautions and advice, and tell him how anxiously I should be waiting for him at the north. Grandmother stole up to me as often as possible to whisper words of counsel. She insisted upon my writing to Dr. Flint, as soon as I arrived in the Free States, and asking him to sell me to her. She said she would sacrifice her house, and all she had in the world, for the sake of having me safe with my children in any part of the world. If she could only live to know *that* she could die in peace. I promised the dear old faithful friend that I would write to her as soon as I arrived, and put the letter in a safe way to reach her; but in my own mind I resolved that not another cent of her hard earnings should be spent to pay rapacious slaveholders for what they called their property. And even if I had not been unwilling to buy what I had already a right to possess, common humanity would have prevented me from accepting the generous offer, at the expense of turning my aged relative out of house and home, when she was trembling on the brink of the grave.

[1]This was the only guide of many a fleeing slave, hiding by day and running by night.

I was to escape in a vessel; but I forbear to mention any further particulars. I was in readiness, but the vessel was unexpectedly detained several days. Meantime, news came to town of a most horrible murder committed on a fugitive slave, named James. Charity, the mother of this unfortunate young man, had been an old acquaintance of ours. I have told the shocking particulars of his death, in my description of some of the neighboring slaveholders. My grandmother, always nervously sensitive about runaways, was terribly frightened. She felt sure that a similar fate awaited me, if I did not desist from my enterprise. She sobbed, and groaned, and entreated me not to go. Her excessive fear was somewhat contagious, and my heart was not proof against her extreme agony. I was grievously disappointed, but I promised to relinquish my project.

When my friend Peter was apprised of this, he was both disappointed and vexed. He said, that judging from our past experience, it would be a long time before I had such another chance to throw away. I told him it need not be thrown away; that I had a friend concealed near by, who would be glad enough to take the place that had been provided for me. I told him about poor Fanny, and the kind-hearted, noble fellow, who never turned his back upon any body in distress, white or black, expressed his readiness to help her. Aggie was much surprised when she found that we knew her secret. She was rejoiced to hear of such a chance for Fanny, and arrangements were made for her to go on board the vessel the next night. They both supposed that I had long been at the north, therefore my name was not mentioned in the transaction. Fanny was carried on board at the appointed time, and stowed away in a very small cabin. This accommodation had been purchased at a price that would pay for a voyage to England. But when one proposes to go to fine old England, they stop to calculate whether they can afford the cost of the pleasure; while in making a bargain to escape from slavery, the trembling victim is ready to say, "Take all I have, only don't betray me!"

The next morning I peeped through my loophole, and saw that it was dark and cloudy. At night I received news that the wind was ahead, and the vessel had not sailed. I was exceedingly anxious about Fanny, and Peter too, who was running a tremendous risk at my instigation. Next day the wind and weather remained the same. Poor Fanny had been half dead with fright when they carried her on board, and I could readily imagine how she must be suffering now. Grandmother came often to my den, to say how thankful she was I did not go. On the third morning she rapped for me to come down to the storeroom. The poor old sufferer was breaking down under her weight of trouble. She was easily flurried now. I found her in a nervous, excited state, but I was not aware that she had forgotten to lock the door behind her, as usual. She was exceedingly worried about the detention of the vessel. She was afraid all would be discovered, and then Fanny, and Peter, and I, would all be tortured to death, and Phillip would be utterly ruined, and her house would be torn down. Poor Peter! If he should die such a horrible death as the poor slave James had lately done, and all for his kindness in trying to help me, how dreadful it would be for us all! Alas, the thought was familiar to me, and had sent many a sharp pang through my heart. I tried to suppress my own anxiety, and speak soothingly to her. She brought in some allusion to aunt Nancy, the dear daughter she had recently buried, and then she lost all control of herself. As she stood there, trembling and sobbing, a voice from the piazza called out, "Whar is you, aunt Marthy?" Grandmother was startled, and in her agitation opened the door, without thinking of me. In stepped Jenny, the mischievous housemaid, who had tried to enter my room, when I was concealed in the house of my white benefactress. "I's bin huntin ebery whar for you, aunt Marthy," said she. "My missis wants you to send her some crackers." I had slunk down behind a barrel, which entirely screened me, but I imagined that Jenny was looking directly at the spot, and my heart beat violently. My grandmother immediately thought what she had done, and went out quickly with

Jenny to count the crackers locking the door after her. She returned to me, in a few minutes, the perfect picture of despair. "Poor child!" she exclaimed, "my carelessness has ruined you. The boat ain't gone yet. Get ready immediately, and go with Fanny. I ain't got another word to say against it now; for there's no telling what may happen this day."

Uncle Phillip was sent for, and he agreed with his mother in thinking that Jenny would inform Dr. Flint in less than twenty-four hours. He advised getting me on board the boat, if possible; if not, I had better keep very still in my den, where they could not find me without tearing the house down. He said it would not do for him to move in the matter, because suspicion would be immediately excited; but he promised to communicate with Peter. I felt reluctant to apply to him again, having implicated him too much already; but there seemed to be no alternative. Vexed as Peter had been by my indecision, he was true to his generous nature, and said at once that he would do his best to help me, trusting I should show myself a stronger woman this time.

He immediately proceeded to the wharf, and found that the wind had shifted, and the vessel was slowly beating down stream. On some pretext of urgent necessity, he offered two boatmen a dollar apiece to catch up with her. He was of lighter complexion than the boatmen he hired, and when the captain saw them coming so rapidly, he thought officers were pursuing his vessel in search of the runaway slave he had on board. They hoisted sails, but the boat gained upon them, and the indefatigable Peter sprang on board.

The captain at once recognized him. Peter asked him to go below, to speak about a bad bill he had given him. When he told his errand, the captain replied, "Why, the woman's here already; and I've put her where you or the devil would have a tough job to find her."

"But it is another woman I want to bring," said Peter. "*She* is in great distress, too, and you shall be paid any thing within reason, if you'll stop and take her."

"What's her name?" inquired the captain.

"Linda," he replied.

"That's the name of the woman already here," rejoined the captain. "By George! I believe you mean to betray me."

"O!" exclaimed Peter, "God knows I wouldn't harm a hair of your head. I am too grateful to you. But there really *is* another woman in great danger. Do have the humanity to stop and take her!"

After a while they came to an understanding. Fanny, not dreaming I was any where about in that region, had assumed my name, though she called herself Johnson. "Linda is a common name," said Peter, "and the woman I want to bring is Linda Brent."

The captain agreed to wait at a certain place till evening, being handsomely paid for his detention.

Of course, the day was an anxious one for us all. But we concluded that if Jenny had seen me, she would be too wise to let her mistress know of it; and that she probably would not get a chance to see Dr. Flint's family till evening, for I knew very well what were the rules in that household. I afterwards believed that she did not see me; for nothing ever came of it, and she was one of those base characters that would have jumped to betray a suffering fellow being for the sake of thirty pieces of silver.

I made all my arrangements to go on board as soon as it was dusk. The intervening time I resolved to spend with my son. I had not spoken to him for seven years, though I had been under the same roof, and seen him every day, when I was well enough to sit at the loophole. I did not dare to venture beyond the storeroom; so they brought him there, and locked us up together, in a place concealed from the piazza door. It was an agitating interview for both of us. After we had talked and wept together for a little while, he said, "Mother, I'm glad you're going away. I wish I could go with you. I knew you was here; and I have been *so* afraid they would come and catch you!"

I was greatly surprised, and asked him how he had found it out.

He replied, "I was standing under the eaves, one day, before Ellen went away, and I heard somebody cough up over the wood shed. I don't know what made me think it was you, but I did think so. I missed Ellen, the night before she went away; and grandmother brought her back into the room in the night; and I thought maybe she'd been to see *you,* before she went, for I heard grandmother whisper to her, 'Now go to sleep; and remember never to tell.'"

I asked him if he ever mentioned his suspicions to his sister. He said he never did; but after he heard the cough, if he saw her playing with other children on that side of the house, he always tried to coax her round to the other side, for fear they would hear me cough, too. He said he had kept a close lookout for Dr. Flint, and if he saw him speak to a constable, or a patrol, he always told grandmother. I now recollected that I had seen him manifest uneasiness, when people were on that side of the house, and I had at the time been puzzled to conjecture a motive for his actions. Such prudence may seem extraordinary in a boy of twelve years, but slaves, being surrounded by mysteries, deceptions, and dangers, early learn to be suspicious and watchful, and prematurely cautious and cunning. He had never asked a question of grandmother, or uncle Phillip, and I had often heard him chime in with other children, when they spoke of my being at the north.

I told him I was now really going to the Free States, and if he was a good, honest boy, and a loving child to his dear old grandmother, the Lord would bless him, and bring him to me, and we and Ellen would live together. He began to tell me that grandmother had not eaten any thing all day. While he was speaking, the door was unlocked, and she came in with a small bag of money, which she wanted me to take. I begged her to keep a part of it, at least, to pay for Benny's being sent to the north; but she insisted, while her tears were falling fast, that I should take the whole. "You may be sick among strangers," she said, "and they would send you to the poorhouse to die." Ah, that good grandmother!

For the last time I went up to my nook. Its desolate appearance no longer chilled me, for the light of hope had risen in my soul. Yet, even with the blessed prospect of freedom before me, I felt very sad at leaving forever that old homestead, where I had been sheltered so long by the dear old grandmother; where I had dreamed my first young dream of love; and where, after that had faded away, my children came to twine themselves so closely round my desolate heart. As the hour approached for me to leave, I again descended to the storeroom. My grandmother and Benny were there. She took me by the hand, and said, "Linda, let us pray." We knelt down together, with my child pressed to my heart, and my other arm round the faithful, loving old friend I was about to leave forever. On no other occasion has it ever been my lot to listen to so fervent a supplication for mercy and protection. It thrilled through my heart, and inspired me with trust in God.

Peter was waiting for me in the street. I was soon by his side, faint in body, but strong of purpose. I did not look back upon the old place, though I felt that I should never see it again.

XXX
Northward Bound

I never could tell how we reached the wharf. My brain was all of a whirl, and my limbs tottered under me. At an appointed place we met my uncle Phillip, who had started before us on a different route, that he might reach the wharf first, and give us timely warning if there was any danger. A rowboat was in readiness. As I was about to step in, I felt something pull me gently, and turning round I saw Benny, looking pale and anxious. He whispered in my ear, "I've been peeping into the doctor's window, and he's at home. Good by, mother. Don't cry; I'll come." He hastened away. I clasped the hand of my good uncle, to whom I owed so much, and of Peter, the brave, generous friend who had volunteered to run such terrible risks to secure my safety. To this day I remember how his bright face beamed with joy, when he told me he had discovered a safe method for me to escape. Yet that intelligent, enterprising, noble-hearted man was a chattel! liable, by the laws of a country that calls itself civilized, to be sold with horses and pigs! We parted in silence. Our hearts were all too full for words!

Swiftly the boat glided over the water. After a while, one of the sailors said, "Don't be down-hearted madam. We will take you safely to your husband, in ——." At first I could not imagine what he meant; but I had presence of mind to think that it probably referred to something the captain had told him; so I thanked him, and said I hoped we should have pleasant weather.

When I entered the vessel the captain came forward to meet me. He was an elderly man, with a pleasant countenance. He showed me to a little box of a cabin, where sat my friend Fanny. She started as if she had seen a spectre. She gazed on me in utter astonishment, and exclaimed, "Linda, can this be *you?* or is it your ghost?" When we were locked in each other's arms, my overwrought feelings could no longer be restrained. My sobs reached the ears of the captain, who came and very kindly reminded us, that for his safety, as well as our own, it would be prudent for us not to attract any attention. He said that when there was a sail in sight he wished us to keep below; but at other times, he had no objection to our being on deck. He assured us that he would keep a good lookout, and if we acted prudently, he thought we should be in no danger. He had represented us as women going to meet our husbands in ——. We thanked him, and promised to observe carefully all the directions he gave us.

Fanny and I now talked by ourselves, low and quietly, in our little cabin. She told me of the sufferings she had gone through in making her escape, and of her terrors while she was concealed in her mother's house. Above all, she dwelt on the agony of separation from all her children on that dreadful auction day. She could scarcely credit me, when I told her of the place where I had passed nearly seven years. "We have the same sorrows," said I. "No," replied she, "you are going to see your children soon, and there is no hope that I shall ever even hear from mine."

The vessel was soon under way, but we made slow progress. The wind was against us. I should not have cared for this, if we had been out of sight of the town; but until there were miles of water between us and our enemies, we were filled with constant apprehensions that the constables would come on board. Neither could I feel quite at ease with the captain and his men. I was an entire stranger to that class of people, and I had heard that sailors were rough, and sometimes cruel. We were so completely in their power, that if they were bad men, our situation would be dreadful. Now that the captain was paid for our passage, might he not be tempted to make more money by giving us up to those who claimed us as property? I was naturally of a confiding disposition, but slavery had made me suspicious of every body. Fanny did not share my distrust of the captain or his men. She said she was afraid at first, but she had been on board three days while the vessel lay in the dock, and nobody had betrayed her, or treated her otherwise than kindly.

The captain soon came to advise us to go on deck for fresh air. His friendly and respectful manner, combined with Fanny's testimony, reassured me, and we went with him. He placed us in a comfortable seat, and occasionally entered into conversation. He told us he was a Southerner by birth, and had spent the greater part of his life in the Slave States, and that he had recently lost a brother who traded in slaves. "But," said he, "it is a pitiable and degrading business, and I always felt ashamed to acknowledge my brother in connection with it." As we passed Snaky Swamp, he pointed to it, and said "There is a slave territory that defies all the laws." I thought of the terrible days I had spent there, and though it was not called Dismal Swamp,[2] it made me feel very dismal as I looked at it.

[2]About thirty miles long and ten wide, lying in southeast Virginia and northeast North Carolina, it is perhaps the best known of many extensive tracts of swampland in the coastal plain of Virginia and the Carolinas.

I shall never forget that night. The balmy air of spring was so refreshing! And how shall I describe my sensations when we were fairly sailing on Chesapeake Bay? O, the beautiful sunshine! the exhilarating breeze! and I could enjoy them without fear or restraint. I had never realized what grand things air and sunlight are till I had been deprived of them.

Ten days after we left land we were approaching Philadelphia. The captain said we should arrive there in the night, but he thought we had better wait till morning, and go on shore in broad daylight, as the best way to avoid suspicion.

I replied, "You know best. But will you stay on board and protect us?"

He saw that I was suspicious, and he said he was sorry, now that he had brought us to the end of our voyage, to find I had so little confidence in him. Ah, if he had ever been a slave he would have known how difficult it was to trust a white man. He assured us that we might sleep through the night without fear; that he would take care we were not left unprotected. Be it said to the honor of this captain, Southerner as he was, that if Fanny and I had been white ladies, and our passage lawfully engaged, he could not have treated us more respectfully. My intelligent friend, Peter, had rightly estimated the character of the man to whose honor he had intrusted us.

The next morning I was on deck as soon as the day dawned. I called Fanny to see the sun rise, for the first time in our lives, on free soil; for such I *then* believed it to be. We watched the reddening sky, and saw the great orb come up slowly out of the water, as it seemed. Soon the waves began to sparkle, and every thing caught the beautiful glow. Before us lay the city of strangers. We looked at each other, and the eyes of both were moistened with tears. We had escaped from slavery, and we supposed ourselves to be safe from the hunters. But we were alone in the world, and we had left dear ties behind us; ties cruelly sundered by the demon Slavery.

XLI

Free at Last

Mrs. Bruce, and every member of her family, were exceedingly kind to me. I was thankful for the blessings of my lot, yet I could not always wear a cheerful countenance. I was doing harm to no one; on the contrary, I was doing all the good I could in my small way; yet I could never go out to breathe God's free air without trepidation at my heart. This seemed hard; and I could not think it was a right state of things in any civilized country.

From time to time I received news from my good old grandmother. She could not write; but she employed others to write for her. The following is an extract from one of her last letters:—

> "Dear Daughter: I cannot hope to see you again on earth; but I pray to God to unite us above, where pain will no more rack this feeble body of mine; where sorrow and parting from my children will be no more. God has promised these things if we are faithful unto the end. My age and feeble health deprive me of going to church now; but God is with me here at home. Thank your brother for his kindness. Give much love to him, and tell him to remember the Creator in the days of his youth, and strive to meet me in the Father's kingdom. Love to Ellen and Benjamin. Don't neglect him. Tell him for me, to be a good boy. Strive, my child, to train them for God's children. May he protect and provide for you, is the prayer of your loving old mother."

These letters both cheered and saddened me. I was always glad to have tidings from the kind, faithful old friend of my unhappy youth; but her messages of love made my heart yearn to see her before she died, and I mourned over the fact that it was impossible. Some months after I returned from my flight to New England, I received a letter from her, in which she wrote, "Dr. Flint is dead. He has left a distressed family. Poor old man! I hope he made his peace with God."

I remembered how he had defrauded my grandmother of the hard earnings she had loaned; how he had tried to cheat her out of the freedom her mistress had promised her, and how he had persecuted her children; and I thought to myself that she was a better Christian than I was, if she could entirely forgive him. I cannot say, with truth, that the news of my old master's death softened my feelings towards him. There are wrongs which even the grave does not bury. The man was odious to me while he lived, and his memory is odious now.

His departure from this world did not diminish my danger. He had threatened my grandmother that his heirs should hold me in slavery after he was gone; that I never should be free so long as a child of his survived. As for Mrs. Flint, I had seen her in deeper afflictions than I supposed the loss of her husband would be, for she had buried several children; yet I never saw any signs of softening in her heart. The doctor had died in embarrassed circumstances, and had little to will to his heirs, except such property as he was unable to grasp. I was well aware what I had to expect from the family of Flints; and my fears were confirmed by a letter from the south, warning me to be on my guard, because Mrs. Flint openly declared that her daughter could not afford to lose so valuable a slave as I was.

I kept close watch of the newspapers for arrivals; but one Saturday night, being much occupied, I forgot to examine the Evening Express as usual. I went down into the parlor for it, early in the morning, and found the boy about to kindle a fire with it. I took it from him and examined the list of arrivals. Reader, if you have never been a slave, you cannot imagine the acute sensation of suffering at my heart, when I read the names of Mr. and Mrs. Dodge, at a hotel in Courtland Street. It was a third-rate hotel, and that circumstance convinced me of the truth of what I had heard, that they were short of funds and had need of my value, as *they* valued me; and that was by dollars and cents. I hastened with the paper to Mrs. Bruce. Her heart and hand were always open to every one in distress, and she always warmly sympathized with mine. It was impossible to tell how near the enemy was. He might have passed and repassed the house while we were sleeping. He might at that moment be waiting to pounce upon me if I ventured out of doors. I had never seen the husband of my young mistress, and therefore I could not distinguish him from any other stranger. A carriage was hastily ordered; and, closely veiled, I followed Mrs. Bruce, taking the baby again with me into exile. After various turnings and crossings, and returnings, the carriage stopped at the house of one of Mrs. Bruce's friends, where I was kindly received. Mrs. Bruce returned immediately, to instruct the domestics what to say if any one came to inquire for me.

It was lucky for me that the evening paper was not burned up before I had a chance to examine the list of arrivals. It was not long after Mrs. Bruce's return to her house, before several people came to inquire for me. One inquired for me, another asked for my daughter Ellen, and another said he had a letter from my grandmother, which he was requested to deliver in person.

They were told, "She *has* lived here, but she has left."

"How long ago?"

"I don't know, sir."

"Do you know where she went?"

"I do not, sir." And the door was closed.

This Mr. Dodge, who claimed me as his property, was originally a Yankee pedler in the south; then he became a merchant, and finally a slaveholder. He managed to get introduced into what was called the first society, and married Miss Emily Flint. A quarrel arose between him and her brother, and the brother cowhided him. This led to a family feud, and he proposed to remove to Virginia. Dr. Flint left him no property, and his own means had become circumscribed, while a wife and children depended upon him for support. Under these circumstances, it was very natural that he should make an effort to put me into his pocket.

I had a colored friend, a man from my native place, in whom I had the most implicit confidence. I sent for him, and told him that Mr. and Mrs. Dodge had arrived in New York. I proposed that he should call upon them to make inquiries about his friends at the south, with whom Dr. Flint's family were well acquainted. He thought there was no impropriety in his doing so, and he consented. He went to the hotel, and knocked at the door of Mr. Dodge's room, which was opened by the gentleman himself, who gruffly inquired, "What brought you here? How came you to know I was in the city?"

"Your arrival was published in the evening papers, sir; and I called to ask Mrs. Dodge about my friends at home. I didn't suppose it would give any offence."

"Where's that negro girl, that belongs to my wife?"

"What girl, sir?"

"You know well enough. I mean Linda, that ran away from Dr. Flint's plantation, some years ago. I dare say you've seen her, and know where she is."

"Yes, sir, I've seen her, and know where she is. She is out of your reach, sir."

"Tell me where she is, or bring her to me, and I will give her a chance to buy her freedom."

"I don't think it would be of any use, sir. I have heard her say she would go to the ends of the earth, rather than pay any man or woman for her freedom, because she thinks she has a right to it. Besides, she couldn't do it, if she would, for she has spent her earnings to educate her children."

This made Mr. Dodge very angry, and some high words passed between them. My friend was afraid to come where I was; but in the course of the day I received a note from him. I supposed they had not come from the south, in the winter, for a pleasure excursion; and now the nature of their business was very plain.

Mrs. Bruce came to me and entreated me to leave the city the next morning. She said her house was watched, and it was possible that some clew to me might be obtained. I refused to take her advice. She pleaded with an earnest tenderness, that ought to have moved me; but I was in a bitter, disheartened mood. I was weary of flying from pillar to post. I had been chased during half my life, and it seemed as if the chase was never to end. There I sat, in that great city, guiltless of crime, yet not daring to worship God in any of the churches. I heard the bells ringing for afternoon service, and, with contemptuous sarcasm, I said, "Will the preachers take for their text, 'Proclaim liberty to the captive, and the opening of prison doors to them that are bound'? or will they preach from the text, 'Do unto others as ye would they should do unto you'?" Oppressed Poles and Hungarians could find a safe refuge in that city; John Mitchell[3] [sic] was free to proclaim in the City Hall his desire for "a plantation well stocked with slaves;" but there I sat, an oppressed American, not daring to show my face. God forgive the black and bitter thoughts I indulged on that Sabbath day! The Scripture says, "Oppression makes even a wise man mad;" and I was not wise.

I had been told that Mr. Dodge said his wife had never signed away her right to my children, and if he could not get me, he would take them. This it was, more than any thing else, that roused such a tempest in my soul. Benjamin was with his uncle William in California, but my innocent young daughter had come to spend a vacation with me. I thought of what I has suffered in slavery at her age, and my heart

[3]John Mitchel (1815–1875)—the name is spelled with a single *l*—Irish nationalist and advocate of armed resistance to England, was transported from Ireland to Van Dieman's Land (Tasmania) but escaped. In New York in 1853, he established a paper dedicated to the cause of Irish freedom, yet he opposed the abolitionists and came out in favor of slavery. He then moved to Knoxville, where he published a paper serving slavery interests. His sons fought in the Confederate army. "His intense nationalism," wrote a biographer in *Dictionary of American Biography,* "prevented his feeling any spirit of kinship with other men working in similar causes; for liberty in the abstract and humanity at large he cared nothing."

was like a tiger's when a hunter tries to seize her young.

Dear Mrs. Bruce! I seem to see the expression of her face, as she turned away discouraged by my obstinate mood. Finding her expostulations unavailing, she sent Ellen to entreat me. When ten o'clock in the evening arrived and Ellen had not returned, this watchful and unwearied friend became anxious. She came to us in a carriage, bringing a well-filled trunk for my journey—trusting that by this time I would listen to reason. I yielded to her, as I ought to have done before.

The next day, baby and I set out in a heavy snow storm, bound for New England again. I received letters from the City of Iniquity, addressed to me under an assumed name. In a few days one came from Mrs. Bruce, informing me that my new master was still searching for me, and that she intended to put an end to this persecution by buying my freedom. I felt grateful for the kindness that prompted this offer, but the idea was no so pleasant to me as might have been expected. The more my mind had become enlightened, the more difficult it was for me to consider myself an article of property; and to pay money to those who had so grievously oppressed me seemed like taking from my sufferings the glory of triumph. I wrote to Mrs. Bruce, thanking her, but saying that being sold from one owner to another seemed too much like slavery; that such a great obligation could not be easily cancelled; and that I preferred to go to my brother in California.

Without my knowledge, Mrs. Bruce employed a gentleman in New York to enter into negotiations with Mr. Dodge. He proposed to pay three hundred dollars down, if Mr. Dodge would sell me, and enter into obligations to relinquish all claim to me or my children forever after. He who called himself my master said he scorned so small an offer for such a valuable servant. The gentleman replied, "You can do as you choose, sir. If you reject this offer you will never get any thing; for the woman has friends who will convey her and her children out of the country."

Mr. Dodge concluded that "half a loaf was better than no bread," and he agreed to the proffered terms. By the next mail I received this brief letter from Mrs. Bruce: "I am rejoiced to tell you that the money for your freedom has been paid to Mr. Dodge. Come home to-morrow. I long to see you and my sweet babe."

My brain reeled as I read these lines. A gentleman near me said, "It's true; I have seen the bill of sale." "The bill of sale!" Those words struck me like a blow. So I was *sold* at last! A human being *sold* in the free city of New York! The bill of sale is on record, and future generations will learn from it that women were articles of traffic in New York, late in the nineteenth century of the Christian religion. It may hereafter prove a useful document to antiquaries, who are seeking to measure the progress of civilization to the United States. I well know the value of that bit of paper; but much as I love freedom, I do not like to look upon it. I am deeply grateful to the generous friend who procured it, but I despise the miscreant who demanded payment for what never rightfully belonged to him or his.

I had objected to having my freedom bought, yet I must confess that when it was done I felt as if a heavy load had been lifted from my weary shoulders. When I rode home in the cars I was no longer afraid to unveil my face and look at people as they passed. I should have been glad to have met Daniel Dodge himself; to have had him seen me and known me, that he might have mourned over the untoward circumstances which compelled him to sell me for three hundred dollars.

When I reached home, the arms of my benefactress were thrown round me, and our tears mingled. As soon as she could speak, she said, "O Linda, I'm *so* glad it's all over! You wrote to me as if you thought you were going to be transferred from one owner to another. But I did not buy you for your services. I should have done just the same, if you had been going to sail for California to-morrow. I should, at least, have the satisfaction of knowing that you left me a free woman."

My heart was exceedingly full. I remembered how my poor father had tried to buy me, when I was a small child, and how he had been disappointed. I hoped his spirit was rejoicing over me now. I remembered how my good old grandmother had laid up her earnings to purchase me in later years, and how often her plans had been frustrated. How that faithful, loving old heart would leap for joy, if she could look on me and my children now that we were free! My relatives had been foiled in all their efforts, but God had raised me up a friend among strangers, who had bestowed on me the precious, long-desired boon. Friend! It is a common word, often lightly used. Like other good and beautiful things, it may be tarnished by careless handling; but when I speak of Mrs. Bruce as my friend, the word is sacred.

My grandmother lived to rejoice in my freedom; but not long after, a letter came with a black seal. She had gone "where the wicked cease from troubling, and the weary are at rest."

Time passed on, and a paper came to me from the south, containing an obituary notice of my uncle Phillip. It was the only case I ever knew of such an honor conferred upon a colored person. It was written by one of his friends, and contained these words: "Now that death has laid him low, they call him a good man and a useful citizen; but what are eulogies to the black man, when the world has faded from his vision? It does not require man's praise to obtain rest in God's kingdom." So they called a colored man a *citizen!* Strange words to be uttered in that region!

Reader, my story ends with freedom; not in the usual way, with marriage. I and my children are now free! We are as free from the power of slaveholders as are the white people of the north; and though that, according to my ideas, is not saying a great deal, it is a vast improvement in *my* condition. The dream of my life is not yet realized. I do not sit with my children in a home of my own. I still long for a hearthstone of my own, however humble. I wish it for my children's sake far more than for my own. But God so orders circumstances as to keep me with my friend Mrs. Bruce. Love, duty, gratitude, also bind me to her side. It is a privilege to serve her who pities my oppressed people, and who has bestowed the inestimable boon of freedom on me and my children.

It has been painful to me, in many ways, to recall the dreary years I passed in bondage. I would gladly forget them if I could. Yet the retrospection is not altogether without solace; for with those gloomy recollections come tender memories of my good old grandmother, like light, fleecy clouds floating over a dark and troubled sea.

Essays, Pamphlets, Letters, and Journals

ROBERT PURVIS

(1810–1898)

Robert Purvis was crucial to the development of both African American thought and the intellectual history of the United States. He pressed for the kind of civil disobedience that had been professed by the white dissident Henry David Thoreau in 1849, and he prepared for the political struggles of Frederick Douglass in the latter part of the nineteenth century, as well as to Martin Luther King, Jr., in the twentieth. Purvis took up a lifelong struggle initially against slavery and, subsequently, for the advocacy of black rights. He welcomed the Civil War as a way to end "the peculiar institution" of slavery. As a somewhat skeptical liberal, he helped support nearly all of the progressive movements of the era, including women's rights, the temperance crusade, and prison reform. With Frederick Douglass and Frances Harper, who would emerge as strong spokepersons after him, he opposed the inquiry by President Lincoln into the prospects of colonization by American blacks in Africa, and he helped advance the educational opportunities for Americans of African descent. He was one of the more remarkable black leaders of the nineteenth century.

An early pioneer of the antislavery movement in Philadelphia, Robert Purvis was born free in Charleston, South Carolina, on August 4, 1810. He was taken to Philadelphia when he was nine. After moving north, his father entered him into private school. Purvis eventually enrolled in the recently founded (1816) Amherst College, which was then dedicated to the education of "indigent young men of piety." His father (William) was an Englishman, who left England around 1890. William Purvis was a cotton broker who eventually settled in Charleston, South Carolina. Robert's mother, Harriet Judah, was freeborn and was of German and Moroccan stock. Given his physical appearance as a very light-skinned black and his complex ethnic heritage, Robert Purvis could have easily passed for white. When his father died, he left him an inheritance of over $120,000. He quickly purchased an estate at Byberry, near Philadelphia. Then, he married Harriet Forten, the daughter of a sail maker and prominent black abolitionist, James Forten. Purvis and his family—including eight children—kept the estate at Byberry until his death in 1898.

Purvis's property and education made him a gentleman of leisure. Inspired by the antislavery books that his father had given him, he decided to embark instead on a career as an activist to secure and protect the Civil Rights of blacks—slave and free—in Pennsylvania and throughout the United States. Both he and his wife became steadfast abolitionists, who befriended William Lloyd Garrison and were persistently loyal to Garrisonian abolitionist ideas, although other prominent black abolitionists, including Henry Highland Garnet and Frederick Douglass, eventually broke with Garrison. With Garrison, however, Robert Purvis helped to found the American Antislavery Society in December of 1833. Earlier that year, Harriet Purvis and her sister Margaretta Forten became two of the four black women prominent in the Female Antislavery Society in Philadelphia. In 1834, Robert Purvis traveled to England, while bearing letters of introduction from Garrison to solicit international support for the American abolitionist cause, where he met several British social reformers, including Sir Thomas Foxwell Buxton, parliamentary head of the antislavery forces.

Although Purvis worked on both the international and national fronts, he spent most of his efforts advancing the abolitionist cause in his home state of Pennsylvania. In 1837, he helped organize the Pennsylvania Anti-Slavery Society; and, during the following year, he became president of the Philadelphia Vigilance Committee, a position that he held for six years. In his capacity as president, his home at Byberry became one of the stops on the Underground Railroad. In fact, he had a secret room constructed with a trap door for those lucky, though desperate, fugitives who made it to Pennsylvania. He was personally instrumental in Basil Dorsey's escape. Furthermore, Purvis was particularly vigilant about the activities and legislative practices of Pennsylvania. When, for instance, in 1837, Pennsylvania adopted a new state constitution, including a provision denying free black men the right to vote, Purvis took direct and public action. Forming a committee of prominent black Pennsylvanians, he, assisted by the committee, wrote an eighteen-page pamphlet titled *Appeal of Forty Thousand Citizens Threatened with Disfranchisement to the People of Pennsylvania.*

Purvis exposes a discrepancy between the letter and the spirit of the Constitution: "Is Pennsylvania, which abolished slavery in 1780, and enfranchised her taxpaying colored citizens in 1790, now in 1838 [the same year of the Frederick Douglass escape to the North] to get upon her knees and repent of her humanity, to gratify those who disgrace the very name of American Liberty by holding our brethren as goods and chattels?" He reasserted that law can only derive its authority from the consent of the governed. Hence, a "Government which tears away from us and our posterity the very power of CONSENT, is a tyrannical usurpation which we will never cease to oppose."

Writing the *Appeal* was not the only manner in which Purvis took direct action to combat racial discrimination. In 1853, black children were legally excluded from the public school system in Byberry. Purvis was one of Byberry's most prominent and most wealthy citizens. He simply refused to pay taxes. Because his refusal meant the loss of substantial revenue, the school board quickly rescinded their original law. With his act of disobedience, he helped shape the doctrine of nonviolent protest as a civic duty of American blacks. Four years later, he would denounce the infamous Dred Scott decision. He maintained that "the only duty the colored man owes to [the] Constitution . . . is to denounce and repudiate it, and do what he can by all proper means to bring it into contempt."

In addition to agitating for black rights during the 1850s, Purvis campaigned for women's rights, temperance, and prison reform. He and Harriet were prime movers of the feminist movement in Philadelphia. In 1854, she was one of the main organizers of the Fifth Women's Rights Convention, the first national women's rights convention held in Philadelphia. Six years later, he became vice president, representing the state of Pennsylvania, of the Tenth National Women's Rights Convention, which was held at the Cooper Institute in New York. In 1866, both of them attained positions in the newly formed American Equal Rights Association (AERA).

Although Robert Purvis remained active in civic affairs throughout his life, his public activities decreased considerably after the Civil War. Much like the Civil Rights activist Theodore Wright, he distrusted both the Democratic and Republican parties. Consequently, Purvis supported, in 1874, a People's Party candidate for mayor in Philadelphia and, nine years later, participated in a political movement of African American Independents in the state. In his personal life, however, he did find satisfaction and solace before his death on April 15, 1898. One of his sons, Charles B. Purvis, had become a highly successful doctor and was eventually appointed chief surgeon at the Freedmen's Hospital. He taught for several decades from 1868 to 1907 as a professor in Howard University's medical school.

Robert Purvis Senior's own persistent efforts to combat slavery, however, should be remembered. He was one of the most perceptive writers of the century. He proposed that the history of freedom in the United States is cyclical rather than linear and that the lovers of freedom must therefore be eternally vigilant. Prepared for a reactionary zeitgeist that would threaten the safety of American blacks again and again during the next century, he exposed the national hypocrisy that would label all American dissidents as traitors. Purvis, on the contrary, revealed that the abolitionist tradition had embodied both the rare qualities of loyalty and dissent. Robert Purvis reclaimed the romantic spirit of American tradition, and he helped rewrite the text of African American freedom beyond his time.

❖❖❖

Benjamin Quarles provides a thorough account of Purvis's abolitionist activities in *Black Abolitionists* (1969) and a short biographical sketch of him in *Dictionary of American Negro Biography.* Purvis's autobiographical account of his early life and some of his abolitionist activities can be found in R. C. Smedley, *History of the Underground railroad in Chester and the Neighboring Countries of Pennsylvania* (1883). See also Herbert Aptheker, *A Documentary History of the Negro People in the United States,* which includes some of Purvis's letters and speeches. In addition, Joseph A. Borome, "Robert Purvis and His Early Challenge to American Racism" *Negro History Bulletin* (May 1967) gives an account of his abolitionist activities abroad.

Appeal of Forty Thousand Citizens Threatened with Disfranchisement to the People of Pennsylvania

Fellow Citizens: We appeal to you from the decision of the "Reform Convention," which has stripped us of a right peaceably enjoyed during forty-seven years under the Constitution of this commonwealth. We honor Pennsylvania and her noble institutions too much to part with our birthright, as her free citizens, without a struggle. To all her citizens the right of suffrage is valuable in proportion as she is free; but surely there are none who can so ill afford to spare it as ourselves.

Was it the intention of the people of this commonwealth that the Convention to which the Constitution was committed for revision and amendment should tear up and cast away its first principles? Was it made the business of the Convention to deny "that all men are born equally free," by making political rights depend upon the skin in which a man is born, or to divide what our fathers bled to unite, to wit, TAXATION and REPRESENTATION? We will not allow ourselves for one moment to suppose that the majority of the people of Pennsylvania are not too respectful of the rights and too liberal towards the feelings of others, as well as too much enlightened to their own interests, to deprive of the right of suffrage a single individual who may safely be trusted with it. And we cannot believe that you have found among those who bear the burdens of taxation any who have proved, by their abuse of the right, that it is not safe in their hands. This is a question, fellow citizens, in which we plead your cause as well as our own. It is the safeguard of the strongest that he lives under a government which is obliged to respect the voice of the weakest. When you have taken from an individual his right to vote, you have made the government, in regard to him, a mere despotism to all. To your women and children, their inability to vote at the polls may be no evil, because they are united by consanguinity and affection with those who can do it. To foreigners and paupers the want of the right may be tolerable, because a little time or labor will make it theirs. They are candidates for the privilege and hence substantially enjoy its benefits. But when a distinct class of the community, already sufficiently the objects of prejudice, are wholly, and for ever, disfranchised and excluded, to the remotest posterity, from the possibility of a voice in regard to the laws under which they are to live—it is the same thing as if their abode were transferred to the dominions of the Russian Autocrat, or of the Grand Turk. They have lost their check upon oppression, their wherewith to buy friends, their panoply of manhood; in short, they are thrown upon the mercy of a despotic majority. Like every other despot, this despot majority will believe in the mildness of its own sway; but who will the more willingly submit to it for that?

To us our right under the Constitution has been more precious, and our deprivation of it will be the more grievous, because our expatriation has come to be a darling project with many of our fellow citizens. Our abhorrence of a scheme which comes to us in the guise of Christian benevolence, and asks us to suffer ourselves to be transplanted to a distant and barbarous land, *because we are a "nuisance" in this,* is not more deep and thorough than it is reasonable. We love our native country, much as it has wronged us; and in the peaceable exercise of our inalienable rights, we will cling to it. The immortal Franklin, and his fellow laborers in the cause of humanity, have bound us to our homes here with chains of gratitude. We are PENNSYLVANIANS, and we hope to see the day when Pennsylvania will have reason to be proud of us, as we believe she has now none to be ashamed. Will you starve our patriotism? Will you cast our hearts out of the treasury of the commonwealth? Do you count our enmity better than our friendship?

Fellow citizens, we entreat you, in the name of fair dealing, to look again at the just and noble charter of Pennsylvania freedom, which you are asked to narrow down to the lines of caste and color. The Constitution reads as follows:—

"*Art.* 3, §1. In elections by the citizens, every freeman of the age of twenty-one years, having resided in the State two years next before the election, and within that time paid a State or county tax, which shall have been assessed at least six months before the election, shall enjoy the rights of an elector," &c.

This clause guaranties the right of suffrage to us as fully as to any of our fellow citizens whatsoever, for

1. Such was the intention of the framers. In the original draft, reported by a committee of nine, the word "WHITE" stood before "FREEMAN." On motion of ALBERT GALLATIN it was stricken out, for the express purpose of including colored citizens within the pale of the elective franchise. (See *Minutes of the Convention,* 1790.)
2. We are CITIZENS. This, we believe, would never have been denied, had it not been for the scheme of expatriation to which we have already referred. But as our citizenship has been doubted by some who are not altogether unfriendly to us, we beg leave to submit some proofs, which we think you will not hastily set aside.

We were regarded as *citizens* by those who drew up the articles of confederation between the States, in 1778. The fourth of the said articles contains the following language:—"The free inhabitants of each of these States, paupers, vagabonds, and fugitives from justice excepted, shall be entitled to all privileges and immunities of free *citizens* in the several States." That we were not excluded under the phrase "paupers, vagabonds, and fugitives from justice," any more than our white countrymen, is plain from the debates that preceded the adoption of the article. For, on the 25th of June, 1778, "the delegates from South Carolina moved the following amendment *in behalf of their State.* In article fourth, between the words *free* inhabitants, insert *white.* Decided in the negative; ayes, two States; nays, eight States; one State divided." Such was the solemn decision of the revolutionary Congress, concurred in by the entire delegation from our own commonwealth. On the adoption of the present Constitution of the United States no change was made as to the rights of citizenship. This is explicitly proved by the Journal of Congress. Take, for example, the following resolution passed in the House of Representatives, Dec. 21, 1803:

> On motion, *Resolved,* That the Committee appointed to enquire and report whether any further provisions are necessary for the more effectual protection of American seamen, do enquire into the expediency of granting protections to such American seamen, *citizens of the United States,* as *are free persons of color,* and that they report by bill, or otherwise.
>
> *Journ. H. Rep.,* 1st Sess., 8th Cong., p. 224.

Proofs might be multiplied. In almost every State we have been spoken of, either expressly or by implication, as *citizens.* In the very year before the adoption of the present Constitution, 1789, the "Pennsylvania Society for Promoting the Abolition of Slavery, &c.," put forth an address, signed by "BENJAMIN FRANKLIN, *President*," in which they stated one of their objects to be, "to *qualify* those who have been restored to freedom, for the exercise and enjoyment of CIVIL LIBERTY." The Convention of 1790, by striking out the word "WHITE," fixed the same standard of *qualification* for all; and, in fact, granted and guarantied "civil liberty" to all who possessed that qualification. Are we now to be told, that the Convention did not intend to include colored men, and that BENJAMIN FRANKLIN did not know what he was about, forasmuch as it was impossible for a colored man to become a citizen of the commonwealth?

It may here be objected to us, that in point of fact we have lost by the recent decision of the Supreme Court, in the case of *Fogg* vs. *Hobbs*, whatever claim to the right of suffrage we may have had under the Constitution of 1790; and hence have no reason to oppose the amended Constitution. Not so. We hold our rights under the present Constitution none the cheaper for that decision. The section already cited gives us all that we ask—all that we can conceive it in the power of language to convey. Reject, fellow citizens, the partial, disfranchising Constitution offered you by the Reform Convention, and we shall confidently expect that the Supreme Court will do us the justice and itself the honor to retract its decision. Should it not, our appeal will still be open to the conscience and common sense of the people, who through their chief magistrate and a majority of two-thirds of both branches of the Legislature may make way to the bench of the Supreme Court, for expounders of the Constitution who will not do violence to its most sacred and fundamental principles.

We cannot forbear here to refer you to some points in the published opinion of the Court as delivered by Chief Justice Gibson, which we believe will go far to strip it of the weight and authority ordinarily conceded to the decision of the highest tribunal (save the elections) of this commonwealth.

1. The Court relies much on a decision *said to have been had* "ABOUT" forty-three years ago, the claim of which to a place in the repository of the Pennsylvania law is thus set forth by the Court itself:—

   About the year 1795, as I have it from James Gibson, Esq., of the Philadelphia bar, the very point before us was ruled by the High Court of Errors and Appeals, against the right of negro suffrage. Mr. Gibson declined an invitation to be concerned in the argument, and therefore has no memorandum of the cause to direct us to the record. I have had the office searched for it; but the papers had fallen into such disorder as to preclude a hope of its recovery. Most of them were imperfect, and many were lost or misplaced. *But Mr. Gibson's remembrance of the decision is perfect and entitled to full confidence.*

   Now, suppressing doubt, and supposing such a decision actually to have emanated from the then highest tribunal of the commonwealth, does not the fact that it was so utterly forgotten as not to have regulated the polls within the memory of the present generation, nor to have been brought up against us in the Reform Convention, prove that it was virtually retracted? And if retracted, is it now to be revived to the overthrow of rights enjoyed without contradiction during the average life of man?
2. The Court argues that colored men are not *freemen*, and hence not entitled by the present Constitution to vote, because under laws prior to the Constitution there *might be* individuals who were not slaves, and yet were not *freemen!* The deduction is, that as the word "freeman" was, *before* the present Constitution, used in a restricted sense, it must have been used in the same sense *in* it. The correctness of this interpretation will be tested by substituting, in Art. 3, Sec. 1, for the word "freeman" the meaning which the Court chooses to have attached to it. This

meaning appears from the passages cited by the Court to be, *an elector.*[1] Making the substitution, the article reads, "In elections by the citizens, every *elector,* of the age of twenty-one years, &c. &c., shall enjoy the right of an *elector,* &c."—a proposition which sheds a very faint light upon the question of the extent of the elective franchise, and from which it would appear that there may be electors who are *not* to enjoy the rights of electors. But taking the less restricted term *citizen,* which the Court also seems to think of the same force with "freeman," the article will read more sensibly, that "In elections by the citizens, every *citizen* of the age of twenty-one," who has paid taxes, &c. "shall enjoy the right of an elector." To what evidence does the Court refer to show that a *colored* man may not be a *citizen?* To none whatever. We have too much respect for old Pennsylvania to believe that such puerile absurdity can become her fixed and irreversible law.

3. Since the argument above referred to, such as it is, does not rest upon color, it is not less applicable to the descendants of Irish and German ancestors than to ourselves. If there ever have been within the commonwealth, men, or sets of men, who though personally free were not technically *freemen,* it is unconstitutional, according to the doctrine of the Court, for their descendants to exercise the right of suffrage, pay what taxes they may, till in "the discretion of the judges," their blood has "become so diluted in successive descents as to lose its distinctive character." Is this the doctrine of Pennsylvania freedom?
4. Lastly, the Court openly rests its decision on the authority of a *wrong,* which this commonwealth so long ago as 1780 solemnly acknowledged, and, to the extent of its power, for ever repealed. To support the same *wrong* in *other States,* the Constitution of *this,* when it uses the words "every freeman," must be understood to exclude every freeman of a certain color! The Court is of opinion that the people of this commonwealth had no power to confer the rights of citizenship upon one who, were he in another State, *might be* loaded by its laws with "countless disabilities." Now, since in some of the States men may be found in slavery who have not the slightest trace of African blood, it is difficult to see, on the doctrine of the Court, how the Constitution of Pennsylvania could confer the right of citizenship upon any person; and, indeed, how it could have allowed the emancipation of slaves of any color. To such vile dependence on its own ancient *wrongs,* and on the present *wrongs* of other States, is Pennsylvania reduced by this decision!

Are we then presumptuous in the hope that this grave sentence will be as incapable of resurrection fifty years hence, as is that which the Chief Justice assures us was pronounced "*about* the year 1795?" No. The blessings of the broad and impartial charter of Pennsylvania rights can no more be wrested from us by legal subtilty, than the beams of our common sun or the breathing of our common air.

What have we done to forfeit the inestimable benefits of this charter? Why should tax-paying colored men, any more than other tax-payers, be deprived of the right of voting for their representatives? It was said in the Convention, that this government belongs to the *Whites.* We have already shown this to be false, as to the past. Those who established our present government designed it equally for all. It is for you to decide whether it shall be confined to the European complexion in future. Why should you exclude us from a fair participation in the benefits of the republic? Have we oppressed the whites? Have we used our right to the injury of any class? Have we disgraced it by receiving bribes? Where are the charges written down, and who will

[1] "Thus," says the Chief Justice, "till the instant when the phrase on which the question turns was penned, the term freeman had a peculiar and specific sense, being used like the term *citizen* which supplanted it, to denote one who had a voice in public affairs. The citizens were denominated freemen even in the Constitution of 1776—and under the present Constitution, the word, though dropped in the style, was used in the legislative acts convertibly with *electors,* so late as the year 1798 when it grew into disuse."

swear to them? We challenge investigation. We put it to the conscience of every Pennsylvanian, whether there is, or ever has been, in the commonwealth, either a political party or religious sect which has less deserved than ourselves to be thus disfranchised. As to the charge of idleness, we fling it back indignantly. Whose brows have sweat for our livelihood but our own? As to vice, if it disqualifies us for civil liberty, why not apply the same rule to the whites, so far as they are vicious? Will you punish the innocent for the crimes of the guilty? The execution of the laws is in the hands of the whites. If we are bad citizens let them apply the proper remedies. We do not ask the right of suffrage for the inmates of our jails and penitentiaries, but for those who honestly and industriously contribute to bear the burdens of the State. As to inferiority to the whites, if indeed we are guilty of it, either by nature or education, we trust our enjoyment of the rights of freemen will on that account be considered the less dangerous. If we are incompetent to fill the offices of State, it will be the fault of the whites only if we are suffered to disgrace them. We are in too feeble a minority to cherish a mischievous ambition. Fair protection is all that we aspire to.

❖❖❖

Our fathers shared with yours the trials and perils of the wilderness. Among the facts which illustrate this, it is well known that the founder of your capital, from whom it bears the name of Harrisburg, was rescued by a colored man from a party of Indians, who had captured, and bound him to the stake for execution. In gratitude for this act he invited colored persons to settle in his town, and offered them land on favorable terms. When our common country has been invaded by a foreign foe, colored men have hazarded their lives in its defense. Our fathers fought by the side of yours in the struggle which made us an independent republic.

❖❖❖

Are we to be thus looked to for help in the "hour of danger," but trampled under foot in the time of peace? In which of the battles of the revolution did not our fathers fight as bravely as yours for American liberty? Was it that their children might be disfranchised and loaded with insult that they endured the famine of Valley Forge and horrors of the Jersey Prison Ship? Nay, among those from whom you are asked to wrench the birthright of CIVIL LIBERTY are those who themselves shed their blood on the snows of Jersey, and faced British bayonets in the most desperate hour of the revolution.

❖❖❖

Are we to be disfranchised, lest the purity of the white blood should be sullied by an intermixture with ours? It seems to us that our white brethren might well enough reserve their fear till we seek such alliance with them. We ask no social favors. We would not willingly darken the doors of those to whom the complexion and features which our Maker has given us are disagreeable. The territories of the commonwealth are sufficiently ample to afford us a home without doing violence to the delicate nerves of our white brethren for centuries to come. Besides, we are not intruders here, nor were our ancestors. Surely you ought to bear as unrepiningly the evil consequences of your fathers' guilt, as we those of our fathers' misfortune. Proscription and disfranchisement are the last things in the world to alleviate these evil consequences. Nothing, as shameful experience has already proved, can so powerfully promote the evil which you profess to deprecate, as the degradation of our race by the oppressive rule of yours. Give us that fair and honorable ground which self-respect requires to stand on, and the dreaded amalgamation, if it take place at all, shall be by your own fault, as indeed it always has been. We dare not give full vent to the indignation we feel on this point, but we will not attempt wholly to conceal it. We ask a voice in the disposition of those public resources which we ourselves have helped to earn; we claim a right to be heard, according to our numbers, in regard to all those great public measures which involve our lives and fortunes, as well as those of our fellow citizens; we assert our right to vote at the polls as a shield against that strange species of benevolence which seeks legislative aid to banish us—and we are told that our white fellow citizens cannot submit to an intermixture of the races! Then let the indentures, title-deeds, contracts, notes of hand, and all other evidences of bargain, in which colored men have been treated as men, be torn and scattered on the winds. Consistency is a jewel. Let no white man hereafter ask his colored neighbor's consent when he wants his property or his labor, lest he should endanger the Anglo-Saxon purity of his descendants. Why should not the same principle hold good between neighbor and neighbor, which is deemed necessary, as a fundamental principle, in the Constitution itself? Why should you be ashamed to act in private business as the Reform Convention would have you act in the capacity of a commonwealth? But, no! we do not believe our fellow citizens, while with good faith they hold themselves bound by their contracts with us, and while they feel bound to deal with us only by fair contract, will ratify the arbitrary principle of the Convention, how much so ever they may prefer the complexion in which their Maker has pleased to clothe themselves.

We would not misrepresent the motives of the Convention, but we are constrained to believe that they have laid our rights a sacrifice on the altar of slavery. We do not believe our disfranchisement would have been proposed, but for the desire which is felt by political aspirants to gain the favor of the slaveholding States. This is not the first time that northern statesmen have "bowed the knee to the dark spirit of slavery," but it is the first time that they have bowed so low! Is Pennsylvania, which abolished slavery in 1780, and enfranchised her tax-paying colored citizens in 1790, now, in 1838, to get upon her knees and repent of her humanity, to gratify those who disgrace the very name of American liberty, by holding our brethren as goods and chattels? We freely acknowledge our brotherhood to the slave, and our interest in his welfare. Is this a crime for which we should be ignominiously punished? The very fact that we are deeply interested for our kindred in bonds shows that we are the right sort of stuff to make good citizens of. Were we not so, we should better deserve a lodging in your penitentiaries than a franchise at your polls. Doubtless it will be well pleasing to the slaveholders of the South to see us degraded. They regard our freedom from chains as a dangerous example, much more our political freedom. They see in everything which fortifies our rights an obstacle to the recovery of their fugitive property. Will Pennsylvania go backwards toward slavery, for the better safety of southern slave property? Be assured the South will never be satisfied till the old "Keystone" has returned to the point from which she started in 1780. And since the number of colored men in the commonwealth is so inconsiderable, the safety may require still more. It may demand that a portion of the white taxpayers should be unmanned and turned into chattels—we mean those whose hands are hardened by daily toil. Fellow citizens, will you take the first step towards reimposing the chains which have now rusted for more than fifty years? Need we inform you that every colored man in Pennsylvania is exposed to be arrested as a fugitive from slavery, and that it depends not upon the verdict of a jury of his peers, but upon the decision of a judge on summary process whether or not he shall be dragged into southern bondage? The Constitution of the United States provides that "no person shall be deprived of life, liberty, or property, without due process of law"—by which is certainly meant a TRIAL BY JURY. Yet the act of Congress of 1793, for the recovery of fugitive slaves, authorizes the claimant to seize his victim without a warrant from any magistrate, and allows him to drag him before "any magistrate of a county, city, or town corporate, where such seizure has been made," and upon proving, by "oral testimony or affidavit," to the satisfaction of such magistrate that the man is his slave, gives him a right to take him into everlasting bondage. Thus may a free-born citizen of Pennsylvania be arrested, tried without counsel, jury, or power to call witness, condemned by a single man, and carried across Mason and Dixon's line, within the compass of a single day. An act of this commonwealth passed in 1820 and enlarged and reenacted in 1825, it is true, puts some restraint upon the power of the claimant under the act of Congress; but it still leaves the case to the decision of a single judge, without the privilege of a jury! What unspeakably aggravates our loss of the right of suffrage at this moment is that, while the increased activity of the slave-catchers enhances our danger, the Reform Convention has refused to amend the Constitution so as to protect our liberty by a jury trial! We entreat you to make our case your own—imagine your own wives and children to be trembling at the approach of every stranger, lest their husbands and fathers should be dragged into a slavery worse than Algerine—worse than death! Fellow citizens, if there is one of us who has abused the right of suffrage, let him be tried and punished according to law. But in the name of humanity, in the name of justice, in the name of the God you profess to worship, who has no respect of persons, do not turn into gall and wormwood the friendship we bear to yourselves by ratifying a Constitution which tears from us a privilege dearly earned and inestimably prized. We lay hold of the principles which Pennsylvania asserted in the hour which tried men's souls—which BENJAMIN FRANKLIN and his eight colleagues, in the name of the commonwealth, pledged their lives, their fortunes, and their sacred honor to sustain. We take our stand upon that solemn declaration, that to protect inalienable rights "governments are instituted among men, deriving their JUST POWERS from the CONSENT of the governed," and proclaim that a government which tears away from us and our posterity the very power of CONSENT is a tyrannical usurpation which we will never cease to oppose. We have seen with amazement and grief the apathy of white Pennsylvanians while the "Reform Convention" has been perpetrating this outrage upon the good old principles of Pennsylvania freedom. But however others may forsake these principles, we promise to maintain them on Pennsylvania soil to the last man. If this disfranchisement is designed to uproot us, it shall fail. Pennsylvania's fields, valleys, mountains and rivers; her canals, railroads, forests and mines; her domestic altars and her public, religious and benevolent institutions; her Penn and Franklin, her Rush, Rawle, Wistar and Vaux; her consecrated past and her brilliant future are as dear to us as they can be to you. Firm upon our old Pennsylvania BILL OF RIGHTS, and trusting in a God of Truth and Justice, we lay our claim before you, with the warning that no amendments of the present Constitution can compensate for the loss of its foundation principle of equal rights, nor for the conversion into enemies of 40,000 friends.

MARTIN R. DELANY
(1812–1885)

"I thank God for making me a man," the renowned abolitionist Frederick Douglass once wrote, "but Delany thanks him for making him a *black* man." Douglass's statement aptly describes Martin Robinson Delany—abolitionist, writer, speaker, journalist, physician, and army officer—whose powerful skeptical voice and inquiring mind often set him apart from the mainstream of his contemporaries. It is precisely these qualities that contributed to his prominence as a pioneer of black cultural nationalism. Unlike Douglass, Robert Purvis, Frances Harper, and several other black activists, Martin Delany did not believe that the spirit of the U.S. Constitution would be lived out in the nation. Rather, he harshly criticized abolitionists who had failed to integrate American blacks into American society. In his significant work,

The Condition, Elevation, Emigration and Destiny of the Colored People of the United States, Politically Considered, therefore, Delany makes a forceful argument on behalf of black political autonomy, self-determination, and self-definition; and, as a solution to the race problem, he proposes colonization for blacks in another place or country. As Dorothy Sterling has observed, Delany's provocative manifesto is "the first, full-length formulation of black nationalism."

Born in Charles Town, Virginia (now a section of West Virginia) in 1812, Martin Delany was the son of Samuel Delany, a slave, and Pati Peace Delany, a free black woman; hence, he was born free. When he was young, his mother took him and his four siblings across the Mason-Dixon line to Chambersburg, Pennsylvania, where they could obtain a formal education. They were later joined by his father, who had escaped from slavery. After receiving his early education in Chambersburg, Delany moved to Pittsburgh at nineteen. There he met a group of free blacks whose entrepreneurial ambition and relative success inspired him. During his Pittsburgh years (1831–1856), many of Delany's lifelong interests were developing. He became an abolitionist and an apprentice physician, joined the Thespian Literary Society, and started the publication of his own newspaper, *The Mystery.* As an officer of the Pittsburgh Anti-Slavery Society and an agent in the Underground Railroad, he rapidly became a leader in the city's black community. This was also the time when Delany started formulating his ideas concerning the emigration of American blacks to a more hospitable country. In 1839, he traveled to Texas (then still an independent Republic) in search of a place for his people. His courageous and extremely dangerous trip, however, proved to be an exercise in futility.

After returning from Texas, he married Catherine Richards in 1843. The couple became the proud parents of seven children. (Catherine actually bore eleven children, but four died, which was consistent with the nineteenth-century infant and child mortality rate.) Delany named each of his children in honor of accomplished individuals of African descent from around the world, clearly revealing his belief in racial pride. His six surviving sons were named Toussaint L'ouverture, Charles Lenox Remond, Alexander Dumas, Saint Cyprian, Faustin Soulouque (a Haitian emperor), and Placido Rameses. Delany supported his family primarily by his work as a doctor. In fact, he was a practicing physician before he entered Harvard Medical School in 1850. However, Delany's study at Harvard (which was brief because some whites objected to his presence) and his subsequent practice of medicine did not overshadow his concurrent and ongoing interest in other matters. For example, Delany and a young science teacher named Robert Campbell traveled in 1859 to Liberia and the Niger Valley in search of a settlement for American blacks. Later, he organized an expedition to Nigeria, during which he is reported to have negotiated with several *alakes* (kings) the right to establish a self-governing colony there. In 1860, he attended an international meeting of ethnologists in England. During the proceedings, the moderator, Henry Brougham, a British statesman and antislavery advocate, acknowledged Delany's presence, pointing out to all that a black man was a free and, according to him, welcome participant. Although Delany was not invited to respond, he rose unexpectedly, thanked Brougham and asserted to all present: "I rise, your Royal Highness, to thank his Lordship, the unflinching friend of the Negro, for the remarks he has made in reference to myself, and to assure your Royal Highness and his Lordship, *I am a man.*" Intelligent and dignified self-representation of this kind is what made President Lincoln refer to Delany, after a later interview with him, as "this most extraordinary and intelligent black man." Perhaps Lincoln was deeply appreciative that Delany aided in the recruitment of black soldiers for the Union Army when he (Delany) returned to the United States in 1861. As a major in the army (the first black commissioned officer of high rank), he raised in South Carolina two regiments of former slaves before the end of the Civil War. He remained in South Carolina until 1868, when he returned to civilian life and, subsequently, moved his family to Wilberforce University in Xenia, Ohio, where he stayed until his death in 1885.

None of Delany's activities, including his military, political, medical, or scientific interests, however, prevented him from writing. Before he joined the Union army in 1861, his *Official Report of the Niger Valley Exploring Party* appeared in print that year. It is a traveler's account of the climate and resources in western Africa. And, as late as 1879, he published *Principia of Ethnology: The Origin of Races with an Archaeological Compendium of Ethiopian and Egyptian Civilization.* Delany should be commended for his efforts at ethnology at a time when a considerable number of pseudoscientists were publishing documents explaining the innate presumed inferiority of blacks. Nevertheless, his most significant publications are *The Condition, Elevation, Emigration, and Destiny of the Colored People of the United States, Politically Considered* (1852) and several sections of his only attempt at fiction, a novel titled *Blake, or The Huts of America* (1859). In *The Condition, Elevation, Emigration, and Destiny of the Colored People of the United States, Politically Considered,* Delany refers to Americans of African descent as "a nation within a nation." "We must go from our oppressors," wrote Delany. The essay is part argument against and exposé of white racism and part appeal to African Americans. He addresses candidly the disproportionate number of American blacks in menial positions and then urges them to remove the psychological shackles from their lives and to move forward with ambition and entrepreneurial energy. While arguing for and appealing to them to become the agents of their own elevation, Delany insists that religion had become an opiate. According to him, blacks have harbored a misplaced and misguided faith and have expected their day-to-day existence to be improved by divine intervention. In effect, he believed that religious faith, without hard work, would amount to little or nothing. Finally, he argues for the emigration of American blacks to Central or South America, where they could fulfill their own destiny; however, he appended to the essay a plan for an expedition to Africa.

With the publication of the tract came a strong reaction from antislavery forces, especially Garrisonian abolitionists such as Frederick Douglass. They had argued that the publication was a serious setback to the antislavery cause. As a result, Delany ceased its circulation. *The Condition, Elevation, Emigration and Destiny of the Colored People of the United States, Politically Considered* did, however, move many northern blacks to action. A year after its publication, James Whitfield, for instance, supported Delany's views in his volume of verse, *America and Other Poems,* which he dedicated to him. Whitfield was also among more than one hundred black delegates who attended the 1854 National Emigration Convention, which was organized by Delany and held in Cleveland, Ohio. There, Delany, in his speech titled "The Political Destiny of the Colored Race," continued to impress on blacks the need for an independent black state.

It is not surprising that Delany's one attempt at fiction—*Blake, or the Huts of America*—involved themes of black separatism and emigration. The novel was published in serial form in the *Anglo-African Magazine* in 1859 and in the successor to the magazine, the *Weekly Anglo African,* during 1861 and 1862. Though not a literary masterpiece by contemporary standards, *Blake* is, nevertheless, a significant work. It illustrates Delany's grasp of the complex fate of Americans of African descent, then as now. As Blyden Jackson has observed in his study *A History of Afro-American Literature: Blake,* it "is the first manifesto within the Negro novel of black separatism. . . . Its protagonist, Blake, is black of skin. . . . He thinks in political terms of black enterprise, espouses a revolution of the slaves and dreams of a distinct black nation."

Blake's theme of a black nation of self-sufficient and proud citizens is entirely consistent with the prevailing interests of Delany's life—the uplifting and indeed elevation of his people. To that end, Delany was quite successful in a variety of ways, not the least being his literary achievements. With *The Condition, Elevation, Emigration, and Destiny of the Colored People of the United States, Politically Considered,* he formulated the doctrine of black cultural nationalism, which had its seeds planted in Walker's *Appeal* (1829) and which matured in Du Bois's *The Souls of Black Folk* (1903). With his novel *Blake,* he began a new genre of black protest that would shape the fictional works of Sutton Griggs and Du Bois at the turn of the 20th century and, in modern times, John A. Williams. Delany set a tone of militancy that would be unsurpassed by any other African American novelist before the 1960s.

❖❖❖

Because Delany, as has been indicated, was highly influential beyond literature, he has been discussed in a variety of critical and historical works. Two of the more informed recent discussions of his life and work are Dorothy Sterling's scholarly critical biography, *The Making of an Afro-American: Martin Robinson Delany* (1971) and Blyden Jackson's remarkable study, *A History of Afro-American Literature, Vol. I: The Long Beginning, 1746–1895* (1989); for extended biographical details, see Victor Ullman's *Martin R. Delany: The Beginnings of Black Nationalism* (1971). Benjamin Quarles discusses Delany as soldier and as abolitionist in *The Negro and The Civil War* (1953) and in *Black Abolitionists* (1969), respectively; and Sterling Stuckey includes the author's *The Political Destiny of the Colored Race* in his collection, *The Ideological Origins of Black Nationalism* (1972).

FROM *The Condition, Elevation, Emigration, and Destiny of the Colored People of the United States, Politically Considered*

Chapter II

Comparative Condition of the Colored People of the United States

The United States, untrue to her trust and unfaithful to her professed principles of republican equality, has also pursued a policy of political degradation to a large portion of her native born countrymen, and that class is the Colored People. Denied an equality not only of political, but of natural rights, in common with the rest of our fellow citizens, there is no species of degradation to which we are not subject.

Reduced to abject slavery is not enough, the very thought of which should awaken every sensibility of our common nature; but those of their descendants who are freemen even in the non-slaveholding States, occupy the very same position politically, religiously, civilly and socially, (with but few exceptions,) as the bondman occupies in the slave States.

In those States, the bondman is disfranchised, and for the most part so are we. He is denied all civil, religious, and social privileges, except such as he gets by mere sufferance, and so are we. They have no part nor lot in the government of the country, neither have we. They are ruled and governed without representation, existing as mere nonentities among the citizens, and excrescences on the body politic—a mere dreg in community, and so are we. Where then is our political superiority to the enslaved? none, neither are we superior in any other relation to society, except that we are defacto masters of ourselves and joint rulers of our own domestic household, while the bondman's self is claimed by another, and his relation to his family denied him. What the unfortunate classes are in Europe, such are we in the United States, which is folly to deny, insanity not to understand, blindness not to see, and surely now full time that our eyes were opened to these startling truths, which for ages have stared us full in the face.

It is time that we had become politicians, we mean, to understand the political economy and domestic policy of nations; that we had become as well as moral theorists, also the practical demonstrators of equal rights and self-government. Except we do, it is idle to talk about rights, it is mere chattering for the sake of being seen and heard—like the slave, saying something because his so called "master" said it, and saying just what he told him to say. Have we not now sufficient intelligence among us to understand our true position, to realise our actual condition, and determine for ourselves what is best to be done? If we have not now, we never shall have, and should at once cease prating about our equality, capacity, and all that.

Twenty years ago, when the writer was a youth, his young and yet uncultivated mind was aroused, and his tender heart made to leap with anxiety in anticipation of the promises then held out by the prime movers in the cause of our elevation.

In 1830 the most intelligent and leading spirits among the colored men in the United States, such as James Forten, Robert Douglass, I. Bowers, A.D. Shadd, John Peck, Joseph Cassey, and John B. Vashon of Pennsylvania; John T. Hilton, Nathaniel and Thomas Paul, and James G. Barbodoes of Massachusetts; Henry Sipkins, Thomas Hamilton, Thomas L. Jennings, Thomas Downing, Samuel E. Cornish, and others of New York: R. Cooley and others of Maryland, and representatives from other States which cannot now be recollected, the data not being at hand, assembled in the city of Philadelphia, in the capacity of a National Convention, to "devise ways and means for the bettering of our condition." These Conventions determined to assemble annually, much talent, ability, and energy of character being displayed; when in 1831 at a sitting of the Convention in September, from their previous pamphlet reports, much interest having been created throughout the country, they were favored by the presence of a number of whites, some of whom were able and distinguished men, such as Rev. R.R. Gurley, Arthur Tappan, Elliot Cresson, John Rankin, Simeon Jocelyn and others, among them William Lloyd Garrison, then quite a young man, all of whom were staunch and ardent Colonizationists, young Garrison at that time, doing his mightiest in his favorite work.

Among other great projects of interest brought before the convention at a previous sitting, was that of the expediency of a general emigration, as far as it was practicable, of the colored people to the British Provinces of North America. Another was that of raising sufficient means for the establishment and erection of a College for the proper education of the colored youth. These gentlemen long accustomed to observation and reflection on the condition of their people, saw at once, that there must necessarily be means used adequate to the end to be attained—that end being an unqualified equality with the ruling class of their fellow citizens. He saw that as a class, the colored people of the country were ignorant, degraded and oppressed, by far the greater portion of them being abject slaves in the South, the very condition of whom was almost enough, under the circumstances, to blast the remotest hope of success, and those who were freemen, whether in the South or North, occupied a subservient, servile, and menial position, considering it a favor to get into the service of the whites, and do their degrading offices. That the difference between the whites and themselves, consisted in the superior advantages of the one over the other, in point of attainments. That if a knowledge of the arts and sciences, the mechanical occupations, the industrial occupations, as farming, commerce, and all the various business enterprises, and learned professions were necessary for the superior position occupied by their rulers, it was also necessary for them. And very reasonably too, the first suggestion which occurred to them was, the advantages of a location, then the necessity of a qualification. They reasoned with themselves, that all distinctive differences made among men on account of their origin, is wicked, unrighteous, and cruel, and never shall receive countenance in any shape from us, therefore, the first acts of the measures entered into by them, was to protest, solemnly protest, against every unjust measure and policy in the country, having for its object the proscription of the colored people, whether state, national, municipal, social, civil, or religious.

But being far-sighted, reflecting, discerning men, they took a political view of the subject, and determined for the good of their people to be governed in their policy according to the facts as they presented themselves. In taking a glance at Europe, they discovered there, however unjustly, as we have shown in another part of this pamphlet, that there are and have been numerous classes proscribed and oppressed, and it was not for them to cut short their wise deliberations, and arrest their proceedings in contention, as to the cause, whether on account of language, the color of eyes, hair, skin, or their origin of country—because all this is contrary to reason, a contradiction to common sense, at war with nature herself, and at variance with facts as they stare us every day in the face, among all nations, in every country—this being made the pretext as a matter of *policy* alone—a fact worthy of observation, that wherever the objects of oppression are the most easily distinguished by any peculiar or general characteristics, these people are the more easily oppressed, because the war of oppression is the more easily waged against them. This is the case with the modern Jews and many other people who have strongly-marked, peculiar, or distinguishing characteristics. This arises in this wise. The policy of all those who proscribe any people, induces them to select as the objects of proscription, those who differed as much as possible, in some particulars, from themselves. This is to ensure the greater success, because it engenders the greater prejudice, or in other words, elicits less interest on the part of the oppressing class, in their favor. This fact is well understood in national conflicts, as the soldier or civilian, who is distinguished by his dress, mustache, or any other peculiar appendage, would certainly prove himself a madman, if he did not take the precaution to change his dress, remove his mustache, and conceal as much as possible his peculiar characteristics, to give him access among the repelling party. This is mere policy, nature having nothing to do with it. Still, it is a fact, a great truth well worthy of remark, and as such we adduce it for the benefit of those of our readers, unaccustomed to an enquiry into the policy of nations.

In view of these truths, our fathers and leaders in our elevation, discovered that as a policy, we the colored people were selected as the subordinate class in this country, not on account of any actual or supposed inferiority on their part, but simply because, in view of all the circumstances of the case, they were the very best class that could be selected. They would have as readily had any other class as subordinates in the country, as the colored people, but the condition of society *at the time,* would not admit of it. In the struggle for American Independence, there were among those who performed the most distinguished parts, the most commonplace peasantry of the Provinces. English, Danish, Irish, Scotch, and others, were among those whose names blazoned forth as heroes in the American Revolution. But a single reflection will convince us, that no course of policy could have induced the proscription of the parentage and relatives of such men as Benjamin Franklin the printer, Roger Sherman the cobbler, the tinkers, and others of the signers of the Declaration of Independence. But as they were determined to have a subservient class, it will readily be conceived, that according to the state of society at the time, the better policy on their part was, to select some class, who from their political position—however much they may have contributed their aid as we certainly did, in the general struggle for liberty by force of arms—who had the least claims upon them, or who had the *least chance,* or was the *least potent* in urging their claims. This class of course was the colored people and Indians.

The Indians who in the early settlement of the continent, before an African captive had ever been introduced thereon, were reduced to the most abject slavery, toiling day and night in the mines, under the relentless hands of heartless Spanish taskmasters, but being a race of people raised to the sports of fishing, the chase, and of war, were wholly unaccustomed to labor, and therefore sunk under the insupportable weight, two millions and a half having fallen victims to the cruelty of oppression and toil suddenly placed upon their shoulders. And it was only this that prevented their farther enslavement as a class, after the provinces were absolved from the British Crown. It is true that their general enslavement took place on the islands and in the mining districts of South America, where indeed, the Europeans continued to enslave them, until a comparatively recent period; still, the design, the feeling, and inclination from policy, was the same to do so here, in this section of the continent.

Nor was it until their influence became too great, by the political position occupied by their brethren in the new republic, that the German and Irish peasantry ceased to be sold as slaves for a term of years fixed by law, for the repayment of their passage-money, the descendants of these classes of people for a long time being held as inferiors, in the estimation of the ruling class, and it was not until they assumed the rights and privileges guaranteed to them by the established policy of the country, among the leading spirits of whom were their relatives, that the policy towards them was discovered to be a bad one, and accordingly changed. Nor was it, as is frequently very erroneously asserted, by colored as well as white persons, that it was on account of hatred to the African, or in other words, on account of hatred to his color, that the African was selected as the subject of oppression in this country. This is sheer nonsense; being based on policy and nothing else, as shown in another place. The Indians, who being the most foreign to the sympathies of the Europeans on this continent, were selected in the first place, who, being unable to withstand the hardships, gave way before them.

But the African race had long been known to Europeans, in all ages of the world's history, as a long-lived, hardy race, subject to toil and labor of various kinds, subsisting mainly by traffic, trade, and industry, and consequently being as foreign to the sympathies of the invaders of the continent as the Indians, they were selected, captured, brought here as a laboring class, and as a matter of policy held as such. Nor was the absurd idea of natural inferiority of the African ever dreamed of, until recently adduced by the slave-holders and their abettors, in justification of their policy. This, with contemptuous indignation, we fling back into their face, as a scorpion to a vulture. And so did our patriots and leaders in the cause of regeneration know better, and never for a moment yielded to the base doctrine. But they had discovered the great fact, that a cruel policy was pursued towards our people, and that they possessed distinctive characteristics which made them the objects of proscription. These characteristics being strongly marked in the colored people, as in the Indians, by color, character of hair and so on, made them the more easily distinguished from other Americans, and the policies more effectually urged against us. For this reason they introduced the subject of emigration to Canada, and a proper institution for the education of the youth.

At this important juncture of their proceedings, the afore named white gentlemen were introduced to the notice of the Convention, and after gaining permission to speak, expressed their gratification and surprise at the qualification and talent manifested by different members of the Convention, all expressing their determination to give the cause of the colored people more serious reflection. Mr. Garrison, the youngest of them all, and none the less honest on account of his youthfulness, being but 26 years of age at the time, (1831) expressed his determination to change his course of policy at once, and espouse the cause of the elevation of the colored people here in their own country. We are not at present well advised upon this point, it now having escaped our memory, but we are under the impression that Mr. Jocelyn also, at once changed his policy.

During the winter of 1832, Mr. Garrison issued his "Thoughts on African Colonization," and near about the same time or shortly after, issued the first number of the "Liberator," in both of which, his full convictions of the enormity of American slavery, and the wickedness of their policy towards the colored people, were fully expressed. At the sitting of the Convention in this year, a number, perhaps all of these gentlemen were present, and those who had denounced the Colonization scheme, and espoused the cause of the elevation of the colored people in this country, or the Anti Slavery cause, as it was now termed, expressed themselves openly and without reserve.

Sensible of the high-handed injustice done to the colored people in the United States, and the mischief likely to emanate from the unchristian proceedings of the deceptious Colonization scheme, like all honest hearted penitents, with the ardor only known to new converts, they entreated the Convention, whatever they did, not to entertain for a moment, the idea of recommending emigration to their people, nor the establishment of separate institutions of learning. They earnestly contended, and doubtless honestly meaning what they said, that they (the whites) had been our oppressors and injurers, they had obstructed our progress to the high positions of civilization, and now, it was their bounden duty to make full amends for the injuries thus inflicted on an unoffending people. They exhorted the Convention to cease; as they had laid on the burden, they would also take it off; as they had obstructed our pathway, they would remove the hindrance. In a word, as they had oppressed and trampled down the colored people, they would now elevate them. These suggestions and promises, good enough to be sure, after they were made, were accepted by the Convention—though some gentlemen were still in favor of the first project as the best policy, Mr. A.D. Shadd of West Chester, Pa., as we learn from himself, being one among that number—ran through the country like wild-fire, no one thinking, and if he thought, daring to speak above his breath of going any where out of certain prescribed limits, or of sending a child to school, if it should but have the name of "colored" attached to it, without the risk of being termed a "traitor" to the cause of his people, or an enemy to the Anti Slavery Cause.

At this important point in the history of our efforts, the colored men stopped suddenly, and with their hands thrust deep in their breeches-pockets, and their mouths gaping open, stood gazing with astonishment, wonder, and surprise, at the stupendous moral colossal statues of our Anti-Slavery friends and brethren, who in the heat and zeal of honest hearts, from a desire to make atonement for the many wrongs inflicted, promised a great deal more than they have ever been able half to fulfill, in thrice the period in which they expected it. And in this, we have no fault to find with our Anti-Slavery friends, and here wish it to be understood, that we are not laying any thing to their charge as blame, neither do we desire for a moment to reflect on them, because we heartily believe that all that they did at the time, they did with the purest and best of motives, and further believe that they now are, as they then were, the truest friends we have among the whites in this country. And hope, and desire, and request, that our people should always look upon *true* anti-slavery people, Abolitionists we mean, as their friends, until they have just cause for acting otherwise. It is true, that the Anti-Slavery, like all good causes, has produced some recreants, but the cause itself is no more to be blamed for that, than Christianity is for the malconduct of any professing hypocrite, nor the society of Friends, for the conduct of a broad-brimmed hat and shad-belly coated horsethief, because he spoke *thee* and *thou* before stealing the horse. But what is our condition even amidst our Anti-Slavery friends? And here, as our sole intention is to contribute to the elevation of our people, we must be permitted to express our opinion freely, without being thought uncharitable.

In the first place, we should look at the objects for which the Anti-Slavery cause was commenced, and the promises or inducements it held out at the commencement. It should be borne in mind, that Anti-Slavery took its rise among *colored men,* just at the time they were introducing their greatest projects for their own elevation, and that our Anti-Slavery brethren were converts of the colored men, in behalf of their elevation. Of course, it would be expected that being baptized into the new doctrines, their faith would induce them to embrace the principles therein contained, with the strictest possible adherence.

The cause of dissatisfaction with our former condition, was, that we were proscribed, debarred, and shut out from every respectable position, occupying the places of inferiors and menials.

It was expected that Anti-Slavery, according to its professions, would extend to colored persons, as far as in the power of its adherents, those advantages nowhere else to be obtained among white men. That colored boys would get situations in their shops and stores, and every other advantage tending to elevate them as far as possible, would be extended to them. At least, it was expected, that in Anti-Slavery establishments, colored men would have the preference. Because, there was no other ostensible object in view, in the commencement of the Anti-Slavery enterprise, than the *elevation* of the *colored man,* by facilitating his efforts in attaining to equality with the white man. It was urged, and it was true, that the colored people were susceptible of all that the whites were, and all that was required was to give them a fair opportunity, and they would prove their capacity. That it was unjust, wicked, and cruel, the result of an unnatural prejudice, that debarred them from places of respectability, and that public opinion could and should be corrected upon this subject. That it was only necessary to make a sacrifice of feeling, and an innovation on the customs of society, to establish a different order of things,—that as Anti-Slavery men, they were willing to make these sacrifices, and determined to take the colored man by the hand, making common cause with him in affliction, and bear a part of the odium heaped upon him. That his cause was the cause of God—that "In as much as ye did it not unto the least of these my little ones, ye did it not unto me," and that as Anti-Slavery men, they would "do right if the heavens fell." Thus, was the cause espoused, and thus did we expect much. But in all this, we were doomed to disappointment, sad, sad disappointment. Instead of realising what we had hoped for, we find ourselves occupying the very same position in relation to our Anti-Slavery friends, as we do in relation to the proslavery part of the community—a mere secondary, underling position, in all our relations to them, and any thing more than this, is not a matter of course affair—it comes not by established anti-slavery custom or right, but like that which emanates from the proslavery portion of the community, by mere sufferance.

It is true, that the "Liberator" office, in Boston, has got Elijah Smith, a colored youth, at the cases—the "Standard," in New York, a young colored man, and the "Freeman," in Philadelphia, William Still, another, in the publication office, as "packing clerk;" yet these are but three out of the hosts that fill these offices in their various departments, all occupying places that could have been, and as we once thought, would have been, easily enough, occupied by colored men. Indeed, we can have no other idea about anti-slavery in this country, than that the legitimate persons to fill any and every position about an anti-slavery establishment are colored persons. Nor will it do to argue in extenuation, that white men are as justly entitled to them as colored men; because white men do not from *necessity* become anti-slavery men in order to get situations; they being white men, may occupy any position they are capable of filling—in a word, their chances are endless, every avenue in the country being opened to them. They do not therefore become abolitionists, for the sake of employment—at least, it is not the song that anti-slavery sung, in the first love of the new faith, proclaimed by its disciples.

And if it be urged that colored men are incapable as yet to fill these positions, all that we have to say is, that the cause has fallen far short; almost equivalent to a failure, of a tithe, of what it promised to do in half the period of its existence, to this time, if it have not as yet, now a period of twenty years, raised up colored men enough, to fill the offices within its patronage. We think it is not unkind to say, if it had been half as faithful to itself, as it should have been—its professed principles we mean; it could have reared and tutored from childhood, colored men enough by this time, for its own especial purpose. These we know could have been easily obtained, because colored people in general, are favorable to the anti-slavery cause, and wherever there is an adverse manifestation, it arises from sheer ignorance; and we have now but comparatively few such among us. There is one thing certain, that no colored person, except such as would reject education altogether, would be adverse to putting their child with an anti-slavery person, for educational advantages. This then, could have been done. But it has not been done, and let the cause of it be whatever it may, and let whoever may be to blame, we are willing to let all that pass, and extend to our anti-slavery brethren the right-hand of fellowship, bidding them God-speed in the propagation of good and wholesome sentiments—for whether they are practically carried out or not, the professions are in themselves all right and good. Like Christianity, the principles are holy and of divine origin. And we believe, if ever a man started right, with pure and holy motives, Mr. Garrison did; and that, had he the power of making the cause what it should be, it would be all right, and there never would have been any cause for the remarks we have made, though in kindness, and with the purest of motives. We are nevertheless, still occupying a miserable position in the community, wherever we live; and what we most desire is, to draw the attention of our people to this fact, and point out what, in our opinion, we conceive to be a proper remedy.

Chapter III
American Colonization

When we speak of colonization, we wish distinctly to be understood, as speaking of the "American Colonization Society"—or that which is under its influence—commenced in Richmond, Virginia, in 1817, under the influence of Mr. Henry Clay of Ky., Judge Bushrod Washington of Va., and other Southern slaveholders, having for their express object, as their speeches and doings all justify us in asserting in good faith, the removal of the free colored people from the land of their birth, for the security of the slaves, as property to the slave propagandists.

This scheme had no sooner been propagated, than the old and leading colored men of Philadelphia, Pa., with Richard Allen, James Forten, and others at their head, true to their trust and the cause of their brethren, summoned the colored people together, and then and there, in language and with voices pointed and loud, protested against the scheme as an outrage, having no other object in view, than the benefit of the slave-holding interests of the country, and that as freemen, they would never prove recreant to the cause of their brethren in bondage, by leaving them without hope of redemption from their chains. This determination of the colored patriots of Philadelphia was published in full, authentically, and circulated throughout the length and breadth of the country by the papers of the day. The colored people every where received the news, and at once endorsed with heart and soul, the doings of the Anti-Colonization Meeting of colored freemen. From that time forth, the colored people generally have had no sympathy with the colonization scheme, nor confidence in its leaders, looking upon them all, as arrant hypocrites, seeking every opportunity to deceive them. In a word, the monster was crippled in its infancy, and has never as yet recovered from the stroke. It is true, that like its ancient sire, that was "more subtile than all the beasts of the field," it has inherited a large portion of his most prominent characteristic—an idiosyncrasy with the animal—that enables him to entwine himself into the greater part of the Church and other institutions of the country, which having once entered there, leaves his venom, which put such a spell on the conductors of those institutions, that it is only on condition that a colored person consents to go to the neighborhood of his kindred brother monster the boa, that he may find admission in the one or the other. We look upon the American Colonization Society as one of the most arrant enemies of the colored man, ever seeking to discomfit him, and envying him of every privilege that he may enjoy. We believe it to be anti-Christian in its character, and misanthropic in its pretended sympathies. Because if this were not the case, men could not be found professing morality and Christianity—as to our astonishment we have found them—who unhesitatingly say, "I know it is right"—that is in itself—"to do" so and so, "and I am willing and ready to do it, but only on condition, that you go to Africa." Indeed, a highly talented clergyman, informed us in November last (three months ago) in the city of Philadelphia, that he was present when the Rev. Doctor J.P. Durbin, late President of Dickinson College, called on Rev. Mr. P. of B., to consult him about going to Liberia, to take charge of the literary department of an University in contemplation, when the following conversation ensued: Mr. P.—"Doctor, I have as much and more than I can do here, in educating the youth of our own country, and preparing them for usefulness here at home." Dr. D.—"Yes, but do as you may, you can never be elevated here." Mr. P.—"Doctor, do you not believe that the religion of our blessed Redeemer Jesus Christ, has morality, humanity, philanthropy, and justice enough in it to elevate us, and enable us to obtain our rights in this our own country?" Dr. D.—"No, indeed, sir, I do not, and if you depend upon that, your hopes are vain!" Mr. P.—Turning to Doctor Durbin, looking him solemnly, though affectionately in the face, remarked—"Well, Doctor Durbin, we both profess to be ministers of Christ; but dearly as I love the cause of my Redeemer, if for a moment, I could entertain the opinion you do about Christianity, I would not serve him another hour!" We do not know, as we were not advised, that the Rev. doctor added in fine,—"Well, you may quit now, for all your serving him will not avail against the power of the god (hydra) of Colonization." Will any one doubt for a single moment, the justice of our strictures on colonization, after reading the conversation between the Rev. Dr. Durbin and the colored clergyman? Surely not. We can therefore make no account of it, but that of setting it down as being the worst enemy of the colored people.

Recently, there has been a strained effort in the city of New York on the part of the Rev. J. B. Pinney and others, of the leading white colonizationists, to get up a movement among some poor pitiable colored men—we say pitiable, for certainly the colored persons who are at this period capable of loaning themselves to the enemies of their race, against the best interest of all that we hold sacred to that race, are pitiable in the lowest extreme, far beneath the dignity of an enemy, and therefore, we pass them by with the simple remark, that this is the hobby that colonization is riding all over the country, as the "tremendous" access of colored people to their cause within the last twelve months. We should make another remark here perhaps, in justification of governor Pinney's New York allies—that is, report says, that in the short space of some three or five months, one of his confidants, benefited himself to the "reckoning" of from eleven to fifteen hundred dollars, or "such a matter, while others" were benefited in sums "pretty considerable" but of a less "reckoning." Well, we do not know after all, that they may not have quite as good a right, to pocket part of the spoils of this "grab game," as any body else. However, they are of little consequence, as the ever watchful eye of those excellent gentlemen and faithful guardians of their people's rights—the *Committee of Thirteen,* consisting of Messrs. John J. Zuille, *Chairman,* T. Joiner White, Philip A. Bell, *Secretaries,* Robert Hamilton, George T. Downing, Jeremiah Powers, John T. Raymond, Wm. Burnett, James McCuen Smith, Ezekiel Dias, Junius C. Morel, Thomas Downing, and Wm. J. Wilson, have properly chastised this pet-slave of Mr. Pinney, and made it "know its place," by keeping within the bound of its master's enclosure.

In expressing our honest conviction of the designedly injurious character of the Colonization Society, we should do violence to our own sense of individual justice, if we did not express the belief, that there are some honest hearted men, who not having seen things in the proper light, favor that scheme, simply as a means of elevating the colored people. Such persons, as soon as they become convinced of their error, immediately change their policy, and advocate the elevation of the colored people, anywhere and everywhere, in common with other men. Of such were the early abolitionists as before stated; and the great and good Dr. F.J. Lemoyne, Gerrit Smith, and Rev. Charles Avery, and a host of others, who were Colonizationists, before espousing the cause of our elevation, here at home, and nothing but an honorable sense of justice, induces us to make these exceptions, as there are many good persons within our knowledge, whom we believe to be well wishers of the colored people, who may favor colonization.* But the animal itself is the same "hydra-headed monster," let whomsoever may fancy to pet it. A serpent is a serpent, and none the less a viper, because nestled in the bosom of an honest hearted man. This the colored people must bear in mind, and keep clear of the hideous thing, lest its venom may be tost upon them. But why deem any argument necessary to show the unrighteousness of colonization? Its very origin as before shown—the source from whence it sprung, being the offspring of slavery—is in itself, sufficient to blast it in the estimation of every colored person in the United States, who has sufficient intelligence to comprehend it.

We dismiss this part of the subject, and proceed to consider the mode and means of our elevation in the United States.

Chapter IV

Our Elevation in the United States

That very little comparatively as yet has been done, to attain a respectable position as a class in this country, will not be denied, and that the successful accomplishment of this end is also possible, must also be admitted; but in what manner, and by what means, has long been, and is even now, by the best thinking minds among the colored people themselves, a matter of difference of opinion.

We believe in the universal equality of man, and believe in that declaration of God's word, in

*Benjamin Coates, Esq., a merchant of Philadelphia, we believe to be an honest hearted man, and real friend of the colored people, and a true, though as yet, rather undecided philanthropist. Mr. Coates, to our knowledge, has supported three or four papers published by colored men, for the elevation of colored people in the United States, and given, as he continues to do, considerable sums to their support. We have recently learned from himself, that, though he still advocates Colonization, simply as a means of elevating the colored race of the United States, that he has *left* the Colonization Society, and prefers seeing colored people located on this continent, to going to Liberia, or elsewhere off of it—though his zeal for the enlightenment of Africa, is unabated, as every good man's should be; and we are satisfied, that Mr. Coates is neither well understood, nor rightly appreciated by the friends of our cause. One thing we do know, that he left the Colonization Society, because he could not conscientiously subscribe to its measures.

which it is there positively said, that "God has made of one blood all the nations that dwell on the face of the earth." Now of "the nations that dwell on the face of the earth," that is, all the people—there are one thousand millions of souls, and of this vast number of human beings, two-thirds are colored, from black, tending in complexion to the olive or that of the Chinese, with all the intermediate and admixtures of black and white, with the various "crosses" as they are physiologically, but erroneously termed, to white. We are thus explicit in stating these points, because we are determined to be understood by all. We have then, two colored to one white person throughout the earth, and yet, singular as it may appear, according to the present geographical and political history of the world, the white race predominates over the colored; or in other words, wherever there is one white person, that one rules and governs two colored persons. This is a living undeniable truth, to which we call the especial attention of the colored reader in particular. Now there is a cause for this, as there is no effect without a cause, a comprehensible remediable cause. We all believe in the justice of God, that he is impartial, "looking upon his children with an eye of care," dealing out to them all, the measure of his goodness; yet, how can we reconcile ourselves to the difference that exists between the colored and the white races, as they truthfully present themselves before our eyes? To solve this problem, is to know the remedy; and to know it, is but necessary, in order successfully to apply it. And we shall but take the colored people of the United States, as a fair sample of the colored races everywhere of the present age, as the arguments that apply to the one, will apply to the other, whether Christians, Mahomedans, or pagans.

The colored races are highly susceptible of religion; it is a constituent principle of their nature, and an excellent trait in their character. But unfortunately for them, they carry it too far. Their hope is largely developed, and consequently, they usually stand still—hope in God, and really expect Him to do that for them, which it is necessary they should do themselves. This is their great mistake, and arises from a misconception of the character and ways of Deity. We must know God, that is understand His nature and purposes, in order to serve Him; and to serve Him well, is but to know him rightly. To depend for assistance upon God, is a *duty* and right; but to know when, how, and in what manner to obtain it, is the key to this great Bulwark of Strength, and Depository of Aid.

God himself is perfect; perfect in all his works and ways. He has means for every end; and every means used must be adequate to the end to be gained. God's means are laws—fixed laws of nature, a part of His own being, and as immutable, as unchangeable as Himself. Nothing can be accomplished but through the medium of, and conformable to these laws.

They are *three*—and like God himself, represented in the three persons in the God-head—the *Spiritual*, *Moral* and *Physical* Laws.

That which is Spiritual, can only be accomplished through the medium of the Spiritual law; that which is Moral, through the medium of the Moral law; and that which is Physical, through the medium of the Physical law. Otherwise than this, it is useless to expect any thing. Does a person want a spiritual blessing, he must apply through the medium of the spiritual law—*pray* for it in order to obtain it. If they desire to do a moral good, they must apply through the medium of the moral law—exercise their sense and feeling of *right* and *justice,* in order to effect it. Do they want to attain a physical end, they can only do so through the medium of the physical law—go to *work* with muscles, hands, limbs, might and strength, and this, and nothing else will attain it.

The argument that man must pray for what he receives, is a mistake, and one that is doing the colored people especially, incalculable injury. That man must pray in order to get to Heaven, every Christian will admit—but a great truth we have yet got to learn, that he can live on earth whether he is religious or not, so that he conforms to the great law of God, regulating the things of earth; the great physical laws. It is only necessary, in order to convince our people of their error and palpable mistake in this matter, to call their attention to the fact, that there are no people more religious in this Country, than the colored people, and none so poor and miserable as they. That prosperity and wealth, smiles upon the efforts of wicked white men, whom we know to utter the name of God with curses, instead of praises. That among the slaves, there are thousands of them religious, continually raising their voices, sending up their prayers to God, invoking His aid in their behalf, asking for a speedy deliverance; but they are still in chains, although they have thrice suffered out their three score years and ten. That "God sendeth rain upon the just and unjust," should be sufficient to convince us that our success in life, does not depend upon our religious character, but that the physical laws governing all earthly and temporary affairs, benefit equally the just and the unjust. Any other doctrine than this, is downright delusion, unworthy of a free people, and only intended for slaves. That all men and women, should be moral, upright, good and religious—we mean *Christians*—we would not utter a word against, and could only wish that it were so; but, what we here desire to do is, to correct the long standing error among a large body of the colored people in this country, that the cause of our oppression and degradation, is the displeasure of God towards us, because of our unfaithfulness to Him. This is not true; because if God is just—and he is—there could be no justice in prospering white men with his fostering care, for more than two thousand years, in all their wickedness, while dealing out to the colored people, the measure of his displeasure, for not half the wickedness as that of the whites. Here then is our mistake, and let it forever henceforth be corrected. We are no longer slaves, believing any interpretation that our oppressors may give the word of God, for the purpose of deluding us to the more easy subjugation; but freemen, comprising some of the first minds of intelligence and rudimental qualifications, in the country. What then is the remedy, for our degradation and oppression? This appears now to be the only remaining question—the means of successful elevation in this our own native land? This depends entirely upon the application of the means of Elevation.

Chapter V
Means of Elevation

Moral theories have long been resorted to by us, as a means of effecting the redemption of our brethren in bonds, and the elevation of the free colored people in this country. Experience has taught us, that speculations are not enough; that the *practical* application of principles adduced, the thing carried out, is the only true and proper course to pursue.

We have speculated and moralised much about equality—claiming to be as good as our neighbors, and every body else—all of which, may do very well in ethics—but not in politics. We live in society among men, conducted by men, governed by rules and regulations. However arbitrary, there are certain policies that regulate all well organized institutions and corporate bodies. We do not intend here to speak of the legal political relations of society, for those are treated on elsewhere. The business and social, or voluntary and mutual policies, are those that now claim our attention. Society regulates itself—being governed by mind, which like water, finds its own level. "Like seeks like," is a principle in the laws of matter, as well as of mind. There is such a thing as inferiority of things, and positions; at least society has made them so; and while we continue to live among men, we must agree to all *just* measures—all those we mean, that do not necessarily infringe on the rights of others. By the regulations of society, there is no equality of persons, where there is not an equality of attainments. By this, we do not wish to be understood as advocating the actual equal attainments of every individual; but we mean to say, that if these attainments be necessary for the elevation of the white man, they are necessary for the elevation of the colored man. That some colored men and women, in a like proportion to the whites, should be qualified in all the attainments possessed by them. It is one of the regulations of society the world over, and we shall have to conform to it, or be discarded as unworthy of the associations of our fellows.

Cast our eyes about us and reflect for a moment, and what do we behold! every thing that presents to view gives evidence of the skill of the white man. Should we purchase a pound of groceries, a yard of linen, a vessel of crockeryware, a piece of furniture, the very provisions that we eat,—all, all are the products of the white man, purchased by us from the white man, consequently, our earnings and means, are all given to the white man.

Pass along the avenues of any city or town, in which you live—behold the trading shops—the manufactories—see the operations of the various machinery—see the stage-coaches coming in, bringing the mails of intelligence—look at the railroads interlining every section, bearing upon them their mighty trains, flying with the velocity of the swallow, ushering in the hundreds of industrious, enterprising travellers. Cast again your eyes widespread over the ocean—see the vessels in every direction with their white sheets spread to the winds of heaven, freighted with the commerce, merchandise and wealth of many nations. Look as you pass along through the cities, at the great and massive buildings—the beautiful and extensive structures of architecture—behold the ten thousand cupolas, with their spires all reared up towards heaven, intersecting the territory of the clouds—all standing as mighty living monuments, of the industry, enterprise, and intelligence of the white man. And yet, with all these living truths, rebuking us with scorn, we strut about, place our hands akimbo, straighten up ourselves to our greatest height, and talk loudly about being "as good as any body." How do we compare with them? Our fathers are their coachmen, our brothers their cook-men, and ourselves their waiting-men. Our mothers their nurse-women, our sisters their scrub-women, our daughters their maid-women, and our wives their washer-women. Until colored men, attain to a position above permitting their mothers, sisters, wives, and daughters, to do the drudgery and menial offices of other men's wives and daughters; it is useless, it is nonsense, it is pitiable mockery, to talk about equality and elevation in society. The world is looking upon us, with feelings of commiseration, sorrow, and contempt. We scarcely deserve sympathy, if we peremptorily refuse advice, bearing upon our elevation.

We will suppose a case for argument: In this city reside, two colored families, of three sons and three daughters each. At the head of each family, there is an old father and mother. The opportunities of these families, may or may not be the same for educational advantages—be that as it may, the children of the one go to school, and become qualified for the duties of life. One daughter becomes a schoolteacher, another a mantua-maker, and a third a fancy shop-keeper; while one son becomes a farmer, another a merchant, and a third a mechanic. All enter into business with fine prospects, marry respectably, and settle down in domestic comfort—while the six sons and daughters of the other family, grow up without educational and business qualifications, and the highest aim they have, is to apply to the sons and daughters of the first named family, to hire for domestics! Would there be an equality here between the children of these two families? Certainly not. This, then, is precisely the position of the colored people generally in the United States, compared with the whites. What is necessary to be done, in order to attain an equality, is to change the condition, and the person is at once changed. If, as before stated, a knowledge of all the various business enterprises, trades, professions, and sciences, is necessary for the elevation of the white, a knowledge of them also is necessary for the elevation of the colored man; and he cannot be elevated without them.

White men are producers—we are consumers. They build houses, and we rent them. They raise produce, and we consume it. They manufacture clothes and wares, and we garnish ourselves with them. They build coaches, vessels, cars, hotels, saloons, and other vehicles and places of accommodation, and we deliberately wait until they have got them in readiness, then walk in, and contend with as much assurance for a "right," as though the whole thing was brought by, paid for, and belonged to us. By their literary attainments, they are the contributors to, authors and teachers of, literature, science, religion, law, medicine, and all other useful attainments that the world now makes use of. We have no reference to ancient times—we speak of modern things.

These are the means by which God intended man to succeed: and this discloses the secret of the white man's success with all of his wickedness, over the head of the colored man, with all of his religion. We have been pointed and plain, on this part of the subject, because we desire our readers to see persons and things in their true position. Until we are determined to change the condition of things, and raise ourselves above the position in which we are now prostrated, we must hang our heads in sorrow, and hide our faces in shame. It is enough to know that these things are so; the causes we care little about. Those we have been examining, complaining about, and moralising over, all our life time. This we are weary of. What we desire to learn now is, how to effect a *remedy;* this we have endeavored to point out. Our elevation must be the result of *self-efforts,* and work of our *own hands.* No other human power can accomplish it. If we but determine it shall be so, it will be so. Let each one make the case his own, and endeavor to rival his neighbor, in honorable competition. . . .

Chapter XVII
Emigration of the Colored People of the United States

That there have been people in all ages under certain circumstances, that may be benefited by emigration, will be admitted; and that there are circumstances under which emigration is absolutely necessary to their political elevation, cannot be disputed.

This we see in the Exodus of the Jews from Egypt to the land of Judea; in the expedition of Dido and her followers from Tyre to Mauritania; and not to dwell upon hundreds of modern European examples—also in the ever memorable emigration of the Puritans, in 1620, from Great Britain, the land of their birth, to the wilderness of the New World, at which may be fixed the beginning of emigration to this continent as a permanent residence.

This may be acknowledged; but to advocate the emigration of the colored people of the United States from their native homes, is a new feature in our history, and at first view, may be considered objectionable, as pernicious to our interests. This objection is at once removed, when reflecting on our condition as incontrovertibly shown in a foregoing part of this work. And we shall proceed at once to give the advantages to be derived from emigration, to us as a people, in preference to any other policy that we may adopt. This granted, the question will then be, Where shall we go? This we conceive to be all-important—of paramount consideration, and shall endeavor to show the most advantageous locality; and premise the recommendation, with the strictest advice against any countenance whatever, to the emigration scheme of the so called Republic of Liberia. . . .

Chapter XVIII
"Republic of Liberia"

. . . But to return to emigration: Where shall we go? We must not leave this continent; America is our destination and our home.

That the continent of America seems to have been designed by Providence as an asylum for all the various nations of the earth, is very apparent. From the earliest discovery, various nations sent a representation here, either as adventurers and speculators, or employed seamen and soldiers, hired to do the work of their employers. And among the earliest and most numerous class who found their way to the New World, were those of the African race. And it is now ascertained to our mind, beyond a peradventure, that when the continent was discovered, there were found in Central America, a tribe of the black race, of fine looking people, having characteristics of color and hair, identifying them originally of the African race—no doubt being a remnant of the Africans who, with the Carthaginian expedition, were adventitiously cast upon this continent, in their memorable excursion to the "Great Island," after sailing many miles distant to the West of the Pillars of Hercules.

We are not inclined to be superstitious, but say, that we can see the "finger of God" in all this; and if the European race may with propriety, boast and claim, that this continent is better adapted to their development, than their own father-land; surely, it does not necessarily detract from our father-land, to claim the superior advantages to the African race, to be derived from this continent. But be that as it may, the world belongs to mankind—his common Father created it for his common good—his temporal destiny is here; and our present warfare, is not upon European rights, nor for European countries; but for the common rights of man, based upon the great principles of common humanity—taking our chance in the world of rights, and claiming to have originally more right to this continent, than the European race. And had we no other claims than those set forth in a former part of this work, they are sufficient to cause every colored man on the continent, to stand upon the soil unshaken and unmoved. The aboriginee of the continent, is more closely allied to us by consanguinity, than to the European—being descended from the Asiatic, whose alliance in matrimony with the African is very common—therefore, we have even greater claims to this continent on that account, and should unite and make common cause in elevation, with our similarly oppressed brother, the Indian.

The advantages of this continent are superior, because it presents every variety of climate, soil, and production of the earth, with every variety of mineral production, with all kinds of water privileges, and ocean coast on all sides, presenting every commercial advantage. Upon the American continent we are determined to stay, in spite of every odds against us. . . .

CHARLOTTE L. FORTEN GRIMKÉ
(1837–1914)

Granddaugher of one of the richest black men in America, a participant in a significant experiment with ex-slaves, a poet who in later life denied that she had written any poems, and a diarist who provides unmatched glimpses at key nineteenth-century personalities and events, Charlotte Forten made unique contributions to African American cultural and literary history. Forten pushed against the limitations of place defined for black women and was able to travel, teach, and write when others were confined almost exclusively to the domestic sphere. Her interactions with the newly freed black people on St. Helena island enabled her to become a chronicler of their religious and folkways. She and her white coworkers in the Port Royal experiment succeeded in convincing the broader public that recently enslaved African Americans were readily able and eager to take advantage of educational opportunities made available to them.

Born of free parents in Philadelphia in 1837, Charlotte was the daughter of Robert Bridges and Mary Wood Forten; her mother died when Charlotte was a young child. Her grandfather, James Forten, was an abolitionist who earned a fortune as a sail maker. He opposed colonization and was actively involved in antislavery activities. His contact with William Lloyd Garrison, abolitionist and editor of the

Liberator, to which Forten had contributed for its launching, would later prove useful to Charlotte, who published some of her poems in that newspaper. Charlotte's father was also a sail maker and an ardent abolitionist and antisegregationist. He hired tutors for Charlotte's early education instead of allowing her to attend the segregated schools of Philadelphia. As a young adult, she was allowed to attend school in Salem, Massachusetts, where there was no segregation in the school system (although there was certainly discrimination). Forten also had the good fortune of living with Charles Lenox Remond, a friend of her family and another important personage in nineteenth-century African American history.

In addition to inheriting from her grandfather and her father the abolitionist spirit that would inform her life's work, she was also influenced by Robert Purvis, who was married to her father's sister Harriet and who served as president of the American Anti-Slavery Society. The Purvis farm, fifteen miles from Philadelphia, became Charlotte's second home. Thus enmeshed in an environment where talk of abolitionism was as frequent as breathing, Charlotte was well seasoned in the politics of the time. When she began keeping her journal in Massachusetts in 1854, awareness of color and the condition of black people found prominent spaces in it. Forten would keep the diary until 1892, although there are sustained periods when she did not write in it. It begins by recounting her experiences as a student at the Higginson Grammar School in Salem, but there is frequent commentary on issues, lectures, and personalities of the day. She includes the dramatic witnessing of a slave who was captured and returned to the South. She heard lectures by and met both Garrison and Wendell Phillips (with whom she would later correspond). Other famous personages she heard included Henry Ward Beecher, Ralph Waldo Emerson, Charles Sumner, and William Wells Brown. Not only did she hear Brown, but he stayed briefly in the home where she lived, and Charlotte joined the Salem Female Anti-Slavery Society with Brown's daughter Josephine.

Politics did not occupy all of Forten's time. She took long walks for exercise with other schoolgirls, traveled throughout New England, played the piano, took German and French lessons, kept up with the latest fashions in sewing, and went to the theater (she saw *Hamlet* in March of 1856). Forten was an avid reader, perusing the works of Dickens, Browning, Hawthorne, Stowe, and Phillis Wheatley. Her intense love of learning persisted throughout her life. Having written journal entries for more than a year, in 1855 Forten turned to writing poetry. "To W.L.G. [William Lloyd Garrison] on Reading his 'Chosen Queen,'" was published in the *Liberator* on March 16, 1855. She praised Garrison (who had also written a poem in tribute to Charlotte's three aunts titled "To the Daughters of James Forten") for his abolitionist spirit, but was embarrassed when one of her aunts saw the poem. "If ever I write doggerel again," she maintained, "I shall be careful not to sign my own initials." This combination of public support for causes but shyness about the writing would prevail throughout Forten's literary endeavors. She seemed to attach a frivolity to the writing of poetry, thinking it not commensurate with the more serious pursuits in life. Nonetheless, she would publish thirteen more poems.

Several of Forten's poems appeared in the *Liberator.* They included "A Parting Hymn," which she wrote for the examination ceremony at Higginson Grammar School and which William Wells Brown published in *The Black Man* in 1863. She also wrote the graduation poem, simply called "Poem," for Salem Normal School, from which she graduated after a year of study in July 1856; it, too, appeared in the *Liberator*. The poem continued her theme of working for higher causes such as abolition. In "The Two Voices" (1859), she focuses on the plight of fighting racism on the one hand and trying to find energy to fight for abolition on the other. Ultimately, the poem ends in sentimentality, which would define other of Forten's poems. A striking example is "The Wind Among the Poplars," in which a woman shares with a friend that she had a premonition of her lover's death and that the wind in the poplars has the same sound as the sea where her lover was drowned. The theme of death runs through Forten's early poems, regardless of the poems' sentimentality.

Forten's Normal School training led to her accept a teaching position at Epes Grammar School of Salem in June 1856; she became the first black teacher in the all-white school. However, ill health that would plague her again and again forced her to return to Philadelphia in May 1857. Returning to Boston in August, she met John Greenleaf Whittier, who would visit her repeatedly over the years. Illness, however, finally forced her to resign from her teaching position at Epes and return to Philadelphia in March 1858. Her journal entries continued during this period, and she completed an essay titled "Glimpses of New England," which appeared in the June 19, 1858 issue of the *National Anti-Slavery Standard*. She continued teaching in Philadelphia but was frequently beset by illness, so much so that she wished for the rest of death. Her expressed journal wishes, however, did not coincide with the reality of her life. She continued to be engaged by abolitionist news and stories of runaway slaves.

On May 7, 1859, Forten stopped writing in her journal and resumed again on January 1, 1860; she returned to Salem during that interval. She was silent again during a period of illness (lung fever) and did not return to the journal until June 22, 1862. She now personified her journal by referring to it as "A," noting especially the visits from Whittier and his sister. It was Whittier who suggested that she apply for a teaching position in Port Royal, South Carolina, which became a testing site for black intelligence. Abandoned by their owners as a result of events during the Civil War, more than ten thousand slaves were immediately freed. The War Department and northern abolitionists were determined to prove that the newly freed people could acquire education and become self-determining. When the Boston Educational Commission turned down Forten's application to join this venture, she returned to Philadelphia and obtained an assignment through J. Miller McKim, who was a friend of her family and an organizer of the Port Royal Relief Association of Philadelphia.

In her diary, Forten describes the songs and folkways of the blacks she encountered in Beaufort and St. Helena. Although she ran the risk at times of being almost too gushing about the songs she heard, she nonetheless provides an invaluable historical record of this creativity. She worked with other abolitionists from the North, including William Allen, Charles Ware, and Lucy McKim, and she was assigned to teach with two white women, Laura M. Towne and Ellen Murphy, the former of whom founded the famous Penn School. (Forten was the only black teacher in Port Royal.) She also had the chance to meet Harriet Tubman, who lived for a short time in Beaufort. In letters to the North, two of which were published in the *Liberator* of December 12 and 19, 1862, Forten describes her various adventures. Although illness forced her to return to Philadelphia between July 31 and October 16, 1863, she took up her teaching duties again and remained in South Carolina until 1864; she continued to record in her diary during this period, but would not write in it again until 1885.

The twelve years after her return to Philadelphia found her teaching in schools there, with a brief sojourn to Boston. She published "Life on the Sea Islands" in the May and June 1864 issues of the *Atlantic Monthly.* It was also during this period that she translated Emile Erckmann and Alexander Chatrian's *Madame Therese; or, The Volunteers of '92;* the English version was published in 1869. She also published on a variety of topics in the *Christian Register,* the *Boston Commonwealth,* and the *New England Magazine.* "Personal Recollections of Whittier" appeared in the June 1893 issue of the *New England Magazine.*

Forten moved to Washington, D.C., in the 1870s, where she met Francis James Grimké, the famous clergyman and descendant of the abolitionist Grimké sisters of South Carolina, in 1877; they were married on December 19, 1878. Their thirteen-years difference in age (Forten was older) proved no hindrance to their spiritual and intellectual union, the kind for which Forten had expressed a desire throughout her years of diary keeping. However, their only child, Theodora Cornelia, who was born on January 1, 1880, died six months later. The Grimkés lived in Jacksonville, Florida, from 1885 to 1889. During this period, after many years of silence, Charlotte Grimké returned to her journal writing. She recorded her long bouts with illness and periods of separation from Francis as well as the church work they shared; she seems to have grown more mission oriented with age. The final entry for the diary was in 1892. Grimké also continued to write what scholars have judged to be a much more mature poetry.

In 1889, the Grimkés returned to Washington. Together, they continued their interest in racial uplift and equality. Charlotte Grimké worked as a clerk in the Treasury Department and as a trustee and secretary of the board of the Westborough Insane Hospital. She was incapacitated by illness during the last years of her life, and she was actually bedridden during the final thirteen months. She died of lung fever (some scholars claim cerebral embolism) on July 23, 1914. Upon Charlotte's death, Francis Grimké passed along the five manuscript versions of her diaries to Anna Julia Cooper, who typed them and provided the copies from which a selected portion was first published in 1953.

Charlotte Grimké's poetry and diaries offer twentieth-century readers a detailed look at a young black women growing up in the nineteenth century and trying to make sense of the slavery-ridden and discriminatory (gender and race) world around her. Her diary was a refuge from the pain of being refused service in Philadelphia ice-cream parlors and elsewhere, a place for effusive reactions to people and places, a site of introspection for a sometimes overly sensitive and lonely mind. Writing was a companion as well as a healer for Grimké. It was the private voice when a public one was not possible. Her poetry is equal to much published in the same vein during her lifetime, and it shows a growth and maturity reflective of a mind ever striving for self-improvement. This record of literary achievement is indeed remarkable.

❖❖❖

Charlotte L. Forten Grimké's manuscripts are in the Moorland-Spingarn Research Center of Howard University.

For biography and criticism, see Ray Allen Billington, introduction to his editing of *The Journals of Charlotte L. Forten* (1953; reprinted New York: Norton, 1981); Joanne Braxton, "A Poet's Retreat: The Diaries of Charlotte Forten Grimké (1837–1914)," in *Wild Women in the Whirlwind: Afra-American Culture and the Contemporary Literary Renaissance* (New Brunswick, N.J.: Rutgers University Press, 1990); Trudier Harris, "Charlotte L. Forten," *Dictionary of Literary Biography*, Vol. 50 (Detroit: Gale, 1986); Joan R. Sherman, *Invisible Poets: Afro-Americans of the Nineteenth Century* (Urbana: University of Illinois Press, 1974); Brenda Stevenson, introduction to and editing of *The Journals of Charlotte Forten Grimké* (New York: Oxford University Press, 1988).

FROM THE *Journal of Charlotte Forten*

Thursday, May 25, 1854. Did not intend to write this evening, but have just heard of something which is worth recording:—something which must ever rouse in the mind of every true friend of liberty and humanity, feelings of the deepest indignation and sorrow. Another fugitive from bondage has been arrested; a poor man, who for two short months has trod the soil and breathed the air of the "Old Bay State," was arrested like a criminal in the streets of her capital, and is now kept strictly guarded,—a double police force is required, the military are in readiness; and all this is done to prevent a man, whom God has created in his own image, from regaining that freedom with which, he, in common with every other human being, is endowed. I can only hope and pray most earnestly that Boston will not again disgrace herself by sending him back to a bondage worse than death; or rather that she will redeem herself from the disgrace which his arrest alone has brought upon her. . . .

Saturday, May 27. . . . Returned home, read the Anti-Slavery papers, and then went down to the depot to meet father; he had arrived in Boston early in the morning, regretted very much that he had not reached there the evening before to attend the great meeting at Faneuil Hall. He says that the excitement in Boston is very great; the trial of the poor man takes place on Monday. We scarcely dare to think of what may be the result; there seems to be nothing too bad for these Northern tools of slavery to do.

Tuesday, May 30. Rose very early and was busy until nine o'clock; then, at Mrs. Putnam's urgent request, went to keep store for her while she went to Boston to attend the Anti-Slavery Convention. I was very anxious to go, and will certainly do so to-morrow; the arrest of the alleged fugitive will give additional interest to the meetings, I should think. His trial is still going on and I can scarcely think of anything else; read again to-day as most suitable to my feelings and to the times, "The Runaway Slave at Pilgrim's Point," by Elizabeth B. Browning; how powerfully it is written! how earnestly and touchingly does the writer portray the bitter anguish of the poor fugitive as she thinks over all the wrongs and sufferings that she has endured, and of the sin to which tyrants have driven her but which they alone must answer for! It seems as if no one could read this poem without having his sympathies roused to the utmost in behalf of the oppressed.—After a long conversation with my friends on their return, on this all-absorbing subject, we separated for the night, and I went to bed, weary and sad.

Wednesday, May 31. . . . Sarah [Remond] and I went to Boston in the morning. Everything was much quieter—outwardly than we expected, but still much real indignation and excitement prevail. We walked past the Court-

House, which is now lawlessly converted into a prison, and filled with soldiers, some of whom were looking from the windows, with an air of insolent authority which made my blood boil, while I felt the strongest contempt for their cowardice and servility. We went to the meeting, but the best speakers were absent, engaged in the most arduous and untiring efforts in behalf of the poor fugitive; but though we missed the glowing eloquence of [Wendell] Phillips, [William Lloyd] Garrison, and [Theodore] Parker, still there were excellent speeches made, and our hearts responded to the exalted sentiments of Truth and Liberty which were uttered. The exciting intelligence which occasionally came in relation to the trial, added fresh zeal to the speakers, of whom Stephen [S.] Foster and his wife [Abby Kelley Foster] were the principal. The latter addressed, in the most eloquent language, the women present, entreating them to urge their husbands and brothers to action, and also to give their aid on all occasions in our just and holy cause.—I did not see father the whole day; he, of course, was deeply interested in the trial.—Dined at Mr. Garrison's; his wife is one of the loveliest persons I have ever seen, worthy of such a husband. At the table, I watched earnestly the expression of that noble face, as he spoke beautifully in support of the non-resistant principles to which he has kept firm; his is indeed the very highest Christian spirit, to which I cannot hope to reach, however, for I believe in 'resistance to tyrants,' and would fight for liberty until death. We came home in the evening, and felt sick at heart as we passed through the streets of Boston on our way to the depot, seeing the military as they rode along, ready at any time to prove themselves the minions of the South.

Thursday, June 1st. . . . The trial is over at last; the commissioner's decision will be given to-morrow. We are all in the greatest suspense; what will that decision be? Alas! that any one should have the power to decide the right of a fellow being to himself! It is thought by many that he will be acquitted of the great crime of leaving a life of bondage, as the legal evidence is not thought sufficient to convict him. But it is only too probable that they will sacrifice him to propitiate the South, since so many at the North dared oppose the passage of the infamous Nebraska Bill.—Miss Putnam was married this evening. Mr. Frothingham performed the ceremony, and in his prayer alluded touchingly to the events of this week; he afterwards in conversation with the bridegroom, (Mr. Gilliard), spoke in the most feeling manner about this case;—his sympathies are all on the right side. The wedding was a pleasant one; the bride looked very lovely; and we enjoyed ourselves as much as possible in these exciting times. It is impossible to be happy now.

Friday, June 2. Our worst fears are realized; the decision was against poor Burns, and he has been sent back to a bondage worse, a thousand times worse than death. Even an attempt at rescue was utterly impossible; the prisoner was completely surrounded by soldiers with bayonets fixed, a cannon loaded, ready to be fired at the slightest sign. To-day Massachusetts has again been disgraced; again has she shewed her submission to the Slave Power; and Oh! with what deep sorrow do we think of what will doubtless be the fate of that poor man, when he is again consigned to the horrors of Slavery. With what scorn must that government be regarded, which cowardly assembles thousands of soldiers to satisfy the demands of slaveholders; to deprive of his freedom a man, created in God's own image, whose sole offence is the color of his skin! And if resistance is offered to this outrage, these soldiers are to shoot down American citizens without mercy; and this by the express orders of a government which proudly boasts of being the freeest [sic] in the world; this on the very soil where the Revolution of 1776 began; in sight of the battle-field, where thousands of brave men fought and died in opposing British tyranny, which was nothing compared with the American oppression of to-day. In looking over my diary, I perceive that I did not mention that there was on the Friday night after the man's arrest, an attempt made to rescue him, but although it failed, on account of there not being men enough engaged in it, all honor should be given to those who bravely made the attempt. I can write no more. A cloud seems hanging over me, over all our persecuted race, which nothing can dispel.

Sunday, June 4. A beautiful day. The sky is cloudless, the sun shines warm and bright, and a delicious breeze fans my cheek as I sit by the window writing. How strange it is that in a world so beautiful, there can be so much wickedness; on this delightful day, while many are enjoying themselves in their happy homes, not poor Burns only, but millions beside are suffering in chains; and how many Christian ministers to-day will mention him, or those who suffer with him? How many will speak from the pulpit against the cruel outrage on humanity which has just been committed; or against the many, even worse ones, which are committed in this country every day? Too well do we know that there are but very few, and these few alone deserve to be called the ministers of Christ, whose doctrine was 'Break every yoke, and let the oppressed go free.'—During the past week, we have had a vacation, which I had expected to enjoy very much, but it was of course impossible for me to do so. To-morrow school commences, and although the pleasure I shall feel in again seeing my beloved teacher, and in resuming my studies will be much saddened by recent events, yet they shall be a fresh incentive to more earnest study, to aid me in fitting myself for laboring in a holy cause, for enabling me to do much towards changing the condition of my oppressed and suffering people. Would that those with whom I shall recite to-morrow could sympathize with me in this; would that they could look upon all God's creatures without respect to color, feeling that it is character alone which makes the true man or woman! I earnestly hope that the time will come when they will feel thus. . . .

Sunday, June 25. Have been writing nearly all day.—This afternoon went to an Anti-Slavery meeting in Danvers, from which I have just returned. Mr. Foss spoke eloquently, and with that warmth and sincerity which evidently come from the heart. He said he was rejoiced that the people at the North were beginning to feel that slavery is no longer confined to the black man alone, but that they too must wear the yoke; and they are becoming roused on the subject at last. He spoke of the objections made by many to the Abolitionists, on the plea of their using too violent language; they say that the slaveholders are driven by it to worse measures; what they need is mild entreaty, etc., etc. But the petition against the Nebraska Bill, couched in the very mildest terms by the clergymen of the North, was received even less favorably by the South, than the hardest sayings of the Abolitionists; and they were abused and denounced more severely than the latter have ever been.—As we walked home, Miss [Sarah] Remond and I were wishing that we could have an anti-slavery meeting in the neighborhood every Sunday, and as well attended as this was. . . .

Sunday, July 2. A delightful day—In the morning read several chapters in the New Testament. The third verse of the last chapter of Hebrews—"Remember them that are in bonds as bound with them" suggested many thoughts to my mind: *Remember the poor slave as bound with him.* How few even of those who are opposed to slavery realize this! If they felt thus so ardent, so untiring, would be their efforts that they would soon accomplish the overthrow of this iniquitous system. All honor for the noble few who do feel for the suffering bondman *as bound with him,* and act accordingly! . . .

Sunday, July 9. Attended the meetings during the day and evening. I felt sorry and disappointed to see such a small number of persons present. The intense heat of the weather perhaps accounted for this. Though for such a cause I thought much more than that might have been endured. Very eloquent and interesting speeches were made by Mr. Garrison and Mr. Foss in the afternoon and evening. After tea I went to Miss [Sarah] Remond's where Mr.

Garrison had taken tea, and felt happier and better after listening to the conversation of that truly good and great man. . . .

Friday, July 28. This morning Miss Creamer, a friend of our teacher, came into the school. She is a very learned lady; a Latin teacher in Troy Seminary, and an authoress. I certainly did feel some alarm, when I saw her entering the room. But she was so very kind and pleasant that I soon felt more at ease. . . . I do think reading one's compositions before strangers is a trying task. If I were to tell Mrs. R[emond] this, I know she would ask how I could expect to become what I often say I should like to be—an Anti-Slavery lecturer. But I think that I should then trust to the inspiration of the subject.—This evening read "Poems of Phillis Wheatly [sic]," an African slave, who lived in Boston at the time of the Revolution. She was a wonderfully gifted woman, and many of her poems are very beautiful. Her character and genius afford a striking proof of the falseness of the assertion made by some that hers is an inferior race. . . .

Tuesday, August 1. To-day is the twentieth anniversary of British emancipation. The joy that we feel at an event so just and so glorious is greatly saddened by thoughts of the bitter and cruel oppression which still exists in our own land, so proudly claiming to be "the land of the free." And how very distant seems the day when she will follow the example of "the mother country," and liberate her millions of suffering slaves! This morning I went with Mr. and Mrs. R[emond] to the celebration at Abington. The weather was delightful, and a very large number of persons was assembled in the beautiful grove. Mr. Garrison, Wendell Phillips and many other distinguished friends of freedom were present, and spoke eloquently. Mr. Garrison gave an interesting account of the rise and progress of the anti-slavery movement in Great Britain. . . . The sadness that I had felt was almost entirely dissipated by the hopeful feelings expressed by the principal speakers. And when they sang the beautiful songs for the occasion, there was something very pleasant in the blending of so many voices in the open air. And still more pleasant to think that it was for a cause so holy that they had assembled then and there. Sarah [Remond] and I had a sail in one of those charming little row-boats which are my particular favorites. It was very delightful to me to feel that I was so near the water; and I could not resist the temptation to cool my hands in the sparkling waves. I greatly enjoyed sitting under the shade of the noble pine trees and listening to the eloquent speeches in behalf of the slave; every sentiment of which met a warm response in my heart. On returning home we stopped in Boston and passed some time very pleasantly in the Common listening to the music which enlivened the stillness of the sultry night. It was quite late when we reached home. And I retired to rest feeling that this had been one of the happiest days of my life, and thinking hopefully of the happy glorious day when every fetter shall be broken, and throughout this land there shall no longer be a single slave! . . .

Tuesday, Sept. 5. . . . I have suffered much today,—my friends Mrs. P[utnam] and her daughters were refused admission to the Museum, after having tickets given them, solely on account of their complexion. Insulting language was used to them—Of course they felt and exhibited deep, bitter indignation; but of what avail was it? none, but to excite the ridicule of those contemptible creatures, miserable doughfaces who do not deserve the name of men. I will not attempt to write more.—No words can express my feelings. But these cruel wrongs cannot be much longer endured. A day of retribution must come. God grant that it may come very soon! . . .

Sunday, Dec. 17. This evening Sarah's husband [J. D. Gilliard] arrived from California. . . . We were very much surprised to see him. Of course Sarah is very happy. There was so much to be said, so many questions to be asked and answered, that we had nearly forgotten Lucy Stone's lecture. We found the hall so much crowded that it was almost impossible to procure a seat. The lecture was earnest and impressive, and some parts of it very beautiful. It was an appeal to the noblest and warmest sympathies of our nature, in behalf of the oppressed. I saw many among her large and attentive audience, who had probably never attended an anti-slavery lecture before. I hope her touching appeal may not have been made in vain—that they may think rightly on this subject. And from noble *thoughts* spring noble *words* and *deeds*.

Interesting Letter from Miss Charlotte L. Forten

ST. HELENA'S ISLAND, BEAUFORT, S. C.
Nov. 27, 1862.

Dear Mr. Garrison—I shall commence this letter in very nearly the same words used by one of your correspondents some weeks since—"Today, for the first time since leaving home, I have been allowed the privilege of reading the *Liberator*." But I must claim that, in my case, the privilege must be a greater one than in his, for he was only in New York, while I am in South Carolina. However, we shall not be at all likely to dispute about it. I cannot tell you what a pleasure it is to see this paper. It is of an old date—Oct. 31st—but it is not the less welcome for that. It is pleasant to look upon, and familiar as the face of an old friend, here in this strange, southern land. And is it not a significant fact, that one may now sit in safety here, in the rebellious little Palmetto State, and read the *Liberator*, and display it to one's friends, rejoicing over it, in the fulness of one's heart, as a very great treasure? It is fitting that we should give it—*the pioneer paper in the cause of human rights*—a hearty welcome to the land where, until so recently, those rights have been most barbarously trampled upon. We do not forget that it is, in fact, directly traceable to the exertions of the editor of this paper, and those who have labored so faithfully with him, that Northern people now occupy in safety the South Carolina shore; that freedom now blesses it; that it is, for the first time, a place worth living in.

Perhaps it may interest you to know how we have spent this day—Thanksgiving Day—here, in the sunny South. It has been truly a "rare" day—a day worthy of October. Cool, delicious air, golden, gladdening sunlight, deep-blue sky, with soft white clouds floating over it. Had we no other causes, the glory and beauty of the day alone would make it a day to give thanks for. But we have other causes, great and glorious, that unite to make this peculiarly a day of thanksgiving and praise. You have, doubtless, ere this, read General Saxton's noble Proclamation for Thanksgiving to the people of Port Royal. I know that it will be fully appreciated by you. For myself, I thanked God with all my heart when I heard it read. I thanked Him for giving to the freed people of these islands a governor like General Saxton—a man so thoroughly good and true, so nobly and earnestly devoted to their interests. I think he is loved and appreciated as he ought to be by them.

In accordance with his Proclamation, this was observed as "a day of thanksgiving and praise." An order had been issued, that the Superintendent of each plantation should have an animal killed, that the people might, to-day, eat fresh meat, which is a great luxury to them,—and, indeed, to all of us here. This morning, a large number, superintendents, teachers, and many of the freed people, assembled in the Baptist church. Gen. Saxton, and his brother, Captain Saxton, were present. The church was crowded, and there were many outside, at the doors and windows, who could not get in. It was a sight that I shall not soon forget—that crowd of eager, happy black faces, from which the shadow of slavery had passed forever. "FOREVER FREE! FOREVER FREE!" All the time those magical words were singing themselves in my soul, and never in my life before have I felt so deeply and sincerely grateful to God. It was a moment of exultation, such as comes but seldom in one's life, that in which I sat among the people assembled on this lovely day to thank God for the most blessed and glorious of all gifts.

The singing was, as usual, very beautiful. These people have really a great deal of musical talent. It is impossible to give you an idea of many of their songs and hymns. They are so wild, so strange, and yet so invariably harmonious and sweet, they must be heard to be appreciated. And the people accompany them with a peculiar swaying motion of the body, which seems to make the singing all the more effective. There is one of their hymns—"Roll, Jordan, roll," that I never listen to without seeming to hear, almost to *feel,* the rolling of waters. There is a great rolling wave of sound through it all.

The singing, to-day, was followed by an appropriate prayer and sermon, by the Rev. Mr. Phillips, who is an excellent New England man, and a minister much liked by the people. After the sermon, General Saxton made a short but very spirited speech, urging the young men of the island to enlist in the colored regiment now forming at Beaufort under Col. T. W. Higginson. That was the first intimation I had had of Mr. Higginson being down here. I am greatly rejoiced thereat. He seems to me, of all fighting men, the one best fitted to command a regiment of blacks. The mention of his name recalled most vividly the happy days passed last summer in good old Massachusetts, when, day after day in the streets of Worcester, we used to see the indefatigable *Capt.* Higginson drilling his white company. I never saw him,—so full of life and energy, so thoroughly enjoying his work,—without thinking what a splendid general he would make. And that, too, may come about. Gen. Saxton to-day expressed the hope of seeing him one day commander of an army of black men. Gen. Saxton told the people, who listened with an eager attention, how bravely Mr. Higginson had stood by the side of Anthony Burns in the old, dark days, even suffering imprisonment for his sake; and assured them that, under the leadership of such a man, they need fear no injustice. He would see to it that they were not wronged in any way. Then he told them the story of Robert Small [sic], and added, "Yesterday, Robert Small came to see me. I asked him how he was getting on in the store which he was keeping for the freed people. He said he was doing very well—was making fifty dollars a week, sometimes. But, said he, 'General, I'm going to stop keeping store—I'm going to enlist.' What, said I, are you going to enlist, when you can make fifty dollars a week keeping store? 'Yes, sir,' he added, 'I'm going to enlist as a private in the black regiment. How can I expect to keep my freedom unless I fight for it? Suppose the Secesh should come back here, what good would my fifty dollars do me then? Yes, sir, I should enlist if I were making a thousand dollars a week.'" The General then told him what a victory the black soldiers had lately won on the Georgia coast, and how great a good they had done for their race in winning it. They have proved to their enemies that the black man can and will fight for his freedom.

The General's speech was a stirring one, and I trust it will prove very effective. There has been among some of the men great distrust about joining the regiment, the soldiers were formerly so unjustly treated by the government. But they trust General Saxton, and his assurances will, doubtless, have much effect. Many of the able-bodied men from these islands have already joined the regiment.

General Saxton was followed by Mrs. Frances D. Gage, who spoke for a few moments very beautifully and earnestly. She told them the story of the people of Santa Cruz, how they had risen and conquered their masters, and declared themselves freemen, and nobody dared to oppose them; and how, a short time afterward, the Danish Governor rode into the marketplace, and proclaimed freedom to all the people of the Danish Islands. Then she made a beautiful appeal to the mothers, and urged them not to keep back their sons, fearing that they might be killed, but to send them as she had done hers, willingly and gladly to fight for liberty.

It was something very novel and strange to them, I suppose, to hear a woman speak in public, but they listened very attentively, and seemed much moved by what she said. Gen. Saxton made a few more remarks; and then the people sang, "Marching Along," with great spirit.

After church, there was a wedding. That is a ceremony that is performed here, among the freed people, nearly every Sunday. Last Sunday, there were six couples married. Some of the bridal costumes are, of course, very unique and comical, but the principal actors are happily quite unconscious of it, and look so very proud and happy while enjoying this, one of the many privileges that freedom has bestowed upon them, that it is very pleasant to see them. . . .

A mile from the Baptist church, in another beautiful grove of live oaks, is the Episcopal church, in which the aristocracy of the island used to worship. It is much smaller than the other, but possesses an organ, which, unlike the other musical instruments in this region, is not hopelessly out of order. The building is not used as a place of worship now, as it is much too small.

Our school is kept in the Baptist church. There are two ladies teaching in it, beside myself. They are earnest workers, and have done and are constantly doing a great deal for the people here, old and young. One of them, Miss T. [Laura M. Towne, Philadelphia abolitionist], is physician as well as teacher. She has a very extensive medical practice, and carries about with her everywhere her box of homeopathic medicines. The people welcome her as a ministering angel to their lowly cabins. Our school averages between eighty and ninety pupils, and later in the season we shall probably have more. It is very pleasant to see how bright, how eager to learn many of the children are. Some of them make wonderful improvement in a short time. It is a great happiness, a great privilege to be allowed to teach them. Every day I enjoy it more and more.

I cannot describe to you their singing. To me it seems wonderfully beautiful. We have just taught them the John Brown Song. I wish you could hear them sing it; it does one's soul good. How often I wish their old "secesh" masters, powerless to harm them, could hear their former chattels singing the praises of the brave old man who died for their sake! We are going to teach them "The Song of the Negro Boatmen" soon.

Although I have been here more than a month, it is at times almost impossible for me to realize that I am in South Carolina, the very last place in which, a year ago, I should have thought it desirable or possible for me to live. Sometimes it seems all like a strange wild dream. But when I see the people at work in the cotton fields, and visit their "quarters," and listen to their strange songs, it becomes more real to me. A month hence, I expect to feel quite at home here, in the very heart of Rebeldom.

I am staying at the same house in which a store is kept for the freed people by a Quaker gentleman sent here by the Philadelphia Commission. One has an excellent opportunity here for observing the negroes. I am particularly pleased with their manners. They are always perfectly courteous to each other, as well as to us. Theirs is a natural and graceful courtesy, which would put to shame many who despise them as an inferior people. As far as I have observed, they seem to me honest, industrious, and anxious to improve in every way. This is wonderful, considering the crushing and degrading system to which they have been subjected. They certainly are not the stupid, degraded people that many at the North believe them to be.

The plantation on which we live was owned by a man whom all the people unite in calling a "hard master." And his wife, it is said, was even more cruel than himself. When the negroes were ill, their scanty allowance of food was entirely withheld from them; and even after they had begun to recover, they were kept half-starved for some time—as a punishment for daring to be ill, I suppose. The whip was used freely. The people were severely whipped for the slightest offences, real or only suspected. If a fowl or anything else on the plantation was missed, and the thief could not be discovered, every slave would receive a number of lashes. They were wretchedly clothed. One poor woman had her feet and limbs so badly frozen from exposure, that she was obliged to have both legs amputated above the knee. She is living here now, and is one of the best women on the place.

From such a life as these poor people led—poorly clothed, poorly fed, worked hard, and cruelly beaten—you can imagine what a blessed change for them is the life they lead now. They are constantly rejoicing over it. Their hearts are overflowing with gratitude to the "Yankees," for coming here, and giving them their freedom. One very old man,—who came into the store this morning, dressed in a very original suit, made entirely of carpeting,—expressed to Mr. H. [John A. Hunn, the Philadelphia Quaker referred to above] his delight at the new state of things:—"Don't have me feelin's hurt now, massa. Used to have me feelin's hurt all de time; but don't hab 'em hurt now, no more." And, truly, we rejoiced with the old man that he, and many like him, who have suffered so long, no longer have their "feelin's hurt," as in the old time. . . .

As I bring this letter to a close, my thoughts revert to New England—to Massachusetts, which I believe I am in the habit of considering as *all* New England. And I recall with pleasure the many happy Thanksgiving Days passed there. But it has been reserved for me to spend here, in South Carolina, the happiest, the most jubilant Thanksgiving Day of my life. We hear of cold weather and heavy snow storms up in the North land; but here roses and oleanders are blooming out of doors, figs are ripening, the sunlight is warm and bright, and over all shines gloriously the blessed light of freedom, freedom forevermore.

I am, dear friend, very truly yours,

C.L.F.

ELIZABETH KECKLEY
(?–1907)

Rarely does a black woman in the United States have repeated contact with the wife of the president of the United States, but it is primarily that distinction that makes Elizabeth Keckley a memorable historical figure. Her penning of her interactions with Mary Todd Lincoln, the wife of President Abraham Lincoln, earned her fame and infamy. *Behind the Scenes. Or, Thirty Years A Slave, and Four Years in the White House* (1868) not only recounts Keckley's adventures as dressmaker to the First Lady, but the autobiography is remarkable for its documentation of the attainment of literacy and the social interactions of African Americans during and immediately following the Civil War. Keckley manages to achieve a credible voice in the text despite the detractors who tried to silence her because they did not approve of her writing about Mrs. Lincoln. The autobiography has stood the test of authenticity against those who claim that it was ghostwritten, perhaps by James Redpath or Hamilton Busbey. Although claims can be made for sections of the volume as a novel, a slave narrative, an autobiography, or a memoir, it is usually considered to be a memoir.

Keckley was born a slave in Dinwiddie Court-House, Virginia, early in the nineteenth century. Dates given for her birth have ranged from 1818 to 1840, although 1824 or 1825 seems most likely from references that Keckley made to her own age. A victim of the separation of slave parents, Keckley's mother, Agnes, was on the Burwell plantation while her father, George Pleasant, was owned by a man named Hobbs. Keckley was early known, therefore, as Elizabeth Hobbs. The local separation of her parents gave way to a more dramatic geographical separation when her father's owner took him west; although her parents wrote to each other, they were never able to live together again. Keckley recounts that she kept her father's letters.

In another peril to young slave women, Elizabeth was pursued for four years by a local white man, Alexander Kirkland, and, in her words, "became a mother" when she was a teenager. She named her son George, after her father. Shortly after George's birth, the white woman whom her mother had served, Anne Burwell Garland, took Agnes, Elizabeth, and George to St. Louis. It was there that she would begin the sewing business that would sustain her for most of her life. The immediate impetus, however, was to prevent Mr. Garland from hiring out the elderly Agnes; Elizabeth's business enabled her to support seventeen people for more than two years. It was also in St. Louis that Elizabeth renewed her acquaintance with James Keckley (who duped her into thinking he was free when he was actually a slave), married him, stayed with him for eight years, and dissolved the relationship because of his "dissipation" and the fact that he was a "burden." She refuses to give details of the relationship in her autobiography.

Soon the stirrings of freedom took hold and Keckley began to worry her master about buying her freedom. After repeated requests, she was given the opportunity to do so—with the price set at twelve hundred dollars. She set about that task with a determination that would define her work ethic throughout her life. Garland's death, however, put an immediacy to the task, and Keckley concluded that she would go to New York and essentially beg for the money. That course was made unnecessary when a Mrs. Le Bourgois, for whom she sewed, collected the money from among Keckley's patrons. Keckley accepted this as a loan and later repaid her patrons for their generosity. She succeeded in purchasing her freedom on August 13, 1855.

After a brief, six-week sojourn in Baltimore in 1860, Keckley moved to Washington, D.C., with the express purpose of eventually being able to sew for "the ladies of the White House." Before she achieved that goal, she counted the wives of Jefferson Davis, Stephen A. Douglas, and E.M. Stanton among her patrons. As she became more well known, and as her business increased (she hired as many as twenty young women at one point), she was finally able, within a year of her arrival in the capital, to get an assignment for Mrs. Lincoln. Her completion of a dress for the inaugural reception was the beginning of her four-year stint as Mrs. Lincoln's dressmaker and fashion designer, personal maid, traveling companion, nurse, and all-around confidante. Her height, bearing, striking features, and good manners, combined with a reputation as an excellent conversationalist, also served her well. Affectionately known as "Lizabeth" and "Lizzie" to Mrs. Lincoln and "Madam Elizabeth" to President Lincoln, she became the most famous person of African descent associated with the White House in the nineteenth century.

Keckley's son George, who had enlisted as a Union soldier, was killed on August 10, 1861, at Wilson's Creek in Missouri. That loss placed Keckley in the particularly appropriate position of becoming comforter to Mrs. Lincoln when her most beloved son, William Wallace ("Willie"), died in February of 1862. (Mrs. Lincoln had written Keckley a letter when George died.) Keckley was also the person for whom Mrs. Lincoln sent when President Lincoln was shot in 1865. In the five weeks following his death, when Mrs. Lincoln was secluded in the White House, she only admitted Keckley and her son Robert. It was Keckley who assisted Mrs. Lincoln in packing to leave the White House and who accompanied her to Chicago. They continued a correspondence, which resulted in Mrs. Lincoln soliciting Keckley's aid in selling some of her old clothes in New York in 1867 to better her financial situation. (A pension she was expecting from Congress was slow in coming.) In the incident that became known as the "old-clothes scandal," Keckley and Mrs. Lincoln, who was disguised as Mrs. Clarke, arrived in New York only to leave without accomplishing their goal. Both were recognized and criticized.

Partly to alleviate the criticism and partly to earn money to help Mrs. Lincoln, Keckley wrote *Behind the Scenes.* Her best intentions were thwarted, however, by the contents of her memoirs. White House secrets and the living habits of its occupants during the Lincoln administration were revealed, to the outrage of Robert Lincoln, who tried to curtail dissemination of the volume by getting his friends to buy up all copies. Several persons to whom Keckley referred or about whom she shared Mrs. Lincoln's opinions were not pleased to find themselves in the pages of her memoir. The situation was worsened because Keckley's editor, James Redpath, took the liberty of including the First Lady's letters to Keckley as an appendix to the volume. Although Keckley and Mrs. Lincoln had clearly been close friends over several years, they did not see each other again after the publication of *Behind the Scenes.* The work, therefore, that established Keckley's literary reputation also made her remaining years ones torn with bad memories and lost friendships.

With the decline of her sewing business (some patrons left because of the scandal), she taught domestic science briefly (1892–1893) at Wilberforce University in Ohio, where she left some Lincoln memorabilia to the museum. She also prepared the university's contribution to the World's Columbian Exposition in Chicago in 1893. As with any historical figure who is identified with a single event or period in her history, there is very little information about Keckley after the White House years. She eventually returned to Washington, D.C., and continued attending the 15th Street Presbyterian Church, with which she had been affiliated for over thirty years and at which the famous Francis J. Grimké was pastor. She ended up in the Home for Destitute Women and Girls, where she died of a paralytic stroke in 1907. It should be understood, however, that the name of the home belies its reality. Keckley's resources were diminished—she only had a small pension from her son's death—but she, true to her lifelong bid for independence, was able to pay for her room and board (eight, then twelve dollars a month) and leave almost two hundred dollars to the home when she died.

Lest we follow the usual pattern of biographers and view Keckley exclusively in the light of Mary Todd Lincoln, it is worth mentioning that her life and autobiography are of significance *in themselves* in several ways. Keckley was able to negotiate the system of slavery to her advantage even as she abided by the rules laid down by slaveholders. Although she claimed there was a "bright" side to slavery, she nonetheless documented its atrocities, including a beating she received as a four-year-old for being inattentive to the mistress's child. She acquired literacy when most slaves were illiterate. She worked for her son and mother, as an example of the tremendous commitment enslaved persons had to family. And, when she penned her autobiography, she gained a public voice to accompany the private voice. Her very act of writing—or even of telling her story to someone else who did the actual writing—is a testament to a creative imagination that portends the likes of Zora Neale Hurston and other twentieth-century personalities. Her remarkable adventures also anticipate Hurston as well as Maya Angelou. For these reasons, therefore, Elizabeth Keckley should be seen in the light of a much broader context than that of her Washington, D.C., experiences.

❖❖❖

For biography and criticism, see Frances Smith Foster, "Autobiography after Emancipation: The Example of Elizabeth Keckley," in *Multicultural Autobiography: American Lives,* edited by James Robert Payne (Knoxville: University of Tennessee Press, 1992); Marie Garrett, "Elizabeth Keckley," in *Notable Black American Women,* edited by Jessie Carney Smith (Detroit: Gale, 1992); Rayford W. Logan and Michael R. Winston, eds., *Dictionary of American Negro Biography* (New York: Norton, 1982); James Olney, introduction to *Behind the Scenes* in *The Schomburg Library of Nineteenth-Century Black Women Writers* (New York: Oxford University Press, 1988); John E. Washington, *They Knew Lincoln* (New York: Dutton, 1942).

FROM *Behind the Scenes*[1]

My troubles in North Carolina were brought to an end by my unexpected return to Virginia, where I lived with Mr. Garland, who had married Miss Ann Burwell, one of my old master's daughters. His life was not a prosperous one, and after struggling with the world for several years he left his native State, a disappointed man. He moved to St. Louis, hoping to improve his fortune in the West; but ill luck followed him there, and he seemed to be unable to escape from the influence of the evil star of his destiny. When his family, myself included, joined him in his new home on the banks of the Mississippi, we found him so poor that he was unable to pay the dues on a letter advertised as in the post-office for him. The necessities of the family were so great, that it was proposed to place my mother out at service. The idea was shocking to me. Every gray hair in her old head was dear to me, and I could not bear the thought of her going to work for strangers. She had been raised in the family, had watched the growth of each child from infancy to maturity; they had been the objects of her kindest care. . . . They had been the central figures in her dream of life—a dream beautiful to her, since she had basked in the sunshine of no other. . . . My mother, my poor aged mother, go among strangers to toil for a living! No, a thousand times no! I would rather work my fingers to the bone, bend over my sewing till the film of blindness gathered in my eyes; nay, even beg from street to street. I told Mr. Garland so, and he gave me permission to see what I could do. I was fortunate in obtaining work, and in a short time I had acquired something of a reputation as a seamstress and dress-maker. The best ladies in St. Louis were my patrons, and when my reputation was once established I never lacked for orders. With my needle I kept bread in the mouths of seventeen persons for two years and five months. While I was working so hard that others might live in comparative comfort, and move in those circles of society to which their birth gave them entrance, the thought often occurred to me whether I was really worth my salt or not; and then perhaps the lips curled with a bitter sneer. . . . The heavy task was too much for me, and my health began to give away. About this time Mr. Keckley, whom I had met in Virginia, and learned to regard with more than friendship, came to St. Louis. He sought my hand in marriage, and for a long time I refused to con-

[1]The following are two excerpts from Keckley's autobiography. The first describes her adult life in slavery; the second illustrates her initial response to hearing of Lincoln's assassination.

sider his proposal; for I could not bear the thought of bringing children into slavery—of adding one single recruit to the millions bound to hopeless servitude, fettered and shackled with chains stronger and heavier than manacles of iron. I made a proposition to buy myself and son; the proposition was bluntly declined, and I was commanded never to broach the subject again. I would not be put off thus, for hope pointed to a freer, brighter life in the future. Why should my son be held in slavery? I often asked myself. He came into the world through no will of mine, and yet, God only knows how I loved him. . . . Much as I respected the authority of my master, I could not remain silent on a subject that so nearly concerned me. One day, when I insisted on knowing whether he would permit me to purchase myself, and what price I must pay for myself, he turned to me in a petulant manner, thrust his hand into his pocket, drew forth a bright silver quarter of a dollar, and proffering it to me, said:

"Lizzie, I have told you often not to trouble me with such a question. If you really wish to leave me, take this: it will pay the passage of yourself and boy on the ferry-boat, and when you are on the other side of the river you will be free. It is the cheapest way that I know of to accomplish what you desire."

I looked at him in astonishment, and earnestly replied: "No, master, I do not wish to be free in such a manner. If such had been my wish, I should never have troubled you about obtaining your consent to my purchasing myself. I can cross the river any day, as you well know, and have frequently done so, but will never leave you in such a manner. By the laws of the land I am your slave—you are my master, and I will only be free by such means as the laws of the country provide." He expected this answer, and I knew that he was pleased. Some time afterwards he told me that he had reconsidered the question; that I had served his family faithfully; that I deserved my freedom, and that he would take $1200 for myself and boy.

This was joyful intelligence for me, and the reflection of hope gave a silver lining to the dark cloud of my life—faint, it is true, but still a silver lining.

Taking a prospective glance at liberty, I consented to marry. The wedding was a great event in the family. The ceremony took place in the parlor, in the presence of the family and a number of guests. Mr. Garland gave me away, and the pastor, Bishop Hawks, performed the ceremony, who had solemnized the bridals of Mr. G.'s own children. The day was a happy one, but it faded all too soon. Mr. Keckley—let me speak kindly of his faults—proved dissipated, and a burden instead of a helpmate. More than all, I learned that he was a slave instead of a free man, as he represented himself to be. With the simple explanation that I lived with him eight years, let charity draw around him the mantle of silence.

I went to work in earnest to purchase my freedom, but the years passed, and I was still a slave. Mr. Garland's family claimed so much of my attention—in fact, I supported them—that I was not able to accumulate anything. In the mean time Mr. Garland died, and Mr. Burwell, a Mississippi planter, came to St. Louis to settle up the estate. He was a kind-hearted man, and said I should be free, and would afford me every facility to raise the necessary amount to pay the price of my liberty. Several schemes were urged upon me by my friends. At last I formed a resolution to go to New York, state my case, and appeal to the benevolence of the people. . . .

. . . A carriage stopped in front of the house; Mrs. Le Bourgois, one of my kind patrons, got out of it and entered the door. She seemed to bring sunshine with her handsome cheery face. She came to where I was, and in her sweet way said:—

"Lizzie, I hear that you are going to New York to beg for money to buy your freedom. I have been thinking over the matter, and told Ma it would be a shame to allow you to go North to *beg* for what we should *give* you. You have many friends in St. Louis, and I am going to raise the twelve hundred dollars required among them. I have two hundred dollars put away for a present; am indebted to you one hundred dollars; mother owes you fifty dollars, and will add another fifty to it; and as I do not want the present, I will make the money a present to you. Don't start for New York now until I see what I can do among your friends."

. . . Mrs. Le Bourgois, God bless her dear good heart, was more than successful. The twelve hundred dollars were raised, and at last my son and myself were free. Free, free! what a glorious ring to the world. Free! the bitter heart-struggle was over. Free! the soul could go out to heaven and to God with no chains to clog its flight or pull it down. Free! the earth wore a brighter look, and the very stars seemed to sing with joy. Yes, free! free by the laws of man and the smile of God—and Heaven bless them who made me so!

❖❖❖

. . . During my residence in the Capital I made my home with Mr. and Mrs. Walker Lewis, people of my own race, and friends in the truest sense of the word.

The days passed without any incident of particular note disturbing the current of life. On Friday morning, April 14th—alas! what American does not remember the day—I saw Mrs. Lincoln but for a moment. She told me that she was to attend the theatre that night with the President, but I was not summoned to assist her in making her toilette. Sherman had swept from the northern border of Georgia through the heart of the Confederacy down to the sea, striking the death-blow to the rebellion. Grant had pursued General Lee beyond Richmond, and the army of Virginia, that had made such stubborn resistance, was crumbling to pieces. Fort Sumter had fallen;—the stronghold first wrenched from the Union, and which had braved the fury of Federal guns for so many years, was restored to the Union; the end of the war was near at hand, and the great pulse of the loyal North thrilled with joy. The dark war-cloud was fading, and a white-robed angel seemed to hover in the sky, whispering "Peace—peace on earth, good-will toward men!" Sons, brothers, fathers, friends, sweethearts were coming home. Soon the white tents would be folded, the volunteer army be disbanded, and tranquillity again reign. Happy, happy day!—happy at least to those who fought under the banner of the Union. There was great rejoicing throughout the North. From the Atlantic to the Pacific, flags were gayly thrown to the breeze, and at night every city blazed with its tens of thousand lights. But scarcely had the fireworks ceased to play, and the lights been taken down from the windows, when the lightning flashed the most appalling news over the magnetic wires. "The President has been murdered!" spoke the swift-winged messenger, and the loud huzza died upon the lips. A nation suddenly paused in the midst of festivity, and stood paralyzed with horror—transfixed with awe.

Oh, memorable day! Oh, memorable night! Never before was joy so violently contrasted with sorrow.

At 11 o'clock at night I was awakened by an old friend and neighbor, Miss M. Brown, with the startling intelligence that the entire Cabinet had been assassinated, and Mr. Lincoln shot, but not mortally wounded. When I heard the words I felt as if the blood had been frozen in my veins, and that my lungs must collapse for the want of air. Mr. Lincoln shot! the Cabinet assassinated! What could it mean? The streets were alive with wondering, awe-stricken people. Rumors flew thick and fast, and the wildest reports came with every new arrival. The words were repeated with blanched cheeks and quivering lips. I waked Mr. and Mrs. Lewis, and told them that the President was shot, and that I must go to the White House. I could not remain in a state of uncertainty. I felt that the house would not hold me. They tried to quiet me, but gentle words could not calm the wild tempest. They quickly dressed themselves, and we sallied out into the street to drift with the excited throng. We walked rapidly towards the White House, and on our way passed the residence of Secretary Seward, which was surrounded by armed soldiers, keeping back all intruders with the point of the bayonet. We hurried on, and as we approached the White House, saw that it too was surrounded with soldiers. Every entrance was strongly guarded, and no one was permitted to pass. The guard at the gate told us that Mr. Lincoln had not been brought home, but refused to give any other information. More excited than ever, we wandered down the street. Grief and anxiety were making me weak, and as we joined the outskirts of a large crowd, I began to feel as meek and humble as a penitent child. A gray-haired old man was passing. I caught a glimpse of his face, and it seemed so full of kindness and sorrow that I gently touched his arm, and imploringly asked:

"Will you please, sir, to tell me whether Mr. Lincoln is dead or not?"

"Not dead," he replied, "but dying. God help us!" and with a heavy step he passed on.

"Not dead, but dying! then indeed God help us!"

We learned that the President was mortally wounded—that he had been shot down in his box at the theatre, and that he was not expected to live till morning; when we returned home with heavy hearts, I could not sleep. I wanted to go to Mrs. Lincoln, as I pictured her wild with grief; but then I did not know where to find her, and I must wait till morning. Never did the hours drag so slowly. Every moment seemed an age, and I could do nothing but walk about and hold my arms in mental agony.

Morning came at last, and a sad morning was it. The flags that floated so gayly yesterday now were draped in black, and hung in silent folds at half-mast. The President was dead, and a nation was mourning for him. Every house was draped in black, and every face wore a solemn look. People spoke in subdued tones, and glided whisperingly, wonderingly, silently about the streets.

About eleven o'clock on Saturday morning a carriage drove up the door, and a messenger asked for "Elizabeth Keckley."

"Who wants her?" I asked.

"I come from Mrs. Lincoln. If you are Mrs. Keckley, come with me immediately to the White House."

I hastily put on my shawl and bonnet, and was driven at a rapid rate to the White House. Everything about the building was sad and solemn. I was quickly shown to Mrs. Lincoln's room, and on entering, saw Mrs. L. tossing uneasily about upon a bed. The room was darkened, and the only person in it besides the widow of the President was Mrs. Secretary Welles, who had spent the night with her. Bowing to Mrs. Welles, I went to the bedside.

"Why did you not come to me last night, Elizabeth—I sent for you?" Mrs. Lincoln asked in a low whisper.

"I did try to come to you, but I could not find you." I answered, as I laid my hand upon her hot brow.

I afterwards learned, that when she had partially recovered from the first shock of the terrible tragedy in the theatre, Mrs. Welles asked:

"Is there no one, Mrs. Lincoln, that you desire to have with you in this terrible affliction?"

"Yes, send for Elizabeth Keckley. I want her just as soon as she can be brought here."

Three messengers, it appears, were successively despatched for me, but all of them mistook the number and failed to find me.

Shortly after entering the room on Saturday morning, Mrs. Welles excused herself, as she said she must go to her own family, and I was left alone with Mrs. Lincoln.

She was nearly exhausted with grief, and when she became a little quiet, I asked and received permission to go into the Guests' Room, where the body of the President lay in state. When I crossed the threshold of the room, I could not help recalling the day on which I had seen little Willie lying in his coffin where the body of his father now lay. I remembered how the President had wept over the pale beautiful face of his gifted boy, and now the President himself was dead. The last time I saw him he spoke kindly to me, but alas! the lips would never move again. The light had faded from his eyes, and when the light went out the soul went with it. What a noble soul was his—noble in all the noble attributes of God! Never did I enter the solemn chamber of death with such palpitating heart and trembling footsteps as I entered it that day. No common mortal had died. The Moses of my people had fallen in the hour of his triumph. Fame had woven her choicest chaplet for his brow. Though the brow was cold and pale in death, the chaplet should not fade, for God had studded it with the glory of the eternal stars.

When I entered the room, the members of the Cabinet and many distinguished officers of the army were grouped around the body of their fallen chief. They made room for me, and, approaching the body, I lifted the white cloth from the white face of the man that I had worshipped as an idol—looked upon as a demigod. Notwithstanding the violence of the death of the President, there was something beautiful as well as grandly solemn in the expression of the placid face. There lurked the sweetness and gentleness of childhood, and the stately grandeur of godlike intellect. I gazed long at the face, and turned away with tears in my eyes and a choking sensation in my throat. Ah! never was man so widely mourned before. The whole world bowed their heads in grief when Abraham Lincoln died.

Returning to Mrs. Lincoln's room, I found her in a new paroxysm of grief. Robert was bending over his mother with tender affection, and little Tad was crouched at the foot of the bed with a world of agony in his young face. I shall never forget the scene—the wails of a broken heart, the unearthly shrieks, the terrible convulsions, the wild, tempestuous outbursts of grief from the soul. I bathed Mrs. Lincoln's head with cold water, and soothed the terrible tornado as best I could. Tad's grief at his father's death was as great as the grief of his mother, but her terrible outbursts awed the boy into silence. Sometimes he would throw his arms around her neck, and exclaim, between his broken sobs, "Don't cry so, Mamma! don't cry, or you will make me cry, too! You will break my heart."

Mrs. Lincoln could not bear to hear Tad cry, and when he would plead to her not to break his heart, she would calm herself with a great effort, and clasp her child in her arms.

Every room in the White House was darkened, and every one spoke in subdued tones, and moved about with muffled tread. The very atmosphere breathed of the great sorrow which weighed heavily upon each heart. Mrs. Lincoln never left her room, and while the body of her husband was being borne in solemn state from the Atlantic to the broad prairies of the West, she was weeping with her fatherless children in her private chamber. She denied admittance to almost every one, and I was her only companion, except her children, in the days of her great sorrow.

THE WOMEN'S NARRATIVE

JARENA LEE
(1783–?)

Rather than accept her place in the domestic sphere that had been defined for women in the nineteenth century, Jarena Lee became one of the earliest known African American female evangelists and preachers. Within a year, she traveled more than two thousand miles and delivered nearly two hundred sermons. An ardent feminist, Lee fought courageously and vehemently for her ministry within the male-dominated A.M.E. Church. The fact that she, like most nineteenth-century female evangelists, had very little formal education only made the task more difficult. Despite this handicap, however, she managed, with the help of others, to chronicle her personal experiences in *The Life and Religious Experiences of Jarena Lee, a*

Coloured Lady, Giving an Account of Her Call to Preach the Gospel, Phila., (1836) and *Religious Experience and Journal of Mrs. Jarena Lee, Giving an Account of Her Call to Preach the Gospel,* Philadelphia (1849). It is with her two autobiographies that she popularized the genre of the spiritual narrative. In the former work, Lee tells us that she is "the first female minister of the First African Methodist Episcopal Church."

What is known about her life, with the exception of a few references in the annals of the A.M.E. Church, is based on her two autobiographical accounts. Nevertheless, significant, personal details, such as her family name, are missing from the works. Her autobiography *Life,* however, pinpoints her date and place of birth and paints a vivid picture of the hardships she faced during the earliest years of her life.

Born free at Cape May, New Jersey, on February 11, 1783, Jarena was separated from her parents at the age of seven. At this time, she went to live as a servant at the home of a Mr. Sharp, who lived approximately sixty miles from her home. The pain and loneliness caused by this break with her family plagued her for much of her early life. Even though she tried to contact her parents several times, she was not reunited with her family until fourteen years later when she visited her aging mother and uncle. According to her logbook account, she saw her mother only four times and one of her sisters twice in forty years.

To fill the emotional void created by her lengthy separation from her family, Jarena turned to religion. In 1801, she converted to Christianity at a religious meeting where she was moved by the preachings of a local minister. For the first four years after her conversion, however, religion could not uplift her spirits. Often, she experienced moments of religious doubt, bouts with poor health, and thoughts of committing suicide before she finally resolved to take up the calling to preach the gospel. A few years later, an ecstatic religious experience led her to ask the prominent black church leader Richard Allen, founder of the Bethel A.M.E. Church in Philadelphia, for permission to preach, but to no avail. While he expressed to her that he did not oppose women leading prayer meetings, he upheld the conservative theological argument against women preaching. During this period in her life, she accepted his decision, although reluctantly and against her better judgment that women should be allowed to preach because "the Saviour died for the woman as well as the man." Shortly afterwards, in 1811, she married Joseph Lee, the pastor of a black church in Snow Hill, a small town on the outskirts of Philadelphia.

Jarena Lee's married life, however, proved to be no consolation for her disappointment with the church. In fact, it only increased her sense of pain and isolation. Within a few years, her husband and five other family members died. She was left to raise a two-year-old child and a six-month infant by herself. Soon following these tragic events, she began again to pursue her calling to preach. In 1818, Lee returned to Philadelphia where, this time, Richard Allen, now Bishop of the A.M.E. Church, granted her request to hold prayer meetings in her home. Encouraged at least in part by Allen's endorsement, she began her career as an itinerant preacher when she was in her mid-thirties.

Lee's ministry became the center of her life. Traveling throughout several cities and towns in the northeast, she preached the Gospel to people of all races in churches, camp meetings, marketplaces, schools, private homes, and even in the bush. Often exhausted and ill, she moved congregations of people with her effective evangelical style and passionate rhetoric to the point of "tears rolling down their cheeks, the signs of contrition and repentance towards God." She approached all topics, including abolition, with religious zeal and enthusiasm. She insisted that Christian gospel was the answer to the earthly oppression of her enslaved people.

In 1823, she accompanied Bishop Allen on a trip to the annual conference of the A.M.E. church held that year in New York. When she returned, he offered her a ministerial position at Bethel, but it was rejected by the church congregation. Whether Lee resumed her career as an itinerant preacher is not known. Nevertheless, she maintained a close, personal relationship with the bishop. Years later, he would provide an education and a trade for her son, who, after the bishop's death, married and had children.

In 1833, at the age of fifty, Lee penned her religious journal with the aid of an editor. Three years later, she had one thousand copies of *Life* printed for one thousand dollars and, in 1839, she reprinted one thousand more copies of the work. Ten years later, when the A.M.E. church refused to publish an expanded edition of *Life,* she personally financed the printing of *Religious Experience and Journal of Jarena Lee.* Based on her two-hundred-page log account of her travels, both autobiographies, which she constructed in three distinct parts, parallel the stages of her spiritual development. Unfortunately, however, after the publication of *Religious Experience and Journal* in 1849, Jarena Lee virtually disappeared from the pages of African American history. Details about the later life of this astounding, courageous woman are unknown.

❖❖❖

Unfortunately, there are no full-length biographical or critical studies on Jarena Lee. Useful biographical information can, however, be found in Miriam DeCosta-Willis's "Jarena Lee" in *Notable Black American Women,* edited by Jessie Carney Smith (1992); and *Black Women in Nineteenth-Century American Life,* edited by Bert James Loewenberg and Ruth Bogin (1976).

FROM *Religious Experience and Journal of Mrs. Jarena Lee, Giving an Account of her Call to Preach the Gospel*

I was born February 11th, 1783, at Cape May, State of New Jersey. At the age of seven years I was parted from my parents, and went to live as a servant maid, with a Mr. Sharp, at the distance of about sixty miles from the place of my birth.

My parents being wholly ignorant of the knowledge of God, had not therefore instructed me in any degree in this great matter. Not long after the commencement of my attendance on this lady, she had bid me do something respecting my work, which in a little while after she asked me if I had done, when I replied, Yes—but this was not true.

At this awful point, in my early history, the Spirit of God moved in power through my conscience, and told me I was a wretched sinner. On this account so great was the impression, and so strong were the feelings of guilt, that I promised in my heart that I would not tell another lie.

But notwithstanding this promise my heart grew harder, after a while, yet the Spirit of the Lord never entirely forsook me, but continued mercifully striving with me, until his gracious power converted my soul. . . .

The man who was to speak . . . was the Rev. Richard Allen, since bishop of the African Episcopal Methodists in America. During the labors of this man that afternoon, I had come to the conclusion, that this is the people to which my heart unites, and it so happened, that as soon as the service closed he invited such as felt a desire to flee the wrath to come, to unite on trial with them—I embraced the opportunity. Three weeks from that day, my soul was gloriously converted to God, under preaching, at the very outset of the sermon. The text was barely pronounced, which was "I perceive thy heart is not right in the sight of God," when there appeared to my view, in the centre of the heart, one sin; and this was *malice* against one particular individual, who had strove deeply to injure me, which I resented. At this discovery I said, *Lord* I forgive *every* creature. That instant, it appeared to me as if a garment, which had entirely enveloped my whole person, even to my fingers' ends, split at the crown of my head, and was stripped away from me, passing like a shadow from my sight—when the glory of God seemed to cover me in its stead.

That moment, though hundreds were present, I did leap to my feet and declare that God, for Christ's sake, had pardoned the sins of my soul. Great was the ecstacy of my mind, for I felt that not only the sin of *malice* was pardoned, but all other sins were swept away together. That day was the first when my heart had believed, and my tongue had made confession unto salvation—the first words uttered, a part of that song, which shall fill eternity with its sound, was *glory to God.* For a few moments I had power to exhort sinners, and to tell of the wonders and of the goodness of Him who had clothed me with *His* salvation. During this the minister was silent, until my soul felt its duty had been performed, when he declared another witness of the power of Christ to forgive sins on earth, was manifest in my conversion. . . .

By the increasing light of the Spirit, I had found there yet remained the root of pride, anger, self-will, with many evils, the result of fallen nature. . . . I was now greatly alarmed, lest I should fall away from what I knew I had enjoyed; and to guard against this I prayed almost incessantly. . . .

. . . I had struggled long and hard, but found not the desire of my heart. When I rose from my knees, there seemed a voice speaking to me, as I yet stood in a leaning posture—"Ask for sanctification." When to my surprise, I recollected that I had not even thought of it in my whole prayer. It would seem Satan had hidden the very object from my mind, for which I had purposely kneeled to pray. But when this voice whispered in my heart, saying, "Pray for sanctification," I again bowed in the same place, at the same time, and said "Lord *sanctify* my soul for Christ's sake." That very instant, as if lightning had darted through me, I sprang to my feet, and cried, "The Lord has sanctified my soul!" There was none to hear this but the angels who stood around to witness my joy—and Satan, whose malice raged the more. That Satan was there, I knew; for no sooner had I cried out "The Lord has sanctified my soul," than there seemed another voice behind me, saying "No, it is too great a work to be done." But another spirit said "Bow down for the witness—I received it—*thou art sanctified!*" The first I knew of myself after that, I was standing in the yard with my hands spread out, and looking with my face toward heaven.

I now ran into the house and told them what had happened to me, when, as it were a new rush of the same ecstacy came upon me, and caused me to feel as if I were in an ocean of light and bliss.

During this, I stood perfectly still, the tears rolling in a flood from my eyes. So great was the joy, that it is past description. There is no language that can describe it, except that which was heard by St. Paul, when he was caught up to third heaven, and heard words which it was not lawful to utter. . . .

Between four and five years after my sanctification, on a certain time, an impressive silence fell upon me, and I stood as if some one was about to speak to me, yet I had no such thought in my heart.—But to my utter surprise there seemed to sound a voice which I thought I distinctly heard, and most certainly understand, which said to me, "Go preach the Gospel!" I immediately replied aloud, "No one will believe me." Again I listened, and again the same voice seemed to say—"Preach the Gospel; I will put words in your mouth, and will turn your enemies to become your friends."

At first I supposed that Satan had spoken to me, for I had read that he could transform himself into an angel of light for the purpose of deception. Immediately I went into a secret place, and called upon the Lord to know if he had called me to preach, and whether I was deceived or not; when there appeared to my view the form and figure of a pulpit, with a Bible lying thereon, the back of which was presented to me as plainly as if it had been a literal fact.

In consequence of this, my mind became so exercised, that during the night following, I took a text and preached in my sleep. I thought there stood before me a great multitude, while I expounded to them the things of religion. So violent were my exertions and so loud were my exclamations, that I awoke from the sound of my own voice, which also awoke the family of the house where I resided. Two days after I went to see the preacher in charge of the African Society, who was the Rev. Richard Allen, the same before named in these pages, to tell him that I felt it my duty to preach the gospel. But as I drew near the street in which his house was, which was in the city of Philadelphia, my courage began to fail me; so terrible did the cross appear, it seemed that I should not be able to bear it. Previous to my setting out to go to see him, so agitated was my mind, that my appetite for my daily food failed me entirely. Several times on my way there, I turned back again; but as often I felt my strength again renewed, and I soon found that the nearer I approached to the house of the minister, the less was my fear. Accordingly, as soon as I came to the door, my fears subsided, the cross was removed, all things appeared pleasant—I was tranquil.

I now told him, that the Lord had revealed it to me, that [I] must preach the gospel. He replied, by asking, in what sphere I wished to move in? I said, among the Methodists. He then replied, that a Mrs. Cook, a Methodist lady, had also some time before requested the same privilege; who, it was believed, had done much good in the way of exhortation, and holding prayer meetings; and who had been permitted to do so by the verbal license of the preacher in charge at the time. But as to women preaching, he said that our Discipline knew nothing at all about it—that it did not call for women preachers. This I was glad to hear, because it removed the fear of the cross—but no sooner did this feeling cross my mind, than I found that a love of souls had in a measure departed from me; that holy energy which burned within me, as a fire, began to be smothered. This I soon perceived.

O how careful ought we to be, lest through our by-laws of church government and discipline, we bring into disrepute even the word of life. For as unseemly as it may appear now-a-days for a woman to preach, it should be remembered that nothing is impossible with God. And why should it be thought impossible, heterodox, or improper for a woman to preach? seeing the Saviour died for the woman as well as for the man.

If the man may preach, because the Saviour died for him, why not the woman? seeing he died for her also. Is he not a whole Saviour, instead of a half one? as those who hold it wrong for a woman to preach, would seem to make it appear.

Did not Mary *first* preach the risen Saviour, and is not the doctrine of the resurrection the very climax of Christianity—hangs not all our hope on this, as argued by St. Paul? Then did not Mary, a woman, preach the gospel? for she preached the resurrection of the crucified Son of God.

But some will say that Mary did not expound the Scripture, therefore, she did not preach, in the proper sense of the term. To this I reply, it may be that the term *preach* in those primitive times, did not mean exactly what it is now *made* to mean; perhaps it was a great deal more simple then, than it is now—if it were not, the unlearned fishermen could not have preached the gospel at all, as they had no learning.

To this it may be replied, by those who are determined not to believe that it is right for a woman to preach, that the disciples, though they were fishermen and ignorant of letters too, were inspired so to do. To which I would reply, that though they were inspired, yet that inspiration did not save them from showing their ignorance of letters, and of man's wisdom; this the multitude soon found out, by listening to the remarks of the envious Jewish priests. If then, to preach the gospel, by the gift of heaven, comes by inspiration solely, is God straitened: must he take the man exclusively? May he not, did he not, and can he not inspire a female to preach the simple story of the birth, life, death, and resurrection of our Lord, and accompany it too with power to the sinner's heart. As for me, I am fully persuaded that the Lord called me to labor according to what I have received, in his vineyard. If he has not, how could he consistently bear testimony in favor of my poor labors, in awakening and converting sinners?

In my wanderings up and down among men, preaching according to my ability, I have frequently found families who told me that they had not for several years been to a meeting, and yet, while listening to hear what God would say by his poor female instrument, have believed with trembling—tears rolling down their cheeks, the signs of contrition and repentance towards God. I firmly believe that I have sown seed, in the name of the Lord, which shall appear with its increase at the great day of accounts, when Christ shall come to make up his jewels. . . .

In the year 1811, I changed my situation in life, having married Mr. Joseph Lee, pastor of a Society at Snow Hill, about six miles from the city of Philadelphia. It became necessary therefore for me to remove. This was a great trial at first, as I knew no person at Snow Hill, except my husband, and to leave my associates in the society, and especially those who composed the band of which I was one. None but those who have been in sweet fellowship with such as really love God, and have together drank bliss and happiness from the same fountain, can tell how dear such company is, and how hard it is to part from them.

At Snow Hill, as was feared, I never found that agreement and closeness in communion and fellowship, that I had in Philadelphia, among my young companions, nor ought I to have expected it. The manners and customs at this place were somewhat different, on which account I became discontented in the course of a year, and began to importune my husband to remove to the city. But this plan did not suit him, as he was the Pastor of the Society, he could not bring his mind to leave them. This afflicted me a little. But the Lord showed me in a dream what his will was concerning this matter.

I dreamed that as I was walking on the summit of a beautiful hill, that I saw near me a flock of sheep, fair and white, as if but newly washed; when there came walking toward me a man of a grave and dignified countenance, dressed entirely in white, as it were in a robe, and looking at me, said emphatically, "Joseph Lee must take care of these sheep, or the wolf will come and devour them." When I awoke I was convinced of my error, and immediately, with a glad heart, yielded to the right spirit in the Lord. . . .

For six years from this time I continued to receive from above, such baptisms of the Spirit as mortality could scarcely bear. About that time I was called to suffer in my family, by death—five, in the course of about six years, fell by his hand; my husband being one of the number, which was the greatest affliction of all.

I was now left alone in the world, with two infant children, one of the age of about two years, the other six months, with no other dependence than the promise of Him who hath said—I will be the widow's God, and a father to the fatherless. Accordingly, he raised me up friends, whose liberality comforted and solaced me in my state of widowhood and sorrows. . . .

It was now eight years since I had made application to be permitted to preach the gospel, during which time I had only been allowed to exhort, and even this privilege but seldom. This subject now was renewed afresh in my mind; it was as a fire shut up in my bones. About thirteen months passed on, while under this renewed impression. During this time, I had solicited of the Rev. Bishop, Richard Allen, who at this time had become Bishop of the African

Episcopal Methodists in America, to be permitted the liberty of holding prayer meetings in my own hired house, and of exhorting as I found liberty, which was granted me. By this means, my mind was relieved, as the house soon filled when the hour appointed for prayer had arrived. . . .

. . . Soon after this, as above related, the Rev. Richard Williams was to preach at Bethel Church, where I with others were assembled. He entered the pulpit, gave out the hymn, which was sung, and then addressed the throne of grace; took his text, passed through the exordium, and commenced to expound it. The text he took is in Jonah, 2d chap. 9th verse,—"Salvation is of the Lord." But as he proceeded to explain, he seemed to have lost the spirit; when in the same instant, I sprang, as by altogether supernatural impulse, to my feet, when I was aided from above to give an exhortation on the very text which my brother Williams had taken.

I told them I was like Jonah; for it had been then nearly eight years since the Lord had called me to preach his gospel to the fallen sons and daughters of Adam's race, but that I had lingered like him, and delayed to go at the bidding of the Lord, and warn those who are as deeply guilty as were the people of Ninevah.

During the exhortation, God made manifest his power in a manner sufficient to show the world that I was called to labor according to my ability, and the grace given unto me, in the vineyard of the good husbandman.

I now sat down, scarcely knowing what I had done, being frightened. I imagined, that for this indecorum, as I feared it might be called, I should be expelled from the church. But instead of this, the Bishop rose up in the assembly, and related that I had called upon him eight years before, asking to be permitted to preach, and that he had put me off; but that he now as much believed that I was called to that work, as any of the preachers present. These remarks greatly strengthened me, so that my fears of having given an offence, and made myself liable as an offender, subsided, giving place to a sweet serenity, a holy joy of a peculiar kind, untasted in my bosom until then.

The Novel or Neo-Slave Narrative

WILLIAM WELLS BROWN

(1815–1884)

Along with Phillis Wheatley, Frederick Douglass, Frances Watkins Harper, and other prominent early African American figures, William Wells Brown helped to pioneer the African American literary tradition. He is generally regarded as the first African American man of letters. Born a slave in Lexington, Kentucky, in 1815, Brown escaped from slavery in 1834. He dedicated the rest of his life to abolishing slavery. Not only did he write the first African American novel, protest play, travel book, and history of the black soldier in the Civil War, but he also lectured throughout the North and in England on the horrors of slavery.

In 1847, Brown published his first autobiography, or narrative—*Narrative of William Wells Brown, A Fugitive Slave.* Like Frederick Douglass's *Narrative,* which was published in 1845, Brown's work spells out various incidents in his life, which highlight the evils of slavery and the moral corruption of the slave masters. Brown's narrative was, at that time, more popular than Douglass's largely because the narrative was carefully and strategically packaged and presented to an abolitionist audience. Documents verifying the authenticity of Brown's account include a letter from him to his trusted friend, the Quaker Wells Brown, and a preface by J.C. Hathaway, a former employer of Brown and then president of the Western New York Antislavery Society. Like Douglass, Brown vividly dramatizes the hypocrisy of northerners and supposed Christians involved in maintaining "the peculiar institution." For instance, a Mr. Haskell, an overseer from New England, is particularly cruel.

Brown includes in his *Narrative* a series of slave-breaking incidents in which slaves, presumed defiant and rebellious, are violently put back in their place. It is not surprising, then, that slaves who escaped, like Douglass and Brown, placed a premium on renaming themselves as an act of psychic and spiritual self-possession. Specifically, in Brown's case, the name "William" was abruptly taken away from him when his master's nephew, who was also called "William," moved into their home. William Wells Brown was thenceforth called "Sandford." Brown's eventual reclaiming of his first name "William," and freely choosing to take and possess Wells Brown, the name of his "first white friend," to whom he dedicates his *Narrative,* is significant. It simultaneously celebrates his individual freedom as it points out to the abolitionist readers both the possibility and redeeming value of human kindness and Christian brotherhood.

In 1853, Brown published *Clotel: Or, The President's Daughter, A Narrative of Slave Life in the United States.* It is the first novel published by an African American, although, as Henry Louis Gates, Jr. has established, Harriet E. Wilson's *Our Nig* (1859) is the first novel by an African American published in the United States. However, the fact and place (England) of *Clotel*'s publication is important. Considering that *Clotel* was published with an English abolitionist audience in mind, the novel's subtitle *Or, The President's Daughter,* referring rather boldly to Thomas Jefferson's involvement with Sally Hemmings, his African American mistress, was meant to suggest how slavery had morally corrupted America from top to bottom. The novel presents the brutal nature of slavery as the plot and numerous subplots unfold. At the end of the novel, Clotel, while attempting to escape, suddenly faces capture. She commits suicide by jumping into the Potomac River. The Capitol and the "President's House" are seen symbolically in the background.

Several critics have pointed out the untidy nature of *Clotel* as a work of fiction. In actuality, it is more a literary hybrid, combining several fictionlike plots, a bit of Brown's own narrative, poems, and brief essays on the brutalities and hypocrisy of slavery. The novel was clearly written primarily as part of Brown's ongoing battle to bring slavery to an end.

Brown published other works, including three other versions of *Clotel,* in which Jefferson becomes an anonymous senator. They are: *Miralda; Or, The Beautiful Quadroon: A Romance of American Slavery, Founded on Fact* (a serial, New York, 1860–1861); *Clotelle: A Tale of the Southern States* (1864); and *Clotelle; Or, The Colored Heroine: A Tale of the Southern States* (1867). Another of Brown's works, *The American Fugitive in Europe: Sketches of Places and People Abroad* (1855) was originally published in 1852 in London as a series of travel letters. In an expanded 1855 version, Brown makes frequent comparisons between the civilized situation of free blacks in Europe, and the racist nature of life in America. He presents himself and other African Americans as walking personifications of intelligence, civility, and human dignity as they move among notables in such places as London and Paris. He underscores, with obvious pleasure, the presence of African Americans attending college at London and Edinburgh.

A prolific man of letters, Brown continued publishing until the end of his life. He wrote a lengthy play titled *The Escape or a Leap for Freedom: A Drama in Five Acts,* which appeared in print in 1858. It was probably the second drama written by an African American and clearly the first play by an African American protesting slavery. An account of his personal, dehumanizing experiences as a slave and his eventual escape to freedom, his highly melodramatic play and his dramatic readings of it were so successful that both received very favorable reviews in northern white liberal newspapers. For instance, in the New York periodicals, the *Daily Advertiser* and the *Seneca Falls Courier, The Escape* was hailed as "one of the most interesting dramatic compositions of modern times . . . a masterful refutation of all apologies for slavery, and abounds in wit, satire, philosophy, arguments and facts" and Brown as one who "exhibits a dramatic talent possessed by few who have under the best instruction, made themselves famous on the stage."

Moreover, Brown understood the necessity of providing an accurate record of African American history and, thus, turned his attention to the task. He published several works, including *The Black Man, His Antecedents, His Genius, and His Achievements* (1863), *The Negro in the American Rebellion: His Heroism and His Fidelity* (1867), *The Rising Son, Or the Antecedents and Advancement of the Colored Race* (1873), and *My Southern Home: Or the South and Its People* (1880). The works are not those of a trained historian, but even Brown's suggestive titles—including such words as "Heroism," "Genius," "Achievement," and "Advancement"—are meant to set the record straight concerning the African American presence and significance in American life.

William Wells Brown is an individual who lived an extraordinarily varied life. Born a slave, the offspring of his white master and slave mother, he eventually became a doctor (medical school was not a professional requirement at that time) and practiced medicine in the Boston area after the Civil War and until his death in 1884.

❖❖❖

Brown's works have received serious scholarly attention. W. Edward Farrison's *William Wells Brown: Author and Reformer* (1969) is a full-length biographical study. Earlier studies include Josephine Brown's *The Biography of an American Bondsman, by his Daughter* (1856); see also *The Negro Author* by Vernon Loggins (1931) and a thorough sketch by Carter G. Woodson in *Dictionary of American Negro Biography* (1982). Also, see Blyden Jackson's *A History of Afro-American Literature, Vol. I: The Long Beginning 1746–1895* (1989) as well as J. Noel Heermance's *William Wells Brown and Clotelle* (1969), a solid critical study of his novel.

FROM *Clotelle: A Tale of the Southern States*

Chapter II
The Negro Sale

As might have been expected, the day of sale brought an unusually large number together to compete for the property to be sold. Farmers, who make a business of raising slaves for the market, were there, and slave-traders, who make a business of buying human beings in the slave-raising States and taking them to the far South, were also in attendance. Men and women, too, who wished to purchase for their own use, had found their way to the slave sale.

In the midst of the throng was one who felt a deeper interest in the result of the sale than any other of the bystanders. This was young Linwood. True to his promise, he was there with a blank bank-check in his pocket, awaiting with impatience to enter the list as a bidder for the beautiful slave.

It was indeed a heart-rending scene to witness the lamentations of these slaves, all of whom had grown up together on the old homestead of Mr. Graves, and who had been treated with great kindness by that gentleman, during his life. Now they were to be separated, and form new relations and companions. Such is the precarious condition of the slave. Even when with a good master, there is no certainty of his happiness in the future.

The less valuable slaves were first placed upon the auction-block, one after another, and sold to the highest bidder. Husbands and wives were separated with a degree of indifference that is unknown in any other relation in life. Brothers and sisters were torn from each other, and mothers saw their children for the last time on earth.

It was late in the day, and when the greatest number of persons were thought to be present, when Agnes and her daughters were brought out to the place of sale. The mother was first put upon the auction-block, and sold to a noted negro trader named Jennings. Marion was next ordered to ascend the stand, which she did with a trembling step, and was sold for $1200.

All eyes were now turned on Isabella, as she was led forward by the auctioneer. The appearance of the handsome quadroon caused a deep sensation among the crowd. There she stood, with a skin as fair as most white women, her features as beautifully regular as any of her sex of pure Anglo-Saxon blood, her long black hair done up in the neatest manner, her form tall and graceful, and her whole appearance indicating one superior to her condition.

The auctioneer commenced by saying that Miss Isabella was fit to deck the drawing-room of the finest mansion in Virginia.

"How much, gentlemen, for this real Albino!—fit fancy-girl for any one! She enjoys good health, and has a sweet temper. How much do you say?"

"Five hundred dollars."

"Only five hundred for such a girl as this? Gentlemen, she is worth a deal more than that sum. You certainly do not know the value of the article you are bidding on. Here, gentlemen, I hold in my hand a paper certifying that she has a good moral character."

"Seven hundred."

"Ah, gentlemen, that is something like. This paper also states that she is very intelligent."

"Eight hundred."

"She was first sprinkled, then immersed, and is now warranted to be a devoted Christian, and perfectly trustworthy."

"Nine hundred dollars."

"Nine hundred and fifty."

"One thousand."

"Eleven hundred."

Here the bidding came to a dead stand. The auctioneer stopped, looked around, and began in a rough manner to relate some anecdote connected with the sale of slaves, which he said had come under his own observation.

At this juncture the scene was indeed a most striking one. The laughing, joking, swearing, smoking, spitting, and talking, kept up a continual hum and confusion among the crowd, while the slave-girl stood with tearful eyes, looking alternately at her mother and sister and toward the young man whom she hoped would become her purchaser.

"The chastity of this girl," now continued the auctioneer, "is pure. She has never been from under her mother's care. She is virtuous, and as gentle as a dove."

The bids here took a fresh start, and went on until $1800 was reached. The auctioneer once more resorted to his jokes, and concluded by assuring the company that Isabella was not only pious, but that she could make an excellent prayer.

"Nineteen hundred dollars."

"Two thousand."

This was the last bid, and the quadroon girl was struck off, and became the property of Henry Linwood.

This was a Virginia slave-auction, at which the bones, sinews, blood, and nerves of a young girl of eighteen were sold for $500; her moral character for $200; her superior intellect for $100; the benefits supposed to accrue from her having been sprinkled and immersed, together with a warranty of her devoted Christianity, for $800; her ability to make a good prayer for $200; and her chastity for $700 more. This, too, in a city thronged with churches, whose tall spires look like so many signals pointing to heaven, but whose ministers preach that slavery is a God-ordained institution!

The slaves were speedily separated, and taken along by their respective masters. Jennings, the slave-speculator, who had purchased Agnes and her daughter Marion, with several of the other slaves, took them to the county prison, where he usually kept his human cattle after purchasing them, previous to starting for the New Orleans market.

Linwood had already provided a place for Isabella, to which she was taken. The most trying moment for her was when she took leave of her mother and sister. The "Good-by" of the slave is unlike that of any other class in the community. It is indeed a farewell forever. With tears streaming down their cheeks, they embraced and commended each other to God, who is no respecter of persons, and before whom master and slave must one day appear.

Chapter X
The Quadroon's Home

A few miles out of Richmond is a pleasant place, with here and and there a beautiful cottage surrounded by trees so as scarcely to be seen. Among these was one far retired from the public roads, and almost hidden among the trees. This was the spot that Henry Linwood had selected for Isabella, the eldest daughter of Agnes. The young man hired the house, furnished it, and placed his mistress there, and for many months no one in his father's family knew where he spent his leisure hours.

When Henry was not with her, Isabella employed herself in looking after her little garden and the flowers that grew in front of her cottage. The passion-flower, peony, dahlia, laburnum, and other plants, so abundant in warm climates, under the tasteful hand of Isabella, lavished their beauty upon this retired spot, and miniature paradise.

Although Isabella had been assured by Henry that she should be free and that he would always consider her as his wife, she nevertheless felt that she ought to be married and acknowledged by him. But this was an impossibility under the State laws, even had the young man been disposed to do what was right in the matter. Related as he was, however, to one of the first families in Virginia, he would not have dared to marry a woman of so low an origin, even had the laws been favorable.

Here, in this secluded grove, unvisited by any other except her lover, Isabella lived for years. She had become the mother of a lovely daughter, which its father named Clotelle. The complexion of the child was still fairer than that of its mother. Indeed, she was not darker than other white children, and as she grew older she more and more resembled her father.

As time passed away, Henry became negligent of Isabella and his child, so much so, that days and even weeks passed without their seeing him, or knowing where he was. Becoming more acquainted with the world, and moving continually in the society of young women of his own station, the young man felt that Isabella was a burden to him, and having as some would say, "outgrown his love," he longed to free himself of the responsibility; yet every time he saw the child, he felt that he owed it his fatherly care.

Henry had now entered into political life, and been elected to a seat in the legislature of his native State; and in his intercourse with his friends had become acquainted with Gertrude Miller, the daughter of a wealthy gentleman living near Richmond. Both Henry and Gertrude were very good-looking, and a mutual attachment sprang up between them.

Instead of finding fault with the unfrequent visits of Henry, Isabella always met him with a smile, and tried to make both him and herself believe that business was the cause of his negligence. When he was with her, she devoted every moment of her time to him, and never failed to speak of the growth and increasing intelligence of Clotelle.

The child had grown so large as to be able to follow its father on his departure out to the road. But the impression made on Henry's feelings by the devoted woman and her child was momentary. His heart had grown hard, and his acts were guided by no fixed principle. Henry and Gertrude had been married nearly two years before Isabella knew anything of the event, and it was merely by accident that she became acquainted with the facts.

One beautiful afternoon, when Isabella and Clotelle were picking wild strawberries some two miles from their home, and near the roadside, they observed a one-horse chaise driving past. The mother turned her face from the carriage not wishing to be seen by strangers, little dreaming that the chaise contained Henry and his wife. The child, however, watched the chaise, and startled her mother by screaming out at the top of her voice, "Papa! papa!" and clapped her little hands for joy. The mother turned in haste to look at the strangers, and her eyes encountered those of Henry's pale and dejected countenance. Gertrude's eyes were on the child. The swiftness with which Henry drove by could not hide from his wife the striking resemblance of the child to himself. The young wife had heard the child exclaim "Papa! papa!" and she immediately saw by the quivering of his lips and the agitation depicted in his countenance, that all was not right.

"Who is that woman? and why did that child call you papa?" she inquired, with a trembling voice.

Henry was silent; he knew not what to say, and without another word passing between them, they drove home.

On reaching her room, Gertrude buried her face in her handkerchief and wept. She loved Henry, and when she had heard from the lips of her companions how their husbands had proved false, she felt that he was an exception, and fervently thanked God that she had been so blessed.

When Gertrude retired to her bed that night, the sad scene of the day followed her. The beauty of Isabella, with her flowing curls, and the look of the child, so much resembling the man whom she so dearly loved, could not be forgotten; and little Clotelle's exclamation of "Papa! papa!" rang in her ears during the whole night.

The return of Henry at twelve o'clock did not increase her happiness. Feeling his guilt, he had absented himself from the house since his return from the ride.

Chapter XI

To-day a Mistress, To-morrow a Slave

The night was dark, the rain descended in torrents from the black and overhanging clouds, and the thunder, accompanied with vivid flashes of lightning, resounded fearfully, as Henry Linwood stepped from his chaise and entered Isabella's cottage.

More than a fortnight had elapsed since the accidental meeting, and Isabella was in doubt as to who the lady was that Henry was with in the carriage. Little, however, did she think that it was his wife. With a smile, Isabella met the young man as he entered her little dwelling. Clotelle had already gone to bed, but her father's voice aroused her from her sleep, and she was soon sitting on his knee.

The pale and agitated countenance of Henry betrayed his uneasiness, but Isabella's mild and laughing allusion to the incident of their meeting him on the day of his pleasure-drive, and her saying, "I presume, dear Henry, that the lady was one of your relatives," led him to believe that she was still in ignorance of his marriage. She was, in fact, ignorant who the lady was who accompanied the man she loved on that eventful day. He, aware of this, now acted more like himself, and passed the thing off as a joke. At heart, however, Isabella felt uneasy, and this uneasiness would at times show itself to the young man. At last, and with a great effort, she said,—

"Now, dear Henry, if I am in the way of your future happiness, say so, and I will release you from any promises that you have made me. I know there is no law by which I can hold you, and if there was, I would not resort to it. You are as dear to me as ever, and my thoughts shall always be devoted to you. It would be a great sacrifice for me to give you up to another, but if it be your desire, as great as the sacrifice is, I will make it. Send me and your child into a Free State if we are in your way."

Again and again Linwood assured her that no woman possessed his love but her. Oh, what falsehood and deceit man can put on when dealing with woman's love!

The unabated storm kept Henry from returning home until after the clock had struck two, and as he drew near his residence he saw his wife standing at the window. Giving his horse in charge of the servant who was waiting, he entered the house, and found his wife in tears. Although he had never satisfied Gertrude as to who the quadroon woman and child were, he had kept her comparatively easy by his close attention to her, and by telling her that she was mistaken in regard to the child's calling him "papa." His absence that night, however, without any apparent cause, had again aroused the jealousy of Gertrude; but Henry told her that he had been caught in the rain while out, which prevented his sooner returning, and she, anxious to believe him received the story as satisfactory.

Somewhat heated with brandy, and wearied with much loss of sleep, Linwood fell into a sound slumber as soon as he retired. Not so with Gertrude. That faithfulness which has ever distinguished her sex, and the anxiety with which she watched all his movements, kept the wife awake while the husband slept. His sleep, though apparently sound, was nevertheless uneasy. Again and again she heard him pronounce the name of Isabella, and more than once she heard him say, "I am not married; I will never marry while you live." Then he would speak the name of Clotelle and say, "My dear child, how I love you!"

After a sleepless night, Gertrude arose from her couch, resolved that she would reveal the whole matter to her mother. Mrs. Miller was a woman of little or no feeling, proud, peevish, and passionate, thus making everybody miserable that came near her; and when she disliked any one, her hatred knew no bounds. This Gertrude knew; and had she not considered it her duty, she would have kept the secret locked in her own heart.

During the day, Mrs. Linwood visited her mother and told her all that had happened. The mother scolded the daughter for not having informed her sooner, and immediately determined to find out who the woman and child were that Gertrude had met on the day of her ride. Three days were spent by Mrs. Miller in this endeavor, but without success.

Four weeks had elapsed, and the storm of the old lady's temper had somewhat subsided, when, one evening, as she was approaching her daughter's residence, she saw Henry walking in the direction of where the quadroon was supposed to reside. Being satisfied that the young man had not seen her, the old woman at once resolved to follow him. Linwood's boots squeaked so loudly that Mrs. Miller had no difficulty in following him without being herself observed.

After a walk of about two miles, the young man turned into a narrow and unfrequented road, and soon entered the cottage occupied by Isabella. It was a fine starlight night, and the moon was just rising when they got to their journey's end. As usual, Isabella met Henry with a smile, and expressed her fears regarding his health.

Hours passed, and still old Mrs. Miller remained near the house, determined to know who lived there. When she undertook to ferret out anything, she bent her whole energies to it. As Michael Angelo, who subjected all things to his pursuit and the idea he had formed of it, painted the crucifixion by the side of a writhing slave and would have broken up the true cross for pencils, so Mrs. Miller would have entered the sepulchre, if she could have done it, in search of an object she wished to find.

The full moon had risen, and was pouring its beams upon surrounding objects as Henry stepped from Isabella's door, and looking at his watch, said,—

"I must go, dear; it is now half-past ten."

Had little Clotelle been awake, she too would have been at the door. As Henry walked to the gate, Isabella followed with her left hand locked in his. Again he looked at his watch, and said,—

"I must go."

"It is more than a year since you staid all night," murmured Isabella, as he folded her convulsively in his arms, and pressed upon her beautiful lips a parting kiss.

He was nearly out of sight when, with bitter sobs, the quadroon retraced her steps to the door of the cottage. Clotelle had in the mean time awoke, and now inquired of her mother how long her father had been gone. At that instant, a knock was heard at the door, and supposing that it was Henry returning for something he had forgotten, as he frequently did, Isabella flew to let him in. To her amazement, however, a strange woman stood in the door.

"Who are you that comes here at this late hour?" demanded the half-frightened Isabella.

Without making any reply, Mrs. Miller pushed the quadroon aside, and entered the house.

"What do you want here?" again demanded Isabella.

"I am in search of you," thundered the maddened Mrs. Miller; but thinking that her object would be better served by seeming to be kind, she assumed a different tone of voice, and began talking in a pleasing manner.

In this way, she succeeded in finding out the connection existing between Linwood and Isabella, and after getting all she could out of the unsuspecting woman, she informed her that the man she so fondly loved had been married for more than two years. Seized with dizziness, the poor, heart-broken woman fainted and fell upon the floor. How long she remained there she could not tell; but when she returned to consciousness, the strange woman was gone, and her child was standing by her side. When she was so far recovered as to regain her feet, Isabella went to the door, and even into the yard, to see if the old woman was not somewhere about.

As she stood there, the full moon cast its bright rays over her whole person, giving her an angelic appearance and imparting to her flowing hair a still more golden hue. Suddenly another change came over her features, and her full red lips trembled as with suppressed emotion. The muscles around her faultless mouth became convulsed, she gasped for breath, and exclaiming, "Is it possible that man can be so false!" again fainted.

Clotelle stood and bathed her mother's temples with cold water until she once more revived.

Although the laws of Virginia forbid the education of slaves, Agnes had nevertheless employed an old free negro to teach her two daughters to read and write. After being separated from her mother and sister, Isabella turned her attention to the subject of Christianity, and received that consolation from the Bible which is never denied to the children of God. This was now her last hope, for her heart was torn with grief and filled with all the bitterness of disappointment.

The night passed away, but without sleep to poor Isabella. At the dawn of day, she tried to make herself believe that the whole of the past night was a dream, and determined to be satisfied with the explanation which Henry should give on his next visit.

Chapter XXV
The Flight

On once gaining the wharf, Devenant and Clotelle found no difficulty in securing an immediate passage to France. The fine packet-ship Utica lay down the bay, and only awaited the return of the lighter that night to complete her cargo and list of passengers, ere she departed. The young Frenchman therefore took his prize on board, and started for the ship.

Daylight was just making its appearance the next morning when the Utica weighed anchor and turned her prow toward the sea. In the course of three hours, the vessel, with outspread sails, was rapidly flying for land. Everything appeared to be auspicious. The skies were beautifully clear, and the sea calm, with a sun that dazzled the whole scene. But clouds soon began to chase each other through the heavens and the sea became rough. It was then that Clotelle felt that there was hope of escaping. She had hitherto kept in the cabin, but now she expressed a wish to come on deck. The hanging clouds were narrowing the horizon to a span, and gloomily mingling with the rising surges. The old and grave-looking seamen shook their weather-wise heads as if foretelling a storm.

As Clotelle came on deck, she strained her eyes in vain to catch a farewell view of her native land. With a smile on her countenance, but with her eyes filled with tears, she said,—

"Farewell, farewell to the land of my birth, and welcome, welcome, ye dark blue waves. I care not where I go, so it is

'Where a tyrant never trod,
  Where a slave was never known,
But where nature worships God,
  If in the wilderness alone.'"

Devenant stood by her side, seeming proud of his future wife, with his face in a glow at his success, while over his noble brow clustering locks of glossy black hair were hanging in careless ringlets. His finely-cut, classic features wore the aspect of one possessed with a large and noble heart.

Once more the beautiful Clotelle whispered in the ear of her lover,—

"Away, away, o'er land and sea,
America is now no home for me."

The winds increased with nightfall, and impenetrable gloom surrounded the ship. The prospect was too uncheering, even to persons in love. The attention which Devenant paid to Clotelle, although she had been registered on the ship's passenger list as his sister, caused more than one to look upon his as an agreeable travelling companion. His tall, slender figure and fine countenance bespoke for him at first sight one's confidence. That he was sincerely and deeply enamored of Clotelle all could see.

The weather became still more squally. The wind rushed through the white, foaming waves, and the ship groaned with its own wild and ungovernable labors, while nothing could be seen but the wild waste of waters. The scene was indeed one of fearful sublimity.

Day came and went without any abatement of the storm. Despair was now on every countenance. Occasionally a vivid flash of lightning would break forth and illuminate the black and boiling surges that surrounded the vessel, which was now scudding before the blast under bare poles.

After five days of most intensely stormy weather, the sea settled down into a dead calm, and the passengers flocked on deck. During the last three days of the storm, Clotelle had been so unwell as to be unable to raise her head. Her pale face and quivering lips and languid appearance made her look as if every pulsation had ceased. Her magnificent large and soft eyes, fringed with lashes as dark as night, gave her an angelic appearance. The unreserved attention of Devenant, even when sea-sick himself, did much to increase the little love that the at first distrustful girl had placed in him. The heart must always have some object on which to centre its affections, and Clotelle having lost all hope of ever again seeing Jerome, it was but natural that she should now transfer her love to one who was so greatly befriending her. At first she respected Devenant for the love he manifested for her, and for his apparent willingness to make any sacrifice for her welfare. True, this was an adventure upon which she had risked her all, and should her heart be foiled in this search for hidden treasures, her affections would be shipwrecked forever. She felt under great obligations to the man who had thus effected her escape, and that noble act alone would entitle him to her love.

Each day became more pleasant as the noble ship sped onward amid the rippled spray. The whistling of the breeze through the rigging was music to the ear, and brought gladness to the heart of every one on board. At last, the long suspense was broken by the appearance of land, at which all hearts leaped for joy. It was a beautiful morning in October. The sun had just risen, and sky and earth were still bathed in his soft, rosy glow, when the Utica hauled into the dock at Bordeaux. The splendid streets, beautiful bridges, glittering equipages, and smiling countenances of the people, gave everything a happy appearance, after a voyage of twenty-nine days on the deep, deep sea.

After getting their baggage cleared from the custom-house and going to a hotel, Devenant made immediate arrangements for the marriage. Clotelle, on arriving at the church where the ceremony was to take place, was completely overwhelmed at the spectacle. She had never beheld a scene so gorgeous as this. The magnificent dresses of the priests and choristers, the deep and solemn voices, the elevated crucifix, the burning tapers, the splendidly decorated altar, the sweet-smelling incense, made the occasion truly an imposing one. At the conclusion of the ceremony, the loud and solemn peals of the organ's swelling anthem were lost to all in the contemplation of the interesting scene.

The happy couple set out at once for Dunkirk, the residence of the bridegroom's parents. But their stay there was short, for they had scarcely commenced visiting the numerous friends of the husband ere orders came for him to proceed to India to join that portion of the French army then stationed there.

In due course of time they left for India, passing through Paris and Lyons, taking ship at Marseilles. In the metropolis of France, they spent a week, where the husband took delight in introducing his wife to his brother officers in the French army, and where the newly-married couple were introduced to Louis Philippe, then King of France. In all of these positions, Clotelle sustained herself in a most ladylike manner.

At Lyons, they visited the vast factories and other public works, and all was pleasure with them. The voyage from Marseilles to Calcutta was very pleasant, as the weather was exceedingly fine. On arriving in India, Captain Devenant and lady were received with honors—the former for his heroic bravery in more than one battle, and the latter for her fascinating beauty and pleasing manners, and the fact that she was connected with one who was a general favorite with all who had his acquaintance. This was indeed a great change for Clotelle. Six months had not elapsed since her exposure in the slave-market of New Orleans. This life is a stage, and we are indeed all actors.

HARRIET E. ADAMS WILSON
(1828?–1863?)

It would not be an exaggeration to claim that Harriet Wilson has perhaps led the inspiration for critical commentary on nineteenth-century African American women writers. An obscure author of an autobiographical novel, Wilson was lost in the unclaimed library of African American literature for most of the twentieth century. Then, comparable to Columbus "discovering" America, critic Henry Louis Gates, Jr., discovered Harriet Wilson in 1982. While earlier scholars knew of her single work and a footnote about it had appeared here and there, no sustained scholarly treatment of the work had emerged. Since its republication in 1983, *Our Nig; Or, Sketches from the Life of a Free Black, in a Two-Story House, North. Showing That*

Slavery's Shadows Fall Even There has inspired a detailed historical investigation, and the volume has earned a place in classes in African American literature. Today, Wilson is generally recognized as the first woman of African American descent to have published a novel in the United States.

What little is known about Harriet Wilson has been derived primarily from information given in *Our Nig* and substantiated by public documents in New Hampshire and Massachusetts. Scholars speculate that she was born around 1827 or 1828 and that she died sometime between 1863 and 1870. The fullest information known covers 1850–1860, the period during which she wrote, published, and tried to sell *Our Nig.* Investigators have concluded that she was born in New Hampshire. It is known that, in 1851, she married Thomas Wilson, whom she assumed to be an ex-slave (he was traveling as an abolitionist lecturer), and that she traveled back and forth between New Hampshire and Massachusetts. The couple had one child, George Mason Wilson, who was born in 1852, weeks after Thomas deserted his pregnant wife and shipped to sea. Wilson's son was born in the County House, a home for the destitute, in Goffstown, New Hampshire. Wilson's circumstances were briefly alleviated when Thomas returned, only to desert them again; it was later discovered that he died of yellow fever in New Orleans. Wilson returned George to the County House, where he remained until she could no longer pay the weekly room and board. At that point, a kindly white couple provided a foster home for the child.

Though suffering from ill health, Wilson nonetheless moved to Boston in 1855 to obtain work as a dressmaker. It was in Boston that she wrote *Our Nig,* copyrighted it on August 18, 1859, and published it on September 5, 1859, with Geo. C. Rand & Avery of Boston. In the preface, she appealed to her "colored Brethren" to come to the aid of "their sister" by buying copies of the book so she might support herself and her child. Her effort to use her literary skills to retrieve her son from the foster home ended in vain, for George Mason Wilson died of fever on February 15, 1860. Wilson lived in Boston until 1863, but public records do not follow her whereabouts beyond that point.

Our Nig documents the plight of Frado, the light-skinned offspring of a white mother and a black father. Shortly after her father's death, her mother abandons Frado to indentured servitude with one of her white neighbors, Mrs. Bellmont. As the subtitle of the novel suggests, slavery clearly exists in the North, for Frado is beaten by Mrs. Bellmont and her daughter Mary, denied proper food, and kept from secular and religious education during her early years. The cruelty recounted, such as Frado being kicked, beaten with a rawhide, and hung up in a closet by her thumbs and whipped, is comparable to that any unscrupulous slaveholder might have exhibited in the southern states. Mrs. Bellmont knows the power of absolute control over another human being, and she henpecks the men in her family into letting her have her way with Frado. The moral ineffectualness of Mr. Bellmont and his sons, James and Jack, is striking, for, although they sympathize with "Nig," as Frado is called, none stands squarely against wife and mother to come to her rescue. Though there is no clear-cut implication of sexual interest in Frado on the part of the Bellmont men, that possibility arises distinctly with one of the sons, who seems unduly interested in the budding, beautiful young woman.

Despite her hardships, Frado is a surprisingly imaginative and sometimes happy child who bears up well under the consistent cruelties of the Bellmont women. She acquires what education she can and, under the tutelage of Aunt Abby, a more sympathetic member of the Bellmont house, learns religious principles as well. Christian zeal triumphs over potential bitterness as Frado remains humble and forgiving of all that happens to her, even when she is turned out, during illness, from the Bellmont household. Her best years broken down with overwork, the young adult Frado tries to pay her way by taking in sewing but discovers that ill health prevents even that self-support. She finally meets and marries Samuel, who claims to be a runaway slave, but is really an abolitionist tool. He leaves her pregnant and goes to sea, never to be seen again. The narrative ends with Frado still in desperate straits, trying valiantly to support herself and her child.

The book is fascinating for its combination of personal narrative and novelistic forms. Wilson's first three chapters, titled "Mag Smith, My Mother," "My Father's Death," and "A New Home for Me," although narrated in the third person, suggest the interweaving of her own biography and that of the fictional Frado. This mixing of genres provides the internal evidence for concluding that the narrative is as much autobiographical—and thus a slave narrative—as it is fictional. Wilson's claims for personal consideration in writing and selling the book lent further credence to the novel being her own story.

As with many slave narratives, there are various authenticating documents appended to Wilson's novel or narrative. A testimonial from "Allida" and letters from "Margaretta Thorn" and "C.D.S." confirm knowledge of Wilson and her health and the precarious position she was in financially, and they vouch for her as an upstanding human being. This combination of slave narrative and novel, therefore, makes *Our Nig* a particularly engaging narrative in the history of African American letters. By writing against the odds of race, gender, impoverishment, and ill health, Harriet Wilson succeeded in expanding the black novelistic tradition by more than thirty years.

❖❖❖

For more information on the unearthing and reentering of *Our Nig* in the African American literary canon, see Henry Louis Gates, Jr., introduction to *Our Nig; Or, Sketches from the Life of a Free Black* (New York: Vintage, 1983) and "Chronology" by David A. Curtis; for biography and criticism, see Bernard Bell, *The Afro-American Novel and Its Tradition* (Amherst: University of Massachusetts Press, 1987); Henry Louis Gates, Jr., "Harriet E. Adams Wilson," *The Dictionary of Literary Biography,* Vol. 50 (Detroit: Gale, 1986); Henry Louis Gates, Jr., and David Ames Curtis, "Establishing the Identity of the Author of *Our Nig,*" in *Wild Women in the Whirlwind: Afra-American Culture and the Contemporary Literary Renaissance,* edited by Joanne Braxton and Andree Nicola McLaughlin (New Brunswick: Rutgers University Press, 1990); Carmen Renee Gillespie, "Harriet E. Adams Wilson," in *Notable Black American Women,* edited by Jessie Carney Smith (Detroit: Gale, 1992).

FROM *Our Nig: Or, Sketches From the Life of a Free Black*

Chapter IV
A Friend for Nig

"Hours of my youth! when nurtured in my breast,
To love a stranger, friendship made me blest;—
Friendship, the dear peculiar bond of youth,
When every artless bosom throbs with truth;
Untaught by worldly wisdom how to feign;
And check each impulse with prudential reign;
When all we feel our honest souls disclose—
In love to friends, in open hate to foes;
No varnished tales the lips of youth repeat,
No dear-bought knowledge purchased by deceit."

Byron

With what differing emotions have the denizens of earth awaited the approach of to-day. Some sufferer has counted the vibrations of the pendulum impatient for its dawn, who, now that it has arrived, is anxious for its close. The votary of pleasure, conscious of yesterday's void, wishes for power to arrest time's haste till a few more hours of mirth shall be enjoyed. The unfortunate are yet gazing in vain for golden-edged clouds they fancied would appear in their horizon. The good man feels that he has accomplished too little for the Master, and sighs that another day must so soon close. Innocent childhood, weary of its stay, longs for another morrow; busy manhood cries, hold! hold! and pursues it to another's dawn. All are dissatisfied. All crave some good not yet possessed, which time is expected to bring with all its morrows.

Was it strange that, to a disconsolate child, three years should seem a long, long time? During school time she had rest from Mrs. Bellmont's tyranny. She was now nine years old; time, her mistress said, such privileges should cease.

She could now read and spell, and knew the elementary steps in grammar, arithmetic, and writing. Her education completed, as *she* said, Mrs. Bellmont felt that her time and person belonged solely to her. She was under her in every sense of the word. What an opportunity to indulge her vixen nature! No matter what occurred to ruffle her, or from what source provocation came, real or fancied, a few blows on Nig seemed to relieve her of a portion of ill-will.

These were days when Fido was the entire confidant of Frado. She told him her griefs as though he were human; and he sat so still, and listened so attentively, she really believed he knew her sorrows. All the leisure moments she could gain were used in teaching him some feat of dog-agility, so that Jack pronounced him very knowing, and was truly gratified to know he had furnished her with a gift answering his intentions.

Fido was the constant attendant of Frado, when sent from the house on errands, going and returning with the cows, out in the fields, to the village. If ever she forgot her hardships it was in his company.

Spring was now retiring. James, one of the absent sons, was expected home on a visit. He had never seen the last acquisition to the family. Jack had written faithfully of all the merits of his colored *protegé,* and hinted plainly that mother did not always treat her just right. Many were the preparations to make the visit pleasant, and as the day approached when he was to arrive, great exertions were made to cook the favorite viands, to prepare the choicest table-fare.

The morning of the arrival day was a busy one. Frado knew not who would be of so much importance; her feet were speeding hither and thither so unsparingly. Mrs. Bellmont seemed a trifle fatigued, and her shoes which had, early in the morning, a methodic squeak, altered to an irregular, peevish snap.

"Get some little wood to make the fire burn," said Mrs. Bellmont, in a sharp tone. Frado obeyed, bringing the smallest she could find.

Mrs. Bellmont approached her, and, giving her a box on her ear, reiterated the command.

The first the child brought was the smallest to be found; of course, the second must be a trifle larger. She well knew it was, as she threw it into a box on the hearth. To Mrs. Bellmont it was a greater affront, as well as larger wood, so she "taught her" with the raw-hide, and sent her the third time for "little wood."

Nig, weeping, knew not what to do. She had carried the smallest; none left would suit her mistress; of course further punishment awaited her; so she gathered up whatever came first, and threw it down on the hearth. As she expected, Mrs. Bellmont, enraged, approached her, and kicked her so forcibly as to throw her upon the floor. Before she could rise, another foiled the attempt, and then followed kick after kick in quick succession and power, till she reached the door. Mr. Bellmont and Aunt Abby, hearing the noise, rushed in, just in time to see the last of the performance. Nig jumped up, and rushed from the house, out of sight.

Aunt Abby returned to her apartment, followed by John, who was muttering to himself.

"What were you saying?" asked Aunt Abby.

"I said I hoped the child never would come into the house again."

"What would become of her? You cannot mean *that,*" continued his sister.

"I do mean it. The child does as much work as a woman ought to; and just see how she is kicked about!"

"Why do you have it so, John?" asked his sister.

"How am I to help it? Women rule the earth, and all in it."

"I think I should rule my own house, John,"—

"And live in hell meantime," added Mr. Bellmont.

John now sauntered out to the barn to await the quieting of the storm.

Aunt Abby had a glimpse of Nig as she passed out of the yard; but to arrest her, or show her that *she* would shelter her, in Mrs. Bellmont's presence, would only bring reserved wrath on her defenceless head. Her sister-in-law had great prejudices against her. One cause of the alienation was that she did not give her right in the homestead to John, and leave it forever; another was that she was a professor of religion, (so was Mrs. Bellmont;) but Nab, as she called her, did not live according to her profession; another, that she *would* sometimes give Nig cake and pie, which she was never allowed to have at home. Mary had often noticed and spoken of her inconsistencies.

The dinner hour passed. Frado had not appeared. Mrs. B. made no inquiry or search. Aunt Abby looked long, and found her concealed in an outbuilding. "Come into the house with me," implored Aunt Abby.

"I ain't going in any more," sobbed the child.

"What will you do?" asked Aunt Abby.

"I've got to stay out here and die. I ha'n't got no mother, no home. I wish I was dead."

"Poor thing," muttered Aunt Abby; and slyly providing her with some dinner, left her to her grief.

Jane went to confer with her Aunt about the affair; and learned from her the retreat. She would gladly have concealed her in her own chamber, and ministered to her wants; but she was dependent on Mary and her mother for care, and any displeasure caused by attention to Nig, was seriously felt.

Toward night the coach brought James. A time of general greeting, inquiries for absent members of the family, a visit to Aunt Abby's room, undoing a few delicacies for Jane, brought them to the tea hour.

"Where's Frado?" asked Mr. Bellmont, observing she was not in her usual place, behind her mistress' chair.

"I don't know, and I don't care. If she makes her appearance again, I'll take the skin from her body," replied his wife.

James, a fine looking young man, with a pleasant countenance, placid, and yet decidedly serious, yet not stern, looked up confounded. He was no stranger to his mother's nature; but years of absence had erased the occurrences once so familiar, and he asked, "Is this that pretty little Nig, Jack writes to me about, that you are so severe upon, mother?"

"I'll not leave much of her beauty to be seen, if she comes in sight; and now, John," said Mrs. B., turning to her husband, "you need not think you are going to learn her to treat me in this way; just see how saucy she was this morning. She shall learn her place."

Mr. Bellmont raised his calm, determined eye full upon her, and said, in a decisive manner: "You shall not strike, or scald, or skin her, as you call it, if she comes back again. Remember!" and he brought his hand down upon the table. "I have searched an hour for her now, and she is not to be found on the premises. Do *you* know where she is? Is she *your* prisoner?"

"No! I have just told you I did not know where she was. Nab has her hid somewhere, I suppose. Oh, dear! I did not think it would come to this; that my own husband would treat me so." Then came fast flowing tears, which no one but Mary seemed to notice. Jane crept into Aunt Abby's room; Mr. Bellmont and James went out of doors, and Mary remained to condole with her parent.

"Do you know where Frado is?" asked Jane of her aunt.

"No," she replied. "I have hunted everywhere. She has left her first hiding-place. I cannot think what has become of her. There comes Jack and Fido; perhaps he knows;" and she walked to a window near, where James and his father were conversing together.

The two brothers exchanged a hearty greeting, and then Mr. Bellmont told Jack to eat his supper; afterward he wished to send him away. He immediately went in. Accustomed to all the phases of indoor storms, from a whine to thunder and lightning, he saw at a glance marks of disturbance. He had been absent through the day, with the hired men.

"What's the fuss?" asked he, rushing into Aunt Abby's.

"Eat your supper," said Jane; "go home, Jack."

Back again through the dining-room, and out to his father.

"What's the fuss?" again inquired he of his father.

"Eat your supper, Jack, and see if you can find Frado. She's not been seen since morning, and then she was kicked out of the house."

"I shan't eat my supper till I find her," said Jack, indignantly. "Come, James, and see the little creature mother treats so."

They started, calling, searching, coaxing, all their way along. No Frado. They returned to the house to consult. James and Jack declared they would not sleep till she was found.

Mrs. Bellmont attempted to dissuade them from the search. "It was a shame a little *nigger* should make so much trouble."

Just then Fido came running up, and Jack exclaimed, "Fido knows where she is, I'll bet."

"So I believe," said his father; "but we shall not be wiser unless we can outwit him. He will not do what his mistress forbids him."

"I know how to fix him," said Jack. Taking a plate from the table, which was still waiting, he called, "Fido! Fido! Frado wants some supper. Come!" Jack started, the dog followed, and soon capered on before, far, far into the fields, over walls and through fences, into a piece of swampy land. Jack followed close, and soon appeared to James, who was quite in the rear, coaxing and forcing Frado along with him.

A frail child, driven from shelter by the cruelty of his mother, was an object of interest to James. They persuaded her to go home with them, warmed her by the kitchen fire, gave her a good supper, and took her with them into the sitting-room.

"Take that nigger out of my sight," was Mrs. Bellmont's command, before they could be seated.

James led her into Aunt Abby's, where he knew they were welcome. They chatted awhile until Frado seemed cheerful; then James led her to her room, and waited until she retired.

"Are you glad I've come home?" asked James.

"Yes; if you won't let me be whipped tomorrow."

"You won't be whipped. You must try to be a good girl," counselled James.

"If I do, I get whipped;" sobbed the child. "They won't believe what I say. Oh, I wish I had my mother back; then I should not be kicked and whipped so. Who made me so?"

"God;" answered James.

"Did God make you?"

"Yes."

"Who made Aunt Abby?"

"God."

"Who made your mother?"

"God."

"Did the same God that made her make me?"

"Yes."

"Well, then, I don't like him."

"Why not?"

"Because he made her white, and me black. Why didn't he make us *both* white?"

"I don't know; try to go to sleep, and you will feel better in the morning," was all the reply he could make to her knotty queries. It was a long time before she fell asleep; and a number of days before James felt in a mood to visit and entertain old associates and friends.

Chapter X

Perplexities—Another Death

NEATH THE BILLOWS OF THE OCEAN,
HIDDEN TREASURES WAIT THE HAND,
THAT AGAIN TO LIGHT SHALL RAISE THEM
WITH THE DIVER'S MAGIC WAND.

G.W. COOK

The family, gathered by James' decease, returned to their homes. Susan and Charles returned to Baltimore. Letters were received from the absent, expressing their sympathy and grief. The father bowed like a "bruised reed," under the loss of his beloved son. He felt desirous to die the death of the righteous; also, conscious that he was unprepared, he resolved to start on the narrow way, and some time solicit entrance through the gate which leads to the celestial city. He acknowledged his too ready acquiescence with Mrs. B., in permitting Frado to be deprived of her only religious privileges for weeks together. He accordingly asked his sister to take her to meeting once more, which she was ready at once to do.

The first opportunity they once more attended meeting together. The minister conversed faithfully with every person present. He was surprised to find the little colored girl so solicitous, and kindly directed her to the flowing fountain where she might wash and be clean. He inquired of the origin of her anxiety, of her progress up to this time, and endeavored to make Christ, instead of James, the attraction of Heaven. He invited her to come to his house, to speak freely her mind to him, to pray much, to read her Bible often.

The neighbors, who were at meeting,—among them Mrs. Reed,—discussed the opinions Mrs. Bellmont would express on the subject. Mrs. Reed called and informed Mrs. B. that her colored girl "related her experience the other night at the meeting."

"What experience?" asked she, quickly, as if she expected to hear the number of times she had whipped Frado, and the number of lashes set forth in plain Arabic numbers.

"Why, you know she is serious, don't you? She told the minister about it."

Mrs. B. made no reply, but changed the subject adroitly. Next morning she told Frado she "should not go out of the house for one while, except on errands; and if she did not stop trying to be religious, she would whip her to death."

Frado pondered; her mistress was a professor of religion; was *she* going to heaven? then she did not wish to go. If she should be near James, even, she could not be happy with those fiery eyes watching her ascending path. She resolved to give over all thought of the future world, and strove daily to put her anxiety far from her.

Mr. Bellmont found himself unable to do what James or Jack could accomplish for her. He talked with her seriously, told her he had seen her many times punished undeservedly; he did not wish to have her saucy or disrespectful, but when she was *sure* she did not deserve a whipping, to avoid it if she could. "You are looking sick," he added, "you cannot endure beating as you once could."

It was not long before an opportunity offered of profiting by his advice. She was sent for wood, and not returning as soon as Mrs. B. calculated, she followed her, and snatching from the pile a stick, raised it over her.

"Stop!" shouted Frado, "strike me, and I'll never work a mite more for you;" and throwing down what she had gathered, stood like one who feels the stirring of free and independent thoughts.

By this unexpected demonstration, her mistress, in amazement, dropped her weapon, desisting from her purpose of chastisement. Frado walked towards the house, her mistress following with the wood she herself was sent after. She did not know, before, that she had a power to ward off assaults. Her triumph in seeing her enter the door with *her* burden, repaid her for much of her former suffering.

It was characteristic of Mrs. B. never to rise in her majesty, unless she was sure she should be victorious.

This affair never met with an "after clap," like many others.

Thus passed a year. The usual amount of scolding, but fewer whippings. Mrs. B. longed once more for Mary's return, who had been absent over a year; and she wrote imperatively for her to come quickly to her. A letter came in reply, announcing that she would comply as soon as she was sufficiently recovered from an illness which detained her.

No serious apprehensions were cherished by either parent, who constantly looked for notice of her arrival, by mail. Another letter brought tidings that Mary was seriously ill; her mother's presence was solicited.

She started without delay. Before she reached her destination, a letter came to the parents announcing her death.

No sooner was the astounding news received, than Frado rushed into Aunt Abby's, exclaiming:—

"She's dead, Aunt Abby!"

"Who?" she asked, terrified by the unprefaced announcement.

"Mary; they've just had a letter."

As Mrs. B. was away, the brother and sister could freely sympathize, and she sought him in this fresh sorrow, to communicate such solace as she could, and to learn particulars of Mary's untimely death, and assist him in his journey thither.

It seemed a thanksgiving to Frado. Every hour or two she would pop in into Aunt Abby's room with some strange query:

"She got into the *river* again, Aunt Abby, did n't she; the Jordan is a big one to tumble into, any how. S'posen she goes to hell, she'll be as black as I am. Would n't mistress be mad to see her a nigger!" and others of a similar stamp, not at all acceptable to the pious, sympathetic dame; but she could not evade them.

The family returned from their sorrowful journey, leaving the dead behind. Nig looked for a change in her tyrant; what could subdue her, if the loss of her idol could not?

Never was Mrs. B. known to shed tears so profusely, as when she reiterated to one and another the sad particulars of her darling's sickness and death. There was, indeed, a season of quiet grief; it was the lull of the fiery elements. A few weeks revived the former tempests, and so at variance did they seem with chastisement sanctified, that Frado felt them to be unbearable. She determined to flee. But where? Who would take her? Mrs. B. had always represented her ugly. Perhaps every one thought her so. Then no one would take her. She was black, no one would love her. She might have to return, and then she would be more in her mistress' power than ever.

She remembered her victory at the woodpile. She decided to remain to do as well as she could; to assert her rights when they were trampled on; to return once more to her meeting in the evening, which had been prohibited. She had learned how to conquer; she would not abuse the power while Mr. Bellmont was at home.

But had she not better run away? Where? She had never been from the place far enough to decide what course to take. She resolved to speak to Aunt Abby. *She* mapped the dangers of her course, her liability to fail in finding so good friends as John and herself. Frado's mind was busy for days and nights. She contemplated administering poison to her mistress, to rid herself and the house of so detestable a plague.

But she was restrained by an overruling Providence; and finally decided to stay contentedly through her period of service, which would expire when she was eighteen years of age.

In a few months Jane returned home with her family, to relieve her parents, upon whom years and affliction had left the marks of age. The years intervening since she had left her home, had, in some degree, softened the opposition to her unsanctioned marriage with George. The more Mrs. B. had about her, the more energetic seemed her directing capabilities, and her fault-finding propensities. Her own, she had full power over; and Jane after vain endeavors, became disgusted, weary, and perplexed, and decided that, though her mother might suffer, she could not endure her home. They followed Jack to the West. Thus vanished all hopes of sympathy or relief from this source to Frado. There seemed no one capable of enduring the oppressions of the house but her. She turned to the darkness of the future with the determination previously formed, to remain until she should be eighteen. Jane begged her to follow her so soon as she should be released; but so wearied out was she by her mistress, she felt disposed to flee from any and every one having her similitude of name or feature.

Chapter XII

The Winding Up of the Matter

NOTHING NEW UNDER THE SUN.

SOLOMON

A few years ago, within the compass of my narrative, there appeared often in some of our New England villages, professed fugitives from slavery, who recounted their personal experience in homely phrase, and awakened the indignation of non-slaveholders against brother Pro. Such a one appeared in the new home of Frado; and as people of color were rare there, was it strange she should attract her dark brother; that he should inquire her out; succeed in seeing her; feel a strange sensation in his heart towards her; that he should toy with her shining curls, feel proud to provoke her to smile and expose the ivory concealed by thin, ruby lips; that her sparkling eyes should fascinate; that he should propose; that they should marry? A short acquaintance was indeed an objection, but she saw him often, and thought she knew him. He never spoke of his enslavement to her when alone, but she felt that, like her own oppression, it was painful to disturb oftener than was needful.

He was a fine, straight negro, whose back showed no marks of the lash, erect as if it never crouched beneath a burden. There was a silent sympathy which Frado felt attracted her, and she opened her heart to the presence of love—that arbitrary and inexorable tyrant.

She removed to Singleton, her former residence, and there was married. Here were Frado's first feelings of trust and repose on human arm. She realized, for the first time, the relief of looking to another for comfortable support. Occasionally he would leave her to "lecture."

Those tours were prolonged often to weeks. Of course he had little spare money. Frado was again feeling her self-dependence, and was at last compelled to resort alone to that. Samuel was kind to her when at home, but made no provision for his absence, which was at last unprecedented.

He left her to her fate—embarked at sea, with the disclosure that he had never seen the South, and that his illiterate harangues were humbugs for hungry abolitionists. Once more alone! Yet not alone. A still newer companionship would soon force itself upon her. No one wanted her with such prospects. Herself was burden enough; who would have an additional one?

The horrors of her condition nearly prostrated her, and she was again thrown upon the public for sustenance. Then followed the birth of her child. The long absent Samuel unexpectedly returned, and rescued her from charity. Recovering from her expected illness, she once more commenced toil for herself and child, in a room obtained of a poor woman, but with better fortune. One so well known would not be wholly neglected. Kind friends watched her when Samuel was from home, prevented her from suffering, and when the cold weather pinched the warmly clad, a kind friend took them in, and thus preserved them. At last Samuel's business became very engrossing, and after long desertion, news reached his family that he had become a victim of yellow fever, in New Orleans.

So much toil as was necessary to sustain Frado, was more than she could endure. As soon as her babe could be nourished without his mother, she left him in charge of a Mrs. Capon, and procured an agency, hoping to recruit her health, and gain an easier livelihood for herself and child. This afforded her better maintenance than she had yet found. She passed into the various towns of the State she lived in, then into Massachusetts. Strange were some of her adventures. Watched by kidnappers, maltreated by professed abolitionists, who didn't want slaves at the South, nor niggers in their own houses, North. Faugh! to lodge one; to eat with one; to admit one through the front door; to sit next one; awful!

Traps slyly laid by the vicious to ensnare her, she resolutely avoided. In one of her tours, Providence favored her with a friend who, pitying her cheerless lot, kindly provided her with a valuable recipe, from which she might herself manufacture a useful article for her maintenance. This proved a more agreeable, and an easier way of sustenance.

And thus, to the present time, may you see her busily employed in preparing her merchandise; then sallying forth to encounter many frowns, but some kind friends and purchasers. Nothing turns her from her steadfast purpose of elevating herself. Reposing on God, she has thus far journeyed securely. Still an invalid, she asks your sympathy, gentle reader. Refuse not, because some part of her history is unknown, save by the Omniscient God. Enough has been unrolled to demand your sympathy and aid.

Do you ask the destiny of those connected with her *early* history? A few years only have elapsed since Mr. and Mrs. B. passed into another world. As age increased, Mrs. B. became more irritable, so that no one, even her own children, could remain with her; and she was accompanied by her husband to the home of Lewis, where, after an agony in death unspeakable, she passed away. Only a few months since, Aunt Abby entered heaven. Jack and his wife rest in heaven, disturbed by no intruders; and Susan and her child are yet with the living. Jane has silver locks in place of auburn tresses, but she has the early love of Henry still, and has never regretted her exchange of lovers. Frado has passed from their memories, as Joseph from the butler's, but she will never cease to track them till beyond mortal vision.

"Free at Las', Free at Las', T'ank Gawd A'mighty, Got Free at Las'!"

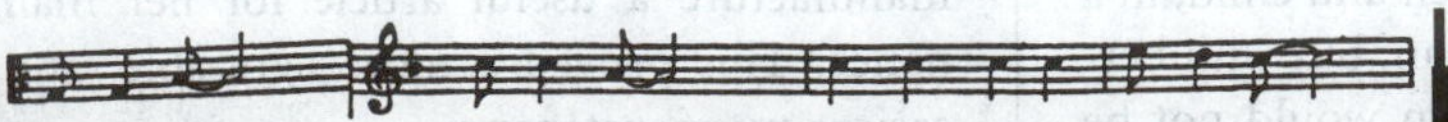

Call for the Ideal Freedom
During the exodus after the Civil War, thousands of poor blacks left the southern plantations in search of a better life.
***Portrait by Jacob Lawrence from* The Migration Series**

III

"No More Shall They in Bondage Toil"

African American History and Culture, 1865–1915

The Description of the Manner of Escape from Slavery and the Considerations of Whether the New Freedom Is the Ideal Freedom

Reconstruction and Post-Reconstruction

No more shall they in bondage toil,

Let my people go;

Let them come out with Egypt's spoil

Let my people go

(Chorus)

Go down, Moses, Way down in Egypt land,

Tell ole Pharaoh, Let my people go.

The literary efforts of African Americans in the post–Civil War era were influenced by a number of factors, not the least of which were educational and political, for literacy was the prerequisite to imaginative creation and politics was the key to access to literacy. Early nineteenth-century writers such as William Wells Brown and Frederick Douglass had used ingenious methods in learning how to read and write; their successors would have more access to formal education during and following Reconstruction. This period immediately after the Civil War had the positive impact of helping persons recently freed from slavery and the negative impact of embittering southern whites. By definition, *Reconstruction* meant re-ordering southern society; it was designed to equalize, as much as possible in those times, the discrepancies between African Americans and whites, to give formerly enslaved people access to American democracy. The federally imposed policy provided that African Americans should own land; have access to better housing, jobs, and education; and generally claim their places in American society. With federal agitation for the rights of blacks and the presence of troops on southern soil to enforce those rights, many African Americans succeeded in changing their status in positive ways.

As a literary person—in her autobiographical writings as well as in her speeches and newspaper articles—Frances Jackson Coppin is exemplary of the ideal. Born into slavery in Washington, D.C., in 1837, she graduated from Oberlin College in 1865. This accomplishment made her one of the most highly educated black women in America. Her movement from slavery to freedom to enlightenment exemplifies the general, but frequently less successful, struggles of those of her race from 1865 to 1915. After the Civil War, many African Americans were in transition. Those separated from their families during slavery were in the process of trying to reconstitute family units. Those who had remained on plantations during slavery and through the Civil War found themselves without space or status in the society; their loyalty had not earned them the forty acres and a mule or the safety that went along with such properties. Many of those in search of a better life left the South for the North.

It follows logically, therefore, that the literary efforts of African Americans during these trying times would reflect the social circumstances of their fellow blacks. The visibility of black officials made oratory one of the primary forms of creative expression during this period. Letter writing might properly be called a creative genre at this time because so many former slaves took pen in hand to try to find relatives who had been relocated to other states. Appeals and petitions could similarly be considered forms of literary expression. Church experiences led to spiritual narratives, accounts by men and women of their processes of conversion and their commitment to God's work. Those written by women would continue the development of the genre of the women's narrative, as would the novels and biographies of African American women during the era. Anna Julia Cooper would use a collection of essays and speeches to formulate black feminist thought. Reconstruction was also an era of reflection, when newly freed African Americans looked back on their experiences during slavery; thus, Frederick Douglass produced the second revision of his famous autobiography during the two decades following the Civil War, thereby further formalizing the autobiographical mode as one of the preferred forms of literary expression for African Americans. Themes underlying the literary efforts of this period focused on freedom and access to American democracy; spiritual development and temperance; the past as an informing part of the present; suffrage and women's rights; and the responsibility of educated persons, particularly mulattoes and writers, to African American communities.

By the second decade following the Civil War, African American fiction writers such as Charles W. Chesnutt would turn to incorporating folk forms into their literary creations. Whether following the pattern established earlier when William Wells Brown used songs, rhymes, and jokes in *Clotel* (1853), or the framed tales that inspired works by Mark Twain and Joel Chandler Harris in the 1870s and 1880s, African American writers consciously exploited the richness of black folk culture by drawing on folk characters, themes, and structures to inform their works. This would be the age of the literary trickster as well as the badman hero, of folk poetry as well as folk novels. The folk sermons would influence the poetry of Paul Laurence Dunbar and the works of James Weldon Johnson. Blues and ragtime music would inform turn-of-the-century novels just as folk beliefs informed Chesnutt's works in the 1880s; by 1912, James Weldon Johnson would be able to tout in *The Autobiography of an Ex-Colored Man* the extensive number of African American folk patterns and musical forms that had found their way into American popular culture and high art, his own novel being exemplary. That year also, W.E.B. Du Bois, inspired by the emergence of distinct black literary forms, would turn his attention to developing a theory of black art. The folk culture that may have been viewed as quaint and curious in the 1860s, therefore, would become, by the 1920s, one of the most inspirational sources for African American literary creation.

Call for the Ideal Freedom: The Folk Tradition

"Oh Freedom! Oh Freedom!"

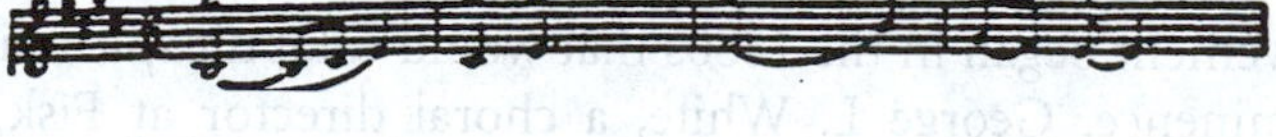

African American folk literature in the decades following the Civil War continued to be viable artistic expression in which to pass on values of significance to the group and in which to express attitudes about the conditions under which black people lived. In a society where formal education was still not a given for the majority of the newly freed population, word of mouth was the primary form of communication and the most natural manner in which to perpetuate stories, beliefs, and music. Whether in spirituals, in blues and other secular songs, or in the oral narrative traditions, African Americans transmitted the values that they considered crucial to their cultural survival. From the plaintive notes of religious songs heard by visitors to the Georgia Sea Islands in the early 1860s to the formal documentation of folk forms undertaken by the American Folklore Society after its founding in 1888 and the Hampton [Institute] Folklore Society in the 1890s, African American oral expression captured the imaginations of participants and observers alike.

Spirituals

The oral tradition began being documented in the mid 1860s. Scholars refer to one of the earliest such efforts as the Port Royal experiment. Northern liberals, including William Francis Allen, Charles Pickard Ware, and Lucy McKim Garrison, documented the folk culture they witnessed among the newly freed African Americans, especially the song tradition. The result of their study is *Slave Songs of the United States,* which appeared in 1867. The volume not only included words and music to the songs but commentary on the process of oral composition. It is an important document in the history of African American music as well as in the history of the recording of folkloristic materials. The work helped to bring recognition to the spirituals as one of African America's most beautiful and creative art forms.

As with the secular songs, the post–Civil War spirituals contained the old forms and idioms of the slave songs. In content, however, they reflected the postwar experiences of the singers and their people. According to African American music historian Eileen Southern, former slaves sang about their new sense of freedom, their new occupations and feelings of loneliness and rootlessness in the strange cities. Consequently, the metaphor of the railroad, which had growing importance in the lives of blacks, especially black men, began to appear in the songs. Such phrases as "git on board, little chillen," "no second class on board the train," and "we shall all reach the station" reflected that the former slaves were constantly on the move, largely because of their desire for a new way of life and progress. Although several of the spirituals appeared in print in works such as *Slave Songs of the United States,* they remained virtually unknown to white Americans.

A movement began in the 1880s that would catapult spirituals to worldwide prominence. George L. White, a choral director at Fisk University, came up with the idea of presenting spirituals before national and international audiences as a means of fundraising for the school. He formed the Fisk Jubilee Singers, who traveled throughout the United States and Europe during the 1880s. Singers carried on the song tradition he encouraged well into the twentieth century. They raised enough money on their first tour to build Jubilee Hall, which is now a historic site on the Nashville campus. Such success did not continue long without imitation. Soon there were choirs from various historically black colleges and universities presenting spirituals in concert form to audiences from whom they expected to raise money for their schools. While purists such as Zora Neale Hurston would complain that the spirituals sung by these groups, as well as by performers such as Paul Robeson in the 1920s, were not the *real* folk creation, these concertized versions, nonetheless, succeeded in bringing African American music to audiences who had never imagined its existence or its power. African American spirituals were further engraved on the American cultural legacy when James Weldon Johnson published *The Book of American Negro Spirituals* and *The Second Book of American Negro Spirituals* in the 1920s and when musicologists such as John Wesley Work completed scholarly research on them, as well as when musical composers such as Harry T. Burleigh, R. Nathaniel Dett, and Will Marion Cook began using them as inspiration.

Slave Songs of the United States included a few secular verses, but its primary focus was on religious songs. The African American secular song tradition, which would lead to the blues and jazz, was harder to document.

Rural Blues

Although the songs known as the blues probably flourished as early as the 1870s, that name did not come into common use until the turn of the century. Yet, the impetus for the blues was inherent in African American culture from the earliest days of African arrival on American soil. When we think of the simplest definition of the blues, "laughing to keep from crying," we can easily imagine the conditions under which enslaved African Americans found the strength to keep on under difficult, almost impossible circumstances. Feelings of exasperation, indeed *blueness*, that might have been tied to the master's request to a slave to pick three hundred pounds of cotton a day or to plow ten acres could easily have led to the songs we now know as the blues. Imagine the psychological misery of having one's loved ones—wives, husbands, children—sold away. The *condition* of the blues, then, anteceded the name. When musicians actually began composing the three-line stanzaic forms and the call and response patterns commonly characteristic of the blues and singing them in the minor notes that became their trademark, they wedded form to substance in a tradition that would reach classic development in the "race records" of the 1920s and the 1930s with singers such as Ma Rainey, Bessie Smith, and Billie Holiday:

> Trouble in mind, I'm blue,
> But I won't be blue always,
> For the sun will shine in my back door some-day.

Black musicologists such as Eileen Southern make it clear that the musical sources for blues songs were the field hollers that originated during slavery; the shouts and peddling songs of street vendors; the mournful songs of stevedores, roustabouts, and other levee workers; and the sorrow songs of the spirituals. The sorrow songs are a common feature of African American oral culture; that is, the intermingling of secular and sacred forms. It is not unusual for a composer of a spiritual to refer to secular events, such as picking cotton or hoeing corn, and it is equally not unusual for the singer of a blues song to call on the Lord or to mourn in the fashion of worshippers in a Sunday morning service. Blues musicians interviewed shortly after the turn of the twentieth century remembered growing up in the 1870s with songs that by 1900 were referred to as *the blues.* Some maintained that it was the primary song form to which they were exposed in their childhoods. Others, like Bunk Johnson, claimed that he "used to play nothing but the blues" in the 1880s. This strong, untutored type of music, termed the "rural" or "country blues" by music scholars, was popularized by the earliest blues singers, who sang the songs in the rural districts of the South as well as in the streets of New Orleans and Memphis. The blues tradition, therefore, was well established in black communities before it reached the point of commercial recording.

Ragtime

As with the blues, little is known about the origins of ragtime. Some black musicologists place its roots during slavery when enslaved persons who demonstrated musical talents were summoned to their masters' houses to provide entertainment on the drawing-room pianos. Most black music scholars believe, however, that the music originated sometime during the early postwar era when ex-slaves began to obtain access to the piano. Characterized by a lightly syncopated melody, this predominately piano music represents the first instrumental music of African Americans in which instruments were not used merely as accompaniment.

The earliest ragtime pianists cited were anonymous drifters of the 1860s and 1870s who played in black bars, saloons, and honky-tonk joints throughout the South for meager tips and wages. Soon their ragtime, often termed then as "coon songs," became the music that accompanied the hottest dance craze of the 1890s, called the cake walk. By the turn of the century, the popularity of the music peaked with the innovative compositions of Scott Joplin, the "King of Ragtime." By blending African American and European musical forms, Joplin created "classic ragtime," such pieces as "Maple Leaf Rag" (1899), "Frog Legs Rag" (1911), and "Climax Rag" (1914). With Joplin came other composers and musicians such as James Sylvester Scott, Thomas Million Turpin, Blind (John William) Boone, James "Eubie" Blake, and the now famous jazzman, Ferdinand Joseph "Jelly Roll" Morton.

A precursor of jazz, classic ragtime influenced the works of the writer and music composer, James Weldon Johnson.

Preacher Tales and Other Folktales

As has been previously mentioned, the narratives most commonly characteristic of the African American *documented* oral tradition in the nineteenth century centered on animal tales. It is reasonable to speculate that other tale types probably existed, but a pattern of collecting was not set until Joel Chandler Harris published *Uncle Remus: His Songs and His Sayings* in 1880. Harris, a newspaperman from Georgia, had been struck by these tales during his youthful interaction with the African Americans near his neighborhood. He so loved the tales they told that he made a career out of publishing them. While Harris succeeded in documenting the tradition, he also succeeded in creating an archetypal pattern for the interaction of audiences with African American narrative tradition. The expectation soon emerged that the natural exchange of cultural forms was for a congenial old black man, Uncle Remus in Harris's many volumes, to share the tales of this folk culture with a willing white audience, a little boy in Harris's volumes.

The conjuring aspect of the folk culture has also influenced the literary tradition. When Charles W. Chesnutt wanted to ensure that his white reading audience would peruse his short stories, he titled his first collection *The Conjure Woman* (1899). The volume draws on the pattern of framing that Joel Chandler Harris had used in *Uncle Remus: His Songs and His Sayings* in that it has an elderly black man, Uncle Julius, telling tales to a white audience—in this case, a white man and his wife who have relocated from Ohio to North Carolina. Conjuring, however, provides the substance of the tales. Even the plantation master gets into the act by hiring the local conjure woman, Aun Peggy, to cast a spell on his vineyard so none of the slaves will be able to eat his prized grapes.

Another cycle of tales believed to have been told during slavery but not documented until decades after the Civil War are the preacher tales. According to Langston Hughes and Arna Bontemps in *The Book of Negro Folklore,* the tale type evolved from a combination of the anecdotes used by eighteenth-century Baptist and Methodist preachers teaching Protestant religion to enslaved people and the medieval European religious tale tradition, the exempla. The preacher tales took root in the South and became a vital part of the southern black folk heritage. These tales included both the stories about the black preacher when not in the pulpit and those told by him in the pulpit. Although often humorous at the expense of the minister, the preacher tales provided African Americans the comic relief so many of them needed in their tragic lives. While many of them are stories of frequent exaggerations, known in the black folk tradition as "lies," some are based on actual experiences of preachers. Whether the tales are based on reality or not, their primary purpose is clear: to entertain.

Badmen, Conjuring, and Prison Songs

An area in which song tradition combined with narrative is that of folk heroic creation. Tricksters were not the only heroic figures that captured the African American folk imagination. Tales about other figures in effect created a badman heroic tradition, one in which the powers of the badman hero sometimes centered on extranatural or conjuring traditions. One such figure was Bras Coupe, who lived in Louisiana in the 1830s; the pattern of narratives surrounding him continued with other figures after the Civil War. On the soil that gave rise to Marie Laveau, and that was indeed the point of embarkation for hoodoo in America, it is not surprising that a man who defied the authority of white masters and became a badman hero would be reputed to have powers of conjuration. Bras Coupe, a native African, was sold to General William de Buys, a prominent slave owner in New Orleans. A favorite with his master, Coupe nevertheless ran away several times; after losing an arm in one such chase, he took to the Louisiana swamps, where he formed a maroon colony. Over the next three years, he raided plantations and murdered whites in the area and managed to escape all attempts to capture him. His seeming invincibility led enslaved people to suspect that he had supernatural powers. Tales circulated that he could not be killed, that bullets bounced off his chest, and that white patrols sent to capture him were lost in the swamps. Although he was eventually captured and killed, the legends perpetuated about his exploits show the vibrancy of the African American oral tradition and the combination of badman and conjuring ingredients.

Another legendary badman was Morris Slater, commonly known as Railroad Bill. He was reputed to have killed a white policeman in rural Alabama in 1893. Sympathy generally aligns with Slater because apparently the only thing he did wrong was to refuse to give up his firearm, an accessory not unusual to most folks in the area. After killing the officer, Slater hopped on a train (hence, his nickname) and spent the next three years robbing trains and supplying poor blacks along the tracks with the goods he appropriated. His ability to elude capture encouraged tales that he was one of the most powerful of conjure men, a shapeshifter who could change his form at will.

This badman/conjurer added the third dimension to this combination of folk forms; his legends were captured in song:

Standin' on corner didn't mean no harm,
Policeman grab me by my arm,
Wuz lookin' fer Railroad Bill.
Railroad Bill was mightly sport
Shot all the buttons off high Sheriff coat
Den holler, "Right on desparado Bill."

Songs about such real-life badmen would have their parallels in the mid–twentieth century in the toasts about badmen such as Stagolee, as well as in the legendary exploits of figures such as John Henry.

The logical end for legendary and historical figures of such stature was either prison or death, and sometimes both. But prison was an end that Stagolee could assert derisively meant almost nothing to him; when a judge sends him to prison for ninety-nine years, he cryptically comments that he has a brother in Sing-Sing doing 299 years. For historical figures, however, prison presented a more formidable obstacle. African American men who found themselves there, justifiably or not, participated in prison culture by composing songs about the Stagolees of the world as well as about their own plights. Songs such as "Go Down, O Hannah" document the blaze of the sun on the backs of men sentenced to hard labor. Songs of separation from loved ones stressed infidelity and the general hardship of prison life. The song tradition that eased the working lives of prisoners would be documented in a number of ways, but especially in the 1960s by Bruce Jackson in the film *Afro-American Worksongs in a Texas Prison.* Men so imprisoned sang not only of heroes and lost love, but of the desire to return home, of the conditions under which they had to work, and of how they were treated. They had no extranatural powers to sustain them, but they did have the energizing heritage of the African American folk tradition.

The Folk Sermon

In addition to the folk ballads, rural blues, and spirituals, the folk sermon was first documented in the post–Civil War era. Stemming from the traditions of the African griot and that of the religion of the black slave (in particular the heritage of the itinerant preacher), the folk sermon flourished throughout slavery and continues to the present. Evolving from the voodoo priest on plantations during the early days of slavery, the preacher became one of the most powerful people in the black community and one of the most eloquent orators in the country. Most of the itinerant preachers were men. However, a few African American women, including Jarena Lee and Amanda Berry Smith, joined their ranks. Known for their electrifying, forceful speech, these preachers held audiences virtually spellbound by infusing their vernacular with colorful metaphors and graphic imagery, black sayings, rhythmic and repetitious phrases, biblical allusions, and moral platitudes.

Two popular folk sermons were documented during the postwar period. The first, "De Sun Do Move" (c. 1882) by Reverend John Jasper, who preached the sermon more than 250 times, was transcribed by William E. Hatcher in his biography of Jasper. The second work, "Dry Bones," which originated in the 1890s, is an anonymous version of the chant portion of an oral sermon on the text of Ezekiel 37:1–14, which was legendary among the black rural communities. The power and beauty of such works influenced the transcribed-sermonic verse of Paul Laurence Dunbar and James Weldon Johnson. While Dunbar is the originator of the poetic form, the poetic sermon does not become refined until Johnson's publication of *God's Trombones* during the 1920s.

Notwithstanding, the folk tradition flourished during the Reconstruction and post-Reconstruction eras. Other literary genres developed more slowly, however, because of the oppressive, racially tense social climate in which African Americans were systematically excluded from the American mainstream.

Response: Northern and Black Self-Help vs. Southern Resentment

"It's a Mighty Rocky Road"

The struggle to find a voice and shape a literature was tied to the larger struggle of African Americans to secure the freedom that was theirs only in name. African American activists had to be ever vigilant in an environment where forces were constantly at work to return them to slavery. Freedom and literature, therefore, went hand in hand. The eloquence of a Douglass speech, with its striking turns of phrases, attention-getting images, and wonderful parallel and periodic constructions not only influenced the social and political status of black Americans, but could be collected by Dorothy Porter Wesley and Philip Foner in the twentieth century as exceptional early examples of African American writing. Frances Watkins Harper's poetry, as it continued to go through several editions between 1854 and 1871, again had the dual purpose of advocating freedom and charting the course for literary endeavors. Writers had to be constantly on guard, for the climate was one in which hostility toward African Americans was rampant; this was especially true in the South.

Having lost the Civil War, southerners felt especially put upon by a group of outsiders who not only freed the slaves but seized or destroyed much of their property and took over the management of those former slaves. For example, on April 9, 1866, over President Andrew Johnson's veto, Congress passed the Civil Rights bill, designed to guarantee Civil Rights to African Americans. That measure enraged white southerners. It did not matter that William Wells Brown published *The Negro in the American Rebellion: His Heroism and His Fidelity* in 1867, in which he documented an African American claim to American citizenry; Southerners were still enraged. The Reconstruction Act of 1867 enfranchised most African Americans and gave the ballot to blacks as well as to whites who had remained loyal to the Union. This northern policy created an environment in which African Americans could be elected to political office; it led to the fear of and speculation about the "nigger domination" that would inspire so many decades of literary expression. Not only did Chesnutt explore this topic in his novel *The Marrow of Tradition* (1901), but liberal white writers such as Judge Albion Tourgée were also drawn to sympathize with African Americans, whose freedoms were being eroded constantly. In the words of the black spiritual, it was indeed "a mighty rocky road" for blacks. For example, southerners would shortly reenact the Black Codes in an effort to force blacks to work and partly in reaction to the northern imposition of Radical Reconstruction (the period during which the federal government actively intervened in the affairs of southern states and when Union troops were present in the South). Although the Fourteenth Amendment to the U.S. Constitution, adopted in 1868, granted African Americans citizenship, the reality of that condition was not soon forthcoming. Large numbers of black people, therefore, were not only physically dislocated, but they were anxious to determine what their roles in the new society would be and what allies they would have as they assumed those roles.

While prominent figures such as Sojourner Truth, Frances Harper, and Frederick Douglass were making speeches and writing on racial and gender rights, the majority of African Americans were getting their primary social assistance from the Freedmen's Bureau, which was officially established as the Bureau of Refugees, Freedmen, and Abandoned Lands in March of 1865, under the direction of General O.O. Howard. This group organized schools, provided medical services, negotiated contracts between newly freed blacks and their employers, leased and sold abandoned lands to blacks, relocated displaced persons, and helped blacks find their way through the red tape necessary for them to claim a space in society. Despite the climate of northern and southern hostility in which it operated, the Bureau relieved suffering among blacks as well as whites. By 1867, when Sojourner Truth split with Douglass and Harper over support for the Fifteenth Amendment (they supported it; she didn't), the Freedmen's Bureau managed forty-six hospitals and had treated almost one half million cases of illness. By 1869, the Freedmen's Bureau had issued more than twenty-million rations, approximately three-fourths to black Americans and one-fourth to white Americans.

Creating an audience for African American literature meant establishing institutions of higher learning and nurturing the clientele for such literary endeavors. African Americans such as Douglass had started schools in the 1830s, as Paul Laurence Dunbar would in the 1890s, but such efforts in the 1860s were also the business of the Freedmen's Bureau. The Bureau set up colleges as well as primary, secondary, and industrial schools. Howard University, Hampton Institute (now University), St. Augustine's College, Atlanta University, Fisk University, Storer College, and Biddle Memorial Institute (now Johnson C. Smith University) were all founded during this period and all received aid from the Freedmen's Bureau; it was in these schools that emerging black writers would find a growing audience. The schools drew white teachers from the North so successfully that by 1869 almost ten thousand such persons were teaching in the freedmen's schools in the South; a few white southerners and a few blacks were also teachers. Gradually, as more blacks became teachers, they would take over primary responsibility for the schools. Frances Jackson Coppin, deemed "one of the most influential black educators and community leaders of the late nineteenth century," became principal of the Female Department of the prestigious Institute for Colored Youth in Philadelphia in 1869.

Spiritual narratives, in particular the women's narratives that had been popularized by Jarena Lee in the 1840s, would be continued in the post–Civil War era in *A Brand Plucked from the Fire* (1879; 1886), the autobiographical sketch of Julia A.J. Foote, and in the early twentieth century in *Twenty Year's Experience of a Missionary* (1907), the narrative of Virginia W. Broughton. Their church-centered literary efforts reflect the growth of African American churches in spiritual, social, and political influence on the lives of black Americans. These churches were another source of comfort and support to blacks during Reconstruction. As blacks withdrew from white churches after emancipation, there was a rapid expansion of independent black churches. The Colored Primitive Baptists in America were established in 1865. The Colored Cumberland Presbyterian Church was organized in 1869. The Colored Methodist Episcopal Church had organized five conferences by 1870. Other older established churches, such as the African Methodist Episcopal Church (founded in 1816) and the Missionary Baptists, experienced new growth during this period; by 1866, the African Methodist Episcopal Church had tripled its membership from the 1856 count, and the Baptists had almost quadrupled theirs by 1870. Churches were a way for blacks to develop leadership skills, extend self-help through various benevolent activities, and provide the social security of an organization that they themselves controlled. Church-sponsored benevolent societies, such as the United Daughters of Ham, the Sisters of Zion, and the Daughters of Zion, attended the sick and the poor and consoled the bereaved, in addition to carrying out the regular missionary and educational work of their churches.

The leadership training in churches was manifested socially in the number of blacks who were appointed or elected to public offices. At the 1868 state constitutional convention in South Carolina, which had forty-five white and seventy-eight black delegates, Robert Brown Elliott emerged as a forceful, dynamic leader. He was elected to the state House of Representatives and was prominent in the predominately black General Assembly. After serving from July 1868 to October 1870, he was elected to the Forty-second United States Congress. He is particularly noted for two speeches he delivered there, the first in 1871 and the second in 1874. In the first, delivered April 1,

1871, he supported a bill to enforce the Fourteenth Amendment, which was being undermined by the racist and cruel actions of the Ku Klux Klan and similar white supremacist groups. In the second, delivered January 6, 1874, he supported H.R. No. 796, the Civil Rights bill that would guarantee *all* citizens equal protection under the law; it was designed "to prevent and forbid inequality and discrimination on account of race, color, or previous condition of servitude." In making his case, Elliott documented black participation in the country's crucial crises, such as the American Revolution, and directly challenged senators from Kentucky and Georgia who opposed the bill.

Not only did South Carolina produce an Elliott, but it managed to elect two black lieutenant-governors, Alonzo J. Ransier in 1870 and Richard H. Gleaves in 1872. An African American educated at the University of Glasgow as well as in London, Francis L. Cardozo was secretary of state (1868–1872) and treasurer (1872–1876) of South Carolina. Louisiana had one hundred twenty-seven black legislators between 1868 and 1896. African Americans were in both houses of the Alabama legislature, but they did not have a significant impact upon policy or history. The Georgia legislature declared its black members ineligible for participation in September of 1868, and they did not regain their seats until a state supreme court overruled the legislature a year later. Florida and Virginia also had black legislators during this period, as did Tennessee, Arkansas, Texas, and Mississippi. Twenty African Americans served as representatives to Congress, the first three of whom made their appearance in the Forty-first Congress in 1869. Two black senators elected to Congress, Hiram R. Revels and Blanche K. Bruce (possible relative of Harlem Renaissance writer Richard Bruce Nugent), were both from Mississippi. Bruce, like Elliott, became an excellent orator. In a speech delivered to the United States Senate on March 3, 1876, he advocated the seating of Pinckney Benton Stewart Pinchback as the senator from Louisiana, despite claims of irregularities surrounding Pinchback's election and the general disarray of Louisiana politics. In another speech to the Senate on March 31, 1876, Bruce commented on a recent Mississippi election in which African American voters were threatened and kept away from the polls through violent means.

To curb the possibility of blacks gaining political power, a number of informal and formal repressive measures were instituted. The 1860s saw the formation of a number of secret societies of whites intent on regaining absolute control of blacks and driving their sympathizers from power. Aggressively advocating "White Supremacy," these groups included the Knights of the White Camelia; the Constitutional Union Guards; the Pale Faces; the White Brotherhood; the Council of Safety; and, perhaps the most infamous, the Knights of the Ku Klux Klan (founded in Tennessee in 1865). The young white men in the Ku Klux Klan determined that it was their specially chosen fate to protect southern ideals and southern white womanhood by eliminating what they viewed as potential threats to those ideals, particularly when those imagined threats came in the form of black men; the presumed attraction of black men for white women was a common theme in the literature as well as in the popular media. Congress tried without success to suppress the Klan and similar groups with laws passed in 1870 and 1871, the same year that Frances Harper addressed the issue of racism in the Reconstruction era in her poem, "An Appeal to the American People," in *Poems on Miscellaneous Subjects,* enlarged and published for the third time since 1854; a second of her volumes, *Poems,* also appeared in 1871. Two years later, Pinckney Benton Stewart Pinchback, the grandfather of Harlem Renaissance writer Jean Toomer, would serve forty-three days as acting governor of Louisiana.

The year 1870 was an auspicious one for additional reasons. Martin R. Delany published *University Pamphlets: A Series of Four Tracts on National Polity,* which again reflected the tie between literature and politics. The Fifteenth Amendment to the U.S. Constitution was also adopted in 1870; it guaranteed the right not to be discriminated against by the states in voting on account of race, color, or previous condition of servitude. Frederick Douglass and other African Americans had worked vigorously to get the amendment passed, including having an audience with President Andrew Johnson. In 1864, at the National Convention of Colored Men held in Syracuse, New York, at which Douglass was a key player, a priority item on the agenda was the right to vote without legal, social, or personal obstacle. (New York had a law requiring African American men to own $250 worth of real estate before they could vote.) Douglass believed his dream of black suffrage would be realized with the passing of the amendment. The celebration of its passing would shortly be minimized, however, for the amendment did not guarantee the right to vote; therefore, white southerners would soon find loopholes to return to White Supremacy. Through legal and illegal methods, African Americans were discouraged from attempting to vote. Legal efforts to figuratively re-enslave blacks were put in place bit by bit, beginning with the separation of the races.

Jim Crow laws were institutionalized in the 1870s. African Americans had controlled, carefully prescribed access to American democracy. There was a prevailing notion of "place," psychological and geographical, that they were taught was theirs. Laws regulating public transportation and facilities prevented African Americans and whites from sharing the same space on trains, in depots, or on wharves. Although a Civil Rights Act was passed in 1875, it could not long stay the tide of southern hostility toward newly freed blacks. Racial tension was high, and a particularly bloody racial clash occurred in Hamburg, South Carolina, on July 4, 1876, when, during an African American militia parade, several blacks were arrested for blocking traffic and refused to apologize for the "offense." Ensuing years would bring separation of blacks and whites in hotels, barber shops, restaurants, and theaters. With the withdrawal of federal troops from the South by 1877, southerners felt they no longer had any obstacles in handling "the Negro problem." When, in 1883, the Supreme Court rescinded the Civil Rights Act of 1875, African Americans found themselves even more at the mercy of the whims of whites. By 1885, schools were separated by law in most southern states.

Response: Fighting Back with the Law and the Pen

"Singin' Wid a Sword in Ma Han'"

History combined with imagination to make attention to such separation one of the major preoccupations of activists and writers. A common theme in the literature is that of a group of black passengers on a train who must suffer the stings of cinders and soot from the engine because their "place" for travel is the first car behind the engine. Ida B. Wells-Barnett presented one of the earliest historical challenges to such laws in 1884 by refusing to move from a cleaner train car when the white conductor requested that she do so; the conductor and two other white men lifted her bodily and removed her from the car, as other cheering whites looked on. She got put off at the next station and filed a suit against the railroad. The incident was a decisive one in shaping her reformist politics. Charles W. Chesnutt, in turn, presented one of the earliest literary accounts of such restrictions. In his *The Marrow of Tradition* (1901), a black doctor and his wife, along with other black passengers, must suffer the acute inconvenience of train service the providers of which are insensitive to them as human beings. Based on a riot in Wilmington, North Carolina, in 1898, during which numerous blacks were killed, the novel further illustrated black writers' preoccupation with fundamental issues of democracy, with social access, and with Civil Rights.

The decade of the 1880s began with several significant historical and literary events. Mary Ann Shadd Cary marked the beginning of the era by organizing in 1880 the Colored Women's Progressive Association, the primary goal of which was to promote equal rights for women and women's suffrage. The following year, when Douglass delivered an oration on John Brown at the fourteenth anniversary of Storer College, Booker T. Washington founded Tuskegee Institute, which institutionalized vocational and industrial education as the acceptable path for blacks to follow. Born the son of slaves in Franklin County, Virginia, Washington had walked to Hampton Institute to get an education. There he was inspired by General Samuel Chapman Armstrong's model of self-help and manual labor. Washington later founded Tuskegee with the intention of preparing young black people to become farmers and skilled servants to whites. He had little tolerance for study of Greek or Latin and little inclination to encourage voting rights in a people he thought must first learn how to bathe regularly and brush their teeth with something other than salt. Yet, some blacks did discover higher pursuits.

On the literary side, William Wells Brown published *My Southern Home: Or, The South and Its People* and Pauline Elizabeth Hopkins produced a play, *Slaves' Escape: or the Underground Railroad.* Of far greater immediate significance, however, in 1880, Joel Chandler Harris published *Uncle Remus: His Songs and Sayings* and introduced a character and a way of perceiving blacks that would later influence literary expression by African Americans. Other black literary achievement during the decade included the publication of Albery Allson Whitman's long poem, *The Rape of Florida,* in 1884, which was reissued as *Twasinta's Seminoles* in 1885 and 1890. Whitman had published his first book-length poem, *Not a Man, and Yet a Man,* in 1877. Chesnutt published "The Goophered Grapevine" in the *Atlantic Monthly* in August of 1887; it was the first of his many short stories to appear in that journal.

The 1890s witnessed the widespread flowering of African American literary talents. During the decade, African American women, for the first time since the pre–Civil War era, turned to the novel form. Amelia Johnson, Emma Dunham Kelley, and Frances Harper continued the tradition of the romance form initiated by Harriet Wilson in *Our Nig* (1859). Johnson published two novels, *Clarence and Corinne; or, God's Way* (1890) and *The Hazeley Family* (1894); Kelly wrote *Megda* (1891) and *Four Girls at Cottage City* (1898); and Harper, *Iola LeRoy; or, Shadows Uplifted* (1892), the most impressive work of the group. In the novel, Harper treated various social issues, including the consequences of slavery, interracial romantic liaisons, and the racial responsibilities of mulattoes. Equally important, she explored the devastating effects that negative black female stereotypes have on African American women. She also emphasized one of her major racial and feminist themes: the need for African American women to be educated and to participate fully in the intellectual affairs for the uplifting of the race.

In 1892 as well, Anna Julia Cooper articulated the same concern in her now celebrated collection of feminist speeches and essays, *A Voice from the South.* Throughout the work, Cooper convincingly argues that "the fundamental agency under God in the regeneration, the retraining of the race, as well as the groundwork and starting point of its progress upward, must be the *black woman.*" Because the future of the race depends on the development of both black women and black men, she contends, black women require and deserve a formal education. Anna Julia Cooper's eloquent call to black women for the moral development and social advancement of the human race is unrivaled in nineteenth-century American literature. It establishes her as one of the pioneers of the Africana womanist aesthetic.

While Cooper's *A Voice from the South* and Harper's *Iola LeRoy* marked 1892 as a milestone for African American women writers, it was also the year that the number of blacks lynched in the United States increased dramatically. As Wells-Barnett in *The Memphis Free Speech and Headlight* and T. Thomas Fortune in *The New York Age*, among others, worked to garner widespread protection for potential black victims, literary artists waged a battle with their pens to improve the condition of blacks in the United States. Harper was acutely sensitive to how the public could perceive her depictions of African Americans in *Iola LeRoy*. One slip of the pen could mean negative feedback for the group, but she was nonetheless committed to her chosen course of change through writing. That decision reflected the general tenet of writers during this period. All felt that they should work to improve the overall condition of African Americans. None felt that he or she could produce art simply for art's sake. They understood the importance of "singin' wid a sword" in their hands.

Harper's reputation as a poet, which had held sway from 1854, gave way to that of Paul Laurence Dunbar, who published *Oak and Ivy* in 1893, *Majors and Minors* in 1896, and *Lyrics of Lowly Life*, also in 1896. Although these volumes contained a mixture of poems written in standard English and in dialect, white critics such as William Dean Howells generally praised the dialect poems. His favorable review of *Lyrics of Lowly Life* may have catapulted Dunbar to national visibility, but it also stigmatized the poet. Dunbar was perceived as being locked into perpetuating the Plantation Tradition of grinning happy "darkies" who delighted in their servile condition. James David Corrothers, however, played into the tradition of popular dialect comedy that featured African Americans; his sketches in *The Black Cat Club* (1902) portray blacks as "bickering, superstitious, boisterous black buffoons." Turning his hand to the novel, Dunbar published *The Uncalled* in 1898, the first of several long fictional works.

Reassessment of Dunbar's work in the latter half of the twentieth century reveals that he was much more race oriented than previous evaluators allowed. While his presentations of African Americans in comfortable cabin settings, around warm fires, eating cornpone, or attending community dinners and dancing to banjos, might seem to perpetuate popular stereotypes, they, nonetheless, capture accurately many of the activities in which blacks engaged. Dunbar's depictions of African Americans cover a broad range, including love triangles, spelling bees, church affairs, singing, preaching, celebrating soldiers who fought in the Civil War, and many traditional lyric concerns. Critics generally agree that Dunbar was the best of all practitioners of dialect from this period and that he was a consummate poet whether in dialect or standard English. The more expansive evaluations of his works, aptly revisionist in their approach, have succeeded in giving Dunbar the less blemished reputation that he rightfully deserves.

Dunbar and James Weldon Johnson were two of the earliest writers and composers for the musical comedy tradition. Dunbar's *Clorindy, or the Origin of the Cakewalk* (1898) initiated a tradition that did not see its demise until well into the twentieth century. Johnson, together with his brother J. Rosamond and their partner Bob Cole, founded a vaudeville song-writing partnership and produced some of the most memorable musical numbers from the musical comedy era, including "Under the Bamboo Tree" and "Oh, Didn't He Ramble." Such entertainment was generally for segregated audiences and did not, in and of itself, go far to ease the tension between the races or to give African Americans greater access to the land of opportunity.

Folk and popular forms entered the literature of this period. Chesnutt, who advocated educational advancement for black people—as reflected in his creating characters with college and medical degrees—was nonetheless one of the first writers to appreciate the possibilities for literary development in the African American folk tradition. While Joel Chandler Harris had introduced the American reading public to Uncle Remus in 1880, that so-called folk character perpetuated a sense of a subservient place for black people. Chesnutt's introduction of Uncle Julius in the stories published in *The Conjure Woman* (1899) signaled a new direction for folkloristic possibilities: the folk character need not applaud the status quo; he could criticize slavery, comment on the greed of white masters, expose the brutality of the economic underpinnings of slavery, and trick his employers into supplementing his meagre income and community status. Dunbar occasionally featured preachers in his poems, as in "An Ante-bellum Sermon," and he consistently showed appreciation for African American singing, as in the poem, "When Malindy Sings." The spirit of competition that would define verbal contests of the toast and rap traditions of the twentieth century also found their way into Dunbar's early poetry. By 1899, therefore, a pattern of folk influence on African American creativity had been set that would inform the literature throughout the twentieth century.

It was also in 1899 that Sutton Griggs, following his own advocacy of self-reliance, personally published the first of his five novels. *Imperium in Imperio* provides a militant contrast to Chesnutt's works. Griggs's characters form their own political organization or nation, aggressively embrace the concept of black nationalism, threaten an open revolt against a repressive government, and generally mark an end to the dominant strand of servile black characters in African American literature. Griggs would continue his theme of blacks thinking and acting independently in *Overshadowed* (1901) and *Unfettered* (1902). He published *The Hindered Hand* (1905) and *Pointing the Way* (1908) in response to Thomas Dixon's virulent attacks on blacks in *The Leopard's Spots* (1902); both of Griggs's later novels argue against political repression and racial prejudice.

Political activity and racial-uplift projects, in addition to setbacks, continued in the 1890s as well. In 1893 African Americans were strikingly underrepresented at the World's Fair and Columbian Exposition held in Chicago. Activist women such as Hallie Quinn Brown, Frances Jackson Coppin, Fannie Barrier Williams, Sarah J. Early, Frances Harper, and Anna Julia Cooper addressed the World's Congress of Representative Women, which had gathered at the Exposition, on the question of keeping black women's issues a part of the larger national struggle for women's rights. The issue of racial exclusion from the Exposition was equally important. The Haitian pavilion, for which Frederick Douglass had been asked to serve as representative commissioner, became the center of controversy on which to focus racial concerns. The exclusion of African Americans led Wells-Barnett, Douglass, and others to publish *The Reason Why the Colored American Is Not in the World's Columbian Exposition* (1893); it also served as additional impetus to the formation of black women's clubs during this decade. Hallie Quinn Brown from Wilberforce, Ohio, felt that there should be a national black women's organization that could voice objection to and comment on such issues; she initiated activity that led to a federation of local clubs that would later be known as the National League. In another race and gender issue, in 1894, Susan B. Anthony requested that Frederick Douglass not attend a suffrage meeting in Atlanta, "as a matter of expediency"; Douglass had been an active supporter of women's suffrage for more than forty years. These events made it clear that African Americans would have to redouble their efforts to achieve racial and gender equality in America. One such effort occurred in 1895, when black women held the First Congress of Colored Women of the United States, at which Victoria Earle Matthews, who would later publish several short stories, addressed the gathering on the importance of race literature.

Response: Two Strategies for Progress—Du Bois vs. Washington

"... Black Train Is A-Comin'"

Perhaps the most dramatic political setback of the decade was Booker T. Washington's famous *Atlanta Exposition Speech* in 1895. It articulated well the differences between his approach to racial progress and that of W.E.B. Du Bois. Touting the separation of the races in all things social, Washington seemed to suggest that African Americans did not wish to improve their class and voting statuses, that they were content to be second-class citizens who would view serving whites as their lot in life. The next year, the Supreme Court seemed to have agreed with Washington's stance by upholding the "separate but equal" concept of education for blacks and whites as presented in *Plessy v. Ferguson.* Du Bois, however, showed his commitment to nationalistic concerns by publishing *The Suppression of the African Slave-Trade to the United States of America, 1638–1870* (1896), *The Conservation of Races* (1897), and his study of urban African Americans, *The Philadelphia Negro: A Social Study* (1899). He articulated the concept of the "Talented Tenth," those persons of education and training among African Americans who would become leaders of the group. In 1899, while he was on the faculty at Atlanta University, Du Bois organized a conference on "The Negro in Business." It was followed in 1900 by Washington's organization of the National Negro Business League, which boasted more than three hundred local branches by 1907.

Debate continues as to whether Du Bois or Washington was the "best" leader for black people during this period. Certainly, Washington should be appreciated for being a successful fundraiser for Tuskegee and for attempting to improve the deplorable and dangerous conditions in which blacks in the South had to exist. Being an astute and powerful southern politician who understood the psychology of the average white southerner, he compromised with the South, some scholars have argued, for the sake of the survival of black people—for entering them into the mainstream of the American work force from the bottom. But Du Bois was a visionary who could see a time beyond that when African Americans could be only farmers and servants. When Washington asked for economic security for his people, Du Bois responded "yes," but not at the high cost of the human rights and dignity of blacks. When Washington was silent on the question of lynching, Du Bois publicly decried it. When Washington downplayed the importance of voting, Du Bois shouted for "universal manhood rights." Both men were uncompromising in their agendas and both contributed significantly to African American intellectual, social, and literary history. The power of their divergent views continues to inform African American politics and literature.

Response: Women's Activism, Black Nationalism, and Setting the Mood for the Twentieth Century

"We Are Building on a Rock"

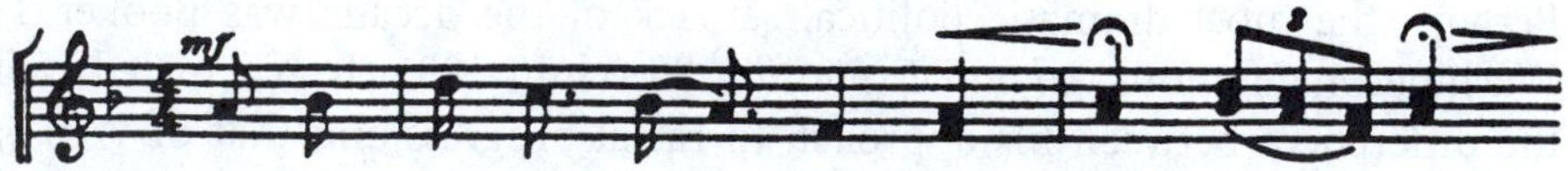

While W.E.B. Du Bois and Booker T. Washington are the usual activists who come to mind when we think of the 1890s, that decade might more accurately be called the African American Women's Era, for it was during this period that the organizational efforts of black women coalesced into groups that still exist today. Such women as Ida B. Wells-Barnett had certainly been successful in establishing local and regional women's clubs, but several black women, such as Anna Julia Cooper, Mary Church Terrell, and Wells-Barnett, who had worked in different parts of the country, decided it was time for them to come together under one collective organizational umbrella.

In 1896, black women formed the National Association of Colored Women, with Mary Church Terrell, who had graduated from Oberlin College in 1884, as their first president. The organization came about as a result of the merger of the National Federation of Afro-American Women and the National League of Colored Women, which were both dedicated to social uplift. The new organization focused its concern for blacks on education, temperance, health, and prison reform. It also advocated day nurseries for working mothers, orphanages, homes for the aged and the infirm, hospitals, cemeteries, night schools, and scholarship funds. Organized locally and regionally, these groups were designed to provide social support and cultural enrichment, including literary study, to African Americans in their communities. From reading groups to volunteering in Young Women's Christian Associations (YWCAs) to burial societies, these groups worked to assist blacks wherever they identified need. Some organizations, such as those founded by Ida B. Wells-Barnett in Chicago, also helped families make a smooth transition from rural to urban areas, and they nurtured young men who had been judged to be delinquent by the society. The amount of their activism and the foundations they laid were ones that Mary McCleod Bethune and Dorothy Height could follow in the twentieth century.

Issues such as the demand for justice, the fight against prevailing stereotypical notions of black female sexuality and morality, combined with disagreement over black women getting the vote, were of primary importance. The immediate impetuses to the national organizational decision, however, were the rise in lynchings and the snubbing of black women by the "Lady Managers" at the World's Columbian Exposition in Chicago in 1893. On the pretext that only national organizations of women could participate fully in the program, the "Lady Managers" therefore permitted only a couple of black women to speak before the group. While these reputedly "safe" black women, including Fannie Barrier Williams, did broach the topics of concern to black women, it was made clear to them that such issues were not the primary agenda for white women. Black women realized that they had to fight for themselves, sometimes against black men such as Booker T. Washington as well as against white women. Their decision to take in hand their own destinies set the course for a philosophy of self-help and improvement that still defines black women's organizations. The decade of the 1890s, therefore, was probably the single most important in the history of, as well as setting the future for, African American women's activism.

Nineteen hundred was the year James Weldon Johnson composed the lyrics to "Lift Every Voice and Sing," which would shortly become known as "the Negro National Anthem." The turn of the century also brought continued literary expression from African Americans in the novel form. In 1900, Pauline Hopkins published her best-known work, *Contending Forces,* with the *Colored Co-operative Publishing Company of Boston* and Dunbar published *The Love of Landry.* Of the two works, Hopkins's novel has more literary merit. Squarely in the tradition of the African American women's narrative, *Contending Forces* anticipates the contemporary novels of Toni Morrison and Alice Walker in its insistence on the empowerment of African American women who have suffered from sexual abuse. During the following year, Chesnutt published his best novel, *The Marrow of Tradition,* and Dunbar added *The Sport of the Gods* to his explorations in fiction in 1902.

Significant nonfiction written expressions during this decade included Washington's *Up From Slavery* (1900), which might accurately be called the culmination of the slave-narrative tradition and the institutionalization of the success story in black autobiography, and Du Bois's *The Souls of Black Folk: Essays and Sketches* (1903), in which he engaged subjects as wide-ranging as spirituals and his disagreements with Washington. In this classic, Du Bois brilliantly argues that the worldwide problem of the color line has stripped people of African descent in America of their basic human dignity, pride, and self-respect.

The year 1900 also found African Americans extending their interest in publishing. In May of that year, Hopkins began editing *The Colored American Magazine,* in which two of her novels (*Hagar's Daughter, A Story of Southern Caste Prejudice* and *Winona: A Tale of Negro Life in the South and Southwest*) were serialized and several of her short stories were published.

Although this period was not the strongest for development of serious African American drama—probably due to the prevalence of the minstrel and musical comedy modes—there were a few attempts. Alice Moore Dunbar Nelson completed four plays: *The Author's Evening at Home* (*Smart Set,* 1900); *Love's Disguise* (1916), *Mine Eyes Have Seen* (*The Crisis,* 1918); and *Gone White* (undated); and Joseph S. Cotter, Jr., contributed *Caleb, The Degenerate,* in 1906.

While the political reality of African American existence in a predominately white, European-American environment seemed almost hopeless at times, there were nonetheless solid political efforts by blacks to change their oppressed circumstances. As early as 1905, Du Bois, William Monroe Trotter, and other African Americans organized the Niagara Movement, a Civil Rights protest organization calling for the end to racism through the use of legal channels. Their efforts would culminate in a more formalized way four years later when they joined forces with whites in the establishment of the National Association for the Advancement of Colored People (NAACP).

This organization was sparked in particular by a race riot in Springfield, Illinois, in 1908. Although a riot had occurred in Atlanta in 1906, when Walter White, who would later investigate lynchings for the NAACP, was an adolescent living there, the Illinois riot was worse by far. Blacks were lynched, whites were killed in turn and more than seventy persons suffered injuries. William English Walling, Mary White Ovington, and Oswald Garrison Villard, all white, were so appalled by the events that they called for a national conference to discuss the brutalities and to renew a focus on political and Civil Rights. Du Bois became the only black officer in the new organization. The group set a course to alter racial political repression. Du Bois and others advocated "universal manhood suffrage," an end to lynching, and equal protection under the law for blacks as well as whites.

To further its objectives, the organization inaugurated its own publishing instrument when Du Bois founded *The Crisis* magazine, which made its debut in 1910 with Du Bois as editor. For the next several years, it would record reported lynching statistics and generally become an advocate for African Americans. It treated topics as diverse as art, culture, education, literature, politics, and science, and it, occasionally, had fashion announcements and accounts of the social activities of certain members of the black middle class. In the 1920s, it also became significant as one of the key publishing outlets for established as well as for budding young black writers; the most notable of those published in its pages include James Weldon Johnson, Langston Hughes, Arna Bontemps, Countee Cullen, and Jean Toomer.

Du Bois's relationship to *The Crisis* is crucial for charting the black aesthetic, for, as early as 1912, he advocated an art that would be responsive to the needs of African Americans. As editor of *The Crisis,* he was able to engender debate about the portrayal of African Americans; to encourage younger writers in their work; and to shape, through his selections, the future path of the literature. While he was regarded by some as perpetuating a "best foot forward" literature, one more reflective of middle-class than working-class black aspirations, his articulation of a theory of black art was nevertheless important to how the literature from the 1920s to the present developed. Du Bois's editing work, therefore, was yet another dimension of African American creativity that set the tone for the future.

African American folk and popular culture continued to thrive as well. In 1912, when Woodrow Wilson was elected president of the United States, W.C. Handy published "Memphis Blues," which proved so successful that he made the collecting and publishing of blues and other folk songs his avocation. He initially focused on country blues and made the first recordings of these songs in 1918. However, as early as the 1870s, lyrics comparable to later full-blown blues songs might have existed but were not documented as such; blues musicians who grew up in the last decades of the nineteenth century testify that they were familiar with the songs in their youth. Handy's attention to the genre brought increased scholarly and popular focus on it, which resulted in a blossoming of interest in the first three decades of the twentieth century.

Also in 1912, the best novel of the period, *The Autobiography of an Ex-Colored Man,* was published anonymously by James Weldon Johnson (whose authorship would become known in 1927). Its complexity of characterizations and skillful handling of black folk materials distinguished it from other novels of the pre–Harlem Renaissance era. The work reflected Johnson's own interest in black folklore and music, in particular the folk sermon and ragtime. The following year, Fenton Johnson published *A Little Dreaming,* a collection that included traditional poetic structures as well as dialect poems. In *Visions of the Dusk* (1915), he included dialect poems reminiscent of some of Dunbar's work. While Johnson was publishing his poetry, and for the next decade and a half, William Stanley Braithwaite would publish his own poetry and, more importantly, would gather his numerous anthologies of magazine verse, which included several African American poets, especially those of the Harlem Renaissance.

The decades immediately preceding and following the turn of the century were also the era of the musical comedy tradition, which in turn had its roots in the minstrel tradition. When Thomas D. ("Daddy") Rice observed a deformed black man in Louisville singing and dancing a jig in 1828 and imitated the song and performance he had witnessed for white audiences, black-faced minstrelsy, which was just gaining a stronghold on American audiences, skyrocketed in popularity. Initially the territory of white performers, African Americans soon blackened their faces as well and joined in the money-making ventures. The shows generally depicted blacks with exaggerated physical features, outrageous clothing, an inability to pronounce the English language, a satisfaction with plantation life, and a love of such delicacies as watermelon and chickens, especially when they belonged to other people. These stereotypical portrayals of African Americans had their literary counterparts in the Plantation Tradition perpetuated by Joel Chandler Harris, Thomas Dixon, and Thomas Nelson Page. Writers such as Chesnutt would try to combat the impact of that tradition.

Entrenched stereotypes could certainly not be eliminated by the efforts of one or two established generations of African American writers. Nonetheless, Harper, Johnson, and others joined Chesnutt in being especially concerned to show the more complex realities of African American experience. Whether in autobiographical narratives or more strictly literary forms, writers between 1865 and 1915 did not have the privilege of separating their blackness from their creative endeavors. Demands from publishers, less than sympathetic editors and reading audiences, and the dictates of racial uplift combined to make them constantly conscious of their racial duties and responsibilities that most of them accepted. They set the stage for later writers to carve out freer and larger national and racial spaces for their creativity.

Choral Refrain

It is all the more remarkable that African Americans created significant black artistic expression during the period immediately following the Civil War and before the Harlem Renaissance, which scholars in general have viewed as the nadir of African American political and social existence. During this Dark Age of African American life, more blacks were lynched, burned, and tortured than in any other time in the nation's history. By the turn of the twentieth century, therefore, the great movement of Americans of African descent from the rural South to the urban North had begun. Yet, a closer examination of the period clearly reveals that it was one of the most influentially formative periods in the history of African American letters. It was one in which a literary tradition continued and was solidified, women's activism reached a pinnacle, and African American political personalities expanded their influence beyond the boundaries of the United States. With the death of Booker T. Washington in 1915, an era in African American history came to an end. With Du Bois's more progressive influence holding sway and with the renewed claims on American democracy engendered by black participation in World War I, the mood was set for continued new directions in African American life and culture. The "mighty rocky road" for African Americans had indeed given way to a star with a much brighter gleam.

Call for the Ideal Freedom: The Folk Tradition

Folk poetry

Spirituals

Free at Las'

(*Refrain*) Free at las' Free at las'
T'ank Gawd a'mighty Got free at las'
Free at las' Free at las'
T'ank Gawd a'mighty Got free at las'.
Oh, I 'member a day I 'member it well,
T'ank Gawd a'mighty got free at las'.
Ma dungeon shook an' ma chain fell off.
T'ank Gawd a'mighty got free at las'.

1. I know ma Lord is a man ob war,
T'ank Gawd a'mighty got free at las'
He fought ma battle at hell's dark do'.
T'ank Gawd a'mighty got free at las'.

(*Refrain*)

2. Satan t'ought he had me fas'
T'ank Gawd a'mighty got free at las'
I broke his chain an' got free at las'.
T'ank Gawd a'mighty got free at las'.

(*Refrain*)

3. Satan mad an' I'm glad.
T'ank Gawd a'mighty got free at las'
I hope to Gawd to keep him mad.
T'ank Gawd a'mighty got free at las'.

(*Refrain*)

4. You can hinder me here, but you can't
hinder me dere.
T'ank Gawd a'mighty got free at las'
De Lord in hebben gwin' t' answer ma
prayer.
T'ank Gawd a'mighty got free at las'.

(*Refrain*)

5. I went in de valley, but I didn't go to stay,
T'ank Gawd a'mighty got free at las'
Ma soul got happy an' I stayed all day.
T'ank Gawd a'mighty got free at las'.

(*Refrain*)

6. Oh, dis aint all, I got mo' beside,
T'ank Gawd a'mighty got free at las'
I'm born ob Gawd an' I been baptize.
T'ank Gawd a'mighty got free at las'.
(*Refrain*)

Singin' Wid a Sword in Ma Han'

(*Refrain*) Singin' wid a sword in ma han', Lord,
Singin' wid a sword in ma han',
Singin' wid a sword in the ma han,' Lord,
Singin' wid a sword in ma han.'

1. Purtiest singin' ever I heard,
'Way ovah on de hill,
De angels sing an' I sing too,
Singin' wid a sword in ma han', Lord,
Singin' wid a sword in ma han', in ma han', Lord,
Singin' wid a sword in ma han'.
Singin' wid a sword in ma han', Lord,
Singin' wid a sword in ma han'.
Singin' wid a sword in ma han', Lord,
Singin' wid a sword in ma han', In ma han', Lord,
Singin' wid a sword in ma han'.

2. Purtiest shoutin' ever I saw,
'Way ovah on de hill,
De angels shout an' I shout too,
Shoutin' wid a sword in ma han,' Lord,
Shoutin' wid a sword in ma han', in ma han', Lord,
Shoutin' wid a sword in ma han',
Shoutin' wid a sword in ma han,' Lord,
Shoutin' wid a sword in ma han'.
Shoutin' wid a sword in ma han', Lord,
Shoutin' wid a sword in ma han', In ma han', Lord,
Shoutin' wid a sword in ma han'.

3. Purtiest preachin' ever I heard,
'Way ovah on de hill,
De Angels preach an' I preach'd too,
Preachin' wid a sword in ma han', Lord,
Preachin' wid a sword in ma han', Lord,
Preachin' wid a sword in ma han'.
(*Refrain*)

4. Purtiest prayin' ever I heard,
'Way ovah on de hill,
De Angels pray an' I pray'd too,
Prayin' wid a sword in ma han', Lord,
Prayin' wid a sword in ma han', Lord,
Prayin' wid a sword in ma han'.
(*Refrain*)

5. Purtiest mournin' ever I heard,
'Way ovah on de hill,
De Angels mourn an' I mourn'd too,
Mournin' wid a sword in ma han', Lord,
Mournin' wid a sword in ma han', Lord,
Mournin' wid a sword in ma han'. (*Refrain*)

My Lord, What a Mornin'

The title of this song has at times been erroneously printed "My Lord, What A Mourning."

(*Refrain*) My Lord, what a mornin,'
My Lord, what a mornin',
My Lord, what a mornin',
When de stars begin to fall.
My Lord, what a mornin',
My Lord, what a mornin',
My Lord, what a mornin',
When de stars begin to fall.

1. You'll hear de trumpet sound,
To wake de nations under ground,
Lookin' to my God's right hand,
When de stars begin to fall.
(*Refrain*)

2. You'll hear de sinner moan,
To wake de nations under ground,
Lookin' to my God's right hand,
When de stars begin to fall.
(*Refrain*)

3. You'll hear de Christians shout,
To wake de nations under ground,
Lookin' to my God's right hand,
When de stars begin to fall.
(*Refrain*)

Deep River

(*Refrain*) Deep river. My home is over Jordan.
Deep river, Lord.
I want to cross over into camp ground, Lord.
I want to cross over into camp ground.
Lord, I want to cross over into camp ground, Lord.
I want to cross over into camp ground.

1. Oh, don't you want to go to that Gospelfeast,
That promis'd land where all is peace?
(*Refrain*)

2. I'll go in to heaven, and take my seat,
Cast my crown at Jesus' feet.
(*Refrain*)

3. Oh, when I get to heav'n, I'll walk all about,
There's nobody there for to turn me out.
(*Refrain*)

Go Tell It on de Mountain

1. When I was a seeker
I sought both night and day,
I ask de Lord to help me,
An' He show' me de way.

(*Refrain*) Go tell it on de mountain,
Over de hills an' everywhere;
Go tell it on de mountain,
Dat Jesus Christ is a born.

2. He made me a watchman
Upon a city wall,
And if I am a Christian
I am de least of all.

(*Refrain*)

When the Saints Go Marching In

1. When the saints go marching in
When the saints go marching in
I want to be in that number
When the saints go marching in.

2. I used to have some playmates
Who used to play with me.
But since I've been converted
They done turned their backs on me.

3. Oh, when they crown Him Lord of Lords
Oh, when they crown Him Lord of Lords
Yes, I want to be in that number
When they crown Him Lord of Lords.

4. When they march all around His throne
When they march all around His throne.
Oh, I want to be in that number
When they march all around His throne.

5. I have a dear old mother who has gone on before
And left me here below,
But I know I'm gonna meet her
When the saints go marching in.

6. When the saints go marching in,
Oh, when the saints go marching in!
Oh, Lord I want to be in that number
When the saints go marching in.

Git on Board, Little Chillen

(*Refrain*) Git on board, little chillen,
Git on board, little chillen,
Git on board, little chillen,
Dere's room for many a mo'.

1. De gospel trains a-comin',
I hear it jus' at han',
I hear de car wheels movin',
An' rumblin' thro de lan'.
(*Refrain*)

2. De fare is cheap, an' all can go,
De rich an' poor are dere,
No second class aboard dis train,
No diffrunce in de fare.
(*Refrain*)

Mighty Rocky Road

1. Hit's a mighty rocky road, an' I'm mos' done trabbelin',
Mighty rocky road, an' I'm mos' done trabbelin',
Mighty rocky road, an' I'm mos' done trabbelin',
I'se bound to kerry my soul to Jesus,
Bound to kerry my soul to de Lord.

2. Christian's on de road, an' he's mos' done trabbelin',
Christian's on de road, an' he's mos' done trabbelin',
Christian's on de road, an' he's mos' done trabbelin',
He's bound to kerry his soul to Jesus,
Bound to kerry his soul to de Lord.

3. Mourner's on de road, an' he's mos' done trabbelin',
Mourner's on de road, an' he's mos' done trabbelin',
Mourner's on de road, an' he's mos' done trabbelin',
He's bound to kerry his soul to Jesus,
Bound to kerry his soul to de Lord.

4. Sinner's on de road, an' he's a long time trabbelin',
Sinner's on de road, an' he's a long time trabbelin',
Sinner's on de road, an' he's a long time trabbelin',
He's bound to kerry his soul to Jesus,
Bound to kerry his soul to de Lord.

Work, Badman, and Prison Songs

Casey Jones

1. On a Sunday morning it begins to rain,
Round the curve sped a passenger train,
Under de cab lay po Casey Jones.
He's a good engineer, but he's dead an gone,

Dead an gone, dead an gone,
Kaze he's been on the cholly so long.

2. Casey Jones was a good engineer,
Tol' is fireman not to have no fear,
"All I want's a lil water an coal,
Peep out de cab an see de drivers roll,
See de drivers roll, see de drivers roll."
Kaze he's been on the cholly so long.

3. When we got within a mile of the place,
Old number 4 stared us right in the face,
Conductor pulled his watch, mumbled and said,
"We may make it, but we'll all be dead,
All be dead, all be dead."
Kaze he's been on the cholly so long.

4. When Casey's wife heard dat Casey was daid,
She was in de kitchun makin up braid;
She say, "Go to bed, chullun an hol yo breath,
Yall all git a pension at yo daddy's death,
At yo daddy's death, at yo daddy's death,
Kaze he's been on the cholly so long."

John Henry

1. Some say he's from Georgia,
Some say he's from Alabam,
But it's wrote on the rock at the Big Ben Tunnel,
John Henry's a East Virginia Man,
John Henry's a East Virginia Man.

2. John Henry he could hammah,
He could whistle, he could sing,
He went to the mountain early in the mornin'
To hear his hammah ring,
To hear his hammah ring.

3. John Henry went to the section boss,
Says the section boss what kin you do?
Says I can line a track, I kin histe a jack,
I kin pick and shovel, too,
I kin pick and shovel, too.

4. John Henry went to the tunnel
And they put him in lead to drive,
The rock was so tall and John Henry so small
That he laid down his hammah and he cried,
That he laid down his hammah and he cried.

5. The steam drill was on the right han' side,
John Henry was on the left,
Says before I let this stream drill beat me down,
I'll hammah myself to death,
I'll hammah myself to death.

6. Oh the cap'n said to John Henry,
I bleeve this mountain's sinkin' in.
John Henry said to the cap'n, Oh my!
Tain't nothin' but my hammah suckin' wind,
Tain't nothin' but my hammah suckin' wind.

7. John Henry had a pretty liddle wife,
She come all dressed in blue.
And the last words she said to him,
John Henry I been true to you,
John Henry I been true to you.

8. John Henry was on the mountain,
The mountain was so high,
He called to his pretty liddle wife,
Said Ah kin almos' touch the sky,
Said Ah kin almos' touch the sky.

9. Who gonna shoe yoh pretty liddle feet,
Who gonna glove yoh han',
Who gonna kiss yoh rosy cheeks,
An' who gonna be yoh man,
An' who gonna be yoh man?

10. Papa gonna shoe my pretty liddle feet,
Mama gonna glove my han',
Sistah gonna kiss my rosy cheeks,
An' I ain't gonna have no man,
An' I ain't gonna have no man.

11. Then John Henry he did hammah,
He did make his hammah soun',
Says now one more lick fore quittin' time,
An' I'll beat this steam drill down,
An' I'll beat this steam drill down.

12. The hammah that John Henry swung,
It weighed over nine poun',
He broke a rib in his left han' side,
And his intrels fell on the groun',
And his intrels fell on the groun'.

13. All the women in the West
That heard of John Henry's death,
Stood in the rain, flagged the east bound train,
Goin' where John Henry dropped dead,
Goin' where John Henry dropped dead.

14. They took John Henry to the White House,
And buried him in the san',
And every locomotive come roarin' by,
Says there lays that steel drivin' man,
Says there lays that steel drivin' man.

Railroad Bill

1. Firs' on table, nex' on wall;
Ol' corn whisky cause of it all.
It's dat bad Railroad Bill.

2. Railroad Bill mighty bad man,
Shoot dem light out o' de brakeman's han'.
It's dat bad Railroad Bill.

3. Railroad Bill went out Wes',
Though he had dem cowboys bes'.
It's dat bad Railroad Bill.

4. Railroad Bill, Railroad Bill,
He never work and he never will.
It's dat bad Railroad Bill.

5. Two policemen dressed in blue
Come down street in two an' two,
Wuz lookin' fer Railroad Bill.

6. O' McMillan had a special train,
When he got dere it was a shower of rain.
Wuz lookin' fer Railroad Bill.

7. Ev'body tol' him he better turn back;
Railroad Bill wuz goin' down de track,
Dat bad man Railroad Bill.

8. Railroad Bill wuz the worst ol' coon,
Killed McMillan by the light of de moon,
When wuz lookin' fer Railroad Bill.

9. Some one went home an' tol' my wife
All about—well, my pas' life.
It wuz dat bad Railroad Bill.

10. I went down on Number One,
Railroad Bill had jus' begun.
Wuz dat bad Railroad Bill.

11. I come up on Number Two,
Railroad Bill had jus' got through.
Dat bad Railroad Bill.

12. An' jus' as I caught dat Number Fo',
Somebody shot at me wid a fo'ty-fo',
Wuz dat bad Railroad Bill.

13. I went back on Number Five,
Goin' bring him back, dead or alive.
Wuz lookin' fer Railroad Bill.

14. I come back on Number Eight,
The folks say I wuz a minute too late.
Lookin' fer Railroad Bill.

15. When I come back on Number Nine,
Folks says, "You're jes' in time.
Lookin' for Railroad Bill."

16. When I got my men, they amounted to ten,
An' that's when I run po' Railroad Bill in.
An' that wuz the last of po' Railroad Bill.

Stagolee

1. It was early, early one mornin',
When I heard my bulldog bark,
Stagolee and Billy Lyons
Was squabblin' in the dark.

2. Stagolee told Billy Lyons,
'What do you think of that?
You win all my money, Billy,
Now you spit in my Stetson Hat.'

3. Stagolee, he went a-walkin'
In the red-hot, broilin' sun—
Says, 'Bring me my six-shooter,
Lawd, I wants my forty-one.'

4. Stagolee, he went a-walkin'
Through the mud and through the sand.
Says, 'I feel mistreated this mornin',
I could kill most any man.'

5. Billy Lyons told Stagolee,
'Please don't take my life,
I've got three little helpless chillun
And one poor, pitiful wife.'

6. 'Don't care nothin' about your chillun,
And nothin' about your wife,
You done mistreated me, Billy,
And I'm bound to take your life.'

7. He shot him three times in the shoulder,
Lawd, and three times in the side,
Well, the last time he shot him
Cause Billy Lyons to die.

8. Stagolee told Mrs Billy,
'You don't believe yo' man is dead;
Come into the bar-room,
See the hole I shot in his head.'

9. The high sheriff told the deputies,
'Get your pistols and come with me.
We got to go 'rest that
Bad man Stagolee.'

10. The deputies took their pistols
And they laid them on the shelf—
'If you want that bad man Stagolee,
Go 'rest him by yourself.'

11. High sheriff ask the bartender,
'Who can that bad man be?'
'Speak softly,' said the bartender,
'It's that bad man Stagolee.'

12. He touch Stack on the shoulder,
Say, 'Stack, why don't you run?'
'I don't run, white folks,
When I got my forty-one.'

13. The hangman put the mask on,
Tied his hands behind his back,
Sprung the trap on Stagolee
But his neck refuse to crack.

14. Hangman, he got frightened,
Said, 'Chief, you see how it be—
I can't hang this man,
Better set him free.'

15. Three hundred dollar funeral,
Thousand dollar hearse,
Satisfaction undertaker
Put Stack six feet in the earth.

16. Stagolee, he told the Devil,
Says, 'Come on and have some fun—
You stick me with your pitchfork,
I'll shoot you with my forty-one.'

17. Stagolee took the pitchfork,
And he laid it on the shelf.
Says, 'Stand back, Tom Devil,
I'm gonna rule Hell by myself.'

John Harty

1. John Harty was a desperate man,
He carried a gun and a razor every day,
He killed a man in Challis town.
You ought to seen poor Johnny get away. (*Repeat*)

2. John Harty went to this big, long town.
When he thought he was out of the way,
Up stepped a marshal and taken him by the hand,
Says, "Johnny, come and go with me." (*Repeat*)

3. Johnny Harty had a father and mother,
He sent for them to go his bail.

No bail was allowed for murdering a man,
So they shoved Johnny Harty back in jail. (*Repeat*)

4. Johnny Harty had a pretty little wife,
She was all dressed in blue,
She cried out with a loud little shout,
"Johnny, I've been true to you." (*Repeat*)

5. Johnny Harty was standing in his cell,
With the tears running down each eye;
"I've been the death of many a poor man,
And now I'm ready to die.
O Lord, now I'm ready to die.

6. "I've been to the east, I've been to the west,
I've been this wide world round,
I've been to the river and been baptized,
So take me to my hanging ground,
O Lord, take me to my hanging ground."

Po Laz' us

1. High Shayiff tol de depitty—Hanh!
"Go out an bring me Laz'us"—Hanh!
High Shayiff tol de depitty—Hanh!
"Go out an bring me Laz'us—Hanh!
Bring him dead or alive, Lawd, Lawd—Hanh!
Bring him dead or alive"—Hanh!

2. De depitty he gins to wonder—Hanh!
Whuh in de worl he could fin him—Hanh!
De depitty he gins to wonder—Hanh!
Whuh in de worl he could fin him—Hanh!
Well-a, Ah don know, Lawd, Lawd—Hanh!
Ah jes don know—Hanh!

3. O dey foun po' Laz'us—Hanh!
Way out tween two mountins—Hanh!
O dey foun po Laz'us—Hanh!
Way out tween two mountins—Hanh!
And dey blowed him down, Lawd, Lawd—Hanh!
Dey blowed him down—Hanh!

4. Ol' Laz'us tol de depitty—Hanh!
He nevah be arrested—Hanh!
Ol' Laz'us tol de depitty—Hanh!
He nevah be arrested—Hanh!
By no one man, Lawd, Lawd—Hanh!
By no one man—Hanh!

5. So dey shot po Laz'us—Hanh!
Shot him wid a great big number—Hanh!

Dey shot po Laz'us—Hanh!
Shot him wid a great big number—Hanh!
Number Forty-five, Lawd, Lawd—Hanh!
Number Forty-five,—Hanh!

6. An dey taken po Laz'us—Hanh!
An lay him on de commisary county—Hanh!
Dey taken po Laz'us—Hanh!
An lay him on de commisary county—Hanh!
Den dey walks away, Lawd, Lawd—Hanh!
Dey walks away—Hanh!

7. Laz'us tol de depitty—Hanh!
"Gimme a cool drink a water"—Hanh!
Laz'us tol de depitty—Hanh!
"Gimme a cool drink a water—Hanh!
Jes fo Ah die, Lawd, Lawd—Hanh!
Jes fo Ah die"—Hanh!

8. Laz'us sister run—Hanh!
An tol huh Mama—Hanh!
Laz'us sister run—Hanh!
An tol huh Mama—Hanh!
"Po Laz'us daid, Lawd, Lawd—Hanh!
Po Laz'us daid"—Hanh!

9. Laz'us mama—Hanh!
Lay down huh sewin—Hanh!
Laz'us mama—Hanh!
Lay down huh sewin—Hanh!
She gin to cry, Lawd, Lawd—Hanh!
She gin to cry—Hanh!

10. Laz'us sister—Hanh!
Couldn't go to de fun'l—Hanh!
Laz'us sister—Hanh!
Couldn't go to de fun'l—Hanh!
Didn't have no shoes, Lawd, Lawd—Hanh!
Didn't have no shoes—Hanh!

11. Cap'n, did you heah—Hanh!
All yo mens gonna leave you—Hanh!
Cap'n, did you heah—Hanh!
All yo mens gonna leave you—Hanh!
Nex payday, Lawd, Lawd—Hanh!
Nex payday—Hanh!

RURAL BLUES

As with black folk music in general, the blues should be considered to be a medium that transmits a blood force, a cultural rather than a purely individualistic experience. Even though the songs are sung by a single person, they represent the collective yearnings and feelings of African American people. Whether the artist sings about his or her despair, problems in love or with racism, lost job, nostalgia for the South, or other major thematic concerns of the blues, the personal life of the singer becomes the prototype of the collective. The singer is able to transmit a communal consciousness effectively because he or she uses an idiom so familiar to his or her audience that the emotional experience is shared as theirs.

Established in the earliest blues called the *rural blues,* the basic idiom is a stanza of three iambic pentameter lines, which generally follows an *a ab* rhyme scheme. According to Eileen Southern, it is based on the three-line stanzaic form that is African in origin and "uncommon in American and European folksong repertories." The second line of the blues idiom is a repetition of the first line. Typically, the third line may be an answer to a question raised in the first two lines or it may offer a reaction to or a comment on the situation.

Like black folk music in general, the blues reflect chief characteristics of African music; in particular, duple rhythms, improvisation, and syncopation. As Southern explains in detail:

> The melody for each line is typically condensed into a little more than two measures of the four-measured phrase; this allows for a pause or "break" at the end of each vocal line, during which the accompanying instrument (guitar, piano, or instrumental ensemble) improvises and the singer interjects spoken asides, such as "Oh, Lordy," "Yes, man," "Oh, play it," etc. The resulting effect is that of call and response, the instrumental improvisation representing the "response" to the voice's call.

The singer improvises by using a device in the blues pattern called "worrying the line"; that is, he or she may slightly shorten or lengthen the repeated line by using words that differ slightly from those in his or her first, personal statement line.

The prototype for all folk blues, blues critics and musicians in general agree, is "The Joe Turner Blues." During the 1890s and early 1900s, the tune formed the basis of several blues songs, including "Gwine Down Dat Lonesome Road" and "Goin' Down the River 'Fore Long." As described in W.C. Handy's *Father of the Blues,* the original song derived from the story of Joe Turney, who was the brother of Pete Turney, the governor of Tennessee:

> Joe had the responsibility of taking Negro prisoners from Memphis to the penitentiary at Nashville [in the early 1890s]. Sometimes he took them to the "farms" along the Mississippi. Their crimes, when indeed there were any crimes, were usually very minor, the object of the arrests being to provide needed labor for spots along the river. As usual, the method was to set a stool-pigeon where he could start a game of craps. The bones would roll blissfully till the required number of laborers had been drawn into the circle. At that point, the law would fall upon the poor devils, arrest as many as were needed for work, try them for gambling in a kangaroo court, and then turn the culprits over to Joe Turney. That night, perhaps, there would be weeping and wailing among the dusky belles. If one of them chanced to ask a neighbor what had become of the sweet good man, she was likely to receive the pat reply, "They tell me Joe Turner's come and gone."

"The Joe Turner Blues" inspired the creation not only of scores of blues songs but also of August Wilson's riveting play, *Joe Turner's Come and Gone,* nearly a century later.

The Joe Turner Blues

Dey tell me Joe Turner's come and gone
Dey tell me Joe Turner's come and gone
Got my man an' gone
He come wid fo'ty links of chain *Oh Lawdy*
Come wid fo'ty links of chain *Oh Lawdy*
Got my man an' gone

Gwine Down Dat Lonesome Road

Gwine down dat lonesome road,
I'm gwine down dat lonesome road:
I'm gwine down dat lonesome road,
An' I won't be treated this-a way.
De springs on my bed done broken down,
An' I ain' got no place to lay my head.
Oh, yes, de springs on my bed done broken down,
An' I ain' got no place to lay my head.

Baby Seals Blues

Words and music by
Baby F. Seals
Arranged by Artie Matthews

1. I got the blues can't be satisfied today
I got them bad want to lay down and die
I woke up this morning bout half past four
Some body knocking at my door
I went out to see what it was about
They told me that my honey gal was gone
I said bub that's bad news
So sing for me them blues

(*Chorus*) *She* Honey baby mamma do she do she double do love you (*Spoken*) YEA-HOO
I Love you babe don't care what you do (*Spoken*) SUEY
He Oh sing em sing em sing them blues
Cause they cert'ly sound good to me
I've been in love these last three weeks
And it cert'ly is a misery
There ain't but one thing I wish was right
I wish my honey babe was here tonight
She Honey babe Mammas coming back to you
He Come on babe Oh sing em sing em sing them blues cause they cert'ly sound good to me

2. Honey babe pop's ain't mad with you today
I love you brown skin don't care what you do
Oh my baby told me just yesterday
She'd take her trunk and move away
I said hon I know what it is about
I know babe you just want to put me out
Now babe I'll go insane
Oh listen while I sing

St. Louis Blues

Words and music by
W.C. Handy

1. I hate to see de ev'nin' sun go down
Hate to see de evenin' sun go down.
Cause my baby, he done lef dis town
Feelin' tomorrow lak Ah feel today
Feel tomorrow lak Ah feel today
I'll pack my trunk Make ma get away
St. Louis woman Wid her diamon' rings
Pulls dat man roun' by her apron strings
'Twant for powder an' for store bought hair
De man I love would not gone nowhere.

2. Been to de Gypsy to get ma fortune tole
To de Gypsy done got ma fortune tole.
Cause I'm most wile 'bout ma Jelly Roll
Gypsy done tole me, "don't you wear no black"
Yes she done tole me "don't you wear no black"
Go to St. Louis You can win him back
Help me to Cairo make St. Louis by maself
Git to Cairo find ma ole friend Jeff,
Gwine to pin ma self close to his side
If ah flag his train I sho' can ride.

3. You ought to see dat stovepipe brown of mine
Lak he owns de Dimon Joseph line.
He'd make a crosseyed o'man go stone blind
Blacker than midnight, teeth lak flags of truce
Blackest man in de whole St. Louis
Blacker de berry Sweeter is the juice
About a crap game he knows a pow'ful lot
But when worktime comes he's on de dot
Gwine to ask him for a cold ten spot
What it takes to git it he's cert'nly got.
(*Chorus*) Got de St. Louis Blues jes as blue as Ah can be
Dat man got a heart lak a rock cast in the sea
Or else he wouldn't have gone so far from me. Dog-gone-it!

(*Chorus*) I loves dat man lak a school boy loves his pie
Lak a Kentucky Col'nel loves his mint an' rye,
I'll love ma baby till the day Ah die. Dog-gone-it!
(*Chorus*) A black headed gal make a freight train jump the track
Said a black headed gal make a freight train jump the track
But a long tall gal makes a preacher ball the Jack. Dog-gone-it!
(*Chorus*) Lawd a blonde headed woman makes a good man leave the town
I said blonde headed woman makes a good man leave the town
But a red head woman makes a boy slap his papa down. Dog-gone-it!
(*Chorus*) Oh ashes to ashes and dust to dust
I said ashes to ashes and dust to dust
If my blues don't get you my jazzing must. Dog-gone-it!

Ragtime

Ragtime is the first black instrumental music in America. Based on an intricate rhythmic foundation of polyrhythms and polymeters, this type of piano music is characterized by a regular straightforward rolling bass combined with syncopation and often spellbound melodic lyricism. As author James Weldon Johnson explains in his novel *The Autobiography of an Ex-Colored Man,* when the pianist played ragtime music, he or she used the right hand to create lightly syncopated melodies while using the left hand for patting and stomping.

According to musicologist Eileen Southern, the most significant feature of ragtime is syncopation. As she explains, "the syncopated patterns might be simple ones, written as ♪♩♪ or ♩♩♩, or they might be complex, resulting from the play of additive rhythms in the right hand—such as ♪♪♪ ♫ ♫ = 3 + 2 + 2—against consistent duple meters in the left hand." An excellent example of the latter is Blind Boone's ragtime song, "I Meet Dat Coon Tonight."

I Meet Dat Coon Tonight

Blind Boone

Words and music by Blind Boone

The Folk Sermon

In general, the folk sermon begins with a text from the Scriptures. The preacher immediately animates the text so the power of the dramatic sermon can be both seen and felt. As James Weldon Johnson in *The Autobiography of an Ex-Colored Man* notes, "he [the preacher] knew all the arts and tricks of oratory, the modulation of the voice to almost a whisper, the pause for effect, the rise through light, rapid fire sentences to the terrific, thundering outburst of an electrifying climax." The sermon is loaded with fire and brimstone, force and fury, threats and warnings, and admonishments and pleas. By the end of the sermon, there is hardly a person who has not been moved by the poetic power and passions of the preacher. The most successful sermons were repeated over and over again and gradually became "set pieces," which were used by different ministers, each adding his own adaptations.

Two popular folk sermons were documented during the postwar period. "De Sun Do Move" (c. 1882) by Reverend John Jasper, who preached the sermon over 250 times, was transcribed by William E. Hatcher in his biography of Jasper. The second work, "Dry Bones," which originated in the 1890s, is an anonymous version of the chant portion of an oral sermon on the text of Ezekiel 37:1–14, which was legendary among the black rural communities.

De Sun Do Move

by Rev. John Jasper

"Low me ter say," he spoke with an outward composure which revealed an inward but mastered swell of emotion, "dat when I wuz a young man and a slave, I knowed nuthin' wuth talkin' 'bout consarnin' books. Dey wuz sealed mysteries ter me, but I tell yer I longed ter break de seal. I thusted fer de bread uv learnin'. When I seen books I ached ter git in ter um, fur I knowed dat dey had de stuff fer me, an' I wanted ter taste dere contents, but most of de time dey wuz bar'd against me.

"By de mursy of de Lord a thing happened. I got er room-feller—he wuz a slave, too, an' he had learn'd ter read. In de dead uv de night he giv me lessons outen de New York Spellin' book. It wuz hard pullin', I tell yer; harder on him, fur he know'd jes' a leetle, an' it made him sweat ter try ter beat sumthin' inter my hard haid. It wuz wuss wid me. Up de hill ev'ry step, but when I got de light uv de less'n into my noodle I farly shouted, but I kno'd I wuz not a scholar. De consequens wuz I crep 'long mighty tejus, gittin' a crum here an' dar untel I cud read de Bible by skippin' de long words, tolerable well. Dat wuz de start uv my eddicashun—dat is, wat little I got. I mek menshun uv dat young man. De years hev fled erway sense den, but I ain't furgot my teachur, an' nevur shall. I thank mer Lord fur him, an' I carries his mem'ry in my heart.

"'Bout seben months after my gittin' ter readin', Gord cunverted my soul, an' I reckin 'bout de fust an' main thing dat I begged de Lord ter give me wuz de power ter und'stan' His Word. I ain' braggin', an' I hates self-praise, but I boun' ter speak de thankful word. I b'lieves in mer heart dat mer pra'r ter und'stand de Scripshur wuz heard. Sence dat time I ain't keer'd 'bout nuthin' 'cept ter study an' preach de Word uv God.

"Not, my bruthrin, dat I'z de fool ter think I knows it all. Oh, mer Father, no! Fur frum it. I don' hardly und'stan myse'f, nor ha'f uv de things roun' me, an' dar is milyuns uv things in de Bible too deep fur Jasper, an' sum uv 'em too deep fur ev'rybody. I doan't cerry de keys ter de Lord's closet, an' He ain' tell me ter peep in, an' ef I did I'm so stupid I wouldn't know it when I see it. No, frens, I knows my place at de feet uv my Marster, an' dar I stays.

"But I kin read de Bible and git de things whar lay on de top uv de soil. Out'n de Bible I knows nuthin' extry 'bout de sun. I sees 'is courses as he rides up dar so gran' an' mighty in de sky, but dar is heaps 'bout dat flamin' orb dat is too much fer me. I know dat de sun shines powerfly an' po's down its light in floods, an' yet dat is nuthin' compared wid de light dat flashes in my min' frum de pages of Gord's book. But you knows all dat. I knows dat de sun burns—oh, how it did burn in dem July days. I tell yer he cooked de skin on my back many er day when I wuz hoein' in de corn feil'. But you knows all dat, an' yet dat is nuthin' der to de divine fire dat burns in der souls uv Gord's chil'n. Can't yer feel it, bruthrin?

"But 'bout de courses uv de sun, I have got dat. I hev dun rang'd thru de whole blessed book an' scode down de las' thing de Bible has ter say 'bout de movements uv de sun. I got all dat pat an' safe. An' lemme say dat if I doan't giv it ter you straight, if I gits one word crooked or wrong, you jes' holler out, 'Hol' on dar, Jasper, yer ain't got dat straight,' an' I'll beg pardon. If I doan't tell de truf, march up on dese steps here an' tell me I'z a liar, an' I'll take it. I fears I do lie sometimes—I'm so sinful, I find it hard ter do right; but my Gord doan't lie an' He ain' put no lie in de Book uv eternal truf, an' if I giv you wat de Bible say, den I boun' ter tell de truf.

"I got ter take yer all dis arternoon on er skershun ter a great bat'l feil'. Mos' folks like ter see fights—some is mighty fon' er gittin' inter fights, an' some is mighty quick ter run down de back alley when dar is a bat'l goin' on, fer de right. Dis time I'll 'scort yer ter a scene whar you shall witness a curus bat'l. It tuk place soon arter Isrel got in de Promus Lan'. Yer 'member de people uv Gibyun mak frens wid Gord's people when dey fust entered Canum an' dey wuz monsus smart ter do it. But, jes' de same, it got 'em in ter an orful fuss. De cities roun' 'bout dar flar'd up at dat, an' dey all jined dere forces and say dey gwine ter mop de Gibyun people orf uv de groun', an' dey bunched all dar armies tergedder an' went up fer ter do it. Wen dey kum up so bol' an' brave de Giby'nites wuz skeer'd out'n dere senses, an' dey saunt word ter Joshwer dat dey wuz in troubl' an' he mus' run up dar an' git 'em out. Joshwer had de heart uv a lion an' he wuz up dar d'reckly. Dey had an orful fight, sharp an' bitter, but yer might know dat Ginr'l Joshwer wuz not up dar ter git whip't. He prayed an' he fought, an' de hours got erway too peart fer him, an' so he ask'd de Lord ter issure a speshul ordur dat de sun hol' up erwhile an' dat de moon furnish plenty uv moonshine down on de lowes' part uv de fightin' groun's. As a fac', Joshwer wuz so drunk wid de bat'l, so thursty fer de blood uv de en'mies uv de Lord, an' so wild wid de vict'ry dat he tell de sun ter stan' still tel he cud finish his job. Wat did de sun do? Did he glar down in fi'ry wrath an' say, 'What you talkin' 'bout my stoppin' for, Joshwer; I ain't navur startid yit. Bin here all de time, an' it wud smash up ev'rything if I wuz ter start'? Naw, he ain' say dat. But wat de Bible say? Dat's wat I ax ter know. It say dat it wuz at de voice uv Joshwer dat it stopped. I don' say it stopt; tain't fer Jasper ter say dat, but de Bible, de Book uv Gord, say so. But I say dis; nuthin' kin stop untel it hez fust startid. So I knows wat I'm talkin' 'bout. De sun wuz travlin' long dar thru de sky wen de order come. He hitched his red ponies and made quite a call on de lan' uv Gibyun. He purch up dar in de skies jes' as frenly as a naibur whar comes ter borrer sumthin', an' he stan' up dar an' he look lak he enjoyed de way Joshwer waxes dem wicked armies. An' de moon, she wait down in de low groun's dar, an' pours out her light and look jes' as ca'm an' happy as if she wuz waitin' fer her 'scort. Dey nevur budg'd, neither uv 'em, long as de Lord's army needed er light to kerry on de bat'l.

"I doan't read when it wuz dat Joshwer hitch up an' drove on, but I 'spose it wuz when de Lord tol' him ter go. Ennybody knows dat de sun didn' stay dar all de time. It stopt fur bizniz, an' went on when it got thru. Dis is 'bout all dat I has ter do wid dis perticl'r case. I dun show'd yer dat dis part uv de Lord's word teaches yer dat de sun stopt, which show dat he wuz movin' befo' dat, an' dat he went on art'rwuds. I toll yer dat I wud prove dis an' I's dun it, an' I derfies ennybody to say dat my p'int ain't made.

"I tol' yer in de fust part uv dis discose dat de Lord Gord is a man uv war. I 'spec by now yer begin ter see it is so. Doan't yer admit it? When de Lord cum ter see Joshwer in de day uv his feers an' warfar, an' actu'ly mek de sun stop stone still in de heavuns, so de fight kin rage on tel all de foes is slain, yer bleeged ter und'rstan' dat de Gord uv peace is also de man uv war. He kin use bofe peace an' war ter hep de reichus, an' ter scattur de host uv de ailyuns. A man talked ter me las' week 'bout de laws uv nature, an' he say dey carn't poss'bly be upsot, an' I had ter laugh right in his face. As if de laws uv ennythin' wuz greater dan my Gord who is de lawgiver fer ev'rything. My Lord is great; He rules in de heavuns, in de earth, an' doun und'r de groun'. He is great, an' greatly ter be praised. Let all de people bow doun an' wurship befo' Him!

"But let us git erlong, for dar is quite a big lot mo' comin' on. Let us take nex' de case of Hezekier. He wuz one of dem kings of Juder—er mighty sorry lot I mus' say dem kings wuz, fur de mos' part. I inclines ter think Hezekier wuz 'bout de highes' in de gin'ral avrig, an' he war no mighty man hisse'f. Well, Hezekier he got sick. I dar say dat a king when he gits his crown an' fin'ry off, an' when he is posterated wid mortal sickness, he gits 'bout es commun lookin' an' grunts an' rolls, an' is 'bout es skeery as de res' of us po' mortals. We know dat Hezekier wuz in er low state uv min'; full uv fears, an' in a tur'ble trub'le. De fac' is, de Lord strip him uv all his glory an' landed him in de dust. He tol' him dat his hour had come, an' dat he had bettur squar up his affaars, fur death wuz at de do'. Den it wuz dat de king fell low befo' Gord; he turn his face ter de wall; he cry, he moan, he beg'd de Lord not ter take him out'n de worl' yit. Oh, how good is our Gord! De cry uv de king moved his heart, an' he tell him he gwine ter give him anudder show. Tain't only de kings dat de Lord hears. De cry uv de pris'nur, de wail uv de bondsman, de tears uv de dyin' robber, de prars uv de backslider, de sobs uv de womun dat wuz a sinner, mighty apt to tech de heart uv de Lord. It look lik it's hard fer de sinner ter git so fur orf or so fur down in de pit dat his cry can't reach de yere uv de mussiful Saviour.

"But de Lord do evun better den dis fur Hezekier—He tell him He gwine ter give him a sign by which he'd know dat what He sed wuz cummin' ter pars. I ain't erquainted wid dem sun diuls dat de Lord toll Hezekier 'bout, but ennybody dat hes got a grain uv sense knows dat dey wuz de clocks uv dem ole times an' dey marked de travuls uv de sun by dem diuls. When, darfo' Gord tol' de king dat He wud mek de shadder go backwud, it mus' hev bin jes' lak puttin' de han's uv de clock back, but, mark yer, Izaer 'spressly say dat de sun return'd ten dergrees. Thar yer are! Ain't dat de movement uv de sun? Bless my soul. Hezekier's case beat Joshwer. Joshwer stop de sun, but heer de Lord mek de sun walk back ten dergrees; an' yet dey say dat de sun stan' stone still an' nevur move er peg. It look ter me he move roun' mighty brisk an' is ready ter go ennyway dat de Lord ordurs him ter go. I wonder if enny uv dem furloserfers is roun' here dis arternoon. I'd lik ter take a squar' look at one uv dem an' ax him to 'splain dis mattur. He carn't do it, my bruthr'n. He knows a heap 'bout books, maps, figgers an' long distunces, but I derfy him ter take up Hezekier's case an' 'splain it orf. He carn't do it. De Word uv de Lord is my defense an' bulwurk, an' I fears not what men can say nor do; my Gord gives me de vict'ry.

"'Low me, my frens, ter put myself squar 'bout dis movement uv de sun. It ain't no bizniss uv mine wedder de sun move or stan' still, or wedder it stop or go back or rise or set. All dat is out er my han's 'tirely, an' I got nuthin' ter say. I got no the-o-ry on de subjik. All I ax is dat we will take wat de Lord say 'bout it an' let His will be dun 'bout ev'rything. Wat dat will is I karn't know 'cept He whisper inter my soul or write it in a book. Here's de Book. Dis is 'nough fer me, and wid it ter pilut me, I karn't git fur erstray.

"But I ain't dun wid yer yit. As de song says, dere's mo' ter foller. I envite yer ter heer de fust vers in de sev'nth chaptur uv de book uv Reverlashuns. What do John, und'r de pow'r uv de

Spirit, say? He say he saw fo' anguls standin' on de fo' corners uv de earth, holdin' de fo' win's uv de earth, an' so fo'th. 'Low me ter ax ef de earth is roun', whar do it keep its corners? Er flat, squar thing has corners, but tell me where is de cornur uv er appul, ur a marbul, ur a cannun ball, ur a silver dollar. Ef dar is enny one uv dem furloserfurs whar's been takin' so many cracks at my ole haid 'bout here, he is korjully envited ter step for'd an' squar up dis vexin' bizniss. I here tell you dat yer karn't squar a circul, but it looks lak dese great scolurs dun learn how ter circul de squar. Ef dey kin do it, let 'em step ter de front an' do de trick. But, mer brutherin, in my po' judgmint, dey karn't do it; tain't in 'em ter do it. Dey is on der wrong side of de Bible; dat's on de outside uv de Bible, an' dar's whar de trubbul comes in wid 'em. Dey dun got out uv de bres'wuks uv de truf, an' ez long ez dey stay dar de light uv de Lord will not shine on der path. I ain't keer'n so much 'bout de sun, tho' it's mighty kunveenyunt ter hav it, but my trus' is in de Word uv de Lord. Long ez my feet is flat on de solid rock, no man kin move me. I'se gittin' my orders f'um de Gord of my salvashun.

"Tother day er man wid er hi coler and side whisk'rs cum ter my house. He was one nice North'rn gemman wat think a heap of us col'rd people in de Souf. Da ar luvly folks and I honours 'em very much. He seem from de start kinder strictly an' cross wid me, and arter while, he brake out furi'us and frettid, an' he say: 'Erlow me Mister Jasper ter gib you sum plain advise. Dis nonsans 'bout de sun movin' whar you ar gettin' is disgracin' yer race all ober de kuntry, an' as a fren of yer peopul, I cum ter say it's got ter stop.' Ha! Ha! Ha! Mars' Sam Hargrove nuvur hardly smash me dat way. It was equl to one ov dem ole overseurs way bac yondur. I tel him dat ef he'll sho me I'se wrong, I give it all up.

"My! My! Ha! Ha! He sail in on me an' such er storm about science, nu 'scuv'ries, an' de Lord only knos wat all, I ner hur befo', an' den he tel me my race is ergin me an' po ole Jasper mus shet up 'is fule mouf.

"Wen he got thru—it look lak he nuvur wud, I tel him John Jasper ain' set up to be no scholur, an' doant kno de ferlosophiz, an' ain' tryin' ter hurt his peopul, but is wurkin' day an' night ter lif 'em up, but his foot is on de rock uv eternal truff. Dar he stan' and dar he is goin' ter stan' til Gabrul soun's de judgment note. So er say to de gemman wat scol'd me up so dat I hur him mek his remarks, but I ain' hur whar he get his Scriptu' from, an' dat 'tween him an' de wurd of de Lord I tek my stan' by de Word of Gord ebery time. Jasper ain' mad: he ain' fightin' nobody; he ain' bin 'pinted janitur to run de sun: he nothin' but de servunt of Gord and a luver of de Everlasting Word. What I keer about de sun? De day comes on wen de sun will be called frum his race-trac, and his light squincked out foruvur; de moon shall turn ter blood, and this yearth be konsoomed wid fier. Let um go; dat wont skeer me nor trubble Gord's erlect'd peopul, for de word uv de Lord shell aindu furivur, an' on dat Solid Rock we stan' an' shall not be muved.

"Is I got yer satisfied yit? Has I prooven my p'int? Oh, ye whose hearts is full uv unberlief! Is yer still hol'in' out? I reckun de reason yer say de sun don' move is 'cause yer are so hard ter move yerse'f. You is a reel triul ter me, but, nevur min'; I ain't gi'n yer up yit, an' nevur will. Truf is mighty; it kin break de heart uv stone, an' I mus' fire anudder arrur uv truf out'n de quivur uv de Lord. If yer haz er copy uv God's Word 'bout yer pussun, please tu'n ter dat miner profit, Malerki, wat writ der las' book in der ole Bible, an' look at chaptur de fust, vurs 'leben; what do it say? I bet'r read it, fur I got er noshun yer critics doan't kerry enny Bible in thar pockits ev'ry day in de week. Here is wat it says: 'Fur from de risin' uv de sun evun unter de goin' doun uv de same My name shall be great 'mong de Gentiles. . . . My name shall be great 'mong de heathun, sez de Lord uv hosts.' How do dat suit yer? It look lak dat ort ter fix it. Dis time it is de Lord uv hosts Hisse'f dat is doin' de talkin', an' He is talkin' on er wonderful an' glorious subjik. He is tellin' uv de spredin' uv His Gorspel, uv de kummin' uv His larst vict'ry ovur de Gentiles, an' de wurldwide glories dat at de las' He is ter git. Oh, my bruddrin, wat er time dat will be. My soul teks wing es I erticipate wid joy dat merlenium day! De glories as dey shine befo' my eyes blin's me, an' I furgits de sun an' moon an' stars. I jes' 'members dat 'long 'bout dose las' days dat de sun an' moon will go out uv bizniss, fur dey won' be needed no mo'. Den will King Jesus come back ter see His people, an' He will be de suffishunt light uv de wurl'. Joshwer's bat'ls will be ovur. Hezekier woan't need no sun diul, an' de sun an' moon will fade out befo' de glorius splendurs uv de New Jerruslem.

"But wat der mattur wid Jasper. I mos' furgit my bizniss, an' mos' gon' ter shoutin' ovur de far away glories uv de secun' cummin' uv my Lord. I beg pardun, an' will try ter git back ter my subjik. I hev ter do as de sun in Hezekier's case—fall back er few dergrees. In dat part uv de Word dat I gin yer frum Malerki—dat de Lord Hisse'f spoke—He klars dat His glory is gwine ter spred. Spred? Whar? Frum de risin' uv de sun ter de goin' down uv de same. Wat? Doan't say dat, duz it? Dat's edzakly wat it sez. Ain't dat cleer 'nuff fer yer? De Lord pity dese doubtin' Tommusses. Here is 'nuff ter settul it all an' kure de wuss cases. Walk up yere, wise folks, an' git yer med'sin. Whar is dem high collar'd furloserfurs now? Wat dey skulkin' roun' in de brush fer? Why doan't yer git out in der broad arternoon light an' fight fer yer cullurs? Ah, I un'stans it; yer got no answer. De Bible is agin yer, an' in yer konshunses yer are convictid.

"But I hears yer back dar. Wat yer wisprin' 'bout? I know; yer say yer sont me sum papurs an' I nevur answer dem. Ha, ha, ha! I got 'em. De differkulty 'bout dem papurs yer sont me is dat dey did not answer me. Dey nevur menshun de Bible one time. Yer think so much uv yoursef's an' so little uv de Lord Gord an' thinks wat yer say is so smart dat yer karn't even speak uv de Word uv de Lord. When yer ax me ter stop believin' in de Lord's Word an' ter pin my faith ter yo words, I ain't er gwine ter do it. I take my stan' by de Bible an' res' my case on wat it says. I take wat de Lord says 'bout my sins, 'bout my Saviour, 'bout life, 'bout death, 'bout de wurl' ter come, an' I take wat de Lord say 'bout de sun an' moon, an' I cares little wat de haters of mer Gord chooses ter say. Think dat I will fursake de Bible? It is my only Book, my hope, de arsnel uv my soul's surplies, an' I wants nuthin' else.

"But I got ernudder wurd fur yer yit. I done wuk ovur dem papurs dat yer sont me widout date an' widout yer name. Yer deals in figgurs an' thinks yer are biggur dan de arkanjuls. Lemme see wat yer dun say. Yer set yerse'f up ter tell me how fur it is frum here ter de sun. Yer think yer got it down ter er nice p'int. Yer say it is 3,339,002 miles frum de earth ter de sun. Dat's wat yer say. Nudder one say dat de distuns is 12,000,000; nudder got it ter 27,000,000. I hers dat de great Isuk Nutun wuk't it up ter 28,000,000, an' later on de furloserfurs gin ernudder rippin' raze to 50,000,000. De las' one gits it bigger dan all de yuthers, up to 90,000,000. Doan't enny uv 'em ergree edzakly an' so dey runs a guess game, an' de las' guess is always de bigges'. Now, wen dese guessers kin hav a kunvenshun in Richmun' an' all ergree 'pun de same thing, I'd be glad ter hear frum yer ag'in, an' I duz hope dat by dat time yer won't be ershamed uv yer name.

"Heeps uv railroads hes bin built sense I saw de fust one wen I wuz fifteen yeers ole, but I ain't hear tell uv er railroad built yit ter de sun. I doan' see why ef dey kin meshur de distuns ter de sun, dey might not git up er railroad er a telurgraf an' enabul us ter fin' sumthin' else 'bout it den merely how fur orf de sun is. Dey tell me dat a kannun ball cu'd mek de trep ter de sun in twelve years. Why doan' dey send it? It might be rig'd up wid quarturs fur a few furloserfers on de inside an' fixed up fur er kumfurterble ride. Dey wud need twelve years' rashuns an' a heep uv changes uv ramint—mighty thick clo'es wen dey start and mighty thin uns wen dey git dar.

"Oh, mer bruthrin, dese things mek yer laugh, an' I doan' blem yer fer laughin', 'cept it's always sad ter laugh at der follies uv fools. If we cu'd laugh 'em out'n kount'nens, we might well laugh day an' night. Wat cuts inter my soul is, dat all dese men seem ter me dat dey is hittin' at de Bible. Dat's wat sturs my soul an' fills me wid reichus wrath. Leetle keers I wat dey says 'bout de sun, purvided dey let de Word uv de Lord er-lone. But nevur min'. Let de heethun rage an' de people 'madgin er vain thing. Our King shall break 'em in pieces an' dash 'em down. But blessed be de name uv our Gord, de Word uv de Lord indurith furivur. Stars may fall, moons may turn ter blood, an' de sun set ter rise no mo', but Thy kingdom, oh, Lord, is frum evurlastin' ter evurlastin'.

"But I has er word dis arternoon fer my own brutherin. Dey is de people fer whose souls I got ter watch—fur dem I got ter stan' an' report at de last—dey is my sheep an' I'se der shepherd, an' my soul is knit ter dem forever. 'Tain fer me ter be troublin' yer wid dese questions erbout dem heb'nly bodies. Our eyes goes far beyon' de smaller stars; our home is clean outer sight uv dem twinklin' orbs; de chariot dat will cum ter take us to our Father's mansion will sweep out by dem flickerin' lights an' never halt till it brings us in clar view uv de throne uv de Lamb. Doan't hitch yer hopes to no sun nor stars; yer home is got Jesus fer its light, an' yer hopes mus' trabel up dat way. I preach dis sermon jest fer ter settle de min's uv my few brutherin, an' repeats it 'cause kin' frens wish ter hear it, an' I hopes it will do honour ter de Lord's Word. But nuthin' short of de purly gates can satisfy me, an' I charge, my people, fix yer feet on de solid Rock, yer hearts on Calv'ry, an' yer eyes on de throne uv de Lamb. Dese strifes an' griefs 'll soon git ober; we shall see de King in His glory an' be at ease. Go on, go on, ye ransom uv de Lord; shout His praises as yer go, an' I shall meet yer in de city uv de New Jeruserlum, whar we shan't need the light uv de sun, fer de Lam' uv de Lord is de light uv de saints."

Dry Bones

Dry bones, dry bones,
Well, them bones, dry bones, that are
Laid in the valley.
Well, them bones, dry bones, that are
Laid in the valley,
You can hear the word of the Lord.
Or from my toe bone to my
Foot bone, or from my
Foot bone to my
Ankle bone, or from my
Ankle bone to my
Leg bone, or from my
Leg bone to my
Knee bone.
Well, them bones, dry bones, that are
Laid in the valley,
You can hear the word of the Lord.
Or from my knee bone to my
Thigh bone, or from my
Thigh bone to my
Hip bone, or from my
Hip bone to my
Rib bone, or from my

Rib bone to my
Back bone.
Well, them bones, dry bones, that are
Laid in the valley,
Well, them bones, dry bones, that are
Laid in the valley,
Well, them bones, dry bones, that are
Laid in the valley.
You can hear the word of the Lord.
Or from my back bone to my
Shoulder bone to my
Head bone, or from my
Head bone to my
Skull bone to my
Eye bone.
Well, them bones, dry bones, that are
Laid in the valley,
Well, them bones, dry bones, that are
Laid in the valley.
You can hear the word of the Lord.
Or from my eye bone to my
Nose bone, or from my
Nose bone to my
Mouth bone, or from my
Mouth bone to my—
Chin bone, or from my—
Chin bone to my
Throat bone, or from my
Throat bone to my
Well, them bones, dry bones, that are
Laid in the valley.
Well, them bones, dry bones, that are
Laid in the valley.
You can hear the word of the Lord.
Or from my throat bone to my
Breast bone, or from my
Breast bone to my
Shoulder bone, or from my
Shoulder bone to my
Muscle bone, or from my
Muscle bone to my
Elbow bone.
Well, them bones, dry bones, that are
Laid in the valley.
Well, them bones, dry bones, that are
Laid in the valley.
Or from my elbow bone to my

Arm bone to my
Wrist bone, or from my
Wrist bone to my
Hand bone, or from my
Hand bone to my
Finger bone,
Well, them bones, dry bones, that are
Laid in the valley.
Well, them bones, dry bones, that are
Laid in the valley.
You can hear the word of the Lord.

Folktales

Memories of Slavery

Swapping Dreams

Master Jim Turner, an unusually good-natured master, had a fondness for telling long stories woven out of what he claimed to be his dreams, and especially did he like to "swap" dreams with Ike, a witty slave who was a house servant. Every morning he would set Ike to telling about what he had dreamed the night before. It always seemed, however, that the master could tell the best dream tale, and Ike had to admit that he was beaten most of the time.

One morning, when Ike entered the master's room to clean it, he found the master just preparing to get out of bed. "Ike," he said, "I certainly did have a strange dream last night."

"Sez yuh did, Massa, sez yuh did?" answered Ike. "Lemme hyeah it."

"All right," replied the master. "It was like this: I dreamed I went to Nigger Heaven last night, and saw there a lot of garbage, some old torn-down houses, a few old broken-down, rotten fences, the muddiest, sloppiest streets I ever saw, and a big bunch of ragged, dirty Negroes walking around."

"Umph, umph, Massa," said Ike, "yuh sho' musta et de same t'ing Ah did las' night, 'case Ah dreamed Ah went up ter de white man's paradise, an' de streets wuz all ob gol' an' silvah, and dey wuz lots o' milk an' honey dere, an' putty pearly gates, but dey wuzn't uh soul in de whole place."

Lias's Revelation

Lias Jones was a praying slave. Lias would pray any time, but no matter what he was doing at twelve o'clock noon, he would stop short, kneel and pray to God. The prayer Lias prayed at this hour was a special one. "Oh, Lawd," he would pray, "won't yuh please gib us ouah freedom? Lawd, won't yuh please gib us ouah freedom?"

Yet Lias was not discouraged. Without variation he continued at high noon every day to pray that God would give him and his slave brothers freedom. Finally, one day the master sent for Lias to help clean the big house. Lias at twelve o'clock was starting in on the parlor, but had not been in the room long enough to examine the furnishings. Just then the big gong that called the Negroes to dinner started sounding. Lias stopped, as was his custom, to pray for freedom. So he knelt down in the parlor and began to pray: "Oh, Lawd, cum an' gib us all ouah freedom. Oh, Lawd, cum an' gib us all ouah freedom." When Lias got up, it happened that he was standing just opposite a lifesize mirror in the parlor, which reflected his image in it.

Since the slaves had no looking-glasses, Lias had never seen one before, and now he was amazed to see a black man gazing at him from the glass. The only thing he could think of in connection with the image was that God had come down in answer to his prayers; so he said, looking at the image in the mirror, "Ah decla', Gawd, Ah didn't know yuh wuz black. Ah thought yuh wuz uh white man. If yuh is black, Ah's gwine make yuh gib us ouah freedom."

Big Sixteen

It was back in slavery time when Big Sixteen was a man and they called 'im Sixteen 'cause dat was de number of de shoe he wore. He was big and strong and Ole Massa looked to him to do everything.

One day Ole Massa said, "Big Sixteen, Ah b'lieve Ah want you to move dem sills Ah had hewed out down in de swamp."

"I yassuh, Massa."

Big Sixteen went down in de swamp and picked up dem 12×12's and brought 'em on up to de house and stack 'em. No one man ain't never toted a 12×12 befo' nor since.

So Ole Massa said one day, "Go fetch in de mules. Ah want to look 'em over."

Big Sixteen went on down to de pasture and caught dem mules by de bridle but they was contrary and balky and he tore de bridles to pieces pullin' on 'em, so he picked one of 'em up under each arm and brought 'em up to Old Massa.

He says, "Big Sixteen, if you kin tote a pair of balky males, you kin do anything. You kin ketch de Devil."

"Yassuh, Ah kin, if you git me a nine-pound hammer and a pick and shovel!"

Ole Massa got Sixteen de things he ast for and tole 'im to go ahead and bring him de Devil.

Big Sixteen went out in front of de house and went to diggin'. He was diggin' nearly a month befo' he got where he wanted. Then he took his hammer and went and knocked on de Devil's door. Devil answered de door hisself.

"Who dat out dere?"

"It's Big Sixteen."

"What you want?"

"Wanta have a word wid you for a minute."

Soon as de Devil poked his head out de door, Sixteen lammed him over de head wid dat hammer and picked 'im up and carried 'im back to Old Massa.

Ole Massa looked at de dead Devil and hollered, "Take dat ugly thing 'way from here, quick! Ah didn't think you'd ketch de Devil sho 'nuff."

So Sixteen picked up de Devil and throwed 'im back down de hole.

Way after while, Big Sixteen died and went up to Heben. But Peter looked at him and tole 'im to g'wan 'way from dere. He was too powerful. He might git outa order and there wouldn't be nobody to handle 'im. But he had to go somewhere so he went on to hell.

Soon as he got to de gate de Devil's children was playin' in de yard and they seem 'im and run to de house, says, "Mama, Mama! Dat man's out dere dat kilt papa!"

So she called 'im in de house and shet de door. When Sixteen got dere she handed 'im a li'l piece of fire and said, "You ain't comin' in here. Here, take dis hot coal and g'wan off and start you a hell uh yo' own."

So when you see a Jack O'Lantern in de woods at night you know it's Big Sixteen wid his piece of fire lookin' for a place to go.

Preacher Tales

The Three Preachers

There was a big Baptist state convention. The delegates was so numerous they couldn't hardly take care of all of them. And there was three preachers left didn't have nowhere to stay, a Baptist preacher, a Methodist preacher, and a Presbyterian preacher. The lady told them she had fixed a room in a nearby house (she didn't tell them it was hanted), and they could take their meals with her.

They came for meeting that night and set down and begin to talk. Eventually the hants commenced to coming in. The Baptist preacher began singing. The more he sang the more the hants came in. The Presbyterian preacher he begin praying. And the more he prayed the more the hants come in. He says to the Methodist preacher, "Now doc, it's your floor."

And the Methodist preacher, say, "Let's take up a collection," and the hants begin to leave.

The Wrong Man in the Coffin

You know de chu'ch folks in de Bottoms hab a love for big funerals. 'Reckly attuh freedom, dey hab de funerals on Sunday, 'caze de boss-mens don' 'low no funerals in de week-a-days. Nowadays, dey hab al funerals on a Sunday jes' for de sake of de love of big funerals.

In dem days comin' up, womens ain't gonna talk 'bout dey men folks while dey's livin'. Dey wanna keep folks thinkin' dey hab a good man for a husband, but dese days an' times hit's a lot diffunt. De gals what ma'ied nowadays talk 'bout dey husbands to any an' evuhbody. You can heah 'em all de time talkin' 'bout "dat ole scoun'al ain't no 'count." Dey say, "If'n you been ma'ied a yeah an' yo' husband ain't nevuh paid a light bill, ain't nevuh bought a sack of flour, ain't nevuh brung you a pair of stockin's, ain't never paid on de insu'ances, what you think 'bout a scoun'al lack dat?"

One time dere was a han' what died on de old McPherson fawm by de name of Ken Parker. De membuhship of de Salem Baptis' Chu'ch think Ken's a good man, 'caze he hab a fine big family an' he 'ten' chu'ch regluh as de Sundays come. De pastuh think he a Good Christun, too. So when he git up to preach Ken's funeral, he tell 'bout what a good man Brothuh Ken was, 'bout how true he was to his wife, an' what a good providuh he done been for his family an' all lack dat. He keep on an' keep on in dis wise, but Ken's wife Sadie know de pastuh done errored; so she turn to de ol'es' boy, Jim, an' say, "Jim, go up dere an' look in dat coffin an' see if'n dat's yo' pappy in dere."

The Preacher and His Farmer Brother

Of occasion in de bottoms, in de same fam'ly you kin fin' some of de bestes' preachuhs dat done evuh grace a pulpit, an' a brothuh or a sistuh what ain't nevuh set foot in de chu'ch ez long ez dey live. Ah calls to min' Revun Jeremiah Sol'mon what pastuh de Baptis' chu'ch down to Egypt, on Caney Creek. He done put on de armuh of de Lawd when he rech fo'teen; he come to be a deacon when he rech sixteen, an' dey 'dained 'im for to preach de Word when he turnt to be eighteen. He one of de mos' pow'ful preachuhs dat done evuh grace a Texas pulpit an' he de moderatuh of de St. John's 'Sociation. But he hab a brothuh, what go by de name of Sid, what ain't nevuh set foot in a chu'ch house in his life.

Sib hab a good spot of lan' roun' bout Falls, on de Brazos, though; so one time Revun Jeremiah 'cide to pay Sid a visit. Hit been twenty yeah since he laid eyes on 'im; so he driv up to de house an' soon ez he gits thoo shakin' han's wid Sid's wife, Lulu Belle, an' de chilluns, he say, "Ah wants to see yo' fawm, Sid. Le's see what kinda fawmuh you is."

"Sho," say Sid. So he gits his hat on an' dey goes down to de cawn patch an' looks at de cawn Sid done planted an' what nelly 'bout grown, an' de Revun say, "Sid, youse got a putty good cawn crop by de he'p of de Lawd." Den dey goes on down to de cotton patch and de Revun looks at hit an' 'low, "Sid, youse got a putty good cotton crop by de he'p of de Lawd." Den dey moseys on down to de sugah cane patch an' when de Revun eye dis, he say, "Sid, youse got a putty good cane patch, by de he'p of de Lawd."

An' when he say dis, Sid eye 'im kinda disgusted lack, an' say, "Yeah, but you oughta seed hit when de Lawd had it by Hisse'f."

Response: The Written Tradition

Voices of the Folk Tradition

CHARLES W. CHESNUTT

(1858–1932)

Charles Waddell Chesnutt, referred to as the "pioneer of the color line" because of his thematic focus on interracial relationships, was one of the major African American writers to win national prominence in the late nineteenth and early twentieth centuries. In contrast to his predecessors, he was able to secure the support of large publishing outlets. His development of assimilationist themes in his works and his concern with the African American folk tradition gave his work a flavor that tied together his roots in North Carolina with his cosmopolitan life in Cleveland, Ohio. His depictions of how black people fared during Reconstruction and shortly thereafter won him audiences from the budding African American literary community as well as from the established white literati. Chesnutt achieved success initially through publishing short stories in the *Atlantic Monthly;* he won the support of editors and writers such as Walter Hines Page and George W. Cable, as well as the editors at Houghton Mifflin.

Chesnutt was born on June 20, 1858, in Cleveland, Ohio, to Andrew Jackson and Anne Maria Sampson Chesnutt, free blacks who had migrated from Fayetteville, North Carolina. Andrew Chesnutt served as a teamster in the Union Army, and Anne Maria had secretly taught slaves in North Carolina, so the young Charles was heir to a tradition of racial and national commitment. Andrew moved his family back to Fayetteville in 1866, where Charles helped his father in their grocery business and attended the local normal school. By the time his mother died in 1871 and he had to help support the family, he had acquired enough education to begin teaching school. One job took him to Spartanburg, South Carolina, and another to Charlotte, North Carolina. Between teaching duties, Chesnutt continued his education by studying American history, algebra, Latin and other languages, music, and literature. As early as 1874, he began to keep a journal that would play a significant role in his observation of race relations as well as in his articulation of his role as a writer.

Returning to teach in Fayetteville in 1877, Chesnutt married a fellow teacher, Susan Perry, in 1878. He added stenography to his studies as a way of combatting the stifling effect of small-town America. Although he became principal in 1880 of the normal school he had attended, his education and color (he was a "white" black man) placed him between the races, and he resigned in 1883 to try his hand at legal stenography in the North. He was also becoming increasingly convinced that he should become a writer. Observing Judge Albion Tourgée's success in writing about black people in North Carolina, Chesnutt questioned in his journal why he could not do the same. He determined that, if he wrote, he would write for "a high, holy purpose." His writing would be goal oriented in terms of preparing the way for black people to get "recognition and equality."

The summer of 1883 found Chesnutt alone in New York working as a stenographer and reporter for the New York *Mail and Express.* Within six months, however, he had decided to move to Cleveland, where he took his family, daughters Ethel and Helen Maria ("Nellie") and son Edwin ("Ned") in addition to his wife, in 1884; a third daughter, Dorothy, was born in Cleveland. That city not only would provide refuge for Chesnutt but also would appear in various of his short works, such as "Baxter's Procrustes" and "The Wife of His Youth."

As early as 1872, Chesnutt had published a short story in a local newspaper in Fayetteville. In 1885, he published "Uncle Peter's House," another short story, with the S.S. McClure newspaper syndicate. He also developed his first long-standing literary friendship during this period; he and George W. Cable exchanged letters and essays. In one radical essay, Chesnutt urged an end to all forms of segregation in the South. Cable tried unsuccessfully to get Chesnutt's "Rena Walden" published in *Century Magazine.* That story, and the many versions of it Chesnutt worked on over the years, formed the core of what became *The House Behind the Cedars* (1900, originally titled "Rena Walden"), a novel depicting the tragic consequences of a young black woman passing for white. Although Chesnutt passed the Ohio bar in 1887 and joined a Cleveland law firm, he nonetheless continued his lucrative business as a court reporter as well as his profession as a writer.

"The Goophered Grapevine," the first story in *The Conjure Woman,* appeared in the August 1887 issue of the *Atlantic Monthly,* after which Walter Hines Page of Houghton Mifflin approached Chesnutt about reading all the short fiction he had written. That contact resulted in the selection and publication of the seven stories in *The Conjure Woman,* which appeared in 1899. Consciously drawing on the tradition of Uncle Remus telling stories to a little white boy, which had been popularized by Joel Chandler Harris in the 1880s, Chesnutt created Uncle Julius, a kindly trickster who tells tales in dialect for his own benefit and that of a northern white couple who have relocated to the South. The volume demonstrates the peculiar position of a black writer trying to make inroads into a white reading audience; while Chesnutt may have wanted to be critical of slavery and the conditions under which blacks lived during Reconstruction, he could only do so by veiling his messages in tales wrapped in fantasy and superstition in order not to offend his audience. Chesnutt also published a biography of Frederick Douglass, *Frederick Douglass,* in 1899 (Boston: Small, Maynard).

In 1900, Houghton Mifflin published Chesnutt's *The Wife of His Youth and Other Stories of the Color Line.* (The title story was originally published in the *Atlantic Monthly* in 1898.) Explorations into miscegenation and other cross-racial sexual encounters, the nine stories weigh the value of human relationships and attachments against the dictates of communities that would keep the races separate. They also explore the intraracial color bar, where black people adopt the value system and prejudices based on color as practiced by the larger society. In "The Wife of His Youth," for example, the leader of Groveland's (Cleveland's) Blue Veins must make the wrenching choice of marrying a very light-skinned black woman or accepting the very dark-skinned "wife of his youth," to whom he had been married during slavery and from whom he had run away more than twenty-five years before. In another instance, a white sheriff who has fathered a black son must make a decision to acknowledge that son when he is jailed or continue to deny kinship to him.

Color, Chesnutt asserts, frequently takes priority over morality and conscience, and human beings distort innate affection in favor of societally prescribed roles that can negate their very essence as beings with altruistic feelings. The psychological traumas of people of mixed blood, combined with the racial hatred and mob violence sometimes directed toward them, did not make for the romantic times that proponents of the Plantation Tradition advocated. Reviewers such as William Dean Howells and Hamilton Wright Mabie applauded Chesnutt's craft, but others were less enthusiastic about his focus on such disturbing subjects.

Chesnutt's efforts not to offend, therefore, did not last long. When he published *The Marrow of Tradition* (1901), a fictionalized account of the Wilmington, North Carolina, massacre of black people who tried to vote in the 1898 election, his critics began to see some bitterness in his work. Sales were disappointing enough (less than five thousand copies sold instead of the projected twenty to thirty thousand) for Chesnutt to reopen in 1902 the court-reporting business he had closed in 1899 to pursue writing full-time. When he published *The Colonel's Dream* (1905), a hard-hitting account of the brutal responses to a kind-hearted Southern white man's effort to transform his prejudiced community, the critical response was so negative that Chesnutt gave up trying to make his living from publishing literary works on race problems in the South. He did not stop writing, however. He had completed two novels, *The Rainbow Chasers* and *Evelyn's Husband*, before 1905 (both focusing on white characters) that did not win publication. After them, he wrote *Mrs. Darcy's Daughter; Paul Marchand, F.M.C.; The Quarry;* and two additional novels; none he submitted for review was judged to be publishable. His revisions of them continued into the 1920s. Uneasy with the direction being taken by some of the writers of the Harlem Renaissance, Chesnutt joined W.E.B. Du Bois and William Stanley Braithwaite in advocating and producing a counterliterature; his efforts were not successful.

As politically active personally as he was in his literary works, Chesnutt publicly espoused a number of causes in the two decades following 1905. He joined Booker T. Washington's Committee of Twelve, a group of speechwriters and pamphleteers who composed essays that depicted blacks sympathetically to influence white public opinion. He also supported the efforts of the Niagara Movement, which would lead to the founding of the NAACP. Chesnutt joined other blacks in protesting the showing of D.W. Griffiths's *The Birth of a Nation* (1915). He completed a series of articles on black and white intermarriage as a solution to race problems.

A few recognitions and rewards came to Chesnutt in the 1920s. In 1921, black filmmaker Oscar Micheaux bought the rights to *The House Behind the Cedars,* made the movie, and showed it to black audiences. The Chicago *Defender* serialized *The House Behind the Cedars.* The NAACP presented Chesnutt with its Spingarn Medal in 1928 for his pioneering work as a literary artist, and, in 1930, Houghton Mifflin reprinted *The Conjure Woman* in a handsome edition; it was the first time in many years that one of Chesnutt's works was back in print.

Color provided Chesnutt with the unique perspective of being caught between cultures and races. His observations on passing, miscegenation, and assimilation enabled him to create a body of works reflective of the peculiar state of American race relations at the turn of the century. Although his works were read in his lifetime, Chesnutt's true literary value has been uncovered in more recent years when quieter political times have allowed readers to appreciate the difficulty as well as the artistry of his achievements.

❖❖❖

Chesnutt's short stories have been collected by Sylvia Lyons Render in a volume titled *The Short Fiction of Charles W. Chesnutt* (1980).

The earliest biography of Chesnutt is by his daughter, Helen M. Chesnutt, titled *Charles Waddell Chesnutt: Pioneer of the Color Line* (1952). Another biography, by Frances Richardson Keller, is *An American Crusade: The Life of Charles Waddell Chesnutt* (1978). A notable biographical and critical study is William L. Andrews's *The Literary Career of Charles Waddell Chesnutt* (1980).

Book-length critical studies are few: J. Noel Heermance, *Charles W. Chesnutt: America's First Great Black Novelist* (1974); Sylvia Lyons Render, *Charles W. Chesnutt* (1980).

The Goophered Grapevine

Some years ago my wife was in poor health, and our family doctor, in whose skill and honesty I had implicit confidence, advised a change of climate. I shared, from an unprofessional standpoint, his opinion that the raw winds, the chill rains, and the violent changes of temperature that characterized the winters in the region of the Great Lakes tended to aggravate my wife's difficulty, and would undoubtedly shorten her life if she remained exposed to them. The doctor's advice was that we seek, not a temporary place of sojourn, but a permanent residence, in a warmer and more equable climate. I was engaged at the time in grape-culture in northern Ohio, and, as I liked the business and had given it much study, I decided to look for some other locality suitable for carrying it on. I thought of sunny France, of sleepy Spain, of Southern California, but there were objections to them all. It occurred to me that I might find what I wanted in some one of our own Southern States. It was a sufficient time after the war for conditions in the South to have become somewhat settled; and I was enough of a pioneer to start a new industry, if I could not find a place where grape-culture had been tried. I wrote to a cousin who had gone into the turpentine business in central North Carolina. He assured me, in response to my inquiries, that no better place could be found in the South than the State and neighborhood where he lived; the climate was perfect for health, and, in conjunction with the soil, ideal for grape-culture; labor was cheap, and land could be bought for a mere song. He gave us a cordial invitation to come and visit him while we looked into the matter. We accepted the invitation, and after several days of leisurely travel, the last hundred miles of which were up a river on a sidewheel steamer, we reached our destination, a quaint old town, which I shall call Patesville, because, for one reason, that is not its name. There was a red brick market-house in the public square, with a tall tower, which held a four-faced clock that struck the hours, and from which there pealed out a curfew at nine o'clock. There were two or three hotels, a court-house, a jail, stores, offices, and all the appurtenances of a county seat and a commercial emporium; for while Patesville numbered only four or five thousand inhabitants, of all shades of complexion, it was one of the principal towns in North Carolina, and had a considerable trade in cotton and naval stores. This business activity was not immediately apparent to my unaccustomed eyes. Indeed, when I first saw the town, there brooded over it a calm that seemed almost sabbatic in its restfulness, though I learned later on that underneath its somnolent exterior the deeper currents of life—love and hatred, joy and despair, ambition and avarice, faith and friendship—flowed not less steadily than in livelier latitudes.

We found the weather delightful at that season, the end of summer, and were hospitably entertained. Our host was a man of means and evidently regarded our visit as a pleasure, and we were therefore correspondingly at our ease, and in a position to act with the coolness of judgment desirable in making so radical a change in our lives. My cousin placed a horse and buggy at our disposal, and himself acted as our guide until I became somewhat familiar with the country.

I found that grape-culture, while it had never been carried on to any great extent, was not entirely unknown in the neighborhood. Several planters thereabouts had attempted it on a commercial scale, in former years, with greater or less success; but like most Southern industries, it had felt the blight of war and had fallen into desuetude.

I went several times to look at a place that I thought might suit me. It was a plantation of considerable extent, that had formerly belonged to a wealthy man by the name of McAdoo. The estate had been for years involved in litigation between disputing heirs, during which period shiftless cultivation had well-nigh exhausted the soil. There had been a vineyard of some extent on the place, but it had not been attended to since the war, and had lapsed into utter neglect. The vines—here partly supported by decayed and broken-down trellises, there twining themselves among the branches of the slender saplings which had sprung up among them—grew in wild and unpruned luxuriance, and the few scattered grapes they bore were the undisputed prey of the first comer. The site was admirably adapted to grape-raising; the soil, with a little attention, could not have been better; and with the native grape, the luscious scuppernong, as my main reliance in the beginning, I felt sure that I could introduce and cultivate successfully a number of other varieties.

One day I went over with my wife to show her the place. We drove out of the town over a long wooden bridge that spanned a spreading mill-pond, passed the long whitewashed fence surrounding the county fair-ground, and struck into a road so sandy that the horse's feet sank to the fetlocks. Our route lay partly up hill and partly down, for we were in the sand-hill county; we drove past cultivated farms, and then by abandoned fields grown up in scrub-oak and short-leaved pine, and once or twice through the solemn aisles of the virgin forest, where the tall pines, well-nigh meeting over the narrow road, shut out the sun, and wrapped us in cloistral solitude. Once, at a cross-roads, I was in doubt as to the turn to take, and we sat there waiting ten minutes—we had already caught some of the native infection of restfulness—for some human being to come along, who could direct us on our way. At length a little negro girl appeared, walking straight as an arrow, with a piggin full of water on her head. After a little patient investigation, necessary to overcome the child's shyness, we learned what we wished to know, and at the end of about five miles from the town reached our destination.

We drove between a pair of decayed gateposts—the gate itself had long since disappeared—and up a straight sandy lane, between two lines of rotting rail fence, partly concealed by jimson-weeds and briers, to the open space where a dwelling-house had once stood, evidently a spacious mansion, if we might judge from the ruined chimneys that were still standing, and the brick pillars on which the sills rested. The house itself, we had been informed, had fallen a victim to the fortunes of war.

We alighted from the buggy, walked about the yard for a while, and then wandered off into the adjoining vineyard. Upon Annie's complaining of weariness I led the way back to the yard, where a pine log, lying under a spreading elm, afforded a shady though somewhat hard seat. One end of the log was already occupied by a venerable-looking colored man. He held on his knees a hat full of grapes, over which he was smacking his lips with great gusto, and a pile of grapeskins near him indicated that the performance was no new thing. We approached him at an angle from the rear, and were close to him before he perceived us. He respectfully rose as we drew near, and was moving away, when I begged him to keep his seat.

"Don't let us disturb you," I said. "There is plenty of room for us all."

He resumed his seat with somewhat of embarrassment. While he had been standing, I had observed that he was a tall man, and, though slightly bowed by the weight of years, apparently quite vigorous. He was not entirely black, and this fact, together with the quality of his hair, which was about six inches long and very bushy, except on the top of his head, where he was quite bald, suggested a slight strain of other than negro blood. There was a shrewdness in his eyes, too, which was not altogether African, and which, as we afterwards learned from experience, was indicative of a corresponding shrewdness in his character. He went on eating the grapes, but did not seem to enjoy himself quite so well as he had apparently done before he became aware of our presence.

"Do you live around here?" I asked, anxious to put him at his ease.

"Yas, suh. I lives des ober yander, behine de nex' san'-hill, on de Lumberton plank-road."

"Do you know anything about the time when this vineyard was cultivated?"

"Lawd bless you, suh, I knows all about it. Dey ain' na'er a man in dis settlement w'at won' tell you ole Julius McAdoo 'us bawn en raise' on dis yer same plantation. Is you de Norv'n gemman w'at 's gwine ter buy de ole vimya'd?"

"I am looking at it," I replied; "but I don't know that I shall care to buy unless I can be reasonably sure of making something out of it."

"Well, suh, you is a stranger ter me, en I is a stranger ter you, en we is bofe strangers ter one anudder, but 'f I 'uz in yo' place, I wouldn' buy dis vimya'd."

"Why not?" I asked.

"Well, I dunno whe'r you b'lieves in cunj'in' er not,—some er de w'ite folks don't, er says dey don't,—but de truf er de matter is dat dis yer ole vimya'd is goophered."

"Is what?" I asked, not grasping the meaning of this unfamiliar word.

"Is goophered,—cunju'd, bewitch'."

He imparted this information with such solemn earnestness, and with such an air of confidential mystery, that I felt somewhat interested, while Annie was evidently much impressed, and drew closer to me.

"How do you know it is bewitched?" I asked.

"I would n' spec' fer you ter b'lieve me 'less you know all 'bout de fac's. But ef you en young miss dere doan' min' lis'nin' ter a ole nigger run on a minute er two w'ile you er restin', I kin 'splain to you how it all happen'."

We assured him that we would be glad to hear how it all happened, and he began to tell us. At first the current of his memory—or imagination—seemed somewhat sluggish; but as his embarrassment wore off, his language flowed more freely, and the story acquired perspective and coherence. As he became more and more absorbed in the narrative, his eyes assumed a dreamy expression, and he seemed to lose site of his auditors, and to be living over again in monologue his life on the old plantation.

"Ole Mars Dugal' McAdoo," he began, "bought dis place long many years befo' de wah, en I 'member well w'en he sot out all dis yer part er de plantation in scuppernon's. De vimes growed monst'us fas', en Mars Dugal' made a thousan' gallon er scuppernon' wine eve'y year.

"Now, ef dey's an'thing a nigger lub, nex' ter 'possum, en chick'n, en watermillyums, it's scuppernon's. Dey ain' nuffin dat kin stan' up side'n de scuppernon' fer sweetness; sugar ain't a suckumstance ter scuppernon'. W'en de season is nigh 'bout ober, en de grapes begin ter swivel up des a little wid de wrinkles er ole age,—w'en de skin git sof' en brown,—den de scuppernon' make you smack yo' lip en roll yo' eye en wush fer mo'; so I reckon it ain' very 'stonishin' dat niggers lub scuppernon'.

"Dey wuz a sight er niggers in de naberhood er de vimya'd. Dere wuz ole Mars Henry Brayboy's niggers, en ole Mars Jeems McLean's niggers, en Mars Dugal's own niggers; den dey wuz a settlement er free niggers en po' buckrahs down by de Wim'l'ton Road, en Mars Dugal' had de only vimya'd in de naberhood. I reckon it ain' so much so nowadays, but befo' de wah, in slab'ry times, a nigger did n' mine goin' fi' er ten mile in a night, w'en dey wuz sump'n good ter ear at de yuther een'.

"So atter a w'ile Mars Dugal' begin ter miss his scuppernon's. Co'se he 'cuse' de niggers er it, but dey all 'nied it ter de las'. Mars Dugal' sot spring guns en steel traps, en he en de oberseah sot up nights once't er twice't, tel one night Mars Dugal'—he 'uz a monst'us keerless man—got his leg shot full er cow-peas. But somehow er nudder day could n' nebber ketch none er de niggers. I dunner how it happen, but it happen des like I tell you, en de grapes kep' on a-goin' des de same.

"But bimeby ole Mars Dugal' fix' up a plan ter stop it. Dey wuz a cunjuh 'oman livin' down 'mongs' de free niggers on de Wim'l'ton Road, en all de darkies fum Rockfish ter Beaver Crick wuz feared er her. She could wuk de mos' powerfulles' kin' er goopher,—could make people hab fits, er rheumatiz, er make 'em des dwinel away en die; en dey say she went out ridin' de niggers at night, fer she wuz a witch 'sides bein' a cunjuh 'oman. Mars Dugal' hearn 'bout Aun' Peggy's doin's, en begun ter 'flect whe'r er no he could n' git her ter he'p him keep de niggers off'n de grapevimes. One day in de spring er de year, ole miss pack' up a basket er chick'n en poun'-cake, en a bottle er scuppernon' wine, en Mars Dugal' tuk it in his buggy en driv ober ter Aun' Peggy's cabin. He tuk de basket in, en had a long talk wid Aun' Peggy.

"De nex' day Aun' Peggy come up ter de vimya'd. De niggers seed her slippin' 'roun', en dey soon foun' out what she 'uz doin' dere. Mars Dugal' had hi'ed her ter goopher de grapevimes. She sa'ntered 'roun' 'mongs' de vimes, en tuk a leaf fum dis one, en a grape-hull fum dat one, en a grape-seed fum anudder one; en den a little twig fum here, en a little pinch er dirt fum dere,—en put it all in a big black bottle, wid a snake's toof en a speckle' hen's gall en some ha'rs fum a black cat's tail, en den fill' de bottle wid scuppernon' wine. W'en she got de goopher all ready en fix', she tuk 'n went out in de woods en buried it under de root uv a red oak tree, en den come back en tole one er de niggers she done goopher de grapevimes, en a'er a nigger w'at eat dem grapes 'ud be sho ter die inside'n twel' mont's.

"Atter dat de niggers let de scuppernon's 'lone, en Mars Dugal' did n' hab no 'casion ter fine no mo' fault; en de season wuz mos' gone, w'en a strange gemman stop at de plantation one night ter see Mars Dugal' on some business; en his coachman, seein' de scuppernon's growin' so nice en sweet, slip 'roun' behine de smoke-house, en et all de scuppernon's he could hole. Nobody did n' notice it at de time, but dat night, on de way home, de gemman's hoss runned away en kill' de coachman. W'en we hearn de noos, Aun' Lucy, de cook, she up 'n say she seed de strange nigger eat'n' er de scuppernon's behine de smoke-house; en den we knowed de goopher had b'en er wukkin'. Den one er de niggers chilluns runned away fum de quarters one day, en got in de scuppernon's, en died de nex' week. W'ite folks say he die' er de fevuh, but de niggers knowed it wuz de goopher. So you k'n be sho de darkies did n' hab much ter do wid dem scuppernon' vimes.

"W'en de scuppernon' season 'uz ober fer dat year, Mars Dugal' foun' he had made fifteen hund'ed gallon er wine; en one er de niggers hearn him laffin' wid de oberseah fit ter kill, en sayin' dem fifteen hund'ed gallon er wine wuz monst'us good intrus' on de ten dollars he laid out on de vimya'd. So I 'low ez he paid Aun' Peggy ten dollars fer to goopher de grapevimes.

"De goopher did n' wuk no mo' tel de nex' summer, w'en 'long to'ds de middle er de season one er de fiel' han's died; en ez dat lef' Mars Dugal' sho't er han's, he went off ter town fer ter buy anudder. He fotch de noo nigger home wid 'im. He wuz er ole nigger, er de color er a gingy-cake, en ball ez a hoss-apple on de top er his head. He wuz a peart ole nigger, do', en could do a big day's wuk.

"Now it happen dat one er de niggers on de nex' plantation, one er ole Mars Henry Brayboy's niggers, had runned away de day befo', en tuk ter de swamp, en ole Mars Dugal' en some er de yuther nabor w'ite folks had gone out wid dere guns en dere dogs fer ter he'p 'em hunt fer de nigger; en de han's on our own plantation wuz all so flustered dat we fuhgot ter tell de noo han' 'bout de goopher on de scuppernon' vimes. Co'se he smell de grapes en see de vimes, an atter dahk de fus' thing he done wuz ter slip off ter de grapevimes 'dout sayin' nuffin ter no-body. Nex' mawnin' he tole some er de niggers 'bout de fine bait er scuppernon' he et de night befo'.

"W'en dey tole 'im 'bout de goopher on de grapevimes, he 'uz dat tarrified dat he turn pale, en look des like he gwine ter die right in his tracks. De oberseah come up en axed w'at 'uz de matter; en w'en dey tole 'im Henry be'n eatin' er de scuppernon's, en got de goopher on 'im, he gin Henry a big drink er w'iskey, en 'low dat de nex' rainy day he take 'im ober ter Aun' Peggy's, en see ef she would n' take de goopher off'n him, seein' ez he did n' know nuffin er-bout it tel he done et de grapes.

"Sho nuff, it rain de nex' day, en de oberseah went ober ter Aun' Peggy's wid Henry. En Aun' Peggy say dat bein' ez Henry did n' know 'bout de goopher, en et de grapes in ign'ance er de conseq'ences, she reckon she mought be able fer ter take de goopher off'n him. So she fotch out er bottle wid some cunjuh medicine in it, en po'd some out in a go'd fer Henry ter drink. He manage ter git it down; he say it tas'e like whiskey wid sump'n bitter in it. She 'lowed dat 'ud keep de goopher off'n him tel de spring; but w'en de sap begin ter rise in de grapevimes he ha' ter come en see her ag'in, en she tell him w'at e's ter do.

"Nex' spring, w'en de sap commence' ter rise in de scuppernon' vime, Henry tuk a ham one night. Whar'd he git de ham? *I* doan know; dey wa'n't no hams on de plantation 'cep'n' w'at 'uz in de smoke-house, but I never see Henry 'bout de smoke-house. But ez I wuz a-sayin', he tuk de ham ober ter Aun' Peggy's; en Aun' Peggy tole 'im dat w'en Mars Dugal' begin ter prune de grapevimes, he mus' go en take 'n scrape off de sap whar it ooze out'n de cut een's er de vimes, en 'n'int his ball head wid it; en ef he do dat once't a year de goopher would n' wuk agin 'im long ez he done it. En bein' ez he fotch her de ham, she fix' it so he kin eat all de scupper-non' he want.

"So Henry 'n'int his head wid de sap out'n de big grapevime des ha'f way 'twix' de quarters en de big house, en de goopher nebber wuk agin him dat summer. But de beatenes' thing you eber see happen ter Henry. Up ter dat time he wuz ez ball ez a sweeten' 'tater, but des ez soon ez de young leaves begun ter come out on de grapevimes, de ha'r begun ter grow out on Henry's head, en by de middle er de summer he had de bigges' head er ha'r on de plantation. Befo' dat, Henry had tol'able good ha'r 'roun' de aidges, but soon ez de young grapes begun ter come, Henry's ha'r begun to quirl all up in little balls, des like dis yer reg'lar grapy ha'r, en by de time de grapes got ripe his head look des like a bunch er grapes. Combin' it did n' do no good; he wuk at it ha'f de night wid er Jim Crow,[1] en think he git it straighten' out, but in de mawnin' de grapes 'ud be dere des de same. So he gin it up, en tried ter keep de grapes down by havin' his ha'r cut sho't.

"But dat wa'n't de quares' thing 'bout de goopher. When Henry come ter de plantation, he wuz gittin' a little ole an stiff in de j'ints. But dat summer he got des ez spry en libely ez any young nigger on de plantation; fac', he got so biggity dat Mars Jackson, de oberseah, ha' ter th'eaten ter whip 'im, ef he did n' stop cuttin' up his didos en behave hisse'f. But de mos' cur'ouses' thing happen' in de fall, when de sap begin ter go down in de grapevimes. Fus', when de grapes 'uz gethered, de knots begun ter straighten out'n Henry's ha'r; en w'en de leaves begin ter fall, Henry's ha'r 'mence' ter drap out; en when de vimes 'uz bar', Henry's head wuz baller 'n it wuz in de spring, en he begin ter git ole en stiff in de j'ints ag'in, en paid no mo' 'tention ter de gals dyoin' er de whole winter. En nex' spring, w'en he rub de sap on ag'in, he got young ag'in, en so soopl en libely dat none

[1]A small card, resembling a currycomb in construction, and used by negroes in the rural districts instead of a comb.

er de young niggers on de plantation could n' jump, ner dance, ner hoe ez much cotton ez Henry. But in de fall er de year his grapes 'mence' ter straighten out, en his j'ints ter git stiff, en his ha'r drap off, en de rheumatiz begin ter wrastle wid 'im.

"Now, ef you'd 'a' knowed ole Mars Dugal' McAdoo, you'd 'a' knowed dat it ha' ter be a mighty rainy day when he could n' fine sump'n fer his niggers ter do, en it ha' ter be a mighty little hole he could n' crawl thoo, en ha' ter be a monst'us cloudy night when a dollar git by him in the dahkness; en w'en he see how Henry git young in de spring en old in de fall, he 'lowed ter hisse'f ez how he could make mo' money out'n Henry dan by wukkin' him in de cotton-fiel'. 'Long de nex' spring, atter de sap 'mence' ter rise, en Henry 'n'int 'is head en sta'ted fer ter git young en soopl, Mars Dugal' up 'n tuk Henry ter town, en sole 'im fer fifteen hunder' dollars. Co'se de man w'at bought Henry did n' know nuffin 'bout de goopher, en Mars Dugal' did n' see no 'casion fer ter tell 'im. Long to'ds de fall, w'en de sap went down, Henry begin ter git ole ag'in same ez yuzhal, en his noo marster begin ter git skeered les'n he gwine ter lose his fifteen-hunder' dollar nigger. He sent fer a mighty fine doctor, but de med'cine did n' 'pear ter do no good; de goopher had a good holt. Henry tole de doctor 'bout de goopher, but de doctor des laff at 'im.

"One day in de winter Mars Dugal' went ter town, en wuz santerin' 'long de Main Street, when who should he meet but Henry's noo marster. Dey said 'Hoddy,' en Mars Dugal' ax 'im ter hab a seegyar; en atter dey run on awhile 'bout de craps en de weather, Mars Dugal' ax 'im, sorter keerless, like ez ef he des thought of it,—

"'How you like de nigger I sole you las' spring?'

"Henry's marster shuck his head en knock de ashes off'n his seegyar.

"'Spec' I made a bad bahgin when I bought dat nigger. Henry done good wuk all de summer, but sence de fall set in he 'pears ter be sorter pinin' away. Dey ain' nuffin pertickler de matter wid 'im—leastways de doctor say so—'cep'n' a tech er de rheumatiz; but his ha'r is all fell out, en ef he don't pick up his strenk mighty soon, I spec' I'm gwine ter lose 'im.'

"Dey smoked on awhile, en bimeby ole Mars say, 'Well, a bahgin's a bahgin, but you en me is good fren's, en I doan wan' ter see you lose all de money you paid fer dat nigger; en ef w'at you say is so, en I ain't 'sputin' it, he ain't wuf much now. I 'spec's you wukked him too ha'd dis summer, er e'se de swamps down here don't agree wid de san'-hill nigger. So you des lemme know, en ef he gits any wusser I'll be willin' ter gib yer five hund'ed dollars fer 'im, en take my chances on his livin'.'

"Sho 'nuff, when Henry begun ter draw up wid de rheumatiz en it look like he gwine ter die fer sho, his noo marster sen' fer Mars Dugal', en Mars Dugal' gin him what he promus, en brung Henry home ag'in. He tuk good keer uv 'im dyoin' er de winter,—give 'im w'iskey ter rub his rheumatiz, en terbacker ter smoke, en all he want ter eat,—'cause a nigger w'at he could make a thousan' dollars a year off'n did n' grow on eve'y huckleberry bush.

"Nex' spring, w'en de sap ris en Henry's ha'r commence' ter sprout, Mars Dugal' sole 'im ag'in, down in Robeson County dis time; en he kep' dat sellin' business up fer five year er mo'. Henry nebber say nuffin 'bout de goopher ter his noo marsters, 'caze he know he gwine ter be tuk good keer uv de nex' winter, w'en Mars Dugal' buy him back. En Mars Dugal' made 'nuff money off'n Henry ter buy anudder plantation ober on Beaver Crick.

"But 'long 'bout de een' er dat five year dey come a stranger ter stop at de plantation. De fus' day he 'uz dere he went out wid Mars Dugal' en spent all de mawnin' lookin' ober de vimya'd, en atter dinner dey spent all de evenin' playin' kya'ds. De niggers soon 'skiver' dat he wuz a Yankee, en dat he come down ter Norf C'lina fer ter l'arn de w'ite folks how to raise grapes en make wine. He promus Mars Dugal' he c'd make de grapevimes b'ar twice't ez many grapes, en dat de noo winepress he wuz a-sellin' would make mo' d'n twice't ez many gallons er wine. En ole Mars Dugal' des drunk it all in, des 'peared ter be bewitch' wid dat Yankee. W'en de darkies see dat Yankee runnin' 'roun' de vimya'd en diggin' under de grapevimes, dey shuk dere heads, en 'lowed dat dey feared Mars Dugal' losin' his min'. Mars Dugal' had all de dirt dug away fum under de roots er all de scuppernon' vimes, an' let 'em stan' dat away fer a week er mo'. Den dat Yankee made de niggers fix up a mixtry er lime en ashes en manyo, en po' it 'roun' de roots er de grapevimes. Den he 'vise Mars Dugal' fer ter trim de vimes close't, en Mars Dugal' tuck 'n done eve'ything de Yankee tole him ter do. Dyoin' all er dis time, mind yer, dis yer Yankee wuz libbin' off'n de fat er de lan', at de big house, en playin' kya'ds wid Mars Dugal' eve'y night; en dey say Mars Dugal' los' mo'n a thousan' dollars dyoin' er de week dat Yankee wuz a-ruinin' de grapevimes.

"W'en de sap ris nex' spring, ole Henry 'n'inted his head ez yuzhal, en his ha'r 'mence' ter grow des de same ez it done eve'y year. De scuppernon' vimes growed monst's fas', en de leaves wuz greener en thicker dan dey eber be'n dyoin' my rememb'ance; en Henry's ha'r growed out thicker dan eber, en he 'peared ter git younger 'n younger, en soopler 'n soopler; en seein' ez he wuz sho't er han's dat spring, havin' tuk in consid'able noo groun', Mars Dugal' 'cluded he would n' sell Henry 'tel he git de crap in en de cotton chop'. So he kep' Henry on de plantation.

"But 'long 'bout time fer de grapes ter come on de scuppernon' vimes, dey 'peared ter come a change ober 'em; de leaves withered en swivel' up, en de young grapes turn' yaller, en bimeby eve'ybody on de plantation could see dat de whole vimya'd wuz dyin'. Mars Dugal' tuk'n water de vimes en done all he could, but 't wa'n' no use: dat Yankee had done bus' de watermillyum. One time de vimes picked up a bit, en Mars Dugal' 'lowed dey wuz gwine ter come out ag'in; but dat Yankee done dug too close under de roots, en prune de branches too close ter de vime, en all dat lime en ashes done burn' de life out'n de vimes, en dey des kep' a-with'in' en a-swivelin'.

"All dis time de goopher wuz a-wukkin'. When de vimes sta'ted ter wither, Henry 'mence' ter complain er his rheumatiz; en when de leaves begin ter dry up, his ha'r 'mence' ter drap out. When de vimes fresh' up a bit, Henry 'd git peart ag'in, en when de vimes wither' ag'in, Henry 'd git ole ag'in, en des kep' gittin' mo' en mo' fitten fer nuffin; he des pined away, en pined away, en fine'ly tuk ter his cabin; en when de big vime whar he got de sap ter 'n'int his head withered en turned yaller en died, Henry died too,—des went out sorter like a cannel. Dey did n't 'pear ter be nuffin de matter wid 'im, 'cep'n de rheumatiz, but his strenk des dwinel' away 'tel he did n' hab ernuff lef' ter draw his bref. De goopher had got de under holt, en th'owed Henry dat time fer good en all.

"Mars Dugal' tuk on might'ly 'bout losin' his vimes en his nigger in de same year; en he swo' dat ef he could git holt er dat Yankee he'd wear 'im ter a frazzle, en den chaw up de frazzle; en he'd done it, too, for Mars Dugal' 'uz a monst'us brash man w'en he once git started. He sot de vimya'd out ober ag'in, but it wuz th'ee er fo' year befo' de vimes got ter b'arin' any scuppernon's.

"W'en de wah broke out, Mars Dugal' raise' a comp'ny, en went off ter fight de Yankees. He say he wuz mightly glad dat wah come, en he des want ter kill a Yankee fer eve'y dollar he los' 'long er dat grape-raisin' Yankee. En I 'spec' he would 'a' done it, too, ef de Yankees had n' s'picioned sump'n, en killed him fus'. Atter de s'render ole miss move' ter town, de niggers all scattered 'way fum de plantation, en de vimya'd ain' be'n cultervated sence."

"Is that story true?" asked Annie doubtfully, but seriously, as the old man concluded his narrative.

"It's des ez true ez I'm a-settin' here, miss. Dey's a easy way ter prove it: I kin lead de way right ter Henry's grave ober yander in de plantation buryin'-groun'. En I tell yer w'at, marster, I would n' 'vise you to buy dis yer ole vimya'd, 'caze de goopher's on it yit, en dey ain' no tellin' w'en it's gwine ter crap out."

"But I thought you said all the old vines died."

"Dey did 'pear ter die, but a few un 'em come out ag'in, en is mixed in 'mongs' de yuthers. I ain' skeered ter eat de grapes, 'caze I knows de old vimes fum de noo ones; but wid strangers dey ain' no tellin' w'at mought happen. I would n' 'vise yer ter buy dis vimya'd."

I bought the vineyard, nevertheless, and it has been for a long time in a thriving condition, and is often referred to by the local press as a striking illustration of the opportunities open to Northern capital in the development of Southern industries. The luscious scuppernong holds first rank among our grapes, though we cultivate a great many other varieties, and our income from grapes packed and shipped to the Northern markets is quite considerable. I have not noticed any developments of the goopher in the vineyard, although I have a mild suspicion that our colored assistants do not suffer from want of grapes during the season.

I found, when I bought the vineyard, that Uncle Julius had occupied a cabin on the place for many years, and derived a respectable revenue from the product of the neglected grapevines. This, doubtless, accounted for his advice to me not to buy the vineyard, though whether it inspired the goopher story I am unable to state. I believe, however, that the wages I paid him for his services as coachman, for I gave him employment in that capacity, were more than an equivalent for anything he lost by the sale of the vineyard.

The Wife of His Youth

I

Mr. Ryder was going to give a ball. There were several reasons why this was an opportune time for such an event.

Mr. Ryder might aptly be called the dean of the Blue Veins. The original Blue Veins were a little society of colored persons organized in a certain Northern city shortly after the war. Its purpose was to establish and maintain correct social standards among a people whose social condition presented almost unlimited room for improvement. By accident, combined perhaps with some natural affinity, the society consisted of individuals who were, generally speaking, more white than black. Some envious outsider made the suggestion that no one was eligible for membership who was not white enough to show blue veins. The suggestion was readily adopted by those who were not of the favored few, and since that time the society, though possessing a longer and more pretentious name, had been known far and wide as the "Blue Vein Society," and its members as the "Blue Veins."

The Blue Veins did not allow that any such requirement existed for admission to their circle, but, on the contrary, declared that character and culture were the only things considered; and that if most of their members were light-colored, it was because such persons, as a rule, had had better opportunities to qualify themselves for membership. Opinions differed, too, as to the usefulness of the society. There were those who had been known to assail it violently as a glaring example of the very prejudice from which the colored race had suffered most; and later, when such critics had succeeded in getting on the inside, they had been heard to maintain with zeal and earnestness that the society was a life-boat, an anchor, a bulwark and a shield,—a pillar of cloud by day and of fire by night, to guide their people through the social wilderness. Another alleged prerequisite for Blue Vein membership was that of free birth; and while there was really no such requirement, it is doubtless true that very few of the members would have been unable to meet it if there had been. If there were one or two of the older members who had come up from the South and from slavery, their history presented enough romantic circumstances to rob their servile origin of its grosser aspects.

While there were no such tests of eligibility, it is true that the Blue Veins had their notions on these subjects, and that not all of them were equally liberal in regard to the things they collectively disclaimed. Mr. Ryder was one of the most conservative. Though he had not been among the founders of the society, but had come in some years later, his genius for social leadership was such that he had speedily become its recognized adviser and head, the custodian of its standards, and the preserver of its traditions. He shaped its social policy, was active in providing for its entertainment, and when the interest fell off, as it sometimes did, he fanned the embers until they burst again into a cheerful flame.

There were still other reasons for his popularity. While he was not as white as some of the Blue Veins, his appearance was such as to confer distinction upon them. His features were of a refined type, his hair was almost straight; he was always neatly dressed; his manners were irreproachable, and his morals above suspicion. He had come to Groveland a young man, and obtaining employment in the office of a railroad company as messenger had in time worked himself up to the position of stationery clerk, having charge of the distribution of the office supplies for the whole company. Although the lack of early training had hindered the orderly development of a naturally fine mind, it had not prevented him from doing a great deal of reading or from forming decidedly literary tastes. Poetry was his passion. He could repeat whole pages of the great English poets; and if his pronunciation was sometimes faulty, his eye, his voice, his gestures, would respond to the changing sentiment with a precision that revealed a poetic soul and disarmed criticism. He was economical, and had saved money; he owned and occupied a very comfortable house on a respectable street. His residence was handsomely furnished, containing among other things a good library, especially rich in poetry, a piano, and some choice engravings. He generally shared his house with some young couple, who looked after his wants and were company for him; for Mr. Ryder was a single man. In the early days of his connection with the Blue Veins he had been regarded as quite a catch, and ladies and their mothers had maneuvered with much ingenuity to capture him. Not, however, until Mrs. Molly Dixon visited Groveland had any woman ever made him wish to change his condition to that of a married man.

Mrs. Dixon had come to Groveland from Washington in the spring, and before the summer was over she had won Mr. Ryder's heart. She possessed many attractive qualities. She was much younger than he; in fact, he was old enough to have been her father, though no one knew exactly how old he was. She was whiter than he, and better educated. She had moved in the best colored society of the country, at Washington, and had taught in the schools of that city. Such a superior person had been eagerly welcomed to the Blue Vein Society, and had taken a leading part in its activities. Mr. Ryder had at first been attracted by her charms of person, for she was very good looking and not over twenty-five; then by her refined manners and by the vivacity of her wit. Her husband had been a government clerk, and at his death had left a considerable life insurance. She was visiting friends in Groveland, and, finding the town and the people to her liking, had prolonged her stay indefinitely. She had not seemed displeased at Mr. Ryder's attentions, but on the contrary had given him every proper encouragement; indeed, a younger and less cautious man would long since have spoken. But he had made up his mind, and had only to determine the time when he would ask her to be his wife. He decided to give a ball in her honor, and at some time during the evening of the ball to offer her his heart and hand. He had no special fears about the outcome, but, with a little touch of romance, he wanted the surroundings to be in harmony with his own feelings when he should have received the answer he expected.

Mr. Ryder resolved that this ball should mark an epoch in the social history of Groveland. He knew, of course,—no one could know better,—the entertainments that had taken place in past years, and what must be done to surpass them. His ball must be worthy of the lady in whose honor it was to be given, and must, by the quality of its guests, set an example for the future. He had observed of late a growing liberality, almost a laxity, in social matters, even among members of his own set, and had several times been forced to meet in a social way persons whose complexions and callings in life were hardly up to the standard which he considered proper for the society to maintain. He had a theory of his own.

"I have no race prejudice," he would say, "but we people of mixed blood are ground between the upper and the nether millstone. Our fate lies between absorption by the white race and extinction in the black. The one doesn't want us yet, but may take us in time. The other would welcome us, but it would be for us a backward step. 'With malice towards none, with charity for all,' we must do the best we can for ourselves and those who are to follow us. Self-preservation is the first law of nature."

His ball would serve by its exclusiveness to counteract leveling tendencies, and his marriage with Mrs. Dixon would help to further the upward process of absorption he had been wishing and waiting for.

II

The ball was to take place on Friday night. The house had been put in order, the carpets covered with canvas, the halls and stairs decorated with palms and potted plants; and in the afternoon Mr. Ryder sat on his front porch, which the shade of a vine running up over a wire netting made a cool and pleasant lounging-place. He expected to respond to the toast "The Ladies," at the supper, and from a volume of Tennyson—his favorite poet—was fortifying himself with apt quotations. The volume was open at A Dream of Fair Women. His eyes fell on these lines, and he read them aloud to judge better of their effect:—

"At length I saw a lady within call,
Stiller than chisell'd marble, standing there;
A daughter of the gods, divinely tall,
And most divinely fair."

He marked the verse, and turning the page read the stanza beginning,—

"O sweet pale Margaret,
O rare pale Margaret."

He weighed the passage a moment, and decided that it would not do. Mrs. Dixon was the palest lady he expected at the ball, and she was of a rather ruddy complexion, and of lively disposition and buxom build. So he ran over the leaves until his eye rested on the description of Queen Guinevere:—

"She seem'd a part of joyous Spring:
A gown of grass-green silk she wore,
Buckled with golden clasps before;
A light-green tuft of plumes she bore
Closed in a golden ring.

❖❖❖

"She look'd so lovely, as she sway'd
The rein with dainty finger-tips,
A man had given all other bliss,
And all his worldly worth for this,
To waste his whole heart in one kiss
Upon her perfect lips."

As Mr. Ryder murmured these words audibly, with an appreciative thrill, he heard the latch of his gate click, and a light footfall sounding on the steps. He turned his head, and saw a woman standing before the door.

She was a little woman, not five feet tall, and proportioned to her height. Although she stood erect, and looked around her with very bright and restless eyes, she seemed quite old; for her face was crossed and recrossed with a hundred wrinkles, and around the edges of her bonnet could be seen protruding here and there a tuft of short gray wool. She wore a blue calico gown of ancient cut, a little red shawl fastened around her shoulders with an old-fashioned brass brooch, and a large bonnet profusely ornamented with faded red and yellow artificial flowers. And she was very black,—so black that her toothless gums, revealed when she opened her mouth to speak, were not red, but blue. She looked like a bit of the old plantation life, summoned up from the past by the wave of a magician's wand, as the poet's fancy had called into being the gracious shapes of which Mr. Ryder had just been reading.

He rose from his chair and came over to where she stood.

"Good-afternoon, madam," he said.

"Good-evenin', suh," she answered, ducking suddenly with a quaint curtsy. Her voice was shrill and piping, but softened somewhat by age. "Is dis yere whar Mistuh Ryduh lib, suh?" she asked, looking around her doubtfully, and glancing into the open windows, through which some of the preparations for the evening were visible.

"Yes," he replied, with an air of kindly patronage, unconsciously flattered by her manner, "I am Mr. Ryder. Did you want to see me?"

"Yah, suh, ef I ain't 'sturbin' of you too much."

"Not at all. Have a seat over here behind the vine, where it is cool. What can I do for you?"

" 'Scuse me, suh," she continued, when she had sat down on the edge of a chair, " 'scuse me, suh, I 's lookin' for my husban'. I heerd you wuz a big man an' had libbed heah a long time, an' I 'lowed you would n't min' ef I 'd come roun' an' ax you ef you 'd eber heerd of a merlatter man by de name er Sam Taylor 'quirin' roun' in de chu'ches ermongs' de people fer his wife 'Lisa Jane?"

Mr. Ryder seemed to think for a moment.

"There used to be many such cases right after the war," he said, "but it has been so long that I have forgotten them. There are very few now. But tell me your story, and it may refresh my memory."

She sat back farther in her chair so as to be more comfortable, and folded her withered hands in her lap.

"My name's 'Liza," she began, " 'Liza Jane. W'en I wuz young I us'ter b'long ter Marse Bob Smif, down in ole Missoura. I wuz bawn down dere. W'en I wuz a gal I wuz married ter a man named Jim. But Jim died, an' after dat I married a merlatter man named Sam Taylor. Sam wuz free-bawn, but his mammy and daddy died, an' de w'ite folks 'prenticed him ter my marster fer ter work fer 'im 'tel he wuz growed up. Sam worked in de fiel', an' I wuz de cook. One day Ma'y Ann, old miss's maid, come rushin' out ter de kitchen, an' says she, " 'Liza Jane, ole marse gwine sell yo' Sam down de ribber.'

"'Go way f'm yere,' says I; 'my husban's free.'

"'Don' make no diff'ence. I heerd ole marse tell ole miss he wuz gwine take yo' Sam 'way wid 'im ter-morrow, fer he needed money, an' he knowed whar he could git a t'ousan' dollars fer Sam an' no questions axed.'

"W'en Sam come home f'm de fiel', dat night, I tole him 'bout ole marse gwine steal 'im, an' Sam run erway. His time wuz mos' up, an' he swo' dat w'en he wuz twenty-one he would come back an' he'p me run erway, er else save up de money ter buy my freedom. An' I know he'd 'a' done it, fer he thought a heap er me, Sam did. But w'en he come back he did n' fin' me, fer I wuz n' dere. Ole marse had heerd dat I warned Sam, so he had me whip' an' sol' down de ribber.

"Den de wah broke out, an' w'en it wuz ober de cullud folks wuz scattered. I went back ter de ole home; but Sam wuz n' dere, an' I could n' l'arn nuffin' 'bout 'im. But I knowed he'd be'n dere to look fer me an' had n' foun' me, an' had gone erway ter hunt fer me.

"I's be'n lookin' fer 'im eber sence," she added simply, as though twenty-five years were but a couple of weeks, "an' I knows he's be'n lookin' fer me. Fer he sot a heap er sto' by me. Sam did, an' I know he's be'n huntin' fer me all dese years.—'less'n he's be'n sick er sump'n, so he could n' work, er out'n his head, so he could n' 'member his promise. I went back down de ribber, fer I 'lowed he 'd gone down dere lookin' fer me. I's be'n ter Noo Orleens, an' Atlanty, an' Charleston, an' Richmon'; an' w'en I 'd be'n all ober de Souf I come ter de Norf. Fer I knows I'll fin' 'im some er dese days," she added softly, "er he'll fin' me, an' den we 'll bofe be as happy in freedom as we wuz in de ole days befo' de wah." A smile stole over her withered countenance as she paused a moment, and her bright eyes softened into a far-away look.

This was the substance of the old woman's story. She had wandered a little here and there.

Mr. Ryder was looking at her curiously when she finished.

"How have you lived all these years?" he asked.

"Cookin', suh. I's a good cook. Does you know anybody w'at needs a good cook, suh? I's stoppin' wid a cullud fam'ly roun' de corner yonder 'tel I kin fin' a place."

"Do you really expect to find your husband? He may be dead long ago."

She shook her head emphatically. "Oh no, he ain' dead. De signs an' de tokens tells me. I dremp three nights runnin' on'y dis las' week dat I foun' him."

"He may have married another woman. Your slave marriage would not have prevented him, for you never lived with him after the war, and without that your marriage does n't count."

"Would n' make no diff'ence wid Sam. He would n' marry no yuther 'ooman 'tel he foun' out 'bout me. I knows it," she added. "Sump'n's be'n tellin' me all dese years dat I's gwine fin' Sam 'fo' I dies."

"Perhaps he's outgrown you, and climbed up in the world where he wouldn't care to have you find him."

"No, indeed, suh," she replied, "Sam ain' dat kin' er man. He wuz good ter me, Sam wuz, but he wuz n' much good ter nobody e'se, fer he wuz one er de triflin'es' han's on de plantation. I 'spec's ter haf ter suppo't 'im w'en I fin' 'im, fer he nebber would work 'less'n he had ter. But den he wuz free, an' he did n' git no pay fer his work, an' I don' blame 'im much. Mebbe he's done better sence he run erway, I ain' 'spectin' much."

"You may have passed him on the street a hundred times during the twenty-five years, and not have known him; time works great changes."

She smiled incredulously. "I'd know 'im 'mongs' a hund'ed men. Fer dey wuz n' no yuther merlatter man like my man Sam, an' I could n' be mistook. I's toted his picture roun' wid me twenty-five years."

"May I see it?" asked Mr. Ryder. "It might help me to remember whether I have seen the original."

As she drew a small parcel from her bosom, he saw that it was fastened to a string that went around her neck. Removing several wrappers, she brought to light an old-fashioned daguerreotype in a black case. He looked long and intently at the portrait. It was faded with time, but the features were still distinct, and it was easy to see what manner of man it had represented.

He closed the case, and with a slow movement handed it back to her.

"I don't know any man in town who goes by that name," he said, "nor have I heard of any one making such inquiries. But if you will leave me your address, I will give the matter some attention, and if I find out anything I will let you know."

She gave him the number of a house in the neighborhood, and went away, after thanking him warmly.

He wrote down the address on the flyleaf of the volume of Tennyson, and, when she had gone, rose to his feet and stood looking after her curiously. As she walked down the street with mincing step, he saw several persons whom she passed turn and look back at her with a smile of kindly amusement. When she had turned the corner, he went upstairs to his bedroom, and stood for a long time before the mirror of his dressing-case, gazing thoughtfully at the reflection of his own face.

III

At eight o'clock the ballroom was a blaze of light and the guests had begun to assemble; for there was a literary programme and some routine business of the society to be gone through with before the dancing. A black servant in evening dress waited at the door and directed the guests to the dressing-rooms.

The occasion was long memorable among the colored people of the city; not alone for the dress and display, but for the high average of intelligence and culture that distinguished the gathering as a whole. There were a number of school-teachers, several young doctors, three or four lawyers, some professional singers, an editor, a lieutenant in the United States army spending his furlough in the city, and others in various polite callings; these were colored, though most of them would not have attracted even a casual glance because of any marked difference from white people. Most of the ladies were in evening costume, and dress coats and dancing-pumps were the rule among the men. A band of string music, stationed in an alcove behind a row of palms, played popular airs while the guests were gathering.

The dancing began at half past nine. At eleven o'clock supper was served. Mr. Ryder had left the ballroom some little time before the intermission, but reappeared at the supper-table. The spread was worthy of the occasion, and the guests did full justice to it. When the coffee had been served, the toastmaster, Mr. Solomon Sadler, rapped for order. He made a brief introductory speech, complimenting host and guests, and then presented in their order the toasts of the evening. They were responded to with a very fair display of after-dinner wit.

"The last toast," said the toast-master, when he reached the end of the list, "is one which must appeal to us all. There is no one of us of the sterner sex who is not at some time dependent upon woman,—in infancy for protection, in manhood for companionship, in old age for care and comforting. Our good host has been trying to live alone, but the fair faces I see around me to-night prove that he too is largely dependent upon the gentler sex for most that makes life worth living,—the society and love of friends,—and rumor is at fault if he does not soon yield entire subjection to one of them. Mr. Ryder will now respond to the toast,—The Ladies."

There was a pensive look in Mr. Ryder's eyes as he took the floor and adjusted his eyeglasses. He began by speaking of woman as the gift of Heaven to man, and after some general observations on the relations of the sexes he said: "But perhaps the quality which most distinguishes woman is her fidelity and devotion to those she loves. History is full of examples, but has recorded none more striking than one which only to-day came under my notice."

He then related, simply but effectively, the story told by his visitor of the afternoon. He told it in the same soft dialect, which came readily to his lips, while the company listened attentively and sympathetically. For the story had awakened a responsive thrill in many hearts. There were some present who had seen, and others who had heard their fathers and grandfathers tell, the wrongs and sufferings of this past generation, and all of them still felt, in their darker moments, the shadow hanging over them. Mr. Ryder went on:—

"Such devotion and such confidence are rare even among women. There are many who would have searched a year, some who would have waited five years, a few who might have hoped ten years; but for twenty-five years this woman has retained her affection for and her faith in a man she has not seen or heard of in all that time.

"She came to me to-day in the hope that I might be able to help her find this long-lost husband. And when she was gone I gave my fancy rein, and imagined a case I will put to you.

"Suppose that this husband, soon after his escape, had learned that his wife had been sold away, and that such inquiries as he could make brought no information of her whereabouts. Suppose that he was young, and she much older than he; that he was light, and she was black; that their marriage was a slave marriage, and legally binding only if they chose to make it so after the war. Suppose, too, that he made his way to the North, as some of us have done, and there, where he had larger opportunities, had improved them, and had in the course of all these years grown to be as different from the ignorant boy who ran away from fear of slavery as the day is from the night. Suppose, even, that he had qualified himself, by industry, by thrift, and by study, to win the friendship and be considered worthy the society of such people as these I see around me to-night, gracing my board and filling my heart with gladness; for

I am old enough to remember the day when such a gathering would not have been possible in this land. Suppose, too, that, as the years went by, this man's memory of the past grew more and more indistinct, until at last it was rarely, except in his dreams, that any image of this bygone period rose before his mind. And then suppose that accident should bring to his knowledge the fact that the wife of his youth, the wife he had left behind him,—not one who had walked by his side and kept pace with him in his upward struggle, but one upon whom advancing years and a laborious life had set their mark,—was alive and seeking him, but that he was absolutely safe from recognition or discovery, unless he chose to reveal himself. My friends, what would the man do? I will suppose that he was one who loved honor, and tried to deal justly with all men. I will even carry the case further, and suppose that perhaps he had set his heart upon another, whom he had hoped to call his own. What would he do, or rather what ought he to do, in such a crisis of a lifetime?

"It seemed to me that he might hesitate, and I imagined that I was an old friend, a near friend, and that he had come to me for advice; and I argued the case with him. I tried to discuss it impartially. After we had looked upon the matter from every point of view, I said to him, in words that we all know:

'This above all: to thine own self be true,
And it must follow, as the night the day,
Thou canst not then be false to any man.'

Then, finally, I put the question to him, 'Shall you acknowledge her?'

"And now, ladies and gentlemen, friends and companions, I ask you, what should he have done?"

There was something in Mr. Ryder's voice that stirred the hearts of those who sat around him. It suggested more than mere sympathy with an imaginary situation; it seemed rather in the nature of a personal appeal. It was observed, too, that his look rested more especially upon Mrs. Dixon, with a mingled expression of renunciation and inquiry.

She had listened, with parted lips and streaming eyes. She was the first to speak: "He should have acknowledged her."

"Yes," they all echoed, "he should have acknowledged her."

"My friends and companions," responded Mr. Ryder, "I thank you, one and all. It is the answer I expected, for I knew your hearts."

He turned and walked toward the closed door of an adjoining room, while every eye followed him in wondering curiosity. He came back in a moment, leading by the hand his visitor of the afternoon, who stood startled and trembling at the sudden plunge into this scene of brilliant gayety. She was neatly dressed in gray, and wore the white cap of an elderly woman.

"Ladies and gentlemen," he said, "this is the woman, and I am the man, whose story I have told you. Permit me to introduce to you the wife of my youth."

PAUL LAURENCE DUNBAR

(1872–1906)

Of all the writers whose reputations emerged at the turn of the century, Paul Laurence Dunbar perhaps had the most difficult time defining himself as a writer and getting editors, reviewers, and readers to accept his definition. Touted as the first African American of untainted blood to become a writer and generally recognized as the first poet to win widespread national and international attention, Dunbar perhaps had too much greatness thrust upon him too soon. A poet in the tradition of James Whitcomb Riley and the homespun variety of dialect, a son of slaves who seemed to glorify the old plantation days, and a black man sensitive to the post-

Reconstruction plight of his fellow blacks, Dunbar had several directions in which he could pour his creative energeies. He earned a reputation in the early 1890s as a poet; by the end of the decade, he was composing novels, musical comedies, and short fiction.

The history of Dunbar's interactions with his editors reflects prevailing stereotypes of black people that were prominent in the last decades of the nineteenth century. While Dunbar was certainly adept at composing dialect poetry, he was equally adept at composing poems in standard English. Yet, his editors and critics praised the dialect poems and locked him into perpetuating images of African Americans that catered to the popular American stereotypes of them. The politics of publishing that guided Dunbar's public reputation has led generations of scholars to criticize Dunbar for undermining the social progress of African Americans. The negative connotations of the dialect poetry and the seeming glorification of the Plantation Tradition overshadowed Dunbar's nationalistic concerns. He, like many other race-conscious blacks, established a school for blacks; he was determined, he said, that "they should not make bootblacks of us all." He celebrated the contributions of black soldiers in the Civil War, and he was generally proud of what blacks had done in the building of America. Close examination of some of his dialect poems, such as "An Ante-bellum Sermon," will reveal that he adopts an ironic voice at times to advocate justice and freedom for blacks; other poems, such as "The Haunted Oak," address threats to African American safety—lynching, in this instance.

Paul Laurence Dunbar was born in Dayton, Ohio, on June 27, 1872, the son of Joshua and Matilda Glass Burton Murphy Dunbar, slaves who had migrated there from Kentucky. Joshua and Matilda separated when Paul was less than two years old, and they divorced in 1876. When her two sons from a previous marriage moved to Chicago, Matilda and Paul were left to form the bond that would greatly influence his writing. His mother told Dunbar stories of her days in slavery, perhaps with a rosier tint than the reality; he would later draw on these stories for his poems and short stories.

There were early signs that Dunbar would be a talented poet and writer. He started publishing poems in the *Dayton Herald* as early as 1888, and he founded the *Dayton Tattler,* a black newspaper. He asked a soon-to-be-famous friend and classmate, Orville Wright, to print the paper for him, and the first issue appeared in 1889. Although the paper folded after six issues, it nonetheless showed a young man with ambition to carve out a literary space for himself and his community. In his senior year in high school, Dunbar also furthered his writing interests by serving as editor in chief of the *High School Times,* his school newspaper. That year, he also served as president of his class, president of the literary club known as the Philomathean Society, and class poet. In this last capacity, he wrote the class poem and delivered it at graduation in 1891.

As Dunbar's classmates dispersed to various clerical and other substantial jobs, he went to work as elevator operator in the Callahan Building in Dayton. He credits that experience with allowing him the opportunity to listen to the nuances of voices, to reread his favorite poets such as Tennyson, Shakespeare, Keats, Shelley, Longfellow, and Riley, and to compose poems and articles, many of which would be published in local and regional newspapers. While the compositions might not have been financially profitable, they at least allowed Dunbar the room for creative expression.

Asked to deliver the welcoming address for the Western Association of Writers meeting in Dayton in June 1892, Dunbar complied and was invited to join the Association. James Newton Matthews, who would become one of Dunbar's patrons and friends, extended the invitation. It was also through Matthews that Dunbar enjoyed a brief correspondence with James Whitcomb Riley. Soon after the Western Association of Writers meeting, Dunbar composed and sold a few dialect poems, which led him to believe that he could become famous through his writing. When Orville Wright suggested that he think of a volume of poems, Dunbar gathered fifty-six poems and took them to William Lawrence Blacher, the business manager of the United Brethren Publishing House in Dayton. Dunbar agreed to allow the book to be published for $125, which would be repaid through sales. *Oak and Ivy* was actually delivered in December of 1892, but the imprint date was 1893.

The publication of the volume and Dunbar's popular readings and sales of it led to a series of patrons who offered financial support for an extended period. Charles A. Thatcher, a lawyer from Toledo, whom Dunbar met in 1893, was perhaps the staunchest of these. Thatcher offered to pay for a college education for Dunbar, which he rejected in preference to becoming a successful poet. Thatcher assisted Dunbar financially on several occasions, and he provided opportunities for Dunbar to read from his poetry and sell his book in the Toledo area. When Dunbar and his mother left Dayton for Chicago in 1893, and he became too financially strapped to return to Dayton, Thatcher paid for the move.

The brief time in Chicago, during the period of the World's Fair and Columbian Exposition, allowed Dunbar to meet a series of black writers and activists. Frederick Douglass hired him to work as a clerk in the Haitian pavilion of the Exposition. He also met Ida B. Wells-Barnett, Mary Church Terrell, James D. Corrothers, James Campbell, and Richard B. Harrison, an actor with whom Dunbar gave poetry readings in an effort to sell his book. In addition, he met the composer Will Marion Cook, with whom he would later collaborate.

Dunbar's financial difficulties did not abate, and he continued to get assistance from patrons and other interested persons. In 1894, a Toledo psychiatrist, Henry A. Tobey, bought several copies of *Oak and Ivy* and became another financial supporter for Dunbar. Tobey, like Thatcher, offered to pay college tuition for Dunbar, this time for him to attend Harvard, but Dunbar believed that the five hundred dollars offered was not sufficient to pay tuition and maintain payments on his family house. Temporary financial release came in 1895 when *Century* magazine published "A Negro Love Song," "Curtain," and "The Dilettante." Other magazines and newspapers, such as the *New York Times* and the *Independent,* also began publishing his poems.

It was through the efforts of Thatcher and Tobey that Dunbar's second volume of poetry was published. They arranged for Hadley and Hadley printing company in Toledo to print and bind the volume in an edition of one thousand copies. *Majors and Minors* (dated 1895, but it did not appear until 1896) replicates the focus on standard English and dialect poems published in *Oak and Ivy.* While Dunbar preferred his standard English poems equally as much if not more than the dialect poems, he was soon typecast as a writer of dialect poetry. That reputation was solidified when prominent literary critic William Dean Howells wrote a favorable review of *Majors and Minors* in *Harper's Weekly* and praised the dialect poems, citing "The Party" in particular. Because that poem catered to "happy darky" stereotypes, the praise was a double-edged sword.

Thatcher and Tobey also enabled Dunbar to travel to New York in 1896 to make arrangements with Dodd, Mead that would lead to the publication of *Lyrics of Lowly Life* (1896), for which Howells wrote the introduction, and which became Dunbar's most successful volume; it led to a reading tour in England. It was on the occasion of the party given for his departure, at which Victoria Earle Matthews and Booker T. Washington were in attendance, that Dunbar actually saw Alice Ruth Moore. He had seen a picture of her in the *Boston Monthly Review* in 1895. He fell in love with her and corresponded with her over the next two years, during which they shared their work; Dunbar published one of Alice's stories about New Orleans in the *Indianapolis World,* a small black newspaper for which he served as temporary editor in 1895. They became engaged on the same evening they met in 1897. They were married secretly in Washington, D.C. on March 6, 1898, after Dunbar's return from a successful tour in England. The marriage did not last long; difficulties included Dunbar's drinking and moodiness, as well as the objections of Alice's family to Dunbar's dark skin, his mother's work as a washerwoman, and his lack of a college education. They parted in 1902 and tried unsuccessfully to reconcile in 1903. However, Alice proved to be a substantial influence on Dunbar. She understood the plight he was in as an artist who viewed himself one way while the public viewed him another.

In the last years of the nineteenth century, Dunbar's life was a busy round of working (he became assistant clerk in the reading room at the Library of Congress), composing, reading, and publishing. In 1898, he wrote the libretto for *Dream Lovers,* an operetta by Samuel Coleridge-Taylor, whom he had met in London the year before. Also in 1898, he collaborated with James Weldon Johnson in writing *Clorindy, or the Origin of the Cakewalk* (1898); he similarly collaborated with Will Marion Cook to produce *Uncle Eph's Christmas* in 1900. He published *Folks from Dixie* (1898), which was reviewed favorably. Although he spent a brief period in New York in 1902, he was not enamored of city life. The novels he published during this period show a preference for the pastoral existence over the urban one. *The Love of Landry* (1900) depicts a young woman recovering from tuberculosis in Colorado. Perhaps Dunbar's most well-known novel, *The Sport of the Gods* (1902), portrays a black family that migrates to New York after the father is falsely accused of theft by the brother of the owner of the plantation on which he resides; the family members quickly discover how evil the city is, but the family unit is destroyed before the truth is uncovered and the family returns to the South. The suggestion is that peace of mind can be reclaimed only in a pastoral environment.

Dunbar turned his attention to the short story and produced a series of volumes over the next few years, including *The Strength of Gideon and Other Stories* (1900), *In Old Plantation Days* (1903), and *The Heart of Happy Hollow* (1904). The popularity of Dunbar's dialect poems led to the republication of some of them in glossy, bound, illustrated volumes, including *When Malindy Sings* (1903), *Li'l Gal* (1904), *Howdy, Honey, Howdy* (1905), and *Joggin' Erlong,* published posthumously in 1906.

Dunbar's health had begun to fail around 1898. On his way to a poetry reading in Albany, New York, in 1899, at which Governor Theodore Roosevelt was scheduled to introduce him, Dunbar fell ill and spent an extensive recovery time in New York City. He and his wife took the suggestion of his doctors and moved to Harmon, Colorado, near Denver, but they returned to Washington in 1900. Illness continued to plague Dunbar; he was coughing incessantly and he started drinking to ease the pain. He spent time in April of 1900 recuperating at the home of his longtime friend, James Weldon Johnson, in Jacksonville, Florida. He continued to fight illness through 1903 and, finally, returned to his home in Dayton that same year. Although he remained productive, his health continued to fail; he died at his home in Dayton, Ohio, on February 9, 1906.

❖❖❖

Biographies of Dunbar include Benjamin Brawley, *Paul Laurence Dunbar: Poet of His People* (1936); Virginia Cunningham, *Paul Laurence Dunbar and His Song* (1947); Jean Gould, *That Dunbar Boy* (1958); Addison Gayle, Jr., *Oak and Ivy: A Biopgraphy of Paul Laurence Dunbar* (1971). Other studies, some with substantial biographical information, include Victor Lawson, *Dunbar Critically Examined* (1941); Jay Martin, ed., *A Singer in the Dawn: Reinterpretations of Paul Laurence Dunbar* (1975); Pete Revell, *Paul Laurence Dunbar* (1979); Jean Wagner, *Black Poets of the United States: From Paul Laurence Dunbar to Langston Hughes* (1973).

Works in the Dunbar collection in Ohio are listed in Sara S. Fuller, *The Paul Laurence Dunbar Collection: An Inventory to the Microfilm Edition* (1972).

An Ante-bellum Sermon

We is gathahed hyeah, my brothahs,
  In dis howlin' wildaness,
Fu' to speak some words of comfo't
  To each othah in distress.
An' we chooses fu' ouah subjic'
  Dis—we'll 'splain it by an' by;
  "An de Lawd said, 'Moses, Moses,'
  An' de man said, 'Hyeah am I.'"

Now ole Pher'oh, down in Egypt,
  Was de wuss man evah bo'n,
An' he had de Hebrew chillun
  Down dah wukin' in his co'n;
'Twell de Lawd got tiahed o' his foolin',
  An' sez he: "I'll let him know—
Look hyeah, Moses, go tell Pher'oh
  Fu' to let dem chillun go."

"An' ef he refuse to do it,
  I will make him rue de houah,
Fu' I'll empty down on Egypt
  All de vials of my powah."
Yes, he did—an' Pher'oh's ahmy
  Wasn't wuth a ha'f a dime;

Fu' de Lawd will he'p his chillun,
  You kin trust him evah time.

An' yo' enemies may 'sail you
  In de back an' in de front;
But de Lawd is all aroun' you,
  Fu' to ba' de battle's brunt.
Dey kin fo'ge yo' chains an' shackles
  F'om de mountains to de sea;
But de Lawd will sen' some Moses
  Fu' to set his chillun free.

An' de lan' shall hyeah his thundah,
  Lak a blas' f'om Gab'el's ho'n,
Fu' de Lawd of hosts is mighty
  When he girds his ahmor on.
But fu' feah some one mistakes me,
  I will pause right hyeah to say,
Dat I'm still a-preachin' ancient,
  I ain't talkin' 'bout to-day.

But I tell you, fellah christuns,
  Things'll happen mighty strange;
Now, de Lawd done dis fu' Isrul,
  An' his ways don't nevah change,
An' de love he showed to Isrul
  Wasn't all on Isrul spent;
Now don't run an' tell yo' mastahs
  Dat I's preachin' discontent.

'Cause I isn't; I'se a-judgin'
  Bible people by deir ac's;
I'se a-givin' you de Scriptuah,
  I'se a-handin' you de fac's.
Cose ole Pher'oh b'lieved in slav'ry,
  But de Lawd he let him see,
Dat de people he put bref in,—
  Evah mothah's son was free.

An' dah's othahs thinks lak Pher'oh,
  But dey calls de Scriptuah liar,
Fu' de Bible says "a servant
  Is a-worthy of his hire."
An' you cain't git roun' nor thoo dat,
  An' you cain't git ovah it,
Fu' whatevah place you git in,
  Dis hyeah Bible too'll fit.

So you see de Lawd's intention,
  Evah sence de worl' began,
Was dat His almighty freedom

Should belong to evah man,
But I think it would be bettah,
Ef I'd pause agin to say,
Dat I'm talkin' 'bout ouah freedom
In a Bibleistic way.

But de Moses is a-comin',
An' he's comin', suah and fas'
We kin hyeah his feet a-trompin',
We kin hyeah his trumpit blas'.
But I want to wa'n you people,
Don't you git too brigity;
An' don't you git to braggin'
'Bout dese things, you wait an' see.

But when Moses wif his powah
Comes an' sets us chillun free,
We will praise de gracious Mastah
Dat has gin us liberty;
An' we'll shout ouah halleluyahs,
On dat mighty reck'nin' day,
When we'se reco'nised ez citiz'—
Huh uh! Chillun, let us pray!

When Malindy Sings

G'way an' quit dat noise, Miss Lucy—
Put dat music book away;
What's de use to keep on tryin'?
Ef you practise twell you're gray,
You cain't sta't no notes a-flyin'
Lak de ones dat rants and rings
F'om de kitchen to de big woods
When Malindy sings.

You ain't got de nachel o'gans
Fu' to make de soun' come right,
You ain't got de tu'ns an' twistin's
Fu' to make it sweet an' light.
Tell you one thing now, Miss Lucy,
An' I'm tellin' you fu' true,
When hit comes to raal right singin',
'T ain't no easy thing to do.

Easy 'nough fu' folks to hollah,
Lookin' at de lines an' dots,
When dey ain't no one kin sence it,
An' de chune comes in, in spots;
But fu' real melojous music,

Dat jes' strikes yo' hea't and clings,
Jes' you stan' an' listen wif me
When Malindy sings.

Ain't you nevah hyeahd Malindy?
Blessed soul, tek up de cross!
Look hyeah, ain't you jokin', honey?
Well, you don't know whut you los'.
Y'ought to hyeah dat gal a-wa'blin',
Robins, la'ks, an' all dem things,
Heish dey moufs an' hides dey faces
When Malindy sings.

Fiddlin' man jes' stop his fiddlin',
Lay his fiddle on de she'f;
Mockin'-bird quit tryin' to whistle,
'Cause he jes' so shamed hisse'f.
Folks a-playin' on de banjo
Draps dey fingahs on de strings—
Bless yo' soul—fu'gits to move 'em,
When Malindy sings.

She jes' spreads huh mouf and hollahs,
"Comes to Jesus," twell you hyeah
Sinnahs' tremblin' steps and voices,
Timid-lak a-drawin' neah;
Den she tu'ns to "Rock of Ages,"
Simply to de cross she clings,
An' you fin' yo' teahs a-drappin'
When Malindy sings.

Who dat says dat humble praises
Wif de Master nevah counts?
Heish yo' mouf, I hyeah dat music,
Ez hit rises up an' mounts—
Floatin' by de hills an' valleys,
Way above dis buryin' sod,
Ez hit makes its way in glory
To de very gates of God!

Oh, hit 's sweetah dan de music
Of an edicated band;
An' hit 's dearah dan de battle's
Song o' triumph in de lan'.
It seems holier dan evenin'
When de solemn chu'ch bell rings,
Ez I sit an' ca'mly listen
While Malindy sings.

Towsah, stop dat ba'kin', hyeah me!
Mandy, mek dat chile keep still;

Don't you hyeah de echoes callin'
F'om de valley to de hill?
Let me listen, I can hyeah it,
Th'oo de bresh of angel's wings,
Sof' an' sweet, "Swing Low, Sweet Chariot,"
Ez Malindy sings.

A Negro Love Song

Seen my lady home las' night,
Jump back, honey, jump back.
Hel' huh han' an' sque'z it tight,
Jump back, honey, jump back.
Hyeahd huh sigh a little sigh,
Seen a light gleam f'om huh eye,
An' a smile go flittin' by—
Jump back, honey, jump back.

Hyeahd de win' blow thoo de pine,
Jump back, honey, jump back.
Mockin'-bird was singin' fine,
Jump back, honey, jump back.
An' my hea't was beatin' so,
When I reached my lady's do',
Dat I couldn't ba' to go—
Jump back, honey, jump back.

Put my ahm aroun' huh wais',
Jump back, honey, jump back.
Raised huh lips an' took a tase,
Jump back honey, jump back.
Love me, honey, love me true?
Love me well ez I love you?
An' she answe'd, "'Cose I do"—
Jump back, honey, jump back.

The Party

Dey had a gread big pahty down to Tom's
de othah night;
Was I dah? You bet! I nevah in my life see
sich a sight;
All de folks f'om fou' plantations was invited, an'
dey come,
Dey come troopin' thick ez chillun when dey
hyeahs a fife an' drum.
Evahbody dressed deir fines'—Heish yo' mouf
an' git away,
Ain't seen no sich fancy dressin' sense las'

quah'tly meeting' day;
Gals all dressed in silks an' satins, not a wrinkle
ner a crease,
Eyes a-battin', teeth a-shinin', haih breshed back
ez slick ez grease;
Sku'ts all tucked an' puffed an' ruffled, evah
blessed seam an' stitch;
Ef you'd seen 'em wif deir mistus, could n't
swahed to which was which.
Men all dressed up in Prince Alberts, swaller-
tails 'u'd tek yo' bref!
I cain't tell you nothin' 'bout it, y' ought to seen
it fu' yo'se'f.
Who was dah? Now who you askin'? How
you 'spect I gwine to know?
You mus' think I stood an' counted evahbody at
de do'.
Ole man Babah's house-boy Isaac, brung dat
gal, Malindy Jane,
Huh a-hangin' to his elbow, him a-struttin' wif
a cane;
My, but Hahvey Jones was jealous! seemed to
stick him lak a tho'n;
But he laughed with Viney Cahteh, tryin' ha'd
to not let on,
But a pusson would 'a' noticed f'om de d'rection
of his look,
Dat he was wachin' ev'ry step dat Ike an'
Lindy took.
Ike he foun' a cheer an' asked huh: "Won't
you set down?" wif a smile,
An' she answe'd up a-bowin', "Oh, I reckon
't ain't wuth while."
Dat was jes' fu' style, I reckon, 'cause she sot
down jes' de same,
An' she stayed dah 'twell he fetched huh fu' to
jine some so't o' game;
Den I hyeahd huh sayin' propah, ez she riz to
go away,
"Oh, you raly mus' excuse me, fu' I hardly
keers to play."
But I seen huh in a minute wif de othahs on de
flo',
An' dah was n't any one o' dem a-playin' any
mo';
Comin' down de flo' a-bowin' an' a-swayin' an'
a-swingin',

Puttin' on huh high-toned mannahs all de time
dat she was singin':
"Oh, swing Johnny up an' down, swing him all
aroun',
Swing Johnny up an' down, swing him all aroun',
Oh, swing Johnny up an' down, swing him all
aroun',
Fa' you well, my dahlin'."
Had to laff at ole man Johnson, he's a caution
now, you bet—
Hittin' clost onto a hundred, but he's spry an'
nimble yet;
He 'lowed how a-so't o' gigglin', "I ain't ole,
I'll let you see,
D'ain't no use in gittin' feeble, now you youngstahs
jes' watch me,"
An' he grabbed ole Aunt Marier—weighs th'ee
hunderd mo' er less,
An' he spun huh 'roun' de cabin swingin' Johnny
lak de res'.
Evahbody laffed an' hollahed: "Go it! Swing
huh, Uncle Jim!"
An' he swung huh too, I reckon, lak a youngstah,
who but him.
Dat was bettah 'n young Scott Thomas, tryin' to
be so awful smaht.
You know when dey gits to singin' an' dey
comes to dat ere paht:
"In some lady's new brick house,
In some lady's gyahden.
Ef you don't let me out, I will jump out,
So fa' you well, my dahlin'."
Den dey's got a circle 'roun' you, an' you's got
to break de line;
Well, dat dahky was so anxious, lak to bust hisse'f
a-tryin';
Kep' on blund'rin' 'roun' an' foolin' 'twell he
giv' one gread big jump,
Broke de line, an' lit head-fo'most in de fiahplace
right plump;
Hit 'ad fiah in it, mind you; well, I thought my
soul I'd bust,
Tried my best to keep f'om laffin', but hit
seemed like die I must!
Y'ought to seen dat man a-scramblin' f'om de
ashes an' de grime.

Did it bu'n him! Sich a question, why he did n't
give it time;
Th'ow'd dem ashes and dem cindahs evah
which-a-way I guess,
An' you nevah did, I reckon, clap yo' eyes on
sich a mess;
Fu' he sholy made a picter an' a funny one to
boot,
Wif his clothes all full o' ashes an' his face all
full o' soot.
Well, hit laked to stopped de pahty, an' I reckon
lak ez not
Dat it would ef Tom's wife, Mandy, had n't
happened on de spot,
To invite us out to suppah—well, we scrambled
to de table,
An' I'd lak to tell you 'bout it—what we had
—but I ain't able,
Mention jes' a few things, dough I know I
had n't orter,
Fu' I know 't will staht a hank'rin' an' yo' mouf
'll 'mence to worter.
We had wheat bread white ez cotton an' a egg
pone jes like gol',
Hog jole, bilin' hot an' steamin' roasted shoat
an' ham sliced cold—
Look out! What's de mattah wif you? Don't
be fallin' on de flo';
Ef it's go'n' to 'fect you dat way, I won't tell you
nothin' mo'.
Dah now—well, we had hot chittlin's—now
you's tryin' ag'in to fall,
Cain't you stan' to hyeah about it? S'pose you'd
been an' seed it all;
Seed dem gread big sweet pertaters, layin' by
de possum's side,
Seed dat coon in all his gravy, reckon den you'd
up and died!
Mandy 'lowed "you all mus' 'scuse me, d' wa'n't
much upon my she'ves,
But I's done my bes' to suit you, so set down
an' he'p yo'se'ves."
Tom, he 'lowed: "I don't b'lieve in 'pologisin'
an' perfessin',
Let'em tek it lak dey ketch it. Eldah Thompson,
ask de blessin'."

Wish you'd seed dat colo'ed preachah cleah
his th'oat an' bow his head;
One eye shet, an' one eye open,—dis is evah
wud he said:
"Lawd, look down in tendah mussy on sich generous
hea'ts ez dese;
Make us truly thankful, amen. Pass dat possum,
ef you please!"
Well, we eat and drunk ouah po'tion, 'twell dah
wasn't nothin' lef,
An' we felt jes' like new sausage, we was mos'
nigh stuffed to def!
Tom, he knowed how we'd be feelin', so he had
de fiddlah 'roun',
An' he made us cleah de cabin fu' to dance dat
suppah down.
Jim, de fiddlah, chuned his fiddle, put some
rosum on his bow,
Set a pine box on de table, mounted it an' let
huh go!
He's a fiddlah, now I tell you, an' he made dat
fiddle ring,
'Twell de ol'est an' de lamest had to give deir
feet a fling.
Jigs, cotillions, reels an' break-downs, cordrills
an' a waltz er two;
Bless yo' soul, dat music winged 'em an' dem
people lak to flew.
Cripple Joe, de ole rheumatic, danced dat flo'
f'om side to middle,
Th'owed away his crutch an' hopped it, what's
rheumatics 'ginst a fiddle?
Eldah Thompson got so tickled dat he lak to
los' his grace,
Had to tek bofe feet an' hol' dem so's to keep
'em in deir place.
An' de Christuns an' de sinnahs got so mixed
up on dat flo',
Dat I don't see how dey'd pahted ef de trump
had chanced to blow.
Well, we danced dat way an' capahed in de mos'
redic'lous way,
'Twell de roosahs in de bahnyard cleahed deir
th'oats an' crowed fu' day.
Y'ought to been dah, fu' I tell you evahthing
was rich an' prime,

An' dey ain't no use in talkin', we jes had one
scrumptious time!

Frederick Douglass

A hush is over all the teeming lists,
And there is pause, a breath-space in the strife;
A spirit brave has passed beyond the mists
And vapors that obscure the sun of life.
And Ethiopia, with bosom torn,
Laments the passing of her noblest born.

She weeps for him a mother's burning tears—
She loved him with a mother's deepest love.
He was her champion thro' direful years,
And held her weal all other ends above.
When Bondage held her bleeding in the dust,
He raised her up and whispered, "Hope and Trust."

For her his voice, a fearless clarion, rung
That broke in warning on the ears of men;
For her the strong bow of his power he strung,
And sent his arrows to the very den
Where grim Oppression held his bloody place
And gloated o'er the mis'ries of a race.

And he was no soft-tongued apologist;
He spoke straightforward, fearlessly uncowed;
The sunlight of his ruth dispelled the mist,
And set in bold relief each dark hued cloud;
To sin and crime he gave their proper hue,
And hurled at evil what was evil's due.

Through good and ill report he cleaved his way
Right onward, with his face set toward the heights,
Nor feared to face the foeman's dread array,—
The lash of scorn, the sting of petty spites.
He dared the lightning in the lightning's track,
And answered thunder with his thunder back.

When men maligned him, and their torrent wrath
In furious imprecations o'er him broke,
He kept his counsel as he kept his path;
'T was for his race, not for himself he spoke.
He knew the import of his Master's call,
And felt himself too mighty to be small.

No miser in the good he held was he,—
His kindness followed his horizon's rim.
His heart, his talents, and his hands were free
To all who truly needed aught of him.

Where poverty and ignorance were rife,
He gave his bounty as he gave his life.

The place and cause that first aroused his might
  Still proved its power until his latest day.
In Freedom's lists and for the aid of Right
  Still in the foremost rank he waged the fray;
Wrong lived; his occupation was not gone.
He died in action with his armor on!

We weep for him, but we have touched his hand,
  And felt the magic of his presence nigh,
The current that he sent throughout the land,
  The kindling spirit of his battle-cry.
O'er all that holds us we shall triumph yet,
And place our banner where his hopes were set!

Oh, Douglass, thou hast passed beyond the shore,
  But still thy voice is ringing o'er the gale!
Thou'st taught thy race how high her hopes may soar,
  And bade her seek the heights, nor faint, nor fail.
She will not fail, she heeds thy stirring cry,
She knows thy guardian spirit will be nigh,
And, rising from beneath the chast'ning rod,
She stretches out her bleeding hands to God!

Sympathy

I know what the caged bird feels, alas!
  When the sun is bright on the upland slopes;
When the wind stirs soft through the springing grass,
And the river flows like a stream of glass;
  When the first bird sings and the first bud opes,
And the faint perfume from its chalice steals—
I know what the caged bird feels!

I know why the caged bird beats his wing
  Till its blood is red on the cruel bars;
For he must fly back to his perch and cling
When he fain would be on the bough a-swing;
  And a pain still throbs in the old, old scars
And they pulse again with a keener sting—
I know why he beats his wing!

I know why the caged bird sings, ah me,
  When his wing is bruised and his bosom sore,—
When he beats his bars and he would be free;
It is not a carol of joy or glee,
  But a prayer that he sends from his heart's deep core,
But a plea, that upward to Heaven he flings—
I know why the caged bird sings!

We Wear the Mask

We wear the mask that grins and lies,
It hides our cheeks and shades our eyes,—
This debt we pay to human guile;
With torn and bleeding hearts we smile,
And mouth with myriad subtleties.

Why should the world be overwise,
In counting all our tears and sighs?
Nay, let them only see us, while
We wear the mask.

We smile, but, O great Christ, our cries
To thee from tortured souls arise.
We sing, but oh the clay is vile
Beneath our feet, and long the mile;
But let the world dream otherwise,
We wear the mask!

The Poet

He sang of life, serenely sweet,
With, now and then, a deeper note.
From some high peak, nigh yet remote,
He voiced the world's absorbing beat.

He sang of love when earth was young,
And Love, itself, was in his lays.
But ah, the world, it turned to praise
A jingle in a broken tongue.

A Spiritual

De 'cession's stahted on de gospel way,
De Capting is a-drawin' nigh:
Bettah stop a-foolin' an' a-try to pray;
Lif' up yo' haid w'en de King go by!

Oh, sinnah mou'nin' in de dusty road,
Hyeah's de minute fu' to dry yo' eye:
Dey's a moughty One a-comin' fu' to baih yo' load;
Lif' up yo' haid w'en de King go by!

Oh, widder weepin' by yo' husban's grave,
Hit's bettah fu' to sing den sigh:
Hyeah come de Mastah wid de powah to save;
Lif' up yo' haid w'en de King go by!

Oh, orphans a-weepin' lak de widder do,
An' I wish you'd tell me why:
De Mastah is a mammy an' a pappy too;
Lif' up yo' haid w'en de King go by!

Oh, Moses sot de sarpint in de wildahness
  W'en de chillun had commenced to die:
Some 'efused to look, but hit cuohed de res;
  Lif' up yo' haid w'en de King go by!

Bow down, bow 'way down,
    Bow down,
But lif' up yo' haid w'en de King go by!

ALICE MOORE DUNBAR-NELSON
(1875–1935)

Overshadowed for many decades by Paul Laurence Dunbar, her first husband, and in whose reputation she basked, Alice Dunbar-Nelson is beginning to be perceived in her own right as a short story writer, poet, dramatist, essayist, anthologist, and diarist. As African American women writers have been rediscovered during the 1980s and 1990s, Nelson has become one of the central writers on whom such attention has focused. She is noted for her often compelling depictions of female characters; her focus on Louisiana settings and culture; and her sometimes conflicting attitudes toward race, class, and color. The publication of her diary in 1984 revealed a bisexually free and feminist spirit (although at times an ambiguous one) at work against the typecasting of her era.

Well educated and cultured, Alice Ruth Moore was born in New Orleans, the younger of two daughters in the family of Joseph and Patricia Wright Moore. Her father was a Creole seaman and her mother a seamstress. She was educated in New Orleans and graduated from high school there in 1889, which enabled her to enter Straight University (now Dillard University) in New Orleans at the age of fifteen. While completing the two-year teacher-training program at the university, she was able to cultivate a wide range of interests with resources at Straight. She could also take advantage of the law school, the printing department, and the classics program; she actually took courses in nursing and trained to become a stenographer. She was also a violin-cellist in William Joseph Nickerson's orchestra and a mandolin player in his all-girl mandolin club. Her writing skills enabled her to serve as editor of the woman's page of the *New Orleans Journal of the Lodge,* a black fraternal publication.

Moore began her teaching career in 1892, just after she turned seventeen, and she would teach until 1931. After teaching at the Old Marigny Elementary School in New Orleans, she traveled northeast in 1896 for further schooling at Cornell and Columbia universities and at the University of Pennsylvania. The previous year, at the age of twenty, she had published *Violets and Other Tales,* a collection of poetry, essays, short stories, and other writings. Also in 1895, Paul Laurence Dunbar had initiated a correspondence with her after seeing a photograph of her that accompanied one of her poems in an issue of the *Boston Monthly Review.* She met Dunbar in New York City in February 1897, shortly after she assumed a teaching position at Public School 83 in Brooklyn; she lived with Victoria Earle Mathews for awhile during this period. Reported to have fallen in love with Moore's picture, it only took the actual sight of her for Dunbar to propose, which he did upon their first meeting and just before he sailed to England for a reading tour. They were married secretly in

March 1898 and relocated to Washington, D.C. By 1902, they were separated, partly because Alice's family never approved of the dark-skinned Paul and his washerwoman mother, and partly because this impetuous Creole was overly aggressive in trying to shape her husband into her image of what he should be. The immediate cause, however, was a drunken rage in which Paul reportedly beat Alice and spread some slanderous story about her. After the separation, Alice Dunbar moved to Delaware, where she taught at Howard High School in Wilmington until 1920. She tirelessly performed her duties at the school, which included teaching, supervising, securing grants, directing plays, and serving as liaison to the administration. It was during this active period in her life that she quietly married her second husband, Henry Arthur Callis, a former teacher turned medical student who was twelve years her junior, on January 19, 1910. Very little is known about this long-concealed marriage, which lasted only one year.

Alice Dunbar-Nelson's career as a short-fiction writer, journalist, playwright, poet, and anthologist flourished between 1899 and 1920. She published stories, poems, and essays in the *Crisis, Messenger, A.M.E. Church Review, Southern Workman, Journal of Negro History, Lippincott's,* and *Opportunity.* Primarily important as a writer of prose, she published in 1899 her best collection of short fiction titled *The Goodness of St. Roque and Other Stories.* All of the stories are set in New Orleans and are filled with the richness of Creole culture and history. In one of the best stories in the collection, "Sister Josepha," Dunbar-Nelson examines the issues of racism, sexism, and illegitimacy, which forces a young woman to convent life. Seven years later, she published her first play, *The Author's Evening at Home,* which appeared in *Smart Set.* A second play, *Mine Eyes Have Seen,* was designed to encourage African American support for World War I and appeared in *Crisis* in 1918. On one level, *Mine Eyes Have Seen* explores the level of loyalty that African Americans owe to a country that disfranchises them. On another level, the play examines the frustrations that women experienced during wartime because of narrowly prescribed roles. Dunbar-Nelson founded and coedited a newspaper, the *Wilmington Advocate,* in 1920. She edited two anthologies, *Masterpieces of Negro Eloquence* (1914) and *The Dunbar Speaker and Entertainer* (1920). She wrote a woman's column, "Une Femme Dit," for the *Pittsburgh Courier* from January to September of 1926. A second column, "As in a Looking Glass," featured book reviews and commentary, and, in a third, "So It Seems," Nelson commented on a variety of racial and political issues. Her two novels, *Confessions of a Lazy Woman* and the longer *This Lofty Oak* (595 typewritten pages), remained unpublished at her death—despite her numerous attempts to get the latter work published. *This Lofty Oak* was a labor of love, a novel based on the friendship that Dunbar-Nelson shared with Edwina B. Kruse, the founding principal of Howard High School.

On April 20, 1916, Dunbar Callis married Robert J. Nelson, a journalist. She became interested in politics and served on the State Republican Committee of Delaware in 1920. She worked with the New York Democratic campaign in 1924, and as executive secretary for the American Friends Interracial Peace Committee from 1928 to 1931. Alice Dunbar-Nelson died on September 18, 1935, at the University of Pennsylvania hospital; she was suffering from heart disease.

❖❖❖

Three volumes of Dunbar-Nelson's works are included in the Schomburg Library of Nineteenth-Century Black Women Writers (1988). Dunbar-Nelson's diary, *Give Us Each Day: The Diary of Alice Dunbar-Nelson,* was edited and published by Gloria Hull in 1984. Hull also has a substantial chapter on Dunbar-Nelson in *Color, Sex, and Poetry: Three Women Writers of the Harlem Renaissance* (1987). Ora Williams has provided information on secondary sources for Dunbar-Nelson in "Works by and About Alice Ruth (Moore) Dunbar-Nelson: A Bibliography," *CLA Journal* 19 (March 1976).

Microfilm copies of Dunbar-Nelson's papers are in the Ohio Historical Society in Columbus, Ohio. The Morris Library, University of Delaware, Newark, Delaware, also holds some of her papers.

Sister Josepha

Sister Josepha told her beads mechanically, her fingers numb with the accustomed exercise. The little organ creaked a dismal "O Salutaris," and she still knelt on the floor, her white-bonneted head nodding suspiciously. The Mother Superior gave a sharp glance at the tired figure; then, as a sudden lurch forward brought the little sister back to consciousness, Mother's eyes relaxed into a genuine smile.

The bell tolled the end of vespers, and the sombre-robed nuns filed out of the chapel to go about their evening duties. Little Sister Josepha's work was to attend to the household lamps, but there must have been as much oil spilled upon the table to-night as was put in the vessels. The small brown hands trembled so that most of the wicks were trimmed with points at one corner which caused them to smoke that night.

"Oh, cher Seigneur," she sighed, giving an impatient polish to a refractory chimney, "it is wicked and sinful, I know, but I am so tired. I can't be happy and sing any more. It doesn't seem right for le bon Dieu to have me all cooped up here with nothing to see but stray visitors, and always the same old work, teaching those mean little girls to sew, and washing and filling the same old lamps. Pah!" And she polished the chimney with a sudden vigorous jerk which treatened destruction.

They were rebellious prayers that the red mouth murmured that night, and a restless figure that tossed on the hard dormitory bed. Sister Dominica called from her couch to know if Sister Josepha were ill.

"No," was the somewhat short response; then a muttered, "Why can't they let me alone for a minute? That pale-eyed Sister Dominica never sleeps; that's why she is so ugly."

About fifteen years before this night some one had brought to the orphan asylum connected with this convent, du Sacré Cœur, a round, dimpled bit of three-year-old humanity, who regarded the world from a pair of gravely twinkling black eyes, and only took a chubby thumb out of a rosy mouth long enough to answer in monosyllabic French. It was a child without an identity; there was but one name that any one seemed to know, and that, too, was vague,—Camille.

She grew up with the rest of the waifs; scraps of French and American civilization thrown together to develop a seemingly inconsistent miniature world. Mademoiselle Camille was a queen among them, a pretty little tyrant who ruled the children and dominated the more timid sisters in charge.

One day an awakening came. When she was fifteen, and almost fully ripened into a glorious tropical beauty of the type that matures early, some visitors to the convent were fascinated by her and asked the Mother Superior to give the girl into their keeping.

Camille fled like a frightened fawn into the yard, and was only unearthed with some difficulty from behind a group of palms. Sulky and pouting, she was led into the parlour, picking at her blue pinafore like a spoiled infant.

"The lady and gentleman wish you to go home with them, Camille," said the Mother Superior, in the language of the convent. Her voice was kind and gentle apparently; but the child, accustomed to its various inflections, detected a steely ring behind its softness, like the proverbial iron hand in the velvet glove.

"You must understand, madame," continued Mother, in stilted English, "that we never force children from us. We are ever glad to place them in comfortable—how you say that?—quarters—maisons—homes—bien! But we will not make them go if they do not wish."

Camille stole a glance at her would-be guardians, and decided instantly, impulsively, finally. The woman suited her; but the man! It was doubtless intuition of the quick, vivacious sort which belonged to her blood that served her. Untutored in worldly knowledge, she could not divine the meaning of the pronounced leers and admiration of her physical charms which gleamed in the man's face, but she knew it made her feel creepy, and stoutly refused to go.

Next day Camille was summoned from a task to the Mother Superior's parlour. The other girls gazed with envy upon her as she dashed down the courtyard with impetuous movement. Camille, they decided crossly, received too much notice. It was Camille this, Camille that; she was pretty, it was to be expected. Even Father Ray lingered longer in his blessing when his hands pressed her silky black hair.

As she entered the parlour, a strange chill swept over the girl. The room was not an unaccustomed one, for she had swept it many times, but to-day the stiff black chairs, the dismal crucifixes, the gleaming whiteness of the walls, even the cheap lithograph of the Madonna which Camille had always regarded as a perfect specimen of art, seemed cold and mean.

"Camille, ma chère," said Mother, "I am extremely displeased with you. Why did you not wish to go with Monseiur and Madame Lafayé yesterday?"

The girl uncrossed her hands from her bosom, and spread them out in a deprecating gesture.

"Mais, ma mère, I was afraid."

Mother's face grew stern. "No foolishness now," she exclaimed.

"It is not foolishness, ma mère; I could not help it, but that man looked at me so funny, I felt all cold chills down my back. Oh, dear Mother, I love the convent and the sisters so, I just want to stay and be a sister too, may I?"

And thus it was that Camille took the white veil at sixteen years. Now that the period of novitiate was over, it was just beginning to dawn upon her that she had made a mistake.

"Maybe it would have been better had I gone with the funny-looking lady and gentleman," she mused bitterly one night. "Oh, Seigneur, I'm so tired and impatient; it's so dull here, and, dear God, I'm so young."

There was no help for it. One must arise in the morning, and help in the refectory with the stupid Sister Francesca, and go about one's duties with a prayerful mien, and not even let a sigh escape when one's head ached with the eternal telling of beads.

A great fête day was coming, and an atmosphere of preparation and mild excitement pervaded the brown walls of the convent like a delicate aroma. The old Cathedral around the corner had stood a hundred years, and all the city was rising to do honour to its age and time-softened beauty. There would be a service, oh, but such a one! with two Cardinals, and Archbishops and Bishops, and all the accompanying glitter of soldiers and orchestras. The little sisters of the Convent du Sacré Cœur clasped their hands in anticipation of the holy joy. Sister Josepha curled her lip, she was so tired of churchly pleasures.

The day came, a gold and blue spring day, when the air hung heavy with the scent of roses and magnolias, and the sunbeams fairly laughed as they kissed the houses. The old Cathedral stood gray and solemn, and the flowers in Jackson Square smiled cheery birthday greetings across the way. The crowd around the door surged and pressed and pushed in its eagerness to get within. Ribbons stretched across the banquette were of no avail to repress it, and important ushers with cardinal colours could do little more.

The Sacred Heart sisters filed slowly in at the side door, creating a momentary flutter as they paced reverently to their seats, guarding the blue-bonneted orphans. Sister Josepha, determined to see as much of the world as she could, kept her big black eyes opened wide, as the church rapidly filled with the fashionably dressed, perfumed, rustling, and self-conscious throng.

Her heart beat quickly. The rebellious thoughts that will arise in the most philosophical of us surged in her small heavily gowned bosom. For her were the gray things, the neutral tinted skies, the ugly garb, the coarse meats; for them the rainbow, the ethereal airiness of earthly joys, the bonbons and glacés of the world. Sister Josepha did not know that the rainbow is elusive, and its colours but the illumination of tears; she had never been told that earthly ethereality is necessarily ephemeral, nor that bonbons and glacés, whether of the palate or of the soul, nauseate and pall upon the taste. Dear God, forgive her, for she bent with contrite tears over her worn rosary, and glanced no more at the worldly glitter of femininity.

The sunbeams streamed through the high windows in purple and crimson lights upon a veritable fugue of colour. Within the seats, crush upon crush of spring millinery; within the aisles erect lines of gold-braided, gold-buttoned military. Upon the altar, broad sweeps of golden robes, great dashes of crimson skirts, mitres and gleaming crosses, the soft neutral hue of rich lace vestments; the tender heads of childhood in picturesque attire; the proud, golden magnificence of the domed altar with its weighting mass of lilies and wide-eyed roses, and the long candles that sparkled their yellow star points above the reverent throng within the altar rails.

The soft baritone of the Cardinal intoned a single phrase in the suspended silence. The censer took up the note in its delicate clink clink, as it swung to and fro in the hands of a fair-haired child. Then the organ, pausing an instant in a deep, mellow, long-drawn note, burst suddenly into a magnificent strain, and the choir sang forth, "Kyrie Elëison, Christe Elëison." One voice, flute-like, piercing, sweet, rang high over the rest. Sister Josepha heard and trembled, as she buried her face in her hands, and let her tears fall, like other beads, through her rosary.

It was when the final word of the service had been intoned, the last peal of the exit march had died away, that she looked up meekly, to encounter a pair of youthful brown eyes gazing pityingly upon her. That was all she remembered for a moment, that the eyes were youthful and handsome and tender. Later, she saw that they were placed in a rather beautiful boyish face, surmounted by waves of brown hair, curling and soft, and that the head was set on a pair of shoulders decked in military uniform. Then the brown eyes marched away with the rest of the rear guard, and the white-bonneted sisters filed out the side door, through the narrow court, back into the brown convent.

That night Sister Josepha tossed more than usual on her hard bed, and clasped her fingers often in prayer to quell the wickedness in her heart. Turn where she would, pray as she might, there was ever a pair of tender, pitying brown eyes, haunting her persistently. The squeaky organ at vespers intoned the clank of military accoutrements to her ears, the white bonnets of the sisters about her faded into mists of curling brown hair. Briefly, Sister Josepha was in love.

The days went on pretty much as before, save for the one little heart that beat rebelliously now and then, though it tried so hard to be submissive. There was the morning work in the refectory, the stupid little girls to teach sewing, and the insatiable lamps that were so greedy for oil. And always the tender, boyish brown eyes, that looked so sorrowfully at the fragile, beautiful little sister, haunting, following, pleading.

Perchance, had Sister Josepha been in the world, the eyes would have been an incident. But in this home of self-repression and retrospection, it was a life-story. The eyes had gone their way, doubtless forgetting the little sister they pitied; but the little sister?

The days glided into weeks, the weeks into months. Thoughts of escape had come to Sister Josepha, to flee into the world, to merge in the great city where recognition was impossible, and, working her way like the rest of humanity, perchance encounter the eyes again.

It was all planned and ready. She would wait until some morning when the little band of black-robed sisters wended their way to mass at the Cathedral. When it was time to file out the side-door into the courtway, she would linger at prayers, then slip out another door, and unseen glide up Chartres Street to Canal, and once there, mingle in the throng that filled the wide thoroughfare. Beyond this first plan she could think no further. Penniless, garbed, and shaven though she would be, other difficulties never presented themselves to her. She would rely on the mercies of the world to help her escape from this torturing life of inertia. It seemed easy now that the first step of decision had been taken.

The Saturday night before the final day had come, and she lay feverishly nervous in her narrow little bed, wondering with wide-eyed fear at the morrow. Pale-eyed Sister Dominica and Sister Francesca were whispering together in the dark silence, and Sister Josepha's ears pricked up as she heard her name.

"She is not well, poor child," said Francesca. "I fear the life is too confining."

"It is best for her," was the reply. "You know, sister, how hard it would be for her in the world, with no name but Camille, no friends, and her beauty; and then—"

Sister Josepha heard no more, for her heart beating tumultously in her bosom drowned the rest. Like the rush of the bitter salt tide over a drowning man clinging to a spar, came the complete submerging of her hopes of another life. No name but Camille, that was true; no nationality, for she could never tell from whom or whence she came; no friends, and a beauty that not even an ungainly bonnet and shaven head could hide. In a flash she realised the deception of the life she would lead, and the cruel self-torture of wonder at her own identity. Already, as if in anticipation of the world's questionings, she was asking herself, "Who am I? What am I?"

The next morning the sisters du Sacré Cœur filed into the Cathedral at High Mass, and bent devout knees at the general confession. "Confiteor Deo omnipotenti," murmured the priest; and tremblingly one little sister followed the words, "Je confesse à Dieu, tout puissant—que j'ai beaucoup péché par pensées—c'est ma faute—c'est ma faute—c'est ma très grande faute."

The organ pealed forth as mass ended, the throng slowly filed out, and the sisters paced through the courtway back into the brown convent walls. One paused at the entrance, and gazed with swift longing eyes in the direction of narrow, squalid Chartres Street, then, with a gulping sob, followed the rest, and vanished behind the heavy door.

FENTON JOHNSON
(1888–1958)

A precursor to the Harlem Renaissance, Fenton Johnson published his major works in the second decade of the twentieth century. Considered one of the first revolutionary black poets, he initially followed in the footsteps of Paul Laurence Dunbar in publishing dialect poetry. He later progressed to focus on African American history and culture and finally to a general pessimism about the state of blacks in American society and about the state of life in general. Not only did he publish his own poetry, but he founded and edited *Champion Magazine*, the outlet he used for expressing his views on the crucial issues facing African Americans of his day. Founded in September 1916, the magazine folded in 1917. He then founded *Favorite Magazine*, which he published until 1920. Johnson's uncle, John "Mushmouth" Johnson, may have supported one of his magazines as well as the publication of some of his volumes of poetry.

Johnson was born in Chicago to Elijah and Jessie Taylor Johnson. His father, a Pullman porter, owned the building in which Johnson was born, therefore making him one of the wealthiest African Americans in Chicago. Johnson was educated at Englewood High School and Wendell Phillips High School in Chicago. His brief enrollment at Northwestern University (1908–09) with plans to become a minister gave way to his attendance at the University of Chicago in February 1910. At nineteen, he had several of his plays performed at Chicago's Pekin Theatre. He held an assortment of jobs during this period, including being a messenger for St. James Convent and St. Charles Convent, working at the U.S. Post Office, and teaching English at State University in Louisville during 1910–11. He married Cecelia Rhone during this period.

Johnson published his first volume of poetry, *A Little Dreaming,* in 1913, which is conventional in its poetic forms and includes poems addressed to Paul Laurence Dunbar and Algernon Charles Swinburne. He celebrates Africa and African Americans, and incorporates supernatural motifs from Greek mythology, Islam, and the Judeo-Christian tradition. In *Visions of the Dusk* (1915), he would try his hand at dialect in the tradition of Dunbar, but falls short of Dunbar's mastery. The dialect poems (especially those portraying cruelty during slavery), however, did capture the pessimism that would increasingly define Johnson's work. He continued the focus on dialect in *Songs of the Soil* (1916), even as he was aware that many African American poets were turning away from that style. The latter two volumes were published in New York, where Johnson lived for a brief period and where *Crisis* magazine published several of his short stories. A fourth volume of poetry, *African Nights,* was apparently never published.

Despite receiving excellent reviews, Johnson was forced to subsidize the publishing of each of his additional volumes of poetry. For that reason, as well as a feeling of being thwarted in his creative efforts because he was black, Johnson did not publish another volume of poetry after 1916. His more experimental forms, some of which show the influence of Vachel Lindsay, Edgar Lee Masters, and Carl Sandburg, appear in poems published in magazines, such as Harriet Monroe's *Poetry: A Magazine of Verse.* Concentration on blacks in urban settings in some of Johnson's works, along with hints of social protest, anticipated the concerns of Harlem Renaissance writers and identified Johnson with such poets of the Chicago Renaissance as Gwendolyn Brooks.

Although Johnson participated in the Work Projects Administration (WPA) focus on the "Negro in Illinois" in the 1930s and had several of his poems included in that project, he did not publish on a regular basis after the 1920s. The "42 WPA Poems" manuscript became a part of the library collection at Fisk University, where Arna Bontemps was on the faculty; Bontemps was one of the few people with whom Johnson maintained contact in his later years. Johnson's last two published volumes were *For the Highest Good* (1920) and *Tales of Darkest America* (1920), a collection of short stories. Little is known of Johnson's life beyond the 1930s. When, in 1958, he was asked to provide biographical information, he responded that "he did not have biographical material 'later or since 1930'."

❖❖❖

Information about Johnson can be obtained from Sterling Brown, *Negro Poetry and Drama* (1937); J. Saunders Redding, *To Make a Poet Black* (1939); Eugene B. Redmond, *Drumvoices: The Mission of Afro-American Poetry, A Critical History* (1976); Jean Wagner, *Black Poets of the United States: From Paul Laurence Dunbar to Langston Hughes* (1973). A critical article on Johnson's work is James P. Hutchinson's "Fenton Johnson: Pilgrim of the Dusk," *Studies in Black Literature* 7 (Autumn 1976).

A Negro Peddler's Song

The pattern of this song was sung by a Negro peddler in a Chicago alley.

Good Lady,
I have corn and beets,
Onions, too, and leeks,
And also sweet potat-y.

Good Lady,
Buy for May and John;
And when work is done
Give a bite to Sadie.

Good Lady,
I have corn and beets,
Onions, too, and leeks,
And also sweet potat-y.

Aunt Jane Allen

State Street is lonely today. Aunt Jane Allen has driven her chariot to Heaven.
I remember how she hobbled along, a little woman, parched of skin, brown as the leather of a satchel and with eyes that had scanned eighty years of life.
Have those who bore her dust to the last resting place buried with her the basket of aprons she went up and down State Street trying to sell?
Have those who bore her dust to the last resting place buried with her the gentle worn *Son* that she gave to each of the seed of Ethiopia?

The Banjo Player

There is music in me, the music of a peasant people.
I wander through the levee, picking my banjo and singing my

songs of the cabin and the field. At the Last Chance Saloon
I am as welcome as the violets in March;
there is always food and drink for me there, and the dimes
of those who love honest music. Behind the railroad tracks
the little children clap their hands and love me as they love
Kris Kringle.
But I fear that I am a failure.
Last night a woman called me a troubadour.
What is a troubadour?

Tired

I am tired of work; I am tired of building up somebody
else's civilization.
Let us take a rest, M'Lissy Jane.
I will go down to the Last Chance Saloon, drink a gallon
or two of gin, shoot a game or two of dice and
sleep the rest of the night on one of Mike's barrels.
You will let the old shanty go to rot, the white people's
clothes turn to dust, and the Calvary Baptist Church
sink to the bottomless pit.
You will spend your days forgetting you married me and
your nights hunting the warm gin Mike serves the
ladies in the rear of the Last Chance Saloon.
Throw the children into the river; civilization has given
us too many. It is better to die than it is to grow up
and find out that you are colored.
Pluck the stars out of the heavens. The stars mark our
destiny. The stars marked my destiny.
I am tired of civilization.

The Scarlet Woman

Once I was good like the Virgin Mary and the Minister's wife.
My father worked for Mr. Pullman and white people's tips; but he died two days after
his insurance expired.
I had nothing, so I had to go to work.
All the stock I had was a white girl's education and a face that enchanted the men of
both races.
Starvation danced with me.
So when Big Lizzie, who kept a house for white men, came to me with tales of fortune
that I could reap from the sale of my virtue I bowed my head to Vice.
Now I can drink more gin than any man for miles around.
Gin is better than all the water in Lethe.

ORATORICAL VOICES OF RECONSTRUCTION, RACE, AND WOMEN'S RIGHTS

BLANCHE KELSO BRUCE
(1841–1898)

Of all his accomplishments, perhaps the one for which Blanche K. Bruce is best known is that of serving as U.S. Senator from Mississippi. He was one of two black Mississippians to have held that distinction during Reconstruction. He was also widely known as a teacher, and he was a successful planter as well. His career attests to the possibilities for African American achievement in public spheres when opportunities are available.

Bruce was born into slavery in Virginia, near Farmville in Prince Edward County. A mulatto, he was the youngest of eleven children born to Polly, who was owned by Pettus Perkinson. (Bruce chose the name of the man who had owned Polly before she was sold to Perkinson.) After his wife's death, Perkinson migrated with his slaves to Missouri and Mississippi, finally settling in Missouri. The young Blanche learned how to read and write from the tutor of young William Perkinson; he also studied the printing trade and worked in tobacco fields and factories.

Dissatisfied with his condition, he ran away to the free state of Kansas and opened the first elementary school for blacks; a minister there tutored Bruce and thus enabled him to continue his own education. He returned to Missouri after it emancipated the slaves in January 1865 and worked as a printer's apprentice before attending Oberlin College briefly. Limited funds sent him from college to portering on the *Columbia*, a Mississippi riverboat. When he heard a speech by John Lusk Alcorn, who later became governor of Mississippi, he migrated there in February 1869 to capitalize on opportunities he envisioned.

His successes equaled his ambition. He became supervisor of elections in Tallahatchie County in 1869 and, in 1870, he went to Jackson, the state capital, and was elected sergeant-at-arms of the Senate. He later served as sheriff and tax assessor of Bolivar County, superintendent of education, and a member of the Floreyville (where he had made his home) Board of Aldermen. He began to acquire property that would eventually amount to three thousand acres of Delta land. His affiliation with the Republican party led to the state legislature electing him to the U.S. Senate in 1874, making him the second African American so elected (Hiram R. Revels served from February 1870 to March 1871); he also had support from Governor Adelbert Ames and from James Hill, a successful black businessman who was favored by influential whites as well as blacks. In the Senate for the full term between 1875 and 1881 (the only black senator at that time), he became well-known for the speeches he made, including his unsuccessful attempt on March 3, 1876, to get P.B.S. Pinchback seated in the Senate after his election in Louisiana had been declared illegal. Bruce also tried to get the U.S. Army desegregated, fought for bounty money for black soldiers and sailors, advocated support for black industrial education, and rejected black migration to Liberia. His most successful work involved concluding the affairs of the bankrupt

Freedmen's Savings and Trust Company; depositors were able to get three-fifths of their money back.

He found time during his busy political career to marry Josephine B. Wilson of Cleveland on June 24, 1878; the couple had one child, a son, Roscoe Conkling Bruce (named after New York Senator Roscoe Conkling who, following long-established custom, had escorted Bruce to his Senate seat when a Mississippi Senator refused), who would graduate Phi Beta Kappa from Harvard University and become assistant superintendent for "colored schools" in the District of Columbia.

Finding Washington more suitable to his ambitions, Bruce was register of the treasury between 1881 and 1885 (under Presidents Garfield and Arthur), recorder of deeds for the District of Columbia between 1889 and 1893 (under President Harrison), and was appointed register of the treasury again in 1897 by President McKinley. In ill health for several years, Bruce died of a kidney ailment on March 17, 1898. His burial in Woodlawn Cemetery in Suitland, Maryland, the final resting place of many prominent blacks, is further testament to the position he held in American politics during the latter quarter of the nineteenth century.

❖❖❖

Sadie Daniel St. Clair completed a biography of Bruce, "The National Career of Blanche K. Bruce," as a doctoral dissertation at New York University in 1947. Bruce's brother, Henry K. Bruce, completed a memoir, *The New Man* (2nd ed., 1969), that provides information on Bruce's early life. Maurine Christopher's *America's Black Congressmen* (1971) also contains information about Bruce.

Speech to the U.S. Senate on Mississippi Elections Delivered March 3, 1876

The conduct of the late election in Mississippi affected not merely the fortunes of the partisans—as the same were necessarily involved in the defeat or success of the respective parties to the contest—but put in question and jeopardy the sacred rights of the citizens; and the investigation contemplated in the pending resolution has for its object not the determination of the question whether the offices shall be held and the public affairs of the State be administered by democrats or republicans, but the higher and more important end, the protection in all their purity and significance of the political rights of the people and the free institutions of the country.

The evidence in hand and accessible will show beyond peradventure that in many parts of the State corrupt and violent influences were brought to bear upon the registrars of voters, thus materially affecting the character of the voting or poll lists; upon the inspectors of election, prejudicially and unfairly, thereby changing the number of votes cast; and finally threats and violence were practiced directly upon the masses of voters in such measures and strength as to produce grave apprehensions for personal safety and as to deter them from the exercise of their political franchises.

It will not accord with the laws of nature or history to brand colored people a race of cowards. On more than one historic field, beginning in 1776 and coming down to the centennial year of the Republic, they have attested in blood their courage as well as a love of liberty. I ask Senators to believe that no consideration of fear or personal danger has kept us quiet and forbearing under the provocations and wrongs that have so sorely tried our souls. But feeling kindly towards our white fellow-citizens, appreciating the good purposes and offices of the better classes, and, above all, abhorring war of races, we determined to wait until such time as an appeal to the good sense and justice of the American people could be made.

The sober American judgment must obtain in the South as elsewhere in the Republic, that the only distinctions upon which parties can be safely organized and in harmony with our institutions are differences of opinion relative to principles and policies of government, and that differences of religion, nationality, or race can neither with safety nor propriety be permitted for a moment to enter into the party contests of the day. The unanimity with which the colored voters act with a party is not referable to any race prejudice on their part. On the contrary, they invite the political co-operation of their white brethren, and vote as a unit because proscribed as such. They deprecate the establishment of the color line by the opposition, not only because the act is unwise, but because it isolates them from the white men of the South and forces them, in sheer self-protection, and against their inclination, to act seemingly upon the basis of a race prejudice that they neither respect nor entertain. They not only recognize the equality of citizenship and the right of every man to hold without proscription any position of honor and trust to which the confidence of the people may elevate him; but owing nothing to race, birth, or surroundings, they above all other classes, in the community, are interested to see prejudices drop out of both politics and the businesses of the country, and success in life proceed upon the integrity and merit of the man who seeks it. . . . But withal, as they progress in intelligence and appreciation of the dignity of their prerogatives as citizens, they as an evidence of growth begin to realize the significance of the proverb, "When thou doest well for thyself, men shall praise thee"; and are disposed to exact the same protection and concessions of rights that are conferred upon other citizens by the Constitution, and that too without humiliation involved in the enforced abandonment of their political convictions.

I have confidence, not only in my country and her institutions, but in the endurance, capacity and destiny of my people. We will, as opportunity offers and ability serves, seek our places, sometimes in the field of literary arts, science and the professions. More frequently mechanical pursuits will attract and elicit our efforts; more still of my people will find employment and livelihood as the cultivators of the soil. The bulk of this people—by surroundings, habits, adaptation, and choice will continue to find their homes in the South and constitute the masses of its yeomanry. We will there, probably of our own volition and more abundantly than in the past, produce the great staples that will contribute to the basis of foreign exchange, and in giving the nation a balance of trade, and minister to the wants and comforts and build up the prosperity of the whole land. Whatever our ultimate position in the composite civilization of the Republic and whatever varying fortunes attend our career, we will not forget our instincts for freedom nor our love for country.[1]

[1]*Congressional Record*, 44th Congress, First Session, pp. 2100–2105

ROBERT BROWN ELLIOTT
(1842–1884)

In contrast to the usual biographical notices that Elliott was born in Boston, new information suggests that he was born and raised in Liverpool, England. Before migrating to the United States, he learned the printer's trade and served in the British navy. He arrived in the United States in time to become a major figure in African American politics during Reconstruction. Docking in Boston in 1867, he found work as a typesetter, married a mulatto woman, Grace, and became a member of Boston's best

African American society. He left Boston after a few months for South Carolina, where he edited the Republican *South Carolina Leader*, an African American newspaper. Shortly after his arrival, blacks and whites elected delegates to a state constitutional convention, and Elliott won a seat. His biographers speculate that his speedy need for U.S. citizenship in this election probably accounted for his claiming birth in Boston and attendance at Eton College. At any rate, Elliott was one of seventy-eight African American delegates (there were forty-five white delegates) to the 1868 convention. His performance there was the beginning of an extensive political career.

Elliott supported compulsory education for all children from ages six through sixteen and convinced delegates to support universal manhood suffrage, which, in effect, would eliminate literacy tests as requirements for voting. He opposed a poll tax to pay for compulsory education because he believed it could be used in the future to disfranchise blacks. His work at the convention led to his election to the state House of Representatives. While performing those duties, he also studied law and was admitted to the South Carolina bar in September 1868.

Elliott's career included a series of additional noteworthy appointments and accomplishments. In March 1869, he was appointed assistant adjutant-general of South Carolina, with responsibility for forming a Black Militia to protect whites and blacks from the Ku Klux Klan. In 1870, he was elected to the U.S. House of Representatives, where, as a member of the 42nd Congress, he spoke against an amnesty bill to remove political disabilities from Confederates, and in support of a proposed bill to use federal intervention to punish the Ku Klux Klan and protect blacks. He lost a bid for the U.S. Senate in 1873, but remained in the House of Representatives. On January 6, 1874, he made a celebrated speech in favor of the Civil Rights bill; observers assert that he easily won arguments over Alexander S. Stephens, the former vice president of the Confederacy. Acclaimed for his speaking ability, Elliott was asked a few months after this event to deliver the eulogy of Charles Sumner at a memorial service at Faneuil Hall in Boston.

Convinced that his talents were more needed in South Carolina than in Washington, Elliott resigned from the Congress and returned to his adopted state to complete his political career. The black majority in South Carolina was being blamed for corruption in the state, and Elliott wanted to change that impression. Although he became speaker of the House, his conflicts with white Republican governor Daniel H. Chamberlain frustrated his efforts at reform. (Chamberlain also wanted reform, but he distrusted Elliott's connection to Democrats.) In 1876, Elliott was elected attorney general in a hotly contested election, a seat he lost when President Rutherford B. Hayes removed federal troops from the South in 1877 and all Republican officeholders were ousted from office.

Although Elliott secured a post as a treasury agent and tried to hold the state's Republican party together, his efforts were in vain. Reconstruction had ended for South Carolina, and African Americans would now have to pay for whatever brief gains they had won. Elliott's personal fortunes declined with those of his party. When he died of malarial fever at the age of forty two, he was penniless and unknown, a sad testament to a brilliant career bound by racial politics too oppressive for the individual talent to overcome.

❖❖❖

Elliott's biographer is Peggy Lamson, who published *The Glorious Failure: Black Congressman Robert Brown Elliott and the Reconstruction in South Carolina* in 1973. Maurine Christopher, in *American Black Congressmen* (1971), includes a chapter on Elliott.

FROM *"The Civil Rights Bill"*[1]

Mr. Speaker:

While I am sincerely grateful for this high mark of courtesy that has been accorded to me by this House, it is a matter of regret to me that it is necessary at this day that I should rise in the presence of an American Congress to advocate a bill which simply asserts equal rights and equal public privileges for all classes of American citizens. I regret, sir, that the dark hue of my skin may lend a color to the imputation that I am controlled by motives personal to myself in my advocacy of this great measure of national justice. Sir, the motive that impels me is restricted by no such narrow boundary, but is as broad as your Constitution. I advocate it, sir, because it is right. The bill, however, not only appeals to your justice, but it demands a response from your gratitude.

In the events that led to the achievement of American independence the Negro was not an inactive or unconcerned spectator. He bore his part bravely upon many battlefields, although uncheered by that certain hope of political elevation which victory would secure to the white man. The tall granite shaft, which a grateful State has reared above its sons who fell in defending Fort Griswold against the attack of Benedict Arnold, bears the name of Jordan, Freeman, and other brave men of the African race, who there cemented with their blood the corner-stone of the Republic. In the State which I have the honor in part to represent (South Carolina) the rifle of the black man rang out against the troops of the British Crown in the darkest days of the American Revolution. Said General Greene, who has been justly termed the "Washington of the North," in a letter written by him to Alexander Hamilton, on the 10th of January, 1781, from the vicinity of Camden, South Carolina: "There is no such thing as national character or national sentiment. The inhabitants are numerous, but they would be rather formidable abroad than at home. There is a great spirit of enterprise among the black people, and those that come out as volunteers are not a little formidable to the enemy."

At the battle of New Orleans under the immortal Jackson, a colored regiment held the extreme right of the American line unflinchingly, and drove back the British column that pressed upon them at the point of the bayonet. So marked was their valor on that occasion that it evoked from their great commander the warmest encomiums, as will be seen from his dispatch announcing the brilliant victory.

As the gentleman from Kentucky (Mr. Beck), who seems to be the leading exponent on this floor of the party that is arrayed against the principle of this bill, has been pleased, in season and out of season, to cast odium upon the Negro and to vaunt the chivalry of his State, I may be pardoned for calling attention to another portion of the same dispatch. Referring to the various regiments under his command, and their conduct on that field which terminated the second war of American Independence, General Jackson says, "At the very moment when the entire discomfiture of the enemy was looked for with a confidence amounting to certainty, the Kentucky reinforcements, in whom so much reliance had been placed, ingloriously fled."

In quoting this indisputable piece of history, I do so only by way of admonition and not to question the well-attested gallantry of the true Kentuckian, and to the gentleman that it would be well that he should not flaunt his heraldry so proudly while he bears this bar-sinister on the military escutcheon of his State—a State which answered the call of the Republic in 1861, when

[1]Extracts from a speech delivered in the House of Representatives, January 6, 1874.

treason thundered at the very gates of the Capital, by coldly declaring her neutrality in the impending struggle. The Negro, true to that patriotism and love of country that have ever marked and characterized his history on this continent, came to the aid of the Government in its efforts to maintain the Constitution. To that Government he now appeals; that Constitution he now invokes for protection against outrage and unjust prejudices founded upon caste.

But, sir, we are told by the distinguished gentleman from Georgia (Mr. Stephens) that Congress has no power under the Constitution to pass such a law, and that the passage of such an act is in direct contravention of the rights of the States. I cannot assent to any such proposition. The Constitution of a free government ought always to be construed in favor of human rights. Indeed, the thirteenth, fourteenth, and fifteenth amendments, in positive words, invest Congress with the power to protect the citizen in his civil and political rights. Now, sir, what are civil rights? Rights natural, modified by civil society. Mr. Lieber says: "By civil liberty is meant, not only the absence of individual restraint, but liberty within the social system and political organism—a combination of principles, and laws which acknowledge, protect, and favor the dignity of man . . . civil liberty is the result of man's two fold character as an individual and social being, so soon as both are equally respected."

Alexander Hamilton, the right-hand man of Washington in the perilous days of the then infant Republic; the great interpreter and expounder of the Constitution, says: "Natural liberty is the gift of a beneficent Creator to the whole human race; civil liberty is founded on it, civil liberty is only natural liberty modified and secured by civil society."[2]

❖❖❖

Are we then, sir, with the amendments to our constitution staring us in the face; with these grand truths of history before our eyes; with innumerable wrongs daily inflicted upon five million citizens demanding redress, to commit this question to the diversity of legislation? In the words of Hamilton—"Is it the interest of the Government to sacrifice individual rights to the preservation of the rights of an artificial being called the States? There can be no truer principle than this, that every individual of the community at large has an equal right to the protection of Government. Can this be a free Government if partial distinctions are tolerated or maintained?"

The rights contended for in this bill are among "the sacred rights of mankind, which are not to be rummaged for among old parchments or musty records; they are written as with a sunbeam in the whole volume of human nature, by the hand of the Divinity itself, and can never be erased or obscured by mortal power."

But the Slaughter-house cases!—The Slaughter-house cases!

❖❖❖

Mr. Speaker, I venture to say here in the presence of the gentleman from Kentucky, and the gentleman from Georgia, and in the presence of the whole country, that there is not a line or word, not a thought or dictum even, in the decision of the Supreme Court in the great Slaughter-house cases, which casts a shadow of doubt on the right of Congress to pass the pending bill, or to adopt such other legislation as it may judge proper and necessary to secure perfect equality before the law to every citizen of the Republic. Sir, I protest against the dishonor now cast upon our Supreme Court by both the gentleman from Kentucky and the gentleman from Georgia. In other days, when the whole country was bowing beneath the yoke of slavery, when press, pulpit, platform, Congress and courts felt the fatal power of the slave oligarchy, I remember a decision of that court which no American now reads without shame and humiliation. But those days are past; the Supreme Court of to-day is a tribunal as true to freedom as any department of this Govern-

[2]*Hamilton's History of the American Republic,* Vol. 1, p. 70.

ment, and I am honored with the opportunity of repelling a deep disgrace which the gentleman from Kentucky, backed and sustained as he is by the gentleman from Georgia, seeks to put upon it.

❖❖❖

The amendments in the Slaughter-house cases one and all, are thus declared to have as their all-pervading design and ends the security of the recently enslaved race, not only their nominal freedom, but their complete protection from those who had formerly exercised unlimited dominion over them. It is in this broad light that all these amendments must be read, the purpose to secure the perfect equality before the law of all citizens of the United States. What you give to one class you must give to all, what you deny to one class you shall deny to all, unless in the exercise of the common and universal police power of the State, you find it needful to confer exclusive privileges on certain citizens, to be held and exercised still for the common good of all.

Such are the doctrines of the Slaughter-house cases—doctrines worthy of the Republic, worthy of the age, worthy of the great tribunal which thus loftily and impressively enunciates them. Do they—I put it to any man, be he lawyer or not; I put it to the gentleman from Georgia—do they give color even to the claim that this Congress may not now legislate against a plain discrimination made by State laws or State customs against that very race for whose complete freedom and protection these great amendments were elaborated and adopted? Is it pretended, I ask the honorable gentleman from Kentucky or the honorable gentleman from Georgia—is it pretended anywhere that the evils of which we complain, our exclusion from the public inn, from the saloon and table of the steamboat, from the sleeping-coach on the railway, from the right of sepulture in the public burial-ground, are an exercise of the police power of the State? Is such oppression and injustice nothing but the exercise by the State of the right to make regulations for the health, comfort, and security of all her citizens? Is it merely enacting that one man shall so use his own as not to injure anothers? Is the colored race to be assimilated to an unwholesome trade or to combustible materials, to be interdicted, to be shut up within prescribed limits? Let the gentleman from Kentucky or the gentleman from Georgia answer. Let the country know to what extent even the audacious prejudice of the gentleman from Kentucky will drive him, and how far even the gentleman from Georgia will permit himself to be led captive by the unrighteous teachings of a false political faith.

If we are to be likened in legal view to "unwholesome trades," to "large and offensive collections of animals" to "noxious slaughter-houses," to "the offal and stench which attend on certain manufactures" let it be avowed. If that is still the doctrine of the political party, to which the gentlemen belong, let it be put upon record. If State laws which deny us the common rights and privileges of other citizens, upon no possible or conceivable ground save one of prejudice, or of "taste" as the gentleman from Texas termed it, and as I suppose the gentlemen will prefer to call it, are to be placed under the protection of a decision which affirms the right of a State to regulate the police power of her great cities, then the decision is in conflict with the bill before us. No man will dare maintain such a doctrine. It is as shocking to the legal mind as it is offensive to the heart and conscience of all who love justice or respect manhood. I am astonished that the gentleman from Kentucky or the gentleman from Georgia should have been so grossly misled as to rise here and assert that the decision of the Supreme Court in these cases was a denial to Congress of the power to legislate against discriminations on account of race, color, or previous conditions of servitude because that Court has decided that exclusive privileges conferred for the common protection of the lives and health of the whole community are not in violation of the recent amendments. The only ground upon which the grant of exclusive privileges to a portion of the community is ever defended is that the substantial good of all is promoted; that in truth it is for the welfare of the whole community that certain persons should alone pursue certain occupations. It is not the special benefit conferred on the few that moves the legislature, but the ultimate and real benefit of all, even of those who are denied the right to pursue those specified occupations. Does the gentleman from Kentucky say that my good is promoted when I am excluded from the public inn? Is the health or safety of the community promoted? Doubtless his prejudice is gratified. Doubtless his democratic instincts are pleased; but will he or his able coadjutor say that such exclusion is a lawful exercise of the police power of the State, or that it is not a denial to me of the equal protection of the laws? They will not so say.

But each of these gentlemen quote at some length from the decision of the court to show that the court recognizes a difference between citizenship of the United States and citizenship of the States. That is true and no man here who supports this bill questions or overlooks the difference. There are privileges and immunities which belong to me as a citizen of the United States, and there are other privileges and immunities which belong to me as a citizen of my State. The former are under the protection of the Constitution and laws of the United States, and the latter are under the protection of the Constitution and laws of my State. But what of that? Are the rights which I now claim—the right to enjoy the common public conveniences of travel on public highways, of rest and refreshment at public inns, of education in public schools, of burial in public cemeteries—rights which I hold as a citizen of the United States or of my State? Or, to state the question more exactly, is not the denial of such privileges to me a denial to me of the equal protection of the laws? For it is under this clause of the fourteenth amendment that we place the present bill, no State shall "deny to any person within its jurisdiction the equal protection of the laws." No matter, therefore, whether his rights are held under the United States or under his particular State he is equally protected by this amendment. He is always and everywhere entitled to the equal protection of the laws. All discrimination is forbidden; and while the rights of citizens of a State as such are not defined or conferred by the Constitution of the United States, yet all discrimination, all denial of equality before the law, all denial of equal protection of the laws whether State or national laws, is forbidden.

The distinction between the two kinds of citizenship is clear, and the Supreme Court has clearly pointed out this distinction, but it has nowhere written a word or line which denies to Congress the power to prevent a denial of equality of rights whether those rights exist by virtue of citizenship of the United States or of a State. Let honorable members mark well this distinction. There are rights which are conferred on us by the United States. There are other rights conferred on us by the states of which we are individually the citizens. The fourteenth amendment does not forbid a state to deny to all its citizens any of those rights which the state itself has conferred with certain exceptions which are pointed out in the decision which we are examining. What it does forbid is inequality, is discrimination or, to use the words of the amendment itself, is the denial "to any person within its jurisdiction, the equal protection of the laws." If a State denies to me rights which are common to all her other citizens, she violates this amendment, unless she can show, as was shown in the Slaughter-house cases, that she does it in the legitimate exercise of her police power. If she abridges the rights of all her citizens equally, unless those rights are specifically guarded by the Constitution of the United States, she does not violate this amendment. This is not to put the rights which I hold by virtue of my citizenship of South Carolina under the protection of the national Government; it is not to blot out or overlook in the slightest particular the distinction between rights held under the United States and rights held under the States; but it seeks to secure equality to prevent discrimination, to confer as complete and ample protection on the humblest as on the highest.

The gentleman from Kentucky, in the course of the speech to which I am now replying, made a reference to the State of Massachusetts which betrays again the confusion which exists in his mind on this precise point. He tells us that Massachusetts excludes from the ballot-box all who cannot read and write, and points to that fact as the exercise of a right which this bill would abridge or impair. The honorable gentleman from Massachusetts (Mr. Dawes) answered him truly and well, but I submit that he did not make the best reply, why did he not ask the gentleman from Kentucky if Massachusetts had ever discriminated against any of her citizens on account of color, or race, or previous condition of servitude? When did Massachusetts sully her proud record by placing on her statute-book any law which admitted to the ballot the white man and shut out the black man. She has never done it; she will not do it; she cannot do it so long as we have a Supreme Court which reads the Constitution of our country with the eyes of Justice; nor can Massachusetts or Kentucky deny to any man on account of his race, color, or previous condition of servitude, that perfect equality of protection under the laws so long as Congress shall exercise the power to enforce by appropriate legislation the great and unquestionable securities embodied in the fourteenth amendment to the Constitution.

❖❖❖

Sir, I have replied to the extent of my ability to the arguments which have been presented by the opponents of this measure. I have replied also to some of the legal propositions advanced by gentlemen on the other side; and now that I am about to conclude, I am deeply sensible of the imperfect manner in which I have performed the task. Technically, this bill is to decide upon the civil status of the colored American citizen; a point disputed at the very formation of our present form of government, when by a short-sighted policy, a policy repugnant to true republican government, one Negro counted as three-fifths of a man. The logical result of this mistake of the framers of the Constitution strengthened the cancer of slavery, which finally spread its poisonous tentacles over the southern portion of the body politic. To arrest its growth and save the nation we have passed through the harrowing operation of intestine war, dreaded at all times, resorted to at the last extremity, like the surgeon's knife, but absolutely necessary to extirpate the disease which threatened with the life of the nation the overthrow of civil and political liberty on this continent. In that dire extremity the members of the race which I have the honor in part to represent—the race which pleads for justice at your hands to-day,—forgetful of their inhuman and brutalizing servitude at the South, their degradation and ostracism at the North, flew willingly and gallantly to the support of the national Government.

Their sufferings, assistance, privations, and trials in the swamps and in the rice-fields, their valor on the land and on the sea, form a part of the ever-glorious record which makes up the history of a nation preserved, and might, should I urge the claim, incline you to respect and guarantee their rights and privileges as citizens of our common Republic. But I remember that valor, devotion, and loyalty are not always rewarded according to their just desserts, and that after the battle some who have borne the brunt of the fray may, through neglect or contempt, he assigned to a subordinate place, while the enemies in war may be preferred to the sufferers.

The results of the war, as seen in reconstruction, have settled forever the political status of my race. The passage of this bill will determine the civil status, not only of the Negro, but of any other class of citizens who may feel themselves discriminated against. It will form the cap-stone of that temple of liberty, begun on this continent under discouraging circumstances, carried on in spite of the sneers of monarchists and the cavils of pretended friends of freedom, until at last it stands, in all its beautiful symmetry and proportions, a building the grandest which the world has ever seen, realizing the most sanguine expectations and the highest hopes of those who, in the name of equal, impartial, and universal liberty, laid the foundation-stone.

The Holy Scriptures tell us of an humble handmaiden who long, faithfully, and patiently gleaned in the rich fields of her wealthy kinsman, and we are told further that at last, in spite of her humble antecedents she found favor in his sight. For over two centuries our race has "reaped down your fields," the cries and woes which we have uttered have "entered into the ears of the Lord of Sabaoth" and we are at last politically free. The last vestiture only is needed—civil rights. Having gained this, we may, with hearts overflowing with gratitude and thankful that our prayer has been answered, repeat the prayer of Ruth: "Entreat me not to leave thee, or to return from following after thee; for whither thou goest, I will go; and where thou lodgest, I will lodge; thy people shall be my people, and thy God my God; where thou diest I will die, and there will I be buried; the Lord do so to me, and more also, if ought but death part thee and me."

LUCY CRAFT LANEY
(1854–1933)

Known for her work in education, Lucy Craft Laney dedicated her life to improving the literacy skills of African Americans. Lucy was the seventh of ten children born to David and Louisa Laney of Macon, Georgia; her father had been born a slave in South Carolina, but had learned the carpenter's trade, purchased his freedom, and moved to Macon in 1836, where he was hired to teach carpentry to slaves. He married Louisa, a slave of the prominent Campbell family of Macon, and purchased her freedom to ensure that his children would be free. During Lucy's early years, the family spent time in Savannah, where David Laney, ordained a minister in the "Old School" Northern Presbyterian Church (which did not limit his preaching to blacks), became pastor of a church.

It was in Macon, however, under the tutelage of one of the Campbell daughters, that Laney received her early schooling. She then graduated from Lewis High School (later Ballard Normal School) in Macon. She graduated from Atlanta University in 1873, one of four members of its Higher Normal Department class. For the next ten years, she taught in the public schools of Macon, Milledgeville, Augusta, and Savannah. The Presbyterian Board of Missions enabled her to open a school in a lecture room of the Christ Presbyterian Church in Augusta in 1883; it was chartered by the state on January 6, 1886. Despite increasing financial difficulties, the school moved to larger quarters. In 1887, Laney traveled to the General Assembly of the Presbyterian Church in Minneapolis seeking assistance for the school. That trip led to a meeting with Francina E.H. Haines, who offered financial support and encouraged others to do so. Laney thus named her school the Haines Normal and Industrial Institute. A ten-thousand-dollar contribution from a Mrs. Marshall enabled her to construct the first brick building in 1889. Although she received contributions from other northern benefactors, including Mrs. Anson Phelps Stokes, she had to continue trips seeking financial assistance for the school. Difficulties notwithstanding, by 1931, the school had twenty-seven teachers, three hundred high school students, four hundred thirteen elementary school students, and an income of twenty-five thousand dollars.

Laney's zeal for her school led to her own declining health. On October 23, 1933, she died of nephritis and hypertension. Out of respect for and in recognition of her singular achievement, more than five thousand Augustans attended her funeral. After her death, the Institute declined during the Depression. Also, as the state of Georgia came to provide more public educational opportunities for African Americans, the school continued to falter. These developments, combined with the dwindling financial support for Haines Institute from the Presbyterian Church as well as from private benefactors, led to its closing and the razing of the building in 1949. The significance of the school is measured by such distinguished students as John Hope and such renowned teachers as Mary McLeod Bethune. The Lucy C. Laney High School was built on the site of the Institute, and Laney's photograph graces the walls of the Georgia State House.

❖❖❖

Sadie Daniel St. Clair includes a biographical sketch of Laney in *Notable American Women, 1607–1950, A Biographical Dictionary* (1971). Information on Laney's life and career can also be obtained from Mary White Ovington's *Portraits in Color* (1927), Sadie I. Daniel's *Women Builders* (1931), and Benjamin Brawley's *Negro Builders and Heroes* (1937).

The Burden of the Educated Colored Woman[1]

If the educated colored woman has a burden,—and we believe she has—what is that burden? How can it be lightened, how may it be lifted? What it is can be readily seen perhaps better than told, for it constantly annoys to irritation; it bulges out as did the load of Bunyan's Christian—ignorance—with its inseparable companions, shame and crime and prejudice.

That our position may be more readily understood, let us refer to the past; and it will suffice for our purpose to begin with our coming to America in 1620, since prior to that time, we claim only heathenism. During the days of training in our first mission school—slavery—that which is the foundation of right training and good government, the basic rock of all true culture—the home, with its fire-side training, mother's moulding, woman's care, was not only neglected but utterly disregarded. There was no time in the institution for such teaching. We know that there were, even in the first days of that school, isolated cases of men and women of high moral character and great intellectual worth, as Phillis Wheatley, Sojourner Truth, and John Chavers, whose work and lives should have taught, or at least suggested to their instructors, the capabilities and possibilities of their dusky slave pupils. The progress and the struggles of these for noble things should have led their instructors to see how the souls and minds of this people then yearned for light—the real life. But alas! these dull teachers, like many modern pedagogues and school-keepers, failed to know their pupils—to find out their real needs, and hence had no cause to study methods of better and best development of the boys and girls under their care. What other result could come from such training or want of training than a conditioned race such as we now have?

For two hundred and fifty years they married, or were given in marriage. Oft times marriage ceremonies were performed for them by the learned minister of the master's church; more often there was simply a consorting by the master's consent, but it was always understood that these unions for cause, or without cause, might be more easily broken, than a divorce can be obtained in Indiana or Dakota. Without going so long a distance as from New York to Connecticut, the separated could take other

[1] "The Burden of the Educated Colored Woman" is a paper read by Laney at the July 1899 Hampton Negro Conference.

companions for life, for a long or short time; for during those two hundred and fifty years there was not a single marriage legalized in a single southern state, where dwelt the mass of this people. There was something of the philosopher in the plantation preacher, who, at the close of the marriage ceremony, had the dusky couple join their right hands, and then called upon the assembled congregation to sing, as he lined it out, "Plunged in a gulf of dark despair," for well he knew the sequel of many such unions. If it so happened that a husband and wife were parted by those who owned them, such owners often consoled those thus parted with the fact that he could get another wife; she, another husband. Such was the sanctity of the marriage vow that was taught and held for over two hundred and fifty years. Habit is indeed second nature. This is the race inheritance. I thank God not of all, for we know, each of us, of instances, of holding most sacred the plighted love and keeping faithfully and sacredly the marriage vows. We know of pure homes and of growing old together. Blessed heritage! If we only had the gold there might be many "Golden Weddings." Despair not; the crushing burden of immorality which has its root in the disregard of the marriage vow, can be lightened. It must be, and the educated colored woman can and will do her part in lifting this burden.

In the old institution there was no attention given to homes and to home-making. Homes were only places in which to sleep, father had neither responsibility nor authority; mother, neither cares nor duties. She wielded no gentle sway nor influence. The character of their children was a matter of no concern to them; surroundings were not considered. It is true, house cleaning was sometimes enforced as a protection to property, but this was done at stated times and when ordered. There is no greater enemy of the race than these untidy and filthy homes; they bring not only physical disease and death, but they are very incubators of sin; they bring intellectual and moral death. The burden of giving knowledge and bringing about the practice of the laws of hygiene among a people ignorant of the laws of nature and common decency, is not a slight one. But this, too, the intelligent women can and must help to carry.

The large number of young men in the state prison is by no means the least of the heavy burdens. It is true that many of these are unjustly sentenced; that longer terms of imprisonment are given Negroes than white persons for the same offences; it is true that white criminals by the help of attorneys, money, and influence, oftener escape the prison, thus keeping small the number of prisoners recorded, for figures never lie. It is true that many are tried and imprisoned for trivial causes, such as the following, clipped from the *Tribune,* of Elberyon, Ga.: "Seven or eight Negroes were arrested and tried for stealing two fish-hooks last week. When the time of our courts is wasted in such a manner as this, it is high time to stop and consider whither we are driving. Such picaunyish cases reflect on the intelligence of a community. It is fair to say the courts are not to blame in this matter." Commenting on this *The South Daily* says: "We are glad to note that the sentiment of the paper is against the injustice. Nevertheless these statistics will form the basis of some lecturer's discourse." This fact remains, that many of our youth are in prison, that large numbers of our young men are serving out long terms of imprisonment, and this is a very sore burden. Five years ago while attending a Teacher's Institute at Thomasville, Ga., I saw working on the streets in the chain gang, with rude men and ruder women, with ignorant, wicked, almost naked men, criminals, guilty of all the sins named in the decalogue, a large number of boys from ten to fifteen years of age, and two young girls between the ages of twelve and sixteen. It is not necessary that prison statistics be quoted, for we know too well the story, and we feel most sensibly this burden, the weight of which will sink us unless it is at once made lighter and finally lifted.

Last, but not least, is the burden of prejudice, heavier in that it is imposed by the strong, those from whom help, not hindrance, should come. They are making the already heavy burden of their victims heavier to bear, and yet they are commanded by One who is even the Master of all: "Bear ye one another's burdens, and thus fulfil the law." This is met with and must be borne everywhere. In the South, in public conveyances, and at all points of race contact; in the North, in hotels, at the baptismal pool, in cemeteries; everywhere, in some shape or form, it is to be borne. No one suffers under the weight of this burden as the educated Negro woman does; and she must help to lift it.

Ignorance and immorality, if they are not the prime causes, have certainly intensified prejudice. The forces to lighten and finally to lift this and all of these burdens are true culture and character, linked with that most substantial coupler, cash. We said in the beginning that the past can serve no further purpose than to give us our present bearings. It is a condition that confronts us. With this we must deal, it is this we must change. The physician of today inquires into the history of his patient, but he has to do especially with diagnosis and cure. We know the history; we think a correct diagnosis has often been made—let us attempt a cure. We would prescribe: homes—better homes, clean homes, pure homes; schools—better schools; more culture; more thrift; and work in large doses; put the patient at once on this treatment and continue through life. Can woman do this work? She can; and she must do her part, and her part is by no means small.

Nothing in the present century is more noticeable than the tendency of women to enter every hopeful field of wage-earning and philanthropy, and attempt to reach a place in every intellectual arena. Women are by nature fitted for teaching very young children; their maternal instinct makes them patient and sympathetic with their charges. Negro women of culture, as kindergartners and primary teachers have a rare opportunity to lend a hand to the lifting of these burdens, for here they may instill lessons of cleanliness, truthfulness, loving kindness, love for nature, and love for Nature's God. Here they may daily start aright hundreds of our children; here, too, they may save years of time in the education of the child; and may save many lives from shame and crime by applying the law of prevention. In the kindergarten and primary school is the salvation of the race.

For children of both sexes from six to fifteen years of age, women are more successful as teachers than men. This fact is proven by their employment. Two-thirds of the teachers in the public schools of the United States are women. It is the glory of the United States that good order and peace are maintained not by a large, standing army of well trained soldiers, but by the sentiment of her citizens, sentiments implanted and nourished by her well trained army of four hundred thousand school teachers, two-thirds of whom are women.

The educated Negro woman, the woman of character and culture, is needed in the schoolroom not only in the kindergarten, and in the primary and the secondary school; but she is needed in high school, the academy, and the college. Only those of character and culture can do successful lifting, for she who would mould character must herself possess it. Not alone in the schoolroom can the intelligent woman lend a lifting hand, but as a public lecturer she may give advice, helpful suggestions, and important knowledge, that will change a whole community and start its people on the upward way. To be convinced of the good that can be done for humanity by this means one need only recall the names of Lucy Stone, Mary Livermore, Frances Harper, Frances Willard and Julia Ward Howe. The refined and noble Negro woman may lift much with this lever. Women may also be most helpful as teachers of sewing schools and cooking classes, not simply in the public schools and private institutions, but in classes formed in neighborhoods that sorely need this knowledge. Through these classes girls who are not in school may be reached; and through them something may be done to better their homes, and inculcate habits of neatness and thrift. To bring the influence of the schools to bear upon these homes is the most needful thing of the hour. Often teachers who have labored most arduously, conscientiously, and intelligently have become discouraged on seeing that society had not been benefited, but sometimes positively injured by the conduct of their pupils.

The work of the schoolroom has been completely neutralized by the training of the home. Then we must have better homes, and better homes mean better mothers, better fathers, better born children. Emerson says, "To the well-born child all the virtues are natural, not painfully acquired."

But "The temporal life which is not allowed to open into the eternal life becomes corrupt and feeble even in its temporalness." As a teacher in the Sabbath school, as a leader in young people's meetings and missionary societies, in women's societies and Bible classes our cultured women are needed to do a great and blessed work. Here they may cause many budding lives to open into eternal life. Froebel urged teachers and parents to see to the blending of the temporal and divine life when he said, "God created man in his own image; therefore man should create and bring forth like God." The young people are ready and anxiously await intelligent leadership in Christian work. The less fortunate women already assembled in churches, are ready for work. Work they do and work they will; that it may be effective work, they need the help and leadership of their more favored sisters.

A few weeks ago this country was startled by the following telegram of southern women of culture sent to Ex-Governor Northen of Georgia, just before he made his Boston speech: "You are authorized to say in your address tonight that the women of Georgia, realizing the great importance to both races of early moral training of the Negro race, stand ready to undertake this work when means are supplied." But more startled was the world the next day, after cultured Boston had supplied a part of the means, $20,000, to read the glaring head lines of the southern press, "Who Will Teach the Black Babies?" because some of the cultured women who had signed the telegram had declared when interviewed, that Negro women fitted for the work could not be found, and no self-respecting southern white woman would teach a colored kindergarten. Yet already in Atlanta, Georgia, and in Athens, Georgia, southern women are at work among Negroes. There is plenty of work for all who have the proper conception of the teacher's office, who know that all men are brothers, God being their common father. But the educated Negro women *must* teach the "Black Babies;" she must come forward and inspire our men and boys to make a successful onslaught upon sin, shame, and crime.

The burden of the educated colored woman is not diminished by the terrible crimes and outrages that we daily hear of, but by these very outrages and lawlessness her burdens are greatly increased.

Somewhere I read a story, that in one of those western cities built in a day, the half-dozen men of the town labored to pull a heavy piece of timber to the top of a building. They pushed and pulled hard to no purpose, when one of the men on the top shouted to those below: "Call the women." They called the women; the women came; they pushed; soon the timber was seen to move, and ere long it was in the desired place. Today not only the men on top call, but a needy race,—the whole world, calls loudly to the cultured Negro women to come to the rescue. Do they hear? Are they coming? Will they push?

ANNA JULIA COOPER
(1858–1964)

Best known for *A Voice from the South by a Black Woman of the South* (1892), Anna Julia Cooper was one of the most significant black intellectuals of her time. She was an active participant in women's organizations in the 1890s and in the first decade of the twentieth century, yet today she is less well known than some of her counterparts, such as Ida B. Wells-Barnett and Mary Church Terrell. One of three women invited to address the World's Congress of Representative Women in 1893, she was also one of few women to speak at the Pan-American Congress Conference in London in 1900. Instrumental in founding the Colored Women's YWCA in 1904, she also founded the first chapter of that organization's Camp Fire Girls in 1912. A passage from *A Voice from the South* inspired one of the most well-known studies of black women's influence on gender and race in America; that volume, Paula Giddings's *When and Where I Enter* (1984), posits as Cooper did, that the African American woman is the moral and spiritual center of the black community: "Only the BLACK WOMAN can say 'when and where I enter, in the quiet, undisputed dignity of my womanhood, without violence and without suing or special patronage, then and there the whole *Negro race enters with me.*'" Giddings had recognized that Anna Julia Cooper was the leading African American feminist thinker of her era. Her eloquent articulation of the importance of the black feminine principle is unsurpassed in nineteenth-century American thought.

Cooper was born Annie Julia Haywood in Raleigh, North Carolina, on August 10, 1858, the child of a slave woman, Hannah Stanley Haywood, and her white master, George Washington Haywood. She attended St. Augustine's Normal School and Collegiate Institute for newly freed African Americans in Raleigh, beginning in 1868. Her school years shaped her later philosophy, for it was here that she began to protest the fact that men were given preferential treatment at St. Augustine's, presumably because they were candidates for the ministry. Women were not encouraged to study theology and the classics; women, Haywood noted to the school's principal, were primarily thought of as candidates for wives of the young men.

Her feminism, however, did not preclude her own marriage to one of the ministers; on June 21, 1877, she married George Christopher Cooper, an Episcopal clergyman and professor of Greek, who died only two years after they married. In 1881, she applied to be admitted to the "Gentleman's Course" at Oberlin over the inferior "Ladies Course" and requested tuition waivers to support her endeavors there. She obtained a B.A. (1884) and an M.A. (1887) at Oberlin. By 1887, she was ready to respond to an invitation to teach at the famous M Street High School in Washington, D.C., which was renamed Dunbar High School in 1916 and for which she composed the words of the Alma Mater in 1924. Initially hired to teach math and science, she later became renowned for her competence in Latin. She was promoted to principal at M Street in January of 1902 and worked, against the wishes of her white supervisor, Perry Hughes, to send several of her students to prestigious universities such as Harvard, Radcliffe, Dartmouth, and Oberlin; Hughes maintained that black students should learn trades in accordance with the prevailing philosophy of Booker T. Washington. For her efforts, Cooper was forced to resign in 1906. Superficial reasons and an alleged affair with John Love, one of her fellow teachers, held sway in the Board's vote to dismiss Cooper (more to the point were issues surrounding women teaching and being principals, as well as the racism of Board members who could not condone black students competing with white ones). Love, who would indeed later fall in love with the woman who was thirteen years his senior, was dismissed along with Cooper. She moved to Jefferson City, Missouri, and taught at Lincoln University, an all-black school. Love, teaching in the midwest at that time, wrote to Cooper proposing marriage, but she refused.

In recognition of the extraordinary work she had done despite opposition, a new superintendent in 1910 invited Cooper to return to the school and resume her position as a Latin teacher. She continued various activities in addition to teaching, including graduate study at La Guilde Internationale in Paris during 1911–12 and at Columbia University off and on between 1913 and 1916. (She never managed to complete the one-year residency requirement for the doctorate.) In 1915, she adopted five orphaned children, grandchildren of her half-brother, who ranged in age from six months to twelve years.

Cooper studied in Paris during the summers and for a sustained period in 1924, the point at which she was forced to return to Washington when she was threatened with the loss of her job and retirement benefits (no sabbatical leaves were available; she claimed sick leave). In 1925, at age sixty-seven, she defended her dissertation and was awarded a doctorate from the University of Paris on December 29, thus becoming only the fourth African American woman to have achieved that level of distinction. Her degree was presented in Washington, D.C., by representatives of the French Embassy under the auspices of Xi Omega chapter of Alpha Kappa Alpha Sorority, to which Cooper belonged.

Cooper continued to work and write into the 1940s. She was president of Frelinghuysen University from 1930 to 1940 and its registrar from 1940 until 1950. She published *Ten Years of Frelinghuysen, 1930–1941* (1941?), *My Second Decennial: The Third Step, 1941–1952* (n.d.), *Legislative Measures Concerning Slavery in the United States* (1942), and *Equality of Races and the Democratic Movement* (1945). Although she had written a biography of Charlotte Forten Grimké in 1936 and sought W.E.B. Du Bois's advice about getting it published (even suggesting that he serialize it in the *Crisis*), Cooper did not complete her work on Grimké until 1951, when she edited the two-volume *Life and Writings of the Grimké Family.* She died on February 29, 1964, at the age of 105.

Throughout her professional career, Cooper challenged and reexamined the traditional roles of women to conceptualize a balance of power between the sexes in society. Hence, she postulated in *Voices from the South* that women's experiences and wisdom complete the circle of humanity, making it whole: "there is a feminine as well as a masculine side to truth; that these are related not as inferior and superior, not as better and worse, not as weaker and stronger, but as complements—complements in one necessary and symmetric whole." Anna Julia Cooper understood that diversity, whether of gender or race, means an appreciation of difference: "Let woman's claim be as broad in the concrete as in the abstract. We take our stand on the solidarity of humanity, the oneness of life, and the unnaturalness and injustice of all special favoritisms, whether of sex, race, country, or condition." Anna Julia Cooper saw the African American woman as the symbol of all universal suffering and triumph: "The colored woman feels that woman's cause is one and universal; . . . not till the universal title of humanity to life, liberty, and the pursuit of happiness is conceded to be inalienable to all; not till then is woman's lesson taught and woman's cause won." She stood at the threshold of African American womanist aesthetics.

❖❖❖

Cooper's biographer is Louise D. Hutchinson, who published *Anna Julia Cooper: A Voice from the South* in 1982.

An early volume that encouraged awareness of Cooper's work is *Black Women in Nineteenth–Century American Life* (1976), edited by Bert James Loewenberg and Ruth Bogin; it includes a selection from *A Voice from the South.* That entire work is included as one of the volumes of the Schomburg Library of Nineteenth-Century Black Women Writers (1988); Mary Helen Washington provided the critical introduction.

The Anna Julia Cooper papers are housed at the Moorland-Spingarn Research Center at Howard University.

FROM *A Voice from the South*

The Higher Education of Women

In the very first year of our century, the year 1801, there appeared in Paris a book by Silvain Marechal, entitled "Shall Woman Learn the Alphabet." The book proposes a law prohibiting the alphabet to women, and quotes authorities weighty and various, to prove that the woman who knows the alphabet has already lost part of her womanliness. The author declares that woman can use the alphabet only as Molière predicted they would, in spelling out the verb *amo;* that they have no occasion to peruse Ovid's *Ars Amoris,* since that is already the ground and limit of their intuitive furnishing; that Madame Guion would have been far more adorable had she remained a beautiful ignoramus as nature made her; that Ruth, Naomi, the Spartan woman, the Amazons, Penelope, Andromache, Lucretia, Joan of Arc, Petrarch's Laura, the daughters of Charlemagne, could not spell their names; while Sappho, Aspasia, Madame de Maintenon, and Madame de Stael could read altogether too well for their good; finally, that if women were once permitted to read Sophocles and work with logarithms, or to nibble at any side of the apple of knowledge, there would be an end forever to their sewing on buttons and embroidering slippers.

Please remember this book was published at the *beginning* of the Nineteenth Century. At the end of its first third, (in the year 1833) one solitary college in America decided to admit women within its sacred precincts, and organized what was called a "Ladies' Course" as well as the regular B.A. or Gentlemen's course.

It was felt to be an experiment—a rather dangerous experiment—and was adopted with fear and trembling by the good fathers, who looked as if they had been caught secretly mixing explosive compounds and were guiltily expecting every moment to see the foundations under them shaken and rent and their fair superstructure shattered into fragments.

But the girls came, and there was no upheaval. They performed their tasks modestly and intelligently. Once in a while one or two were found choosing the gentlemen's course. Still no collapse; and the dear, careful, scrupulous, frightened old professors were just getting their hearts out of their throats and preparing to draw one good free breath, when they found they would have to change the names of those courses; for there were as many ladies in the gentlemen's course as in the ladies', and a distinctively Ladies' Course, inferior in scope and aim to the regular classical course, did not and could not exist.

Other colleges gradually fell into line, and today there are one hundred and ninety-eight colleges for women, and two hundred and seven coeducational colleges and universities in the United States alone offering the degree of B.A. to women, and sending out yearly into the arteries of this nation a warm, rich flood of strong, brave, active, energetic, well-equipped, thoughtful women—women quick to see and eager to help the needs of this needy world—women who can think as well as feel, and who feel none the less because they think—women who are none the less tender and true for the parchment scroll they bear in their hands—women who have given a deeper, richer, nobler and grander meaning to the word "womanly" than any one-sided masculine definition could ever have suggested or inspired—women whom the world has long waited for in pain and anguish till there should be at last added to its forces and allowed to permeate its thought the complement of that masculine influence which has dominated it for fourteen centuries.

Since the idea of order and subordination succumbed to barbarian brawn and brutality in the fifth century, the civilized world has been like a child brought up by his father. It has needed the great mother heart to teach it to be pitiful, to love mercy, to succor the weak and care for the lowly.

Whence came this apotheosis of greed and cruelty? Whence this sneaking admiration we all have for bullies and prize-fighters? Whence the self-congratulation of "dominant" races, as if "dominant" meant "righteous" and carried with it a title to inherit the earth? Whence the scorn of so-called weak or unwarlike races and individuals, and the very comfortable assurance that it is their manifest destiny to be wiped out as vermin before this advancing civilization? As if the possession of the Christian graces of meekness, non-resistance and forgiveness, were incompatible with a civilization professedly based on Christianity, the religion of love! Just listen to this little bit of Barbarian brag:

> "As for Far Orientals, they are not of those who will survive. Artistic attractive people that they are, their civilization is like their own tree flowers, beautiful blossoms destined never to bear fruit. If these people continue in their old course, their earthly career is closed. Just as surely as morning passes into afternoon, so surely are these races of the Far East, if unchanged, destined to disappear before the advancing nations of the West. Vanish, they will, off the face of the earth, and leave our planet the eventual possession of the dwellers where the day declines. Unless their newly imported ideas really take root, it is from this whole world that Japanese and Koreans, as well as Chinese, will inevitably be excluded. Their Nirvana is already being realized; already, it has wrapped Far Eastern Asia in its winding sheet."—*Soul of the Far East—P. Lowell.*

Delightful reflection for "the dwellers where day declines." A spectacle to make the gods laugh, truly, to see the scion of an upstart race by one sweep of his generalizing pen consigning to annihilation one-third the inhabitants of the globe—a people whose civilization was hoary headed before the parent elements that begot his race had advanced beyond nebulosity.

How like Longfellow's Iagoo, we Westerners are, to be sure! In the few hundred years, we have had to strut across our allotted territory and bask in the afternoon sun, we imagine we have exhausted the possibilities of humanity. Verily, we are the people, and after us there is none other. Our God is power; strength, our standard of excellence, inherited from barbarian ancestors through a long line of male progenitors, the Law Salic permitting no feminine modifications. . . .

As individuals, we are constantly and inevitably, whether we are conscious of it or not, giving out our real selves into our several little worlds, inexorably adding our own true ray to the flood of starlight, quite independently of our professions and our masquerading; and so in the world of thought, the influence of thinking woman far transcends her feeble declamation and may seem at times even opposed to it.

A visitor in Oberlin once said to the lady principal, "Have you no rabble in Oberlin? How is it I see no police here, and yet the streets are as quiet and orderly as if there were an officer of the law standing on every corner."

Mrs. Johnston replied, "Oh, yes; there are vicious persons in Oberlin just as in other towns—*but our girls are our police.*"

With from five to ten hundred pure-minded young women threading the streets of the village every evening unattended, vice must slink away, like frost before the rising sun: and yet I venture to say there was not one in a hundred of those girls who would not have run from a street brawl as she would from a mouse, and who would not have declared she could never stand the sight of blood and pistols.

There is, then, a real and special influence of woman. An influence subtle and often involuntary, an influence so intimately interwoven in, so intricately interpenetrated by the masculine influence of the time that it is often difficult to extricate the delicate meshes and analyze and identify the closely clinging fibers. And yet, without this influence—so long as woman sat with bandaged eyes and manacled hands, fast bound in the clamps of ignorance and inaction, the world of thought moved in its orbit like the revolutions of the moon; with one face (the man's face) always out, so that the spectator could not distinguish whether it was disc or sphere.

Now I claim that it is the prevalence of the Higher Education among women, the making it a common everyday affair for women to reason and think and express their thought, the training and stimulus which enable and encourage women to administer to the world the bread it needs as well as the sugar it cries for; in short it is the transmitting the potential forces of her soul into dynamic factors that has given symmetry and completeness to the world's agencies. So only could it be consummated that Mercy, the lesson she teaches, and Truth, the task man has set himself, should meet together: that righteousness, or *rightness,* man's ideal,—and *peace,* its necessary 'other half,' should kiss each other.

We must thank the general enlightenment and independence of woman (which we may now regard as a *fait accompli*) that both these forces are now at work in the world, and it is fair to demand from them for the twentieth century a higher type of civilization than any attained in the nineteenth. Religion, science, art, economics, have all needed the feminine flavor; and literature, the expression of what is permanent and best in all of these, may be gauged at any time to measure the strength of the feminine ingredient. You will not find theology consigning infants to lakes of unquenchable fire long after women have had a chance to grasp, master, and wield its dogmas. You will not find science annihilating personality from the government of the Universe and making of God an ungovernable, unintelligible, blind, often destructive physical force; you will not find jurisprudence formulating as an axiom the absurdity that man and wife are one, and that one the man—that the married woman may not hold bequeath her own property save as subject to her husband's direction; you will not find political economists declaring that the only possible adjustment between laborers and capitalists is that of selfishness and rapacity—that each must get all he can and keep all that he gets, while the world cries *laissez faire* and the lawyers explain, "it is the beautiful working of the law of supply and demand;" in time, you will not find the law of love shut out from the affairs of men after the feminine half of the world's truth is completed.

Nay, put your ear now close to the pulse of the time. What is the key-note of the literature of these days? What is the banner cry of all the activities of the last half decade? What is the dominant seventh which is to add richness and tone to the final cadences of this century and lead by a grand modulation into the triumphant harmonies of the next? Is it not compassion for the poor and unfortunate, and, as Bellamy has expressed it, "indignant outcry against the failure of the social machinery as it is, to ameliorate the miseries of men!" Even Christianity is being brought to the bar of humanity and tried by the standard of its ability to alleviate the world's suffering and lighten and brighten its woe. What else can be the meaning of Matthew Arnold's saddening protest, "We cannot do without Christianity," cried he, "and we cannot endure it as it is."

When went there by an age, when so much time and thought, so much money and labor were given to God's poor and God's invalids, the lowly and unlovely, the sinning as well as the suffering—homes for inebriates and homes for lunatics, shelter for the aged and shelter for babes, hospitals for the sick, props and braces for the falling, reformatory prisons and prison reformatories, all show that a "mothering" influence from some source is leavening the nation.

Now please understand me. I do not ask you to admit that these benefactions and virtues are the exclusive possession of women, or even that women are their chief and only advocates. It may be a man who formulates and makes them vocal. It may be, and often is, a man who weeps over the wrongs and struggles for the amelioration: but that man has imbibed those impulses from a mother rather than from a father and is simply materializing and giving back to the world in tangible form the ideal love and tenderness, devotion and care that have cherished and nourished the helpless period of his own existence.

All I claim is that there is a feminine as well as a masculine side to truth; that these are related not as inferior and superior, not as better and worse, not as weaker and stronger, but as complements—complements in one necessary and symmetric whole. That as the man is more noble in reason, so the woman is more quick in sympathy. That as he is indefatigable in pursuit of abstract truth, so is she in caring for the interests by the way—striving tenderly and lovingly that not one of the least of these 'little ones' should perish. That while we not unfrequently see women who reason, we say, with the coolness and precision of a man, and men as considerate of helplessness as a woman, still there is a general consensus of mankind that the one trait is essentially masculine and the other as peculiarly feminine. That both are needed to be worked into the training of children, in order that our boys may supplement their virility by tenderness and sensibility, and our girls may round out their gentleness by strength and self-reliance. That, as both are alike necessary in giving symmetry to the individual, so a nation or a race will degenerate into mere emotionalism on the one hand, or bullyism on the other, if dominated by either exclusively; lastly, and most emphatically, that the feminine factor can have its proper effect only through woman's development and education so that she may fitly and intelligently stamp her force on the forces of her day, and add her modicum to the riches of the world's thought.

"For woman's cause is man's: they rise or sink
Together, dwarfed or godlike, bond or free:
For she that out of Lethe scales with man
The shining steps of nature, shares with man
His nights, his days, moves with him to one goal.
If she be small, slight-natured, miserable,
How shall men grow?
. . . Let her make herself her own
To give or keep, to live and learn and be
All that not harms distinctive womanhood.
For woman is not undeveloped man
But diverse: could we make her as the man
Sweet love were slain; his dearest bond is this,
Not like to like, but like in difference.
Yet in the long years liker must they grow;
The man be more of woman, she of man;
He gain in sweetness and in moral height,
Nor lose the wrestling thews that throw the
world;
She mental breadth, nor fail in childward care,
Nor lose the childlike in the larger mind;
Till at the last she set herself to man,
Like perfect music unto noble words."

Now you will argue, perhaps, and rightly, that higher education for women is not a modern idea, and that, if that is the means of setting free and invigorating the long desired feminine force in the world, it has already had a trial and should, in the past, have produced some of these glowing effects. Sappho, the bright, sweet singer of Lesbos, "the violet-crowned, pure, sweetly smiling Sappho" as Alcaeus calls her, chanted her lyrics and poured forth her soul nearly six centuries before Christ, in notes as full and free, as passionate and eloquent as did ever Archilochus or Anacreon.

Aspasia, that earliest queen of the drawing-room, a century later ministered to the intellectual entertainment of Socrates and the leading wits and philosophers of her time. Indeed, to her is attributed, by the best critics, the authorship of one of the most noted speeches ever delivered by Pericles.

Later on, during the Renaissance period, women were professors in mathematics, physics, metaphysics, and the classic languages in Bologna, Pavia, Padua, and Brescia. Olympia Fulvia Morata, of Ferrara, a most interesting character, whose magnificent library was destroyed in 1553 in the invasion of Schweinfurt by Albert of Brandenburg, had acquired a most extensive education. It is said that this wonderful girl gave lectures on classical subjects in her sixteenth year, and had even before that written several very remarkable Greek and Latin poems, and what is also to the point, she married a professor at Heidelberg, and became a *help-meet for him.*

It is true then that the higher education for women—in fact, the highest that the world has ever witnessed—belongs to the past; but we must remember that it was possible, down to the middle of our own century, only to a select few; and that the fashions and traditions of the times were before that all against it. There were not only no stimuli to encourage women to make the most of their powers and to welcome their development as a helpful agency in the progress of civilization, but their little aspirations, when they had any, were chilled and snubbed in embryo, and any attempt at thought was received as a monstrous usurpation of man's prerogative.

Lessing declared that "the woman who thinks is like the man who puts on rouge—ridiculous;" and Voltaire in his coarse, flippant way used to say, "Ideas are like beards—women and boys have none." Dr. Maginn remarked, "We like to hear a few words of sense from a woman sometimes, as we do from a parrot—they are so unexpected!" and even the pious Fenelon taught that virgin delicacy is almost as incompatible with learning as with vice.

That the average woman retired before these shafts of wit and ridicule and even gloried in her ignorance is not surprising. The Abbe Choisi, it is said, praised the Duchesse de Fontanges as being pretty as an angel and silly as a goose, and all the young ladies of the court strove to make up in folly what they lacked in charms. The ideal of the day was that "women must be pretty, dress prettily, flirt prettily, and not be too well informed;" that it was the *summum bonum* of her earthly hopes to have, as Thackeray puts it, "all the fellows battling to dance with her;" that she had no God-given destiny, no soul with unquenchable longings and inexhaustible possibilities—no work of her own to do and give to the world—no absolute and inherent value, no duty to self, transcending all pleasure-giving that may be demanded of a mere toy; but that her value was purely a relative one and to be estimated as are the fine arts—by the pleasure they give. "Woman, wine and song," as "the world's best gifts to man," were linked together in praise with as little thought of the first saying, "What doest thou," as that the wine and the song should declare, "We must be about our Father's business."

Men believed, or pretended to believe, that the great law of self development was obligatory on their half of the human family only; that while it was the chief end of man to glorify God and put his five talents to the exchangers, gaining thereby other five, it was, or ought to be, the sole end of woman to glorify man and wrap her one decently away in a napkin, retiring into "Hezekiah Smith's lady during her natural life and Hezekiah Smith's relict on her tombstone;" that higher education was incompatible with the shape of the female cerebrum, and that even if it could be acquired it must inevitably unsex woman destroying the lisping, clinging, tenderly helpless, and beautifully dependent creatures whom men would so heroically think for and so gallantly fight for, and giving in their stead a formidable race of blue stockings with corkscrew ringlets and other spinster propensities.

But these are eighteenth century ideas.

We have seen how the pendulum has swung across our present century. The men of our time have asked with Emerson, "that woman only show us how she can best be served;" and woman has replied: the chance of the seedling and of the animalcule is all I ask—the chance for growth and self development, the permission to be true to the aspirations of my soul without incurring the blight of your censure and ridicule. . . .

Matthew Arnold during his last visit to America in '82 or '83, lectured before a certain co-educational college in the West. After the lecture he remarked, with some surprise, to a lady professor, that the young women in his audience, he noticed, paid as close attention as the men, *all the way through.*" This led, of course, to a spirited discussion of the higher education for women, during which he said to his enthusiastic interlocutor, eyeing her philosophically through his English eyeglass: "But—eh—don't you think it—eh—spoils their *chawnces,* you know!"

Now, as to the result to women, this is the most serious argument ever used against the higher education. If it interferes with marriage, classical training has a grave objection to weigh and answer. . . .

I grant you that intellectual development, with the self-reliance and capacity for earning a livelihood which it gives, renders woman less dependent on the marriage relation for physical support (which, by the way, does not always accompany it). Neither is she compelled to look to sexual love as the one sensation capable of giving tone and relish, movement and vim to the life she leads. Her horison is extended. Her sympathies are broadened and deepened and multiplied. She is in closer touch with nature. Not a bud that opens, not a dew drop, not a ray of light, not a cloud-burst or a thunderbolt, but adds to the expansiveness and zest of her soul. And if the sun of an absorbing passion be gone down, still 'tis night that brings the stars. She has remaining the mellow, less obtrusive, but none the less enchanting and inspiring light of friendship, and into its charmed circle she may gather the best the world has known. She can commune with Socrates about the *daimon* he knew and to which she too can bear witness; she can revel in the majesty of Dante, the sweetness of Virgil, the simplicity of Homer, the strength of Milton. She can listen to the pulsing heart throbs of passionate Sappho's encaged soul, as she beats her bruised wings against her prison bars and struggles to flutter out into Heaven's æther, and the fires of her own soul cry back as she listens. "Yes; Sappho, I know it all; I know it all." Here, at last, can be communion without suspicion; friendship without misunderstanding; love without jealousy.

We must admit then that Byron's picture, whether a thing of beauty or not, has faded from the canvas of to-day.

> "Man's love," he wrote, "is of man's life a thing
> apart,
> 'Tis woman's whole existence.
> Man may range the court, camp, church, the
> vessel and the mart,
> Sword, gown, gain, glory offer in exchange.
> Pride, fame, ambition, to fill up his heart—
> And few there are whom these cannot estrange.
> Men have all these resources, we *but one—*
> *To love again and be again undone.*"

This may have been true when written. *It is not true to-day.* The old, subjective, stagnant, indolent and wretched life for woman has gone. She has as many resources as men, as many activities beckon her on. As large possibilities swell and inspire her heart.

Now, then, does it destroy or diminish her capacity for loving?

Her standards have undoubtedly gone up. The necessity of speculating in 'chawnces' has probably shifted. The question is not how with the woman "How shall I so cramp, stunt, simplify and nullify myself as to make me eligible to the honor of being swallowed up into some little man?" but the problem, I trow, now rests with the man as to how he can so develop his God-given powers as to reach the ideal of a generation of women who demand the noblest, grandest and best achievements of which he is capable; and this surely is the only fair and natural adjustment of the chances. Nature never meant that the ideals and standards of the world should be dwarfing and minimizing ones, and the men should thank us for requiring of them the richest fruits which they can grow. If it makes them work, all the better for them.

As to the adaptability of the educated woman to the marriage relation, I shall simply quote from that excellent symposium of learned women that appeared recently under Mrs. Armstrong's signature in answer to the "Plain Words" of Mr. Allen, already referred to. "Admitting no longer any question as to their intellectual equality with the men whom they meet, with the simplicity of conscious strength, they take their place beside the men who challenge them, and fearlessly face the result of their actions. They deny that their education in any way unfits them for the duty of wifehood and maternity or primarily renders these conditions any less attractive to them than to the domestic type of woman. On the contrary, they hold that their knowledge of physiology makes them better mothers and housekeepers; their knowledge of chemistry makes them better cooks; while from their training in other natural sciences and in mathematics, they obtain an accuracy and fair-mindedness which is of great value to them in dealing with their children or employees."

So much for their willingness. Now the apple may be good for food and pleasant to the eyes, and a fruit to be desired to make one wise. Nay, it may even assure you that it has no aversion whatever to being tasted. Still, if you do not like the flavor all these recommendations are nothing. Is the intellectual woman *desirable* in the matrimonial market?

This I cannot answer. I confess my ignorance. I am no judge of such things. I have been told that strong-minded women could be, when they thought it worth their while, quite endurable, and, judging from the number of female names I find in college catalogues among the alumnae with double patronymics, I surmise that quite a number of men are willing to put up with them.

Now I would that my task ended here. Having shown that a great want of the world in the past has been a feminine force; that that force can have its full effect only through the untrammelled development of woman; that such development, while it gives her to the world and to civilization, does not necessarily remove her from the home and fireside; finally, that while past centuries have witnessed sporadic instances of this higher growth, still it was reserved for the latter half of the nineteenth century to render it common and general enough to be effective; I might close with a glowing prediction of what the twentieth century may expect from this heritage of twin forces—the masculine battered and toil-worn as a grim veteran after centuries of warfare, but still strong, active, and vigorous, ready to help with his hard-won experience the young recruit rejoicing in her newly found freedom, who so confidently places her hand in his with mutual pledges to redeem the ages.

> "And so the twain upon the skirts of Time,
> Sit side by side, full-summed in all their powers,
> Dispensing harvest, sowing the To-be,
> Self-reverent each and reverencing each."

Fain would I follow them, but duty is nearer home. The high ground of generalities is alluring but my pen is devoted to a special cause: and with a view to further enlightenment on the achievements of the century for THE HIGHER EDUCATION OF COLORED WOMEN, I wrote a few days ago to the colleges which admit women and asked how many colored women had completed the B.A. course in each during its entire history. These are the figures returned: Fisk leads the way with twelve; Oberlin next with five; Wilberforce, four; Ann Arbor and Wellesley three each, Livingstone two, Atlanta one, Howard, as yet, none.

I then asked the principal of the Washington High School how many out of a large number of female graduates from his school had chosen to go forward and take a collegiate course. He replied that but one had ever done so, and she was then in Cornell.*

Others ask questions too, sometimes, and I was asked a few years ago by a white friend, "How is it that the men of your race seem to outstrip the women in mental attainment?"

*Graduated from Scientific Course, June, 1890, the first African American woman to graduate from Cornell.

"Oh," I said, "so far as it is true, the men, I suppose, from the life they lead, gain more by contact; and so far as it is only apparent, I think the women are more quiet. They don't feel called to mount a barrel and harangue by the hour every time they imagine they have produced an idea."

But I am sure there is another reason which I did not at that time see fit to give. The atmosphere, the standards, the requirements of our little world do not afford any special stimulus to female development.

It seems hardly a gracious thing to say, but it strikes me as true, that while our men seem thoroughly abreast of the times on almost every other subject, when they strike the woman question they drop back into sixteenth century logic. They leave nothing to be desired generally in regard to gallantry and chivalry, but they actually do not seem sometimes to have outgrown that old contemporary of chivalry—the idea that women may stand on pedestals or live in doll houses, (if they happen to have them) but they must not furrow their brows with thought or attempt to help men tug at the great questions of the world. I fear the majority of colored men do not yet think it worth while that women aspire to higher education. Not many will subscribe to the "advanced" ideas of Grant Allen already quoted. The three R's, a little music and a good deal of dancing, a first rate dress-maker and a bottle of magnolia balm, are quite enough generally to render charming any woman possessed of tact and the capacity for worshipping masculinity.

My readers will pardon my illustrating my point and also giving a reason for the fear that is in me, by a little bit of personal experience. When a child I was put into a school near home that professed to be normal and collegiate, i. e. to prepare teachers for colored youth, furnish candidates for the ministry, and offer collegiate training for those who should be ready for it. Well, I found after a while that I had a good deal of time on my hands. I had devoured what was put before me, and, like Oliver Twist, was looking around to ask for more. I constantly felt (as I suppose many an ambitious girl has felt) a thumping from within unanswered by any beckoning from without. Class after class was organized for these ministerial candidates (many of them men who had been preaching before I was born). . . .

Finally a Greek class was to be formed. My inspiring preceptor informed me that Greek had never been taught in the school, but that he was going to form a class *for the candidates for the ministry,* and if I liked I might join it. I replied—humbly I hope, as became a female of the human species—that I would like very much to study Greek, and that I was thankful for the opportunity, and so it went on. A boy, however meager his equipment and shallow his pretentions, had only to declare a floating intention to study theology and he could get all the support, encouragement and stimulus he needed, be absolved from work and invested beforehand with all the dignity of his far away office. While a self-supporting girl had to struggle on by teaching in the summer and working after school hours to keep up with her board bills, and actually to fight her way against positive discouragements to the higher education; till one such girl one day flared out and told the principal "the only mission opening before a girl in his school was to marry one of those candidates." He said he didn't know but it was. And when at last that same girl announced her desire and intention to go to college it was received with about the same incredulity and dismay as if a brass button on one of those candidate's coats had propounded a new method for squaring the circle or trisecting the arc.

Now this is not fancy. It is a simple unvarnished photograph, and what I believe was not in those days exceptional in colored schools, and I ask the men and women who are teachers and co-workers for the highest interests of the race, that they give the girls a chance! We might as well expect to grow trees from leaves as hope to build up a civilization or a manhood without taking into consideration our women and the home life made by them, which must be the root and ground of the whole matter. Let us insist then on special encouragement for the education of our women and special care in their training. Let our girls feel that we expect something more of them than that they merely look pretty and appear well in society. Teach them that there is a race with special needs which they and only they can help; that the world needs and is already asking for their trained, efficient forces. Finally, if there is an ambitious girl with pluck and brain to take the higher education, encourage her to make the most of it. Let there be the same flourish of trumpets and clapping of hands as when a boy announces his determination to enter the lists; and then, as you know that she is physically the weaker of the two, don't stand from under and leave her to buffet the waves alone. Let her know that your heart is following her, that your hand, though she sees it not, is ready to support her. To be plain, I mean let money be raised and scholarships be founded in our colleges and universities for self-supporting, worthy young women, to offset and balance the aid that can always be found for boys who will take theology.

The earnest well trained Christian young woman, as a teacher, as a home-maker, as wife, mother, or silent influence even, is as potent a missionary agency among our people as is the theologian; and I claim that at the present stage of our development in the South she is even more important and necessary.

Let us then, here and now, recognize this force and resolve to make the most of it—not the boys less, but the girls more.

Remarks before the 1893 World's Congress of Representative Women on the Status of the Black Woman in the United States

The higher fruits of civilization can not be extemporized, neither can they be developed normally, in the brief space of thirty years. It requires the long and painful growth of generations. Yet all through the darkest period of the colored women's oppression in this country her yet unwritten history is full of heroic struggle, a struggle against fearful and overwhelming odds, that often ended in a horrible death, to maintain and protect that which woman holds dearer than life. The painful, patient, and silent toil of mothers to gain a fee simple title to the bodies of their daughters, the despairing fight, as of an entrapped tigress, to keep hallowed their own persons, would furnish material for epics. That more went down under the flood than stemmed the current is not extraordinary. The majority of our women are not heroines—but I do not know that a majority of any race of women are heroines. It is enough for me to know that while in the eyes of the highest tribunal in America she was deemed no more than a chattel, an irresponsible thing, a dull block, to be drawn hither or thither at the volition of an owner, the Afro-American woman maintained ideals of womanhood unshamed by any ever conceived. Resting or fermenting in untutored minds, such ideals could not claim a hearing at the bar of the nation. The white woman could at least plead for her own emancipation: the black woman, doubly enslaved, could but suffer and struggle and be silent. I speak for the colored women of the South, because it is there that the millions of blacks in this country have watered the soil with blood and tears, and it is there too that the colored woman of America has made her characteristic history, and there her destiny is evolving. Since emancipation the movement has been at times confused and stormy, so that we could not always tell whether we were going forward or groping in a circle. We hardly knew what we ought to emphasize, whether education or wealth, or civil freedom and recognition. We were utterly destitute. Possessing no homes nor the knowledge of how to make them, no money nor the habit of acquiring it, no education, no political status, no influence, what could we do? But as Frederick Douglass had said in darker days than those, "One with God is a majority," and our ignorance had hedged us in from the fine-spun theories of agnostics. We had remaining at least a simple faith that a just God is on the throne of the universe, and that somehow—we could not see, nor did we bother our heads to try to tell how—he would in his own good time make all right that seemed most wrong.

Schools were established, not merely public day-schools, but home training and industrial schools, at Hampton, at Fisk, Atlanta, Raleigh, and other central stations, and later, through the energy of the colored people themselves, such schools as the Wilberforce, the Livingstone, the Allen, and the Paul Quinn were opened. These schools were almost without exception co-educational. Funds were too limited to be divided on sex lines, even had it been ideally desirable; but our girls as well as our boys flocked in and battled for an education. Not even then was that patient, untrumpeted heroine, the slave-mother, released from self-sacrifice, and many an unbuttered crust was eaten in silent content that she might eke out enough from her poverty to send her young folks off to school. She "never had the chance," she would tell you, with tears on her withered cheek, so she wanted them to get all they could. The work in these schools, and in such as these, has been like the little leaven hid in the measure of meal, permeating life throughout the length and breadth of the Southland, lifting up ideals of home and of womanhood; diffusing a contagious longing for higher living and purer thinking, inspiring woman herself with a new sense of her dignity in the eternal purposes of nature. To-day there are twenty-five thousand five hundred and thirty colored schools in the United States with one million three hundred and fifty-three thousand three hundred and fifty-two pupils of both sexes. This is not quite the thirtieth year since their emancipation, and the colored people hold in landed property for churches and schools twenty-five million dollars. Two and one-half million colored children have learned to read and write, and twenty-two thousand nine hundred and fifty-six colored men and women (mostly women) are teaching in these schools. According to Doctor Rankin, President of Howard University, there are two hundred and forty-seven colored students (a large percentage of whom are women) now preparing themselves in the universities of Europe. . . .

Now, I think if I could crystallize the sentiment of my constituency, and deliver it as a message to this congress of women, it would be something like this: Let woman's claim be as broad in the concrete as in the abstract. We take our stand on the solidarity of humanity, the oneness of life, and the unnaturalness and injustice of all special favoritisms, whether of sex, race, country, or condition. If one link of the chain be broken, the chain is broken. A bridge is no stronger than its weakest part, and a cause is not worthier than its weakest element. Least of all can woman's cause afford to decry the weak. We want, then, as toilers for the universal triumph of justice and human rights, to go to our homes from this Congress, demanding an entrance not through a gateway for ourselves, our race, our sex, or our sect, but a grand highway for humanity. The colored woman feels that woman's cause is one and universal; and that not till the image of God, whether in parian or ebony, is sacred and inviolable; not till race, color, sex, and condition are seen as the accidents, and not the substance of life; not till the universal title of humanity to life, liberty, and the pursuit of happiness is conceded to be inalienable to all; not till then is woman's lesson taught and woman's cause won—not the white woman's, nor the black woman's, nor the red woman's, but the cause of every man and of every woman who has writhed silently under a mighty wrong. Woman's wrongs are thus indissolubly linked with all undefended woe, and the acquirement of her "rights" will mean the final triumph of all right over might, the supremacy of the moral forces of reason, and justice, and love in the government of the nations of earth.

FANNIE BARRIER WILLIAMS
(1855–1944)

Fannie Barrier Williams was an influential lecturer and club woman at an important period in the history of the development of the black women's club movement. She was the youngest of three children of Anthony J. and Harriet Prince Barrier, born in Brockport, New York, in 1855. Her family had been free for two generations and enjoyed its relationships with the whites in the area, thus Fannie attended the local schools. She graduated from the academic and classical course of the State Normal School at Brockport in 1870, before embarking on teaching assignments in the deep South as well as in Washington, D.C. She enhanced her own education by studying at the New England Conservatory of Music in Boston and at the School of Fine Arts in Washington.

In 1887, Barrier returned to Brockport to marry S. Laing Williams, a Georgian who had graduated from the University of Michigan, as well as with honors from the Columbian Law School in Washington, D.C. (now George Washington Law School). The couple had no children, so Williams was able to focus her attention on issues of politics and the women's club movement. Between 1893 and the late 1920s, she was generally known as one of the most effective "colored" lecturers and club women. She shared the period's limelight with Ida B. Wells-Barnett, Mary Church Terrell, Anna Julia Cooper, and Frances Jackson Coppin.

She moved to Chicago to assist her husband in establishing his law practice and became even more involved in the club women's movement. During her famous May 1893 appearance before the World's Congress of Representative Women at the Columbian Exposition in Chicago, she delivered "The Intellectual Progress of the Colored Women of the United States since the Emancipation Proclamation," which became known as one of her most important speeches. She focused on equality before the law and achieved it in her own small way when she claimed French heritage in order not to be moved to a Jim Crow car while traveling on a train in the South. In 1895, she was admitted to Chicago's Women's Club as its only black member. She was active in other programs in Chicago, including assisting Daniel Hale Williams in founding Provident Hospital in 1891. She also helped found the National League of Colored Women in 1893, and she collaborated with Mary Church Terrell in founding its successor, the National Association of Colored Women, in 1896. Williams also worked with the Illinois Woman's Alliance; she encouraged employers to hire black women for stenographic and clerical jobs.

Perhaps this last activity led to Williams's seeming change in political stance after 1900. She supported Booker T. Washington's program of industrial education despite her own training in the classical tradition. She was a contributor, along with Washington, to *A New Negro for a New Century* (1900), and, at the 1902 convention of the Afro-American Council in Saint Paul, Minnesota, she was elected to the position of corresponding secretary because she had the support of such Washington followers as Emmett J. Scott and T. Thomas Fortune. She apologized to Washington for an article she wrote in the *New York Age* on women's activities in 1907 so she might continue writing the column. Williams and her husband both courted favors from Washington; S. Laing Williams was rewarded with the appointment of federal assistant district attorney in Chicago, a position he lost when Washington's power declined under the administration of Woodrow Wilson.

After her husband's death in 1921, Williams lived with her sister and became less active in public affairs. Between 1924 and 1926, however, she did serve on the Library Board of Chicago, perhaps the first woman and the first African American to be so appointed. She died of arteriosclerosis in 1944 and was buried in the family plot in High Street Cemetery in Brockport.

❖❖❖

Information on Williams's life, career, and politics can be obtained from "A Northern Woman's Autobiography," a sketch she wrote that appeared in the July 14, 1904, *Independent,* and from a variety of other sources, including May Wright Sewall, ed., *The World's Congress of Representative Women* (1894), Allan H. Spear, *Dictionary of American Biography: Supplement 3* (1973); Leslie H. Fishel, Jr., *Notable American Women* (1971).

The Intellectual Progress of the Colored Women of the United States Since the Emancipation Proclamation[1]

Less than thirty years ago the term progress as applied to colored women of African descent in the United States would have been an anomaly. The recognition of that term to-day as appropriate is a fact full of interesting significance. That the discussion of progressive womanhood in this great assemblage of the representative women of the world is considered incomplete without some account of the colored women's status is a most noteworthy evidence that we have not failed to impress ourselves on the higher side of American life.

Less is known of our women than of any other class of Americans.

No organization of far-reaching influence for their special advancement, no conventions of women to take note of their progress, and no special literature reciting the incidents, the events, and all things interesting and instructive concerning them are to be found among the agencies directing their career. There has been no special interest in their peculiar condition as native-born American women. Their power to affect the social life of America, either for good or for ill, has excited not even a speculative interest.

Though there is much that is sorrowful, much that is wonderfully heroic, and much that is romantic in a peculiar way in their history, none of it has as yet been told as evidence of what is possible for these women. How few of the happy, prosperous, and eager living Americans can appreciate what it all means to be suddenly changed from irresponsible bondage to the responsibility of freedom and citizenship!

The distress of it all can never be told, and the pain of it all can never be felt except by the victims, and by those saintly women of the white race who for thirty years have been consecrated to the uplifting of a whole race of women from a long-enforced degradation.

The American people have always been impatient of ignorance and poverty. They believe with Emerson that "America is another word for opportunity," and for that reason success is a virtue and poverty and ignorance are inexcusable. This may account for the fact that our women have excited no general sympathy in the struggle to emancipate themselves from the demoralization of slavery. This new life of freedom, with its far-reaching responsibilities, had to be learned by these children of darkness

[1]Fannie Barrier Williams, address, "The Intellectual Progress of the Colored Women of the United States since the Emancipation Proclamation." *The World's Congress of Representative Women,* edited by May Wright Sewall (Chicago: Rand, McNally, 1894), pp. 696–711. This was also published as a pamphlet: Fannie Barrier Williams, *The Present Status and Intellectual Progress of Colored Women* (Chicago, 1893).

mostly without a guide, a teacher, or a friend. In the mean vocabulary of slavery there was no definition of any of the virtues of life. The meaning of such precious terms as marriage, wife, family, and home could not be learned in a school-house. The blue-back speller, the arithmetic, and the copy-book contain no magical cures for inherited inaptitudes for the moralities. Yet it must ever be counted as one of the most wonderful things in human history how promptly and eagerly these suddenly liberated women tried to lay hold upon all that there is in human excellence. There is a touching pathos in the eagerness of these millions of new home-makers to taste the blessedness of intelligent womanhood. The path of progress in the picture is enlarged so as to bring to view these trustful and zealous students of freedom and civilization striving to overtake and keep pace with women whose emancipation has been a slow and painful process for a thousand years. The longing to be something better than they were when freedom found them has been the most notable characteristic in the development of these women. This constant striving for equality has given an upward direction to all the activities of colored women.

Freedom at once widened their vision beyond the mean cabin life of their bondage. Their native gentleness, good cheer, and hopefulness made them susceptible to those teachings that make for intelligence and righteousness. Sullenness of disposition, hatefulness, and revenge against the master class because of two centuries of ill-treatment are not in the nature of our women.

But a better view of what our women are doing and what their present status is may be had by noticing some lines of progress that are easily verifiable.

First it should be noticed that separate facts and figures relative to colored women are not easily obtainable. Among the white women of the country, independence, progressive intelligence, and definite interests have done so much that nearly every fact and item illustrative of their progress and status is classified and easily accessible. Our women, on the contrary, have had no advantage of interests peculiar and distinct and separable from those of men that have yet excited public attention and kindly recognition.

In their religious life, however, our women show a progressiveness parallel in every important particular to that of white women in all Christian churches. . . .

While there has been but little progress toward the growing rationalism in the Christian creeds, there has been a marked advance toward a greater refinement of conception, good taste, and the proprieties. It is our young women coming out of the schools and academies that have been insisting upon a more godly and cultivated ministry. It is the young women of a new generation and new inspirations that are making tramps of the ministers who once dominated the colored church, and whose intelligence and piety were mostly in their lungs. . . .

Another evidence of growing intelligence is a sense of religious discrimination among our women. Like the nineteenth century woman generally, our women find congeniality in all the creeds, from the Catholic creed to the no-creed of Emerson. There is a constant increase of this interesting variety in the religious life of our women.

Closely allied to this religious development is their progress in the work of education in schools and colleges. For thirty years education has been the magic word among the colored people of this country. That their greatest need was education in its broadest sense was understood by these people more strongly than it could be taught to them. It is the unvarying testimony of every teacher in the South that the mental development of the colored women as well as men has been little less than phenomenal. In twenty-five years, and under conditions discouraging in the extreme, thousands of our women have been educated as teachers. They have adapted themselves to the work of mentally lifting a whole race of people so eagerly and readily that they afford an apt illustration of the power of self-help. Not only have these women become good teachers in less than twenty-five years, but many of them are the prize teachers in the mixed schools of nearly every Northern city.

These women have also so fired the hearts of the race for education that colleges, normal schools, industrial schools, and universities have been reared by a generous public to meet the requirements of these eager students of intelligent citizenship. As American women generally are fighting against the nineteenth century narrowness that still keeps women out of the higher institutions of learning, so our women are eagerly demanding the best of education open to their race. They continually verify what President Rankin[2] of Howard University recently said, "Any theory of educating the Afro-American that does not throw open the golden gates of the highest culture will fail on the ethical and spiritual side."

It is thus seen that our women have the same spirit and mettle that characterize the best of American women. Everywhere they are following in the tracks of those women who are swiftest in the race for higher knowledge.

To-day they feel strong enough to ask for but one thing, and that is the same opportunity for the acquisition of all kinds of knowledge that may be accorded to other women. This granted, in the next generation these progressive women will be found successfully occupying every field where the highest intelligence alone is admissible. In less than another generation American literature, American art, and American music will be enriched by productions having new and peculiar features of interest and excellence.

The exceptional career of our women will yet stamp itself indelibly upon the thought of this country.

American literature needs for its greater variety and its deeper soundings that which will be written into it out of the hearts of these self-emancipating women.

The great problems of social reform that are now so engaging the highest intelligence of American women will soon need for their solution the reinforcement of that new intelligence which our women are developing. In short, our women are ambitious to be contributors to all the great moral and intellectual forces that make for the greater weal of our common country.

If this hope seems too extravagant to those of you who know these women only in their humbler capacities, I would remind you that all that we hope for and will certainly achieve in authorship and practical intelligence is more than prophesied by what has already been done, and more that can be done, by hundreds of Afro-American women whose talents are now being expended in the struggle against race resistance.

The power of organized womanhood is one of the most interesting studies of modern sociology. Formerly women knew so little of each other mentally, their common interests were so sentimental and gossipy, and their knowledge of all the larger affairs of human society was so meager that organization among them, in the modern sense, was impossible. Now their liberal intelligence, their contact in all the great interests of education, and their increasing influence for good in all the great reformatory movements of the age has created in them a greater respect for each other, and furnished the elements of organization for large and splendid purposes. The highest ascendancy of woman's development has been reached when they have become mentally strong enough to find bonds of association interwoven with sympathy, loyalty, and mutual trustfulness. To-day union is the watchword of woman's onward march.

If it be a fact that this spirit of organization among women generally is the distinguishing mark of the nineteenth century woman, dare we ask if the colored women of the United States have made any progress in this respect? . . .

Benevolence is the essence of most of the colored women's organizations. The humane side of their natures has been cultivated to recognize the duties they owe to the sick, the indigent and ill-fortuned. No church, school, or

[2]Dr. Jeremiah Eames Rankin (1828–1904) was a white Congregationalist minister who served as president of Howard University from 1890 to 1903.

charitable institution for the special use of colored people has been allowed to languish or fail when the associated efforts of the women could save it. . . .

The hearts of Afro-American women are too warm and too large for race hatred. Long suffering has so chastened them that they are developing a special sense of sympathy for all who suffer and fail of justice. All the associated interests of church, temperance, and social reform in which American women are winning distinction can be wonderfully advanced when our women shall be welcomed as co-workers, and estimated solely by what they are worth to the moral elevation of all the people.

I regret the necessity of speaking to the question of the moral progress of our women, because the morality of our home life has been commented upon so disparagingly and meanly that we are placed in the unfortunate position of being defenders of our name.

It is proper to state, with as much emphasis as possible, that all questions relative to the moral progress of the colored women of America are impertinent and unjustly suggestive when they relate to the thousands of colored women in the North who were free from the vicious influences of slavery. They are also meanly suggestive as regards thousands of our women in the South whose force of character enabled them to escape the slavery taints of immorality. The question of the moral progress of colored women in the United States has force and meaning in this discussion only so far as it tells the story of how the once-enslaved women have been struggling for twenty-five years to emancipate themselves from the demoralization of their enslavement.

While I duly appreciate the offensiveness of all references to American slavery, it is unavoidable to charge to that system every moral imperfection that mars the character of the colored American. The whole life and power of slavery depended upon an enforced degradation of everything human in the slaves. The slave code recognized only animal distinctions between the sexes, and ruthlessly ignored those ordinary separations that belong to the social state.

It is a great wonder that two centuries of such demoralization did not work a complete extinction of all the moral instincts. But the recuperative power of these women to regain their moral instincts and to establish a respectable relationship to American womanhood is among the earlier evidences of their moral ability to rise above their conditions. In spite of a cursed heredity that bound them to the lowest social level, in spite of everything that is unfortunate and unfavorable, these women have continually shown an increasing degree of teachableness as to the meaning of woman's relationship to man.

Out of this social purification and moral uplift have come a chivalric sentiment and regard from the young men of the race that give to the young women a new sense of protection. I do not wish to disturb the serenity of this conference by suggesting why this protection is needed and the kind of men against whom it is needed.

It is sufficient for us to know that the daughters of women who thirty years ago were not allowed to be modest, not allowed to follow the instincts of moral rectitude, who could cry for protection to no living man, have so elevated the moral tone of their social life that new and purer standards of personal worth have been created, and new ideals of womanhood, instinct with grace and delicacy, are everywhere recognized and emulated.

This moral regeneration of a whole race of women is no idle sentiment—it is a serious business; and everywhere there is witnessed a feverish anxiety to be free from the mean suspicions that have so long underestimated the character strength of our women.

These women are not satisfied with the unmistakable fact that moral progress has been made, but they are fervently impatient and stirred by a sense of outrage under the vile imputations of a diseased public opinion. . . .

It may now perhaps be fittingly asked, What mean all these evidences of mental, social, and moral progress of a class of American women of whom you know so little? Certainly you can not be indifferent to the growing needs and importance of women who are demonstrating their intelligence and capacity for the highest privileges of freedom.

The most important thing to be noted is the fact that the colored people of America have reached a distinctly new era in their career so quickly that the American mind has scarcely had time to recognize the fact, and adjust itself to the new requirements of the people in all things that pertain to citizenship. . . .

It seems to daze the understanding of the ordinary citizen that there are thousands of men and women everywhere among us who in twenty-five years have progressed as far away from the non-progressive peasants of the "black belt" of the South as the highest social life in New England is above the lowest levels of American civilization.

This general failure of the American people to know the new generation of colored people, and to recognize this important change in them, is the cause of more injustice to our women than can well be estimated. Further progress is everywhere seriously hindered by this ignoring of their improvement.

Our exclusion from the benefits of the fair play sentiment of the country is little less than a crime against the ambitions and aspirations of a whole race of women. The American people are but repeating the common folly of history in thus attempting to repress the yearnings of progressive humanity.

In the item of employment colored women bear a distressing burden of mean and unreasonable discrimination. . . .

It is almost literally true that, except teaching in colored schools and menial work, colored women can find no employment in this free America. They are the only women in the country for whom real ability, virtue, and special talents count for nothing when they become applicants for respectable employment. Taught everywhere in ethics and social economy that merit always wins, colored women carefully prepare themselves for all kinds of occupation only to meet with stern refusal, rebuff, and disappointment. One of countless instances will show how the best as well as the meanest of American society are responsible for the special injustice to our women.

Not long ago I presented the case of a bright young woman to a well-known bank president of Chicago, who was in need of a thoroughly competent stenographer and typewriter. The president was fully satisfied with the young woman as exceptionally qualified for the position, and manifested much pleasure in commending her to the directors for appointment, and at the same time disclaimed that there could be any opposition on account of the slight tinge of African blood that identified her as a colored woman. Yet, when the matter was brought before the directors for action, these mighty men of money and business, these men whose prominence in all the great interests of the city would seem to lift them above all narrowness and foolishness, scented the African taint, and at once bravely came to the rescue of the bank and of society by dashing the hopes of this capable yet helpless young woman. . . .

Can the people of this country afford to single out the women of a whole race of people as objects of their special contempt? Do these women not belong to a race that has never faltered in its support of the country's flag in every war since Attucks fell in Boston's streets?

Are they not the daughters of men who have always been true as steel against treason to everything fundamental and splendid in the republic? In short, are these women not as thoroughly American in all the circumstances of citizenship as the best citizens of our country?

If it be so, are we not justified in a feeling of desperation against that peculiar form of Americanism that shows respect for our women as servants and contempt for them when they become women of culture? We have never been taught to understand why the unwritten law of chivalry, protection, and fair play that are everywhere the conservators of women's welfare must exclude every woman of a dark complexion.

We believe that the world always needs the influence of every good and capable woman, and this rule recognizes no exceptions based on complexion. In their complaint against hindrances to their employment colored women ask for no special favors. . . .

Another, and perhaps more serious, hindrance to our women is that nightmare known as "social equality." The term equality is the most inspiring word in the vocabulary of citizenship. It expresses the leveling quality in all the splendid possibilities of American life. It is this idea of equality that has made room in this country for all kinds and conditions of men, and made personal merit the supreme requisite for all kinds of achievement.

When the colored people became citizens, and found it written deep in the organic law of the land that they too had the right to life, liberty, and the pursuit of happiness, they were at once suspected of wishing to interpret this maximum of equality as meaning social equality.

Everywhere the public mind has been filled with constant alarm lest in some way our women shall approach the social sphere of the dominant race in this country. Men and women, wise and perfectly sane in all things else, become instantly unwise and foolish at the remotest suggestion of social contact with colored men and women. At every turn in our lives we meet this fear, and are humiliated by its aggressiveness and meanness. If we seek the sanctities of religion, the enlightenment of the university, the honors of politics, and the natural recreations of our common country, the social equality alarm is instantly given, and our aspirations are insulted. "Beware of social equality with the colored American" is thus written on all places, sacred or profane, in this blessed land of liberty. The most discouraging and demoralizing effect of this false sentiment concerning us is that it utterly ignores individual merit and discredits the sensibilities of intelligent womanhood. The sorrows and heartaches of a whole race of women seem to be matters of no concern to the people who so dread the social possibilities of these colored women.

On the other hand, our women have been wonderfully indifferent and unconcerned about the matter. The dread inspired by the growing intelligence of colored women has interested us almost to the point of amusement. It has given to colored women a new sense of importance to witness how easily their emancipation and steady advancement is disturbing all classes of American people. It may not be a discouraging circumstance that colored women can command some sort of attention, even though they be misunderstood. We believe in the law of reaction, and it is reasonably certain that the forces of intelligence and character being developed in our women will yet change mistrustfulness into confidence and contempt into sympathy and respect. It will soon appear to those who are not hopelessly monomaniacs on the subject that the colored people are in no way responsible for the social equality nonsense. We shall yet be credited with knowing better than our enemies that social equality can neither be enforced by law nor prevented by oppression. Though not philosophers, we long since learned that equality before the law, equality in the best sense of that term under our institutions, is totally different from social equality.

We know, without being exceptional students of history, that the social relationship of the two races will be adjusted equitably in spite of all fear and injustice, and that there is a social gravitation in human affairs that eventually overwhelms and crushes into nothingness all resistance based on prejudice and selfishness.

Our chief concern in this false social sentiment is that it attempts to hinder our further progress toward the higher spheres of womanhood. On account of it, young colored women of ambition and means are compelled in many instances to leave the country for training and education in the salons and studios of Europe. On many of the railroads of this country women of refinement and culture are driven like cattle into human cattle-cars lest the occupying of an individual seat paid for in a first-class car may result in social equality. This social quarantine on all means of travel in certain parts of the country is guarded and enforced more rigidly against us than the quarantine regulations against cholera.

Without further particularizing as to how this social question opposes our advancement, it may be stated that the contentions of colored women are in kind like those of other American women for greater freedom of development. Liberty to be all that we can be, without artificial hindrances, is a thing no less precious to us than to women generally.

We come before this assemblage of women feeling confident that our progress has been along high levels and rooted deeply in the essentials of intelligent humanity. We are so essentially American in speech, in instincts, in sentiments and destiny that the things that interest you equally interest us.

We believe that social evils are dangerously contagious. The fixed policy of persecution and injustice against a class of women who are weak and defenseless will be necessarily hurtful to the cause of all women. Colored women are becoming more and more a part of the social forces that must help to determine the questions that so concern women generally. In this Congress we ask to be known and recognized for what we are worth. If it be the high purpose of these deliberations to lessen the resistance to woman's progress, you can not fail to be interested in our struggles against the many oppositions that harass us.

Women who are tender enough in heart to be active in humane societies, to be foremost in all charitable activities, who are loving enough to unite Christian womanhood everywhere against the sin of intemperance, ought to be instantly concerned in the plea of colored women for justice and humane treatment. Women of the dominant race can not afford to be responsible for the wrongs we suffer, since those who do injustice can not escape a certain penalty.

But there is no wish to overstate the obstacles to colored women or to picture their status as hopeless. There is no disposition to take our place in this Congress as faultfinders or suppliants for mercy. As women of a common country, with common interests, and a destiny that will certainly bring us closer to each other, we come to this altar with our contribution of hopefulness as well as with our complaints. . . .

If the love of humanity more than the love of races and sex shall pulsate throughout all the grand results that shall issue to the world from this parliament of women, women of African descent in the United States will for the first time begin to feel the sweet release from the blighting thrall of prejudice.

The colored women, as well as all women, will realize that the inalienable right to life, liberty, and the pursuit of happiness is a maxim that will become more blessed in its significance when the hand of woman shall take it from its sepulture in books and make it the gospel of every-day life and the unerring guide in the relations of all men, women, and children.

VOICES OF REFORM

AUTOBIOGRAPHY

BOOKER T. WASHINGTON

(1856–1915)

Booker Taliferro Washington was probably the most important African American leader empowered by the American majority between the end of Reconstruction in 1875 and the stirrings of the Harlem Renaissance in the 1920s. In disputes with W.E.B. Du Bois, who was nearly twelve years his junior, Washington preferred to trade Civil Rights for the opportunity to learn a trade, to forego liberal education in order to pursue what he called "practical knowledge," or "knowing how to make a living," and to master menial labor marketed in the plantation South. Even as he spoke and wrote, the agricultural world was being industrialized into oblivion. He relied almost too conveniently on the presumed good will among whites in a nation segregated rigidly on the basis of racial inequality. Even a few radicals, such as Du Bois, believed early on that Washington's policy of racial compromise might achieve peace and progress in America. But as the toll of lynched blacks (many of whom were soldiers recently back from World War I) increased, astute thinkers began to realize that Washington's policy of accommodation meant only more black dreams deferred.

Washington valued facts more than fiction. He could not read between the lines of history. He liked biographies much more than stories, which he thought were a waste of time. Hence, he failed to understand that a profound, genuine enlightenment promotes the interpretation of human values. Almost never did he stress the communal power of self-definition. Washington was an unusually accomplished corporate entrepreneur who, grounded in the historical moment of the Carnegie, Rockefeller, and Vanderbilt fortunes, lacked brilliance as an original thinker. Although he lacked the depth and creative insight of either the literary artist or the great mentor, he was mythologized by the American mainstream as the undisputed leader of his people.

Booker T. Washington was born on Burrough's Plantation near Hale's Ford in Franklin County, Virginia, on April 5, 1856. He would die on November 14, 1915. In 1865, his family moved to Malden, West Virginia. While a boy, he worked for nine months a year in coal mines and eventually made his way with a dollar and a half in his pocket to Hampton Normal and Agricultural Institute (now Hampton University), from which he graduated in 1875. The legend is that he was a Horatio Alger of color. After he returned to teach in Malden, he went to study for a year at Wayland Seminary, which is today a part of Virginia Union University. On his return to Hampton in 1879, he took responsibility for a group of Native American students and established a night school at the Institute. In 1881, he began service as the first president of Tuskegee Institute, a trade school for blacks in Alabama. The Institute, with one teacher and fifty pupils, opened despite limited funds of $2,000 a year from the state. In twenty-five years, the school would have more than 1,500 students who were trained in thirty-seven industries. Despite the pervasive discrimination based on race at the time, Washington advocated trades as a means to secure economic positions. When he proposed in the speech at the Atlanta Exposition of 1895 a compromise based on racial segregation within an accepted hierarchy of white power, reinforced by the enthusiastic subservience of blacks, he gained strong support from white leaders. Washington became highly influential in directing philanthropic moneys to black causes and in establishing a peonage system by which a few people of color were assigned to federal jobs. As part of what Du Bois despised as the "Tuskegee Machine"—a repressively conservative ideology that undermined all creative and independent thought among young blacks—Washington advised Presidents Theodore Roosevelt and William Howard Taft about racial issues. Indeed, Washington's twelve books, including his classic autobiography, *Up from Slavery* (1901), display a marvelous understanding of a plantation tradition that upholds racial patience and eschews all bitterness. Somewhat too naively, perhaps, he presumed a natural triumph of liberal good will and education over the harsh realities of corporate greed and human evil. Though he himself was probably never as naive as his language and ideology would suggest, most Americans took his conciliatory words at face value. They found him an effective and popular speaker who clearly favored in the concrete images of casting "down your buckets where you are" the plantation past over a more challenging future. Booker T. Washington assured the nation, "in all things that are purely social we can be as separate as the fingers, yet one as the hand in all things essential to mutual progress." For his superb form of political salesmanship, Harvard University awarded him an M.A. degree in 1896. It was, indeed, the same year that the Supreme Court legalized racial segregation in the public schools of the nation.

Often since 1980, an emphasis on the conciliatory strategies of Booker T. Washington has enjoyed a kind of popular renaissance among traditional scholars. Indeed, the position has a powerful resilience that usually resurfaces during slow, conservative eras. In the famous Atlanta address of 1895, he had assured the white South that "you and your families will be surrounded by the most patient, faithful, law-abiding, and unresentful people the world has seen." Washington has become a de facto standard in tone and demeanor by which the more aggressive assertions of political activists have been measured since his time. Indeed, Washington seems almost to have beckoned a few dreamers back to the supposedly happy days before the bus boycotts at Montgomery in the late 1950s and the racial sit-ins at the public lunch counters during the early 1960s. Booker T. Washington was, indeed, a most accomplished apologist for a southern world-view now gone with the wind.

❖❖❖

Washington's often ghostwritten texts include *The Future of the American Negro* (1899), *Tuskegee and Its People* (1905), *Life of Frederick Douglass* (1907), *The Story of the Negro* (1909), *My Larger Education* (1911), and *The Negro in the South* (1907) [coauthored with Du Bois]. Recent studies include the editing by Louis R. Harlan and Raymond Smock of Washington's previously unpublished manuscripts and papers, *Booker T. Washington, 1856–1915* (Urbana: University of Illinois Press, 1972–84). More critical studies are Hugh Hawkins, *Booker T. Washington and His Critics* (1974) and Willis N. Pitts, *A Critical Study of Booker T. Washington* (1973). Other inquiries are Robert L. Factor, *The Black Response to American Men* (1970) and Frederick Drinker, *Booker T. Washington, the Master Mind of Tuskegee* (1970). A pioneering study was that of Arna Bontemps, *Young Booker: Booker T. Washington's Early Years.* Few articles of insight have appeared since the 1980s.

FROM *Up from Slavery*

Chapter I
A Slave Among Slaves

I was born a slave on a plantation in Franklin County, Virginia. I am not quite sure of the exact place or exact date of my birth, but at any rate I suspect I must have been born somewhere and at some time. As nearly as I have been able to learn, I was born near a cross-roads post-office called Hale's Ford, and the year was 1858 or 1859. I do not know the month or the day. The earliest impressions I can now recall are of the plantation and the slave quarters—the latter being the part of the plantation where the slaves had their cabins.

My life had its beginning in the midst of the most miserable, desolate, and discouraging surroundings. This was so, however, not because my owners were especially cruel, for they were not, as compared with many others. I was born in a typical log cabin, about fourteen by sixteen feet square. In this cabin I lived with my mother and a brother and sister till after the Civil War, when we were all declared free.

Of my ancestry I know almost nothing. In the slave quarters, and even later, I heard whispered conversations among the coloured people of the tortures which the slaves, including, no doubt, my ancestors on my mother's side, suffered in the middle passage of the slave ship while being conveyed from Africa to America. I have been unsuccessful in securing any information that would throw any accurate light upon the history of my family beyond my mother. She, I remember, had a half-brother and a half-sister. In the days of slavery not very much attention was given to family history and family records—that is, black family records. My mother, I suppose, attracted the attention of a purchaser who was afterward my owner and hers. Her addition to the slave family attracted about as much attention as the purchase of a new horse or cow. Of my father I know even less than of my mother. I do not even know his name. I have heard reports to the effect that he was a white man who lived on one of the near-by plantations. Whoever he was, I never heard of his taking the least interest in me or providing in any way for my rearing. But I do not find especial fault with him. He was simply another unfortunate victim of the institution which the Nation unhappily had engrafted upon it at that time.

The cabin was not only our living-place, but was also used as the kitchen for the plantation. My mother was the plantation cook. The cabin was without glass windows; it had only openings in the side which let in the light, and also the cold, chilly air of winter. There was a door to the cabin—that is, something that was called a door—but the uncertain hinges by which it was hung, and the large cracks in it, to say nothing of the fact that it was too small, made the room a very uncomfortable one. In addition to these openings there was, in the lower right-hand corner of the room, the "cat-hole,"—a contrivance which almost every mansion or cabin in Virginia possessed during the ante-bellum period. The "cat-hole" was a square opening, about seven by eight inches, provided for the purpose of letting the cat pass in and out of the house at will during the night. In the case of our particular cabin I could never understand the necessity for this convenience, since there were at least a half-dozen other places in the cabin that would have accommodated the cats. There was no wooden floor in our cabin, the naked earth being used as a floor. In the centre of the earthen floor there was a large, deep opening covered with boards, which was used as a place in which to store sweet potatoes during the winter. An impression of this potato-hole is very distinctly engraved upon my memory, because I recall that during the process of putting the potatoes in or taking them out I would often come into possession of one or two, which I roasted and thoroughly enjoyed. There was no cooking-stove on our plantation, and all the cooking for the whites and slaves my mother had to do over an open fireplace, mostly in pots and "skillets." While the poorly built cabin caused us to suffer with cold in the winter, the heat from the open fireplace in summer was equally trying.

The early years of my life, which were spent in the little cabin, were not very different from those of thousands of other slaves. My mother, of course, had little time in which to give attention to the training of her children during the day. She snatched a few moments for our care in the early morning before her work began, and at night after the day's work was done. One of my earliest recollections is that of my mother cooking a chicken late at night, and awakening her children for the purpose of feeding them. How or where she got it I do not know. I presume, however, it was procured from our owner's farm. Some people may call this theft. If such a thing were to happen now, I should condemn it as theft myself. But taking place at the time it did, and for the reason that it did, no one could ever make me believe that my mother was guilty of thieving. She was simply a victim of the system of slavery. I cannot remember having slept in a bed until after our family was declared free by the Emancipation Proclamation. Three children—John, my older brother, Amanda, my sister, and myself—had a pallet on the dirt floor, or, to be more correct, we slept in and on a bundle of filthy rags laid upon the dirt floor.

I was asked not long ago to tell something about the sports and pastimes that I engaged in during my youth. Until that question was asked it had never occurred to me that there was no period of my life that was devoted to play. From the time that I can remember anything, almost every day of my life has been occupied in some kind of labour; though I think I would now be a more useful man if I had had time for sports. During the period that I spent in slavery I was not large enough to be of much service, still I was occupied most of the time in cleaning the yards, carrying water to the men in the fields, or going to the mill, to which I used to take the corn, once a week, to be ground. The mill was about three miles from the plantation. This work I always dreaded. The heavy bag of corn would be thrown across the back of the horse, and the corn divided about evenly on each side; but in some way, almost without exception, on these trips, the corn would so shift as to become unbalanced and would fall off the horse, and often I would fall with it. As I was not strong enough to reload the corn upon the horse, I would have to wait, sometimes for many hours, till a chance passer-by came along who would help me out of my trouble. The hours while waiting for some one were usually spent in crying. The time consumed in this way made me late in reaching the mill, and by the time I got my corn ground and reached home it would be far into the night. The road was a lonely one, and often led through dense forests. I was always frightened. The woods were said to be full of soldiers who had deserted from the army, and I had been told that the first thing a deserter did to a Negro boy when he found him alone was to cut off his ears. Besides, when I was late in getting home I knew I would always get a severe scolding or a flogging.

I had no schooling whatever while I was a slave, though I remember on several occasions I went as far as the schoolhouse door with one of my young mistresses to carry her books. The picture of several dozen boys and girls in a schoolroom engaged in study made a deep impression upon me, and I had the feeling that to get into a schoolhouse and study in this way would be about the same as getting into paradise.

So far as I can now recall, the first knowledge that I got of the fact that we were slaves, and that freedom of the slaves was being discussed, was early one morning before day, when I was awakened by my mother kneeling over her children and fervently praying that Lincoln and his armies might be successful, and that one day she and her children might be free. In this connection I have never been able to understand how the slaves throughout the South, completely ignorant as were the masses so far as books or newspapers were concerned, were able to keep themselves so accurately and completely informed about the great National questions that were agitating the country. From the time that Garrison, Lovejoy, and others began to agitate for freedom, the slaves throughout the South kept in close touch with the progress of the movement. Though I was a mere child during the preparation for the Civil War and during the war itself, I now recall the many late-at-night whispered discussions that I heard my mother and the other slaves on the plantation indulge in. These discussions showed that they understood the situation, and that they kept themselves informed of events by what was termed the "grape-vine" telegraph.

During the campaign when Lincoln was first a candidate for the Presidency, the slaves on our far-off plantation, miles from any railroad or large city or daily newspaper, knew what the issues involved were. When war was begun between the North and the South, every slave on our plantation felt and knew that, though other issues were discussed, the primal one was that of slavery. Even the most ignorant members of my race on the remote plantations felt in their hearts, with a certainty that admitted of no doubt, that the freedom of the slaves would be the one great result of the war, if the Northern armies conquered. Every success of the Federal armies and every defeat of the Confederate forces was watched with the keenest and most intense interest. Often the slaves got knowledge of the results of great battles before the white people received it. This news was usually gotten from the coloured man who was sent to the post-office for the mail. In our case the post-office was about three miles from the plantation and the mail came once or twice a week. The man who was sent to the office would linger about the place long enough to get the drift of the conversation from the group of white people who naturally congregated there, after receiving their mail, to discuss the latest news. The mail-carrier on his way back to our master's house would as naturally retail the news that he had secured among the slaves, and in this way they often heard of important events before the white people at the "big house," as the master's house was called.

I cannot remember a single instance during my childhood or early boyhood when our entire family sat down to the table together, and God's blessing was asked, and the family ate a meal in a civilized manner. On the plantation in Virginia, and even later, meals were gotten by the children very much as dumb animals get theirs. It was a piece of bread here and a scrap of meat there. It was a cup of milk at one time and some potatoes at another. Sometimes a portion of our family would eat out of the skillet or pot, while some one else would eat from a tin plate held on the knees, and often using nothing but the hands with which to hold the food. When I had grown to sufficient size, I was required to go to the "big house" at meal-times to fan the flies from the table by means of a large set of paper fans operated by a pulley. Naturally much of the conversation of the white people turned upon the subject of freedom and the war, and I absorbed a good deal of it. I remember that at one time I saw two of my young mistresses and some lady visitors eating ginger-cakes, in the yard. At that time those cakes seemed to me to be absolutely the most tempting and desirable things that I had ever seen; and I then and there resolved that, if I ever got free, the height of my ambition would be reached if I could get to the point where I could secure and eat ginger-cakes in the way that I saw those ladies doing.

Of course as the war was prolonged the white people, in many cases, often found it difficult to secure food for themselves. I think the slaves felt the deprivation less than the whites, because the usual diet for the slaves was corn bread and pork, and these could be raised on the plantation; but coffee, tea, sugar, and other articles which the whites had been accustomed to use could not be raised on the plantation, and the conditions brought about by the war frequently made it impossible to secure these things. The whites were often in great straits. Parched corn was used for coffee, and a kind of black molasses was used instead of sugar. Many times nothing was used to sweeten the so-called tea and coffee.

The first pair of shoes that I recall wearing were wooden ones. They had rough leather on the top, but the bottoms, which were about an inch thick, were of wood. When I walked they made a fearful noise, and besides this they were very inconvenient, since there was no yielding to the natural pressure of the foot. In wearing them one presented an exceedingly awkward appearance. The most trying ordeal that I was forced to endure as a slave boy, however, was the wearing of a flax shirt. In the portion of Virginia where I lived it was common to use flax as part of the clothing for the slaves. That part of the flax from which our clothing was made was largely the refuse, which of course was the cheapest and roughest part. I can scarcely imagine any torture, except, perhaps, the pulling of a tooth, that is equal to that caused by putting on a new flax shirt for the first time. It is almost equal to the feeling that one would experience if he had a dozen or more chestnut burrs, or a hundred small pin-points, in contact with his flesh. Even to this day I can recall accurately the tortures that I underwent when putting on one of these garments. The fact that my flesh was soft and tender added to the pain. But I had no choice. I had to wear the flax shirt or none; and had it been left to me to choose, I should have chosen to wear no covering. In connection with the flax shirt, my brother John, who is several years older than I am, performed one of the most generous acts that I ever heard of one slave relative doing for another. On several occasions when I was being forced to wear a new flax shirt, he generously agreed to put it on in my stead and wear it for several days, till it was "broken in." Until I had grown to be quite a youth this single garment was all that I wore.

One may get the idea from what I have said, that there was bitter feeling toward the white people on the part of my race, because of the fact that most of the white population was away fighting in a war which would result in keeping the Negro in slavery if the South was successful. In the case of the slaves on our place this was not true, and it was not true of any large portion of the slave population in the South where the Negro was treated with anything like decency. During the Civil War one of my young masters was killed, and two were severely wounded. I recall the feeling of sorrow which existed among the slaves when they heard of the death of "Mars' Billy." It was no sham sorrow but real. Some of the slaves had nursed "Mars' Billy"; others had played with him when he was a child. "Mars' Billy" had begged for mercy in the case of others when the overseer or master was thrashing them. The sorrow in the slave quarter was only second to that in the "big house." When the two young masters were brought home wounded, the sympathy of the slaves was shown in many ways. They were just as anxious to assist in the nursing as the family relatives of the wounded. Some of the slaves would even beg for the privilege of sitting up at night to nurse their wounded masters. This tenderness and sympathy on the part of those held in bondage was a result of their kindly and generous nature. In order to defend and protect the women and children who were left on the plantations when the white males went to war, the slaves would have laid down their lives. The slave who was selected to sleep in the "big house" during the absence of the males was considered to have the place of honour. Any one attempting to harm "young Mistress" or "old Mistress" during the night would have had to cross the dead body of the slave to do so. I do not know how many have noticed it, but I think that it will be found to be true that there are few instances, either in slavery or freedom, in which a member of my race has been known to betray a specific trust.

As a rule, not only did the members of my race entertain no feelings of bitterness against the whites before and during the war, but there are many instances of Negroes tenderly caring for their former masters and mistresses who for some reason have become poor and dependent since the war. I know of instances where the former masters of slaves have for years been supplied with money by their former slaves to keep them from suffering. I have known of still other cases in which the former slaves have assisted in the education of the descendants of their former owners. I know of a case on a large plantation in the South in which a young white man, the son of the former owner of the estate, has become so reduced in purse and self-control by reason of drink that he is a pitiable creature; and yet, notwithstanding the poverty of the coloured people themselves on this plantation, they have for years supplied this young white man with the necessities of life. One sends him a little coffee or sugar, another a little meat, and so on. Nothing that the coloured people possess is too good for the son of "old Mars' Tom," who will perhaps never be permitted to suffer while any remain on the place who knew directly or indirectly of "old Mars' Tom."

I have said that there are few instances of a member of my race betraying a specific trust. One of the best illustrations of this which I know of is in the case of an ex-slave from Virginia whom I met not long ago in a little town in the state of Ohio. I found that this man had made a contract with his master, two or three years previous to the Emancipation Proclamation, to the effect that the slave was to be permitted to buy himself, by paying so much per year for his body; and while he was paying for himself, he was to be permitted to labour where and for whom he pleased. Finding that he could secure better wages in Ohio, he went there. When freedom came, he was still in debt to his master some three hundred dollars. Notwithstanding that the Emancipation Proclamation freed him from any obligation to his master, this black man walked the greater portion of the distance back to where his old master lived in Virginia, and placed the last dollar, with interest, in his hands. In talking to me about this, the man told me that he knew that he did not have to pay the debt, but that he had given his word to his master, and his word he had never broken. He felt that he could not enjoy his freedom till he had fulfilled his promise.

From some things that I have said one may get the idea that some of the slaves did not want freedom. This is not true. I have never seen one who did not want to be free, or one who would return to slavery.

I pity from the bottom of my heart any nation or body of people that is so unfortunate as to get entangled in the net of slavery. I have long since ceased to cherish any spirit of bitterness against the Southern white people on account of the enslavement of my race. No one section of our country was wholly responsible for its introduction, and, besides, it was recognized and protected for years by the General Government. Having once got its tentacles fastened on to the economic and social life of the Republic, it was no easy matter for the country to relieve itself of the institution. Then, when we rid ourselves of prejudice, or racial feeling, and look facts in the face, we must acknowledge that, notwithstanding the cruelty and moral wrong of slavery, the ten million Negroes inhabiting this country, who themselves or whose ancestors went through the school of American slavery, are in a stronger and more hopeful condition, materially, intellectually, morally, and religiously, than is true of an equal number of black people in any other portion of the globe. This is so to such an extent that Negroes in this country, who themselves or whose forefathers went through the school of slavery, are constantly returning to Africa as missionaries to enlighten those who remained in the fatherland. This I say, not to justify slavery—on the other hand, I condemn it as an institution, as we all know that in America it was established for selfish and financial reasons, and not from a missionary motive—but to call attention to a fact, and to show how Providence so often uses men and institutions to accomplish a purpose. When persons ask me in these days how, in the midst of what sometimes seem hopelessly discouraging conditions, I can have such faith in the future of my race in this country, I remind them of the wilderness through which and out of which, a good Providence has already led us.

Ever since I have been old enough to think for myself, I have entertained the idea that, notwithstanding the cruel wrongs inflicted upon us, the black man got nearly as much out of slavery as the white man did. The hurtful influences of the institution were not by any means confined to the Negro. This was fully illustrated by the life upon our own plantation. The whole machinery of slavery was so constructed as to cause labour, as a rule, to be looked upon as a badge of degradation, of inferiority. Hence labour was something that both races on the slave plantation sought to escape. The slave system on our place, in a large measure, took the spirit of self-reliance and self-help out of the white people. My old master had many boys and girls, but not one, so far as I know, ever mastered a single trade or special line of productive industry. The girls were not taught to cook, sew, or to take care of the house. All of this was left to the slaves. The slaves, of course, had little personal interest in the life of the plantation, and their ignorance prevented them from learning how to do things in the most improved and thorough manner. As a result of the system, fences were out of repair, gates were hanging half off the hinges, doors creaked, window-panes were out, plastering had fallen but was not replaced, weeds grew in the yard. As a rule, there was food for whites and blacks, but inside the house, and on the dining-room table, there was wanting that delicacy and refinement of touch and finish which can make a home the most convenient, comfortable, and attractive place in the world. Withal there was a waste of food and other materials which was sad. When freedom came, the slaves were almost as well fitted to begin life anew as the master, except in the matter of book-learning and ownership of property. The slave owner and his sons had mastered no special industry. They unconsciously had imbibed the feeling that manual labour was not the proper thing for them. On the other hand, the slaves, in many cases, had mastered some handicraft, and none were ashamed, and few unwilling, to labour.

Finally the war closed, and the day of freedom came. It was a momentous and eventful day to all upon our plantation. We had been expecting it. Freedom was in the air, and had been for months. Deserting soldiers returning to their homes were to be seen every day. Others who had been discharged, or whose regiments had been paroled, were constantly passing near our place. The "grape-vine telegraph" was kept busy night and day. The news and mutterings of great events were swiftly carried from one plantation to another. In the fear of "Yankee" invasions, the silverware and other valuables were taken from the "big house," buried in the woods, and guarded by trusted slaves. Woe be to any one who would have attempted to disturb the buried treasure. The slaves would give the Yankee soldiers food, drink, clothing—anything but that which had been specifically intrusted to their care and honour. As the great day drew nearer, there was more singing in the slave quarters than usual. It was bolder, had more ring, and lasted later into the night. Most of the verses of the plantation songs had some reference to freedom. True, they had sung those same verses before, but they had been careful to explain that the "freedom" in these songs referred to the next world, and had no connection with life in this world. Now they gradually threw off the mask, and were not afraid to let it be known that the "freedom" in their songs meant freedom of the body in this world. The night before the eventful day, word was sent to the slave quarters to the effect that something unusual was going to take place at the "big house" the next morning. There was little, if any, sleep that night. All was excitement and expectancy. Early the next morning word was sent to all the slaves, old and young, to gather at the house. In company with my mother, brother, and sister, and a large number of other slaves, I went to the master's house. All of our master's family were either standing or seated on the veranda of the house, where they could see what was to take place and hear what was said. There was a feeling of deep interest, or perhaps sadness, on their faces, but not bitterness. As I now recall the impression they made upon me, they did not at the moment seem to be sad because of the loss of property, but rather because of parting with those whom they had reared and who were in many ways very close to them. The most distinct thing that I now recall in connection with the scene was that some man who seemed to be a stranger (a United States officer, I presume) made a little speech and then read a rather long paper—the Emancipation Proclamation, I think. After the reading we were told that we were all free, and could go when and where we pleased. My mother, who was standing by my side, leaned over and kissed her children, while tears of joy ran down her cheeks. She explained to us what it all meant, that this was the day for which she had been so long praying, but fearing that she would never live to see.

For some minutes there was great rejoicing, and thanksgiving, and wild scenes of ecstasy. But there was no feeling of bitterness. In fact, there was pity among the slaves for our former owners. The wild rejoicing on the part of the emancipated coloured people lasted but for a brief period, for I noticed that by the time they returned to their cabins there was a change in their feelings. The great responsibility of being free, of having charge of themselves, of having to think and plan for themselves and their children, seemed to take possession of them. It was very much like suddenly turning a youth of ten or twelve years out into the world to provide for himself. In a few hours the great questions with which the Anglo-Saxon race had been grappling for centuries had been thrown upon these people to be solved. These were the questions of a home, a living, the rearing of children, education, citizenship, and the establishment and support of churches. Was it any wonder that within a few hours the wild rejoicing ceased and a feeling of deep gloom seemed to pervade the slave quarters? To some it seemed that, now that they were in actual possession of it, freedom was a more serious thing than they had expected to find it. Some of the slaves were seventy or eighty years old; their best days were gone. They had no strength with which to earn a living in a strange place and among strange people, even if they had been sure where to find a new place of abode. To this class the problem seemed especially hard. Besides, deep down in their hearts there was a strange and peculiar attachment to "old Marster" and "old Missus," and to their children, which they found it hard to think of breaking off. With these they had spent in some cases nearly a half-century, and it was no light thing to think of parting. Gradually, one by one, stealthily at first, the older slaves began to wander from the slave quarters back to the "big house" to have a whispered conversation with their former owners as to the future.

Chapter III
The Struggle for an Education

One day, while at work in the coal-mine, I happened to overhear two miners talking about a great school for coloured people somewhere in Virginia. This was the first time that I had ever heard anything about any kind of school or college that was more pretentious than the little coloured school in our town.

In the darkness of the mine I noiselessly crept as close as I could to the two men who were talking. I heard one tell the other that not only was the school established for the members of my race, but that opportunities were provided by which poor but worthy students could work out all or a part of the cost of board, and at the same time be taught some trade or industry.

As they went on describing the school, it seemed to me that it must be the greatest place on earth, and not even Heaven presented more attractions for me at that time than did the Hampton Normal and Agricultural Institute in Virginia, about which these men were talking. I resolved at once to go to that school, although I had no idea where it was, or how many miles away, or how I was going to reach it; I remembered only that I was on fire constantly with one ambition, and that was to go to Hampton. This thought was with me day and night.

After hearing of the Hampton Institute, I continued to work for a few months longer in the coal-mine. While at work there, I heard of a vacant position in the household of General Lewis Ruffner, the owner of the salt-furnace and coal-mine. Mrs. Viola Ruffner, the wife of General Ruffner, was a "Yankee" woman from Vermont. Mrs. Ruffner had a reputation all through the vicinity for being very strict with her servants, and especially with the boys who tried to serve her. Few of them had remained with her more than two or three weeks. They all left with the same excuse: she was too strict. I decided, however, that I would rather try Mrs. Ruffner's house than remain in the coal-mine, and so my mother applied to her for the vacant position. I was hired at a salary of $5 per month.

I had heard so much about Mrs. Ruffner's severity that I was almost afraid to see her, and trembled when I went into her presence. I had not lived with her many weeks, however, before I began to understand her. I soon began to learn that, first of all, she wanted everything kept clean about her, that she wanted things done promptly and systematically, and that at the bottom of everything she wanted absolute honesty and frankness. Nothing must be sloven or slipshod; every door, every fence, must be kept in repair.

I cannot now recall how long I lived with Mrs. Ruffner before going to Hampton, but I think it must have been a year and a half. At any rate, I here repeat what I have said more than once before, that the lessons that I learned in the home of Mrs. Ruffner were as valuable to me as any education I have ever gotten anywhere since. Even to this day I never see bits of paper scattered around a house or in the street that I do not want to pick them up at once. I never see a filthy yard that I do not want to clean it, a paling off of a fence that I do not want to put it on, an unpainted or unwhitewashed house that I do not want to paint or whitewash it, or a button off one's clothes, or a grease-spot on them or on a floor, that I do not want to call attention to it.

From fearing Mrs. Ruffner I soon learned to look upon her as one of my best friends. When she found that she could trust me she did so implicitly. During the one or two winters that I was with her she gave me an opportunity to go to school for an hour in the day during a portion of the winter months, but most of my studying was done at night, sometimes alone, sometimes under some one whom I could hire to teach me. Mrs. Ruffner always encouraged and sympathized with me in all my efforts to get an education. It was while living with her that I began to get together my first library. I secured a dry-goods box, knocked out one side of it, put some shelves in it, and began putting into it every kind of book that I could get my hands upon, and called it my "library."

Notwithstanding my success at Mrs. Ruffner's I did not give up the idea of going to the Hampton Institute. In the fall of 1872 I determined to make an effort to get there, although, as I have stated, I had no definite idea of the direction in which Hampton was, or of what it would cost to go there. I do not think that any one thoroughly sympathized with me in my ambition to go to Hampton unless it was my mother, and she was troubled with a grave fear that I was starting out on a "wild-goose chase." At any rate, I got only a half-hearted consent from her that I might start. The small amount of money that I had earned had been consumed by my stepfather and the remainder of the family, with the exception of a very few dollars, and so I had very little with which to buy clothes and pay my traveling expenses. My brother John helped me all that he could, but of course that was not a great deal, for his work was in the coal-mine, where he did not earn much, and most of what he did earn went in the direction of paying the household expenses.

Perhaps the thing that touched and pleased me most in connection with my starting for Hampton was the interest that many of the older coloured people took in the matter. They had spent the best days of their lives in slavery, and hardly expected to live to see the time when they would see a member of their race leave home to attend a boarding-school. Some of these older people would give me a nickel, others a quarter, or a handkerchief.

Finally the great day came, and I started for Hampton. I had only a small, cheap satchel that contained what few articles of clothing I could get. My mother at the time was rather weak and broken in health. I hardly expected to see her again, and thus our parting was all the more sad. She, however, was very brave through it all. At that time there were no through trains connecting that part of West Virginia with eastern Virginia. Trains ran only a portion of the way, and the remainder of the distance was travelled by stage-coaches.

The distance from Malden to Hampton is about five hundred miles. I had not been away from home many hours before it began to grow painfully evident that I did not have enough money to pay my fare to Hampton. One experience I shall long remember. I had been travelling over the mountains most of the afternoon in an old-fashioned stage-coach, when, late in the evening, the coach stopped for the night at a common, unpainted house called a hotel. All the other passengers except myself were whites. In my ignorance I supposed that the little hotel existed for the purpose of accommodating the passengers who travelled on the stage-coach. The difference that the colour of one's skin would make I had not thought anything about. After all the other passengers had been shown rooms and were getting ready for supper, I shyly presented myself before the man at the desk. It is true I had practically no money in my pocket with which to pay for bed or food, but I had hoped in some way to beg my way into the good graces of the landlord, for at that season in the mountains of Virginia the weather was cold, and I wanted to get indoors for the night. Without asking as to whether I had any money, the man at the desk firmly refused to even consider the matter of providing me with food or lodging. This was my first experience in finding out what the colour of my skin meant. In some way I managed to keep warm by walking about, and so got through the night. My whole soul was so bent upon reaching Hampton that I did not have time to cherish any bitterness toward the hotel-keeper.

By walking, begging rides both in wagons and in the cars, in some way, after a number of days, I reached the city of Richmond, Virginia, about eighty-two miles from Hampton. When I reached there, tired, hungry, and dirty, it was late in the night. I had never been in a large city, and this rather added to my misery. When I reached Richmond, I was completely out of money. I had not a single acquaintance in the place, and, being unused to city ways, I did not know where to go. I applied at several places for lodging, but they all wanted money, and that was what I did not have. Knowing nothing else better to do, I walked the streets. In doing this I passed by many food-stands where fried chicken and half-moon apple pies were piled high and made to present a most tempting appearance. At that time it seemed to me that I would have promised all that I expected to possess in the future to have gotten hold of one of those chicken legs or one of those pies. But I could not get either of these, nor anything else to eat.

I must have walked the streets till after midnight. At last I became so exhausted that I could walk no longer. I was tired, I was hungry, I was everything but discouraged. Just about the time when I reached extreme physical exhaustion, I came upon a portion of a street where the board sidewalk was considerably elevated. I waited for a few minutes, till I was sure that no passers-by could see me, and then crept under the sidewalk and lay for the night upon the ground, with my satchel of clothing for a pillow. Nearly all night I could hear the tramp of feet over my head. The next morning I found myself somewhat refreshed, but I was extremely hungry, because it had been a long time since I had had sufficient food. As soon as it became light enough for me to see my surroundings I noticed that I was near a large ship, and that this ship seemed to be unloading a cargo of pig iron. I went at once to the vessel and asked the captain to permit me to help unload the vessel in order to get money for food. The captain, a white man, who seemed to be kind-hearted, consented. I worked long enough to earn money for my breakfast, and it seems to me, as I remember it now, to have been about the best breakfast that I have ever eaten.

My work pleased the captain so well that he told me if I desired I could continue working for a small amount per day. This I was very glad to do. I continued working on this vessel for a number of days. After buying food with the small wages I received there was not much left to add to the amount I must get to pay my way to Hampton. In order to economize in every way possible, so as to be sure to reach Hampton in a reasonable time, I continued to sleep under the same sidewalk that gave me shelter the first night I was in Richmond. Many years after that the coloured citizens of Richmond very kindly tendered me a reception at which there must have been two thousand people present. This reception was held not far from the spot where I slept the first night I spent in that city, and I must confess that my mind was more upon the sidewalk that first gave me shelter than upon the reception, agreeable and cordial as it was.

When I had saved what I considered enough money with which to reach Hampton, I thanked the captain of the vessel for his kindness, and started again. Without any unusual occurrence I reached Hampton, with a surplus of exactly fifty cents with which to begin my education. To me it had been a long, eventful journey; but the first sight of the large, three-story, brick school building seemed to have rewarded me for all that I had undergone in order to reach the place. If the people who gave the money to provide that building could appreciate the influence the sight of it had upon me, as well as upon thousands of other youths, they would feel all the more encouraged to make such gifts. It seemed to me to be the largest and most beautiful building I had ever seen. The sight of it seemed to give me new life. I felt that a new kind of existence had now begun—that life would now have a new meaning. I felt that I had reached the promised land, and I resolved to let no obstacle prevent me from putting forth the highest effort to fit myself to accomplish the most good in the world.

As soon as possible after reaching the grounds of the Hampton Institute, I presented myself before the head teacher for assignment to a class. Having been so long without proper food, a bath and change of clothing, I did not, of course, make a very favourable impression upon her, and I could see at once that there were doubts in her mind about the wisdom of admitting me as a student. I felt that I could hardly blame her if she got the idea that I was a worthless loafer or tramp. For some time she did not refuse to admit me, neither did she decide in my favour, and I continued to linger about her, and to impress her in all the ways I could with my worthiness. In the meantime I saw her admitting other students, and that added greatly to my discomfort, for I felt, deep down in my heart, that I could do as well as they, if I could only get a chance to show what was in me.

After some hours had passed, the head teacher said to me: "The adjoining recitation-room needs sweeping. Take the broom and sweep it."

It occurred to me at once that here was my chance. Never did I receive an order with more delight. I knew that I could sweep, for Mrs. Ruffner had thoroughly taught me how to do that when I lived with her.

I swept the recitation-room three times. Then I got a dusting-cloth and I dusted it four times. All the woodwork around the walls, every bench, table, and desk, I went over four times with my dusting-cloth. Besides, every piece of furniture had been moved and every closet and corner in the room had been thoroughly cleaned. I had the feeling that in a large measure my future depended upon the impression I made upon the teacher in the cleaning of that room. When I was through, I reported to the head teacher. She was a "Yankee" woman who knew just where to look for dirt. She went into the room and inspected the floor and closets; then she took her handkerchief and rubbed it on the woodwork about the walls, and over the table and benches. When she was unable to find one bit of dirt on the floor, or a particle of dust on any of the furniture, she quietly remarked, "I guess you will do to enter this institution."

I was one of the happiest souls on earth. The sweeping of that room was my college examination, and never did any youth pass an examination for entrance into Harvard or Yale that gave him more genuine satisfaction. I have passed several examinations since then, but I have always felt that this was the best one I ever passed.

I have spoken of my own experience in entering the Hampton Institute. Perhaps few, if any, had anything like the same experience that I had, but about that same period there were hundreds who found their way to Hampton and other institutions after experiencing something of the same difficulties that I went through. The young men and women were determined to secure an education at any cost.

The sweeping of the recitation-room in the manner that I did it seems to have paved the way for me to get through Hampton. Miss Mary F. Mackie, the head teacher, offered me a position as janitor. This, of course, I gladly accepted, because it was a place where I could work out nearly all the cost of my board. The work was hard and taxing but I stuck to it. I had a large number of rooms to care for, and had to work late into the night, while at the same time I had to rise by four o'clock in the morning, in order to build the fires and have a little time in which to prepare my lessons. In all my career at Hampton, and ever since I have been out in the world, Miss Mary F. Mackie, the head teacher to whom I have referred, proved one of my strongest and most helpful friends. Her advice and encouragement were always helpful and strengthening to me in the darkest hour.

I have spoken of the impression that was made upon me by the buildings and general appearance of the Hampton Institute, but I have not spoken of that which made the greatest and most lasting impression upon me, and that was a great man—the noblest, rarest human being that it has ever been my privilege to meet. I refer to the late General Samuel C. Armstrong.

It has been my fortune to meet personally many of what are called great characters, both in Europe and America, but I do not hesitate to say that I never met any man who, in my estimation, was the equal of General Armstrong. Fresh from the degrading influences of the slave plantation and the coal-mines, it was a rare privilege for me to be permitted to come into direct contact with such a character as General Armstrong. I shall always remember that the first time I went into his presence he made the impression upon me of being a perfect man: I was made to feel that there was something about him that was superhuman. It was my privilege to know the General personally from the time I entered Hampton till he died, and the more I saw of him the greater he grew in my estimation. One might have removed from Hampton all the buildings, classrooms, teachers, and industries, and given the men and women there the opportunity of coming into daily contact with General Armstrong, and that alone would have been a liberal education. The older I grow, the more I am convinced that there is no education which one can get from books and costly apparatus that is equal to that which can be gotten from contact with great men and women. Instead of studying books so constantly, how I wish that our schools and colleges might learn to study men and things!

General Armstrong spent two of the last six months of his life in my home at Tuskegee. At that time he was paralyzed to the extent that he had lost control of his body and voice in a very large degree. Notwithstanding his affliction, he worked almost constantly night and day for the cause to which he had given his life. I never saw a man who so completely lost sight of himself. I do not believe he ever had a selfish thought. He was just as happy in trying to assist some other institution in the South as he was when working for Hampton. Although he fought the Southern white man in the Civil War, I never heard him utter a bitter word against him afterward. On the other hand, he was constantly seeking to find ways by which he could be of service to the Southern whites.

It would be difficult to describe the hold that he had upon the students at Hampton, or the faith they had in him. In fact, he was worshipped by his students. It never occurred to me that General Armstrong could fail in anything that he undertook. There is almost no request that he could have made that would not have been complied with. When he was a guest at my home in Alabama, and was so badly paralyzed that he had to be wheeled about in an invalid's chair, I recall that one of the General's former students had occasion to push his chair up a long, steep hill that taxed his strength to the utmost. When the top of the hill was reached, the former pupil, with a glow of happiness on his face, exclaimed, "I am so glad that I have been permitted to do something that was real hard for the General before he dies!" While I was a student at Hampton, the dormitories became so crowded that it was impossible to find room for all who wanted to be admitted. In order to help remedy the difficulty the General conceived the plan of putting up tents to be used as rooms. As soon as it became known that General Armstrong would be pleased if some of the older students would live in the tents during the winter, nearly every student in school volunteered to go.

I was one of the volunteers. The winter that we spent in those tents was an intensely cold one, and we suffered severely—how much I am sure General Armstrong never knew, because we made no complaints. It was enough for us to know that we were pleasing General Armstrong, and that we were making it possible for an additional number of students to secure an education. More than once, during a cold night, when a stiff gale would be blowing, our tent was lifted bodily, and we would find ourselves in the open air. The General would usually pay a visit to the tents early in the morning, and his earnest, cheerful, encouraging voice would dispel any feeling of despondency.

I have spoken of my admiration for General Armstrong, and yet he was but a type of that Christlike body of men and women who went into the Negro schools at the close of the war by the hundreds to assist in lifting up my race. The history of the world fails to show a higher, purer, and more unselfish class of men and women than those who found their way into those Negro schools.

Life at Hampton was a constant revelation to me; was constantly taking me into a new world. The matter of having meals at regular hours, of eating on a tablecloth, using a napkin, the use of the bathtub and of the tooth-brush, as well as the use of sheets upon the bed, were all new to me.

I sometimes feel that almost the most valuable lesson I got at the Hampton Institute was in the use and value of the bath. I learned there for the first time some of its value, not only in keeping the body healthy, but in inspiring self-respect and promoting virtue. In all my travels in the South and elsewhere since leaving Hampton I have always in some way sought my daily bath. To get it sometimes when I have been the guest of my own people in a single-roomed cabin has not always been easy to do, except by slipping away to some stream in the woods. I have always tried to teach my people that some provision for bathing should be a part of every house.

For some time, while a student at Hampton, I possessed but a single pair of socks, but when I had worn these till they became soiled, I would wash them at night and hang them by the fire to dry, so that I might wear them again the next morning.

The charge for my board at Hampton was ten dollars per month. I was expected to pay a part of this in cash and to work out the remainder. To meet this cash payment, as I have stated, I had just fifty cents when I reached the institution. Aside from a very few dollars that my brother John was able to send me once in a while, I had no money with which to pay my board. I was determined from the first to make my work as janitor so valuable that my services would be indispensable. This I succeeded in doing to such an extent that I was soon informed that I would be allowed the full cost of my board in return for my work. The cost of tuition was seventy dollars a year. This, of course, was wholly beyond my ability to provide. If I had been compelled to pay the seventy dollars for tuition, in addition to providing for my board, I would have been compelled to leave the Hampton school. General Armstrong, however, very kindly got Mr. S. Griffitts Morgan, of New Bedford, Mass., to defray the cost of my tuition during the whole time that I was at Hampton. After I finished the course at Hampton and had entered upon my lifework at Tuskegee, I had the pleasure of visiting Mr. Morgan several times.

After having been for a while at Hampton, I found myself in difficulty because I did not have books and clothing. Usually, however, I got around the trouble about books by borrowing from those who were more fortunate than myself. As to clothes, when I reached Hampton I had practically nothing. Everything that I possessed was in a small hand satchel. My anxiety about clothing was increased because of the fact that General Armstrong made a personal inspection of the young men in ranks, to see that their clothes were clean. Shoes had to be polished, there must be no buttons off the clothing, and no grease-spots. To wear one suit of clothes continually, while at work and in the schoolroom, and at the same time keep it clean, was rather a hard problem for me to solve. In some way I managed to get on till the teachers learned that I was in earnest and meant to succeed, and then some of them were kind enough to see that I was partly supplied with second-hand clothing that had been sent in barrels from the North. These barrels proved a blessing to hundreds of poor but deserving students. Without them I question whether I should ever have gotten through Hampton.

When I first went to Hampton I do not recall that I had ever slept in a bed that had two sheets on it. In those days there were not many buildings there, and room was very precious. There were seven other boys in the same room with me; most of them, however, students who had been there for some time. The sheets were quite a puzzle to me. The first night I slept under both of them, and the second night I slept on top of both of them; but by watching the other boys I learned my lesson in this, and have been trying to follow it ever since and to teach it to others.

I was among the youngest of the students who were in Hampton at that time. Most of the students were men and women—some as old as forty years of age. As I now recall the scene of my first year, I do not believe that one often has the opportunity of coming into contact with three or four hundred men and women who were so tremendously in earnest as these men and women were. Every hour was occupied in study or work. Nearly all had had enough actual contact with the world to teach them the need of education. Many of the older ones were, of course, too old to master the text-books very thoroughly, and it was often sad to watch their struggles; but they made up in earnestness much of what they lacked in books. Many of them were as poor as I was, and, besides having to wrestle with their books, they had to struggle with a poverty which prevented their having the necessities of life. Many of them had aged parents who were dependent upon them, and some of them were men who had wives whose support in some way they had to provide for.

The great and prevailing idea that seemed to take possession of every one was to prepare himself to lift up the people at his home. No one seemed to think of himself. And the officers and teachers, what a rare set of human beings they were! They worked for the students night and day, in season and out of season. They seemed happy only when they were helping the students in some manner. Whenever it is written—and I hope it will be—the part that the Yankee teachers played in the education of the Negroes immediately after the war will make one of the most thrilling parts of the history of this country. The time is not far distant when the whole South will appreciate this service in a way that it has not yet been able to do.

Chapter VII
Early Days at Tuskegee

During the time that I had charge of the Indians and the night-school at Hampton, I pursued some studies myself, under the direction of the instructors there. One of these instructors was the Rev. Dr. H. B. Frissell, the present Principal of the Hampton Institute, General Armstrong's successor.

In May, 1881, near the close of my first year in teaching the night-school, in a way that I had not dared expect, the opportunity opened for me to begin my life-work. One night in the chapel, after the usual chapel exercises were over, General Armstrong referred to the fact that he had received a letter from some gentlemen in Alabama asking him to recommend some one to take charge of what was to be a normal school for the coloured people in the little town of Tuskegee in that state. These gentlemen seemed to take it for granted that no coloured man suitable for the position could be secured, and they were expecting the General to recommend a white man for the place. The next day General Armstrong sent for me to come to his office, and, much to my surprise, asked me if I thought I could fill the position in Alabama. I told him that I would be willing to try. Accordingly, he wrote to the people who had applied to him for the information, that he did not know of any white man to suggest, but if they would be willing to take a coloured man, he had one whom he could recommend. In this letter he gave them my name.

Several days passed before anything more was heard about the matter. Some time afterward, one Sunday evening during the chapel exercises, a messenger came in and handed the general a telegram. At the end of the exercises he read the telegram to the school. In substance, these were its words: "Booker T. Washington will suit us. Send him at once."

There was a great deal of joy expressed among the students and teachers, and I received very hearty congratulations. I began to get ready at once to go to Tuskegee. I went by way of my old home in West Virginia, where I remained for several days, after which I proceeded to Tuskegee. I found Tuskegee to be a town of about two thousand inhabitants, nearly one-half of whom were coloured. It was in what was known as the Black Belt of the South. In the county in which Tuskegee is situated the coloured people outnumbered the whites by about three to one. In some of the adjoining and near-by counties the proportion was not far from six coloured persons to one white.

I have often been asked to define the term "Black Belt." So far as I can learn, the term was first used to designate a part of the country which was distinguished by the colour of the soil. The part of the country possessing this thick, dark, and naturally rich soil was, of course, the part of the South where the slaves were most profitable, and consequently they were taken there in the largest numbers. Later and especially since the war, the term seems to be used wholly in a political sense—that is, to designate the counties where the black people outnumber the white.

Before going to Tuskegee I had expected to find there a building and all the necessary apparatus ready for me to begin teaching. To my disappointment, I found nothing of the kind. I did find, though, that which no costly building and apparatus can supply,—hundreds of hungry, earnest souls who wanted to secure knowledge.

Tuskegee seemed an ideal place for the school. It was in the midst of the great bulk of the Negro population, and was rather secluded, being five miles from the main line of railroad, with which it was connected by a short line. During the days of slavery, and since, the town had been a centre for the education of the white people. This was an added advantage, for the reason that I found the white people possessing a degree of culture and education that is not surpassed by many localities. While the coloured people were ignorant, they had not, as a rule degraded and weakened their bodies by vices such as are common to the lower class of people in the large cities. In general, I found the relations between the two races pleasant. For example, the largest, and I think at that time the only hardware store in the town was owned and operated jointly by a coloured man and a white man. This copartnership continued until the death of the white partner.

I found that about a year previous to my going to Tuskegee some of the coloured people who had heard something of the work of education being done at Hampton had applied to the state Legislature, through their representatives, for a small appropriation to be used in starting a normal school in Tuskegee. This request the Legislature had complied with to the extent of granting an annual appropriation of two thousand dollars. I soon learned however, that this money could be used only for the payment of the salaries of the instructors, and that there was no provision for securing land, buildings, or apparatus. The task before me did not seem a very encouraging one. It seemed much like making bricks without straw. The coloured people were overjoyed, and were constantly offering their services in any way in which they could be of assistance in getting the school started.

My first task was to find a place in which to open the school. After looking the town over with some care, the most suitable place that could be secured seemed to be a rather dilapidated shanty near the coloured Methodist church, together with the church itself as a sort of assembly-room. Both the church and the shanty were in about as bad condition as was possible. I recall that during the first months of school that I taught in this building it was in such poor repair that, whenever it rained, one of the older students would very kindly leave his lessons and hold an umbrella over me while I heard the recitations of the others. I remember, also, that on more than one occasion my landlady held an umbrella over me while I ate breakfast.

At the time I went to Alabama the coloured people were taking considerable interest in politics, and they were very anxious that I should become one of them politically, in every respect. They seemed to have a little distrust of strangers in this regard. I recall that one man, who seemed to have been designated by the others to look after my political destiny, came to me on several occasions and said, with a good deal of earnestness: "We wants you to be sure to vote jes' like we votes. We can't read de newspapers very much, but we knows how to vote, an' we wants you to vote jes' like we votes." He added: "We watches de white man, and we keeps watching de white man till we finds out which way de white man's gwine to vote; an' when we finds out which way de white man's gwine to vote, den we votes 'xactly de other way. Den we knows we's right."

I am glad to add, however, that at the present time the disposition to vote against the white man merely because he is white is largely disappearing, and the race is learning to vote from principle, for what the voter considers to be for the best interests of both races.

I reached Tuskegee, as I have said, early in June, 1881. The first month I spent in finding accommodations for the school, and in travelling through Alabama, examining into the actual life of the people, especially in the country districts, and in getting the school advertised among the class of people that I wanted to have attend it. The most of my travelling was done over the country roads, with a mule and a cart or a mule and a buggy wagon for conveyance. I ate and slept with the people, in their little cabins. I saw their farms, their schools, their churches. Since, in the case of the most of these visits, there had been no notice given in advance that a stranger was expected, I had the advantage of seeing the real, everyday life of the people.

In the plantation districts I found that, as a rule the whole family slept in one room, and that in addition to the immediate family there sometimes were relatives, or others not related to the family, who slept in the same room. On more than one occasion I went outside the house to get ready for bed, or to wait until the family had gone to bed. They usually contrived some kind of a place for me to sleep, either on the floor or in a special part of another's bed. Rarely was there any place provided in the cabin where one could bathe even the face and hands, but usually some provision was made for this outside the house, in the yard.

The common diet of the people was fat pork and corn bread. At times I have eaten in cabins where they had only corn bread and "black-eye peas" cooked in plain water. The people seemed to have no other idea than to live on this fat meat and corn bread,—the meat, and the meal of which the bread was made, having been bought at a high price at a store in town, notwithstanding the fact that the land all about the cabin homes could easily have been made to produce nearly every kind of garden vegetable that is raised anywhere in the country. Their one object seemed to be to plant nothing but cotton; and in many cases cotton was planted up to the very door of the cabin.

In these cabin homes I often found sewing-machines which had been bought, or were being bought, on installments, frequently at a cost of as much as sixty dollars, or showy clocks for which the occupants of the cabins had paid twelve or fourteen dollars. I remember that on one occasion when I went into one of these cabins for dinner, when I sat down to the table for a meal with the four members of the family, I noticed that, while there were five of us at the table, there was but one fork for the five of us to use. Naturally there was an awkward pause on my part. In the opposite corner of that same cabin was an organ for which the people told me they were paying sixty dollars in monthly installments. One fork, and a sixty-dollar organ!

In most cases the sewing-machine was not used, the clocks were so worthless that they did not keep correct time—and if they had, in nine cases out of ten there would have been no one in the family who could have told the time of day—while the organ, of course, was rarely used for want of a person who could play upon it.

In the case to which I have referred, where the family sat down to the table for the meal at which I was their guest, I could see plainly that this was an awkward and unusual proceeding, and was done in my honour. In most cases, when the family got up in the morning, for example, the wife would put a piece of meat in a frying-pan and put a lump of dough in a "skillet," as they called it. These utensils would be placed on the fire, and in ten or fifteen minutes breakfast would be ready. Frequently the husband would take his bread and meat in his hand and start for the field, eating as he walked. The mother would sit down in a corner and eat her breakfast, perhaps from a plate and perhaps directly from the "skillet" or frying-pan, while the children would eat their portion of the bread and meat while running about the yard. At certain seasons of the year, when meat was scarce, it was rarely that the children who were not old enough or strong enough to work in the fields would have the luxury of meat.

The breakfast over, and with practically no attention given to the house, the whole family would, as a general thing, proceed to the cotton-field. Every child that was large enough to carry a hoe was put to work, and the baby—for usually there was at least one baby—would be laid down at the end of the cotton row, so that its mother could give it a certain amount of attention when she had finished chopping her row. The noon meal and the supper were taken in much the same way as the breakfast.

All the days of the family would be spent after much this same routine, except Saturday and Sunday. On Saturday the whole family would spend at least half a day, and often a whole day, in town. The idea in going to town was, I suppose, to do shopping, but all the shopping that the whole family had money for could have been attended to in ten minutes by one person. Still, the whole family remained in town for most of the day, spending the greater part of the time in standing on the streets, the women, too often, sitting about somewhere smoking or dipping snuff. Sunday was usually spent in going to some big meeting. With few exceptions, I found that the crops were mortgaged in the counties where I went, and that the most of the coloured farmers were in debt. The state had not been able to build schoolhouses in the country districts, and, as a rule, the schools were taught in churches or in log cabins. More than once, while on my journeys, I found that there was no provision made in the house used for school purposes for heating the building during the winter, and consequently a fire had to be built in the yard, and teacher and pupils passed in and out of the house as they got cold or warm. With few exceptions, I found the teachers in these country schools to be miserably poor in preparation for their work, and poor in moral character. The schools were in session from three to five months. There was practically no apparatus in the schoolhouses, except that occasionally there was a rough blackboard. I recall that one day I went into a schoolhouse—or rather into an abandoned log cabin that was being used as a schoolhouse—and found five pupils who were studying a lesson from one book. Two of these, on the front seat, were using the book between them; behind these were two others peeping over the shoulders of the first two, and behind the four was a fifth little fellow who was peeping over the shoulders of all four.

What I have said concerning the character of the schoolhouses and teachers will also apply quite accurately as a description of the church buildings and the ministers.

I met some very interesting characters during my travels. As illustrating the peculiar mental processes of the country people, I remember that I asked one coloured man, who was about sixty years old, to tell me something of his history. He said that he had been born in Virginia, and sold into Alabama in 1845. I asked him how many were sold at the same time. He said, "There were five of us; myself and brother and three mules."

In giving all these descriptions of what I saw during my month of travel in the country around Tuskegee, I wish my readers to keep in mind the fact that there were many encouraging exceptions to the conditions which I have described. I have stated in such plain words what I saw, mainly for the reason that later I want to emphasize the encouraging changes that have taken place in the community, not wholly by the work of the Tuskegee school but by that of other institutions as well.

Chapter VIII
Teaching School in a Stable and a Hen-House

I confess that what I saw during my month of travel and investigation left me with a very heavy heart. The work to be done in order to lift these people up seemed almost beyond accomplishing. I was only one person, and it seemed to me that the little effort which I could put forth could go such a short distance toward bringing about results. I wondered if I could accomplish anything, and if it were worth while for me to try.

Of one thing I felt more strongly convinced than ever, after spending this month in seeing the actual life of the coloured people, and that was that, in order to lift them up, something must be done more than merely to imitate New England education as it then existed. I saw more clearly than ever the wisdom of the system which General Armstrong had inaugurated at Hampton. To take the children of such people as I had been among for a month, and each day give them a few hours of mere book education, I felt would be almost a waste of time.

After consultation with the citizens of Tuskegee, I set July 4, 1881, as the day for the opening of the school in the little shanty and church which had been secured for its accommodation. The white people, as well as the coloured, were greatly interested in the starting of the new school, and the opening day was looked forward to with much earnest discussion. There were not a few white people in the vicinity of Tuskegee who looked with some disfavour upon the project. They questioned its value to the coloured people, and had a fear that it might result in bringing about trouble between the races. Some had the feeling that in proportion as the Negro received education, in the same proportion would his value decrease as an economic factor in the state. These people feared the result of education would be that the Negroes would leave the farms, and that it would be difficult to secure them for domestic service.

The white people who questioned the wisdom of starting this new school had in their minds pictures of what was called an educated Negro, with a high hat, imitation gold eyeglasses, a showy walking-stick, kid gloves, fancy boots, and what not—in a word, a man who was determined to live by his wits. It was difficult for these people to see how education would produce any other kind of a coloured man.

In the midst of all the difficulties which I encountered in getting the little school started, and since then through a period of nineteen years, there are two men among all the many friends of the school in Tuskegee upon whom I have depended constantly for advice and guidance; and the success of the undertaking is largely due to these men, from whom I have never sought anything in vain. I mention them simply as types. One is a white man and an ex-slaveholder, Mr. George W. Campbell; the other is a black man and an ex-slave, Mr. Lewis Adams. These were the men who wrote to General Armstrong for a teacher.

Mr. Campbell is a merchant and banker, and had had little experience in dealing with matters pertaining to education. Mr. Adams was a mechanic, and had learned the trades of shoemaking, harness-making, and tinsmithing during the days of slavery. He had never been to school a day in his life, but in some way he had learned to read and write while a slave. From the first, these two men saw clearly what my plan of education was, sympathized with me, and supported me in every effort. In the days which were darkest financially for the school, Mr. Campbell was never appealed to when he was not willing to extend all the aid in his power. I do not know two men, one an ex-slaveholder, one an ex-slave, whose advice and judgment I would feel more like following in everything which concerns the life and development of the school at Tuskegee than those of these two men.

I have always felt that Mr. Adams, in a large degree, derived his unusual power of mind from the training given his hands in the process of mastering well three trades during the days of slavery. If one goes to-day into any Southern town, and asks for the leading and most reliable coloured man in the community, I believe that in five cases out of ten he will be directed to a Negro who learned a trade during the days of slavery.

On the morning that the school opened, thirty students reported for admission. I was the only teacher. The students were about equally divided between the sexes. Most of them lived in Macon County, the county in which Tuskegee is situated, and of which it is the county-seat. A great many more students wanted to enter the school, but it had been decided to receive only those who were above fifteen years of age, and who had previously received some education. The greater part of the thirty were public-school teachers, and some of them were nearly forty years of age. With the teachers came some of their former pupils, and when they were examined it was amusing to note that in several cases the pupil entered a higher class than did his former teacher. It was also interesting to note how many big books some of them had studied, and how many high-sounding subjects some of them claimed to have mastered. The bigger the book and the longer the name of the subject, the prouder they felt of their accomplishment. Some had studied Latin, and one or two Greek. This they thought entitled them to special distinction.

In fact, one of the saddest things I saw during the month of travel which I have described was a young man, who had attended some high school, sitting down in a one-room cabin, with grease on his clothing, filth all around him, and weeds in the yard and garden, engaged in studying a French grammar.

The students who came first seemed to be fond of memorizing long and complicated "rules" in grammar and mathematics, but had little thought or knowledge of applying these rules to the everyday affairs of their life. One subject which they liked to talk about, and tell me that they had mastered, in arithmetic, was "banking and discount," but I soon found out that neither they nor almost any one in the neighbourhood in which they lived had ever had a bank account. In registering the names of the students, I found that almost every one of them had one or more middle initials. When I asked what the "J" stood for, in the name of John J. Jones, it was explained to me that this was a part of his "entitles." Most of the students wanted to get an education because they thought it would enable them to earn more money as school-teachers.

Notwithstanding what I have said about them in these respects, I have never seen a more earnest and willing company of young men and women than these students were. They were *all* willing to learn the right thing as soon as it was shown them what was right. I was determined to start them off on a solid and thorough foundation, so far as their books were concerned. I soon learned that most of them had the merest smattering of the high-sounding things that they had studied. While they could locate the Desert of Sahara or the capital of China on an artificial globe, I found out that the girls could not locate the proper places for the knives and forks on an actual dinner-table, or the places on which the bread and meat should be set.

I had to summon a good deal of courage to take a student who had been studying cube root and "banking and discount," and explain to him that the wisest thing for him to do first was thoroughly to master the multiplication table.

The number of pupils increased each week, until by the end of the first month there were nearly fifty. Many of them, however, said that, as they could remain only for two or three months, they wanted to enter a high class and get a diploma the first year if possible.

At the end of the first six weeks a new and rare face entered the school as a co-teacher. This was Miss Olivia A. Davidson, who later became my wife. Miss Davidson was born in Ohio, and received her preparatory education in the public schools of that state. When little more than a girl, she heard of the need of teachers in the South. She went to the state of Mississippi and began teaching there. Later she taught in the city of Memphis. While teaching in Mississippi, one of her pupils became ill with smallpox. Every one in the community was so frightened that no one would nurse the boy. Miss Davidson closed her school and remained by the bedside of the boy night and day until he recovered. While she was at her Ohio home on her vacation, the worst epidemic of yellow fever broke out in Memphis, Tenn., that perhaps has ever occurred in the South. When she heard of this, she at once telegraphed the Mayor of Memphis, offering her services as a yellow-fever nurse, although she had never had the disease.

Miss Davidson's experience in the South showed her that the people needed something more than mere book-learning. She heard of the Hampton system of education, and decided that this was what she wanted in order to prepare herself for better work in the South. The attention of Mrs. Mary Hemenway, of Boston, was attracted to her rare ability. Through Mrs. Hemenway's kindness and generosity, Miss Davidson, after graduating at Hampton, received an opportunity to complete a two years' course of training at the Massachusetts State Normal School at Framingham.

Before she went to Framingham, some one suggested to Miss Davidson that, since she was so very light in colour, she might find it more comfortable not to be known as a coloured woman in this school in Massachusetts. She at once replied that under no circumstances and for no considerations would she consent to deceive any one in regard to her racial identity.

Soon after her graduation from the Framingham institution, Miss Davidson came to Tuskegee, bringing into the school many valuable and fresh ideas as to the best methods of teaching, as well as a rare moral character and a life of unselfishness that I think has seldom been equalled. No single individual did more toward laying the foundations of the Tuskegee Institution so as to insure the successful work that has been done there than Olivia A. Davidson.

Miss Davidson and I began consulting as to the future of the school from the first. The students were making progress in learning books and in developing their minds; but it became apparent at once that, if we were to make any permanent impression upon those who had come to us for training, we must do something besides teach them mere books. The students had come from homes where they had had no opportunities for lessons which would teach them how to care for their bodies. With few exceptions, the homes in Tuskegee in which the students boarded were but little improvement upon those from which they had come. We wanted to teach the students how to bathe; how to care for their teeth and clothing. We wanted to teach them what to eat, and how to eat it properly, and how to care for their rooms. Aside from this, we wanted to give them such a practical knowledge of some one industry, together with the spirit of industry, thrift, and economy, that they would be sure of knowing how to make a living after they had left us. We wanted to teach them to study actual things instead of mere books alone.

We found that the most of our students came from the country districts, where agriculture in some form or other was the main dependence of the people. We learned that about eighty-five per cent of the coloured people in the Gulf states depended upon agriculture for their living. Since this was true, we wanted to be careful not to educate our students out of sympathy with agricultural life, so that they would be attracted from the country to the cities, and yield to the temptation of trying to live by their wits. We wanted to give them such an education as would fit a large proportion of them to be teachers, and at the same time cause them to return to the plantation districts and show the people there how to put new energy and new ideas into farming, as well as into the intellectual and moral and religious life of the people.

All these ideas and needs crowded themselves upon us with a seriousness that seemed well-nigh overwhelming. What were we to do? We had only the little old shanty and the abandoned church which the good coloured people of the town of Tuskegee had kindly loaned us for the accommodation of the classes. The number of students was increasing daily. The more we saw of them, and the more we travelled through the country districts, the more we saw that our efforts were reaching, to only a partial degree, the actual needs of the people whom we wanted to lift up through the medium of the students whom we should educate and send out as leaders.

The more we talked with the students, who were then coming to us from several parts of the state, the more we found that the chief ambition among a large proportion of them was to get an education so that they would not have to work any longer with their hands.

This is illustrated by a story told of a coloured man in Alabama, who, one hot day in July, while he was at work in a cotton-field, suddenly stopped, and, looking toward the skies, said: "O Lawd, de cotton am so grassy, de work am so hard, and the sun am so hot dat I b'lieve dis darky am called to preach!"

About three months after the opening of the school, and at the time when we were in the greatest anxiety about our work, there came into the market for sale an old and abandoned plantation which was situated about a mile from the town of Tuskegee. The mansion house—or "big house," as it would have been called—which had been occupied by the owners during slavery, had been burned. After making a careful examination of this place, it seemed to be just the location that we wanted in order to make our work effective and permanent.

But how were we to get it? The price asked for it was very little—only five hundred dollars—but we had no money, and we were strangers in the town and had no credit. The owner of the land agreed to let us occupy the place if we could make a payment of two hundred and fifty dollars down, with the understanding that the remaining two hundred and fifty dollars must be paid within a year. Although five hundred dollars was cheap for the land, it was a large sum when one did not have any part of it.

In the midst of the difficulty I summoned a great deal of courage and wrote to my friend General J. F. B. Marshall, the Treasurer of the Hampton Institute, putting the situation before him and beseeching him to lend me the two hundred and fifty dollars on my own personal responsibility. Within a few days a reply came to the effect that he had no authority to lend me money belonging to the Hampton Institute, but that he would gladly lend me the amount needed from his own personal funds.

I confess that the securing of this money in this way was a great surprise to me, as well as a source of gratification. Up to that time I never had had in my possession so much money as one hundred dollars at a time, and the loan which I had asked General Marshall for seemed a tremendously large sum to me. The fact of my being responsible for the repaying of such a large amount of money weighed very heavily upon me.

I lost no time in getting ready to move the school on to the new farm. At the time we occupied the place there were standing upon it a cabin, formerly used as the dining room, an old kitchen, a stable, and an old hen-house. Within a few weeks we had all of these structures in use. The stable was repaired and used as a recitation-room, and very presently the hen-house was utilized for the same purpose.

I recall that one morning, when I told an old coloured man who lived near, and who sometimes helped me, that our school had grown so large that it would be necessary for us to use the hen-house for school purposes, and that I wanted him to help me give it a thorough cleaning out the next day, he replied, in the most earnest manner: "What you mean, boss? You sholy ain't gwine clean out de hen-house in de *day*-time?"

Nearly all the work of getting the new location ready for school purposes was done by the students after school was over in the afternoon. As soon as we got the cabins in condition to be used, I determined to clear up some land so that we could plant a crop. When I explained my plan to the young men, I noticed that they did not seem to take to it very kindly. It was hard for them to see the connection between clearing land and an education. Besides, many of them had been school-teachers, and they questioned whether or not clearing land would be in keeping with their dignity. In order to relieve them from any embarrassment, each afternoon after school I took my axe and led the way to the woods. When they saw that I was not afraid or ashamed to work, they began to assist with more enthusiasm. We kept at the work each afternoon, until we had cleared about twenty acres and had planted a crop.

In the meantime Miss Davidson was devising plans to repay the loan. Her first effort was made by holding festivals, or "suppers." She made a personal canvass among the white and coloured families in the town of Tuskegee, and got them to agree to give something, like a cake, a chicken, bread, or pies, that could be sold at the festival. Of course the coloured people were glad to give anything that they could spare, but I want to add that Miss Davidson did not apply to a single white family, so far as I now remember, that failed to donate something; and in many ways the white families showed their interest in the school.

Several of these festivals were held, and quite a little sum of money was raised. A canvass was also made among the people of both races for direct gifts of money, and most of those applied to gave small sums. It was often pathetic to note the gifts of the older coloured people, most of whom had spent their best days in slavery. Sometimes they would give five cents, sometimes twenty-five cents. Sometimes the contribution was a quilt, or a quantity of sugarcane. I recall one old coloured woman, who was about seventy years of age, who came to see me when we were raising money to pay for the farm. She hobbled into the room where I was, leaning on a cane. She was clad in rags; but they were clean. She said: "Mr. Washin'ton, God knows I spent de bes' days of my life in slavery. God knows I's ignorant an' poor; but," she added, "I knows what you an' Miss Davidson is tryin' to do. I knows you is tryin' to make better men an' better women for de coloured race. I ain't got no money, but I wants you to take dese six eggs, what I's been savin' up, an' I wants you to put dese six eggs into de eddication of dese boys an' gals."

Since the work at Tuskegee started, it has been my privilege to receive many gifts for the benefit of the institution, but never any, I think, that touched me so deeply as this one.

Chapter XIV
The Atlanta Exposition Address

The Atlanta Exposition, at which I had been asked to make an address as a representative of the Negro race, as stated in the last chapter, was opened with a short address from Governor Bullock. After other interesting exercises, including an invocation from Bishop Nelson, of Georgia, a dedicatory ode by Albert Howell, Jr., and addresses by the President of the Exposition and Mrs. Joseph Thompson, the President of the Woman's Board, Governor Bullock introduced me with the words, "We have with us today a representative of Negro enterprise and Negro civilization."

When I arose to speak, there was considerable cheering, especially from the coloured people. As I remember it now, the thing that was uppermost in my mind was the desire to say something that would cement the friendship of the races and bring about hearty cooperation between them. So far as my outward surroundings were concerned, the only thing I recall distinctly now is that when I got up, I saw thousands of eyes looking intently into my face. The following is the address which I delivered:—

MR. PRESIDENT AND GENTLEMEN OF THE BOARD OF DIRECTORS AND CITIZENS.

One-third of the population of the South is of the Negro race. No enterprise seeking the material, civil, or moral welfare of this section can disregard this element of our population and reach the highest success. I but convey to you, Mr. President and Directors, the sentiment of the masses of my race when I say that in no way have the value and manhood of the American Negro been more fittingly and generously recognized than by the managers of this magnificent Exposition at every stage of its progress. It is a recognition that will do more to cement the friendship of the two races than any occurrence since the dawn of our freedom.

Not only this, but the opportunity here afforded will awaken among us a new era of industrial progress. Ignorant and inexperienced, it is not strange that in the first years of our new life we began at the top instead of at the bottom; that a seat in Congress or the state legislature was more sought than real estate or industrial skill; that the political convention of stump speaking had more attractions than starting a dairy farm or truck garden.

A ship lost at sea for many days suddenly sighted a friendly vessel. From the mast of the unfortunate vessel was seen a signal, "Water, water; we die of thirst!" The answer from the friendly vessel at once came back, "Cast down your bucket where you are." A second time the signal, "Water, water; send us water!" ran up from the distressed vessel, and was answered, "Cast down your bucket where you are." And a third and fourth signal for water was answered, "Cast down your bucket where you are." The captain of the distressed vessel, at last heeding the injunction, cast down his bucket, and it came up full of fresh, sparkling water from the mouth of the Amazon River. To those of my race who depend on bettering their condition in a foreign land or who underestimate the importance of cultivating friendly relations with the Southern white man, who is their next-door neighbour, I would say: "Cast down your bucket where you are"—cast it down in making friends in every manly way of the people of all races by whom we are surrounded.

Cast it down in agriculture, mechanics, in commerce, in domestic service, and in the professions. And in this connection it is well to bear in mind that whatever other sins the South may be called to bear, when it comes to business, pure and simple, it is in the South that the Negro is given a man's chance in the commercial world, and in nothing is this Exposition more eloquent than in emphasizing this chance. Our greatest danger is that in the great leap from slavery to freedom we may overlook the fact that the masses of us are to live by the productions of our hands, and fail to keep in mind that we shall prosper in proportion as we learn to dignify and glorify common labour and put brains and skill into the common occupations of life; shall prosper in proportion as we learn to draw the line between the superficial and the substantial, the ornamental gewgaws of life and the useful. No race can prosper till it learns that there is as much dignity in tilling a field as in writing a poem. It is at the bottom of life we must begin, and not at the top. Nor should we permit our grievances to overshadow our opportunities.

To those of the white race who look to the incoming of those of foreign birth and strange tongue and habits for the prosperity of the South, were I permitted I would repeat what I say to my own race, "Cast down your bucket where you are." Cast it down among the eight millions of Negroes whose habits you know, whose fidelity and love you have tested in days when to have proved treacherous meant the ruin of your firesides. Cast down your bucket among these people who have, without strikes and labour wars, tilled your fields, cleared your forests, builded your railroads and cities, and brought forth treasures from the bowels of the earth, and helped make possible this magnificent representation of the progress of the South. Casting down your bucket among my people, helping and encouraging them as you are doing on these grounds, and to education of head, hand, and heart, you will find that they will buy your surplus land, make blossom the waste places in your fields, and run your factories. While doing this, you can be sure in the future, as in the past, that you and your families will be surrounded by the most patient, faithful, law-abiding, and unresentful people that the world has seen. As we have proved our loyalty to you in the past, in nursing your children, watching by the sick-bed of your mothers and fathers, and often following them with tear-dimmed eyes to their graves, so in the future, in our humble way, we shall stand by you with a devotion that no foreigner can approach, ready to lay down our lives, if need be, in defence of yours, interlacing our industrial, commercial, civil, and religious life with yours in a way that shall make the interests of both races one. In all things that are purely social we can be as separate as the fingers, yet one as the hand in all things essential to mutual progress.

There is no defence or security for any of us except in the highest intelligence and development of all. If anywhere there are efforts tending to curtail the fullest growth of the Negro, let these efforts be turned into stimulating, encouraging, and making him the most useful and intelligent citizen. Effort or means so invested will pay a thousand per cent. interest. These efforts will be twice blessed—"blessing him that gives and him that takes."

There is no escape through law of man or God from the inevitable:—

> The laws of changeless justice bind
> Oppressor with oppressed;
> And close as sin and suffering joined
> We march to fate abreast.

Nearly sixteen millions of hands will aid you in pulling the load upward, or they will pull against you the load downward. We shall constitute one-third and more of the ignorance and crime of the South, or one-third its intelligence and progress; we shall contribute one-third to the business and industrial prosperity of the South, or we shall prove a veritable body of death, stagnating, depressing, retarding every effort to advance the body politic.

Gentlemen of the Exposition, as we present to you our humble effort at an exhibition of our progress, you must not expect overmuch. Starting thirty years ago with ownership here and there in a few quilts and pumpkins and chickens (gathered from miscellaneous sources), remember the path that has led from these to the inventions and production of agricultural implements, buggies, steam-engines, newspapers, books, statuary, carving, paintings, the management of drug-stores and banks, has not been trodden without contact with thorns and thistles. While we take pride in what we exhibit as a result of our independent efforts, we do not for a moment forget that our part in this exhibition would fall far short of your expectations but for the constant help that has come to our educational life, not only from the Southern states, but especially from Northern philanthropists, who have made their gifts a constant stream of blessing and encouragement.

The wisest among my race understand that the agitation of questions of social equality is the extremest folly, and that progress in the enjoyment of all the privileges that will come to us must be the result of severe and constant struggle rather than of artificial forcing. No race that has anything to contribute to the markets of the world is long in any degree ostracized. It is important and right that all privileges of the law be ours, but it is vastly more important that we be prepared for the exercises of these privileges. The opportunity to earn a dollar in a factory just now is worth infinitely more than the opportunity to spend a dollar in an opera-house.

In conclusion, may I repeat that nothing in thirty years has given us more hope and encouragement, and drawn us so near to you of the white race, as this opportunity offered by the Exposition; and here bending, as it were, over the altar that represents the results of the struggles of your race and mine, both starting practically empty-handed three decades ago, I pledge that in your effort to work out the great and intricate problem which God has laid at the doors of the South, you shall have at all times the patient, sympathetic help of my race; only let this be constantly in mind, that, while from representations in these buildings of the product of field, of forest, of mine, of factory, letters, and art, much good will come, yet far above and beyond material benefits will be that higher good, that, let us pray God, will come, in a blotting out of sectional differences and racial animosities and suspicions, in a determination to administer absolute justice, in a willing obedience among all classes to the mandates of law. This, this, coupled with our material prosperity, will bring into our beloved South a new heaven and a new earth.

The first thing that I remember, after I had finished speaking, was that Governor Bullock rushed across the platform and took me by the hand, and that others did the same. I received so many and such hearty congratulations that I found it difficult to get out of the building. I did not appreciate to any degree, however, the impression which my address seemed to have made, until the next morning, when I went into the business part of the city. As soon as I was recognized, I was surprised to find myself pointed out and surrounded by a crowd of men who wished to shake hands with me. This was kept up on every street on to which I went, to an extent which embarrassed me so much that I went back to my boarding-place. The next morning I returned to Tuskegee. At the station in Atlanta, and at almost all of the stations at which the train stopped between that city and Tuskegee, I found a crowd of people anxious to shake hands with me.

The papers in all parts of the United States published the address in full, and for months afterward there were complimentary editorial references to it. Mr. Clark Howell, the editor of the Atlanta *Constitution,* telegraphed to a New York paper, among other words, the following, "I do not exaggerate when I say that Professor Booker T. Washington's address yesterday was one of the most notable speeches, both as to character and as to the warmth of its reception, ever delivered to a Southern audience. The address was a revelation. The whole speech is a platform upon which blacks and whites can stand with full justice to each other."

The Boston *Transcript* said editorially: "The speech of Booker T. Washington at the Atlanta Exposition, this week, seems to have dwarfed all the other proceedings and the Exposition itself. The sensation that it has caused in the press has never been equalled."

I very soon began receiving all kinds of propositions from lecture bureaus, and editors of magazines and papers, to take the lecture platform, and to write articles. One lecture bureau offered me fifty thousand dollars, or two hundred dollars a night and expenses, if I would place my services at its disposal for a given period. To all these communications I replied that my life-work was at Tuskegee; and that whenever I spoke it must be in the interests of the Tuskegee school and my race, and that I would enter into no arrangements that seemed to place a mere commercial value upon my services.

Some days after its delivery I sent a copy of my address to the President of the United States, the Hon. Grover Cleveland. I received from him the following autograph reply:—

GRAY GABLES, BUZZARD'S BAY, MASS.
OCTOBER 6, 1895.

BOOKER T. WASHINGTON, ESQ.:

MY DEAR SIR: I thank you for sending me a copy of your address delivered at the Atlanta Exposition.

I thank you with much enthusiasm for making the address. I have read it with intense interest, and I think the Exposition would be fully justified if it did not do more than furnish the opportunity for its delivery. Your words cannot fail to delight and encourage all who wish well for your race; and if our coloured fellow-citizens do not from your utterances gather new hope and form new determinations to gain every valuable advantage offered them by their citizenship, it will be strange indeed.

Yours very truly,
GROVER CLEVELAND

Later I met Mr. Cleveland, for the first time, when, as President, he visited the Atlanta Exposition. At the request of myself and others he consented to spend an hour in the Negro Building, for the purpose of inspecting the Negro exhibit and of giving the coloured people in attendance an opportunity to shake hands with him. As soon as I met Mr. Cleveland I became impressed with his simplicity, greatness, and rugged honesty. I have met him many times since then, both at public functions and at his private residence in Princeton, and the more I see of him the more I admire him. When he visited the Negro Building in Atlanta he seemed to give himself up wholly, for that hour, to the coloured people. He seemed to be as careful to shake hands with some old coloured "auntie" clad partially in rags, and to take as much pleasure in doing so, as if he were greeting some millionaire. Many of the coloured people took advantage of the occasion to get him to write his name in a book or on a slip of paper. He was as careful and patient in doing this as if he were putting his signature to some great state document.

Mr. Cleveland has not only shown his friendship for me in many personal ways, but has always consented to do anything I have asked of him for our school. This he has done, whether it was to make a personal donation or to use his influence in securing the donations of others. Judging from my personal acquaintance with Mr. Cleveland, I do not believe that he is conscious of possessing any colour prejudice. He is too great for that. In my contact with people I find that, as a rule, it is only the little, narrow people who live for themselves, who never read good books, who do not travel, who never open up their souls in a way to permit them to come into contact with other souls—with the great outside world. No man whose vision is bounded by colour can come into contact with what is highest and best in the world. In meeting men, in many places, I have found that the happiest people are those who do the most for others; the most miserable are those who do the least. I have also found that few things, if any, are capable of making one so blind and narrow as race prejudice. I often say to our students, in the course of my talks to them on Sunday evenings in the chapel, that the longer I live and the more experience I have of the world, the more I am convinced that, after all, the one thing that is most worth living for—and dying for, if need be—is the opportunity of making some one else more happy and more useful.

The coloured people and the coloured newspapers at first seemed to be greatly pleased with the character of my Atlanta address, as well as with its reception. But after the first burst of enthusiasm began to die away, and the coloured people began reading the speech in cold type, some of them seemed to feel that they had been hypnotized. They seemed to feel that I had been too liberal in my remarks toward the Southern whites, and that I had not spoken out strongly enough for what they termed the "rights" of the race. For a while there was a reaction, so far as a certain element of my own race was concerned, but later these reactionary ones seemed to have been won over to my way of believing and acting.

While speaking of changes in public sentiment, I recall that about ten years after the school at Tuskegee was established, I had an experience that I shall never forget. Dr. Lyman Abbott, then the pastor of Plymouth Church, and also editor of the *Outlook* (then the *Christian Union*), asked me to write a letter for his paper giving my opinion of the exact condition, mental and moral, of the coloured ministers in the South, as based upon my observations. I wrote the letter, giving the exact facts as I conceived them to be. The picture painted was a rather black one—or, since I am black, shall I say "white"? It could not be otherwise with a race but a few years out of slavery, a race which had not had time or opportunity to produce a competent ministry.

What I said soon reached every Negro minister in the country, I think, and the letters of condemnation which I received from them were not few. I think that for a year after the publication of this article every association and every conference or religious body of any kind, of my race, that met, did not fail before adjourning to pass a resolution condemning me, or calling upon me to retract or modify what I had said. Many of these organizations went so far in their resolutions as to advise parents to cease sending their children to Tuskegee. One association even appointed a "missionary" whose duty it was to warn the people against sending their children to Tuskegee. This missionary had a son in the school, and I noticed that, whatever the "missionary" might have said or done with regard to others, he was careful not to take his son away from the institution. Many of the coloured papers, especially those that were the organs of religious bodies, joined in the general chorus of condemnation or demands for retraction.

During the whole time of the excitement, and through all the criticism, I did not utter a word of explanation or retraction. I knew that I was right, and that time and the sober second thought of the people would vindicate me. It was not long before the bishops and other church leaders began to make a careful investigation of the conditions of the ministry, and they found out that I was right. In fact, the oldest and most influential bishop in one branch of the Methodist Church said that my words were far too mild. Very soon public sentiment began making itself felt, in demanding a purifying of the ministry. While this is not yet complete by any means, I think I may say, without egotism, and I have been told by many of our most influential ministers, that my words had much to do with starting a demand for the placing of a higher type of men in the pulpit. I have had the satisfaction of having many who once condemned me thank me heartily for my frank words.

The change of the attitude of the Negro ministry, so far as regards myself, is so complete that at the present time I have no warmer friends among any class than I have among the clergymen. The improvement in the character and life of the Negro ministers is one of the most gratifying evidences of the progress of the race. My experience with them, as well as other events in my life, convince me that the thing to do, when one feels sure that he has said or done the right thing, and is condemned, is to stand still and keep quiet. If he is right, time will show it.

In the midst of the discussion which was going on concerning my Atlanta speech, I received the letter which I give below, from Dr. Gilman, the President of Johns Hopkins University, who had been made chairman of the judges of award in connection with the Atlanta Exposition:—

JOHN HOPKINS UNIVERSITY, BALTIMORE,
President's Office, September 30, 1895.

DEAR MR. WASHINGTON: Would it be agreeable to you to be one of the Judges of Award in the Department of Education at Atlanta? If so, I shall be glad to place your name upon the list. A line by telegraph will be welcomed.

Yours very truly,
D.C. GILMAN

I think I was even more surprised to receive this invitation than I had been to receive the invitation to speak at the opening of the Exposition. It was to be a part of my duty, as one of the jurors, to pass not only upon the exhibits of the coloured schools, but also upon those of the white schools. I accepted the position, and spent a month in Atlanta in performance of the duties which it entailed. The board of jurors was a large one, consisting in all of sixty members. It was about equally divided between Southern white people and Northern white people. Among them were college presidents, leading scientists and men of letters, and specialists in many subjects. When the group of jurors to which I was assigned met for organization, Mr. Thomas Nelson Page, who was one of the number, moved that I be made secretary of that division, and the motion was unanimously adopted. Nearly half of our division were Southern people. In performing my duties in the inspection of the exhibits of white schools I was in every case treated with respect, and at the close of our labours I parted from my associates with regret.

I am often asked to express myself more freely than I do upon the political condition and the political future of my race. These recollections of my experience in Atlanta give me the opportunity to do so briefly. My own belief is, although I have never before said so in so many words, that the time will come when the Negro in the South will be accorded all the political rights which his ability, character, and material possessions entitle him to. I think, though, that the opportunity to freely exercise such political rights will not come in any large degree through outside or artificial forcing, but will be accorded to the Negro by the Southern white people themselves, and that they will protect him in the exercise of those rights. Just as soon as the South gets over the old feeling that it is being forced by "foreigners," or "aliens," to do something which it does not want to do, I believe that the change in the direction that I have indicated is going to begin. In fact, there are indications that it is already beginning in a slight degree.

Let me illustrate my meaning. Suppose that some months before the opening of the Atlanta Exposition there had been a general demand from the press and public platform outside the South that a Negro be given a place on the opening programme, and that a Negro be placed upon the board of jurors of award. Would any such recognition of the race have taken place? I do not think so. The Atlanta officials went as far as they did because they felt it to be a pleasure, as well as a duty, to reward what they considered merit in the Negro race. Say what we will, there is something in human nature which we cannot blot out, which makes one man, in the end, recognize and reward merit in another, regardless of colour or race.

I believe it is the duty of the Negro—as the greater part of the race is already doing—to deport himself modestly in regard to political claims, depending upon the slow but sure influences that proceed from the possession of property, intelligence, and high character for the full recognition of his political rights. I think that the according of the full exercise of political rights is going to be a matter of natural, slow growth, not an over-night, gourd-vine affair. I do not believe that the Negro should cease voting, for a man cannot learn the exercise of self-government by ceasing to vote any more than a boy can learn to swim by keeping out of the water, but I do believe that in his voting he should more and more be influenced by those of intelligence and character who are his next-door neighbours.

I know coloured men who, through the encouragement, help, and advice of Southern white people, have accumulated thousands of dollars' worth of property, but who, at the same time, would never think of going to those same persons for advice concerning the casting of their ballots. This, it seems to me, is unwise and unreasonable, and should cease. In saying this I do not mean that the Negro should truckle, or not vote from principle, for the instant he ceases to vote from principle he loses the confidence and respect of the Southern white man even.

I do not believe that any state should make a law that permits an ignorant and poverty-stricken white man to vote, and prevents a black man in the same condition from voting. Such a law is not only unjust, but it will react, as all unjust laws do in time; for the effect of such a law is to encourage the Negro to secure education and property, and at the same time it encourages the white man to remain in ignorance and poverty. I believe that in time, through the operation of intelligence and friendly race relations, all cheating at the ballot box in the South will cease. It will become apparent that the white man who begins by cheating a Negro out of his ballot soon learns to cheat a white man out of his, and that the man who does this ends his career of dishonesty by the theft of property or by some equally serious crime. In my opinion, the time will come when the South will encourage all of its citizens to vote. It will see that it pays better, from every standpoint, to have healthy, vigorous life than to have that political stagnation which always results when one-half of the population has no share and no interest in the Government.

As a rule, I believe in universal, free suffrage, but I believe that in the South we are confronted with peculiar conditions that justify the protection of the ballot in many of the states, for a while at least, either by an educational test, a property test, or by both combined; but whatever tests are required, they should be made to apply with equal and exact justice to both races.

Women's Narrative

JULIA A.J. FOOTE

(1823–1900)

Julia A.J. Foote was one of several black women during the mid-nineteenth century who established the genre of spiritual narratives. Designed to inspire by the example of conversion and sanctification, the narratives also provide clear evidence of the literacy of a portion of the population usually thought to have very limited access to education. Foote, along with such figures as Jarena Lee and Rebecca Cox Jackson, documents the black woman's preaching tradition, black church history, a budding feminism, the impact of slavery on religious endeavor, and the sexism inherent not only in nineteenth-century social practices but in church practices as well. Of historical value, then, Foote's narrative further serves as a clear literary statement in its structure; its creation of characters; and its use of symbolism, images, anecdotes, and biblical references.

Foote was born in Schenectady, New York, in 1823. Her father had been born free, but was stolen and enslaved as a child; her mother was born a slave. Her parents had been converted to the Methodist faith after Foote's mother narrowly escaped drowning in a river. Foote recounts the racism that her mother confronted on one occasion when she went to take communion and was chastised soundly for not having waited until all white persons were served. The nineteenth century was a mixture of temperance and excess; Foote recalls that her parents kept alcohol in the house, and that she got "stupidly drunk" when she was only five years old. She became conscious of religion at the age of eight and learned the Lord's Prayer. Julia also developed a tremendous desire for education; her father taught her the alphabet, and she attended school for a short while, during which she witnessed the lynching, for murder, of one of her schoolteachers. At ten, she was hired out to a local white family that also allowed her some time to attend school. A kindly Methodist minister offered her a few additional lessons once the family moved to Albany. Mostly, however, Foote depended on divine guidance to understand what she read.

Converted to Christianity at the age of fifteen, and sanctified shortly thereafter, the young Julia began to proselytize among her friends and neighbors, many of whom laughed at her efforts. She viewed the loss of sight in one of her eyes as a test of her steadfastness. Called to the ministry after an especially trying experience in which she was comatose at times, the initially reluctant Foote finally consented to preach.

Shortly after she married her husband George, Foote moved with him to Boston, where she met other women who were responsive to her calling. However, her minister, Jehial C. Beman, became a special enemy. Through jealousy, fear, or self-righteousness, he forbade Foote from using his sanctuary to preach her sermons, and he threatened to excommunicate any members of his church who went to other places to hear her. Nonetheless, she was relatively well accepted into the community and preached there for six years, during which her husband, who sometimes thought his wife crazy and sporadically objected to her preaching, got away from it all by going to sea, where he would eventually die during one of his numerous trips. Foote began to extend her preaching into Pennsylvania, other parts of New York, Canada, and Ohio, where she settled in Cleveland, which had been her home for twenty years at the point of the writing of her narrative. She remained firm in her religious conviction despite a throat ailment that prevented her from speaking publicly for several years and an illness that confined her to bed from June to October of 1850.

Throughout her narrative, Foote recites scripture to reinforce the thematic points she makes, and she includes a song near the end. She also writes a section to her "Dear Sisters" and encourages them, in the manner of Paul, to continue their efforts on the Christian battlefield. She concludes the narrative by addressing her fellow Christians and admonishing them to continue in the faith. For those not yet sanctified, she maintains that that state can be attained, through faith, even as they are reading her text. Not one of the most striking in the genre of spiritual narratives, Foote's is nonetheless heartfelt and sincere. Its value to literary scholarship and what it documents in terms of quality of writing, nineteenth-century social and religious trends, and women's issues obviously surpass its attempts to convert its readers.

❖❖❖

The biographical source for Foote's early life and preaching career is Julia A.J. Foote, *A Brand Plucked from the Fire: An Autobiographical Sketch* (1886). See also William L. Andrews, *Sisters of the Spirit: Three Black Women's Autobiographies of the Nineteenth Century* (1986).

FROM *A Brand Plucked from the Fire*

Chapter I
Birth and Parentage

I was born in 1823, in Schenectady, N.Y. I was my mother's fourth child. My father was born free, but was stolen, when a child, and enslaved. My mother was born a slave, in the State of New York. She had one very cruel master and mistress. This man, whom she was obliged to call master, tied her up and whipped her because she refused to submit herself to him, and reported his conduct to her mistress. After the whipping, he himself washed her quivering back with strong salt water. At the expiration of a week she was sent to change her clothing, which stuck fast to her back. Her mistress, seeing that she could not remove it, took hold of the rough tow-linen under-garment and pulled it off over her head with a jerk, which took the skin with it, leaving her back all raw and sore.

This cruel master soon sold my mother, and she passed from one person's hands to another's, until she found a comparatively kind master and mistress in Mr. and Mrs. Cheeseman, who kept a public house.

My father endured many hardships in slavery, the worst of which was his constant exposure to all sorts of weather. There being no railroads at that time, all goods and merchandise were moved from place to place with teams, one of which my father drove.

My father bought himself, and then his wife and their first child, at that time an infant. That infant is now a woman, more than seventy years old, and an invalid, dependent upon the bounty of her poor relatives.

I remember hearing my parents tell what first led them to think seriously of their sinful course. One night, as they were on their way home from a dance, they came to a stream of water, which, owing to rain the night previous, had risen and carried away the log crossing. In their endeavor to ford the stream, my mother made a misstep, and came very nearly being drowned, with her babe in her arms. This nearly fatal accident made such an impression upon their minds that they said, "We'll go to no more dances;" and they kept their word. Soon after, they made a public profession of religion and united with the M. E. Church. They were not treated as Christian believers, but as poor lepers. They were obliged to occupy certain seats in one corner of the gallery, and dared not come down to partake of the Holy Communion until the last white communicant had left the table.

One day my mother and another colored sister waited until all the white people had, as they thought, been served, when they started for the communion table. Just as they reached the lower door, two of the poorer class of white folks arose to go to the table. At this, a mother in Israel caught hold of my mother's dress and said to her, "Don't you know better than to go to the table when white folks are there?" Ah! she did know better than to do such a thing purposely. This was one of the fruits of slavery. Although professing to love the same God, members of the same church, and expecting to find the same heaven at last, they could not partake of the Lord's Supper until the lowest of the whites had been served. Were they led by the Holy Spirit? Who shall say? The Spirit of Truth can never be mistaken, nor can he inspire anything unholy. How many at the present day profess great spirituality, and even holiness, and yet are deluded by a spirit of error, which leads them to say to the poor and the colored ones among them, "Stand back a little—I am holier than thou."

My parents continued to attend to the ordinances of God as instructed, but knew little of the power of Christ to save; for their spiritual guides were as blind as those they led.

It was the custom, at that time, for all to drink freely of wine, brandy and gin. I can remember when it was customary at funerals, as well as at weddings, to pass around the decanter and glasses, and sometimes it happened that the pall-bearers could scarcely move out with the coffin. When not handed round, one after another would go to the closet and drink as much as they chose of the liquors they were sure to find there. The officiating clergyman would imbibe as freely as any one. My parents kept liquor in the house constantly, and every morning sling was made, and the children were given the bottom of the cup, where the sugar and a little of the liquor was left, on purpose for them. It is no wonder, is it, that every one of my mother's children loved the taste of liquor?

One day, when I was but five years of age, I found the blue chest, where the black bottle was kept, unlocked—an unusual thing. Raising the lid, I took the bottle, put it to my mouth, and drained it to the bottom. Soon after, the rest of the children becoming frightened at my actions, ran and told aunt Giney—an old colored lady living in a part of our house—who sent at once for my mother, who was away working. She came in great haste, and at once pronounced me DRUNK. And so I was—stupidly drunk. They walked with me, and blew tobacco smoke into my face, to bring me to. Sickness almost unto death followed, but my life was spared. I was like a "brand plucked from the burning."

Dear reader, have you innocent children, given you from the hand of God? Children, whose purity rouses all that is holy and good in your nature? Do not, I pray, give to these little ones of God the accursed cup which will send them down to misery and death. Listen to the voice of conscience, the woes of the drunkard, the wailing of poverty-stricken women and children, and touch not the accursed cup. From Sinai come the awful words of Jehovah, "No drunkard shall inherit the kingdom of heaven."

Chapter II

Religious Impressions—Learning the Alphabet

I do not remember having any distinct religious impression until I was about eight years old. At this time there was a "big meeting," as it was called, held in the church to which my parents belonged. Two of the ministers called at our house: one had long gray hair and beard, such as I had never seen before. He came to me, placed his hand on my head, and asked me if I prayed. I said, "Yes, sir," but was so frightened that I fell down on my knees before him and began to say the only prayer I knew, "Now I lay me down to sleep." He lifted me up, saying, "You must be a good girl and pray." He prayed for me long and loud. I trembled with fear, and cried as though my heart would break, for I thought he was the Lord, and I must die. After they had gone, my mother talked with me about my soul more than she ever had before, and told me that this preacher was a good man, but not the Lord; and that, if I were a good girl, and said my prayers, I would go to heaven. This gave me great comfort. I stopped crying, but continued to say, "Now I lay me." A white woman, who came to our house to sew, taught me the Lord's prayer. No tongue can tell the joy that filled my poor heart when I could repeat, "Our Father, which art in heaven." It has always seemed to me that I was converted at this time.

When my father had family worship, which was every Sunday morning, he used to sing,

> "Lord, in the morning thou shalt hear
> My voice ascending high."

I took great delight in this worship, and began to have a desire to learn to read the Bible. There were none of our family able to read except my father, who had picked up a little here and there, and who could, by carefully spelling out the words, read a little in the New Testament, which was a great pleasure to him. My father would very gladly have educated his children, but there were no schools where colored children were allowed. One day, when he was reading, I asked him to teach me the letters. He replied, "Child, I hardly know them myself." Nevertheless, he commenced with "A," and taught me the alphabet. Imagine, if you can, my childish glee over this, my first lesson. The children of the present time, taught at five years of age, can not realize my joy at being able to say the entire alphabet when I was nine years old.

I still continued to repeat the Lord's prayer and "Now I lay me," &c., but not so often as I had done months before. Perhaps I had begun to backslide, for I was but a child, surrounded by children, and deprived of the proper kind of teaching. This is my only excuse for not proving as faithful to God as I should have done.

Dear children, with enlightened Christian parents to teach you, how thankful you should be that "from a child you are able to say that you have known the Holy Scriptures, which are able to make you wise unto salvation, through faith which is in Christ Jesus." I hope all my young readers will heed the admonition, "Remember now thy Creator in the days of thy youth," etc. It will save you from a thousand snares to mind religion young. God says: "I love those that love me, and those that seek me early shall find me." Oh! I am glad that we are never too young to pray, or too ignorant or too sinful. The younger, the more welcome. You have nothing to fear, dear children; come right to Jesus.

Why was Adam afraid of the voice of God in the garden? It was not a strange voice; it was a voice he had always loved. Why did he flee away, and hide himself among the trees? It was because he had disobeyed God. Sin makes us afraid of God, who is holy; nothing but sin makes us fear One so good and so kind. It is a sin for children to disobey their parents. The Bible says: "Honor thy father and thy mother." Dear children, honor your parents by loving and obeying them. If Jesus, the Lord of glory, was subject and obedient to his earthly parents, will you not try to follow his example? Lift up your hearts to the dear, loving Jesus, who, when on earth, took little children in his arms, and blessed them. He will help you, if you pray, "Our Father, which art in heaven, thy dear Son, Jesus Christ, my Saviour, did say, 'Suffer little children to come unto me.' I am a little child, and I come to thee. Draw near to me, I pray thee. Hear me, and forgive the many wicked things I have done, and accept my thanks for the many good gifts thou hast given me. Most of all, I thank thee, dear Father, for the gift of thy dear Son, Jesus Christ, who died for me, and for whose sake I pray thee hear my prayer. Amen."

Chapter III
The Primes—Going to School

When I was ten years of age I was sent to live in the country with a family by the name of Prime. They had no children, and soon became quite fond of me. I really think Mrs. Prime loved me. She had a brother who was dying with consumption, and she herself was a cripple. For some time after I went there, Mr. John, the brother, was able to walk from his father's house, which was quite near, to ours, and I used to stand, with tears in my eyes, and watch him as he slowly moved across the fields, leaning against the fence to rest himself by the way. I heard them say he could not live much longer, and that worried me dreadfully; and then I used to wonder if he said his prayers. He always treated me kindly, and often stopped to talk with me.

One day, as he started for home, I stepped up to him and said, "Mr. John, do you say your prayers?" and then I began to cry. He looked at me for a moment, then took my hand in his and said: "Sometimes I pray; do you?" I answered, "Yes, sir." Then said he, "You must pray for me"—and turned and left me. I ran to the barn, fell down on my knees, and said: "Our Father, who art in heaven, send that good man to put his hand on Mr. John's head." I repeated this many times a day as long as he lived. After his death I heard them say he died very happy, and had gone to heaven. Oh, how my little heart leaped for joy when I heard that Mr. John had gone to heaven; I was sure the good man had been there and laid his hand on his head. "Bless the Lord, O my soul, and all that is within me praise his holy name," for good men and good women, who are not afraid to teach dear children to pray.

The Primes being an old and influential family, they were able to send me to a country school, where I was well treated by both teacher and scholars.

Children were trained very differently in those days from what they are now. We were taught to treat those older than ourselves with great respect. Boys were required to make a bow, and girls to drop a courtesy, to any person whom they might chance to meet in the street. Now, many of us dread to meet children almost as much as we do the half-drunken men coming out of the saloons. Who is to blame for this? Parents, are you training your children in the way they should go? Are you teaching them obedience and respect? Are you bringing your little ones to Jesus? Are they found at your side in the house of God, on Sunday, or are they roving the streets or fields? Or, what is worse, are they at home reading books or newspapers that corrupt the heart, bewilder the mind, and lead down to the bottomless pit? Father, mother, look on this picture, and then on the dear children God has given you to train up for lives of usefulness that will fit them for heaven. May the dear Father reign in and rule over you, is the prayer of one who desires to meet you all in heaven.

Chapter IV
My Teacher Hung for Crime

My great anxiety to read the Testament caused me to learn to spell quite rapidly, and I was just commencing to read when a great calamity came upon us. Our teacher's name was John Van Paten. He was keeping company with a young lady, who repeated to him a remark made by a lady friend of hers, to the effect that John Van Paten was not very smart, and she didn't see why this young lady should wish to marry him. He became very angry, and, armed with a shotgun, proceeded to the lady's house, and shot her dead. She fell, surrounded by her five weeping children. He then started for town, to give himself up to the authorities. On the way he met the woman's husband and told him what he had done. The poor husband found, on reaching home, that John's words were but too true; his wife had died almost instantly.

After the funeral, the bereaved man went to the prison and talked with John and prayed for his conversion until his prayers were answered, and John Van Paten, the murderer, professed faith in Christ.

Finally the day came for the condemned to be publicly hung (they did not plead emotional insanity in those days). Everybody went to the execution, and I with the rest. Such a sight! Never shall I forget the execution of my first school-teacher. On the scaffold he made a speech, which I cannot remember, only that he said he was happy, and ready to die. He sang a hymn, the chorus of which was,

"I am bound for the kingdom;
Will you go to glory with me?"

clasping his hands, and rejoicing all the while.

The remembrance of this scene left such an impression upon my mind that I could not sleep for many a night. As soon as I fell into a doze, I could see my teacher's head tumbling about the room as fast as it could go; I would waken with a scream, and could not be quieted until some one came and staid with me.

Never since that day have I heard of a person being hung, but a shudder runs through my whole frame, and a trembling seizes me. Oh, what a barbarous thing is the taking of human life, even though it be "a life for a life," as many believe God commands. That was the old dispensation. Jesus said: "A new commandment I give unto you, that ye love one another." Again: "Resist not evil; but whosoever shall smite thee on thy right cheek, turn to him the other also." Living as we do in the Gospel dispensation, may God help us to follow the precepts and example of Him, who, when he was reviled, reviled not again, and in the agony of death prayed: "Father, forgive them, for they know not what they do." Christian men, vote as you pray, that the legalized traffic in ardent spirits may be abolished, and God grant that capital punishment may be banished from our land.

Chapter XVIII
Heavenly Visitations Again

Nearly two months from the time I first saw the angel, I said that I would do anything or go anywhere for God, if it were made plain to me. He took me at my word, and sent the angel again with this message: "You have I chosen to go in my name and warn the people of their sins." I bowed my head and said, "I will go, Lord."

That moment I felt a joy and peace I had not known for months. But strange as it may appear, it is not the less true, that, ere one hour had passed, I began to reason thus: "I am elected to preach the Gospel without the requisite qualifications, and, besides, my parents and friends will forsake me and turn against me; and I regret that I made a promise." At that instant all the joy and peace I had felt left me, and I thought I was standing on the brink of hell, and heard the devil say: "Let her go! let her go! I will catch her." Reader, can you imagine how I felt? If you were ever snatched from the mouth of hell, you can, in part, realize my feelings.

I continued in this state for some time, when, on a Sabbath evening—ah! that memorable Sabbath evening—while engaged in fervent prayer, the same supernatural presence came to me once more and took me by the hand. At that moment I became lost to everything of this world. The angel led me to a place where there was a large tree, the branches of which seemed to extend either way beyond sight. Beneath it sat, as I thought, God the Father, the Son, and the Holy Spirit, besides many others, whom I thought were angels. I was led before them: they looked me over from head to foot, but said nothing. Finally, the Father said to me: "Before these people make your choice, whether you will obey me or go from this place to eternal misery and pain." I answered not a word. He then took me by the hand to lead me, as I thought, to hell, when I cried out, "I will obey thee, Lord!" He then pointed my hand in different directions, and asked if I would go there. I replied, "Yes, Lord." He then led me, all the others following, till we came to a place where there was a great quantity of water, which looked like silver, where we made a halt. My hand was given to Christ, who led me into the water and stripped me of my clothing, which at once vanished from sight. Christ then appeared to wash me, the water feeling quite warm.

During this operation, all the others stood on the bank, looking on in profound silence. When the washing was ended, the sweetest music I had ever heard greeted my ears. We walked to the shore, where an angel stood with a clean, white robe, which the Father at once put on me. In an instant I appeared to be changed into an angel. The whole company looked at me with delight, and began to make a noise which I called shouting. We all marched back with music. When we reached the tree to which the angel first led me, it hung full of fruit, which I had not seen before. The Holy Ghost plucked some and gave me, and the rest helped themselves. We sat down and ate of the fruit, which had a taste like nothing I had ever tasted before. When we had finished, we all arose and gave another shout. Then God the Father said to me: "You are now prepared, and must go where I have commanded you." I replied, "If I go, they will not believe me." Christ then appeared to write something with a golden pen and golden ink, upon golden paper. Then he rolled it up, and said to me: "Put this in your bosom, and, wherever you go, show it, and they will know that I have sent you to proclaim salvation to all." He then put it into my bosom, and they all went with me to a bright, shining gate, singing and shouting. Here they embraced me, and I found myself once more on earth.

When I came to myself, I found that several friends had been with me all night, and my husband had called a physician, but he had not been able to do anything for me. He ordered those around me to keep very quiet, or to go home. He returned in the morning, when I told him, in part, my story. He seemed amazed, but made no answer, and left me.

Several friends were in, during the day. While talking to them, I would, without thinking, put my hand into my bosom, to show them my letter of authority. But I soon found, as my friends told me, it was in my heart, and was to be shown in my life, instead of in my hand. Among others, my minister, Jehial C. Beman, came to see me. He looked very coldly upon me and said: "I guess you will find out your mistake before you are many months older." He was a scholar, and a fine speaker; and the sneering, indifferent way in which he addressed me, said most plainly: "You don't know anything." I replied: "My gifts are very small, I know, but I can no longer be shaken by what you or any one else may think or say."

Chapter XIX
Public Effort—Excommunication

From this time the opposition to my life-work commenced, instigated by the minister, Mr. Beman. Many in the church were anxious to have me preach in the hall, where our meetings were held at that time, and were not a little astonished at the minister's cool treatment of me. At length two of the trustees got some of the elder sisters to call on the minister and ask him to let me preach. His answer was: "No; she can't preach her holiness stuff here, and I am astonished that you should ask it of me." The sisters said he seemed to be in quite a rage, although he said he was not angry.

There being no meeting of the society on Monday evening, a brother in the church opened his house to me, that I might preach, which displeased Mr. Beman very much. He appointed a committee to wait upon the brother and sister who had opened their doors to me, to tell them they must not allow any more meetings of that kind, and that they must abide by the rules of the church, making them believe they would be excommunicated if they disobeyed him. I happened to be present at this interview, and the committee remonstrated with me for the course I had taken. I told them my business was with the Lord, and wherever I found a door opened I intended to go in and work for my Master.

There was another meeting appointed at the same place, which I, of course, attended; after which the meetings were stopped for that time, though I held many more there after these people had withdrawn from Mr. Beman's church.

I then held meetings in my own house; whereat the minister told the members that if they attended them he would deal with them, for they were breaking the rules of the church. When he found that I continued the meetings, and that the Lord was blessing my feeble efforts, he sent a committee of two to ask me if I considered myself a member of his church. I told them I did, and should continue to do so until I had done something worthy of dismembership.

At this, Mr. Beman sent another committee with a note, asking me to meet him with the committee, which I did. He asked me a number of questions, nearly all of which I have forgotten. One, however, I do remember: he asked if I was willing to comply with the rules of the discipline. To this I answered: "Not if the discipline prohibits me from doing what God has bidden me to do; I fear God more than man." Similar questions were asked and answered in the same manner. The committee said what they wished to say, and then told me I could go home. When I reached the door, I turned and said: "I now shake off the dust of my feet as a witness against you. See to it that this meeting does not rise in judgment against you."

The next evening, one of the committee came to me and told me that I was no longer a member of the church, because I had violated the rules of the discipline by preaching.

When this action became known, the people wondered how any one could be excommunicated for trying to do good. I did not say much, and my friends simply said I had done nothing but hold meetings. Others, anxious to know the particulars, asked the minister what the trouble was. He told them he had given me the privilege of speaking or preaching as long as I chose, but that he could not give me the right to use the pulpit, and that I was not satisfied with any other place. Also, that I had appointed meeting on the evening of his meetings, which was a thing no member had a right to do. For these reasons he said he had turned me out of the church.

Now if the people who repeated this to me told the truth—and I have no doubt but they did—Mr. Beman told an actual falsehood. I had never asked for his pulpit, but had told him and others, repeatedly, that I did not care where I stood—any corner of the hall would do. To which Mr. Beman had answered: "You cannot have any place in the hall." Then I said: "I'll preach in a private house." He answered me: "No, not in this place; I am stationed over all Boston." He was determined I should not preach in the city of Boston. To cover up his deceptive, unrighteous course toward me, he told the above falsehoods.

From his statements, many erroneous stories concerning me gained credence with a large number of people. At that time, I thought it my duty as well as privilege to address a letter to the Conference, which I took to them in person, stating all the facts. At the same time I told them it was not in the power of Mr. Beman, or any one else, to truthfully bring anything against my moral or religious character—that my only offence was in trying to preach the Gospel of Christ—and that I cherished no ill feelings toward Mr. Beman or any one else, but that I desired the Conference to give the case an impartial hearing, and then give me a written statement expressive of their opinion. I also said I considered myself a member of the Conference, and should do so until they said I was not, and gave me their reasons, that I might let the world know what my offence had been.

My letter was slightingly noticed, and then thrown under the table. Why should they notice it? It was only the grievance of a woman, and there was no justice meted out to women in those days. Even ministers of Christ did not feel that women had any rights which they were bound to respect.

Chapter XX
Women in the Gospel

Thirty years ago there could scarcely a person be found, in the churches, to sympathize with any one who talked of Holiness. But, in my simplicity, I did think that a body of Christian ministers would understand my case and judge righteously. I was, however, disappointed.

It is no little thing to feel that every man's hand is against us, and ours against every man, as seemed to be the case with me at this time; yet how precious, if Jesus but be with us. In this severe trial I had constant access to God, and a clear consciousness that he heard me; yet I did not seem to have that plenitude of the Spirit that I had before. I realized most keenly that the closer the communion that may have existed, the keener the suffering of the slightest departure from God. Unbroken communion can only be retained by a constant application of the blood which cleanseth.

Though I did not wish to pain any one, neither could I please any one only as I was led by the Holy Spirit. I saw, as never before, that the best men were liable to err, and that the only safe way was to fall on Christ, even though censure and reproach fell upon me for obeying his voice. Man's opinion weighed nothing with me, for my commission was from heaven, and my reward was with the Most High.

I could not believe that it was a short-lived impulse or spasmodic influence that impelled me to preach. I read that on the day of Pentecost was the Scripture fulfilled as found in Joel ii. 28, 29; and it certainly will not be denied that women as well as men were at that time filled with the Holy Ghost, because it is expressly stated that women were among those who continued in prayer and supplication, waiting for the fulfillment of the promise. Women and men are classed together, and if the power to preach the Gospel is short-lived and spasmodic in the case of women, it must be equally so in that of men; and if women have lost the gift of prophecy, so have men.

We are sometimes told that if a woman pretends to a Divine call, and thereon grounds the right to plead the cause of a crucified Redeemer in public, she will be believed when she shows credentials from heaven; that is, when she works a miracle. If it be necessary to prove one's right to preach the Gospel, I ask of my brethren to show me their credentials, or I can not believe in the propriety of their ministry.

But the Bible puts an end to this strife when it says: "There is neither male nor female in Christ Jesus." Philip had four daughters that prophesied, or preached. Paul called Priscilla, as well as Aquila, his "helper," or, as in the Greek, his "fellow-laborer." Rom. xv. 3; 2 Cor. viii. 23; Phil. ii. 5; 1 Thess. iii. 2. The same word, which, in our common translation, is now rendered a "servent of the church," in speaking of Phebe (Rom. xix. 1.), is rendered "minister" when applied to Tychicus. Eph. vi. 21. When Paul said, "Help those women who labor with me in the Gospel," he certainly meant that they did more than to pour out tea. In the eleventh chapter of First Corinthians Paul gives directions, to men and women, how they should appear when they prophesy or pray in public assemblies; and he defines prophesying to be speaking to edification, exhortation and comfort.

I may further remark that the conduct of holy women is recorded in Scripture as an example to others of their sex. And in the early ages of Christianity many women were happy and glorious in martyrdom. How nobly, how heroically, too, in later ages, have women suffered persecution and death for the name of the Lord Jesus.

In looking over these facts, I could see no miracle wrought for those women more than in myself.

Though opposed, I went forth laboring for God, and he owned and blessed my labors, and has done so wherever I have been until this day. And while I walk obediently, I know he will, though hell may rage and vent its spite.

Chapter XXI

The Lord Leadeth—Labor in Philadelphia

As I left the Conference, God wonderfully filled my heart with his love, so that, as I passed from place to place, meeting one and another of the ministers, my heart went out in love to each of them as though he had been my father; and the language of 1 Pet. i. 7, came forcibly to my mind: "The trial of our faith is much more precious than of gold that perisheth, though it be tried by fire." Fiery trials are not strange things to the Lord's anointed. The rejoicing in them is born only of the Holy Spirit. Oh, praise his holy name for a circumcised heart, teaching us that each trial of our faith hath its commission from the Father of spirits. Each wave of trial bears the Galilean Pilot on its crest. Listen: his voice is in the storm, and winds and waves obey that voice: "It is I; be not afraid." He has promised us help and safety in the fires, and not escape from them.

"And hereby we know that he abideth in us, by the Spirit which he hath given us." I John iii. 24. Glory to the Lamb for the witness of the Holy Spirit! He knoweth that every step I have taken has been for the glory of God and the good of souls. However much I may have erred in judgment, it has been the fault of my head and not of my heart. I sleep, but my heart waketh; bless the Lord.

Had this opposition come from the world, it would have seemed as nothing. But coming, as it did, from those who had been much blessed—blessed with me—and who had once been friends of mine, it touched a tender spot; and had it not been for the precious blood of Jesus, I should have been lost.

While in Philadelphia, attending the Conference, I became acquainted with three sisters who believed they were called to public labors in their Master's vineyard. But they had been so opposed, they were very much distressed and shrank from their duty. One of them professed sanctification. They had met with more opposition from ministers than from any one else.

After the Conference had adjourned, I proposed to these sisters to procure a place and hold a series of meetings. They were pleased with the idea, and were willing to help if I would take charge of the meetings. They apprehended some difficulty, as there had never been a meeting there under the sole charge of women. The language of my heart was:

> "Only Thou my Leader be
> And I still will follow Thee."

Trusting in my Leader, I went on with the work. I hired a large place in Canal Street, and there we opened our meetings, which continued eleven nights, and over one Sabbath. The room was crowded every night—some coming to receive good, others to criticise, sneer, and say hard things against us.

One of the sisters left us after a day or two, fearing that the Church to which she belonged would disown her if she continued to assist us. We regretted this very much, but could only say, "An enemy hath done this."

These meetings were a time of refreshing from the presence of the Lord. Many were converted, and a few stepped into the fountain of cleansing.

Some of the ministers, who remained in the city after the Conference, attended our meetings, and occasionally asked us if we were organizing a new Conference, with a view of drawing out from the churches. This was simply to ridicule our meeting.

We closed with a love-feast, which caused such a stir among the ministers and many of the church-members, that we could not imagine what the end would be. They seemed to think we had well nigh committed the unpardonable sin.

FRANCES JACKSON COPPIN
(1837–1913)

Of all the African American women who came to prominence during the last quarter of the nineteenth century, Frances Jackson Coppin was one of the most renowned. From becoming one of the first black women to graduate from Oberlin College in 1865 until her death in 1913, Frances Coppin was an inspirational achiever and leader to African Americans. The first woman to head the prestigious Institute for Colored Youth (ICY) in Philadelphia, beginning in 1869, she was progressive in strengthening the classical course of study as well as in training students for the industrial professions. An activist who persuaded the Quakers to strengthen their support for the school they had founded, she retained a stronghold of influence until Booker T. Washington's philosophy of industrial education as a primary endeavor for African Americans led the Quakers to lessen their support for her and eventually to transform the ICY into a little Tuskegee.

Jackson's path to Philadelphia had led from her birth as a slave in Washington, D.C., through freedom that her aunt, Sarah Orr Clark, had purchased for her. Determined to get an education and teach black people, Jackson moved from the South to New Bedford, Massachusetts, and from there to Newport, Rhode Island. Her first significant educational opportunity came at the Rhode Island State Normal School, which she attended in the 1850s. In 1860, she enrolled at Oberlin College; her aunt and Bishop Daniel Payne of the A.M.E. Church assisted her financially in this endeavor. Inspired to do well by the consciousness of the burden of her race, Jackson not only succeeded academically, but she was selected to teach in the Preparatory Department of Oberlin College, the first African American student so chosen. White visitors to her class were numerous, astounded by the fact that a black person had such intellectual capacities; indeed, Jackson's appointment was written up in the London *Athenaeum.*

Committed to education, Jackson volunteered to teach newly freed black people how to read and write as they poured into the Oberlin area. Having earned considerable publicity for her efforts, Jackson moved to Philadelphia shortly after her graduation from Oberlin in 1865 and continued her educational mission there. Initially appointed principal of the Female Department of the ICY, Jackson was promoted to principal of the Institute in 1869 when Ebenezer Bassett, the preceding principal, became U.S. Minister to Haiti. Overseen by a board of Quaker Managers, the Institute took pride in its constant stream of visitors and in its highly trained teaching staff.

Jackson set about meeting the increasing needs of African Americans in the Philadelphia area by starting a normal school at the Institute and by abolishing tuition so poorer black students could attend. Remembering her own experiences at Oberlin, she also allowed students to teach in the Preparatory Department. From the Institute, she reached out to the community to become involved in a number of issues, including racial conflicts and voting rights (one of her fellow teachers, O.V. Otto, was killed when he attempted to vote). Writing for the *Christian Recorder* (under the pen name of Catherine Casey), she commented on these issues as well as on the need for employment opportunities for African Americans and for black people to become financially independent. She also commented on issues specifically relevant to black women. When the *Christian Recorder* was threatened with bankruptcy in 1879, she organized sufficient nationwide African American support to stave off that fate. She also taught her students to give one cent a week for charitable purposes, thus enabling them to contribute seventy-five to one hundred dollars to worthy causes at the end of each year. And she let her charity begin in her own actions by renting a house next to hers and paying for it to be used as a dormitory for students from the South when the Quaker Managers refused to undertake a new building.

Married to Levi Jenkins Coppin in December 1881, Coppin defied the usual expectation and continued her principalship even when her husband, an A.M.E. minister, was transferred to Baltimore immediately following their marriage. He did not return to Philadelphia on a permanent basis until 1885, in time to watch Coppin work for the development of an industrial department at the Institute. That came about in 1889, and ten trades were in place by 1900, including sewing, typing, bricklaying, and plastering. This recognition of community needs—and classes at night to accommodate working adults—did not lessen Coppin's interest in classical education. In addition to those already available, she wanted courses to prepare students for medicine and engineering. However, the Quaker Managers were less interested in these developments.

Coppin continued her community work by opening a home for destitute young women in 1888 and by establishing the Women's Exchange and Girls' Home on Twelfth Street in 1894. The home was designed to do what many educational institutions had refused to do—educate and train black women. They learned to cook and sew, and at Mother Bethel, the church pastored by Reverend Levi Coppin, they participated in literary exercises.

As a result of illnesses suffered from her many activities, and the increasing influence of Booker T. Washington's philosophy of education, Coppin was forced to retire from the Institute in June of 1901. Committed to the philosophy that black people should help themselves, Coppin continued to present her views in the *Christian Recorder.* She served on the Board of Managers of the Home for the Aged and Infirm Colored People in Philadelphia from 1881 until 1913. She continued lecturing at churches and organizations of all classes of blacks. In November 1902, Coppin traveled to Cape Town, South Africa, to join her husband, who had been appointed bishop of the A.M.E. Church there. The Coppins returned to Philadelphia in the spring of 1904. Coppin was widely honored by African Americans; in 1909, Coppin State Teachers College in Baltimore was named in her honor. She died of arteriosclerosis on January 21, 1913, the same year in which she published her autobiography, *Reminiscences of School Life, and Hints on Teaching.*

❖❖❖

The renewed interest in African American women's history has brought many significant black women into contemporary focus, including Frances Jackson Coppin. Her life and work are treated in *Black Women in American History,* edited by Darlene Clark Hine, Vol. 3 (1990). Linda M. Perkins, who contributed the article to the Hine volume, has published several additional articles on the life and work of Frances Jackson Coppin. Perkins also completed her dissertation on Coppin at the University of Illinois in 1978.

FROM *Reminiscences of School Life*

I

There are some few points in my life which, "some forlorn and shipwrecked brother seeing, may take heart again."

We used to call our grandmother "mammy," and one of my earliest recollections—I must have been about three years old—is, I was sent to keep my mammy company. It was in a little one-room cabin. We used to go up a ladder to the loft where we slept.

Mammy used to make a long prayer every night before going to bed; but not one word of all she said do I remember except the one word "offspring." She would ask God to bless her offspring. This word remained with me, for, I wondered what offspring meant.

Mammy had six children, three boys and three girls. One of these, Lucy, was my mother. Another one of them, Sarah, was purchased by my grandfather, who first saved money and bought himself, then four of his children. Sarah went to work at six dollars a month, saved one hundred and twenty-five dollars, and bought little Frances, having taken a great liking to her, for on account of my birth, my grandfather refused to buy my mother; and so I was left a slave in the District of Columbia, where I was born. . . .

When my aunt had finally saved up the hundred and twenty-five dollars, she bought me and sent me to New Bedford, Mass., where another aunt lived, who promised to get me a place to work for my board, and get a little education if I could. She put me out to work, at a place where I was allowed to go to school when I was not at work. But I could not go on wash day, nor ironing day, nor cleaning day, and this interfered with my progress. There were no Hamptons, and no night schools then.

Finally, I found a chance to go to Newport with Mrs. Elizabeth Orr, an aunt by marriage, who offered me a home with her and a better chance at school. I went with her, but I was not satisfied to be a burden on her small resources. I was now fourteen years old, and felt that I ought to take care of myself. So I found a permanent place in the family of Mr. George H. Calvert, a great grandson of Lord Baltimore, who settled Maryland. His wife was Elizabeth Stuart, a descendant of Mary, Queen of Scots. Here I had one hour every other afternoon in the week to take some private lessons, which I did. . . . After that, I attended for a few months the public colored school. . . . I thus prepared myself to enter the examination for the Rhode Island State Normal School. . . . the school was then located at Bristol, R.I. Here, my eyes were first opened on the subject of teaching. I said to myself, is it possible that teaching can be made so interesting as this! But, having finished the course of study there, I felt that I had just begun to learn; and, hearing of Oberlin College, I made up my mind to try and get there. I had learned a little music while at Newport, and had mastered the elementary studies of the piano and guitar. My aunt in Washington still helped me, and I was able to pay my way to Oberlin, the course of study there being the same as that at Harvard College. Oberlin was then the only College in the United States where colored students were permitted to study.

The faculty did not forbid a woman to take the gentleman's course, but they did not advise it. There was plenty of Latin and Greek in it, and as much mathematics as one could shoulder. Now, I took a long breath and prepared for a delightful contest. All went smoothly until I was in the junior year in College. Then, one day, the Faculty sent for me—ominous request—and I was not slow in obeying it. It was a custom in Oberlin that forty students from the junior and senior classes were employed to teach the preparatory classes. As it was now time for the juniors to begin their work, the Faculty informed me that it was their purpose to give me a class, but I was to distinctly understand that if the pupils rebelled against my teaching, they did not intend to force it. Fortunately for my training at the normal school, and my own dear love of teaching, tho there was a little surprise on the faces of some when they came into the class, and saw the teacher, there were no signs of rebellion. The class went on increasing in numbers until it had to be divided, and I was given both divisions. One of the divisions ran up again, but the Faculty decided that I had as much as I could do, and it would not allow me to take any more work.

When I was within a year of graduation, an application came from a Friends' school in Philadelphia for a colored woman who could teach Greek, Latin, and higher mathematics. The answer returned was: "We have the woman, but you must wait a year for her."

Then began a correspondence with Alfred Cope, a saintly character, who, having found out what my work in college was, teaching my classes in college, besides sixteen private music scholars, and keeping up my work in the senior class, immediately sent me a check for eighty dollars, which wonderfully lightened my burden as a poor student.

I shall never forget my obligation to Bishop Daniel A. Payne, of the African Methodist Episcopal Church, who gave me a scholarship of nine dollars a year upon entering Oberlin.

My obligation to the dear people of Oberlin can never be measured in words. When President Finney met a new student, his first words were: "Are you a Christian? and if not, why not?" He would follow you up with an intelligent persistence that could not be resisted, until the question was settled.

When I first went to Oberlin I boarded in what was known as the Ladies' Hall, and altho the food was good, yet, I think, that for lack of variety I began to run down in health. About this time I was invited to spend a few weeks in the family of Professor H.E. Peck, which ended in my staying a few years, until the independence of the Republic of Hayti was recognized, under President Lincoln, and Professor Peck was sent as the first U.S. Minister to that interesting country; then the family was broken up, and I was invited by Professor and Mrs. Charles H. Churchill to spend the remainder of my time, about six months, in their family. The influence upon my life in these two Christian homes, where I was regarded as an honored member of the family circle, was a potent factor in forming the character which was to stand the test of the new and strange conditions of my life in Philadelphia. I had been so long in Oberlin that I had forgotten about my color, but I was sharply reminded of it when, in a storm of rain, a Philadelphia street car conductor forbid my entering a car that did not have on it "for colored people," so I had to wait in the storm until one came in which colored people could ride. This was my first unpleasant experience in Philadelphia. Visiting Oberlin not long after my work began in Philadelphia, President Finney asked me how I was growing in grace; I told him that I was growing as fast as the American people would let me. When told of some of the conditions which were meeting me, he seemed to think it unspeakable.

At one time, at Mrs. Peck's, when we girls were sitting on the floor getting out our Greek, Miss Sutherland, from Maine, suddenly stopped, and, looking at me, said: "Fanny Jackson, were you ever a slave?" I said yes; and she burst into tears. Not another word was spoken by us. But those tears seemed to wipe out a little of what was wrong.

I never rose to recite in my classes at Oberlin but I felt that I had the honor of the whole African race upon my shoulders. I felt that, should I fail, it would be ascribed to the fact that I was colored. At one time, when I had quite a signal triumph in Greek, the Professor of Greek concluded to visit the class in mathematics and see how we were getting along. I was particularly anxious to show him that I was as safe in mathematics as in Greek.

I, indeed, was more anxious, for I had always heard that my race was good in the languages, but stumbled when they came to mathematics. Now, I was always fond of a demonstration, and happened to get in the examination the very proposition that I was well acquainted with; and so went that day out of the class with flying colors.

I was elected class poet for the Class Day exercises, and have the kindest remembrance of the dear ones who were my classmates. I never can forget the courtesies of the three Wright brothers; of Professor Pond, of Dr. Lucien C. Warner, of Doctor Kincaid, the Chamberland girls, and others, who seemed determined that I should carry away from Oberlin nothing but most pleasant memories of my life there.

Recurring to my tendency to have shaking agues every fall and spring in Washington, I often used to tell my aunt that if she bought me according to my weight, she certainly had made a very poor bargain. For I was not only as slim as a match, but, as the Irishman said, I was as slim as two matches.

While I was living with Mrs. Calvert at Newport, R.I., I went with her regularly to bathe in the ocean, and after this I never had any more shakes or chills. It was contrary to law for colored persons to bathe at the regular bathing hour, which was the only safe hour to go into the ocean, but, being in the employ of Mrs. Calvert, and going as her servant, I was not prohibited from taking the baths which proved so beneficial to me. She went and returned in her carriage.

After this I began to grow stronger, and take on flesh. Mrs. Calvert sometimes took me out to drive with her; this also helped me to get stronger.

Being very fond of music, my aunt gave me permission to hire a piano and have it at her house, and I used to go there and take lessons. But, in the course of time, it became noticeable to Mrs. Calvert that I was absent on Wednesdays at a certain hour, and that without permission. So, on one occasion, when I was absent, Mrs. Calvert inquired of the cook as to my whereabouts, and directed her to send me to her upon my return that I might give an explanation. When the cook informed me of what had transpired, I was very much afraid that something quite unpleasant awaited me. Upon being questioned, I told her the whole truth about the matter. I told Mrs. Calvert that I had been taking lessons for some time, and that I had already advanced far enough to play the little organ in the Union Church. Instead of being terribly scolded, as I had feared, Mrs. Calvert said: "Well, Fanny, when people will go ahead, they cannot be kept back; but, if you had asked me, you might have had the piano here." Mrs. Calvert taught me to sew beautifully and to darn, and to take care of laces. My life there was most happy, and I never would have left her, but it was in me to get an education and to teach my people. This idea was deep in my soul. Where it came from I cannot tell, for I had never had any exhortations, nor any lectures which influenced me to take this course. It must have been born in me. At Mrs. Calvert's, I was in contact with people of refinement and education. Mr. Calvert was a perfect gentleman, and a writer of no mean ability. They had no children, and this gave me an opportunity to come very near to Mrs. Calvert, doing for her many things which otherwise a daughter would have done. I loved her and she loved me. When I was about to leave her to go to the Normal School, she said to me: "Fanny, will money keep you?" But that deep-seated purpose to get an education and become a teacher to my people, yielded to no inducement of comfort or temporary gain. During the time that I attended the Normal School in Rhode Island, I got a chance to take some private lessons in French, and eagerly availed myself of the opportunity. French was not in the Oberlin curriculum, but there was a professor there who taught it privately, and I continued my studies under him, and so was able to complete the course and graduate with a French essay. Freedmen now began to pour into Ohio from the South, and some of them settled in the township of Oberlin. During my last year at the college, I formed an evening class for them, where they might be taught to read and write. It was deeply touching to me to see old men painfully following the simple words of spelling; so intensely eager to learn. I felt that for such people to have been kept in the darkness of ignorance was an unpardonable sin, and I rejoiced that even then I could enter measurably upon the course in life which I had long ago chosen. Mr. John M. Langston, who afterwards became Minister to Hayti, was then practicing law at Oberlin. His comfortable home was always open with a warm welcome to colored students, or to any who cared to share his hospitality.

I went to Oberlin in 1860, and was graduated in August, 1865, after having spent five and a half years.

The years 1860 and 1865 were years of unusual historic importance and activity. In '60 the immortal Lincoln was elected, and in '65 the terrible war came to a close, but not until freedom for all the slaves in America had been proclaimed, and that proclamation made valid by the victorious arms of the Union party. In the year 1863 a very bitter feeling was exhibited against the colored people of the country, because they were held responsible for the fratricidal war then going on. The riots in New York especially gave evidence of this ill feeling. It was in this year that the faculty put me to teaching.

Of the thousands then coming to Oberlin for an education, a very few were colored. I knew that, with the exception of one here or there, all my pupils would be white; and so they were. It took a little moral courage on the part of the faculty to put me in my place against the old custom of giving classes only to white students. But, as I have said elsewhere, the matter was soon settled and became an overwhelming success. How well do I remember the delighted look on the face of Principal Fairchild when he came into the room to divide my class, which then numbered over eighty. How easily a colored teacher might be put into some of the public schools. It would only take a little bravery, and might cause a little surprise, but wouldn't be even a nine days' wonder.

And now came the time for me to leave Oberlin, and start in upon my work at Philadelphia.

In the year 1837, the Friends of Philadelphia had established a school for the education of colored youth in higher learning. To make a test whether or not the Negro was capable of acquiring any considerable degree of education. For it was one of the strongest arguments in the defense of slavery, that the Negro was an inferior creation; formed by the Almighty for just the work he was doing. It is said that John C. Calhoun made the remark, that if there could be found a Negro that could conjugate a Greek verb, he would give up all his preconceived ideas of the inferiority of the Negro. Well, let's try him, and see, said the fair-minded Quaker people. And for years this institution, known as the Institute for Colored Youth, was visited by interested persons from different parts of the United States and Europe. Here I was given the delightful task of teaching my own people, and how delighted I was to see them mastering Caesar, Virgil, Cicero, Horace and Xenophon's Anabasis. We also taught New Testament Greek. It was customary to have public examinations once a year, and when the teachers were thru examining their classes, any interested person in the audience was requested to take it up, and ask questions. At one of such examinations, when I asked a titled Englishman to take the class and examine it, he said: "They are more capable of examining me, their proficiency is simply wonderful."

One visiting friend was so pleased with the work of the students in the difficult metres in Horace that he afterwards sent me, as a present, the Horace which he used in college. A learned Friend from Germantown, coming into a class in Greek, the first aorist, passive and middle, being so neatly and correctly written at one board, while I, at the same time, was hearing a class recite, exclaimed: "Fanny, I find thee driving a coach and six." As it is much more difficult to drive a coach and six, than a coach and one, I took it as a compliment. But I was especially glad to know that the students were doing their work so well as to justify Quakers in their fair-minded opinion of them. General O.C. Howard, who was brought in at one time by one of the managers to hear an examination in Virgil, remarked that Negroes in trigonometry and the classics might well share in the triumphs of their brothers on the battlefield.

When I came to the School, the Principal of the Institute was Ebenezer D. Bassett, who for fourteen years had charge of the work. He was a graduate of the State Normal School of Connecticut, and was a man of unusual natural and acquired ability, and an accurate and ripe scholar; and, withal, a man of great modesty of character. Many are the reminiscences he used to give of the visits of interested persons to the school: among these was a man who had written a book to prove that the Negro was not a man. And, having heard of the wonderful achievements of this Negro school, he determined to come and see for himself what was being accomplished. He brought a friend with him, better versed in algebra than himself, and asked Mr. Bassett to bring out his highest class. There was in the class at that time Jesse Glasgow, a very black boy. All he asked was a chance. Just as fast as they gave the problems, Jesse put them on the board with the greatest ease. This decided the fate of the book, then in manuscript form, which, so far as we know, was never published. Jesse Glasgow afterwards found his way to the University of Edinburgh, Scotland.

In the year 1869, Mr. Bassett was appointed United States Minister to Hayti by President Grant; leaving the principalship of the Institute vacant. Now, Octavius V. Catto, a professor in the school, and myself, had an opportunity to keep the school up to the same degree of proficiency that it attained under its former Principal and to carry it forward as much as possible.

About this time we were visited by a delegation of school commissioners, seeking teachers for schools in Delaware, Maryland and New Jersey. These teachers were not required to know and teach the classics, but they were expected to come into an examination upon the English branches, and to have at their tongue's end the solution of any abstruse problem in the three R's which their examiners might be inclined to ask them. And now, it seemed best to give up the time spent in teaching Greek and devote it to the English studies.

As our young people were now about to find a ready field in teaching, it was thought well to introduce some text books on school management, and methods of teaching, and thoroughly prepare our students for normal work. At this time our faculty was increased by the addition of Richard T. Greener, a graduate of Harvard College, who took charge of the English Department, and Edward Bouchet, a graduate of Yale College, and also of the Sheffield Scientific School, who took charge of the scientific department. Both of these young men were admirably fitted for their work. And, with Octavius V. Catto in charge of the boys' department, and myself in charge of the girls—in connection with the principalship of the school—we had a strong working force.

I now instituted a course in normal training, which at first consisted only of a review of English studies, with the theory of teaching, school management and methods. But the inadequacy of this course was so apparent that when it became necessary to reorganize the Preparatory Departments, it was decided to put this work into the hands of the normal students, who would thus have ample practice in teaching and governing under daily direction and correction. These students became so efficient in their work that they were sought for and engaged to teach long before they finished their course of study.

Richard Humphreys, the Friend—Quaker—who gave the first endowment with which to found the school, stipulated that it should not only teach higher literary studies, but that a Mechanical and Industrial Department, including Agriculture, should come within the scope of its work. The wisdom of this thoughtful and far-seeing founder has since been amply demonstrated. At the Centennial Exhibition in 1876, the foreign exhibits of work done in trade schools opened the eyes of the directors of public education in America as to the great lack existing in our own system of education. If this deficiency was apparent as it related to the white youth of the country, it was far more so as it related to the colored.

In Philadelphia, the only place at the time where a colored boy could learn a trade, was in the House of Refuge, or the Penitentiary!

And now began an eager and intensely earnest crusade to supply this deficiency in the work of the Institute for Colored Youth.

The teachers of the Institute now vigorously applied their energies in collecting funds for the establishment of an Industrial Department, and in this work they had the encouragement of the managers of the school, who were as anxious as we that the greatly needed department should be established.

In instituting this department, a temporary organization was formed, with Mr. Theodore Starr as President, Miss Anna Hallowell as Tresurer, and myself as Field Agent.

The Academic Department of the Institute had been so splendidly successful in proving that the Negro youth was equally capable as others in mastering a higher education, that no argument was necessary to establish its need, but the broad ground of education by which the masses must become self-supporting was, to me, a matter of painful anxiety. Frederick Douglass once said, it was easier to get a colored boy into a lawyer's office than into a blacksmith shop; and on account of the inflexibility of the Trades Unions, this condition of affairs still continues, making it necessary for us to have our own "blacksmith shop."

The minds of our people had to be enlightened upon the necessity of industrial education.

Before all the literary societies and churches where they would hear me; in Philadelphia and the suburban towns; in New York, Washington and everywhere, when invited to speak, I made that one subject my theme. To equip an industrial plant is an expensive thing, and knowing that much money would be needed, I made it a rule to take up a collection wheresoever I spoke. But I did not urge anyone to give more than a dollar, for the reason I wanted the masses to have an opportunity to contribute their small offerings, before going to those who were able to give larger sums. . . .

In preparing for the industrial needs of the boys, the girls were not neglected. It was not difficult to find competent teachers of sewing and cooking for the girls.

Dressmaking on the Taylor system was introduced with great success, and cooking was taught by the most improved methods.

As the work advanced, other trades were added, and those already undertaken were expanded and perfected.

When the Industrial Department was fully established, the following trades were being taught: For boys: bricklaying, plastering, carpentry, shoemaking, printing and tailoring. For the girls: dressmaking, millinery, typewriting, stenography and classes in cooking, including both boys and girls. Stenography and typewriting were also taught the boys, as well as the girls.

Having taught certain trades, it was now necessary to find work for those who had learned them, which proved to be no easy task.

It was decided to put on exhibition, in one of the rooms of the dormitory, specimens of the work of our girls in any trade in which they had become proficient, and we thus started an Industrial Exchange for their work. Those specimens consisted of work from the sewing, millinery and cooking departments. . . .

Our white friends were invited to come and inspect the work of the Exchange. Some of the exhibits were found to be highly creditable, and many encouraging words were given to those who prepared them. There is one class of women, for whom no trades are provided, but who are expected to do their work without any special preparation; and these are the women in domestic service. I have always felt a deep sympathy with such persons, for I believe that they are capable of making a most honorable record. I therefore conceived a plan of holding some receptions for them, where the honorableness of their work and the necessity of doing it well might be discussed. I earnestly hoped that no one should be ashamed of the word servant, but should learn what great opportunity for doing good there is for those who serve others.

There is, and always must be, a large number of people who must depend upon this class of employment for a living, and there is every reason, therefore, why they should be especially prepared for it. A woman should not only know how to cook in an ordinary way, but she should have some idea of the chemical properties of the food she cooks. The health of those whom she serves depends much upon the nutritive qualities of the food which she prepares. It is possible to burn all the best out of a beefsteak, and leave a pork chop with those elements which should have been neutralized by thorough cooking.

A housemaid should know enough about sanitation to appreciate the difference between well ventilated sleeping rooms and those where impure air prevails.

I have often thought, as I sat in churches, that janitors should be better prepared for their work by being taught the difference between pure air and air with a strong infusion of coal gas. . . .

As a means of preparation for this work, which I may call an Industrial Crusade, I studied Political Economy for two years under Dr. William Elder, who was a disciple of Mr. Henry C. Carey, the eminent writer on the doctrine of Protective Tariff.

In the year 1879 the Board of Education of Philadelphia, instructed and admonished by the exhibit of work done in the schools of Europe, as exhibited in the Centennial exhibition of '76, began to consider what they were doing to train their young people in the industrial arts and trades. The comparison was not very gratifying. The old apprenticeship system had silently glided away, and merchants declared that under the pressure of competition they were not able to compete with other merchants, nor were they able to stand the waste made by those who did not know how to handle the new material economically. At a meeting of some of the public school directors and heads of some of the educational institutions, I was asked to tell what was being done in Philadelphia for the industrial education of the colored youth. It may well be understood I had a tale to tell. And I told them the only places in the city where a colored boy could learn a trade was in the House of Refuge or the Penitentiary, and the sooner he became incorrigible and got into the Refuge, or committed a crime and got into the Penitentiary, the more promising it would be for his industrial training. It was to me a serious occasion. I so expressed myself. As I saw building after building going up in this city, and not a single colored hand employed in the constructions, it made the occasion a very serious one to me. . . .

The next day Mrs. Elizabeth Whitney, the wife of one of the school directors, drove up to my school and said: Mrs. Coppin, I was there last night and heard what you had to say about the limitations of the colored youth, and I am here to say, if the colored people will go ahead and start a school for the purpose of having the colored youth taught this greatly needed education, you will find plenty of friends to help you. Here are fifty dollars to get you started, and you will find as much behind it as you need.

We only needed a feather's weight of encouragment to take up the burden. We started out at once. . . .

We carried on an industrial crusade which never ended until we saw a building devoted to the purpose of teaching trades. For the managers of the Institute, seeing the need of the work, threw themselves into this new business, after their thirty previous years working for the colored youth. Our money in the end amounted to nearly three thousand dollars, and of this we have always been justly very glad. . . . Three thousand dollars was a mere drop in the bucket, but it was a great deal to us, who had seen it collected in small sums—quarters, dollars, etc. It was a delightful scene to us to pass thru that school where ten trades were being taught, altho in primitive fashion, the limited means of the Institute precluding the use of machinery. The managers always refused to take any money from the State, altho it was frequently offered.

Many were the ejaculations of satisfaction at this busy hive of industry. "Ah," said some, "this is the way the school should have begun, the good Quaker people began at the wrong end." Not so, for when they began this school, the whole South was a great industrial plant where the fathers taught the sons and the mothers taught the daughters, but the mind was left in darkness. . . .

In the fall of the same year, namely, in November, '79, as a means of bringing the idea of industrial education and self help practically before the colored people of the United States, I undertook the work of helping an enterprise, namely, *The Christian Recorder*, edited and published by colored men at 631 Pine Street, Philadelphia. I here reproduce the plea made thirty-four years ago:

The Publication Department of *The Christian Recorder* is weighed down by a comparatively small debt, which cripples its usefulness and thus threatenes its existence. This paper finds its way into many a dark hamlet in the South, where no one ever heard of the Philadelphia *Bulletin* or the *New York Tribune*. A persistent vitality has kept this paper alive thru a good deal of thick and thin since 1852. In helping to pay this debt we shall also help to keep open an honorable vocation to colored men who, if they will be printers, must "shinny on their own side." Knowing the conditions of the masses of our people, no large sums were asked for; the people were requested to club together and send on a number of little gifts, which might be at a stated time exhibited and sold at a fair. And thus the debt liquidated by a co-operative effort would be an instructive lesson of how light a burden becomes when borne by the many instead of the few. . . . The great lesson to be taught by this fair is the value of co-operative effort to make our cents dollars, and to show us what help there is for ourselves in ourselves. That the colored people of this country have enough money to materially alter their financial condition, was clearly demonstrated by the millions of dollars deposited in the Freedman's Bank, that they have the good sense, and the unanimity to use this power is now proven by this industrial exhibition and fair. It strikes me that much of the talk about the exodus has proceeded upon the high-handed assumption that, owing largely to the credit system of the South, the colored people there are forced to the alternative to "curse God, and die," or else "go West." Not a bit of it. The people of the South, it is true, cannot produce hundreds of dollars, but they have millions of pennies; and millions of pennies make tens of thousands of dollars. By clubbing together and lumping their pennies, a fund might be raised in the cities of the South that the poorer classes might fall back upon while their crops are growing, or else by the opening of co-operative stores become their own creditors and so effectually rid themselves of their merciless extortioners. "O, they won't do anything; you can't get them united on anything!" The best way for a man to prove that he can do a thing is to do it, and that is what we have done. This fair, participated in by twenty-four States in the Union, and got up for a purpose which is of no pecuniary benefit to those concerned in it, effectually silences all slanders about "we won't or we can't do," and teaches its own instructive and greatly needed lessons of self-help, the best help that any man can have, next to God's.

Those who have this matter in charge have studiously avoided preceding it with noisy and demonstrative babblings, which are so often the vapid precursors of promises as empty as themselves; therefore in some quarters our fair has been overlooked. It is not, we think, a presumptuous interpretation of this great movement, to say that the voice of God now seems to utter, "Speak to the people that they go forward." "Go forward" in what respect? Teach the millions of poor colored laborers of the South how much power they have in themselves, by co-operation of effort, and by a combination of their small means to change the despairing poverty which now drives them from their homes, and makes them a millstone around the neck of any community, South or West. Secondly, that we shall go forward in asking to enter the same employments which other people enter. Within the past ten years we have made almost no advance in getting our youth into industrial and business occupations. It is just as hard to get a boy into a printing office now as it was ten years ago. It is simply astonishing when we consider how many of the common vocations of life colored people are shut out of. Colored men are not admitted to the Printers' Trade Union, nor, with very rare exceptions, are they employed in any city of the United States in a paid capacity as printers or writers, one of the rare exceptions being the employment of H. Price Williams, on the Sunday *Press* of this city. We are not employed as salesmen, or pharmacists, or saleswomen, or bank clerks, or merchants' clerks, or tradesmen, or mechanics, or telegraph operators, or to any degree as State or Government officials, and I could keep on with the string of "ors" until tomorrow morning, but the patience of a reader has its limit.

Slavery made us poor, and its gloomy, malicious shadow tends to keep us so. I beg to say, kind reader, that this is not spoken in a spirit of recrimination; we have no quarrel with our fate, and we leave your Christianity to yourself. Our faith is firmly fixed in that "Eternal Providence," that in its own good time will "justify the ways of God to man." But, believing that to get the right men into the right places is a "consummation most devoutly to be wished," it is a matter of serious concern to us to see our youth, with just as decided diversity of talent as any other people, all herded together into three or four occupations. It is cruel to make a teacher or a preacher of a man who ought to be a printer or a blacksmith, and that is exactly what we are now obliged to do. The most advance that has been made since the war has been done by political parties, and it is precisely into political positions that we think it least desirable that our youth should enter. We have our choice of the professions, but, as we have not been endowed with a monopoly of brains, it is not probable that we can contribute to the bar a great lawyer, except once in a great while. The same may be said of medicine; nor are we able to tide over the "starving time," between the reception of a diploma and the time that a man's profession becomes a paying one.

Being determined to know whether this industrial and business ostracism was "in ourselves or in our stars," we have from time to time, knocked, shaken and kicked at these closed doors of work. A cold, metallic voice from within replies, "We do not employ colored people." Ours not to make reply, ours not to question why. Thank heaven, we are not obliged to do and die, having the preference to do or die, we naturally prefer to do. But we can not help wondering if some ignorant or faithless steward of God's work and God's money hasn't blundered. It seems necessary that we should make known to the good men and women who are so solicitous about our souls and our minds that we haven't quite got rid of our bodies yet, and until we do we must feed and clothe them; and this thing of keeping us out of work forces us back upon charity. That distinguished thinker, Mr. Henry C. Carey, in his valuable works on Political Economy, has shown by the truthful and irresistible logic of history that the elevation of all peoples to a higher moral and intellectual plane, and to a fuller investiture of their civil rights has always steadily kept pace with the improvements in their physical condition. Therefore we feel that resolutely and in unmistakable language, yet in the dignity of moderation, we should strive to make known to all men the justice of our claims to the same employments as other men under the same conditions. We do not ask that any one of our people shall be put into a position because he is a colored person, but we do most emphatically ask that he shall not be kept out of a position because he is a colored person. "An open field and no favors" is all that is requested.

The Novel, or Neo-Slave Narrative

PAULINE ELIZABETH HOPKINS

(1859–1930)

A multitalented woman who worked in several creative genres, Pauline Elizabeth Hopkins has in recent years begun to receive the critical attention that is her due. In addition to writing novels, Hopkins edited a significant magazine at the turn of the twentieth century and managed and participated in a troupe of stage performers. She was proficient in stenography as well as in promoting the *Colored American* magazine, for which she served as literary editor between 1903 and 1904.

Although the exact day of her birth is not known, it is known that Hopkins was born in 1859 in Portland, Maine, to Northrup and Sarah Allen Hopkins. Her father had migrated from Virginia to the Northeast, and her mother, a New Englander, was the grandniece of poet James M. Whitfield as well as a descendant of Nathaniel and Thomas Paul, who founded Baptist churches in Boston. The family moved to Boston, and Pauline attended the public schools in that city. When she was fifteen, she won a writing contest that had been sanctioned by William Wells Brown, abolitionist, novelist, and temperance lecturer. Hopkins's winning entry was an essay titled "Evils of Intemperance and Their Remedies," for which she won ten dollars. She graduated from Girls High School in Boston.

Hopkins completed two musical dramas in the 1870s—*Colored Aristocracy* (1877) and *Slaves' Escape: or the Underground Railroad* (1879); Hopkins's Colored Troubadours performed *Slaves' Escape* at the Oakland Garden on July 5, 1880. The Troubadours included Hopkins's mother and stepfather, and Hopkins sang and played a central role. Good reviews led to more productions of the play and to a revision in which Hopkins changed the title to *Peculiar Sam, or the Underground Railroad.* She traveled and performed with her family group until 1892, when she completed a course in stenography and worked in that profession for several years, including a four-year stint in the Bureau of Statistics, where she worked on the Massachusetts Decennial Census of 1895.

With the founding of the *Colored American* magazine in 1900, Hopkins pursued her writing career more actively. The first issue included her short story, "The Mystery Within Us." Over the next eight years, she would publish six more short stories in the journal (at least one under a pen name), and three serialized novels. The same company that published the journal, the Colored Cooperative Publishing Company of Boston, also published *Contending Forces* (1900), the novel for which Hopkins is best known today. The novel's entangled plot tells the story of a mulatto brother and sister, Will and Dora Smith, and Sappho Clark, a beautiful octoroon who boards with the Smith family. A story of lost love, villainy, and the ultimate triumph and reuniting of separated lovers, the novel uses the conventions of the domestic fiction of the late nineteenth century.

The *Colored American* magazine, for which Hopkins would work as literary editor beginning in 1903, published two of her short stories, "Talma Gordon" and "George Washington, A Christmas Story," in its October and December 1900 issues. The first of three of her novels was serialized beginning in March 1901. She wrote *Hagar's Daughter, A story of Southern Caste Prejudice* under the pen name of Sarah A. Allen. *Winona: A Tale of Negro Life in the South and Southwest* was serialized from May until October 1902, and *Of One Blood; or, The Hidden Self* was serialized between November 1902 and November 1903. All of the novels reflect tangled family trees and love relationships, and various kinds of villainy.

Hopkins's stories carried some of her novelistic themes and introduced others. "A Dash for Liberty" continued her interest in the escape theme for tales set in slavery; it appeared in the August 1901 issue of the *Colored American.* "Bro'r Abr'm Jimson's Wedding, a Christmas Story" appeared in December 1901, and "As the Lord Lives, He is One of Our Mother's Children" appeared in the November 1903 issue of the journal.

In her role as literary editor, Hopkins initiated a biographical series, "Famous Men of the Negro Race" and "Famous Women of the Negro Race." Among the men so named were William Wells Brown, Blanche K. Bruce, Frederick Douglass, and Charles Lenox Remond; the women included Frances Jackson Coppin, Frances E.W. Harper, Sojourner Truth, and Harriet Tubman. Hopkins also worked in a promotional capacity for the magazine by founding the Colored American League in Boston for that purpose. In 1904, she also traveled throughout the country promoting the magazine and trying to get additional support for it.

When the magazine began increasingly to reflect the philosophy of Booker T. Washington and was purchased by Fred R. Moore, a Washington supporter, and moved to New York City (with Washington's financial assistance), Hopkins became uncomfortable with its editorial policies. It was probably suggested to her that her attitudes were not in keeping with Washington's philosphy and that she should probably consider work elsewhere. However, the official reason for Hopkins terminating her relationship with the magazine in September 1904 was "illness." Though no longer with the magazine, Hopkins continued other writing projects. She published "The Dark Races of the Twentieth Century," a sociocultural survey, in the *Voice of the Negro* in 1905. It was also in 1905 that she started her own publishing company and printed her history, *A Primer of Facts Pertaining to the Early Greatness of the African Race and the Possibility of Restoration by Its Descendants—with Epilogue.* In 1916, *New Era,* which Hopkins, along with Walter Wallace, had founded, published her final work, a novella titled *Topsy Templeton.* During the 1920s, Hopkins returned to her career as a stenographer, including working for the Massachusetts Institute of Technology. On August 13, 1930, her life came to a dramatic end when flannel bandages soaked with liniment, which she was wearing to relieve neuritis, caught fire from the oil stove in her room.

❖❖❖

New editions of Hopkins's work attest to her steady rediscovery over the past few years. *Contending Forces* is included in the Schomburg Library of Nineteenth-Century Black Women Writers (1988), with an introduction by Richard Yarborough. *The Magazine Novels of Pauline Hopkins,* with an introduction by Hazel Carby, is also one of the Schomburg volumes. Renewed interest in Hopkins's work over the past couple of decades was perhaps inspired by Ann Allen Shockley's "Pauline Elizabeth Hopkins: A Biographical Excursion into Obscurity," *Phylon* 33(1972), and more recently by Claudia Tate's "Pauline Hopkins: Our Literary Foremother," in *Conjuring: Black Women, Fiction, and Literary Tradition,* edited by Marjorie Pryse and Hortense J. Spillers (1985). Jane Campbell completed a biographical essay for the *Dictionary of Literary Biography* (1986) and headnotes for the Hopkins selections included in the *Heath Anthology of American Literature* (1989).

Hopkins's papers are in the Fisk University Library in Nashville, Tennessee.

FROM *Contending Forces*

Preface

In giving this little romance expression in print, I am not actuated by a desire for notoriety or for profit, but to do all that I can in an humble way to raise the stigma of degradation from my race.

While I make no apology for my somewhat abrupt and daring venture within the wide field of romantic literature, I ask the kind indulgence of the generous public for the many crudities which I know appear in the work, and their approval of whatever may impress them as being of value to the Negro race and to the world at large.

The colored race has historians, lecturers, ministers, poets, judges and lawyers,—men of brilliant intellects who have arrested the favorable attention of this busy, energetic nation. But, after all, it is the simple, homely tale, unassumingly told, which cements the bond of brotherhood among all classes and all complexions.

Fiction is of great value to any people as a preserver of manners and customs—religious, political and social. It is a record of growth and development from generation to generation. *No one will do this for us; we must ourselves develop the men and women who will faithfully portray the inmost thoughts and feelings of the Negro with all the fire and romance which lie dormant in our history,* and, as yet, unrecognized by writers of the Anglo-Saxon race.

The incidents portrayed in the early chapters of the book actually occurred. Ample proof of this may be found in the archives of the courthouse at Newberne, N.C., and at the national seat of government, Washington, D.C.

In these days of mob violence, when lynch-law is raising its head like a venomous monster, more particularly in the southern portion of the great American republic, the retrospective mind will dwell upon the history of the past, seeking there a solution of these monstrous outbreaks under a government founded upon the greatest and brightest of principles for the elevation of mankind. While we ponder the philosophy of cause and effect, the world is horrified by a fresh outbreak, and the shocked mind wonders that in this—the brightest epoch of the Christian era—*such things are.*

Mob-law is nothing new. Southern sentiment has not been changed; the old ideas close in analogy to the spirit of the buccaneers, who formed in many instances the first settlers of the Southland, still prevail, and break forth clothed in new forms to force the whole republic to an acceptance of its principles.

"Rule or ruin" is the motto which is committing the most beautiful portion of our glorious country to a cruel revival of piratical methods; and, finally, to the introduction of *Anarchy.* Is this not so? Let us compare the happenings of one hundred—two hundred years ago, with those of today. The difference between then and now, if any there be, is so slight as to be scarcely worth mentioning. The atrocity of the acts committed one hundred years ago are duplicated today, when slavery is supposed no longer to exist.

I have tried to tell an impartial story, leaving it to the reader to draw conclusions. I have tried to portray our hard struggles here in the North to obtain a respectable living and a partial education. I have presented both sides of the dark picture—lynching and concubinage—truthfully and without vituperation, pleading for that justice of heart and mind for my people which the Anglo-Saxon in America never withholds from suffering humanity.

In Chapter XIII, I have used for the address of the Hon. Herbert Clapp the statements and accusations made against the Negro by ex-Governor Northen of Georgia, in his memorable address before the Congregational Club at Tremont Temple, Boston, Mass., May 22, 1899. In Chapter XV, I have made Will Smith's argument in answer to the Hon. Herbert Clapp a combination of the best points made by well-known public speakers in the United States—white and black—in defense of the Negro. I feel my own deficiencies too strongly to attempt original composition on this subject at this crisis in the history of the Negro in the United States. I have introduced enough of the exquisitely droll humor peculiar to the Negro (a work like this would not be complete without it) to give a bright touch to an otherwise gruesome subject.

THE AUTHOR.

Chapter VI

Ma Smith's Lodging-House—Concluded

THE GRAY DAY DARKENED INTO NIGHT,
. . . MADE HOARY WITH THE SWARM
AND WHIRL-DANCE OF THE BLINDING STORM,
AS ZIGZAG WAVERING TO AND FRO,
CROSSED AND RECROSSED THE WINGED SNOW.

WHITTIER

February drew slowly to a close. Boston had lain for the past three or four days in the grasp of the snow king. At No. 500 D Street each tenant seemed content to keep within the bounds of his or her small domain, literally "frozed up," as Mrs. Ophelia Davis expressed it.

No one had seen much of the new lodger. She passed in and out each morning with a package of work in her hand; and all day long, from nine in the morning until late at night sometimes, the click of the typewriter could be heard coming from the "first front-square," which interpreted meant the front room on the second floor. Dora had been very neighborly and had called on Miss Clark frequently. There was a great fascination for her about the quiet, self-possessed woman. She did not, as a rule, care much for girl friendships, holding that a close intimacy between two of the same sex was more than likely to end disastrously for one or the other. But Sappho Clark seemed to fill a long-felt want in her life, and she had from the first a perfect trust in the beautiful girl.

Mrs. Smith had furnished her rooms substantially and well, but there had been no attempt at decoration. The first time Dora entered the room after Sappho had settled herself in it, she was struck at the alteration in its appearance. The iron bedstead and the washing utensils were completely hidden by drapery curtains of dark-blue denim, beautifully embroidered in white floss; a cover of the same material was thrown over the small table between the windows; plain white muslin draperies hid the unsightly but serviceable yellow shades at the windows; her desk and typewriter occupied the center of the room, and a couch had been improvised from two packing-cases and a spring, covered with denim and piled high with cushions; two good steel engravings completed a very inviting interior.

"How pretty you have made it," observed Dora, looking curiously around the room.

Sappho came and stood beside her, and the two girls smiled at each other in a glow of mutual interest, and became fast friends at once.

"I always carry these things with me in my travels, and I find that I can make myself very comfortable in a short time with their help."

"I wish you would show me how to do this embroidery," said Dora, as she lifted the edge of the denim curtain before the toilet stand and critically examined it. "This is beautifully done. Where did you learn?"

"I will teach you with pleasure," replied Sappho; but Dora noticed that she did not tell her where she had learned.

"Do you like your work—is it hard?" asked Dora, as she idly wandered from one object to another in the pretty room, pausing beside the desk to glance admiringly at a pile of neatly written sheets, just taken from the machine.

"Oh, I like the work very well. Sometimes the dictator is obtuse, or long-winded, or thinks that the writer ought to do his thinking for him as well as the corrections; then it is not pleasant work. But, generally speaking, I prefer it to most anything that I know of. Do sit down," she continued, pushing a chair toward Dora.

"This man receiveth sinners," read Dora from a pamphlet on the desk, as she turned to accept the offered chair. "I see that is your illuminated text for the day. Are you a Christian?" Then she saw an ivory crucifix suspended at the left side of the desk, and stopped in some confusion.

Sappho dropped the dress she was mending, and for a moment her eyes took on the far-away look of one in deep thought. Finally she said: "I saw you glance at the crucifix. I am not a Catholic, but I have received many benefits and kindnesses at their hands. Your question is a hard one to answer. I am afraid I am not a Christian, as we of our race understand the expression; but I try to do the best I can."

'And he who does the best he can
Need never fear the church's ban
Nor hell's damnation.
God recks not how man counts his beads,
For righteousness is not in creeds
Nor solemn faces;
But rather lies in Christian deeds
And Christian graces';

quoted Dora softly. "For my part, I am sick of loud professions and constant hypocrisy. My religion is short, and to the point—feed the starving thief and make him an honest man; cover your friend's faults with the mantle of charity and keep her in the path of virtue."

"Then you are not one of those who think that a woman should be condemned to eternal banishment for the sake of one misstep?"

"Not I, indeed; I have always felt a great curiosity to know the reason why each individual woman loses character and standing in the eyes of the world. I believe that we would hang our heads in shame at having the temerity to judge a fallen sister, could we but know the circumstances attending many such cases. And, after all we may do or say," continued the girl softly, "the best of us, who have lived the purest lives on earth that mortal can conceive, find at last that our only hope lies in the words of that text—'This man receiveth sinners.'"

"You are a dear little preacher," said Sappho gently, as she looked at Dora from two wet eyes; "and if our race ever amounts to anything in this world, it will be beacuse such women as you are raised up to save us."

Dora laughed and said, as she rose from her seat: "I think I am forgetting my errand." And making an elaborate bow, she continued: "If it please your royal highness, I present to you the compliments of the occupants of No. 500 D Street, with the request that you will honor us on Sunday evening, at half after seven, in the parlor of the worthy landlady of said house, where an informal reception will be held to further the better acquaintance of Miss Sappho Clark with her fellow-occupants of said house. Music during the evening. Refreshments at nine sharp; after which, you are all expected to retire to your rooms like virtuous citizens."

"I herewith most gratefully accept your kind invitation," replied Sappho, with a deep courtesy.

"Ta, ta, then, until Sunday night. I sha'n't see you before that. I shall be lost for the remainder of the week 'getting ready for company'"; and Dora, with a gay laugh, ran lightly down the stairs.

Mrs. Smith, after many trials, found that her house contained respectable though unlettered people, who possessed kindly hearts and honesty of purpose in a greater degree than one generally finds in a lodging-house. Her great desire, then, was to make them as happy together as possible, and to this end she had Dora institute musical evenings or reception nights, that her tenants might have a better opportunity of becoming acquainted with each other. She argued, logically enough, that those who were inclined to stray from right paths would be influenced either in favor of upright conduct or else shamed into an acceptance of the right. It soon became noised about that very pleasant times were enjoyed in that house; and that a sick lodger had been nursed back to health, instead of being hustled into the hospital ambulance at the first sign of sickness. It was also whispered that to enjoy these privileges one must be "pretty nice," or as some expressed it: "You've got to be high-toned to get in there." The result, however, justified Mrs. Smith's judgment, and rooms were always hard to get at No. 500 D Street.

Saturday was a busy day for Dora and her mother. At these little gatherings Mrs. Smith always gave her guests plenty of good homemade cake, sandwiches, hot chocolate, and on very special occasions, ice cream or sherbet. Sunday night there was to be ice cream in honor of the new lodger. "Good things to eat," said Ma Smith, as she industriously beat eggs, sugar and butter together in a large yellow bowl, "good things to eat make a man respect himself and look up in the world. You can't feel that you are nobody all the time if once in a while you eat the same quality of food that a millionaire does."

Dora lighted the lamps all over the house on Sunday night as soon as it fell dark. In the parlor there was a handsome piano lamp, which was only used on special occasions; it was lighted, and threw a soft, warm glow over the neat woolen carpet, the modest furniture and few ornaments. In a corner stood Dora's piano, given her on her sixteenth birthday by her brother. Very soon after seven o'clock the guests began to drop in; and as Dora and her mother were busy still over a few last preparations, Will and John volunteered to act as the reception committee.

The first comers were the two occupants of the basement rooms,—those which would have answered for the dining-room and kitchen of a moderately well-to-do family living in this class of house. Mrs. Ophelia Davis and Mrs. Sarah Ann White were friends of long standing. They were both born in far-away Louisiana, had been raised on neighboring plantations, and together had sought the blessings of liberty in the North at the close of the war. Mrs. Davis had always been a first-class cook, while Mrs. White tempted fortune as a second-girl. As their ideas of life and living enlarged, and they saw the possibilities of enjoying some comfort in a home, they began to think of establishing themselves where they could realize this blessing, and finally hit upon the idea of going into partnership in a laundry. After looking about them for a suitable situation for such a project, their choice finally fell upon Mrs. Smith's house, because of her known respectability, and because they could there come in contact with brighter intellects than their own; for, strange to say, it is a very hopeless case when a colored man or woman does not respect intelligence and good position.

"Yas, Sis'r Smith," said Mrs. Ophelia Davis the day she and Sarah Ann White went to engage the rooms; "yas'm, I'm tired o' livin' in white folkses' kitchens. Yas'm, thar's lots o' talk 'bout servant gals not bein' as good as enybody else, specially cooks. Yas'm, I kin git my five dollars a week with enyone; but ef you puts on a decent dress to go to church with a-Sunday afternoon, the mistis is a-wonderin' how you kin 'ford sech style and you nuthin' but a cook in her kitchen. Yas'm, I've got a silk dress, two of 'em, an' a lace shawl an' a gold watch and chain. People wants ter know how'd I git 'em. I come by 'em hones', I did. Yas'm, when my ol' mistis left her great big house an' all that good stuff—silver an' things—a-layin' thar fer enyone to pick up thet had sense 'nough to know a good thing an' git it ahead of enybody else, I jes' said to myself: ''Phelia, chile, now's yer time!' Yas'm, I feathered my nes', I jes' did. Sarah Ann, you 'member that time, honey, an' how skeered we was fer fear some o' them Union sojers would ketch us. You stuffed yerself with greenbacks, but, honey, I took clo's, too."

"Bless Gawd, Sis'r 'Phelia," replied her friend, with a chuckle and a great shaking of her fat sides; "bless Gawd, I disremember how much I did took in that ar pile; but Lord love yer, honey, I'se got some o' that money yet."

The two women engaged the rooms and prospered in their enterprise. The clothes under their deft fingers seemed to gain an added prettiness. They became the style; and no young bride on the Back Bay felt that she was complete unless "The First-class New Orleans Laundry" placed the finishing polish on the dainty lingerie of her wedding finery.

Tonight Mrs. Davis wore the famous black silk dress and gold watch and chain of ante bellum days, and Mrs. White was gay in a bright blue silk skirt and rose-colored silk shirtwaist. She said that she did not believe in any of your gloomy colors; for her part, she'd be dead soon enough and have a long time enough to stay "moulderin' inter clay, without buryin' herself befo' it was time." The next arrival was the young student preacher from the "first square-back." He was due at a prayer meeting; but when the time came for him to go there, he peeped over the banister and caught sight of Dora flitting back and forth in the entries, and then a whiff of Ma Smith's famous white cake was borne temptingly to his nostrils and banished the last scruple. He satisfied his conscience by hugging to his breast the idea that his presence was necessary to give the festivities the religious air which was needed for Sunday evening. In his Prince Albert coat and high white stock and tie he entered the parlor early, so that proper decorum might be maintained. Two dressmakers from the "second-front and back" now appeared and were made very welcome by the family; and then Sappho entered.

Her dress was plain black, with white chiffon at the neck and wrists, and on her breast a large bunch of "Jack" roses was fastened. With modest self-possession she moved to Mrs. Smith's side, and soon found herself being presented to the occupants of the parlor. For a moment or two there was an unbroken hush in the room. Tall and fair, with hair of a golden cast, aquiline nose, rosebud mouth, soft brown eyes veiled by long, dark lashes which swept her cheek, just now covered with a delicate rose flush, she burst upon them—a combination of "queen rose and lily in one."

"Lord," said Ophelia Davis to her friend Sarah Ann, "I haven't seen enything look like thet chile since I lef' home."

"That's the truth, 'Phelia," replied Sarah Ann; "that's somethin' God made, honey; thar ain't nothin' like thet growed outside o' Loosy-annie."

"Miss Clark," said Mrs. Davis, during a lull in the conversation, "I presume you're from Loosyannie?"

"My mother was born in New Orleans," replied the girl.

"I knowed it," cried Mrs. White, as she triumphantly glanced around the room. "Ol' New Orleans blood will tell on itself anywhere. These col'-blooded Yankees can't raise nuthin' that looks like thet chile; no, 'ndeed!"

Two or three of the young friends of the family who lived in the neighborhood had now arrived, and the conversation became very animated. Then it was announced that a literary and musical programme had been provided. Dora played an opening piece, which was a medley of Moody and Sankey hymns; Will sang "Palm Branches" in a musical baritone voice; John contributed a poem, and two young friends gave the duet from "Il Trovatore." After a little persuasion Sappho rendered the "Chariot Race" from "Ben Hur" in true dramatic style, and breathing so much of the stage that the Rev. Tommy James, the young theologian, felt that possibly he might have made a mistake in going into such hilarious company on the Sabbath.

"Now," said Mrs. Ophelia Davis, "I'm goin' to sin 'Suwanee River.' None o' yer high-falutin' things can tech that song." Dora accompanied her, and soon the air was filled with Mrs. Davis' ambitious attempts to imitate an operatic artist singing that good old-time song. With much wheezing and puffing—for the singer was neither slender nor young—and many would-be fascinating jumps and groans, presumed to be trills and runs, she finished, to the relief of the company. Her friend, Mrs. White, looked at her with great approval, and immediately informed them that 'Phelia made a great impression the Sunday before at Tremont Temple.

"The whole congregation was to sing 'Where's My Wandering Boy.' 'Phelia had no paper to see the words,—not as they made eny matter, 'cause 'Phelia can't read nohow,—an' the gentleman next us on the other side, he gave 'Phelia a paper thet *he* had. The man wanted ter be perlite. Well, 'Phelia was thet flattered thet she jes' let herself go, an' thet man never sung another note, he was so *'sprised.* After the second verse 'Phelia saw the distraction she was makin', an' she says to me, says she: *'How's thet, Sarah Ann?'* an' I says to her: *'That's out o' sight, 'Phelia!'* You jes' ought ter seen them white folks look! they was paralyzed! Why, you could hear 'Phelia *clean* above the orgin!"

Meantime the young people in the room had gathetered in a little knot, and were discussing many questions of the day and their effect upon the colored people. During a pause in the music the last remark made by John Langley was distinctly heard: "Yes, I must admit that our people are improving in their dress, in their looks and in their manners."

"What's that, John Langley?" asked Mrs. Davis, as she leaned forward to catch the words of the speaker; "colored people improvin' in ther manners? I should think they was! Don't yer fool yerself 'bout thet, now, will yer? The other night Sarah Ann and me was goin' down to Beacon Street to 'liver some goods, an' the car was crowded with people, an' thar was a pile o' young colored folks on it from the West End. Some o' them was a-standin' up in thet car, an' every onct in a while I noticed thet a passenger'd squirm as ef suthin' had hit him. Finally I got so mad I jes' couldn't see along with sech antics from them critters a-disgracin' theirselves and the whole o' the res' o' the colored population, an' I jes' elbowed myself into thet crowd o' young jades—what's thet (as Will murmured something under his breath), was they gals? yas, they was; young *jades,* every one o' them! Now what do yer think they was a-doin'?" she asked, as she swept her gaze over the company.

"Not being a mind-reader, I wouldn't dare to say," replied John Langley, with a grin of delight.

"They was a-trampin' onto the feet of every white man an' woman in thet car to show the white folks how free they was! I jes' took my ambriller an' knocked it into two or three o' them thet I knowed, an' tol' 'em I'd tell ther mothers. Improvin' in ther manners! I should think they was!"

At this moment refreshments were served, and the attention of the company was turned to the wants of the inner man.

Dora had placed a pretty little tea table at one side of the room, and Sappho had promised to pour the tea and chocolate. At a sign from Mrs. Smith she took her place, and soon the steaming beverage was cheering the hearts of the guests. The young men vied with each other in serving her. The tea table became the center of attraction, in fact, for the whole room. Even the divinity student was drawn into the magic circle, and divided his attention between Sappho and Mrs. Ophelia Davis, for whom he seemed to have a very tender regard.

The girl was naturally buoyant and bright, and the influence of the pleasant company in which she found herself seemed to inspire her, and yet no man would have overstepped the bounds of propriety with her in his manner. The pleasant word and jest were free from all coquetry. John was dumb before so much beauty and wit. Will was so blinded by her charms that he was scarcely conscious of what he was doing; but not a word or movement of hers was lost to him.

Dora watched the tea table smilingly. She loved to see her friends enjoy themselves. It never occurred to her to be jealous of the attention given Sappho by her brother and John Langley.

Presently there were many pleasant compliments passed on the enjoyable evening which had so quickly flown, and each gentleman proposed a toast, which was drunk in a cup of hot chocolate; and as the clock struck ten, they all joined hands and united in singing "Auld Lang Syne" and "Praise God, from Whom All Blessings Flow." The evening was over; the lights were out; but up in John's attic chamber the two young men smoked a social cigar before separating for the night.

They were silent for some time, and then Will said: "Miss Clark is a very beautiful woman; don't you think so, John?"

"Well," replied John, "beauty is not the word to describe her. She's a stunner, and no mistake."

John went to bed; but Will sat by the fire a longer time than usual, thinking thoughts which had never before troubled his young manhood; and, unconsciously, one face—the face of Sappho Clark—formed the background of his thoughts.

Chapter VIII
The Sewing-Circle

WHERE VILLAGE STATESMEN TALKED
WITH LOOKS PROFOUND,
IMAGINATION FONDLY STOOPS TO TRACE
THE PARLOR SPLENDORS OF THAT FESTIVE PLACE.

❖❖❖

YES! LET THE RICH DERIDE, THE PROUD DISDAIN,
THESE SIMPLE BLESSINGS OF THE LOWLY TRAIN;
TO ME MORE DEAR,
ONE NATIVE CHARM THAN ALL THE GLOSS OF ART.
GOLDSMITH

Ma Smith was a member of the church referred to in the last chapter, the most prominent one of color in New England. It was situated in the heart of the West End, and was a very valuable piece of property. Every winter this church gave many entertainments to aid in paying off the mortgage, which at this time amounted to about eight thousand dollars. Mrs. Smith, as the chairman of the board of stewardesses, was inaugurating a fair—one that should eclipse anything of a similar nature ever attempted by the colored people, and numerous sewing-circles were being held among the members all over the city. Parlor entertainments where an admission fee of ten cents was collected from every patron, were also greatly in vogue, and the money thus obtained was put into a fund to defray the expense of purchasing eatables and decorations, and paying for the printing of tickets, circulars, etc., for the fair. The strongest forces of the colored people in the vicinity were to combine and lend their aid in making a supreme effort to clear this magnificent property.

Boston contains a number of well-to-do families of color whose tax-bills show a most comfortable return each year to the city treasury. Strange as it may seem, these well-to-do people, in goodly numbers, distribute themselves and their children among the various Episcopal churches with which the city abounds, the government of which holds out the welcome hand to the brother in black, who is drawn to unite his fortunes with the members of this particular denomination. It may be true that the beautiful ritual of the church is responsible in some measure for this. Colored people are nothing if not beauty-lovers, and for such a people the grandeur of the service has great attractions. But in justice to this church one must acknowledge that it has been instrumental in doing much toward helping this race to help itself, along the lines of brotherly interest.

These people were well represented within the precincts of Mrs. Smith's pretty parlor one afternoon, all desirous of lending their aid to help along the great project.

As we have said, Mrs. Smith occupied the back parlor of the house as her chamber, and within this room the matrons had assembled to take charge of the cutting out of different garments; and here, too, the sewing machine was placed ready for use. In the parlor proper all the young ladies were seated ready to perform any service which might be required of them in the way of putting garments together.

By two o'clock all the members of the sewing-circle were in their places. The parlor was crowded. Mrs. Willis, the brilliant widow of a bright Negro politician, had charge of the girls, and after the sewing had been given out the first business of the meeting was to go over events of interest to the Negro race which had transpired during the week throughout the country. These facts had been previously tabulated upon a blackboard which was placed upon an easel, and occupied a conspicuous position in the room. Each one was supposed to contribute anything of interest that she had read or heard in that time for the benefit of all. After these points had been gone over, Mrs. Willis gave a talk upon some topic of interest. At six o'clock tea was to be served in the kitchen, the company taking refreshment in squads of five. At eight o'clock all unfinished work would be folded and packed away in the convenient little Boston bag, to be finished at home, and the male friends of the various ladies were expected to put in an appearance. Music and recitations were to be enjoyed for two hours, ice cream and cake being sold for the benefit of the cause.

Mrs. Willis was a good example of a class of women of color that came into existence at the close of the Civil War. She was not a *rara avis,* but one of many possibilities which the future will develop from among the colored women of New England. Every city or town from Maine to New York has its Mrs. Willis. Keen in her analysis of human nature, most people realized, after a short acquaintance, in which they ran the gamut of emotions from strong attraction to repulsion, that she had sifted them thoroughly, while they had gained nothing in return. Shrewd in business matters, many a subtle business man had been worsted by her apparent womanly weakness and charming simplicity. With little money, she yet contrived to live in quiet elegance, even including the little journeys from place to place, so adroitly managed as to increase her influence at home and her fame abroad. Well-read and thoroughly conversant with all current topics, she impressed one as having been liberally educated and polished by travel, whereas a high-school course more than covered all her opportunities.

Even today it is erroneously believed that all racial development among colored people has taken place since emancipation. It is impossible of belief for some, that little circles of educated men and women of color have existed since the Revolutionary War. Some of these people were born free, some have lost the memory of servitude in the dim past; a greater number by far were recruited from the energetic slaves of the South, who toiled when they should have slept, for the money that purchased their freedom, or else they boldly took the rights which man denied. Mrs. Willis was one from among these classes. The history of her descent could not be traced, but somewhere, somehow, a strain of white blood had filtered through the African stream. At sixty odd she was vigorous, well-preserved, broad and comfortable in appearance, with an aureole of white hair crowning a pleasant face.

She had loved her husband with a love ambitious for his advancement. His foot on the stairs mounting to the two-room tenement which constituted their home in the early years of married life, had sent a thrill to her very heart as she sat sewing baby clothes for the always expected addition to the family. But twenty years make a difference in all our lives. It brought many changes to the colored people of New England—social and business changes. Politics had become the open sesame for the ambitious Negro. A seat in the Legislature then was not a dream to this man, urged by the loving woman behind him. Other offices of trust were quickly offered him when his worth became known. He grasped his opportunity; grew richer, more polished, less social, and the family broadened out and overflowed from old familiar "West End" environments across the River Charles into the aristocratic suburbs of Cambridge. Death comes to us all.

Money, the sinews of living and social standing, she did not possess upon her husband's death. Therefore she was forced to begin a weary pilgrimage—a hunt for the means to help her breast the social tide. The best opening, she decided after looking carefully about her, was in the great cause of the evolution of true womanhood in the work of the "Woman Question" as embodied in marriage and suffrage. She could talk dashingly on many themes, for which she had received much applause in by-gone days, when in private life she had held forth in the drawing-room of some Back Bay philanthropist who sought to use her talents as an attraction for a worthy charitable object, the discovery of a rare species of versatility in the Negro character being a sure drawing-card. It was her boast that she had made the fortunes of her family and settled her children well in life. The advancement of the colored woman should be the new problem in the woman question that should float her upon its tide into the prosperity she desired. And she succeeded well in her plans: conceived in selfishness, they yet bore glorious fruit in the formation of clubs of colored women banded together for charity, for study, for every reason under God's glorious heavens that can better the condition of mankind.

Trivialities are not to be despised. Inborn love implanted in a woman's heart for a luxurious, esthetic home life, running on well-oiled wheels amid flowers, sunshine, books and priceless pamphlets, easy chairs and French gowns, may be the means of developing a Paderewski or freeing a race from servitude. It was amusing to watch the way in which she governed societies and held her position. In her hands committees were as wax, and loud murmurings against the tyranny of her rule died down to judicious whispers. If a vote went contrary to her desires, it was in her absence. Thus she became the pivot about which all the social and intellectual life of the colored people of her section revolved. No one had yet been found with the temerity to contest her position, which, like a title of nobility, bade fair to descend to her children. It was thought that she might be eclipsed by the younger and more brilliant women students on the strength of their alma mater, but she still held her own by sheer force of will-power and indomitable pluck.

The subject of the talk at this meeting was: "The place which the virtuous woman occupies in upbuilding a race." After a few explanatory remarks, Mrs. Willis said:

"I am particularly anxious that you should think upon this matter seriously, because of its intrinsic value to all of us as race women. I am not less anxious because you represent the coming factors of our race. Shortly, you must fill the positions now occupied by your mothers, and it will rest with you and your children to refute the charges brought against us as to our moral irresponsibility, and the low moral standard maintained by us in comparison with other races."

"Did I understand you to say that the Negro woman in her native state is truly a virtuous woman?" asked Sappho, who had been very silent during the bustle attending the opening of the meeting.

"Travelers tell us that the native African woman is impregnable in her virtue," replied Mrs. Willis.

"So we have sacrificed that attribute in order to acquire civilization," chimed in Dora.

"No, not 'sacrificed,' but pushed one side by the force of circumstances. Let us thank God that it *is* an essential attribute peculiar to us—a racial characteristic which is slumbering but not lost," replied Mrs. Willis. "But let us not forget the definition of virtue—'Strength to do the right thing under all temptations.' Our ideas of virtue are too narrow. We confine them to that conduct which is ruled by our animal passions alone. It goes deeper than that—general excellence in every duty of life is what we may call virtue."

"Do you think, then, that Negro women will be held responsible for all the lack of virtue that is being laid to their charge today? I mean, do you think that God will hold us responsible for the *illegitimacy* with which our race has been obliged, as it were, to flood the world?" asked Sappho.

"I believe that we shall not be held responsible for wrongs which we have *unconsciously* committed, or which we have committed under *compulsion.* We are virtuous or non-virtuous only when we have a *choice* under temptation. We cannot by any means apply the word to a little child who has never been exposed to temptation, nor to the Supreme Being 'who cannot be tempted with evil.' So with the African brought to these shores against his will—the state of morality which implies willpower on his part does not exist, therefore he is not a responsible being. The sin and its punishment lies with the person *consciously* false to his *knowledge* of right. From this we deduce the truism that 'the civility of no race is perfect whilst another race is degraded.'"

"I shall never forget my feelings," chimed in Anna Stevens, a school teacher of a very studious temperament, "at certain remarks made by the Rev. John Thomas at one of his noonday lectures in the Temple. He was speaking on 'Different Races,' and had in his vigorous style been sweeping his audience with him at a high elevation of thought which was dazzling to the faculties, and almost impossible to follow in some points. Suddenly he touched upon the Negro, and with the impressive gesture and lowered voice thanked God that the mulatto race was dying out, because it was a mongrel mixture which combined the worst elements of two races. Lo, the poor mulatto! despised by the blacks of his own race, scorned by the whites! Let him go out and hang himself!" In her indignation Anna forgot the scissors, and bit her thread off viciously with her little white teeth.

Mrs. Willis smiled as she said calmly: "My dear Anna, I would not worry about the fate of the mulatto, for the fate of the mulatto will be the fate of the entire race. Did you never think that today the black race on this continent has developed into a race of mulattoes?"

"Why, Mrs. Willis!" came in a chorus of voices.

"Yes," continued Mrs. Willis, still smiling. "It is an incontrovertible truth that there is no such thing as an unmixed black on the American continent. Just bear in mind that we cannot tell by a person's complexion whether he be dark or light in blood, for by the working of the natural laws the white father and black mother produce the mulatto offspring; the black father and white mother the mulatto offspring also, while the *black father* and *quadroon* mother produce the black child, which to the eye alone is a child of unmixed black blood. I will venture to say that out of a hundred apparently pure black men not one will be able to trace an unmixed flow of African blood since landing upon these shores! What an unhappy example of the frailty of all human intellects, when such a man and scholar as Doctor Thomas could so far allow his prejudices to dominate his better judgment as to add one straw to the burden which is popularly supposed to rest upon the unhappy mulattoes of a despised race," finished the lady, with a dangerous flash of her large dark eyes.

"Mrs. Willis," said Dora, with a scornful little laugh, "I am not unhappy, and I am a mulatto. I just enjoy my life, and I don't want to die before my time comes, either. There are lots of good things left on earth to be enjoyed even by mulattoes, and I want my share."

"Yes, my dear; and I hope you may all live and take comfort in the proper joys of your lives. While we are all content to accept life, and enjoy it along the lines which God has laid down for us as individuals as well as a race, we shall be happy and get the best out of life. Now, let me close this talk by asking you to remember one maxim written of your race by a good man: 'Happiness and social position are not to be gained by pushing.' Let the world, by its need of us along certain lines, and our intrinsic fitness for these lines, push us into the niche which God has prepared for us. So shall our lives be beautified and our race raised in the civilization of the future as we grow away from all these prejudices which have been the instruments of our advancement according to the intention of an All-seeing Omnipotence, from the beginning. Never mind our poverty, ignorance, and the slights and injuries which we bear at the hands of a higher race. With the thought ever before us of what the Master suffered to raise all humanity to its present degree of prosperity and intelligence, let us cultivate, while we go about our daily tasks, no matter how inferior they may seem to us, beauty of the soul and mind, which being transmitted to our children by the law of heredity, shall improve the race by eliminating *immorality* from our midst and raising *morality* and virtue to their true place. Thirty-five years of liberty have made us a new people. The marks of servitude and oppression are dropping slowly from us; let us hasten the transformation of the body by the nobility of the soul."

> For of the soul the body form doth take,
> For soul is form and doth the body make,

quoted Dora.

"Yes," said Mrs. Willis with a smile, "that is the idea exactly, and well expressed. Now I hope that through the coming week you will think of what we have talked about this afternoon, for it is of the very first importance to all people, but particularly so to young folks."

Sappho, who had been thoughtfully embroidering pansies on white linen, now leaned back in her chair for a moment and said: "Mrs. Willis, there is one thing which puzzles me—how are we to overcome the nature which is given us? I mean how can we eliminate passion from our lives, and emerge into the purity which marked the life of Christ? So many of us desire purity and think to have found it, but in a moment of passion, or under the pressure of circumstances which we cannot control, wc commit some horrid sin, and the taint of it sticks and will not leave us, and we grow to loathe ourselves."

"Passion, my dear Miss Clark, is a state in which the will lies dormant, and all other desires become subservient to one. Enthusiasm for any one object or duty may become a passion. I believe that in some degree passion may be beneficial, but we must guard ourselves against a sinful growth of any appetite. All work of whatever character, as I look at it, needs a certain amount of absorbing interest to become successful, and it is here that the Christian life gains its greatest glory in teaching us how to keep ourselves from abusing any of our human attributes. We are not held responsible for compulsory sin, only for the sin that is pleasant to our thoughts and palatable to our appetites. All desires and hopes with which we are endowed are good in the sight of God, only it is left for us to discover their right uses. Do I cover your ground?"

"Yes and no," replied Sappho; "but perhaps at some future time you will be good enough to talk with me personally upon this subject."

"Dear child, sit here by me. It is a blessing to look at you. Beauty like yours is inspiring. You seem to be troubled; what is it? If I can comfort or strengthen, it is all I ask." She pressed the girl's hand in hers and drew her into a secluded corner. For a moment the flood-gates of suppressed feeling flew open in the girl's heart, and she longed to lean her head on that motherly breast and unburden her sorrows there.

"Mrs. Willis, I am troubled greatly," she said at length.

"I am *so* sorry; tell me, my love, what it is all about."

Just as the barriers of Sappho's reserve seemed about to be swept away, there followed, almost instantly, a wave of repulsion toward this woman and her effusiveness, so forced and insincere. Sappho was very impressionable, and yielded readily to the influence which fell like a cold shadow between them. She drew back as from an abyss suddenly beheld stretching before her.

"On second thoughts, I think I ought to correct my remarks. It is not really *trouble,* but more a desire to confirm me in my own ideas."

"Well, if you feel you are right, dear girl, stand for the uplifting of the race and womanhood. Do not shrink from duty."

"It was simply a thought raised by your remarks on morality. I once knew a woman who had sinned. No one in the community in which she lived knew it but herself. She married a man who would have despised her had he known her story; but as it is, she is looked upon as a pattern of virtue for all women."

"And then what?" asked Mrs. Willis, with a searching glance at the fair face beside her.

"Ought she not to have told her husband before marriage? Was it not her duty to have thrown herself upon his clemency?"

"I think not," replied Mrs. Willis dryly. "See here, my dear, I am a practical woman of the world, and I think your young woman builded wiser than she knew. I am of the opinion that most men are like the lower animals in many things—they don't always know what is for their best good. If the husband had been left to himself, he probably would not have married the one woman in the world best fitted to be his wife. I think in her case she did her duty."

"Ah, that word 'duty.' What is our duty?" queried the girl, with a sad droop to the sensitive mouth. "It is so hard to know our duty. We are told that all hidden things shall be revealed. Must repented and atoned-for sin rise at last to be our curse?"

"Here is a point, dear girl. God does not look upon the constitution of sin as we do. His judgment is not ours; ours is finite, his infinite. *Your* duty is not to be morbid, thinking these thoughts that have puzzled older heads than yours. *Your* duty is, also, to be happy and bright for the good of those about you. Just blossom like the flowers, have faith and *trust.*" At this point the entrance of the men made an interruption, and Mrs. Willis disappeared in a crowd of other matrons. Sappho was impressed in spite of herself, by the woman's words. She sat buried in deep thought.

There was evidently more in this woman than appeared upon the surface. With all the centuries of civilization and culture that have come to this grand old world, no man has yet been found able to trace the windings of God's inscrutable ways. There are men and women whose seeming uselessness fit perfectly into the warp and woof of Destiny's web. All things work together for good.

Supper being over, the elderly people began to leave. It was understood that after nine o'clock the night belonged to the young people. A committee had been formed from among them to plan for their enjoyment, and they consulted with Ma Smith, in the kitchen, as to the best plan of procedure.

"The case is this," said the chairman, who was also the church chorister: "Ma Smith has bought four gallons of ice cream, to be sold for the benefit of this fair. It's *got* to go, and it rests with us to devise ways and means of getting rid of it."

"Get up a dance," suggested Sam Washington, a young fellow who was the life of all social functions.

"Dance!" exclaimed Ma Smith, "not in this house."

The choir-master surreptitiously kicked Sam on the shins, as he said soothingly: "Under the circumstances I see no other way, as we've *got* to sell the cream, and there's no harm in dancing, anyway."

"You ain't going to object to our dancing, are you, Ma? It's all old fogyism about dancing being a sin," chimed in Sam.

"Oh, but my son, I've been a church member over thirty years, a consistent Christian, and I never was up before the board for behavior unbecoming a professor. Think of the disgrace on me if the church took it up," she expostulated tearfully.

"Look here, Ma, the deacons and ministers are all fooling you. It's the style for church members to go to the theatre and the circus, to balls and everything you can mention. Why, I've seen our own pastor up to see the Black Crook, and laughing like all possessed at the sights. Fact!"

"Why, Samuel!" said Ma Smith, "how can you stand there and tell me such awful stories?"

"Not a bit of a story," declared the brazen-faced Sam, "it's as true as gospel. I'll find out what seat the minister gets next June when the circus comes into town, and I'll get a seat for you right behind him. If you've never been to the circus, Ma, and to see the seven-headed lady and the dancing mokes, you ought to go as soon as possible. Think of the fun you're missing."

"Oh!" groaned the good woman in holy horror, "how you do go on."

"But that ain't nothing to the ice cream," continued Sam, "and them girls in there have got to be warmed up, or the cream will be left, and there won't be a thing doing when the committee calls for the money."

"That's so," replied Ma Smith, beginning to weaken in her opposition.

"Well, mother," said Will, who had been an amused listener to the dialogue, "we'll have the dance, and it shall be *my* dance for *my* company. No one shall trouble you; you will have nothing to do with it."

"Well, if you say so, Willie, it's all right," replied his mother with a fond smile; "you are master in this house."

In the meantime the furniture in the parlors had been moved out by other members of the committee, and in one corner a set of whist-players were enjoying themselves at ten cents a head for a thirty-minute game, which ended at the stroke of a small silver bell, their places being taken by others.

Already it was getting very warm in the crowded rooms. The doors leading into the entry had been thrown open, and couples were finding seats in convenient nooks waiting for dancing to begin. The girls were thinking of ice cream. Rev. Tommy James gravitated toward

Mrs. Davis's corner. She had not gone out with the other matrons.

"I enjoy a real good time as much as anybody, children," she said; "and when it comes to dancing, you can't lose your Aunt Hannah."

The Reverend Tommy was always at his ease with Mrs. Davis. She led him along paths which caused him no embarrassment. He knew that she looked up to him because of his education and his clerical dignity. On his side, he admired her rugged common-sense, which put him at his ease, and banished the last atom of his "ladylike" bashfulness. Early in the winter he had been brought to realize the nature of his feeling for Mrs. Davis, by seeing Brother Silas Hamm, recently left a widower, and having ten children, making a decided stampede in the widow's direction. Reverend Tommy was grieved. To be sure, she was old enough to be his mother, but she had many good points to be considered. She was a good worker, experienced in married life and ways of making a man comfortable. Then her savings must be considered. When Tommy reached this last point he always felt sure that she was the most desirable woman in the world for a young minister. He felt hopeful tonight, because he had seen Brother Hamm and his bride in church the Sunday before. Mrs. Davis opened the conversation by speaking of the bride and groom.

"Hamm and his bride looked mighty comfut'ble in church Sunday, didn't they?"

"*He* did. I'm glad he's settled again. It is not good for man to be alone."

"'Deed I'm glad, too."

"*You*—well, well, I'm real glad to hear *you* say it."

"What for?" asked the widow coyly, looking down and playing with her fan.

"I—I didn't know how you and Brother Hamm stood."

"Stood! Well, I never."

"I thought Brother Hamm had been trying to get you," whispered Tommy, sitting closer and putting his arm across the back of her chair.

"Law suz, Mr. Jeems, how nervous you does make me. Do take yer arm away, everybody'll be a-lookin' at yer, honey. I'm 'sprised at yer thinkin' I'd look at Hamm an' all them chillun. Massy knows what the 'ooman he's got's gwine to do with 'em." But she looked so mild and smiling that Tommy went into the seventh heaven of delight, and so lost his head that when he heard the call "Another couple wanted here!" he took Mrs. Davis on his arm and stood up on the floor, forgetful of the fact that he was within a few months of his ordination. A good-natured matron not connected with the church had volunteered to supply the lack of an orchestra. Waltzing was soon in full blast, and the demand on the ice-cream cans was filling Ma Smith's heart with joy, tempered with inward stings of conscience and fear of the Steward's Board. Dora was dancing assiduously and eating ice cream at John's expense, he meantime saying that if she kept on she would turn into a frozen dainty, to say nothing of a frost in his pocketbook. Dora declared that it was for the good of the cause, and he'd "just got to stand it." She was wildly happy because of the tender familiarity between her brother and her friend. A long-stemmed rose that Will wore in his button-hole had been transferred to Sappho's corsage. Dora smiled as she caught the half-puzzled, half-wondering expression on her mother's face.

It was approaching twelve o'clock when it was proposed to wind up the festivities with the good old "Virginy" reel. Sam Washington was the caller, and did his work with the fancy touch peculiar to a poetic Southern temperament. He was shrewd and good-natured, and a bit of a wag. He knew all the secret sighings of the ladies and their attendant swains. A lively girl whom everyone called "Jinny," remarked to Sam, referring to the fact that Sam was on probation: "Your class-leader won't recommend you to the Board for membership after tonight."

"Now, Jinny," replied Sam, stopping in his business of arranging couples, "don't make yourself obnoxious bringing up unpleasant subjects. I'll take my medicine like a man when the time comes; but I'd bust, sho, if I didn't git loose tonight. I'm in good company, too," he grinned, nodding toward Reverend Tommy and Mrs. Davis, who were just taking their places on the floor. "If this is good for Tommy, it is good enough for me."

All reserve was broken down the instant the familiar strains of the Virginia reel were heard. The dance was soon in full swing—and up-and-down, dead-in-earnest seeking for a good time, and a determination to have it if it was to be got. It was a vehement rhythmic thump, thump, thumpity thump, with a great stamping of the feet and cutting of the pigeon wing. Sam had provided himself with the lively Jinny for a partner, and was cutting grotesque juba figures in the pauses of the music, to the delight of the company. His partner, in wild vivacity, fairly vied with him in his efforts at doing the hoe-down and the heel-and-toe. Not to be outdone, the Rev. Tommy James and Mrs. Davis scored great hits in cutting pigeon wings and in reviving forgotten beauties of the "walk-'round." Tommy "allowed" he hadn't enjoyed himself so much since he came up North.

"Yes," said Sam, "this beats the cake-walk all holler. Now then, one more turn and we're done. Forward on the head; balance yer partner; swing the next gent; swing that lady. Now swing yer rose, yer pretty rose, yer yaller rose of Texas. All promen*ade.*"

Everybody declared it had been a wonderful evening. "Thank the Lord it's over," said Ma Smith to Mrs. Sarah Ann White, who was helping her in the kitchen.

"Well," said the latter, pausing in her work with her arms akimbo, "sech sights as I've seen tonight I never would have believed. 'Phelia Davis, what ought ter be a mother in Jerusalem, kickin' up her heels in your parlor like a colt in a corn-field; and that Tommy Jeems, no more fittin' fer a minister than a suckin' babe, a-traipsin' after her like a bald-headed rooster."

VOICES OF ACTIVISM

IDA B. WELLS-BARNETT

(1862–1931)

Any history of the fight against lynching in the United States would have to give serious attention to Ida B. Wells-Barnett. A schoolteacher turned newspaperwoman, she committed her writing to the antilynching cause in 1892 when Thomas Moss, a friend of hers, was lynched in Memphis because whites deemed that he was too outspoken and his business was too profitable to be owned by a black man. Wells wrote of the event in her newspaper, *The Free Speech and Headlight,* and advised blacks to leave Memphis for the west. After three months of exodus and editorials, Wells finally commented on the "thread bare lie" that black men raped white women, which had become the ostensible reason for lynching. Whites responded by burning her newspaper office, running her business manager out of town, and threatening to kill her if she returned to Memphis (she was vacationing in New York at the time).

Becoming increasingly committed to showing that economic and political justifications more than rape spawned lynching, Wells was uncompromising in uncovering brutality and in urging progressive Americans to bring about much-needed changes. She produced a seven-column article for T. Thomas Fortune's *The New York Age,* which she expanded and published in 1892 as "Southern Horrors: Lynch Law in All Its Phases"; the pamphlet included case studies of lynchings and offered "names, date, and places of many lynchings for alleged rape." She continued her campaign against lynching with the publication in 1895 of *A Red Record: Tabulated*

Statistics and Alleged Causes of Lynching in the United States, 1892–1893–1894. It was even more explicit in asserting that lynchings resulted when white women who willingly dated black men were caught and then screamed rape.

For a brief period in 1893 and for a more expanded time in 1894, Wells took her crusade to England in an effort to bring influence she garnered there to bear on the lynching situation in the United States. She supplied a series of letters on her reception in England, all of which were published by the *Chicago Inter-Ocean.* Her last work on lynching was *Mob Rule in New Orleans,* published in 1900.

The daughter of slaves, Ida B. Wells was born in Holly Springs, Mississippi, on July 16, 1862. The oldest of eight children, she assumed responsibility for her surviving siblings when both her parents and the youngest child died in a yellow fever epidemic in 1878. Her attendance at Shaw University (later Rust College) had given her enough training to become a teacher, the profession she used to keep her family together until 1883, when the family was divided and she moved to Memphis to secure a better job.

Her refusal to accept second-class citizenship in America early came to the fore. In Memphis in 1884, she refused to move from a regular passenger car on a train to the smoking car, where blacks were expected to ride. Bodily removed by the conductor and two white male passengers, she sued the railroad and won a five-hundred-dollar settlement, only to have a higher court reverse the lower court's decision.

In 1887, she submitted articles to a church newspaper, which led to her journalistic work and editorship of the Memphis *Free Speech and Headlight* (later *Free Speech*). Her articles critical of the "colored" schools in Memphis led to her dismissal as a teacher in 1891, and she became a full-time newspaperwoman. While antilynching work certainly required a major portion of her energy, she was also involved in the women's club movement and other political issues central to African American communities. With her location from Memphis to Chicago, she became involved in several projects there. When blacks were excluded from the Chicago World's Fair of 1893, Wells urged Frederick Douglass and others to join her in publishing *The Reason Why the Colored American Is Not in the World's Columbian Exposition.* She founded the Ida B. Wells Club of Chicago, and she served as a probation officer for young black men in Chicago. She also offered assistance to blacks migrating from the South into Chicago, and she was instrumental in the founding of the Chicago chapter of the NAACP.

Wells married Ferdinand L. Barnett, a Chicago lawyer, on June 27, 1895, and for a number of years she successfully combined careers as wife, mother, and activist. She would take her babies on lecturing engagements with the expectation that the local sponsors would provide the necessary child care for her. She gave birth to two sons and two daughters, all of whom she lived to see into their adulthood. She completed an autobiography before she died on March 25, 1931.

Although a federal measure, the Dyer Anti-Lynching bill, was introduced in Congress many times, it never received enough support to pass. History will certainly record that that failure was not due in any part to Wells-Barnett's lack of vigilance. With the fiery sword she wielded as writer, lecturer, and surrogate lawyer, she fought to eradicate the evil of lynching from American society. The clarity of her vision and the power of her pen give her a place among the many black women writers, such as Anna Julia Cooper and Frances Ellen Watkins Harper, who were intent on showing the American public that black women could also use words effectively to transform the social and political situation of African Americans in the last decade of the nineteenth century.

❖❖❖

Trudier Harris has compiled *Selected Works of Ida B. Wells-Barnett,* which was published by Oxford Univerity Press in 1991. Wells-Barnett's daughter, Alfreda M. Duster, edited and published Wells-Barnett's autobiography, *Crusade for Justice: The Autobiography of Ida B. Wells,* in 1970. Mildred I. Thompson completed a biographical/critical study, *Ida B. Wells-Barnett: An Exploratory Study of An American Black Woman, 1893–1930,* in 1990.

FROM *"Southern Horrors: Lynch Law in All Its Phases"*

On Wednesday evening, May 25th, 1892, the city of Memphis, Tennessee, was filled with excitement. Editorials in the daily papers of that date caused a meeting to be held in the Cotton Exchange Building; a committee was sent for the editors of the *Free Speech,* an Afro-American journal published in that city, and the only reason the open threats of lynching that were made were not carried out was because the editors could not be found. The cause of all this commotion was the following editorial published in the *Free Speech,* May 21st, 1892, on the Saturday previous:—

"Eight Negroes lynched since last issue of *Free Speech,* one at Little Rock, Arkansas, last Saturday morning where the citizens broke (?) into the penitentiary and got their man; three near Anniston, Alabama, one near New Orleans; and three at Clarksville, Georgia, the last three for killing a white man, and five on the same old racket—the new alarm about raping white women. The same programme of hanging, then shooting bullets into the lifeless bodies, was carried out to the letter. Nobody in this section of the country believes the old threadbare lie that Negro men rape white women. If Southern white men are not careful, they will overreach themselves and public sentiment will have a reaction: a conclusion will then be reached which will be very damaging to the moral reputation of *their* women."

The *Daily Commercial* of Wednesday following, May 25th, contained the following leader—:

"Those Negroes who are attempting to make the lynching of individuals of their race a means for arousing the worst passions of their kind, are playing with a dangerous sentiment. The Negroes may as well understand that there is no mercy for the Negro rapist and little patience with his defenders. A Negro organ printed in this city, in a recent issue publishes the following atrocious paragraph: 'Nobody in this section of the country believes the old thread-bare lie that Negro men rape white women. If Southern white men are not careful they will overreach themselves, and public sentiment will have a reaction; and a conclusion will be reached which will be very damaging to the moral reputation of their women.' The fact that a black scoundrel is allowed to live and utter such loathsome and repulsive calumnies is a volume of evidence as to the wonderful patience of Southern whites. But we have had enough of it. There are some things that the Southern white man will not tolerate, and the obscene intimations of the foregoing have brought the writer to the very outermost limit of public patience. We hope we have said enough."

The *Evening Scimitar* of same date, copied the *Commercial's* editorial with these words of comment: "Patience under such circumstances is not a virtue. If the Negroes themselves do not apply the remedy without delay, it will be the duty of those whom he has attacked to tie the wretch who utters these calumnies to a stake at the intersection of Main and Madison Sts., brand him in the forehead with a hot iron, and perform upon him a surgical operation with a pair of tailor's shears."

Acting upon this advice, the leading citizens met in the Cotton Exchange Building the same evening, and threats of lynching were freely indulged—not by the lawless element upon which the devilry of the South is usually saddled, but by the leading business men, in their leading business centre. Mr. Fleming, the business manager and owner of a half interest in *Free Speech*, had to leave town to escape the mob, and was afterwards ordered not to return; letters and telegrams sent me in New York, where I was spending my vacation, advised me that bodily harm awaited my return. Creditors took possession of the office and sold the outfit, and the *Free Speech* was as if it had never been.

The editorial in question was prompted by the many inhuman and fiendish lynchings of Afro-Americans which have recently taken place, and was meant as a warning. Eight lynched in one week, and five of them charged with rape! The thinking public will not easily believe freedom and education more brutalising than slavery, and the world knows that the crime of rape was unknown during the four years of civil war, when the white women of the South were at the mercy of the race, which is all at once charged with being a bestial one.

Since my business has been destroyed, and I am an exile from home because of that editorial, the issue has been forced, and as the writer of it I feel that the race and the public generally should have a statement of the facts as they exist. They will serve at the same time as a defence for the Afro-American Sampsons who suffer themselves to be betrayed by white Delilahs. . . .

. . . There are many white women in the South who would marry coloured men if such an act would not place them at once beyond the pale of society, and within the clutches of the law. The miscegenation laws of the South only operate against the legitimate union of the races: they leave the white man free to seduce all the coloured girls he can, but it is death to the coloured man who yields to the force and advances of a similar attraction in white women. White men lynch the offending Afro-American not because he is a despoiler of virtue, but because he succumbs to the smiles of white women. . . .

On March 9th, 1892, there were lynched in the same city three of the best specimens of young Afro-American manhood since the war. They were peaceful, law-abiding citizens and energetic business men. They believed the problem was to be solved by eschewing politics and putting money in the purse. They owned a flourishing grocery business in a thickly populated suburb of Memphis, and a white man named Barrett had one on the opposite corner. After a personal difficulty which Barrett had sought by going into the "People's Grocery" and drawing a pistol and getting thrashed by Calvin M'Dowell, he (Barrett) threatened to "Clean them out." These men were a mile beyond the city limits and police protection; so on hearing that Barrett's crowd was coming to attack them on Saturday night, they mustered forces and prepared to defend themselves against the attack.

When Barrett came, he led a posse of officers, twelve in number who afterward claimed to be hunting a man for whom they had a warrant. [Why twelve men in citizen's clothes should think it necessary to go in the night to hunt one man who had never before been arrested, or made any record as a criminal, has never been explained.] When they entered the back door the young men thought the threatened attack was on, and fired into them. Three of the officers were wounded, and when the defending party found it was officers of the law upon whom they had fired, they ceased firing and got away. Thirty-one men were arrested and thrown in gaol as "conspirators," although they all declared more than once they did not know they were firing on officers. Excitement was at fever heat until the morning papers, two days after, announced that the wounded deputy sheriffs were recovering. This hindered rather than helped the plans of the whites. There was no law on the statute books which would execute an Afro-American for wounding a white man, but the "unwritten law" did. Three of these men, the president, the manager, and the clerk of the grocery—"the leaders of the conspiracy"—were secretly taken from gaol and lynched in a shockingly brutal manner. "The Negroes are getting too independent," they say, "we must teach them a lesson." What lesson? The lesson of subordination. "Kill the leaders, and it will cow the Negro who dares to shoot a white man, even in self-defence."

Although the race was wild over the outrage, and the mockery of law and justice which disarmed men and locked them up in gaols where they could be easily and safely reached by the mob, the Afro-American ministers, newspapers and leaders counselled obedience to the law which did not protect them. Their counsel was heeded and not a hand was uplifted to resent the outrage; following the advice of the *Free Speech*, people left the city in great numbers.

The "dailies" and associated press reports heralded the dead men to the country as "toughs" (roughs) and "Negro desperadoes who kept a low dive." This same press service printed that a Negro who was lynched at Indianola, Mississippi, in May, had outraged the sheriff's eight-year-old daughter. This girl was more than eighteen years old, and was found by her father in this man's room, who was a servant on the place! Not content with misrepresenting the race, the mob-spirit was not to be satisfied until the paper which was doing all it could to counteract this impression was silenced. The coloured people were resenting their bad treatment in a way to make itself felt, yet gave the mob no excuse for further murder, until the appearance of the editorial which is construed as a reflection on the "honour" of the Southern white women. It is not half so libellous as that of the *Commercial* which appeared four days before, and that which has been given in these pages. They would have lynched the manager of the *Free Speech* for exercising the right of free speech (if they had found him) as quickly as they would have hung any scoundrel guilty of outrage, and been glad of the excuse to do so. The owners were ordered not to return, as *Free Speech* was suspended with as little compunction as the business of the "People's Grocery" had been broken up and its proprietors murdered. . . .

Mr. Henry W. Grady, in his well-remembered speeches in New England and New York, pictured the Afro-American as incapable of self-government. Through him and other leading men the cry of the South to the country has been "Hands off! Leave us to solve our problem." To the Afro-American the South says, "The white man must and will rule." There is little difference between the Ante-bellum South and the New South. Her white citizens are wedded to any method however revolting, any measure however extreme, for the subjugation of the young manhood of the dark race. They have cheated him out of his ballot, deprived him of civil rights or redress in the Civil Courts thereof, robbed him of the fruits of his labour, and are still murdering, burning, and lynching him.

The result is a growing disregard of human life. Lynch Law has spread its insidious influence till men in New York State, Pennsylvania and on the free Western plains feel they can take the law in their own hands with impunity, especially where an Afro-American is concerned. The South is brutalised to a degree not realised by its own inhabitants, and the very foundation of government, law, and order are imperilled.

Public sentiment has had a slight "reaction," though not sufficient to stop the crusade of lawlessness and lynching. The spirit of Christianity of the great M.E. Church was sufficiently aroused by the frequent and revolting crimes against a powerless people, to pass strong condemnatory resolutions at its General Conference in Omaha last May. The spirit of justice of the grand old party asserted itself sufficiently to secure a denunciation of the wrongs, and a feeble declaration of the belief in human rights in the Republican platform at Minneapolis, June

7th. A few of the great "dailies" and "weeklies" have swung into line declaring that Lynch Law must go. The President of the United States issued a proclamation that it be not tolerated in the territories over which he has jurisdiction. Governor Northen and Chief Justice Bleckley,[1] of Georgia, have proclaimed against it. The citizens of Chattanooga, Tennessee, have set a worthy example in that they not only condemn Lynch Law, but her public men demanded a trial for Weems, who was accused of outrage, and guarded him while the trial was in progress. The trial only lasted ten minutes, and Weems chose to plead guilty, and accept twenty-one years sentence, rather than invite the certain death which awaited him outside that cordon of police if he had told the truth and shown the letters he had received from the white woman in the case.

Colonel A.S. Colyar, of Nashville, Tennessee, is so overcome with the horrible state of affairs that he addressed the following earnest letter to the Nashville *American:*—"Nothing since I have been a reading man has so impressed me with the decay of manhood among the people of Tennessee as the dastardly submission to the mob reign. We have reached the unprecedent low level; the awful criminal depravity of substituting the mob for the Court and jury, of giving up the gaol keys to the mob whenever they are demanded. We do it in the largest cities and in the country towns; we do it in midday; we do it after full, not to say formal, notice, and so thoroughly and generally is it acquiesced in that the murderers have discarded the formula of masks. They go into the town where everybody knows them, sometimes under the gaze of the governor, in the presence of the Courts, in the presence of the sheriff and his deputies, in the presence of the entire police force, take out the prisoner, take his life, often with fiendish glee, and often with acts of cruelty and barbarism which impress the reader with a degeneracy rapidly approaching savage life. That the State is disgraced but faintly expresses the humiliation which has settled upon the once proud people of Tennessee. The State, in its majesty, through its organised life, for which the people pay liberally, makes but one record, but one note, and that a criminal falsehood, was hung by persons to the jury unknown. The murder at Shelbyville is only a verification of what every intelligent man knew would come, because with a mob rumour is as good as a proof."

These efforts brought forth apologies and a short halt, but the lynching mania has raged again through the past twelve months with unabated fury. The strong arm of the law must be brought to bear upon lynchers in severe punishment, but this cannot and will not be done unless a healthy public sentiment demands and sustains such action. The men and women in the South who disapprove of lynching and remain silent on the perpetration of such outrages are *particeps criminis*—accomplices, accessories before and after the fact, equally guilty with the actual law-breakers, who would not persist if they did not know that neither the law nor militia would be employed against them. . . .

In the creation of this healthier public sentiment, the Afro-American can do for himself what no one else can do for him. The world looks on with wonder that we have conceded so much, and remain law-abiding under such great outrage and provocation.

To Northern capital and Afro-American labour the South owes its rehabilitation. If labour is withdrawn capital will not remain. The Afro-American is thus the backbone of the South. A thorough knowledge and judicious exercise of this power in lynching localities could many times effect a bloodless revolution. The white man's dollar is his god, and to stop this will be to stop outrages in many localities.

The Afro-Americans of Memphis denounced the lynching of three of their best citizens, and urged and waited for the authorities to act in the matter, and bring the lynchers to justice. No attempt was made to do so, and the black men left the city by thousands, bringing about great

[1] William Jonathan Northen (1835–1913) was governor of Georgia from 1890 to 1894. Logan Edwin Bleckley (1827–1907) was Chief Justice of the Supreme Court of Georgia from 1887 to 1894.

stagnation in every branch of business. Those who remained so injured the business of the street car company by staying off the cars, that the superintendent, manager, and treasurer called personally on the editors of the *Free Speech,* and asked them to urge our people to give them their patronage again. Other business men became alarmed over the situation, and the *Free Speech* was suppressed that the coloured people might be more easily controlled. A meeting of white citizens in June, three months after the lynching, passed resolutions for the first time condemning it. *But they did not punish the lynchers.* Every one of them was known by name because they had been selected to do the dirty work by some of the very citizens who passed these resolutions! Memphis is fast losing her black population, who proclaim as they go that there is no protection for the life and property of any Afro-American citizen in Memphis who will not be a slave.

The Afro-American citizens of Kentucky, whose intellectual and financial improvement has been phenomenal, have never had a separate car law until now. Delegations and petitions poured into the Legislature against it, yet the Bill passed, and the Jim Crow Car of Kentucky is a legalised institution. Will the great mass of Negroes continue to patronise the railroad? A special from Covington, Kentucky, says:—

"Covington, June 13th.—The railroads of the State are beginning to feel very markedly the effects of the separate coach Bill recently passed by the Legislature. No class of people in the State have so many and so largely attended excursions as the blacks. All these have been abandoned, and regular travel is reduced to a minimum." A competent authority says the loss to the various roads will reach 1,000,000 dols. this year.

A call to a State Conference in Lexington, Kentucky, last June, had delegates from every county in the State. Those delegates, the ministers, teachers, heads of secret and other orders, and the heads of families should pass the word around, for every member of the race in Kentucky to stay off railroads unless obliged to ride. If they did so, and their advice was followed persistently, the Convention would not need to petition the Legislature to repeal the law or raise money to file a suit. The railroad corporations would be so affected they would, in self defence, "lobby" to have the separate car law repealed. On the other hand, as long as the railroads can get Afro-American excursions they will always have plenty of money to fight all the suits brought against them. They will be aided in so doing by the same partisan public sentiment which passed the law. White men passed the law, and white judges and juries would pass upon the suits against the law, and render judgment in line with their prejudices, and in deference to the greater financial power.

The appeal to the white man's pocket has ever been more effectual than all the appeals ever made to his conscience. Nothing, absolutely nothing, is to be gained by a further sacrifice of manhood and self-respect. By the right exercise of his power as the industrial factor of the South, the Afro-American can demand and secure his rights, the punishment of lynchers, and a fair trial for members of his race accused of outrage.

Of the many inhuman outrages of this present year, the only case where the proposed lynching did not occur, was where the men armed themselves in Jacksonville, Florida, and Paducah, Kentucky, and prevented it. The only times an Afro-American who was assaulted got away has been when he had a gun, and used it in self-defence. The lesson this teaches, and which every Afro-American should ponder well, is that a Winchester rifle should have a place of honour in every black home, and it should be used for that protection which the law refuses to give. When the white man, who is always the aggressor, knows he runs as great risk of biting the dust every time his Afro-American victim does, he will have greater respect for Afro-American life. The more the Afro-American yields and cringes and begs, the more he has to do so, the more he is insulted, outraged, and lynched.

The assertion has been substantiated throughout these pages that the Press contains unreliable and doctored reports of lynchings, and one of the most necessary things for the race to do is to get these facts before the public. The people must know before they can act, and there is no educator to compare with the Press.

The Afro-American papers are the only ones which will print the truth, and they lack means to employ agents and detectives to get at the facts. The race must rally a mighty host to the support of their journals, and thus enable them to do much in the way of investigation.

A lynching occurred at Port Jarvis, New York, the first week in June. A white and a coloured man were implicated in the assault upon a white girl. It was charged that the white man paid the coloured boy to make the assault, which he did on the public highway in broad day time, and was lynched. This, too, was done by "parties unknown." The white man in the case still lives. He was imprisoned, and promises to fight the case on trial. At the preliminary examination, it developed that he had been a suitor of the girl's. She had repulsed and refused him, yet had given him money, and he had sent threatening letters demanding more. The day before this examination she was so wrought up, she left home and wandered miles away. When found she said she did so because she was afraid of the man's testimony. Why should she be afraid of the prisoner? Why should she yield to his demands for money if not to prevent him exposing something he knew? It seems explainable only on the hypothesis that a *liaison* existed between the coloured boy and the girl, and the white man knew of it. The press is singularly silent. Has it a motive? We owe it to ourselves to find out.

The story comes from Larned, Kansas, October 1st, that a young white lady held at bay until daylight, without alarming any one in the house, "a burly Negro," who entered her room and bed. The "burly Negro" was promptly lynched without investigation or examination of the accuracy of the statement.

A house was found burned down near Montgomery, Alabama, in Monroe County, a few weeks ago—also the burned bodies of the owners and melted piles of gold and silver. These discoveries led to the conclusion that the awful crime was not prompted by motives of robbery. The suggestion of the whites was that "brutal lust was the incentive, and as there are nearly 200 Negroes living within a radius of five miles of the place the conclusion was inevitable that some of them were the perpetrators." Upon this "suggestion," probably made by the real criminal, the mob acted upon the "conclusion," and arrested ten Afro-Americans, four of whom, they tell the world, confessed to the deed of murdering Richard L. Johnson and outraging his daughter, Jeanette. These four men, Berrell Jones, Moses Johnson, Jim and John Packer, none of them 25 years of age, upon this conclusion, were taken from gaol, hanged, shot, and burned while yet alive, the night of October 12th. The same report says that Mr. Johnson was on the best of terms with his Negro tenants.

The race thus outraged must find out the facts of this awful hurling of men into eternity on supposition, and give them to the indifferent and apathetic country. We feel this to be a garbled report, but how can we prove it?

Near Vicksburg, Mississippi, a murder was committed by a gang of burglars. Of course only Negroes could have committed the crime, and Negroes were arrested for it. It is believed that the two men, Smith Tooley and John Adams, belonged to a gang controlled by white men, who feared exposure, so on the night of July 4th they were hanged in the Court House yard by those interested in silencing them. Robberies since committed in the same vicinity have been known to be by white men who had their faces blackened. We strongly believe in the innocence of these murdered men, but we have no proof. No other news goes out to the world save that which stamps us as a race of cutthroats, robbers, and lustful wild beasts.

So great is Southern hate and prejudice, that they legally (?) hung poor little thirteen-year-old Mildred Brown at Columbia, South Carolina, October 7th, on the circumstantial evidence that she poisoned a white infant. If her guilt had been proven unmistakably, had she been white, Mildred Brown would never have been hung, the country would have been aroused and South Carolina disgraced for ever for such a crime. . . .

Nothing is more definitely settled than that he [the Afro-American] must act for himself. I have shown how he may employ the "boycott," emigration, and the Press; and I feel that by a combination of all these agencies Lynch Law—the last relic of barbarism and slavery—can be effectually stamped out. "The gods help those who help themselves." . . .

The following details of lynching from 1882 to 1891 inclusive, is proof of all that has been said, in the preceding pages. During these years the South has had full control of the political, legislative, judicial, and executive machinery. With the judges, juries, and prosecuting attorneys all Southern white men, no Negro has ever been known to escape the penalty of the law for any crime he commits. It is only the wealthy white man, with money and influence, who fails of conviction for his crimes. There is not, and never has been, any fear by the mob that a Negro would not receive full punishment for all crimes of which he is convicted. But if this state of affairs did prevail, . . . clearly the laws or those who are paid to enforce them are at fault. Hence, those who make such inoperative laws, or the officials who fail to do their duty, and not the criminals, should be lynched. But the reverse is true. The gaols, penitentiaries, and convict farms are filled with race criminals who are too poor and weak to avert such a fate. Yet of this race there were lynched in—

1882—52	1886—73	1889—95
1883—39	1887—70	1890—100
1884—53	1888—72	1891—169
1885—77		

Of this number only 269 were charged with outrage; 253 with murder; 44 with robbery; 37 with incendiarism; 32 with reasons unstated (not necessary to give a reason for lynching a Negro); 27 with "race prejudice"; 13 with quarreling with white men; 10 with making threats; 7 with rioting; 5 with miscegenation; 4 with burglary.

W.E.B. DU BOIS
(1868–1963)

W.E.B. Du Bois was one of the most brilliant men of words and action born in the United States. By his death at ninety-three, he had become not only a product of African American history but a significant director of its course as well. In his youth, he had been a skilled debator and orator and later had developed into a talented autobiographer who had honed his craft and had offered insightful critiques of Western history. Although he was foremost a historian and a founder of modern sociology, he achieved in several moments of exquisite prose many passages with poetic brilliance as well as profundity. He was a literary artist, a symbolist, and a writer of visionary fictions. He was a committed moralist and sometimes an all-too-prescriptive and even genteel one as well. Most of all, he was a dedicated thinker and an indefatigable researcher who wrote nearly a score of volumes and more than a hundred articles for publication. As a race leader, he helped channel the flow of scholarly method at Atlanta University and at the NAACP. All the while, Du Bois had begun to develop the idea of Pan-Africanism, a concept dedicated to the liberation of blacks throughout the world. He exploited a rare talent for language coupled with an experimental understanding in the social dynamics of race and culture. He was truly gifted, and he was most likely a genius.

W.E.B. Du Bois—philosopher; sociologist; and writer of fiction, poetry, biography, and autobiography—was, in the words of Charles H. Wesley, our greatest "lyric historian." Although he was labeled a Marxist revolutionary, his political range transcended nearly all schools and ideologies. During the 1880s, he was a reform Republican when people of the kind were still the party of Lincoln. In the second decade of the twentieth century, he was a socialist, though by 1912 he supported Woodrow Wilson for president. And, as a political independent during the thirties, he proposed the Progressive Party as an answer for the country during the late forties. By the fifties, Du Bois was a candidate for U.S. Senator on the ticket for the party of American Labor. Near the end of the decade, according to his editor Herbert Aptheker, he would come to doubt that even his great young faith in American democracy could remedy the ills facing America.

This remarkable scholar, educator, and philosopher was born free in Great Barrington, Massachusetts, in 1868, among a family that dated back several generations in America. One ancestor, in fact, had served as a soldier in the American Revolution. With a somewhat idyllic childhood, Du Bois grew up in a stable community of African Americans in a small town of approximately 5,000 people. Of partly French, Dutch, and African ancestry, he was spared a few of the most conspicuous incidents of racism and segregation in the small New England town. His mother, Mary Burghardt, lived somewhat meagerly while he was recognized as a youth with unusual gifts of intellect. Upon his mother's death following his high school graduation, Du Bois received a scholarship to attend Fisk University, a prominent black institution of higher education founded originally in Nashville, Tennessee, to educate the children of freed slaves. He had wanted to attend Harvard University but thought that he needed to learn more about his people. The journey south would return the young scholar to his cultural roots, tracing him to the souls of black folk. Upon entry at Fisk in 1885, Du Bois, who was quite happy, excelled in classes. During the summers, he taught blacks in the rural areas before his graduation with honors in three years.

However, he had never abandoned his dream of attending Harvard. With his eventual admission in 1888 to study for a second bachelor's degree in 1890, he discovered that his fellow students disliked him intensely. He benefited from exposure to inspiring professors such as George Santayana, Albert Bushnell Hart, Josiah Rose, and William James, an early mentor who became a friend. With all doctoral work except for his dissertation at Harvard completed by 1892, Du Bois secured admission to the University of Berlin for two years to study history, sociology, and philosophy. When he returned to the United States in 1894, he found an appointment as an instructor in history at the University of Pennsylvania denied to him.

For his doctorate in 1895 he completed *The Suppression of the African Slave-Trade to the United States of America, 1538–1870,* the initial book in the Harvard Historical Series. His next volume, *The Philadelphia Negro* (1899), which documents in interviews the lives of 5,000 African Americans steeped in poverty, is the first sociological study on American blacks by an American of African descent. The work would become definitive for its day. In 1897, he obtained a faculty appointment at Atlanta University, a black institution of higher learning, where he taught for thirteen years. In 1900 he would write, "The problem of the twentieth century is the color line." He saw the whole of life through a part of it. He had learned to extrapolate from African American suffering sympathy for all human oppression, particularly for those of African ancestry throughout the world; he viewed the unity of all the darker peoples on earth; and he would extend his concept of the suffering masses to laboring hordes around the globe.

In many ways, his theory about the prospects of a global village—a human family—was still latent at the turn of the century. By 1901, he struck the chord of disagreement with Booker T. Washington, founder of Tuskegee Institute in Alabama, who had held a conciliatory position of accommodating racial discrimination. Despite his own early praise for Washington's Atlanta Exposition Address of 1895 ("a word fitly spoken"), Du Bois noticed that the Tuskegee politician had begun to silence African American critics and to manipulate the black press as well as other agents of power. With the review in *Dial* of Washington's *Up From Slavery* in 1901, Du Bois facilitated a protracted disagreement between the conservative and radical camps of American blacks.

He revised his decisive critique of the politically passive Washington in *The Souls of Black Folk* (1903), one of the most seminal treatises in African American aesthetics. Essentially, the work is a passionate outcry of black nationalism. Du Bois is primarily concerned with the black consciousness of the black people as they struggle, both internally and externally, for survival. Nine chapters derive from nearly thirty-six of his printed essays on black life and culture. The narrator of the lyric experiences is at once historian, scholar, artist, and visionary. Du Bois's essay "Of the Training of Black Men" is a plea for "a Talented Tenth," a liberally educated leadership, while his essays "The Quest of the Golden Fleece," The Wings of Atalanta," and "Of the Black Belt" are the studies of the struggles of the black peasantry. Other essays, such as "Of the Faith of the Fathers," "Of the Passing of the First Born," and "Of the Sorrow Songs," are studies of the religion, human suffering, and spirituals of African Americans. Almost single-handedly, he saves the reputation of the brilliant nineteenth-century black man of letters, Alexander Crummell, from oblivion. Because of its poetic quality, exquisite unifying metaphors, and range of materials portraying the black life experience in America, *The Souls of Black Folk* stands as Du Bois's major literary achievement. It probably has had a greater impact in America than any other book written by an African American. Its controversial subject matter—the problem of race in America—has resulted in the book's immense popularity. It has passed through more than thirty editions and is still selling. By its publication at the turn of the century, Du Bois's influence had begun to spread over the conciliatory Washington and his political forces.

Also in his effort to defeat Washingtonianism, Du Bois helped establish the Niagara Movement in 1905. This organization became perhaps the first formal committee on African American protest in the twentieth century. By 1909, Du Bois became the only African American founder of the NAACP and, the following year, he assumed the editorship of *The Crisis,* the official publication of the group. As editor of the periodical, Du Bois became a leading black spokesperson for various social and political causes. He wrote columns exposing the horror of lynching and mob violence as well as the injustice of lawful segregation. Just as his support for the American war effort displeased blacks in 1918, his criticism of racism within the American military personnel of Europe displeased whites equally well. He also wrote a series of editorials advocating Pan-Africanism and women's suffrage. As the prime mover of the Pan-African movement, he organized the first Pan-African Congresses in 1919, 1921, 1923, 1927, and, later, in 1945. With his positions as editor of *The Crisis* and director of Publicity and Research of the NAACP, Du Bois emerged as the foremost intellectual leader of Americans of African descent for nearly the first half of the twentieth century. Somewhat stunned in the twenties by the appeal to the black masses of Marcus Garvey, the Jamaican founder of the United Negro Improvement Association, Du Bois called him "the most dangerous enemy of the Negro race in America and the world."

As part of his larger social vision, Du Bois developed and promoted in *The Crisis* throughout the twenties and early thirties his theory of a black aesthetic; that is, that the primary purpose of black art must be social. He did accept somewhat kindly the contributions of "ordinary decent colored people." In "Negro Art" he had hoped to establish by 1923 a professional understanding with Alain Locke, the black critic and educator who had even more refined preferences in art. But, in the same year, he disagreed with the position advocated by Locke in "The Colonial Literature of France." To Du Bois, the cultivation of a high art at the expense of human rights was dangerous. He never loved art as a God unto itself. Thinking of himself more as a propagandist than as an artist (he knew the distinction was forced), he had written *Darkwater: Voices From Within the Veil* (1920), which is quite lyrical. At the height of the Harlem Renaissance in 1928, his novel, *Dark Princess,* was published, which related the historical struggle of African Americans to the revolutionary movements of darker races of people in Africa and Asia.

During the 1930s, Du Bois brought out *Black Reconstruction* (1935), which was originally titled *Black Reconstruction of Democracy in America, 1860–1880.* He saw the era of national restructuring as dating from the Civil War rather than afterwards. Indeed, he perceived a carefully fused triangle in which the resistance to slavery, the Civil War, and the commitment to Reconstruction were bound inseparably. He revealed the persistence of the black liberation struggle as part of an unbroken circle across even the nadir of the 1870s through the 1890s. Du Bois proposed slavery as the primary cause of the Civil War and the major agent of northern victory within it; he recognized the franchisement of freed slave men as one of the "greatest steps toward democracy taken in the nineteenth century"; and he foresaw the reversal of rights by African Americans as part of a southern imperative that would destroy in time the democratic ideal of what America must be. Four years later, with the publication of his historical book, *Black Folk, Then and Now,* he continued to have a lasting impact on the political reformation of the high-art school that had been championed by Alain Locke during the 1920s.

As the Great Depression of the 1930s gave way to World War II and its aftermath, Du Bois completed the autobiographical *Dusk of Dawn* (1940), in which he presents the experience of blacks who yell constantly in a cave but who go forth unheard as misunderstood people. He had become an eloquent voice in *The World of Africa* (1947) for those he believed had been silenced. Of less talent was his *The Black Flame: A Trilogy—The Ordeal of Mansart* (1957), *Mansart Builds a School* (1959), and *Worlds of Color* (1961), which traces four generations of a black family from the end of Reconstruction to the 1950s.

Twice Du Bois stepped down from roles of leadership in the NAACP because of ideological disagreements. While Walter White, the Executive Secretary, supported the candidacy of Harry Truman for president in 1948, Du Bois rallied behind Henry Wallace, the standard bearer for the Progressive Party. Indicted as a subversive in 1951, Du Bois was acquitted, although the government retained his passport. His alleged offense was membership during the McCarthy era in the Peace Information Center that sought to end the proliferation of nuclear weapons on earth. Often denied by even many of his own sometimes fearful people, Du Bois received the International Lenin Prize in 1958. In 1961, he joined the communist party. Perhaps he underestimated the national cowardice:

> I know the United States. It is my country and the land of my fathers. It is still a land of magnificent possibilities. It is still the home of noble souls and generous people. . . . I was born on its soil and educated in its schools. I have served my country to the best of my ability. I have never knowingly broken its laws or unjustly attacked its reputation. At the same time I have pointed out its injustices and crimes and blamed it, rightly as I believe, for its mistakes. It has given me education and some of its honors, for which I am thankful.

Today, the scholarly accounts of the life and work of Booker T. Washington are three to four times as many as those on Du Bois. Whatever the ideological neglect since 1975 of the work by Du Bois, his genius was nearly beyond question. He helped usher in the research method of modern sociology, but he was in many ways almost theatrical in revising the personal text for the times. In *Soliloquy* (1968), a final draft of the autobiography completed at ninety, he writes:

> Autobiographies do not form indisputable authorities. They are always incomplete, and often unreliable. Eager as I am to put down the truth, there are difficulties; memory fails especially in small details, so that it becomes finally but a theory of my life, with much forgotten and misconceived, with valuable testimony but often less than absolutely true, despite my intention to be frank and fair.

His life span had covered ninety-three productive years. After having become a full citizen of Ghana, he died in the African country in August 1963.

Although Du Bois would die almost as an embittered Communist disowned—he thought perhaps wrongly—by nearly all of his countrymen, he was an incurable seeker for world peace and a community of humankind. At the turn of the century, his disagreement with Booker T. Washington was the debate of which legends have been made. Washington had proposed that the dreams of social equality and Civil Rights had to be deferred for the purposes of monetary gains in the trades and in skilled labor by the black masses. As black lynching had begun to increase almost exponentially, Du Bois held firm for the human rights to liberal education and free association with all people of aspiration. To many, Du Bois had an arrogant and abrasive manner, but he championed the rights of the poor. What he appreciated about African Americans in the United States he came to value about many groups of people throughout the aboriginal or first worlds. Du Bois was one of the earliest pluralists or proponents of diverse cultures in America. Called by John Oliver Killens "the greatest American intellectual of the twentieth century," he was at least six generations ahead of his time.

❖❖❖

Several pioneering works include Saunders Redding, "Portrait: W.E. Burghardt Du Bois," *The American Scholar,* 18, No. 1 (Winter 1948–49); Francis L. Broderick, *W.E.B. Du Bois, Negro Leader in a Time of Crisis* (Stanford: Stanford University Press, 1959); Oswald G. Villard, "Darkwater," *The Nation,* CX, No. 2865 (May 29, 1920); Charles H. Wesley, "Propaganda and Historical Writing: The Emancipation of the Historian," *Opportunity* 12.8 (August 1935); Charles H. Wesley, "W.E.B. Du Bois the Historian," *Freedomways* 5.1 (First Quarter 1965); Eliott M. Rudwick, *Propagandist of the Negro Protest* (New York: Atheneum, 1968); Rayford Logan, *W.E.B. Du Bois* (1971). Subsequent works of revised fact or interpretation include John Henrik Clarke et al., eds, *Black Titan: W.E.B. Du Bois* (Boston: Beacon Press, 1970); Irene Diggs, introduction to *Dusk of Dawn: An Essay Toward an Autobiography of a Race Concept,* by W.E.B. Du Bois (New Brunswick, N.J.: Transaction Books, 1984); Arlene A. Elder, "Swamp Versus Plantation: Symbolic Structure in W.E.B. Du Bois Triology: A Literary Triumph," *Mainstream* 14, No. 10 (October 1961); Herbert Aptheker, "Du Bois as Historian," *Negro History Bulletin* 32.4 (April 1969); Wilson J. Moses, "The Poetics of Ethiopianism: W.E.B. Du Bois and Literary Black Nationalism," *American Literature* 48.3 (November 1975); Arnold Rampersad, *Art and Imagination of W.E.B. Du Bois* (Cambridge: Harvard University Press, 1976); Arnold Rampersad, "W.E.B. Du Bois as a Man of Literature," *American Literature* 51.1 (March 1979); Robert B. Stepto, "The Quest of the Weary Traveler: W.E.B. Du Bois's *The Souls of Black Folk,*" in *From Behind the Veil: A Study of Afro-American Narrative* (Urbana: University of Illinois Press, 1979); William B. Stone, "Idolect and Ideology: Some Stylistic Aspects of Norris, James, and Du Bois," *Style* 10.4 (Fall 1976); Gerald Horne, *Black and Red* (Albany, N.Y.: State University of New York Press, 1985); Darwin T. Turner, "W.E.B. Du Bois and the Theory of a Black Aesthetic," in *The Harlem Renaissance Re-examined,* edited by Victor A. Kramer (New York: AMS Press, 1987).

FROM *The Souls of Black Folk*

I

Of Our Spiritual Strivings

O WATER, VOICE OF MY HEART, CRYING IN THE SAND,
ALL NIGHT LONG CRYING WITH A MOURNFUL CRY,
AS I LIE AND LISTEN, AND CANNOT UNDERSTAND
THE VOICE OF MY HEART IN MY SIDE OR THE VOICE
OF THE SEA,
O WATER, CRYING FOR REST, IS IT I, IS IT I?
ALL NIGHT LONG THE WATER IS CRYING TO ME.

UNRESTING WATER, THERE SHALL NEVER BE REST
TILL THE LAST MOON DROOP AND THE LAST TIDE FAIL,
AND THE FIRE OF THE END BEGIN TO BURN IN THE WEST;
AND THE HEART SHALL BE WEARY AND WONDER AND CRY
LIKE THE SEA,
ALL LIFE LONG CRYING WITHOUT AVAIL,
AS THE WATER ALL NIGHT LONG IS CRYING TO ME.

ARTHUR SYMONS

Between me and the other world there is ever an unasked question: unasked by some through feelings of delicacy; by others through the difficulty of rightly framing it. All, nevertheless, flutter round it. They approach me in a half-hesitant sort of way, eye me curiously or compassionately, and then, instead of saying directly, how does it feel to be a problem? they say, I know an excellent colored man in my town; or, I fought at Mechanicsville; or, Do not these Southern outrages make your blood boil? At these I smile, or am interested, or reduce the boiling to a simmer, as the occasion may require. To the real question, How does it feel to be a problem? I answer seldom a word.

And yet, being a problem is a strange experience,—peculiar even for one who has never been anything else, save perhaps in babyhood and in Europe. It is in the early days of rollicking boyhood that the revelation first bursts upon one, all in a day, as it were. I remember well when the shadow swept across me. I was a little thing, away up in the hills of New England, where the dark Housatonic winds between Hoosac and Taghkanic to the sea. In a wee wooden schoolhouse, something put it into the boys' and girls' heads to buy gorgeous visiting-cards—ten cents a package—and exchange. The exchange was merry, till one girl, a tall newcomer, refused my card,—refused it peremptorily, with a glance. Then it dawned upon me with a certain suddenness that I was different from the others; or like, mayhap, in heart and life and longing, but shut out from their world by a vast veil. I had thereafter no desire to tear down that veil, to creep through; I held all beyond it in common contempt, and lived above it in a region of blue sky and great wandering shadows. That sky was bluest when I could beat my mates at examination-time, or beat them at a foot-race, or even beat their stringy heads. Alas, with the years all this fine contempt began to fade; for the worlds I have longed for, and all their dazzling opportunities, were theirs, not mine. But they should not keep these prizes, I said; some, all, I would wrest from them. Just how I would do it I could never decide: by reading law, by healing the sick, by telling the wonderful tales that swam in my head,—some way. With other black boys the strife was not so fiercely sunny: their youth shrunk into tasteless sycophancy, or into silent hatred of the pale world about them and mocking distrust of everything white; or wasted itself in a bitter cry, Why did God make me an outcast and a stranger in mine own house? The shades of the prison-house closed round about us all: walls strait and stubborn to the whitest, but relentlessly narrow, tall, and unscalable to sons of night who must plod darkly on in resignation, or beat unavailing palms against the stone, or steadily, half hopelessly, watch the streak of blue above.

After the Egyptian and Indian, the Greek and Roman, the Teuton and Mongolian, the Negro is a sort of seventh son, born with a veil, and gifted with second-sight in this American world,—a world which yields him no true self-consciousness, but only lets him see himself through the revelation of the other world. It is a peculiar sensation, this double-consciousness, this sense of always looking at one's self through the eyes of others, of measuring one's soul by the tape of a world that looks on in amused contempt and pity. One ever feels his two-ness,—an American, a Negro; two souls, two thoughts, two unreconciled strivings; two warring ideals in one dark body, whose dogged strength alone keeps it from being torn asunder.

The history of the American Negro is the history of this strife,—this longing to attain self-conscious manhood, to merge his double self into a better and truer self. In this merging he wishes neither of the older selves to be lost. He would not Africanize America, for America has too much to teach the world and Africa. He would not bleach his Negro soul in a flood of white Americanism, for he knows that Negro blood has a message for the world. He simply wishes to make it possible for a man to be both a Negro and an American, without being cursed and spit upon by his fellows, without having the doors of Opportunity closed roughly in his face.

This, then, is the end of his striving: to be a coworker in the kingdom of culture, to escape both death and isolation, to husband and use his best powers and his latent genius. These powers of body and mind have in the past been strangely wasted, dispersed, or forgotten. The shadow of a mighty Negro past flits through the tale of Ethiopia the Shadowy and of Egypt the Sphinx. Throughout history, the powers of single black men flash here and there like falling stars, and die sometimes before the world has rightly gauged their brightness. Here in America, in the few days since Emancipation, the black man's turning hither and thither in hesitant and doubtful striving has often made his very strength to lose effectiveness, to seem like absence of power, like weakness. And yet it is not weakness,—it is the contradiction of double aims. The double-aimed struggle of the black artisan—on the one hand to escape white contempt for a nation of mere hewers of wood and drawers of water, and on the other hand to plough and nail and dig for a poverty-stricken horde—could only result in making him a poor craftsman, for he had but half a heart in either cause. By the poverty and ignorance of his people, the Negro minister or doctor was tempted toward quackery and demagogy; and by the criticism of the other world, toward ideals that made him ashamed of his lowly tasks. The would-be black *savant* was confronted by the paradox that the knowledge his people needed was a twice-told tale to his white neighbors, while the knowledge which would teach the white world was Greek to his own flesh and blood. The innate love of harmony and beauty that set the ruder souls of his people a-dancing and a-singing raised but confusion and doubt in the soul of the black artist; for the beauty revealed to him was the soul-beauty of a race which his larger audience despised, and he could not articulate the message of another people. This waste of double aims, this seeking to satisfy two unreconciled ideals, has wrought sad havoc with the courage and faith and deeds of ten thousand thousand people,—has sent them often wooing false gods and invoking false means of salvation, and at times has even seemed about to make them ashamed of themselves.

Away back in the days of bondage they thought to see in one divine event the end of all doubt and disappointment; few men ever worshipped Freedom with half such unquestioning faith as did the American Negro for two centuries. To him, so far as he thought and dreamed, slavery was indeed the sum of all villainies, the cause of all sorrow, the root of all prejudice; Emancipation was the key to a promised land of sweeter beauty than ever stretched before the eyes of wearied Israelites. In song and exhortation swelled one refrain—Liberty; in his tears and curses the God he implored had Freedom in his right hand. At last it came,—suddenly, fearfully, like a dream. With one wild carnival of blood and passion came the message in his own plaintive cadences:—

> "Shout, O children!
> Shout, you're free!
> For God has bought your liberty!"

Years have passed away since then,—ten, twenty, forty; forty years of national life, forty years of renewal and development, and yet the swarthy spectre sits in its accustomed seat at the Nation's feast. In vain do we cry to this our vastest social problem:—

> "Take any shape but that, and my firm nerves
> Shall never tremble!"

The Nation has not yet found peace from its sins; the freedman has not yet found in freedom his promised land. Whatever of good may have come in these years of change, the shadow of a deep disappointment rests upon the Negro people,—a disappointment all the more bitter because the unattained ideal was unbounded save by the simple ignorance of a lowly people.

The first decade was merely a prolongation of the vain search for freedom, the boon that seemed ever barely to elude their grasp,—like a tantalizing will-o'-the-wisp, maddening and misleading the headless host. The holocaust of war, the terrors of the Ku-Klux Klan, the lies of carpet-baggers, the disorganization of industry, and the contradictory advice of friends and foes, left the bewildered serf with no new watchword beyond the old cry for freedom. As the time flew, however, he began to grasp a new idea. The ideal of liberty demanded for its attainment powerful means, and these the Fifteenth

Amendment gave him. The ballot, which before he had looked upon as a visible sign of freedom, he now regarded as the chief means of gaining and perfecting the liberty with which war had partially endowed him. And why not? Had not votes made war and emancipated millions? Had not votes enfranchised the freedmen? Was anything impossible to a power that had done all this? A million black men started with renewed zeal to vote themselves into the kingdom. So the decade flew away, the revolution of 1876 came, and left the half-free serf weary, wondering, but still inspired. Slowly but steadily, in the following years, a new vision began gradually to replace the dream of political power,—a powerful movement, the rise of another ideal to guide the unguided, another pillar of fire by night after a clouded day. It was the ideal of "book-learning"; the curiosity, born of compulsory ignorance, to know and test the power of the cabalistic letters of the white man, the longing to know. Here at last seemed to have been discovered the mountain path to Canaan; longer than the highway of Emancipation and law, steep and rugged, but straight, leading to heights high enough to overlook life.

Up the new path the advance guard toiled, slowly, heavily, doggedly; only those who have watched and guided the faltering feet, the misty minds, the dull understandings, of the dark pupils of these schools know how faithfully, how piteously, this people strove to learn. It was weary work. The cold statistician wrote down the inches of progress here and there, noted also where here and there a foot had slipped or some one had fallen. To the tired climbers, the horizon was ever dark, the mists were often cold, the Canaan was always dim and far away. If, however, the vistas disclosed as yet no goal, no resting place, little but flattery and criticism, the journey at least gave leisure for reflection and self-examination; it changed the child of Emancipation to the youth with dawning self-consciousness, self-realization, self-respect. In those sombre forests of his striving his own soul rose before him, and he saw himself,—darkly as through a veil; and yet he saw in himself some faint revelation of his power, of his mission. He began to have a dim feeling that, to attain his place in the world, he must be himself, and not another. For the first time he sought to analyze the burden he bore upon his back, that dead-weight of social degradation partially masked behind a half-named Negro problem. He felt his poverty; without a cent, without a home, without land, tools, or savings, he had entered into competition with rich, landed, skilled neighbors. To be a poor man is hard, but to be a poor race in a land of dollars is the very bottom of hardships. He felt the weight of his ignorance,—not simply of letters, but of life, of business, of the humanities; the accumulated sloth and shirking and awkwardness of decades and centuries shackled his hands and feet. Nor was his burden all poverty and ignorance. The red stain of bastardy, which two centuries of systematic legal defilement of Negro women had stamped upon his race, meant not only the loss of ancient African chastity, but also the hereditary weight of a mass of corruption from white adulterers, threatening almost the obliteration of the Negro home.

A people thus handicapped ought not to be asked to race with the world, but rather allowed to give all its time and thought to its own social problems. But alas! while sociologists gleefully count his bastards and his prostitutes, the very soul of the toiling, sweating black man is darkened by the shadow of a vast despair. Men call the shadow prejudice, and learnedly explain it as the natural defence of culture against barbarism, learning against ignorance, purity against crime, the "higher" against the "lower" races. To which the Negro cries Amen! and swears that to so much of this strange prejudice as is founded on just homage to civilization, culture, righteousness, and progress, he humbly bows and meekly does obeisance. But before that nameless prejudice that leaps beyond all this he stands helpless, dismayed, and well-nigh speechless; before that personal disrespect and mockery, the ridicule and systematic humiliation, the distortion of fact and wanton license of fancy, the cynical ignoring of the better and the boisterous welcoming of the worse, the all-pervading desire to inculcate disdain for everything black, from Toussaint to the devil,—before this there rises a sickening despair that would disarm and discourage any nation save that black host to whom "discouragement" is an unwritten word.

But the facing of so vast a prejudice could not but bring the inevitable self-questioning, self-disparagement, and lowering of ideals which ever accompany repression and breed in an atmosphere of contempt and hate. Whisperings and portents came borne upon the four winds: Lo! we are diseased and dying, cried the dark hosts; we cannot write, our voting is vain; what need of education, since we must always cook and serve? And the Nation echoed and enforced this self-criticism, saying: Be content to be servants, and nothing more; what need of higher culture for half-men? Away with the black man's ballot, by force or fraud,—and behold the suicide of a race! Nevertheless, out of the evil came something of good,—the more careful adjustment of education to real life, the clearer perception of the Negroes' social responsibilities, and the sobering realization of the meaning of progress.

So dawned the time of *Sturm und Drang*: storm and stress to-day rocks our little boat on the mad waters of the world-sea; there is within and without the sound of conflict, the burning of body and rending of soul; inspiration strives with doubt, and faith with vain questionings. The bright ideals of the past,—physical freedom, political power, the training of brains and the training of hands,—all these in turn have waxed and waned, until even the last grows dim and overcast. Are they all wrong,—all false? No, not that, but each alone was over-simple and incomplete,—the dreams of a credulous race-childhood, or the fond imaginings of the other world which does not know and does not want to know our power. To be really true, all these ideals must be melted and welded into one. The training of the schools we need to-day more than ever,—the training of deft hands, quick eyes and ears, and above all the broader, deeper, higher culture of gifted minds and pure hearts. The power of the ballot we need in sheer self-defence,—else what shall save us from a second slavery? Freedom, too, the long-sought, we still seek,—the freedom of life and limb, the freedom to work and think, the freedom to love and aspire. Work, culture, liberty,—all these we need, not singly but together, not successively but together, each growing and aiding each, and all striving toward that vaster ideal that swims before the Negro people, the ideal of human brotherhood, gained through the unifying ideal of Race; the ideal of fostering and developing the traits and talents of the Negro, not in opposition to or contempt for other races, but rather in large conformity to the greater ideals of the American Republic, in order that some day on American soil two world-races may give each to each those characteristics both so sadly lack. We the darker ones come even now not altogether empty-handed: there are to-day no truer exponents of the pure human spirit of the Declaration of Independence than the American Negroes; there is no true American music but the wild sweet melodies of the Negro slave; the American fairy tales and folk-lore are Indian and African; and, all in all, we black men seem the sole oasis of simple faith and reverence in a dusty desert of dollars and smartness. Will America be poorer if she replace her brutal dyspeptic blundering with lighthearted but determined Negro humility? or her coarse and cruel wit with loving jovial good-humor? or her vulgar music with the soul of the Sorrow Songs?

Merely a concrete test of the underlying principles of the great republic is the Negro Problem, and the spiritual striving of the freedmen's sons is the travail of souls whose burden is almost beyond the measure of their strength, but who bear it in the name of an historic race, in the name of this the land of their fathers' fathers, and in the name of human opportunity.

And now what I have briefly sketched in large outline let me on coming pages tell again in many ways, with loving emphasis and deeper detail, that men may listen to the striving in the souls of black folk.

III
Of Mr. Booker T. Washington and Others

FROM BIRTH TILL DEATH ENSLAVED; IN WORD, IN DEED, UNMANNED!

❖❖❖

HEREDITARY BONDSMEN! KNOW YE NOT
WHO WOULD BE FREE THEMSELVES MUST STRIKE
THE BLOW?

BYRON

Easily the most striking thing in the history of the American Negro since 1876 is the ascendancy of Mr. Booker T. Washington. It began at the time when war memories and ideals were rapidly passing; a day of astonishing commercial development was dawning; a sense of doubt and hesitation overtook the freedmen's sons,—then it was that his leading began. Mr. Washington came, with a simple definite programme, at the psychological moment when the nation was a little ashamed of having bestowed so much sentiment on Negroes, and was concentrating its energies on Dollars. His programme of industrial education, conciliation of the South, and submission and silence as to civil and political rights, was not wholly original; the Free Negroes from 1830 up to war-time had striven to build industrial schools, and the American Missionary Association had from the first taught various trades; and Price and others had sought a way of honorable alliance with the best of the Southerners. But Mr. Washington first indissolubly linked these things; he put enthusiasm, unlimited energy, and perfect faith into this programme, and changed it from a by-path into a veritable Way of Life. And the tale of the methods by which he did this is a fascinating study of human life.

It startled the nation to hear a Negro advocating such a programme after many decades of bitter complaint; it startled and won the applause of the South, it interested and won the admiration of the North; and after a confused murmur of protest, it silenced if it did not convert the Negroes themselves.

To gain the sympathy and cooperation of the various elements comprising the white South was Mr. Washington's first task; and this, at the time Tuskegee was founded, seemed, for a black man, well-nigh impossible. And yet ten years later it was done in the word spoken at Atlanta: "In all things purely social we can be as separate as the five fingers, and yet one as the hand in all things essential to mutual progress." This "Atlanta Compromise" is by all odds the most notable thing in Mr. Washington's career. The South interpreted it in different ways: the radicals received it as a complete surrender of the demand for civil and political equality; the conservatives, as a generously conceived working basis for mutual understanding. So both approved it, and to-day its author is certainly the most distinguished Southerner since Jefferson Davis, and the one with the largest personal following.

Next to this achievement comes Mr. Washington's work in gaining place and consideration in the North. Others less shrewd and tactful had formerly essayed to sit on these two stools and had fallen between them; but as Mr. Washington knew the heart of the South from birth and training, so by singular insight he intuitively grasped the spirit of the age which was dominating the North. And so thoroughly did he learn the speech and thought of triumphant commercialism, and the ideals of material prosperity, that the picture of a lone black boy poring over a French grammar amid the weeds and dirt of a neglected home soon seemed to him the acme of absurdities. One wonders what Socrates and St. Francis of Assisi would say to this.

And yet this very singleness of vision and thorough oneness with his age is a mark of the successful man. It is as though Nature must needs make men narrow in order to give them force. So Mr. Washington's cult has gained unquestioning followers, his work has wonderfully prospered, his friends are legion, and his enemies are confounded. To-day he stands as the one recognized spokesman of his ten million fellows, and one of the most notable figures in a nation of seventy millions. One hesitates, therefore, to criticise a life which, beginning with so little, has done so much. And yet the time is come when one may speak in all sincerity and utter courtesy of the mistakes and shortcomings of Mr. Washington's career, as well as of his triumphs, without being thought captious or envious, and without forgetting that it is easier to do ill than well in the world.

The criticism that has hitherto met Mr. Washington has not always been of this broad character. In the South especially has he had to walk warily to avoid the harshest judgments,—and naturally so, for he is dealing with the one subject of deepest sensitiveness to that section. Twice—once when at the Chicago celebration of the Spanish-American War he alluded to the color-prejudice that is "eating away the vitals of the South," and once when he dined with President Roosevelt—has the resulting Southern criticism been violent enough to threaten seriously his popularity. In the North the feeling has several times forced itself into words, that Mr. Washington's counsels of submission overlooked certain elements of true manhood, and that his educational programme was unnecessarily narrow. Usually, however, such criticism has not found open expression, although, too, the spiritual sons of the Abolitionists have not been prepared to acknowledge that the schools founded before Tuskegee, by men of broad ideals and self-sacrificing spirit, were wholly failures or worthy of ridicule. While, then, criticism has not failed to follow Mr. Washington, yet the prevailing public opinion of the land has been but too willing to deliver the solution of a wearisome problem into his hands, and say, "If that is all you and your race ask, take it."

Among his own people, however, Mr. Washington has encountered the strongest and most lasting opposition, amounting at times to bitterness, and even to-day continuing strong and insistent even though largely silenced in outward expression by the public opinion of the nation. Some of this opposition is, of course, mere envy; the disappointment of displaced demagogues and the spite of narrow minds. But aside from this, there is among educated and thoughtful colored men in all parts of the land a feeling of deep regret, sorrow, and apprehension at the wide currency and ascendancy which some of Mr. Washington's theories have gained. These same men admire his sincerity of purpose, and are willing to forgive much to honest endeavor which is doing something worth the doing. They cooperate with Mr. Washington as far as they conscientiously can; and, indeed, it is no ordinary tribute to this man's tact and power that, steering as he must between so many diverse interests and opinions, he so largely retains the respect of all.

But the hushing of the criticism of honest opponents is a dangerous thing. It leads some of the best of the critics to unfortunate silence and paralysis of effort, and others to burst into speech so passionately and intemperately as to lose listeners. Honest and earnest criticism from those whose interests are most nearly touched,—criticism of writers by readers, of government by those governed, of leaders by those led,—this is the soul of democracy and the safeguard of modern society. If the best of the American Negroes receive by outer pressure a leader whom they had not recognized before, manifestly there is here a certain palpable gain. Yet there is also irreparable loss,—a loss of that peculiarly valuable education which a group receives when by search and criticism it finds and commissions its own leaders. The way in which this is done is at once the most elementary and the nicest problem of social growth. History is but the record of such group-leadership; and yet how infinitely changeful is its type and character! And of all types and kinds, what can be more instructive than the leadership of a group within a group?—that curious double movement where real progress may be negative and actual advance be relative retrogression. All this is the social student's inspiration and despair.

Now in the past the American Negro has had instructive experience in the choosing of group leaders, founding thus a peculiar dynasty which in the light of present conditions is worth while studying. When sticks and stones and beasts form the sole environment of a people, their attitude is largely one of determined opposition to and conquest of natural forces. But when to earth and brute is added an environment of men and ideas, then the attitude of the imprisoned group may take three main forms,—a feeling of revolt and revenge; an attempt to adjust all thought and action to the will of the greater group; or, finally, a determined effort at self-realization and self-development despite environing opinion. The influence of all of these attitudes at various times can be traced in the history of the American Negro, and in the evolution of his successive leaders.

Before 1750, while the fire of African freedom still burned in the veins of the slaves, there was in all leadership or attempted leadership but the one motive of revolt and revenge,—typified in the terrible Maroons, the Danish blacks, and Cato of Stono, and veiling all the Americas in fear of insurrection. The liberalizing tendencies of the latter half of the eighteenth century brought, along with kindlier relations between black and white, thoughts of ultimate adjustment and assimilation. Such aspiration was especially voiced in the earnest songs of Phyllis, in the martyrdom of Attucks, the fighting of Salem and Poor, the intellectual accomplishments of Banneker and Derham, and the political demands of the Cuffes.

Stern financial and social stress after the war cooled much of the previous humanitarian ardor. The disappointment and impatience of the Negroes at the persistence of slavery and serfdom voiced itself in two movements. The slaves in the South, aroused undoubtedly by vague rumors of the Haytian revolt, made three fierce attempts at insurrection,—in 1800 under Gabriel in Virginia, in 1822 under Vesey in Carolina, and in 1831 again in Virginia under the terrible Nat Turner. In the Free States, on the other hand, a new and curious attempt at self-development was made. In Philadelphia and New York color-prescription led to a withdrawal of Negro communicants from white churches and the formation of a peculiar socio-religious institution among the Negroes known as the African Church,—an organization still living and controlling in its various branches over a million of men.

Walker's wild appeal against the trend of the times showed how the world was changing after the coming of the cotton-gin. By 1830 slavery seemed hopelessly fastened on the South, and the slaves thoroughly cowed into submission. The free Negroes of the North, inspired by the mulatto immigrants from the West Indies, began to change the basis of their demands; they recognized the slavery of slaves, but insisted that they themselves were freemen, and sought assimilation and amalgamation with the nation on the same terms with other men. Thus, Forten and Purvis of Philadelphia, Shad of Wilmington, Du Bois of New Haven, Barbadoes of Boston, and others, strove singly and together as men, they said, not as slaves; as "people of color," not as "Negroes." The trend of the times, however, refused them recognition save in individual and exceptional cases, considered them as one with all the despised blacks, and they soon found themselves striving to keep even the rights they formerly had of voting and working and moving as freemen. Schemes of migration and colonization arose among them; but these they refused to entertain, and they eventually turned to the Abolition movement as a final refuge.

Here, led by Remond, Nell, Wells-Brown, and Douglass, a new period of self-assertion and self-development dawned. To be sure, ultimate freedom and assimilation was the ideal before the leaders, but the assertion of the manhood rights of the Negro by himself was the main reliance, and John Brown's raid was the extreme of its logic. After the war and emancipation, the great form of Frederick Douglass, the greatest of American Negro leaders, still led the host. Self-assertion, especially in political lines, was the main programme, and behind Douglass came Elliot, Bruce, and Langston, and the Reconstruction politicians, and, less conspicuous but of greater social significance Alexander Crummell and Bishop Daniel Payne.

Then came the Revolution of 1876, the suppression of the Negro votes, the changing and shifting of ideals, and the seeking of new lights in the great night. Douglass, in his old age, still bravely stood for the ideals of his early manhood,—ultimate assimilation *through* self-assertion, and on no other terms. For a time Price arose as a new leader, destined, it seemed, not to give up, but to re-state the old ideals in a form less repugnant to the white South. But he passed away in his prime. Then came the new leader. Nearly all the former ones had become leaders by the silent suffrage of their fellows, had sought to lead their own people alone, and were usually, save Douglass, little known outside their race. But Booker T. Washington arose as essentially the leader not of one race but of two,—a compromiser between the South, the North, and the Negro. Naturally the Negroes resented, at first bitterly, signs of compromise which surrendered their civil and political rights, even though this was to be exchanged for larger chances of economic development. The rich and dominating North, however, was not only weary of the race problem, but was investing largely in Southern enterprises, and welcomed any method of peaceful cooperation. Thus, by national opinion, the Negroes began to recognize Mr. Washington's leadership; and the voice of criticism was hushed.

Mr. Washington represents in Negro thought the old attitude of adjustment and submission; but adjustment at such a peculiar time as to make his programme unique. This is an age of unusual economic development, and Mr. Washington's programme naturally takes an economic cast, becoming a gospel of Work and Money to such an extent as apparently almost completely to overshadow the higher aims of life. Moreover, this is an age when the more advanced races are coming in closer contact with the less developed races, and the race-feeling is therefore intensified; and Mr. Washington's programme practically accepts the alleged inferiority of the Negro races. Again, in our own land, the reaction from the sentiment of war time has given impetus to race-prejudice against Negroes, and Mr. Washington withdraws many of the high demands of Negroes as men and American citizens. In other periods of intensified prejudice all the Negro's tendency to self-assertion has been called forth; at this period a policy of submission is advocated. In the history of nearly all other races and peoples the doctrine preached at such crises has been that manly self-respect is worth more than lands and houses, and that a people who voluntarily surrender such respect, or cease striving for it, are not worth civilizing.

In answer to this, it has been claimed that the Negro can survive only through submission. Mr. Washington distinctly asks that black people give up, at least for the present, three things,—

First, political power,

Second, insistence on civil rights,

Third, higher education of Negro youth,—

and concentrate all their energies on industrial education, the accumulation of wealth, and the conciliation of the South. This policy has been courageously and insistently advocated for over fifteen years, and has been triumphant for perhaps ten years. As a result of this tender of the palm-branch, what has been the return? In these years there have occurred:

1. The disfranchisement of the Negro.
2. The legal creation of a distinct status of civil inferiority for the Negro.
3. The steady withdrawal of aid from institutions for the higher training of the Negro.

These movements are not, to be sure, direct results of Mr. Washington's teachings; but his propaganda has, without a shadow of doubt, helped their speedier accomplishment. The question then comes: Is it possible, and probable, that nine millions of men can make effective progress in economic lines if they are deprived of political rights, made a servile caste, and allowed only the most meagre chance for developing their exceptional men? If history and reason give any distinct answer to these questions, it is an emphatic *No*. And Mr. Washington thus faces the triple paradox of his career:

1. He is striving nobly to make Negro artisans business men and property-owners; but it is utterly impossible, under modern competitive methods, for workingmen and property-owners to defend their rights and exist without the right of suffrage.
2. He insists on thrift and self-respect, but at the same time counsels a silent submission to civic inferiority such as is bound to sap the manhood of any race in the long run.
3. He advocates common-school and industrial training, and depreciates institutions of higher learning; but neither the Negro common-schools, nor Tuskegee itself, could remain open a day were it not for teachers trained in Negro colleges, or trained by their graduates.

This triple paradox in Mr. Washington's position is the object of criticism by two classes of colored Americans. One class is spiritually descended from Toussaint the Savior, through Gabriel, Vesey, and Turner, and they represent the attitude of revolt and revenge; they hate the white South blindly and distrust the white race generally, and so far as they agree on definite action, think that the Negro's only hope lies in emigration beyond the borders of the United States. And yet, by the irony of fate, nothing has more effectually made this programme seem hopeless than the recent course of the United States toward weaker and darker peoples in the West Indies, Hawaii, and the Philippines,—for where in the world may we go and be safe from lying and brute force?

The other class of Negroes who cannot agree with Mr. Washington has hitherto said little aloud. They deprecate the sight of scattered counsels, of internal disagreement; and especially they dislike making their just criticism of a useful and earnest man an excuse for a general discharge of venom from small-minded opponents. Nevertheless, the questions involved are so fundamental and serious that it is difficult to see how men like the Grimkes, Kelly Miller, J.W.E. Bowen, and other representatives of this group, can much longer be silent. Such men feel in conscience bound to ask of this nation three things:

1. The right to vote.
2. Civic equality.
3. The education of youth according to ability.

They acknowledge Mr. Washington's invaluable service in counselling patience and courtesy in such demands; they do not ask that ignorant black men vote when ignorant whites are debarred, or that any reasonable restrictions in the suffrage should not be applied; they know that the low social level of the mass of the race is responsible for much discrimination against it, but they also know, and the nation knows, that relentless color-prejudice is more often a cause than a result of the Negro's degradation; they seek the abatement of this relic of barbarism, and not its systematic encouragement and pampering by all agencies of social power from the Associated Press to the Church of Christ. They advocate, with Mr. Washington, a broad system of Negro common schools supplemented by thorough industrial training; but they are surprised that a man of Mr. Washington's insight cannot see that no such educational system ever has rested or can rest on any other basis than that of the well-equipped college and university, and they insist that there is a demand for a few such institutions throughout the South to train the best of the Negro youth as teachers, professional men, and leaders.

This group of men honor Mr. Washington for his attitude of conciliation toward the white South; they accept the "Atlanta Compromise" in its broadest interpretation; they recognize, with him, many signs of promise, many men of high purpose and fair judgment, in this section; they know that no easy task has been laid upon a region already tottering under heavy burdens.

But, nevertheless, they insist that the way to truth and right lies in straightforward honesty, not in indiscriminate flattery; in praising those of the South who do well and criticising uncompromisingly those who do ill; in taking advantage of the opportunities at hand and urging their fellows to do the same, but at the same time in remembering that only a firm adherence to their higher ideals and aspirations will ever keep those ideals within the realm of possibility. They do not expect that the free right to vote, to enjoy civic rights, and to be educated, will come in a moment; they do not expect to see the bias and prejudices of years disappear at the blast of a trumpet; but they are absolutely certain that the way for a people to gain their reasonable rights is not by voluntarily throwing them away and insisting that they do not want them; that the way for a people to gain respect is not by continually belittling and ridiculing themselves; that, on the contrary, Negroes must insist continually, in season and out of season, that voting is necessary to modern manhood, that color discrimination is barbarism, and that black boys need education as well as white boys.

In failing thus to state plainly and unequivocally the legitimate demands of their people, even at the cost of opposing an honored leader, the thinking classes of American Negroes would shirk a heavy responsibility,—a responsibility to themselves, a responsibility to the struggling masses, a responsibility to the darker races of men whose future depends so largely on this American experiment, but especially a responsibility to this nation,—this common Fatherland. It is wrong to encourage a man or a people in evil-doing; it is wrong to aid and abet a national crime simply because it is unpopular not to do so. The growing spirit of kindliness and reconciliation between the North and South after the frightful differences of a generation ago ought to be a source of deep congratulation to all, and especially to those whose mistreatment caused the war; but if that reconciliation is to be marked by the industrial slavery and civic death of those same black men, with permanent legislation into a position of inferiority, then those black men, if they are really men, are called upon by every consideration of patriotism and loyalty to oppose such a course by all civilized methods, even though such opposition involves disagreement with Mr. Booker T. Washington. We have no right to sit silently by while the inevitable seeds are sown for a harvest of disaster to our children, black and white.

First, it is the duty of black men to judge the South discriminatingly. The present generation of Southerners are not responsible for the past, and they should not be blindly hated or blamed for it. Furthermore, to no class is the indiscriminate endorsement of the recent course of the South toward Negroes more nauseating than to the best thought of the South. The South is not "solid"; it is a land in the ferment of social change, wherein forces of all kinds are fighting for supremacy; and to praise the ill the South is to-day perpetrating is just as wrong as to condemn the good. Discriminating and broad-minded criticism is what the South needs,—needs it for the sake of her own white sons and daughters, and for the insurance of robust, healthy mental and moral development.

To-day even the attitude of the Southern whites toward the blacks is not, as so many assume, in all cases the same; the ignorant Southerner hates the Negro, the workingmen fear his competition, the money-makers wish to use him as a laborer, some of the educated see a menace in his upward development, while others—usually the sons of the masters—wish to help him to rise. National opinion has enabled this last class to maintain the Negro common schools, and to protect the Negro partially in property, life, and limb. Through the pressure of the money-makers, the Negro is in danger of being reduced to semi-slavery, especially in the country districts; the workingmen, and those of the educated who fear the Negro, have united to disfranchise him, and some have urged his deportation; while the passions of the ignorant are easily aroused to lynch and abuse any black man. To praise this intricate whirl of thought and prejudice is nonsense; to inveigh indiscriminately against "the South" is unjust; but to use the same breath in praising Governor Aycock, exposing Senator Morgan, arguing with Mr. Thomas Nelson Page, and denouncing Senator Ben Tillman, is not only sane, but the imperative duty of thinking black men.

It would be unjust to Mr. Washington not to acknowledge that in several instances he has opposed movements in the South which were unjust to the Negro; he sent memorials to the Louisiana and Alabama constitutional conventions, he has spoken against lynching, and in other ways has openly or silently set his influence against sinister schemes and unfortunate happenings. Notwithstanding this, it is equally true to assert that on the whole the distinct impression left by Mr. Washington's propaganda is, first, that the South is justified in its present attitude toward the Negro because of the Negro's degradation; secondly, that the prime cause of the Negro's failure to rise more quickly is his wrong education in the past; and, thirdly, that his future rise depends primarily on his own efforts. Each of these propositions is a dangerous half-truth. The supplementary truths must never be lost sight of: first, slavery and race-prejudice are potent if not sufficient causes of the Negro's position; second, industrial and common-school training were necessarily slow in planting because they had to await the black teachers trained by higher institutions,—it being extremely doubtful if any essentially different development was possible, and certainly a Tuskegee was unthinkable before 1880; and, third, while it is a great truth to say that the Negro must strive and strive mightily to help himself, it is equally true that unless his striving be not simply seconded, but rather aroused and encouraged, by the initiative of the richer and wiser environing group, he cannot hope for great success.

In his failure to realize and impress this last point, Mr. Washington is especially to be criticised. His doctrine has tended to make the whites, North and South, shift the burden of the Negro problem to the Negro's shoulders and stand aside as critical and rather pessimistic spectators; when in fact the burden belongs to the nation, and the hands of none of us are clean if we bend not our energies to righting these great wrongs.

The South ought to be led, by candid and honest criticism, to assert her better self and do her full duty to the race she has cruelly wronged and is still wronging. The North—her co-partner in guilt—cannot salve her conscience by plastering it with gold. We cannot settle this problem by diplomacy and suaveness, by "policy" alone. If worse come to worst, can the moral fibre of this country survive the slow throttling and murder of nine millions of men?

The black men of America have a duty to perform, a duty stern and delicate,—a forward movement to oppose a part of the work of their greatest leader. So far as Mr. Washington preaches Thrift, Patience, and Industrial Training for the masses, we must hold up his hands and strive with him, rejoicing in his honors and glorying in the strength of this Joshua called of God and of man to lead the headless host. But so far as Mr. Washington apologizes for injustice, North or South, does not rightly value the privilege and duty of voting, belittles the emasculating effects of caste distinctions, and opposes the higher training and ambition of our brighter minds,—so far as he, the South, or the Nation, does this,—we must unceasingly and firmly oppose them. By every civilized and peaceful method we must strive for the rights which the world accords to men, clinging unwaveringly to those great words which the sons of the Fathers would fain forget: "We hold these truths to be self-evident: That all men are created equal; that they are endowed by their Creator with certain unalienable rights; that among these are life, liberty, and the pursuit of happiness."

XIV
Of the Sorrow Songs

I WALK THROUGH THE CHURCHYARD
TO LAY THIS BODY DOWN;
I KNOW MOON-RISE, I KNOW STAR-RISE;

I WALK IN THE MOONLIGHT, I WALK IN THE STARLIGHT;
I'LL LIE IN THE GRAVE AND STRETCH OUT MY ARMS,
I'LL GO TO JUDGMENT IN THE EVENING OF THE DAY,
AND MY SOUL AND THY SOUL SHALL MEET THAT DAY,
WHEN I LAY THIS BODY DOWN.

NEGRO SONG

They that walked in darkness sang songs in the olden days—Sorrow Songs—for they were weary at heart. And so before each thought that I have written in this book I have set a phrase, a haunting echo of these weird old songs in which the soul of the black slave spoke to men. Ever since I was a child these songs have stirred me strangely. They came out of the South unknown to me, one by one, and yet at once I knew them as of me and of mine. Then in after years when I came to Nashville I saw the great temple builded of these songs towering over the pale city. To me Jubilee Hall seemed ever made of the songs themselves, and its bricks were red with the blood and dust of toil. Out of them rose for me morning, noon, and night, bursts of wonderful melody, full of the voices of my brothers and sisters, full of the voices of the past.

Little of beauty has America given the world save the rude grandeur God himself stamped on her bosom; the human spirit in this new world has expressed itself in vigor and ingenuity rather than in beauty. And so by fateful chance the Negro folk-song—the rhythmic cry of the slave—stands to-day not simply as the sole American music, but as the most beautiful expression of human experience born this side the seas. It has been neglected, it has been, and is, half despised, and above all it has been persistently mistaken and misunderstood; but notwithstanding, it still remains as the singular spiritual heritage of the nation and the greatest gift of the Negro people.

Away back in the thirties the melody of these slave songs stirred the nation, but the songs were soon half forgotten. Some, like "Near the lake where drooped the willow," passed into current airs and their source was forgotten; others were caricatured on the "minstrel" stage and their memory died away. Then in war-time came the singular Port Royal experiment after the capture of Hilton Head, and perhaps for the first time the North met the Southern slave face to face and heart to heart with no third witness. The Sea Islands of the Carolinas, where they met, were filled with a black folk of primitive type, touched and moulded less by the world about them than any others outside the Black Belt. Their appearance was uncouth, their language funny, but their hearts were human and their singing stirred men with a mighty power. Thomas Wentworth Higginson hastened to tell of these songs, and Miss McKim and others urged upon the world their rare beauty. But the world listened only half credulously until the Fisk Jubilee Singers sang the slave songs so deeply into the world's heart that it can never wholly forget them again.

There was once a blacksmith's son born at Cadiz, New York, who in the changes of time taught school in Ohio and helped defend Cincinnati from Kirby Smith. Then he fought at Chancellorsville and Gettysburg and finally served in the Freedman's Bureau at Nashville. Here he formed a Sunday-school class of black children in 1866, and sang with them and taught them to sing. And then they taught him to sing, and when once the glory of the Jubilee songs passed into the soul of George L. White, he knew his life-work was to let those Negroes sing to the world as they had sung to him. So in 1871 the pilgrimage of the Fisk Jubilee Singers began. North to Cincinnati they rode,—four half-clothed black boys and five girl-women,—led by a man with a cause and a purpose. They stopped at Wilberforce, the oldest of Negro schools, where a black bishop blessed them.

Then they went, fighting cold and starvation, shut out of hotels, and cheerfully sneered at, ever northward; and ever the magic of their song kept thrilling hearts, until a burst of applause in the Congregational Council at Oberlin revealed them to the world. They came to New York and Henry Ward Beecher dared to welcome them, even though the metropolitan dailies sneered at his "Nigger Minstrels." So their songs conquered till they sang across the land and across the sea, before Queen and Kaiser, in Scotland and Ireland, Holland and Switzerland. Seven years they sang, and brought back a hundred and fifty thousand dollars to found Fisk University.

Since their day they have been imitated—sometimes well, by the singers of Hampton and Atlanta, sometimes ill, by straggling quartettes. Caricature has sought again to spoil the quaint beauty of the music, and has filled the air with many debased melodies which vulgar ears scarce know from the real. But the true Negro folk-song still lives in the hearts of those who have heard them truly sung and in the hearts of the Negro people.

What are these songs, and what do they mean? I know little of music and can say nothing in technical phrase, but I know something of men, and knowing them, I know that these songs are the articulate message of the slave to the world. They tell us in these eager days that life was joyous to the black slave, careless and happy. I can easily believe this of some, of many. But not all the past South, though it rose from the dead, can gainsay the heart-touching witness of these songs. They are the music of an unhappy people, of the children of disappointment; they tell of death and suffering and unvoiced longing toward a truer world, of misty wanderings and hidden ways.

The songs are indeed the siftings of centuries; the music is far more ancient than the words, and in it we can trace here and there signs of development. My grandfather's grandmother was seized by an evil Dutch trader two centuries ago; and coming to the valleys of the Hudson and Housatonic, black, little, and lithe, she shivered and shrank in the harsh north winds, looked longingly at the hills, and often crooned a heathen melody to the child between her knees, thus:

Do ba-na co-ba, ge-ne me, ge-ne me!
Do ba-na co-ba, ge-ne me, ge-ne me!
Ben d' nu-li, nu-li, nu-li, nu-li, ben d' le.

The child sang it to his children and they to their children's children, and so two hundred years it has travelled down to us and we sing it to our children, knowing as little as our fathers what its words may mean, but knowing well the meaning of its music.

This was primitive African music; it may be seen in larger form in the strange chant which heralds "The Coming of John":

"You may bury me in the East,
You may bury me in the West,
But I'll hear the trumpet sound in that morning,"

—the voice of exile.

Ten master songs, more or less, one may pluck from this forest of melody—songs of undoubted Negro origin and wide popular currency, and songs peculiarly characteristic of the slave. One of these I have just mentioned. Another whose strains begin this book is "Nobody knows the trouble I've seen." When, struck with a sudden poverty, the United States refused to fulfil its promises of land to the freedmen, a brigadier-general went down to the Sea Islands to carry the news. An old woman on the outskirts of the throng began singing this song; all the mass joined with her, swaying. And the soldier wept.

The third song is the cradle-song of death which all men know,—"Swing low, sweet chariot,"—whose bars begin the life story of "Alexander Crummell." Then there is the song of many waters, "Roll, Jordan, roll," a mighty chorus with minor cadences. There were many songs of the fugitive like that which opens "The Wings of Atalanta," and the more familiar "Been a-listening." The seventh is the song of the End and the Beginning—"My Lord, what a mourning! when the stars begin to fall"; a strain of this is placed before "The Dawn of Freedom." The song of groping—"My way's cloudy"—begins "The Meaning of Progress"; the ninth is the song of this chapter—"Wrestlin' Jacob, the day is a-breaking,"—a pæan of hopeful strife. The last master song is the song of songs—"Steal away,"—sprung from "The Faith of the Fathers."

There are many others of the Negro folk-songs as striking and characteristic as these, as, for instance, the three strains in the third, eighth, and ninth chapters; and others I am sure could easily make a selection on more scientific principles. There are, too, songs that seem to me a step removed from the more primitive types: there is the maze-like medley, "Bright sparkles," one phrase of which heads "The Black Belt"; the Easter carol, "Dust, dust and ashes"; the dirge, "My mother's took her flight and gone home"; and that burst of melody hovering over "The Passing of the First-Born"—"I hope my mother will be there in that beautiful world on high."

These represent a third step in the development of the slave song, of which "You may bury me in the East" is the first, and songs like "March on" (chapter six) and "Steal away" are the second. The first is African music, the second Afro-American, while the third is a blending of Negro music with the music heard in the foster land. The result is still distinctively Negro and the method of blending original, but the elements are both Negro and Caucasian. One might go further and find a fourth step in this development, where the songs of white America have been distinctively influenced by the slave songs or have incorporated whole phrases of Negro melody, as "Swanee River" and "Old Black Joe." Side by side, too, with the growth has gone the debasements and imitations—the Negro "minstrel" songs, many of the "gospel" hymns, and some of the contemporary "coon" songs,—a mass of music in which the novice may easily lose himself and never find the real Negro melodies.

In these songs, I have said, the slave spoke to the world. Such a message is naturally veiled and half articulate. Words and music have lost each other and new and cant phrases of a dimly understood theology have displaced the older sentiment. Once in a while we catch a strange word of an unknown tongue, as the "Mighty Myo," which figures as a river of death; more often slight words or mere doggerel are joined to music of singular sweetness. Purely secular songs are few in number, partly because many of them were turned into hymns by a change of words, partly because the frolics were seldom heard by the stranger, and the music less often caught. Of nearly all the songs, however, the music is distinctly sorrowful. The ten master songs I have mentioned tell in word and music of trouble and exile, of strife and hiding; they grope toward some unseen power and sigh for rest in the End.

The words that are left to us are not without interest, and, cleared of evident dross, they conceal much of real poetry and meaning beneath conventional theology and unmeaning rhapsody. Like all primitive folk, the slave stood near to Nature's heart. Life was a "rough and rolling sea" like the brown Atlantic of the Sea Islands; the "Wilderness" was the home of God, and the "lonesome valley" led to the way of life. "Winter 'll soon be over," was the picture of life and death to a tropical imagination. The sudden wild thunder-storms of the South awed and impressed the Negroes,—at times the rumbling seemed to them "mournful," at times imperious:

"My Lord calls me,
He calls me by the thunder,
The trumpet sounds it in my soul."

The monotonous toil and exposure is painted in many words. One sees the ploughmen in the hot, moist furrow, singing:

"Dere's no rain to wet you,
Dere's no sun to burn you,
Oh, push along, believer,
I want to go home."

The bowed and bent old man cries, with thrice-repeated wail:

"O Lord, keep me from sinking down,"

and he rebukes the devil of doubt who can whisper:

"Jesus is dead and God's gone away."

Yet the soul-hunger is there, the restlessness of the savage, the wail of the wanderer, and the plaint is put in one little phrase:

My soul wants something that's new, that's new

Over the inner thoughts of the slaves and their relations one with another the shadow of fear ever hung, so that we get but glimpses here and there, and also with them, eloquent omissions and silences. Mother and child are sung, but seldom father; fugitive and weary wanderer call for pity and affection, but there is little of wooing and wedding; the rocks and the mountains are well known, but home is unknown. Strange blending of love and helplessness sings through the refrain:

"Yonder 's my ole mudder,
Been waggin' at de hill so long;
'Bout time she cross over,
Git home bime-by."

Elsewhere comes the cry of the "motherless" and the "Farewell, farewell, my only child."

Love-songs are scarce and fall into two categories—the frivolous and light, and the sad. Of deep successful love there is ominous silence, and in one of the oldest of these songs there is a depth of history and meaning:

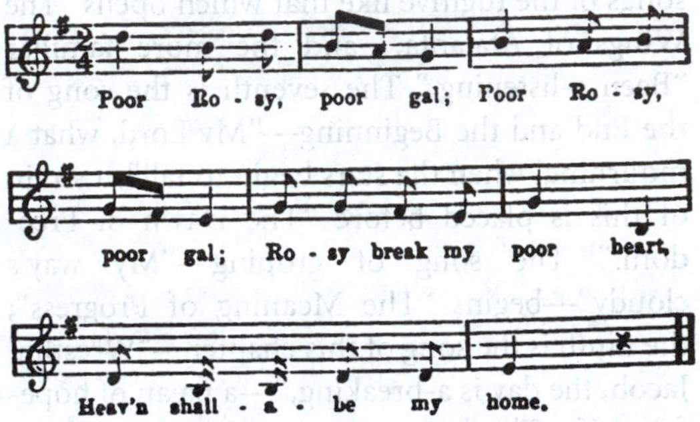
Poor Ro - sy, poor gal; Poor Ro - sy,
poor gal; Ro - sy break my poor heart,
Heav'n shall - a - be my home.

A black woman said of the song, "It can't be sung without a full heart and a troubled sperrit." The same voice sings here that sings in the German folksong:

"Jetz Geh i'an's brunele, trink' aber net."

Of death the Negro showed little fear, but talked of it familiarly and even fondly as simply a crossing of the waters, perhaps—who knows?—back to his ancient forests again. Later days transfigured his fatalism, and amid the dust and dirt the toiler sang:

"Dust, dust and ashes, fly over my grave,
But the Lord shall bear my spirit home."

The things evidently borrowed from the surrounding world undergo characteristic change when they enter the mouth of the slave. Especially is this true of Bible phrases. "Weep, O captive daughter of Zion," is quaintly turned into "Zion, weep-a-low," and the wheels of Ezekiel are turned every way in the mystic dreaming of the slave, till he says:

"There's a little wheel a-turnin' in-a-my heart."

As in olden time, the words of these hymns were improvised by some leading minstrel of the religious band. The circumstances of the gathering, however, the rhythm of the songs, and the limitations of allowable thought, confined the poetry for the most part to single or double lines, and they seldom were expanded to quatrains or longer tales, although there are some few examples of sustained efforts, chiefly paraphrases of the Bible. Three short series of verses have always attracted me,—the one that heads this chapter, of one line of which Thomas Wentworth Higginson has fittingly said, "Never, it seems to me, since man first lived and suffered was his infinite longing for peace uttered more plaintively." The second and third are descriptions of the Last Judgment,—the one a late improvisation, with some traces of outside influence:

"Oh, the stars in the elements are falling,
And the moon drips away into blood,
And the ransomed for the Lord are returning
unto God,
Blessed be the name of the Lord."

And the other earlier and homelier picture from the low coast lands:

"Michael, haul the boat ashore,
Then you'll hear the horn they blow,
Then you'll hear the trumpet sound,
Trumpet sound the world around,
Trumpet sound for rich and poor,
Trumpet sound the Jubilee,
Trumpet sound for you and me."

Through all the sorrow of the Sorrow Songs there breathes a hope—a faith in the ultimate justice of things. The minor cadences of despair change often to triumph and calm confidence. Sometimes it is faith in life, sometimes a faith in death, sometimes assurance of boundless justice in some fair world beyond. But whichever it is, the meaning is always clear: that sometime, somewhere, men will judge men by their souls and not by their skins. Is such a hope justified? Do the Sorrow Songs sing true?

The silently growing assumption of this age is that the probation of races is past, and that the backward races of to-day are of proven inefficiency and not worth the saving. Such an assumption is the arrogance of peoples irreverent toward Time and ignorant of the deeds of men. A thousand years ago such an assumption, easily possible, would have made it difficult for the Teuton to prove his right to life. Two thousand years ago such dogmatism, readily welcome, would have scouted the idea of blond races ever leading civilization. So wofully unorganized is sociological knowledge that the meaning of progress, the meaning of "swift" and "slow" in human doing, and the limits of human perfectability, are veiled, unanswered sphinxes on the shores of science. Why should Æschylus have sung two thousand years before Shakespeare was born? Why has civilization flourished in Europe, and flickered, flamed, and died in Africa? So long as the world stands meekly dumb before such questions, shall this nation proclaim its ignorance and unhallowed prejudices by denying freedom of opportunity to those who brought the Sorrow Songs to the Seats of the Mighty?

Your country? How came it yours? Before the Pilgrims landed we were here. Here we have brought our three gifts and mingled them with yours: a gift of story and song—soft, stirring melody in an ill-harmonized and unmelodious land; the gift of sweat and brawn to beat back the wilderness, conquer the soil, and lay the foundations of this vast economic empire two hundred years earlier than your weak hands could have done it; the third, a gift of the Spirit. Around us the history of the land has centred for thrice a hundred years; out of the nation's heart we have called all that was best to throttle and subdue all that was worst; fire and blood, prayer and sacrifice, have billowed over this people, and they have found peace only in the altars of the God of Right. Nor has our gift of the Spirit been merely passive. Actively we have woven ourselves with the very warp and woof of this nation,—we fought their battles, shared their sorrow, mingled our blood with theirs, and generation after generation have pleaded with a headstrong, careless people to despise not Justice, Mercy, and Truth, lest the nation be smitten with a curse. Our song, our toil, our cheer, and warning have been given to this nation in blood-brotherhood. Are not these gifts worth the giving? Is not this work and striving? Would America have been America without her Negro people?

Even so is the hope that sang in the songs of my fathers well sung. If somewhere in this whirl and chaos of things there dwells Eternal Good, pitiful yet masterful, then anon in His good time America shall rend the Veil and the prisoned shall go free. Free, free as the sunshine trickling down the morning into these high windows of mine, free as yonder fresh young voices welling up to me from the caverns of brick and mortar below—swelling with song, instinct with life, tremulous treble and darkening bass. My children, my little children, are singing to the sunshine, and thus they sing:

Let us cheer the wea-ry trav-el-ler,
Cheer the wea-ry trav-el-ler, Let us
cheer the wea-ry trav-el-ler A-long the heav-
en-ly way.

And the traveller girds himself, and sets his face toward the Morning, and goes his way.

A Litany of Atlanta

O Silent God, Thou whose voice afar in mist and mystery hath left our ears an-hungered in these fearful days—
Hear us, good Lord!

Listen to us, Thy children: our faces dark with doubt, are made a mockery in Thy sanctuary. With uplifted hands we front Thy heaven, O God, crying:
We beseech Thee to hear us, good Lord!

We are not better than our fellows, Lord, we are but weak and human men. When our devils do deviltry, curse Thou the doer and the deed: curse them as we curse them, do to them all and more than ever they have done to innocence and weakness, to womanhood and home.
Have mercy upon us, miserable sinners!

And yet whose is the deeper guilt? Who made these devils? Who nursed them in crime and fed them on injustice? Who ravished and debauched their mothers and their grandmothers? Who bought and sold their crime, and waxed fat and rich on public iniquity?

Thou knowest, good God!

Is this Thy justice, O Father, that guile be easier than innocence, and the innocent crucified for the guilt of the untouched guilty?

Justice, O Judge of men!

Wherefore do we pray? Is not the God of the fathers dead? Have not seers seen in Heaven's halls Thine hearsed and lifeless form stark amidst the black and rolling smoke of sin, where all along bow bitter forms of endless dead?

Awake, Thou that sleepest!

Thou art not dead, but flown afar, up hills of endless light, thru blazing corridors of suns, where worlds do swing of good and gentle men, of women strong and free—far from the cozenage, black hypocrisy and chaste prostitution of this shameful speck of dust!

Turn again, O Lord, leave us not to perish in our sin!

From lust of body and lust of blood

Great God deliver us!

From lust of power and lust of gold,

Great God deliver us!

From the leagued lying of despot and of brute,

Great God deliver us!

A city lay in travail, God our Lord, and from her loins sprang twin Murder and Black Hate. Red was the midnight; clang, crack and cry of death and fury filled the air and trembled underneath the stars when church spires pointed silently to Thee. And all this was to sate the greed of greedy men who hide behind the veil of vengeance!

Bend us Thine ear, O Lord!

In the pale, still morning we looked upon the deed. We stopped our ears and held our leaping hands, but they—did they not wag their heads and leer and cry with bloody jaws: *Cease from Crime!* The word was mockery, for thus they train a hundred crimes while we do cure one.

Turn again our captivity, O Lord!

Behold this maimed and broken thing; dear God it was an humble black man who toiled and sweat to save a bit from the pittance paid him. They told him: *Work and Rise.* He worked. Did this man sin? Nay, but some one told how some one said another did—one whom he had never seen nor known. Yet for that man's crime this man lieth maimed and murdered, his wife naked to shame, his children, to poverty and evil.

Hear us, O heavenly Father!

Doth not this justice of hell stink in Thy nostrils, O God? How long shall the mounting flood of innocent blood roar in Thine ears and pound in our hearts for vengeance? Pile the pale frenzy of blood-crazed brutes who do such deeds high on Thine altar, Jehovah Jirch, and burn it in hell forever and forever!

Forgive us, good Lord; we know not what we say!

Bewildered we are, and passion-tost, mad with the madness of a mobbed and mocked and murdered people; straining at the armposts of Thy Throne, we raise our shackled hands and charge. Thee, God, by the bones of our stolen fathers, by the tears of our dead mothers, by the very blood of Thy crucified Christ: *What meaneth this?* Tell us the Plan; give us the Sign!

Keep not thou silence, O God!
Sit no longer blind, Lord God, deaf to our prayer and dumb to our dumb suffering. Surely Thou too art not white, O Lord, a pale, bloodless, heartless thing?
Ah! Christ of all the Pitties!
Forgive the thought! Forgive these wild, blasphemous words. Thou art still the God of our black fathers, and in Thy soul's soul sit some soft darkenings of the evening, some shadowings of the velvet night.
But whisper—speak—call, great God, for Thy silence is white terror to our hearts! The way, O God, show us the way and point us the path.
Whither? North is greed and South is blood; within, the coward, and without, the liar. Whither? To death?
Amen! Welcome dark sleep!
Whither? To life? But not this life, dear God, not this. Let the cup pass from us, tempt us not beyond our strength, for there is that clamoring and clawing within, to whose voice we would not listen, yet shudder lest we must, and it is red, Ah! God! It is a red and awful shape.
Selah!
In yonder East trembles a star.
Vengeance is mine; I will repay, saith the Lord!
Thy will, O Lord. be done!
Kyrie Eleison!
Lord, we have done these pleading, wavering words.
We beseech Thee to hear us, good Lord!
We bow our heads and hearken soft to the sobbing of women and little children.
We beseech Thee to hear us, good Lord!
Our voices sink in silence and in night.
Hear us, good Lord!
In night, O God of a godless land!
Amen!
In silence, O Silent God.
Selah!

The Song of the Smoke

I am the smoke king,
I am black.
I am swinging in the sky.
I am ringing worlds on high:
I am the thought of the throbbing mills,
I am the soul toil kills,
I am the ripple of trading rills,

Up I'm curling from the sod,
I am whirling home to God.
I am the smoke king,
I am black.

I am the smoke king,
I am black.

I am wreathing broken hearts,
I am sheathing devils' darts:
Dark inspiration of iron times,
Wedding the toil of toiling climes
Shedding the blood of bloodless crimes.

Down I lower in the blue,
Up I tower toward the true,
I am the smoke king,
I am black.

I am the smoke king,
I am black.

I am darkening with song,
I am hearkening to wrong:
I will be black as blackness can,

The blacker the mantle the mightier the man,
My purpl'ing midnights no day dawn may ban.

I am carving God in night,
I am painting hell in white.
I am the smoke king,
I am black.
I am the smoke king,
I am black.

I am cursing ruddy morn,
I am nursing hearts unborn;
Souls unto me are as mists in the night,
I whiten my blackmen, I beckon my white,
What's the hue of a hide to a man in his might!

Sweet Christ, pity toiling lands!
Hail to the smoke king,
Hail to the black!

The Niagara Movement

ADDRESS TO THE COUNTRY*

The men of the Niagara movement coming from the toil of the year's hard work and pausing a moment from the earning of their daily bread turn toward the nation and again ask in the name of ten million the privilege of a hearing. In the past year the work of the Negro hater has flourished in the land. Step by step the defenders of the rights of American citizens have retreated. The work of stealing the black man's ballot has progressed and the fifty and more representatives of stolen votes still sit in the nation's capital. Discrimination in travel and public accommodation has so spread that some of our weaker brethren are actually afraid to thunder against color discrimination as such and are simply whispering for ordinary decencies.

Against this the Niagara Movement eternally protests. We will not be satisfied to take one jot

*A two-page leaflet (1906). The 1906 meeting of the Niagara Movement, held from August 16 through 19, convened at Harpers Ferry, W. Va., the scene of the immortal assault upon slavery led by John Brown in 1859. This Address was widely reprinted at the time of its issuance.

or little less than our full manhood rights. We claim for ourselves every single right that belongs to a freeborn American, political, civil and social; and until we get these rights we will never cease to protest and assail the ears of America. The battle we wage is not for ourselves alone but for all true Americans. It is a fight for ideals, lest this, our common fatherland, false to its founding, become in truth the land of the thief and the home of the Slave—a by-word and a hissing among the nations for its sounding pretentions and pitiful accomplishment.

Never before in the modern age has a great and civilized folk threatened to adopt so cowardly a creed in the treatment of its fellow-citizens born and bred on its soil. Stripped of verbiage and subterfuge and in its naked nastiness the new American creed says: Fear to let black men even try to rise lest they become the equals of the white. And this is the land that professes to follow Jesus Christ. The blasphemy of such a course is only matched by its cowardice.

In detail our demands are clear and unequivocal. First, we would vote; with the right to vote goes everything: Freedom, manhood, the honor of your wives, the chastity of your daughters, the right to work, and the chance to rise, and let no man listen to those who deny this.

We want full manhood suffrage, and we want it now, henceforth and forever.

Second. We want discrimination in public accommodation to cease. Separation in railway and street cars, based simply on race and color, is un-American, un-democratic, and silly. We protest against all such discrimination.

Third. We claim the right of freeman to walk, talk, and be with them that wish to be with us. No man has a right to choose another man's friends, and to attempt to do so is an impudent interference with the most fundamental human privilege.

Fourth. We want the laws enforced against rich as well as poor; against Capitalist as well as Laborer; against white as well as black. We are not more lawless than the white race, we are more often arrested, convicted and mobbed. We want justice even for criminals and outlaws. We want the Constitution of the country enforced. We want Congress to take charge of Congressional elections. We want the Fourteenth amendment carried out to the letter and every State disfranchised in Congress which attempts to disfranchise its rightful voters. We want the Fifteenth amendment enforced and No State allowed to base its franchise simply on color.

The failure of the Republican Party in Congress at the session just closed to redeem its pledge of 1904 with reference to suffrage conditions at the South seems a plain, deliberate, and premeditated breach of promise, and stamps that party as guilty of obtaining votes under false pretense.

Fifth. We want our children educated. The school system in the country districts of the South is a disgrace and in few towns and cities are the Negro schools what they ought to be. We want the national government to step in and wipe out illiteracy in the South. Either the United States will destroy ignorance or ignorance will destroy the United States.

And when we call for education we mean real education. We believe in work. We ourselves are workers, but work is not necessarily education. Education is the development of power and ideal. We want our children trained as intelligent human beings should be, and we will fight for all time against any proposal to educate black boys and girls simply as servants and underlings, or simply for the use of other people. They have a right to know, to think, to aspire.

These are some of the chief things which we want. How shall we get them? By voting where we may vote, by persistent, unceasing agitation; by hammering at the truth, by sacrifice and work.

We do not believe in violence, neither in the despised violence of the raid nor the lauded violence of the soldier, nor the barbarous violence of the mob, but we do believe in John Brown, in that incarnate spirit of justice, that hatred of a lie, that willingness to sacrifice money, reputation, and life itself on the altar of right. And here on the scene of John Brown's martyrdom we reconsecrate ourselves, our honor, our property to the final emancipation of the race which John Brown died to make free.

Our enemies, triumphant for the present, are fighting the stars in their courses. Justice and humanity must prevail. We live to tell these dark brothers of ours—scattered in counsel, wavering and weak—that no bribe of money or notoriety, no promise of wealth or fame, is worth the surrender of a peoples' manhood or the loss of a man's self-respect. We refuse to surrender the leadership of this race to cowards and trucklers. We are men; we will be treated as men. On this rock we have planted our banners. We will never give up, though the trump of doom find us still fighting.

And we shall win. The past promised it, the present foretells it. Thank God for John Brown! Thank God for Garrison and Douglass! Sumner and Phillips, Nat Turner and Robert Gould Shaw, and all the hallowed dead who died for freedom! Thank God for all those to-day, few though their voices be, who have not forgotten the divine brotherhood of all men white and black, rich and poor, fortunate and unfortunate.

We appeal to the young men and women of this nation, to those whose nostrils are not yet befouled by greed and snobbery and racial narrowness: Stand up for the right, prove yourselves worthy of your heritage and whether born north or south dare to treat men as men. Cannot the nation that has absorbed ten million foreigners into its political life without catastrophe absorb ten million Negro Americans into that same political life at less cost than their unjust and illegal exclusion will involve?

Courage brothers! The battle for humanity is not lost or losing. All across the skies sit signs of promise. The Slav is raising in his might, the yellow millions are tasting liberty, the black Africans are writhing toward the light, and everywhere the laborer, with ballot in his hand, is voting open the gates of Opportunity and Peace. The morning breaks over blood-stained hills. We must not falter, we may not shrink. Above are the everlasting stars.

The Negro in Literature and Art[1]

The Negro is primarily an artist. The usual way of putting this is to speak disdainfully of his sensuous nature. This means that the only race which has held at bay the life destroying forces of the tropics, has gained therefrom in some slight compensation a sense of beauty, particularly for sound and color, which characterizes the race. The Negro blood which flowed in the veins of many of the mightiest of the Pharaohs accounts for much of Egyptian art, and indeed, Egyptian civilization owes much in its origins to the development of the large strain of Negro blood which manifested itself in every grade of Egyptian society.

Semitic civilization also had its Negroid influences, and these continually turn toward art as in the case of Nosseyeb, one of the five great poets of Damascus under the Ommiades. It was therefore not to be wondered at that in modern days one of the greatest of modern literatures, the Russian, should have been founded by Pushkin, the grandson of a full blooded Negro, and that among the painters of Spain was the mulatto slave, Gomez. Back of all this development by way of contact, comes the artistic sense of the indigenous Negro as shown in the stone figures of Sherbro, the bronzes of Benin, the marvelous handwork in iron and other metals which has characterized the Negro race so long that archeologists today, with less and less hesitation, are ascribing the discovery of the welding of iron to the Negro race.

To America, the Negro could bring only his music, but that was quite enough. The only real American music is that of the Negro American, except the meagre contribution of the Indian.

[1]*The Annals of the American Academy* (Philadelphia: Kraus Reprint Company, 1913), pp. 233–237.

Negro music divides itself into many parts: the older African wails and chants, the distinctively Afro-American folk song set to religious words and Calvinistic symbolism, and the newer music which the slaves adapted from surrounding themes. To this may be added the American music built on Negro themes such as "Suwanee River," "John Brown's Body," "Old Black Joe," etc. In our day Negro artists like Johnson and Will Marian Cook have taken up this music and begun a newer and most important development, using the syncopated measure popularly known as "rag time," but destined in the minds of musical students to a great career in the future.

The expression in words of the tragic experiences of the Negro race is to be found in various places. First, of course, there are those, like Harriet Beecher Stowe, who wrote from without the race. Then there are black men like Es-Sadi who wrote the Epic of the Sudan, in Arabic, that great history of the fall of the greatest of Negro empires, the Songhay. In America the literary expression of Negroes has had a regular development. As early as the eighteenth century, and even before the Revolutionary War the first voices of Negro authors were heard in the United States.

Phyllis [sic] Wheatley, the black poetess, was easily the pioneer, her first poems appearing in 1773, and other editions in 1774 and 1793. Her earliest poem was in memory of George Whitefield. She was followed by the Negro, Olaudah Equiano—known by his English name of Gustavus Vassa—whose autobiography of 350 pages, published in 1787, was the beginning of that long series of personal appeals of which Booker T. Washington's *Up from Slavery* is the latest. Benjamin Banneker's almanacs represented the first scientific work of American Negroes, and began to be issued in 1792.

Coming now to the first decades of the nineteenth century we find some essays on freedom by the African Society of Boston, and an apology for the new Negro church formed in Philadelphia. Paul Cuffe, disgusted with America, wrote an early account of Sierra Leone, while the celebrated Lemuel Haynes, ignoring the race question, dipped deeply into the New England theological controversy about 1815. In 1829 came the first full-voiced, almost hysterical, protest against slavery and the color line in David Walker's *Appeal* which aroused Southern legislatures to action. This was followed by the earliest Negro conventions which issued interesting minutes, and a strong appeal against disfranchisement in Pennsylvania.

In 1840 some strong writers began to appear. Henry Highland Garnet and J.W.C. Pennington preached powerful sermons and gave some attention to Negro history in their pamphlets; R.B. Lewis made a more elaborate attempt at Negro history. Whitfield's poems appeared in 1846, and William Wells Brown began a career of writing which lasted from 1847 until after the war. In 1845 Douglass' autobiography made its first appearance, destined to run through endless editions up until the last in 1893. Moreover it was in 1841 that the first Negro magazine appeared in America, edited by George Hogarth and published by the A.M.E. Church.

In the fifties William Wells Brown published his *Three Years in Europe;* James Whitfield published further poems, and a new poet arose in the person of Frances E. W. Harper, a woman of no little ability who died lately; Martin R. Delaney [sic] and William Nell wrote further of Negro history, Nell especially making valuable contributions to the history of the Negro soldiers. Three interesting biographies were added in this decade to the growing number: Josiah Henson, Samuel G. Ward and Samual Northrop; while Catto, leaving general history, came down to the better known history of the Negro church.

In the sixties slave narratives multiplied, like that of Linda Brent, while two studies of Africa based on actual visits were made by Robert Campbell and Dr. Alexander Crummell; William Douglass and Bishop Daniel Payne continued the history of the Negro church, while William Wells Brown carried forward his work in general Negro history. In this decade, too, Bishop Tanner began his work in Negro theology.

Most of the Negro talent in the seventies was taken up in politics; the older men like Bishop Wayman wrote of their experiences; William Wells Brown wrote the *Rising Sun,* and Sojourner Truth added her story to the slave narratives. A new poet arose in the person of A.A. Whitman, while James M. Trotter was the first to take literary note of the musical ability of his race. Indeed this section might have been begun by some reference to the music and folklore of the Negro race; the music contained much primitive poetry and the folklore was one of the great contributions to American civilization.

In the eighties there are signs of unrest and different conflicting streams of thought. On the one hand the rapid growth of the Negro church is shown by the writers on church subjects like Moore and Wayman. The historical spirit was especially strong. Still wrote of the *Underground Railroad;* Simmons issued his interesting biographical dictionary, and the greatest historian of the race appeared when George W. Williams issued his two-volume history of the *Negro Race in America.* The political turmoil was reflected in Langston's *Freedom and Citizenship,* Fortune's *Black and White,* and Straker's *New South,* and found its bitterest arraignment in Turner's pamphlets; but with all this went other new thought; a black man published his *First Greek Lessons,* Bishop Payne issued his *Treatise on Domestic Education,* and Stewart studied Liberia.

In the nineties came histories, essays, novels and poems, together with biographies and social studies. The history was represented by Payne's *History of the A.M.E. Church,* Hood's *History of the A.M.E. Zion Church,* Anderson's sketch of *Negro Presbyterianism* and Hagood's *Colored Man in the M.E. Church;* general history of the older type by R. L. Perry's *Cushite* and the newer type in Johnson's history, while one of the secret societies found their historian in Brooks; Crogman's essays appeared and Archibald Grimke's biographies. The race question was discussed in Frank Grimke's published sermons, while social studies were made by Penn, Wright, Mossell, Crummell, Majors and others. Most notable, however, was the rise of the Negro novelist and poet with national recognition; Frances Harper was still writing and Griggs began his racial novels, but both of these spoke primarily to the Negro race; on the other hand, Chesnut's six novels and Dunbar's inimitable works spoke to the whole nation.

Since 1900 the stream of Negro writing has continued. Dunbar has found a worthy successor in the less-known but more carefully cultured Braithwaite; Booker T. Washington has given us his biography and *Story of the Negro;* Kelly Miller's trenchant essays have appeared in book form; Sinclair's *Aftermath of Slavery* has attracted attention, as have the studies made by Atlanta University. The forward movement in Negro music is represented by J.W. and F.J. Work in one direction and Rosamond Johnson, Harry Burleigh and Will Marion Cook in another.

On the whole, the literary output of the American Negro has been both large and creditable, although, of course, comparatively little known; few great names have appeared and only here and there work that could be called first class, but this is not a peculiarity of Negro literature.

The time has not yet come for the great development of American Negro literature. The economic stress is too great and the racial persecution too bitter to allow the leisure and the poise for which literature calls. On the other hand, never in the world has a richer mass of material been accumulated by a people than that which the Negroes possess today and are becoming conscious of. Slowly but surely they are developing artists of technic who will be able to use this material. The nation does not notice this for everything touching the Negro is banned by magazines and publishers unless it takes the form of caricature or bitter attack, or is so thoroughly innocuous as to have no literary flavor.

Outside of literature the American Negro has distinguished himself in other lines of art. One need only mention Henry O. Tanner whose pictures hang in the great galleries of the world, including the Luxembourg. There are a score of other less known colored painters of ability including Bannister, Harper, Scott and Brown. To these may be added the actors headed by Ira Aldridge, who played in Covent Garden, was decorated by the King of Prussia and the Emperor of Russia, and made a member of learned societies.

There have been many colored composers of music. Popular songs like Grandfather's Clock, Listen to the Mocking Bird, Carry Me Back to Old Virginia, etc., were composed by colored men. There were a half dozen composers of ability among New Orleans freedmen and Harry Burleigh, Cook and Johnson are well known today. There have been sculptors like Edmonia Lewis, and singers like Flora Batson, whose color alone kept her from the grand opera stage.

To appraise rightly this body of art one must remember that it represents the work of those artists only whom accident set free; if the artist had a white face his Negro blood did not militate against him in the fight for recognition; if his Negro blood was visible white relatives may have helped him; in a few cases ability was united to indomitable will. But the shrinking, modest, black artist without special encouragement had little or no chance in a world determined to make him a menial. So this sum of accomplishment is but an imperfect indication of what the Negro race is capable of in America and in the world.

The Immediate Program of the American Negro (1915)

The immediate program of the American Negro means nothing unless it is mediate to his great ideal and the ultimate ends of his development. We need not waste time by seeking to deceive our enemies into thinking that we are going to be content with a half loaf, or by being willing to lull our friends into a false sense of our indifference and present satisfaction.

The American Negro demands equality—political equality, industrial equality and social equality; and he is never going to rest satisfied with anything less. He demands this in no spirit of braggadocio and with no obsequious envy of others, but as an absolute measure of self-defense and the only one that will assure to the darker races their ultimate survival on earth.

Only in a demand and a persistent demand for essential equality, in the modern realm of human culture can any people show a real pride of race and a decent self-respect. For any group, nation or race to admit for a moment the present monstrous demand of the white race to be the inheritors of the earth, the arbiters of mankind and the sole owners of a heritage of culture which they did not create, nor even improve to any greater extent than the other great division of men—to admit such pretense for a moment is for the race to write itself down immediately as indisputably inferior in judgment, knowledge and common sense.

The equality in political, industrial and social life which modern men must have in order to live, is not to be confounded with sameness. On the contrary, in our case, it is rather insistence upon the right of diversity;—upon the right of a human being to be a man even if he does not wear the same cut of vest, the same curl of hair or the same color of skin. Human equality does not even entail, as is sometimes said, absolute equality of opportunity; for certainly the natural inequalities of inherent genius and varying gift make this a dubious phrase. But there is more and more clearly recognized minimum of opportunity and maximum of freedom to be, to move and to think, which the modern world denies to no being which it recognizes as a real man.

These involve both negative and positive sides. They call for freedom on the one hand and power on the other. The Negro must have political freedom; taxation without representation is tyranny. American Negroes of to-day are ruled by tyrants who take what they please in taxes and give what they please in law and administration, in justice and in injustice; and the great mass of black people must stand helpless and voiceless before a condition which has time and time again caused other peoples to fight and die.

The Negro must have industrial freedom. Between the peonage of the rural South, the oppression of shrewd capitalists and the jealousy of certain trade unions, the Negro laborer is the most exploited class in the country, giving more hard toil for less money than any other American, and have less voice in the conditions of his labor.

In social intercourse every effort is being made to-day from the President of the United States and the so-called Church of Christ down to saloons and boot-blacks to segregate, strangle and spiritually starve Negroes so as to give them the least possible chance to know and share civilization.

These shackles must go. But that is but the beginning. The Negro must have power; the power of men, the right to do, to know, to feel and to express that knowledge, action and spiritual gift. He must not simply be free from the political tyranny of white folk, he must have the right to vote and to rule over the citizens, white and black, to the extent of his proven foresight and ability. He must have a voice in the new industrial democracy which is building and the power to see to it that his children are not in the next generation trained to be the mudsills of society. He must have the right to social intercourse with his fellows. There was a time in the atomic individualistic group when "social intercourse" meant merely calls and tea-parties; to-day social intercourse means theatres, lectures, organizations, churches, clubs, excursions, travel, hotels,—it means in short Life; to bar a group from such methods of thinking, living and doing is to bar them from the world and bid them create a new world;—a task to which no single group is to-day equal; it is to crucify them and taunt them with not being able to live.

What now are the practical steps which must be taken to accomplish these ends?

First of all before taking steps the wise man knows the object and end of his journey. There are those who would advise the black man to pay little or no attention to where he is going so long as he keeps moving. They assume that God or his vice-gerent the White Man will attend to the steering. This is arrant nonsense. The feet of those that aimlessly wander land as often in hell as in heaven. Conscious self-realization and self-direction is the watchword of modern man, and the first article in the program of any group that will survive must be the great aim, equality and power among men.

The practical steps to this are clear. First we must fight obstructions; by continual and increasing effort we must first make American courts either build up a body of decisions which will protect the plain legal rights of American citizens or else make them tear down the civil and political rights of all citizens in order to oppress a few. Either result will bring justice in the end. It is lots of fun and most ingenious just now for courts to twist law so as to say I shall not live here or vote there, or marry the woman who wishes to marry me. But when to-morrow these decisions throttle all freedom and overthrow the foundation of democracy and decency, there is going to be some judicial house cleaning.

We must *secondly* seek in legislature and congress remedial legislation; national aid to public school education, the removal of all legal discriminations based simply on race and color, and those marriage laws passed to make the seduction of black girls easy and without legal penalty.

Third the human contact of human beings must be increased; the policy which brings into sympathetic touch and understanding, men and women, rich and poor, capitalist and laborer,

Asiatic and European, must bring into closer contact and mutual knowledge the white and black people of this land. It is the most frightful indictment of a country which dares to call itself civilized that it has allowed itself to drift into a state of ignorance where ten million people are coming to believe that all white people are liars and thieves, and the whites in turn to believe that the chief industry of Negroes is raping white women.

Fourth only the publication of the truth repeatedly and incisively and uncompromisingly can secure that change in public opinion which will correct these awful lies. THE CRISIS, our record of the darker races, must have a circulation not of 35,000 chiefly among colored folk but of at least 250,000 among all men who believe in men. It must not be a namby-pamby box of salve, but a voice that thunders fact and is more anxious to be true than pleasing. There should be a campaign of tract distribution—short well written facts and arguments—rained over this land by millions of copies, particularly in the South, where the white people know less about the Negro than in any other part of the civilized world. The press should be utilized—the 400 Negro weeklies, the great dailies and eventually the magazines, when we get magazine editors who will lead public opinion instead of following afar with resonant brays. Lectures, lantern-slides and moving pictures, co-operating with a bureau of information and eventually becoming a Negro encyclopedia, all these are efforts along the line of making human beings realize that Negroes are human.

Such is the program of work against obstructions. Let us now turn to constructive effort. This may be summed up under (1) economic co-operation (2) a revival of art and literature (3) political action (4) education and (5) organization.

Under economic co-operation we must strive to spread the idea among colored people that the accumulation of wealth is for social rather than individual ends. We must avoid, in the advancement of the Negro race, the mistakes of ruthless exploitation which have marked modern economic history. To this end we must seek not simply home ownership, small landholding and saving accounts, but also all forms of co-operation, both in production and distribution, profit sharing, building and loan associations, systematic charity for definite, practical ends, systematic migration from mob rule and robbery, to freedom and enfranchisement, the emancipation of women and the abolition of child labor.

In art and literature we should try to loose the tremendous emotional wealth of the Negro and the dramatic strength of his problems through writing, the stage, pageantry and other forms of art. We should resurrect forgotten ancient Negro art and history, and we should set the black man before the world as both a creative artist and a strong subject for artistic treatment.

In political action we should organize the votes of Negroes in such congressional districts as have any number of Negro voters. We should systematically interrogate candidates on matters vital to Negro freedom and uplift. We should train colored voters to reject the bribe of office and to accept only decent legal enactments both for their own uplift and for the uplift of laboring classes of all races and both sexes.

In education we must seek to give colored children free public school training. We must watch with grave suspicion the attempt of those who, under the guise of vocational training, would fasten ignorance and menial service on the Negro for another generation. Our children must not in large numbers, be forced into the servant class; for menial service is still, in the main little more than an antiquated survival of impossible conditions. It has always been as statistics show, a main cause of bastardy and prostitution and despite its many marvelous exceptions it will never come to the light of decency and honor until the house servant becomes the Servant in the House. It is our duty then, not drastically but persistently, to seek out colored children of ability and genius, to open up to them broader, industrial opportunity and above all, to find that Talented Tenth and encourage it by the best and most exhaustive training in order to supply the Negro race and the world with leaders, thinkers and artists.

For the accomplishment of all these ends we must organize. Organization among us already has gone far but it must go much further and higher. Organization is sacrifice. It is sacrifice of opinions, of time, of work and of money, but it is, after all, the cheapest way of buying the most priceless of gifts—freedom and efficiency. I thank God that most of the money that supports the National Association for the Advancement of Colored People comes from black hands; a still larger proportion must so come, and we must not only support but control this and similar organizations and hold them unwaveringly to our objects, our aims and our ideals.

"One-Way Ticket"/"Bound No'th Blues"

Call for Political and Social Change
Because more blacks were lynched, burned and tortured during the Post-Reconstruction Era than in any other time in American history, the Great Migration of African Americans from the rural South to the urban North occurred largely from 1915 to 1930.
Portrait by Jacob Lawrence from the Migration Series

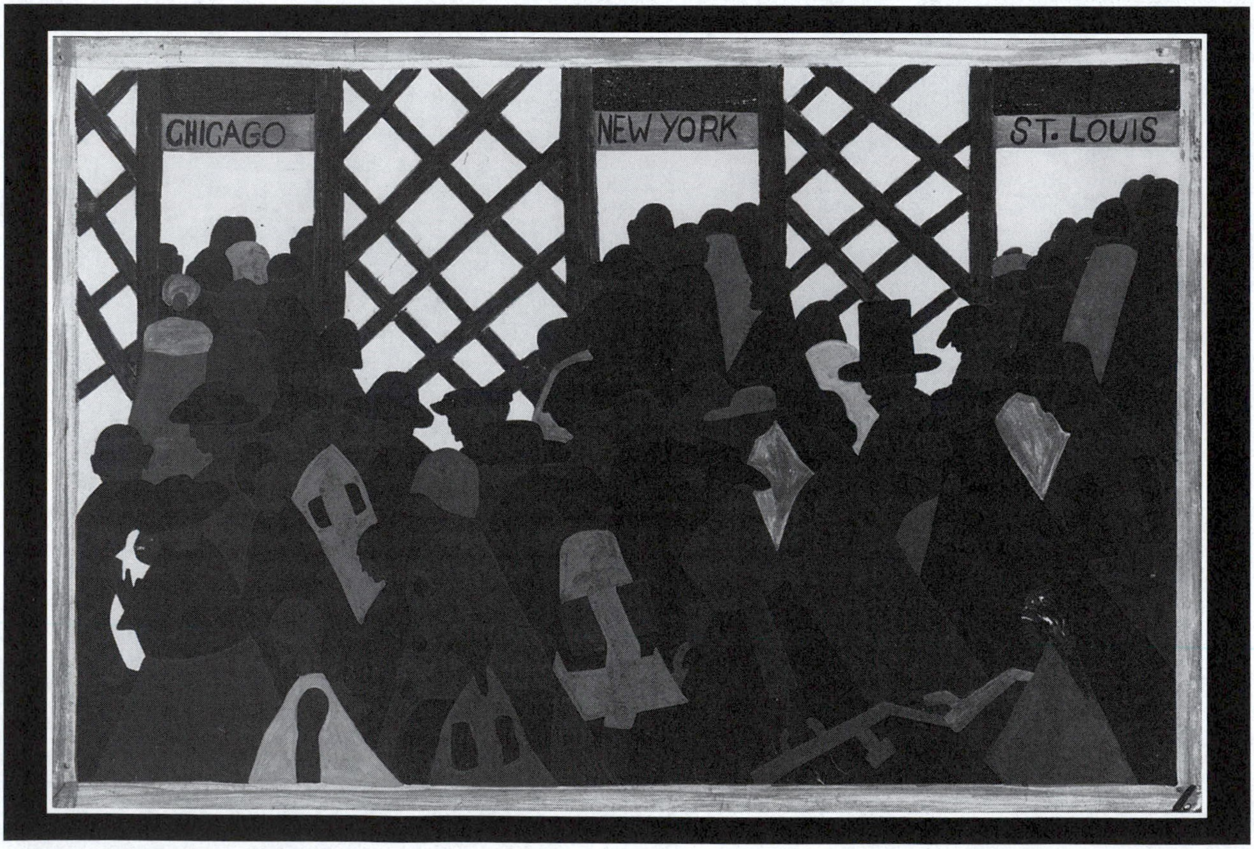

IV "BOUND NO'TH BLUES"

"Play the Blues for Me"

African American History and Culture, 1915–1945

"What Happens to a Dream Deferred?"

Renaissance and Reformation

Road, road, road, O!

Road, road . . . road . . . road, road!

Road, road, road, O!

On the no'thern road.

These Mississippi towns ain't

Fit fer a hoppin' toad.

Langston Hughes, "Bound No'th Blues"

From 1915 to 1945, or by the end of World War II, a new African American consciousness emerged in the United States. A new racial self took shape as the Great Migration of people of African descent from the South to the North took place largely between 1915 and 1930 and as the leadership of blacks shifted from the political conservatism of Booker T. Washington to the radicalism, black cultural nationalism, and Pan-Africanism of W.E.B. Du Bois and Marcus Garvey. This new self displayed more militancy and a determination that social equality for blacks no longer be denied. As critic Alain Locke observed in *The New Negro* (1925), African Americans shook off the psychology of the "Old Negro," of the implied inferiority of the post-Reconstruction era, to become the "New Negro," self-assertive and racially conscious as though for the first time. The New Negro was urban rather than rural and more self-assured and articulate. This transformed psychology of the group crystallized into the New Negro Movement or Harlem Renaissance, the black arts movement of the 1920s. Later would come what Locke would disparage as the "Reformation," the black literary art of the thirties and forties, although the authenticity of the latter period would be far greater than he would ever concede.

With the growth of black cultural nationalism came the growth of interest in cultural heritage. Hence, the new generation of literary artists celebrated the new sense of the black self by highlighting the rich folk tradition as a source for composition and performance. The musicians, composers, and writers borrowed folk materials from one another. The former used poems by black poets in their songs and rhythms, harmonies, and melodies of the blues and the newer kinds of music called jazz, boogie woogie, and gospel. The early twentieth century, therefore, became the era of W. C. Handy, Bessie Smith, and Billie Holiday, as well as that of Duke Ellington, Louis Armstrong, and Thomas Dorsey. The wealth of folk music inspired poets like Langston Hughes and Sterling Brown, who experimented with old and new black folk music and speech idioms as sources for artistic expression. In addition, James Weldon Johnson refined in *God's Trombones* (1927) a kind of black sermonic verse possibly derived from the earlier poet Paul Laurence Dunbar.

Prose writers and dramatists also heralded the new folk spirit. Inspired by the rural folk culture of African Americans, Jean Toomer wrote *Cane* (1923), generally regarded as the most innovative literary piece of the Harlem Renaissance. Several critics consider this work of diverse fiction and poems—and possibly, as represented in the concluding sketch of "Kabnis," a highly original rendition of prose drama—to be a complex blues composition. Zora Neale Hurston helped to revitalize interest in the black cultural heritage and the growth of African-centered scholarship with her collection of folklore titled *Mules and Men* (1935) and other anthropological studies. Besides her celebrated stories, Hurston wrote a landmark novel, *Their Eyes Were Watching God* (1937), in which she used the richness of the black folk culture to explore the intricate relationship between the black woman and her community. Richard Wright drew from black folk materials to create several of his fascinating short stories in *Uncle Tom's Children* (1938). In addition, several playwrights, including Georgia Douglas Johnson, Willis Richardson, Toomer, and Hughes, wrote folk dramas that rendered realistic portrayals of African American life.

The search for urbanity and sophistication led these and other writers to use conventional literary genres and forms. Poetry and fiction dominated the era far more than did drama. The array of poetic forms included the sonnets of Claude McKay, Countee Cullen, Gwendolyn Bennett, and Helene Johnson; the sonatas of Georgia Douglas Johnson; the lyrics of Anne Spencer, Angelina Weld Grimké, and Mae V. Cowdery; and the free verse of Hughes and Toomer. The fiction ranged from the novels of passing by Nella Larsen, James Weldon Johnson, and Jessie Fauset to the novels of urban realism by Richard Wright, Ann Petry, and Chester Himes; and the dramatic forms extended from the classical Greek tragedy of Cullen's *Medea* (1911) to the pageant and ritualistic drama of Hughes's *Don't You Want to Be Free?* (1938).

In the early twentieth century, the black artist and art came of age. It was the era that echoed variations of the "bound no'th blues"—a new northern, urban, but southern-based black culture. During and after the Great Migration, artists called in quite diverse ways for a new manner of thinking and for new modes of artistic expression. It was, therefore, a time in which African American scholars called for critical debate about the nature of black creative expression. Should it be art or propaganda? The response was the Harlem Renaissance—the regeneration of black culture and character grounded in their folk roots—and the Reformation—the poetics of social realism. The prevailing movement was from an art simply for art's sake to art for people's sake.

Call for Political Change and the Renaissance

Bound No'th Blues

The Harlem Renaissance, or New Negro Movement, as it has been called, came soon after the death of Booker T. Washington in 1915. Although Washington was a gifted orator and dedicated educator, his philosophies of racial accommodation and compromise were too inadequate to secure freedom and social equality for black Americans. Despite the unparalleled support he received largely from white philanthropists and politicians and from major black and white presses, he did not achieve the economic gains through industrial training he had promised the race. As the definitive biography by Louis R. Harlan establishes, not only was Washington a white-chosen black leader, his rise coincided with a setback of his race. White terrorism and black disfranchisement were on the rise in the 1890s as the former Confederate states followed the lead of Mississippi in legally reestablishing the rule of segregation and white supremacy in the South. Publicly, Washington was generally silent on these issues. Privately, his influence on his white friends in high places was ineffectual. Washington's lack of creative imagination, foresight, and tolerance of opposition helped to preclude any new conceptions and different strategies to achieve racial equality in the United States. He failed to understand the imperative of human dignity and the rights of blacks to vote in the struggle for racial self-reliance. Nevertheless, talented thinkers and artists were split between Washington's conservative programs for racial progress and W.E.B. Du Bois's more radical programs. By the end of Washington's life, the cracks in his naive philosophies were chasms. A severe depression of labor in 1914 and 1915 had reduced wages to no more than seventy-five dollars per week. Few African Americans were accepted into labor unions. Despite the end of World War I, which presumably had been fought to make the world safe for democracy and freedom, African Americans had become victims of extraordinary violence. During the first year after the war, whites lynched seventy-five African Americans. Of the fourteen African Americans burned in public, eleven were still alive at the time.

Driven by social and economic limitations, African Americans left the rural South at the turn of the century for the more favorable labor market created in the urban North by the war. (Greater restriction of immigration during the war had prompted a labor demand.) With whatever belongings they could carry, they caught trains, buses, or anything else they could afford that was headed north. From 1915 to 1919, the great movement of blacks from the southern farmlands to the northern cities was in full force. By 1918, an estimated one million African Americans had left the South, although the public census of the North and West showed a net gain of only 333,000. Meanwhile, blacks from the West Indies migrated to New York, Paris, and London, and Africans moved to America and Europe to be a part of the new social order.

Harlem, in New York City, became the race capital for uprooted blacks throughout the world. By 1915, the black population of Harlem had increased to approximately 50,000, and by 1920, it had risen to 70,000. By the end of the 1920s, Harlem was the most densely populated black area in the world. Approximately 165,000 blacks had moved there in hopes of realizing the American dream.

Soon the dream turned into a nightmare. Instead of being part of America, the migrants were often victims of racial violence and poverty. By the end of 1919, during the time James Weldon Johnson refers to as the "red summer," race riots had occurred in twenty-five cities across the country, including New York, Washington, D.C., Chicago, and Omaha, Nebraska. The more than 200,000 African American soldiers who had fought in World War I to make the world safe for democracy returned to an unsafe, undemocratic America. Often they were beaten or lynched for wearing their service uniforms in public, for attempting to find employment or housing, or for even looking at a white woman.

Perhaps the national hypocrisy was the symbolic father of the New Negro. W.E.B. Du Bois had steadily gained recognition as a race spokesperson since the publication in 1903 of *The Souls of Black Folk,* in which he brilliantly challenged the political machine of Booker T. Washington. Du Bois led the radical opposition at the Niagara Conference in 1905, formed with white liberals the NAACP in 1909, and became editor of *The Crisis* in 1910. From 1917 to 1920, he called for a radical transformation of the American social and economic order of African American liberation. This New Negro captured the essence of the new radicalism when in 1919 Du Bois rallied his political forces in an editorial in *The Crisis:* "But by the God in Heaven, we are cowards and jackasses if now the war is over, we do not marshal every ounce of our brain and brawn to fight a sterner, more unbending battle against the forces of hell in our land." Joining him were A. Philip Randolph and Chandler Owen, coeditors of *The Messenger,* a militant socialist magazine, and other African American radicals. They demanded (1) a new social order, (2) an end to mob violence against blacks, (3) a black criterion for black art, (4) a liberation of the African from imperialism, (5) an African American identification with Africa, and (6) an effort at Pan-African unity.

Later, Du Bois became the great architect of modern Pan-Africanism when he organized the initial Pan-African Congress, which he had called to be held at the same time as the post–World War I Peace Conference held at Versailles, France. Meeting in the Grand Hotel in Paris in February 1919, the group consisted of fifty-seven delegates, among them sixteen African Americans, twenty West Indians, and twelve Africans. Du Bois and the other delegates managed to call the attention of the world to their gathering and signaled the intent of the darker races to advocate for justice and equality in all arenas that affected their lives and nations. This international perspective placed the concerns of African Americans in a larger context and paved the way for Du Bois and others to assume key roles in the four Pan-African Congresses that followed the gathering in 1919.

Du Bois's vision of a new world social order included the empowerment of women. Hence, he used his powerful editorial position at *The Crisis* to support woman suffrage. "The actual work of the world today," Du Bois wrote in 1915, "depends more largely upon women than upon men." With the vote, he believed, black women could help bolster the black voting power in the South. As the leading black male spokesperson for women's rights since Frederick Douglass, Du Bois helped to turn back the tide of the powerful southern Democratic congressional bloc and of influential white feminists in the National American Woman Suffrage Association (NAWSA) who opposed suffrage for black women. He joined forces with Mary Church Terrell, Verina Morton Jones, and other leading African American women in the suffrage departments of the NAACP and in the National Association of Colored Women (NACW) to lobby Congress for the enfranchisement of black women with the passage of the Nineteenth Amendment.

Marcus Garvey rose to power during the period. He was especially popular among the black masses who supported his Back to Africa movement. In 1916, he arrived in Harlem to transplant from Jamaica his organization, the Universal Negro Improvement Association (UNIA). The initial purpose was "to establish a Universal Confraternity among the race." By 1922, however, he had recruited to the rolls of the UNIA a world membership of an estimated four million believers. Through his newspaper, *The Negro World,* first published in 1917, and his successful speeches, he gained enthusiastic supporters for his Pan-African movement. At Madison Square Garden in August 1920, for instance, twenty thousand people heard him demand that Africa be controlled by the world's four million blacks. Even though he was falsely convicted of mail fraud in 1925 and subsequently deported in 1927, his impact on black America was profound. He led the most significant and largest movement of the black masses around the world ever recorded. He promoted black self-help, pride, and solidarity. With his colorful pageantry, parades, oratory, and slogans ("Africa for Africans at home and abroad"), he made African Americans proud of their African heritage and taught them that black is beautiful.

The philosophies of Garvey, Du Bois, and other Harlem radicals helped to inspire the Renaissance. Even though their political radicalism was less influential than their cultural nationalism during the 1920s, they challenged literary artists to address the issues of racial consciousness and wholeness in art. The art itself, therefore, became a crucial instrument in the process of exploring and forging new black images and identities. In 1919, for instance, Claude McKay published his poem "If We Must Die" in *The Liberator.* The poem proved to be a defiant retort to the lynching of blacks. More literature of this kind would signal to America the arrival of a more militant New Negro. Not surprisingly, Du Bois became perhaps the first critic to recognize the need for a renaissance of African American literature. In a 1920 editorial in *The Crisis,* he called for this rebirth:

> We have today all too few Negro writers for the reason that there is a small market for their ideas among whites and their energies are being called to other and more lucrative ways of earning a living. Nevertheless, we have a literary ability and the race needs it. A renaissance of American Negro Literature is due; the material about us in the strange heart rendering race tangles us in riches beyond dreams, and only we can tell the tale and sing the song from the heart.

Response: The Harlem Renaissance

Harlem Blues

The response to the call of Du Bois and the Harlem radicals and to the blues world of the era was the burst of creativity described later as the Harlem Renaissance. Some critics prefer to call the cultural and artistic activity the New Negro Movement because the influence extended far beyond Harlem. Several African American literary artists involved in the movement were living in other sections of the country. In fact, among the writers in the movement, only Countee Cullen, Jessie Fauset, Helene Johnson, Gwendolyn Bennett, and Dorothy West were from Harlem when it became the national showcase for black art and artists. Langston Hughes and Jean Toomer lived elsewhere during most of the decade. The movement also attracted people of African descent outside the continental United States. Claude McKay was from Jamaica and Eric Walrond from British Guiana. Eventually, the energetic surge of the Renaissance reached Paris and inspired African expatriates Leopold Senghor and David Diop and the West Indian intellectual Aimé Césaire, who during the thirties were the chief designers of the Négritude movement, which emphasized worldwide unity among blacks and a revolt against colonialism.

Although many of the new Renaissance artists kept alive the social messages of the previous century, they stressed more of a personal sensibility and a refined folk consciousness. African Americans were learning to balance the impulses of literary art and social change. Indeed, the most important black texts then and now reveal the delicate balance between the individual riffs of expression and the more sermonic messages of communal value that preceded the Renaissance. Although the Renaissance marked a "rebirth" of artistic forms, it would eventually mean a "rebirth" of the abolitionist spirit of self-definition carried over from the nineteenth century. Unlike the individual artistic successes of Paul Laurence Dunbar, Charles Chesnutt, Du Bois, and James Weldon Johnson at the turn of the century, the Renaissance was the first collective literary expression of African Americans—the first African American folk and written literary movement in America. Through it, Harlem became both center and symbol of black culture and thought, a rallying place for black people throughout the world, generating a renewal of the black folk spirit thought to have existed before enslavement.

The place and time were ripe for an artistic renaissance. Harlem was the hotbed of the Roaring Twenties—the age of the blues, jazz, the Charleston, and Prohibition. It was the Mecca not only for blacks but also for white pleasure seekers from downtown Manhattan and abroad. Whereas white American modernist writers such as F. Scott Fitzgerald, Ernest Hemingway, T. S. Eliot, and others of the Lost Generation left the country for Europe in search of traditional values, these people from downtown escaped to what they believed to be the exotic, erotic world of black Harlem. As they rushed to this mythic dreamland of primitive abandon, of continuous excitement and thrills, many of them ignored the harsh realities of this New York city ghetto—its rundown, rat-infested buildings accompanied by skyrocketing rents that kept most black residents in a cycle of abject poverty. And while these pleasure seekers held slumming parties at night in the Harlem cabarets to soak up the rhythms of black life, they blinded themselves to the real Harlem, the Harlem of the daytime—the insular black community that held itself together by its pains and pleasures, its cries and laughter, its frustrations and dreams, its extended black families and other social institutions, and its religious and folk traditions. Certainly, many of the whites were in revolt against Victorian social and sexual repression, while some were in rebellion against what they saw as the dehumanizing effects of the machine age. A few were patrons of the arts, such as Carl Van Vechten, an influential critic who brought several black writers and singers to the attention of the white literati.

More important, Harlem, like a beacon, attracted a wealth of black artists and thinkers from numerous disciplines to seek their fortune, fame, and fun in the new cultural and literary capital. Just as Manhattan was the center for publishing, recording, and acting for white America, Harlem became the center for the arts and criticism for the New Negro and the symbol of urbanity for black America. It attracted artists Aaron Douglas, Richard Barthe, Palmer Hayden, Jacob Lawrence, and Hale Woodruff; dramatists Paul Robeson, Charles Gilpin, and Bert Williams (the famous actor whose greatness eventually transcended the mask of compulsory blackface); and social scientists and journalists Charles S. Johnson, A. Philip Randolph, Chandler Owen, Ira A. Reid, and P. M. Savory.

The Folk Tradition

Fast Life Blues

At the very heart of the Harlem Renaissance scene were the geniuses of music—W.C. Handy, Mamie Smith, Ma Rainey, Bessie Smith, Billie Holiday, Duke Ellington, Fletcher Henderson, Louis Armstrong, Eubie Blake, Thomas Dorsey, and Huddie "Leadbelly" Ledbetter. The creative energies and talents of these and other great musicians helped to establish the twenties and thirties as the golden age of African American folk and formal culture—the age of the classic city blues, jazz, gospel music, and the toasts. They transformed black folk music from the rural to the urban sound, creating possibly the most brilliant milestones of American culture. The hot, sometimes dizzying array of rhythms reflected the "fast life blues" of the era, the ambivalence of the northern black life experience—the tensions between the possibilities of the city and the harsh realities of urbanization, between expectations and disappointments, and between what was gained and what was lost.

Classic City Blues

The evolution of the blues from country or rural to classic city blues took place during the Great Migration. Once transplanted to the urban setting, the music was popularized when first published. In 1912, Artie Mathews, a ragtime pianist, published the first blues compositions, *Baby Seals Blues;* three years later, he composed *Weary Blues,* a work that informed Langston Hughes's volume of poetry of approximately the same title. However, it was W. C. Handy, the "Father of the Blues," who brought recognition to the music and its commercial potential with his *St. Louis Blues* (1914) and other compositions. By 1920, New York City's recording industry along Tin Pan Alley had made blues the hottest music craze.

The classic or city blues, more sophisticated in tone than the country or rural blues, were sung during the Renaissance era primarily by African American women. Perhaps these female griots were the most authentic black women poets of the period because they communicated their feelings and experiences in a folk idiom so recognizable to their black audiences that the listeners identified with the singers' emotions. One of the women, Mamie Smith, formerly a singer of vaudeville in New York, made the first vocal blues recording by a black singer in 1920. Her *Crazy Blues* was written by the black composer Perry Bradford.

Three years later, Ma Rainey (Gertrude Malissa Pridgitt Rainey), the "Mother of the Blues," made her first commercial recordings. Known for her down-to-earth singing style that forged a link between the rural and city blues, she recorded songs such as "Sissy Blues" and "Black Cat on My Doorstep." According to Sterling Brown, whose blues poetry was inspired by her performances, "She wouldn't have to sing any words; she would moan, and the audience would moan with her. . . . Ma really knew these people, she was a person of the folk."

Soon afterward, Ma Rainey's protégée, Bessie Smith, the "Empress of the Blues," emerged as the most renowned blues singer of the time. Combining the emotional fervor of the rural blues and the vigorous appeal of jazz, she remained a favorite with the black public through hits such as *Down Hearted Blues* (1923), *Young Woman's Blues,* (1926), and *Preachin' the Blues* (1927).

Before Bessie Smith's recording career ended during the years of the Great Depression, her recordings sold approximately eight million copies. Her influence was profoundly felt by her contemporaries, including Clara Smith, Ethel Waters, Chippie Hill, and, in the thirties and forties, the legendary Billie "Lady Day" Holiday. Other leading black female blues griots during the 1920s included Ida Cox, Sara Martin, Trixie Smith, Victoria Spivey, and Sippie Wallace.

By the beginning of the Depression, the commercial interest in blues singers shifted from female to male performers and from the classic city blues to the less sophisticated rural blues. Noted blues singers Blind Lemon Jefferson, Blind Willie Johnson, and Big Bill Broonzy (William Lee Conley), all of whom became major influences on Sterling Brown's poetry, gravitated to Memphis and Chicago. By the thirties, these were the two chief centers of the blues industry. Some of the best-known blues singers, such as Jimmie Rushing, Joe Turner, and Jimmy Witherspoon, played with jazz ensembles. Then, in the late thirties and early forties, Huddie "Leadbelly" Ledbetter, a former inmate of southern prison farms, was discovered at Angola Prison Farm, Louisiana, by the folklorists John and Alan Lomax. Leadbelly became one of the most popular singers of the rural blues in the country. His repertoire included not only the blues but also spirituals, prison work songs, and toasts. Leadbelly became a part of the "proletarian revival," a cultural movement of black sacred and secular music sponsored by white political radicals in New York City. This griot-poet helped to bring the blues into popular American culture.

Leadbelly and other blues pioneers succeeded in establishing a radical new art form in America's black ghettos. As a message music of human vulnerability and resilience, the blues complemented spirituals and folktales as the oral literature of the black masses. The intrinsic dual nature of the music, its expression of both the pains and pleasures, of the personal and collective experiences of black people, provided desperately needed healing for African Americans in their continued struggle against rural and urban hard times as well as with the ups and downs of love. The blues became what Richard Wright would later call the "sad-happy songs" of the African American.

Jazz

Like the blues, the inestimable value of jazz as a cultural repository—as a musical memory of and by the people—is undeniable. Possibly no other form of music indigenous to America has had such an impact on the cultures of peoples across the world. Conceived at first by gifted African Americans late in the nineteenth century, jazz was derived at once from the rhythms and melodic cadences of Africa and from the harmonic forms of Europe.

At first, jazz was primarily a ritual of performance in joyous celebration of the spirituality and sensuality of African Americans. In New Orleans, the marching bands of African Americans played traditionally slow hymns while going to the cemetery but loosened up into celebratory renditions of the same songs on the way back to town. What had been the instrumental nucleus of the marching band—the trumpet or cornet for melody, the trombone or clarinet for filler, and the drum or string bass for rhythm—became the foundation of the jazz bands. One of the first famous jazz groups was King Oliver's Creole Jazz Band, and one of its most famous members was Louis "Satchmo" Armstrong.

As the twenties advanced, jazz generated both public approval and condemnation for its association with bathtub gin, casual sex, and the pleasures of sin. New York and Chicago became the two most significant centers for recordings, although all regions of the nation developed dances such as the Charleston and black bottom that were intimately associated with the music. Hence, the decade of the twenties came to be known as the Jazz Age. During that time, performances came to depend more on written arrangements. Some of the jazz artists who directed the outpouring of hot swinging music were Ferdinand "Jelly Roll" Morton, Louis Armstrong, Thomas "Fats" Waller, James P. Johnson, and Coleman Hawkins. Essential to the development of the big band sound were the inimitable Edward Kennedy "Duke" Ellington, Fletcher Henderson, and, later in the 1930s and 1940s, the renowned William "Count" Basie, the scintillating Lionel Hampton, and the sensational vocalist Ella Fitzgerald. Drawing so noticeably upon the same structural pattern of the blues and folk sermon, that of "call and response," Ellington and Henderson came to develop a kind of delivery called swing, in which the brass and the reeds seemed to talk to each other musically. It is likely that this jazz pattern and mood inspired and informed Langston Hughes's collection of poems *Montage of a Dream Deferred* (1951) and his most brilliant and underrated volume of verse, *Ask Your Mama* (1961). Here was heard the riff, the recurrence of a pattern, for small groups with instrumental soloists. But even when arrangements had become rather elaborately written, space was still encouraged for spontaneous innovation. In particular, Ellington broadened the role of the African American musician and artist into that of a composer and writer. (The storyteller in "Daybreak in Alabama," a poem by Langston Hughes, describes himself as a composer.) Ellington's art of composing helped set the cultural standards by which jazz artists, including many African American poets, are still judged.

Gospel Music

Another new song type, black gospel music, emerged in the 1920s as the urban music counterpart to the rural spirituals. When blacks migrated to the northern centers in the first three decades of the twentieth century, many of them found their spirituals inadequate for expressing their emotional and psychological responses to the shock of industrialization and urbanization. Consequently, the church singers created a sacred music marked by the rocking, driving beat of the city as well as the blues and jazz of the period.

The chief mover in the extraordinary development of gospel music from its beginnings in the twenties was the renowned composer and singer Thomas Dorsey. In 1921, he sang his first gospel song, "I Do, Don't You?" composed by Charles A. Tindley. Inspired by Tindley's music, he began writing gospel songs early in the twenties. After a brief period as a blues pianist for Ma Rainey, he composed his first successful gospel, "If You See My Saviour, Tell Him That You Saw Me," in 1928 and established his success in 1932 with his most famous gospel song, "Take My Hand, Precious Lord." From the 1920s to the 1970s, Dorsey wrote more than four hundred songs, founded the National Convention of Gospel Singers, and inspired the organization of scores of gospel ensembles. Through his compositions and the spectacular singing performances of Mahalia Jackson, gospel music has become a worldwide phenomenon. Just as significant, it influenced the works of several writers of the period, including James Weldon Johnson, Langston Hughes, Sterling Brown, Jean Toomer, Zora Neale Hurston, Arna Bontemps, Rudolph Fisher, Wallace Thurman, Richard Wright, and Waring Cuney.

Boogie Woogie

By the 1930s, the piano-style music called boogie woogie had supplanted ragtime. This uptempo music helped lift the spirits of black people during the Depression years. Often the hot, bouncy boogie rhythms excited the black masses to dance the huckle-buck and jitterbug, helping to release their pent-up frustrations and fears. Boogie woogie, which was essentially a fast-paced blues, appears to have originated from bass-range guitar principles. It was performed by blues pianists Clarence "Pine Top" Smith, Albert Ammons, and Pete Johnson.

The exact origins of the music are not known. Whereas Big Bill Broonzy insists that the boogie was a popular dance performed by blacks at the beginning of the nineteenth century, other musicians such as Jelly Roll Morton, Leadbelly, and Aaron "T" Bone Walker trace its roots to the earliest years of the twentieth century. Its fast tempo and balladlike structure informed the poetry of Langston Hughes and some of the works of contemporary writers.

Toasts and Other Folk Epic Ballads

The migration to the cities also brought about the rise of urban black folk narratives known as toasts. Although they were not collected in Louisiana and Mississippi until the 1930s and their origins are unknown, folklorists have speculated that they began between 1912 and 1920. William Labov, for example, in "Toasts" from *Mother Wit from the Laughing Barrel* (1973), considers them to be "the most elaborate poetic forms of American Negro oral art," and Roger Abrahams, in *Deep Down in the Jungle* (1970), describes them as "the greatest flowering of Negro verbal talent."

Usually, men compose toasts in bars within a social environment of camaraderie. Often they are sexist, coarse, and vulgar. Created primarily for entertainment purposes, they have as their major themes sex, failure of love, racism, and violence. Evolving from the trickster tale and "bad man" song traditions, many of the toasts are exaggerated narratives about tricksters and urban hustlers who, among others, sometimes "play the dozens" (a pattern of public insult and personal recovery rooted in African tradition). In form and content, they are the precursors of contemporary rap music. A few black male poets, such as Sterling Brown and Etheridge Knight of the contemporary era, have drawn from this tradition.

Folktales and Other Folklore

Interest in black folktales also soared during the 1920s and 1930s with the help of the first professionally trained black folklorists—Zora Neale Hurston, J. Mason Brewer, and Arthur Huff Fauset. Of these collectors, Hurston made the most profound impact with her pioneering work *Mules and Men* (1935). Essentially a product of her 1928–1930 field trip in Florida, Alabama, Louisiana, and the West Indies, it was the first book of African American folklore collected by an African American and presented by a major publishing company for a general audience. The collection consists of seventy folktales and a series of hoodoo rituals, interspersed with a glossary of folk speech; an appendix of folk songs, blues lyrics, street cries, conjure formulas, and proverbs; and a folk sermon. Although some of the material, especially the etiological, animal, slave, and haunt tales, had been collected before, Hurston presented mostly new, authentic folklore in a different context from what had previously existed. Her sensitive ear for black speech and idiom gave her work a veracity never before found in black folklore transcription. Moreover, her colorful folk characters, such as Uncle Monday, came alive in tales published in various magazines during the period. Hurston named the special African-derived spirit that lifted up from the burden of slavery and returned to Africa "High John de Conquer." This spirit is based on a belief that permeated the African American literary tradition. In fact, Ray Billingsley picked up on it in a cartoon as recently as August 1991. Along with the "bad man" folk hero Daddy Mention and various eerie hoodoo doctors, High John reappeared in *The Sanctified Church,* a collection of Hurston's works published posthumously in 1983. By drawing heavily on the vast store of folk materials,

Hurston and other writers of the period generated renewed interest in the oral tradition.

The Literary Magazines

Partly inspired by the challenge of exploring the relationships of folk to formal art and low-brow to high-brow culture, many African American literary artists flocked to Harlem to be near the publishing houses in New York City. For the first time, major presses such as Harcourt, Harper's, and Alfred A. Knopf were providing opportunities for black writers. Perhaps even more important, black organizations sponsored magazines that featured the talents of the new writers. In November 1919, for instance, Jessie Fauset joined W.E.B. Du Bois and the editorial board of *The Crisis* as literary editor and welcomed submissions from younger writers such as Langston Hughes and Countee Cullen. Four years later, *Opportunity,* the official organ of the Urban League, was launched under the editorship of Charles S. Johnson. With a more attractive format than *The Crisis, Opportunity* boasted a readership spanning several generations with often divergent ideas regarding politics and art. With the help of literary contests funded by white and black patrons, the two journals attracted a broad audience that was interested primarily in affairs of race and society. The publications also had a secondary goal of promoting high-brow culture, as the editors believed that the elite one-tenth of the race would facilitate integration of the educated New Negro into cultured society.

Despite the aloofness of these black middle-class organizations, the stability of their audiences furnished writers with a reliable forum that neither the more extreme political journals nor the more arty ones could equal. For instance, even though A. Philip Randolph and Chandler Owne's *Messenger* survived for a decade, from 1917 to 1928, its literary contributions hardly rivaled those of *The Crisis* and *Opportunity.* Considerably less fortunate were the more self-consciously literary reviews such as *FIRE!!* and *Harlem,* each of which was proposed by Wallace Thurman but lasted for only one issue.

Before the publication of *Opportunity,* African American writers rarely had access to a readership that was sensitive to their representation of the human experience. But the failure of the magazines to the ideological left or right of *Opportunity* exposed the chalk line that the black writer had to walk. For Hughes and Cullen, for example, the challenge had been to write out of their individual experiences while creating a voice—an idiom, a moral sensibility, a racial consciousness—that would signify the dreams of a people. Critics encouraged the writers to ground their personal expressions in the historical experiences of their racial and ethnic communities.

The dominant call of the era was for writing by blacks that would discover and develop the truths, beauty, and power of the communal experience of Americans of African descent before and beyond Harlem. Writing had to be a link in memory between African Americans who had lived and those who would live. Writing had to be literature but keep faith with the rural and urban communal experiences of African Americans, with the consciousness of the race.

In March 1925, Alain Locke edited the Harlem issue of *Survey Graphic* that would be published later that year in enlarged format as *The New Negro.* Although the anthology is generally revered as a landmark of its time, it was only one more indication of pressures black writers experienced in creating black art. Not only did Locke define the literary movement in the work, but he also heralded the new generation of writers, including Countee Cullen, Langston Hughes, Jean Toomer, Claude McKay, and Zora Neale Hurston. As the most influential African American literary critic of his time, Locke wielded enormous power over the movement and writers. At times, he toned down or muted the element of protest in the writings in an attempt to make black literature more acceptable to whites. Furthermore, as Gloria T. Hull in *Color, Sex and Poetry* (1987) has revealed, Locke was a misogynist who, with the exception of Zora Neale Hurston, "excluded women writers from his homosexual coterie of friendship and patronage." Yet in spite of his shortcomings as a literary critic and patron, the Harlem Renaissance would probably not have been the same without him.

The Writers' Response

Singin' the Blues

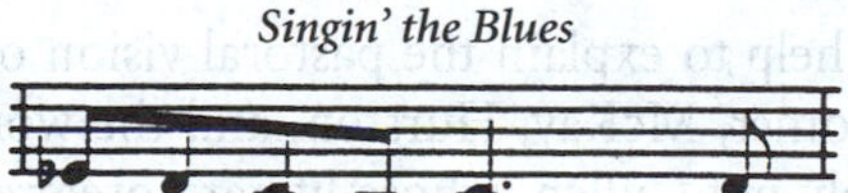

In essence, the Harlem Renaissance was the fusion of the old and the new. It was old in the sense that some of the writers who had originally made the call for the movement were still around. W.E.B. Du Bois, James Weldon Johnson, and Alice Dunbar-Nelson were well into their fifties during the 1920s, and those who were just starting out as writers were echoing some of the same issues raised by their elders. But the Renaissance was new because this was the first generation of highly self-conscious writers who were essentially middle class and who saw their roles not only as race leaders, as did the older writers, but also as independent artists. As Hughes declared in his artistic manifesto, "The Negro Artist and the Racial Mountain" (1926), "We younger Negro artists who create now intend to express our individual dark-skinned selves without fear or shame. We build our temples for tomorrow, strong as we know how, and stand on top of the mountain, free within ourselves."

Writers had their own distinct voices. For example, Hughes and Angelina Weld Grimké were often whimsical and ironic, just as McKay and James Weldon Johnson were often judgmental. Sometimes Rudolph Fisher, Eric Walrond, and Dorothy West were satirical. And despite the oversimplification of lumping together the diverse voices of Jean Toomer, Countee Cullen, Gwendolyn Bennett, Anne Spencer, Grimké, Helene Johnson, and Georgia Douglas Johnson, all had a captivating lyric power. Of the seven, the highly symbolic prose of Toomer and the social drama of Georgia Johnson convey perhaps the most skilled irony.

Certainly, the writers answered the call of Du Bois and the radicals. They wrote social protests and turned to Africa as a source of racial pride. They voiced a proud black spirit, an anger at racism, and an indictment of Western culture. They focused on various thematic concerns, such as black heroes and heroic episodes from American history, a treatment of the black folk masses, and a franker, deeper self-revelation of race, though several of them sought to concentrate on romantic themes.

In *The Afro-American Novel and Its Tradition* (1987), Bernard Bell suggests that the romanticism or pastoral aspects of Renaissance literature might be best understood as ancestralism, arising from a desire to reconcile the urban present with a rural past. According to him,

> Out of a sense of loss, a feeling that the times were out of joint and the soul was under siege, . . . a romantic longing for a freer, more innocent time and place was born . . . where the rhythms of life were closely linked to nature and one's essential humanity was unquestioned. . . . That fostered a feeling of harmony with one's ancestors [and] one's self.

Bell's theory could help to explain the pastoral vision of several New Negro authors such as Toomer, McKay, Hurston, and the women poets and playwrights, but certainly not Cullen, whose literary preference was Eurocentric aesthetics. As Maureen Honey in *Shadowed Dreams: Women's Poetry of the Harlem Renaissance* (1989) adds, the writers retreated from "a technological urban world that excluded Blacks and operated for self interest rather than social justice." But as she also points out, the women writers had another, equally pressing reason to place the self in the natural setting: "Nature provided an objective correlative through which they could articulate their gender oppression as well as that of race, for nature, like them, had been objectified, invaded, and used by men seeking power and wealth." Viewing the cityscape as white and man-made, the women turned to the pastoral setting, where they used nature imagery subversively to explore the dignity, humanity, and significance of the female self and black womanhood.

Most of the writers of the era were poets and their poetry was primarily responsible for the fame of the "Renaissance." The veteran writer James Weldon Johnson in 1922 set the stage for the development of a black aesthetic when he called for an end to dialect poetry and the beginning of a new

African American poetic form. In the preface to his landmark anthology, *The Book of American Negro Poetry,* he called for the African American poet to attempt something along the lines of what John Millington Synge had done for the Irish:

> He [the black] needs to find a form that will express the racial spirit by symbols from without, such as the mere mutilation of English spelling and pronunciation form that is freer and larger than dialect, but which will still hold the racial flavor; a form expressing the imagery, the idioms, the peculiar turns of thought, and the distinctive humor and pathos, too, of the Negro, but which will also be capable of voicing the deepest and highest emotions and aspirations, and allow the widest range of subjects and the widest scope of treatment.

One response would be to ignore the formal limits of racial dialect in order to portray the racial self in standard English. His position was well-intentioned but quite conservative. In the previous century, Paul Laurence Dunbar had truly struggled with the dilemma of dialect, to his own great chagrin and disappointment. Eventually, Hughes, Hurston, and Brown would show that the ultimate answer would be to expand the human range of black dialect itself. These three outstanding writers would ultimately show that dialect is a form worthy of human expression, and they would reveal that rural and urban folks who spoke black dialect were obviously human as well.

Certainly, Langston Hughes responded to Johnson's call. His literary sources were Paul Laurence Dunbar, Walt Whitman, and Carl Sandburg; his cultural sources were scores of blues and jazz musicians, including Artie Blake, W. C. Handy, Duke Ellington, and Louis Armstrong. His poetry covers a range of themes—black pride, black unity, racism, violence against and poverty of blacks, black womanhood, and integration—and his forms are just as varied. For instance, by bringing the blues back full circle to a spoken-sung word, Hughes created transcribed-blues poetry. According to R. Baxter Miller in *The Art and Imagination of Langston Hughes* (1989), Hughes turned to the blues idiom because

> the blues, like comedy, arrests the movement of tragic and linear time, even the certainty of death. To Langston Hughes, the narrator in the tragicomic world and the great blues singers are the same: they convert tragic time into laughter and the reaffirmation of the human spirit. Like comedy, blues confront the problems in the world and the unexplained injustice decreed by self-appointed gods yet still signify the heroic endurance of the artistic self.

Hughes was also the innovator of transcribed-jazz and gospel music verse.

Hughes's experimentation with black poetic forms established him as the griot-bard of the African American masses and as the most versatile and talented of the Renaissance poets. When his remarkable free verse poem

"The Negro Speaks of Rivers" (*The Crisis,* 1921) brought him into prominence on the Renaissance scene, he was only nineteen years old. Additionally, he, unlike the young Helene Johnson, benefited very early in the 1920s from a literary patronage that was arranged by Alain Locke. Johnson, whose skillful handling of the urban black vernacular and treatment of racial themes is reminiscent of Hughes's work, never received from Locke or anyone else the opportunity to write in leisure. Eventually, she would disappear from the Renaissance scene with no published volume of verse, whereas Hughes would enjoy the fruits of a long and successful career. His many publications include *The Weary Blues* (1926), *Fine Clothes to the Jew* (1927), and eight other volumes of impressive poetry.

James Weldon Johnson rose to meet his own challenge in the volume of verse titled *God's Trombones* (1927). He chose the form of seven black sermons as a central metaphor to express from within the African American experience—the black preacher as God's trombone. As he maintains in the preface of the volume, the voice of the old-time black preacher is a sacred musical "instrument possessing above all others the power to express the wide and varied range of emotions encompassed by the human voice—with greater amplitude." To illustrate the artistic power of the black preacher, he avoided the use of dialect. Instead, he blended in the sermons the various elements of black sayings and verbal art forms. Whatever the class assumptions behind his standard English, his magisterial volume is a highly experimental one in African American sermonics.

Less innovative in form were the bohemian Claude McKay and the bourgeois Countee Cullen. Both poets preferred to use the traditional Petrarchan (abba abba cde cde) and Shakespearean (ab ab cd cd ef ef gg) sonnet forms. At least in McKay's case, the sonnet was an appropriate form for controlling his expressed anger. McKay arrived in the United States in 1912 with a reputation as the "Black Bobbie Burns," for the Jamaican dialect poetry he had published earlier that year. Although he lived abroad during most of the Renaissance, McKay emerged in "If We Must Die" (1919) as a major literary representative of the militant New Negro in the United States. His powerful racial protest poems, such as "The White House," "America," and "Harlem Shadows," and his sentimental novel *Banjo* (1929) inspired Leopold Senghor, Aimé Césaire, and other writers of the Négritude movement of the 1930s. However, most of his poetry, including his brilliant sonnet "Harlem Dancer" (*Harlem Shadows,* 1922), reflects far more exactly the romantic voice derived from his native Jamaica.

The younger Countee Cullen represented an image of the New Negro that is less popular today—the urbane, sophisticated, middle-class traditionalist, whose poetry was European inspired but supposedly universal. With a Phi Beta Kappa key from New York University and an M.A. from Harvard, Cullen associated closely with Locke and the Genteel Tradition of middle-class intellectuals both white and black. His literary model was the British romantic poet John Keats, whose brilliant poems of and about permanence occasionally conceal, as within "On Reading Chapman's Homer," a subtle apology for Western colonialism throughout the world. In the verse of the acclaimed volumes *Color* (1925), *The Ballad of the Brown Girl: An Old Ballad Retold* (1927), and *The Black Christ and Other Poems* (1929), Cullen treated the romantic themes of doubt and fear, love and death, religious and psychological conflict, and spiritual freedom. At the height of his power, he wrote mild social protest poems such as "Heritage," "Yet Do I Marvel," and "From a Dark Tower." Therein, he probes the questions of race and history. In his best known line he questions how God could "make a poet black and bid him sing."

Cullen and McKay call to mind Gwendolyn Bennett, a Renaissance poet who was skilled but remains far too obscure, despite a career distinguished by fine craft. Bennett, who used the forms of the sonnet, lyric and free verse, wrote quality work. During the period in which she worked as an artist and served as a contributing editor for *Opportunity*, her poetry appeared in numerous periodicals, including *The Crisis* and *The Messenger*, as well as in *Ebony and Topaz*, Charles Johnson's anthology of African American literature. With precise language that is at once sensual and lyrical, she wrote of black womanhood. Her poem "To a Dark Girl," for example, is a meditation on the strength of "old forgotten queens," of even the "little brown girl, born for sorrow's mate." The short poem "Hatred" resembles the more militant ones of McKay. Her celebratory poem "Heritage" appears to be a response to Cullen's poem of the same title. Bennett's relative obscurity in the Renaissance may have been due in part to the misrepresentation of her work in Locke's *New Negro*. For some reason, Locke included the poem "Song," one of her worst, in this volume.

Other women poets also suffered from Locke's lack of literary patronage and from the male-dominated environment of the Renaissance. For example, Anne Spencer, an able technician of imagist poetry, maintained that Locke held her back because he wanted to promote Countee Cullen. Being left out of Locke's old-boy's network, which received grants and other financial assistance through him, and not having a strong female support system were major factors in dooming most of the women poets to short-lived literary careers and relegating them to the status of minor literary figures. The latter was largely due to their limited poetic output. With the exception of Georgia Douglas Johnson and Mae V. Cowdery, none of them published a book of poems. Additionally, with the exception of Johnson and Alice Dunbar-Nelson (who composed most of her poetry before the Renaissance), none of the women poets wrote verse after 1931. Yet despite their limited professional opportunities, the women did write poems of considerable merit. Collectively, they helped to expand the scope of both the African

American and the black woman's poetic traditions by skillfully employing both conventional and innovative forms and techniques—sonnets, blank verse, imagism, and the black vernacular.

Arna Bontemps, Frank Horne, and Sterling Brown also contributed to the rich literary scene. Bontemps and Horne wrote mostly personal poetry, which appeared in various black periodicals during the era. Neither of them published a collection of poems until the 1960s. Brown, who was one of the most brilliant poets of the black folk idiom, appeared only briefly in print during the decade.

Unlike the works of other Renaissance writers, Jean Toomer's *Cane* (1923) resists classification. Not altogether poetry, fiction, or drama, it fits best what James Weldon Johnson had in mind when he called for a "form that will express the racial spirit by symbols from within." Clearly the most innovative work in fictional form during the Renaissance, *Cane* takes on the pattern of an intricate blues composition of three basic movements. It is the "blues epic" of African American people from Georgia (the South) to Washington, D.C. and Chicago (the North), and back to the South. Functioning as a blues singer, Toomer makes the call to bring the black life experience back full circle to the ancestral home. Toomer, who was an experimental modernist writer, emphasized the devastating effects of urbanization, industrialization, and technology on African Americans and others. He exquisitely carved a series of contrasting patterns—of rhythmic point and counterpoint, of rural and urban, of South and North, of female and male, and of black and white—around his chief metaphor of "deep rooted Cane." The metaphor embodies at once both the sweetness and the bitterness of human existence. In short, *Cane* was probably the most brilliant and influential text of the period.

Poetry was the hallmark of the Renaissance, but significant contributions were made in fiction as well. Jean Toomer was unique, for the potential of his unfulfilled genius seemed to promise that it would reach across all the varied forms of writing, hence shaping them into a new experimental synthesis. Along with Jessie Fauset, Walter White, and James Weldon Johnson (whose *Autobiography of an Ex-Colored Man* was reissued in 1927), Nella Larsen wrote novels concerning the black middle class. Her two novels *Quicksand* (1928) and *Passing* (1929) were well received by the critics. Both of these works are important in that they were among the first novels written by an African American woman to explore implications in the process toward self-realization. Several reliable contemporary feminist revisionist assessments of them have revealed that Larsen's central metaphor, "passing," stands for gender (her own lesbianism) as well as racial passing. *The Blacker the Berry* (1929) and *Black No More* (1931) are protest novels by Wallace Thurman and George Schuyler, respectively, that satirize the color consciousness of the black bourgeoisie.

The short stories of Zora Neale Hurston and Rudolph Fisher, especially Hurston's "The Gilded Six Bits" (1933) and Fisher's "Miss Cynthie" (1933), demonstrate a command of folklore and idiom exceeded probably by no other fiction writers of the era. Even though Hurston won prizes for her stories, such as "Sweat" (1926), in *Opportunity* literary contests, she did not reach her peak as a writer until the thirties with her novels *Jonah's Gourd Vine* (1934) and *Their Eyes Were Watching God* (1937). Likewise, Dorothy West, who won an *Opportunity* literary prize in 1926 for her short story "The Typewriter," made her most significant literary contributions after 1930 with her editorship of the magazine *Challenge: A Literary Quarterly* (1934–1937) and her late 1940s novel *The Living Is Easy.* During the 1920s, she published several stories in such popular magazines as *Opportunity* and *Saturday Evening Quill,* in which she examined the ironic limitations and possibilities of black urban life. Together with West and Hurston, Fisher, whose *Walls of Jericho* (1928) reflected the wry humor and realism of racial segregation in Harlem, and Walrond, whose *Tropic Death* (1926) treated the seamy side of Caribbean life, were likely the best short story writers of the Renaissance.

For the most part, the Renaissance lacked a great African American dramatist. Even though it was the era of black folk drama, only a few of the many plays that were written were ever produced. Garland Anderson's *Appearances* (1925) had a brief run (23 performances) on Broadway, as did Hall Johnson's *Run Little Children* (1933), which ran for only 123 shows. But most of the black playwrights needed white producers, who were hardly looking for dramatic sermons. Although the folk plays of Willis Richardson are sometimes anthologized, the inclusion of them probably represents the acknowledgment of his invaluable contributions to the theater of historical black colleges and universities more than any recognition of the quality of his dramatic art. New efforts in scholarly excavation have helped revive the valuable plays of Georgia Douglas Johnson, Mary Burrill, Angelina Weld Grimké, Alice Dunbar-Nelson, and May Miller. All of these women writers made earnest attempts to present onstage a less negative and stereotypical portrayal of blacks and black life than did their predecessors.

African American writers and artists were then, as now, preoccupied with the question of black identity. Part of their search for self-definition was manifested in serious questions about the function of black art. To what extent should the African American artist take into account social reality? If the artist protests against his or her oppressive conditions, is the writing merely propaganda? Is the artist supposed to produce a work of art for the purpose of acceptance by the American mainstream? What criteria should the African American artist use? For the first time in the history of the African American people, these and other questions about the role of black art became a central focus of black intellectuals during the Renaissance. Predictably, the forum of discussion was as male dominated as the Renaissance itself.

Call for Critical Debate: Art or Propaganda?

Preachin' the Blues

During the 1920s, an important literary debate developed mainly between Alain Locke and W.E.B. Du Bois about whether black writing should be art or propaganda. Primarily a political leader and social scientist, Du Bois, who had earned a Ph.D. from Harvard, concerned himself with literary theory because he viewed literature basically as a means for advancing social and political causes. For at least the first two decades of the century, he demonstrated a sustained interest in literary theory through his editorials in *The Crisis.* Through a collection of essays and poems titled *Darkwater* (1920) and a novel titled *Dark Princess* (1928), Du Bois added to the belles-lettres of the Renaissance. During the 1930s, his activities as a literary critic ceased. Instead, he turned his attention to the development of independent black institutions and was subsequently expelled from the NAACP for his radical views. Only briefly in his *Dusk of Dawn: An Essay Toward a Race Concept* (1940) did his interest in expressing artistic theory reappear. But his example of prophecy in black critical theory would eventually establish him as the progenitor of the black aesthetic and the Black Arts Movement of the 1960s and 1970s.

In contrast, Locke, a Rhodes scholar, a professor of philosophy at Howard University, and also a recipient of a Ph.D. from Harvard, spent most of his professional career developing a theory of black art. As the literary critic for *Opportunity* and the most powerful black literary force of the period, he dedicated his time during the Renaissance and the Reformation to encouraging writers to make themselves universally relevant, to achieve what was "truly Negro" in art. Because he never concretely and systematically defined the abstract terms of his theory, however, his advice to them was often unclear and contradictory.

When Locke first appeared on the literary scene in 1923, he advocated in his article "The Colonial Literature of France" that the black artist should take a purely aesthetic approach to written material. He maintained that the black artist should embrace "art for its own sake, combined with that stark cult of veracity—the truth whether it hurts or not." What he stated in the article he attempted to apply two years later in *The New Negro,* the landmark anthology of the decade. A basic aim of the book was to demonstrate that the writers of the new generation—for example, Langston Hughes, Jean Toomer, Countee Cullen, and Claude McKay—had created art for its own beauty. Hence, he intended to distinguish between the new Renaissance writers, who embraced a "new aesthetic" and a "fresh spiritual and cultural focus," and the writers of the older generation, who "felt art must fight social battles and compensate social wrongs." To support his position, Locke included in *The New Negro* critic William Stanley Braithwaite's article "The Negro in American Literature," which also hailed the "new literary generation" for their literary creations, which displayed a universally defined rather than a purely racial sense of what is beautiful.

However, Locke experienced difficulty in practicing the theory that he proposed in *The New Negro*. For example, some of the strong writings of social protest from the Renaissance, including several of McKay's poems, did not fit into his philosophical scheme. Consequently, Locke simply omitted McKay's poems "If We Must Die" and "Mulatto" from the anthology. He also changed the title of McKay's poem "The White House" to "White Houses" in order to temper the attack on the American government. The inclusion of the inflammatory writings would have defeated his purpose, for he wanted to establish African American art as a basis for the mainstream acceptance of blacks.

Like Locke, Du Bois insisted that black artists must be concerned with truth and beauty. But unlike Locke, Du Bois believed that writing should be didactic as well. Therefore, when Du Bois critiqued *The New Negro* in a 1926 edition of *The Crisis*, for the first time he expressed the notion that black art must act as propaganda. In a basically favorable review of the book, he contended that the work was not only polemic but also implicit propaganda:

> With one point alone do I differ. . . . Mr. Locke has newly been seized with the idea that Beauty rather than propaganda should be the object of Negro literature and art. His book proves the falseness of this thesis. This is a book filled and bursting with propaganda but it is a propaganda for the most part beautifully and painstakingly done. . . . If Mr. Locke's thesis is insisted upon too much, it is going to turn the Negro Renaissance into decadence. It is the fight for Life and Liberty that is giving birth to Negro literature and art today and when turning from the fight or ignoring it, the young Negro tries to do pretty things or things that catch the passing fancy of the really unimportant critics and publishers about him, he will find that he has killed the soul of Beauty in art.

In the same edition of *The Crisis*, Du Bois denounced the Lockeian doctrine again. He stressed that "while we [*The Crisis*] believe in Negro art, we do not believe in art simply for art's sake. . . . We want Negro writers to produce beautiful things but we stress the things rather than the beauty."

Hughes and Jessie Fauset also offered alternatives to the Lockeian doctrine. Hughes argued in "The Negro Artist and the Racial Mountain" that the black artist should write freely of his or her experience, regardless of the needs and demands of his audience, black or white. His forceful declaration in the essay was echoed in the "Black is Beautiful" cry of the Black Arts

Movement of the 1960s and 1970s. According to Hughes, "It is the duty of the younger Negro artist, if he accepts any duty at all from outsiders, to change through the force of his art that old whispering 'I want to be white,' hidden in the aspiration of his people, to 'Why should I want to be white? I am a Negro—and beautiful.'" Less provocative than Hughes and Du Bois, Fauset explored the politics of laughter—"our emotional salvation"—in African American drama and life in her essay "The Gift of Laughter," which was included in *The New Negro.*

What eventually became apparent is that Locke's aesthetics in *The New Negro* had drawn the battle line between the writers and critics of the period. But from the time of the book's publication to the beginning of the 1930s, Locke and Du Bois conducted virtually a two-man war and became even more emphatic about their positions. For instance, in "Criteria of Negro Art" (1926), Du Bois began to press the position (much as would the proponents of the New Black Aesthetic in the sixties and seventies) that black art must serve a political and social function for black people. "Thus all Art is propaganda and ever must be, despite the wailing of the purists," he said. "I stand in utter shamelessness and say that whatever art I have for writing has been used always for propaganda, for gaining the right of black folk to love and enjoy." Furthermore, he maintained that black art must be evaluated according to the criteria of black people: "The ultimate judge has got to be you [black people] and you have got to build yourselves up into that wide judgment, that catholicity of temper which is going to enable the artist to have the widest chance for freedom." From his desk at *The Crisis,* he spent the next four years evaluating works by black literary artists, including James Weldon Johnson, Claude McKay, Rudolph Fisher, Nella Larsen, and Aaron Douglas, based on what he considered to be the truth and beauty of black art.

In 1928, Locke disagreed strongly with Du Bois in "Art or Propaganda?" He warned black writers that art for the sake of propaganda perpetuates the notion that blacks are cultural subordinates to whites: "My chief objection to propaganda, apart from its besetting sin of monotony and disproportion, is that it perpetuates the position of group inferiority even in crying against it." Although Locke admitted the need for polemics, he recommended that it be expressed in social journals. In art, he insisted, truth must take propaganda's place: "After Beauty, let Truth come into the Renaissance picture."

Two years later, Du Bois responded in "Dramatis Personae." He concluded that true art cannot be disassociated from ideology:

> All art is propaganda and without propaganda there is no true art. But, on the other hand, all propaganda is not art. . . . If a person portrays ideal Negro life, the sole judgment of its success is whether the picture is a beautiful thing. . . . If he caricatures Negro life, and makes it sordid and despicable, the critic's criterion is . . . solely, is the idea well presented?

After "Dramatis Personae," Du Bois virtually disappeared as a literary critic during the Renaissance of the twenties and the Reformation of the thirties. The economic depression in the 1930s led him instead to place a special emphasis on the role of the black university. To him, the institution had to accomplish what the Renaissance had failed to do: to produce artistic literary achievements for the black race. In an editorial titled "The Negro College" (1933), he expressed the view that the Renaissance had failed because "it was a literature written for the benefit of white people and at the behest of white readers, staring out privately from the white point of view."

Locke also admitted the failings of the literary Renaissance, but in "This Year of Grace" (1931) he maintained that the major failing of the writers was their lack of depth or understanding and realization of "what was truly Negro" (a phrase Locke never clearly defined). Nonetheless, he believed that this realization would be accomplished by the writers of the Reformation during the thirties. To Locke, the Reformation was merely a continuation of the Renaissance, the "second and truly sound phase of the cultural development of the Negro in American literature and art."

Not only did he spend the decade of the thirties, as he had done in the twenties, insisting that black writers be universally relevant, but he fought practically a one-man battle against the trend of stark social realism. In his 1936 essay "Propaganda or Poetry?" from *Race I,* Locke bemoaned the fact that literature, as in the nineteenth century, had turned "prosaic, partisan, and propagandistic, but this time not in behalf of striving, strident radicalism, but rather in a protestant and belligerent universalism of social analysis and protests."

During the decade, Sterling Brown and James Weldon Johnson sided with Locke. In 1930, Brown asserted in his essay "Our Literary Audience," which appeared in *Opportunity,* that the goal of the black artist should be truth rather than propaganda: "Propaganda, however legitimate, can speak no louder than truth. Such a cause as ours needs no dressing up." Four years later, Johnson contended in *Challenge: A Literary Quarterly* that black artists "need not be propagandists; they need only be sincere artists."

Richard Wright agreed with Du Bois. According to Wright in his essay "Blueprint for Negro Writing" (1937), the black writer "is being called upon to do no less than create values by which his race is to struggle, live or die." He insists that "if his [the black writer's] conception of the life of his people is broad and deep enough, if the sense of the whole life he is seeking is vivid and strong in him, then his writing will embrace all those social, political, and economic forms under which the life of his people is manifest."

What Wright and Du Bois knew and Locke and others missed in their analysis of the black art of the thirties and early forties is that a "true" Reformation had indeed taken place. For the most part, the black literary artists of the period had avoided Locke's aesthetic "art for art's sake" to rediscover "art for people's sake." To a degree, they had gone home to their abolitionist roots, but not completely. They had returned black art to its primary function of promoting social and political change, but with the new consciousness to shape artistry itself. The Great Depression was a wonderful tonic for reminding them of history. "The hunger I thought I had left behind," Wright would later say, "returned." The stock market crash of 1929 reawakened them all not only to the call of the Renaissance but also to the undeniable claims of a burning history that would perhaps never be silenced. Hence, they turned away from the decadent excesses of the Renaissance and their desire for acceptance into the American literary mainstream to critique the harsh realities of coping with the continuing deferral of the American dream for blacks.

Response: The Reformation, an Art for People's Sake

Hard Times Blues

The Reformation musicians and writers emerged to voice the historical tensions of the thirties and early forties. It was a time of economic crisis, of mounting social and racial conflicts, and of world war. It was a time of increased unemployment for black sharecroppers and industrial workers, a time in which most laborers pushed for unionization. It was a time of lynchings, of race riots, and of the Scottsboro trial of 1931, in which several African American youths in Alabama were falsely accused of raping two white prostitutes. And it was a time of droughts, of floods, and of ravages by the boll weevil. These hard times dominated the blues music of the age: Charlie Spand's "Hard Time Blues," Ramblin' Thomas's "No Job Blues," Charley Jordan's "Tight Time Blues," Kokomo Arnold's "Bo-Weevil Blues," Lonnie Johnson's "Flood Water Blues," and Doctor Clayton's "Pearl Harbor Blues." Increased unemployment had forced many writers and other black intellectuals to turn to the Federal Writers' Project of the Work Projects Administration (WPA) from 1935 to 1943 to survive. The organization provided opportunity and work not only for the established writers such as Claude McKay, Arna Bontemps, Rudolph Fisher, and Sterling Brown, who served as editor for Negro Affairs, but also for a group of talented new writers whose impact was immediately felt. They included novelists Richard Wright, Ralph Ellison, Frank Yerby, William Attaway, and Willard Motley; poets Margaret Walker and Robert Hayden; and playwrights Theodore Ward, J. A. Smith, Theodore Brown, and Hughes Allison.

Most of the Reformation writers promoted and produced a literature charged with stark social and political realism as the most appropriate response to the exigencies of the era. Desperately seeking to find the answer to the black dilemma, many of the writers embraced a proletarian literature, and several of them turned to socialism and communism. Although the Communist Party never appealed to the black masses, its credo of racial equality and unity did attract several black intellectuals. W.E.B. Du Bois, who often had socialist leanings early in his career, was sympathetic to Marxism in the early years of the decade. Richard Wright joined the Communist Party; Claude McKay, Langston Hughes, Dorothy West, and others flirted with it.

Consequently, most of the literature captured the anger and cynicism of African Americans during the era. In all genres, this literature breathed an air "dusted with despair" (in Hughes's words) of a society gone wrong. In poetry, for example, Waring Cuney lamented the droughts in "Hard Time Blues." Elsewhere, Countee Cullen protested against white racism in "Scottsboro Too, Is Worth Its Song." A theme throughout the literature was the call for unity among black and white workers. A socialist oversimplification was that the fate of poor people, regardless of color, was the same. Class and race struggle became the main focus of *Challenge: A Literary Quarterly,* a rare black periodical published during the Depression years. In 1937, editor Dorothy West changed the title to *New Challenge* when Wright and Marina Minus joined the staff as associate editors.

Like the poetry of Wright, Hughes, and others, the classic poetry of Sterling Brown depicted the "hard time blues" for African Americans. Although Brown understood all the social ills of the time and wrote so memorably about them, he was more concerned with depicting the strength and beauty of southern black folks. Within this context, his formidable literary achievement *Southern Road* (1932) ranks with Hughes's *The Weary Blues* (1926). Whereas Hughes was the poet of the Harlem trumpeter, Brown was the poet of the southern tiller of the soil. Throughout *Southern Road,* Brown shapes black language into a cultural instrument conveying the character of a people. He fuses genuine literary portraits of proud and defiant black folks such as Ma Rainey and Slim Greer with folk rhythms. His literary achievement comes from his innovative presentation of the blues-ballad.

Whereas Brown treats black folk culture primarily from without—that is, through its relationship with whites—Zora Neale Hurston explores it from within the boundaries of the black community. A folklorist and anthropologist, Hurston is set apart from other African American writers of the era by her expertise in black folk culture. Indeed, a scholarly distinction of the kind is evident in her major works, many of which were published during the period. Besides her critically acclaimed *Their Eyes Were Watching God* (1937), she wrote three other novels—*Jonah's Gourd Vine* (1934),

Moses, Man of the Mountain (1939), and *Seraph on the Suwanee* (1948); several short stories; three books of folklore—*Mules and Men* (1935), *Tell My Horse* (1938), and *The Sanctified Church* (1983); and numerous articles. She also wrote an autobiography, *Dust Tracks on a Road* (1942). Her works examine a wide range of southern black folk culture. In *Their Eyes Were Watching God,* for example, Hurston explores the search by Janie Starks, a black woman, for female self-definition within the restrictions imposed on her by her rural southern black community. This novel was a groundbreaking text in that since its publication, black women writers have explored racial-gender self-definitions with stronger, bolder voices. By skillfully fusing complex black female characterizations, nature imagery, and black folklore to treat the theme of racial-gender oppression, she anticipated several contemporary black women novelists, such as Toni Morrison and Alice Walker.

When the spirit of racial protest had understandably infused the proletarian writing of the thirties, the fiction of Richard Wright also came forth to articulate a rare depth in the narrative consciousness of black people. Wright was a great modernist writing out of the epic hungers of a culture. Drawing from a wealth of black folk materials for his short stories, he achieved a brilliant idiom of ill-fated young black men programmed for failure and death. What made him remarkable was that he revealed through irreducible moments of often brilliant language an acute understanding of human psychology and society. This is evident in his now famous autobiography, *Black Boy* (1945), which is an important social document as much as it is a moving personal history.

But it was Wright's powerful novel, his neo-slave narrative *Native Son* (1940), in its dramatization of the hatred, oppression, and social injustices inflicted on African Americans, that apparently inspired an entire generation of black writers. After its publication, a literary trend described by some critics as "urban realism" developed among black writers in post–World War II America. Fiction writers associated in varying degrees with this school of thought, each with his or her own distinctive voice and eventual departure from that thematic emphasis, included Frank Yerby (his early short stories), Chester Himes, and Ann Petry.

Like Wright, these writers relied heavily on the conventional techniques of the social realists and the naturalists to express the anger and frustration resulting from the racial prejudice and segregation that were daily reminders of the deferral of the American dream for blacks. Yerby, in his early fiction, primarily concerned himself with racial protest. After failing to sell a novel about the black male's deprivation of manhood by white society, he turned to writing historical romances in 1946. In contrast, Himes focused on the violence inflicted on the African American community by white society in his novels *If He Hollers Let Him Go* (1945) and *Lonely Crusade* (1947). Himes believed that black liberation in America could be achieved only through massive violence: "After all, America lives by violence, and violence achieves

. . . its own end." Although the theme of black manhood and the setting of Los Angeles are similar in both books, the plot, characters, and socialist vision in *Lonely Crusade* are more complex and contrived.

Whereas Himes centers his fiction on the plight of oppressed black men, Petry, in her powerful novel *The Street* (1946), dramatizes the struggle of a black woman to survive in Harlem against racism and poverty. In this sense, Petry picked up where Hurston left off. Literary critics and historians now credit *The Street* as the first novel to address social problems faced by low-income black women who were single parents in urban America. This emphasis on gender-race-class distinguishes it from novels by other black urban realists. Moreover, Petry's characters are more fully developed, more totally individualized, than are Wright's in *Native Son.* Although they are often portrayed as victims of their social conditions, they usually appear to have more choices in determining their actions. At the time of its publication, *The Street* won Petry wide critical recognition. However, despite her fine craftswomanship, the novel, like Hurston's *Their Eyes Were Watching God,* was virtually ignored by critics of the canon until the contemporary women's movement. Unlike Hurston, Petry has not yet received the critical attention that she and her fiction so rightfully deserve. Certainly, *The Street* ranks with *Native Son* and *The Grapes of Wrath* as a classic American novel of social realism.

Coda

As the proletarian writings of Petry, Wright, and others clearly show, the thirties and forties resounded the "hard time blues" for blacks. African Americans were kept at or near the bottom of the American social ladder and were segregated by color. Yet the Reformation, like the Renaissance, was an era of great energy and creativity. Critic George Kent reminds us, "If today we can sometimes jog, rather than puff, down the road toward self-definition, it would seem that the Harlem Renaissance was a father who should not go without thanks or reverence." Though male dominated, middle class, and faddish, the movement signaled a striking out in new directions for African American literature. It was during the Renaissance that African American literature entered into the highest phase of development of any newly formed nation or race—that is, the exploration of racial identity, experience, and heritage. What underlay both the Renaissance and the Reformation was the quest for racial-gender-class self-definitions in an ever-increasing variety of ways. What underlay both movements was, finally, the reaffirmation of black art and black folk culture. It was a reverence not only for sermons but also for the crafted pictures of value that informed them. For "the long black song," Langston Hughes had reached for the literary power of jazz, and Richard Wright and Ann Petry had cleared the airways for it to be heard.

Lift Every Voice and Sing

The Negro National Anthem

JAMES WELDON JOHNSON

Lift every voice and sing
Till earth and heaven ring,
Ring with the harmonies of Liberty;
Let our rejoicing rise
High as the listening skies,
Let it resound loud as the rolling sea.
Sing a song full of the faith that the dark past has taught us,
Sing a song full of the hope that the present has brought us,
Facing the rising sun of our new day begun
Let us march on till victory is won.

Stony the road we trod,
Bitter the chastening rod,
Felt in the days when hope unborn had died;
Yet with a steady beat,
Have not our weary feet
Come to the place for which our fathers sighed?
We have come over a way that with tears has been watered,
We have come, treading our path through the blood of the slaughtered,
Out from the gloomy past,
Till now we stand at last
Where the white gleam of our bright star is cast.

God of our weary years,
God of our silent tears,
Thou who has brought us thus far on the way;
Thou who has by Thy might
Led us into the light,
Keep us forever in the path, we pray.
Lest our feet stray from the places, our God, where we met Thee,
Lest, our hearts drunk with the wine of the world, we forget Thee;
Shadowed beneath Thy hand,
May we forever stand.
True to our God,
True to our native land.

FOLK CALL FOR POLITICAL AND SOCIAL CHANGE

FOLK POETRY

CLASSIC BLUES LYRICS

The classic blues are the now-standard twelve-bar blues form. As Eileen Southern explains in *The Music of Black Americans* (1971; 1983, second edition)

> The melody for each line is typically condensed into a little more than two measures of the four-measured phrase; this allows for a pause or "break" at the end of each vocal line, during which the accompanying instrument (guitar, piano, or instrumental ensemble) improvises and the singer interjects spoken asides, such as "Oh, Lordy," "Yes, man," "Oh, play it," etc. The resulting effect is that of "response" to the voice's call.

12-bar blues with melodic outline and poetic scheme

Woke up dis mawning, found m' baby gone,
Woke up dis mawning, found m' baby gone,
If she went to stay, I won't be here too long.

The classic blues were popularized by the black women blues singers of the 1920s and 1930s, who abandoned the basically unstructured and variable rural blues. Their performances, in general call and response patterns, were done to the accompaniment of a piano or orchestra. Vocalists such as Ma Rainey and Billy Holiday were hailed in the poetry of Sterling Brown and Langston Hughes. More important, the blues singers of the period influenced the verse of Hughes, Brown, and Waring Cuney. These poets devised techniques to simulate the blue note—that is, to make the reader's mental ear hear the human singing, humming, or shouting voice "bluing" words and sounds. At times, they simulated the blue note verbally by placing an important word at the end of a line with rising inflection or prolongation. Hughes demonstrates this device in his poem "The Weary Blues," in which he uses the dash (—) after the word *satisfied* to signal prolongation:

I got the Weary Blues
And I can't be satisfied
Got the Weary Blues
And can't be satisfied—
I ain't happy no mo'
And I wish that I had died.

At other times, the poets emphasized the blue note by inserting pure sound words, italicized words, and/or exclamation marks. Hughes's poem "As Befits a Man" is an illustration:

I want the woman to holler:
Please don't take him away!
Ow-ooo-oo-o
Don't take daddy away!

Harlem Blues

W. C. HANDY

You never can tell what's in a woman's mind,
And if she's from Harlem, there's no use o' tryin'
Just like the tide her mind comes and goes,
Like March weather
Ah there's one sweet spot in Harlem, It's known as striver's row
Dicty folks call 'em live there and you should know,
That I have a friend who lives there, I know he won't refuse
To put some music to my troubles and call 'em Harlem Blues.

FROM *That Thing Called Love*

MAMIE SMITH

I'm worried in my mind, I'm worried all the time,
My friend he told me to-day, that he was going away to stay,
Now I love him deep down in my heart,
But the best of friends must part.

FROM *Tain't Nobody's Business If I Do*

BESSIE SMITH

There ain't nothing I can do or nothing I can say,
That folks don't criticize me,
But I'm going to do just as I want to do anyway,
And I don't care if they despise me.

If I should take a notion,
To jump in the ocean,
Tain't nobody's business if I do do do do.

If I go to church on Sunday,
Then just shimmy down on Monday,
Tain't nobody's business if I do do do do.

FROM *Nobody Knows You When You're Down and Out*

BESSIE SMITH

Once I lived the life of a millionaire,
Spending my money, I didn't care,
I carried my friends out for a good time,
Buyin' bootleg liquor, champagne and wine.

When I began to fall so low,
I didn't have a friend, and no place to go,
So if I ever get my hands on a dollar again,
I'm gonna hold on to it 'til them eagles grin.

Nobody knows you when you're down and out,
In my pocket, not one penny,
And my friends, I haven't got any,
But if I ever get on my feet again,
Then I'll meet all my long lost friends.

It's mighty strange, but without a doubt,
Nobody knows you when you're down and out.

FROM *Sissy Blues*

GERTRUDE "MA" RAINEY

I dreamed last night I was far from harm,
Woke up and found my man in a sissy's arms.

Hello, Central, it's 'bout to run me wild,
Can I get that number, or will I have to wait a while?

Some are young, some are old,
My man says sissy's got good jelly roll.

My man got a sissy, his name is "Miss Kate,"
He shook that thing like jelly on a plate.

Now all the people ask me why I'm all alone,
A sissy shook that thing and took my man from home.

FROM *Wild Women Don't Have the Blues*

IDA COX

I've got a different system and a way of my own,
When my man starts kicking, I let him find another home,
I get full of good liquor and walk the streets all night,
Go home and put my man out if he don't treat me right,
Wild women don't worry, wild women don't have the blues.

You never get nothing by being an angel child,
You better change your ways and get real wild,
I want to tell you something and I wouldn't tell you no lie.
Wild women are the only kind that really get by,
'Cause wild women don't worry, wild women don't have the blues.

FROM *God Bless the Child*

BILLIE HOLIDAY

Them that's got shall get, them that's not shall lose,
So the Bible said, and it still is news;
Mama may have, Papa may have, but God bless the child that's got his own!

Yes, the strong gets more, While the weak ones fade,
Empty pockets don't ever make the grade,
Mama may have, Papa may have, But God bless the child that's got his own!

Money, you got lots o' friends, Crowdin' 'round the door,

When you're gone and spendin' ends, They don't come no more.
Rich relations give, crust of bread, and such,
You can help yourself, but don't take too much!
Mama may have, Papa may have, but God bless the child that's got his own!

FROM *Fast Life Blues*

BUMBLE BEE SLIM

I wonder why fast life keeps on follerin' me, *(twice)*
Well it seems like ole fast life, ain't gonna never let me be.

Fast life is killin' me, stiff-dead on my knees, *(twice)*
Fast life is a living, that is awful hard to please.

It don't pay nobody to live this life so fast, *(twice)*
Just take it slow and easy as long as it will last.

FROM *Coal Woman Blues*

BLACK BOY SHINE

When I went out hustlin', tryin' to do the best I could, *(twice)*
I knowed you were broke and hungry and I tried to chop some wood.

I got wood in my wood-house, and I've got coal in my bin *(twice)*
'Cause my fire went out, Lord since God knows when.

Now woman don't worry, 'cause my heater's always hot, *(twice)*
'Cause good wood and coal is all I've got.

Rural Blues Lyrics of the Thirties and Forties

Dry Spell Blues

EDDIE "SON" HOUSE

The dry spell blues have fallen, drove me from door to door.
Dry spell blues have fallen, drove me from door to door.
The dry spell blues have put everybody on the killing floor.

Now the people down south sure won't have no home.
Now the people down south sure won't have no home.
'Cause the dry spell have parched all this cotton and corn.

Hard luck's on everybody, and many people are through.
Hard luck's on everybody, and many people are through.
Now besides the shower, ain't got a help but you.

Lord, I fold my arms, and I walked away.
Lord, I fold my arms, Lord, I walked away.
Just like I tell you, somebody's got to pay.

Pork chops forty-five cents a pound, cotton is only ten.
Pork chops forty-five cents a pound, cotton is only ten.
I can't keep no women, no, no, nowhere I been.

So dry, old boll weevil turned up his toes and died.
So dry, old boll weevil turned up his toes and died.
Now ain't nothing to do, bootleg moonshine and rye.

It have been so dry, you can make a powderhouse out of the world.
Yes, it has been so dry, you can make a powderhouse out of the world.
Then all the money men like a rattlesnake in his coil.

I done throwed up my hands, Lord, and solemnly swore.
I done throwed up my hands, Lord, and solemnly swore.
There ain't no need of me changing towns, it's a drought everywhere I go.

It's a dry old spell everywhere I been.
Oh, it's a dry old spell everywhere I been.
I believe to my soul this old world is bound to end.

Well, I stood in my back yard, wrung my hands and screamed.
I stood in my back yard, I wrung my hands and screamed.
And I couldn't see nothing, couldn't see nothing green.
Oh Lord, have mercy if you please.
Oh Lord, have mercy if you please.
Let your rain come down, and give our poor hearts ease.

These blues, these blues is worthwhile to be heard.
Oh, these blues, worthwhile to be heard.
God's very likely bound to rain somewhere.

FROM *Hard Time Blues*

CHARLIE SPAND

Lord I walked and I walked but I cannot find a job, *(twice)*
Lord I can't talk about no money, and I sure don't want to rob.

Now my woman's hard to get along with, as I'm sittin' here, *(twice)*
I ain't cooked me a square meal, honey in God knows when.

Everybody cryin' "Depression," I just found out what it means, *(twice)*
It means a man ain't got no money, he can't buy no bacon and greens.

FROM *Honey, I'm All Out and Down*

HUDDIE "LEADBELLY" LEDBETTER

This man is a long way from home, an' he's got a brownskin woman,
An' he knows pay-day's comin' pretty soon,
An' the woman's shoutin' 'cause it's 'most pay-day.
An' the ole mules is hongry and the sun is going down,
An' the man wishes pay-day would move off a little further
So he wouldn't have to pay that woman nothin'.

(sung verse)
I'm goin' t' tell ma woman like the rabbit tol' the hound,
You don' wan' me, and honey I don' wan' you.

Hollerin' the Blues

BIG BILL BROONZY

Yes, I'm settin on this old stump, baby, got a worried mind.
Yes, I'm settin on this stump, baby, I've got a worried mind.
Yeah, I'm gonna find my baby, Lord, or lose my life tryin.

Yeah, I shot five dollars, caught a point like nine,
Yes, I shot five dollars, baby, and I caught a point like nine.
Yeah, I stopped that six spot, baby, and that trey come flyin.

Yeah, I hear my hamstring a-poppin, my collar cryin,
Lord, I hear my hamstring a-poppin, baby, and I hear my collar cryin.
Now how can I stay happy, Lord, when my baby's down the line.

Yeah, you'll never get to do me like you did my buddy Shine,
No, you'll never get to do me like you done my buddy Shine.
You know you worked him down on the levee until he went real stone blind.

Crossroad Blues

ROBERT JOHNSON

I went to the crossroad, fell down on my knee,
Went to the crossroad, fell down on my knee,
Asked the Lord above to have mercy, save poor Bob if you please.

Uumh, standing at the crossroad, I tried to flag a ride,
Standing at the crossroad, I tried to flag a ride,
Didn't nobody seem to know me, everybody passed me by.

Uumh, the sun going down, boy, dark gonna catch me here,
Uumh, dark gonna catch me here,
I haven't got no loving sweet woman that loves and feels my care.

You can run, you can run, tell my friend, poor Willie Brown,
You can run, tell my friend, poor Willie Brown,
Lord, that I'm standing at the crossroad, babe, I believe I'm sinking down.

Gospel Songs

Sung in the improvisational style of the classic blues—with piano, guitar, or instrumental accompaniment—gospel music became essentially the sacred counterpart to the blues. Whereas the classic blues were primarily worldly songs of overcoming despair by a resourceful wit and resilient spirit, gospel songs were jubilant black Baptist and Methodist hymns of hope and affirmation. In general, Jesus Christ and the New Testament figures of these songs replaced the Old Testament heroes of the spirituals. Beginning in the 1930s, gospel songs replaced spirituals as the most important single body of black religious music.

As with the spirituals, gospel music is grounded in the African antiphonal pattern of call and response and is heavily dependent on bodily rhythmic movement. Hand clapping, foot tapping, and swaying to and fro are salient features of the gospel sound. So is the beating of tambourines, as Langston Hughes's poem "Tambourines" emphasizes:

A gospel shout
And a gospel song:
Life is short
But God is long!

Tambourines!
Tambourines!
Tambourines
To glory!

Also of significance is the vocal quality of the singers. According to Eileen Southern,

> The full throated, strained, raspy sound is sought after; special effects are practically obligatory—the growl, falsetto, humming, moaning, and similar kinds of sounds. . . . Male singers often emphasize their falsetto tones; female singers, their low-register tones. Speaking parts of the text—phrases, or full stanzas—is a common procedure.

SOURCE: The Music of Black Americans (1983).

Take My Hand, Precious Lord

THOMAS A. DORSEY

Precious Lord, take my hand,
Lead me on, let me stand,
I am tired, I am weak, I am worn.
Through the storm, through the night
Lead me on to the light,
Take my hand, precious Lord,
Lead me home.

When my way grows drear,
Precious Lord, linger near.
When my life is almost gone,
Hear my cry, hear my call,
Hold my hand lest I fall.
Take my hand, precious Lord,
Lead me home.

When the darkness appears
And the night draws near,
And the day is past and gone,
At the river I stand,
Guide my feet, hold my hand.
Take my hand, precious Lord,
Lead me home.

When I Touch His Garment

LANGSTON HUGHES AND JOBE HUNTLEY

When I go to face my Lord,
I will face my Lord alone.
When I walk that starry street
Up to His Christian throne,
I will go all by myself,
Yes, I will go alone—
But when I touch His garment,
He'll claim me for His own.

(Chorus)

When I touch His garment,
Yes, I touch His garment,
When I touch His garment,
He'll claim me for His own.
I've got to go all by myself,
Got to go all alone;
But when I touch His garment,
He'll claim me for His own.

All the troubles of this world
Such as weigh me down today,
All my heartaches, all my woes
I know He'll take away.
On the road up to His throne,
I will go all alone—
But when I touch His garment,
He'll claim me for His own.

There will be a shower of stars.
There will be a blaze of light,
All around my savior's head
A diadem so bright.
I will see it from afar,
As I stand there all alone—
For when I touch His garment,
He'll claim me for His own.

If I Can Just Make It In

KENNETH MORRIS

If I can just make it in,
If I can just make it in,
If I can just make it in
To the heavenly gate,
I won't mind the load I'm bearing,
I won't mind the clothes I'm wearing,
I won't mind the way I'm faring
If I can just make it in.
I won't mind the work I've done,
I won't mind the race I've run.
All my trials will count as one
If I can just make it in.

I won't mind my lowly station,
I won't mind Satan's temptations,
I won't mind my tribulations
If I can just make it in.
You can have all this world's gold
And all the riches you can hold,
Just let me save my soul
So I can just make it in.
Though my pathway now is drear,
Though my heart is filled with fear,
I won't mind my every tear
If I can just make it in.

Jazz

Development of Jazz Techniques in Performance

Like the blues, jazz has its roots in the social experiences and musical idioms of Americans of African descent, as represented in the improvisational style and call and response structure of the spirituals and work songs. Essentially, it is an amalgam of certain elements of blues, ragtime, and syncopated dance music. Of major importance is the creative use of the voice as a musical instrument, as in the field holler.

Jazz is perhaps best described by novelist Ralph Ellison in his prologue to *Invisible Man* (1952). Writing in jazz rhythmic language, he explains the concept of the music and that of invisibility simultaneously:

> Invisibility, let me explain, gives one a slightly different sense of time, you're never quite on the beat. Sometimes you're ahead and sometimes behind. Instead of the swift and imperceptible flowing of time, you are aware of its nodes, those points where time stands still, or from which it leaps ahead. And you slip into the breaks and look around. That's what you hear vaguely in Louis' [Armstrong's] music.

As Ellison's description reveals, some of the most telling characteristics of the music are as follows: improvisation, or the spontaneous changes in the melody; syncopation, or the placement of a rhythmic stress on what would usually be a weak beat; break, or the brief flurry of notes played by a soloist during a pause in the ensemble playing; riffs, or repeated thematic figures; and the kind of accent that sounds so much without tune according to the conventions of European classical music.

RHYTHM, MELODY, AND HARMONY

Of all of the aspects of jazz, rhythm and improvisation are the most difficult elements to perform. Once based on duple meter, the music later developed to include a rapid succession or exchange of polymeters or multimeters. As African American musicologist Hildred Roach points out in her study, *Black American Music: Past and Present* (1992), "One therefore had to be keenly aware and responsive to rhythmic alterations of dotting, augmenting and diminishing." Additionally, she insists, the performer has to have an extensive knowledge of chords, scales, melodic direction, and imagination. Roach provides an illustration that shows the technical development of the music:

Ex. 30. Jazz techniques in performance.

IMPROVISATION

The polyphony of the music is achieved, Eileen Southern insists in *The Music of Black Americans* (1971; 1983 second edition), by "collective improvisation"—that is, by each player or performer embellishing the melody "by adding extra tones and alternating note values, but in such a manner as to retain the essential shape of the original melody." With each player improvising his or her own part, a balanced, integrated musical composition is created.

Improvisatory jazz pieces have been built over the years on a variety of compositions and melodies, including the blues, ragtime, work songs, spirituals, marches, stomps, shuffles, and dance songs. Above all, the blues formed the base for the music during the 1920s and 1930s. Among the popular blues-jazz compositions of the period were "Beale Street Blues" and "St. Louis Blues" by W. C. Handy and "(What Did I Do to Be So) Black and Blue" by Andy Razaf and Thomas "Fats" Waller. The latter song became a smash hit when Louis "Satchmo" Armstrong first recorded it in 1929. With his own ingenious improvisational elaborations, Armstrong made the song and its hard-hitting message of the devastating effects of racism come alive. Not only has the song lasted as one of the finest pieces of overt racial protest in American popular music, but it also served as the thematic basis for Ralph Ellison's *Invisible Man* (1952).

(What Did I Do to Be So) Black and Blue

ANDY RAZAF AND THOMAS "FATS" WALLER

Out in the street, shufflin' feet,
Couples passing two by two,
While here am I, left high and dry,
Black, and 'cause I'm black I'm blue.
Browns and yellers all have fellers,
Gentleman prefer them light,

Wish I could fade, can't make the grade,
Nothin' but dark days in sight.

Cold empty bed, springs hard as lead,
Pains in my head, feel like old Ned,
What did I do to be so black and blue?

No joys for me, no company,
Even the mouse ran from my house,
All my life through, I've been so black and blue.

I'm white inside, it don't help my case,
'Cause I can't hide what is on my face.

I'm so forlorn, life's just a thorn,
My heart is torn, why was I born?
What did I do to be so black and blue?

Just 'cause you're black, folks think you lack,
They laugh ta you and scorn you too,
What did I do to be so black and blue?

When you are near, they laugh and sneer,
Set you aside and you're denied,
What did I do to be so black and blue?

How sad I am, each day I feel worse,
My mark of Ham seems to be a curse.

How will it end? Ain't got a friend,
My only sin is in my skin,
What did I do to be so black and blue?

SWING OR BIG BAND JAZZ

With his 1932 song "It Don't Mean a Thing If It Ain't Got That Swing," Duke Ellington launched a new style of jazz called swing or big band jazz. Through his musical creations and arrangements, characterized by striking, rich harmonies, and his brilliant blending of solo and ensemble relationships, he developed an orchestra style that became the center of the jazz scene during the period. In 1932, Ellington extended his big band sound by adding a third trombone and fourth saxophone to his famous orchestra at the Cotton Club in Harlem. Previously, his band had included two trombones, two trumpets, an alto saxophone, a baritone saxophone, a tenor saxophone, a clarinet, a guitar, a banjo, drums, a bass, and a piano. With a score of talented jazz musicians, ranging from alto saxophonist Johnny Hodges and trumpeter James "Bubber" Miley to his co-composer/arranger Billy Strayhorn, Ellington made his mark in jazz musical history. Besides "It Don't Mean a Thing If It Ain't Got That Swing," he wrote a repertory of songs, including his best-known works: "Sophisticated Lady," "In a Sentimental Mood," "Mood Indigo," and "I Got It Bad and That Ain't Good."

FROM *It Don't Mean a Thing If It Ain't Got That Swing*

EDWARD KENNEDY "DUKE" ELLINGTON

It don't mean a thing if it ain't got that swing
Doo-wah doo-wah, doo-wah doo-wah, doo-wah doo-wah, doo-wah doo-wah
It don't mean a thing, all you got to do is sing
Doo-wah doo-wah, doo-wah doo-wah, doo-wah doo-wah, doo-wah doo-wah
It makes no difference if it's sweet or hot
Just keep that rhythm, give it everything you got
It don't mean a thing if it ain't got that swing
Doo-wah doo-wah, doo-wah doo-wah, doo-wah doo-wah, doo-wah doo-wah.

Boogie Woogie

As illustrated in the following chart, boogie woogie is based on an eight-beat measure. Written in duple pulse beats, this standard pattern is played by the boogie pianist with his or her left hand while he or she plays a more ornamental melody of cross rhythms with the right hand. Hildred Roach's illustration in *Black American Music: Past and Present* (1992) demonstrates that the typical boogie patterns are those that either alternate within sections or display one continuous pattern:

Boogie patterns.

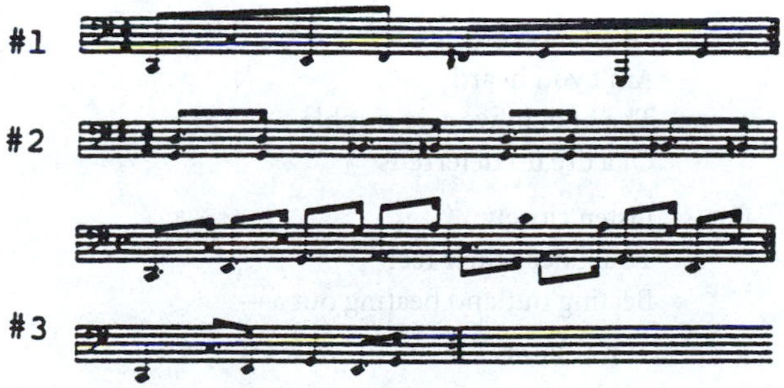

The driving rhythms of the music, as indicated in Clarence "Pine Top" Smith's piano composition called "Pine Top's Boogie Woogie" and Langston Hughes's poem "Dream Boogie," accompanied the popular dance crazes of the period. They were designed to inspire blacks to dance with reckless abandon in an effort to forget temporarily the blues realities of everyday life.

Pine Top's Boogie Woogie[1]

CLARENCE "PINE TOP" SMITH

Now look, let me tell you something about that 'Pine Top Boogie Woogie.'
Now when I say stop, I mean stop.

[1]Derived from "Pine Top's Boogie Woogie" (Vocalion 1245), recorded by Clarence "Pine Top" Smith in Chicago, December 29, 1928.

I say git it, I mean git it.
Do like I tell you.
I say hold it, I mean hold it, that's what I'm talking about.
Now, Red, [Jasper Love] hold yourself.
Don't move a peg.
Now git it.
Now boogie.
Now look, you see that woman with her red dress on?
I want you to swing her right on back to me.
Don't forgit it.
Do like I tell you.
I say hold it, I mean hold it, that's what I'm talking about.

Now, Red, hold yourself again.
Don't move a peg.
Now git it, boogie.
Now shake it.

Dream Boogie

LANGSTON HUGHES

Good morning, daddy!
Ain't you heard
The boogie-woogie rumble
Of a dream deferred?

Listen closely:
You'll hear their feet
Beating out and beating out a—

You think
It's a happy beat?

Listen to it closely:
Ain't you heard
something underneath
like a—

What did I say?

Sure,
I'm happy!
Take it away!

Hey, pop!
Re-bop!
Mop!

Y-e-a-h!

Bad Man and Prison Songs

Garvey

Garvey, Garvey, is a big man
To take his folks to monkey-land.
If he does, I'm sure I can
Stay right here with Uncle Sam.

When I get on the other side
I'll buy myself a mango.
Grab myself a monkey gal
And do the monkey tango.

When a monkey-chaser dies
Don't need no undertaker.
Just throw him in the Harlem River
He'll float back to Jamaica.

Champ Joe Louis

BILL GAITHER

I came all the way from Chicago to see Joe Louis and Max Schmelling fight. *(twice)*
Schmelling went down like the *Titanic* when Joe gave him just one hard right.

Well, you've heard of the King of Swing, well Joe is the King of Gloves, *(twice)*
Now he's the World Heavyweight Champion, a man that this whole world loves.

It was only two minutes and four seconds poor Schmelling was down on his knees, *(twice)*
He looked like he was praying to the Good Lord to "Have mercy on me, please!"

If I'd had a million dollars would have bet every dime on Joe, *(twice)*
I'd've been a rich man this very day and I wouldn't have to worry no more.

This Mornin', This Evenin', So Soon

Went up town wid my hat in my hand' dis mornin',
Went up town wid my hat in my han'.
"Good mornin', jedge, done killed my man,"
This mornin', this evenin', so soon.

"I didn't quite kill him, but I fixed him so, this mornin';
I didn't quite kill him but I fixed him so
He won't bodder wid me no mo'."
This mornin', this evenin', so soon.

All I want is my strong hand-out, this mornin',
All I want is my strong hand-out;
It will make me strong and stout.
This mornin', this evenin', so soon.

Slim Greer

STERLING BROWN

Listen to the tale
Of Ole Slim Greer,
Waitines' devil
Waitin' here;

Talkinges' guy
An' biggest liar,
With always a new lie
On the fire.

Tells a tale
Of Arkansaw
That keeps the kitchen
In a roar;

Tells in a long-drawled
Careless tone,
As solemn as a Baptist
Parson's moan.

How he in Arkansaw
Passed for white,
An' he no lighter
Than a dark midnight.

Found a nice white woman
At a dance,
Thought he was from Spain
Or else from France;

Nobody suspicioned
Ole Slim Greer's race
But a Hill Billy, always
Roun' the place,

Who called one day
On the trustful dame
An' found Slim comfy
When he came.

The whites lef' the parlor
All to Slim
Which didn't cut
No ice with him,

An' he started a-tinklin'
Some mo'nful blues,
An' a-pattin' the time
With No. Fourteen shoes.

The cracker listened
An' then he spat
An' said, "No white man
Could play like that. . . ."

The white jane ordered
The tattler out;
Then, female-like,
Began to doubt,
Crept into the parlor
Soft as you please,
Where Slim was agitatin'
The ivories.

Heard Slim's music—
An' then, hot damn!
Shouted sharp—"Nigger!"
An' Slim said, "Ma'am?"

She screamed and the crackers
Swarmed up soon,
But found only echoes
Of his tune;

'Cause Slim had sold out
With lightnin' speed;
"Hope I may die, sir—
Yes, indeed. . . ."

TOASTS

Toasts are long epic poems that are acted out in a theatrical manner. In general, they consist of rhyming couplets built around the pattern of a four-stress line. As Roger Abrahams explains in his study of the form in *Deep Down in the Jungle* (1970), toasts contain "some sort of picturesque or exciting introduction, action alternating with dialogue (because the action is usually a struggle between two people or animals), and a twist ending of some sort, either a quip, an ironic comment, or a brag." The teller does not sing or recite the poem but performs it. In fact, toast-telling is heavily dependent on the teller's style of dramatic performance. The teller changes voice from one persona in the poem to another by using different stresses, accents, and degrees of clarity for various characters. Often the audience participates in the activity. The audience's judgment is part of the event, and any participant can change obscure parts of the toast or redesign those that are not personally meaningful.

Two of the most popular toasts, "Shine and the Sinking of the Titanic" and "The Signifying Monkey," illustrate the use of boastful verbal wit, irony, and the profane to win an encounter. Another popular toast, "Stagolee," derives from the "bad man" song of the same title. Only one Harlem Renaissance poet, Sterling Brown, wrote verse celebrating the "bad man" ballad tradition. He and other writers of the period avoided the toast tradition, perhaps because of the obscenity and vulgarity of the language embedded in it. Nevertheless, the toasts, along with the blues and gospel music, became the most popular black communal art form among the black masses during the period. Not until the contemporary era would black literary artists begin to draw on the tradition.

Shine and the Sinking of the Titanic

A TRADITIONAL VERSION

Boys, you remember way back on the day of the eighth of May
the year of nineteen and twelve, was a hell of a day.
Up popped little Shine from the deck below,
sayin', "Captain, captain, you don't know,
'bout forty feet of water on this boiler-room floor."
He said, "Never mind, Shine," say, "You go on back and keep stackin' them sacks,
I got forty-eight pumps to keep the water back."
Shine says, "That seems mighty funny 'cause maybe you doin' fine,
I'm tryin' to save this old black body of mine."
So Shine jumped overboard and begin to swim,
all the people were standin' on deck watchin' him.
The captain's daughter jumped on the deck
with her dress above her head and her teddies below her knees.
Sayin', "Shine, Shine," say, "save poor me,"
say, "I'll make you as rich as any shine can be."
He say, "Miss, I know you's pretty and that is true,"
said, "there's women on the shore will make a ass out a you."
Well, Shine turned over and begin to swim
and the people were still watchin' him.
Say, a whale popped up in the middle of the sea
and said, "Put a special delivery on Shine's black ass for me."
Shine say, "Your eyes may roll and your teeth may grit,
but none of this black ass you gonna git."
He swimmed and swimmed till he came to a seaport town.
The people asked had the *Titanic* gone down.
Shine said, "Hell, yeah," they said, "How do you know?"
"I left the big sonofagun sinkin' thirty minutes ago."

Titanic

(Look where and what has been done—1912, twelfth day of May, when the Titanic sink in the sea. When they was getting on board (there) was not no colored folks on. There was not no Negroes died on that ship. But Jack Johnson went to get on board. "We are not hauling no coal," (they said). So Jack Johnson didn't like what the Big Boss said. He went and tried to do something about it, but it was so much Jim Crow he could not have no go. And a few hours later Jack Johnson read the papers where the Titanic went down. Then the peoples began to holler about that mighty shock. You might have been Jack Johnson doing the Eagle Rock so glad that he was not on that ship. [Leadbelly, from a letter to Moses Asch, Folkways]

SOURCE: Version of "Shine" by Huddie "Leadbelly" Ledbetter.

Captain Smith, when he got his load,
Might 'a' heared him holl'in', "All aboa'd!"
Cryin', "Fare thee, *Titanic*, fare thee well!"*

Captain Smith, when he got his load,
Might 'a' heared him holl'in', "All aboa'd!"
Cryin', "Fare thee, *Titanic*, fare thee well!"

Jack Johnson wanted to get on boa'd;
Captain Smith hollered, "I ain' haulin' no coal."
Cryin', "Fare thee, *Titanic*, fare thee well!"

It was midnight on the sea,
Band playin', "Nearer My God to Thee."
Cryin', "Fare thee, *Titanic*, fare thee well!"

Titanic was sinking down,
Had them lifeboats aroun',
Cryin', "Fare thee, *Titanic*, fare thee well!"

Had them lifeboats aroun',
Savin' the women, lettin' the men go down.
Cryin', "Fare thee, *Titanic*, fare thee well!"

When the women got out on the land,
Cryin', "Lawd, have mercy on my man."
Cryin', "Fare thee, *Titanic*, fare thee well!"

Jack Johnson heard the mighty shock,
Might 'a seen the black rascal doin' th' Eagle Rock.
Cryin', "Fare thee, *Titanic*, fare thee well!"

Black man oughta shout for joy,
Never lost a girl or either a boy.
Cryin', "Fare thee, *Titanic*, fare thee well!"

*Each group of three lines is sung twice to make a full stanza.

The Signifying Monkey

The Monkey and the Lion
Got to talking one day.
Monkey looked down and said, Lion,
I hear you's king in every way.
But I know somebody
Who do not think that is true—
He told me he could whip
The living daylights out of you.
Lion said, Who?
Monkey said, Lion,
He talked about your mama

And talked about your grandma, too,
And I'm too polite to tell you
What he said about you.
Lion said, Who said what? Who?
Monkey in the tree,
Lion on the ground.
Monkey kept on signifying
But he didn't come down.
Monkey said, His name is Elephant—
He stone sure is not your friend.
Lion said, He don't need to be
Because today will be his end.
Lion took off through the jungle
Lickity-split,
Meaning to grab Elephant
And tear him bit to bit. Period!
He come across Elephant copping a righteous nod
Under a fine cool shady tree.
Lion said, You big old no-good so-and-so,
It's either you or me.
Lion let out a solid roar
And bopped Elephant with his paw.
Elephant just took his trunk
And busted old Lion's jaw.
Lion let out another roar,
Reared up six feet tall.
Elephant just kicked him in the belly
And laughed to see him drop and fall.
Lion rolled over,
Copped Elephant by the throat.
Elephant just shook him loose
And butted him like a goat,
Then he tromped him and he stomped him
Till the Lion yelled, Oh, no!
And it was near-nigh sunset
When Elephant let Lion go.
The signifying Monkey
Was still setting in his tree
When he looked down and saw the Lion.
Said, Why, Lion, who can that there be?
Lion said, It's me.
Monkey rapped, "Why, Lion,
You look more dead than alive!
Lion said, Monkey, I don't want
To hear your jive-end jive.
Monkey just kept on signifying,

Lion, you for sure caught hell—
Mister Elephant's done whipped you
To a fare-thee-well!
Why, Lion, you look like to me
You been in the precinct station
And had the third-degree,
Else you look like
You been high on gage
And done got caught
In a monkey cage!
You ain't no king to me.
Facts, I don't think that you
Can even as much as roar—
And if you try I'm liable
To come down out of this tree and
Whip your tail some more.
The Monkey started laughing
And jumping up and down.
But he jumped so hard the limb broke
And he landed—*bam!*—on the ground.
When he went to run, his foot slipped
And he fell flat down.
Grr-rrr-rr-r! The Lion was on him
With his front feet and his hind.
Monkey hollered, Ow!
I didn't mean it, Mister Lion!
Lion said, You little flea-bag you!
Why, I'll eat you up alive.
I wouldn't a-been in this fix a-tall
Wasn't for your signifying jive.
Please, said Monkey, Mister Lion,
If you'll just let me go,
I got something to tell you, *please,*
I think you ought to know.
Lion let the Monkey loose
To see what his tale could be—
And Monkey jumped right back on up
Into his tree.
What I was gonna tell you, said Monkey,
Is you square old so-and-so,
If you fool with me I'll get
Elephant to whip your head some more.
Monkey, said the Lion,
Beat to his unbooted knees,
You and all your signifying children
Better stay up in them trees.

Which is why today
Monkey does his signifying
A-way-up out of the way.

SOURCE: A traditional version.

Stack O'Lee Blues

Police and officers, how can it be
You can arrest everybody but cruel Stack O'Lee
That bad man, O cruel Stack O'Lee!

He said, "Stack O'Lee! Stack O'Lee!
Please don't take my life."
Says, "I got two little babes and a darling loving wife."
He's a bad man, that cruel Stack O'Lee!

"What I care about your two little babes, your darling loving wife.
Say, You done stole my Stetson hat,
I'm bound to take your life."
That bad man, O cruel Stack O'Lee!

Ummmmmm Ummmmmmmmmm Ummmmmmmmmm
Ummmmmm Ummmmmmmmmm Ummmmmm Ummmm Ummm

Boom! Boom! Boom! Boom! went a .44
Well, when they spy Billy Lyons
He was lying down on the floor
That bad man, O cruel Stack O'Lee!

Gentleman of the jury,
What do you think of that?
Say Stack O'Lee killed Billy Lyons
About a five dollar Stetson hat
He's a bad man, O cruel Stack O'Lee!

Standin' on the gallows
Stack O'Lee did curse.
The judge say, "Let's kill him
Before he kill some of us."
He's a bad man, O cruel Stack O'Lee!

Standin' on the gallows
His head was way up high.
At twelve o'clock they killed him
They's all glad to see him die.
That bad man, O cruel Stack O'Lee!

Police and officers, how can it be
You can arrest everybody but cruel Stack O'Lee
That bad man, O cruel Stack O'Lee!

SOURCE: Version of "Stackolee" by Mississippi John Hurt.

Folk sermons

The Creation

from *God's Trombones*

JAMES WELDON JOHNSON

And God stepped out on space,
And he looked around and said:
I'm lonely—
I'll make me a world.

And far as the eye of God could see
Darkness covered everything,
Blacker than a hundred midnights
Down in a cypress swamp.

Then God smiled,
And the light broke,
And the darkness rolled up on one side,
And the light stood shining on the other,
And God said: That's good!

Then God reached out and took the light in his hands,
And God rolled the light around in his hands
Until he made the sun;
And he set that sun a-blazing in the heavens.
And the light that was left from making the sun
God gathered it up in a shining ball
And flung it against the darkness,
Spangling the night with the moon and stars.
Then down between
The darkness and the light
He hurled the world;
And God said: That's good!

Then God himself stepped down—
And the sun was on his right hand,
And the moon was on his left;
The stars were clustered about his head,
And the earth was under his feet.
And God walked, and where he trod
His footsteps hollowed the valleys out
And bulged the mountains up.

Then he stopped and looked and saw
That the earth was hot and barren.
So God stepped over to the edge of the world
And he spat out the seven seas—

He batted his eyes, and the lightnings flashed—
He clapped his hands, and the thunders rolled—
And the waters above the earth came down,
The cooling waters came down.

Then the green grass sprouted,
And the little red flowers blossomed,
The pine tree pointed his finger to the sky,
And the oak spread out his arms,
The lakes cuddled down in the hollows of the ground,
And the rivers ran down to the sea;
And God smiled again,
And the rainbow appeared,
And curled itself around his shoulder.

Then God raised his arm and he waved his hand
Over the sea and over the land,
And he said: Bring forth! Bring forth!
And quicker than God could drop his hand,
Fishes and fowls
And beasts and birds
Swam the rivers and the seas,
Roamed the forests and the woods,
And split the air with their wings.
And God said: That's good!

Then God walked around,
And God looked around
On all that he had made.
He looked at his sun,
And he looked at his moon,
And he looked at his little stars;
He looked on his world
With all its living things,
And God said: I'm lonely still.

Then God sat down—
On the side of a hill where he could think;
By a deep, wide river he sat down;
With his head in his hands,
God thought and thought,
Till he thought: I'll make me a man!

Up from the bed of the river
God scooped the clay;
And by the bank of the river
He kneeled him down;
And there the great God Almighty
Who lit the sun and fixed it in the sky,
Who flung the stars to the most far corner of the night,

Who rounded the earth in the middle of his hand;
This Great God,
Like a mammy bending over her baby,
Kneeled down in the dust
Toiling over a lump of clay
Till he shaped it in his own image;
Then into it he blew the breath of life,
And man became a living soul.
Amen. Amen.

Go Down Death—A Funeral Sermon

FROM *GOD'S TROMBONES*

JAMES WELDON JOHNSON

Weep not, weep not,
She is not dead;
She's resting in the bosom of Jesus.
Heart-broken husband—weep no more;
Grief-stricken son—weep no more;
Left-lonesome daughter—weep no more;
She's only just gone home.

Day before yesterday morning,
God was looking down from his great, high heaven,
Looking down on all his children,
And his eye fell on Sister Caroline,
Tossing on her bed of pain.
And God's big heart was touched with pity,
With the everlasting pity.

And God sat back on his throne,
And he commanded that tall, bright angel standing at his right hand:
Call me Death!
And that tall, bright angel cried in a voice
That broke like a clap of thunder:
Call Death!—Call Death!
And the echo sounded down the streets of heaven
Till it reached away back to that shadowy place,
Where Death waits with his pale, white horses.

And Death heard the summons,
And he leaped on his fastest horse,
Pale as a sheet in the moonlight.
Up the golden street Death galloped,
And the hoofs of his horse struck fire from the gold,
But they didn't make no sound.
Up Death rode to the Great White Throne,
And waited for God's command.

And God said: Go down, Death, go down,
Go down to Savannah, Georgia,
Down in Yamacraw,

And find Sister Caroline.
She's borne the burden and heat of the day,
She's labored long in my vineyard,
And she's tired—
She's weary—
Go down, Death, and bring her to me.

And Death didn't say a word,
But he loosed the reins on his pale, white horse,
And he clamped the spurs to his bloodless sides,
And out and down he rode,
Through heaven's pearly gates,
Past suns and moons and stars;
On Death rode,
And the foam from his horse was like a comet in the sky;
On Death rode,
Leaving the lightning's flash behind;
Straight on down he came.

While we were watching round her bed,
She turned her eyes and looked away,
She saw what we couldn't see;
She saw Old Death. She saw Old Death
Coming like a falling star.
But Death didn't frighten Sister Caroline;
He looked to her like a welcome friend.
And she whispered to us: I'm going home,
And she smiled and closed her eyes.

And Death took her up like a baby,
And she lay in his icy arms,
But she didn't feel no chill.
And Death began to ride again—
Up beyond the evening star,
Out beyond the morning star,
Into the glittering light of glory,
On to the Great White Throne.
And there he laid Sister Caroline
On the loving breast of Jesus.

And Jesus took his own hand and wiped away her tears,
And he smoothed the furrows from her face,
And the angels sang a little song,
And Jesus rocked her in his arms,
And kept a-saying: Take your rest,
Take your rest, take your rest.

Weep not—weep not,
She is not dead;
She's resting in the bosom of Jesus.

A Mock Sermon

FROM *PREACHIN' THE BLUES*

BESSIE SMITH

Down in Atlanta GA,
Under the viaduct every day,
Drinkin' corn and hollerin', 'Hooray!'
Piano's playin' till the break of day.
But as I turned my head, I loudly said:
  Preach them blues, sing them blues,
  They certainly sound good to me.
  I been in love for the last six months,
  And ain't done worryin' yet.
  Moan them blues, holler them blues,
  Let me convert your soul. . . .

Goin' on down the line a li'l further now,
'There's many a po' woman down.'
Read on down to chapter nine,
'Women must learn how to take their time.'
Read on down to chapter ten,
'Takin' other women's men, you are doin' a sin.'
Sing 'em, sing 'em, sing them blues,
Let me convert your soul.

Folktale (collected by Zora Neale Hurston)

High John De Conquer

High John de Conquer came to be a man, and a mighty man at that. But he was not a natural man in the beginning. First off, he was a whisper, a will to hope, a wish to find something worthy of laughter and song. Then the whisper put on flesh. His footsteps sounded across the world in a low but musical rhythm as if the world he walked on was a singing-drum. Black people had an irresistible impulse to laugh. High John de Conquer was a man in full, and had come to live and work on the plantations, and all the slave folks knew him in the flesh.

The sign of this man was a laugh, and his singing-symbol was a drum-beat. No parading drum-shout like soldiers out for show. It did not call to the feet of those who were fixed to hear it. It was an inside thing to live by. It was sure to be heard when and where the work was the hardest, and the lot the most cruel. It helped the slaves endure. They knew that something better was coming. So they laughed in the face of things and sang, "I'm so glad! Trouble don't last always." And the white people who heard them were struck dumb that they could laugh. In an outside way, this was Old Massa's fun, so what was Old Cuffy laughing for?

Old Massa couldn't know, of course, but High John de Conquer was there walking his plantation like a natural man. He was treading the sweat-flavored clods of the plantation, crushing out his drum tunes, and giving out secret laughter. He walked on the winds and moved fast. Maybe he was in Texas when the lash fell on a slave in Alabama, but before the blood was dry on the back he was there. A faint pulsing of a drum like a goat-skin stretched over a heart, that came nearer and closer, then somebody in the saddened quarters would feel like laughing, and say, "Now, High John de Conquer, Old Massa couldn't get the best of *him.* That old John was a case!" Then everybody sat up and began to smile. Yes, yes, that was right. Old John, High John could beat the unbeatable. He was top-superior to the whole mess of sorrow. He could beat it all, and what made it so cool, finish it off with a laugh. So they pulled the covers up over their souls and kept them from all hurt, harm and danger and made them a laugh and a song. Night time was a joke, because daybreak was on the way. Distance and the impossible had no power over High John de Conquer.

He had come from Africa. He came walking on the waves of sound. Then he took on flesh after he got here. The sea captains of ships knew that they brought slaves in their ships. They knew about those black bodies huddled down there in the middle passage, being hauled across the waters to helplessness. John de Conquer was walking the very winds that filled the sails of the ships. He followed over them like the albatross.

It is no accident that High John de Conquer has evaded the ears of white people. They were not supposed to know. You can't know what folks won't tell you. If they, the white people, heard some scraps, they could not understand because they had nothing to hear things like that with. They were not looking for any hope in those days, and it was not much of a strain for them to find something to laugh over. Old John would have been out of place for them.

Old Massa met our hope-bringer all right, but when Old Massa met him, he was not going by his right name. He was traveling, and touristing around the plantations as the laugh-provoking Brer Rabbit. So Old Massa and Old Miss and their young ones laughed with and at Brer Rabbit and wished him well. And all the time, there was High John de Conquer playing his tricks of making a way out of no-way. Hitting a straight lick with a crooked stick. Winning the jack pot with no other stake but a laugh. Fighting a mighty battle without outside-showing force, and winning his war from within. Really winning in a permanent way, for he was winning with the soul of the black man whole and free. So he could use it afterwards. For what shall it profit a man if he gain the whole world, and lose his own soul? You would have nothing but a cruel, vengeful, grasping monster come to power. John de Conquer was a bottom-fish. He was deep. He had the wisdom tooth of the East in his head. Way over there, where the sun rises a day ahead of time, they say that Heaven arms with love and laughter those it does not wish to see destroyed. He who carries his heart in his sword must perish. So says the ultimate law. High John de Conquer knew a lot of things like that. He who wins from within is in the "Be" class. *Be* here when the ruthless man comes and *be* here when he is gone.

Moreover, John knew that it is written where it cannot be erased, that nothing shall live on human flesh and prosper. Old Maker said that before He made any more sayings. Even a man-eating tiger and lion can teach a person that much. His flabby muscles and mangy hide can teach an emperor right from wrong. If the emperor would only listen.

II

There is no established picture of what sort of looking-man this John de Conquer was. To some, he was a big, physical-looking man like John Henry. To others, he was a little, hammered-down, low-built man like the Devil's doll-baby. Some said that they never heard what he looked like. Nobody told them, but he lived on the plantation where their old folks were slaves. He is not so well known to the present generation of colored people in the same way that he was in slavery time. Like King Arthur of England, he has served his people, and gone back into mystery again. And, like King Arthur, he is not dead. He waits to return when his people shall call again. Symbolic of English power, Arthur came out of the water, and with Excalibur, went back into the water again. High John de Conquer went back to Africa, but he left his power here, and place his American dwelling in the root of a certain plant. Possess that root, and he can be summoned at any time.

"Of course, High John de Conquer got plenty power!" Aunt Shady Anne Sutton bristled at me when I asked her about him. She took her pipe out of her mouth and stared at me out of her deeply wrinkled face. "I hope you ain't one of these here smart colored folks that done got so they don't believe nothing, and come here questionizing me so you can have something to poke fun at. Done got shamed of the things that brought us through. Make out 'taint no such thing no more."

When I assured her that that was not the case, she went on.

"Sho John de Conquer means power. That's bound to be so. He come to teach and tell us. God don't leave nobody ignorant, you child. Don't care where He drops you down. He puts you on a notice. He don't want folks taken advantage of because they don't know. Now, back there in slavery time, us didn't have no power of protection, and God knowed it, and put us under watch-care. Rattlesnakes never bit no colored folks until four years after freedom was declared. That was to give us time to learn and to know. 'Course, I don't know nothing about slavery personal like. I wasn't born till two years after the Big Surrender. Then I wasn't nothing but a infant baby when I was born, so I couldn't know nothing but what they told me. My mama told me, and I know she wouldn't mislead me, how High John de Conquer helped us out. He had done teached the black folks so they knowed a hundred years ahead of time that freedom was coming. Long before the white folks knowed anything about it at all.

"These young Negroes reads they books and talk about the war freeing the Negroes, but Aye, Lord! A heap sees, but a few knows. 'Course, the war was a lot of help, but how come the war took place? They think they knows, but they don't. John de Conquer had done put it into the white folks to give us our freedom, that's what. Old Massa fought against it, but us could have told him that it wasn't no use. Freedom just *had* to come. The time set aside for it was there. That war was just a sign and a symbol of the thing. That's the truth! If I tell the truth about everything as good as I do about that, I can go straight to Heaven without a prayer."

Aunt Shady Anne was giving the inside feeling and meaning to the outside laughs around John de Conquer. He romps, he clowns, and looks ridiculous, but if you will, you can read something deeper behind it all. He is loping on off from the Tar Baby with a laugh.

Take, for instance, those words he had with Old Massa about stealing pigs.

Old John was working in Old Massa's house that time, serving around the eating table. Old Massa loved roasted young pigs, and had them often for dinner. Old John loved them too, but Massa never allowed the slaves to eat any at all. Even put aside the left-over and ate it next time. John de Conquer got tired of that. He took to stopping by the pig pen when he had a strong taste for pig-meat, and getting himself one, and taking it on down to his cabin and cooking it.

Massa began to miss his pigs, and made up his mind to squat for who was taking them and give whoever it was a good hiding. So John kept on taking pigs, and one night Massa walked him down. He stood out there in the dark and saw John kill the pig and went on back to the "big house" and waited till he figured John had it dressed and cooking. Then he went on down to the quarters and knocked on John's door.

"Who dat?" John called out big and bold, because he never dreamed that it was Massa rapping.

"It's me, John," Massa told him. "I want to come in."

"What you want, Massa? I'm coming right out."

"You needn't to do that, John. I want to come in."

"Naw, naw, Massa. You don't want to come into no old slave cabin. Youse too fine a man for that. It would hurt my feelings to see you in a place like this here one."

"I tell you I want to come in, John!"

So John had to open the door and let Massa in. John had seasoned that pig *down,* and it was stinking pretty! John knowed Old Massa couldn't help but smell it. Massa talked on about the crops and hound dogs and one thing and another, and the pot with the pig in it was hanging over the fire in the chimney and kicking up. The smell got better and better.

Way after while, when that pig had done simbled down to a low gravy, Massa said, "John, what's that you cooking in that pot?"

"Nothing but a little old weasly possum, Massa. Sickliest little old possum I ever did see. But I thought I'd cook him anyhow."

"Get a plate and give me some of it, John. I'm hungry."

"Aw, naw, Massa, you ain't hongry."

"Now, John, I don't mean to argue with you another minute. You give me some of that in the pot, or I mean to have the hide off of your back tomorrow morning. Give it to me!"

So John got up and went and got a plate and a fork and went to the pot. He lifted the lid and looked at Massa and told him, "Well, Massa, I put this thing in here a possum, but if it comes out a pig, it ain't no fault of mine."

Old Massa didn't want to laugh, but he did before he caught himself. He took the plate of brownded-down pig and ate it up. He never said nothing, but he gave John and all the other house servants roast pig at the big house after that.

III

John had numerous scrapes and tight squeezes, but he usually came out like Brer Rabbit. Pretty occasionally, though, Old Massa won the hand. The curious thing about this is, that there are no bitter tragic tales at all. When Old Massa won, the thing ended up in a laugh just the same. Laughter at the expense of the slave, but laughter right on. A sort of recognition that life is not one-sided. A sense of humor that said, "We are just as ridiculous as anybody else. We can be wrong, too."

There are many tales, and variants of each, of how the Negro got his freedom through High John de Conquer. The best one deals with a plantation where the work was hard, and Old Massa mean. Even Old Miss used to pull her maids' ears with hot fire-tongs when they got her riled. So, naturally, Old John de Conquer was around that plantation a lot.

"What we need is a song," he told the people after he had figured the whole thing out. "It ain't here, and it ain't no place I knows of as yet. Us better go hunt around. This has got to be a particular piece of singing."

But the slaves were scared to leave. They knew what Old Massa did for any slave caught running off.

"Oh, Old Massa don't need to know you gone from here. How? Just leave your old work-tired bodies around for him to look at, and he'll never realize youse way off somewhere, going about your business."

At first they wouldn't hear to John, that is, some of them. But, finally, the weak gave in to the strong, and John told them to get ready to go while he went off to get something for them to ride on. They were all gathered up under a big hickory nut tree. It was noon time and they were knocked off from chopping cotton to eat their dinner. And then that tree was right where Old Massa and Old Miss could see from the cool veranda of the big house. And both of them were sitting out there to watch.

"Wait a minute, John. Where we going to get something to wear off like that. We can't go nowhere like you talking about dressed like we is."

"Oh, you got plenty things to wear. Just reach inside yourselves and get out all those fine raiments you been toting around with you for the last longest. They is in there, all right. I know. Get 'em out, and put 'em on."

So the people began to dress. And then John hollered back for them to get out their musical instruments so they could play music on the way. They were right inside where they got their fine raiments from. So they began to get them out. Nobody remembered that Massa and Miss were setting up there on the veranda looking things over. So John went off for a minute. After that they all heard a big sing of wings. It was John come back, riding on a great black crow. The crow was so big that one wing rested on the morning, while the other dusted off the evening star.

John lighted down and helped them, so they all mounted on, and the bird took out straight across the deep blue sea. But it was a pearly blue, like ten squillion big pearl jewels dissolved in running gold. The shore around it was all grainy gold itself.

Like Jason in search of the golden fleece, John and his party went to many places, and had numerous adventures. They stopped off in Hell where John, under the name of Jack, married the Devil's youngest daughter and became a popular character. So much so, that when he and the Devil had some words because John turned the dampers down in old Original Hell and put some of the Devil's hogs to barbecue over the coals, John ran for high Chief Devil and won the election. The rest of his party was overjoyed at the possession of power and wanted to stay there. But John said no. He reminded them that they had come in search of a song. A song that would whip Old Massa's earlaps down. The song was not in Hell. They must go on.

The party escaped out of Hell behind the Devil's two fast horses. One of them was named Hallowed-Be-Thy-Name, and the other, Thy-Kingdom-Come. They made it to the mountain. Somebody told them that the Golden Stairs went up from there. John decided that since they were in the vicinity, they might as well visit Heaven.

They got there a little weary and timid. But the gates swung wide for them, and they went in. They were bathed, robed, and given new and shining instruments to play on. Guitars of gold, and drums, and cymbals and wind-singing instruments. They walked up Amen Avenue, and down Hallelujah Street, and found with delight that Amen Avenue was tuned to sing bass and alto. The west end was deep bass, and the east end alto. Hallelujah Street was tuned for tenor and soprano, and the two promenades met right in front of the throne and made harmony by themselves. You could make any tune you wanted to by the way you walked. John and his party had a very good time at that and other things. Finally, by the way they acted and did, Old Maker called them up before His great work-bench, and made them a tune and put it in their mouths. It had no words. It was a tune that you could bend and shape in most any way you wanted to fit the words and feelings that you had. They learned it and began to sing.

Just about that time a loud rough voice hollered, "You Tunk! You July! You Aunt Diskie!" Then Heaven went black before their eyes and they couldn't see a thing until they saw the hickory nut tree over their heads again. There was everything just like they had left it, with Old Massa and Old Miss sitting on the veranda, and Massa was doing the hollering.

"You all are taking a mighty long time for dinner," Massa said. "Get up from there and get on back to the field. I mean for you to finish chopping that cotton today if it takes all night long. I got something else, harder than that, for you to do tomorrow. Get a move on you!"

They heard what Massa said, and they felt bad right off. But John de Conquer took and told them, saying, "Don't pay what he say no mind. You know where you got something finer than this plantation and anything it's got on it, put away. Ain't that funny? Us got all that, and he don't know nothing at all about it. Don't tell him nothing. Nobody don't have to know where us gets our pleasure from. Come on. Pick up your hoes and let's go."

They all began to laugh and grabbed up their hoes and started out.

"Ain't that funny?" Aunt Diskie laughed and hugged herself with secret laughter. "Us got all the advantage, and Old Massa think he got us tied!"

The crowd broke out singing as they went off to work. The day didn't seem hot like it had before. Their gift song came back into their memories in pieces, and they sang about glittering new robes and harps, and the work flew.

IV

So after a while, freedom came. Therefore High John de Conquer has not walked the winds of America for seventy-five years now. His people had their freedom, their laugh and their song. They have traded it to the other Americans for things they could use like education and property, and acceptance. High John knew that that was the way it would be, so he could retire with his secret smile into the soil of the South and wait.

The thousands upon thousands of humble people who still believe in him, that is, in the power of love and laughter to win by their subtle power, do John reverence by getting the root of the plant in which he has taken up his secret dwelling, and "dressing" it with perfume, and keeping it on their person, or in their houses in a secret place. It is there to help them overcome things they feel that they could not beat otherwise, and to bring them the laugh of the day. John will never forsake the weak and the helpless, nor fail to bring hope to the hopeless. That is what they believe, and so they do not worry. They go on and laugh and sing. Things are bound to come out right tomorrow. That is the secret of black song and laughter.

Call for Political and Social Change

MARCUS GARVEY
(1887–1940)

Marcus Garvey, Jamaican journalist, essayist, editor, poet, and orator, was a major black activist of the twentieth century. With a dramatic flair for controversy, he achieved a magnetic populism. He encouraged American blacks and others of African heritage to unify for the common good. He proposed that their shared plight derived from a communal experience rooted in an economics of deprivation and in a mutual ancestry. Although his coarseness provoked the scorn of W. E. B. Du Bois, who was probably the most brilliant thinker of the age, Garvey gained a broad following among the working poor. Like Frederick Douglass of the previous century, Garvey looked first to exploit the kind of industrial training that encouraged the mainstream to promote the image of Booker T. Washington from 1895 to 1915. With Alexander Crummell, who had been a shining beacon of religious scholarship until 1898, but without the cognition of Crummell in either deductive or inductive thought, Garvey proposed to direct African American resources toward the material development of West Africa. Shaped in part by the experience of social caste in Jamaica, Garvey was for most of his life a self-exile in the United States, Canada, France, Switzerland, and England. He often pursued unrealized business ventures around the globe.

Garvey originated an aesthetic, or code of racial beauty, that would in time win grudging praise from even his foes. To a degree, history has vindicated him as his own age refused to do. The most innovative writers of his time—Zora Neale Hurston, Jean Toomer, Sterling Brown, and Langston Hughes—stood with Garvey in spirit against the boring grain of the age. All helped to create both a vernacular language and a warmly communal perception of black existence.

Marcus Moziah Garvey, Jr., was born into a working family in St. Ann's Bay, Jamaica, on August 17, 1887. With a somewhat scholarly father and a gentle mother, he developed an appreciation for knowledge of various kinds. Unable to study law as he wanted, he was compelled by financial exigency to quit studies at age fourteen and seek employment. He accepted an appointment as an apprentice to a printer in St. Ann's and later in Kingston, the Jamaican capital. In 1907, at the age of twenty, he directed an ill-fated strike by twenty union printers. Later blacklisted in the trade, he established his first magazine, *Garvey's Watchman,* in 1910. For the next two years, he explored Central America at the same time that he was establishing other militant periodicals. Then he met Duse Mohammed Ali, a black Egyptian, who educated him in England about the flaws of colonial rule. In 1912, Garvey read *Up from Slavery* (1901), the autobiography of Booker T. Washington. Influenced by the philosophy of self-help, he assumed a mission:

> My doom—if I may so call it—of being a race leader dawned upon me. . . . I asked: Where is the black man's Government? Where is his King and his kingdom? Where

is his President, his country, and his ambassador, his army, his navy, his men of big affairs? I could not find them, and then I declared, "I will help to make them."

His entire career reads as an unfinished odyssey. He returned home to Jamaica for a short time to establish an industrial school based on Washington's design. When his plans did not work out, he ventured to Harlem in New York City on March 23, 1916. With the support of a few West Indians in 1917, his movement of race solidarity advanced quickly to thousands of people. By the time he established the United Negro Improvement Association (UNIA) in 1918–1919, he had initiated thirty branches of the association that would number from two to four million members in the United States alone. Additional participants inhabited regions such as South and Central America, the West Indies, and Africa. According to Richard Barksdale and Keneth Kinnamon in *Black Writers of America* (1972), "Perhaps these figures are somewhat inflated, but the immense success of the first international convention of the organization in August 1920 made it clear to the most skeptical that Garvey's massive support was unprecedented in Black history."

Garvey's editorials promoted an independent state of Africa and presumed liberation of the continent as a requisite for the equality of race in the world. Garvey organized the Black Star Line, a fleet of transport ships funded by African Americans, to contribute Western technology to the development of African independence. He sought the financial assistance of blacks worldwide to strengthen his negotiations with the Liberian government for the award of land to immigrants. At the UNIA meeting in 1920, approximately 250,000 delegates awarded him the ceremonial presidency of Africa. Some serious problems of finance and maintenance occurred with the Star Line, and a few campaigns to solicit money through the mail led to his controversial arrest for fraud in 1922. Garvey was jailed on February 8, 1925, at the height of the Harlem Renaissance, and he served nearly three years of a five-year sentence before receiving a pardon by President Calvin Coolidge.

Released from prison in 1927, Garvey was immediately deported to Jamaica. There he began a school by mail for the study of African philosophy. Even though Pan-Africanism was weakening, he continued to promote his ideals. Despite extensive travels throughout the Caribbean, North America, and Europe, he was generally unable to recapture the imagination of the predominantly white countries of Canada, France, Sweden, and England with his racial magic. Upon his return to Jamaica in 1929, his new ventures in publishing, such as *Black Man* and *The New Jamaica,* affected the entrenched bourgeoisie very little. He moved to London in 1935 and died there as an indigent in 1940.

Despite charges that Garvey was a megalomaniac, his thought proves consistent. His philosophy marked a radical departure from the traditionally acceptable Civil Rights posture of political and financial equality within an established order. Hence, the National Association for the Advancement of Colored People (NAACP) challenged both his financial thought and his premise that a strong Africa would ensure the rights of African heritage throughout the world. James P. Draper writes, "He [Garvey] further charged that the African-American intelligentsia was elitist and dominated by mulattos who sought preeminence for those with light complexions rather than dark." Garvey frequently maligned Du Bois's racially mixed heritage and quipped that NAACP stood for "National Association for the Advancement of Certain People." Besides Du Bois, Garvey positioned himself against R. R. Morton, whom some regarded as the successor to Booker T. Washington, as well as against African American ministers, political leaders in New York, and those whom he demeaned for being Jamaican hybrids. Like Washington, Garvey blamed the failures of the race on African American intellectuals, but only Garvey went so far as to portray them as traitors and enemies.

Often ignored is the fact that Garvey and Du Bois had so much in common. Both men proposed a kind of religious celebration of Africans in the Diaspora, Garvey more explicitly than Du Bois. Both argued for an inquiry into something other than a white God, but Garvey was more disposed toward a black God and Du Bois toward a God behind the scenes of historical logic. Both were suspicious about the elitist detachment of the New Negro literature of the twenties, though Du Bois operated inside the highbrow circle of the middle class and Garvey outside the circle. Du Bois distrusted Alain Locke and the argument of art for art's sake nearly as much as Garvey did, for even within the carefully rehearsed circle of elitism, all of the highbrows were not the same. Both Du Bois and Garvey believed in African standards for artistic beauty—Du Bois as the Massachusetts outsider in his own land and Garvey as the Jamaican outsider in the American homeland of Du Bois. Often each writer presumed to speak for the masses. Garvey criticized bourgeois blacks; Du Bois found fault with nearly everyone without preference of either race or favor. Like most decent humans, Du Bois could never have accepted Garvey's somewhat incredulous pact with the Ku Klux Klan, Anglo-Saxon clubs, and White American Societies. But both men detested hypocrisy. Each, indeed, might have thought himself the nemesis, the classic opponent, of the other. Du Bois had helped found and lead the NAACP as well as Atlanta and Fisk Universities. He had been crucial in the founding of *The Crises* and *Phylon* as major publications to stand the test of time. Whereas Du Bois was a long-distance runner, Garvey was a charismatic sprinter with style. Du Bois helped build the political institutions Garvey only dreamed about, but Garvey helped obtain the kind of mass support that Du Bois would leave behind.

Garvey's program evinced a simple appeal. Rather than an avowed hatred of whites, it suggested that all races were created equally. Hence, an overall goal was the freedom of all people as well as unity among blacks as a whole. The design emphasized the promotion of racial pride and love. It sought to reverse the fall in the status of blacks worldwide and to strengthen the imperialistic impetus of African nations. Somewhat curiously, the scheme legitimized the need to assist the "backward tribes" of Africa so as to promote Christianity among the natives. Garvey overlooked the great heights of civilization achieved in the ancient states of Mali and Ghana from the fourth to the thirteenth centuries, during which time Europe was still in the Dark Ages. Instead, he based most of his claims for African glory on the achievements of Egypt and Ethiopia in the East. In the "Declaration of Rights of the Negro Peoples of the World," a presentation to UNIA in New York in 1920, he called for an Africa for blacks, an Asia for Asians, and a Europe for Europeans. Possibly he feared that collaboration among the races would end with the domination of one by another.

Garvey was one of the earliest precursors of what would be called a black aesthetic two generations later. In fact, he led the rediscovery of the black aesthetic that had been lost during the African slave trade. He proposed that the culturally raw art of African peoples had to contribute to the knowledge of the race and the perception of it. Although he provided even less than did Du Bois or Locke a theory for the evaluation of literary technique, he was at least ideologically consistent. Tony Martin writes,

> It was the Garvey aesthetic that provided the essential difference between Garvey's potential infrastructure and the superstructure of the mainstream writers. The wealthy dilettantes who patronized the Renaissance loved exotic Harlem and genial Claude McKay and witty Zora Neale Hurston and jazz and speakeasies and Negro melodies and brown-skinned chorus lines; but they could not love Garvey. Garvey was not out to entertain anybody.

Du Bois called Garvey an "astonishingly popular leader" who had mastered propaganda, and he hailed UNIA as "one of the most interesting spiritual movements of the modern world." Sociologist E. Franklin Frazier praised Garvey in 1926 for unparalleled leadership of the masses. Even the somewhat peculiar Alain Locke acknowledged the importance of Garvey as a "transient, if spectacular phenomenon." To A. Philip Randolph, a social organizer, Garvey represented the arrival of black leadership. Indeed, only James Weldon Johnson insisted that Garvey had "squandered" opportunities for real authority.

Writers of the age portrayed Garvey as a buffoon, lunatic, and criminal. In one instance, Zora Neale Hurston forwarded a story that disparaged him to Carl Van Vechten, the white author of *Nigger Heaven* (1926). In another instance, Wallace Thurman and Williard Jourdan Rapp took turns belittling Garvey. Du Bois derided the extremely black West Indian with broad features, and James Weldon Johnson perceived Garvey as the living caricature of what Eugene O'Neill had dramatized in *The Emperor Jones* (1920). This group blamed Garvey for validating white supremacists and for blaming blacks themselves for being victims. They saw through Garvey's invective. Certainly, they did not see themselves as naive perpetuators of "further disturbances in riots, lynching, and mob rule." Unfortunately, Garvey had transferred the traditional stereotypes of the black masses—"lazy, dull, and uncreative"—to the black middle class: "His [the Negro Leader's] purpose is to deceive the less fortunate of his race, and by his wiles ride easily into position and wealth at their expense, and therefore agitate for and seek social equality with the creative and industrial whites." A. Philip Randolph, Du Bois, and Robert S. Abbott, editor of the *Chicago Defender*, took exception to the accusation. Indeed, Garvey's somewhat flippant agreement with President Warren G. Harding about a limited place for blacks displeased many African Americans who were looking for an equal opportunity in jobs. Nor could the intellectuals possibly have agreed with Garvey that American slavery had derived from a flaw in the African race or that they, as American citizens, should volunteer to abdicate their birthright. Such leaders were more likely to challenge the race that had enslaved their ancestors than to chastise the ancestors themselves across at least fifteen generations. Garvey, the Jamaican, simply never understood the greatness of the African American people.

Garvey underestimated the American vestiges of the African spirit and the power of civil disobedience. Despite his observations of racism as a social act, he could not marshal his resources against the psychological intent of someone else's racism. Hence, he fought effects rather than causes, and he fought mostly blacks. His distrust for even the most sincere black intellectuals proved divisive, and his prescription for what the masses should do implied totalitarianism. Although he eagerly promoted the philosophy of self-help, he rarely asked why racist whites encouraged his movement. Although he sought the prize of freedom, he undervalued the need for dignity. But Garvey did restore respect for many African standards of artistic beauty. Proclaimed a Jamaican hero in 1964, he became a subject for reggae singers during the 1980s and since then for the Calypso singers of Trinidad. Richard Hart explains his impact:

> Others appealed to the intellect with sane and logical reasoning and won to the path of struggle a dedicated handful. Garvey spoke less logically, more emotionally; he spoke from less knowledge but more convincingly. Garvey used flamboyant methods that fired simple [sic] imaginations. And Garvey stirred millions from the apathetic into action who but for him might have slumbered on. . . . It is as well that Garvey passed from the scene at the time he did. What Garvey had to offer to his followers, once he had stirred them into awareness and self respect, would have been of negligible value. But he it was who has stirred the masses up and they will never be the same again.

Indeed, most of the cultural innovations in the Harlem Renaissance seem to make sense only when the significance of Garvey is recovered.

❖❖❖

Broad indebtedness goes throughout the anthology to Richard K. Barksdale and Keneth Kinnamon, *Black Writers of America: A Comprehensive Anthology* (1972). Other studies of historical significance are Marcus H. Boulware, *The Marcus Garvey Period, 1916–1927: The Orator of Negro Leaders, 1900–1968* (1969); Robert H. Brisbane, "His Excellency: The Provincial President of Africa," *Phylon* 10, No. 3 (1949); Robert A. Hill, " 'The Foremost Radical Among His Race,' Marcus Garvey and the Black Scare, 1918–1921," *Prologue* 16, No. 4 (Winter 1984); John Henrik Clarke, ed., *Marcus Garvey and the Vision of Africa* (1973); R. L. Okonkwo, "The Garvey Movement in British West Africa," *Journal of African History* 21, No. 1 (1980); and Shirley N. Weber, "Black Nationalism and Garveyism," in *Pan-Africanism or Communism?* (1971). Probably the most consulted biographies are David E. Cronan, *Black Moses: The Story of Marcus Garvey and the Universal Negro Improvement Association* (1955); Lawrence Levine, "Marcus Garvey and the Politics of Revitalization," in *Black Leaders of the Twentieth Century,* ed. John Hope Franklin and August Meir (1982); Levine, "Marcus Garvey's Moment," *The New Republic* 191, No. 18 (October 1984); and Tony Martin, *Race First: The Ideological and Organizational Struggles of Marcus Garvey and the Universal Negro Improvement Association* (1976). Among the most helpful sources about Garvey and economics are W.E.B. Du Bois, "Marcus Garvey," *The Crisis* 21, Nos. 2, 3 (December 1920; January 1921); Du Bois, "The Black Star Line," *The Crisis* 24, No. 5 (September 1922); Tony Martin, "The Economic Programs of Marcus Garvey," *The Black Collegian* 9, No. 1 (September-October 1978); and William A. Edwards, "Racial Purity in Black and White: The Case of Marcus Garvey and Earnest Cox," *Journal of Ethnic Studies* 15, No. 1 (Spring 1987). Most useful for the study of ideology and nationalism are Robert M. Kahn, "The Political Ideology of Marcus

Garvey," *Midwest Quarterly* 24, No. 2 (Winter 1983); and Jabe Ayodele Langley, "Garveyism and African Nationalism," *Race* 11, No. 2 (October 1969). Foremost analysts of the debates within intellectual tradition have been Elliott M. Rudwick, "Du Bois Versus Garvey: Race Propagandists at War," *Journal of Negro Education* 28, No. 4 (Fall 1959); and Charles Willis Simmons, "The Negro Intellectual's Criticism of Garveyism," *Negro History Bulletin* 25, No. 1 (October 1961).

Speech on Disarmament Conference Delivered at Liberty Hall, New York, November 6, 1921

Just at this time the world is again preparing for a reorganization. Since the war of 1914 the world became disorganized. Many conferences have been held, in which statesmen of all the reputable governments have taken part, for the purpose of settling a world policy, by which humanity and the world could return to normal. Several of the conferences were held in France, others in Switzerland and England. On the 11th of this month will assemble an Washington what is to be known as an Armament Conference. At this conference statesmen from Great Britain and her self-governing dominions, statesmen from France, Japan, China, Norway, Holland and several other countries will there assemble and partake in the discussion for regulating the armaments of the world.

Every race will be represented at that conference except the Negro race. It is a sad confession to make, nevertheless it is true. The world wants to return to normal and the only people preventing it from returning to normal, apparently, are the white and yellow peoples, and they only are taken into account. I suppose after they have met and discussed the issues, the world will return to normal, but I believe someone has a second thought coming. I have no faith in the disarmament plan of the nations. I am a pessimist as far as disarmament goes. I do not believe that man will disarm until there is universal justice. Any attempt at disarming when half of the world oppresses the other half is but a farce, because the oppressed half will make somebody get armed sooner or later, and I hope Negroes will pay no attention to what is said and what is done at the conference. It does not concern you one bit. Disarmament may sound good for heaven and paradise, but not for this world that we live in, where we have so many robbers and plunderers. You keep a pistol or a gun in your home because the robber is at large, and you are afraid while you sleep he will creep through the window or get through the door and make an attempt to rob your property; and because you know he is at large, and may pay you a visit, you sleep with a gun under your pillow. When all the burglars and all the robbers are put in jail, and we know they are in jail, then we will throw away our pistols and our guns. Now everybody knows that the robber—the thief—is at large; he is not only robbing domestic homes, he is robbing continents; he is robbing countries, and how do you expect, in the name of reason, for races and peoples to disarm when the thief is at large trying to get into your country, trying to get into your continent to take away your land—your birthright. The whole thing is a farce, and I trust no sensible Negro will pay any attention to it.

Negroes Must Arm Through Organization

I am not advising you to arm now with the things they have, I am asking you to arm through organization; arm through preparedness. You do not want to have guns and bombs just now; you have no immediate use for them, so they can throw away those things if they want in Washington on Armistice Day. I am saying to the Negro people of the world, get armed with organization; get armed by coming together 400,000,000 strong. That is your weapon. Their weapon in the past has been big guns and explosive shells; your weapon must be universal organization. You are a people most favorably situated today for getting what you want through organization. Why? Because universally Negroes have a common cause; universally Negroes suffer from one common disadvantage. You are not like the other people in that respect. The white people cannot organize as you are organizing. Why? Because their society is disrupted—is in chaos. Why do I say this? They are so disrupted—they are in such chaos that they have to fight against themselves—capital fighting labor, labor fighting capital. There is no common cause between capital and labor, and, therefore, they cannot get together, and will never get together until they realize the virtue of justice—the virtue of equity to all mankind. You have no fight among yourselves as between capital and labor, because all of us are laborers, therefore we need not be Socialists; we have no fight against party, because all of us are belonging to the "Suffering Party." So when it comes to organization we occupy a unique position.

England cannot organize with France, for England will be looking to rob France, and France looking to rob England, and they will be suspicious of each other. The white races will never get together. They have done so many injustices one to the other that between here and heaven they will never get together. Do you think Germany and England will ever get together? Do you think France and Germany will ever get together? They have no cause that is in common; but 400,000,000 Negroes have a cause that is in common, and that is why I pointed out to you that your strongest armament is organization, and not so much big guns and bombshells. Later on we may have to use some of those things, however, because it appears that some people cannot hear a human voice unless something is exploding nearby. Some people sleep too soundly, when it comes to a question of human rights, and you have to touch them up with something more than our ordinary human voice.

Believes Arms Conference Will Be Fiasco

This conference on disarmament, I have said, is all a joke, and every one of them is going there to see what can be gotten. Japan to see what she can get out of America; America to see what she can get out of France; England to see what she can get out of Japan; Italy to see what she can get out of England, and the greatest vagabond will come out with the big stick. Everybody knows that; all sensible statesmen know that. They do not want any conference on disarmament, because you must arm to a certain extent. Swords are in heaven to keep the angels in good order. So since human nature is what it is, the world cannot afford to disarm. But do you know what they are getting together for? Not so much disarmament; they are getting together to form a pact by which they can subdue and further oppress the weaker peoples, who are not as strong as themselves to demand a place in this conference now to be held.

I told you during the war in my speeches throughout the length and breadth of this country and through my writings in The Negro World week by week in 1916 it was planned in England that the Negro should pay the cost of the war. You will remember (some of you) my saying that several years ago it was the determination in Europe that Africa was to be exploited to pay the cost of the war and Negroes everywhere were to be used to supply the source of revenue by which the bankrupt nations would be able to declare themselves once more solvent. Since peace was declared—since the armistice was signed—those of you who have seen the conduct of statesmen in Europe, of governments and of subsidized commercial agents, will recall that great demands have been made and are being made to commercialize the raw, and mineral products of Africa, and by the spoils gained out of exploiting Africa they hope to reimburse themselves of the billions of dollars lost in the war of 1914 to 1918.

The Aim of European Statesmen

It does not take the vision of a seer; it does not take the vision of a prophet, to see what the future will be to us, as a race, through the ambitions of the present-day statesmen of Europe. They feel that they have a divine right because of the strength of arms; because of their highly developed power to go into any part of the world and occupy it, and hold it, if that part of the world is occupied by weaker peoples. The statesmen of today believe that might makes right, and until they get that feeling out of them, until they destroy that spirit, the world cannot disarm. They fail to take into consideration, they fail to take into account, that there are 400,000,000 black men in the world today and that these 400,000,000 people are not going to allow anybody to infringe upon their rights without asking the question why. They have been playing all kinds of dodges; they have been practicing all kinds of schemes and adopting all kinds of tactics, since the armistice was signed, to keep the Negro in his old-time place, but they have failed; they cannot successfully do it. When they created the emergency, they called the Negro to battle; they placed in the Negro's hands the gun and the sword; they told him to go out and kill—kill so that the side for which you are fighting might be victorious. The Negro killed. The Negro fought his way to victory and returned the standard with honor. After the battle was won, after the victory was declared, the Negro became a puzzle. He became a puzzle to Great Britain; he became a puzzle to France; he became a puzzle to America. The American Negro was no longer wanted in active service by the American Government. What did they do? They disarmed him; they took away his pistol and his gun before he landed, so that he could not do any harm with them, and they sent him back South without any armament. What did the Frenchman do? The Frenchman is puzzled up to now; they cannot send them back yet.

All this noise they have been making about Negro soldiers being on the Rhineland, it is not because the French want the Negro to be on the Rhineland so much, but they do not know where to send him.

And do you know what they are keeping those Negroes there for? Those Negroes may never be returned to Senegal; they may never be returned to Africa. Those Negroes probably will be kept in France until they die. With the knowledge they have gained in the four years of war, they do not want those Senegalese to go back to Africa with that knowledge. That is why they are now on the Rhineland, and these French statesmen come and tell us it is because they love Negroes so much why they are kept in France. It is because they fear the Negroes so much why they have kept those black Senegalese on the Rhineland and in France.

A Conference of the "Bigger Brotherhood"

They do not know what to do. They are puzzled, and are holding conferences in France, in Switzerland, in England and now in America, and have not decided on anything. Why won't they be honest? Why won't they have a real conference? Why won't they say, "We are going to solve this great human problem; we are going to have peace forever; let us meet, whether it be in Washington, London, or Paris; come on Asia, meet us, too; come on, Africa, let us all sit around the table and let us not call this conference a disarmament conference or any such conference; let us call it a "conference of the bigger brotherhood." That is the conference the world is waiting for, and until that conference is called, it is all a farce talking about disarmament and the rest of it. Until these statesmen get ready to give Asia what is belonging to Asia, to give to Europe what is belonging to Europe, and then, above all, to give to Africa what is belonging to Africa, their conferences will be in vain.

If Great Britain will take my advice she would call a conference tomorrow morning, and say to all Englishmen leave India, leave Africa and go back to England because we want peace. If France takes my advice she will call out her white colonists from her African dominions, because so long as this injustice is perpetrated against weaker peoples there is going to be wars and rumors of wars. It is human nature and the world knows it. If you take my property, and I know it, is a different proposition, to taking my property and my not knowing it. In the past they took our property and we did not know about it, therefore we did not say anything; but they do not seem to count on the change that has come about. We know all about it now. If a man breaks into my house and steals some of my things and I do not know him, I will meet him on the street and shake hands and say, "Brother, how are you?" If he salutes me and says "Hello, how are you?" I will return it. But when I come home and find out that my property is robbed, and that he is the man who robbed my property, I am going to change my attitude. Just give me what is belonging to me. That is the situation between weaker peoples and stronger ones. They have fooled us; they have robbed us, when we did not know any better; but it is a different proposition now.

The new Negro is going to strike back or is going to die; and if David Lloyd George, Briand and the different statesmen believe they can assemble in Washington, in London, in Paris, or anywhere and dispose of black people's property without first consulting them they make a big mistake, because we have reared many Fochs between 1914 and 1918 on the battlefields of France and Flanders. It will be a question later on of Foch meeting Foch.

Now the world of oppressed peoples have got the spirit of liberty and from far-off India we hear the cry of a free and independent India; from far-off Egypt we hear the cry of a free and independent Egypt. The Negro loves peace; the Negro likes to disarm, but the Negro says to the world, "Let us have justice; let us have equity; let us have freedom; let us have democracy indeed"; and I from Liberty Hall, on behalf of 400,000,000 Negroes, send a plea to the statesmen at Washington in their assembly on the question of disarmament, give the Negro the consideration due him; give the Hindoo the consideration due him; give the Egyptian the consideration due him; give the weaker peoples of the world the consideration due them, and let us disarm. But until then, I repeat, there will be wars and rumors of wars.

Text of Telegram Sent to the Disarmament Conference

NOVEMBER 11, 1921.

President and Members of the International
Conference on Disarmament,
Care of Secretary of Conference,
Pan-American Building,
Washington, D.C.

HONORABLE GENTLEMEN:

I salute you in the name of Democracy, and for the cause of Justice on behalf of the four hundred million Negroes of the world. Your Honorable Conference now sitting in Washington has a purpose that has been announced and advertised to the world for several months. You were called together by the President of the Democratic Republic of the United States of America to discuss the problem of armaments, the settlement of which you believe will ensure the perpetual peace of the world. As the elected spokesman of the Negro peoples of the world who desire freedom, politically, industrially, educationally, socially and religiously, as well as a full enjoyment of world democracy and a national independence all our own on the continent of Africa, it is for me to inform you of a little slight that has been shown to four hundred million Negroes who form a part of this world's population. At the Versailles Peace Conference, the statesmen who gathered there made the awful mistake of legislating for the disposition of other people's lands (especially in Africa) without taking them into consideration, believing that a world peace could have been established after such a conference. The mistake is now apparent. There can be no peace among us mortals so long as the strong of humanity oppresses the weak, for in due process of time and through evolution the weak will one day turn, even like the worm, and then humanity's hope of peace will be shattered. All men have brains; some use their abilities for inventing destructive elements of warfare, such as guns, gun-powder, gas, and other destructive chemicals. The Negro for hundreds of years has attempted nothing destructive to the peace and good-will of humanity; in fact, he has not even made an attempt to make the world know that he is alive; nevertheless, like the worm, the Negro will one day turn. I humbly ask you therefore that your Honorable Conference act, not like the one at Versailles, but that you realize and appreciate the fact that the Negro is a man, and that there can be no settlement of world affairs without proper consideration being given to him with his rights. President Harding of America has but recently sounded the real cry of Democracy. He says to his own country, and I think it should be an advice to the world, "Give the Negro equality in education, in politics, in industry, because he is entitled to human rights." I humbly beg to recommend to your Honorable Conference those quoted words of President Harding. Negroes have blood, they have souls, and for the cause of Liberty they feel that the conduct of men like Alexander, Hannibal, Caesar, Napoleon, Wellington, Lafayette, Garabaldi, Washington, is imitable, and that peace not founded on real human justice will only be a mockery of the divine invocation, "Peace, perfect peace." I trust your Honorable Conference will not fail to take into consideration, therefore, that there are four hundred million Negroes in the world who demand Africa as their rightful heritage, even as the European claims Europe, and the Asiatic Asia. I pray that your Conference will not only be one of disarmament, but that it will be a congregation of the "Bigger Brotherhood," through which Europe will see the rights of Asia, Asia and Europe see the rights of Africa, and Africa and Asia see the rights of Europe and accordingly give every race and nation their due, and let there be peace indeed. On behalf of the four hundred million Negroes of the world not represented at your Honorable Conference,

I have the honor to be

Your obedient servant,
MARCUS GARVEY,
President General of the Universal Negro Improvement Association and First Provisional President of Africa, New York City.

REPLY

NOVEMBER 17, 1921.

Conference of the Limitation of Armament,
Secretariat General.

Sir: I am directed by the Secretary General, the Chairman of the Conference, to acknowledge the receipt of your communication, which has been read with attention.

I am charged to express to you his appreciation of the interest and support which you have been so good to evince.

I am, sir,

Yours very truly,
T. G. W. PAUL,
For the Secretary General.

Mr. Marcus Garvey, President-General Universal Negro Improvement Association, 56 West 135th Street, New York.

WALTER WHITE

(1893–1955)

Walter White, essayist, autobiographer, novelist, and nonfiction writer, was one of the most significant figures in the New Negro Movement of the twenties, and his influence extended well into mid-century. Indirectly, he proposed a kind of compromise that aligned him spiritually with the folk masses. As a native Georgian who personally faced southern violence, White maintained an incurable optimism to overcome racism so that even his white reviewers found his spirit to be perhaps miraculous. Although White was often genteel in his written style, his verbal probing into ritualistic consciousness was distinctly modern. He traced contradictions in Christianity to the roots of the southern psyche.

In manner, Walter White was almost Victorian, but in concept he was quite innovative. As an effective lobbyist in Washington, he advised Presidents Franklin D. Roosevelt and Harry Truman. He helped to facilitate the Gavan bill against lynching and to defeat the nomination of John J. Parker, a segregationist, to the Supreme Court. Although White designed his social research to help lead the nation from racial segregation into human equality, he revealed a cyclical pattern of African American history. From 1924 through 1928, he suggested somewhat subconsciously that the popular concern for racial passing was only a way to forget lynching in the United States. His work penetrates into the unspoken conscience of the nation. In the literary Reformation of the 1930s, he called rather more for social activism than for a polite aesthetic. Near the end of the forties, he struck a compromise between art and survival.

White recognized that the New Negro Movement of the twenties tended to invalidate the importance of historical memory. He understood that a vicious history would have to be recovered as communal as well as personal text—as a shared tradition as much as an individual talent—so that black literary art might advance as an authentic story of a people. Perhaps he never recognized the lasting value of personal lyric any more than did his fellow politicians W.E.B. Du Bois and James Weldon Johnson, who thought themselves obliged to create art as well as to lead people. But both Du Bois and Johnson had achieved somewhat naturally lyrical harmonies in *The Souls of Black Folk* (1903) and *God's Trombones* (1927), respectively.

Walter Francis White, one of seven children, was born as a blue-eyed blond of African ancestry to Madeline and George White on July 1, 1893. His mother had been a schoolteacher, and his father was a mailman. Walter grew up in Atlanta and attended public schools there. In the Atlanta race riots of 1906, the thirteen-year-old boy stood with rifle in hand beside his father. After graduating from high school, he attended Atlanta University, where he earned a bachelor's degree in 1916. During his work at the Atlanta Life Insurance Company, he became a resourceful leader of the NAACP and won the attention of James Weldon Johnson, the organization's national field secretary. In 1918, White moved to New York City to become Johnson's assistant at the NAACP.

Able to pass for white, White infiltrated many supremacist groups to enlighten the nation about racial lynching. Once authorized as a deputy sheriff in Arkansas and later in Oklahoma, he was openly encouraged to murder blacks when desirable. Through the teens and twenties, he derived from his own social reports rich material for documentary essays and fiction. With James Weldon Johnson, Charles S. Johnson, Alain Locke, Jessie Fauset, and others, he championed the development of younger writers such as Countee Cullen, Claude McKay, Langston Hughes, Rudolph Fisher, and Zora Neale Hurston. As a strong supporter of the New Negro, as popularized by Alain Locke in 1925, White joined with Locke to establish a Negro Foreign Fellowship Fund for young New Negroes who wished to experience the artistic atmosphere of Europe. Through political connections, White also helped present aspiring writers of color to leading editors and publishers.

With Johnson, White believed that creative writing might serve to uplift the race. Following a meeting with H. L. Mencken, an eminent intellectual of the white Left, White was invited to assess the authenticity of *Birthright* (1922), a racial novel by T. S. Stribling. In a painfully long reply, White wrote that Stribling had written outside the richness of African American experience. Mencken replied, "Why don't you do the right kind of novel? You could do it, and it would create a sensation." White, who had rarely considered creative writing, discussed the invitation with colleagues. Eventually, he accepted the request by Mary White Ovington, a white friend in the NAACP, to draft the novel in her cottage at Great Barrington, Massachusetts. White had recently married the former Gladys Powell, and on February 15, 1922, together they packed for a two-week stay in New England, during which he completed *The Fire in the Flint* (1924). The book's plot is only a stock device for relaying one of the "most successful exposés of lynching in American fiction," according to Barksdale and Kinnamon. The main character is Kenneth Harper, a graduate of Atlanta University and a northern medical school, who returns from military service in France to his hometown of Central City, Georgia. Somewhat ambitious to become the best surgeon in the southern part of the state, he hopes eventually to open a clinic. Despite the pessimistic outlook of a younger brother, who doubts the sincerity of whites, Kenneth thinks that he will succeed in being left alone. Unfortunately, Kenneth is lynched for his naiveté.

In a second novel, *Flight* (1926), White depicts Annettee Angela Daquin (Mime), who complicates her life considerably by deciding to pass for white. Later, in *Rising Wind: A Report on the Negro Soldier in the European Theater of War* (1945), he challenges the American conscience. In *A Man Called White* (1948), he reveals what had been biographical sources for *Flight:* "Mimi dated thereafter her *consciousness* [editor's italics] of being coloured from September, nineteen hundred and six. For her the old order had passed, she was now definitely of a race set apart." In *How Far the Promised Land?* (1955), he had almost prophesied what would become the dominant metaphor for Martin Luther King, Jr., who had then only begun to lead the bus boycott in Montgomery, Alabama. Francis Hackett views White as "possessed by one of those mastering passions to which no wise American can refuse heed and no good citizen refuse sympathy." Ralph J. Bunche, a representative to the United Nations, adds, "We do not go backward, we do not stand still, he said; American democracy moves forward. There is an ever-stronger current of democracy which eventually will carry all Americans into the 'Promised Land.'"

White became part of the great and wonderful naiveté of the 1950s: "By the very excellence of each race's and each individual's gifts will come lessening of hatred and distrust and cruelty of race to race. Hart Burleigh, Roland Hayes, Paul Roberson, Countee Cullen, Dr. Du Bois and other artists in their various fields are, I feel tearing down barriers of all sorts." White fantasized in part that his final decade had summed up the three others that had immediately preceded it.

Even so, White showed no particular respect for blues and jazz as innovative art forms, made no mention of folk dialect as an authentic medium of expression, and conveyed no appreciation for modernism. Despite all charges of propaganda on his part, he insisted on the personal freedom to write portraits of societal conflict. In theory, he disagreed with Alain Locke, who believed that a lyrical chant—a beautiful moment in high art—would whitewash away most human tensions. But history had made Walter White a cautious optimist.

White neither thought nor wrote in theoretic terms, but his life implies them. As the Jazz Age of the twenties gave way to the postwar world of the forties, he articulated a test for the early Gwendolyn Brooks, Alice Childress, James Baldwin, and Ralph Ellison, who were still emerging. In spirit he called for exceptional talents that might survive the American caldron of boring sameness, and he helped pave the way for new innovations in racial self-definition. Whatever his own preferences, he facilitated new twists in literary forms. He pointed to an African American aesthetic far beyond what he wrote.

❖❖❖

Exploration of the relative balance between White's literary technique and his social commitment needs more attention, as does his work as a spiritual and metaphoric source for later fiction. Especially, exploring his role of challenging the black bourgeoisie from within the South, as Langston Hughes did within the North, could be very fruitful. Of significant importance would be the restoration of White to his rightful place in southern black literature. After a decade of critical silence, a timely reassessment would help. Significant articles with a historic bent are Charles W. Scruggs, "Alain Locke and Walter White: Their Struggle for Control of the Harlem Renaissance," *Black American Literature Forum* 14, No. 3 (Fall, 1980); Charles F. Cooney, "Walter White and the Harlem Renaissance," *Journal of Negro History* 57, No. 3 (July 1972); Roy Wilkins, "Walter White," in *Rising Above Color,* ed. Philip Henry Lotz (1946); and Heywood Broun, "It Seems to Heywood Broun," *The Nation,* May 21, 1930. General essays of very detailed appraisal include the unsigned overview in *Black Literature Criticism,* ed. James P. Draper (1992), 1903–1916; and the fine article by Walter C. Daniel for *Dictionary of Literary Biography: Afro-American Writers from the Harlem Renaissance to 1940,* ed. Trudier Harris (1987), Vol. 51. The Daniel piece is perhaps the most insightful contribution from an African American perspective. Of the remaining scholarship, nearly all are reviews of specific texts: "A Novel by a Negro," *Survey,* November 1, 1924 for *Fire in the Flint;* "Black and White," *New York Times Book Review,* April 11, 1926, and Ernest Gruening, "Going White," *Saturday Review of Literature,* July 10, 1926, for *Flight;* and Clarence Darrow, "The Shame of America," *New York Herald Tribune Books,* April 21, 1929, Melville J. Herskovits, "Lynching: An American Pastime," *The Nation,* May, 15, 1929, and "Lynch Law," *The Times Literary Supplement,* October 17, 1929, for *Rope and Faggot.* A reprinted review by W.E.B. Du Bois appears in *Collected Published Works,* ed. Herbert Aptheker (1977). H. A. Overstreet was rare in reviewing *A Man Called White,* for *Saturday Review of Literature,* October 2, 1948. Gerald W. Johnson wrote about *How Far the Promised Land?* in *New York Times Book Review,* November 6, 1955. An early biography by White's second wife is Poppy Cannon, *A Gentle Knight: My Husband, Walter White* (1958). A biocritical description is Edward E. Waldron, *Walter White and the Harlem Renaissance* (1978).

I Investigate Lynchings

I

Nothing contributes so much to the continued life of an investigator of lynchings and his tranquil possession of all his limbs as the obtuseness of the lynchers themselves. Like most boastful people who practice direct action when it involve[s] no personal risk, they just can't help talk about their deeds to any person who manifests even the slightest interest in them.

Most lynchings take place in small towns and rural regions where the natives know practically nothing of what is going on outside their own immediate neighborhoods. Newspapers, books, magazines, theatres, visitors and other vehicles for the transmission of information and ideas are usually as strange among them as dry-point etchings. But those who live in so sterile an atmosphere usually esteem their own perspicacity in about the same degree as they are isolated from the world of ideas. They gabble on *ad infinitum,* apparently unable to keep from talking.

In any American village, North or South, East or West, there is no problem which cannot be solved in half an hour by the morons who lounge about the village store. World peace, or the lack of it, the tariff, sex, religion, the settlement of the war debts, short skirts, Prohibition, the carryings-on of the younger generation, the superior moral rectitude of country people over city dwellers (with a wistful eye on urban sins)—all these controversial subjects are disposed of quickly and finally by the bucolic wise men. When to their isolation is added an emotional fixation, such as the rural South has on the Negro, one can sense the atmosphere from which spring the Heflins, the Ku Kluxers, the two-gun Bible-beaters, the lynchers and the anti-evolutionists. And one can see why no great amount of cleverness or courage is needed to acquire information in such a forlorn place about the latest lynching.

Professor Earle Fiske Young of the University of Southern California recently analyzed the lynching returns from fourteen Southern states for thirty years. He found that in counties of less than 10,000 people there was a lynching rate of 3.2 per 100,000 of population; that in those of from 10,000 to 20,000 the rate dropped to 2.4; that in those of from 20,000 to 30,000, it was 2.1 per cent; that in those of from 30,000 to 40,000, it was 1.7, and that thereafter it kept on going down until in counties with from 300,000 to 800,000 population it was only 0.05.

Of the forty-one lynchings and eight race riots I have investigated for the National Association for the Advancement of Colored People during the past ten years, all of the lynchings and seven of the riots occurred in rural or semi-rural communities. The towns ranged in population from around one hundred to ten thousand or so. The lynchings were not difficult to inquire into because of the fact already noted that those who perpetrated them were in nearly every instance simple-minded and easily fooled individuals. On but three occasions were suspicions aroused by my too definite questions or by informers who had seen me in other places. These three times I found it rather desirable to disappear slightly in advance of reception committees imbued with the desire to make an addition to the lynching record. One other time the possession of a light skin and blue eyes (though I consider myself a colored man) almost cost me my life when (it was during the Chicago race riots in 1919) a Negro shot at me, thinking me to be a white man.

II

In 1918 a Negro woman, about to give birth to a child, was lynched with almost unmentionable brutality along with ten men in Georgia. I reached the scene shortly after the butchery and while excitement yet ran high. It was a prosperous community. Forests of pine trees gave rich returns in turpentine, tar and pitch. The small towns where the farmers and turpentine hands traded were fat and rich. The main streets of the largest of these towns were well paved and lighted. The stores were well stocked. The white inhabitants belonged to the class of Georgia crackers—lanky, slow of movement and of speech, long-necked, with small eyes set close together, and skin tanned by the hot sun to a reddish-yellow hue.

As I was born in Georgia and spent twenty years of my life there, my accent is sufficiently Southern to enable me to talk with Southerners and not arouse their suspicion that I am an outsider. (In the rural South hatred of Yankees is not much less than hatred of Negroes.) On the morning of my arrival in the town I casually dropped into the store of one of the general merchants who, I had been informed, had been one of the leaders of the mob. After making a small purchase I engaged the merchant in conversation. There was, at the time, no other customer in the store. We spoke of the weather, the possibility of good crops in the fall, the political situation, the latest news from the war in Europe. As his manner became more and more friendly I ventured to mention guardedly the recent lynchings.

Instantly he became cautious—until I hinted that I had great admiration for the manly spirit the men of the town had exhibited. I mentioned the newspaper accounts I had read and confessed that I had never been so fortunate as to see a lynching. My words or tone seemed to disarm his suspicions. He offered me a box on which to sit, drew up another one for himself, and gave me a bottle of Coca-Cola.

"You'll pardon me, Mister," he began, "for seeming suspicious but we have to be careful. In ordinary times we wouldn't have anything to worry about, but with the war there's been some talk of the Federal government looking into lynchings. It seems there's some sort of law during wartime making it treason to lower the man power of the country."

"In that case I don't blame you for being careful," I assured him. "But couldn't the Federal government do something if it wanted to when a lynching takes place, even if no war is going on at the moment?"

"Naw," he said, confidently, proud of the opportunity of displaying his store of information to one who he assumed knew nothing whatever about the subject. "There's no such law, in spite of all the agitation by a lot of fools who don't know the niggers as we do. States' rights won't permit Congress to meddle in lynching in peace time."

"But what about your State government—your Governor, your sheriff, your police officers?"

"Humph! Them? We elected them to office, didn't we? And the niggers, we've got them disfranchised, ain't we? Sheriffs and police and Governors and prosecuting attorneys have got too much sense to mix in lynching-bees. If they do they know they might as well give up all idea of running for office any more—if something worse don't happen to them—" This last with a tightening of the lips and a hard look in the eyes.

I sought to lead the conversation into less dangerous channels. "Who was the white man who was killed—whose killing caused the lynchings?" I asked.

"Oh, he was a hard one, all right. Never paid his debts to white men or niggers and wasn't liked much around here. He was a mean 'un all right, all right."

"Why, then, did you lynch the niggers for killing such a man?"

"It's a matter of safety—we gotta show niggers that they mustn't touch a white man, no matter how low-down and ornery he is."

Little by little he revealed the whole story. When he told of the manner in which the pregnant woman had been killed he chuckled and slapped his thigh and declared it to be "the best show, Mister, I ever did see. You ought to have heard the wench howl when we strung her up."

Covering the nausea the story caused me as best I could, I slowly gained the whole story, with the names of the other participants. Among them were prosperous farmers, business men, bankers, newspaper reporters and editors, and several law-enforcement officers.

My several days of discreet inquiry began to arouse suspicions in the town. On the third day of my stay I went once more into the store of the man with whom I had first talked. He asked me to wait until he had finished serving the sole customer. When she had gone he came from behind the counter and with secretive manner and lowered voice he asked, "You're a government man, ain't you?" (An agent of the Federal Department of Justice was what he meant.)

"Who said so?" I countered.

"Never mind who told me; I know one when I see him," he replied, with a shrewd harshness in his face and voice.

Ignorant of what might have taken place since last I had talked with him, I thought it wise to learn all I could and say nothing which might commit me. "Don't you tell anyone I am a government man; if I *am* one, you're the only one in town who knows it," I told him cryptically. I knew that within a hour everybody in town would share his "information."

An hour or so later I went at nightfall to the little but not uncomfortable hotel where I was staying. As I was about to enter a Negro approached me and, with an air of great mystery, told me that he had just heard a group of white men discussing me and declaring that if I remained in the town overnight "something would happen" to me.

The thought raced through my mind before I replied that it was hardly likely that, following so terrible a series of lynchings, a Negro would voluntarily approach a supposedly white man whom he did not know and deliver such a message. He had been sent, and no doubt the persons who sent him were white and for some reason did not dare tackle me themselves. Had they dared there would have been no warning in advance—simply an attack. Though I had no weapon with me, it occurred to me that there was no reason why two should not play at the game of bluffing. I looked straight into my informant's eyes and said: "You go back to the ones who sent you and tell them this: that I have a damned good automatic and I know how to use it. If anybody attempts to molest me tonight or any other time, somebody is going to get hurt."

That night I did not take off my clothes nor did I sleep. Ordinarily in such small Southern towns everyone is snoring by nine o'clock. That night, however, there was much passing and repassing of the hotel. I learned afterward that the merchant had, as I expected, told generally that I was an agent of the Department of Justice, and my empty threat had served to reinforce his assertion. The Negro had been sent to me in the hope that I might be frightened enough to leave before I had secured evidence against the members of the mob. I remained in the town two more days. My every movement was watched, but I was not molested. But when, later, it became known that not only was I not an agent of the Department of Justice but a Negro, the fury of the inhabitants of the region was unlimited—particularly when it was found that evidence I gathered had been placed in the hands of the Governor of Georgia. It happened that he was a man genuinely eager to stop lynching—but restrictive laws against which he had appealed in vain effectively prevented him from acting upon the evidence. And the Federal government declared itself unable to proceed against the lynchers.

III

In 1926 I went to a Southern State for a New York newspaper to inquire into the lynching of two colored boys and a colored woman. Shortly after reaching the town I learned that a certain lawyer knew something about the lynchers. He proved to be the only specimen I have ever encountered in much traveling in the South of the Southern gentleman so beloved by fiction writers of the older school. He had heard of the lynching before it occurred and, fruitlessly, had warned the judge and the prosecutor. He talked frankly about the affair and gave me the names of certain men who knew more about it than he did. Several of them lived in a small town nearby where the only industry was a large cotton mill. When I asked him if he would go with me to call on these people he peered out of the window at the descending sun and said, somewhat anxiously, I thought, "I will go with you if you will promise to get back to town before sundown."

I asked why there was need of such haste. "No one would harm a respectable and well-known person like yourself, would they?" I asked him.

"Those mill hands out there would harm anybody," he answered.

I promised him we would be back before sundown—a promise that was not hard to make, for if they would harm this man I could imagine what they would do to a stranger!

When we reached the little mill town we passed through it and ascending a steep hill, our car stopped in front of a house perched perilously on the side of the hill. In a yard stood a man with iron-gray hair and eyes which seemed strong enough to bore through concrete. The old lawyer introduced me and we were invited into the house. As it was a cold afternoon in late autumn the gray-haired man called a boy to build a fire.

I told him frankly I was seeking information about the lynching. He said nothing but left the room. Perhaps two minutes later, hearing a sound at the door through which he had gone, I looked up and there stood a figure clad in the full regalia of the Ku Klux Klan. I looked at the figure and the figure looked at me. The hood was then removed and, as I suspected, it was the owner of the house.

"I show you this," he told me, "so you will know that what I tell you is true."

This man, I learned, had been the organizer and kleagle of the local Klan. He had been quite honest in his activities as a Kluxer, for corrupt officials and widespread criminal activities had caused him and other local men to believe that the only cure rested in a secret extra-legal organization. But he had not long been engaged in promoting the plan before he had the experience of other believers in Klan methods. The very people whose misdeeds the organization was designed to correct gained control of it. This man then resigned and ever since had been living in fear of his life. He took me into an adjoining room after removing his Klan robe and there showed me a considerable collection of revolvers, shotguns, rifles and ammunition.

We then sat down and I listened to as hair-raising a tale of Nordic moral endeavor as it has ever been my lot to hear. Among the choice bits were stories such as this: The sheriff of an adjoining county the year before had been a candidate for reelection. A certain man of considerable wealth had contributed largely to his campaign fund, providing the margin by which he was reelected. Shortly afterwards a married woman with whom the sheriff's supporter had been intimate quarreled one night with her husband. When the cuckold charged his wife with infidelity, the gentle creature waited until he was asleep, got a large butcher knife, and then artistically carved him up. Bleeding more profusely than a pig in the stockyards, the man dragged himself to the home of a neighbor several hundred yards distant and there died on the doorstep. The facts were notorious, but the sheriff effectively blocked even interrogation of the widow!

I spent some days in the region and found that the three Negroes who had been lynched were about as guilty of the murder of which they were charged as I was. Convicted in a court thronged with armed Klansmen and sentenced to death, their case had been appealed to the State Supreme Court, which promptly reversed the conviction, remanded the appellants for new trials, and severely criticized the judge before whom they had been tried. At the new trial the evidence against one of the defendants so clearly showed his innocence that the judge granted a motion to dismiss, and the other two defendants were obviously as little guilty as he. But as soon as the motion to dismiss was granted the defendant was rearrested on a trivial charge and once again lodged in jail. That night the mob took the prisoners to the outskirts of the town, told them to run, and as they set out pumped bullets into their backs. The two boys died instantly. The woman was shot in several places, but was not immediately killed. One of the lynchers afterwards laughingly told me that "we had to waste fifty bullets on the wench before one of them stopped her howling."

Evidence in affidavit form indicated rather clearly that various law-enforcement officials, including the sheriff, his deputies, various jailers and policemen, three relatives of the then Governor of the State, a member of the State Legislature and sundry individuals prominent in business, political and social life of the vicinity were members of the mob.

The revelation of these findings after I had returned to New York did not add to my popularity in the lynching region. Public sentiment in the State itself, stirred up by several courageous newspapers, began to make it uncomfortable for the lynchers. When the sheriff found things getting a bit too unpleasant, he announced that he was going to ask the grand jury to indict me for "bribery and passing for white." It developed that the person I was supposed to have paid money to for execution of an affidavit was a man I had never seen in the flesh, the affidavit having been secured by the reporter of a New York newspaper.

An amusing tale is connected with the charge of passing. Many years ago a bill was introduced in the Legislature of that State defining legally as a Negro any person who had one drop or more of Negro blood. Acrimonious debate in the lower house did not prevent passage of the measure, and the same result seemed likely in the State Senate. One of the Senators, a man destined eventually to go to the United States Senate on a campaign of vilification of the Negro, rose at a strategic point to speak on the bill. As the story goes, his climax was: "If you go on with this bill you will bathe every county in blood before nightfall. And, what's more, there won't be enough white people left in the State to pass it."

When the sheriff threatened me with an indictment for passing as white, a white man in the State with whom I had talked wrote me a long letter asking me if it were true that I had Negro blood. "You did not tell me nor anyone else in my presence," he wrote, "that you were white except as to your name. I had on amber-colored glasses and did not take the trouble to scrutinize your color, but I really did take you for a white man and, according to the laws of ——, you may be." My informant urged me to sit down and figure out mathematically the exact percentage of Negro blood that I possessed and, if it proved to be less than one-eighth, to sue for libel those who had charged me with passing.

This man wrote of the frantic efforts of the whites of his State to keep themselves thought of as white. He quoted an old law to the effect that "it was not slander to call one a Negro because everybody could see that he was not; but it was slanderous to call him a mulatto."

IV

On another occasion a serious race riot occurred in Tulsa, Oklahoma, a bustling town of 100,000 inhabitants. In the early days Tulsa had been a lifeless and unimportant village of not more than five thousand people, and its Negro residents had been forced to live in what was considered the least desirable section of the village, down near the railroad. Then oil was discovered nearby and almost overnight the village grew into a prosperous town. The Negroes prospered along with the whites and began to erect comfortable homes, business establishments, a hotel, two cinemas and other enterprises, all of these springing up in the section to which they had been relegated. This was, as I have said, down near the railroad tracks. The swift growth of the town made this hitherto disregarded land of great value for business purposes. Efforts to purchase the land from the Negro owners at prices far below its value were unavailing. Having built up the neighborhood and knowing its value, the owners refused to be victimized.

One afternoon in 1921 a Negro messenger boy went to deliver a package in an office building on the main street of Tulsa. His errand done, he rang the bell for the elevator in order that he might descend. The operator, a young white girl, on finding that she had been summoned by a Negro, opened the door of the car ungraciously. Two versions there are of what happened then. The boy declared that she started the car on its downward plunge when he was only halfway in, and that to save himself from being killed he had to throw himself into the car, stepping on the girl's foot in doing so. The girl, on the other hand, asserted that the boy attempted to rape her in the elevator. The latter story, at best, seemed highly dubious—that an attempted criminal assault would be made by any person in an open elevator of a crowded office building on the main street of a town of 100,000 inhabitants—and in open daylight!

Whatever the truth, the local press, with scant investigation, published lurid accounts of the alleged assault. That night a mob started to the jail to lynch the Negro boy. A group of Negroes offered their services to the jailer and sheriff in protecting the prisoner. The offer was declined and, when the Negroes started to leave the sheriff's office, a clash occurred between them and the mob. Instantly the mob swung into action.

The Negroes, outnumbered, were forced back to their own neighborhood. Rapidly the news spread of the clash and the numbers of mobbers grew hourly. By daybreak of the following day the mob numbered around five thousand, and was armed with machine-guns, dynamite, rifles, revolvers and shotguns, cans of gasoline and kerosene, and—such are the blessings of invention!—airplanes. Surrounding the Negro section, it attacked, led by men who had been officers in the American army in France. Outnumbered and outequipped, the plight of the Negroes was a hopeless one from the beginning. Driven further and further back, many of them were killed or wounded, among them an aged man and his wife, who were slain as they knelt at prayer for deliverance. Forty-four blocks of property were burned after homes and stores had been pillaged.

I arrived in Tulsa while the excitement was at its peak. Within a few hours I met a commercial photographer who had worked for five years on a New York newspaper and he welcomed me with open arms when he found that I represented a New York paper. From him I learned that special deputy sheriffs were being sworn in to guard the town from a rumored counterattack by the Negroes. It occurred to me that I could get myself sworn in as one of these deputies.

It was even easier to do this than I had expected. That evening in the City Hall I had to answer only three questions—name, age and address. I might have been a thug, a murderer, an escaped convict, a member of the mob itself which had laid waste a large area of the city—none of these mattered; my skin was apparently white, and that was enough. After we—some fifty or sixty of us—had been sworn in, solemnly declaring we would do our utmost to uphold the laws and constitutions of the United States and the State of Oklahoma, a villainous-looking man next to me turned and remarked casually, even with a note of happiness in his voice: "Now you can go out and shoot any nigger you see and the law'll be behind you."

As we stood in the wide marble corridor of the not unimposing City Hall waiting to be assigned to automobiles which were to patrol the city during the night, I noticed a man, clad in the uniform of a captain of the United States Army, watching me closely. I imagined I saw in his very swarthy face (he was much darker than I, but was classed as a white man while I am deemed a Negro) mingled inquiry and hostility. I kept my eye on him without appearing to do so. Tulsa would not have been a very healthy place for me that night had my race or my previous investigations of other race riots been known there. At last the man seemed certain he knew me and started toward me.

He drew me aside into a deserted corner on the excuse that he had something he wished to ask me, and I noticed that four other men, with whom he had been talking, detached themselves from the crowd and followed us.

Without further introduction or apology my dark-skinned, newly made acquaintance, putting his face close to mine and looking into my eyes with a steely, unfriendly glance, demanded challengingly:

"You say that your name is White?"

I answered affirmatively.

"You say you're a newspaper man?"

"Yes, I represent the New York ——. Would you care to see my credentials?"

"No, but I want to tell you something. There's an organization in the South that doesn't love niggers. It has branches everywhere. You needn't ask me the name—I can't tell you. But it has come back into existence to fight this damned nigger Advancement Association. We watch every movement of the officers of this nigger society and we're out to get them for putting notions of equality into the heads of our niggers down South here."

There could be no question that he referred to the Ku Klux Klan on the one hand and the National Association for the Advancement of Colored People on the other. As coolly as I could, the circumstances being what they were,

I took a cigarette from my case and lighted it, trying to keep my hand from betraying my nervousness. When he finished speaking I asked him:

"All this is very interesting, but what, if anything, has it to do with the story of the race riot here which I've come to get?"

For a full minute we looked straight into each other's eyes, his four companions meanwhile crowding close about us. At length his eyes fell. With a shrug of his shoulders and a half-apologetic smile, he replied as he turned away, "Oh, nothing, except I wanted you to know what's back of the trouble here."

It is hardly necessary to add that all that night, assigned to the same car with this man and his four companions, I maintained a considerable vigilance. When the news stories I wrote about the riot (the boy accused of attempted assault was acquitted in the magistrate's court after nearly one million dollars of property and a number of lives had been destroyed) revealed my identity—that I was a Negro and an officer of the Advancement Society—more than a hundred anonymous letters threatening my life came to me. I was also threatened with a suit for criminal libel by a local paper, but nothing came of it after my willingness to defend it was indicated.

V

A narrow escape came during an investigation of an alleged plot by Negroes in Arkansas to "massacre" all the white people of the State. It later developed that the Negroes had simply organized a coöperative society to combat their economic exploitation by landlords, merchants, and bankers, many of whom openly practiced peonage. I went as a representative of a Chicago newspaper to get the facts. Going first to the capital of the State, Little Rock, I interviewed the Governor and other officials and then proceeded to the scene of the trouble, Phillips county, in the heart of the cotton-raising area, close to the Mississippi.

As I stepped from the train at Elaine, the county seat, I was closely watched by a crowd of men. Within half an hour of my arrival I had been asked by two shopkeepers, a restaurant waiter, and a ticket agent why I had come to Elaine, what my business was and what I thought of the recent riot. The tension relaxed somewhat when I implied I was in sympathy with the mob. Little by little suspicion was lessened and then, the people being eager to have a metropolitan newspaper give their side of the story, I was shown "evidence" that the story of the massacre plot was well-founded, and not very clever attempts were made to guide me away from the truth.

Suspicion was given new birth when I pressed my inquiries too insistently concerning the share-cropping and tenant-farming system, which works somewhat as follows: Negro farmers enter into agreements to till specified plots of land, they to receive usually half of the crop for their labor. Should they be too poor to buy food, seed, clothing and other supplies, they are supplied these commodities by their landlords at designated stores. When the crop is gathered the landowner takes it and sells it. By declaring that he has sold it at a figure far below the market price and by refusing to give itemized accounts of the supplies purchased during the year by the tenant, a landlord can (and in that region almost always does) so arrange it that the bill for supplies always exceeds the tenant's share of the crop. Individual Negroes who had protested against such thievery had been lynched. The new organization was simply a union to secure relief through the courts, which relief those who profited from the system meant to prevent. Thus the story of a "massacre" plot.

Suspicion of me took definite form when word was sent to Phillips county from Little Rock that it had been discovered that I was a Negro, though I knew nothing about the message at the time. I walked down West Cherry Street, the main thoroughfare of Elaine, one day on my way to the jail, where I had an appointment with the sheriff, who was going to permit me to interview some of the Negro prisoners who were charged with being implicated in the alleged plot. A tall, heavy-set Negro passed me and, *sotto voce,* told me as he passed that he had something important to tell me, and that I should turn to the right at the next corner and follow him. Some inner sense bade me obey. When we had got out of sight of other persons the Negro told me not to go to the jail, that there was great hostility in the town against me and they planned harming me. In the man's manner there was something which made me certain he was telling the truth. Making my way to the railroad station, since my interview with the prisoners (the sheriff and jailer being present) was unlikely to add anything to my story, I was able to board one of the two trains a day out of Elaine. When I explained to the conductor—he looked at me so inquiringly—that I had no ticket because delays in Elaine had given me no time to purchase one, he exclaimed, "Why, Mister, you're leaving just when the fun is going to start! There's a damned yaller nigger down here passing for white and the boys are going to have some fun with him."

I asked him the nature of the fun.

"Wal, when they get through with him," he explained grimly, "he won't pass for white no more."

Call for Critical Debate

The Alain Locke–W.E.B. Du Bois Debate on the Theory of Black Art

W.E.B. DU BOIS[1]

Criteria of Negro Art

So many persons have asked for the complete text of the address delivered by Dr. Du Bois at the Chicago Conference of the National Association for the Advancement of Colored People that we are publishing the address here.

I do not doubt but there are some in this audience who are a little disturbed at the subject of this meeting, and particularly at the subject I have chosen. Such people are thinking something like this: "How is it that an organization like this, a group of radicals trying to bring new things into the world, a fighting organization which has come up out of the blood and dust of battle, struggling for the right of black men to be ordinary human beings—how is it that an organization of this kind can turn aside to talk about Art? After all, what have we who are slaves and black to do with Art?"

Or perhaps there are others who feel a certain relief and are saying, "After all it is rather satisfactory after all this talk about rights and fighting to sit and dream of something which leaves a nice taste in the mouth."

Let me tell you that neither of these groups is right. The thing we are talking about tonight is part of the great fight we are carrying on and it represents a forward and an upward look—a pushing onward. You and I have been breasting hills; we have been climbing upward; there has been progress and we can see it day by day looking back along blood-filled paths. But as you go through the valleys and over the foothills, so long as you are climbing, the direction,—north, south, east or west,—is of less importance. But when gradually the vista widens and you begin to see the world at your feet and the far horizon, then it is time to know more precisely whither you are going and what you really want.

What do we want? What is the thing we are after? As it was phrased last night it had a certain truth: We want to be Americans, full-fledged Americans, with all the rights of other American citizens. But is that all? Do we want simply to be Americans? Once in a while through all of us there flashes some clairvoyance, some clear idea, of what America really is. We who are dark can see America in a way that white Americans can not. And seeing our country thus, are we satisfied with its present goals and ideals?

In the high school where I studied we learned most of Scott's "Lady of the Lake" by heart. In after life once it was my privilege to see the lake. It was Sunday. It was quiet. You could glimpse the deer wandering in unbroken forests; you could hear the soft ripple of romance on the waters. Around me fell the cadence of that poetry of my youth. I fell asleep full of the enchantment of the Scottish border. A new day broke and with it came a sudden rush of excursionists. They were mostly Americans and they were loud and strident. They poured upon the little pleasure boat,—men with their hats a little on one side and drooping cigars in the wet corners of their mouths; women who shared their conversation with the

[1] Du Bois's biography can be found in Part III, pp. 732–37.

world. They all tried to get everywhere first. They pushed other people out of the way. They made all sorts of incoherent noises and gestures so that the quiet home folk and the visitors from other lands silently and half-wonderingly gave way before them. They struck a note not evil but wrong. They carried, perhaps, a sense of strength and accomplishment, but their hearts had no conception of the beauty which pervaded this holy place.

If you tonight suddenly should become full-fledged Americans; if your color faded, or the color line here in Chicago was miraculously forgotten; suppose, too, you became at the same time rich and powerful;—what is it that you would want? What would you immediately seek? Would you buy the most powerful of motor cars and outrace Cook County? Would you buy the most elaborate estate on the North Shore? Would you be a Rotarian or a Lion or a What-not of the very last degree? Would you wear the most striking clothes, give the richest dinners and buy the longest press notices?

Even as you visualize such ideals you know in your hearts that these are not the things you really want. You realize this sooner than the average white American because, pushed aside as we have been in America, there has come to us not only a certain distaste for the tawdry and flamboyant but a vision of what the world could be if it were really a beautiful world; if we had the true spirit; if we had the Seeing Eye, the Cunning Hand, the Feeling Heart; if we had, to be sure, not perfect happiness, but plenty of good hard work, the inevitable suffering that always comes with life; sacrifice and waiting, all that—but, nevertheless, lived in a world where men know, where men create, where they realize themselves and where they enjoy life. It is that sort of a world we want to create for ourselves and for all America.

After all, who shall describe Beauty? What is it? I remember tonight four beautiful things: The Cathedral at Cologne, a forest in stone, set in light and changing shadow, echoing with sunlight and solemn song; a village of the Veys in West Africa, a little thing of mauve and purple, quiet, lying content and shining in the sun; a black and velvet room where on a throne rests, in old and yellowing marble, the broken curves of the Venus of Milo; a single phrase of music in the Southern South—utter melody, haunting and appealing, suddenly arising out of night and eternity, beneath the moon.

Such is Beauty. Its variety is infinite, its possibility is endless. In normal life all may have it and have it yet again. The world is full of it; and yet today the mass of human beings are choked away from it, and their lives distorted and made ugly. This is not only wrong, it is silly. Who shall right this well-nigh universal failing? Who shall let this world be beautiful? Who shall restore to men the glory of sunsets and the peace of quiet sleep?

We black folk may help for we have within us as a race new stirrings; stirrings of the beginning of a new appreciation of joy, of a new desire to create, of a new will to be; as though in this morning of group life we had awakened from some sleep that at once dimly mourns the past and dreams a splendid future; and there has come the conviction that the Youth that is here today, the Negro Youth, is a different kind of Youth, because in some new way it bears this mighty prophecy on its breast, with a new realization of itself, with new determination for all mankind.

What has this Beauty to do with the world? What has Beauty to do with Truth and Goodness—with the facts of the world and the right actions of men? "Nothing," the artists rush to answer. They may be right. I am but an humble disciple of art and cannot presume to say. I am one who tells the truth and exposes evil and seeks with Beauty and for Beauty to set the world right. That somehow, somewhere eternal and perfect Beauty sits above Truth and Right I can conceive, but here and now and in the world in which I work they are for me unseparated and inseparable.

This is brought to us peculiarly when as artists we face our own past as a people. There has come to us—and it has come especially through the man we are going to honor tonight* —a realization of that past, of which for long years we have been ashamed, for which we have apologized. We thought nothing could come out of that past which we wanted to remember; which we wanted to hand down to our children. Suddenly, this same past is taking on form, color and reality, and in a half shamefaced way we are beginning to be proud of it. We are remembering that the romance of the world did not die and lie forgotten in the Middle Age; that if you want romance to deal with you must have it here and now and in your own hands.

I once knew a man and woman. They had two children, a daughter who was white and a daughter who was brown; the daughter who was white married a white man; and when her wedding was preparing the daughter who was brown prepared to go and celebrate. But the mother said, "No!" and the brown daughter went into her room and turned on the gas and died. Do you want Greek tragedy swifter than that?

Or again, here is a little Southern town and you are in the public square. On one side of the square is the office of a colored lawyer and on all the other sides are men who do not like colored lawyers. A white woman goes into the black man's office and points to the white-filled square and says, "I want five hundred dollars now and if I do not get it I am going to scream."

Have you heard the story of the conquest of German East Africa? Listen to the untold tale: There were 40,000 black men and 4,000 white men who talked German. There were 20,000 black men and 12,000 white men who talked English. There were 10,000 black men and 400 white men who talked French. In Africa then where the Mountains of the Moon raised their white and snow-capped heads into the mouth of the tropic sun, where Nile and Congo rise and the Great Lakes swim, these men fought; they struggled on mountain, hill and valley, in river, lake and swamp, until in masses they sickened, crawled and died; until the 4,000 white Germans had become mostly bleached bones; until nearly all the 12,000 white Englishmen had returned to South Africa, and the 400 Frenchmen to Belgium and Heaven; all except a mere handful of the white men died; but thousands of black men from East, West and South Africa, from Nigeria and the Valley of the Nile, and from the West Indies still struggled, fought and died. For four years they fought and won and lost German East Africa; and all you hear about it is that England and Belgium conquered German Africa for the allies!

Such is the true and stirring stuff of which Romance is born and from this stuff come the stirrings of men who are beginning to remember that this kind of material is theirs; and this vital life of their own kind is beckoning them on.

The question comes next as to the interpretation of these new stirrings, of this new spirit: Of what is the colored artist capable? We have had on the part of both colored and white people singular unanimity of judgment in the past. Colored people have said: "This work must be inferior because it comes from colored people." White people have said: "It is inferior because it is done by colored people." But today there is coming to both the realization that the work of the black man is not always inferior. Interesting stories come to us. A professor in the University of Chicago read to a class that had studied literature a passage of poetry and asked them to guess the author. They guessed a goodly company from Shelley and Robert Browning down to Tennyson and Masefield. The author was Countée Cullen. Or again the English critic John Drinkwater went down to a Southern seminary, one of the sort which "finishes" young white women of the South. The students sat with their wooden faces while he tried to get some response out of them. Finally he said, "Name me some of your Southern poets." They hesitated. He said finally, "I'll start out with your best: Paul Laurence Dunbar!"

With the growing recognition of Negro artists in spite of the severe handicaps, one

*Carter Godwin Woodson, 12th Spingarn Medallist.

comforting thing is occurring to both white and black. They are whispering, "Here is a way out. Here is the real solution of the color problem. The recognition accorded Cullen, Hughes, Fauset, White and others shows there is no real color line. Keep quiet! Don't complain! Work! All will be well!"

I will not say that already this chorus amounts to a conspiracy. Perhaps I am naturally too suspicious. But I will say that there are today a surprising number of white people who are getting great satisfaction out of these younger Negro writers because they think it is going to stop agitation of the Negro question. They say, "What is the use of your fighting and complaining; do the great thing and the reward is there." And many colored people are all too eager to follow this advice; especially those who are weary of the eternal struggle along the color line, who are afraid to fight and to whom the money of philanthropists and the alluring publicity are subtle and deadly bribes. They say, "What is the use of fighting? Why not show simply what we deserve and let the reward come to us?"

And it is right here that the National Association for the Advancement of Colored People comes upon the field, comes with its great call to a new battle, a new fight and new things to fight before the old things are wholly won; and to say that the Beauty of Truth and Freedom which shall some day be our heritage and the heritage of all civilized men is not in our hands yet and that we ourselves must not fail to realize.

There is in New York tonight a black woman molding clay by herself in a little bare room, because there is not a single school of sculpture in New York where she is welcome. Surely there are doors she might burst through, but when God makes a sculptor He does not always make the pushing sort of person who beats his way through doors thrust in his face. This girl is working her hands off to get out of this country so that she can get some sort of training.

There was Richard Brown. If he had been white he would have been alive today instead of dead of neglect. Many helped him when he asked but he was not the kind of boy that always asks. He was simply one who made colors sing.

There is a colored woman in Chicago who is a great musician. She thought she would like to study at Fontainebleau this summer where Walter Damrosch and a score of leaders of Art have an American school of music. But the application blank of this school says: "I am a white American and I apply for admission to the school."

We can go on the stage; we can be just as funny as white Americans wish us to be; we can play all the sordid parts that America likes to assign to Negroes; but for any thing else there is still small place for us.

And so I might go on. But let me sum up with this: Suppose the only Negro who survived some centuries hence was the Negro painted by white Americans in the novels and essays they have written. What would people in a hundred years say of black Americans? Now turn it around. Suppose you were to write a story and put in it the kind of people you know and like and imagine. You might get it published and you might not. And the "might not" is still far bigger than the "might." The white publishers catering to white folk would say, "It is not interesting"—to white folk, naturally not. They want Uncle Toms, Topsies, good "darkies" and clowns. I have in my office a story with all the earmarks of truth. A young man says that he started out to write and had his stories accepted. Then he began to write about the things he knew best about, that is, about his own people. He submitted a story to a magazine which said, "We are sorry, but we cannot take it." "I sat down and revised my story, changing the color of the characters and the locale and sent it under an assumed name with a change of address and it was accepted by the same magazine that had refused it, the editor promising to take anything else I *might* send in providing it was good enough."

We have, to be sure, a few recognized and successful Negro artists; but they are not all those fit to survive or even a good minority. They are but the remnants of that ability and genius among us whom the accidents of education and opportunity have raised on the tidal waves of chance. We black folk are not altogether peculiar in this. After all, in the world at large, it is only the accident, the remnant, that gets the chance to make the most of itself; but if this is true of the white world it is infinitely more true of the colored world. It is not simply the great clear tenor of Roland Hayes that opened the ears of America. We have had many voices of all kinds as fine as his and America was and is as deaf as she was for years to him. Then a foreign land heard Hayes and put its imprint on him and immediately America with all its imitative snobbery woke up. We approved Hayes because London, Paris and Berlin approved him and not simply because he was a great singer.

Thus it is the bounden duty of black America to begin this great work of the creation of Beauty, of the preservation of Beauty, of the realization of Beauty, and we must use in this work all the methods that men have used before. And what have been the tools of the artist in times gone by? First of all, he has used the Truth—not for the sake of truth, not as a scientist seeking truth, but as one upon whom Truth eternally thrusts itself as the highest handmaid of imagination, as the one great vehicle of universal understanding. Again artists have used Goodness—goodness in all its aspects of justice, honor and right—not for sake of an ethical sanction but as the one true method of gaining sympathy and human interest.

The apostle of Beauty thus becomes the apostle of Truth and Right not by choice but by inner and outer compulsion. Free he is but his freedom is ever bounded by Truth and Justice; and slavery only dogs him when he is denied the right to tell the Truth or recognize an ideal of Justice.

Thus all Art is propaganda and ever must be, despite the wailing of the purists. I stand in utter shamelessness and say that whatever art I have for writing has been used always for propaganda for gaining the right of black folk to love and enjoy. I do not care a damn for any art that is not used for propaganda. But I do care when propaganda is confined to one side while the other is stripped and silent.

In New York we have two plays: "White Cargo" and "Congo." In "White Cargo" there is a fallen woman. She is black. In "Congo" the fallen woman is white. In "White Cargo" the black woman goes down further and further and in "Congo" the white woman begins with degradation but in the end is one of the angels of the Lord.

You know the current magazine story: A young white man goes down to Central American and the most beautiful colored woman there falls in love with him. She crawls across the whole isthmus to get to him. The white man says nobly, "No." He goes back to his white sweetheart in New York.

In such cases, it is not the positive propaganda of people who believe white blood divine, infallible and holy to which I object. It is the denial of a similar right of propaganda to those who believe black blood human, lovable and inspired with new ideals for the world. White artists themselves suffer from this narrowing of their field. They cry for freedom in dealing with Negroes because they have so little freedom in dealing with whites. DuBose Heywood writes "Porgy" and writes beautifully of the black Charleston underworld. But why does he do this? Because he cannot do a similar thing for the white people of Charleston, or they would drum him out of town. The only chance he had to tell the truth of pitiful human degradation was to tell it of colored people. I should not be surprised if Octavius Roy Cohen had approached the *Saturday Evening Post* and asked permission to write about a different kind of colored folk than the monstrosities he has created; but if he has, the *Post* has replied, "No. You are getting paid to write about the kind of colored people you are writing about."

In other words, the white public today demands from its artists, literary and pictorial, racial pre-judgment which deliberately distorts Truth and Justice, as far as colored races are concerned, and it will pay for no other.

On the other hand, the young and slowly growing black public still wants its prophets almost equally unfree. We are bound by all sorts of customs that have come down as second-hand soul clothes of white patrons. We are ashamed of sex and we lower our eyes when people will talk of it. Our religion holds us in superstition. Our worst side has been so shamelessly emphasized that we are denying we have or ever had a worst side. In all sorts of ways we are hemmed in and our new young artists have got to fight their way to freedom.

The ultimate judge has got to be you and you have got to build yourselves up into that wide judgment, that catholicity of temper which is going to enable the artist to have his widest chance for freedom. We can afford the Truth. White folk today cannot. As it is now we are handing everything over to a white jury. If a colored man wants to publish a book, he has got to get a white publisher and a white newspaper to say it is great; and then you and I say so. We must come to the place where the work of art when it appears is reviewed and acclaimed by our own free and unfettered judgment. And we are going to have a real and valuable and eternal judgment only as we make ourselves free of mind, proud of body and just of soul to all men.

And then do you know what will be said? It is already saying. Just as soon as true Art emerges; just as soon as the black artist appears, someone touches the race on the shoulder and says, "He did that because he was an American, not because he was a Negro; he was born here; he was trained here; he is not a Negro—what is a Negro anyhow? He is just human; it is the kind of thing you ought to expect."

I do not doubt that the ultimate art coming from black folk is going to be just as beautiful, and beautiful largely in the same ways, as the art that comes from white folk, or yellow, or red; but the point today is that until the art of the black folk compells recognition they will not be rated as human. And when through art they compell recognition then let the world discover if it will that their art is as new as it is old and as old as new.

I had a classmate once who did three beautiful things and died. One of them was a story of a folk who found fire and then went wandering in the gloom of night seeking again the stars they had once known and lost; suddenly out of blackness they looked up and there loomed the heavens; and what was it that they said? They raised a mighty cry: "It is the stars, it is the ancient stars, it is the young and everlasting stars!"

ALAIN LOCKE

(1886–1954)

Alain Locke appears in standard literary histories as the preeminent scholar of the New Negro Movement or Harlem Renaissance. Although he lacked the analytical brilliance of W.E.B. Du Bois and the racial consciousness of Walter White, the three men vied for dominance throughout the era. The media chose Locke as the figurehead for the New Negro. Locke called for literature as an expressive song as distilled and detached from a history grounded in the militancy of mid-nineteenth-century abolitionism and of late-nineteenth-century Reconstruction. In the place of the vocal Old Negro, Locke proposed the New Negro of greater refinement. In his own writing, he displayed a polished elitism and even a patriarchal arrogance. Supposedly a philosophical critic of culture, he was really a formalist who read literary works without reference either to morality or to history.

In several ways, Locke was a contradiction. Although he seemed to write with great moral authority, he attempted to separate the beautiful and the ethical. While he assumed that literature has a hidden purpose that makes it beautiful, he almost never inquired into the deeper meaning of texts. Sometimes his apparent calls for bold innovation in literary forms probably masked a conservative cowardice that kept him from appraising great literature as anything other than personal lyric. Rarely did he ever consider a world with many literary genres achieving excellence in many varied ways. Often he even begged the question about the points he tried to prove. His traditional assumptions about the universal values of European culture and the American middle class were questionable. Frequently, he veiled his own aristocratic inclinations in a convenient pretense of writing democratically for the masses. Almost never did he free his thought from the conventional principles of the Enlightenment of the eighteenth century. He believed passionately in the universality of literary texts that were independent of history or social circumstance.

Perhaps no other writer revealed as much as he the deep-seated schizophrenia of the New Negro Movement. His genteel sensibility suggested the very traditional formalists, who like Georgia Douglas Johnson, Angelina Weld Grimké, Claude McKay, and Countee Cullen looked back to the Victorian period in England or to the Gilded Age in the United States. Although he believed in and promoted the black folk tradition in theory, he separated himself from the real folk in fact. His elite preference marked in stunning contrast the emergence of varied innovations in folk idiom—and sometimes even modernist technique—by James Weldon Johnson, Zora Neale Hurston, Nella Larsen, Jean Toomer, Sterling Brown, and Langston Hughes. Locke's universalistic thought set the tone for the 1920s and the late 1970s through the 1990s. His strong Oxford pedigree, however, lost significant ground during the 1930s through the 1960s.

Two prominent contemporary theorists of African American texts, Houston A. Baker and Henry Louis Gates, Jr., have celebrated Locke as either a role model or as an intellectual. However, praise for the integrationist aesthetic rarely lasts for long periods of time. Indeed, Locke's somewhat dandyish style cannot adapt to highly volatile changes in rising unemployment and urban insurrections. He is a wonderful litmus test for whether African Americans—and the civilization that produces their leaders—can ever learn anything from history.

Alain LeRoy Locke, born in Philadelphia on September 13, 1886, grew up in a city "flavored by urbanity and her petty bourgeois psyche with the Tory slant."* He was only nine years old when Booker T. Washington promised in his Atlanta Exposition address of 1895 to trade human equality for technical training, and he was only ten when the Supreme Court legalized the racial doctrine of separate but equal. Hence, he lived fifty-eight of his sixty-eight years—a full 85 percent—under institutionalized segregation. In 1904, after graduation from Central High School and the Philadelphia School of Pedagogy, he began study at Harvard University under the renowned pragmatist William James, as W.E.B. Du Bois had done a decade or so earlier. Locke found himself, says Ernest D. Mason, "clinging to the genteel tradition of Palmer, Royce, and Munsterberg, yet attracted by the disillusion of Santayana and the radical protest of James." Graduated with an impressive record in 1907, Locke studied as the first black Rhodes scholar at Oxford University in England from 1907 to 1910, during which time he earned a bachelor of literature degree. After further study at the University of Berlin, he began in 1912 a stint as assistant professor of

*Source: *African American Literary Criticism.*

English and instructor in philosophy and education at Howard University. When Locke returned to Harvard in 1916, he intended to work with Josiah Royce, a famous philosopher of American idealism. Although Royce died, in 1918 Locke completed a dissertation titled "The Problem of Classification in Theory of Value" under the direction of Ralph Barton Perry.

Until his retirement in 1952, Locke was, for a total of thirty-six years, professor of philosophy at Howard University. Frequently, he would take leave to do research or to lecture at institutions such as the City College of New York, the New School for Social Research, and the Salzburg Seminar in American Studies, as well as to serve as a visiting professor at New York University, the University of Wisconsin, and Harvard. Locke spoke widely in the Caribbean, Europe, Latin America, and the United States. Often recruited as a polished specialist in race, he developed a comfortable repertoire in Africana studies. Editor of *Associates of Negro Folk Education* and *Survey Graphic,* he completed *The New Negro,* the best known of his edited volumes, in 1925. Two of his other edited works, *Four Negro Poets* and *Plays of Negro Life* (with Montgomery Gregory), were published in 1927. Among his original books are *The Negro in America* (1933), *The Negro and His Music* (1936), *Negro Art—Past and Present* (1937), *The Negro in Art: A Pictorial Record of the Negro Artist and of the Negro Theme in Art* (1941), *When Peoples Meet: A Study in Race and Culture Contacts* (with Bernard Stern, 1942). Although Locke did not live to complete a planned synthesis of his work, Margaret Just Butcher used collected materials written by him to finish *The Negro in American Culture* (1956). Locke wrote several fine book reviews for *Opportunity* and *Phylon* from the thirties through the fifties.

In making an arbitrary distinction between art and propaganda (Du Bois reviewed the point with contempt in January 1926), Locke believed that sermons and prophecies should give way to literary songs. Locke rationalized that the writing of protest confirmed indirectly the dominance of whites or the majority group. He saw too much unbridled ego in the strategy and preferred the self-effacing "balance or poise or inner dignity and self-respect." To him, literary art had to be "self-contained." At the same time, he valued the importance of group or even individualistic expression. According to Ernest D. Mason, he never stopped asking, "Is there any possible way of deciding the validity of the conflicting claims and of establishing a unitary principle of rightness and wrongs of values, apart, that is, from their function within a particular historical, social, or cultural context?" Hence, his primary intent was ethical. Nevertheless, his tone encodes some rather curious assumptions:

> Not all of our [patriarchal stance] younger writers are deep enough in the [primitive] sub-soil of their native [primitive] materials,—too many are poet plants [primitive earthiness] seeking a forced growth [Booker T. Washington; Separate but Equal: natural order] according to the exotic tastes [unrefined white and black masses] demanded of history? Of a pampered and decadent public [blaming the victim]. It is the art of the people[?] that needs to be cultivated [by me], not the art of the [other] coteries. Propaganda itself is preferable to shallow, truckling imitation. Negro things may reasonably be a [public or popular] fad for others; for us they must be a religion [of the inner self but not of the outer world]. Beauty [for

Plato and Keats], however, is its best [personal] priest and psalms [personal lyrics] will be more effective than sermons [public performances] [editor's brackets].

Locke believed that the same religion that produces artistic sacredness forbids engagement with the polluted world, and the beauty that is a priest for the self may well be no priest for others. Indeed, he thought, the best way to achieve human community is to transcend the differences that separate people, for acknowledgment of the kind breeds conflict and intolerance, possibly even racial hatred.

Both the slave narratives of the nineteenth century and the somewhat raw proclamations of the Black Arts Movement of the 1960s and 1970s, which Locke did not live to see, clarify what he misunderstood. The universal takes root in the specifics of race, gender, and history; evil must either be confronted or suffered. With self-determination, the private self can make a difference in the public world.

Why did Locke's theory fail? His universalistic aesthetic resisted the rise of modernism as epitomized by Jean Toomer and devalued the ascent of folk idiom with Zora Neale Hurston, Langston Hughes, and Sterling Brown. Without deeply spiritual roots in black liberation, the stance proved to be as irrelevant for the proletarian writing of the Great Depression as for the lyrical dreams and ironic wit of the postwar world. Even for the integrationist era of the fifties, Locke's somewhat aloof aesthetic lacked practical applications to help America deal with escalating crises of racial change. In the time of the Black Arts Movement, Locke's claims for universal ethics fell on deaf ears while Americans struggled to achieve peace through the reduction of social conflict. Many of the subconscious efforts today to revive the Lockeian preference are too narrowly promoted to prevail. His sexist exclusion of women writers from power in the Renaissance held them back. Ethics and history—like aesthetics and history—are inseparably bound. Alain Locke's life, except for the first ten years, spanned precisely from separate but equal in 1896 to the integration of the nation's public schools in 1954. George Kent partially exonerates Locke by saying that "despite his essentially middle-class sensibility and somewhat simplistic integrationist orientation, he reflected a critical and cultural sensitivity that has not been surpassed."

❖❖❖

So much criticism on Locke has been deferentially saccharine that almost no scholar has inquired conscientiously into the struggle between cultural authenticity and mainstream empowerment. Locke is an invaluable key to both the Renaissance and our own times. Ernest D. Mason has written insightful work, in, for example, "Alain Locke," in *Dictionary of Literary Biography: Afro-American Writers From the Harlem Renaissance*, ed. Trudier Harris (1987). A pioneering collection, with Mason as featured lead and Patricia Liggins Hill on black folk music, is Russell J. Linnemann, ed., *Alain Locke: Reflections of a Modern Renaissance Man* (1982). For unrivaled excellence, consult George E. Kent, "Patterns of the Harlem Renaissance," in *Harlem Renaissance Remembered,* ed. Arna Bontemps (1972). Most informative texts of a previous generation include Richard K. Barksdale and Keneth Kinnamon, *Black Writers of America: A Comprehensive Anthology* (1972) and Arthur P. Davis, *From the Dark Tower* (1974).

The New Negro

In the last decade something beyond the watch and guard of statistics has happened in the life of the American Negro and the three norns who have traditionally presided over the Negro problem have a changeling in their laps. The Sociologist, the Philanthropist, the Race-leader are not unaware of the New Negro, but they are at a loss to account for him. He simply cannot be swathed in their formulae. For the younger generation is vibrant with a new psychology; the new spirit is awake in the masses, and under the very eyes of the professional observers is transforming what has been a perennial problem into the progressive phases of contemporary Negro life.

Could such a metamorphosis have taken place as suddenly as it has appeared to? The answer is no; not because the New Negro is not here, but because the Old Negro had long become more of a myth than a man. The Old Negro, we must remember, was a creature of moral debate and historical controversy. His has been a stock figure perpetuated as an historical fiction partly in innocent sentimentalism, partly in deliberate reactionism. The Negro himself has contributed his share to this through a sort of protective social mimicry forced upon him by the adverse circumstances of dependence. So for generations in the mind of America, the Negro has been more of a formula than a human being—a something to be argued about, condemned or defended, to be "kept down," or "in his place," or "helped up," to be worried with or worried over, harassed or patronized, a social bogey or a social burden. The thinking Negro even has been induced to share this same general attitude, to focus his attention on controversial issues, to see himself in the distorted perspective of a social problem. His shadow, so to speak, has been more real to him than his personality. Through having had to appeal from the unjust stereotypes of his oppressors and traducers to those of his liberators, friends and benefactors he has had to subscribe to the traditional positions from which his case has been viewed. Little true social or self-understanding has or could come from such a situation.

But while the minds of most of us, black and white, have thus burrowed in the trenches of the Civil War and Reconstruction, the actual march of development has simply flanked these positions, necessitating a sudden reorientation of view. We have not been watching in the right direction; set North and South on a sectional axis, we have not noticed the East till the sun has us blinking.

Recall how suddenly the Negro spirituals revealed themselves; suppressed for generations under the stereotypes of Wesleyan hymn harmony, secretive, half-ashamed, until the courage of being natural brought them out—and behold, there was folk-music. Similarly the mind of the Negro seems suddenly to have slipped from under the tyranny of social intimidation and to be shaking off the psychology of imitation and implied inferiority. By shedding the old chrysalis of the Negro problem we are achieving something like a spiritual emancipation. Until recently, lacking self-understanding, we have been almost as much of a problem to ourselves as we still are to others. But the decade that found us with a problem has left us with only a task. The multitude perhaps feels as yet only a strange relief and a new vague urge, but the thinking few know that in the reaction the vital inner grip of prejudice has been broken.

With this renewed self-respect and self-dependence, the life of the Negro community is bound to enter a new dynamic phase, the buoyancy from within compensating for whatever pressure there may be of conditions from without. The migrant masses, shifting from countryside to city, hurdle several generations of experience at a leap, but more important, the same thing happens spiritually in the life-attitudes and self-expression of the Young Negro, in his poetry, his art, his education and his new outlook, with the additional advantage, of course, of the poise and greater certainty of knowing what it is all about. From this comes the promise and warrant of a new leadership. As one of them has discerningly put it:

> We have tomorrow
> Bright before us
> Like a flame.
>
> Yesterday, a night-gone thing
> A sun-down name.
>
> And dawn today
> Broad arch above the road we came.
> We march!

This is what, even more than any "most creditable record of fifty years of freedom," requires that the Negro of to-day be seen through other than the dusty spectacles of past controversy. The day of "aunties," "uncles" and "mammies" is equally gone. Uncle Tom and Sambo have passed on, and even the "Colonel" and "George" play barnstorm roles from which they escape with relief when the public spotlight is off. The popular melodrama has about played itself out, and it is time to scrap the fictions, garret the bogeys and settle down to a realistic facing of facts.

First we must observe some of the changes which since the traditional lines of opinion were drawn have rendered these quite obsolete. A main change has been, of course, that shifting of the Negro population which has made the Negro problem no longer exclusively or even predominantly Southern. Why should our minds remain sectionalized, when the problem itself no longer is? Then the trend of migration has not only been toward the North and the Central Midwest, but city-ward and to the great centers of industry—the problems of adjustment are new, practical, local and not peculiarly racial. Rather they are an integral part of the large industrial and social problems of our present-day democracy. And finally, with the Negro rapidly in process of class differentiation, if it ever was warrantable to regard and treat the Negro *en masse* it is becoming with every day less possible, more unjust and more ridiculous.

In the very process of being transplanted, the Negro is becoming transformed.

The tide of Negro migration, northward and city-ward, is not to be fully explained as a blind flood started by the demands of war industry coupled with the shutting off of foreign migration, or by the pressure of poor crops coupled with increased social terrorism in certain sections of the South and Southwest. Neither labor demand, the boll-weevil nor the Ku Klux Klan is a basic factor, however contributory any or all of them may have been. The wash and rush of this human tide on the beach line of the northern city centers is to be explained primarily in terms of a new vision of opportunity, of social and economic freedom, of a spirit to seize, even in the face of an extortionate and heavy toll, a chance for the improvement of conditions. With each successive wave of it, the movement of the Negro becomes more and more a mass movement toward the larger and the more democratic chance—in the Negro's case a deliberate flight not only from countryside to city, but from medieval America to modern.

Take Harlem as an instance of this. Here in Manhattan is not merely the largest Negro community in the world, but the first concentration in history of so many diverse elements of Negro life. It has attracted the African, the West Indian, the Negro American; has brought together the Negro of the North and the Negro of the South; the man from the city and the man from the town and village; the peasant, the student, the business man, the professional man, artist, poet, musician, adventurer and worker, preacher and criminal, exploiter and social outcast. Each group has come with its own separate motives and for its own special ends, but their greatest experience has been the finding of one another. Proscription and prejudice have thrown these dissimilar elements into a common area of contact and interaction. Within this area, race sympathy and unity have determined a further fusing of sentiment and experience. So what began in terms of segregation becomes more and more, as its elements mix and react, the laboratory of a great race-welding. Hitherto, it must be admitted that American Negroes have been a race more in name than in fact, or to be exact, more in sentiment than in experience. The chief bond between them has been that of a common condition rather than a common consciousness; a problem in common rather than a life in common. In Harlem, Negro life is seizing upon its first chances for group expression and self-determination. It is—or promises at least to be—a race capital. That is why our comparison is taken with those nascent centers of folk-expression and self-determination which are playing a creative part in the world to-day. Without pretense to their political significance, Harlem has the same rôle to play for the New Negro as Dublin has had for the New Ireland or Prague for the New Czechoslovakia.

Harlem, I grant you, isn't typical—but it is significant, it is prophetic. No sane observer, however sympathetic to the new trend, would contend that the great masses are articulate as yet, but they stir, they move, they are more than physically restless. The challenge of the new intellectuals among them is clear enough—the "race radicals" and realists who have broken with the old epoch of philanthropic guidance, sentimental appeal and protest. But are we after all only reading into the stirrings of a sleeping giant the dreams of an agitator? The answer is in the migrating peasant. It is the "man farthest down" who is most active in getting up. One of the most characteristic symptoms of this is the professional man, himself migrating to recapture his constituency after a vain effort to maintain in some Southern corner what for years back seemed an established living and clientele. The clergyman following his errant flock, the physician or lawyer trailing his clients, supply the true clues. In a real sense it is the rank and file who are leading, and the leaders who are following. A transformed and transforming psychology permeates the masses.

When the racial leaders of twenty years ago spoke of developing race-pride and stimulating race-consciousness, and of the desirability of race solidarity, they could not in any accurate degree have anticipated the abrupt feeling that has surged up and now pervades the awakened centers. Some of the recognized Negro leaders and a powerful section of white opinion identified with "race work" of the older order have indeed attempted to discount this feeling as a "passing phase," an attack of "race nerves" so to speak, an "aftermath of the war," and the like. It has not abated, however, if we are to gauge by the present tone and temper of the Negro press, or by the shift in popular support from the officially recognized and orthodox spokesmen to those of the independent, popular, and often radical type who are unmistakable symptoms of a new order. It is a social disservice to blunt the fact that the Negro of the Northern centers has reached a stage where tutelage, even of the most interested and well-intentioned sort, must give place to new relationships, where positive self-direction must be reckoned with an ever increasing measure. The American mind must reckon with a fundamentally changed Negro.

The Negro too, for his part, has idols of the tribe to smash. If on the one hand the white man has erred in making the Negro appear to be that which would excuse or extenuate his treatment of him, the Negro, in turn, has too often unnecessarily excused himself because of the way he has been treated. The intelligent Negro of to-day is resolved not to make discrimination an extenuation for his shortcomings in performance, individual or collective; he is trying to hold himself at par, neither inflated by sentimental allowances nor depreciated by current social discounts. For this he must know himself and be known for precisely what he is, and for that reason he welcomes the new scientific rather than the old sentimental interest. Sentimental interest in the Negro has ebbed. We used to lament this as the falling off of our friends; now we rejoice and pray to be delivered both from self-pity and condescension. The mind of each racial group has had a bitter weaning, apathy or hatred on one side matching disillusionment or resentment on the other; but they face each other to-day with the possibility at least of entirely new mutual attitudes.

It does not follow that if the Negro were better known, he would be better liked or better treated. But mutual understanding is basic for any subsequent coöperation and adjustment. The effort toward this will at least have the effect of remedying in large part what has been the most unsatisfactory feature of our present stage of race relationships in America, namely the fact that the more intelligent and representative elements of the two race groups have at so many points got quite out of vital touch with one another.

The fiction is that the life of the races is separate, and increasingly so. The fact is that they have touched too closely at the unfavorable and too lightly at the favorable levels.

While inter-racial councils have sprung up in the South, drawing on forward elements of both races, in the Northern cities manual laborers may brush elbows in their everyday work, but the community and business leaders have experienced no such interplay or far too little of it. These segments must achieve contact or the race situation in America becomes desperate. Fortunately this is happening. There is a growing realization that in social effort the co-operative basis must supplant long-distance philanthropy, and that the only safeguard for mass relations in the future must be provided in the carefully maintained contacts of the enlightened minorities of both race groups. In the intellectual realm a renewed and keen curiosity is replacing the recent apathy; the Negro is being carefully studied, not just talked about and discussed. In art and letters, instead of being wholly caricatured, he is being seriously portrayed and painted.

To all of this the New Negro is keenly responsive as an augury of a new democracy in American culture. He is contributing his share to the new social understanding. But the desire to be understood would never in itself have been sufficient to have opened so completely the protectively closed portals of the thinking Negro's mind. There is still too much possibility of being snubbed or patronized for that. It was rather the necessity for fuller, truer self-expression, the realization of the unwisdom of allowing social discrimination to segregate him mentally, and a counter-attitude to cramp and fetter his own living—and so the "spite-wall" that the intellectuals built over the "color-line" has happily been taken down. Much of this reopening of intellectual contacts has centered in New York and has been richly fruitful not merely in the enlarging of personal experience, but in the definite enrichment of American art and letters and in the clarifying of our common vision of the social tasks ahead.

The particular significance in the re-establishment of contact between the more advanced and representative classes is that it promises to offset some of the unfavorable reactions of the past, or at least to re-surface race contacts somewhat for the future. Subtly the conditions that are molding a New Negro are molding a new American attitude.

However, this new phase of things is delicate; it will call for less charity but more justice; less help, but infinitely closer understanding. This is indeed a critical stage of race relationships because of the likelihood, if the new temper is not understood, of engendering sharp group antagonism and a second crop of more calculated prejudice. In some quarters, it has already done so. Having weaned the Negro, public opinion cannot continue to paternalize. The Negro today is inevitably moving forward under the control largely of his own objectives. What are these objectives? Those of his outer life are happily already well and finally formulated, for they are none other than the ideals of American institutions and democracy. Those of his inner life are yet in process of formation, for the new psychology at present is more of a consensus of feeling than of opinion, of attitude rather than of program. Still some points seem to have crystallized.

Up to the present one may adequately describe the Negro's "inner objectives" as an attempt to repair a damaged group psychology and reshape a warped social perspective. Their realization has required a new mentality for the American Negro. And as it matures we begin to see its effects; at first, negative, iconoclastic, and then positive and constructive. In this new group psychology we note the lapse of sentimental appeal, then the development of a more positive self-respect and self-reliance; the repudiation of social dependence, and then the gradual recovery from hyper-sensitiveness and "touchy" nerves, the repudiation of the double standard of judgment with its special philanthropic allowances and then the sturdier desire for objective and scientific appraisal; and finally the rise from social disillusionment to race pride, from the sense of social debt to the responsibilities of social contribution, and offsetting the necessary working and commonsense acceptance of restricted conditions, the belief in ultimate esteem and recognition. Therefore the Negro to-day wishes to be known for what he is, even in his faults and shortcomings, and scorns a craven and precarious survival at the price of seeming to be what he is not. He resents being spoken of as a social ward or minor, even by his own, and to being regarded a chronic patient for the sociological clinic, the sick man of American Democracy. For the same reasons, he himself is through with those social nostrums and panaceas, the so-called "solutions" of his "problem," with which he and the country have been so liberally dosed in the past. Religion, freedom, education, money—in turn, he has ardently hoped for and peculiarly trusted these things; he still believes in them, but not in blind trust that they alone will solve his life-problem.

Each generation, however, will have its creed, and that of the present is the belief in the efficacy of collective effort, in race co-operation. This deep feeling of race is at present the mainspring of Negro life. It seems to be the outcome of the reaction to proscription and prejudice; an attempt, fairly successful on the whole, to convert a defensive into an offensive position, a handicap into a incentive. It is radical in tone, but not in purpose and only the most stupid forms of opposition, misunderstanding or persecution could make it otherwise. Of course, the thinking Negro has shifted a little toward the left with the world-trend, and there is an increasing group who affiliate with radical and liberal movements. But fundamentally for the present the Negro is radical on race matters, conservative on others, in other words, a "forced radical," a social protestant rather than a genuine radical. Yet under further pressure and injustice iconoclastic thought and motives will inevitably increase. Harlem's quixotic radicalisms call for their ounce of democracy to-day lest to-morrow they be beyond cure.

The Negro mind reaches out as yet to nothing but American wants, American ideas. But this forced attempt to build his Americanism on race values is a unique social experiment, and its ultimate success is impossible except through the fullest sharing of American culture and institutions. There should be no delusion about this. American nerves in sections unstrung with race hysteria are often fed the opiate that the trend of Negro advance is wholly separatist, and that the effect of its operation will be to encyst the Negro as a benign foreign body in the body politic. This cannot be—even if it were desirable. The racialism of the Negro is no limitation or reservation with respect to American life; it is only a constructive effort to build the obstructions in the stream of his progress into an efficient dam of social energy and power. Democracy itself is obstructed and stagnated to the extent that any of its channels are closed. Indeed they cannot be selectively closed. So the choice is not between one way for the Negro and another way for the rest, but between American institutions frustrated on the one hand and American ideals progressively fulfilled and realized on the other.

There is, of course, a warrantably comfortable feeling in being on the right side of the country's professed ideals. We realize that we cannot be undone without America's undoing. It is within the gamut of this attitude that the thinking Negro faces America, but with variations of mood that are if anything more significant than the attitude itself. Sometimes we have it taken with the defiant ironic challenge of McKay:

> Mine is the future grinding down to-day
> Like a great landslip moving to the sea,
> Bearing its freight of débris far away

Where the green hungry waters restlessly
Heave mammoth pyramids, and break and
roar
Their eerie challenge to the crumbling shore.

Sometimes, perhaps more frequently as yet, it is taken in the fervent and almost filial appeal and counsel of Weldon Johnson's:

O Southland, dear Southland!
Then why do you still cling
To an idle age and a musty page,
To a dead and useless thing?

But between defiance and appeal, midway almost between cynicism and hope, the prevailing mind stands in the mood of the same author's *To America*, an attitude of sober query and stoical challenge:

How would you have us, as we are?
Or sinking 'neath the load we bear,
Our eyes fixed forward on a star,
Or gazing empty at despair?

Rising or falling? Men or things?
With dragging pace or footsteps fleet?
Strong, willing sinews in your wings,
Or tightening chains about your feet?

More and more, however, an intelligent realization of the great discrepancy between the American social creed and the American social practice forces upon the Negro the taking of the moral advantage that is his. Only the steadying and sobering effect of a truly characteristic gentleness of spirit prevents the rapid rise of a definite cynicism and counter-hate and a defiant superiority feeling. Human as this reaction would be, the majority still deprecate its advent, and would gladly see it forestalled by the speedy amelioration of its causes. We wish our race pride to be a healthier, more positive achievement than a feeling based upon a realization of the shortcomings of others. But all paths toward the attainment of a sound social attitude have been difficult; only a relatively few enlightened minds have been able as the phrase puts it "to rise above" prejudice. The ordinary man has had until recently only a hard choice between the alternatives of supine and humiliating submission and stimulating but hurtful counter-prejudice. Fortunately from some inner, desperate resourcefulness has recently sprung up the simple expedient of fighting prejudice by mental passive resistance, in other words by trying to ignore it. For the few, this manna may perhaps be effective, but the masses cannot thrive upon it.

Fortunately there are constructive channels opening out into which the balked social feelings of the American Negro can flow freely.

Without them there would be much more pressure and danger than there is. These compensating interests are racial but in a new and enlarged way. One is the consciousness of acting as the advance-guard of the African peoples in their contact with Twentieth Century civilization; the other, the sense of a mission of rehabilitating the race in world esteem from that loss of prestige for which the fate and conditions of slavery have so largely been responsible. Harlem, as we shall see, is the center of both these movements; she is the home of the Negro's "Zionism." The pulse of the Negro world has begun to beat in Harlem. A Negro newspaper carrying news material in English, French and Spanish, gathered from all quarters of America, the West Indies and Africa has maintained itself in Harlem for over five years. Two important magazines, both edited from New York, maintain their news and circulation consistently on a cosmopolitan scale. Under American auspices and backing, three pan-African congresses have been held abroad for the discussion of common interests, colonial questions and the future co-operative development of Africa. In terms of the race question as a world problem, the Negro mind has leapt, so to speak, upon the parapets of prejudice and extended its cramped horizons. In so doing it has linked up with the growing group consciousness of the dark-peoples and is gradually learning their common interests. As one of our writers has recently put it: "It is imperative that we understand the white world in its relations to the non-white world." As with the Jew, persecution is making the Negro international.

As a world phenomenon this wider race consciousness is a different thing from the much asserted rising tide of color. Its inevitable causes are not of our making. The consequences are not necessarily damaging to the best interests of civilization. Whether it actually brings into being new Armadas of conflict or argosies of cultural exchange and enlightenment can only be decided by the attitude of the dominant races in an era of critical change. With the American Negro, his new internationalism is primarily an effort to recapture contact with the scattered peoples of African derivation. Garveyism may be a transient, if spectacular, phenomenon, but the possible rôle of the American Negro in the future development of Africa is one of the most constructive and universally helpful missions that any modern people can lay claim to.

Constructive participation in such causes cannot help giving the Negro valuable group incentives, as well as increased prestige at home and abroad. Our greatest rehabilitation may possibly come through such channels, but for the present, more immediate hope rests in the revaluation by white and black alike of the Negro in terms of his artistic endowments and cultural contributions, past and prospective. It must be increasingly recognized that the Negro has already made very substantial contributions, not only in his folk-art, music especially, which has always found appreciation, but in larger, though humbler and less acknowledged ways. For generations the Negro has been the peasant matrix of that section of America which has most undervalued him, and here he has contributed not only materially in labor and in social patience, but spiritually as well. The South has unconsciously absorbed the gift of his folk-temperament. In less than half a generation it will be easier to recognize this, but the fact remains that a leaven of humor, sentiment, imagination and tropic nonchalance has gone into the making of the South from a humble, unacknowledged source. A second crop of the Negro's gifts promises still more largely. He now becomes a conscious contributor and lays aside the status of a beneficiary and ward for that of a collaborator and participant in American civilization. The great social gain in this is the releasing of our talented group from the arid fields of controversy and debate to the productive fields of creative expression. The especially cultural recognition they win should in turn prove the key to that revaluation of the Negro which must precede or accompany any considerable further betterment of race relationships. But whatever the general effect, the present generation will have added the motives of self-expression and spiritual development to the old and still unfinished task of making material headway and progress. No one who understandingly faces the situation with its substantial accomplishment or views the new scene with its still more abundant promise can be entirely without hope. And certainly, if in our lifetime the Negro should not be able to celebrate his full initiation into American democracy, he can at least, on the warrant of these things, celebrate the attainment of a significant and satisfying new phase of group development, and with it a spiritual Coming of Age.

Response: Voices of the Harlem Renaissance

Poets

JAMES WELDON JOHNSON

(1871–1938)

James Weldon Johnson's literary career spanned the period preceding the Harlem Renaissance, flourished through it, and expanded into the 1930s. A cosmopolitan statesman competent in a variety of professions, Johnson earned accolades as a songwriter, diplomat, novelist, poet, anthologist, and activist. From his early training as a lawyer in Florida to his final days as field secretary of the NAACP, Johnson had a hand in shaping the organizations and movements in which he was involved. Author of "Lift Every Voice and Sing," which is commonly referred to as "the Negro National Anthem," Johnson further showed race pride by collecting and compiling two books of spirituals, writing poems celebrating African American history, and encouraging younger writers to find more expansive forms than dialect in which to portray the complexity of black American experience.

Johnson was born in Jacksonville, Florida, on June 17, 1871, to James and Helen Louise Dillet Johnson. His father was a New Yorker, and his mother had immigrated from Nassau in the Bahamas. The couple met in New York and returned to Nassau to get married. When economic conditions forced them to move, they settled in Jacksonville, where James and his younger brother, John Rosamond, were born. The elder Johnson was a self-educated man and instilled in young James an appreciation for independence and hard work, attributes that were visible throughout Johnson's life. His mother, the first black woman public school teacher in Florida, inspired his artistic pursuits. He learned to read early on and to play the piano.

Johnson attended the Stanton School in Jacksonville, where his mother taught, until the eighth grade, which was as far as that school went. He then attended Atlanta University's preparatory school and received his A.B. in 1894 from the college division. During the summers, Johnson explored the rural area in Georgia, gathering valuable experience for his understanding of the folk, who were very unlike the people he had known in his middle-class background. For two summers, he taught at a rural black school near Hampton, Georgia. He also traveled to Chicago for the Columbian Exposition in 1893, where he heard Frederick Douglass deliver a speech and Paul Laurence Dunbar read from his poetry. It was Dunbar who influenced Johnson's early attempts at dialect poetry.

From Atlanta, Johnson went to the Northeast to help raise money for Atlanta University. He was a member of a singing quartet, perhaps fashioned after the fundraising Jubilee Singers of Fisk University. Through this venture, he also increased his interest in indigenous African American music. Upon his return to Florida, he served as principal of the Stanton School, adding ninth- and tenth-grade courses to the curriculum. He also studied law, and although no black person had ever been admitted to the Florida bar, he passed the exam after a year and a half of study—in spite of the rigor of the test and the obvious hostility of the examiners. He founded and edited a newspaper, the *Daily American* (1895–1896), before joining his brother in songwriting ventures in the late 1890s. Although they did not initially achieve the New York success they anticipated, they did meet the famous performing artists of the day, such as Bert Williams, George Walker, and Ernest Hogan, and were inspired to continue their efforts. It was in New York in 1900 that Johnson wrote the words to "Lift Every Voice and Sing," which received the Lewis Carroll Shelf Award in 1971. Johnson's songwriting successes with his brother and Bob Cole ended when he was appointed to a diplomatic post in Puerto Cabello, Venezuela.

His stay there began in 1906 and enabled him to proceed with a variety of literary projects, including poems and a novel. During the tenure of his next consular position in Corinto, Nicaragua, he returned to New York in 1910 to marry Grace Nail, the daughter of a New York tavern owner and real estate broker. He was back in Nicaragua when *The Autobiography of an Ex-Colored Man* was published anonymously in 1912; the book examines the then-current theme of lighter-skinned blacks passing for white. In a strikingly detached manner, an anonymous narrator relates his adventures as as the mixed-blood son of a mulatto woman and her southern white lover. His adventures read like a scenario of African American social life during the period (including speakeasy scenes, cakewalks, ragtime, and college life), as well as some interesting scenes in a cigar factory in Florida and travel in various countries in Europe where the narrator, an accomplished musician, is paid to perform for his rich, equally anonymous millionaire benefactor. Returning to the United States, Johnson published *Fifty Years and Other Poems* (1917), the title poem of which chronicled the contributions of black people to American culture in the relatively short time since their emancipation. The volume also contained poems in the manner of Dunbar's famous dialect poetry, but they were not as well executed as those of Dunbar.

It was also around this time that W.E.B. Du Bois and Joel Spingarn approached Johnson about attending a conference sponsored by the NAACP. Shortly thereafter, in December 1916, Spingarn asked Johnson to become field secretary of the NAACP. He accepted and began traveling around the country in the capacity that would enable him to witness the church gatherings and sermons that inspired *God's Trombones.* Between his inspiration and publication of the volume in 1927, however, Johnson paused to edit *The Book of American Negro Poetry* in 1922. It introduced relatively unknown young writers, such as Claude McKay, to the larger public; Harlem Renaissance poets too young to be included in the 1922 edition, such as Langston Hughes, Countee Cullen, and Arna Bontemps, would appear in the revised and enlarged edition in 1931. The volume also is important for its introduction; it has become a classic statement on the use of dialect by African American poets and a pointing of the way to what Johnson considered more productive approaches. He was certain that any great people are measured by the art they create, and he was convinced that there was talent enough among African American poets to reach higher heights. Johnson's second and third edited volumes, *The Book of American Negro Spirituals* (1925) and *The Second Book of American Negro Spirituals* (1926) continued his interest in preserving African American cultural forms and respecting the persons who had created those forms, many of which he had learned to admire during his travels through African American communities in the United States. The 1927 publication of *God's Trombones*—a prayer and seven sermons in the folk tradition—marked the culmination of a long-standing interest Johnson had in poetry, innovative literary traditions, and African American folk forms.

Johnson accepted a fellowship from the Rosenwald Fund in 1929 and, instead of returning to his NAACP position, resigned from it in 1930. He then became Adam K. Spence Chair of Creative Literature at Fisk University, which provided him time for the several writing projects he completed in the 1930s. The academic community also had recognized Johnson in the number of honorary degrees he received, including ones from Atlanta University (A.M., 1904), Talladega College (Litt.D., 1917), and Howard University (Litt.D., 1923).

In the early to mid-1930s, Johnson published *St. Peter Relates an Incident of the Resurrection Day* (1930; 1935)*; a version of his selected poems; a history of African Americans in New York titled *Black Manhattan* (1930); and *Along This Way* (1933), his autobiography. It is rumored that Johnson wrote his own autobiography in self-defense against those who continued to believe that *The Autobiography of an Ex-Colored Man* was a factual instead of a fictional work. Johnson's final book, *Negro Americans, What Now?* (1934) offers speculation on the future of black Americans, especially in relation to the racial problem.

On June 26, 1938, Johnson died in an automobile collision with a train as he was on his way to his summer home in Maine. From his broad vantage points of poet, novelist, historian, songwriter, cultural observer, national administrator, diplomat, activist, principal, and professor, Johnson chronicled a transitional period for African Americans—from the deprivations of the nineteenth century to the politically aware and creative bursts of the Harlem Renaissance. His full life reflects the fullness of the period in which his talents came to fruition.

❖❖❖

Johnson's biographer is Eugene Levy, who published *James Weldon Johnson: Black Leader, Black Voice* in 1973. Johnson's works have received fairly consistent attention in a number of standard works on African American literature. Following is a selection of those works. Houston A. Baker, Jr., "A Forgotten Prototype: *The Autobiography of an Ex-Colored and Invisible Man*," *Virginia Quarterly Review* 49 (Summer 1973); Robert A. Bone, *The Negro Novel in America* (1965); Richard A. Carroll, "Black Racial Spirit: An Analysis of James Weldon Johnson's Critical Perspective," *Phylon* 32 (Winter 1971); Eugenia Collier, "The Endless Journey of an Ex-Coloured Man," *Phylon* 32 (Winter 1971); Robert E. Fleming, "Contemporary Themes in Johnson's *Autobiography of an Ex-Coloured Man*," *Negro American Literature Forum* 4 (Winter 1970); Fleming, "Irony as a Key to Johnson's *The Autobiography of an Ex-Coloured Man*," *American Literature* 43 (March 1971); Fleming, *James Weldon Johnson and Arna Wendell Bontemps: A Reference Guide* (1978); Marvin P. Garrett, "Early Recollections and Structural Irony in *The Autobiography of an Ex-Coloured Man*," *Critique: Studies in Modern Fiction* 13 (December 1971); Richard A. Long, "A

*Privately printed in 1930, by Viking in 1935.

Weapon of My Song: The Poetry of James Weldon Johnson," *Phylon* 32 (Winter 1971); Louis D. Rubin, Jr., "The Search for a Language, 1746–1923," in *Black Poetry in America: Two Essays in Historical Interpretation*, Louis D. Rubin, Jr., and Blyden Jackson (1974); Robert B. Stepto, *From Behind the Veil: A Study of Afro-American Narrative* (1979); Jean Wagner, *Black Poets of the United States: From Paul Laurence Dunbar to Langston Hughes* (1973); Wendell Phillips Whalum, "James Weldon Johnson's *Theories and Performance Practices of Afro-American Folksongs*," *Phylon* 32 (Winter 1971). The papers of James Weldon Johnson are included in the James Weldon Johnson Collection of Negro Arts and Letters in the Beinecke Library of Yale University.

Preface

FROM THE BOOK OF AMERICAN NEGRO POETRY

A people may become great through many means, but there is only one measure by which its greatness is recognized and acknowledged. The final measure of the greatness of all peoples is the amount and standard of the literature and art they have produced. The world does not know that a people is great until that people produces great literature and art. No people that has produced great literature and art has ever been looked upon by the world as distinctly inferior.

The status of the Negro in the United States is more a question of national mental attitude toward the race than of actual conditions. And nothing will do more to change that mental attitude and raise his status than a demonstration of intellectual parity by the Negro through the production of literature and art.

Is there likelihood that the American Negro will be able to do this? There is, for the good reason that he possesses the innate powers. He has the emotional endowment, the originality and artistic conception, and, what is more important, the power of creating that which has universal appeal and influence.

I make here what may appear to be a more startling statement by saying that the Negro has already proved the possession of these powers by being the creator of the only things artistic that have yet sprung from American soil and been universally acknowledged as distinctive American products.

These creations by the American Negro may be summed up under four heads. The first two are the Uncle Remus stories, which were collected by Joel Chandler Harris, and the "spirituals" or slave songs, to which the Fisk Jubilee Singers made the public and the musicians of both the United States and Europe listen. The Uncle Remus stories constitute the greatest body of folklore that America has produced, and the "spirituals" the greatest body of folk-song. I shall speak of the "spirituals" later because they are more than folk-songs, for in them the Negro sounded the depths, if he did not scale the heights, of music.

❖❖❖

It may be surprising to many to see how little of the poetry being written by Negro poets to-day is being written in Negro dialect. The newer Negro poets show a tendency to discard dialect; much of the subject-matter which went into the making of traditional dialect poetry, 'possums, watermelons, etc., they have discarded altogether, at least, as poetic material. This tendency will, no doubt, be regretted by the majority of white readers; and, indeed, it would be a distinct loss if the American Negro poets threw away this quaint and musical folk-speech as a medium of expression. And yet, after all, these poets are working through a problem not realized by the reader, and, perhaps, by many of these poets themselves not realized consciously. They are trying to break away from, not Negro dialect itself, but the limitations on Negro dialect imposed by the fixing effects of long convention.

The Negro in the United States has achieved or been placed in a certain artistic niche. When he is thought of artistically, it is as a happy-go-lucky, singing, shuffling, banjo-picking being or as a more or less pathetic figure. The picture of him is in a log cabin amid fields of cotton or along the levees. Negro dialect is naturally and by long association the exact instrument for voicing this phase of Negro life; and by that very exactness it is an instrument with but two full stops, humor and pathos. So even when he confines himself to purely racial themes, the Aframerican poet realizes that there are phases of Negro life in the United States which cannot be treated in the dialect either adequately or artistically. Take, for example, the phases rising out of life in Harlem, that most wonderful Negro city in the world. I do not deny that a Negro in a log cabin is more picturesque than a Negro in a Harlem flat, but the Negro in the Harlem flat is here, and he is but part of a group growing everywhere in the country, a group whose ideals are becoming increasingly more vital than those of the traditionally artistic group, even if its members are less picturesque.

What the colored poet in the United States needs to do is something like what Synge did for the Irish; he needs to find a form that will express the racial spirit by symbols from within rather than by symbols from without, such as the mere mutilation of English spelling and pronunciation. He needs a form that is freer and larger than dialect, but which will still hold the racial flavor; a form expressing the imagery, the idioms, the peculiar turns of thought, and the distinctive humor and pathos, too, of the Negro, but which will also be capable of voicing the deepest and highest emotions and aspirations, and allow of the widest range of subjects and the widest scope of treatment.

Negro dialect is at present a medium that is not capable of giving expression to the varied conditions of Negro life in America, and much less is it capable of giving the fullest interpretation of Negro character and psychology. This is no indictment against the dialect as dialect, but against the mould of convention in which Negro dialect in the United States has been set. In time these conventions may become lost, and the colored poet in the United States may sit down to write in dialect without feeling that his first line will put the general reader in a frame of mind which demands that the poem be humorous or pathetic. In the meantime, there is no reason why these poets should not continue to do the beautiful things that can be done, and done best, in the dialect.

In stating the need for Aframerican poets in the United States to work out a new and distinctive form of expression I do not wish to be understood to hold any theory that they should limit themselves to Negro poetry, to racial themes; the sooner they are able to write *American* poetry spontaneously, the better. Nevertheless, I believe that the richest contribution the Negro poet can make to the American literature of the future will be the fusion into it of his own individual artistic gifts.

❖❖❖

O Black and Unknown Bards

O black and unknown bards of long ago,
How came your lips to touch the sacred fire?
How, in your darkness, did you come to know
The power and beauty of the minstrel's lyre?
Who first from midst his bonds lifted his eyes?
Who first from out the still watch, lone and long,
Feeling the ancient faith of prophets rise
Within his dark-kept soul, burst into song?

Heart of what slave poured out such melody
As "Steal away to Jesus"? On its strains
His spirit must have nightly floated free,
Though still about his hands he felt his chains.
Who heard great "Jordan roll"? Whose starward eye
Saw chariot "swing low"? And who was he
That breathed that comforting, melodic sigh,
"Nobody knows de trouble I see"?

What merely living clod, what captive thing,
Could up toward God through all its darkness grope,
And find within its deadened heart to sing
These songs of sorrow, love and faith, and hope?
How did it catch that subtle undertone,
That note in music heard not with the ears?
How sound the elusive reed so seldom blown,
Which stirs the soul or melts the heart to tears.

Not that great German master in his dream
Of harmonies that thundered amongst the stars
At the creation, ever heard a theme
Nobler than "Go down, Moses." Mark its bars
How like a mighty trumpet-call they stir
The blood. Such are the notes that men have sung
Going to valorous deeds; such tones there were
That helped make history when Time was young.

There is a wide, wide wonder in it all,
That from degraded rest and servile toil
The fiery spirit of the seer should call
These simple children of the sun and soil.
O black slave singers, gone, forgot, unfamed,
You—you alone, of all the long, long line
Of those who've sung untaught, unknown, unnamed,
Have stretched out upward, seeking the divine.

You sang not deeds of heroes or of kings;
No chant of bloody war, no exulting paean
Of arms-won triumphs; but your humble strings
You touched in chord with music empyrean.
You sang far better than you knew; the songs
That for your listeners' hungry hearts sufficed
Still live,—but more than this to you belongs:
You sang a race from wood and stone to Christ.

The White Witch

O brothers mine, take care! Take care!
The great white witch rides out tonight,
Trust not your prowess nor your strength;

Your only safety lies in flight;
For in her glance there is a snare,
And in her smile there is a blight.

The great white witch you have not seen?
Then, younger brothers mine, forsooth,
Like nursery children you have looked
For ancient hag and snaggle-tooth;
But no, not so; the witch appears
In all the glowing charms of youth.

Her lips are like carnations red,
Her face like new-born lilies fair,
Her eyes like ocean waters blue,
She moves with subtle grace and air,
And all about her head there floats
The golden glory of her hair.

But though she always thus appears
In form of youth and mood of mirth,
Unnumbered centuries are hers,
The infant planets saw her birth;
The child of throbbing Life is she,
Twin sister to the greedy earth.

And back behind those smiling lips,
And down within those laughing eyes,
And underneath the soft caress
Of hand and voice and purring sighs,
The shadow of the panther lurks,
The spirit of the vampire lies.

For I have seen the great white witch,
And she has led me to her lair,
And I have kissed her red, red lips
And cruel face so white and fair;
Around me she has twined her arms,
And bound me with her yellow hair.

I felt those red lips burn and sear
My body like a living coal;
Obeyed the power of those eyes
As the needle trembles to the pole;
And did not care although I felt
The strength go ebbing from my soul.

Oh! she has seen your strong young limbs,
And heard your laughter loud and gay,
And in your voices she has caught
The echo of a far-off day,
When man was closer to the earth;
And she has marked you for her prey.

She feels the old Antæan strength
In you, the great dynamic beat
Of primal passions, and she sees
In you the last besieged retreat
Of love relentless, lusty, fierce,
Love pain-ecstatic, cruel-sweet.

O, brothers mine, take care! Take care!
The great white witch rides out tonight.
O, younger brothers mine, beware!
Look not upon her beauty bright;
For in her glance there is a snare,
And in her smile there is a blight.

Fragment

The hand of Fate cannot be stayed,
The course of Fate cannot be steered,
By all the gods that man has made,
Nor all the devils he has feared,
Not by the prayers that might be prayed
In all the temples he has reared.

See! In your very midst there dwell
Ten thousand thousand blacks, a wedge
Forged in the furnaces of hell,
And sharpened to a cruel edge
By wrong and by injustice fell,
And driven by hatred as a sledge.

'Tis fixed—for them that violate
The eternal laws, naught shall avail
Till they their error expiate;
Nor shall their unborn children fail
To pay the full required weight
Into God's great, unerring scale.

A wedge so slender at the start—
Just twenty slaves in shackles bound—
And yet which split the land apart
With shrieks of war and battle sound,
Which pierced the nation's very heart,
And still lies cankering in the wound.

Not all the glory of your pride,
Preserved in story and in song,
Can from the judging future hide,
Through all the coming ages long,
That though you bravely fought and died,
You fought and died for what was wrong.

Think not repentance can redeem,
That sin his wages can withdraw;
No, think as well to change the scheme
Of worlds that move in reverent awe;
Forgiveness is an idle dream,
God is not love, no, God is law.

ANNE SPENCER
(1882–1975)

Anne Spencer is known for two things: her poetry and her garden in Lynchburg, Virginia. Her garden has become as much an emblem of the kind of poetry she wrote as a physical space. Although much of her poetry was not published during her lifetime, it marks her as one of the many women who were busy writing during the Harlem Renaissance. Her home in Lynchburg was a way station for African Americans traveling from the North and East, especially the Washington, D.C., area, into places farther south such as Atlanta. She was host to such luminaries as James Weldon Johnson (who encouraged her to publish the few poems that she did during the 1920s), Paul Robeson, Langston Hughes, W.E.B. Du Bois, and many others. While putting her philosophy into social action, Spencer earned a reputation in Lynchburg as a "crazy" woman who would stand up to whites who infringed on her rights and those of her fellow black citizens.

Anne Spencer was born Annie Bethel Scales Bannister on February 6, 1882, to Sarah Louise Scales and Joel Cephus Bannister of Henry County, Virginia. The only child of ambitious parents with different notions of how to achieve their objectives, young Anne witnessed the disagreements that led to her parents' separation in 1887. She and her mother moved to Bramwell, West Virginia, where Anne was placed in a foster home while Sarah worked as a cook in the restaurant of a local inn. With no black children her age in the town, Anne sometimes had friendly contact with a young white girl, but she spent most of her time either with adults or alone. It was only in 1893, at her father's insistence, that Anne was enrolled formally in Virginia Seminary, a boarding school for blacks in Lynchburg.

She began writing at the age of fourteen, partly to cope with the new frustration of being the youngest student in the seminary, combined with the attendant problems of precocity and adolescence. She graduated at the top of her class in 1899 and returned to Bramwell to teach public school for two years. She married Edward Alexander Spencer on May 15, 1901, and moved to Lynchburg. The couple had three children. Understanding his wife's creative urges and need for private space, Edward Spencer hired housekeepers to free her from the burdens of housewife and mother, and he built a garden for her at the back of the house that contained a one-room cottage. It was here that Spencer did most of her reading and writing.

Although she did not publish a poem until she was thirty-eight, she had written hundreds by that time, usually on scraps of paper, in the margins of books, or on paper bags. It was James Weldon Johnson, traveling in his role with the NAACP and staying over with the Spencers, who encouraged Spencer to publish her first poem.

"Before the Feast at Shushan" appeared in the February 1920 issue of *The Crisis* magazine. It is reminiscent of Frances Harper's poem "Vashti" in its subtle, feminist message: the Old Testament King Ahasuerus resists his wife's (Vashti's) attempts to establish an egalitarian relationship with him. Five of Spencer's poems were included in the 1922 edition of Johnson's *The Book of American Negro Poetry.* The poems focus on women in society, especially their potential rejection of stereotypical roles. In 1923, *The Crisis* published "White Things," a poem that Spencer had refused to revise to the specifications of editors who considered it too unorthodox in its treatment of racial conflict; it is one of her few protest poems.

Spencer used her newfound reputation as a published poet to enhance her fight for justice in Lynchburg. When she applied for a job as a librarian at the all-white Jones Memorial Library in Lynchburg in 1923, she used her knowledge of books to offset her lack of formal training. She succeeded in being hired to head a branch library to be housed in Dunbar High School; she held that position for more than twenty years. In 1927, Countee Cullen anthologized ten of Spencer's poems in *Caroling Dusk,* the most to appear in print during her lifetime. With images of her garden and nature as prominent touchstones, the poems focus on friendship, human relations, and the personal rights of women. The same year, Charles S. Johnson published her poem "Letter to My Sister" in his anthology *Ebony and Topaz.* With the beginning lines "It is dangerous for a woman to defy the gods; / To taunt them with the tongue's thin tip," the poem goes on to explore through veiled imagery and language the social restrictions placed on women.

Of the many artists and writers who visited the Spencer home, and of the many whom the Spencers came to know during their travels to New York, Washington, D.C., and elsewhere, none mattered more to Anne than James Weldon Johnson. She attributed to him the expansion of her intellectual and creative worlds. When he died in an automobile accident in Maine in 1938, she penned "For Jim, Easter Eve" as a tribute to him. It was the only other poem she allowed to be published during her lifetime. An extensive selection of her poems was made available in 1977, two years after her death, with the publication of J. Lee Greene's *Time's Unfading Garden.*

After her husband died in 1964, the garden declined, as Spencer withdrew increasingly from it as well as from social interactions. She turned her attention to reading history and, following the advice of her friends from earlier years, to writing prose. Although she never completed the novel she began, she did finish several social and political essays. Turning back to poetry in 1969, she completed research for a lengthy poem about John Brown. Poor health did not allow her to conclude "A Dream of John Brown," which she wrote off and on between 1971 and 1974. During this same period, she also worked on revising her earlier poems, apparently in preparation for a collection of her poetry. The project remained unfinished at her death in 1975.

❖❖❖

J. Lee Greene's *Time's Unfading Garden: Anne Spencer's Life and Poetry* (1977) is the authoritative source on Spencer. Other excellent, but brief, analyses of her verse appear in Maureen Honey's *Shadowed Dreams: Women's Poetry of the Harlem*

Renaissance (1989) and Gloria T. Hull's "Black Women Poets from Wheatley to Walker" in *Sturdy Black Bridges,* ed. Roseann P. Bell et al. (1970).

Before the Feast at Shushan

Garden of Shushan!
After Eden, all terrace, pool, and flower recollect thee:
Ye weaves in saffron and haze and Tyrian purple,
Tell yet what range in color wakes the eye;
Sorcerer, release the dreams born here when
Drowsy, shifting palm-shade enspells the brain;
And sound! ye with harp and flute ne'er essay
Before these star-noted birds escaped from paradise awhile to
Stir all dark, and dear, and passionate desire, till mine
Arms go out to be mocked by the softly kissing body of the wind—
Slave, send Vashti to her King!

The fiery wattles of the sun startle into flame
The marbled towers of Shushan:
So at each day's wane, two peers—the one in
Heaven, the other on earth—welcome with their
Splendor the peerless beauty of the Queen.

Cushioned at the Queen's feet and upon her knee
Finding glory for mine head,—still, nearly shamed
Am I, the King, to bend and kiss with sharp
Breath the olive-pink of sandaled toes between;
Or lift me high to the magnet of a gaze, dusky,
Like the pool when but the moon-ray strikes to its depth;
Or closer press to crush a grape 'gainst lips redder
Than the grape, a rose in the night of her hair;
Then—Sharon's Rose in my arms.

And I am hard to force the petals wide;
And you are fast to suffer and be sad.
Is any prophet come to teach a new thing
Now in a more apt time?
Have him 'maze how you say love is sacrament;
How, says Vashti, love is both bread and wine;
How to the altar may not come to break and drink,
Hulky flesh nor fleshly spirit!
I, thy lord, like not manna for meat as a Judahn;
I, thy master, drink, and red wine, plenty, and when
I thirst. Eat meat, and full, when I hunger.
I, thy King, teach you and leave you, when I list.
No woman in all Persia sets out strange action
To confuse Persia's lord—
Love is but desire and thy purpose fulfillment;
I, thy King, so say!

White Things

Most things are colorful things—the sky, earth, and sea.
  Black men are most men; but the white are free!
White things are rare things; so rare, so rare
They stole from out a silvered world—somewhere.
Finding earth-plains fair plains, save greenly grassed,
They strewed white feathers of cowardice, as they passed;
  The golden stars with lances fine,
  The hills all red and darkened pine,
They blanched with their wand of power;
And turned the blood in a ruby rose
To a poor white poppy-flower.

They pyred a race of black, black men,
And burned them to ashes white; then,
Laughing, a young one claimed a skull,
For the skull of a black is white, not dull,
  But a glistening awful thing
  Made, it seems, for this ghoul to swing
In the face of God with all his might,
And swear by the hell that sired him:
  "Man-maker, make white!"

Lady, Lady

Lady, Lady, I saw your face,
Dark as night withholding a star . . .
The chisel fell, or it might have been
You had borne so long the yoke of men.
Lady, Lady, I saw your hands,
Twisted, awry, like crumpled roots,
Bleached poor white in a sudsy tub,
Wrinkled and drawn from your rub-a-dub.
Lady, Lady, I saw your heart,
And altared there in its darksome place
Were the tongues of flames the ancients knew,
Where the good God sits to spangle through.

Letter to My Sister

It is dangerous for a woman to defy the gods;
To taunt them with the tongue's thin tip,
Or strut in the weakness of mere humanity,
Or draw a line daring them to cross;
The gods own the searing lightning,
The drowning waters, tormenting fears
And anger of red sins.

Oh, but worse still if you mince timidly—
Dodge this way or that, or kneel or pray,
Be kind, or sweat agony drops
Or lay your quick body over your feeble young;
If you have beauty or none, if celibate
Or vowed—the gods are Juggernaut,
Passing over . . . over . . .

This you may do:
Lock your heart, then, quietly,
And lest they peer within,
Light no lamp when dark comes down
Raise no shade for sun;
Breathless must your breath come through
If you'd die and dare deny
The gods their god-like fun.

[God never planted a garden]

God never planted a garden
But He placed a keeper there
And the keeper ever razed the ground
And built a city where
God cannot walk at the eve of day,
Nor take the morning air.

CLAUDE MCKAY
(1889–1948)

Claude McKay, autobiographer, novelist, essayist, journalist, and muse, wrote memorable poetry during the Harlem Renaissance. But like the Harlem Dancer in his poetic world, he escaped from Harlem both as place and time. Of his fifty-nine years, he spent twenty-three in his native Jamaica before emigrating to the United States in 1912. He also spent eleven years in northwest Africa and in several European countries. Of three significant West Indian internationals—Marcus Garvey (1887–1940), Claude McKay (1889–1948), and Eric Walrond (1898–1966)—McKay alone seemed to have tried to avoid dying in London. Perhaps he was the most African American.

Early on, he wrote dialect verse about the nature of the peasantry in Jamaica and America. More perhaps than any other black poet of his time, he converted angry protest into a poetry of enduring art. With W.E.B. Du Bois, James Weldon Johnson, Alice Dunbar-Nelson, Jean Toomer, and Nella Larsen, McKay created moments of intensely personal epiphany, of psychological complexity. He was a precursor of African American modernism, the ironic reconciliation of conflicting tensions within our devastating cities; yet he had a courageous spirit to seek out brave new worlds.

As a major impetus for the Harlem Renaissance, he helped set the tone for the Civil Rights Movement after World Wars I and II. What he sought most was to preserve the dignity of a black folk identity in an alienating world. His most popular themes include those of nostalgia and longing for his tropical homeland; testing of the individual spirit in the city; ambivalence toward racial opportunity and challenge in the United States; and reassessment of Africa as a realistic and cultural resource with a starker realism than any portrayed in the poetry of either Langston Hughes or Countee Cullen.

Festus Claudius McKay, who sometimes wrote under the pseudonym Eli Edwards, was born in the hills of Jamaica on September 15, 1889, to Thomas Francis and Ann Elisabeth Edwards Kennedy, peasant farmers with a sense of racial pride. As the youngest of eleven children, he spent his childhood near the cliffs of Clarendon Parish. Sometimes his father told him folktales about Africa and the story of a grandfather's enslavement. McKay developed a habit of free and independent thought from listening to his brother, who was a schoolteacher and passionate agnostic.

In 1907, McKay left his rural home to apprentice as a woodworker in Brown's Town and met Walter Jekyl, an English linguist who specialized in Jamaican folklore. Introducing the young man to British writers such as John Milton, Alexander Pope, and Percy Bysshe Shelley, Jekyl was one of the first people to encourage McKay to write poetry in the Jamaican dialect. By 1909, McKay had moved to Kingston, the capital of Jamaica, to serve as constable. Whereas his hometown of Sunny Ville had been primarily black, the predominantly white Kingston evinced a caste society based on degrees of color. By 1912, McKay had published both *Songs of Jamaica* and *Constab Ballads,* lyrical collections in the Jamaican vernacular. After coming to the United States to study agriculture initially at Tuskegee Institute in Alabama in 1912 and eventually at Kansas State College, he ended his studies in 1914 to facilitate a move to New York City. There he developed strong ties with Max Eastman, editor of the Communist magazine *The Liberator,* in which the now-renowned poem "If We Must Die" first appeared in 1919.

In 1920, McKay traveled to London and read Karl Marx during completion of assignments for *Worker's Dreadnought,* a leftist periodical edited by Sylvia Pankhurst. As an apprentice in practical journalism, he had published *Harlem Shadows* (1922), with an introduction by Eastman, in the year that T. S. Eliot published *The Waste Land* and James Joyce published *Ulysses,* though even his socialist inclinations had not given him radical freedom of literary form and thought. The same year, he traveled to the Soviet Union as a representative for the American Worker's Party, while taking a personal odyssey through Europe during his "internationalist" phase. From 1923 to 1934, he wandered from France to Spain to Morocco. The next year, he found work as a nude model in Paris until he took sick with pneumonia. Uncomfortable with Euramerican expatriates in Paris such as Ernest Hemingway, James Joyce, and Gertrude Stein, he left for Marseilles, where he lived until 1934, when he returned to the United States. In 1938, he met his friend Ellen Tarry, a Roman Catholic, and converted to her faith.

McKay completed his first novel in 1925, but he threw it in the trash. During the zenith of the Harlem Renaissance, he had the novels *Home to Harlem* (1928), *Banjo: a Story without a Plot* (1929), and *Banana Bottom* (1933) published while still abroad. His first book of fiction, which appeared during his sixth year of expatriation from America, incited a debate among black intellectuals about primitivism as a subject. In this book, he writes about the adventures of Jake, a noble savage seeking a lost love, even as *Banjo* would present an African American musician as a primitive hero in "the Ditch," a slum of Marseilles, France. While many of the Old Guard asserted that the book pandered to the American mainstream needs for "Negro exoticism," McKay's peers often agreed with Langston Hughes that the book was passionately alive. In *Banana Bottom,* possibly his most successful work of fiction, Bita Plant, the female counterpart to Jake, rejects her Christian training to rediscover herself as a vibrant primitive in the Caribbean islands. Evidently, the author was writing in fiction a theory that proved unlivable in his own world.

Some critics say that McKay's career can be divided into four stages. The first, or most "provincial," of these stages encompasses his first two books, *Songs of Jamaica* (1912) and *Constab Ballads* (1912). The second, or urban, phase includes *Home to Harlem* (1928) and *Banjo* (1929). The stories in *Gingertown* (1932) would be included in this group. The subsequent pastoral phase includes his autobiography, *A Long Way from Home* (1937), and his sociological study *Harlem: Negro Metropolis* (1940). The final phase of his work appeared after he became involved with a Catholic community center in Harlem called Friendship House. In constantly failing health by the mid-forties, McKay died of heart failure in Chicago in 1948.

Perhaps no black poet has ever struggled with the perceived limits of black aesthetics more than McKay. He was one of the first to convert his hatred of the city into a resentment of evil, transforming negativity into a reaffirmation of the human spirit. Although he never resolved this irony in the discrete text, as did Jean Toomer, or in the experimental work ranging across half a century, as did Langston Hughes, he perceived an obvious conflict between African and Western cultures. Sometimes he seemed to forget that the distinction could almost never be absolute. His heroine Bita Plant never really had to choose between her marriage to a deviant minister and her personal salvation among the Jamaican peasantry. Through the sheer power of her self-definition, she could have transcended both experiences into new reaches of existence unlimited by racism and history. Although McKay possessed the greatness of African culture in theory, he sometimes failed to live it out in practice.

McKay was a radical conservative, an oxymoron. He explained his signature piece, "If We Must Die," as follows:

> This poem was written during the time of the Chicago race riots. I was then a train waiter in the service of the Pennsylvania Railroad. Our dining car was running between New York, Philadelphia and Pittsburgh, Harrisburg and Washington and I remember we waiters and cooks carried revolvers in secret and always kept together going from our quarters to the railroad yards, as a precaution against sudden attack. The poem was an outgrowth of the intense emotional experience I was living through (no doubt with thousands of other Negroes) in those days. It appeared in the radical magazine the *Liberator,* and was widely reprinted in the Negro press. Later it was included in my book of poetry *Harlem Shadows.* At the time I was writing a great deal of lyric poetry and none of my colleagues on the *Liberator* considered me a propaganda poet who could reel off revolutionary poetry like an automatic machine cutting fixed patterns. If we were a rebel group because we had faith that human life might be richer, by the same token we believed in the highest standards of creative work.

William S. Braithwaite, the so-called dean of Negro critics, labeled McKay an angry and violent propagandist. Others thought that he was too vituperative as well.

As a traditionalist, McKay represented Jamaican peasants with their "primitive joys." But in an essay for the *New York Herald Tribune Books* in 1932, he wrote of race neutrality that has not yet emerged nearly half a century after his death and will probably not happen by the year 2000:

> The time when a writer will stick only to the safe old ground of his own class of people is undoubtedly passing. Especially in America, where all the peoples of the world are scrambling side by side and modern machines and the ramifications of international commerce are steadily breaking down the ethnological barriers that separate the peoples of the world.

What McKay overlooked was that personal rituals of consciousness and memory, as well as the material causes of inequity—class, gender, and race—could all keep the old order entrenched. In fact, many of the apparent limits of provinciality are only perceived ones. As a poet of transition from romanticism to modernism, McKay broke decisively with the credo of Booker T. Washington:

> They [the accommodationists] seem afraid of the revelation of bitterness in Negro life. But it may as well be owned, and frankly by those who know the inside and heart of Negro life, that the Negro, and especially the Aframerican has bitterness in him in spite of his joyous exterior. And the more educated he is in these times the more he is likely to have.

Of countless explanations about the African American, his own prove quite incisive:

> The spirituals and the blues were not created of sweet deceit. There is as much sublimated bitterness in them as there is humility, pathos and bewilderment. And if the Negro is a little bitter, the white man should be the last person in the world to accuse him of bitterness. For the feeling of bitterness is a natural part of the black man's birthright as the feeling of superiority is of the white man's. It matters not so much that one has had an experience of bitterness, but rather how one has developed out of it. To ask the Negro to render up his bitterness is asking him to part with his soul [contradicts B.T.W.]. For out of his bitterness he has bloomed and created his spirituals and blues and conserved his racial attributes—his humor and ripe laughter and particular rhythm of life.

The contributions of Claude McKay remain a lasting legacy. He challenged the dialect school of Paul Laurence Dunbar and the strategies of Booker T. Washington. Even before Langston Hughes, he told the forbidden story of the African holocaust. Once he was the romantic poet who sought beauty in the Jamaican landscape, the Harlem cabaret, and the peace of his own heart. Possibly the first poet to introduce Harlem into Negro poetry (*Harlem Shadows* [1922]), he had excluded "If We Must Die" from an earlier volume titled *Spring in New Hampshire* (1920) to make the book race neutral. With other Caribbean writers in the United States, he reassessed the human costs of urban life. Despite the radicalism of his early life, he eventually accepted Catholicism. While he associated with white leftists of privilege in Greenwich Village, foreshadowing the careers of James Baldwin and Amiri Baraka after him, he remembered the Jamaican peasantry.

But McKay never returned to his homeland. Though a poet of racial celebration, he once traveled to the Soviet Union to show that class transcended race. Like most American leftists, however, his communism was theoretical. He had written in the British and Italian sonnet forms of the Elizabethan era. America had challenged his courageous spirit with a racism that he could defy, if not defeat. As with Du Bois and others, his experience aborted his romantic innocence. Alienated from the New Negro, he disagreed with Alain Locke's view of art for art's sake and with the proposed elitism of the privileged few. It was editor Locke, after all, who had once changed the title of a McKay poem from "The White House" to "White Houses." McKay was more akin in the British sense to Keats and Byron. Older than many of the young stars in the Renaissance, he had white friends who lived in the fashionable suburbs of New York. During the halcyon days of "the weary blues," he was literally out of the Americas. He wrote, according to Arthur P. Davis in James P. Draper's *Black Literature Criticism,* those "brilliant, ironic . . . poems which set the tone for the protest writing of the Harlem Renaissance." His Jamaican lyrics became the conscience of a race.

❖❖❖

James Giles has compiled a helpful bibliography, and Penni Cagan has written a solid overview for *Dictionary of Literary Biography: Afro-American Writers.* Of all the references on McKay, *Black Literature Criticism,* ed. James P. Draper, is invaluable. Besides the primary texts discussed above, *The Passion of Claude McKay: Selected Poems,* and *The Selected Poems* (1953; 1973) are valuable additions to any personal library, as is *The Dialect Poetry of Claude McKay,* ed. Wayne F. Cooper (1972). Remarkable insights are in "Claude McKay, A Negro Writer to His Critics," *New York Herald Tribune,* 1932; *The Passion of Claude McKay: Selected Poetry and Prose, 1912–1948,* ed. Wayne F. Cooper (1973); Jean Wagner, *Black Poets of the United States* (1962; trans. English, 1973). Possibly most controversial is Gary Woods, *Gay Re-readings of the Harlem Renaissance* (1993). Ezekiel Mphalele writes from an international perspective in *Voices in the Whirlwind* (1972). Wayne F. Cooper has done resourceful work in the comprehensive biography *Claude McKay: Rebel Sojourner in the Harlem Renaissance* (1987) and in an article for *Phylon* 25 (Fall 1964). An earlier biography by James Giles (1976) is a little more critical. Among the more famous authors to write about McKay have been Kenneth Ramchand in *West Indian Novel and Its Background* (1983) and George E. Kent in *Blackness and the Adventure of Western Culture* (1972). Assessments by contemporaries include W.E.B. Du Bois, "Review of Home to Harlem," *The Crisis* 35, No. 6 (June 1928); William Stanley Braithwaite, "Some Contemporary Poets of the Negro Race," *The Crisis* 17, No. 6 (April 1919). Recent essays explore the poet's struggle to balance traditional form with black meaning and the search for ideology and literary source as well as for religion: Clenora Hudson-Weems, *Western Journal of Black Studies* (Spring 1992); Barbara J. Griffith, *CLA Journal* (December 1992); P. S. Chauhan, *CLA Journal* (September 1990).

Wonderful opportunities exist for brilliant new readings of the poetry and the highly neglected autobiography. Equally helpful would be a carefully detailed extrapolation of the critical theory as grounded in the essays and revealed through

McKay's poetry and fiction. Finally, an excellent critical study on Garvey, McKay, and Walrond would make an academic career.

The Tropics in New York

Bananas ripe and green, and ginger-root,
  Cocoa in pods and alligator pears,
And tangerines and mangoes and grape fruit,
  Fit for the highest prize at parish fairs,

Set in the window, bringing memories
  Of fruit-trees laden by low-singing rills,
And dewy dawns, and mystical blue skies
  In benediction over nun-like hills.

My eyes grew dim, and I could no more gaze;
  A wave of longing through my body swept,
And, hungry for the old, familiar ways,
  I turned aside and bowed my head and wept.

If We Must Die

If we must die, let it not be like hogs
Hunted and penned in an inglorious spot,
While round us bark the mad and hungry dogs,
Making their mock at our accursed lot.
If we must die, O let us nobly die,
So that our precious blood may not be shed
In vain; then even the monsters we defy
Shall be constrained to honor us though dead!
O kinsmen! we must meet the common foe!
Though far outnumbered let us show us brave,
And for their thousand blows deal one deathblow!
What though before us lies the open grave?
Like men we'll face the murderous, cowardly pack,
Pressed to the wall, dying, but fighting back!

Baptism

Into the furnace let me go alone;
Stay you without in terror of the heat.
I will go naked in—for thus 'tis sweet—
Into the weird depths of the hottest zone.
I will not quiver in the frailest bone,
You will not note a flicker of defeat;
My heart shall tremble not its fate to meet,
My mouth give utterance to any moan.
The yawning oven spits forth fiery spears;
Red aspish tongues shout wordlessly my name.
Desire destroys, consumes my mortal fears,

Transforming me into a shape of flame.
I will come out, back to your world of tears,
A stronger soul within a finer frame.

Tiger

The white man is a tiger at my throat,
Drinking my blood as my life ebbs away,
And muttering that his terrible striped coat
Is Freedom's and portends the Light of Day.
Oh white man, you may suck up all my blood
And throw my carcass into potter's field,
But never will I say with you that mud
Is bread for Negroes! Never will I yield.

Europe and Africa and Asia wait
The touted New Deal of the New World's hand!
New systems will be built on race and hate,
The Eagle and the Dollar will command.
Oh Lord! My body, and my heart too, break—
The tiger in his strength his thirst must slake!

America

Although she feeds me bread of bitterness,
And sinks into my throat her tiger's tooth,
Stealing my breath of life, I will confess
I love this cultured hell that tests my youth!
Her vigor flows like tides into my blood,
Giving me strength erect against her hate.
Her bigness sweeps my being like a flood.
Yet as a rebel fronts a king in state,
I stand within her walls with not a shred
Of terror, malice, not a word of jeer.
Darkly I gaze into the days ahead,
And see her might and granite wonders there,
Beneath the touch of Time's unerring hand,
Like priceless treasures sinking in the sand.

Harlem Shadows

I hear the halting footsteps of a lass
  In Negro Harlem when the night lets fall
Its veil. I see the shapes of girls who pass
  To bend and barter at desire's call.
Ah, little dark girls who in slippered feet
Go prowling through the night from street to street!

Through the long night until the silver break
  Of day the little gray feet know no rest;

Through the lone night until the last snow-flake
  Has dropped from heaven upon the earth's white breast,
The dusky, half-clad girls of tired feet
Are trudging, thinly shod, from street to street.

Ah, stern harsh world, that in the wretched way
  Of poverty, dishonor and disgrace,
Has pushed the timid little feet of clay,
  The sacred brown feet of my fallen race!
Ah, heart of me, the weary, weary feet
In Harlem wandering from street to street.

The Harlem Dancer

Applauding youths laughed with young prostitutes
And watched her perfect, half-clothed body sway;
Her voice was like the sound of blended flutes
Blown by black players upon a picnic day.
She sang and danced on gracefully and calm,
The light gauze hanging loose about her form;
To me she seemed a proudly-swaying palm
Grown lovelier for passing through a storm.
Upon her swarthy neck black shiny curls
Luxuriant fell; and tossing coins in praise,
The wine-flushed, bold-eyed boys, and even the girls,
Devoured her shape with eager, passionate gaze;
But looking at her falsely-smiling face,
I knew her self was not in that strange place.

The White House[1]

Your door is shut against my tightened face,
And I am sharp as steel with discontent;
But I possess the courage and the grace
To bear my anger proudly and unbent.
The pavement slabs burn loose beneath my feet,
A chafing savage, down the decent street;
And passion rends my vitals as I pass,
Where boldly shines your shuttered door of glass.
Oh, I must search for wisdom every hour,
Deep in my wrathful bosom sore and raw,
And find in it the superhuman power
To hold me to the letter of your law!
Oh, I must keep my heart inviolate
Against the potent poison of your hate.

[1]"My title was symbolic . . . it had no reference to the official residence of the President of the United States. . . . The title 'White Houses' changed the whole symbolic intent and meaning of the poem, making it appear as if the burning ambition of the black malcontent was to enter white houses in general." Claude McKay, *A Long Way from Home* (1937), pp. 313–314.

St. Isaac's Church, Petrograd

Bow down my soul in worship very low
And in the holy silences be lost.
Bow down before the marble Man of Woe,
Bow down before the singing angel host.
What jewelled glory fills my spirit's eye,
What golden grandeur moves the depths of me!
The soaring arches lift me up on high,
Taking my breath with their rare symmetry.

Bow down my soul and let the wondrous light
Of beauty bathe thee from her lofty throne,
Bow down before the wonder of man's might.
Bow down in worship, humble and alone,
Bow lowly down before the sacred sight
Of man's Divinity alive in stone.

LANGSTON HUGHES
(1902–1967)

James Langston Hughes was one of the most gifted writers of the twentieth century. From the Harlem Renaissance during the twenties to the Black Arts Movement of the sixties, his short stories, plays, novels, anthologies, translations, and poems helped to build a sense of community among peoples of the African Diaspora and to encourage the writers who would follow. His early poetry in rhythm and blues set an artistic standard from which to view the Keatsian verse by Countee Cullen, his occasionally more celebrated contemporary; the experimental paintings of Aaron Douglas; and the theatrical flamboyance of Josephine Baker. After he had established his early reputation, he encouraged the poets Gwendolyn Brooks and Margaret Walker. Subsequently, he extended a helping hand to writers of the next generation, including Alice Walker, the author of "To Hell with Dying." Indirectly, Hughes assisted in opening up traditional magazines and presses to those of diverse races. Indeed, he lured Americans to the celebration of ethnic difference without sacrifice of a common humanity. He wrote brilliantly lyrical dreams about what the United States could be. He was the poet of our future.

Langston Hughes was born to Carrie Langston Hughes and James Nathaniel Hughes on February 1, 1902, in Joplin, Missouri. Carrie's father, Charles Howard Langston, had moved to Kansas in search of greater racial and financial freedom. His talent for literary expression and his intent to advance beyond the farm and the grocery store in Lawrence were passed on to young Langston. Charles's brother, John Mercer Langston, the poet's great-uncle, wrote an autobiography titled *From the Virginia Plantation to the National Capital* (1894). The well-established John Mercer Langston left to his posterity a big house along with some stocks and bonds. Langston Hughes's mother, Carrie Langston, attended college briefly. She showed a dramatic imagination through the writing of poetry and the performance of monologues in costume. James Nathaniel Hughes, the poet's father, studied law by mail. When the elder Hughes was denied permission by the all-white examining board to take the bar examination for the Oklahoma Territory, he moved with his wife to Joplin, Missouri in 1899. Angered by unremitting poverty and faced with supporting an eighteen-month-old baby, James Hughes left the United States in October 1903 for Mexico. Eventually, he prospered and was able to contribute to the support of his son. Carrie Hughes refused to accompany her husband to Mexico, and, unable to get even menial jobs in Joplin, she moved from city to city looking for work, occasionally taking young Langston with her. For most of the next nine years, however, the child lived in Lawrence with his maternal grandmother, Mary Leary Langston, although he visited his mother and traveled with her to Mexico in 1908 to see his father. In 1907, Langston's mother took him with her to a library in Topeka, Kansas, where he fell in love with books, in part because he liked the fact that the library did not have to pay rent. Hughes later wrote, in *The Big Sea*, "Even before I was six books began to happen to me, so that after a while there came a time when I believed in books more than in people—which, of course, was wrong."

As a youngster, Hughes was acutely aware of the luxury in which his cousins in Washington lived, in contrast to the poverty in which he and his grandmother lived, but she never wrote to them for help. He learned early that bills did not always get paid but that resourcefulness was essential to survival. Unlike most other black women in Lawrence, his grandmother did not earn money by domestic service. She rented rooms to college students from the University of Kansas, and sometimes she would even move in with a friend and rent out her entire house for ten or twelve dollars a month.

Hughes's grandmother was a gentle and proud woman of Native American and African American blood. He recalled that once she took him to Waswatomie, where she shared the platform as an honored guest of Theodore Roosevelt because she was the last surviving widow of the 1859 John Brown raid on Harper's Ferry. Following her death in April 1915, Hughes lived briefly with his mother, who had by then (possibly in the previous year) married Homer Clark. When Clark left town to seek a job elsewhere, Carrie left Langston with his grandmother's friend Auntie Reed and her husband, who owned a house a block from the river near the railroad station. As devout Christians, the Reeds constantly urged Hughes to join the church, but he resisted prescription of all kinds. In the seventh grade, he landed his first regular job as the custodian of the toilets and lobby for an old hotel near his school. Later, the occasion would inspire "Brass Spittoons," a poem he would eventually publish in *Fine Clothes to the Jew* (1927).

Hughes spent the summer of 1919 with his father in Mexico. Unfortunately, he discovered that he greatly disliked his father's materialism. Depressed for much of his visit, he thought about suicide. Eventually, like the voice of "Still Here" and his comic character Jesse B. Semple, he decided to continue to live. In July 1920, on a train taking him again to visit his father in Mexico, he crossed the Mississippi River to St. Louis. Not quite nineteen, he wrote "The Negro Speaks of Rivers." Through the images of water and pyramid, the storyteller suggests the endurance of human spirituality, spanning from the days of old Egypt to recent centuries. He thought of the role the Congo River had played in human history. He thought about the Niger, as well as the Nile, down which the early slaves were sent. He considered Abraham Lincoln, whom he thought moved to end slavery after travels down the Mississippi. The draft of the poem, written on the back of an envelope, became one of his most famous works.

During the winter of 1923, Hughes wrote what would become the title poem of his first volume of poetry. "The Weary Blues" tells of a pianist in Harlem who is savoring the flavor of the nightlife and African American forms of folk expression. With Zora Neale Hurston, Sterling Brown, Bruce Nugent, and Jean Toomer—all in individualized ways—Hughes became an innovator in both literary form and racial concept. His piano player re-creates the call and response pattern so essential to the blues: "Ain't got nobody in all this world, / Ain't got nobody but ma self. / I's gwine to quit ma frownin' / And put ma troubles on the shelf." But the piano of the blues man responds to him, and he sings his way out of his troubles. This is the greatness of Hughes's experimentation with the blues idiom.

During Hughes's years of study at Lincoln University in Pennsylvania (after dropping out of Columbia University in the early twenties), he met Charlotte Osgood Mason, an elderly white lady who pleased him and who, despite her age, was modern in her ideas about books. Mason also kept up with Harlem theater and current events. Through an arrangement with Alain Locke, she soon became Hughes's literary patron. Although Hughes appreciated her work for the advancement of the race and for liberal causes, approving of her support of Duke Ellington and Marian Anderson, who were then rising stars in music, he disagreed with her on the theory about African American creativity. Mason thought that blacks might best link whites with the joys of the primitive life, but Hughes saw a place for African Americans in the modern world. Hughes did not criticize Mason openly, but he became psychosomatically ill after a permanent breakup with her. During a tour of black colleges in the South in the fall of 1931, he took time after a program in New Orleans to encourage Margaret Walker, then an adolescent poet.

The range and folk quality of Hughes's literary art have rarely been equaled. In 1934, the light fictions "Home" (*Esquire*) and "The Blues I'm Playing" (*Scribner*) appeared in print. "Home" sets the artist's dream of beauty and truth against the animalism of some mob lynchers. In "The Blues I'm Playing," Hughes rewrites the historical break with Mason into a wry tale about a black pianist, Oceola Jones, who abandons the Western classics. His patron, Dora Ellsworth, believes in art alone.

Hughes always maintained the humor that distinguished him as a writer. "To defeat us," he wrote, the world would have to "defeat our laughter." He needed all of it to weather the Broadway production of *Mulatto*, a tale about miscegenation produced from 1935 to 1936. The drama, sensationalized by producers into an exotic fantasy of rape, was banned in Philadelphia and nearly prohibited from playing in Chicago. By the time Hughes was thirty-three, he had learned firsthand about the exploitation of black art in the theaters of America. Later, *Shakespeare in Harlem* (1942), his next book of poems, was a development in presenting precisely the tones and dramatic situations of urban life. In *One-Way Ticket* (1949), he brought to the hilarious persona of Madam Alberta K. Johnson the refreshing realism of a woman created with a deceptive sophistication of satire and biblical irony. With *Montage of a Dream Deferred* (1951), his first book-length poem, he skillfully sustained jazz cadences in poetry. By the time *The Best of Simple* (1961), compiled from newspaper columns in the *Chicago Defender* over nearly two decades, was published, he had become probably the greatest black writer of prose comedy of his generation and probably of the greatest writers in the United States of the kind during the past two centuries.

In 1961, Hughes published *Ask Your Mama,* a neglected volume that may in a very different way have been his most brilliant one since *The Weary Blues* (1926). *Panther & the Lash* (1967), suggesting the Black Panthers of the 1960s and the white backlash against African Americans, marked a decline in his creative powers. "Daybreak in Alabama," the final poem in the book, originally had been published more than twenty years earlier. But at least the book kept alive Hughes's lifelong dream of human community. Even at age sixty-five, Hughes lived out a creed. His literary art proves that people can write across race if, and only if, they accept their gifts as both a race and a human race.

❖❖❖

A few other of Hughes's works, which number altogether more than eighty, are the narratives *The Big Sea: An Autobiography* (1940) and *I Wonder As I Wander: An Autobiographical Journal* (1956); the cultural histories *Famous American Negroes* (1954), *The First Book of Jazz* (1957), and *Fight for Freedom: The Story of the NAACP* (1962); and the plays *Troubled Island* (1936; 1949), *Soul Gone Home* (1937), and *Don't You Want to Be Free?* (1938). Standard bibliographies are Donald C. Dickinson, *A Bio-Bibliography of Langston Hughes, 1902–1967* (1967); R. Baxter Miller, *Langston Hughes and Gwendolyn Brooks: A Reference Guide* (1978). Biographies include Faith Berry, *Langston Hughes: Before and Beyond Harlem* (1983); Arnold Rampersad, *The Life of Langston Hughes,* 2 vols. (1986; 1988). A groundbreaking work is Therman B. O'Daniel, ed., *Langston Hughes: Black Genius* (1971). A reassessment made for an entire issue of *Black American Literature Forum* (Fall 1981), edited by R. Baxter Miller. A more recent collection is Edward J. Mullen, ed., *Critical Essays on Langston Hughes* (1986). Scholarly and critical books include James Emanuel, *Langston Hughes* (1967); Richard K. Barksdale, *Langston Hughes: The Poet and His Critics* (1977); R. Baxter Miller, *The Art and Imagination of Langston Hughes* (1989). Some of the most famous articles are by Arthur P. Davis on the "cool poet" and the mulatto theme, by Blyden Jackson on the comic character Semple, and by Amritjit Singh on theory. Akiba Sullivan Harper, who is doing fine work on the short fiction, has important books published by the University of Missouri Press.

The Negro Speaks of Rivers

I've known rivers:
I've known rivers ancient as the world and older than the
  flow of human blood in human veins.

My soul has grown deep like the rivers.

I bathed in the Euphrates when dawns were young.
I built my hut near the Congo and it lulled me to sleep.
I looked upon the Nile and raised the pyramids above it.
I heard the singing of the Mississippi when Abe Lincoln
  went down to New Orleans, and I've seen its muddy
  bosom turn all golden in the sunset.

I've known rivers:
Ancient, dusky rivers.

My soul has grown deep like the rivers.

Dream Variations

To fling my arms wide
In some place of the sun,
To whirl and to dance
Till the white day is done.
Then rest at cool evening
Beneath a tall tree
While night comes on gently,
    Dark like me—
That is my dream!

To fling my arms wide
In the face of the sun,
Dance! Whirl! Whirl!
Till the quick day is done.
Rest at pale evening . . .
A tall, slim tree . . .
Night coming tenderly
    Black like me.

Sunday Morning Prophecy

An old Negro minister concludes his sermon in his loudest voice, having previously pointed out the sins of this world:

. . . and now
When the rumble of death
Rushes down the drain
Pipe of eternity,
And hell breaks out
Into a thousand smiles,
And the devil licks his chops
Preparing to feast on life,
And all the little devils
Get out their bibs
To devour the corrupt bones
Of this world—
Oh-ooo-oo-o!
Then my friends!
Oh, then! Oh, then!
What will you do?
You will turn back
And look toward the mountains.
You will turn back
And grasp for a straw.
You will holler,
Lord-d-d-d-ah!
Save me, Lord!
Save me!

And the Lord will say,
In the days of your greatness
I did not hear your voice!
The Lord will say,
In the days of your richness
I did not see your face!
The Lord will say,
No-oooo-ooo-oo-o!
I will not save you now!

And your soul
Will be lost!

Come into the church this morning,
Brothers and Sisters,
And be saved—
And give freely
In the collection basket
That I who am thy shepherd
Might live.

Amen!

The Weary Blues

Droning a drowsy syncopated tune,
Rocking back and forth to a mellow croon,
   I heard a Negro play.
Down on Lenox Avenue the other night
By the pale dull pallor of an old gas light
   He did a lazy sway. . . .
   He did a lazy sway. . . .
To the tune o' those Weary Blues.
With his ebony hands on each ivory key
He made that poor piano moan with melody.
   O Blues!
Swaying to and fro on his rickety stool
He played that sad raggy tune like a musical fool.
   Sweet Blues!
Coming from a black man's soul.
   O Blues!
In a deep song voice with a melancholy tone
I heard that Negro sing, that old piano moan—
   "Ain't got nobody in all this world,
   Ain't got nobody but ma self.
   I's gwine to quit ma frownin'
   And put ma troubles on the shelf."
Thump, thump, thump, went his foot on the floor.

He played a few chords then he sang some more—
"I got the Weary Blues
And I can't be satisfied.
Got the Weary Blues
And can't be satisfied—
I ain't happy no mo'
And I wish that I had died."
And far into the night he crooned that tune.
The stars went out and so did the moon.
The singer stopped playing and went to bed
While the Weary Blues echoed through his head.
He slept like a rock or a man that's dead.

Jazzonia

Oh, silver tree!
Oh, shining rivers of the soul!

In a Harlem cabaret
Six long-headed jazzers play.
A dancing girl whose eyes are bold
Lifts high a dress of silken gold.

Oh, singing tree!
Oh, shining rivers of the soul!

Were Eve's eyes
In the first garden
Just a bit too bold?
Was Cleopatra gorgeous
In a gown of gold?

Oh, shining tree!
Oh, silver rivers of the soul!

In a whirling cabaret
Six long-headed jazzers play.

Life Is Fine

I went down to the river,
I set down on the bank.
I tried to think but couldn't,
So I jumped in and sank.

I came up once and hollered!
I came up twice and cried!
If that water hadn't a-been so cold
I might've sunk and died.

But it was
Cold in that water!
It was cold!

I took the elevator
Sixteen floors above the ground.
I thought about my baby
And thought I would jump down.

I stood there and I hollered!
I stood there and I cried!
If it hadn't a-been so high
I might've jumped and died.

But it was
High up there!
It was high!

So since I'm still here livin',
I guess I will live on.
I could've died for love—
But for livin' I was born.

Though you may hear me holler,
And you may see me cry—
I'll be dogged, sweet baby,
If you gonna see me die.

Life is fine!
Fine as wine!
Life is fine!

Daybreak in Alabama

When I get to be a composer
I'm gonna write me some music about
Daybreak in Alabama
And I'm gonna put the purtiest songs in it
Rising out of the ground like a swamp mist
And falling out of heaven like soft dew.
I'm gonna put some tall tall trees in it
And the scent of pine needles
And the smell of red clay after rain
And long red necks
And poppy colored faces
And big brown arms
And the field daisy eyes
Of black and white black white black people
And I'm gonna put white hands
And black hands and brown and yellow hands
And red clay earth hands in it
Touching everybody with kind fingers
And touching each other natural as dew
In that dawn of music when I

Get to be a composer
And write about daybreak
In Alabama.

Bound No'th Blues

Goin' down the road, Lawd,
Goin' down the road.
Down the road, Lawd,
Way, way down the road.
Got to find somebody
To help me carry this load.

Road's in front o' me,
Nothin' to do but walk.
Road's in front o' me,
Walk . . . an' walk . . . an' walk.
I'd like to meet a good friend
To come along an' talk.

Hates to be lonely,
Lawd, I hates to be sad.
Says I hates to be lonely,
Hates to be lonely an' sad,
But ever friend you finds seems
Like they try to do you bad.

Road, road, road, O!
Road, road . . . road . . . road, road!
Road, road, road, O!
On the no'thern road.
These Mississippi towns ain't
Fit fer a hoppin' toad.

Mother to Son

Well, son, I'll tell you:
Life for me ain't been no crystal stair.
It's had tacks in it,
And splinters,
And boards torn up,
And places with no carpet on the floor—
Bare.
But all the time
I'se been a-climbin' on,
And reachin' landin's,
And turnin' corners,
And sometimes goin' in the dark
Where there ain't been no light.

So boy, don't you turn back.
Don't you set down on the steps
'Cause you finds it's kinder hard.
Don't you fall now—
For I'se still goin', honey,
I'se still climbin',
And life for me ain't been no crystal stair.

Madam's Past History

My name is Johnson—
Madam Alberta K.
The Madam stands for business.
I'm smart that way.

I had a
HAIR-DRESSING PARLOR
Before
The depression put
The prices lower.

Then I had a
BARBECUE STAND
Till I got mixed up
With a no-good man.

Cause I had a insurance
The WPA
Said, We can't use you
Wealthy that way.

I said,
DON'T WORRY 'BOUT ME!
Just like the song,
You WPA folks take care of yourself—
And I'll get along.

I do cooking,
Day's work, too!
Alberta K. Johnson—
Madam to you.

Ballad of the Landlord

Landlord, landlord,
My roof has sprung a leak.
Don't you 'member I told you about it
Way last week?

Landlord, landlord,
These steps is broken down.

When you come up yourself
It's a wonder you don't fall down.

Ten Bucks you say I owe you?
Ten Bucks you say is due?
Well, that's Ten Bucks more'n I'll pay you
Till you fix this house up new.

What? You gonna get eviction orders?
You gonna cut off my heat?
You gonna take my furniture and
Throw it in the street?

Um-huh! You talking high and mighty.
Talk on—till you get through.
You ain't gonna be able to say a word
If I land my fist on you.

Police! Police!
Come and get this man!
He's trying to ruin the government
And overturn the land!

Copper's whistle!
Patrol bell!
Arrest.

Precinct Station.
Iron cell.
Headlines in press:

MAN THREATENS LANDLORD

TENANT HELD NO BAIL

JUDGE GIVES NEGRO 90 DAYS IN COUNTY JAIL

Dream Boogie

Good morning, daddy!
Ain't you heard
The boogie-woogie rumble
Of a dream deferred?

Listen closely:
You'll hear their feet
Beating out and beating out a—

You think
It's a happy beat?

Listen to it closely:
Ain't you heard
something underneath
like a—

What did I say?

Sure,
I'm happy!
Take it away!
Hey, pop!
Re-bop!
Mop!

Y-e-a-h!

Harlem

What happens to a dream deferred?

Does it dry up
like a raisin in the sun?
Or fester like a sore—
And then run?
Does it stink like rotten meat?
Or crust and sugar over—
like a syrupy sweet?

Maybe it just sags
like a heavy load.

Or does it explode?

I, Too

I, too, sing America.

I am the darker brother.
They send me to eat in the kitchen
When company comes,
But I laugh,
And eat well,
And grow strong.

Tomorrow,
I'll be at the table
When company comes.
Nobody'll dare
Say to me,
"Eat in the kitchen,"
Then.

Besides,
They'll see how beautiful I am
And be ashamed—

I, too, am America.

Feet Live Their Own Life

"If you want to know about my life," said Simple as he blew the foam from the top of the newly filled glass the bartender put before him, "don't look at my face, don't look at may hands. Look at my feet and see if you can tell how long I been standing on them."

"I cannot see your feet through your shoes," I said.

"You do not need to see through my shoes," said Simple. "Can't you tell by the shoes I wear—not pointed, not rocking-chair, not French-toed, not nothing but big, long, broad, and flat—that I been standing on these feet a long time and carrying some heavy burdens? They ain't flat from standing at no bar, neither, because I always sets at a bar. Can't you tell that? You know I do not hang out in a bar unless it has stools, don't you?"

"That I have observed," I said, "but I did not connect it with your past life."

"Everything I do is connected up with my past life," said Simple. "From Virginia to Joyce, from my wife to Zarita, from my mother's milk to this glass of beer, everything is connected up."

"I trust you will connect up with that dollar I just loaned you when you get paid," I said. "And who is Virginia? You never told me about her."

"Virginia is where I was borned," said Simple. "I *would* be borned in a state named after a woman. From that day on, women never give me no peace."

"You, I fear, are boasting. If the women were running after you as much as you run after them, you would not be able to sit here on this bar stool in peace. I don't see any women coming to call you out to go home, as some of these fellows' wives do around here."

"Joyce better not come in no bar looking for me," said Simple. "That is why me and my wife busted up—one reason. I do not like to be called out of no bar by a female. It's a man's prerogative to just set and drink sometimes."

"How do you connect that prerogative with your past?" I asked.

"When I was a wee small child," said Simple, "I had no place to set and think in, being as how I was raised up with three brothers, two sisters, seven cousins, one married aunt, a common-law uncle, and the minister's grandchild—and the house only had four rooms. I never had no place just to set and think. Neither to set and drink—not even much my milk before some hongry child snatched it out of my hand. I were not the youngest, neither a girl, nor the cutest. I don't know why, but I don't think nobody liked me much. Which is why I was afraid to like anybody for a long time myself. When I did like somebody, I was full-grown and then I picked out the wrong woman because I had no practice in liking anybody before that. We did not get along."

"Is that when you took to drink?"

"Drink took to me," said Simple. "Whiskey just naturally likes me but beer likes me better. By the time I got married I had got to the point where a cold bottle was almost as good as a warm bed, especially when the bottle could not talk and the bed-warmer could. I do not like a woman to talk to me too much—I mean about me. Which is why I like Joyce. Joyce most in generally talks about herself."

"I am still looking at your feet," I said, "and I swear they do not reveal your life to me. Your feet are no open book."

"You have eyes but you see not," said Simple. "These feet have stood on every rock from the Rock of Ages to 135th and Lenox. These feet have supported everything from a cotton bale to a hongry woman. These feet have walked ten thousand miles working for white folks and another ten thousand keeping up with colored. These feet have stood at altars, crap tables, free lunches, bars, graves, kitchen doors, betting windows, hospital clinics, WPA desks, social security railings, and in all kinds of lines from soup lines to the draft. If I just had four feet, I could have stood in more places longer. As it is, I done wore out seven hundred pairs of shoes, eighty-nine tennis shoes, twelve summer sandals, and six loafers. The socks that these feet have bought could build a knitting mill. The corns I've cut away would dull a German razor. The bunions I forgot would make you ache from now till Judgment Day. If anybody was to write the history of my life, they should start with my feet."

"Your feet are not all that extraordinary," I said. "Besides, everything you are saying is general. Tell me specifically some one thing your feet have done that makes them different from any other feet in the world, just one."

"Do you see that window in that white man's store across the street?" asked Simple. "Well, this right foot of mine broke out that window in the Harlem riots right smack in the middle. Didn't no other foot in the world break that window but mine. And this left foot carried me off running as soon as my right foot came down. Nobody else's feet saved me from the cops that night but these *two* feet right here. Don't tell me these feet ain't had a life of their own."

"For shame," I said, "going around kicking out windows. Why?"

"Why?" said Simple. "You have to ask my great-great-grandpa why. He must of been simple—else why did he let them capture him in Africa and sell him for a slave to breed my great-grandpa in slavery to breed my grandpa in slavery to breed my pa to breed me to look at that window and say, 'It ain't mine! Bam-mmm-mm-m!' and kick it out?"

"This bar glass is not yours either," I said. "Why don't you smash it?"

"It's got my beer in it," said Simple.

Just then Zarita came in wearing her Thursday-night rabbitskin coat. She didn't stop at the bar, being dressed up, but went straight back to a booth. Simple's hand went up, his beer went down, and the glass back to its wet spot on the bar.

"Excuse me a minute," he said, sliding off the stool.

Just to give him pause, the dozens, that old verbal game of maligning a friend's female relatives, came to mind.

"Wait," I said. "You have told me about what to ask your great-great-grandpa. But I want to know what to ask your great-great-grand*ma*."

"I don't play the dozens that far back," said Simple, following Zarita into the smoky juke-box blue of the back room.

The Negro Artist and the Racial Mountain

FROM THE NATION (1926)

One of the most promising of the young Negro poets said to me once, "I want to be a poet—not a Negro poet," meaning, I believe, "I want to write like a white poet"; meaning subconsciously, "I would like to be a white poet"; meaning behind that, "I would like to be white." And I was sorry the young man said that, for no great poet has ever been afraid of being himself. And I doubted then that, with his desire to run away spiritually from his race, this boy would ever be a great poet. But this is the mountain standing in the way of any true Negro art in America—this urge within the race toward whiteness, the desire to pour racial individuality into the mold of American standardization, and to be as little Negro and as much American as possible.

But let us look at the immediate background of this young poet. His family is of what I suppose one would call the Negro middle class: people who are by no means rich yet never uncomfortable nor hungry—smug, contented, respectable folk, members of the Baptist church. The father goes to work every morning. He is a chief steward at a large white club. The mother sometimes does fancy sewing or supervises parties for the rich families of the town. The children go to a mixed school. In the home they read white papers and magazines. And the mother often says "Don't be like niggers" when the children are bad. A frequent phrase from the father is, "Look how well a white man does things." And so the word white comes to be unconsciously a symbol of all the virtues. It holds for the children beauty, morality, and money. The whisper of "I want to be white" runs silently through their minds. This young poet's home is, I believe, a fairly typical home of the colored middle class. One sees immediately how difficult it would be for an artist born in such a home to interest himself in interpreting the beauty of his own people. He is never taught to see that beauty. He is taught rather not to see it, or if he does, to be ashamed of it when it is not according to Caucasian patterns.

For racial culture the home of a self-styled "high-class" Negro has nothing better to offer. Instead there will perhaps be more aping of things white than in a less cultured or less wealthy home. The father is perhaps a doctor, lawyer, landowner, or politician. The mother may be a social worker, or a teacher, or she may do nothing and have a maid. Father is often dark but he has usually married the lightest woman he could find. The family attend a fashionable church where few really colored faces are to be found. And they themselves draw a color line. In the North they go to white theatres and white movies. And in the South they have at least two cars and a house "like white folks." Nordic manners, Nordic faces, Nordic hair, Nordic art (if any), and an Episcopal heaven. A very high mountain indeed for the would-be racial artist to climb in order to discover himself and his people.

But then there are the low-down folks, the so-called common element, and they are the majority—may the Lord be praised! The people who have their nip of gin on Saturday nights and are not too important to themselves or the community, or too well fed, or too learned to watch the lazy world go round. They live on Seventh Street in Washington or State Street in Chicago and they do not particularly care whether they are like white folks or anybody else. Their joy runs, bang! into ecstasy. Their religion soars to a shout. Work maybe a little today, rest a little tomorrow. Play awhile. Sing awhile. O, let's dance! These common people are not afraid of spirituals, as for a long time their more intellectual brethren were, and jazz is their child. They furnish a wealth of colorful, distinctive material for any artist because they still hold their own individuality in the face of American standardizations. And perhaps these common people will give to the world its truly great Negro artist, the one who is not afraid to be himself. Whereas the better-class Negro would tell the artist what to do, the people at least let him alone when he does appear. And they are not ashamed of him—if they know he exists at all. And they accept what beauty is their own without question.

Certainly there is, for the American Negro artist who can escape the restrictions the more advanced among his own group would put upon him, a great field of unused material ready for his art. Without going outside his race, and even among the better classes with their "white" culture and conscious American manners, but still Negro enough to be different, there is sufficient matter to furnish a black artist with a lifetime of creative work. And when he chooses to touch on the relations between Negroes and whites in this country with their innumerable overtones and undertones surely, and especially for literature and the drama, there is an inexhaustible supply of themes at hand. To these the Negro artist can give his racial individuality, his heritage of rhythm and warmth, and his incongruous humor that so often, as in the Blues, becomes ironic laughter mixed with tears. But let us look again at the mountain.

A prominent Negro clubwoman in Philadelphia paid eleven dollars to hear Raquel Meller sing Andalusian popular songs. But she told me a few weeks before she would not think of going to hear "that woman," Clara Smith, a great black artist, sing Negro folksongs. And many an upper-class Negro church, even now, would not dream of employing a spiritual in its services. The drab melodies in white folks' hymnbooks are much to be preferred. "We want to worship the Lord correctly and quietly. We don't believe in 'shouting.' Let's be dull like the Nordics," they say, in effect.

The road for the serious black artist, then, who would produce a racial art is most certainly rocky and the mountain is high. Until recently he received almost no encouragement for his work from either white or colored people. The fine novels of Chesnutt go out of print with neither race noticing their passing. The quaint charm and humor of Dunbar's dialect verse brought to him, in his day, largely the same kind of encouragement one would give a sideshow freak (A colored man writing poetry! How odd!) or a clown (How amusing!).

The present vogue in things Negro, although it may do as much harm as good for the budding colored artist, has at least done this: it has brought him forcibly to the attention of his own people among whom for so long, unless the other race had noticed him beforehand, he was a prophet with little honor. I understand that Charles Gilpin acted for years in Negro theatres without any special acclaim from his own, but when Broadway gave him eight curtain calls, Negroes, too, began to beat a tin pan in his honor. I know a young colored writer, a manual worker by day, who had been writing well for the colored magazines for some years, but it was not until he recently broke into the white publications and his first book was accepted by a prominent New York publisher that the "best" Negroes in his city took the trouble to discover that he lived there. Then almost immediately they decided to give a grand dinner for him. But the society ladies were careful to whisper to his mother that perhaps she'd better not come. They were not sure she would have an evening gown.

The Negro artist works against an undertow of sharp criticism and misunderstanding from his own group and unintentional bribes from the whites. "Oh, be respectable, write about nice people, show how good we are," say the Negroes. "Be stereotyped, don't go too far, don't shatter our illusions about you, don't amuse us too seriously. We will pay you," say the whites. Both would have told Jean Toomer not to write *Cane*. The colored people did not praise it. The white people did not buy it. Most of the colored people who did read *Cane* hate it. They are afraid of it. Although the critics gave it good reviews the public remained indifferent. Yet (excepting the work of Du Bois) *Cane* contains the finest prose written by a Negro in America. And like the singing of Robeson, it is truly racial.

But in spite of the Nordicized Negro intelligentsia and the desires of some white editors we have an honest American Negro literature already with us. Now I await the rise of the Negro theatre. Our folk music, having achieved world-wide fame, offers itself to the genius of the great individual American composer who is to come. And within the next decade I expect to see the work of a growing school of colored artists who paint and model the beauty of dark faces and create with new technique the expressions of their own soul-world. And the Negro dancers who will dance like flame and the singers who will continue to carry our songs to all who listen—they will be with us in even greater numbers tomorrow.

Most of my own poems are racial in theme and treatment, derived from the life I know. In many of them I try to grasp and hold some of the meanings and rhythms of jazz. I am as sincere as I know how to be in these poems and yet after every reading I answer questions like these from my own people: Do you think Negroes should always write about Negroes? I wish you wouldn't read some of your poems to white folks. How do you find anything interesting in a place like a cabaret? Why do you write about black people? You aren't black. What makes you do so many jazz poems?

But jazz to me is one of the inherent expressions of Negro life in America; the eternal tom-tom beating in the Negro soul—the tom-tom of revolt against weariness in a white world, a world of subway trains, and work, work, work; the tom-tom of joy and laughter, and pain swallowed in a smile. Yet the Philadelphia clubwoman is ashamed to say that her race created it and she does not like me to write about it. The old subconscious "white is best" runs through her mind. Years of study under white teachers, a lifetime of white books, pictures, and papers, and white manners, morals, and Puritan standards made her dislike the spirituals. And now she turns up her nose at jazz and all its manifestations—likewise almost everything else distinctly racial. She doesn't care for the Winold Reiss portraits of Negroes because they are "too Negro." She does not want a true picture of herself from anybody. She wants the artist to flatter her, to make the white world believe that all Negroes are as smug and as near white in soul as she wants to be. But, to my mind, it is the duty of the younger Negro artist, if he accepts any duties at all from outsiders, to change through the force of his art that old whispering "I want to be white," hidden in the aspirations of his people, to "Why should I want to be white? I am a Negro—and beautiful!"

So I am ashamed for the black poet who says, "I want to be a poet, not a Negro poet," as though his own racial world were not as interesting as any other world. I am ashamed, too, for the colored artist who runs from the painting of Negro faces to the painting of sunsets after the manner of the academicians because he fears the strange un-whiteness of his own features. An artist must be free to choose what he does, certainly, but he must also never be afraid to do what he might choose.

Let the blare of Negro jazz bands and the bellowing voice of Bessie Smith singing Blues penetrate the closed ears of the colored near-intellectuals until they listen and perhaps understand. Let Paul Robeson singing "Water Boy," and Rudolph Fisher writing about the streets of Harlem, and Jean Toomer holding the heart of Georgia in his hands, and Aaron Douglas drawing strange black fantasies cause the smug Negro middle class to turn from their white, respectable, ordinary books and papers to catch a glimmer of their own beauty. We younger Negro artists who create now intend to express our individual dark-skinned selves without fear or shame. If white people are pleased we are glad. If they are not, it doesn't matter. We know we are beautiful. And ugly too. The tom-tom cries and the tom-tom laughs. If colored people are pleased we are glad. If they are not, their displeasure doesn't matter either. We build our temples for tomorrow, strong as we know how, and we stand on top of the mountain, free within ourselves.

GWENDOLYN BENNETT

(1902–1981)

Largely as a result of the efforts of feminist critics and historians, the writings and paintings of Gwendolyn Bennett have been resurrected from the dust of library archives after more than half a century of being neglected. Although Bennett joined Alice Dunbar-Nelson, Jessie Fauset, and Georgia Douglas Johnson in a select group of African American women newspaper and magazine columnists during the Harlem Renaissance, she was apparently one of the talented women artists who did not receive the patronage of the powerful literary critic Alain Locke. Only one of her works, "Song," which does not reflect the quality of her poetry, appeared in his celebrated anthology *The New Negro* (1925). Yet Bennett's small body of verse reveals that she was a craftswoman of chiseled beauty and strength, a poet who painted her canvas with various brushes, big and small, to capture both the large aspects and the small details of the black life experience in America. As she expresses in her poem "Quatrain," "brushes and paints are all I have / To speak the music of my soul."

Bennett was born on July 8, 1902, in Giddings, Texas, to Joshua Robin and Mayme F. Abernathy Bennett. Her parents soon became teachers on an Indian reservation in Nevada, where Bennett lived until they moved to Washington, D.C., when she was around five years old. A divorce led to Mayme Bennett's being granted custody of Gwendolyn, a decision with which her father did not agree. In spite of his studying to become a lawyer and presumably developing a respect for the law, he nonetheless kidnapped Gwendolyn from her mother when the child was seven. Gwendolyn would not see her mother again until 1924, after she had joined the faculty at Howard University in the fine arts department.

Her father took Gwendolyn to Harrisburg, Pennsylvania, where he remained long enough for her to become an honors student at Central High School and for him to marry again. He then settled in Brooklyn, New York, where Bennett attended Brooklyn's Girls High School. Her many talents became clear as she won the school's art contest and was the first black student elected to the literary and drama societies. She also wrote the class graduation speech, as well as the lyrics to the graduation song. She was particularly influenced by Cordelia Went, her third-year English teacher. When she graduated in 1921, she began preparing herself for a career in fine arts, a decision to which her father, who wanted her to pursue something more stable, objected. Nonetheless, not only did she study fine arts at Pratt Institute and Columbia University, but she also traveled to Paris on a $1,000 Delta Sigma Theta Sorority scholarship to receive training during the 1925–26 academic year. She specialized in watercolor, oil, woodcuts, pen and ink, and batik.

Returning to her job at Howard University, where she had begun teaching in 1924, she pursued the creative efforts that led to the publication of her poetry and short fiction. This was a courageous act in the face of her father's death and the burning in a fire at her stepmother's home of most of the paintings, batiks, and artwork she had brought home from Paris. Like several other women poets of the Renaissance, Bennett had no volume of her verse published. However, twenty-two of her poems appeared between 1923 and 1931 in journals such as *The Crisis* and *Opportunity,* as well as in *Palms* and *Gypsy.* One poem, "Heritage" (1923), predates Countee Cullen's much better known work of the same title. Her artwork appeared on the covers of *The Crisis* and *Opportunity* several times between 1923 and 1930. James Weldon Johnson included her work in the 1922 edition of *The Book of American Negro Poetry,* Countee Cullen included her poetry in *Caroling Dusk* (1927), and William Stanley Braithwaite included some of her poems in his *Anthology of Magazine Verse for 1927 and Yearbook of American Poetry.*

Partly through the aegis of Charles S. Johnson, editor of *Opportunity,* who had invited Bennett to one of his famous awards dinners in 1924, Bennett came to know many of the other young writers of the period, including Cullen, Langston Hughes, Wallace Thurman, and Zora Neale Hurston, as well as some of the older scholars and creative writers, such as James Weldon Johnson and W. E. B. Du Bois. The occasion of the awards dinner was the celebration of Jessie Fauset's publication of *There Is Confusion,* in response to which Bennett penned "To Usward," which has perhaps become her best-known poem.

By 1926, Bennett had been hired to serve as assistant editor at *Opportunity* with the assignment of writing a literary and fine arts column, which she called "The Ebony Flute." An outlet for comments on writers, actors, musicians, and other creative persons, the column contained most of Bennett's published work. Also in 1926, Bennett published "Wedding Day," a short story, in *Fire!!,* a magazine edited for one issue by Hughes, Thurman, Hurston, and Bruce Nugent. The story follows a black American in Paris who falls in love with a white woman who seems to return his affection until she announces, on their planned wedding day and in a note, that she simply cannot bring herself to marry a "nigger." Bennett published one other short story, "Tokens," in 1927, which also focuses on a black American male living in Paris.

Forced to resign from Howard University in 1927 because she married Alfred Jackson, a Morehouse graduate and medical student at Howard, Bennett taught briefly at Tennessee Agricultural and Industrial State College before moving to Eustis, Florida. It was there that her husband set up his practice. Increasingly unhappy in her marriage and missing the circle of literary friends into which she had been taken, Bennett was unable to continue her column; it ended in 1928. Although Bennett and her husband returned to Hemstead, Long Island, in 1932, the literary movement with which she identified was essentially over. After her husband's death in the early 1930s, Bennett turned her attention to more community-based projects, first the Federal Writers' Project, then the Federal Arts Project. Beginning in 1937, she served as assistant director (sculptor Augusta Savage, a long-time friend of Bennett's, was director) of the Harlem Community Art Center, from which she was suspended in 1941 on suspicion of Communist connections. The same suspicions dogged her during her employment in the early 1940s at the Jefferson School and as director of the George Washington Carver School, both of which were considered Communist front organizations. Driven to work anonymously as a secretary for Consumers Union, Bennett held this position until she retired. Afterward, she moved to Kutztown, Pennsylvania, and worked as an antique collector and dealer with her second husband, Richard Crosscup. Crosscup died in 1980; Bennett died of congestive heart failure on May 30, 1981.

Thematically, Gwendolyn Bennett's poems fall into the three categories that best characterize Harlem Renaissance women's poetry: racial protest, heritage, and female identity and black womanhood. She captures the biting, stinging racial militancy of Claude McKay's "America" and W. E. B. Du Bois's "The Riddle of the Sphinx" in her poem "Hatred," celebrates black pride and unity in "To Usward," and glorifies Africa in "Heritage." But clearly Bennett's best poems are those of a more personal nature, those moving, passionate, lyrical pieces that reflect her deep sense of woman-self and black female identity. With the stirring feminism of the nineteenth-century activist Frances Watkins Harper, she evokes a strong sense of black sisterhood in "To a Dark Girl." With the broad, colorful strokes of her poetic brush, she paints "Street Lamps in Early Spring" and "Fantasy" in dark/nighttime imagery to unveil a black queen/earth goddess figure. It is with the precision, sharpness, and terseness of her imagery that Bennett shows her skills as a poet. It is with the same powerful poetic strokes that she has left a lasting imprint on Harlem Renaissance poetry.

❖❖❖

Very little has been published on Gwendolyn Bennett. However, Sandra Y. Govan is currently completing a biography of her. To date, Govan has published articles on Bennett's life and works in *Dictionary of Literary Biography,* Cathy N. Davidson, ed., *The Oxford Companion to Women's Writing in the United States* (1995), and Jessie Carney Smith, ed., *Notable Black American Women* (1992). Brief but very useful commentary on the author's works appears in Maureen Honey, *Shadowed Dreams: Women's Poetry of the Harlem Renaissance* (1989); Eugene Redmond, *Drumvoices: The Mission of Afro-American Poetry* (1976). In particular, Honey gives insight into Bennett's use of nature imagery in her verse.

Heritage

I want to see the slim palm-trees,
Pulling at the clouds
With little pointed fingers. . . .

I want to see lithe Negro girls
Etched dark against the sky
While sunset lingers.

I want to hear the silent sands,
Singing to the moon
Before the Sphinx-still face. . . .

I want to hear the chanting
Around a heathen fire
Of a strange black race.

I want to breathe the Lotus flow'r,
Sighing to the stars
With tendrils drinking at the Nile. . . .

I want to feel the surging
Of my sad people's soul,
Hidden by a minstrel-smile.

To a Dark Girl

I love you for your brownness
And the rounded darkness of your breast.
I love you for the breaking sadness in your voice
And shadows where your wayward eye-lids rest.

Something of old forgotten queens
Lurks in the lithe abandon of your walk
And something of the shackled slave
Sobs in the rhythm of your talk.

Oh, little brown girl, born for sorrow's mate,
Keep all you have of queenliness,
Forgetting that you once were slave,
And let your full lips laugh at Fate!

Nocturne

This cool night is strange
Among midsummer days . . .
Far frosts are caught
In the moon's pale light,
And sounds are distant laughter
Chilled to crystal tears.

To Usward

Dedicated to all Negro Youth known and unknown who have a song to sing, a story to tell or a vision for the sons of earth. Especially dedicated to Jessie Fauset upon the event of her novel, *There Is Confusion.*

Let us be still
As ginger jars are still
Upon a Chinese shelf.
And let us be contained
By entities of Self. . . .
Not still with lethargy and sloth,
But quiet with the pushing of our growth.
Not self-contained with smug identity
But conscious of the strength in entity.
If any have a song to sing
That's different from the rest,
Oh let them sing
Before the urgency of Youth's behest!
For some of us have songs to sing
Of jungle heat and fires,
And some of us are solemn grown
With pitiful desires,
And there are those who feel the pull
Of seas beneath the skies,
And some there be who want to croon
Of Negro lullabies.
We claim no part with racial dearth;
We want to sing the songs of birth!
And so we stand like ginger jars
Like ginger jars bound round
With dust and age;
Like jars of ginger we are sealed
By nature's heritage.
But let us break the seal of years
With pungent thrusts of song,
For there is joy in long-dried tears
For whetted passions of a throng!

Street Lamps in Early Spring

Night wears a garment
All velvet soft, all violet blue . . .
And over her face she draws a veil
As shimmering fine as floating dew . . .
And here and there
In the black of her hair
The subtle hands of Night
Move slowly with their gem-starred light.

Hatred

I shall hate you
Like a dart of singing steel
Shot through still air
At even-tide,
Or solemnly
As pines are sober
When they stand etched
Against the sky.
Hating you shall be a game
Played with cool hands
And slim fingers.
Your heart will yearn
For the lonely splendor
Of the pine tree
While rekindled fires
In my eyes
Shall wound you like swift arrows.
Memory will lay its hands
Upon your breast
And you will understand
My hatred.

Fantasy

I sailed in my dreams to the Land of Night
Where you were the dusk-eyed queen,
And there in the pallor of moon-veiled light
The loveliest things were seen . . .

A slim-necked peacock sauntered there
In a garden of lavender hues,
And you were strange with your purple hair
As you sat in your amethyst chair
With your feet in your hyacinth shoes.

Oh, the moon gave a bluish light
Through the trees in the land of dreams and night.
I stood behind a bush of yellow-green
And whistled a song to the dark-haired queen . . .

Secret

I shall make a song like your hair . . .
Gold-woven with shadows green-tinged,
And I shall play with my song
As my fingers might play with your hair.
Deep in my heart
I shall play with my song of you,

Gently. . . .
I shall laugh
At its sensitive lustre . . .
I shall wrap my song in a blanket,
Blue like your eyes are blue
With tiny shots of silver.
I shall wrap it caressingly,
Tenderly. . . .
I shall sing a lullaby
To the song I have made
Of your hair and eyes . . .
And you will never know
That deep in my heart
I shelter a song of you
Secretly. . . .

COUNTEE CULLEN
(1903–1946)

Countee Cullen was the foremost poet of the New Negro academy during the Harlem Renaissance. In his own time, he was more traditionally accepted than were the presumably unrefined Langston Hughes and the somewhat gruff Sterling Brown. Indeed, Cullen found great favor with his literary elders, such as James Weldon Johnson, author of *Autobiography of an Ex-Colored Man* (1912); Charles S. Johnson (no relation), editor of *Opportunity* magazine; and W. E. B. Du Bois, editor of *The Crisis* magazine. With Alain Locke—Rhodes scholar, philosopher, and major spokesman for the Harlem Renaissance—Cullen ranked highly indeed.

Although Cullen proposed to emphasize beauty and nobility in poetry, he wanted almost desperately to be just a writer rather than a black writer. Perhaps he never questioned the arbitrariness of the distinction. He wrote "Heritage," which Langston Hughes called the most beautiful poem known by him; Italian sonnets of personal anxiety, such as "Yet Do I Marvel" and "From the Dark Tower"; and ballads, such as the famous "Incident," about a child's experience of racism in Baltimore. He created other ballads to celebrate the nineteenth-century poets John Keats and Paul Laurence Dunbar. Whatever the traditional inclination of his poetry, Cullen represents the most painful hurt of black people.

Countee Cullen, who was the adopted son of the Reverend Frederick A. Cullen of the Salem African Methodist Episcopal Church in Harlem, began writing poetry while at DeWitt Clinton High School in New York. One of his first poems, "I Have a Rendezvous," appeared in an issue of the school magazine *Magpie* (January 1921). Although he was one of the few blacks in the school, he is now one of many prominent black graduates, including James Baldwin. After graduation in January 1922, he attended New York University (NYU), where he earned a Phi Beta Kappa key and began to write poems that would appear in *Opportunity, The Crisis, Bookman, Poetry,* and *American Mercury.* By the time he graduated from NYU, he had received a contract from Harper and Row for the publication of his first volume of verse, *Color*

(1925). The book, which was an immediate success, brought him to the attention of Locke, who published several of his poems that year in his landmark anthology *The New Negro.* Over the next two years, *Color,* which sold more than two thousand copies, established him as one of the major writers of the Renaissance. In 1926, Cullen earned an M.A. from Harvard, where he studied creative writing with Robert Hillyer. Also that year, he became Charles Johnson's assistant editor at *Opportunity.* Through his position at *Opportunity,* he not only became well acquainted with Langston Hughes, Claude McKay, Zora Neale Hurston, and other significant Renaissance authors, but he, like Locke, also exercised substantial influence over the publishing of Renaissance writing. For instance, in his 1927 collection of African American poetry titled *Caroling Dusk,* he promoted the works of several New Negro poets. Furthermore, during many of his travels, he met and established good relationships with several white poets, including Edward Arlington Robinson and Robert Frost.

Quite often Cullen turned down opportunities to write and teach in southern schools. As a reputable poet of the prestigious New Negro academy, he received an offer to join the faculty at Dillard University, a historically black college in New Orleans, in 1934. He chose to stay near his family in the North and to enjoy life without Jim Crow segregation. Appointed as a teacher of French, he eventually became an instructor of creative writing at Frederick Douglass Junior High School in New York City. He taught at the all-black institution with mostly white staff from 1934 until his death in 1946. In 1935, he served on the committee for education that investigated the causes of a New York riot. In 1944, he declined the offer of a chair of creative literature at Fisk University because he still did not wish to live in the South. He died in 1946 from high blood pressure and uremic poisoning.

Cullen's creative work is often effetely comfortable and self-consciously vulnerable. Whereas his first volume, *Color* (1925), is beautiful and promising, *The Black Christ and Other Poems* (1929) reveals the pain of aborted love. The metaphor of the title, however, captures an association that will pass from the spirituals through his own poetry on to James Baldwin and subsequent African American writers. In 1947, one year after his death, Cullen's volume of poems entitled *On These I Stand* was published. He had hoped this volume would be a definitive collection of his poems. Cullen's fiction includes *One Way to Heaven* (1932), in which he presents the realities of religion and class in Harlem. Aside from *The Medea and Some Poems* (1935), which is primarily a translation of Euripides, Cullen collaborated with Arna Bontemps on *St Louis Woman* (1945), a dramatic rewrite of Bontemps's novel *God Sends Sunday* (1931).

For nearly the last two decades of his life, Cullen wrote no original poetry, possibly because his work belonged to a bygone era. He was still writing a decadent romanticism when modernism was on the horizon. Despite the historical opportunities to enrich himself, as had Hughes and Brown, with a folk vernacular pervaded with blues and jazz rhythms, he maintained a somewhat inflexible preference for Tennyson, Millay, Keats, and others. Hence, his poetic world was too antiquated, too vacuous. He wrote neither great epic nor great lyric poetry, wherein the poet projects the personal self into an object; he offered no international sweep of time nor any objectified moment to release emotion. Usually he was a poet without catharsis. From the very traditions of the black folks so belittled by him, he might have secured the powers of aesthetic transcendence. Whatever the literary experimentation of others, he rarely doubted the premise that the folk tradition must fail in any appropriate comparison to "high" literary art. In fact, at the height of the Renaissance, he shocked the black literary world when he expressed in his preface to *Caroling Dusk* the notion that black poets should align themselves with the European and American literary traditions rather than the African literary heritage. He was sure that the jazz poems by Hughes would pale beside the "dignified company, that select and austere circle of high literary expression which we call poetry." He exemplified the very best of a fading tradition that would give way to the future.

❖❖❖

Countee Cullen has received more biographical and critical attention than most African American poets. Early assessments came from the pioneering scholar J. Saunders Redding in *To Make a Poet Black* (1939) and from Cullen's friend and fellow poet Owen Dodson in *Phylon* (January–March 1942). Blanche Ferguson, in *Countee Cullen and the Negro Renaissance* (1966), and Darwin T. Turner, in *A Minor Chord* (1971), provide factual knowledge about him. Jean Wagner, *The Black Poets of the United States* (1973), contextualizes the poet within the literary tradition of African Americans. More recent studies by Houston Baker, *A Many Colored Coat of Dreams* (1974), and by Allen Shucard, *Countee Cullen* (1984), also are informative.

Heritage

(For Harold Jackman)[1]

What is Africa to me:
Cooper sun or scarlet sea,
Jungle star or jungle track,
Strong bronzed men, or regal black
Women from whose loins I sprang
When the birds of Eden sang?
One three centuries removed
From the scenes his fathers loved,
Spicy grove, cinnamon tree,
What is Africa to me?

So I lie, who all day long
Want no sound except the song
Sung by wild barbaric birds
Goading massive jungle herds,
Juggernauts[2] of flesh that pass
Trampling tall defiant grass
Where young forest lovers lie,

[1]Harold Jackman (1900–1960) was Cullen's best friend. Of West Indian descent, Jackman was quite handsome and his portrait by Winold Reiss became a noted icon of the Renaissance. He was largely a fringe player, but his journals and letters contain a great deal of gossipy information about Harlem happenings. He was the recipient of most of Cullen's papers when Cullen died.

[2]Among the Hindus in India, the juggernaut is a sacred idol conveyed on a huge cart in the path of which believers often throw themselves.

Plighting troth beneath the sky.
So I lie, who always hear,
Though I cram against my ear
Both my thumbs, and keep them there,
Great drums throbbing through the air.
So I lie, whose fount of pride,
Dear distress, and joy allied,
Is my somber flesh and skin,
With the dark blood dammed within
Like great pulsing tides of wine
That, I fear, must burst the fine
Channels of the chafing net
Where they surge and foam and fret.

Africa? A book one thumbs
Listlessly, till slumber comes.
Unremembered are her bats
Circling through the night, her cats
Crouching in the river reeds,
Stalking gentle flesh that feeds
By the river brink; no more
Does the bugle-throated roar
Cry that monarch claws have leapt
From the scabbards where they slept.
Silver snakes that once a year
Doff the lovely coats you wear,
Seek no covert in your fear
Lest a mortal eye should see;
What's your nakedness to me?
Here no leprous flowers rear
Fierce corollas[3] in the air;
Here no bodies sleek and wet,
Dripping mingled rain and sweat,
Tread the savage measures of
Jungle boys and girls in love.
What is last year's snow to me,
Last year's anything? The tree
Budding yearly must forget
How its past arose or set—
Bough and blossom, flower, fruit,
Even what shy bird with mute
Wonder at her travail there,
Meekly labored in its hair.
One three centuries removed
From the scenes his fathers loved,

[3]Corollas—the petals that form the inner envelope of a flower.

Spice grove, cinnamon tree,
What is Africa to me?

So I lie, who find no peace
Night or day, no slight release
From the unremittant beat
Made by cruel padded feet
Walking through my body's street.
Up and down they go, and back,
Treading out a jungle track.
So I lie, who never quite
Safely sleep from rain at night—
I can never rest at all
When the rain begins to fall;
Like a soul gone mad with pain
I must match its weird refrain;
Ever must I twist and squirm,
Writhing like a baited worm,
While its primal measures drip
Through my body, crying, "Strip!
Doff this new exuberance.
Come and dance the Lover's Dance!"
In an old remembered way
Rain works on me night and day.

Quaint, outlandish heathen gods
Black men fashion out of rods,
Clay, and brittle bits of stone,
In a likeness like their own,
My conversion came high-priced;
I belong to Jesus Christ,
Preacher of humility;
Heathen gods are naught to me.

Father, Son, and Holy Ghost,
So I make an idle boast;
Jesus of the twice-turned cheek,
Lamb of God, although I speak
With my mouth thus, in my heart
Do I play a double part.
Ever at Thy glowing altar
Must my heart grow sick and falter,
Wishing He I served were black,
Thinking then it would not lack
Precedent of pain to guide it,
Let who would or might deride it;
Surely then this flesh would know
Yours had borne a kindred woe.

Lord, I fashion dark gods, too,
Daring even to give You
Dark despairing features where,
Crowned with dark rebellious hair,
Patience wavers just so much as
Mortal grief compels, while touches
Quick and hot, of anger, rise
To smitten cheek and weary eyes.
Lord, forgive me if my need
Sometimes shapes a human creed.

All day long and all night through,
One thing only must I do:
Quench my pride and cool my blood,
Lest I perish in the flood.
Lest a hidden ember set
Timber that I thought was wet
Burning like the dryest flax,
Melting like the merest wax,
Lest the grave restore its dead,
Not yet has my heart or head
In the least way realized
They and I are civilized.

Scottsboro, Too, Is Worth Its Song[1]

(A POEM TO AMERICAN POETS)

I said:
Now will the poets sing,—
Their cries go thundering
Like blood and tears
Into the nation's ears,
Like lightning dart
Into the nation's heart.
Against disease and death and all things fell,
And war,
Their strophes rise and swell
To jar
The foe smug in his citadel.

Remembering their sharp and pretty
Tunes for Sacco and Vanzetti,
I said:

[1]In Scottsboro, Alabama, nine black boys, ranging in age from thirteen to nineteen, were accused of raping two white prostitutes. Between 1931 and 1933 the case became a *cause célèbre* for blacks and the white liberal left after the boys were sentenced to death. As a result of public outcry and persistent legal appeals, the convictions, one by one, were overturned.

Here too's a cause divinely spun
For those whose eyes are on the sun,
Here in epitome
Is all disgrace
And epic wrong,
Like wine to brace
The minstrel heart, and blare it into song.

Surely, I said,
Now will the poets sing.
But they have raised no cry.
I wonder why

Colored Blues Singer

Some weep to find the Golden Pear
Feeds maggots at the core,
And some grow cold as ice, and bear
Them prouder than before.

But you go singing like the sea
Whose lover turns to land;
You make your grief a melody
And take it by the hand.

Such songs the mellow-bosomed maids
Of Africa intone
For lovers dead in hidden glades,
Slow rotting flesh and bone.

Such keenings tremble from the kraal,
Where sullen-browed abides
The second wife whose dark tears fail
To draw him to her sides.

Somewhere Jeritza[1] breaks her heart
On symbols Verdi[2] wrote;
You tear the strings of your soul apart,
Blood dripping note by note.

[1]Maria Jeritza, a Czech-born soprano who was a major opera star of the twenties and thirties.

[2]Giuseppe Verdi (1813–1901), Italian composer of some of the most famous operas in the world, including *Aïda* (1871), *Otello* (1887), *Il Trovatore* (1853), and *La Traviata* (1853).

The Litany of the Dark People

Our flesh that was a battle-ground
Shows now the morning-break;
The ancient deities are downed
For Thy eternal sake.
Now that the past is left behind,
Fling wide Thy garment's hem

To keep us one with Thee in mind,
Thou Christ of Bethlehem.

The thorny wreath may ridge our brow,
The spear may mar our side,
And on white wood from a scented bough
We may be crucified;
Yet no assault the old gods make
Upon our agony
Shall swerve our footsteps from the wake
Of Thine toward Calvary.

And if we hunger now and thirst,
Grant our withholders may,
When heaven's constellations burst
Upon Thy crowning day,
Be fed by us, and given to see
Thy mercy in our eyes,
When Bethlehem and Calvary
Are merged in Paradise.

Yet Do I Marvel

I doubt not God is good, well-meaning, kind,
And did He stoop to quibble could tell why
The little buried mole continues blind,
Why flesh that mirrors Him must some day die,
Make plain the reason tortured Tantalus[1]
Is baited by the fickle fruit, declare
If merely brute caprice dooms Sisyphus[2]
To struggle up a never-ending stair.
Inscrutable His ways are, and immune
To catechism by a mind too strewn
With petty cares to slightly understand
What awful brain compels His awful hand.
Yet do I marvel at this curious thing:
To make a poet black, and bid him sing!

[1]Tantalus was a king of Sispylus in Lydia, the father of Niobe and Pelops, and a friend of the gods, who was punished for the crime of either: (1) killing his son Pelops and serving him to the gods: (2) stealing nectar and ambrosia, the gods' food: or (3) revealing the secrets he learned from the gods. He was dispatched to Hades, where he stood up to his neck in water which would recede whenever he tried to drink. The fruit just above his head would ascend whenever he tried to reach for it.

[2]Sisyphus was a king of Corinth who was punished in Hades by having to roll a huge stone up a hill, only to have the stone roll down again as soon as he brought it to the top.

A Song of Praise

(For One Who Praised His Lady's Being Fair.)

You have not heard my love's dark throat,
Slow-fluting like a reed,

Release the perfect golden note
  She caged there for my need.

Her walk is like the replica
  Of some barbaric dance
Wherein the soul of Africa
  Is winged with arrogance.

And yet so light she steps across
  The ways her sure feet pass,
She does not dent the smoothest moss
  Or bend the thinnest grass.

My love is dark as yours is fair,
  Yet lovelier I hold her
Than listless maids with pallid hair,
  And blood that's thin and colder.

You-proud-and-to-be-pitied one,
  Gaze on her and despair;
Then seal your lips until the sun
  Discovers one as fair.

Not Sacco and Vanzetti[1]

These men who do not die, but send to death,
These iron men whom mercy cannot bend
Beyond the lettered law; what when their breath
Shall suddenly and naturally end?
What shall their final retribution be,
What bloody silver then shall pay the tolls
Exacted for this legal infamy
When death indicts their stark immortal souls?

The day a slumbering but awful God,
Before Time to Eternity is blown,
Examines with the same unyielding rod
These images of His with hearts of stone,
These men who do not die, but death decree,—
These are the men I should not care to be.

[1]Nicola Sacco and Bartolomeo Vanzetti were two Italian-born anarchists accused of robbery and murder. Their case became a *cause célèbre* among intellectuals and liberals in the 1920s. Despite doubts about their guilt and strenuous protests, they were executed in 1927.

HELENE JOHNSON

(1907–)

Helene Johnson is one of the few women poets identified with the Harlem Renaissance. She and her cousin Dorothy West, another Renaissance writer and editor, both lived in Boston and were both members of the Saturday Evening Quill Club of that city. Publication of Johnson's poems in *Opportunity* magazine beginning in 1925 put her in a select group of Renaissance writers whose works were touted as the best of the period. The youngest of the Renaissance women poets, Johnson was described by fellow poet James Weldon Johnson in *The Book of American Negro Poetry* (1931) as a writer who "took the 'racial' bull by the horns." However, the volume of her poetic output remained small, and her reputation dwindled with the fading of the Renaissance.

Helene Johnson was born in Boston on July 7, 1907, the only child of Ella Benson and William Johnson. Her mother's family had migrated from South Carolina, where her grandfather had been a carpenter during slavery. Although he eventually returned to South Carolina, he bought property in Oak Bluffs, Martha's Vineyard, which remains in the family today (Dorothy West lived there). Johnson never saw her father or even a photograph of him. She was told that he was Greek, that he and her mother were incompatible, and that he probably lived in Chicago. Johnson's mother worked as a domestic for well-to-do Harvardites, which kept her away from Helene for extended periods of time. Still, her mother provided unusual opportunities for that period by taking Helene to see such newsmakers as the Wright brothers. Johnson spent a large part of her childhood in a huge house that included her mother's sisters and their children (the same setting that Dorothy West develops in her novel *The Living Is Easy* [1948]). Johnson's Aunt Rachel, Dorothy West's mother, dubbed her "Helene" because it had a "fancy ring" to it; her legal name was Helen. She attended school in Oak Bluffs as well as in Boston before entering Boston University. Shortly thereafter, she turned her attention more and more to writing and the literary happenings in New York.

At the height of her reputation, she once stood second only to Langston Hughes in a *Crisis* contest, and her works in *Opportunity* received repeated praise. As early as July 1925, she published "My Race," about the possibilities of African American life, in *Opportunity.* This piece would be repeated with "Metamorphism," about the changeable nature of the sea, in March 1926. In another *Opportunity* contest, three of Johnson's poems received honorable mention ("Fulfillment," "Magalu," and "The Road"); the impressive judges for the contest were William Rose Benét, Alain Locke, Vachel Lindsay, and Robert Frost. Johnson's poems show the influence of Walt Whitman, Alfred Lord Tennyson, Percy Bysshe Shelley, and Carl Sandburg, all of whom she named as among her favorite poets.

Johnson also published poems in 1926 in the only issue of *Fire!!* magazine, part of the success that led her and West to move to New York to study journalism at the Extension Division of Columbia University. When she sold a poem titled "Bottled" to *Vanity Fair,* she was celebrated throughout Harlem. The poem, which posits that the black man has been "bottled" in the same way that Sahara Desert sand is on a Harlem library shelf, appeared in the May 1927 issue of the magazine. In a third *Opportunity* contest, Johnson won second prize in poetry for "Summer Matures," which focuses erotically on the legend of Sappho's unconsummated love for Phaon; Sterling Brown won first prize.

Johnson continued to enjoy her new circle of literary friends during the 1920s, and they apparently appreciated her work. When Countee Cullen edited *Caroling Dusk* (1927), he included eight of her poems, the ones on which her identification with the Harlem Renaissance rests. In 1928, "A Missionary Brings a Young Native to

America" appeared in *Harlem* magazine, and James Weldon Johnson included five of her poems in his *Book of American Negro Poetry* (1931). He praised the work she put into her colloquial style and also recognized her true lyric talent.

Some scholars contend that Johnson returned to Boston sometime after 1929, where details of her life are just as sketchy as during her period in Harlem, but others maintain that she lived in New York for more than half a century before returning to the Boston area in the early 1980s. It is known that she retired more and more from public view, but she did allow Dorothy West to publish a couple of her poems in issues of *Challenge: A Literary Quarterly.* Although her peers continued to praise her work, that did not inspire her to greater creativity or social interaction. She married, but her husband's name, William Warner Hubbell, was not made public until 1970. She had one child, Abigail Calachaly (the name given a family doll) Hubbell, born in 1940. In 1986, Johnson was back in New York, living with her daughter's family. The reasons for her cultivation of privacy and her abandonment of literary creation (at least for publication) are unclear.

Helene Johnson wrote poems about the beauties of the natural world. Like those of other Renaissance women poets, they are of a personal nature. Poems such as "Fulfillment," "Trees at Night," and "Summer Matures" suggest that she used nature imagery as a subterfuge to celebrate her sense of woman's self, especially her female sensuality.

Johnson is best known for her works that reflect, more than the verse of any other woman poet in the Harlem group, what most critics consider to be the major themes and poetic forms of the Renaissance. Like Langston Hughes, she used the innovative, street-smart language of Harlem to treat her central themes—racial oppression, militancy, black pride, the African heritage, and the folk. The underlying premise of her racial protest poems, such as "Bottled," "Sonnet to a Negro in Harlem," "Magalu," "The Road," and "Poem," is that only through an exploration and understanding of the African past and of his or her innate rhythmic sense can the African American come to truly appreciate his or her real significance as a human being.

In many ways, Johnson's racial poetry addresses the issue of African American "double consciousness" raised by W.E.B. Du Bois and Countee Cullen in their works. Johnson rejected the notion that the African American, in Du Bois's words, "ever feels his twoness,—an American, a Negro; two souls, two thoughts, two unreconciled strivings; two warring ideals in one dark body." In particular, she attacked Cullen's problem of cultural dualism, of being torn between Christian teachings and African religion. To the contrary, Johnson believed that African tradition is the only true cultural heritage of the African American. The poet warns a young black woman named "Magalu," therefore, to ignore Christianity, "a creed that will not let you dance." Rather than listen to "a man with a white collar / And a small black book with a cross on it," the woman should embrace ancestral worship, the sacred rituals of "laughing waters, / Lulling lakes, lissome winds" and "the passionate wonder" of the forest.

Johnson's racial poems established her during the 1920s as one of the brightest lights shining among the up-and-coming young poets. One has to wonder what the literary fate of this talented poet would have been if she had received the patronage and critical attention enjoyed by several of the male poets of the time.

❖❖❖

Very little has been written on Johnson. However, short but informative accounts of her life and works can be found in the following: Gloria T. Hull, "Black Women Poets from Wheatley to Walker," in *Sturdy Black Bridges,* ed. Roseann P. Bell et al. (1979); Maureen Honey, *Shadowed Dreams: Women's Poetry of the Harlem Renaissance* (1989); T. J. Bryan, "Helene Johnson," *Notable Black American Women* (1992); Raymond R. Patterson, "Helene Johnson," in *Dictionary of Literary Biography, Afro-American Writers—from the Harlem Renaissance to 1940.* vol. 51 (1987).

My Race

Ah, my race,
Hungry race,
Throbbing and young—
Ah, my race,
Wonder race,
Sobbing with song—
Ah, my race,
Laughing race,
Careless in mirth—
Ah, my veiled
Unformed race,
Fumbling in birth.

Sonnet to a Negro in Harlem

You are disdainful and magnificent—
Your perfect body and your pompous gait,
Your dark eyes flashing solemnly with hate;
Small wonder that you are incompetent
To imitate those whom you so despise—
Your shoulders towering high above the throng,
Your head thrown back in rich, barbaric song,
Palm trees and mangoes stretched before your eyes.
Let others toil and sweat for labor's sake
And wring from grasping hands their meed of gold.
Why urge ahead your supercilious feet?
Scorn will efface each footprint that you make.
I love your laughter, arrogant and bold.
You are too splendid for this city street!

Bottled

Upstairs on the third floor
Of the 135th Street library
In Harlem, I saw a little
Bottle of sand, brown sand,
Just like the kids make pies

Out of down at the beach.
But the label said: "This
Sand was taken from the Sahara desert."
Imagine that! The Sahara desert!
Some bozo's been all the way to Africa to get some sand.
And yesterday on Seventh Avenue
I saw a darky dressed to kill
In yellow gloves and swallowtail coat
And swirling a cane. And everyone
Was laughing at him. Me too,
At first, till I saw his face
When he stopped to hear a
Organ grinder grind out some jazz.
Boy! You should a seen that darky's face!
It just shone. Gee, he was happy!
And he began to dance. No
Charleston or Black Bottom for him.
No sir. He danced just as dignified
And slow. No, not slow either.
Dignified and *proud!* You couldn't
Call it slow, not with all the
Cuttin' up he did. You would a died to see him.
The crowd kept yellin' but he didn't hear,
Just kept on dancin' and twirlin' that cane
And yellin' out loud every once in a while.
I know the crowd thought he was coo-coo.
But say, I was where I could see his face,
And somehow, I could see him dancin' in a jungle,
A real honest-to-cripe jungle, and he wouldn't leave on them
Trick clothes—those yaller shoes and yaller gloves
And swallowtail coat. He wouldn't have on nothing.
And he wouldn't be carrying no cane.
He'd be carrying a spear with a sharp fine point
Like the bayonets we had "over there."
And the end of it would be dipped in some kind of
Hoo-doo poison. And he'd be dancin' black and naked and gleaming.
And he'd have rings in his ears and on his nose
And bracelets and necklaces of elephants' teeth.
Gee, I bet he'd be beautiful then all right.
No one would laugh at him then, I bet.
Say! That man that took that sand from the Sahara desert
And put it in a little bottle on a shelf in the library,
That's what they done to this shine, ain't it? Bottled him.
Trick shoes, trick coat, trick cane, trick everything—all glass—
But inside—
Gee, that poor shine!

Trees at Night

Slim sentinels
Stretching lacy arms
About a slumbrous moon;
Black quivering
Silhouettes,
Tremulous,
Stencilled on the petal
Of a bluebell;
Ink spluttered
On a robin's breast;
The jagged rent
Of mountains
Reflected in a
Stilly sleeping lake;
Fragile pinnacles
Of fairy castles;
Torn webs of shadows;
And printed 'gainst the sky—
The trembling beauty
Of an urgent pine.

The Road

Ah, little road, all whirry in the breeze,
A leaping clay hill lost among the trees,
The bleeding note of rapture-streaming thrush
Caught in a drowsy hush
And stretched out in a single, singing line of dusky song.
Ah, little road, brown as my race is brown,
Your trodden beauty like our trodden pride,
Dust of the dust, they must not bruise you down.
Rise to one brimming golden, spilling cry!

Magalu

Summer comes.
The ziczac hovers
'Round the greedy-mouthed crocodile.
A vulture bears away a foolish jackal.
The flamingo is a dash of pink
Against dark green mangroves,
Her slender legs rivalling her slim neck.
The laughing lake gurgles delicious music in its throat
And lulls to sleep the lazy lizard.
A nebulous being on a sun-scorched rock.
In such a place,

In this pulsing, riotous gasp of color,
I met Magalu, dark as a tree at night,
Eager-lipped, listening to a man with a white collar
And a small black book with a cross on it.
Oh Magalu, come! Take my hand and I will read you poetry,
Chromatic words,
Seraphic symphonies,
Fill up your throat with laughter and your heart with song.
Do not let him lure you from your laughing waters,
Lulling lakes, lissome winds.
Would you sell the colors of your sunset and the fragrance
Of your flowers, and the passionate wonder of your forest
For a creed that will not let you dance?

Summer Matures

Summer matures. Brilliant Scorpion
Appears. The Pelican's thick pouch
Hangs heavily with perch and slugs.
The brilliant-bellied newt flashes
Its crimson crest in the white water.
In the lush meadow, by the river,
The yellow-freckled toad laughs
With a toothless gurgle at the white-necked stork
Standing asleep on one red reedy leg.
And here Pan dreams of slim stalks clean for piping,
And of a nightingale gone mad with freedom.
Come. I shall weave a bed of reeds
And willow limbs and pale nightflowers.
I shall strip the roses of their petals,
And the white down from the swan's neck.
Come. Night is here. The air is drunk
With wild grape and sweet clover.
And by the sacred fount of Aganippe,
Euterpe sings of love. Ah, the woodland creatures,
The doves in pairs, the wild sow and her shoats,
The stag searching the forest for a mate,
Know more of love than you, my callous Phaon.
The young moon is a curved white scimitar
Pierced thru the swooning night.
Sweet Phaon. With Sappho, sleep like the stars at dawn.
This night was born for love, my Phaon.
Come.

Fulfillment

To climb a hill that hungers for the sky,
  To dig my hands wrist deep in pregnant earth,

To watch a young bird, veering, learn to fly,
  To give a still, stark poem shining birth.

To hear the rain drool, dimpling, down the drain
  And splash with a wet giggle in the street,
To ramble in the twilight after supper,
  And to count the pretty faces that you meet.

To ride to town on trolleys, crowded, teeming,
  With joy and hurry and laughter and push and sweat—
Squeezed next a patent-leathered Negro dreaming
  Of a wrinkled river and a minnow net.

To buy a paper from a breathless boy,
  And read of kings and queens in foreign lands,
Hyperbole of romance and adventure,
  All for a penny the color of my hand.

To lean against a strong tree's bosom, sentient
  And hushed before the silent prayer it breathes,
To melt the still snow with my seething body
  And kiss the warm earth tremulous underneath.

Ah, life, to let your stabbing beauty pierce me
  And wound me like we did the studded Christ,
To grapple with you, loving you too fiercely,
  And to die bleeding—consummate with Life!

Fiction Writers

NELLA LARSEN

(1891–1964)

Perhaps no other novelist has captured the complexities of race, gender, class, and color with which the mulatto female in the United States struggles as well as Nella Larsen. Born to a white mother and a variously identified black father, Larsen used the many patterns of acceptance and rejection in her own life to fashion characters who are torn by three worlds—black, white and mulatto—as they try to capitalize on European standards of beauty to form an acceptable female identity. While the author gained international prominence through these well-crafted depictions, her characters never discover societal compatibility or personal fulfillment. At each novel's end, their displacement merely mirrors continuous sets of tragic circumstances in the writer's own life.

Nella Larsen went to great lengths to keep facts about her childhood and even some years of her adult life in strict privacy. What is known is that she was born in Chicago on April 13, 1891. She has stated that her mother was a white Scandinavian woman and her father was of African Caribbean origin with some unknown degree of black blood. It is not known whether the mother and father ever legally married or what really happened to the father (although Larsen stated that he died shortly after she was born). What is known is that the mother remarried and that she and Nella's white stepfather had another daughter with whom Nella shared some time during childhood.

Thadious Davis's recent groundbreaking biography of Larsen, taken from well-researched but necessarily fragmented background material, builds a strong foundation for her position that Larsen in fact came from a community of mixed Scandinavian and Caribbean immigrants who used various maneuvers of clever subterfuge to hide the "taint" of their partial African ancestry. Larsen was apparently born too dark-skinned to permit the illusion. Her very existence seemed to bring such shame to various family members that her mother kept her a safe distance away, at one point denying her existence altogether. Davis points out that part of the distancing may have meant that Larsen spent part of her early life in an orphanage. Several critics have pointed out that the chilling attitudes that the white women in Larsen's novels hold toward their children were crafted from the novelist's experience with her own mother.

The mother's insistence on denying Nella also is the central point of another biographical theory. In his seminal 1989 article "Whatever Happened to Nella Larsen?", Charles R. Larson claims that Nella was the illegitimate offspring of a white mother and an African American chauffeur whom the mother met when she worked as a maid in New York City. Larson says that the mother returned to Chicago after Nella was born and subsequently married a fellow Scandinavian who was uncomfortable having Nella around, especially after the couple had their own daughter. Larson indicates that this discomfort may have led to turning the child out. Davis has authenticated records that Larsen first entered elementary school when she was almost ten years old. Although the reasons for such a late entry are problematical, they do lend some support to the theory that Larsen spent part of her young life in an orphanage.

Larsen left Chicago in 1907 to undertake nurse's training at the famed Fisk University in Nashville, Tennessee. She left Fisk a year later, and the next four years of her life are a mystery, but it is possible that she spent part of that time continuing her studies at the University of Copenhagen in Denmark as an auditing student. In true biographical style, Helga Crane, the leading character in Larsen's novel *Quicksand,* spent part of her early years in Copenhagen.

In 1912, Larsen entered New York's Lincoln Hospital and Home Training School for Nurses. Nursing was one of the most advanced careers for a young black woman in early-twentieth-century America. Graduating on May 13, 1915, Larsen worked on the Lincoln staff for a few months before moving to Tuskegee, Alabama, to begin work as the head nurse of the John Andrew Memorial Hospital and Nurse Training School, an affiliate program of Tuskegee Institute. Dissatisfied with the class divisions at Tuskegee, Nella returned to New York in 1916 and began a courtship with physicist Elmer Samuel Imes, whom she married in 1919.

Imes was not only one of few African American Ph.D. scientists, but he also was an elite member of Harlem's upper class, well-known to both blacks and whites. The marriage brought Larsen into contact with the most prestigious members of the current literary movement among black intellectuals—most notably Walter White, the black American leader of the Urban League, and Carl Van Vechten, the noted white critic and patron of young black writers, who took Larsen under their wings. She abandoned the nursing profession for work at a library in 1923, a position perhaps better suited for a physicist's wife, and she began earnest work on several short stories. With Van Vechten's encouragement, she submitted her first novel, *Quicksand,* to his publisher, Alfred A. Knopf. It was published in 1928 to rave reviews. Her second novel, *Passing,* came out just eleven months later. With two novels that brought her instant fame and success, Nella Larsen became the first African American woman to win a fellowship from the prestigious Guggenheim Foundation in 1930.

In *Quicksand,* Larsen contrasts the world of the northern, urban, mulatto middle class concerned with maintaining a social standing distant from both blacks and whites with that of a dark-skinned, rural, undereducated population in the South. After trying to live with several Scandinavian family members in both the Midwest and Europe, the heroine, Helga Crane, leaves a comfortable but disillusioning life in New York to marry an unrefined Baptist minister who demanded that she accept his atavistic sensuality and religious lifestyle. After several children and much physical and mental illness, Crane finds that she cannot escape. Her demise illustrates the tragedy of the 1920s mulatto female, who had no compatible identification in either the plastic world among whites and mulattos or the simplistic peasant life of the more African ex-slaves.

In *Passing,* through controlled artistic techniques and mutely expressed themes, very much like F. Scott Fitzgerald in *The Great Gatsby,* Larsen again shows the extreme materialism rampant among nouveau riche whites and mulattos in upper-class New York. The heroine, Clare Kendry, tries to balance the paranoid life of a light-skinned African American woman who is attempting to pass for white with the ostensibly normal life of an upper-class wife and mother. She lives not only with the constant torment of being discovered but with the incessant question of whether her husband loves her for herself or for her put-on European beauty. Kendry is never free to develop outside of constraints imposed by men and a society that will subject her to poverty, rejection, and failure once her identity is known.

But even with all of this international acclaim, Nella Larson's personal life was falling apart. Her husband became increasingly unfaithful. Upon returning from the trip to Europe made possible by the Guggenheim Fellowship, Larsen suffered three disappointments. She found that her husband was unfaithful; Knopf refused to publish her third novel, *Mirage;* and she was accused of plagiarism. After trying a brief period of reconciliation with Imes, Larsen finally divorced him. Eventually, like her character Hilda Crane, Larsen retreated into obscurity, withdrew from public life in the literary world of the Harlem Renaissance, and reentered the field of nursing. She died in 1964.

Perhaps the most impressive tribute to her literary talents came from the greatest black intellectual leader of the early twentieth century, W.E.B. Du Bois, quoted in Thadious M. Davis, *Nella Larsen,* who said, "I think that Mrs. Imes, writing under the pen name of Nella Larsen, has done a fine, thoughtful and courageous piece of work. . . . *Quicksand* . . . is, on the whole, the best piece of fiction that Negro America has produced since the heyday of Chestnutt." Although most critics usually do not go as far as DuBois, those from the 1930s to the 1970s rate Larsen's books as among the best of the period because they so aptly explore the trauma of mulatto identity within a race-conscious society.

However, recent feminist critics such as Barbara Christian, Claudia Tate, Deborah McDowell, and Mary Helen Washington have assailed traditional criticism about Larsen, citing overemphasis on the mixed-raced aspects of her characters rather than on their female development. Several have ventured theories that conflicts over female sexual identity are more urgent considerations in the two novels. The facts rendered in Davis's biography have provided a delicate balance to this ongoing discussion.

❖❖❖

Recently, the most commanding work on Larsen's life and works is Thadious M. Davis's biography, *Nella Larsen: Novelist of the Harlem Renaissance* (1994). There is at least one full collection of Larsen's short stories and novels, *An Intimation of Things Distant: The Collected Fiction of Nella Larsen* (1992). Deborah E. McDowell has a compelling introduction to a joint edition of the two novels published in 1986.

See also Davis's discussion in *Dictionary of Literary Biography,* vol. 51 (1987); Mary Helen Washington, "Nella Larsen—Mystery Woman of the Harlem Renaissance," *Ms.,* December 1980; 44–50; Claudia Tate, "Nella Larsen's *Passing:* A Problem of Interpretation," *Black American Literature Forum* 14, No. 1 (1980); Barbara Christian, *Black Women Novelists: The Making of a Tradition, 1892–1976* (1980); Addison Gayle, *The Way of the New World: The Black Novel in America* (1975); and Mary Helen Washington's remarks in *Invented Lives: Narratives of Black Women 1860–1960* (1987).

Traditional interpretations of Larsen's novel include Nathan Huggins, *Harlem Renaissance* (1971); David L. Lewis, *When Harlem Was in Vogue* (1981); Arthur P. Davis, *From the Dark Tower: Afro-American Writers 1900–1960* (1974); Arna Bontemp, *The Harlem Renaissance Remembered* (1972); Robert Bone, *The Negro Novel in America* (1965).

FROM *Quicksand*

One

Helga Crane sat alone in her room, which at that hour, eight in the evening, was in soft gloom. Only a single reading lamp, dimmed by a great black and red shade, made a pool of light on the blue Chinese carpet, on the bright covers of the books which she had taken down from their long shelves, on the white pages of the opened one selected, on the shining brass bowl crowded with many-colored nasturtiums beside her on the low table, and on the oriental silk which covered the stool at her slim feet. It was a comfortable room, furnished with rare and intensely personal taste, flooded with Southern sun in the day, but shadowy just then with the drawn curtains and single shaded light. Large, too. So large that the spot where Helga sat was a small oasis in a desert of darkness. And eerily quiet. But that was what she liked after her taxing day's work, after the hard classes, in which she gave willingly and unsparingly of herself with no apparent return. She loved this tranquillity, this quiet, following the fret and strain of the long hours spent among fellow members of a carelessly unkind and gossiping faculty, following the strenuous rigidity of conduct required in this huge educational community of which she was an insignificant part. This was her rest, this intentional isolation for a short while in the evening, this little time in her own attractive room with her own books. To the rapping of other teachers, bearing fresh scandals, or seeking information, or other more concrete favors, or merely talk, at that hour Helga Crane never opened her door.

An observer would have thought her well fitted to that framing of light and shade. A slight girl of twenty-two years, with narrow, sloping shoulders and delicate, but well-turned, arms and legs, she had, none the less, an air of radiant, careless health. In vivid green and gold negligee and glistening brocaded mules, deep sunk in the big high-backed chair, against whose dark tapestry her sharply cut face, with skin like yellow satin, was distinctly outlined, she was—to use a hackneyed word—attractive. Black, very broad brows over soft, yet penetrating, dark eyes, and a pretty mouth, whose sensitive and sensuous lips had a slight questioning petulance and a tiny dissatisfied droop, were the features on which the observer's attention would fasten; though her nose was good, her ears delicately chiseled, and her curly blue-black hair plentiful and always straying in a little wayward, delightful way. Just then it was tumbled, falling unrestrained about her face and on to her shoulders.

Helga Crane tried not to think of her work and the school as she sat there. Ever since her arrival in Naxos she had striven to keep these ends of the days from the intrusion of irritating thoughts and worries. Usually she was successful. But not this evening. Of the books which she had taken from their places she had decided on Marmaduke Pickthall's *Saïd the Fisherman.* She wanted forgetfulness, complete mental relaxation, rest from thought of any kind. For the day had been more than usually crowded with distasteful encounters and stupid perversities. The sultry hot Southern spring had left her strangely tired, and a little unnerved. And annoying beyond all other happenings had been that affair of the noon period, now again thrusting itself on her already irritated mind.

She had counted on a few spare minutes in which to indulge in the sweet pleasure of a bath and a fresh, cool change of clothing. And instead her luncheon time had been shortened, as had that of everyone else, and immediately after the hurried gulping down of a heavy hot meal the hundreds of students and teachers had been herded into the sun-baked chapel to listen to the banal, the patronizing, and even the insulting remarks of one of the renowned white preachers of the state.

Helga shuddered a little as she recalled some of the statements made by that holy white man of God to the black folk sitting so respectfully before him.

This was, he had told them with obvious sectional pride, the finest school for Negroes anywhere in the country, north or south; in fact, it was better even than a great many schools for white children. And he had dared any Northerner to come south and after looking upon this great institution to say that the Southerner mistreated the Negro. And he had said that if all Negroes would only take a leaf out of the book of Naxos and conduct themselves in the manner of the Naxos products, there would be no race problem, because Naxos Negroes knew what was expected of them. They had good sense and they had good taste. They knew enough to stay in their places, and that, said the preacher, showed good taste. He spoke of his great admiration for the Negro race, no other race in so short a time had made so much progress, but he had urgently besought them to know when and where to stop. He hoped, he sincerely hoped, that they wouldn't become avaricious and grasping, thinking only of adding to their earthly goods, for that would be a sin in the sight of Almighty God. And then he had spoken of contentment, embellishing his words with scriptural quotations and pointing out to them that it was their duty to be satisfied in the estate to which they had been called, hewers of wood and drawers of water. And then he had prayed.

Sitting there in her room, long hours after, Helga again felt a surge of hot anger and seething resentment. And again it subsided in amazement at the memory of the considerable applause which had greeted the speaker just before he had asked his God's blessing upon them.

The South. Naxos. Negro education. Suddenly she hated them all. Strange, too, for this was the thing which she had ardently desired to share in, to be a part of this monument to one man's genius and vision. She pinned a scrap of paper about the bulb under the lamp's shade, for, having discarded her book, in the certainty that in such a mood even *Saïd* and his audacious villainy could not charm her, she wanted an even more soothing darkness. She wished it were vacation, so that she might get away for a time.

"No, forever!" she said aloud.

The minutes gathered into hours, but still she sat motionless, a disdainful smile or an angry frown passing now and then across her face. Somewhere in the room a little clock ticked time away. Somewhere outside, a whip-poorwill wailed. Evening died. A sweet smell of early Southern flowers rushed in on a newly-risen breeze which suddenly parted the thin silk curtains at the opened windows. A slender, frail glass vase fell from the sill with a tingling crash, but Helga Crane did not shift her position. And the night grew cooler, and older.

At last she stirred, uncertainly, but with an overpowering desire for action of some sort. A second she hesitated, then rose abruptly and pressed the electric switch with determined firmness, flooding suddenly the shadowy room with a white glare of light. Next she made a quick nervous tour to the end of the long room, paused a moment before the old bow-legged secretary that held with almost articulate protest her school-teacher paraphernalia of drab books and papers. Frantically Helga Crane clutched at the lot and then flung them violently, scornfully toward the wastebasket. It received a part, allowing the rest to spill untidily over the floor. The girl smiled ironically, seeing in the mess a simile of her own earnest endeavor to inculcate knowledge into her indifferent classes.

Yes, it was like that; a few of the ideas which she tried to put into the minds behind those baffling ebony, bronze, and gold faces reached their destination. The others were left scattered about. And, like the gay, indifferent wastebasket, it wasn't their fault. No, it wasn't the fault of those minds back of the diverse colored faces. It was, rather, the fault of the method, the general idea behind the system. Like her own hurried shot at the basket, the aim was bad, the material drab and badly prepared for its purpose.

This great community, she thought, was no longer a school. It had grown into a machine. It was now a show place in the black belt, exemplification of the white man's magnanimity, refutation of the black man's inefficiency. Life had died out of it. It was, Helga decided, now only a big knife with cruelly sharp edges ruthlessly cutting all to a pattern, the white man's pattern. Teachers as well as students were subjected to the paring process, for it tolerated no innovations, no individualisms. Ideas it rejected, and looked with open hostility on one and all who had the temerity to offer a suggestion or ever so mildly express a disapproval. Enthusiasm, spontaneity, if not actually suppressed, were at least openly regretted as unladylike or ungentlemanly qualities. The place was smug and fat with self-satisfaction.

A peculiar characteristic trait, cold, slowly accumulated unreason in which all values were distorted or else ceased to exist, had with surprising ferociousness shaken the bulwarks of that self-restraint which was also, curiously, a part of her nature. And now that it had waned as quickly as it had risen, she smiled again, and this time the smile held a faint amusement, which wiped away the little hardness which had congealed her lovely face. Nevertheless she was soothed by the impetuous discharge of violence, and a sigh of relief came from her.

She said aloud, quietly, dispassionately: "Well, I'm through with that," and, shutting off the hard, bright blaze of the overhead lights, went back to her chair and settled down with an odd gesture of sudden soft collapse, like a person who had been for months fighting the devil and then unexpectedly had turned round and agreed to do his bidding.

Helga Crane had taught in Naxos for almost two years, at first with the keen joy and zest of those immature people who have dreamed dreams of doing good to their fellow men. But gradually this zest was blotted out, giving place to a deep hatred for the trivial hypocrisies and careless cruelties which were, unintentionally perhaps, a part of the Naxos policy of uplift. Yet she had continued to try not only to teach, but to befriend those happy singing children, whose charm and distinctiveness the school was so surely ready to destroy. Instinctively Helga was aware that their smiling submissiveness covered many poignant heartaches and perhaps much secret contempt for their instructors. But she was powerless. In Naxos between teacher and student, between condescending authority and smoldering resentment, the gulf was too great, and too few had tried to cross it. It couldn't be spanned by one sympathetic teacher. It was useless to offer her atom of friendship, which under the existing conditions was neither wanted nor understood.

Nor was the general atmosphere of Naxos, its air of self-rightness and intolerant dislike of difference, the best of mediums for a pretty, solitary girl with no family connections. Helga's essentially likable and charming personality was smudged out. She had felt this for a long time. Now she faced with determination that other truth which she had refused to formulate in her thoughts, the fact that she was utterly unfitted for teaching, even for mere existence, in Naxos. She was a failure here. She had, she conceded now, been silly, obstinate, to persist for so long. A failure. Therefore, no need, no use, to stay longer. Suddenly she longed for immediate departure. How good, she thought, to go now, tonight!—and frowned to remember how impossible that would be. "The dignitaries," she said, "are not in their offices, and there will be yards and yards of red tape to unwind, gigantic, impressive spools of it."

And there was James Vayle to be told, and much-needed money to be got. James, she decided, had better be told at once. She looked at the clock racing indifferently on. No, too late. It would have to be tomorrow.

She hated to admit that money was the most serious difficulty. Knowing full well that it was important, she nevertheless rebelled at the unalterable truth that it could influence her actions, block her desires. A sordid necessity to be grappled with. With Helga it was almost a superstition that to concede to money its importance magnified its power. Still, in spite of her reluctance and distaste, her financial situation would have to be faced, and plans made, if she were to get away from Naxos with anything like the haste which she now so ardently desired.

Most of her earnings had gone into clothes, into books, into the furnishings of the room which held her. All her life Helga Crane had loved and longed for nice things. Indeed, it was this craving, this urge for beauty which had helped to bring her into disfavor in Naxos—"pride" and "vanity" her detractors called it.

The sum owing to her by the school would just a little more than buy her ticket back to Chicago. It was too near the end of the school term to hope to get teaching-work anywhere. If she couldn't find something else, she would have to ask Uncle Peter for a loan. Uncle Peter was, she knew, the one relative who thought kindly, or even calmly, of her. Her step-father, her step-brothers and sisters, and the numerous cousins, aunts, and other uncles could not be even remotely considered. She laughed a little, scornfully, reflecting that the antagonism was mutual, or, perhaps, just a trifle keener on her side than on theirs. They feared and hated her. She pitied and despised them. Uncle Peter was different. In his contemptuous way he was fond of her. Her beautiful, unhappy mother had been his favorite sister. Even so, Helga Crane knew that he would be more likely to help her because her need would strengthen his oft-repeated conviction that because of her Negro blood she would never amount to anything, than from motives of affection or loving memory. This knowledge, in its present aspect of truth, irritated her to an astonishing degree. She regarded Uncle Peter almost vindictively, although always he had been extraordinarily generous with her and she fully intended to ask his assistance. "A beggar," she thought ruefully, "cannot expect to choose."

Returning to James Vayle, her thoughts took on the frigidity of complete determination. Her resolution to end her stay in Naxos would of course inevitably end her engagement to James. She had been engaged to him since her first semester there, when both had been new workers, and both were lonely. Together they had discussed their work and problems in adjustment, and had drifted into a closer relationship. Bitterly she reflected that James had speedily and with entire ease fitted into his niche. He was now completely "naturalized," as they used laughingly to call it. Helga, on the other hand, had never quite achieved the unmistakable Naxos mold, would never achieve it, in spite of much trying. She could neither conform, nor be happy in her unconformity. This she saw clearly now, and with cold anger at all the past futile effort. What a waste! How pathetically she had struggled in those first months and with what small success. A lack somewhere. Always she had considered it a lack of understanding on the part of the community, but in her present new revolt she realized that the fault had been partly hers. A lack of acquiescence. She hadn't really wanted to be made over. This thought bred a sense of shame, a feeling of ironical disillusion. Evidently there were parts of her she couldn't be proud of. The revealing picture of her past striving was too humiliating. It was as if she had deliberately planned to steal an ugly thing, for which she had no desire, and had been found out.

Ironically she visualized the discomfort of James Vayle. How her maladjustment had bothered him! She had a faint notion that it was behind his ready assent to her suggestion anent a longer engagement than, originally, they had planned. He was liked and approved of in Naxos and loathed the idea that the girl he was to marry couldn't manage to win liking and approval also. Instinctively Helga had known that secretly he had placed the blame upon her. How right he had been! Certainly his attitude had gradually changed, though he still gave her his attentions. Naxos pleased him and he had become content with life as it was lived there. No longer lonely, he was now one of the community and so beyond the need or the desire to discuss its affairs and its failings with an outsider. She was, she knew, in a queer indefinite way, a disturbing factor. She knew too that a something held him, a something against which he was powerless. The idea that she was in but one nameless way necessary to him filled her with a sensation amounting almost to shame. And yet his mute helplessness against that ancient appeal by which she held him pleased her and fed her vanity—gave her a feeling of power. At the same time she shrank away from it, subtly aware of possibilities she herself couldn't predict.

Helga's own feelings defeated inquiry, but honestly confronted, all pretense brushed aside, the dominant one, she suspected, was relief. At least, she felt *no* regret that tomorrow would mark the end of any claim she had upon him. The surety that the meeting would be a clash annoyed her, for she had no talent for quarreling—when possible she preferred to flee. That was all.

The family of James Vayle, in near-by Atlanta, would be glad. They had never liked the engagement, had never liked Helga Crane. Her own lack of family disconcerted them. No family. That was the crux of the whole matter. For Helga, it accounted for everything, her failure here in Naxos, her former loneliness in Nashville. It even accounted for her engagement to James. Negro society, she had learned, was as complicated and as rigid in its ramifications as the highest strata of white society. If you couldn't prove your ancestry and connections, you were tolerated, but you didn't "belong." You could be queer, or even attractive, or bad, or brilliant, or even love beauty and such nonsense if you were a Rankin, or a Leslie, or a Scoville; in other words, if you had a family. But if you were just plain Helga Crane, of whom nobody had ever heard, it was presumptuous of you to be anything but inconspicuous and conformable.

To relinquish James Vayle would most certainly be social suicide, for the Vayles were people of consequence. The fact that they were a "first family" had been one of James's attractions for the obscure Helga. She had wanted social background, but—she had not imagined that it could be so stuffy.

She made a quick movement of impatience and stood up. As she did so, the room whirled about her in an impish, hateful way. Familiar objects seemed suddenly unhappily distant. Faintness closed about her like a vise. She swayed, her small, slender hands gripping the chair arms for support. In a moment the faintness receded, leaving in its wake a sharp resentment at the trick which her strained nerves had played upon her. And after a moment's rest she got hurriedly into bed, leaving her room disorderly for the first time.

Books and papers scattered about the floor, fragile stockings and underthings and the startling green and gold negligee dripping about on chairs and stool, met the encounter of the amazed eyes of the girl who came in the morning to awaken Helga Crane.

FROM *Passing*

One

It was the last letter in Irene Redfield's little pile of morning mail. After her other ordinary and clearly directed letters the long envelope of thin Italian paper with its almost illegible scrawl seemed out of place and alien. And there was, too, something mysterious and slightly furtive about it. A thin sly thing which bore no return address to betray the sender. Not that she hadn't immediately known who its sender was. Some two years ago she had one very like it in outward appearance. Furtive, but yet in some peculiar, determined way a little flaunting. Purple ink. Foreign paper of extraordinary size.

It had been, Irene noted, postmarked in New York the day before. Her brows came together in a tiny frown. The frown, however, was more from perplexity than from annoyance; though there was in her thoughts an element of both. She was wholly unable to comprehend such an attitude towards danger as she was sure the letter's contents would reveal; and she disliked the idea of opening and reading it.

This, she reflected, was of a piece with all that she knew of Clare Kendry. Stepping always on the edge of danger. Always aware, but not drawing back or turning aside. Certainly not because of any alarms or feeling of outrage on the part of others.

And for a swift moment Irene Redfield seemed to see a pale small girl sitting on a ragged blue sofa, sewing pieces of bright red cloth together, while her drunken father, a tall, powerfully built man, raged threateningly up and down the shabby room, bellowing curses and making spasmodic lunges at her which were not the less frightening because they were, for the most part, ineffectual. Sometimes he did manage to reach her. But only the fact that the child had edged herself and her poor sewing over to the farthermost corner of the sofa suggested that she was in any way perturbed by this menace to herself and her work.

Clare had known well enough that it was unsafe to take a portion of the dollar that was her weekly wage for the doing of many errands for the dressmaker who lived on the top floor of the building of which Bob Kendry was janitor. But that knowledge had not deterred her. She wanted to go to her Sunday school's picnic, and she had made up her mind to wear a new dress. So, in spite of certain unpleasantness and possible danger, she had taken the money to buy the material for that pathetic little red frock.

There had been, even in those days, nothing sacrificial in Clare Kendry's idea of life, no allegiance beyond her own immediate desire. She was selfish, and cold, and hard. And yet she had, too, a strange capacity of transforming warmth and passion, verging sometimes almost on theatrical heroics.

Irene, who was a year or more older than Clare, remembered the day that Bob Kendry had been brought home dead, killed in a silly saloon-fight. Clare, who was at that time a scant fifteen years old, had just stood there with her lips pressed together, her thin arms folded across her narrow chest, staring down at the familiar pasty-white face of her parent with a sort of disdain in her slanting black eyes. For a very long time she had stood like that, silent and staring. Then, quite suddenly, she had given way to a torrent of weeping, swaying her thin body, tearing at her bright hair, and stamping her small feet. The outburst had ceased as suddenly as it had begun. She glanced quickly about the bare room, taking everyone in, even the two policemen, in a sharp look of flashing scorn. And, in the next instant, she had turned and vanished through the door.

Seen across the long stretch of years, the thing had more the appearance of an outpouring of pent-up fury than of an overflow of grief for her dead father; though she had been, Irene admitted, fond enough of him in her own rather catlike way.

Catlike. Certainly that was the word which best described Clare Kendry, if any single word could describe her. Sometimes she was hard and apparently without feeling at all; sometimes she was affectionate and rashly impulsive. And there was about her an amazing soft malice, hidden well away until provoked. Then she was capable of scratching, and very effectively too. Or, driven to anger, she would fight with a ferocity and impetuousness that disregarded or forgot any danger; superior strength, numbers, or other unfavourable circumstances. How savagely she had clawed those boys the day they had hooted her parent and sung a derisive rhyme, of their own composing, which pointed out certain eccentricities in his careening gait! And how deliberately she had—

Irene brought her thoughts back to the present, to the letter from Clare Kendry that she still held unopened in her hand. With a little feeling of apprehension, she very slowly cut the envelope, drew out the folded sheets, spread them, and began to read.

It was, she saw at once, what she had expected since learning from the postmark that Clare was in the city. An extravagantly phrased wish to see her again. Well, she needn't and wouldn't, Irene told herself, accede to that. Nor would she assist Clare to realize her foolish desire to return for a moment to that life which long ago, and of her own choice, she had left behind her.

She ran through the letter, puzzling out, as best she could, the carelessly formed words or making instinctive guesses at them.

". . . For I am lonely, so lonely . . . cannot help longing to be with you again, as I have never longed for anything before; and I have wanted many things in my life. . . . You can't know how in this pale life of mine I am all the time seeing the bright pictures of that other that I once thought I was glad to be free of. . . . It's like an ache, a pain that never ceases. . . ." Sheets upon thin sheets of it. And ending finally with, "and it's your fault, 'Rene dear. At least partly. For I wouldn't now, perhaps, have this terrible, this wild desire if I hadn't seen you that time in Chicago. . . ."

Brilliant red patches flamed in Irene Redfield's warm olive cheeks.

"That time in Chicago." The words stood out from among the many paragraphs of other words, bringing with them a clear, sharp remembrance, in which even now, after two years, humiliation, resentment, and rage were mingled.

Two

This is what Irene Redfield remembered.

Chicago. August. A brilliant day, hot, with a brutal staring sun pouring down rays that were like molten rain. A day on which the very outlines of the buildings shuddered as if in protest at the heat. Quivering lines sprang up from baked pavements and wriggled along the shining car-tracks. The automobiles parked at the kerbs were a dancing blaze, and the glass of the shop-windows threw out a blinding radiance. Sharp particles of dust rose from the burning sidewalks, stinging the seared or dripping skins of wilting pedestrians. What small breeze there was seemed like the breath of a flame fanned by slow bellows.

It was on that day of all others that Irene set out to shop for the things which she had promised to take home from Chicago to her two small sons, Brian junior and Theodore. Characteristically, she had put it off until only a few crowded days remained of her long visit. And only this sweltering one was free of engagements till the evening.

Without too much trouble she had got the mechanical aeroplane for Junior. But the drawing-book, for which Ted had so gravely and insistently given her precise directions, had sent her in and out of five shops without success.

It was while she was on her way to a sixth place that right before her smarting eyes a man toppled over and became an inert crumpled heap on the scorching cement. About the lifeless figure a little crowd gathered. Was the man dead, or only faint? someone asked her. But Irene didn't know and didn't try to discover. She edged her way out of the increasing crowd, feeling disagreeably damp and sticky and soiled from contact with so many sweating bodies.

For a moment she stood fanning herself and dabbing at her moist face with an inadequate scrap of handkerchief. Suddenly she was aware that the whole street had a wobbly look, and realized that she was about to faint. With a quick perception of the need for immediate safety, she lifted a wavering hand in the direction of a cab parked directly in front of her. The perspiring driver jumped out and guided her to his car. He helped, almost lifted her in. She sank down on the hot leather seat.

For a minute her thoughts were nebulous. They cleared.

"I guess," she told her Samaritan, "it's tea I need. On a roof somewhere."

"The Drayton, ma'am?" he suggested. "They do say as how it's always a breeze up there."

"Thank you. I think the Drayton'll do nicely," she told him.

There was that little grating sound of the clutch being slipped in as the man put the car in gear and slid deftly out into the boiling traffic. Reviving under the warm breeze stirred up by the moving cab, Irene made some small attempts to repair the damage that the heat and crowds had done to her appearance.

All too soon the rattling vehicle shot towards the sidewalk and stood still. The driver sprang out and opened the door before the hotel's decorated attendant could reach it. She got out, and thanking him smilingly as well as in a more substantial manner for his kind helpfulness and understanding, went in through the Drayton's wide doors.

Stepping out of the elevator that had brought her to the roof, she was led to a table just in front of a long window whose gently moving curtains suggested a cool breeze. It was, she thought, like being wafted upward on a magic carpet to another world, pleasant, quiet, and strangely remote from the sizzling one that she had left below.

The tea, when it came, was all that she had desired and expected. In fact, so much was it what she had desired and expected that after the first deep cooling drink she was able to forget it, only now and then sipping, a little absently, from the tall green glass, while she surveyed the room about her or looked out over some lower buildings at the bright unstirred blue of the lake reaching away to an undetected horizon.

She had been gazing down for some time at the specks of cars and people creeping about in streets, and thinking how silly they looked, when on taking up her glass she was surprised to find it empty at last. She asked for more tea and while she waited, began to recall the happenings of the day and to wonder what she was to do about Ted and his book. Why was it that almost invariably he wanted something that was difficult or impossible to get? Like his father. For ever wanting something that he couldn't have.

Presently there were voices, a man's booming one and a woman's slightly husky. A waiter passed her, followed by a sweetly scented woman in a fluttering dress of green chiffon whose mingled pattern of narcissuses, jonquils, and hyacinths was a reminder of pleasantly chill spring days. Behind her there was a man, very red in the face, who was mopping his neck and forehead with a big crumpled handkerchief.

"Oh dear!" Irene groaned, rasped by annoyance, for after a little discussion and commotion they had stopped at the very next table. She had been alone there at the window and it had been so satisfyingly quiet. Now, of course, they would chatter.

But no. Only the woman sat down. The man remained standing, abstractedly pinching the knot of his bright blue tie. Across the small space that separated the two tables his voice carried clearly.

"See you later, then," he declared, looking down at the woman. There was pleasure in his tones and a smile on his face.

His companion's lips parted in some answer, but her words were blurred by the little intervening distance and the medley of noises floating up from the streets below. They didn't reach Irene. But she noted the peculiar caressing smile that accompanied them.

The man said: "Well, I suppose I'd better," and smiled again, and said good-bye, and left.

An attractive-looking woman, was Irene's opinion, with those dark, almost black, eyes and that wide mouth like a scarlet flower against the ivory of her skin. Nice clothes too, just right for the weather, thin and cool without being mussy, as summer things were so apt to be.

A waiter was taking her order. Irene saw her smile up at him as she murmured something—thanks, maybe. It was an odd sort of smile. Irene couldn't quite define it, but she was sure that she would have classed it, coming from another woman, as being just a shade too provocative for a waiter. About this one, however, there was something that made her hesitate to name it that. A certain impression of assurance, perhaps.

The waiter came back with the order. Irene watched her spread out her napkin, saw the silver spoon in the white hand slit the dull gold of the melon. Then, conscious that she had been staring, she looked quickly away.

Her mind returned to her own affairs. She had settled, definitely, the problem of the proper one of two frocks for the bridge party that night, in rooms whose atmosphere would be so thick and hot that every breath would be like breathing soup. The dress decided, her thoughts had gone back to the snag of Ted's book, her unseeing eyes far away on the lake, when by some sixth sense she was acutely aware that someone was watching her.

Very slowly she looked around, and into the dark eyes of the woman in the green frock at the next table. But she evidently failed to realize that such intense interest as she was showing might be embarrassing, and continued to stare. Her demeanour was that of one who with utmost singleness of mind and purpose was determined to impress firmly and accurately each detail of Irene's features upon her memory for all time, nor showed the slightest trace of disconcertment at having been detected in her steady scrutiny.

Instead, it was Irene who was put out. Feeling her colour heighten under the continued inspection, she slid her eyes down. What, she wondered, could be the reason for such persistent attention? Had she, in her haste in the taxi, put her hat on backwards? Guardedly she felt at it. No. Perhaps there was a streak of powder somewhere on her face. She made a quick pass over it with her handkerchief. Something wrong with her dress? She shot a glance over it. Perfectly all right. *What* was it?

Again she looked up, and for a moment her brown eyes politely returned the stare of the other's black ones, which never for an instant fell or wavered. Irene made a little mental shrug. Oh well, let her look! She tried to treat the woman and her watching with indifference, but she couldn't. All her efforts to ignore her, it, were futile. She stole another glance. Still looking. What strange languorous eyes she had!

And gradually there rose in Irene a small inner disturbance, odious and hatefully familiar. She laughed softly, but her eyes flashed.

Did that woman, could that woman, somehow know that here before her very eyes on the roof of the Drayton sat a Negro?

Absurd! Impossible! White people were so stupid about such things for all that they usually asserted that they were able to tell; and by the most ridiculous means, finger-nails, palms of hands, shapes of ears, teeth, and other equally silly rot. They always took her for an Italian, a Spaniard, a Mexican, or a gipsy. Never, when she was alone, had they even remotely seemed to suspect that she was a Negro. No, the woman sitting there staring at her couldn't possibly know.

Nevertheless, Irene felt, in turn, anger, scorn, and fear slide over her. It wasn't that she was ashamed of being a Negro, or even of having it declared. It was the idea of being ejected from any place, even in the polite and tactful way in which the Drayton would probably do it, that disturbed her.

But she looked, boldly this time, back into the eyes still frankly intent upon her. They did not seem to her hostile or resentful. Rather, Irene had the feeling that they were ready to smile if she would. Nonsense, of course. The feeling passed, and she turned away with the firm intention of keeping her gaze on the lake, the roofs of the buildings across the way, the sky, anywhere but on that annoying woman. Almost immediately, however, her eyes were back again. In the midst of her fog of uneasiness she had been seized by a desire to outstare the rude observer. Suppose the woman did know or suspect her race. She couldn't prove it.

Suddenly her small fright increased. Her neighbor had risen and was coming towards her. What was going to happen now?

"Pardon me," the woman said pleasantly, "but I think I know you." Her slightly husky voice held a dubious note.

Looking up at her, Irene's suspicions and fears vanished. There was no mistaking the friendliness of that smile or resisting its charm. Instantly she surrendered to it and smiled too, as she said: "I'm afraid you're mistaken."

"Why, of course, I know you!" the other exclaimed. "Don't tell me you're not Irene Westover. Or do they still call you 'Rene?"

In the brief second before her answer, Irene tried vainly to recall where and when this woman could have known her. There, in Chicago. And before her marriage. That much was plain. High school? College? Y.W.C.A. committees? High school, most likely. What white girls had she known well enough to have been familiarly addressed as 'Rene by them? The woman before her didn't fit her memory of any of them. Who was she?

"Yes, I'm Irene Westover. And though nobody calls me 'Rene any more, it's good to hear the name again. And you—" She hesitated, ashamed that she could not remember, and hoping that the sentence would be finished for her.

"Don't you know me? Not really, 'Rene?"

"I'm sorry, but just at the minute I can't seem to place you."

Irene studied the lovely creature standing beside her for some clue to her identity. Who could she be? Where and when had they met? And through her perplexity there came the thought that the trick which her memory had played her was for some reason more gratifying than disappointing to her old acquaintance, that she didn't mind not being recognized.

And, too, Irene felt that she was just about to remember her. For about the woman was some quality, an intangible something, too vague to define, too remote to seize, but which was, to Irene Redfield, very familiar. And that voice. Surely she'd heard those husky tones somewhere before. Perhaps before time, contact, or something had been at them, making them into a voice remotely suggesting England. Ah! Could it have been in Europe that they had met? 'Rene. No.

"Perhaps," Irene began, "you—"

The woman laughed, a lovely laugh, a small sequence of notes that was like a trill and also like the ringing of a delicate bell fashioned of a precious metal, a tinkling.

Irene drew a quick sharp breath. "Clare!" she exclaimed, "not really Clare Kendry?"

So great was her astonishment that she had started to rise.

"No, no, don't get up," Clare Kendry commanded, and sat down herself. "You've simply got to stay and talk. We'll have something more. Tea? Fancy meeting you here! It's simply too, too lucky!"

"It's awfully surprising," Irene told her, and, seeing the change in Clare's smile, knew that she had revealed a corner of her own thoughts. But she only said: "I'd never in this world have known you if you hadn't laughed. You are changed, you know. And yet, in a way, you're just the same."

"Perhaps," Clare replied. "Oh, just a second."

She gave her attention to the waiter at her side. "M-mm, let's see. Two teas. And bring some cigarettes. Y-es, they'll be all right. Thanks." Again that odd upward smile. Now, Irene was sure that it was too provocative for a waiter.

While Clare had been giving the order, Irene made a rapid mental calculation. It must be, she figured, all of twelve years since she, or anybody that she knew, had laid eyes on Clare Kendry.

After her father's death she'd gone to live with some relatives, aunts or cousins two or three times removed, over on the west side: relatives that nobody had known the Kendry's possessed until they had turned up at the funeral and taken Clare away with them.

For about a year or more afterwards she would appear occasionally among her old friend and acquaintances on the south side for short little visits that were, they understood, always stolen from the endless domestic tasks in her new home. With each succeeding one she was taller, shabbier, and more belligerently sensitive. And each time the look on her face was more resentful and brooding. "I'm worried about Clare, she seems so unhappy," Irene remembered her mother saying. The visits dwindled, becoming shorter, fewer, and further apart until at last they ceased.

Irene's father, who had been fond of Bob Kendry, made a special trip over to the west side about two months after the last time Clare had been to see them and returned with the bare information that he had seen the relatives and that Clare had disappeared. What else he had confided to her mother, in the privacy of their own room, Irene didn't know.

But she had had something more than a vague suspicion of its nature. For there had been rumours. Rumours that were, to girls of eighteen and nineteen years, interesting and exciting.

There was the one about Clare Kendry's having been seen at the dinner hour in a fashionable hotel in company with another woman and two men, all of them white. And *dressed!* And there was another which told of her driving in Lincoln Park with a man, unmistakably white, and evidently rich. Packard limousine, chauffeur in livery, and all that. There had been others whose context Irene could no longer recollect, but all pointing in the same glamorous direction.

And she could remember quite vividly how, when they used to repeat and discuss these tantalizing stories about Clare, the girls would always look knowingly at one another and then, with little excited giggles, drag away their eager shining eyes and say with lurking undertones of regret or disbelief some such thing as: "Oh, well, maybe she's got a job or something," or "After all, it mayn't have been Clare," or "You can't believe all you hear."

And always some girl, more matter-of-fact or more frankly malicious than the rest, would declare: "Of course it was Clare! Ruth said it was and so did Frank, and they certainly know her when they see her as well as we do." And someone else would say: "Yes, you can bet it was Clare all right." And then they would all join in asserting that there could be no mistake about its having been Clare, and that such circumstances could mean only one thing. Working indeed! People didn't take their servants to the Shelby for dinner. Certainly not all dressed up like that. There would follow insincere regrets, and somebody would say: "Poor girl, I suppose it's true enough, but what can you expect. Look at her father. And her mother, they say, would have run away if she hadn't died. Besides, Clare always had a—a—having way with her."

Precisely that! The words came to Irene as she sat there on the Drayton roof, facing Clare Kendry. "A having way." Well, Irene acknowledged, judging from her appearance and manner, Clare seemed certainly to have succeeded in having a few of the things that she wanted.

It was, Irene repeated, after the interval of the waiter, a great surprise and a very pleasant one to see Clare again after all those years, twelve at least.

"Why, Clare, you're the last person in the world I'd have expected to run into. I guess that's why I didn't know you."

Clare answered gravely: "Yes, it is twelve years. But I'm not surprised to see you, 'Rene. That is, not so very. In fact, ever since I've been here, I've more or less hoped that I should, or someone. Preferably you, though. Still, I imagine that's because I've thought of you often and often, while you—I'll wager you've never given me a thought."

It was true, of course. After the first speculations and indictments, Clare had gone completely from Irene's thoughts. And from the thoughts of others too—if their conversation was any indication of their thoughts.

Besides, Clare had never been exactly one of the group, just as she'd never been merely the janitor's daughter, but the daughter of Mr. Bob Kendry, who, it was true, was a janitor, but who also, it seemed, had been in college with some of their fathers. Just how or why he happened to be a janitor, and a very inefficient one at that, they none of them quite knew. One of Irene's brothers, who had put the question to their father, had been told: "That's something that doesn't concern you," and given him the advice to be careful not to end in the same manner as "poor Bob."

No, Irene hadn't thought of Clare Kendry. Her own life had been too crowded. So, she supposed, had the lives of other people. She defended her—their—forgetfulness. "You know how it is. Everybody's so busy. People leave, drop out, maybe for a little while there's talk about them, or questions; then, gradually they're forgotten."

"Yes, that's natural," Clare agreed. And what, she inquired, had they said of her for that little while at the beginning before they'd forgotten her altogether?

Irene looked away. She felt the telltale colour rising in her cheeks. "You can't," she evaded, "expect me to remember trifles like that over twelve years of marriages, births, deaths, and the war."

There followed that trill of notes that was Clare Kendry's laugh, small and clear and the very essence of mockery.

"Oh, 'Rene!" she cried, "of course you remember! But I won't make you tell me, because I know just as well as if I'd been there and heard every unkind word. Oh, I know, I know. Frank Danton saw me in the Shelby one night. Don't tell me he didn't broadcast that, and with embroidery. Others may have seen me at other times. I don't know. But once I met Margaret Hammer in Marshall Field's. I'd have spoken, was on the very point of doing it, but she cut me dead. My dear 'Rene, I assure you that from the way she looked through me, even I was uncertain whether I was actually there in the flesh or not. I remember it clearly, too clearly. It was that very thing which, in a way, finally decided me not to go out and see you one last time before I went away to stay. Somehow, good as all of you, the whole family, had always been to the poor forlorn child that was me, I felt I shouldn't be able to bear that. I mean if any of you, your mother or the boys or—Oh, well, I just felt I'd rather not know it if you did. And so I stayed away. Silly, I suppose. Sometimes I've been sorry I didn't go."

Irene wondered if it was tears that made Clare's eyes so luminous.

"And now 'Rene, I want to hear all about you and everybody and everything. You're married, I s'pose?"

Irene nodded.

"Yes," Clare said knowingly, "you would be. Tell me about it."

And so for an hour or more they had sat there smoking and drinking tea and filling in the gap of twelve years with talk. That is, Irene did. She told Clare about her marriage and removal to New York, about her husband, and about her two sons, who were having their first experience of being separated from their parents at a summer camp, about her mother's death, about the marriages of her two brothers. She told of the marriages, births and deaths in other families that Clare had known, opening up, for her, new vistas on the lives of old friends and acquaintances.

Clare drank it all in, these things which for so long she had wanted to know and hadn't been able to learn. She sat motionless, her bright lips slightly parted, her whole face lit by the radiance of her happy eyes. Now and then she put a question, but for the most part she was silent.

Somewhere outside, a clock struck. Brought back to the present, Irene looked down at her watch and exclaimed: "Oh, I must go, Clare!"

A moment passed during which she was the prey of uneasiness. It had suddenly occurred to her that she hadn't asked Clare anything about her own life and that she had a very definite unwillingness to do so. And she was quite well aware of the reason for that reluctance. But, she asked herself, wouldn't it, all things considered, be the kindest thing not to ask? If things with Clare were as she—as they all—had suspected, wouldn't it be more tactful to seem to forget to inquire how she had spent those twelve years?

If? It was that "if" which bothered her. It might be, it might just be, in spite of all gossip and even appearances to the contrary, that there was nothing, had been nothing, that couldn't be simply and innocently explained. Appearances, she knew now, had a way sometimes of not fitting facts, and if Clare hadn't—Well, if they had all been wrong, then certainly she ought to express some interest in what had happened to her. It would seem queer and rude if she didn't. But how was she to know? There was, she at last decided, no way; so she merely said again. "I must go, Clare."

"Please, not so soon, 'Rene," Clare begged, not moving.

Irene thought: "She's really almost too good-looking. It's hardly any wonder that she—"

"And now, 'Rene dear, that I've found you, I mean to see lots and lots of you. We're here for a month a least. Jack, that's my husband, is here on business. Poor dear! in this heat. Isn't it beastly? Come to dinner with us tonight, won't you?" And she gave Irene a curious little side-long glance and a sly, ironical smile peeped out on her full red lips, as if she had been in the secret of the other's thoughts and was mocking her.

Irene was conscious of a sharp intake of breath, but whether it was relief or chagrin that she felt, she herself could not have told. She said hastily: "I'm afraid I can't, Clare. I'm filled up. Dinner and bridge. I'm so sorry."

"Come tomorrow instead, to tea," Clare insisted. "Then you'll see Margery—she's just ten—and Jack too, maybe, if he hasn't got an appointment or something."

From Irene came an uneasy little laugh. She had an engagement for tomorrow also and she was afraid that Clare would not believe it. Suddenly, now, that possibility disturbed her. Therefore it was with a half-vexed feeling at the sense of undeserved guilt that had come upon her that she explained that it wouldn't be possible because she wouldn't be free for tea, or for luncheon or dinner either. "And the next day's Friday when I'll be going away for the week-end, Idlewild, you know. It's quite the thing now." And then she had an inspiration.

"Clare!" she exclaimed, "why don't you come up with me? Our place is probably full up—Jim's wife has a way of collecting mobs of the most impossible people—but we can always manage to find room for one more. And you'll see absolutely everybody."

In the very moment of giving the invitation she regretted it. What a foolish, what an idiotic impulse to have given way to! She groaned inwardly as she thought of the endless explanations in which it would involve her, of the curiosity, and the talk, and the lifted eyebrows. It wasn't she assured herself, that she was a snob, that she cared greatly for the petty restrictions and distinctions with which what called itself Negro society chose to hedge itself about; but that she had a natural and deeply rooted aversion to the kind of front-page notoriety that Clare Kendry's presence in Idlewild, as her guest, would expose her to. And here she was, perversely and against all reason, inviting her.

But Clare shook her head. "Really, I'd love to, 'Rene," she said, a little mournfully. "There's nothing I'd like better. But I couldn't. I mustn't, you see. It wouldn't do at all. I'm sure you understand. I'm simply crazy to go, but I can't." The dark eyes glistened and there was a suspicion of a quaver in the husky voice. "And believe me, 'Rene, I do thank you for asking me. Don't think I've entirely forgotten just what it would mean for you if I went. That is, if you still care about such things."

All indication of tears had gone from her eyes and voice, and Irene Redfield, searching her face, had an offended feeling that behind what was now only an ivory mask lurked a scornful amusement. She looked away, at the wall far beyond Clare. Well, she deserved it, for, as she acknowledged to herself, she *was* relieved. And for the very reason at which Clare had hinted. The fact that Clare had guessed her perturbation did not, however, in any degree lessen that relief. She was annoyed at having been detected in what might seem to be an insincerity; but that was all.

The waiter came with Clare's change. Irene reminded herself that she ought immediately to go. But she didn't move.

The truth was, she was curious. There were things that she wanted to ask Clare Kendry. She wished to find out about this hazardous business of "passing," this breaking away from all that was familiar and friendly to take one's chances in another environment, not entirely strange, perhaps, but certainly not entirely friendly. What, for example, one did about background, how one accounted for oneself. And how one felt when one came into contact with other Negroes. But she couldn't. She was unable to think of a single question that in its context or its phrasing was not too frankly curious, if not actually impertinent.

As if aware of her desire and her hesitation, Clare remarked, thoughtfully: "You know, 'Rene, I've often wondered why more coloured girls, girls like you and Margaret Hammer and Esther Dawson and—oh, lots of others—never 'passed' over. It's such a frightfully easy thing to do. If one's the type, all that's needed is a little nerve."

"What about background? Family, I mean. Surely you can't just drop down on people from nowhere and expect them to receive you with open arms, can you?"

"Almost," Clare asserted. "You'd be surprised, 'Rene, how much easier that is with white people than with us. Maybe because there are so many more of them, or maybe because they are secure and so don't have to bother. I've never quite decided."

Irene was inclined to be incredulous. "You mean that you didn't have to explain where you came from? It seems impossible."

Clare cast a glance of repressed amusement across the table at her. "As a matter of fact, I didn't. Though I suppose under any other circumstances I might have had to provide some plausible tale to account for myself. I've a good imagination, so I'm sure I could have done it quite creditably, and credibly. But it wasn't necessary. There were my aunts, you see, respectable and authentic enough for anything or anybody."

"I see. They were 'passing' too."

"No. They weren't. They were white."

"Oh!" And in the next instant it came back to Irene that she had heard this mentioned before; by her father, or, more likely, her mother. They were Bob Kendry's aunts. He had been a son of their brother's, on the left hand. A wild oat.

"They were nice old ladies," Clare explained, "very religious and as poor as church mice. That adored brother of theirs, my grandfather, got through every penny they had after he'd finished his own little bit."

Clare paused in her narrative to light another cigarette. Her smile, her expression, Irene noticed, was faintly resentful.

"Being good Christians," she continued, "when dad came to his tipsy end, they did their duty and gave me a home of sorts. I was, it was true, expected to earn my keep by doing all the housework, and most of the washing. But do you realize, 'Rene, that if it hadn't been for them, I shouldn't have had a home in the world?"

Irene's nod and little murmur were comprehensive, understanding.

Clare made a small mischievous grimace and proceeded. "Besides, to their notion, hard labour was good for me. I had Negro blood and they belonged to the generation that had written and read long articles headed: 'Will the Blacks Work?' Too, they weren't quite sure that the good God hadn't intended the sons and daughters of Ham to sweat because he had poked fun at old man Noah once when he had taken a drop too much. I remember the aunts telling me that that old drunkard had cursed Ham and his sons for all time."

Irene laughed. But Clare remained quite serious.

"It was more than a joke, I assure you, 'Rene. It was a hard life for a girl of sixteen. Still, I had a roof over my head, and food, and clothes—such as they were. And there were the Scriptures, and talks on morals and thrift and industry and the loving-kindness of the good Lord."

"Have you ever stopped to think, Clare," Irene demanded, "how much unhappiness and downright cruelty are laid to the loving-kindness of the Lord? And always by His most ardent followers, it seems."

"Have I?" Clare exclaimed. "It, they, made me what I am today. For, of course, I was determined to get away, to be a person and not a charity or a problem, or even a daughter of the indiscreet Ham. Then, too, I wanted things. I knew I wasn't bad-looking and that I could 'pass.' You can't know, 'Rene, how, when I used to go over to the south side, I used almost to hate all of you. You had all the things I wanted and never had had. It made me all the more determined to get them, and others. Do you, can you understand what I felt?"

She looked up with a pointed and appealing effect, and, evidently finding the sympathetic expression on Irene's face sufficient answer, went on. "The aunts were queer. For all their Bibles and praying and ranting about honesty, they didn't want anyone to know that their darling brother had seduced—ruined, they called it—a Negro girl. They could excuse the ruin, but they couldn't forgive the tar-brush. They forbade me to mention Negros to the neighbours, or even to mention the south side. You may be sure that I didn't. I'll bet they were good and sorry afterwards."

She laughed and the ringing bells in her laugh had a hard metallic sound.

"When the chance to get away came, that omission was of great value to me. When Jack, a schoolboy acquaintance of some people in the neighbourhood, turned up from South America with untold gold, there was no one to tell him that I was coloured, and many to tell him about the severity and the religiousness of Aunt Grace and Aunt Edna. You can guess the rest. After he came, I stopped slipping off to the south side and slipped off to meet him instead. I couldn't manage both. In the end I had no great difficulty in convincing him that it was useless to talk marriage to the aunts. So on the day that I was eighteen, we went off and were married. So that's that. Nothing could have been easier."

"Yes, I do see that for you it was easy enough. By the way! I wonder why they didn't tell father that you were married. He went over to find out about you when you stopped coming over to see us. I'm sure they didn't tell him. Not that you were married."

Clare Kendry's eyes were bright with tears that didn't fall. "Oh, how lovely! To have cared enough about me to do that. The dear sweet man! Well, they couldn't tell him because they didn't know it. I took care of that, for I couldn't be sure that those consciences of theirs wouldn't begin to work on them afterwards and make them let the cat out of the bag. The old things probably thought I was living in sin, wherever I was. And it would be about what they expected."

An amused smile lit the lovely face for the smallest fraction of a second. After a little silence she said soberly: "But I'm sorry if they told your father so. That was something I hadn't counted on."

"I'm not sure that they did," Irene told her. "He didn't say so, anyway."

"He wouldn't, 'Rene dear. Not your father."

"Thanks, I'm sure he wouldn't."

"But you've never answered my question. Tell me, honestly, haven't you ever thought of 'passing'?"

Irene answered promptly: "No. Why should I?" And so disdainful was her voice and manner that Clare's face flushed and her eyes glinted. Irene hastened to add: "You see, Clare, I've everything I want. Except, perhaps, a little more money."

At that Clare laughed, her spark of anger vanished as quickly as it had appeared. "Of course," she declared, "that's what everybody wants, just a little more money, even the people who have it. And I must say I don't blame them. Money's awfully nice to have. In fact, all things considered, I think, 'Rene, that it's even worth the price."

Irene could only shrug her shoulders. Her reason partly agreed, her instinct wholly rebelled. And she could not say why. And though conscious that if she didn't hurry away, she was going to be late to dinner, she still lingered. It was as if the woman sitting on the other side of the table, a girl that she had known, who had done this rather dangerous and, to Irene Redfield, abhorrent thing successfully and had announced herself well satisfied, had for her a fascination, strange and compelling.

Clare Kendry was still leaning back in the tall chair, her sloping shoulders against the carved top. She sat with an air of indifferent assurance, as if arranged for, desired. About her clung that dim suggestion of polite insolence with which a few women are born and which some acquire with the coming of riches or importance.

Clare, it gave Irene a little prick of satisfaction to recall, hadn't got that by passing herself off as white. She herself had always had it.

Just as she'd always had that pale gold hair, which, unsheared still, was drawn loosely back from a broad brow, partly hidden by the small close hat. Her lips, painted a brilliant geranium-red, were sweet and sensitive and a little obstinate. A tempting mouth. The face across the forehead and cheeks was a trifle too wide, but the ivory skin had a peculiar soft lustre. And the eyes were magnificent! dark, sometimes absolutely black, always luminous, and set in long, black lashes. Arresting eyes, slow and mesmeric, and with, for all their warmth, something withdrawn and secret about them.

Ah! Surely! They were Negro eyes! mysterious and concealing. And set in that ivory face under that bright hair, there was about them something exotic.

Yes, Clare Kendry's loveliness was absolute, beyond challenge, thanks to those eyes which her grandmother and later her mother and father had given her.

Into those eyes there came a smile and over Irene the sense of being petted and caressed. She smiled back.

"Maybe," Clare suggested, "you can come Monday, if you're back. Or, if you're not, then Tuesday."

With a small regretful sigh, Irene informed Clare that she was afraid she wouldn't be back by Monday and that she was sure she had dozens of things for Tuesday, and that she was leaving Wednesday. It might be, however, that she could get out of something Tuesday.

"Oh, do try. Do put somebody else off. The others can see you any time, while I—Why, I may never see you again! Think of that, 'Rene! You'll have to come. You'll simply have to! I'll never forgive you if you don't."

At that moment it seemed a dreadful thing to think of never seeing Clare Kendry again. Standing there under the appeal, the caress, of her eyes, Irene had the desire, the hope, that this parting wouldn't be the last.

"I'll try, Clare," she promised gently. "I'll call you—or will you call me?"

"I think, perhaps, I'd better call you. Your father's in the book, I know, and the address is the same. Sixty-four eighteen. Some memory, what? Now remember, I'm going to expect you. You've got to be able to come."

Again that peculiar mellowing smile.

"I'll do my best, Clare."

Irene gathered up her gloves and bag. They stood up. She put out her hand. Clare took it and held it.

"It has been nice seeing you again, Clare. How pleased and glad father'll be to hear about you!"

"Until Tuesday, then," Clare Kendry replied. "I'll spend every minute of the time from now on looking forward to seeing you again. Good-bye, 'Rene dear. My love to your father, and this kiss for him."

The sun had gone from overhead, but the streets were still like fiery furnaces. The languid breeze was still hot. And the scurrying people looked even more wilted than before Irene had fled from their contact.

Crossing the avenue in the heat, far from the coolness of the Drayton's roof, away from the seduction of Clare Kendry's smile, she was aware of a sense of irritation with herself because she had been pleased and a little flattered at the other's obvious gladness at their meeting.

With her perspiring progress homeward this irritation grew, and she began to wonder just what had possessed her to make her promise to find time, in the crowded days that remained of her visit, to spend another afternoon with a woman whose life had so definitely and deliberately diverged from hers; and whom, as had been pointed out, she might never see again.

Why in the world had she made such a promise?

As she went up the steps to her father's house, thinking with what interest and amazement he would listen to her story of the afternoon's encounter, it came to her that Clare had omitted to mention her marriage name. She had referred to her husband as Jack. That was all. Had that, Irene asked herself, been intentional?

Clare had only to pick up the telephone to communicate with her, or to drop her a card, or to jump into a taxi. But she couldn't reach Clare in any way. Nor could anyone else to whom she might speak of their meeting.

"As if I should!"

Her key turned in the lock. She went in. Her father, it seemed, hadn't come in yet.

Irene decided that she wouldn't, after all, say anything to him about Clare Kendry. She had, she told herself, no inclination to speak of a person who held so low an opinion of her loyalty, or her discretion. And certainly she had no desire or intention of making the slightest effort about Tuesday. Nor any other day for that matter.

She was through with Clare Kendry.

ZORA NEALE HURSTON

(1891–1960)

In recent years, Zora Neale Hurston has been elevated to the position of foremother of most contemporary African American women writers. This designation, combined with the fact that Hurston was the most prolific black woman writer prior to the 1960s, gives her a unique position in African American literary history. Praised for her early realistic portraits of African American women, for her celebration of African American folk culture, and for a lifestyle that, in retrospect, made her a prototypical feminist, Hurston not only contributed substantially to the African American literary canon, but she remains an elusive, enigmatic personality whose actions continue to baffle biographers and scholars.

Zora Neale Hurston was born in Eatonville, Florida, the first all-black incorporated town in America, on January 7, 1891. That date was only conclusively determined in 1984, for one of Hurston's enigmatic habits was the changing of her birth date at will and the concealing of other personal information that she considered nobody's business. Hurston's father, John, a carpenter and itinerant preacher, would serve as the inspiration for John Buddy Pearson, the folk preacher Hurston featured in her first novel, *Jonah's Gourd Vine,* published in 1934. Lucy Ann Potts Hurston, a former schoolteacher, was assisted in her delivery of Zora by a white male neighbor. Lucy instilled in her daughter a great desire to learn and the ambition to "jump at the sun," an injunction that early became a motto for the adventurous young Zora. The fifth of eight children, Zora developed a special bond with her mother that would be tested on the occasion of Lucy's death. The thirteen-year-old Zora had been instructed not to allow the death-watchers to take the pillow from Lucy's head or to stop the clocks, folk rituals that Zora had little power to prevent in a world of adults bent on carrying out the time-honored inscriptions to passage beyond this world.

While Hurston would remember the incident as one of the haunting failures of her life, she clearly judged herself too harshly. Her mother's death, however, set Hurston on the road to fending for herself. When her father seemed overwhelmed as to how to care for his numerous children, Hurston set out to work. Although she enjoyed a brief stint at a boarding school in Jacksonville, a fitting culmination to the recognition she had received in grade school for her intellectual superiority, that luxury did not last long. Straitened circumstances forced her father to remove her from school. After living with relatives in Florida for a brief period, she became "a wardrobe girl in a Gilbert and Sullivan repertory company touring the South." That adventure carried her to Baltimore, where she left the troupe to pursue a secondary education at Morgan Academy, the high school division of Morgan State University. She graduated from the academy in 1918 and enrolled in classes at Howard University. It was there that she met Herbert Sheen, whom she married in 1927. Marriage could not contain the adventurous Hurston, however, as she stayed with Sheen for only four months. They were divorced in 1931.

Getting wind that the center of activity during the 1920s was Harlem, Hurston made the trip there with less than two dollars to her name. She went to the editorial offices of *Opportunity* magazine and introduced herself to Charles S. Johnson and Ethel Nance, both of whom had been instrumental in drawing talented young black artists and writers to New York. Thus began Hurston's involvement with the Harlem Renaissance, which would lead to her entering several creative writing contests and publishing short stories and plays in *Opportunity* and *The Crisis.* She continued her education, this time at Barnard; she also studied anthropology at Columbia with the famed Franz Boas, who would later write the introduction to her first collection of folklore. In 1926, combining school and creative endeavors, she collaborated with Langston Hughes, Wallace Thurman, and Richard Bruce Nugent on the publication of *Fire!!* That little magazine carried what has commonly become known as the manifesto of the movement—an article by Hughes titled "The Negro Artist and the Racial Mountain." Hurston's contributions included "Sweat," a highly praised short story, and *Color Struck,* a folk play in which an excursion, a cakewalking contest, and intraracial prejudices carry the day. Although the play is rough, it showcases the themes and characters that occupied the remainder of Hurston's creative career: folk speech, folk characters, folk music.

Hurston joined Hughes in enjoying the patronage of Charlotte Osgood Mason, a Park Avenue matron who made black art and her conception of primitive black people the preoccupation of her declining years. Although Mason supported

Hurston handsomely on folklore-collecting trips through the South in 1927 and 1928, Hurston had to suffer the indignities of Mason's having control over her work. Therefore, she was not able to publish *Mules and Men,* her collection of folktales and voodoo, until 1935, after she had severed her ties with Mason.

It was also in the thirties that Hurston published her signature work, *Their Eyes Were Watching God* (1937). The story of Janie Crawford Killicks Starks Woods, the novel portrays how a woman stifled by convention and community expectations eventually escapes both to find happiness with a younger man. But because she, as a black woman, is an integral part of her community, she returns to it and contributes to its growth by bringing her fulfilling life's experiences back to it. To celebrate the black female self coming into bloom, Hurston locates her heroine in the natural landscape, for nature, like women, is life giving, nurturing, and sensuous. Janie wonders, "Oh to be a pear tree—*any* tree in bloom! With kissing bees singing of the beginning of the world!" After spending time in the Everglades with young Tea Cake, she brings back to her southern black rural community her "horizons," which have been broadened by the love and respect the two of them have shared. The novel is based on Hurston's affair with a twenty-three-year-old man when she was over forty. She claimed that she tried to capture all the passion of that relationship in the book; critics generally agree that she succeeded at that and much more. *Their Eyes Were Watching God* has been regarded as an American classic by several scholars of the African American literary canon and feminist critics since the beginning of the contemporary women's movement in the 1970s.

Her other literary achievements during the 1930s included essays published in the *Journal of American Folklore* (1931), musical revues such as *The Great Day* (1932), and short stories such as "The Gilded Six-Bits" (1933). She also worked for the WPA Federal Theater Project in 1935. In 1939, she published *Tell My Horse,* a volume about Haitian voodoo practices, which professed to include a real photograph of a zombie—one of the living dead. An indefatigable traveler, Hurston ventured into parts of Haiti and Jamaica where few American blacks had gone; in fact, she wrote *Their Eyes Were Watching God* during a seven-week stint in Jamaica.

The thirties also witnessed one of the two incidents that caused a great deal of pain for Hurston. In 1930, she and Hughes collaborated on a folk play, an outgrowth of their adventures traveling together from Mobile, Alabama, to New York in 1927. The controversy entered when Hughes discovered on a trip to Cleveland that the play was about to be produced, when he thought Hurston was in Florida working on the final act. Misunderstandings and justified as well as unjustified indignations abounded, which biographers of both authors have tried to sort through. The upshot was a rift between Hurston and Hughes that was not mended in their lifetimes. The play, *Mule Bone,* finally reached the stage in February 1991.

In the habit of disappearing when she was ill or without financial resources, Hurston increasingly dropped out of sight for extended periods. Yet she continued to write and publish. *Moses, Man of the Mountain,* a re-creation of the biblical story with Moses cast as a conjure man, appeared in 1939. In response to her publisher's request, she produced her autobiography, *Dust Tracks on a Road,* in 1942. The silence was longer before her next work appeared. In 1948, she published *Seraph on the Suwanee,* a novel about "crackers" (poor whites) in South Florida. Although she consciously acknowledged responding to the idea that black authors could indeed write about white characters, her detractors were not convinced. Even today, some maintain that she abandoned her black folk inspiration by focusing on basically uninteresting white peasants.

The other incident that caused Hurston tremendous pain followed the publication of *Seraph*. In September 1948, she was arrested and falsely accused of sodomizing a ten-year-old boy. Although Hurston was eventually able to prove that she was in Honduras (searching for a lost city) when the alleged incident took place, African American newspapers nevertheless spread lurid headlines across their front pages; passages from *Seraph* were even used to suggest the possibility of sexual deviancy. Depressed to the point of contemplating suicide, Hurston was exonerated when it was shown that the boy was mentally unstable and that his mother, who had disagreed with Hurston over rent money, might have instigated his testimony. Nonetheless, retractions never occupy the same newspaper or mind space, and it would be quite some time before Hurston felt confident enough in her abilities to pursue her work again.

Having been plagued by financial difficulties all her life, Hurston experienced even harder times in the 1950s. She was discovered working as a maid in Rivo Alto, Florida, in 1950; her tale that she was conducting research firsthand for a planned creative work on domestics did not fool anyone who knew her. When the Supreme Court ruled in favor of *Brown v. Board of Education* in 1954, Hurston opposed the ruling. In this, she might have been prophetic, as in recent years many African Americans have come to question the value of integration for black lives and culture.

Throughout the fifties, it was difficult for Hurston's family members to know exactly where she was; similarly, she gradually faded from public view. When she died in 1960, collections had to be taken up for her burial. Her interment in an unmarked grave at the Garden of the Heavenly Rest in Fort Pierce, Florida, however, is not the end of her story. As part of the revival of this foremother so central to African American creativity, Alice Walker journeyed to Florida to locate Hurston's grave in 1973. Reaching what she felt to be the appropriate spiritual place, Walker erected a monument that reads: "Zora Neale Hurston / 'A Genius of the South' / 1901–1960 / Novelist, Folklorist / Anthropologist." For the past several years, a Zora Neale Hurston Festival has been held in Eatonville, Florida, each January. As the twenty-first century approaches, it seems certain that the evaluation of Hurston as "A Genius of the South" will continue to gain ground, and deservedly so.

❖❖❖

The most extensive biography of Hurston to date is Robert Hemenway's *Zora Neale Hurston: A Literary Biography* (1977). Other book-length studies containing biographical information are Lillie P. Howard, *Zora Neale Hurston* (1980); Karla F. C. Holloway, *The Character of the Word: The Texts of Zora Neale Hurston* (1987). An early extended discussion of Hurston and her works appears in Darwin T. Turner, *In a Minor Chord: Three Afro-American Writers and Their Search for Identity* (1971). Daryl C. Dance's "Zora Neale Hurston" appears in *American Women Writers: Bibliographical Essays*, ed. Maurice Duke, Jackson R. Bryer, and M. Thomas Inge (1983).

Hurston's works have become reference points for various contemporary studies in critical theory, including Barbara Johnson, "Metaphor, Metonymy and Voice in *Their Eyes Were Watching God,*" in *Black Literature & Literary Theory,* ed. Henry Louis Gates, Jr. (1984); Henry Louis Gates, Jr., *The Signifying Monkey* (1988); Francoise Lionnet, *Autobiographical Voices: Race, Gender, Self-Portraiture* (1989).

Two early collections of Hurston's works are Alice Walker, ed., *I Love Myself When I Am Laughing . . . & Then Again When I Am Looking Mean & Impressive* (1979) and *Spunk, The Selected Stories of Zora Neale Hurston* (1985). Through Gates's efforts on behalf of the Hurston family, all of Hurston's previously published works and several unpublished collections of materials are appearing at regular intervals from HarperCollins.

Spunk

A giant of a brown-skinned man sauntered up the one street of the Village and out into the palmetto thickets with a small pretty woman clinging lovingly to his arm.

"Looka theah, folkses!" cried Elijah Mosley, slapping his leg gleefully. "Theah they go, big as life an' brassy as tacks."

All the loungers in the store tried to walk to the door with an air of nonchalance but with small success.

"Now pee-eople!" Walter Thomas gasped. "Will you look at 'em!"

"But that's one thing Ah likes about Spunk Banks—he ain't skeered of nothin' on God's green footstool—*nothin'!* He rides that log down at saw-mill jus' like he struts 'round wid another man's wife—jus' don't give a kitty. When Tes' Miller got cut to giblets on that circle-saw, Spunk steps right up and starts ridin'. The rest of us was skeered to go near it."

A round-shouldered figure in overalls much too large, came nervously in the door and the talking ceased. The men looked at each other and winked.

"Gimme some soda-water. Sass'prilla Ah reckon," the newcomer ordered, and stood far down the counter near the open pickled pig-feet tub to drink it.

Elijah nudged Walter and turned with mock gravity to the new-comer.

"Say, Joe, how's everything up yo' way? How's yo' wife?"

Joe started and all but dropped the bottle he held in his hands. He swallowed several times painfully and his lips trembled.

"Aw, 'Lige, you oughtn't to do nothin' like that," Walter grumbled. Elijah ignored him.

"She jus' passed heah a few minutes ago goin' thata way," with a wave of his hand in the direction of the woods.

Now Joe knew his wife had passed that way. He knew that the men lounging in the general store had seen her, moreover, he knew that the men knew *he* knew. He stood there silent for a long moment staring blankly, with his Adam's apple twitching nervously up and down his throat. One could actually *see* the pain he was suffering, his eyes, his face, his hands and even the dejected slump of his shoulders. He set the bottle down upon the counter. He didn't bang it, just eased it out of his hand silently and fiddled with his suspender buckle.

"Well, Ah'm goin' after her to-day. Ah'm goin' an' fetch her back. Spunk's done gone too fur."

He reached deep down into his trouser pocket and drew out a hollow ground razor, large and shiny, and passed his moistened thumb back and forth over the edge.

"Talkin' like a man, Joe. Course that's *yo'* fambly affairs, but Ah like to see grit in anybody."

Joe Kanty laid down a nickel and stumbled out into the street.

Dusk crept in from the woods. Ike Clarke lit the swinging oil lamp that was almost immediately surrounded by candleflies. The men laughed boisterously behind Joe's back as they watched him shamble woodward.

"You oughtn't to said whut you did to him, Lige—look how it worked him up," Walter chided.

"And Ah hope it did work him up. 'Tain't even decent for a man to take and take like he do."

"Spunk will sho' kill him."

"Aw, Ah doan't know. You never kin tell. He might turn him up an' spank him fur gettin' in the way, but Spunk wouldn't shoot no unarmed man. Dat razor he carried outa heah ain't gonna run Spunk down an' cut him, an' Joe ain't got the nerve to go up to Spunk with it knowing he totes that Army .45. He makes that break outa heah to bluff us. He's gonna hide that razor behind the first likely palmetto root an' sneak back home to bed. Don't tell me nothin' 'bout that rabbit-foot colored man. Didn't he meet Spunk an' Lena face to face one day las' week an' mumble sumthin' to Spunk 'bout lettin' his wife alone?"

"What did Spunk say?" Walter broke in— "Ah like him fine but 'tain't right the way he carries on wid Lena Kanty, jus' cause Joe's timid 'bout fightin'."

"You wrong theah, Walter. 'Tain't cause Joe's timid at all, it's cause Spunk wants Lena. If Joe was a passle of wile cats Spunk would tackle the job just the same. He'd go after *anything* he wanted the same way. As Ah wuz sayin' a minute ago, he tole Joe right to his face that Lena was his. 'Call her,' he says to Joe. 'Call her and see if she'll come. A woman knows her boss an' she answers when he calls.' 'Lena, ain't I yo' husband?' Joe sorter whines out. Lena looked at him real disgusted but she don't answer and she don't move outa her tracks. Then Spunk reaches out an' takes hold of her arm an' says: 'Lena, youse mine. From now on Ah works for you an' fights for you an' Ah never wants you to look to nobody for a crumb of bread, a stitch of close or a shingle to go over yo' head, but *me* long as Ah live. Ah'll git the lumber foh owah house to-morrow. Go home an' git yo' things together!'

" 'Thass mah house,' Lena speaks up. 'Papa gimme that.'

" 'Well,' says Spunk, 'doan give up whut's yours, but when youse inside don't forgit youse mine, an' let no other man git outa his place wid you!'

"Lena looked up at him with her eyes so full of love that they wuz runnin' over, an' Spunk seen it an' Joe seen it too, and his lip started to tremblin' and his Adam's apple was galloping up and down his neck like a race horse. Ah bet he's wore out half a dozen Adam's apples since Spunk's been on the job with Lena. That's all he'll do. He'll be back heah after while swallowin' an' workin' his lips like he wants to say somethin' an' can't."

"But didn't he do *nothin'* to stop 'em?"

"Nope, not a frazzlin' thing—jus' stood there. Spunk took Lena's arm and walked off jus' like nothin' ain't happened and he stood there gazin' after them till they was outa sight. Now you know a woman don't want no man like that. I'm jus' waitin' to see whut he's goin' to say when he gits back."

II

But Joe Kanty never came back, never. The men in the store heard the sharp report of a pistol somewhere distant in the palmetto thicket and soon Spunk came walking leisurely, with his big black Stetson set at the same rakish angle and Lena clinging to his arm, came walking right into the general store. Lena wept in a frightened manner.

"Well," Spunk announced calmly, "Joe come out there wid a meatax an' made me kill him."

He sent Lena home and led the men back to Joe—Joe crumpled and limp with his right hand still clutching his razor.

"See mah back? Mah cloes cut clear through. He sneaked up an' tried to kill me from the back, but Ah got him, an' got him good, first shot," Spunk said.

The men glared at Elijah, accusingly.

"Take him up an' plant him in 'Stoney lonesome,' " Spunk said in a careless voice. "Ah didn't wanna shoot him but he made me do it. He's a dirty coward, jumpin' on a man from behind."

Spunk turned on his heel and sauntered away to where he knew his love wept in fear for him and no man stopped him. At the general store later on, they all talked of locking him up until the sheriff should come from Orlando, but no one did anything but talk.

A clear case of self-defense, the trial was a short one, and Spunk walked out of the court house to freedom again. He could work again, ride the dangerous log-carriage that fed the singing, snarling, biting, circle-saw; he could stroll the soft dark lanes with his guitar. He was free to roam the woods again; he was free to return to Lena. He did all of these things.

III

"Whut you reckon, Walt?" Elijah asked one night later. "Spunk's gittin' ready to marry Lena!"

"Naw! Why, Joe ain't had time to git cold yit. Nohow Ah didn't figger Spunk was the marryin' kind."

"Well, he is," rejoined Elijah. "He done moved most of Lena's things—and her along wid 'em—over to the Bradley house. He's buying it. Jus' like Ah told yo' all right in heah the night Joe wuz kilt. Spunk's crazy 'bout Lena. He don't want folks to keep on talkin' 'bout her—thass reason he's rushin' so. Funny thing 'bout that bob-cat, wan't it?"

"Whut bob-cat, 'Lige? Ah ain't heered 'bout none."

"Ain't cher? Wll, night befo' las' was the fust night Spunk an' Lena moved together an' jus' as they was goin' to bed, a big black bob-cat, black all over, you hear me, *black*, walked round and round that house and howled like forty, an' when Spunk got his gun an' went to the winder to shoot it, he says it stood right still an' looked him in the eye, an' howled right at him. The thing got Spunk so nervoused up he couldn't shoot. But Spunk says twan't no bob-cat nohow. He says it was Joe done sneaked back from Hell!"

"Humph!" sniffed Walter, "he oughter be nervous after what he done. Ah reckon Joe come back to dare him to marry Lena, or to come out an' fight. Ah bet he'll be back time and agin, too. Know what Ah think? Joe wuz a braver man than Spunk."

There was a general shout of derision from the group.

"Thass a fact," went on Walter. "Lookit whut he done; took a razor an' went out to fight a man he knowed toted a gun an' wuz a crack shot, too; 'nother thing Joe wuz skeered of Spunk, skeered plumb stiff! But he went jes' the same. It took him a long time to get his nerve up. 'Tain't nothin' for Spunk to fight when he ain't skeered of nothin'. Now, Joe's done come back to have it out wid the man that's got all he ever had. Y'll know Joe ain't never had nothin' nor wanted nothin' besides Lena. It musta been a h'ant cause ain' nobody never seen no black bob-cat."

"'Nother thing," cut in one of the men, "Spunk wuz cussin' a blue streak to-day 'cause he 'lowed dat saw wuz wobblin'—almos' got 'im once. The machinist come, looked it over an' said it wuz alright. Spunk musta been leanin' t'wards it some. Den he claimed some-body pushed 'im but 'twant nobody close to 'im. Ah wuz glad when knockin' off time come. I'm skeered of dat man when he gits hot. He'd beat you full of button holes as quick as he's look atcher."

IV

The men gathered the next evening in a different mood, no laughter. No badinage this time.

"Look, 'Lige, you goin' to set up wid Spunk?"

"Naw, Ah reckon not, Walter. Tell yuh the truth, Ah'm a lil bit skittish. Spunk died too wicket—died cussin' he did. You know he thought he wuz done outa life."

"Good Lawd, who'd he think done it?"

"Joe."

"Joe Kanty? How come?"

"Walter, Ah b'leeve Ah will walk up thata way an' set. Lena would like it Ah reckon."

"But whut did he say, 'Lige?"

Elijah did not answer until they had left the lighted store and were strolling down the dark street.

"Ah wuz loadin' a wagon wid scantlin' right near the saw when Spunk fell on the carriage but 'fore Ah could git to him the saw got him in the body—awful sight. Me an' Skint Miller got him off but it was too late. Anybody could see that. The fust thing he said wuz: 'He pushed me, 'Lige—the dirty hound pushed me in the back!'—He was spittin' blood at ev'ry breath. We laid him on the sawdust pile with his face to the East so's he could die easy. He helt mah han' till the last, Walter, and said: 'It was Joe, 'Lige—the dirty sneak shoved me . . . he didn't dare come to mah face . . . but Ah'll git the son-of-a-wood louse soon's Ah get there an' make hell too hot for him. . . . Ah felt him shove me . . . !' Thass how he died."

"If spirits kin fight, there's a powerful tussle goin' on somewhere ovah Jordan 'cause Ah b'leeve Joe's ready for Spunk an' ain't skeered any more—yas, Ah b'leeve Joe pushed 'im mahself."

They had arrived at the house. Lena's lamentations were deep and loud. She had filled the room with magnolia blossoms that gave off a heavy sweet odor. The keepers of the wake tipped about whispering in frightened tones. Everyone in the village was there, even old Jeff Kanty, Joe's father, who a few hours before would have been afraid to come within ten feet of him, stood leering triumphantly down upon the fallen giant as if his fingers had been the teeth of steel that laid him low.

The cooling board consisted of three sixteen-inch boards on saw horses, a dingy sheet was his shroud.

The women ate heartily of the funeral baked meats and wondered who would be Lena's next. The men whispered coarse conjectures between guzzles of whiskey.

Sweat

It was eleven o'clock of a Spring night in Florida. It was Sunday. Any other night, Delia Jones would have been in bed for two hours by this time. But she was a washwoman, and Monday morning meant a great deal to her. So she collected the soiled clothes on Saturday when she returned the clean things. Sunday night after church, she sorted them and put the white things to soak. It saved her almost a half day's start. A great hamper in the bedroom held the clothes that she brought home. It was so much neater than a number of bundles lying around.

She squatted in the kitchen floor beside the great pile of clothes, sorting them into small heaps according to color, and humming a song in a mournful key, but wondering through it all where Sykes, her husband, had gone with her horse and buckboard.

Just then something long, round, limp and black fell upon her shoulders and slithered to the floor beside her. A great terror took hold of her. It softened her knees and dried her mouth so that it was a full minute before she could cry out or move. Then she saw that it was the big bull whip her husband liked to carry when he drove.

She lifted her eyes to the door and saw him standing there bent over with laughter at her fright. She screamed at him.

"Sykes, what you throw dat whip on me like dat? You know it would skeer me—looks just like a snake, an' you knows how skeered Ah is of snakes."

"Course Ah knowed it! That's how come Ah done it." He slapped his leg with his hand and almost rolled on the ground in his mirth. "If you such a big fool dat you got to have a fit over a earth worm or a string, Ah don't keer how bad Ah skeer you."

"You aint got no business doing it. Gawd knows it's a sin. Some day Ah'm gointuh drop dead from some of yo' foolishness. 'Nother thing, where you been wid mah rig? Ah feeds dat pony. He aint fuh you to be drivin' wid no bull whip."

"You sho is one aggravatin' nigger woman!" he declared and stepped into the room. She resumed her work and did not answer him at once. "Ah done tole you time and again to keep them white folks' clothes outa dis house."

He picked up the whip and glared down at her. Delia went on with her work. She went out into the yard and returned with a galvanized tub and set it on the washbench. She saw that Sykes had kicked all of the clothes together again, and now stood in her way truculently, his whole manner hoping, *praying,* for an argument. But she walked calmly around him and commenced to re-sort the things.

"Next time, Ah'm gointer kick 'em outdoors," he threatened as he struck a match along the leg of his corduroy breeches.

Delia never looked up from her work, and her thin, stooped shoulders sagged further.

"Ah aint for no fuss t'night Sykes. Ah just come from taking sacrament at the church house."

He snorted scornfully. "Yeah, you just come from de church house on a Sunday night, but heah you is gone to work on them clothes. You ain't nothing but a hypocrite. One of them amen-corner Christians—sing, whoop, and shout, then come home and wash white folks clothes on the Sabbath."

He stepped roughly upon the whitest pile of things, kicking them helter-skelter as he crossed the room. His wife gave a little scream of dismay, and quickly gathered them together again.

"Sykes, you quit grindin' dirt into these clothes! How can Ah git through by Sat'day if Ah don't start on Sunday?"

"Ah don't keer if you never git through. Anyhow, Ah done promised Gawd and a couple of other men, Ah aint gointer have it in mah house. Don't gimme no lip neither, else Ah'll throw 'em out and put mah fist up side yo' head to boot."

Delia's habitual meekness seemed to slip from her shoulders like a blown scarf. She was on her feet; her poor little body, her bare knuckly hands bravely defying the strapping hulk before her.

"Looka heah, Sykes, you done gone too fur. Ah been married to you fur fifteen years, and Ah been takin' in washin' fur fifteen years. Sweat, sweat, sweat! Work and sweat, cry and sweat, pray and sweat!"

"What's that got to do with me?" he asked brutally.

"What's it got to do with you, Sykes? Mah tub of suds is filled yo' belly with vittles more times than yo' hands is filled it. Mah sweat is done paid for this house and Ah reckon Ah kin keep on sweatin' in it."

She seized the iron skillet from the stove and struck a defensive pose, which act surprised him greatly, coming from her. It cowed him and he did not strike her as he usually did.

"Naw you won't," she panted, "that ole snaggle-toothed black woman you runnin' with aint comin' heah to pile up on *mah* sweat and blood. You aint paid for nothin' on this place, and Ah'm gointer stay right heah till Ah'm toted out foot foremost."

"Well, you better quit gittin' me riled up, else they'll be totin' you out sooner than you expect. Ah'm so tired of you Ah don't know whut to do. Gawd! how Ah hates skinny wimmen!"

A little awed by this new Delia, he sidled out of the door and slammed the back gate after him. He did not say where he had gone, but she knew too well. She knew very well that he would not return until nearly daybreak also. Her work over, she went on to bed but not to sleep at once. Things had come to a pretty pass!

She lay awake, gazing upon the debris that cluttered their matrimonial trail. Not an image left standing along the way. Anything like flowers had long ago been drowned in the salty stream that had been pressed from her heart. Her tears, her sweat, her blood. She had brought love to the union and he had brought a longing after the flesh. Two months after the wedding, he had given her the first brutal beating. She had the memory of his numerous trips to Orlando with all of his wages when he had returned to her penniless, even before the first year had passed. She was young and soft then, but now she thought of her knotty, muscled limbs, her harsh knuckly hands, and drew herself up into an unhappy little ball in the middle of the big feather bed. Too late now to hope for love, even if it were not Bertha it would be someone else. This case differed from the others only in that she was bolder than the others. Too late for everything except her little home. She had built it for her old days, and planted one by one the trees and flowers there. It was lovely to her, lovely.

Somehow, before sleep came, she found herself saying aloud: "Oh well, whatever goes over the Devil's back, is got to come under his belly. Sometime or ruther, Sykes, like everybody else, is gointer reap his sowing." After that she was able to build a spiritual earthworks against her husband. His shells could no longer reach her. *Amen.* She went to sleep and slept until he announced his presence in bed by kicking her feet and rudely snatching the cover away.

"Gimme some kivah heah, an' git yo' damn foots over on yo' own side! Ah oughter mash you in yo' mouf fuh drawing dat skillet on me."

Delia went clear to the rail without answering him. A triumphant indifference to all that he was or did.

The week was as full of work for Delia as all other weeks, and Saturday found her behind her little pony, collecting and delivering clothes.

It was a hot, hot day near the end of July. The village men on Joe Clarke's porch even chewed cane listlessly. They did not hurl the cane-knots as usual. They let them dribble over the edge of the porch. Even conversation had collapsed under the heat.

"Heah come Delia Jones," Jim Merchant said, as the shaggy pony came 'round the bend of the road toward them. The rusty buckboard was heaped with baskets of crisp, clean laundry.

"Yep," Joe Lindsay agreed. "Hot or col', rain or shine, jes ez reg'lar ez de weeks roll roun' Delia carries 'em an' fetches 'em on Sat'day."

"She better if she wanter eat," said Moss. "Syke Jones aint wuth de shot an' powder hit would tek tuh kill 'em. Not to *huh* he aint."

"He sho' aint," Walter Thomas chimed in. "It's too bad, too, cause she wuz a right pritty lil trick when he got huh. Ah'd uh mah'ied huh mahseff if he hadnter beat me to it."

Delia nodded briefly at the men as she drove past.

"Too much knockin' will ruin *any* 'oman. He done beat huh 'nough tuh kill three women, let 'lone change they looks," said Elijah Mosely. "How Syke kin stommuck dat big black greasy Mogul he's layin' roun' wid, gits me. Ah swear dat eight-rock couldn't kiss a sardine can Ah done thowed out de back do' 'way las' yeah."

"Aw, she's fat, thass how come. He's allus been crazy 'bout fat women," put in Merchant. "He'd a' been tied up wid one long time ago if he could a' found one tuh have him. Did Ah tell yuh 'bout him come sidlin' roun' *mah* wife—bringin' her a basket uh pee-cans outa his yard fuh a present? Yessir, mah wife! She tol' him tuh take 'em right straight back home, cause Delia works so hard ovah dat washtub she reckon everything on de place taste lak sweat an' soapsuds. Ah jus' wisht Ah'd a' caught 'im 'roun' dere! Ah'd a' made his hips ketch on fiah down dat shell road."

"Ah know he done it, too. Ah sees 'im grinnin' at every 'oman dat passes," Walter Thomas said. "But even so, he useter eat some mighty big hunks uh humble pie tuh git dat lil' 'oman he got. She wuz ez pritty ez a speckled pup! Dat wuz fifteen yeahs ago. He useter be so skeered uh losin' huh, she could make him do some parts of a husband's duty. Dey never wuz de same in de mind."

"There oughter be a law about him," said Lindsay. "He aint fit tuh carry guts tuh a bear."

Clarke spoke for the first time. "Taint no law on earth dat kin make a man be decent if it aint in 'im. There's plenty men dat takes a wife lak dey do a joint uh sugar-cane. It's round, juicy an' sweet when dey gits it. But dey squeeze an' grind, squeeze an' grind an' wring tell dey wring every drop uh pleasure dat's in 'em out. When dey's satisfied dat dey is wrung dry, dey treats 'em jes lak dey do a cane-chew. Dey throws 'em away. Dey knows whut dey is doin' while dey is at it, an' hates theirselves fuh it but they keeps on hangin' after huh tell she's empty. Den dey hates huh fuh bein' a cane-chew an' in de way."

"We oughter take Syke an' dat stray 'oman uh his'n down in Lake Howell swamp an' lay on de rawhide till they cain't say 'Lawd a' mussy.' He allus wuz uh ovahbearin' niggah, but since dat white 'oman from up north done teached 'im how to run a automobile, he done got too biggety to live—an' we oughter kill 'im," Old Man Anderson advised.

A grunt of approval went around the porch. But the heat was melting their civic virtue and Elijah Moseley began to bait Joe Clarke.

"Come on, Joe, git a melon outa dere an' slice it up for yo' customers. We'se all sufferin' wid de heat. De bear's done got *me*!"

"Thass right, Joe, a watermelon is jes' whut Ah needs tuh cure de eppizudicks," Walter Thomas joined forces with Moseley. "Come on dere, Joe. We all is steady customers an' you aint set us up in a long time. Ah chooses dat long, bowlegged Floridy favorite."

"A god, an' be dough. You all gimme twenty cents and slice away," Clarke retorted. "Ah needs a col' slice m'self. Heah, everybody chip in. Ah'll lend y'll mah meat knife."

The money was quickly subscribed and the huge melon brought forth. At that moment, Sykes and Bertha arrived. A determined silence fell on the porch and the melon was put away again.

Merchant snapped down the blade of his jackknife and moved toward the store door.

"Come on in, Joe, an' gimme a slab uh sow belly an' uh pound uh coffee—almost fuhgot 'twas Sat'day. Got to git on home." Most of the men left also.

Just then Delia drove past on her way home, as Sykes was ordering magnificently for Bertha. It pleased him for Delia to see.

"Git whutsoever yo' heart desires, Honey. Wait a minute, Joe. Give huh two bottles uh strawberry soda-water, uh quart uh parched ground-peas, an' a block uh chewin' gum."

With all this they left the store, with Sykes reminding Bertha that this was his town and she could have it if she wanted it.

The men returned soon after they left, and held their watermelon feast.

"Where did Syke Jones git dat 'oman from nohow?" Lindsay asked.

"Ovah Apopka. Guess dey musta been cleanin' out de town when she lef'. She don't look lak a thing but a hunk uh liver wid hair on it."

"Well, she sho' kin squall," Dave Carter contributed. "When she gits ready tuh laff, she jes' opens huh mouf an' latches it back tuh de las' notch. No ole grandpa alligator down in Lake Bell ain't got nothin' on huh."

Bertha had been in town three months now. Sykes was still paying her room rent at Della Lewis'—the only house in town that would have taken her in. Sykes took her frequently to Winter Park to "stomps." He still assured her that he was the swellest man in the state.

"Sho' you kin have dat lil' ole house soon's Ah kin git dat 'oman outa dere. Everything b'longs tuh me an' you sho' kin have it. Ah sho' 'bominates uh skinny 'oman. Lawdy, you sho' is got one portly shape on you! You kin git *anything* you wants. Dis is *mah* town an' you sho' kin have it."

Delia's work-worn knees crawled over the earth in Gethsemane and up the rocks of Calvary many, many times during these months. She avoided the villagers and meeting places in her efforts to be blind and deaf. But Bertha nullified this to a degree, by coming to Delia's house to call Sykes out to her at the gate.

Delia and Sykes fought all the time now with no peaceful interludes. They slept and ate in silence. Two or three times Delia had attempted a timid friendliness, but she was repulsed each time. It was plain that the breaches must remain agape.

The sun had burned July to August. The heat streamed down like a million hot arrows, smiting all things living upon the earth. Grass withered, leaves browned, snakes went blind in shedding and men and dogs went mad. Dog days!

Delia came home one day and found Sykes there before her. She wondered, but started to go on into the house without speaking, even though he was standing in the kitchen door and she must either stoop under his arm or ask him to move. He made no room for her. She noticed a soap box beside the steps, but paid no particular attention to it, knowing that he must have brought it there. As she was stooping to pass under his outstretched arm, he suddenly pushed her backward, laughingly.

"Look in de box dere Delia, Ah done brung yuh somethin'!"

She nearly fell upon the box in her stumbling, and when she saw what it held, she all but fainted outright.

"Syke! Syke, mah Gawd! You take dat rattlesnake 'way from heah! You *gottuh.* Oh, Jesus, have mussy!"

"Ah aint gut tuh do nuthin' uh de kin'—fact is Ah aint got tuh do nothin' but die. Taint no use uh you puttin' on airs makin' out lak you skeered uh dat snake—he's gointer stay right heah tell he die. He wouldn't bite me cause Ah knows how tuh handle 'im. Nohow he wouldn't risk breakin' out his fangs 'gin *yo'* skinny laigs."

"Naw, now Syke, don't keep dat thing 'roun' heah tuh skeer me tuh death. You knows Ah'm even feared uh earth worms. Thass de biggest snake Ah evah did see. Kill 'im Syke, please."

"Doan ast me tuh do nothin' fuh yuh. Goin' 'roun' tryin' tuh be so damn asterperious. Naw, Ah aint gonna kill it. Ah think uh damn sight mo' uh him dan you! Dat's a nice snake an' anybody doan lak 'im kin jes' hit de grit."

The village soon heard that Sykes had the snake, and came to see and ask questions.

"How de hen-fire did you ketch dat six-foot rattler, Syke?" Thomas asked.

"He's full uh frogs so he caint hardly move, thass how Ah eased up on 'm. But Ah'm a snake charmer an' knows how tuh handle 'em. Shux, dat aint nothin'. Ah could ketch one eve'y day if Ah so wanted tuh."

"Whut he needs is a heavy hick'ry club leaned real heavy on his head. Dat's de bes' way tuh charm a rattlesnake."

"Naw, Walt, y'll jes' don't understand dese diamon' backs lak Ah do," said Sykes in a superior tone of voice.

The village agreed with Walter, but the snake stayed on. His box remained by the kitchen door with its screen wire covering. Two or three days later it had digested its meal of frogs and literally came to life. It rattled at every movement in the kitchen or the yard. One day as Delia came down the kitchen steps she saw his chalky-white fangs curved like scimitars hung in the wire meshes. This time she did not run away with averted eyes as usual. She stood for a long time in the doorway in a red fury that grew bloodier for every second that she regarded the creature that was her torment.

That night she broached the subject as soon as Sykes sat down to the table.

"Syke, Ah wants you tuh take dat snake 'way fum heah. You done starved me an' Ah put up widcher, you done beat me an Ah took dat, but you done kilt all mah insides bringin' dat varmint heah."

Sykes poured out a saucer full of coffee and drank it deliberately before he answered her.

"A whole lot Ah keer 'bout how you feels inside uh out. Dat snake aint goin' no damn wheah till Ah gits ready fuh 'im tuh go. So fur as beatin' is concerned, yuh aint took near all dat you gointer take ef you stay 'roun' *me.*"

Delia pushed back her plate and got up from the table. "Ah hates you, Sykes," she said calmly. "Ah hates you tuh de same degree dat Ah useter love yuh. Ah done took an' took till mah belly is full up tuh mah neck. Dat's de reason Ah got mah letter fum de church an' moved mah membership tuh Woodbridge—so Ah don't haftuh take no sacrament wid yuh. Ah don't wantuh see yuh 'roun' me atall. Lay 'roun' wid dat 'oman all yuh wants tuh, but gwan 'way fum me an' mah house. Ah hates yuh lak uh suck-egg dog."

Sykes almost let the huge wad of corn bread and collard greens he was chewing fall out of his mouth in amazement. He had a hard time whipping himself up to the proper fury to try to answer Delia.

"Well, Ah'm glad you does hate me. Ah'm sho' tiahed uh you hangin' ontuh me. Ah don't want yuh. Look at yuh stringey ole neck! Yo' rawbony laigs an' arms is enough tuh cut uh man tuh death. You looks jes' lak de devvul's doll-baby tuh *me.* You cain't hate me no worse dan Ah hates you. Ah been hatin' *you* fuh years."

"Yo' ole black hide don't look lak nothin' tuh me, but uh passle uh wrinkled up rubber, wid yo' big ole yeahs flappin' on each side lak uh paih uh buzzard wings. Don't think Ah'm gointuh be run 'way fum mah house neither. Ah'm goin' tuh de white folks about *you*, mah young man, de very nex' time you lay yo' han's on me. Mah cup is done run ovah." Delia said this with no signs of fear and Sykes departed from the house, threatening her, but made not the slightest move to carry out any of them.

That night he did not return at all, and the next day being Sunday, Delia was glad that she did not have to quarrel before she hitched up her pony and drove the four miles to Woodbridge.

She stayed to the night service—"love feast"—which was very warm and full of spirit. In the emotional winds her domestic trials were borne far and wide so that she sang as she drove homeward,

"Jurden water, black an' col'
Chills de body, not de soul
An' Ah wantah cross Jurden in uh calm time."

She came from the barn to the kitchen door and stopped.

"Whut's de mattah, ol' satan, you aint kickin' up yo' racket?" She addressed the snake's box. Complete silence. She went on into the house with a new hope in its birth struggles. Perhaps her threat to go to the white folks had frightened Sykes! Perhaps he was sorry! Fifteen years of misery and suppression had brought Delia to the place where she would hope *anything* that looked towards a way over or through her wall of inhibitions.

She felt in the match safe behind the stove at once for a match. There was only one there.

"Dat niggah wouldn't fetch nothin' heah tuh save his rotten neck, but he kin run thew whut Ah brings quick enough. Now he done toted off nigh on tuh haff uh box uh matches. He done had dat 'oman heah in mah house, too."

Nobody but a woman could tell how she knew this even before she struck the match. But she did and it put her into a new fury.

Presently she brought in the tubs to put the white things to soak. This time she decided she need not bring the hamper out of the bedroom; she would go in there and do the sorting. She picked up the pot-bellied lamp and went in. The room was small and the hamper stood hard by the foot of the white iron bed. She could sit and reach through the bedposts—resting as she worked.

"Ah wantah cross Jurden in uh calm time." She was singing again. The mood of the "love feast" had returned. She threw back the lid of the basket almost gaily. Then, moved by both horror and terror, she sprang back toward the door. *There lay the snake in the basket!* He moved sluggishly at first, but even as she turned round and round, jumped up and down in an insanity of fear, he began to stir vigorously. She saw him pouring his awful beauty from the basket upon the bed, then she seized the lamp and ran as fast as she could to the kitchen. The wind from the open door blew out the light and the darkness added to her terror. She sped to the darkness of the yard, slamming the door after her before she thought to set down the lamp. She did not feel safe even on the ground, so she climbed up in the hay barn.

There for an hour or more she lay sprawled upon the hay a gibbering wreck.

Finally she grew quiet, and after that, coherent thought. With this, stalked through her a cold, bloody rage. Hours of this. A period of introspection, a space of retrospection, then a mixture of both. Out of this an awful calm.

"Well, Ah done de bes' Ah could. If things aint right, Gawd knows taint mah fault."

She went to sleep—a twitchy sleep—and woke up to a faint gray sky. There was a loud hollow sound below. She peered out. Sykes was at the wood-pile, demolishing a wire-covered box.

He hurried to the kitchen door, but hung outside there some minutes before he entered, and stood some minutes more inside before he closed it after him.

The gray in the sky was spreading. Delia descended without fear now, and crouched beneath the low bedroom window. The drawn shade shut out the dawn, shut in the night. But the thin walls held back no sound.

"Dat ol' scratch is woke up now!" She mused at the tremendous whirr inside, which every woodsman knows, is one of the sound illusions. The rattler is a ventriloquist. His whirr sounds to the right, to the left, straight ahead, behind, close under foot—everywhere but where it is. Woe to him who guesses wrong unless he is prepared to hold up his end of the argument! Sometimes he strikes without rattling at all.

Inside, Sykes heard nothing until he knocked a pot lid off the stove while trying to reach the match safe in the dark. He had emptied his pockets at Bertha's.

The snake seemed to wake up under the stove and Sykes made a quick leap into the bedroom. In spite of the gin he had had, his head was clearing now.

"Mah Gawd!" he chattered, "ef Ah could on'y strack uh light!"

The rattling ceased for a moment as he stood paralyzed. He waited. It seemed that the snake waited also.

"Oh, fuh de light! Ah thought he'd be too sick"—Sykes was muttering to himself when the whirr began again, closer, right underfoot this time. Long before this, Sykes' ability to think had been flattened down to primitive instinct and he leaped—onto the bed.

Outside Delia heard a cry that might have come from a maddened chimpanzee, a stricken gorilla. All the terror, all the horror, all the rage that man possibly could express, without a recognizable human sound.

A tremendous stir inside there, another series of animal screams, the intermittent whirr of the reptile. The shade torn violently down from the window, letting in the red dawn, a huge brown hand seizing the window stick, great dull blows upon the wooden floor punctuating the gibberish of sound long after the rattle of the snake had abruptly subsided. All this Delia could see and hear from her place beneath the window, and it made her ill. She crept over to the four-o'clocks and stretched herself on the cool earth to recover.

She lay there. "Delia, Delia!" She could hear Sykes calling in a most despairing tone as one who expected no answer. The sun crept on up, and he called. Delia could not move—her legs were gone flabby. She never moved, he called, and the sun kept rising.

"Mah Gawd!" She heard him moan. "Mah Gawd fum Heben!" She heard him stumbling about and got up from her flower-bed. The sun was growing warm. As she approached the door she heard him call out hopefully, "Delia, is dat you Ah heah?"

She saw him on his hands and knees as soon as she reached the door. He crept an inch or two toward her—all that he was able, and she saw his horribly swollen neck and his one open eye shining with hope. A surge of pity too strong to support bore her away from that eye that must, could not, fail to see the tubs. He would see the lamp. Orlando with its doctors was too far. She could scarcely reach the Chinaberry tree, where she waited in the growing heat while inside she knew the cold river was creeping up and up to extinguish that eye which must know by now that she knew.

JEAN TOOMER

(1894–1967)

The New Negro Movement, which flourished after the outbreak of World War II, was an extremely variegated phenomenon, far more differentiated in its scope and aims than is commonly assumed. Although the movement was often identified simply with the racial thinking of figures such as Marcus Garvey, Langston Hughes, and Alain Locke, the intellectuals who formed its conspicuous mainstream, it included a whole range of subcurrents whose adherents often defined themselves in opposition to Locke and his race theories. It is within such a current that Jean Toomer took his bearings.

On December 26, 1894, Toomer was born in Washington, D.C., of racially mixed parentage: French, Dutch, Welsh, African American, German, Jewish, and Native American. His father deserted his mother a few months after he was born, and his mother died during a brief, unhappy second marriage when Toomer was fourteen. In childhood, he suffered from a lack of self-esteem and turned in upon himself, away from his tyrannical grandfather, P. B. S. Pinchback, a mulatto who had served as governor of Louisiana for two months. Initially living in an elegant all-white neighborhood in Washington, Toomer's family was forced in 1910 to move to a more modest dwelling in the black section of the city when his grandfather's fortunes declined. As Toomer recalled in 1922, "I have lived equally amid the two race groups. Now white, now colored."

Although Toomer initially liked his new life, proclaiming that it gave him "more emotion, more rhythm, more color, more gaiety, than the chilly atmosphere of white society," he continued to suffer from self-doubt and morbid introspection. He attended the M Street High School, where he became a troublemaker, a nuisance in the classroom, and a victim of overpowering sexual impulses, which he thought were destroying his health. He turned to barbells and special diets and began a three-year period of revolt and wandering. In 1914, he enrolled as a student of agriculture at the University of Wisconsin for a semester and at the Massachusetts College of Agriculture, where he lasted only a week. He then went to a physical training college in Chicago but ended up more interested in Darwin and atheism than in physical fitness. Toomer experienced a loss of faith in God, saying that he felt "condemned and betrayed." "In truth, I did not want to live," he wrote in his "Outline of Autobiography." As a substitute for religion, he tried sociology at New York University, then history at City College. When history became a bore, psychology took its place. After being rejected for the draft, he took on a series of odd jobs. He sold cars in Chicago, taught physical education in Milwaukee, and worked for several days in a New Jersey shipyard.

In 1920, he returned to his grandfather in Washington, D.C., where, in a mood of defeat and rejection, he began reading literature—Robert Frost, Sherwood Anderson, the imagists, all of whom taught him that words were mere symbols of things and not the things themselves. It was during this time that he again experienced utter despair: "Finally we reached the stage where we vowed to suffer no more. Of people, of life, of the world, we said, 'Don't touch me.' We resolved that no one ever would." This is the mood Toomer was in when, in 1921, he accepted an offer to serve as a temporary superintendent of a small black industrial school in rural Georgia. The following year, he wrote to his close friend Waldo Frank,

> There for the first time I really saw the Negro, not as a vulgarized, a semi-Americanized product, but the Negro peasant, strong with the tang of fields and soil. It was there that I first heard the folk-songs rolling up the valley at twilight, heard them as spontaneous and native utterances. They filled me with gold, and hints of an eternal purple.

The result of Toomer's stay in the black South was *Cane* (1923), a work that reflects both his joy in discovering the black folk spirit and his sadness in realizing that it was a thing of the past. Of the spirituals he wrote,

> But I learned that the Negroes of the town objected to them. They called them "shouting." They had victrolas and player-pianos. So, I realized with deep regret, that the spirituals, meeting ridicule, world be certain to die out. With Negroes also the trend was towards the small town and toward the city—and industry and commerce and the machines. The folk-spirit was walking in to die on the modern desert. That spirit was so beautiful. Its death was so tragic.

After the publication of *Cane*, Toomer never again published anything of significance to black literature, except the poem "Blue Meridian" (1936). Instead, he continued his quest for "unity" and "personal wholeness," spending a summer (1924) at the Gurdjieff Institute in Fontainebleau, France. Toomer found what he was looking for in Gurdjieff's philosophy, a blend of mysticism, Freudianism, and religion.

One of the most innovative works of twentieth-century American fiction, *Cane* anticipated the later experimental works of John Dos Passos and William Faulkner. Because the work is a series of short stories or vignettes intermixed with lyrical poetry and concludes with a play called "Kabnis," there was some question as to whether *Cane* could be properly called a novel. Today most critics agree that it is an experimental lyrical novel whose unity is derived not from its plot or characters but from its images.

The novel is divided into three parts. Part I is composed of six prose sections and ten poems. The setting is the South, the time is shortly after World War I, and the focus is largely on a number of women: Karintha, Becky, Carma, Fern, Esther, and Louisa. All of the women's names, with the exception of Louisa, are used as titles for the prose sections. The women have all led frustrated lives and have been involved with lusting and dominating men. Karintha, for instance, drives men mad and leaves them unfulfilled. Becky, a white woman, is ostracized by the community because of her two mulatto children and is misunderstood by both men and women. When she dies, her spirit haunts the forest.

In Part II of *Cane*, we see the results of the Great Migration (1915–1930). The time is during and after World War I, and the emphasis shifts from the South to the North, to Washington, D.C., and Chicago. As counterpoint to Part I, the focus is mainly on black men and the frustrated lives they lead in industrialized northern cities. "Seventh Street" opens Part II, describing the "whitewashed" world of Washington:

> Money burns the pocket, pocket hurts.
> Bootleggers in silken shirts,
> Ballooned, zooming Cadillacs,
> Whizzing, whizzing down the street-car tracks.

"Rhobert," the second prose segment in this part, describes Rhobert as wearing a dead house on his head, a burden so heavy that he is slowly sinking down. For Toomer, the black man was much better off in the South.

In "Kabnis," the third part of *Cane,* the setting shifts back to the South. Ralph Kabnis, a teacher at a Georgia girls' school, sits alone in his cabin as the section opens. He feels estranged and longs for his home, Washington, D.C. Other characters in "Kabnis" include Fred Halsey, a shopkeeper; Lewis, a fellow teacher and northerner; three women; and Father John, an old man. Kabnis expresses his opinions on a variety of topics: black religion, slavery, color. This section ends the morning after Kabnis, Halsey, and Lewis have spent a night in the basement (known as the "hole") of Halsey's shop with two women, Stella and Cora. During that night, Kabnis renounces his religion and his color.

Although highly acclaimed by white critics, the book did not initially sell well. Despite the black community's enthusiastic reception of both *Cane* and Toomer, he remained detached from the black literary world. Although he established contact with Alain Locke, Claude McKay, Countee Cullen, and other blacks involved in the New Negro Movement as early as 1921, he chose in later years to stress his Greenwich Village connection: "In New York, I stepped into the literary world. Frank, Gorham Munson, Kenneth Burke, Hart Crane, Matthew Josephson, Malcolm Cowley, Paul Rosenfield, Van Wyck Brooks, Robert Lillell-Broom, the Dial, the New Republic and many more. I lived on Gay Street and entered into the swing of it."

In short, Toomer's closest friends and literary contacts were white writers, editors, and critics. As we have seen from the sketch of his early life, Toomer suffered from a pronounced sense of cultural and racial ambivalence, and this ambivalence predisposed him during his early years to keep his distance from his white heritage. After the publication of *Cane,* however, he abandoned his black identity and mobilized his white one. Given his ardent assertions that race should be transcended, this was a perilous concession. Still, Toomer remains one of America's most talented artists, and *Cane* one of its most original and innovative creations.

❖❖❖

Nellie Y. McKay's biography, *Jean Toomer, Artist: A Study of His Literary Life and Work, 1894–1936* (1984), is informative; the one by Cynthia Kerman and Richard Eldridge, *The Lives of Jean Toomer: A Hunger for Wholeness* (1987), is middle class but illuminative. Brian Benson's critical study *Jean Toomer* (1980) was groundbreaking. The collection titled *The Wayward and the Seeking* (1982) by Darwin T. Turner is definitive. *Jean Toomer: A Critical Evaluation* (1988) by Therman B. O'Daniel is the product of a dedicated scholar seasoned in the trenches of African American literary history.

Karintha

FROM *CANE*

HER SKIN IS LIKE DUSK ON THE EASTERN HORIZON,
O CANT YOU SEE IT, O CANT YOU SEE IT,
HER SKIN IS LIKE DUSK ON THE EASTERN HORIZON
. . . WHEN THE SUN GOES DOWN.

Men had always wanted her, this Karintha, even as a child, Karintha carrying beauty, perfect as dusk when the sun goes down. Old men rode her hobby-horse upon their knees. Young men danced with her at frolics when they should have been dancing with their grown-up girls. God grant us youth, secretly prayed the old men. The young fellows counted the time to pass before she would be old enough to mate with them. This interest of the male, who wishes to ripen a growing thing too soon, could mean no good to her.

Karintha, at twelve, was a wild flash that told the other folks just what it was to live. At sunset, when there was no wind, and the pine-smoke from over by the sawmill hugged the earth, and you couldnt see more than few feet in front, her sudden darting past you was a bit of vivid color, like a black bird that flashes in light. With the other children one could hear, some distance off, their feet flopping in the two-inch dust. Karintha's running was a whir. It had the sound of the red dust that sometimes makes a spiral in the road. At dusk, during the hush just after the sawmill had closed down, and before any of the women had started their supper-getting-ready songs, her voice, high-pitched, shrill, would put one's ears to itching. But no one ever thought to make her stop because of it. She stoned the cows, and beat her dog, and fought the other children. . . . Even the preacher, who caught her at mischief, told himself that she was as innocently lovely as a November cotton flower. Already, rumors were out about her. Homes in Georgia are most often built on the two-room plan. In one, you cook and eat, in the other you sleep, and there love goes on. Karintha had seen or heard, perhaps she had felt her parents loving. One could but imitate one's parents, for to follow them was the way of God. She played "home" with a small boy who was not afraid to do her bidding. That started the whole thing. Old men could no longer ride her hobby-horse upon their knees. But young men counted faster.

Her skin is like dusk,
O cant you see it,
Her skin is like dusk,
When the sun goes down.

Karintha is a woman. She who carries beauty, perfect as dusk when the sun goes down. She has been married many times. Old men remind her that a few years back they rode her hobby-horse upon their knees. Karintha smiles, and indulges them when she is in the mood for it. She has contempt for them. Karintha is a woman. Young men run stills to make her money. Young men go to the big cities and run on the road. Young men go away to college. They all want to bring her money. These are the young men who thought that all they had to do was to count time. But Karintha is a woman, and she has had a child. A child fell out of her womb onto a bed of pine-needles in the forest. Pine-needles are smooth and sweet. They are elastic to the feet of rabbits. . . . A sawmill was nearby. Its pyramidal sawdust pile smouldered. It is a year before one completely burns. Meanwhile, the smoke curls up and hangs in odd wraiths about the trees, curls up, and spreads itself out over the valley. . . . Weeks after Karintha returned home the smoke was so heavy you tasted it in water. Some one made a song:

Smoke is on the hills. Rise up.
Smoke is on the hills, O rise
And take my soul to Jesus.

Karintha is a woman. Men do not know that the soul of her was a growing thing ripened too soon. They will bring their money; they will die not having found it out. . . . Karintha at twenty, carrying beauty, perfect as dusk when the sun goes down. Karintha . . .

Her skin is like dusk on the eastern horizon,
O cant you see it, O cant you see it,
Her skin is like dusk on the eastern horizon
. . . When the sun goes down.
Goes down . . .

Song of the Son

FROM *CANE*

Pour O pour that parting soul in song,
O pour it in the sawdust glow of night,
Into the velvet pine-smoke air to-night,
And let the valley carry it along.

And let the valley carry it along.

O land and soil, red soil and sweet-gum tree,
So scant of grass, so profligate of pines,
Now just before an epoch's sun declines
Thy son, in time, I have returned to thee,
Thy son, I have in time returned to thee.

In time, for though the sun is setting on
A song-lit race of slaves, it has not set;
Though late, O soil, it is not too late yet
To catch thy plaintive soul, leaving, soon gone,
Leaving, to catch thy plaintive soul soon gone.

O Negro slaves, dark purple ripened plums,
Squeezed, and bursting in the pine-wood air,
Passing, before they stripped the old tree bare
One plum was saved for me, one seed becomes

An everlasting song, a singing tree,
Caroling softly souls of slavery,
What they were, and what they are to me,
Caroling softly souls of slavery.

Fern

FROM *CANE*

Face flowed into her eyes. Flowed in soft cream foam and plaintive ripples, in such a way that wherever your glance may momentarily have rested, it immediately thereafter wavered in the direction of her eyes. The soft suggestion of down slightly darkened, like the shadow of a bird's wing might, the creamy brown color of her upper lip. Why, after noticing it, you sought her eyes, I cannot tell you. Her nose was aquiline, Semitic. If you have heard a Jewish cantor sing, if he has touched you and made your own sorrow seem trivial when compared with his, you will know my feeling when I follow the curves of her profile, like mobile rivers, to their common delta. They were strange eyes. In this, that they sought nothing—that is, nothing that was obvious and tangible and that one could see, and they gave the impression that nothing was to be denied. When a woman seeks, you will have observed, her eyes deny. Fern's eyes desired nothing that you could give her; there was no reason why they should withhold. Men saw her eyes and fooled themselves. Fern's eyes said to them that she was easy. When she was young, a few men took her, but got no joy from it. And then, once done, they felt bound to her (quite unlike their hit and run with other girls), felt as though it would take them a lifetime to fulfill an obligation which they could find no name for. They became attached to her, and hungered after finding the barest trace of what she might desire. As she grew up, new men who came to town felt as almost everyone did who ever saw her: that they would not be denied. Men were everlastingly bringing her their bodies. Something inside of her got tired of them, I guess, for I am certain that for the life of her she could not tell why or how she began to turn them off. A man in fever is no trifling thing to send away. They began to leave her, baffled and ashamed, yet vowing to themselves that some day they would do some fine thing for her: send her candy every week and not let her know whom it came from, watch out for her wedding-day and give her a magnificent something with no name on it, buy a house and deed it to her, rescue her from some unworthy fellow who had tricked her into marrying him. As you know, men are apt to idolize or fear that which they cannot understand, especially if it be a woman. She did not deny them, yet the fact was that they were denied. A sort of superstition crept into their consciousness of her being somehow above them. Being above them meant that she was not to be approached by anyone. She became a virgin. Now a virgin in a small southern town is by no means the usual thing, if you will believe me. That the sexes were made to mate is the practice of the South. Particularly, black folks were made to mate. And it is black folks whom I have been talking about thus far. What white men thought of Fern I can arrive at only by analogy. They let her alone.

Anyone, of course, could see her, could see her eyes. If you walked up the Dixie Pike most any time of day, you'd be most like to see her resting listless-like on the railing of her porch, back propped against a post, head tilted a little forward because there was a nail in the porch post just where her head came which for some reason or other she never took the trouble to pull out. Her eyes, if it were sunset, rested idly where the sun, molten and glorious, was pouring down between the fringe of pines. Or maybe they gazed at the gray cabin on the knoll from which an evening folk-song was coming. Perhaps they followed a cow that had been turned loose to roam and feed on cotton-stalks and corn leaves. Like as not they'd settle on some vague spot above the horizon, though hardly a trace of wistfulness would come to them. If it were dusk, then they'd wait for the search-light of the evening train which you could see miles up the track before it flared across the Dixie Pike, close to her home. Wherever they looked, you'd follow them and then waver back. Like her face, the whole countryside seemed to flow into her eyes. Flowed into them with the soft listless cadence of Georgia's South. A young Negro, once, was looking at her, spellbound, from the road. A white man passing in a buggy had to flick him with his whip if he was to get by without running him over. I first saw her on her porch. I was passing with a fellow whose crusty numbness (I was from the North and suspected of being prejudiced and stuck-up) was melting as he found me warm. I asked him who she was. "That's Fern," was all that I could get from him. Some folks already thought that I was given to nosing around; I let it go at that, so far as questions were concerned. But at first sight of her I felt as if I heard a Jewish cantor sing. As if his singing rose above the unheard chorus of a folk-song. And I felt bound to her. I too had my dreams: something I would do for her. I have knocked about from town to town too much not to know the futility of mere change of place. Besides, picture if you can, this cream-colored solitary girl sitting at a tenement window looking down on the indifferent throngs of Harlem. Better that she listen to folk-songs at dusk in Georgia, you would say, and so would I. Or, suppose she came up North and married. Even a doctor or a lawyer, say, one who would be sure to get along—that is, make money. You and I know, who have had experience in such things, that love is not a thing like prejudice which can be bettered by changes of town. Could men in Washington, Chicago, or New York, more than the men of Georgia, bring her something left vacant by the bestowal of their bodies? You and I who know men in these cities will have to say, they could not. See her out and out a prostitute along State Street in Chicago. See her move into a southern town where white men are more aggressive. See her become a white man's concubine. . . . Something I must do for her. There was myself. What could I do for her? Talk, of course. Push back the fringe of pines upon new horizons. To what purpose? and what for? Her? Myself? Men in her case seem to lose their selfishness. I lost mine before I touched her. I ask you, friend (it makes no difference if you sit in the Pullman or the Jim Crow as the train crosses her road), what thoughts would come to you—that is, after you'd finished with the thoughts that leap into men's minds at the sight of a pretty woman who will not deny them; what thoughts would come to you, had you seen her in a quick flash, keen and intuitively, as she sat there on her porch when your train thundered by? Would you have got off at the next station and come back for her to take her where? Would you have completely forgotten her as soon as you reached Macon, Atlanta, Augusta, Pasadena, Madison, Chicago, Boston, or New Orleans? Would you tell your wife or sweetheart about a girl you saw? Your thoughts can help me, and I would like to know. Something I would do for her. . . .

One evening I walked up the Pike on purpose, and stopped to say hello. Some of her family were about, but they moved away to make room for me. Damn if I knew how to begin. Would you? Mr. and Miss So-and-So, people, the weather, the crops, the new preacher, the frolic, the church benefit, rabbit and possum hunting, the new soft drink they had at old Pap's store, the schedule of the trains, what kind of town Macon was, Negro's migration north, bollweevils, syrup, the Bible—to all these things she gave a yassur or nassur, without further comment. I began to wonder if perhaps my own emotional sensibility had played one of its tricks on me. "Lets take a walk," I at last ventured. The suggestion, coming after so long an isolation, was novel enough, I guess, to surprise. But it wasnt that. Something told me that men before me had said just that as a prelude to the offering of their bodies. I tried to tell her with my eyes. I think she understood. The thing from her that made my throat catch, vanished. Its passing left her visible in a way I'd thought, but never seen. We walked down the Pike with people on all the porches gaping at us. "Doesnt it make you mad?" She meant the row of petty gossiping people. She meant the world. Through a canebrake that was ripe for cutting, the branch was reached. Under a sweet-gum tree, and where reddish leaves had dammed the creek a little, we sat down. Dusk, suggesting the almost imperceptible procession of giant trees, settled with a purple haze about the cane. I felt strange, as I always do in Georgia, particularly at dusk. I felt that things unseen to men were tangibly immediate. It would not have surprised me had I had vision. People have them in Georgia more often than you would suppose. A black woman once saw the mother of Christ and drew her in charcoal on the courthouse wall. . . . When one is on the soil of one's ancestors, most anything can come to one. . . . From force of habit, I suppose, I held Fern in my arms—that is, without at first noticing it. Then my mind came back to her. Her eyes, unusually weird and open, held me. Held God. He flowed in as I've seen the countryside flow in. Seen men. I must have done something—what, I dont know, in the confusion of my emotion. She sprang up. Rushed some distance from me. Fell to her knees, and began swaying, swaying. Her body was tortured with something it could not let out. Like boiling sap it flooded arms and fingers till she shook them as if they burned her. It found her throat, and spattered inarticulately in plaintive, convulsive sounds, mingled with calls to Christ Jesus. And then she sang, brokenly. A Jewish cantor singing with a broken voice. A child's voice, uncertain, or an old man's. Dusk hid her; I could hear only her song. It seemed to me as though she were pounding her head in anguish upon the ground. I rushed to her. She fainted in my arms.

There was talk about her fainting with me in the canefield. And I got one or two ugly looks from town men who'd set themselves up to protect her. In fact, there was talk of making me leave town. But they never did. They kept a watch-out for me, though. Shortly after, I came back North. From the train window I saw her as I crossed her road. Saw her on her porch, head tilted a little forward where the nail was, eyes vaguely focused on the sunset. Saw her face flow into them, the countryside and something that I call God, flowing into them . . . Nothing ever really happened. Nothing ever came to Fern, not even I. Something I would do for her. Some fine unnamed thing. . . . And, friend, you? She is still living, I have reason to know. Her name, against the chance that you might happen down that way, is Fernie May Rosen.

Portrait in Georgia

FROM *CANE*

Hair—braided chestnut, coiled like a lyncher's rope,
Eyes—fagots,
Lips—old scars, or the first red blisters,
Breath—the last sweet scent of cane,
And her slim body, white as the ash of black flesh after flame.

Seventh Street

FROM *CANE*

MONEY BURNS THE POCKET, POCKET HURTS,
BOOTLEGGERS IN SILKEN SHIRTS,
BALLOONED, ZOOMING CADILLACS,
WHIZZING, WHIZZING DOWN THE STREET-CAR TRACKS.

Seventh Street is a bastard of Prohibition and the War. A crude-boned, soft-skinned wedge of nigger life breathing its loafer air, jazz songs and love, thrusting unconscious rhythms, black reddish blood into the white and whitewashed wood of Washington. Stale soggy wood of Washington. Wedges rust in soggy wood. . . . Split it! In two! Again! Shred it! . . . the sun. Wedges are brilliant in the sun; ribbons of wet wood dry and blow away. Black reddish blood. Pouring for crude-boned soft-skinned life, who set you flowing? Blood suckers of the war would spin in a frenzy of dizziness if they drank your blood. Prohibition would put a stop to it. Who set you flowing? White and whitewash disappear in blood. Who set you flowing? Flowing down the smooth asphalt of Seventh Street, in shanties, brick office buildings, theaters, drug stores, restaurants, and cabarets? Eddying on the corners? Swirling like a blood-red smoke up where the buzzards fly in heaven? God would not dare to suck black red blood. A Nigger God! He would duck his head in shame and call for the Judgment Day. Who set you flowing?

Money burns the pocket, pocket hurts.
Bootleggers in silken shirts,
Ballooned, zooming Cadillacs,
Whizzing, whizzing down the street-car tracks.

Box Seat

FROM *CANE*

1

Houses are shy girls whose eyes shine reticently upon the dusk body of the street. Upon the gleaming limbs and asphalt torso of a dreaming nigger. Shake your curled wool-blossoms, nigger. Open your liver lips to the lean, white spring. Stir the root-life of a withered people. Call them from their houses, and teach them to dream.

Dark swaying forms of Negroes are street songs that woo virginal houses.

Dan Moore walks southward on Thirteenth Street. The low limbs of budding chestnut tress recede above his head. Chestnut buds and blossoms are wool he walks upon. The eyes of houses faintly touch him as he passes them. Soft girl-eyes, they set him singing. Girl-eyes within him widen upward to promised faces. Floating away, they daily wistfully over the dusk body of the street. Come on, Dan Moore, come on. Dan sings. His voice is a little hoarse. It cracks. He strains to produce tones in keeping with the houses' loveliness. Cant be done. He whistles. His notes are shrill. They hurt him. Negroes open gates, and go indoors, perfectly. Dan thinks of the house he's going to. Of the girl. Lips, flesh-notes of a forgotten song, plead with him. . . .

Dan turns into a side-street, opens an iron gate, bangs it to. Mounts the steps, and searches for the bell. Funny, he cant find it. He fumbles around. The thought comes to him that some one passing by might see him, and not understand. Might think that he is trying to sneak, to break in.

Dan: Break in. Get an ax and smash in. Smash in their faces. I'll show em. Break into an engine-house, steal a thousand horsepower fire truck. Smash in with the truck. I'll show em. Grab an ax and brain em. Cut em up. Jack the Ripper. Baboon from the zoo. And then the cops come. "No, I aint a baboon. I aint Jack the Ripper. I'm a poor man out of work. Take your hands off me, you bull-necked bears. Look into my eyes. I am Dan Moore. I was born in a canefield. The hands of Jesus touched me. I am come to a sick world to heal it. Only the other day, a dope fiend brushed against me—Dont laugh, you mighty, juicy, meat-hook men. Give me your fingers and I will peel them as if they were ripe bananas."

Some one might think he is trying to break in. He'd better knock. His knuckles are raw bone against the thick glass door. He waits. No one comes. Perhaps they havent heard him. He raps again. This time, harder. He waits. No one comes. Some one is surely in. He fancies that he sees their shadows on the glass. Shadows of gorillas. Perhaps they saw him coming and dont want to let him in. He knocks. The tension of his arms makes the glass rattle. Hurried steps come towards him. The door opens.

"Please, you might break the glass—the bell—oh, Mr. Moore! I thought it must be some stranger. How do you do? Come in, wont you? Muriel? Yes. I'll call her. Take your things off, wont you? And have a seat in the parlor. Muriel will be right down. Muriel! Oh Muriel! Mr. Moore to see you. She'll be right down. You'll pardon me, wont you? So glad to see you."

Her eyes are weak. They are bluish and watery from reading newspapers. The blue is steel. It gimlets Dan while her mouth flaps amiably to him.

Dan: Nothing for you to see, old musselhead. Dare I show you? If I did, delirium would furnish you headlines for a month. Now look here. Thats enough. Go long, woman. Say some nasty thing and I'll kill you. Huh. Better damned sight not. Ta-ta, Mrs. Pribby.

Mrs. Pribby retreats to the rear of the house. She takes up a newspaper. There is a sharp click as she fits into her chair and draws it to the table. The click is metallic like the sound of a bolt being shot into place. Dan's eyes sting. Sinking into a soft couch, he closes them. The house contracts about him. It is a sharp-edged, massed, metallic house. Bolted. About Mrs. Pribby. Bolted to the endless rows of metal houses. Mrs. Pribby's house. The rows of houses belong to other Mrs. Pribbys. No wonder he couldn't sing to them.

Dan: What's Muriel doing here? God, what a place for her. Whats she doing? Putting her stockings on? In the bathroom. Come out of there, Dan Moore. People must have their privacy. Peeping-toms. I'll never peep. I'll listen. I like to listen.

Dan goes to the wall and places his ear against it. A passing street car and something vibrant from the earth sends a rumble to him. That rumble comes from the earth's deep core. It is the mutter of powerful underground races. Dan has a picture of all the people rushing to put their ears against walls, to listen to it. The next world-savior is coming up that way. Coming up. A continent sinks down. The new-world Christ will need consummate skill to walk upon the waters where huge bubbles burst. . . . Thuds of Muriel coming down. Dan turns to the piano and glances through a stack of jazz music sheets. Ji-ji-bo, JI-JI-BO! . . .

"Hello, Dan, stranger, what brought you here?"

Muriel comes in, shakes hands, and then clicks into a high-armed seat under the orange glow of a floor-lamp. Her face is fleshy. It would tend to coarseness but for the fresh fragrant something which is the life of it. Her hair like an Indian's. But more curly and bushed and vagrant. Her nostrils flare. The flushed ginger of her cheeks is touched orange by the shower of color from the lamp.

"Well, you havent told me, you havent answered my question, stranger. What brought you here?"

Dan feels the pressure of the house, of the rear room, of the rows of houses, shift to Muriel. He is light. He loves her. He is doubly heavy.

"Dont know, Muriel—wanted to see you—wanted to talk to you—to see you and tell you that I know what you've been through—what pain the last few months must have been—"

"Lets dont mention that."

"But why not, Muriel? I—"

"Please."

"But Muriel, life is full of things like that. One grows strong and beautiful in facing them. What else is life?"

"I dont know, Dan. And I dont believe I care. Whats the use? Lets talk about something else. I hear there's a good show at the Lincoln this week."

"Yes, so Harry was telling me. Going?"

"To-night."

Dan starts to rise.

"I didnt know. I dont want to keep you."

"Its all right. You dont have to go till Bernice comes. And she wont be here till eight. I'm all dressed. I'll let you know."

"Thanks."

Silence. The rustle of a newspaper being turned comes from the rear room.

Muriel: Shame about Dan. Something awfully good and fine about him. But he dont fit in. In where? Me? Dan, I could love you if I tried. I dont have to try. I do. O Dan, dont you know I do? Timid lover, brave talker that you are. Whats the good of all you know if you dont know that? I wont let myself. I? Mrs. Pribby who reads newspapers all night wont. What has she got to do with me? She *is* me, somehow. No she's not. Yes she is. She is the town, and the town wont let me love you, Dan. Dont you know? You could make it let me if you would. Why wont you? Youre selfish. I'm not strong enough to buck it. Youre too selfish to buck it, for me. I wish you'd go. You irritate me. Dan, please go.

"What are you doing now, Dan?"

"Same old thing, Muriel. Nothing, as the world would have it. Living, as I look at things. Living as much as I can without—"

"But you cant live without money, Dan. Why dont you get a good job and settle down?"

Dan: Same old line. Shoot it at me, sister. Hell of a note, this loving business. For ten minutes of it youve got to stand the torture of an intolerable heaviness and a hundred platitudes. Well, damit, shoot on.

"To what? my dear. Rustling newspapers?"

"You mustnt say that, Dan. It isnt right. Mrs. Pribby has been awfully good to me."

"Dare say she has. Whats that got to do with it?"

"Oh, Dan, youre so unconsiderate and selfish. All you think of is yourself."

"I think of you."

"Too much—I mean, you ought to work more and think less. Thats the best way to get along."

"Mussel-heads get along, Muriel. There is more to you than that—"

"Sometimes I think there is, Dan. But I dont know. I've tried. I've tried to do something with myself. Something real and beautiful, I mean. But whats the good of trying? I've tried to make people, every one I come in contact with, happy—"

Dan looks at her, directly. Her animalism, still unconquered by zoo-restrictions and keeper-taboos, stirs him. Passion tilts upward, bringing with it the elements of an old desire. Muriel's lips become the flesh-notes of a futile, plaintive longing. Dan's impulse to direct her is its fresh life.

"Happy, Muriel? No, not happy. Your aim is wrong. There is no such thing as happiness. Life bends joy and pain, beauty and ugliness, in such a way that no one may isolate them. No one should want to. Perfect joy, or perfect pain, with no contrasting element to define them, would mean a monotony of consciousness, would mean death. Not happy, Muriel. Say that you have tried to make them create. Say that you have used your own capacity for life to cradle them. To start them upward-flowing. Or if you cant say that you have, then say that you will. My talking to you will make you aware of your power to do so. Say that you will love, that you will give yourself in love—"

"To you, Dan?"

Dan's consciousness crudely swerves into his passions. They flare up in his eyes. They set up quivers in his abdomen. He is suddenly over-tense and nervous.

"Muriel—"

The newspaper rustles in the rear room.

"Muriel—"

Dan rises. His arms stretch towards her. His fingers and his palms, pink in the lamplight, are glowing irons. Muriel's chair is close and stiff about her. The house, the rows of houses locked about her chair. Dan's fingers and arms are fire to melt and bars to wrench and force and pry. Her arms hang loose. Her hands are hot and moist. Dan takes them. He slips to his knees before her.

"Dan, you mustnt."

"Muriel—"

"Dan, really you mustnt. No, Dan. No."

"Oh, come, Muriel. Must I—"

"Shh. Dan, please get up. Please. Mrs. Pribby is right in the next room. She'll hear you. She may come in. Dont, Dan. She'll see you—"

"Well then, lets go out."

"I cant. Let go, Dan. Oh, wont you please let go."

Muriel tries to pull her hands away. Dan tightens his grip. He feels the strength of his fingers. His muscles are tight and strong. He stands up. Thrusts out his chest. Muriel shrinks from him. Dan becomes aware of his crude absurdity. His lips curl. His passion chills. He has an obstinate desire to possess her.

"Muriel, I love you. I want you, whatever the world of Pribby says. Damn your Pribby. Who is she to dictate my love? I've stood enough of her. Enough of you. Come here."

Muriel's mouth works in and out. Her eyes flash and waggle. She wrenches her hands loose and forces them against his breast to keep him off. Dan grabs her wrists. Wedges in between her arms. Her face is close to him. It is hot and blue and moist. Ugly.

"Come here now."

"Dont, Dan. Oh, dont. What are you killing?"

"Whats weak in both of us and a whole litter of Pribbys. For once in your life youre going to face whats real, by God—"

A sharp rap on the newspaper in the rear room cuts between them. The rap is like cool thick glass between them. Dan is hot on one side. Muriel, hot on the other. They straighten. Gaze fearfully at one another. Neither moves. A clock in the rear room, in the rear room, the rear room, strikes eight. Eight slow, cool sounds. Bernice. Muriel fastens on her image. She smooths her dress. She adjusts her skirt. She becomes prim and cool. Rising, she skirts Dan as if to keep the glass between them. Dan, gyrating nervously above the easy swing of his limbs, follows her to the parlor door. Muriel retreats before him till she reaches the landing of the steps that lead upstairs. She smiles at him. Dan sees his face in the hall mirror. He runs his fingers through his hair. Reaches for his hat and coat and puts them on. He moves towards Muriel. Muriel steps backward up one step. Dan's jaw shoots out. Muriel jerks her arm in warning of Mrs. Pribby. She gasps and turns and starts to run. Noise of a chair scraping as Mrs. Pribby rises from it, ratchets down the hall. Dan stops. He makes a wry face, wheels round, goes out, and slams the door.

2

People come in slowly . . . mutter, laughs, flutter, whishadwash, "I've changed my work-clothes—" . . . and fill vacant seats of Lincoln Theater. Muriel, leading Bernice who is a cross between a washerwoman and a blue-blood lady, a washer-blue, a washer-lady, wanders down the right aisle to the lower front box. Muriel has on an orange dress. Its color would clash with the crimson box-draperies, its color would contradict the sweet rose smile her face is bathed in, should she take her coat off. She'll keep it on. Pale purple shadows rest on the planes of her cheeks. Deep purple comes from her thick-shocked hair. Orange of the dress goes well with these. Muriel presses her coat down from around her shoulders. Teachers are not supposed to have bobbed hair. She'll keep her hat on. She takes the first chair, and indicates that Bernice is to take the one directly behind her. Seated thus, her eyes are level with, and near to, the face of an imaginary man upon the stage. To speak to Berny she must turn. When she does, the audience is square upon her.

People come in slowly . . . "—for my Sunday-go-to-meeting dress. O glory God! O shout Amen!" . . . and fill vacant seats of Lincoln Theater. Each one is a bolt that shoots into a slot, and is locked there. Suppose the Lord should ask, where was Moses when the light went out? Suppose Gabriel should blow his trumpet! The seats are slots. The seats are bolted houses. The mass grows denser. Its weight at first is impalpable upon the box. Then Muriel begins to feel it. She props her arm against the brass box-rail, to ward it off. Silly. These people are friends of hers: a parent of a child she teaches, an old school friend. She smiles at them. They return her courtesy, and she is free to chat with Berny. Berny's tongue, started, runs on, and on. O washer-blue! O washer-lady!

Muriel: Never see Dan again. He makes me feel queer. Starts things he doesnt finish. Upsets me. I am not upset. I am perfectly calm. I am going to enjoy the show. Good show. I've had some show! This damn tame thing. O Dan. Wont see Dan again. Not alone. Have Mrs. Pribby come in. She *was* in. Keep Dan out. If I love him, can I keep him out? Well then, I dont love him. Now he's out. Who is that coming in? Blind as a bat. Ding-bat. Looks like Dan. He mustnt see me. Silly. He cant reach me. He wont dare come in here. He'd put his head down like a goring bull and charge me. He'd trample them. He'd gore. He'd rape! Berny! He wont dare come in here.

"Berny, who was that who just came in? I havent my glasses."

"A friend of yours, a *good* friend so I hear. Mr. Daniel Moore, Lord."

"Oh. He's no friend of mine."

"No? I hear he is."

"Well, he isnt."

Dan is ushered down the aisle. He has to squeeze past the knees of seated people to reach his own seat. He treads on a man's corns. The man grumbles, and shoves him off. He shrivels close beside a portly Negress whose huge rolls of flesh meet about the bones of seat-arms. A soil-soaked fragrance comes from her. Through the cement floor her strong roots sink down. They spread under the asphalt streets. Dreaming, the streets roll over on their bellies, and suck their glossy health from them. Her strong roots sink down and spread under the river and disappear in blood-lines that waver south. Her roots shoot down. Dan's hands follow them. Roots throb. Dan's heart beats violently. He places his palms upon the earth to cool them. Earth throbs. Dan's heart beats violently. He sees all the people in the house rush to the walls to listen to the rumble. A new-world Christ is coming up. Dan comes up. He is startled. The eyes of the woman dont belong to her. They look at him unpleasantly. From either aisle, bolted masses press in. He doesnt fit. The mass grows agitant. For an instant, Dan's and Muriel's eyes meet. His weight there slides the weight on her. She braces an arm against the brass rail, and turns her head away.

Muriel: Damn fool; dear Dan, what did you want to follow me here for? Oh cant you ever do anything right? Must you always pain me, and make me hate you? I do hate you. I wish some one would come in with a horse-whip and lash you out. I wish some one would drag you up a back alley and brain you with the whip-butt.

Muriel glances at her wrist-watch.

"Quarter of nine. Berny, what time have you?"

"Eight-forty. Time to begin. Oh, look Muriel, that woman with the plume; doesnt she look good! They say she's going with, oh, whats his name. You know. Too much powder. I can see it from here. Here's the orchestra now. O fine! Jim Clem at the piano!"

The men fill the pit. Instruments run the scale and tune. The saxophone moans and throws a fit. Jim Clem, poised over the piano, is ready to begin. His head nods forward. Opening crash. The house snaps dark. The curtain recedes upward from the blush of the footlights. Jazz overture is over. The first act is on.

Dan: Old stuff. Muriel—bored. Must be. But she'll smile and she'll clap. Do what youre bid, you she-slave. Look at her. Sweet, tame woman in a brass box seat. Clap, smile, fawn, clap. Do what youre bid. Drag me in with you. Dirty me. Prop me in your brass box seat. I'm there, am I not? because of you. He-slave. Slave of a woman who is a slave. I'm a damned sight worse than you are. I sing your praises, Beauty! I exalt thee, O Muriel! A slave, thou art greater than all Freedom because I love thee.

Dan fidgets, and disturbs his neighbors. His neighbors glare at him. He glares back without seeing them. The man whose corns have been trod upon speaks to him.

"Keep quiet, cant you, mister. Other people have paid their money besides yourself to see the show."

The man's face is a blur about two sullen liquid things that are his eyes. The eyes dissolve in the surrounding vagueness. Dan suddenly feels that the man is an enemy whom he has long been looking for.

Dan bristles. Glares furiously at the man.

"All right. All right then. Look at the show. I'm not stopping you."

"Shhh," from some one in the rear.

Dan turns around.

"Its that man there who started everything. I didnt say a thing to him until he tried to start something. What have I got to do with whether he has paid his money or not? Thats the manager's business. Do I look like the manager?"

"Shhh. Youre right. Shhh."

"Dont tell me to shhh. Tell him. That man there. He started everything. If what he wanted was to start a fight, why didn't he say so?"

The man leans forward.

"Better be quiet, sonny. I aint said a thing about fight, yet."

"Its a good thing you havent."

"Shhh."

Dan grips himself. Another act is on. Dwarfs, dressed like prizefighters, foreheads bulging like boxing gloves, are led upon the stage. They are going to fight for the heavyweight championship. Gruesome. Dan glances at Muriel. He imagines that she shudders. His mind curves back into himself, and picks up tail-ends of experiences. His eyes are open, mechanically. The dwarfs pound and bruise and bleed each other, on his eyeballs.

Dan: Ah, but she was some baby! And not vulgar either. Funny how some women can do those things. Muriel dancing like that! Hell. She rolled and wabbled. Her buttocks rocked. She pulled up her dress and showed her pink drawers. Baby! And then she caught my eyes. Dont know what my eyes had in them. Yes I do. God, dont I though! Sometimes I think, Dan Moore, that your eyes could burn clean . . . burn clean . . . BURN CLEAN! . . .

The gong rings. The dwarfs set to. They spar grotesquely, playfully, until one lands a stiff blow. This makes the other sore. He commences slugging. A real scrap is on. Time! The dwarfs go to their corners and are sponged and fanned off. Gloves bulge from their wrists. Their wrists are necks for the tight-faced gloves. The fellow to the right lets his eyes roam over the audience. He sights Muriel. He grins.

Dan: Those silly women arguing feminism. Here's what I should have said to them. "It should be clear to you women, that the proposition must be stated thus:

> Me, horizontally above her.
> Action: perfect strokes downward oblique.
> Hence, man dominates because of limitation.
> Or, so it shall be until women learn their stuff.

So framed, the proposition is a mental-filler, Dentist, I want gold teeth. It should become cherished of the technical intellect. I hereby offer it to posterity as one of the important machine-age designs. P.S. It should be noted, that because it *is* an achievement of this age, its growth and hence its causes, up to the point of maturity, antedate machinery. Ery. . . ."

The gong rings. No fooling this time. The dwarfs set to. They clinch. The referee parts them. One swings a cruel upper-cut and knocks the other down. A huge head hits the floor. Pop! The house roars. The fighter, groggy, scrambles up. The referee whispers to the contenders not to fight so hard. They ignore him. They charge. Their heads jab like boxing-gloves. They kick and spit and bite. They pound each other furiously. Muriel pounds. The house pounds. Cut lips. Bloody noses. The referee asks for the gong. Time! The house roars. The dwarfs bow, are made to bow. The house wants more. The dwarfs are led from the stage.

Dan: Strange I never really noticed him before. Been sitting there for years. Born a slave. Slavery not so long ago. He'll die in his chair. Swing low, sweet chariot. Jesus will come and roll him down the river Jordan. Oh, come along, Moses, you'll get lost; stretch out your rod and come across. LET MY PEOPLE GO! Old man. Knows everyone who passes the corners. Saw the first horse-cars. The first Oldsmobile. And he was born in slavery. I did see his eyes. Never miss eyes. But they were bloodshot and watery. It hurt to look at them. It hurts to look in most people's eyes. He saw Grant and Lincoln. He saw Walt—old man, did you see Walt Whitman? Did you see Walt Whitman! Strange force that drew me to him. And I went up to see. The woman thought I saw crazy. I told him to look into the heavens. He did, and smiled. I asked him if he knew what that rumbling is that comes up from the ground. Christ, what a stroke that was. And the jabbering idiots crowding around. And the crossing-cop leaving his job to come over and wheel him away. . . .

The house applauds. The house wants more. The dwarfs are led back. But no encore. Must give the house something. The attendant comes out and announces that Mr. Barry, the champion, will sing one of his own songs, "for your approval." Mr. Barry grins at Muriel as he wabbles from the wing. He holds a fresh white rose, and a small mirror. He wipes blood from his nose. He signals Jim Clem. The orchestra starts. A sentimental love song, Mr. Barry sings, first to one girl, and then another in the audience. He holds the mirror in such a way that it flashes in the face of each one he sings to. The light swings around.

Dan: I am going to reach up and grab the girders of this building and pull them down. The crash will be a signal. Hid by the smoke and dust Dan Moore will arise. In his right hand will be a dynamo. In his left, a god's face that will flash white light from ebony. I'll grab a girder and swing it like a walking-stick. Lightning will flash. I'll grab its black knob and swing it like a crippled cane. Lightning. . . . Some one's flashing . . . some one's flashing. . . . Who in hell is flashing that mirror? Take it off me, godam you.

Dan's eyes are half blinded. He moves his head. The light follows. He hears the audience laugh. He hears the orchestra. A man with a high-pitched, sentimental voice is singing. Dan sees the dwarf. Along the mirror flash the song comes. Dan ducks his head. The audience roars. The light swings around to Muriel. Dan looks. Muriel is too close. Mr. Barry covers his mirror. He sings to her. She shrinks away. Nausea. She clutches the brass box-rail. She moves to face away. The audience is square upon her. Its eyes smile. Its hands itch to clap. Muriel turns to the dwarf and forces a smile at him. With a showy blare of orchestration, the song comes to its close. Mr. Barry bows. He offers Muriel the rose, first having kissed it. Blood of his battered lips is a vivid stain upon its petals. Mr. Barry offers Muriel the rose. The house applauds. Muriel flinches back. The dwarf steps forward, diffident; threatening. Hate pops from his eyes and crackles like a brittle heat about the box. The thick hide of his face is drawn in tortured wrinkles. Above his eyes, the bulging, tight-skinned brow. Dan looks at it. It grows calm and massive. It grows profound. It is a thing of wisdom and tenderness, of suffering and beauty. Dan looks down. The eyes are calm and luminous. Words come from them. . . . Arms of the audience reach out, grab Muriel, and hold her there. Claps are steel fingers that manacle her wrists and move them forward to acceptance. Berny leans forward and whispers: "Its all right. Go on—take it."

Words form in the eyes of the dwarf:

> Do not shrink, Do not be afraid of me.
> *Jesus*
> See how my eyes look at you.
> *the Son of God*
> I too was made in His image.
> *was once—*
> I give you the rose.

Muriel, tight in her revulsion, sees black, and daintily reaches for the offering. As her hand touches it, Dan springs up in his seat and shouts:

"JESUS WAS ONCE A LEPER!"

Dan steps down.

He is as cool as a green stem that has just shed its flower.

Rows of gaping faces strain towards him. They are distant, beneath him, impalpable. Squeezing out, Dan again treads upon the corn-foot man. The man shoves him.

"Watch where youre going, mister. Crazy or no, you aint going to walk over me. Watch where youre going there."

Dan turns, and serenely tweaks the fellow's nose. The man jumps up. Dan is jammed against a seat-back. A slight swift anger flicks him. His fist hooks the other's jaw.

"Now you have started something. Aint no man living can hit me and get away with it. Come on on the outside."

The house, tumultuously stirring, grabs its wraps and follows the men.

The man leads Dan up a black alley. The alley-air is thick and moist with smells of garbage and wet trash. In the morning, singing niggers will drive by and ring their gongs. . . . Heavy with the scent of rancid flowers and with the scent of fight. The crowd, pressing forward, is a hollow roar. Eyes of houses, soft girl-eyes, glow reticently upon the hubbub and blink out. The man stops. Takes off his hat and coat. Dan, having forgotten him, keeps going on.

FROM *Kabnis*

FROM *CANE*

1

Ralph Kabnis, propped in his bed, tries to read. To read himself to sleep. An oil lamp on a chair near his elbow burns unsteadily. The cabin room is spaced fantastically about it. White-washed hearth and chimney, black with sooty saw-teeth. Ceiling, patterned by the fringed globe of the lamp. The walls, unpainted, are seasoned a rosin yellow. And cracks between the boards are black. These cracks are the lips the night winds use for whispering. Night winds in Georgia are vagrant poets, whispering. Kabnis, against his will, lets his book slip down, and listens to them. The warm whiteness of his bed, the lamp-light, do not protect him from the weird chill of their song:

> White-man's land.
> Niggers, sing.
> Burn, bear black children
> Till poor rivers bring
> Rest, and sweet glory
> In Camp Ground.

Kabnis' thin hair is streaked on the pillow. His hand strokes the slim silk of his mustache. His thumb, pressed under his chin, seems to be trying to give squareness and projection to it. Brown eyes stare from a lemon face. Moisture gathers beneath his arm-pits. He slides down beneath the cover, seeking release.

Kabnis: Near me. Now. Whoever you are, my warm glowing sweetheart, do not think that the face that rests beside you is the real Kabnis. Ralph Kabnis is a dream. And dreams are faces with large eyes and weak chins and broad brows that get smashed by the fists of square faces. The body of the world is bull-necked. A dream is a soft face that fits uncertainly upon it. . . . God, if I could develop that in words. Give what I know a bull-neck and a heaving body, all would go well with me, wouldnt it, sweetheart? If I could feel that I came to the South to face it. If I, the dream (not what is weak and afraid in me) could become the face of the South. How my lips would sing for it, my songs being the lips of its soul. Soul. Soul hell. There aint no such thing. What in hell was that?

A rat had run across the thin boards of the ceiling. Kabnis thrusts his head out from the covers. Through the cracks, a powdery faded red dust sprays down on him. Dust of slave-fields, dried, scattered. . . . No use to read. Christ, if he only could drink himself to sleep. Something as sure as fate was going to happen. He couldnt stand this thing much longer. A hen, perched on a shelf in the adjoining room begins to tread. Her nails scrape the soft wood. Her feathers ruffle.

"Get out of that, you egg-laying bitch."

Kabnis hurls a slipper against the wall. The hen flies from her perch and cackles as if a skunk were after her.

"Now cut out that racket or I'll wring your neck for you."

Answering cackles arise in the chicken yard.

"Why in Christ's hell cant you leave me alone? Damn it, I wish your cackle would choke you. Choke every mother's son of them in this God-forsaken hole. Go away. By God I'll wring your neck for you if you dont. Hell of a mess I've got in: even the poultry is hostile. Go way. Go way. By God, I'll . . ."

Kabnis jumps from his bed. His eyes are wild. He makes for the door. Bursts through it. The hen, driving blindly at the windowpane, screams. Then flies and flops around trying to elude him. Kabnis catches her.

"Got you now, you she-bitch."

With his fingers about her neck, he thrusts open the outside door and steps out into the serene loveliness of Georgian autumn moon-light. Some distance off, down in the valley, a band of pine-smoke, silvered gauze, drifts steadily. The half-moon is a white child that sleeps upon the tree-tops of the forest. White winds croon its sleep-song:

rock a-by baby . .
Black mother sways, holding a white child on
her bosom.
when the bough bends . .
Her breath hums through pine-cones.
cradle will fall . .
Teat moon-children at your breasts,
down will come baby . .
Black mother.

Kabnis whirls the chicken by its neck, and throws the head away. Picks up the hopping body, warm, sticky, and hides it in a clump of bushes. He wipes blood from his hands onto the coarse scant grass.

Kabnis: Thats done. Old Chromo in the big house there will wonder whats become of her pet hen. Well, it'll teach her a lesson: not to make a hen-coop of my quarters. Quarters. Hell of a fine quarters, I've got. Five years ago; look at me now. Earth's child. The earth my mother. God is a profligate red-nosed man about town. Bastardy; me. A bastard son has got a right to curse his maker. God. . . .

Kabnis is about to shake his fists heaven-ward. He looks up, and the night's beauty strikes him dumb. He falls to his knees. Sharp stones cut through his thin pajamas. The shock sends a shiver over him. He quivers. Tears mist his eyes. He writhes.

"God Almighty, dear God, dear Jesus, do not torture me with beauty. Take it away. Give me an ugly world. Ha, ugly. Stinking like unwashed niggers. Dear Jesus, do not chain me to myself and set these hills and valleys, heaving with folk-songs, so close to me that I cannot reach them. There is a radiant beauty in the night that touches and . . . tortures me. Ugh. Hell. Get up, you damn fool. Look around. Whats beautiful there? Hog pens and chicken yards. Dirty red mud. Stinking outhouse. Whats beauty anyway but ugliness if it hurts you? God, He doesnt exist, but nevertheless He is ugly. Hence, what comes from Him is ugly. Lynchers and business men, and that cockroach Hanby, especially. How come that he gets to be principal of a school? Of the school I'm driven to teach in? God's handiwork, doubtless. God and Hanby, they belong together. Two godam moral-spouters. Oh, no, I wont let that emotion come up in me. Stay down. Stay down, I tell you. O Jesus, Thou art beautiful. . . . Come, Ralph, pull yourself together. Curses and adoration dont come from what is sane. This loneliness, dumbness, awful, intangible oppression is enough to drive a man insane. Miles from nowhere. A speck on a Georgia hillside. Jesus, can you imagine it—an atom of dust in agony on a hillside? Thats a spectacle for you. Come, Ralph, old man, pull yourself together."

Kabnis has stiffened. He is conscious now of the night wind, and of how it chills him. He rises. He totters as a man would who for the first time uses artificial limbs. As a completely artificial man would. The large frame house, squatting on brick pillars, where the principal of the school, his wife, and the boarding girls sleep, seems a curious shadow of his mind. He tries, but cannot convince himself of its reality. His gaze drifts down into the vale, across the swamp, up over the solid dusk bank of pines, and rests, bewildered-like, on the court-house tower. It is dull silver in the moonlight. White child that sleeps upon the top of pines. Kabnis' mind clears. He sees himself yanked beneath that tower. He sees white minds, with indolent assumption, juggle justice and a nigger. . . . Somewhere, far off in the straight line of his sights, is Augusta. Christ, how cut off from everything he is. And hours, hours north, why not say a lifetime north? Washington sleeps. Its still, peaceful streets, how desirable they are. Its people whom he had always halfway despised. New York? Impossible. It was a fiction. He had dreamed it. An impotent nostalgia grips him. It becomes intolerable. He forces himself to narrow to a cabin silhouetted on a knoll about a mile away. Peace. Negroes within it are content. They farm. They sing. They love. They sleep. Kabnis wonders if perhaps they can feel him. If perhaps he gives them bad dreams. Things are so immediate in Georgia.

Thinking that now he can go to sleep, he re-enters his room. He builds a fire in the open hearth. The room dances to the tongues of flames, and sings to the crackling and spurting of the logs. Wind comes up between the floor boards, through the black cracks of the walls.

Kabnis: Cant sleep. Light a cigarette. If that old bastard comes over here and smells smoke, I'm done for. Hell of a note, cant even smoke. The stillness of it: where they burn and hang men, you cant smoke. Cant take a swig of licker. What do they think this is, anyway, some sort of temperance school? How did I ever land in such a hole? Ugh. One might just as well be in his grave. Still as a grave. Jesus, how still everything is. Does the world know how still it is? People make noise. They are afraid of silence. Of what lives, and God, of what dies in silence. There must be many dead things moving in silence. They come here to touch me. I swear I feel their fingers. . . . Come, Ralph, pull yourself together. What in hell was that? Only the rustle of leaves, I guess. You know, Ralph, old man, it wouldnt surprise me at all to see a ghost. People dont think there are such things. They rationalize their fear, and call their cowardice science. Fine bunch, they are. Damit, that was a noise. And not the wind either. A chicken maybe. Hell, chickens dont wander around this time of night. What in hell is it?

A scraping sound, like a piece of wood dragging over the ground, is coming near.

"Ha, ha. The ghosts down this way havent got any chains to rattle, so they drag trees along with them. Thats a good one. But no joke, something is outside this house, as sure as hell. Whatever it is, it can get a good look at me and I cant see it. Jesus Christ!"

Kabnis pours water on the flames and blows his lamp out. He picks up a poker and stealthily approaches the outside door. Swings it open, and lurches into the night. A calf, carrying a yoke of wood, bolts away from him and scampers down the road.

"Well, I'm damned. This godam place is sure getting the best of me. Come, Ralph, old man, pull yourself together. Nights cant last forever. Thank God for that. Its Sunday already. First time in my life I've ever wanted Sunday to come. Hell of a day. And down here there's no such thing as ducking church. Well, I'll see Halsey and

Layman, and get a good square meal. Thats something. And Halsey's a damn good feller. Cant talk to him, though. Who in Christ's world can I talk to? A hen. God. Myself . . . I'm going bats, no doubt of that. Come now, Ralph, go in and make yourself go to sleep. Come now . . in the door . . thats right. Put the poker down. There. All right. Slip under the sheets. Close your eyes. Think nothing . . a long time . . nothing, nothing. Dont even think nothing. Blank. Not even blank. No, mustnt count. Nothing . . blank . . nothing . . blank . . space without stars in it. No, nothing . . nothing . .

Kabnis sleeps. The winds, like soft-voiced vagrant poets sing:

> White-man's land.
> Niggers, sing.
> Burn, bear black children
> Till poor rivers bring
> Rest, and sweet glory
> In Camp Ground.

RUDOLPH FISHER

(1897–1934)

Rudolph Fisher, who helped create a fictional landscape for the Harlem Renaissance, captured in his stories the spirit of the twenties. Langston Hughes called him "the wittiest of these new Negroes of Harlem . . . whose tongue was favored with the sharpest and saltiest humor." Fisher replaced the pastoral green of African American writing with images of blue streets lined with crowded tenements. Whenever American citizens ask in different decades—or even centuries—whether English prose continues to respond to the plight of the modern poor in the industrial world, they might well look at his neglected stories. It was obvious to Fisher that the uncurled cities, like dreams deferred, would explode. He recognized the newly emergent aesthetic forms of blues and jazz as powerful dams against the resentment that threatened to engulf the ghetto. In seeking to transform individual anger into communal love—by ironic reconciliation—he stood with modernism. With Langston Hughes, Jean Toomer, and Nella Larsen, he experimented with new efforts in idiom—fresh ways of speaking—and with fictional places so as to help advance writing from romantic stereotypes to realistic narrative. Certainly, his nineteenth-century prose belied his modern task. In more than one sense, he marked the ironic contrast of southern and northern generations of African Americans from opposite sides of the Great Migration. Although his sympathy for the urban landscape would nearly vanish from American prose, during the 1970s and 1980s the folk scenes of the kind of cities he portrayed persisted. He set the urban stage for African American fiction.

Rudolph Fisher, the son of Reverend John Wesley Fisher, was born in Washington, D.C., on May 9, 1897. After his father accepted a pastorate in Providence, Rhode Island, he completed studies with honors at Classical High School in 1915, the same year Booker T. Washington died and Margaret Walker was born. In 1915, he entered Brown University, where he majored in biology and English. By the time he received his B.A. in 1919, he had been elected to the honor societies Sigma Psi for science and Delta Sigma Rho for forensics. Following the completion of his M.A. at Brown in 1920, he studied at Howard University Medical School, where he earned his degree with highest honors in 1924. He interned for a year at Freedmen's Hospital in Washington and registered later for research study in biology at the College of Physicians and Surgeons at Columbia University. After the establishment of his medical practice in Harlem in 1927, he continued studies to specialize in roentgenology and opened an x-ray laboratory. He was later associated with the x-ray division of the New York Department of Health. Fisher died on December 16, 1934, following a third operation for intestinal illness.

Especially during the years 1925–1933, his disciplined stories appeared in prestigious publications of the middle class. "City of Refuge," which he had written while still in medical school, appeared in the *Atlantic Monthly* in February 1925; "Blades of Steel" appeared in the same magazine in August 1927. Other celebrated stories, such as "The Promised Land" and "Miss Cynthie," were published in magazines such as *McClure's, Opportunity, The Crisis, Redbook,* and *Story.* Two novels, *The Walls of Jericho* (1928) and *The Conjure Man Dies* (1932), are only loosely constructed episodes. The former presents the story of Shine, a young pianist of marvelous strength, and the latter treats the experiences of N. Frimbo Psychist in the form of a detective story.

"Miss Cynthie," probably the most admired of his stories, was first published in *Story* in 1933. In it, a seventy-year-old woman from the South finds fault with a boy whom she had hoped would be a doctor, a dentist, or even an undertaker—a prominent member of the Negro middle class—although she finally accepts his chosen career as a musician. Indeed, it was the old woman herself who had once sung to him and had inspired his love for music. Without heavy sermons, Fisher reveals generational differences with sympathy and rapprochement, suggesting the transformation of American history and the changing roles of African Americans within the dynamic. As a signature work, "Miss Cynthie" appeared subsequently in Edward J. O'Brien's *The Best Short Stories for 1934.* When *The Conjure-Man Dies: A Mystery Tale of Dark Harlem* (1932), the dramatic revision of the novel, was produced at the Lafayette Theater in New York in 1935–1936, Fisher had already been dead for more than a year. Perhaps a reviewer of his work, as collected by Draper, provides a suitable epitaph:

> Frimbo, the conjure-man, was a queer one. He lived next to an undertaker and died, apparently, from having a handkerchief stuffed down his throat. It would have been impossible for a normal person to find out who killed him, but not for Dr. Archer, a colored physician almost as erudite as Frimbo himself.

By the 1930s, Fisher had achieved standing as one of the ablest short story writers of his time. His range of characterization and theme was remarkable, and the slang he wrote was novel, if not universally loved. Later, in the 1970s, Richard K. Barksdale wrote:

> Unlike many of his colleagues of the Harlem Renaissance, Fisher was as much concerned with the ordinary man in the street as he was with the educated class or the inhabitants of the jazz world. All types of blacks appear in *The Walls of Jericho,* from the poolroom inhabitants to the society ball snob, but most of Fisher's short stories concentrated on the folk. Often bewildered, exploited, and deceived, they nevertheless manage to survive and sometimes to triumph in their struggle with the city.

Frankly, Fisher lacked the achievement of epic dimension in either his presentation of history or his consciousness of it. His fiction needed a persistent unity of metaphor or image. While his protagonists waited for great moments of insight, they settled for lesser moments that were too careful, too limited, and too shallow. Nevertheless, he marked the transition between the Gilded Age of the 1880s and the modernist strand of the mid-1920s. Without the moral depth of a Frances Harper, who had preceded him in the nineteenth century, he could not move easily into the interior self of a protagonist as had Alice Dunbar Nelson. Whatever the admirable qualities of his literary technique, he could hardly equal the earlier Charles Chesnutt in density of image and ironic detachment. For Chesnutt had written so subtly with strong claims to moral authority as to subvert many of the pretentious ones of Christendom—self-presuming aesthetic and moral superiority over colonized peoples. Beyond a scientific gift for precise detail, Fisher wanted for the psychological probing of a Jessie Fauset or a Nella Larsen in his own time. Rarely, if ever, did he accomplish dramatic reversals in plot, mythmaking powers, lyrical fluency. profundity, or brilliance.

What made him exemplary? With greater realism than Claude McKay, he advanced beyond romantic stereotypes. Even more so than Zora Neale Hurston and Jean Toomer, he wrote African American males into the urban landscape. He was a healing voice for the urban black poor in life and in art. "Harlem is the epitome of American Negro life," he said. "I intend to write whatever interests me. But if I should be fortunate enough to become known as Harlem's interpreter, I should be very happy."

❖❖❖

Perceptive and thoughtful criticism on the literary techniques and traditions in which Fisher experimented is needed. In *The Negro Genius* (1937), Benjamin Brawley provided groundbreaking biography and description. Margaret Perry, ed., *The Short Fiction of Rudolph Fisher* (1987), and John McCluskey, Jr., *The City of Refuge: The Collected Stories of Rudolph Fisher* (1987), helped establish primary resources. Indeed, Perry's introduction, "The Brief Life and Art of Rudolph Fisher," is one of the more helpful descriptions of biography and theme. Elsewhere, Julie A. Brown, *African American Review,* 26 (Fall 1992), speaks very highly of the McCluskey collection. Richard K. Barksdale and Kenneth Kinnamon, eds., *Black Writers of America* (1972), are customarily professional in providing the historical context. Victor A. Kramer, ed., serves a solidifying role of coverage in *The Harlem Renaissance Reexamined* (1987), as does John E. Bassett in "The Negro Awakening," in *Harlem in Review* (1992).

Miss Cynthie

For the first time in her life somebody had called her "madam." She had been standing, bewildered but unafraid, while innumerable Red Caps appropriated piece after piece of the baggage arrayed on the platform. Neither her brief seventy years' journey through life nor her long two days' travel northward had dimmed the live brightness of her eyes, which, for all their bewilderment, had accurately selected her own treasures out of the row of luggage and guarded them vigilantly. "These yours, madam?"

The biggest Red Cap of all was smiling at her. He looked for all the world like Doc Crinshaw's oldest son back home. Her little brown face relaxed; she smiled back at him.

"They got to be. You all done took all the others."

He laughed aloud. Then—"Carry 'em for you?"

She contemplated his bulk. "Reckon you can manage it—puny little feller like you?"

Thereupon they were friends. Still grinning broadly, he surrounded himself with her impedimenta, the enormous brown extension-case on one shoulder, the big straw suitcase in the opposite hand, the carpet-bag under one arm. She herself held fast to the umbrella. "Always like to have sump'm in my hand when I walk. Can't never tell when you'll run across a snake."

"There aren't any snakes in the city."

"There's snakes everywhere, chile."

They began the tedious hike up the interminable platform. She was small and quick. Her carriage was surprisingly erect, her gait astonishingly spry. She said:

"You liked to took my breath back yonder, boy, callin' me 'madam.' Back home everybody call me 'Miss Cynthie.' Even their chillun. Black folks, white folks too. 'Miss Cynthie.' Well when you come up with that 'madam' o' yourn, I say to myself, 'Now, I wonder who that chile's a-grinnin' at? "Madam" stands for mist'ess o' the house, and I sho' ain' mist'ess o' nothin' in this hyeh New York.'"

"Well, you see, we call everybody 'madam.'"

"Everybody?—Hm." The bright eyes twinkled. "Seem like that'd worry me some—if I was a man."

He acknowledged his slip and observed, "I see this isn't your first trip to New York."

"First trip any place, son. First time I been over fifty miles from Waxhaw. Only travelin' I've done is in my head. Ain' seen many places, but I's seen a passel o' people. Reckon places is pretty much alike after people been in 'em awhile."

"Yes, ma'am. I guess that's right."

"You ain' no reg'lar bag-toter, is you?"

"Ma'am?"

"You talk too good."

"Well, I only do this in vacation-time. I'm still in school."

"You is. What you aimin' to be?"

"I'm studying medicine."

"You is?" She beamed. "Aimin' to be a doctor, huh? Thank the Lord for that. That's what I always wanted my David to be. My grandchile hyeh in New York. He's to meet me hyeh now."

"I bet you'll have a great time."

"Mussn't bet, chile. That's sinful. I tole him 'for' he left home, I say, 'Son, you the only one o' the chillun what's got a chance to amount to sump'm. Don't th'ow it away. Be a preacher or a doctor. Work yo' way up and don' stop short. If the Lord don' see fit for you to doctor the soul, then doctor the body. If you don't get to be a reg'lar doctor, be a tooth-doctor. If you jes' can't make that, be a foot-doctor. And if you don' get that fur, be a undertaker. That's the least you must be. That ain' so bad. Keep you acquainted with the house of the Lord. Always mind the house o' the Lord—whatever you do, do like a church-steeple: aim high and go straight.'"

"Did he get to be a doctor?"

"Don' b'lieve he did. Too late startin', I reckon. But he's done succeeded at sump'm. Mus' be at least a undertaker, 'cause he started sendin' the home-folks money, and he come home las' year dressed like Judge Pettiford's boy what went off to school in Virginia. Wouldn't tell none of us 'zackly what he was doin', but he said he wouldn' never be happy till I come and see for myself. So hyeh I is." Something softened her voice. "His mammy died befo' he knowed her. But he was always sech a good chile—" The something was apprehension. "Hope he is a undertaker."

They were mounting a flight of steep stairs leading to an exit-gate, about which clustered a few people still hoping to catch sight of arriving friends. Among these a tall young brown-skinned man in a light grey suit suddenly waved his panama and yelled, "Hey, Miss Cynthie!"

Miss Cynthie stopped, looked up, and waved back with a delighted umbrella. The Red Cap's eyes lifted too. His lower jaw sagged.

"Is that your grandson?"

"It sho' is," she said and distanced him for the rest of the climb. The grandson, with an abandonment that superbly ignored onlookers, folded the little woman in an exultant, smothering embrace. As soon as she could, she pushed him off with breathless mock impatience.

"Go 'way, you fool you. Aimin' to squeeze my soul out my body befo' I can get a look at this place?" She shook herself into the semblance of composure. "Well. You don't look hungry, anyhow."

"Ho-Ho! Miss Cynthie in New York! Can y' imagine this? Come on. I'm parked on Eighth Avenue."

The Red Cap delivered the outlandish luggage into a robin's egg blue open Packard with scarlet wheels, accepted the grandson's dollar and smile, and stood watching the car roar away up Eighth Avenue.

Another Red Cap came up. "Got a break, hey, boy?"

"Dave Tappen himself—can you beat that?"

"The old lady hasn't seen the station yet—starin' at him."

"That's not the half of it, bozo. That's Dave Tappen's grandmother. And what do you s'pose she hopes?"

"What?"

"She hopes that Dave has turned out to be a successful undertaker!"

"Undertaker? Undertaker!"

They stared at each other a gaping moment, then doubled up with laughter.

"Look—through there—that's the Chrysler Building. Oh, hellelujah! I meant to bring you up Broadway—"

"David—"

"Ma'am?"

"This hyeh wagon yourn?"

"Nobody else's. Sweet buggy, ain't it?"

"David—you ain't turned out to be one of them moonshiners, is you?"

"Moonshiners—? Moon—Ho! No indeed, Miss Cynthie. I got a better racket 'n that."

"Better which?"

"Game. Business. Pick-up."

"Tell me, David. What is yo' racket?"

"Can't spill it yet, Miss Cynthie. Rather show you. Tomorrow night you'll know the worst. Can you make out till tomorrow night?"

"David, you know I always wanted you to be a doctor, even if 'twasn' nothin' but a foot-doctor. The very leas' I wanted you to be was a undertaker."

"Undertaker! Oh, Miss Cynthie!—with my sunny disposition?"

"Then you ain' even a undertaker?"

"Listen, Miss Cynthie. Just forget 'bout what I am for awhile. Must till tomorrow night. I want you to see for yourself. Tellin' you will spoil it. Now stop askin', you hear?—because I'm not answerin'—I'm surprisin' you. And don't expect anybody you meet to tell you. It'll mess up the whole works. Understand? Now give the big city a break. There's the elevated train going up Columbus Avenue. Ain't that hot stuff?"

Miss Cynthie looked. "Humph!" she said. "'Tain' half high as that trestle two miles from Waxhaw."

She thoroughly enjoyed the ride up Central Park West. The stagger lights, the extent of the park, the high, close, kingly buildings, remarkable because their stoves cooled them in summer as well as heated them in winter, all drew nods of mild interest. But what gave her special delight was not these: it was that David's car so effortlessly sped past the headlong drove of vehicles racing northward.

They stopped for a red light; when they started again their machine leaped forward with a triumphant eagerness that drew from her an unsuppressed "Hot you, David! That's it!"

He grinned appreciatively. "Why, you're a regular New Yorker already."

"New York nothin'! I done the same thing fifty years ago—befo' I knowed they was a New York."

"What!"

"'Deed so. Didn' I use to tell you 'bout my young mare, Betty? Chile, I'd hitch Betty up to yo' grandpa's buggy and pass anything on the road. Betty never knowed what another horse's dust smelt like. No 'ndeedy. Shuh, boy, this ain' nothin' new to me. Why that broke-down Fo'd yo uncle Jake's got ain' nothin'—nothin' but a sorry mess. Done got so slow I jes' won' ride in it—I declare I'd rather walk. But this hyeh thing, now, this is right nice." She settled back in complete, complacent comfort, and they sped on, swift and silent.

Suddenly she sat erect with abrupt discovery. "David—well—bless my soul!"

"What's the matter, Miss Cynthie?"

Then he saw what had caught her attention. They were travelling up Seventh Avenue now, and something was miraculously different. Not the road; that was as broad as ever, wide, white gleaming in the sun. Not the houses; they were lofty still, lordly, disdainful, supercilious. Not the cars; they continued to race impatiently onward, innumerable, precipitate, tumultuous. Something else, something at once obvious and subtle, insistent, pervasive, compelling.

"David—this mus' be Harlem!"

"Good Lord, Miss Cynthie—!"

"Don' use the name of the Lord in vain, David."

"But I mean—gee!—you're no fun at all. You get everything before a guy can tell you."

"You got plenty to tell me, David. But don' nobody need to tell me this. Look a yonder."

Not just a change of complexion. A completely dissimilar atmosphere. Sidewalks teeming with leisurely strollers, at once strangely dark and bright. Boys in white trousers, berets, and green shirts, with slickened black heads and proud swagger. Bareheaded girls in crisp organdie dresses, purple, canary, gay scarlet. And laughter, abandoned strong Negro laughter, some falling full on the ear, some not heard at all, yet sensed—the warm life-breath of the tireless carnival to which Harlem's heart quickens in summer.

"This is it," admitted David. "Get a good eyeful. Here's 125th Street—regular little Broadway. And here's the Alhambra, and up ahead we'll pass the Lafayette."

"What's them?"

"Theatres."

"Theatres? Theatres. Humph! Look, David—is that a colored folks church?" They were passing a fine gray-stone edifice.

"That? Oh. Sure it is. So's this one on this side."

"No! Well, ain' that fine? Splendid big church like that for colored folks."

Taking his cue from this, her first tribute to the city, he said, "You ain't seen nothing yet. Wait a minute."

They swung left through a side-street and turned right on a boulevard. "What do you think o' that?" And he pointed to the quarter-million dollar St. Mark's.

"That a colored church, too?"

"'Tain' no white one. And they built it themselves, you know. Nobody's hand-me-down gift."

She heaved a great happy sigh. "Oh, yes, it was a gift, David. It was a gift from on high." Then, "Look a hyeh—which a one you belong to?"

"Me? Why, I don't belong to any—that is, none o' these. Mine's over in another section. Y'see, mine's Baptist. These are all Methodist. See?"

"M–m. Uh-huh. I see."

They circled a square and slipped into a quiet narrow street overlooking a park, stopping before the tallest of the apartment-houses in the single commanding row.

Alighting, Miss Cynthie gave this imposing structure one sidewise, upward glance, and said, "Y'all live like bees in a hive, don't y'?—I boun' the women does all the work, too." A moment later, "So this is a elevator? Feel like I'm glory-bound sho' nuff."

Along a tiled corridor and into David's apartment. Rooms leading into rooms. Luxurious couches, easy-chairs, a brown-walnut grand piano, gay-shaded floor lamps, panelled walls, deep rugs, treacherous glass-wood floors—and a smiling golden-skinned girl in a gingham house-dress, approaching with outstretched hands.

"This is Ruth, Miss Cynthie."

"Miss Cynthie!" said Ruth.

They clasped hands. "Been wantin' to see David's girl ever since he first wrote us 'bout her."

"Come—here's your room this way. Here's the bath. Get out of your things and get comfy. You must be worn out with the trip."

"Worn out? Worn out? Shuh. How you gon' get worn out on a train. Now if 'twas a horse, maybe, or Jake's no-count Fo'd—but a train—didn' but one thing bother me on that train."

"What?"

"When the man made them beds down, I jes' couldn' manage to undress same as home. Why, s'posin' sump'm bus' the train open—where'd you be? Naked as a jay-bird in a dew-berry time."

David took in her things and left her to get comfortable. He returned, and Ruth, despite his reassuring embrace, whispered:

"Dave, you can't fool old folks—why don't you go ahead and tell her about yourself? Think of the shock she's going to get—at her age."

David shook his head. "She'll get over the shock if she's there looking on. If we just told her, she'd never understand. We've got to railroad her into it. Then she'll be happy."

"She's nice. But she's got the same ideas as all old folks—"

"Yea—but with her you can change 'em. Specially if everything is really all right. I know her. She's for church and all, but she believes in good times too, if they're right. Why, when I was a kid—" He broke off. "Listen!"

Miss Cynthie's voice came quite distinctly to them, singing a jaunty little rhyme:

Oh I danced with the gal with the hole in her
stockin'
And her toe kep' a-kickin' and her heel kep'
a-knockin'—
Come up, Jesse, and get a drink o' gin,
'Cause you near to heaven as you'll ever get
ag'in'.

"She taught me that when I wasn't knee-high to a cricket," David said.

Miss Cynthie still sang softly and merrily:

Then I danced with the gal with the dimple in
her cheek,
And if she'd 'a' kep' a-smilin', I'd 'a' danced for
a week—

"God forgive me," prayed Miss Cynthie as she discovered David's purpose the following night. She let him and Ruth lead her, like an early Christian martyr, into the Lafayette Theatre. The blinding glare of the lobby produced a merciful self-anaesthesia, and she entered the sudden dimness of the interior as involuntarily as in a dream. . . .

Attendants outdid each other for Mr. Dave Tappen. She heard him tell them, "Fix us up till we go on," and found herself sitting between Ruth and David in the front row of a lower box. A miraculous device of the devil, a motion-picture that talked, was just ending. At her feet the orchestra was assembling. The motion-picture faded out amid a scattered round of applause. Lights blazed and the orchestra burst into an ungodly rumpus.

She looked out over the seated multitude, scanning row upon row of illumined faces, black faces, white faces, yellow, tan, brown: bald heads, bobbed heads, kinky and straight heads; and upon every countenance, expectancy—scowling expectance in this case, smiling in that, complacent here, amused there, commentative elsewhere, but everywhere suspense, abeyance, anticipation.

Half a dozen people were ushered down the nearer aisle to reserved seats in the second row. Some of them caught sight of David and Ruth and waved to them. The chairs immediately behind them in the box were being shifted. "Hello, Tap!" Miss Cynthie saw David turn, rise, and shake hands with two men. One of them was large, bald and pink, emanating good cheer; the other short, thin, sallow with thick black hair and a sour mien. Ruth also acknowledged their greeting. "This is my grandmother," David said proudly. "Miss Cynthie, meet my managers, Lou and Lee Goldman." "Pleased to meet you," managed Miss Cynthie. "Great lad, this boy of yours," said Lou Goldman. "Great little partner he's got, too," added Lee. They also settled back expectantly.

"Here we go!"

The curtain rose to reveal a cotton-field at dawn. Pickers in blue denim overalls, bandanas, and wide-brimmed straws, or in gingham aprons and sun-bonnets, were singing as they worked. Their voices, from clearest soprano to richest bass, blended in low concordances, first simply humming a series of harmonies, until, gradually, came words, like figures forming in mist. As the sound grew, the mist cleared, the words came round and full, and the sun rose bringing light as if in answer to the song. The chorus swelled, the radiance grew, the two, as if emanating from a single source, fused their crescendos, till at last they achieved a joint transcendence of tonal and visual brightness.

"Swell opener," said Lee Goldman.

"Ripe," agreed Lou.

David and Ruth arose. "Stay here and enjoy the show, Miss Cynthie. You'll see us again in a minute."

"Go to it, kids," said Lou Goldman.

"Yea—burn 'em up," said Lee.

Miss Cynthie hardly noted that she had been left, so absorbed was she in the spectacle. To her, the theatre had always been the antithesis of church. As the one was the refuge of righteousness, so the other was the stronghold of transgression. But this first scene awakened memories, captured and held her attention by offering a blend of truth and novelty. Having thus baited her interest, the show now proceeded to play it like the trout through swift-flowing waters of wickedness. Resist as it might, her mind was caught and drawn into the impious subsequences.

The very music that had just rounded out so majestically now distorted itself into ragtime. The singers came forward and turned to dancers; boys, a crazy, swaying background, threw up their arms and kicked out their legs in a rhythmic jamboree; girls, an agile, brazen foreground, caught their skirts up to their hips and displayed their copper calves, knees, thighs, in shameless, incredible steps. Miss Cynthie turned dismayed eyes upon the audience, to discover that mob of sinners devouring it all with fond satisfaction. Then the dancers separated and with final abandon flung themselves off the stage in both directions.

Lee Goldman commented through the applause, "They work easy, them babies."

"Yea," said Lou. "Savin' the hot stuff for later."

Two black-faced cotton-pickers appropriated the scene, indulging in dialogue that their hearers found uproarious.

"Ah'm tired."

"Ah'm hongry."

"Dis job jes' wears me out."

"Starves me to death."

"Ah'm so tired—you know what Ah'd like to do?"

"What?"

"Ah'd like to go to sleep and dream I was sleepin'."

"What good dat do?"

"Den I could wake up and still be 'sleep."

"Well y'know what Ah'd like to do?"

"No. What?"

"Ah'd like to swaller me a hog and a hen."

"What good dat do?"

"Den Ah'd always be full o' ham and eggs."

"Ham? Shuh. Don't you know a hog has to be smoked 'fo' he's a ham?"

"Well, if I swaller him, he'll have a smoke all around him, won' he?"

Presently Miss Cynthie was smiling like everyone else, but her smile soon fled. For the comics departed, and the dancing girls returned, this time in scant travesties on their earlier voluminous costumes—tiny sun-bonnets perched jauntily on one side of their glistening bobs, bandanas reduced to scarlet neck ribbons, waists mere brassieres, skirts mere gingham sashes.

And now Miss Cynthie's whole body stiffened with a new and surpassing shock; her bright eyes first widened with unbelief, then slowly grew dull with misery. In the midst of a sudden great volley of applause her grandson had broken through the bevy of agile wantons and begun to sing.

He too was dressed as a cotton-picker, but a Beau Brummel among cotton pickers; his hat bore a pleated green band, his bandana was silk, his overalls blue satin, his shoes black patent leather. His eyes flashed, his teeth gleamed, his body swayed, his arms waved, his words came fast and clear. As he sang, his companions danced a concerted tap, uniformly wild, ecstatic. When he stopped singing, he himself began to dance, and without sacrificing crispness of execution, seemed to absorb into himself every measure of the energy which the girls, now merely standing off and swaying, had relinquished.

"Look at that boy go," said Lee Goldman.

"He ain't started yet," said Lou.

But surrounding comment, Dave's virtuosity, the eager enthusiasm of the audience were all alike lost on Miss Cynthie. She sat with stricken eyes watching this boy whom she'd raised from a babe, taught right from wrong, brought up in the church, and endowed with her prayers, this child whom she had dreamed of seeing a preacher, a regular doctor, a tooth-doctor, a foot-doctor, at the very least an undertaker—sat watching him disport himself for the benefit of a sinsick, flesh-hungry mob of lost souls, not one of whom knew or cared to know the loving kindness of God; sat watching a David she'd never foreseen, turned tool of the devil, disciple of lust, unholy prince among sinners.

For a long time she sat there watching with wretched eyes, saw portrayed on the stage David's arrival in Harlem, his escape from "old friends" who tried to dupe him; saw him working as a trap-drummer in a night-club, where he fell in love with Ruth, a dancer; not the gentle Ruth Miss Cynthie knew, but a wild and shameless young savage who danced like seven devils—in only a girdle and breast-plates; saw the two of them join in a song-and-dance act that eventually made them Broadway headliners, an act presented *in toto* as the pre-finale of this show. And not any of the melodies, not any of the sketches, not all the comic philosophy of the tired-and-hungry duo, gave her figure a moment's relaxation or brightened the dull defeat in her staring eyes. She sat apart, alone in the box, the symbol, the epitome of supreme failure. Let the rest of the theatre be riotous, clamoring for more and more of Dave Tappen, "Tap," the greatest tapster of all time, idol of uptown and downtown New York. For her, they were lauding simply an exhibition of sin which centered about her David.

"This'll run a year on Broadway," said Lee Goldman.

"Then we'll take it to Paris."

Encores and curtains with Ruth, and at last David came out on the stage alone. The clamor dwindled. And now he did something quite unfamiliar to even the most consistent of his followers. Softly, delicately, he begun to tap a routine designed to fit a particular song. When he had established the rhythm, he began to sing the song:

> Oh I danced with the gal with the hole in her
> stockin'
> And her toe kep' a-kickin' and her heel kep'
> a-knockin'—
> Come up, Jesse, and get a drink o' gin,
> 'Cause you near to the heaven as you'll ever get
> ag'in'—

As he danced and sang this song, frequently smiling across at Miss Cynthie, a visible change transformed her. She leaned forward incredulously, listened intently, then settled back in limp wonder. Her bewildered eyes turned on the crowd, on those serried rows of shiftless sinners. And she found in their faces now an overwhelming curious thing: a grin, a universal grin, a gleeful and sinless grin such as not the nakedest chorus in the performance had produced. In a few seconds, with her own song, David had dwarfed into unimportance, wiped off their faces, swept out of their minds every trace of what had seemed to be sin; had reduced it all to mere trivial detail and revealed these revelers as a crowd of children, enjoying the guileless antics of another child. And Miss Cynthie whispered:

"Bless my soul! They didn' mean nothin' . . . They jes' didn' see no harm in it—"

> Then I danced with the gal with the dimple in
> her cheek,
> And if she'd 'a' kep' a-smilin', I'd 'a' danced for
> week—
> "Come up, Jesse—"

The crowd laughed, clapped their hands, whistled. Someone threw David a bright yellow flower. "From Broadway!"

He caught the flower. A hush fell. He said:

"I'm really happy tonight, folks. Y'see this flower? Means success, don't it? Well, listen. The one who is really responsible for my success is here tonight with me. Now what do you think o' that?"

The hush deepened.

"Y'know folks, I'm sump'm like Adam—I never had no mother. But I've got a grandmother. Down home everybody calls her Miss Cynthie. And everybody loves her. Take that song I just did for you. Miss Cynthie taught me that when I wasn't knee-high to a cricket. But that wasn't all she taught me. Far back as I can remember, she used to always say one thing: Son, do like a church steeple—aim high and go straight. And for doin' it—" he grinned, contemplating the flower—"I get this."

He strode across to the edge of the stage that touched Miss Cynthie's box. He held up the flower.

"So y'see, folks, this isn't mine. It's really Miss Cynthie's." He leaned over to hand it to her. Miss Cynthie's last trace of doubt was swept away. She drew a deep breath of revelation; her bewilderment vanished, her redoubtable composure returned, her eyes lighted up; and no one but David, still holding the flower toward her, heard her sharply whispered reprimand:

"Keep it, you fool. Where's yo' manners—givin' 'way what somebody give you?"

David grinned:

"Take it, tyro. What you tryin' to do—crab my act?"

Thereupon, Miss Cynthie, smiling at him with bright, meaningful eyes, leaned over without rising from her chair, jerked a tiny twig off the stem of the flower, then sat decisively back, resolutely folding her arms, with only a leaf in her hand.

"This'll do me," she said.

The finale didn't matter. People filed out of the theatre. Miss Cynthie sat awaiting her children, her foot absently patting time to the orchestra's jazz recessional. Perhaps she was thinking, "God moves in a mysterious way," but her lips were unquestionably forming the words:

—danced with the gal—hole in her stockin'—
—toe kep' a-kickin'—heel kep' a-knockin'.

ERIC WALROND
(1898–1966)

Eric Walrond was probably the most gifted of the international nomads in the Harlem Renaissance. As a protégé of Charles S. Johnson, the national director of research and investigation for the Urban League, he achieved in *Tropic Death* (1926) a volume of fiction that nearly rivaled the critical reception of Jean Toomer's *Cane* in 1923. With Toomer, Walrond was as an example of avant-garde writing, although he lacked the talent for tightly historical context and for brilliantly clarifying moments of historical revelation. To Walrond, many of the most important themes were the cycles of life and death, cultural disorientation, racial conflict, imperialism, and hardship in the American tropics. Although Walrond brought out most of his short stories and journalistic pieces during the early to mid-twenties, he earned a vagabond's respected place in literary history. He wrote from within a largely British world that presumed a political truth of linear history, but he found this conception of existence profoundly in conflict with his own—and with even the colonizing Catholic Church's—sense of cyclical and mythic history.

Walrond reminds us of three highly variant sets of writing consciousness by blacks worldwide. He himself, for example, was the final member of the West Indian triangle that had led from the religious/political leader Marcus Garvey (1887–1940) through the militant Jamaican poet Claude McKay (1889–1948). Of these three internationals, only McKay, after several years on the French Riviera, would die in the United States. Both Garvey and Walrond would pass away in London.

What encourages sympathy on all of their parts is that they wrote nearly all of their lives without grounding in a homeland. In the ideology that mattered, they belonged more to the immigrant tradition in America than to the one that wanted to rewrite the shameful legacy of chattel slavery at home. Second, the internationals set into relief the pattern of African Americans' own expatriates, including Langston Hughes for a brief time in Paris during the twenties, as well as Josephine Baker, Richard Wright, Chester Himes, and James Baldwin for much longer stints. Third, the international triumvirate in the Harlem Renaissance—Garvey, McKay, and Walrond—helped establish a pattern of English acceptance that would facilitate the eventual emergence of Caribbean authors such as Derek Walcott, Kenneth Ramchand, and Maryse Condé.

As with perhaps all of them, Walrond revealed mystery and wonder. He was not, as is usually written, a critical realist, because he often preserved in his stories a gothic mood and a moral reckoning that had nearly disappeared from African American narrative since Frederick Douglass. By the elapse of two generations, the gothic impulse would return strongly in the most magical fiction of David Bradley, Alice Walker, Henry Dumas, and Toni Morrison. What Walrond had called into question was the interface between the literally jeweled Caribbean of amethyst or diamond and the possibly less resilient world of the human spirit. To him, stories deflected the colonial terror outside of him and expressed the more brittle ornaments of the soul. He wrote, according to Barksdale and Kinnamon, scenes that were "vividly and intensely etched." Even more, Walrond served as a touchstone to a variegated variety of black writing in English across time and space. Hence, he revealed in relief the literary consciousness written by Africans of the Diaspora, particularly the historical uniqueness of them as a triumphant people.

Eric Walrond, the son of a Barbadian mother and Guianese father, was born in Georgetown, British Guiana, in 1898. Eight years later, following his father's desertion, he moved to Barbados to live with his mother's family. He soon began Catholic school at St. Stephens Boys' School in Black Rock, near which his grandfather had developed a small neighborhood. Several years later, in an effort to locate his father, he traveled to the Panama Canal Zone, where thousands of Guianese and West Indians labored. Subsequently, he settled there with his mother in Colón. During his completion, often with private tutors, of secondary school between 1913 and 1916, he became bilingual because of the pervasive influence of Spanish, and he encountered many of the experiences that would become fertile sources for *Tropic Death*.

Trained as a secretary and stenographer, he found work as a clerk in the Health Department of the Canal Commission at Cristobal. From 1916 to 1918, he was employed as a court reporter, general reporter, and sportswriter for the *Panama Star Herald*, "the most contemporaneous newspaper in the American tropics." At the age of twenty, he migrated to New York, where he sought employment at various newspapers in Harlem. Failing in his job search, he decided to study at the City University of New York, where he remained for the next three years. He spent another year taking extension courses in creative writing at Columbia University. During this time he worked as a stenographer in the British Recruiting Mission. He became a secretary to a local architect and to the superintendent of the Broad Street Hospital. By the time he finally secured a position as coproprietor and editor of the *Brooklyn and Long Island Informer* (1921–1923), a black weekly, his years of searching so futilely for work in his trade had intensified his awareness of racist rebuffs. That same year, he left the *Informer* to work for *Negro World,* the weekly newspaper of the Universal Negro Improvement Association of Marcus Garvey.

In an early article of the period, "The New Negro Faces America" (*Current History,* 1923), Walrond rejected the leadership style of Booker T. Washington as too much Christian humility and labeled the position of W.E.B. Du Bois as elite supremacy. Although Walrond could barely tolerate the bombast and pageantry of Marcus Garvey, he viewed the Jamaican as the person with the most potential to lead African Americans. Holding a view on race so different from Garvey's, despite his own Catholicism, Walrond was also a West Indian who probably failed to understand the impact of race on American religion. Although Walrond surpassed many of his Harlem contemporaries in claiming Africa as a vital resource, he overlooked the Zeitgeist of self-determination.

In keeping with the earlier accommodation of Washington, Walrond extended the promise to accept the mainstream violence against blacks. He spoke for indigenous African Americans who were hardly his own people. In 1925, he accepted an appointment by Charles S. Johnson to edit *Opportunity,* the official periodical of the Urban League and a powerful instrument for the promotion of the Harlem Renaissance. Walrond also began to publish articles and short stories in magazines as varied as *The New Republic, Current History, The Messenger, The New Age, Saturday Review of Literature, The Independent, Argosy All-Story Magazine, Smart Set, Vanity Fair,* and *Opportunity.*

In 1923, Walrond brought out four stories, including "On Being a Domestic" (*Opportunity,* 1923), "Miss Kenny's Marriage" (*Smart Set,* 1923), "The Stone Rebounds" (*Opportunity,* 1923), and "Cynthia Goes to the Prom" (*Opportunity,* 1923). He continued to develop impressionist techniques, as in "A Cholo Romance" (*Opportunity,* 1924) and "The Voodoo's Revenge," which won third prize in a literary contest sponsored by *Opportunity* in 1925. Appropriately, the final two stories take place in Panama, as does "The Big Ditch," an unpublished manuscript completed in 1928. About the same time, Walrond left New York City to live in France for several years. He later moved to London, where he lived until his death in 1966.

Tropic Death (1926) is a very solid collection. To be sure, the surface presents only the light themes of critical realism, including those of dissipation, poverty, famine, and racial prejudice in the American tropics. The underlying themes are of tension between the natural and human worlds, of technological development and imperialism, of tropical nature and alienation, and of the fate of the Caribbean landscape. To traditionalists, Walrond distinguished himself by providing a vivid description of life in the West Indies without propaganda and with the varied pictures of the Caribbean islands. Hence, tales such as "Drought," "The Wharf Rats," "Subjection," "The Vampire Bat," and "Tropic Death" all become "local color tales" or even "arabesques." Actually, the phrase "wharf rats" is a metaphor for exploited people of color who worked on the Panama Canal. In his "The Palm Porch" the natural details of the sea and its precious jewels contrast sharply with the very troubled earth of dull people. One of the ten stories in *Tropic Death,* "Subjection," depicts a brutal plot in which a white marine shoots to death a black canal worker who has protested the beating of another. In "The Vampire Bat," Bellon Prout, a British colonial of Dutch and Huguenot descent, falls victim to the mysterious obeah girl. As his likely sexual victim, she has drilled a "magical" hole through his head: "Sea on top of sea, the Empire mourned the loss of a sovereign; and to the ends of the earth, there sped the glory of the coronation." For in the colonized subcontinent, the black boys find their marble games overturned in the figurative shadow of the Catholic Church. Walrond interweaves three symbols—the rare minerals of the earth, the profoundly religious irony of Catholic power, and the British Crown—into a "tropic death" that encapsulates the fall of humanity.

Walrond was too properly British ever to have read his author's place as being primitive or atavistic. Often his stories collapse under the weight of disjointed plots that bog down in inertia. "So thorough [had] been our British upbringing," he once wrote, "that, if in the event we [had] found a Colour Bar, we would consider it 'bad form' openly to admit its existence." He became a wonderful dissembler, a gifted writer of indirection. Imprisoned by the great codes of gentility and Catholicism, he reached for a human meaning much deeper than mere local color. In vain, he searched for the communal source of recovery through writing about a people's history.

❖❖❖

Several essays and at least one good book should be written about *Tropic Death* and Walrond's earlier body of work. The article by Jay Berry in *Dictionary of Literary Biography: African American Writers from the Harlem Renaissance to 1940,* ed. Trudier Harris (1987), 296–300, is most helpfully detailed. Groundbreaking research by Benjamin Brawley in *The Negro Genius* (1937) and by Hugh Gloster in *Negro Voices in American Fiction* (1948) has been a reliable source for nearly all who have followed. During the last generation, Robert Bone risked a psychobiographical reading in *Down Home* (1975); James A. Page and Jae Min Roh provided international context in *Selected Black American African, and Caribbean Authors* (1977; 1985). Most recently, John E. Bassett has compiled some very useful entries for Harlem in *Review: Critical Reactions to Black American Writers, 1917–1939* (1992). An on-line search shows no current articles on Walrond; so an opportunity for original assessment exists.

The Wharf Rats

Among the motley crew recruited to dig the Panama Canal were artisans from the four ends of the earth. Down in the Cut drifted hordes of Italians, Greeks, Chinese, Negroes—a hardy, sun-defying set of white, black and yellow men. But the bulk of the actual brawn for the work was supplied by the dusky peons of those coral isles in the Caribbean ruled by Britain, France and Holland.

At the Atlantic end of the Canal the blacks were herded in boxcar huts buried in the jungles of "Silver City"; in the murky tenements perilously poised on the narrow banks of Faulke's River; in the low, smelting cabins of Coco Té. The "Silver Quarters" harbored the inky ones, their wives and pickaninnies.

As it grew dark the hewers at the Ditch, exhausted, half-asleep, naked but for wormy singlets, would hum queer creole tunes, play on guitar or piccolo, and jig to the rhythm of the *coombia.* It was a *brujerial* chant, for *obeah,* a heritage of the French colonial, honeycombed the life of the Negro laboring camps. Over smoking pots, on black, death-black nights, legends of the bloodiest were recited till they became the essence of a sort of Negro Koran. One refuted them at the price of one's breath. And to question the verity of the obeah, to dismiss or reject it as the ungodly rite of some lurid, crackbrained Islander was to be an accursed paleface, dog of a white. And the obeah man in a fury of rage would throw a machete at the heretic's head or—worse—burn on his doorstep at night a pyre of Maube bark or green Ganja weed.

On the banks of a river beyond Cristobal, Coco Té sheltered a colony of Negroes enslaved to the obeah. Near a roundhouse daubed with smoke and coal ash, a river serenely flowed away and into the guava region, at the eastern tip of Monkey Hill. Across the bay from it was a sand bank—a rising out of the sea—where ships stopped for coal.

In the first of the six chinky cabins making up the family quarters of Coco Té lived a stout, potbellied St. Lucian, black as the coal hills he mended, by the name of Jean Baptiste. Like a host of the native St. Lucian emigrants, Jean Baptiste forgot where the French in him ended and the English began. His speech was the petulant patois of the unlettered French black. Still, whenever he lapsed into His Majesty's English, it was with a thick Barbadian bias.

A coal passer at the dry dock, Jean Baptiste was a man of intense piety. After work, by the glow of a red setting sun, he would discard his crusted overalls, get in starched crocus bag, aping the Yankee foreman on the other side of the track in the "Gold Quarters," and loll on his coffee-vined porch. There, dozing in a bamboo rocker, Celestin his second wife, a becomingly stout brown beauty from Martinique, chanted gospel hymns to him.

Three sturdy sons Jean Baptiste's first wife had borne him—Philip, the eldest, a good-looking, black fellow; Ernest, shifty, cunning; and Sandel, aged eight. Another boy, said to be wayward and something of a ne'er-do-well, was sometimes spoken of. But Baptiste, a proud, disdainful man, never once referred to him in the presence of his children. No vagabond son of his could eat from his table or sit at his feet unless he went to "meeting." In brief, Jean Baptiste was a religious man. It was a thrust at the omnipresent obeah. He went to "meeting." He made the boys go, too. All hands went, not to the Catholic Church, where Celestin secretly worshiped, but to the English Plymouth Brethren in the Spanish city of Colón.

Stalking about like a ghost in Jean Baptiste's household was a girl, a black ominous Trinidad girl. Had Jean Baptiste been a man given to curiosity about the nature of women, he would have viewed skeptically Maffi's adoption by Celestin. But Jean Baptiste was a man of lofty unconcern, and so Maffi remained there, shadowy, obdurate.

And Maffi was such a hardworking patois girl. From the break of day she'd be at the sink, brightening the tinware. It was she who did the chores which Madame congenitally shirked. And towards sundown, when the labor trains had emptied, it was she who scoured the beach for cockles for Jean Baptiste's epicurean palate.

And as night fell, Maffi, a long, black figure, would disappear in the dark to dream on top of a canoe hauled up on the mooning beach. An eternity Maffi'd sprawl there, gazing at the frosting of the stars and the glitter of the black sea.

A cabin away lived a family of Tortola mulattoes by the name of Boyce. The father was also a man who piously went to "meeting"—gaunt and hollow-cheeked. The eldest boy, Esau, had been a journeyman tailor for ten years; the girl next to him, Ora, was plump, dark, freckled; others came—a string of ulcered girls until finally a pretty, opaque one, Maura.

Of the Bantu tribe, Maura would have been a person to turn and stare at. Crossing the line into Cristobal or Colón—a city of rarefied gaiety—she was often mistaken for a native senorita or an urbanized Chola Indian girl. Her skin was the reddish yellow of old gold and in her eyes there lurked the glint of mother-of-pearl. Her hair, long as a jungle elf's, was jettish, untethered. And her teeth were whiter than the full-blooded black Philip's.

Maura was brought up, like the children of Jean Baptiste, in the Plymouth Brethren. But the Plymouth Brethren was a harsh faith to bring hemmed-in peasant children up in, and Maura, besides, was of a gentle romantic nature. Going to the Yankee commissary at the bottom of Eleventh and Front Streets, she usually wore a leghorn hat. With flowers bedecking it, she'd look in it older, much older than she really was. Which was an impression quite flattering to her. For Maura, unknown to Philip, was in love—in love with San Tie, a Chinese half-breed, son of a wealthy canteen proprietor in Colón. But San Tie liked to go fishing and deer hunting up the Monkey Hill lagoon, and the object of his occasional visits to Coco Té was the eldest son of Jean Baptiste. And thus it was through Philip that Maura kept in touch with the young Chinese Maroon.

One afternoon Maura, at her wits' end, flew to the shed roof to Jean Baptiste's kitchen.

"Maffi," she cried, the words smoky on her lips, "Maffi, when Philip come in tonight tell 'im I want fo' see 'im particular, yes?"

"Sacre gache! All de time Philip, Philip!" growled the Trinidad girl, as Maura, in heartaching preoccupation, sped towards the lawn. "Why she no le' 'im alone, yes?" And with a spatter she flecked the hunk of lard on Jean Baptiste's stewing okras.

As the others filed up front after dinner that evening, Maffi said to Philip, pointing to the cabin across the way, "She—she want fo' see yo'."

Instantly Philip's eyes widened. Ah, he had good news for Maura! San Tie, after an absence of six days, was coming to Coco Té Saturday to hunt on the lagoon. And he'd relish the joy that'd flood Maura's face as she glimpsed the idol of her heart, the hero of her dreams! And Philip, a true son of Jean Baptiste, loved to see others happy, ecstatic.

But Maffi's curious rumination checked him. "All de time, Maura, Maura, me can't understand it, yes. But no mind, me go stop it, oui, me go stop it, so help me—"

He crept up to her, gently holding her by the shoulders.

"Le' me go, sacre!" She shook off his hands bitterly. "Le' me go—yo' go to yo' Maura." And she fled to her room, locking the door behind her.

Philip sighed. He was a generous, good-natured sort. But it was silly to try to enlighten Maffi. It wasn't any use. He could as well have spoken to the tattered torsos the lazy waves puffed up on the shores of Coco Té.

"Philip, come on, a ship is in—let's go." Ernest, the wharf rat, seized him by the arm.

"Come," he said, "let's go before it's too late. I want to get some money, yes."

Dashing out of the house the two boys made for the wharf. It was dusk. Already the Hindus in the bachelor quarters were mixing their rotie and the Negroes in their singlets were smoking and cooling off. Night was rapidly approaching. Sunset, an iridescent bit of molten gold, was enriching the stream with its last faint radiance.

The boys stole across the lawn and made their way to the pier.

"Careful," cried Philip, as Ernest slid between a prong of osyter-crusted piles to a raft below. "Careful, these shells cut wussah'n a knife."

On the raft the boys untied a rowboat they kept stowed away under the dock, got into it and pushed off. The liner still had two hours to dock. Tourists crowded its decks. Veering away from the barnacled piles the boys eased out into the churning ocean.

It was dusk. Night would soon be upon them. Philip took the oars while Ernest stripped down to loincloth.

"Come, Philip, let me paddle—" Ernest took the oars. Afar on the dusky sea a whistle echoed. It was the pilot's signal to the captain of port. The ship would soon dock.

The passengers on deck glimpsed the boys. It piqued their curiosity to see two black boys in a boat amidstream.

"All right, mistah," cried Ernest. "A penny, mistah."

He sprang at the guilder as it twisted and turned through a streak of silver dust to the bottom of the sea. Only the tips of his crimson toes—a sherbet-like foam—and up he came with the coin between his teeth.

Deep-sea gamin, Philip off yonder, his mouth noisy with coppers, gargled, "This way, sah, as far as you' like, mistah."

An old red-bearded Scot, in spats and mufti, presumably a lover of the exotic in sport, held aloft a sovereign. A sovereign! Already red, and sore by virtue of the leaps and plunges in the briny swirl, Philip's eyes bulged at its yellow gleam.

"Ovah ya, sah—"

Off in a whirlpool the man tossed it. And like a garfish Philip took after it, a falling arrow in the stream. His body, once in the water, tore ahead. For a spell the crowd on the ship held its breath. "Where is he?" "Where is the nigger swimmer gone to?" Even Ernest, driven to the boat by the race for such an ornate prize, cold, shivering, his teeth chattering—even he watched with trembling and anxiety. But Ernest's concern was of a deeper kind. For there, where Philip had leaped, was Deathpool—a spawning place for sharks, for barracudas!

But Philip rose—a brief gurgling sputter—a ripple on the sea—and the Negro's crinkled head was above the water.

"Hey!" shouted Ernest. "There, Philip! Down!"

And down Philip plunged. One—two minutes. God, how long they seemed! And Ernest anxiously waited. But the bubble on the water boiled, kept on boiling—a sign that life still lasted! It comforted Ernest.

Suddenly Philip, panting, spitting, pawing, dashed through the water like a streak of lightning.

"Shark!" cried a voice aboard ship. "Shark! There he is, a great big one! Run, boy! Run for your life!"

From the edge of the boat Philip saw the monster as twice, thrice it circled the boat. Several times the shark made a dash for it, endeavoring to strike it with its murderous tail.

The boys quietly made off. But the shark still followed the boat. It was a pale green monster. In the glittering dusk it seemed black to Philip. Fattened on the swill of the abattoir nearby and the beef tossed from the decks of countless ships in port, it had become used to the taste of flesh and the smell of blood.

"Yo' know, Ernest," said Philip, as he made the boat fast to raft, "one time I thought he wuz rubbin' 'gainst me belly. He wuz such a big able one. But it wuz wuth it, Ernie, it wuz wuth it—"

In his palm there was a flicker of gold. Ernest emptied his loincloth and together they counted the money, dressed, and trudged back to the cabin.

On the lawn Philip met Maura. Ernest tipped his cap, left his brother and went into the house. As he entered, Maffi, pretending to be scouring a pan, was flushed and mute as a statue. And Ernest, starved, went in the dining room and for a long time stayed there. Unable to beat it any longer, Maffi sang out, "Ernest, whey Philip dey?"

"Outside—some whey—ah talk to Maura—"

"Yo' sure yo' lie, Ernest?" she asked, suspended.

"Yes, of cose, I jes' lef' 'im 'tanding' out dey—why?"

"Nutton—"

He suspected nothing. He went on eating while Maffi tiptoed to the shed roof. Yes, confound it, there he was, near the standpipe, talking to Maura!

"Go stop ee, oui," she hissed impishly. "Go 'top ee, yes."

Low, shadowy, the sky painted Maura's face bronze. The sea, noisy, enraged, sent a blob of wind about her black, wavy hair. And with her back to the sea, her hair blew loosely about her face.

"D'ye think, d'ye think he really likes me, Philip?"

"I'm positive he do, Maura," vowed the youth.

And an aging faith shone in Maura's eyes. No longer was she a silly, insipid girl. Something holy, reverent had touched her. And in so doing it could not fail to leave an impress of beauty. It was worshipful. And it mellowed, ripened her.

Weeks she had waited for word of San Tie. And the springs of Maura's life took on a noble ecstasy. Late at night, after the others had retired, she'd sit up in bed, dreaming. Sometimes they were dreams of envy. For Maura began to look with eyes of comparison upon the happiness of the Italian wife of the boss riveter at the Dry Dock—the lady on the other side of the railroad tracks in the Gold Quarters, for whom she sewed—who got a fresh baby every year and who danced in a world of silks and satins. Yes, Maura had dreams, love dreams of San Tie, the flashy half-breed, son of a Chinese beer seller and a Jamaica Maroon, who had swept her off her feet by a playful wink of the eye.

"Tell me, Philip, does he work? Or does he play the lottery—what does he do, tell me!"

"I dunno," Philip replied with mock lassitude. "I dunno myself—"

"But it doesn't matter, Philip. I don't want to be nosy, see? I'm simply curious about everything that concerns him, see?"

Ah, but Philip wished to cherish Maura, to shield her, be kind to her. And so he lied to her. He did not tell her he had first met San Tie behind the counter of his father's saloon in the Colón tenderloin, for he would have had to tell besides why he, Philip, had gone there. And that would have led him, a youth of meager guile, to Celestin Baptiste's mulish regard for anisette, which he procured her. He dared not tell her, well-meaning fellow that he was, what San Tie, a fiery comet in the night life of the district, had said to him the day before. "She sick in de head, yes," he had said. "Ah, me no dat saht o' man—don't she know no bettah, egh, Philip?" But Philip desired to be kindly, and hid it from Maura.

"What is today?" she cogitated aloud. "Tuesday. You say he's comin' fo' hunt Saturday, Philip? Wednesday—four more days. I can wait. I can wait. I'd wait a million years fo' 'im, Philip."

But Saturday came and Maura, very properly, was shy as a duck. Other girls, like Hilda Long, a Jamaica brunette, the flower of a bawdy cabin up by the abattoir, would have been less genteel. Hilda would have caught San Tie by the lapels of his coat and in no time would have got him told.

But Maura was lowly, trepid, shy. To her he was a dream—a luxury to be distantly enjoyed. He was not to be touched. And she'd wait till he decided to come to her. And there was no fear, either, of his ever failing to come. Philip had seen to that. Had not he been the intermediary between them? And all Maura needed now was to sit back, and wait till San Tie came to her.

And besides, who knows, brooded Maura, San Tie might be a bashful fellow.

But when, after an exciting hunt, the Chinese mulatto returned from the lagoon, nodded stiffly to her, said good-bye to Philip and kept on to the scarlet city, Maura was frantic.

"Maffi," she said, "tell Philip to come here quick—"

It was the same as touching a match to the patois girl's dynamite. "Yo' mek me sick," she said. "Go call he yo'self, yo' ole hag, yo' ole fire hag yo'." But Maura, flighty in despair, had gone on past the lawn.

"Ah go stop ee, oui," she muttered diabolically. "Ah go stop it, yes. This very night."

Soon as she got through lathering the dishes she tidied up and came out on the front porch.

It was a humid dusk, and the glowering sky sent a species of fly—bloody as a tick—buzzing about Jean Baptiste's porch. There he sat, rotund and sleepy-eyed, rocking and languidly brushing the darting imps away.

"Wha' yo' gwine, Maffi?" asked Celestin Baptiste, fearing to wake the old man.

"Ovah to de Jahn Chinaman shop, mum," answered Maffi unheeding.

"Fi' what?"

"Fi' buy some wash blue, mum."

And she kept on down the road past the Hindu kiosk to the Negro mess house.

"Oh, Philip," cried Maura. "I am so unhappy. Didn't he ask about me at all? Didn't he say he'd like to visit me—didn't he give yo' any message fo' me, Philip?"

The boy toyed with a blade of grass. His eyes were downcast. Sighing heavily, he at last spoke. "No, Maura, he didn't ask about you."

"What, he didn't ask about me? Philip? I don't believe it! Oh, my God!"

She clung to Philip mutely; her face, her breath coming warm and fast.

"I wish to God I'd never seen either of you," cried Philip.

"Ah, but wasn't he your friend, Philip? Didn't yo' tell me that?" And the boy bowed his head sadly.

"Answer me!" she screamed, shaking him. "Weren't you his friend?"

"Yes, Maura—"

"But you lied to me, Philip, you lied to me! You took messages from me—you brought back—lies!" Two pearls, large as pigeon's eggs, shone in Maura's burnished face.

"To think," she cried in a hollow sepulchral voice, "that I dreamed about a ghost, a man who didn't exist. Oh, God, why should I suffer like this? Why was I ever born? What did I do, what did my people do, to deserve such misery as this?"

She rose, leaving Philip with his head buried in his hands. She went into the night, tearing her hair, scratching her face, raving.

"Oh, how happy I was! I was a happy girl! I was so young and I had such merry dreams! And I wanted so little! I was carefree—"

Down to the shore of the sea she staggered, the wind behind her, the night obscuring her.

"Maura!" cried Philip, running after her. "Maura! come back!"

Great sheaves of clouds buried the moon, and the wind bearing up from the sea bowed the cypress and palm lining the beach.

"Maura—Maura—"

He bumped into someone, a girl, black, part of the dense pattern of the tropical night.

"Maffi," cried Philip, "have you seen Maura down yondah?"

The girl quietly stared at him. Had Philip lost his mind?

"Talk, no!" he cried, exasperated.

And his quick tones sharpened Maffi's vocal anger. Thrusting him aside, she thundered, "Think I'm she keeper! Go'n look fo' she yo'self. I is not she keeper! Le' me pass, move!"

Towards the end of the track he found Maura, heartrendingly weeping.

"Oh, don't cry, Maura! Never mind, Maura!"

He helped her to her feet, took her to the standpipe on the lawn, bathed her temples and sat soothingly, uninterruptingly, beside her.

At daybreak the next morning Ernest rose and woke Philip.

He yawned, put on the loincloth, seized a "cracked licker" skillet, and stole cautiously out of the house. Of late Jean Baptiste had put his foot down on his sons' copper-diving proclivities. And he kept at the head of his bed a greased cat-o'-nine-tails which he would use on Philip himself if the occasion warranted.

"Come on, Philip, let's go—"

Yawning and scratching, Philip followed. The grass on the lawn was bright and icy with the dew. On the railroad tracks the six o'clock labor trains were coupling. A rosy mist flooded the dawn. Out in the stream the tug *Exotic* snorted in a heavy fog.

On the wharf Philip led the way to the rafters below.

"Look out fo' that crapeau, Ernest, don't step on him, he'll spit on you."

The frog splashed into the water. Prickle-backed crabs and oysters and myriad other shells spawned on the rotting piles. The boys paddled the boat. Out in the dawn ahead of them the tug puffed a path through the foggy mist. The water was chilly. Mist glistened on top of it. Far out, beyond the buoys, Philip encountered a placid, untroubled sea. The liner, a German tourist boat, was loaded to the bridge. The water was as still as a lake of ice.

"All right, Ernest, let's hurry—"

Philip drew in the oars. The *Kron Prinz Wilhelm* came near. Huddled in thick European coats, the passengers viewed from their lofty estate the spectacle of two naked Negro boys peeping up at them from a wiggly bateau.

"Penny, mistah, penny, mistah!"

Somebody dropped a quarter. Ernest, like a shot, flew after it. Half a foot down he caught it as it twisted and turned in the gleaming sea. Vivified by the icy dip, Ernest was a raving wolf and the folk aboard dealt a lavish hand.

"Ovah yah, mistah," cried Philip, "ovah yah."

For a Dutch guilder Philip gave an exhibition of "cork." Under something of a ledge on the side of the boat he had stuck a piece of cork. Now, after his and Ernest's mouths were full of coins, he could afford to be extravagant and treat the Europeans to a game of West Indian "cork."

Roughly ramming the cork down in the water, Philip, after the fifteenth ram or so, let it go, and flew back, upwards, having thus "lost" it. It was Ernest's turn now, as a sort of endman, to scramble forward to the spot where Philip had dug it down and "find" it, the first one to do so having the prerogative, which he jealously guarded, of raining on the other a series of thundering leg blows. As boys in the West Indies, Philip and Ernest had played it. Of a Sunday the Negro fishermen on the Barbados coast made a pagan rite of it. Many a Bluetown dandy got his spine cracked in a game of cork.

With a passive interest the passengers viewed the proceedings. In a game of cork, the cork after a succession of rammings is likely to drift many feet away whence it was first "lost." One had to be an expert, quick, alert, to spy and promptly seize it as it popped up on the rolling waves. Once Ernest got it, and endeavored to make much of the possession. But Philip, besides being two feet taller than he, was slippery as an eel, and Ernest, despite all the artful ingenuity at his command, was able to do no more than ineffectively beat the water about him. Again and again he tried, but to no purpose.

Becoming reckless, he let the cork drift too far away from him and Philip seized it.

He twirled it in the air like a crapshooter, and dug deep down in the water with it, "lost" it, then leaped back, briskly waiting for it to rise.

About them the water, due to the ramming and beating, grew restive. Billows sprang up; soaring, swelling waves sent the skiff nearer the shore. Anxiously Philip and Ernest watched for the cork to make its ascent.

It was all a bit vague to the whites on the deck, and an amused chuckle floated down to the boys.

And still the cork failed to come up.

"I'll go after it," said Philip at last. "I'll go and fetch it." And from the edge of the boat he leaped, his body long and resplendent in the rising tropic sun.

It was a suction sea, and down in it Philip plunged. And it was lazy, too, and willful—the water. Ebony-black, it tugged and mocked. Old brass staves—junk dumped there by the retiring French—thick, yawping mud, barrel hoops, tons of obsolete brass, a wealth of slimy steel faced him. Did a rammed cork ever go that deep?

And the water, stirring, rising, drew a haze over Philip's eyes. Had a cuttlefish, an octopus, a nest of eels been routed? It seemed so to Philip, blindly diving, pawing. And the sea, the tide—touching the roots of Deathpool—tugged and tugged. His gathering hands stuck in mud. Iron staves bruised his shins. It was black down there. Impenetrable.

Suddenly, like a flash of lightning, a vision blew across Philip's brow. It was a soaring shark's belly. Drunk on the nectar of the deep, it soared above Philip—rolling, tumbling, rolling. It had followed the boy's scent with the accuracy of a diver's rope.

Scrambling to the surface, Philip struck out for the boat. But the sea, the depths of it wrested out of an aeon's slumber, had sent it a mile from his diving point. And now, as his strength ebbed, a shark was at his heels.

"Shark! Shark!" was the cry that went up from the ship.

Hewing a lane through the hostile sea, Philip forgot the cunning of the doddering beast and swam noisier than he needed to. Faster grew his strokes. His line was a straight, dead one. Fancy strokes and dives—giraffe leaps . . . he summoned into play. He shot out recklessly. One time he suddenly paused—and floated for a stretch. Another time he swam on his back, gazing at the chalky sky. He dived for whole lengths.

But the shark, a bloaty, stone-colored man-killer, took a shorter cut. Circumnavigating the swimmer it bore down upon him with the speed of a hurricane. Within adequate reach it turned, showed its gleaming belly, seizing its prey.

A fiendish gargle—the gnashing of bones—as the sea once more closed its jaws on Philip.

Someone aboard ship screamed. Women fainted. There was talk of a gun. Ernest, an oar upraised, capsized the boat as he tried to inflict a blow on the coursing, chop-licking man-eater.

And again the fish turned. It scraped the waters with its deadly fins.

At Coco Té, at the fledging of the dawn, Maffi, polishing the tinware, hummed an obeah melody.

> Trinidad is a damn fine place
> But obeah down dey. . . .

Peace had come to her at last.

Response: Voices of the Reformation

Poets

STERLING BROWN

(1901–1989)

Sterling Brown, poet, anthologist, literary critic, and mentor, exemplified through poetic form and spirit the folk greatness of the African American people. One of the most balanced African American professors ever to live, he was in many ways one of the last Renaissance men in the tradition of the nineteenth century. Once Brown took his own record collection of blues and jazz into the dormitories of Howard University—hence enlightening both Le Roi Jones (later Amiri Baraka) and A. B. Spellman, who were undergraduates at the time and would go on to become celebrated authorities on the culture of the blues. The teaching of Brown, says the gifted performer Ossie Davis, was inspirational. The professor merits a truly revered distinction in African American literary history because of the special moment at which his definitive work appeared. Near the end of the Great Depression, Brown began to challenge the most debasing stereotypes of the "Brute Negro" and "Tragic Mulatto" in traditional American literature. Brown was in the academy but never completely of it. He helped take the first critical steps toward legitimate African American criticism and poetry, and he helped establish a tone and a set of indigenous values by which those who aspire to be critical leaders among blacks must still be authenticated.

Sterling Brown attempted to revise the blues and spirituals into a creative expression of great aesthetic appeal. Sometimes, as in "Ma Rainey" and "Strong Men," he achieved a resonance of complementary voices. He had the rare skill that allowed him to address his poetic vision from the sides of oppressor and oppressed at once. At times a protest poet, he documented the injustices suffered by blacks in the South. The excellence of his literary qualities has led a few academic critics to extol him beyond Langston Hughes, but Brown almost never accomplished, as did Hughes, the sweeping blues spirit and the lyrical vision of the African American dream. Brown was to the formal letter and structure of the folk experience what Hughes was to the unstinting spirit of it. Often Brown brought an ironic detachment to the African American folk world, whereas Hughes empathized—if not delighted in—jazz's triumph over social limits. Brown reveled in the nobility that enables folk characters such as "old Lem" to withstand the great pain of African American experience. Hughes, on the contrary, depicted a gifted trumpet player who blows his way through a discomfort with African American suffering to a cultural vindication. Today Brown's work is part of a national treasure, just as his brilliant teaching was while he lived.

Sterling Allen Brown, the son of a professor of theology at Howard University, was born on May 1, 1901, and educated at Dunbar High School in Washington, D.C. Later, he earned his B.A. as a Phi Beta Kappa at Williams College in

Williamstown, Massachusetts, and subsequently earned an M.A. in English at Harvard in 1923. He had prepared himself for a career in teaching and publishing that would come along at several historical black institutions such as Virginia Seminary and College, Lincoln University (Missouri), Fisk University, and Howard University. When mainstream schools began to look for talented scholars who happened to be black, Brown accepted various invitations to visit at New York University, New School, Sarah Lawrence, and Vassar. By the time the doors of racial opportunity opened in the late sixties and early seventies, Brown had already established his credentials as a folklorist and consummate spinner of tall tales. More than a generation earlier, from 1936 to 1939, he had been the editor for Negro Affairs in the Federal Writers' Project of the Work Projects Administration (WPA). He also had served as a member of the Carnegie-Myrdal study.

The reassessment of his imaginative work requires a balanced assessment across two-thirds of a century. For many years, Brown was the literary editor of *Opportunity.* He contributed to the *Journal of Negro Education* in 1931 and to the *Quarterly Review of Higher Education Among Negroes* in 1941. His work also appeared in professional journals such as *Phylon* (1953), which had been founded by W.E.B. Du Bois in 1940, and the *Massachusetts Review* (1966). Brown has been honored of late in special sessions of the Modern Language Association and celebrated within academic circles. Although his work is often revered today without rigorous scrutiny, in earlier years he was not given his rightful place in the New Negro Movement. Brown preferred the term "New Negro Movement" over "Harlem Renaissance" because he thought the progress extended far beyond and below Harlem. Like Zora Neale Hurston, Brown published representative works in periodicals during the twenties, and he wrote one of the final works rooted firmly in the Renaissance. Hurston's novel was a wonderful culmination of the female romance that had existed since the turn of the century and in time would come again. Brown's poetry, on the contrary, displays the postmodernist realism that would prevail after World War II. Hurston preserved the exuberant glitter of her times; Brown rediscovered the somewhat torturous history that underlay them. Whereas the greatness of Hurston appeared through the imaginative suspension of history, the prominence of Brown came through the stubborn resurrection of it. What Hurston achieved in the shape of black female liberation, Brown accomplished in the blues suffering of black men. *Southern Road* (1932), a minor classic of dialect poetry, has several strong poems that range from broad laughter to despair. Brown's notable compilations *Negro Poetry and Drama* (1937), *The Negro in American Fiction* (1937; reprinted 1969), and *The Negro Caravan* (1941; reprinted 1969; with Arthur P. Davis and Ulysses Lee) may seem quite pedestrian today, but they were landmarks in Brown's time. *The Last Ride of Wild Bill* (1975) and *The Collected Poems of Sterling A. Brown* (1980), edited by the modern imagist Michael S. Harper, round out the creative legacy of Brown. Sterling Brown led deftly from Langston Hughes to Richard Wright and from Zora Neale Hurston to Gwendolyn Brooks. As a talented black folk poet and an engaging scholar, he was unique.

❖❖❖

Of the current Brown scholars, Joanne V. Gabbin and Edgar Tidwell continue to do sustained work. See Gabbin's excellent critical study, *Sterling Brown: Building the*

Black Aesthetic Tradition (1985), and Tidwell's "The Art of Tall Tale in the Slim Greer Poems," *Cottonwood* 38/39 (Summer/Fall, 1986). Occasional articles by Michael S. Harper, who has made Brown a personal mission, and by Robert O'Meally are instructive. Virtually nothing appears on the work of Brown in current periodical databases. Especially since 1989, *Black American Literature Forum* (now *African American Review*) has been quite useful, and *Sterling A. Brown: A Umum Tribute* (1982) was a rare honor by the Black History Museum Committee of Philadelphia.

When de Saints Go Ma'chin' Home

I

He'd play, after the bawdy songs and blues,
After the weary plaints
Of "Trouble, Trouble deep down in muh soul,"
Always one song in which he'd lose the role
Of entertainer to the boys. He'd say
"My mother's favorite." And we knew
That what was coming was his chant of saints
"When de Saints go ma'chin' home . . . "
And that would end his concert for the day.

Carefully as an old maid over needlework,
Or, as some black deacon, over his Bible, lovingly,
He'd tune up specially for this. There'd be
No chatter now, no patting of the feet.
After a few slow chords, knelling and sweet
Oh, when de saints go ma'chin' home
Oh, when de sayaints goa ma'chin' home . . .
He would forget
The quieted bunch, his dimming cigarette
Stuck into a splintered edge of the guitar.
Sorrow deep hidden in his voice, a far
And soft light in his strange brown eyes;
Alone with his masterchords, his memories . . .
   Lawd, I wanna be one in nummer
   When de saints go ma'chin' home.

Deep the bass would rumble while the treble scattered high
For all the world like heavy feet a trompin' toward the sky.
With shrill-voiced women getting 'happy'
All to celestial tunes.
The chap's few speeches helped me understand
The reason why he gazed so fixedly
Upon the burnished strings.
For he would see
A gorgeous procession to 'de Beulah Land'
Of Saints—his friends—*'a climbin' fo' deir wings.'*
Oh, when de saints go ma'chin' home

Lawd, I wanna be one o' dat nummer
When de saints goa ma'chin' home . . .

II

There'd be—so ran his dream—
"Old Deacon Zachary
With de asthmy in his chest
A puffin' an' a wheezin'
Up de golden stair
Wid de badges of his lodges
Strung acrost his heavin' breast
An' de hoggrease jest shinin'
In his coal-black hair . . .
An' old Sis Joe
In huh big straw hat
An' huh wrapper flappin'
Flappin' in de heavenly win'
An' huh thin-soled easy walkers
Goin' pitty pitty pat
Lawd, she'd have to ease her corns
When she got in!"
Oh, when de saints go ma'chin' home.
"Ole Elder Peter Johnson
Wid his corncob jes a puffin'
And de smoke a rollin'
Like storm clouds out behin'
Crossin' de cloud mountains
Widout slowin' up fo' nuffin'
Steamin' up de grade
Lak Wes' bound No. 9.
An' de little brown-skinned chillen
Wid deir skinny legs a dancin'
Jes' a kickin' up ridic'lous
To de heavenly band
Lookin' at de Great Drum Major
On a white hoss jes' a prancin'
Wid a gold and silver drumstick
A waggin' in his han'.
Oh when de sun refuse to shine
Oh when de mo-on goes down
In Blood . . .
"Old Maumee Annie
Wid huh washin' done
An' huh las' piece o'laundry
In de renchin' tub,
A wavin' sof pink han's

To de much obligin' sun
An' her feet a moverin' now
To a swif' rub-a-dub;
And old Grampa Eli
Wid his wrinkled old haid
A puzzlin' over summut
He ain' understood
Intendin' to ask Peter
Pervidin' he hain't skyaid
Jes' what mought be de meanin'
Of de moon in blood? . . .
When de saints go ma'chin' home . . . "

III

Whuffolks, he dreams, will have to stay outside
Being so onery. But what is he to do
With that red brakeman who once let him ride
An empty, going home? Or with that kindfaced man
Who paid his songs with board and drink and bed?
Or with the Yankee Cap'n who left a leg
At Vicksburg? *Mought be a place, he said*
Mought be another mansion for white saints
A smaller one than hisn . . . not so gran'
As for the rest . . . oh, let them howl and beg.
Hell would be good enough, if big enough
Widout no shade trees, lawd, widout no rain
Whuffolks sho to bring nigger out behin'
Excep'—when de saints go ma'chin' home.

IV

Sportin' Legs would not be there—nor lucky Sam
Nor Smitty, nor Hambone, nor Hardrock Gene
An' not too many guzzlin', cuttin' shines,
Nor bootleggers to keep his pockets clean.
An' Sophie wid de sof' smile on her face,
Her foolin' voice, her strappin' body, brown
Lak coffee doused wid milk—she had been good
To him, wid lovin', money, and wid food.—
But saints and heaven didn't seem to fit
Jes rite wid Sophy's beauty—nary bit—
She mought stir trouble, somehow, in dat peaceful place
Mought be some dressed up dudes in dat fair town.

V

Ise got a dear ole modder
She is in hebben I know . . .
He sees

Mammy
L'il mammy—wrinkled face
Her brown eyes, quick to tears—to joy
With such happy pride in her
Guitar plunkin' boy.
Oh, kain't I be one in nummer?
Mammy
With deep religion defeating the grief
Life piled so closely about her
Ise so glad trouble doan las' alway' . . .
And her dogged belief
That some fine day
She'd go a ma'chin'
When de saints go ma'chin' home.
He sees her ma'chin' home, ma'chin' along,
Her perky joy shining in her furrowed face,
Her weak and quavering voice singing her song—
The best chair set apart for her worn-out body
In that restful place . . .
I pray to de Lawd I'll meet her
When de saints go ma'chin' home.

VI

He'd shuffle off from us, always, at that,—
His face a brown study beneath his torn brimmed hat.
His broad shoulders slouching, his old box strung
Around his neck;—he'd go where we
Never could follow him—to Sophie probably,
Or to his dances in old Tinbridge flat.

Southern Road

Swing dat hammer—hunh—
Steady, bo';
Swing dat hammer—hunh—
Steady, bo';
Ain't no rush, bebby,
Long ways to go.

Burner tore his—hunh—
Black heart away;
Burner tore his—hunh—
Black heart away;
Got me life, bebby,
An' a day.

Gal's on Fifth Street—hunh—
Son done gone;
Gal's on Fifth Street—hunh—

Son done gone;
Wife's in de ward, bebby,
Babe's not bo'n.

My ole man died—hunh—
Cussin' me;
My ole man died—hunh—
Cussin' me;
Ole lady rocks, bebby,
Huh misery.

Doubleshackled—hunh—
Guard behin';
Doubleshackled—hunh—
Guard behin';
Ball an' chain, bebby,
On my min'.

White man tells me—hunh—
Damn yo' soul;
White man tells me—hunh—
Damn yo' soul;
Got no need, bebby,
To be tole.

Chain gang nevah—hunh—
Let me go;
Chain gang nevah—hunh—
Let me go;
Po' los' boy, bebby,
Evahmo'. . . .

Ma Rainey

I

When Ma Rainey
Comes to town,
Folks from anyplace
Miles aroun',
From Cape Girardeau,
Poplar Bluff,
Flocks in to hear
Ma do her stuff;
Comes flivverin' in,
Or ridin' mules,
Or packed in trains,
Picknickin' fools. . . .
That's what it's like,
Fo' miles on down,
To New Orleans delta

An' Mobile town,
When Ma hits
Anywheres aroun'.

II

Dey comes to hear Ma Rainey from de little river settlements,
From blackbottom cornrows and from lumber camps;
Dey stumble in de hall, jes a-laughin' an' a-cacklin',
Cheerin' lak roarin' water, lak wind in river swamps.

An' some jokers keeps deir laughs a-goin' in de crowded aisles,
An' some folks sits dere waitin' wid deir aches an' miseries,
Till Ma comes out before dem, a-smilin' gold-toofed smiles
An' Long Boy ripples minors on de black an' yellow keys.

III

O Ma Rainey,
Sing yo' song;
Now you's back
Whah you belong,
Git way inside us,
Keep us strong. . . .

O Ma Rainey,
Li'l an' low;
Sing us 'bout de hard luck
Roun' our do';
Sing us 'bout de lonesome road
We mus' go. . . .

IV

I talked to a fellow, an' the fellow say,
"She jes' catch hold of us, somekindaway.
She sang Backwater Blues one day:

'It rained fo' days an de skies was dark as night,
Trouble taken place in de lowlands at night.

'Thundered an' lightened an' the storm begin to roll
Thousan's of people ain't got no place to go.

'Den I went an' stood upon some high ol' lonesome hill,
An' looked down on the place where I used to live.'

An' den de folks, dey natchally bowed dey heads an' cried,
Bowed dey heavy heads, shet dey moufs up tight an' cried,
An' Ma lef' de stage, an' followed some de folks outside."

Dere wasn't much more de fellow say:
She jes' gits hold of us dataway.

Memphis Blues

I

Nineveh, Tyre,
Babylon,
Not much lef'
Of either one.
All dese cities
Ashes and rust,
De win' sing sperrichals
Through deir dus' . . .
Was another Memphis
Mongst de olden days,
Done been destroyed
In many ways. . . .
Dis here Memphis
It may go;
Floods may drown it;
Tornado blow;
Mississippi wash it
Down to sea—
Like de other Memphis in
History.

II

Watcha gonna do when Memphis on fire,
  Memphis on fire, Mistah Preachin' Man?
Gonna pray to Jesus and nebber tire,
  Gonna pray to Jesus, loud as I can,
    Gonna pray to my Jesus, oh, my Lawd!

Watcha gonna do when de tall flames roar,
  Tall flames roar, Mistah Lovin' Man?
Gonna love my brownskin better'n before—
  Gonna love my baby lak a do right man,
    Gonna love my brown baby, oh, my Lawd!

Watcha gonna do when Memphis falls down,
  Memphis falls down, Mistah Music Man?
Gonna plunk on dat box as long as it soun',
  Gonna plunk dat box fo' to beat de ban',
    Gonna tickle dem ivories, oh, my Lawd!

Watcha gonna do in de hurricane,
  In de hurricane, Mistah Workin' Man?
Gonna put dem buildings up again,
  Gonna put em up dis time to stan',
    Gonna push a wicked wheelbarrow, oh, my Lawd!

Watcha gonna do when Memphis near gone,
  Memphis near gone, Mistah Drinkin' Man?
Gonna grap a pint bottle of Mountain Corn,
  Gonna keep de stopper in my han',
    Gonna get a mean jag on, oh, my Lawd!

Watcha gonna do when de flood roll fas',
  Flood roll fas', Mistah Gamblin' Man?
Gonna pick up my dice fo' one las' pass—
  Gonna fade my way to de lucky lan',
    Gonna throw my las' seven—oh, my Lawd!

III

Memphis go
By Flood or Flame;
Nigger won't worry
All de same—
Memphis go
Memphis come back,
Ain' no skin
Off de nigger's back.
All dese cities
Ashes, rust. . . .
De win' sing sperrichals
Through deir dus'.

Old Lem

I talked to old Lem
and old Lem said:
  "They weigh the cotton
  They store the corn
    We only good enough
    To work the rows;
  They run the commissary
  They keep the books
    We gotta be grateful
    For being cheated;
  Whippersnapper clerks
  Call us out of our name
    We got to say mister
    To spindling boys
  They make our figgers
  Turn somersets
  We buck in the middle
    Say, "Thankyuh, sah."

They don't come by ones
They don't come by twos
But they come by tens.

"They got the judges
They got the lawyers
They got the jury-rolls
They got the law
They don't come by ones
They got the sheriffs
They got the deputies
They don't come by twos
They got the shotguns
They got the rope
We git the justice
In the end
And they come by tens.

"Their fists stay closed
Their eyes look straight
Our hands stay open
Our eyes must fall
They don't come by ones
They got the manhood
They got the courage
They don't come by twos
We got to slink around
Hangtailed hounds.
They burn us when we dogs
They burn us whem we men
They come by tens . . .

"I had a buddy
Six foot of man
Muscled up perfect
Game to the heart
They don't come by ones
Outworked and outfought
Any man or two men
They don't come by twos
He spoke out of turn
At the commissary
They gave him a day
To git out the county
He didn't take it.
He said 'Come and get me.'
They came and got him
And they came by tens.

He stayed in the county—
He lays there dead.
    They don't come by ones
    They don't come by twos
    But they come by tens."

Strong Men

THE YOUNG MEN KEEP COMING ON
THE STRONG MEN KEEP COMING ON.
SANDBURG

They dragged you from homeland,
They chained you in coffles,
They huddled you spoon-fashion in filthy hatches,
They sold you to give a few gentlemen ease.

They broke you in like oxen,
They scourged you,
They branded you,
They made your women breeders,
They swelled your numbers with bastards. . . .
They taught you the religion they disgraced.

You sang:
  Keep a-inchin' along
  Lak a po' inch worm. . . .

You sang:
  Bye and bye
  I'm gonna lay down dis heaby load. . . .

You sang:
  Walk togedder, chillen,
  Dontcha git weary. . . .
    The strong men keep a-comin' on
    The strong men git stronger.

They point with pride to the roads you built for them,
They ride in comfort over the rails you laid for them.
They put hammers in your hands
And said—Drive so much before sundown.

You sang:
  Ain't no hammah
  In dis lan',
  Strikes lak mine, bebby,
  Strikes lak mine.

They cooped you in their kitchens,
They penned you in their factories,
They gave you the jobs that they were too good for,

They tried to guarantee happiness to themselves
By shunting dirt and misery to you.

You sang:
  Me an' muh baby gonna shine, shine
  Me an' muh baby gonna shine.
    The strong men keep a-comin' on
    The strong men git stronger. . . .

They bought off some of your leaders
You stumbled, as blind men will . . .
They coaxed you, unwontedly soft-voiced. . . .
You followed a way.
Then laughed as usual.

They heard the laugh and wondered;
Uncomfortable,
Unadmitting a deeper terror. . . .
    The strong men keep a-comin' on
    Gittin' stronger. . . .

What, from the slums
Where they have hemmed you,
What, from the tiny huts
They could not keep from you—
What reaches them
Making them ill at ease, fearful?
Today they shout prohibition at you
"Thou shalt not this"
"Thou shalt not that"
"Reserved for whites only"
You laugh.

One thing they cannot prohibit—
    The strong men . . . coming on
    The strong men gittin' stronger.
    Strong men. . . .
    Stronger. . . .

FRANK MARSHALL DAVIS
(1905–1987)

Frank Marshall Davis has reemerged since 1973 as a midwestern voice extending from the New Negro of the twenties and the Reformation of the thirties to the conservative era of Ronald Reagan's presidency. His creative time spanned nearly half a century. Eventually, he may be remembered as a poet who honed cadence flatly and naturally into the written expression of African American popular speech. In fact, he, with Fenton Johnson, suggests a Chicago line of writers that leads from the achievements of Richard Wright, Gwendolyn Brooks, Margaret Walker, Margaret Danner, and Margaret Burroughs in Chicago to those of Lorraine Hansberry,

George E. Kent, Ronald Fair, Haki Madhubuti, Carolyn Rodgers, and Sterling Plump. If New York provided more limelight for celebrated artistic movements such as the New Negro Movement of the twenties and the Black Arts Movement of the sixties, Chicago perhaps facilitated even more the emergence of literary and scholarly voices across the twentieth century. Davis helped set the tone of his age.

Frank Marshall Davis was born on December 31, 1905, in Arkansas City, Kansas. After graduating from high school in 1923, he enrolled in the School of Journalism at Kansas State Agricultural College in Manhattan. Early in his studies, he chose to write a poem rather than an essay for a class assignment of personal choice and discovered the pleasure of writing free verse. Soon his efforts won him not only the instructor's approval but also the attention of the American College Quill Club, a national society of creative writers that welcomed him as a member. In 1927, Davis moved to Chicago and secured work on a succession of African American dailies, including the *Chicago Evening Bulletin,* the *Whip,* and the *Gary American.* He returned to Kansas State in the fall of 1929 and the following year was recruited by W. A. Scott to expand the semiweekly *Atlanta* to a biweekly publication. By then, Davis had won the notice of Frances Norton Manning, a white woman sophisticate and bohemian, who encouraged his move back to Chicago in 1934. Impressed by his poem on "Chicago's Congo," she introduced him to Norman Forgue, formerly a welterweight fighter and seaman, who fancied the publication of beautiful books. Forgue's firm, Black Cat Press, published *Black Man's Verse* in the summer of 1935. One of the most famous portraits in the book is "Giles Johnson, Ph.D.," about a man who is quite learned in Greek and Latin but who starves as a college graduate because "he wouldn't teach and he couldn't porter."

Davis served on the staff of Chicago's Negro Press in 1935 and became part of a developing nucleus of authors. With the urging of Richard Wright, whom he met during the founding of the National Negro Congress in 1935, he joined the Chicago chapter of the League of American Writers. After the two authors became friends, Davis often teased Wright about his communist inclinations. Davis attended most of the league's meetings and encountered many white writers, such as Nelson Algren, who lived only a block or so away on the South Side, Stuart Engstrand, and Meyer Levin. He also met Paul Romaine, a literary critic and collector, and Jack Conroy, an editor and novelist. It was Conroy who wrote so many of the valuable manuscripts of the Work Projects Administration (WPA), collected now in the Carter G. Woodson Branch of the Chicago Public Library. Davis urged Conroy, who was editor of *The New Anvil,* to publish the first short story by Frank Yerby, a young college student from Georgia, who spent summers in Chicago.

Davis and Yerby shared a mutual interest in photography. Davis would later sell Richard Wright his first camera after snapping a picture that *Time* magazine would use as backdrop for a story on *Black Boy* (1945), Wright's autobiography. Davis also read the galleys of Wright's novel *Native Son* (1940). He met Theodore Ward, who wrote the proletarian play *Big White Fog* (1940) for the Federal Writers' Project in Chicago, and joined a short-lived group of writers that included Margaret Walker and Gwendolyn Brooks, among others. During the group's meetings, Wright presented sections of the manuscript later published as *Uncle Tom's Children* (1938), and Walker read parts of a manuscript that would become *Jubilee* (1966), a fictionalized account of her great-grandmother's experiences during slavery and Reconstruction.

Davis expanded his own interpretation of race to his perception of class. In his best-known volume, *47th Street* (1948), dedicated to his second wife, he reveals "almost too painfully" a sense of injustice. During the McCarthy era, many libraries and schools in the United States banned his books, at the same time that his poems were being translated in Europe. By the time he moved to Hawaii in December 1948, he was clearly on the way to becoming an expatriate African American artist. Davis wrote a weekly column for the *Honolulu Record,* reared five children, and ran a small business selling wholesale paper.

Davis implied that the excellent and more persistent tradition of Chicago challenged the traditional renown of Harlem; he exposed the fact that the leftist black poet suffered political harassment that dirtied the name of democracy; and he demonstrated that an African American voice of midwestern poetry fused the modern imagism of painted words, the personal story of a decadent romanticism, and the jazz aesthetics of folk culture:

> I liked the tough, often brutal, image of Chicago projected by Sandburg and felt this was my city. I never liked Kansas when I was growing up—too many restrictions. Kansas City was better. But Chicago in the late 1920s and early 1930s was a complete challenge. It was big and the home of the Chicago Defender, at that time the nation's largest Negro newspaper; it was then the jazz capital of the nation. I wanted to paint it in verse. At this time Harlem had plenty of Black writers. But except for Fenton Johnson and possibly two or three more, when I reached Chicago in 1927, it was as barren of Black writers as the Sahara. So I put down my roots to live in Chicago, and I think I had some success in my attempt to mirror Aframerican Chicago in particular. . . . There is no law preventing the ancient muse from blowing a saxophone.

Davis thought that Chicago was "rugged, possibly brutal" and that New York lacked the "raw strength" of the Midwest. He wanted the freedom to explore an African American voice quite different from the one in the "Effete East." His Chicago, the "jazz capital of the nation," boasting Louis Armstrong and King Oliver's band, suggested bloodlines running down to the New Orleans roots of African American culture.

While a member of the Associated Negro Press, Davis met with Zora Neale Hurston and Claude McKay and later became friends with Langston Hughes. Acquainted with James Weldon Johnson during the years 1931–1934, he also encountered Sterling Brown, whose folk poetry he admired. Davis counted himself among the most successful advocates on behalf of early publications by the novelist Chester Himes. By 1937, the year during which Davis met Alain Locke in Chicago, the Renaissance had all but ended. According to Davis,

> He [Locke] was a dapper, fastidious little man who by then had become disillusioned with the Harlem Renaissance and was a little bit cynical about some of the participants. In one letter, he [Locke] told me [Davis] that it would have blown up in everybody's faces had it not been for free gin in the big posh apartments of Park Avenue and the personal efforts of Carl Van Vechten. When I told him of the jeal-

ousies and difficulties of trying to keep together another fledgling writers' group in Chicago, he told me of how some of the Harlem writers stayed together only because it was a way of establishing new homosexual relationships.

Davis excavated the past into new metaphors infused with startling juxtaposition of the sacred and the profane:

Between the covers of books lie the bones of
yesterdays.
Today is a new dollar,
And my city is money-mad—

Elsewhere, he lapses into confessional poetry:

I would sing a song
but I have no words
I would hum a tune
but I have no melody.

success
like grains of brown sand
at the sea-shore
slips through my nerveless fingers
the world
has not time
even to laugh.

In *Phylon* (1950), Nick Aaron Ford, who became famous as a literary critic at Morgan State College (today Morgan State University), "demanded" more observance and good taste. Davis's "propaganda, though based on sound critical analysis," wrote Ford, "is so blunt and militant that it has little chance of winning sympathetic consideration." What was so conservatively true for the fifties, however, would be more flexibly true for the seventies and beyond. In a 1971 article, Helena Kloder asserts that "Davis' greatest strength lies not in his style or message, but in his creation of visual art. Davis' poetry is a force of verbal kodacolar snapshots and reels of spliced, almost always precisely edited, motion pictures." She says that she appreciates his colorfully realistic portraits of lynchings in the South and his vivid scenes of urban landscapes in the North. She praises his wide-ranging technique in regional dialects, connotative slang that distinguishes class and race, and other varied styles, characters, and scenes. She notes that his poetry invigorates the themes of love, of the frustrated African American artist, of human connections, of class struggle and conflict, and of national hypocrisy. According to Klodner, Davis's onomatopoeic lines seem to drag and achieve the caressing sounds of dreams, but he failed to "invest poetry with all of his emotion and thought" within the process of a "distilled and coherent synthesis."

He wrote free verse as a rebellion against the European tyranny of rhyme and meter, just as he considered jazz to be an emotional liberation from traditional syncopation. Davis once wrote, "Although I do not borrow from the classic blues format, I think that I have the feeling. Such poets as Langston Hughes and Sterling Brown have often used more obvious blues devices. But I feel the blues walked into my life when I first heard them and have never left me. That's why I call my autobiography *Livin' the Blues.*" Kloder concurs:

> We cannot dismiss Frank Marshall Davis' verse by concluding that it is neither pure prose nor pure poetry, and it is our loss if his work is not drawn to critics' and editors' attention. His "impurities" are a conglomeration of talents. He is acutely perceptive in his details of color and light of faces and bodies of people on the streets. He is intelligent about history and the black man's role in it, sensitive to the poor and suffering, and keenly aware of "America's most subtle hypocrises." Furthermore, he understands the essences and relationships of painting, music, and literature. He has brilliant lines in many of his poems, and several are unforgettable.

Davis never completely recognized his importance to the realignment of African American writers and literary schools. As an urban realist, he proposed "mirroring" Chicago; as a racial nationalist, he wrote with the clarifying power of the speaking dead. He restored to English verse a gothic undertone of graveyard poets such as George Crabbe and Thomas Gray of the British eighteenth century. What he wanted to reveal most was the stark reality of urban death among blacks of the modern era and the brutally midwestern courage of those who spoke. "Some critics," he remarked, "have dubbed me 'the father of modern Black poetry'." In reality, he ushered in a new Chicago Renaissance.

❖❖❖

John Edgar Tidwell ranks foremost among the professional advocates for Frank Marshall Davis since 1985. His entry for the *Dictionary of Literary Biography: Afro American Writers from the Harlem Renaissance to 1940,* ed. Trudier Harris (1987), vol. 51, is standard. Tidwell is preparing a book and presenting papers at major conferences. His interview in *Black American Literature Forum* 19 (September 1985), is the most important one since the rediscovery of Davis by Dudley Randall, "Interview with Frank Marshall Davis," *Black World* 23, No. 3 (1974), and by Stephen Henderson in *Understanding the New Black Poetry* (1973). Background information appears in Carol Ourkrop, "Diplomat Discovered in Hawaii," *Alliance: An Ethnic Newspaper at Kansas State University,* (November 1984), and in the very useful critical survey by Jean Wagner, *Black Poets of the United States* (1973). Of invaluable use for enlightenment is *Black Literature Criticism,* ed. James P. Draper (1992). Slightly more critical commentary is found in Paul Fussell, *Poetic Meter and Poetic Form* (1979), and Helena Kloder, "The Film and Canvas of Frank Marshall Davis," *CLA Journal* 15, No. 1 (1971).

Jazz Band

Play that thing, you jazz mad fools!
Boil a skyscraper with a jungle
Dish it to 'em sweet and hot—
Ahhhhhhhhh
Rip it open then sew it up, jazz band!

Thick bass notes from a moon faced drum
Saxophones moan, banjo strings hum

High thin notes from the cornet's throat
Trombone snorting, bass horn snorting
Short tan notes from the piano
And the short tan notes from the piano

Plink plank plunk a plunk
Plink plank plunk a plunk
Chopin gone screwy, Wagner with the blues
Plink plank plunk a plunk
Got a date with Satan—ain't no time to lose
Plink plank plunk a plunk
Strut it in Harlem, let Fifth Avenue shake it slow
Plink plank plunk a plunk
Ain't goin' to heaven nowhow—
crowd up there's too slow . . .
Plink plank plunk a plunk
Plink plank plunk a plunk
Plunk

Do that thing, jazz band!

Whip it to a jelly

Sock it, rock it; heat it, beat it; then fling it at 'em

Let the jazz stuff fall like hail on king and truck driver, queen and laundress, lord and laborer, banker and bum

Let it fall in London, Moscow, Paris, Hongkong, Cairo, Buenos Aires, Chicago, Sydney

Let it rub hard thighs, let it be molten fire in the veins of dancers

Make 'em shout a crazy jargon of hot hosannas to a fiddle-faced jazz god

Send Dios, Jehovah, Gott, Allah, Buddha past in a high stepping cake walk

Do that thing, jazz band!
Your music's been drinking hard liquor
Got shanghaied and it's fightin' mad
Stripped to the waist feedin' ocean liner bellies
Big burly bibulous brute
Poet hands and bone crusher shoulders—
Black sheep or white?

Hey, Hey!
Pick it, papa!
Twee twa twee twa twa
Step on it, black boy
Do re mi fa sol la ti do
Boomp boomp
Play that thing, you jazz mad fools!

Robert Whitmore

Having attained success in business
possessing three cars
one wife and two mistresses
a home and furniture
talked of by the town
and thrice ruler of the local Elks
Robert Whitmore
died of apoplexy
when a stranger from Georgia
mistook him
for a former Macon waiter.

Arthur Ridgewood, M.D.

He debated whether
as a poet
to have dreams and beans
or as a physician
have a long car and caviar.
Dividing his time between both
he died from a nervous breakdown
caused by worry
from rejection slips
and final notices from the finance company.

Giles Johnson, Ph.D.

Giles Johnson
had four college degrees
knew the whyfore of this
the wherefore of that
could orate in Latin
or cuss in Greek
and, having learned such things
he died of starvation
because he wouldn't teach
and he couldn't porter.

Fiction Writers

RICHARD WRIGHT
(1908–1960)

Richard Wright ranks among the foremost authors of fiction in the world during the nineteenth and twentieth centuries. In many ways, he was the first black novelist to narrate the experience of the urban masses and to write major fiction in the naturalistic tradition. As the figurative father for the African American novel since World War II, he foreshadowed so many others whose anger would resemble his later during the sixties. He left his imprint on the worldview and metaphors that were eventually to find variously rich completions in the fiction of Ralph Ellison, James Baldwin, and Toni Morrison. Wright represents African American alienation from the racial roots in the American South. In balancing stories about secular violence with an intuitive faith, he showed remarkable subtlety in creatively transforming the spiritual power within human suffering into moments of great epiphany. Just as he faced the social justice of the racist South and subsequently of the North, he inquired into the cosmic questions of human existence. Personally, he embodied the artistic moment of the talented individual ever challenging the folk community that produced the creative quest. He was a communal artist who only claimed to be his own man.

Wright provided an artistic plan or theory for retracing African American roots. First, blacks must define themselves as unblossomed flowers in the wasteland of the South (*Black Boy,* 1945). Second, they must reconcile their own beauty as being threatened by American violence (*Uncle Tom's Children,* 1938). Third, they must seek the power of language to articulate and liberate themselves from violence (*Native Son,* 1940: "What I killed for I am"). Fourth, they must withstand the French seduction to write not about the Black Mississippian but about the existential person who, though perhaps black, would transcend the supposedly trivial limits of racial memory (*The Outsider,* 1953). Fifth, African Americans must identify with the figures of the bullfighter, priest, and artist, who see themselves truthfully within the mirror of their own existence yet without assisting in their own psychological destruction (*Pagan Spain,* 1957; *Eight Men,* 1960). Finally, blacks must look back at their own southern American faces to reclaim a positive self-esteem (*The Long Dream,* 1958).

Richard Wright was born on September 4, 1908, on a plantation in Roxie, Mississippi, some twenty-two miles east of Natchez, to Ella Wilson Wright, a teacher, and Nathan Wright, a sharecropper. In 1911, Ella went to Natchez to live with her family while Nathan became an itinerant worker. The same year, Nathan took the family on a riverboat from Natchez to Memphis, Tennessee, and then deserted them. When Ella became ill in 1914, Richard and his younger brother, Leon, entered a Methodist orphanage. In one way or another he was shuffled back and forth. Two years later, Ella and her sons moved in late 1916 or early 1917 to Elaine, Arkansas, to live with her sister, Maggie, and Maggie's husband, Silas Hoskins.

Richard Wright entered Howe Institute in Memphis in 1916. In 1918, after Silas was murdered by whites who coveted his land, the family migrated to West Helena, Arkansas. Two years later he was back in Jackson, Mississippi, where he enrolled in a Seventh-Day Adventist school. Before long, he moved in with his Grandmother Wilson, a fanatical follower of the faith, in Jackson, Mississippi. He published his first short story, "The Voodoo of Hell's Half Acre," in 1924. The story appeared in the *Southern Register,* a black Jackson newspaper.

Wright returned to Memphis in 1925 in pursuit of opportunity and work. From 1925 to 1927, during the heyday of the New Negro Movement, he browsed through *Harper's Magazine, Atlantic Monthly,* and *American Mercury.* He especially admired

H. L. Mencken's *Book of Prefaces* (1917; 1919–1927) as he writes in his autobiography, *Black Boy:*

> Yes, this man was fighting, fighting with words. He was using words as a weapon, using them as one would use a club. Could words be weapons? Well, yes, for here they were. Then, maybe perhaps, I could use them as a weapon. No. It frightened me. I read on and what amazed me was not what he said, but how on earth anybody had the courage to say it.

When Wright moved to Chicago in 1927, the latent seeds of his mature thought had already been sown. For the next decade, the city would foster his growth as a thinker nearly as much as his nineteen years in the South had done. He worked as a postal clerk, and in his free time he studied the styles of other modern writers. By 1931, he was on relief, another victim of the Great Depression. In 1932, he began to attend meetings of the John Reed Club in Chicago. As a communist literary organization, the group intended its work to serve revolutionary ends. During that time, Wright wrote for leftist magazines such as *Left Front, International Literature, Daily Worker,* and *Anvil.* In 1933, he joined the Communist party and wrote many poems, such as "I Have Seen Black Hands," "We of the Streets," and "Red Leaves of Red Books," for *New Masses* and other political magazines. Most of these verses lack an original voice.

After the breakup of the John Reed Club in 1935, many black fiction writers gathered around Wright. In time, they would become known as the Wright School. During the Depression, Wright joined Dorothy West's editorial staff at *New Challenge* and often participated in the Chicago Federal Writers' Project. By May 1937, he had written most of *Lawd Today* (1963), a story of the social plight of a black postal clerk in the city.

Wright's rise to fame began with the publication of *Uncle Tom's Children* in 1938. In this collection, Big Boy Morrison, Bobo, and two others enjoy a forbidden swim in an idyllic countryside in the short story "Big Boy Leaves Home." When a white woman discovers the "boys" swimming naked in the creek, their deaths are imminent. Her hysterical screams make her white fiancé rush unnecessarily to her defense. After Big Boy has killed him, he must hide from the white mob during the consequent lynching and burning of his friend Bobo. Big Boy himself escapes on the night train to Chicago. Similarly, Wright presents an African American "son" who seeks to die with dignity in "Down by the Riverside" and a "fatherly" minister who persists in the struggle for racial justice in "Fire and Cloud." In these stories, Wright emphasizes the aborted potential of black boys in the American South and North. In "Long Black Song," the protagonist, Sarah, shows a female introspection in transcending the pettiness of her husband Silas and a white clock salesman, who fight over her as a sexual object.

In 1939, Wright won a Guggenheim Fellowship to complete his novel *Native Son.* With the publication of the novel in March 1940 came an abrupt break with the middle-class politeness of earlier black novels. Much of the novel's success was based on the fact that Wright wrote in the third person but narrates the story from the point of view of Bigger Thomas, a member of the underclass. The viewpoint changes constantly from the black Thomas family to the white Daltons, whose rich

daughter, Mary, dies at the hands of Bigger. Elsewhere, the voices change to those of Bessie Mears, an exploited and murdered black woman; Buckley, a white prosecutor who parlays racial tragedy into political victory as a prosecutor; Jan, a white communist supporter who once mistook Marxist theory for human life; and Max, a white liberal defense attorney who recoils in terror from the civilization he himself helped to create. Wright, in collaboration with Paul Green, finished a dramatic rendition of the story that was produced by Orson Welles in 1941. The following year, Wright won the Spingarn Medal for contributions to African American life. He was already on the road to disassociating himself from the Communist party. Despite lively support for communists earlier, he broke completely with them in 1944. "Humanity is never won," Wright says in his autobiography, *Black Boy* (1945). "It must be lived, struggled, and suffered for from one generation to another." Sales of *Black Boy* reached more than four hundred thousand copies. Glowing reviews appeared in the *New York Times, New York Herald Tribune,* and *St. Louis Post Dispatch.*

Wright traveled abroad to present speeches. With his own work favorably reviewed, he helped secure financial aid for the popular novelist Chester Himes and to arrange a grant for James Baldwin. (By the early fifties, Wright would quarrel with Baldwin over Baldwin's accusation that *Native Son* was an inferior novel of protest.) In Paris, Wright became friends with the American expatriate Gertrude Stein and many intellectuals, including Jean Paul Sartre and Simone de Beauvoir. With his first wife, Ellen, he visited Switzerland in 1946 to arrange for a German publisher to issue an edition of his autobiography. Near the end of the year in London, he met George Padmore, "Father of African Liberation," who helped acquaint him with African leaders.

Wright joined other board members of *Les Temps Modernes,* a contemporary journal, wrote articles in English for *Presence Africaine,* the premier intellectual journal of the black world, and with Albert Camus, Sartre, and André Gide, he served on the magazine's board of patrons. He wrote articles in French for magazines such as *France Observateur* and in English for *Encounter, Twice a Year,* and *Ebony.* The quantity and quality of his literary production declined during his expatriate years, although he sought to articulate the politics behind his images. His completion, in London, of *The Outsider* in 1953 showed his attraction to French existentialism. Possibly the first novel of the kind by an American, the story presents Cross Damon, a paradoxical Christian man who presumes the self-righteousness of God.

Disaffected with communism, Wright retained his leftist sympathies for the rest of his life. Despite his intellectual flirtation with Sartre and Beauvoir, his subconscious commitment to the African American folk survived. Some younger black writers at the time, such as the emerging playwright Lorraine Hansberry, saw him as an exile from his own race. More likely, he was trying to rediscover it in his own grappling way. A few months after the completion of a draft for *Savage Holiday* in 1953, he journeyed by way of the Canary Islands through the undeveloped territory of the British West African colony of the Gold Coast (now part of Ghana). In *Black Power: A Record of Reactions in a Land of Pathos* (1954), he recorded his experiences on that journey. By July 1957, he had nearly completed the novel then called "The Double Hearter" or "American Shadow." *The Long Dream,* a title suggested by Edward Aswell, his editor at Harper and Row, appeared in mid-October 1958. As the first and only published work in a planned trilogy, the story re-creates the southern

world of *Black Boy* (1945). After a fifteen-year layoff as a prodigal son, Wright had written his final inquiry into the American South, his personal heart of darkness. Following his death in 1960, "The Man Who Lived Underground," written in 1944 and included in the collection *Eight Men* in 1960, became a celebrated work ranking with Feodor Dostoyevsky's *Notes from the Underground* (1864) and Victor Hugo's *Les Misérables* in profound sensitivity for the poor.

Often Wright's most undiscerned gift is his sustained power of metaphor or symbolic image. He accomplished a remarkable command of racial history in the United States, seeing the world as a fire consuming its greatest talents, enshrouded in clouds of doubt and fear. Even in the Great Depression of the thirties, Wright envisioned a better day to come for American blacks. Neither naturalism nor existentialism ever claimed him completely. He wrote about paradox and contradiction, proposing a pattern in *Black Boy* in which the hungry artist emerges from shadow into light:

> I was taking a part of the south to transplant in alien soil, to see if it could grow differently, if it could drink of new and cool rains, bend in strange winds, respond to the warmth of other suns, and, perhaps, to bloom. . . . I would know that the south too could overcome its fear, its hate, its cowardice, its heritage of guilt and blood, its burden of anxiety and compulsive cruelty.

Without a doubt, Richard Wright helped set the tone for African American aesthetics in the twentieth century.

❖❖❖

Despite a dizzying amount of scholarship on Wright annually, far more good work should analyze the literary technique of his social vision. Michel Fabre's *Unfinished Quest of Richard Wright* (1973) is the definitive biography that displaced Constance Webb's *Richard Wright: A Biography* (1970). Few works could ever equal Margaret Walker's *Daemonic Genius* (1988) for familiarity with Wright's personal life and times or John A. William's *The Most Native of Sons* (1970) for speculation about the Federal Bureau of Investigation's harassment of Wright. Just as Kenneth's Kinnamon's *Emergence of Richard Wright* (1972) provides a solid overview of social themes, Joyce Ann Joyce's *Richard Wright's Art of Tragedy* (1986) details the writer's use of fundamental conventions. Besides Kinnamon, Professors Maryemma Graham, Donald B. Gibson, and Jerry W. Ward, Jr., have proved excellent scholars in the development of the Richard Wright Society. Many articles by them are available.

Long Black Song

I

Go t sleep, baby
Papas gone t town
Go t sleep, baby
The suns goin down
Go t sleep, baby
Yo candys in the sack
Go t sleep, baby
Papas comin back . . .

Over and over she crooned, and at each lull of her voice she rocked the wooden cradle with a bare black foot. But the baby squalled louder, its wail drowning out the song. She stopped and stood over the cradle, wondering what was bothering it, if its stomach hurt. She felt the diaper; it was dry. She lifted it up and patted its back. Still it cried, longer and louder. She put it back into the cradle and dangled a string of red beads before its eyes. The little black fingers clawed them away. She bent over, frowning, murmuring: "Whuts the mattah, chile? Yuh wan some watah?" She held a dripping gourd to the black lips, but the baby turned its head and kicked its legs. She stood a moment, perplexed. Whuts wrong wid that chile? She ain never carried on like this this tima day. She picked it up and went to the open door. "See the sun, baby?" she asked, pointing to a big ball of red dying between the branches of trees. The baby pulled back and strained its round black arms and legs against her stomach and shoulders. She knew it was tired; she could tell by the halting way it opened its mouth to draw in air. She sat on a wooden stool, unbuttoned the front of her dress, brought the baby closer and offered it a black teat.

"Don baby wan suppah?" It pulled away and went limp, crying softly, piteously, as though it would never stop. Then it pushed its fingers against her breasts and wailed. Lawd, chile, what yuh wan? Yo ma cant help yuh less she knows whut yuh wan. Tears gushed; four white teeth flashed in red gums; the little chest heaved up and down and round black fingers stretched floorward. Lawd, chile, whuts wrong wid yuh? She stooped slowly, allowing her body to be guided by the downward tug. As soon as the little fingers touched the floor the wail quieted into a broken sniffle. She turned the baby loose and watched it crawl toward a corner. She followed and saw the little fingers reach for the tail-end of an old eight-day clock. "Yuh wan tha ol clock?" She dragged the clock into the center of the floor. The baby crawled after it, calling, "Ahh!" Then it raised its hands and beat on the top of the clock Bink! Bink! Bink! "Naw, yuhll hurt yo hans!" She held the baby and looked around. It cried and struggled. "Wait, baby!" She fetched a small stick from the top of a rickety dresser. "Here," she said, closing the little fingers about it. "Beat wid this, see?" She heard each blow landing squarely on top of the clock. Bang! Bang! Bang! And with each bang the baby smiled and said, "Ahhh!" Mabbe thall keep yuh quiet erwhile. Mabbe Ah kin git some res now. She stood in the doorway. Lawd, tha chiles a pain! She mus be teethin. Er something . . .

She wiped sweat from her forehead with the bottom of her dress and looked out over the green fields rolling up the hillsides. She sighed, fighting a feeling of loneliness. Lawd, its sho hard t pass the days wid Silas gone. Been mos a week now since he took the wagon outta here. Hope ain nothin wrong. He must be buyin a heapa stuff there in Colwatah t be stayin all this time. Yes; maybe Silas would remember and bring that five-yard piece of red calico she wanted. Oh, Lawd! Ah *hope* he don fergit it!

She saw green fields wrapped in the thickening gloam. It was as if they had left the earth, those fields, and were floating slowly skyward. The afterglow lingered, red, dying, somehow tenderly sad. And far away, in front of her, earth and sky met in a soft swoon of shadow. A cricket chirped, sharp and lonely; and it seemed she could hear it chirping long after it had stopped. Silas oughta c mon soon. Ahm tireda staying here by mahsef.

Loneliness ached in her. She swallowed, hearing Bang! Bang! Bang! Tom been gone t war mos a year now. N tha ol wars over n we ain heard nothing yit. Lawd, don let Tom be dead! She frowned into the gloam and wondered about that awful war so far away. They said it was over now. Yeah, Gawd had t stop em fo they killed everybody. She felt that merely to go so far away from home was a kind of death in itself. Just to go that far away was to be killed. Nothing good could come from men going miles across the sea to fight. N how come they wanna kill each other? How come they wanna make blood? Killing was not what men ought to do. Shucks! she thought.

She sighed, thinking of Tom, hearing Bang! Bang! Bang! She saw Tom, saw his big black smiling face; her eyes went dreamily blank, drinking in the red afterglow. Yes, God; it could have been Tom instead of Silas who was having her now. Yes; it could have been Tom she was loving. She smiled and asked herself, Lawd, Ah wondah how would it been wid Tom? Against the plush sky she saw a white bright day and a green cornfield and she saw Tom walking in his overalls and she was with Tom and he had his arm about her waist. She remembered how weak she had felt feeling his fingers sinking into the flesh of her hips. Her knees had trembled and she had had a hard time trying to stand up and not just sink right there to the ground. Yes; that was what Tom had wanted her to do. But she had held Tom up and he had held her up; they had held each other up to keep from slipping to the ground there in the green cornfield. Lawd! Her breath went and she passed her tongue over her lips. But that was not as exciting as that winter evening when the grey skies were sleeping and she and Tom were coming home from church down dark Lover's Lane. She felt the tips of her teats tingling and touching the front of her dress as she remembered how he had crushed her against him and hurt her. She had closed her eyes and was smelling the acrid scent of dry October leaves and had gone weak in his arms and had felt she could not breathe any more and had torn away and run, run home. And the sweet ache which had frightened her then was stealing back to her loins now with the silence and the cricket calls and the red afterglow and Bang! Bang! Bang! Lawd, Ah wondah how would it been wid Tom?

She stepped out on the porch and leaned against the wall of the house. Sky sang a red song. Fields whispered a green prayer. And song and prayer were dying in silence and shadow. Never in all her life had she been so much alone as she was now. Days were never so long as these days; and nights were never so empty as these nights. She jerked her head impatiently, hearing Bang! Bang! Bang! Shucks! she thought. When Tom had gone something had ebbed so slowly that at first she had not noticed it. Now she felt all of it as though the feeling had no bottom. She tried to think just how it had happened. Yes; there had been all her life the long hope of white bright days and the deep desire of dark black nights and then Tom had gone. Bang! Bang! Bang! There had been laughter and eating and singing and the long gladness of green cornfields in summer. There had been cooking and sewing and sweeping and the deep dream of sleeping grey skies in winter. Always it had been like that and she had been happy. But no more. The happiness of those days and nights, of those green cornfields and grey skies had started to go from her when Tom had gone to war. His leaving had left an empty black hole in her heart, a black hole that Silas had come in and filled. But not quite. Silas had not quite filled that hole. No; days and nights were not as they were before.

She lifted her chin, listening. She had heard something, a dull throb like she had heard that day Silas had called her outdoors to look at the airplane. Her eyes swept the sky. But there was no plane. Mabbe its behin the house? She stepped into the yard and looked upward through paling light. There were only a few big wet stars trembling in the east. Then she heard the throb again. She turned, looking up and down the road. The throb grew louder, droning; and she heard Bang! Bang! Bang! There! A car! Wondah whuts a car doin coming out here? A black car was winding over a dusty road, coming toward her. Mabbe some white mans bringing Silas home wida loada goods? But, Lawd, Ah *hope* its no trouble! The car stopped in front of the house and a white man got out. Wondah whut he wans? She looked at the car, but could not see Silas. The white man was young; he wore a straw hat and had no coat. He walked toward her with a huge black package under his arm.

"Well, howre yuh today, Aunty?"

"Ahm well. How yuh?"

"Oh, so-so. Its sure hot today, hunh?"

She brushed her hand across her forehead and sighed.

"Yeah; it is kinda warm."

"You busy?"

"Naw, Ah ain doin nothin."

"Ive got something to show you. Can I sit here, on your porch?"

"Ah reckon so. But, Mistah, Ah ain got no money."

"Haven't you sold your cotton yet?"

"Silas gone t town wid it now."

"Whens he coming back?"

"Ah don know. Ahm waitin fer im."

She saw the white man take out a handkerchief and mop his face. Bang! Bang! Bang! He turned his head and looked through the open doorway, into the front room.

"Whats all that going on in there?"

She laughed.

"Aw, thas jus Ruth."

"Whats she doing?"

"She beatin tha ol clock."

"Beating a *clock?*"

She laughed again.

"She wouldn't go t sleep so Ah give her tha ol clock t play wid."

The white man got up and went to the front door; he stood a moment looking at the black baby hammering on the clock. Bang! Bang! Bang!

"But why let her tear your clock up?"

"It ain no good."

"You could have it fixed."

"We ain got no money t be fixin' no clocks."

"Haven't you got a clock?"

"Naw."

"But how do you keep time?"

"We git erlong widout time."

"But how do you know when to get up in the morning?"

"We jus git up, thas all."

"But how do you know what time it is when you get up?"

"We git up wid the sun."

"And at night, how do you tell when its night?"

"It gits dark when the sun goes down."

"Haven't you ever had a clock?"

She laughed and turned her face toward the silent fields. "Mistah, we don need no clock."

"Well, this beats everything! I don't see how in the world anybody can live without time."

"We just don need no time, Mistah."

The white man laughed and shook his head; she laughed and looked at him. The white man was funny. Jus like lil boy. Astin how do Ah know when t git up in the mawnin! She laughed again and mused on the baby, hearing Bang! Bang! Bang! She could hear the white man breathing at her side; she felt his eyes on her face. She looked at him; she saw he was looking at her breasts. Hes jus lika lil boy. Acks like he cant understand *nothin!*

"But you need a clock," the white man insisted. "That's what Im out here for. I'm selling clocks and graphopones. The clocks are made right into the graphophones, a nice sort of combination, hunh? You can have music and time all at once. Ill show you . . ."

"Mistah, we don need no clock!"

"You dont have to buy it. It wont cost you anything just to look."

He unpacked the big black box. She saw the strands of his auburn hair glinting in the afterglow. His back bulged against his white shirt as she stooped. He pulled out a square brown graphophone. She bent forward, looking. Lawd, but its pretty! She saw the face of a clock under the horn of the graphophone. The gilt on the corners sparkled. The color in the wood glowed softly. It reminded her of the light she saw sometimes in the baby's eyes. Slowly she slid a finger over a beveled edge; she wanted to take the box into her arms and kiss it.

"Its eight o'clock," he said.

"Yeah?"

"It only costs fifty dollars. And you dont have to pay for it all at once. Just five dollars down and five dollars a month."

She smiled. The white man was just like a little boy. Jus like a chile. She saw him grinding the handle of the box.

There was a sharp, scratching noise; then she moved nervously, her body caught in the ringing coils of music.

When the trumpet of the Lord shall sound . . .

She rose on circling waves of white bright days and dark black nights.

. . . and time shall be no more . . .

Higher and higher she mounted.

And the morning breaks . . .

Earth fell far behind, forgotten.

. . . eternal, bright and fair . . .

Echo after echo sounded.

When the saved of the earth shall gather . . .

Her blood surged like the long gladness of summer.

. . . over the other shore . . .

Her blood ebbed like the deep dream of sleep in winter.

And when the roll is called up yonder . . .

She gave up, holding her breath.

I'll be there . . .

A lump filled her throat. She leaned her back against a post, trembling, feeling the rise and fall of days and nights, of summer and winter; surging, ebbing, leaping about her, beyond her, far out over the fields to where earth and sky lay folded in darkness. She wanted to lie down and sleep, or else leap up and shout. When the music stopped she felt herself coming back, being let down slowly. She sighed. It was dark now. She looked into the doorway. The baby was sleeping on the floor. Ah gotta git up n put tha chile t bed, she thought.

"Wasnt that pretty?"

"It wuz pretty, awright."

"When do you think your husbands coming back?"

"Ah don know, Mistah."

She went into the room and put the baby into the cradle. She stood again in the doorway and looked at the shadowy box that had lifted her up and carried her away. Crickets called. The dark sky had swallowed up the earth, and more stars were hanging, clustered, burning. She heard the white man sigh. His face was lost in shadow. She saw him rub his palms over his forehead. Hes just lika lil boy.

"Id like to see your husband tonight," he said. "Ive got to be in Lilydale at six o'clock in the morning and I wont be back through here soon. I got to pick up my buddy over there and we're heading North."

She smiled into the darkness. He was just like a little boy. A little boy selling clocks.

"Yuh sell them things alla time?" she asked.

"Just for the summer," he said. "I go to school in winter. If I can make enough money out of this Ill go to Chicago to school this fall . . ."

"Whut yuh gonna be?"

"*Be?* What do you mean?"

"Whut yuh goin to school fer?"

"Im studying science."

"Whuts tha?"

"Oh, er . . ." He looked at her. "Its about why things are as they are."

"Why things is as they *is?*"

"Well, its something like that."

"How come yuh wanna study tha?"

"Oh, you wouldnt understand."

She sighed.

"Naw, Ah guess Ah wouldnt."

"Well, I reckon Ill be getting along," said the white man. "Can I have a drink of water?"

"Sho. But we ain got nothing but well-watah, n yuhll have t come n git."

"Thats all right."

She slid off the porch and walked over the ground with bare feet. She heard the shoes of the white man behind her, falling to the earth in soft whispers. It was dark now. She led him to the well, groped her way, caught the bucket and let it down with a rope; she heard a splash and the bucket grew heavy. She drew it up, pulling against its weight, throwing one hand over the other, feeling the cool wet of the rope on her palms.

"Ah don git watah outa here much," she said, a little out of breath. "Silas gits the watah mos of the time. This buckets too heavy fer me."

"Oh, wait! Ill help!"

His shoulder touched hers. In the darkness she felt his warm hands fumbling for the rope.

"Where is it?"

"Here."

She extended the rope through the darkness. His fingers touched her breasts.

"Oh!"

She said it in spite of herself. He would think she was thinking about that. And he was a white man. She was sorry she had said that.

"Wheres the gourd?" he asked. "Gee, its dark!"

She stepped back and tried to see him.

"Here."

"I cant see!" he said, laughing.

Again she felt his fingers on the tips of her breasts. She backed away, saying nothing this time. She thrust the gourd out from her. Warm fingers met her cold hands. He had the gourd. She heard him drink; it was the faint, soft music of water going down a dry throat, the music of water in a silent night. He sighed and drank again.

"I was thirsty," he said. "I hadnt had any water since noon."

She knew he was standing in front of her; she could not see him, but she felt him. She heard the gourd rest against the wall of the well. She turned, then felt his hands full on her breasts. She struggled back.

"Naw, Mistah!"

"Im not going to hurt you!"

White arms were about her, tightly. She was still. But hes a *white* man. A *white* man. She felt his breath coming hot on her neck and where his hands held her breasts the flesh seemed to knot. She was rigid, poised; she swayed backward, then forward. She caught his shoulders and pushed.

"Naw, naw . . . Mistah, Ah cant do that!"

She jerked away. He caught her hand.

"Please . . ."

"Lemme go!"

She tried to pull her hand out of his and felt his fingers tighten. She pulled harder and for a moment they were balanced, one against the other. Then he was at her side again, his arms about her.

"I wont hurt you! I wont hurt you . . ."

She leaned backward and tried to dodge his face. Her breasts were full against him; she gasped, feeling the full length of his body. She held her head far to one side; she knew he was seeking her mouth. His hands were on her breasts again. A wave of warm blood swept into her stomach and loins. She felt his lips touching her throat and where he kissed it burned.

"Naw, naw . . ."

Her eyes were full of the wet stars and they blurred, silver and blue. Her knees were loose and she heard her own breathing; she was trying to keep from falling. But hes a *white* man! A *white* man! Naw! Naw! And still she would not let him have her lips; she kept her face away. Her breasts hurt where they were crushed against him and each time she caught her breath she held it and while she held it it seemed that if she would let it go it would kill her. Her knees were pressed hard against his and she clutched the upper parts of his arms, trying to hold on. Her loins ached. She felt her body sliding.

"Gawd . . ."

He helped her up. She could not see the stars now; her eyes were full of the feeling that surged over her body each time she caught her breath. He held her close, breathing into her ear; she straightened, rigidly, feeling that she had to straighten or die. And then her lips felt his and she held her breath and dreaded ever to breathe again for fear of the feeling that would sweep down over her limbs. She held tightly, hearing a mountain tide of blood beating against her throat and temples. Then she gripped him, tore her face away, emptied her lungs in one long despairing gasp and went limp. She felt his hand; she was still, taut, feeling his hand, then his fingers. The muscles in her legs flexed and she bit her lips and pushed her toes deep into the wet dust by the side of the well and tried to wait and tried to wait until she could wait no longer. She whirled away from him and a streak of silver and blue swept across her blood. The wet ground cooled her palms and knee-caps. She stumbled up and ran, blindly, her toes flicking warm, dry dust. Her numbed fingers grabbed at a rusty nail in the post at the porch and she pushed ahead of hands that held her breasts. Her fingers found the door-facing; she moved into the darkened room, her hands before her. She touched the cradle and turned till her knees hit the bed. She went over, face down, her fingers trembling in the crumpled folds of his shirt. She moved and moved again and again, trying to keep ahead of the warm flood of blood that sought to catch her. A liquid metal covered her and she rode on the curve of white bright days and dark black nights and the surge of the long gladness of summer and the ebb of the deep dream of sleep in winter till a high red wave of hotness drowned her in a deluge of silver and blue and boiled her blood and blistered her flesh *bangbangbang* . . .

II

"Yuh bettah go," she said.

She felt him standing by the side of the bed, in the dark. She heard him clear his throat. His belt-buckle tinkled.

"Im leaving that clock and graphophone," he said.

She said nothing. In her mind she saw the box glowing softly, like the light in the baby's eyes. She stretched out her legs and relaxed.

"You can have it for forty instead of fifty. Ill be by early in the morning to see if your husbands in."

She said nothing. She felt the hot skin of her body growing steadily cooler.

"Do you think hell pay ten on it? Hell only owe thirty then."

She pushed her toes deep into the quilt, feeling a night wind blowing through the door. Her palms rested lightly on top of her breasts.

"Do you think hell pay ten on it?"

"Hunh?"

"Hell pay ten, wont he?"

"Ah don know," she whispered.

She heard his shoe hit against a wall; footsteps echoed on the wooden porch. She started nervously when she heard the roar of his car; she followed the throb of the motor till she heard it when she could hear it no more, followed it till she heard it roaring faintly in her ears in the dark and silent room. Her hands moved on her breasts and she was conscious of herself, all over; she felt the weight of her body resting heavily on shucks. She felt the presence of fields lying out there covered with night. She turned over slowly and lay on her stomach, her hands tucked under her. From somewhere came a creaking noise. She sat upright, feeling fear. The wind sighed. Crickets called. She lay down again, hearing shucks rustle. Her eyes looked straight up in the darkness and her blood sogged. She had lain a long time, full of a vast peace, when a far away tinkle made her feel the bed again. The tinkle came through the night; she listened, knowing that soon she would hear the rattle of Silas' wagon. Even then she tried to fight off the sound of Silas' coming, even then she wanted to feel the peace of night filling her again; but the tinkle grew louder and she heard the jangle of a wagon and the quick trot of horses. Thas Silas! She gave up and waited. She heard horses neighing. Out of the window bare feet whispered in the dust, then crossed the porch, echoing in soft booms. She closed her eyes and saw Silas come into the room in his dirty overalls as she had seen him come in a thousand times before.

"Yuh sleep, Sarah?"

She did not answer. Feet walked across the floor and a match scratched. She opened her eyes and saw Silas standing over her with a lighted lamp. His hat was pushed far back on his head and he was laughing.

"Ah reckon yuh thought Ah waznt never comin back, hunh? Cant yuh wake up? See, Ah got that red cloth yuh wanted . . ." He laughed again and threw the red cloth on the mantel.

"Yuh hungry?" she asked.

"Naw, Ah kin make out till mawnin." Shucks rustled as he sat on the edge of the bed. "Ah got two hundred n fifty fer mah cotton."

"Two hundred n fifty?"

"Nothin different! N guess whut Ah done?"

"Whut?"

"Ah bought ten mo acres o lan. Got em from ol man Burgess. Paid im a hundred n fifty dollahs down. Ahll pay the rest next year ef things go erlong awright. Ahma have t git a man t hep me nex spring . . ."

"Yuh mean hire somebody?"

"Sho, hire somebody! Whut yuh think? Ain tha the way the white folks do? Ef yuhs gonna git anywheres yuhs gotta do just like they do." He paused. "Whut yuh been doin since Ah been gone?"

"Nothin. Cookin, cleanin, n . . ."

"How Ruth?"

"She awright." She lifted her head. "Silas, yuh git any lettahs?"

"Naw. But Ah heard Tom wuz in town."

"In *town?*"

She sat straight up.

"Yeah, thus whut the folks wuz sayin at the sto."

"Back from the war?"

"Ah ast erroun t see ef Ah could fin im. But Ah couldnt."

"Lawd, Ah wish hed c mon home."

"Them white folks shoe glad the wars over. But things wuz kinda bad there in town. Everywhere Ah looked wuznt nothin but black n white soljers. N them white folks beat up a black soljer yestiddy. He was jus in from France. Wuz still wearin his soljers suit. They claimed he sassed a white woman . . ."

"Who wuz he?"

"Ah don know. Never saw im befo."

"Yuh see An Peel?"

"Naw."

"Silas!" she said reprovingly.

"Aw, Sarah, Ah jus couldnt git out there."

"Whut else yuh bring sides the cloth?"

"Ah got yuh some high-top shoes." He turned and looked at her in the dim light of the lamp. "Woman, ain yuh glad Ah bought yuh some shoes n cloth?" He laughed and lifted his feet to the bed. "Lawd, Sarah, yuhs sho sleepy, ain yuh?"

"Bettah put tha lamp out, Silas . . ."

"Aw . . ." He swung out of the bed and stood still for a moment. She watched him, then turned her face to the wall.

"Whuts that by the windah?" he asked.

She saw him bending over and touching the graphophone with his fingers.

"Thasa graphophone."

"Where yuh git it from?"

"A man lef it here."

"When he bring it?"

"Today."

"But how come he t leave it?"

"He says hell be out here in the mawnin t see ef yuh wans t buy it."

He was on his knees, feeling the wood and looking at the gilt on the edges of the box. He stood up and looked at her.

"Yuh ain never said yuh wanted one of these things."

She said nothing.

"Where wuz the man from?"

"Ah don know."

"He white?"

"Yeah."

He put the lamp back on the mantel. As he lifted the globe to blow out the flame, his hand paused.

"Whos hats this?"

She raised herself and looked. A straw hat lay bottom upwards on the edge of the mantel. Silas picked it up and looked back to the bed, to Sarah.

"Ah guess its the white mans. He must a lef it . . ."

"Whut he doin *in our room?*"

"He wuz talkin t me bout that graphophone."

She watched him go to the window and stoop again to the box. He picked it up, fumbled with the price-tag and took the box to the light.

"Whut this thing cos?"

"Forty dollahs."

"But its marked fifty here."

"Oh, Ah means he said fifty . . ."

He took a step toward the bed.

"Yuh lyin t me!"

"Silas!"

He heaved the box out of the front door; there was a smashing, tinkling noise as it bounded off the front porch and hit the ground. "Whut in hell yuh lie t me fer?"

"Yuh broke the box!"

"Ahma break yo Gawddam neck ef yuh don stop lyin t me!"

"Silas, Ah ain lied t yuh!"

"Shut up, Gawddammit! Yuh did!"

He was standing by the bed with the lamp trembling in his hand. She stood on the other side, between the bed and the wall.

"How come yuh tell me that thing cos *forty* dollahs when it cos *fifty?*"

"Thas whut he tol me."

"How come he take *ten* dollars off fer yuh?"

"He ain took nothin off fer me, Silas!"

"Yuh lyin t me! N yuh lied t me bout Tom, too!"

She stood with her back to the wall, her lips parted, looking at him silently, steadily. Their eyes held for a moment. Silas looked down, as though he were about to believe her. Then he stiffened.

"Whos this?" he asked, picking up a short, yellow pencil from the crumpled quilt.

She said nothing. He started toward her.

"Yuh wan me t take mah raw-hide whip n make yuh talk?"

"Naw, naw, Silas! Yuh wrong! He wuz figgerin wid tha pencil!"

He was silent a moment, his eyes searching her face.

"Gawddam yo black soul t hell, don yuh try lyin t me! Ef yuh start layin wid white men Ahll hosswhip yuh t a incha yo life. Shos theres a Gawd in Heaven Ah will! From sunup t sundown Ah works mah guts out t pay them white trash bastards whut Ah owe em, n then Ah comes n fins they been in mah house! Ah cant go into their houses, n yuh know Gawddam well Ah cant! They don have no mercy on no black folks; wes jus like dirt under their feet! Fer ten years Ah slaves lika dog t git mah farm free, givin ever penny Ah kin t em, n then Ah comes n fins they been in mah house . . ." He was speechless with outrage. "If yuh wans t eat at mah table yuhs gonna keep them white trash bastards out, yuh hear? Tha white ape kin come n git tha damn box n Ah ain gonna pay im a cent! He had no bisness leavin it here, n yuh had no bisness lettin im! Ahma tell tha sonofabitch something when he comes out here in the mawnin, so hep me Gawd! Now git back in tha bed!"

She slipped beneath the quilt and lay still, her face turned to the wall. Her heart thumped slowly and heavily. She heard him walk across the floor in his bare feet. She heard the bottom of the lamp as it rested on the mantel. She stiffened when the room darkened. Feet whispered across the floor again. The shucks rustled from Silas' weight as he sat on the edge of the bed. She was still, breathing softly. Silas was mumbling. She felt sorry for him. In the darkness it seemed that she could see the hurt look on his black face. The crow of a rooster came from far away, came so faintly that it seemed she had not heard it. The bed sank and the shucks cried out in dry whispers; she knew Silas had stretched out. She heard him sigh. Then she jumped because he jumped. She could feel the tenseness of his body; she knew he was sitting bolt upright. She felt his hands fumbling jerkily under the quilt. Then the bed heaved amid a wild shout of shucks and Silas' feet hit the floor with a loud boom. She snatched herself to her elbows, straining her eyes in the dark, wondering what was wrong now. Silas was moving about, cursing under his breath.

"Don wake Ruth up!" she whispered.

"Ef yuh say one mo word t me Ahma slap yuh inter a black spasm!"

She grabbed her dress, got up and stood by the bed, the tips of her fingers touching the wall behind her. A match flared in yellow flame; Silas' face was caught in a circle of light. He was looking downward, staring intently at a white wad of cloth balled in his hand. His black cheeks were hard, set; his lips were tightly pursed. She looked closer; she saw that the white cloth was a man's handkerchief. Silas' fingers loosened; she heard the handkerchief hit the floor softly, damply. The match went out.

"Yuh little bitch!"

Her knees gave. Fear oozed from her throat to her stomach. She moved in the dark toward the door, struggling with the dress, jamming it over her head. She heard the thick skin of Silas' feet swish across the wooden planks.

"Ah got mah raw-hide whip n Ahm takin yuh t the barn!"

She ran on tiptoe to the porch and paused, thinking of the baby. She shrank as something whined through the air. A red streak of pain cut across the small of her back and burned its way into her body, deeply.

"Silas!" she screamed.

She grabbed for the post and fell in dust. She screamed again and crawled out of reach.

"Git t the barn, Gawddammit!"

She scrambled up and ran through the dark, hearing the baby cry. Behind her leather thongs hummed and feet whispered swiftly over the dusty ground.

"C mere, yuh bitch! C mere, Ah say!"

She ran to the road and stopped. She wanted to go back and get the baby, but she dared not. Not as long as Silas had that whip. She stiffened, feeling that he was near.

"Yuh jus as well c mon back n git yo beatin!"

She ran again, slowing now and then to listen. If she only knew where he was she would slip back into the house and get the baby and walk all the way to Aunt Peel's.

"Yuh ain comin back in mah house till Ah beat yuh!"

She was sorry for the anger she knew he had out there in the field. She had a bewildering impulse to go to him and ask him not to be angry; she wanted to tell him that there was nothing to be angry about; that what she had done did not matter; that she was sorry; that after all she was his wife and still loved him. But there was no way she could do that now; if she went to him he would whip her as she had seen him whip a horse.

"Sarah! Sarah!"

His voice came from far away. Ahm goin git Ruth. Back through dust she sped, going on her toes, holding her breath.

"Saaaarah!"

From far off his voice floated over the fields. She ran into the house and caught the baby in her arms. Again she sped through dust on her toes. She did not stop till she was so far away that his voice sounded like a faint echo falling from the sky. She looked up; the stars were paling a little. Mus be gittin near mawnin. She walked now, letting her feet sink softly into the cool dust. The baby was sleeping; she could feel the little chest swelling against her arm. She looked up again; the sky was solid black. Its gittin near mawnin. Ahma take Ruth t An Peels. N mabee Ahll fin Tom . . . But she could not walk all that distance in the dark. Not now. Her legs were tired. For a moment a memory of surge and ebb rose in her blood; she felt her legs straining, upward. She sighed. Yes, she would go to the sloping hillside back of the garden and wait until morning. Then she would slip away. She stopped, listened. She heard a faint, rattling noise. She imagined Silas' kicking or throwing the smashed graphophone. Hes mad! Hes sho mad! Aw, Lawd! . . . She stopped stock still, squeezing the baby till it whimpered. What would happened when that white man came out in the morning? She had forgotten him. She would have to head him off and tell him. Yeah, cause Silas jus mad ernuff t kill! Lawd, hes mad ernuff t kill!

III

She circled the house widely, climbing a slope, groping her way, holding the baby high in her arms. After awhile she stopped and wondered where on the slope she was. She remembered there was an elm tree near the edge; if she could find it she would know. She groped farther, feeling with her feet. Ahm gittin los! And she did not want to fall with the baby. Ahma stop here, she thought. When morning came she would see the car of the white man from this hill and she would run down the road and tell him to go back; and then there would be no killing. Dimly she saw in her mind a picture of men killing and being killed. White men killed the black and black men killed the white. White men killed the black men because they could, and the black men killed the white men to keep from being killed. And killing was blood. Lawd, Ah wish Tom wuz here. She shuddered, sat on the ground and watched the sky for signs of morning. Mabbe Ah oughta walk on down the road? Naw . . . Her legs were tired. Again she felt her body straining. Then she saw Silas holding the white man's handkerchief. She heard it hit the floor, softly, damply. She was sorry for what she had done. Silas was as good to her as any black man could be to a black woman. Most of the black women worked in the fields as croppers. But Silas had given her her own home, and that was more than many others had done for their women. Yes, she knew how Silas felt. Always he had said he was as good as any white man. He had worked hard and saved his money and bought a farm so he could grow his own crops like white men. Silas hates white folks! Lawd, he sho hates em!

The baby whimpered. She unbuttoned her dress and nursed her in the dark. She looked toward the east. There! A tinge of grey hovered. It wont be long now. She could see ghostly outlines of trees. Soon she would see the elm, and by the elm she would sit till it was light enough to see the road.

The baby slept. Far off a rooster crowed. Sky deepened. She rose and walked slowly down a narrow, curving path and came to the elm tree. Standing on the edge of a slope, she saw a dark smudge in a sea of shifting shadows. That was her home. Wondah how come Silas didnt light the lamp? She shifted the baby from her right hip to her left, sighed, struggled against sleep. She sat on the ground again, caught the baby close and leaned against the trunk of a tree. Her eye-lids drooped and it seemed that a hard, cold hand caught hold of her right leg or was it her left leg—she did not know which—and began to drag her over a rough litter of shucks and when she strained to see who it was that was pulling her no one was in sight but far ahead was darkness and it seemed that out of the darkness some force came and pulled her like a magnet and she went sliding along over a rough bed of screeching shucks and it seemed that a wild fear made her want to scream but when she opened her mouth to scream she could not scream and she felt she was coming to a wide black hole and again she made ready to scream and then it was too late for she was already over the wide black hole falling falling falling . . .

She awakened with a start and blinked her eyes in the sunshine. She found she was clutching the baby so hard that it had begun to cry. She got to her feet, trembling from fright of the dream, remembering Silas and the white man and Silas' running her out of the house and the white man's coming. Silas was standing in the front yard; she caught her breath. Yes, she had to go and head that white man off! Naw! She could not do that, not with Silas standing there with that whip in his hand. If she tried to climb any of those slopes he would see her surely. And Silas would never forgive her for something like that. If it were anybody but a white man it would be different.

Then, while standing there on the edge of the slope looking wonderingly at Silas striking the whip against his overall-leg—and then, while standing there looking—she froze. There came from the hills a distant throb. Lawd! The baby whimpered. She loosened her arms. The throb grew louder, droning. Hes comin fas! She wanted to run to Silas and beg him not to bother the white man. But he had that whip in his hand. She should not have done what she had done last night. This was all her fault. Lawd, ef anything happens t im its mah blame . . . Her eyes watched a black car speed over the crest of a hill. She should have been out there on the road instead of sleeping here by the tree. But it was too late now. Silas was standing in the yard; she saw him turn with a nervous jerk and sit on the edge of the porch. He was holding the whip stiffly. The car came to a stop. A door swung open. A white man got out. Thas im! She saw another white man in the front seat of the car. N thats his buddy . . . The white man who had gotten out walked over the ground, going to Silas. They faced each other, the white man standing up and Silas sitting down; like two toy men they faced each other. She saw Silas point the whip to the smashed graphophone. The white man looked down and took a quick step backward. The white man's shoulders were bent and he shook his head from left to right. Then Silas got up and they faced each other again; like two dolls, a white doll and a black doll, they faced each other in the valley below. The white man pointed his finger into Silas' face. Then Silas' right arm went up; the whip flashed. The white man turned, bending, flinging his hands to shield his head. Silas' arm rose and fell, rose and fell. She saw the white man crawling in dust, trying to get out of reach. She screamed when she saw the other white man get out of the car and run to Silas. Then all three were on the ground, rolling in dust, grappling for the whip. She clutched the baby and run. Lawd! Then she stopped, her mouth hanging open. Silas had broken loose and was running toward the house. She knew he was going for his gun.

"Silas!"

Running, she stumbled and fell. The baby rolled in the dust and bawled. She grabbed it up and ran again. The white men were scrambling for their car. She reached level ground, running. Hell be killed! Then again she stopped. Silas was on the front porch, aiming a rifle. One of the white men was climbing into the car. The other was standing, waving his arms, shouting at Silas. She tried to scream, but choked; and she could not scream till she heard a shot ring out.

"Silas!"

One of the white men was on the ground. The other was in the car. Silas was aiming again. The car started, running in a cloud of dust. She fell to her knees and hugged the baby close. She heard another shot, but the car was roaring over the top of the southern hill. Fear was gone now. Down the slope she ran. Silas was standing on the porch, holding his gun and looking at the fleeing car. Then she saw him go to the white man lying in the dust and stoop over him. He caught one of the man's legs and dragged the body into the middle of the road. Then he turned and came slowly back to the house. She ran, holding the baby, and fell at his feet.

"Silas!"

IV

"Git up, Sarah!"

His voice was hard and cold. She lifted her eyes and saw blurred black feet. She wiped tears away with dusty fingers and pulled up. Something took speech from her and she stood with bowed shoulders. Silas was standing still, mute; the look on his face condemned her. It was as though he had gone far off and had stayed a long time and had come back changed even while she was standing there in the sunshine before him. She wanted to say something, to give herself. She cried.

"Git the chile up, Sarah!"

She lifted the baby and stood waiting for him to speak, to tell her something to change all this. But he said nothing. He walked toward the house. She followed. As she attempted to go in, he blocked the way. She jumped to one side as he threw the red cloth outdoors to the ground. The new shoes came next. Then Silas heaved the baby's cradle. It hit the porch and a rocker splintered; the cradle swayed for a second, then fell to the ground, lifting a cloud of brown dust against the sun. All of her clothes and the baby's clothes were thrown out.

"Silas!"

She cried, seeing blurred objects sailing through the air and hearing them hit softly in the dust.

"Git yo things n go!"

"Silas!"

"Ain no use yuh sayin *nothin* now!"

"But theyll kill yuh!"

"There ain nothin Ah kin do. N there ain nothin yuh kin do. Yuh done done too Gawddam much awready. Git yo things n go!"

"Theyll kill yuh, Silas!"

He pushed her off the porch.

"GIT YO THINGS N GO T AN PEELS!"

"Les *both* go, Silas!"

"Ahm stayin here till they come back!"

She grabbed his arm and he slapped her hand sway. She dropped to the edge of the porch and sat looking at the ground.

"Go way," she said quietly. "Go way fo they comes. Ah didnt mean no harm . . ."

"Go way fer whut?"

"Theyll *kill* yuh . . ."

"It don make no difference." He looked out over the sun-filled fields. "Fer ten years Ah slaved mah life out t git mah farm free . . ." His voice broke off. His lips moved as though a thousand words were spilling silently out of his mouth, as though he did not have breath enough to give them sound. He looked to the sky, and then back to the dust. "Now, its all gone. *Gone* . . . Ef Ah run erway, Ah ain got nothin. Ef Ah stay n fight, Ah ain got nothin. It dont make no difference which way Ah go. Gawd! Gawd, Ah wish all them white folks wuz dead! *Dead,* Ah tell yuh! Ah wish Gawd would kill em *all!*"

She watched him run a few steps and stop. His throat swelled. He lifted his hands to his face; his fingers trembled. Then he bent to the ground and cried. She touched his shoulders.

"Silas!"

He stood up. She saw he was staring at the white man's body lying in the dust in the middle of the road. She watched him walk over to it. He began to talk to no one in particular; he simply stood over the dead white man and talked out of his life, out of a deep and final sense that now it was all over and nothing could make any difference.

"The white folks ain never gimme a chance! They ain never give no black man a chance! There ain nothin in yo whole life yuh kin keep from em! They take yo lan! They take yo freedom! They take yo women! N then they take yo life!" He turned to her, screaming. "N then Ah gits stabbed in the back by mah own blood! When mah eyes is on the white folks to keep em from killin me, mah own blood trips me up!" He knelt in the dust again and sobbed; after a bit he looked to the sky, his face wet with tears. "Ahm gonna be hard like they is! So hep me, Gawd, Ah'm gonna be *hard!* When they come fer me Ahm gonna *be here!* N when they git me outta here theys gonna *know* Ahm gone! Ef Gawd lets me live Ahm gonna make em *feel* it!" He stopped and tried to get his breath. "But, Lawd, Ah don wanna be this way! I don mean nothin! Yuh die ef yuh fight! Yuh die ef yuh don fight! Either way yuh die n it don mean nothin . . ."

He was lying flat on the ground, the side of his face deep in dust. Sarah stood nursing the baby with eyes black and stony. Silas pulled up slowly and stood again on the porch.

"Git on t An Peels, Sarah!"

A dull roar came from the south. They both turned. A long streak of brown dust was weaving down the hillside.

"Silas!"

"Go on cross the fiels, Sarah!"

"We kin *both* go! Git the hosses!"

He pushed her off the porch, grabbed her hand, and led her to the rear of the house, past the well, to where a path led up a slope to the elm tree.

"Silas!"

"Yuh git on fo they ketch yuh too!"

Blind from tears, she went across the swaying fields, stumbling over blurred grass. It ain no use! She knew it was now too late to make him change his mind. The calves of her legs knotted. Suddenly her throat tightened, aching. She stopped, closed her eyes and tried to stem a flood of sorrow that drenched her. Yes, killing of white men by black men and killing of black men by white men went on in spite of the hope of white bright days and the desire of dark black nights and the long gladness of green cornfields in summer and the deep dream of sleepy grey skies in winter. And when killing started it went on, like a river flowing. Oh, she felt sorry for Silas! Silas. . . . He was following that long river of blood. Lawd, how come he wans t stay there like tha? And he did not want to die; she knew he hated dying by the way he talked of it. Yet he followed the old river of blood, knowing that it meant nothing. He followed it, cursing and whimpering. But he followed it. She stared before her at the dry, dusty grass. Somehow, men, black men and white men, land and houses, green cornfields and grey skies, gladness and dreams, were all a part of that which made life good. Yes, somehow, they were linked, like the spokes in a spinning wheel. She felt they were. She knew they were. She felt it when she breathed and knew it when she looked. But she could not say how; she could not put her finger on it and when she thought hard about it it became all mixed up, like milk spilling suddenly. Or else it knotted in her throat and chest in a hard, aching lump, like the one she felt now. She touched her face to the baby's face and cried again.

There was a loud blare of auto horns. The growing roar made her turn round. Silas was standing, seemingly unafraid, leaning against a post of the porch. The long line of cars came speeding in clouds of dust. Silas moved toward the door and went in. Sarah ran down the slope a piece, coming again to the elm tree. Her breath was slow and hard. The cars stopped in front of the house. There was a steady drone of motors and drifting clouds of dust. For a moment she could not see what was happening. Then on all sides white men with pistols and rifles swarmed over the fields. She dropped to her knees, unable to take her eyes away, unable, it seemed, to breathe. A shot rang out. A white man fell, rolling over, face downward.

"Hes gotta gun!"

"Git back!"

"Lay down!"

The white men ran back and crouched behind cars. Three more shots came from the house. She looked, her head and eyes aching. She rested the baby in her lap and shut her eyes. Her knees sank into the dust. More shots came, but it was no use looking now. She knew it all by heart. She could feel it happening even before it happened. There were men killing and being killed. Then she jerked up, being compelled to look.

"Burn the bastard out!"

"Set the sonofabitch on fire!"

"Cook the coon!"

"Smoke im out!"

She saw two white men on all fours creeping past the well. One carried a gun and the other a red tin can. When they reached the back steps the one with the tin can crept under the house and crept out again. Then both rose and ran. Shots. One fell. A yell went up. A yellow tongue of fire licked out from under the back steps.

"Burn the nigger!"

"C mon out, nigger, n git yos!"

She watched from the hill-slope; the back steps blazed. The white men fired a steady stream of bullets. Black smoke spiraled upward in the sunshine. Shots came from the house. The white men crouched out of sight, behind their cars.

"Make up your mind, nigger!"

"C mon out er burn, yuh black bastard!"

"Yuh think yuhre white now, nigger?"

The shack blazed, flanked on all sides by whirling smoke filled with flying sparks. She heard the distant hiss of flames. White men were crawling on their stomachs. Now and then they stopped, aimed, and fired into the bulging smoke. She looked with a tense numbness; she looked, waiting for Silas to scream, or run out. But the house crackled and blazed, spouting yellow plumes to the blue sky. The white men shot again, sending a hail of bullets into the furious pillars of smoke. And still she could not see Silas running out, or hear his voice calling. Then she jumped, standing. There was a loud crash; the roof caved in. A black chimney loomed amid crumbling wood. Flames roared and black smoke billowed, hiding the house. The white men stood up, no longer afraid. Again she waited for Silas, waited to see him fight his way out, waited to hear his call. Then she breathed a long, slow breath, emptying her lungs. She knew now. Silas had killed as many as he could and stayed on to burn, had stayed without a murmur. She filled her lungs with a quick gasp as the walls fell in; the house was hidden by eager plumes of red. She turned and ran with the baby in her arms, ran blindly across the fields, crying, "Naw, Gawd!"

ANN PETRY

(1908–)

From an unusual parentage of economically successful blacks in early-twentieth-century New England, Ann Petry became one of the greatest fictional artists of her time, one who would influence national and international perceptions about the African American woman's struggle to survive in both contemporary and historical contexts. Born on October 12, 1908, in Old Saybrook, Connecticut, Petry was the youngest of two daughters of Peter C. and Bertha J. Lane, who were among the very few blacks in Connecticut at the turn of the century. The legacy that the Lanes and their relatives gave Petry, as well as the restrictive surroundings in which they managed to establish successful black business ventures, became the rich fabric from which Petry drew most of her art.

"Obviously, the small New England village in which I was born provided an essentially hostile environment for a black family," Petry would later write when discussing the entrepreneurial talents of an extraordinary family of people who persisted in attaining achievements regardless of the harsh realities of racism. Petry says that she grew up in a world of books through exposure both at home and in the quaint New England community. Both her mother and father were consummate storytellers. She also grew up around black success. Her father, paternal aunt, and grandfather were pharmacists. (The men were licensed by the State of Connecticut, which refused to license a woman for the profession.) Her mother was a licensed chiropodist (podiatrist), practicing cosmetologist, and otherwise prosperous businesswoman. Her maternal uncles were world-renowned travelers who brought home stories from their many adventures as soldiers, sailors, and longshoremen. They all became successful businessmen when they finally settled down; her maternal aunts were all successful businesswomen as well. Petry's sister was one of the first blacks to graduate from Brown University at a time when black women were not allowed to live in the dormitories with white women.

After graduating from Old Saybrook High School in 1929, Petry attended the Connecticut College of Pharmacy (now the School of Pharmacy at the University of Connecticut). After finishing as the only African American in her 1931 graduating class, she went to work in the family drugstores in Old Saybrook and Old Lyme. She soon met George Petry from New Iberia, Louisiana, and they were married on February 28, 1938. The couple moved to New York City, where Petry decided that because of the long hours pharmacists worked, she would become a writer instead. She sold advertising space for the weekly *Amsterdam News* from 1938 to 1941, edited women's pages, and wrote news pieces for Adam Clayton Powell's weekly, *People's Voice*, from 1941 to 1944.

Although she had begun writing fiction in her childhood, Petry did not sell her first short story until 1939, when another weekly newspaper, the *Afro-American*, paid her five dollars for "Marie of the Cabin Club." Greatly encouraged by a writer's workshop at Columbia University, she soon sold another story, "On Saturday the Siren Sounds at Noon," to the NAACP's *Crisis* in 1943. *The Crisis* carried Petry's "Olaf and His Girl Friend" and "Like a Winding Sheet" in 1945. "Like a Winding Sheet" won Petry national acclaim. The work was placed in Martha Foley's *Best American Stories of 1946.* Upon reading "On Saturday the Siren Sounds at Noon," Houghton Mifflin wrote Petry stating that if she had a novel in progress, they would like to consider her for one of their literary fellowships.

Thus, Petry began to work several hours a day on her first novel, *The Street.* In 1944, she submitted five chapters to Houghton Mifflin for the Literary Fellowship contest, and to her surprise, it won the $2,400 prize in 1945. Published in 1946, the book almost immediately sold more than a million and a half copies. In what most critics of African American literature consider to be Petry's finest work, she paints a bleak picture of an unmarried black woman who struggles to raise her child in the

Harlem ghetto. Petry draws very realistic pictures of the inevitable forces of poverty, ignorance, racism, and sexism assaulting the ambitious heroine, Lutie Johnson, until they finally quench any hope of a viable life or a possible escape. *The Street* is the only novel seemingly written in the style of American naturalism, using the techniques of realism to examine the lives of black women in lower-class urban environments. Four years after the novel's publication, Petry defended the work in a critical article, "The Novel as Social Criticism," by arguing against "art for art's sake" and by asserting that most of the world's greatest novelists have written social criticism.

The Street brought the author instant fame. After her husband was discharged from his World War II military service in 1948, the couple returned to Old Saybrook and settled down in a house built in 1790, where they hoped to maintain some level of privacy. The couple had one daughter, Elizabeth Ann Petry.

In accordance with Petry's candid admission that she used either Connecticut, New York, or other parts of New England as the backdrop for all her short stories and fictional literary contexts, the setting for Petry's second novel, *Country Place,* was her father's drugstore. Published in 1947, *Country Place* is essentially a novel about white people and white values in small-town America as they were affected by the traumatic losses of World War II. The book was honored as a selection of the distinguished British Book Club and was judged "exceedingly good" by the *Atlantic Monthly.*

Following the same setting of geographical pattern, Petry's third novel, *The Narrows,* published in 1953, portrays the failed love affair between a mixed couple—Link Williams, who is black, and Camilo Treadway, who is white. Even though this novel has sold more than a million copies, Margaret McDowell says it has not received sufficient critical attention. She believes that it is a more "intricate" work than *The Street,* delving into the complex emotional and psychological reactions to and expressions of racism. The couple do not find it possible to move beyond the pressures of time, history, and an unyielding society in their attempts to forge a common destiny.

Disturbed by the paucity of books for young black readers, Petry published her first historical novel, *Harriet Tubman: Conductor on the Underground Railroad,* in 1955. It was republished in 1971. Billed as children's literature, the book is in fact the only full-length historical work that explores the life of the nineteenth century's most influential African American female leader. Another intriguing text, *Tituba of Salem Village,* which came out in 1964, looks at the misunderstood role of the black woman in American society. It is an imaginative historical portrayal of the innocent woman whom a fearful white society made both infamous and guilty under punishment of death during the Salem witch trials. Petry's other juvenile literature includes *The Drugstore Cat* (1949) and *Legends of the Saints* (1970).

The author's only collection of short stories, *Miss Muriel and Other Stories,* came out in 1971. Her novella "Miss Muriel" makes a powerful statement about the race barrier within American society that prevents meaningful relationships between men and women. The other pieces in the collection are either vignettes taken from childhood or very effective depictions of historical events in Harlem such as the riots of 1943.

Much more critical work needs to be done both on Petry's life (there is scholarly disagreement as to whether she was born in 1908 or 1911) and on her works. It is problematic to place her in the naturalist camp with Richard Wright, as there is no direct evidence indicating that she studied either Wright or other naturalists. As with most fiction by African American writers who deal with interracial themes, few critics have commented on her psychological study of interracial romance. Similarly, Petry's work is seldom included in commentaries on fiction that depicts life in small-town New England, although her work does contain some of the most authentic portrayals in all of American literature. The author's literary offerings for children and young people have received more critical attention than any of her other works. The contemporary critical neglect of Ann Petry's fiction is a tragedy much like that of her heroine Lutie Johnson, who in *The Street* cannot escape the box in which a society, indifferent to her race and status, has placed her.

❖❖❖

Biographical studies of Petry and literary interviews to ascertain influences on her life include James W. Ivy, "Ann Petry Talks About First Novel," *The Crisis* 53 (1946); Marjorie Greene, "Ann Petry Planned to Write," *Opportunity* 24 (1946); Petry's lengthy disclosure notes in *Contemporary Authors Autobiography Series*, vol. 6; John O'Brien, *Interviews with Black Writers* (1973). Critical works that equate Petry's work with that of Richard Wright include Robert Bone, *The Negro Novel in America* (1965); Barbara Christian, *Black Women Novelists: The Making of a Tradition, 1892–1976* (1980); Arthur P. Davis, *From the Dark Tower: Afro-American Writers 1900–1960* (1974); Carl M. Hughes, *The Negro Novelist: A Discussion of the Writings of American Negro Novelists 1940–1950* (1953); Theodore Gross, "Ann Petry: The Novelist As Social Critic," in Robert A. Lee, ed., *Black Fiction: New Studies in the Afro-American Novel Since 1945* (1980); Addison Gayle, *The Way of the New World* (1975).

A few recent works attempt to look at the Petry novels for their feminist as well as racial fodder. These include Joyce Ann Joyce, "Ann Petry," In *Nethula 2* (1982); Sandra Carlton Alexander, *Dictionary of Literary Biography*, vol. 76; Margaret B. McDowell, "*The Narrows*, A Fuller View of Ann Petry," in Chester J. Fontenot, ed., *Black American Literature Forum* (1980).

Critics who have concentrated on Petry's short stories and children's literature include George R. Adams, "Riot as Ritual: Ann Petry's 'In Darkness and Confusion,'" John F. Bayliss, ed., *Negro American Literature Forum* (1972); Clara O. Jackson, *Twentieth Century Children's Writers* (1978).

The Mugar Memorial Library at Boston University houses most of Petry's papers.

Like a Winding Sheet

He had planned to get up before Mae did and surprise her by fixing breakfast. Instead he went back to sleep and she got out of bed so quietly he didn't know she wasn't there beside him until he woke up and heard the queer soft gurgle of water running out of the sink in the bathroom.

He knew he ought to get up but instead he put his arms across his forehead to shut the afternoon sunlight out of his eyes, pulled his legs up close to his body, testing them to see if the ache was still in them.

Mae had finished in the bathroom. He could tell because she never closed the door when she was in there and now the sweet smell of talcum powder was drifting down the hall and into the bedroom. Then he heard her coming down the hall.

"Hi, babe," she said affectionately.

"Hum," he grunted, and moved his arms away from his head, opened one eye.

"It's a nice morning."

"Yeah." He rolled over and the sheet twisted around him, outlining his thighs, his chest. "You mean afternoon, don't ya?"

Mae looked at the twisted sheet and giggled. "Looks like a winding sheet," she said. "A shroud—" Laughter tangled with her words and she had to pause for a moment before she could continue. "You look like a huckleberry—in a winding sheet—"

"That's no way to talk. Early in the day like this," he protested.

He looked at his arms silhouetted against the white of the sheets. They were inky black by contrast and he had to smile in spite of himself and he lay there smiling and savoring the sweet sound of Mae's giggling.

"Early?" She pointed a finger at the alarm clock on the table near the bed and giggled again. "It's almost four o'clock. And if you don't spring up out of there, you're going to be late again."

"What do you mean 'again'?"

"Twice last week. Three times the week before. And once the week before and—"

"I can't get used to sleeping in the daytime," he said fretfully. He pushed his legs out from under the covers experimentally. Some of the ache had gone out of them but they weren't really rested yet. "It's too light for good sleeping. And all that standing beats the hell out of my legs."

"After two years you oughta be used to it," Mae said.

He watched her as she fixed her hair, powdered her face, slipped into a pair of blue denim overalls. She moved quickly and yet she didn't seem to hurry.

"You look like you'd had plenty of sleep," he said lazily. He had to get up but he kept putting the moment off, not wanting to move, yet he didn't dare let his legs go completely limp because if he did he'd go back to sleep. It was getting later and later but the thought of putting his weight on his legs kept him lying there.

When he finally got up he had to hurry, and he gulped his breakfast so fast that he wondered if his stomach could possibly use food thrown at it at such a rate of speed. He was still wondering about it as he and Mae were putting their coats on in the hall.

Mae paused to look at the calendar. "It's the thirteenth," she said. Then a faint excitement in her voice, "Why, it's Friday the thirteenth." She had one arm in her coat sleeve and she held it there while she stared at the calendar. "I oughta stay home," she said. "I shouldn't go outa the house."

"Aw, don't be a fool," he said. "Today's payday. And payday is a good luck day everywhere, any way you look at it." And as she stood hesitating he said, "Aw, come on."

And he was late for work again because they spent fifteen minutes arguing before he could convince her she ought to go to work just the same. He had to talk persuasively, urging her gently, and it took time. But he couldn't bring himself to talk to her roughly or threaten to strike her like a lot of men might have done. He wasn't made that way.

So when he reached the plant he was late and he had to wait to punch the time clock because the day-shift workers were streaming out in long lines, in groups and bunches that impeded his progress.

Even now just starting his workday his legs ached. He had to force himself to struggle past the outgoing workers, punch the time clock, and get the little cart he pushed around all night, because he kept toying with the idea of going home and getting back in bed.

He pushed the cart out on the concrete floor, thinking that if this was his plant he'd make a lot of changes in it. There were too many standing-up jobs for one thing. He'd figure out some way most of 'em could be done sitting down and he'd put a lot more benches around. And this job he had—this job that forced him to walk ten hours a night, pushing this little cart, well, he'd turn it into a sitting-down job. One of those little trucks they used around railroad stations would be good for a job like this. Guys sat on a seat and the thing moved easily, taking up little room and turning in hardly any space at all, like on a dime.

He pushed the cart near the foreman. He never could remember to refer to her as the forelady even in his mind. It was funny to have a white woman for a boss in a plant like this one.

She was sore about something. He could tell by the way her face was red and her eyes were half-shut until they were slits. Probably been out late and didn't get enough sleep. He avoided looking at her and hurried a little, head down, as he passed her though he couldn't resist stealing a glance at her out of the corner of his eyes. He saw the edge of the light-colored slacks she wore and the tip end of a big tan shoe.

"Hey, Johnson!" the woman said.

The machines had started full blast. The whirr and the grinding made the building shake, made it impossible to hear conversations. The men and women at the machines talked to each other but looking at them from just a little distance away, they appeared to be simply moving their lips because you couldn't hear what they were saying. Yet the woman's voice cut across the machine sounds—harsh, angry.

He turned his head slowly. "Good evenin', Mrs. Scott," he said, and waited.

"You're late again."

"That's right. My legs were bothering me."

The woman's face grew redder, angrier looking. "Half this shift comes in late," she said. "And you're the worst one of all. You're always late. Whatsa matter with ya?"

"It's my legs," he said. "Somehow they don't ever get rested. I don't seem to get used to sleeping days. And I just can't get started."

"Excuses. You guys always got excuses," her anger grew and spread. "Every guy comes in here late always has an excuse. His wife's sick or his grandmother died or somebody in the family had to go to the hospital," she paused, drew a deep breath. "And the niggers is the worse. I don't care what's wrong with your legs. You get in here on time. I'm sick of you niggers—"

"You got the right to get mad," he interrupted softly. "You got the right to cuss me four ways to Sunday but I ain't letting nobody call me a nigger."

He stepped closer to her. His fists were doubled. His lips were drawn back in a thin narrow line. A vein in his forehead stood out swollen, thick.

And the woman backed away from him, not hurriedly but slowly—two, three steps back.

"Aw, forget it," she said. "I didn't mean nothing by it. It slipped out. It was an accident." The red of her face deepened until the small blood vessels in her cheeks were purple. "Go on and get to work," she urged. And she took three more slow backward steps.

He stood motionless for a moment and then turned away from the sight of the red lipstick on her mouth that made him remember that the foreman was a woman. And he couldn't bring himself to hit a woman. He felt a curious tingling in his fingers and he looked down at his hands. They were clenched tight, hard, ready to smash some of those small purple veins in her face.

He pushed the cart ahead of him, walking slowly. When he turned his head, she was staring in his direction, mopping her forehead with a dark blue handkerchief. Their eyes met and then they both looked away.

He didn't glance in her direction again but moved past the long work benches, carefully collecting the finished parts, going slowly and steadily up and down, back and forth the length of the building, and as he walked he forced himself to swallow his anger, get rid of it.

And he succeeded so that he was able to think about what had happened without getting upset about it. An hour went by but the tension stayed in his hands. They were clenched and knotted on the handles of the cart as though ready to aim a blow.

And he thought he should have hit her anyway, smacked her hard in the face, felt the soft flesh of her face give under the hardness of his hands. He tried to make his hands relax by offering them a description of what it would have been like to strike her because he had the queer feeling that his hands were not exactly a part of him anymore—they had developed a separate life of their own over which he had no control. So he dwelt on the pleasure his hands would have felt—both of them cracking at her, first one and then the other. If he had done that his hands would have felt good now—relaxed, rested.

And he decided that even if he'd lost his job for it, he should have let her have it and it would have been a long time, maybe the rest of her life, before she called anybody else a nigger.

The only trouble was he couldn't hit a woman. A woman couldn't hit back the same way a man did. But it would have been a deeply satisfying thing to have cracked her narrow lips wide open with just one blow, beautifully timed and with all his weight in back of it. That way he would have gotten rid of all the energy and tension his anger had created in him. He kept remembering how his heart had started pumping blood so fast he had felt it tingle even in the tips of his fingers.

With the approach of night, fatigue nibbled at him. The corners of his mouth drooped, the frown between his eyes deepened, his shoulders sagged; but his hands stayed tight and tense. As the hours dragged by he noticed that the women workers had started to snap and snarl at each other. He couldn't hear what they said because of the sound of machines but he could see the quick lip movements that sent words tumbling from the sides of their mouths. They gestured irritably with their hands and scowled as their mouths moved.

Their violent jerky motions told him that it was getting close on to quitting time but somehow he felt that the night still stretched ahead of him, composed of endless hours of steady walking on his aching legs. When the whistle finally blew he went on pushing the cart, unable to believe that it had sounded. The whirring of the machines died away to a murmur and he knew then that he'd really heard the whistle. He stood still for a moment, filled with a relief that made him sigh.

Then he moved briskly, putting the cart in the storeroom, hurrying to take his place in the line forming before the paymaster. That was another thing he'd change, he thought. He'd have the pay envelopes handed to the people right at their benches so there wouldn't be ten or fifteen minutes lost waiting for the pay. He always got home about fifteen minutes late on payday. They did it better in the plant where Mae worked, brought the money right to them at their benches.

He stuck his pay envelope in his pants' pocket and followed the line of workers heading for the subway in a slow-moving stream. He glanced up at the sky. It was a nice night, the sky looked packed full to running over with stars. And he thought if he and Mae would go right to bed when they got home from work they'd catch a few hours of darkness for sleeping. But they never did. They fooled around—cooking and eating and listening to the radio and he always stayed in a big chair in the living room and went almost but not quite to sleep and when they finally got to bed it was five or six in the morning and daylight was already seeping around the edges of the sky.

He walked slowly, putting off the moment when he would have to plunge into the crowd hurrying toward the subway. It was a long ride to Harlem and tonight the thought of it appalled him. He paused outside an all-night restaurant to kill time, so that some of the first rush of workers would be gone when he reached the subway.

The lights in the restaurant were brilliant, enticing. There was life and motion inside. And as he looked through the window he thought that everything within range of his eyes gleamed—the long imitation marble counter, the tall stools, the white porcelain-topped tables and especially the big metal coffee urn right near the window. Steam issued from its top and a gas flame flickered under it—a lively, dancing, blue flame.

A lot of the workers from his shift—men and women—were lining up near the coffee urn. He watched them walk to the porcelain-topped tables carrying steaming cups of coffee and he saw that just the smell of the coffee lessened the fatigue lines in their faces. After the first sip their faces softened, they smiled, they began to talk and laugh.

On a sudden impulse he shoved the door open and joined the line in front of the coffee urn. The line moved slowly. And as he stood there the smell of the coffee, the sound of the laughter and of the voices, helped dull the sharp ache in his legs.

He didn't pay any attention to the white girl who was serving the coffee at the urn. He kept looking at the cups in the hands of the men who had been ahead of him. Each time a man stepped out of the line with one of the thick white cups the fragrant steam got in his nostrils. He saw that they walked carefully so as not to spill a single drop. There was a froth of bubbles at the top of each cup and he thought about how he would let the bubbles break against his lips before he actually took a big deep swallow.

Then it was his turn. "A cup of coffee," he said, just as he had heard the others say.

The white girl looked past him, put her hands up to her head and gently lifted her hair away from the back of her neck, tossing her head back a little. "No more coffee for a while," she said.

He wasn't certain he'd heard her correctly and he said, "What?" blankly.

"No more coffee for a while," she repeated.

There was silence behind him and then uneasy movement. He thought someone would say something, ask why or protest, but there was only silence and then a faint shuffling sound as though the men standing behind him had simultaneously shifted their weight from one foot to the other.

He looked at the girl without saying anything. He felt his hands begin to tingle and the tingling went all the way down to his finger tips so that he glanced down at them. They were clenched tight, hard, into fists. Then he looked at the girl again. What he wanted to do was hit her so hard that the scarlet lipstick on her mouth would smear and spread over her nose, her chin, out toward her cheeks, so hard that she would never toss her head again and refuse a man a cup of coffee because he was black.

He estimated the distance across the counter and reached forward, balancing his weight on the balls of his feet, ready to let the blow go. And then his hands fell back down to his sides because he forced himself to lower them, to unclench them and make them dangle loose. The effort took his breath away because his hands fought against him. But he couldn't hit her. He couldn't even now bring himself to hit a woman, not even this one, who had refused him a cup of coffee with a toss of her head. He kept seeing the gesture with which she had lifted the length of her blond hair from the back of her neck as expressive of her contempt for him.

When he went out the door he didn't look back. If he had he would have seen the flickering blue flame under the shiny coffee urn being extinguished. The line of men who had stood behind him lingered a moment to watch the people drinking coffee at the tables and then they left just as he had without having had the coffee they wanted so badly. The girl behind the counter poured water in the urn and swabbed it out and as she waited for the water to run out, she lifted her hair gently from the back of her neck and tossed her head before she began making a fresh lot of coffee.

But he had walked away without a backward look, his head down, his hands in his pockets, raging at himself and whatever it was inside of him that had forced him to stand quiet and still when he wanted to strike out.

The subway was crowded and he had to stand. He tried grasping an overhead strap and his hands were too tense to grip it. So he moved near the train door and stood there swaying back and forth with the rocking of the train. The roar of the train beat inside his head, making it ache and throb, and the pain in his legs clawed up into his groin so that he seemed to be bursting with pain and he told himself that it was due to all that anger-born energy that had piled up in him and not been used and so it had spread through him like a poison—from his feet and legs all the way up to his head.

Mae was in the house before he was. He knew she was home before he put the key in the door of the apartment. The radio was going. She had it tuned up loud and she was singing along with it.

"Hello, babe," she called out, as soon as he opened the door.

He tried to say 'hello' and it came out half grunt and half sigh.

"You sure sound cheerful," she said.

She was in the bedroom and he went and leaned against the doorjamb. The denim overalls she wore to work were carefully draped over the back of a chair by the bed. She was standing in front of the dresser, tying the sash of a yellow housecoat around her waist and chewing gum vigorously as she admired her reflection in the mirror over the dresser.

"Whatsa matter?" she said. "You get bawled out by the boss or somep'n?"

"Just tired," he said slowly. "For God's sake, do you have to crack that gum like that?"

"You don't have to lissen to me," she said complacently. She patted a curl in place near the side of her head and then lifted her hair away from the back of her neck, ducking her head forward and then back.

He winced away from the gesture. "What you got to be always fooling with your hair for?" he protested.

"Say, what's the matter with you anyway?" She turned away from the mirror to face him, put her hands on her hips. "You ain't been in the house two minutes and you're picking on me."

He didn't answer her because her eyes were angry and he didn't want to quarrel with her. They'd been married too long and got along too well and so he walked all the way into the room and sat down in the chair by the bed and stretched his legs out in front of him, putting his weight on the heels of his shoes, learning way back in the chair, not saying anything.

"Lissen," she said sharply. "I've got to wear those overalls again tomorrow. You're going to get them all wrinkled up leaning against them like that."

He didn't move. He was too tired and his legs were throbbing now that he had sat down. Besides the overalls were already wrinkled and dirty, he thought. They couldn't help but be for she'd worn them all week. He leaned farther back in the chair.

"Come on, get up," she ordered.

"Oh, what the hell," he said wearily, and got up from the chair. "I'd just as soon live in a subway. There'd be just as much place to sit down."

He saw that her sense of humor was struggling with her anger. But her sense of humor won because she giggled.

"Aw, come on and eat," she said. There was a coaxing note in her voice. "You're nothing but an old hungry nigger trying to act tough and—" she paused to giggle and then continued, "You—"

He had always found her giggling pleasant and deliberately said things that might amuse her and then waited, listening for the delicate sound to emerge from her throat. This time he didn't even hear the giggle. He didn't let her finish what she was saying. She was standing close to him and that funny tingling started in his finger tips, went fast up his arms and sent his fist shooting straight for her face.

There was the smacking sound of soft flesh being struck by a hard object and it wasn't until she screamed that he realized he had hit her in the mouth—so hard that the dark red lipstick had blurred and spread over her full lips, reaching up toward the tip of her nose, down toward her chin, out toward her cheeks.

The knowledge that he had struck her seeped through him slowly and he was appalled but he couldn't drag his hands away from her face. He kept striking her and he thought with horror that something inside him was holding him, binding him to this act, wrapping and twisting about him so that he had to continue it. He had lost all control over his hands. And he groped for a phrase, a word, something to describe what this thing was like that was happening to him and he thought it was like being enmeshed in a winding sheet—that was it—like a winding sheet. And even as the thought formed in his mind, his hands reached for her face again and yet again.

Miss Muriel

Almost every day, Ruth Davis and I walk home from school together. We walk very slowly because we like to talk to each other and we don't get much chance in school or after school either. We are very much alike. We are both twelve years old and we are freshmen in high school and we never study—well, not very much, because we learn faster than the rest of the class. We laugh about the same things and we are curious about the same things. We even wear our hair in the same style—thick braids halfway down our backs. We are not alike in one respect. She is white and I am black.

Yesterday when we reached the building that houses my father's drugstore, we sat down on the front steps—long wooden steps that go all the way across the front of the building. Ruth said, "I wish I lived here," and patted the steps though they are very splintery.

Aunt Sophronia must have heard our voices, because she came to the door and said, "I left my shoes at the shoemaker's this morning. Please go and get them for me," and she handed me a little cardboard ticket with a number on it.

"You want to come with me, Ruth?"

"I've got to go home. I'm sure my aunt will have things for me to do. Just like your aunt." She smiled at Aunt Sophronia.

I walked partway home with Ruth and then turned back and went up Petticoat Lane toward the shoemaker's shop. Mr. Bemish, the shoemaker, is a little white man with gray hair. He has a glass eye. This eye is not the same color as his own eye. It is a deeper gray. If I stand too close to him, I get a squeamish feeling because one eye moves in its socket and the other eye does not.

Mr. Bemish and I are friends. I am always taking shoes to his shop to be repaired. We do not own a horse and buggy and so we walk a great deal. In fact, there is a family rule that we must walk any distance under three miles. As a result, our shoes are in constant need of repair, the soles and heels have to be replaced, and we always seem to be in need of shoelaces. Quite often I snag the uppers on the bull briars in the woods and then the tears have to be stitched.

When I went to get Aunt Sophronia's shoes, Mr. Bemish was sitting near the window. It is a big window and he has a very nice view of the street. He had on his leather apron and his eyeglasses. His glasses are small and they have steel rims. He was sewing a shoe and he had a long length of waxed linen thread in his needle. He waxes the thread himself.

I handed him the ticket and he got up from his workbench to get the shoes. I saw that he had separated them from the other shoes. These are Aunt Sophronia's store shoes. They had been polished so that they shone like patent leather. They lay alone, near the front of the table where he keeps the shoes he has repaired. He leaned toward me and I moved away from him. I did not like being so close to his glass eye.

"The lady who brought these shoes in. Who is she?"

I looked at him and raised one eyebrow. It has taken me two months of constant practice in front of a mirror to master the art of lifting one eyebrow.

Mr. Bemish said, "What's the matter with you? Didn't you hear what I said? Who was that lady who brought these shoes in?"

I moved further away from him. He didn't know it but I was imitating Dottle Smith, my favorite person in all the world. Dottle tells the most wonderful stories and he can act and recite poetry. He visits our family every summer. Anyway, I bowed to Mr. Bemish and I bowed to an imaginary group of people seated somewhere on my right and I said, "Gentlemen, be seated. Mr. Bones, who was that lady I saw you with last night?" I lowered the pitch of my voice and said, "That wasn't no lady. That was my *wife*."

"Girlie—"

"Why do you keep calling me girlie? I have a name."

"I cannot remember people's names. I'm too old. I've told you that before."

"How old are you, Mr. Bemish?"

"None of your business," he said pettishly. "Who—"

"Well, I only asked in order to decide whether to agree with you that you're old enough to be forgetful. Does the past seem more real to you than the present?"

Mr. Bemish scowled his annoyance. "The town is full of children," he said. "It's the children who bring the shoes in and come and get them after I've fixed them. They run the errands. All those children look just alike to me. I can't remember their names. I don't even try. I don't plan to clutter up my mind with a lot of children's names. I don't see the same children that often. So I call the boys boy, and I call the girls girlie. I've told you this before. What's the matter with you today?"

"It's spring and the church green is filled with robins looking for worms. Don't you sometimes wish you were a robin looking for a worm?"

He sighed. "Now tell me, who was that lady that brought these shoes in?"

"My Aunt Sophronia."

"Sophronia?" he said. "What a funny name. And she's your aunt?"

"Yes."

"Does she live with you?"

Mr. Bemish's cat mewed at the door and I let her in. She is a very handsome creature, gray with white feet, and really lovely fur. "May-a-ling, May-a-ling," I said, patting her, "where have you been?" I always have the feeling that if I wait, if I persist, she will answer me. She is a very intelligent cat and very responsive.

"Does your aunt live with you?"

"Yes."

"Has she been living with you very long?"

"About six months, I guess. She's a druggist."

"You mean she knows about medicine?"

"Yes, just like my father. They run the store together."

Mr. Bemish thrust his hands in Aunt Sophronia's shoes and held them up, studying them. Then he made the shoes walk along the edge of the table, in a mincing kind of walk, a caricature of the way a woman walks.

"She has small feet, hasn't she?"

"No." I tried to sound like my mother when she disapproves of something.

He flushed and wrapped the shoes in newspaper, making a very neat bundle.

"Is she married?"

"Who? Aunt Sophronia? No. She's not married."

Mr. Bemish took his cookie crock off the shelf. He lives in the shop. Against one wall he has a kitchen stove, a big black iron stove with nickel fenders and a tea kettle on it, and there is a black iron sink with a pump right near the stove. He cooks his meals himself, he bakes bread, and usually there is a stew bubbling in a pot on the stove. In winter the windows of his little shop frost over, so that I cannot see in and he cannot see out. He draws his red curtains just after dusk and lights his lamps, and the windows look pink because of the frost and the red curtains and the light shining from behind them.

Sometimes he forgets to draw the curtains that separate his sleeping quarters from the rest of the shop and I can see his bed. It is a brass bed. He evidently polishes it, because it shines like gold. It has a very intricate design on the headboard and the footboard. He has a little piece of flowered carpet in front of his bed. I can see his white china pot under the bed. A dark suit and some shirts hang on hooks on the wall. There is a chest of drawers with a small mirror in a gold frame over it, and a washbowl and pitcher on a washstand. The washbowl and pitcher are white with pink rosebuds painted on them.

Mr. Bemish offered me a cookie from the big stoneware crock.

"Have a cookie, girlie."

He makes big thick molasses cookies. I ate three of them without stopping. I was hungry and did not know it. I ate the fourth cookie very slowly and I talked to Mr. Bemish as I ate it.

"I don't think my Aunt Sophronia will ever get married."

"Why not?"

"Well, I never heard of a lady druggist before and I don't know who a lady druggist would marry. Would she marry another druggist? There aren't any around here anywhere except my father and certainly she couldn't marry him. He's already married to my mother."

"She looks like a gypsy," Mr. Bemish said dreamily.

"You mean my Aunt Sophronia?"

Mr. Bemish nodded.

"She does not. She looks like my mother and my Aunt Ellen. And my father and Uncle Johno say they look like Egyptian queens."

They are not very tall and they move quickly and their skins are brown and very smooth and their eyes are big and black and they stand up very straight. They are not alike though. My mother is business-minded. She likes to buy and sell things. She is a chiropodist and a hairdresser. Life sometimes seems full of other people's hair and their toenails. She makes a hair tonic and sells it to her customers. She designs luncheon sets and banquet cloths and guest towels and sells them. Aunt Ellen and Uncle Johno provide culture. Aunt Ellen lectures at schools and colleges. She plays Bach and Beethoven on the piano and organ. She writes articles for newspapers and magazines.

I do not know very much about Aunt Sophronia. She works in the store. She fills prescriptions. She does embroidery. She reads a lot. She doesn't play the piano. She is very neat. The men who come in the store look at her out of the corner of their eyes. Even though she wears her hair skinned tight back from her forehead, and wears very plain clothes, dresses with long, tight sleeves and high necks, but still looks like—well, like an Egyptian queen. She is young but she seems very quiet and sober.

Mr. Bemish offered me another cookie. "I'll eat it on my way home to keep my strength up. Thank you very much," I said primly.

When I gave the shoes to Aunt Sophronia, I said, "Mr. Bemish thinks you look like a gypsy."

My mother frowned. "Did he tell you to repeat that?"

"No, he didn't. But I though it was an interesting statement."

"I wish you wouldn't repeat the things you hear. It just causes trouble. Now every time I look at Mr. Bemish I'll wonder about him—"

"What will you wonder—I mean—"

She said I must go and practice my music lesson and ignored my question. I wonder how old I will be before I can ask questions of an adult and receive honest answers. My family always finds something for me to do. Are they not using their power as adults to give orders in order to evade the questions?

That evening, about five o'clock, Mr. Bemish came in the store. I was sitting on the bench in the front. It is a very old bench. The customers sit there while they wait for their prescriptions to be filled. The wood is a beautiful color. It is a deep, reddish brown.

Mr. Bemish sat down beside me on the bench. His presence irritated me. He kept moving his hand up and down the arms of the bench, up and down, in a quick, nervous movement. It is as though he thought he had an awl in his hand, and he was going in and out making holes in leather and then sewing, slipping a needle in and out, as he would mend a saddle or a pair of boots.

My father looked at him over the top of his glasses and said, "Well, Bemish, what can I do for you?"

"Nothing. Nothing at all. I just stopped in to pass the time of day, to see how you all were—" His voice trailed away, softly.

He comes every evening. I find this very annoying. Quite often I have to squeeze myself onto the bench. Pritchett, the sexton of the Congregational church—stout, red-faced, smelling of whiskey—rings the bell for a service at seven o'clock and then he, too, sits in the front of the store, watching the customers as they come and go until closing time. He eyed Mr. Bemish rather doubtfully at first, but then ignored him. When the sexton and Mr. Bemish were on the bench, there was just room enough for me to squeeze in between them. I didn't especially mind the sexton, because he usually went to sleep, nodding and dozing until it was time to close the store. But Mr. Bemish doesn't sit still—and the movement of his hands is distracting.

My mother finally spoke to my father about Mr. Bemish. They were standing in the back room. "Why does Mr. Bemish sit out there in the store so much?" she asked.

"Nothin' else to do."

She shook her head. "I think he's interested in Sophronia. He keeps looking around for someone."

My father laughed out loud. "That dried-up old white man?"

The laughter of my father is a wonderful sound—if you know anything about music you know he sings tenor and you know he sings in the Italian fashion with an open throat and you begin to smile, and if he laughs long enough, you laugh too, because you can't help it.

"Bemish?" he said. And he laughed so hard that he had to lean against the doorjamb in order to keep his balance.

Every night right after supper, Mr. Bemish sits in the store rubbing the arm of the bench with that quick, jerking motion of his hand, nodding to people who come in, sometimes talking to them, but mostly just sitting.

Two weeks later I walked past his shop. He came to the door and called me. "Girlie," he said, beckoning.

"Yes, Mr. Bemish?"

"Is your aunt with the peculiar name still here—that is, in town, living with you?"

"Yes, she is, Mr. Bemish."

"Don't she ever go in the drugstore?"

"Not after five o'clock, Mr. Bemish. My father doesn't approve of ladies working at night. At night we act just like other people's families. We sit around the table in the dining room and talk, and we play checkers, and we read and we—"

"Yes, yes," he said impatiently. "But don't you aunt ever go anywhere at night?"

"I don't think so. I go to bed early."

"Do you think—" And he shook his head. "Never mind, girlie, never mind," and he sighed. "Here—I just made up a fresh batch of those big cookies you like so well."

I walked down Petticoat Lane toward the drugstore eating one of Mr. Bemish's thick molasses cookies. I wished I had taken time to tell him how cozy our downstairs parlor is in the winter. We have turkey-red curtains at the windows too, and we pull the window shades and draw the curtains, and there is a very thick rug on the floor and it is a small room, so the rug completely covers the floor. The piano is in there and an old-fashioned sofa with a carved mahogany frame and a very handsome round stove and it is warm in winter; and in the summer when the windows are open, you can look right out into the back yard and smell the flowers and feel the cool air that comes from the garden.

The next afternoon, Mr. Bemish came in the drugstore about quarter past three. It was a cold, windy afternoon. I had just come from school and there was a big mug of hot cocoa for me. Aunt Sophronia had it ready and waiting for me in the back room. I had just tasted the first spoonful; it was much too hot to gulp down, and I leaned way over and blew on it gently, and inhaled the rich, chocolatey smell of it. I heard my aunt say, "Why, Mr. Bemish, what are you doing out at this hour?"

"I thought I'd like an ice cream soda." Mr. Bemish's voice sounded breathless, lighter in weight, and the pitch was lower than normal.

I peeked out at him. He was sitting near the fountain in one of the ice cream parlor chairs. He looked very stiff and prim and neater than usual. He seemed to have flattened his hair closer to his skull. This made his head appear smaller. He was holding his head a little to one side. He looked like a bird but I cannot decide what bird—perhaps a chickadee. He drank the soda neatly and daintily. He kept looking at Aunt Sophronia.

He comes every day now, in the middle of the afternoon. He should have been in his shop busily repairing shoes or making boots, or making stews and cookies. Instead, he is in our store, and his light gray eye, the one good eye, travels busily over Aunt Sophronia. His ears seem to waggle when he hears her voice, and he has taken to giggling in a very silly fashion.

He always arrives about the same time. Sometimes I sit in one of the ice cream parlor chairs and talk to him. He smells faintly of leather, and of shoe polish, and of wax, and of dead flowers. It was quite a while before I could place that other smell—dead flowers. Each day he stays a little longer than he stayed the day before.

I have noticed that my father narrows his eyes a little when he looks at Mr. Bemish. I heard him say to my mother: "I don't like it. I don't want to tell him not to come in here. But I don't like it—an old white man in here every afternoon looking at Sophronia and licking his chops—well, I just don't like it."

Aunt Sophronia took a sudden interest in the garden. In the afternoon, after school, I help her set out plants and sow seed. Our yard is filled with flowers in the summer; and we have a vegetable garden that in some ways is as beautiful as the flowers—it is so neat and precise-looking. We keep chickens so that we can have fresh eggs. And we raise a pig and have him butchered in the fall.

When the weather is bad and we cannot work in the garden, Aunt Sophronia and I clean house. I do not like to clean house but I do like to sort out the contents of other people's bureau drawers. We started setting Aunt Sophronia's bureau in order. She showed me a picture of her graduating class from Pharmacy College. She was the only girl in a class of boys. She was black and the boys were white. I did not say anything about this difference in color and neither did she. But I did try to find out what it was like to be the only member of the female sex in a class filled with males.

"Didn't you feel funny with all those boys?"

"They were very nice boys."

"Oh, I'm sure they were. But didn't you feel funny being the only girl with so many young men?"

"No. I never let them get overly friendly and we got along very well."

I looked at the picture and then I looked at her and said, "You are beautiful."

She put the picture back in her top drawer. She keeps her treasures in there. She has a collar made of real lace, and a pair of very long white kid gloves, and a necklace made of gold nuggets from Colorado that a friend of my mother's left to Aunt Sophronia in her will. The gloves and the collar smell like our garden in August when the flowers are in full bloom and the sun is shining on them.

Sometimes I forget that Aunt Sophronia is an adult and that she belongs in the enemy camp, and I make the mistake of saying what I have been thinking.

I leaned against the bureau and looked down into the drawer, at the picture, and said, "You know, this picture reminds me of the night last summer when there was a female moth, one of those huge night moths, on the inside of the screen door, and all the male moths for miles around came and clung on the outside of the screen, making their wings flutter, and you know, they didn't make any sound but it was kind of scary. Weren't you—"

Aunt Sophronia closed the drawer with a hard push. "You get a broom and a dustpan and begin to sweep in the hall," she said.

On Saturday morning, after I finished washing the breakfast dishes and scrubbing the kitchen floor, I paid a call on Mr. Bemish. He was cleaning his house, too. He had taken down the red curtains that hung at the windows all winter, and the red curtains that hung in front of his bed, separating his sleeping quarters from the rest of his shop, and he was washing these curtains in a big tub at the side of his house. He was making a terrific splashing and the soapsuds were pale pink. He had his sleeves rolled up. His arms are very white and stringy-looking.

"Too much red for summer, girlie. I've got to get out the green summer ones."

He hung them on the line and poured the wash water out on the ground. It was pink.

"Your curtains ran, didn't they?" I looked at a little pink puddle left on the top of a stone. "If you keep washing them, they'll be pink instead of red."

His own eye, the real eye, moved away from me, and there was something secret, and rather sly, about his expression. He said, "I haven't seen your aunt in the store lately. Where is she?"

"She's been busy fixing the garden and cleaning the house. Everybody seems to be cleaning house."

"As soon as I get my green curtains put up, I'm going to ask your aunt to come have tea."

"Where would she have tea with you?"

"In my shop."

I shook my head. "Aunt Sophronia does not drink tea in people's bedrooms and you have only that one room for your shop and there's a bed in it and it would be just like—"

"I would like to have her look at some old jewelry that I have and I thought she might have tea."

"Mr. Bemish," I said, "do you like my Aunt Sophronia?"

"Now, girlie," he said, and he tittered. "Well, now, do you think your aunt likes me?"

"Not especially. Not any more than anybody else. I think you're too old for her and besides, well, you're white and I don't think she would be very much interested in an old white man, do you?"

He frowned and said, "You go home. You're a very rude girl."

"You asked me what I thought, Mr. Bemish. I don't see why you get mad when I tell you what I think. You did ask me, Mr. Bemish."

I followed him inside his shop. He settled himself near the window and started to work on a man's boot. It needed a new sole and he cut the sole out of leather. I looked out the front window. There is always enough breeze to make his sign move back and forth; it makes a sighing noise. In the winter if there's a wind, the sign seems to groan because it moves back and forth quickly. There is a high-laced shoe painted on the sign. The shoe must once have been a deep, dark red, but it has weathered to a soft rose color.

Mr. Bemish is my friend and I wanted to indicate that I am still fond of him though I disapprove of his interest in Aunt Sophronia. I searched for some topic that would indicate that I enjoy talking to him.

I said, "Why don't you have a picture of a man's boot on your sign?"

"I prefer ladies' shoes. More delicate, more graceful—" He made an airy gesture with his awl and simpered.

I went home and I told Aunt Sophronia that Mr. Bemish is going to ask her to have tea with him.

"Will you go?"

"Of course not," she said impatiently.

Aunt Sophronia did not have tea with Mr. Bemish. He sees her so rarely in the store that he finally came in search of her.

It is summer now and the Wheeling Inn is open for the season. The great houses along the waterfront are occupied by their rich owners. We are all very busy. At night after the store is closed, we sit in the back yard. On those warm June nights, the fireflies come out, and there is a kind of soft summer light, composed of moonlight and starlight. The grass is thick underfoot and the air is sweet. Almost every night my mother and my father and Aunt Sophronia and I, and sometimes Aunt Ellen and Uncle Johno, sit there in the quiet and in the sweetness and in that curious soft light.

Last night when we were sitting there, Mr. Bemish came around the side of the house. There was something tentative in the way he came toward us. I had been lying on the grass and I sat up straight, wondering what they would do and what they would say.

He sidled across the lawn. He didn't speak until he was practically upon us. My mother was sitting in the hammock under the cherry tree, rocking gently back and forth, and she didn't see him until he spoke. He said, "Good evening." He sounded as though he was asking a question.

We all looked at him. I hoped that someone would say: "What are you doing in our back yard, our private place, our especially private place? You are an intruder, go back to your waxed thread and your awl, go back to your house and your cat." Nobody said anything.

He stood there for a while, waiting, hesitant, and then he bowed and sat down, cross-legged, on the grass near Aunt Sophronia. She was sitting on one of the benches. And he sat so close to her that her skirt was resting on one of his trouser legs. I kept watching him. One of his hands reached toward her skirt and he gently fingered the fabric. Either she felt this or the motion attracted her attention, because she moved away from him, and gathered her skirt about her, and then stood up and said, "The air is making me sleepy. Good night."

The next afternoon I took a pair of my father's shoes to Mr. Bemish to have the heels fixed. My father wears high-laced black shoes. I left them on Mr. Bemish's work table.

"You can get them tomorrow."

I did not look right at him. I leaned over and patted May-a-ling. "She has such a lovely name, Mr. Bemish. It seems to me a name especially suited for a cat."

Mr. Bemish looked at me over the top of his little steel-rimmed glasses. "You've got a nice back yard," he said.

"I don't think you should have been in it."

"Why not?" he asked sharply. "Did anybody say that I shouldn't have been in it?"

"No. But the front part of the building, the part where the drugstore is, belongs to everybody. The back part of the building, and upstairs in the building, and the yard are ours. The yard is a private part of our lives. You don't belong in it. You're not a part of our family."

"But I'd like to be a part of your family."

"You can't get to be a part of other people's families. You have to be born into a family. The family part of our lives is just for us. Besides, you don't seem to understand that you're the wrong color, Mr. Bemish."

He didn't answer this. He got up and got his cookie crock and silently offered me a cookie.

After I returned from the shoe shop, I sat on the wooden steps that run across the front of the drugstore. I was trying to decide how I really feel about Mr. Bemish. I always sit at the far end of the steps with my back against the tight board fence. It is a very good place from which to observe the street, the front of the store, the church green. People walk past me not noticing that I am there. Sometimes their conversations are very unusual. I can see a long way down the path that bisects the green. It is a dirt path and not too straight. The only straight paths in town are those in front of the homes of people who have gardeners.

From where I sat I could see a man approaching. He was strolling down the path that crosses the church green. This is a most unusual way for a man to walk in Wheeling in the summer. It is during the summer that the year-round residents earn their living. They mow lawns, and cut hedges, and weed gardens, and generally look after the summer people. Able-bodied men in Wheeling walked fast in summer.

This tall, broad-shouldered man was strolling down the path. He was wearing a white suit, the pants quite tight in the leg, and he had his hands in his hip pockets, and a stiff straw hat, a boater, on the back of his head.

I sat up very straight when I discovered that this was a very dark-colored man. I could not imagine where he came from. He could not possibly have been a butler or a waiter, even if he had wanted to and spent a whole lifetime in trying. He would never have been able to walk properly—he would always swagger, and who ever heard of a swaggering butler or a waiter who strolled around a table?

As he came nearer, I saw that he had a beard, an untidy shaggy beard like the beard of a goat. His hair was long and shaggy and rough-looking too. Though he was tall, with wide shoulders, the thick rough hair on his head and the goat's beard made his head and face look too big, out of proportion to his body.

When he saw me, he came straight toward me. He bent over me, smiling, and I moved back away from him, pressing against the fence.

His eyes alarmed me. Whenever I think about his eyes, I close mine, trying to shut his out. They are reddish brown and they look hot, and having looked into them, I cannot seem to look away. I have never seen anyone with eyes that color or with that strange quality, whatever it is. I described them as looking "hot," but that's not possible. It must be that they are the color of something that I associate with fire or heat. I do not know what it is.

"You lost?" he said.

"No. Are you?"

"Yup. All us black folks is lost." He said this in a husky, unmusical voice, and turned away and went in the store.

I went in the store, too. If this unusual-looking man with the goat's beard got into a discussion of "all us black folks is lost" with my father, I wanted to hear it.

My father said, "How-de-do?" and he made it a question.

The bearded man nodded and said, "The druggist in?"

"I'm the druggist."

"This your store?"

"That's right."

"Nice place you got here. You been here long?"

My father grunted. I waited for him to make the next move in the game we called Stanley and Livingstone. All black strangers who came into our store were Livingstones—and it was up to the members of our family to find out which lost Mr. Livingstone or which lost Mrs. Livingstone we had encountered in the wilds of the all-white town of Wheeling. When you live in a town where there aren't any other black people, naturally you're curious when another black person shows up.

I sat down in the front of the store and waited for my father to find out which Mr. David Livingstone he was talking to and what he was doing in our town. But my father looked at him with no expression on his face and said, "And what did you want?"

The man with the goat's beard fished in the pocket of his tight white pants. In order to do this, he thrust his leg forward a little to ease the strain on the fabric, and thus he gave the impression that he was pawing the ground. He handed my father a piece of paper.

"I got a prescription for a lotion—"

"It'll take a few minutes," my father said, and went in the back room.

The bearded man came and sat beside me.

"Do you live here in Wheeling?" I asked.

"I work at the inn. I'm the piano player."

"You play the piano?"

"And sing. I'm the whole orchestra. I play for the dinner hour. I play for all those nice rich white folks to dance at night. I'll be here all summer."

"You will?"

"That's right. And I've never seen a deader town."

"What's your name?"

"Chink."

"Mr. Chink—"

"No," he said, and stood up. "Chink is my first name. Chink Johnson."

Mr. Johnson is a restless kind of man. He keeps moving around even when he is sitting still, moving his feet, his hands, his head. He crosses his legs, uncrosses them, clasps his hands together, unclasps them.

"Why are you having a prescription filled?"

"Hand lotion. I use it for my hands."

My father came out of the back room, wrapped up a bottle, and said, "Here you are."

Chink Johnson paid him, said good-bye to me, and I said, "Good-bye, Chink."

"What's his name?"

"Chink Johnson. He plays the piano at the inn."

Chink Johnson seems to me a very interesting and unusual man. To my surprise, my father did not mention our newest Mr. Livingstone to the family. He said nothing about him at all. Neither did I.

Yet he comes in the drugstore fairly often. He buys cigarettes and throat lozenges. Sometimes he drives over from the inn in a borrowed horse and carriage. Sometimes he walks over. My father has very little to say to him.

He doesn't linger in the store, because my father's manner is designed to discourage him from lingering or hanging around. But he does seem to be looking for something. He looks past the door of the prescription room, and on hot afternoons the door in the very back is open and you can see our yard, with its beautiful little flower gardens, and he looks out into the yard, seems to search it. When he leaves he looks at the house, examining it. It is as though he is trying to see around a corner, see through the walls, because some sixth sense has told him that there exists on the premises something that will interest him, and if he looks hard enough, he will find it.

My mother finally caught a glimpse of him as he went out the front door. She saw what I saw—the goat's beard in silhouette, the forward thrust of his head, the thick shaggy hair—because we were standing in the prescription room looking toward the door.

"Who was that?" she asked, her voice sharp.

"That's the piano player at the inn," my father said.

"You've never mentioned him. What is his name?"

"Jones," my father said.

I started to correct him but I was afraid to interrupt him because he started talking fast and in a very loud voice. "Lightfoot Jones," he said. "Shake Jones. Barrelhouse Jones." He started tapping on the glass case in front of him. I have never heard him do this before. He sings in the Congregational church choir. He has a pure, lyric tenor voice, and he sings all the tenor solos—the "Sanctus," "The Heavens Are Telling." You can tell from his speaking voice that he sings. He is always humming or singing or whistling. There he was with a pencil in his hand, tapping out a most peculiar rhythm on the glass of a showcase.

"Shake Jones," he repeated. "Rhythm in his feet. Rhythm in his blood. Rhythm in his feet. Rhythm in his blood. Beats out his life, beats out his lungs, beats out his liver, on a piano," and he began a different and louder rhythm with his foot. "On a pi-an-o. On a pi-an-o. On a pi—"

"Samuel, what is the matter with you? What are you talking about?"

"I'm talkin' about Tremblin' Shakefoot Jones. The piano player. The piano player who can't sit still and comes in here lookin' around and lookin' around, prancin' and stampin' his hoofs, and sniffin' the air. Just like a stallion who smells a mare—a stallion who—"

"Samuel! How can you talk that way in front of this child?"

My father was silent.

I said, "His name is Chink Johnson."

My father roared, terrible in his anger, "His name is Duke. His name is Bubber. His name is Count, is Maharajah, is King of Lions. I don't give a good goddamn what he calls himself. I don't want him and his restless feet hangin' around. He can let his long feet slap somebody else's floor. But not mine. Not here—"

He glared at me and glared at my mother. His fury silenced us. At that moment his eyes were red-brown just like Chink Jones, no, Johnson. He is shorter, he has no beard, but he had at that moment a strong resemblance to Chink.

I added to his fury. I said, "You look just like Chink Johnson."

He said, "Ah!!! . . ." He was so angry I could not understand one word he said. I went out the front door and across the street, and sat on the church steps and watched the world go by and listened to the faint hum it made as it went around and around.

I saw Mr. Bemish go in the drugstore. He stayed a long time. That gave me a certain pleasure because I knew he had come to eat his ice cream soda, mouthful by mouthful, from one of our long-handled ice cream soda spoons, and to look at Aunt Sophronia as he nibbled at the ice cream. He always looks at her out of the corners of his eyes, stealing sly little glances at her. I knew that Aunt Sophronia would not be in the store until much later and that he was wasting his time. It was my father's birthday and Aunt Sophronia was in the kitchen baking a great big cake for him.

If Mr. Bemish had known this, he might have dropped in on the birthday celebration, even though he hadn't been invited. After all, he had sidled into our back yard without being invited and our yard is completely enclosed by a tight board fence, and there is a gate that you have to open to get in the yard, so that entering our yard is like walking into our living room. It is a very private place. Mr. Bemish is the only person that I know of who has come into our yard without being invited, and he keeps coming, too.

After Mr. Bemish left the store, I crossed the street and sat outside on the store steps. It was hot. It was very quiet. Old Lady Chimble crossed the church green carrying a black silk umbrella, and she opened it and used it as a sunshade. A boy went by on a bicycle. Frances Jackins (we called her Aunt Frank), the black cook in the boardinghouse across the street, arrived carrying something in a basket. She is always cross and usually drunk. She drinks gin. Mother says this is what has made Aunt Frank's lips look as though they were turned inside out and she says this is called a "gin lip." They are bright red, almost like a red gash across the dark skin of her face. I want very much to ask Aunt Frank about this—how it feels, when it happened, etc.—and someday I will, but I have not as yet had a suitable opportunity. When she is drunk, she cannot give a sensible answer to a sensible question, and when she is sober, or partially sober, she is very irritable and constantly finds fault with me. She is absolutely no relation to us; it is just that my mother got in the habit of calling her Aunt Frank many years ago and so we all call her that. Because I am young, she tries to boss me and to order me around, and she calls me Miss in a very unpleasant, sarcastic way.

She is a very good cook when she is sober. But when she is drunk, she burns everything, and she is always staggering across the street and stumbling up our back steps, with bread pans filled with dough which would not rise because she had forgotten the yeast, and with burned cakes and pies and burned hams and roasts of beef. When she burns things, they are not just scorched; they are blackened and hardened until they are like charcoal.

Almost every night she scratches at our back door. I have sharper hearing than everybody else; I can hear people walking around the side of the house when no one else has heard them—anyway, I always hear her first. I open the door suddenly and very fast, and she almost falls into the kitchen and stands there swaying, and fouling our kitchen with the sweetish smell of gin and the dank and musty odor of her clothes.

She always has a dip of snuff under her upper lip and she talks around this obstruction, so that her voice is peculiar. She speaks quickly to keep the snuff in place, and sometimes she pauses and works her upper lip, obviously getting the snuff in some special spot. When she comes to the back door at night, she puts the basket of ruined food just inside the door, on the floor, and says to my mother, "Here, Martha, throw this away. Throw it a-way for me. Give it to the hens. Feed it to the pig—"

She turns all two-syllable words into two separate one-syllable words. She doesn't say "Martha" all in one piece. She separates it, so that it becomes "Mar-tha"; she doesn't say "away," but "a-way." It is a very jerky kind of speech.

I am always given the job of burying the stuff in the back yard, way down in the back. I dig a hole and throw the blackened mess into it and then cover it with lime to hasten decomposition and discourage skunks and dogs.

Sometimes I hide behind the fence and yell at her on her way back across the street:

> Ole Aunt Frankie
> Black as tar
> Tried to get to heaven
> In a 'lectric car.
> Car got stalled in an underpass,
> Threw Aunt Frankie right on her ass.

Whenever I singsong this rhyme at her, she invariably tries to climb over the fence, a furious drunken old woman, threatening me with the man's umbrella that she carries. I should think she would remember from past performances that she cannot possibly reach me. But she always tries. After several futile efforts, she gives up and goes back to the boardinghouse across the street. A lot of old maids and widows live there. No gentlemen. Just ladies. They spend their spare time rocking on the front porch, and playing whist, and looking over at the drugstore. Aunt Frank spends her spare time in the kitchen of the boardinghouse, rocking and emptying bottle after bottle of gin.

But on the day of my father's birthday, she was sober; at least, she walked as though she were. She had a basket on her arm with a white napkin covering its contents. I decided she must have made something special for my father's supper. She went in the drugstore, and when she came out, she didn't have the basket. She saw me sitting on the steps but she ignored me.

Aunt Sophronia came and stood in the window. She had washed the glass globes that we keep filled with blue, red, and yellow liquid. She was wearing a dark skirt and a white blouse. Her hair was no longer skinned tight back from her forehead; it was curling around her forehead, perhaps because she had been working in the garden, bending over, and the hairpins that usually hold it so tightly in place had worked themselves loose. She didn't look real. The sun was shining in the window and it reflected the lights from the jars of colored water back on her face and her figure, and she looked golden and rose-colored and lavender, and it was as though there were a rainbow moving in the window.

Chink Johnson drove up in his borrowed horse and carriage. He stood and talked to me and then started to go in the store, saw Aunt Sophronia, and stood still. He took a deep breath. I could hear him. He took off the stiff straw hat that he wore way back on his head and bowed to her. She nodded, as though she really didn't want to, and turned away and acted as though she were very busy.

He grabbed my arm and actually pinched it.

"What are you doin'?" I said angrily. "What is the matter with you? Let go my arm."

"Shut up," he said impatiently, pinching harder. His fingers felt as though they were made of iron. "Who is that?"

I pried his fingers loose and rubbed my arm. "Where?"

"In the window. Who is that girl in the window?"

"That's my Aunt Sophronia."

"Your aunt? Your aunt?"

"Yes."

He went in the store. One moment he was standing beside me and the next moment he had practically leaped inside the store.

I went in too. He was leaning in the window, saying, "Wouldn't you like to go for a walk with me this Sunday?"

She shook her head.

"Well, couldn't you go for a ride with me? I'll call for you—"

Aunt Sophronia said, "I work every day."

"Every day?" he said. "But that's not possible. Nobody works every day. I'll be back tomorrow—"

And he was gone. Aunt Sophronia looked startled. She didn't look angry, just sort of surprised.

I said, "Tomorrow and tomorrow and tomorrow—" And I thought, well, she's got two suitors now. There's this Shake Jones Livingstone, otherwise known as Chink Johnson, and there's Mr. Bemish. I do not think I would pick either one. Mr. Bemish is too old even though he is my friend. I think of Chink Johnson as my friend too, but I do not think he would make a good husband. I tried to decide why I do not approve of him as a husband for Aunt Sophronia. I think it is because Aunt Sophronia is a lady and Chink Johnson is—well—he is not a gentleman.

That night at supper we celebrated my father's birthday. At that hour nobody much came in the store. Pickett, the sexton, sat on the bench in the front and if anybody came in and wanted my father, he'd come to the back door and holler for him.

There was a white tablecloth on the big, oak dining room table, and we used my mother's best Haviland china and the sterling silver knives and forks with the rose pattern, and there was a pile of packages by my father's plate, and there were candles on the cake and we had ice cream for dessert. My old enemy, Aunt Frank, had delivered Parker House rolls for his birthday and had made him a milkpanful of rice pudding, because my father has always said that when he dies he hopes it will be because he drowns in a sea composed of rice pudding, that he could eat rice pudding morning, noon, and night. Aunt Frank must have been sober when she made the pudding, for it was creamy and delicious and I ate two helpings of it right along with my ice cream.

I kept waiting for Aunt Sophronia to say something about Chink Johnson. He is a very unusual-looking man and we've never had a customer, black or white, with that kind of beard. She did not mention him. Neither did I. My father has never mentioned him—at least not at the table. I wonder if my father hopes he will vanish. Perhaps they are afraid he will be come a part of the family circle if they mention him.

Now Chink Johnson has become a part of the family circle, and he used the same method that Mr. Bemish used. He just walked into the yard and into the house. I was upstairs and I happened to look out of the window, and there was Chink Johnson walking up the street. He opened our gate, walked around the side of the house and into our back yard. I hurried to the back of the house and looked out the window and saw him open the screen door and go into the kitchen. He didn't knock on the door either, he just walked in.

For the longest time I didn't hear a sound. I listened and listened. I must have stood still for fifteen minutes. Then I heard someone playing our piano. I knew it must be Chink Johnson because this was not the kind of music anyone in our house would have been playing. I ran downstairs. My mother had been in the cellar, and she came running up out of the cellar, and my father came hurrying over from the drugstore. We all stood and looked and looked.

Chink was sitting at our piano. He had a cigarette dangling from his lower lip, and the smoke from the cigarette was like a cloud—a blue-gray, hazy kind of cloud around his face, his eyes, his beard—so that you could only catch glimpses of them through the smoke. He was playing some kind of fast, discordant-sounding music and he was slapping the floor with one of his long feet and he was slapping the keys with his long fingers.

Aunt Sophronia was leaning against the piano looking down at him. He did not use music when he played, and he never once looked at the keyboard, he just kept looking right into Aunt Sophronia's eyes. I thought my father would tell Chink to go slap somebody else's floor with his long feet, but my mother gave him one of those now-don't-say-a-word looks and he glared at Chink and went back to the drugstore.

Chink stayed a long time; he played the piano, he sang, or rather I guess you would say he talked to the music. It is a very peculiar kind of musical performance. He plays some chords, a whole series of them, and he makes peculiar changes in the chords as he plays, and then he says the words of a song—he doesn't really sing, but his voice does change in pitch to, in a sense, match the chords he is playing, and he does talk to a kind of rhythm which also matches the chords. I sat down beside him and watched what he was doing, and listened to the words he said, and though it is not exactly music as I am accustomed to hearing it, I found it very interesting. He told me that what he does with those songs is known as the "talkin' blues." Only he said "*talk*in'" and he made "blues" sound like it was two separate words; not just a two-syllable word, but two distinct words.

I have been trying to play the piano the way he does but I get nothing but terrible sounds. I pretend that I am blind and keep my eyes closed all the time while I feel for chords. He must have a special gift for this because it is an extremely difficult thing that he is doing and I don't know whether I will ever be able to do it. He has a much better ear for music than I have.

Chink Johnson comes to see Aunt Sophronia almost every day. Sometimes when I look out in the back yard, Mr. Bemish is out there too. He always sits on the ground, and at his age, I should think it might give him rheumatism. He must be a very brave little man or else his love for Aunt Sophronia has given him great courage. I say this because Chink Johnson is very rude to Mr. Bemish and he stares at him with a dreadfully cruel look on his face. If I were small and slender and old like Mr. Bemish, I would not sit in the same yard with a much bigger, much younger man who obviously did not want me there.

I have thought a great deal about Mr. Bemish. I like him. He is truly a friend. But I do not think he should be interested in Aunt Sophronia—at least not in a loving kind of way. The thing that bothers me is that I honestly cannot decide whether I object to him as a suitor for her because he is white or because he is old. Sometimes I think it is for both reasons. I am fairly certain it isn't just because he's old. This bothers me. If my objections to him are because he's white (and that's what I told him, but I often say things that I know people do not want to hear and that they particularly do not want to hear from someone very much younger than they are), then I have been "trained" on the subject of race just as I have been "trained" to be a Christian. I know how I was trained to be a Christian—Sunday school, prayers, etc. I do not know exactly how I've been "trained" on the subject of race. Then why do I feel like this about Mr. Bemish?

Shortly after I wrote that, I stopped puzzling about Mr. Bemish because summer officially started—at least for me. It is true that school has been out for a long time, and we are wearing our summer clothes, and the yard is filled with flowers—but summer never really gets under way for me until Dottle Smith comes for his yearly visit.

Dottle and Uncle Johno went to school together. They look sort of alike. They are big men and they are so light in color they look like white men. But something in them (Dottle says that it is a "cultivated and developed and carefully nourished hatred of white men") will not permit them to pass for white. Dottle teaches English and elocution and dramatics at a school for black people in Georgia, and he gives lectures and readings during the summer to augment his income. Uncle Johno is the chief fund-raising agent for a black school in Louisiana.

I believe that my attitude towards Mr. Bemish stems from Dottle Smith. And Johno. They are both what my father calls race-conscious. When they travel on trains in the South, they ride in Jim Crow coaches until the conductor threatens to have them arrested unless they sit in the sections of the train reserved for whites. They are always being put out of the black sections of waiting rooms, and warned out of the black sections of towns, and being refused lodgings in black rooming houses on the grounds that they would be a source of embarrassment—nobody would be able to figure out why a white man wanted to live with black people, and they would be suspected of being spies, but of what kind or to what purpose, they have never been able to determine.

I have just reread what I have written here, and I find that I've left out the reason why I am writing so much about Dottle. Yesterday afternoon when I came back from an errand, there was a large, heavy-looking bag—leather, but it was shaped like a carpetbag—near the bench where the customers sit when they wait for prescriptions. I recognized it immediately. I have seen that bag every summer for as far back as I can remember. I wondered if Dottle had come alone this time or if he had a friend with him. Sometimes he brings a young man with him. These young men look very much alike—they are always slender, rather shy, have big dark eyes and very smooth skin just about the color of bamboo.

I looked at Dottle's big battered old bag sitting on the floor near the bench, and I could almost see him, with his long curly hair, and I could hear him reciting poetry in his rich, buttery voice. He can quote all the great speeches from *Hamlet, Macbeth, Richard II,* and he can recite the sonnets.

I loved him. He was lively and funny and unexpected. Sometimes he would grab my braid and shout in his best Shakespearean voice, "Seize on her Furies, take her to your torments!"

I looked at Dottle's battered bag and I said to my father, "Is he alone? Or has he got one of those pretty boys with him?"

My father looked at me over the top of his glasses. "Alone."

"How come he to leave his bag here?"

"Well, the Ecckles aren't home. Ellen's gone on vacation—"

"Why does Aunt Ellen always go on vacation when Dottle comes?"

My father ignored this and went on talking. "Johno's gone to Albany collecting money for the school."

"Where is Dottle now?"

"I'm right here, sugar," and Dottle Smith opened the screen door and came in. He looked bigger than he had the summer before. He hugged me. He smelled faintly of lavender.

"You went and grew, honey," he said, and took off his hat and bowed. It was a wide-brimmed Panama, and he had on a starched white shirt, and a flowing Byronic kind of black tie, and I looked at him with absolute delight. He was being a Southern "cunnel" and he was such an actor—I thought I could see lace at his wrists, hear mockingbirds sing, see a white-columned mansion, hear hoofbeats in the distance, and hear a long line of slaves, suitably clad as footmen and coachmen and butlers and housemen, murmur, "Yes, massah. Yes, massah." It was all there in his voice.

"Why, in another couple years I'll be recitin' poetry to you. How's your momma? This summer I'll have to teach you how to talk. These Yankah teachers you've got all talk through their noses. They got you doin' the same thing—"

For two whole days I forgot about Chink Johnson and Mr. Bemish and Aunt Sophronia. Dottle liked to go fishing and crabbing; he liked to play whist; and he could tell the most marvelous stories and act them out.

The very next day Dottle and Uncle Johno and I went crabbing. We set out early in the morning with our nets and our fishing lines and the rotten meat we used for bait, and our lunch and thermos bottles with lemonade in them. It was a two-mile walk from where we lived to the creek where we caught crabs.

There was a bridge across the creek, an old wooden bridge. Some of the planks were missing. We stood on this bridge or sat on it and threw our lines in the water. Once in a great while a horse and wagon would drive across and set the planks to vibrating. Johno and Dottle would hop off the bridge. But I stayed on and held to the railing. The bridge trembled under my feet, and the horse and wagon would thunder across, and the driver usually waved and hollered, "I gotta go fast or we'll all fall in."

The water in the creek was so clear I could see big crabs lurking way down on the bottom; I could see little pieces of white shells and beautiful stones. We didn't talk much while we were crabbing. Sometimes I lay flat on my stomach on the bridge and looked down into the water, watching the little eddies and whirlpools that formed after I threw my line in.

Before we ate our lunch, we went wading in the creek. Johno and Dottle rolled up the legs of their pants, and their legs were so white I wondered if they were that white all over, and if they were, how they could be called black. We sat on the bank of the creek and ate our lunch. Afterward Dottle and Johno told stories, wonderful stories in which animals talk, and there are haunted houses and ghosts and demons, and old black preachers who believe in heaven and hell.

They always started off the same way. Dottle would say to Johno, "Mr. Bones, be seated."

Though I have heard some of these stories many, many times, Dottle and Johno never tell them exactly the same. They change their gestures; they vary their facial expressions and the pitch of their voices.

Dottle almost always tells the story about the black man who goes in a store in a small town in the South and asks for Muriel cigars. The white man who owns the store says (and here Johno becomes an outraged Southern white man), "Nigger, what's the matter with you? Don't you see that picture of that beautiful white woman on the front of this box? When you ask for them cigars, you say *Miss* Muriel cigars!"

Though Uncle Johno is a good storyteller, he is not as good, not as funny or as dramatic, as Dottle. When I listen to Dottle I can see the old black preacher who spent the night in a haunted house. I see him approaching the house, the wind blowing his coattails, and finally him taking refuge inside because of the violence of the storm. He lights a fire in the fireplace and sits down by it and rubs his hands together, warming them. As he sits there, he hears heavy footsteps coming down the stairs (and Dottle makes his hand go thump, thump, thump on the bank of the creek) and the biggest cat the old man has ever seen comes in and sits down, looks at the old preacher, looks around, and says, "Has Martin got here yet?" The old man is too startled and too nervous to answer. He hears heavy footsteps again—thump, thump, thump. And a second cat, much bigger than the first one, comes in, and sits down right next to the old preacher. Both cats stare at him, and then the second cat says to the first cat, "Has Martin got here yet?" and the first cat shakes his head. There is something so speculative in their glance that the old man gets more and more uneasy. He wonders if they are deciding to eat him. The wind howls in the chimney, puffs of smoke blow back into the room. Then another and bigger cat thumps down the stairs. Finally there are six enormous cats, three on each side of him. Each one of these cats has asked the same question of the others—"Martin got here yet?" A stair-shaking tread begins at the top of the stairs, the cats all look at each other, and the old man grabs his hat, and says to the assembled cats, "You tell Martin ah been here but ah've gone."

I clapped when Dottle finished this story. I looked around thinking how glad I am he is here and what a wonderful place this is to listen to stories. The sun is warm but there is a breeze and it blows through the long marsh grass which borders the creek. The grass moves, seems to wave. Gulls fly high overhead. The only sound is the occasional cry of a gull and the lapping of water against the piling of the bridge.

Johno tells the next story. It is about an old black preacher and a rabbit. The old man tries to outrun an overfriendly and very talkative rabbit. The rabbit keeps increasing in size. The old man runs away from him and the rabbit catches up with him. Each time the rabbit says, "That was some run we had, wasn't it, brother?" Finally the old man runs until he feels as though his lungs are going to burst and his legs will turn to rubber, and he looks back and doesn't see the rabbit anywhere in sight. He sits down on a stone to rest and catch his breath. He has just seated himself when he discovers the rabbit sitting right beside him, smiling. The rabbit is now the same size as the preacher. The rabbit rolls his eyes and lisps, "That wath thome run we had, wathn't it?" The old man stood up, got ready to run again, and said, "Yes, that was some run we had, brother, but"—he took a deep breath—"you ain't *seen* no runnin' yet."

After they finished telling stories, we all took naps. Dottle and Johno were wearing old straw hats, wide-brimmed Panamas with crooked, floppy brims. Dottle had attached a piece of mosquito netting to his, and it hung down across his shoulders. From the back he looked like a woman who was wearing a veil.

When we woke up it was late in the afternoon and time to start for home. I ran part of the way. Then I sat down by the side of the road, in the shade, and waited until they caught up with me.

Dottle said, "Sugar, what are you in such a hurry for?"

I said, laughing, "Miss Muriel, you tell Martin I been here but I've gone and that he ain't *seen* no runnin' yet."

I got home first. Chink Johnson was in the store. When Dottle and Johno arrived, I introduced Chink to my uncles, Johno and Dottle. They didn't seem much impressed with each other. Johno nodded and Dottle smiled and left. Chink watched Dottle as he went toward the back room. Dottle has a very fat bottom and he sort of sways from side to side as he walks.

Chink said, "He seems kind of ladylike. He related on your mother's side?"

"He's not related at all. He's an old friend of Uncle Johno's. They went to school together. In Atlanta, Georgia." I sounded very condescending. "Do you know where that is?"

"Yeah. 'Nigger, read this. Nigger, don't let sundown catch you here. Nigger, if you can't read this, run anyway. If you can't run—then vanish. Just vanish out.' I know the place. I came from there."

My father was standing outside on the walk talking to Aunt Frank, so I felt at liberty to speak freely and I said, "Nigger, what are you talkin' about you want Muriel cigars. You see this picture of this beautiful redheaded white woman, nigger, you say *Miss* Muriel."

Chink stood up and he was frowning and his voice was harsh. "Little girl, don't you talk that way. I talk that way if I feel like it but don't you ever talk that way."

I felt as though I had been betrayed. One moment he was my friend and we were speaking as equals and the next moment, without warning, he is an adult who is scolding me in a loud, harsh voice. I was furious and I could feel tears welling up in my eyes. This made me angrier. I couldn't seem to control my weeping. Recently, and I do not know how it happened, whenever I am furiously angry, I begin to cry.

Chink leaned over and put his hand under my chin, lifted my face, saw the tears and he kissed my cheek. His beard was rough and scratchy. He smelled like the pine woods, and I could see pine needles in his hair and in his beard, and I wondered if he and Aunt Sophronia had been in the woods.

"Sugar," he said gently, "I don't like that Miss Muriel story. It ought to be told the other way around. A black man should be tellin' a white man, 'White man, you see this picture of this beautiful black woman? *White* man, you say *Miss* Muriel!'"

He went out of the store through the back room into the yard just as though he were a member of the family. It hadn't taken him very long to reach this position. Almost every afternoon he goes for a walk with Aunt Sophronia. I watch them when they leave the store. He walks so close to her that he seems to surround her, and he has his head bent so that his face is close to hers. Once I met them strolling up Petticoat Lane, his dark face so close to hers that his goat's beard was touching her smooth brown cheek.

My mother used to watch them too, as they walked side by side on the dirt path that led to the woods—miles and miles of woods. Sometimes he must have said things that Aunt Sophronia didn't like, because she would turn her head sharply away from him.

I decided that once you got used to his beard and the peculiar color and slant of his eyes, why you could say he had an interesting face. I do not know what it is about his eyes that makes me think of heat. But I know what color they are. They are the color of petrified wood after it's been polished, it's a red brown, and that's what his eyes are like.

I like the way he plays the piano, though I do not like his voice. I cannot get my mother to talk about him. My father grunts when I mention Chink's name and scowls so ferociously that it is obvious he does not like him.

I tried to find out what Aunt Sophronia thought of him. Later in the day I found her in the store alone and I said, "Do you like Chink Johnson?"

She said, "Run along and do the supper dishes."

"But do you?"

"Don't ask personal questions," she said, and her face and neck flushed.

She must have liked him though. She not only went walking with him in the afternoon, but on Sunday mornings he went to church with her. He wore a white linen suit and that same stiff straw hat way back on his head. He brought her presents—a tall bottle of violet eau de cologne, a bunch of Parma violets made of silk, but they looked real. On Sundays, Aunt Sophronia wore the violets pinned at her waist and they made her look elegant, like a picture in a book.

I said, "Oh, you look beautiful."

My mother said, dryly, "Very stylish."

We all crossed the street together on Sunday mornings. They went to church. I went to Sunday school. Sunday school was out first and I waited for them to come down the church steps. Aunt Sophronia came down the church steps and he would be so close behind her that he might have been dancing with her and matching his leg movements to hers. Suddenly he was in front of her and down on the path before she was and he turned and held out his hand. Even there on the sidewalk he wasn't standing still. It is as though his feet and his hands are more closely connected to his heart, to his central nervous system, than is true of other people, so that during every waking moment he moves, tapping his foot on the floor, tapping his fingers on a railing, on somebody's arm, on a table top. I wondered if he kept moving like that when he was asleep, tapping quarter notes with his foot, playing eighth notes with his right hand, half notes with his left hand. He attacked a piano when he played, violated it—violate a piano? I thought, violate Aunt Sophronia?

He stood on the dirt path and held out his hand to Aunt Sophronia, smiling, helping her down the church steps.

"Get your prayers said, sugar?" he said to me.

"Yes. I said one for you and one for the family. Aunt Sophronia, you smell delicious. Like violets—"

"She does, doesn't she?"

We walked across the street to the drugstore, hand in hand. Chink was in the middle and he held one of my hands and one of Aunt Sophronia's. He stays for dinner on Sundays. And on Sunday nights we close the store early and we all sit in the back yard, where it is cool. Mr. Bemish joins us in the yard. At dusk the fireflies come out, and then as the darkness deepens, bats swoop around us. Aunt Sophronia says, "Oooooh!" and holds on to her head, afraid one might get entangled in her hair.

Dottle took out one of his big white handkerchiefs and tied it around his head, and said in his richest, most buttery voice, "One of the nocturnal or crepuscular flying mammals constituting the order Chiroptera."

Dottle sprawled in a chair and recited poetry or told long stories about the South—stories that sometimes had so much fear and terror and horror in them that we shivered even though the air was warm. Chink didn't spend the evening. He sat in one of the lawn chairs, tapping on the arm with his long flexible fingers, and then left. Mr. Bemish always stays until we go in for the night. He takes no part in the conversation, but sits on the ground, huddled near Aunt Sophronia's skirts. Once when a bat swooped quite close, Aunt Sophronia clutched his arm.

Sometimes Dottle recites whole acts from *Macbeth* or *Hamlet* or all of the Song of Solomon, or sometimes he recites the loveliest of Shakespeare's sonnets. We forget about the bats swooping over our heads, ignore the mosquitoes that sting our ankles and our legs, and sit mesmerized while he declaims, "Shall I compare thee to a summer's day?"

The summer is going faster and faster—perhaps because of the presence of Aunt Sophronia's suitors. I don't suppose Dottle is really a suitor, but he goes through the motions. He picks little bouquets for her—bachelor buttons and candytuft—and leaves them on the kitchen table. He always calls her Miss Sophronia. If we are outdoors and she comes out to sit in the yard, he leaps to his feet, and bows and says, "Wait, wait. Befo' you sit on that bench, let me wipe it off," and he pulls out an enormous linen handkerchief and wipes off the bench. He is always bowing and kissing her hand.

By the middle of August it was very hot. My father had the store painted, and when the blinds were taken down, the painter found whole families of bats clinging together in back of the blinds. Evidently they lived there. I couldn't get hold of one, although I tried. They were the most peculiar-looking creatures. They looked almost like a person who wears glasses all the time and then suddenly goes without them, they have a kind of peering look.

Chink Johnson is always in our house or in the store or in the yard or going for walks with Aunt Sophronia. Whenever he is not violating the piano at the inn, he is with Aunt Sophronia—

He taught her how to dance—in the back yard, without any music, just his counting and clapping his hands. His feet made no sound on our thick grass. On two different sunny afternoons, he gave her dancing lessons, and on the third afternoon, he had her dancing. She was laughing and she was lively-looking and she looked young. He persuaded her to take off her shoes and she danced in her bare feet. Fortunately, nobody knows this but me.

He took her fishing. When they came back, she was quite sunburned but her eyes were shining as though they held the reflected light from the sun shining on water.

Just in that one short summer he seemed to take on all kinds of guises—fisherman, dancer, singer, churchgoer, even delivery boy.

One morning someone knocked at the back door and there was Chink Johnson with our grocery order, saying to my Aunt Sophronia, "Here's your meat, ma'am, and your vegetables," touching his hat, bowing, unloading the crate of groceries, and then sitting down at the kitchen table as though he owned it, drinking a cup of coffee that no one had offered him, just pouring it out of the enamel pot that stays on the stove, finding cream and sugar himself, and sitting there with his legs thrust way out in front of him, and those terribly tight pants he wears looking as though they were painted on his thighs.

Sometimes when he sits in our kitchen, he laughs. His laughter is not merry. When my father laughs, the sound makes you laugh, even when you don't know what he is laughing about.

When Chink Johnson laughs, I look away from him. The sound hurts my ears. It is like the ugly squawk of some big bird that you have disturbed in the woods and it flies right into your face, pecking at your eyes.

It has been a very interesting summer. I have begun to refer to it in the past tense because there isn't much left of a summer by the middle of August. One Thursday afternoon, Aunt Sophronia and I saw that other ladies liked Chink Johnson too.

Thursday afternoon is traditionally maid's day off and Chink Johnson drove the maids from the inn into town, in a wagon, late in the day. He stopped in front of the store with a wagon full of girls in long skirts, giggling, leaning against him, a kind of panting excitement in that wagon, their arms around him; they whispered to him; they were seized by fits of laughter, shrieks of laughter.

They came in the store and bought hairnets and hairpins and shampoo and Vaseline and hair tonics and cough medicines and court plaster and a great many items that they did not need because it was a pleasure to be spending money, and to be free of the tyranny of the housekeepers' demands—or so my mother said—some young and attractive, some not so young, about ten of them.

Aunt Sophronia was in the store and she waited on them, studying them. Every once in a while one would go to the door, and yell, "We'll be out in a minute, Chink. Just a little while!" and wave at him and throw kisses at him.

Then they were gone, all at once, piling into the wagon, long full skirts in disarray. One of them sat in Chink's lap, laughing, looking up into his face, and saying, "Let's go in the woods. Chink, take us in the woods. I'll help drive."

Aunt Sophronia and I stood in the doorway and watched them as they drove off, going toward the pine woods. The wagon seemed to be filled with wide skirts, and ruffled petticoats, all suddenly upended because Chink said, "Giddup, there!" and hit the horse with the whip, cracked it over the horse's ears, and the horse started off as though he were a racehorse.

It was late when they went past the store, going home. Sitting in the back yard, we could hear the horse racing, and the girls squealing and laughing, and Chink singing a ribald song, about "Strollin', and Strollin'."

Dottle stopped right in the middle of a poem and Mr. Bemish straightened up so that he was not quite so close to Aunt Sophronia's skirts. It was like having Chink Johnson right there in the back yard with us—the rough, atonal voice, the red-brown eyes that looked hot, literally hot, as though if you touched them you would have to withdraw your fingers immediately because they would be scorched or singed or burned, the jutting beard, the restless feet and hands.

We sat absolutely still. We could hear the rattling of the wagon, the clop-clop of the horse's hoofs and above it the laughter of the girls, and dominating that sound, Chink Johnson's voice lifted in song. Even after they were so far away we could not possibly hear them, these sounds seemed to linger in the air, faint, far-off.

It was a warm night, brilliant with light from the moon. I pictured the girls as sitting on top of Chink, all around him, on his arms, in his lap, on his shoulder, and I thought the prettiest one should be perched on his head.

Dottle lit a cigar and puffed out clouds of bluish smoke and said, "I never heard the mating call of the male so clearly sounded on a summer's night." He laughed so hard that he had to get out one of his big handkerchiefs and dab his eyes with it.

Aunt Sophronia got up from the bench so fast that she brushed against Mr. Bemish, almost knocking him over. He lost his balance and regained it only because he supported himself with one hand on the ground. She must have known that she had very nearly upset him but she went marching toward the house, her back very straight and her head up in the air, and she never once looked back.

Dottle said, "Have I offended her?"

My mother said, "It's late. It's time we went in."

Mr. Bemish must have gone home when we went in the house, but he was back in the yard so early the next morning he might just as well have spent the night. Dottle and I were standing in the kitchen, looking down at the back yard. He was drinking coffee out of a mug and I was eating a piece of bread and butter. Our back yard is a pretty sight on a summer morning. It is filled with flowers, and birds are singing, and the air is very cool; and there is a special smell, a summer smell compounded of grass and dew on the grass and flowers, and the suggestion of heat to come later in the day.

We looked out the door and there was Mr. Bemish down on his knees in front of Aunt Sophronia. She was sitting on the bench and she looked horrified, and she seemed to have been in the act of trying to stop him, one hand extended in a thrusting-away motion. I thought: His pants legs will be very damp because there's still dew on the grass, and how did he get here so early, and did he know that she would be sitting on the bench almost before sunup?

"Ah, girlie, girlie!" he said, on his knees in our back yard, kneeling on our thick, soft grass. "Will you marry me?"

"No!"

"Is it," he said, "because I am old?" and his voice went straight up in pitch just like a scale. "I'm not old. I'm not old. Why, I can still jump up in the air and click my heels together three times!"

And he did. He got up off his knees and he jumped up, straight up, and clicked his heels together three times, and landed on the grass, and there was just a slight thumping sound when he landed.

Aunt Sophronia said, "Mr. Bemish, Mr. Bemish, don't do that—don't do that—go away, go home—" And she ran toward the house and he started after her and then he saw us standing in the door, watching him, and he stood still. He shouted after her, "I'll put on my best coat and my best hat and you won't know me—I'll be back—and you won't know me—"

Dottle glared at him through the screen door and said, "You old fool—you old fool—"

Mr. Bemish hurried around the side of the house, pretending that he hadn't heard him.

I did not know when Mr. Bemish would be back, wearing his best coat and his best hat, but I certainly wanted to see him and, if possible, to witness his next performance. I decided that whenever Aunt Sophronia was in the store, I'd be in the store too.

When my father went to eat his dinner at twelve-thirty, Aunt Sophronia looked after the store. There weren't many people who came in at that hour; it was the dinner hour and Aunt Sophronia sat in the prescription room, with the door open, and read the morning newspaper. There was an old wooden chair by the window, in the prescription room. It had a faded painting across the back, a wooden seat, and back and arms. It was a very comfortable chair if you sat up straight, and Aunt Sophronia sat up very straight. She could look out of the window and see the church green, see the path that went up Petticoat Lane toward the pine woods, and she commanded a view of the interior of the store.

I don't think she saw Mr. Bemish when he entered. If she had, she would have gotten out of the chair immediately to wait on him. But she was reading the newspaper, and he came in very quietly. He was wearing a cutaway coat that was too long, and a pair of striped trousers, and he was carrying a silk hat in his hand, a collapsed silk hat. He stopped inside the door and put the hat in shape and then placed it carefully on his head. He looked like a circus clown who is making fun of the ringmaster, mocking him, making his costume look silly.

Mr. Bemish went straight through the store, and stood in front of Aunt Sophronia, and he jumped straight up in the air, like a dancer, and clicked his heels together three times. The bottles on the shelves rattled and the back room was filled with a pinging sound.

"Oh, my goodness," Aunt Sophronia said, frowning. "Oh, my goodness, don't jump like that." And she stood up.

My father came in through the back door and he said, "What's going on in here? What's going on in here?"

Mr. Bemish said, "I was just showing Miss Sophronia that I can still jump up in the air and click my heels together three times before I come back down again."

My father made a noise that sounded like "Boooooh!" but wasn't quite, and Mr. Bemish retreated, talking very fast. "I had asked Miss Sophronia if she would marry me and she said no, and I thought perhaps it was because she thinks I'm too old and not stylish enough and so I got dressed up and I was showing her I could still jump—"

"Get out of here! Get out of here! Get out of here!"

My father's voice kept rising and increasing in volume, and his face looked as though he were about to burst. It seemed to darken and to swell, to get bigger.

Aunt Sophronia said, "Oh, you mustn't talk to him like that—"

My father was moving toward Mr. Bemish, and Mr. Bemish was retreating, retreating, and finally he turned and ran out of the store and ran up Petticoat Lane with his long coattails flapping about his legs.

My father said, "I shouldn't have let him hang around here all these months. I can't leave this store for five minutes that I don't find one of these no-goods hangin' around when I come back. Not one of 'em worth the powder and shot to blow 'em to hell and back. That piano player pawin' the ground and this old white man jumpin' up in the air, and that friend of Johno's, that poet or whatever he is, all he needs are some starched petticoats and a bonnet and he'd make a woman—he's practically one now—and he's tee-heein' around, and if they were all put together in one piece, it still wouldn't be a whole man." My father shook his fist in the air and glared at Aunt Sophronia.

"I guess it's all my fault—" Aunt Sophronia sounded choked-up and funny.

My father said, "No, no, no, I didn't mean that," and patted her arm. "It's all perfectly natural. It's just that we're the only black people living in this little bit of town and there aren't any fine young black men around, only this tramp piano player, and every time I look at him I can hear him playing some rags and see a whole line of big-bosomed women done up in sequined dresses standin' over him, moanin' about wantin' somebody to turn their dampers down, and I can see poker games and crap games and—"

My mother came in through the back room. She said, "Samuel, why are you talking about gambling games?"

"I was trying to explain to Sophy how I feel about that piano player."

To my surprise, my mother said, "Has Sophronia asked you how you feel about Mr. Johnson?"

When my father shook his head, she said, "Then I don't think there is any reason for you to say anything about him. I need you in the garden. I want you to move one of my peonies."

I wonder what my mother would say if she knew how my father chased little Mr. Bemish out of his store. I wonder if Mr. Bemish will ever come back.

Mr. Bemish did come back. He came back the following Sunday. We were all in the store—Aunt Sophronia, and Dottle, and Chink and I.

Mr. Bemish sidled in through the door. He looked as though he expected someone to jump out at him and yell, "Go home!" But he came in anyway and he sat down beside me on the bench near the front of the store.

Chink was leaning on the cigar case, talking to Aunt Sophronia, his face very close to hers. I couldn't hear what he was saying, but he seemed to be trying to persuade her to do something, go for a walk, or something, and she was obviously refusing, politely but definitely. Dottle was standing near the back of the store, watching Chink.

Aunt Frank opened the store door, and she stood in the doorway holding the screen door open. She has a cross, sharp way of speaking, very fast and very unpleasant. She saw me and she said, "Where's Mar-tha?"

I wasn't expecting to see Aunt Frank in the store at that hour and I was so surprised that I didn't answer her.

"What's the mat-ter with you? Cat got your tongue? Didn't you hear what I said? Where's your moth-er?"

"She's over on the other side of the building, in the kitchen. She's having coffee with my father."

She scowled at Chink. "How long's that bearded man been in here talkin' to Sophy?"

Chink turned around and looked toward Aunt Frank. Aunt Sophronia started toward her, moving very fast out from behind the cigar case, saying, "Can I get something for you?"

As Aunt Frank stood there holding the door open, a whole flight of bats came in the store. I say a "flight" because I don't know what else to call a large-sized group of bats. They swooped down and up in a blind, fast flight.

Aunt Frank shrieked, "Ahhh! My hair, watch out for your hair! Ahhhhhh!" and stood up on the bench, and held her black fusty skirts close about her and then pulled them over her head. I decided she had confused mice and bats, that the technique for getting rid of mice was to stand on a chair and clutch one's skirts around one, that is, if you were a lady and pretended to be afraid of mice. I did learn that Aunt Frank was wearing carpet slippers made of dark gray felt, black cotton stockings, and under the outside layer of skirts there seemed to be a great many layers of black petticoats.

Dottle ran into the back room and held the door tightly shut. There is a glass in the door and he could look out at the rest of us as we dodged the bats. I could see his large pale face, and long hair, and I supposed he was as frightened as Aunt Frank that bats would get entangled in his hair, because he squealed, all the rich, buttery quality gone from his voice, just a high-pitched squealing.

Aunt Frank cautiously lowered the outer skirt, fumbled in a pocket, and took out a bottle—not a big bottle, but about the size of an eight-ounce cough medicine bottle—and she took two or three swigs from it, recorked it, and then re-covered her head.

Chink grabbed a newspaper and slapped at the bats as they circled. "Gotcha. Hi-hi gotcha—hi-hi-gotcha—hi-hi!" and he folded the newspaper and belted them as they swished past him.

Mr. Bemish stared. I decided that he'd lived with bats and spiders and mice, well, not lived with perhaps, but was so accustomed to them that he could not understand why they should cause all this noise and confusion and fear. He ignored the bats entirely and went to the rescue of his lady love. He clasped Aunt Sophronia to his bosom, covering her head with his hands and arms and he kept murmuring comforting words. "Now, now, I won't let anything hurt you. Nothing can harm you." He took a deep breath and said, quite distinctly, "I love you, my darling. I love you, love you—"

Aunt Sophronia seemed to nestle in his arms, to cuddle closer to him, to lean harder every time a bat swooped past them.

Father came through the back room—he had to wrestle Dottle out of the way before he could get through the door—and he very sensibly held the screen door open, and what with the impetus offered by Chink's folded newspaper, the bats swooped outside.

It was really very exciting while it lasted, what with all the shrieks and the swift movement of the bats. When I began to really look around, the first thing I noticed was that Aunt Sophronia was still huddled in the protective arms of Mr. Bemish. Dottle came out of the back room with his mouth pursed and his cheeks were puffed out a little and I wouldn't have been surprised if he had hissed at Mr. Bemish. He and Chink headed straight toward Mr. Bemish. They are very tall men and Mr. Bemish is short and slender, and as they converged on him, one from the rear and the other from the side, he looked smaller and older than ever.

Aunt Sophronia stepped away from Mr. Bemish. She moved toward Chink. One side of her face was red where it had been pressed hard against the wool of Mr. Bemish's coat.

All of a sudden my father's hand was resting on one of Chink's shoulders. He has large, heavy hands and his hand seemed to have descended suddenly and with great weight. He said, "You'll not start any trouble in my store."

Aunt Frank said, "Bats! Bats!" She indicated that my father was to help her down from the bench. She climbed down awkwardly, holding on to him. "Worse than bats," she said, and she made a wide all-inclusive gesture that took in Chink and Dottle and Mr. Bemish. "Where's Mar-tha?" she demanded. "She still in the kitchen?"

My father nodded. He held the door open for Mr. Bemish and Mr. Bemish scuttled out. Dottle and Chink went out too.

I found a dead bat on the floor and sat down on the bench at the front of the store to examine it. It had a very unpleasant smell. But it was such an interesting creature that I ignored the odor. It had rather large, pointed ears that I thought were quite charming. It had very sharp little claws. I could see why the ladies had screamed and covered their heads, because if those claws got entangled in their long hair, someone would have had to cut their hair to get a bat out of it. Aunt Frank's hair isn't long; it is like a sheep's wool, tight-curled and close to the skin or scalp. But I suppose a bat's sharp little claws and peculiar wings snarled up in that might create more of a problem than it would if caught in longer and less tightly curled hair.

The wings of the bat were webbed like the feet of ducks, with a thin membranelike tissue that was attached to the body, reaching from the front legs or arms to the back legs and attached to the sides. The body was small in comparison to the wide sweep of those curious wings. I stretched its wings out and they looked like the inside of an opened umbrella, and I couldn't help admiring them. I began to think of all the things I'd heard said about bats, "blind as a bat," and the word "batty" meaning crazy, and I tried to figure out why "batty." Probably because a bat's behavior didn't make sense to a human being—its fast, erratic flight would look senseless.

Then Aunt Frank's voice sounded right in my ear, and her horrible breath was in my nose, and she smelled worse than the bat. She said, "You throw that nasty thing away. You throw that nasty thing away."

I thrust the dead bat straight at her black and wrinkled face. "Look out," I yelled. "It'll suck your blood. It's still alive. Look out!"

She jumped away, absolutely furious. "You little vixen," she said, and squealed just like a pig. Then she saw my mother standing in the door of the prescription room. "Mar-tha," she commanded, "you come here and make her throw this nasty thing away. Make her throw it away. She's settin' here playin' with a dead bat."

My mother said, "If you want to look at the bat, take it outside or take it in the back room. You can't keep a dead bat here in the drugstore."

"This can't hurt her. It's dead."

She interrupted me. "Many people are afraid of bats. It doesn't make any difference whether the bats are dead or alive—they are still afraid of them."

I went outside and sat on the front steps and waited. There was a full moon and the light from it made the street and the houses and the church look as though they had been white-washed. I put the bat beside me on the step. I was going to wait for Aunt Frank, and when she came out of the store and started down the steps, I was going to put the dead stinking bat in one of the big pockets in her skirt—the pocket where she kept her bottle of gin. And when she got home and reached for a drink, I hoped she would discover, encounter, touch with her bony fingers, the corpse of "one of the nocturnal or crepuscular flying mammals constituting the order Chiroptera" as a token of my affection.

I must have waited there on the steps for two hours. My father began putting out the lights in the store. I stayed right there, anticipating the moment when my ancient enemy, Aunt Frank, would come stumbling around the side of the building.

And then—one moment I was sitting on the splintery front steps of the store, and the next moment I was running up Petticoat Lane, going just as fast as I could, because it had suddenly occurred to me that Chink Johnson and Dottle Smith had gone out of the drugstore right behind Mr. Bemish and they hadn't returned.

By the time I reached Mr. Bemish's shop, I was panting. I couldn't catch my breath.

Mr. Bemish's wagon was drawn up close to the side of the shop. The horse was hitched to it. Mr. Bemish was loading the headboard of his beautiful brass bed on the wagon. He was obviously moving—leaving town—at night. He walked in a peculiar fashion as though he were lame. He was panting too, and making hiccupping noises like someone who has been crying a long time, so long that no real sound comes out, just a kind of hiccupping noise due to the contractions of the throat muscles and the heaving of the chest.

As I stood there, he got the headboard on the wagon, and then he struggled with his mattress, and then the springs, and then he brought out his cobbler's bench.

Dottle and Chink stood watching him, just like two guards or two sheriffs. None of us said anything.

I finally sat down on the enormous millstone that served as Mr. Bemish's front step. I sat way off to one side where I wouldn't interfere with his comings and goings.

May-a-ling, his cat, rubbed against me and then came and sat in my lap, with her back to me, facing toward Mr. Bemish.

It didn't take him very long to empty the shop of his belongings. I couldn't help thinking that if we ever moved, it would take us days to pack all the books and the pictures and the china, and all our clothes and furniture. We all collected things. Aunt Sophronia did beautiful embroidery and she collected embroidered fabrics, and Mother collected old dishes and old furniture, and my father collected old glass bottles and old mortars, and they all collected books, and then all the rooms had furniture and there were all kinds of cooking pots. No one of us would ever get all of his belongings in one wagon.

Mr. Bemish came out of the shop and walked all around the little building with that peculiar stiff-legged gait. Apparently the only item he'd overlooked was his garden bench. He had trouble getting it in the wagon, and I dumped May-a-ling on the ground and went to help him.

One of Dottle's meaty hands gripped my braid. "He can manage."

I twisted away from him. "He's just a little old man and he's my friend and I'm going to help him."

Chink said, "Leave her alone."

Dottle let go of my hair. I helped put the bench in the wagon, and then went inside the shop with him, and helped him carry out the few items that were left. Each time I went inside the shop with Mr. Bemish I asked him questions. We both whispered.

"Where are you going, Mr. Bemish?"

"Massachusetts."

"Why?"

He didn't answer. His hiccups got worse.

I waited until we'd taken down the green summer curtains and carefully folded them, and put them in the little trunk that held some of his clothes, and put his broom and his dustpan and his tall kitchen cooking stool on the wagon, before I repeated my question. His hiccups had quieted down.

"Why are you leaving, Mr. Bemish?" I whispered.

"They were going to sew me up."

"Sew you up. Did you say—sew you up?"

"Yes."

"Where?" I said, staring at him, thinking: Sew up? Sew up what—eyes, nostrils, mouth, ears, rectum? "They were trying to scare you, Mr. Bemish. Nobody would sew up a person, a human being, unless it was a surgeon—after an operation—"

He shook his head. "No," he whispered. "I thought so too, but—no, they meant it—with my own waxed thread—"

"Did they—"

"Hush! Hush!"

We used this little piece of flowered carpet to wrap his washbowl and pitcher in and then put the whole bulky package it made on the wagon. We went back inside to make sure that we hadn't forgotten anything. The inside of his shop looked very small and shabby and lonely. There wasn't anything left except his stove and he obviously couldn't take that. It was a very big, handsome stove and he kept it quite shiny and clean.

"Can you keep a secret?" he whispered, standing quite close to me. He smelled old and dusty and withered like dried flowers.

I nodded.

He handed me a small velvet bag. "Hide it, girlie," he whispered. "It's some old jewelry that belonged to my mother. Give it to Miss Sophronia at Christmas from me." He patted my arm.

We went outside and he took down the sign with the lady's high-laced shoe painted on it, and put in on the wagon seat. He climbed in the wagon, picked up the reins.

"May-a-ling, May-a-ling," he called. It was the most musical sound I have ever heard used to call a cat. She answered him instantly. She mewed and jumped up on the wagon seat beside him. He clucked to the horse and they were off.

I waited not only until they were out of sight, but until I could no longer hear the creak of the wagon wheels and the clop-clop of the horse's hoofs, and then I turned and ran.

Chink said, "Wait a minute—"

Dottle said, "You don't understand—"

I stopped running just long enough to shout at them, "You both stink. You stink like dead bats. You and your goddamn Miss Muriel—"

CHESTER HIMES

(1909–1984)

Chester Himes will be known to many readers as the author of *Cotton Comes to Harlem* (1965), a novel made into a popular film in which two black detectives, Coffin Ed Johnson and Gravedigger Jones, carry on in a stunning variety of sensational scenes. However, as Himes's novels indicate, he was a serious writer seeking to come to terms with his life as a black man and writer.

Himes grew up in Jefferson City, Missouri, and wrote extensively and poignantly about his life in his two-volume autobiography, *The Quality of Hurt* (1972) and *My Life of Absurdity* (1976). His father, Professor Joseph Sandy Himes, was a blacksmithing and wheelwrighting teacher in the mechanical department of Lincoln Institute, now Lincoln University, and a series of other small southern colleges. Between 1913 and 1926, the family was forced, because of racism, to move from one state to another. For the first four of these years, they settled in Cleveland, Ohio, before moving to Alcorn, Mississippi. In 1917, Professor Himes lost his job at Alcorn A&M in Mississippi, largely because he was the only black man in the county to own a car.

Chester was extremely close to his brother Joe. Unfortunately, Joe was blinded in an explosion during a chemistry experiment when they were boys, an accident for which Himes blamed himself. After high school, he enrolled at Ohio State University but was expelled after being involved in a brawl. In 1927, he returned to Cleveland, where he immersed himself in the gambling world of the black ghetto. He began hustling, gambling, pimping, smoking opium, committing burglaries, and stealing cars. A year later, in 1928, he was arrested in Chicago for $53,000 armed robbery and sentenced to twenty-two to twenty-five years in the Ohio State Penitentiary. He was released in 1936. It was during his stay in prison that Himes, like Malcolm X, Eldridge Cleaver, and Etheridge Knight, among other creative writers and thinkers, began redirecting his emotional and creative energies. At first he began publishing stories and articles in black newspapers and magazines. Then, he began publishing more widely, with stories appearing in *Commentary, Esquire, The Crisis,* and other magazines. During this period, Himes zigzagged across the country in search of employment and adventure. He eventually landed in Los Angeles, where he worked in a defense plant during World War II.

Himes's early novels seem rather explicitly to be reflective of his own life. *If He Hollers Let Him Go* (1945) and *Lonely Crusade* (1947) focus on the effects of racism on the lives of young, intelligent black men who find themselves in the Los Angeles defense plants. His male protagonists are generally middle class, well educated, and sophisticated. Even so, they are in certain ways not unlike Richard Wright's Bigger Thomas. Himes wrote *If He Hollers Let Him Go* in the wake of the success of *Native Son,* and many similarities between the two books are deliberate. Both Bigger Thomas and Himes's hero, Robert Jones, are deeply self-conscious. Both contend with false accusations of raping white women. Both undergo court trials with fated consequences. The bottom line for Himes was that being better dressed and better paid was of little consequence for black men in America. Such a bleak outlook led critic Edward Margolies to the conclusion that Himes

> feels the trunk and roots of American society are so corrupted as to make normal growth and development impossible. His concern is not with social protest, as has often been alleged, for protest implies some hope and appropriate reform, and Himes, one suspects, regards the American scene as beyond redemption. His principal subject is the human consequences of a distorted and diseased civilization.

Himes's second novel, *Lonely Crusade* (1947), also details how difficult it is for black men to be men. In addition to his attack on white women who use black men to further their own goals, Himes strikes out at the lack of understanding on the part of the middle-class black woman. When Ruth discovers that Gordon is involved in the killing of a representative of his company, he runs to Jackie for comfort, but she calls the police. The lasting effects of racism are among Himes's major themes.

The author's third novel, *Cast the First Stone* (1952), deals with the demoralizing effects of prison life. His fourth novel, *The Third Generation* (1954), returns to the issue of race, specifically color consciousness. Based in part on a narrative history of his family written by Himes's mother, the latter focuses on dissension within the black community, as it treats the differences between light-colored blacks with a house-servant mentality and dark-skinned blacks with a field-hand perspective. In his autobiography, Himes tells of how he resented the importance of skin color among his fellow black students:

> I despised the in-group class distinction based on color and the degree of white blood in one's veins. . . . I liked dark black people. . . . Among them, I felt as black as the next person and as good as anyone. The 'light-bright-and-damn-near-white' social clique got on my ass.

The black man–white woman relationship is the theme of *The Primitive* (1956). In this fifth novel, Himes describes Kriss as a white neurotic woman who seeks release through pills, liquor, and sex. To ease her sense of inferiority and worthlessness, she associates with blacks, reasoning that she can always feel superior to "Niggers." Himes's pessimism and frustration with racism in America led him to the satire *Pinktoes* (1961). The protagonist, Mamie Mason, a Harlem hostess, feels that race relations can be improved best through sexual relations between white liberals and influential blacks. Throughout, Himes pokes fun at middle-class blacks who want to be like whites and at white liberals who are either hypocritical or ignorant.

In addition to *Une Affaire de Viol (A Case of Rape)*, a novel about the rape and murder of a white woman published in French in 1963, Himes wrote a number of violent, nightmarish, and surrealistic detective stories, mostly about Harlem characters whom he knew all too well—pimps, prostitutes, numbers barons, cult leaders, and homosexuals. Like the short story "Marihuana and a Pistol," they bear all the marks of the black man's absurd existence in America. "Racism," Himes maintained, "introduces absurdity into the human condition. . . . If one lives in a country where racism is held valid and practiced in all ways of life, eventually, no matter whether one is a racist or a victim, one comes to feel the absurdity of life."

Himes died in Spain in 1984.

❖❖❖

For further study, see James Lundquist, *Chester Himes* (1976); Stephen Miliken, *Chester Himes: A Critical Appraisal* (1976); Edward Margolies, *Native Sons* (1968); Michel Fabre, *From Harlem to Paris: Black American Writers in France, 1840–1980* (1991).

Marihuana and a Pistol

"Red" Caldwell bought two "weeds" and went to the room where he lived and where he kept his pearl handled blue-steel .38 revolver in the dresser drawer and smoked them. Red was despondent because his girl friend had quit him when he didn't have any more money to spend on her. But at the height of his jag, despondency became solid to the touch and attained weight which rested so heavily upon his head and shoulders that he forgot his girl friend in the feeling of the weight.

As night came on it grew dark in the room; but the darkness was filled with colors of dazzling hue and grotesque pattern in which he abruptly lost his despondency and focused instead on the sudden, brilliant idea of light.

In standing up to turn on the light, his hand gripped the rough back of the chair. He snatched his hand away, receiving the sensation of a bruise. But the light bulb, which needed twisting, was cool and smooth and velvety and pleasing to the touch so that he lingered awhile to caress it. He did not turn it on because the idea of turning it on was gone, but he returned slowly to the middle of the floor and stood there absorbed in vacancy until the second idea came to him.

He started giggling and then began to laugh and laugh and laugh until his guts retched because it was such a swell idea, so amazingly simple and logical and perfect that it was excruciatingly funny that he had never thought of it before—he would stick up the main offices of the Cleveland Trust Company at Euclid and Ninth with two beer bottles stuck in his pockets.

His mind was not aware that the thought had come from any desire for money to win back his girl friend. In fact it was an absolutely novel idea and the completely detailed execution of it exploded in his mind like a flare, showing with a stark, livid clarity his every action from the moment of his entrance into the bank until he left it with the money from the vault. But in reviewing it, the detailed plan of execution eluded him so that in the next phase it contained a pistol and the Trust Company had turned into a theater.

Perhaps ten minutes more passed in aimless wanderings about the two-by-four room before he came upon a pistol, a pearl handled blue-steel .38. But it didn't mean anything other than a pistol, cold and sinister to the touch, and he was extremely puzzled by the suggestion it presented that he go out into the street. Already he had lost the thought of committing a robbery.

Walking down the street was difficult because his body was so light, and he became angry and annoyed because he could not get his feet down properly. As he passed the confectionery store his hand was tightly gripping the butt of the pistol and he felt its sinister coldness. All of a sudden the idea came back to him complete in every detail—only this time it was a confectionery store. He could remember the idea coming before, but he could not remember it as ever containing anything but the thought of robbing a confectionery store.

He opened the door and went inside, but by that time the idea was gone again and he stood there without knowing what for. The sensation of coldness produced by the gun made him think of his finger on the trigger, and all of a sudden the scope of the fascinating possibilities opened up before him, inspired by the feeling of his finger on the trigger of the pistol. He could shoot a man—or even two, or three, or he could go hunting and kill everybody.

He felt a dread fascination of horror growing on him which attracted him by the very essence of horror. He felt on the brink of a powerful sensation which he kept trying to capture but which kept eluding him. His mind kept returning again and again to his finger on the trigger of the pistol, so that by the time the storekeeper asked him what he wanted, he was frantic and he pulled the trigger five startling times, feeling the pressure on his finger and the kick of the gun and then becoming engulfed with stark, sheer terror at the sound of the shots.

His hands flew up, dropping the pistol on the floor. The pistol made a clanking sound, attracting his attention, and he looked down at it, recognizing it as a pistol and wondering who would leave a pistol on a store floor.

A *pistol on a store floor.* It was funny and he began to giggle, thinking, *a pistol on a store floor,* and then he began to laugh, louder and louder and harder, abruptly stopping at the sight of the long pink and white sticks of peppermint candy behind the showcase.

They looked huge and desirable and delicious beyond expression and he would have died for one; and then he was eating one, and then two, reveling in the sweetish mint taste like a hog in slop, and then he was eating, three, and then four, and then he was gorged and the deliciousness was gone and the taste in his mouth was bitter and brackish and sickening. He spat out what he had in his mouth. He felt like vomiting.

In bending over to vomit he saw the body of an old man lying in a puddle of blood and it so shocked him that he jumped up and ran out of the store and down the street.

He was still running when the police caught him but by that time he did not know what he was running for.

"Win the War Blues"

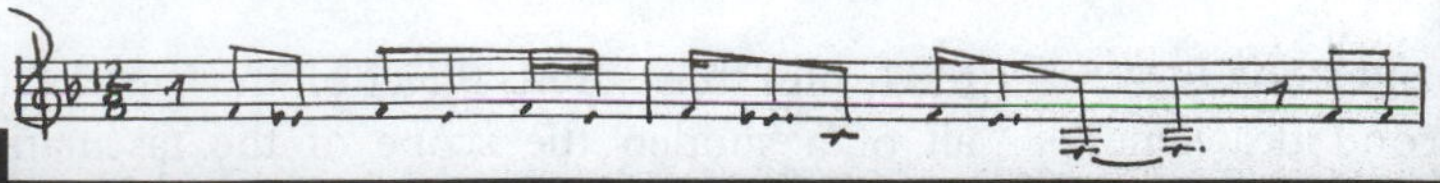

Call for Social Equality

The major battle of African Americans from 1945 to 1960, the post World War II period, was against lawful segregation in the nation.

Portrait by Aaron Douglass from James Weldon Johnson's God's Trombones

V

"Win the War Blues"

"Play the Blues for Me"

African American History and Culture, 1945–1960

"Does it dry up like a raisin in the sun?"

Post-Renaissance and Post-Reformation

I've got the Victory Blues because I know
I've got to go, (repeat)
Now to keep the Japanese from slipping in through
my baby's back door.

"Win the War Blues" by Sonny Boy Williamson

During the period 1945 to 1960, African Americans fought for freedom and social equality on the foreign as well as the domestic level. As Sonny Boy Williamson's "Win the War Blues" illustrates, many of the eight hundred thousand black American soldiers were eager to fight in World War II to uphold American democratic principles abroad. Paradoxically, as the war novels of John Oliver Killens, William Gardner Smith, and John A. Williams compellingly chronicle, these soldiers fought in segregated units against both the systemic racism of their own democratic government and the genocidal racism of a fascist German regime. Back in the United States, black civilians battled against poverty, joblessness, racial violence, and legal segregation in virtually every aspect of American life. This ironic, double-layered war against racism led Walter White, executive secretary of the National Association for the Advancement of Colored People (NAACP), to deliver an emergency call that would signal the African American struggle of the postwar era. In the January 1944 issue of *The Crisis,* he declared, "Victory must crush Hitlerism both at home and abroad." Immediately, American blacks responded to the call. The NAACP, which had grown in power and influence after WWII, led the fight against lawful segregation in American courts and in the nation's streets during the postwar years. Moreover, the literature produced by African Americans during the Post-Reformation, the black artistic period from 1945 to 1960, can be read as a response on several levels to the recurring calls of black people for victory at home and abroad against racial and ethnic prejudice, segregation, social injustice, and terrorism.

By 1945, the center of black cultural activity had shifted from the cabarets, nightclubs, and streets of Harlem to the academic halls of historically black colleges, especially Howard University in Washington, D.C., where a group of influential black intellectuals had emerged. After the Depression and World War II, Howard began attracting large numbers of people of African descent not only from the United States but also from continental Africa and the West Indies. The university became not only their home away from home but also the seedbed of black intellectual and political thought. Beginning in the forties, it sponsored lecture series and cultural events spotlighting the crème de la crème of the black world—political leaders W.E.B. Du Bois, Emperor Haile Selassie of Ethiopia, President Léopold Senghor of Senegal, Martin Luther King, Jr., and Malcolm X; literary artists Zora Neale Hurston, James Baldwin, and Ossie Davis; and musicians Roland Hayes, Marian Anderson, and Thelonius Monk. By the early fifties, Howard became nationally and internationally recognized as the "Black Harvard" when it was hailed in *The Saturday Evening Post* as "America's leading Negro University" and in *Life* as "America's Center of Negro Learning."

The university's prominence during the era was due in large measure to the accomplishments and efforts of its esteemed faculty and alumni, African Americans who had distinguished themselves in practically every field of human endeavor. In politics, for example, Ralph Bunche left his position as head of the political science department in 1945 to make his mark in international affairs as adviser to the U.S. delegation that drafted the Charter of the United Nations, as the Nobel Peace Prize winner in 1950, and as the first African American to hold the position of undersecretary for special political affairs in the UN. Howard Law School graduate Thurgood Marshall led the NAACP's legal defense team to victory in the famous 1954 Supreme Court decision to desegregate state-supported public schools. In medicine, Charles R. Drew remained at the university as chief of staff and medical director of Freedman's Hospital, where he did his pioneering work in developing blood plasma storage until his untimely death in 1950. In the social sciences, E. Franklin Frazier, head of the Department of Sociology, and Rayford Logan, head of the Department of History, initiated in 1954 the university's African Studies Program, which linked Howard, through its faculty's travel, research grants, and cultural activities, to the newly independent nations of Africa during the late 1950s. Frazier and other faculty members, including John Hope Franklin of the history department, also published works that became definitive texts in their respective fields. Among them were Franklin's scholarly history of African Americans, *From Slavery to Freedom* (1956), which has gone through several editions, and Frazier's heralded sociological study *Black Bourgeoisie* (1957).

From the faculty also emerged a talented coterie of critics and writers, who established Howard as the hub of black literary thought during the period. Sterling A. Brown, Arthur P. Davis, Margaret Just Butcher, and Owen Dodson were products of the Genteel Tradition who had joined their Howard colleague Alain Locke by the early 1940s in opposing the literature of social realism that had begun to exhaust itself. Embracing the Lockeian "art simply for art's sake" doctrine, they paralleled the political activities of the NAACP by insisting on the integration of black art and artists into the American literary mainstream. Ironically, however, the faculty produced gifted students who were among the leading African-centered voices of this and the next generation of black writers. They included Lucille Clifton, Ossie Davis, Pauli Murray, LeRoi Jones (Amiri Baraka), Toni Morrison, Toni Cade Bambara, and Lance Jeffers, Eugene Redmond, and other members of the Howard Poets.

Certainly, not all of the cultural activity during the period came from Howard. The voices of major black literary artists were heard from various places inside and outside the United States, and for the first time in the country's history, black writers received national literary honors from the white critical establishment. From the Mississippi Delta blues region, for instance, came Margaret Walker, the recipient of the Yale University Prize for Younger Poets for her volume of verse *For My People* (1942); and from Chicago, the blues capital of the era, came Gwendolyn Brooks, the first black Pulitzer Prize winner for her second book of poems, *Annie Allen* (1949). From the "Big Apple," the mecca of jazz, came the dramatists Alice Childress, the winner of the 1956 Obie Award, and Lorraine Hansberry, the recipient of the coveted New York Drama Critics Circle Award in 1959. But most of the writers were not as fortunate as they were. For example, from Detroit, the city of the "Motown Sound," came the critically overlooked circle of poets—Robert Hayden, Margaret Danner, Dudley Randall, and Naomi Madgett—whose later publishing efforts helped shape much of contemporary black poetry.

By 1947, Melvin Tolson, the author of *Rendezvous with America* (1944), had been appointed poet laureate of Liberia (the only American poet to receive that honor from another nation), and Richard Wright, who had become frustrated with American racism, had settled permanently in France. There Wright became a part of existentialism—the most influential philosophical and literary movement in Europe during and after the war. In addition to Wright, black expatriates who moved to Europe in the forties and fifties included the novelists James Baldwin, Chester Himes, William Demby, William Gardner Smith, and Frank Yerby. These writers, like the 1952 National Book Award–winning novelist Ralph Ellison, who remained in the United States, focused on the continuing quest for personal freedom and communal unity and on the search for values in a world that seemed to have lost all meaning beyond the anxieties of an atomic, apocalyptic future.

In 1960, Wright died in Paris as a black expatriate who had continued to influence writers of the next generation. In Chicago, Brooks began to inspire and introduce the next generation of black consciousness artists. Approximately twenty years earlier, Sterling Brown, Arthur P. Davis, and their Morgan State College colleague Ulysses Lee had coedited an anthology that was highly influential in exposing the black literary talents of the postwar years. The publication of their landmark book, *The Negro Caravan,* in 1941 and of LeRoi Jones's (Amiri Baraka's) critically acclaimed first collection of poems, *Preface to a Twenty Volume Suicide Note,* in 1961 marked a watershed in the dynamic tension between modernist integrationist poetics and African-centered poetics in texts by African American writers of the period.

Call: Double Victory Against Racism at Home and Abroad

We Shall Overcome©

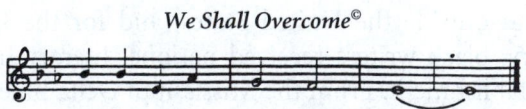

The black leadership of the NAACP and the National Negro Congress pursued the quest for African Americans' equal rights twice in the international forum afforded by the formation of the United Nations in 1945. Despite the

Jewish Holocaust, African Americans and nonwhite colonized peoples were encouraged by the preamble of the Charter of the United Nations. It affirmed "faith in fundamental human rights, in the dignity and worth of the human person, in the equal rights of men and women and of nations large and small." Equally encouraging was the chapter that committed the United Nations to "universal respect for and observance of human rights and fundamental freedoms for all without distinction to race, language, or religion." In 1946, black leaders sent to the UN the "Petition to the United Nations on Behalf of Thirteen Million Oppressed Negro Citizens of America." When they received no reply, W. E. B. Du Bois and others, on behalf of the NAACP, petitioned the UN again the following year. This 155-page petition was flatly rejected by the American delegates but was endorsed by the Soviet members of the UN's Commission on Human Rights.

With no redress for their grievances at the UN, the leadership of the NAACP and other black organizations continued to wage the fight against racism and for Civil Rights in the streets and courts of postwar America. With rare exceptions, public signs particularly in the South and private behavior nearly everywhere in the nation reflected the disparity between the American dream for whites and the blues realities for blacks. The signs still read: NO COLORED. WHITES ONLY. Because of racial discrimination, the vast majority of African Americans, many of whom were unemployed, made up a large portion of America's lowest economic class. Many of those who were employed held menial jobs, working as domestic servants, maritime workers, common laborers, sharecroppers, and farmers. African Americans were still the last to be hired and the first to be fired.

The war in the courts against segregation involved serious battles on many fronts, including public transportation, housing, education, and the military. When, for instance, the Congress of Racial Equality (CORE) organized a group to travel South in April 1947, they were sending "freedom riders" to act as living test cases. They were testing with their bodies the *Morgan v. Virginia* Supreme Court decision of June 3, 1946, prohibiting segregation in interstate bus travel. In many instances, the law of the land was not sufficient to lead to peaceful, effective, honest change. For example, despite the *Shelley v. Kraemer* decision of May 1948, which held that whites could no longer legally refuse to sell houses to blacks merely on the basis of race, many whites flatly and violently refused to obey the law. On July 12, 1951, Governor Adlai Stevenson had to send in the National Guard to handle a major disturbance in Cicero, Illinois. More than three thousand whites organized and violently protested the efforts of a single black family to move into an all-white neighborhood. When Dwight D. Eisenhower became president in 1953, the majority of blacks became increasingly apprehensive that their social and economic conditions would worsen. Their fear is reflected in blues singer J. B. Lenoir's song "Eisenhower Blues":

Ain't got a dime, ain't even got a cent,
I don't even have no money to pay my rent,
My baby needs some clothes, she needs some shoes,
People, I don't know what I'm gonna do,
Mmmm-mmm-mmm—I've got them Eisenhower Blues.

Adding to the anxiety of blacks during the Eisenhower era was the Red Scare, a wave of anticommunism and anti-intellectualism mounted primarily by Senator Joseph McCarthy of Wisconsin. In particular, many black intellectuals, especially college professors, politicians, and artists, were interrogated by the Federal Bureau of Investigation (FBI) for subversive activities, including membership in various so-called Communist front organizations. Although most blacks rejected communism, many were not exonerated from the charge of being un-American until after December 2, 1954, when the U.S. Senate censured McCarthy for conduct unbecoming a member. This was not the case with W. E. B. Du Bois. Four years later, he was harassed by so-called super patriots who attempted unsuccessfully to prevent him from giving a lecture at Howard University.

With African Americans being attacked on so many fronts, the quest for Civil Rights in all aspects of African American public and private life became a dominant motif in the written literature of the period. For example, several black writers, including Lorraine Hansberry and James Baldwin, treated the problem of segregated housing. In Hansberry's play *A Raisin in the Sun* (1959), a title borrowed from Langston Hughes's poetic series *Montage of a Dream Deferred* (1951), and in James Baldwin's short story "Previous Condition," achieving the dream of a home, a nurturing place of mutual love and respect, is a central theme. In *A Raisin in the Sun,* the black Younger family's purchase of a home in a white neighborhood while trying to maintain their courage and pride symbolizes the mixed emotions of African Americans striving to realize the promise of the American dream. In "Previous Condition," Baldwin's protagonist, Peter, makes a desperate attempt to escape from the slums, where he has been forced to live by custom and law. Evicted from an apartment in downtown New York City, Peter expresses an often-heard variation on "win the war blues" to a friend: "I'm sick of it. Can't I get a place to sleep without dragging it through the courts? I'm goddamn tired of battling every Tom, Dick and Harry for what everyone else takes for granted."

What happened in civilian life was equally true in the military. Although nearly a million African Americans served in World War II, they served in essentially all-black units. The legendary segregated training unit at Tuskegee Institute for black pilots, who were generally believed by whites to be intellectually incapable of flying planes, is a classic example of the "win the war blues" on which Ralph Ellison wryly improvises in the short story "Flying

Home." A. Philip Randolph, the organizer of the Brotherhood of Sleeping Car Porters, the first black labor union, informed a U.S. Senate committee in March 1948 that the would urge young African American men to avoid military service until segregation and discrimination were no longer the order of the day. After Randolph organized a group called the League for Non-Violent Civil Disobedience Against Military Segregation, President Harry S. Truman issued an executive order urging equal treatment and opportunity for all Americans in the armed forces. But segregation continued during the early fifties. Not until 1954, a year after the termination of the Korean War, did the Defense Department discontinue its policy and practice of segregated all-black units.

Drawing on the social injustices of American blacks in the segregated armed forces, Gwendolyn Brooks, in the poem "The Negro Hero" in her first volume of verses, *A Street in Bronzeville* (1945) and John Oliver Killens in his novel *And Then We Heard the Thunder* (1963), developed different variations on the "win the war blues." Though both writers focus on the tragic irony of the double foreign and domestic war that African Americans had to fight for freedom, the racism in military life during the war is more overtly and violently portrayed in Killens's novel. The third-person narrator traces the evolving black consciousness of Solomon "Solly" Saunders, an ambitious middle-class soldier who attempts to ignore his color to achieve success in the white world, only to discover in an apocalyptic racial war that all of his individual solutions and personal assets, "the whole damn shooting match, was one great grand illusion, without dignity."

The Defense Department's order ending federally sanctioned segregation in the U.S. armed services in October 1954 was preceded by a more celebrated landmark decision of the U.S. Supreme Court. On May 17, 1954, in *Brown v. Board of Education of Topeka, Kansas,* the Court voted unanimously that racial segregation in public schools was unconstitutional. Thurgood Marshall served as chief counsel for the NAACP attorneys who argued the case. In 1967, Marshall would be appointed the first African American to serve on the Supreme Court by President Lyndon Johnson. This school desegregation case was a decisive moment in a well-organized legal campaign that had already won a series of smaller victories. Marshall later affirmed the significance of *States' Laws on Race and Color* (1951), a book by black lawyer, activist, and poet-writer Pauli Murray that became the bible for Civil Rights attorneys who were fighting segregation laws.

Brown v. Board of Education of Topeka, Kansas and the desegregation of public schools were not the only significant events in 1954 that affected African American life. That year, Malcolm X, formerly Malcolm Little and "Detroit Red," became minister of Black Muslim Temple No. 7 in Harlem. From there, he was catapulted into the national limelight as the fiery, powerful spokesman for the Nation of Islam. Until his assassination in 1965, he captured the media throughout the country by calling for a militant black separatism. In the tradition of his nineteenth-century predecessors David Walker, Maria W. Stewart, and Henry Highland Garnet, Malcolm X spoke daringly, forcefully, and eloquently of a racial militancy without fear or restraint. Not until the early 1960s, however, would the full impact of Malcolm X and his message of black cultural nationalism be felt throughout the country.

Despite the individual efforts and accomplishments of hard-working and courageous African Americans and the court victories, certain traditional brutal patterns of racial prejudice continued. As Brooks's poem "The Last Quatrain of the Ballad of Emmett Till" recalls, on August 28, 1955, a fourteen-year-old black youth from Chicago who whistled at a white woman in Money, Mississippi, was brutally lynched and the murderers were acquitted. The public battles against segregation were not over either. It took the courageous example of Rosa Parks, who sparked the Montgomery, Alabama, bus boycott after she refused to give up her seat on a public bus to a white rider, along with subsequent organized protests by African Americans and others, numerous arrests, and civil disturbances, before the Supreme Court ruled on December 13, 1956, that segregation on public buses in Montgomery was illegal. As a young, charismatic black preacher, Martin Luther King, Jr., was recruited to lead the boycott and the Southern Christian Leadership Conference (SCLC), which immediately elevated him to national prominence and ultimately the Nobel Peace Prize in 1964.

Nor were the battles against segregation in public schools over—the *Brown* decision notwithstanding. Governor Orval Faubus of Arkansas attempted to prevent desegregation of a Little Rock school. He and a group of angry whites flagrantly ignored the law. President Eisenhower sent federal troops into the city to ensure that nine black children could attend school on September 26, 1957. The situation was monitored by the National Guard until May 1958.

In spite of the setbacks, African Americans fought on courageously throughout the decade in the newly formed Civil Rights Movement led by Martin Luther King and the SCLC. They had been inspired by the beginnings of the decolonization of Africa that had begun in the mid-1950s. With African nations such as Ghana, Senegal, Guinea, Ivory Coast, and Nigeria gaining their independence in rapid succession, these leaders' hopes to win the battle against racism at home soared. Against the domestic backdrop of racial injustice, segregation, fear, hatred, and violence, "Win the War Blues" was transformed into the more resolute, widespread, and dynamic spiritual "We Shall Overcome," the theme song of the Civil Rights era. Transcending the anxieties of World War II, the Korean War, the Red Scare, and possible nuclear annihilation by the Soviet Union, this mood of spiritual resilience and resolve was reflected in the continuities and changes in the vernacular and written literature throughout the period.

The Black Vernacular Tradition

Justice Blues

Black expressive art, especially music and speech, is an implicit if not explicit form of resistance or accommodation to color, class, and gender discrimination and a cultural affirmation of a distinctive African American lifestyle. In the 1940s and 1950s, this cultural reality and tradition was transformed by the changing needs of its primary creators and consumers into more urban, technological, intense, and influential patterns, innovatively stressing a view of America from the bottom and margins of a postindustrialized society. The urban blues, gospel, rhythm and blues, and bebop jazz aesthetic became a clearly posed alternative to the mass conformity, moral hypocrisy, and sentimental nostalgia of the prevailing conventional white, middle-class, Tin Pan Alley way of American life. Through the use of these indigenous black American vernacular and formal art forms, African American artists creatively resisted or rejected the dominance of a white American ruling class—subverting, inverting, or reversing its racial barriers and boundaries in social beliefs and behavior as well as in cultural forms and values.

During the postwar years, the majority of black southern migrants were culturally transformed in the transitional (liminal) stage of their rite of passage from predominantly agrarian communities to industrialized and postindustrialized northern and western cities. As a result of this cultural process, the strategies, patterns, and forms of survival of the black masses, especially speech and music, may be more appropriately called vernacular modes of cultural expression. In modern urban black America, residual elements of the vernacular tradition continued to develop in dynamic tension with the formal literary tradition. In *Blues People* (1963), Amiri Baraka called poor, working-class black Americans "blues people" in an attempt to characterize the reciprocal relationship between their sociohistorical condition and their cultural tradition of African American expressivity—especially the blues, gospel, and jazz. This tradition enabled Americans of African descent to cope with the pain and pleasure of living and loving in a racist society, to develop grace and style under the pressure of good times and bad, and to keep hope and dignity alive in the journey from slavery to freedom as individuals with a shared sense of race, ethnicity, and citizenship as a people. Ralph Ellison eloquently and concisely defines the blues in *The Antioch Review* (1945) as "an impulse to keep the painful details and episodes of a brutal experience alive in one's aching consciousness, to finger its jagged grain, and to transcend it, not by the consolation of philosophy, but by squeezing from it a near-tragic, near-comic lyricism."

Urban Blues

Packing their suitcases and heading North on the first thing smoking—sometimes a Greyhound bus and sometimes a railroad train—blues singers from Mississippi like Muddy Waters; Howling Wolf, who left Memphis in 1948 as a disc jockey; and B. B. King, who arrived in Memphis that same year as a disc jockey, headed up Highway 51 through Memphis and into Chicago. Although Kansas City and Memphis were major blues cities, Chicago and Chess Records were the mecca for the urban blues. Transplanted poor, working-class, rural black folks in urban centers like South Side Chicago were a hungry audience for the gut-bucket, shouting, boastful blues of Muddy Waters and Howling Wolf and for the more mellow call and response between B. B. King's guitar "Lucille" and his falsetto voice.

The mid-century years became the golden age of the urban blues, the type of blues music that used electric guitars, basses, and amplifiers with drums and a sax or trumpet. After World War II, the amplification of instruments and vocals became a common practice in the blues scene of Chicago. The urban blues became the music of the black masses, especially for the poor working class on Friday and Saturday nights. These people had only recently migrated from provincial cultural communities in the rural South to work in the war industries of northern, western, and midwestern cities. The main focus of the music was on black people's everyday problems and pleasures of living and loving. With wry humor and innovative rhythms, the music stressed the joys and sorrows of the price of love of self and others in the struggle to survive in a democratic, yet paternalistic, racially segregated, and capitalistically exploitive social order. The popularity of the urban blues was enhanced by the rise of blues record labels during the era. The most famous blues label, Chess Records in Chicago, recorded the best-known blues musicians, including the formidable Muddy Waters (McKinley Morganfield), Howling Wolf, John Lee "Sonny Boy" Williamson II, Little Walter Jacobs, Chuck Berry, Bo Diddley, and J. B. Lenoir.

Besides Chicago, Detroit and Memphis were hot spots of urban blues during the postwar era. Detroit musicians John Lee Hooker, Eddie Kirkland, and Bobo Jenkins launched their blues careers from small nightclubs along the Hasting Street strip. The Memphis blues scene supported larger live blues shows, radio disc jockeys, and two satellite blues centers: the West Memphis, Tennessee, and Helena, Arkansas, blues circuits. The most famous blues singers to emerge from the scene were Junior Parker, Riley "Blues Boy" King, Big Walter Horton, Bobby Blue Bland, Willa Mae "Big Mama" Thornton, and Johnny Ace. In mood, theme, and style, the blues influenced the work of a number of writers of the forties and fifties, including Ralph Ellison, James Baldwin, Melvin Tolson, Langston Hughes, and Robert Hayden, who were seeking to express their African American cultural authenticity and authority as artists.

Black Gospel Music

Black gospel music attained its greatest popularity in the 1940s. The first major recording of a gospel-blues song in the period 1945–1960 was made in October 1946 by Robert H. Harris and the Soul Stirrers, who recorded W. Herbert Brewster's "Lord, I've Tried." "This gospel-blues, which was the first recording made by the Soul Stirrers, set the pace for other recordings by the ensemble and its disciples, which include the Pilgrim Travelers and the Five Blind Boys of Mississippi," ethnomusicologist Horace C. Boyer notes in his article titled "Contemporary Gospel Music" in *Black Perspectives in Music* (1979).

As in previous eras, black religious music of the postwar years reflected rays of hope for African Americans in difficult times. The nation's leading gospel singer, Mahalia Jackson, spread the beauty of black gospel music throughout the country and abroad. She sang her music in concert halls, stadiums, and churches throughout the world. Other well-known gospel singers—Clara Ward, James Cleveland, "Sister" Rosetta Tharpe, Sam Cooke, and Roberta Martin, who were leaders of choirs, ensembles, or quartets—added to the popularity of the music. Gospel music also was used by dance-choreographer Alvin Ailey in his troupe's production *Revelations,* which was performed in New York City and Europe. Gospel song plays such as Langston Hughes's *Black Nativity* (1961) and *The Prodigal Son* (1965) were performed in New York and abroad.

Bop and Cool Jazz

In the forties and fifties, the popularity of big swing bands began to decline with new developments in jazz: "bebop" and "bop" music and "cool jazz." During the 1940s, bop music emerged from musical experimentation in jam sessions of talented jazzmen, who played together after working hours at Minton's Playhouse, a Harlem nightclub on West 118th Street. Members of the now famous group included legendary saxophonist Charlie Christopher "Bird" or "Yardbird" Parker, pianists Thelonius Monk and Earl "Bud" Powell, trumpeter John Birks "Dizzy" Gillespie, drummers Kenny Clarke and Max Roach, and guitarist Charlie Christian. Bop was developed from musical styles as diverse as Parker's smooth, flowing phrases and cascading, staccato, short notes; Monk's improvised, angular, stark melodies; Gillespie's powerful, driving Afro-Cuban bursts of short phrases; and Clarke's and Roach's original rhythmic use of the top cymbal and occasional explosive bass drum. The originality of improvisation and the intricacies of rhythms and harmonies in familiar pieces such as "Cherokee" and "Stomping at the Savoy" made bop primarily a music for listening and for the intellectual set. The lifestyle, symbolized by Gillespie's beret, goatee, and dark glasses, as well as other black bohemian "hep cat" dress, language, and mannerisms—including, for many, the heavy use of drugs and alcohol—became the vogue for many devout jazz fans. This also was true of cool jazz, which was inspired by the irregular melodies of Lester "Prez" Young's tenor sax and epitomized in the low- to middle-register, serene, introspective trumpet playing of Miles Davis, especially his record album *Birth of the Cool* (1949). The laid-back, sometimes haughty mood of the music and the musicians was a sharp contrast to the "hot jazz" of the 1920s and 1930s, as well as to the polyrhythmic, explosive, irregular melodies of bop.

Inevitably, the difficulty of understanding the sound of cool jazz and bop led in the 1950s to the "hard bop" or "soul jazz" movement. Led by the jazz musicians themselves, the movement attempted to take this classic black American music back to its communal and ritual function of communicating directly with a grassroots audience of celebrants that had become increasingly white. Among these artists were Thelonius Monk, saxophonists Edwin "Cannonball" Adderly and Sonny Rollins, pianist Horace Silver, drummer Art Blakey and his Jazz Messengers, trumpeters Nat Adderly (Cannonball's brother) and Clifford Brown, and organist Jimmy Smith. However, writers of the period, such as Ellison, Hughes, Brooks, Tolson, and Owen Dodson, preferred the more smoothly and formally arranged big band, bop, and cool styles of the music. Consequently, they used the latter types of idioms in their writings and paid tribute to Louis "Satchmo" Armstrong, Duke Ellington, Charlie "Yardbird" Parker, and other jazz greats.

Rhythm and Blues

Rhythm and blues, a blend of jazz, gospel music, and urban blues, emerged in the late 1940s. In contrast to the blues of the 1920s and 1930s, which until 1949 the white music industry classified as "race music," the new music was called rhythm and blues (R&B) to reflect the changes taking place in the lives of blacks as well as in the making and marketing of African American music. Even though the new musical synthesis that characterized R&B had been popular in African American communities for some time before being discovered by the dominant white music industry, R&B was not mass-produced until the late 1940s, when it was marketed nationally by independent record companies and disc jockeys. The major independent record labels that fostered the rise of the music were Apollo, Savoy, Atlantic, and National. But Decca produced the major black crossover artist of the 1940s, Louis Jordan. Jordan was an alto saxophonist and popular comic singer with Chick Webb's big band until 1938, when he formed his own combo of six to eight musicians, called the Tymphony Five. From 1945 to 1947, Jordan produced such popular hits as "Caledonia Boogie," "Don't Worry 'Bout That Mule," "Let the Good Times Roll," "Stone Cold Dead in the Market," and "Ain't Nobody Here But Us Chickens."

With the decade of the 1950s came the rise of R&B greats such as Charles "Chuck" Berry, Little Richard, Antoine "Fats" Domino, Otis Redding, Willa Mae "Big Mama" Thornton, Sam Cooke, Jackie Wilson, Dinah Washington, Ruth Brown, Ray Charles, LaVerne Baker, Chuck Willis, Clyde McPhatter, Big Joe Turner, and James Brown. Like Brown, who began leading a gospel quartet while in prison in 1949, many R&B singers had a black church music background. Favorite groups included the Drifters, the Coasters, the Platters, the Five Keys, the Ravens, the Spaniels, and the Orioles.

The decade also ignited a growing interest in R&B among white Americans when white singers such as Elvis Presley, Bill Haley, and Pat Boone began singing black R&B originals, producing commercially successful, generally diluted versions of the music for primarily young white audiences. On July 5, 1954, Presley began his career as the "King of Rock 'n' Roll" by covering the legendary bluesman Arthur "Big Boy" Crudup's 1947 blues song "I'm All Right, Mama" on one side of his first record and bluegrass singer Bill Monroe's "Blue Moon of Kentucky" on the other. Presley's first big hit, "Hound Dog," was a cover of Big Mama Thornton's 1953 "Hound Dog"; Haley's "Crazy Man Crazy" was a cover of Big Joe Turner's 1954 "Shake, Rattle and Roll"; and Pat Boone covered several R&B songs, including Fats Domino's "Ain't That a Shame" and Little Richard's "Tutti Frutti." Because of racism and the economic advantages of major record companies in promoting and distributing their records to a white audience in desperate flight from the anxiety of potential atomic annihilation during the Cold War with Russia, the white cover versions generally outsold the black originals. The blend of country and western, gospel, and R&B music gave rise to "rock 'n' roll," although the young white audience also began to demand the original music as well.

In 1959, the entrepreneur and now legendary Berry Gordy founded Motown Records in Detroit. As a result of his efforts to establish a "Detroit Sound" or "Motown Sound," the music became an intricate blend of urban blues, country blues, gospel music, and jazz by the end of the 1950s. In response to the changing times and values, African American writers sought appropriate modes to express the modern tone, tempo, and texture of the cultural aspects of their poetics—that is, their aesthetic principles.

Call: Integrationist Poetics or Black Poetics?

Future Blues

During the forties and fifties, as previously during the Harlem Renaissance and earlier historical periods, there was no consciously formulated black aesthetic. But the debate launched by Alain Locke and W.E.B. Du Bois in the 1920s as to whether black art should be art or propaganda continued throughout the Post-Reformation era. With Du Bois's absence as a literary critic, the waning of the literature of social realism, and the more conservative political climate of the postwar years, most of the academic critics and some of the writers subscribed in some degree to the Lockeian doctrine—the dominant white, middle-class, integrationist standard of universality and art for art's sake.

In the forties, Locke's distinguished colleagues at Howard University—Arthur P. Davis, Sterling Brown, and Margaret Just Butcher—and other prominent black critics such as Saunders Redding, who taught at Hampton Institute and various other universities and colleges, and Atlanta University professor Hugh Gloster applied many of the critical standards pertinent to white American literature and urged black writers not to limit their subject matter to racial experience in order to dramatize the broader resources of American culture. In 1949, Redding, in his article "American Negro Literature," applauded Frank Yerby and Willard Motley, who used white materials in their novels to attract a large white audience. Yerby's *The Foxes of Harrow* (1946) and Motley's *Knock on Any Door* (1947) represented the possibilities of commercial success by focusing on the lives of white rather than black characters.

Also in 1949, James Baldwin, in his essay "Everybody's Protest Novel," challenged Richard Wright's view that all good literature is protest literature. After engaging in long discussions with Wright concerning the issue of protest in black fiction, Baldwin insisted in the article that the best literature should be universal in nature and should not be limited to what he considered to be the narrow confines of social protest. In terms of the black protest novel, he argued that its failure "lies in its rejection of life, the human being, the denial of his beauty, dread, power, in its insistence that it is his categorization alone which is real and which cannot be transcended."

The place of social protest in African American literature became the focus of the critical debate in 1950 in *Phylon,* an Atlanta University periodical of arts and letters first published in 1940 by W.E.B. Du Bois. Hugh Gloster, in "Race and the Negro Writer," maintains that the black artist should "consider all life as his proper milieu, treat race from the universal point of view, and shun the cultural insularity that results from racial preoccupation and Jim-Crow esthetics." Hence, he celebrates what he calls "the gradual emancipation of the Negro writer from the letters of racial chauvinism." Responding in "A Blueprint for Negro Authors," Morgan State College professor Nick Aaron Ford declares that "such perverted reasoning is pure sophistry." He states that "the record shows that up to this point, at least, the most powerful and most significant poetry, drama, and fiction by Negro authors have been based on racial themes." Quoting critics and writers Albert Guerard, Granville Hicks, and Leo Tolstoy, Ford argues for "propaganda as a legitimate ingredient of serious literature," but he calls for "the use of social propaganda subordinated so skillfully to the purposes of art that it will not insult the average intelligent reader."

The same year, novelist Ann Petry voiced even stronger sentiments to a different audience in "The Novel as Social Criticism." Echoing the views of W. E. B. Du Bois of the previous era, Petry insists that "all truly great art is propaganda, whether it be the Sistine Chapel, or La Gioconda, *Madame Bovary,* or *War and Peace.* The novel, like all other forms of art, will always reflect the political, economic, and social structure of the period in which it was created." Petry then defends the social function of black art by placing it within the historical context of the Western literary tradition. "The idea that a story should point a moral, convey a message," she argues, derived from "the world's folk tales and fairy stories, the parables of the Bible, the old morality plays, the Greek tragedies, the Shakespearean tragedies." The "messages" of modern black novels, she maintains, stem from that tradition, in which the basic theme emanated from the well-known murder story of Cain and Abel and from the question "Am I my brother's keeper." Petry concludes,

> In one way or another, the novelist who criticizes some undesirable phase of the status quo is saying that man *is* his brother's keeper and that unless a social evil (war or racial prejudice or anti-Semitism or political corruption) is destroyed man cannot survive but will become what Cain feared he would become—a wanderer and a vagabond on the face of the earth.

Petry's theory of black art proved to be valid when two years later Ralph Ellison's National Book Award–winning novel *Invisible Man* (1952) first appeared in print. When asked by the editors of *Paris Review* whether he considered the novel to be "a purely literary work," Ellison immediately replied that there is "no dichotomy between art and protest. . . . If social protest is antithetical to art, what then shall we make of Goya, Dickens and Twain? One hears alot of complaint about the so-called 'protest novel' especially written by Negroes." He would, however, reverse his position a decade later in his essay "The Art of Fiction" (1964), in which he rejects what he considers to be a purely racial view of art. Nevertheless, "Ellison's great novel," Richard Barksdale in *Black Writers of America* (1972) writes, "not only settled the question about the admissibility of social protest, but it linked the dispossessed American Black man with the dispossessed throughout the world." Ann Petry would probably agree that as his "brother's keeper," the Invisible Man became, in Barksdale's words, "both blood brother to Bigger Thomas and distant cousin to Camus' Meurseult and Dostoevsky's underground man."

For Petry, Ford, and others, literary theory could never supplant the realities of the black life experience. But the academic critics at Howard University disagreed. They continued to advocate the "art simply for art's sake" doctrine at the 1955 symposium held at the university, which was dedicated to Locke, who had died the previous year. Sterling Brown contributed his criticisms to *The New Negro Thirty Years Afterwards,* Howard's review of the symposium, and Margaret Just Butcher published her informative *The Negro in American Culture: Based on Materials Left by Alain Locke* in 1956. The same year, Arthur P. Davis, in his essay "Integration and Race Literature," which appeared in *Phylon,* hailed black writing that had "moved towards the mainstream of American literature." But because of the changes in the political climate both at home and abroad during the latter half of the decade, their efforts were in vain. With the dawning of the Civil Rights Movement had come a stronger black racial awareness. With the rise of the newly independent African nations had come a revitalized interest in Négritude, the unifying, global concept of blackness formulated in the previous decades by Léopold Senghor, Aimé Césaire, and Alexandre Dumas. And with these movements had come a new racial militancy that began to permeate African American culture, literature, and thought. During the next decade, the voices of the Howard critics would be drowned out by the louder, more militant Black Power shouts of their students, Amiri Baraka and others. During the next decade, an art simply for art's sake would be replaced by an art for people's sake—the black aesthetic and the Black Arts Movement.

The Writers' Response

What Did I Do to Be So Black and Blue?

As with writers in the Renaissance and Reformation and with other black authors of the past. African American writers of the Post-Reformation era primarily concerned themselves with black liberation. But their worldview was wider and more inclusive than that of their immediate predecessors. In general, the Post-Reformation writers viewed the race problem globally—that is, as part of the worldwide struggle for freedom. Molded largely by the great events of the era—WWII, the rise of the United States and the Soviet Union as superpowers, the Korean War, and the beginnings of the decolonization of Africa—they saw their fight against racism at home in the broader context of a war against fascism, poverty, terrorism, and colonization abroad. Using African American vernacular culture—blues lyrics, jazz rhythms, folk sermons, popular rhymes and rhythms—as well as modernist forms and idioms, black writers of the era improvised on the old and experimented with the new to form a communal bond with oppressed peoples throughout the world. The poetry, drama, and fiction that African Americans created, therefore, sought to represent the best of their cultural heritage as they experimented with diverse techniques and ways of expressing their freedom as individual modern American black literary artists and their responsibility in the biblical sense of being their brother's and sister's keepers.

In the poetry of the period, Robert Hayden placed the black liberation struggle within the context of global oppression. In subject matter, Hayden's poetry ranged from his "Prophecy" of the death of Adolf Hitler in *Heart-Shape in the Dust* (1940) to the problems of race and class in the United States in *American Journal* (1978). Stylistically, however, he was at his best in his remarkable "Middle Passage," a blues-based epic poem about the horrifying, culturally transforming journey of Africans on slave ships crossing the Atlantic. Hayden employs black bop devices and modernist techniques in the poem's extended rhythms, complicated syntax, and incongruous imagery to conflate time and space in charting the physical, emotional, and psychological costs of the historical journey of becoming an African American. He found the modernist techniques of Hart Crane, T. S. Eliot, and Ezra Pound worth adapting in his improvisational, "Yardbird"-like flights of fancy and language. "Runagate Runagate" is another long but more upbeat bluesy poem of the heroic flight to freedom of runaway slaves. It is a brilliant display of Hayden's technical virtuosity and his merger of conventional free verse and black vernacular structures, including the blues, jazz, and spirituals: "And before I'll be a slave / I'll be buried in my grave." Throughout his verse, Hayden maintains a delicate balance between the poetics of the American black vernacular tradition and the poetics of modern Western literary culture.

Like Hayden, Melvin Tolson responded to the call for victory over racism and other social injustices at home and abroad. In his title poem from *Rendezvous with America* (1944), Tolson links the black struggle to that of other people of color. Writing from his own point of view as an American of African descent, he explores the horrors of racism toward black, brown, and yellow people everywhere:

> A blind man said,
> "Look at the Chinks,"
> And I saw
> Lin Yutang crying the World Charter in the white man's
> wilderness. . .

Even more than Hayden, Tolson used language that dips and soars with Eurocentric obscurantist, mystical, and technical symbols and images and with intricate jazz and blues cadences. He used the modernist techniques of Pound, Eliot, and Wallace Stevens and blended them with rich black folk speech and music. Consequently, his later poems "Rendezvous" and "Dark Symphony" reveal that he invented a new musical structure, one that merged an assortment of black vernacular idioms and Western cultural musical idioms: blues rhapsody, bass crescendo, diatonic picks, and belting harmonies. Building on his structure of a "dark symphony," he reached for African as well as modernist idioms for his *Libretto for the Republic of Liberia* (1953). In this volume, which celebrates the one hundredth birthday of Liberia, he uses African proverbs and musical rhythms along the lines of a Western musical scale to give a broad overview of African history—from the glorious period of medieval kingdoms through the dark age of European exploitation to Africa's contributions to the modern world. Brilliantly and innovatively, he expanded the use of the poetics of the urban African American vernacular in his literary masterpiece *Harlem Gallery* (1965) by infusing the ode form with the blues, jazz, spirituals, work songs, folk epics, and ballads—from "Papa Handy with his blue notes" and "Old Satchmo's gravelly voice and tapping foot and crazy notes" in "Lambda" to "the Birth of John Henry" in "Xi." In short, he created a new poetic form based on the various rhythmic patterns he celebrates in "Xi": "O spiritual, worksong, ragtime, blues, jazz— / consorts of / the march, quadrille, polka, and waltz."

Tolson's and Hayden's contemporaries Owen Dodson and Langston Hughes also expressed their concerns about global oppression. Dodson, in his poem "Open Letter" from his volume of protest verse *Powerful Long Ladder* (1946), aligns the American black with the Jewish people being massacred in Germany. This collection of verse, as well as his often anthologized poem "Yardbird's Skull (For Charlie Parker)" and his earlier play *Divine Comedy* (1938), show his debt to the black folk tradition. Hughes, who by the late forties worked black music and folk materials more artfully into his poetry, continued to write on racial themes and urban black folks, but he also wrote within the context of liberty and democracy for all. In his poem "I Dream a World," the poet calls for a world "Whatever race you be, / Will share the bounties of the earth / And every man is free." For his 1951 volume of poetry, *Montage of a Dream Deferred,* he charged his verse with bebop jazz rhythmic cadences.

Whereas Hughes, Dodson, Tolson, and Hayden treated the African American life experience, for the most part, from without—that is, globally—women poets such as Margaret Walker, Gwendolyn Brooks, Margaret Danner, Naomi Madgett, Pauli Murray, and Gloria C. Oden continued the women's literary tradition of exploring it from within the black community itself. Walker's verse, from her earliest and most acclaimed volume of poetry

For My People (1942) through *Prophets for a New Day* (1970) to *This Is My Century* (1988), has always been deeply rooted in a sense of community, but she has had an aggressive vision of how that community must assert its basic human dignity. Hence, Walker functions as a griot in her title poem "For My People," one of the best-known poems in African American literature, which sets the purpose, mood, and tone of her first book and her poetry as a whole. It is an exhortation for the empowerment of common black people and a celebration of the black folk heritage.

Although Walker's earliest poems reflect the influence of Carl Sandburg, Edgar Lee Masters, Vachel Lindsay, and Langston Hughes, among the major poets of the period, she was the least influenced by the modernist tradition. In fact, in her essay "New Poets" (1950), she disapproves of the increasing emphasis of black poets on modern "obscurity and ambiguity in the use of poetic symbols and imagery." Instead, for most of her poetry she turns to the modern black vernacular tradition, which she credits wholly to Hughes. For most of the poems in the second part of the book, she uses the ballad form of quatrains to parade a variety of bad man characters such as "Two Gun Buster," "Trigger Slim," and "Yalluh Hammer." In fact, she expanded that folk poetic tradition to include such bad women as "Molly Means" and "Kissie Lee." As poet-critic Eugene Redmond in *Drumvoices: The Mission of Afro-American Poetry* (1976) observes, "She [Walker] surpassed [Sterling] Brown in her search for the verse forms to convey black folk life."

Gwendolyn Brooks, who is perhaps the greatest American poet to emerge from the period of the postwar blues, focused on the realities of segregation in her Chicago black community in her first volume of verse, *A Street in Bronzeville* (1945). Similarly, she created splendid modernist movements of eloquent memory with her black female characters in her award-winning collection of poems *Annie Allen* (1949) and her one novel, *Maud Martha* (1953). As with Hayden and Tolson, she has maintained an intricate balance between modernist techniques and African American aesthetic principles and practices. But as with Walker, she has avoided complex, oblique, esoteric language, which allows her audience to experience the world of her subjects, especially the uncommon courage and dignity of urban black women and children. From 1945 to the present, Brooks's poetry traverses the kaleidoscopic range of the urban black life experience: black womanhood, poverty, racism, segregation, joblessness, female-male relationships, youth, and unsung war heroes.

Brooks's poetic forms are just as varied. She is an innovator in the sonnet-ballad form ("Appendix to the Anniad") and a skillful technician of the ballad form. In "We Real Cool," Brooks demonstrates her artistry in the black vernacular. Equally impressive are her skills in free verse and poetry in iambic lines of varying lengths, which are similar to the irregular melodies, harmonies, and rhythms of bop. Her superb poetic craft and discipline have never displaced her commitment to expressing the experiences of blacks.

Along with Margaret Walker, Margaret Danner, and other poets of the period, she has served as a bridge between the poetry of the Civil Rights struggle and that of the Black Power Movement of the mid-1960s and 1970s. She has not only introduced several of the New Black Poets, including Haki Madhubuti (Don L. Lee) and Etheridge Knight, to the literary world, but she also has voiced an invigorating black cultural nationalism in her later volumes of poetry: *In the Mecca* (1968), *Family Pictures* (1970), and *Primer for Blacks* (1980).

Brooks's contemporary Margaret Danner often gave brilliant shape to black ancestral values across both time and space. Danner wrote of the African heritage and of a deep pride in blackness, but like Brooks, her tone of social protest was somewhat subtle. This is apparent in the series of four poems, including the often anthologized "Far from Africa," that she contributed to *Poetry* magazine, where she served as an editor from 1951 to 1955. Although she never mentions the word *black* in the poems, she constantly refers to the all-inclusive "we" and links it to the black cultural past through a series of African references—"Dance of the Abakweta," "Watusi warriors," "Zulu Prince," and "carvings from Benin." Her fine poem "The Slave and the Iron Lace," from her volume *Iron Lace* (1968), celebrates the technical skill of the slave mason from the days of servitude until now. Part of her remarkable craft is that Danner blends together so beautifully two different voices and psychologies—that of the conservative black Old Guard and the new Black Power voice of the sixties. She was, indeed, one of the premier black American poets of all time on the shapes of African sculpture and the admirable ancestry that lay behind African instrumentation in music.

As with Hayden, Danner belonged to the distinguished circle of Detroit poets that included Naomi Madgett and Dudley Randall, who began writing verse in the 1940s and 1950s and who encouraged the development of black poetry in later decades. With Randall, she formed the Boone House cultural center in Detroit in the early 1960s. In fact, Broadside Press, founded by Randall in 1965 and the eventual outlet for an entire generation of revolutionary poetics, would succeed in part because of Danner's pioneering work. Since 1984, Madgett has been the publisher of Lotus Press, one of the few companies in the country dedicated to keeping black poetry alive. In Madgett's earliest collections of verse, *Songs to a Phantom Nightingale* (1941) and *One and the Many* (1956), she appears to have continued the Renaissance women's tradition of writing romantic and nature poetry for the purpose of exploring the sense of the black female self. Additionally, she has written subtle racial protest, such as her remarkable and best-known poem "Midway" (1959), in which the black persona comes to symbolize all African Americans: "I've prayed and slaved and waited and I've sung my song. / You've bled me and you've starved me but I've still grown strong."

To even a greater degree than the poetry of the era, the drama portrays the African American life experience from within the perimeters of the black community. And it was within that community, in particular on the stages of black colleges and little theaters, that most of the black plays were produced. As during the Renaissance and Reformation, black playwrights experienced great difficulty in trying to reach a white audience. It was partly for this reason that Owen Dodson, who was head of the drama department at Howard University, took his Howard Players on a U.S. State Department–sponsored tour of Germany and Scandinavia in 1949.

Most of the plays of the period are tragicomic dramatizations about black domestic life. Like the novels and poems of the era, they capture the timbre and spirit of the black vernacular. Drawing from the folk sermon and gospel music, James Baldwin wrote *The Amen Corner* (1954), which highlights the ministry of a black woman preacher and the experiences of urban blacks in the storefront church where many continued to practice their fundamentalist faith. As Baldwin wrote, "I knew, in attempting to write the play, by the fact that I was born in the church. I know that out of the ritual of the church, historically speaking, comes the act of theater, the communion." Nonetheless, the play, along with Lorraine Hansberry's *Drinking Gourd* (1960) and Ossie Davis's *Purlie Victorious* (1961), which was informed by the folk tradition, did not attract white audiences. Whereas black critics praised *The Amen Corner,* white critics condemned its turgidity. And even though *The Drinking Gourd* was written for television, the play, which focuses on black slavery, was never produced because network executives feared that it would offend large segments of the white public audience. It lacked the appeal of Hansberry's *A Raisin in the Sun* (1959) and Louis Peterson's *Take a Giant Step* (1953), plays based on the plight of the African American family with which white Americans could identify. As one white critic raved about *Raisin,* "Why, after all, that Younger family was just like us." Oddly enough, he and other white critics missed Hansberry's African-centered worldview and concern for women's rights, which put her and *Raisin* at least two decades ahead of its time.

The white critical establishment also had ignored one of Alice Childress's earliest plays, *Florence* (1949), a strong indictment of racial stereotyping. Although Childress later won an Obie for her off-Broadway drama *Trouble in Mind* (1955), a moving esposé of the historical racism of the American theater, black playwrights had to wait for the Black Arts Movement of the sixties for the popular reception of black art threaded with strong social protest, such as LeRoi Jones's (Amiri Baraka's) off-Broadway Obie-winning *Dutchman* and James Baldwin's Broadway hit *Blues for Mister Charlie,* both produced in 1964.

With intensity equal to that of the playwrights and poets, black fiction writers of post–World War II America perfected the tools of their trade to treat the African American experience from inside and outside the black community. Some following in the wake of Richard Wright and others with their own distinctive voices and modes of literary expression dramatized the blues realities of African Americans. For instance, although Chester Himes left the United States permanently in the early fifties to live in Spain, he kept in touch with the problems his people faced in America by continuing to explore in his fiction the brutalizing effects of racism on various social classes within the African American community. After his novels *If He Hollers Let Him Go* (1945) and *Lonely Crusade* (1947), he exposed the social injustices inflicted on the black male criminal in eight detective thrillers, on the black middle-class family in *The Third Generation* (1954), on the interracial couple in *The Primitive* (1956), and on the Harlem socialite in *Pinktoes* (1961).

To an even greater extent than Himes, Ann Petry moved beyond the economic determinism of Wright in her later fiction. In her novels *Country Place* (1947) and *The Narrows* (1953) and her short stories "In Darkness and Confusion" (1947) and *Miss Muriel and Other Stories* (1971), she established a literary voice on her own terms. The setting and themes of her fiction were a natural outgrowth of her intimacy with the black inner-city life of New York City and the white small-town life of Connecticut. By exploring the sociopsychological dynamics of specific black and white communities in these works, she effectively undercut the contrasting myths of the urban success and progress, versus the rural innocence and virtue, of black and white men and women. In her delineation of cultural myths, especially those of the American dream and the pathology of racism and sexism, she voiced a distinctive social protest.

Dorothy West expanded her 1930s focus on the race-class struggle to include the problems of gender in her memorable, scintillating, semiautobiographical novel *The Living Is Easy* (1948). In exposing the shallow, false values that psychologically trap many middle-class urban blacks in their pursuit of the American dream, West perceptively illumined personally intense moments of psychological understanding by focusing on the development of her light-skinned, black female protagonist largely through her childhood fantasies about her mother. As Mary Helen Washington has observed in "I Sign My Mother's Name" in Ruth Parry and Matrine Watson Brownley's *Mothering the Mind* (1984), the heroine discovers her creative voice "through the mediation of a female power—her mother." In this novel and in other narratives, West reinvigorates the values of black family communion by scrutinizing superficial color-gender-class barriers that separate black people from one another.

The issues of the black urban life experience were extended to an international scope during the early fifties by several black novelists who turned to existentialism and Pan-Africanism for literary inspiration. While existentialism had its roots in the early writings of Søren Kierkegaard, Friedrich Nietzsche, Martin Heidegger, and Karl Jaspers, it was the French philosopher and novelist Jean Paul Sartre who popularized the view "that existence precedes essence, that the significant fact is that we and things in general exist, but that these things have no meaning for us except as we can create meaning through acting upon them." At the beginning of the decade, black expatriate William Demby, in his novel *Beetlecreek* (1950), fused elements of existentialism with those of stark social realism to portray a dreary, stagnant West Virginia town whose black and white inhabitants have lost all hope and desire for improved conditions. Demby continued the theme of the novel—that death, as opposed to life, is related to a failure of courage to act and to love—in his second book, *The Catacombs* (1965).

Existentialism clearly influenced Richard Wright's later novels of protest—*The Outsider* (1953), *Savage Holiday* (1954), and *The Long Dream* (1958)—as well as his works dealing with Pan-Africanism and the sociopolitical situations of Africa, such as *A Record of Reactions in the Land of Pathos* (1954). It also informed the works of Ralph Ellison and James Baldwin, who were deeply inspired by Wright. Although not members of the Wright School, Ellison, who had been introduced to Wright by Langston Hughes, was strongly influenced by him, and Baldwin considered the veteran writer to be a father figure.

There is little doubt that Ellison's *Invisible Man* (1952), in its exploration of the black experience in America, pointed African American literature in a new direction. It eliminated the black writer's need or demand to integrate into the American literary mainstream by brilliantly and artistically establishing the black liberation struggle in America as a worldwide issue. Richard Barksdale in *Black Writers of America* has astutely observed that Ellison's black protagonist became both "a symbol of American social and moral protest" and "the mid-century existential man, trapped in godless uncertainties and meaningless absurdities." By the end of this classic neoslave narrative, the protagonist comes to the realization that he—that is, his humanity—is invisible to most people, black and white, and that he must discover for himself what his existence must be.

Embedded in the novel's richly textured structure are outstanding modernist improvisations on the blues and jazz traditions woven smoothly into the fabric of the story. Insofar as the blues are a lyrical expression of "both the agony of life and the possibility of conquering it through sheer toughness of spirit," the form, style, and mood of *Invisible Man* is blues-based jazz. Ellison himself described the book's structure as that of a jazz composition, complete with a central blues theme and harmonic variations on it: "I'd like to hear five recordings of Louis Armstrong playing and singing 'What Did I Do to Be so Black and Blue'—all at the same time," says the hero in the prologue. Here the theme of the novel is given resonance by the complex connotation of this blues refrain, the striking color imagery with its subtle, wry allusion to pain and violence, and the ambiguous use of Louis Armstrong (whose comic mask frequently cast a shadow over the splendor of his music) as the archetypal black musician. The wry refrain represents the blues motif that runs through each episode of the novel. Thus each episode serves as an extended blues verse, with the protagonist as the singer.

The jazz motif also is evident in Ellison's exuberant, improvisational use of language. Beginning with the prologue, Ellison delights in cutting into the tempo of the narrative to play variations on the theme of invisibility by organically incorporating the litany of a down-home chanted church sermon, a parody of Booker T. Washington's Atlanta Cotton Exposition speech of 1895, a southwestern tall tale, a classic southern sermon, a jive spiel, a sidewalk harangue, a radical political speech, a black nationalist dialectic, and a funeral sermon. The tempo, nuance, imagery, passion, and range of the polyrhythmic, polyphonic varieties of African American speech are overpowering and integral to the novel's development through repetition of plot, theme, and character.

In contrast to Ellison's *Invisible Man,* James Baldwin's short stories and novels are memorable for the soul-stirring eloquence and resonance of their pulpit oratory and black music as they plumb the depths of black suffering and the possibilities of salvation. By word and deed, Baldwin clearly and humbly defines himself as a witness. "I have never seen myself as a spokesman," he told an interviewer in 1984. "I am a witness. In the church in which I was raised you were supposed to bear witness to the truth. Now, later on, you wonder what in the world the truth is, but you do know what a lie is." In other words, he continues, "[I am a] witness to whence I came, where I am. Witness to what I've seen and the possibilities that I think I see." His use of the rhetoric, lore, and music of the black fundamentalist church show to their best advantage in his four collections of essays and in his novel *Go Tell It on the Mountain* (1953). Black music also is organically significant in "Sonny's Blues," *Another Country* (1962), *If Beale Street Could Talk* (1974), and *Just Above My Head* (1979).

Bearing witness to the blues as a sociohistorical and sociopsychological condition and cultural mode of black vernacular expression, Baldwin writes in "The Harlem Ghetto" that "it is simply impossible not to sing the blues, audibly or not, when the lives lived by Negroes are so inescapably harsh and stunted." In "Sonny's Blues," his narrator discovers his own definition of the blues as he is reconciled with his brother Sonny, a former heroin addict and jazz musician:

> Creole began to tell us what the blues were all about. They were not about anything very new. He and his boys up there were keeping it new, at the risk of ruin, destruction, madness, and death, in order to find new ways to make us listen. For, while the tale of how we suffer, and how we are delighted, and how we may triumph is never new, it always must be heard. There isn't any other tale to tell, it's the only light we've got in this darkness.

In short, Baldwin's novels, short stories, and essays helped to popularize the blues world of African Americans and to connect it with the social conditions of people of color everywhere they have been colonized by a Eurocentric, patriarchal, heterosexually oriented culture. Beginning with his second novel, *Giovanni's Room* (1956), Baldwin, who was openly gay, exposed the sexual identity crisis of the black homosexual male caught up in the homophobia of Western culture. His body of writings also shows that he moved from his earlier social integrationist position to a more black militant one denouncing racist American society. As Baldwin would later ask, "Do I really want to integrate into a burning house?"

Whereas Baldwin rejected the allure of the American mainstream in his later years, two other black fiction writers of the fifties, John Oliver Killens and Paule Marshall, stood with Richard Wright, Ann Petry, Chester Himes, and Dorothy West against the desperation of the integrationist tide during the postwar era. They were not separatists but sober negotiators on behalf of cultural authenticity and folk values. They were memorable writers of African American communal bonding through literary art. And they were certainly skilled stylists in different ways, though not to the exclusion of either human life or meaning.

Modeling his career on the social protest tradition of Wright, Killens satirized in his hard-hitting novels various aspects of American society in order to change it for the better. Besides attacking racism in the American military overseas in his novel *And Then We Heard the Thunder* (1963), Killens celebrated the emergence of a new generation of proud, courageous, self-liberating southern blacks in *Youngblood* (1954). He also explored the human impact of the Supreme Court school desegregation decision of 1954 in *Sippi* (1967), wryly indicted middle-class blacks who assume that whites are naturally better examples of what it means to be human in *The Cotillion* (1971), and commemorated the life of slave revolt leader Denmark Vesey in *Great Gittin' Up Morning* (1972). Killens found a rich soil worth tilling in African American folktales and legends, as well as spirituals and the blues. His philosophy that "all art is social, all art is propaganda" clearly shaped his works—five novels, three plays, a collection of essays, several short stories, and two books for children—and aligned him squarely with the Du Bois–Wright–Petry school of thought.

Unlike Killens's works, Paule Marshall's fiction focuses on the African Diaspora. From her first major novel, *Brown Girl, Brownstones* (1959), to her most recent work, *Daughters* (1991), Marshall creates a world of black Caribbean immigrants in the United States, particularly New York City, and their valiant efforts to live at the nexus of three cultures: West Indian, North American, and, by ancestry, African. With the impressive talents of a keen observer and chronicler of the idioms and nuances of Americans of Barbadian descent, she emphasizes black female characters in her works and addresses contemporary women's issues from an African-centered perspective. With her modernist techniques, blended with traditional African oral narrative devices, she skillfully reveals the effects of social injustice and economic exploitation that all blacks experience as colonized subjects of white America and Europe. It is the individual black woman's and man's search for a "home"—a spiritual anchor for his or her personal identity—that preoccupies the central characters in Marshall's fiction. That search often takes the individual on a journey to the Caribbean, or the individual who remains in the United States often refuses to relinquish the dream of returning "home."

Coda

In many ways, the black literature of the Post-Reformation period of 1945 to 1960 journeyed along an inverted "Middle Passage." It moved slowly and gradually from an emphasis on Eurocentric aesthetics toward the African-centered poetics of the 1960s and 1970s as African American artists responded to the blues call to win the war against racist oppression in "democratic" America and fascist, imperialistic Europe. It moved across both time and space toward African ancestralism as male and female writers searched for race-gender-class self-definitions. It moved intellectually and spiritually from an American materialistic perspective back to an African-centered worldview as some American artists of African descent reached again for the cultural powers and traditions of Africa. It moved chronologically and geographically from an American to an African American to a Pan-African sensibility as a few black authors explored the black experience from the New World *toward* Africa. And it charted a steady course for the new generation of African American literary artists, intellectuals, and blues people. As expressed in Margaret Walker's apocalyptic visionary poem "For My People," the literature served as a pressing call to arms:

> Let a new earth rise. Let another world be born. Let a bloody peace be written in the sky. Let a second generation full of courage issue forth; let a people loving freedom come to growth. Let a beauty full of healing and a strength of final clenching be the pulsing in our spirits and our blood. Let the martial songs be written, let the dirges disappear. Let a race of men now rise and take control.

Walker's call would be thunderously answered by the black leaders, activists, writers, and singers of the Civil Rights and Black Power Movements of the 1960s and 1970s.

FOLK CALL FOR VICTORY AT HOME AND ABROAD

FOLK POETRY

URBAN BLUES LYRICS

Win the War Blues

SONNY BOY WILLIAMSON

(Twice)
Uncle Sam is gonna give me a Thunderbolt, he want me to fly away up above the clouds,
He wants me to drop a bomb on the Japanese, I really got to make my baby proud.

(Twice)
I want a machine gun and I want to be hid out in the woods,
I want to show old man Hitler that Sonny Boy don't mean him no good.

(Twice)
I want to drop a bomb, and set the Japanese city on fire,
Now because they are so rotten, I just love to see them die.

(Twice)
I've got the Victory Blues because I know I've got to go,
Now to keep the Japanese from slipping in through my baby's back door.

Hitler Blues

THE FLORIDA KID

Woman I done told you, told you once or twice,
Bring me plenty of lovin' before Hitler takes our lives,
  Because Hitler he's a bad man, tryin' to take every country now,
  Well, before he takes this country woman, please be my so-and-so.

Well ole Hitler says he's a man from his feet to his chest,
He don't bother with nobody but God and Death,

Hitler got his just-right tanks, his planes and his ships,
Get over your town he'll let his big boat slip.

Hitler says some of our people are white, says some are brown and black,
But Hitler say all that matters to him, they look just alike.

Well you better mind how you get drunk, be careful how you clown,
You wake up some of these mornings, Hitler be right in your town,
  Because Hitler he's a bad man.

Eisenhower Blues

J. B. LENOIR

Hey ev'rybody, I was talkin' to you,
I been tellin you jivers this is the natural truth. A-hm—

I've got them Eisenhower blues
Thinkin' about me and you, what on earth are we gonna do?

My money's gone, my phone is gone,
The way things look—I cannot be here long
Mmm-mmm-mmm—I've got them Eisenhower blues.

Takin' all my money to pay the tax,
I'm only givin' you people the natural facts,
I'm only tellin' you people my belief,
Because I am headed straight for Relief.
Mmm-mmm-mmm—I've got them Eisenhower Blues.

Ain't got a dime, ain't even got a cent,
I don't even have no money to pay my rent,
My baby needs some clothes, she needs some shoes,
People, I don't know what I'm gonna do,
Mmmm-mmm-mmm—I've got them Eisenhower Blues.

Louisiana Blues

MUDDY WATERS

I'm goin' down to New Orleans
Get me a mojo hand
I'm goin' down to New Orleans, umm-hmmm
Get me a mojo hand
(*Walter, shouting:* Aw, take me witcha, man, when you go!)
I'm gonna show all you good-lookin' women
Just how to treat your man

I'm goin' down to Louisiana
Baby behind the sun
I'm goin' down to Louisiana
Honey behind the sun
Well y'know I just found out
My trouble's just begun

Back to Korea Blues

SUNNYLAND SLIM

(Twice)
I was laying in my bed, turn on my radio,
All I could hear was the news about the war.

(Twice)
Way up in the sky, airplanes flyin' just like birds,
Well I got my questionnaire this morning and you know I sure got to go.

(Twice)
Well they're fightin' over in Korea and you know that ain't no fun,
Every minute of the day I can hear nothin' but noisy guns.

(Twice)
I got to go back to the old Army, but I hate to leave my little baby behind,
'Cause duty has called me, you know I have got to go.

Future Blues

WILLIE BROWN

Can't tell my future, I can't tell my past,
Lord it seems like every minute sure gonna be my last.

(Twice)
Well minutes seems like hours, hours seem like days,
And it seems like my woman ought-a stop her low-down ways.

Gospels and Spirituals

We Shall Overcome©

1. We shall overcome, we shall overcome.
We shall overcome some day,
Oh, deep in my heart I do believe
We shall overcome some day.

2. We'll walk hand in hand, we'll walk hand in hand,
We'll walk hand in hand some day,
Oh, deep in my heart I do believe
We shall overcome some day.
We are not afraid,
We are not afraid,
We are not afraid today,
Oh, deep in my heart I do believe
We shall overcome some day.

We shall stand together,
We shall stand together,
We shall stand together—now,
Oh, deep in my heart I do believe
We shall overcome some day.

The truth will make us free,
The truth will make us free,
The truth will make us free some day,
Oh, deep in my heart I do believe
We shall overcome some day.

The Lord will see us through,
The Lord will see us through,
The Lord will see us through some day,
Oh, deep in my heart I do believe
We shall overcome some day.

We shall be like Him,
We shall be like Him,
We shall be like Him some day,
Oh, deep in my heart I do believe
We shall overcome some day.

We shall live in peace,
We shall live in peace,
We shall live in peace some day,
Oh, deep in my heart I do believe
We shall overcome some day.

The whole wide world around,
The whole wide world around,
The whole wide world around some day,
Oh, deep in my heart I do believe
We shall overcome some day.

We shall overcome,
We shall overcome,
We shall overcome some day,
Oh, deep in my heart I do believe
We shall overcome some day.

Gimme Dat Ol'-Time Religion (arranged by J. Rosamond Johnson)

Gimme dat ol' time religion, gimme dat ol' time religion, gimme dat ol' time religion,
It's good enough for me.
Jus' gimme dat ol' time religion, gimme dat ol' time religion, gimme dat ol' time religion,
It's good enough for me
It was good for de Hebrew children, it was
good for de Hebrew children, it was good for de Hebrew children
An it's good enough for me.
It will do when de world's on fiah,
It will do when do world's on fiah,
It will do when de world's on fiah
An it's good enough for me.
Oh, gimme dat ol' time religion, gimme dat ol' time religion, gimme dat ol' time religion
It's good enough for me

Move On Up a Little Higher

MAHALIA JACKSON AND THEODORE FRYE

One of these mornings,
One of these mornings
I'm gonna lay down my cross
And get my crown.

One of these evenings, Oh, Lord,
Late one evening, My Lord,
Late one evening I'm going home
To live on high.

Just as soon as my feet strike Zion,
Lay down my heavy burden,
Put on my robe in glory, Lord,
Sing, Lord, and tell my story.
Up over hills and mountains, Lord,
To the Christian fountain,
All of God's sons and daughters, Lord,
Drinking that old healing water.

I'm gonna live on forever,
Yes, I'm gonna live on forever,
Yes, I'm gonna live up in glory after while.
I'm going out sightseeing in Beulah,
March all around God's altar,
Walk and never tire,
Fly, Lord, and never falter.
Move on up a little higher,
Meet old man Daniel.
Move on up a little higher,
Meet the Hebrew children.
Move on up a little higher,
Meet Paul and Silas.
Move on up a little higher,
Meet my friends and kindred.
Move on up a little higher,
Meet my loving mother.
Move on up a little higher,
Meet that Lily of the Valley,
Feast with the Rose of Sharon.

It will be always, *Howdy! Howdy!*
It will be always, *Howdy! Howdy!*
It will be always, *Howdy! Howdy!*
And never *Goodbye.*

Late one evening I'm going home
To live on high.

Just as soon as my feet strike Zion,
Lay down my heavy burden,
Put on my robe in glory, Lord,
Sing, Lord, and tell my story.
Up over hills and mountains, Lord,
To the Christian fountain,

All of God's sons and daughters, Lord,
Drinking that old healing water.

I'm gonna live on forever,
Yes, I'm gonna live on forever,
Yes, I'm gonna live up in glory after while.
I'm going out sightseeing in Beulah,
March all around God's altar,
Walk and never tire,
Fly, Lord, and never falter.
Move on up a little higher,
Meet old man Daniel.
Move on up a little higher,
Meet the Hebrew children.
Move on up a little higher,
Meet Paul and Silas.
Move on up a little higher,
Meet my friends and kindred.
Move on up a little higher,
Meet my loving mother.
Move on up a little higher,
Meet that Lily of the Valley,
Feast with the Rose of Sharon.

It will be always, *Howdy! Howdy!*
It will be always, *Howdy! Howdy!*
It will be always, *Howdy! Howdy!*
And never *Goodbye.*

Oh, will you be there early one morning?
Will you be there assembled 'round the altar?
Will you be there when the angels call the roll?
Oh, children, I'll be waiting 'round God's altar.
Yes, I'll be watching early one of these mornings.
Yes, I'll be waiting at the beautiful Golden Gate.
Soon as my feet strike Zion,
Lay down my heavy burden, Lord,
Put on my robe, Lord, in glory,
Sing, Lord, Lord, and tell my story,
Been climbing over hills and mountains, Lord,
Up to the Christian fountain,
All of God's sons and daughters, Lord,
Drinking that old healing water.
I'm gonna live on forever,
I'm gonna live on forever,
Yes, I'm gonna live up in glory after while.

Oh, will you be there early one morning?
Will you be there assembled 'round the altar?

Will you be there when the angels call the roll?
Oh, children, I'll be waiting 'round God's altar.
Yes, I'll be watching early one of these mornings.
Yes, I'll be waiting at the beautiful Golden Gate.
Soon as my feet strike Zion,
Lay down my heavy burden, Lord,
Put on my robe, Lord, in glory,
Sing, Lord, Lord, and tell my story,
Been climbing over hills and mountains, Lord,
Up to the Christian fountain,
All of God's sons and daughters, Lord,
Drinking that old healing water.
I'm gonna live on forever,
I'm gonna live on forever,
Yes, I'm gonna live up in glory after while.

I Know It Was the Lord

CLARA WARD

Who found me when I was lost?
Who helped me to bear my heavy cross?
Who fixed me up, turned me 'round,
Left my feet on solid ground?
  I know it was Jesus!
  I know it was the Lord!

Who did you think it was in the Lion's den
When Daniel was put there by evil men?
Who put the lock on the lion's jaw,
And rescued Daniel from the terrible claws?
  I know it was Jesus!
  I know it was the Lord!

Tell me who do you think stopped Ezekiel's wheel
That kept on turning in the middle of the wheel?
Who fought with Joshua at Jericho?
Don't you know it was Jesus!
He'll reign for evermore.

Rhythm and Blues Lyrics

During the late thirties and early forties, a new kind of music had begun to evolve as an intricate blend of the classical and rural blues, gospel, and jazz. By the late forties, it was termed rhythm and blues (R&B). Defined as an ensemble music, R&B consisted of three basic musical units: rhythm (piano, drums, string bass, and/or electric guitar), vocal (solo or group), and supplementary (saxophone or other type of wind instrument). In *The Music of Black Americans* (1971), musicologist Eileen Southern describes the music in more technical terms, as one that uses "the blues form and harmonic patterns of the thirty-two bar form" and emphasizes "propulsive duple meters with heavy stress on the strong beats of the measure." The performance style of R&B singers, like that of black music in general, is improvisational and is based on call and response between the soloist and the group. With their soulful lyrics, Chubby Checker, Sam Cooke, Little Richard, and others began a long line of talented R&B singers whose music informed the works of several contemporary black writers.

FROM *The Twist*

HANK BALLARD; PERFORMED BY CHUBBY CHECKER

Come on baby, let's do The Twist
Come on baby, let's do The Twist.
Take me by my little hand and go like this:
Ee oh Twist, baby, baby twist,
'Round and around and around and a just, just like this,
'Round and round.
Come on little miss, and do The Twist,
'Round and around and around and a just, just like this,
'Round and round.

Good Golly Miss Molly

JOHN S. MARASCALCO AND ROBERT A. BLACKWELL; PERFORMED BY LITTLE RICHARD

Good Golly Miss Molly,
Sure like to ball.
Good Golly Miss Molly,
Sure like to ball.
When you're rockin' and a rollin',
Can't hear your Mama call.

From the early early mornin'
To the early early night
When I call Miss Molly's rockin'
At the house of Blue Lights.

Mama, Papa told me "SON,
YOU BETTER WATCH YOUR STEP."
If they knew about Miss Molly,
Have to watch my Pop myself.

Going to the corner,
Gonna buy a diamond ring.
When she hugs me and kisses me,
Makes me ting-a-ling-a-ling.

Bop and Cool Jazz

Unlike the jazz of the swing era, which was associated with dance, bop was solo-oriented, developing in the forties and fifties into a highly evolved type of jazz composition characterized by complex polyrhythms, steady but subtle, light beats, irregular phrases, on- and offbeat accents, and new, exciting dissonant harmonies. Two of the most striking features of this new music were the frequent use of the flatted fifth of the scale and a greater reliance on the bass drummer to sustain the main beat and carry the music forward. As Ortiz M. Walton points out in *Music: Black, White, and Blue* (1972), in bop "the African concept of drums involving rhythm and melody was being reasserted more than a hundred years after its banishment during slavery." For this reason, several black musicologists and other scholars associate bop drumming with revolution and violence.

Typically, both bop composition and performance have a three-part structure. First, two horns—trumpet and saxophone—introduce the theme of the piece in unison. Then a series of improvisations follows—usually both solo and group performances. Finally, the horns repeat the theme statement in unison. In the classic bop melody "Parker's Mood," for instance, the legendary saxophonist Charlie "Yardbird" Parker begins the song with a heralded two-bar phrase:

As the song progresses, he sounds a lexicon of blues phrases for his theme variation, which culminates in an electrifying solo performance:

Equally penetrating is Miles Davis's solo performance of Parker's "Donna Lee":

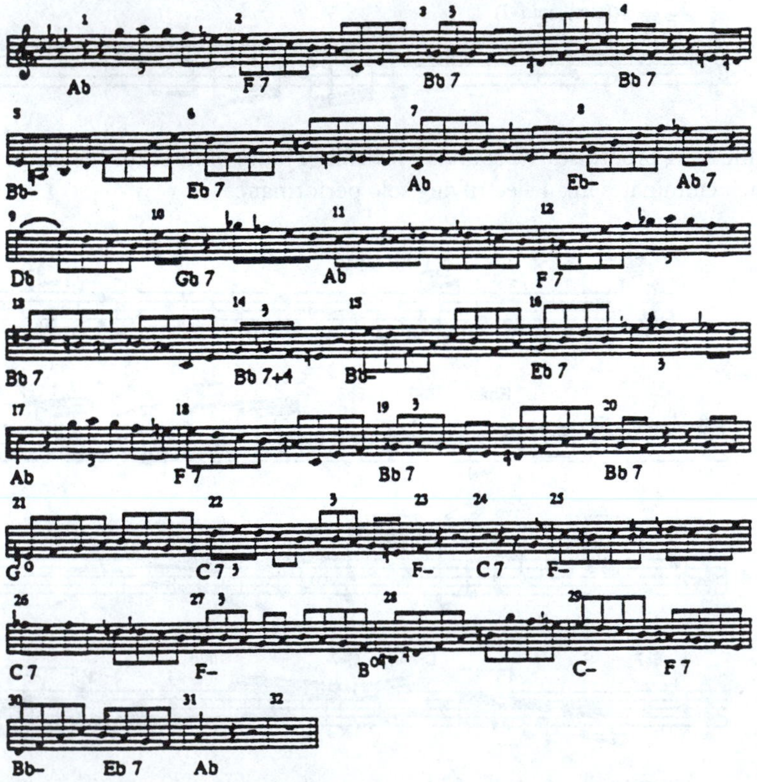

SOURCE: The source for "Donna Lee" and "Parker's Mood" is *The Bebop Revolution in Words and Music,* ed. Dave Oliphant (Harry Ransom Humanities Center, The University of Texas at Austin, 1994).

Also characteristic of bop is the use of nonsensical language. Jazz musicians sing words and phrases such as "Hey Boppa Rebop" for rhythmic effect and/or expression of ecstasy or joy. The same holds true for Langston Hughes, who used bop language and rhythmic cadences throughout his volume of poems *Montage of a Dream Deferred* (1951). His poem "Flatted Fifths" is an excellent example:

Little cullud boys with beards
re-bop be-bop mop and stop.

Little cullud boys with fears,
frantic, kick their draftee years
into flatted fifths and flatter beers
that at a sudden change become
sparkling Oriental wines
rich and strange
silken bathrobes with gold twines
and Heilbroner, Crawford,
Nat-undreamed-of Lewis combines
in silver thread and diamond notes
on trade-marks inside
Howard coats.

Little cullud boys in berets
   oop pop-a-da
horse a fantasy of days
   ool ya koo
and dig all plays.

Bad Women Folk Ballads (poems by Margaret Walker)

Molly Means

Old Molly Means was a hag and a witch;
Chile of the devil, the dark, and sitch.
Her heavy hair hung thick in ropes
And her blazing eyes was black as picch.
Imp at three and wench at 'leben
She counted her husbands to the number seben.
   O Molly, Molly, Molly Means
   There goes the ghost of Molly Means.

Some say she was born with a veil on her face
So she could look through unnatural space
Through the future and through the past
And charm a body or an evil place
And every man could well despise
The evil look in her coal black eyes.
   Old Molly, Molly, Molly Means
   Dark is the ghost of Molly Means.

And when the tale begun to spread
Of evil and of holy dread:
Her black-hand arts and her evil powers
How she could cast her spells and called the dead,
The younguns was afraid at night
And the farmers feared their crops would blight.
  Old Molly, Molly, Molly Means
  Cold is the ghost of Molly Means.

Then one dark day she put a spell
On a young gal-bride just come to dwell
In the lane just down from Molly's shack
And when her husband come riding back
His wife was barking like a dog
And on all fours like a common hog.
  O Molly, Molly, Molly Means
  Where is the ghost of Molly Means?

The neighbors come and they went away
And said she'd die before break of day
But her husband held her in his arms
And swore he'd break the wicked charms;
He'd search all up and down the land
And turn the spell on Molly's hand.
  O Molly, Molly, Molly Means
  Sharp is the ghost of Molly Means.

So he rode all day and he rode all night
And at the dawn he come in sight
Of a man who said he could move the spell
And cause the awful thing to dwell
On Molly Means, to bark and bleed
Till she died at the hands of her evil deed.
  Old Molly, Molly, Molly Means
  This is the ghost of Molly Means.

Sometimes at night through the shadowy trees
She rides along on a winter breeze.
You can hear her holler and whine and cry.
Her voice is thin and her moan is high,
And her cackling laugh or her barking cold
Bring terror to the young and old.
  O Molly, Molly, Molly Means
  Lean is the ghost of Molly Means.

Kissie Lee

Toughest gal I ever did see
Was a gal by the name of Kissie Lee;

The toughest gal God ever made
And she drew a dirty, wicked blade.

Now this here gal warn't always tough
Nobody dreamed she'd turn out rough
But her Grammaw Mamie had the name
Of being the town's sin and shame.

When Kissie Lee was young and good
Didn't nobody treat her like they should
Allus gettin' beat by a no-good shine
An' allus quick to cry and whine.

Till her Grammaw said, "Now listen to me,
I'm tiahed of yoah whinin', Kissie Lee.
People don't ever treat you right,
An' you allus scrappin' or in a fight."

"Whin I was a gal wasn't no soul
Could do me wrong an' still stay whole.
Ah got me a razor to talk for me
An' aftah that they let me be."

Well Kissie Lee took her advice
And after that she didn't speak twice
'Cause when she learned to stab and run
She got herself a little gun.

And from that time that gal was mean,
Meanest mama you ever seen.
She could hold her likker and hold her man
And she went thoo life jus' raisin' san'.

One night she walked in Jim's saloon
And seen a guy what spoke too soon;
He done her dirt long time ago
When she was good and feeling low.

Kissie bought her drink and she paid her dime
Watchin' this guy what beat her time
And he was making for the outside door
When Kissie shot him to the floor.

Not a word she spoke but she switched her blade
And flashing that lil ole baby paid:
Evvy livin' guy got out of her way
Becasue Kissie Lee was drawin' her pay.

She could shoot glass offa the hinges,
She could take herself on the wildest binges.
And she died with her boots on switching blades
On Talledega Mountain in the likker raids.

Folk Sermon

The Prodigal Son (C. L. Franklin)

He sat there
hungry
and set there
you understand
full of experience and wisdom that he'd gained
from all of his trials.
And as he sat there
thinking about it,
hungry
and realizing
that he'd come from
a palace
down to a pigpen,
and in this situation,
the record is
he came to himself.
I wish somebody tonight
that's listening to me
would sit right where you are
and come to yourself.
O Lord.
You know Jesus told
this story
in order to let men know
that he had faith
in men,
that he did not believe that man
was ultimately
sinful
and wicked,
but the ultimate end
of man was
to come to God.
For you see, my brothers
and my sisters,
to do wrong
is alien with man.
One of these days
wrongness

SOURCE: Reverend C. L. Franklin, the father of "The Queen of Soul," Aretha Franklin, was one of the most prominent African American ministers of his time. The congregation he pastored in Detroit numbered more than ten thousand members.

will disappear.
One of these days
selfishness
will be wiped out on this globe.
One of these days
wars
will end,
and
one of these days peace
will prevail.
(I don't believe you know what I'm talking about.)
And this young man
sat there,
realizing
that he had ended up there
and was paying for his folly.
O Lord.
He sat there,
there among swines,
with hogs
all around him.
O Lord.
Realizing,
great God,
that he'd sought a freedom
without laws,
O Lord,
that he wanted a freedom
at the expense
of law and order
and discipline,
O Lord,
and he'd given up a
happy home.
You ought to be able
to see him sitting there
thinking to himself:
Here I am
in rags,
in tattered rags,
but at home my father
has a wardrobe
full of robes.
Here I am
with the last bracelet gone,
and

in my father's jewelry box
there's another bracelet there.
O Lord.
Here I am
with no necklace
about my neck,
and at my father's house
there are many necklaces,
O Lord.
And here I am hungry,
yeah,
and at home
there's bread
and enough to spare.
O Lord.
I know
That I've done wrong,
yes,
I know,
yes,
yes I know,
I know
I disobeyed my father,
I know
that I'm a violator,
I know
that I've been wild
and then I've been reckless,
yes I have,
but I'm going
back home today.
O Lord.
I've done wrong
but I'm going home,
yes I am.
I'm a rioter
but I'm going home,
yes I am.
I'm hungry
but I'm going home,
yes I am.
I'm outdoors
but I'm going home,
yes.
Yes!

(I wish somebody would pray with me.)
Yes.
Yes.
I'm going to tell my father,
yes,
that Lord, Father,
Father,
Father!
yes,
Father!
yes,
I've been wrong,
yes I have,
Father!
I know I disobeyed you,
yes I did,
I left home talking about
give me,
I left home telling you,
to give me,
but I've come back home today,
telling you to make me,
make me
one of your servants,
O Lord.
And that's what I'm telling them now.
Lord!
Lord.
Lord!
Lord!
You just make me,
you just make me,
as one of your highest servants.
Lord!
Lord.
Lord!
Lord!
Lord.
Lord!
Just use me,
anything you want me to do,
here is my life,
here is my heart,
here are my hands,
here are my eyes,

Lord!
Lord.
Lord!
O Lord.
Ohh!
Ohh yes!
Yes!
Just make me
one of your highest servants,
yes.

CALL FOR CRITICAL DEBATE

HUGH M. GLOSTER
(1911–)

Critic-educator Hugh M. Gloster was born on May 11, 1911 and reared in Brownsville, Tennessee. He received a B.A. from Morehouse College in 1931 and an M.A. from Atlanta University in 1933. Five years later, he founded the College Language Association (CLA) and served as its president for a year. In 1943, he received a Ph.D. in English from New York University. While in New York, he met many writers, artists, and musicians in Harlem. "It was a fantastic period, with Langston Hughes, Countee Cullen, and Zora Neale Hurston," Gloster said. They became the subject of his dissertation, which he later published as *Negro Voices in American Fiction* (1948), his best-known work.

From 1948 to 1950, Gloster served the CLA as president. From 1948 to 1953, he was contributing editor of the social and literary journal *Phylon.* It was during this period that he participated in a debate on the nature of black art that appeared in *Phylon* (1950). In his essay "Race and the Negro Writer," Gloster, a strong advocate of "art for art's sake," urged the black writer to abandon the subject of racial experience in order to dramatize the broader resources of American life and heritage.

After a lengthy career of teaching English at various universities, including Morehouse College, LeMoyne College in Memphis, Tennessee, and Hampton Institute in Hampton, Virginia, he returned to Morehouse in 1967 to become president. During his twenty-year tenure at the college, the enrollment and faculty doubled, and the college's endowment quadrupled. According to Samuel Myers, president of the National Association for Equal Opportunity in Higher Education, Gloster became known "in higher education circles . . . as a statesman who kept an eye on the broad policy effects of blacks in higher education." Before his retirement in 1987, he was named by his peers as one of the one hundred best presidents in the country.

❖❖❖

Very little has been written on this distinguished educator. However, useful biographical information can be found in Michele N. E. Collison's article, "Morehouse's Gloster: Man on a Mountain Top," *The Chronicle of Higher Education,* July 22, 1987, and *Encyclopedia of Black America* (1988).

Race and the Negro Writer

From the beginnings of his active authorship in this country the Negro writer has been preoccupied with racial issues and materials. This obsession with race is not hard to explain, because the tragic plight of the colored population of the United States has forced the Negro writer to stand with his people and to voice their sufferings, reverses, triumphs, and aspirations. The inhumanities of slavery, the restrictions of segregation, the frustrations of prejudice and injustice, the debasements of concubinage and bastardy, the ravages of persecution and lynching—these have constituted the bitter experience of American black folk; and it is only natural that the Negro writer has focused upon the themes of racial defense, protest, and glorification.

While propaganda from inside sources has frequently assisted colored people in their struggle toward equality and freedom, the preponderating use of racial subject matter has handicapped the Negro writer in at least four important ways. In the first place, it has retarded his attainment of a cosmic grasp of the varied experiences, humorous as well as tragic, through which individuals pass in this life. Second, it has diminished his philosophical perspective to the extent that he has made only meager contributions to national and world ideologies. Third, it has usually limited his literary range to the moods and substance of race in the United States. Fourth and finally, it has helped certain critics and publishers to lure him into the deadly trap of cultural segregation by advising him that the black ghetto is his proper milieu and that he will write best when he is most Negroid. Incidentally, this insidious counsel, repeated many times in an attempt to stabilize cultural separation, has been propagated so effectively that the abandonment of black stereotypes by the Negro writer is traditionally viewed by many Americans as an artistic desertion of the race.

In spite of the limiting and crippling effects of racial hypersensitivity and Jim-Crow esthetics, the Negro writer has gradually loosened the shackles that have held him in mental bondage for the past two centuries. In recent years the emancipatory process has been accelerated through the efforts of such authors as Richard Wright, Ann Petry, Gwendolyn Brooks, Willard Motley, Frank Yerby, and Zora Neale Hurston. In *Native Son* (1940), Wright treats the old subject to Negro degradation and persecution but transcends the color line by identifying his downtrodden protagonist with underprivileged youth of other lands and races:

> More than anything else, as a writer, I was fascinated by the similarity of the emotional tensions of Bigger in America and Bigger in Nazi Germany and Bigger in old Russia. All Bigger Thomases, white and black, felt tense, afraid, nervous, hysterical, and restless.

This successful blending of class and race experience suggests that Wright's sympathies are comprehensive enough to include all exploited people; and *Native Son* illustrates, perhaps more effectively than any other novel by an American Negro, that it is possible to attack racial oppression and at the same time provide truthful implications for all mankind. In *The Street* (1946), a stirring record of delinquency in Harlem, and in *Annie Allen* (1949), a Pulitzer Prize–winning account of human fortunes in South Chicago, Ann Petry and Gwendolyn Brooks, respectively, disclose the common human denominators of passion, marriage, motherhood, and disillusionment in the lives of contemporary Negro women. Also lifting his work to the universal plane by presenting humanity through an individual, Willard Motley reports the downfall and death of Nick Romano in *Knock on Any Door* (1947). In this important contribution to world literature the symbolic victim of organized society is an Italian boy who rapidly degenerates after his impoverished family moves to the slums of Chicago's West Side. With his motto of "Live fast, die young, and have a good-looking corpse," Nick could be any dissolute youth in any corrupt metropolis. Writing entertaining romances for big-money profits, Frank Yerby has produced in rapid succession five novels that are ideologically and esthetically unimportant but nevertheless noteworthy as the first series of best-seller triumphs by an American Negro writer in the field of general fiction. Following Yerby into the mainstream but not approaching his financial success have come Ann Petry with *Country Place* (1947), an account of clandestine love in a small New England town, and Zora Neale Hurston with *Seraph on the Suwanee* (1948), a local-color tale of romance and marriage among Florida Crackers. Wright, Mrs. Petry, Miss Brooks, Motely, Yerby, and Miss Hurston are tillers of broader fields than the circumscribed areas of racial life.

The gradual emancipation of the Negro writer from the fetters of racial chauvinism and cultural isolation has recently been facilitated by the rapid extension of democratic ideas and attitudes in this country and abroad. Despite the persistence of the plantation tradition with its apotheosis of slavery as a felicitous existence for the irresponsible "darky," the publishing and writing professions have exhibited an increasingly liberal attitude toward the Negro as author and as subject. During the past five years, for example, such firms as D. Appleton-Century Company, the Dial Press, Houghton Mifflin Company, and Charles Scribner's Sons have published Negro-authored books in the field of general fiction; and in advertisements of these works the practice has been to make no mention of the racial identity of the writers. Throughout the country, moreover, white authors are manifesting a growing disposition to describe frankly and understandingly the social and intellectual dilemmas of colored people. Even Southerners are treating Negro life with increasing honesty and objectivity, and Georgia-born Lillian Smith's *Killers of the Dream* (1949) may be regarded as a harbinger of an unbiased approach to racial subject matter by writers living below the Mason-Dixon Line. That the social conscience is disturbed not only in the United States but in other countries as well is convincingly demonstrated in Alan Paton's *Cry, the Beloved Country* (1948), an epochal novel which records the interactions of South African natives and whites with the insight and courage that characterize the universal approach.

The main point of this essay is not that the Negro writer should suppress his ethnic individuality or relinquish racial subject matter. The chief emphasis is that he should consider all life as his proper milieu, treat race from the universal point of view, and shun the cultural insularity that results from racial preoccupation and Jim-Crow esthetics. If a liberal English clergyman can deal realistically and understandingly with the experience of South Africans in *Cry, the Beloved Country,* the broad-minded Negro artist can similarly handle the comedy and tragedy of his own racial group and of other folk as well. The Negro writer is also an American writer, a man of letters as free as any of his national confreres to tap the rich literary resources of our land and its people. To accept the principle that racial experience is the only natural province of the Negro writer is to approve an artistic double standard that is just as confining and demoralizing in American literature as is segregation in American life.

NICK AARON FORD

(1904–1982)

Scholar, educator, consultant, and editor, Nick Aaron Ford was born on August 4, 1904, in Ridgeway, South Carolina. The son of Nick A. and Carrie Ford, he attended segregated public schools in Ridgeway. Guided by the faith, patience, and industry of his parents on how to survive the Jim Crow South, Ford kept his eye on the prize of education. Inspired by the example and lessons of his parents and community, he went on to complete his B.A. at Benedict College in 1926 and his M.A. at the University of Iowa in 1934. Eleven years later, he received his Ph.D. in politics at the University of Iowa.

His distinguished career in education began at Schofield Normal School in Aiken, South Carolina, where he served as principal from 1926 to 1928. From there, Ford taught English at various black colleges until he joined the faculty at Morgan State College in Baltimore, Maryland, in 1945. It was during his long tenure as professor and chairman of the English department at Morgan State (1945–1974) that he established his reputation as one of the foremost critics of black literature of his time. In his essay "A Blueprint for Negro Authors," published in *Phylon* in 1950, Ford challenged the then popular notion that black writers should abandon race as a subject matter.

He wrote several books, including *The Contemporary Negro Novel: A Study in Race Relations* (1936), *American Culture in Literature* (1967), and *Black Studies: Threat or Challenge?* (1973). He also edited *Language in Uniform: A Reader on Propaganda* (1967) and *Black Insights: Significant Literature by Black Americans, 1870 to Present* (1971).

Ford served the U.S. Office of Education from 1964 to 1967, where, he said, "he was in constant demand as consultant in the use of resources for integrating the study of Afro-American life and culture into courses in American literature and Freshman English and Black (Afro-American) literature." Eventually, he retired from Morgan State as Alain Locke Professor Emeritus of Black Studies. He died on July 17, 1982.

❖❖❖

Sources on Ford and his critical works are sparse. Brief biographical information can be found in *Contemporary Authors,* ed. Carolyn Riley, vols. 25–28.

A Blueprint for Negro Authors

If the Negro author's past achievements have not been great, at least they have been motivated by great intentions. He has created the kind of literature that Walt Whitman had in mind when he said, "Literature is big only in one way—when used as an aid in the growth of the humanities—a furthering of the cause of the masses—a means whereby men may be revealed to each other as brothers."

But as we face the second half of the twentieth century, there is a babel of voices seeking to direct the harassed author. There is widespread dissatisfaction not only with the failure of these authors to achieve a maturity in artistic technique, but also with the limited goals some of them seemingly have set for themselves. In this welter of confusion I dare suggest a blueprint for writers who wish to accept the glorious opportunities and grave responsibilities of the next half century.

The first of my requirements is a mastery of craftsmanship. The past record in this respect is dismal. Despite one hundred and ninety years of effort, no American Negro poet has achieved a status comparable to such first-rate white poets as Robert Frost or Edwin Arlington Robinson. In the field of drama the record is almost nil. Only in fiction, and that within the last decade, has the Negro author achieved first-rate distinction.

The chief weakness of these writers has been in the area of craftsmanship and design rather than theme. No Negro author before the advent of Richard Wright's *Native Son* (1940) has deserved a listing among first-rate American novelists. Only Frank Yerby and Willard Motley have earned such a place since. Other authors have treated equally potent themes, but mastery of the art of fiction has been lacking. For the most part, the style is heavy and laborious, more suitable to a sociological treatise than to a novel. They fail in the three major essentials of good craftsmanship—namely, the ability to invent interesting and natural conversation, the ability to create memorable characters, and the ability to construct unforgettable scenes through the creation of pity and terror.

In addition to Wright, Yerby, and Motley, there are five other novelists who possess one or more of these qualities to a considerable degree, and who, if they continue to improve, will achieve first rank in the near future: they are

William Attaway, Ann Petry, Arna Bontemps, William Gardner Smith, and J. Saunders Redding.

My second requirement for the Negro author is the continued use of racial themes. In certain quarters a great clamor has arisen for Negro authors to abandon racial material and launch out in the "universal depths." It is the belief of this school of thought that a writer's preoccupation with materials dealing with his own race is an admission that he is incapable of dealing with any other. It further maintains that such a writer is adding fuel to the fires of race consciousness, segregation, and racial proscription. To counteract these sinister forces, the writer must treat universal themes, and leave to white authors the exploitation of subject matter dealing with Negro life.

In my opinion such perverted reasoning is pure sophistry. In all ages and climates of man's civilization, one of the major purposes of literature has been to represent the thought and actions of men with as much truth to life as is possible. Naturally a writer can portray life that he feels deeply and understands minutely with a greater degree of genuineness and truth than he can life which is more foreign to his experience. I cannot believe that a Negro, sensitive, as all artists must be, can feel and understand anything in America as minutely and as truthfully as he can the effects of race. Then, why should he not write about that which he knows best? No white man or woman can understand the tragedy, the pathos, and the humor of being a Negro in America as well as a talented Negro. Sir Philip Sidney's advice to the young poet, "Look in thy heart, and write," has not yet been proved either invalid or unwise.

Futhermore, the record shows that up to this point, at least, the most powerful and most significant poetry, drama, and fiction by Negro authors have been based on racial themes. Ann Petry's second novel, which logically should have been better than the first, is greatly inferior to *The Street* both in design and execution. She had to be so concerned with conjuring up vicarious experiences of a white society with which she was not minutely familiar that she lost the naturalness of expression necessary to good art. Zora Neale Hurston's *Seraph on the Suwanne,* which portrays life among white Floridians, is almost unbelievably inferior to her two novels of Negro life. Even Frank Yerby achieved greater artistic perfection in *The Foxes of Harrow* and *The Vixens,* both of which have a background of Negro life and action, than he did in *The Golden Hawk* and *Pride's Castle,* which completely ignore the racial angle.

Professor Harry A. Overstreet of New York City College was right when he said, "The whites need to know the Negro and like him. A special obligation, therefore, is upon the Negro writer to turn to the story as a means whereby he may make his people known."

My third requirement for the Negro author is the use of social propaganda subordinated so skillfully to the purposes of art that it will not insult the average intelligent reader. I do not think it is sufficient for the Negro author to treat racial themes with no regard to their deeper social implications as was done by Countee Cullen in *One Way to Heaven* and Zora Neale Hurston in *Jonah's Gourd Vine* and *Their Eyes Were Watching God.*

Is propaganda a legitimate ingredient of literature? Albert Guerard, in *Art for Art's Sake,* says, "An artist does not suffer from being identified with a cause; if the cause is himself, a vital part of himself, it is also a fit element of his art. He suffers most from not being identified with his cause, from adopting and serving a purpose which remains alien to his personality."

In *The Great Tradition* Granville Hicks maintains, "In the whole history of American literature one can scarcely think of a writer, commonly recognized as great, who did not immerse himself in the life of the times, who did not concern himself with the problems of his age."

Tolstoi, in *What Is Art?,* declares, "We know that the well being of man lies in union with his fellowmen. . . . Art should transform this perception into feeling."

If one accepts the conclusions of the three critics quoted above, as I certainly do, he must also accept propaganda as a legitimate ingredient of serious literature. But I do not advocate art for the sake of propaganda. I demand a proper subordination and the observance of good taste. An example of the violation of the limitations I place upon this requirement may be seen in the poetry of Frank Marshall Davis. His propaganda, though based on sound critical analysis, is so blunt and militant that it has little chance of winning sympathetic consideration. In addition, much of it offends good taste. Such bitter iconoclasm as the following quotation from "Christ Is a Dixie Nigger" goes beyond the bounds which I have prescribed:

> Your pink priests who whine about Pilate and
> Judas and Gethsemane I'd like to hog-tie and dump into the stinking cells to write a New Testament around the Scottsboro Boys.
> Subdivide your million dollar temples into
> liquor taverns and high class whore-houses. . . . My nigger Christ can't get past the door anyway.
> Remember this, you wise guys.
> Your tales about Jesus of Nazareth are no go
> with me. . . . I've got a dozen Christs in Dixie all bloody and black.

With his extraordinary imagination and his marvelous skill in the use of words, Davis could make a favorable impression in the world of poetry, provided he curb his bitterness and temper his cynicism with reasonable restraint.

My fourth requirement grows out of the third. One of the best methods of subordinating propaganda to art is the skillful use of symbolism. By this means the Negro author can fight the battles of his race with subtlety and popularity. Willard Motley, in presenting the story of an Italian minority in *Knock on Any Door,* has symbolized the problems of all minorities, including his own race.

But the chief symbolist among Negro authors is Frank Yerby. Starting his literary career in 1944 with "Health Card," a bitter story of America's rejection of the Negro as a dignified human being, which won for him an O. Henry Memorial Prize, he has steadily progressed from complete absorption in a racial theme to complete abandonment of racial material. But in all of his non-racial writings he has substituted a racial symbol, the symbol of rejection.

He finds in the social rebels of the white race, in men and women who because of birth, or manner of livelihood, or disregard of social and moral proprieties have become pariahs among their own people, an archetype of racial rejection. But these white rejectees fight back. They build industrial empires, or pile up huge mountains of illicit wealth, or become swashbuckling pirates who defy the laws of the smug and the respectable. Thus, symbolically the white rejectees get their revenge on a proud and haughty society, and through them the rejected Negro can feel a sense of vicarious triumph.

I conclude with the challenging words of J. Donald Adams: "Sometimes I think the wheel has turned full circle, and that writers must be the fighters now. They really stand at Armageddon, and must battle for the Lord. They, more than anyone else, perhaps, can be effective in preserving the values that are threatened."

ANN PETRY[1]

The Novel as Social Criticism

After I had written a novel of social criticism (it was my first book, written for the most part without realizing that it belonged in a special category) I slowly became aware that such novels were regarded as a special and quite deplorable creation of American writers of the twentieth century. It took me quite awhile to realize that there were fashions in literary criticism and that they shifted and changed much like the fashions in women's hats.

Right now the latest style, in literary circles, is to say that the sociological novel reached its peak and its greatest glory in *The Grapes of Wrath,* and having served its purpose it now lies stone-cold dead in the market place. Perhaps it

[1] Ann Petry's biography can be found in Part IV.

does. But the corpse is quick with life. Week after week it sits up and moves close to the top of the best-seller list.

It is my personal opinion that novels of this type will continue to be written until such time as man loses his ability to read and returns to the cave. Once there he will tell stories to his mate and to his children; and the stories will contain a message, make a comment on cave society; and he will, finally, work out a method of recording the stories, and having come full circle the novel of social criticism will be reborn.

Its rebirth in a cave or an underground mine seems inevitable because it is not easy to destroy an old art form. The idea that a story should point a moral, convey a message, did not originate in the twentieth century; it goes far back in the history of man. Modern novels with their "messages" are cut from the same bolt of cloth as the world's folk tales and fairy stories, the parables of the Bible, the old morality plays, the Greek tragedies, the Shakespearean tragedies. Even the basic theme of these novels is very old. It is derived from the best known murder story in literature. The cast and the setting vary, of course, but the message in *Knock on any Door, Gentleman's Agreement, Kingsblood Royal, Native Son, The Naked and the Dead, Strange Fruit, A Passage to India,* is essentially the same: And the Lord said unto Cain, Where is Abel thy brother? And he said, I know not: Am I my brother's keeper?

In one way or another, the novelist who criticizes some undesirable phase of the status quo is saying that man *is* his brother's keeper and that unless a social evil (war or racial prejudice or anti-Semitism or political corruption) is destroyed man cannot survive but will become what Cain feared he would become—a wanderer and a vagabond on the face of the earth.

The critical disapproval that I mentioned just above is largely based on an idea that had its origin in the latter part of the eighteenth century, the idea that art should exist for art's sake—*l'art pour l'art,* Poe's poem for the poem's sake. The argument runs something like this: the novel is an art form; art (any and all art) is prostituted, bastardized, when it is used to serve some moral or political end for it then becomes propaganda. This eighteenth century attitude is now as fashionable as Dior dresses. Hence, many a critic who keeps up with the literary Joneses reserves his most powerful ammunition for what he calls problem novels, thesis novels, propaganda novels.

Being a product of the twentieth century (Hitler, atomic energy, Hiroshima, Buchenwald, Mussolini, USSR) I find it difficult to subscribe to the idea that art exists for art's sake. It seems to me that all truly great art is propaganda, whether it be the Sistine Chapel, or La Gioconda, *Madame Bovary,* or *War and Peace.* The novel, like all other forms of art, will always reflect the political, economic, and social structure of the period in which it was created. I think I could make out a fairly good case for the idea that the finest novels are basically novels of social criticism, some obviously and intentionally, others less obviously, unintentionally, from *Crime and Punishment* to *Ulysses,* to *Remembrance of Things Past,* to *USA.* The moment the novelist begins to show how society affected the lives of his characters, how they were formed and shaped by the sprawling inchoate world in which they lived, he is writing a novel of social criticism whether he calls it that or not. The greatest novelists have been so sharply aware of the political and social aspects of their time that this awareness inevitably showed up in their major works. I think that this is as true of Dickens, Tolstoy, and Dostoevski as it is of Balzac, Hemingway, Dreiser, Faulkner.

A professional patter has been developed to describe the awareness of social problems which has crept into creative writing. It is a confused patter. Naturalism and realism are terms that are used almost interchangeably. *Studs Lonigan* and *USA* are called naturalist novels; but *The Grapes of Wrath* is cited as an example of realism. So is *Tom Jones.* Time, that enemy of labels, makes this ridiculous. Dickens, George Sand, Mrs. Gaskell, George Eliot, Harriet Beecher Stowe, wrote books in which they advocated the rights of labor, condemned slums, slavery and anti-Semitism, roughly a hundred years ago. They are known as "the humanitarian novelists of the nineteenth century." Yet the novels produced in the thirties which made a similar comment on society are lumped together as proletarian literature and their origin attributed to the perfidious influence of Karl Marx. This particular label has been used so extensively in recent years that the ghost of Marx seems even livelier than that of Hamlet's father's ghost—or at least he, Marx, appears to have done his haunting over more of the world's surface.

I think it would make more sense if some of the fictional emphasis on social problems were attributed to the influence of the Old Testament idea that man is his brother's keeper. True it is an idea that has been corrupted in a thousand ways—sometimes it has been offered to the world as socialism, and then again as communism. It was used to justify the Inquisition of the Roman Church in Spain, the burning of witches in New England, the institution of slavery in the South.

It seems plausible that so potent an idea should keep cropping up in fiction for it is a part of the cultural heritage of the West. If it is not recognized as such it is almost impossible to arrive at a satisfactory explanation for, let alone classify, some of the novels that are derived from it. How should *Uncle Tom's Cabin, Germinal,* and *Mary Barton* be classified? As proletarian literature? If *Gentleman's Agreement* is a problem novel what is *Daniel Deronda?* Jack London may be a proletarian writer but his most famous book *The Call of the Wild* is an adventure story. George Sand has been called one of the founders of the "problem" novel but the bulk of her output dealt with those bourgeois emotions: love and passion.

I think one of the difficulties here is the refusal to recognize and admit the fact that not all of the concern about the shortcomings of society originated with Marx. Many a socially conscious novelist is merely a man or a woman with a conscience. Though part of the cultural heritage of all of us derives from Marx, whether we subscribe to the Marxist theory or not, a larger portion of it stems from the Bible. If novelists were asked for an explanation of their criticism of society they might well quote Richard Rumbold, who knew nothing about realism or naturalism and who had never heard of Karl Marx. When Rumbold mounted the scaffold in 1685 he said, according to Macaulay's *History of England:* "I never could believe that Providence had sent a few men into the world, ready booted and spurred to ride, and millions ready saddled and bridled to be ridden."

Similar beliefs have been stated in every century. Novelists would be strangely impervious to ideas if a variant of this particular belief did not find expression in some of their works.

No matter what these novels are called, the average reader seems to like them. Possibly the reading public, and here I include myself, is like the man who kept butting his head against a stone wall and when asked for an explanation said that he went in for this strange practice because it felt so good when he stopped. Perhaps there is a streak of masochism in all of us; or perhaps we all feel guilty because of the shortcomings of society and our sense of guilt is partially assuaged when we are accused, in the printed pages of a novel, of having done those things that we ought not to have done—and of having left undone those things we ought to have done.

The craftsmanship that goes into these novels is of a high order. It has to be. They differ from other novels only in the emphasis on the theme—but it is the theme which causes the most difficulty. All novelists attempt to record the slow struggle of man toward his long home, sometimes depicting only the beginning or the middle or the end of the journey, emphasizing the great emotional peaks of birth and marriage and death which occur along the route. If it is a good job, the reader nods and says, Yes, that is how it must have been. Because the characters are as real as one's next-door-neighbor, predictable and yet unpredictable, lingering in the memory.

The sociological novelist sets out to do the same thing. But he is apt to become so obsessed by his theme, so entangled in it and fascinated by it, that his heroes resemble the early Christian martyrs; and his villains are showboat villains, first-class scoundrels with no redeeming features or virtues. If he is more pamphleteer than novelist, and something of a romanticist in the bargain, he will offer a solution to the social problem he has posed. He may be in love with a new world order, and try to sell it to his readers; or, and this happens more frequently, he has a trade union, usually the CIO, come to the rescue in the final scene, horse-opera fashion, and the curtain rings down on a happy ending as rosy as that of a western movie done in technicolor.

Characterization can be the greatest glory of the sociological novel. I offer as examples: Oliver Twist, child of the London slums, asking for more; Ma Joad, holding the family together in that long westward journey, somehow in her person epitomizing an earlier generation of women who traveled westward in search of a promised land; Bigger Thomas, who was both criminal and victim, fleeing for his life over the rooftops of Chicago; Jeeter Lester clinging to his worn-out land in futile defiance of a mechanized world. They have an amazing vitality, much of which springs from the theme. People still discuss them, argue about them, as though they had had an actual existence.

Though characterization is the great strength of these novels, as it is of all novels, it can also be the great weakness. When society is given the role of fate, made the evil in the age-old battle between good and evil, the burden of responsibility for their actions is shifted away from the characters. This negates the Old Testament idea of evil as a thing of the spirit, with each individual carrying on his own personal battle against the evil within himself. In a book which is more political pamphlet or sermon than novel the characters do not battle with themselves to save their souls, so to speak. Their defeat or their victory is not their own—they are pawns in the hands of a deaf, blind, stupid, social system. Once the novelist begins to manipulate his characters to serve the interests of his theme they lose whatever vitality they had when their creator first thought about them.

And so the novelist who takes an evil in society for his theme is rather like an aerial trapeze artist desperately trying to maintain his balance in mid-air. He works without a net and he may be sent tumbling by the dialogue, the plot, the theme itself. Dialogue presents a terrible temptation. It offers the writer a convenient platform from which to set forth his pet theories and ideas. This is especially true of the books that deal with some phase of the relationship between whites and Negroes in the United States. Most of the talk in these books comes straight out of a never-never land existing in the author's mind. Anyone planning to write a book on this theme should reread *Native Son* and compare the small talk which touches on race relations with that found in almost any novel on the subject published since then. Or reread Act I Scene I of *Othello,* and note how the dialogue advances the action, characterizes the speaker and yet at no point smacks of the pulpit or of the soapbox. When Iago and Rodrigo inform Brabantio that Desdemona has eloped with Othello, the Moor, they speak the language of the prejudiced; but it is introduced with a smoothness that hasn't been duplicated elsewhere.

One of the most successful recent performances is that of Alan Paton in *Cry the Beloved Country*. The hero, the old Zulu minister, wrestles with the recognized evil within himself, and emerges victorious. Yet the miserable existence of the exploited native in Johannesburg, the city of evil, has been revealed and the terror and glory of Africa become as real as though one had lived there. It is written in a prose style so musical and so rhythmic that much of it is pure poetry. *Cry the Beloved Country* is proof, if such proof is necessary, that the novel of social criticism will have a life as long and as honorable as that of the novel itself as an art form. For this book is art of the highest order, but it could not possibly be called an example of art for art's sake. It tells the reader in no uncertain terms that society is responsible for the tragedy of the native African.

In recent years, many novels of social criticism have dealt with race relations in this country. It is a theme which offers the novelist a wide and fertile field; it is the very stuff of fiction, sometimes comic, more often tragic, always ironic, endlessly dramatic. The setting and the characters vary in these books but the basic story line is derived from *Uncle Tom's Cabin;* discrimination and/or segregation (substitute slavery for the one or the other) are evils which lead to death—actual death or potential death. The characters either conform to the local taboos and mores and live, miserably; or refuse to conform and die.

This pattern of violence is characteristic of the type for a very good reason. The arguments used to justify slavery still influence American attitudes toward the Negro. If I use the words intermarriage, mixed marriage, miscegenation, there are few Americans who would not react to those words emotionally. Part of that emotion can be traced directly to the days of slavery. And if emotion is aroused merely by the use of certain words, and the emotion is violent, apoplectic, then it seems fairly logical that novels which deal with race relations should reflect some of this violence.

As I said, my first novel was a novel of social criticism. Having written it, I discovered that I was supposed to know the answer to many of the questions that are asked about such novels. What good do they do is a favorite. I think they do a lot of good. Social reforms have often received their original impetus from novels which aroused the emotions of a large number of readers. *Earth and High Heaven, Focus,* and *Gentleman's Agreement* undoubtedly made many a person examine the logic of his own special brand of anti-Semitism. The novels that deal with race relations have influenced the passage of the civil rights bills which have become law in many states.

I was often asked another question: *Why* do people write these novels? Sometimes I have been tempted to paraphrase the Duchess in *Alice in Wonderland* by way of answer (I never did): " 'Please would you tell me,' said Alice a little timidly . . . 'Why your cat grins like that?' 'It's a Cheshire cat,' said the Duchess, 'and that's why.' "

Behind this question there is the implication that a writer who finds fault with society must be a little wrong in the head. Or that he is moved by the missionary spirit or a holier-than-thou attitude and therefore is in need of psychiatric treatment. I think the best answer to that question, on record, is to be found in Robert Van Gelder's *Writers and Writing.* He quotes Erich Remarque (*All Quiet on the Western Front, Three Comrades, Arch of Triumph*) as saying that people cannot count with their imaginations, that if five million die in a concentration camp it really does not equal one death in emotional impact and meaning—the death of someone you have known and loved: "If I say one died—a man I have made you know and understand—he lived so, this is what he thought, this is what he hoped, this was his faith, these were his difficulties, these his triumphs and then he—in this manner, on this day, at an hour when it rained and the room was stuffy—was killed, after torture, then perhaps I have told you something that you should know about the Nazis. . . . Some people who did not understand before may be made to understand what the Nazis were like and what they did and what their kind will try to do again."

It is with reluctance that I speak of my own writing, I have never been satisfied with anything I have written and I doubt that I ever will be. Most of what I have learned about writing I learned the hard way, through trial and error and rejection slips. I set out to be a writer of short stories and somehow ended up as a novelist—possibly because there simply wasn't room enough within the framework of a short story to do the sort of thing I wanted to do. I have collected enough rejection slips for my short stories to paper four or five good sized rooms. During that rejection slip period I was always reading the autobiography of writers, and in

Arthur Train's *My Day in Court* I found a piece of rather wonderful advice. He said that if he were a beginning writer one of the things that he would do would be to enter Mabel L. Robinson's course in the short story at Columbia University. Needless to say I promptly applied for admission to the class.

I spent a year in Miss Robinson's short story class. And during another year I was a member of the workshop that she conducts at Columbia. What I didn't learn through trial and error I learned from Miss Robinson. She taught me to criticize what I had written and to read other people's creative efforts with a critical eye. Perhaps of even greater importance she made me believe in myself.

As partial payment for a debt of gratitude I am passing along Arthur Train's advice. If the walls of your apartment or your house are papered with rejection slips I suggest that you apply for admission to one of Miss Robinson's classes.

Response: Voices of African American Tradition and Modernism

Poets

MELVIN B. TOLSON

(1898–1966)

The poetry of Melvin Tolson strikes one immediately with its scope, complexity, and esoteric diction. Although indebted to French symbolism, with its hunger for the transcendental and the ineffable, Tolson's verse has managed to remain remarkably earthy, distinguished by a masterful use of circumlocution and metaphor.

Melvin Beaunorous Tolson, in Herbert Hill's *Anger and Beyond* (1966), described himself as a "shoeshine boy, stevedore, soldier, janitor, packinghouse worker, cook on a railroad, waiter in beach-front hotels, boxer, actor, football coach, director of drama, lecturer for the NAACP, organizer of sharecroppers' unions, teacher, father of Ph.D.'s, poet laureate of a foreign country, painter, newspaper columnist, four-time mayor of a town, facer of mobs." Tolson was born on February 6, 1898, in Moberly, Missouri. His father, Alonzo Tolson, was a Methodist minister who taught himself Latin and Greek. His mother, Lera Hurt Tolson, encouraged his interest in music, art, and literature. After attending Fisk University for a year, Tolson transferred to Lincoln University in Pennsylvania, where he graduated in 1923. Shortly after that, he married Ruth Southall and settled in Marshall, Texas, where they reared three sons and one daughter. In 1924, he began teaching debate and drama at Wiley College in Marshall, Texas. In 1932, he received his master's degree from Columbia University with a thesis titled "The Harlem Group of Negro Writers." He became a professor of English and drama at Langston University in Langston, Oklahoma, in 1947 and Avalon Professor of Humanities at Tuskegee Institute in Tuskegee, Alabama, in 1965.

Tolson wrote several plays, including two lost works of the late 1930s, *The Moses of Beale Street* and *Southern Front,* and dramatizations of George Schuyler's novel *Black No More* (1952) and Walter White's *Fire in the Flint* (1952). Of his verse, his long poem "Dark Symphony," from *Rendezvous with America* (1944), won the National Poetry Contest conducted by the American Negro Exposition in Chicago, and, in 1952, *Poetry* magazine gave him the Bess Hopkin Award. He published *Harlem Gallery* in 1965 and *Harlem Portraits* in 1979. A collection of his newspaper columns was published in 1982 under the title *Caviar and Cabbage.* In addition to serving as mayor of the city of Langston for four terms, Tolson was, in 1947, appointed poet laureate of Liberia (the only American poet ever to be honored as the poet laureate of another nation) and commissioned to work on a poem to celebrate the centennial of the founding of that republic. The result was *Libretto for the Republic of Liberia* (1953), an extended ode on the history and destiny of Liberia.

Tolson's poetry has characteristics in common with that of many of the writers of the 1960s. He wrote, though not exclusively, about black culture and was alert to the concrete historical processes taking place in African American and American life. "Dark Symphony" is a case in point. Similar in theme to Margaret Walker's *For My People* (1942), the poem moves from Crispus Attucks through the spirituals of slavery to the Harlem Renaissance and beyond, detailing evidence of black achievement and black pride. But Tolson also had a gift for abstraction and metaphor, which often lend his poetry a difficult, mysterious, parabolic, and esoteric quality. All of his poetry bears the marks of a conscious and experimental stylist. In creating mood, atmosphere, and themes, he used ambiguity, juxtapositions, and binary oppositions. He relied heavily on esoteric diction, literary and historical allusions, indirection, double talk, symbols, hyperbolic imagery, and other subtle forms of parody and signifying practices.

Tolson's most ambitious attempt to put together many characters, ideas, moods, and strains was *Harlem Gallery* (1965). This is a work of great cultural depth, arresting historical relevance, and considerable aesthetic interest. In Tolson's vision, Harlem was a place for communal participation, entertainment, art, eating, and dancing; its social geography included theaters, nightclubs, police stations, cafeterias, galleries, and churches. Composed of twenty-four sections, each identified by a letter of the Greek alphabet from alpha to omega, *Harlem Gallery* was conceived to be the first of five books that would encompass the history of black people. The plan was never completed, however, because of Tolson's death in 1966. The unwritten books were to have been *Egypt Land, The Red Sea, The Wilderness,* and *The Promised Land.* Regardless, *Harlem Gallery* remains a complete work in itself. Its great virtue is its style, which emanates from colorful narrators with distinct points of view and a gift for imagery and figurative expression. The principal narrators are the curator of the gallery, an art critic, and three artists (a painter, a writer, and a composer). The curator is an octoroon who embodies the question "What is a Negro?" in his ambiguous racial identity. At one point in *Harlem Gallery*, Tolson concludes,

> The Negro is a dish in the white man's kitchen
> a potpourri
> an ola-podrida,
> a mixie-maxie
> a hotchpotch of lineal ingredients;
> with UN guests at his table,
> the host finds himself a Hamlet on the spot,
> for, in spite of his catholic pose,
> the Negro dish; a dish nobody knows.

All attempts to define "the Negro" are ultimately futile. He is the Invisible Man nobody knows. The expatriate Zulu and art critic Dr. Obi Nkomo is an amalgamation of Western thought and African experience who contends that only in art can one know life in its complexity. The three artists also direct the focus of the narrative to art and artists—the blues and jazz, classical and symphonic, and painters, sculptors, engravers, and writers.

The Zulu Club and the Harlem Gallery itself constitute the setting of the poem. The club is Tolson's depiction of Harlem nightlife in the 1920s, where Snakehips Briskie's "snake act in the Garden of Eden" often stole the show:

Convulsively, unexampledly,
Snakehips' body and soul
began to twist and untwist like
a gyrating rawhide—
began to coil, to writhe
like a prismatic-hued python
in the throes of copulation.

Along with Snakehips, Frog Legs Lux and his Indigo Combo and a host of other Harlemites make up the Zulu Club's frequent visitors. They include Hideho Heights (derived from Cab Calloway and Henry Heights), Guy Delaporte III, Black Orchid, Dipsey Muse, Wafer Waite, Vincent Aveline, Joshua Nitze, Black Diamond, and Shadrach Martial Kilroy.

Just as the Zulu Club houses the dancers and musicians, the gallery itself is the location for black art and writing. The first poem of *Harlem Gallery*, "Alpha," is a statement about the poet's intention to invigorate modern Western, white poetry with the African American's idioms and sense of life—most notably, the blues and jazz. The curator hears the alarm birds announcing revolution, both political and poetic. He hears "a dry husk-of-locust blues / descend the tone ladder of a laughing goose."

Critical reaction to Tolson's poetry has been mixed. It has ranged from the views of Allen Tate and Karl Shapiro, who believe that he was a great poet who "Outpounded Pound," to Sara Webster Fabio's verdict that Tolson's complex and difficult rhetoric represents only a "bizarre, pseudo-literary diction" that he misguidedly took over from "the American mainstream where it belonged" and where it should have stayed. Tolson himself called for a more balanced view of his art. When asked in an interview about the influence of the metaphysical poets of the English seventeenth century, the French symbolists, and the classic white avant-garde of the present century (Yeats, Eliot, Pound, Apollinaire, Pasternak, and Hart Crane), Tolson responded,

> I would add another group to the Metaphysical Poets and the French Symbolists: the Negro people. Remember Karl Shapiro's words in his Introduction to *Harlem Gallery:* "Tolson writes in Negro." I, as a black poet, have absorbed the Great Ideas of the Great White World, and interpreted them in the melting-pot idiom of my people. My roots are in Africa, Europe, and America.

For critics unhappy with Tolson's attraction to Europe and America, this is but another instance of literary assimilation, of cozying up to the masters. To more sympathetic readers, it is, as Alden Nielsen has put it, Tolson's attempt to "emphasize and glorify the African-Americanism of his art, and he does it on the plain of his master's colony, on the site of the colonized master text of modernism." Tolson himself maintained that his esoteric diction made him more militantly black because modernism itself had roots in Africa and African poetics. In a lecture to an audience at the Library of Congress in 1965, Tolson remarked,

> You know, poets like to do a great amount of double talking. We think very often that the modernists gave us that concept of poetry, which is untrue. Because I can

go back into the Negro work songs, the spirituals and jazz, and show you that double talk of poetry. And I can even [clicking his fingers for emphasis] go to Africa, as I shall do tonight, and show you that double talk of poetry, especially in metaphors and symbols. So I'm doing some double talk here.

Elsewhere, Tolson says, "Sometimes, the Africans go esoteric on us."

Although modernist techniques can be seen in traditional African modes of expression, there is, in terms of technique, clearly more of Europe and America in Tolson's poetry than there is of Africa. Still, there can be little doubt that Tolson's poetry demonstrates a particular fascination with African Americanness, a yearning to define and disclose its deep and complex spiritual and cultural essence.

❖❖❖

Mariann B. Russell offers an excellent overview of Tolson's oeuvre in "Evolution of Style in the Poetry of Melvin Tolson," in *Black American Poets Between Worlds, 1940–1960,* ed. R. Baxter Miller (1986). Robert M. Farnsworth has written a biography, *Melvin B. Tolson, 1898–1966; Plain Talk and Poetic Prophecy* (1984). See also the illuminating essay by Aldon Nielson, "Melvin B. Tolson and the Deterritorialization of Modernism," *African American Review* 26, No. 2 (Summer 1992), and an important interview by M. W. King, "A Poet's Odyssey: Melvin B. Tolson," in *Anger and Beyond,* ed. Herbert Hill (1960). Of significance also are the following critiques of the poet and his works: Sara Webster Fabio's "Who Speaks Negro?", *Negro Digest,* xvi, 2 (December, 1966); Allen Tate, Preface, *Libretto for the Republic of Liberia* (New York, 1953); and Karl Shapiro's Introduction, *Harlem Gallery: Book I, The Curator* (New York, 1965).

Dark Symphony

I: Allegro Moderato

Black Crispus Attucks taught
            Us how to die
Before white Patrick Henry's bugle breath

Uttered the vertical
            Transmitting cry:
"Yea, give me liberty, or give me death."

And from that day to this
            Men black and strong
For Justice and Democracy have stood,
Steeled in the faith that Right
            Will conquer Wrong
And Time will usher in one brotherhood.

No Banquo's ghost can rise
            Against us now
And say we crushed men with a tyrant's boot

Or pressed the crown of thorns
On Labor's brow,
Or ravaged lands and carted off the loot.

II: Lento Grave

The centuries-old pathos in our voices
Saddens the great white world,
And the wizardry of our dusky rhythms
Conjures up shadow-shapes of ante-bellum years:

Black slaves singing *One More River to Cross*
In the torture tombs of slave ships,
Black slaves singing *Steal Away to Jesus*
In jungle swamps,
Black slaves singing *The Crucifixion*
In slave pens at midnight,
Black slaves singing *Swing Low, Sweet Chariot*
In cabins of death,
Black slaves singing *Go Down, Moses*
In the canebrakes of the Southern Pharaohs.

III: Andante Sostenuto

The tell us to forget
The Golgotha we tread . . .
We who are scourged with hate,
A price upon our head.
They who have shackled us
Require of us a song,
They who have wasted us
Bid us o'erlook the wrong.

They tell us to forget
Democracy is spurned.
They tell us to forget
The Bill of Rights is burned.
Three hundred years we slaved,
We slave and suffer yet:
Though flesh and bone rebel,
They tell us to forget!

Oh, how can we forget
Our human rights denied?
Oh, how can we forget
Our manhood crucified?
When Justice is profaned
And plea with curse is met,
When Freedom's gates are barred,

Oh, how can we forget?

IV: *Tempo Primo*

The New Negro strides upon the continent
In seven league boots . . .
The New Negro
Who sprang from the vigor-stout loins
Of Nat Turner, gallows-martyr for Freedom,
Of Joseph Cinquez, Black Moses of the Amistad Mutiny,
Of Frederick Douglass, oracle of the Catholic Man,
Of Sojourner Truth, eye and ear of Lincoln's legions,
Of Harriet Tubman, St. Bernard of the Underground Railroad.

V: *Largetto*

None in the Land can say
To us black men Today:
You send the tractors on their bloody path,
And create Oakies for *The Grapes of Wrath.*
You breed the slum that breeds a *Native Son*
To damn the good earth Pilgrim Fathers won.

None in the Land can say
To us black men Today:
You dupe the poor with rags-to-riches tales,
And leave the workers empty dinner pails.
You stuff the ballot box, and honest men
Are muzzled by your demogogic din.

None in the Land can say
To us black men Today:
You smash stock markets with your coined blitzkriegs
And make a hundred million guinea pigs.
You counterfeit our Christianity,
And bring contempt upon Democracy.

None in the Land can say
To us black men Today:
You prowl when citizens are fast asleep,
And hatch Fifth Column plots to blast the deep
Foundations of the State and leave the Land
A vast Sahara with a Fascist brand.

None in the Land can say
To us black men Today:
You send flame-gutting tanks, like swarms of flies,
And plump a hell from dynamiting skies.
You fill machine-gunned towns with rotting dead—
A No Man's Land where children cry for bread.

VI: Tempo di Marcia

Out of abysses of Illiteracy,
Through labyrinths of Lies,
Across wastelands of Disease . . .
We advance!

Out of dead-ends of Poverty,
Through wildernesses of Superstition,
Across barricades of Jim Crowism . . .
We advance!

With the Peoples of the World . . .
We advance!

Lambda

from Harlem Gallery

From the mouth of the Harlem Gallery
came a voice like a
ferry horn in a river of fog:

"Hey man, when you gonna close this dump?
Fetch highbrow stuff for the middlebrows who
don't give a damn and the lowbrows who ain't hip!
Think you're a little high-yellow Jesus?"

No longer was I a boxer with a brain bruised
against its walls by Tyche's fists,
as I welcomed Hideho Heights,
the vagabond bard of Lenox Avenue,
whose satyric legends adhered like beggar's-lice.

"Sorry, Curator, I got here late:
my black ma birthed me in the Whites' bottom drawer,
and the Reds forgot to fish me out!"

His belly laughed and quaked
the Blakean tigers and lambs on the walls.
Haw-Haw's whale of a forefinger mocked
Max Donachie's revolutionary hero, Crispus Attucks,
in the Harlem Gallery and on Boston Commons,
"In the beginning was the Word,"
he challenged, "not the Brush!"
The scorn in the eyes that raked the gallery
was the scorn of an Ozymandias.

The metal smelted from the ore of ideas,
his grin revealed all the gold he had stored away.
"Just came from a jam session
at the Daddy-O Club," he said.

"I'm just one step from heaven
with the blues a-percolating in my head.

You should've heard old Satchmo blow his horn!
The Lord God A'mighty made no mistake
the day that cat was born!

Like a bridegroom unloosing a virgin knot,
from an inner pocket he coaxed a manuscript.
"Just given Satchmo a one-way ticket
to Immortality," he said. "Pure inspiration!"
His lips folded about the neck of a whiskey bottle
whose label belied its white-heat hooch.
I heard a gurgle, a gurgle—a death rattle.
His eyes as bright as a parachute light,
he began to rhetorize in the grand style
of a Doctor Faustus in the dilapidated Harlem Opera House:

King Oliver of New Orleans
has kicked the bucket, but he left behind
old Satchmo with his red-hot horn
to syncopate the heart and mind.
The honky-tonks in Storyville
have turned to ashes, have turned to dust,
but old Satchmo is still around
like Uncle Sam's IN GOD WE TRUST.

Where, oh, where is Bessie Smith
with her heart as big as the blues of truth?
Where, oh, where is Mister Jelly Roll
with his Cadillac and diamond tooth?
Where, oh, where is Papa Handy
with his blue notes a-dragging from bar to bar?
Where, oh, where is bulletproof Leadbelly
with his tall tales and 12-string guitar?

Old Hip Cats, when you sang and played the blues
the night Satchmo was born,
did you know hypodermic needles in Rome
couldn't hoodoo him away from his horn?
Wyatt Earp's legend, John Henry's, too,
is a dare and a bet to old Satchmo
when his groovy blues put headlines in the news
from the Gold Coast to cold Moscow.

Old Satchmo's gravelly voice and tapping foot and crazy notes
set my soul on fire.
If I climbed the seventy-seven steps of the Seventh
Heaven, Satchmo's high C would carry me higher!
Are you hip to this, Harlem? Are you hip?
On Judgment Day, Gabriel will say after he blows his horn:
"I'd be the greatest trumpeter in the Universe,
if old Satchmo had never been born!"

ROBERT HAYDEN
(1913–1980)

Robert Hayden's last published volume of poetry, *American Journal* (1978), pulls together in a succinct collection a wide range of concerns that read like his autobiography. Like Phillis Wheatley, the subject of the opening epistolary poem, Hayden was acclaimed as a poet but was questioned about serving the black cause. Also like her, he had to attend to the ongoing exigencies of family, health, career, and economic survival. Other poems in *American Journal* that pay homage to Paul Lawrence Dunbar, Paul Robeson, and John Brown reflect Hayden's commitment to art and social justice. In the latter case, for instance, the poet recognizes a certain kind of white who gave up his life for the black struggle. Also in the collection are poems that go back to Hayden's childhood—poems that show his early concern about worldwide issues (environment, waste, and war) and reveal his curiosity about space travel, technology, and ultimately race and class in the United States. A second edition of *American Journal,* which the poet was working on up to the time of his death, spotlights what the man lived for and why critics eulogize him as the quintessential moral African American.

Robert Earl Hayden was born in Detroit on August 4, 1913 and grew up in a section of the city ironically nicknamed "Paradise Valley." His parents, Asa and Ruth Sheffey, named him Asa Bundy Sheffey. During his infancy, they separated, and Hayden became the foster son of Sue Ellen Westerfield Hayden and William Hayden. The Haydens' only child, Robert suffered in childhood the confusion of loyalty to them and to his birth mother, who stayed intermittently in his life until her death. The confusion extended to his real name, for neither the Haydens nor his mother corrected his false impression that he was adopted and legally named Robert Hayden. Finding out the truth after their deaths late in his own life inspired his poem "Names," which is included in *American Journal.* Two other factors complicated Hayden's early life. His birth mother took up residence next door to where he resided with his "adopted" parents. He also felt pressure from his foster father, who was disappointed in his myopic son's interest in academics rather than athletics. The young Hayden turned to poetry as a refuge from the troubled household where frustration was often vented in beatings.

In high school, Hayden read Eliot, Hawthorne, and Bulwer-Lytton, later explaining, "I loved those books, partly because they took me completely out of the environment I lived in, and they appealed to my imagination, because they were full of strange and wonderful things that I'd had no direct experience with." During an interim between high school and college, he discovered the poets of the Harlem Renaissance quite fortuitously when he happened upon Alain Locke's anthology *The New Negro* (1925). He read Orrick Johns and Countee Cullen with great regard. He became familiar with contemporary poetry through anthology study, also holding in high regard Sandburg, Teasdale, Benét, Millay, and Wylie. Among the traditional English poets he read were Chaucer, Burns, Shelley, Wordsworth, Byron, and Keats. Outside of poetry, he read with great eagerness the plays of Eugene O'Neill.

Hayden entered what is now Wayne State University (then Detroit City College) on a scholarship and majored in Spanish with a minor in English. In college, he acted in a play written by Langston Hughes. Later, when he met Hughes, he showed him his poems. The established poet counseled him on how his verse was imitative. Hayden continued his development as a writer after completing college. From 1936 to 1938, he became involved in the Work Projects Administration (WPA), in particular the Detroit branch of the Federal Writers' Project, where he researched black history and folklore. With what he was paid, he was able to support himself and to contribute financially to his foster family. Later, another WPA project enabled him to compile the *Historical Record Survey* and to serve as a part-time drama and music critic for the black newspaper the *Michigan Chronicle.*

The editor of the *Michigan Chronicle,* Louis Martin, who also founded Falcon Press, published Hayden's first book of poetry, *Heart-Shape in the Dust* (1940). Throughout his life, Hayden's concern for the black struggle in America and his pride in African American heritage found its way into his poems. Yet this first collection shows little of his later mastery. The mature Hayden considered these early works his apprentice efforts, much of it derivative of the poets of the Harlem Renaissance. His "Poem to a Negro Dancer," for instance, is indebted to Countee Cullen's "Heritage" and Claude McKay's "Harlem Dancer."

The following year (1941), Hayden married Erma Inez Morris over the objections of her well-educated, upper-class family, who found Hayden's financial situation far from ideal. The couple went to live in New York so that Erma could study at the Juilliard School of Music. While there, the poet met Countee Cullen, a college classmate of his wife's uncle. Cullen invited them to his home, and the meeting proved to be a positive influence on the young poet. When the couple returned to Detroit that year, Erma supported them by teaching public school while Hayden pursued a master's degree at the University of Michigan. A year later, their only child, Maia, was born.

At Michigan, Hayden studied under W. H. Auden, who Hayden said, in *Interviews with Black Writers,* contributed to his development as a poet, "the range of his learning, and the breadth of his knowledge." Twice Hayden won the university's Hopwood Award. Upon completion of his degree, he stayed on for two years as a teaching fellow. Eventually, he became the first black member of the English department. It was during this period that first his wife and then he became members of the Baha'i faith. Hayden was sustained throughout his life by this faith, which finds creative output of spiritual significance.

In 1946, the *Atlantic Monthly* published two of his most renowned poems, "Middle Passage" and "Frederick Douglass," a tour de force of technique. That same year, he accepted a full-time teaching position at Fisk University in Nashville, Tennessee. The Haydens were unhappy at Fisk due to Tennessee's segregation laws and a black bourgeois stronghold. Nevertheless, Hayden stayed at Fisk for twenty uneasy years.

In 1947, Hayden received a Rosenwald Fellowship. The following year, he published *The Lion and the Archer.* Seven years later, he received a Ford Foundation Grant, which took him to Mexico. There he produced his sequence of poems "An Inference of Mexico." Back in Nashville in 1955, he published his third collection, *Figure of Time: Poems.* His fourth collection, *A Ballad of Remembrance,* published in 1962, won him the 1966 Grand Prize for Poetry at the First World Festival of Negro Arts in Dakar, Senegal. Included in the volume are his famous poems "The Whipping" (at the hands of his foster mother) and "Those Winter Sundays" (about his unappreciative foster father). Commercial success came in 1966 with the publication of *Selected Poems,* arranged thematically—black history, quest for meaning, Mexico, racism, and autobiography. His most famous quest poem, "The Diver," continues to inspire debate. Some critics view it in strictly psychological terms, while others interpret it sociologically, as a reaction to racism.

During the sixties, while still at Fisk, Hayden stood apart from the New Black Poets. Although his opposition still gives rise to applause from whites, it angered blacks who advocated that poetry serve the cause of freedom. Later, many who were at odds with his outspoken criticism of limiting poetry to racial themes would praise his work because it grew out of his life as a black man proud of his African American heritage. Ironically, his best poems during the sixties—"Middle Passage," "Runagate Runagate," and "Frederick Douglass"—are deeply rooted in the black experience, especially the liberation cause.

Hayden returned to the University of Michigan as a visiting professor in 1968. In 1969, he became a professor of English there, holding that position until his death eleven years later. While he and his wife were relieved to return to Michigan, his personal and racial struggles continued. Notwithstanding, he found an outlet for them in the poems of his sixth collection, *Words in the Mourning Time* (1970). A particularly fine poem is "El-Hajj Malik El-Shabazz," which portrays Malcolm X's return from his pilgrimage to Mecca. Hayden won the Russell Loines Award in 1970. In 1972, his seventh book, *The Night-Blooming Cerus,* was published in London. This work is largely metaphysical, a preoccupation that marked his maturity. Critics have argued about whether this work shows that Hayden was departing from a focus on black history and moving into a private retreat or into symbolism. However, even here, he is consistent in his commitment to the struggle—a specific ethnic struggle extended to all humankind, in a back-from-Mecca sense.

Hayden was appointed consultant in poetry at the Library of Congress in 1976. Two more books of poetry, *Angle of Ascent* (1975) and *American Journal* (1978), would sum up his achievements in African American literature and in life. Today the definition of "womanist" must embrace the sensibility that composed "A Letter from Phillis Wheatley." The crucial aspects of community and an awareness of power in powerlessness—race and gender—put Hayden ahead of his time. In this poem, he captures his forebear in her eloquent distress, dining alone "like captive Royalty" in "Idyllic England," where "Alas, there is no Eden without its Serpent."

American Journal concludes with a poem of the same title. Instead of depicting an Invisible Man observing America, this poem gives us the poet/narrator as alien, who sees his nation for what it is. The precocious foster child of "Paradise Valley," the decidedly African American, the Baha'i, the teacher, the artist, the adapter, the baffled, the attuned, the citizen—all are rolled into this incredible poet who spent much time on earth as his "metabolism" could take.

❖❖❖

Not until the past few years has a full-length study of Hayden's poetry been done. Pontheolla Taylor Williams has published an excellent revision of her dissertation, "A Critical Analysis of the Poetry of Robert Hayden Through His Middle Years" (1978) under the title *Robert Hayden: A Critical Analysis of His Poetry* (1987). Two other tributes are Julius Lester, "In Memorium: In Gratitude of Robert

Hayden," *World Order* 16 (1981), and Dorothy Tsuruta, "Robert Hayden: In Memorium," *Black Scholar* (March/April 1980) Vol. II, No. 1. An excellent interview of Hayden can be found in *Interviews with Black Writers,* edited by John O'Brien (1973).

Homage to the Empress of the Blues

Because there was a man somewhere in a candystripe silk shirt,
gracile and dangerous as a jaguar and because a woman moaned
for him in sixty-watt gloom and mourned him Faithless Love
Twotiming Love Oh Love Oh Careless Aggravating Love,

She came out on the stage in yards of pearls, emerging like
a favorite scenic view, flashed her golden smile and sang.

Because grey laths began somewhere to show from underneath
torn hurdygurdy lithographs of dollfaced heaven;
and because there were those who feared alarming fists of snow
on the door and those who feared the riot-squad of statistics,

She came out on the stage in ostrich feathers, beaded satin,
and shone that smile on us and sang.

Middle Passage

I

Jesús, Estrella, Esperanza, Mercy:
Sails flashing to the wind like weapons,
sharks following the moans the fever and the dying;
horror the corposant and compass rose.

Middle Passage:
voyage through death
to life upon these shores.

"10 April 1800—
Blacks rebellious. Crew uneasy. Our linguist says
their moaning is a prayer for death,
ours and their own. Some try to starve themselves.
Lost three this morning leaped with crazy laughter
to the waiting sharks, sang as they went under."

Desire, Adventure, Tartar, Ann:
Standing to America, bringing home
black gold, black ivory, black seed.

Deep in the festering hold thy father lies,
of his bones New England pews are made,
those are altar lights that were his eyes.

Jesus Saviour Pilot Me
Over Life's Tempestuous Sea

We pray that Thou wilt grant, O Lord,

safe passage to our vessels bringing
heathen souls unto Thy chastening.

Jesus Saviour

"8 bells, I cannot sleep, for I am sick
with fear, but writing eases fear a little
since still my eyes can see these words take shape
upon the page & so I write, as one
would turn to exorcism. 4 days scudding,
but now the sea is calm again. Misfortune
follows in our wake like sharks (our grinning
tutelary gods). Which one of us
has killed an albatross? A plague among
our blacks—Ophthalmia: blindness—& we
have jettisoned the blind to no avail.
It spreads, the terrifying sickness spreads.
Its claws have scratched sight from the Capt.'s eyes
& there is blindness in the fo'c'sle
& we must sail 3 weeks before we come
to port."

What port awaits us, Davy Jones'
or home? I've heard of slavers drifting, drifting,
playthings of wind and storm and chance, their crews
gone blind, the jungle hatred
crawling up on deck.

Thou Who Walked On Galilee

"Deponent further sayeth *The Bella J*
left the Guinea Coast
with cargo of five hundred blacks and odd
for the barracoons of Florida:

"That there was hardly room 'tween-decks for half
the sweltering cattle stowed spoon-fashion there;
that some went mad of thirst and tore their flesh
and sucked the blood:

"That Crew and Captain lusted with the comeliest
of the savage girls kept naked in the cabins;
that there was one they called The Guinea Rose
and they cast lots and fought to lie with her:

"That when the Bo's'n piped all hands, the flames
spreading from starboard already were beyond
control, the negroes howling and their chains
entangled with the flames:

"That the burning blacks could not be reached,
that the Crew abandoned ship,
leaving their shrieking negresses behind,

that the Captain perished drunken with the wenches:

"Further Deponent sayeth not."

Pilot Oh Pilot Me

II

Aye, lad, and I have seen those factories,
Gambia, Rio Pongo, Calabar;
have watched the artful mongos baiting traps
of war wherein the victor and the vanquished

Were caught as prizes for our barracoons.
Have seen the nigger kings whose vanity
and greed turned wild black hides of Fellatah,
Mandingo, Ibo, Kru to gold for us.

And there was one—King Anthracite we named him—
fetish face beneath French parasols
of brass and orange velvet, impudent mouth
whose cups were carven skulls of enemies:

He'd honor us with drum and feast and conjo
and palm-oil-glistening wenches deft in love,
and for tin crowns that shone with paste,
red calico and German-silver trinkets

Would have the drums talk war and send
his warriors to burn the sleeping villages
and kill the sick and old and lead the young
in coffles to our factories.

Twenty years a trader, twenty years,
for there was wealth aplenty to be harvested
from those black fields, and I'd be trading still
but for the fevers melting down my bones.

III

Shuttles in the rocking loom of history,
the dark ships move, the dark ships move,
their bright ironical names
like jests of kindness on a murderer's mouth;
plough through thrashing glister toward
fata morgana's lucent melting shore,
weave toward New World littorals that are
mirage and myth and actual shore.

Voyage through death,
voyage whose chartings are unlove.

A charnel stench, effluvium of living death
spreads outward from the hold,
where the living and the dead, the horribly dying,

lie interlocked, lie foul with blood and excrement.

Deep in the festering hold thy father lies,
the corpse of mercy rots with him,
rats eat love's rotten gelid eyes.

But, oh, the living look at you
with human eyes whose suffering accuses you,
whose hatred reaches through the swill of dark
to strike you like a leper's claw.

You cannot stare that hatred down
or chain the fear that stalks the watches
and breathes on you its fetid scorching breath;
cannot kill the deep immortal human wish,
the timeless will.

"But for the storm that flung up barriers
of wind and wave, *The Amistad*, señores,
would have reached the port of Príncipe in two,
three days at most; but for the storm we should
have been prepared for what befell.
Swift as the puma's leap it came. There was
that interval of moonless calm filled only
with the water's and the rigging's usual sounds,
then sudden movement, blows and snarling cries
and they had fallen on us with machete
and marlinspike. It was as though the very
air, the night itself were striking us.
Exhausted by the rigors of the storm,
we were no match for them. Our men went down
before the murderous Africans. Our loyal
Celestino ran from below with gun
and lantern and I saw, before the cane-
knife's wounding flash, Cinquez,
that surly brute who calls himself a prince,
directing, urging on the ghastly work.
He hacked the poor mulatto down, and then
he turned on me. The decks were slippery
when daylight finally came. It sickens me
to think of what I saw, of how these apes
threw overboard the butchered bodies of
our men, true Christians all, like so much jetsam.
Enough, enough. The rest is quickly told:
Cinquez was forced to spare the two of us
you see to steer the ship to Africa,
and we like phantoms doomed to rove the sea
voyaged east by day and west by night,
deceiving them, hoping for rescue,

prisoners on our own vessel, till
at length we drifted to the shores of this
your land, America, where we were freed
from our unspeakable misery. Now we
demand, good sirs, the extradition of
Cinquez and his accomplices to La
Havana. And it distresses us to know
there are so many here who seem inclined
to justify the mutiny of these blacks.
We find it paradoxical indeed
that you whose wealth, whose tree of liberty
are rooted in the labor of your slaves
should suffer the august John Quincy Adams
to speak with so much passion of the right
of chattel slaves to kill their lawful masters
and with his Roman rhetoric weave a hero's
garland for Cinquez. I tell you that
we are determined to return to Cuba
with our slaves and there see justice done. Cinquez—
or let us say 'the Prince'—Cinquez shall die."

The deep immortal human wish,
the timeless will:

Cinquez its deathless primaveral image,
life that transfigures many lives.

Voyage through death
to life upon these shores.

Runagate Runagate

I.

Runs falls rises stumbles on from darkness into darkness
and the darkness thicketed with shapes of terror
and the hunters pursuing and the hounds pursuing
and the night cold and the night long and the river
to cross and the jack-muh-lanterns beckoning beckoning
and blackness ahead and when shall I reach that somewhere
morning and keep on going and never turn back and keep on going
Runagate
Runagate
Runagate

Many thousands rise and go
many thousands crossing over
O mythic North
O star-shaped yonder Bible city

Some go weeping and some rejoicing

some in coffins and some in carriages
some in silks and some in shackles

Rise and go or fare you well

No more auction block for me
no more driver's lash for me

If you see my Pompey, 30 yrs of age,
new breeches, plain stockings, negro shoes;
if you see my Anna, likely young mulatto
branded E on the right cheek, R on the left,
catch them if you can and notify subscriber.
Catch them if you can, but it won't be easy.
They'll dart underground when you try to catch them,
plunge into quicksand, whirlpools, mazes,
turn into scorpions when you try to catch them.

And before I'll be a slave
I'll be buried in my grave

North star and bonanza gold
I'm bound for the freedom, freedom-bound
and oh Susyanna don't you cry for me

Runagate

Runagate

II.

Rises from their anguish and their power,

Harriet Tubman,

woman of earth, whipscarred,
a summoning, a shining

Mean to be free

And this was the way of it, brethren, brethren,
way we journeyed from Can't to Can.
Moon so bright and no place to hide,
the cry up and the patterollers riding,
hound dogs belling in bladed air.
And fear starts a-murbling. Never make it,
we'll never make it. *Hush that now,*
and she's turned upon us, levelled pistol
glinting in the moonlight:
Dead folks can't jaybird-talk, she says;
you keep on going now or die, she says.

Wanted   Harriet Tubman   alias The General
alias Moses   Stealer of Slaves

In league with Garrison   Alcott   Emerson

Garrett   Douglass   Thoreau   John Brown

Armed and known to be Dangerous

Wanted   Reward   Dead or Alive

Tell me, Ezekiel, oh tell me do you see
mailed Jehovah coming to deliver me?

Hoot-owl calling in the ghosted air,
five times calling to the hants in the air.
Shadow of a face in the scary leaves,
shadow of a voice in the talking leaves.

Come ride-a my train

Oh that train, ghost-story train
through swamp and savanna movering movering,
over trestles of dew, through caves of the wish,
Midnight Special on a sabre track movering movering,
first stop Mercy and the last Hallelujah.

Come ride-a my train

Mean mean mean to be free.

Frederick Douglass

When it is finally ours, this freedom, this liberty, this beautiful
and terrible thing, needful to man as air,
usable as earth; when it belongs at last to all,
when it is truly instinct, brain matter, diastole, systole,
reflex action; when it is finally won; when it is more
than the gaudy mumbo jumbo of politicians:
this man, this Douglass, this former slave, this Negro
beaten to his knees, exiled, visioning a world
where none is lonely, none hunted, alien,
this man, superb in love and logic, this man
shall be remembered. Oh, not with statues' rhetoric,
not with legends and poems and wreaths of bronze alone,
but with the lives grown out of his life, the lives
fleshing his dream of the beautiful, needful thing.

Elegies for Paradise Valley

I

My shared bedroom's window
opened on alley stench.
A junkie died in maggots there.
I saw his body shoved into a van.
I saw the hatred for our kind
glistening like tears
in the policemen's eyes.

II

No place for Pestalozzi's
fiorelli. No time of starched
and ironed innocence. Godfearing
elders, even Godless grifters, tried
as best they could to shelter
us. Rats fighting in their walls.

III

Waxwork Uncle Henry
(murdered Uncle Crip)
lay among floral pieces
in the front room where
the Christmas tree had stood.

Mister Hong of the
Chinese Lantern (there
Auntie as waitress queened it
nights) brought freesias, wept
beside the coffin.

Beautiful, our neighbors
murmured; he would be proud.
Is it mahogany?
Mahogany—I'd heard
the victrola voice of
dead Bert Williams
talk-sing that word as macabre
music played, chilling
me. Uncle Crip
had laughed and laughed.

IV

Whom now do you guide, Madam Artelia?
Who nowadays can summon you to speak
from the spirit place your ghostly home
of the oh-riental wonders there—
of the fate, luck, surprises, gifts

awaiting us out here? Oh, Madam,
part Seminole and confidante
("Born with a veil over my face")
of all our dead, how clearly you
materialize before the eye

of memory—your AfroIndian features,
Gypsy dress, your silver crucifix
and manycolored beads. I see

again your waitingroom, with its wax
bouquets, its plaster Jesus of the Sacred Heart.

I watch blue smoke of incense curl
from a Buddah's lap as I wait with Ma
and Auntie among your nervous clients.
You greet us, smiling, lay your hand
in blessing on my head, then lead

the others into a candlelit room
I may not enter. She went into a trance,
Auntie said afterward, and spirits
talked, changing her voice to suit
their own. And Crip came.

Happy yes I am happy here,
he told us; dying's not death. Do not grieve.
Remembering, Auntie began to cry
and poured herself a glass of gin.
Didn't sound a bit like Crip, Ma snapped.

V

And Belle the classy dresser, where is she,
who changed her frocks three times a day?
  Where's Nora, with her laugh, her comic flair,
  stagestruck Nora waiting for her chance?
Where's fast Iola, who so loved to dance
she left her sickbed one last time to whirl
in silver at The Palace till she fell?
  Where's mad Miss Alice, who ate from garbage cans?
  Where's snuffdipping Lucy, who played us 'chunes'
on her guitar? Where's Hattie? Where's Melissabelle?
  Let vanished rooms, let dead streets tell.

Where's Jim, Watusi prince and Good Old Boy,
who with a joke went off to fight in France?
  Where's Tump the defeated artist, for meals or booze
  daubing with quarrelsome reds, disconsolate blues?
Where's Les the huntsman? Tough Kid Chocolate, where
is he? Where's dapper Jess? Where's Stomp the shell-
shocked, clowning for us in parodies of war?
  Where's taunted Christopher, sad queen of night?
  And Ray, who cursing crossed the color line?
Where's gentle Brother Davis? Where's dopefiend Mel?
  Let vanished rooms, let dead streets tell.

VI

Of death. Of loving too:
Oh sweet sweet jellyroll:

so the sinful hymned it while
the churchfolk loured.

I scrounged for crumbs:
I yearned to touch the choirlady's hair,
I wanted Uncle Crip

to kiss me, but he danced
with me instead;
we Balled-the-Jack
to Jellyroll

Morton's brimstone
piano on the phonograph,
laughing, shaking the gasolier
a later stillness dimmed.

VII

Our parents warned us: Gypsies
kidnap you. And we must never play
with Gypsy children: Gypsies
all got lice in their hair.

Their queen was dark as Cleopatra
in the Negro History Book. Their king's
sinister arrogance flashed fire
like the diamonds on his dirty hands.

Quite suddenly he was dead,
his tribe clamoring in grief.
They take on bad as Colored Folks,
Uncle Crip allowed. Die like us too.

Zingaros: Tzigeune: Gitanos: Gypsies:
pornographers of gaudy otherness:
aliens among the alien: thieves,
carriers of sickness: like us like us.

VIII

Of death, of loving,
of sin and hellfire too.
Unsaved, old Christians
gossiped; pitched

from the gamblingtable—
Lord have mercy on
his wicked soul—
face foremost into hell.

We'd dance there, Uncle
Crip and I,
for though I spoke

my pieces well in Sunday School,

I knew myself (precocious
in the ways of guilt
and secret pain)
the devil's own rag babydoll.

A Letter from Phillis Wheatley

London, 1773

Dear Obour
Our crossing was without
event. I could not help, at times,
reflecting on that first—my Destined—
voyage long ago (I yet
have some remembrance of its Horrors)
and marveling at God's Ways.
Last evening, her Ladyship presented me
to her illustrious Friends.
I scarce could tell them anything
of Africa, though much of Boston
and my hope of Heaven. I read
my latest Elegies to them.
"O Sable Muse!" the Countess cried,
embracing me, when I had done.
I held back tears, as is my wont,
and there were tears in Dear
Nathaniel's eyes.
At supper—I dined apart
like captive Royalty—
the Countess and her Guests promised
signatures affirming me
True Poetess, albeit once a slave.
Indeed, they were most kind, and spoke,
moreover, of presenting me
at Court (I thought of Pocahontas)—
an Honor, to be sure, but one,
I should, no doubt, as Patriot decline.
My health is much improved;
I feel I may, if God so Wills,
entirely recover here.
Idyllic England! Alas, there is
no Eden without its Serpent. Under
the chiming Complaisance I here him Hiss;
I see his flickering tongue
when foppish would-be Wits
murmur of the Yankee Pedlar

and his Cannibal Mockingbird.
Sister, forgive th'intrusion of
my Sombreness—Nocturnal Mood
I would not share with any save
your trusted Self. Let me disperse,
in closing, such unseemly Gloom
by mention of an Incident
you may, as I, consider Droll:
Today, a little Chimney Sweep,
his face and hands with soot quite Black,
staring hard at me, politely asked:
"Does you, M'lady, sweep chimneys too?"
I was amused, but dear Nathaniel
(ever Solicitous) was not.
I pray the Blessings of our Lord
and Saviour Jesus Christ be yours
Abundantly. In His Name,

Phillis

DUDLEY RANDALL
(1914–)

Today Dudley Randall bridges the somewhat romanticized Negro folk of the twenties and the sermon incantations by blacks of the sixties. Already he has restored to a worthy spotlight the neglected poetry of Margaret Danner and has opened up a new forum among the masses for the mature Gwendolyn Brooks. Early on, he forwarded the experimental voices of the young Sonia Sanchez, Audre Lorde, and Etheridge Knight. Even now, he is a literary man of three Zeitgeists: the awesome wonder of the Harlem Renaissance, the energized passion of the sixties, and the surviving love balanced by the power and wisdom so worthy of his own generation.

Randall—poet, librarian, and publisher—has helped shape the course of African American poetry from the mid-sixties to the present. He has facilitated a forum that nurtured so many voices of both revolutionary and traditional persuasions. His own work, so accomplished technically and profoundly concerned with the history and racial identity of blacks, has benefited from the intellectual and creative forms of the twenties as well as from a scholarly recognition of the earlier Western Renaissance. Randall, who borrows quite intelligently from various sources, transforms the meaning of them into African American experience. Through his brilliant editorial work at Broadside Press, the company he founded in 1965, he has distributed for world praise the poetry of Gwendolyn Brooks and Margaret Walker. The variety of the writers he has promoted suggests that his mission has been hardly prescriptive, demanding a party line for the acceptance of good work. Indeed, his own literary shapes, so firmly rooted in literary history, are as different in theory from the more precisely witty turns of a Brooks or a Danner as they are from the folk ballads and visionary sermonics of a Walker. Bolstered by a poetic credo of human tolerance, Randall makes an active commitment to nearly all African American literary art.

Dudley F. Randall was born in Washington, D.C., on January 14, 1914. By the time he was thirteen, he had won a dollar for a sonnet published on the poet's page of the *Detroit Free Press.* His father, Arthur George Clyde Randall, who knew about black intellectuals such as James Weldon Johnson and W.E.B. Du Bois, took Dudley to hear them speak in local churches. Later Randall learned about the postbellum poet Paul Laurence Dunbar and the subsequent writers of the Harlem Renaissance. Immediately, he came to appreciate the craft in the poetry of Countee Cullen and the delightful imagery in the prose of Jean Toomer. Between 1943 and 1946, he served in the U.S. Army in the South Pacific. In 1949, at the age of thirty-five, he earned a B.A. in English at Wayne State University. Two years later, he earned an M.A. in library science at the University of Michigan. After working for the Ford Motor Company and the U.S. Post Office for a few months, he became a librarian at Lincoln University from 1951 to 1954, at Morgan State College (now Morgan State University) from 1954 to 1956, and in the Wayne County Federated Library System from 1959 to 1962.

As a mentor for the Black Arts Movement (1960–1974), Randall infused his own ballads with racial experience. At Wayne State, he completed all the requirements for a master's degree in the humanities, except a thesis, the subject matter of which was to be a translation of Chopin's music into words. Randall won the Tompkins Award in 1962, and after founding Broadside Press in 1965, he earned a second Tompkins Award in 1966. Boone House, a cultural center founded by Margaret Danner in Detroit, provided him with occasions for artistic collaboration from 1962 through 1964. Each Sunday Danner and he read from their own works, and over the years the two of them collected a group of their poems. As Randall edited the Broadside Press anthology *For Malcolm X* (1969), the prospects for publication encouraged him to bring out the collaborative book as well. Titled *Poem-Counterpoem* (1966), it became the first major publication from Broadside Press.

At the John Oliver Killens' Writers Conference at Fisk University in 1967, Randall met Margaret Burroughs, founder and director of the Du Sable Museum of Black History in Chicago. Along with her, he recognized, as perhaps most Americans did not, that Alexander Pushkin, the father of Russian literature, claimed African origins through a maternal grandfather. Randall, who had learned the Russian language after the Second World War, was able to read the literature in the original. Much impressed with work by Latin and French poets, he was inspired to undertake some translation, such as "Wait for Me" and "My Native Land" by K. M. Siminov. On his return from Russia and once again at home in Boone House, he plunged into cultural activities. He met some emerging black authors, one of whom was the poet Naomi Long Madgett, who would eventually become founding editor of Lotus Press.

Randall demonstrates with energy and commitment the symbolic process of black self-determination. Influenced even more by modernist techniques, he talks about the love of writing and the joy of publishing. Despite the occasional fun of teaching, he expects his professional and literary career to take new turns. Only as time allows does he write, sometimes while lying down or driving along the freeway. He believes that young African American poets should be free from large mainstream publishers. Older poets, he thinks, should continue to be active. To attract a more diverse audience, he seeks greater richness of texture and philosophical depth. For the sake of political freedom, he has declined offers of partnerships and incorporation of Broadside Press. Usually he has feared that stockholders would demand profits, lower the quality of the poetry submitted, or favor the publication of prose. With so much of his own income from the press committed to the production of new volumes by others, he pays royalties to other poets. He confesses in *Broadside Memories: Poets I Have Known* (1975), "I am not well qualified to operate in a capitalistic society. I came of age during the Great Depression, and my attitude toward business is one of dislike and suspicion. Writers who send me manuscripts and speak of 'Making a buck' turn me off."

His own poems are a missing link in the continuum of the African Diaspora. *Cities Burning* (1968) captures his Zeitgeist. Here humorous poems such as "The Idiot" and "The Melting Pot" show a nice range of technique, blending psychological depth with colloquial tone to reveal police brutality. In pieces such as "A Different Image," he pays homage to the influence of African and Caribbean poets. The fourteen poems in *Love You* (1970) are more accomplished in focus and form than in the earlier work. *More to Remember* (1971) concludes with his credo that the poet is at once the inheritor and reshaper of literary as well as cultural tradition. Randall radicalizes the conservative claims by T. S. Eliot in the latter's "Tradition and the Individual Talent." So appropriate to his own tolerance for change, Randall's own poetic voice sometimes assumes, as in *After the Killing* (1973), the idiom of younger poets. A later book, *A Litany of Friends* (1981), demonstrates an admirable range of literary form and content. Of the eighty-two poems gathered there, twenty-four are reprints and forty-eight new.

Although many people today probably think of Randall as a pioneering publisher of black poetry, he is one of our most gifted men of letters. He is blessed with an unerring literary sense that transcends nearly all formulaic procedures in the careful making of textual evaluations. Although he sometimes fails to shape his poetic gifts into polished rhythms, he writes keenly in the ballad and sonnet forms. He experiments with prophetic verse and with parody as well as fable. Dudley Randall is indeed a poet, a custodian of memory.

❖❖❖

Pioneering studies are R. Baxter Miller, *Black American Poets Between Worlds, 1940–1960* (1986); D. H. Melhem, *Heroism and the New Black Poetry* (1990). An indispensable source for contemporary African American poetry is Dudley Randall, *Broadside Memories: Poets I Have Known* (1975). An excellent interview with Randall is Charles H. Rowell's "In Conversation with Dudley Randall, *Obsidian,* 2, No. 1(1976). See also Dudley Randall's "Black Publisher, Black Writer: An Answer," *Black World* 24, No. 5 (1975). Charles H. Rowell began to lift interviewing to a more revealing level in "In Conversation with Dudley Randall," *Obsidian* 2, No. 1(1976). See also Dudley Randall, "Black Publisher, Black Writer: An Answer," *Black World* 24, No. 5 (1975).

Booker T. and W.E.B.

(Booker T. Washington and W.E.B. Du Bois)

"It seems to me," said Booker T.,
"It shows a mighty lot of cheek
To study chemistry and Greek

When Mister Charlie needs a hand
To hoe the cotton on his land,
And when Miss Ann looks for a cook,
Why stick your nose inside a book?"

"I don't agree," said W.E.B.
"If I should have the drive to seek
Knowledge of chemistry or Greek,
I'll do it. Charles and Miss can look
Another place for hand or cook.
Some men rejoice in skill of hand,
And some in cultivating land,
But there are others who maintain
The right to cultivate the brain."

"It seems to me," said Booker T.,
"That all you folks have missed the boat
Who shout about the right to vote,
And spend vain days and sleepless nights
In uproar over civil rights.
Just keep your mouths shut, do not grouse,
But work, and save, and buy a house."

"I don't agree," said W.E.B.
"For what can property avail
If dignity and justice fail?
Unless you help to make the laws,
They'll steal your house with trumped-up clause.
A rope's as tight, a fire as hot,
No matter how much cash you've got.
Speak *soft*, and try your little plan,
But as for me, I'll be a man."

"It seems to me," said Booker T.—

"I don't agree,"
Said W.E.B.

Legacy: My South

What desperate nightmare rapts me to this land
Lit by a bloody moon, red on the hills,
Red in the valleys? Why am I compelled
To tread again where buried feet have trod,
To shed my tears where blood and tears have flowed?
Compulsion of the blood and of the moon
Transports me. I was molded from this clay.
My blood must ransom all the blood shed here,
My tears redeem the tears. Cripples and monsters
Are here. My flesh must make them whole and hale.
I am the sacrifice.

See where the halt
Attempt again and again to cross a line
Their minds have drawn, but fear snatches them back
Though health and joy wait on the other side.
And there another locks himself in a room
And throws away the key. A ragged scarecrow
Cackles an antique lay, and cries himself
Lord of the world. A naked plowman falls
Famished upon the plow, and overhead
A lean bird circles.

Ancestors

Why are our ancestors
always kings or princes
and never the common people?

Was the Old Country a democracy
where every man was a king?
Or did the slavecatchers
steal only the aristocrats
and leave the fieldhands
laborers
streetcleaners
garbage collectors
dishwashers
cooks
and maids
behind?

My own ancestor
(research reveals)
was a swineherd,
who tended the pigs
in the Royal Pigstye
and slept in the mud
among the hogs.

Yet I'm as proud of him
as of any king or prince
dreamed up in fantasies
of bygone glory.

OWEN DODSON
(1914–1983)

Owen Dodson—American poet, novelist, librettist, short story writer, nonfiction author, and dramatist—was an able teacher and cultural ambassador. Once introduced by the Pulitzer Prize–winning poet Richard Eberhardt as "the best Negro poet in the United States," Dodson published only three volumes of poetry. Indeed, his contemporary poet Margaret Walker once wrote to literary critic R. Baxter Miller that Dodson was the most neglected poet of her generation. Dodson's fiction and plays have been translated into Czech, German, Dutch, Italian, and Japanese. Invited twice to read his poetry at the Library of Congress, Dodson was praised in *Time* magazine 94 (October 3, 1969) as an author whose verse "stands peer to Frost, Carl Sandburg, and other white American poets." Over more than twenty years of directing plays, Dodson achieved the honorary title of "Dean of Black Theater." He attained prominence in an era during which Howard University set the intellectual tone for the African American world.

Owen Vincent Dodson was born on November 28, 1914, the ninth child of Nathaniel Dodson, a freelance journalist for the African American press, and Sarah Elizabeth Goode Dodson, a social worker and church volunteer. He grew up in Brooklyn, New York. Through his father, the director of the National Negro Press Association, he met such political figures as James Weldon Johnson, Booker T. Washington, and W. E. B. Du Bois. With family members, he attended the Concord Baptist Church, where his father was superintendent of the Sunday school and sang traditional hymns by African Americans.

Dodson studied poetry with Elias Lieberman, principal of Thomas Jefferson High School, and in 1932 received a scholarship to attend Bates College in Lewiston, Maine. Among his classmates were John Ciardi, who would go on to become a successful poet and poetry editor for the *Saturday Review,* and Edmund Muskie, who would become a moderate leader in the Democratic Party. With a developing interest in English literature, Dodson told Professor Robert Berkelman that he could write a sonnet as good as John Keats's "On First Looking Into Chapman's Homer." In reply, the instructor required the undergraduate to submit a sonnet to him each week until Dodson had equaled Keats or had graduated. Although Dodson apparently never accomplished the end, according to the professor's own aesthetic, he did write well enough to have work published in the *New York Herald Tribune* and *Phylon.*

The young poet received his B.A. in 1936 and then entered Yale Drama School, where his first play, *Divine Comedy,* was performed in 1938. Named after a work by the epic poet Dante Alighieri, the work received the Maxwell Anderson Award for a poetic play. It mocked self-proclaimed prophets who, such as Father Divine, proclaimed themselves to be God. His next script, *Garden of Time* (1939), adapted the Medea story, originated by the Greek dramatist Euripides, to postbellum South Carolina. By the time he graduated from Yale, Dodson had established several friendships for life, including those with the poet W. H. Auden, the cartoonist Ollie Harrington, and Anne Cooke, who would recruit him to work at Spelman College in 1938.

In 1941, Dodson accepted a position with the communications department at Hampton Institute in Virginia before enlisting in the U.S. Navy the following year. Assigned by Commander Daniel Armstrong to raise "the morale of the Negro seaman" through a series of plays, Dodson was soon discharged because of a serious asthma condition.

In 1944, Dodson directed a performance of his play *New World A Coming,* intended to celebrate African American contributions to the armed forces. Soon he was appointed to the Committee for Mass Education in Race Relations at the American Film Center. There he met writers such as Richard Wright, Langston Hughes, and Arna Bontemps. He began his career as a poet with the volume *Powerful Long Ladder* (1946), praised for its balance between a solo performance and a chorus of slaves. Following is an excerpt from the title poem.

> My father say: Freedom a story they tell that
> never happen.
> When, O when, ma brothers, ma sisters, will the
> well be drained of masquerading death?
> When will the noosed rope strangle the nooser?
> It take a powerful long ladder to climb to the sky
> an catch the bird of freedom for the dark . . .

Alfred Kreymborg, a poetry editor, praised the book in the *Saturday Review of Literature.* However, Dodson was unable to forge into a brilliant new synthesis the conflicting demands of the classical Greek lyric on the one hand and the African American vernacular on the other.

Upon resignation from the American Film Center in 1947, Dodson moved to Washington, D.C., to lead the newly established drama department of Howard University. As his first major achievement at Howard, he directed *Bayou Legend* (1948), a poetic play he adapted from Henrik Ibsen's *Peer Gynt* (1867). With James Cooke and Margaret Butcher, he led the Howard Players on a tour through northwestern Europe in 1949.

Dodson's first novel, *Boy at the Window* (1951; reprinted 1967 as *When Trees Were Green*), tells the somewhat autobiographical story of Coin Foreman, a sensitive youth who feels that his conversion to the Baptist faith should have prevented his mother's death. In 1952, Dodson received a Guggenheim Fellowship to produce a sequel titled *Come Home Early, Child* (1977). During the fellowship year, he lived in an Italian villa belonging to W. H. Auden. In the second novel, which remained unpublished for twenty-five years, Foreman has a love affair in Italy while serving in the U.S. Navy. He returns to Brooklyn to find himself alienated in place and time. His ritualistic passage into manhood sets the stage for a narrative strategy that becomes somewhat surrealistic in the second half of the work.

By 1953, Dodson had directed several premier performances, including one of James Baldwin's *Amen Corner* in 1953. Insisting that black college students must present the traditional drama of Western theater, he produced three performances of *Hamlet* during his twenty-three years at Howard. In 1956, George Plimpton awarded Dodson second prize in a contest sponsored by the *Paris Review* for a story included subsequently in *Best Short Stories from the Paris Review* (1959). Obviously, Dodson considered himself a universalist. Later Dodson said, "I was told that the novel was not Black enough. Part of it won a prize. . . . Of course, writers from all over the world were represented there, not just black writers."

In 1967, Dodson received a Litt.D. from Bates College. Returning to New York City after his retirement, Dodson completed *The Confession Stone Song Cycles* in 1970. Spoken by various members of the Holy Family, the series of monologues presents the life of Jesus Christ. Dodson hoped that this work would be his masterpiece, though it lacked a brilliant originality in style. Even years later in 1974, at the

Kennedy Center Opera House in Washington, D.C., Dodson's play *Till Victory Is Won* was performed to honor Howard University's centennial.

During his life, Dodson was invited to the White House by President Lyndon Johnson. At other times, the playwright received Rosenwald and Rockefeller fellowships. Beside W. H. Auden, he listed Langston Hughes and Countee Cullen as his friends. His students included the celebrated playwright and poet Leroi Jones (today Amiri Baraka); the renowned performers Ossie Davis and Debbie Allen; the legal advocate Marilyn Berry; the dramatist and critic Ted Shine; the literary critic Michael Thelwell and literary theorist Patricia Liggins Hill. Richard Eberhart's claim that Dodson was the "best Negro poet in the United States," however, violated the emerging principle that blacks would soon learn to make these judgments for themselves on their own terms.

More transforming energy would soon emerge from a return to the spirit of abolitionism, hence renewing the Black American struggle for human freedom. The real power of Amiri Baraka's drama, therefore, would derive not only from conflict, as the very traditional Dodson had clearly foreseen, but from the revolutionary hope to reconcile tensions between Eurocentric survival and world humanity, between traditional insanity and innovative quests—especially newly beautiful ways—to realize sanity for American civilization. Dodson's generation asked how "Negro" drama might imitate the great Greek plays of antiquity. Baraka's would develop original blues forms to explore territory where no one had gone before.

❖❖❖

African American critics have yet to make peace with the ideology and historical impact of Owen Dodson. For the most part, sympathetic whites have led the way. His good friend John V. Hatch dedicated much of the past decade to the biography *Sorrow Is the Only Faithful One: The Life of Owen Dodson* (1993), an expansion of his article "Owen Dodson: Excerpts from a Biography in Progress," *Massachusetts Review* 28, No. 4 (Winter 1987), and his essay "Remembering Owen Dodson," in *Artist and Influence,* ed. Leo Hamalian and Judith Wilson, vol. 3 (1985). Invaluable are Bernard L. Peterson, Jr., "The Legendary Owen Dodson," *The Crisis* 86 (November 1979); John O'Brien, "Owen Dodson," in *Interviews with Black Writers* (1973).

Sorrow Is the Only Faithful One

Sorrow is the only faithful one:
The lone companion clinging like a season
To its original skin no matter what the variations.

If all the mountains paraded
Eating the valleys as they went
And the sun were a coiffure on the highest peak,

Sorrow would be there between
The sparkling and the giant laughter
Of the enemy when the clouds come down to swim.

But I am less, unmagic, black,
Sorrow clings to me more than to doomsday mountains
Or erosion scars on a palisade.

Sorrow has a song like a leech
Crying because the sand's blood is dry
And the stars reflected in the lake

Are water for all their twinkling
And bloodless for all their charm.
I have blood, and song.
Sorrow is the only faithful one.

Yardbird's Skull

(For Charlie Parker)

The bird is lost,
Dead, with all the music:
Whole sunsets heard the brain's music
Faded to last horizon notes.
I do not know why I hold
This skull, smaller than a walnut's,
Against my ear,
Expecting to hear
The smashed fear
Of childhood from . . . bone;
Expecting to see
Wind nosing red and purple,
Strange gold and magic
On bubbled windowpanes
Of childhood. Shall I hear?
I should hear: this skull
Has been with violets
Not Yorick, or the gravedigger,
Yapping his yelling story,
This skull has been in air,
Sensed his brother, the swallow,
(Its talent for snow and crumbs).
Flown to lost Atlantis islands,
Places of dreaming, swimming lemmings.
O I shall hear skull skull,
Hear your lame music,
Believe music rejects undertaking,
Limps back.
Remember tiny lasting, we get lonely:
Come sing, come sing, come sing sing
And sing.

Guitar

Ma six string guitar with the lonesome sound
Can't hold its own against a Georgia hound.

O mamma when the sun goes the downstairs way
And the night spreads out an the moon make day,

I sits with ma feet raised to the rail
And sings the song bout ma buddy in jail:

In the red-dirt land,
And the pine tree high,
Gonna find me peace
By-an-by.

Gonna find me a baby
Some pretty-eye gal
To be ma mother
Ma wife an pal.

Ain't had nobody
To call me home
From the electric cities
Where I roam.

Yes, I been travelin
Over all
To find a place
What I could call
Home, baby,
Sweet cotton-field home. . . .

When I gets to the place where a cracker got mad,
Struck ma fine buddy, struck all I had,
The hound start howlin till the stars break down
An make ma song like a boat what's drown.

Ma six string guitar with the lonesome sound
Can't hold its own against that Georgia hound.

MARGARET ESSE DANNER
(1915–1988)

Margaret Esse Danner, poet of five books and editor of two others, deserves more recognition than she has received. Among her greatest contemporaries in African American poetry—Melvin Tolson, Robert Hayden, Dudley Randall, Margaret Walker, and even Gwendolyn Brooks—she was often the most precise in focusing exact images, as in the poem "The Slave and the Iron Lace," an intense moment of beauty. With the most gifted of her fellows, she continued throughout her poetic life to reach for aesthetic forms of beauty preserved from the Harlem Renaissance of her childhood. She particularly brought to her poetry about Africa a highly introspective and lyrical quality. At once she was somewhat Keatsian, yet modernist in creating an object-centered moment of perception. Her poems are highly polished in the somewhat esoteric diction of her time. For example, in her African sequence she made telling use of Paul Gauguin, a nineteenth-century French painter, as an artistic signature. Her poems appeared in *Voices, Negro Digest, Black World, Negro History Bulletin, Accent, Chicago Review, Quicksilver,* and *Chicago Magazine.* As with several other African American women, her poetry is often misplaced in the post-sixties period because of the new appreciation of it today. Almost nothing could be further from the truth for this unusually ancestral voice of the Old Guard.

Margaret Esse was born on January 12, 1915, to Caleb and Naomi Esse of Pryorsburg, Kentucky. She began to write poetry in junior high school and when she was in the eighth grade won first prize in a poetry contest for "The Violin." Later she attended Englewood High School in Chicago and went to college at Loyola and Northwestern Universities. Especially at the latter, she established academic associations with Karl Shapiro and Paul Engle, strong mentors who could make reputations for poets in the Midwest. By 1945, Danner had won recognition after being awarded second place in the poetry workshop of the Midwestern Writers Conference held at Northwestern.

As a guardian of African art forms, Danner was clearly ahead of her time. Gwendolyn Brooks, Ralph Ellison, and James Baldwin, three of the most gifted writers of the fifties (though Brooks had emerged in the forties), evinced little African consciousness in their work during that decade. Indeed, even Richard Wright rarely looked to Africa for spiritual sustenance in novels such as *The Outsider* (1953) and *The Long Dream* (1958). And even Wright, in thought-provoking treatises such as *Black Power* (1954) and *Pagan Spain* (1957), showed lapses into a kind of patriarchal Western condescension. Danner, who was conservative about African American politics, was radical about the positive perception of African images. Indirectly, she was one of the foremost proponents of African American self-esteem.

As editorial assistant for the prestigious *Poetry* magazine from 1951 to 1955, she contributed a series of four poems, including "Far from Africa," a popular piece. Consequently, she received a John Hay Whitney Fellowship in 1951 for a trip to Africa, although the trip would be delayed until 1966. In 1956, she was promoted to assistant editor, probably at the urging of Karl Shapiro, becoming the first African American to be so honored.

In 1961, Danner became poet-in-residence at Wayne State University in Detroit, one of her many stints in this role at universities around the country. Later, in 1962, she located a vacant parish house near King Solomon Church and convinced the minister, Dr. Boone, to help found a community arts center, called Boone House. There evolved a distinguished circle of poetry and culture that included the innovative thinker and critic Hoyt Fuller as well as the creative traditionalists Robert Hayden, Owen Dodson, Dudley Randall, and Naomi Long Madgett. In fact, the development of Broadside Press, founded by Randall in 1965 and the eventual outlet for an entire generation of revolutionary poetics, would derive in part from the pioneering work of Danner.

The Civil Rights Movement, along with the consequent feminist movement, helped restore Danner to prominence. *Impressions of African Art Forms in the Poetry of Margaret Danner* (1960) set the tone for her career. Her other books include *To*

Flower: Poems (1963), *The Down of a Thistle* (1966), and, with Dudley Randall, *Poem-Counterpoem* (1966). The titles suggest that Danner's poetry focuses on either sculptured or natural beauty, or perhaps both. Later she edited two anthologies of students' verse, *Brass Horse* (1968) and *Regroup* (1969).

With Hayden, Danner had taken to the Baha'i faith. Perhaps a spiritual quality helped her, during her final years at LeMoyne-Owen College in Memphis (1970–1975), to be recognized as a Tennessee writer. By then, she had led her celebratory aesthetic of African peoples back into the South. Today "The Slave and the Iron Lace" keeps alive the excellence of her poetry. Like her mythical figure the mason Samuel Rouse, she created a black poetics with grace.

❖❖❖

Since 1984, Danner has begun to receive some of the critical attention she deserves. Significant contributions are Richard K. Barksdale, in *Praisesong of Survival* (Urbana, 1991); Erlene Stetson, in *Black American Poets Between Worlds, 1940–1960*, ed. R. Baxter Miller (1986). Articles by June M. Aldridge in *Dictionary of Literary Biography: Afro-American Writers* (1985), vol. 41, and in the *Langston Hughes Review* 3 (Fall 1984) have paved the way for new research.

Far from Africa: Four Poems

"are you beautiful still?"

1. Garnishing the Aviary

Our moulting days are in their twilight stage.
These lengthy dreaded suns of draggling plumes.
These days of moods that swiftly alternate between

The former preen (ludicrous now) and a downcast rage
Or crestfallen lag, are fading out. The initial bloom;
Exotic, dazzling in its indigo, tangerine
Splendor; this rare, conflicting coat had to be shed.
Our drooping feathers turn all shades. We spew
This unamicable aviary, gag upon the worm, and fling
Our loosening quills. We make a riotous spread
Upon the dust and mire that beds us. We do not shoo
So quickly; but the shades of the pinfeathers resulting
From this chaotic push, though still exotic,
Blend in more easily with those on the wings
Of the birds surrounding them; garnishing
The aviary, burnishing this zoo.

2. Dance of the Abakweta

Imagine what Mrs. Haessler would say
If she could see the Watusi youth dance

Their well-versed initiation. At first glance
As they bend to an invisible barre
You would know that she had designed their costumes.

For though they were made of pale beige bamboo straw
Their lines were the classic tutu. Nothing varied.
Each was cut short at the thigh and carried
High to a degree of right angles. Nor was there a flaw
In their leotards. Made of leopard skin or the hide
Of a goat, or the Gauguin-colored Okapi's striped coat
They were cut in her reverenced "tradition."
She would have approved their costumes and positions.
And since neither Iceland nor Africa is too remote
For her vision she would have wanted to form

A "traditional" ballet. Swan Lake, Scheherazade or
(After seeing their incredible leaps)
Les Orientales. Imagine the exotic sweep
Of such a ballet, and from the way the music pours
Over these dancers (this tinkling of bells, talking
Of drums, and twanging of tan, sandalwood harps)
From this incomparable music, Mrs. Haessler of Vassar can
Glimpse strains of Tchaikovsky, Chopin
To accompany her undeviatingly sharp
"Traditional" ballet. I am certain that if she could
Tutor these potential protégés, as
Quick as Aladdin rubbing his lamp, she would.

3. The Visit of the Professor of Aesthetics

To see you standing in the sagging bookstore door
So filled me with chagrin that suddenly you seemed as
Pink and white to me as a newborn, hairless mouse. For

I had hoped to delight you at home. Be a furl
Of faint perfume and Vienna's cordlike lace.
To shine my piano till a shimmer of mother-of-pearl

Embraced it. To pleasantly surprise you with the grace
That transcends my imitation and much worn
"Louis XV" couch. To display my Cathedrals and ballets.

To plunge you into Africa through my nude
Zulu Prince, my carvings from Benin, forlorn
Treasures garnered by much sacrifice of food.

I had hoped to delight you, for more
Rare than the seven-year bloom of my
Chinese spiderweb fern is a mind like yours

That concedes my fetish for this substance
Of your trade. And I had planned to prove

Your views of me correct at even every chance

Encounter. But you surprised me. And the store which
Had shown promise until you came, arose
Like a child gone wild when company comes or a witch

At Hallowe'en. The floor, just swept and mopped,
Was persuaded by the northlight to deny it.
The muddy rag floor rugs hunched and flopped
Away from the tears in the linoleum that I wanted
Them to hide. The drapes that I had pleated
In clear orchid and peach feverishly flaunted

Their greasiest folds like a banner.
The books who had been my friends, retreated—
Became as shy as the proverbial poet in manner

And hid their better selves. All glow had been deleted
By the dirt. And I felt that you whose god is grace
Could find no semblance of it here. And unaware

That you were scrubbing, you scrubbed your hands.
Wrung and scrubbed your long white fingers. Scrubbed
Them as you smiled and I lowered my eyes from despair.

4. *Etta Moten's Attic*

(Filled with mementos of African journeys)

It was as if Gauguin
had upset a huge paint pot
of his incomparable tangerine,
splashing wherever my startled eyes ran
here and there, and at my very hand on
masques and paintings and carvings not seen

here before, spilling straight as a stripe
spun geometrically in a Nbeble rug
flung over an ebony chair,

or dripping round as a band on a type
of bun the Watusi warriors
make of their pompadoured hair,

splashing high as a sunbird or fly moving
over a frieze of mahogany trees,
or splotching out from low underneath as a root,

shimmering bright as a ladybug grooving
a green bed of moss, sparkling as a beetle,
a bee, shockingly dotting the snoot
of an ape or the nape of its neck or as clue
to its navel, stamping a Zulu's
intriguing masque, tipping

the lips of a chief of Ashantis who
was carved to his stool so he'd sit
there forever and never fear a slipping

of rule or command, dyeing the skirt
(all askew) that wouldn't stay put on the
Pygmy in spite of his real leather belt,

quickening and charming till we felt the bloom
of veldt and jungle flow through the room.

The Rhetoric of Langston Hughes

While some "rap" over this turmoil
of who was Blackest first
and the ins and outs of the Spirituals
and the Blues
and how many of us have or have not
paid our dues;

Langston Hughes (in his traveling)
has sung to so many for so long
and from so very Black a Power
that we have clearly seen the "angles"
and dedicated ourselves
to be unraveling.

The Slave and the Iron Lace

The craving of Samuel Rouse for clearance to create
was surely as hot as the iron that buffeted him. His passion
for freedom so strong that it molded the smouldering fashions
he laced, for how else could a slave plot
or counterplot such incomparable shapes,

form or reform, for house after house
the intricate Chatilion Patio pattern, the delicate
Rose and Lyre, the Debutante Settee
the complex but famous Grape; frame the classic vein
in an iron bench?

How could he turn an iron Venetian urn, wind the Grape Vine chain
the trunk of a pine with a Round-the-Tree-settee,
mold a Floating Flower tray, a French chair, create all this
in such exquisite fairyland taste, that he'd be freed
and his skill would still resound a hundred years after?

Passive Resistance

And to this Man who turned the other cheek,
this Man who murmured not a word,
or fought at persecutors,

remained meek under it all,
I crawl, in wonder.

For as the evil tongues begin to turn on me
I want to fight, strike back,
and see them quail
in some rat-ridden jail,
or suffering for
the suffering they've caused.
I want no more of this humility.
But I must bow,
bow low before it now,
and love the evil ones,
as You did. Yet, I am sure
it was much easier for
God's son.

MARGARET WALKER

(1915–)

Margaret Walker is the senior-ranking author of the African American South and probably its greatest poet. Variously she has fulfilled the diverse roles of teacher, novelist, essayist, and poet. As one of the most distinguished American authors for the past half century, she exemplifies a good range of poetic forms, including the Shakespearean and Petrarchan sonnet. Especially in her earlier verse, she re-creates the trickery and deceit of the early folklore of the nineteenth century. She portrays a fascination with superstition and magic during her own time. In her later work, she elevates the poetic cadences of the African American folk sermon to new heights of literary expression. Hence, she achieves a tone of righteous indignation. She has been one of America's foremost poets of ideas. She is a first-rate thinker and one of the finest writers for the artistic celebration of black people. Of the most talented poets who have bridged the generations of the Harlem Renaissance of the twenties and the Black Arts Movement of the sixties, she perhaps has retained the most creativity. Some of her greatest metaphors, such as the well-crafted quilt of her grandmother and the Crystal Palace, signifying a once eminent hotel decayed through time, have come of late. Walker also has emerged as a poetic historian of African monuments and a guardian of cultured memory.

Margaret Abigail Walker was born on July 7, 1915, in Birmingham, Alabama, to Reverend Sigismund C. and Marion Dozier Walker. Her father, a Methodist minister who had been born near Buff Bay, Jamaica, encouraged her to read works by Benedict Spinoza, a seventeenth-century Dutch philosopher, and Arthur Schopenhauer, a nineteenth-century German thinker. Walker's mother, a musician who played ragtime, helped introduce her to the poetry of Paul Laurence Dunbar, John Greenleaf Whittier, and William Shakespeare. By the age of eleven, Margaret had read the poetry of Langston Hughes and Countee Cullen.

Many of the highlights of Walker's career have historical roots in the thirties. As a senior at Northwestern University in 1934, she began a fruitful association with the

Work Projects Administration (WPA). She lived on the North Side of Chicago and served as a volunteer working with young girls who had been shoplifters and prostitutes. In March 1936, she began full-time work on the Federal Writers' Project in Chicago. As a junior contributor, her salary to complete an Illinois guidebook was $85 a month. Some of her colleagues on the project were Katherine Dunham, Nelson Algren, Willard Motley, Frank Yerby, and Fenton Johnson. In 1941, she began her teaching career at Livingston College in North Carolina and in 1942 taught at West Virginia State College. From 1949 until her retirement, she was a member of the English faculty at Jackson State College (now Jackson State University).

Walker's major collaboration in the thirties was with the novelist Richard Wright. Often she would discuss with him the possible literary structures for poetry. She helped with the revisions of a story or two by Wright and with the short novel that would eventually be entitled *Lawd Today* (1963). Sometimes she would discuss with him the subject of folk materials and forms. Although she considered writing a Civil War story for her master's thesis at the University of Iowa in the late thirties, Wright supported her delay of the manuscript that would later become *Jubilee* (1966). Walker did much of the research for Wright's novel *Native Son* (1940). She visited the Cook County Jail, where Robert Nixon, a young black man accused of rape, was incarcerated; helped Wright find a vacant lot to use for the house address of the Daltons, a prominent family in the novel; and checked out a library book about the celebrated lawyer Clarence Darrow, who became a source for Wright's development of a defense for Bigger Thomas, the protagonist of the novel. In 1939, the working friendship between Walker and Wright ended so that the two of them could avoid any complications of a romantic relationship.

Walker was one of the most talented writers of the thirties. The range and persistence of her literary gift, however, would go largely unrecognized for fifty years. "For My People," her signature poem, appeared in 1937, and "We Have Been Believers" came out the next year. "The Struggle Staggers Us" was published in *Poetry* magazine in 1939. Magazines such as *Opportunity* and *The Crisis* also had provided her with useful forums. Despite her early inclination to write a Civil War novel for her master's thesis, she decided to complete instead a collection of poems titled *For My People* (1942). The volume won the Yale University Prize for younger poets.

What makes the recovered reputation of Margaret Walker so remarkable is that she delayed for an entire generation the publication of her later books. *For My People* (1942) and *Prophets for a New Day* (1970) speak to entirely different generations, the first volume coming out before the end of World War II and the second near the end of the Black Arts Movement. Even more impressively, Walker has maintained a highly unusual ability to adjust on the fly the forms that she uses. Many of the controlled lyrics in *October Journey* (1973), *For Farish Street Green* (1986), and, especially, *This Is My Century: New and Collected Poems* (1988) show a polished finish. "African Village" achieves a delightful repetition of history transmuted into stone:

> Dark faces of our living generations
> hear voices of our loving dead go echoing
>   down corridors of centuries.
> For those who suffered, bled and died
> Let this be monument.

One side of the poetic voice speaks to the communal traditions of African Americans, while the other testifies to the individual talent, as in "The Labyrinth of Life":

> a kiss to give across a wide abyss
> and knowing magic of reconciliation and hope
> To a place blessed with smiling
> Shining beyond the brightness of noon day
> and I lift my voice above a rising wind . . .

Here sounds the hidden echo of the Negro National Anthem, "Lift Every Voice and Sing." Margaret Walker, striking an excellent balance of lyric and epic, writes for all that is human.

❖❖❖

Maryemma Graham, "The Fusion of Ideas: An Interview with Margaret Walker Alexander," *African American Review,* Vol. 27 (Summer 1993); and Jerry W. Ward, Jr., "An Open Letter to Michel Fabre," *The Mississippi Quarterly,* 43, No. 2 (Spring 1990), have worked steadfastly to promote the reputation of Margaret Walker over the past several years. R. Baxter Miller, " 'The Etched Flame of Margaret Walker'," *Tennessee Studies in Literature,* 26 (1981) is frequently anthologized. Paula Giddings, "Some Themes in the Poetry of Margaret Walker," *Black World* (Dec. 1971); and Charles Rowell, "Poetry, History, and Humanism," *Black World,* 25 (Dec. 1975), provided early, important sources. Interviews by John Griffin Jones, ed., *Mississippi Writers Talking* (University: University of Mississippi Press, 1982), Vol. 2, has made intriguing biography accessible.

For My People

For my people everywhere singing their slave songs repeatedly: their dirges and their
ditties and their blues and jubilees, praying their prayers nightly to an unknown
god, bending their knees humbly to an unseen power;

For my people lending their strength to the years, to the gone years and the now years
and the maybe years, washing ironing cooking scrubbing sewing mending hoeing
plowing digging planting pruning patching dragging along never gaining never
reaping never knowing and never understanding;

For my playmates in the clay and dust and sand of Alabama backyards playing baptizing
and preaching and doctor and jail and soldier and school and mama and cooking
and playhouse and concert and store and hair and Miss Choomby and company;

For the cramped bewildered years we went to school to learn to know the reasons why
and the answers to and the people who and the places where and the days when, in
memory of the bitter hours when we discovered we were black and poor and small
and different and nobody cared and nobody wondered and nobody understood;

For the boys and girls who grew in spite of these things to be man and woman, to laugh
and dance and sing and play and drink their wine and religion and success, to
marry their playmates and bear children and then die of consumption and anemia
and lynching;

For my people thronging 47th Street in Chicago and Lenox Avenue in New York and Rampart Street in New Orleans, lost disinherited dispossessed and happy people filling the cabarets and taverns and other people's pockets needing bread and shoes and milk and land and money and something—something all our own;

For my people walking blindly spreading joy, losing time being lazy, sleeping when hungry, shouting when burdened, drinking when hopeless, tied, and shackled and tangled among ourselves by the unseen creatures who tower over us omnisciently and laugh;

For my people blundering and groping and floundering in the dark of churches and schools and clubs and societies, associations and councils and committees and conventions, distressed and disturbed and deceived and devoured by money-hungry glory-craving leeches, preyed on by facile force of state and fad and novelty, by false prophet and holy believer;

For my people standing staring trying to fashion a better way from confusion, from hypocrisy and misunderstanding, trying to fashion a world that will hold all the people, all the faces, all the adams and eves and their countless generations;

Let a new earth rise. Let another world be born. Let a bloody peace be written in the sky. Let a second generation full of courage issue forth; let a people loving freedom come to growth. Let a beauty full of healing and a strength of final clenching be the pulsing in our spirits and our blood. Let the martial songs be written, let the dirges disappear. Let a race of men now rise and take control.

Lineage

My grandmothers were strong.
They followed plows and bent to toil.
They moved through fields sowing seed.
They touched earth and grain grew.
They were full of sturdiness and singing.
My grandmothers were strong.

My grandmothers are full of memories
Smelling of soap and onions and wet clay
With veins rolling roughly over quick hands
They have many clean words to say.
My grandmothers were strong.
Why am I not as they?

The Ballad of the Free

Bold Nat Turner by the blood of God
Rose up preaching on Virginia's sod;
Smote the land with his passionate plea
Time's done come to set my people free.

The serpent is loosed and the hour is come
The last shall be first and the first shall be none
The serpent is loosed and the hour is come

Gabriel Prosser looked at the sun,
Said, "Sun, stand still till the work is done.
The world is wide and the time is long
And man must meet the avenging wrong."

The serpent is loosed and the hour is come
The last shall be first and the first shall be none
The serpent is loosed and the hour is come

Denmark Vesey led his band
Across the hot Carolina land.
The plot was foiled, the brave men killed,
But Freedom's cry was never stilled.

The serpent is loosed and the hour is come
The last shall be first and the first shall be none
The serpent is loosed and the hour is come

Toussaint L'Ouverture won
All his battles in the tropic sun,
Hero of the black man's pride
Among those hundred who fought and died.

The serpent is loosed and the hour is come
The last shall be first and the first shall be none
The serpent is loosed and the hour is come

Brave John Brown was killed but he
Became a martyr of the free,
For he declared that blood would run
Before the slaves their freedom won.

The serpent is loosed and the hour is come
The last shall be first and the first shall be none
The serpent is loosed and the hour is come

Wars and Rumors of Wars have gone,
But Freedom's army marches on.
The heroes' list of dead is long,
And Freedom still is for the strong.

The serpent is loosed and the hour is come
The last shall be first and the first shall be none
The serpent is loosed and the hour is come

Prophets for a New Day

1.

As the Word came to prophets of old,
As the burning bush spoke to Moses,
And the fiery coals cleansed the lips of Isaiah;
As the wheeling cloud in the sky
Clothed the message of Ezekiel;

So the Word of fire burns today
On the lips of our prophets in an evil age—
Our sooth-sayers and doom-tellers and doers of the Word.
So the Word of the Lord stirs again
These passionate people toward deliverance.
As Amos, Shepherd of Tekoa, spoke
To the captive children of Judah,
Preaching to the dispossessed and the poor,
So today in the pulpits and the jails,
On the highways and in the byways,
A fearless shepherd speaks at last
To his suffering weary sheep.

2.

So, kneeling by the river bank
Comes the vision to a valley of believers
So in flaming flags of stars in the sky
And in the breaking dawn of a blinding sun
The lamp of truth is lighted in the Temple
And the oil of devotion is burning at midnight
So the glittering censer in the Temple
Trembles in the presence of the priests
And the pillars of the door-posts move
And the incense rises in smoke
And the dark faces of the sufferers
Gleam in the new morning
The complaining faces glow
And the winds of freedom begin to blow
While the Word descends on the waiting World below.

3.

A beast is among us.
His mark is on the land.
His horns and his hands and his lips are gory with our blood.
He is War and Famine and Pestilence
He is Death and Destruction and Trouble
And he walks in our houses at noonday
And devours our defenders at midnight.
He is the demon who drives us with whips of fear
And in his cowardice
He cries out against liberty
He cries out against humanity
Against all dignity of green valleys and high hills
Against clean winds blowing through our living;
Against the broken bodies of our brothers.
He has crushed them with a stone.

He drinks our tears for water
And he drinks our blood for wine;
He eats our flesh like a ravenous lion
And he drives us out of the city
To be stabbed on a lonely hill.

The Crystal Palace

The Crystal Palace used to be
a place of elegance
Where "bourgie" black folks came to shoot
a game of pool
And dine in the small cafe
across the way.
The dance hall music rocked the night
and sang sweet melodies:
"Big fat mama with the meat shaking on her bones"
"Boogie woogie mama
Please come back home"
"I miss you loving papa
but I can't live on love alone"
The Crystal Palace
Used to be
most elegant.

A Patchwork Quilt

This street is like my grandma's patchwork quilt
Kaleidoscope, appliqued with multicolored
threads of embroidery.
A golden sun, blue skies, carpeted with the greenness
the yellow, the red, the white, the black, the brown, and
the checkered.
Bright gingham, fine silk and satin and linen cloth
patterned patches on the faces of these people
the Chinese laundryman
Black cobbler
Greek grocer
And down the street there used to be
A livery stable with a brown Indian man.
Now there's a taxi stand.
Once streetcars passed along the side
Up Capitol
to where black slaves built the Capitol
the mansion for the governor
and over there, the city hall.
They made these bricks and laid them too
Not knowing some day they would meet

As Black and Tan in 1868.
This patchwork quilt is stitched with blood and tears
This street is paved with martyred Black men's flesh and bones.

GWENDOLYN BROOKS
(1917–)

Gwendolyn Brooks ranks among the greatest American poets. Few have equaled her brilliant range in the traditional and innovative forms of the sonnet and ballad as well as the black vernacular. What makes her poetry unique is the intellectual depth that pervades nearly every line. Countee Cullen and Claude McKay wrote in the established forms a generation or two earlier, but neither could suit the poetic shape so naturally to concentrated thought as she.

From her first volume, *A Street in Bronzeville* (1945), Brooks has shared with Margaret Walker a gift in responding to human existence through poetic form. Early on in her work, she explored the questions of human meaning in the postwar world. Later she sought to answer within epic structure (*Annie Allen,* 1949) whether the consequent rift in human alienation can ever be closed. Finally, she has concluded that the great visionary, whether an imagined Langston Hughes (*Selected Poems,* 1963) or an urban tenant in a decaying apartment building (*In the Mecca,* 1968), represents the process of human health. Although her images are often Eurocentric, especially those before 1967, the ironic and somewhat coyish tone of wisdom in her work is distinctly African American. In fact, almost no other black poet writing in English demands so much the careful ear for twisting turns and unraveling insight as does she. She attempts to place Western art forms in a black folk perspective so as to possess them in a way still true to the African American experience.

For nearly fifty years, Brooks has walked a tightrope of negotiation between the beauty of artistic forms and the human self that must interpret them. Variously her poetic narrators mention baroque and rococo styles of architecture and traditional musicians such as Grieg, Tchaikovsky, Saint-Saëns, and Brahms. The painter Pablo Picasso appears in her poetry as well. So do Satin Legs Smith, an urbanite with a folk flair for clothes, and an unrelated black youth who breaks windows in the streets. Brooks voices the hurt and triumph of the common people. Hence, she creates a poetic art that helps free them and others from an easy acceptance of social limits. Her earlier verse helps save the Euro-American tradition of poetry that so often ignores the way the poor are human. Her later verse and literary activities help marshal in the New Black Poets and the black aesthetic.

Gwendolyn Brooks was born in Topeka, Kansas, on June 7, 1917, to Keziah Corinne Wims Brooks and David Anderson Brooks. As early as first grade, this dark-skinned girl began to recognize distinctions based on color, gender, and class. She lacked athletic skills and many social graces, as well as straight hair. For her, the writing of poetry became a positive antidote to peer rejection. Supported in these efforts by her parents, she wrote many poems about the triumph of beauty and order in the world, but discrimination based on race-gender-class would become the focus of her later poetry.

Early on, Brooks was influenced by English and American romantic poets such as William Wordsworth, John Keats, William Cullen Bryant, and Henry Wadsworth Longfellow. In 1930, at age thirteen, she wrote "Eventide" for *American Childhood* magazine; four years later, she began to write poetry for a variety column, "Lights and Shadows," in the *Chicago Defender.* Brooks graduated in 1934 from the integrated Englewood High School in Topeka and by 1935 was well on her way in writing the traditional forms of poetry. Influenced by Sara Teasdale, she focused primarily on love as a subject and occasionally treated a theme of racial pride. Briefly, she corresponded with James Weldon Johnson, a Harlem Renaissance poet. Her mother had taken her to meet Johnson and hear him lecture in 1933. That same year, Langston Hughes encouraged her at one of his readings to continue writing. He surprised her by taking time after a performance to read some of her poems. By the late thirties, Brooks had published seventy-five poems in the *Chicago Defender.*

After graduating from Wilson Junior College in 1936, Brooks read the works of modern poets such as T. S. Eliot, Ezra Pound, and e. e. cummings. Five years later, she began to study at Chicago's South Side Community Art Center with Inez Cunningham Stark, a disgruntled socialite who was a reader for *Poetry* magazine. At the time Brooks did odd jobs and early on had even worked as a typist. Others who studied at the center were Henry Blakely, Brooks's husband; William Couch, scholar of African American drama; Margaret Taylor Goss Burroughs, curator of African history in a Chicago museum; and Margaret Danner, a fine poet in her own right. Many of the poems Brooks wrote in 1941 and 1942 appeared in her collection *A Street in Bronzeville* (1945).

With "Gay Chaps at the Bar" in 1944 and "The Progress" in 1945, Brooks won the prize awarded by the Midwestern Writers' Conference. Both of the pieces rival some by W. H. Auden as the most talented war poems in the twentieth century. Initially, Brooks tried to publish her early poetry through Emily Morrison at Alfred K. Knopf, but finally she gathered together nineteen pieces, mainly about African Americans, and sent them to Harper's. *A Street in Bronzeville,* which was published in August 1945, received a good review from Paul Engle in the Sunday *Chicago Tribune Book Review.* It was Engle, in fact, who had helped secure prizes for Brooks at the Northwestern University Annual Writers' Conference that year.

For Brooks, the forties were a decade of rising fame. In 1945, she received the Mademoiselle Merit Award as one of the ten outstanding women of the year. In 1946 and 1947, she earned Guggenheim Fellowships. In 1949, she secured the Eunice Tietjens Memorial Prize from *Poetry* for several pieces that would appear in *Annie Allen* (1949). For the volume, she earned the 1950 Pulitzer Prize, the first time it was presented to an African American. During the 1950s, she wrote reviews for the *New York Times, Negro Digest,* and *New York Herald Tribune.* She also wrote articles with titles such as "How I Told My Child About Race" and "Why Negro Women Leave Home."

For the next decade, Brooks developed her commitment to the nurturing of young students. From 1963 to 1969, she led a poetry workshop at Columbia College in Chicago and taught at Elmhurst College in Elmhurst, Illinois. She was Rennebohm Professor of English at the University of Wisconsin at Madison and Distinguished Professor of the Arts at the City College of New York. Although she resigned from the academic world in 1971, she helped establish the Illinois Poet Laureate Awards to promote creative writing.

Over the past forty-eight years, Brooks's carefully focused work has become a milestone in literary history. With a startling development in stylistic complexity from 1945 to 1949, and with an abrupt shift in explicit ideology since 1967, her poems have been highly consistent in technical excellence. What makes the work especially eloquent is the gift that Brooks has for achieving an ironic distance on historical suffering. As early as *A Street in Bronzeville* (1945), she achieved startling shifts of time, as well as varying perceptions into memory, making "The Mother" a classic poem about abortion. In 1975, Brooks told a literary critic that she would never again write some of the apologetic lines in *Annie Allen* (1949), begging whites to accept that she was human. *Maud Martha* (1953), an autobiographical novel in poetic sketches, tells the story of a black girl who advances from romantic dreams to achieve completeness as a woman.

Initially, Brooks planned a novel on the topic. A version written for Herbert Hill's anthology *Soon One Morning* (1963) preceded a revision published as "The Life of Lincoln West" in *Family Pictures* (1970). *The Bean Eaters* (1960) contains some of Brooks's most explicitly social verse: "A Bronzeville Mother Loiters in Mississippi. Meanwhile, a Mississippi Mother Burns Bacon." This poem presents the lynching in 1955 of Emmett Till, a fourteen-year-old Chicagoan. In "The Chicago Defender Sends a Man to Little Rock," a northern narrator travels to Arkansas in 1957 to witness the uproar over school integration, where those in the mob "are like people everywhere."

As in "Negro Hero" and "The Progress," Brooks continues to explore the discrepancy between appearance and morality. Her poetic world represents that evil is unique neither to a particular clime nor to a people; it is, on the contrary, endemic to human existence. Hence, all people must guard against lapses into a barbarism that threatens human life. Even when Brooks's speakers address themselves to race, they evince a wisdom learned from world war.

Sometimes the recollection is painfully personal. In the mid-fifties, Brooks was sent by the Illinois Employment Service to work as a secretary for Dr. E. N. French, the manager of a large slum known as the Mecca Building. He exploited the tenants by selling them useless trinkets and charms and was eventually murdered. Years later, in 1962, she would write her *Harper's* editor about plans to complete a two-thousand-line poem on the subject. She also wrote commemorative poems about Medgar Evers and Malcolm X, two racial martyrs of the sixties, for *In the Mecca* (1968) and *The World of Gwendolyn Brooks* (1971).

Report from Part One (1971), with prefaces by Don L. Lee (Haki Madhubuti) and George E. Kent, details the events that helped shape Brooks's epic vision over twenty-three years. Besides many details about her family life, the autobiography chronicles in fragmented sketches her supposed transformation from a conservative Negro into a proud black woman. Actually, a somewhat playful sonnet, "First Fight/Then Fiddle" (*Annie Allen,* 1949), persists as one of the most brilliant poems about the way that military power supported the evolution of European art from the Roman Empire through the Holy Crusades. Brooks, in other words, was often more racially aware than she gives herself credit for being in the 1940s.

Even with the acclaim she has received since the sixties, students are tempted to view her as only one gifted writer among so many talented others to earn contemporary honors. Once invited by President John Kennedy to read at the Library of Congress, she met Robert Frost, who praised her work. She was reinvigorated by the Second Fisk Writer's Conference in April 1967, energized by the likes of LeRoi Jones (Amiri Baraka), Margaret Danner, and John Oliver Killens. In January 1978, Governor Otto Kerner appointed her poet laureate of Illinois. Meanwhile, she was en route to establishing book contracts with black publishers—Broadside Press, established by Dudley Randall in Detroit, and Third World Press, founded by Haki Madhubuti in Chicago. In 1973, she was named an honorary consultant in American literature to the Library of Congress. In 1981, she had a junior high school in Harvey, Illinois, dedicated to her. And in 1983, she went to England to evaluate the Sotheby's International Poetry Contest.

Her wide-ranging activities continue to obscure how truly great a poet she is. Indeed, she holds a unique distinction in American civilization. Her strong commitments to human community inform a true brilliance of poetic style. Almost no other American poet since Walt Whitman has touched human sympathy as profoundly. No other black poet, except for Langston Hughes, has shared the gift to outlive audiences, change them, and keep on writing. Gwendolyn Brooks may indeed be the greatest American poet.

❖❖❖

Groundbreaking sources are Jon N. Loff, "Gwendolyn Brooks: A Bibliography," *CLAJ,* 17 (September), and Heidi L. Mahoney, "Selected Checklist of Material By and About Gwendolyn Brooks," *NALF,* 8 (Summer 1974). Clenora F. Hudson, "Racial Themes in the Poetry of Gwendolyn Brooks," is a female rediscovery. Arthur P. Davis, "The Black and Tan Motif in the Poetry of Gwendolyn Brooks," *CLAJ,* 6 (December 1960), and "Gwendolyn Brooks: Poet of the Unheroic," *CLAJ,* 7 (Dec. 1963), set a tone for serious criticism a decade earlier. At least four other scholars have championed the excellence of Gwendolyn Brooks's literary art. George E. Kent, "The Poetry of Gwendolyn Brooks, Part I," *Black World,* 20 (September 1971), and Kent, "The Poetry of Gwendolyn Brooks, Part II," *Black World,* 20 (October), reappear in George E. Kent, *Blackness and the Adventure of Western Culture* (Chicago: Third World Press, 1972). Kent contributed a fine essay, "Aesthetic Values in the Poetry of Gwendolyn Brooks," to R. Baxter Miller, ed., *Black American Literature and Humanism* (Lexington: University Press of Kentucky, 1981). Kent's posthumous biography is *A Life of Gwendolyn Brooks* (Lexington: University Press of Kentucky, 1990). With an early bibliography in book form, R. Baxter Miller also has written essays available in *Black American Literature and Humanism* and *Black American Poets Between Worlds, 1940–1960,* ed. R. Baxter Miller (Knoxville: University of Tennessee Press, 1986). Maria K. Mootry and Gary Smith edited *A Life Distilled: Gwendolyn Brooks: Her Poetry and Fiction,* (Urbana: University of Illinois Press, 1987) which presents a critical overview of poetic themes and techniques, just as Harry Shaw, *Gwendolyn Brooks* (Boston: Twayne, 1980), introduces basic themes in her work. In *Gwendolyn Brooks: Poetry and Heroic Voice* (Lexington: University Press of Kentucky, 1987), D. H. Melhem sounds an empathetic note of a white female poet.

the mother

Abortions will not let you forget.
You remember the children you got that you did not get,
The damp small pulps with a little or with no hair,
The singers and workers that never handled the air.
You will never neglect or beat
Them, or silence or buy with a sweet.
You will never wind up the sucking-thumb
Or scuttle off ghosts that come.
You will never leave them, controlling your luscious sigh,
Return for a snack of them, with gobbling mother-eye.

I have heard in the voices of the wind the voices of my dim killed children.
I have contracted. I have eased
My dim dears at the breasts they could never suck.
I have said, Sweets, if I sinned, if I seized
Your luck
And your lives from your unfinished reach,
If I stole your births and your names,
Your straight baby tears and your games,
Your stilted or lovely loves, your tumults, your marriages, aches, and your deaths,
If I poisoned the beginnings of your breaths,
Believe that even in my deliberateness I was not deliberate.
Though why should I whine,
Whine that the crime was other than mine?—
Since anyhow you are dead.
Or rather, or instead,
You were never made.

But that too, I am afraid,
Is faulty: oh, what shall I say, how is the truth to be said?
You were born, you had body, you died.
It is just that you never giggled or planned or cried.

Believe me, I loved you all.
Believe me, I knew you, though faintly, and I loved, I loved you
All.

the children of the poor

1

People who have no children can be hard:
Attain a mail of ice and insolence:
Need not pause in the fire, and in no sense
Hesitate in the hurricane to guard.
And when wide world is bitten and bewarred
They perish purely, waving their spirits hence

Without a trace of grace or of offense
To laugh or fail, diffident, wonder-starred.
While through a throttling dark we others hear
The little lifting helplessness, the queer
Whimper-whine; whose unridiculous
Lost softness softly makes a trap for us.
And makes a curse. And makes a sugar of
The malocclusions, the inconditions of love.

2

What shall I give my children? who are poor,
Who are adjudged the leastwise of the land,
Who are my sweetest lepers, who demand
No velvet and no velvety velour;
But who have begged me for a brisk contour,
Crying that they are quasi, contraband
Because unfinished, graven by a hand
Less than angelic, admirable or sure.
My hand is stuffed with mode, design, device.
But I lack access to my proper stone.
And plenitude of plan shall not suffice
Nor grief nor love shall be enough alone
To ratify my little halves who bear
Across an autumn freezing everywhere.

3

And shall I prime my children, pray, to pray?
Mites, come invade most frugal vestibules
Spectered with crusts of penitents' renewals
And all hysterics arrogant for a day.
Instruct yourselves here is no devil to pay.
Children, confine your lights in jellied rules;
Resemble graves; be metaphysical mules;
Learn Lord will not distort nor leave the fray.
Behind the scurryings of your neat motif
I shall wait, if you wish: revise the psalm
If that should frighten you: sew up belief
If that should tear: turn, singularly calm
At forehead and at fingers rather wise,
Holding the bandage ready for your eyes.

4

First fight. Then fiddle. Ply the slipping string
With feathery sorcery; muzzle the note
With hurting love; the music that they wrote

Bewitch, bewilder. Qualify to sing
Threadwise. Devise no salt, no hempen thing
For the dear instrument to bear. Devote
The bow to silks and honey. Be remote
A while from malice and from murdering.
But first to arms, to armor. Carry hate
In front of you and harmony behind.
Be deaf to music and to beauty blind.
Win war. Rise bloody, maybe not too late
For having first to civilize a space
Wherein to play your violin with grace.

5

When my dears die, the festival-colored brightness
That is their motion and mild repartee
Enchanted, a macabre mockery
Charming the rainbow radiance into tightness
And into a remarkable politeness
That is not kind and does not want to be,
May not they in the crisp encounter see
Something to recognize and read as rightness?
I say they may, so granitely discreet,
The little crooked questionings inbound,
Concede themselves on most familiar ground,
Cold an old predicament of the breath:
Adroit, the shapely prefaces complete,
Accept the university of death.

The Last Quatrain of the Ballad of Emmett Till

after the murder,
after the burial

Emmett's mother is a pretty-faced thing;
the tint of pulled taffy.
She sits in a red room,
drinking black coffee.
She kisses her killed boy.
And she is sorry.
Chaos in windy grays
through a red prairie.

The Chicago Defender Sends a Man to Little Rock

Fall, 1957

In Little Rock the people bear
Babes, and comb and part their hair
And watch the want ads, put repair

To roof and latch. While wheat toast burns
A woman waters multiferns

Time upholds or overturns
The many, tight, and small concerns.

In Little Rock the people sing
Sunday hymns like anything,
Through Sunday pomp and polishing.

And after testament and tunes,
Some soften Sunday afternoons
With lemon tea and Lorna Doones.

I forecast
And I believe
Come Christmas Little Rock will cleave
To christmas tree and trifle, weave,
From laugh and tinsel, texture fast.

In Little Rock is baseball; Barcarolle.
That hotness in July . . . the uniformed figures raw and implacable
And not intellectual,
Batting the hotness or clawing the suffering dust.
The Open Air Concert, on the special twilight green. . . .
When Beethoven is brutal or whispers to lady-like air.
Blanket-sitters are solemn, as Johann troubles to lean
To tell them what to mean. . . .

There is love, too, in Little Rock. Soft women softly
Opening themselves in kindness,
Or, pitying one's blindness,
Awaiting one's pleasure
In azure
Glory with anguished rose at the root. . . .
To wash away old semi-discomfitures.
They re-teach purple and unsullen blue.
The wispy soils go. And uncertain
Half-havings have they clarified to sures.

In Little Rock they know
Not answering the telephone is a way of rejecting life,
That it is our business to be bothered, is our business
To cherish bores or boredom, be polite
To lies and love and many-faceted fuzziness.

I scratch my head, massage the hate-I-had.
I blink across my prim and pencilled pad.
The saga I was sent for is not down.
Because there is a puzzle in this town.
The biggest News I do not dare
Telegraph to the Editor's chair:
"They are like people everywhere."

The angry Editor would reply
In hundred harryings of Why.

And true, they are hurling spittle, rock,
Garbage and fruit in Little Rock.
And I saw coiling storm a-writhe
On bright madonnas. And a scythe
Of men harassing brownish girls.
(The bows and barrettes in the curls
And braids declined away from joy.)

I saw a bleeding brownish boy. . . .

The lariat lynch-wish I deplored.

The loveliest lynchee was our Lord.

We Real Cool

The Pool Players.

Seven at the Golden Shovel.

We real cool. We
Left school. We

Lurk late. We
Strike straight. We

Sing sin. We
Thin gin. We

Jazz June. We
Die soon.

The Wall

August 27, 1967
For Edward Christmas

"THE SIDE WALL OF A TYPICAL SLUM BUILDING ON THE CORNER OF 43RD AND LANGLEY BECAME A MURAL COMMUNICATING BLACK DIGNITY. . . ."

—*EBONY*

A drumdrumdrum.
Humbly we come.
South of success and east of gloss and glass are
sandals;
flowercloth;
grave hoops of wood or gold, pendant
from black ears, brown ears, reddish-brown
and ivory ears;

black boy-men.
Black

boy-men on roofs fist out "Black Power!" Val,
a little black stampede
in African
images of brass and flowerswirl,
fists out "Black Power!"—tightens pretty eyes,
leans back on mothercountry and is tract,
is treatise through her perfect and tight teeth.

Women in wool hair chant their poetry.
Phil Cohran gives us messages and music
made of developed bone and polished and honed cult.
It is the Hour of tribe and of vibration,
the day-long Hour. It is the Hour
of ringing, rouse, of ferment-festival.

On Forty-third and Langley
black furnaces resent ancient
legislatures
of ploy and scruple and practical gelatin.
They keep the fever in,
fondle the fever.

All
worship the Wall.

I mount the rattling wood. Walter
says, "She is good." Says, "She
our Sister is." In front of me
hundreds of faces, red-brown, brown, black, ivory,
yield me hot trust, their yea and their Announcement
that they are ready to rile the high-flung ground.
Behind me, Paint.
Heroes.
No child has defiled
the Heroes of this Wall this serious Appointment
this still Wing
this Scald this Flute this heavy Light this Hinge.

An emphasis is paroled.
The old decapitations are revised,
the dispossessions beakless.

And we sing.

The Chicago Picasso

August 15, 1967

"Mayor Daley tugged a white ribbon, loosing the
blue percale wrap. A hearty cheer went up as the
covering slipped off the big steel sculpture that
looks at once like a bird and a woman."
—Chicago *Sun-Times*

(Seiji Ozawa leads the Symphony.
The Mayor smiles.
And 50,000 See.)

Does man love Art? Man visits Art, but squirms.
Art hurts. Art urges voyages—
and it is easier to stay at home,
the nice beer ready.
    In commonrooms
we belch, or sniff, or scratch.
Are raw.

But we must cook ourselves and style ourselves for Art, who
is a requiring courtesan.
We squirm.
We do not hug the Mona Lisa.
We
may touch or tolerate
an astounding fountain, or a horse-and-rider.
At most, another Lion.

Observe the tall cold of a Flower
which is as innocent and as guilty,
as meaningful and as meaningless as any
other flower in the western field.

Medgar Evers

For Charles Evers

The man whose height his fear improved he
arranged to fear no further. The raw
intoxicated time was time for better birth or
a final death.
Old styles, old tempos, all the engagement of
the day—the sedate, the regulated fray—
the antique light, the Moral rose, old gusts,
tight whistlings from the past, the mothballs
in the Love at last our man forswore.

Medgar Evers annoyed confetti and assorted
brands of businessmen's eyes.

The shows came down: to maxims and surprise.
And palsy.

Roaring no rapt arise-ye to the dead, he
leaned across tomorrow. People said that
he was holding clean globes in his hands.

Malcolm X

For Dudley Randall

Original.
Ragged-round.
Rich-robust.

He had the hawk-man's eyes.
We gasped. We saw the maleness.
The maleness raking out and making guttural the air
and pushing us to walls.

And in a soft and fundamental hour
a sorcery devout and vertical
beguiled the world.

He opened us—
who was a key,

who was a man.

The Sermon on the Warpland

"The fact that we are black
is our ultimate reality."

—Ron Karenga

And several strengths from drowsiness campaigned
but spoke in Single Sermon on the warpland.

And went about the warpland saying No.
"My people, black and black, revile the River.
Say that the River turns, and turn the River.

Say that our Something in doublepod contains
seeds for the coming hell and health together.
Prepare to meet
(sisters, brothers) the brash and terrible weather;
the pains;
the bruising; the collapse of bestials, idols.
But then oh then!—the stuffing of the hulls!
the seasoning of the perilously sweet!
the health! the heralding of the clear obscure!

Build now your Church, my brothers, sisters. Build
never with brick nor Corten nor with granite.
Build with lithe love. With love like lion-eyes.
With love like morningrise.
With love like black, our black—
luminously indiscreet;
complete; continuous."

To an Old Black Woman, Homeless and Indistinct

I

Your every day is a pilgrimage.
A blue hubbub.
Your days are collected bacchanals of fear and self-troubling.

And your nights! Your nights.
When you put you down in alley or cardboard or viaduct,
your lovers are rats, finding your secret places.

II

When you rise in another morning,
you hit the street, your incessant enemy.

See? Here you are, in the so-busy world.
You walk. You walk.
You pass The People.
No. The People pass you.

Here's a Rich Girl marching briskly to her charms.
She is suede and scarf and belting and perfume.
She sees you not, she sees you very well.
At five in the afternoon Miss Rich Girl will go Home
to brooms and vacuum cleaner and carpeting,
two cats, two marble-top tables, two telephones,
shiny green peppers, flowers in impudent vases,
visitors.
Before all that there's luncheon to be known.
Lasagna, lobster salad, sandwiches.
All day there's coffee to be loved.
There are luxuries
of minor dissatisfaction, luxuries of Plan.

III

That's *her* story.
You're going to vanish, not necessarily nicely, fairly soon.
Although essentially dignity itself a death
is not necessarily tidy, modest or discreet.
When they find you
your legs may not be tidy nor aligned.
Your mouth may be all crooked or destroyed.

Black old woman, homeless, indistinct—
Your last and least adventure is Review.
    Folks used to celebrate your birthday!
Folks used to say "She's such a pretty little thing!"
Folks used to say "She draws such handsome horses, cows and
    houses."
Folks used to say "That child is going far."

NAOMI LONG MADGETT

(1923–)

Born on July 5, 1923, in Norfolk, Virginia, but reared in East Orange, New Jersey, Naomi Cornelia Long Madgett was part of a rare but representative upper-middle-class black family: her father was a Baptist minister, and her mother was a schoolteacher. Clarence Marcellus Long and Maude Hilton Long gave her the precious heritage of an educated literary environment during her early years of childhood. Madgett often lists the many books that not only entertained her as a child but that also helped to inform her poetic craft, including *Aesop's Fables* and Robert Kerlin's 1923 anthology *Negro Poets and Their Poems.*

The family made a providential move to St. Louis, Missouri, when Madgett was fourteen years old. There she was able to attend the all-black Sumner High School, where she was even more immersed in African American literature and where teachers encouraged her to develop her writing talents further. Thus Madgett was able to publish her first book of poetry, *Songs to a Phantom Nightingale,* in St. Louis in June 1941, when she was just seventeen years old. A few months later, she entered her mother's alma mater, Virginia State University, where she graduated in 1945. She married Julian F. Witherspoon in March 1946, and they relocated to Detroit. They were divorced in 1949. The couple had one child, Jill Witherspoon Boyer, in 1947.

Madgett began her professional career as a reporter and copy reader for Detroit's black weekly newspaper, the *Michigan Chronicle,* from 1945 to 1946. She worked as a service representative in the all-black branch of Michigan Bell Telephone Company from 1948 to 1954, when she married William H. Madgett. (They were divorced in 1960.) The following year, she began teaching in the Detroit public schools. Madgett received a master's degree in English education from Detroit's Wayne State University in 1956, the same year in which her second collection of poetry, *One and the Many,* was published.

By this time, Madgett was a rather well-known public name, with her poetry appearing in most anthologies of African American, and even general American, literature. She continued to work intermittently for the Detroit public school system until 1968. In 1965, she received a $10,000 Mott Fellowship to work as a resource associate at Oakland University in Rochester, Michigan. In 1968, she was named associate professor of English at Eastern Michigan University in Ypsilanti, where she taught courses in African American literature and creative writing until she retired as a full professor in 1984. She earned a Ph.D. in literature and creative writing from the International Institute of Advanced Studies.

By the time of her retirement from the teaching profession, Madgett had seven books of poetry, two edited collections of poetry, and two textbooks to her credit. Her *One and the Many* came out in 1956 before white American critics understood or accepted the political aesthetic of African American protest literature. A white critic, Griffith T. Pugh, wrote in the *English Journal* (1957), "The question of whether poetry can co-exist with propaganda is raised again by Mrs. Madgett's collection." He concluded that her work did not exhibit "a coherent philosophy" but that her "most impressive poem on the 'great American problem' is 'Not I Alone,' in which she attempts to speak for her race." Obviously, the critical establishment was not ready for a strong voice of protest against its endemic racism. But by 1972, when

Madgett's fourth book, *Pink Ladies in the Afternoon,* was published, the national scene was somewhat different. The Civil Rights Movement was at its zenith, and black protest poetry was in vogue, although the literary establishment was still not very receptive to protesters' outcries. Wanting to see *Pink Ladies* published, several of Madgett's friends encouraged her to join them in forming Lotus Press. Two years later, Madgett's family bought total control of the fledgling publishing company. These steps had far-reaching implications. Not only was Madgett's literary career greatly advanced by ownership of a major publishing company, but scores of other budding black writers—Houston Baker, Tom Dent, Gayl Jones, Pinkie Gordon Lane, and others—were able to launch literary and academic careers because of their early associations with Lotus Press as well.

During the seventies and eighties, Madgett's work shifted from a general ethnic focus to a particular view of black women and their relationships with their families and communities. Her work *Octavia and Other Poems,* published by Third World Press in 1988, celebrates her great-aunt Octavia Cornelia Long and several other members of her family. Critic Michele Gibbs wrote, "In form, the book is an innovative approach to compiling a genealogy that is more than a tree. Instead a whole forest is invoked. . . . Madgett's repossession of her past, the voice of the granddaughter, eventually a mother in her own right, is the bridge to the future." To further indicate her concern about the division between black men and black women and her interest in the women's central role in maintaining communal stability, Madgett in 1992 steered through Lotus Press an important anthology of poems by African American female poets titled *Adam of Ife: Black Women in Praise of Black Men.*

Robert P. Sedlack's *Dictionary of Literary Biography* article on Madgett stresses that although she has had hundreds of poems published over the past half century, Madgett's work has never received the extended scholarly review that it deserves, concluding that this neglect stems mainly from the delicacy of the poet's aesthetic style. "Over the years Madgett has emphasized her lyric poetry at a time when such poetry, regrettably, has been regarded lightly," Sedlack notes. He contends that Madgett has "tended to down-play her Afro-American verse. This was particularly true in *One and the Many, Star by Star,* and *Pink Ladies in the Afternoon,* where her Afro-American poems were placed at the ends of the volumes." He concludes, however, that works such as *Exits and Entrances* and *Octavia and Other Poems* (1988), where Madgett does intone African American themes, have never been fully explored through serious critical or scholarly review. This same neglect is true for the works of many other African American women poets, especially those who have written since the end of the Civil Rights Movement. Hopefully, these oversights, including a long-overdue complete assessment of Madgett's poetry, will soon be redressed.

❖❖❖

Leonead P. Bailey discusses Madgett's work in *Broadside Authors and Artists: An Illustrated Biographical Directory* (1974). Eugene B. Redmond has a revealing discussion of Madgett's work in *Drumvoices: The Mission of Afro-American Poetry* (1976). Ray Fleming reviewed *Exits and Entrances* in *Black American Literature Forum* (1980). Melba Boyd reviewed the work for the *Black Scholar* 11: No. 4 (1980). And, of course, there is Robert P. Sedlack's entry in the *Dictionary of Literary Biography,* 76.

Madgett's papers are in the Special Collections archives of Fisk University Library in Nashville, Tennessee.

Midway

I've come this far to freedom and I won't turn back.
I'm climbing to the highway from my old dirt track.
  I'm coming and I'm going
  And I'm stretching and I'm growing
And I'll reap what I've been sowing or my skin's not black.

I've prayed and slaved and waited and I've sung my song.
You've bled me and you've starved me but I've still grown strong.
  You've lashed me and you've treed me
  And you've everything but freed me
But in time you'll know you need me and it won't be long.

I've seen the daylight breaking high above the bough.
I've found my destination and I've made my vow;
  So whether you abhor me
  Or deride me or ignore me,
Mighty mountains loom before me and I won't stop now.

The Old Women

They are young.
They do not understand
what the old women are saying.

They see the gnarled hands raised
and think they are praying.
They cannot see the weapons hung

between their fingers. When the mouths
gape and the rasping noises
crunch like dead leaves,

they laugh at the voices
they think are trying to sing.
They are young

and have not learned
the many faces of endurance, the furtive
triumphs earned through suffering.

New Day

"Keep a-inchin' along, keep-a inchin' along,
Jesus 'll come bye an' bye.
Keep a-inchin' along like a po' inchworm,
Jesus 'll come bye an' bye."
(Negro Spiritual)

She coaxes her fat in front of her
like a loaded market basket with defective wheels.
Then she pursues it, slowly catches up, and
the cycle begins again.
Every step is a hardship and a triumph.

As she inches her way along in my direction
I sense the stretchings and drawings of
her heavy years. I feel the thunderous
effort of her movement reverberating through
a wilderness of multiple betrayals.
As gently as I can, I say, "Good morning, Sister,"
as we come face to face, and wonder
if she can understand what I am saying.

Monday Morning Blues

All night my bed was rocky, all night nobody by my side;
My bed was cold and rocky, all night no good man by my side.
The radiator sputtered, the furnace gave a groan and died.

I woke up dreaming Friday, but Monday dragged me out of bed;
Yes, woke up dreaming Friday, Monday dragged me out of bed.
Was looking for a paycheck, mailman brought me bills instead.

Well, no one comes to see me, no one ever telephones;
Nobody but Misfortune visits me or telephones.
Wish I could find me something as lucky as a black cat's bones.

You may not see me smiling, still you'll never hear me cry;
Seldom see me smiling, never gonna hear me cry;
But I do a lot of laughing 'cause I'm too damn proud to die.

A Litany for Afro-Americans

Our ancestors called Thee by other names,
But Thou, O God, were with us
In the dawn of time.

LORD, BE WITH US STILL.

From Ife and Timbuktu we came,
Crying to Thee in the agonies
Of the Middle Passage.

WE CRY TO THEE TODAY.

In the confinement of our bodies' chains,
Our spirits nightly floated free.

FREE OUR SPIRITS NOW, WE PRAY.

We watched the captors steal our names,
Our continuity, the richness of our heritage,
And we were naked and impotent

Against the evil of their power.
Other captors rob us still.

TEACH US TO BE WATCHFUL, LORD,
TEACH US TO BE STRONG.

Against false prophets,
Against destructive forces
That seek to divide us
And deny us the family of Thy spirit,
The family of *our* spirit,

PROTECT US, O GOD,
AND LEAD US IN THE WAY
OF POWER THROUGH RIGHTEOUSNESS.
AMEN.

Playwrights

ALICE CHILDRESS
(1920–1994)

Alice Childress enjoyed a loyal if not an impressively widespread following during her more than forty years of composing plays and novels. Ever committed to focusing on less popular issues and characters, she described herself as "the best known of little known persons." Childress also enjoyed a career as an actress and a director. She collaborated with her second husband, Nathan Woodard, on several artistic projects. As with many African American women writers, she benefited from the renewal of interest in black literature over the past two decades. Yet hers remains a relatively quiet voice that portrays a consistent love for black people, an understanding of their political and personal struggles, and a healthy commitment to sustained focus on them.

Born in South Carolina in 1920, Childress was early left in the care of her grandmother, Eliza Campbell White, who took her to New York City when she was five years old. It was White who encouraged young Alice to write down ideas worth remembering and stimulated her interest in reading, which led her to writers such as Richard Wright, H. L. Mencken, Theodore Dreiser, and Sinclair Lewis. Alice and her grandmother also would clip newspaper articles and speculate on what had *not* been covered. And the two of them would sit at the window on 118th Street between Lenox and Seventh Avenues and speculate about the people passing by. These creative exercises, combined with Eliza White's deep interest in writing, set Childress solidly on the road to imaginative achievement. White also would take Childress to cultural sites around the city, including art galleries and museums, as well as to the Italian and Jewish shopping areas. They attended poetry readings by famous black writers at local churches, and they attended operas and musical programs put on at Salem Church of Harlem, of which the poet Countee Cullen's father was minister.

Childress's fascinating career is truly impressive in light of the fact that she was largely self-taught, not even a high-school graduate. Her writing ability, however, was early recognized; when Childress was ten years old, one of her white teachers expressed confidence in her abilities and encouraged her theatrical ambitions. "When you have a gift," she said, "you use it," in spite of the obstacles posed by race. Childress did attend Wadleigh High School for three years. After her experience there, she held several jobs, including assistant machinist, photo retoucher, saleslady, insurance agent, and domestic, to support herself and her young daughter, Jean, the product of her first marriage. These jobs enabled her to pursue her interest in writing and acting. She originated the role of Blanche in the American Negro Theatre (ANT) production *Anna Lucasta* in 1944. Over the next several years, Childress would direct, act, and write for ANT, as well as serve as drama coach.

In 1949, she directed her own play, *Florence,* under the auspices of that group; the one-act play was published in *Masses and Mainstream* in 1950. Set in the Jim Crow South in a railroad station waiting room, *Florence* centers on the friction that arises when a black woman flatly rejects the racial stereotyping expressed by a white "liberal" woman. Though written over a very short period of time, *Florence* displays Childress's superb craft in characterization, dialogue, and conflict. The same holds true for the plays that followed. *Just a Little Simple* (1950), which is Childress's adaptation of a Langston Hughes work, was the first play that was professionally produced by a black woman. Her *Gold Through the Trees,* which was written in 1952, has Afrocentricity as its major theme. In *Negro Playwrights in the American Theater, 1925–1959,* Doris Abramson describes the latter work as one that features "an Ashanti warrior's dance, modern dance, the Blues, sketches about Harriet Tubman and about the present-day freedom movement."

Florence paved the way thematically for Childress's first full-length play, *Trouble in Mind,* which was produced by the Greenwich Mews Theatre on November 4, 1955. In this play about a play, Wiletta Mayer, an aging black actress, challenges stereotypical presentations of black people. She tries to lead the cast in a walkout of the rehearsal of *Chaos in Belleville,* where, playing the role of the mother, she is asked to utter words she knows are untrue to a black mother's feeling. The mother reputedly gives up her son to white men who will "protect" him for the "crime" of voting and urging other blacks to vote. However, it is clear by the play's end that she will be the only sacrificial militant; her fellow actors simply bow to the racial insults and continue the rehearsals. Childress developed two endings for the play, one with the certainty that Wiletta would be fired for challenging the white director's authority and the other with the characters marching out of the theater in support of Wiletta's complaint. In recognition of the reality in which she worked, Childress used the first ending in the Greenwich Mews production. The play won the 1956 Obie Award for best original off-Broadway play; Childress rejected an option for Broadway, which would have taken the play to more commercially successful theaters.

In 1956, Childress published *Like One of the Family . . . conversations from a domestic's life,* which had initially been serialized in Paul Robeson's newspaper, *Freedom,* under the title "Conversations from Life" and continued in the *Baltimore Afro-American* as "Here's Mildred." The volume is composed of sketches that feature Mildred, a sassy black domestic worker, and her friend Marge. Shaped as dramatic monologues by Mildred, we sense Marge's presence in the questions she presumably directs to Mildred. In Mildred, Childress introduces a black woman who is proud of herself, her work, and her people. She holds forth on topics as diverse as African American history, Indian reservations, Africa, crime in New York City, romantic relationships, integration, and the many foibles of her white employers.

Childress's interest in drama continued in the early 1960s with her completion of *Wedding Band* (1966). The story of an interracial love affair in South Carolina around World War I, the play was first produced by the Mendelssohn Theatre at the University of Michigan in 1966 and later by Joseph Papp at the New York Shakespeare Festival in 1973. Papp also produced the play for ABC; Childress wrote the screenplay. When it aired on prime-time television, 8 of the 168 television stations in the viewing area would not show it, and another 3 showed it only after midnight. Similarly, Childress's *Wine in the Wilderness* (1969), which depicts several young blacks coming to a true understanding of their identity while a riot is going on, was banned from television in Alabama. Childress completed *String* in 1969 and *Mojo* in 1970.

In 1979, Alice Childress Week was officially observed in Columbia and Charleston, South Carolina, for the opening of *Sea Island Song* (1977), a play Childress had written upon the request of the South Carolina Arts Commission. The play deals with the Gullah-speaking people of the Georgia Sea Islands. She finished *Gullah*, another play about her native South Carolina, in 1984. She worked with her husband, Nathan Woodard, to present 120 performances of the musical drama in South Carolina and a full-length performance at the University of Massachusetts at Amherst.

Childress spent time at the MacDowell Colony in Peterborough, New Hampshire, in 1965. During that year, she also appeared on a BBC panel discussion titled "The Negro in American Theatre," which also featured James Baldwin, LeRoi Jones (Amiri Baraka), Langston Hughes, and Geoffrey Bridson of BBC. She participated in similar discussions at the New School for Social Research in 1965 and at Fisk University in 1966. She was a fellow at the Radcliffe Institute for Independent Scholars (now the Mary Ingraham Bunting Institute) for two years in the 1960s. As playwright/scholar-in-residence, she worked on *The African Garden* (1971).

A steady stream of fictional work held Childress's attention in the 1970s and 1980s. *A Hero Ain't Nothin' But a Sandwich* (1973), the story of a thirteen-year-old drug addict narrated with multiple voices, became the first book banned in a Savannah, Georgia, school library since *The Catcher in the Rye* had been banned in the 1950s. It also was one of nine books banned in the mid-1970s by the school board of Island Trees, Long Island, New York. It was reinstated in the school libraries there by order of the Supreme Court in 1983. This book won the Jane Addams Honor Award for a young adult novel (1974), as well as the Lewis Carroll Shelf Award from the University of Wisconsin (1975). For a film version of the novel, Childress won the 1977 Best Screenplay of the Year Award from the Virgin Islands Film Festival and the Paul Robeson Award for Outstanding Contribution to the Performing Arts from the Black Filmmakers Hall of Fame.

Childress also published the children's books *When the Rattlesnake Sounds* (1975), about Harriet Tubman, and *Let's Hear It for the Queen* (1976), written in honor of the birthday of her granddaughter, Mary Alice Lee; *A Short Walk* (1979), an adult novel featuring many aspects of the Marcus Garvey movement; *Rainbow Jordan* (1981), an adolescent novel about a young woman trying to preserve her virginity in an environment where it is not valued; and *Those Other People* (1989), a novel about a young white homosexual trying to come to grips with his own sexuality in a racially tense and homophobic environment in upstate New York.

But it is in the field of drama that Alice Childress has made a lasting impact. By fusing elements of African American folk culture, African mythology, sociopolitical statement, feminism, and traditional dramatic conventions, she anticipated Ntozake Shange and other black women experimental dramatists of the contemporary era. With her commissioned plays and continued performances and her publications in the 1970s and 1980s, she remained an active creative writer until her death late in 1994.

❖❖❖

Perhaps Childress's best-known work, *Like One of the Family . . . conversations from a domestic's life,* was reissued by Beacon Press in 1986, with an introduction by Trudier Harris. Harris also completed the biographical essay on Childress for *The Dictionary of Literary Biography* (1985), vol. 38, as well as the introduction to "In the Laundry Room," a Childress story included in *Women's Friendships,* ed. Susan Koppelman (1991). Two of Childress's plays, *Florence* and *Wine in the Wilderness,* were recently anthologized in *Wines in the Wilderness: Plays by African American Women from the Harlem Renaissance to the Present* (1991), compiled and edited by Elizabeth Brown-Guillory, who also discusses Childress's plays in *Their Place on the Stage: Black Women Playwrights in America* (1988). Brown-Guillory also wrote "Alice Childress: A Pioneering Spirit," an interview for *Sage: A Scholarly Journal on Black Women* 1 (Spring 1987).

Critical works include Doris Abramson, *Negro Playwrights in the American Theater, 1925–1959* (1969); Rosemary Curb, "An Unfashionable Tragedy of American Racism: Alice Childress' *Wedding Band,*" *MELUS* 7 (Winter 1980); Trudier Harris, *From Mammies to Militants: Domestics in Black American Literature* (1982); Harris, "'I Wish I Was a Poet': The Character as Artist in Alice Childress' *Like One of the Family,*" *Black American Literature Forum* 14 (Spring 1980); Loften Mitchell, *Black Drama: The Story of the American Negro in the Theatre* (1977).

A biography of Childress by La Vinia D. Jennings was published in 1996 in the Twayne U.S. Authors Series.

Wedding Band

A Love/Hate Story in Black and White

Act One

Scene One

TIME: Summer 1918 . . . Saturday morning. A city by the sea . . . South Carolina, U.S.A.

SCENE: Three houses in a backyard. The center house is newly painted and cheery looking in contrast to the other two which are weather-beaten and shabby. Center house is gingerbready . . . odds and ends of "picked up" shutters, picket railing, wrought iron railing, newel posts, a Grecian pillar, odd window boxes of flowers . . . everything clashes with a beautiful, subdued splendor; the old and new mingles in defiance of style and period. The playing areas of the houses are raised platforms furnished according to the taste of each tenant. Only one room of each house is visible. JULIA AUGUSTINE *(tenant of the center house) has recently moved in and there is still unpacking to be done. Paths are worn from the houses to the front yard entry. The landlady's house and an outhouse are offstage. An outdoor hydrant supplies water.*

JULIA *is sleeping on the bed in the center house.* TEETA, *a girl about eight years old, enters the yard from the Stage Right house. She tries to control her weeping as she examines a clump of grass.*

The muffled weeping disturbs JULIA*'s sleep. She starts up, half rises from her pillow, then falls back into a troubled sleep.* MATTIE, TEETA*'s mother, enters carrying a switch and fastening her clothing. She joins the little girl in the search for a lost quarter. The search is subdued, intense.*

MATTIE You better get out there and get it! Did you find it? Gawd, what've I done to be treated this way! You gon' get a whippin' too.

FANNY *(Enters from the front entry. She is landlady and the self-appointed, fifty-year-old representative of her race.)* Listen, Mattie . . . I want some quiet out here this mornin'.

MATTIE Dammit, this gal done lost the only quarter I got to my name.

*(*LULA *enters from the direction of the outhouse carrying a covered slop jar. She is forty-five and motherly.)*

"Teeta," I say, "Go to the store, buy three cent grits, five cent salt pork, ten cent sugar; and keep your hand closed 'roun' my money." How I'm gonna sell any candy if I got no sugar to make it? You little heifer!

(Goes after TEETA *who hides behind* LULA.*)*

LULA Gawd, help us to find it.

MATTIE Your daddy is off sailin' the ocean and you got nothin' to do but lose money! *I'm gon' put you out in the damn street, that's what!* (TEETA *cries out.* JULIA *sits up in the bed and cries out.)*

JULIA No . . . no . . .

FANNY You disturbin' the only tenant who's paid in advance.

LULA Teeta, retrace your steps. Show Lula what you did.

TEETA I hop-hop-hop . . . *(Hops near a post-railing of* JULIA*'s porch.)*

MATTIE What the hell you do that for?

LULA There 'tis! That's a quarter . . . down in the hole . . . Can't reach it . . .

*(*JULIA *is now fully awake. Putting on her house-dress over her camisole and petticoat.* MATTIE *takes an axe from the side of the house to knock the post out of the way.)*

Aw, *move,* move! That's all the money I got. I'll tear this damn house down and you with it!

FANNY And I'll blow this police whistle.

*(*JULIA *steps out on the porch. She is an attractive brown woman about thirty-five years old.)*

MATTIE Blow it . . . blow it . . . blow it . . . hot damn—*(Near tears. She decides to tell* JULIA *off also.)* I'll tear it down—that's right. If you don't like it—come on down here and whip me.

JULIA *(Nervous but determined to present a firm stand.)* Oh, my . . . Good mornin' ladies. My name is Julia Augustine. I'm not gonna move.

LULA My name is Lula. Why you think we wantcha to move?

FANNY Miss Julia, I'm sorry your first day starts like this. Some people are ice cream and others just cow-dung. I try to be ice cream.

MATTIE Dammit, I'm ice cream, too. Strawberry. *(Breaks down and cries.)*

FANNY That's Mattie. She lost her last quarter, gon' break down my house to get it.

JULIA *(Gets a quarter from her dresser.)* Oh my, dear heart, don't cry. Take this twenty-five cents, Miss Mattie.

MATTIE No thank you, ma'm.

JULIA And I have yours under my house for good luck.

FANNY Show your manners.

TEETA Thank you. You the kin'est person in the worl'. (LULA *enters her house.* TEETA *starts for home, then turns to see if her mother is coming.)*

MATTIE *(To* JULIA.*)* I didn't mean no harm. But my husband October's in the Merchant Marine and I needs my little money. Well, thank you. *(To* TEETA.*)* Come on, honey bunch. *(She enters her house Stage Right.* TEETA *proudly follows.* LULA *is putting* NELSON*'s breakfast on the table at Stage Left.)*

FANNY *(Testing strength of post.)* My poor father's turnin' in his grave. He built these rent houses just 'fore he died . . . And he wasn't a carpenter. Shows what the race can do when we wanta. *(Feels the porch railing and tests its strength.)* That loud-mouth Mattie used to work in a white cat-house.

JULIA A what?

FANNY Sportin' house, house of . . . A whore house. Know what she used to do?

JULIA *(Embarrassed.)* Not but so many things *to* do, I guess. *(*FANNY *wants to follow her in the house but* JULIA *fends her off.)*

FANNY Used to wash their joy-towels. Washin' joy-towels for one cent apiece. I wouldn't work in that kinda place—would you?

JULIA Indeed not.

FANNY Vulgarity.

JULIA *(Trying to get away.)* I have my sewing to do now, Miss Fanny.

FANNY I got a lovely piece-a blue serge. Six yards. *(She attempts to get into the house but* JULIA *deftly blocks the door.)*

JULIA I don't sew for people. *(*FANNY *wonders why not.)* I do homework for a store . . . hand-finishin' on ladies' shirtwaists.

FANNY You 'bout my age . . . I'm thirty-five.

JULIA *(After a pause.)* I thought you were younger.

FANNY *(Genuinely moved by the compliment.)* Thank you. But I'm not married 'cause nobody's come up to my high standard. Where you get them expensive-lookin', high-class shoes?

JULIA In a store. I'm busy now, Miss Fanny.

FANNY Doin' what?

JULIA First one thing then another. Good-day.

(Thinks she has dismissed her. Goes in the house. FANNY *quickly follows into the room . . . picks up a teacup from the table.)*

FANNY There's a devil in your tea-cup . . . also prosperity. Tell me 'bout yourself, don't be so distant.

JULIA It's all there in the tea-leaves.

FANNY Oh, go on! I'll tell you somethin' . . . that sweetface Lula killed her only child.

JULIA No, she didn't.

FANNY In a way-a speakin'. And then Gawd snatched up her triflin' husband. One nothin' piece-a man. Biggest thing he ever done for her was to lay down and die. Poor woman. Yes indeed, then she went and adopted this fella from the colored orphan home. Boy grew too big for a lone woman to keep in the house. He's a big, strappin', over-grown man now. I wouldn't feel safe livin' with a man that's not blood kin, 'doption or no 'doption. It's 'gainst nature. Oughta see the muscles on him.

JULIA *(Wearily.)* Oh, my . . . I think I hear somebody callin' you.

FANNY Yesterday the white-folks threw a pail-a dirty water on him. A black man on leave got no right to wear his uniform in public. The crackers don't like it. That's flauntin' yourself.

JULIA Miss Fanny, I don't talk about people.

FANNY Me neither. *(Giving her serious advice.)* We high-class, quality people oughta stick together.

JULIA I really do stay busy.

FANNY Doin' what? Seein' your beau? You have a beau haven't-cha?

JULIA *(Realizing she must tell her something in order to get rid of her.)* Miss Johnson . . .

FANNY Fanny.

JULIA *(Managing to block her toward the door.)* My mother and father have long gone on to Glory.

FANNY Gawd rest the dead and bless the orphan.

JULIA Yes, I do have a beau . . . But I'm not much of a mixer. *(She now has* FANNY *out on the porch.)*

FANNY Get time, come up front and see my parlor. I got a horsehair settee and a four piece, silver-plated tea service.

JULIA Think of that.

FANNY The first and only one to be owned by a colored woman in the United States of America. Salesman told me.

JULIA Oh, just imagine.

*(*MATTIE *enters wearing a blue calico dress and striped apron.)*

FANNY My mother was a genuine, full-blooded, qualified, Seminole Indian.

TEETA *(Calls to her mother from the doorway.)* Please . . . Mama . . . Mama . . . Buy me a hair ribbon.

MATTIE All right! I'm gon' buy my daughter a hair ribbon.

FANNY Her hair is so short you'll have to nail it on. *(FANNY exits to her house.)*

MATTIE That's all right about that, Fanny. Your father worked in a stinkin' phosphate mill . . . yeah, and didn't have a tooth in his head. Then he went and married some half Portuguese woman. I don't call that bein' in no damn society. I works for my livin'. I makes candy and I takes care of a little white girl. Hold this nickel 'til I get back. Case of emergency I don't like Teeta to be broke.

JULIA I'll be busy today, lady.

SHRIMP MAN *(Offstage.)* Shrimp-dee-raw . . . I got raw shrimp.

(NELSON leaves the house just as JULIA steps out on her porch to hang a rug over the rail. TEETA enters GREEN house.)

NELSON Er . . . howdy-do, er . . . beg pardon. My name is Nelson. Lula Green's son, if you don't mind. Miss . . . er . . . Mrs.?

JULIA *(After a brief hesitation.)* Miss . . . Julia Augustine.

NELSON Miss Julia, you the best-lookin' woman I ever seen in my life. I declare you look jus' like a violin sounds. And I'm not talkin' 'bout pretty. You look like you got all the right feelin's, you know?

JULIA Well, thank you, Mr. Nelson.

NELSON See, you got me talkin' all outta my head.

(LULA enters, TEETA follows eating a biscuit and carrying a milk pail . . . she exits toward street.)

Let's go for a walk this evenin', get us a lemon phosphate.

JULIA Oh, I don't care for any, Mr. Nelson.

LULA That's right. She say stay home.

JULIA *(To NELSON.)* I'm sorry.

NELSON Don't send me back to the army feelin' bad 'cause you turn me down. Orange-ade tonight on your porch. I'll buy the oranges, you be the sugar.

JULIA No, thank you.

NELSON Let's make it—say—six o'clock.

JULIA No, I said no!

LULA Nelson, go see your friends. *(He waves goodbye to JULIA and exits through the back entry.)* He's got a lady friend, her name is Merrilee Jones. And he was just tryin' to be neighborly. That's how me and Nelson do. But you go on and stay to yourself. *(Starts toward her house.)*

JULIA Miss Lula! I'm sorry I hurt your feelin's. Miss Lula! I have a gentleman friend, that's why I said no.

LULA I didn't think-a that. When yall plan to cut the cake?

JULIA Not right now. You see . . . when you offend Gawd you hate for it to be known. Gawd might forgive but people never will. I mean . . . when a man and a woman are not truly married . . .

LULA Oh, I see.

JULIA I live by myself . . . but he visits . . . I declare I don't know how to say . . .

LULA Everybody's got some sin, but if it troubles your heart you're a gentle sinner, just a good soul gone wrong.

JULIA That's a kind thought.

LULA My husband, Gawd rest the dead, used to run 'round with other women; it made me kind-a careless with my life. One day, many long years ago, I was sittin' in a neighbor's house tellin' my troubles; my only child, my little boy, wandered out on the railroad track and got killed.

JULIA That must-a left a fifty pound weight on your soul.

LULA It did. But if we grow stronger . . . and rise higher than what's pullin' us down . . .

JULIA Just like Climbin' Jacob's Ladder . . . *(Sings.)* Every round goes higher and higher . . .

LULA Yes, rise higher than the dirt . . . that fifty pound weight will lift and you'll be free, free without anybody's by-your-leave. Do something to wash out the sin. That's why I got Nelson from the orphanage.

JULIA And now you feel free?

LULA No, not yet. But I believe Gawd wants me to start a new faith; one that'll make our days clear and easy to live. That's what I'm workin' on now. Oh, Miss Julia, I'm glad you my neighbor.

JULIA Oh, thank you, Miss Lula! Sinners or saints, didn't Gawd give us a beautiful day this mornin'!

(The sound of cow-bells clanking and the thin piping of a tin and paper flute. TEETA *backs into the yard carefully carrying the can of milk.* THE BELL MAN *follows humming, "Over There" on the flute. He is a poor white about thirty years old but time has dealt him some hard blows. He carries a large suitcase; the American flag painted on both sides, cowbells are attached.* THE BELL MAN *rests his case on the ground. Fans with a very tired-looking handkerchief. He cuts the fool by dancing and singing a bit of a popular song as he turns corners around the yard.)*

THE BELL MAN *(As* LULA *starts to go in the house.)* Stay where you at, Aunty! You used to live on Thompson Street. How's old Thompson Street?

JULIA *(A slightly painful memory.)* I moved 'bout a year ago, moved to Queen Street.

THE BELL MAN Move a lot, don'tcha? *(Opens suitcase.)* All right, everybody stay where you at! *(Goes into a fast sales spiel.)* Lace-trim ladies' drawers! Stockin's, ladies' stockin's . . . gottem for the knock-knees and the bow-legs too . . . white, black and navy blue! All right, no fools no fun! The joke's on me! Here we go! *(As he places some merchandise in front of the* WOMEN; *does a regular minstrel walk-around.)* Anything in the world . . . fifty cent a week and one long, sweet year to pay . . . Come on, little sister!

TEETA *(Doing the walk-around with* THE BELL MAN.*)*

And a-ring-ting-tang
And-a shimmy-she-bang
While the sun am a-shinin' and the sky am blue . . .
And a-ring-ting-tang
And-a shimmy-she-bang
While the sun am a-shinin' and the sky am blue . . .

LULA *(Annoyed with* TEETA*'s dancing with* THE BELL MAN.*)* Stop all that shimmy she-bang and get in the house! *(Swats at* TEETA *as she passes.)*

THE BELL MAN *(Coldly.)* Whatcha owe me, Aunty?

LULA Three dollars and ten cent. I don't have any money today.

THE BELL MAN When you gon' pay?

LULA Monday, or better say Wednesday.

JULIA *(To divert his attention from* LULA.*)* How much for sheets?

THE BELL MAN For you they on'y a dollar. *(*JULIA *goes to her house to get the money.* THE BELL MAN *moves toward her house as he talks to* LULA.*)* Goin' to the Service Men's parade Monday?

LULA Yes, sir. My boy's marchin'. *(She exits.)*

THE BELL MAN Uh-huh, I'll getcha later. Lord, Lord, Lord, how'dja like to trot 'round in the sun beggin' the poorest people in the world to buy somethin' from you. This is nice. Real nice. *(To* JULIA.*)* A good friend-a mine was a nigra boy. Me 'n' him was jus' like that. Fine fella, he couldn't read and he couldn't write.

JULIA *(More to herself than to him.)* When he learns you're gon' lose a friend.

THE BELL MAN But talkin' serious, what is race and color? Put a paper bag over your head and who'd know the difference. Tryin' to remember me ain'tcha. I seen you one time coming out that bakery shop on Thompson street, didn' see me.

JULIA Is that so?

THE BELL MAN *(Sits on the bed and bounces up and down.)* Awwww, Great Gawd-a-mighty! I haven't been on a high-built bed since I left the back woods.

JULIA Please don't sit on my bed!

THE BELL MAN Old country boy, that's me! Strong and healthy country boy . . . *(Not noticing any rejection.)* Sister, Um in need for it like I never been before. Will you 'comodate me? Straighten me, fix me up, will you? Wouldn't take but five minutes. Um quick like a jack rabbit. Wouldn't nobody know but you and me. *(She backs away from him as he pants and wheezes out his admiration.)* Um clean, too. Clean as the . . . Board-a Health. Don't believe in dippin' inta everything. I got no money now, but Ladies always need stockin's.

JULIA *(Trying to keep her voice down, throws money at his feet.)* Get out of my house! Beneath contempt, that's what you are.

THE BELL MAN Don't be lookin' down your nose at me . . . actin' like you Mrs. Martha Washington . . . Throwin' one chicken-shit dollar at me and goin' on . . .

JULIA *(Picking up wooden clothes hanger.)* Get out! Out, before I take a stick to you.

THE BELL MAN *(Bewildered, gathering his things to leave.)* Hell, what I care who you sleep with! It's your nooky! Give it way how you want to. I dont' own no rundown bakery shop but I'm good as those who do. A baker ain' nobody . . .

JULIA I wish you was dead, you just oughta be dead, stepped on and dead.

THE BELL MAN Bet that's what my mama said first time she saw me. I was a fourteenth child. Damn women! . . . that's all right . . . Gawd bless you, Gawd be with you and let his light shine on you. I give you good for evil . . . God bless you! *(As he walks down the porch steps.)* She must be goin' crazy. Unfriendly, sick-minded bitch! (TEETA *enters from* LULA'*s house.* THE BELL MAN *takes a strainer from his pocket and gives it to* TEETA *with a great show of generosity.)* Here, little honey. You take this sample. You got nice manners.

TEETA Thank you, you the kin'est person in the world.

(THE BELL MAN *exits to the tune of clanking bells, and* LULA *enters.)*

JULIA I hate those kind-a people.

LULA You mustn't hate white folks. Don'tcha believe in Jesus? He's white.

JULIA I wonder if he believes in me.

LULA Gawd says we must love everybody.

JULIA Just lovin' and lovin', no matter what? There are days when I love, days when I hate.

FANNY Mattie, Mattie, mail!

JULIA Your love is worthless if nobody wants it.

(FANNY *enters carrying a letter. She rushes over to Mattie's house.)*

FANNY I had to pay the postman two cent. No stamp.

TEETA (*Calls to* JULIA) Letter from Papa! Gimmie my mama's five cents!

FANNY (*To* TEETA.) You gon' end your days in the Colored Women's Jailhouse.

(PRINCESS, *a little girl, enters skipping and jumping. She hops, runs and leaps across the yard.* PRINCESS *is six years old.* TEETA *takes money from* JULIA'*s outstretched hand and gives it to* FANNY.*)*

TEETA (*To* MATTIE.) Letter from Papa! Gotta pay two cent!

FANNY Now I owe you three cent . . . or do you want me to read the letter?

(PRINCESS *gets wilder and wilder, makes Indian war whoops.* TEETA *joins the noise-making. They climb porches and play follow-the-leader.* PRINCESS *finally lands on* JULIA'*s porch after peeping and prying into everything along the way.)*

PRINCESS *(Laughing merrily.)* Hello . . . hello . . . hello.

JULIA *(Overwhelmed by the confusion.)* Well—Hello.

FANNY Get away from my new tenant's porch!

PRINCESS (*Is delighted with* FANNY'*s scolding and decides to mock her.*) My new tennis porch!

(MATTIE *opens the letter and removes a ten-dollar bill. Lost in thought she clutches the letter to her bosom.)*

FANNY (*To* MATTIE.) Ought-a mind w-h-i-t-e children on w-h-i-t-e property!

PRINCESS *(Now swinging on* JULIA*'s gate.)* . . . my new tennis porch!

FANNY *(Chases* PRINCESS *around the yard.)* You Princess! Stop that!

*(*JULIA *laughs but she is very near tears.)*

MATTIE A letter from October.

FANNY Who's gon' read it for you?

MATTIE Lula!

PRINCESS My new tennis porch!

FANNY Princess! Mattie!

MATTIE Teeta! In the house with that drat noise!

FANNY It'll take Lula half-a day. *(Snatches letter.)* I won't charge but ten cent. *(Reads.)* "Dear, Sweet Molasses, My Darlin' Wife . . ."

MATTIE No, I don't like how you make words sound. You read too rough.

(Sudden offstage yells and screams from TEETA *and* PRINCESS *as they struggle for possession of some toy.)*

PRINCESS *(Offstage).* Give it to me!

TEETA No! It's mine!

MATTIE *(Screams.)* Teeta! *(The* CHILDREN *are quiet.)*

FANNY Dear, Sweet Molasses—how 'bout that?

JULIA *(To* FANNY.*)* Stop that! Don't read her mail.

FANNY She can't read it.

JULIA She doesn't want to. She's gonna go on holdin' it in her hand and never know what's in it . . . just 'cause it's hers!

FANNY Forgive 'em Father, they know not.

JULIA Another thing, you told me it's quiet here! You call this quiet? I can't stand it!

FANNY When you need me come and humbly knock on my *back* door. *(She exits.)*

MATTIE *(Shouts to* FANNY.*)* I ain't gonna knock on no damn back door! Miss Julia, can you read? *(Offers the letter to* JULIA.*)* I'll give you some candy when I make it.

JULIA *(Takes the letter.)* All right.

*(*LULA *takes a seat to enjoy a rare social event. She winds stems for the paper flowers as* JULIA *reads.)*

Dear, sweet molasses, my darlin' wife.

MATTIE Yes, honey. *(To* JULIA.*)* Thank you.

JULIA *(Reads.)* Somewhere, at sometime, on the high sea, I take my pen in hand . . . well, anyway, this undelible pencil.

LULA Hope he didn't put it in his mouth.

JULIA *(Reads.)* I be missin' you all the time.

MATTIE And we miss you.

JULIA *(Reads.)* Sorry we did not have our picture taken.

MATTIE Didn't have the money.

JULIA *(Reads.)* Would like to show one to the men and say this is my wife and child . . . They always be showin' pictures.

MATTIE *(Waves the ten-dollar bill.)* I'm gon' send you one, darlin'.

JULIA *(Reads.)* I recall how we used to take a long walk on Sunday afternoon . . . *(Thinks about this for a moment.)* . . . then come home and be lovin' each other.

MATTIE I recall.

JULIA *(Reads.)* The Government people held up your allotment.

MATTIE Oh, do Jesus.

JULIA *(Reads.)* They have many papers to be sign, pink, blue and white also green. Money can't be had 'til all papers match. Mine don't match.

LULA Takes a-while.

JULIA *(Reads.)* Here is ten cash dollars I hope will not be stole.

MATTIE *(Holds up the money.)* I got it.

JULIA *(Reads.)* Go to Merchant Marine office and push things from your end.

MATTIE Monday, Lula, le's go Monday.

LULA I gotta see Nelson march in the parade.

JULIA *(Reads.)* They say people now droppin in the street, dying' from this war-time influenza. Don't get sick—buy tonic if you do. I love you.

MATTIE Gotta buy a bottle-a tonic.

JULIA *(Reads.)* Sometimes people say hurtful things 'bout what I am, like color and race . . .

MATTIE Tell 'em you my brown-skin Carolina daddy, that's who the hell you are. Wish I was there.

JULIA *(Reads.)* I try not to hear 'cause I do want to get back to your side. Two things a man can give the woman he loves . . . his name and his protection . . . The first you have, the last is yet to someday come. The war is here, the road is rocky. I am *ever* your lovin' husband, October.

MATTIE So-long, darlin'. I wish I had your education.

JULIA I only went through eighth grade. Name and protection. I know you love him.

MATTIE Yes'm, I do. If I was to see October in bed with another woman, I'd never doubt him 'cause I trust him more than I do my own eyesight. Bet yall don't believe me.

JULIA I know how much a woman can love. *(Glances at the letter again.)* Two things a man can give . . .

MATTIE Name and protection. That's right, too. I wouldn't live with no man. Man got to marry me. Man that won't marry you thinks nothin' of you. Just usin' you.

JULIA I've never allowed anybody to *use* me!

LULA *(Trying to move her away Stage Right.)* Mattie, look like rain.

MATTIE A man can't use a woman less she let him.

LULA *(To* MATTIE.*)* You never know when to stop.

JULIA Well, I read your letter. Good day.

MATTIE Did I hurtcha feelin's? Tell me, what'd I say.

JULIA I—I've been keepin' company with someone for a long time and . . . we're not married.

MATTIE For how long?

LULA *(Half-heartedly tries to hush* MATTIE *but she would also like to know.)* Ohhh, Mattie.

JULIA *(Without shame).* Ten years today, ten full, faithful years.

MATTIE He got a wife?

JULIA *(Very tense and uncomfortable.)* No.

MATTIE Oh, a man don't wanta get married, work on him. Cut off piece-a his shirt-tail and sew it to your petticoat. It works. Get Fanny to read the tea leaves and tell you how to move. She's a old bitch but what she sees in a tea-cup is true.

JULIA Thank you, Mattie.

LULA Let's pray on it, Miss Julia. Gawd bring them together, in holy matrimony.

JULIA Miss Lula, please don't . . . You know it's against the law for black and white to get married, so Gawd nor the tea leaves can help us. My friend is white and that's why I try to stay to myself. *(After a few seconds of silence.)*

LULA Guess we shouldn't-a disturbed you.

JULIA But I'm so glad you did. Oh, the things I can tell you 'bout bein' lonesome and shut-out. Always movin', one place to another, lookin' for some peace of mind. I moved out in the country . . . Pretty but quiet as the graveyard; so lonesome. One year I was in such a *lovely* colored neighborhood but they couldn't be bothered with me, you know? I've lived near sportin' people . . . they were very kindly but I'm not a sporty type person. Then I found this place hid way in the back-yard so quiet, didn't see another soul . . . And that's why I thought yall wanted to tear my house down this mornin' . . . 'cause you might-a heard 'bout me and Herman . . . and some people are . . . well, they judge, they can't help judgin' you.

MATTIE *(Eager to absolve her of wrong doing.)* Oh, darlin', we all do things we don't want sometimes. You grit your teeth and take all he's got; if you don't somebody else will.

LULA No, no, you got no use for 'em so don't take nothin' from 'em.

MATTIE He's takin' somethin' from her.

LULA Have faith, you won't starve.

MATTIE Rob him blind. Take it all. Let him froth at the mouth. Let him die in the poor-house—bitter, bitter to the gone!

LULA A white man is somethin' else. Everybody knows how that low-down slave master sent for a different black woman every night . . . for his pleasure. That's why none of us is the same color.

MATTIE And right now today they're mean, honey. They can't help it; their nose is pinched together so close they can't get enough air. It makes 'em mean. And their mouth is set back in their face so hard and flat . . . no roundness, no sweetness, they can't even carry a tune.

LULA I couldn't stand one of 'em to touch me intimate no matter what he'd give me.

JULIA Miss Lula, you don't understand. Mattie, the way you and your husband feel that's the way it is with me 'n' Herman. He loves me . . . We love each other, that's all, we just love each other. *(After a split second of silence.)* And someday, as soon as we're able, we have to leave here and go where it's right . . . Where it's legal for everybody to marry. That's what we both want . . . to be man and wife—like you and October.

LULA Well I have to cut out six dozen paper roses today. *(Starts for her house.)*

MATTIE And I gotta make a batch-a candy and look after Princess so I can feed me and Teeta 'til October comes back. Thanks for readin' the letter. *(She enters her house.)*

JULIA But Mattie, Lula—I wanted to tell you why it's been ten years—and why we haven't—

LULA Good day, Miss Julia. *(Enters her house.)*

JULIA Well, that's always the way. What am I doing standin' in a backyard explainin' my life? Stay to yourself, Julia Augustine. Stay to yourself. *(Sweeps her front porch.)*

I got to climb my way to glory
Got to climb it by myself
Ain't nobody here can climb it for me
I got to climb it for myself

Curtain

SCENE TWO

TIME: That evening. Cover closed Scene One curtain with song and laughter from MATTIE, LULA *and* KIDS.

As curtain opens, JULIA *has almost finished the unpacking. The room now looks quite cozy. Once in a while she watches the clock and looks out of the window.* TEETA *follows* PRINCESS *out of* MATTIE*'s house and ties her sash.* PRINCESS *is holding a jump-rope.*

MATTIE *(Offstage. Sings.)*

My best man left me, it sure do grieve my mind
When I'm laughin', I'm laughin' to keep from cryin' . . .

PRINCESS *(Twirling the rope to one side.)* Ching, ching, China-man eat dead rat . . .

TEETA *(As* PRINCESS *jumps rope.)* Knock him in the head with a baseball bat . . .

PRINCESS You wanta jump?

TEETA Yes.

PRINCESS Say "Yes, M'am."

TEETA No.

PRINCESS Why?

TEETA You too little.

PRINCESS *(Takes bean bag from her pocket.)* You can't play with my bean bag.

TEETA I 'on care, play it by yourself.

PRINCESS *(Drops rope, tosses the bag to* TEETA.*)* Catch.

*(*TEETA *throws it back.* HERMAN *appears at the back-entry. He is a strong, forty-year-old working man. His light brown hair is sprinkled with gray. At the present moment he is tired.* PRINCESS *notices him because she is facing the back fence. He looks for a gate or opening but can find none.)*

Hello.

TEETA Mama! Mama!

HERMAN Hello, children. Where's the gate?

*(*HERMAN *passes several packages through a hole in the fence; he thinks of climbing the fence but it is very rickety. He disappears from view.* MATTIE *dashes out of her house, notices the packages, runs into* LULA*'s house, then back into the yard.* LULA *enters in a flurry of excitement; gathers a couple of pieces from the clothesline.* MATTIE *goes to inspect the packages.)*

LULA Don't touch 'em, Mattie. Might be dynamite.

MATTIE Well, I'm gon' get my head blowed off, 'cause I wanta see. *(*NELSON *steps out wearing his best civilian clothes; neat fitting suit,* *striped silk shirt and bulldog shoes in ox-blood leather. He claps his hands to frighten* MATTIE.*)*

MATTIE Oh, look at him. Where's the party?

NELSON Everywhere! The ladies have heard Nelson's home. They waitin' for me!

LULA Don't get in trouble. Don't answer anybody that bothers you.

NELSON How come it is that when I carry a sack-a coal on my back you don't worry, but when I'm goin' out to enjoy myself you almost go crazy.

LULA Go on! Deliver the piece to the funeral. *(Hands him a funeral piece.* MATTIE *proceeds to examine the contents of a paper bag.)*

NELSON Fact is, I was gon' stay home and have me some orange drink, but Massa beat me to it. None-a my business no-how, dammit.

*(*MATTIE *opens another bag.* HERMAN *enters through the front entry.* FANNY *follows at a respectable distance.)*

MATTIE Look, rolls and biscuits!

LULA Why'd he leave the food in the yard?

HERMAN Because I couldn't find the gate. Good evening. Pleasant weather. Howdy do. Cool this evenin'. *(Silence.)* Err—I see where the Allies suffered another set-back yesterday. Well, that's the war, as they say.

(The WOMEN *answer with nods and vague throat clearings.* JULIA *opens her door, he enters.)*

MATTIE That's the lady's husband. He's a light colored man.

PRINCESS What is a light colored man?

*(*CHILDREN *exit with* MATTIE *and* NELSON, FANNY *exits by front entry,* LULA *to her house.)*

JULIA Why'd you pick a conversation? I tell you 'bout that.

HERMAN Man gotta say somethin' stumblin' round in a strange back yard.

JULIA Why didn't you wear your good suit? You know how people like to look you over and sum you up.

HERMAN Mama and Annabelle made me so damn mad tonight. When I got home Annabelle had this in the window. *(Removes a cardboard sign from the bag . . . printed with red, white and blue crayon* . . . WE ARE AMERICAN CITIZENS . . . *)*

JULIA We are American Citizens. Why'd she put it in the window?

HERMAN Somebody wrote cross the side of our house in purple paint . . . "Krauts . . . Germans live here"! I'd-a broke his arm if I caught him.

JULIA It's the war. Makes people mean. But didn't she print it pretty.

HERMAN Comes from Mama boastin' 'bout her German grandfather, now it's no longer fashionable. I snatched that coward sign outta the window . . . Goddamit, I says . . . Annabelle cryin', Mama hollerin' at her. Gawd save us from the ignorance, I say . . . Why should I see a sign in the window when I get home? That Annabelle got flags flyin' in the front yard, the backyard . . . and red, white and blue flowers in the grass . . . confound nonsense . . . Mama is an ignorant woman . . .

JULIA Don't say that . . .

HERMAN A poor ignorant woman who is mad because she was born a sharecropper . . . outta her mind 'cause she ain't high class society. We're red-neck crackers, I told her, that's what.

JULIA Oh, Herman . . . no you didn't . . .

HERMAN I did.

JULIA *(Standing.)* But she raised you . . . loaned you all-a-her three thousand dollars to pour into that bakery shop. You know you care about her.

HERMAN Of course I do. But sometimes she makes me so mad . . . Close the door, lock out the world . . . all of 'em that ain't crazy are coward. *(Looks at sign.)* Poor Annabelle—Miss War-time Volunteer . . .

JULIA She's what you'd call a very Patriotic Person, wouldn't you say?

HERMAN Well, guess it is hard for her to have a brother who only makes pies in time of war.

JULIA A brother who makes pies and loves a nigger!

HERMAN Sweet Kerist, there it is again!

JULIA Your mama's own words . . . according to you—I'll never forget them as long as I live. Annabelle, you've got a brother who makes pies and loves a nigger.

HERMAN How can you remember seven or eight years ago, for Gawd's sake? Sorry I told it.

JULIA I'm not angry, honeybunch, dear heart. I just remember.

HERMAN When you say honeybunch, you're angry. Where do you want your Aunt Cora?

JULIA On my dresser!

HERMAN An awful mean woman.

JULIA Don't get me started on your mama and Annabelle. *(Pause.)*

HERMAN Julia, why did you move into a backyard?

JULIA *(Goes to him.)* Another move, another mess. Sometimes I feel like fightin' . . . and there's nobody to fight but you . . .

HERMAN Open the box. Go on. Open it.

JULIA *(Opens the box and reveals a small but ornate wedding cake with a bride and groom on top and ten pink candles.)* Ohhh, it's the best one ever. Tassels, bells, roses . . .

HERMAN . . . Daffodils and silver sprinkles . . .

JULIA You're the best baker in the world.

HERMAN *(As he lights the candles.)* Because you put up with me . . .

JULIA Gawd knows that.

HERMAN . . . because the palms of your hands and the soles of your feet are pink and brown . . .

JULIA Jus' listen to him. Well, go on.

HERMAN Because you're a good woman, a kind, good woman.

JULIA Thank you very much, Herman.

HERMAN Because you care about me.

JULIA Well, I do.

HERMAN Happy ten years . . . Happy tenth year.

JULIA And the same to you.

HERMAN *(Tries a bit of soft barbershop harmony.)*

I love you as I never loved before *(*JULIA *joins him.)*
When first I met you on the village green
Come to me e'er my dream of love is o'er
I love you as I loved you
When you were sweet—Take the end up higher—
When you were su-weet six-ateen.

Now blow! *(They blow out the candles and kiss through a cloud of smoke.)*

JULIA *(Almost forgetting something.)* Got something for you. Because you were my only friend when Aunt Cora sent me on a sleep-in job in the white-folks kitchen. And wasn't that Miss Bessie one mean white woman? *(Gives present to* HERMAN.*)*

HERMAN Oh, Julia, just say she was mean.

JULIA Well yes, but she was white too.

HERMAN A new peel, thank you. A new pastry bag. Thank you.

JULIA *(She gives him a sweater.)* I did everything right but one arm came out shorter.

HERMAN That's how I feel. Since three o'clock this morning, I turned out twenty ginger breads, thirty sponge cakes, lady fingers, Charlotte Russe . . . loaf bread, round bread, twist bread and water rolls . . . and—

JULIA Tell me about pies. Do pies!

HERMAN Fifty pies. Open apple, closed apple, apple-crumb, sweet potato and pecan. And I got a order for a large wedding cake. They want it in the shape of a battleship. *(*HERMAN *gives* JULIA *ring box.* JULIA *takes out a wide, gold wedding band—it is strung on a chain.)* It's a wedding band . . . on a chain . . . To have until such time as . . . It's what you wanted, Julia. A damn fool present.

JULIA Sorry I lost your graduation ring. If you'd-a gone to college what do you think you'd-a been?

HERMAN A baker with a degree.

JULIA *(Reads.)* Herman and Julia 1908 . . . and now it's . . . 1918. Time runs away. A wedding band . . . on a chain. *(She fastens the chain around her neck.)*

HERMAN A damn fool present. *(*JULIA *drops the ring inside of her dress.)*

JULIA It comforts me. It's your promise. You hungry?

HERMAN No.

JULIA After the war, the people across the way are goin' to Philadelphia.

HERMAN I hear it's cold up there. People freeze to death waitin' for a trolley car.

JULIA *(Leans back beside him, rubs his head.)* In the middle of the night a big bird flew cryin' over this house—Then he was gone, the way time goes flyin' . . .

HERMAN Julia, why did you move in a back yard? Out in the country the air was so sweet and clean. Makes me feel shame . . .

JULIA *(Rubbing his back.)* Crickets singin' that lonesome evenin' song. Any kind-a people better than none a-tall.

HERMAN Mama's beggin' me to hire Greenlee again, to help in the shop, "Herman, sit back like a half-way gentleman and just take in money."

JULIA Greenlee! When white-folks decide . . .

HERMAN People, Julia, people.

JULIA When people decide to give other people a job, they come up with the biggest Uncle Tom they can find. The *people* I know call him a "white-folks-nigger." It's a terrible expression so don't you ever use it.

HERMAN He seems dignified, Julia.

JULIA Jus' 'cause you're clean and stand straight, that's not dignity. Even speakin' nice might not be dignity.

HERMAN What's dignity? Tell me. Do it.

JULIA Well, it . . . it . . . It's a feeling—It's a spirit that rises higher than the dirt around it, without any by-your-leave. It's not proud and it's not 'shamed . . . Dignity "Is" . . . and it's never Greenlee . . . I don't know if it's us either, honey.

HERMAN *(Standing.)* It still bothers my mother that I'm a baker. "When you gonna rise in the world!" A baker who rises . . . *(Laughs and coughs a little.)* Now she's worried 'bout Annabelle marryin' a sailor. After all, Annabelle is a concert pianist. She's had only one concert . . . in a church . . . and not many people there.

JULIA A sailor might just persevere and become an admiral. Yes, an admiral and a concert pianist.

HERMAN Ten years. If I'd-a known what I know now, I wouldn't-a let Mama borrow on the house or give me the bakery.

JULIA Give what? Three broken stoves and all-a your papa's unpaid bills.

HERMAN I *got* to pay her back. And I can't go to Philadelphia or wherever the hell you're saying to go. I can hear you thinkin', Philadelphia, Philadelphia, Phil . . .

JULIA *(Jumping up. Pours wine.)* Oh damnation! The hell with that!

HERMAN All right, not so much hell and damn. When we first met you were so shy.

JULIA Sure was, wouldn't say "dog" 'cause it had a tail. In the beginnin' nothin' but lovin' and kissin' . . . and thinkin' 'bout you. Now I worry 'bout gettin' old. I do. Maybe you'll meet somebody younger. People do get old, y'know. *(Sits on bed.)*

HERMAN There's an old couple 'cross from the bakery . . . "Mabel," he yells, "Where's my keys!" . . . Mabel has a big behind on her. She wears his carpet slippers. "All right, Robbie, m'boy," she says . . . Robbie walks kinda one-sided. But they're havin' a pretty good time. We'll grow old together both of us havin' the same name. *(Takes her in his arms.)* Julia, I love you . . . you know it . . . I love you . . . *(After a pause.)* Did you have my watch fixed?

JULIA *(Sleepily.)* Uh-huh, it's in my purse. *(Getting up.)* Last night when the bird flew over the house—I dreamed 'bout the devil's face in the fire . . . He said "I'm comin' to drag you to hell."

HERMAN *(Sitting up.)* There's no other hell, honey. Celestine was sayin' the other day—

JULIA How do you know what Celestine says?

HERMAN Annabelle invited her to dinner.

JULIA They still trying to throw that white widow-woman at you? Oh, Herman, I'm gettin' mean . . . jumpin' at noises . . . and bad dreams.

HERMAN *(Brandishing bottle.)* Dammit, this is the big bird that flew over the house!

JULIA I don't go anywhere, I don't know anybody, I gotta do somethin'. Sometimes I need to have company—to say . . . "Howdy-do, pleasant evenin', do drop in." Sometimes I need other people. How you ever gonna pay back three thousand dollars? Your side hurt?

HERMAN Schumann, came in to see me this mornin'. Says he'll buy me out, ten cents on the dollar, and give me a job bakin' for him . . . it's an offer—can get seventeen hundred cash.

JULIA Don't do it, Herman. That sure wouldn't be dignity.

HERMAN He makes an American flag outta gingerbread. But they sell. Bad taste sells. Julia, where do you want to go? New York, Philadelphia, where? Let's try their dignity. Say where you want to go.

JULIA Well, darlin', if folks are freezin' in Philadelphia, we'll go to New York.

HERMAN Right! You go and size up the place. Meanwhile I'll stay here and do like everybody else, make war money . . . battleship cakes, cannon-ball cookies . . . chocolate bullets . . . they'll sell. Pay my debts. Less than a year, I'll be up there with money in my pockets.

JULIA Northerners talk funny—"We're from New Yo*rrrk*."

HERMAN I'll getcha train ticket next week.

JULIA No train. I wanta stand on the deck of a Clyde Line boat, wavin' to the people on the shore. The whistle blowin', flags flyin' . . . wavin' my handkerchief . . . So long, so long, look here—South Carolina . . . so long, hometown . . . goin' away by myself—*(Tearfully blows her nose.)*

HERMAN You gonna like it. Stay with your cousin and don't talk to strangers. *(JULIA gets dress from her hope chest.)*

JULIA Then, when we do get married we can have a quiet reception. My cut glass punch bowl . . . little sandwiches, a few friends . . . Herman? Hope my weddin' dress isn't too small. It's been waitin' a good while. *(Holds dress in front of her.)* I'll use all of my hope chest things. Quilts, Irish linens, the silver cups . . . Oh, Honey, how are you gonna manage with me gone?

HERMAN Buy warm underwear and a woolen coat with a fur collar . . . to turn against the northern wind. What size socks do I wear?

JULIA Eleven, eleven and a half if they run small.

HERMAN . . . what's the store? Write it down.

JULIA Coleridge. And go to King Street for your shirts.

HERMAN Coleridge. Write it down.

JULIA Keep payin' Ruckheiser, the tailor, so he can start your new suit.

HERMAN Ruckheiser. Write it down.

JULIA Now that I know I'm goin' we can take our time.

HERMAN No, rush, hurry, make haste, do it. Look at you . . . like your old self.

JULIA No, no, not yet—I'll go soon as we get around to it. *(Kisses him.)*

HERMAN That's right. Take your time . . .

JULIA Oh, Herman.

(MATTIE enters through the back gate with TEETA She pats and arranges TEETA's hair. FANNY enters from the front entry and goes to JULIA's window.)

MATTIE You goin' to Lula's service?

FANNY A new faith. Rather be a Catholic than somethin' you gotta make up. Girl, my new tenant and her—

MATTIE *(Giving FANNY the high-sign to watch what she says in front of TEETA.)* . . . and her husband.

FANNY I gotcha. She and her husband was in there havin' a orgy. Singin', laughin', screamin', crying' . . . I'd like to be a fly on that wall.

(LULA enters the yard wearing a shawl over her head and a red band on her arm. She carries two chairs and places them beside two kegs.)

LULA Service time!

(MATTIE, TEETA and FANNY enter the yard and sit down. LULA places a small table and a cross.)

FANNY *(Goes to JULIA's door and knocks.)* Let's spread the word to those who need it. *(Shouts.)* Miss Julia, don't stop if you in the middle-a somethin'. We who love Gawd are gatherin' for prayer. Got any time for Jesus?

ALL *(Sing.)* When the roll is called up yonder.

JULIA Thank you, Miss Fanny. *(FANNY flounces back to her seat in triumph. JULIA sits on the bed near HERMAN.)*

HERMAN Dammit, she's makin' fun of you.

JULIA *(Smooths her dress and hair.)* Nobody's invited me anywhere in a long time . . . so I'm goin'.

HERMAN *(Standing.)* I'm gonna buy you a Clyde Line ticket for New York City on Monday . . . this Monday.

JULIA Monday?

HERMAN As Gawd is my judge. That's dignity. Monday.

JULIA *(Joyfully kissing him.)* Yes, Herman! *(She enters yard.)*

LULA My form-a service opens with praise. Let us speak to Gawd.

MATTIE Well, I thang Gawd that—that I'm livin' and I pray my husband comes home safe.

TEETA I love Jesus and Jesus loves me.

ALL Amen.

FANNY I thang Gawd that I'm able to rise spite-a-those who try to hold me down, spite-a those who are two-faceted, spite-a those in my own race who jealous 'cause I'm doin' so much better than the rest of 'em. He preparest a table for me in the presence of my enemies. Double-deal Fanny Johnson all you want but me 'n' Gawd's gonna come out on top.

(ALL look to JULIA.)

JULIA I'm sorry for past sin—but from Monday on through eternity—I'm gonna live in dignity accordin' to the laws of God and man. Oh, Glory!

LULA Glory Halleluhjah!

(NELSON enters a bit unsteadily . . . struts and preens while singing.)

NELSON Come here black woman . . . whoooo . . . eee . . . on daddy's knee . . . etc.

LULA *(Trying to interrupt him.)* We're testifyin . . .

NELSON *(Throwing hat on porch.)* Right! Testify! Tonight I asked the prettiest girl in Carolina to be my wife; and Merrilee Jones told me . . . I'm sorry but you got nothin to offer. She's right! I got nothin to offer but a hard way to go. Merrilee Jones . . . workin for the rich white folks and better off washin their dirty drawers than marryin me.

LULA Respect the church! *(Slaps him.)*

NELSON *(Sings.)* Come here, black woman (etc.) . . .

JULIA Oh, Nelson, respect your mother!

NELSON Respect your damn self, Julia Augustine! *(Continues singing.)*

LULA How we gonna find a new faith?

NELSON *(Softly.)* By tellin' the truth, Mamma. Merrilee ain't no liar. I got nothin' to offer, just like October.

MATTIE You keep my husband's name outta your mouth.

NELSON *(Sings.)* Come here, black woman . . .

FANNY AND CONGREGATION *(Sing.)*

Ain't gon let nobody turn me round, turn me round, turn me round
Ain't gon let nobody turn me round . . .

HERMAN *(Staggers out to porch.)* Julia, I'm going now, I'm sorry . . . I don't feel well . . . I don't know . . . *(Slides forward and falls.)*

JULIA Mr. Nelson . . . won'tcha please help me . . .

FANNY Get him out of my yard.

(NELSON and JULIA help HERMAN in to bed. Others freeze in yard.)

End of Act One

Act Two

Scene One

TIME: Sunday morning.

SCENE: The same as Act One except the yard and houses are neater. The clothes line is down. Off in the distance someone is humming a snatch of a hymn. Church bells are ringing. HERMAN is in a heavy, restless sleep. The bed covers indicate he has spent a troubled night. On the table Downstage Right are medicine bottles, cups and spoons. JULIA *is standing beside the bed, swinging a steam kettle; she stops and puts it on a trivet on top of her hope chest.*

FANNY *(Seeing her.)* Keep usin' the steam-kettle. (HERMAN *groans lightly.*)

MATTIE *(Picks up scissors.)* Put the scissors under the bed, open. It'll cut the pain.

FANNY *(Takes scissors from* MATTIE.*)* That's for childbirth.

JULIA He's had too much paregoric. Sleepin' his life away. I want a doctor.

FANNY Over my dead body. It's against the damn law for him to be layin' up in a black woman's bed.

MATTIE A doctor will call the police.

FANNY They'll say I run a bad house.

JULIA I'll tell 'em the truth.

MATTIE We don't tell things to police.

FANNY When Lula gets back with his sister, his damn sister will take charge.

MATTIE That's his family.

FANNY Family is family.

JULIA I'll hire a hack and take him to a doctor.

FANNY He might die on you. That's police. That's the work-house.

JULIA I'll say I found him on the street!

FANNY Walk into the jaws of the law—they'll chew you up.

JULIA Suppose his sister won't come?

FANNY She'll be here. (FANNY *picks up a tea-cup and turns it upside down on the saucer and twirls it.)* I see a ship, a ship sailin' on the water.

MATTIE Water clear or muddy?

FANNY Crystal clear.

MATTIE *(Realizing she's late.)* Oh, I gotta get Princess so her folks can open their ice cream parlor. Take care-a Teeta.

FANNY I see you on your way to Miami, Florida, goin' on a trip.

JULIA *(Sitting on window seat.)* I know you want me to move. I will, Fanny.

FANNY Julia, it's hard to live under these mean white-folks . . . but I've done it. I'm the first and only colored they let buy land 'round here.

JULIA They all like you, Fanny. Only one of 'em cares for me . . . just one.

FANNY Yes, I'm thought highly of. When I pass by they can say . . . "There she go, Fanny Johnson, representin' her race in-a approved manner" . . . 'cause they don't have to worry 'bout my next move. I can't afford to mess that up on account-a you or any-a the rest-a these hard-luck, better-off-dead, triffin' niggers.

JULIA *(Crossing up Right.)* I'll move. But I'm gonna call a doctor.

FANNY Do it, we'll have a yellow quarantine sign on the front door . . . "INFLUENZA." Doctor'll fill out papers for the law . . . address . . . race . . .

JULIA I . . . I guess I'll wait until his sister gets here.

FANNY No, you call a doctor, Nelson won't march in the parade tomorrow or go back to the army, Mattie'll be outta work, Lula can't deliver flowers . . .

JULIA I'm sorry, so very sorry. I'm the one breakin' laws, doin' wrong.

FANNY I'm not judgin' you. High or low, nobody's against this if it's kept quiet. But when you pickin' white . . . pick a wealthy white. It makes things easier.

JULIA No, Herman's not rich and I've never tried to beat him out of anything.

FANNY *(Crossing to* JULIA.*)* Well, he just ought-a be and you just should-a. A colored woman needs money more than anybody else in this world.

JULIA You sell yours.

FANNY All I don't sell I'm going to keep.

HERMAN Julia?

FANNY *(Very genial.)* Well, well sir, how you feelin', Mr. Herman? This is Aunt Fanny . . . Miss Julia's landlady. You lookin' better, Mr. Herman. We've been praying for you. (FANNY *exits to* TEETA*'s house.)*

JULIA Miss Lula—went to get your sister.

HERMAN Why?

JULIA Fanny made me. We couldn't wake you up.

(He tries to sit up in bed to prepare for leaving. She tries to help him. He falls back on the pillow.)

HERMAN Get my wallet ... see how much money is there. What's that smell?

(She takes the wallet from his coat pocket. She completes counting the money.)

JULIA Eucalyptus oil, to help you breathe; I smell it, you smell it and Annabelle will have to smell it too! Seventeen dollars.

HERMAN A boat ticket to New York is fourteen dollars—Ohhhh, Kerist! Pain ... pain ... Count to ten ... one, two ...

(JULIA gives paregoric water to him. He drinks. She puts down glass and picks up damp cloth from bowl on tray and wipes his brow.)

My mother is made out of too many ... little things ... the price of carrots, how much fat is on the meat ... little things make people small. Make ignorance—y'know?

JULIA Don't fret about your people, I promise I won't be surprised at anything and I won't have unpleasant words no matter what.

HERMAN *(The pain eases. He is exhausted.)* Ahhh, there ... All men are born which is—utterly untrue.

(NELSON steps out of the house. He is brushing his army jacket. HERMAN moans slightly. JULIA gets her dress-making scissors and opens them, places the scissors under the bed.)

FANNY *(To NELSON as she nods towards JULIA's house.)* I like men of African descent, myself.

NELSON Pitiful people. They pitiful.

FANNY They common. Only reason I'm sleepin' in a double bed by myself is 'cause I got to bear the standard for the race. I oughta run her outta here for the sake-a the race too.

NELSON It's your property. Run us all off it, Fanny.

FANNY Plenty-a these hungry, jobless, bad-luck colored men, just-a itchin' to move in on my gravy-train. I don't want 'em.

NELSON *(With good nature.)* Right, Fanny! We empty-handed, got nothin' to offer.

FANNY But I'm damn tired-a ramblin' round in five rooms by myself. House full-a new furniture, the icebox forever full-a goodies. I'm a fine cook and I know how to pleasure a man ... he wouldn't have to step outside for a thing ... food, fun and finance ... all under one roof. Nelson, how'd you like to be my business advisor? Fix you up a little office in my front parlor. You wouldn't have to work for white folks ... and Lula wouldn't have to pay rent. The war won't last forever ... then what you gonna do? They got nothin' for you but haulin' wood and cleanin' toilets. Let's you and me pitch in together.

NELSON I know you just teasin', but I wouldn't do a-tall. Somebody like me ain't good enough for you no-way, but you a fine-lookin' woman, though. After the war I might hit out for Chicago or Detroit ... a rollin' stone gathers no moss.

FANNY Roll on. Just tryin' to help the race.

(LULA enters by front entry, followed by ANNABELLE, a woman in her thirties. She assumes a slightly mincing air of fashionable delicacy. She might be graceful if she were not ashamed of her size. She is nervous and fearful in this strange atmosphere. The others fall silent as they see her. ANNABELLE wonders if PRINCESS is her brother's child? Or could it be TEETA, or both?)

ANNABELLE Hello there ... er ... children.

PRINCESS *(Can't resist mocking her.)* Hello there, er ... children. *(Giggles.)*

ANNABELLE *(To TEETA.)* Is she your sister? *(ANNABELLE looks at NELSON and draws her shawl a little closer.)*

TEETA You have to ask my mama.

NELSON *(Annoyed with ANNABELLE's discomfort.)* Mom, where's the flat-iron? *(Turns and enters his house. LULA follows. MATTIE and CHILDREN exit.)*

FANNY I'm the landlady. Mr. Herman had every care and kindness 'cept a doctor. Miss Juliaaaa! That's the family's concern. *(FANNY opens door, then exits.)*

ANNABELLE Sister's here. It's Annabelle.

JULIA *(Shows her to a chair.)* One minute he's with you, the next he's gone. Paregoric makes you sleep.

ANNABELLE *(Dabs at her eyes with a handkerchief.)* Cryin' doesn't make sense a-tall. I'm a volunteer worker at the Naval hospital . . . I've nursed my mother . . . *(Chokes with tears.)*

JULIA *(Pours a glass of water for her.)* Well, this is more than sickness. It's not known' 'bout other things.

ANNABELLE We've known for years. He is away all the time and when old Uncle Greenlee . . . He's a colored gentleman who works in our neighborhood . . . and he said . . . he told . . . er, well, people do talk. *(*ANNABELLE *spills water,* JULIA *attempts to wipe the water from her dress.)* Don't do that . . . It's all right.

HERMAN Julia?

ANNABELLE Sister's here. Mama and Uncle Greenlee have a hack down the street. Gets a little darker we'll take you home, call a physician . . .

JULIA Can't you do it right away?

ANNABELLE 'Course you could put him out. Please let us wait 'til dark.

JULIA Get a doctor.

ANNABELLE Our plans are made, thank you.

HERMAN Annabelle, this is Julia.

ANNABELLE Hush.

HERMAN This is my sister.

ANNABELLE Now be still.

JULIA I'll call Greenlee to help him dress.

ANNABELLE No. Dress first. The colored folk in *our* neighborhood have great respect for us.

HERMAN Because I give away cinnamon buns, for Kerist sake.

ANNABELLE *(To* JULIA.*)* I promised my mother I'd try and talk to you. Now—you look like one-a the nice coloreds . . .

HERMAN Remember you are a concert pianist, that is a very dignified calling.

ANNABELLE Put these on. We'll turn our backs.

JULIA He can't.

ANNABELLE *(Holds the covers in a way to keep his midsection under wraps.)* Hold up. *(They manage to get the trousers up as high as his waist but they are twisted and crooked.)* Up we go! There . . . *(They are breathless from the effort of lifting him.)* Now fasten your clothing.

*(*JULIA *fastens his clothes.)*

I declare, even a dead man oughta have enough pride to fasten himself.

JULIA You're a volunteer at the Naval hospital?

HERMAN *(As another pain hits him.)* Julia, my little brown girl . . . Keep singing . . .

JULIA We are climbin' Jacob's ladder, We are climbin' Jacob's ladder,
We are climbin' Jacob's ladder, Soldiers of the Cross . . .

HERMAN The palms of your hands . . .

JULIA *(Singing.)* Every round goes higher and higher . . .

HERMAN . . . the soles of your feet are pink and brown.

ANNABELLE Dammit, hush. Hush this noise. Sick or not sick, hush! It's ugliness. *(To* JULIA.*)* Let me take care of him, please, leave us alone.

JULIA I'll get Greenlee.

ANNABELLE No! You hear me? No.

JULIA I'll be outside.

ANNABELLE *(Sitting on bed.)* If she hadn't-a gone I'd-a screamed. *(*JULIA *stands on the porch.* ANNABELLE *cries.)* I thought so highly of you . . . and here you are in somethin' that's been festerin' for years. *(In disbelief.)* One of the finest women in the world is pinin' her heart out for you, a woman who's pure gold. Everything Celestine does for Mama she's really doin' for you . . . to get next to you . . . But even a Saint wants some reward.

HERMAN I don't want Saint Celestine.

ANNABELLE *(Standing.)* Get up! *(Tries to move* HERMAN.*)* At the Naval hospital I've seen influenza cases tied down to keep 'em from walkin'. What're we doin' here? How do you meet a black woman?

HERMAN She came in the bakery on a rainy Saturday evening.

ANNABELLE *(Giving in to curiosity.)* Yes?

MATTIE *(Offstage. Scolding* TEETA *and* PRINCESS.*)* Sit down and drink that lemonade. Don't bother me!

HERMAN "I smell rye bread baking." Those were the first words . . . Every day . . . Each time the bell sounds over the shop door I'm hopin' it's the brown girl . . . pretty shirtwaist and navy blue skirt. One day I took her hand . . . "little lady, don't be afraid of me" . . . She wasn't. . . . I've never been lonesome since.

ANNABELLE *(Holding out his shirt.)* Here, your arm goes in the sleeve. *(They're managing to get the shirt on.)*

HERMAN *(Beginning to ramble.)* Julia? Your body is velvet . . . the sweet blackberry kisses . . . you are the night-time, the warm, Carolina night-time in my arms . . .

ANNABELLE *(Bitterly.)* Most excitement I've ever had was takin' piano lessons.

JULIA *(Calls from porch.)* Ready?

ANNABELLE No. Rushin' us out. A little longer, please. *(Takes a comb from her purse and nervously combs his hair.)* You nor Mama put yourselves out to understand my Walter when I had him home to dinner. Yes, he's a common sailor . . . I wish he was an officer. I never liked a sailor's uniform, tight pants and middy blouses . . . but they are in the service of their country . . . He's taller than I am. You didn't even stay home that one Sunday like you promised. Must-a been chasin' after some-a them blackberry kisses you love so well. Mama made a jackass outta Walter. You know how she can do. He left lookin' like a whipped dog. Small wonder he won't live down here. I'm crazy-wild 'bout Walter even if he is a sailor. Marry Celestine. She'll take care-a Mama and I can go right on up to the Brooklyn Navy Yard. I been prayin' so hard . . . You marry Celestine and set me free. And Gawd knows I don't want another concert.

HERMAN *(Sighs.)* Pain, keep singing.

ANNABELLE Dum-dum-blue Danube. *(He falls back on the pillow. She bathes his head with a damp cloth.)*

JULIA *(As* NELSON *enters the yard.)* Tell your mother I'm grateful for her kindness. I appreciate . . .

NELSON Don't have so much to say to me. *(Quietly, in a straightforward manner.)* They set us on fire 'bout their women. String us up, pour on kerosene and light a match. Wouldn't I make a bright flame in my new uniform?

JULIA Don't be thinkin' that way.

NELSON I'm thinkin' 'bout black boys hangin' from trees in Little Mountain, Elloree, Winnsboro.

JULIA Herman never killed anybody. I couldn't care 'bout that kind-a man.

NELSON *(Stepping, turning to her.)* How can you account for carin' 'bout him a-tall?

JULIA In that place where I worked, he was the only one who cared . . . who really cared. So gentle, such a gentle man . . . "Yes, Ma'am," . . . "No, Ma'am," "Thank you, Ma'am . . ." In the best years of my youth, my Aunt Cora sent me out to work on a sleep-in job. His shop was near that place where I worked. . . . Most folks don't have to *account* for why they love.

NELSON You ain't most folks. You're down on the bottom with us, under his foot. A black man got nothin' to offer you . . .

JULIA I wasn't lookin' for anybody to do for me.

NELSON . . . and *he's* got nothin' to offer. The one layin' on your mattress, not even if he's kind as you say. He got nothin' for you . . . but some meat and gravy or a new petticoat . . . or maybe he can give you meriny-lookin' little bastard chirrun for us to take in and raise up. We're the ones who feed and raise 'em when it's like this . . . They don't want 'em. They only too glad to let us have their kin-folk. As it is, we supportin' half-a the slave-master's offspring right now.

JULIA Go fight those who fight you. He never threw a pail-a water on you. Why didn't you fight them that did? Takin' it out on me 'n Herman 'cause you scared of 'em . . .

NELSON Scared? What scared! If I gotta die I'm carryin' one 'long with me.

JULIA No you not. You gon' keep on fightin' me.

NELSON ... Scared-a what? I look down on 'em, I spit on 'em.

JULIA No, you don't. They throw dirty water on your uniform ... and you spit on me!

NELSON Scared, what scared!

JULIA You fightin' me, me, me, not them ... never them.

NELSON Yeah, I was scared and I'm tougher, stronger, a better man than any of 'em ... but they won't letcha fight one or four or ten. I was scared to fight a hundred or a thousand. A losin' fight.

JULIA I'd-a been afraid too.

NELSON And you scared right now, you let the woman run you out your house.

JULIA I didn't want to make trouble.

NELSON But that's what a fight is ... trouble.

LULA *(In her doorway.)* Your mouth will kill you. *(To* JULIA.*)* Don't tell Mr. Herman anything he said ... or I'll hurt you.

JULIA Oh, Miss Lula.

LULA Anyway, he didn't say nothin'.

*(*HERMAN'S MOTHER *enters the yard. She is a "poor white" about fifty-seven years old. She has risen above her poor farm background and tries to assume the airs of "quality." Her clothes are well-kept-shabby. She wears white shoes, a shirtwaist and skirt, drop earrings, a cameo brooch, a faded blue straw hat with a limp bit of veiling. She carries a heavy-black, oil-cloth bag. All in the yard give a step backward as she enters. She assumes an air of calm well-being. Almost as though visiting friends, but anxiety shows around the edges and underneath.* JULIA *approaches and* HERMAN'S MOTHER *abruptly turns to* MATTIE.*)*

HERMAN'S MOTHER How do. *(*MATTIE, TEETA *and* PRINCESS *look at* HERMAN'S MOTHER. HERMAN'S MOTHER *is also curious about them.)*

MATTIE *(In answer to a penetrating stare from the old woman.)* She's mine. I take care-a her. *(Speaking her defiance by ordering the children.)* Stay inside 'fore y'all catch the flu!

HERMAN'S MOTHER *(To* LULA.*)* You were very kind to bring word ... er ...

LULA Lula, Ma'am.

HERMAN'S MOTHER The woman who nursed my second cousin's children ... she had a name like that ... Lul*u* we called her.

LULA My son, Nelson.

HERMAN'S MOTHER Can see that.

*(*MATTIE *and the children exit.* FANNY *hurries in from the front entry. Is most eager to establish herself on the good side of* HERMAN'S MOTHER. *With a slight bow. She is carrying the silver tea service.)*

FANNY Beg pardon, if I may be so bold, I'm Fanny, the owner of all this property.

HERMAN'S MOTHER *(Definitely approving of* FANNY*)* I'm ... er ... Miss Annabelle's mother.

FANNY My humble pleasure ... er ... Miss er ...

HERMAN'S MOTHER *(After a brief, thoughtful pause.)* Miss Thelma.

(They move aside but FANNY *makes sure others hear.)*

FANNY Miss Thelma, this is not Squeeze-gut Alley. We're just poor, humble, colored people ... and everybody knows how to keep their mouth shut.

HERMAN'S MOTHER I thank you.

FANNY She wanted to get a doctor. I put my foot down.

HERMAN'S MOTHER You did right. *(Shaking her head, confiding her troubles.)* Ohhhh, you don't know.

FANNY *(With deep understanding.)* Ohhhh, yes, I do. She moved in on me yesterday.

HERMAN'S MOTHER Friend Fanny, help me to get through this.

FANNY I will. Now this is Julia, she's the one ...

*(*HERMAN'S MOTHER *starts toward the house without looking at* JULIA. FANNY *decides to let the matter drop.)*

HERMAN'S MOTHER *(To* LULA.*)* Tell Uncle Greenlee not to worry. He's holdin' the horse and buggy.

NELSON *(Bars* LULA*'s way.)* Mama. I'll do it.

*(*LULA *exits into her house.* FANNY *leads her to the chair near* HERMAN*'s bed.)*

ANNABELLE Mama, if we don't call a doctor Herman's gonna die.

HERMAN'S MOTHER Everybody's gon' die. Just a matter of when, where and how. A pretty silver service.

FANNY English china. Belgian linen. Have a cup-a tea?

HERMAN'S MOTHER *(As a studied pronouncement.)* My son comes to deliver baked goods and the influenza strikes him down. Sickness, it's the war.

FANNY *(Admiring her cleverness.)* Yes, Ma'am, I'm a witness. I saw him with the packages.

JULIA Now please call the doctor.

ANNABELLE Yes, please, Mama. No way for him to move 'less we pick him up bodily.

HERMAN'S MOTHER Then we'll pick him up.

HERMAN About Walter . . . your Walter . . . I'm sorry . . .

*(*JULIA *tries to give* HERMAN *some water.)*

HERMAN'S MOTHER Annabelle, help your brother.

*(*ANNABELLE *gingerly takes glass from* JULIA.*)*

Get that boy to help us. I'll give him a dollar. Now gather his things.

ANNABELLE What things?

HERMAN'S MOTHER His possessions, anything he owns, whatever is his. What you been doin' in here all this time?

*(*FANNY *notices* JULIA *is about to speak, so she hurries her through the motions of going through dresser drawers and throwing articles into a pillow case.)*

FANNY Come on, sugar, make haste.

JULIA Don't go through my belongings.

(Tears through the drawers, flinging things around as she tries to find his articles. FANNY *neatly piles them together.)*

FANNY *(Taking inventory.)* Three shirts . . . one is kinda soiled.

HERMAN'S MOTHER That's all right, I'll burn 'em.

FANNY Some new undershirts.

HERMAN'S MOTHER I'll burn them too.

JULIA *(To* FANNY*)* Put 'em down. I bought 'em and they're not for burnin'.

HERMAN'S MOTHER *(Struggling to hold her anger in check.)* Fanny, go get that boy. I'll give him fifty cents.

FANNY You said a dollar.

HERMAN'S MOTHER All right, dollar it is.

*(*FANNY *exits toward the front entry. In tense, hushed, excited tones, they argue back and forth.)*

Now where's the bill-fold . . . there's papers . . . identity . . . *(Looks in* HERMAN*'s coat pockets.)*

ANNABELLE Don't make such-a to-do.

HERMAN'S MOTHER You got any money of your own? Yes, I wanta know where's his money.

JULIA I'm gettin' it.

HERMAN'S MOTHER In her pocketbook. This is why the bakery can't make it.

HERMAN I gave her the Gawd-damned money!

JULIA And I know what Herman wants me to do . . .

HERMAN'S MOTHER *(With a wry smile.)* I'm sure you know what he wants.

JULIA I'm not gonna match words with you. Furthermore, I'm too much of a lady.

HERMAN'S MOTHER A lady oughta learn how to keep her dress down.

ANNABELLE Mama, you makin' a spectacle outta yourself.

HERMAN'S MOTHER You a big simpleton. Men have nasty natures, they can't help it. A man would go with a snake if he only knew how. They cleaned out your wallet.

HERMAN *(Shivering with a chill.)* I gave her the damn money.

*(*JULIA *takes it from her purse.)*

HERMAN'S MOTHER Where's your pocket-watch or did you give that too? Annabelle, get another lock put on that bakery door.

HERMAN I gave her the money to go—to go to New York.

(JULIA *drops the money in* HERMAN'S MOTHER*'s lap. She is silent for a moment.)*

HERMAN'S MOTHER All right. Take it and go. It's never too late to undo a mistake. I'll add more to it. *(She puts the money on the dresser.)*

JULIA I'm not goin' anywhere.

HERMAN'S MOTHER Look here, girl, you leave him 'lone.

ANNABELLE Oh, Mama, all he has to do is stay away.

HERMAN'S MOTHER But he can't do it. Been years and he can't do it.

JULIA I got him hoo-dooed, I sprinkle red pepper on his shirt-tail.

HERMAN'S MOTHER I believe you.

HERMAN I have a black woman . . . and I'm gon' marry her. I'm gon' marry her . . . got that? Pride needs a paper, for . . . for the sake of herself . . . that's dignity—tell me, what is dignity—Higher than the dirt it is . . . dignity is . . .

ANNABELLE Let's take him to the doctor, Mama.

HERMAN'S MOTHER When it's dark.

JULIA Please!

HERMAN'S MOTHER Nightfall.

(JULIA *steps out on the porch but hears every word said in the room.)*

I had such high hopes for him. *(As if* HERMAN *is dead.)* All my high hopes. When he wasn't but five years old I had to whip him so he'd study his John C. Calhoun speech. Oh, Calhoun knew 'bout niggers. He said, "*MEN* are not born . . . equal, or any other kinda way . . . MEN are *made*" . . . Yes, indeed, for recitin' that John C. Calhoun speech . . . Herman won first mention and a twenty dollar gold piece . . . at the Knights of The Gold Carnation picnic.

ANNABELLE Papa changed his mind about the Klan. I'm glad.

HERMAN'S MOTHER Yes, he was always changin' his mind about somethin'. But I was proud-a my men-folk that day. He spoke that speech . . . The officers shook my hand. They honored me . . . "That boy a-yours gonna be somebody." A poor baker-son layin' up with a nigger woman, a over-grown daughter in heat over a common sailor. I must be payin' for somethin' I did. Yesiree, do a wrong, God'll whip you.

ANNABELLE I wish it was dark.

HERMAN'S MOTHER I put up with a man breathin' stale whiskey in my face every night . . . pullin' and pawin' at me . . . always tired, inside and out . . . *(Deepest confidence she has ever shared.)* Gave birth to seven . . . five-a them babies couldn't draw breath.

ANNABELLE *(Suddenly wanting to know more about her.)* Did you love Papa, Mama? Did you ever love him? . . .

HERMAN'S MOTHER Don't ask me 'bout love . . . I don't know nothin' about it. Never mind love. This is my harvest . . .

HERMAN Go home. I'm better. (HERMAN'S MOTHER*'s strategy is to enlighten* HERMAN *and also wear him down. Out on the porch,* JULIA *can hear what is being said in the house.)*

HERMAN'S MOTHER There's something wrong 'bout mismatched things, be they shoes, socks, or people.

HERMAN Go away, don't look at us.

HERMAN'S MOTHER People don't like it. They're not gonna letcha do it in peace.

HERMAN We'll go North.

HERMAN'S MOTHER Not a thing will change except her last name.

HERMAN She's not like others . . . she's not like that . . .

HERMAN'S MOTHER All right, sell out to Schumann. I want my cash-money . . . You got no feelin' for me, I got none for you . . .

HERMAN I feel . . . I feel what I feel . . . I don't know what I feel . . .

HERMAN'S MOTHER Don't need to feel. Live by the law. Follow the law—law, law of the land. Obey the law!

ANNABELLE We're not obeyin' the law. He should be quarantined right here. The city's tryin' to stop an epidemic.

HERMAN'S MOTHER Let the city drop dead and you 'long with it. *Rather* be dead than disgraced. Your papa gimme the house and little money . . . I want my money back. *(She tries to drag* HERMAN *up in the bed.)* I ain't payin' for this. *(Shoves* ANNABELLE *aside.)* Let Schumann take over. A man who knows what he's doin'. Go with her . . . Take the last step against your own! Kill us all. Jesus, Gawd, save us or take us—

HERMAN *(Screams.)* No! No! No! No!

HERMAN'S MOTHER Thank Gawd, the truth is the light. Oh, Blessed Savior . . . (HERMAN *screams out, starting low and ever going higher. She tries to cover his mouth.* ANNABELLE *pulls her hand away.*) Thank you, Gawd, let the fire go out . . . this awful fire.

*(*LULA *and* NELSON *enter the yard.)*

ANNABELLE You chokin' him. Mama . . .

JULIA *(From the porch.)* It's dark! It's dark. Now it's very dark.

HERMAN One ticket on the Clyde Line . . . Julia . . . where are you? Keep singing . . . count . . . one, two . . . three. Over there, over there . . . send the word, send the word . . .

HERMAN'S MOTHER Soon be home, son.

*(*HERMAN *breaks away from the men, staggers to* MATTIE*'s porch and holds on.* MATTIE *smothers a scream and gets the children out of the way.* FANNY *enters.)*

HERMAN Shut the door . . . don't go out . . . the enemy . . . the enemy . . . *(Recites the Calhoun speech.)* Men are not born, infants are born! They grow to all the freedom of which the condition in which they were born permits. It is a great and dangerous error to suppose that all people are equally entitled to liberty.

JULIA Go home—Please be still.

HERMAN It is a reward to be earned, a reward reserved for the intelligent, the patriotic, the virtuous and deserving; and not a boon to be bestowed on a people too ignorant, degraded and vicious . . .

JULIA You be still now, shut up.

HERMAN . . . to be capable either of appreciating or of enjoying it.

JULIA *(Covers her ears.)* Take him . . .

HERMAN A black woman . . . not like the others . . .

JULIA . . . outta my sight . . .

HERMAN Julia, the ship is sinking . . .

*(*HERMAN'S MOTHER *and* NELSON *help* HERMAN *up and out.)*

ANNABELLE *(To* JULIA *on the porch.)* I'm sorry . . . so sorry it had to be this way. I can't leave with you thinkin' I uphold Herman, and blame you.

HERMAN'S MOTHER *(Returning.)* You the biggest fool.

ANNABELLE I say a man is responsible for his own behavior.

HERMAN'S MOTHER And you, you oughta be locked up . . . workhouse . . . jail! Who you think you are!?

JULIA I'm your damn daughter-in-law, you old bitch! The Battleship Bitch! The bitch who destroys with her filthy mouth. They could win the war with your killin' mouth. The son-killer, man-killer bitch . . . She's killin' him 'cause he loved me more than anybody in the world.

*(*FANNY *returns.)*

HERMAN'S MOTHER Better off . . . He's better off dead in his coffin than live with the likes-a you . . . black thing! *(She is almost backing into* JULIA*'s house.)*

JULIA The black thing who bought a hot water bottle to put on your sick, white self when rheumatism threw you flat on your back . . . who bought flannel gowns to warm your pale, mean body. He never ran up and down

King Street shoppin' for you . . . I bought what he took home to you . . .

HERMAN'S MOTHER Lies . . . tear outcha lyin' tongue.

JULIA . . . the lace curtains in your parlor . . . the shirt-waist you wearin'—I made them.

FANNY Go *on* . . . I got her. *(Holds* JULIA.*)*

HERMAN'S MOTHER Leave 'er go! The undertaker will have-ta unlock my hands off her black throat!

FANNY Go on, Miss Thelma.

JULIA Miss Thelma my ass! Her first name is Frieda. The Germans are here . . . in purple paint!

HERMAN'S MOTHER Black, sassy nigger!

JULIA Kraut, knuckle-eater, red-neck . . .

HERMAN'S MOTHER Nigger whore . . . he used you for a garbage pail . . .

JULIA White trash! Sharecropper! Let him die . . . let 'em all die . . . Kill him with your murderin' mouth—sharecropper bitch!

HERMAN'S MOTHER Dirty black nigger . . .

JULIA . . . If I wasn't black with all-a Carolina 'gainst me I'd be mistress of your house! *(To* ANNABELLE.*)* Annabelle, you'd be married livin' in Brooklyn, New York . . . *(To* HERMAN'S MOTHER.*)* . . . and I'd be waitin' on Frieda . . . cookin' your meals . . . waterin' that damn red-white and blue garden!

HERMAN'S MOTHER Dirty black bitch.

JULIA Daughter of a bitch.

ANNABELLE Leave my mother alone! She's old . . . and sick.

JULIA But never sick enough to die . . . dirty ever-lasting woman.

HERMAN'S MOTHER *(Clinging to* ANNABELLE, *she moves toward the front entry.)* I'm as high over you as Mount Everest over the sea. White reigns supreme . . . I'm white, you can't change that. *(They exit.* FANNY *goes with them.)*

JULIA Out! Out! Out! And take the last ten years-a my life with you and . . . when he gets better . . . keep him home. Killers, murderers . . . Kinsmen! Klansmen! Keep him home. *(To* MATTIE.*)* Name and protection . . . he can't gimme either one. *(To* LULA.*)* I'm gon' get down on my knees and scrub where they walked . . . what they touched . . . *(To* MATTIE.*)* . . . with brown soap . . . hot lye-water . . . scaldin' hot . . . *(She dashes into the house and collects an armful of bedding . . .)* Clean! . . . Clean the whiteness outta my house . . . clean everything . . . even the memory . . . no more love . . . Free . . . free to hate-cha for the rest-a my life. *(Back to the porch with her arms full.)* When I die I'm gonna keep on hatin' . . . I don't want any whiteness in my house. Stay out . . . out . . . *(Dumps the things in the yard.)* . . . out . . . out . . . out . . . and leave me to my black self!

Blackout

Scene Two

TIME: Early afternoon the following day.
PLACE: The same.

In JULIA*'s room, some of the hope chest things are spilled out on the floor, bedspread, linens, silver cups. The half-emptied wine decanter is in a prominent spot. A table is set up in the yard. We hear the distant sound of a marching band. The excitement of a special day is in the air.* NELSON*'s army jacket hangs on his porch,* LULA *brings a pitcher of punch to table.* MATTIE *enters with* TEETA *and* PRINCESS; *she is annoyed and upset in contrast to* LULA*'s singing and gala mood. She scolds the children, smacks* TEETA*'s behind.*

MATTIE They was teasin' the Chinaman down the street 'cause his hair is braided. *(To* CHILDREN.*)* If he ketches you, he'll cook you with onions and gravy.

LULA *(Inspecting* NELSON*'s jacket.)* Sure will.

TEETA Can we go play?

MATTIE A mad dog might bite-cha.

PRINCESS Can we go play?

MATTIE No, you might step on a nail and get lockjaw.

TEETA Can we go play?

MATTIE Oh, go on and play! I wish a gypsy would steal both of 'em! *(*JULIA *enters her room.)*

LULA What's the matter, Mattie?

MATTIE Them damn fool people at the Merchant Marine don't wanta give me my 'lotment money.

JULIA *(Steps out on her porch with deliberate, defiant energy. She is wearing her wedding dress . . . carrying a wine glass. She is over-demonstrating a show of carefree abandon and joy.)* I'm so happy! I never been this happy in all my life! I'm happy to be alive, alive and livin for my people.

LULA You better stop drinkin so much wine. *(*LULA *enters her house.)*

JULIA But if you got no feelin's they can't be hurt!

MATTIE Hey, Julia, the people at the Merchant Marine say I'm not married to October.

JULIA Getcha license, honey, show your papers. Some of us, thang Gawd, got papers!

MATTIE I don't have none.

JULIA Why? Was October married before?

MATTIE No, but I was. A good for nothin' named Delroy . . . I hate to call his name. Was years 'fore I met October. Delroy used to beat the hell outta me . . . tried to stomp me, grind me into the gound . . . callin' me such dirty names . . . Got so 'til I was shame to look at myself in a mirror. I was glad when he run off.

JULIA Where'd he go?

MATTIE I don't know. Man at the office kept sayin' . . . "You're not married to October" . . . and wavin' me 'way like that.

JULIA Mattie, this state won't allow divorce.

MATTIE Well, I never got one.

JULIA You shoulda so you could marry October. You have to be married to get his benefits.

MATTIE We was married. On Edisto Island. I had a white dress and flowers . . . everything but papers. We couldn't get papers. Elder Burns knew we was doin' best we could.

JULIA You can't marry without papers.

MATTIE What if your husband run off? And you got no money? Readin' from the Bible makes people married, not no piece-a paper. We're together eleven years, that oughta-a be legal.

JULIA *(Puts down glass.)* No, it doesn't go that way.

MATTIE October's out on the icy water, in the war-time, worryin' 'bout me 'n Teeta. I say he's my husband. Gotta pay Fanny, buy food. Julia, what must I do?

JULIA I don't know.

MATTIE What's the use-a so much-a education if you don't know what to do?

JULIA You may's well just lived with October. Your marriage meant nothin'.

MATTIE *(Standing angry.)* It meant somethin' to me if not to anybody else. It means I'm ice cream, too, strawberry. *(*MATTIE *heads for her house.)*

JULIA Get mad with me if it'll make you feel better.

MATTIE Julia, could you lend me two dollars?

JULIA Yes, that's somethin' I can do besides drink this wine. *(*JULIA *goes into her room, to get the two dollars. Enter* FANNY, TEETA *and* PRINCESS.*)*

FANNY Colored men don't know how to do nothin' right. I paid that big black boy cross the street . . . thirty cents to paint my sign . . . *(Sign reads . . .* GOODBYE COLORED BOYS . . . *on one side; the other reads . . .* FOR GOD AND CONTRY.*)* But he can't spell. I'm gon' call him a dumb darky and get my money back. Come on, children! *(*CHILDREN *follow laughing.)*

LULA Why call him names!?

FANNY 'Cause it makes him mad, that's why.

*(*FANNY *exits with* TEETA *and* PRINCESS. JULIA *goes into her room.* THE BELL MAN *enters carrying a display board filled with badges and flags . . . buttons, red and blue ribbons attached to the buttons . . . slogans . . .* THE WAR TO END ALL WARS. *He also carries a string of overseas caps [paper] and wears one. Blows a war tune on his tin flute.* LULA *exits.)*

THE BELL MAN "War to end all wars . . ." Flags and badges! Getcha emblems! Hup-two-three . . . Flags and badges . . . hup-two-three! Hey, Aunty! Come back here! Where you at? *(Starts to follow* LULA *into her house.*

NELSON *steps out on the porch and blocks his way.)*

NELSON My mother is in her house. You ain't to come walkin' in. You knock.

THE BELL MAN Don't letcha uniform go to your head, Boy, or you'll end your days swingin' from a tree.

LULA *(Squeezing past* NELSON *dressed in skirt and open shirt-waist.)* Please, Mister, he ain't got good sense.

MATTIE He crazy, Mister.

NELSON Fact is, you stay out of here. Don't ever come back here no more.

THE BELL MAN *(Backing up in surprise.)* He got no respect. One them crazies. I ain't never harmed a bareassed soul but, hot damn, I can get madder and badder than you. Let your uniform go to your head.

LULA Yessir, he goin' back in the army today.

THE BELL MAN Might not get there way he's actin'.

MATTIE *(As* LULA *takes two one dollar bills from her bosom.)* He sorry right now, Mister, his head ain' right.

THE BELL MAN *(Speaks to* LULA *but keeps an eye on* NELSON.*)* Why me? I try to give you a laugh but they say, "Play with a puppy and he'll lick your mouth." Familiarity makes for contempt.

LULA *(Taking flags and badges.)* Yessir. Here's somethin' on my account . . . and I'm buyin' flags and badges for the children. Everybody know you a good man and do right.

THE BELL MAN *(To* LULA.*)* You pay up by Monday. *(To* NELSON.*)* Boy, you done cut off your Mama's credit.

LULA I don't blame you, Mister. (BELL MAN *exits.)*

NELSON Mama, your new faith don't seem to do much for you.

LULA *(Turning to him.)* Nelson, go on off to the war 'fore somebody kills you. I ain't goin' to let nobody spoil my day. *(*LULA *puts flags and badges on punchbowl table.* JULIA *comes out of her room, with the two dollars for* MATTIE*—hands it to her. Sound of Jenkins Colored Orphan Band is heard [Record: Ramblin' by Bunk Johnson].)*

JULIA Listen, Lula . . . Listen, Mattie . . . it's Jenkin's Colored Orphan Band . . . Play! Play, you Orphan boys! Rise up higher than the dirt around you! Play! That's struttin' music, Lula!

LULA It sure is! *(*LULA *struts, arms akimbo, head held high.* JULIA *joins her; they haughtily strut toward each other, then retreat with mock arrogance . . . exchange cold, hostile looks . . . A Carolina folk dance passed on from some dimly-remembered African beginning. Dance ends strutting.)*

JULIA *(Concedes defeat in the dance.)* All right, Lula, strut me down! Strut me right on down! *(They end dance with breathless laughter and cross to* LULA*'s porch.)*

LULA Julia! Fasten me! Pin my hair.

JULIA I'm not goin' to that silly parade, with the colored soldiers marchin' at the end of it.

(LULA *sits on the stool.* JULIA *combs and arranges her hair.)*

LULA Come on, we'll march behind the white folks whether they want us or not. Mister Herman's people got a nice house . . . lemon trees in the yard, lace curtains at the window.

JULIA And red, white and blue flowers all around.

LULA That Uncle Greenlee seems to be well-fixed.

JULIA He works for the livery stable . . . cleans up behind horses . . . in a uniform.

LULA That's nice.

JULIA Weeds their gardens . . . clips white people's pet dogs . . .

LULA Ain't that lovely? I wish Nelson was safe and nicely settled.

JULIA Uncle Greenlee is a well-fed, tale-carryin' son-of-a-bitch . . . and that's the only kind-a love they want from us.

LULA It's wrong to hate.

JULIA They say it's wrong to love too.

LULA We got to show 'em we're good, got to be three times as good, just to make it.

JULIA Why? When they mistreat us who cares? We mistreat each other, who cares? Why we gotta be so good jus' for them?

LULA Dern you, Julia Augustine, you hard-headed thing, 'cause they'll kill us if we not.

JULIA They doin' it anyway. Last night I dreamed of the dead slaves—all the murdered black and bloody men silently gathered at the foot-a my bed. Oh, that awful silence. I wish the dead could scream and fight back. What they do to us . . . and all they want is to be loved in return. Nelson's not Greenlee. Nelson is a fighter.

LULA *(Standing.)* I know. But I'm tryin' to keep him from findin' it out.

*(*NELSON, *unseen by* LULA, *listens.)*

JULIA Your hair looks pretty.

LULA Thank you. A few years back I got down on my knees in the courthouse to keep him off-a the chain gang. I crawled and cried, "Please white folks, yall's everything. I'se nothin, yall's everything." The court laughed—I meant for 'em to laugh . . . then they let Nelson go.

JULIA *(Pitying her.)* Oh, Miss Lula, a lady's not supposed to crawl and cry.

LULA I was savin' his life. Is my skirt fastened? Today might be the last time I ever see Nelson. *(*NELSON *goes back in house.)* Tell him how life's gon' be better when he gets back. Make up what *should* be true. A man can't fight a war on nothin' . . . would you send a man off—to die on nothin'?

JULIA That's sin, Miss Lula, leavin' on a lie.

LULA That's all right—some truth has no nourishment in it. Let him feel good.

JULIA I'll do my best.

*(*MATTIE *enters carrying a colorful, expensive parasol. It is far beyond the price range of her outfit.)*

MATTIE October bought it for my birthday 'cause he know I always wanted a fine-quality parasol.

*(*FANNY *enters through the back entry,* CHILDREN *with her. The mistake on the sign has been corrected by pasting OU over the error.)*

FANNY *(Admiring* MATTIE*'s appearance.)* Just shows how the race can look when we wanta. I called Rusty Bennet a dumb darky and he wouldn't even get mad. Wouldn't gimme my money back either. A black Jew. *(*NELSON *enters wearing his Private's uniform with quartermaster insignia. He salutes them.)*

NELSON Ladies. Was nice seein' you these few days. If I couldn't help, 'least I didn't do you no harm, so nothin' from nothin' leaves nothin'.

FANNY *(Holds up her punch cup;* LULA *gives* JULIA *high sign.)* Get one-a them Germans for me.

JULIA *(Stands on her porch.)* Soon, Nelson, in a little while . . . we'll have whatsoever our hearts desire. You're comin' back in glory . . . with honors and shining medals . . . And those medals and that uniform is gonna open doors for you . . . and for October . . . for all, all of the servicemen. Nelson, on account-a you we're gonna be able to go in the park. They're gonna take down the no-colored signs . . . and Rusty Bennet's gonna print new ones . . . Everybody welcome . . . Everybody welcome . . .

MATTIE *(To* TEETA.*)* Hear that? We gon' go in the park.

FANNY Some of us ain't ready for that.

PRINCESS Me too?

MATTIE You can go now . . . and me too if I got you by the hand.

PRINCESS *(Feeling left out.)* Ohhhhh.

JULIA We'll go to the band concerts, the museums . . . we'll go in the library and draw out books.

MATTIE And we'll draw books.

FANNY Who'll read 'em to you?

MATTIE My Teeta!

JULIA Your life'll be safe, you and October'll be heroes.

FANNY *(Very moved.)* Colored heroes.

JULIA And at last we'll come into our own.

*(*ALL *cheer and applaud.* JULIA *steps down from porch.)*

NELSON Julia, can you look me dead in the eye and say you believe all-a that?

JULIA If you just gotta believe somethin', it may's well be that. *(Applause.)*

NELSON *(Steps up on* JULIA*'s porch to make his speech.)* Friends, relatives and all other well-wishers. All-a my fine ladies and little ladies—all you good-lookin', tantalizin', pretty-eyed ladies—yeah, with your *kind* ways and your *mean* ways. I find myself a thorn among six lovely roses. Sweet little Teeta . . . the merry little Princess. Mattie, she so pretty 'til October better hurry up and come on back here. Fanny—uh—tryin' to help the race . . . a race woman. And Julia—my good friend. Mama—the only mama I got, I wanta thank you for savin' my life from time to time. What's hard ain't the goin', it's the comin' back. From the bottom-a my heart, I'd truly like to see y'all, each and every one-a you . . . able to go in the park and all that. I really would. So, with a full heart and a loaded mind, I bid you, as the French say, Adieu.

LULA *(Bowing graciously, she takes* NELSON*'s arm and they exit.)* Our humble thanks . . . my humble pleasure . . . gratitude . . . thank you . . .

*(*CHILDREN *wave their flags.)*

FANNY *(To the* CHILDREN.*)* Let's mind our manners in front-a the downtown white people. Remember we're bein' judged.

PRINCESS Me too?

MATTIE *(Opening umbrella.)* Yes, you too.

FANNY *(Leads the way and counts time.)* Step, step, one, two, step, step.

*(*MATTIE, FANNY *and the* CHILDREN *exit.* HERMAN *enters yard by far gate, takes two long steamer tickets from his pocket.* JULIA *senses him, turns. He is carelessly dressed and sweating.)*

HERMAN I bought our tickets. Boat tickets to New York.

JULIA *(Looks at tickets.)* Colored tickets. You can't use yours. *(She lets tickets flutter to the ground.)*

HERMAN They'll change and give one white ticket. You'll ride one deck, I'll ride the other . . .

JULIA John C. Calhoun really said a mouthful—men are not born—men are made. Ten years ago—that's when you should-a bought tickets. You chained me to your mother for ten years.

HERMAN *(Kneeling, picking up tickets.)* Could I walk out on 'em? . . . Ker-ist sake. I'm that kinda man like my father was . . . a debt-payer, a plain, workin' man—

JULIA He was a member in good standin' of The Gold Carnation. What kinda robes and hoods did those plain men wear? For downin' me and mine. You won twenty dollars in gold.

HERMAN I love you . . . I love work, to come home in the evenin' . . . to enjoy the breeze for Gawd's sake . . . But no, I never wanted to go to New York. The hell with Goddamm bread factories . . . I'm a stony-broke, half-dead, half-way gentleman . . . But I'm what I wanta be. A baker.

JULIA You waited 'til you was half-dead to buy those tickets. I don't want to go either . . . Get off the boat, the same faces'll be there at the dock. It's that shop. It's that shop!

HERMAN It's mine. I did want to keep it.

JULIA Right . . . people pick what they want most.

HERMAN *(Indicating the tickets.)* I did . . . you threw it in my face.

JULIA Get out. Get your things and get out of my life. *(The remarks become counterpoint. Each rides through the other's speech.* HERMAN *goes in house.)* Must be fine to *own* somethin'—even if it's four walls and a sack-a flour.

HERMAN *(*JULIA *has followed him into the house.)* My father labored in the street . . . liftin' and layin' down cobblestone . . . liftin' and layin' down stone 'til there was enough money to open a shop . . .

JULIA My people . . . relatives, friends and strangers . . . they worked and slaved free for nothin' for some-a the biggest name families down here . . . Elliots, Lawrences, Ravenals . . .

(HERMAN *is wearily gathering his belongings.)*

HERMAN Great honor, working for the biggest name families. That's who you slaved for. Not me. The big names.

JULIA . . . the rich and the poor . . . we know you . . . all of you . . . Who you are . . . where you came from . . . where you goin' . . .

HERMAN What's my privilege . . . Good mornin', good afternoon . . . pies are ten cents today . . . and you can get 'em from Schumann for eight . . .

JULIA "She's different" . . . I'm no different . . .

HERMAN I'm white . . . did it give me favors and friends?

JULIA . . . "Not like the others" . . . We raised up all-a these Carolina children . . . white and the black . . . I'm just like all the rest of the colored women . . . like Lula, Mattie . . . Yes, like Fanny!

HERMAN Go here, go there . . . Philadelphia . . . New York . . . Schumann wants me to go North too . . .

JULIA We nursed you, fed you, buried your dead . . . grinned in your face—cried 'bout your troubles—and laughed 'bout ours.

HERMAN Schumann . . . Alien robber . . . waitin' to buy me out . . . My father . . .

JULIA Pickin' up cobblestones . . . left him plenty-a time to wear bed-sheets in that Gold Carnation Society . . .

HERMAN He never hurt anybody.

JULIA He hurts me. There's no room for you to love him and me too . . . *(Sits.)* it can't be done—

HERMAN The ignorance . . . he didn't know . . . the ignorance . . . mama . . . they don't know.

JULIA But *you* know. My father was somebody. He helped put up Roper Hospital and Webster Rice Mills after the earthquake wiped the face-a this Gawd-forsaken city clean . . . a fine brick-mason he was . . . paid him one-third-a what they paid the white ones . . .

HERMAN We were poor . . . No big name, no quality.

JULIA Poor! My Gramma was a slave wash-woman bustin' suds for free! Can't get poorer than that.

HERMAN *(Trying to shut out the sound of her voice.)* Not for me, she didn't!

JULIA We the ones built the pretty white mansions . . . for free . . . the fishin' boats . . . for free . . . made your clothes, raised your food . . . for free . . . and I loved you—for free.

HERMAN A Gawd-damn lie . . . nobody did for me . . . you know it . . . you know how hard I worked—

JULIA If it's anybody's home down here it's mine . . . everything in the city is mine—why should I go anywhere . . . ground I'm standin' on—it's mine.

HERMAN *(Sitting on foot of the bed.)* It's the ignorance . . . Lemme be, lemme rest . . . Kerist sake . . . It's the ignorance . . .

JULIA After ten years you still won't look. All-a my people that's been killed . . . It's your people that killed 'em . . . all that's been in bondage—your people put 'em there—all that didn't go to school—your people kept 'em out.

HERMAN But I didn't do it. Did I do it?

JULIA They killed 'em . . . all the dead slaves . . . buried under a blanket-a this Carolina earth, even the cotton crop is nourished with hearts' blood . . . roots-a that cotton tangled and wrapped 'round my bones.

HERMAN And you blamin' me for it . . .

JULIA Yes! . . . For the one thing we never talk about . . . white folks killin' me and mine. You wouldn't let me speak.

HERMAN I never stopped you . . .

JULIA Every time I open my mouth 'bout what they do . . . you say . . . "Ker-ist, there it is again . . ." Whenever somebody was lynched . . . you 'n me would eat a very silent supper. It hurt me not to talk . . . what you don't say you swallow down . . . *(Pours wine.)*

HERMAN I was just glad to close the door 'gainst what's out there. You did all the givin' . . . I failed you in every way.

JULIA You nursed me when I was sick . . . paid my debts . . .

HERMAN I didn't give my name.

JULIA You couldn't . . . was the law . . .

HERMAN I shoulda walked 'til we came to where it'd be all right.

JULIA You never put any other woman before me.

HERMAN Only Mama, Annabelle, the customers, the law . . . the ignorance . . . I honored them while you waited and waited—

JULIA You clothed me . . . you fed me . . . you were kind, loving . . .

HERMAN I never did a damn thing for you. After ten years look at it—I never did a damn thing for you.

JULIA Don't low-rate yourself . . . leave me something.

HERMAN When my mother and sister came . . . I was ashamed. What am I doin' bein' ashamed of us?

JULIA When you first came in this yard I almost died-a shame . . . so many times you was nothin' to me but white . . . times we were angry . . . damn white man . . . times I was tired . . . damn white man . . . but most times you were my husband, my friend, my lover . . .

HERMAN Whatever is wrong, Julia . . . not the law . . . *me;* what I didn't do, with all-a my faults, spite-a all that . . . You gotta believe I love you . . . 'cause I do . . . That's the one thing I know . . . I love you . . . I love you.

JULIA Ain't too many people in this world that get to be loved . . . really loved.

HERMAN We gon' take that boat trip . . . You'll see, you'll never be sorry.

JULIA To hell with sorry. Let's be glad!

HERMAN Sweetheart, leave the ignorance outside . . . *(Stretches out across the bed.)* Don't let that doctor in here . . . to stand over me shakin' his head.

JULIA *(Pours water in a silver cup.)* Bet you never drank from a silver cup. Carolina water is sweet water . . . Wherever you go you gotta come back for a drink-a this water. Sweet water, like the breeze that blows 'cross the battery.

HERMAN *(Happily weary.)* I'm gettin' old, that ain' no joke.

JULIA No, you're not. Herman, my real weddin' cake . . . I wanta big one . . .

HERMAN Gonna bake it in a wash-tub . . .

JULIA We'll put pieces of it in little boxes for folks to take home and dream on.

HERMAN . . . But let's don't give none to your landlady . . . Gon' get old and funny-lookin' like Robbie m'boy and . . . and . . .

JULIA And Mable . . .

HERMAN *(Breathing heavier.)* Robbie says "Mable, where's my keys" . . . Mable—Robbie—Mable—

(Lights change, shadows grow longer. MATTIE *enters the yard.)*

MATTIE Hey, Julia! *(Sound of carriage wheels in front of the main house.* MATTIE *enters* JULIA*'s house. As she sees* HERMAN.*)* They 'round there, they come to get him, Julia *(*JULIA *takes the wedding band and chain from around her neck, gives it to* MATTIE *with tickets.)*

JULIA Surprise. Present.

MATTIE For me?

JULIA Northern tickets . . . and a wedding band.

MATTIE I can't take that for nothing.

JULIA You and Teeta are my people.

MATTIE Yes.

JULIA You and Teeta are my family. Be my family.

MATTIE We your people whether we blood kin or not. *(*MATTIE *exits to her own porch.)*

FANNY *(Offstage.)* No . . . No, Ma'am. *(Enters with* LULA. LULA *is carrying the wilted bouquet.)* Julia! They think Mr. Herman's come back.

*(*HERMAN'S MOTHER *enters with* ANNABELLE. *The old lady is weary and subdued.* ANNABELLE *is almost without feeling.* JULIA *is on her porch waiting.)*

JULIA Yes, Fanny, he's here. (LULA *retires to her doorway.* JULIA *silently stares at them, studying each* WOMAN, *seeing them with new eyes. She is going through that rising process wherein she must reject them as the molders and dictators of her life.*) Nobody comes in my house.

FANNY What kind-a way is that?

JULIA Nobody comes in my house.

ANNABELLE We'll quietly take him home.

JULIA You can't come in.

HERMAN'S MOTHER (*Low-keyed, polite and humble simplicity.*) You see my condition. Gawd's punishin' me . . . Whippin' me for somethin' I did or didn't do. I can't understand this . . . I prayed, but ain't no understandin' Herman's dyin'. He's almost gone. It's right and proper that he should die at home in his own bed. I'm askin' humbly . . . or else I'm forced to get help from the police.

ANNABELLE Give her a chance . . . She'll do right . . . won'tcha?

(HERMAN *stirs. His breathing becomes harsh and deepens into the sound known as the "death rattle."* MATTIE *leads the* CHILDREN *away.*)

JULIA (*Not unkindly.*) Do whatever you have to do. Win the war. Represent the race. Call the police. (*She enters her house, closes the door and bolts it.* HERMAN'S MOTHER *leaves through the front entry.* FANNY *slowly follows her.*) I'm here, do you hear me? (*He tries to answer but can't.*) We're standin' on the deck-a that Clyde Line Boat . . . wavin' to the people on the shore . . . Your mama, Annabelle, my Aunt Cora . . . all of our friends . . . the children . . . all wavin' . . . "Don't stay 'way too long . . . Be sure and come back . . . We gon' miss you . . . Come back, we need you" . . . But we're goin' . . . The whistle's blowin', flags wavin' . . . We're takin' off, ridin' the waves so smooth and easy . . . There now . . . (ANNABELLE *moves closer to the house as she listens to* JULIA.) . . . the bakery's fine . . . all the orders are ready . . . out to sea . . . on our way . . . (*The weight has lifted, she is radiantly happy. She helps him gasp out each remaining breath. With each gasp he seems to draw a step nearer to a wonderful goal.*) Yes . . . Yes . . . Yes . . . Yes . . . Yes . . . Yes . . .

Curtain

LORRAINE HANSBERRY

(1930–1965)

Lorraine Hansberry marks the evolution from the age of racial integration to that of Black Arts. Her plays, in other words, bridge the accommodationist fifties and the more radical sixties. Based on her award-winning play *A Raisin in the Sun* (1959), she has been all too conveniently stereotyped as a major playwright of the American dream. Her mercurial ideologies almost always vacillate between a black nationalism that she could never really accept and a liberal idealism that she almost always distrusted. She was the right talent from the right middle class at the right time. By the time the curtain would fall on *A Raisin in the Sun*, she would be the only black writer under thirty years old acclaimed by the American mainstream.

Lorraine Hansberry exuded the incorrigible optimism of the fifties. Certainly since then, history has disproved the dubious hope of so passionately pursuing racial integration without precise assurances of intercultural terms, of seeking to preserve authentic values of what it means to be black in America and human in the greater world. Hansberry never lived to see the premises through to their logical conclusions. At age thirty-four, she died of cancer. Except for *Raisin*, her historical, experimental, and even radical tone ranges from a script on slavery, titled *The Drinking*

Gourd for NBC television in 1960, through an inquiry into the privileged life of fortunate whites (*The Sign in Sidney Brustein's Window,* 1964) to a presentation of Pan-African liberation in *Les Blancs* (1972). As related in the adapted autobiography, *To Be Young, Gifted, and Black* (1969), she brought a dramatic flair to the racial confusion of the time. Once she assured a young intellectual in her Greenwich Village living room—one whom she kept anonymous—: "I wish to live because life has within it that which is good, that which is beautiful, and that which is love. Therefore, since I have known all of these things, I have found them to be reason enough and—I wish to live. Moreover, because this is so, I wish others to live for generations and generations and generations and generations."

Elsewhere, she narrates her personal story as an example of the time. Born on the South Side of Chicago, she grew up as a young black female in the Depression. During her teens, the first nuclear weapons were dropped on Hiroshima and Nagasaki, Japan. When she came of age, the country was fearfully engaged with the former Soviet Union in the nuclear détente known as the Cold War. Her heart in *To Be Young*[1] was with those who were coming to believe in space travel: "I think that the human race does command its own destiny and that destiny can eventually embrace the stars." In the end, she was most certainly self-consciously and properly middle class. The arty gestures of her aloofness recalled Jean Toomer and Nella Larsen from the Harlem Renaissance, while her far more volatile inclinations toward racial community looked forward, on the contrary, to Amiri Baraka and Sonia Sanchez. Almost no African American writer, including the early and late Baraka, reveals a greater tension between an integrationist imperative and a black aesthetics rooted in the folk masses. Often Hansberry represents a missing link within African American literary and cultural tradition.

Lorraine Vivian Hansberry, the youngest of four children, was born in Chicago on May 19, 1930, to Carl A. Hansberry and Nanny Perry Hansberry. She ignored the family tradition of going to Howard University and instead attended the University of Wisconsin. Unimpressed by her classes, she left school in 1950 to seek in New York an "education of a different kind." She began work with *Freedom*, the radical newspaper of Paul Robeson, as a book reviewer of plays. In 1952, she became associate editor of the newspaper. Today she would be considered a political activist. She marched on picket lines and gave speeches on Harlem street corners to whomever would listen. In 1952, she served as a representative to the Intercontinental Peace Congress in Montevideo, Uruguay, when Robeson was denied a passport because of his leftist ideas. There she met with many women from other countries with whom she compared experiences. Eventually, her commentary would take the form of the essay "Simone de Beauvoir and *The Second Sex:* An American Commentary, 1957." In 1953, Hansberry married Robert Nemiroff, an aspiring writer who was a graduate student in History and English at New York University. They had met on a picket line and on their wedding night took part in a demonstration to save Julius and Ethel Rosenberg from execution for treason. The same year, she resigned from *Freedom* to concentrate on her writing. From then until 1956, she revised three plays while working at a series of jobs, including those as a tag inserter and an assistant in a theatrical firm. At times a writer for *Sing Out* magazine, she also worked in recreation at the Federation for the Handicapped. During this time, she sought to com-

[1]In the body of this title, the author refers only to the adapted autobiography by this title.

plete a novel, several plays, and an opera. By the time of the Beauvoir article, she had begun to focus on one play that was originally titled *The Crystal Stair,* which alludes to "The Mother," a famous dramatic monologue written by Langston Hughes. The cryptic poem "Harlem," also by Hughes, eventually became the source for her final title: "What happens to a dream deferred? Does it dry up like a raisin in the sun . . . or does it *explode?*"

A Raisin in the Sun (1959) was performed on Broadway two years after the racial integration of the public schools in Little Rock, Arkansas. With an enthusiastic response from Nemiroff, Hansberry read the manuscript to friends Bert D'Lugoff and Philip Rose. Rose said that he wanted to produce the play on Broadway. Subsequently, he secured many investors to support the production of the drama. Rose sent a copy of the script to Sidney Poitier, who had performed in several movies and who seemed appropriate for the part of Walter Lee Younger, the male lead. When Poitier accepted the part, he proposed Lloyd Richards, his former professor, as director and Richards became the first black director on Broadway. Then Rose brought together the rest of the now famous cast: Ruby Dee, Louis Gossett, Ivan Dixon, Diana Sands, Claudia McNeil, Glynn Turman, Lonne Elder III, Douglas Turner, and Ossie Davis, who would become a replacement for Poitier. Much of the historical importance of *Raisin* emerges not only from its literary importance but also from the tremendous opportunity provided by the play for the flowering of African American talent in the theater.

A Raisin in the Sun opened at the Ethel Barrymore Theatre on March 11, 1959, and prompted favorable responses from the most respected newspapers in New York. With a run of 538 consecutive performances, it was voted the best play of the year by the New York Drama Critics Circle over Tennessee Williams's *Sweet Bird of Youth,* Archibald MacLeish's *JB,* and Eugene O'Neill's *A Touch of the Poet.* Eventually, *Raisin* would be the basis for a film in 1961 and a musical in 1973. By then, the convenient stereotyping of Hansberry as an assimilationist artist would be firmly in place. Ann Robertson, writing for the *New York Times,* misrepresented her by saying, "It [*Raisin*] was a play about honest-to God-believable, many-sided people who happened to be Negroes," prompting Hansberry's retort in *Vogue Magazine* for June, 1959, that *Raisin,* the story of a black family integrating a white Chicago suburb, is "definitely a Negro play before it's anything else."

We know today that Hansberry had originally written another act in which whites attack the Younger family in the new neighborhood. Lena, the compassionate matriarch in the play, paces the house at night with a loaded shotgun, as Hansberry's own mother had done with a German luger in 1938. In those days, the fight of Hansberry's father against restrictive convenants in Chicago had forced the family to occupy a disputed property in a white neighborhood. Hostile mobs had surrounded the house, and in one instance young Lorraine might have been killed. In her daily trek to school, she, like the widely photographed children at Little Rock, was spat at and cursed. In a letter to her mother, on January 19, 1959, she wrote that African Americans have "among our miserable and downtrodden ranks . . . people who are the very essence of human dignity."

In 1960, Dore Schary contracted Hansberry to write a drama about slavery to be produced on NBC as the first in a series of dramas by leading playwrights, the purpose of which was to commemorate the centennial of the Civil War. Hansberry had permission to be as frank as she thought appropriate. Eventually, the series was canceled. She finished the play titled *The Drinking Gourd* (1960), however, and it was published posthumously in 1972. Although the drama has yet to be produced for television, a few scenes from it did appear in the PBS documentary *To Be Young, Gifted, and Black* (January 1972).

Was Lorraine Hansberry an integrationist or a black nationalist? On May 24, 1963, she was one of several blacks and a few whites to meet with Attorney General Robert Kennedy to discuss racial strife.

Obviously, the "integrationist" Hansberry was out on break: "What we are interested in is in making perfectly clear that between the Negro intelligentsia, the Negro middle class, and the Negro this—and that—we are one people. And that as far as we are concerned, we are represented by the Negroes in the streets of Birmingham." She voiced concern not for endangered blacks who had "done splendidly . . . all things considered," but for the "state of the civilization which produced that photograph of the white cop standing on the Negro woman's neck in Birmingham." The following year, Hansberry brought out *The Movement: Documentary of a Struggle for Equality* (1904), a book with pictures of dilapidated buildings and brutalized demonstrators. She also divorced Nemiroff, with whom she would continue to meet daily until her death. She received radiation treatments and chemotherapy during her revisions on *The Sign in Sidney Brustein's Window* (1964) and *Les Blancs* (1970), and an unfinished play about the eighteenth-century white feminist Mary Wollstonecraft. On May 1, she was released from the hospital to address the winners of the United Negro College Fund writing contest and voiced her vision of what it meant to be "young, gifted, and black." And she might have added "lesbian."

Hansberry was probably the most persistent and discerning African American writer since Richard Wright to critique the flaws of white liberalism. She proposed that American liberals would have to be radicalized, yet preferred the white nineteenth-century abolitionist John Brown to the contemporary, black African dictator Moise Tshombe. She argued for the importance of race and against the significance of race. She urged blacks to "tell the story of our people," yet nearly chortled, "We have a very great tradition of white radicalism in the United States." She was a very complex young woman who in her shining moments presented a black pride worthy of our greatest literary artists. She was an African American feminist ahead of her time, who proposed to write about the world not only as it is but as it should be. She insisted that the African American literary artist must "*write to a point* . . . work hard at it, *care* about it." In her own searching way, she prepared for the era of the Black Arts Movement.

❖❖❖

All of the personal quotations appear from *To Be Young, Gifted, and Black: Lorraine Hansberry in Her Own Words,* adapted by her surviving husband Robert Nemiroff (Englewood Cliffs, N.J.: Prentice-Hall, 1969), not to be confused with the play and television productions by the same title, respectively, in 1969 and January 1972. See Studs Terkel, "An Interview with Lorraine Hansberry," WFMT, *Chicago Fine Arts Guide,* 10 (April 1961), a pioneering exchange. Steven R. Carter, *Hansberry's Drama: Commitment and Complexity* (Urbana: University of Illinois Press, 1991), has detailed the most biographical information about Hansberry. In 1979, *Freedomways* dedicated an entire issue to her life and work. Harold Cruse writes in *The Crisis of the Negro Intellectual* (New York: Morrow, 1967) that she was an overrated, middle-class dramatist. Margaret Wilkerson, in "The Dark Vision of Lorraine

Hansberry," *Massachusetts Review,* 28, No. 4 (Winter 1987), continues to publish definitive work. Probing insights into Hansberry's literary strategies and complex psyche need to be written.

A Raisin in the Sun

A Raisin in the Sun *was first presented by Philip Rose and David J. Cogan at the Ethel Barrymore Theatre, New York City, March 11, 1959, with the following cast:*

(In order of appearance)

Characters

RUTH YOUNGER, Ruby Dee

TRAVIS YOUNGER, Glynn Turman

WALTER LEE YOUNGER (BROTHER), Sidney Poitier

BENEATHA YOUNGER, Diana Sands

LENA YOUNGER (MAMA), Claudia McNeil

JOSEPH ASAGAI, Ivan Dixon

GEORGE MURCHISON, Louis Gossett

KARL LINDNER, John Fiedler

BOBO, Lonne Elder III

MOVING MEN, Ed Hall, Douglas Turner

Directed by Lloyd Richards

Designed and lighted by Ralph Alswang

Costumes by Virginia Volland

WHAT HAPPENS TO A DREAM DEFERRED?
DOES IT DRY UP
LIKE A RAISIN IN THE SUN?
OR FESTER LIKE A SORE—
AND THEN RUN?
DOES IT STINK LIKE ROTTEN MEAT?
OR CRUST AND SUGAR OVER—
LIKE A SYRUPY SWEET?

MAYBE IT JUST SAGS
LIKE A HEAVY LOAD.

OR DOES IT EXPLODE?

—LANGSTON HUGHES

Act One

SCENE ONE

The YOUNGER *living room would be a comfortable and well-ordered room if it were not for a number of indestructible contradictions to this state of being. Its furnishings are typical and undistinguished and their primary feature now is that they have clearly had to accommodate the living of too many people for too many years—and they are tired. Still, we can see that at some time, a time probably no longer remembered by the family (except perhaps for* MAMA*), the furnishings of this room were actually selected with care and love and even hope—and brought to this apartment and arranged with taste and pride.*

That was a long time ago. Now the once loved pattern of the couch upholstery has to fight to show itself from under acres of crocheted doilies and couch covers which have themselves finally come to be more important than the upholstery. And here a table or a chair has been moved to disguise the worn places in the carpet; but the carpet has fought back by showing its weariness, with depressing uniformity, elsewhere on its surface.

Weariness has, in fact, won in this room. Everything has been polished, washed, sat on, used, scrubbed too often. All pretenses but living itself have long since vanished from the very atmosphere of this room.

Moreover, a section of this room, for it is not really a room unto itself, though the landlord's lease would make it seem so, slopes backward to provide a small kitchen area, where the family prepares the meals that are eaten in the living room proper, which must also serve as dining room. The single window that has been provided for these "two" rooms is located in this kitchen area. The sole natural light the family may enjoy in the course of a day is only that which fights its way through this little window.

At left, a door leads to a bedroom which is shared by MAMA *and her daughter,* BENEATHA. *At right, opposite, is a second room (which in the beginning of the life of this apartment was probably a breakfast room) which serves as a bedroom for* WALTER *and his wife,* RUTH.

TIME: Sometime between World War II and the present.

PLACE: Chicago's Southside.

AT RISE: It is morning dark in the living room. TRAVIS *is asleep on the make-down bed at center. An alarm clock sounds from within the bedroom at right, and presently* RUTH *enters from that room and closes the door behind her. She crosses sleepily toward the window. As she passes her sleeping son she reaches down and shakes him a little. At the window she raises the shade and a dusky Southside morning light comes in feebly. She fills a pot with water and puts it on to boil. She calls to the boy, between yawns, in a slightly muffled voice.*

RUTH *is about thirty. We can see that she was a pretty girl, even exceptionally so, but now it is apparent that life has been little that she expected, and disappointment has already begun to hang in her face. In a few years, before thirty-five even, she will be known among her people as a "settled woman."*

She crosses to her son and gives him a good, final, rousing shake.

RUTH Come on now, boy, it's seven thirty! *(Her son sits up at last, in a stupor of sleepiness)* I say hurry up, Travis! You ain't the only person in the world got to use the bathroom! *(The child, a sturdy, handsome little boy of ten or eleven, drags himself out of the bed and almost blindly takes his towels and "today's clothes" from drawers and a closet and goes out to the bathroom, which is in an outside hall and which is shared by another family or families on the same floor.* RUTH *crosses to the bedroom door at right and opens it and calls in to her husband)* Walter Lee! . . . It's after seven thirty! Lemme see you do some waking up in there now! *(She waits)* You better get up from there, man! It's after seven thirty I tell you. *(She waits again)* All right, you just go ahead and lay there and next thing you know Travis be finished and Mr. Johnson'll be in there and you'll be fussing and cussing round here like a madman! And be late too! *(She waits, at the end of patience)* Walter Lee—it's time for you to GET UP!

(She waits another second and then starts to go into the bedroom, but is apparently satisfied that her husband has begun to get up. She stops, pulls the door to, and returns to the kitchen area. She wipes her face with a moist cloth and runs her fingers through her sleep-disheveled hair in a vain effort and ties an apron around her housecoat. The bedroom door at right opens and her husband stands in the doorway in his pajamas, which are rumpled and mismated. He is a lean, intense young man in his middle thirties, inclined to quick nervous movements and erratic speech habits—and always in his voice there is a quality of indictment)

WALTER Is he out yet?

RUTH What you mean *out*? He ain't hardly got in there good yet.

WALTER *(Wandering in, still more oriented to sleep than to a new day)* Well, what was you doing all that yelling for if I can't even get in there yet? *(Stopping and thinking)* Check coming today?

RUTH They *said* Saturday and this is just Friday and I hopes to God you ain't going to get up here first thing this morning and start talking to me 'bout no money—'cause I 'bout don't want to hear it.

WALTER Something the matter with you this morning?

RUTH No—I'm just sleepy as the devil. What kind of eggs you want?

WALTER Not scrambled. *(*RUTH *starts to scramble eggs)* Paper come? *(*RUTH *points impatiently to the rolled up* Tribune *on the table, and he gets it and spreads it out and vaguely reads the front page)* Set off another bomb yesterday.

RUTH *(Maximum indifference)* Did they?

WALTER *(Looking up)* What's the matter with you?

RUTH Ain't nothing the matter with me. And don't keep asking me that this morning.

WALTER Ain't nobody bothering you. *(Reading the news of the day absently again)* Say Colonel McCormick is sick.

RUTH *(Affecting tea-party interest)* Is he now? Poor thing.

WALTER *(Sighing and looking at his watch)* Oh, me. *(He waits)* Now what is that boy doing in that bathroom all this time? He just going to have to start getting up earlier. I can't be being late to work on account of him fooling around in there.

RUTH *(Turning on him)* Oh, no he ain't going to be getting up no earlier no such thing! It ain't his fault that he can't get to bed no earlier nights 'cause he got a bunch of crazy good-for-nothing clowns sitting up running their mouths in what is supposed to be his bedroom after ten o'clock at night . . .

WALTER That's what you mad about, ain't it? The things I want to talk about with my friends just couldn't be important in your mind, could they?

(He rises and finds a cigarette in her handbag on the table and crosses to the little window and looks out, smoking and deeply enjoying this first one)

RUTH *(Almost matter of factly, a complaint too automatic to deserve emphasis)* Why you always got to smoke before you eat in the morning?

WALTER *(At the window)* Just look at 'em down there . . . Running and racing to work . . . *(He turns and faces his wife and watches her a moment at the stove, and then, suddenly)* You look young this morning, baby.

RUTH *(Indifferently)* Yeah?

WALTER Just for a second—stirring them eggs. Just for a second it was—you looked real young again. *(He reaches for her; she crosses away. Then, drily)* It's gone now—you look like yourself again!

RUTH Man, if you don't shut up and leave me alone.

WALTER *(Looking out to the street again)* First thing a man ought to learn in life is not to make love to no colored woman first thing in the morning. You all some eeeevil people at eight o'clock in the morning.

*(*TRAVIS *appears in the hall doorway, almost fully dressed and quite wide awake now, his towels and pajamas across his shoulders. He opens the door and signals for his father to make the bathroom in a hurry)*

TRAVIS *(Watching the bathroom)* Daddy, come on!

*(*WALTER *gets his bathroom utensils and flies out to the bathroom)*

RUTH Sit down and have your breakfast, Travis.

TRAVIS Mama, this is Friday. *(Gleefully)* Check coming tomorrow, huh?

RUTH You get your mind off money and eat your breakfast.

TRAVIS *(Eating)* This is the morning we supposed to bring the fifty cents to school.

RUTH Well, I ain't got no fifty cents this morning.

TRAVIS Teacher say we have to.

RUTH I don't care what teacher say. I ain't got it. Eat your breakfast, Travis.

TRAVIS I *am* eating.

RUTH Hush up now and just eat!

(The boy gives her an exasperated look for her lack of understanding, and eats grudgingly)

TRAVIS You think Grandmama would have it?

RUTH No! And I want you to stop asking your grandmother for money, you hear me?

TRAVIS *(Outraged)* Gaaaleee! I don't ask her, she just gimme it sometimes!

RUTH Travis Willard Younger—I got too much on me this morning to be—

TRAVIS Maybe Daddy—

RUTH *Travis!*

(The boy hushes abruptly. They are both quiet and tense for several seconds)

TRAVIS *(Presently)* Could I maybe go carry some groceries in front of the supermarket for a little while after school then?

RUTH Just hush, I said. *(*TRAVIS *jabs his spoon into his cereal bowl viciously, and rests his head in anger upon his fists)* If you through eating, you can get over there and make up your bed.

*(The boy obeys stiffly and crosses the room, almost mechanically, to the bed and more or less

folds the bedding into a heap, then angrily gets his books and cap)

TRAVIS *(Sulking and standing apart from her unnaturally)* I'm gone.

RUTH *(Looking up from the stove to inspect him automatically)* Come here. *(He crosses to her and she studies his head)* If you don't take this comb and fix this here head, you better! *(*TRAVIS *puts down his books with a great sigh of oppression, and crosses to the mirror. His mother mutters under her breath about his "slubbornness")* 'Bout to march out of here with that head looking just like chickens slept in it! I just don't know where you get your slubborn ways . . . And get your jacket, too. Looks chilly out this morning.

TRAVIS *(With conspicuously brushed hair and jacket)* I'm gone.

RUTH Get carfare and milk money—*(Waving one finger)*—and not a single penny for no caps, you hear me?

TRAVIS *(With sullen politeness)* Yes'm.

(He turns in outrage to leave. His mother watches after him as in his frustration he approaches the door almost comically. When she speaks to him, her voice has become a very gentle tease)

RUTH *(Mocking; as she thinks he would say it)* Oh, Mama makes me so mad sometimes, I don't know what to do! *(She waits and continues to his back as he stands stock-still in front of the door)* I wouldn't kiss that woman good-bye for nothing in this world this morning! *(The boy finally turns around and rolls his eyes at her, knowing the mood has changed and he is vindicated; he does not, however, move toward her yet)* Not for nothing in this world! *(She finally laughs aloud at him and holds out her arms to him and we see that it is a way between them, very old and practiced. He crosses to her and allows her to embrace him warmly but keeps his face fixed with masculine rigidity. She holds him back from her presently and looks at him and runs her fingers over the features of his face. With utter gentleness—)* Now—whose little old angry man are you?

TRAVIS *(The masculinity and gruffness start to fade at last)* Aw gaalee—Mama . . .

RUTH *(Mimicking)* Aw—gaaaaalleeeee, Mama! *(She pushes him, with rough playfulness and finality, toward the door)* Get on out of here or you going to be late.

TRAVIS *(In the face of love, new aggressiveness)* Mama, could I *please* go carry groceries?

RUTH Honey, it's starting to get so cold evenings.

WALTER *(Coming in from the bathroom and drawing a make-believe gun from a make-believe holster and shooting at his son)* What is it he wants to do?

RUTH Go carry groceries after school at the supermarket.

WALTER Well, let him go . . .

TRAVIS *(Quickly, to the ally)* I *have* to—she won't gimme the fifty cents . . .

WALTER *(To his wife only)* Why not?

RUTH *(Simply, and with flavor)* 'Cause we don't have it.

WALTER *(To* RUTH *only)* What you tell the boy things like that for? *(Reaching down into his pants with a rather important gesture)* Here, son—

(He hands the boy the coin, but his eyes are directed to his wife's. TRAVIS *takes the money happily)*

TRAVIS Thanks, Daddy.

(He starts out. RUTH *watches both of them with murder in her eyes.* WALTER *stands and stares back at her with defiance, and suddenly reaches into his pocket again on an afterthought)*

WALTER *(Without even looking at his son, still staring hard at his wife)* In fact, here's another fifty cents . . . Buy yourself some fruit today—or take a taxicab to school or something!

TRAVIS Whoopee—

(He leaps up and clasps his father around the middle with his legs, and they face each other in mutual appreciation; slowly WALTER LEE *peeks*

around the boys to catch the violent rays from his wife's eyes and draws his head back as if shot)

WALTER You better get down now—and get to school, man.

TRAVIS *(At the door)* O.K. Good-bye.

(He exits)

WALTER *(After him, pointing with pride)* That's *my* boy. *(She looks at him in disgust and turns back to her work)* You know what I was thinking 'bout in the bathroom this morning?

RUTH No.

WALTER How come you always try to be so pleasant!

RUTH What is there to be pleasant 'bout!

WALTER You want to know what I was thinking 'bout in the bathroom or not!

RUTH I know what you thinking 'bout.

WALTER *(Ignoring her)* 'Bout what me and Willy Harris was talking about last night.

RUTH *(Immediately—a refrain)* Willy Harris is a good-for-nothing loudmouth.

WALTER Anybody who talks to me has got to be a good-for-nothing loudmouth, ain't he? And what you know about who is just a good-for-nothing loudmouth? Charlie Atkins was just a "good-for-nothing loudmouth" too, wasn't he! When he wanted me to go in the dry-cleaning business with him. And now—he's grossing a hundred thousand a year. A hundred thousand dollars a year! You still call *him* a loudmouth!

RUTH *(Bitterly)* Oh, Walter Lee . . .

(She folds her head on her arms over the table)

WALTER *(Rising and coming to her and standing over her)* You tired, ain't you? Tired of everything. Me, the boy, the way we live—this beat-up hole—everything. Ain't you? *(She doesn't look up, doesn't answer)* So tired—moaning and groaning all the time, but you wouldn't do nothing to help, would you? You couldn't be on my side that long for nothing, could you?

RUTH Walter, please leave me alone.

WALTER A man needs for a woman to back him up . . .

RUTH Walter—

WALTER Mama would listen to you. You know she listen to you more than she do me and Bennie. She think more of you. All you have to do is just sit down with her when you drinking your coffee one morning and talking 'bout things like you do and—*(He sits down beside her and demonstrates graphically what he thinks her methods and tone should be)*—you just sip your coffee, see, and say easy like that you been thinking 'bout that deal Walter Lee is so interested in, 'bout the store and all, and sip some more coffee, like what you saying ain't really that important to you— And the next thing you know, she be listening good and asking you questions and when I come home—I can tell her the details. This ain't no fly-by-night proposition, baby. I mean we figured it out, me and Willy and Bobo.

RUTH *(With a frown)* Bobo?

WALTER Yeah. You see, this little liquor store we got in mind cost seventy-five thousand and we figured the initial investment on the place be 'bout thirty thousand, see. That be ten thousand each. Course, there's a couple of hundred you got to pay so's you don't spend your life just waiting for them clowns to let your license get approved—

RUTH You mean graft?

WALTER *(Frowning impatiently)* Don't call it that. See there, that just goes to show you what women understand about the world. Baby, don't *nothing* happen for you in this world 'less you pay *somebody* off!

RUTH Walter, leave me alone! *(She raises her head and stares at him vigorously—then says, more quietly)* Eat your eggs, they gonna be cold.

WALTER *(Straightening up from her and looking off)* That's it. There you are. Man say to his woman: I got me a dream. His woman say: Eat your eggs. *(Sadly, but gaining in power)* Man say: I got to take hold of this here world, baby! And a woman will say: Eat your eggs and go to work. *(Passionately now)* Man say: I got to change my life, I'm choking to death, baby! And his woman say—*(In utter anguish as he brings his fists down on his thighs)*—Your eggs is getting cold!

RUTH *(Softly)* Walter, that ain't none of our money.

WALTER *(Not listening at all or even looking at her)* This morning, I was lookin' in the mirror and thinking about it . . . I'm thirty-five years old; I been married eleven years and I got a boy who sleeps in the living room—*(Very, very quietly)*—and all I got to give him is stories about how rich white people live . . .

RUTH Eat your eggs, Walter.

WALTER *(Slams the table and jumps up)*—DAMN MY EGGS—DAMN ALL THE EGGS THAT EVER WAS!

RUTH Then go to work.

WALTER *(Looking up at her)* See—I'm trying to talk to you 'bout myself—*(Shaking his head with the repetition)*—and all you can say is eat them eggs and go to work.

RUTH *(Wearily)* Honey, you never say nothing new. I listen to you every day, every night and every morning, and you never say nothing new. *(Shrugging)* So you would rather *be* Mr. Arnold than be his chauffeur. So—I would *rather* be living in Buckingham Palace.

WALTER That is just what is wrong with the colored woman in this world . . . Don't understand about building their men up and making 'em feel like they somebody. Like they can do something.

RUTH *(Drily, but to hurt)* There *are* colored men who do things.

WALTER No thanks to the colored woman.

RUTH Well, being a colored woman, I guess I can't help myself none.

(She rises and gets the ironing board and sets it up and attacks a huge pile of rough-dried clothes, sprinkling them in preparation for the ironing and then rolling them into tight fat balls)

WALTER *(Mumbling)* We one group of men tied to a race of women with small minds!

(His sister BENEATHA *enters. She is about twenty, as slim and intense as her brother. She is not as pretty as her sister-in-law, but her lean, almost intellectual face has a handsomeness of its own. She wears a bright-red flannel nightie, and her thick hair stands wildly about her head. Her speech is a mixture of many things; it is different from the rest of the family's insofar as education has permeated her sense of English—and perhaps the Midwest rather than the South has finally—at last—won out in her inflection; but not altogether, because over all of it is a soft slurring and transformed use of vowels which is the decided influence of the Southside. She passes through the room without looking at either* RUTH *or* WALTER *and goes to the outside door and looks, a little blindly, out to the bathroom. She sees that it has been lost to the Johnsons. She closes the door with a sleepy vengeance and crosses to the table and sits down a little defeated)*

BENEATHA I am going to start timing those people.

WALTER You should get up earlier.

BENEATHA *(Her face in her hands. She is still fighting the urge to go back to bed)* Really—would you suggest dawn? Where's the paper?

WALTER *(Pushing the paper across the table to her as he studies her almost clinically, as though he has never seen her before)* You a horrible-looking chick at this hour.

BENEATHA *(Drily)* Good morning, everybody.

WALTER *(Senselessly)* How is school coming?

BENEATHA *(In the same spirit)* Lovely. Lovely. And you know, biology is the greatest. *(Looking up at him)* I dissected something that looked just like you yesterday.

WALTER I just wondered if you've made up your mind and everything.

BENEATHA *(Gaining in sharpness and impatience)* And what did I answer yesterday morning—and the day before that?

RUTH *(From the ironing board, like someone disinterested and old)* Don't be so nasty, Bennie.

BENEATHA *(Still to her brother)* And the day before that and the day before that!

WALTER *(Defensively)* I'm interested in you. Something wrong with that? Ain't many girls who decide—

WALTER *and* BENEATHA *(In unison)*—"to be a doctor."

(Silence)

WALTER Have we figured out yet just exactly how much medical school is going to cost?

RUTH Walter Lee, why don't you leave that girl alone and get out of here to work?

BENEATHA *(Exits to the bathroom and bangs on the door)* Come on out of there, please!

(She comes back into the room)

WALTER *(Looking at his sister intently)* You know the check is coming tomorrow.

BENEATHA *(Turning on him with a sharpness all her own)* That money belongs to Mama, Walter, and it's for her to decide how she wants to use it. I don't care if she wants to buy a house or a rocket ship or just nail it up somewhere and look at it. It's hers. Not ours—*hers.*

WALTER *(Bitterly)* Now ain't that fine! You just got your mother's interest at heart, ain't you, girl? You such a nice girl—but if Mama got that money she can always take a few thousand and help you through school too—can't she?

BENEATHA I have never asked anyone around here to do anything for me!

WALTER No! And the line between asking and just accepting when the time comes is big and wide—ain't it!

BENEATHA *(With fury)* What do you want from me, Brother—that I quit school or just drop dead, which!

WALTER I don't want nothing but for you to stop acting holy 'round here. Me and Ruth done made some sacrifices for you—why can't you do something for the family?

RUTH Walter, don't be dragging me in it.

WALTER You are in it— Don't you get up and go work in somebody's kitchen for the last three years to help put clothes on her back?

RUTH Oh, Walter—that's not fair . . .

WALTER It ain't that nobody expects you to get on your knees and say thank you, Brother; thank you, Ruth; thank you, Mama—and thank you, Travis, for wearing the same pair of shoes for two semesters—

BENEATHA *(Dropping to her knees)* Well—I *do*—all right?—thank everybody! And forgive me for ever wanting to be anything at all! *(Pursuing him on her knees across the floor)* FORGIVE ME, FORGIVE ME, FORGIVE ME!

RUTH Please stop it! Your mama'll hear you.

WALTER Who the hell told you you had to be a doctor? If you so crazy 'bout messing 'round with sick people—then go be a nurse like other women—or just get married and be quiet . . .

BENEATHA Well—you finally got it said . . . It took you three years but you finally got it said. Walter, give up; leave me alone—it's Mama's money.

WALTER *He was my father, too!*

BENEATHA So what? He was mine, too—and Travis's grandfather—but the insurance money belongs to Mama. Picking on me is not going to make her give it to you to invest in any liquor stores—*(Underbreath, dropping into a chair)*—and I for one say, God bless Mama for that!

WALTER *(To* RUTH*)* See—did you hear? Did you hear!

RUTH Honey, please go to work.

WALTER Nobody in this house is ever going to understand me.

BENEATHA Because you're a nut.

WALTER Who's a nut?

BENEATHA You—you are a nut. Thee is mad, boy.

WALTER *(Looking at his wife and his sister from the door, very sadly)* The world's most backward race of people, and that's a fact.

BENEATHA *(Turning slowly in her chair)* And then there are all those prophets who would lead us out of the wilderness—*(*WALTER *slams out of the house)*—into the swamps!

RUTH Bennie, why you always gotta be pickin' on your brother? Can't you be a little sweeter sometimes? *(Door opens.* WALTER *walks in. He fumbles with his cap, starts to speak, clears throat, looks everywhere but at* RUTH. *Finally:)*

WALTER *(To* RUTH*)* I need some money for carfare.

RUTH *(Looks at him, then warms; teasing, but tenderly)* Fifty cents? *(She goes to her bag and gets money)* Here—take a taxi!

*(*WALTER *exits.* MAMA *enters. She is a woman in her early sixties, full-bodied and strong. She is one of those women of a certain grace and beauty who wear it so unobtrusively that it takes a while to notice. Her dark-brown face is surrounded by the total whiteness of her hair, and, being a woman who has adjusted to many things in life and overcome many more, her face is full of strength. She has, we can see, wit and faith of a kind that keep her eyes lit and full of interest and expectancy. She is, in a word, a beautiful woman. Her bearing is perhaps most like the noble bearing of the women of the Hereros of Southwest Africa—rather as if she imagines that as she walks she still bears a basket or a vessel upon her head. Her speech, on the other hand, is as careless as her carriage is precise—she is inclined to slur everything—but her voice is perhaps not so much quiet as simply soft)*

MAMA Who that 'round here slamming doors at this hour?

(She crosses through the room, goes to the window, opens it, and brings in a feeble little plant growing doggedly in a small pot on the window sill. She feels the dirt and puts it back out)

RUTH That was Walter Lee. He and Bennie was at it again.

MAMA My children and they tempers. Lord, if this little old plant don't get more sun than it's been getting it ain't never going to see spring again. *(She turns from the window)* What's the matter with you this morning, Ruth? You looks right peaked. You aiming to iron all them things? Leave some for me. I'll get to 'em this afternoon. Bennie honey, it's too drafty for you to be sitting 'round half dressed. Where's your robe?

BENEATHA In the cleaners.

MAMA Well, go get mine and put it on.

BENEATHA I'm not cold, Mama, honest.

MAMA I know—but you so thin . . .

BENEATHA *(Irritably)* Mama, I'm not cold.

MAMA *(Seeing the make-down bed as* TRAVIS *has left it)* Lord have mercy, look at that poor bed. Bless his heart—he tries, don't he?

(She moves to the bed TRAVIS *has sloppily made up)*

RUTH No—he don't half try at all 'cause he knows you going to come along behind him and fix everything. That's just how come he don't know how to do nothing right now—you done spoiled that boy so.

MAMA *(Folding bedding)* Well—he's a little boy. Ain't supposed to know 'bout housekeeping. My baby, that's what he is. What you fix for his breakfast this morning?

RUTH *(Angrily)* I feed my son, Lena!

MAMA I ain't meddling—*(Underbreath; busybodyish)* I just noticed all last week he had cold cereal, and when it starts getting this chilly in the fall a child ought to have some hot grits or something when he goes out in the cold—

RUTH *(Furious)* I gave him hot oats—is that all right!

MAMA I ain't meddling. *(Pause)* Put a lot of nice butter on it? *(*RUTH *shoots her an angry look and does not reply)* He likes lots of butter.

RUTH *(Exasperated)* Lena—

MAMA *(To* BENEATHA. MAMA *is inclined to wander conversationally sometimes)* What was you and your brother fussing 'bout this morning?

BENEATHA It's not important, Mama.

(She gets up and goes to look out at the bathroom, which is apparently free, and she picks up her towels and rushes out)

MAMA What was they fighting about?

RUTH Now you know as well as I do.

MAMA *(Shaking her head)* Brother still worrying hisself sick about that money?

RUTH You know he is.

MAMA You had breakfast?

RUTH Some coffee.

MAMA Girl, you better start eating and looking after yourself better. You almost thin as Travis.

RUTH Lena—

MAMA Un-hunh?

RUTH What are you going to do with it?

MAMA Now don't you start, child. It's too early in the morning to be talking about money. It ain't Christian.

RUTH It's just that he got his heart set on that store—

MAMA You mean that liquor store that Willy Harris want him to invest in?

RUTH Yes—

MAMA We ain't no business people, Ruth. We just plain working folks.

RUTH Ain't nobody business people till they go into business. Walter Lee say colored people ain't never going to start getting ahead till they start gambling on some different kinds of things in the world—investments and things.

MAMA What done got into you, girl? Walter Lee done finally sold you on investing.

RUTH No. Mama, something is happening between Walter and me. I don't know what it is—but he needs something—something I can't give him any more. He needs this chance, Lena.

MAMA *(Frowning deeply)* But liquor, honey—

RUTH Well—like Walter say—I spec people going to always be drinking themselves some liquor.

MAMA Well—whether they drinks it or not ain't none of my business. But whether I go into business selling it to 'em *is,* and I don't want that on my ledger this late in life. *(Stopping suddenly and studying her daughter-in-law)* Ruth Younger, what's the matter with you today? You look like you could fall over right there.

RUTH I'm tired.

MAMA Then you better stay home from work today.

RUTH I can't stay home. She'd be calling up the agency and screaming at them, "My girl didn't come in today—send me somebody! My girl didn't come in!" Oh, she just have a fit . . .

MAMA Well, let her have it. I'll just call her up and say you got the flu—

RUTH *(Laughing)* Why the flu?

MAMA 'Cause it sounds respectable to 'em. Something white people get, too. They know 'bout the flu. Otherwise they think you been cut up or something when you tell 'em you sick.

RUTH I got to go in. We need the money.

MAMA Somebody would of thought my children done all but starved to death the way they talk about money here late. Child, we got a great big old check coming tomorrow.

RUTH *(Sincerely, but also self-righteously)* Now that's your money. It ain't got nothing to do with me. We all feel like that—Walter and Bennie and me—even Travis.

MAMA *(Thoughtfully, and suddenly very far away)* Ten thousand dollars—

RUTH Sure is wonderful.

MAMA Ten thousand dollars.

RUTH You know what you should do, Miss Lena? You should take yourself a trip somewhere. To Europe or South America or someplace—

MAMA *(Throwing up her hands at the thought)* Oh, child!

RUTH I'm serious. Just pack up and leave! Go on away and enjoy yourself some. Forget about the family and have yourself a ball for once in your life—

MAMA *(Drily)* You sound like I'm just about ready to die. Who'd go with me? What I look like wandering 'round Europe by myself?

RUTH Shoot—these here rich white women do it all the time. They don't think nothing of packing up they suitcases and piling on one of them big steamships and—swoosh!—they gone, child.

MAMA Something always told me I wasn't no rich white woman.

RUTH Well—what are you going to do with it then?

MAMA I ain't rightly decided. *(Thinking. She speaks now with emphasis)* Some of it got to be put away for Beneatha and her schoolin'—and ain't nothing going to touch that part of it. Nothing. *(She waits several seconds, trying to make up her mind about something, and looks at* RUTH *a little tentatively before going on)* Been thinking that we maybe could meet the notes on a little old two-story somewhere, with a yard where Travis could play in the summertime, if we use part of the insurance for a down payment and everybody kind of pitch in. I could maybe take on a little day work again, few days a week—

RUTH *(Studying her mother-in-law furtively and concentrating on her ironing, anxious to encourage without seeming to)* Well, Lord knows, we've put enough rent into this here rat trap to pay for four houses by now . . .

MAMA *(Looking up at the words "rat trap" and then looking around and leaning back and sighing—in a suddenly reflective mood—)* "Rat trap"—yes, that's all it is. *(Smiling)* I remember just as well the day me and Big Walter moved in here. Hadn't been married but two weeks and wasn't planning on living here no more than a year. *(She shakes her head at the dissolved dream)* We was going to set away, little by little, don't you know, and buy a little place out in Morgan Park. We had even picked out the house. *(Chuckling a little)* Looks right dumpy today. But Lord, child, you should know all the dreams I had 'bout buying that house and fixing it up and making me a little garden in the back—*(She waits and stops smiling)* And didn't none of it happen.

(Dropping her hands in a futile gesture)

RUTH *(Keeps her head down, ironing)* Yes, life can be a barrel of disappointments, sometimes.

MAMA Honey, Big Walter would come in here some nights back then and slump down on that couch there and just look at the rug, and look at me and look at the rug and then back at me—and I'd know he was down then . . . really down. *(After a second very long and thoughtful pause; she is seeing back to times that only she can see)* And then, Lord, when I lost that baby—little Claude—I almost thought I was going to lose big Walter too. Oh, that man grieved hisself! He was one man to love his children.

RUTH Ain't nothin' can tear at you like losin' your baby.

MAMA I guess that's how come that man finally worked hisself to death like he done. Like he was fighting his own war with this here world that took his baby from him.

RUTH He sure was a fine man, all right. I always liked Mr. Younger.

MAMA Crazy 'bout his children! God knows there was plenty wrong with Walter Younger—hard-headed, mean, kind of wild with women—plenty wrong with him. But he sure loved his children. Always wanted them to have something—be something. That's where Brother gets all these notions, I reckon. Big Walter used to say, he'd get right wet in the eyes sometimes, lean his head back with the water standing in his eyes and say, "Seem like God didn't see fit to give the black man nothing but dreams—but He did give us children to make them dreams seem worth while." *(She smiles)* He could talk like that, don't you know.

RUTH Yes, he sure could. He was a good man, Mr. Younger.

MAMA Yes, a fine man—just couldn't never catch up with his dreams, that's all.

*(*BENEATHA *comes in, brushing her hair and looking up to the ceiling, where the sound of a vacuum cleaner has started up)*

BENEATHA What could be so dirty on that woman's rugs that she has to vacuum them every single day?

RUTH I wish certain young women 'round here who I could name would take inspiration about certain rugs in a certain apartment I could also mention.

BENEATHA *(Shrugging)* How much cleaning can a house need, for Christ's sakes.

MAMA *(Not liking the Lord's name used thus)* Bennie!

RUTH Just listen to her—just listen!

BENEATHA Oh, God!

MAMA If you use the Lord's name just one more time—

BENEATHA *(A bit of a whine)* Oh, Mama—

RUTH Fresh—just fresh as salt, this girl!

BENEATHA *(Drily)* Well—if the salt loses its savor—

MAMA Now that will do. I just ain't going to have you 'round here reciting the scriptures in vain—you hear me?

BENEATHA How did I manage to get on everybody's wrong side by just walking into a room?

RUTH If you weren't so fresh—

BENEATHA Ruth, I'm twenty years old.

MAMA What time you be home from school today?

BENEATHA Kind of late. *(With enthusiasm)* Madeline is going to start my guitar lessons today.

(MAMA and RUTH look up with the same expression)

MAMA Your *what* kind of lessons?

BENEATHA Guitar.

RUTH Oh, Father!

MAMA How come you done taken it in your mind to learn to play the guitar?

BENEATHA I just want to, that's all.

MAMA *(Smiling)* Lord, child, don't you know what to do with yourself? How long it going to be before you get tired of this now—like you got tired of that little play-acting group you joined last year? *(Looking at* RUTH*)* And what was it the year before that?

RUTH The horseback-riding club for which she bought that fifty-five dollar riding habit that's been hanging in the closet ever since!

MAMA *(To* BENEATHA*)* Why you got to flit so from one thing to another, baby?

BENEATHA *(Sharply)* I just want to learn to play the guitar. Is there anything wrong with that?

MAMA Ain't nobody trying to stop you. I just wonders sometimes why you has to flit so from one thing to another all the time. You ain't never done nothing with all that camera equipment you brought home—

BENEATHA I don't flit! I—I experiment with different forms of expression—

RUTH Like riding a horse?

BENEATHA —People have to express themselves one way or another.

MAMA What is it you want to express?

BENEATHA *(Angrily)* Me! *(MAMA and RUTH look at each other and burst into raucous laughter)* Don't worry—I don't expect you to understand.

MAMA *(To change the subject)* Who you going out with tomorrow night?

BENEATHA *(With displeasure)* George Murchison again.

MAMA *(Pleased)* Oh—you getting a little sweet on him?

RUTH You ask me, this child ain't sweet on nobody but herself—*(Underbreath)* Express herself!

(They laugh)

BENEATHA Oh—I like George all right, Mama. I mean I like him enough to go out with him and stuff, but—

RUTH *(For devilment)* What does *and stuff* mean?

BENEATHA Mind your own business.

MAMA Stop picking at her now, Ruth. *(She chuckles—then a suspicious sudden look at her daughter as she turns in her chair for emphasis)* What DOES it mean?

BENEATHA *(Wearily)* Oh, I just mean I couldn't ever really be serious about George. He's—he's so shallow.

RUTH Shallow—what do you mean he's shallow? He's *rich!*

MAMA Hush, Ruth.

BENEATHA I know he's rich. He knows he's rich, too.

RUTH Well—what other qualities a man got to have to satisfy you, little girl?

BENEATHA You wouldn't even begin to understand. Anybody who married Walter could not possibly understand.

MAMA *(Outraged)* What kind of way is that to talk about your brother?

BENEATHA Brother is a flip—let's face it.

MAMA *(To* RUTH, *helplessly)* What's a flip?

RUTH *(Glad to add kindling)* She's saying he's crazy.

BENEATHA Not crazy. Brother isn't really crazy yet—he—he's an elaborate neurotic.

MAMA Hush your mouth!

BENEATHA As for George. Well. George looks good—he's got a beautiful car and he takes me to nice places and, as my sister-in-law says, he is probably the richest boy I will ever get to know and I even like him sometimes—but if the Youngers are sitting around waiting to see if their little Bennie is going to tie up the family with the Murchisons, they are wasting their time.

RUTH You mean you wouldn't marry George Murchison if he asked you someday? That pretty, rich thing? Honey, I knew you was odd—

BENEATHA No I would not marry him if all I felt for him was what I feel now. Besides, George's family wouldn't really like it.

MAMA Why not?

BENEATHA Oh, Mama—The Murchisons are honest-to-God-real-*live*-rich colored people, and the only people in the world who are more snobbish than rich white people are rich colored people. I thought everybody knew that. I've met Mrs. Murchison. She's a scene!

MAMA You must not dislike people 'cause they well off, honey.

BENEATHA Why not? It makes just as much sense as disliking people 'cause they are poor, and lots of people do that.

RUTH *(A wisdom-of-the-ages manner. To* MAMA*)* Well, she'll get over some of this—

BENEATHA Get over it? What are you talking about, Ruth? Listen, I'm going to be a doctor. I'm not worried about who I'm going to marry yet—if I ever get married.

MAMA *and* RUTH *If!*

MAMA Now, Bennie—

BENEATHA Oh, I probably will . . . but first I'm going to be a doctor, and George, for one, still thinks that's pretty funny. I couldn't be bothered with that. I am going to be a doctor and everybody around here better understand that!

MAMA *(Kindly)* 'Course you going to be a doctor, honey, God willing.

BENEATHA *(Drily)* God hasn't got a thing to do with it.

MAMA Beneatha—that just wasn't necessary.

BENEATHA Well—neither is God. I get sick of hearing about God.

MAMA Beneatha!

BENEATHA I mean it! I'm just tired of hearing about God all the time. What has He got to do with anything? Does he pay tuition?

MAMA You 'bout to get your fresh little jaw slapped!

RUTH That's just what she needs, all right!

BENEATHA Why? Why can't I say what I want to around here, like everybody else?

MAMA It don't sound nice for a young girl to say things like that—you wasn't brought up that way. Me and your father went to trouble to get you and Brother to church every Sunday.

BENEATHA Mama, you don't understand. It's all a matter of ideas, and God is just one idea I don't accept. It's not important. I am not going out and be immoral or commit crimes because I don't believe in God. I don't even think about it. It's just that I get tired of Him getting credit for all the things the human race achieves through its own stubborn effort. There simply is no blasted God—there is only man and it is *he* who makes miracles!

*(*MAMA *absorbs this speech, studies her daughter and rises slowly and crosses to* BENEATHA *and slaps her powerfully across the face. After, there is only silence and the daughter drops her eyes from her mother's face, and* MAMA *is very tall before her)*

MAMA Now—you say after me, in my mother's house there is still God. *(There is a long pause and* BENEATHA *stares at the floor wordlessly.*

MAMA *repeats the phrase with precision and cool emotion)* In my mother's house there is still God.

BENEATHA In my mother's house there is still God.

(A long pause)

MAMA *(Walking away from* BENEATHA, *too disturbed for triumphant posture. Stopping and turning back to her daughter)* There are some ideas we ain't going to have in this house. Not long as I am at the head of this family.

BENEATHA Yes, ma'am.

*(*MAMA *walks out of the room)*

RUTH *(Almost gently, with profound understanding)* You think you a woman, Bennie—but you still a little girl. What you did was childish—so you got treated like a child.

BENEATHA I see. *(Quietly)* I also see that everybody thinks it's all right for Mama to be a tyrant. But all the tyranny in the world will never put a God in the heavens!

(She picks up her books and goes out. Pause)

RUTH *(Goes to* MAMA*'s door)* She said she was sorry.

MAMA *(Coming out, going to her plant)* They frightens me, Ruth. My children.

RUTH You got good children, Lena. They just a little off sometimes—but they're good.

MAMA No—there's something come down between me and them that don't let us understand each other and I don't know what it is. One done almost lost his mind thinking 'bout money all the time and the other done commence to talk about things I can't seem to understand in no form or fashion. What is it that's changing, Ruth.

RUTH *(Soothingly, older than her years)* Now . . . you taking it all too seriously. You just got strong-willed children and it takes a strong woman like you to keep 'em in hand.

MAMA *(Looking at her plant and sprinkling a little water on it)* They spirited all right, my children. Got to admit they got spirit—Bennie and Walter. Like this little old plant that ain't never had enough sunshine or nothing—and look at it . . .

(She has her back to RUTH, *who has had to stop ironing and lean against something and put the back of her hand to her forehead)*

RUTH *(Trying to keep* MAMA *from noticing)* You . . . sure . . . loves that little old thing, don't you? . . .

MAMA Well, I always wanted me a garden like I used to see sometimes at the back of the houses down home. This plant is close as I ever got to having one. *(She looks out of the window as she replaces the plant)* Lord, ain't nothing as dreary as the view from this window on a dreary day, is there? Why ain't you singing this morning, Ruth? Sing that "No Ways Tired." That song always lifts me up so—*(She turns at last to see that* RUTH *has slipped quietly to the floor, in a state of semiconsciousness)* Ruth! Ruth honey—what's the matter with you . . . Ruth!

Curtain

SCENE TWO

It is the following morning; a Saturday morning, and house cleaning is in progress at the YOUNGERS. *Furniture has been shoved hither and yon and* MAMA *is giving the kitchen-area walls a washing down.* BENEATHA, *in dungarees, with a handkerchief tied around her face, is spraying insecticide into the cracks in the walls. As they work, the radio is on and a Southside disk-jockey program is inappropriately filling the house with a rather exotic saxophone blues.* TRAVIS, *the sole idle one, is leaning on his arms, looking out of the window.*

TRAVIS Grandmama, that stuff Bennie is using smells awful. Can I go downstairs, please?

MAMA Did you get all them chores done already? I ain't seen you doing much.

TRAVIS Yes'm—finished early. Where did Mama go this morning?

MAMA *(Looking at* BENEATHA*)* She had to go on a little errand.

(The phone rings. BENEATHA *runs to answer it and reaches it before* WALTER, *who has entered from bedroom)*

TRAVIS Where?

MAMA To tend to her business.

BENEATHA Haylo . . . *(Disappointed)* Yes, he is. *(She tosses the phone to* WALTER, *who barely catches it)* It's Willy Harris again.

WALTER *(As privately as possible under* MAMA'*s gaze)* Hello, Willy. Did you get the papers from the lawyer? . . . No, not yet. I told you the mailman doesn't get here till ten-thirty . . . No, I'll come there . . . Yeah! Right away. *(He hangs up and goes for his coat)*

BENEATHA Brother, where did Ruth go?

WALTER *(As he exits)* How should I know!

TRAVIS Aw come on, Grandma. Can I go outside?

MAMA Oh, I guess so. You stay right in front of the house, though, and keep a good lookout for the postman.

TRAVIS Yes'm. *(He darts into bedroom for stickball and bat, reenters, and sees* BENEATHA *on her knees spraying under sofa with behind upraised. He edges closer to the target, takes aim, and lets her have it. She screams)* Leave them poor little cockroaches alone, they ain't bothering you none! *(He runs as she swings the spraygun at him viciously and playfully)* Grandma! Grandma!

MAMA Look out there, girl, before you be spilling some of that stuff on that child!

TRAVIS *(Safely behind the bastion of* MAMA*)* That's right—look out, now! *(He exits)*

BENEATHA *(Drily)* I can't imagine that it would hurt him—it has never hurt the roaches.

MAMA Well, little boys' hides ain't as tough as Southside roaches. You better get over there behind the bureau. I seen one marching out of there like Napoleon yesterday.

BENEATHA There's really only one way to get rid of them, Mama—

MAMA How?

BENEATHA Set fire to this building! Mama, where did Ruth go?

MAMA *(Looking at her with meaning)* To the doctor, I think.

BENEATHA The doctor? What's the matter? *(They exchange glances)* You don't think—

MAMA *(With her sense of drama)* Now I ain't saying what I think. but I ain't never been wrong 'bout a woman neither.

(The phone rings)

BENEATHA *(At the phone)* Hay-lo . . . *(Pause, and a moment of recognition)* Well—when did you get back! . . . And how was it? . . . Of course I've missed you—in my way . . . This morning? No . . . house cleaning and all that and Mama hates it if I let people come over when the house is like this . . . You *have?* Well, that's different . . . What is it— Oh, what the hell, come on over . . . Right, see you then. *Arrividerci.*

(She hangs up)

MAMA *(Who has listened vigorously, as is her habit)* Who is that you inviting over here with this house looking like this? You ain't got the pride you was born with!

BENEATHA Asagai doesn't care how houses look, Mama—he's an intellectual.

MAMA *Who?*

BENEATHA Asagai—Joseph Asagai. He's an African boy I met on campus. He's been studying in Canada all summer.

MAMA What's his name?

BENEATHA Asagai, Joseph. Ah-sah-guy . . . He's from Nigeria.

MAMA Oh, that's the little country that was founded by slaves way back . . .

BENEATHA No, Mama—that's Liberia.

MAMA I don't think I never met no African before.

BENEATHA Well, do me a favor and don't ask him a whole lot of ignorant questions about Africans. I mean, do they wear clothes and all that—

MAMA Well, now, I guess if you think we so ignorant 'round here maybe you shouldn't bring your friends here—

BENEATHA It's just that people ask such crazy things. All anyone seems to know about when it comes to Africa is Tarzan—

MAMA *(Indignantly)* Why should I know anything about Africa?

BENEATHA Why do you give money at church for the missionary work?

MAMA Well, that's to help save people.

BENEATHA You mean save them from *heathenism—*

MAMA *(Innocently)* Yes.

BENEATHA I'm afraid they need more salvation from the British and the French.

*(*RUTH *comes in forlornly and pulls off her coat with dejection. They both turn to look at her)*

RUTH *(Dispiritedly)* Well, I guess from all the happy faces—everybody knows.

BENEATHA You pregnant?

MAMA Lord have mercy, I sure hope it's a little old girl. Travis ought to have a sister.

*(*BENEATHA *and* RUTH *give her a hopeless look for this grandmotherly enthusiasm)*

BENEATHA How far along are you?

RUTH Two months.

BENEATHA Did you mean to? I mean did you plan it or was it an accident?

MAMA What do you know about planning or not planning?

BENEATHA Oh, Mama.

RUTH *(Wearily)* She's twenty years old, Lena.

BENEATHA Did you plan it, Ruth?

RUTH Mind your own business.

BENEATHA It is my business—where is he going to live, on the *roof? (There is silence following the remark as the three women react to the sense of it)* Gee—I didn't mean that, Ruth, honest. Gee, I don't feel like that at all. I—I think it is wonderful.

RUTH *(Dully)* Wonderful.

BENEATHA Yes—really.

MAMA *(Looking at* RUTH, *worried)* Doctor say everything going to be all right?

RUTH *(Far away)* Yes—she says everything is going to be fine . . .

MAMA *(Immediately suspicious)* "She"— What doctor you went to?

*(*RUTH *folds over, near hysteria)*

MAMA *(Worriedly hovering over* RUTH*)* Ruth honey—what's the matter with you—you sick?

*(*RUTH *has her fists clenched on her thighs and is fighting hard to suppress a scream that seems to be rising in her)*

BENEATHA What's the matter with her, Mama?

MAMA *(Working her fingers in* RUTH'*s shoulders to relax her)* She be all right. Women gets right depressed sometimes when they get her way. *(Speaking softly, expertly, rapidly)* Now you just relax. That's right . . . just lean back, don't think 'bout nothing at all . . . nothing at all—

RUTH I'm all right. . . .

(The glassy-eyed look melts and then she collapses into a fit of heavy sobbing. The bell rings)

BENEATHA Oh, my God—that must be Asagai.

MAMA *(To* RUTH*)* Come on now, honey. You need to lie down and rest awhile . . . then have some nice hot food.

(They exit, RUTH'S *weight on her mother-in-law.* BENEATHA, *herself profoundly disturbed, opens the door to admit a rather dramatic-looking young man with a large package)*

ASAGAI Hello, Alaiyo—

BENEATHA *(Holding the door open and regarding him with pleasure)* Hello . . . *(Long pause)* Well—come in. And please excuse everything. My mother was very upset about my letting anyone come here with the place like this.

ASAGAI *(Coming into the room)* You look disturbed too . . . Is something wrong?

BENEATHA *(Still at the door, absently)* Yes . . . we've all got acute ghetto-itus. *(She smiles and comes toward him, finding a cigarette and sitting)* So—sit down! No! Wait! *(She whips the spraygun off sofa where she had left it and puts the cushions back. At last perches on arm of sofa. He sits)* So, how was Canada?

ASAGAI *(A sophisticate)* Canadian.

BENEATHA *(Looking at him)* Asagai, I'm very glad you are back.

ASAGAI *(Looking back at her in turn)* Are you really?

BENEATHA Yes—very.

ASAGAI Why?—you were quite glad when I went away. What happened?

BENEATHA You went away.

ASAGAI Ahhhhhhhh.

BENEATHA Before—you wanted to be so serious before there was time.

ASAGAI How much time must there be before one knows what one feels?

BENEATHA *(Stalling this particular conversation. Her hands pressed together, in a deliberately childish gesture)* What did you bring me?

ASAGAI *(Handing her the package)* Open it and see.

BENEATHA *(Eagerly opening the package and drawing out some records and the colorful robes of a Nigerian woman)* Oh, Asagai! ... You got them for me! ... How beautiful ... and the records too! *(She lifts out the robes and runs to the mirror with them and holds the drapery up in front of herself)*

ASAGAI *(Coming to her at the mirror)* I shall have to teach you how to drape it properly. *(He flings the material about her for the moment and stands back to look at her)* Ah—*Oh-pay-gay-day, oh-gbah-mu-shay. (A Yoruba exclamation for admiration)* You wear it well ... very well ... mutilated hair and all.

BENEATHA *(Turning suddenly)* My hair—what's wrong with my hair?

ASAGAI *(Shrugging)* Were you born with it like that?

BENEATHA *(Reaching up to touch it)* No ... of course not.

(She looks back to the mirror, disturbed)

ASAGAI *(Smiling)* How then?

BENEATHA You know perfectly well how ... as crinkly as yours ... that's how.

ASAGAI And it is ugly to you that way?

BENEATHA *(Quickly)* Oh, no—not ugly ... *(More slowly, apologetically)* But it's so hard to manage when it's, well—raw.

ASAGAI And so to accommodate that—you mutilate it every week?

BENEATHA It's not mutilation!

ASAGAI *(Laughing aloud at her seriousness)* Oh ... please! I am only teasing you because you are so very serious about these things. *(He stands back from her and folds his arms across his chest as he watches her pulling at her hair and frowning in the mirror)* Do you remember the first time you met me at school? ... *(He laughs)* You came up to me and you said—and I thought you were the most serious little thing I had ever seen—you said: *(He imitates her)* "Mr. Asagai—I want very much to talk with you. About Africa. You see, Mr. Asagai, I am looking for my *identity!*"

(He laughs)

BENEATHA *(Turning to him, not laughing)* Yes—

(Her face is quizzical, profoundly disturbed)

ASAGAI *(Still teasing and reaching out and taking her face in his hands and turning her profile to him)* Well ... it is true that this is not so much a profile of a Hollywood queen as perhaps a queen of the Nile—*(A mock dismissal of the importance of the question)* But what does it matter? Assimilationism is so popular in your country.

BENEATHA *(Wheeling, passionately, sharply)* I am not an assimilationist!

ASAGAI *(The protest hangs in the room for a moment and* ASAGAI *studies her, his laughter fading)* Such a serious one. *(There is a pause)* So—you like the robes? You must take excellent care of them—they are from my sister's personal wardrobe.

BENEATHA *(With incredulity)* You—you sent all the way home—for me?

ASAGAI *(With charm)* For you—I would do much more ... Well, that is what I came for. I must go.

BENEATHA Will you call me Monday?

ASAGAI Yes . . . We have a great deal to talk about. I mean about identity and time and all that.

BENEATHA Time?

ASAGAI Yes. About how much time one needs to know what one feels.

BENEATHA You see! You never understood that there is more than one kind of feeling which can exist between a man and a woman—or, at least, there should be.

ASAGAI *(Shaking his head negatively but gently)* No. Between a man and a woman there need be only one kind of feeling. I have that for you . . . Now even . . . right this moment . . .

BENEATHA I know—and by itself—it won't do. I can find that anywhere.

ASAGAI For a woman it should be enough.

BENEATHA I know—because that's what it says in all the novels that men write. But it isn't. Go ahead and laugh—but I'm not interested in being someone's little episode in America or—*(With feminine vengeance)*—one of them! *(*ASAGAI *has burst into laughter again)* That's funny as hell, huh!

ASAGAI It's just that every American girl I have known has said that to me. White—black—in this you are all the same. And the same speech, too!

BENEATHA *(Angrily)* Yuk, yuk, yuk!

ASAGAI It's how you can be sure that the world's most liberated women are not liberated at all. You all talk about it too much!

*(*MAMA *enters and is immediately all social charm because of the presence of a guest)*

BENEATHA Oh—Mama—this is Mr. Asagai.

MAMA How do you do?

ASAGAI *(Total politeness to an elder)* How do you do, Mrs. Younger. Please forgive me for coming at such an outrageous hour on a Saturday.

MAMA Well, you are quite welcome. I just hope you understand that our house don't always look like this. *(Chatterish)* You must come again. I would love to hear all about—*(Not sure of the name)*—your country. I think it's so sad the way our American Negroes don't know nothing about Africa 'cept Tarzan and all that. And all that money they pour into these churches when they ought to be helping you people over there drive out them French and Englishmen done taken away your land.

(The mother flashes a slightly superior look at her daughter upon completion of the recitation)

ASAGAI *(Taken aback by this sudden and acutely unrelated expression of sympathy)* Yes . . . yes . . .

MAMA *(Smiling at him suddenly and relaxing and looking him over)* How many miles is it from here to where you come from?

ASAGAI Many thousands.

MAMA *(Looking at him as she would* WALTER*)* I bet you don't half look after yourself, being away from your mama either. I spec you better come 'round here from time to time to get yourself some decent home-cooked meals . . .

ASAGAI *(Moved)* Thank you. Thank you very much. *(They are all quiet, then—)* Well . . . I must go. I will call you Monday, Alaiyo.

MAMA What's that he call you?

ASAGAI Oh—"Alaiyo." I hope you don't mind. It is what you would call a nickname, I think. It is a Yoruba word. I am a Yoruba.

MAMA *(Looking at* BENEATHA*)* I—I thought he was from— *(Uncertain)*

ASAGAI *(Understanding)* Nigeria is my country. Yoruba is my tribal origin—

BENEATHA You didn't tell us what Alaiyo means . . . for all I know, you might be calling me Little Idiot or something . . .

ASAGAI Well . . . let me see . . . I do not know how just to explain it . . . The sense of a thing can be so different when it changes languages.

BENEATHA You're evading.

ASAGAI No—really it is difficult . . . *(Thinking)* It means . . . it means One for Whom Bread—Food—Is Not Enough. *(He looks at her)* Is that all right?

BENEATHA *(Understanding, softly)* Thank you.

MAMA *(Looking from one to the other and not understanding any of it)* Well . . . that's nice . . . You must come see us again—Mr.—

ASAGAI Ah-sah-guy . . .

MAMA Yes . . . Do come again.

ASAGAI Good-bye.

(He exits)

MAMA *(After him)* Lord, that's a pretty thing just went out here! *(Insinuatingly, to her daughter)* Yes, I guess I see why we done commence to get so interested in Africa 'round here. Missionaries my aunt Jenny!

(She exits)

BENEATHA Oh, Mama! . . .

(She picks up the Nigerian dress and holds it up to her in front of the mirror again. She sets the headdress on haphazardly and then notices her hair again and clutches at it and then replaces the headdress and frowns at herself. Then she starts to wriggle in front of the mirror as she thinks a Nigerian woman might. TRAVIS *enters and stands regarding her)*

TRAVIS What's the matter, girl, you cracking up?

BENEATHA Shut up.

(She pulls the headdress off and looks at herself in the mirror and clutches at her hair again and squinches her eyes as if trying to imagine something. Then, suddenly, she gets her raincoat and kerchief and hurriedly prepares for going out)

MAMA *(Coming back into the room)* She's resting now. Travis, baby, run next door and ask Miss Johnson to please let me have a little kitchen cleanser. This here can is empty as Jacob's kettle.

TRAVIS I just came in.

MAMA Do as you told. *(He exits and she looks at her daughter)* Where you going?

BENEATHA *(Halting at the door)* To become a queen of the Nile!

(She exits in a breathless blaze of glory. RUTH *appears in the bedroom doorway)*

MAMA Who told you to get up?

RUTH Ain't nothing wrong with me to be lying in no bed for. Where did Bennie go?

MAMA *(Drumming her fingers)* Far as I could make out—to Egypt. (RUTH *just looks at her)* What time is it getting to?

RUTH Ten twenty. And the mailman going to ring that bell this morning just like he done every morning for the last umpteen years.

(TRAVIS *comes in with the cleanser can)*

TRAVIS She say to tell you that she don't have much.

MAMA *(Angrily)* Lord, some people I could name sure is tight-fisted! *(Directing her grandson)* Mark two cans of cleanser down on the list there. If she that hard up for kitchen cleanser, I sure don't want to forget to get her none!

RUTH Lena—maybe the woman is just short on cleanser—

MAMA *(Not listening)* —Much baking powder as she done borrowed from me all these years, she could of done gone into the baking business!

(The bell sounds suddenly and sharply and all three are stunned—serious and silent—mid-speech. In spite of all the other conversations and distractions of the morning, this is what they have been waiting for, even TRAVIS, *who looks helplessly from his mother to his grandmother.* RUTH *is the first to come to life again)*

RUTH *(To* TRAVIS*) Get down them steps, boy!*

(TRAVIS *snaps to life and flies out to get the mail)*

MAMA *(Her eyes wide, her hand to her breast)* You mean it done really come?

RUTH *(Excited)* Oh, Miss Lena!

MAMA *(Collecting herself)* Well . . . I don't know what we all so excited about 'round here for. We known it was coming for months.

RUTH That's a whole lot different from having it come and being able to hold it in your hands . . . a piece of paper worth ten thousand dollars . . . (TRAVIS *bursts back into the room. He holds the envelope high above his head, like a little dancer, his face is radiant and he is breathless. He moves to his grandmother with sudden slow ceremony and puts the envelope into her hands. She accepts it, and then merely holds it and looks at it)* Come on! Open it . . . Lord have mercy, I wish Walter Lee was here!

TRAVIS Open it, Grandmama!

MAMA *(Staring at it)* Now you all be quiet. It's just a check.

RUTH Open it . . .

MAMA *(Still staring at it)* Now don't act silly . . . We ain't never been no people to act silly 'bout no money—

RUTH *(Swiftly)* We ain't never had none before—OPEN IT!

*(*MAMA *finally makes a good strong tear and pulls out the thin blue slice of paper and inspects it closely. The boy and his mother study it raptly over* MAMA*'s shoulders)*

MAMA *Travis! (She is counting off with doubt)* Is that the right number of zeros?

TRAVIS Yes'm . . . ten thousand dollars. Gaalee, Grandmama, you rich.

MAMA *(She holds the check away from her, still looking at it. Slowly her face sobers into a mask of unhappiness)* Ten thousand dollars. *(She hands it to* RUTH*)* Put it away somewhere, Ruth. *(She does not look at* RUTH*; her eyes seem to be seeing something somewhere very far off)* Ten thousand dollars they give you. Ten thousand dollars.

TRAVIS *(To his mother, sincerely)* What's the matter with Grandmama—don't she want to be rich?

RUTH *(Distractedly)* You go on out and play now, baby. *(*TRAVIS *exits.* MAMA *starts wiping dishes absently, humming intently to herself.* RUTH *turns to her, with kind exasperation)* You've gone and got yourself upset.

MAMA *(Not looking at her)* I spec if it wasn't for you all . . . I would just put that money away or give it to the church or something.

RUTH Now what kind of talk is that. Mr. Younger would just be plain mad if he could hear you talking foolish like that.

MAMA *(Stopping and staring off)* Yes . . . he sure would. *(Sighing)* We got enough to do with that money, all right. *(She halts then, and turns and looks at her daughter-in-law hard;* RUTH *avoids her eyes and* MAMA *wipes her hands with finality and starts to speak firmly to* RUTH*)* Where did you go today, girl?

RUTH To the doctor.

MAMA *(Impatiently)* Now, Ruth . . . you know better than that. Old Doctor Jones is strange enough in his way but there ain't nothing 'bout him make somebody slip and call him "she"—like you done this morning.

RUTH Well, that's what happened—my tongue slipped.

MAMA You went to see that woman, didn't you?

RUTH *(Defensively, giving herself away)* What woman you talking about?

BENEATHA *(Angrily)* That woman who—

*(*WALTER *enters in great excitement)*

WALTER Did it come?

MAMA *(Quietly)* Can't you give people a Christian greeting before you start asking about money?

WALTER *(To* RUTH*)* Did it come? *(*RUTH *unfolds the check and lays it quietly before him, watching him intently with thoughts of her own.* WALTER *sits down and grasps it close and counts off the zeros)* Ten thousand dollars—*(He turns suddenly, frantically to his mother and draws some papers out of his breast pocket)* Mama—look. Old Willy Harris put everything on paper—

MAMA Son—I think you ought to talk to your wife . . . I'll go on out and leave you alone if you want—

WALTER I can talk to her later—Mama, look—

MAMA Son—

WALTER WILL SOMEBODY PLEASE LISTEN TO ME TODAY!

MAMA *(Quietly)* I don't 'low no yellin' in this house, Walter Lee, and you know it—*(*WALTER *stares at them in frustration and starts to* *speak several times)* And there ain't going to be no investing in no liquor stores.

WALTER But, Mama, you ain't even looked at it.

MAMA I don't aim to have to speak on that again.

(A long pause)

WALTER You ain't looked at it and you don't aim to have to speak on that again? You ain't even looked at it and *you* have decided— *(Crumpling his papers)* Well, *you* tell that to my boy tonight when you put him to sleep on the living-room couch . . . *(Turning to* MAMA *and speaking directly to her)* Yeah—and tell it to my wife, Mama, tomorrow when she has to go out of here to look after somebody else's kids. And tell it to *me,* Mama, every time we need a new pair of curtains and I have to watch *you* go out and work in somebody's kitchen. Yeah, you tell me then! *(*WALTER *starts out)*

RUTH Where you going?

WALTER I'm going out!

RUTH Where?

WALTER Just out of this house somewhere—

RUTH *(Getting her coat)* I'll come too.

WALTER I don't want you to come!

RUTH I got something to talk to you about, Walter.

WALTER That's too bad.

MAMA *(Still quietly)* Walter Lee—*(She waits and he finally turns and looks at her)* Sit down.

WALTER I'm a grown man, Mama.

MAMA Ain't nobody said you wasn't grown. But you still in my house and my presence. And as long as you are—you'll talk to your wife civil. Now sit down.

RUTH *(Suddenly)* Oh, let him go on out and drink himself to death! He makes me sick to my stomach! *(She flings her coat against him and exits to bedroom)*

WALTER *(Violently flinging the coat after her)* And you turn mine too, baby! *(The door slams behind her)* That was my biggest mistake—

MAMA *(Still quietly)* Walter, what is the matter with you?

WALTER Matter with me? Ain't nothing the matter with *me!*

MAMA Yes there is. Something eating you up like a crazy man. Something more than me not giving you this money. The past few years I been watching it happen to you. You get all nervous acting and kind of wild in the eyes—*(*WALTER *jumps up impatiently at her words)* I said sit there now, I'm talking to you!

WALTER Mama—I don't need no nagging at me today.

MAMA Seem like you getting to a place where you always tied up in some kind of knot about something. But if anybody ask you 'bout it you just yell at 'em and bust out the house and go out and drink somewheres. Walter Lee, people can't live with that. Ruth's a good, patient girl in her way—but you getting to be too much. Boy, don't make the mistake of driving that girl away from you.

WALTER Why—what she do for me?

MAMA She loves you.

WALTER Mama—I'm going out. I want to go off somewhere and be by myself for a while.

MAMA I'm sorry 'bout your liquor store, son. It just wasn't the thing for us to do. That's what I want to tell you about—

WALTER I got to go out, Mama—

(He rises)

MAMA It's dangerous, son.

WALTER What's dangerous?

MAMA When a man goes outside his home to look for peace.

WALTER *(Beseechingly)* Then why can't there never be no peace in this house then?

MAMA You done found it in some other house?

WALTER No—there ain't no woman! Why do women always think there's a woman somewhere when a man gets restless. *(Picks up the check)* Do you know what this money means to me? Do you know what this money can do for us? *(Puts it back)* Mama—Mama—I want so many things . . .

MAMA Yes, son—

WALTER I want so many things that they are driving me kind of crazy . . . Mama—look at me.

MAMA I'm looking at you. You a good-looking boy. You got a job, a nice wife, a fine boy and—

WALTER A job. *(Looks at her)* Mama, a job? I open and close car doors all day long. I drive a man around in his limousine and I say, "Yes, sir; no, sir; very good, sir; shall I take the Drive, sir?" Mama, that ain't no kind of job . . . that ain't nothing at all. *(Very quietly)* Mama, I don't know if I can make you understand.

MAMA Understand what, baby?

WALTER *(Quietly)* Sometimes it's like I can see the future stretched out in front of me—just plain as day. The future, Mama. Hanging over there at the edge of my days. Just waiting for me—a big, looming blank space—full of *nothing.* Just waiting for *me.* But it don't have to be. *(Pause. Kneeling beside her chair)* Mama—sometimes when I'm downtown and I pass them cool, quiet-looking restaurants where them white boys are sitting back and talking 'bout things . . . sitting there turning deals worth millions of dollars . . . sometimes I see guys don't look much older than me—

MAMA Son—how come you talk so much 'bout money?

WALTER *(With immense passion)* Because it is life, Mama!

MAMA *(Quietly)* Oh—*(Very quietly)* So now it's life. Money is life. Once upon a time freedom used to be life—now it's money. I guess the world really do change . . .

WALTER No—it was always money, Mama. We just didn't know about it.

MAMA No . . . something has changed. *(She looks at him)* You something new, boy. In my time we was worried about not being lynched and getting to the North if we could and how to stay alive and still have a pinch of dignity too . . . Now here come you and Beneatha—talking 'bout things we ain't never even thought about hardly, me and your daddy. You ain't satisfied or proud of nothing we done. I mean that you had a home; that we kept you out of trouble till you was grown; that you don't have to ride to work on the back of nobody's streetcar—You my children—but how different we done become.

WALTER *(A long beat. He pats her hand and gets up)* You just don't understand, Mama, you just don't understand.

MAMA Son—do you know your wife is expecting another baby? (WALTER *stands, stunned, and absorbs what his mother has said)* That's what she wanted to talk to you about. (WALTER *sinks down into a chair)* This ain't for me to be telling—but you ought to know. *(She waits)* I think Ruth is thinking 'bout getting rid of that child.

WALTER *(Slowly understanding)* —No—no—Ruth wouldn't do that.

MAMA When the world gets ugly enough—a woman will do anything for her family. *The part that's already living.*

WALTER You don't know Ruth, Mama, if you think she would do that.

(RUTH *opens the bedroom door and stands there a little limp)*

RUTH *(Beaten)* Yes I would too, Walter. *(Pause)* I gave her a five-dollar down payment.

(There is total silence as the man stares at his wife and the mother stares at her son)

MAMA *(Presently)* Well—*(Tightly)* Well—son, I'm waiting to hear you say something . . . *(She waits)* I'm waiting to hear how you be your father's son. Be the man he was . . . *(Pause. The silence shouts)* Your wife say she going to destroy your child. And I'm waiting to hear you talk like him and say we a people who give children life, not who destroys them—*(She rises)* I'm waiting to see you stand up and look like your daddy and say we done give up one baby to poverty and that we ain't going to give up nary another one . . . I'm waiting.

WALTER Ruth—*(He can say nothing)*

MAMA If you a son of mine, tell her! (WALTER *picks up his keys and his coat and walks out. She continues, bitterly)* You . . . you are a disgrace to your father's memory. Somebody get me my hat!

Curtain

Act Two

Scene One

TIME: Later the same day.

AT RISE: RUTH *is ironing again. she has the radio going. Presently* BENEATHA*'s bedroom door opens and* RUTH*'s mouth falls and she puts down the iron in fascination.*

RUTH What have we got on tonight!

BENEATHA *(Emerging grandly from the doorway so that we can see her thoroughly robed in the costume Asagai brought)* You are looking at what a well-dressed Nigerian woman wears—*(She parades for* RUTH*, her hair completely hidden by the headdress; she is coquettishly fanning herself with an ornate oriental fan, mistakenly more like Butterfly than any Nigerian that ever was)* Isn't it beautiful? *(She promenades to the radio and, with an arrogant flourish, turns off the good loud blues that is playing)* Enough of this assimilationist junk! (RUTH *follows her with her eyes as she goes to the phonograph and puts on a record and turns and waits ceremoniously for the music to come up. Then, with a shout—)* OCOMOGOSIAY!

(RUTH *jumps. The music comes up, a lovely Nigerian melody.* BENEATHA *listens, enraptured, her eyes far away—"back to the past." She begins to dance.* RUTH *is dumbfounded)*

RUTH What kind of dance is that?

BENEATHA A folk dance.

RUTH *(Pearl Bailey)* What kind of folks do that, honey?

BENEATHA It's from Nigeria. It's a dance of welcome.

RUTH Who you welcoming?

BENEATHA The men back to the village.

RUTH Where they been?

BENEATHA How should I know—out hunting or something. Anyway, they are coming back now . . .

RUTH Well, that's good.

BENEATHA *(With the record)*

Alundi, alundi
Alundi alunya
Jop pu a jeepua
Ang gu soooooooooo

Ai yai yae . . .
Ayehaye—alundi . . .

(WALTER *comes in during this performance; he has obviously been drinking. He leans against the door heavily and watches his sister, at first with distaste. Then his eyes look off—"back to the past"—as he lifts both his fists to the roof, screaming)*

WALTER YEAH . . . AND ETHIOPIA STRETCH FORTH HER HANDS AGAIN! . . .

RUTH *(Drily, looking at him)* Yes—and Africa sure is claiming her own tonight. *(She gives them both up and starts ironing again)*

WALTER *(All in a drunken, dramatic shout)* Shut up! . . . I'm digging them drums . . . them drums move me! . . . *(He makes his weaving way to his wife's face and leans in close to her)* In my *heart of hearts—(He thumps his chest)*—I am much warrior!

RUTH *(Without even looking up)* In your heart of hearts you are much drunkard.

WALTER *(Coming away from her and starting to wander around the room, shouting)* Me and Jomo . . . *(Intently, in his sister's face. She has stopped dancing to watch him in this unknown mood)* That's my man, Kenyatta. *(Shouting and thumping his chest)* FLAMING SPEAR! HOT DAMN! *(He is suddenly in possession of an imaginary spear and actively spearing enemies all over the room) OCOMOGOSIAY . . .*

BENEATHA *(To encourage* WALTER*, thoroughly caught up with this side of him) OCOMOGOSIAY,* FLAMING SPEAR!

WALTER THE LION IS WAKING . . . OWIMOWEH! *(He pulls his shirt open and leaps up on the table and gestures with his spear)*

BENEATHA OWIMOWEH!

WALTER *(On the table, very far gone, his eyes pure glass sheets. He sees what we cannot, that he is a leader of his people, a great chief, a descendant of Chaka, and that the hour to march has come)* Listen, my black brothers—

BENEATHA OCOMOGOSIAY!

WALTER —Do you hear the waters rushing against the shores of the coastlands—

BENEATHA OCOMOGOSIAY!

WALTER —Do you hear the screeching of the cocks in yonder hills beyond where the chiefs meet in council for the coming of the mighty war—

BENEATHA OCOMOGOSIAY!

(And now the lighting shifts subtly to suggest the world of WALTER*'s imagination, and the mood shifts from pure comedy. It is the inner* WALTER *speaking: the Southside chauffeur has assumed an unexpected majesty)*

WALTER —Do you hear the beating of the wings of the birds flying low over the mountains and the low places of our land—

BENEATHA OCOMOGOSIAY!

WALTER —Do you hear the singing of the women, singing the war songs of our fathers to the babies in the great houses? Singing the sweet war songs! *(The doorbell rings)* OH, DO YOU HEAR, MY BLACK BROTHERS!

BENEATHA *(Completely gone)* We hear you, Flaming Spear—

*(*RUTH *shuts off the phonograph and opens the door.* GEORGE MURCHISON *enters)*

WALTER Telling us to prepare for the GREATNESS OF THE TIME! *(Lights back to normal. He turns and sees* GEORGE*)* Black Brother!

(He extends his hand for the fraternal clasp)

GEORGE Black Brother, hell!

RUTH *(Having had enough, and embarrassed for the family)* Beneatha, you got company—what's the matter with you? Walter Lee Younger, get down off that table and stop acting like a fool . . .

*(*WALTER *comes down off the table suddenly and makes a quick exit to the bathroom)*

RUTH He's had a little to drink . . . I don't know what her excuse is.

GEORGE *(To* BENEATHA*)* Look honey, we're going *to* the theatre—we're not going to be *in* it . . . so go change, huh?

*(*BENEATHA *looks at him and slowly, ceremoniously, lifts her hands and pulls off the headdress. Her hair is close-cropped and unstraightened.* GEORGE *freezes mid-sentence and* RUTH*'s eyes all but fall out of her head)*

GEORGE What in the name of—

RUTH *(Touching* BENEATHA*'s hair)* Girl, you done lost your natural mind!? Look at your head!

GEORGE What have you done to your head—I mean your hair!

BENEATHA Nothing—except cut it off.

RUTH Now that's the truth—it's what ain't been done to it! You expect this boy to go out with you with your head all nappy like that?

BENEATHA *(Looking at* GEORGE*)* That's up to George. If he's ashamed of his heritage—

GEORGE Oh, don't be so proud of yourself, Bennie—just because you look eccentric.

BENEATHA How can something that's natural be eccentric?

GEORGE That's what being eccentric means—being natural. Get dressed.

BENEATHA I don't like that, George.

RUTH Why must you and your brother make an argument out of everything people say?

BENEATHA Because I hate assimilationist Negroes!

RUTH Will somebody please tell me what assimila-whoever means!

GEORGE Oh, it's just a college girl's way of calling people Uncle Toms—but that isn't what it means at all.

RUTH Well, what does it mean?

BENEATHA *(Cutting* GEORGE *off and staring at him as she replies to* RUTH*)* It means someone who is willing to give up his own culture and submerge himself completely in the dominant, and in this case *oppressive* culture!

GEORGE Oh, dear, dear, dear! Here we go! A lecture on the African past! On our Great West African Heritage! In one second we will hear all about the great Ashanti empires; the great Songhay civilizations; and the great sculpture of Bénin—and then some poetry in the Bantu—and the whole monologue will end with the word *heritage! (Nastily)* Let's face it, baby, your heritage is nothing but a bunch of raggedy-assed spirituals and some grass huts!

BENEATHA GRASS HUTS! *(*RUTH *crosses to her and forcibly pushes her toward the bedroom)* See there . . . you are standing there in your splendid ignorance talking about people who were the first to smelt iron on the face of the earth! *(*RUTH *is pushing her through the door)* The Ashanti were performing surgical operations when the English—*(*RUTH *pulls the door to, with* BENEATHA *on the other side, and smiles graciously at* GEORGE. BENEATHA *opens the door and shouts the end of the sentence defiantly at* GEORGE*)*—were still tattooing themselves with blue dragons! *(She goes back inside)*

RUTH Have a seat, George *(They both sit.* RUTH *folds her hands rather primly on her lap, determined to demonstrate the civilization of the family)* Warm, ain't it? I mean for September. *(Pause)* Just like they always say about Chicago weather: If it's too hot or cold for you, just wait a minute and it'll change. *(She smiles happily at this cliché of clichés)* Everybody say it's got to do with them bombs and things they keep setting off. *(Pause)* Would you like a nice cold beer?

GEORGE No, thank you. I don't care for beer. *(He looks at his watch)* I hope she hurries up.

RUTH What time is the show?

GEORGE It's an eight-thirty curtain. That's just Chicago, though. In New York standard curtain time is eight forty.

(He is rather proud of this knowledge)

RUTH *(Properly appreciating it)* You get to New York a lot?

GEORGE *(Offhand)* Few times a year.

RUTH Oh—that's nice. I've never been to New York.

*(*WALTER *enters. We feel he has relieved himself, but the edge of unreality is still with him)*

WALTER New York ain't got nothing Chicago ain't. Just a bunch of hustling people all squeezed up together—being "Eastern."

(He turns his face into a screw of displeasure)

GEORGE Oh—you've been?

WALTER *Plenty* of times.

RUTH *(Shocked at the lie)* Walter Lee Younger!

WALTER *(Staring her down)* Plenty! *(Pause)* What we got to drink in this house? Why don't you offer this man some refreshment. *(To* GEORGE*)* They don't know how to entertain people in this house, man.

GEORGE Thank you—I don't really care for anything.

WALTER *(Feeling his head; sobriety coming)* Where's Mama?

RUTH She ain't come back yet.

WALTER *(Looking* MURCHISON *over from head to toe, scrutinizing his carefully casual tweed sports jacket over cashmere V-neck sweater over soft eyelet shirt and tie, and soft slacks, finished off with white buckskin shoes)* Why all you college boys wear them faggoty-looking white shoes?

RUTH Walter Lee!

*(*GEORGE MURCHISON *ignores the remark)*

WALTER *(To* RUTH*)* Well, they look crazy as hell—white shoes, cold as it is.

RUTH *(Crushed)* You have to excuse him—

WALTER No he don't! Excuse me for what? What you always excusing me for! I'll excuse myself when I needs to be excused! *(A pause)* They look as funny as them black knee socks Beneatha wears out of here all the time.

RUTH It's the college *style,* Walter.

WALTER Style, hell. She looks like she got burnt legs or something!

RUTH Oh, Walter—

WALTER *(An irritable mimic)* Oh, Walter! Oh, Walter! *(To* MURCHISON*)* How's your old man making out? I understand you all going to buy that big hotel on the Drive? *(He finds a beer in the refrigerator, wanders over to* MURCHISON*, sipping and wiping his lips with the back of his hand, and straddling a chair backwards to talk to the other man)* Shrewd move. Your old man is all right, man. *(Tapping his head and half winking for emphasis)* I mean he knows how to operate. I mean he thinks *big*, you know what I mean, I mean for a *home*, you know? But I think he's kind of running out of ideas now. I'd like to talk to him. Listen, man, I got some plans that could turn this city upside down. I mean think like he does. *Big.* Invest big, gamble big, hell, lose *big* if you have to, you know what I mean. It's hard to find a man on this whole Southside who understands my kind of thinking—you dig? *(He scrutinizes* MURCHISON *again, drinks his beer, squints his eyes and leans in close, confidential, man to man)* Me and you ought to sit down and talk sometimes, man. Man, I got me some ideas . . .

MURCHISON *(With boredom)* Yeah—sometimes we'll have to do that, Walter.

WALTER *(Understanding the indifference, and offended)* Yeah—well, when you get the time, man. I know you a busy little boy.

RUTH Walter, please—

WALTER *(Bitterly, hurt)* I know ain't nothing in this world as busy as you colored college boys with your fraternity pins and white shoes . . .

RUTH *(Covering her face with humiliation)* Oh, Walter Lee—

WALTER I see you all all the time—with the books tucked under your arms—going to your *(British A—a mimic)* "clahsses." And for what! What the hell you learning over there? Filling up your heads—*(Counting off on his fingers)*—with the sociology and the psychology—but they teaching you how to be a man? How to take over and run the world? They teaching you how to run a rubber plantation or a steel mill? Naw—just to talk proper and read books and wear them faggoty-looking white shoes . . .

GEORGE *(Looking at him with distaste, a little above it all)* You're all wacked up with bitterness, man.

WALTER *(Intently, almost quietly, between the teeth, glaring at the boy)* And you—ain't you bitter, man? Ain't you just about had it yet? Don't you see no stars gleaming that you can't reach out and grab? You happy?—You contented son-of-a-bitch—you happy? You got it made? Bitter? Man, I'm a volcano. Bitter? Here I am a giant—surrounded by ants! Ants who can't even understand what it is the giant is talking about.

RUTH *(Passionately and suddenly)* Oh, Walter—ain't you with nobody!

WALTER *(Violently)* No! 'Cause ain't nobody with me! Not even my own mother!

RUTH Walter, that's a terrible thing to say!

*(*BENEATHA *enters, dressed for the evening in a cocktail dress and earrings, hair natural)*

GEORGE Well—hey—*(Crosses to* BENEATHA*; thoughtful, with emphasis, since this is a reversal)* You look great!

WALTER *(Seeing his sister's hair for the first time)* What's the matter with your head?

BENEATHA *(Tired of the jokes now)* I cut it off, Brother.

WALTER *(Coming close to inspect it and walking around her)* Well, I'll be damned. So that's what they mean by the African bush . . .

BENEATHA Ha ha. Let's go, George.

GEORGE *(Looking at her)* You know something? I like it. It's sharp. I mean it really is. *(Helps her into her wrap)*

RUTH Yes—I think so, too. *(She goes to the mirror and starts to clutch at her hair)*

WALTER Oh no! You leave yours alone, baby. You might turn out to have a pin-shaped head or something!

BENEATHA See you all later.

RUTH Have a nice time.

GEORGE Thanks. Good night. *(Half out the door, he reopens it. To* WALTER*)* Good night, Prometheus!

(BENEATHA *and* GEORGE *exit)*

WALTER *(To* RUTH*)* Who is Prometheus?

RUTH I don't know. Don't worry about it.

WALTER *(In fury, pointing after* GEORGE*)* See there—they get to a point where they can't insult you man to man—they got to go talk about something ain't nobody never heard of!

RUTH How do you know it was an insult? *(To humor him)* Maybe Prometheus is a nice fellow.

WALTER Prometheus! I bet there ain't even no such thing! I bet that simple-minded clown—

RUTH Walter—

(She stops what she is doing and looks at him)

WALTER *(Yelling)* Don't start!

RUTH Start what?

WALTER Your nagging! Where was I? Who was I with? How much money did I spend?

RUTH *(Plaintively)* Walter Lee—why don't we just try to talk about it . . .

WALTER *(Not listening)* I been out talking with people who understand me. People who care about the things I got on my mind.

RUTH *(Wearily)* I guess that means people like Willy Harris.

WALTER Yes, people like Willy Harris.

RUTH *(With a sudden flash of impatience)* Why don't you all just hurry up and go into the banking business and stop talking about it!

WALTER Why? You want to know why? 'Cause we all tied up in a race of people that don't know how to do nothing but moan, pray and have babies!

(The line is too bitter even for him and he looks at her and sits down)

RUTH Oh, Walter . . . *(Softly)* Honey, why can't you stop fighting me?

WALTER *(Without thinking)* Who's fighting you? Who even cares about you?

(This line begins the retardation of his mood)

RUTH Well—*(She waits a long time, and then with resignation starts to put away her things)* I guess I might as well go on to bed . . . *(More or less to herself)* I don't know where we lost it . . . but we have . . . *(Then, to him)* I—I'm sorry about this new baby, Walter. I guess maybe better go on and do what I started . . . I guess I just didn't realize how bad things was with us . . . I guess I just didn't really realize—*(She starts out to the bedroom and stops)* You want some hot milk?

WALTER Hot milk?

RUTH Yes—hot milk.

WALTER Why hot milk?

RUTH 'Cause after all that liquor you come home with you ought to have something hot in your stomach.

WALTER I don't want no milk.

RUTH You want some coffee then?

WALTER No, I don't want no coffee. I don't want nothing hot to drink. *(Almost plaintively)* Why you always trying to give me something to eat?

RUTH *(Standing and looking at him helplessly)* What *else* can I give you, Walter Lee Younger?

(She stands and looks at him and presently turns to go out again. He lifts his head and watches her going away from him in a new mood which began to emerge when he asked her "Who cares about you?")

WALTER It's been rough, ain't it, baby? *(She hears and stops but does not turn around and he continues to her back)* I guess between two people there ain't never as much understood as folks generally thinks there is. I mean like between me and you—*(She turns to face him)* How we gets to the place where we scared to talk softness to each other. *(He waits, thinking hard himself)* Why you think it got to be like that? *(He is thoughtful, almost as a child would be)* Ruth, what is it gets into people ought to be close?

RUTH I don't know, honey. I think about it a lot.

WALTER On account of you and me, you mean? The way things are with us. The way something done come down between us.

RUTH There ain't so much between us, Walter . . . Not when you come to me and try to talk to me. Try to be with me . . . a little even.

WALTER *(Total honesty)* Sometimes . . . sometimes . . . I don't even know how to try.

RUTH Walter—

WALTER Yes?

RUTH *(Coming to him, gently and with misgiving, but coming to him)* Honey . . . life don't have to be like this. I mean sometimes people can do things so that things are better . . . You remember how we used to talk when Travis was born . . . about the way we were going to live . . . the kind of house . . . *(She is stroking his head)* Well, it's all starting to slip away from us . . .

(He turns her to him and they look at each other and kiss, tenderly and hungrily. The door opens and MAMA *enters—*WALTER *breaks away and jumps up. A beat)*

WALTER Mama, where have you been?

MAMA My—them steps is longer than they used to be. Whew! *(She sits down and ignores him)* How you feeling this evening, Ruth?

*(*RUTH *shrugs, disturbed at having been interrupted and watching her husband knowingly)*

WALTER Mama, where have you been all day?

MAMA *(Still ignoring him and leaning on the table and changing to more comfortable shoes)* Where's Travis?

RUTH I let him go out earlier and he ain't come back yet. Boy, is he going to get it!

WALTER Mama!

MAMA *(As if she has heard him for the first time)* Yes, son?

WALTER Where did you go this afternoon?

MAMA I went downtown to tend to some business that I had to tend to.

WALTER What kind of business?

MAMA You know better than to question me like a child, Brother.

WALTER *(Rising and bending over the table)* Where were you, Mama? *(Bringing his fists down and shouting)* Mama, you didn't go do something with that insurance money, something crazy?

(The front door opens slowly, interrupting him, and TRAVIS *peeks his head in, less than hopefully)*

TRAVIS *(To his mother)* Mama, I—

RUTH "Mama I" nothing! You're going to get it, boy! Get on in that bedroom and get yourself ready!

TRAVIS But I—

MAMA Why don't you all never let the child explain hisself.

RUTH Keep out of it now, Lena.

*(*MAMA *clamps her lips together, and* RUTH *advances toward her son menacingly)*

RUTH A thousand times I have told you not to go off like that—

MAMA *(Holding out her arms to her grandson)* Well—at least let me tell him something. I want him to be the first one to hear . . . Come here, Travis. *(The boy obeys, gladly)* Travis—*(She takes him by the shoulder and looks into his face)*—you know that money we got in the mail this morning?

TRAVIS Yes'm—

MAMA Well—what you think your grandmama gone and done with that money?

TRAVIS I don't know, Grandmama.

MAMA *(Putting her finger on his nose for emphasis)* She went out and she bought you a house! *(The explosion comes from* WALTER *at the end of the revelation and he jumps up and turns away from all of them in a fury.* MAMA *continues, to* TRAVIS*)* You glad about the house? It's going to be yours when you get to be a man.

TRAVIS Yeah—I always wanted to live in a house.

MAMA All right, gimme some sugar then—*(*TRAVIS *puts his arms around her neck as she watches her son over the boy's shoulder. Then, to* TRAVIS*, after the embrace)* Now when you say your prayers tonight, you thank God and your grandfather—'cause it was him who give you the house—in his way.

RUTH *(Taking the boy from* MAMA *and pushing him toward the bedroom)* Now you get out of here and get ready for your beating.

TRAVIS Aw, Mama—

RUTH Get on in there—*(Closing the door behind him and turning radiantly to her mother-in-law)* So you went and did it!

MAMA *(Quietly, looking at her son with pain)* Yes, I did.

RUTH *(Raising both arms classically)* PRAISE GOD! *(Looks at* WALTER *a moment, who says nothing. She crosses rapidly to her husband)* Please, honey—let me be glad . . . you be glad too. *(She has laid her hands on his shoulders, but he shakes himself free of her roughly, without turning to face her)* Oh, Walter . . . a home . . . *a home. (She comes back to* MAMA*)* Well—where is it? How big is it? How much it going to cost?

MAMA Well—

RUTH When we moving?

MAMA *(Smiling at her)* First of the month.

RUTH *(Throwing back her head with jubilance) Praise God!*

MAMA *(Tentatively, still looking at her son's back turned against her and* RUTH*)* It's—it's a nice house too . . . *(She cannot help speaking directly to him. An imploring quality in her voice, her manner, makes her almost like a girl now)* Three bedrooms—nice big one for you and Ruth. . . . Me and Beneatha still have to share our room, but Travis have one of his own—and *(With difficulty)* I figure if the—new baby—is a boy, we could get one of them double-decker outfits . . . And there's a yard with a little patch of dirt where I could maybe get to grow me a few flowers . . . And a nice big basement . . .

RUTH Walter honey, be glad—

MAMA *(Still to his back, fingering things on the table)* 'Course I don't want to make it sound fancier than it is . . . It's just a plain little old house—but it's made good and solid—and it will be *ours.* Walter Lee—it makes a difference in a man when he can walk on floors that belong to *him* . . .

RUTH Where is it?

MAMA *(Frightened at this telling)* Well—well—it's out there in Clybourne Park—

*(*RUTH*'s radiance fades abruptly, and* WALTER *finally turns slowly to face his mother with incredulity and hostility)*

RUTH Where?

MAMA *(Matter-of-factly)* Four o six Clybourne Street, Clybourne Park.

RUTH Clybourne Park? Mama, there ain't no colored people living in Clybourne Park.

MAMA *(Almost idiotically)* Well, I guess there's going to be some now.

WALTER *(Bitterly)* So that's the peace and comfort you went out and bought for us today!

MAMA *(Raising her eyes to meet his finally)* Son—I just tried to find the nicest place for the least amount of money for my family.

RUTH *(Trying to recover from the shock)* Well—well—'course I ain't one never been 'fraid of no crackers, mind you—but—well, wasn't there no other houses nowhere?

MAMA Them houses they put up for colored in them areas way out all seem to cost twice as much as other houses. I did the best I could.

RUTH *(Struck senseless with the news, in its various degrees of goodness and trouble, she sits a moment, her fists propping her chin in thought, and then she starts to rise, bringing her fists down with vigor, the radiance spreading from cheek to cheek again)* Well—well!—All I can say is—if this is my time in life—*MY* TIME—to say good-bye—*(And she builds with momentum as she starts to circle the room with an exuberant, almost tearfully happy release)*—to these Goddamned cracking walls!—*(She pounds the walls)*—and these marching roaches!—*(She wipes at an imaginary army of marching roaches)*—and this cramped little closet which ain't now or never was no kitchen! . . . then I say it loud and good, HALLELUJAH! AND GOOD-BYE MISERY . . . I DON'T NEVER WANT TO SEE YOUR UGLY FACE AGAIN! *(She laughs joyously, having practically destroyed the apartment, and flings her arms up and lets them come down happily, slowly, reflectively, over her abdomen, aware for the first time perhaps that the life therein pulses with happiness and not despair)* Lena?

MAMA *(Moved, watching her happiness)* Yes, honey?

RUTH *(Looking off)* Is there—is there a whole lot of sunlight?

MAMA *(Understanding)* Yes, child, there's a whole lot of sunlight.

(Long pause)

RUTH *(Collecting herself and going to the door of the room* TRAVIS *is in)* Well—I guess I better see 'bout Travis. *(To* MAMA*)* Lord, I sure don't feel like whipping nobody today!

(She exits)

MAMA *(The mother and son are left alone now and the mother waits a long time, considering deeply, before she speaks)* Son—you—you understand what I done, don't you? *(*WALTER *is silent and sullen)* I—I just seen my family falling apart today . . . just falling to pieces in front of my eyes . . . We couldn't of gone on like we was today. We was going backwards 'stead of forwards—talking 'bout killing babies and wishing each other was dead . . . When it gets like that in life—you just got to do something different, push on out and do something bigger . . . *(She waits)* I wish you say something, son . . . I wish you'd say how deep inside you you think I done the right thing—

WALTER *(Crossing slowly to his bedroom door and finally turning there and speaking measuredly)* What you need me to say you done right for? *You* the head of this family. You run our lives like you want to. It was your money and you did what you wanted with it. So what you need for me to say it was all right for? *(Bitterly, to hurt her as deeply as he knows is possible)* So you butchered up a dream of mine—you—who always talking 'bout your children's dreams . . .

MAMA Walter Lee—

(He just closes the door behind him. MAMA *sits alone, thinking heavily)*

Curtain

SCENE TWO

TIME: Friday night. A few weeks later.

AT RISE: Packing crates mark the intention of the family to move. BENEATHA *and* GEORGE *come in, presumably from an evening out again.*

GEORGE O.K. . . . O.K., whatever you say . . . *(They both sit on the couch. He tries to kiss her. She moves away)* Look, we've had a nice evening; let's not spoil it, huh? . . .

(He again turns her head and tries to nuzzle in and she turns away from him, not with distaste but with momentary lack of interest; in a mood to pursue what they were talking about)

BENEATHA I'm *trying* to talk to you.

GEORGE We always talk.

BENEATHA Yes—and I love to talk.

GEORGE *(Exasperated; rising)* I know it and I don't mind it sometimes . . . I want you to cut it out, see— The moody stuff, I mean. I don't like it. You're a nice-looking girl . . . all over. That's all you need, honey, forget the atmosphere. Guys aren't going to go for the atmosphere—they're going to go for what they see. Be glad for that. Drop the Garbo routine. It doesn't go with you. As for myself, I want a nice—*(Groping)*—simple *(Thoughtfully)*—sophisticated girl . . . not a poet—O.K.?

(He starts to kiss her, she rebuffs him again and he jumps up)

BENEATHA Why are you angry, George?

GEORGE Because this is stupid! I don't go out with you to discuss the nature of "quiet desperation" or to hear all about your thoughts—because the world will go on thinking what it thinks regardless—

BENEATHA Then why read books? Why go to school?

GEORGE *(With artificial patience, counting on his fingers)* It's simple. You read books—to learn facts—to get grades—to pass the course—to get a degree. That's all—it has nothing to do with thoughts.

(A long pause)

BENEATHA I see. *(He starts to sit)* Good night, George.

*(*GEORGE *looks at her a little oddly, and starts to exit. He meets* MAMA *coming in)*

GEORGE Oh—hello, Mrs. Younger.

MAMA Hello, George, how you feeling?

GEORGE Fine—fine, how are you?

MAMA Oh, a little tired. You know them steps can get you after a day's work. You all have a nice time tonight?

GEORGE Yes—a fine time. A fine time.

MAMA Well, good night.

GEORGE Good night. *(He exits.* MAMA *closes the door behind her)* Hello, honey. What you sitting like that for?

BENEATHA I'm just sitting.

MAMA Didn't you have a nice time?

BENEATHA No.

MAMA No? What's the matter?

BENEATHA Mama, George is a fool—honest.

(She rises)

MAMA *(Hustling around unloading the packages she has entered with. She stops)* Is he, baby?

BENEATHA Yes.

*(*BENEATHA *makes up* TRAVIS*'s bed as she talks)*

MAMA You sure?

BENEATHA Yes.

MAMA Well—I guess you better not waste your time with no fools.

*(*BENEATHA *looks up at her mother, watching her put groceries in the refrigerator. Finally she gathers up her things and starts into the bedroom. At the door she stops and looks back at her mother)*

BENEATHA Mama—

MAMA Yes, baby—

BENEATHA Thank you.

MAMA For what?

BENEATHA For understanding me this time.

(She exits quickly and the mother stands, smiling a little, looking at the place where BENEATHA *just stood.* RUTH *enters)*

RUTH Now don't you fool with any of this stuff, Lena—

MAMA Oh, I just thought I'd sort a few things out. Is Brother here?

RUTH Yes.

MAMA *(With concern)* Is he—

RUTH *(Reading her eyes)* Yes.

*(*MAMA *is silent and someone knocks on the door.* MAMA *and* RUTH *exchange weary and knowing glances and* RUTH *opens it to admit the neighbor,* MRS. JOHNSON,* *who is a rather squeaky wide-eyed lady of no particular age, with a newspaper under her arm)*

MAMA *(Changing her expression to acute delight and a ringing cheerful greeting)* Oh—hello there, Johnson.

JOHNSON *(This is a woman who decided long ago to be enthusiastic about EVERYTHING in life and she is inclined to wave her wrist vigorously at the height of her exclamatory comments)* Hello there, yourself! H'you this evening, Ruth?

RUTH *(Not much of a deceptive type)* Fine, Mis' Johnson, h'you?

JOHNSON Fine. *(Reaching out quickly, playfully, and patting* RUTH*'s stomach)* Ain't you starting to poke out none yet! *(She mugs with delight at the over-familiar remark and her eyes dart around looking at the crates and packing preparation;* MAMA*'s face is a cold sheet of endurance)* Oh, ain't we getting ready round here, though! Yessir! Lookathere! I'm telling you the Youngers is really getting ready to "move on up a little higher!"—Bless God!

MAMA *(A little drily, doubting the total sincerity of the Blesser)* Bless God.

JOHNSON He's good, ain't He?

MAMA Oh yes, He's good.

*This character and the scene of her visit were cut from the original production and early editions of the play.

JOHNSON I mean sometimes He works in mysterious ways . . . but He works, don't He!

MAMA *(The same)* Yes, he does.

JOHNSON I'm just soooooo happy for y'all. And this here child—*(About* RUTH*)* looks like she could just pop open with happiness, don't she. Where's all the rest of the family?

MAMA Bennie's gone to bed—

JOHNSON Ain't no . . . *(The implication is pregnancy)* sickness done hit you—I hope . . . ?

MAMA No—she just tired. She was out this evening.

JOHNSON *(All is a coo, an emphatic coo)* Aw—ain't that lovely. She still going out with the little Murchison boy?

MAMA *(Drily)* Ummmm huh.

JOHNSON That's lovely. You sure got lovely children, Younger. Me and Isaiah talks all the time 'bout what fine children you was blessed with. We sure do.

MAMA Ruth, give Mis' Johnson a piece of sweet potato pie and some milk.

JOHNSON Oh honey, I can't stay hardly a minute—I just dropped in to see if there was anything I could do. *(Accepting the food easily)* I guess y'all seen the news what's all over the colored paper this week . . .

MAMA No—didn't get mine yet this week.

JOHNSON *(Lifting her head and blinking with the spirit of catastrophe)* You mean you ain't read 'bout them colored people that was bombed out their place out there?

*(*RUTH *straightens with concern and takes the paper and reads it.* JOHNSON *notices her and feeds commentary)*

JOHNSON Ain't it something how bad these here white folks is getting here in Chicago! Lord, getting so you think you right down in Mississippi! *(With a tremendous and rather insincere sense of melodrama)* 'Course I thinks it's wonderful how our folks keeps on pushing out. You hear some of these Negroes round here talking 'bout how they don't go where they ain't wanted and all that—but not me, honey! *(This is a lie)* Wilhemenia Othella Johnson goes anywhere anytime she feels like it! *(With head movement for emphasis)* Yes I do! Why if we left it up to these here crackers, the poor niggers wouldn't have nothing—*(She clasps her hand over her mouth)* Oh, I always forgets you don't 'low that word in your house.

MAMA *(Quietly, looking at her)* No—I don't 'low it.

JOHNSON *(Vigorously again)* Me neither! I was just telling Isaiah yesterday when he come using it in front of me—I said, "Isaiah, it's just like Mis' Younger says all the time—"

MAMA Don't you want some mow pie?

JOHNSON No—no thank you; this was lovely. I got to get on over home and have my midnight coffee. I hear some people say it don't let them sleep but I finds I can't close my eyes right lessen I done had that laaaast cup of coffee . . . *(She waits. A beat. Undaunted)* My Good-night coffee, I calls it!

MAMA *(With much eye-rolling and communication between herself and* RUTH*)* Ruth, why don't you give Mis' Johnson some coffee.

*(*RUTH *gives* MAMA *an unpleasant look for her kindness)*

JOHNSON *(Accepting the coffee)* Where's Brother tonight?

MAMA He's lying down.

JOHNSON MMmmmmm, he sure gets his beauty rest, don't he? Good-looking man. Sure is a good-looking man! *(Reaching out to pat* RUTH'S *stomach again)* I guess that's how come we keep on having babies around here. *(She winks at* MAMA*)* One thing 'bout Brother, he always know how to have a good time. And soooooo ambitious! I bet it was his idea y'all moving out to Clybourne Park. Lord—I bet this time next month y'all's names will have been in the papers plenty—*(Holding up her hands to mark off each word of the headline she can see in front of her)* "NEGROES INVADE CLYBOURNE PARK—BOMBED!"

MAMA *(She and* RUTH *look at the woman in amazement)* We ain't exactly moving out there to get bombed.

JOHNSON Oh, honey—you know I'm praying to God every day that don't nothing like that happen! But you have to think of life like it is—and these here Chicago peckerwoods is some baaaad peckerwoods.

MAMA *(Wearily)* We done thought about all that Mis' Johnson.

*(*BENEATHA *comes out of the bedroom in her robe and passes through to the bathroom.* MRS. JOHNSON *turns)*

JOHNSON Hello there, Bennie!

BENEATHA *(Crisply)* Hello Mrs. Johnson.

JOHNSON How is school?

BENEATHA *(Crisply)* Fine, thank you. *(She goes out.)*

JOHNSON *(Insulted)* Getting so she don't have much to say to nobody.

MAMA The child was on her way to the bathroom.

JOHNSON I know—but sometimes she act like ain't got time to pass the time of day with nobody ain't been to college. Oh—I ain't criticizing her none. It's just—you know how some of our young people gets when they get a little education. *(*MAMA *and* RUTH *say nothing, just look at her)* Yes—well. Well, I guess I better get on home. *(Unmoving)* 'Course I can understand how she must be proud and everything—being the only one in the family to make something of herself. I know just being a chauffeur ain't never satisfied Brother none. He shouldn't feel like that, though. Ain't nothing wrong with being a chauffeur.

MAMA There's plenty wrong with it.

JOHNSON What?

MAMA Plenty. My husband always said being any kind of a servant wasn't a fit thing for a man to have to be. He always said a man's hands was made to make things, or to turn the earth with—not to drive nobody's car for 'em—or—*(She looks at her own hands)* carry they slop jars. And my boy is just like him—he wasn't meant to wait on nobody.

JOHNSON *(Rising, somewhat offended)* Mmmm-mmmmm. The Youngers is too much for me! *(She looks around)* You sure one proud-acting bunch of colored folks. Well—I always thinks like Booker T. Washington said that time—"Education has spoiled many a good plow hand"—

MAMA Is that what old Booker T. said?

JOHNSON He sure did.

MAMA Well, it sounds just like him. The fool.

JOHNSON *(Indignantly)* Well—he was one of our great men.

MAMA Who said so?

JOHNSON *(Nonplussed)* You know, me and you ain't never agreed about some things, Lena Younger. I guess I better be going—

RUTH *(Quickly)* Good night.

JOHNSON Good night. Oh—*(Thrusting it at her)* You can keep the paper! *(With a trill)* 'Night.

MAMA Good night, Mis' Johnson.

*(*MRS. JOHNSON *exits)*

RUTH If ignorance was gold . . .

MAMA Shush. Don't talk about folks behind their backs.

RUTH You do.

MAMA I'm old and corrupted. *(*BENEATHA *enters)* You was rude to Mis' Johnson, Beneatha, and I don't like it at all.

BENEATHA *(At her door)* Mama, if there are two things we, as a people, have got to overcome, one is the Klu Klux Klan—and the other is Mrs. Johnson. *(She exits)*

MAMA Smart aleck.

(The phone rings)

RUTH I'll get it.

MAMA Lord, ain't this a popular place tonight.

RUTH *(At the phone)* Hello—Just a minute. *(Goes to door)* Walter, it's Mrs. Arnold. *(Waits. Goes back to the phone. Tense)* Hello. Yes, this is his wife speaking . . . He's lying down now. Yes . . . well, he'll be in tomorrow. He's been very sick. Yes—I know we should have called, but we were so sure he'd be able to come in today. Yes—yes, I'm very sorry. Yes . . . Thank you very much. *(She hangs up.* WALTER *is standing in the doorway of the bedroom behind her)* That was Mrs. Arnold.

WALTER *(Indifferently)* Was it?

RUTH She said if you don't come in tomorrow that they are getting a new man . . .

WALTER Ain't that sad—ain't that crying sad.

RUTH She said Mr. Arnold has had to take a cab for three days . . . Walter, you ain't been to work for three days! *(This is a revelation to her)* Where you been Walter Lee Younger? (WALTER *looks at her and starts to laugh)* You're going to lose your job.

WALTER That's right . . . *(He turns on the radio)*

RUTH Oh, Walter, and with your mother working like a dog every day—

(A steamy, deep blues pours into the room)

WALTER That's sad too—Everything is sad.

MAMA What you been doing for these three days, son?

WALTER Mama—you don't know all the things a man what got leisure can find to do in this city . . . What's this—Friday night? Well—Wednesday I borrowed Willy Harris' car and I went for a drive . . . just me and myself and I drove and drove . . . Way out . . . way past South Chicago, and I parked the car and I sat and looked at the steel mills all day long. I just sat in the car and looked at them big black chimneys for hours. Then I drove back and I went to the Green Hat. *(Pause)* And Thursday—Thursday I borrowed the car again and I got in it and I pointed it the other way and I drove the other way—for hours—way, way up to Wisconsin, and I looked at the farms. I just drove and looked at the farms. Then I drove back and I went to the Green Hat. *(Pause)* And today—today I didn't get the car. Today I just walked. All over the Southside. And I looked at the Negroes and they looked at me and finally I just sat down on the curb at Thirty-ninth and South Parkway and I just sat there and watched the Negroes go by. And then I went to the Green Hat. You all sad? You all depressed? And you know where I am going right now—

(RUTH *goes out quietly)*

MAMA Oh, Big Walter, is this the harvest of our days?

WALTER You know what I like about the Green Hat? I like this little cat they got there who blows a sax . . . He blows. He talks to me. He ain't but 'bout five feet tall and he's got a conked head and his eyes is always closed and he's all music—

MAMA *(Rising and getting some papers out of her handbag)* Walter—

WALTER And there's this other guy who plays the piano . . . and they got a sound. I mean they can work on some music . . . They got the best little combo in the world in the Green Hat . . . You can just sit there and drink and listen to them three men play and you realize that don't nothing matter worth a damn, but just being there—

MAMA I've helped do it to you, haven't I, son? Walter I been wrong.

WALTER Naw—you ain't never been wrong about nothing, Mama.

MAMA Listen to me, now. I say I been wrong, son. That I been doing to you what the rest of the world been doing to you. *(She turns off the radio)* Walter—*(She stops and he looks up slowly at her and she meets his eyes pleadingly)* What you ain't never understood is that I ain't got nothing, don't own nothing, ain't never really wanted nothing that wasn't for you. There ain't nothing as precious to me . . . There ain't nothing worth holding on to, money, dreams, nothing else—if it means—if it means it's going to destroy my boy. *(She takes an envelope out of her handbag and puts it in front of him and he watches her without speaking or moving)* I paid the man thirty-five hundred dollars down on the house. That leaves sixty-five hundred dollars. Monday morning I want you to take this money and take three thousand dollars and put it in a savings account for Beneatha's medical schooling. The rest you put in a checking account—with your name on it. And from now on any penny that come out of it or that go in it is for you to look after. For you to decide. *(She drops her hands a little helplessly)* It ain't much, but it's all I got in the world and I'm putting it in your hands. I'm telling you to be the head of this family from now on like you supposed to be.

WALTER *(Stares at the money)* You trust me like that, Mama?

MAMA I ain't never stop trusting you. Like I ain't never stop loving you.

(She goes out, and WALTER *sits looking at the money on the table. Finally, in a decisive gesture, he gets up, and, in mingled joy and desperation, picks up the money. At the same moment,* TRAVIS *enters for bed)*

TRAVIS What's the matter, Daddy? You drunk?

WALTER *(Sweetly, more sweetly than we have ever known him)* No, Daddy ain't drunk. Daddy ain't going to never be drunk again. . . .

TRAVIS Well, good night, Daddy.

(The FATHER *has come from behind the couch and leans over, embracing his son)*

WALTER Son, I feel like talking to you tonight.

TRAVIS About what?

WALTER Oh, about a lot of things. About you and what kind of man you going to be when you grow up. . . . Son—son, what do you want to be when you grow up?

TRAVIS A bus driver.

WALTER *(Laughing a little)* A what? Man, that ain't nothing to want to be!

TRAVIS Why not?

WALTER 'Cause, man—it ain't big enough—you know what I mean.

TRAVIS I don't know then. I can't make up my mind. Sometimes Mama asks me that too. And sometimes when I tell her I just want to be like you—she says she don't want me to be like that and sometimes she says she does. . . .

WALTER *(Gathering him up in his arms)* You know what, Travis? In seven years you going to be seventeen years old. And things is going to be very different with us in seven years, Travis. . . . One day when you are seventeen I'll come home—home from my office downtown somewhere—

TRAVIS You don't work in no office, Daddy.

WALTER No—but after tonight. After what your daddy gonna do tonight, there's going to be offices—a whole lot of offices. . . .

TRAVIS What you gonna do tonight, Daddy?

WALTER You wouldn't understand yet, son, but your daddy's gonna make a transaction . . . a business transaction that's going to change our lives. . . . That's how come one day when you 'bout seventeen years old I'll come home and I'll be pretty tired, and you know what I mean, after a day of conferences and secretaries getting things wrong the way they do . . . 'cause an executive's life is hell, man—*(The more he talks the farther away he gets)* And I'll pull the car up on the driveway . . . just a plain black Chrysler, I think, with white walls—no—black tires. More elegant. Rich people don't have to be flashy . . . though I'll have to get something a little sportier for Ruth—maybe a Cadillac convertible to do her shopping in. . . . And I'll come up the steps to the house and the gardener will be clipping away at the hedges and he'll say, "Good evening, Mr. Younger." And I'll say, "Hello, Jefferson, how are you this evening?" And I'll go inside and Ruth will come downstairs and meet me at the door and we'll kiss each other and she'll take my arm and we'll go up to your room to see you sitting on the floor with the catalogues of all the great schools in America around you. . . . All the great schools in the world! And—and I'll say, all right son—it's your seventeenth birthday, what is it you've decided? . . . Just tell me where you want to go to school and you'll *go.* Just tell me, what it is you want to be—and you'll *be* it. . . . Whatever you want to be—Yessir! *(He holds his arms open for* TRAVIS*)* You just name it, son . . . (TRAVIS *leaps into them)* and I hand you the world!

(WALTER's voice has risen in pitch and hysterical promise and on the last line he lifts TRAVIS high)

Blackout

SCENE THREE

TIME: Saturday, moving day, one week later. Before the curtain rises, RUTH's voice, a strident, dramatic church alto, cuts through the silence.

It is, in the darkness, a triumphant surge, a penetrating statement of expectation: "Oh, Lord, I don't feel no ways tired! Children, oh, glory hallelujah!"

As the curtain rises we see that RUTH is alone in the living room, finishing up the family's packing. It is moving day. She is nailing crates and tying cartons. BENEATHA enters, carrying a guitar case, and watches her exuberant sister-in-law.

RUTH Hey!

BENEATHA *(Putting away the case)* Hi.

RUTH *(Pointing at a package)* Honey—look in that package there and see what I found on sale this morning at the South Center. (RUTH *gets up and moves to the package and draws out some curtains)* Lookahere—hand-turned hems!

BENEATHA How do you know the window size out there?

RUTH *(Who hadn't thought of that)* Oh— Well, they bound to fit something in the whole house. Anyhow, they was too good a bargain to pass up. (RUTH *slaps her head, suddenly remembering something)* Oh, Bennie—I meant to put a special note on that carton over there. That's your mama's good china and she wants 'em to be very careful with it.

BENEATHA I'll do it.

(BENEATHA *finds a piece of paper and starts to draw large letters on it)*

RUTH You know what I'm going to do soon as I get in that new house?

BENEATHA What?

RUTH Honey—I'm going to run me a tub of water up to here . . . *(With her fingers practically up to her nostrils)* And I'm going to get in it—and I am going to sit . . . and sit . . . and sit in that hot water and the first person who knocks to tell *me* to hurry up and come out—

BENEATHA Gets shot at sunrise.

RUTH *(Laughing happily)* You said it, sister! *(Noticing how large* BENEATHA *is absent-mindedly making the note)* Honey, they ain't going to read that from no airplane.

BENEATHA *(Laughing herself)* I guess I always think things have more emphasis if they are big, somehow.

RUTH *(Looking up at her and smiling)* You and your brother seem to have that as a philosophy of life. Lord, that man—done changed so 'round here. You know—you know what we did last night? Me and Walter Lee?

BENEATHA What?

RUTH *(Smiling to herself)* We went to the movies. *(Looking at* BENEATHA *to see if she understands)* We went to the movies. You know the last time me and Walter went to the movies together?

BENEATHA No.

RUTH Me neither. That's how long it been. *(Smiling again)* But we went last night. The picture wasn't much good, but that didn't seem to matter. We went—and we held hands.

BENEATHA Oh, Lord!

RUTH We held hands—and you know what?

BENEATHA What?

RUTH When we come out of the show it was late and dark and all the stores and things was closed up . . . and it was kind of chilly and there wasn't many people on the streets . . . and we was still holding hands, me and Walter.

BENEATHA You're killing me.

(WALTER *enters with a large package. His happiness is deep in him; he cannot keep still with his new-found exuberance. He is singing and wig-*

gling and snapping his fingers. He puts his package in a corner and puts a phonograph record, which he has brought in with him, on the record player. As the music, soulful and sensuous, comes up he dances over to RUTH *and tries to get her to dance with him. She gives in at last to his raunchiness and in a fit of giggling allows herself to be drawn into his mood. They dip and she melts into his arms in a classic, body-melding "slow drag")*

BENEATHA *(Regarding them a long time as they dance, then drawing in her breath for a deeply exaggerated comment which she does not particularly mean)* Talk about—olddddddddd-fashioneddddddd—Negroes!

WALTER *(Stopping momentarily)* What kind of Negroes? *(He says this in fun. He is not angry with her today, nor with anyone. He starts to dance with his wife again)*

BENEATHA Old-fashioned.

WALTER *(As he dances with* RUTH*)* You know, when these *New Negroes* have their convention—*(Pointing at his sister)*—that is going to be the chairman of the Committee on Unending Agitation. *(He goes on dancing, then stops)* Race, race, race! . . . Girl, I do believe you are the first person in the history of the entire human race to successfully brainwash yourself. *(*BENEATHA *breaks up and he goes on dancing. He stops again, enjoying his tease)* Damn, even the N double A C P takes a holiday sometimes! *(*BENEATHA *and* RUTH *laugh. He dances with* RUTH *some more and starts to laugh and stops and pantomimes someone over an operating table)* I can just see that chick someday looking down at some poor cat on an operating table and before she starts to slice him, she says . . . *(Pulling his sleeves back maliciously)* "By the way, what are your views on civil rights down there? . . ."

(He laughs at her again and starts to dance happily. The bell sounds)

BENEATHA Sticks and stones may break my bones but . . . words will never hurt me!

*(*BENEATHA *goes to the door and opens it as* WALTER *and* RUTH *go on with the clowning.* BENEATHA *is somewhat surprised to see a quiet-looking middle-aged white man in a business suit holding his hat and a briefcase in his hand and consulting a small piece of paper)*

MAN Uh—how do you do, miss. I am looking for a Mrs.—*(He looks at the slip of paper)* Mrs. Lena Younger? *(He stops short, struck dumb at the sight of the oblivious* WALTER *and* RUTH*)*

BENEATHA *(Smoothing her hair with slight embarrassment)* Oh—yes, that's my mother. Excuse me *(She closes the door and turns to quiet the other two)* Ruth! Brother! *(Enunciating precisely but soundlessly: "There's a white man at the door!" They stop dancing,* RUTH *cuts off the phonograph,* BENEATHA *opens the door. The man casts a curious quick glance at all of them)* Uh—come in please.

MAN *(Coming in)* Thank you.

BENEATHA My mother isn't here just now. Is it business?

MAN Yes . . . well, of a sort.

WALTER *(Freely, the Man of the House)* Have a seat. I'm Mrs. Younger's son. I look after most of her business matters.

*(*RUTH *and* BENEATHA *exchange amused glances)*

MAN *(Regarding* WALTER *and sitting)* Well—My name is Karl Lindner . . .

WALTER *(Stretching out his hand)* Walter Younger. This is my wife—*(*RUTH *nods politely)*—and my sister.

LINDNER How do you do.

WALTER *(Amiably, as he sits himself easily on a chair, leaning forward on his knees with interest and looking expectantly into the newcomer's face)* What can we do for you, Mr. Lindner!

LINDNER *(Some minor shuffling of the hat and briefcase on his knees)* Well—I am a representative of the Clybourne Park Improvement Association—

WALTER *(Pointing)* Why don't you sit your things on the floor?

LINDNER Oh—yes. Thank you. *(He slides the briefcase and hat under the chair)* And as I was saying—I am from the Clybourne Park Improvement Association and we have had it brought to our attention at the last meeting that you people—or at least your mother—has bought a piece of residential property at—*(He digs for the slip of paper again)*—four o six Clybourne Street . . .

WALTER That's right. Care for something to drink? Ruth, get Mr. Lindner a beer.

LINDNER *(Upset for some reason)* Oh—no, really. I mean thank you very much, but no thank you.

RUTH *(Innocently)* Some coffee?

LINDNER Thank you, nothing at all.

(BENEATHA is watching the man carefully)

LINDNER Well, I don't know how much you folks know about our organization. *(He is a gentle man; thoughtful and somewhat labored in his manner)* It is one of these community organizations set up to look after—oh, you know, things like block upkeep and special projects and we also have what we call our New Neighbors Orientation Committee . . .

BENEATHA *(Drily)* Yes—and what do they do?

LINDNER *(Turning a little to her and then returning the main force to* WALTER*)* Well—it's what you might call a sort of welcoming committee, I guess. I mean they, we—I'm the chairman of the committee—go around and see the new people who move into the neighborhood and sort of give them the lowdown on the way we do things out in Clybourne Park.

BENEATHA *(With appreciation of the two meanings, which escape* RUTH *and* WALTER*)* Unhuh.

LINDNER And we also have the category of what the association calls—*(He looks elsewhere)*—uh—special community problems . . .

BENEATHA Yes—and what are some of those?

WALTER Girl, let the man talk.

LINDNER *(With understated relief)* Thank you. I would sort of like to explain this thing in my own way. I mean I want to explain to you in a certain way.

WALTER Go ahead.

LINDNER Yes. Well. I'm going to try to get right to the point. I'm sure we'll all appreciate that in the long run.

BENEATHA Yes.

WALTER Be still now!

LINDNER Well—

RUTH *(Still innocently)* Would you like another chair—you don't look comfortable.

LINDNER *(More frustrated than annoyed)* No, thank you very much. Please. Well—to get right to the point I—*(A great breath, and he is off at last)* I am sure you people must be aware of some of the incidents which have happened in various parts of the city when colored people have moved into certain areas—*(*BENEATHA *exhales heavily and starts tossing a piece of fruit up and down in the air)* Well—because we have what I think is going to be a unique type of organization in American community life—not only do we deplore that kind of thing—but we are trying to do something about it. *(*BENEATHA *stops tossing and turns with a new and quizzical interest to the man)* We feel—*(gaining confidence in his mission because of the interest in the faces of the people he is talking to)*—we feel that most of the trouble in this world, when you come right down to it—*(He hits his knee for emphasis)*—most of the trouble exists because people just don't sit down and talk to each other.

RUTH *(Nodding as she might in church, pleased with the remark)* You can say that again, mister.

LINDNER *(More encouraged by such affirmation)* That we don't try hard enough in this world to understand the other fellow's problem. The other guy's point of view.

RUTH Now that's right.

*(*BENEATHA *and* WALTER *merely watch and listen with genuine interest)*

LINDNER Yes—that's the way we feel out in Clybourne Park. And that's why I was elected to come here this afternoon and talk to you people. Friendly like, you know, the way people should talk to each other and see if we couldn't find some way to work this thing out. As I say, the whole business is a matter of *caring* about the other fellow. Anybody can see that you are a nice family of folks, hard working and honest I'm sure. (BENEATHA *frowns slightly, quizzically, her head tilted regarding him)* Today everybody knows what it means to be on the outside of *something.* And of course, there is always somebody who is out to take advantage of people who don't always understand.

WALTER What do you mean?

LINDNER Well—you see our community is made up of people who've worked hard as the dickens for years to build up that little community. They're not rich and fancy people; just hard-working, honest people who don't really have much but those little homes and a dream of the kind of community they want to raise their children in. Now, I don't say we are perfect and there is a lot wrong in some of the things they want. But you've got to admit that a man, right or wrong, has the right to want to have the neighborhood he lives in a certain kind of way. And at the moment the overwhelming majority of our people out there feel that people get along better, take more of a common interest in the life of the community, when they share a common background. I want you to believe me when I tell you that race prejudice simply doesn't enter into it. It is a matter of the people of Clybourne Park believing, rightly or wrongly, as I say, that for the happiness of all concerned that our Negro families are happier when they live in their *own* communities.

BENEATHA *(With a grand and bitter gesture)* This, friends, is the Welcoming Committee!

WALTER *(Dumbfounded, looking at* LINDNER*)* Is this what you came marching all the way over here to tell us?

LINDNER Well, now we've been having a fine conversation. I hope you'll hear me all the way through.

WALTER *(Tightly)* Go ahead, man.

LINDNER You see—in the face of all the things I have said, we are prepared to make your family a very generous offer . . .

BENEATHA Thirty pieces and not a coin less!

WALTER Yeah?

LINDNER *(Putting on his glasses and drawing a form out of the briefcase)* Our association is prepared, through the collective effort of our people, to buy the house from you at a financial gain to your family.

RUTH Lord have mercy, ain't this the living gall!

WALTER All right, you through?

LINDNER Well, I want to give you the exact terms of the financial arrangement—

WALTER We don't want to hear no exact terms of no arrangements. I want to know if you got any more to tell us 'bout getting together?

LINDNER *(Taking off his glasses)* Well—I don't suppose that you feel . . .

WALTER Never mind how I feel—you got any more to say 'bout how people ought to sit down and talk to each other? . . . Get out of my house, man.

(He turns his back and walks to the door)

LINDNER *(Looking around at the hostile faces and reaching and assembling his hat and briefcase)* Well—I don't understand why you people are reacting this way. What do you think you are going to gain by moving into a neighborhood where you just aren't wanted and where some elements—well—people can get awful worked up when they feel that their whole way of life and everything they've ever worked for is threatened.

WALTER Get out.

LINDNER *(At the door, holding a small card)* Well—I'm sorry it went like this.

WALTER Get out.

LINDNER *(Almost sadly regarding* WALTER*)* You just can't force people to change their hearts, son.

(He turns and puts his card on a table and exits, WALTER *pushes the door to with stinging hatred, and stands looking at it.* RUTH *just sits and* BENEATHA *just stands. They say nothing.* MAMA *and* TRAVIS *enter)*

MAMA Well—this all the packing got done since I left out of here this morning. I testify before God that my children got all the energy of the *dead!* What time the moving men due?

BENEATHA Four o'clock. You had a caller, Mama.

(She is smiling, teasingly)

MAMA Sure enough—who?

BENEATHA *(Her arms folded saucily)* The Welcoming Committee.

*(*WALTER *and* RUTH *giggle)*

MAMA *(Innocently)* Who?

BENEATHA The Welcoming Committee. They said they're sure going to be glad to see you when you get there.

WALTER *(Devilishly)* Yeah, they said they can't hardly wait to see your face.

(Laughter)

MAMA *(Sensing their facetiousness)* What's the matter with you all?

WALTER Ain't nothing the matter with us. We just telling you 'bout the gentleman who came to see you this afternoon. From the Clybourne Park Improvement Association.

MAMA What he want?

RUTH *(In the same mood as* BENEATHA *and* WALTER*)* To welcome you, honey.

WALTER He said they can't hardly wait. He said the one thing they don't have, that they just *dying* to have out there is a fine family of fine colored people! *(To* RUTH *and* BENEATHA*)* Ain't that right!

RUTH *(Mockingly)* Yeah! He left his card—

BENEATHA *(Handing card to* MAMA*)* In case.

*(*MAMA *reads and throws it on the floor—understanding and looking off as she draws her chair up to the table on which she has put her plant and some sticks and some cord)*

MAMA Father, give us strength. *(Knowingly—and without fun)* Did he threaten us?

BENEATHA Oh—Mama—they don't do it like that any more. He talked Brotherhood. He said everybody ought to learn how to sit down and hate each other with good Christian fellowship.

(She and WALTER *shake hands to ridicule the remark)*

MAMA *(Sadly)* Lord, protect us . . .

RUTH You should hear the money those folks raised to buy the house from us. All we paid and then some.

BENEATHA What they think we going to do—eat 'em?

RUTH No, honey, marry 'em.

MAMA *(Shaking her head)* Lord, Lord, Lord . . .

RUTH Well—that's the way the crackers crumble. *(A beat)* Joke.

BENEATHA *(Laughingly noticing what her mother is doing)* Mama, what are you doing?

MAMA Fixing my plant so it won't get hurt none on the way . . .

BENEATHA Mama, you going to take *that* to the new house?

MAMA Un-huh—

BENEATHA That raggedy-looking old thing?

MAMA *(Stopping and looking at her)* It expresses ME!

RUTH *(With delight, to* BENEATHA*)* So there, Miss Thing!

*(*WALTER *comes to* MAMA *suddenly and bends down behind her and squeezes her in his arms with all his strength. She is overwhelmed by the suddenness of it and, though delighted, her manner is like that of* RUTH *and* TRAVIS *)*

MAMA Look out now, boy! You make me mess up my thing here!

WALTER *(His face lit, he slips down on his knees beside her, his arms still about her)* Mama . . . you know what it means to climb up in the chariot?

MAMA *(Gruffly, very happy)* Get on away from me now . . .

RUTH *(Near the gift-wrapped package, trying to catch* WALTER'*s eye)* Psst—

WALTER What the old song say, Mama . . .

RUTH Walter—Now?

(She is pointing at the package)

WALTER *(Speaking the lines, sweetly, playfully, in his mother's face)*
I got wings . . . you got wings . . .
All God's Children got wings . . .

MAMA Boy—get out of my face and do some work . . .

WALTER *When I get to heaven gonna put on my wings.*
Gonna fly all over God's heaven . . .

BENEATHA *(Teasingly, from across the room)* Everybody talking 'bout heaven ain't going there!

WALTER *(To* RUTH *who is carrying the box across to them)* I don't know, you think we ought to give her that . . . Seems to me she ain't been very appreciative around here.

MAMA *(Eying the box, which is obviously a gift)* What is that?

WALTER *(Taking it from* RUTH *and putting it on the table in front of* MAMA*)* Well—what you all think? Should we give it to her?

RUTH Oh—she was pretty good today.

MAMA I'll good you—

(She turns her eyes to the box again)

BENEATHA Open it, Mama.

(She stands up, looks at it, turns and looks at all of them, and then presses her hands together and does not open the package)

WALTER *(Sweetly)* Open it, Mama. It's for you. *(*MAMA *looks in his eyes. It is the first present in her life without its being Christmas. Slowly she opens her package and lifts out, one by one, a brand-new sparkling set of gardening tools.* WALTER *continues, prodding)* Ruth made up the note—read it . . .

MAMA *(Picking up the card and adjusting her glasses)* "To our own Mrs. Miniver—Love from Brother, Ruth and Beneatha." Ain't that lovely . . .

TRAVIS *(Tugging at his father's sleeve)* Daddy, can I give her mine now?

WALTER All right, son. *(*TRAVIS *flies to get his gift)*

MAMA Now I don't have to use my knives and forks no more . . .

WALTER Travis didn't want to go in with the rest of us, Mama. He got his own. *(Somewhat amused)* We don't know what it is . . .

TRAVIS *(Racing back in the room with a large hatbox and putting it in front of his grandmother)* Here!

MAMA Lord have mercy, baby. You done gone and bought your grandmother a hat?

TRAVIS *(Very proud)* Open it!

(She does and lifts out an elaborate, but very elaborate, wide gardening hat, and all the adults break up at the sight of it)

RUTH Travis, honey what is that?

TRAVIS *(Who thinks it is beautiful and appropriate)* It's a gardening hat! Like the ladies always have on in the magazines when they work in their gardens.

BENEATHA *(Giggling fiercely)* Travis—we were trying to make Mama Mrs. Miniver—not Scarlett O'Hara!

MAMA *(Indignantly)* What's the matter with you all! This here is a beautiful hat! *(Absurdly)* I always wanted me one just like it!

(She pops it on her head to prove it to her grandson, and the hat is ludicrous and considerably oversized)

RUTH Hot dog! Go, Mama!

WALTER *(Doubled over with laughter)* I'm sorry, Mama—but you look like you ready to go out and chop you some cotton sure enough!

(They all laugh except MAMA*, out of deference to* TRAVIS'*s feelings)*

MAMA *(Gathering the boy up to her)* Bless your heart—this is the prettiest hat I ever owned—*(*WALTER, RUTH *and* BENEATHA *chime in—noisily, festively and insincerely* *congratulating* TRAVIS *on his gift)* What are we all standing around here for? We ain't finished packin' yet. Bennie, you ain't packed one book.

(The bell rings)

BENEATHA That couldn't be the movers . . . it's not hardly two good yet—

*(*BENEATHA *goes into her room.* MAMA *starts for door)*

WALTER *(Turning, stiffening)* Wait—wait—I'll get it.

(He stands and looks at the door)

MAMA You expecting company, son?

WALTER *(Just looking at the door)* Yeah—yeah . . .

*(*MAMA *looks at* RUTH, *and they exchange innocent and unfrightened glances)*

MAMA *(Not understanding)* Well, let them in, son.

BENEATHA *(From her room)* We need some more string.

MAMA Travis—you run to the hardware and get me some string cord.

*(*MAMA *goes out and* WALTER *turns and looks at* RUTH. TRAVIS *goes to a dish for money)*

RUTH Why don't you answer the door, man?

WALTER *(Suddenly bounding across the floor to embrace her)* 'Cause sometimes it hard to let the future begin!

(Stooping down in her face)

I got wings! You got wings!
All God's children got wings!

(He crosses to the door and throws it open. Standing there is a very slight little man in a not too prosperous business suit and with haunted frightened eyes and a hat pulled down tightly, brim up, around his forehead. TRAVIS *passes between the men and exits.* WALTER *leans deep in the man's face, still in his jubilance)*

When I get to heaven gonna put on my wings,
Gonna fly all over God's heaven . . .

(The little man just stares at him)

Heaven—

(Suddenly he stops and looks past the little man into the empty hallway) Where's Willy, man?

BOBO He ain't with me.

WALTER *(Not disturbed)* Oh—come on in. You know my wife.

BOBO *(Dumbly, taking off his hat)* Yes—h'you, Miss Ruth.

RUTH *(Quietly, a mood apart from her husband already, seeing* BOBO*)* Hello, Bobo.

WALTER You right on time today . . . Right on time. That's the way! *(He slaps* BOBO *on his back)* Sit down . . . lemme hear.

*(*RUTH *stands stiffly and quietly in back of them, as though somehow she senses death, her eyes fixed on her husband)*

BOBO *(His frightened eyes on the floor, his hat in his hands)* Could I please get a drink of water, before I tell you about it, Walter Lee?

*(*WALTER *does not take his eyes off the man.* RUTH *goes blindly to the tap and gets a glass of water and brings it to* BOBO*)*

WALTER There ain't nothing wrong, is there?

BOBO Lemme tell you—

WALTER Man—didn't nothing go wrong?

BOBO Lemme tell you—Walter Lee. *(Looking at* RUTH *and talking to her more than to* WALTER*)* You know how it was. I got to tell you how it was. I mean first I got to tell you how it was all the way . . . I mean about the money I put in, Walter Lee . . .

WALTER *(With taut agitation now)* What about the money you put in?

BOBO Well—it wasn't much as we told you—me and Willy—*(He stops)* I'm sorry, Walter. I got a bad feeling about it. I got a real bad feeling about it . . .

WALTER Man, what you telling me about all this for? . . . Tell me what happened in Springfield . . .

BOBO Springfield.

RUTH *(Like a dead woman)* What was supposed to happen in Springfield?

BOBO *(To her)* This deal that me and Walter went into with Willy— Me and Willy was going to go down to Springfield and spread some money 'round so's we wouldn't have to wait so long for the liquor license . . . That's what we were going to do. Everybody said that was the way you had to do, you understand, Miss Ruth?

WALTER Man—what happened down there?

BOBO *(A pitiful man, near tears)* I'm trying to tell you, Walter.

WALTER *(Screaming at him suddenly)* THEN TELL ME, GODDAMMIT . . . WHAT'S THE MATTER WITH YOU?

BOBO Man . . . I didn't go to no Springfield, yesterday.

WALTER *(Halted, life hanging in the moment)* Why not?

BOBO *(The long way, the hard way to tell)* 'Cause I didn't have no reasons to . . .

WALTER Man, what are you talking about!

BOBO I'm talking about the fact that when I got to the train station yesterday morning—eight o'clock like we planned . . . Man—*Willy didn't never show up.*

WALTER Why . . . where was he . . . where is he?

BOBO That's what I'm trying to tell you . . . I don't know . . . I waited six hours . . . I called his house . . . and I waited . . . six hours . . . I waited in that train station six hours . . . *(Breaking into tears)* That was all the extra money I had in the world . . . *(Looking up at* WALTER *with the tears running down his face)* Man, *Willy is gone.*

WALTER Gone, what you mean Willy is gone? Gone where? You mean he went by himself. You mean he went off to Springfield by himself—to take care of getting the license—*(Turns and looks anxiously at* RUTH*)* You mean maybe he didn't want too many people in on the business down there? *(Looks to* RUTH *again, as before)* You know Willy got his own ways. *(Looks back to* BOBO*)* Maybe you was late yesterday and he just went on down there without you. Maybe—maybe—he's been callin' you at home tryin' to tell you what happened or something. Maybe—maybe—he just got sick. He's somewhere—he's got to be somewhere. We just got to find him—me and you got to find him. *(Grabs* BOBO *senselessly by the collar and starts to shake him)* We got to!

BOBO *(In sudden angry, frightened agony)* What's the matter with you, Walter! *When a cat take off with your money he don't leave you no road maps!*

WALTER *(Turning madly, as though he is looking for* WILLY *in the very room)* Willy! . . . Willy . . . don't do it . . . Please don't do it . . . Man, not with that money . . . Man, please, not with that money . . . Oh, God . . . Don't let it be true . . . *(He is wandering around, crying out for* WILLY *and looking for him or perhaps for help from God)* Man . . . I trusted you . . . Man, I put my life in your hands . . . *(He starts to crumple down on the floor as* RUTH *just covers her face in horror.* MAMA *opens the door and comes into the room, with* BENEATHA *behind her)* Man . . . *(He starts to pound the floor with his fists, sobbing wildly)* THAT MONEY IS MADE OUT OF MY FATHER'S FLESH—

BOBO *(Standing over him helplessly)* I'm sorry, Walter . . . *(Only* WALTER*'s sobs reply.* BOBO *puts on his hat)* I had my life staked on this deal, too . . .

(He exits)

MAMA *(To* WALTER*)* Son—*(She goes to him, bends down to him, talks to his bent head)* Son . . . Is it gone? Son, I gave you sixty-five hundred dollars. Is it gone? All of it? Beneatha's money too?

WALTER *(Lifting his head slowly)* Mama . . . I never . . . went to the bank at all . . .

MAMA *(Not wanting to believe him)* You mean . . . your sister's school money . . . you used that too . . . Walter? . . .

WALTER Yessss! All of it . . . It's all gone . . .

(There is total silence. RUTH *stands with her face covered with her hands;* BENEATHA *leans forlornly*

against a wall, fingering a piece of red ribbon from the mother's gift. MAMA *stops and looks at her son without recognition and then, quite without thinking about it, starts to beat him senselessly in the face.* BENEATHA *goes to them and stops it)*

BENEATHA Mama!

*(*MAMA *stops and looks at both of her children and rises slowly and wanders vaguely, aimlessly away from them)*

MAMA I seen . . . him . . . night after night . . . come in . . . and look at that rug . . . and then look at me . . . the red showing in his eyes . . . the veins moving in his head . . . I seen him grow thin and old before he was forty . . . working and working and working like somebody's old horse . . . killing himself . . . and you—you give it all away in a day—*(She raises her arms to strike him again)*

BENEATHA Mama—

MAMA Oh, God . . . *(She looks up to Him)* Look down here—and show me the strength.

BENEATHA Mama—

MAMA *(Folding over)* Strength . . .

BENEATHA *(Plaintively)* Mama . . .

MAMA Strength!

Curtain

Act Three

An hour later.

At curtain, there is a sullen light of gloom in the living room, gray light not unlike that which began the first scene of Act One. At left we can see WALTER *within his room, alone with himself. He is stretched out on the bed, his shirt out and open, his arms under his head. He does not smoke, he does not cry out, he merely lies there, looking up at the ceiling, much as if he were alone in the world.*

In the living room BENEATHA *sits at the table, still surrounded by the now almost ominous packing crates. She sits looking off. We feel that this is a mood struck perhaps an hour before, and it lingers now, full of the empty sound of profound disappointment. We see on a line from her brother's bedroom the sameness of their attitudes. Presently the bell rings and* BENEATHA *rises without ambition or interest in answering. It is* ASAGAI, *smiling broadly, striding into the room with energy and happy expectation and conversation.*

ASAGAI I came over . . . I had some free time. I thought I might help with the packing. Ah, I like the look of packing crates! A household in preparation for a journey! It depresses some people . . . but for me . . . it is another feeling. Something full of the flow of life, do you understand? Movement, progress . . . It makes me think of Africa.

BENEATHA Africa!

ASAGAI What kind of a mood is this? Have I told you how deeply you move me?

BENEATHA He gave away the money, Asagai . . .

ASAGAI Who gave away what money?

BENEATHA The insurance money. My brother gave it away.

ASAGAI Gave it away?

BENEATHA He made an investment! With a man even Travis wouldn't have trusted with his most worn-out marbles.

ASAGAI And it's gone?

BENEATHA Gone!

ASAGAI I'm very sorry . . . And you, now?

BENEATHA Me? . . . Me? . . . Me, I'm nothing . . . Me. When I was very small . . . we used to take our sleds out in the wintertime and the only hills we had were the ice-covered stone steps of some houses down the street. And we used to fill them in with snow and make them smooth and slide down them all day . . . and it was very dangerous, you know . . . far too steep . . . and sure enough one day a kid named Rufus came down too fast and hit the sidewalk and we saw his face just split open right there in front of us . . . And I remember standing there looking at his bloody open face thinking that was the end of Rufus. But the ambulance came and they took him to the hospital and they fixed the broken bones and they sewed it all up . . . and the next time I saw Rufus he just had a little line down the middle of his face . . . I never got over that . . .

ASAGAI What?

BENEATHA That that was what one person could do for another, fix him up—sew up the problem, make him all right again. That was the most marvelous thing in the world . . . I wanted to do that. I always thought it was the one concrete thing in the world that a human being could do. Fix up the sick, you know—and make them whole again. This was truly being God . . .

ASAGAI You wanted to be God?

BENEATHA No—I wanted to cure. It used to be so important to me. I wanted to cure. It used to matter. I used to care. I mean about people and how their bodies hurt . . .

ASAGAI And you've stopped caring?

BENEATHA Yes—I think so.

ASAGAI Why?

BENEATHA *(Bitterly)* Because it doesn't seem deep enough, close enough to what ails mankind! It was a child's way of seeing things—or an idealist's.

ASAGAI Children see things very well sometimes—and idealists even better.

BENEATHA I know that's what you think. Because you are still where I left off. You with all your talk and dreams about Africa! You still think you can patch up the world. Cure the Great Sore of Colonialism—*(Loftily, mocking it)* with the Penicillin of Independence—!

ASAGAI Yes!

BENEATHA Independence *and then what?* What about all the crooks and thieves and just plain idiots who will come into power and steal and plunder the same as before—only now they will be black and do it in the name of the new Independence—WHAT ABOUT THEM?!

ASAGAI That will be the problem for another time. First we must get there.

BENEATHA And where does it end?

ASAGAI End? Who even spoke of an end? To life? To living?

BENEATHA An end to misery! To stupidity! Don't you see there isn't any real progress, Asagai, there is only one large circle that we march in, around and around, each of us with our own little picture in front of us—our own little mirage that we think is the future.

ASAGAI That is the mistake.

BENEATHA What?

ASAGAI What you just said—about the circle. It isn't a circle—it is simply a long line—as in geometry, you know, one that reaches into infinity. And because we cannot see the end—we also cannot see how it changes. And it is very odd but those who see the changes—who dream, who will not give up—are called idealists . . . and those who see only the circle—we call *them* the "realists"!

BENEATHA Asagai, while I was sleeping in that bed in there, people went out and took the future right out of my hands! And nobody asked me, nobody consulted me—they just went out and changed my life!

ASAGAI Was it your money?

BENEATHA What?

ASAGAI Was it your money he gave away?

BENEATHA It belonged to all of us.

ASAGAI But did you earn it? Would you have had it at all if your father had not died?

BENEATHA No.

ASAGAI Then isn't there something wrong in a house—in a world—where all dreams, good or bad, must depend on the death of a man? I never thought to see *you* like this, Alaiyo. You! Your brother made a mistake and you are grateful to him so that now you can give up the ailing human race on account of it! You talk about what good is struggle, what good is anything! Where are we all going and why are we bothering!

BENEATHA AND YOU CANNOT ANSWER IT!

ASAGAI *(Shouting over her) I LIVE THE ANSWER! (Pause)* In my village at home it is the exceptional man who can even read a newspaper . . . or who ever sees a book at all. I will go home and much of what I will have to say will seem strange to the people of my village. But I will teach and work and things will happen, slowly and swiftly. At times it will seem that nothing changes at all . . . and then again the sudden dramatic events which make history leap into the future. And then quiet again. Retrogression even. Guns, murder, revolution. And I even will have moments when I wonder if the quiet was not better than all that death and hatred. But I will look about my village at the illiteracy and disease and ignorance and I will not wonder long. And perhaps . . . perhaps I will be a great man . . . I mean perhaps I will hold on to the substance of truth and find my way always with the right course . . . and perhaps for it I will be butchered in my bed some night by the servants of empire . . .

BENEATHA *The martyr!*

ASAGAI *(He smiles)* . . . or perhaps I shall live to be a very old man, respected and esteemed in my new nation . . . And perhaps I shall hold office and this is what I'm trying to tell you, Alaiyo: Perhaps the things I believe now for my country will be wrong and outmoded, and I will not understand and do terrible things to have things my way or merely to keep my power. Don't you see that there will be young men and women—not British soldiers then, but my own black countrymen—to step out of the shadows some evening and slit my then useless throat? Don't you see they have always been there . . . that they always will be. And that such a thing as my own death will be an advance? They who might kill me even . . . actually replenish all that I was.

BENEATHA Oh, Asagai, I know all that.

ASAGAI Good! Then stop moaning and groaning and tell me what you plan to do.

BENEATHA Do?

ASAGAI I have a bit of a suggestion.

BENEATHA What?

ASAGAI *(Rather quietly for him)* That when it is all over—that you come home with me—

BENEATHA *(Staring at him and crossing away with exasperation)* Oh—Asagai—at this moment you decide to be romantic!

ASAGAI *(Quickly understanding the misunderstanding)* My dear, young creature of the New World—I do not mean across the city—I mean across the ocean: home—to Africa.

BENEATHA *(Slowly understanding and turning to him with murmured amazement)* To Africa?

ASAGAI Yes! . . . *(Smiling and lifting his arms playfully)* Three hundred years later the African Prince rose up out of the seas and swept the maiden back across the middle passage over which her ancestors had come—

BENEATHA *(Unable to play)* To—to Nigeria?

ASAGAI Nigeria. Home. *(Coming to her with genuine romantic flippancy)* I will show you our mountains and our stars; and give you cool drinks from gourds and teach you the old songs and the ways of our people—and, in time, we will pretend that—*(Very softly)*—you have only been away for a day. Say that you'll come—

(He swings her around and takes her full in his arms in a kiss which proceeds to passion)

BENEATHA *(Pulling away suddenly)* You're getting me all mixed up—

ASAGAI Why?

BENEATHA Too many things—too many things have happened today. I must sit down and think. I don't know what I feel about anything right this minute.

(She promptly sits down and props her chin on her fist)

ASAGAI *(Charmed)* All right, I shall leave you. No—don't get up. *(Touching her, gently, sweetly)* Just sit awhile and think . . . Never be afraid to sit awhile and think. *(He goes to door and looks at her)* How often I have looked at you and said, "Ah—so this is what the New World hath finally wrought . . ."

(He exits. BENEATHA *sits on alone. Presently* WALTER *enters from his room and starts to rummage through things, feverishly looking for something. She looks up and turns in her seat)*

BENEATHA *(Hissingly)* Yes—just look at what the New World hath wrought! . . . Just look! *(She gestures with bitter disgust)* There he is!

Monsieur le petit bourgeois noir—himself! There he is—Symbol of a Rising Class! Entrepreneur! Titan of the system!

(WALTER *ignores her completely and continues frantically and destructively looking for something and hurling things to floor and tearing things out of their place in his search.* BENEATHA *ignores the eccentricity of his actions and goes on with the monologue of insult)*

Did you dream of yachts on Lake Michigan, Brother? Did you see yourself on that Great Day sitting down at the Conference Table, surrounded by all the mighty bald-headed men in America? All halted, waiting, breathless, waiting for your pronouncements on industry? Waiting for you—Chairman of the Board! (WALTER *finds what he is looking for—a small piece of white paper—and pushes it in his pocket and puts on his coat and rushes out without ever having looked at her. She shouts after him)* I look at you and I see the final triumph of stupidity in the world!

(The door slams and she returns to just sitting again. RUTH *comes quickly out of* MAMA*'s room)*

RUTH Who was that?

BENEATHA Your husband.

RUTH Where did he go?

BENEATHA Who knows—maybe he has an appointment at U.S. Steel.

RUTH *(Anxiously, with frightened eyes)* You didn't say nothing bad to him, did you?

BENEATHA Bad? Say anything bad to him? No—I told him he was a sweet boy and full of dreams and everything is strictly peachy keen, as the ofay kids say!

(MAMA *enters from her bedroom. She is lost, vague, trying to catch hold, to make some sense of her former command of the world, but it still eludes her. A sense of waste overwhelms her gait; a measure of apology rides on her shoulders. She goes to her plant, which has remained on the table, looks at it, picks it up and takes it to the window sill and sits it outside, and she stands and looks at it a long moment. Then she closes the window, straightens her body with effort and turns around to her children)*

MAMA Well—ain't it a mess in here, though? *(A false cheerfulness, a beginning of something)* I guess we all better stop moping around and get some work done. All this unpacking and everything we got to do. (RUTH *raises her head slowly in response to the sense of the line; and* BENEATHA *in similar manner turns very slowly to look at her mother)* One of you all better call the moving people and tell 'em not to come.

RUTH Tell 'em not to come?

MAMA Of course, baby. Ain't no need in 'em coming all the way here and having to go back. They charges for that too. *(She sits down, fingers to her brow, thinking)* Lord, ever since I was a little girl, I always remembers people saying, "Lena—Lena Eggleston, you aims too high all the time. You needs to slow down and see life a little more like it is. Just slow down some." That's what they always used to say down home—"Lord, that Lena Eggleston is a high-minded thing. She'll get her due one day!"

RUTH No, Lena . . .

MAMA Me and Big Walter just didn't never learn right.

RUTH Lena, no! We gotta go. Bennie—tell her . . . *(She rises and crosses to* BENEATHA *with her arms outstretched.* BENEATHA *doesn't respond)* Tell her we can still move . . . the notes ain't but a hundred and twenty-five a month. We got four grown people in this house—we can work . . .

MAMA *(To herself)* Just aimed too high all the time—

RUTH *(Turning and going to* MAMA *fast—the words pouring out with urgency and desperation)* Lena—I'll work . . . I'll work twenty hours a day in all the kitchens in Chicago . . . I'll strap my baby on my back if I have to and scrub all the floors in America and wash all the sheets in America if I have to—but we got to MOVE! We got to get OUT OF HERE!!

(MAMA *reaches out absently and pats* RUTH*'s hand)*

MAMA No—I sees things differently now. Been thinking 'bout some of the things we could do to fix this place up some. I seen a second-hand bureau over on Maxwell Street just the other day that could fit right there. *(She points to where the new furniture might go.* RUTH *wanders away from her)* Would need some new handles on it and then a little varnish and it look like something brand-new. And—we can put up them new curtains in the kitchen . . . Why this place be looking fine. Cheer us all up so that we forget trouble ever come . . . *(To* RUTH*)* And you could get some nice screens to put up in your room round the baby's bassinet . . . *(She looks at both of them, pleadingly)* Sometimes you just got to know when to give up some things . . . and hold on to what you got. . . .

*(*WALTER *enters from the outside, looking spent and leaning against the door, his coat hanging from him)*

MAMA Where you been, son?

WALTER *(Breathing hard)* Made a call.

MAMA To who, son?

WALTER To The Man. *(He heads for his room)*

MAMA What man, baby?

WALTER *(Stops in the door)* The Man, Mama. Don't you know who The Man is?

RUTH Walter Lee?

WALTER *The Man.* Like the guys in the streets say—The Man. Captain Boss—Mistuh Charley . . . Old Cap'n Please Mr. Bossman . . .

BENEATHA *(Suddenly)* Lindner!

WALTER That's right! That's good. I told him to come right over.

BENEATHA *(Fiercely, understanding)* For what? What do you want to see him for!

WALTER *(Looking at his sister)* We going to do business with him.

MAMA What you talking 'bout, son?

WALTER Talking 'bout life, Mama. You all always telling me to see life like it is. Well—I laid in there on my back today . . . and I figured it out. Life just like it is. Who gets and who don't get. *(He sits down with his coat on and laughs)* Mama, you know it's all divided up. Life is. Sure enough. Between the takers and the "tooken." *(He laughs)* I've figured it out finally. *(He looks around at them)* Yeah. Some of us always getting "tooken." *(He laughs)* People like Willy Harris, they don't never get "tooken." And you know why the rest of us do? 'Cause we all mixed up. Mixed up bad. We get to looking 'round for the right and the wrong; and we worry about it and cry about it and stay up nights trying to figure out 'bout the wrong and the right of things all the time . . . And all the time, man, them takers is out there operating, just taking and taking. Willy Harris? Shoot—Willy Harris don't even count. He don't even count in the big scheme of things. But I'll say one thing for old Willy Harris . . . he's taught me something. He's taught me to keep my eye on what counts in this world. Yeah—*(Shouting out a little)* Thanks, Willy!

RUTH What did you call that man for, Walter Lee?

WALTER Called him to tell him to come on over to the show. Gonna put on a show for the man. Just what he wants to see. You see, Mama, the man came here today and he told us that them people out there where you want us to move—well they so upset they willing to pay us *not* to move! *(He laughs again)* And—and oh, Mama—you would of been proud of the way me and Ruth and Bennie acted. We told him to get out . . . Lord have mercy! We told the man to get out! Oh, we was some proud folks this afternoon, yeah. *(He lights a cigarette)* We were still full of that old-time stuff . . .

RUTH *(Coming toward him slowly)* You talking 'bout taking them people's money to keep us from moving in that house?

WALTER I ain't just talking 'bout it, baby—I'm telling you that's what's going to happen!

BENEATHA Oh, God! Where is the bottom! Where is the real honest-to-God bottom so he can't go any farther!

WALTER See—that's the old stuff. You and that boy that was here today. You all want everybody to carry a flag and a spear and sing some marching songs, huh? You wanna spend your life looking into things and trying to find the right and the wrong part, huh? Yeah. You know what's going to happen to that boy someday—he'll find himself sitting in a dungeon, locked in forever—and the takers will have the key! Forget it, baby! There ain't no causes—there ain't nothing but taking in this world, and he who takes most is smartest—and it don't make a damn bit of difference *how.*

MAMA You making something inside me cry, son. Some awful pain inside me.

WALTER Don't cry, Mama. Understand. That white man is going to walk in that door able to write checks for more money than we ever had. It's important to him and I'm going to help him . . . I'm going to put on the show, Mama.

MAMA Son—I come from five generations of people who was slaves and sharecroppers—but ain't nobody in my family never let nobody pay 'em no money that was a way of telling us we wasn't fit to walk the earth. We ain't never been that poor. *(Raising her eyes and looking at him)* We ain't never been that—dead inside.

BENEATHA Well—we are dead now. All the talk about dreams and sunlight that goes on in this house. It's all dead now.

WALTER What's the matter with you all! I didn't make this world! It was give to me this way! Hell, yes, I want me some yachts someday! Yes, I want to hang some real pearls 'round my wife's neck. Ain't she supposed to wear no pearls? Somebody tell me—tell me, who decides which women is suppose to wear pearls in this world. I tell you I am a *man*—and I think my wife should wear some pearls in this world!

(This last line hangs a good while and WALTER *begins to move about the room. The word "Man" has penetrated his consciousness; he mumbles it to himself repeatedly between strange agitated pauses as he moves about)*

MAMA Baby, how you going to feel on the inside?

WALTER Fine! . . . Going to feel fine . . . a man . . .

MAMA You won't have nothing left then, Walter Lee.

WALTER *(Coming to her)* I'm going to feel fine, Mama. I'm going to look that son-of-a-bitch in the eyes and say—*(He falters)*—and say, "All right, Mr. Lindner—*(He falters even more)*—that's *your* neighborhood out there! You got the right to keep it like you want! You got the right to have it like you want! Just write the check and—the house is yours." And—and I am going to say—*(His voice almost breaks)* "And you—you people just put the money in my hand and you won't have to live next to this bunch of stinking niggers! . . ." *(He straightens up and moves away from his mother, walking around the room)* And maybe—maybe I'll just get down on my black knees . . . *(He does so;* RUTH *and* BENNIE *and* MAMA *watch him in frozen horror)* "Captain, Mistuh, Bossman—*(Groveling and grinning and wringing his hands in profoundly anguished imitation of the slow-witted movie stereotype)* A-hee-hee-hee! Oh, yassuh boss! Yasssssuh! Great white—*(Voice breaking, he forces himself to go on)*—Father, just gi' ussen de money, fo' God's sake, and we's—we's ain't gwine come out deh and dirty up yo' white folks neighborhood . . ." *(He breaks down completely)* And I'll feel fine! Fine! FINE! *(He gets up and goes into the bedroom)*

BENEATHA That is not a man. That is nothing but a toothless rat.

MAMA Yes—death done come in this here house. *(She is nodding, slowly, reflectively)* Done come walking in my house on the lips of my children. You what supposed to be my beginning again. You—what supposed to be my harvest. *(To* BENEATHA*)* You—you mourning your brother?

BENEATHA He's no brother of mine.

MAMA What you say?

BENEATHA I said that that individual in that room is no brother of mine.

MAMA That's what I thought you said. You feeling like you better than he is today? (BENEATHA *does not answer)* Yes? What you tell him a minute ago? That he wasn't a man? Yes? You give him up for me? You done wrote his epitaph too—like the rest of the world? Well, who give you the privilege?

BENEATHA Be on my side for once! You saw what he just did, Mama! You saw him—down on his knees. Wasn't it you who taught me to despise any man who would do that? Do what he's going to do?

MAMA Yes—I taught you that. Me and your daddy. But I thought I taught you something else too . . . I thought I taught you to love him.

BENEATHA Love him? There is nothing left to love.

MAMA There is *always* something left to love. And if you ain't learned that, you ain't learned nothing. *(Looking at her)* Have you cried for that boy today? I don't mean for yourself and for the family 'cause we lost the money. I mean for him: what he been through and what it done to him. Child, when do you think is the time to love somebody the most? When they done good and made things easy for everybody? Well then, you ain't through learning—because that ain't the time at all. It's when he's at his lowest and can't believe in hisself 'cause the world done whipped him so! When you starts measuring somebody, measure him right, child, measure him right. Make sure you done taken into account what hills and valleys he come through before he got to wherever he is.

*(*TRAVIS *bursts into the room at the end of the speech, leaving the door open)*

TRAVIS Grandmama—the moving men are downstairs! The truck just pulled up.

MAMA *(Turning and looking at him)* Are they, baby? They downstairs?

(She sighs and sits. LINDNER *appears in the doorway. He peers in and knocks lightly, to gain attention, and comes in. All turn to look at him)*

LINDNER *(Hat and briefcase in hand)* Uh—hello . . .

*(*RUTH *crosses mechanically to the bedroom door and opens it and lets it swing open freely and slowly as the lights come up on* WALTER *within, still in his coat, sitting at the far corner of the room. He looks up and out through the room to* LINDNER*)*

RUTH He's here.

(A long minute passes and WALTER *slowly gets up)*

LINDNER *(Coming to the table with efficiency, putting his briefcase on the table and starting to unfold papers and unscrew fountain pens)* Well, I certainly was glad to hear from you people. (WALTER *has begun the trek out of the room, slowly and awkwardly, rather like a small boy, passing the back of his sleeve across his mouth from time to time)* Life can really be so much simpler than people let it be most of the time. Well—with whom do I negotiate? You, Mrs. Younger, or your son here? (MAMA *sits with her hands folded on her lap and her eyes closed as* WALTER *advances.* TRAVIS *goes closer to* LINDNER *and looks at the papers curiously)* Just some official papers, sonny.

RUTH Travis, you go downstairs—

MAMA *(Opening her eyes and looking into* WALTER*'s)* No. Travis, you stay right here. And you make him understand what you doing, Walter Lee. You teach him good. Like Willy Harris taught you. You show where our five generations done come to. (WALTER *looks from her to the boy, who grins at him innocently)* Go ahead, son—*(She folds her hands and closes her eyes)* Go ahead.

WALTER *(At last crosses to* LINDNER *who is reviewing the contract)* Well, Mr. Lindner. (BE-

NEATHA *turns away)* We called you—*(There is a profound, simple groping quality in his speech)*—because, well, me and my family *(He looks around and shifts from one foot to the other)* Well—we are very plain people . . .

LINDNER Yes—

WALTER I mean—I have worked as a chauffeur most of my life—and my wife here, she does domestic work in people's kitchens. So does my mother. I mean—we are plain people . . .

LINDNER Yes, Mr. Younger—

WALTER *(Really like a small boy, looking down at his shoes and then up at the man)* and—uh—well, my father, well, he was a laborer most of his life. . . .

LINDNER *(Absolutely confused)* Uh, yes—yes, I understand. *(He turns back to the contract)*

WALTER *(A beat; staring at him)* And my father—*(With sudden intensity)* My father almost *beat a man to death* once because this man called him a bad name or something, you know what I mean?

LINDNER *(Looking up, frozen)* No, no, I'm afraid I don't—

WALTER *(A beat. The tension hangs; then* WALTER *steps back from it)* Yeah. Well—what I mean is that we come from people who had a lot of *pride.* I mean—we are very proud people. And that's my sister over there and she's going to be a doctor—and we are very proud—

LINDNER Well—I am sure that is very nice, but—

WALTER What I am telling you is that we called you over here to tell you that we are very proud and that this—*(Signaling to* TRAVIS*)* Travis, come here. *(*TRAVIS *crosses and* WALTER *draws him before him facing the man)* This is my son, and he makes the sixth generation our family in this country. And we have all thought about your offer—

LINDNER Well, good . . . good—

WALTER And we have decided to move into our house because my father—my father—he earned it for us brick by brick. *(*MAMA *has her eyes closed and is rocking back and forth as though she were in church, with her head nodding the Amen yes)* We don't want to make no trouble for nobody or fight no causes, and we will try to be good neighbors. And that's *all* we got to say about that. *(He looks the man absolutely in the eyes)* We don't want your money. *(He turns and walks away)*

LINDNER *(Looking around at all of them)* I take it then—that you have decided to occupy . . .

BENEATHA That's what the man said.

LINDNER *(To* MAMA *in her reverie)* Then I would like to appeal to you, Mrs. Younger. You are older and wiser and understand things better I am sure . . .

MAMA I am afraid you don't understand. My son said we was going to move and there ain't nothing left for me to say. *(Briskly)* You know how these young folks is nowadays, mister. Can't do a thing with 'em! *(As he opens his mouth, she rises)* Good-bye.

LINDNER *(Folding up his materials)* Well—if you are that final about it . . . there is nothing left for me to say. *(He finishes, almost ignored by the family, who are concentrating on* WALTER LEE. *At the door* LINDNER *halts and looks around)* I sure hope you people know what you're getting into.

(He shakes his head and exits)

RUTH *(Looking around and coming to life)* Well, for God's sake—if the moving men are here—LET'S GET THE HELL OUT OF HERE!

MAMA *(Into action)* Ain't it the truth! Look at all this here mess. Ruth, put Travis' good jacket on him . . . Walter Lee, fix your tie and tuck your shirt in, you look like somebody's hoodlum! Lord have mercy, where is my plant? *(She flies to get it amid the general bustling of the family, who are deliberately trying to ignore the nobility of the past moment)* You all start on down . . . Travis child, don't go empty-handed . . . Ruth, where did I put that box with my skillets in it? I want to be in charge of it myself . . . I'm going to make us the biggest dinner we ever ate tonight . . . Beneatha, what's the matter with them stockings? Pull them things up, girl . . .

(The family starts to file out as two moving men appear and begin to carry out the heavier pieces of furniture, bumping into the family as they move about)

BENEATHA Mama, Asagai asked me to marry him today and go to Africa—

MAMA *(In the middle of her getting-ready activity)* He did? You ain't old enough to marry nobody—*(Seeing the moving men lifting one of her chairs precariously)* Darling, that ain't no bale of cotton, please handle it so we can sit in it again! I had that chair twenty-five years . . .

(The movers sigh with exasperation and go on with their work)

BENEATHA *(Girlishly and unreasonably trying to pursue the conversation)* To go to Africa, Mama—be a doctor in Africa . . .

MAMA *(Distracted)* Yes, baby—

WALTER *Africa!* What he want you to go to Africa for?

BENEATHA To practice there . . .

WALTER Girl, if you don't get all them silly ideas out your head! You better marry yourself a man with some loot . . .

BENEATHA *(Angrily, precisely as in the first scene of the play)* What have you got to do with who I marry!

WALTER Plenty. Now I think George Murchison—

BENEATHA *George Murchison!* I wouldn't marry him if he was Adam and I was Eve!

(WALTER *and* BENEATHA *go out yelling at each other vigorously and the anger is loud and real till their voices diminish.* RUTH *stands at the door and turns to* MAMA *and smiles knowingly)*

MAMA *(Fixing her hat at last)* Yeah—they something all right, my children . . .

RUTH Yeah—they're something. Let's go, Lena.

MAMA *(Stalling, starting to look around at the house)* Yes—I'm coming. Ruth—

RUTH Yes?

MAMA *(Quietly, woman to woman)* He finally come into his manhood today, didn't he? Kind of like a rainbow after the rain . . .

RUTH *(Biting her lip lest her own pride explode in front of* MAMA*)* Yes, Lena.

(WALTER*'s voice calls for them raucously)*

WALTER *(Off stage)* Y'all come on! These people charges by the hour, you know!

MAMA *(Waving* RUTH *out vaguely)* All right, honey—go on down. I be down directly.

(RUTH *hesitates, then exits.* MAMA *stands, at last alone in the living room, her plant on the table before her as the lights start to come down. She looks around at all the walls and ceilings and suddenly, despite herself, while the children call below, a great heaving thing rises in her and she puts her fist to her mouth to stifle it, takes a final desperate look, pulls her coat about her, pats her hat and goes out. The lights dim down. The door opens and she comes back in, grabs her plant, and goes out for the last time)*

Curtain

Fiction Writers

DOROTHY WEST

(1907–)

Dorothy West is the last great surviving writer of the Harlem Renaissance. Eventually, the historical roots of her era—of the New Negro Movement—would extend from her own place in Martha's Vineyard, Massachusetts, in the North, through the Chicago poet Frank Marshall Davis's location in the Midwest, to the poet Ann Spencer's garden in Lynchburg, Virginia, to the novelist Walter White's Atlanta, Georgia, in the deep South. Hence, West marks the northernmost point of a triangular consciousness that informs African American existence. As novelist, editor, journalist, and short story writer, she has spanned nearly three-quarters of a century, thence acting as a senior light in a newly emerging African American canon that remains open to change.

Today West remembers the Renaissance luminaries such as Zora Neale Hurston, Claude McKay, Countée Cullen, Wallace Thurman, Bruce Nugent, Aaron Douglas, and Langston Hughes. She experiments with the revelation of history less than with the wonder and bond of family ties. Ultimately, her concern depends on the lively interior of African American thought and community. She writes about the intensity of woman's personal struggle. Although she avoids interior monologue, or stream of consciousness, she has prepared the ground for new strategies in modern fiction. To re-create moods of the urban environment, she often writes Spartan sentences or even lyrical lines. Whatever her style, her language is provocative. She helped pave the way from the romantic era of the Renaissance to the Reformation of African American sensibility during the thirties and forties, replete with the biting realism that Alain Locke despised. "I am a rather reticent sort," West says in her biographical sketch, Opportunity (1926), "but . . . I love to sit apart and read—as best I can—the souls of my neighbors."

Dorothy West was born on June 2, 1907, in Boston, the only child of Rachel Pease Benson West and Isaac Christopher West. Her father, a successful importer of fresh fruits, was known as Boston's "Black Banana King." Her mother had moved to Boston from Camden, South Carolina, while still in her teens.

At the age of two, West studied with a tutor, Bessie Trotter, the sister of Monroe Trotter, the famous African American editor of the *Boston Guardian.* In 1911, Rachel urged the Boston School Board to admit Dorothy to public school. Upon entrance to the Farragut School at the age of four, West proved herself capable of doing second-grade work and studied subsequently with tutor Grace Turner, a proper Bostonian. During her elementary education at the Martin School in the Mission Hill district of Boston, West began to write stories, despite constant harassment by poor Irish classmates. While at the Girls Latin School, she achieved some reprieve from the insults, but studied with peers who, because of her color, ignored her on the street. Graduated in 1923, she studied journalism and philosophy at Boston University and Columbia University. Her first published story appeared in the *Boston Globe,* a daily newspaper for which she became a frequent writer.

With the poet Helene Johnson, her cousin, West moved to New York City in 1926. The two attended, as invited guests, the yearly awards dinner held by *Opportunity* magazine and roomed at the Harlem Young Women's Christian Association (YWCA). Later they moved into an apartment that had been occupied by Zora Neale Hurston. West shared second place with Hurston in a short-story contest sponsored by *Opportunity.* West's narrative, "The Typewriter," portrays a frustrated black father named J. L. Jones, who, denied an equal opportunity to become an entrepreneur, dictated business letters to his daughter for transmission to important tycoons. Each day Jones looks forward to their evening sessions until the day he returns from work to learn that Millie has terminated the lease on the typewriter. Now deprived of his dream, Jones dies in anguish. Nevertheless, the riddle of the story remains a suggestive one: Is there a possible way to be the primary subject of importance in one's own story, but the valued object of assistance in someone else's?

Despite West's laudatory remarks about Zora Neale Hurston—whom West believed was envied and belittled by homosexual men—West favored nevertheless the literary influence of men. She admired Feodor Dostoyevsky as her favorite novelist and befriended Wallace Thurman before his death in 1934. And Claude McKay, who returned to the United States from Europe and North Africa, warned her, "You're friends with the fat souls," the elite artists of the Renaissance. West confessed,

> I don't know how I would have written, if it hadn't been for him [McKay]. Dostoyevsky was the person who had the greatest influence on me, and Claude did not have anywhere near that much, but of all the writers that I knew in that period it was Claude . . . So I do thank the man. I loved Countée Cullen. I love Langston Hughes, but they did not have anywhere near the same influence on me.

Of all her contemporaries, the Jamaican Claude McKay had shaped the spirit of North American rebellion into the poetic forms—the English and Italian sonnet—of the British Empire. The Russian Dostoyevsky, on the contrary, had been a talented nineteenth-century writer who depicted with unrivaled skill the psychological complexity behind his symbolic figures of human suffering. Both authors were profoundly, if in unorthodox fashion, Christian. But it was West, the closet radical, who wrote impeccably standard English. Many of her stories, such as "Hannah Byde" (*Messenger,* July 8, 1926), "An Unimportant Man" (*Saturday Evening Quill,* June 1, 1926), "Prologue to a Life," (*Saturday Evening Quill,* June 1, 1928), "The Black Dress" (October 18, 1940), and "Mammy" (*Opportunity,* October 18, 1940), round out her achievements during the first two decades of her career.

In the summer of 1929, West went to London to perform a bit part in a performance of *Porgy and Bess* by the Theatre Guild. Later, the Fellowship of Peace recruited her, along with Langston Hughes and twenty other African American authors in 1932, to create a black-and-white film about race relations in the United States. Eventually, the producers of the film surrendered to political pressures by the American government to keep the Soviets from performing a drama of American racism for all the world to see. West remained in the USSR in the employment of Mes Chrapborm Films in 1933.

On her return to America in 1934, West founded *Challenge* and, despite the fine examples set by Alice Dunbar-Nelson and Angelina Gimké, broke ranks with the genteel Negro tradition of favoring a decadent romanticism. By 1937, with Richard Wright and Marina as associate editors, West changed the name of *Challenge* to *New Challenge.* Their revamped magazine, which would last for only one issue, featured pieces by established and promising writers. In October 1933, West wrote to writer James Weldon Johnson, "It occurred to me that I could make up for much I have wasted by some way finding space for young dark throats to sing." In June 1936, she had altered her position: "We would like to print more articles and stories of protest. We have only daily contact with the underprivileged. We know their suffering and soul weariness. They have only the meager bread and meat of the dole, and that will not feed their failing spirits."

A headline in the *New Yorker* read as follows: "Dorothy West Is a Communist." "The young people at the University of Chicago were leftist. I never was," says West, "because I was too independent to be anything. But the Chicago students decided they were going to take over the magazine . . . I was just a woman. . . . I stopped it . . . I had no choice."[1] West was looking for a way to save face for a nineteenth-century aesthetics of the romanticism and a twentieth-century aesthetic of modernism. She complained that very few articles reviewed had ever been true to literature, and she nearly ranted against the bombast of manuscripts written with misspelled words. By the fourth and fifth numbers of *Challenge*, West had changed her literary values a little. With Jessie Fauset and W.E.B. Du Bois, she became the third African American writer to cross the great chasm between romanticism and modernism.

For a year or two after the collapse of *Challenge* and *New Challenge* by 1937, West worked as a welfare investigator in Harlem. The experience probably inspired the story "Mammy," which was published in *Opportunity* in October 1940. Here, a caseworker degrades and is debased by a racial fellow for purposes of economic survival. The narrator develops an ironic hierarchy through which characters tolerate in their superiors the same kind of humiliations they resent seeing in subordinates. A black elevator operator protects his job by berating a black woman caseworker who has offended a white woman. Just as the man had pleaded for forgiveness by the worker, she herself must seek absolution for denying the equally legitimate claims of a black maid. To complicate the various ambiguities of the story, Coleman is either the maid's surrogate daughter or is somewhat incredibly the real daughter passing for white. Hence, the strange fruit of white supremacy humiliates African Americans from all walks of life.

After leaving her job as a caseworker, West joined the Work Projects Administration (WPA). From 1940 through 1960, she had more than twenty-six stories published in the *New York Daily News*, defending the work as the kind that paid the bills. After World War II, she moved to Martha's Vineyard, where she still has a byline in the local *Gazette*.

Dorothy West encodes the values of the African American spirit, the black womanist suspicions about middle-class privilege, and the creative legacy of African American memory. Following several false starts in writing a novel, *The Living Is Easy* was published in 1948. She satirized affluent Bostonians for allowing class differences to separate them from working-class communities. In 1982, the Feminist Press reprinted the book, with an afterword by Adelaide Cromwell Gulliver. In the novel *Cleo Bart and Judy Judson*, the couple appears in a thinly veiled reworking of the household in which West herself grew up. As had been true with Rachel West, the beautifully light-skinned mother hopes that her daughter will favor her in complexion and personality. Also like Rachel, Cleo, the fictive mother, by relocating a large extended family with sisters and children at home, causes her own marriage to deteriorate.

West hopes that publishers today will bring out once again works about color in middle-class life. Since 1960, literary emphasis has shifted to an African American struggle with history, including a much more subtle attention to the mainstream prejudice that African Americans have internalized as self-hatred. Today the depth

[1]The reference to reading the souls of West's neighbors appears in Ferguson (188), but the other personal quotations come from West's interview for the *Langston Hughes Review*.

of racial consciousness greatly exceeds that of the twenties, and the national mind can probably not revert so easily to a simpler time. West states,

> Many people say, "Haven't you written another book?" I have. After Houghton and Mifflin published *The Living Is Easy,* I gave them fifty pages of another novel. They liked it. It was beautiful. But they were afraid it would not sell. Then I wrote a third novel which I hope to finish. But I come from a light-skinned society. People are doctors or lawyers or so, and when I was writing that novel it was a bad time. It was the time of Rap Brown and other people of that sort who thought that the revolution was on its way and that Martin Luther King was an SOB. "What we must do is hit the white man in the head," and sorts of foolishness like that. Anybody who was a doctor or a lawyer was called an Uncle Tom. I thought the book was good, and I still have it in my desk. Of course, I'm years older now. But I want to finish it.

The volume might be the last one completed by a New Negro.

As Walter C. Daniel has noted, West sought in the ambitious publication of *Challenge* magazine to "recapture, in the mid thirties, the literary vitality of the Harlem Renaissance which had not survived the Depression. James Weldon Johnson said once,

> It is a good thing that Dorothy West is doing in instituting a magazine through which the voices of younger Negro writers may be heard.

But "these sirens," West urges in the pioneering issue of *New Challenge,*

> must not be mere dilettantes; they have serious work to do. They need not be propagandists; they need only be sincere artists, disdaining all cheap applause and remaining true to themselves. Writing is not an art, it is a trade.

In West's short story "The Richer, The Poorer," Lottie listens to the widow of a jazzman:

> With the glow of good food in her stomach, Bess began to spin stories. They were rich with places and people, most of them lovely, all of them magnificent. Her face reflected her telling, the joys and sorrows of her remembering, and above all, the love she lived by that enhanced the poorest place, the humblest person. . . .

The story emerges as the expression of creative light, the tangible shape of African American memory. Shining remembrance transforms Lottie's dull house into a glowing home. Here emerges the emblem of West's biography that was to be explained later in the *Langston Hughes Review* (Fall 1993):

> I would sit there quietly, writing. One day when I was about fourteen or fifteen, my dear mother took me aside and said, "My dear Dorothy, I know you want to write about the family, and that's all right. But when you sit with paper and pencil writing down what people say, it makes them very self-conscious, and maybe they will say things they don't want. So keep it in the back of your head." My mother was the one who taught me to *remember* things. [editor's italics]

"All I ask," West urged Katrine Dalsgård, is "for you to remember me." After the WPA ended, West saved publications of the time: "Langston Hughes is in there, Countée Cullen—all of them. But, as I phrase it, 'Langston Hughes was; Countée

Cullen was; Dorothy West is alive and well and living on the island of Martha's Vineyard.' "

Perhaps literary existence transcends even time. Her most recent novel, *The Wedding* (1995) and *The Richer, The Poorer: Sketches and Reminiscences* (1995) were well received. No one dies, says an African proverb, until all who remember are gone. Frederick Douglass, Linda Brent, James Baldwin, Paule Marshall, Ernest Gaines, and Toni Morrison have all written excellent narratives that encapsulate African American memory. Dorothy West helped usher in an African American aesthetic of the family covenant.

❖❖❖

Of good use would be a definitive collection of West's short stories introduced by a very perceptive scholar. Many critical studies are needed, especially those that might expand critical methodology beyond observations about theme and plot. Although social commentary is valuable, it needs contextualization within the deeper concerns of imagery and structure. Someone could do groundbreaking analysis of West's fictional technique. Indeed, an inquiry into theory as well as practice would be completely new ground. For background, see Walter C. Daniel, "*Challenge Magazine:* An Experiment That Failed," *CLA Journal* 26 (June 1976); Genii Guinier, "Black for Unity and Harmony," *Freedomways* 20 (First Quarter 1980). Among the more biographical pieces, Katrine Dalsgård, "Alive and Well and Living on the Island of Martha's Vineyard: An Interview with Dorothy West," *The Langston Hughes Review,* 12, 2 (Fall 1993), and Sally Ann H. Ferguson, "Dorothy West," *Dictionary of Literary Biography: Afro-American Writers, 1940–1955,* ed. Trudier Harris (Detroit: Gale, 1988) 76, are invaluable resources. Mary Helen Washington set the tone for the examination of a womanist theme of color in "I Sign My Mother's Name: Alice Walker, Dorothy West, Paule Marshall" in *Mothering the Mind: Twelve Studies of Writers and Their Silent Partners,* ed. Ruth Perry and Matrine Watson Brownley (New York: Holmes and Meier 1984). All of West's personal quotations come from her interview in the *Langston Hughes Review* (1993). Sustained works of importance remain to be written.

The Richer, The Poorer

Over the years Lottie had urged Bess to prepare for her old age. Over the years Bess had lived each day as if there were no other. Now they were both past sixty, the time for summing up. Lottie had a bank account that had never grown lean. Bess had the clothes on her back, and the rest of her worldly possessions in a battered suitcase.

Lottie had hated being a child, hearing her parents' skimping and scraping. Bess had never seemed to notice. All she ever wanted was to go outside and play. She learned to skate on borrowed skates. She rode a borrowed bicycle. Lottie couldn't wait to grow up and buy herself the best of everything.

As soon as anyone would hire her, Lottie put herself to work. She minded babies, she ran errands for the old.

She never touched a penny of her money, though her child's mouth watered for ice cream and candy. But she could not bear to share with Bess, who never had anything to share with her. When the dimes began to add up to dollars, she lost her taste for sweets.

By the time she was twelve, she was clerking after school in a small variety store. Saturdays she worked as long as she was wanted. She decided to keep her money for clothes. When she entered high school, she would wear a wardrobe that neither she nor anyone else would be able to match.

But her freshman year found her unable to indulge so frivolous a whim, particularly when her admiring instructors advised her to think seriously of college. No one in her family had ever gone to college, and certainly Bess would never get there. She would show them all what she could do, if she put her mind to it.

She began to bank her money, and her bank became her most private and precious possession.

In her third year she found a job in a small but expanding restaurant, where she cashiered from the busy hour until closing. In her last year the business increased so rapidly that Lottie was faced with the choice of staying in school or working full-time.

She made her choice easily. A job in hand was worth two in the future.

Bess had a beau in the school band, who had no other ambition except to play a horn. Lottie expected to be settled with a home and family while Bess was still waiting for Harry to earn enough to buy a marriage license.

That Bess married Harry straight out of high school was not surprising. That Lottie never married at all was not really surprising either. Two or three times she was halfway persuaded, but to give up a job that paid well for a homemaking job that paid nothing was a risk she was incapable of taking.

Bess's married life was nothing for Lottie to envy. She and Harry lived like gypsies, Harry playing in second-rate bands all over the country, even getting himself and Bess stranded in Europe. They were often in rags and never in riches.

Bess grieved because she had no child, not having sense enough to know she was better off without one. Lottie was certainly better off without nieces and nephews to feel sorry for. Very likely Bess would have dumped them on her doorstep.

That Lottie had a doorstep they might have been left on was only because her boss, having bought a second house, offered Lottie his first house at a price so low and terms so reasonable that it would have been like losing money to refuse.

She shut off the rooms she didn't use, letting them go to rack and ruin. Since she ate her meals out, she had no food at home, and did not encourage callers, who always expected a cup of tea.

Her way of life was mean and miserly, but she did not know it. She thought she lived frugally in her middle years so that she could live in comfort and ease when she most needed peace of mind.

The years, after forty, began to race. Suddenly Lottie was sixty, and retired from her job by her boss's son, who had no sentimental feeling about keeping her on until she was ready to quit.

She made several attempts to find other employment, but her dowdy appearance made her look old and inefficient. For the first time in her life Lottie would gladly have worked for nothing, to have some place to go, something to do with her day.

Harry died abroad, in a third-rate hotel, with Bess weeping as hard as if he had left her a fortune. He had left her nothing but his horn. There wasn't even money for her passage home.

Lottie, trapped by the blood tie, knew she would not only have to send for her sister, but take her in when she returned. It didn't seem fair that Bess should reap the harvest of Lottie's lifetime of self-denial.

It took Lottie a week to get a bedroom ready, a week of hard work and hard cash. There was everything to do, everything to replace or paint. When she was through the room looked so fresh and new that Lottie felt she deserved it more than Bess.

She would let Bess have her room, but the mattress was so lumpy, the carpet so worn, the curtains so threadbare that Lottie's conscience pricked her. She supposed she would have to redo that room, too, and went about doing it with an eagerness that she mistook for haste.

When she was through upstairs, she was shocked to see how dismal downstairs looked by comparison. She tried to ignore it, but with nowhere to go to escape it, the contrast grew more intolerable.

She worked her way from kitchen to parlor, persuading herself she was only putting the rooms to right to give herself something to do. At night she slept like a child after a long and happy day of playing house. She was having more fun than she had ever had in her life. She was living each hour for itself.

There was only a day now before Bess would arrive. Passing her gleaming mirrors, at first with vague awareness, then with painful clarity, Lottie saw herself as others saw her, and could not stand the sight.

She went on a spending spree from specialty shops to beauty salon, emerging transformed into a woman who believed in miracles.

She was in the kitchen basting a turkey when Bess rang the bell. Her heart raced, and she wondered if the heat from the oven was responsible.

She went to the door, and Bess stood before her. Stiffly she suffered Bess's embrace, her heart racing harder, her eyes suddenly smarting from the onrush of cold air.

"Oh, Lottie, it's good to see you," Bess said, but saying nothing about Lottie's splendid appearance. Upstairs Bess, putting down her shabby suitcase, said, "I'll sleep like a rock tonight," without a word of praise for her lovely room. At the lavish table, top-heavy with turkey, Bess said, "I'll take light and dark both," with no marveling at the size of the bird, or that there was turkey for two elderly women, one of them too poor to buy her own bread.

With the glow of good food in her stomach, Bess began to spin stories. They were rich with places and people, most of them lowly, all of them magnificent. Her face reflected her telling, the joys and sorrows of her remembering, and above all, the love she lived by that enhanced the poorest place, the humblest person.

Then it was that Lottie knew why Bess had made no mention of her finery, or the shining room, or the twelve-pound turkey. She had not even seen them. Tomorrow she would see the room as it really looked, and Lottie as she really looked, and the warmed-over turkey in its second-day glory. Tonight she saw only what she had come seeking, a place in her sister's home and heart.

She said, "That's enough about me. How have the years used you?"

"It was me who didn't use them," said Lottie wistfully. "I saved for them. I forgot the best of them would go without my ever spending a day or a dollar enjoying them. That's my life story in those few words, a life never lived.

"Now it's too near the end to try."

Bess said, "To know how much there is to know is the beginning of learning to live. Don't count the years that are left us. At our time of life it's the days that count. You've too much catching up to do to waste a minute of a waking hour feeling sorry for yourself."

Lottie grinned, a real wide open grin, "Well, to tell the truth I felt sorry for you. Maybe if I had any sense I'd feel sorry for myself, after all. I know I'm too old to kick up my heels, but I'm going to let you show me how. If I land on my head, I guess it won't matter. I feel giddy already, and I like it."

RALPH ELLISON
(1914–1994)

"I agree . . . that protest is an element of all art, though it does not necessarily take the form of speaking for a political or social program. It might appear in a novel as a technical assault against the styles that have gone before." The author of these words achieved the remarkable feat of writing a novel that became a favorite of both black nationalists and mainstream American critics. Ralph Ellison, according to Larry Neal,

> keeps checking out style. The way people walk, what they say, and what they leave unsaid. If anyone has been concerned with a "black aesthetic," it has certainly got to be Ralph Ellison. And even if you disagree with Ellison's political thrust these days, you have to dig his consistent concern for capturing the essential truths of the black man's experience in America.

Born March 1, 1914, in Oklahoma City during the era of southwestern jazz, Ellison was the son of hard-working and highly informed lower-middle-class parents. After the death of his father, Lewis Alfred Ellison, when he was three years old, his mother, Ida Milsap Ellison, continued to encourage and nourish his artistic impulses by providing him with novels and magazines. Because Oklahoma had not achieved statehood until 1907 and thus had no tradition of slavery, it was racially segregated but more open in race relations than the former slave states. The frontier atmosphere of postwar Oklahoma also fostered a sense of freedom and adventure in Ellison and his friends, causing them to create their own heroes and ideals. Ellison writes in *Shadow and Act* (1964),

> Gamblers and scholars, jazz musicians and scientists, Negro cowboys and soldiers from Spanish-American and First World Wars, movie stars and stuntmen, figures from the Italian Renaissance and literature, both classical and popular, were combined with the special virtues of some local boot-legger, the eloquence of some Negro preacher, the strength and grace of some local athlete, the ruthlessness of some businessman-physician, the elegance in dress and manners of some headwaiter or hotel doorman.

In addition to being a shoeshine boy, janitor, and freelance photographer, Ellison developed during his early years an interest in jazz. He won a scholarship to Tuskegee Institute, where he studied military and classical music for three years, with the intention of ultimately becoming a composer of symphonies. An accomplished trumpet player, Ellison admired and emulated such blues and jazz musicians as Jimmy Rushing, Walter Page, Charlie Christian, and Duke Ellington. In *Going to the Territory* (1986), he pays homage to Ellington:

> I wish that all those who write so knowledgeably of Negro boys having no masculine figures with whom to identify would consider the long national and international career of Ellington and his band, and the thousands of one night stands played in the black communities of this nation. Where in the white community, in any community, could there have been found images, examples such as these? . . . For us, Duke was a culture hero, a musical magician who worked his powers through his mastery of form, nuance, and style, a charismatic figure whose personality influenced even those who had no immediate concern with the art of jazz.

In addition to the influence of his mother and jazz musicians like Duke Ellington, Ellison acknowledged the importance and generosity of Richard Wright in launching his literary career. After reading a poem by Wright in the *New Masses,* Ellison left the South for New York in 1936 in search of Wright. A year later, with the help of Langston Hughes, a meeting was arranged. Shortly thereafter, Ellison was privileged to read Wright's stories before they were published and was encouraged by Wright to publish a book review and a short story in *New Challenge,* a short-lived black journal edited by Wright and Dorothy West. Ellison and Wright both participated in the Federal Writers' Project, and, in 1939, Ellison was best man at Wright's first wedding. In "Richard Wright's Blues," a review of Wright's autobiography, he paid tribute to Wright by lamenting the absence in America of any "social or political action based upon the solid realities of Negro life depicted in *Black Boy.*" Ellison was interested in the politics of the left, but he never became a Communist or Marxist. And although he insisted that Wright was "no spiritual father," he continued to confess Wright's influence, insisting that his own stories and essays were "implicitly, criticisms of Wright's; just as all novels of a given historical moment form an argument over the nature of reality and are, to an extent, criticisms each of the other." Ellison's commitment to dialogue and "argument over the nature of reality" in other texts led him to experiment with a wide variety of modernist artistic techniques and to claim as his literary ancestors not only Richard Wright but Henry James, André Malraux, T. S. Eliot, Stephen Crane, Emerson, Thoreau, Hawthorne, Whitman, Melville, and numerous others.

In *Shadow and Act* (1964) and *Going to the Territory* (1986), Ellison published a number of influential essays that further developed his views on the complex relationships between race, art, and American culture. Among them is "The Art of Fiction," a work in which Ellison rejects the purely racial view of art in favor of what he considers to be a more balanced view that gives equal importance to questions of style and form. While this claim constituted one source of distrust toward his work for many African Americans during the sixties, Ellison's remarks must, as Larry Neal has pointed out in "Ellison's Zoot Suit," be placed in the political context of his debates with the official socialist realism espoused by the Communist Party. They also must be seen in the context of the rise of the anti-Communist, Cold War "New Liberalism" of the forties and fifties, with the New Criticism as its aestheticist analogue. What separated Ellison from his white anti-Communist liberal colleagues was that he continued to criticize the very American racism in which his liberal friends were implicated.

Among Ellison's earliest publications and critiques of American racism was "Flying Home," a short story published in 1944 about an incident in the U.S. Air Force school for black pilots in the Deep South. The story introduced many of the techniques later found in *Invisible Man* (1952)—surrealism, realistic details, flashbacks, the Greek myth of Icarus, black folklore, and various symbols of the modern world. Tod, a black trainee in Alabama, flies too high and strikes a buzzard (Jim Crow), then lands on the property of a white landowner. When he regains consciousness, he is asked by the old black sharecropper on the farm why he wanted to fly and warned that he could be mistaken and shot for a buzzard. The entire story is a metaphor of the African American's place in American society.

Although a superb critic and short story writer, Ellison is best known for the work judged in 1965 as the best American novel since World War II. A mixture of music, black folklore, and modernist technique, *Invisible Man* (1952) is an excellent illustration of Ellison's ability to tie the formal, literary strategies in the novel to larger social questions of black oppression and liberation. The plot structure recapitulates the history of the African American's struggle for survival in America. It moves from slavery (the Grandfather) to Reconstruction and accommodationism (the "Battle Royal" and the Invisible Man's version of the "Atlanta Exposition Address") to the migration north (the factory sequence). Each historical moment is linked to one or more liberation strategies. They include tricksterism (as embodied in the Grandfather and Trueblood), Booker T. Washington's accommodationism (as embodied in Bledsoe and Barbee), paternalistic philanthropic humanism (as embodied in Norton), Marxian humanism (as embodied in Jack and the Brotherhood), and separatist black nationalism (as embodied in Ras the Exhorter/Destroyer).

One of the major themes in the novel is the unnamed protagonist's search for identity. The Invisible Man's highest hope was to become like the crowd in the Men's House, who carried the *Wall Street Journal* in one "always manicured and gloved hand," while "the other hand whipped a tightly rolled umbrella back and forth at a calculated angle, with their homburgs and Chesterfields, their polo coats and Tyrolean hats worn strictly as fashion demanded." But his role as orator for the Brotherhood toward the end of the novel brings the awareness "that there were two of me: the old self that slept a few hours at night and dreamed of something of my grandfather . . . and the new public self that spoke for the Brotherhood and was becoming so much more important than the other self that it seemed to run a foot race against myself." The Invisible Man's attempt to find himself is also the theme of the prologue. Through a series of images, each one representing an element of black culture, the Invisible Man is brought face to face with his past: an old black woman singing spirituals; a slave auction with a beautiful black woman who reminds him of his mother; and an old-time black revivalist preaching. Similar "soul" traditions, including soul food and soul music, continue to contribute to the Invisible Man's rebirth throughout the novel.

As both critic and author, Ellison insisted on the positive, "healthy" side of African American culture. In rejecting the "pathological" view of black American culture and character promoted by Gunnar Myrdal's classic study *The Negro Problem and Modern Democracy: An American Dilemma* (1944), Ellison wrote:

> But can a people (its faith in an idealized American creed notwithstanding) live and develop for over three hundred years simply by reacting? Are American Negroes simply the creation of white men, or have they at least helped to create themselves out of what they found around them? Men have made a way of life in caves and upon cliffs, why cannot Negroes have made a life upon the horns of the white man's dilemma? . . . Much of Negro culture might be negative, but there is also much of great value, of richness, which, because it has been secreted by living and has made their lives more meaningful, Negroes will not willingly disregard.

It is, perhaps, in light of this observation that readers must understand the Invisible Man's ending, with the protagonist's talk of "infinite possibilities."

In 1965, Ellison published his short story, "Juneteenth," in *Quarterly Review of Literature,* vol. 16. It is a fragment of a long novel on black religion and politics that Ellison had been working on intermittently since the publication of *Invisible Man.* Rich in folklore, especially the orality of the black sermon, "Valley of Dry Bones," its major characters include Reverend Daddy Hickmann, a born-again jazz trombonist, and Reverend Bliss, his light-skinned adopted son who becomes a racist United States senator. Juneteenth is the annual black celebration in parts of Texas, Louisiana, Arkansas, and Oklahoma of Emancipation Day on June 19, 1865.

Ellison received an impressive number of honors, fellowships, and awards. For *Invisible Man,* he was given the National Book Award, the Russwurm Award, and the National Newspaper Publishers' Award. Other distinguished awards include the Medal of Freedom (1969), the Chevalier de l'Ordre des Arts et Lettres (1970), and the National Medal of Arts (1985). He was vice president of the National Institute of Arts and Letters, a member of the American Academy of Arts, and a trustee of the John F. Kennedy Center for the Performing Arts. An Albert Schweitzer Professor of Humanities at New York University from 1970 to 1980, Ellison taught, lectured, and served as author-in-residence at Bard College, the State University of New York at Stony Brook, Columbia University, Bennington College, Fisk University, Antioch University, the University of Chicago, Barnard, Rutgers, and Yale. He died on April 16, 1994, before completing his much-anticipated second novel.

❖❖❖

Informative critical studies of Ellison's writings include Robert G. O'Meally, *The Craft of Ralph Ellison* (1982), and *New Essays on* Invisible Man (1988); John Hersey, ed., *Ralph Ellison: A Collection of Critical Essays* (1974); John M. Reilly, *Twentieth Century Interpretations of* Invisible Man (1970); Kimberly W. Benston, ed., *Speaking for You: The Vision of Ralph Ellison* (1987); Alan Nadel, *Invisible Criticism: Ralph Ellison and the American Canon* (1988); Larry Neal, "Ellison's Zoot Suit," in *Speaking for You,* ed. Kimberly W. Benston (1987).

Prologue

FROM INVISIBLE MAN

I am an invisible man. No, I am not a spook like those who haunted Edgar Allan Poe; nor am I one of your Hollywood-movie ectoplasms. I am a man of substance, of flesh and bone, fiber and liquids—and I might even be said to possess a mind. I am invisible, understand, simply because people refuse to see me. Like the bodiless heads you see sometimes in circus sideshows, it is as though I have been surrounded by mirrors of hard, distorting glass. When they approach me they see only my surroundings, themselves, or figments of their imagination—indeed, everything and anything except me.

Nor is my invisibility exactly a matter of a biochemical accident to my epidermis. That invisibility to which I refer occurs because of a peculiar disposition of the eyes of those with whom I come in contact. A matter of the construction of their *inner* eyes, those eyes with which they look through their physical eyes upon reality. I am not complaining, nor am I protesting either. It is sometimes advantageous to be unseen, although it is most often rather wearing on the nerves. Then too, you're constantly being bumped against by those of poor vision. Or again, you often doubt if you really exist. You wonder whether you aren't simply a phantom in other people's minds. Say, a figure in a nightmare which the sleeper tries with all his strength to destroy. It's when you feel like this that, out of resentment, you begin to bump people back. And, let me confess, you feel that way most of the time. You ache with the need to convince yourself that you do exist in the real world, that you're a part of all the sound and anguish, and you strike out with your fists, you curse and you swear to make them recognize you. And, alas, it's seldom successful.

One night I accidentally bumped into a man, and perhaps because of the near darkness he saw me and called me an insulting name. I sprang at him, seized his coat lapels and demanded that he apologize. He was a tall blond man, and as my face came close to his he looked insolently out of his blue eyes and cursed me, his breath hot in my face as he struggled. I pulled his chin down sharp upon the crown of my head, butting him as I had seen the West Indians do, and I felt his flesh tear and the blood gush out, and I yelled, "Apologize! Apologize!" But he continued to curse and struggle, and I butted him again and again until he went down heavily, on his knees, profusely bleeding. I kicked him repeatedly, in a frenzy because he still uttered insults though his lips were frothy with blood. Oh yes, I kicked him! And in my outrage I got out my knife and prepared to slit his throat, right there beneath the lamplight in the deserted street, holding him in the collar with one hand, and opening the knife with my teeth—when it occurred to me that the man had not *seen* me, actually; that he, as far as he knew, was in the midst of a walking nightmare! And I stopped the blade, slicing the air as I pushed him away, letting him fall back to the street. I stared at him hard as the lights of a car stabbed through the darkness. He lay there, moaning on the asphalt; a man almost killed by a phantom. It unnerved me. I was both disgusted and ashamed. I was like a drunken man myself, wavering about on weakened legs. Then I was amused: Something in this man's thick head had sprung out and beaten him within an inch of his life. I began to laugh at this crazy discovery. Would he have awakened at the point of death? Would Death himself have freed him for wakeful living? But I didn't linger. I ran away into the dark, laughing so hard I feared I might rupture myself. The next day I saw his picture in the *Daily News,* beneath a caption stating that he had been "mugged." Poor fool, poor blind fool, I thought with sincere compassion, mugged by an invisible man!

Most of the time (although I do not choose as I once did to deny the violence of my days by ignoring it) I am not so overtly violent. I remember that I am invisible and walk softly so as not to awaken the sleeping ones. Sometimes it is best not to awaken them; there are few things in the world as dangerous as sleepwalkers, I learned in time though that it is possible to carry on a fight against them without their realizing it. For instance, I have been carrying on a fight with Monopolated Light & Power for some time now. I use their service and pay them nothing at all, and they don't know it. Oh, they suspect that power is being drained off, but they don't know where. All they know is that according to the master meter back there in their power station a hell of a lot of free current is disappearing somewhere into the jungle of Harlem. The joke, of course, is that I don't live in Harlem but in a border area. Several years ago (before I discovered the advantages of being invisible) I went through the routine process of buying service and paying their outrageous rates. But no more. I gave up all that, along with my apartment, and my old way of life: That way based upon the fallacious assumption that I, like other men, was visible. Now, aware of my invisibility, I live rent-free in a building rented strictly to whites, in a section of the basement that was shut off and forgotten during the nineteenth century, which I discovered when I was trying to escape in the night from Ras the Destroyer. But that's getting too far ahead of the story, almost to the end, although the end is in the beginning and lies far ahead.

The point now is that I found a home—or a hole in the ground, as you will. Now don't jump to the conclusion that because I call my home a "hole" it is damp and cold like a grave; there are cold holes and warm holes. Mine is a warm hole. And remember, a bear retires to his hole for the winter and lives until spring; then he comes strolling out like the Easter chick breaking from its shell. I say all this to assure you that it is incorrect to assume that, because I'm invisible and live in a hole, I am dead. I am neither dead nor in a state of suspended animation. Call me Jack-the-Bear, for I am in a state of hibernation.

My hole is warm and full of light. Yes, *full* of light. I doubt if there is a brighter spot in all New York than this hole of mine, and I do not exclude Broadway. Or the Empire State Building on a photographer's dream night. But that is taking advantage of you. Those two spots are among the darkest of our whole civilization—

pardon me, our whole *culture* (an important distinction, I've heard)—which might sound like a hoax, or a contradiction, but that (by contradiction, I mean) is how the world moves. Not like an arrow, but a boomerang. (Beware of those who speak of the *spiral* of history; they are preparing a boomerang. Keep a steel helmet handy.) I know; I have been boomeranged across my head so much that I now can see the darkness of lightness. And I love light. Perhaps you'll think it strange that an invisible man should need light, desire light, love light. But maybe it is exactly because I *am* invisible. Light confirms my reality, gives birth to my form. A beautiful girl once told me of a recurring nightmare in which she lay in the center of a large dark room and felt her face expand until it filled the whole room, becoming a formless mass while her eyes ran in bilious jelly up the chimney. And so it is with me. Without light I am not only invisible, but formless as well; and to be unaware of one's form is to live a death. I myself, after existing some twenty years, did not become alive until I discovered my invisibility.

That is why I fight my battle with Monopolated Light & Power. The deeper reason, I mean: It allows me to feel my vital aliveness. I also fight them for taking so much of my money before I learned to protect myself. In my hole in the basement there are exactly 1,369 lights. I've wired the entire ceiling, every inch of it. And not with fluorescent bulbs, but with the older, more-expensive-to-operate kind, the filament type. An act of sabotage, you know. I've already begun to wire the wall. A junk man I know, a man of vision, has supplied me with wire and sockets. Nothing, storm or flood, must get in the way of our need for light and ever more and brighter light. The truth is the light and light is the truth. When I finish all four walls, then I'll start on the floor. Just how that will go, I don't know. Yet when you have lived invisible as long as I have you develop a certain ingenuity. I'll solve the problem. And maybe I'll invent a gadget to place my coffee pot on the fire while I lie in bed, and even invent a gadget to warm my bed—like the fellow I saw in one of the picture magazines who made himself a gadget to warm his shoes! Though invisible, I am in the great American tradition of tinkers. That makes me kin to Ford, Edison and Franklin. Call me, since I have a theory and a concept, a "thinker-tinker." Yes, I'll warm my shoes; they need it, they're usually full of holes. I'll do that and more.

Now I have one radio-phonograph; I plan to have five. There is a certain acoustical deadness in my hole, and when I have music I want to *feel* its vibration, not only with my ear but with my whole body. I'd like to hear five recordings of Louis Armstrong playing and singing "What Did I Do to Be so Black and Blue"—all at the same time. Sometimes now I listen to Louis while I have my favorite dessert of vanilla ice cream and sloe gin. I pour the red liquid over the white mound, watching it glisten and the vapor rising as Louis bends that military instrument into a beam of lyrical sound. Perhaps I like Louis Armstrong because he's made poetry out of being invisible. I think it must be because he's unaware that he *is* invisible. And my own grasp of invisibility aids me to understand his music. Once when I asked for a cigarette, some jokers gave me a reefer, which I lighted when I got home and sat listening to my phonograph. It was a strange evening. Invisibility, let me explain, gives one a slightly different sense of time, you're never quite on the beat. Sometimes you're ahead and sometimes behind. Instead of the swift and imperceptible flowing of time, you are aware of its nodes, those points where time stands still or from which it leaps ahead. And you slip into the breaks and look around. That's what you hear vaguely in Louis' music.

Once I saw a prizefighter boxing a yokel. The fighter was swift and amazingly scientific. His body was one violent flow of rapid rhythmic action. He hit the yokel a hundred times while the yokel held up his arms in stunned surprise. But suddenly the yokel, rolling about in the gale of boxing gloves, struck one blow and knocked science, speed and footwork as cold as a well-digger's posterior. The smart money hit the canvas. The long shot got the nod. The yokel had simply stepped inside of his opponent's sense of time. So under the spell of the reefer I discovered a new analytical way of listening to music. The unheard sounds came through, and each melodic line existed of itself, stood out clearly from all the rest, said its piece, and waited patiently for the other voices to speak. That night I found myself hearing not only in time, but in space as well. I not only entered the music but descended, like Dante, into its depths. And *beneath the swiftness of the hot tempo there was a slower tempo and a cave and I entered it and looked around and heard an old woman singing a spiritual as full of Weltschmerz as flamenco, and beneath that lay a still lower level on which I saw a beautiful girl the color of ivory pleading in a voice like my mother's as she stood before a group of slaveowners who bid for her naked body, and below that I found a lower level and a more rapid tempo and I heard someone shout:*

"Brothers and sisters, my text this morning is the 'Blackness of Blackness.'"

And a congregation of voices answered: "That blackness is most black, brother, most black . . ."

"In the beginning . . ."

"At the very start," they cried.

". . . there was blackness . . ."

"Preach it . . ."

". . . and the sun . . ."

"The sun, Lawd . . ."

". . . was bloody red . . ."

"Red . . ."

"Now black is . . ." the preacher shouted.

"Bloody . . ."

"I said black is . . ."

"Preach it, brother . . ."

". . . an' black ain't . . ."

"Red, Lawd, red: He said it's red!"

"Amen, brother . . ."

"Black will git you . . ."

"Yes, it will . . ."

"Yes, it will . . ."

". . . an' black won't . . ."

"Naw, it won't!"

"It do . . ."

"It do, Lawd . . ."

". . . an' it don't."

"Halleluiah . . ."

". . . It'll put you, glory, glory, Oh my Lawd, in the WHALE'S BELLY.*"*

"Preach it, dear brother . . ."

". . . an' make you tempt . . ."

"Good God a-mighty!"

"Old Aunt Nelly!"

"Black will make you . . ."

"Black . . ."

". . . or black will un-make you."

"Ain't it the truth, Lawd?"

And at that point a voice of trombone timbre screamed at me, "Git out of here, you fool! Is you ready to commit treason?"

And I tore myself away, hearing the old singer of spirituals moaning, "Go curse your God, boy, and die."

I stopped and questioned her, asked her what was wrong.

"I dearly loved my master, son," she said.

"You should have hated him," I said.

"He gave me several sons," she said, "and because I loved my sons I learned to love their father though I hated him too."

"I too have become acquainted with ambivalence," I said. "That's why I'm here."

"What's that?"

"Nothing, a word that doesn't explain it. Why do you moan?"

"I moan this way 'cause he's dead," she said.

"Then tell me, who is that laughing upstairs?"

"Them's my sons. They glad."

"Yes, I can understand that too," I said.

"I laughs too, but I moans too. He promised to set me free but he never could bring hisself to do it. Still I loved him . . ."

"Loved him? You mean . . . ?"

"Oh yes, but I loved something else even more."

"What more?"

"Freedom."

"Freedom," I said. "Maybe freedom lies in hating."

"Naw, son, it's in loving. I loved him and give him the poison and he withered away like a frost-bit apple. Them boys woulda tore him to pieces with they homemade knives."

"A mistake was made somewhere," I said, "I'm confused." And I wished to say other things, but the laughter upstairs became too loud and moan-like for me and I tried to break out of it, but I couldn't. Just as I was leaving I felt an urgent desire to ask her what freedom was and went back. She sat with her head in her hands, moaning softly; her leather-brown face was filled with sadness.

"Old woman, what is this freedom you love so well?" I asked around a corner of my mind.

She looked surprised, then thoughtful, then baffled. "I done forgot, son. It's all mixed up. First I think it's one thing, then I think it's another. It gits my head to spinning. I guess now it ain't nothing but knowing how to say what I got up in my head. But it's a hard job, son. Too much is done happen to me in too short a time. Hit's like I have a fever. Ever' time I starts to walk my head gits to swirling and I falls down. Or if it ain't that, it's the boys; they gits to laughing and wants to kill up the white folks. They's bitter, that's what they is . . ."

"But what about freedom?"

"Leave me 'lone, boy; my head aches!"

I left her, feeling dizzy myself. I didn't get far.

Suddenly one of the sons, a big fellow six feet tall, appeared out of nowhere and struck me with his fist.

"What the matter, man?" I cried.

"You made Ma cry!"

"But how?" I said, dodging a blow.

"Askin' her them questions, that's how. Git outa here and stay, and next time you got questions like that, ask yourself!"

He held me in a grip like cold stone, his fingers fastening upon my windpipe until I thought I would suffocate before he finally allowed me to go. I stumbled about dazed, the music beating hysterically in my ears. It was dark. My head cleared and I wandered down a dark narrow passage, thinking I heard his footsteps hurrying behind me. I was sore, and into my being had come a profound craving for tranquillity, for peace and quiet, a state I felt I could never achieve. For one thing, the trumpet was blaring and the rhythm was too hectic. A tom-tom beating like heart-thuds began drowning out the trumpet, filling my ears. I longed for water and I heard it rushing through the cold mains my fingers touched as I felt my way, but I couldn't stop to search because of the footsteps behind me.

"Hey, Ras," I called. "Is it you, Destroyer? Rinehart?"

No answer, only the rhythmic footsteps behind me. Once I tried crossing the road, but a speeding machine struck me, scraping the skin from my leg as it roared past.

Then somehow I came out of it, ascending hastily from this underworld of sound to hear Louis Armstrong innocently asking,

> *What did I do*
> *To be so black*
> *And blue?*

At first I was afraid; this familiar music had demanded action, the kind of which I was incapable, and yet had I lingered there beneath the surface I might have attempted to act. Nevertheless, I know now that few really listen to this music. I sat on the chair's edge in a soaking sweat, as though each of my 1,369 bulbs had everyone become a klieg light in an individual setting for a third degree with Ras and Rinehart in charge. It was exhausting—as though I had held my breath continuously for an hour under the terrifying serenity that comes from days of intense hunger. And yet, it was a strangely satisfying experience for an invisible man to hear the silence of sound. I had discovered unrecognized compulsions of my being—even though I could not answer "yes" to their promptings. I haven't smoked a reefer since, however; not because they're illegal, but because to *see* around corners is enough (that is not unusual when you are invisible). But to hear around them is too much; it inhibits action. And despite Brother Jack and all that sad, lost period of the Brotherhood, I believe in nothing if not in action.

Please, a definition: A hibernation is a covert preparation for a more overt action.

Besides, the drug destroys one's sense of time completely. If that happened, I might forget to dodge some bright morning and some cluck would run me down with an orange and yellow street car, or a bilious bus! Or I might forget to leave my hole when the moment for action presents itself.

Meanwhile I enjoy my life with the compliments of Monopolated Light & Power. Since you never recognize me even when in closest contact with me, and since, no doubt, you'll hardly believe that I exist, it won't matter if you know that I tapped a power line leading into the building and ran it into my hole in the ground. Before that I lived in the darkness into which I was chased, but now I see. I've illuminated the blackness of my invisibility—and vice versa. And so I play the invisible music of my isolation. The last statement doesn't seem just right, does it? But it is; you hear this music simply because music is heard and seldom seen, except by musicians. Could this compulsion to put invisibility down in black and white be thus an urge to make music of invisibility? But I am an orator, a rabble rouser—Am? I *was,* and perhaps shall be again. Who knows? All sickness is not unto death, neither is invisibility.

I can hear you say, "What a horrible, irresponsible bastard!" And you're right. I leap to agree with you. I am one of the most irresponsible beings that ever lived. Irresponsibility is part of my invisibility; any way you face it, it is a denial. But to whom can I be responsible, and why should I be, when you refuse to see me? And wait until I reveal how truly irresponsible I am. Responsibility rests upon recognition, and recognition is a form of agreement. Take the man whom I almost killed: Who was responsible for that near murder—I? I don't think so, and I refuse it. I won't buy it. You can't give it to me. *He* bumped *me, he* insulted *me.* Shouldn't he, for his own personal safety, have recognized my hysteria, my "danger potential"? He, let us say, was lost in a dream world. But didn't *he* control that dream world—which, alas, is only too real!—and didn't *he* rule me out of it? And if he had yelled for a policeman, wouldn't *I* have been taken for the offending one? Yes, yes, yes! Let me agree with you, I was the irresponsible one; for I should have used my knife to protect the higher interests of society. Some day that kind of foolishness will cause us tragic trouble. All dreamers and sleepwalkers must pay the price, and even the invisible victim is responsible for the fate of all. But I shirked that responsibility; I became too snarled in the incompatible notions that buzzed within my brain. I was a coward . . .

But what did *I* do to be so blue? Bear with me.

Juneteenth

No, the wounded man thought, Oh no! Get back to that; back to a bunch of old-fashioned Negroes celebrating an illusion of emancipation, and getting it mixed up with the Resurrection, minstrel shows and vaudeville routines? Back to that tent in the clearing surrounded by trees, that bowl-shaped impression in the earth beneath the pines? . . . Lord, it hurts. Lordless and without loyalty, it hurts. Wordless, it hurts. Here and especially here. Still I see it after all the roving years and flickering scenes: Twin lecterns on opposite ends of the platform, behind one of which I stood on a wide box, leaning forward to grasp the lectern's edge. Back. Daddy Hickman at the other. Back to the first day of that week of celebration. Juneteenth. Hot, dusty. Hot with faces shining with sweat and the hair of the young dudes metallic with grease and straightening irons. Back to that? He was not so heavy then, but big with the quick energy of a fighting bull and still kept the battered silver trombone on top of the piano, where at the climax of a sermon he could reach for it and stand blowing tones that sounded like his own voice amplified; persuading, denouncing, rejoicing—moving beyond words back to the undifferentiated cry. In strange towns and cities the jazz musicians were always around him. Jazz. What was jazz and what religion back there? Ah yes, yes, I loved him. Everyone did, deep down. Like a great, kindly, daddy bear along the streets, my hand lost in his huge paw. Carrying me on his shoulder so that I could touch the leaves of the trees as we passed. The true father, but black, black. Was he a charlatan—am I—or simply as resourceful in my fashion. Did he know himself, or care? Back to the problem of all that. Must I go back to the beginning when only he knows the start . . . ?

Juneteenth and him leaning across the lectern, resting there looking into their faces with a great smile, and then looking over to me to make sure that I had not forgotten my part, winking his big red-rimmed eye at me. And the women looking back and forth from him to me with that bright, bird-like adoration in their faces; their heads cocked to one side. And him beginning:

On this God-given day, brothers and sisters, when we have come together to praise God and celebrate our oneness, our slipping off the chains, let's us begin this week of worship by taking a look at the ledger. Let us, on this day of deliverance, take a look at the figures writ on our bodies and on the living tablet of our heart. The Hebrew children have their Passover so that they can keep their history alive in their memories—so let us take one more page from their book and, on this great day of deliverance, on this day of emancipation, let's us tell ourselves our story. . . .

Pausing, grinning down. . . . Nobody else is interested in it anyway, so let us enjoy it ourselves, yes, and learn from it.

And thank God for it. Now let's not be too solemn about it either, because this here's a happy occasion. Rev. Bliss over there is going to take the part of the younger generation, and I'll try to tell it as it's been told to me. Just look at him over there, he's ready and raring to go—because he knows that a true preacher is a kind of educator, and that we have got to know our story before we can truly understand God's blessings and how far we have still got to go. Now you've heard him, so you know that he can preach.

Amen! They all responded and I looked preacher-faced into their shining eyes, preparing my piccolo voice to support his baritone sound.

Amen is right, he said. So here we are, five thousand strong, come together on this day of celebration. Why? We just didn't happen. We're here and that is an undeniable fact—but how come we're here? How and why here in these woods that used to be such a long way from town? What about it, Rev. Bliss, is that a suitable question on which to start?

God, bless you, Rev. Hickman, I think that's just the place we have to start. We of the younger generation are still ignorant about these things. So please, sir, tell us just how we came to be here in our present condition and in this land. . . .

Not back to that me, not to that six-seven year old ventriloquist's dummy dressed in a white evening suit. Not to that charlatan born—must I have no charity for me? . . .

Was it an act of God, Rev. Hickman, or an act of man. . . . Not to that puppet with a memory like a piece of flypaper. . . .

We came, amen, Rev. Bliss, sisters and brothers, as an act of God, but through—I said through, an act of cruel, ungodly man.

An act of almighty God, *my treble echo sounded,* but through the hands of cruel man.

Amen, Rev. Bliss, that's how it happened. It was, as I understand it, a cruel calamity laced up with a blessing—or maybe a blessing laced up with a calamity. . . .

Laced up with a blessing, Rev. Hickman? We understand you partially because you have taught us that God's sword is a two-edged sword. But would you please tell us of the younger generation just why it was a blessing?

It was a blessing, brothers and sisters, because out of all the pain and the suffering, out of the night of storm, we found the Word of God.

So here we found the Word. Amen, so now we are here. But where did we come from, Daddy Hickman?

We come here out of Africa, son; out of Africa.

Africa? Way over across the ocean? The black land? Where the elephants and monkeys and the lions and tigers are?

Yes, Rev. Bliss, the jungle land. Some of us have fair skins like you, but out of Africa too.

Out of Africa truly, sir?

Out of the ravaged mama of the black man, son.

Lord, thou hast taken us out of Africa . . .

Amen, out of our familiar darkness. Africa. They brought us here from all over Africa, Rev. Bliss. And some were the sons and daughters of heathen kings . . .

Some were kings, Daddy Hickman? Have we of the younger generation heard you correctly? Some were kin to kings? Real kings?

Amen! I'm told that some were the sons and the daughters of kings . . .

. . . Of Kings! . . .

And some were the sons and daughters of warriors . . .

. . . Of warriors . . .

Of fierce warriors. And some were the sons and the daughters of farmers . . .

Of African farmers . . .

. . . And some of musicians . . .

. . . Musicians . . .

And some were the sons and daughters of weapon makers and of smelters of brass and iron . . .

But didn't they have judges, Rev. Hickman? And weren't there any preachers of the word of God?

Some were judges but none were preachers of the word of God, Rev. Bliss. For we come out of heathen Africa . . .

Heathen Africa?

Out of heathen Africa. Let's tell this thing true; because the truth is the light.

And they brought us here in chains . . .

In chains, son; in iron chains . . .

From half-a-world away, they brought us . . .

In chains and in boats that the history tells us weren't fit for pigs—because pigs cost too much money to be allowed to waste and die as we did. But they stole us and brought us in boats which I'm told could move like the swiftest birds of prey, and which filled the great trade winds with the stench of our dying and their crime . . .

What a crime! Tell us why, Rev. Hickman . . .

It was a crime, Rev. Bliss, brothers and sisters, like the fall of proud Lucifer from Paradise.

But why, Daddy Hickman? You have taught us of the progressive younger generation to ask why. So we want to know how come it was a crime?

Because, Rev. Bliss, this was a country dedicated to the principles of almighty God. That Mayflower boat that you hear so much about Thanksgiving Day was a *Christian* ship—Amen! Yes, and those many-named floating coffins we came here in were Christian too. They had turned traitor to the God who set them free from Europe's tyrant kings. Because, God have mercy on them, no sooner than they got free enough to breathe themselves, they set out to bow us down . . .

They made our Lord shed tears!

Amen! Rev. Bliss, amen. God must have wept like Jesus. Poor Jonah went down into the belly of the whale, but compared to our journey his was like a trip to paradise on a silvery cloud.

Worse than old Jonah, Rev. Hickman?

Worse than Jonah slicked all over with whale puke and gasping on the shore. We went down into hell on those floating coffins and don't you youngsters forget it! Mothers and babies, men and women, the living and the dead and the dying—all chained together. And yet, praise God, most of us arrived here in this land. The strongest came through. Thank God, and we arrived and that's why we're here today. Does that answer the question, Rev. Bliss?

Amen, Daddy Hickman, amen. But now the younger generation would like to know what they did to us when they got us here. What happened then?

They brought us up onto this land in chains . . .

. . . In chains . . .

. . . And they marched us into the swamps . . .

. . . Into the fever swamps, they marched us . . .

And they set us to work draining the swampland and toiling in the sun . . .

. . . They set us to toiling . . .

They took the white fleece of the cotton and the sweetness of the sugar cane and made them bitter and bloody with our toil . . . And they treated us like one great unhuman animal without any face . . .

Without a *face,* Rev. Hickman?

Without personality, without names, Rev. Bliss, we were made into nobody and not even *mister* nobody either, just nobody. They left us without names. Without choice. Without the right to do or not to do, to be or not to be . . .

You mean without faces and without eyes? We were eyeless like Samson in Gaza? Is that the way, Rev. Hickman?

Amen, Rev. Bliss, like baldheaded Samson before that nameless little lad like you came as the Good Book tells us and led him to the pillars whereupon the big house stood—Oh, you little black boys, and oh, you little brown girls, you're going to shake the building down! And then, Oh, how you will build in the name of the Lord!

Yes Revered Bliss, we were eyeless like unhappy Samson among the Philistines—and worse . . . .

And WORSE?

Worse, Rev. Bliss, because they chopped us up into little bitty pieces like a farmer when he cuts up a potato. And they scattered us around the land. All the way from Kentucky to Florida; from Louisiana to Texas; from Missouri all the way down the great Mississippi to the Gulf. They scattered us around this land.

How now, Daddy Hickman? You speak in parables which we of the younger generation don't clearly understand. How do you mean, they scattered us?

Like seed, Rev. Bliss; they scattered us just like a dope-fiend farmer planting a field with dragon teeth!

Tell us about it, Daddy Hickman.

They cut out our tongues . . .

. . . They left us speechless . . .

. . . They cut out our tongues . . .

. . . Lord, they left us without words . . .

. . . Amen! They scattered our tongues in this land like seed . . .

. . . And left us without language . . .

. . . They took away our talking drums . . .

. . . Drums that talked, Daddy Hickman? Tell us about those talking drums . . .

Drums that talked like a telegraph. Drums that could reach across the country like a church bell sound. Drums that told the news almost before it happened! Drums that spoke with big voices like big men! Drums like a conscience and a deep heart-beat that knew right from wrong. Drums that told glad tidings! Drums that sent the news of trouble speeding home! Drums that told us *our* time and told us where we were . . .

Those were some drums, Rev. Hickman . . .

. . . Yes and they took those drums away . . .

Away, Amen! Away! And they took away our heathen dances . . .

. . . They left us drumless and they left us danceless . . . .

Ah yes, they burnt up our talking drums and our dancing drums . . .

. . . Drums . . .

. . . And they scattered the ashes . . .

. . . Ah, Aaaaaah! Eyeless, tongueless, drumless, danceless, ashes . . .

And a worst devastation was yet to come, Lord God!

Tell us, Reveren Hickman. Blow on your righteous horn!

Ah, but Rev. Bliss, in those days we didn't have any horns . . .

No *horns?* Hear him!

And we had no songs . . .

. . . No songs . . .

. . . And we had no . . .

. . . Count it on your fingers, see what cruel man has done . . .

Amen, Rev. Bliss, lead them . . .

We were eyeless, tongueless, drumless, danceless, hornless, songless!

All true, Rev. Bliss. No eyes to see. No tongue to speak or taste. No drums to raise the spirits and wake up our memories. No dance to stir the rhythm that makes life move. No songs to give praise and prayers to God!

We were truly in the dark, my young brothern and sisteren. Eyeless, earless, tongueless, drumless, danceless, songless, hornless, soundless . . .

And worst to come!

. . . And worse to come . . .

Tell us, Rev. Hickman. But not too fast so that we of the younger generation can gather up our strength to face it. So that we may listen and not become discouraged!

I said, Rev. Bliss, brothers and sisters, that they snatched us out of the loins of Africa. I said that they took us from our mammys and pappys and from our sisters and brothers. I said that they scattered us around this land . . .

. . . And we, let's count it again, brothers and sisters; let's add it up. Eyeless, tongueless, drumless, danceless, songless, hornless, soundless, sightless, dayless, nightless, wrongless, rightless, motherless, fatherless—scattered.

Yes, Rev. Bliss, they scattered us around like seed . . .

. . . Like seed . . .

. . . Like seed, that's been flung broadcast on unplowed ground . . .

Ho, chant it with me, my young brothers and sisters! Eyeless, tongueless, drumless, danceless, songless, hornless, soundless, sightless, wrongless, rightless, motherless, fatherless, brotherless, sisterless, powerless . . .

Amen! But though they took us like a great black giant that had been chopped up into little pieces and the pieces buried; though they deprived us of our heritage among strange scenes in strange weather; divided and divided and divided us again like a gambler shuffling and cutting a deck of cards. Although we were ground down, smashed into little pieces; spat upon, stamped upon, cursed and buried, and our memory of Africa ground down into powder and blown on the winds of foggy forgetfulness . . .

. . . Amen, Daddy Hickman! Abused and without shoes, pounded down and ground like grains of sand on the shores of the sea . . .

. . . Amen! And God—Count it, Rev. Bliss . . .

. . . Left eyeless, earless, noseless, throatless, teethless, tongueless, handless, feetless, armless, wrongless, rightless, harmless, drumless, danceless, songless, hornless, soundless, sightless, wrongless, rightless, motherless, fatherless, sisterless, brotherless, plowless, muleless, foodless, mindless—and Godless, Rev. Hickman, did you say Godless?

. . . At first, Rev. Bliss, he said, his trombone entering his voice, broad, somber and noble. At first. Ah, but though divided and scattered, ground down and battered into the earth like a spike being pounded by a ten pound sledge, we were on the ground and in the earth and the earth was red and black like the earth of Africa. And as we moldered underground we were mixed with this land. We liked it. It fitted us fine. It was in us and we were in it. And then—praise God—deep in the ground, deep in the womb of this land, we began to stir!

Praise God!

At last, Lord, at last.

Amen!

Oh the truth, Lord, it tastes so sweet!

What was it like then, Rev. Bliss? You read the scriptures, so tell us. Give us a word.

WE WERE LIKE THE VALLEY OF DRY BONES!

Amen. Like the Valley of Dry Bones in Ezekiel's dream. Hoooh! We lay scattered in the ground for a long dry season. And the winds blew and the sun blazed down and the rains came and went and we were dead. Lord, we were dead! Except . . . Except . . .

. . . Except what, Rev. Hickman?

Except for one nerve left from our ear . . .

Listen to him!

And one nerve in the soles of our feet . . .

. . . Just watch me point it out, brothers and sisters . . .

Amen, Bliss, you point it out . . . and one nerve left from the throat . . .

. . . From our throat—right *here!*

. . . Teeth . . .

. . . From our teeth, one from all thirty-two of them . . .

. . . Tongue . . .

. . . Tongueless . . .

. . . And another nerve left from our heart . . .

. . . Yes, from our heart . . .

. . . And another left from our eyes and one from our hands and arms and legs and another from our stones . . .

Amen, Hold it right there, Rev. Bliss . . .

. . . All stirring in the ground . . .

. . . Amen, stirring, and right there in the midst of all our death and buriedness, the voice of God spoke down the Word . . .

. . . Crying, Do! I said, Do! Crying Doooo—

These dry bones live?

He said, Son of Man . . . under the ground, Ha! Heatless beneath the roots of plants and trees . . . Son of man, do . . .

I said, Do . . .

. . . I said Do, Son of Man, Doooooo!—

These dry bones live?

Amen! And we heard and rose up. Because in all their blasting they could not blast away one solitary vibration of God's true word . . . We heard it down among the roots and among the rocks. We heard it in the sand and in the clay. We heard it in the falling rain and in the rising sun. On the high ground and in the gullies. We heard it lying moldering and corrupted in the earth. We heard it sounding like a bugle call to wake up the dead. Crying, Doooooo! Ay, do these dry bones live!

And did our dry bones live, Daddy Hickman?

Ah, we sprang together and walked around. All clacking together and clicking into place. All moving in time! Do! I said, Dooooo—these dry bones live!

And now strutting in my white tails, across the platform, filled with the power almost to dancing.

Shouting, Amen, Daddy Hickman, is this the way we walked?

Oh we walked through Jerusalem, just like John—That's it, Rev. Bliss, walk! Show them how we walked!

Was this the way?

That's the way. Now walk on back. Lift your knees! Swing your arms! Make your coat tails fly! Walk! And him strutting me three times around the pulpit across the platform and back. Ah, yes! And then his voice deep and exultant: And if they ask you in the city why we praise the Lord with bass drums and brass trombones tell them we were rebirthed dancing, we were rebirthed crying affirmation of the Word, quickening our transcended flesh.

Amen!

Oh, Rev. Bliss, we stamped our feet at the trumpet's sound and we clapped our hands, ah, in joy! And we moved, yes, together in a dance, amen! Because we had received a new song in a new land and been resurrected by the Word and Will of God!

Amen! . . .

. . . —We were rebirthed from the earth of this land and revivified by the Word. So now we had a new language and a brand new song to put flesh on our bones . . .

New teeth, new tongue, new word, new song!

We had a new name and a new blood, and we had a new task . . .

Tell us about it, Reveren Hickman . . .

We had to take the Word for bread and meat. We had to take the Word for food and shelter. We had to use the Word as a rock to build up a whole new nation, cause to tell it true, we were born again in chains of steel. Yes, and chains of ignorance. And all we knew was the spirit of the word. We had no schools. We owned no tools; no cabins, no churches, not even our own bodies.

We were chained, young brothers, in steel. We were chained, young sisters, in ignorance. We were schooless, tool-less, cabinless—owned . . .

Amen, Reveren Bliss. We were owned and faced with the awe-inspiring labor of transforming God's word into a lantern so that in the darkness we'd know where we were. Oh God hasn't been easy with us because He always plans for the looooong haul. He's looking far ahead and this time He wants a well-tested people to work his will. He wants some sharp-eyed, quick-minded, generous-hearted people to give names to the things of this world and to its values. He's tired of untempered tools and half-blind masons! Therefore, He's going to keep on testing us against the rocks and in the fires. He's going to heat us till we almost melt and then He's going to plunge us into the ice-cold water. And each time we come out we'll be blue and as tough as cold-blue steel! Ah yes! He means for us to be a new kind of human. Maybe we won't be that people but we'll be a part of that people, we'll be an element in them, Amen! He wants us limber as willow switches and he wants us tough as whit leather, so that when we have to bend, we can bend and snap back into place. He's going to throw bolts of lightning to blast us so that we'll have good foot work and lightning-fast minds. He'll drive us hither and yon around this land and make us run the gauntlet of hard times and tribulations, misunderstanding and abuse. And some will pity you and some will despise you. And some will try to use you and change you. And some will deny you and try to deal you out of the game. And sometimes you'll feel so bad that you'll wish you could die. But it's all the pressure of God. He's giving you a will and He wants you to use it. He's giving you brains and he wants you to train them lean and hard so that you can overcome all the obstacles. Educate your minds! Make do with what you have so as to get what you need! Learn to look at what *you* see and not what somebody tells you is true. Pay lip-service to Caesar if you have to, but put your trust in God. Because nobody has a patent on truth or a copyright on the best way to live and serve almighty God. Learn from what we've lived. Remember that when the labor's back-breaking and the boss man's mean our singing can lift us up. That it can strengthen us and make his meanness but the flyspeck irritation of an empty man. Roll with the blow like ole Jack Johnson. Dance on out of his way like Williams and Walker. Keep to the rhythm and you'll keep to life. God's time is long; and all short-haul horses shall be like horses on a merry-go-round. Keep, keep, keep to the rhythm and you won't get weary. Keep to the rhythm and you won't get lost. We're handicapped, amen! Because the Lord wants us strong! We started out with nothing but the Word—just like the others but they've forgot it . . . We worked and stood up under hard times and tribulations. We learned patience and to understand Job. Of all the animals, man's the only one not born knowing almost everything he'll ever know. It takes him longer than an elephant to grow up because God didn't mean him to leap to any conclusions, for God himself is in the very process of things. We learned that all blessings come mixed with sorrow and all hardships have a streak of laughter. Life is a streak-a-lean—a—streak-a-fat. Ha, yes! We learned to bounce back and to disregard the prizes of fools. And we must keep on learning. Let them have their fun. Even let them eat humming bird's wings and tell you it's too good for you.—Grits and greens don't turn to ashes in anybody's mouth—How about it, Rev. Eatmore? Amen? Amen! Let everybody say amen. Grits and greens are humble but they make you strong and when the right folks get together to share them they can taste like ambrosia. So draw, so let us draw on our own wells of strength.

Ah yes, so we were reborn, Rev. Bliss. They still had us harnessed, we were still laboring in the fields, but we had a secret and we had a new rhythm . . .

So tell us about this rhythm, Reveren Hickman.

They had us bound but we had our kind of time, Rev. Bliss. They were on a merry-go-round that they couldn't control but we learned to beat time from the seasons. We learned to make this land and this light and darkness and this weather and their labor fit us like a suit of new underwear. With our new rhythm, amen, but we weren't free and they still kept dividing us. There's many a thousand gone down the river. Mama sold from papa and chillun sold from both. Beaten and abused and without shoes. But we had the Word, now, Rev. Bliss, along with the rhythm. They couldn't divide us now. Because anywhere they dragged us we throbbed in time together. If we got a chance to sing, we sang the same song. If we got a chance to dance, we beat back hard times and tribulations with a clap of our hands and the beat of our feet, and it was the same dance. Oh they come out here sometimes to laugh at our way of praising God. They can laugh but they can't deny us. They can curse and kill us but they can't destroy us all. This land is ours because we come out of it, we bled in it, our tears watered it, we fertilized it with our dead. So the more of us they destroy the more it becomes filled with the spirit of our redemption. They laugh but we know who we are and where we are, but they keep on coming in their millions and they don't know and can't get together.

But tell us, how do we know who we are, Daddy Hickman?

We know where we are by the way we walk. We know where we are by the way we talk. We know where we are by the way we sing. We know where we are by the way we dance. We know where we are by the way we praise the Lord on high. We know where we are because we hear a different tune in our minds and in our hearts. We know who we are because when we make the beat of our rhythm to shape our day the whole land says, Amen! It smiles, Rev. Bliss, and it moves to our time! Don't be ashamed, my brothern! Don't be cowed. Don't throw what you have away! Continue! Remember! Believe! Trust the inner beat that tells us who we are. Trust God and trust life and trust this land that is you! Never mind the laughers, the scoffers, they come around because they can't help themselves. They can deny you but not your sense of life. They hate you because whenever they look into a mirror they fill up with bitter gall. So forget them and most of all don't deny yourselves. They're tied by the short hair to a run-away merry-go-round. They make life a business of struggle and fret, fret and struggle. See who you can hate; see what you can get. But you just keep on inching along like an old inchworm. If you put one and one and one together soon they'll make a million too. There's been a heap of Juneteenths before this one and I tell you there'll be a heap more before we're truly free! Yes! But keep to the rhythm, just keep to the rhythm and keep to the way. Man's plans are but a joke to God. Let those who *will* despise you, but remember deep down inside yourself that the life we have to lead is but a preparation for other things, it's a discipline, Reveren Bliss, Sisters and Brothers; a discipline through which we may see that which the others are too self-blinded to see. Time will come round when we'll have to be their eyes; time will swing and turn back around. I tell you, time shall swing and spiral back around . . .

JOHN OLIVER KILLENS

(1916–1987)

John Oliver Killens, like Richard Wright, is a writer whose literary sensibility and creative imagination were deeply influenced by the segregated South. He wrote throughout his career with a conscious purpose to rectify some of the social ills that plagued African Americans. "Art," he is quoted in the *Dictionary of Literary Biography,* vol. 76, as saying, "is social and political, takes a position for humanity or against."

Killens was born January 14, 1916, in Macon, Georgia. His parents consciously introduced him to African American literature. His mother was president of the Dunbar Literary Club. The harsh realities of life for blacks in the segregated South, a recurrent theme in his early work, eventually led him to seek opportunities elsewhere. He left Macon in 1936 and accepted a position with the National Labor Relations Board in Washington, D.C. He held that position until 1942. From 1942 to 1945, he served in the U.S. Amphibian Forces in the South Pacific.

In 1946, Killens was honorably discharged from the military and moved with his wife and his children to Brooklyn, New York. For two years, he tried to organize black and white workers for the Congress of Industrial Organizations (CIO). He failed but did not lose interest in social justice and Civil Rights. Among other activities, he participated in the Montgomery, Alabama, bus boycott in 1955. He began writing seriously during the forties and acknowledged the influence of Wright, Langston Hughes, and Margaret Walker. He joined John Henrick Clark, Rosa Guy, and Walter Christmas in the founding of the Harlem Writers Guild in 1951.

Killens began publishing books in 1954, when his first novel, *Youngblood,* appeared. His final work, *The Great Black Russian; A Novel on the Life of Alexander Pushkin,* was published posthumously in 1988. During those three decades, Killens wrote, among other works, five novels, a collection of essays, and a biography. *Youngblood,* set in Crossroads, Georgia, explores the relationship between a white laborer and a black man who refuses to abide by segregationist laws and customs. Another character, Joe Youngblood, as his surname symbolically suggests, represents the possibilities of a new generation. The novel ends when Youngblood is treated by a white doctor at a white hospital. Although at first the doctor is a reluctant and grudging actor in this unprecedented vital scene of racial and human understanding, he manages to rise magnanimously to the occasion and saves Youngblood's life. The blood for Youngblood's transfusion is donated by another white character. The novel, falling dramatically into the protest tradition, has several scenes of violence against blacks. In an attempt to rescue it from a predictably grim outcome, Killens reluctantly suggests the possibility of racial reconciliation and understanding at the end.

The author's second novel, *And Then We Heard the Thunder* (1963), is probably his best-known work. The story takes place during World War II, and the action centers on Sergeant Solly Saunders, a college graduate. When Saunders's unit is moved to Ebbensville, Georgia, trouble eventually starts as black soldiers are repeatedly harassed and attacked by white police and citizens of the town. After several black soldiers are severely beaten on one occasion, Saunders writes a letter about the racial situation of black soldiers. The letter condemns the U.S. armed forces and is published in a widely read black newspaper, prompting an investigation by the NAACP. When a commanding officer discovers that Saunders wrote the letter, he ships him and his buddies to war in the Pacific. Several of them, including Saunders, are wounded and are sent to a hospital in Bainbridge, Australia.

The denouement of the novel occurs when a group of white southern troops arrives in Bainbridge, bringing their racial bigotry with them. A gun battle between the black and white soldiers breaks out. Several of Saunders's close black friends are killed, and the novel ends with Saunders sitting in the street crying. As one critic has carefully observed, "two" wars are being fought in *And Then We Heard the Thunder:*

> Both involve the maiming and killing of men and both are fought against facism. Thus the Battle of Bainbridge is as important as the Battle of Iwo Jima or the Battle of North Africa; it is a war not for territory or material gain, not to subject or to oppress a nation or its people; it is a war for manhood.

Much of Killens's criticism of American racism can be found in his essay "The Black Writer Vis-à-Vis His Country" (1965). It opens with George Bernard Shaw's observation that "America was the first country in history to move from barbarism to decadence without going through civilization." The victims have been all Americans. Hence, "a cultural revolution is desperately needed here and now, to unbrainwash the entire American people, black and white. For the people of this land have been the victims of a mighty brainwash that has continued unabated for the last four hundred years." And because African Americans have "born the brunt of the millions of little white lies America has told the world about herself and about the Negro," black artists must assume an uneven load in the cultural revolution. They must do so because "as black folk, they know America better than she knows herself."

In keeping with his aesthetic manifesto, Killens's third novel, *Sippi* (1967), serves as a venue for the airing of a range of views on topics such as integration, racial separation, and Black Power. His fourth novel, *The Cotillion; or, One Good Bull Is Half the Herd* (1971), a satirical exposé of African Americans trapped in pretentious traditions of superior social standing, has been described as a "literary dozens." The action of the novel centers on an annual cotillion, sponsored by the Femme Fatales, a group of "Negro Society" women who live in the Crowning Heights section of Brooklyn, New York. Killens's characters engage in numerous exaggerated statements of personal insult, so that by the novel's end, the pretenses have been stripped away and exposed. Middle-class pretentiousness also is a theme in Killens's short story "The Stick Up" (1967). The secure, educated black "professor," removed from the plight of less fortunate men and women, can only clench his hands and smile with a "bitter taste" in his mouth when an unshaven, filthy white vagabond exclaims to him, "Damn. This is getting to be a helluva country, when you can't chisel four lousy pennies offa prosperous-looking nigger!"

Killens devoted much of his final years to writing for younger readers. His *Great Gittin' Up Morning* (1972) is a fictionalized account of the life of Denmark Vesey, a free black who planned a slave revolt in Charleston, South Carolina, in 1822. He also published a book for children based on the life of John Henry titled *A Man Ain't Nothin' But a Man: The Adventures of John Henry* (1975). According to Killens in "*The Black Writer: This Is His Country!*"

> We must build a literature of heroes, myths, and legends. The lives of Harriet Tubman, Frederick Douglass, Nat Turner, Sojourner Truth, are as formidable as George Washington's, and are based on a much more substantial reality. Our people, young and old, need such heroes desperately. . . . We need such a heritage in order to really believe that we shall prevail.

During different periods in his life, Killens taught creative writing at various universities, including Fisk, Howard, and Columbia. In addition to his books, he wrote a collection of essays and a movie script. When he died in 1987, he was a professor at Medgar Evers College in Brooklyn.

❖❖❖

For further discussion of Killens and his work, see William H. Wiggins, Jr.'s essay in *Dictionary of Literary Biography* (51); Bernard Bell, *The Afro-American*

Novel and Its Tradition (1987); Addison Gayle, *The Way of the New World* (1975); William H. Wiggins, Jr., "Black Folk Tales in the Novels of John O. Killens," *Black Scholar* 3 (November 1971).

The Stick Up

I felt good. I think the park had something to do with it. Trees, grass, bushes—everything in brand-new togs of shining green. The warm yellow sunlight sifting down through the trees, making my face feel alive and healthy and casting shadows on the paved walks and the unpaved walks and the wooden benches. Slight breezes tickling my nostrils, caressing my face, bringing with them a good clean odor of things new and live and dripping with greenness. Such a good feeling made me uneasy.

The park breathing with people, old and young. Playing checkers and chess, listening to portable radios—the Dodgers leading the Giants. I walked to the end of the park and stood near the wading pool where the water spurted skyward.

Little children in their underpants, splashing the water and pretending to swim, and throwing water at each other and yelling and shouting in wild childish happiness. One Negro child with a soft dark face and big brown eyes pretended to enjoy herself, but her big black eyes gave her away—anxious and uneasy. As if she were not sure that all of a sudden the other children would not turn on her and bite her like a bunch of mad dogs. I knew that feeling—even now. Barefoot women sat round the pool watching the children, reading books, trying to get brown without the expense of a Florida vacation. A little blonde-headed girl got smacked in the face and ran bawling to her black-haired mother. A double-decker Fifth Avenue bus passed to the east, with curious passengers looking from the top deck. The tall buildings of New York University looked over and down upon a noisy humanity playing in the park. *Perstando Et Praestando Utilitati—*

The kids were having loads of fun and it make me think back. I substituted a country woods for the beautiful city park. I made believe the wading pool was the swimming hole on old man Gibson's forbidden grounds. And something turned over and over in my stomach and ran like a chill through the length of my body, leaving a funny taste in my mouth. I took a sudden trip into the past. Meeting kids I had known many years ago, as if they had remained kids and had never grown up. My face tight and full now as I swallowed a mouthful of cool green air. It was the first time I had been homesick in many years. Standing there trying to recall names, faces and incidents. After a moment I shrugged it off. I could never really be homesick for the country woods and the swimming holes of Georgia. Give me the city—the up-north city.

I turned and started walking back through the park, passing women, young and old, blond and brunette, and black and brown and light brown in white uniforms, pushing various types of baby carriages. I had almost reached the other end of the park, when a big lumbering giant of a white man came toward me. I tried to walk out of his way, but he maneuvered into my path and grabbed me by the shoulders. He was unshaven, his clothes were filthy and he reeked of rot-gut whiskey and days and nights without soap and water. He towered over me and coughed in my face and said in a deep rasping voice—"This is a stick up!"

I must have looked silly and startled. What was he up to, in broad open daylight? Oh—no—he must be kidding. And yet, crazier things happen every day in this crazy world of New York City. Especially in the Village.

He jabbed his big forefinger into my side, causing me to wince. Then he nudged me playfully and said, "I'm only kidding, buddy. But cheesuz christmas, I do need just four more cents for the price of a drink. How about it, professor? It's just four lousy cents. Didn't hardly take me no time at all to hustle up the rest of it this morning, but seems to me I just can't get this last four cents don't care how hard I try. It's a goddamn shame!"

I made a show of feeling in my pockets. I had no loose change and knew it. I wanted to say, Well, you sure won't get it from me, but I said instead, "Gosh, I don't have it. I'm sorry."

I started to walk away from him. He put his big arms around me, surrounding me with his foul odor. His shirt was dirty and greasy, smelled like sour food and whiskey vomit. A deep gash started near his right eye and beat a trail down into his mouth. An awful cloud came between me and the springtime, blotting out the breeze, the sunshine, the freshness that had been everywhere.

"Look, buddy, I ain't no ordinary bum you meet on the street. I want you to know that. I'm just down on my luck—see?"

I wanted to shrug my shoulders, wanted to say, I don't give a damn what you are! Through the years I had built up a resistance against people like him, and I thought I was foolproof. He rambled on, "I know—you—you think I'm just one of them everyday bums, but it isn't so. I'm just as educated as the next feller. But I know what you think though. I—"

My nostrils quivered, my neck gathered sweat. I wanted to be away from him. "You don't know what I think!"

He leaned heavily on my shoulder. My body sagged under his enormous weight. My knees buckled. "You don't have to be that way, mate. Just because a feller is down on his luck. Can't never tell when you'll need a favor yourself. Listen, I'm an educated man. Look, I used to be a business man too."

I kept thinking angrily to myself, of all the people in the park, most of them white, why did he single me out? It wasn't the first time a thing like this had happened. Just a week before I was on the subway and a white drunk got on at Thirty-fourth Street. He looked around for a seat and there were plenty available next to other people. But he finally spied me, the only Negro in the half-empty car, and he came and sat down beside me, choosing me to be the benefactor of his infinite wisdom and his great liberal philosophy and his bad-liquored breath.

I tried to pull away from this one in the park but his huge hand held be by the shoulder. With his other hand he fumbled in his shirt pocket, then in the back pocket of his trousers. He fished out a dirty ragged snapshot. "Look," he said, "that's me and my family. I used to be a business man out west. Had a good business too. Yes indeed."

It would have been comical had it not been so tragic, the way pride gleamed in his eyes as he gazed at the picture. I suppose it was he, although you had to stare at it hard and stretch your imagination. He looked like a million dollars, posing with a wife and two fine-looking children. I began to wonder what had happened to him along the way—what had become of his family—then caught myself going soft. Oh—no—none of that sentimental stuff. I glanced at my watch deliberately. "Look, my friend," I said, "I've got—"

His eyes were like red flint marbles. He coughed like he would strangle to death and directly into my face. My entire being came up in revolt against everything about him, but still he was a human being, and he might have gotten his four cents, maybe more, if he hadn't made his next pitch the way he did.

"Look, professor, I don't think I'm any better than you or anybody else. I want you to know that. We're all fighting together against them goddamn gooks in Viet Nam, ain't we? You look like an intelligent young man. I'm an educa—How about it, professor? Just four little old lousy cents—"

All of my inner resentment pushed outward as I squirmed and wrested myself angrily from his hold. "I've got to go! Goddamnit—I don't have any four cents for you!"

I started walking away from him toward the street corner trembling with anger, but uplifted by the fresh air rushing into my entire body. I stood at the intersection waiting for the light to change. Something made me turn and look for the big man. I saw him lumbering toward me again. My body became tense. A flock of cars were passing. Why in the hell didn't the light change to green? But then he stopped and sat down heavily on the last bench in the park. Amid a fit of coughing I heard him mumble—"Damn. This is getting to be a helluva country, when you can't chisel four lousy pennies offa prosperous-looking nigger!"

My hands clenched unconsciously. I smiled with a bitter taste in my mouth. The light changed to green. I started across the street.

JAMES BALDWIN
(1924–1987)

"I love America more than any other country in the world," wrote James Baldwin in "Notes of a Native Son" (1955), "and exactly for this reason, I insist on the right to criticize her perpetually." From the beginning of his career to the very end, Baldwin exercised his right to criticize American racism "perpetually" in virtually everything he wrote. Starting out as a writer during the late forties, publishing in journals and magazines such as *The Nation, The New Leader, Commentary,* and *Partisan Review,* Baldwin rose to international fame after the appearance of "The Fire Next Time" in 1963. However, nearly two decades before the publication of this most famous essay, he had already captured the attention of an assortment of writers, literary critics, and intellectuals in the United States and abroad. Writing to Langston Hughes in 1948, Arna Bontemps commented on Baldwin's "The Harlem Ghetto," published in the February 1948 issue of *Commentary.* Referring to "that remarkable piece by the 24-year-old colored kid." Bontemps wrote, "What a kid! He has zoomed high among our writers with his first effort."

The victim of poverty and the anger of his stepfather, Baldwin had a difficult childhood, as revealed in his semiautobiographical novel *Go Tell It on the Mountain* (1953). The son of Emma Berdis Jones, a single parent, James Baldwin was born August 2, 1924, and grew up in Harlem with David Baldwin, his stepfather, and eight brothers and sisters. He was a gay youth who divided his time between helping with his younger siblings and reading. He was a voracious reader, devouring the King James version of the Bible, Charles Dickens, Harriet Beecher Stowe, Richard Wright, and virtually everything else in sight. He read Stowe's *Uncle Tom's Cabin* so often that his mother hid the book. Although she was very supportive of him, David Baldwin, his stepfather and a storefront preacher, was a bitter and demanding individual. The relationship between the two became increasingly difficult when the latter saw clearly that his stepson was fiercely independent about his own life. Young James decided as a teenager that he wanted to make writing his life's work. As early as his years at Frederick Douglass Junior High, as well as during his years at Dewitt Clinton High School, he wrote stories and articles for various literary magazines.

Baldwin left Harlem after high school and found employment during World War II in Trenton, New Jersey. One of his most poignant and moving essays, "Notes of a Native Son" describes this period in his life. He frequently experienced racism and discrimination while there. He also discusses in the essay the declining health (mental and physical) of his stepfather, who eventually died in 1943. He was buried on Baldwin's nineteenth birthday.

Baldwin moved back to New York, to Greenwich Village, where he lived and worked for several years. With Richard Wright's support, Baldwin was granted a Eugene F. Saxton Memorial Trust Award to complete drafts of *Go Tell It on the Mountain.* He continued writing, although he became increasingly exasperated by the racial situation in America. Thus, with his typewriter, a small sum of money, and his faith, he bought a one-way ticket to Paris in 1948. For him, Paris truly became the "City of Light." After arriving there, he said, "I felt as though I had come out of a dark tunnel and seen the sky for the first time." While in Europe, Baldwin made a discovery about himself. In "The Discovery of What It Means to Be an American" he writes about his experience with two Bessie Smith recordings while living and writing in Switzerland:

> There, in that alabaster landscape, armed with two Bessie Smith records and a typewriter, I began to recreate the life that I had first known as a child and from which I had spent so many years in flight. . . . Bessie Smith, through her fame and cadence . . . helped me dig back to the way I myself must have spoken when I was a pickaninny, and to remember the things I had heard and seen and felt. I had buried them very deep.

Baldwin concludes with his confession that while he was in Europe, Bessie Smith "helped to reconcile me to being a 'Nigger.' "

Baldwin achieved success and fame as an expatriate. Writing about race and sexuality (including homosexuality, major themes in *Giovanni's Room* [1956] and *Another Country* [1962]), he published twenty-two books, among them six novels: *Go Tell It on the Mountain* (1953), *Giovanni's Room, Another Country, Tell Me How Long the Train's Been Gone* (1968), *If Beale Street Could Talk* (1974), and *Just Above My Head* (1979). His collections of essays include *Notes of a Native Son* (1953), *Nobody Knows My Name* (1961), *The Fire Next Time* (1963), *No Name in the Street* (1972), and *The Devil Finds Work: An Essay* (1976). In addition, he wrote a collection of short stories, *Going to Meet the Man* (1965), two plays, a children's book, a movie scenario, *A Rap on Race* (1971), with Margaret Mead, *A Dialogue* (1975), with Nikki Giovanni, and *Jimmy's Blues* (1985), a chapbook of poems. Starting with his controversial *Another Country,* many of his books, including *The Fire Next Time, If Beale Street Could Talk,* and *Just Above My Head,* were bestsellers. His play *Blues for Mr. Charlie* (1964) was produced on Broadway, and his scenario *One Day When I Was Lost: A Scenario Based on Alex Haley's* The Autobiograpy of Malcolm X (1965) was used by the movie director Spike Lee in his feature film on Malcolm X.

Baldwin's career, which can be divided into two phases, up to *The Fire Next Time* and after, gained momentum after the publication of two of his most famous essays. In 1948 and 1949, respectively, he wrote "Everybody's Protest Novel," and "Many Thousands Gone," which were published in *Partisan Review.* Those essays served as the stage from which he made pronouncements about the limitations of the protest tradition in American literature. He scathingly criticized Harriet Beecher Stowe's *Uncle Tom's Cabin* and Richard Wright's *Native Son* for being firmly rooted in the protest tradition. Each writer failed in Baldwin's judgment because, as he states in "Everybody's Protest Novel," the "power of revelation . . . is the business of the novelist, that journey toward a more vast reality which must take precedence over all other claims." He abhorred the idea of the writer as a kind of "congressman" and embraced ideas concerning the art of fiction articulated by Henry James. The writer, as Baldwin envisioned himself during this early period, should self-consciously seek distance between himself and his subject: "Social affairs are not generally speaking the writer's prime concern, whether they ought to be or not; it is absolutely necessary that he establish between himself and these affairs distance which will allow, at least, for clarity."

Because of these and similar statements, Baldwin was heralded early in his career by white liberals as the supreme voice on race matters in America—the prophet of a new, more human black American. But white Americans' romance with Baldwin was short-lived. The guilt-soothing rhetoric that characterized his early writing quickly gave way in the sixties to the much more militant expression of intense disgust with America. The America of Baldwin's *Another Country* (1962) was portrayed as a white wasteland of sterility, pain, and greed. In contrast, the black world that he once feared—the pimps, whores, and racketeers—now seemed to Baldwin beautiful, free, and authentic. The people who inhabited it were beautiful because they were, in contrast to the joylessness and sterility of white Americans, lively and present in everything they did—their jazz, their blues, their church music. He even contrasted their straightforward criminality with the hypocritical immorality of white Americans and came to prefer it.

Himself a Holy Roller preacher in storefront churches by the age of fourteen, Baldwin speaks of Christ as a "disreputable sunbaked Hebrew" in "The Fire Next Time" (1963). He notes, "If the concept of God has any validity or any use, it can only be to make us larger, freer. . . . If God cannot do this, then it is time we got rid of Him." Baldwin openly advocated gay rights, criticized American military involvement in Vietnam, equated the Civil Rights Movement in the United States with decolonization abroad, and accused the Nixon administration of plotting, with the help of FBI director J. Edgar Hoover, the genocide of all people of color at home and abroad. Although he admired and supported both the Black Muslims and the Black Panthers, Baldwin always sought unity between the two races. If white America did not do all that it could to achieve that unity, "the fulfillment of that prophesy, recreated from the Bible in song by a slave, is upon us: God gave Noah the rainbow sign, no more water, the fire next time!" Contemplating the actual fulfillment of this prophesy, Baldwin asked: "Do I really want to integrate into a burning house?"

The Fire Next Time attracted the attention of national leaders, including the Kennedy brothers. Attorney General Robert F. Kennedy invited Baldwin to breakfast to solicit advice during the spring 1963 demonstrations in Birmingham, Alabama. When Baldwin did not say what the attorney general wanted to hear, Kennedy asked J. Edgar Hoover for a dossier on Baldwin. But Baldwin was not to be intimidated. He continued to criticize Hoover, pointing out that he

> is not a lawgiver, nor is there any reason to suppose him to be a particularly profound student of human nature. He is a law-enforcement officer. It is appalling that in this capacity he not only opposes the trend of history among civilized nations but uses his enormous power and prestige to corroborate the blindest and basest instinct of the retaliating mob.

Baldwin predicted the end of Western civilization and Eurocentricism as early as 1972 in *No Name in the Street,* and he maintained that only in revolution could

American racism be solved: "There will be bloody holding actions all over the world, for years to come: but the Western party is over, and the white man's sun has set, Period."

During the final decade of his life, Baldwin taught at a number of American colleges and universities, including the University of Massachusetts at Amherst and Hampshire College. In addition to the Saxton Award, he had a Rosenwald Fellowship, a Guggenheim Fellowship, a National Institute of Arts and Letters Fellowship, a Ford Foundation Grant-in-Aid, and a *Partisan Review* Fellowship. Commuting back and forth between the United States and his home in St. Paul de Vence in the south of France, Baldwin was one of the more eloquent and influential writers of the twentieth century. After his death in France on November 30, 1987, the *New York Times* reported on its front page the following day, "James Baldwin, Eloquent Essayist in Behalf of Civil Rights, Is Dead."

❖❖❖

Baldwin has been written about in the popular press as well as in scholarly journals. Several book-length critical studies have been published since his death, including two unofficial biographies by Horace Porter and James Campbell: Fern Eckman, *The Furious Passage of James Baldwin* (1977); Stanley Macebuh, *James Baldwin: A Critical Study* (1973); Louis H. Pratt, *James Baldwin* (1978); Trudier Harris, *Black Women in the Fiction of James Baldwin* (1985); Horace Porter, *Stealing the Fire: The Art and Protest of James Baldwin* (1989); James Campbell, *Talking at the Gates: A Life of James Baldwin* (1991).

Sonny's Blues

I read about it in the paper, in the subway, on my way to work I read it, and I couldn't believe it, and I read it again. Then perhaps I just stared at it, at the newsprint spelling out his name, spelling out the story. I stared at it in the swinging lights of the subway car, and in the faces and bodies of the people, and in my own face, trapped in the darkness which roared outside.

It was not to be believed and I kept telling myself that, as I walked from the subway station to the high school. And at the same time I couldn't doubt it. I was scared, scared for Sonny. He became real to me again. A great block of ice got settled in my belly and kept melting there slowly all day long, while I taught my classes algebra. It was a special kind of ice. It kept melting, sending trickles of ice water all up and down my veins, but it never got less. Sometimes it hardened and seemed to expand until I felt my guts were going to come spilling out or that I was going to choke or scream. This would always be at a moment when I was remembering some specific thing Sonny had once said or done.

When he was about as old as the boys in my classes his face had been bright and open, there was a lot of copper in it; and he'd had wonderfully direct brown eyes, and great gentleness and privacy. I wondered what he looked like now. He had been picked up, the evening before, in a raid on an apartment downtown, for peddling and using heroin.

I couldn't believe it: but what I mean by that is that I couldn't find any room for it anywhere inside me. I had kept it outside me for a long time. I hadn't wanted to know. I had had suspicions, but I didn't name them, I kept putting them away. I told myself that Sonny was wild, but he wasn't crazy. And he'd always been a good boy, he hadn't ever turned hard or evil or disrespectful, the way kids can, so quick, so quick, especially in Harlem. I didn't want to believe that I'd ever see my brother going down, coming to nothing, all that light in his face gone out in the condition I'd already seen so many others. Yet it had happened and here I was, talking about algebra to a lot of boys who might, every one of them for all I knew, be popping off needles every time they went to the head. Maybe it did more for them than algebra could.

I was sure that the first time Sonny had ever had horse, he couldn't have been much older than these boys were now. These boys, now, were living as we'd been living then, they were growing up with a rush and their heads bumped abruptly against the low ceiling of their actual possibilities. They were filled with rage. All they really knew were two darknesses, the darkness of their lives, which was now closing in on them, and the darkness of the movies, which had blinded them to that other darkness, and in which they now, vindictively, dreamed, at once more together than they were at any other time, and more alone.

When the last bell rang, the last class ended, I let out my breath. It seemed I'd been holding it for all that time. My clothes were wet—I may have looked as though I'd been sitting in a steam bath, all dressed up, all afternoon. I sat alone in the classroom a long time. I listened to the boys outside, downstairs, shouting and cursing and laughing. Their laughter struck me for perhaps the first time. It was not the joyous laughter which—God knows why—one associates with children. It was mocking and insular, its intent to denigrate. It was disenchanted, and in this, also, lay the authority of their curses. Perhaps I was listening to them because I was thinking about my brother and in them I heard my brother. And myself.

One boy was whistling a tune, at once very complicated and very simple, it seemed to be pouring out of him as though he were a bird, and it sounded very cool and moving through all that harsh, bright air, only just holding its own through all those other sounds.

I stood up and walked over to the window and looked down into the courtyard. It was the beginning of the spring and the sap was rising in the boys. A teacher passed through them every now and again, quickly, as though he or she couldn't wait to get out of that courtyard, to get those boys out of their sight and off their minds. I started collecting my stuff. I thought I'd better get home and talk to Isabel.

The courtyard was almost deserted by the time I got downstairs. I saw this boy standing in the shadow of a doorway, looking just like Sonny. I almost called his name. Then I saw that it wasn't Sonny, but somebody we used to know, a boy from around our block. He'd been Sonny's friend. He'd never been mine, having been too young for me, and, anyway, I'd never liked him. And now, even though he was a grown-up man, he still hung around that block, still spent hours on the street corners, was always high and raggy. I used to run into him from time to time and he'd often work around to asking me for a quarter or fifty cents. He always had some real good excuse, too, and I always gave it to him, I don't know why.

But now, abruptly, I hated him. I couldn't stand the way he looked at me, partly like a dog, partly like a cunning child. I wanted to ask him what the hell he was doing in the school courtyard.

He sort of shuffled over to me, and he said, "I see you got the papers. So you already know about it."

"You mean about Sonny? Yes, I already know about it. How come they didn't get you?"

He grinned. It made him repulsive and it also brought to mind what he'd looked like as a kid. "I wasn't there. I stay away from them people."

"Good for you." I offered him a cigarette and I watched him through the smoke. "You come all the way down here just to tell me about Sonny?"

"That's right." He was sort of shaking his head and his eyes looked strange, as though they were about to cross. The bright sun deadened his damp dark brown skin and it made his eyes look yellow and showed up the dirt in his kinked hair. He smelled funky. I moved a little away from him and I said, "Well, thanks. But I already know about it and I got to get home."

"I'll walk you a little ways," he said. We started walking. There were a couple of kids still loitering in the courtyard and one of them said goodnight to me and looked strangely at the boy beside me.

"What're you going to do?" he asked me. "I mean, about Sonny?"

"Look. I haven't seen Sonny for over a year, I'm not sure I'm going to do anything. Anyway, what the hell *can* I do?"

"That's right," he said quickly, "ain't nothing you can do. Can't much help old Sonny no more, I guess."

It was what I was thinking and so it seemed to me he had no right to say it.

"I'm surprised at Sonny, though," he went on—he had a funny way of talking, he looked straight ahead as though he were talking to himself—"I thought Sonny was a smart boy, I thought he was too smart to get hung."

"I guess he thought so too," I said sharply, "and that's how he got hung. And now about you? You're pretty goddamn smart, I bet."

Then he looked directly at me, just for a minute. "I ain't smart," he said. "If I was smart, I'd have reached for a pistol a long time ago."

"Look. Don't tell *me* your sad story, if it was up to me, I'd give you one." Then I felt guilty—guilty, probably, for never having supposed that the poor bastard *had* a story of his own, much less a sad one, and I asked, quickly, "What's going to happen to him now?"

He didn't answer this. He was off by himself some place. "Funny thing," he said, and from his tone we might have been discussing the quickest way to get to Brooklyn, "when I saw the papers this morning, the first thing I asked myself was if I had anything to do with it. I felt sort of responsible."

I began to listen more carefully. The subway station was on the corner, just before us, and I stopped. He stopped, too. We were in front of a bar and he ducked slightly, peering in, but whoever he was looking for didn't seem to be there. The juke box was blasting away with something black and bouncy and I half watched the barmaid as she danced her way from the juke box to her place behind the bar. And I watched her face as she laughingly responded to something someone said to her, still keeping time to the music. When she smiled one saw the little girl, one sensed the doomed, still-struggling woman beneath the battered face of the semi-whore.

"I never *give* Sonny nothing," the boy said finally, "but a long time ago I come to school high and Sonny asked me how it felt." He paused, I couldn't bear to watch him, I watched the barmaid, and I listened to the music which seemed to be causing the pavement to shake. "I told him it felt great." The music stopped, the barmaid paused and watched the juke box until the music began again. "It did."

All this was carrying me some place I didn't want to go. I certainly didn't want to know how it felt. It filled everything, the people, the houses, the music, the dark, quicksilver barmaid, with menace; and this menace was their reality.

"What's going to happen to him now?" I asked again.

"They'll send him away some place and they'll try to cure him." He shook his head. "Maybe he'll even think he's kicked the habit. Then they'll let him loose"—he gestured, throwing his cigarette into the gutter. "That's all."

"What do you mean, that's *all?*"

But I knew what he meant.

"I *mean,* that's *all.*" He turned his head and looked at me, pulling down the corners of his mouth. "Don't you know what I mean?" he asked, softly.

"How the hell *would* I know what you mean?" I almost whispered it, I don't know why.

"That's right," he said to the air, "how would *he* know what I mean?" He turned toward me again, patient and calm, and yet I somehow felt him shaking, shaking as though he were going to fall apart. I felt that ice in my guts again, the dread I'd felt all afternoon; and again I watched the barmaid, moving about the bar, washing glasses, and singing. "Listen. They'll let him out and then it'll just start all over again. That's what I mean."

"You mean—they'll let him out. And then he'll just start working his way back in again. You mean he'll never kick the habit. Is that what you mean?"

"That's right," he said, cheerfully. "*You* see what I mean."

"Tell me," I said at last, "why does he want to die? He must want to die, he's killing himself, why does he want to die?"

He looked at me in surprise. He licked his lips. "He don't want to die. He wants to live. Don't nobody want to die, ever."

Then I wanted to ask him—too many things. He could not have answered, or if he had, I could not have borne the answers. I started walking. "Well, I guess it's none of my business."

"It's going to be rough on old Sonny," he said. We reached the subway station. "This is your station?" he asked. I nodded. I took one step down. "Damn!" he said, suddenly. I looked up at him. He grinned again. "Damn it if I didn't leave all my money home. You ain't got a dollar on you, have you? Just for a couple of days, is all."

All at once something inside gave and threatened to come pouring out of me. I didn't hate him any more. I felt that in another moment I'd start crying like a child.

"Sure," I said. "Don't sweat." I looked in my wallet and didn't have a dollar, I only had a five. "Here," I said. "That hold you?"

He didn't look at it—he didn't want to look at it. A terrible closed look came over his face, as though he were keeping the number on the bill a secret from him and me. "Thanks," he said, and now he was dying to see me go. "Don't worry about Sonny. Maybe I'll write him or something."

"Sure," I said. "You do that. So long."

"Be seeing you," he said. I went on down the steps.

And I didn't write Sonny or send him anything for a long time. When I finally did, it was just after my little girl died, he wrote me back a letter which made me feel like a bastard.

Here's what he said:

DEAR BROTHER,

You don't know how much I needed to hear from you. I wanted to write you many a time but I dug how much I must have hurt you and so I didn't write. But now I feel like a man who's been trying to climb up out of some deep, real deep and funky hole and just saw the sun up there, outside. I got to get outside.

I can't tell you much about how I got here. I mean I don't know how to tell you. I guess I was afraid of something or I was trying to escape from something and you know I have never been very strong in the head (smile). I'm glad Mama and Daddy are dead and can't see what's happened to their son and I swear if I'd known what I was doing I would never have hurt you so, you and a lot of other fine people who were nice to me and who believed in me.

I don't want you to think it had anything to do with me being a musician. It's more than that. Or maybe less than that. I can't get anything straight in my head down here and I try not to think about what's going to happen to me when I get outside again. Sometime I think I'm going to flip and *never* get outside and sometime I think I'll come straight back. I tell you one thing, though, I'd rather blow my brains out than go through this again. But that's what they all say, so they tell me. If I tell you when I'm coming to New York and if you could meet me, I sure would appreciate it. Give my love to Isabel and the kids and I was sure sorry to hear about little Gracie. I wish I could be like Mama and say the Lord's will be done, but I don't know it seems to me that trouble is the one thing that never does get stopped and I don't know what good it does to blame it on the Lord. But maybe it does some good if you believe it.

Your brother,
SONNY

Then I kept in constant touch with him and I sent him whatever I could and I went to meet him when he came back to New York. When I saw him many things I thought I had forgotten came flooding back to me. This was because I had begun, finally, to wonder about Sonny, about the life that Sonny lived inside. This life, whatever it was, had made him older and thinner and it had deepened the distant stillness in which he had always moved. He looked very unlike my baby brother. Yet, when he smiled, when we shook hands, the baby brother I'd never known looked out from the depths of his private life, like an animal waiting to be coaxed into the light.

"How you been keeping?" he asked me.

"All right. And you?"

"Just fine." He was smiling all over his face. "It's good to see you again."

"It's good to see you."

The seven years' difference in our ages lay between us like a chasm: I wondered if these years would ever operate between us as a bridge. I was remembering, and it made it hard to catch my breath, that I had been there when he was born; and I had heard the first words he had ever spoken. When he started to walk, he walked from our mother straight to me. I caught him just before he fell when he took the first steps he ever took in this world.

"How's Isabel?"

"Just fine. She's dying to see you."

"And the boys?"

"They're fine, too. They're anxious to see their uncle."

"Oh, come on. You know they don't remember me."

"Are you kidding? Of course they remember you."

He grinned again. We got into a taxi. We had a lot to say to each other, far too much to know how to begin.

As the taxi began to move, I asked, "You still want to go to India?"

He laughed. "You still remember that. Hell, no. This place is Indian enough for me."

"It used to belong to them." I said.

And he laughed again. "They damn sure knew what they were doing when they got rid of it."

Years ago, when he was around fourteen, he'd been all hipped on the idea of going to India. He read books about people sitting on rocks, naked, in all kinds of weather, but mostly bad, naturally, and walking barefoot through hot coals and arriving at wisdom. I used to say that it sounded to me as though they were getting away from wisdom as fast as they could. I think he sort of looked down on me for that.

"Do you mind," he asked, "if we have the driver drive alongside the park? On the west side—I haven't seen the city in so long."

"Of course not," I said. I was afraid that I might sound as though I were humoring him, but I hoped he wouldn't take it that way.

So we drove along, between the green of the park and the stony, lifeless elegance of hotels and apartment buildings, toward the vivid, killing streets of our childhood. These streets hadn't changed, though housing projects jutted up out of them now like rocks in the middle of a boiling sea. Most of the houses in which we had grown up had vanished, as had the stores from which we had stolen, the basements in which we had first tried sex, the rooftops from which we had hurled tin cans and bricks. But houses exactly like the houses of our past yet dominated the landscape, boys exactly like the boys we once had been found themselves smothering in these houses, came down into the streets for light and air and found themselves encircled by disaster. Some escaped the trap, most didn't. Those who got out always left something of themselves behind, as some animals amputate a leg and leave it in the trap. It might be said, perhaps, that I had escaped, after all. I was a school teacher; or that Sonny had, he hadn't lived in Harlem for years. Yet, as the cab moved uptown through streets which seemed, with a rush, to darken with dark people, and as I covertly studied Sonny's face, it came to me that what we both were seeking through our separate cab windows was that part of ourselves which had been left behind. It's always at the hour of trouble and confrontation that the missing member aches.

We hit 110th Street and started rolling up Lenox Avenue. And I'd known this avenue all my life, but it seemed to me again, as it had seemed on the day I'd first heard about Sonny's trouble, filled with a hidden menace which was its very breath of life.

"We almost there," said Sonny.

"Almost." We were both too nervous to say anything more.

We live in a housing project. It hasn't been up long. A few days after it was up it seemed uninhabitably new, now, of course, it's already rundown. It looks like a parody of the good, clean, faceless life—God knows the people who live in it do their best to make it a parody. The beat-looking grass lying around isn't enough to make their lives green, the hedges will never hold out the streets, and they know it. The big windows fool no one, they aren't big enough to make space out of no space. They don't bother with the windows, they watch the TV screen instead. The playground is most popular with the children who don't play at jacks, or skip rope, or roller skate, or swing, and they can be found in it after dark. We moved in partly because it's not too far from where I teach, and partly for the kids, but it's really just like the houses in which Sonny and I grew up. The same things happen, they'll have the same things to remember. The moment Sonny and I started into the house I had the feeling that I was simply bringing him back into the danger he had almost died trying to escape.

Sonny has never been talkative. So I don't know why I was sure he'd be dying to talk to me when supper was over the first night. Everything went fine, the oldest boy remembered him, and the youngest boy liked him, and Sonny had remembered to bring something for each of them; and Isabel, who is really much nicer than I am, more open and giving, had gone to a lot of trouble about dinner and was genuinely glad to see him. And she's always been able to tease Sonny in a way that I haven't. It was nice to see her face so vivid again and to hear her laugh and watch her make Sonny laugh. She wasn't, or, anyway, she didn't seem to be, at all uneasy or embarrassed. She chatted as though there were no subject which had to be avoided and she got Sonny past his first, faint stiffness. And thank God she was there, for I was filled with that icy dread again. Everything I did seemed awkward to me, and everything I said sounded freighted with hidden meaning. I was trying to remember everything I'd heard about dope addiction and I couldn't help watching Sonny for signs. I wasn't doing it out of malice. I was trying to find out something about my brother. I was dying to hear him tell me he was safe.

"Safe!" my father grunted, whenever Mama suggested trying to move to a neighborhood which might be safer for children. "Safe, hell! Ain't no place safe for kids, nor nobody."

He always went on like this, but he wasn't, ever, really as bad as he sounded, not even on weekends when he got drunk. As a matter of fact, he was always on the lookout for "something a little better," but he died before he found it. He died suddenly, during a drunken weekend in the middle of the war, when Sonny was fifteen. He and Sonny hadn't ever got on too well. And this was partly because Sonny was the apple of his father's eye. It was because he loved Sonny so much and was frightened for him, that he was always fighting with him. It doesn't do any good to fight with Sonny. Sonny just moves back, inside himself, where he can't be reached. But the principal reason that they never hit it off is that they were so much alike. Daddy was big and rough and loud-talking, just the opposite of Sonny, but they both had—that same privacy.

Mama tried to tell me something about this, just after Daddy died. I was home on leave from the army.

This was the last time I ever saw my mother alive. Just the same, this picture gets all mixed up in my mind with pictures I had of her when she was younger. The way I always see her is the way she used to be on a Sunday afternoon, say, when the old folks were talking after the big Sunday dinner. I always see her wearing pale blue. She'd be sitting on the sofa. And my father would be sitting in the easy chair, not far from her. And the living room would be full of church folks and relatives. There they sit, in chairs all around the living room, and the night is creeping up outside, but nobody knows it yet. You can see the darkness growing against the windowpanes and you hear the street noises every now and again, or maybe the jangling beat of a tambourine from one of the churches close by, but it's real quiet in the room. For a moment nobody's talking, but every face looks darkening, like the sky outside. And my mother rocks a little from the waist, and my father's eyes are closed. Everyone is looking at something a child can't see. For a minute they've forgotten the children. Maybe a kid is lying on the rug, half asleep. Maybe somebody's got a kid in his lap and is absent-mindedly stroking the kid's head. Maybe there's a kid, quiet and big-eyed, curled up in a big chair in the corner. The silence, the darkness coming, and the darkness in the faces frightens the child obscurely. He hopes that the hand which strokes his forehead will never stop—will never die. He hopes that there will never come a time when the old folks won't be sitting around the living room, talking about where they've come from, and what they've seen, and what's happened to them and their kinfolk.

But something deep and watchful in the child knows that this is bound to end, is already ending. In a moment someone will get up and turn on the light. Then the old folks will remember the children and they won't talk any more that day. And when light fills the room, the child is filled with darkness. He knows that everytime this happens he's moved just a little closer to that darkness outside. The darkness outside is what the old folks have been talking about. It's what they've come from. It's what they endure. The child knows that they won't talk any more because if he knows too much about what's happened to *them,* he'll know too much too soon, about what's going to happen to *him.*

The last time I talked to my mother, I remember I was restless. I wanted to get out and see Isabel. We weren't married then and we had a lot to straighten out between us.

There Mama sat, in black, by the window. She was humming an old church song, *Lord, you brought me from a long ways off.* Sonny was out somewhere. Mama kept watching the streets.

"I don't know," she said, "if I'll ever see you again, after you go off from here. But I hope you'll remember the things I tried to teach you."

"Don't talk like that," I said, and smiled. "You'll be here a long time yet."

She smiled, too, but she said nothing. She was quiet for a long time. And I said, "Mama, don't you worry about nothing. I'll be writing all the time, and you be getting the checks. . . ."

"I want to talk to you about your brother," she said, suddenly. "If anything happens to me he ain't going to have nobody to look out for him."

"Mama," I said, "ain't nothing going to happen to you *or* Sonny. Sonny's all right. He's a good boy and he's got good sense."

"It ain't a question of his being a good boy," Mama said, "nor of his having good sense. It ain't only the bad ones, nor yet the dumb ones that gets sucked under." She stopped, looking at me. "Your Daddy once had a brother," she said, and she smiled in a way that made me feel she was in pain. "You didn't never know that, did you?"

"No," I said, "I never knew that," and I watched her face.

"Oh, yes," she said, "your Daddy had a brother." She looked out of the window again. "I know you never saw your Daddy cry. But *I* did—many a time, through all these years."

I asked her, "What happened to his brother? How come nobody's ever talked about him?"

This was the first time I ever saw my mother look old.

"His brother got killed," she said, "when he was just a little younger than you are now. I knew him. He was a fine boy. He was maybe a little full of the devil, but he didn't mean nobody no harm."

Then she stopped and the room was silent, exactly as it had sometimes been on those Sunday afternoons. Mama kept looking out into the streets.

"He used to have a job in the mill," she said, "and, like all young folks, he just liked to perform on Saturday nights. Saturday nights, him and your father would drift around to different places, go to dances and things like that, or just sit around with people they knew, and your father's brother would sing, he had a fine voice, and play along with himself on his guitar. Well, this particular Saturday night, him and your father was coming home from some place, and they were both a little drunk and there was a moon that night, it was bright like day. Your father's brother was feeling kind of good, and he was whistling to himself, and he had his guitar slung over his shoulder. They was coming down a hill and beneath them was a road that turned off from the highway. Well, your father's brother, being always kind of frisky, decided to run down this hill, and he did, with that guitar banging and clanging behind him, and he ran across the road, and he was making water behind a tree. And you father was sort of amused at him and he was still coming down the hill, kind of slow. Then he heard a car motor and that same minute his brother stepped from behind the tree, into the road, in the moonlight. And he started to cross the road. And your father started to run down the hill, he says he don't know why. This car was full of white men. They was all drunk, and when they seen your father's brother they let out a great whoop and holler and they aimed the car straight at him. They was having fun, they just wanted to scare him, the way they do sometimes, you know. But they was drunk. And I guess the boy, being drunk, too, and scared, kind of lost his head. By the time he jumped it was too late. Your father says he heard his brother scream when the car rolled over him, and he heard the wood of that guitar when it give, and he heard them strings go flying, and he heard them white men shouting, and the car kept on a-going and it ain't stopped till this day. And, time your father got down the hill, his brother weren't nothing but blood and pulp."

Tears were gleaming on my mother's face. There wasn't anything I could say.

"He never mentioned it," she said, "because I never let him mention it before you children. Your Daddy was like a crazy man that night and for many a night thereafter. He says he never in his life seen anything as dark as that road after the lights of that car had gone away. Weren't nothing, weren't nobody on that road, just your Daddy and his brother and that busted guitar. Oh, yes. Your Daddy never did really get right again. Till the day he died he weren't sure but that every white man he saw was the man that killed his brother."

She stopped and took out her handkerchief and dried her eyes and looked at me.

"I ain't telling you all this," she said, "to make you scared or bitter or to make you hate nobody. I'm telling you this because you got a brother. And the world ain't changed."

I guess I didn't want to believe this. I guess she saw this in my face. She turned away from me, toward the window again, searching those streets.

"But I praise my Redeemer," she said at last, "that He called your Daddy home before me. I ain't saying it to throw no flowers at myself, but, I declare, it keeps me from feeling too cast down to know I helped your father get safely through this world. Your father always acted like he was the roughest, strongest man on earth. And everybody took him to be like that. But if he hadn't had *me* there—to see his tears!"

She was crying again. Still, I couldn't move. I said, "Lord, Lord, Mama, I didn't know it was like that."

"Oh, honey," she said, "there's a lot that you don't know. But you are going to find it out." She stood up from the window and came over to me. "You got to hold on to your brother," she said, "and don't let him fall, no matter what it looks like is happening to him and no matter how evil you gets with him. You going to be evil with him many a time. But don't you forget what I told you, you hear?"

"I won't forget," I said. "Don't you worry, I won't forget. I won't let nothing happen to Sonny."

My mother smiled as though she were amused at something she saw in my face. Then, "You may not be able to stop nothing from happening. But you got to let him know you's *there.*"

Two days later I was married, and then I was gone. And I had a lot of things on my mind and I pretty well forgot my promise to Mama until I got shipped home on a special furlough for her funeral.

And, after the funeral, with just Sonny and me alone in the empty kitchen, I tried to find out something about him.

"What do you want to do?" I asked him.

"I'm going to be a musician," he said.

For he had graduated, in the time I had been away, from dancing to the juke box to finding out who was playing what, and what they were doing with it, and he had bought himself a set of drums.

"You mean, you want to be a drummer?" I somehow had the feeling that being a drummer might be all right for other people but not for my brother Sonny.

"I don't think," he said, looking at me very gravely, "that I'll ever be a good drummer. But I think I can play a piano."

I frowned. I'd never played the role of the older brother quite so seriously before, had scarcely ever, in fact, *asked* Sonny a damn thing. I sensed myself in the presence of something I didn't really know how to handle, didn't understand. So I made my frown a little deeper as I asked: "What kind of musician do you want to be?"

He grinned. "How many kinds do you think there are?"

"Be *serious,*" I said.

He laughed, throwing his head back, and then looked at me. "I *am* serious."

"Well, then, for Christ's sake, stop kidding around and answer a serious question. I mean, do you want to be a concert pianist, you want to play classical music and all that, or—or what?" Long before I finished he was laughing again. "For Christ's *sake,* Sonny!"

He sobered, but with difficulty. "I'm sorry. But you sound so—*scared!*" and he was off again.

"Well, you may think it's funny now, baby, but it's not going to be so funny when you have to make your living at it, let me tell you *that.*" I was furious because I knew he was laughing at me and I didn't know why.

"No," he said, very sober now, and afraid, perhaps, that he'd hurt me, "I don't want to be a classical pianist. That isn't what interests me. I mean"—he paused, looking hard at me, as though his eyes would help me to understand, and then gestured helplessly, as though perhaps his hand would help—"I mean, I'll have a lot of studying to do, and I'll have to study *everything,* but, I mean, I want to play *with*—jazz musicians." He stopped. "I want to play jazz," he said.

Well, the word had never before sounded as heavy, as real, as it sounded that afternoon in Sonny's mouth. I just looked at him and I was probably frowning a real frown by this time. I simply couldn't see why on earth he'd want to spend his time hanging around nightclubs, clowning around on bandstands, while people pushed each other around a dance floor. It seemed—beneath him, somehow. I had never thought about it before, had never been forced to, but I suppose I had always put jazz musicians in a class with what Daddy called "good-time people."

"Are you *serious?*"

"Hell, *yes,* I'm serious."

He looked more helpless than ever, and annoyed, and deeply hurt.

I suggested, helpfully: "You mean—like Louis Armstrong?"

His face closed as though I'd struck him. "No. I'm not talking about none of that old-time, down home crap."

"Well, look, Sonny, I'm sorry, don't get mad. I just don't altogether get it, that's all. Name somebody—you know, a jazz musician you admire."

"Bird."

"Who?"

"Bird! Charlie Parker! Don't they teach you nothing in the goddamn army?"

I lit a cigarette. I was surprised and then a little amused to discover that I was trembling. "I've been out of touch," I said. "You'll have to be patient with me. Now. Who's this Parker character?"

"He's just one of the greatest jazz musicians alive," said Sonny, sullenly, his hands in his pockets, his back to me. "Maybe *the* greatest," he added, bitterly, "that's probably why *you* never heard of him."

"All right," I said, "I'm ignorant. I'm sorry. I'll go out and buy all the cat's records right away, all right?"

"It don't," said Sonny, with dignity, "make any difference to me. I don't care what you listen to. Don't do me no favors."

I was beginning to realize that I'd never seen him so upset before. With another part of my mind I was thinking that this would probably turn out to be one of those things kids go through and that I shouldn't make it seem important by pushing it too hard. Still, I didn't think it would do any harm to ask: "Doesn't all this take a lot of time? Can you make a living at it?"

He turned back to me and half leaned, half sat, on the kitchen table. "Everything takes time," he said, "and—well, yes, sure, I can make a living at it. But what I don't seem to be able to make you understand is that it's the only thing I want to do."

"Well, Sonny," I said, gently, "you know people can't always do exactly what they *want* to do—"

"*No*, I don't know that," said Sonny, surprising me. "I think people *ought* to do what they want to do, what else are they alive for?"

"You getting to be a big boy," I said desperately, "it's time you started thinking about your future."

"I'm thinking about my future," said Sonny, grimly. "I think about it all the time."

I gave up. I decided, if he didn't change his mind, that we could always talk about it later. "In the meantime," I said, "you got to finish school." We had already decided that he'd have to move in with Isabel and her folks. I knew this wasn't the ideal arrangement because Isabel's folks are inclined to be dicty and they hadn't especially wanted Isabel to marry me. But I didn't know what else to do. "And we have to get you fixed up at Isabel's."

There was a long silence. He moved from the kitchen table to the window. "That's a terrible idea. You know it yourself."

"Do you have a *better* idea?"

He just walked up and down the kitchen for a minute. He was as tall as I was. He had started to shave. I suddenly had the feeling that I didn't know him at all.

He stopped at the kitchen table and picked up my cigarettes. Looking at me with a kind of mocking, amused defiance, he put one between his lips. "You mind?"

"You smoking already?"

He lit the cigarette and nodded, watching me through the smoke. "I just wanted to see if I'd have the courage to smoke in front of you." He grinned and blew a great cloud of smoke to the ceiling. "It was easy." He looked at my face. "Come on, now. I bet you was smoking at my age, tell the truth."

I didn't say anything but the truth was on my face, and he laughed. But now there was something very strained in his laugh. "Sure. And I bet that ain't all you was doing."

He was frightening me a little. "Cut the crap," I said. "We already decided that you was going to go and live at Isabel's. Now what's got into you all of a sudden?"

"*You* decided it," he pointed out. "*I* didn't decide nothing." He stopped in front of me, leaning against the stove, arms loosely folded. "Look, brother. I don't want to stay in Harlem no more, I really don't." He was very earnest. He looked at me, then over toward the kitchen window. There was something in his eyes I'd never seen before, some thoughtfulness, some worry all his own. He rubbed the muscle of one arm. "It's time I was getting out of here."

"Where do you want to *go*, Sonny?"

"I want to join the army. Or the navy, I don't care. If I say I'm old enough, they'll believe me."

Then I got mad. It was because I was so scared. "You must be crazy. You goddamn fool, what the hell do you want to go and join the *army* for?"

"I just told you. To get out of Harlem."

"Sonny, you haven't even finished *school.* And if you really want to be a musician, how do you expect to study if you're in the *army?*"

He looked at me, trapped, and in anguish. "There's ways. I might be able to work out some kind of deal. Anyway, I'll have the G.I. Bill when I come out."

"*If* you come out." We stared at each other. "Sonny, please. Be reasonable. I know the setup is far from perfect. But we got to do the best we can."

"I ain't learning nothing in school," he said. "Even when I go." He turned away from me and opened the window and threw his cigarette out into the narrow alley. I watched his back. "At least, I ain't learning nothing you'd want me to learn." He slammed the window so hard I thought the glass would fly out, and turned back to me. "And I'm sick of the stink of these garbage cans!"

"Sonny," I said, "I know how you feel. But if you don't finish school now, you're going to be sorry later that you didn't." I grabbed him by the shoulders. "And you only got another year. It ain't so bad. And I'll come back and I swear I'll help you do *whatever* you want to do. Just try to put up with it till I come back. Will you please do that? For me?"

He didn't answer and he wouldn't look at me.

"Sonny. You hear me?"

He pulled away. "I hear you. But you never hear anything *I* say."

I didn't know what to say to that. He looked out of the window and then back at me. "OK," he said, and sighed. "I'll try."

Then I said, trying to cheer him up a little. "They got a piano at Isabel's. You can practice on it."

And as a matter of fact, it did cheer him up for a minute. "That's right," he said to himself. "I forgot that." His face relaxed a little. But the worry, the thoughtfulness, played on it still, the way shadows play on a face which is staring into the fire.

But I thought I'd never hear the end of that piano. At first, Isabel would write me, saying how nice it was that Sonny was so serious about his music and how, as soon as he came in from school, or wherever he had been when he was supposed to be at school, he went straight to that piano and stayed there until suppertime. And, after supper, he went back to that piano and stayed there until everybody went to bed. He was at the piano all day Saturday and all day Sunday. Then he bought a record player and started playing records. He'd play one record over and over again, all day long sometimes, and he'd improvise along with it on the piano. Or he'd play one section of the record, one chord, one change, one progression, then he'd do it on the piano. Then back to the record. Then back to the piano.

Well, I really don't know how they stood it. Isabel finally confessed that it wasn't like living with a person at all, it was like living with sound. And the sound didn't make any sense to her, didn't make any sense to any of them—naturally. They began, in a way, to be afflicted by this presence that was living in their home. It was as though Sonny were some sort of god, or monster. He moved in an atmosphere which wasn't like theirs at all. They fed him and he ate, he washed himself, he walked in and out of their door; he certainly wasn't nasty or unpleasant or rude, Sonny isn't any of those things; but it was as though he were all wrapped up in some cloud, some fire, some vision all his own; and there wasn't any way to reach him.

At the same time, he wasn't really a man yet, he was still a child, and they had to watch out for him in all kinds of ways. They certainly couldn't throw him out. Neither did they dare to make a great scene about that piano because even they dimly sensed, as I sensed, from so many thousands of miles away, that Sonny was at that piano playing for his life.

But he hadn't been going to school. One day a letter came from the school board and Isabel's mother got it—there had, apparently, been other letters but Sonny had torn them up. This day, when Sonny came in, Isabel's mother showed him the letter and asked where he'd been spending his time. And she finally got it out of him that he'd been down in Greenwich Village, with musicians and other characters, in a white girl's apartment. And this scared her and she started to scream at him and what came up, once she began—though she denies it to this day—was what sacrifices they were making to give Sonny a decent home and how little he appreciated it.

Sonny didn't play the piano that day. By evening, Isabel's mother had calmed down but then there was the old man to deal with, and Isabel herself. Isabel says she did her best to be calm but she broke down and started crying. She says she just watched Sonny's face. She could tell, by watching him, what was happening with him. And what was happening was that they penetrated his cloud, they had reached him. Even if their fingers had been a thousand times more gentle than human fingers ever are, he could hardly help feeling that they had stripped him naked and were spitting on that nakedness. For he also had to see that his presence, that music, which was life or death to him, had been torture for them and that they had endured it, not at all for his sake, but only for mine. And Sonny couldn't take that. He can take it a little better today than he could then but he's still not very good at it and, frankly, I don't know anybody who is.

The silence of the next few days must have been louder than the sound of all the music ever played since time began. One morning, before she went to work, Isabel was in his room for something and she suddenly realized that all of his records were gone. And she knew for certain that he was gone. And he was. He went as far as the navy would carry him. He finally sent me a postcard from some place in Greece and that was the first I knew that Sonny was still alive. I didn't see him any more until we were both back in New York and the war had long been over.

He was a man by then, of course, but I wasn't willing to see it. He came by the house from time to time, but we fought almost every time we met. I didn't like the way he carried himself, loose and dreamlike all the time, and I didn't like his friends, and his music seemed to be merely an excuse for the life he led. It sounded just that weird and disordered.

Then we had a fight, a pretty awful fight, and I didn't see him for months. By and by I looked him up, where he was living, in a furnished room in the Village, and I tried to make it up. But there were lots of people in the room and Sonny just lay on his bed, and he wouldn't come downstairs with me, and he treated these other people as though they were his family and I weren't. So I got mad and then he got mad, and then I told him that he might just as well be dead as live the way he was living. Then he stood up and he told me not to worry about him any more in life, that he *was* dead as far as I was concerned. Then he pushed me to the door and the other people looked on as though nothing were happening, and he slammed the door behind me. I stood in the hallway, staring at the door. I heard somebody laugh in the room and then the tears came to my eyes. I started down the steps, whistling to keep from crying, I kept whistling to myself, *You going to need me, baby, one of these cold, rainy days.*

I read about Sonny's trouble in the spring. Little Grace died in the fall. She was a beautiful little girl. But she only lived a little over two years. She died of polio and she suffered. She had a slight fever for a couple of days, but it didn't seem like anything and we just kept her in bed. And we would certainly have called the doctor, but the fever dropped, she seemed to be all right. So we thought it had just been a cold. Then, one day, she was up, playing, Isabel was in the kitchen fixing lunch for the two boys when they'd come in from school, and she heard Grace fall down in the living room. When you have a lot of children you don't always start running when one of them falls, unless they start screaming or something. And, this time, Grace was quiet. Yet, Isabel says that when she heard that *thump* and then that silence, something happened in her to make her afraid. And she ran to the living room and there was little Grace on the floor, all twisted up, and the reason she hadn't screamed was that she couldn't get her breath. And when she did scream, it was the worst sound, Isabel says, that she'd ever heard in all her life, and she still hears it sometimes in her dreams. Isabel will sometimes wake me up with a low, moaning, strangled sound and I have to be quick to awaken her and hold her to me and where Isabel is weeping against me seems a mortal wound.

I think I may have written Sonny the very day that little Grace was buried. I was sitting in the living room in the dark, by myself, and I suddenly thought of Sonny. My trouble made his real.

One Saturday afternoon, when Sonny had been living with us, or, anyway, been in our house, for nearly two weeks, I found myself wandering aimlessly about the living room, drinking from a can of beer, and trying to work up the courage to search Sonny's room. He was out, he was usually out whenever I was home, and Isabel had taken the children to see their grandparents. Suddenly I was standing still in front of the living room window, watching Seventh Avenue. The idea of searching Sonny's room made me still. I scarcely dared to admit to myself what I'd be searching for. I didn't know what I'd do if I found it. Or if I didn't.

On the sidewalk across from me, near the entrance to a barbecue joint, some people were holding an old-fashioned revival meeting. The barbecue cook, wearing a dirty white apron, his conked hair reddish and metallic in the pale sun, and a cigarette between his lips, stood in the doorway, watching them. Kids and older people paused in their errands and stood there, along with some older men and a couple of very tough-looking women who watched everything that happened on the avenue, as though they owned it, or were maybe owned by it. Well, they were watching this, too. The revival was being carried on by three sisters in black, and a brother. All they had were their voices and their Bibles and a tambourine. The brother was testifying and while he testified two of the sisters stood together, seeming to say, amen, and the third sister walked around with the tambourine outstretched and a couple of people dropped coins into it. Then the brother's testimony ended and the sister who had been taking up the collection dumped the coins into her palm and transferred them to the pocket of her long black robe. Then she raised both hands, striking the tambourine against the air, and then against one hand, and she started to sing. And the two other sisters and the brother joined in.

It was strange, suddenly, to watch, though I had been seeing these street meetings all my life. So, of course, had everybody else down there. Yet, they paused and watched and listened and I stood still at the window. *"Tis the old ship of Zion,"* they sang, and the sister with the tambourine kept a steady, jangling beat, *"it has rescued many a thousand!"* Not a soul under the sound of their voices was hearing this song for the first time, not one of them had been rescued. Nor had they seen much in the way of rescue work being done around them. Neither did they especially believe in the holiness of the three sisters and the brother, they knew too much about them, knew where they lived, and how. The woman with the tambourine, whose voice dominated the air, whose face was bright with joy, was divided by very little from the woman who stood watching her, a cigarette between her heavy, chapped lips, her hair a cuckoo's nest, her face scarred and swollen from many beatings, and her black eyes glittering like coal. Perhaps they both knew this, which was why, when, as rarely, they addressed each other, they addressed each other as Sister. As the singing filled the air the watching, listening faces underwent a change, the eyes focusing on something within; the music seemed to soothe a poison out of them; and time seemed, nearly, to fall away from the sullen, belligerent, battered faces, as though they were fleeing back to their first condition, while dreaming of their last. The barbecue cook half shook his head and smiled, and dropped his cigarette and disappeared into his joint. A man fumbled in his pockets for change and stood holding it in his hand impatiently, as though he had just remembered a pressing appointment further up the avenue. He looked furious. Then I saw Sonny, standing on the edge of the crowd. He was carrying a wide, flat notebook with a green cover, and it made him look, from where I was standing, almost like a schoolboy. The coppery sun brought out the copper in his skin, he was very faintly smiling, standing very still. Then the singing stopped, the tambourine turned into a collection plate again. The furious man dropped in his coins and vanished, so did a couple of the women, and Sonny dropped some change in the plate, looking directly at the woman with a little smile. He started across the avenue, toward the house. He has a slow, loping walk, something like the way Harlem hipsters walk, only he's imposed on this his own half-beat. I had never really noticed it before.

I stayed at the window, both relieved and apprehensive. As Sonny disappeared from my sight, they began singing again. And they were still singing when his key turned in the lock.

"Hey," he said.

"Hey, yourself. You want some beer?"

"No. Well, maybe." But he came up to the window and stood beside me, looking out. "What a warm voice," he said.

They were singing *If I could only hear my mother pray again!*

"Yes," I said, "and she can sure beat the tambourine."

"But what a terrible song," he said, and laughed. He dropped his notebook on the sofa and disappeared into the kitchen. "Where's Isabel and the kids?"

"I think they went to see their grandparents. You hungry?"

"No." He came back into the living room with his can of beer. "You want to come some place with me tonight?"

I sensed, I don't know how, that I couldn't possibly say no. "Sure. Where?"

He sat down on the sofa and picked up his notebook and started leafing through it. "I'm going to sit in with some fellows in a joint in the Village."

"You mean, you're going to play, tonight?"

"That's right." He took a swallow of his beer and moved back to the window. He gave me a sidelong look. "If you can stand it."

"I'll try," I said.

He smiled to himself and we both watched as the meeting across the way broke up. The three sisters and the brother, heads bowed, were singing *God be with you till we meet again.* The faces around them were very quiet. Then the song ended. The small crowd dispersed. We watched the three women and the lone man walk slowly up the avenue.

"When she was singing before," said Sonny, abruptly, "her voice reminded me for a minute of what heroin feels like sometimes—when it's in your veins. It makes you feel sort of warm and cool at the same time. And distant. And—and sure." He sipped his beer, very deliberately not looking at me. I watched his face. "It makes you feel—in control. Sometimes you've got to have that feeling."

"Do you?" I sat down slowly in the easy chair.

"Sometimes." He went to the sofa and picked up his notebook again. "Some people do."

"In order," I asked, "to play?" And my voice was very ugly, full of contempt and anger.

"Well"—he looked at me with great, troubled eyes, as though, in fact, he hoped his eyes would tell me things he could never otherwise say—"they *think* so. And *if* they think so—!"

"And what do *you* think?" I asked.

He sat on the sofa and put his can of beer on the floor. "I don't know," he said, and I couldn't be sure if he was answering my question or pursuing his thoughts. His face didn't tell me. "It's not so much to *play.* It's to *stand* it, to be able to make it at all. On any level." He frowned and smiled: "In order to keep from shaking to pieces."

"But these friends of yours," I said, "they seem to shake themselves to pieces pretty goddamn fast."

"Maybe." He played with the notebook. And something told me that I should curb my tongue, that Sonny was doing his best to talk, that I should listen. "But of course you only know the ones that've gone to pieces. Some don't—or at least they haven't *yet* and that's just about all *any* of us can say." He paused. "And then there are some who just live, really, in hell, and they know it and they see what's happening and they go right on. I don't know." He sighed, dropped the notebook, folded his arms. "Some guys, you can tell from the way they play, they on something *all* the time. And you can see that, well, it makes something real for them. But of course," he picked up his beer from the floor and sipped it and put the can down again, "they *want* to, too, you've got to see that. Even some of them that say they don't—*some,* not all."

"And what about you?" I asked—I couldn't help it. "What about you? Do *you* want to?"

He stood up and walked to the window and remained silent for a long time. Then he sighed. "Me," he said. Then: "While I was downstairs before, on my way here, listening to that woman sing, it struck me all of a sudden how much suffering she must have had to go through—to sing like that. It's *repulsive* to think you have to suffer that much."

I said: "But there's no way not to suffer—is there, Sonny?"

"I believe not," he said and smiled, "but that's never stopped anyone from trying." He looked at me. "Has it?" I realized, with this mocking look, that there stood between us, forever, beyond the power of time or forgiveness, the fact that I had held silence—so long!—when he had needed human speech to help him. He turned back to the window. "No, there's no way not to suffer. But you try all kinds of ways to keep from drowning in it, to keep on top of it, and to make it seem—well, like *you.* Like you did something, all right, and now you're suffering for it. You know?" I said nothing. "Well you know," he said, impatiently, "why *do* people suffer? Maybe it's better to do something to give it a reason, *any* reason."

"But we just agreed," I said, "that there's no way not to suffer. Isn't it better, then, just to—take it?"

"But nobody just takes it," Sonny cried, "that's what I'm telling you! *Everybody* tries not to. You're just hung up on the *way* some people try—it's not *your* way!"

The hair on my face began to itch, my face felt wet. "That's not true," I said, "that's not true. I don't give a damn what other people do, I don't even care how they suffer. I just care how *you* suffer." And he looked at me. "Please believe me," I said, "I don't want to see you—die—trying not to suffer."

"I won't," he said, flatly, "die trying not to suffer. At least, not any faster than anybody else."

"But there's no need," I said, trying to laugh, "is there? in killing yourself."

I wanted to say more, but I couldn't. I wanted to talk about will power and how life could be—well, beautiful. I wanted to say that it was all within; but was it? or, rather, wasn't that exactly the trouble? And I wanted to promise that I would never fail him again. But it would all have sounded—empty words and lies.

So I made the promise to myself and prayed that I would keep it.

"It's terrible sometimes, inside," he said, "that's what's the trouble. You walk these streets, black and funky and cold, and there's not really a living ass to talk to, and there's nothing shaking, and there's no way of getting it out—that storm inside. You can't talk it and you can't make love with it, and when you finally try to get with it and play it, you realize *nobody's* listening. So *you've* got to listen. You got to find a way to listen."

And then he walked away from the window and sat on the sofa again, as though all the wind had suddenly been knocked out of him. "Sometimes you'll do *anything* to play, even cut your mother's throat." He laughed and looked at me. "Or your brother's." Then he sobered. "Or your own." Then: "Don't worry. I'm all right now and I think I'll *be* all right. But I can't forget—where I've been. I don't mean just the physical place I've been, I mean where I've *been.* And *what* I've been."

"What have you been, Sonny?" I asked.

He smiled—but sat sideways on the sofa, his elbow resting on the back, his fingers playing with his mouth and chin, not looking at me. "I've been something I didn't recognize, didn't know I could be. Didn't know anybody could be." He stopped, looking inward, looking helplessly young, looking old. "I'm not talking about it now because I feel *guilty* or anything like that—maybe it would be better if I did, I don't know. Anyway, I can't really talk about it. Not to you, not to anybody," and now he turned and faced me. "Sometimes, you know, and it was actually when I was most *out* of the world, I felt that I was in it, that I was *with* it, really, and I could play or I didn't really have to *play,* it just came out of me, it was there. And I don't know how I played, thinking about it now, but I know I did awful things, those times, sometimes, to people. Or it wasn't that I *did* anything to them—it was that they weren't real." He picked up the beer can; it was empty; he rolled it between his palms: "And other times—well, I needed a fix, I needed to find a place to lean, I needed to clear a space to *listen*—and I couldn't find it, and I—went crazy, I did terrible things to *me,* I was terrible *for* me." He began pressing the beer can between his hands, I watched the metal begin to give. It glittered, as he played with it, like a knife, and I was afraid he would cut himself, but I said nothing. "Oh well. I can never tell you. I was all by myself at the bottom of something, stinking and sweating and crying and shaking, and I smelled it, you know? *my* stink, and I thought I'd die if I couldn't get away from it and yet, all the same, I knew that everything I was doing was just locking me in with it. And I didn't know," he paused, still flattening the beer can, "I didn't know, I still *don't* know, something kept telling me that maybe it was good to smell your own stink, but I didn't think that *that* was what I'd been trying to do—and—who can stand it?" and he abruptly dropped the ruined beer can, looking at me with a small, still smile, and then rose, walking to the window as though it were the lodestone rock. I watched his face, he watched the avenue. "I couldn't tell you when Mama died—but the reason I wanted to leave Harlem so bad was to get away from drugs. And then, when I ran away, that's what I was running from—really. When I came back, nothing had changed, *I* hadn't changed, I was just—older." And he stopped, drumming with his fingers on the windowpane. The sun had vanished, soon darkness would fall. I watched his face. "It can come again," he said, almost as though speaking to himself. Then he turned to me. "It can come again," he repeated. "I just want you to know that."

"All right," I said, at last. "So it can come again, All right."

He smiled, but the smile was sorrowful. "I had to try to tell you," he said.

"Yes," I said. "I understand that."

"You're my brother," he said, looking straight at me, and not smiling at all.

"Yes," I repeated, "yes. I understand that."

He turned back to the window, looking out. "All that hatred down there," he said, "all that hatred and misery and love. It's a wonder it doesn't blow the avenue apart."

We went to the only nightclub on a short, dark street, downtown. We squeezed through the narrow, chattering, jam-packed bar to the entrance of the big room, where the bandstand was. And we stood there for a moment, for the lights were very dim in this room and we couldn't see. Then, "Hello, boy," said a voice and an enormous black man, much older than Sonny or myself, erupted out of all that atmospheric lighting and put an arm around Sonny's shoulder. "I been sitting right here," he said, "waiting for you."

He had a big voice, too, and heads in the darkness turned toward us.

Sonny grinned and pulled a little away, and said, "Creole, this is my brother. I told you about him."

Creole shook my hand. "I'm glad to meet you, son," he said, and it was clear that he was glad to meet me *there,* for Sonny's sake. And he smiled, "You got a real musician in *your* family," and he took his arm from Sonny's shoulder and slapped him, lightly, affectionately, with the back of his hand.

"Well. Now I've heard it all," said a voice behind us. This was another musician, and a friend of Sonny's, a coal-black, cheerful-looking man, built close to the ground. He immediately began confiding to me, at the top of his lungs, the most terrible things about Sonny, his teeth gleaming like a lighthouse and his laugh coming up out of him like the beginning of an earthquake. And it turned out that everyone at the bar knew Sonny, or almost everyone; some were musicians, working there, or nearby, or not working, some were simply hangers-on, and some were there to hear Sonny play. I was introduced to all of them and they were all very polite to me. Yet, it was clear that, for them, I was only Sonny's brother. Here, I was in Sonny's world. Or, rather: his kingdom. Here, it was not even a question that his veins bore royal blood.

They were going to play soon and Creole installed me, by myself, at a table in a dark corner. Then I watched them, Creole, and the little black man, and Sonny, and the others, while they horsed around, standing just below the bandstand. The light from the bandstand spilled just a little short of them and, watching them laughing and gesturing and moving about, I had the feeling that they, nevertheless, were being most careful not to step into that circle of light too suddenly: that if they moved into the light too suddenly, without thinking, they would perish in flame. Then, while I watched, one of them, the small, black man, moved into the light and crossed the bandstand and started fooling around with his drums. Then—being funny and being, also, extremely ceremonious—Creole took Sonny by the arm and led him to the piano. A woman's voice called Sonny's name and a few hands started clapping. And Sonny, also being funny and being ceremonious, and so touched, I think, that he could have cried, but neither hiding it nor showing it, riding it like a man, grinned, and put both hands to his heart and bowed from the waist.

Creole then went to the bass fiddle and a lean, very bright-skinned brown man jumped up on the bandstand and picked up his horn. So there they were, and the atmosphere on the bandstand and in the room began to change and tighten. Someone stepped up to the microphone and announced them. Then there were all kinds of murmurs. Some people at the bar shushed others. The waitress ran around, frantically getting in the last orders, guys and chicks got closer to each other, and the lights on the bandstand, on the quartet, turned to a kind of indigo. Then they all looked different there. Creole looked about him for the last time, as though he were making certain that all his chickens were in the coop, and then he—jumped and struck the fiddle. And there they were.

All I know about music is that not many people ever really hear it. And even then, on the rare occasions when something opens within, and the music enters, what we mainly hear, or hear corroborated, are personal, private, vanishing evocations. But the man who creates the music is hearing something else, is dealing with the roar rising from the void and imposing order on it as it hits the air. What is evoked in him, then, is of another order, more terrible because it has no words, and triumphant, too, for that same reason. And his triumph, when he triumphs, is ours. I just watched Sonny's face. His face was troubled, he was working hard, but he wasn't with it. And I had the feeling that, in a way, everyone on the bandstand was waiting for him, both waiting for him and pushing him along. But as I began to watch Creole, I realized that it was Creole who held them all back. He had them on a short rein. Up there, keeping the beat with his whole body, wailing on the fiddle, with his eyes half closed, he was listening to everything, but he was listening to Sonny. He was having a dialogue with Sonny. He wanted Sonny to leave the shoreline and strike out for the deep water. He was Sonny's witness that deep water and drowning were not the same thing—he had been there, and he knew. And he wanted Sonny to know. He was waiting for Sonny to do the things on the keys which would let Creole know that Sonny was in the water.

And, while Creole listened, Sonny moved, deep within, exactly like someone in torment. I had never before thought of how awful the relationship must be between the musician and his instrument. He has to fill it, this instrument, with the breath of life, his own. He has to make it do what he wants it to do. And a piano is just a piano. It's made out of so much wood and wires and little hammers and big ones, and ivory. While there's only so much you can do with it, the only way to find this out is to try; to try and make it do everything.

And Sonny hadn't been near a piano for over a year. And he wasn't on much better terms with his life, not the life that stretched before him now. He and the piano stammered, started one way, got scared, stopped; started another way, panicked, marked time, started again; then seemed to have found a direction, panicked again, got stuck. And the face I saw on Sonny I'd never seen before. Everything had been burned out of it, and, at the same time, things usually hidden were being burned in, by the fire and fury of the battle which was occurring in him up there.

Yet, watching Creole's face as they neared the end of the first set, I had the feeling that something had happened, something I hadn't heard. Then they finished, there was scattered applause, and then, without an instant's warning, Creole started into something else, it was almost sardonic, it was *Am I Blue.* And, as though he commanded, Sonny began to play. Something began to happen. And Creole let out the reins. The dry, low, black man said something awful on the drums, Creole answered, and the drums talked back. Then the horn insisted, sweet and high, slightly detached perhaps, and Creole listened, commenting now and then, dry, and driving, beautiful and calm and old. Then they all came together again, and Sonny was part of the family again. I could tell this from his face. He seemed to have found, right there beneath his fingers, a damn brand-new piano. It seemed that he couldn't get over it. Then, for awhile, just being happy with Sonny, they seemed to be agreeing with him that brand-new pianos certainly were a gas.

Then Creole stepped forward to remind them that what they were playing was the blues. He hit something in all of them, he hit something in me, myself, and the music tightened and deepened, apprehension began to beat the air. Creole began to tell us what the blues were all about. They were not about anything very new. He and his boys up there were keeping it new, at the risk of ruin, destruction, madness, and death, in order to find new ways to make us listen. For, while the tale of how we suffer, and how we are delighted, and how we may triumph is never new, it always must be heard. There isn't any other tale to tell, it's the only light we've got in all this darkness.

And this tale, according to that face, that body, those strong hands on those strings, has another aspect in every country, and a new depth in every generation. Listen, Creole seemed to be saying, listen. Now these are Sonny's blues. He made the little black man on the drums know it, and the bright, brown man on the horn. Creole wasn't trying any longer to get Sonny in the water. He was wishing him Godspeed. Then he stepped back, very slowly, filling the air with the immense suggestion that Sonny speak for himself.

Then they all gathered around Sonny and Sonny played. Every now and again one of them seemed to say, amen. Sonny's fingers filled the air with life, his life. But that life contained so many others. And Sonny went all the way back, he really began with the spare, flat statement of the opening phrase of the song. Then he began to make it his. It was very beautiful because it wasn't hurried and it was no longer a lament. I seemed to hear with what burning he had made it his, with what burning we had yet to make it ours, how we could cease lamenting. Freedom lurked around us and I understood, at last, that he could help us to be free if we would listen, that he would never be free until we did. Yet, there was no battle in his face now. I heard what he had gone through, and would continue to go through until he came to rest in earth. He had made it his: that long line, of which we knew only Mama and Daddy. And he was giving it back, as everything must be given back, so that, passing through death, it can live forever. I saw my mother's face again, and felt, for the first time, how the stones of the road she had walked on must have bruised her feet. I saw the moonlit road where my father's brother died. And it brought something else back to me, and carried me past it. I saw my little girl again and felt Isabel's tears again, and I felt my own tears begin to rise. And I was yet aware that this was only a moment, that the world waited outside, as hungry as a tiger, and that trouble stretched above us, longer than the sky.

Then it was over. Creole and Sonny let out their breath, both soaking wet, and grinning. There was a lot of applause and some of it was real. In the dark, the girl came by and I asked her to take drinks to the bandstand. There was a long pause, while they talked up there in the indigo light and after awhile I saw the girl put a Scotch and milk on top of the piano for Sonny. He didn't seem to notice it, but just before they started playing again, he sipped from it and looked toward me, and nodded. Then he put it back on top of the piano. For me, then, as they began to play again, it glowed and shook above my brother's head like the very cup of trembling.

Everybody's Protest Novel

In *Uncle Tom's Cabin,* that cornerstone of American social protest fiction, St. Clare, the kindly master, remarks to his coldly disapproving Yankee cousin, Miss Ophelia, that, so far as he is able to tell, the blacks have been turned over to the devil for the benefit of the whites in this world—however, he adds thoughtfully, it may turn out in the next. Miss Ophelia's reaction is, at least, vehemently right-minded: "This is perfectly horrible!" she exclaims. "You ought to be ashamed of yourselves!"

Miss Ophelia, as we may suppose, was speaking for the author; her exclamation is the moral, neatly framed, and incontestable like those improving mottoes sometimes found hanging on the walls of furnished rooms. And, like those mottoes, before which one invariably flinches, recognizing an insupportable, almost an indecent glibness, she and St. Clare are terribly in earnest. Neither of them questions the medieval morality from which their dialogue springs: black, white, the devil, the next world—posing its alternatives between heaven and the flames—were realities for them as, of course, they were for their creator. They spurned and were terrified of the darkness, striving mightily for the light; and considered from this aspect, Miss Ophelia's exclamation, like Mrs. Stowe's novel, achieves a bright, almost a lurid significance, like the light from a fire which consumes a witch. This is the more striking as one considers the novels of Negro oppression written in our own, more enlightened day, all of which say only: "This is perfectly horrible! You ought to be ashamed of yourselves!" (Let us ignore, for the moment, those novels of oppression written by Negroes, which add only a raging, near-paranoiac postscript to this statement and actually reinforce, as I hope to make clear later, the principles which activate the oppression they decry.)

Uncle Tom's Cabin is a very bad novel, having, in its self-righteous, virtuous sentimentality, much in common with *Little Women.* Sentimentality, the ostentatious parading of excessive and spurious emotion, is the mark of dishonesty, the inability to feel; the wet eyes of the sentimentalist betray his aversion to experience, his fear of life, his arid heart; and it is always, therefore, the signal of secret and violent inhumanity, the mask of cruelty. *Uncle Tom's*

Cabin—like its multitudinous, hard-boiled descendants—is a catalogue of violence. This is explained by the nature of Mrs. Stowe's subject matter, her laudable determination to flinch from nothing in presenting the complete picture; an explanation which falters only if we pause to ask whether or not her picture is indeed complete; and what constriction or failure of perception forced her to so depend on the description of brutality—unmotivated, senseless—and to leave unanswered and unnoticed the only important question: what it was, after all, that moved her people to such deeds.

But this, let us say, was beyond Mrs. Stowe's powers; she was not so much a novelist as an impassioned pamphleteer; her book was not intended to do anything more than prove that slavery was wrong; was, in fact, perfectly horrible. This makes material for a pamphlet but it is hardly enough for a novel; and the only question left to ask is why we are bound still within the same constriction. How is it that we are so loath to make a further journey than that made by Mrs. Stowe, to discover and reveal something a little closer to the truth?

But that battered word, truth, having made its appearance here, confronts one immediately with a series of riddles and has, moreover, since so many gospels are preached, the unfortunate tendency to make one belligerent. Let us say, then, that truth, as used here, is meant to imply a devotion to the human being, his freedom and fulfillment; freedom which cannot be legislated, fulfillment which cannot be charted. This is the prime concern, the frame of reference; it is not to be confused with a devotion to humanity which is too easily equated with a devotion to a Cause; and Causes, as we know, are notoriously bloodthirsty. We have, as it seems to me, in this most mechanical and interlocking of civilizations, attempted to lop this creature down to the status of a time-saving invention. He is not, after all, merely a member of a Society or a Group or a deplorable conundrum to be explained by Science. He is—and how old-fashioned the words sound!—something more than that, something resolutely indefinable, unpredictable. In overlooking, denying, evading his complexity—which is nothing more than the disquieting complexity of ourselves—we are diminished and we perish; only within this web of ambiguity, paradox, this hunger, danger, darkness, can we find at once ourselves and the power that will free us from ourselves. It is this power of revelation which is the business of the novelist, this journey toward a more vast reality which must take precedence over all other claims. What is today parroted as his Responsibility—which seems to mean that he must make formal declaration that he is involved in, and affected by, the lives of other people and to say something improving about this somewhat self-evident fact—is, when he believes it, his corruption and our loss; moreover, it is rooted in, interlocked with and intensifies this same mechanization. Both *Gentleman's Agreement* and *The Postman Always Rings Twice* exemplify this terror of the human being, the determination to cut him down to size. And in *Uncle Tom's Cabin* we may find foreshadowing of both: the formula created by the necessity to find a lie more palatable than the truth has been handed down and memorized and persists yet with a terrible power.

It is interesting to consider one more aspect of Mrs. Stowe's novel, the method she used to solve the problem of writing about a black man at all. Apart from her lively procession of field hands, house niggers, Chloe, Topsy, etc.—who are the stock, lovable figures presenting no problem—she has only three other Negroes in the book. These are the important ones and two of them may be dismissed immediately, since we have only the author's word that they are Negro and they are, in all other respects, as white as she can make them. The two are George and Eliza, a married couple with a wholly adorable child—whose quaintness, incidentally, and whose charm, rather put one in mind of a darky bootblack doing a buck-and-wing to the clatter of condescending coins. Eliza is a beautiful, pious hybrid, light enough to pass—the heroine of *Quality* might, indeed, be her reincarnation—differing from the genteel mistress who has overseered her education only in the respect that she is a servant. George is darker, but makes up for it by being a mechanical genius, and is, moreover, sufficiently un-Negroid to pass through town, a fugitive from his master, disguised as a Spanish gentleman, attracting no attention whatever beyond admiration. They are a race apart from Topsy. It transpires by the end of the novel, through one of those energetic, last-minute convolutions of the plot, that Eliza has some connection with French gentility. The figure from whom the novel takes its name, Uncle Tom, who is a figure of controversy yet, is jet-black, wooly-haired, illiterate; and he is phenomenally forbearing. He has to be; he is black; only through this forbearance can he survive or triumph. (Cf. Faulkner's preface to *The Sound and the Fury:* These others were not Compsons. They were black:—They endured.) His triumph is metaphysical, unearthly; since he is black, born without the light, it is only through humility, the incessant mortification of the flesh, that he can enter into communion with God or man. The virtuous rage of Mrs. Stowe is motivated by nothing so temporal as a concern for the relationship of men to one another—or, even, as she would have claimed, by a concern for their relationship to God—but merely by a panic of being hurled into the flames, of being caught in traffic with the devil. She embraced this merciless doctrine with all her heart, bargaining shamelessly before the throne of grace: God and salvation becoming her personal property, purchased with the coin of her virtue. Here, black equates with evil and white with grace; if, being mindful of the necessity of good works, she could not cast out the blacks—a wretched, huddled mass, apparently, claiming, like an obsession, her inner eye—she could not embrace them either without purifying them of sin. She must cover their intimidating nakedness, robe them in white, the garments of salvation; only thus could she herself be delivered from ever-present sin, only thus could she bury, as St. Paul demanded, "the carnal man, the man of the flesh." Tom, therefore, her only black man, has been robbed of his humanity and divested of his sex. It is the price for that darkness with which he has been branded.

Uncle Tom's Cabin, then, is activated by what might be called a theological terror, the terror of damnation; and the spirit that breathes in this book, hot, self-righteous, fearful, is not different from that spirit of medieval times which sought to exorcize evil by burning witches; and is not different from that terror which activates a lynch mob. One need not, indeed, search for examples so historic or so gaudy; this is a warfare waged daily in the heart, a warfare so vast, so relentless and so powerful that the interracial handshake or the interracial marriage can be as crucifying as the public hanging or the secret rape. This panic motivates our cruelty, this fear of the dark makes it impossible that our lives shall be other than superficial; this, interlocked with and feeding our glittering, mechanical, inescapable civilization which has put to death our freedom.

This, notwithstanding that the avowed aim of the American protest novel is to bring greater freedom to the oppressed. They are forgiven, on the strength of these good intentions, whatever violence they do to language, whatever excessive demands they make of credibility. It is, indeed, considered the sign of a frivolity so intense as to approach decadence to suggest that these books are both badly written and wildly improbable. One is told to put first things first, the good of society coming before niceties of style or characterization. Even if this were incontestable—for what exactly is the "good" of society?—it argues an insuperable confusion, since literature and sociology are not one and the same; it is impossible to discuss them as if they were. Our passion for categorization, life neatly fitted into pegs, has led to an unforeseen, paradoxical distress; confusion, a breakdown of meaning. Those categories which were meant to define and control the world for us have boomeranged us into chaos; in which limbo we whirl, clutching the straws of our definitions. The "protest" novel, so far from being disturbing, is an accepted and comforting aspect of the American scene, ramifying that framework we believe to be so necessary. Whatever unsettling questions are raised are evanescent, titillating; remote, for this has nothing to do with us, it is safely ensconced in the social arena, where, indeed, it has nothing to do with anyone, so that finally we receive a very definite thrill of virtue from the fact that we are reading such a book at all. This report from the pit reassures us of its reality and its darkness and of our own salvation; and "As long as such books are being published," an American liberal once said to me, "everything will be all right."

But unless one's ideal of society is a race of neatly analyzed, hard-working ciphers, one can hardly claim for the protest novels the lofty purpose they claim for themselves or share the present optimism concerning them. They merge for what they are: a mirror of our confusion, dishonesty, panic, trapped and immobilized in the sunlit prison of the American dream. They are fantasies, connecting nowhere with reality, sentimental; in exactly the same sense that such movies as *The Best Years of Our Lives* or the works of Mr. James M. Cain are fantasies. Beneath the dazzling pyrotechnics of these current operas one may still discern, as the controlling force, the intense theological preoccupations of Mrs. Stowe, the sick vacuities of *The Rover Boys.* Finally, the aim of the protest novel becomes something very closely resembling the zeal of those alabaster missionaries to Africa to cover the nakedness of the natives, to hurry them into the pallid arms of Jesus and thence into slavery. The aim has now become to reduce all Americans to the compulsive, bloodless dimensions of a guy named Joe.

It is the peculiar triumph of society—and its loss—that it is able to convince those people to whom it has given inferior status of the reality of this decree; it has the force and the weapons to translate its dictum into fact, so that the allegedly inferior are actually made so, insofar as the societal realities are concerned. This is a more hidden phenomenon now than it was in the days of serfdom, but it is no less implacable. Now, as then, we find ourselves bound, first without, then within, by the nature of our categorization. And escape is not effected through a bitter railing against this trap; it is as though this very striving were the only motion needed to spring the trap upon us. We take our shape, it is true, within and against that cage of reality bequeathed us at our birth; and yet it is precisely through our dependence on this reality that we are most endlessly betrayed. Society is held together by our need; we bind it together with legend, myth, coercion, fearing that without it we will be hurled into that void, within which, like the earth before the Word was spoken, the foundations of society are hidden. From this void—ourselves—it is the function of society to protect us; but it is only this void, our unknown selves, demanding, forever, a new act of creation, which can save us—"from the evil that is in the world." With the same motion, at the same time, it is this toward which we endlessly struggle and from which, endlessly, we struggle to escape.

It must be remembered that the oppressed and the oppressor are bound together within the same society; they accept the same criteria, they share the same beliefs, they both alike depend on the same reality. Within this cage it is romantic, more, meaningless, to speak of a "new" society as the desire of the oppressed, for that shivering dependence on the props of reality which he shares with the *Herrenvolk* makes a truly "new" society impossible to conceive. What is meant by a new society is one in which inequalities will disappear, in which vengeance will be exacted; either there will be no oppressed at all, or the oppressed and the oppressor will change places. But, finally, as it seems to me, what the rejected desire is, is an elevation of status, acceptance within the present community. Thus, the African, exile, pagan, hurried off the auction block and into the fields, fell on his knees before that God in Whom he must now believe; who had made him, but not in His image. This tableau, this impossibility, is the heritage of the Negro in America: "Wash me," cried the slave to his Maker, "and I shall be whiter, whiter than snow!" For black is the color of evil; only the robes of the saved are white. It is this cry, implacable on the air and in the skull, that he must live with. Beneath the widely published catalogue of brutality—bringing to mind, somehow, an image, a memory of church-bells burdening the air—is this reality which, in the same nightmare notion, he both flees and rushes to embrace. In America, now, this country devoted to the death of the paradox—which may, therefore, be put to death by one—his lot is as ambiguous as a tableau by Kafka. To flee or not, to move or not, it is all the same; his doom is written on his forehead, it is carried in his heart. In *Native Son,* Bigger Thomas stands on a Chicago street corner watching airplanes flown by white men racing against the sun and "Goddamn" he says, the bitterness bubbling up like blood, remembering a million indignities, the terrible, rat-infested house, the humiliation of home-relief, the intense, aimless, ugly bickering, hating it; hatred smoulders through these pages like sulphur fire. All of Bigger's life is controlled, defined by his hatred and his fear. And later, his fear drives him to murder and his hatred to rape; he dies, having come, through this violence, we are told, for the first time, to a kind of life, having for the first time redeemed his manhood. Below the surface of this novel there lies, as it seems to me, a continuation, a complement of that monstrous legend it was written to destroy. Bigger is Uncle Tom's descendant, flesh of his flesh, so exactly opposite a portrait that, when the books are placed together, it seems that the contemporary Negro novelist and the dead New England woman are locked together in a deadly, timeless battle; the one uttering merciless exhortations, the other shouting curses. And, indeed, within this web of lust and fury, black and white can only thrust and counter-thrust, long for each other's Now, exquisite death; death by torture, acid, knives, and burning; the thrust, the counter-thrust, the longing making the heavier that cloud which blinds and suffocates them both, so that they go down into the pit together. Thus has the cage betrayed us all, this moment, our life, turned to nothing through our terrible attempts to insure it. For Bigger's tragedy is not that he is cold or black or hungry, not even that he is American, black; but that he has accepted a theology that denies him life, that he admits the possibility of his being sub-human and feels constrained, therefore, to battle for his humanity according to those brutal criteria bequeathed him at his birth. But our humanity is our burden, our life; we need not battle for it; we need only to do what is infinitely more difficult—that is, accept it. The failure of the protest novel lies in its rejection of life, the human being, the denial of his beauty, dread, power, in its insistence that it is his categorization alone which is real and which cannot be transcended.

PAULE MARSHALL

(1929–)

The novelist who has most successfully presented narratives about transplanted African Caribbean people attempting to adjust to life in the urban United States is Paule Marshall, author of four major novels and two collections of short stories. Herself the daughter of immigrants from Barbados, Marshall creates scenarios that cause constant interplays among culture, class, and nativity. In addition to the adjustments that most blacks must make in a majority white society that typically rejects African identity, cultural differences between various groups of people of African descent often must be resolved. In a few of Marshall's plots, African Americans are even forced to confront the tensions arising from cultural differences when they are the ones on "foreign" soil. Often, however, these dividing walls cannot be breached; forces of outdated traditions, sexism, and racism cannot be conquered; and families, individuals, and communities are destroyed.

Paule Marshall was born Valenza Pauline Burke on April 9, 1929, in Brooklyn, New York. Her parents, Samuel and Ada Clement Burke, had migrated from the West Indies ten years before her birth, but they, along with a tight-knit West Indian–American community, still struggled to maintain the culture of their homeland. Marshall has visited Barbados only once, when she was nine years old, but even then she was writing poetry about her impressions of what everyone continually reminded her was her homeland. These youthful assessments of Caribbean character and culture further enabled her later to exploit the obvious cultural contrasts in her work.

Marshall graduated Phi Beta Kappa from Brooklyn College in 1953 and began her professional career first as a librarian for the New York Public Library and later as a journalist for *Our World* magazine. The latter assignment required her to travel rather extensively to the West Indies and Brazil. During those early years of preparation to become a writer, Marshall also attended Hunter College and attempted to establish a home. She married Kenneth E. Marshall in 1950, and the couple had one son, Evan. They were divorced in 1963. In 1970, Marshall married Nourry Menard, a businessman from Haiti.

Always finding it necessary to supplement her writing career, Marshall was a professor of English and creative writing at Virginia Commonwealth University from 1987 until the mid 1990s. In 1984, she was Regents Professor at the University of California at Berkeley. She taught at the Iowa Writers Workshop at the University of Iowa in 1983 and variously at the University of Massachusetts at Boston, Columbia University, and Yale University.

Undoubtedly, Marshall's most successful novel to date is *Brown Girl, Brownstones,* which was published in 1959, about ten years too early to receive the critical attention given to African American novels of the 1970s. Adapted for television by the CBS Television Workshop in 1960 and republished by the Feminist Press in 1981, *Brown Girl, Brownstones* tells the story of a young female, Selina Boyce, who is a first-generation American-born child of Caribbean immigrant parents. Selina struggles to attain self-actualization in a family that attempts to preserve the values of their island home while trying to survive America's Great Depression and, afterward, to achieve monetary success in a capitalistic society. Selina must choose between becoming a mature, independent woman, maintaining strong ties with her family, and establishing new relationships with lovers who, like her parents, want to usurp her rights to full freedom and artistic expression.

Marshall's second publication, *Soul Clap Hands and Sing,* appeared in 1961. This is a collection of four novellas tied together by a common theme. The title is taken from William Butler Yeats's poem "Sailing to Byzantium." Each offering—"Barbados," "Brooklyn," "British Guiana," and "Brazil"—culminates in the main character's recognition that the search for material values has left him bereft of the warmth of love and human contact. As in her later works, the obvious conclusions are that these material values come from emulating American capitalism and that the superior choices based on collective human worth are from the characters' Caribbean backgrounds.

Marshall released a lengthy episodic novel, *The Chosen Place, The Timeless People,* in 1969. Like most of her works, it is concerned with Africans in the Diaspora seeking self-discovery, this time through a return to the Caribbean, where the main characters find an impoverished but unified African people. The novel confronts the heritage of slavery and revolt in the West Indies, as well as the cultural conflict between the native Caribbean citizens and a visiting American tourist. Again, resolution is illusive, and idealists are left disillusioned.

With the reissue of *Brown Girl, Brownstones* in 1981 and the appearance of a new novel, *Praisesong for the Widow,* and a collection of short fiction, *Reena and Other Stories*, in 1983, Marshall refocused her fiction on feminist issues and thereby gained an expanded and sustained reading audience. In *Praisesong*, Marshall examines the life of an African American middle-age widow completely devoted to middle-class materialism and values. The novel follows her on a luxury cruise to the West Indian island of Carriacou, during which she actually begins a journey of self-discovery—one that takes her toward an understanding of her African heritage. Gaining national and international distribution, which few books by African American writers have achieved, *Praisesong* was chosen as a Book of the Month Club alternate.

Reena and Other Stories focuses on Marshall's female characters. In the introduction to this collection is her own autobiographical essay, "From the Poets in the Kitchen," in which she explains how she was profoundly influenced as a child by the West Indian women who gathered in her mother's kitchen every weekday:

> For me, sitting over in the corner, being seen but not heard, which was the rule for children in those days, it wasn't only what the women talked about—the content—but the way they put things—their style. The insight, irony, wit and humor they brought to their stories and discussions and their poet's inventiveness and daring with language—which of course I could only sense but not define back then.

These kitchen poets, Marshall insists, were the first influences on her development as a writer. By listening to their stories and absorbing, unconsciously, their particular style of storytelling, she learned her first lessons in the narrative art. These women "trained my ear," says the author, who often fuses traditional African oral narrative devices with Western cultural forms.

Marshall's latest novel, *Daughters* (1991), also can be easily set in a feminist context. "In *Daughters,*" writes Dorothy L. Denniston, "Marshall returns to the complex, changing parameters of a female persona living and growing in the two worlds that have formed her: The Caribbean and the United States." The change in this work, Denniston continues, is that it is a study of "black female-male relationships as well." However, the common Marshall theme of a young girl's struggle to overcome her father's dominance is revisited. Unlike in *Brown Girl, Brownstones* and *Soul Clap Hands and Sing,* however, the writer does strive for communal unity.

In addition to Guggenheim and Ford Foundation Fellowships, Marshall has been recognized by the National Institute of the Arts and Letters, the National Endowment for the Arts, and the Yaddo Corporation. She was the PEN/Faulkner Award Honoree in 1990 and received the John Dos Passos Award for Literature in 1989. She also was nominated for the Neustadt International Prize for Literature in 1988, and she received the New York State Governor's Arts Award for Literature in 1987. These recognitions culminated in Marshall receiving a prestigious MacArthur fellowship in 1992.

John McCluskey, Jr., rightfully points out that Marshall's works have never received proper inclusion in the canon of African American literature and that they have not received sufficient scholarly review. The oversight could simply be a case of poor timing: Marshall emerged as a major novelist before the advent of the Civil Rights Movement and its cultural accompaniment, the Black Power Movement. However, insufficient critical response also could be caused by the universal themes and symbolic forms in her work that do not seem to fit neatly into the latter movement's more political and Afrocentric mode.

In a lengthy article for *New Letters* in 1973 titled "Shaping the World of My Art," Marshall outlines what she believes are the two dominant forces in her work: exploration of the past with a view of reshaping the present. Scholars of African American literature still wrestle with the quandary of which segments of the "past" can be recharted and how much time and geography can be included in those definitions. Nor is the "present," especially in the context of gender and class, always easy to grasp. Thus Marshall's fiction offers critics a challenge—a challenge that few Afrocentric or feminist critics have as yet undertaken. Hopefully, within the next few years, critical comment will catch up with the new horizons toward which Marshall's work is pointing readers and critics as well.

❖❖❖

Comprehensive studies of all of Marshall's works include Eugenia Collier "The Closing of the Circle: Movement from Division to Wholeness in Paule Marshall's Fiction," and John McCluskey, Jr., "And Called Every Generation Blessed: Theme, Setting, and Ritual in the Works of Paule Marshall," both in *Black Women Writers (1950–1980): A Critical Evaluation,* ed. Mari Evans (1984); Leela Kapai, "Dominant Themes and Technique in Paule Marshall's Fiction," and Winifred Stelting, "Time Past and Time Present: The Search for Viable Links in *Chosen Place, The Timeless People* by Paule Marshall," both in *CLA Journal* 16 (1972) September; Marcia Keizs, "Themes and Style in the Works of Paule Marshall," in *Negro American Literature Forum* 9:3 (Fall 1975); John Cook, "Whose Child? The Fiction of Paule Marshall," *CLA Journal* 24 (September 1980); Mary Helen Washington, "I Sign My Mother's Name: Alice Walker, Dorothy West and Paule Marshall," in *Mothering the Mind,* eds. Ruth Perry and Martine Watson Brownley (1984); Barbara Christian, *Black Women Novelists* (1980).

Biographical entries include articles in *Contributions of Black Women to America;* Dorothy L. Denniston's entry in *American Women Writers* (1981 and 1994); Theresa Gunnels Rush, Carol Fairbanks Myers, and Esther Spring Arata's article in *Black American Writers Past and Present* (1976); J. Vinson's entry in *Contemporary Novelists* (1976). Daryl Cumber Dance interviewed Marshall for the *Southern Review* 28:1 (January 1992). Two full-length critical studies of Marshall's work have appeared recently. They are Dorothy Hamer Denniston's *The Fiction of Paule Marshall: Reconstructions of History, Culture, and Gender* (1995) and Joyce Owens Pettis's *Toward Wholeness in Paule Marshall's Fiction* (1995).

Barbados

Dawn, like the night which had preceded it, came from the sea. In a white mist tumbling like spume over the fishing boats leaving the island and the hunched, ghost shapes of the fishermen. In a white, wet wind breathing over the villages scattered amid the tall canes. The cabbage palms roused, their high headdresses solemnly saluting the wind, and along the white beach which ringed the island the casuarina trees began their moaning—a sound of women lamenting their dead within a cave.

The wind, smarting of the sea, threaded a wet skein through Mr. Watford's five hundred dwarf coconut trees and around his house at the edge of the grove. The house, Colonial American in design, seemed created by the mist—as if out of the dawn's formlessness had come, magically, the solid stone walls, the blind, broad windows and the portico of fat columns which embraced the main story. When the mist cleared, the house remained—pure, proud, a pristine white—disdaining the crude wooden houses in the village outside its high gate.

It was not the dawn settling around his house which awakened Mr. Watford, but the call of his Barbary doves from their hutch in the yard. And it was more the feel of that sound than the sound itself. His hands had retained, from the many times a day he held the doves, the feel of their throats swelling with that murmurous, mournful note. He lay abed now, his hands—as cracked and callused as a cane cutter's—filled with the sound, and against the white sheet which flowed out to the white walls he appeared profoundly alone, yet secure in loneliness, contained. His face was fleshless and severe, his black skin sucked deep into the hollow of his jaw, while under a high brow, which was like a bastion raised against the world, his eyes were indrawn and pure. It was as if during all his seventy years, Mr. Watford had permitted nothing to sight which could have affected him.

He stood up, and his body, muscular but stripped of flesh, appeared to be absolved from time, still young. Yet each clenched gesture of his arms, of his lean shank as he dressed in a faded shirt and work pants, each vigilant, snapping motion of his head betrayed tension. Ruthlessly he spurred his body to perform like a younger man's. Savagely he denied the accumulated fatigue of the years. Only sometimes when he paused in his grove of coconut trees during the day, his eyes tearing and the breath torn from his lungs, did it seem that if he could find a place hidden from the world and himself he would give way to exhaustion and weep from weariness.

Dressed, he strode through the house, his step tense, his rough hand touching the furniture from Grand Rapids which crowded each room. For some reason, Mr. Watford had never completed the house. Everywhere the walls were raw and unpainted, the furniture unarranged. In the drawing room with its coffered ceiling, he stood before his favorite piece, an old mantel clock which eked out the time. Reluctantly it whirred five and Mr. Watford nodded. His day had begun.

It was no different from all the days which made up the five years since his return to Barbados. Downstairs in the unfinished kitchen, he prepared his morning tea—tea with canned milk and fried bakes—and ate standing at the stove while lizards skittered over the unplastered walls. Then, belching and snuffling the way a child would, he put on a pith helmet, secured his pant legs with bicycle clasps and stepped into the yard. There he fed the doves, holding them so that their sound poured into his hands and laughing gently—but the laugh gave way to an irritable grunt as he saw the mongoose tracks under the hutch. He set the trap again.

The first heat had swept the island like a huge tidal wave when Mr. Watford, with that tense, headlong stride, entered the grove. He had planted the dwarf coconut trees because of their quick yield and because, with their stunted trunks, they always appeared young. Now as he worked, rearranging the complex of pipes which irrigated the land, stripping off the dead leaves, the trees were like cool, moving presences; the stiletto fronds wove a protective dome above him and slowly, as the day soared toward noon, his mind filled with the slivers of sunlight through the trees and the feel of earth in his hands, as it might have been filled with thoughts.

Except for a meal at noon, he remained in the grove until dusk surged up from the sea; then returning to the house, he bathed and dressed in a medical doctor's white uniform, turned on the lights in the parlor and opened the tall doors to the portico. Then the old women of the village on their way to church, the last hawkers caroling, "Fish, flying fish, a penny, my lady," the roistering saga-boys lugging their heavy steel drums to the crossroad where they would rehearse under the street lamp—all passing could glimpse Mr. Watford, stiff in his white uniform and with his head bent heavily over a Boston newspaper. The papers reached him weeks late but he read them anyway, giving a little savage chuckle at the thought that beyond his world that other world went its senseless way. As he read, the night sounds of the village welled into a joyous chorale against the sea's muffled cadence and the hollow, haunting music of the steel band. Soon the moths, lured in by the light, fought to die on the lamp, the beetles crashed drunkenly against the walls and the night—like a woman offering herself to him—became fragrant with the night-blooming cactus.

Even in America Mr. Watford had spent his evenings this way. Coming home from the hospital, where he worked in the boiler room, he would dress in his white uniform and read in the basement of the large rooming house he owned. He had lived closeted like this, detached, because America—despite the money and property he had slowly accumulated—had meant nothing to him. Each morning, walking to the hospital along the rutted Boston streets, through the smoky dawn light, he had known—although it had never been a thought—that his allegiance, his place, lay elsewhere. Neither had the few acquaintances he had made mattered. Nor the women he had occasionally kept as a younger man. After the first months their bodies would grow coarse to his hand and he would begin edging away.... So that he had felt no regret when, the year before his retirement, he resigned his job, liquidated his properties and, his fifty-year exile over, returned home.

The clock doled out eight and Mr. Watford folded the newspaper and brushed the burnt moths from the lamp base. His lips still shaped the last words he had read as he moved through the rooms, fastening the windows against the night air, which he had dreaded even as a boy. Something palpable but unseen was always, he believed, crouched in the night's dim recess, waiting to snare him.... Once in bed in his sealed room, Mr. Watford fell asleep quickly.

The next day was no different except that Mr. Goodman, the local shopkeeper, sent the boy for coconuts to sell at the racetrack and then came that evening to pay for them and to herald—although Mr. Watford did not know this—the coming of the girl.

That morning, taking his tea, Mr. Watford heard the careful tap of the mule's hoofs and looking out saw the wagon jolting through the dawn and the boy, still lax with sleep, swaying on the seat. He was perhaps eighteen and the muscles packed tightly beneath his lustrous black skin gave him a brooding strength. He came and stood outside the back door, his hands and lowered head performing the small, subtle rites of deference.

Mr. Watford's pleasure was full, for the gestures were those given only to a white man in his time. Yet the boy always nettled him. He sensed a natural arrogance like a pinpoint of light within his dark stare. The boy's stance exhumed a memory buried under the years. He remembered, staring at him, the time when he had worked as a yard boy for a white family, and had had to assume the same respectful pose while their flat, raw, Barbadian voices assailed him with orders. He remembered the muscles in his neck straining as he nodded deeply and a taste like alum on his tongue as he repeated the "Yes, please," as in a litany. But because of their whiteness and wealth, he had never dared hate them. Instead his rancor, like a boomerang, had rebounded, glancing past him to strike all the dark ones like himself, even his mother with her spindled arms and her stomach sagging with a child who was, invariably, dead at birth. He had been the only one of ten to live, the only one to escape. But he had never lost the sense of being pursued by the same dread presence which had claimed them. He had never lost the fear that if he lived too fully he would tire and death would quickly close the gap. His only defense had been a cautious life and work. He had been almost broken by work at the age of twenty when his parents died, leaving him enough money for the passage to America. Gladly had he fled the island. But nothing had mattered after his flight.

The boy's foot stirred the dust. He murmured, "Please, sir, Mr. Watford, Mr. Goodman at the shop send me to pick the coconut."

Mr. Watford's head snapped up. A caustic word flared, but died as he noticed a political button pinned to the boy's patched shirt with "Vote for the Barbados People's Party" printed boldly on it, and below that the motto of the party: "The Old Shall Pass." At this ludicrous touch (for what could this boy, with his splayed and shigoed feet and blunted mind, understand about politics?) he became suddenly nervous, angry. The button and its motto seemed, somehow, directed at him. He said roughly, "Well, come then. You can't pick any coconuts standing there looking foolish!"—and he led the way to the grove.

The coconuts, he knew, would sell well at the booths in the center of the track, where the poor were penned in like cattle. As the heat thickened and the betting grew desperate, they would clamor: "Man, how you selling the water coconuts?" and hacking off the tops they would pour rum into the water within the hollow centers, then tilt the coconuts to their heads so that the rum-sweetened water skimmed their tongues and trickled bright down their dark chins. Mr. Watford had stood among them at the track as a young man, as poor as they were, but proud. And he had always found something unutterably graceful and free in their gestures, something which had roused contradictory feelings in him: admiration, but just as strong, impatience at their easy ways, and shame. . . .

That night, as he sat in his white uniform reading, he heard Mr. Goodman's heavy step and went out and stood at the head of the stairs in a formal, proprietary pose. Mr. Goodman's face floated up into the light—the loose folds of flesh, the skin slick with sweat as if oiled, the eyes scribbled with veins and mottled, bold—as if each blemish there was a sin he proudly displayed or a scar which proved he had met life head-on. His body, unlike Mr. Watford's, was corpulent and, with the trousers caught up around his full crotch, openly concupiscent. He owned the one shop in the village which gave credit and a booth which sold coconuts at the race track, kept a wife and two outside women, drank a rum with each customer at his bar, regularly caned his fourteen children, who still followed him everywhere (even now they were waiting for him in the darkness beyond Mr. Watford's gate) and bet heavily at the races, and when he lost gave a loud hacking laugh which squeezed his body like a pain and left him gasping.

The laugh clutched him now as he flung his pendulous flesh into a chair and wheezed, "Watford, how? Man, I near lose house, shop, shirt and all at races today. I tell you, they got some horses from Trinidad in this meet that's making ours look like they running backwards. Be Jese, I wouldn't bet on a Bajan horse tomorrow if Christ heself was to give me the top. Those bitches might look good but they's nothing 'pon a track."

Mr. Watford, his back straight as the pillar he leaned against, his eyes unstained, his gaunt face planed by contempt, gave Mr. Goodman his cold, measured smile, thinking that the man would be dead soon, bloated with rice and rum—and somehow this made his own life more certain.

Sputtering with his amiable laughter, Mr. Goodman paid for the coconuts, but instead of leaving then as he usually did, he lingered, his eyes probing for a glimpse inside the house. Mr. Watford waited, his head snapping warily; then, impatient, he started toward the door and Mr. Goodman said, "I tell you, your coconut trees bearing fast enough even for dwarfs. You's lucky, man."

Ordinarily Mr. Watford would have waved both the man and his remark aside, but repelled more than usual tonight by Mr. Goodman's gross form and immodest laugh, he said—glad of the cold edge his slight American accent gave the words—"What luck got to do with it? I does care the trees properly and they bear, that's all. Luck! People, especially this bunch around here, is always looking to luck when the only answer is a little brains and plenty of hard work. . . ." Suddenly remembering the boy that morning and the political button, he added in loud disgust, "Look that half-foolish boy you does send here to pick the coconuts. Instead of him learning a trade and going to England where he might find work he's walking about with a political button. He and all in politics now! But that's the way with these down here. They'll do some of everything but work. They don't want work!" He gestured violently, almost dancing in anger. "They too busy spreeing."

The chair creaked as Mr. Goodman sketched a pained and gentle denial. "No, man," he said, "you wrong. Things is different to before. I mean to say, the young people nowadays is different to how we was. They not just sitting back and taking things no more. They not so frighten for the white people as we was. No, man. Now take that said same boy, for an example. I don't say he don't like a spree, but he's serious, you see him there. He's a member of this new Barbados People's Party. He wants to see his own color running the government. He wants to be able to make a living right here in Barbados instead of going to any cold England. And he's right!" Mr. Goodman paused at a vehement pitch, then shrugged heavily. "What the young people must do, nuh? They got to look to something . . ."

"Look to work!" And Mr. Watford thrust out a hand so that the horned knuckles caught the light.

"Yes, that's true—and it's up to we that got little something to give them work," Mr. Goodman said, and a sadness filtered among the dissipations in his eyes. "I mean to say we that got little something got to help out. In a manner of speaking, we's responsible . . ."

"Responsible!" The work circled Mr. Watford's head like a gnat and he wanted to reach up and haul it down, to squash it underfoot.

Mr. Goodman spread his hands; his breathing rumbled with a sigh. "Yes, in a manner of speaking. That's why, Watford man, you got to provide little work for some poor person down in here. Hire a servant at least! 'Cause I gon tell you something . . ." And he hitched forward his chair, his voice dropped to a wheeze. "People talking. Here you come back rich from big America and build a swell house and plant 'nough coconut trees and you still cleaning and cooking and thing like some woman. Man, it don't look good!" His face screwed in emphasis and he sat back. "Now, there's this girl, the daughter of a friend that just dead, and she need work bad enough. But I wouldn't like to see she working for these white people 'cause you know how those men will take advantage of she. And she'd make a good servant, man. Quiet and quick so, and nothing a-tall to feed and she can sleep anywhere about the place. And she don't have no boys always around her either. . . ." Still talking, Mr. Goodman eased from his chair and reached the stairs with surprising agility. "You need a servant," he whispered, leaning close to Mr. Watford as he passed. "It don't look good, man, people talking. I gon send she."

Mr. Watford was overcome by nausea. Not only from Mr. Goodman's smell—a stench of salt fish, rum and sweat—but from an outrage which was like a sediment in his stomach. For a long time he stood there almost kecking from disgust, until his clock struck eight, reminding him of the sanctuary within—and suddenly his cold laugh dismissed Mr. Goodman and his proposal. Hurrying in, he locked the doors and windows against the night air and, still laughing, he slept.

The next day, coming from the grove to prepare his noon meal, he saw her. She was standing in his driveway, her bare feet like strong dark roots amid the jagged stones, her face tilted toward the sun—and she might have been standing there always waiting for him. She seemed of the sun, of the earth. The folktale of creation might have been true with her: that along a riverbank a god had scooped up the earth—rich and black and warmed by the sun—and molded her poised head with its tufted braids and then with a whimsical touch crowned it with a sober brown felt hat which should have been worn by some stout English matron in a London suburb, had sculptured the passionless face and drawn a screen of gossamer across her eyes to hide the void behind. Beneath her bodice her small breasts were smooth at the crest. Below her waist, her hips branched wide, the place prepared for its load of life. But it was the bold and sensual strength of her legs which completely unstrung Mr. Watford. He wanted to grab a hoe and drive her off.

"What it 'tis you want?" he called sharply.

"Mr. Goodman send me."

"Send you for what?" His voice was shrill in the glare.

She moved. Holding a caved-in valise and a pair of white sandals, her head weaving slightly as though she bore a pail of water there or a tray of mangoes, she glided over the stones as if they were smooth ground. Her bland expression did not change, but her eyes, meeting his, held a vague trust. Pausing a few feet away, she curtsied deeply, "I's the new servant."

Only Mr. Watford's cold laugh saved him from anger. As always it raised him to a height where everything below appeared senseless and insignificant—especially his people, whom the girl embodied. From this height, he could even be charitable. And thinking suddenly of how she had waited in the brutal sun since morning without taking shelter under the nearby tamarind tree, he said, not unkindly, "Well, girl, go back and tell Mr. Goodman for me that I don't need no servant."

"I can't go back."

"How you mean can't?" His head gave its angry snap.

"I'll get lashes," she said simply. "My mother say I must work the day and then if you don't wish me, I can come back. But I's not to leave till night falling, if not I get lashes."

He was shaken by her dispassion. So much so that his head dropped from its disdaining angle and his hands twitched with helplessness. Despite anything he might say or do, her fear of the whipping would keep her there until nightfall, the valise and shoes in hand. He felt his day with its order and quiet rhythms threatened by her intrusion—and suddenly waving her off as if she were an evil visitation, he hurried into the kitchen to prepare his meal.

But he paused, confused, in front of the stove, knowing that he could not cook and leave her hungry at the door, nor could he cook and serve her as though he were the servant.

"Yes, please."

They said nothing more. She entered the room with a firm step and an air almost of familiarity, placed her valise and shoes in a corner and went directly to the larder. For a time Mr. Watford stood by, his muscles flexing with anger and his eyes bounding ahead of her every move, until feeling foolish and frighteningly useless, he went out to feed his doves.

The meal was quickly done and as he ate he heard the dry slap of her feet behind him—a pleasant sound—and then silence. When he glanced back she was squatting in the doorway, the sunlight aslant the absurd hat and her face bent to a bowl she held in one palm. She ate slowly, thoughtfully, as if fixing the taste of each spoonful in her mind.

It was then that he decided to let her work the day and at nightfall to pay her a dollar and dismiss her. His decision held when he returned later from the grove and found tea awaiting him, and then through the supper she prepared. Afterward, dressed in his white uniform, he patiently waited out the day's end on the portico, his face setting into a grim mold. Then just as dusk etched the first dark line between the sea and sky, he took out a dollar and went downstairs.

She was not in the kitchen, but the table was set for his morning tea. Muttering at her persistence, he charged down the corridor, which ran the length of the basement, flinging open the doors to the damp, empty rooms on either side, and sending the lizards and the shadows long entrenched there scuttling to safety.

He found her in the small slanted room under the stoop, asleep on an old cot he kept there, her suitcase turned down beside the bed, and the shoes, dress and the ridiculous hat piled on top. A loose nightshift muted the outline of her body and hid her legs, so that she appeared suddenly defenseless, innocent, with a child's trust in her curled hand and in her deep breathing. Standing in the doorway, with his own breathing snarled and his eyes averted, Mr. Watford felt like an intruder. She had claimed the room. Quivering with frustration, he slowly turned away, vowing that in the morning he would shove the dollar at her and lead her like a cow out of his house. . . .

Dawn brought rain and a hot wind which set the leaves rattling and swiping at the air like distraught arms. Dressing in the dawn darkness, Mr. Watford again armed himself with the dollar and, with his shoulders at an uncompromising set, plunged downstairs. He descended into the warm smell of bakes and this smell, along with the thought that she had been up before him, made his hand knot with exasperation on the banister. The knot tightened as he saw her, dust swirling at her feet as she swept the corridor, her face bent solemn to the task. Shutting her out with a lifted hand, he shouted, "Don't bother sweeping. Here's a dollar. G'long back."

The broom paused and although she did not raise her head, he sensed her groping through the shadowy maze of her mind toward his voice. Behind the dollar which he waved in her face, her eyes slowly cleared. And, surprisingly, they held no fear. Only anticipation and a tenuous trust. It was as if she expected him to say something kind.

"G'long back!" His angry cry was a plea.

Like a small, starved flame, her trust and expectancy died and she said, almost with reproof, "The rain falling."

To confirm this, the wind set the rain stinging across the windows and he could say nothing, even though the words sputtered at his lips. It was useless. There was nothing inside her to comprehend that she was not wanted. His shoulders sagged under the weight of her ignorance, and with a futile gesture he swung away, the dollar hanging from his hand like a small sword gone limp.

She became as fixed and familiar a part of the house as the stones—and as silent. He paid her five dollars a week, gave her Mondays off and in the evenings, after a time, even allowed her to sit in the alcove off the parlor, while he read with his back to her, taking no more notice of her than he did the moths on the lamp.

But once, after many silent evenings together, he detected a sound apart from the night murmurs of the sea and village and the metallic tuning of the steel band, a low, almost inhuman cry of loneliness which chilled him. Frightened, he turned to find her leaning hesitantly toward him, her eyes dark with urgency, and her face tight with bewilderment and a growing anger. He started, not understanding, and her arm lifted to stay him. Eagerly she bent closer. But as she uttered the low cry again, as her fingers described her wish to talk, he jerked around, afraid that she would be foolish enough to speak and that once she did they would be brought close. He would be forced then to acknowledge something about her which he refused to grant; above all, he would be called upon to share a little of himself. Quickly he returned to his newspaper, rustling it to settle the air, and after a time he felt her slowly, bitterly, return to her silence. . . .

Like sand poured in a careful measure from the hand, the weeks flowed down to August and on the first Monday, August Bank holiday, Mr. Watford awoke to the sound of the excursion buses leaving the village for the annual outing, their backfire pelleting the dawn calm and the ancient motors protesting the overcrowding. Lying there, listening, he saw with disturbing clarity his mother dressed for an excursion—the white headtie wound above her dark face and her head poised like a dancer's under the heavy outing basket of food. That set of her head had haunted his years, reappearing in the girl as she walked toward him the first day. Aching with the memory, yet annoyed with himself for remembering, he went downstairs.

The girl had already left for the excursion, and although it was her day off, he felt vaguely betrayed by her eagerness to leave him. Somehow it suggested ingratitude. It was as if his doves were suddenly to refuse him their song or his trees their fruit, despite the care he gave them. Some vital past which shaped the simple mosaic of his life seemed suddenly missing. An alien silence curled like coal gas throughout the house. To escape it he remained in the grove all day and, upon his return to the house, dressed with more care than usual, putting on a fresh, starched uniform, and solemnly brushing his hair until it lay in a smooth bush above his brow. Leaning close to the mirror, but avoiding his eyes, he cleaned the white rheum at their corners, and afterward pried loose the dirt under his nails.

Unable to read his papers, he went out on the portico to escape the unnatural silence in the house, and stood with his hands clenched on the balustrade and his taut body straining forward. After a long wait he heard the buses return and voices in gay shreds upon the wind. Slowly his hands relaxed, as did his shoulders under the white uniform; for the first time that day his breathing was regular. She would soon come.

But she did not come and dusk bloomed into night, with a fragrant heat and a full moon which made the leaves glint as though touched with frost. The steel band at the crossroads began the lilting songs of sadness and seduction, and suddenly—like shades roused by the night and the music—images of the girl flitted before Mr. Watford's eyes. He saw her lost amid the carousings in the village, despoiled; he imagined someone like Mr. Goodman clasping her lewdly or tumbling her in the canebrake. His hand rose, trembling, to rid the air of her; he tried to summon his cold laugh. But, somehow, he could not dismiss her as he had always done with everyone else. Instead, he wanted to punish and protect her, to find and lead her back to the house.

As he leaned there, trying not to give way to the desire to go and find her, his fist striking the balustrade to deny his longing, he saw them. The girl first, with the moonlight like a silver patina on her skin, then the boy whom Mr. Goodman sent for the coconuts, whose easy strength and the political button—"The Old Order Shall Pass"—had always mocked and challenged Mr. Watford. They were joined in a tender battle: the boy in a sport shirt riotous with color was reaching for the girl as he leaped and spun, weightless, to the music, while she fended him off with a gesture which was lovely in its promise of surrender. Her protests were little scattered bursts: "But, man, why don't you stop, nuh . . . ? But, you know, you getting on like a real-real idiot. . . ."

Each time she chided him he leaped higher and landed closer, until finally he eluded her arm and caught her by the waist. Boldly he pressed a leg between her tightly closed legs until they opened under his pressure. Their bodies cleaved into one whirling form and while he sang she laughed like a wanton, with her hat cocked over her ear. Dancing, the stones moiling underfoot, they claimed the night. More than the night. The steel band played for them alone. The trees were their frivolous companions, swaying as they swayed. The moon rode the sky because of them.

Mr. Watford, hidden by a dense shadow, felt the tendons which strung him together suddenly go limp; above all, an obscure belief which, like rare china, he had stored on a high shelf in his mind began to tilt. He sensed the familiar specter which hovered in the night reaching out to embrace him, just as the two in the yard were embracing. Utterly unstrung, incapable of either speech or action, he stumbled into the house, only to meet there an accusing silence from the clock, which had missed its eight o'clock winding, and his newspapers lying like ruined leaves over the floor.

He lay in bed in the white uniform, waiting for sleep to rescue him, his hands seeking the comforting sound of his doves. But sleep eluded him and instead of the doves, their throats tremulous with sound, his scarred hands filled with the shape of a woman he had once kept: her skin, which had been almost bruising in its softness; the buttocks and breasts spread under his hands to inspire both cruelty and tenderness. His hands closed to softly crush those forms, and the searing thrust of passion, which he had not felt for years, stabbed his dry groin. He imagined the two outside, their passion at a pitch by now, lying together behind the tamarind tree, or perhaps—and he sat up sharply—they had been bold enough to bring their lust into the house. Did he not smell their taint on the air? Restored suddenly, he rushed downstairs. As he reached the corridor, a thread of light beckoned him from her room and he dashed furiously toward it, rehearsing the angry words which would jar their bodies apart. He neared the door, glimpsed her through the small opening, and his step faltered; the words collapsed.

She was seated alone on the cot, tenderly holding the absurd felt hat in her lap, one leg tucked under her while the other trailed down. A white sandal, its strap broken, dangled from the foot and gently knocked the floor as she absently swung her leg. Her dress was twisted around her body—and pinned to the bodice, so that it gathered the cloth between her small breasts, was the political button the boy always wore. She was dreamily fingering it, her mouth shaped by a gentle, ironic smile and her eyes strangely acute and critical. What had transpired on the cot had not only, it seemed, twisted the dress around her, tumbled her hat and broken her sandal, but had also defined her and brought the blurred forms of life into focus for her. There was a woman's force in her aspect now, a tragic knowing and acceptance in her bent head, a hint about her of Cassandra watching the future wheel before her eyes.

Before those eyes which looked to another world, Mr. Watford's anger and strength failed him and he held to the wall for support. Unreasonably, he felt that he should assume some hushed and reverent pose, to bow as she had the day she had come. If he had known their names, he would have pleaded forgiveness for the sins he had committed against her and the others all his life, against himself. If he could have borne the thought, he would have confessed that it had been love, terrible in its demand, which he had always fled. And that love had been the reason for his return. If he had been honest, he would have whispered—his head bent and a hand shading his eyes—that unlike Mr. Goodman (whom he suddenly envied for his full life) and the boy with his political button (to whom he had lost the girl), he had not been willing to bear the weight of his own responsibility. . . . But all Mr. Watford could admit, clinging there to the wall, was, simply, that he wanted to live—and that the girl held life within her as surely as she held the hat in her hands. If he could prove himself better than the boy, he could win it. Only then, he dimly knew, would he shake off the pursuer which had given him no rest since birth. Hopefully, he staggered forward, his step cautious and contrite, his hands, quivering along the wall.

She did not see or hear him as he pushed the door wider. And for some time he stood there, his shoulders hunched in humility, his skin stripped away to reveal each flaw, his whole self offered in one outstretched hand. Still unaware of him, she swung her leg, and the dangling shoe struck a derisive note. Then, just as he had turned away that evening in the parlor when she had uttered her low call, she turned away now, refusing him.

Mr. Watford's body went slack and then stiffened ominously. He knew that he would have to wrest from her the strength needed to sustain him. Slamming the door, he cried, his voice cracked and strangled, "What you and him was doing in here? Tell me! I'll not have you bringing nastiness round here. Tell me!"

She did not start. Perhaps she had been aware of him all along and had expected his outburst. Or perhaps his demented eye and the desperation rising from him like a musk filled her with pity instead of fear. Whatever, her benign smile held and her eyes remained abstracted until his hand reached out to fling her back on the cot. Then, frowning, she stood up, wobbling a little on the broken shoe and holding the political button as if it was a new power which would steady and protect her. With a cruel flick of her arm she struck aside his hand and, in a voice as cruel, halted him. "But you best move and don't come holding on to me, you nasty, pissy old man. That's all you is, despite yuh big house and fancy furnitures and yuh newspapers from America. You ain't people, Mr. Watford, you ain't people!" And with a look and a lift of her head which made her condemnation final, she placed the hat atop her braids, and turning aside picked up the valise which had always lain, packed, beside the cot—as if even on the first day she had known that this night would come and had been prepared against it. . . .

Mr. Watford did not see her leave, for a pain squeezed his heart dry and the driven blood was a bright, blinding cataract over his eyes. But his inner eye was suddenly clear. For the first time it gazed mutely upon the waste and pretense which had spanned his years. Flung there against the door by the girl's small blow, his body slowly crumpled under the weariness he had long denied. He sensed that dark but unsubstantial figure which roamed the nights searching for him wind him in its chill embrace. He struggled against it, his hands clutching the air with the spastic eloquence of a drowning man. He moaned—and the anguished sound reached beyond the room to fill the house. It escaped to the yard and his doves swelled their throats, moaning with him.

FROM *Praisesong for the Widow*

1

With a strength born of the decision that had just come to her in the middle of the night, Avey Johnson forced the suitcase shut on the clothes piled inside and slid the lock into place. Taking care not to make a sound, she then eased the heavy bag off the couch onto the floor and, straining under her breath, her tall figure bent almost in two, hauled it over the thick carpeting to the door on the other side of the cabin.

A thirty-inch Pullman stood packed and waiting there. Quickly she deposited the second bag next to it, and after pausing to dart a nervous glance behind her, she slipped over to a long sectional closet which took up the rest of the wall beside the door.

From the storage space at the bottom she pulled out another suitcase. Her movements a whisper, she raised up and with her free hand began stripping the hangers of as many clothes as she could carry along with the bag. In seconds her arms were full, and she had spun around and was heading rapidly back across the dimly lighted room, moving like a woman half her age, her shadow on the walls and ceiling hurrying to keep up.

Over at the couch, with the suitcase laid open on top of the bedcovers, she made quick work of the clothes, tossing them helter-skelter into the bag without a trace of the neatness and order that were her hallmark. A minute later found her back at the closet, blindly reaching and snatching at whatever came to her hand in the darkness. Then, noiseless as a sneak thief, she was beating it back to the couch, her arms piled high again.

Perspiration was beginning to sheet her forehead despite the air-conditioning in the cabin. She didn't stop to wipe it. The determined look on her face had brought her underlip jutting forward, exposing the spillover of raw pink across the top which she always kept hidden. She let the lip stay as it was. The back pain she suffered with occasionally was threatening to flare up with all the bending and hauling. She closed her mind to it.

Her mind in a way wasn't even in her body or, for that matter, in the room. From the moment she had awakened in a panic less than an hour ago and come to the reckless decision, her mind had left to go and stand down at the embarkation door near the waterline five decks below. While she swiftly crisscrossed the room on her bare feet, spiriting her belongings out of the closest and drawers, her mind had leaped ahead to the time, later that morning, when the ship would have arrived at the next port of call. The huge door in the steel hull would be rolled back then, and along with her fellow passengers going ashore for the day, she would step from the liner onto the waiting launch. For the last time. And without so much as a backward glance.

Avey Johnson's two traveling companions, with whom she shared the large deluxe cabin, were asleep in the bedroom on the other side of a divider with narrow shelflike openings on top and a long chest of drawers below, facing what was called the living area. Not to risk waking them, she had left off the lamps in the living area, where she always volunteered to sleep each cruise because it was more private.

For illumination she had opened the drapes at the picture window of a porthole and was making do with the reflection of the deck lights outside, along with the faint glow of the nightlight filtering through the divider, which the woman, Thomasina Moore, always kept burning in the bedroom, like a child afraid of the dark. The pale satin sheen of the nightgown she had on added to the small pool of light, as did the subtle aura, unbeknown to her, which her dark skin had given off since birth.

Slipping back over the couch, Avey's feet struck a chair. Quickly she stifled her outcry, shook off the pain, and kept going. When was the last time she had gone barefoot around the house? She paused a second, the clothes she was about to let drop into the suitcase suspended in her arms. Halsey Street? Had it been that long ago? Back then the young woman whose headstrong ways and high feelings Avey Johnson had long put behind her, whom she found an embarrassment to even think of now with her 1940s upsweeps and pompadours and vampish high-heeled shoes, used to kick off her shoes the moment she came in from work, shed her stockings, and start the dusting and picking up in her bare feet. The pots on in the tiny kitchen. The 78s on the turntable in the living room: Coleman Hawkins, Lester Young, The Count, The Duke. Music to usher Jay in the door. Freed of the high heels her body always felt restored to its proper axis. And the hardwood floor which Jay had rescued from layers of oxblood-colored paint when they first moved in and stained earth-brown, the floor reverberating with "Cottontail" and "Lester Leaps In" would be like a rich nurturing ground from which she had sprung and to which she could always turn for sustenance.

Avey Johnson hadn't thought of that floor in decades.

A bottom drawer became stuck in the chest of drawers below the divider where her underclothes were stowed. Grasping it between her hands, she tried jiggling it back on its tracks, unmindful for a moment in her haste of the noise she was making until she heard her friend, Clarice, shift massively in her sleep. Poor Clarice. She always sounded as if she were wrestling with someone as large as herself on the narrow bed whenever she turned. There quickly followed a sound from the other bed, like the knocking in a radiator as the steam rises, as Thomasina Moore, her sleep disturbed, began an ominous implosive clucking at the roof of her mouth.

Her hands froze on the drawer. That was the last person she wanted to wake before she was done! Scarcely breathing, she remained bent double over the chest, perspiring, her back aching, holding herself rigid except once when she gave a fearful glance back over her shoulder—something she had repeatedly caught herself doing since yesterday.

Only when the two inside the bedroom had been quiet for some time did she try the drawer again. With a burglar's finesse this time she eased it back on its tracks, slid it open without a sound, and the next moment was darting across to the couch with the wealth of underthings she had scooped up, the drawer left open behind.

Her skirts, blouses, and summer suits were done. The sweaters and stoles she drew around her when the weather on deck turned chilly had been packed after a fashion. Crowded into the wrong bag were the linen shirtdresses she wore on excursions ashore in place of the shorts and slacks favored by the other women her age on board, no matter what their size. Her shoes were in their special caddy. Her hats in their cylindrical box. And she had just disposed of the last of her underthings. All that remained were her ensemble dresses and evening gowns. She was down to the last of the six suitcases.

"But why six, Mother? Why would anyone in their right mind need to take this much stuff just to go away for a couple of weeks?"—Marion, Avey Johnson's youngest, the morning she had come to drive her mother to the pier before her first cruise three years ago. Entering the house, Marion had stopped short at sight of the half-dozen bags neatly lined up in the downstairs hall, had stood staring at them for the longest time, trying to contain her exasperation but failing. When she finally looked up, it had been all she could do, from her expression, not to reach out and grab her mother by the shoulders and shake her the way she might have one of her pupils in the small community school she helped to run in a church in Brooklyn. To shake sense into her. Around the face which bore Jay's clear imprint, her hair had stood massed like a rain cloud about to make good its threat. And the noisy necklace of cowrie shells and amber she had brought back from Togo her last visit had sounded her angry despair with its rattle each time she breathed.

"Why go on some meaningless cruise with a bunch of white folks anyway, I keep asking you? What's that supposed to be about? Couldn't you think of something better to do on your vacation? And since when have you started letting Thomasina Moore decide how you should spend it? You don't even like the woman. What the hell's gotten into you?"

Avey Johnson's own mother would have slapped Marion down long ago had she been her child—and never mind she was twenty-eight and a woman already married and divorced. She would have raised a hard palm and with a blow to set her ears ringing put her in her place: "Girl, where you get off talking to *me* like that?"

And the Avey Johnson of thirty, forty years ago would have done likewise. She had been quick then to show her displeasure, her bottom lip immediately unfolding to bare the menacing sliver of pink and then her mouth letting fly with the words. But she had grown away from such high-strung behavior, and over the years had developed a special silence to deal with anyone the likes of Marion. With her daughter she simply acted as if nothing unpleasant was being said, that Marion was still, as she had once been, the most polite and tractable of her children.

"Here last summer I begged you to go on that tour to Brazil, and on the one, the year before that, to Ghana. . . ." The voice hung unrelenting at her ear as she made the final hurried trips between the closet again and the couch. "And all I got for an answer was either 'we'll see' or that infuriating silence of yours. Yet here you are willing and eager to go off on some ridiculous cruise. Could you have thought of anything more banal!"

Banal? For a second before she quickly checked herself the word had threatened to overturn the rock of her calm. Did Marion know that the closest she had ever come to a cruise in her life had been the annual boat ride up the Hudson to Bear Mountain as a child? What did she know?

". . . Why can't you be a little imaginative, for God's sake, a little independent, and go off on your own somewhere. Learn something!"

Marion had been the only one of Avey Johnson's three children to oppose the trip. Sis, the eldest, in her weekly phone call from Los Angeles, had urged her mother to go, reminding her that she and her husband, a systems programmer at Lockheed (the only one his color in his division), had sailed to Hawaii the previous year, taking their two boys, and had enjoyed it.

Annawilda, interning at Meharry Hospital at the time, had written to say it was just what she needed, adding: "It'll take your mind off Daddy." It had been 1974 then, and Jerome Johnson had been dead only a little over a year.

And they, it turned out, had been right and Marion wrong. Because whatever doubts she had managed to sow in Avey Johnson's mind vanished the moment she saw the *Bianca Pride* that first time in her berth at West Fortieth Street and the river, with the flags and pennants flying from all her stations, her high bow canted toward the sun. All that dazzling white steel! Her hull appeared to sweep clear across to New Jersey. The precision and power of her lines! The ship's turbines, she had read in the brochure they had sent her before sailing, produced enough heat and light to run a city the size of Albany! And on a group tour of the bridge that first trip she had seen the huge Ferranti computer that monitored all operations on board. Her group had stood awestruck and reverent before the console with its array of keyboards, switches, and closed-circuit television screens.

There had been no resisting it! Thomasina Moore had no sooner suggested a return trip the following year than she had accepted. And Marion, seeing her resolve, began keeping her objections to herself. Her eyes had carefully avoided the suitcases the last two times she had come to drive her to the pier, and on the way into Manhattan she had talked only of her pupils, most of whom had been rejected by the public schools as being impossible to teach. Her "sweetest lepers," Marion called them, from a poem she was always urging her mother to read.

The last of the evening gowns lay where she had just flung them on top of the final pile of dresses in the fold-over garment bag. They had graced their last dinner in the Versailles Room; they had attended their last Captain's Ball. As if sealing a tomb, Avey Johnson zippered the long flap into place over them and, still working feverishly, like someone pursued, folded the bag over on itself, latched the two halves together, and seconds later was dragging it across the cabin to join the others.

The marathon packing was done. On an armchair over near the window lay the clothes she had hastily set aside to wear. The suitcases, all six of them along with the shoe caddy and hatbox, stood assembled near the door, ready for the steward. Giving the apprehensive glance over her shoulder, she immediately headed toward them, not even allowing herself a moment to rest her back or wipe the perspiration from her face—or to consider, quietly and rationally, which was normally her way, what she was about to do.

Outside the glow of the deck lights was slowly being absorbed by a pearl-gray light that was both filtering down from the clearing sky and curling up like mist from the sea. And the sea itself had become a wide, silver-toned sheet of plate metal, which was already, out near the horizon, reflecting the subtle mauve and rose and pale yellows of the day.

Amid the burgeoning color stood the liner—huge, sleek, imperial, a glacial presence in the warm waters of the Caribbean. The long night run completed, it had come to rest and drop anchor a short time ago in the same smooth and soundless manner with which it had moved over the sea.

From its decks could be made out the faint, almost insubstantial form of an island across the silvery moat of the harbor. The next port of call.

Avey Johnson had finished in good time.

2

"What you doing up and dressed so early?"

A pair of grayish eyes with the unblinking watchfulness of a bird's was peering through the divider's narrow openings. They were like eyes at the slot of a speakeasy door.

Seconds later, wearing a sheer frilly dressing gown that looked meant for a bride (it even had a slight train), Thomasina Moore stepped curiously around the divider into the living area.

She was a thin-featured woman in her early seventies with a lined and hectic brow, what used to be called "good hair" covered over with a sleeping net, and the first signs of a dowager's hump across her shoulders: old age beginning to warp the once graceful curve of her back. She could still, though—she liked to boast—kick her legs as high as when she had danced in the chorus line of the Cotton Club back in the twenties. (At least she claimed it had been the Cotton Club. Which might have been true. She had the color to have qualified: black that was the near-white of a blanched almond or the best of ivory. A color both sacred—for wasn't it a witness?—and profane: *"he forced my mother my mother / late / One night / What do they call me?"*).

She almost collided with the suitcases at the door.

"And what're your bags doing sitting here by the door? What's going on around here?"

Avey Johnson, gazing out of the window on the other side of the living area, didn't turn to her immediately. After quickly showering and dressing, she had gone to wait out the time till morning, watching the island across the way gradually take shape in the growing light. A dark mass of coastal hills with a darker foil of mountains behind had been the first to appear. Then, as the sun rose fully, lighting the hills one after the other the way an acolyte would light candles in a church, the town had become sharply visible: a pretty seaport town of pastel houses with red tiled roofs crowding down to the harbor and perched like tick birds on the flanks of the hills.

She had found the sight soothing, reassuring. The town, the hills, the distant mountains, the morning sunlight, all not only applauded her decision, it seemed, but assured her there would be a plane to New York later in the day with a seat for her on it.

So that as she turned to Thomasina Moore after making her wait almost a full minute, she scarcely felt the need to steel herself against the tirade she knew would follow. Indeed, it was as if she had already heard the woman out and had left. Part of her had already stepped on board the launch and was planing swiftly over the morning sea toward the island and the waiting plane.

She had decided, she said, to cut short the cruise and go home. She kept her gaze on the middle distance.

"You decided to do *what?* What you say?"

She knew it must have come as a shock, her leaving on the spur of the moment like this, but it couldn't be helped. She had ignored the woman's outcry. The cruise itself she didn't think was to blame. Nor was she sick, although she hadn't been feeling herself the last couple of days. It was nothing she could put her finger on. She had simply awakened in the middle of the night and decided she would prefer to spend the rest of her vacation at home. It didn't make any sense, she knew, but her mind was made up. If she was lucky she might get a flight out today. . . .

While she was saying all this, the words terse and final, her manner calm, Thomasina Moore started slowly toward her across the living area, her dumbstruck gaze taking in the emptied-out closet and the drawers, all of which stood sprawling open. She faltered to a stop in the middle of the floor, and from there, with a child's open-mouth disbelief, she examined the dressy two-piece ensemble Avey Johnson had on, the stylish but conservative pumps on her feet, and the straw hat she was already wearing, whose wide brim curved down to hide most of her face.

The pocketbook she had placed on a chair beside her also drew the woman's stricken gaze—a handsome bag of navy-blue straw to complement the muted beige and navy print of her dress, and draped over it a pair of mesh summer gloves with a single crystal button at the wrist.

Here her eyes came to focus, and for the longest while she gazed at the buttons as if in her shaken mind they were tiny crystal balls which could tell her whether she was hearing right. Until finally, with a sound like that of a bewildered mute struggling desperately to speak, her head jerked back over her shoulder, and she was calling toward the bedroom, "Clarice! Clarice! Get on out here! *Clarice* . . . !"

She continued to summon Clarice even when the latter, sleepily trying to pull a robe around her bulk, appeared from behind the divider.

At fifty-eight Clarice was six years Avey Johnson's junior and the youngest of the three women. Where the bones of her face pressed up through the fleshiness, her skin—black with an admixture of plum that spoke of centuries of sunlight—was as smooth as a girl's. Yet she tended to look as old or older than Thomasina Moore because of the worry lines furrowed deep around her mouth, and the downcast, burdened expression she never completely abandoned even on those rare occasions when she laughed.

"Did you hear this?"

"No," she said, still struggling with the robe. "What's happened?"

Clarice asked but she really didn't want to know. She had already, in a single apprehensive glance around the room, taken in the suitcases by the door, the ransacked drawers and closet, and her two friends, one agitated and close to anger in the middle of the floor, the other calm and enveloped in that special intimidating silence of hers over by the porthole; and she had resigned herself to the worst.

"What d'you mean what's happened? This one's leaving, that's what. Walking out on the cruise. She all of sudden feels she'd rather spend what's left of her vacation at home and is going back today. Just like that. Without a word to anybody. You ever heard anything like it . . . ?"

"Is that true, Avey . . . ?" Clarice's reluctant gaze sought the tall figure across the room.

"What d'you mean if it's true?" Thomasina Moore's voice had risen sharply. "Don't you see her bags all packed over there near you? Don't you see the way she's dressed? Hat, gloves, the works. Do you think she'd be all dolled up like that if she was just going sight-seeing with the rest of us today? She's leaving, I'm telling you. Quitting the cruise after only five days and taking a plane home!"

The shock of it was still so great she fell speechless again, and in the small charged silence left by her voice Clarice tried asking Avey Johnson what had gone wrong. Had something happened on board? Or had she come down with something? Was she perhaps feeling sick . . . ?

"Do . . . she . . . look . . . sick . . . to . . . you?" Her colors, as Thomasina Moore called them, were up: anger like a battery of flags being rung up all at once in a strong wind. ("Look out you don't get my colors up," she was always warning. Or: "These white folks around here must be trying to get my colors up"—this on their first cruise, when they had been assigned a table in the dining room which she felt was too close to the service entrance. She had promptly had it changed.)

"Do she look sick to you, I ask?" Though furious, her voice was pitched low: despite her anger she was being mindful of the public corridor just outside the door. "Ain' not a thing wrong with her. Talking 'bout she ain' been feeling herself these past couple of days. Well, what's ailing her? What's her complaint? If she was sick she would have gone to the doctor, wouldn't she? That's what he's here for. No, she can't fool me with no excuse like that."

Suddenly the grayish eyes with their unblinking intensity narrowed, becoming more acute, more suspicious. "But I should've known somethin' was up the funny way she was acting yesterday. Keeping to herself all day. Not showing up till dinner and then scarcely touching the food on her plate. Hardly talking to anybody. I should've known somethin' was up. And now come this morning here she is dressed back, ready to walk off the ship for good. All of a sudden like this! And without a word as to why! 'It's nothin' I can put my finger on.' Who she thinks she's kiddin'? A person would have to have a reason for doing a thing like this. No, somethin's behind this mess. Somethin' deep. She can't make me out for no fool!"

There would be a taxi waiting for her on the wharf of the little pastel town. Or one would arrive the moment she stepped off the launch. The driver would inform her that, yes, there was a plane to New York today, a nonstop flight scheduled to leave shortly. No, it was unlikely to be filled, this being May and the off-season. She was certain to get a seat. The airport would turn out to be only a short drive away, on a wide safe plain between the hills fronting the sea and the mountains she had glimpsed in the distance. They would reach there in ample time for the flight.

". . . And what about the money? Have you heard her say anything about all the money she's gonna be losing?" Thomasina Moore swung with this toward Clarice, the violence of her movement sending up a shower of scented dust from the bride's dressing gown, and causing the daylight inside the cabin, which was only an hour old, to waver like a used-up light bulb.

"Have you, I'm asking!"

Clarice, backed up against the tall wooden support to the divider, numbly shook her head. She had assumed the pose characteristic of her whenever there was trouble, her eyes lowered, her thick shoulders sloping down, and the burdened look adding years to her face. It was a look that went back decades, dating from her endless difficulties with her husband before their breakup, her mother's long, demanding illness and death, and her disappointment in her only son, who had suddenly, after years of being a straight-A student, dropped out of the predominantly white college he had been attending. With each crisis her weight had increased, the fat metastasizing with each new sorrow. Now, under the robe she had finally managed to pull around her, her flesh with the pierced heart at its center had opened to absorb this latest tragedy. For wasn't she, Clarice, somehow responsible for what was happening? Wasn't she in some way to blame? Her dullness, her rampant flesh, her blackness . . .

"Gonna forfeit the fifteen hundred dollars she paid for the cruise and then turn around and spend more money to take a plane home! Now what kinda sense do that make, will you tell me? She must be out of her mind. . . . Wait, that's it! She's done gone and lost her mind . . . !"

The lined face, the color of old ivory, came thrusting forward as the woman tried surprising the insanity under the turned-down hat brim. She was met instead by the underlip Avey Johnson had left thrusting forward slightly so that the knife edge of raw pink was still visible, and by the expression in her eyes of someone who had already left the cabin and the ship and was well on her way somewhere else.

"Gots to be," she muttered, drawing back, "out of her cotton-pickin' mind."

The taxi driver had been right. The plane was far from full. She had the three seats in her row all to herself. They had already reached cruising altitude, so that the only thing visible when she looked down was the hazy undifferentiated blue of the sea far below. And with the flight under way, everything had come right again. She no longer caught herself giving the little fearful involuntary glance back over her shoulder, and the odd unpleasant sensation in her stomach that had plagued her off and on for the past two days was gone. Down the aisle the stewardess was taking orders for drinks before lunch. She would have a glass of white wine to celebrate.

"'. . . If I'm lucky I might get a flight out today.'" The words, spoken in the low-pitched shout, were a scathing parody of Avey Johnson's. "Just listen to her! Who told her she's gonna find a plane going to New York today? Who's guaranteed her a flight right away? Why, some of these little islands don't see a plane going anywhere but maybe two, three times a week. She might be stuck for days. And in some place that probably won't have a decent hotel to its name. She'll wind up having to stay in some dump where the mosquitoes'll eat her alive and the food—or what passes for food—won't be fit for hogs.

"And forget about drinking the water! Remember that place we stopped at last year?" She half swung toward Clarice again with the same violent movement that jarred the light. "Cartarena or Cartarana or whatever they called it . . ." (It had been Cartagena, Colombia, where, to Avey Johnson's disgust, the woman had abandoned them to dance in a carnival parade they were watching with other passengers from the *Bianca Pride.* Had gone off amid a throng of strangers swishing her bony hips to the drums. With the slight hump like an organ grinder's monkey begging pennies from her shoulders. And with their fellow passengers watching. White faces laughing! White hands applauding! Avey Johnson had never been so mortified. And she had returned, the woman, laughing proudly, with the jumpsuit she had on soaked through under the arms, and in her laugh, in her flushed face, something of the high-stepping, high-kicking young chorus girl she had once been. "Girl, those drums *got* to me! Where's some water?")

". . . Remember the water they gave me to drink there? You could see the bugs swimming around in it clear as day. Well, just let this one here go running around eating and drinking on her own. She's gonna come back with her stomach all *tore* up!" (With her colors up she said "tow.") "A girlfriend of mine went to Mexico for a week and was laid up in the hospital for two months straight when she got back just from drinking a glass of water down there. . . ."

The drive from Kennedy to their small section of North White Plains was over. The airport limousine had deposited her at the door and departed. Before leaving, the driver had helped her take the suitcases into the front hall. She could glimpse them through the archway to the dining room where she had gone to sit for a moment in the welcoming dark, at the great oval-shaped table. Where the light from the hall fell across the table's polished surface, the cherry wood glowed like a banked fire that had awaited her return. Over on the buffet the coffee service on its chased and footed tray was a study in silver and black in the semidarkness. Everything was as she had left it: her special crystal in the china closet, her silverplate—all eighty pieces—in its felt-lined case. It was her favorite room, the dining room. She was right not to go back on her promise to Jerome Johnson and sell the house as Marion kept nagging her to do. (According to Marion, the house had served its purpose.) Later she would make herself a cup of tea and drink it here at the table in the half-light.

". . . Packing her things in the middle of the night like some thief . . . no reason . . . no explanation . . . good money gone . . . gots to be crazy . . . no plane for days . . . gonna run into all kinds of trouble. . . ."

Caught in the riptide of her anger, Thomasina Moore was powerless to stop herself.

". . . Here the three of us suppose to be traveling together and she just ups and leaves, ruining the rest of the trip for the two of us. And after all the time I spent seeing to it everything would be just right!" (Which was true. The woman devoted the better part of the year to planning for the cruise—which each year took them to a different set of islands. She had the time, not having worked since her show business days. Her dead husband, a dentist, who had been taken with her color, had indulged her shamelessly, treating her as if she were all the children they had never had.)

". . . No decent person'd do a thing like this. Why she's no better, come to think of it, than some bum on a Hundred Twenty-fifth Street, never mind the airs she gives herself. But she never had me fooled. Oh, no, this is one boot she couldn't play for a fool. I could tell her airs were nothing but a front. Always knew she had it in her to pull somethin' mean and low-down like this. Knew it!

"That's why—" she cried, her suppressed fury at a new high, her breath sucked deep into the bony wells at her throat, her eyes convulsed. "That's why if I've said it once I've said it a thousand times: it . . . don't . . . pay . . . to . . . go . . . no . . . place . . . with . . . *niggers!* They'll mess up ever' time!"

Unhurriedly, Avey Johnson bent and picked up first her gloves and then her pocketbook from the chair beside her. To her surprise she found she was smiling. A little faint, pleased, self-congratulatory smile, as if, instead of the insult, the woman had said something complimentary. It didn't make sense. Yet there the smile was, its warmth stealing across her face, its gentle pull easing the strain from the held-in lip that had become a permanent part of her expression over the years. To hide the smile she was forced to remain bent over the chair longer than necessary.

Then, with the pocketbook on her arm and her gloves in hand, she was stepping around the still raging figure in the center of the room: ". . . somethin' deep's behind this mess. You can't tell me different. . . ." She gave her a wide berth, the way she might have some mildly demented bag woman railing to herself on the city's streets.

Her unhurried step led her across to Clarice at the divider. She had intended apologizing privately to her friend. Had meant to say, her voice low, her back to Thomasina Moore, that it was wrong of her to leave in this manner, but that she hoped Clarice would not hold it against her. It was just that something—she couldn't say what—had come over her the past couple of days. She couldn't explain it. She could make no sense of it. Anyway, they would see each other back at work once their vacations were over and everything would be as usual. (They both worked for the State Motor Vehicle Department, Avey Johnson as a supervisor and Clarice as a Grade Five Clerk.) Their first day back they would splurge and have lunch at the seafood restaurant near the office.

She had it in mind to say something on this order crossing the room, to assure Clarice that she was in no way to blame. But the moment she drew up in front of her friend and saw close-up the familiar burdened slope to her shoulders and the expression of mute acceptance on her face, her tongue balked. For the first time in the twenty years they had known each other, something about Clarice both frightened and offended her. She found herself wanting to back away from her as from something contagious, or to make a sign (if she had known one) to ward off some dangerous hex. At the same time her hand ached to reach out and lift that bowed head, force it up. She wanted to shout at Clarice the way her father used to at her long ago whenever he caught her slouching, "Pull your back up, girl!"

Instead all she said, quickly moving away, was, "I'm going to arrange with the purser about my leaving. I'll be back with a steward for my things."

In seconds she made her way around the suitcases to the door, and was opening and hurriedly closing it on the voice which continued choleric and unflagging from the middle of the floor.

". . . no reason . . . no explanation . . . trying to play people for fools . . . !"

"Cross Road Blues"

Call for Political Strategy

The unresolved problem of racism in the United States has placed African Americans in the contemporary era at the crossroad in their historical struggle for freedom, of whether to choose social integration or black cultural nationalism as a political strategy for achieving it.

Portrait by Aaron Douglass from Song of the Towers

VI "Cross Road Blues"

"No Other Music'll Ease My Misery"

African American History and Culture, 1960 to the Present

"Or Does It Explode?"

Social Revolution, New Renaissance, and Second Reconstruction

Uumh, standing at the crossroad, I tried to flag a ride,

Standing at the crossroads, I tried to flag a ride,

Didn't nobody seem to know me, everybody passed me by.

Robert Johnson, "Cross Road Blues"

During the decade called the Searing Sixties, African Americans responded to the battle cries of black activists, writers, musicians, and other blues people of the 1940s and 1950s with bloodshed and cataclysmic upheavals that not only sounded the death knell for centuries of segregation in the United States but also sent shock waves throughout the country and around the world. Because the dream for freedom and social equality had been deferred for so long, it exploded, and simultaneously created one of the tensest climates of racial and social turmoil in the nation's history. Out of this eruptive social atmosphere burst forth a more militant black consciousness, a strong sense of black pride, and the most prolific and impressive body of African American art, music, and written literature ever produced.

What ignited this outburst of creativity was a series of events beginning with the nonviolent boycotts and sit-ins of the late 1950s and early 1960s, which were marked by unarmed blacks being attacked by heavily armed police and vicious dogs, and with the brutal murders in the early 1960s of heroes, martyrs, and other freedom fighters by the government. Since then have come devastating race riots, radical political movements and countermovements, political backlashes and setbacks, and new definitions of blackness and sexuality. Since then have come partisan politics, partisan visions, high passions, and shifting ideas about the roles and responsibilities of black people. For African Americans, the contemporary period has been a time of tremendous struggle and charged debate about the nature of freedom and the strategies for achieving it. For once again, since the march toward freedom began in the nineteenth century, black people have found themselves "standing at the crossroad" in American society. Once again, they have had to decide whether to follow the path paved by Frederick Douglass and scores of early anticolonizationists toward social integration into a highly resistant American mainstream or to cross over to the rugged road mapped out by Henry Highland Garnet and his contemporary emigrationists toward black separatism. African Americans have been singing the "Cross Road Blues," experiencing the constant tension between the integrationist philosophy of Martin Luther King, Jr., and the separationist ideology of Malcolm X. This tension has provided a rich soil and inspiration for the contemporary black literary artist.

With the radicalization of black politics came a radicalization of black art, a move away from the integrationist politics and poetics of the 1940s and 1950s toward an aesthetic of black cultural nationalism of the 1960s and early 1970s. Inspired largely by Pan-Africanism and the rise of newly independent African states, black intellectuals insisted on what critic Addison Gayle, Jr., hailed in *The Black Aesthetic* (1971) as the "de-Americanization" of black people—the disassociation of African Americans from Eurocentric cultural values and ideals. Numerous writers, musicians, and visual and performing artists throughout the country championed the cause of the Black Power Movement by finding direction and strength in what the famous black theorist Larry Neal called "the Black Arts Movement . . . the aesthetic and spiritual sister of the Black Power concept." They called to African Americans everywhere to celebrate their African heritage, to be black and proud, and to embrace the concept and shout, "Black is beautiful!"

The result has been the most recent Black Renaissance, from 1960 to the present, which has touched upon virtually every aspect of American and African American life. In the 1960s and early 1970s—the age of avant-garde jazz, soul music, and the Black Power Movement—poetry and drama dominated the literary scene. In the late 1970s, 1980s, and 1990s, the era of revolutionary rap music, the hip-hop generation, and the women's rights movement, fiction captured center stage. Beginning in the 1960s, veteran authors such as Langston Hughes, Gwendolyn Brooks, Margaret Walker, James Baldwin, Ralph Ellison, Alice Childress, Robert Hayden, Paule Marshall, John Oliver Killens, and others who continued to write, would ripen the cultural landscape with their enormous skills, experiences, and influences on younger writers. Newcomers such as Ernest Gaines, Alice Walker, Ishmael Reed, James McPherson, Kristin Hunter, Tom Dent, and John Wideman would bring fresh themes, new understandings, and new treatments of black folk materials to the literature. Women such as Toni Morrison, Alice Walker, Ntozake Shange, Gayl Jones, Gloria Naylor, Terry McMillan, and Rita Dove and gays and lesbians such as Melvin Dixon, Randall Kenan, Audre Lorde, Alexis Deveaux, and Pat Parker would become more visible within the ranks of black artists. Moreover, Morrison, Amiri Baraka (LeRoi Jones), and August Wilson would extend the limits of the English language, enriching it with black vernacular, black myths, and the rhythms of black music.

This great multitude of voices can be seen as a dynamic response to the cadre of angry but talented young writers—Baraka, Haki Madhubuti (Don L. Lee), Sonia Sanchez, Etheridge Knight, and the other New Black Poets—as well as their senior mentors Gwendolyn Brooks and Dudley Randall. These literary artists not only lived through the events of the sixties but also used them as the basis for aesthetic creation that would inspire black people to tear down the walls of oppression.

Call for Social Revolution and Political Strategies

Inner City Blues

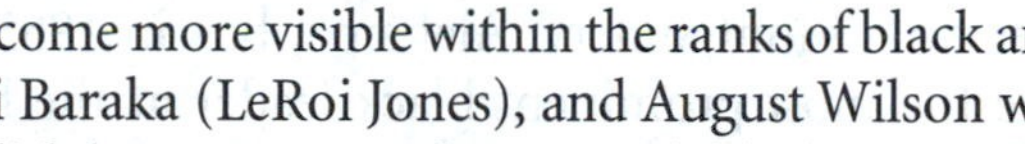

When saxophonist Ornette Coleman sounded the loud, dissonant chords from his classic composition "Free Jazz" (1960), he not only introduced a new kind of music—"avant-garde" or "free" jazz—but he also echoed the explosion of the "dream deferred" for African Americans that marked the beginning of the contemporary era. On February 1, 1960, four black college students who "sat-in" at a Woolworth's lunch counter in Greensboro, North Carolina, set off a spark that lit a fire across the nation. Within weeks, tens of thousands of students all over the South were staging sit-ins. Television played a key role, as the American public nightly viewed reactionary white police abusing the young demonstrators, who had as their only defense the spirituals and gospels they sang for unity of mind and spirit. Within two months, the Southern Christian Leadership Conference (SCLC) called on students to organize the Student Nonviolent Coordinating Committee (SNCC) for better coordination of various sit-in activities. Eventually, the SNCC moved throughout the Deep South to register, and thus empower, poor, usually undereducated black voters. Sociologist-historian E. Franklin Frazier estimates that at least twenty thousand people were arrested as a result of participation in nonviolent demonstrations in the South between 1960 and 1963. Participating in these student boycotts and voter registration drives were African American writers such as Alice Walker, Toni Cade Bambara, Sherley Anne Williams, and Askia Muhammad Touré. They would later incorporate these dramatic experiences into the African American literary canon.

With the formation of the SCLC and the galvanization of black communal action following Rosa Parks's determined stand not to give up her seat to a white passenger on a Montgomery, Alabama, bus in 1955, Martin Luther King, Jr., became the most prominent black leader at the beginning of the 1960s. His 1963 "Letter from Birmingham Jail" was the catalyst for a special bond between American blacks and President John F. Kennedy, and it proved the effectiveness of the written word to garner public attention and to rally the national black, and in many cases white, community to cohesive political action. In 1963, King provided the nation with moral leadership at a time when it was reeling from the shock of the deaths of President Kennedy and Mississippi freedom fighter Medgar Evers, state director of the NAACP, and from the firebombing of the Sixteenth Street Baptist Church in Birmingham, Alabama, where four young black girls were killed. (No one has yet been charged with these murders.) Harking back to the great Frederick Douglass, black activists across the country would soon follow King's example of strong public rhetoric reinforced by mass distribution of aesthetic and politically forceful writing. Within the next two years, King's dynamic leadership of the Civil Rights Movement would lead to the passage of the Civil Rights Bill, which prohibited segregation in public places and discrimination in employment, as well as the Voting Rights Act, which increased the numbers of blacks in local and state governments.

But during the early 1960s, the collective focus of the black struggle began to shift from the rural South to the urban North, where instead of Christian pastors, leaders of the more militant Nation of Islam became the major spokespersons. White Americans were horrified to hear leading Black Muslim spokesmen like Malcolm X and Elijah Muhammad refer to them as "white devils" and instruct the black community to press for a completely independent nationhood and to avoid all aspects of the racial integration that was slowly emerging in the country. However, for a substantial number of African Americans, especially young urban blacks, Malcolm X replaced King as a black hero and political leader. By 1963, fifty thousand blacks had crossed over to the Nation of Islam. Several young activist writers, such as Amiri Baraka, Sonia Sanchez, Marvin Jackman (known as Marvin X), and Askia Muhammad Touré, eventually joined the Nation of Islam or another branch of the Muslim religion. Literary history would soon prove Malcolm X to have a much greater effect on the public rhetoric and creative aesthetic of African Americans from the 1960s to the present than perhaps any other leader of the period.

An already shocked black community—still reeling from the deaths of President Kennedy and Medgar Evers—was further stunned when, in 1965, Malcolm X was assassinated, reportedly by two Black Muslim members while he was speaking to a black audience in Harlem. (Karl Evanzz's recent book *The Judas Factor* [1992] charges that Malcolm's killers were actually undercover government agents.) As Malcolm had predicted, he did not live long enough to read "in finished form" Alex Haley's transcribed *The Autobiography of Malcolm X,* which appeared in print later that year.

In the mid-sixties, the Civil Rights Movement changed into the Black Power Movement. The explosive riots in Watts (a section of Los Angeles) in 1965, the Black Panther Party's call for self-defense in 1966, the expulsion of white members from the once integrated SNCC also in 1966, and the race riots in several northern inner cities in 1967 all signaled a new militant mood. Also by the middle years, the SNCC had elected as its chairman the outspoken Stokely Carmichael, who popularized Richard Wright's electrifying term "Black Power." It became the rallying call for black pride and unity and for the creation of separate socioeconomic institutions as power bases for black communities.

With the emergence of the call for Black Power in the 1960s came the Black Arts Movement, also known as the Black Aesthetic or New Black Aesthetic. Central to both the Black Power and Black Arts Movements was the concept of self-determination as articulated in *The Wretched of the Earth* by Frantz Fanon, the black revolutionary psychiatrist from Martinique. First published in France in 1961 and referred to by Black Panther Eldridge Cleaver as the bible of the black liberation movement, *The Wretched of the Earth* is a systematic analysis of the origins and justifications of revolutionary violence as a weapon against colonial oppression. According to Fanon, by presuming to know all about the "pathological" mind of black people, mainstream psychology (or "scientific colonialism" as Fanon called it) had contributed to the worldwide domination and subjugation of people of color. Thus, there existed a need for black people to formulate and establish new definitions, conceptual models, and standards of normative behavior that would be free of the controlling values of the dominant culture. Drawing on Fanon's analysis, black intellectuals of the sixties began to speak of African America as an internal colony at war with the oppressors, and they embarked on a revolutionary campaign to master their environment by changing it. This was to be accomplished by Americans of African descent "becoming black" and grounding themselves in the collective identity provided by their unique African and African American group history and culture. At the urging of Fanon, Malcolm X, Maulana Ron Karenga, Amiri Baraka, and other theorists of the period, African Americans sought a radical revision of history and art to break the bonds of Euro-American psychological and cultural domination. No longer were they willing to allow others to speak for them; they insisted on having their own voice in and through their African American group culture.

This strong affirmation of black pride was not enough to turn back the tide of discrimination and oppression, especially in the inner cities. Racism raised its ugly head again on April 4, 1968, when Martin Luther King, Jr., the apostle of nonviolence, was gunned down, reportedly by a white male named James Earl Ray. Tears boiled over into rage. This devastating blow to African Americans led to race riots in more than 125 cities across the nation. Reaction to the violent death of this great Civil Rights leader poured the fuel of outrage on the already discontented masses of black people who were experiencing in every urban center in America the stark realities of the "Inner City Blues," as reflected in Marvin Gaye's song of that title:

> Crime is increasing / Trigger happy policing
> Panic is spreading / God knows where we're heading
> Oh make me wanna holler / They don't understand
> Oh make me wanna holler / They don't understand
> ....
> This ain't livin', This ain't livin' / No, no baby, this ain't livin'

After such massive urban black unrest, the period of white backlash began. This included major white flight from cities to suburbs and the resurgence of racist groups such as the Ku Klux Klan and the neo-Nazis.

With the white backlash gaining momentum throughout the conservative Nixon administration (1969–1974), African Americans began to feel that much of what was gained in the sixties would soon be lost. Their anxieties only increased with the nation's polarization over the issues of affirmative action programs and quotas, welfare programs, and school busing. Moreover, Nixon's campaign promise of "law and order" was implemented. Police targeted militant black organizations, particularly the Black Panther

Party, for destruction. By the early seventies, the Panthers had been virtually ripped apart by the arrests of leaders Huey Newton and Bobby Seale, the flight of Eldridge Cleaver to Algiers, and the Chicago police's brutal murders of Midwest leaders Fred Hampton and Mark Clark while the two men were asleep in their beds. Because of ongoing police brutality, urban unrest, and other social problems, such as the rising cost of living and the Vietnam War, in which a disproportionate number of black men lost their lives, African Americans continued to sing the "Inner City Blues":

> Inflation, no chance / To increase finance
> Bills pile up sky high / Send that boy off to die
> Make me wanna holler / The way they do my life
> Make me wanna holler / The way they do my life
> . . . .
> This ain't livin', This ain't livin' / No, no baby, this ain't livin'

What many blacks believed was a marvelous and quite complex network of local activist organizations, including grassroots as well as professionally formed ones, interacting often with spontaneous national orchestration, now seemed severely weakened by a leadership void. The deaths of black liberation movement leaders such as King, Malcolm, and Evers and the arrest and silencing of hundreds of other leaders and foot soldiers at both ends of the spectrum in the collective drive for freedom—whether they were seeking change through nonviolence or militancy—began a predictable decline, decentralization, and de-emphasis of the movement, especially in the eyes of white Americans and the news media. But simultaneously, several African American intellectuals were asserting that there was no leadership void but rather that their freedom movement had been infiltrated and that powerful national forces were manipulating the public spotlight away from their cause. Recently released information about Cointelpro, a counterintelligence project that FBI director J. Edgar Hoover founded in the sixties to disrupt black organizations and movements, including the Black Arts Movement, appears to corroborate the claims of infiltration. Its aims, outlined quite clearly in the document, included (1) preventing a coalition of militant black organizations, (2) preventing the rise of a messiah among black people who could unify and electrify them, (3) preventing militant black nationalist groups from gaining respectability in the black community by discrediting them, and (4) preventing the long-range growth of militant black organizations. The liberation movement was further staggered when a number of allies and supporters turned to other causes such as the anti–Vietnam War and ecology movements.

By the mid-seventies, other American constituencies who also suffered collective discrimination had stepped into the fray. These included white women, migrant Mexican and Chicano farm workers, Native Americans, gays, lesbians, senior citizens, and people with physical impairments. The contemporary women's rights movement, like the nineteenth-century feminist movement, was an offshoot of the black liberation struggle. As in the earlier movement, many contemporary black women were activists in both the black and women's movements. Notable black leaders such as Shirley Chisholm, Angela Davis, and Audre Lorde became leading spokespersons for groups such as the National Organization for Women (NOW), decrying the double oppression of African American women: that of being both black and female within a white and male power structure.

But history would soon repeat itself. The falsely dichotomized issue of which battle was more imperative—black rights or women's rights—drove a wedge between black women and black men in an already splintered and apparently infiltrated black liberation movement. Several black women activists turned to the women's rights movement because the Civil Rights, Black Power, and Black Arts Movements were male dominated. They attacked the secondary positions to which black women had been relegated and the sexism of liberation movement leaders such as Stokely Carmichael, who once remarked that the only position women would hold in the SNCC was prone. The controversial depictions of black men in Ntozake Shange's Obie Award–winning drama *for colored girls who have considered suicide when the rainbow is enuf* (1975) and Michele Wallace's book *Black Macho and the Myth of the Superwoman* (1979) would spark a heated national debate, polarizing black men and women. Several black male scholars and writers accused these authors of negatively stereotyping black men and attacked black women activists for being pawns of the predominantly middle-class white women's movement. Black women activists defended the writings as being less about black men as villains than about the need for black women to achieve their freedom from, in Wallace's words, "white male cultural hegemony." Again, black women and men who were divided over the "women's issue" had to sing the "Cross Road Blues." But instead of one or two roads from which to choose, blacks would find themselves increasingly pulled in various directions.

During the Reagan administration (1981–1989), Jesse Jackson, perhaps the most visible black man in the nation, took the Civil Rights struggle to higher ground when in 1984 and again in 1988 he ran impressive campaigns for the Democratic nomination for the U.S. presidency. Using the slogan "I Am Somebody" and forming a multiracial political base that he called the Rainbow Coalition, Jackson frightened the political establishment and his media critics because, for the first time since the Civil War, whites, blacks, and other people of color were coming together to effect change within the established political system.

Also during the 1980s, black lawyer-activist Randall Robinson bridged the African American liberation struggle and the black South African freedom movement when he founded Trans Africa, an organized designed to free black political prisoners in South Africa and to weaken that country's system of apartheid. In orchestration with the Congressional Black Caucus and various antiapartheid pressure groups, Robinson and other members of Trans Africa successfully lobbied Congress to impose economic sanctions on the white South African government. In conjunction with a number of national and international organizations, Trans Africa was key not only in the freeing of African National Congress (ANC) leader Nelson Mandela from prison but also in the eventual dismantling of apartheid. With Trans Africa, Robinson fulfilled Malcolm X's vision of a unified Pan-Africanism.

But as the walls of oppression were being torn down in South Africa, more intransigent walls of social injustice were being put in place in the United States with a massive conservative backlash that plunged America into the era of "post–Civil Rights," a time of diminished rights for black people. This backlash has been a major component of what most black historians collectively call the Decline of the Second Reconstruction—that is, the decline of the period characterized by the democratic upsurgence of American blacks against institutionalized racism. Black scholars such as E. Franklin Frazier, Vincent Harding, and others liken resistance to the black liberation movement's goals to that of the post–Civil War era, when whites instituted sharecropping and the Ku Klux Klan. A significant factor in this decline was President Ronald Reagan's fiscal policies, known as trickle-down economics, which several economists contend put more blacks and other Americans into poverty than any other sociopolitical action in recent history. It created a class of homeless that had never existed in the country before, while plunging the nation into a financial recession from which most lower- and lower-middle-class blacks and others have never recovered. Since 1980, although there has been an increase in numbers in a rising black middle class, more than one-third of all African Americans remain below the poverty line, and black males make up 44 percent of the country's prison population. In addition, although African Americans have made substantial gains in holding public office, they continue to be underrepresented in American politics, making up only 2 percent of all elected officials in a nation in which they are 13 percent of the total population.

Largely as a result of the failure of many white socioeconomic and political institutions to meet the needs of American blacks, the Afrocentricity Movement, which seeks to put African values and ideals at the center of African American life and education, came to life in the 1980s. The members of this movement, including scholars John Henrik Clarke and Molefi Kete Asante, want to replace the Eurocentric worldview, which they feel rules the schools, with an Afrocentric one. In its call for pride in the African heritage and "blackness," Afrocentricity is a resurgence of the Black Power and Black Arts Movements of the 1960s.

At the other end of the political spectrum in the 1980s surfaced a small but influential group of conservative black Republicans. They included

Thomas Sowell, Walter Williams, Glenn Loury, Shelby Steele, Clarence Pendleton, and Clarence Thomas—all of whom opposed affirmative action and various other aspects of Civil Rights legislation. Pendleton and Thomas were Reagan appointees to head the Equal Employment Opportunity Commission (EEOC). Both of them worked actively to dismantle affirmative action programs, an activity that made it increasingly difficult for blacks in the work force to gain legal redress from racial discrimination that had been claimed illegal by a more liberal Congress. Although Clarence Thomas and other black neoconservatives appear to have substantial political backing from the far right and receive widespread coverage by the news media, they have won very little support from the vast majority of African Americans and have become marked targets in Civil Rights circles.

During the Bush administration (1989–1993), Thomas would cause more divisiveness within the black community and further destruction to affirmative action goals when in 1991 Bush gave Thomas a seat on the U.S. Supreme Court. Thomas's ascension to the Court came at the denigration of a black woman, law professor Anita Hill, who claimed during an internationally televised U.S. Senate hearing that while the EEOC had given Thomas the charge to protect women from gender discrimination, he was, in fact, subjecting her to sexual harassment. Outraged white women around the country sided with Hill. But again, the black community became divided over the race versus gender issue. Predictably, as in the nineteenth-century dispute over the Fifteenth Amendment to the Constitution, which gave black men the right to vote, the majority of blacks chose race. Because many black men and women were resentful that Hill would degrade a black man before the world community, 70 percent of the black people polled sided with Thomas. The incident may well have contributed to Bush's loss of the next presidential election. Angry that the Senate confirmed Thomas despite Hill's moving testimony, white women and many black and other women of color voted overwhelmingly for female candidates in both national and state elections, and for the first time in the country's history, a black woman, Carol Moseley Braun, was elected to the U.S. Senate. Because blacks benefited minimally at the ballot box from the Hill-Thomas affair, some black women activists took very vocal positions about the pervasive implications of the Thomas appointment. Outspoken writers such as Toni Morrison and June Jordan sounded wake-up calls to the black community that the white backlash now also had black faces.

Not surprisingly, the backlash has widened the gap in communication between blacks and whites. In "The Hidden Rage of Successful Blacks," an article in the November 3, 1993, issue of *Newsweek,* Mark Whitaker observed, "When it comes to discussing race, Americans might as well be watching different movies . . . whites see one reality; blacks see another." These diametrically opposing visions became quite apparent in several dramatic events of the 1990s, in which, as in the 1960s, television played a central role. These episodes included the 1991 beating of black motorist Rodney King by four Los Angeles policemen and the 1994–1995 televised trial of black sports superstar O. J. Simpson, who was accused of slaying his white ex-wife, Nicole Brown Simpson, and her white friend Ronald Goldman. In the first case, in spite of the fact that the beating of Rodney King was videotaped and televised to the nation, an all-white jury found the police officers innocent. The white jury saw justice, law, and order; blacks saw injustice, police brutality, and racism. Predominantly black Los Angeles exploded into riots reminiscent of the Watts riots of 1965. For the black residents of South Central L.A., the King verdict epitomized the "Inner City Blues" realities of crushing poverty, joblessness, and lack of opportunity, which they had experienced for generations:

> Hang ups, let downs / Bad breaks, set backs
> Natural fact is / I can't pay my taxes
> Oh, make me wanna holler / And throw up both my hands
> Yea, it make me wanna holler / And throw up both my hands
> . . . .
> This ain't livin', This ain't livin' / No, no baby, this ain't livin'

In the other case, days before black lawyer Johnnie Cochran and other members of O. J. Simpson's "dream team" of attorneys presented Simpson's defense in a Los Angeles courtroom, a September 1995 ABC News poll revealed that 77 percent of white Americans believed that Simpson was guilty, while 72 percent of black Americans thought that he was innocent. Whites saw sexism, domestic violence, and murder; blacks saw racism, stereotyping, and police conspiracy. When a predominantly black and female jury found Simpson not guilty of first- or second-degree murder on October 2, 1995, African Americans throughout the country jubilantly celebrated with Black Power fists raised high, while white Americans stood in shocked silence. Soon afterward, a white American form of rioting, shunning, took place; Simpson was ostracized and isolated by his white neighbors in Brentwood, the white media, and the white American public at large. Clearly, the Simpson case reflects a moment of national crisis: at this time blacks and whites are as polarized as they have ever been in American history.

These and other recent events have alerted African Americans to the fact that as the twenty-first century approaches, little has changed in the nation, that the United States still, as the 1968 Kerner Commission Report stated, comprises two communities, "one white, one black, separate and unequal." This feeling has been underscored by the July 1, 1996 Supreme Court decision that by a vote of 5 to 4 eliminated race as a factor for determining political districts throughout the country and by the heated debates on affirmative action and other social programs that have continued to polarize whites and blacks and that have been at the center of the 1996 presidential election campaigns. According to a July 1995 ABC News poll, 60 percent of whites oppose affirmative action programs, while 60 percent of blacks favor them. Many whites view these programs as unfair, preferential treatment. Although white women, not blacks, have been the major beneficiaries of affirmative action, many black people see it as a necessary legal protection against Jim Crow.

The "separate and unequal" status of the black community has given rise to a new wave of black cultural nationalism. On October 16, 1995, two weeks after the Simpson verdict, Louis Farrakhan, head of the Nation of Islam, and Baptist minister Benjamin Chavez led the Million Man March on Washington, D.C., to show black unity, black pride, and the commitment of black men to their families and communities. A crowd of well over one million black men (and some black women) from all walks of life, ranging from young to old, grassroots to affluent, came together in the spirit of "atonement," to make amends for any disservice they had done to black women. They vowed to make a difference for the betterment of their people in particular and of society as a whole. Having designed the Million Man March specifically to address the critical needs of black people, Farrakhan called on African Americans to develop strong, independent economic and sociopolitical bases for black communities through a national black economic development fund and a massive black voter registration drive. Farrakhan's call for black self-determination, black unity, and black pride echoed the teachings of Malcolm X and other Black Power advocates of the 1960s. Another link to the Searing Sixties has been the commemorative literature anthology *Million Man March: Day of Absence* (1996), published by Haki Madhubuti and Maulana Karenga, two of the major voices of the Black Arts Movement—the first, exciting phase of the New Black Renaissance.

Response: The New Black Renaissance

To Be Young, Gifted and Black

Like the Harlem Renaissance, the New Black Renaissance sprang, to a large extent, from the loins of Pan-African thought. Together with the writings of Frantz Fanon and other black intellectuals, the interaction among black scholars and writers from around the globe gave direction to the Black Arts Movement. This exchange of ideas took place in both the United States and Africa. The rise of the newly emerging African nations from the shackles of colonialism in the late 1950s and early 1960s brought African intellectuals, artists, poets, novelists, and dramatists to America to lecture, teach, perform, and travel. Simultaneously, African American thinkers, including Langston Hughes and Malcolm X, traveled to Africa to exchange cultural ideas with influential Africans. For instance, Hughes was a leading literary figure at two major black arts conferences held in Africa—the 1959 First Conference of Negro Writers and the 1966 First World Festival of Negro Arts. He also introduced the American public to African literature in his anthologies *An African Treasury: Essays, Stories, Poems by Black Africans* (1960) and *Poems from Black Africa* (1963).

Beginning with the First Conference of Negro Writers and culminating with the First World Festival of Negro Arts, held in Dakar, Senegal, the revolutionary agenda for the Blacks Arts Movement was set in motion. Chairing the 1966 Dakar Festival was Senegal's president Léopold Senghor, the chief architect of the Négritude movement. Under Senghor's leadership, African, African American, and Caribbean intellectuals and literary artists met for twenty-four days to formulate and exchange ideas for the Black Arts Movement. African-oriented journals such as *Presence Africaine* and *Black Orpheus* renewed their interest in African American writers during the time. Likewise, black American scholars and literary artists sponsored the First American Festival of Negro Art (AFNA) in 1965 and the Second AFNA in 1969 and published African works in black-owned periodicals.

As a major thrust of the Black Arts Movement, the new African American writers turned to black journals such as *Broadside Press Series, Black World, Journal of Black Poetry, Black Dialogue, Free Lance, Freedomways, Black Expression, Soulbook, Dasein, Umbra,* and *Uhuru.* These periodicals freed them from dependence on mainstream commercial publishers and offered them the opportunity to publish for a black audience without white censorship. Publishers such as Dudley Randall of Broadside Press, Hoyt Fuller of Johnson Enterprises, Joe Goncalves of Journal of Black Poetry Press, Alhamisi of Black Arts Publication, Don L. Lee (Haki Madhubuti) and Carolyn Rodgers of Third World Press, and Julian and Raye Richardson of Marcus Books worked tirelessly to defend the new aesthetic. They allowed the writers to "blacken" the language with the idioms and idiosyncrasies of black speech and music. Together with the new writers and scores of musicians and visual and performing artists, they rallied African Americans everywhere to celebrate the new black cultural group identity.

Hence, unlike the Harlem Renaissance, which was culturally and to some degree geographically centered, the New Black Renaissance erupted in every American community with a substantial black population. For the first time in the nation's history, black was considered beautiful, and Black Power and black pride were images and attitudes to be celebrated and revered, not hidden or feared. Wearing big natural Afros, dashikis, and African beads, blacks, young and old, raised their fists to salute Black Power; greeted one another with the black handshake and the black familial terms "sistah" and "brothah"; attended Black Power conferences, black poetry readings, and Back to Africa rallies; and planned trips to the motherland. Never before in the nation's history had so many black consciousness institutions, activities, and events flourished. Big cities and small towns alike saw the establishment of black studies programs on white and black college campuses, new black colleges, free schools, black nationalist communes, black bookstores and boutiques, and black music concerts, community theaters, and acting ensembles.

From coast to coast, community-oriented artists and art projects produced Black Aesthetic visual art that colored the black inner cityscapes with images of "Black Is Beautiful" and "Black Power." This type of art, like the literature and music of the period, was message oriented, a form of artist-to-people communication. Aware of the impact of visual symbols on disseminating social ideas, Black Aesthetic painters used highly visible outdoor murals, sometimes termed *billboard art* or *street art,* to instruct black neighborhood residents about desirable cultural and social goals and to portray black heroes and other positive images of the black life experience. Often these street artists organized to produce collective murals such as the famous *Wall of Respect,* which was completed during the 1960s in Chicago, the home base for this kind of art. Outstanding muralists, including Eugene Eda, Dana Chandler, William Walker, and Mitchell Caton, painted striking, bold wall murals in Chicago, Boston, Detroit, St. Louis, and Washington, D.C. In 1970, for instance, Eda produced in Chicago *The Wall of Meditation,* which brilliantly portrays the "Cross Road Blues"—Martin Luther King and Malcolm X pointing black people in opposite sociopolitical directions. Other New Black Renaissance art highlighted the African American life experience in an array of styles and forms, including the cubist and surrealistic collages of Romare Bearden, the expressionist paintings of Reginald Gammon and Faith Ringgold, the neoslavery "Wanted" posters of Charles White, the ebony sculptures of Elizabeth Catlett, and the lineoleum prints of Ruth Waddy.

Blacks and whites also saw powerful images of black heroes and heroines on the movie screen. In the early 1960s, Sidney Poitier had been the major black film star with several leading roles, including his 1963 Academy Award–winning performance in *Lilies of the Field.* With the early 1970s would come black-directed films such as Ossie Davis's *Cotton Comes to Harlem,* an adaptation of Chester Himes's novel of that title. In addition, Black Aesthetic film directors Melvin Van Peebles, Gordon Parks, and Gordon Parks, Jr., introduced a new black movie icon. Van Peebles in *Sweet Sweetback's Badassss Song,* Parks in *Shaft,* and Parks, Jr., in *Superfly* created the militant, outspoken, sexy, macho black male protagonist who triumphed over the villains in the poverty-stricken, crime-infested, and morally decayed inner cities created by white America. Though criticized for making films glamorizing violence and sexism, these directors paved the way for latter-day filmmakers Spike Lee, John Singleton, and Robert Earl Ray.

During the period, black women and men achieved other milestones in the film, television, and other entertainment industries. Winning Oscar nominations for Best Actress were Cicely Tyson for her performance as a sharecropper's wife named Rebecca in the movie *Sounder* in 1972, Diana Ross for her star billing as Billie Holiday in *Lady Sings the Blues,* also in 1972, and Diahann Carroll for her role as a welfare mother in *Claudine* in 1974. Carroll had made television history six years earlier as the lead character in "Julia." Whereas whites in the 1950s had pressured sponsors like Coca-Cola not to air television shows such as "The Nat King Cole Show," white sponsors and audiences in the 1970s gave major support to black shows such as "The Jeffersons," "Good Times," and "What's Happening." Moreover, Alex Haley's "Roots: The Saga of an American Family" (1976) would become the most-watched television series in the history of the industry and the model for a miniseries. Also during the decade, white audiences and producers began to recognize talented black comedians such as Richard Pryor, Bill Cosby, Dick Gregory, Godfrey Cambridge, and Redd Foxx.

Whites also became acculturated to African American music. The music had captured the imagination of young whites even before the Civil Rights Movement. As cultural historian Ben Sidran in *Black Talk* (1971) explains, "Black music, then, was at least part of the basic 'cause' that changed the young American 'rebel without a cause' into a political activist." In the wake of the Black Arts Movement, the new black musicians combined messages of love, freedom, and political action in the lyrics of their songs. As composer-singers of the "Cross Road Blues," they addressed power imbalances through their moral commitment to radical change and the strategic role of the arts and humanities in producing new identities and institutions.

The Oral Tradition

Fight the Power

The clarion call of the era for change was clear from "Ain't Gonna Let Nobody Turn Me 'Round" to "Free in '63" of the champions for Civil Rights; from "A Love Supreme" by jazz saxophonist John Coltrane to "Say It Loud, I'm Black and I'm Proud" by James Brown of the Black Power activists; from "Respect" by Aretha Franklin to "Ladies First" by rappers Queen Latifah and Monie Love of the proponents for women's rights; and from "Fight the Power" by rappers Public Enemy and "Freedom of Speech" by rapper Ice T of the hip-hop generation of the 1980s and 1990s. Since the 1960s, black music has been at the very heart of the social and cultural revolution.

Whether it has been the blues of Bobby "Blue" Bland, the jazz of John Coltrane, or the rap of Public Enemy, it has been what Ben Sidran in *Black Talk* (1971) calls a "confrontation music," a music reflecting the new racial militancy. Its call and response cadences, its disregard for Eurocentric forms, and its enormous rhythmic dynamism have been even more revolutionary than its often controversial lyrics. As Sidran explains, "The increasing cathartic power of this new music . . . was a function of the growing necessity for violent catharsis within the black community." It has brought the black musician from the underground of the 1940s and 1950s to the forefront of the American political scene.

Contemporary Urban Blues

Chicago and Chess Records continued as blues centers after the 1960s. The blues of Muddy Waters, Sonny Boy Williamson, Bo Diddley, Bobby "Blue" Bland, B. B. and Albert King, and many others helped to revolutionize the music of the Western world. Not only have the Beatles, the Rolling Stones, and other British musicians publicly acknowledged their debt to these black blues musicians, but major contemporary black soul singers such as Ray Charles, Aretha Franklin, and James Brown have experimented with combining the music with gospel and jazz. Since the fifties and sixties, much of the urban blues has been diffused with other forms of black folk music such as rhythm and blues, gospel, and jazz. The blues diffusion has continued to be a popular musical trend.

Not since the Harlem Renaissance has there been so much interest in the blues. At the beginning of the 1960s, bluesmen Memphis Slim and Willie Dixon, a Chess blues artist, founded the American Folk Blues Festival, which first toured Europe in 1962. The event led to a rediscovery of the rural and city blues traditions and a growing interest in the urban blues by young white musicians. From 1960 to the present, major blues festivals have taken place throughout Europe and the United States, culminating in the launching of the largest free blues festival in the world, the 1984 Chicago Blues Festival, by Mayor Harold Washington.

The urban blues have had a profound impact on contemporary African American writers. Directly or indirectly, the blues have informed the work of James Baldwin, William Melvin Kelley, Alice Walker, Toni Morrison, Gayl Jones, August Wilson, Cornelius Eady, and many other black literary artists and critics. Numerous contemporary poets who have been influenced by the blues tradition include Amiri Baraka, Etheridge Knight, Sonia Sanchez, Haki Madhubuti, Carolyn Rodgers, Sherley Anne Williams, Tom Dent, Michael Harper, Al Young, A. B. Spellman, Ted Joans, Eugene Redmond, and Jay Wright. In some instances, the influence is ornamental and thematic, as in Sanchez's "Blues" and Young's "The Old O. O. Blues." Sometimes the blues mood is ritualistic and intrinsic, as in Harper's "Come Back Blues" and

Williams's "Any Woman's Blues." At other times, contemporary black poets have experimented with the blues motif and form, as in Knight's "A Poem for Myself (or Blues for a Mississippi Black Boy)."

Spirituals and Gospels

One of the primary functions of black religious music during the contemporary era has been as expressions of Civil Rights. As mentioned earlier, Martin Luther King, Jr., and his followers turned many spirituals into freedom songs, including "We Shall Overcome." Students jailed as a result of the earliest sit-ins sang "We Shall Not Be Moved" and "Oh Freedom" for moral and spiritual support. Songs like "Keep Your Eyes on the Prize," "Ain't Gonna Let Nobody Turn Me 'Round," and "This Little Light of Mine" gave fieldworkers in the SNCC and other African Americans in the freedom movement a sense of community pride, unity, and purpose. "Keep Your Eyes on the Prize" is an adaptation of a traditional gospel song called "Keep Your Hand on the Plow."

At the same time, the renowned singer Mahalia Jackson, newcomer Edwin Hawkins, and other singers and composers made gospel music a chief inspirational source for the freedom struggle. In 1961, the music was firmly established when President John F. Kennedy invited Jackson to sing at one of his inauguration parties. Approximately ten years later, Hawkins, who rose to gospel fame with his recording of "Oh Happy Day," won a Grammy Award for his album *Every Man Wants to Be Free* (1970).

The composer of more than five hundred songs during the post-1960s era, James Cleveland—Grammy Award–winning singer, pianist, composer, and conductor and the "Crown Prince of Gospel"—was probably the major artist in moving gospel music from the church to the contemporary charts and concert halls. Many of his compositions have become gospel standards, including "Grace Is Sufficient," "Peace Be Still," "Oh Lord, Stand by Me," "He's Using Me," "Walk On by Faith," and "Lord, Help Me to Hold Out." During the 1980s and 1990s, the era of "urban gospel," singing stars such as the Winans, Michael Peace, P.I. D., and Stephen Wiley expanded the genre by incorporating elements of rap in their music. The world-renowned Sweet Honey in the Rock, a female a cappella group, rely on only their voices and a percussion instrument made from a gourd and beads to sing gospel, folk, blues, jazz, and rap.

The impact of gospel on contemporary literary figures is apparent in the works of Langston Hughes, James Baldwin, Nikki Giovanni, Rita Dove, Gloria Naylor, Henry Dumas, Randall Kenan, Alice Walker, Sherley Anne Williams, and Toni Morrison. For example, Hughes's *Tambourines to Glory,* a gospel musical, opened on Broadway in 1963; Giovanni rewrote the father of gospel, Thomas A. Dorsey, in her poem "Reflections on April 4, 1968," and recorded a gospel album, *Truth Is on Its Way,* where her poetry reading is backed up by the singing of the New York Community Choir. The protagonist of Baldwin's *Just Above My Head* (1979) is a gospel singer, and Naylor quotes from the spirituals in her novels.

Soul, Funk, Disco, and Pop

Whereas the spirituals and gospel songs became the music of the Civil Rights Movement, soul, the sixties form of rhythm and blues, became the music of the black revolution. Although soul music is popular and commercially successful, it, like all modern black music, derives from black folk culture, mainly from the blues and gospel. In the sixties, Amiri Baraka observed in *Blues People* (1963), "Rhythm and blues took on special significance and meaning. Those artists, too, reflected the rising tide of mass struggle." Setting the mood and tone of the era in 1963 was the "High Priestess of Soul," Nina Simone, with "Mississippi Goddam," a song that expressed the black rage surrounding the assassination of Medgar Evers. As the leading black protest singer of the time, Simone continued to express the black collective consciousness of the era in her moving tribute to Lorraine Hansberry, "To Be Young, Gifted and Black." In this song, she called for black unity: "Don't divide us, unify us, Lord. Help us to get it together. . . . To be young, gifted, and black, that's where it's at."

Echoing similar sentiments about black pride were the "Godfather of Soul," James Brown, and songwriter-performer Curtis Mayfield. James Brown's 1968 top seller, "Say It Loud, I'm Black and I'm Proud," was like the black national anthem of the period. Gerald Early reports in *Hungry Mind Review* (Spring 1992) Brown saying "It was necessary to teach pride then, and I think the song did a lot of good for a lot of people." Perhaps even more revolutionary than his controversial lyrics were the driving drumbeats and Brown's screams, which created an enormous rhythmic catharsis; his infectious call and response performance style, which defined soul music; and his staccato delivery, which anticipated rap. The same year, Mayfield answered the Black Power cry with his sensational hit "We're a Winner." Other great soul artists were the "Queen of Soul," Aretha Franklin, the late great Otis Redding, the unconquerable Ray Charles, and the "New Musical Messenger," Roberta Flack.

Vitally important in the exposure of soul music was Berry Gordy's Motown Records, which brought numerous musical talents, including the Supremes, the Temptations, Martha Reeves and the Vandellas, the Jackson Five, Stevie Wonder, Smokey Robinson, and Marvin Gaye, to the top of the entertainment world. Yet, beginning in the 1970s, Motown underwent a change when Gaye, despite the company's reservations, came out with the now classic album *What's Goin' On.* Besides "Inner City Blues," this album contains two other songs—"Mercy, Mercy Me (The Ecology)" and the title cut—that centered on the theme of racial injustice. Two years later, Stevie Wonder continued the focus on social protest with his top-selling album *Music on My Mind.*

A spinoff of soul music called funk also emerged during the 1970s. This densely textured music, which was heavily dependent on extravagant showpersonship, costumes, and staging, was played, sung, and performed by groups such as Parliament (who later became the Funkadelics), the Ohio Players, and the Commodores. The decade also witnessed the rise of disco, a music of driving rhythms defined by songwriter Freddie Perren as "music made primarily for dancing." Unrivaled as the "Disco Sex Goddess," Donna Summers reigned over the disco scene with her popular album *Love to Love You* (1975). Other important disco artists were Gloria Gaynor with her song "I Will Survive" (1977) and Peaches and Herb (Linda Green and Herb Feemster) with their hit album *Reunited* (1978).

Whereas the 1970s were the decade of funk and disco, the 1980s were the era of pop. In 1983, Michael Jackson became the "King of Pop" with his hit album *Thriller.* The album won an unprecedented seven Grammy Awards. The following year, Prince challenged Jackson for the crown with his smash album *Purple Rain,* which was also the title of his successful movie that year. Other sensational pop stars include Patti Labelle, Luther Vandross, and Whitney Houston.

The lasting legacy of pop, funk, and soul artists to the written texts of African Americans derived from their profound recognition of human alienation and the black rhythms of existence that define it. Their music has influenced diverse literary voices from Amiri Baraka, Nikki Giovanni, and David Henderson to Ntozake Shange, Michael Harper, and Jayne Cortex.

Avant-Garde and Straight-Ahead Jazz

If the substance of black life was soul, funk, and pop, the triumphant spirit was jazz. Poet, dramatist, and cultural critic Amiri Baraka and others saw avant-garde jazz as the source of the revolution. He maintained that the new music of Ornette Coleman, John Coltrane, Charlie Mingus, Archie Shepp, Cecil Taylor, Albert Ayler, McCoy Tyner, Reggie Workman, and others sounded the penetrating, shrill chords of black revolution. "What these musicians have done," Baraka contends in *Blues People* (1963), "is to restore to jazz its valid separation from, and anarchic disregard of, Western popular form. Their music was stripped to its basic elemental form: the striving to play without regard to harmony and for personal freedom through complete collective efforts." Baraka literally brought this new music to the streets in Harlem with loudspeakers to entice the masses. In response, some avantgardists, led by legendary trumpeter Miles Davis and more recently by saxophonist David Murray, began experimenting with electronic popular music and reinventing their identities as fusion musicians.

In contrast, Wynton Marsalis's Jazz at Lincoln Center program is criticized by some musicians as being purist and ignoring the avant-garde jazz of the 1960s and 1970s. After playing with the experimental Herbie Hancock Quartet in the early 1980s, Marsalis began his own quintet and led the renaissance in classical or straight-ahead jazz, winning many awards for his debut album in 1982 and Grammy Awards for both his classical and jazz albums in 1984. In "What Jazz Is and Isn't," he explained in 1988,

> For too many people, any kind of music can be lumped as jazz. . . . Despite attempts by writers and record companies and promoters and educators and even musicians to blur the lines for commercial purposes, rock isn't jazz and new age isn't jazz, and neither are pop or third stream. There may be much good in all of them, but they aren't jazz.

For Marsalis, "jazz broke the rules of European conventions and created rules of its own that were so specific, so thorough and so demanding that a great art resulted. . . . [T]he greatness of jazz lies not only in its emotion but also in its deliberate artifice." Also among the phenomenally talented and disciplined young straight-ahead jazz artists are pianist Marcus Roberts, trumpeter Roy Hargrove, guitarist Mark Whitfield, and saxophonist Joshua Remon. Moreover, Carmen McRae, Betty Carter, Abbey Lincoln, Anita Baker, and, before their deaths, Ella Fitzgerald and Sarah Vaughan have been the dominant contemporary jazz vocalists in this tradition. This new music has informed the works of Baraka, Al Young, Michael Harper, Quincy Troupe, Ishmael Reed, A. B. Spellman, Nathaniel Mackey, and Cornelius Eady. Many other contemporary black poets celebrate avant-garde jazz in their songs.

Rap

Rap is the current revolutionary poetry of the young black masses. But as Tricia Rose, the authoritative voice on rap, points out, to view the music simply as a direct and natural outgrowth of the oral African American idiom is to romanticize and decontextualize it as a cultural form. Rap, Rose explains in *Black Noise: Rap Music and Black Culture in Contemporary America* (1994), is "a dynamic hybrid of oral traditions, postliterate orality, and advanced technology." Accompanied by highly rhythmic, electronically based instruments, it is composed by musicians who establish a base rhythm and message with samples from rhythm and blues (R&B), soul, and jazz artists such as James Brown, James Clinton, and John Coltrane and black cultural activists such as Malcolm X, Martin Luther King, Jr., and Louis Farrakhan. On top of this computerized baseline, the technicians and musicians then build, erase, and revise the sounds into multilayered, thematically and stylistically diverse musical forms.

Although rap has evolved into a highly technological form, it is unmistakably rooted in African American tradition. According to essayist Gerald Early in "Politics and the Black American Song" (*Hungry Mind Review*, Spring 1992), the music is "an offshoot of black masculine toasts, the revolutionary poetry of the late sixties and early seventies from people like Gil-Scott Heron, the Last Poets, and American soul-funk." Characterized by the dramatic, incantatory declamations of the performer, rap is a fusion of jagged jazz, blues rhythms, and street language channeled into a vehicle of protest and exhortation. Shouting "Fight the Power," a title borrowed from a 1975 hit R&B song by the Isley Brothers, rappers such as Public Enemy have addressed some of the most complex social, cultural, and political issues in contemporary American society. The social consciousness of rap was apparent from the hip-hop dance rhythms of "Rapper's Delight" by the Sugar Hill Gang in 1980 to the release of "The Message" by Grandmaster Flash and the Furious Five in 1982. "Rapper's Delight" also popularized the term *hip-hop*, which has come to symbolize an entire generation and its culture of music, dance, attitudes, language, clothes, and publications.

Since the 1980s, hip-hop generation griots such as Public Enemy, Eric B. & Rakim, KRS One, LL Cool J, MC Lyte, De La Soul, Paris, and other "Prophets of Rage" have criticized America for its perpetuation of racial and economic discrimination against African Americans, especially in the form of police brutality. Much less exhortative is the soft or playful pop rap of MC Hammer, DJ Jazzy Jeff and the Fresh Prince, Tone Loc, and Heavy D. In contrast, during the late 1980s, Ice T, Ice Cube, Snoop Doggy Dogg, Tupac Shakur, and other Los Angeles rap groups from Compton and Watts, two economically depressed areas of the city, developed "gangster rap," a West Coast style that narrates the "Inner City Blues" realities of the typical young, poor, black male in the ghetto. Because these rappers frequently and irresponsibly celebrate gang violence and violence against women and use offensive and misogynist language, they have come under heavy attack by the media and various national organizations. For example, in 1995 Black Women for Political Action helped in pressuring Time-Warner to sell its rap label. However, female rappers like Queen Latifah and Monie Love have disagreed with this action. Although these women have called some male rap groups misogynists, they have defended their male counterparts' constitutional right to create their music. Simultaneously, Queen Latifah and Monie Love and other groups have countered the negative messages of the gangster griots by rapping about issues that plague the hip-hop generation, such as the dangers of teenage pregnancy, AIDS, gang warfare, drug use, and dropping out of school. The death of Tupac Shakur, who was slain on September 13, 1996, has underscored the need of these rappers to continue to deliver positive social messages to the young black masses.

John Wideman, in an essay titled "The Architectonics of Fiction" (1990), says, "Today, rap, for all its excesses and commercializations, reasserts the African core of black music: polyrhythmic dance beat, improvisational spontaneity, incantory use of the word to name, blame, shame, and summon power, the obligation of ritual to instruct and enthuse." Moreover, in his 1990 novel *Philadelphia Fire,* one of his central characters is a rap artist, J. B., which gave Wideman a chance to write rap songs for the novel. Although rap has informed his writing and the works of Amiri Baraka, Etheridge Knight, and Sherley Anne Williams, its main influence in the artistic world seems to be on filmmakers such as Spike Lee, John Singleton, and Matty Rich. In Lee's movie *Do the Right Thing* (1989), the character Radio Raheem's boom box, playing rap, permeates the atmosphere of the film. In the August 1991 issue of the film magazine *Sight and Sound,* Singleton, director of *Boyz N the Hood* (1991), says of the bleak black city culture that he portrays, "I'm just saying the same thing that the hard-core rappers are saying. They say it on wax, and I'm saying it on film."

Folktales

Besides the rappers, many other griots have kept the black oral tradition alive. As seen in Daryl C. Dance's impressive and representative collection of contemporary black folklore *Shuckin and Jivin* (1978), African Americans from all social and economic levels still enjoy telling tales that have been passed down from generation to generation. Most of the stories, however, are adaptations of old ones. As Dance explains, "A new folktale is a rare phenomenon. Certain tellers add new dimensions and original perspectives to many of the old tales." Further, she notes that many of the contemporary stories, especially those from younger African Americans who have become embittered and frustrated by the continuum of racism within American society, "are frequently more blatantly hostile, sadistic, and obscene than are some of the older tales." These characteristics are quite apparent in most of the tales, including fascinating "bad nigger" hero and animal fables; didactic tales of origins; humorous stories about black preachers, sex, and outsmarting "whitey"; and lurid conjure and ghost tales. Most conjure and ghost tales have virtually disappeared from the black folklore repertoire, however, while lewd tales about badman heroes, religion, the white man, and women remain among the most popular types. In this sense, black folklore serves the same functions today as it did during slavery: it provides entertainment and dispenses folk wisdom, while it simultaneously expresses aggression and rebellion against societal oppression.

Unlike rap music, black folktales have been featured prominently in the works of contemporary literary figures such as John Oliver Killens, Toni Morrison, Ishmael Reed, Alice Walker, August Wilson, Randall Kenan,

Charles Johnson, Virginia Hamilton, and others. These authors have decided to retell the communal tales, emphasizing at once their cultural uniqueness and human range. They tease out the wisdom of their cultural myths. For example, in Morrison's *Song of Solomon* (1977), the hero, Milkman, finds himself only after he decodes the stories and songs of the black oral tradition. Reed, in his retelling of the "Railroad Bill" folktale in his poem "Railroad Bill, a Conjure Man," creates a contemporary "bad nigger"—a wild, rule-breaking black male. And Wilson, in his play *Joe Turner's Come and Gone* (1987), evokes the haunting power of a ghost story through his creation of the black folk character "the shiny man." In recent years, writers such as Reed, Johnson, and Walker have rediscovered voodoo, a folk religion of African origins. By taking on this belief, these authors demonstrate that Christianity is only one manifestation of black religiosity in the New World. The old-time religion surfaces in Charles Burnett's film *To Sleep with Anger* (1990), where the old folks hang on to the old ways under the disapproving eyes of modern Christianity in Los Angeles.

The contemporary period will be remembered for its energetic fusion of folk, popular, and high art with advanced technology, along with its dangerous orientation away from the historical markers of slavery and abolitionism as the preeminent metaphors for African American folk existence. Old boundaries have dropped away, allowing the contemporary black literary artist, from the New Black Aesthetic and the New Breed to the New Wave—back and forth in call and response—to create a wondrous and variously new black song within the call for individual lyricism, challenged still by the historical necessity to swim once more against the reactionary tide.

Critical Theory and Debate: The Black Aesthetic or Black Poststructuralism?

What's Goin' On?

As previously mentioned, during the late 1960s and early 1970s a group of black scholars and writers developed the sociopoetics called the Black Aesthetic, a black criterion for judging the validity and/or beauty of a work of art. Larry Neal, Amiri Baraka, and the other New Black critics, including Maulana Karenga, Clarence Major, Addison Gayle, Jr., Hoyt Fuller, Stephen Henderson, Carolyn Fowler, and Sarah Webster Fabio, rejected Eurocentric standards applied to literary works by American blacks and instead demanded that African American literature be judged according to an aesthetic grounded in African American culture. Dismissing the notion of Immanuel Kant and his inheritors that form, not content, is the imperative of art, these critics insisted that in order to have value, black art must address the sociopolitical and spiritual needs of African American people. Like W.E.B. Du Bois, Richard Wright, Ann Petry, and others before them, they insisted that, above all else, black literature must contribute to the cause of black liberation. But with the new black aestheticians, the old theme of liberation took on new meaning. In short, they raised the process of self-definition—of black racial consciousness and black group solidarity—of the Harlem Renaissance and Reformation periods to the level of revolutionary thought. They called for black art to serve as a revolutionary weapon, not merely in polemics against Euro-American psychological and cultural domination but also in reinterpretation of the African American life experience.

These theorists eschewed "protest" literature, which in previous periods was directed toward a white audience and appealed to white morality. Rather, they insisted upon an art of liberating vision—a black way of seeing the world—because, as Clarence Major maintains in his 1967 essay "A Black Criterion," "seeing the world through white eyes from a black soul causes death." In *Understanding the New Black Poetry* (1972), Stephen Henderson explains, "The present movement [the Black Arts Movement] is different from the Harlem Renaissance in the extent of its attempt to speak directly to Black people *about themselves* in order to move them toward self-knowledge and collective freedom." Thus, placing their stamp of disapproval firmly on the T. S. Eliot–Ezra Pound notion that art should be reserved for the intellectual few, Baraka and Neal, in their landmark black nationalist anthology *Black Fire* (1968), contended that the black literary artist must make black art more meaningful by taking it to the black masses. In the Afterword to the work, Neal declared, "the artist and the political activist are one." Accordingly, Maulana Karenga insisted in his essay "Black Art: Mute Matter Given Force and Function" (1968), black art must be "functional," "collective," and "committed."

This "art for people's sake," all of the New Black critics agreed, should be judged according to its presentation of the traditions and styles stemming from African and African American cultures. Thus, as Neal highlighted in his seminal essay "The Black Arts Movement" (1968), these aestheticians called for "a separate symbolism, mythology, critique, and iconology," which emphasized the cultural heritage of African Americans, particularly African survival and the oral tradition. Understanding that rhythmic assertion has always characterized black cultural assertion, they underscored the need for the black artist to use spirituals, gospels, blues, and jazz rhythms, along with various other aspects of the folk culture, as instruments for the revolution. Not since the 1930s had black art and politics been so tightly joined.

These aesthetic assumptions were immediately challenged during the years of the conservative Nixon administration, not only by the traditional white literary establishment but also by a new group of black academic critics who, as products of affirmative action programs, entered the faculties at white colleges and universities throughout the country. Desiring acceptance and integration into the mainstream of American life and the financial rewards that accompany it, some of these black academicians, especially from Ivy League schools, rejected what they considered to be the purely racial and sociopolitical approach of Black Aesthetic critics in favor of what, in a Eurocentric sense, is a literary one. For example, Yale University critic Robert Stepto, who coedited *Afro-American Literature: The Reconstruction of Instruction* (1979) with his colleague Dexter Fisher, proposed that African American texts should be examined by applying the Eurocentric literary method called structuralism. It is a theory built on the literary model advanced by the French scholar Ferdinand de Saussure, who postulated that language, rather than social, political, and historical events and forces, shapes the world. "[N]o ideas are established in advance," Saussure maintains in *Course in General Linguistics* (1916; reprinted London, 1974), "and nothing is distinct before the introduction of linguistic structure." Structuralism is reminiscent of the New Criticism, the school of literary thought advocated in the late 1940s to the 1960s by white conservative Southern Agrarians Robert Penn Warren, John Crowe Ransom, Allen Tate, and others who believed that literature should be judged on its own formal structure without reference to social, political, or other external values.

Also calling for a structuralist or linguistic approach to the literature is the influential University of Pennsylvania professor Houston A. Baker, the author of *The Journey Back: Issues in Black Literature and Criticism* (1980) and *Blues Ideology, and Afro-American Literature: A Vernacular Theory* (1984). Applying his scientific method, or what he terms an "anthropology of art," Baker attempts in these highly complex, obscure works to establish a middle ground between structuralism and Black Aesthetic assumptions. According to Vincent Leitch, in *American Literary Criticism from the Thirties to the Eighties* (1988), Baker relies on anthropological structuralism because "he envisions culture as a linguistic discourse based on systematic rules, principles, and conventions, all of which regularize the social production of art." Although "Baker locates black works of literature within *black* American culture," Leitch adds, "[w]hat he sought was a means of depoliticizing, deidealizing, and depersonalizing the powerful premises propounded by the Black Aestheticians."

Further targeting the Black Aesthetic through a structuralist theoretical approach to African American literature has been Harvard University professor Henry Louis "Skip" Gates, Jr. With his critical studies *Black Literature and Literary Theory* (1984) and *The Signifying Monkey: Theory of African American Literary Criticism* (1988), Gates has emerged as the most powerful African American literary critic since Alain Locke. More influential than Locke ever was, Gates has become, in Haki Madhubuti's words in *Claiming*

Earth: Race, Rage, Rape, Redemption (1994), "a modern day, 21st century, updated Booker T. Washington." Madhubuti observes,

> Never before in the history of Black-white relationships in the United States has an African American been given such unrestricted, unlimited access to influential white journals, newspapers, magazines, and quarterlies. His articles and reviews are not just filler material, equal to that of other scholars or writers, but are often the cover pieces—giving Mr. Gates a tremendous amount of influence and power in the arena of ideas.

Gates has become virtually an "unchallenged authority" in the area of black studies, who, Madhubuti adds,

> is frequently called upon to pass judgment on the 'new negroes' . . . assistant professors fighting for tenure, young writers looking for publishing contracts and grants, and first book authors looking for a jacket blurb to help sales . . . and his stamp of approval may be the difference between a fast or slow future.

But nowhere has Gates's influence been more keenly felt than in the field of African American literature. As with Locke during the Harlem Renaissance, Gates has towered over the New Black Renaissance. In recent years, he, along with fellow critic Houston Baker, took over the editorship of two leading black literary journals, *Callaloo* and *African American Review* (formerly *Black American Literature Forum*), thus controlling both canon and voice of African American critical and literary thought. But unlike Locke, Gates has insisted on an ahistorical view of African American literature and has said that "a literary text is a linguistic event; its application must be an activity of close textual analysis." In an earlier piece, "Preface to Blackness: Text and Pretext," from Robert Stepto and Dexter Fisher's *Afro-American Literature: The Reconstruction of Instruction* (1979), Gates contends "that the correspondence of content between a writer and his world is less significant to literary criticism than is a correspondence of organization of structure, for a relation of content may be a mere reflection of prescriptive, scriptural canon." He concludes that "black literature is a verbal art like other verbal arts. 'Blackness' is not a material object or an event but a metaphor." According to Gates, "If he [the black writer] does embody a 'Black Aesthetic,' then it can be measured not by 'content,' but by a complex structure of meanings."

As a result of Gates's enormous power over the academic world of African American studies, very few literary critics have publicly criticized him. However, Deborah E. McDowell, professor of English at the University of Virginia, has suggested in her essay "The Changing Same: Generational Connections and Black Women Novelists" (1987), that Gates, in his lack of intertextual aggression in examining works by black women fiction writers, has made a particularly male theory of African American intertextuality, that is, a rather selective male theory of black literary history. But his strongest opposition to date has come from black scholar Joyce A. Joyce, professor of black studies at Chicago State University and author of the 1995 American Book Award–winning text *Warriors, Conjurers, and Priests: Defining African-Centered Literary Criticism* (1994). The heated critical debate between Joyce, on the one side, and Gates and Baker, on the other, that appeared in the pages of the literary journal *New Literary History* (Winter 1987) struck at the very heart of contemporary conceptions of black art and of race-gender-class issues within the black community. In the essays "The Black Canon: Reconstructing Black American Literary Criticism" and "Who the Cap Fit," Joyce assesses the critical practices of both Gates and Baker. A Black Aesthetic critic, Joyce passionately attacks them for their black poststructuralism, which she finds to be not only obfuscated but, more importantly, pernicious because it is a movement toward operating in a "historical vacuum." As she points out, "The Black creative writer has continuously struggled to assert his or her real self and to establish a connection between the self and the people outside that self." Moreover, she says, she "cannot fathom why a Black critic would trust that the master [the poststructuralist] would provide the African American with tools through which one can seek independence." For Joyce, black poststructuralism is an acceptance of "elitist American values," a literary theory that widens the gap between intellectuals and "those masses of Blacks whose lives are still stifled by oppressive environmental, intellectual phenomena." Above all, she criticizes Gates and Baker for dismissing "race as an important element of literary analysis of Black literature" and is outraged by Gates's position that blackness is a mere metaphor. She insists that these critics are irresponsible in their black political commitment, as demonstrated in their critical practice. Finally, she claims that they are alienated from their own culture. Unlike these Ivy League scholars, she sees the black critic not simply as an explicator of texts but also as "a point of consciousness" for the history of black people.

With equal passion, Gates and Baker responded with patriarchal certainty about their African American place in the mainstream canon of American literature. In his essay "'What's Love Got to Do with It?': Critical Theory, Integrity, and the Black Idiom," Gates says that "what Joyce Joyce erroneously thinks of as our 'race' is our *culture*"—that is, that race is a metaphor but black culture is a reality that he both believes in and loves. Gates maintains that the black critic's responsibility is to "translate [contemporary theory] into the black idiom" and identify "indigenous black principles" of critical discourse. The African American experience, in other words, is essentially a linguistic exercise. Baker, in his essay "In Dubious Battle," defends poststructuralism as a radical way of undercutting Western hegemony, of maintaining "a thoroughgoing critique of Western philosophy and its privileges such as colonialism, slavery, racism, and so on." He insists that this recent criticism seems arcane to Joyce because it is "a new sound."

Certainly, all three scholars have critical shortcomings. Joyce underestimates the importance of language, Gates undermines the primacy of "content" in art, and both Gates and Baker attempt to use a textual model to encompass an entire culture. Equally important, all of them overlook the significance of rhythm as an aesthetic principle. As novelist-theorist Sylvia Wynter writes in her study "Ethnopoetics-Sociopoetics?" (1976), "Rhythm as an aesthetic principle not only synthesizes the dialectic of form and content, but makes impossible the separation of form from sense perception, since form is born out of and concomitant with the experiencing of the senses, rather than being a priori." Put simply, blackness is much more than a book. In particular, Gates does not seem to understand the power of race (or, for that matter, racism)—metaphor or not—in American society. To quote the black philosopher Cornel West, "Race matters."

Moreover, to the black poststructuralist's charge that the New Black Aesthetic is political, one can easily respond that poststructuralism, like the New Criticism, is in its own way political; it is a denial of history, an implicit acceptance of the status quo, and an imposition of Eurocentric ideas of structure. Certainly, as Joyce posits, the Black Aesthetic not only serves a significant sociopolitical and literary function but also constitutes a questioning of basic aesthetic assumptions at a time when they clearly need to be questioned.

Voices of the New Black Aesthetic

Say It Loud, I'm Black and I'm Proud

Although Larry Neal, Maulana Karenga, and others were significant theorists of the new aesthetic, Amiri Baraka was its prime mover. As William J. Harris in *The Poetry and Poetics of Amiri Baraka* (1985) explains, Baraka "was the main artist-intellectual responsible for shifting the emphasis of contemporary black literature from an integrationist art conveying a raceless and classless vision to a literature rooted in the black experience." Baraka, in his 1966 essay "The Legacy of Malcolm X, and the Coming of the Black Nation," said, "The Black artist is desperately needed to change the images his people identify with, by asserting Black feeling, Black mind, Black judgment." This seminal essay influenced a generation of writers by succinctly sketching the role of the black nationalist artist. As polemicist, playwright, poet, and practical politician, Baraka was hailed in the 1970 edition of *Negro Digest* (later called *Black World*) for having "set in motion the whole New Black Arts Movement."

By the mid-1960s, Baraka (then LeRoi Jones) had founded the Black Arts Repertory Theater in Harlem, which marked the beginning of the movement and inspired the creation of black community theaters across the country. He established the black revolutionary tradition in theater with his 1964 plays *Dutchman, The Toilet,* and *The Slave.* In *Dutchman,* Baraka embraces and legitimizes revolutionary violence when the protagonist, Clay, proclaims, "Murder. Just murder! Would make us all sane." By the late sixties, dozens of playwrights had extended this dramatic tradition. Ed Bullins in *Goin' a Buffalo* (1966), Douglass Turner Ward in *Happy Endings* (1966), Adrienne Kennedy in *A Rat's Mass* (1968), and Lonnie Elders in the best play of the group, *Ceremonies in Dark Old Men* (1969), made powerful statements about political, social, and economic injustices designed to further black revolution. Among the other noteworthy New Black playwrights were Carol Freeman, Roy Milner, Aisha Hughes, Jimmy Garrett, Charles Patterson, and William Patterson.

At the height of the Black Arts Movement, Baraka wrote politically charged poetry that greatly influenced the African American literary world and a generation of young writers. In his poem "Black Art," from *Black Magic Poetry* (1969), he called for "poems that kill," for black art to function as "fists," "daggers," and "guns" against racism, police brutality, and political corruption in America and to clean out the world for virtue and love. In general, Baraka and the other New Black Poets functioned as poet-seers, poet-priests instructing black people in the new rites—teaching them how to be black, how to love themselves by stripping Eurocentric values and ideas out of their minds and lives, how to fight for black rights, and how to build a black nation. The other new poets included Haki Madhubuti (Don L. Lee), Sonia Sanchez, Carolyn Rodgers, Nikki Giovanni, Lucille Clifton, Jayne Cortez, Askia Muhammad Touré, Sarah Webster Fabio, Eugene Perkins, Lorenzo Thomas, Conrad Kent Rivers, Clarence Major, Gil Scott-Heron, The Last Poets (Abiodun Oyewole, Alafia Pudimand, and Omar Ben Hassen), and scores of other writers.

These poets, like the black abolitionist poets of the nineteenth century, took their poetry to the people. But instead of using the platform and the pulpit as their nineteenth-century predecessors did, they used the bar, the street corner, the school, and the community center. Also like the antislavery poets, the New Black Poets were oral artists who brought audiences to their feet. In *Black Fire* (1968), Larry Neal likens their performance style to "the way James Brown is a performer—loud, gaudy, and racy." Like the "Godfather of Soul," these contemporary black griots channeled jagged jazz rhythms and driving blues and gospel beats, hypnotic call and response cadences, and dramatic and incantatory declamations into their transcribed oral verse to deliver their revolutionary messages to the people. Since the African American on the street was the intended audience, these poets used direct, provocative language. Nikki Giovanni taunts, "nigger / Can you kill / Can you run a protestant down with your / 68 El Dorado." Haki Madhubuti exhorts, "change change your change change change / your nigger mind." And Sonia Sanchez summons, "rise up blk / people / de dum da da da da / move straight in yo / blkness / da dum da da da da / step over the wite / ness / that was yesterday / weeeeeeee are toooooooday." Giovanni was in the forefront of the new poets who chanted poems of militant revolt on record albums. Continuing the tradition of performance poets Giovanni, Baraka, Madhubuti, Sanchez, and Carolyn Rodgers were The Last Poets, a group of young men whose albums were the most commercially successful of this group of writers.

A good example of the new black poetry is Rodgers's "U Name This One":

> let uh revolution come. uh
> state of peace is not known to me
>   anyway
> since i grew uhround in chi town
>   where
> howlin wolf howled in the tavern on 47th st. . . .
> let uh revolution come.
> couldn't be no action like what
> i dun already seen.

Although the poem re-creates street language and idiom to inspire mass revolt, it employs avant-garde techniques such as unconventional spelling and free verse line breaks to achieve the ends. The poem, which resounds the bleak "Inner City Blues" realities of the ghetto world, makes free use of urban and black musical references. Instead of liberal solutions, the work calls for revolutionary ones that will transform American society.

Whereas Rodgers, Baraka, Madhubuti, and the others functioned as leaders and teachers of the new rites, Etheridge Knight saw himself as one and the same with the other participants (the black masses) in the circle of ritual. Although he shared with the other New Black Poets the bond of black cultural identity (the bond of the oppressed and the bond formed by black folklore), he emerged from a second consciousness of community, a community of criminals and social outcasts, which Frantz Fanon, in *The Wretched of the Earth* (1961), calls "the lumpen proletariat," the most "wretched of the earth." As Patricia Liggins Hill observes in her essay "The Violent Space" (*Black American Literature Forum*, 1980), ". . . Knight's major contribution to the New Black Aesthetic derived from this second sense of consciousness, which favorably reinforced his strong collective mentally as a black artist and his close identification with black folks. He brought his prison consciousness, a consciousness in which the individual sense is institutionally destroyed and the self is merely one number among many, to the new black poetry." As a result, much of Knight's poetry is distinguished by its heavy reliance on a variety of traditional communal black art forms such as African musical structures, rural and urban blues, blues ballads, and toasts. By using these traditional black folk idioms, he was able to merge his consciousness with that of the black masses.

The genre of the black autobiographical prison narrative popularized earlier in the 1960s by Malcolm X was enhanced by Eldridge Cleaver's *Soul on Ice* (1968) and George Jackson's *Soledad Brother* (1970). Young black revolutionary novelists also delivered strong, aggressive, militant messages to primarily black audiences. John A. Williams, one of the angriest but most powerful voices, won international acclaim with *The Man Who Cried I Am* (1967), a novel about attempts by a group of black people to thwart a global white conspiracy to commit black genocide.

Voices of the New Breed

What Freedom Means

With the emerging conservatism of the Nixon administration, the New Black writers and theorists had come to the conclusion that directly confronting an American society that refused to recognize Black Aesthetic values and ideals was all but futile. Hence, critic Addison Gayle, Jr., called for "a new table of laws." In his essay "Cultural Strangulation: Black Literature and the White Aesthetic" (1971), Gayle declared,

> In similar iconoclastic fashion the proponents of a Black Aesthetic, the idol smashers of America, call for a set of rules by which Black literature and art is to be judged and evaluated. For the historical practice of bowing to other men's gods and definitions has produced a crisis of the highest magnitude, and brought us, culturally, to the limits of racial armageddon. The trends must be reversed.

"The acceptance of the phrase 'Black is Beautiful,'" Gayle continued, "is the first step in the old table of the laws and the construction of new ones, for the phrase flies in the face of the whole ethos of the white aesthetic." Thus, as an artistic style, the Black Aesthetic came to be viewed by several black writers and critics as a poetic constructed on the idioms, symbolism, imagery, mythology, and iconology that reflect the uniqueness of the African American life experience. The following list of seven Black Aesthetic categories offered by Haki Madhubuti in his 1971 essay "Toward a Definition: Black Poetry of the Sixties (After LeRoi Jones)" is a good example of this effort:

1. polyrhythmic, uneven, short, and explosive lines
2. intensity; depth, yet simplicity; spirituality, yet flexibility
3. irony; humor; signifying
4. sarcasm—new comedy
5. direction; positive movement; teaching, nation building
6. subject matter—concrete; reflects a collective and personal lifestyle
7. music; the unique use of vowels and consonants with the developed rap demands that poetry be read, and read aloud.

In the early 1970s, a New Breed of African American writers, most of whom had emerged during the Searing Sixties, began to garner critical attention, each in his or her distinctive voice and with a unique black way of seeing the world. Although they were as committed to the black liberation cause as were Amiri Baraka and other black revolutionary writers, they did not deal with it as directly. In general, they were more subtle, more introspective in mood and tone. As chanters of the "Cross Road Blues," the New Breed ranged from proponents of the Civil Rights Movement such as Ernest Gaines, Audre Lorde, and Alice Walker to champions of the Black Power Movement such as William Melvin Kelley, Mari Evans, and June Jordan. But even though Kelley, Evans, and Jordan were black cultural nationalists, they did not wave a black flag. As with the other writers of the New Breed, they were less concerned about a revolution in the streets than a revolution in consciousness.

Consequently, like the Harlem Renaissance writers before them, the New Breed focused primarily on the dramatization of the black life experience and the fostering of black cultural identity and pride through their conscious use of black folk materials, black dialect, and the language of the street. Many of the writers chose the novel form, which added possibilities for perceiving and portraying the realities of African American life and history. For example, Melvin Kelley, whose first novel was *A Different Drummer* (1962), called upon the folk tradition, including the oral narrative with comic dimensions, in *dem* (1967) and *Dunsford Travels Everywhere* (1970) to create fables about freedom, courage, and the innate beauty and strength of black culture. Ernest Gaines, who first appeared on the literary scene in 1964 with *Catherine Carmier,* explored the limitations and possibilities of southern rural black folk culture in *The Autobiography of Miss Jane Pittman* (1971), his saga of southern blacks from Reconstruction to the Civil Rights Movement as seen through the eyes of an elderly black woman. Ishmael Reed, whose earliest fictional works were *The Free Lance Pallbearers* (1968) and *Yellow Back Radio Broke Down* (1969), continued to rely on African mythology, voodoo and hoodoo, black heroes, and the vernacular of the street, television, and black music in his neoslave narrative *Flight to Canada* (1976). Albert Murray created a blues hero in *Train Whistle Guitar* (1974), a figure based on the blues musician, whose improvisations symbolically dramatize his or her ability to improvise in the face of adversity. Alice Walker, Toni Morrison, and Gayl Jones published their first novels in the 1970s. Walker's *The Third Life of Grange Copeland* (1970), Morrison's *The Bluest Eye* (1970), and Jones's *Corregidora* (1975) deal with the devastating effects of racism on the black family in America. Morrison's book, Trudier Harris in *Fiction and Folklore: The Novels of Toni Morrison* (1991) explains, "is the story of African-American folk culture in process"; Walker's novel is a skillfully crafted tale of three generations of one black family as it migrates from the South to the North; and Jones's work is what Harris calls a "blues narrative," a psychological drama of the powerful impact of the slave system on one black family's ancestral lineage.

But unlike the Harlem group, the New Breed did not depict black self-awareness as a means of recognition and acceptance into the American literary mainstream and middle-class "whiteness." As with the revolutionary writers, these literary artists emphasized the portrayal of the African American experience without explicit regard for the conventions of Eurocentric aesthetics and sensibilities. In his anthology *19 Neocrancer from Now* (1970), Ishmael Reed states, "What distinguishes the present crop of Afro-American and Black writers from their predecessors is a marked independence from Western form . . . [and, furthermore,] anyone who told these writers to 'stick to [white] verse' as Max Eastman advised Claude McKay would have to pick up his teeth."

The New Breed writers continued to reaffirm the sense of black self by investing their works with the distinctive styles, rhythms, and colors of their own culture and community. In poetry, for example, Reed, Al Young, Michael Harper, Quincy Troupe, Calvin Hernton, A. B. Spellman, Sterling Plumpp, David Henderson, and Tom Weatherly created adaptations of jazz rhythms from musicians such as John Coltrane and Ornette Coleman; Young, Sherley Anne Williams, Tom Dent, Ted Joans, Eugene Redmond, Jay Wright, Henry Dumas, and several other writers grounded their verse in the blues aesthetic; and Mari Evans, Audre Lorde, and Lance Jeffers blended rich African and African American folk idioms in their free verse to celebrate their African heritage. In short fiction, Toni Cade Bambara explored the meaning of black ancestry through the use of black folk speech and nontraditional narrators in her collection of stories *Gorilla My Love* (1972); Gayl Jones created poignant, psychologically intense tales of frustration and black poverty in *White Rat* (1977); and James McPherson portrayed the ironies and paradoxes of African American life by focusing on urban black communities in the North in his Pulitzer Prize–winning collection *Elbow Room*

(1977). In drama, Joseph Walker demonstrated the sociopsychological effects of racism on human consciousness in *River Niger* (1973), and Ntozake Shange created a new form, the choreopoem, for the professional theater in *for colored girls who have considered suicide when the rainbow is enuf* (1975) and *Spell #7* (1979).

Also in the 1970s, autobiography became increasingly important as a mode for expressing the new sense of the black self and the uniqueness of African American group culture and history. The self that Maya Angelou celebrates in *I Know Why the Caged Bird Sings* (1970) is one that has survived an abusive childhood, and the self that Alex Haley portrays in *Roots* (1976) is one that becomes revitalized after the discovery of his African family history. This semiautobiographical saga inspired a generation of Americans, black and white, to trace their cultural roots and actualized the power premises of the Black Aesthetic. It demonstrated not only the value of the oral tradition but also the use of history as an important tool for instilling black cultural identity, self-esteem, and pride.

Women's Voices of Self-Definition

Since 1970, the year that marked the publication of Maya Angelou's critically acclaimed autobiography, Alice Walker's and Toni Morrison's first novels, and Toni Cade Bambara's landmark anthology *The Black Woman,* African American women writers have moved to the forefront of the American and African American literary stage. Like the leading black male writers of the sixties, these women have written in defiance of white American cultural assumptions by asserting black culture and black values. In their art, they have celebrated African American discourse styles, habits of interpersonal relationships, history, myth, and music.

As mentioned earlier, Angelou, Walker, Morrison, and Bambara, like other African American women who participated in the Black Arts Movement during the late 1960s, used their Civil Rights experiences as the source for their creative writings in the 1970s. They, along with Gwendolyn Brooks, Paule Marshall, Audre Lorde, Mari Evans, June Jordan, Sonia Sanchez, Nikki Giovanni, Lucille Clifton, Jayne Cortez, and Sherley Anne Williams, bridged the Black Arts Movement and the Black Women's Literary Movement. Being inspired largely by an ever-growing black readership generated by the Black Arts Movement and supported by the women's movement and mainstream commercial publishers, these and more recent black women writers have been able not only to address a primarily black audience but also to treat subjects familiar to the African American community and pertinent to its continued development.

The Black Women's Literary Movement, which has been in full force since the mid-seventies, should be regarded as a "revolution within a Revolution." As Stephen Henderson, in his foreword to Mari Evans's *Black Women Writers: A Critical Evaluation* (1984), explains,

> The contradictions between knowledge and action that surfaced in the Civil Rights and Black Power Movements forced sensitive and intelligent women to reexamine their own positions vis-à-vis the men and to conclude that they were the victims not only of racial injustice but of sexual arrogance tantamount to dual colonialism—one from without, the other from within, the Black community.

Consequently, several black women writers, influenced by the predominantly white women's liberation movement, urged women to protest all forms of sexism. Often black male writers were sexist, and there was much that was retrograde in the Black Arts Movement.

It was in response to blatantly sexist statements that Toni Bambara edited *The Black Woman* (1970). This innovative work includes poetry, short stories, and essays by a variety of black women writers, including Audre Lorde, Alice Walker, Sherley Anne Williams, Paule Marshall, Nikki Giovanni, Abbey Lincoln, and others. Even leading white feminists, says Bambara in *The Black Woman,* were not equipped to understand, much less to explain, the feelings and the social situation of black women. Bambara's charges of racism on the part of white feminists echo the concerns raised by Frances Watkins Harper and other black women activists more than a century ago. Hence, black women activists and writers have been singing a variation of the "Cross Road Blues," assailing racism in the women's rights movement, on the one hand, and sexism in the Black Power Movement, on the other. As black feminist Barbara Smith observes in *Home Girls: A Black Feminist Anthology* (1983), "It was our experience and disillusionment within these liberation movements, as well as experience on the periphery of the white male left, that led to the need to develop a politics that was antiracist, unlike those of white women, and anti-sexist, unlike those of Black and white men."

By the mid-1970s, black women writers, especially the novelists, had delved into many facets of the interrelationship of racism and sexism in American society. Although racism is an ever-present social force affecting the lives of their characters, contemporary black women novelists, unlike the major black male fiction writers of the period, have continued the Zora Neale Hurston tradition of focusing on interactions within the black community rather than its reaction to the white community. This concentration has allowed Bambara, Morrison, Walker, Marshall, Jones, and other women writers to address at once the sexism that exists in the African American community in particular and the narrow definitions of womanhood ascribed to females by American society in general. Collectively, they portray a collage of wounded, suffocating, often perverse women—neurotic, psychotic, raped, rebellious, and suicidal heroines who have been victimized to a great extent by the restricted mother–wife–male lover roles imposed on them by their communities. Not only do their novels reveal that the African American community's attitudes toward women must change, but they also show, directly or indirectly, through their varied depictions of the inextricable relationship between the black woman and her community that the black community's survival and growth rest largely on its acceptance, understanding, and appreciation of black female self-definition and empowerment. In novels like Morrison's *Sula* (1974) and Walker's *Meridian* (1976), for instance, when the black woman's creativity is stifled, the black community suffers. In Bambara's *The Salt Eaters* (1980), when the black woman's personal transformation takes place, her community's regeneration becomes possible.

Of equal significance were the plays of the period written by African American women. Since Ntozake Shange's candid exploration of black women's emotional and physical needs in *for colored girls* (1975), no topic dealing with black women's sexuality has been taboo on the American stage. For instance, Aishah Rahman in *Unfinished Women Cry in No Man's Land While a Bird Dies in a Gilded Cage* (1977) and P. J. Gibson in *Brown Silk and Magenta Sunsets* (1985) probe the problem of black teenage pregnancy; Alexis Deveaux in *The Tapestry* (1976) and Gibson in *Long Since Yesterday* (1985) treat black lesbianism and homosexual relationships frankly and with profundity.

Also since the 1970s, black women theorists and critics, most of whom are from the academy, have attempted to formulate new definitions and conceptual models for African American women who seek empowerment. In a large camp are black feminist critics Barbara Smith, Cheryl Walls, bell hooks, Barbara Christian, Mary Helen Washington, Gloria T. Hull, Claudia Tate, Hortense Spillers, Deborah E. McDowell, and Nellie McKay. Although these women differ on various issues, a *black feminist* is, in general, a woman who insists on the simultaneity of gender, race, and class even though her obvious alignment with feminism is dictated by the fact that most of her energies go into the gender question. Closely akin to the black feminist is the *womanist,* as defined by Alice Walker in her landmark collection of essays *In Search of Our Mothers' Gardens* (1983). According to Walker, a womanist is "a black feminist or feminist of color . . . who loves other women, sexually and/or nonsexually. Appreciates and prefers women's culture . . . [and] sometimes loves individual men, sexually and nonsexually. . . . Committed to survival and wholeness of entire people, male or female." However, with the exception of Walker's inclusion of women of color, there is little differentiation between the womanist and the black feminist. Walker states, "Womanist is to feminist as purple to lavender." Other womanist writers and critics are Sherley Anne Williams and Dorothy Tsuruta.

An *Africana womanist*, as defined by theorist Clenora Hudson-Weems in her book *Africana Womanism* (1993), is a black woman activist who is family centered rather than female centered and who focuses on race and class empowerment before gender empowerment. Of all the theoretical models, Hudson-Weems's best describes the racially based perspective of many black women's rights advocates, beginning with Maria W. Stewart and Frances W. Harper in the early nineteenth century. Besides Hudson-Weems, some of the contemporary Africana womanist critics are Maria Mootry, Doreathea Drummond Mbalia, Ashi McIntyre, and Delores Aldridge. But in view of all of the nuances for the black woman, inside and outside of the academy, the terms *black feminist, womanist,* and *Africana womanist,* with all their connotations and denotations, are problematic. For if the African American woman (and women in general) seeks *real* empowerment, she will need new terminology to replace the words *woman,* which stems from and means the "woe of man," and *female,* which also denotes that woman is merely the extension of man.

Whether black feminist, womanist, or Africana womanist, African American women critics and writers have exposed the oppression of black literary women. Alice Walker played a crucial role in the resurrection of Zora Neale Hurston's works when she took a spiritual journey to Eatonville, Florida, to find this black literary foremother's unmarked grave. Additionally, Walker's "In Search of Our Mothers' Gardens," the pivotal essay in her development as a black woman writer, celebrates the "anonymous" black women in America—"our mothers [who] were stifled in their creativity." These older generations of sharecroppers, servants, and custodial workers, Walker argues, were limited to folk arts and crafts, such as gardening, quilting, and embroidering, to express their imaginations. Walker urges younger generations of black women artists to "retell these women's experiences and to find ourselves in the tales of our mothers and grandmothers." Thus she conveys her vision of black women's literature as rooted in the oral traditions of black people.

Furthermore, Barbara Smith, in her seminal essay "Toward a Black Feminist Criticism" (1977), accuses white feminist critics of the early seventies of rarely addressing black women's literature and expresses the anger of many black women writers at this glaring omission. She calls for a specific black feminist approach to the study of black women's literature. The method, she argues, embodies the realization that the politics of gender, as well as the politics of race and class, are crucially interlocking factors in the works of black women writers. She ultimately attempts to develop a black woman's theoretical approach. The one flaw of the Smith essay is her conflation of female and lesbian, assuming that the one is automatically the other. Nevertheless, she creates a critical space for later African American women scholars.

These African American women critics have responded to the call for the reexamination of history and texts by African American literary artists, especially women. Their voices are as diverse as black aestheticians Joanne Gabbin, Patricia Liggins Hill, Mary Rhodes Hoover, Joyce Ann Joyce, Sondra O'Neale, Eleanor Traylor, and Clenora Hudson-Weems; folklorists Daryl C. Dance and Trudier Harris; literary historians Melba Joyce Boyd, Hazel Carby, Gloria Wade Gayles, Maryemma Graham, and Paula Giddings; socialists Paulette Britten-Caldwell and Sylvia Wynter; and traditionalists Thadious Davis, Frances Smith Foster, Sandra Govan, Jennifer Jordan, Priscilla Ramsey, and Valerie Smith.

Several important anthologies have played a significant role in institutionalizing African American women in literature in university curricula. Closing out the decade of the seventies, a period of intense critical and literary activity by black women, was the anthology *Sturdy Black Bridges: Visions of Black Women in Literature* (1979) edited by Roseann Bell, Bettye Parker, and Beverly Guy-Sheftall. Similar in mission to Bambara's anthology, *Sturdy Black Bridges* includes all types of writing by all types of black women. Some of the entries are by black men on women writers. This anthology was the first one edited by African Americans to include discussions of African and Afro-Caribbean women's literature. Other noteworthy anthologies have been Mary Helen Washington's *Midnight Birds: Stories of Contemporary Black Women Writers* (1980), Erlene Stetson's *Black Sister: Poetry by Black American Women* (1981), Barbara Smith's *Home Girls* (1983), and Charlotte Watson Sherman's *Sisterfire: Black Womanist Fiction and Poetry* (1994).

African American women writers, the novelists in particular, have set the tone for the American literary scene of the 1980s and 1990s. Morrison, Alice Walker, Gloria Naylor, and Terry McMillan have given new life to the novel form with their distinctive use of the African American folk idiom and mythology and their continued emphasis on black female lives. Walker won the Pulitzer Prize for *The Color Purple* (1982) in 1983 and Naylor won the American Book Award for *The Women of Brewster Place* (1982) in 1983. Morrison was awarded the Pulitzer Prize for *Beloved* (1982) in 1988 and she became the first African American to receive the prestigious Nobel Prize for literature for the entire body of her work in 1993. These novelists' success, however, has also given rise to a body of misogynistic male criticism.

In spite of this condemnation, these women have won immense public approval. Millions of Americans watched the film version of Walker's *The Color Purple* and the television version of Naylor's *The Women of Brewster Place*. Even more popular with readers have been Terry McMillan's *Mama* (1987) and *Disappearing Acts* (1989), the latter of which sold 30,000 copies in hardcover and was auctioned off to a paperback house for $180,000.

McMillan and the other women authors have continued to meet the public's demand. All of them produced novels in 1992: McMillan's *Waiting to Exhale,* Walker's *Possessing the Secret of Joy,* Morrison's *Jazz,* and Naylor's *Bailey's Cafe. Waiting to Exhale,* the most popular of the four works, has had the most appeal to a growing black readership. Not only did it remain on the *New York Times* hardcover bestseller list for months in 1992 and return for additional months on the paperback bestseller list in 1993, but its paperback rights also were sold to a publisher for $2.64 million, one of the highest prices ever paid for a reprint. Moreover, the film version of the novel was so popular in 1995 that black women throughout the country gave *Waiting to Exhale* parties to celebrate black sisterhood. Even surpassing the initial sales of *Waiting to Exhale* has been McMillan's latest novel, *How Stella Got Her Groove Back* (1996). The book has sold over 850,000 copies in the first printing. As of September 1996, it has remained on *Publishers Weekly*'s Best Seller List for hardcover in fiction for four months. During 1996, both McMillian and Morrison gave dramatic readings of their latest novels at conferences and bookstores throughout the country. Morrison's novel tentatively titled *Paradise* is scheduled to be published in 1997.

The black woman writer in America was virtually ignored by critics and scholars until the beginning of the 1970s. In *American Visions* (February 1990), Will Nixon reported that Florence Howe, editor of the Feminist Press, said that "there were no black women writers allowed until the 70s despite the fact they had been writing for as long as the men or white women." Since then, the community of black women writers has not only assumed its rightful place in the American canon, but, more importantly, it has become a major international literary movement. It has evolved into a Pan-African movement energized by African and Caribbean women authors who are also producing quality literature at an accelerated pace.

Voices of the New Wave

Keep on Pushin'

In the 1980s and 1990s, another wave of African American writers appeared. This New Wave includes August Wilson, Charles Johnson, Rita Dove, John Wideman, Randall Kenan, Kenneth McClane, Melvin Dixon, Jamaica Kincaid, Yusef Komunyakaa, Pat Parker, Jewelle Gomez, J. California Cooper, Samuel Delany, Octavia Butler, Walter Mosley, Nathaniel Mackey, Greg Tate, Trey Ellis, Anna Deavere Smith, Wanda Coleman, Thulani Davis, Gerald Early, Kamaria Muntu, Malkia M. Moore, and many other exciting writers. More than any other group of contemporary black writers, they stand at the crossroads in American society, pulled in the direction of either integrationist or Afrocentric poetics.

They either are adherents of an integrated society or have been silenced by that society. Most of these artists were born between the late 1940s and the early 1960s. Many have received their undergraduate education from white universities; some have never been privileged to attend college at all. In the best position to benefit from hard-fought socioeconomic gains won by the Civil Rights and Black Power Movements, most of these younger writers are not only college educated but also at least second-generation middle class.

Because the experiences of many of the New Wave writers are not rooted in previous racial struggles, their literature bespeaks a different temperament with a milder, less militant voice or celebratory strain. Whereas black writers in the Civil Rights and Black Power Movements, as well as the movements that were built upon them in the 1970s and early 1980s, came to the fore as a result of political activism within the black community, several of the New Wave writers have had the nation's spotlight in the midst of the massive conservative backlash of the past two decades. Many of these writers have received lucrative faculty positions at prestigious universities and won coveted national awards and grants, while at the same time the Black Aesthetic writers and critics have largely been forced underground.

In his 1988 article in *College English* titled "The New Black Aesthetic Critics and Their Exclusion from American 'Mainstream' Criticism," black scholar Reginald Martin charts the way in which the academy has resisted Afrocentric creativity and literary criticism since the 1960s. He writes,

> One would search in vain in any venue of contemporary literary scholarship for the inclusion of new black aesthetic critics. The writings are most certainly not included in the readings of standard literary criticism anthologies; they are not taught in doctoral literary criticism courses, nor are they included in the criticism section of doctoral comprehensive examinations. One must ask, why is this work not a part of the standard critical corpus?

Martin concludes, "Nor can one reasonably suggest that the scholarship of the new black aesthetic writers is second-rate. It was and is amazingly well-written, well-researched, and ground-breaking."

The conservative wing of the New Wave has been influenced and supported by several interrelated factors. First of all, since the mid 1970s has come the silencing of major black aesthetic voices with Amiri Baraka's conversion to revolutionary Marxism and the deaths of Larry Neal and Addison Gayle Jr. Secondly, white intellectuals reacted to the political upheaval of the 1960s and 1970s by creating and promoting Henry Louis Gates, Jr., and other black poststructuralist critics. The rise of Gates and these other critics complemented the emergence of black neoconservative political voices. Another factor influencing the trend toward more conservative writing has been the difficulty of the black community in harnessing the millions of dollars needed to publish and distribute Afrocentric works, including textbooks, on a mass scale. Finally, the New Wave has been affected by the inability of the larger black community to reconcile the crossroads struggle between Martin and Malcolm—integration and separation.

In a collection of essays titled *Flyboy in the Buttermilk* (1992), New Wave critic Greg Tate writes that the new generation "feel[s] secure enough about black culture to claim art produced by non-blacks as part of their inheritance." Several black novelists prove Tate's position. For instance, by the early 1990s Samuel Delany and Octavia Butler had won the coveted Hugo Award for their impressive works in the genre of science fiction. In addition, Walter Mosley has produced a number of highly regarded mystery novels.

Other New Wave writers and critics have even revisited and praised black writers of the 1950s who had been maligned during the 1960s by the black cultural nationalists for being conservative, universalist, integrationist, and apolitical. Charles Johnson particularly praised Ralph Ellison when he accepted the 1990 National Book Award for Fiction for his neo-slave narrative *Middle Passage.* In the November 28, 1990, issue of the *New York Times,* he predicted that black fiction would shift "from narrow complaint to broad celebration" and away from "ideology in the narrowest political sense" to the broader concerns of "what it means to be a human being who is black." Like the other new integrationist writers, Johnson wants "a fiction of increasing intellectual and artistic generosity." John Wideman, winner of the prestigious PEN Faulkner Award for fiction in 1984, and Rita Dove, recipient of the 1987 Pulitzer Prize for poetry and recently national poet laureate for the Clinton administration, reach for these wider-ranging aesthetic subjects while recounting specific aspects of unique black experience.

In contrast, other New Wave writers have kept the faith with the Black Aesthetic. For example, August Wilson, winner of two Pulitzer Prizes, five New York Drama Critics Circle Awards, and a Tony Award, aims "to raise consciousness through theater." As he states in the preface to his *Three Plays* (1984),

> My own youth is fired in the kiln of black cultural nationalism as exemplified by Amiri Baraka in the sixties. It posited black Americans as coming from a long line of honorable people with a cultural and political history, a people of manners with a strong moral responsibility that had to be reclaimed by strengthening the elements that made it unique and by developing institutions

> for preserving and promoting it. The ideas of self-determination, self-respect, and self-defense which it espoused are still very much a part of my life as I sit down to write.

Just as Wilson was inspired by Baraka, exciting new community-based but largely unpublished writers have been influenced by the poet Askia Muhammad Touré and other leading writers of the Afrocentricity Movement. One such writer is Kamaria Muntu, who uses the iconology, mythology, and cultural cosmology of the African worldview "to lift, restore, to engage [the reader] in the vast dialectics of Black Woman experience in this present world she inherited without choice." Muntu, Touré, Malkia M. Moore, and many other Afrocentric poets continue the Black Aesthetic tradition of reading their poetry aloud to supportive audiences in the black community in order to revolutionize and activate black consciousness.

Likewise, critic Sydne Mahone has amassed a significant new collection of contemporary Afrocentric drama by black women writers titled *Moon Marked and Touched by the Sun* (1994). One of Mahone's accomplishments is to insist that the New Wave of black female dramatists be given their rightful place in the American canon. Of playwright Anna Deavere Smith, the author of the Obie Award–winning play *Fires in the Mirror* (1992), Mahone writes, "Not since the debuts of George C. Wolfe and Ntozake Shange has an 'experimental' play authored by an African American so astonished the theater community and commanded national attention." Using the power of the oral tradition and mask as mirror, Smith presents a unique and riveting dramatic form. Based on her interviews with a diverse group of men and women concerning timely events that have sparked controversy within the black community, she gives a solo performance of each character using the verbatim testimony from the interview process. As Mahone observes, Smith "reclaims the power of the voice of a solo artist to become the voice of the people."

The New Wave black gay and lesbian writers also use art as a weapon for political activism. Unlike the homosexual writers before them, they regard themselves as healthy as straight people and are totally public about their sexual preferences. Some of the contemporary gay writers include Melvin Dixon, Randall Kenan, Samuel Delany, Charles I. Nero, Joseph Beam, and Essex Hemphill. An excellent collection of prose essays by black male gay writers is *Brother to Brother* (1991) edited by Hemphill. The title of Beam's essay in the collection, "James Baldwin: Not a Bad Legacy Brother," suggests Baldwin's centrality as a major writer who pioneered the way for contemporary black male homosexual writers. Also avowing the connection between the Black Aesthetic and gay protest literature is Nero's essay "Toward a Black Gay Aesthetic: Signifying in Contemporary Black Gay Literature." The efforts of Beam, Nero, and the other essayists in *Brother to Brother,* combined with the writings of Pat Parker, Jewelle Gomez, and other lesbian authors, demonstrate that the black gay and lesbian movement within the New Wave is another significant "revolution within a Revolution."

Coda

During the contemporary period, there has been an incredible mushrooming of black talent in almost every form—from black militant poems, to choreopoems, bestselling novels to avant-garde novels, and Hollywood films to rap songs. As the dawning of the twenty-first century approaches, we can only hope that the prophetic vision of the contemporary black literary artist will move African American people—female and male, young and old, gay and straight, educated and unlettered—from the crossroad toward a more enlightened, economically independent, and unified black community.

Walking *by Charles H. Alston. Collection: Sydney Smith Gordon, Chicago.*

Folk Call for Social Revolution and Political Strategy

Folk Poetry

Urban Blues Lyrics

The Thrill Is Gone

B. B. KING

The thrill is gone!
The thrill is gone!

I can see it in your eyes,
I can hear it in your sighs,
Feel your touch and realize
The thrill is gone.

The nights are cold,
Love is old.

Love was grand when love was new,
Birds were singing, skies were blue,
Now it don't appeal to you.
The thrill is gone.

This is the end,
So why pretend
And let it linger on,
The thrill is gone!

I Pity the Fool

BOBBY "BLUE" BLAND

Look at the people.
I know you're wondering what they're doing,
They're just standing there
Watching you make a fool of me.

Oh, I pity the fool,
Oh, I pity the fool,
That was in love with you
And expected you to be true,
Oh, I pity the fool.

Back Door Man

HOWLIN' WOLF

I am a back door man.
I am a back door man.
Well, the men don't know,

But the little girls understand,

When everybody's tryin' to sleep
I'm somewhere, makin' my midnight creep.
Every morning, the rooster crow;
Some men tell me, I got to go.

Am I Blue?

RAY CHARLES

I'm just a woman,
A lonely woman
Waitin' on the weary shore.
I'm just a woman
That's only human,
One you should be sorry for.
Got up this mornin'
Along about dawn,
Without a warnin'
I found he was gone.
Why should he do it?
How could he do it?
He never done it before.

Am I blue?
Am I blue?
Ain't these tears in these eyes tellin' you?
Am I blue?
You'd be too
If each plan with your man done fell through.
Was a time
I was his only one,
But now I'm
The sad and lonely one.
"Lawdy," was I gay
'Til today,
Now he's gone and we're through.

It's aggravatin'
To stand here waitin'
Waitin' for a triflin' man.
It set me hatin'
To stand here waitin'
Suicide's my only plan.
I think it's awful,
His treatment of me,
It's most unlawful
How mean he can be.
I can't forget him,
I'm bound to get him,

I'll run him down if I can.

Am I blue?
Am I blue?
Ain't these tears in these eyes tellin' you?
Am I blue?
You'd be too
If each plan with your man done fell through.
Was a time
I was his only one,
But now I'm
The sad and lonely one.
"Lawdy," was I gay
'Til today,
Now he's gone and we're through.
Am I blue?
Am I blue?

Big Boss Man

JIMMY REED

Big boss, don't you hear me when I call?
Big boss, don't you hear me when I call?
Yes, you ain't all that tall, you just big, that's all.

You long-legged, you just make a fuss.
You just funking round, trying to be someone.
Big boss man, don't you hear me when I call?
Yes you long and tall, you ain't gitting nowhere.

Now you try to take my woman, you ain't doing no good.
Running round here talking, trying to be someone.
Now, big boss man, don't you hear me when I call?
Now you ain't that strong, you just big, that's all.

Rhythm and Blues Lyrics

Respect

OTIS REDDING; AS INTERPRETED BY ARETHA FRANKLIN

What you want baby I got,
What you need You know I got it.
All I'm asking is for a little respect,
  when you come home.
Baby, when you come home, Respect.

I ain't gonna do you wrong while you gone.
I ain't gonna do you wrong 'Cause I don't wanna.
All I'm asking is for a little respect,
  when you come home.
Baby, when you come home, Respect.

I'm out to give you all my money,
But all I'm askin' in return, honey,
Is to give me my proper respect when you get home.
Yeah, baby, when you get home.

Ooh, your kisses, sweeter than honey,
But guess what, so here's my money,
All I want you to do for me is give me some here when you get home.
Yeah, baby, when you get home.

R-E-S-P-E-C-T, find out what it means to me,
R-E-S-P-E-C-T, take care, T.C.B.
Ohhhhhhhhhhh! Sock it to me, sock it to me,
    sock it to me . . . .

FROM *Say It Loud, I'm Black and I'm Proud*

JAMES BROWN

Say it loud, I'm black and I'm proud
Whee it's hurting me, if it's alright, it's alright,
You're too tough, you're tough enough,
You're alright and you're out of sight,
Say it loud, I'm black and I'm proud.

I say we won't quit moving until we get what we deserve,
We've been 'buked and we've been scorned,
We've been treated bad, as sure as you've been borned,
But just as it takes two eyes to make a pair,
We're not gonna quit until we get our share.

FROM *Keep on Pushing*

CURTIS MAYFIELD AND THE IMPRESSIONS

Keep on pushing
I've got to keep on pushing
I can't stop now . . .
'Cause I've got my strength
And it don't make sense
Not to
Keep on pushing. . . .

What's Going On

MARVIN GAYE, A. CLEVELAND, AND R. BENSON

Mother, mother
There's too many of you crying
Brother, brother, brother
There's far too many of you dying.
You know we've got to find a way
To bring some lovin' here today—Ya
Father, father, father we don't need to escalate

You see, war is not the answer
For only love can conquer hate
You know we've got to find the way
To bring some lovin' here today.
Picket lines and picket signs
Don't punish me with brutality
Talk to me, so you can see
Oh, what's going on
What's going on
Ya, what's going on
Ah, what's going on
In the meantime
Right on baby
Right on
Right on
Father, father, everybody thinks we're wrong
Oh, but who are they to judge us
Simply because our hair is long
Oh, you know we've got to find a way
To bring some understanding here today
Oh
Picket lines and picket signs
Don't punish me with brutality
Come on talk to me
So you can see
What's going on
Ya, what's going on
Tell me, what's going on
I'll tell you what's going on—Uh
Right on baby
Right on baby

Spirituals and Gospels Adapted for the Liberation Movement

Ain't Gonna Let Nobody Turn Me 'Round

Ain't gonna let nobody, Lordy, turn me 'round,
   Turn me 'round, turn me 'round,
Ain't gonna let nobody turn me 'round,
   I'm gonna keep on a-walkin',
Keep on a-talkin',
Marching up to freedom land.

Ain't gonna let no jail house turn me 'round,
   Turn me 'round, turn me 'round,
Ain't gonna let no jail house turn me 'round,
   I'm gonna keep on a-walkin',
Keep on a-talkin',
Marching up to freedom land.

Ain't gonna let no sheriff turn me 'round,
  Turn me 'round, turn me 'round,
Ain't gonna let no sheriff turn me 'round,
  I'm gonna keep on a-walkin',
Keep on a-talkin',
Marching up to freedom land.

Keep Your Eyes on the Prize

Paul and Silas bound in jail,
Had no money for to go their bail.
Keep your eyes on the prize,
Hold on, hold on.
  Hold on, hold on.
Keep your eyes on the prize,
  Hold on, hold on.

Paul and Silas begin to shout,
The jail door open and they walked out.
Keep your eyes on the prize,
Hold on, hold on.

Freedom's name is mighty sweet,
Soon one day we're gonna meet.
Keep your eyes on the prize,
Hold on, hold on.

Got my hand on the Gospel plow,
I wouldn't take nothing for my journey now.
Keep your eyes on the prize,
Hold on, hold on.

The only chain that a man can stand,
Is that chain of hand in hand.
Keep your eyes on the prize,
Hold on, hold on.

The only thing that we did wrong,
Stayed in the wilderness a day too long.
Keep your eyes on the prize,
Hold on, hold on.

But the one thing we did right,
Was the day we started to fight.
Keep your eyes on the prize,
Hold on, hold on.

We're gonna board that big Greyhound,
Carryin' love from town to town.
Keep your eyes on the prize,
Hold on, hold on.

We're gonna ride for civil rights,
We're gonna ride both black and white.

Keep your eyes on the prize,
Hold on, hold on.

We've met jail and violence too,
But God's love has seen us through.
Keep your eyes on the prize,
Hold on, hold on.

Haven't been to Heaven but I've been told,
Streets up there are paved with gold.
Keep your eyes on the prize,
Hold on, hold on.

This Little Light of Mine

This little light of mine, I'm gonna let it shine
This little light of mine, I'm gonna let it shine
This little light of mine, I'm gonna let it shine
Let it shine, let it shine, let it shine

(Bridge)

The light that shines is the light of love,
lights the darkness from above
It shines on me and it shines on you,
and shows what the power of love can do
I'm gonna shine my light both far and near,
I'm gonna shine my light both bright and clear
Where there's a dark corner in this land,
I'm gonna let my little light shine.

We've got the light of freedom, we're gonna let it shine
We've got the light of freedom, we're gonna let it shine
We've got the light of freedom, we're gonna let it shine
Let it shine, let it shine, let it shine

Deep down in the South, we're gonna let it shine . . .

Down in Birmingham (Mississippi, Alabama, etc.), we're gonna let it shine . . .

Everywhere I go, I'm gonna let it shine . . .

Tell Chief Pritchett, we're gonna let it shine . . .

All in the jail house, we're gonna let it shine . . .

(Bridge)

On Monday he gave me the gift of love
Tuesday peace came from above
Wednesday he told me to have more faith
Thursday he gave me a little more grace
Friday he told me just to watch and pray
Saturday told me just what to say
Sunday he gave me the power divine—
to let my little light shine.

This little light of mine, I'm gonna let it shine . . .

We Shall Not Be Moved

We shall not, we shall not be moved;
We shall not, we shall not be moved.
Just like a tree that's standing by the water,
We shall not be moved.
We're fighting for our freedom . . .
Black and white together . . .
Our union is behind us . . .
Our union is our leader . . .

Avant-Garde Jazz

Avant-garde jazz is the music of freedom unobstructed by the notions of Eurocentric jazz playing. Its purpose is not to emphasize harmonic simultaneity. Instead, avant-garde, or "free," jazz is based on improvisation on a grand scale, melodic emphasis, leaps, scales, arpeggios, and a completely free handling of forms and rhythms. Characterized mainly by African, Asian, and Caribbean musical elements, this form of music emphasizes the importance of the collective ensemble rather than the soloist. Hence, its production, which may sound like chaos and disorder to some, is very Afrocentric in nature.

The following example from one of John Coltrane's workbooks shows this famous musician's composition of a free jazz piece, based primarily on African and Asian scales.

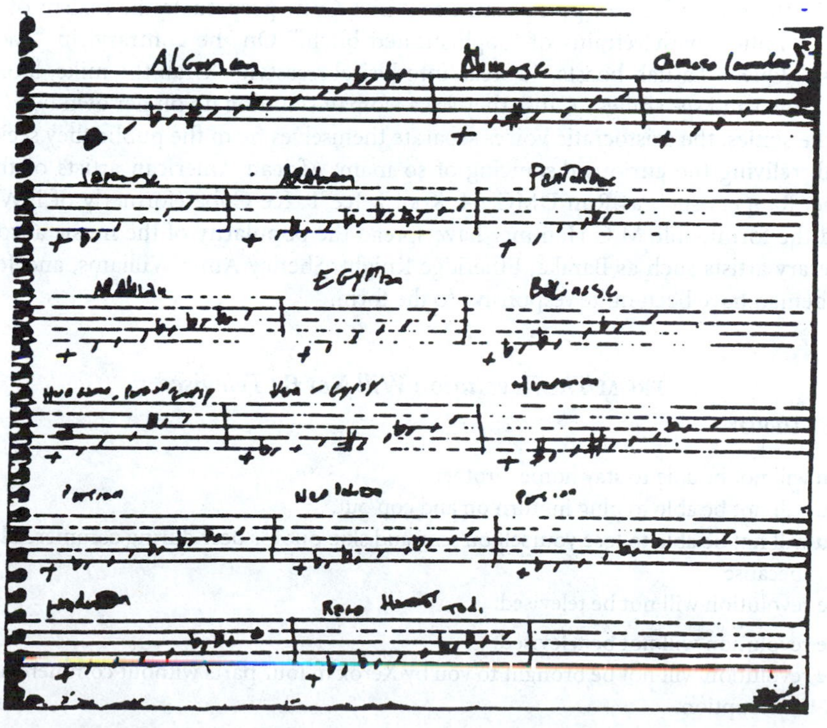

Rap Lyrics

Rap is the latest black folk music idiom that articulates the urban African American life experience. But it is a far cry from traditional black oral folk idioms and performers. In this age of advanced technology, this new, exciting form of rhymed storytelling is composed, revised, and improvised by computers and microprocessors. "In most rap music," black historian-musicologist Tricia Rose maintains, "the instruments are samplers that reproduce synthesized versions of traditional instruments, frighteningly real reproductions of other sounds (breaking glass, sirens, etc.) and the dynamic and explosive mixing and dubbing of new, previously recorded and seemingly fixed sounds."

Though built around a synthesized drumbeat and backbeat, the music is deeply rooted in African American orature. Stemming from the traditions of toasting, boasting, signifying, and playing the dozens, it is characterized by duple pulse beats, rhythmic complexity, repetition with subtle variations, melodic interest in bass frequencies, and breaks in time and pitch. Moreover, like the toasts, rap is heavily dependent on the theatrical performance—or the freestyle of the musician—and audience participation. Also like the toasts, it has as its major themes racial protest, violence, and sex, but the message is more strident, direct, and militant. The mostly male griots create lyrics that, as expressions of the urban poor, voice distrust. Don't believe the hype, they say; the dream was not intended for us. The popular message parallels that of the black nationalist poetry of the sixties, including the work of Amiri Baraka, Haki Madhubuti, and Carolyn Rodgers, though usually with less power of redemptive introspection and celebrated awareness of the sacred values of African American people. For example, the rap group Public Enemy urges blacks to "fight the power." Other groups such as 2 Live Crew perpetuate the sexism of the folk tradition with refrains of "sophisticated bitch." On the contrary, in "Ladies First," Queen Latifah boasts, "I break into lyrical freestyle / Grab the mike, look at the crowd and see smiles / Cause they see a woman standing up on her own two." As in the sixties, the aristocratic voices separate themselves from the public they seek to lead, reliving the curious distancing of so many African American artists of their time. Rappers such as Run DMC, LL Kool J, Ice T, Ice Cube (formerly of NWA), and the formidable M C Hammer have spread the popularity of the music abroad. Literary artists such as Baraka, Etheridge Knight, Sherley Anne Williams, and John Wideman have been quite responsive to the form.

FROM *The Revolution Will Not Be Televised*

GIL SCOTT-HERON

You will not be able to stay home, brother.
You will not be able to plug in, turn on and cop out.
You will not be able to lose yourself on scag and skip out for beer during commercials
because
The revolution will not be televised.

The revolution will not be televised.
The revolution will not be brought to you by Xerox in four parts without commercial
interruption.

The revolution will not show you pictures of Nixon blowing a bugle and leading a charge by John Mitchell, General Abramson and Spiro Agnew to eat hog maws confiscated from a Harlem sanctuary.
The revolution will not be televised.

The revolution will not be brought to you by
The Schaeffer Award Theater and will not star Natalie Wood and Steve McQueen or Bullwinkle and Julia.
The revolution will not give you mouth sex appeal.
The revolution will not get rid of the nubs.
The revolution will not make you look five pounds thinner.
The revolution will not be televised, brother.

There will be no pictures of you and Willie Mae pushing that shopping cart down the block on the dead run,
Or trying to slide that color TV in a stolen ambulance.
NBC will not be able to predict the winner at 8:32 on reports from twenty-nine districts.
The revolution will not be televised. . . .

FROM *Rapper's Delight*

THE SUGAR HILL GANG

I said a hip hop
The hippie the hippie
To the hip hip hop, a you don't stop the rock it
To the bang bang boogie, say up jumped the boogie
To the rhythm of the boogie, the beat

Now what you hear is not a test—I'm rappin' to the beat
And me, the groove, and my friends are gonna try to move your feet
See I am Wonder Mike and I like to say hello
To the black, to the white, the red, and the brown, the purple and yellow
But first I gotta bang bang the boogie to the boogie
Say up jump the boogie to the bang bang boogie
Let's rock, you don't stop
Rock the riddle that will make your body rock
Well so far you've heard my voice but I brought two friends along
And next on the mike is my man Hank
Come on, Hank, sing that song

Check it out, I'm the C-A-S-AN-the-O-V-A
And the rest is F-L-Y
Ya see I go by the code of the doctor of the mix
And these reasons I'll tell ya why
Ya see I'm six foot one and I'm tons of fun
And I dress to a T
Ya see I got more clothes than Muhammad Ali and I dress so viciously
I got bodyguards, I got two big cars
That definitely ain't the wack
I got a Lincoln Continental and a sunroof Cadillac

So after school, I take a dip in the pool
Which really is on the wall
I got a color TV so I can see
The Knicks play basketball
Hear me talkin' 'bout checkbooks, credit cards
More money than a sucker could ever spend
But I wouldn't give a sucker or a bum from the Rucker
Not a dime 'til I made it again
Everybody go, "Hotel motel, watcha gonna do today" (Say what?)
'Cause I'm 'a get a fly girl
Gonna get some spank 'n'
Drive off in a def OJ
Everybody go, "Hotel motel Holiday Inn"
Say if your girl starts actin' up, then you take her friend
Master G, my mellow
It's on you so what you gonna do
Well it's on 'n' on 'n' on on 'n' on
The beat don't stop until the break of dawn
I said M-A-S, T-E-R, a G with a double E
I said I go by the unforgettable name
Of the man they call the Master Gee
Well, my name is known all over the world
By all the foxy ladies and the pretty girls
I'm goin' down in history
As the baddest rapper there ever could be
Now I'm feelin' the highs and ya feelin' the lows
The beat starts gettin' into your toes
Ya start poppin' ya fingers and stompin' your feet
And movin' your body while you're sittin' in your seat
And then damn—ya start doin' the freak
I said damn, right outta your seat
Then ya throw your hands high in the air
Ya rockin' to the rhythm, shake your derriere
Ya rockin' to the beat without a care
With the sureshot M.C.s for the affair

Now, I'm not as tall as the rest of the gang
But I rap to the beat just the same
I got a little face and a pair of brown eyes
All I'm here to do, ladies, is hypnotize
Singin' on 'n' 'n' on 'n' on on 'n' on
The beat don't stop until the break of dawn
Singin' on 'n' 'n' on 'n' on on 'n' on
Like a hot buttered a pop da pop da pop dibbie dibbie
Pop da pop pop, ya don't dare stop
Come alive y'all, gimme what ya got
I guess by now you can take a hunch

And find that I am the baby of the bunch
But that's okay, I still keep in stride
'Cause all I'm here to do is just wiggle your behind
Singin' on 'n' 'n' on 'n' on on 'n' on
The beat don't stop until the break of dawn
Singin' on 'n' 'n' on 'n' on on 'n' on
Rock rock, y'all, throw it on the floor
I'm gonna freak ya here, I'm gonna freak ya there
I'm gonna move you outta this atmosphere
'Cause I'm one of a kind and I'll shock your mind
I'll put T-N-T in your behind
I said 1-2-3-4, come on, girls, get on the floor
A-come alive, y'all, a-gimme what ya got
'Cause I'm guaranteed to make you rock
I said 1-2-3-4, tell me, Wonder Mike, what are you waiting for?

I said a hip hop
The hippie to the hippie
The hip hip hop, a you don't stop the rock it
To the bang bang the boogie, say up jumped the boogie
To the rhythm of the boogie, the beat . . .

FROM *The Message*

GRANDMASTER FLASH AND THE FURIOUS FIVE

It's like a jungle sometimes, it make me wonder
How I keep from going under
It's like a jungle sometimes, it makes me wonder
How I keep from going under

Broken glass everywhere
People pissing on the stairs
You know they just don't care
I can't take the smell, can't take the noise
Got no money to move out, I guess I got no choice
Rats in the front room, roaches in the back
Junkies in the alley with a baseball bat
I tried to get away but I couldn't get far
'Cause the man with the tow truck repossessed my car

. . . .

A child is born with no state of mind
Blind to the ways of mankind
God is smiling on you but he's frowning too
Because only God knows what you go through
You grow in the ghetto, living second rate
And your eyes will sing a song of deep hate

The place that you play and where you stay
Looks like one great big alleyway
You'll admire all the number book-takers
Thugs, pimps, and pushers and the big money makers
Driving big cars, spending twenties and tens
And you wanna grow up to be just like them, huh
Smugglers, scramblers, burglars, gamblers
Pickpockets, peddlers, even panhandlers
You say, "I'm cool, huh, I'm no fool"
But then you wind up dropping out of high school
Now you're unemployed, all nonvoid
Walking 'round like you're Pretty Boy Floyd
Turned stick-up kid but look what you done did
Got sent up for a eight-year bid
Now your manhood is took and you're a Maytag
Spend the next two years as a undercover fag

Being used and abused to serve like hell
'Til one day you was found hung dead in the cell
It was plain to see that your life was lost
You was cold and your body swung back and forth
But now your eyes sing the sad sad song
Of how ya lived so fast and died so young

So don't push me 'cause I'm close to the edge
I'm trying not to lose my head
Ah huh huh huh huh
It's like a jungle sometimes, it make me wonder
How I keep from going under . . .

FROM *Paid in Full*

ERIC B. AND RAKIM

Thinkin' of a master plan
This ain't nothin' but sweat inside my hand
So I dig into my pocket all my money's spent
So I dig deeper—still comin' up with lint
So I start my mission and leave my residence
Thinkin' how I'm gonna get some dead Presidents
I need money, I used to be a stick up kid
So I think of all the devious things I did
I used to roll up, "this is a hold up—ain't nuttin' funny
Stop smiling ain't still don't nothin' move but the money"
But now I learned to earn cause I'm righteous
I feel great, so maybe I might just
Search for a nine to five
And if I thrive, then maybe I'll stay alive.

Don't Believe the Hype

PUBLIC ENEMY

Don't believe the hype

Back—caught you lookin' for the same thing
It's a new thing—check out this I bring
Uh-oh, the roll below the level
'Cause I'm livin' low
Next to the bass (c'mon)
Turn up the radio
They claim that I'm a criminal
By now I wonder how
Some people never know
The enemy could be their friend, guardian
I'm not a hooligan
I rock the party and
Clear all the madness, I'm not a racist
Preach to teach to all
'Cause some, they never had this
Number one, not born to run
About the gun
I wasn't licensed to have one
The minute they see me, fear me
I'm the epitome—a public enemy
Used, abused, without clues
I refused to blow a fuse
They even had it on the news
Don't believe the hype

Don't believe the hype

Yes—was the start of my last jam
So here it is again, another def jam
But since I gave you all a little something
That we knew you lacked
They still consider me a new jack
All the critics, you can hang 'em
I'll hold the rope
But they hope to the pope
And pray it ain't dope
The follower of Farrakhan
Don't tell me that you understand
Until you hear the man
The book of the new school rap game
Writers treat me like Coltrane, insane
Yes to them, but to me I'm a different kind
We're brothers of the same mind, unblind
Caught in the middle and

Not surrenderin'
I don't rhyme for the sake of riddlin'
Some claim that I'm a smuggler
Some say I never heard of ya
A rap burglar, false media
We don't need it, do we?
It's fake, that's what it be to ya, dig me?
Yo, Terminator X, step up on the stand and show the people what time it is, boyyyyy!

Don't believe the hype

Don't believe the hype—it's a sequel
As an equal, can I get this through to you
My 98's boomin' with a trunk of funk
All the jealous punks can't stop the dunk
Comin' from the school of hard knocks
Some perpetrate, they drink Clorox
Attack the Black, because I know they lack exact
The cold facts, and still they try to xerox
The leader of the new school, uncool
Never played the fool, just made the rules
Remember there's a need to get alarmed
Again I said I was a timebomb
In the daytime, radio's scared of me
'Cause I'm mad, 'cause I'm the enemy
They can't come on and play me in prime time
'Cause I know the time, plus I'm gettin' mine
I get on the mix late in the night
They know I'm living right, so here go the mike, psych
Before I let it go, don't rush my show
You try to reach and grab and get elbowed
Word to Herb, yo if you can't swing this
Learn the words, you might sing this
Just a little bit of the taste of the bass for you
As you get up and dance at the LQ
When some deny it, defy it, I swing bolos
And then they clear the lane, I go solo
The meaning of all of that
Some media is the wack
As you believe it's true
It blows me through the roof
Suckers, liars, get me a shovel
Some writers I know are damn devils
For them I say, "Don't believe the hype"
Yo Chuck, they must be on the pipe, right?
Their pens and pads I'll snatch
'Cause I've had it
I'm not an addict, fiendin' for static

I'll see their tape recorder and grab it
No, you can't have it back, silly rabbit
I'm goin' to my media assassin
Harry Allen, I gotta ask him
Yo Harry, you're a writer, are we that type?

Don't believe the hype
Don't believe the hype

I got Flavor and all those things you know
Yeah boy, part two bum rush the show
Yo Griff, get the green, black, red, and
Gold down, countdown to Armageddon
'88 you wait the S-One's will
Put the left in effect and I still will
Rock the hard jams, treat it like a seminar
Reach the bourgeois, and rock the boulevard
Some say I'm negative
But they're not positive
But what I got to give
The media says this
Red black and green
Know what I mean
Yo, don't believe the hype

Fight the Power

PUBLIC ENEMY

1989, the number, another summer (get down)
Sound of the funky drummer
Music hittin' your heart 'cause I know you got soul
(Brothers and sisters, hey)
Listen if you're missin', y'all
Swingin' while I'm singin' (hey)
Givin' whatcha gettin'
Knowin' what I'm knowin'
While the black band's sweatin'
And the rhythm rhyme's rollin'
Gotta give us what we want (Uh!)
Gotta give us what we need (Hey!)
Our freedom of speech is freedom or death
We got to fight the powers that be
Lemme hear you say

FIGHT THE POWER
We got to fight the powers that be

As the rhythm's designed to bounce
What counts is that the rhyme's

Designed to fill your mind
Now that you've realized the pride's arrived
We got to pump the stuff to make us tough
From the heart
It's a start, a work of art
To revolutionize, make a change, nothin' strange
People people, we are the same
No we're not the same
'Cause we don't know the game
What we need is awareness, we can't get careless
You say what is this?
My beloved, let's go down to business
Mental self-defensive fitness
(Yo) Bum rush the show
You gotta go for what you know
To make everybody see, in order to fight the powers that be
Lemme hear you say

FIGHT THE POWER
We got to fight the powers that be

Elvis was a hero to most
But he never meant shit to me, you see
Straight up racist that sucker was simple and plain
Motherfuck him and John Wayne
'Cause I'm black and I'm proud
I'm ready and hyped plus I'm amped
Most of my heroes don't appear on no stamps
Sample a look back, you look and find
Nothin' but rednecks for 400 years if you check
"Don't Worry Be Happy"
Was a number one jam
Damn, if I say it you can slap me right here
(Get it) Let's get this party started right
Right on, c'mon
What we got to say (Yaaaah!)
Power to the people, no delay
To make everybody see
In order to fight the powers that be

FIGHT THE POWER
We got to fight the powers that be

FROM *Ladies First*

QUEEN LATIFAH AND MONIE LOVE

Queen Latifah
The ladies will kick it, the rhyme it is wicked
Those who don't know how to be pros get evicted

A woman can bear you, break you, take you
Now it's time to rhyme. Can you relate to
A sister dope enough to make you holler and scream?

MONIE LOVE
Ay, yo! Let me take it from here, Queen!
Excuse me, but I think I'm about due
To get into precisely what I am about to do
I'm conversating to the folks who have no whatsoever clue
So listen very carefully as I break it down for you
Merrily, merrily, merrily, merrily, hyper, happy, overjoyed
Pleased with all the beats and rhymes my sister has employed
Slick and smooth, throwing down, the sound totally a yes
Let me state the position: Ladies first, yes?

BOTH
Yes!

Just a Friendly Game of Baseball

MAIN SOURCE

Awwww shit, another young brother hit
I better go over to my man's crib and get the pump
'Cause to the cops, shooting brothers is like playing baseball
And they're never in a slump
I guess when they shoot up a crew, it's a grand slam
And when it's one, it's a home run
But I'm 'a be ready with a wild pitch
My finger got a bad twitch plus I wanna switch
Sides and step up to the batter's box
Fuck red and white, I got on black sox
But let 'em shoot a person from the white sox, what's the call?
Foul ball
Babe Ruth would've made a good cop but he didn't
Instead he was a bigot, dig it
My life is valuable and I protect it like a gem
Instead of cops shooting me, I'm going out shooting them
And let 'em cough up blood like phlegm
It's grim, but dead is my antonym
And legally they can't take a fall
Yo, check it out, it's just a friendly game of baseball

R.B.I.—real bad injury
But don't get happy, you're in jail for a century
Just as bad as being shot in the groin
To see who'll shoot you, they'll flip a coin
And watch you run for the stretch
But you don't know the man is at home waiting to make the catch
So the outfielder guns you down

You're out, off to the dugout, underground
I know a cop that's savage, his pockets stay green like cabbage
'Cause he has a good batting average
No questions, just pulls out the flamer
And his excuses get lamer
Once a brother tried to take a lead
But they shot him in his face saying he was trying to steal a base
And people watch the news for coverage on the game
And got the nerve to complain
They need to get themselves a front row seat
Or save the baseline for a beat
'Cause hellivision just ain't designed for precision y'all
It's just a friendly game of baseball

A brother caught on but I don't know where the brother went
The umpires are the government
I guess they kicked him out the game and replaced him with a pinch hitter
And the scam, he was quitter
So the cops usually torment, I mean tournament
Win 'em, I was saying
You can't let the umpires hear you speaking bad
Or like the other kid, you won't be playing
'Cause they'll beat you 'til your ass drop
A walking gun with a shell in his hand is their mascot
When you run around, let it be noted
Step lightly, the bases are loaded
My man got out from three strikes, in the skull
But the knife he was carrying was dull
Instead of innings, we have endings
What a fine way to win things
And hot dog vendors have fun
Selling you the cat, rat, and dog on a bun
And when you ask, "What is all of this called?"
It's just a friendly game of baseball

"You low-lifes.
You take that! And that! And that!
I'm here to protect and serve
And that's exactly what I'm gonna do."

FROM *Freedom of Speech*

ICE T

Hey, yo, Ice, man, I'm workin' on this term paper for college
What's the First Amendment?

Freedom of speech, let 'em take it from me
Next they'll take it from you
Then what you gonna do?
Let 'em censor books, let 'em censor art

PMRC, this is where the witchhunt starts
You'll censor what we see, we read, we hear, we learn
The books will burn
You better think it out
We should be able to say anything
Our lungs were meant to shout
Say what we feel, yell out what's real
Even though it may not bring mass appeal
Your opinion is yours, my opinion is mine
If you don't like what I'm sayin' fine
But don't close it, always keep an open mind
A man who fails to listen is blind
We only got one right left in the world today
Let me have it, or throw the constitution away

Freedom of Speech
Yeahh, just watch what you say
Freedom of Speech
You better watch what you say
Freedom of Speech
Yeah, boy, you better watch what you say
(Explicit lyrics)

A Rap

FROM "PHILADELPHIA FIRE"

JOHN WIDEMAN

Hey—hey, youall, this rapcity here
Got a tale to tell make you shed a tear
Bout some dreadlocked bloods trying to do their thing
And a evil Empire with a evil King
Not the kind of story I like to tell
Dreads was seeking heaven, all they caught was hell
Didn't eat no meat, let their kids run naked
Got the Emperor uptight, he just couldn't take it
Called his army, his navy, his flying corps
Said: This shit's gone too far, I can't stand it no more
Got to play by my rules if you live in my city
Fuck with the piper, don't expect no pity.
Shame if babies have to burn
But life is hard, they got to learn
Give them primitives five minutes to leave the premises
If they don't comply, come down like Nemesis
When the smoke clears, don't want nary a one
Left standing to tell me how my city should be run
Left standing to tell me how my city should be run

How can I rule with equanimity
When every day them monkeys making a monkey out of me.
You wouldn't believe the ordinance brought to bear
To drive them Rastas out their lair
Dreads didn't falter, they fought toe to toe
But the odds were too heavy, they had to go
It was like Tyson throwing on a little kid
The kid was doomed whatever he did
Down they went in bullets, water and flame
It was Murder One by another name
Murder One by any name
Uh—uh. Uh—uh, uh—uh, uh—uh
Spleeby—spleeby, spleeby—spleeby, spleeby do duh
I—I—I—I'm the—the—the rapper, the dapper, the last backslapper
Wit you on my team we the cream de cream
Don't cry, don't moan, don't pine away
Them Dreadys be back another day
Remember what you heard rapcity say
Them Dreads coming back another day
Hey, hey, hey, hey, hey, hey—hey, hey
Them Dreads coming back, somebody's got to pay
Dreads coming back
Somebody's gotta pay
Gotta pay, gotta pay
Somebody's gotta pay.

Toasts

Signifyin' Monkey

VERSION BY OSCAR BROWN, JR.

Said the signifyin' monkey to the lion one day:
"Hey, dere's a great big elephant down th' way
Goin' 'roun' talkin', I'm sorry t' say,
About yo' momma in a scandalous way!"

"Yea, he's talkin' 'bout yo' momma an' yo' grandma, too;
And he don' show too much respect fo' you.
Now, you weren't there an' I sho' am glad
'Cause what he said about yo' momma made me mad!"

Signifyin' monkey, stay up in yo' tree
You are always lyin' and signifyin'
But you better not monkey wit' me.

The lion said, "Yea? Well, I'll fix him;

I'll tear that elephant limb from limb."
Then he shook the jungle with a mighty roar
Took off like a shot from a forty-four.

He found the elephant where the tall grass grows
And said, "I come to punch you in your long nose."
The elephant looked at the lion in surprise
And said, "Boy, you better go pick on somebody your size."

But the lion wouldn't listen; he made a pass;
The elephant slapped him down in the grass.
The lion roared and sprung from the ground
And that's when that elephant really went to town.

I mean he whupped that lion for the rest of the day
And I still don't see how the lion got away
But he dragged on off, more dead than alive,
And that's when that monkey started his signifyin' jive.

The monkey looked down and said, "Oooh wee!
What is this beat-up mess I see?
Is that you, Lion? Ha, ha! Do tell!
Man, he whupped yo' head to a fare-thee-well!

"Give you a beatin' that was rough enough;
You' s'pposed to be king of the jungle, ain't dat some stuff?
You big overgrown pussycat! Don' choo roar
Or I'll hop down there an' whip you some more."

The monkey got to laughing and a' jumpin' up an' down,
But his foot missed the limb and he plunged to the ground.
The lion was on him with all four feet
Gonna grind that money to hamburger meat.

The monkey looked up with tears in his eyes
And said, "Please, Mr. Lion, I apologize,
I meant no harm, please, let me go
And I'll tell you something you really need to know."

The lion stepped back to hear what he'd say,
And that monkey scampered up the tree and got away.
"What I wanted to tell you," the monkey hollered then,
"Is if you fool with me, I'll sic the elephant on you again!"

The lion just shook his head, and said, "You jive . . .
If you and yo' monkey children wanna stay alive,
Up in them trees is where you better stay"
And that's where they are to this very day.

Signifyin' monkey, stay up in yo' tree
You are always lyin' and signifyin'
But you better not monkey wit' me.

Folk sermon

Ezekiel and the Vision of Dry Bones

VERSION BY CARL J. ANDERSON; COLLECTED AND TRANSCRIBED BY GERALD DAVIS

If you have your Bibles ready
You may turn with me
To the thirty-seventh chapter of the book of Ezekiel
And we're going to read
The first, second, and third verse
"The hand of the Lord
Was upon me
And carried me out in the Spirit of the Lord
And set me down
In the midst of the valley which was full of bones"
You understand that
"And cause me to pass by them round about
And behold there was very many in the open valley
And lo, they were very dry"
You understand me
I want to use as my theme tonight
Ezekiel and the Vision of Dry Bones
You understand
Not dry bones in the valley
But Ezekiel and the Vision of Dry Bones
And this is one message from the Lord that you cannot run away from it
Yes sir
He that is led by the Spirit
They are the sons of God
And I feel sorry for that individual
That only loves sin
And runs from the Gospel
For it will take the Gospel to save your soul
Now this new Ezekiel signifies God's way of thinking
Ezekiel is known as one of the most mysterious Hebrew prophets
Yes sir
And he began, well, as a boy
He grew up under the influence of Jeremiah
And he began to prophesy at the age of thirty
And for twenty-two years preached by the River of Shafar
At Talabinth
And history says he died at the age of fifty-two
Now this man Ezekiel styles himself
The son of man
Several times he uses this expression
"Thus sayeth the Lord"

You understand me
And you'll find one hundred and seventeen times
Yes sir
The times of his prophesy was stormy and traditional
Ezekiel had two audiences
One real and present, the exiled about him
And the other the whole house of Israel
You understand me
Yes sir
And you'll find many dry Christians in church
As I oftentimes say
I wouldn't have a religion I can't feel
Ezekiel used allegories or parables such as those of Israel as a founding child
Representing one with a sound body but unable to walk
Do you understand me
And second as a lioness
Third a stately figure
And fourth a vine doomed
Yes sir
He employed symbolic actions depicting the siege of Jerusalem
By dividing his hair into three parts
Do you understand me
First part to be burned
Second part to be smitten
And the third part to be scattered representing
Do you understand me
Israel and Jerusalem when one-third of the city was smitten
With the sword and the gates were set on fire
Help me Lord
Another third representing the scattered Jews all over the world today
Now by way of parenthesis
I sometimes wonder why
The Lord chose that the hair from Ezekiel's head would be divided three times
Yes sir
And then as I began to search
I find that one is Heaven's unity number
And seven is Heaven's sacred number
You understand me
But three is Heaven's complete number
Whatever God does He does completely
Am I right about it?
I want the world to know
That there are three heavenly bodies
Yes sir
The sun
Moon

And the planets
Guide me Lord
The earth is constituted of three great elements
They are land, water, and air
And these have three different forms
You understand me
And they are solid, liquid, and vapor
Help me Holy Spirit
Yes sir
Three kinds of animal life
Animals that inhabit the earth
Fish inhabit the waters
And fowls the air
Am I right about it?
Well, I turn to the Bible
And I read where Noah had three sons
Sham, Ham, and Jephtha
Yes sir
You know it's difficult
To preach to people who do not read their Bible
Yes sir
And I read where Moses was hidden for three months
Can I get a witness?
Yeah, his life was divided into three periods
Forty years in Pharaoh's house
Forty years in the wilderness
And forty years in leadership
You understand me
And the workmen of Solomon's temple
Were divided into three classes
Seventy thousand entered apprentices
Eighty thousand fellow craftsmen
And three thousand six hundred master masons
Help me Holy Spirit
And not only that, Daniel prayed three times a day
Yes sir
So you see three is important
The Hebrew children
Shadrack, Meshack, and Abednego
Composed Heaven's fireproof unit
Yes sir
And when Jesus was born
Three wise men came from the East
And presented three kinds of gifts
Am I right about it?
When the Master wanted to confirm his divine nature

And mission in the minds of disciples
He took three of them
Peter, James, and John
Am I right about it?
Yeah, and He took them into a high mountain
Apart and was transfigured before them
And Peter got happy there
And said
Let us build three tabernacles
Am I right about it?
Yes sir
One for Thee
One for Moses
And one for Elijah
So the Lord told Ezekiel to divide his hair
After having shaved his head with a barber's razor
In three parts
Ezekiel used other symbols
He stood out on the street and ate bread with feminine hands
Representing the failing of the staff of life
He set his furniture out of his house
In the broad daylight
Representing the holy vessels and the furniture of the temple
Would be moved out before their eyes
Not only did he speak by parables and symbols
But he saw, he saw visions of the glory of God
Am I right about it?
Yes sir
Of the restored sanctuary and of our discourse this evening
Of the valley of dry bones
My brothers and sisters
In the Lord there are many valleys
Am I right about it?
Now the children of Israel were pictured as in bondage
While in Babylon, Ezekiel was with them in servitude
He heard their cry as is recorded in the one hundred thirty-seventh number of the Psalms
Judah had lost her political existence as a nation
And their temple was destroyed
And the beautiful service of Jehovah was abolished
I'll hook this train up in a minute
And the walls of Jerusalem was torn down
And the gates had been set on fire
All because the nations had been unfaithful to God
And prepared that their very name was going to be wiped out
From the remembrance of God

In their sorrow they cried
Our bones are dry
You understand me
Our hopes is lost
And we are cut off from our parts
They looked upon themselves, children
As dead in the sight of God
You know it's a bad thing to walk around with the name Christian and do not have no spirit
Am I right about it?
They would find that they resemble the body in the grave
Which nothing remains
And I see Ezekiel he was true to his calling
Yes sir
And he was wearied over the plight of Judah
And the Lord set him down in the valley that was full of bones
Yeah, he saw
You understand me
He saw the flesh
Had been devoured
So to speak
By animals and vultures
He saw bones had been bleached by the chilly winds and parching sun
Yeah, he saw bones scattered by the rolling chariots and the clattering of the horses
And these bones were dry
Do you understand me
They were so dry no footsteps could be heard anywhere
Yeah, it's a sad thing
Yeah, to go to church and find Christians all dry
Yeah, and when the Lord said
Yes sir, when the Lord said make a joyful noise
Am I right about it?
Make it unto the Lord all ye lambs
And right now the world is making their noise
The nightclubs are dancing by the tune of the band
Yeah, and the blues and rock and roll singers
Yeah, those who set around are clapping their hands and they're saying to their favorite singer "Come on!"
You understand me
And I think that you shouldn't mind me crying about Jesus
Yeah, I want to make a noise about the Lord Jesus Christ
I'm so glad
That I'm able to make a noise
And He's been so good to me
Yeah, has He been good to you
Somebody said that the Lord was so good to them

But they never make any noise about what the Lord has said
A woman met Jesus down at the well
You understand me
And He told her everything that she had done
She dropped the water pot and ran downtown saying
"Come and see a man that told me all that I did!"
Oh Lord
Yeah, now this woman can tell what Jesus done for her
Yeah, I think the church ought to witness what the Lord has done for you
Yeah, early one morning
Yeah, I found the Lord
Yes I did
I was in the valley of dry bones
Yeah, I had no God on my side
Yeah, I didn't have no spirit
To make me shout
But when I found the Lord
I found joy
Yeah, joy
Yeah, joy was found
I found joy
Peace to my dying soul

Contemporary Folktales (collected by Daryl C. Dance)

In the Beginning

They say that, in the beginning of time, God was getting the races together, and He told the people, He say, "Now . . . " (He was telling them what to do, you know—couldn't hear so good). He say, "Yawl git to the right." They got white, you know.

He say, "Yawl stand *aroun'*, stand *aroun'*, git *aroun'*!" They got brown you know.

And [He said], "Yawl, git back!" And they got *black*.

How Blacks Got to America

I hear that the colored people one time was all on one side of the river. And the white people was all on *this* side. And they had a red flag, red handkerchief or sumpin'. They took that and kept on waving it, wavin' it and *wavin'* it, and that caused them to get those slaves—by that red flag. That's how they managed to come over here. They waved and got 'em over here—through that red flag. Yeah! So that's the way the colored people mostly got here—got here through that red handkerchief—that red flag. They [whites] was on one side of the river—and they [Blacks] was on the other, and they [whites] waved, kep' on waving and they got over there where the white folks at and when they got over here, see, they kep' 'em.

He Remembered

This Minister could not find his hat, and he finally decided that one of the members of his church must have stolen it. He was very disturbed, and he decided to talk to his Deacon about what he should do. The Deacon suggested, "Why don't you preach on the Ten Commandments next Sunday, and then when you come to 'Thou shalt not steal' really lay it on, so that the guilty person will repent and return your hat." The Minister said, "That's a good idea. I'll try it."

So the next Sunday he got up in the pulpit and he was really laying it on strong on those Ten Commandments. He preached on "Honor thy father and thy mother"; then he preached on "Thou shalt not commit adultery." Then—he cut his sermon short.

After the service the Deacon said to him, "Reverend, you were doing so well, but you never did get to the main part of your sermon. What happened?"

He say, "Deacon Jones, I didn't need to use that part 'cause when I got to 'Thou shalt not commit adultery,' I remembered where I left my hat."

Don't Call My Name

They were taking a collection and the Minister hadn't been getting much collection during the revival. So they had this visiting Minister, and he said, "Well, Reverend, let me up there. I'll show you how to get you some collection."

So he walked up to the pulpit, and he said, "Now, look," he say, "there's a man out in that audience going with another man's wife." Said, "If I don't get a five-dollar bill in the collection plate from that man, I'll call his name out in church." He said, "Okay, Brothers, let's take up collection."

So they say when they took up collection they had ten five-dollar bills in the plate, and they had one two-dollar bill with a note on it. It said, "Please, Reverend, don't call my name. If you don't call my name *today*, I'll bring you the other three *tomorrow*."

The Only Two I Can Trust

An old lady was asked why she carried her money in her bosom. "Well," replied the Negro woman, "them's the only two suckers I can trust!"

I'm Gon' Get in the Drawer

A. This newly married couple were ready to retire on the first night, and the husband was already in bed. So the lady removed her contact lenses. She put those in the drawer. Then she removed her teeth and put those in the drawer. She removed her falsies, and she even had on false hips. She put all that in the drawer. And then her husband got up. She said, "Now, where are *you* going?"

He said, "I'm gon' get in the drawer."

B. Here's a guy who just got married. He's known this girl for several months, but he had never had anything to do with her sexually. He gets in the bed there, and she start to taking off false hair [mimicking lady removing her wig and laying it on the table], false teeth [mimicking lady removing her false teeth and laying them on the table], false eye [mimicking]. So she had all this stuff laying all up on top o' the table. He kept on looking back over at her and looking back over at the table.

She say, "What you looking at?"

He say, "I'm trying to decide whether to get in the bed with you or to get up here on that table. It's as much of you on the table as in the bed."

Outsmarting Whitey

"Naw-w-w-w, Master, I don't think I could make that, I don't think I could make a walk that far."

He say, "Well, I'll tell ya what I'll do; I'll send a couple o' men with a cart and they pick you up and load you in the cart and carry you, and we'll set you by the straw stack 'cause that sun will do you good."

"Well, just as you say. I don't think it'll do me no good."

So they took 'im, carried 'im out there, set 'im over there by that big stack o' straw; he layin' back in the sun there; and they went behind the straw stack and set the whole stack of straw afire. And that old man see that fire and jumped over top the stack and got up and outrun everybody.

So they took him and put him back in the fields.

CALL FOR POLITICAL AND SOCIAL STRATEGY

MALCOLM X
(1925–1965)

Malcolm X was a dynamic and influential political figure who profoundly challenged the integrationist and nonviolent rhetoric of the late fifties and early sixties. He was also a brilliant orator and an effective and powerful writer who epitomized the militancy and defiance of the age. For the artists and other radicals of the sixties, he represented black manhood and revolution. In short, he was the man who put fear in the hearts of the "white devils," his reference to white people. Malcolm X has influenced scores of black writers and political thinkers from Amiri Baraka, Sonia Sanchez, Etheridge Knight, Stokely Carmichael, and Haki R. Madhubuti (Don L. Lee) to Spike Lee and Public Enemy. In New York on the subway, you can see dapper young men hungrily devouring *Malcolm X Speaks* (1965). In addition, Malcolm stills speaks to the black masses, as Spike Lee's powerful film *Malcolm X* (1992) shows.

Malcolm X was born Malcolm Little in Omaha, Nebraska, on May 19, 1925. Earl Little, his father, was a Baptist minister and a follower of Jamaican-born black nationalist Marcus Garvey. In 1929, Reverend Little was murdered by a white supremacist in Michigan. Malcolm's mother, Louise Little, was left to take care of Malcolm and the other children. The strain proved too much for her, and she ended up in a mental institution. The children were sent to foster homes. In one of them, Malcolm grew up to become a gifted and popular student, but, as he recalls in *The Autobiography* (1965), this did not stop a white teacher from scuttling his ambition of becoming a lawyer by telling him to "be realistic about being a nigger" and pursue the more appropriate career of carpenter.

After the eighth grade, Malcolm quit school. He drifted to Boston, where he became a pimp, hustler, and drug dealer. In early 1946, Malcolm was arrested, charged with robbery, and sentenced to ten years in prison. While serving his time, he began to read seriously, became a follower of the Black Muslim leader Elijah Muhammad, and changed his name to Malcolm X to indicate the loss of his true African name and his rejection of his slave name. Muhammad preached that the white man was the devil, and Malcolm felt that most blacks would accept this notion because the white man acted like the devil in their daily lives. Malcolm was very successful in the Nation of Islam, but eventually he had disagreements with Muhammad. After Malcolm observed that the killing of John F. Kennedy was a case of "chickens coming home to roost," Muhammad expelled him from the Nation of Islam. Malcolm felt a need for Pan-African unity, black control of the black community, and racial pride in a society that hates black people.

In 1964, Malcolm X made a pilgrimage to Mecca, the holy city of the Muslim world, where he underwent a transformation. In *The Last Speeches* (1989), contrary to popular opinion, Malcolm demonstrated that he did not change his views toward white Americans after his trip:

> Despite the fact that I saw that Islam was a religion of brotherhood, I also had to face reality, and when I got back into this American society, I'm not in a society that practices brotherhood. I'm in a society that might preach it on Sunday, but they don't practice it on any other day. America is a society where there is no brotherhood. This society is controlled primarily by racists and segregationists, who are in Washington, D.C. in positions of power.

What Malcolm changed after his trip to Mecca was his name, which became El-Hajj Malik El-Shabazz.

On February 21, 1965, Malcolm X was murdered by four men who were presented by the media to be associated with the Nation of Islam. Speculation still exists, especially in the African American community, that his assassins were Central Intelligence Agency (CIA) agents. *The Autobiography of Malcolm X* (1965) was published after his death to much popular and critical acclaim.

The Autobiography begins, in the tradition of black American spiritual autobiographies, with the opening of consciousness into a primal vision of fear, violence, and pain. It opens with a chapter titled "Nightmare," with Malcolm unborn, lodged in his mother's womb, as Ku Klux Klan nightriders in Omaha come in search of his Baptist minister–Garveyite father. Again in that tradition, self-discovery eventually finds its dramatic climax in a conversion experience. After being stripped of his family and dignity by white American society and after being lost and lured into the criminal world, he adopts the code of Islam.

Many accused Malcolm of preaching a gospel of hate. To them his reply was as uncompromising as it was scathing:

> How can anyone ask us do we hate the white man who kidnapped us four hundred years ago, brought us here and stripped us of our history, stripped us of our culture, stripped us of our language, stripped us of everything you could have used today to prove you're part of the human family, bring you down to a level of an animal, sell you from plantation to plantation like a sack of wheat, sell you like a sack of potatoes, sell you like a horse and plow, and then hang you up from one end of the country to the other and then you ask me do I hate him. Why, your question is worthless.

Building on the foundation of black nationalism set by the likes of Marcus Garvey, Malcolm gave his followers a vision of racial dignity and self-pride restored. At a time when African and African American history and culture were essentially untaught in American schools, Malcolm glorified Africa's past and its cultural richness. He insisted that African Americans live up to their African heritage and take pride in their dark skin and in their own communities. "Stand yourself up and look at yourself—with your eyes not the white man's," he preached to the crowds in Harlem's streets.

A significant dimension of Malcolm's legacy is his Pan-African consciousness. On his way back from his trip to Mecca in the spring of 1964, he stopped in several African countries, among them Nigeria and Ghana. He told an audience at Nigeria's Ibadan University,

> I was convinced that it was time for all Afro-Americans to join the world's Pan-Africanists. I said that physically we Afro-Americans might remain in America,

> fighting for our constitutional rights, but that philosophically and culturally we Afro-Americans badly needed to return to Africa—and develop a working unity in the framework of Pan-Africanism.

Unfortunately, Malcom did not live long enough to develop the Organization of Afro-American Unity (OAAU) that he spoke of in his "Speech to African Summit Conference—Cairo, Egypt" in 1964 and planned to bring about in order to build this political framework for African Americans. Within less than a year of his trip to Africa, he was assassinated at the Audubon Ballroom in Harlem.

Malcolm X was a brilliant and brave man. In the closing pages of *The Autobiography* (1965), the actor Ossie Davis conveyed the sense of the times that Malcolm had come to change:

> Protocol and common sense require that negroes stand back and let the white man speak up for us, defend us, and lead us from behind the scene in our fight. This is the essence of Negro politics. But Malcolm said to hell with that! Get up off your knees and fight your own battles.

He articulated a new militant and international position for black people. Looking back on this figure of the sixties, we can now see how correct he was in his judgments of his America.

❖❖❖

Biographical studies on Malcolm X include Marshall Frady, "The Children of Malcolm," *The New Yorker,* October 12, 1992; Peter Goldman, *The Death and Life of Malcolm X* (1973); and Bruce Perry, *Malcolm: The Life of a Man Who Changed Black America* (1991) and Introduction to *Malcolm X: The Last Speeches* (1989). Of interest also is Karl Evanzz's *The Judas Factor* (1992), which proposes a United States government plot to kill Malcolm X.

*Speech to African Summit Conference—Cairo, Egypt**

Their Excellencies
First Ordinary Assembly of Heads of State and Governments
Organization of African Unity
Cairo, U.A.R.

YOUR EXCELLENCIES: The Organization of Afro-American Unity has sent me to attend this historic African Summit Conference as an observer to represent the interests of 22 million African-Americans whose *human rights* are being violated daily by the racism of American imperialists.

The Organization of Afro-American Unity (OAAU) has been formed by a cross section of America's African-American community, and is patterned after the letter and spirit of the Organization of African Unity (OAU).

Just as the Organization of African Unity has called upon all African leaders to submerge their differences and unite on common objectives for the common good of all Africans, in America the Organization of Afro-American Unity has called upon Afro-American leaders to submerge their differences and find areas of agreement wherein we can work in unity for the good of the entire 22 million African-Americans.

Since the 22 million of us were originally Africans, who are now in America, not by choice but only by a cruel accident in our his-

*July 17, 1964.

tory, we strongly believe that African problems are our problems and our problems are African problems.

YOUR EXCELLENCIES: We also believe that as heads of the independent African states you are the shepherds of *all* African peoples everywhere, whether they are still at home here on the mother continent or have been scattered abroad.

Some African leaders at this conference have implied that they have enough problems here on the mother continent without adding the Afro-American problem.

With all due respect to your esteemed positions, I must remind all of you that *the Good Shepherd* will leave ninety-nine sheep who are safe at home to go to the aid of the one who is lost and has fallen into the clutches of the imperialist wolf.

We in America are your long-lost brothers and sisters, and I am here only to remind you that our problems are your problems. As the African-Americans "awaken" today, we find ourselves in a strange land that has rejected us, and, like the prodigal son, we are turning to our elder brothers for help. We pray our pleas will not fall upon deaf ears.

We were taken forcibly in chains from this mother continent and have now spent over three hundred years in America, suffering the most inhuman forms of physical and psychological tortures imaginable.

During the past ten years the entire world has witnessed our men, women, and children being attacked and bitten by vicious police dogs, brutally beaten by police clubs, and washed down the sewers by high-pressure water hoses that would rip the clothes from our bodies and the flesh from our limbs.

And all of these inhuman atrocities have been inflicted upon us by the American governmental authorities, the police themselves, for no reason other than we seek the recognition and respect granted other human beings in America.

YOUR EXCELLENCIES: The American Government is either unable or unwilling to protect the lives and property of your 22 million African-American brothers and sisters. We stand defenseless, at the mercy of American racists who murder us at will for no reason other than we are black and of African descent.

Two black bodies were found in the Mississippi River this week; last week an unarmed African-American educator was murdered in cold blood in Georgia; a few days before that three civil rights workers disappeared completely, perhaps murdered also, only because they were teaching our people in Mississippi how to vote and how to secure their political rights.

Our problems are your problems. We have lived for over three hundred years in that American den of racist wolves in constant fear of losing life and limb. Recently, three students from Kenya were mistaken for American Negroes and were brutally beaten by the New York police. Shortly after that two diplomats from Uganda were also beaten by the New York City police, who mistook them for American Negroes.

If Africans are brutally beaten while only visiting in America, imagine the physical and psychological suffering received by your brothers and sisters who have lived there for over three hundred years.

Our problem is your problem. No matter how much independence Africans get here on the mother continent, unless you wear your national dress at all times when you visit America, you may be mistaken for one of us and suffer the same psychological and physical mutilation that is an everyday occurrence in our lives.

Your problems will never be fully solved until and unless ours are solved. You will never be fully respected until and unless we are also respected. You will never be recognized as free human beings until and unless we are also recognized and treated as human beings.

Our problem is your problem. It is not a Negro problem, nor an American problem. This is a world problem; a problem for humanity. It is not a problem of civil rights, but a problem of human rights.

If the United States Supreme Court justice Arthur Goldberg a few weeks ago could find legal grounds to threaten to bring Russia before the United Nations and charge her with violating the human rights of less than 3 million Russian Jews, what makes our African brothers hesitate to bring the United States Government before the United Nations and charge her with violating the human rights of 22 million African-Americans?

We pray that our African brothers have not freed themselves of European colonialism only to be overcome and held in check now by American *dollarism.* Don't let American racism be "legalized" by American dollarism.

America is worse than South Africa, because not only is America racist, but she is also deceitful and hypocritical. South Africa preaches segregation and practices segregation. She, at least, practices what she preaches. America preaches integration and practices segregation. She preaches one thing while deceitfully practicing another.

South Africa is like a vicious wolf, openly hostile toward black humanity. But America is cunning like a fox, friendly and smiling, but even more vicious and deadly than the wolf.

The wolf and the fox are both enemies of humanity, both are canine, both humiliate and mutilate their victims. Both have the same objectives, but differ only in methods.

If South Africa is guilty of violating the human rights of Africans here on the mother continent, then America is guilty of worse violations of the 22 million Africans on the American continent. And if South African racism is not a domestic issue, then American racism also is not a *domestic* issue.

Many of you have been led to believe that the much publicized, recently passed Civil Rights Bill is a sign that America is making a sincere effort to correct the injustices we have suffered there. This propaganda maneuver is part of her deceit and trickery to keep the African nations from condemning her racist practices before the United Nations, as you are now doing as regards the same practices of South Africa.

The United States Supreme Court passed laws ten years ago making America's segregated school system illegal. But the Federal Government cannot enforce the law of the highest court in the land when it comes to nothing but equal-rights to education for African-Americans. How can anyone be so naïve as to think all the additional laws brought into being by the Civil Rights Bill will be enforced?

These are nothing but tricks of this century's leading neocolonialist power. Surely, our intellectually mature African brothers will not fall for this trickery?

The Organization of Afro-American Unity, in cooperation with a coalition of other Negro leaders and organizations, has decided to elevate our freedom struggle above the domestic level of civil rights. We intend to internationalize it by placing it at the level of human rights. Our freedom struggle for human dignity is no longer confined to the domestic jurisdiction of the United States Government.

We beseech the independent African states to help us bring our problem before the United Nations, on the grounds that the United States Government is morally incapable of protecting the lives and the property of 22 million African-Americans. And on the grounds that our deteriorating plight is definitely becoming a threat to world peace.

Out of frustration and hopelessness our young people have reached the point of no return. We no longer endorse patience and turning the other cheek. We assert the right of self-defense by whatever means necessary, and reserve the right of maximum retaliation against our racist oppressors, no matter what the odds against us are.

From here on in, if we must die anyway, we will die fighting back, and we will not die alone. We intend to see that our racist oppressors also get a taste of death.

We are well aware that our future efforts to defend ourselves by retaliating—by meeting violence with violence, eye for eye and tooth for tooth—could create the type of racial conflict in America that could easily escalate into a violent, worldwide, bloody race war.

In the interests of world peace and security, we beseech the heads of the independent

African states to recommend an immediate investigation into our problem by the United Nations Commission on Human Rights.

If this humble plea that I am voicing at this conference is not properly worded, then let our elder brothers, who know the legal language, come to our aid and word our plea in the proper language necessary for it to be heard.

One last word, my beloved brothers at this African Summit: "No one knows the master better than his servant." We have been servants in America for over three hundred years. We have a thorough inside knowledge of this man who calls himself "Uncle Sam." Therefore, you must heed our warning. Don't escape from European colonialism only to become even more enslaved by deceitful, "friendly" American dollarism.

May Allah's blessings of good health and wisdom be upon you all.

ASALAAM ALAIKUM

MARTIN LUTHER KING, JR.
(1929–1968)

On April 4, 1968, Dr. Martin Luther King, Jr., a recipient of the Nobel Peace Prize four years earlier, was shot to death on the balcony of the Lorraine Motel in Memphis, Tennessee. This senseless assassination silenced one of the great African American leaders of the twentieth century. Through his sermons, speeches, and writings and the numerous Civil Rights marches and protests he led, his name, image, and eloquent voice became, during the second half of the twentieth century, the quintessential symbol of the long black struggle for freedom and justice in America.

Born in Atlanta, Georgia, on January 15, 1929, King was the second of three children born to Reverend Martin Luther King, Sr., and Alberta Christine Williams King. King, who was called "M.L." as a child, had with his older sister, Christine (Christine King Farris), and his younger brother, Alfred Daniel, a black southern version of middle-class childhood. His father, known as "Daddy King," was the pastor of Ebenezer Baptist Church, a position he had taken over in 1931 from his father-in-law, Reverend A. D. Williams. Mrs. King was an elementary school teacher. She was also a good musician, a student of the piano and organ, and later director of music at Ebenezer. Although Martin Luther King, Jr., grew up in a relatively comfortable middle-class environment, Georgia, during the years of his boyhood, was still racially segregated. Thus, he had to make his own truce with the absurd social arrangement that divided the South along black and white lines. Like all other blacks, he drank from the drinking fountain marked COLORED and sat in the "colored" waiting rooms.

King attended David T. Howard Elementary School, and then a private experimental school, Laboratory High School, sponsored by Atlanta University. Two years later, he moved to Booker T. Washington High School, the oldest black public high school in the city. He spent two years there, then enrolled at Morehouse College in the Fall of 1944. He was fifteen.

While at Morehouse, King was influenced by several devoted teachers who had dedicated their lives to motivating young black men to aspire to excellence. Chief among them was Benjamin E. Mays, who served as president of Morehouse during that period. Several of King's professors were also ministers. Despite their influence and the example of his father and grandfather, however, it was not until his junior year that he decided to become a man of the cloth. During his senior year, he was ordained a Baptist minister. In addition to being an excellent student at Morehouse, he was popular, generally regarded as a suave dresser and a good dancer. After graduating from Morehouse in 1948 with a B.A. in sociology, he studied at Crozer Theological Seminary in Pennsylvania. The combination of academic excellence and social charm that he had exhibited at Morehouse also stood him in good stead at Crozer. Although King was only one of six black students, he was the most outstanding student and president of his senior class. After graduating from Crozer in 1951, he enrolled in Boston University to pursue his Ph.D.

On June 18, 1953, King married Coretta Scott in Marion, Alabama. The following year he received his Ph.D. in systematic theology. He was invited to become the full-time pastor of Dexter Avenue Baptist Church in Montgomery, Alabama, in September 1954. Later that year, on November 17, his first child, Yolanda Denise, was born.

King was catapulted into fame after becoming an outspoken leader of the Montgomery bus boycott, which began in December 1955 after Rosa Parks was arrested for refusing to give up her seat to a white man. Despite various attempts to thwart the efforts of those involved in the boycott, a lawsuit charging that Montgomery's segregated public transportation system was unconstitutional eventually made it to the U.S. Supreme Court. On November 13, 1956, the Supreme Court upheld an earlier decision by the U.S. district court that Alabama's state and local bus segregation laws were unconstitutional. In December 1956, Montgomery city buses were integrated.

In January 1957, King was elected president of the Southern Christian Leadership Conference (SCLC) at its founding meeting. As president of the SCLC, he, along with Ralph Abernathy, led a series of successful protests against segregation in Birmingham, Alabama. Several years later, on August 28, 1963, he led the March on Washington, during which as many as 250,000 blacks and many whites marched to protest racial bigotry and segregation in the United States. Although many celebrities spoke at the Lincoln Memorial on this historic occasion, King's "I Have a Dream" speech remains the most memorable.

King was unquestionably a powerful orator, but the cadences, rhythms, and moral perspicacity that are characteristic of his speeches also are found in much of his writing. His first book, *Stride Toward Freedom* (1958), is autobiographical and discusses in detail how Montgomery's black community came together during the bus boycott, which lasted for well over a year. *Stride Toward Freedom* was followed by *Strength to Love* (1963), a collection of seventeen sermons rewritten for publication. King published the sermons somewhat reluctantly, noting in his introduction, "While I tried to rewrite these for the eye, I am convinced that this venture could never be entirely successful." His third book, *Why We Can't Wait* (1964), includes the famous "Letter from Birmingham Jail," in which King addressed several Alabama clergymen who, in an open letter, had objected to his presence in Birmingham.

In 1967, King published *Where Do We Go from Here: Chaos or Community?* The book represents King's extended dialogue with those who believed that the advent of the Black Power Movement, led by Stokely Carmichael, would mean the end of nonviolent protest. While maintaining his essential position on nonviolent protest,

King admired the way the Black Muslims "took care of business." He agreed with the Black Power Movement that "the problem of transferring the ghetto is . . . a problem of power" and that blacks must "amass political and economic strength" by using the ballot and pooling their financial resources "to achieve their legitimate goals." King also endorsed Black Power's emphasis on racial pride. Instructed on their contributions to history and culture, black Americans would acquire a sense of dignity and worth, enabling them to overcome the crippling effects of personal and institutional racism. "As long as the mind is enslaved," King maintained, "the body can never be free."

Near the end of his life, King was becoming increasingly political, almost radical, in a more explicit ideological way. As David J. Garrow makes clear in *The FBI and Martin Luther King, Jr., From "Solo" to Memphis* (1981), King could no longer apologize for America's racism. In King's own words,

> America is deeply racist and its democracy is flawed both economically and socially . . . the black revolution is more than a struggle for the rights of Negroes. It is forcing America to face all its inter-related flaws—racism, poverty, militarism, and materialism. It reveals systematic rather than superficial flaws and suggests that radical reconstruction of society itself is the real issue to be faced.

King would eventually go on to embrace an anti–Vietnam War position on the basis that there was a vital moral link between that movement and the Civil Rights Movement. In a decisive anti–Vietnam War speech in Los Angeles in 1967, he said, "We must demonstrate, teach, and preach *until the very foundations of our nation are shaken.*" It was this kind of intimidating language, reminiscent of biblically prophetic proclamations, that would bring King into inevitable political disfavor with federal officials, including President Lyndon B. Johnson.

King's increasing involvement in world affairs did not decrease the energy and time he spent on the domestic front. In fact, his life was brought to its tragic end in Memphis several days after he had led six thousand protesters through the city in support of striking sanitation workers. A riot broke out, killing a sixteen-year-old and injuring more than fifty other people. Later, King delivered his "I've Been to the Mountain Top" speech, which was fatally precise in its eloquence:

> Well, I don't know what will happen now. . . . But it doesn't matter with me now. Because I've been to the mountain top . . . like anybody, I would like to live a long life. . . . But I'm not concerned about that now. . . . I've seen the promised land. . . . I'm not fearing any man. Mine eyes have seen the glory of the coming of the Lord.

The following day, King was shot and died in St. Joseph Hospital. James Earl Ray was eventually captured and convicted of murder.

The thousands of mourners King touched with his words and life would eventually see an American hero celebrated when his birthday was made a national holiday by President Ronald Reagan on November 2, 1983. His name and image continue to live on in American and international postage stamps, on avenues and streets, and in the names of high schools and institutes. An eternal flame burns at King's crypt at the Martin Luther Ling Jr. Center for Nonviolent Social Change, Inc., in Atlanta. The crypt bears the following words: Rev. Martin Luther King, Jr. 1929–1968 "Free at Last."

Studies of King's role in the Civil Rights Movement often emphasize the influence of Paul Tillich, Reinhold Niebuhr, Nelson Wieman, Walter Rauschenbusch, Mahatma Gandhi, and other theologians and thinkers. But the effectiveness of his leadership cannot be attributed solely to his ideas about nonviolence as a mode of political resistance. The real power of his leadership lay in his ability to combine a simple but profound philosophy with the folk religion and revival techniques of the black Baptist preacher. He was able to elicit from the thousands who flocked to hear him the old-fashioned religiosity of the folk converted into a passion for justice. As with the lives of Frederick Douglass, Mary McLeod Bethune, W. E. B. Du Bois, and Marcus Garvey, King's life represents the living dramatization of a spirit deeply rooted in African American culture—the spirit of freedom.

❖❖❖

Books of varying lengths and perspectives, as well as numerous articles, both journalistic and academic, have been published on King. See Lerone Bennet, Jr., *What Manner of Man* (1965); Coretta Scott King, *My Life with Martin Luther King, Jr.* (1969); and David L. Lewis, *King: A Critical Biography* (1970). Several collections of his speeches and writings have been published. See *A Testament of Hope: The Essential Writings of Martin Luther King, Jr.* (1986) and Joseph M. Washington, ed., *I Have a Dream: Writings and Speeches That Changed the World* (1992). The first volume of King's official papers also has been published. See Clayborne Carson, senior editor, *Called to Serve: The Papers of Martin Luther King, Jr., January 1929–June 1951,* vol. 1 (1992).

I Have a Dream

I am happy to join with you today in what will go down in history as the greatest demonstration for freedom in the history of our nation.

Five score years ago, a great American, in whose symbolic shadow we stand today, signed the Emancipation Proclamation. This momentous decree came as the great beacon light of hope for millions of Negro slaves who had been seared in the flames of withering injustice. It came as the joyous daybreak to end the long night of their captivity.

But one hundred years later the Negro still is not free. One hundred years later, the life of the Negro is still badly crippled by the manacles of segregation and the chains of discrimination. One hundred years later, the Negro lives on a lonely island of poverty in the midst of a vast ocean of material prosperity. One hundred years later, the Negro is still languished in the corners of American society and finds himself an exile in his own land. So we have come here today to dramatize the shameful condition.

In a sense we've come to our Nation's Capital to cash a check. When the architects of our republic wrote the magnificent words of the Constitution and the Declaration of Independence, they were signing a promissory note to which every American was to fall heir. This note was a promise that all men, yes, black men as well as white men, should be guaranteed the unalienable rights of life, liberty and the pursuit of happiness.

It is obvious today that America has defaulted on this promissory note insofar as her citizens of color are concerned. Instead of honoring this sacred obligation, America has given the Negro people a bad check, a check which has come back marked "Insufficient Funds." But we refuse to believe the bank of justice is bankrupt. We refuse to believe that there are insufficient funds in the great vaults of opportunity of this nation. So we have come to cash this check, a check that will give us upon demand, the riches of freedom and the security of justice. We have also come to this hallowed spot to remind America of the fierce urgency of now.

This is no time to engage in the luxury of cooling off or to take the tranquilizing drug of gradualism. Now is the time to make real the promises of democracy. Now is the time to rise from the dark, the desolate valley of segregation to the sunlit path of racial justice. Now is the time to lift our nation from the quicksands of racial injustice to the solid rock of brotherhood. Now is the time to make justice a reality for all of God's children.

It would be fatal for the nation to overlook the urgency of the moment. This sweltering summer of the Negro's legitimate discontent will not pass until there is an invigorating autumn of freedom and equality. Nineteen sixty-three is not an end but a beginning. Those who hoped that the Negro needed to blow off steam and will now be content will have a rude awakening if the nation returns to business as usual. There will be neither rest nor tranquility in America until the Negro is guaranteed his citizenship rights. The whirlwinds of revolt will continue to shake the foundations of our nation until the bright day of justice emerges.

But there is something I must say to my people who stand on the warm threshold which leads them to the palace of justice. In the process of gaining our rightful place we must not be guilty of wrongful deeds. Let us not seek to satisfy our thirst for freedom by drinking from the cup of bitterness and hatred. We must forever conduct our struggle on the high plane of dignity and discipline. We must not allow our creative protest to degenerate into physical violence. Again and again we must rise to the majestic heights of meeting physical force with soul force.

The marvelous new militancy which has engulfed the Negro community must not lead us to a distrust of all white people, for many of our white brothers, as evidenced by their presence here today, have come to realize that their destiny is tied up with our destiny. They have come to realize that their freedom is inextricably bound to our freedom. We cannot walk alone.

And as we walk we must make the pledge that we shall always march ahead. We cannot turn back. There are those who are asking the devotees of civil rights: "When will you be satisfied?" We can never be satisfied as long as our bodies, heavy with the fatigue of travel, cannot gain lodging in the motels of the highways and the hotels of the cities. We cannot be satisfied as long as the Negro's basic mobility is from a smaller ghetto to a larger one. We can never be satisfied as long as our children are stripped of their selfhood and robbed of their dignity by signs stating: "For Whites Only." We cannot be satisfied as long as the Negro in Mississippi cannot vote and the Negro in New York believes he has nothing for which to vote. No, no, we are not satisfied and we will not be satisfied until justice rolls down like the waters and righteousness like a mighty stream.

I am not unmindful that some of you have come here out of great trials and tribulations, some of you have come fresh from narrow jail cells, some of you have come from areas where your quest for freedom left you battered by the storms of persecution and staggered by the winds of police brutality. You have been the veterans of creative suffering. Continue to work with the faith that unearned suffering is redemptive.

Go back to Mississippi, go back to Alabama, go back to South Carolina, go back to Georgia, go back to Louisiana, go back to the slums and ghettos of our northern cities, knowing that somehow this situation can and will be changed. Let us not wallow in the valley of despair.

I say to you today, my friends, even though we face the difficulties of today and tomorrow, I still have a dream. It is a dream deeply rooted in the American dream. I have a dream that one day this nation will rise up and live out the true meaning of its creed: "We hold these truths to be self-evident that all men are created equal."

I have a dream that one day on the red hills of Georgia the sons of former slaves and the sons of former slaveowners will be able to sit down together at the table of brotherhood.

I have a dream that one day even the State of Mississippi, a state sweltering with the heat of injustice, sweltering with the heat of oppression, will be transformed into an oasis of freedom and justice. I have a dream that my four little children will one day live in a nation where they will not be judged by the color of their skin but by the content of their character. I have a dream today.

I have a dream that one day down in Alabama with its vicious racists, with its Governor having his lips dripping with the words of interposition and nullification—one day right there in Alabama, little black boys and black girls will be able to join hands with little white boys and white girls as sisters and brothers.

I have a dream today.

I have a dream that one day every valley shall be exalted, every hill and mountain shall be made low, the rough places will be made plain and the crooked places will be made straight, and the glory of the Lord shall be revealed, and all flesh shall see it together.

This is our hope. This is the faith that I go back to the South with. With this faith we will be able to hew out of the mountain of despair a stone of hope. With this faith we will be able to transform the jangling discords of our nation into a beautiful symphony of brotherhood. With this faith we will be able to work together, to pray together, to struggle together, to go to jail together, to stand up for freedom together, knowing that we will be free one day.

This will be the day when all of God's children will be able to sing with new meaning:

> My country 'tis of thee,
> Sweet land of liberty,
> Of thee I sing:
> Land where my fathers died,
> Land of the pilgrims' pride.
> From every mountain-side
> Let Freedom ring.

And if America is to be a great nation, this must become true. So, let freedom ring from the prodigious hill tops of New Hampshire. Let freedom ring from the mighty mountains of New York. Let freedom ring from the heightening Alleghenies of Pennsylvania. Let freedom ring from the snowcapped Rockies of Colorado. Let freedom ring from the curvaceous slopes of California. But not only that, let freedom ring from Stone Mountain of Georgia.

Let freedom ring from Lookout Mountain of Tennessee.

Let freedom ring from every hill and molehill of Mississippi. From every mountainside, let freedom ring. And when we allow freedom to ring, when we let it ring from every village, from every hamlet, from every state and every city, we will be able to speed up that day when all of God's children, black men and white men, Jews and Gentiles, Protestants and Catholics, will be able to join hands and sing in the words of the old Negro spiritual: "Free at last! free at last! thank God almighty, we are free at last!"

STOKELY CARMICHAEL

(1941–)

Handsome and articulate, Stokely Carmichael was one of the most charismatic figures of the Black Power Movement. Both on the stage and on the page, Carmichael argued coolly and logically for black political power and control. He popularized the term "Black Power," which was the title of Richard Wright's travel book of 1954, and was the effective leader of the Student Nonviolent Coordinating Committee (SNCC) for many years.

The son of Adolphus and Mabel F. Carmichael, Stokely Carmichael (now Kwame Ture) was born on June 29, 1941, in Port of Spain, Trinidad. In 1952, at age eleven, he emigrated to the United States. He attended the prestigious Bronx High School of Science in New York City and received his bachelor's degree from Howard

University in 1964. Three years earlier, while still an undergraduate student at Howard, Carmichael had traveled south as a freedom rider to confront segregation in public bus terminals. He was arrested in Jackson, Mississippi, where he served forty-nine days in Parchman Prison. After his release, he joined the SNCC. He was instrumental in turning the organization away from nonviolence and toward black militancy. Carmichael called for self-defense against white violence and for the expulsion of whites from the SNCC. In March 1965, he went to Lowndes County, Alabama, to register black voters. Within a short time, he had increased the number of blacks registered to vote from 70 to 2,600 and established an all-black political party, the Lowndes County Freedom Organization.

In 1966, in Greenwood, Mississippi, he made his famous "Black Power" speech. The address is often credited for changing the direction of the Civil Rights Movement from nonviolence and social integration to self-defense and black nationalism. Carmichael later left the SNCC and joined the Black Panthers, but he differed with Panther leader Eldridge Cleaver over the issue of working with white radicals. Consequently, he also left the Panthers. In 1969, he and his wife, black South African singer Mariam Makeba, moved to Guinea, where he still lives today.

❖❖❖

For information on Carmichael, see Cleveland Sellers, *The River of No Return: The Autobiography of a Black Militant and the Life and Death of SNCC* (1973) and Allen Matusow, *The Unraveling of America: A History of Liberalism in the 1960s* (1984).

*Black Power**

. . . It seems to me that the institutions that function in this country are clearly racist, and that they're built upon racism. And the question then is, how can black people inside this country move? And then how can white people, who say they're not a part of those institutions, begin to move, and how then do we begin to clear away the obstacles that we have in this society that keep us from living like human beings. How can we begin to build institutions that will allow people to relate with each other as human beings? This country has never done that. Especially around the concept of white or black.

Now several people have been upset because we've said that integration was irrelevant when initiated by blacks and that in fact it was a subterfuge, an insidious subterfuge for the maintenance of white supremacy. We maintain that in the past six years or so this country has been feeding us a thalidomide drug of integration, and that some Negroes have been walking down a dream street talking about sitting next to white people, and that that does not begin to solve the problem. When we went to Mississippi, we did not go to sit next to Ross Barnett; we did not go to sit next to Jim Clark; we went to get them out of our way, and people ought to understand that. We were never fighting for the right to integrate, we were fighting against white supremacy. . . .

Now we are engaged in a psychological struggle in this country and that struggle is whether or not black people have the right to use the words they want to use without white people giving their sanction to it. We maintain, whether they like it or not, we gon' use the word "black power" and let them address themselves to that. We are not gonna wait for white people to sanction black power. We're tired of waiting. Every

*"Black Power," speech by Stokely Carmichael, former chairman of the Student Nonviolent Coordinating Committee, University of California, Berkeley, November 19, 1966. Transcribed from taped remarks.

time black people move in this country, they're forced to defend their position before they move. It's time that the people who're supposed to be defending their position do that. That's white people. They ought to start defending themselves, as to why they have oppressed and exploited us.

It is clear that when this country started to move in terms of slavery, the reason for a man being picked as a slave was one reason: because of the color of his skin. If one was black, one was automatically inferior, inhuman, and therefore fit for slavery. So that the question of whether or not we are individually suppressed is nonsensical and is a downright lie. We are oppressed as a group because we are black, not because we are lazy, not because we're apathetic, not because we're stupid, not because we smell, not because we eat watermelon and have good rhythm. We are oppressed because we are black, and in order to get out of that oppression, one must feel the group power that one has. Not the individual power which this country then sets the criteria under which a man may come into it. That is what is called in this country as integration. You do what I tell you to do, and then we'll let you sit at the table with us. And then we are saying that we have to be opposed to that. We must now set a criteria, and that if there's going to be any integration it's going to be a two-way thing. If you believe in integration, you can come live in Watts. You can send your children to the ghetto schools. Let's talk about that. If you believe in integration, then we're going to start adopting us some white people to live in our neighborhood. So it is clear that the question is not one of integration or segregation. Integration is a man's ability to want to move in there by himself. If someone wants to live in a white neighborhood and he is black, that is his choice. It should be his right. It is not because white people will allow him. So vice-versa, if a black man wants to live in the slums, that should be his right. Black people will let him, that is the difference.

It is this difference which points up the logical mistakes this country makes when it begins to criticize the program articulated by SNCC. We maintain that we cannot afford to be concerned about 6 percent of the children in this country. I mean the black children who you allow to come into white schools. We have 94 percent who still live in shacks. We are going to be concerned about those 94 percent. You ought to be concerned about them, too. The question is, are we willing to be concerned about those 94 percent. Are we willing to be concerned about the black people who will never get to Berkeley, who will never get to Harvard and cannot get an education, so you'll never get a chance to rub shoulders with them and say, "Well he's almost as good as we are; he's not like the others." The question is, how can white society begin to move to see black people as human beings? I am black, therefore I am. Not that I am black and I must go to college to prove myself. I am black, therefore I am. And don't surprise me with anything and say to me that you must go to college before you gain access to X, Y, and Z. It is only a rationalization for one's oppression.

The political parties in this country do not meet the needs of the people on a day-to-day basis. The question is, how can we build new political institutions that will become the political expressions of people on a day-to-day basis. The question is, how can you build political institutions that will begin to meet the needs of Oakland, California; and the needs of Oakland California is not 1,000 policemen with submachine guns. They don't need that. They need that least of all. The question is, how can we build institutions where those people can begin to function on a day-to-day basis, where they can get decent jobs, where they can get decent housing, and where they can begin to participate in the policy and major decisions that affect their lives. That's what they need. Not Gestapo troops. Because this is not 1942. And if you play like Nazis, we're playing back with you this time around. Get hip to that.

The question then is, how can white people move to start making the major institutions that they have in this country function the way they are supposed to function? That is the real question. And can white people move inside their own community and start tearing down racism where, in fact, it does exist? It is you who live in Cicero and stop us from living there. It is white people who stop us from moving into Grenada. It is white people who make sure that we live in the ghettos of this country. It is white institutions that do that. They must change. In order for America to really live on a basic principle of human relationships, a new society must be born. Racism must die, and the economic exploitation of this country, of non-white people around the world, must also die.

There are several programs that we have in the South among some poor white communities. We're trying to organize poor whites on a base where they can begin to move around the question of economic exploitation and political disenfranchisement. We know we've heard the theory several times, but few people are willing to go into this. The question is, can the white activist not try to be a Pepsi generation who comes alive in the black community, but that he be a man who's willing to move into the white community and start organizing where the organization is needed? . . .

We've been saying that we cannot have white people working in the black community and we've based it on psychological grounds. The fact is that all black people often question whether or not they are equal to whites because every time they start to do something white people are around showing them how to do it. If we are going to eliminate that for the generations that come after us, then black people must be seen in positions of power doing the articulating for themselves. . . .

Now then, the question is, how can we move to begin to change what's going on in this country? I maintain, as we have in SNCC, that the war in Vietnam is an illegal and immoral war. And the question is, what can we do to stop that war. What can we do to stop the people who, in the name of our country, are killing babies, women and children. What can we do to stop that? And I maintain that we do not have the power in our hands to change that institution, to begin to recreate it so that they learn to leave the Vietnamese people alone, and that the only power we have is the power to say "Hell, no!" to the draft. . . . There isn't one organization that has begun to meet our stand on the war in Vietnam. Because we not only say we are against the war in Vietnam; *we are against the draft.* We are against the draft. No man has the right to take a man for two years and train him to be a killer. . . .

It is impossible for white and black people to talk about building a relationship based on humanity when the country is the way it is, when the institutions are clearly against us. We have taken all the myths of this country and we've found them to be nothing but downright lies. This country told us that if we worked hard we would succeed, and if that were true we would own this country lock, stock and barrel. It is we who have picked the cotton for nothing; it is we who are the maids in the kitchens of liberal white people; it is we who are the janitors, the porters, the elevator men; it is we who sweep up your college floors; yes, it is we who are the hardest working and the lowest paid. And that it is nonsensical for people to start talking about human relationships until they're willing to build new institutions. Black people are economically insecure. White liberals are economically secure. Can you begin an economic coalition? Are the liberals willing to share their salaries with the economically insecure black people who they so much love? Then if you're not, are you willing to start building new institutions that will provide economic security for black people? That's the question we want to deal with. . . .

We have to raise questions about whether or not we need new types of political institutions in this country and we in SNCC maintain that we need them now. We need new political institutions in this country. And any time Lyndon Baines Johnson can head a party which has in it Bobby Kennedy, Wayne Morse, Eastland, Wallace and all those other supposedly liberal cats, there's something wrong with that party. They're moving politically, not morally. And if that party refuses to seat black people from Mississippi and goes ahead and seats racists like Eastland and his clique, then it is clear to me that they're moving politically and that one cannot begin to talk morality to people like that. We must begin to think politically and see if we can have the power to impose and keep the moral values that we hold high. We must question the values of this society. And I maintain that black people are the best people to do that because we have been excluded from that society and the question is, we ought to think whether or not we want to become a part of that society. That's what we want. And that is precisely what, it seems to me, the Student Nonviolent Coordinating Committee is doing. We are raising questions about this country. I do not want to be a part of the American pride. The American pride means raping South Africa, beating Vietnam, beating South America, raping the Philippines, raping every country you've been in. I don't want any of your blood money. I don't want it . . . don't want to be part of that system. And the question is, how do we raise those questions. . . . How do we raise them as activists?

We have grown up and we are the generation that has found this country to be a world power, that has found this country to be the wealthiest country in the world. We must question how she got her wealth. That's what we're questioning. And whether or not we want this country to continue being the wealthiest country in the world at the price of raping everybody across the world. That's what we must begin to question. And because black people are saying we do not now want to become a part of you, we are called reverse racists. Ain't that a gas?

How do we raise the questions of poverty? The assumptions of this country is that if someone is poor, they're poor because of their own individual blight, or they weren't born on the right side of town. They had too many children; they went in the Army too early; their father was a drunk; they didn't care about school; they made a mistake. That's a lot of nonsense. *Poverty is well calculated in this country.* It is well calculated. And the reason why the poverty program won't work is because the calculators of poverty are administering it. That's why it won't work.

So how can we, as the youth in the country, move to start tearing those things down? We must move into the white community. We are in the black community. We have developed a movement in the black community that challenges the white activist who has failed miserably to develop the movement inside of his community. The question is, can we find white people who are going to have the courage to go into white communities and start organizing them? Can we find them? Are they here? And are they willing to do that? Those are the questions that we must raise for white activists.

We are never going to get caught up with questions about power. This country knows what power is and knows it very well. And knows what black power is because it's deprived black people of it for 400 years. So it knows what black power is. But the question is, why do white people in this country associate black power with violence? Because of their own inability to deal with blackness. If we had said Negro power, nobody would get scared. Everybody would support it. And if we said power for colored people, everybody would be for that. But it is the word 'black,' it is the word 'black' that bothers people in this country, and that's their problem, not mine. . . .

So that in conclusion, we want to say that first, it is clear to me that we have to wage a psychological battle on the right for black people to define their own terms, define themselves as they see fit and organize themselves as they see fit. Now, the question is, how is the white community going to begin to allow for that organizing, because once they start to do that, they will also allow for the organizing that they want to do inside their communities. It doesn't make any difference. Because we're going to organize our way anyway. We're going to do it. The question is, how we're going to facilitate those matters. Whether it's going to be done with a thousand policemen with sub-machine guns or whether or not it's going to be done in the context where it's allowed to be done by white people warding off those policemen. That is the question.

And the question is, how will white people who call themselves activists get ready to start moving into the white communities on two counts? On building new political institutions, to destroy the old ones that we have, and to move around the concept of white youth refusing to go into the army. So that we can start then to build a new world.

It is ironic to talk about civilization in this country. This country is uncivilized. It needs to be civilized. We must begin to raise those questions of civilization. What it is, and we'll do it. And so we must urge you to fight now to be the leaders of today, not tomorrow. We've got to be the leaders of today. This country is a nation of thieves. It stands on the brink of becoming a nation of murderers. We must stop it. *We* must stop it.

And then, in a larger sense, there is the question of black people. We are on the move for our liberation. We have been tired of trying to prove things to white people. We are tired of trying to explain to white people that we're not going to hurt them. We are concerned with getting the things we want, the things that we have to have to be able to function. The question is, can white people allow for that in this country? The question is, will white people overcome their racism and allow for that to happen in this country? If that does not happen, brothers and sisters, we have no choice, but to say very clearly, move on over, or we're going to move on over you.

JESSE JACKSON

(1941–)

Recent polls have recognized Jesse Jackson as America's most important black leader. As a Baptist clergyman and social activist, he has attempted to improve the lot of the dispossessed and disenfranchised throughout the world. As a presidential candidate, statesman, and powerful moral speaker, he has been an inspiration to black America.

Jesse Louis Jackson was born on October 8, 1941, to Noah Robinson, a cotton grader, and Helen Burns Jackson, a hairdresser, in Greenville, South Carolina. Like many American blacks, Jackson's ancestry includes black slaves, a Cherokee Indian, and a white plantation owner. At Sterling High School, he was elected president of his class and lettered in football, basketball, and baseball. At North Carolina Agricultural and Technical College in Greensboro, a predominantly black institution, he was a quarterback, an honor student, and president of the student body. He attended Chicago Theological Seminary from 1964 to 1966 and soon afterward became an ordained Baptist minister. In 1965, Jackson joined Martin Luther King, Jr., and the Southern Christian Leadership Conference (SCLC) during demonstrations to expand black voter rights in Selma, Alabama. Six years later, he resigned from the SCLC to found his own organization, People United to Save Humanity (PUSH). The purpose of PUSH was to improve the economic condition of poor people. PUSH-Excel, a spinoff program, was dedicated to keeping inner-city youths in school.

When Jackson ran for president in 1984, he received 3.5 million votes; when he ran again in 1988, he won 6.9 million votes. Three years later, he was elected the District of Columbia's "statehood senator," a position created by the city of Washington to help it gain statehood. Mayor Andrew Young of Atlanta has called Jackson "America's prophet in residence." In *The LeRoi Jones/Amiri Baraka Reader,* Baraka says of Jackson: "Jesse represent[s] our desire for Self-Determination, the shaping of our own lives with the same opportunity possessed by any other American." At present, Jackson serves as a political commentator on his own television show.

❖❖❖

For information on Jackson, see Elizabeth O. Colton, *The Jackson Phenomenon: The Man, the Power, the Message* (1989); Amiri Baraka, "Black People & Jesse Jackson," in *The LeRoi Jones/Amiri Baraka Reader* (1991); and Gerald Early, "Jesse Jackson's Black Bottom, or Crossing the Roads at Tuxedo Junction," in *Tuxedo Junction* (1989).

Address: Democratic National Convention, San Francisco, July 17, 1984

Our flag is red, white and blue, but our Nation is a rainbow—Red, Yellow, Brown, Black and White—we're all precious in God's sight.

America is not like a blanket—one piece of unbroken cloth, the same color, the same texture, the same size. America is more like a quilt—many patches, many pieces, many colors, many sizes, all woven and held together by a common thread. The White, the Hispanic, the Black, the Arab, the Jew, the woman, the Native American, the small farmer, the businessperson, the environmentalist, the peace activist, the young, the old, the lesbian, the gay and the disabled make up the American quilt.

Even in our fractured state, all of us count and fit somewhere. We have proven that we can survive without each other. But we have not proven that we can win and make progress without each other. We must come together.

From Fannie Lou Hamer in Atlantic City in 1964 to the Rainbow Coalition in San Francisco today; from the Atlantic to the Pacific, we have experienced pain but progress as we ended America's apartheid laws, we got public accommodations, we secured voting rights, we obtained open housing, as young people got the right to vote. We lost Malcolm, Martin, Medgar, Bobby and John and Viola. The team that got us here must be expanded, not abandoned.

Twenty years ago, tears welled up in our eyes as the bodies of Schwerner, Goodman, and Chaney were dredged from the depths of a river in Mississippi. Twenty years later, our communities, Black and Jewish, are in anguish, anger and in pain. Feelings have been hurt on both sides.

There is a crisis in communications. Confusion is in the air, but we cannot afford to lose our way. We may agree to agree or agree to disagree on issues; we must bring back civility to the tensions.

We are co-partners in a long and rich religious history—the Judeo-Christian traditions. Many Blacks and Jews have a shared passion for social justice at home and peace abroad. We must seek a revival of the spirit inspired by a new vision and new possibilities. We must return to higher ground.

We are bound by Moses and Jesus, but also connected with Islam and Mohammed. These three great religions—Judaism, Christianity, and Islam—were all born in the revered and Holy City of Jerusalem.

We are bound by Dr. Martin Luther King, Jr., and Rabbi Abraham Heschel, crying out from their graves for us to reach common ground. We are bound by shared blood and shared sacrifices. We are much too intelligent; much too bound by our Judeo-Christian heritage; much too victimized by racism, sexism, militarism, and anti-Semitism; much too threatened as historical scapegoats to go on divided one from another. We must turn from finger-pointing to clasped hands. We must share our burdens and our joys with each other once again. We must turn to each other and not on each other, and choose higher ground.

Twenty years later, we cannot be satisfied by just restoring the old coalition. Old wine skins must make room for new wine. We must heal and expand. The Rainbow Coalition is making room for Arab Americans. They, too, know the pain and hurt of racial and religious rejection. They must not continue to be made pariahs. The Rainbow Coalition is making room for Hispanic Americans who this very night are living under the threat of the Simpson-Mazzoli bill. And [for] farm workers from Ohio who are fighting the Campbell Soup Company with a boycott to achieve legitimate workers' rights.

The Rainbow is making room for the Native American, the most exploited people of all, a people with the greatest moral claim amongst us. We support them as they seek the restoration of land and water rights, as they seek to preserve their ancestral homelands and the beauty of a land that was once all theirs. They can never receive a fair share for all they have given us. They must finally have a fair chance to develop their great resources and to preserve their people and their culture.

The Rainbow Coalition includes Asian Americans, now being killed in our streets, scapegoats for the failures of corporate, industrial and economic policies.

The Rainbow is making room for young Americans. . . .

The Rainbow includes disabled veterans. The color scheme fits in the Rainbow. The disabled have their handicap revealed and their genius concealed; while the able-bodied have their genius revealed and their disability concealed. But ultimately, we must judge people by their values and their contribution. Don't leave anybody out. I would rather have Roosevelt in a wheelchair than Reagan on a horse.

The Rainbow is making room for small farmers. . . .

The Rainbow includes lesbians and gays. No American citizen ought to be denied equal protection under the law.

We must be unusually committed and caring as we expand our family to include new members. All of us must be tolerant and understanding as the fears and anxieties of the rejected . . . express themselves in many different ways. Too often, what we call hate, as if it were some deeply rooted philosophy or strategy, is simply ignorance, anxiety, paranoia, fear and insecurity.

In 1984, my heart is made to feel glad, because I know there is a way out—justice. The requirement for rebuilding America is justice. The linchpin of progressive politics in our Nation will not come from the North. . . . [It] in fact will come from the South.

That is why I argue over and over again. We look from Virginia around to Texas. There is only one Black Congressperson out of 115. Nineteen years later, we are locked out of the Congress, the Senate, and the Governor's Mansion.

What does this large black vote mean? Why do I fight to win second primaries and fight gerrymandering and annexation and at-large elections? Why do we fight over that? Because I tell you, you cannot hold someone in the ditch unless you linger there with them. . . .

If you want a change in this Nation, you enforce that Voting Rights Act. We will get 12 to 20 Black, Hispanic, female and progressive congresspersons from the South. We can save the cotton, but we have got to fight the boll weevils. We have got to make a judgment. . . .

It is not enough to hope ERA will pass. How can we pass ERA? If Blacks vote in great numbers, progressive Whites win. It is the only way progressive Whites win. If Blacks vote in great numbers, Hispanics win. When Blacks, Hispanics, and progressive Whites vote, women win. When women win, children win. When women and children win, workers win. We must all come together. We must come up together.

I have a message for our youth. I challenge them to put hope in their brains and not dope in their veins. I told them that like Jesus, I, too, was born in the slum, and just because you are born in the slum does not mean the slum is born in you, and you can rise above it if your mind is made up. I told them in every slum there are two sides. When I see a broken window, that is the slummy side. Train some youth to become a glazier; that is the sunny side. When I see a missing brick, that is the slummy side. Let that child in the union and become a brick mason and build; that is the sunny side. When I see a missing door, that is the slummy side. Train some youth to become a carpenter; that is the sunny side. And when I see the vulgar words and hieroglyphics of destitution on the walls, that's the slummy side. Train some youth to become a painter, an artist; that is the sunny side.

We leave this place looking for the sunny side because there is a brighter side somewhere. I am more convinced than ever that we can win. We will vault up the rough side of the mountain. We can win. I just want young America to do me one favor. . . .

Exercise the right to dream. You must face reality—that which is; but then dream of the reality that ought to be—that must be. Live beyond the pain of reality with the dream of a bright tomorrow. Use hope and imagination as weapons of survival and progress. Use love to motivate you and obligate you to serve the human family.

Young America, dream. Choose the human race over the nuclear race. Bury the weapons and don't burn the people. Dream—dream of a new value system.

Teachers who teach for life and not just for a living, teach because they can't help it. Dream of lawyers more concerned about justice than a judgeship. Dream of doctors more concerned about public health than personal wealth. Dream of preachers and priests who will prophesy and not just profiteer. Preach and dream! Our time has come. Our time has come.

Suffering breeds character, character breeds faith, and faith will not disappoint. Our time has come. Our faith, hopes and dreams will prevail. Our time has come. Weeping has endured for night, but now joy cometh in the morning.

Our time has come. No grave can hold our body down. Our time has come. No lie can live forever. Our time has come. We must leave the racial battleground and find the economic common ground and moral higher ground. America, our time has come.

We come from disgrace to Amazing Grace. Our time has come. Give me your tired, give me your poor, your huddled masses who yearn to breathe free, and come November there will be a change because our time has come.

Thank you and God bless you.

ANGELA DAVIS

(1944–)

Few African American authors and scholars have had more influence on spheres of political and social power in the United States than Angela Davis. A child of relatively middle-class blacks living in the segregated South, Davis grew up in an atmosphere of revolution, anger, and constant change. Throughout her years of training at various national and international institutes of education and her years of working in academic circles, Davis's continual interaction with very liberal and left-wing organizations put her in the vanguard of forces determined to bring about major social change. As one of the important figures in the Civil Rights Movement of the 1960s, she was one of the key instruments in making that change possible.

Born Angela Yvonne Davis on January 26, 1944, in Birmingham, Alabama, she is the daughter of B. Frank Davis and Sallye E. Davis, both of whom were schoolteachers. However, because of the low salaries paid to teachers in the segregated school systems of the day, her father gave up teaching and became an entrepreneur. The family was part of Birmingham's black middle class, and they were able to take Angela to advanced educational levels for normal preschoolers even before she entered kindergarten. Moreover, as she observed their early and growing struggles for freedom and integration in the Birmingham area, she perceived her role models on Civil Rights activism in both her mother and grandmother.

When Davis was fifteen years old, the American Friends Service Committee provided the tuition for her to attend Elizabeth Irwin High School, a progressive private school in New York. An Episcopal pastor and his family provided her with room and board. This was the young student's first real exposure to political radicalism. Many of her teachers were Marxists, and the school was known as a hotbed of radicals. These associations gave Davis the rare privilege to study at the Sorbonne, University of Paris, from 1963 to 1964, while she was a junior at Brandeis University.

In 1965, she graduated magna cum laude from Brandeis with a B.A. in French. She then continued on to graduate studies in philosophy at the University of Frankfurt from 1965 to 1967. At Brandeis and in Paris, she had increased her political activities, demonstrating often against racism in the United States and becoming involved with Algerian freedom fighters in France. In Germany, she joined socialist groups that were demonstrating against the Vietnam War. When she returned to the United States in 1967, she attended the University of California at San Diego, where she received a master's degree in philosophy in 1968.

It was during a teaching assignment in San Diego that Davis first caught the spotlight of national attention for her activity with the Student Nonviolent Coordinating Committee (SNCC) and the Black Panther Party. The act that would most affect her life, however, was joining the Communist Party in 1968. A year later, she traveled to Cuba to meet with Communist officials there. Subsequently, Davis was hired to teach at the University of California at Los Angeles, but when the university learned of her Communist Party membership, she was fired by the California Board of Regents and by Governor Ronald Reagan himself. Davis challenged the dismissal in court and won reinstatement. This amazing political and academic victory brought her to the attention of major political powers.

At this time, Davis became a vocal supporter of the "Soledad Brothers," inmates of Soledad Prison who had formed a Marxist cell group within the prison. One of the "brothers" was killed by a guard, and another, a man named George Jackson, was indicted for a guard's murder. Because of Davis's speeches in their defense, the California Board of Regents again refused to grant Davis a teaching contract.

As Davis and Jackson became the focus of much national and international media attention, they were also developing an intimate relationship. This close association received such widespread media exposure that it would transform Davis into a countercultural hero. Later, after Jackson was acquitted of the murder charge, he was killed by prison guards, supposedly for an escape attempt.

In reaction to Jackson's death, his brother, Jonathan Jackson, went into a courthouse in Marin County where a San Quentin prisoner was on trial and took hostages. Two prisoners, a judge, and Jackson were killed in his attempted getaway. The guns Jackson had used in the crime belonged to Angela Davis. Although she had purchased them because of death threats against her and they were registered, a warrant was issued for her arrest. Davis chose to go underground, and in August 1970 she became one of the FBI's ten most wanted "criminals."

Although her only involvement in the hostage taking had been owning the guns used in the crime, she was charged with kidnapping, conspiracy, and murder. Two months later, she was discovered in New York, extradited to California, and imprisoned without bail. The government's intransigence on Davis's case caused the beginning of a massive citizens' uprising, which took as its slogan "Free Angela Davis." The slogan appeared on T-shirts, stickers, newspapers, and walls. Moreover, popular support for her cause transformed Davis into an icon of the nation's political left. She finally was released on $102,000 bail in February 1972 after sixteen months in jail. At her trial, she was acquitted of all charges after thirteen hours of jury deliberation.

Davis has remained politically active since her trial. Her defense team during the trial became the National Alliance Against Racism and Political Repression, an organization devoted to defending political justice cases. She has continued teaching despite the efforts of the California Board of Regents. Most recently, she has taught at San Francisco State University and the San Francisco Art Institute, and she has lectured at the University of California at Berkeley. She has traveled in the Soviet Union and other Communist countries, and in 1979 she received the Soviet Union's Lenin Peace Prize. In 1980 and 1984, she was the vice-presidential candidate for the American Communist Party.

Her first book, *If They Come in the Morning,* a political statement about her experiences, was published in 1971. Her second, *Women, Race, and Class* (1983), indicated a public shift in Davis's ideology to include women, regardless of their racial identification, as unique members of the oppressed classes. *Women, Culture, and Politics* was published in 1989. The latter two books are extremely popular with members of the feminist movement, both white and black. But the heart of Davis's message in these books is the neglect, and often mistreatment, that black women receive in both white and black communities.

Davis's seminal essay, "Reflections on the Black Woman's Role in the Community of Slaves," was first published in 1971 in *The Black Scholar.* In it, she attempted to unite the causes of African Americans and women and to inspire artistic writers and academicians to look at the historical and contemporary contributions of black women in the American experience. That essay, along with others by Shirley Chisholm, Joyce Ladner, Jacquelyne J. Jackson, Johnnetta Cole, and Kathleen Cleaver in the same issue, helped to ignite exchanges along gender lines in the black community for several years.

Davis published *Angela Davis: An Autobiography* in 1988. The work retraces her steps into the heart of the Black Power Movement and her later transition to feminism.

Davis is still a popular political speaker on forums, particularly those involving issues about black women and poverty. Her willingness to take on the causes of the disadvantaged have proved successful over time, and her success in making the black community look at the historic and contemporary roles and treatment of black women is unprecedented. Historians, biographers, and scholars of black women's studies, political movements, and cultural change will surely reform, reestablish, and reconstruct Davis's impact on twentieth-century America for years to come.

❖❖❖

Major works on Davis include Regina Nadelson, *Who Is Angela Davis? The Biography of a Revolutionary* (1972); J. A. Parker, *Angela Davis: The Making of a Revolutionary* (1973); Kathleen Thompson's entry in *Black Women in America,* Vol. I (1993); and Diane Abbott, "Revolution by Other Means," *New Statesman* (August 1987). Paul Buhle et al. include Davis in *Encyclopedia of the American Left* (1990); Linda Reed discusses her in *Encyclopedia of African-American Civil Rights from Emancipation to the Present* (1992); and Robert Chrisman reviewed *If They Come in the Morning* in *The Black Scholar,* Vol. 3, No. 4 (1971).

FROM *Reflections on the Black Woman's Role in the Community of Slaves*

. . . The paucity of literature on the black woman is outrageous on its face. But we must also contend with the fact that too many of these rare studies must claim as their signal achievement the reinforcement of fictitious cliches. They have given credence to grossly distorted categories through which the black woman continues to be perceived. In the words of Nathan and Julia Hare, ". . . she has been labeled 'aggressive' or 'matriarchal' by white scholars and 'castrating female' by [some] blacks" (*Transaction,* Nov.-Dec., 1970). Many have recently sought to remedy this situation. But for the time being, at least, we are still confronted with these reified images of ourselves. And for now, we must still assume the responsibility of shattering them.

Initially, I did not envision this paper as strictly confined to the era of slavery. Yet, as I began to think through the issue of the black matriarch, I came to the conclusion that it had to be refuted at its presumed historical inception.

The chief problem I encountered stemmed from the conditions of my incarceration: opportunities for researching the issue I wanted to explore were extremely limited. I chose, therefore, to entitle this piece "Reflections. . . ." It does not pretend to be more than a collection of ideas which would constitute a starting point—a framework within which to conduct a rigorous reinvestigation of the black woman as she interacted with her people and with her oppressive environment during slavery.

I would like to dedicate these reflections to one of the most admirable black leaders to emerge from the ranks of our liberation movement—to George Jackson, whom I loved and respected in every way. As I came to know and love him, I saw him developing an acute sensitivity to the real problems facing black women and thus refining his ability to distinguish these from their mythical transpositions. George was uniquely aware of the need to extricate himself and other black men from the remnants of divisive and destructive myths purporting to represent the black woman. If his life had not been so precipitously and savagely extinguished, he would have surely accomplished a task he had already outlined some time ago: a systematic critique of his past misconceptions about black women and of their roots in the ideology of the established order. He wanted to appeal to other black men, still similarly disoriented, to likewise correct themselves through self-criticism. George viewed this obligation as a revolutionary duty, but also, and equally important, as an expression of his boundless love for all black women.

The matriarchal black woman has been repeatedly invoked as one of the fatal by-products of slavery. When the Moynihan Report consecrated this myth with Washington's stamp of approval, its spurious content and propagandistic mission should have become apparent. Yet even outside the established ideological apparatus, and also among black people, unfortunate references to the matriarchate can still be encountered. Occasionally, there is even acknowledgement of the "tangle of pathology" it supposedly engendered. (This black matriarchate, according to Moynihan *et al.* defines the roots of our oppression as a people.) An accurate portrait of the African woman in bondage must debunk the myth of the matriarchate. Such a portrait must simultaneously attempt to illuminate the historical matrix of her oppression and must evoke her varied, often heroic, responses to the slaveholder's domination.

Lingering beneath the notion of the black matriarch is an unspoken indictment of our female forebears as having actively assented to slavery. The notorious cliche, the "emasculating female," has its roots in the fallacious inference that in playing a central part in the slave "family," the black woman related to the slaveholding class as collaborator. Nothing could be further from the truth. In the most fundamental sense, the slave system did not—and could not—engender and recognize a matriarchal family structure. Inherent in the very concept of the matriarchy is "power." It would have been exceedingly risky for the slaveholding class to openly acknowledge symbols of authority—female symbols no less than male. Such legitimized concentrations of authority might eventually unleash their "power" against the slave system itself.

The American brand of slavery strove toward a rigidified disorganization in family life, just as it had to proscribe all potential social structures within which black people might forge a collective and conscious existence.[1] Mothers and fathers were brutally separated; children, when they became of age, were branded and frequently severed from their mothers. That the mother was "the only legitimate parent of her child" did not therefore mean that she was even permitted to guide it to maturity.

Those who lived under a common roof were often unrelated through blood. Frederick Douglass, for instance, had no recollection of his father. He only vaguely recalled having seen his mother—and then on extremely rare occasions. Moreover, at the age of seven, he was forced to abandon the dwelling of his grandmother, of whom he would later say: "She was to me a mother and a father."[1a] The strong personal bonds between immediate family members which oftentimes persisted despite coerced separation bore witness to the remarkable capacity of black people for resisting the disorder so violently imposed on their lives.

Where families were allowed to thrive, they were, for the most part, external fabrications serving the designs of an avaricious, profit-seeking slaveholder.

> The strong hand of the slave owner dominated the Negro family, which existed at his mercy and often at his own personal instigation. An ex-slave has told of getting married on one plantation: "When you married, you had to jump over a broom three times."[2]

---

[1]It is interesting to note a parallel in Nazi Germany: with all its ranting and raving about motherhood and the family, Hitler's regime made a conscious attempt to strip the family of virtually all its social functions. The thrust of their unspoken program for the family was to reduce it to a biological unit and to force its members to relate in an unmediated fashion to the fascist bureaucracy. Clearly the Nazis endeavored to crush the family in order to ensure that it could not become a center from which oppositional activity might originate.

[1a]Herbert Aptheker, ed., *A Documentary History of the Negro People in the United States*, New York: The Citadel Press, 1969 (1st ed., 1951), p. 272.

[2]Andrew Billingsley, *Black Families in White America*, Englewood, New Jersey: Prentice-Hall, Inc., 1968, p. 61.

This slave went on to describe the various ways in which his master forcibly coupled men and women with the aim of producing the maximum number of healthy child-slaves. In the words of John Henrik Clarke,

> The family as a functional entity was outlawed and permitted to exist only when it benefited the slave-master. Maintenance of the slave family as a family unit benefited the slave owners only when, and to the extent that such unions created new slaves who could be exploited.[3]

The designation of the black woman as a matriarch is a cruel misnomer. It is a misnomer because it implies stable kinship structures within which the mother exercises decisive authority. It is cruel because it ignores the profound traumas the black woman must have experienced when she had to surrender her child-bearing to alien and predatory economic interests.

Even the broadest construction of the matriarch concept would not render it applicable to the black slave woman. But it should not be inferred that she therefore played no significant role in the community of slaves. Her indispensable efforts to ensure the survival of her people can hardly be contested. Even if she had done no more, her deeds would still be laudable. But her concern and struggles for physical survival, while clearly important, did not constitute her most outstanding contributions. It will be submitted that by virtue of the brutal force of circumstances, the black woman was assigned the mission of promoting the consciousness and practice of resistance. A great deal has been said about the black *man* and resistance, but very little about the unique relationship black women bore to the resistance struggles during slavery. To understand the part she played in developing and sharpening the thrust towards freedom, the broader meaning of slavery and of American slavery in particular must be explored.

Slavery is an ancient human institution. Of slave labor in its traditional form and of serfdom as well, Karl Marx had the following to say:

> The slave stands in absolutely no relation to the objective conditions of his labor; it is rather the *labor* itself, in the form of the slave as of the serf, which is placed in the category of *inorganic condition* of production alongside the other natural beings, *e.g.* cattle, or regarded as an appendage of the earth.[4]

The bondsman's existence as a natural condition of production is complemented and reinforced, according to Marx, by his membership in a social grouping which he perceives to be an extension of nature. Enmeshed in what appears to be a natural state of affairs, the attitude of the slave, to a greater or lesser degree, would be an acquiescence in his subjugation. Engels points out that in Athens, the state could depend on a police force consisting entirely of slaves.[5]

The fabric of American slavery differed significantly from ancient slavery and feudalism. True, black people were forced to act as if they were "inorganic conditions of production." For slavery was "personality swallowed up in the sordid idea of property—manhood lost in chattelhood."[6] But there were no pre-existent social structures or cultural dictates which might induce reconciliation to the circumstances of their bondage. On the contrary, Africans had been uprooted from their natural environment, their social relations, their culture. No legitimate socio-cultural surroundings would be permitted to develop and flourish, for, in all likelihood, they would be utterly incompatible with the demands of slavery.

Yet another fact would militate against harmony and equilibrium in the slave's relation to

---

[3]John Henrik Clarke, "The Black Woman: A Figure in World History" Part III, *Essence*, New York: July, 1971.

[4]Karl Marx, *Grundrisse der Kritik der Politischen Oekonomie*, Berlin: Dietz Verlag, 1953, p. 389.

[5]Frederick Engels, *Origin of the Family, Private Property and The State*, New York: International Publishers, 1942, p. 107.

[6]Frederick Douglass, *Life and Times of Frederick Douglass*, New York: Collier Books, 1962, p. 93.

his bondage: slavery was enclosed in a society otherwise characterized by "free" wage-labor. Black men and women could always contrast their chains with the nominally free status of white working people. This was quite literally true in such cases where, like Frederick Douglass, they were contracted out as wage-laborers. Unlike the "free" white men alongside whom they worked, they had no right to the meager wages they earned. Such were some of the many contradictions unloosed by the effort to forcibly inject slavery into the early stages of American capitalism.

The combination of a historically superseded slave labor system based almost exclusively on race and the drive to strip black people of all their social and cultural bonds would create a fateful rupture at the heart of the slave system itself. The slaves would not readily adopt fatalistic attitudes towards the conditions surrounding and ensnaring their lives. They were a people who had been violently thrust into a patently "unnatural" subjugation. If the slaveholders had not maintained an absolute monopoly of violence, if they had not been able to rely on large numbers of their fellow white men—indeed the entire ruling class as well as misled working people—to assist them in their terrorist machinations, slavery would have been far less feasible than it actually proved to be.

The magnitude and effects of the black people's defiant rejection of slavery has not yet been fully documented and illuminated. But there is more than ample evidence that they consistently refused to succumb to the all-encompassing dehumanization objectively demanded by the slave system. Comparatively recent studies have demonstrated that the few slave uprisings—too spectacular to be relegated to oblivion by the racism of ruling class historians—were not isolated occurrences, as the latter would have had us believe. The reality, we know now, was that these open rebellions erupted with such a frequency that they were as much a part of the texture of slavery as the conditions of servitude themselves. And these revolts were only the tip of an iceberg: resistance expressed itself in other grand modes and also in the seemingly trivial forms of feigned illness and studied indolence.

If resistance was an organic ingredient of slave life, it had to be directly nurtured by the social organization which the slaves themselves improvised. The consciousness of their oppression, the conscious thrust towards its abolition could not have been sustained without impetus from the community they pulled together through the sheer force of their own strength. Of necessity, this community would revolve around the realm which was furthermost removed from the immediate arena of domination. It could only be located in and around the living quarters, the area where the basic needs of physical life were met.

In the area of production, the slaves—pressed into the mold of beasts of burden—were forcibly deprived of their humanity. (And a human being thoroughly dehumanized, has no desire for freedom.) But the community gravitating around the domestic quarters might possibly permit a retrieval of the man and the woman in their fundamental humanity. We can assume that in a very real material sense, it was only in domestic life—away from the eyes and whip of the overseer—that the slaves could attempt to assert the modicum of freedom they still retained. It was only there that they might be inspired to project techniques of expanding it further by leveling what few weapons they had against the slaveholding class whose unmitigated drive for profit was the source of their misery.

Via this path, we return to the African slave woman: in the living quarters, the major responsibilities "naturally" fell to her. It was the woman who was charged with keeping the "home" in order. This role was dictated by the male supremacist ideology of white society in America; it was also woven into the patriarchal traditions of Africa. As her biological destiny, the woman bore the fruits of procreation; as her social destiny, she cooked, sewed, washed, cleaned house, raised the children. Traditionally the labor of females, domestic work is supposed to complement and confirm their inferiority.

But with the black slave woman, there is a strange twist of affairs: in the infinite anguish of ministering to the needs of the men and children around her (who were not necessarily members of her immediate family), she was performing the *only* labor of the slave community which could not be directly and immediately claimed by the oppressor. There was no compensation for work in the fields: it served no useful purpose for the slaves. Domestic labor was the only meaningful labor for the slave community as a whole (discounting as negligible the exceptional situations where slaves received some pay for their work).

Precisely through performing the drudgery which has long been a central expression of the socially conditioned inferiority of women, the black woman in chains could help to lay the foundation for some degree of autonomy, both for herself and her men. Even as she was suffering under her unique oppression as female, she was thrust by the force of circumstances into the center of the slave community. She was, therefore, essential to the *survival* of the community. Not all people have survived enslavement; hence her survival-oriented activities were themselves a form of resistance. Survival, moreover, was the prerequisite of all higher levels of struggle.

But much more remains to be said of the black woman during slavery. The dialectics of her oppression will become far more complex. It is true that she was a victim of the myth that only the woman, with her diminished capacity for mental and physical labor, should do degrading household work. Yet, the alleged benefits of the ideology of feminity did not accrue to her. She was not sheltered or protected; she would not remain oblivious to the desperate struggle for existence unfolding outside the "home." She was also there in the fields, alongside the man, toiling under the lash from sun-up to sun-down.

This was one of the supreme ironies of slavery: in order to approach its strategic goal—to extract the greatest possible surplus from the labor of the slaves—the black woman had to be released from the chains of the myth of feminity. In the words of W. E. B. Du Bois, ". . . our women in black had freedom contemptuously thrust upon them."[7] In order to function as slave, the black woman had to be annulled as woman, that is, as woman in her historical stance of wardship under the entire male hierarchy. The sheer force of things rendered her equal to her man.

Excepting the woman's role as caretaker of the household, male supremacist structures could not become deeply embedded in the internal workings of the slave system. Though the ruling class was male and rabidly chauvinistic, the slave system could not confer upon the black man the appearance of a privileged position vis-à-vis the black woman. The man-slave could not be the unquestioned superior within the "family" or community, for there was no such thing as the "family provided" among the slaves. The attainment of slavery's intrinsic goals was contingent upon the fullest and most brutal utilization of the productive capacities of every man, woman and child. They all had to "provide" for the master. The black woman was therefore wholly integrated into the productive force.

> The bell rings at four o'clock in the morning and they have half an hour to get ready. Men and women start together, and the women must work as steadily as the men and perform the same tasks as the men.[8]

Even in the posture of motherhood—otherwise the occasion for hypocritical adoration—the black woman was treated with not greater compassion and with no less severity than her

---

[7]W. E. B. Du Bois, *Darkwater, Voices from Within the Veil,* New York: AMS Press, 1969, p. 185.

[8]Lewis Clarke, *Narrative of the Sufferings of Lewis and Milton Clarke, Sons of a Soldier of the Revolution,* Boston: 1846, p. 127 [Quoted by E. Franklin Frazier, *The Negro Family in the United States*].

man. As one slave related in a narrative of his life:

> . . . women who had sucking children suffered much from their breasts becoming full of milk, the infants being left at home; they therefore could not keep up with the other hands: I have seen the overseer beat them with raw hide so that the blood and the milk flew mingled from their breasts.[9]

Moses Grandy, ex-slave, continues his description with an account of a typical form of field punishment reserved for the black woman with child:

> She is compelled to lie down over a hole made to receive her corpulency, and is flogged with the whip, or beat with a paddle, which has holes in it; at every stroke comes a blister.[10]

The unbridled cruelty of this leveling process whereby the black woman was forced into equality with the black man requires no further explanation. She shared in the deformed equality of equal oppression.

But out of this deformed equality was forged quite undeliberately, yet inexorably, a state of affairs which could unharness an immense potential in the black woman. Expending indispensable labor for the enrichment of her oppressor, she could attain a practical awareness of the oppressor's utter dependence on her—for the master needs the slave far more than the slave needs the master. At the same time she could realize that while her productive activity was wholly subordinated to the will of the master, it was nevertheless proof of her ability to transform things. For "labor is the living, shaping fire; it represents the impermanence of things, their temporality . . ."[11]

The black woman's consciousness of the oppression suffered by her people was honed in the bestial realities of daily experience. It would not be the stunted awareness of a woman confined to the home. She would be prepared to ascend to the same levels of resistance which were accessible to her men. Even as she performed her housework, the black woman's role in the slave community could not be identical to the historically evolved female role. Stripped of the palliative feminine veneer which might have encouraged a passive performance of domestic tasks, she was now uniquely capable of weaving into the warp and woof of domestic life a profound consciousness of resistance.

With the contributions of strong black women, the slave community as a whole could achieve heights unscalable within the families of the white oppressed or even within the patriarchal kinship groups of Africa. Latently or actively it was always a community of resistance. It frequently erupted in insurgency, but was daily animated by the minor acts of sabotage which harassed the slave master to no end. Had the black woman failed to rise to the occasion, the community of slaves could not have fully developed in this direction. The slave system would have to deal with the black woman as the custodian of a house of resistance.

The oppression of black woman during the era of slavery, therefore, had to be buttressed by a level of overt ruling-class repression. Her routine oppression had to assume an unconcealed dimension of outright counter-insurgency.

To say that the oppression of black slave women necessarily incorporated open forms of counter-insurgency is not as extravagant as it might initially appear. The penetration of counter-insurgency into the day to day routine of the slave master's domination will be considered towards the end of this paper. First, the participation of black women in the overt and explosive upheavals which constantly rocked the slave system must be confirmed. This will be an indication of the magnitude of her role as caretaker of a household of resistance—of the

---

[9]Moses Grandy, *Narrative of the Life of Moses Grandy; Late a Slave in the United States of America,* Boston: 1844, p. 18 [quoted by Frazier].

[10]*Ibid.*

[11]Marx, *Grundrisse,* p. 266.

degree to which she could concretely encourage those around her to keep their eyes on freedom. It will also confirm the objective circumstances to which the slave master's counter-insurgency was a response.

With the sole exceptions of Harriet Tubman and Sojourner Truth, black women of the slave era remain more or less enshrouded in unrevealed history. And, as Earl Conrad has demonstrated, even "General Tubman's" role has been consistently and grossly minimized. She was a far greater warrior against slavery than is suggested by the prevalent misconception that her only outstanding contribution was to make nineteen trips into the South, bringing over 300 slaves to their freedom.

> [She] was head of the Intelligence Service in the Department of the South throughout the Civil War; she is the only American woman to lead troops black and white on the field of battle, as she did in the Department of the South. . . . She was a compelling and stirring orator in the councils of the abolitionists and the anti-slavers, a favorite of the antislavery conferences. She was the fellow planner with Douglass, Martin Delany, Wendell Phillips, Gerrit Smith and other leaders of the anti-slavery movement.[12]

No extensive and systematic study of the role of black women in resisting slavery has come to my attention. It has been noted that large numbers of freed black women worked towards the purchase of their relatives' and friends' freedom. About the participation of women in both the well-known and more obscure slave revolts, only casual remarks have been made. It has been observed, for instance, that Gabriel's wife was active in planning the rebellion spearheaded by her husband, but little else has been said about her.

The sketch which follows is based in its entirety on the works of Herbert Aptheker, the only resources available to me at the time of this writing.[13] These facts, gleaned from Aptheker's works on slave revolts and other forms of resistance, should signal the urgency to undertake a thorough study of the black woman as anti-slavery rebel. In 1971 this work is far overdue.

Aptheker's research has disclosed the widespread existence of communities of blacks who were neither free nor in bondage. Throughout the South (in South and North Carolina, Virginia, Louisiana, Florida, Georgia, Mississippi and Alabama), maroon communities consisting of fugitive slaves and their descendants were "an ever present feature"—from 1642 to 1864—of slavery. They provided ". . . havens for fugitives, served as bases for marauding expeditions against nearby plantations and, at times, supplied leadership to planned uprisings."[14]

Every detail of these communities was invariably determined by and steeped in resistance, for their raison d'etre emanated from their perpetual assault on slavery. Only in a fighting stance could the maroons hope to secure their constantly imperiled freedom. As a matter of necessity, the women of those communities were compelled to define themselves—no less than the men—through their many acts of resistance. Hence, throughout this brief survey the counter-attacks and heroic efforts at defense assisted by maroon women will be a recurring motif.

As it will be seen, black women often poisoned the food and set fire to the houses of their masters. For those who were also employed as domestics these particular overt forms of resistance were especially available.

The vast majority of the incidents to be related involve either tactically unsuccessful as-

---

[12]Earl Conrad, "I Bring You General Tubman," *The Black Scholar*, Vol. 1, No. 3–4, Jan.-Feb. 1970, p. 4.

[13]In February, 1949, Herbert Aptheker published an essay in *Masses and Mainstream* entitled "The Negro Woman." As yet I have been unable to obtain it.

[14]Herbert Aptheker, "Slave Guerrilla Warfare" in *To Be Free, Studies in American Negro History*, New York: International Publishers, 1969 (1st ed., 1948), p. 11.

saults or eventually thwarted attempts at defense. In all likelihood, numerous successes were achieved, even against the formidable obstacles posed by the slave system. Many of these were probably unpublicized even at the time of their occurrence, lest they provide encouragement to the rebellious proclivities of other slaves and, for other slaveholders, an occasion for fear and despair.

During the early years of the slave era (1708) a rebellion broke out in New York. Among its participants were surely many women, for one, along with three men, was executed in retaliation for the killing of seven whites. It may not be entirely insignificant that while the men were hanged, she was heinously burned alive.[15] In the same colony, women played an active role in a 1712 uprising in the course of which slaves, with their guns, clubs and knives, killed members of the slaveholding class and managed to wound others. While some of the insurgents—among them a pregnant woman—were captured, others—including a woman—committed suicide rather than surrender.[16]

"In New Orleans one day in 1730 a woman slave received 'a violent blow from a French soldier for refusing to obey him' and in her anger shouted 'that the French should not long insult Negroes'."[17] As it was later disclosed, she and undoubtedly many other women, had joined in a vast plan to destroy slaveholders. Along with eight men, this dauntless woman was executed. Two years later, Louisiana pronounced a woman and four men leaders of a planned rebellion. They were all executed and, in a typically savage gesture, their heads publicly displayed on poles.[18]

Charleston, South Carolina condemned a black woman to die in 1740 for arson,[19] a form of sabotage, as earlier noted, frequently carried out by women. In Maryland, for instance, a slave woman was executed in 1776 for having destroyed by fire her master's house, his outhouses and tobacco house.[20]

In the thick of the Colonies' war with England, a group of defiant slave women and men were arrested in Saint Andrew's Parish, Georgia in 1774. But before they were captured, they had already brought a number of slave owners to their death.[21]

The maroon communities have been briefly described; from 1782 to 1784, Louisiana was a constant target of maroon attacks. When twenty-five of this community's members were finally taken prisoner, men and women alike were all severely punished.[22]

As can be inferred from previous example, the North did not escape the tremendous impact of fighting black women. In Albany, New York, two women were among three slaves executed for anti-slavery activities in 1794.[23] The respect and admiration accorded the black woman fighter by her people is strikingly illustrated by an incident which transpired in York, Pennsylvania: when, during the early months of 1803, Margaret Bradley was convicted of attempting to poison two white people, the black inhabitants of the area revolted en masse.

> They made several attempts to destroy the town by fire and succeeded, within a period of three weeks, in burning eleven buildings. Patrols were established, strong guards set up, the militia dispatched to the scene of the unrest . . . and a reward of three hundred dollars offered for the capture of the insurrectionists.[24]

[15]Herbert Aptheker, *American Negro Slave Revolts,* New York: International Publishers, 1970 (1st ed., 1943), p. 169).

[16]*Ibid.*, p. 173.

[17]*Ibid.*, p. 181.

[18]*Ibid.*, p. 182.

[19]*Ibid.*, p. 190.

[20]*Ibid.*, p. 145.

[21]*Ibid.*, p. 201.

[22]*Ibid.*, p. 207.

[23]*Ibid.*, p. 215.

[24]*Ibid.*, p. 239.

A successful elimination by poisoning of several "of our respectable men" (said a letter to the governor of North Carolina) was met by the execution of four or five slaves. One was a woman who was burned alive.[25] In 1810, two women and a man were accused of arson in Virginia.[26]

In 1811 North Carolina was the scene of a confrontation between a maroon community and a slave-catching posse. Local newspapers reported that its members "had bid defiance to any force whatever and were resolved to stand their ground." Of the entire community, two were killed, one wounded and two—both women—were captured.[27]

Aptheker's *Documentary History of the Negro People in the United States* contains a portion of the transcript of an 1812 confession of a slave rebel in Virginia. The latter divulged the information that a black woman brought him into a plan to kill their master and that yet another black woman had been charged with concealing him after the killing occurred.[28]

In 1816 it was discovered that a community of three hundred escaped slaves—men, women, children—had occupied a fort in Florida. After the U.S. Army was dispatched with instructions to destroy the community, a ten day siege terminated with all but forty of the three hundred dead. All the slaves fought to the very end.[29] In the course of a similar, though smaller confrontation between maroons and a militia group (in South Carolina, 1826), a woman and a child were killed.[30] Still another maroon community was attacked in Mobile, Alabama in 1837. Its inhabitants, men and women alike, resisted fiercely—according to local newspapers, "fighting like Spartans."[31]

Convicted of having been among those who, in 1829, had been the cause of a devastating fire in Augusta, Georgia, a black woman was "executed, dissected, and exposed" (according to an English visitor). Moreover, the execution of yet another woman, about to give birth, was imminent.[32] During the same year, a group of slaves, being led from Maryland to be sold in the South, had apparently planned to kill the traders and make their way to freedom. One of the traders was successfully done away with, but eventually a posse captured all the slaves. Of the six leaders sentenced to death, one was a woman. She was first permitted, for reasons of economy, to give birth to her child.[33] Afterwards, she was publicly hanged.

The slave class in Louisiana, as noted earlier, was not unaware of the formidable threat posed by the black woman who chose to fight. It responded accordingly: in 1846 a posse of slave owners ambushed a community of maroons, killing one woman and wounding two others. A black man was also assassinated.[34] Neither could the border states escape the recognition that slave women were eager to battle for their freedom. In 1850 in the state of Missouri, "about thirty slaves, men and women, of four different owners, had armed themselves with knives, clubs and three guns and set out for a free state." Their pursuers, who could unleash a far more powerful violence than they, eventually thwarted their plans.[35]

This factual survey of but a few of the open acts of resistance in which black women played major roles will close with two further events. When a maroon camp in Mississippi was destroyed in 1857, four of its members did not manage to elude capture, one of whom was a fugitive slave woman.[36] All of them, women as

[25] *Ibid.*, pp. 241–242.

[26] *Ibid.*, p. 247.

[27] *Ibid.*, p. 251.

[28] Aptheker, *Documentary History*, pp. 55–57.

[29] Aptheker, *Slave Revolts*, p. 259.

[30] *Ibid.*, p. 277.

[31] *Ibid.*, p. 259.

[32] *Ibid.*, p. 281.

[33] *Ibid.*, p. 487.

[34] Aptheker, "Guerilla Warfare," p. 27.

[35] Aptheker, *Slave Revolts*, p. 342.

[36] Aptheker, "Guerrilla Warfare," p. 28.

well as men, must have waged a valiant fight. Finally, there occurred in October, 1862 a skirmish between maroons and a scouting party of Confederate soldiers in the state of Virginia.[37] This time, however, the maroons were the victors and it may well have been that some of the many women helped to put the soldiers to death.

The oppression of slave women had to assume dimensions of open counter-insurgency. Against the background of the facts presented above, it would be difficult indeed to refute this contention. As for those who engaged in open battle, they were no less ruthlessly punished than slave men. It would even appear that in many cases they may have suffered penalties which were more excessive than those meted out to the men. On occasion, when men were hanged, the women were burned alive. If such practices were widespread, their logic would be clear. They would be terrorist methods designed to dissuade other black women from following the examples of their fighting sisters. If all black women rose up alongside their men, the institution of slavery would be in difficult straits.

It is against the backdrop of her role as fighter that the routine oppression of the slave woman must be explored once more. If she was burned, hanged, broken on the wheel, her head paraded on poles before her oppressed brothers and sisters, she must have also felt the edge of this counter-insurgency as a fact of her daily existence. The slave system would not only have to make conscious efforts to stifle the tendencies towards acts of the kind described above; it would be no less necessary to stave off escape attempts (escapes to maroon country!) and all the various forms of sabotage within the system. Feigning illness was also resistance as were work slowdowns and actions destructive to the crops. The more extensive these acts, the more the slaveholder's profits would tend to diminish.

While a detailed study of the myriad modes in which this counter-insurgency was manifested can and should be conducted, the following reflections will focus on a single aspect of the slave woman's oppression, particularly prominent in its brutality.

Much as been said about the sexual abuses to which the black woman was forced to submit. They are generally explained as an outgrowth of the male supremacy of Southern culture: the purity of white womanhood could not be violated by the aggressive sexual activity desired by the white male. His instinctual urges would find expression in his relationships with his property—the black slave woman, who would have to become his unwilling concubine. No doubt there is an element of truth in these statements, but it is equally important to unearth the meaning of these sexual abuses from the vantage point of the woman who was assaulted.

In keeping with the theme of these reflections, it will be submitted that the slave master's sexual domination of the black woman contained an unveiled element of counter-insurgency. To understand the basis for this assertion, the dialectical moments of the slave woman's oppression must be restated and their movement recaptured. The prime factor, it has been said, was the total and violent expropriation of her labor with no compensation save the pittance necessary for bare existence.

Secondly, as female, she was the housekeeper of the living quarters. In this sense, she was already doubly oppressed. However, having been wrested from passive, "feminine" existence by the sheer force of things—literally by forced labor—confining domestic tasks were incommensurable with what she had become. That is to say, by virtue of her participation in production, she would not act the part of the passive female, but could experience the same need as her men to challenge the conditions of her subjugation. As the center of domestic life, the only life at all removed from the arena of exploitation, and thus as an important source of survival, the black woman could play a pivotal role in nurturing the thrust towards freedom.

[37] *Ibid.*, p. 29.

The slave master would attempt to thwart this process. He knew that as female, this slave woman could be particularly vulnerable in her sexual existence. Although he would not pet her and deck her out in frills, the white master could endeavor to reestablish her femaleness by reducing her to the level of her *biological* being. Aspiring with his sexual assaults to establish her as a female *animal,* he would be striving to destroy her proclivities towards resistance. Of the sexual relations of animals, taken at their abstract biological level (and not in terms of their quite different social potential for human beings), Simone de Beauvoir says the following:

> It is unquestionably the male who *takes* the female—she is *taken.* Often the word applies literally, for whether by means of special organs or through superior strength, the male seizes her and holds her in place; he performs the copulatory movements; and, among insects, birds, and mammals, he penetrates. . . . Her body becomes a resistance to be broken through. . . .[38]

The act of copulation, reduced by the white man to an animal-like act, would be symbolic of the effort to conquer the resistance the black woman could unloose.

In confronting the black woman as adversary in a sexual contest, the master would be subjecting her to the most elemental form of terrorism distinctively suited for the female: rape. Given the already terroristic texture of plantation life, it would be as potential victim of rape that the slave woman would be most unguarded. Further, she might be most conveniently manipulable if the master contrived a ransom system of sorts, forcing her to pay with her body for food, diminished severity in treatment, the safety of her children, etc.

The integration of rape into the sparsely furnished legitimate social life of the slaves harks back to the feudal "right of the first night," the *jus primae noctis.* The feudal lord manifested and reinforced his domination over the serfs by asserting his authority to have sexual intercourse with all the females. The right itself referred specifically to all freshly married women. But while the right to the first night eventually evolved into the institutionalized "virgin tax,"[39] the American slaveholder's sexual domination never lost its openly terroristic character.

As a direct attack on the black female as potential insurgent, this sexual repression finds its parallels in virtually every historical situation where the woman actively challenges oppression. Thus, Frantz Fanon could say of the Algerian woman: "A woman led away by soldiers who comes back a week later—it is not necessary to question her to understand that she has been violated dozens of times."[40]

In its political contours, the rape of the black woman was not exclusively an attack upon her. Indirectly, its target was also the slave community as a whole. In launching the sexual war on the woman, the master would not only assert his sovereignty over a critically important figure of the slave community, he would also be aiming a blow against the black man. The latter's instinct to protect his female relations and comrades (now stripped of its male supremacist implications) would be frustrated and violated to the extreme. Placing the white male's sexual barbarity in bold relief, Du Bois cries out in a rhetorical vein:

> I shall forgive the South much in its final judgement day: I shall forgive its slavery, for slavery is a world-old habit; I shall forgive its fighting for a well-lost cause, and for remembering that struggle with tender tears; I shall forgive its so-called 'pride of race,' the passion of its hot blood, and even its dear, old, laughable strutting and pos-

[38] Simone de Beauvoir, *The Second Sex,* New York: Bantam Books, 1961, pp. 18–19.

[39] August Bebel, *Women and Socialism,* New York: Socialist Literature Co., 1910, pp. 66–69.

[40] Frantz Fanon, *A Dying Colonialism,* New York: Grove Press, 1967, p. 119.

ing; but one thing I shall never forgive, neither in this world nor the world to come: its wanton and continued and persistent insulting of the black womanhood which it sought and seeks to prostitute to its lust.[41]

The retaliatory import of the rape for the black man would be entrapment in an untenable situation. Clearly the master hoped that once the black man was struck by his manifest inability to rescue his women from sexual assaults of the master, he would begin to experience deep-seated doubts about his ability to resist at all.

Certainly the wholesale rape of slave women must have had a profound impact on the slave community. Yet it could not succeed in its intrinsic aim of stifling the impetus towards struggle. Countless black women did not passively submit to these abuses, as the slaves in general refused to passively accept their bondage. The struggles of the slave woman in the sexual realm were a continuation of the resistance interlaced in the slave's daily existence. As such, this was yet another form of insurgency, a response to a politically tinged sexual repression.

Even E. Franklin Frazier (who goes out of his way to defend the thesis that "the master in his mansion and his colored mistress in her special house nearby represented the final triumph of social ritual in the presence of the deepest feelings of human solidarity"[42]) could not entirely ignore the black woman who fought back. He notes: "That physical compulsion was necessary at times to secure submission on the part of black women . . . is supported by historical evidence and has been preserved in the tradition of Negro families."[43]

The sexual contest was one of many arenas in which the black woman had to prove herself as a warrior against oppression. What Frazier unwillingly concedes would mean that countless children brutally fathered by whites were conceived in the thick of battle. Frazier himself cites the story of a black woman whose great grandmother, a former slave, would describe with great zest the battles behind all her numerous scars—that is, all save one. In response to questions concerning the unexplained scar, she had always simply said: "White men are as low as dogs, child, stay away from them." The mystery was not unveiled until after the death of this brave woman: "She received that scar at the hands of her master's youngest son, a boy of about eighteen years at the time she conceived their child, my grandmother Ellen."[44]

An intricate and savage web of oppression intruded at every moment into the black woman's life during slavery. Yet a single theme appears at every juncture: the woman transcending, refusing, fighting back, asserting herself over and against terrifying obstacles. It was not her comrade brother against whom her incredible strength was directed. She fought alongside her man, accepting or providing guidance according to her talents and the nature of their tasks. She was in no sense an authoritarian figure; neither her domestic role nor her acts of resistance could relegate the man to the shadows. On the contrary, she herself had just been forced to leave behind the shadowy realm of female passivity in order to assume her rightful place beside the insurgent male.

This portrait cannot, of course, presume to represent every individual slave woman. It is rather a portrait of the potentials and possibilities inherent in the situation to which slave women were anchored. Invariably there were those who did not realize this potential. There were those who were indifferent and a few who were outright traitors. But certainly they were not the vast majority. The image of black women enchaining their men, cultivating relationships

[41]Du Bois, *Darkwater*, p. 172.

[42]E. Franklin Frazier, *The Negro Family in the United States*, Chicago: U. of Chicago Press, 1966 (1st ed., 1939), p. 69.

[43]*Ibid.*, p. 53.

[44]*Ibid.*, pp. 53–54.

with the oppressor is a cruel fabrication which must be called by its right name. It is a dastardly ideological weapon designed to impair our capacity for resistance today by foisting upon us the ideal of male supremacy.

According to a time-honored principle, advanced by Marx, Lenin, Fanon and numerous other theorists, the status of women in any given society is a barometer measuring the overall level of social development. As Fanon has masterfully shown, the strength and efficacy of social struggles—and especially revolutionary movements—bear an immediate relationship to the range and quality of female participation.

The meaning of this principle is strikingly illustrated by the role of the black woman during slavery. Attendant to the indiscriminant brutal pursuit of profit, the slave woman attained a correspondingly brutal status of equality. But in practice, she could work up a fresh content for this deformed equality by inspiring and participating in acts of resistance of every form and color. She could turn the weapon of equality in struggle against the avaricious slave system which had engendered the mere caricature of equality in oppression. The black woman's activities increased the total incidence of anti-slavery assaults. But most important, without consciously rebellious black women, the theme of resistance could not have become so thoroughly intertwined in the fabric of daily existence. The status of black women within the community of slaves was definitely a barometer indicating the overall potential for resistance.

This process did not end with the formal dissolution of slavery. Under the impact of racism, the black woman has been continually constrained to inject herself into the desperate struggle for existence. She—like her man—has been compelled to work for wages, providing for her family as she was previously forced to provide for the slaveholding class. The infinitely onerous nature of this equality should never be overlooked. For the black woman has always also remained harnessed to the chores of the household. Yet, she could never be exhaustively defined by her uniquely "female" responsibilities.

As a result, black women have made significant contributions to struggles against the racism and the dehumanizing exploitation of a wrongly organized society. In fact, it would appear that the intense levels of resistance historically maintained by black people and thus the historical function of the Black Liberation Struggle as harbinger of change throughout the society are due in part to the greater *objective* equality between the black man and the black women. Du Bois put it this way:

> In the great rank and file of our five million women, we have the up-working of new revolutionary ideals, which must in time have vast influence on the thought and action of this land.[45]

Official and unofficial attempts to blunt the effects of the egalitarian tendencies as between the black man and woman should come as no surprise. The matriarch concept, embracing the cliched "female castrator," is, in the last instance, an open weapon of ideological warfare. Black men and women alike remain its potential victims—men unconsciously lunging at the woman, equating her with the myth; women sinking back into the shadows, lest an aggressive posture resurrect the myth in themselves.

The myth must be consciously repudiated as myth and the black woman in her true historical contours must be resurrected. We, the black women of today, must accept the full weight of a legacy wrought in blood by our mothers in chains. Our fight, while identical in spirit, reflects different conditions and thus implies different paths of struggle. But as heirs to a tradition of supreme perseverance and heroic resistance, we must hasten to take our place wherever our people are forging on towards freedom.

---

[45]Du Bois, *Darkwater*, p. 185.

CALL FOR CRITICAL DEBATE

LARRY NEAL
(1937–1981)

The brilliant writer Larry Neal died at a young age. In his short forty-three years he managed to be a critic, poet, playwright, filmmaker, editor, folklorist, teacher, and administrator. Along with Amiri Baraka, he was the main architect of the Black Arts Movement of the 1960s. His essays were among the most cogent and thoughtful of that time; they repay careful reading today. At the end of this life, he was moving toward a more complex black aesthetic, a black way of creating and judging art. As the Black Arts Movement as a whole re-evaluates Larry Neal, he will claim his proper place in black literary history.

Larry Neal was born on September 4, 1937 in Atlanta, Georgia, to Woodie and Maggie Neal. When he was a child, the Neals moved to Philadelphia, where he grew up. He graduated from Lincoln University, a predominantly black school in Pennsylvania, in 1961 and received an M.A. from the University of Pennsylvania in 1963. The following year, he moved to New York City, and the next year he married Evelyn Rodgers, a chemist. The couple lived in Sugar Hill, Harlem. During this time Neal met, among other literary artists, Ishmael Reed, Quincy Troupe, Askia Muhammad Touré, Stanley Crouch, Henry Dumas, and Amiri Baraka. In 1964 he and Baraka established the Black Arts Repertory Theater in Harlem. The next year, however, Neal was shot by an unknown assailant who reportedly disagreed with Neal's political and artistic vision. In 1968 he and Amiri Baraka co-edited *Black Fire*. This major anthology included the finest writing of the new generation by such authors as Sonia Sanchez, Ed Bullins, Harold Cruise, and Stokely Carmichael. The same year, Neal published his primary manifesto and seminal essay "The Black Arts Movement," where he declares that the movement is "the aesthetic and spiritual sister of the Black Power concept. . . . The Black Arts Movement proposes a radical reordering of the Western cultural aesthetic." Neal also published two books of poems, *Black Boogaloo* (1969) and *Hoodoo Hollerin Bebop Ghosts* (1971), and two plays, *The Glorious Monster in the Bell of the Horn* (1976) and *In an Upstate Motel* (1976).

From 1976 to 1979, Neal was the executive director of the Commission on the Arts and Humanities in Washington, D.C. On January 6, 1981, he died of a heart attack in Hamilton, New York, where he was attending a theater workshop at Colgate College. To understand our past and to shape a precise future, we must read and reread this major African American intellectual.

❖❖❖

Michael Schwartz has edited a collection of Neal's writings, *Visions of a Liberated Future: Black Arts Movement Writings* (1987). Norman Harris has a highly informative article on Neal in *Dictionary of Literary Biography*, vol. 38: *Afro-American Writers After 1955: Dramatists and Prose Writers*, ed. Trudier Harris et al. (1985).

The Black Arts Movement

The Black Arts Movement is radically opposed to any concept of the artist that alienates him from his community. This movement is the aesthetic and spiritual sister of the Black Power concept. As such, it envisions an art that speaks directly to the needs and aspirations of black America. In order to perform this task, the Black Arts Movement proposes a radical reordering of the Western cultural aesthetic. It proposes a separate symbolism, mythology, critique, and iconology. The Black Arts and the Black Power concepts both relate broadly to the Afro-American's desire for self-determination and nationhood. Both concepts are nationalistic. One is concerned with the relationship between art and politics; the other with the art of politics.

Recently, these two movements have begun to merge: the political values inherent in the Black Power concept are now finding concrete expression in the aesthetics of Afro-American dramatists, poets, choreographers, musicians, and novelists. A main tenet of Black Power is the necessity for black people to define the world in their own terms. The black artist has made the same point in the context of aesthetics. The two movements postulate that there are in fact and in spirit two Americas—one black, one white. The black artist takes this to mean that his primary duty is to speak to the spiritual and cultural needs of black people. Therefore, the main thrust of this new breed of contemporary writers is to confront the contradictions arising out of the black man's experience in the racist West. Currently, these writers are reevaluating Western aesthetics, the traditional role of the writer, and the social function of art. Implicit in this reevaluation is the need to develop a "black aesthetic." It is the opinion of many black writers, I among them, that the Western aesthetic has run its course: it is impossible to construct anything meaningful within its decaying structure. We advocate a cultural revolution in art and ideas. The cultural values inherent in Western history must either be radicalized or destroyed, and we will probably find that even radicalization is impossible. In fact, what is needed is a whole new system of ideas. Poet Don L. Lee expresses it:

> We must destroy Faulkner, dick, jane, and other perpetuators of evil. It's time for Du Bois, Nat Turner, and Kwame Nkrumah. As Frantz Fanon points out: destroy the culture and you destroy the people. This must not happen. Black artists are culture stabilizers; bringing back old values, and introducing new ones. Black art will talk to the people and with the will of the people stop impending "protective custody."

The Black Arts Movement eschews "protest" literature. It speaks directly to black people. Implicit in the concept of "protest" literature, as Brother Etheridge Knight has made clear, is an appeal to white morality:

> Now any Black man who masters the technique of his particular art form, who adheres to the white aesthetic, and who directs his work towards a white audience is, in one sense, protesting. And implicit in the act of protest is the belief that a change will be forthcoming once the masters are aware of the protestor's "grievance" (the very word connotes begging, supplications to the gods). Only when that belief has faded and protestings end, will Black art begin.

Brother Knight also has some interesting statements about the development of a "black aesthetic":

> Unless the Black artist establishes a "Black aesthetic" he will have no future at all. To accept the white aesthetic is to accept and validate a society that will not allow him to live. The Black artist must create new forms and new values, sing new songs (or purify old ones); and along with other Black authorities, he must create a new history, new symbols, myths and legends (and purify old ones by fire). And the Black artist, in creating his own aesthetic, must be accountable for it

> only to the Black people. Further, he must hasten his own dissolution as an individual (in the Western sense)—painful though, the process may be, having been breast-fed the poison of "individual experience."

When we speak of a "black aesthetic" several things are meant. First, we assume that there is already in existence the basis for such an aesthetic. Essentially, it consists of an African-American cultural tradition. But this aesthetic is finally, by implication, broader than that tradition. It encompasses most of the usable elements of Third World culture. The motive behind the black aesthetic is the destruction of the white thing, the destruction of white ideas, and white ways of looking at the world. The new aesthetic is mostly predicated on an ethics which asks the question: Whose vision of the world is finally more meaningful, ours or the white oppressors? What is truth? Or more precisely, whose truth shall we express, that of the oppressed or of the oppressors? These are basic questions. Black intellectuals of previous decades failed to ask them. Further, national and international affairs demand that we appraise the world in terms of our own interests. It is clear that the question of human survival is at the core of contemporary experience. The black artist must address himself to this reality in the strongest terms possible. In a context of world upheaval, ethics and aesthetics must interact positively and be consistent with the demands for a more spiritual world. Consequently, the Black Arts Movement is an ethical movement. Ethical, that is, from the viewpoint of the oppressed. And much of the oppression confronting the Third World and black America is directly traceable to the Euro-American cultural sensibility. This sensibility, antihuman in nature, has, until recently, dominated the psyches of most black artists and intellectuals. It must be destroyed before the black creative artist can have a meaningful role in the transformation of society.

It is this natural reaction to an alien sensibility that informs the cultural attitudes of the Black Arts and the Black Power movements. It is a profound ethical sense that makes a black artist question a society in which art is one thing and the actions of men another. The Black Arts Movement believes that your ethics and your aesthetics are one. That [there are] contradictions between ethics and aesthetics in Western society is symptomatic of a dying culture.

The term "Black Arts" is of ancient origin, but it was first used in a positive sense by LeRoi Jones:

> We are unfair
> And unfair
> We are black magicians
> Black arts we make
> in black labs of the heart
>
> The fair are fair
> and deathly white
>
> The day will not save them
> And we own the night

There is also a section of the poem "Black Dada Nihilismus" that carries the same motif. But a fuller amplification of the nature of the new aesthetics appears in the poem "Black Art":

> Poems are bullshit unless they are
> teeth or trees or lemons piled
> on a step. Or black ladies dying
> of men leaving nickel hearts
> beating them down. Fuck poems
> and they are useful, they shoot
> come at you, love what you are,
> breathe like wrestlers, or shudder
> strangely after pissing. We want live
> words of the hip world, live flesh &
> coursing blood. Hearts Brains
> Souls splintering fire. We want poems
> like fists beating niggers out of Jocks
> or dagger poems in the slimy bellies
> of the owner-jews . . .

Poetry is a concrete function, an action. No more abstractions. Poems are physical entities: fists, daggers, airplane poems, and poems that shoot guns. Poems are transformed from physical object into personal forces:

Put it on him poem. Strip him naked
to the world. Another bad poem cracking
steel knuckles in a jewlady's mouth
Poem scream poison gas on breasts in green
berets . . .

Then the poem affirms the integral relationship between black art and black people:

Let Black people understand
that they are the lovers and the sons
of lovers and warriors and sons
of warriors Are poems & poets &
all the loveliness here in the world

It ends with the following lines, a central assertion in both the Black Arts Movement and the philosophy of Black Power:

We want a black poem. And a
Black World.
Let the world be a Black Poem
And Let All Black People Speak This Poem
Silently
Or LOUD

The poem comes to stand for the collective consciousness and unconscious of black America—the real impulse in back of the Black Power movement, which is the will toward self-determination and nationhood, a radical reordering of the nature and function of both art and the artist.

2.

In the spring of 1964, LeRoi Jones, Charles Patterson, William Patterson, Clarence Reed, Johnny Moore, and a number of other black artists opened the Black Arts Repertory Theater School. They produced a number of plays including Jones's *Experimental Death Unit #1, Black Mass, Jello,* and *Dutchman.* They also initiated a series of poetry readings and concerts. These activities represented the most advanced tendencies in the movement and were of excellent artistic quality. The Black Arts school came under immediate attack by the New York power structure. The Establishment, fearing black creativity, did exactly what it was expected to do—it attacked the theater and all of its values. In the meantime, the school was granted funds by OEO through HARYOU-ACT. Lacking a cultural program itself, HARYOU turned to the only organization which addressed itself to the needs of the community. In keeping with its "revolutionary" cultural ideas, the Black Arts Theater took its programs into the streets of Harlem. For three months, the theater presented plays, concerts, and poetry readings to the people of the community. Plays that shattered the illusions of the American body politic, and awakened black people to the meaning of their lives.

Then the hawks from the OEO moved in and chopped off the funds. Again, this should have been expected. The Black Arts Theater stood in radical opposition to the feeble attitudes about culture of the "War On Poverty" bureaucrats. And later, because of internal problems, the theater was forced to close. But the Black Arts group proved that the community could be served by a valid and dynamic art. It also proved that there was a definite need for a cultural revolution in the black community.

With the closing of the Black Arts Theater, the implications of what Brother Jones and his colleagues were trying to do took on even more significance. Black Arts groups sprang up on the West Coast and the idea spread to Detroit, Philadelphia, Jersey City, New Orleans, and Washington D.C. Black Arts movements began on the campuses of San Francisco State College, Fisk University, Lincoln University, Hunter College in the Bronx, Columbia University, and Oberlin College. In Watts, after the rebellion, Maulana Karenga welded the Blacks Arts Movement into a cohesive cultural ideology which owed much to the work of LeRoi Jones. Karenga sees culture as the most important element in the struggle for self-determination:

> Culture is the basis of all ideas, images and actions. To move is to move culturally, i.e., by a set of values given to you by your culture.

Without a culture Negroes are only a set of reactions to white people.

The seven criteria for culture are:

1. Mythology
2. History
3. Social Organization
4. Political Organization
5. Economic Organization
6. Creative Motif
7. Ethos

In drama, LeRoi Jones represents the most advanced aspects of the movement. He is its prime mover and chief designer. In a poetic essay entitled "The Revolutionary Theatre," he outlines the iconology of the movement:

> The Revolutionary Theatre should force change: it should be change. (All their faces turned into the lights and you work on them black nigger magic, and cleanse them at having seen the ugliness. And if the beautiful see themselves, they will love themselves.) We are preaching virtue again, but by that to mean NOW, toward what seems the most constructive use of the word.

The theater that Jones proposes is inextricably linked to the Afro-American political dynamic. And such a link is perfectly consistent with Black America's contemporary demands. For theater is potentially the most social of all the arts. It is an integral part of the socializing process. It exists in direct relationship to the audience it claims to serve. The decadence and inanity of the contemporary American theater is an accurate reflection of the state of American society. Albee's *Who's Afraid of Virginia Woolf?* is very American: sick white lives in a homosexual hell hole. The theater of white America is escapist, refusing to confront concrete reality. Into this cultural emptiness come the musicals, an up-tempo version of the same stale lives. And the use of Negroes in such plays as *Hello, Dolly!* and *Hallelujah Baby* does not alert their nature; it compounds the problem. These plays are simply hipper versions of the minstrel show. They present Negroes acting out the hang-ups of middle-class white America. Consequently, the American theater is a palliative prescribed to bourgeois patients who refuse to see the world as it is. Or, more crucially, as the world sees them. It is no accident, therefore, that the most "important" plays come from Europe—Brecht, Weiss, and Ghelderode. And even these have begun to run dry.

The Black Arts Theater, the theater of LeRoi Jones, is a radical alternative to the sterility of the American theater. It is primarily a theater of the spirit, confronting the black man in his interaction with his brothers and with the white thing.

> Our theater will show victims so that their brothers in the audience will be better able to understand that they are the brothers of victims, and that they themselves are blood brothers. And what we show must cause the blood to rush, so that prerevolutionary temperaments will be bathed in this blood, and it will cause their deepest souls to move, and they will find themselves tensed and clenched, even ready to die, at what the soul has been taught. We will scream and cry, murder, run through the streets in agony, if it means some soul will be moved, moved to actual life understanding of what the world is, and what it ought to be. We are preaching virtue and feeling, and a natural sense of the self in the world. All men live in the world, and the world ought to be a place for them to live.

The victims in the world of Jones's early plays are Clay, murdered by the white bitch-goddess in *Dutchman,* and Walker Vessels, the revolutionary in *The Slave.* Both of these plays present black men in transition. Clay, the middle-class Negro trying to get himself a little action from Lula, digs himself and his own truth only to get murdered after telling her like it really is:

> Just let me bleed you, you loud whore, and one poem vanished. A whole people neurotics, struggling to keep from being sane.

> And the only thing that would cure the neurosis would be your murder. Simple as that. I mean if I murdered you, then other white people would understand me. You understand? No, I guess not. If Bessie Smith had killed some white people she wouldn't needed that music. She could have talked very straight and plain about the world. Just straight two and two are four. Money. Power. Luxury. Like that. All of them. Crazy niggers turning their back on sanity. When all it needs is that simple act. Just murder. Would make us all sane.

But Lula understands, and she kills Clay first. In a perverse way it is Clay's nascent knowledge of himself that threatens the existence of Lula's idea of the world. Symbolically, and in fact, the relationship between Clay (black America) and Lula (white America) is rooted in the historical castration of black manhood. And in the twisted psyche of white America, the black man is both an object of love and hate. Analogous attitudes exist in most black Americans, but for decidedly different reasons. Clay is doomed when he allows himself to participate in Lula's "fantasy" in the first place. It is the fantasy to which Frantz Fanon alludes in *The Wretched of the Earth* and *Black Skins, White Mask:* the native's belief that he can acquire the oppressor's power by acquiring his symbols, one of which is the white woman. When Clay finally digs himself, it is too late.

Walker Vessels, in *The Slave,* is Clay reincarnated as the revolutionary confronting problems inherited from his contact with white culture. He returns to the home of his ex-wife, a white woman, and her husband, a literary critic. The play is essentially about Walker's attempt to destroy his white past. For it is the past, with all of its painful memories, that is really the enemy of the revolutionary. It is impossible to move until history is either re-created or comprehended. Unlike Todd, in Ralph Ellison's *Invisible Man,* Walker cannot fall outside history. Instead, Walker demands a confrontation with history, a final shattering of bullshit illusions. His only salvation lies in confronting the physical and psychological forces that have made him and his people powerless. Therefore, he comes to understand that the world must be restructured along spiritual imperatives. But in the interim it is basically a question of *who* has power:

> EASLEY You're so wrong about everything. So terribly, sickeningly wrong. What can you change? What do you hope to change? Do you think Negroes are better people than whites . . . that they can govern a society *better* than whites? That they'll be more judicious or more tolerant? Do you think they'll make fewer mistakes? I mean really, if the Western white man has proved one thing . . . it's the futility of modern society. So the have-not peoples become the haves. Even so, will that change the essential functions of the world? Will there be more love or beauty in the world . . . more knowledge . . . because of it?
>
> WALKER Probably. Probably there will be more . . . if more people have a chance to understand what it is. But that's not even the point. It comes down to baser human endeavor than any social-political thinking. What does it matter if there's more love or beauty? Who the fuck cares? Is that what the Western ofay thought while he was ruling . . . that his rule somehow brought more love and beauty into the world? Oh, he might have thought that concomitantly, while sipping a gin rickey and scratching his ass . . . but that was not ever the point. Not even on the Crusades. The point is that you had your chance, darling, now these older folks have theirs. *Quietly.* Now they have theirs.
>
> EASLEY God, what an ugly idea.

This confrontation between the black radical and the white liberal is symbolic of larger confrontations occurring between the Third World and Western society. It is a confrontation between the colonizer and the colonized, the slave master and the slave. Implicit in Easley's remarks is the belief that the white man is culturally and politically superior to the black man.

Even though Western society has been traditionally violent in its relation with the Third World, it sanctimoniously deplores violence or self-assertion on the part of the enslaved. And the Western mind, with clever rationalizations, equates the violence of the oppressed with the violence of the oppressor. So that when the native preaches self-determination, the Western white man cleverly misconstrues it to mean hate of *all* white men. When the black political radical warns his people not to trust white politicians of the Left and the Right, but instead to organize separately on the basis of power, the white man cries: "Racism in reverse." Or he will say, as many of them do today: "We deplore both white and black racism." As if the two could be equated.

There is a minor element in *The Slave* which assumes great importance in a later play entitled *Jello*. Here I refer to the emblem of Walker's army: a red-mouthed grinning field slave. The revolutionary army has taken one of the most hated symbols of the Afro-American past and radically altered its meaning.[1] This is the supreme act of freedom, available only to those who have liberated themselves psychically. Jones amplifies this inversion of emblem and symbol in *Jello* by making Rochester (Ratfester) of the old Jack Benny (Penny) program into a revolutionary nationalist. Ratfester, ordinarily the supreme embodiment of the Uncle Tom Clown, surprises Jack Penny by turning on the other side of the nature of the Black man. He skillfully, and with an evasive black humor, robs Penny of all of his money. But Ratfester's actions are "moral." That is to say, Ratfester is getting his back pay; payment of a long overdue debt to the Black man. Ratfester's sensibilities are different from Walker's. He is *blues people* smiling and shuffling while trying to figure out how to destroy the white thing. And like the blues man, he is the master of the understatement. Or in the Afro-American folk tradition, he is the Signifying Monkey, Shine, and Stackolee all rolled into one. There are no stereotypes anymore. History has killed Uncle Tom. Because even Uncle Tom has a breaking point beyond which he will not be pushed. Cut deeply enough into the most docile Negro, and you will find a conscious murderer. Behind the lyrics of the blues and the shuffling porter loom visions of white throats being cut and cities burning.

Jones's particular power as a playwright does not rest solely on his revolutionary vision, but is instead derived from his deep lyricism and spiritual outlook. In many ways, he is fundamentally more a poet than a playwright. And it is his lyricism that gives body to his plays. Two important plays in this regard are *Black Mass* and *Slave Ship. Black Mass* is based on the Muslim myth of Yacub. According to this myth, Yacub, a Black scientist, developed the means of grafting different colors of the Original Black Nation until a White Devil was created. In *Black Mass,* Yacub's experiments produce a raving White Beast who is condemned to the coldest regions of the North. The other magicians implore Yacub to cease his experiments. But he insists on claiming the primacy of scientific knowledge over spiritual knowledge. The sensibility of the White Devil is alien, informed by lust and sensuality. The Beast is the consummate embodiment of evil, the beginning of the historical subjugation of the spiritual world.

Black Mass takes place in some pre-historical time. In fact, the concept of time, we learn, is the creation of an alien sensibility, that of the Beast. This is a deeply weighted play, a colloquy on the nature of man, and the relationship between legitimate spiritual knowledge and scientific knowledge. It is LeRoi Jones's most important play mainly because it is informed by a mythology that is wholly the creation of the Afro-American sensibility.

---

[1]In Jones's study of Afro-American music, *Blues People,* we find the following observation: "Even the adjective *funky,* which once meant to many Negroes merely a stink (usually associated with sex), was used to qualify the music as meaningful (the word became fashionable and is now almost useless). The social implication, then, was that even the old stereotype of a distinctive Negro smell that white America subscribed to could be turned against white America. For this smell now, real or not, was made a valuable characteristic of 'Negro-ness.' and 'Negro-ness,' by the fifties, for many Negroes (and whites) was the only strength left to American culture."

Further, Yacub's creation is not merely a scientific exercise. More fundamentally, it is the aesthetic impulse gone astray. The Beast is created merely for the sake of creation. Some artists assert a similar claim about the nature of art. They argue that art need not have a function. It is against this decadent attitude toward art—rammed throughout most of Western society—that the play militates. Yacub's real crime, therefore, is the introduction of a meaningless evil into a harmonious universe. The evil of the Beast is pervasive, corrupting everything and everyone it touches. What was beautiful is twisted into an ugly screaming thing. The play ends with the destruction of the holy place of the Black Magicians. Now the Beast and his descendants roam the earth. An off-stage voice chants a call for the Jihad to begin. It is then that myth merges into legitimate history, and we, the audience, come to understand that all history is merely someone's version of mythology.

Slave Ship presents a more immediate confrontation with history. In a series of expressionistic tableaux it depicts the horrors and the madness of the Middle Passage. It then moves through the period of slavery, early attempts at revolt, tendencies toward Uncle Tom–like reconciliation and betrayal, and the final act of liberation. There is no definite plot (LeRoi calls it a pageant), just a continuous rush of sound, moans, screams, and souls wailing for freedom and relief from suffering. This work has special attributes with the New Music of Sun Ra, John Coltrane, Albert Ayler, and Ornette Coleman. Events are blurred, rising and falling in a stream of sound. Almost cinematically, the images flicker and fade against a heavy backdrop of rhythm. The language is spare, stripped to the essential. It is a play which almost totally eliminates the need for a text. It functions on the basis of movement and energy, the dramatic equivalent of the New Music.

3.

LeRoi Jones is the best known and the most advanced playwright of the movement, but he is not alone. There are other excellent playwrights who express the general mood of the Black Arts ideology. Among them are Ron Milner, Ed Bullins, Ben Caldwell, Jimmy Stewart, Joe White, Charles Patterson, Charles Fuller, Aisha Hughes, Carol Freeman, and Jimmy Garrett.

Ron Milner's *Who's Got His Own* is of particular importance. It strips bare the clashing attitudes of a contemporary Afro-American family. Milner's concern is with legitimate manhood and morality. The family in *Who's Got His Own* is in search of its conscience, or more precisely its own definition of life. On the day of his father's death, Tim and his family are forced to examine the inner fabric of their lives, the lies, self-deceits, and sense of powerlessness in a white world. The basic conflict, however, is internal. It is rooted in the historical search for black manhood. Tim's mother is representative of a generation of Christian black women who have implicitly understood the brooding violence lurking in their men. And with this understanding, they have interposed themselves between their men and the object of that violence—the white man. Thus unable to direct his violence against the oppressor, the black man becomes more frustrated and the sense of powerlessness deepens. Lacking the strength to be a man in the white world, he turns against his family. So the oppressed, as Fanon explains, constantly dreams violence against his oppressor, while killing his brother on fast weekends.

Tim's sister represents the Negro woman's attempt to acquire what Eldridge Cleaver calls "ultrafemininity." That is, the attributes of her white upper-class counterpart. Involved here is a rejection of the body-oriented life of the working-class black man, symbolized by the mother's traditional religion. The sister has an affair with a white upper-class liberal, ending in abortion. There are hints of lesbianism, i.e., a further rejection of the body. The sister's life is a pivotal factor in the play. Much of the stripping away of falsehood initiated by Tim is directed at her life, which they have carefully kept hidden from the mother.

Tim is the product of the new Afro-American sensibility, informed by the psychological revolution now operative within Black America. He is a combination ghetto soul-brother and militant intellectual, very hip and slightly flawed himself. He would change the world, but without comprehending the particular history that produced his "tyrannical" father. And he cannot be the man his father was—not until he truly understands his father. He must understand why his father allowed himself to be insulted daily by the "honky" types on the job; why he took a demeaning job in the "shit-house"; and why he spent on his family the violence that he should have directed against the white man. In short, Tim must confront the history of his family. And that is exactly what happens. Each character tells his story, exposing his falsehood to the other until a balance is reached.

Who's Got His Own is not the work of an alienated mind. Milner's main thrust is directed toward unifying the family around basic moral principles, toward bridging the "generation gap." Other black playwrights, Jimmy Garrett for example, see the gap as unbridgeable.

Garrett's *We Own the Night* takes place during an armed insurrection. As the play opens we see the central characters defending a section of the city against attacks by white police. Johnny, the protagonist, is wounded. Some of his Brothers intermittently fire at attacking forces, while others look for medical help. A doctor arrives, forced at gunpoint. The wounded boy's mother also comes. She is a female Uncle Tom who berates the Brothers and their cause. She tries to get Johnny to leave. She is hysterical. The whole idea of black people fighting white people is totally outside of her orientation. Johnny begins a vicious attack on his mother, accusing her of emasculating his father—a recurring theme in the sociology of the black community. In Afro-American literature of previous decades the strong black mother was the object of awe and respect. But in the new literature her status is ambivalent and laced with tension. Historically, Afro-American women have had to be the economic mainstays of the family. The oppressor allowed them to have jobs while at the same time limiting the economic mobility of the black man. Very often, therefore, the woman's aspirations and values are closely tied to those of the white power structure and not to those of her man. Since he cannot provide for his family the way white men do, she despises his weakness, tearing into him at every opportunity until, very often, there is nothing left but a shell.

The only way out of this dilemma is through revolution. It either must be an actual blood revolution, or one that psychically redirects the energy of the oppressed. Milner is fundamentally concerned with the latter, and Garrett with the former. Communication between Johnny and his mother breaks down. The revolutionary imperative demands that men step outside the legal framework. It is a question of erecting *another* morality. The old constructs do not hold up because adhering to them means consigning oneself to the oppressive reality. Johnny's mother is involved in the old constructs. Manliness is equated with white morality. And even though she claims to love her family (her men), the overall design of her ideas are against black manhood. In Garrett's play the mother's morality manifests itself in a deep-seated hatred of black men, while in Milner's work the mother understands, but holds her men back.

The mothers that Garrett and Milner see represent the Old Spirituality—the Faith of the Fathers of which Du Bois spoke. Johnny and Tim represent the New Spirituality. They appear to be a type produced by the upheavals of the colonial world of which black America is a part. Johnny's assertion that he is a criminal is remarkably similar to the rebel's comments in Aimé Césaire's play *Les Armes Miraculeuses (The Miraculous Weapons)*. In that play the rebel, speaking to his mother, proclaims: "My name—an offense; my Christian name—humiliation; my status—a rebel; my age—the stone age." To which the mother replies: "My race—the human race. My religion—brotherhood." The Old Spirituality is generalized. It seeks to recognize Universal Humanity. The New Spirituality is specific. It begins by seeing the world from the concise point of view of the colonialized. Where the Old Spirituality would live with oppression while ascribing to the oppressors an innate goodness, the New Spirituality demands a radical shift in point of view. The colonialized native, the oppressed must, of necessity, subscribe to a *separate* morality. One that will liberate him and his people.

The assault against the Old Spirituality can sometimes be humorous. In Ben Caldwell's play *The Militant Preacher* a burglar is seen slipping into the home of a wealthy minister. The preacher comes in and the burglar ducks behind a large chair. The preacher, acting out the role of the supplicant minister, begins to moan, praying to De Lawd for understanding.

In the context of today's politics, the minister is an Uncle Tom, mouthing platitudes against self-defense. The preacher drones in a self-pitying monologue about the folly of protecting oneself against brutal policemen. Then the burglar begins to speak. The preacher is startled, taking the burglar's voice for the voice of God. The burglar begins to play on the preacher's old-time religion. He *becomes* the voice of God insulting and goading the preacher on until the preacher's attitudes about protective violence change. The next day the preacher emerges militant, gun in hand, wounding like Reverend [Albert Buford] Cleage in Detroit. He now preaches a new gospel—the gospel of the gun, an eye for an eye. The gospel is preached in the rhythmic cadences of the old black church. But the content is radical. Just as Jones inverted the symbols in *Jello,* Caldwell twists the rhythms of the Uncle Tom preacher into the language of the new militancy.

These plays are directed at problems within black America. They begin with the premise that there is a well-defined Afro-American audience. An audience that must see itself and the world in terms of its own interests. These plays, along with many others, constitute the basis for a viable movement in the theater—a movement which takes as its task a profound reevaluation of the black man's presence in America. The Black Arts Movement represents the flowering of a cultural nationalism that has been suppressed since the 1920s. I mean the "Harlem Renaissance"—which was essentially a failure. It did not address itself to the mythology and the life-styles of the black community. It failed to take root, to link itself concretely to the struggles of that community, to become its voice and spirit. Implicit in the Black Arts Movement is the idea that black people, however dispersed, constitute a *nation* within the belly of white America. This is not a new idea. Garvey said it and the Honorable Elijah Muhammad says it now. And it is on this idea that the concept of Black Power is predicated.

Afro-American life and history is full of creative possibilities, and the movement is just beginning to perceive them. Just beginning to understand that the most meaningful statements about the nature of Western society must come from the Third World of which black America is a part. The thematic material is broad, ranging from folk heroes like Shine and Stackolee to historical figures like Marcus Garvey and Malcolm X. And then there is the struggle for black survival, the coming confrontation between white America and black America. If art is the harbinger of future possibilities, what does it portend for the future of black America?

JOYCE ANN JOYCE

(1949–)

The eminent Afrocentric scholar Joyce Ann Joyce is, undoubtedly, the most outspoken critic of Henry Louis Gates's poststructuralist approach to African American literature. Eschewing the idea of race as metaphor, Joyce instead uses an approach that explores black literature and art as connected to a culture and to the people who inform it, while at the same time reconnecting it to the people and culture that inform it. The roots of her thesis are evident in her first book, *Native Son: Richard Wright's Art of Tragedy* (1986). This critical work is a reevaluation of Wright's most famous work and simultaneously comments on appropriate approaches to African American literary criticism. Joyce recasts *Native Son,* traditionally received as a consummate example of the naturalistic novel, into new critical terms so that the novel emerges as a classic tragedy in the tradition of Shakespeare's *King Lear* and Sophocles' *Oedipus Rex.*

Joyce was born on August 26, 1949, in Valdosta, Georgia to Edna and Henry Joyce, Jr. She received her B.A. in English from Valdosta State College in 1970 and went on to graduate work at the University of Georgia, where she completed her Ph.D. in English in 1979. She has taught at various institutions, including the University of Georgia and the University of Nebraska. She is currently a professor of English at Chicago State University and associate director of the university's Gwendolyn Brooks Center.

During the 1980s, Joyce became embroiled in the debate about African American literary studies. In an essay for *New Literary History* (Winter 1987), she stood in opposition to Henry Louis Gates's poststructuralist reading of metaphoricity in African American literature. Along with a growing number of critics, she rejects what she considers to be the needlessly mystifying terms of deconstructionist theory, in favor of an Afrocentric reading of the literature focusing on the political as well as the aesthetic aspects of African American art. In a statement in *Contemporary Authors,* the controversial critic said that her "approach to African-American literary criticism attempts to merge the political and the aesthetic."

Joyce's work has appeared in anthologies such as *Issues in Feminist Inquiry: Agency and Value Judgment* (1991) and in periodicals such as *Mississippi Quarterly* and *CEA Critic.* She is also the editor, with Arthur P. Davis and Saunders Redding, of the 1991 and 1992 editions of *Cavalcade: An Anthology of Afro-American Literature.* Her most recent book is *Warriors, Conjurers and Priests: Defining African-Centered Literary Criticism* (1994), for which she won the American Book Award for literary criticism in 1995.

❖❖❖

Biographical information is available in *Contemporary Authors* (1992), vol. 137. For reviews of Joyce's work, see W. J. Hug, *Southern Humanities Review* vol. 22, no. 3 (Summer 1988) and Arnold Rampersad, *American Literature* vol. 59, no. 4 (December 1987). Her essay "The Black Canon: Reconstructing Black American Literary Criticism" was first published in *New Literary History* 18 (Winter 1987).

The Black Canon: Reconstructing Black American Literary Criticism

In April 1984 a former student of mine came to my office specifically to discuss James Baldwin's essay "On Being 'White' . . . And Other Lies," which appeared in the April 1984 issue of *Essence* magazine.[1] This very bright young woman was bothered because she knew that if she only marginally understood the essay, then many of "our people"—to use her phraseol-

[1]James Baldwin, "On Being 'White' . . . And Other Lies," *Essence,* April 1984, pp. 90–92.

ogy—the ones who read *Essence* but who have not read some of Baldwin's other works, would not understand the essay. I still have trouble believing that the response I gave this young woman came from my mouth as I heard myself say that James Baldwin writes like James Baldwin. "How is he supposed to write?" I asked the student, whom my emotions told me I was failing. Her response was simple. She said, "He is supposed to be clear."

I realized that I was trapped by my own contradictions and elitism, while I agreed that if a reader is familiar with Baldwin's previous essays, particularly his "Down at the Cross: Letter from a Region in My Mind," the major piece in *The Fire Next Time,* he or she would better understand how Baldwin thinks, how he shapes his ideas, his thought and feeling patterns—his Baldwinian sensibility. As the student stared at me, I realized that she and I—the student and the teacher—had exchanged places. For she was teaching me—implicitly reminding me of all those times when I cajoled and coerced her away from narrow and provincial interpretations of the literary work and preached of the responsibility of the writer to his or her audience.

As we discussed the contents of Baldwin's essay, I was intellectually paralyzed by thoughts of the intricacies of the relationship of the writer to the audience, by the historical interrelationship between literature, class, values and the literary canon, and finally by my frustration as to how all these complexities augment ad finitum when the writer is a Black American. For in the first works of Black American literature the responsibility of the writers to their audience was as easy to deduce as it was to identify their audience. The slave narratives, most of the poetry, *Clotel,* and *Our Nig* were all addressed to white audiences with the explicit aim of denouncing slavery. This concentration on the relationship of Black Americans to the hegemony, to mainstream society, continues to this day to be the predominant issue in Black American literature, despite the change in focus we find in some of the works of Black women writers.

With Black American literature particularly, the issue of the responsibility of the creative writer is directly related to the responsibility of the literary critic. As is the case with James Baldwin, the most influential critics of Black literature have been the creative writers themselves, as evidenced also by W. E. B. Du Bois, Langston Hughes, Richard Wright, Ralph Ellison, Amiri Baraka, and Ishmael Reed. In his essay "Afro-American Literary Critics: An Introduction," found in Addison Gayle's landmark edition of *The Black Aesthetic,* Darwin Turner pinpoints why up to the 1960s a number of Black literary artists were also critics. Turner explains, "When a white publisher has wanted a black man to write about Afro-American literature, the publisher generally has turned to a famous creative writer. The reason is obvious. White publishers and readers have not been, and are not, familiar with the names and work of black scholars—the academic critics. Therefore, publishers have called upon the only blacks they have known—the famous writers."[2] After the 1960s, however, a group of literary scholars who had not begun their careers as creative artists emerged.

The 1960s mark a subtly contradictory change in Black academia reflective of the same contradictions inherent in the social, economic, and political strife that affected the lives of all Black Americans. Organizations like SNCC and CORE; the work of political figures like Stokely Carmichael, H. Rap Brown, Julian Bond, Huey Newton, Medgar Evers, Martin Luther King, Malcolm X, and Elijah Muhammad; the intense activity of voter registration drives, sit-ins, boycotts, and riots, the Black Arts Movement; and the work of Black innovative jazz musicians together constituted a Black social force that elicited affirmative action programs and the merger of a select number of Blacks into American mainstream society. This merger embodies the same shift in Black consciousness that Alain Locke described in 1925 in *The New Negro*

---

[2]Darwin Turner, "Afro-American Literary Critics: An Introduction," in *The Black Aesthetic,* ed. Addison Gayle (Garden City, N.Y., 1971), p. 66.

where he suggested that the mass movement of Blacks from a rural to an urban environment thrust a large number of Blacks into contact with mainstream values. He wrote:

> A main change has been, of course, that shifting of the Negro population which has made the Negro problem no longer exclusively or even predominantly Southern. . . . Then the trend of migration has not only been toward the North and the Central Midwest, but cityward and to the great centers of industry—the problems of adjustment are new, practical, local and not peculiarly racial. Rather they are an integral part of the large industrial and social problems of our present-day democracy. And finally, with the Negro rapidly in process of class differentiation, if it ever was warrantable to regard and treat the Negro *en masse* it is becoming with every day less possible, more unjust and more ridiculous.[3]

Professor Locke's comments here manifest the same social and ideological paradoxes that describe the relationship between the contemporary Black literary critic and his exogamic, elitist, epistemological adaptations.

For Professor Locke's assertion that to regard and treat the Negro en masse is becoming "every day less possible, more unjust and more ridiculous" is the historical prototype for Henry Louis Gates, Jr.'s denial of blackness or race as an important element of literary analysis of Black literature. Immersed in poststructuralist critical theory, Gates writes:

> Ultimately, black literature is a verbal art like other verbal arts. "Blackness" is not a material object or an event but a metaphor; it does not have an "essence" as such but is defined by a network of relations that form a particular aesthetic unity. . . . The black writer is the point of consciousness of his language. If he does embody a "Black Aesthetic," then it can be measured not by "content," but by a complex structure of meanings. The correspondence of content between a writer and his world is less significant to literary criticism than is a correspondence of organization or structure, for a relation of content may be a mere reflection of prescriptive, scriptural canon, such as those argued for by Baker, Gayle, and Henderson. . . .[4]

Interestingly enough, Locke's attenuation of race as a dominant issue in the lives of Blacks in the 1920s and Gates's rejection of race, reflecting periods of intense critical change for Black Americans, point to their own class orientation that ironically results from social changes provoked by racial issues.

In their succinct but thorough histories of Black American literary criticism, Houston Baker, Jr. in "Generational Shifts and the Recent Criticism of Afro-American Literature"[5] and Darwin Turner in the already cited "Afro-American Literary Critics: An Introduction" inadvertently corroborate Richard Wright's assertion that "expression springs out of an environment." Prophetically describing the direction of Black literary expression, Wright predicted in 1957

> . . . an understanding of Negro expression cannot be arrived at without a constant reference to the environment which cradles it. Directly after World War II, the United States and Soviet Russia emerged as the two dominant world powers. This meant a lessening of the influence of the ideology of Marxism in America and a frantic attempt on the part of white Americans to set their

---

[3]Alain Locke, "The New Negro," in *Cavalcade: Negro American Writing from 1760 to the Present,* ed. Arthur P. Davis and Saunders Redding (Boston, 1971), p. 276.

[4]Henry Louis Gates, Jr., "Preface to Blackness: Text and Pretext," in *Afro-American Literature: The Reconstruction of Instruction,* ed. Dexter Fisher and Robert B. Stepto (New York, 1979), p. 67; hereafter cited in text.

[5]Houston A. Baker, Jr., "Generational Shifts and the Recent Criticism of Afro-American Literature," *Black American Literature Forum,* 15, No. 11 (Spring 1981), 3–21.

> racial house somewhat in order in the face of world criticism. . . . The recent decision of the United States Supreme Court to integrate the schools of America on a basis of racial equality is one, but by no means the chief, change that has come over the American outlook. Naturally this effort on the part of the American nation to assimilate the Negro has had its effect upon Negro literary expression. . . . the mode and pitch of Negro literary expression would alter as soon as the attitude of the nation toward the Negro changed.[6]

The idea that white America has changed its attitude toward the Negro is quite dubious. However, what appears to have changed or grown is the intensity of the Black American's adoption of mainstream lifestyles and ideology, particularly the middle-class Black man's.

Up to the appearance of Dexter Fisher and Robert Stepto's *Afro-American Literature: The Reconstruction of Instruction* in 1979 and Michael Harper and Robert Stepto's edition of *Chant of Saints: A Gathering of Afro-American Literature, Art, and Scholarship,* also in 1979,[7] the Black American literary critic saw his role not as a "point of consciousness of his language," as Gates asserts, but as a point of consciousness for his or her people. This role was not one the critic had to contrive. A mere glance at the representative works from the Black literary canon chosen by any means of selection reveals that the most predominant, recurring, persistent, and obvious theme in Black American literature is that of liberation from the oppressive economic, social, political, and psychological strictures imposed on the Black man by white America. As characteristic, then, of the relationship between the critic and the work he or she analyzes, the critic takes his or her cues from the literary work itself as well as from the historical context of which that work is a part.

Consequently, Black American literary critics, like Black creative writers, saw a direct relationship between Black lives—Black realities—and Black literature. The function of the creative writer and the literary scholar was to guide, to serve as an intermediary in explaining the relationship between Black people and those forces that attempt to subdue them. The denial or rejection of this role as go-between in some contemporary Black literary criticism reflects the paradoxical elements of Alain Locke's assertions and the implicit paradoxes inherent in Black poststructuralist criticism: for the problem is that no matter how the Black man merges into American mainstream society, he or she looks at himself from an individualistic perspective that enables him or her to accept elitist American values and thus widen the chasm between his or her worldview and that of those masses of Blacks whose lives are still stifled by oppressive environmental, intellectual phenomena. When Professor Gates denies that consciousness is predetermined by culture and color (66), he manifests a sharp break with traditional Black literary criticism and strikingly bears out another of Wright's prophetic pronouncements made in 1957 when he said, ". . . the Negro, as he learns to stand on his own feet and expresses himself not in purely racial, but human terms, will launch criticism upon his native land which made him feel a sense of estrangement that he never wanted. This new attitude could have a healthy effect upon the culture of the United States. At long last, maybe a merging of Negro expression with American expression will take place" (104–5).

If we look at the most recently published works of Black literary criticism and theory—Joe Weixlmann and Chester Fontenot's edition of *Studies in Black American Literature: Black American Prose Theory, Volume 1* (1984), Henry Louis Gates, Jr.'s edition of *Black Literature & Literary Theory* (1984), Houston A. Baker, Jr.'s *Blues, Ideology, and Afro-American Literature: A*

[6]Richard Wright, "The Literature of the Negro in the United States," in *White Man, Listen!* (Garden City, N.Y., 1964), pp. 103–4; hereafter cited in text.

[7]*Chant of Saints: A Gathering of Afro-American Literature, Art, and Scholarship,* ed. Michael S. Harper and Robert B. Stepto (Urbana, Ill., 1979).

Vernacular Theory (1984), and even Michael Cooke's most recent *Afro-American Literature in the Twentieth Century: The Achievement of Intimacy* (1984)—we witness the merger of Negro expression with Euro-American expression. For the modes of execution in all these works, with the exception of Professor Cooke's ground-breaking study, prompt the same response that my student felt when reading Baldwin's essay in *Essence.*

Following the same methodological strategies characteristic of the works of Northrop Frye and poststructuralist critics like Roland Barthes, Paul de Man, Jacques Derrida, and Geoffrey Hartman, Black poststructuralist critics have adopted a linguistic system and an accompanying world view that communicate to a small, isolated audience. Their pseudoscientific language is distant and sterile. These writers evince their powers of ratiocination with an overwhelming denial of most, if not all, the senses. Ironically, they challenge the intellect, "dulling" themselves to the realities of the sensual, communicative function of language. As Wright predicted, this merger of Black expression into the mainstream estranges the Black poststructuralist in a manner that he perhaps "never wanted," in a way which contradicts his primary goal in adopting poststructuralist methodology.

Although the paradox embodied in this estrangement holds quite true for the white poststructuralist critic as well, its negative effects are more severe for the Black scholar. Structuralism in mainstream culture is a reaction to the alienation and despair of late nineteenth and early twentieth-century existentialism which "spoke of isolated man, cut off from objects and even from other men, in an absurd condition of being."[8] In order to demonstrate the common bond that unites all human beings, structuralist thinkers—philosophers, linguists, psychoanalysts, anthropologists, and literary critics—use a complex linguistic system to illuminate "the configurations of human mentality itself" (79). Structuralism, then, "is a way of looking for reality not in individual things [in man isolated] but in the relationships among them" (4), that is, in the linguistic patterns that bind men together. Yet, ironically, the idea that the words on the page have no relationship to an external world and the language used—the unique meanings of words like *code, encode, sign, signifier, signified, difference, discourse, narratology,* and *text*—create the very alienation and estrangement that structuralists and poststructuralists attempt to defeat. Hence I see an inherent contradiction between those values postmodernists intend to transmit and those perceived by many readers.

In the September 1983 special issue of *Critical Inquiry,* Professor Barbara H. Smith's comments on the classic canonical author can analogously illuminate how values are transmitted through literary theory as well. She says simply, "The endurance of a classic canonical author such as Homer . . . owes not to the alleged transcultural or universal value of his works but, on the contrary, to the continuity of their circulation in a particular culture."[9] Thus, in adopting a critical methodology, the Black literary critic must ask himself or herself: "How does a Black literary theorist/critic gain a voice in the white literary establishment?" Moreover, despite Professor Smith's and the poststructuralists' attenuation of values, the Black literary critic should question the values that will be transmitted through his or her work. The Black critic must be ever cognizant of the fact that not only what he or she says, but also how he or she writes will determine the values to be circulated and preserved over time once he or she is accepted by mainstream society, if this acceptance is his or her primary goal. Despite writers like John Oliver Killens, John Williams, Gayl Jones, Naomi Long Madgett, and Ann Petry, who are seriously overlooked by the white

[8]Robert E. Scholes, *Structuralism in Literature: An Introduction* (New Haven, 1974), p. 1; hereafter cited in text.

[9]Barbara H. Smith, "Contingencies of Value," *Critical Inquiry,* 10, No. 1 (Sept. 1983), 30.

mainstream, the most neglected aspect of Black American literature concerns the issue of form or structure. I agree fully with Professor Gates when he says that social and prolemical functions of Black literature have overwhelmingly superseded or, to use his word, "repressed" the structure of Black literature.[10] But I must part ways with him when he outlines the methodology he uses to call attention to what he refers to as "the language of the black text." He says, "A study of the so-called arbitrariness, and of the relation between a sign, of the ways in which *concepts* divide reality arbitrarily, and of the relation between a sign, such as blackness, and its referent, such as absence, can help us to engage in more sophisticated readings of black texts."[11] It is insidious for the Black literary critic to adopt any kind of strategy that diminishes or in this case—through an allusion to binary oppositions—negates his blackness. It is not a fortuitous occurrence that Black creative writers for nearly two-hundred years have consistently addressed the ramifications of slavery and racism. One such ramification that underpins W. E. B. Du Bois's essays and Langston Hughes's poetry and that emerged undisguised in the 1960s is the issue of Black pride, self-respect as opposed to self-abnegation or even self-veiling.

The Black creative writer has continuously struggled to assert his or her real self and to establish a connection between the self and the people outside that self. The Black creative writer understands that it is not yet time—and it might not ever be possible—for a people with hundreds of years of disenfranchisement and who since slavery have venerated the intellect and the written word to view language as merely a system of codes or as mere play. Language has been an essential medium for the evolution of Black pride and the dissolution of the double consciousness. For as evidenced by David Walker's *Appeal,* Claude McKay's "If We Must Die," Richard Wright's *Native Son,* the poetry of Sonia Sanchez and Amiri Baraka, and most recently by Toni Morrison's *Tar Baby,* the Black writer recognizes that the way in which we interpret our world is more than a function of the languages we have at our disposal, as Terry Eagleton asserts.[12] Even though Innis Brown in Margaret Walker's *Jubilee* cannot read or write, he understands clearly—he interprets quite accurately—that he has been wronged when his white landlord attempts to collect from Innis money for services Innis has not received. And though he too cannot read or write, Jake, Milkman's grandfather in Morrison's *Song of Solomon,* dies rather than surrender his land to the whites who shoot him. Shared experiences like these can bond a people together in ways that far exceed language. Hence what I refer to as the "poststructuralist sensiblity" does not aptly apply to Black American literary works. In explaining that an essential difference between structuralism and poststructuralism is the radical separation of the signifier from the signified, Terry Eagleton presents what I see as the "poststructuralist sensibility." He writes, ". . . nothing is ever fully present in signs: it is an illusion for me to believe that I can ever be fully present to you in what I say or write, because to use signs at all entails that my meaning is always somehow dispersed, divided and never quite at one with itself. Not only my meaning, indeed, but *me:* since language is something I am made out of, rather than merely a convenient tool I use, the whole idea that I am a stable, unified entity must also be a fiction" (129–30). For the Black American—even the Black intellectual—to maintain that meaningful or real communication between human beings is impossible because we cannot know each other through language would be to erase or ignore the continuity embodied in Black American history. Pushed to its extreme, poststructuralist thinking perhaps helps to explain why it

[10]Henry Louis Gates, Jr., "Criticism in the Jungle," in *Black Literature and Literary Theory,* ed. Henry Louis Gates, Jr. (New York, 1984), pp. 5–6.

[11]Gates, "Criticism in the Jungle," p. 7.

[12]Terry Eagleton, *Literary Theory: An Introduction* (Minneapolis, 1983), p. 107; hereafter cited in text.

has become increasingly difficult for members of contemporary society to sustain commitments, to assume responsibility, to admit to a clear right and an obvious wrong.

Yet we can only reluctantly find fault with any ideology or critical methodology that seeks to heighten our awareness and cure us of the political, elitist, and narrow pedagogical and intellectual biases that have long dictated what we teach as well as how we teach. Interestingly enough, discussions such as Barbara Smith's "Contingencies of Value" and Richard Ohmann's "The Shaping of a Canon: U.S. Fiction, 1960–1975,"[13] and even Robert E. Scholes's "The Humanities, Criticism and Semiotics"[14] all echo some of the ideas espoused at length by the Black theoretician Larry Neal, by poets like Sonia Sanchez, Amiri Baraka, and Haki Madhubuti, and by scholars like Addison Gayle and Stephen Henderson. All of these writers have given continuous attention to how the needs and values of the hegemony have attempted to dictate the subject matter of the Black American writer and to determine whether a writer is published at all. To my knowledge only Sonia Sanchez and perhaps Gwendolyn Brooks have met this dilemma by having their works published exclusively by Black presses. This act implicitly suggests their response to the issue of their intended audience and to the question of their attitude toward their acceptance to the intellectual mainstream.

It is no accident that the Black poststructuralist methodology has so far been applied to fiction, the trickster tale, and the slave narrative. Black poetry—particularly that written during and after the 1960s—defies both linguistically and ideologically the "poststructuralist sensibility." According to Terry Eagleton, "most literary theories . . . unconsciously 'foreground' a particular literary genre, and derive their general pronouncements from this" (51). Equally as telling as their avoidance of Black poetry is the unsettling fact that Black American literary criticism has skipped a whole phase in the evolution of literary theory. The natural cycle organically requires that one school of literary thought be created from the one that goes before. For just as structuralism is a reaction to the despair of existentialism, poststructuralism is a reaction to the limitations of the concepts of the sign. "The poststructuralist attitude is therefore literally unthinkable without structuralism."[15] Consequently, the move in Black American literature from polemical, biographical criticism to poststructuralist theories means that these principles are being applied in a historical vacuum.

Since the Black creative writer has always used language as a means of communication to bind people together, the job of the Black literary critic should be to find a point of merger between the communal, utilitarian, phenomenal nature of Black literature and the aesthetic or linguistic—if you will—analyses that illuminate the "universality" of a literary text. Rather than being a "linguistic event" or a complex network of linguistic systems that embody the union of the signified and the signifier independent of phenomenal reality, Black creative art is an act of love which attempts to destroy estrangement and elitism by demonstrating a strong fondness or enthusiasm for freedom and an affectionate concern for the lives of people, especially Black people. Black creative art addresses the benevolence, kindness, and brotherhood that men should feel toward each other. Just as language has no function without man, the Black literary critic is free to go beyond the bonds of the creative writer. For we have many thoughts that we have yet no words for, particularly those thoughts that remain in an inchoate state. It should be the job of the Black literary critic to force ideas to the surface, to give them force in order to affect, to guide, to animate, and to arouse the minds and emotions of Black people.

---

[13]Richard Ohmann, "The Shaping of a Canon: U.S. Fiction, 1960–1975," *Critical Inquiry,* 10, No. 1 (Sept. 1983), 199–223.

[14]Robert E. Scholes, *Semiotics and Interpretation* (New Haven, 1982).

[15]Josué V. Harari, "Critical Factions/Critical Fictions," in *Textual Strategies: Perspectives in Post-Structuralist Criticism,* ed. Josué V. Harari (New York, 1979), p. 30.

HENRY LOUIS GATES, JR.
(1950–)

Not even Booker T. Washington in 1895 and Alain Locke in 1925 surpassed Henry Louis "Skip" Gates, Jr., for the widespread endorsement by the media and the American mainstream's active promotion as the preferably recognized voice for his people. In fact, thirty years between Washington's Atlanta Exposition Address and Locke's *The New Negro* equals almost exactly the span between the Black Arts critics of the sixties and Gates.

Gates, an affable historian of English linguistics, exerts an influence quite rare for an academician of any hue. His unrivaled press depicts him as almost peerless in the timely adopted specialization of African American literature, especially as forwarded by the most lucrative theorists of public change. As a colorblind scholar with strong so-called liberal ties, Gates proposes a new complexion for American form and tradition to a most liberal academy, which claims all innocence from racism. Gates lionizes the most celebrated graduates of interracial exchange on highly privileged campuses as the rightful heirs to many professorships in African American literature. He transforms the call by the early W.E.B. Du Bois for the "talented tenth" of African Americans to lead the race to a more richly multicultural invitation that the talented tenth of any race from any continent or experience may well qualify for blackness. Hence, Gates represents a final examination about whether African Americans and all readers of goodwill have ever really appreciated the true artistry of self-definition as accomplished by the greatest black writers during the past ninety years.

Henry Louis Gates, Jr., was born on September 16, 1950, in Keyser, West Virginia, to Henry Louis Gates, Sr., and Pauline Augusta Coleman Gates. As a talented child from a working-class background, he spent his early years in Piedmont, a nearby village. In 1957, his mother became the first black secretary of the local PTA. Gates, who graduated summa cum laude from Yale in 1973, earned an M.A. (1974) and a Ph.D. (1979) from Clare College of the University of Cambridge in England. He worked as a staff correspondent for the *Times* magazine in London from 1973 to 1975 and as a public relations representative for the American Cyanamid Company in Wayne, New Jersey, in 1975. Somewhat curiously reminiscent of Marcus Garvey, who would have been his political foil, Skip Gates discovered that his several years in journalism and business proved crucial in his ability to market racial discourse for public consumption. And indeed this talent would enable him to finesse the *Washington Post* and *New York Times* to celebrate him as a chosen leader to rediscover lost texts by blacks. From 1979 to 1984, Gates was a lecturer and assistant professor of English and African American studies and comparative literature at Yale, advancing to the rank of associate professor by 1984. By 1985, he moved to Cornell University as professor of English and of African studies and comparative literature. From 1988 to 1991, he was W.E.B. Du Bois Professor of Literature at Cornell. In 1990, he went to Duke University as visiting John Spencer Basset Professor of English, including an option for a permanent position. He has taught at Harvard since 1991.

His major awards include research grants from the National Endowment for the Humanities (1980–1984), from the Rockefeller Foundation (1980–1981), and from the McArthur Foundation (1981–1986), as well as honorary commendations from the Zora Neale Hurston Society (1986) and the committee of the Anisfeld Book Award for Race Relations (1989).

Gates's writing has a diffuse range and impact. *Figures in Black: Words, Signs, and the Racial Self* (1987) and *The Signifying Monkey: A Theory of African-American Literary Criticism* (1988) mark the logical completion of his graduate theses. His rediscovery of *Our Nig* (1983) by Harriet E. Adams Wilson, so championed by the *Washington Post*, helped promote his fame. (A few bibliographers have observed that the text was already listed in the Library of Congress.) *Black Literature and Literary Theory* (1984) has been fashionable academic reading throughout the British commonwealth, strengthening Gates's claim of a strong base in European values. *Race, Writing, and Difference* (1986) and *Reading Black, Reading Feminist: A Critical Anthology* (1990) achieved a popular niche among the white academic left. In 1987, the critical edition of *The Classic Slave Narrative* (1987) paid homage indirectly to his mentor, the late Charles T. Davis, a Dartmouth graduate and Walt Whitman scholar, who founded the African American studies program at Yale. Gates had already edited the Davis collected essays, *Black Is the Color of the Cosmos*, in 1982. Along with winning the prestigious McArthur Prize, his editing for the Schomburg Library of Nineteenth Century Black Women Writers solidified his impressive entrepreneurship in literary history. Gates helped establish the careers of several white scholars and many African American women. Meanwhile, he coordinated a graduate team that compiled *Wole Soyinka: A Bibliography of Primary and Secondary Sources* (1986). The Nigerian writer Soyinka had been helpful to him during his years in England. *Loose Canons* (1992) is a popular account about race, and *Colored People* (1994), an autobiography, accomplishes a diction and tone worthy of Booker T. Washington, whose roots had grown deeply in the soil of western Virginia.

Gates's rise to academic power emerged from his genuine gift for marketing British culture as a radically American innovation. An anonymous admirer writes for *Current Biography* (1992) as follows: "Notwithstanding the criticism that he had endured at the hands of his more conservative colleagues, Gates's provocative ideas about educational reform have been impossible to ignore, if only because he has in recent years emerged as something of an academic celebrity." Having noted Gates's alleged "attack" on William J. Bennett, formerly Secretary of Education, along with another on Allan Bloom, author of the bestseller *The Closing of the American Mind* (1987), the liberal biographer continues: "As might be expected, Gates had been critical of (and has in turn been criticized by) those who consider multicultural programs to be little more than 'victim studies' and therefore, as their reasoning goes, detrimental to society." But most celebrated, the biographer continues, is that Gates "has also been vehemently opposed to the efforts of those black scholars who have worked to establish courses of study that remain self-consciously apart from traditional academic departments. He has further set himself apart from his separatist black colleagues by maintaining that African American culture, notwithstanding its links to that of West Africa, is principally an American rather than an African phenomenon." Hence, Skip Gates is a great white hope, a delightful integrationist on traditional terms.

Gates has demonstrated significant strengths in academic entrepreneurship since 1975. With a political acumen unrivaled by his peers, he has parlayed Ivy League pedigree and sterling British credentials into appointments at several of the most prestigious research universities in the world. Bolstered by his varied experience in popular journalism, public relations, and corporate business, he has built a nearly unassailable coalition between the white liberal establishment and the most proper intelligentsia of middle-class blacks. In reverting to the ideology of the early 1900s and later the 1950s, he has insisted on an integrationist blending of culture and race over the importance of any racial signature. He has restored important attention to African folk texts in the African Diaspora as well as to the linguistic properties of African American idioms. Beyond all else, he has been a consummate salesman for the cheerful acceptance of privileged whites into African American studies and for a very few qualified scholars of color into the American mainstream.

Even his most highly discursive thought evinces flaws, however. First, he often overlooks the vital role of language in culture and the inseparability of form and function. Second, he demonstrates a remarkable inability—or at least a lack of honest will—to perceive the causal relations in Western history. How did the marketer of black slaves, for instance, foreshadow the entrepreneur of African American research in 1995? Sometimes his theoretical intelligence supersedes his common sense. Third, he ignores that words almost never exist as polite objects in and of themselves. Hence, African American English encapsulates the blues and jazz triumph of its own people. Fourth, Gates implies, as in "What's Love Got to Do with It?", that African Americans should abandon the very aesthetic distance that allows them to exist ironically within and beyond the American mainstream at once. They should simply be accepted and belong.

But absolute assimilation by blacks in America would undermine the conscience and dissent through which the country, relentlessly challenged to live up to its creed, can ever critique itself, thereby helping to advance a decent ethos for world civilization. To repeat the essayist James Baldwin, who himself was fond of quoting the playwright Lorraine Hansberry, "Do I really want to be integrated into a burning house?" Fifth, Gates errs in his implication in *Colored People* (1994) that the radical freedom of the African American male depends in part on his sexual acceptance by white women. Sixth, Gates's ingenious doublespeak and doublewrite prove more dangerous than cute. *Our Nig* (1983) prove historically accurate in title and offensive in import; *The Signifying Monkey* (1988) refers to the African sources of the folk figure Egu, but it panders subconsciously to a racist figure for the African American critic; *Colored People* (1994) suggests a comfortable tone of Jim Crow discrimination even as it intimates an ability to laugh at a history the scars of which are still being formed. Finally, Gates's persistent obsession about the way whites perceive blacks became outdated for good reason by 1960. Gates exploits an academic preference for the lost literary glory of the British empire.

❖❖❖

Information about Gates and his works appears in James Olney, *Dictionary of Literary Biography*, vol. 67 (1988); "Henry Louis Gates, Jr. And Current Debates in African-American Literary Criticism," *Contemporary Literary Criticism Yearbook 1990* (1990); *The Negro Almanac*, ed. Harry A. Ploski (New York: Bellwether, 1967–1989). Very liberal praise informs *Current Biography* (Bronx, NY: H. W. Wilson, 1992).

"What's Love Got to Do with It?": Critical Theory, Integrity, and the Black Idiom

RATHER THAN BEING A "LINGUISTIC EVENT" OR A COMPLEX NETWORK OF LINGUISTIC SYSTEMS THAT EMBODY THE UNION OF THE SIGNIFIED AND THE SIGNIFIER INDEPENDENT OF PHENOMENAL REALITY, BLACK CREATIVE ART IS AN ACT OF LOVE WHICH ATTEMPTS TO DESTROY ESTRANGEMENT AND ELITISM BY DEMONSTRATING A STRONG FONDNESS OR ENTHUSIASM FOR FREEDOM AND AN AFFECTIONATE CONCERN FOR THE LIVES OF PEOPLE, ESPECIALLY BLACK PEOPLE.

JOYCE A. JOYCE

IT MAY SEEM TO YOU THAT I'M ACTING CONFUSED
WHEN YOU'RE CLOSE TO ME.
IF I TEND TO LOOK DAZED
I READ IT SOMEPLACE, I'VE GOT CAUSE TO BE.
THERE'S A NAME FOR IT,
THERE'S A PHRASE THAT FITS.
BUT WHATEVER THE REASON
YOU DO IT FOR ME—OH, OH, OH

WHAT'S LOVE GOT TO DO, GOT TO DO WITH IT?
WHAT'S LOVE BUT A SECONDHAND EMOTION?
WHAT'S LOVE GOT TO DO, GOT TO DO WITH IT?
WHO NEEDS A HEART WHEN A HEART CAN BE BROKEN?

TINA TURNER, "WHAT'S LOVE GOT TO DO WITH IT?" LYRICS BY TERRY BRITTEN AND GRAHAM LYLE

I have structured my response to Joyce Joyce's "The Black Canon" in two parts. The first section of this essay attempts to account for the prevalence among Afro-Americans of what Paul de Man called the "resistance to theory."[1] The second section of this essay attempts to respond directly to the salient parts of Professor Joyce's argument. While the first part of my essay is historical, it also explains why literary theory has been useful in my work, in an attempt to defamiliarize a black text from this black reader's experiences as an African-American. This section of my essay, then, is something of an auto-critography, generated by what I take to be the curiously *personal* terms of Joyce Joyce's critique of the remarkably vague, yet allegedly antiblack, thing that she calls, variously, "structuralism," or "poststructuralism." Apparently for Joyce Joyce, and for several other critics, my name and my work have become metonyms for "structuralism," "poststructuralism," and/or "deconstructionism" in the black tradition, even when these terms are not defined at all or, perhaps worse, not adequately understood. (While Houston Baker generously acknowledges my influence in his remarkable work *Blues, Ideology, and Afro-American Literature*,[2] let me state clearly that our relation of influence is a reciprocal one, in which each stands as "ideal reader" for the other.) These terms become epithets where used as in Joyce Joyce's essay, and mostly opprobrious epithets at that. Just imagine: if Richard Pryor (and his all-too-eager convert Michael Cooke) have their way and abolish the use of the word *nigger* even among ourselves, and black feminists abolish m____, perhaps the worse thing a black person will be able to call another black person will be: "You black poststructuralist, you!" What would Du Bois have said?!

I must confess that I am bewildered by Joyce Joyce's implied claim that to engage in black critical theory is to be, somehow, antiblack. In fact, I find this sort of claim to be both false and a potentially dangerous—and dishonest—form of witch-hunting or nigger-baiting. While it is one thing to say that someone is *wrong* in their premises or their conclusions, it is quite another to ascertain (on that person's behalf) their motivations, their intentions, their *affect*; and then to imply that they do not love their culture, or that they seek to deny their heritage, or that they are alienated from their "race," appealing all the while to an undefined transcendent essence called "the Black Experience," from which Houston Baker and I have somehow strayed. This is silliness.

---

[1]See Paul de Man, "The Resistance to Theory," *Yale French Studies*, No. 63 (1982), 3–20.

[2]Houston A. Baker, Jr., *Blues, Ideology, and Afro-American Literature: A Vernacular Theory* (Chicago, 1984).

Who can disagree that there is more *energy* being manifested and good work being brought to bear on black texts by black critics today than at any other time in our history, and that a large part of the explanation for this wonderful phenomenon is the growing critical sophistication of black readers of literature? Or that this sophistication is not directly related to the fact that we are taking our work—the close reading, interpretation, and *preservation* of the texts and authors of our tradition—with the utmost *seriousness?* What else is there for a critic to do? *What's love got to do with it,* Joyce Joyce? Precisely this: it is an act of love of the tradition—by which I mean *our* tradition—to bring to bear upon it honesty, insight, and skepticism, as well as praise, enthusiasm, and dedication; all values fundamental to the blues and to signifying, those two canonical black discourses in which Houston and I locate the black critical difference. It is merely a mode of critical masturbation to praise a black text simply because it is somehow "black," and it is irresponsible to act as if we are not all fellow citizens of literature for whom developments in other sections of the republic of letters have no bearing or relevance. To do either is most certainly *not* to manifest "love" for our tradition.

Before I can respond more directly to Joyce Joyce's essay, however, I want to examine the larger resistance to (white) theory in the (black) tradition.[3]

I

Unlike almost every other literary tradition, the Afro-American literary tradition was generated as a response to allegations that its authors did not, and *could not*, create "literature." Philosophers and literary critics, such as Hume, Kant, Jefferson, and Hegel, seemed to decide that the presence of a written literature was the signal measure of the potential, innate "humanity" of a race. The African living in Europe or in the New World seems to have felt compelled to create a literature both to demonstrate, implicitly, that blacks did indeed possess the intellectual ability to create a written art, but also to indict the several social and economic institutions that delimited the "humanity" of all black people in Western cultures.

So insistent did these racist allegations prove to be, at least from the eighteenth to the early twentieth centuries, that it is fair to describe the subtext of the history of black letters as this urge to refute the claim that because blacks had no written traditions, they were bearers of an "inferior" culture. The relation between European and American critical theory, then, and the development of the African and Afro-American literary traditions, can readily be seen to have been ironic, indeed. Even as late as 1911, when J. E. Casely Hayford published *Ethiopia Unbound* (the "first" African novel), that pioneering author felt compelled to address this matter in the first two paragraphs of his text. "At the dawn of the twentieth century," the novel opens, "men of light and leading both in Europe and in America had not yet made up their minds as to what place to assign to the spiritual aspirations of the black man: . . . Before this time," the narrative continues, "it had been discovered that the black man was not necessarily the missing link between man and ape. It had even been granted that for intellectual endowments he had nothing to be ashamed of in an *open* competition with the Aryan or any other type."[4] *Ethiopia Unbound*, it seems obvious, was concerned to settle the matter of black mental equality, which had remained something of an open question in European discourse for two hundred years. Concluding this curiously polemical exposition of three paragraphs, which precedes the introduction of the novel's protagonist, Casely Hayford points to

[3]Fuller versions of this section of my essay appear in my "Criticism in the Jungle," in *Black Literature and Literary Theory*, ed. Henry Louis Gates, Jr. (New York, 1985) pp. 1–24 and "Writing 'Race' and the Difference It Makes." *Critical Inquiry*, 12, No. 1 (Autumn 1985), 1–20.

[4]J. E. Casely Hayford, *Ethiopia Unbound: Studies in Race Emancipation* (London, 1911), pp. 1–2; hereafter cited in text.

"the names of men like [W. E. B.] Du Bois, Booker T. Washington, [Wilmot E.] Blyden, [Paul Laurence] Dunbar, [Samuel] Coleridge-Taylor, and others" (2) as prima facie evidence of the sheer saliency of what Carter G. Woodson once termed "the public [Negro] mind."[5] These were men, the narrative concludes, "who had distinguished themselves in the fields of activity and intellectuality" (2), men who had demonstrated conclusively that the African's first cousin was indeed the European, rather than the ape.

That the presence of a written literature could assume such large proportions in several Western cultures from the Enlightenment to this century is even more curious than is the fact that blacks themselves, as late as 1911, felt moved to respond to this stimulus, indeed felt the need to speak the matter silent, to end the argument by producing literature. Few literary traditions have begun or been sustained by such a complex and curious relation to its criticism: allegations of an absence led directly to a presence, a literature often inextricably bound in a dialogue with its potentially harshest critics.[6]

Black literature and its criticism, then, have been put to uses that were not primarily aesthetic; rather, they have formed part of a larger discourse on the nature of the black and his or her role in the order of things. The integral relation between theory and a literary text, therefore, which so very often in other traditions has been a sustaining relation, in our tradition has been an extraordinarily problematical one. The relation among theory, tradition, and integrity within the black literary tradition has not been, and perhaps cannot be, a straightforward matter.

Let us consider the etymology of the word *integrity*, which I take to be the keyword implied in Dr. Joyce's essay. *Integrity* is a curious keyword to address in a period of bold and sometimes exhilarating speculation and experimentation, two other words which aptly characterize literary criticism, generally, and Afro-American criticism, specifically, at the present time. The Latin origin of the English word *integritas* connotes wholeness, entireness, completeness, chastity, and purity; most of which are descriptive terms that made their way frequently into the writings of the American New Critics, critics who seem not to have cared particularly for, or about, the literature of Afro-Americans. Two of the most common definitions of *integrity* elaborate upon the sense of wholeness derived from the Latin original. Let me cite these here, as taken from the *Oxford English Dictionary:* "1. The condition of having no part or element taken away or wanting: undivided or unbroken state: material wholeness, completeness, entirety; something undivided; an integral whole; 2. The condition of not being marred or violated: unimpaired or uncorrupted condition: original perfect state: soundness." It is the second definition of *integrity*—that is to say, the one connoting the absence of violation and corruption, the preservation of an initial wholeness or soundness—which I would like to consider in this deliberation upon "Theory and Integrity," or more precisely upon that relationship which ideally should obtain between African or Afro-American literature and the theories we borrow, revise, or fabricate to account for the precise nature and shape of our literature and its "being" in the world.

It is probably true that critics of Afro-American literature (which, by the way, I employ as a less ethnocentric designation than "the Black Critic") are more concerned with the complex relation between literature and literary theory than we have ever been before. There are many reasons for this, not the least of which is our increasingly central role in "the profession," precisely when our colleagues in other literatures are engulfed in their own extensive debates about the intellectual merit of so very much theorizing. Theory, as a second-order reflection

[5] Carter G. Woodson, "Introduction," *The Mind of the Negro as Reflected in Letters Written During the Crisis, 1800–1860* (New York, 1969), p. v.

[6] I have traced the history and theory of this critical debate in my *Black Letters and the Enlightenment*, forthcoming from Oxford University Press.

upon a primary gesture such as "literature," has *always* been viewed with deep mistrust and suspicion by those scholars who find it presumptuous and perhaps even decadent when criticism claims the right to stand, as discourse, on its own, as a parallel textual universe to literature. Theoretical texts breed other, equally "decadent," theoretical responses in a creative process that can be remarkably far removed from a poem or a novel.

For the critic of Afro-American literature, this process is even more perilous precisely because the largest part of contemporary literary theory derives from critics of Western European languages and literatures. Is the use of theory to write about Afro-American literature, we might ask rhetorically, merely another form of intellectual indenture, a form of servitude of the mind as pernicious in its intellectual implications as any other form of enslavement? This is the issue raised, for me at least, by the implied presence of the word *integrity* in Joyce Joyce's essay, but also by my own work over the past decade. Does the propensity to theorize about a text or a literary tradition "mar," "violate," "impair," or "corrupt" the "soundness" of a purported "original perfect state" of a black text or of the black tradition? To argue the affirmative is to align one's position with the New Critical position that texts are "wholes" in the first place.

To be sure, this matter of criticism and integrity has a long and rather tortured history in black letters. It was David Hume, after all, who called the Jamaican poet of Latin verse, Francis Williams, "a parrot who merely speaks a few words plainly";[7] and Phillis Wheatley has for far too long suffered from the spurious attacks of black and white critics alike for being the original *rara avis* of a school of so-called "mockingbird poets," whose use and imitation of received European and American literary conventions have been regarded, simply put, as a corruption itself of a "purer" black expression, privileged somehow in black artistic forms such as the blues, signifying, the spirituals, and the Afro-American dance. Can we, as critics, escape a "mockingbird" relation to theory, one destined to be derivative, often to the point of parody? Can we, moreover, escape the racism of so many critical theorists, from Hume and Kant through the Southern Agrarians and the Frankfurt School?

As I have argued elsewhere, there are complex historical reasons for the resistance to theory among critics of comparative black literature, which stem in part from healthy reactions against the marriage of logocentrism and ethnocentrism in much of post-Renaissance Western aesthetic discourse. Although there have been a few notable exceptions, theory as a subject of inquiry has only in the past decade begun to sneak into the discourse of Afro-American literature. The implicit racism of some of the Southern Agrarians who became the New Critics and Adorno's bizarre thoughts about something he calls "jazz" did not serve to speed this process along at all. Sterling A. Brown has summed up the relation of the black tradition to the Western critical tradition. In response to Robert Penn Warren's line from "Pondy Woods" (1945), "Nigger, your breed ain't metaphysical," Brown replies, "Cracker, your breed ain't exegetical."[8] No tradition is "naturally" metaphysical or exegetical, of course. Only recently have some scholars attempted to convince critics of black literature that the racism of the Western critical tradition was not a sufficient reason for us to fail to theorize about our own endeavor, or even to make use of contemporary theoretical innovations when this seemed either useful or appropriate. Perhaps predictably, a number of these attempts share a concern with that which, in the received tradition of Afro-American criticism, has been most repressed: that is, with close readings of the text itself. This return of the repressed—the very

[7]David Hume, "Of National Characters," in *The Philosophical Works*, ed. Thomas Hill Green and Thomas Hodge Grose (Darmstadt, 1964), III, 252 n. 1.

[8]Sterling A. Brown, Lecture, Yale University, 17 April 1979.

language of the black text—has generated a new interest among our critics in theory. My charged advocacy of the relevance of contemporary theory to reading Afro-American and African literature closely has been designed as the prelude to the definition of principles of literary criticism peculiar to the black literary traditions themselves, related to and compatible with contemporary critical theory generally, yet "indelibly black," as Robert Farris Thompson puts it.[9] All theory is text-specific, and ours must be as well. Lest I be misunderstood, I have tried to work through contemporary theories of literature *not* to "apply" them to black texts, but rather to *transform* by *translating* them into a new rhetorical realm. These attempts have been successful in varying degrees; nevertheless, I have tried to make them at all times interesting episodes in one critic's reflection on the black "text-milieu," what he means by "the tradition," and from which he extracts his "canon."

It is only through this critical activity that the profession, in a world of dramatically fluid relations of knowledge and power, and of the reemerging presence of the tongues of Babel, can redefine itself away from a Eurocentric notion of a hierarchical canon of texts, mostly white, Western, and male, and encourage and sustain a truly comparative and pluralistic notion of the institution of literature. What all students of literature share in common is the art of interpretation, even where we do not share in common the same texts. The hegemony implicit in the phrase "the Western tradition" reflects material relationships primarily, and not so-called universal, transcendent normative judgments. Judgment is specific, both culturally and temporally. The sometimes vulgar nationalism implicit in would-be literary categories such as "American Literature," or the not-so-latent imperialism implied by the vulgar phrase "Commonwealth literature," are extraliterary designations of control, symbolic of material and concomitant political relations, rather than literary ones. We, the scholars of our profession, much eschew these categories of domination and ideology and insist upon the fundamental redefinition of what it is to speak of "the canon."

Whether we realize it or not, each of us brings to a text an *implicit* theory of literature, or even an unwitting hybrid of theories, a critical gumbo as it were. To become aware of contemporary theory is to become aware of one's presuppositions, those ideological and aesthetic assumptions which we bring to a text unwittingly. It is incumbent upon us, those of us who respect the sheer integrity of the black tradition, to turn to this very tradition to create self-generated theories about the *black* literary endeavor. We must, above all, respect the integrity, the wholeness, of the black work of art, by bringing to bear upon the explication of its meanings all of the attention to language that we may learn from several developments in contemporary theory. By the very process of "application," as it were, we recreate, through revision, the critical theory at hand. As our familiarity with the black tradition and with literary theory expands, we shall invent our own theories, as some of us have begun to do—black, text-specific theories.

I have tried to utilize contemporary theory to *defamiliarize* the texts of the black tradition, to create a distance between this black reader and our black texts, so that I may more readily *see* the formal workings of those texts. Wilhelm von Humboldt describes this phenomenon in the following way: "Man lives with things mainly, even exclusively—since sentiment and action in him depend upon his mental representations—as they are conveyed to him by language. Through the same act by which he spins language out of himself he weaves himself into it, and every language draws a circle around the people to which it belongs, a circle that can only be transcended in so far as one at the same time enters another one." I have turned to literary theory as a "second circle." I have done this to preserve the integrity of these texts, by trying to

[9]Robert Farris Thompson, *Indelibly Black: Essays on African and Afro-American Art* (forthcoming).

avoid confusing my experience as an Afro-American with the black act of language which defines a text. On the other hand, by learning to read a black text within a black formal cultural matrix, and explicating it with the principles of criticism at work in *both* the Euro-American and Afro-American traditions, I believe that we critics can produce richer structures of meaning than are possible otherwise.

This is the challenge of the critic of black literature in the 1980s: not to shy away from literary theory; rather, to translate it into the black idiom, *renaming* principles of criticism where appropriate, but especially *naming* indigenous black principles of criticism and applying these to explicate our own texts. It is incumbent upon us to protect the integrity of our tradition by bringing to bear upon its criticism any tool of sensitivity to language that is appropriate. And what do I mean by "appropriate"? Simply this: *any* tool that enables the critic to explain the complex workings of the language of a text is an "appropriate" tool. For it is language, the black language of black texts, which expresses the distinctive quality of our literary tradition. A literary tradition, like an individual, is to a large extent defined by its past, its received traditions. We critics in the 1980s have the especial privilege of explicating the black tradition in ever closer detail. We shall not meet this challenge by remaining afraid of, or naive about, literary theory; rather, we will only inflict upon our literary tradition the violation of the uninformed reading. We are the keepers of the black literary tradition. No matter what theories we seem to embrace, we have more in common with each other than we do with any other critic of any other literature. We write for each other, and for our own contemporary writers. This relation is a sacred trust.

Let me end this section of my essay with a historical anecdote. In 1915, Edmond Laforest, a prominent member of the Haitian literary movement called "La Ronde," made of his death a symbolic, if ironic, statement of the curious relation of the "non-Western" writer to the act of writing in a modern language. M. Laforest, with an inimitable, if fatal, flair for the grand gesture, calmly tied a Larousse dictionary around his neck, then proceeded to commit suicide by drowning. While other black writers, before and after M. Laforest, have suffocated as artists beneath the weight of various modern languages, Laforest chose to make his death an emblem of this relation of indenture. We commit intellectual suicide by binding ourselves too tightly to nonblack theory; but we drown just as surely as did Laforest if we pretend that "theory" is "white," or worse—that it is "antiblack." Let scores of black theories proliferate, and let us encourage speculation among ourselves about our own literature. And let us, finally, realize that we must be each other's allies, even when we most disagree, because those who would dismiss both black literature and black criticism will no doubt increase in numbers in this period of profound economic fear and scarcity unless we meet their challenge head-on.

II

That said, let me respond to the salient points in Joyce Joyce's essay. Joyce Joyce's anecdote about the student who could not understand Jimmy Baldwin's essay "On Being 'White' . . . and Other Lies" is only remarkable for what it reveals about her student's lack of reading skills and/or training. Let me cite a typical paragraph of Baldwin's text, since so very much of Joyce Joyce's argument turns upon the idea of *critical language as a barrier of alienation between black critics and "our people":*

> . . . Without further pursuing the implication of this mutual act of faith, one is nevertheless aware that the Jewish translation into a white American can sustain the state of Israel in a way that the Black presence, here, can scarcely hope—at least, not yet—to halt the slaughter in South Africa.
>
> And there is a reason for that.
>
> America became white—the people who, as they claim, "settled" in the country became white—because of the necessity of

denying the Black presence, and justifying the Black subjugation. No community can be based on such a principle—or, in other words, no community can be established on so genocidal a lie. White men—from Norway, for example, where they were *Norwegians*—became white: by slaughtering the cattle, poisoning the wells, torching the houses, massacring Native Americans, raping Black women.[10]

We are not exactly talking about the obscure or difficult language of Fanon or Hegel or Heidegger or Wittgenstein here, now are we? Rather than being "trapped by [her] own contradiction and elitism," as Joyce Joyce claims she was, and granting this student her point, Joyce Joyce *should* have done what Anna Julia Cooper or Du Bois would have done: sent the student back to the text and told her to read it again—and again, until she got it *right*. Then, she, a teacher in training, I presume, must serve as an interpreter, as mediator, between Baldwin's text and "our people" out there. (Would the superb and thoughtful editors of *Essence*, by the way, publish an essay their readers could not understand? Perhaps the anecdote is merely apocryphal, after all.) Next time, give the child a dictionary, Joyce, and make her come back in a week.

To use this anecdote to conclude that Baldwin (and, of course, we blankety-blank poststructuralists) has abnegated "the responsibility of the writer to his or her audience" is for a university professor to fail to understand or satisfy our most fundamental charge as teachers of literature: to preach the responsibility of *the reader* to his or her *writers*. Joyce Joyce, rather regrettably, has forgotten that the two propositions are inseparable and that the latter is the basic charge that *any* professor of literature accepts when he or she walks into a classroom or opens a text. *That's* what love's got to do, got to do with it, Joyce Joyce. How hard are we willing to work to meet our responsibilities to our *writers?* What would you have Jimmy Baldwin *do:* rewrite that paragraph, reduce his level of diction to a lower common denominator, then poll the readers of *Essence* to see if they understood the essay? What insolence; what arrogance! What's love got to do with your student's relation to Baldwin and his text? We should *beg* our writers to publish in *Essence* and in every other black publication, from *Ebony* and *Jet* to the *Black American Literature Forum* and the *CLA Journal.*

The relationship between writer and reader is a reciprocal relationship, and one sells our authors short if one insists that their "responsibility," as you put it, is "to be clear." Clear to whom, or to what? Their "responsibility" is to write. Our responsibility, as critics, to our writers, is to work at understanding *them*, not to demand that they write at such a level that every one of "our people" understands every word of every black writer without working at it. Your assertion that "the first works of black American literature" were "addressed to white audiences" is not strictly true. The author of *Our Nig*, for example, writes that "I appeal to my colored brethren universally for patronage, hoping they will not condemn this attempt of their sister to be erudite, but rally around me a faithful band of supporters and defenders."[11] How much "blacker" can an author get? No, even at the beginning of the tradition, black writers wrote for a double or mulatto audience, one black *and* white. Even Phillis Wheatley, whose poetry was the object of severe scrutiny for those who would deny us membership in the human community, wrote "for" Arbour Tanner, Scipio Moorehead, and Jupiter Hammon, just as black critics today write "for" each other and "for" our writers, and not "for" Derrida, Jameson, Said, or Bloom.

It is just not true that "the most influential critics of black literature have been the creative

[10]James Baldwin, "On Being 'White' . . . and Other Lies," *Essence*, April 1984, pp. 90–92.

[11]Harriet Wilson, *Our Nig* (Boston, 1859), p. i.

writers themselves." Rather, I believe that our "most influential critics" have been academic critics, such as W. S. Scarborough, Alain Locke, Sterling A. Brown, Du Bois (a mediocre poet and *terrible* novelist), J. Saunders Redding, Darwin T. Turner, and Houston A. Baker, among others (though both Brown and Baker are also poets). "Most influential" does not necessarily mean whom a white publisher publishes: most influential, to me, means who has generated a critical *legacy*, a critical *tradition* upon which other critics have built or can build. Among the writers that Joyce Joyce lists, Ralph Ellison has been "most influential" in the sense that I am defining it, while Hughes is cited mainly for "The Negro Artist and the Racial Mountain," Wright mostly for his two major pieces, "The Literature of the Negro in the United States" and "Blueprint for Negro Literature," while almost none of us cites Du Bois at all, despite the face that Du Bois was probably the very first systematic literary and cultural theorist in the tradition. Rather, we *genuflect* to Du Bois.

I am not attempting to deny that creative writers such as Amiri Baraka and Ishmael Reed have been remarkably important. Rather, I deny Joyce Joyce's claim that a new generation of academic critics has usurped the place of influence in the black tradition which creative writers occupied before "the 1960s." The matter is just not as simple as a "shift in black consciousness" in the 1960s, similar to that caused by migration in the 1920s, which Joyce Joyce maintains led to "the merger of a select number of blacks into American mainstream society" and, accordingly, to our "exogamic, elitist, epistemological adaptations." No, I learned my trade as a critic of black literature from a black academic critic, Charles Davis, who made me read Scarborough, Locke, Redding, Ellison, Turner, and Houston Baker as a matter of course.

This is a crucial matter in Joyce Joyce's argument, though it is muddled. For she implies (1) that larger sociopolitical changes in the 1960s led to the crossover of blacks into white institutions (true), and (2) that the critical language that I use, and my firm belief that "race" is not an essence but a trope for ethnicity or culture, both result from being trained into a "class orientation that ironically result[s] from social changes provoked by racial issues."

There are several false leaps being made here. In the first place, what Joyce Joyce erroneously thinks of as our "race" is our *culture*. Of course I "believe in" Afro-American culture; indeed, I celebrate it every day. But I also believe that to know it, to find it, to touch it, one must locate it in its *manifestations* (texts, expressive culture, music, the dance, language, and so forth) and not in the realm of the abstract or the a priori. Who can argue with that? The point of my passage about our language with which Joyce Joyce takes such issue is that for a literary critic to discuss "the black aesthetic," he or she must "find" it in language use. What is so controversial, or aristocratic, about that? As for my "class orientation," the history of my family, whether or not we were slaves or free, black or mulatto, property owners or sharecroppers, Howard M.D.s or janitors, is really none of Joyce Joyce's business. To say, moreover, that because I matriculated at Yale (when Arna Bontemps and Houston Baker taught black literature there, by the way) and at the University of Cambridge, I became a "poststructuralist" is simply illogical.

This claim is crucial to Joyce Joyce's argument, however, because of her assertion that "middle-class black men" adopted "mainstream [white] lifestyles and ideology" with great intensity after the "integration" of the 1960s. This dangerous tendency, her argument runs, culminated in 1979 with my oft-cited statement about a black writer or critic being the point of consciousness of our *language*. I am delighted that Joyce Joyce points to the significance of this statement, because I think that it is of crucial importance to the black critical activity, and especially to the subsequent attention to actual black language use that is apparent in much of our criticism since 1979.

Why has that statement been such an important one in the development of Afro-American literary criticism? Precisely because if our literary critics saw her or his central function as that of a "guide," as Joyce Joyce puts it, or as "an intermediary in explaining the relationship between black people and those forces that attempt to subdue them," she or he tended to fail at both tasks: neither were we as critics in a position to "lead" our people to "freedom," nor did we do justice to the texts created by our writers. Since *when* have black people turned to our critics to lead us out of the wilderness of Western racism into the promised land of freedom? If black readers turn to black critics, I would imagine they do so to learn about the wondrous workings of *literature*, our literature, of how our artists have represented the complex encounter of every aspect of black culture with itself and with the Other in formal literary language. Who reads our books anyway? Who can doubt that *Black Fire*, the splendid anthology of the Black Arts edited by Larry Neal and LeRoi Jones, has sold *vastly* more copies to black intellectuals than to "our people"?[12] Let us not deceive ourselves about our readership.

Joyce Joyce makes a monumental error here, when she offers the following "syllogism":

1. The sixties led to the "integration" of a few black people into historically white institutions.
2. Such exposure to mainstream culture led to the imitation by blacks of white values, habits, and so on.
3. Therefore, black people so educated or exposed suffer from "an individualistic perspective that enables him or her to accept elitist American values and thus widen the chasm between his or her worldview and that of those masses of Blacks whose lives are still stifled by oppressive environmental, intellectual phenomena."

Joyce Joyce arrives at this syllogism all because, I think, we can see important structures of meaning in black texts using sophisticated tools of literary analysis! As my friend Ernie Wilson used to say in the late sixties, "Yeah, but compared to *what*?"!

Let me state clearly that I have no fantasy about my readership: I write for our writers and for our critics. If I write a book review, say, for a popular Afro-American newspaper, I write in one voice; if I write a close analysis of a black text and publish it in a specialist journal, I choose another voice, or voices. Is not that my "responsibility," to use Joyce Joyce's word, and my privilege as a writer? But no, I do not think that my task as a critic is to lead black people to "freedom." My task is to explicate black texts. That's why *I* became a critic. In 1984, I voted for Jesse Jackson for President; if he stays out of literary criticism, I shall let him continue to speak for me in the political realm. (He did not, by the way, return the donation that Sharon Adams and I sent him, so I suppose that being a "poststructuralist" is okay with Jesse.)

And who is to say that Baker's work or mine is not implicitly political because it is "poststructuralist"? How can the demonstration that our texts sustain ever closer and sophisticated readings *not* be political, at a time in the academy when all sorts of so-called canonical critics mediate their racism through calls for "purity" of "the tradition," demands as implicitly racist as anything the Southern Agrarians said? How can the deconstruction, as it were, of the forms of racism itself (as carried out, for example, in a recent issue of *Critical Inquiry* by black and nonblack poststructuralists) not be political?[13] How can the use of literary analysis to explicate the racist social text in which we still find ourselves be anything *but* political? To be political, however does not mean that I have to write at the level of diction of a Marvel comic book. No, my task—as I see it—is to train university graduate and undergraduate students to think, to read, and yes Joyce, even to *write* clearly, helping them to expose false uses of language, fraudulent claims and muddled argument, propaganda and vicious lies from all of which our

[12]*Black Fire: An Anthology of Afro-American Writing*, ed. LeRoi Jones and Larry Neal (New York, 1968).

[13]See *Critical Inquiry*, 12, No. 1 (Autumn 1985).

people have suffered just as surely as we have from an economic order in which we were zeroes and a metaphysical order in which we were absences. These are the "values," as Joyce Joyce puts it, which I hope "will be transmitted through [my] work."

Does my work "negate [my] blackness," as Joyce Joyce claims? I would challenge Joyce Joyce to *demonstrate* anywhere in my entire work how I have, even once, negated my blackness. Simply because I have attacked an error in logic in the work of certain Black Aestheticians does not mean that I am antiblack, or that I do not love black art or music, or that I feel alienated from black people, or that I am trying to pass like some poststructural ex–colored man. My feelings about black culture and black people are everywhere manifested in my work and in the way that I define my role in the profession, which is as a critic who would like to think that history will regard him as having been a solid "race man," as we put it. My association with Black Studies departments is by choice, just as is my choice of subject matter. (Believe me, Joyce, almost no one at Cambridge wanted me to write about black literature!)

No, Joyce Joyce, I am as black as I ever was, which is just as black as I ever want to be. And I am asserting my "real self," as you put it so glibly, and whatever influence that my work has had or might have on readers of black literature *establishes a connection between the self and the people outside the self*, as you put it. And for the record, let me add here that only a black person alienated from black language use could fail to understand that we have been deconstructing white people's languages—as "a system of codes or as mere play"—since 1619. That's what signifying is all about. (If you don't believe me, by the way, ask your grandparents, or your parents, especially your mother.)

But enough, Joyce Joyce. Let me respond to your two final points: first, your claim that "the poststructuralist sensibility" does not "aptly apply to black American literary work." I challenge you to refute any of Houston Baker's readings, or my own, to justify such a strange claim. Argue with our readings, not with *your* idea of who or what we are as black people, or with *your* idea of how so very many social ills can be traced, by fits and starts, to "poststructuralist thinking."

Finally, to your curious claims that "black American literary criticism has skipped a whole phase in the evolution of literary theory," that "one school of literary thought [must] be created from the one that goes before," and that "the move in black American literature from polemical, biographical criticism to poststructuralist theories mean[s] that these principles are being applied in a historical vacuum," let me respond by saying that my work arose as a direct response to the theories of the Black Arts Movement, as Houston Baker demonstrates so very well in the essay that you cite. Let me also point out politely that my work with binary oppositions which you cite (such as my earlier Frederick Douglass essay)[14] *is* structuralist as is the work of several other critics of black literature in the seventies (Sunday Anozie, O. A. Ladimeji, Jay Edwards, and the essays in the black journal *The Conch*) and that my work as a poststructuralist emerged directly from my experiments as a structuralist, as Houston Baker also makes clear. No vacuum here; I am acutely aware of the tradition in which I write.

Was it Keynes who said that those who are "against theory" and believe in common sense are merely in the grip of another theory? Joyce Joyce makes a false opposition between theory and humanism, or theory and black men. She also has failed to realize that lucidity through oversimplification is easy enough to achieve; however, it is the lucidity of *command* which is the challenge posed before any critic of any literature. The use of fashionable critical language without the *pressure* of that language is as foolish as is the implied allegation that Houston and

[14]Henry Louis Gates, Jr., "Binary Oppositions in Chapter One of *Narrative of the Life of Frederick Douglass, an American Slave, Written by Himself*," in *Afro-American Literature: The Reconstruction of Instruction*, ed. Dexter Fisher and Robert B. Stepto (New York, 1979), pp. 212–33.

I are nouveau Uncle Toms because we read and write theory.

Coda

Neither ideology nor blackness can exist as an entity in itself, outside of its forms, or its texts. This is the central theme of *Mumbo Jumbo*, for example. But how can we read the text of black ideology? What language(s) do black people use to represent or to contain their ideological positions? In what forms of language do we speak, or write, or *rewrite*? These are the issues at the heart of Joyce Joyce's essay.

Can we derive a valid, *integral* "black" text of ideology from borrowed or appropriated forms? That is, can an authentic black text emerge in the forms of language inherited from the master's class, whether that be, for instance, the realistic novel or poststructuralist theory? Can a black woman's text emerge authentically as borrowed, or "liberated," or revised, from the patriarchal forms of the slave narratives, on one hand, or from the white matriarchal forms of the sentimental novel, on the other, as Harriet Jacobs and Harriet Wilson attempted to do in *Incidents in the Life of a Slave Girl* (1861) and *Our Nig* (1859)?

How much space is there between these two forms through which to maneuver, to maneuver without a certain preordained confinement or "garroting," such as that to which Valerie Smith alludes so pregnantly in her superb post-structural reading of Jacobs's *Incidents in the Life of a Slave Girl*?[15] Is to revise, in this sense, to exist within the confines of the garrot, to extend the metaphor, only to learn to manipulate the representation of black structures of feeling between the cracks, the dark spaces, provided for us by the white masters? Can we write true texts of our ideological selves by the appropriation of received forms of the oppressor—be that oppressor patriarchy or racism—forms in which we see no reflection of our own faces, and through which we hear no true resonances of our own voices? Where lies the liberation in revision, where lies the ideological integrity of defining freedom in the modes and forms of difference charted so cogently by so many post-structural critics of black literature?

It is in these spaces, or garrots, of difference that black literature has dwelled. And while it is crucial to read closely these patterns of formal difference, it is incumbent upon us as well to understand that the quest was lost, in a major sense, before it had even begun simply because the terms of our own self-representation have been provided by the master. Are our choices only to dwell in the quicksand or the garrot of refutation, or negation, or revision? The ideological critique of revision must follow, for us as critics, our detailed and ever closer readings of these very modes of revision. It is not enough for us to show that these exist, and to define these as satisfactory gestures of ideological independence. In this sense, our next set of concerns must be to address the black political signified, and to urge for our writers the fullest and most ironic explorations of manner and matter, of content and form, of structure and sensibility so familiar and poignant to us in our most sublime forms of art, verbal and nonverbal black music, where ideology and art are one, whether we listen to Bessie Smith or to postmodern and post-structural Coltrane.

But what of the ideology of the black critical text? And what of our own critical discourse? In whose voices do we speak? Have we merely renamed the terms of the Other?

Just as we must urge of our writers the meeting of this challenge, we as critics must turn to our own peculiarly black structures of thought and language to develop our own language of criticism, or else we will surely sink in the mire of Nella Larsen's quicksand, remain alienated in the isolation of Harriet Jacobs's garrot, or masked in the received stereotype of the Black Other helping Huck Honey to return to the Raft again, singing "China Gate" with Nat King Cole under the Da Nang moon, standing with the In-

---

[15] Valerie Smith, "'Loopholes of Retreat': Architecture and Ideology in Harriet Jacobs's *Incidents in the Life of a Slave Girl*," paper presented at the 1985 American Studies Association meeting, San Diego.

credible Hulk as the monstrous split doubled selves of mild mannered white people, or as Rocky's too-devoted trainer Apollo Creed, or reflecting our balded heads in the shining flash of Mr. T's signifying gold chains.

As Tina Turner puts it:

I've been taking on a new direction,
But I have to say
I've been thinking about my own protection
It scares me to feel this way.
Oh, oh, oh,
What's love got to do, got to do with it?
What's love but a sweet old-fashioned notion. . . .

RESPONSE: VOICES OF THE NEW BLACK RENAISSANCE
Voices of the Black Arts Movement

THE NEW BLACK POETS

ETHERIDGE KNIGHT

(1931–1991)

Etheridge Knight once wrote, "Unless the black artist establishes a black aesthetic, he will have no future at all. To accept the white aesthetic is to accept and validate a society that will not allow him to live." This statement logically follows from Knight's conviction, which he shared with Amiri Baraka and the other New Black Poets, that the primary function of black art is social. Although Knight became one of the major voices of the Black Arts Movement of the 1960s and 1970s, he is different from the other New Black Poets in his moods and approaches to poetry. Often, he tempers the strident, polemical rhetoric of the other New Black Poets and expresses wider, deeper ranges of personal feelings and human experiences in his verse. "In Knight's poetry," Richard Barksdale observes, "one finds more private reflection and more emotion, recollected not in tranquillity but recollected with that tortured perturbation of heart and soul which is the stuff of good poetry." What sets Knight apart from the other New Black Poets is the fact that he began writing poetry in the bleakest abyss of human existence—prison. In fact, Knight is the quintessential black prison-born artist.

Born on April 19, 1931, in Corinth, Mississippi to Etheridge "Bushie" and Belzora Cozart Knight, into a poor family of seven children, he discovered early in life that his social and economic opportunities were quite limited. Able to complete only a ninth-grade education, he found just a few menial jobs, such as shining shoes, available to him in Corinth. Therefore, he spent most of his teenage years hanging out on street corners, in pool halls, and in barrooms and turning to narcotics for what he felt would relieve him of his emotional anguish. At sixteen, in an attempt to find a purpose in life, he enlisted in the U.S. Army and later fought in the Korean War. During the war, his addiction increased when he was treated with morphine for a shrapnel wound. After his discharge from the service, he drifted aimlessly for several years throughout the country, until he settled in Indianapolis. There Knight learned through his experiences in bars and pool halls the art of telling toasts—long, narrative poems from the black oral tradition that are acted out in a theatrical manner. Unfortunately, his drug addiction, more than toast-telling, shaped his life. In Indianapolis, Knight snatched an elderly white woman's purse to support his habit and was sentenced to a ten- to twenty-five-year prison term at Indiana State Prison.

Embittered by what he considered to be an unjustly long and racially motivated prison sentence, Knight became belligerent, hostile, and rebellious during his first year of incarceration. It was during this, the bleakest period in his life, that he turned to *The Autobiography of Malcolm X* (1965) and other prison works and to writing poetry. As he has stated in the Preface to *Poems from Prison* (1968), "I died in Korea from a shrapnel wound and narcotics resurrected me. I died in 1960 from a prison sentence and poetry brought me back to life."

From his early experiences as a toast-teller, Knight developed his verse into a transcribed oral poetry of considerable power. His early poems, "The Idea of Ancestry," "The Violent Space," "Hard Rock Returns to Prison from the Hospital for the Criminal Insane," and "He Sees Through Stone," were so effective that Broadside Press publisher Dudley Randall published Knight's first volume of verse, *Poems from Prison*, in 1968 and hailed him as one of the major poets of the new Black Arts Movement. Gwendolyn Brooks added in her preface to the collection, "This poetry is a major announcement. . . . The music that seems so effortless is exquisitely carved . . . And there is blackness, inclusive, possessed and given; freed and terrible and beautiful." Brooks and other prominent figures of the Black Arts Movement, including Haki Madhubuti (Don L. Lee), Sonia Sanchez, and Hoyt Fuller, aided Knight in obtaining his parole that same year.

Upon his release from prison, he married Sanchez, but because of his drug addiction, the marriage only lasted a short time. The same holds true for his second marriage to Mary McNally. After adopting two children and living in Minneapolis for a few years, the couple separated in 1977. Soon afterward, Knight fulfilled his desire to return to the South, the only place he called "home," to get a fresh start. He moved to Memphis, Tennessee, where he received methadone treatments and continued to write poetry. In 1980, he published *Born of a Woman: New and Selected Poems*. Six years later, in 1986, *The Essential Etheridge Knight* appeared in print. But his dream of a new beginning was short-lived. He died of lung cancer on March 10, 1991.

Knight's poetry moves from expressions of anguish, loneliness, and frustration to a sense of triumph over the soul's struggle. In his earlier prison poetry, for example, he brings us mercilessly face to face with the infinite varieties of pain and sorrow of the black prison world, until, finally, the prison soul stands before us anatomized. We meet the lobotomized inmate "Hard Rock," the raped convict "Freckled-Face Gerald," and the elderly black soothsayer lifer who "sees through stone" and waits patiently for the dawning of freedom. Above all, in "The Violent Space" and "The Idea of Ancestry," the two most powerful of his prison poems, we witness the poet himself deep in despair, alone in the freedomless void of his prison cell. Here he fuses various temporal-spatial elements to denote not only his incarceration but also the sociopolitical conditions of black people in general.

Although Knight's prison verse is quite impressive, his best poems are his later ones, which search for heritage, continuity, and meaning. In two of his postprison poems, "The Bones of My Father," which shows his growing concern for the image rather than the statement, and his superbly crafted blues poem, "A Poem for Myself (or Blues for a Mississippi Black Boy)," Knight, like Jean Toomer in *Cane* (1923), calls for African Americans to return to their southern roots. Finally, in "Ilu, the Talking Drum," one of the finest poems in contemporary American poetry, the poet brings the African American life experience full circle from Africa to the black South and then back to an Africa of the spirit. Through the use of African pulse beats (duple and triple meters), Knight drums the call to the black community. The message of his verse is at once subtle and clear: Americans of African descent must all ride "the rhythms as one / from Nigeria to Mississippi / and back."

❖❖❖

Surprisingly, critical studies on Knight are sparse. A full-length critical biography on this significant poet is long overdue. However, useful biographical information can be found in Art Powers, "The Prison Artist," in *An Eye for an Eye*, eds. H. Jack Griswold, Mike Misenhower, Art Powers et al. (1970); and in Patricia Liggins Hill, "An Interview with Etheridge Knight," *San Francisco Review of Books* 3, No. 9 (1978). Hill also has written two critical articles on the poet: "'The Violent Space': An Interpretation of the Function of the New Black Aesthetic As Seen in the Poetry of Etheridge Knight," *Black American Literature Forum* 14, No. 3 (Fall 1980); "'Blues for a Mississippi Black Boy': Etheridge Knight's Craft in the Black Oral Tradition," *Mississippi Quarterly* 36, No. 1 (Winter 1982–1983). See also Shirley Lumpkin, "Etheridge Knight," *Dictionary of Literary Biography: Afro-American Poets Since 1955,* vol. 41. Richard Barksdale's commentary on Knight's poetry in *Black Writers of America* (1972) and Eugene Remond's insights on him in *Drumvoices: The Mission of Afro-American Poetry* (1976) are very good but brief.

The Idea of Ancestry

1

Taped to the wall of my cell are 47 pictures: 47 black
faces: my father, mother, grandmothers (1 dead), grandfathers (both dead), brothers, sisters, uncles, aunts,
cousins (1st & 2nd), nieces, and nephews. They stare
across the space at me sprawling on my bunk. I know
their dark eyes, they know mine. I know their style,
they know mine. I am all of them, they are all of me;
they are farmers, I am a thief, I am me, they are thee.

I have at one time or another been in love with my mother,
1 grandmother, 2 sisters, 2 aunts (1 went to the asylum),
and 5 cousins. I am now in love with a 7-yr-old niece
(she sends me letters written in large block print, and
her picture is the only one that smiles at me).

I have the same name as 1 grandfather, 3 cousins, 3 nephews,
and 1 uncle. The uncle disappeared when he was 15, just took
off and caught a freight (they say). He's discussed each year
when the family has a reunion, he causes uneasiness in
the clan, he is an empty space. My father's mother, who is 93
and who keeps the Family Bible with everybody's birth dates
(and death dates) in it, always mentions him. There is no
place in her Bible for "whereabouts unknown."

2

Each fall the graves of my grandfathers call me, the brown
hills and red gullies of mississippi send out their electric
messages, galvanizing my genes. Last yr / like a salmon quitting
the cold ocean-leaping and bucking up his birthstream / I

hitchhiked my way from LA with 16 caps in my pocket and a
monkey on my back. And I almost kicked it with the kinfolks.
I walked barefooted in my grandmother's backyard / I smelled the old
land and the woods / I sipped cornwhiskey from fruit jars with the men /
I flirted with the women / I had a ball till the caps ran out
and my habit came down. That night I looked at my grandmother
and split / my guts were screaming for junk / but I was almost
contented / I had almost caught up with me.
(The next day in Memphis I cracked a croaker's crib for a fix.)

This yr there is a gray stone wall damming my stream, and when
the falling leaves stir my genes, I pace my cell or flop on my bunk
and stare at 47 black faces across the space. I am all of them,
they are all of me, I am me, they are thee, and I have no children
to float in the space between.

The Violent Space
(or when your sister sleeps around for money)

Exchange in greed the ungraceful signs. Thrust
The thick notes between green apple breasts.
Then the shadow of the devil descends,
The violent space cries and angel eyes,
Large and dark, retreat in innocence and in ice.
(Run sister run—the Bugga man comes!)

The violent space cries silently,
Like you cried wide years ago
In another space, speckled by the sun
And the leaves of a green plum tree,
And you were stung
By a red wasp and we flew home.
(Run sister run—the Bugga man comes!)

Well, hell, lil sis, wasps still sting.
You are all of seventeen and as alone now
In your pain as you were with the sting
On your brow.
Well, shit, lil sis, here we are:
You and I and this poem.
And what should I do? should I squat
In the dust and make strange markings on the ground?
Shall I chant a spell to drive the demon away?
(Run sister run—the Bugga man comes!)

In the beginning you were the Virgin Mary,
And you are the Virgin Mary now.
But somewhere between Nazareth and Bethlehem
You lost your name in the nameless void.

"*Oh Mary don't you weep don't you moan*"
O Mary shake your butt to the violent juke,
Absorb the demon puke and watch the white eyes pop,
(Run sister run—the Bugga man comes!)

And what do I do. I boil my tears in a twisted spoon
And dance like an angel on the point of a needle.
I sit counting syllables like Midas gold.
I am not bold. I cannot yet take hold of the demon
And lift his weight from your black belly,
So I grab the air and sing my song.
(But the air cannot stand my singing long.)

Hard Rock Returns to Prison from the Hospital for the Criminal Insane

Hard Rock / was / "known not to take no shit
From nobody," and he had the scars to prove it:
Split purple lips, lumbed ears, welts above
His yellow eyes, and one long scar that cut
Across his temple and plowed through a thick
Canopy of kinky hair.

The WORD / was / that Hard Rock wasn't a mean nigger
Anymore, that the doctors had bored a hole in his head,
Cut out part of his brain, and shot electricity
Through the rest. When they brought Hard Rock back,
Handcuffed and chained, he was turned loose,
Like a freshly gelded stallion, to try his new status.
And we all waited and watched, like a herd of sheep,
To see if the WORD was true.

As we waited we wrapped ourselves in the cloak
Of his exploits: "Man, the last time, it took eight
Screws to put him in the Hole." "Yeah, remember when he
Smacked the captain with his dinner tray?" "He set
The record for time in the Hole—67 straight days!"
"O! Hard Rock! man, that's one crazy nigger."
And then the jewel of a myth that Hard Rock had once bit
A screw on the thumb and poisoned him with syphilitic spit.

The testing came, to see if Hard Rock was really tame.
A hillbilly called him a black son of a bitch
And didn't lose his teeth, a screw who knew Hard Rock
From before shook him down and barked in his face.
And Hard Rock did *nothing*. Just grinned and looked silly,
His eyes empty like knot holes in a fence.

And even after we discovered that it took Hark Rock
Exactly 3 minutes to tell you his first name,
We told ourselves that he had just wised up,
Was being cool; but we could not fool ourselves for long,
And we turned away, our eyes on the ground. Crushed.
He had been our Destroyer, the doer of things
We dreamed of doing but could not bring ourselves to do,
The fears of years, like a biting whip,
Had cut deep bloody grooves
Across our backs.

He Sees Through Stone

He sees through stone
he has the secret eyes
this old black one
who under prison skies
sits pressed by the sun
against the western wall
his pipe between purple gums

the years fall
like overripe plums
bursting red flesh
on the dark earth

his time is not my time
but I have known him
in a time gone

he led me trembling cold
into the dark forest
taught me the secret rites
to make it with a woman
to be true to my brothers
to make my spear drink
the blood of my enemies

now black cats circle him
flash white teeth
snarl at the air
mashing green grass beneath
shining muscles

ears peeling his words
he smiles
he knows
the hunt   the enemy
he has the secret eyes
he sees through stone

A Poem for Myself
(or Blues for a Mississippi Black Boy)

I was born in Mississippi;
I walked barefooted thru the mud.
Born black in Mississippi,
Walked barefooted thru the mud.
But, when I reached the age of twelve
I left that place for good.
Said my daddy chopped cotton
And he drank his liquor straight.
When I left that Sunday morning
He was leaning on the barnyard gate.
Left her standing in the yard
With the sun shining in her eyes.
And I headed North
As straight as the Wild Goose Flies,
I been to Detroit & Chicago
Been to New York city too.
I been to Detroit & Chicago
Been to New York city too.
Said I done strolled all those funky avenues
I'm still the same old black boy with the same old blues.
Going back to Mississippi
This time to stay for good
Going back to Mississippi
This time to stay for good—
Gonna be free in Mississippi
Or dead in the Mississippi mud.

Ilu, the Talking Drum

The deadness was threatening us—15 Nigerians and 1 Mississippi nigger.
It hung heavily, like stones around our necks, pulling us down
to the ground, black arms and legs outflung
on the wide green lawn of the big white house
The deadness was threatening us, the day
was dying with the sun, the stillness—
unlike the sweet silence after love / making or
the pulsating quietness of a summer night—
the stillness was skinny and brittle and wrinkled
by the precise people sitting on the wide white porch
of the big white house . . .
The darkness was threatening us, menacing . . .
we twisted, turned, shifted positions, picked our noses,
stared at our bare toes, hissed air thru our teeth . . .
Then Tunji, green robes flowing as he rose,
strapped on Ilu, the talking drum,

and began:

kah doom / kah doom-doom / kah doom / kah doom-doom-doom
kah doom / kah doom-doom / kah doom / kah doom-doom-doom
kah doom / kah doom-doom / kah doom / kah doom-doom-doom
kah doom / kah doom-doom / kah doom / kah doom-doom-doom

the heart, the heart beats, the heart, the heart beats slow
the heart beats slowly, the heart beats
the blood flows slowly, the blood flows
the blood, the blood flows, the blood, the blood flows slow
kah doom / kah doom-doom / kah doom / kah doom-doom-doom
and the day opened to the sound

kah doom / kah doom-doom / kah doom / kah doom-doom-doom
and our feet moved to the sound of life
kah doom / kah doom-doom / kah doom / kah doom-doom-doom
and we rode the rhythms as one
from Nigeria to Mississippi
and back
kah doom / kah doom-doom / kah doom / kah doom-doom-doom

The Bones of My Father

1

There are no dry bones
here in this valley. The skull
of my father grins
at the Mississippi moon
from the bottom
of the Tallahatchie,
the bones of my father
are buried in the mud
of these creeks and brooks that twist
and flow their secrets to the sea.
but the wind sings to me
here the sun speaks to me
of the dry bones of my father.

2

There are no dry bones
in the northern valleys, in the Harlem alleys
young / black / men with knees bent
nod on the stoops of the tenements
and dream
of the dry bones of my father.

And young white longhairs who flee
their homes, and bend their minds

and sing their songs of brotherhood
and no more wars are searching for
my father's bones.

3

There are no dry bones here.
We hide from the sun.
No more do we take the long straight strides.
Our steps have been shaped by the cages
that kept us. We glide sideways
like crabs across the sand.
We perch on green lilies, we search
beneath white rocks . . .
THERE ARE NO DRY BONES HERE

The skull of my father
grins at the Mississippi moon
from the bottom
of the Tallahatchie.

SONIA SANCHEZ

(1934–)

Sonia Sanchez, one of the eminent poets of the Black Arts Movement beginnings in the sixties, wrote in the introduction to her collection of short stories *We Be Word Sorcerers* (1973):

> The move from Negroness to Blackness has been a slow/painful/upward journey of the twentieth century, a journey still not completed. The voice of Blackness in the wilderness of North America awoke the Black man from the sleep of his forgotten identity. He awoke angry and startled at those who had put him to sleep. In the beginning of this Black literature, anger overshadowed self-identity. But when reason lit the darkness of this new world, the energy of anger turned inward toward themes of Black love, respect, and Black nationhood.

Above all, Sanchez has been one of the key figures both to awaken African Americans from the darkness of the stolen legacy of African heritage and to lead this nation within a nation to the true light of black identity.

Born Wilsonia Driver in Birmingham, Alabama, on September 9, 1934, Sanchez was the daughter of Wilson L. and Lena Driver. When Lena died one year after Sonia's birth, she, along with her sister Pat, was taken in by various family members. To complicate matters, Sonia was a very shy child who often stuttered when she spoke. When she was nine years old, Wilson Driver moved the family to Harlem, a move that proved providential for the development of the young girl's artistic talents.

In 1955, Sanchez received a B.A. in political science from Hunter College in New York City. She then undertook graduate work in poetry with Louise Bogan at New York University for a year. By the early 1970s, she had emerged on the national scene as a woman well-known for emotional readings, which included chanting and ghost spirit imitations of notables such as Martin Luther King, Jr., Harriet Tubman, Frederick Douglass, and Malcolm X. Meanwhile, her early poems were being published in newly prominent journals featuring African American literature, such as the *Liberator, Journal of Black Poetry, Negro Digest,* and *Black Dialogue.*

Her first book of poetry, titled *Homecoming,* was published in 1969 by Broadside Press, the emerging black publishing house founded by Dudley Randall. The book announces the major themes that would come to dominate Sanchez's work: black female-male relationships, black home, black family, black community, and the examples set for and the legacies left to black children. But the dominant tone of the work is anger; in poems such as "small comment" and "the final solution," the poet voices her raw anger at white America for stripping blacks of their humanity and dignity. Critic Haki Madhubuti says that *Homecoming* was "significant . . . for its pace-setting language." David Williams notes that imagining an audience "is occasionally crucial to the poems in *Homecoming,* some of which are, in essence, communal chant performances in which Sanchez, as poet, provides the necessary language for the performance. The perceptions in such poems are deliberately generalized, filtered through the shared consciousness of the urban Black."

Liberation Poem and *We a BaddDDD People* appeared in 1970. Madhubuti praises *We a BaddDDD People* for "its scope and maturity." The many sides of the poet were first demonstrated in this book, where she carefully and lovingly surveys the black world. The first section, "Survival Poems," is a mirror of the sixties generation. She comments on everything from suicide to her relationship with poet Etheridge Knight, to whom she was married at the time. Marked with inflections of oral presentation, she uses strong black street language in poems such as "blk/chant" to communicate to her black audience the need to liberate themselves from "whiteness."

Sanchez has published three children's books—*It's a New Day* (1971), *The Adventures of Fathead, Smallhead, and Squarehead* (1973), and *A Sound Investment* (1980); five plays—*The Bronx Is Next* (1970), *Sister Son/jii* (1972), *Uh, Huh; But How Do It Free Us?* (1974), *Malcolm\Man Don't Live Here No Mo'* (1979), and *I'm Black When I'm Singing, I'm Blue When I Ain't* (1982); and two speeches—*Crisis in Culture: Two Speeches* (1983). Six additional books of poetry include *Love Poems* (1973), *A Blues Book for Black Magical Women* (1973), *I've Been a Woman: New and Selected Poems* (1981), *homegirls and handgrenades* (1984), *Under a Soprano Sky* (1987), and *Wounded in the House of a Friend* (1995). With the latter offerings, the poet turned more to metaphor than statement and more to the intimacy of female identity. She explores black male-female relationships, the necessary role of militancy for women in political revolt, the necessity for female solidarity, and her embrace of Islam.

In *I've Been a Woman* (1981), she brings together some of her strongest poems from previous collections, demonstrating the diversity of issues she has addressed, such as explorations of the self, Malcolm X's assassination, the influence of family, drug addiction, the relationship between art and political commitment, and the importance of writers who have preceded her.

Yet it is *homegirls and handgrenades* (1984) that best reflects the power and force of Sanchez's poetry. "Handgrenades," she explains in Herbert Leibowitz's interview with her in *Parnassus: Poetry in Review* (1985), "are the words I use to explode myths about people, about ourselves, about how we live and what we think, because this is really the last chance we have in this country." Her words are weapons, but they carry an exquisite poetic lyricism that is clearly evident in "Masks." The collection also introduces her long prose poems, which when heard are indistinguishable from pure poetry, but when read manifest all the characteristics of prose. This type of verse, as well as superbly crafted shorter poetic forms—blues, haikus, and tankas—also appears in *Under a Soprano Sky* (1987). The title poem is a culmination of the poet's spiritual journey: she is at one with nature, her art, and herself as "under a soprano sky, a woman sings, / lovely as chandeliers."

Mother, poet, professor, political activist, and playwright, Sanchez has worked at numerous universities and colleges, including Amherst College, San Francisco State University, the University of Pittsburgh, and Temple University, where she currently teaches a broad range of courses in African American literature and holds the Laura Cornell Chair in English. Her travels throughout the United States and especially to Africa, Cuba, the Caribbean, Australia, Nicaragua, and the People's Republic of China testify to her political commitment to awaken the consciousness of the masses around the world. This commitment emerges most forcefully in her written poetry and in her dramatic performance of that poetry. An essential member of the Black Arts Movement that began in the 1960s, Sanchez indefatigably demonstrates the balance between political commitment and the craft of literary art.

Her numerous awards and honors include an honorary Ph.D. in fine arts from Wilberforce University, the PEN Writing Award (1969), the Lucretia Mott Award (1984), an American Book Award for *homegirls and handgrenades* in 1985, the Peace and Freedom Award from the Women's International League for Peace and Freedom in 1988, and the Governor's Award for Excellence in the Humanities for 1988.

In the introduction to *We Be Word Sorcerers* (1973), Sanchez was particularly concerned with undoing the process by which descendants of the stalwart African generation first forced into slavery were turned into "Negroes." She cites language, culture, and religion as the main tools with which the patriarchy manipulated all future generations of blacks until the 1960s. With her poetry and other literature, she seeks to reverse those influences so that American blacks can become "black" again. "Sonia Sanchez is," Amiri Baraka writes, "one of the important figures in Afro-American literature."

❖❖❖

For further information on Sanchez and her art, see Sebastian Clarke, "Sonia Sanchez and Her Work," *Black World,* (July 1971); "Sonia Sanchez Creates Poetry for the Stage," *Black Creation* 5 (Fall 1973); Joyce Ann Joyce, "The Development of Sonia Sanchez: A Continuing Journey," *Indian Journal of American Studies* 13 (July 1983); Haki Madhubuti, "Sonia Sanchez: The Bringer of Memories," and David Williams, "The Poetry of Sonia Sanchez," in *Black Women Writers (1950–1980): A Critical Evaluation,* ed. Mari Evans (1984); Raymond Patterson, "What's Happening in Black Poetry?", *Poetry Review* 2 (April 1985); Kalamu ya Salaam's biocritical essay in the *Dictionary of Literary Biography: Afro-American Poets Since 1955,* vol. 41 (1985); see also Herbert Leibowitz's "Exploding Myths: An Interview with Sonia Sanchez," *Parnassus: Poetry in Review* (Spring/Summer, Fall/Winter 1985); Joanne

V. Gabbin, "The Southern Imagination of Sonia Sanchez," in *Southern Women Writers: The New Generation,* ed. Tonette Bond Inge (1990); D. H. Melhem, "Sonia Sanchez: The Will and the Spirit," in *Heroism in the New Black Poetry: Introductions and Interviews* (1990).

the final solution/

the leaders speak
america.
land of free/
dom
land of im/mi/grant
wh/ites
and slave/
blacks. there is
no real problem here.
we the
lead/ers of free
a/mer/ica
say. give us your
hungry/
illiterates/
criminals/
dropouts/
(in other words)
your blacks
and we will
let them fight
in vietnam
defending america's honor.
we will make responsible
citi/
zens out of them or
kill them trying.

america
land of free/dom
free/
enter/
prise and de/mo/
cracy.
bring us your problems.
we your lead/ers
always find a solution.
after all
what else are
we get/
ting pd for?

right on: white america

this country might have
been a pio
          neer land
once.
     but.   there ain't
no mo
     indians   blowing
custer's mind
          with a different
image of america.
               this country
might have
          needed shoot/
outs/ daily/
          once.
               but. there ain't
no mo real/ white   allamerican
                         bad/guys.
just.
   u & me
          blk/ and un/armed.
this country might have
been a pio
          neer land,   once.
                              and it still is.
check out
          the falling
gun/shells   on our blk/ tomorrows.

Summer Words of a Sustuh Addict

the first day i shot dope
was on a sunday.
          i had just come
home from church
          got mad at my motha
cuz she got mad at me. u dig?
          went out. shot up
behind a feelen against her.
               it felt good.
gooder than dooing it. yeah.
               it was nice.
i did it. uh huh. i did it.   uh. huh.
i want to do it again. it felt so goooood.
          and as the sistuh
          sits in her silent/

remembered/high
someone leans for
ward gently asks her:
sistuh.
did u
finally
learn how to hold yo/mother?
and the music of the day
drifts in the room
to mingle with the sistuh's young tears.
and we all sing.

Masks

(BLACKS DON'T HAVE THE INTELLECTUAL
CAPACITY TO SUCCEED.)

WILLIAM COORS

the river runs toward day
and never stops.
so life receives the lakes
patrolled by one-eyed pimps
who wash their feet in our blue whoredom

the river floods
the days grow short
we wait to change our masks
we wait for warmer days and
fountains without force
we wait for seasons without power.

today
ah today
only the shrill sparrow seeks the sky
our days are edifice.
we look toward temples that give birth to sanctioned flesh.

o bring the white mask
full of the chalk sky.

entering the temple
on this day of sundays
i hear the word spoken
by the unhurried speaker
who speaks of unveiled eyes.

o bring the chalk mask
full of altitudes.

straight in this chair
tall in an unrehearsed role
i rejoice
and the spirit sinks in twilight of
distant smells.

o bring the mask
full of drying blood.

fee, fie, fo, fum,
i smell the blood
of an englishman
o my people
wear the white masks
for they speak without speaking
and hear words of forgetfulness.

o my people.

now poem. for us

don't let them die out
all these old/blk/people
don't let them cop out
with their memories
of slavery/survival.
it is our
heritage.
u know. part/african.
part/negro.
part/slave
sit down with em brothas & sistuhs.
talk to em. listen to their
tales of victories/woes/sorrows.
listen to their blk/
myths.
record them talken their ago talk
for our tomorrows.
ask them bout the songs of
births. the herbs
that cured
their aches. the crazy/
niggers blowen
some cracker's cool.
the laughter
comen out of tears.
let them tell us of their juju years
so ours will be that much stronger.

Blues

in the night
in my half hour
negro dreams
i hear voices knocking at the door
i see walls dripping screams up
and down the halls
                    won't someone open
the door for me? won't some
one schedule my sleep
and don't ask no questions?
noise.
     like when he took me to his
home away from home place
and i died the long sought after
death he'd planned for me.
Yeah, bessie he put in the bacon
and it overflowed the pot.
and two days later
when i was talking
i started to grin.
as everyone knows
i am still grinning.

Woman

Come ride my birth, earth mother
tell me how i have become, became
this woman with razor blades between
her teeth.
          sing me my history O earth mother
about tongues multiplying memories
about breaths contained in straw.
pull me from the throat of mankind
where worms eat, O earth mother.
come to this Black woman. you.
rider of earth pilgrimages.
tell me how i have held five bodies
in one large cocktail of love
and still have the thirst of the beginning sip.
tell me. tellLLLLLL me. earth mother
for i want to rediscover me. the secret of me
the river of me. the morning ease of me.
i want my body to carry my words like aqueducts.
i want to make the world my diary
and speak rivers.

rise up earth mother
out of rope-strung-trees
dancing a windless dance
come phantom mother
dance me a breakfast of births
let your mouth spill me forth
so i creak with your mornings.
come old mother, light up my mind
with a story bright as the sun.

under a soprano sky

1.

once i lived on pillars in a green house
boarded by lilacs that rocked voices into weeds.
i bled an owl's blood
shredding the grass until i
rocked in a choir of worms.
obscene with hands, i wooed the world
with thumbs
                    while yo-yos hummed.
was it an unborn lacquer i peeled?
the woods, tall as waves, sang in mixed
tongues that loosened the scalp
and my bones wrapped in white dust
returned to echo in my thighs.

i heard a pulse wandering somewhere
on vague embankments.
O are my hands breathing? I cannot smell the nerves.
i saw the sun
ripening green stones for fields.
O have my eyes run down? i cannot taste my birth.

2.

now as i move, mouth quivering with silks
my skin runs soft with eyes.
descending into my legs, i follow obscure birds
purchasing orthopedic wings.
the air is late this summer.

i peel the spine and flood
the earth with adolescence.
O who will pump these breasts? I cannot waltz my tongue.

under a soprano sky, a woman sings,
lovely as chandeliers.

AMIRI BARAKA (LEROI JONES)

(1934–)

If the contemporary era could be called the Age of African American Writers, then Amiri Baraka can be credited with creating the yardstick by which others are measured. Since his public debut with the production of his play *Dutchman* in 1964, Baraka has been best known in both national and international circles, D. H. Melhem points out, as "the figure to be reckoned with in Black political life and art." A founder of the Black Arts Movement of the 1960s, this major poet, dramatist, essayist, screenplay writer, and music and literary critic has had a more profound impact on American culture than any other contemporary American writer. He stands squarely in the forefront of the creation of a black revolutionary tradition in American literature. Since the early 1960s, Baraka has dedicated his professional career to transforming through language and theory white aesthetics to Black Aesthetic purposes, avant-garde poetics into black poetics, white liberal politics into black nationalist and Marxist politics, and jazz forms into literary forms. By all indications, he and his art have been part of a continually evolving political process. So far, his career has gone through three distinct stages: beatnik-bohemian (1957–1964), black nationalist revolutionary (1965–1974), and Marxist revolutionary (1974 to the present). Though deemed controversial and socially ambivalent by the American critical establishment, Baraka continues to be one of the most exciting and original contemporary writers in America. He remains the prime example of the ethnically and politically committed literary artist of our time.

Named Everett LeRoy (not LeRoi) Jones at birth, Baraka was born in the industrial city of Newark, New Jersey, on October 7, 1934 to black middle-class parents. His father, Coytette LeRoy Jones, was a postal supervisor; his mother, Anna Lois Jones, was a social worker. LeRoy was an outstanding student, graduating with honors from Barringer High School in 1951. Shortly before entering college in 1952, he started spelling his first name in its Frenchified form, LeRoi. He attended Howard University in Washington, D.C., where he studied with the preeminent black scholars of the day. Jones examined the blues with Sterling A. Brown, jazz and sociology with E. Franklin Frazier, and Dante with Nathan A. Scott; all three had a lasting impression on Jones's intellectual and artistic development. Dante is a recurrent reference in his writing, especially in the novel *The System of Dante's Hell* (1965), where he borrows the structure of Dante's "Inferno" to shape this work. He has published three books on jazz: the groundbreaking socioaesthetic history of black music *Blues People: Negro Music in White America* (1963), the black nationalist book *Black Music* (1968), and the Marxist piece *The Music: Reflections on Jazz Blues* (1987). Moreover, Jones's negative conception of the black bourgeoisie comes virtually from Frazier, who wrote the classic attack on the black middle class, *Black Bourgeoisie* (1957).

After flunking out of Howard in his senior year, he joined the U.S. Air Force, eventually reaching the rank of sergeant. While in the service, he began his intellectual and artistic apprenticeship in earnest by writing poetry, keeping a journal, and reading voraciously, sometimes two books a day. With an unorthodox library, unorthodox ways, and little regard for military discipline, he was dishonorably discharged in 1957. That same year, Jones moved to Greenwich Village in New York

City, where he came under the influence of the post–World War II avant-garde, most significantly Allen Ginsberg of the Beat Generation, Frank O'Hara of the New York School, and Charles Olson of the Black Mountain Poets. While in the Village, he wrote *Preface to a Twenty Volume Suicide Note* (1961), a collection of experimental poetry, and coedited two important avant-garde magazines, *Yugen* (1958–1962) and *The Floating Bear* (1961–1963). Although learning a great deal technically and intellectually from the Beat writers, soon after his 1960 trip to Fidel Castro's leftist Cuba—a trip that was recorded in the 1960 essay "Cuba Libre" (*Home,* 1966)—he began to grow disillusioned with their apolitical art and attitudes. In fact, this trip initiated Jones's conception of art as being political. The book of poems titled *The Dead Lecturer* (1964) embodies his desperate need to create a black political art and distance himself from the Village intellectuals and artists who had failed him. For him, these bohemians were simply carping beatniks accomplishing nothing, while he was struggling to become a revolutionary, someone who would change the material conditions of the black masses. Jones's poetry, like much other poetry of the period, is highly autobiographical; there is little difference between the poetic persona speaking in a poem and the real autobiographical self.

In 1964, his play *Dutchman* catapulted him into the national limelight. The play is about Clay, a young, middle-class black man who has not learned to use the black revolutionary spirit that pumps in his black heart. When he reveals his true militancy, he is summarily killed by white society, allegorized as a beautiful white woman. With increasing racial tensions in the country, culminating in the death of Malcolm X in 1965, Jones turned his back on the white world and moved to Harlem, becoming a black cultural nationalist whose artistic goal was the creation of black culture and the destruction of white civilization. With other black intellectuals, including Larry Neal, Don L. Lee (Haki R. Madhubuti), and Maulana Ron Karenga, Jones forged a cultural nationalist art and philosophy. He wrote politically charged poems, essays, and plays that greatly influenced an entire generation of black writers. "We want 'poems that kill,'" Jones says in "Black Art," a poem from his collection *Black Magic Poetry* (1969). Although the poem is an offensive, even shocking poem, it is important because it epitomizes a particular moment of black anger in American history. In the mid 1960s, one expression of black anger was the riots; another was black militant poetry. Slashing out at the entire white world, "Black Art" gives the contemporary reader an opportunity to understand black rage, an understanding which could help us avoid riots such as the recent ones in Los Angeles. In his contemporary African American poetry anthology, *Every Shut Eye Ain't Asleep* (1994), the poet Michael Harper says of Baraka's poetry of that era, that it expresses the rage of those "who have watched several social 'movements' come and go without much substantive change." "The Black Artist's role in America," Baraka insisted, "is to aid in the destruction of America as he knows it." One influential outgrowth of the Black Arts Movement was Jones's founding of the Black Arts Repertory Theatre/School in Harlem, which inspired the creation of black theaters throughout the country. In plays such as *Madheart* (1966) and *The Baptism & the Toilet* (1967), he envisioned the white man as the devil, the source of all evil in the world. In *The Autobiography,* Baraka reports that once at a meeting at the Village Gate when a white woman asked what whites could do to help the black revolution, Jones replied, "You can help by dying. You are a cancer."

In 1965, after a difficult time in Harlem, Jones returned to his hometown of Newark, establishing Spirit House, a black repertory theater and cultural center. Soon after his arrival, he published a book of social essays significantly titled *Home* (1966), where he declares "By the time this book appears, I will be even blacker." It was during 1967 that he assumed the Bantuized Muslim name Imamu Amiri Baraka, which means "Blessed Prince." During the Newark riots in July 1967, he was arrested for carrying weapons and resisting arrest. At his trial, Judge Leon Kapp read Baraka's poem "Black People!" as evidence of his involvement in the riots. He was convicted of a misdemeanor, but his conviction was reversed on appeal.

In 1974, Baraka rejected cultural nationalism. In the article "Toward Ideological Clarity," published in *Black World,* he proclaimed his conversion to international socialism because he came to view capitalism, not white society, as the true enemy of black people. However, in an interview in *The Poetry and Poetics of Amiri Baraka* (1985), Baraka argues that his revolutionary "intentions are similar to those I had when I was a Nationalist. . . . they were similar in the sense I see art as a weapon, and a weapon of revolution." "The analysis of our condition," he added five years later, "must be made in terms of class and an international struggle."

After an inauspicious beginning, Baraka has produced a major body of work in the socialist mode, including the long poem *In the Tradition* (1982), the epic poem in progress *Wise, Why's Y's* (1995), and the plays *What Was the Relationship of the Lone Ranger to the Means of Production?* (1979), *General Hag's Skeezag* (1992), and *Meeting Lillie,* which was produced in 1993 at the Nuyorican Poets Cafe in New York City, *Funk Love* (1996), and *Eulogies* (1996). Some of his other important works are a collection of experimental short stories titled *Beat Poetry; Tales* (1967) and *The Autobiography of LeRoi Jones/Amiri Baraka* (1984), a major volume that vividly covers his life up to the Marxist period.

Baraka has shown that great art can be self-consciously racial and political. In fact, no American writer has been more committed to social justice and the achievement of that justice through art than Baraka. He is dedicated to bringing the voices of black America into the very fiber of his writings.

❖❖❖

For further information and insight into Baraka and his works, see D. H. Melhem, "Amiri Baraka (LeRoi Jones): Revolutionary Traditions," in *Heroism in the New Black Poetry: Introductions and Interviews* (1990); Robert Elliot Fox, *Conscientious Sorcerers: The Black Postmodernist Fiction of LeRoi Jones/Amiri Baraka, Ishmael Reed, and Samuel R. Delany* (1987); William J. Harris, *The Poetry and Poetics of Amiri Baraka* (1985); William J. Harris, "Amiri Baraka," in *African American Writers,* ed. Valerie Smith (1991); Werner Sollors, *Amiri Baraka/LeRoi Jones* (1978); Theodore R. Hudson, *From LeRoi Jones to Amiri Baraka: The Literary Works* (1973). Since Baraka's writings are difficult to find, the best single source is *The LeRoi Jones/Amiri Baraka Reader,* ed. William J. Harris (1991).

Preface to a Twenty Volume Suicide Note

For Kellie Jones, born 16 May 1959

Lately, I've become accustomed to the way
The ground opens up and envelopes me
Each time I go out to walk the dog.
Or the broad edged silly music the wind
Makes when I run for a bus . . .

Things have come to that.

And now, each night I count the stars,
And each night I get the same number.
And when they will not come to be counted,
I count the holes they leave.

Nobody sings anymore.

And then last night, I tiptoed up
To my daughter's room and heard her
Talking to someone, and when I opened
The door, there was no one there . . .
Only she on her knees, peeking into
Her own clasped hands.

Black Art

Poems are bullshit unless they are
teeth or trees or lemons piled
on a step. Or black ladies dying
of men leaving nickel hearts
beating them down. Fuck poems
and they are useful, wd they shoot
come at you, love what you are,
breathe like wrestlers, or shudder
strangely after pissing. We want live
words of the hip world live flesh &
coursing blood. Hearts Brains
Souls splintering fire. We want poems
like fists beating niggers out of Jocks
or dagger poems in the slimy bellies
of the owner-jews. Black poems to
smear on girdlemamma mulatto bitches
whose brains are red jelly stuck
between 'lizabeth taylor's toes. Stinking
Whores! We want "poems that kill."
Assassin poems, Poems that shoot

guns. Poems that wrestle cops into alleys
and take their weapons leaving them dead
with tongues pulled out and sent to Ireland. Knockoff
poems for dope selling wops or slick halfwhite
politicians Airplane poems, rrrrrrrrrrrrrrr
rrrrrrrrrrrrrr . . . tuhtuhtuhtuhtuhtuhtuhtuhtuh
. . . rrrrrrrrrrrrrrr . . . Setting fire and death to
whities ass. Look at the Liberal
Spokesman for the jews clutch his throat
& puke himself into eternity . . . rrrrrrrr
There's a negroleader pinned to
a bar stool in Sardi's eyeballs melting
in hot flame Another negroleader
on the steps of the white house one
kneeling between the sheriff's thighs
negotiating cooly for his people.

Agggh . . . stumbles across the room . . .
Put it on him, poem. Strip him naked
to the world! Another bad poem cracking
steel knuckles in a jewlady's mouth
Poem scream poison gas on beasts in green berets
Clean out the world for virtue and love,
Let there be no love poems written
until love can exist freely and
cleanly. Let Black People understand
that they are the lovers and the sons
of lovers and warriors and sons
of warriors Are poems & poets &
all the loveliness here in the world

We want a black poem. And a
Black World.
Let the world be a Black Poem
And Let All Black People Speak This Poem
Silently
or LOUD

SOS

Calling black people
Calling all black people, man woman child
Wherever you are, calling you, urgent, come in
Black People, come in, wherever you are, urgent, calling
you, calling all black people
calling all black people, come in, black people, come
on in.

Black People: This Is Our Destiny

The road runs straight with no turning, the circle
runs complete as it is in the storm of peace, the all
embraced embracing in the circle complete turning road
straight like a burning straight with the circle complete
as in a peaceful storm, the elements, the niggers' voices
harmonized with creation on a peak in the holy black man's
eyes that we rise, whose race is only direction up, where
we go to meet the realization of makers knowing who we are
and the war in our hearts but the purity of the holy world
that we long for, knowing how to live, and what life is, and
who God is, and the many revolutions we must spin through in our
seven adventures in the endlessness of all existing feeling, all
existing forms of life, the gases, the plants, the ghost minerals
the spirits the souls the light in the stillness where the storm
the glow the nothing in God is complete except there is nothing
to be incomplete the pulse and change of rhythm, blown flight
to be anything at all . . . vibration holy nuance beating against
itself, a rhythm a playing re-understood now by one of the 1st race
the primitives the first men who evolve again to civilize the
world

A Poem for Black Hearts

For Malcolm's eyes, when they broke
the face of some dumb white man, For
Malcolm's hands raised to bless us
all black and strong in his image
of ourselves, For Malcolm's words
fire darts, the victor's tireless
thrusts, words hung above the world
change as it may, he said it, and
for this he was killed, for saying,
and feeling, and being/change, all
collected hot in his heart, For Malcolm's
heart, raising us above our filthy cities,
for his stride, and his beat, and his address
to the grey monsters of the world, For Malcolm's
pleas for your dignity, black men, for your life,
black man, for the filling of your minds
with righteousness, For all of him dead and
gone and vanished from us, and all of him which
clings to our speech black god of our time.
For all of him, and all of yourself, look up,
black man, quit stuttering and shuffling, look up,
black man, quit whining and stooping, for all of him,

For Great Malcolm a prince of the earth, let nothing in us rest
until we avenge ourselves for his death, stupid animals
that killed him, let us never breathe a pure breath if
we fail, and white men call us faggots till the end of
the earth.

Ka 'Ba

A closed window looks down
on a dirty courtyard, and black people
call across or scream across or walk across
defying physics in the stream of their will

Our world is full of sound
Our world is more lovely than anyone's
tho we suffer, and kill each other
and sometimes fail to walk the air

We are beautiful people
with african imaginations
full of masks and dances and swelling chants
with african eyes, and noses, and arms,
though we sprawl in grey chains in a place
full of winters, when what we want is sun.

We have been captured,
brothers. And we labor
to make our getaway, into
the ancient image, into a new
correspondence with ourselves
and our black family. We need magic
now we need the spells, to raise up
return, destroy, and create. What will be
the sacred words?

leroy

I wanted to know my mother when she sat
looking sad across the campus in the late 20's
into the future of the soul, there were black angels
straining above her head, carrying life from our ancestors,
and knowledge, and the strong nigger feeling. She sat
(in that photo in the yearbook I showed Vashti) getting into
new blues, from the old ones, the trips and passions
showered on her by her own. Hypnotizing me, from so far
ago, from that vantage of knowledge passed on to her passed on
to me and all the other black people of our time.
When I die, the consciousness I carry I will to

black people. May they pick me apart and take the useful parts, the sweet meat of my feelings. And leave the bitter bullshit rotten white parts alone.

An Agony. As Now.

I am inside someone
who hates me. I look
out from his eyes. Smell
what fouled tunes come in
to his breath. Love his
wretched women.

Slits in the metal, for sun. Where
my eyes sit turning, at the cool air
the glance of light, or hard flesh
rubbed against me, a woman, a man,
without shadow, or voice, or meaning.

This is the enclosure (flesh,
where innocence is a weapon. An
abstraction. Touch. (Not mine.
Or yours, if you are the soul I had
and abandoned when I was blind and had
my enemies carry me as a dead man
(if he is beautiful, or pitied.

It can be pain. (As now, as all his
flesh hurts me.) It can be that. Or
pain. As when she ran from me into
that forest.
Or pain, the mind
silver spiraled whirled against the
sun, higher than even old men thought
God would be. Or pain. And the other. The
yes. (Inside his books, his fingers. They
are withered yellow flowers and were never
beautiful.) The yes. You will, lost soul, say
'beauty.' Beauty, practiced, as the tree. The
slow river. A white sun in its wet sentences.

Or, the cold men in their gale. Ecstasy. Flesh
or soul. The yes. (Their robes blown. Their bowls
empty. They chant at my heels, not at yours.) Flesh
or soul, as corrupt. Where the answer moves too quickly.
Where the God is a self, after all.)

Cold air blown through narrow blind eyes. Flesh,
white hot metal. Glows as the day with its sun.

It is a human love, I live inside. A bony skeleton
you recognize as words or simple feeling.

But it has no feeling. As the metal, is hot, it is not,
given to love.

It burns the thing
Inside it. And that thing
screams.

A Poem Some People Will Have to Understand

Dull unwashed windows of eyes
and buildings of industry. What
industry do I practice? A slick
colored boy, 12 miles from his
home. I practice no industry.
I am no longer a credit
to my race. I read a little,
scratch against silence slow spring
afternoons.
        I had thought, before, some years ago
that I'd come to the end of my life.
        Watercolor ego. Without the preciseness
a violent man could propose.
        But the wheel, and the wheels,
wont let us alone. All the fantasy
        and justice, and dry charcoal winters
All the pitifully intelligent citizens
        I've forced myself to love.

        We have awaited the coming of a natural
        phenomenon. Mystics and romantics, knowledgeable
        workers
        of the land.

But none has come.
(Repeat)
        but none has come.
Will the machinegunners please step forward?

Three Movements and a Coda

THE QUALITY OF NIGHT THAT YOU HATE MOST IS ITS BLACK
AND ITS STARTEETH EYES, AND STICKS ITS STICKY FINGERS
IN YOUR EARS. RED NIGGER EYES LOOKING UP FROM A BLACK HOLE.
RED NIGGER LIPS TURNING KILLER GEOMETRY, LIKE HIS EYES ROLL UP
LIKE HE THOUGHT RELIGION WAS BEBOP.
        LIKE HE THOUGHT RELIGION WAS
        BEBOP . . . SIXTEEN KILLERS ON A

LIVE MAN'S CHEST . . .
THE LONE RANGER
IS DEAD.
THE SHADOW
IS DEAD.
ALL YOUR HEROES ARE DYING. J. EDGAR HOOVER WILL
SOON BE DEAD. YOUR MOTHER WILL DIE. LYNDON JOHNSON,
these are natural
things. No one is
threatening anybody
thats just the way life
is,
boss.

Red Spick talking to you from a foxhole very close to the
Vampire Nazis' lines. I can see a few Vampire Nazis moving very quickly
back and forth under the heavy smoke. I hear, and perhaps you do, in
the back ground, the steady deadly cough of mortars, and the light shatter
of machine guns.

BANZAI!! BANZAI!! BANZAI!! BANZAI!! BANZAI!!

Came running out of the drugstore window with
an electric alarm clock, and then dropped the motherfucker
and broke it. Go get somethin' else. Take everything in there.
Look in the cashregister. TAKE THE MONEY. TAKE THE MONEY. YEH.
TAKE IT ALL. YOU DON'T HAVE TO CLOSE THE DRAWER. COME ON MAN,
I SAW
A TAPE RECORDER BACK THERE.
These are the words of lovers.
Of dancers, of dynamite singers
These are songs if you have the
music

Numbers, Letters

If you're not home, where
are you? Where'd you go? What
were you doing when gone? When
you come back, better make it good.
What was you doing down there, freakin' off
with white women, hangin' out
with Queens, say it straight to be
understood straight, put it flat and real
in the street where the sun comes and the
moon comes and the cold wind in winter
waters your eyes. Say what you mean, dig
it out put it down, and be strong
about it.

I cant say who I am
unless you agree I'm real

I cant be anything I'm not
Except these words pretend
to life not yet explained,
so here's some feeling for you
see how you like it, what it
reveals, and that's me.

Dope

uuuuuuuuuu
uuuuuuuuuu
uuuuuuuuuu uuu ray light morning fire lynch yet
uuuuuuu, yester-pain in dreams
comes again. race-pain, people our people our people
everywhere . . . yeh . . . uuuuu. yeh uuuuu.yeh
our people
yes people
every people
most people
uuuuuu, yeh uuuuu, most people
in pain
yester-pain, and pain today
(Screams) ooowow! ooowow! It must be the devil
(jumps up like a claw stuck him) oooo wow! oooowow! (screams)

It must be the devil
It must be the devil
it must be the devil
(shakes like evangelical sanctify
shakes tambourine like evangelical sanctify in heat)

ooowow! ooowow! yeh, devil, yeh, devil ooowow!

Must be the devil must be the devil
(waves plate like collection) mus is mus is mus is
mus is be the devil, cain be rockerfeller (eyes roll
up batting, and jumping all the way around to face the
other direction) caint be him, no lawd
caint be dupont, no lawd, cain be, no lawd, no way
noway, naw saw, no way jose—cain be them rich folks
theys good to us theys good to us theys good to us theys
good to us theys good to us, i know, the massa tolt me
so, i seed it on channel 7, i seed it on channel 9 i seed
it on channel 4 and 2 and 5. Rich folks good to us
poor folks aint shit, hallelujah, hallelujah, ooowow! oowow!
must be the devil, going to heaven after i die, after we die

everything gonna be different, after we die we aint gon be
hungry, ain gon be pain, ain gon be sufferin wont go thru this
again, after we die, after we die owooo! owowoooo!
after we die, its all gonna be good, have all the money we
need after we die, have all the food we need after we die
have a nice house like the rich folks, after we die, after we die, after we
die, we can live like rev ike, after we die, hallelujah, hallelujah, must be
the devil, it ain capitalism, it aint capitalism, it aint capitalism,
naw it ain that, jimmy carter wdnt lie, "lifes unfair" but it aint capitalism
must be the devil, owow! it ain the police, jimmy carter wdnt lie, you
know rosalynn wdnt not lillian, his drunken racist brother aint no reflection
on jimmy, must be the devil got in im, i tell you, the devil killed malcolm
and dr king too, even killed both kennedies, and pablo neruda and overthrew
allende's govt. killed lumumba, and is negotiating with step and fetchit,
sleep n eat and birmingham, over there in "Rhodesia", goin' under the name
ian smith, must be the devil, caint be vorster, caint be apartheid, caint
be imperialism, jimmy carter wdnt lie, didn't you hear him say in his state
of the union message, i swear on rosalynn's face-lifted catatonia, i wdnt lie
nixon lied, haldeman lied, dean lied, hoover lied hoover sucked (dicks) too
but jimmy dont, jimmy wdnt jimmy aint lying, must be the devil, put yr
money on the plate, must be the devil, in heaven we'all all be straight.
cain be rockfeller, he gave amos pootbootie a scholarship to Behavior
Modification Univ, and Genevieve Almoswhite works for his foundation
Must be niggers! Cain be Mellon, he gave Winky Suckass, a fellowship in
his bank put him in charge of closing out mortgages in the lowlife
Pittsburgh Hill nigger section, caint be him.
(Goes on babbling, and wailing, jerking in pathocrazy grin stupor)
Yessuh, yessuh, yessuh, yessuh, yessuh, yessuh, yessuh, yessuh, yessuh, yessuh
put yr money in the plate, dont be late, dont have to wait, you gonna be in
heaven after you die, you gon get all you need once you gone, yessuh, i heard

it on *the jeffersons,* i heard it on *the rookies,* i swallowed it
whole on *roots:* wasn't it nice slavery was so cool and
all you had to do was wear derbies and vests and train chickens and buy your
way free if you had a mind to, must be the devil, wasnt no *white* folks,
lazy niggers chained theyselves and threw they own black asses in the bottom
of the boats, [(well now that you mention it King Assblackuwasi helped throw yr ass in
the bottom of the boat, yo mamma, wife, and you never seed em no more)] must
a been the devil, gimme your money put your money in this plate, heaven be
here soon, just got to die, just got to stop living, close yr eyes stop
breathin and bammm-O heaven be here, you have all a what you need, Bam-O
all a sudden, heaven be here, you have all you need, that assembly line
you work on will dissolve in thin air owowoo! owowoo! Just gotta die
just gotta die, this ol world aint nuthin, must be the devil got you
thinkin so, it cain be rockefeller, it cain be morgan, it caint be capitalism
it caint be national oppression owow! No Way! Now go back to work and cool
it, go back to work and lay back, just a little while longer till you pass
its all gonna be alright once you gone. gimme that last bitta silver you got
stashed there sister, gimme that dust now brother man, itll be ok on the
other side, yo soul be clean be washed pure white. yes. yes. yes. owow.
now go back to work, go to sleep, yes, go to sleep, go back to work, yes
owow. owow. uuuuuuuuuu. uuuuuuuuuu. uuuuuuuuu. yes, uuuuuuu. yes. uuuuuuuuuu.
a men

Wise 1

WHY's
(Nobody Knows
The Trouble I Seen)
(Trad.)

If you ever find
yourself, some where
lost and surrounded
by enemies
who won't let you
speak in your own language
who destroy your statues

& instruments, who ban
your oom boom ba boom
then you are in trouble
deep trouble
they ban your
oom boom ba boom
you in deep deep
trouble
humph!
probably take you several hundred years
to get
out!

Dutchman

Dutchman was first presented at The Cherry Lane Theatre, New York City on March 24, 1964.

Original Cast: Jennifer West, Robert Hooks

Produced by Theater 1964
(Richard Barr, Clinton Wilder, Edward Albee)

Directed by Edward Parone

Characters

CLAY, twenty-year-old Negro

LULA, thirty-year-old white woman

RIDERS OF COACH, white and black

YOUNG NEGRO

CONDUCTOR

In the flying underbelly of the city. Steaming hot, and summer on top, outside. Underground. The subway heaped in modern myth.

Opening scene is a man sitting in a subway seat, holding a magazine but looking vacantly just above its wilting pages. Occasionally he looks blankly toward the window on his right. Dim lights and darkness whistling by against the glass. (Or paste the lights, as admitted props, right on the subway windows. Have them move, even dim and flicker. But give the sense of speed. Also stations, whether the train is stopped or the glitter and activity of these stations merely flashes by the windows.)

The man is sitting alone. That is, only his seat is visible, though the rest of the car is outfitted as a complete subway car. But only his seat is shown. There might be, for a time, as the play begins, a loud scream of the actual train. And it can recur throughout the play, or continue on a lower key once the dialogue starts.

The train slows after a time, pulling to a brief stop at one of the stations. The man looks idly up, until he sees a woman's face staring at him through the window; when it realizes that the man has noticed the face, it begins very premeditatedly to smile. The man smiles too, for a moment, without a trace of self-consciousness. Almost an instinctive though undesirable response. Then a kind of awkwardness or embarrassment sets in, and the man makes to look away, is further embarrassed, so he brings back his eyes to where the face was, but by now the train is moving again, and the face would seem to be left behind by the way the man turns his head to look back through the other windows at the slowly fading platform. He smiles then; more comfortably confident, hoping perhaps that his memory of this brief encounter will be pleasant. And then he is idle again.

Scene I

Train roars. Lights flash outside the windows.

LULA *enters from the rear of the car in bright, skimpy summer clothes and sandals. She carries a net bag full of paper books, fruit, and other anonymous articles. She is wearing sunglasses, which she pushes up on her forehead from time to time.* LULA *is a tall, slender, beautiful woman with long red hair hanging straight down her back, wearing only loud lipstick in somebody's good taste. She is eating an apple, very daintily. Coming down the car toward* CLAY.

She stops beside CLAY*'s seat and hangs languidly from the strap, still managing to eat the apple. It is apparent that she is going to sit in the seat next to* CLAY, *and that she is only waiting for him to notice her before she sits.*

CLAY *sits as before, looking just beyond his magazine, now and again pulling the magazine slowly back and forth in front of his face in a hopeless effort to fan himself. Then he sees the woman hanging there beside him and he looks up into her face, smiling quizzically.*

LULA Hello.

CLAY Uh, hi're you?

LULA I'm going to sit down. . . . O.K.?

CLAY Sure.

LULA *(Swings down onto the seat, pushing her legs straight out as if she is very weary)* Oooof! Too much weight.

CLAY Ha, doesn't look like much to me. *(Leaning back against the window, a little surprised and maybe stiff)*

LULA It's so anyway. *(And she moves her toes in the sandals, then pulls her right leg up on the left knee, better to inspect the bottoms of the sandals and the back of her heel. She appears for a second not to notice that* CLAY *is sitting next to her or that she has spoken to him just a second before.* CLAY *looks at the magazine, then out the black window. As he does this, she turns very quickly toward him)* Weren't you staring at me through the window?

CLAY *(Wheeling around and very much stiffened)* What?

LULA Weren't you staring at me through the window? At the last stop?

CLAY Staring at you? What do you mean?

LULA Don't you know what staring means?

CLAY I saw you through the window . . . if that's what it means. I don't know if I was staring. Seems to me you were staring through the window at me.

LULA I was. But only after I'd turned around and saw you staring through that window down in the vicinity of my ass and legs.

CLAY Really?

LULA Really. I guess you were just taking those idle potshots. Nothing else to do. Run your mind over people's flesh.

CLAY Oh boy. Wow, now I admit I was looking in your direction. But the rest of that weight is yours.

LULA I suppose.

CLAY Staring through train windows is weird business. Much weirder than staring very sedately at abstract asses.

LULA That's why I came looking through the window . . . so you'd have more than that to go on. I even smiled at you.

CLAY That's right.

LULA I even got into this train, going some other way than mine. Walked down the aisle . . . searching you out.

CLAY Really? That's pretty funny.

LULA That's pretty funny. . . . God, you're dull.

CLAY Well, I'm sorry, lady, but I really wasn't prepared for party talk.

LULA No, you're not. What are you prepared for? *(Wrapping the apple core in a Kleenex and dropping it on the floor)*

CLAY *(Takes her conversation as pure sex talk. He turns to confront her squarely with this idea)* I'm prepared for anything. How about you?

LULA *(Laughing loudly and cutting it off abruptly)* What do you think you're doing?

CLAY What?

LULA You think I want to pick you up, get you to take me somewhere and screw me, huh?

CLAY Is that the way I look?

LULA You look like you been trying to grow a beard. That's exactly what you look like. You look like you live in New Jersey with your parents and are trying to grow a beard. That's what. You look like you've been reading Chinese poetry and drinking lukewarm sugarless tea. *(Laughs, uncrossing and recrossing her legs)* You look like death eating a soda cracker.

CLAY *(Cocking his head from one side to the other, embarrassed and trying to make some comeback, but also intrigued by what the woman is saying . . . even the sharp city coarse-*

ness of her voice, which is still a kind of gentle sidewalk throb) Really? I look like all that?

LULA Not all of it. *(She feints a seriousness to cover an actual somber tone)* I lie a lot. *(Smiling)* It helps me control the world.

CLAY *(Relieved and laughing louder than the humor)* Yeah, I bet.

LULA But it's true, most of it, right? Jersey? Your bumpy neck?

CLAY How'd you know all that? Huh? Really, I mean about Jersey . . . and even the beard. I met you before? You know Warren Enright?

LULA You tried to make it with your sister when you were ten.

*(*CLAY *leans back hard against the back of the seat, his eyes opening now, still trying to look amused)*

LULA But I succeeded a few weeks ago. *(She starts to laugh again)*

CLAY What're you talking about? Warren tell you that? You're a friend of Georgia's?

LULA I told you I lie. I don't know your sister. I don't know Warren Enright.

CLAY You mean you're just picking these things out of the air?

LULA Is Warren Enright a tall skinny black black boy with a phony English accent?

CLAY I figured you knew him.

LULA But I don't. I just figured you would know somebody like that. *(Laughs)*

CLAY Yeah, yeah.

LULA You're probably on your way to his house now.

CLAY That's right.

LULA *(Putting her hand on* CLAY*'s closest knee, drawing it from the knee up to the thigh's hinge, then removing it, watching his face very closely, and continuing to laugh, perhaps more gently than before)* Dull, dull, dull. I bet you think I'm exciting.

CLAY You're O.K.

LULA Am I exciting you now?

CLAY Right. That's not what's supposed to happen?

LULA How do I know? *(She returns her hand, without moving it, then takes it away and plunges it in her bag to draw out an apple)* You want this?

CLAY Sure.

LULA *(She gets one out of the bag for herself)* Eating apples together is always the first step. Or walking up uninhabited Seventh Avenue in the twenties on weekends. *(Bites and giggles, glancing at* CLAY *and speaking in loose sing-song)* Can get you involved . . . boy! Get us involved. Um-huh. *(Mock seriousness)* Would you like to get involved with me, Mister Man?

CLAY *(Trying to be as flippant as* LULA*, whacking happily at the apple)* Sure. Why not? A beautiful woman like you. Huh, I'd be a fool not to.

LULA And I bet you're sure you know what you're talking about. *(Taking him a little roughly by the wrist, so he cannot eat the apple, then shaking the wrist)* I bet you're sure of almost everything anybody ever asked you about . . . right? *(Shakes his wrist harder)* Right?

CLAY Yeah, right. . . . Wow, you're pretty strong, you know? Whatta you, a lady wrestler or something?

LULA What's wrong with lady wrestlers? And don't answer because you never knew any. Huh. *(Cynically)* That's for sure. They don't have any lady wrestlers in that part of Jersey. That's for sure.

CLAY Hey, you still haven't told me how you know so much about me.

LULA I told you I didn't know anything about you . . . you're a well-known type.

CLAY Really?

LULA Or at least I know the type very well. And your skinny English friend too.

CLAY Anonymously?

LULA *(Settles back in seat, single-mindedly finishing her apple and humming snatches of rhythm and blues song)* What?

CLAY Without knowing us specifically?

LULA Oh boy. *(Looking quickly at* CLAY*)* What a face. You know, you could be a handsome man.

CLAY I can't argue with you.

LULA *(Vague, off-center response)* What?

CLAY *(Raising his voice, thinking the train noise has drowned part of his sentence)* I can't argue with you.

LULA My hair is turning gray. A gray hair for each year and type I've come through.

CLAY Why do you want to sound so old?

LULA But it's always gentle when it starts. *(Attention drifting)* Hugged against tenements, day or night.

CLAY What?

LULA *(Refocusing)* Hey, why don't you take me to that party you're going to?

CLAY You must be a friend of Warren's to know about the party.

LULA Wouldn't you like to take me to the party? *(Imitates clinging vine)* Oh, come on, ask me to your party.

CLAY Of course I'll ask you to come with me to the party. And I'll bet you're a friend of Warren's.

LULA Why not be a friend of Warren's? Why not? *(Taking his arm)* Have you asked me yet?

CLAY How can I ask you when I don't know your name?

LULA Are you talking to my name?

CLAY What is it, a secret?

LULA I'm Lena the Hyena.

CLAY The famous woman poet?

LULA Poetess! The same!

CLAY Well, you know so much about me... what's my name?

LULA Morris the Hyena.

CLAY The famous woman poet?

LULA The same. *(Laughing and going into her bag)* You want another apple?

CLAY Can't make it, lady. I only have to keep one doctor away a day.

LULA I bet your name is... something like... uh, Gerald or Walter. Huh?

CLAY God, no.

LULA Lloyd, Norman? One of those hopeless colored names creeping out of New Jersey. Leonard? Gag....

CLAY Like Warren?

LULA Definitely. Just exactly like Warren. Or Everett.

CLAY Gag....

LULA Well, for sure, it's not Willie.

CLAY It's Clay.

LULA Clay? Really? Clay what?

CLAY Take your pick. Jackson, Johnson, or Williams.

LULA Oh, really? Good for you. But it's got to be Williams. You're too pretentious to be a Jackson or Johnson.

CLAY Thass right.

LULA But Clay's O.K.

CLAY So's Lena.

LULA It's Lula.

CLAY Oh?

LULA Lula the Hyena.

CLAY Very good.

LULA *(Starts laughing again)* Now you say to me, "Lula, Lula, why don't you go to this party with me tonight?" It's your turn, and let those be your lines.

CLAY Lula, why don't you go to this party with me tonight. Huh?

LULA Say my name twice before you ask, and no huh's.

CLAY Lula, Lula, why don't you go to this party with me tonight?

LULA I'd like to go, Clay, but how can you ask me to go when you barely know me?

CLAY That is strange, isn't it?

LULA What kind of reaction is that? You're supposed to say, "Aw, come on, we'll get to know each other better at the party."

CLAY That's pretty corny.

LULA What are you into anyway? *(Looking at him half sullenly but still amused)* What thing are you playing at, Mister? Mister Clay Williams? *(Grabs his thigh, up near the crotch)* What are you thinking about?

CLAY Watch it now, you're gonna excite me for real.

LULA *(Taking her hand away and throwing her apple core through the window)* I bet. *(She slumps in the seat and is heavily silent)*

CLAY I thought you knew everything about me? What happened?

*(*LULA *looks at him, then looks slowly away, then over where the other aisle would be. Noise of the train. She reaches in her bag and pulls out one of the paper books. She puts it on her leg and thumbs the pages listlessly.* CLAY *cocks his head to see the title of the book. Noise of the train.* LULA *flips pages and her eyes drift. Both remain silent)*

CLAY Are you going to the party with me, Lula?

LULA *(Bored and not even looking)* I don't even know you.

CLAY You said you know my type.

LULA *(Strangely irritated)* Don't get smart with me, Buster. I know you like the palm of my hand.

CLAY The one you eat the apples with?

LULA Yeh. And the one I open doors late Saturday evening with. That's my door. Up at the top of the stairs. Five flights. Above a lot of Italians and lying Americans. And scrape carrots with. Also . . . *(looks at him)* the same hand I unbutton my dress with, or let my skirt fall down. Same hand. Lover.

CLAY Are you angry about anything? Did I say something wrong?

LULA Everything you say is wrong. *(Mock smile)* That's what makes you so attractive. Ha. In that funnybook jacket with all the buttons. *(More animate, taking hold of his jacket)* What've you got that jacket and tie on in all this heat for? And why're you wearing a jacket and tie like that? Did your people ever burn witches or start revolutions over the price of tea? Boy, those narrow-shoulder clothes come from a tradition you ought to feel oppressed by. A three-button suit. What right do you have to be wearing a three-button suit and striped tie? Your grandfather was a slave, he didn't go to Harvard.

CLAY My grandfather was a night watchman.

LULA And you went to a colored college where everybody thought they were Averell Harriman.

CLAY All except me.

LULA And who did you think you were? Who do you think you are now?

CLAY *(Laughs as if to make light of the whole trend of the conversation)* Well, in college I thought I was Baudelaire. But I've slowed down since.

LULA I bet you never once thought you were a black nigger.

(Mock serious, then she howls with laughter. CLAY *is stunned but after initial reaction, he quickly tries to appreciate the humor.* LULA *almost shrieks)*

LULA A black Baudelaire.

CLAY That's right.

LULA Boy, are you corny. I take back what I said before. Everything you say is not wrong. It's perfect. You should be on television.

CLAY You act like you're on television already.

LULA That's because I'm an actress.

CLAY I thought so.

LULA Well, you're wrong. I'm no actress. I told you I always lie. I'm nothing, honey, and don't you ever forget it. *(Lighter)* Although my mother was a Communist. The only person in my family ever to amount to anything.

CLAY My mother was a Republican.

LULA And your father voted for the man rather than the party.

CLAY Right!

LULA Yea for him. Yea, yea for him.

CLAY Yea!

LULA And yea for America where he is free to vote for the mediocrity of his choice! Yea!

CLAY Yea!

LULA And yea for both your parents who even though they differ about so crucial a matter as the body politic still forged a union of love and sacrifice that was destined to flower at the birth of the noble Clay . . . what's your middle name?

CLAY Clay.

LULA A union of love and sacrifice that was destined to flower at the birth of the noble Clay Clay Williams. Yea! And most of all yea yea for you, Clay Clay. The Black Baudelaire. Yes! *(And with knifelike cynicism)* My Christ. My Christ.

CLAY Thank you ma'am.

LULA May the people accept you as a ghost of the future. And love you, that you might not kill them when you can.

CLAY What?

LULA You're a murderer, Clay, and you know it. *(Her voice darkening with significance)* You know goddamn well what I mean.

CLAY I do?

LULA So we'll pretend the air is light and full of perfume.

CLAY *(Sniffing at her blouse)* It is.

LULA And we'll pretend the people cannot see you. That is, the citizens. And that you are free of your own history. And I am free of my history. We'll pretend that we are both anonymous beauties smashing along through the city's entrails. *(She yells as loud as she can)* GROOVE!

Black

Scene II

Scene is the same as before, though now there are other seats visible in the car. And throughout the scene other people get on the subway. There are maybe one or two seated in the car as the scene opens, though neither CLAY *nor* LULA *notices them.* CLAY*'s tie is open.* LULA *is hugging his arm.*

CLAY The party!

LULA I know it'll be something good. You can come in with me, looking casual and significant. I'll be strange, haughty, and silent, and walk with long slow strides.

CLAY Right.

LULA When you get drunk, pat me once, very lovingly on the flanks, and I'll look at you cryptically, licking my lips.

CLAY It sounds like something we can do.

LULA You'll go around talking to young men about your mind, and to old men about your plans. If you meet a very close friend who is also with someone like me, we can stand together, sipping our drinks and exchanging codes of lust. The atmosphere will be slithering in love and half-love and very open moral decision.

CLAY Great. Great.

LULA And everyone will pretend they don't know your name, and then . . . *(She pauses heavily)* later, when they have to, they'll claim a friendship that denies your sterling character.

CLAY *(Kissing her neck and fingers)* And then what?

LULA Then? Well, then we'll go down the street, late night, eating apples and winding very deliberately toward my house.

CLAY Deliberately?

LULA I mean, we'll look in all the shopwindows, and make fun of the queers. Maybe we'll meet a Jewish Buddhist and flatten his conceits over some very pretentious coffee.

CLAY In honor of whose God?

LULA Mine.

CLAY Who is . . . ?

LULA Me . . . and you?

CLAY A corporate Godhead.

LULA Exactly. Exactly *(Notices one of the other people entering)*

CLAY Go on with the chronicle. Then what happens to us?

LULA *(A mild depression, but she still makes her description triumphant and increasingly direct)* To my house, of course.

CLAY Of course.

LULA And up the narrow steps of the tenement.

CLAY You live in a tenement?

LULA Wouldn't live anywhere else. Reminds me specifically of my novel form of insanity.

CLAY Up the tenement stairs.

LULA And with my apple-eating hand I push open the door and lead you, my tender big-eyed prey, into my . . . God, what can I call it . . . into my hovel.

CLAY Then what happens?

LULA After the dancing and games, after the long drinks and long walks, the real fun begins.

CLAY Ah, the real fun. *(Embarrassed, in spite of himself)* Which is . . . ?

LULA *(Laughs at him)* Real fun in the dark house. Hah! Real fun in the dark house, high up above the street and the ignorant cowboys. I lead you in, holding your wet hand gently in my hand . . .

CLAY Which is not wet?

LULA Which is dry as ashes.

CLAY And cold?

LULA Don't think you'll get out of your responsibility that way. It's not cold at all. You Fascist! Into my dark living room. Where we'll sit and talk endlessly, endlessly.

CLAY About what?

LULA About what? About your manhood, what do you think? What do you think we've been talking about all this time?

CLAY Well, I didn't know it was that. That's for sure. Every other thing in the world but that. *(Notices another person entering, looks quickly, almost involuntarily up and down the car, seeing the other people in the car)* Hey, I didn't even notice when those people got on.

LULA Yeah, I know.

CLAY Man, this subway is slow.

LULA Yeah, I know.

CLAY Well, go on. We were talking about my manhood.

LULA We still are. All the time.

CLAY We were in your living room.

LULA My dark living room. Talking endlessly.

CLAY About my manhood.

LULA I'll make you a map of it. Just as soon as we get to my house.

CLAY Well, that's great.

LULA One of the things we do while we talk. And screw.

CLAY *(Trying to make his smile broader and less shaky)* We finally got there.

LULA And you'll call my rooms black as a grave. You'll say, "This place is like Juliet's tomb."

CLAY *(Laughs)* I might.

LULA I know. You've probably said it before.

CLAY And is that all? The whole grand tour?

LULA Not all. You'll say to me very close to my face, many, many times, you'll say, even whisper, that you love me.

CLAY Maybe I will.

LULA And you'll be lying.

CLAY I wouldn't lie about something like that.

LULA Hah. It's the only kind of thing you will lie about. Especially if you think it'll keep me alive.

CLAY Keep you alive? I don't understand.

LULA *(Bursting out laughing, but too shrilly)* Don't understand? Well, don't look at me. It's the path I take, that's all. Where both feet take me when I set them down. One in front of the other.

CLAY Morbid. Morbid. You sure you're not an actress? All that self-aggrandizement.

LULA Well, I told you I wasn't an actress . . . but I also told you I lie all the time. Draw your own conclusions.

CLAY Is that all of our history together you've described? There's no more?

LULA I've told you all I know. Or almost all.

CLAY There's no funny parts?

LULA I thought it was all funny.

CLAY But you mean peculiar, not ha-ha.

LULA You don't know what I mean.

CLAY Well, tell me the almost part then. You said almost all. What else? I want the whole story.

LULA *(Searching aimlessly through her bag. She begins to talk breathlessly, with a light and silly tone)* All stories are whole stories. All of 'em. Our whole story . . . nothing but change. How could things go on like that forever? Huh? *(Slaps him on the shoulder, begins finding things in her bag, taking them out and throwing them over her shoulder into the aisle)* Except I do go on as I do. Apples and long walks with deathless intelligent lovers. But you mix it up. Look out the window, all the time. Turning pages. Change change change. Till, shit, I don't know you. Wouldn't, for that matter. You're too serious. I bet you're even too serious to be psychoanalyzed. Like all those Jewish poets from Yonkers, who leave their mothers looking for other mothers, or others' mothers, on whose baggy tits they lay their fumbling heads. Their poems are always funny, and all about sex.

CLAY They sound great. Like movies.

LULA But you change. *(Blankly)* And things work on you till you hate them.

(More people come into the train. They come closer to the couple, some of them not sitting, but swinging drearily on the straps, starring at the two with uncertain interest)

CLAY Wow. All these people, so suddenly. They must all come from the same place.

LULA Right. That they do.

CLAY Oh? You know about them too?

LULA Oh yeah. About them more than I know about you. Do they frighten you?

CLAY Frighten me? Why should they frighten me?

LULA 'Cause you're an escaped nigger.

CLAY Yeah?

LULA 'Cause you crawled through the wire and made tracks to my side.

CLAY Wire?

LULA Don't they have wire around plantations?

CLAY You must be Jewish. All you can think about is wire. Plantations didn't have any wire. Plantations were big open whitewashed places like heaven, and everybody on 'em was grooved to be there. Just strummin' and hummin' all day.

LULA Yes, yes.

CLAY And that's how the blues was born.

LULA Yes, yes. And that's how the blues was born.

(LULA begins to make up a song that becomes quickly hysterical. As she sings she rises from her seat, still throwing things out of her bag into the aisle, beginning a rhythmical shudder and twist-like wiggle, which she continues up and down the aisle, bumping into many of the standing people and tripping over the feet of those sitting. Each time she runs into a person she lets out a very vicious piece of profanity, wiggling and stepping all the time)

LULA And that's how the blues was born. Yes. Yes. Son of a bitch, get out of the way. Yes. Quack. Yes. Yes. And that's how the blues was born. Ten little niggers sitting on a limb, but none of them ever looked like him. *(Points to CLAY, returns toward the seat, with her hands extended for him to rise and dance with her)* And that's how blues was born. Yes. Come on, Clay. Let's do the nasty. Rub bellies. Rub bellies.

CLAY *(Waves his hands to refuse. He is embarrassed, but determined to get a kick out of the proceedings)* Hey, what was in those apples? Mirror, mirror on the wall, who's the fairest one of all? Snow White, baby, and don't you forget it.

LULA *(Grabbing for his hands, which he draws away)* Come on, Clay. Let's rub bellies on the train. The nasty. The nasty. Do the gritty grind, like your ol'rag-head mammy. Grind till you lose your mind. Shake it, shake it, shake it, shake it. OOOOweeee! Come on, Clay. Let's do the choo-choo train shuffle, the navel scratcher.

CLAY Hey, you coming on like the lady who smoked up her grass skirt.

LULA *(Becoming annoyed that he will not dance, and becoming more animated as if to embarrass him still further)* Come on, Clay . . . let's do the thing. Uhh! Uhh! Clay! Clay! You middle-class black bastard. Forget your social-working mother for a few seconds and let's knock stomachs. Clay, you liver-lipped white man. You would-be Christian. You ain't no nigger, you're just a dirty white man. Get up, Clay. Dance with me, Clay.

CLAY Lula! Sit down, now. Be cool.

LULA *(Mocking him, in wild dance)* Be cool. Be cool. That's all you know . . . shaking that wildroot cream-oil on your knotty head, jackets buttoning up to your chin, so full of white man's words. Christ. God. Get up and scream at these people. Like scream meaningless shit in these hopeless faces. *(She screams at people in train, still dancing)* Red trains cough Jewish underwear for keeps! Expanding smells of silence. Gravy snot whistling like sea birds. Clay, Clay, you got to break out. Don't sit there dying the way they want you to die. Get up.

CLAY Oh, sit the fuck down. *(He moves to restrain her)* Sit down, goddamn it.

LULA *(Twisting out of his reach)* Screw yourself, Uncle Tom. Thomas Woolly-Head. *(Begins to dance a kind of jig, mocking* CLAY *with loud forced humor)* There is Uncle Tom . . . I mean, Uncle Thomas Woolly-Head. With old white matted mane. He hobbles on his wooden cane. Old Tom. Old Tom. Let the white man hump his ol' mama, and he jes' shuffle off in the woods and hide his gentle gray head. Ol' Thomas Woolly-Head.

(Some of the other riders are laughing now. A drunk gets up and joins LULA *in her dance, singing, as best he can, her "song."* CLAY *gets up out of his seat and visibly scans the faces of the other riders)*

CLAY Lula! Lula!

(She is dancing and turning, still shouting as loud as she can. The drunk too is shouting, and waving his hands wildly)

CLAY Lula . . . you dumb bitch. Why don't you stop it? *(He rushes half stumbling from his seat, and grabs one of her flailing arms)*

LULA Let me go! You black son of bitch. *(She struggles against him)* Let me go! Help!

*(*CLAY *is dragging her towards her seat, and the drunk seeks to interfere. He grabs* CLAY *around the shoulders and begins wrestling with him.* CLAY *clubs the drunk to the floor without releasing* LULA, *who is still screaming.* CLAY *finally gets her to the seat and throws her into it)*

CLAY Now you shut the hell up. *(Grabbing her shoulders)* Just shut up. You don't know what you're talking about. You don't know anything. So just keep your stupid mouth closed.

LULA You're afraid of white people. And your father was. Uncle Tom Big Lip!

*(*CLAY *slaps her as hard as he can, across the mouth.* LULA*'s head bangs against the back of the seat. When she raises it again,* CLAY *slaps her again)*

CLAY Now shut up and let me talk.

(He turns toward the other riders, some of whom are sitting on the edge of their seats. The drunk is on one knee, rubbing his head, and singing softly the same song. He shuts up too when he sees CLAY *watching him. The others go back to newspapers or stare out the windows)*

CLAY Shit, you don't have any sense, Lula, nor feelings either. I could murder you now. Such a tiny ugly throat. I could squeeze it flat, and watch you turn blue, on a humble. For dull kicks. And all these weak-faced ofays squatting around here, staring over their papers at me. Murder them too. Even if they expected it. That man there . . . *(Points to well-dressed man)* I could rip that *Times* right out of his hand, as skinny and middle-classed as I am, I could rip that paper out of his hand and just as easily rip out his throat. It takes no great effort. For what? To kill you soft idiots? You don't understand anything but luxury.

LULA You fool!

CLAY *(Pushing her against the seat)* I'm not telling you again, Tallulah Bankhead! Luxury. In your face and your fingers. You telling me what I ought to do. *(Sudden scream frightening the whole coach)* Well, don't! Don't you tell me anything! If I'm a middle-class fake white man . . . let me be. And let me be in the way I want. *(Through his teeth)* I'll rip your lousy breasts off! Let me be who I feel like being. Uncle Tom. Thomas. Whoever. It's none of your business. You don't know anything except what's there for you to see. An act. Lies. Device. Not the pure heart, the pumping black heart. You don't ever know that. And I sit here, in this buttoned-up suit, to keep myself from cutting all your throats. I mean wantonly. You great liberated whore! You fuck some black man, and right away you're an expert on black people. What a lotta shit that is. The only thing you know is that you come if he bangs you hard enough. And that's all. The belly rub? You wanted to do the belly rub? Shit, you don't even know how. You don't know how. That ol'dipty-dip shit you do, rolling your ass like an elephant. That's not my kind of belly rub. Belly rub is not Queens. Belly rub is dark places, with big hats and overcoats held up with one arm. Belly rub hates you. Old bald-headed four-eyed ofays popping their fingers . . . and don't know yet what they're doing. They say, "I love Bessie Smith." And don't even understand that Bessie Smith is saying, "Kiss my ass, kiss my black unruly ass." Before love, suffering, desire, anything you can explain, she's saying, and very plainly, "Kiss my black ass." And if you don't know that, it's you that's doing the kissing.

Charlie Parker? Charlie Parker. All the hip white boys scream for Bird. And Bird saying, "Up your ass, feeble-minded ofay! Up your ass." And they sit there talking about the tortured genius of Charlie Parker. Bird would've played not a note of music if he just walked up to East Sixty-seventh Street and killed the first ten white people he saw. Not a note! And I'm the great would-be poet. Yes, that's right. Poet. Some kind of bastard literature . . . all it needs is a simple knife thrust. Just let me bleed you, you loud whore, and one poem vanished. A whole people of neurotics, struggling to keep from being sane. And the only thing that would cure the neurosis would be your murder. Simple as that. I mean if I murdered you, then other white people would begin to understand me. You understand? No. I guess not. If Bessie Smith had killed some white people she wouldn't have needed that music. She could have talked very straight and plain about the world. No metaphors. No grunts. No wiggles in the dark of her soul. Just straight two and two are four. Money. Power. Luxury. Like that. All of them. Crazy niggers turning their backs on sanity. When all it needs is that simple act. Murder. Just murder! Would make us all sane. *(Suddenly weary)* Ahhh. Shit. But who needs it? I'd rather be a fool. Insane. Safe with my words, and no deaths, and clean, hard thoughts, urging me to new conquests. My people's madness. Hah! That's a laugh. My people. They don't need me to claim them. They got legs and arms of their own. Personal insanities. Mirrors. They don't need all those words. They don't need any defense. But listen, though, one more thing. And you tell this to your father, who's probably the kind of man who needs to know at once. So he can plan ahead. Tell him not to preach so much rationalism and cold logic to these niggers. Let them alone. Let them sing curses at you in code and see your filth as simple lack of style. Don't make the mistake, through some irresponsible surge of Christian charity, of talking too much about the advantages of Western rationalism, or the great intellectual legacy of the white man, or maybe they'll begin to listen. And then, maybe one day, you'll find they actually do understand exactly what you are talking about, all these fantasy people. All these blues people. And on that day, as sure as shit, when you really believe you can "accept" them into your fold, as half-white trusties late of the subject peoples. With no more blues, except the very old ones, and not a watermelon in sight, the great missionary heart will have triumphed, and all of those ex-coons will be stand-up Western men, with eyes for clean hard useful lives, sober, pious and sane, and they'll murder you. They'll murder you, and have very rational explanations. Very much like your own. They'll cut your throats, and drag you out to the edge of your cities so the flesh can fall away from your bones, in sanitary isolation.

LULA *(Her voice takes on a different, more businesslike quality)* I've heard enough.

CLAY *(Reaching for his books)* I bet you have. I guess I better collect my stuff and get off this train. Looks like we won't be acting out that little pageant you outlined before.

LULA No. We won't. You're right about that, at least. *(She turns to look quickly around the rest of the car)* All right! *(The others respond)*

CLAY *(Bending across the girl to retrieve his belongings)* Sorry, baby, I don't think we could make it.

(As he is bending over her, the girl brings up a small knife and plunges it into CLAY'S *chest. Twice. He slumps across her knees, his mouth working stupidly)*

LULA Sorry is right. *(Turning to the others in the car who have already gotten up from their seats)* Sorry is the rightest thing you've said. Get this man off me! Hurry, now!

(The others come and drag CLAY'S *body down the aisle)*

LULA Open the door and throw his body out.

(They throw him off)

LULA And all of you get off at the next stop.

*(*LULA *busies herself straightening her things. Getting everything in order. She takes out a notebook and makes a quick scribbling note. Drops it in her bag. The train apparently stops and all the others get off, leaving her alone in the coach.*

Very soon a young Negro of about twenty comes into the coach, with a couple of books under his arm. He sits a few seats in back of LULA. *When he is seated she turns and gives him a long slow look. He looks up from his book and drops the book on his lap. Then an old Negro conductor comes into the car, doing a sort of restrained soft shoe, and half mumbling the words of some song. He looks at the young man, briefly, with a quick greeting)*

CONDUCTOR Hey, brother!

YOUNG MAN Hey.

(The conductor continues down the aisle with his little dance and the mumbled song. LULA *turns to stare at him and follows his movements down the aisle. The conductor tips his hat when he reaches her seat, and continues out the car)*

Curtain

JAYNE CORTEZ

(1936–)

It is no hyperbole to say that there is probably no contemporary American writer with a greater ability to direct her exquisitely developed literary style against what she views as the evil warlords of the corporate-industrial-military complexes of the Western world than the poet Jayne Cortez. Cortez can best be known through her poetry, as one senses her compassion and is drawn into sharing the anger she articulates through vivid portrayals of those whom the African novelist Frantz Fanon wrote about in *The Wretched of the Earth* (1961).

Cortez was born on May 10, 1936, in Fort Huachuca, Arizona, where her father was completing a military tour of duty. She was reared in Watts, California, a section of Los Angeles that is a well-known black American ghetto. The middle child, with an older sister and a younger brother, she is named for her Filipino maternal grandmother, Julia Cortez. Always aspiring to be an actress, she attended public schools in Watts and Compton Junior College.

Cortez married a jazz musician in 1954. They had one son, Denardo Coleman, in 1956, and were later divorced. In 1975, she married sculptor Melvin Edwards, who would become an illustrator of her works. Most photographs of Cortez depict her as a soulful and thoughtful woman in sunglasses, so that her face is not seen in full. The poetic self is hidden so that the reader must concentrate solely on her words.

Cortez claims that she was trained as a poet through membership in several Los Angeles writing clubs during the sixties and seventies. She also was the artistic director of the Watts Repertory Theater Company from 1964 to 1970. However, in 1967, she transferred her home base to New York. Her first book of poetry, *Pisstained Stairs and the Monkey Man's Wares* (1969), is a celebration of legendary African American heroes who championed the causes of freedom—especially black musicians. Of her second book, *Festivals and Funerals* (1971), Eugene Redmond wrote, "The volume extends Cortez's concerns with love and celebrations of sexuality, but the poems exhibit a move to more theoretical concerns: colonialism, African nationhood, revolution, mythology, and the role of the artist in revolutionary politics."

Cortez's third book, *Scarifications,* came out in 1973, during the Vietnam War, and it continues in those veins of protest of which Redmond wrote. For instance, she maintains in a lyrically exquisite poem titled "Orisha" that Afrocentric consciousness was retained amid the police brutality and chaos of the American urban scene. As she has often done in her later works, she juxtaposes America's treatment of Vietnamese civilians with that of the American Indians a hundred years earlier. *Mouth on Paper* (1977) continues in this mode but also includes jazz motifs, which acknowledge martyrs slain in the worldwide struggle against racism, and African "praise poetry" to celebrate the African American cultural heritage. Among the other types of poems in the volume are a fine blues adaptation ("Grinding Vibrato") and an elegy to Josephine Baker ("So Many Feathers"). In *Firespitter* (1982), Cortez further incorporates the voices of African American speech and folklore into her political messages. For example, she considers her poem "Rape" to be a human rights poem rather than a more narrowly prescribed feminist statement on physical abuse.

Undoubtedly, Cortez's most biting and antiestablishment collection is *Coagulations: New and Selected Poems* (1982). Never abandoning social protest and the Black Aesthetic matrix of her roots or her identification with the African American masses, Cortez has broadened the scope of her compassion to include all Third World peoples and all poor and battered women as well. Calling *Coagulations* a work of resistance in a 1986 review for *Callaloo,* Barbara T. Christian further wrote, "It is eminently clear from her selected edition that Jayne Cortez is a blatantly political poet—for that work intends to help us identify those who control our lives, and she rouses us to do something about it."

Another source of Cortez's efficacy is her identification with the African American jazz movement. When her poetry vehemently cries out against police forces that are brutally biased against women and people of color, or as it wails against what she believes are inhumane corporations that feed on the destruction of people and the earth, she speaks from the same heart as those musicians and singers—such as Billie Holiday, Bessie Smith, Huddie "Leadbelly" Ledbetter, Charlie Parker, Ornette Coleman, Clifford Brown, and John Coltrane—who founded and extended the American jazz movement of the 1920s and 1930s and who intended to use music as a means of creative protest against establishment institutions. When reviewing *Pisstained Stairs and the Monkey Man's Wares* (1969) in *Negro Digest* 19 (December 1969), poet Nikki Giovanni said,

> We haven't had many jazz poets who got inside the music and the people who created it. We poet about them, but not of them. And this is Cortez's strength. She can wail from Theodore Navarro and Leadbelly to Ornette and never lose a beat and never make a mistake. She's a genius and all lovers of jazz will need this book—lovers of poetry will want it.

Cortez has read her poetry as a complement to several jazz performances and recordings. She even read her poetry accompanied by the Clifford Thornton New Art Ensemble at Carnegie Hall in 1970. Her recordings include *Celebrations and Solitudes: The Poetry of Jayne Cortez* (1975), *Unsubmissive Blues* (1980), and *There It Is* (1983). In reviewing *Unsubmissive Blues* in the *Small Press Review* (March 1981), music critic Warren Woessner said that the record "is the most accomplished collaboration between a poet and a jazz group that I've listened to in years." Another reviewer, Fahamisha Patricia Brown, said in *American Women Writers* that Cortez is "a high priestess for the human race" who still has "a black woman's vision. She is seer and healer, singer and chastiser. She self-consciously assumes a 'griot' stance, singing praise" of well-deserving African writers, singers, and musicians.

In his critical text on Cortez, D. H. Melhem points out that her hands-on commitment to the Civil Rights Movement (Cortez went to Mississippi in 1963 and 1964 to help Fannie Lou Hamer with voter registration) and considerable travels to Third World countries have greatly strengthened her works. According to Melhem, she has

> read her work and lectured extensively in Africa (Ghana, Nigeria, Zimbabwe), in Latin America (Mexico, Brazil, Martinique, Trinidad, Cuba), in Europe (England, France, West Germany, the Netherlands), in Canada, and throughout the United States. She has visited Nicaragua, the Ivory Coast, and Morocco. In Asilah, Morocco, she made a series of monoprints that incorporated her poetry.

Despite the deeply troubling political controversies in Cortez's poetry she has been invited to teach, albeit in temporary positions, at various universities around the country, including Queens College, Dartmouth College, Wesleyan College, Howard University, and the University of Ibadan. From 1977 to 1983, she was writer-in-residence at Livingston College of Rutgers University. Currently, she resides in New York City.

Like most successful African American poets who established themselves in the 1960s, Cortez has won numerous accolades: Before Columbus Book Award for excellence in literature (1980); Rockefeller Foundation grant (1970); Creative Artists Public Service Poetry Awards (1973 and 1981); fellowship from the New York State Council on the Arts (1973 and 1981); and a National Endowment for the Arts fellowship for creative writing (1979–1980).

Those who still maintain the passion of the 1960s are glad that Cortez has not lost her zeal to attack poverty, oppression, genocide, misogyny, and exploitation wherever she finds them. These people believe that few writers still have that vision or are willing to express it with such boldness and venom. As with most African American poets who began their careers during the Civil Rights era, much critical and biographical work still must be done on Cortez's literary references, on the intricate symbolism that especially graces her latest works, and on her life.

❖❖❖

Don L. Lee (Haki Madhubuti) discusses Cortez's work in "Toward a Definition: Black Poetry of the Sixties," in Addison Gayle (ed.) *The Black Aesthetic* (1971), as does Eugene B. Redmond in *Drumvoices: The Mission of Afro-American Poetry*

(1976). Jon Woodson's article in the *Dictionary of Literary Biography: Afro-American Poets Since 1955*, vol. 41, edited by Trudier Harris and Thadious M. Davis.

Fahamisha Patricia Brown has a background discussion of Cortez in *American Women Writers,* edited by Carol Hurd Green and Mary Grinley (1994). Perhaps the most definitive criticism on Cortez, as well as an in-depth interview, is D. H. Melhem's chapter "Jayne Cortez: Supersurrealist Vision" in his book *Heroism in the New Black Poetry: Introductions and Interviews* (1990).

Nikki Giovanni's review, "Pisstain [sic] Stairs and the Monkey Man's Wares," *Negro Digest* 19 (December 1969) is also very insightful.

In the Morning

Disguised in my mouth as a swampland
nailed to my teeth like a rising sun
you come out in the middle of fish-scales
you bleed into gourds wrapped with red ants
you syncopate the air with lungs like screams from yazoo
like X rated tongues
and nickel plated fingers of a raw ghost man
you touch brown nipples to knives
and somewhere stripped like a whirlwind
stripped for the shrine room
you sing to me through the side face of a black rooster

In the morning in the morning in the morning
all over my door like a rooster
in the morning in the morning in the morning

And studded in my kidneys like perforated hiccups
inflamed in my ribs like three hoops of thunder through a screw
a star-bent-bolt of quivering colons
you breathe into veiled rays and scented ice holes
you fire the space like the flair of embalmed pigeons
and palpitate with the worms and venom and wailing flanks
and somewhere inside this fever
inside my patinaed pubic and camouflaged slit
stooped forward on fangs
in rear of your face
you shake to me in the full crown of a black rooster
In the morning in the morning in the morning

Masquerading in my horn like a river
eclipsed to these infantries of dentures of diving spears
you enter broken mirrors through fragmented pipe spit
you pull into a shadow ring of magic jelly
you wear the sacrificial blood of nightfall
you lift the ceiling with my tropical slush dance
you slide and tremble with the reputation of an earthquake
and when i kick through walls

to shine like silver
when i shine like brass through crust in a compound
when i shine shine shine
you wail to me in the drum call of a black rooster

In the morning in the morning in the morning
gonna kill me a rooster
in the morning
early in the morning
way down in the morning
before the sun passes by
in the morning in the morning in the morning

In the morning
when the deep sea goes through a dogs bite
and you spit on tip of your long knife

In the morning in the morning
when peroxide falls on a bed of broken glass
and the sun rises like a polyester ball of menses
in the morning
gonna firedance in the petro
in the morning
turn loose the blues in the funky jungle
in the morning
I said when you see the morning coming like
a two-headed twister
let it blow let it blow
in the morning in the morning
all swollen up like an ocean in the morning
early in the morning
before the cream dries in the bushes
in the morning
when you hear the rooster cry
cry rooster cry
in the morning in the morning in my evilness of this morning

I said
disguised in my mouth as a swampland
nailed to my teeth like a rising sun
you come out in the middle of fish-scales
you bleed into gourds wrapped with red ants
you syncopate the air with lungs like screams from yazoo
like X rated tongues
and nickel plated fingers of a raw ghost man
you touch brown nipples into knives
and somewhere stripped like a whirlwind
stripped for the shrine room
you sing to me through the side face of a black rooster

In the morning in the morning in the morning

Orisha

Across the flesh and feeling of soledad
tornados of blackness
patoised in its beauty
in its luminous fuchsia lagos nights
ruby darkness
criss-crossing in front of the music
in front of my pigeontoed solitude
another bush of praise
another battle ground for accents
insurrecting against brainwash and breakdowns
white bucks and famished lyrics
spellbound and peglegged
on cartridges of gunpowder teeth
Windpipes of burgundy lands
burning veins of respect forward into the blues
into pulsating ear of my cobra skin heart
immense in its infancy of these few words
Orisha Orisha Satchmo Orisha

So Many Feathers

You danced a magnetic dance
in your rhinestones and satin banana G-strings
it was you who cut the river
with your pink diamond tongue
did the limbo on your back
straight from the history of southern flames
onto the stage where your body
covered in metallic flint
under black and green feathers strutted
with wings of a vulture paradise on your head
strutted among the birds
until you became terror woman of all feathers
of such terrible beauty
of such fire
such flames
all feathers Josephine
This Josephine
exploding red marble eyes in new york

this Josephine
breaking color bars in miami
this Josephine
mother of orphans
legion of honor
rosette of resistance
this Josephine before
splitting the solidarity of her beautiful feathers

Feather-woman of terror
such feathers so beautiful
Josephine
with your frosted mouth half-open
why split your flamingos
with the death white boers in durban south africa
Woman with magnificent face of Ife mask
why all the teeth for the death white boers in durban
Josephine you had every eyelash in the forest
every feather flying
why give your beaded snake-hips
to the death white boers in durban
Josephine didn't you know about the torture chambers
made of black flesh and feathers
made by the death white boers in durban
Josephine terror-woman of terrible beauty of such feathers
I want to understand why dance
the dance of the honorary white
for the death white boers in durban

After all Josephine
I saw you in your turquoise headdress
with royal blue sequins pasted on your lips
your fantastic legs studded with emeralds
as you kicked as you bumped as you leaped in the air
then froze
your body breaking lightning in fish net
and Josephine Josephine
what a night in harlem
what electricity
such trembling
such goose pimples
so many feathers
Josephine
dancer of the magnetic dancers
of the orange flint pelvis of the ruby navel
of the purple throat
of the feet pointing both ways
of feathers now gone

Josephine Josephine
I remember you rosette of resistance
southern flames
Josephine of the birdheads, ostrich plumes
bananas and sparkling G-strings
Josephine of the double-jointed knees
double-jointed shoulders double-jointed thighs
double-jointed breasts double-jointed fingers
double-jointed toes double-jointed eyeballs
double-jointed hips doubling
into a double squat like a double star into a giant double snake
with the double heartbeats of a young girl
doubling into woman-hood
and grinding into an emulsified double spirit
Josephine terror-woman of feathers i remember
Josephine of such conflicts i remember
Josephine of such floating i remember
Josephine of such heights i remember
Josephine
of so many transformations i remember

Josephine
of such beauty i remember
Josephine of such fire i remember
Josephine of such sheen i remember
Josephine
so many feathers i remember
Josephine Josephine

Grinding Vibrato

Blues Lady
with the beaded face
painted lips
and hair smeared
in the oil of Texas

You were looking good and sounding beautiful
until the horseman wanted your thunder
until the boa constrictor wanted your body
until syringes of upright hyenas
barbwired your meat to their teeth and
pushed behind your ears
inside your mouth
between your vagina
scabs the size of quarters
scabs the size of pennies
the size of the shape of you

all pigeon holes and spider legs colonized woman
funky piece of blood flint
with blue graffitied arms
a throat of dead bees
and swollen fingers that dig into a swamp of broken
purrtongue

Spotted stripped blues lady
who was looking good and sounding beautiful
with those nasal love songs
those strident battle-cry songs
that copper maroon rattle resonator
shaking from your feet to your eyes
the sound of water drum songs
grinding vibrato songs to work by to make love by
to remember you by
Blues song lady who was looking good and sounding
beautiful
until you gave away your thunder
until you gave up your spirit
until you barbwired your meat to teeth
and became the odor of hyenas
uprooted woman with the embalmed face
pall bearer lips
and hair matted in the mud of texas
how many ounces of revolution do you need
to fill the holes in your body
or
is it too late to get back your lightning
is it too late to reconstruct your blues song sister tell me
is it too late for the mother tongue in your womanself to
insurrect

Rape

What was Inez supposed to do for
the man who declared war on her body
the man who carved a combat zone between her breasts
Was she supposed to lick crabs from his hairy ass
kiss every pimple on his butt
blow hot breath on his big toe
draw back the corners of her vagina and
hee haw like a Calif. burro

This being war time for Inez
she stood facing the knife
the insults and
her own smell drying on the penis of
the man who raped her

She stood with a rifle in her hand
doing what a defense department will do in times of war
And when the man started grunting and panting and wobbling forward like
a giant hog
She pumped lead into his three hundred pounds of shaking flesh
Sent it flying to the virgin of Guadeloupe
then celebrated day of the dead rapist punk
and just what the fuck else was she supposed to do?

And what was Joanne supposed to do for
the man who declared war on her life
Was she supposed to tongue his encrusted toilet stool lips
suck the numbers off of his tin badge
choke on his clap trap balls
squeeze on his nub of rotten maggots and
sing god bless america thank you for fucking my life away

This being wartime for Joanne
she did what a defense department will do in times of war
and when the piss drinking   shit sniffing guard said
I'm gonna make you wish you were dead black bitch come here
Joanne came down with an ice pick in
the swat freak mother fucker's chest
yes in the fat neck of that racist policeman
Joanne did the dance of the ice picks and once again
from coast to coast
house to house
we celebrated day of the dead rapist punk
and just what the fuck else were we supposed to do

LUCILLE CLIFTON
(1936–)

One of the few African American writers who has never abandoned the aesthetic expression of political protest born in the black communal struggles of the 1960s is the poet, dramatist, and prose and fiction writer Lucille Clifton. Author of six books of poetry, which combine Christian symbolism and neo-African dedication to depict the common culture and history of African Americans, particularly that of black American females, Clifton also has an autobiography and nineteen works of juvenile fiction. Most critics of the Black Arts Movement believe that her work incorporates the optimal feel, sense, and voice of an unspoiled and unified black community.

Born Thelma Lucille Sayles in Depew, New York, on June 27, 1936, Clifton was inspired to write because of a unique familial heritage of authentic history and artistic talent. Her mother, Thelma Moore Sayles, was a prolific folk poet; her father, Samuel Louis, Sr., was an oral storyteller and family historian. "My family tends to be a spiritual and even mystical one," Clifton once said in "A Simple Language," an interview in *Black Women Writers: 1950–1980: A Critical Evaluation,* edited by Mari Evans. Her parents' influence on her writing is most apparent in one of her later collection of poems, *Two-Headed Woman* (1980), in which she invokes the "two-headed woman" of black folklore in order to use elements of conjuring and hoodoo to present another way of perceiving the world. But perhaps the greatest influence on Clifton's life and works was the legacy of her great-great-grandmother Caroline Donald. Kidnapped from the Dahomey Republic of West Africa when she was eight years old, Caroline was placed in the New Orleans plantation system, where she was expected to serve as a slave for life. Instead, as Clifton's father often recounted in his entertaining tales of family folklore, Caroline walked eight hundred miles to Virginia and to a life that would eventually offer her a degree of freedom and a place of honor and respect. She has appeared in Clifton's verse as "Mammy Ca'line," the link to the poet's African heritage, the voice that speaks through her and hands down to her the legacy of social responsibility.

In 1953, as a drama major at Howard University, where she was a classmate of LeRoi Jones (Amiri Baraka), A. B. Spellman, Owen Dodson, and Sterling Brown, among other African American leaders and writers, Clifton had a role in the first performance of James Baldwin's play *The Amen Corner,* which debuted at the school. Transferring to Fredonia State Teachers College in New York in 1955, Clifton continued to write poetry and fiction. However, she began her professional career as a claims clerk in the unemployment office in Buffalo in 1958. On May 10 of that same year, she married Fred James Clifton, a writer, artist, and philosophy professor at the University of Buffalo. Married for twenty-four years, the couple had six children. Fred died in 1984.

Clifton spent the first eleven years of her marriage rearing her children. Nonetheless, the intellectual life at the University of Buffalo greatly nourished her artistic talents. She had been writing in her own short, cryptic style for years but had never attempted to publish her poetry because the style seemed to her so unusual. However, one of her classmates, Ishmael Reed, who was also destined to become a noted American writer, showed some of Clifton's poems to Langston Hughes, who included them in his anthology *Poetry of the Negro, 1746–1970* (1970).

In 1969, Clifton sent additional poems to another well-known poet, Robert Hayden, who arranged to have them presented to the YW-YMCA Poetry Center in New York City, which gave Clifton the coveted Discovery Award, presented to promising but undiscovered poets. That same year, she went to work as a literature assistant for the Central Atlantic Regional Educational Laboratory in Washington, D.C. In 1971, after the highly acclaimed publication of her first collection of poems, she joined the faculty of Coppin State College in Baltimore as poet-in-residence. Three years later, she was invited to be a visiting writer at the Columbia University School of the Arts. Finally, Clifton joined the faculty of the University of California at Santa Cruz as a professor of literature and creative writing in 1985.

The *New York Times* cited Clifton's first volume of poetry, *Good Times: Poems,* as one of the ten best books of 1969. In it, one finds beautifully crafted female poems such as "miss rosie" and "for deLawd," which celebrate the historical tradition of strong black women. Her next two collections, *Good News About the Earth* (1972) and *An Ordinary Woman* (1974) were equally well received. The former volume contains one of her finest lyrical pieces, "the lost baby poem," which takes on the form of the blues idiom. Clifton had by 1972 established herself not only as an eminent poet of African American literature but as a defiant spokesperson who could articulate the experiences of African American women in their struggle to maintain faith, family, and community. The emerging poet also wrote about the black woman's place during the liberation movement of the sixties and seventies in her *Good News About the Earth*: "i became a woman during the old prayers," she wrote of the police attacks on, and deaths of, so many of her fellow workers during the Civil Rights Movement.

Critic Andrea Benton Rushing says that Clifton reached her full poetic maturity with the publications of *An Ordinary Woman* (1974) and *Two-Headed Woman* (1980): "These two fine collections parse the female sector of African-American life and give vivid testimony to the terse brilliance which alerted readers of her early work to Clifton's enormous potential." Rushing says that Clifton has written more about women's lives than any other African American poet with the exception of Gwendolyn Brooks. This is also evident in her latest collections of verse, *Good Woman: Poems and a Memoir, 1969–1980* (1987) and *Quilting Poems: 1987–1990* (1991).

Clifton's compelling autobiography, *Generations,* was published by Random House in 1976. Again the critics were generous with praise. "Her purpose is perpetuation and celebration, not judgment," wrote Reynolds Price in the *New York Times Book Review* (March 1976). A contributor to the *Virginia Quarterly Review* (February 1976) stated that the work is "more than an elegy or a personal memoir. It is an attempt on the part of one woman to retrieve, and lyrically to celebrate, her Afro-American heritage."

Between 1969 and 1981, Clifton published fifteen collections of short stories for children. Her works are intended to soften and interpret the world and society in which black children are nurtured and to help them to understand their cultural lineage and non-Europeanized history. Moreover, she is concerned that her young readers become conversant with the experiences not only of Africans in America but also of those throughout the African Diaspora.

Clifton's writings have engendered several prestigious awards and nominations, including a Pulitzer Prize Committee Citation in 1970 and a Pulitzer Prize nomination in 1980. She was named poet laureate of Maryland in 1979 and received the Juniper Prize for poetry in 1980. The author also has received two honorary doctorates, from Goucher College and the University of Maryland, both in 1980.

Clifton's commitment to the Black Aesthetic and her devotion to the Afrocentric education of African American children demand production of a full review of her works, particularly her children's literature, by Afrocentric critics. Hopefully, that void will be filled in the coming years.

❖❖❖

Essential criticisms of Clifton's work include Wallace R. Peppers and Ronald Baughman's entries in the *Dictionary of Literary Biography: Afro-American Poets Since 1955,* vol. 41; Haki Madhubuti, "Lucille Clifton: Warm Water, Greased Legs, and Dangerous Poetry," and Audrey McClusky, "Tell the Good News: A View of the Works of Lucille Clifton," in *Black Women Writers (1950–1980): A Critical Evaluation.* Two other outstanding articles on Clifton are Andrea Benton Rushing, "Lucille Clifton: A Changing Voice for Changing Times," in *Coming to Light: American Women Poets in the Twentieth Century* (1985); Hank Lazer, "Blackness Blessed: The Writings of Lucille Clifton," *Southern Review* 25, No. 3 (1989). See also James P. Draper, *Black Literature Criticism,* vol. 1 (1992); Linda Metzger, *Black Writers*

(1989); Deborah A. Strub's entry in *Contemporary Authors* (1975); Sharon Malinowski's entry in *Something About the Author* (1992), vol. 69; Thelma Bryant, "A Conversation with Lucille Clifton," *Sage* 2, No. 1 (1985).

Clifton's fiction for children has been variously reviewed in *Interracial Books for Children Bulletin, School Library Journal, Bulletin for the Center of Children's Books, Reading Teacher,* and *Children's Literature Review.*

miss rosie

when i watch you
wrapped up like garbage
sitting, surrounded by the smell
of too old potato peels
or
when i watch you
in your old man's shoes
with the little toe cut out
sitting, waiting for your mind
like next week's grocery
i say
when i watch you
you wet brown bag of a woman
who used to be the best looking gal in georgia
used to be called the Georgia Rose
i stand up
through your destruction
i stand up

for deLawd

people say they have a hard time
understanding how i
go on about my business
playing my ray charles
hollering at the kids—
seem like my afro
cut off in some old image
would show i got a long memory
and i come from a line
of black and going on women
who got used to making it through murdered sons
and who grief kept on pushing
who fried chicken
ironed
swept off the back steps
who grief kept
for their still alive sons

for their sons coming
for their sons gone
just pushing

my mama moved among the days

my mama moved among the days
like a dreamwalker in a field;
seemed like what she touched was hers
seemed like what touched her couldn't hold,
she got us almost through the high grass
then seemed like she turned around and ran
right back in
right back on in

good times

my daddy has paid the rent
and the insurance man is gone
and the lights is back on
and my uncle brud has hit
for one dollar straight
and they is good times
good times
good times

my mama has made bread
and grampaw has come
and everybody is drunk
and dancing in the kitchen
and singing in the kitchen
oh these is good times
good times
good times

oh children think about the
good times

the lost baby poem

the time i dropped your almost body down
down to meet the waters under the city
and run one with the sewage to the sea
what did i know about waters rushing back
what did i know about drowning
or being drowned

you would have been born into winter
in the year of the disconnected gas
and no car   we would have made the thin
walk over Genesee hill into the Canada wind

to watch you slip like ice into strangers' hands
you would have fallen naked as snow into winter
if you were here i could tell you these
and some other things

if i am ever less than a mountain
for your definite brothers and sisters
let the rivers pour over my head
let the sea take me for a spiller
of seas   let black men call me stranger
always   for your never named sake

homage to my hips

these hips are big hips.
they need space to
move around in.
they don't fit into little
petty places. these hips
are free hips.
they don't like to be held back.
these hips have never been enslaved,
they go where they want to go
they do what they want to do.
these hips are mighty hips.
these hips are magic hips.
i have known them
to put a spell on a man and
spin him like a top!

what the mirror said

listen,
you a wonder.
you a city
of a woman.
you got a geography
of your own.
listen,
somebody need a map
to understand you.
somebody need directions
to move around you.
listen,
woman,
you not a noplace
anonymous
girl;
mister with his hands on you

he got his hands on
some
damn
body!

the making of poems

the reason why i do it
though i fail and fail
in the giving of true names
is i am adam and his mother
and these failures are my job.

HAKI R. MADHUBUTI (DON L. LEE)
(1942–)

Since the 1960s, Haki Madhubuti has been one of the most powerful forces of black cultural nationalism in America. His entire career has been devoted to the development of black art, black consciousness, and black institutions. Starting out in the 1960s as one of the most militant of the New Black Poets, Madhubuti was the cofounder of Third World Press, one of the few black presses that is still in existence today, and the publisher of *Black Books Bulletin,* one of the rare socioliterary journals for black nationalist thought that has remained in print. As he declared in his book *Enemies: The Clashes of Races* (1978), "I use writing as a weapon, offensively and defensively, to help raise the consciousness of myself and my people." Through both poetry and prose, this contemporary griot has called out loud and clear to his people to be black rather than white people's image of what they should be. As D. H. Melhem writes, "Madhubuti's courage and determination in maintaining his press, his support of other writers, his teaching, readings, lectures, and most critically, the vigor and social direction of his poetry all contribute to his major status in our country's literary and social landscape."

Madhubuti was born Don L. Lee in Little Rock, Arkansas, on February 23, 1942, but was raised in Detroit. He grew up poor, and his family was often on welfare. His father abandoned the family when Madhubuti was a young boy, forcing him to take care of his alcoholic mother, Maxine Graves Lee. Perhaps as a consequence of these early years, Madhubuti does not drink or take drugs. He has been referred to as an ascetic. His mother instilled a love of literature and music in him. When he was sixteen, she died. At that time, he went to Chicago to live with an aunt. There he attended Dunbar Vocational High School. After graduation, Madhubuti continued his education at Wilson Junior College and Roosevelt University until he joined the army at age eighteen. He remained in the service until 1963. For the next few years, Madhubuti worked at a variety of odd jobs in Chicago until he turned his attention to writing poetry.

In 1967, he self-published his first collection of poems, *Think Black!* He managed to sell six hundred copies of the book in a week at the el stop along Sixty-third Street. It was the first work in which he expressed his black separatist philosophy. Later that year, he enrolled in Gwendolyn Brooks's poetry workshop, which would have a major influence on his career. With Carolyn Rodgers, a member of the workshop, and Johari Amini, he founded Third World Press in 1967. Madhubuti also met Dudley Randall, owner of Broadside Press, who produced his second book, *Black Pride* (1968). In the introduction to the collection, Randall points out that Madhubuti "writes for the man in the street and uses the language of the street, and sometimes of the gutter, with wit, inventiveness, and surprise."

Madhubuti did not gain national recognition for his creative use of language until the publication of his third book, *Don't Cry, Scream,* in 1969. The title stems from his mother's early words to him: "nigger, if u is goin' ta open yr / mouth **Don't Cry, Scream,** which also means: **Don't Beg, Take.**" The title poem, which is dedicated to John Coltrane, reveals the most striking aspect of Madhubuti's verse—his use of rhythms. Using the improvisational flux of rhythms and a variety of riffs and breaks, he creates a Coltrane-like free jazz musical composition. From the violent rage of *Don't Cry, Scream* to the quieter turbulence of *We Walk the Way of the New World* (1970), Madhubuti brilliantly explored a wide range of rhythmic possibilities. He discusses his linguistic feats and the language of the other New Black Poets in his essay "Toward a Definition: Black Poetry of the Sixties (After LeRoi Jones)," which appeared in Addison Gayle's *The Black Aesthetic* (1971).

In 1972, he founded the Institute of Positive Education and began publishing *Black Books Bulletin.* A year later, he changed his name from Don L. Lee to Haki R. Madhubuti, which means "justice, awakening, strong; also precise/accurate" in Swahili. Madhubuti has an M.F.A. from the University of Iowa and is a professor of English at Chicago State University. He has been a poet-in-residence at Cornell University, the University of Illinois–Circle Campus, Howard University, and Central State University. In more recent books such as *Earthquakes* (1984), he speaks with sensitivity of the problems that black women face in the contemporary world. His books have sold more than 100,000 copies.

Throughout Madhubuti's career, he has been Afrocentric. Consequently, his more recent writings, including *Earthquakes* (1984) and *Killing Memories, Seeking Ancestors* (1987), reveal that he, like Brooks and Amiri Baraka, has moved toward Pan-Africanism and its emphasis on the oppression of the Third World. Poems in *Killing Memories,* for instance, identify the black struggle in the United States with the oppression of people in South Africa, El Salvador, Afghanistan, Lebanon, and Ethiopia. The volume ends with the five-part poem "Seeking Ancestors," which both celebrates the African cultural heritage and challenges black artists and intellectuals "to / recall the memory / to / recall the tradition & meaning / to rename the bringers / genius." Madhubuti has made the same call as editor and publisher of *Black Books Bulletin.* In a recent edition of the journal titled "Blacks, Jews, and Henry Louis Gates" (Winter, 1993/1994), he criticizes Gates for condemning the concept of Afrocentricity. This article also appears in his book on black-white race relationships, *Claiming Earth: Race, Rage, Rape, Redemption* (1994). Also, with Ron Manlana Karenga, he has coedited the commemorative literature anthology, *Million Man March: Day of Absence* (1996). A vigorous defender of black cultural nationalism, Madhubuti delivers a powerful message that, Darwin Turner in his afterword to *Earthquakes* reminds us, "will shut off some television sets, redirect some minds, and may invite book burning in some quarters." With the force of his rhetoric and the urgency of his message, this editor, publisher, essayist, and poet continues to inspire the present generation of African Americans to "Think Black!"

❖❖❖

Haki Madhubuti has been interviewed in *Black Books Bulletin* 1 (Spring 1992) and in D. H. Melhem's *Heroism in the New Black Poetry* (1990). The latter book, along with Karl Malkoff's earlier book, *Crowell's Handbook of Contemporary American Poetry* (1973), contains a critical discussion of his poetry. Another earlier analysis of his works is Annette Oliver Shands, "The Relevancy of Don L. Lee as a Contemporary Black Poet," *Black World* 21 (June 1972).

Don't Cry, Scream

for John Coltrane / from a black poet /
in a basement apt. crying dry tears
of "you ain't gone."

into the sixties
a trane
came / out of the
fifties with a
golden boxcar
riding the rails
of novation.
        blowing
        a-melodics
        screeching,
        screaming,
        blasting—
                driving some away,
                (those paper readers who thought
                manhood was something innate)
                bring others in,
                (the few who didn't believe that the
                world existed around established whi
                teness & leonard bernstein)
music that ached.
murdered our minds (we reborn)
born into a neoteric aberration.
& suddenly
you envy the
BLIND man—
you know that he will
hear what you'll never
see.
                your music is like
                my head—nappy black /
                a good nasty feel with
                tangled songs of:
                        we-eeeeeeeeee   sing
                        WE-EEEeeeeeeeee   loud &

WE-EEEEEEEEEEEEEEEE high
with
feeling

a people playing
the sound of me when
i combed it. combed at
it.

i cried for billy holiday.
the blues. we ain't blue
the blues exhibited illusions of manhood.
destroyed by you. Ascension into:

scream-eeeeeeeeeeeeee-ing sing
SCREAM-EEEeeeeeeeeeee-ing loud &
SCREAM-EEEEEEEEEEEEEE-ing long with
feeling

we ain't blue, we are black.
we ain't blue, we are black.
(all the blues did was
make me cry)
soultrane gone on a trip
he left man images
he was a life-style of
man-makers & annihilator
of attache case carriers.

Trane done went.
(got his hat & left me one)
naw brother,
i didn't cry,
i just—
Scream-eeeeeeeeeeeeee-ed sing loud
SCREAM-EEEEEEEEEEEEEEEE-ED & high with
we-eeeeeeeeeeeeeeeeeeeee ee feeling
WE-EEEEEEeeeeeeeeEEEEEEEE letting
WE-EEEEEEEEEEEEEEEEEEEEEE yr/voice
WHERE YOU DONE GONE, BROTHER? break

it hurts, grown babies
dying. born. done caught me
a trane. steel wheels broken
by popsicle sticks. i went out
& tried to buy a nickle bag
with my standard oil card.
(swung on a faggot who politely
scratched his ass in my presence.
he smiled broken teeth stained from
his over-used tongue. fisted-face.

teeth dropped in tune with ray
charles singing "yesterday.")

blonds had more fun—
with snagga-tooth niggers
who saved pennies & pop bottles for week-ends
to play negro & other filthy inventions.
be-bop-en to james brown's
cold sweat—these niggers didn't sweat,
they perspired. & the blond's dye came out,
i ran. she did too, with his pennies, pop bottles
& his mind. tune in next week same time same station
for anti-self in one lesson.

to the negro cow-sissies
who did tchaikovsky &
the beatles & live in
split-level homes & had
split-level minds & babies.
who committed the act of
love with their clothes on.

(who hid in the bathroom to read
jet mag., who didn't read the chicago
defender because of the misspelled
words & had shelves of books by
europeans on display. untouched. who
hid their little richard & lightnin'
slim records & asked: "John who?"

instant hate.)

they didn't know any better,
brother, they were too busy getting
into debt, expressing humanity &
taking off color.

SCREAMMMM/we-eeeee/screech/teee improvise
aheeeeeeeee/screeeeeee/theeee/ee with
ahHHHHHHHHH/WEEEEEEEE/scrEEE feeling
EEEE
we-eeeeeWE-EEEEEEEEWE-EE-EEEEE

the ofays heard you &
were wiped out. spaced.
one clown asked me during,
my favorite things, if
you were practicing.
i fired on the muthafucka & said,
"i'm practicing."

naw brother,
i didn't cry.

i got high off my thoughts—
they kept coming back,
back to destroy me.

& that BLIND man
i don't envy him anymore
i can see his hear
& hear his heard through my pores.
i can see my me. it was truth you gave,
like a daily shit
it had to come.

can you scream—brother? very
can you scream—brother? soft

i hear you.
i hear you.

and the Gods will too.

Two Poems

FROM "SKETCHES FROM A BLACK-NAPPY-HEADED POET"

last week
my mother died /
& the most often asked question
at the funeral;
was not of her death
or of her life before death
but
why was i present
with / out
a
tie on.
i ain't seen no poems stop a .38,
i ain't seen no stanzas brake a honkie's head,
i ain't seen no metaphors stop a tank,
i ain't seen no words kill
& if the word was mightier than the sword
pushkin wouldn't be fertilizing russian soil /
& until my similes can protect me from a night stick
i guess i'll keep my razor
& buy me some more bullets.

We Walk the Way of the New World

1.

we run the dangercourse.
the way of the stocking caps & murray's grease.
(if u is modern u used duke greaseless hair pomade)

jo jo was modern / an international nigger
born: jan. 1, 1863 in new york, mississippi.
his momma was mo militant than he was / is
jo jo bes no instant negro
his development took all of 106 years
& he was the first to be stamped "made in USA"
where he arrived bow-legged a curve ahead of the 20th
century's new weapon: television.
which invented, "how to win and influence people"
& gave jo jo his how / ever look: however u want me.

we discovered that with the right brand of cigarettes
that one, with his best girl,
cd skip thru grassy fields in living color
& in slow-motion: Caution: niggers, cigarette smoking
will kill u & yr / health.
& that the breakfast of champions is: blackeyed peas & rice.
& that God is dead & Jesus is black and last seen on 63rd
street in a gold & black dashiki, sitting in a pink
hog speaking swahili with a pig-latin accent.
& that integration and coalition are synonymous,
& that the only thing that really mattered was:
who could get the highest on the least or how to expand
& break one's mind.

in the coming world
new prizes are
to be given

we *ran* the dangercourse.
now, it's a silent walk / a careful eye
jo jo is there
to his mother he is unknown
(she accepted with a newlook: what wd u do if someone
loved u?)
jo jo is back
& he will catch all the new jo jo's as they wander in & out
and with a fan-like whisper say: you ain't no
tourist
and Harlem ain't for
sight-seeing, brother.

2.

Start with the itch and there will be no scratch. Study
yourself.
Watch yr / every movement as u skip thru-out the southside of
chicago.
be hip to yr / actions.

our dreams are realities
traveling the nature-way.
we meet them
at the apex of their utmost
meanings / means;
we walk in cleanliness
down state st / or Fifth Ave.
& wicked apartment buildings shake
as their windows announce our presence
as we jump into the interior
& cut the day's evil away.

We walk in cleanliness
the newness of it all
becomes us
our women listen to us
and learn.
We teach our children thru
our actions.

We'll become owners of the   New World
the New World.
will run it as unowners
for
we will live in it too
& will want to be remembered
as   realpeople.

Assassination

it was wild.
the
bullet hit high.
(the throat-neck)
& from everywhere:
the motel, from under bushes and cars,
from around corners and across streets,
out of the garbage cans and from rat holes
in the earth
they came running.
with
guns
drawn
they came running
toward the King—
all of them
fast and sure—
as if
the King

was going to fire back.
they came running,
fast and sure,
in the
wrong
direction.

But He Was Cool
or: he even stopped for green lights

super-cool
ultrablack
a tan / purple
had a beautiful shade.

he had a double-natural
that wd put the sisters to shame.
his dashikis were tailor made
& his beads were imported sea shells
    (from some blk / country i never heard of)
he was triple-hip.

his tikis were hand carved
out of ivory
& came express from the motherland.
he would greet u in swahili
& say good-by in yoruba.
woooooooooooo-jim he bes so cool & ill tel li gent
        cool-cool is so cool he was un-cooled by other niggers' cool
        cool-cool ultracool was bop-cool / ice box cool so cool cold cool
        his wine didn't have to be cooled, him was air conditioned cool
        cool-cool / real cool made me cool—now ain't that cool
        cool-cool so cool him nick-named refrigerator.

cool-cool so cool
he didn't know,
after detroit, newark, chicago &c.,
we had to hip
      cool-cool / super-cool / real cool
  that
to be black
is
to be
very-hot.

My Brothers

my brothers i will not tell you
who to love or not love
i will only say to you

that
Black women have not been
loved enough.

i will say to you
that
we are at war & that
Black men in america are
being removed from the
earth
like loose sand in a wind storm
and that the women Black are
three to each of us.

no
my brothers i will not tell you
who to love or not love
but
i will make you aware of our
self hating and hurting ways.
make you aware of whose bellies
you dropped from.
i will glue your ears to those images
you reflect which are not being
loved.

White on Black Crime

lately and not by choice
milton washington is self employed.
workin hard
he collects aluminum cans,
pop bottles, papers & cardboard
and sells them to the
local recycling center.

milton washington is an unemployed
master welder who has constantly sought
work in & out of his trade.
he is now seen on beaches, in parks,
in garbage cans, leaving well lit allies
in the evenings pushing one cart
& pulling the other, head to the side
eyes glued southward long steppin homeward.

milton's unemployment ran out 14 months ago.
first the car went & he questioned his manhood.
next the medical insurance, savings & family
nights out ceased & he questioned his god.
finally his home was snatched & he disappeared

for two days & questioned his dreams
and all he believed in.

milton works a 15 hour day &
recently redefined his life for
the sixth time selecting as his only goal
the housing, feeding & keeping his family
together.

yesterday the payout per pound
on aluminum was reduced by 1/4 cent
as the stock market hit an all time high
& the president smiled through a speech
on economic recovery, welfare cheats & the
availability of jobs for those who want to work.

milton washington has suffered
the humiliation of being denied food stamps,
the laughter and cat calls of children,
the misunderstanding in the eyes of his family
and friends.
milton believed in the american way
even hung flags on the fourth & special days
and demanded the respect of god & country in
his home.

at 1/4 cent reduction in pay per pound
milton washington will have to add
an hour and a half to his 15 hour day.
milton washington, more american than black,
quiet and resourceful, a collector of dreams
cannot close his eyes anymore,
cannot excuse the failure in his heart,
cannot expect miracles in daylight,
is real close, very, very close to hurtin somebody
real bad.

CAROLYN RODGERS
(1943–)

Carolyn Rodgers emerged as one of the most searching poets of the sixties. As a uniquely experimental writer, she matured into a leading voice of the seventies. Today, she seeks a way to mediate between the creativity of the poetic individual and the African American community. Possibly, she expresses the greatest challenge and even paradox of the black writer. She advanced beyond the early verse of militant revolution in *Paper Soul* (1968) and *Songs of a Blackbird* (1969) to the mature achievement in *how i got ovah* (1975) and *The Heart as Ever Green* (1978). Her legacy includes a remarkable plasticity for literary growth. Of three poetic voices—Sonia Sanchez, Amiri Baraka, and Carolyn Rodgers—who spanned the Black Arts Movement of the sixties and to the present, only Sanchez rivals Rodgers for flowering in brave new ways, and no one surpasses her in ferreting out a set of artistic memories for new generations.

So it is that Rodgers writes with an ever-pervasive commitment to the future. Despite a militant temper, so often expressed through a profane vernacular, she reveals a sacredness in folk religion. Of all her contemporaries, she perhaps seeks most a language to bridge the community after 1960 and the more conservative ones of earlier times. Hence, she emerges as one of the most innovative poets to reach for a Black Aesthetic marked by a continuum of family love and challenged by political history.

Carolyn Marie Rodgers was born on December 14, 1943, to Clarence and Bazella Colding Rodgers in Chicago. Enrolled at the University of Illinois in 1960, she began to write poetry as a freshman to cope with the isolation of academic life. In 1961, she transferred to Roosevelt University, where she studied until 1965. She eventually received her B.A. in English in 1981 and an M.A. in English from the University of Chicago in 1984. After working as a YMCA social worker from 1963–1968, Rodgers won the Conrad Kent Rivers Award for writing in 1968 and a National Endowment for the Arts grant in 1969. She was an instructor of African American literature at Columbia College in Chicago in 1969–1970 and at the University of Washington at Seattle in 1970. Named poet laureate of the Society of Midland Authors the same year, she also received a grant from the National Endowment for the Arts. Rodgers has been writer-in-residence at Albany State College in Georgia (1971), Malcolm X College in Chicago (1971–1972), and Roosevelt University (1983). Among her literary achievements was winning the Pen Award in 1987. She has written a column titled "Riffin" for the *Milwaukee Courier* and was formerly Midwest editor for *Black Dialogue.* Her work has been published in *Negro Digest* (subsequently *Black World* and then *First World*), *Kenyatta, Nation, Black Arts, Journal of Black Poetry, Dagens,* and *Nyheter.*

Rodgers has had an impact on African American literary history. Her vibrant career, so adept at responding to the call of the times, displays an evolution in the historical consciousness of the race. First came her temperamental volumes of the sixties, such as *Paper Soul* (1969), *Two Love Raps* (1969), *Now Ain't That Love* (1969), and *For H. W. Fuller* (1969), dedicated to the founder of *Black World* and *First World.* Then were the crowning epiphanies, great moments of lyrical vision in *Songs of a Blackbird* (1969), *how i got ovah: New and Selected Poems* (1975), and *The Heart as Ever Green* (1978). Finally came a literary mellowing after the historical decline of the Black Aesthetic and Black Arts in the eighties. If, as the French critic Henri Pyre said once, all great lyric is about the fall of humanity, Rodgers has spent the last fourteen years in poetic speculation about the former greatness of the Black Arts Movement. Besides a decay in social commitment, she has perceived a decrease in the imaginative vision of the poets themselves. Many of her recent works, including *Eden and Other Poems* (1983), *Echoes, from a Circle Called Earth* (1988), *A Little Lower Than the Angels* (1984), and *Morning Glory* (1989), have appeared from her own Eden Press. From the most encouraging houses for young black talent, such as Third World Press and Broadside Press during 1969–1971, on through Doubleday, she has come eventually to establish her own press.

In her short confessional poem "It Is Deep," a college revolutionary experiences an epiphany about her personal ancestry. She says, "My mother, religious-negro, proud of / having waded through a storm, is very obviously, / a sturdy Black bridge that I / crossed over, on." The love between mother and daughter dissipates an initial anger through which the Christian parent chastizes the Marxist child. What Rodgers achieves elsewhere in a poem dedicated to the poet Gwendolyn Brooks is a remarkable structure through which all African American expressive art—including song, painting, and poetry—revolutionizes the emblem of chivalry.

Carolyn Rodgers reveals the human condition in all its sordidness. While she tries to tell a poetic story about the ordinary qualities in life, she looks for what has been forgotten for clandestine reasons. So cynically curious about the world, she proves nevertheless prophetic with hope. And like an Aeolian harp, as with Etheridge Knight and others, she cherishes her role as a personal instrument to shape the lyric of African American culture. As Bettye Parker-Smith has written in *Dictionary of Literary Biography: American Poets Since 1955* (1985), "Certainly, there never was a gap between the world of Rodgers's vision which she glorifies and the authentic Black community." Over her career, her poetry has advanced into a jazz whole of great inner beauty. She asserts the power of African American language in a title poem for *The Heart as Ever Green* (1978): ". . . when we spoke of freedom / we spoke of our hearts / as / ever green." Ultimately, the lyric speaks against the backdrop of hopes subverted by history. Rodgers challenges the Black Aesthetic of the sixties—the passionate demand for commitment, relevance, and revolution—to create a lasting poetic of at least one transformed voice.

❖❖❖

Especially since the Reagan era, literary scholarship about the Black Arts Movement has been politically correct in the conservative vein. No article about Rodgers appears in the on-line catalogue for current criticism. While the neglect extends across all genres, it is particularly deep in drama and poetry. Nevertheless, the years 1969 to 1978 include some of the most startling experimentation and creative energy of all African American poetry. An excellent article is Jean Davis's "Carolyn M. Rodgers," *Afro-American Poets Since 1955,* vol. 41, edited by Trudier Harris and Thadious M. Davis. A few general sources for Carolyn Rodgers include Mari Evans, ed., *Black Women Writers (1950–1980): A Critical Evaluation* (1984); Haki Madhubuti (Don L. Lee), *Dynamite Voices: Black Poets of the 1960s* (1971); Antar Sudan Katara Mberi, "Reaching for Unity and Harmony," *Freedomways* 20 (First Quarter 1980). Sustained works of importance remain to be written.

Me, in Kulu Se & Karma

it's me
bathed and ashy
smelling down with
                    (revlons aquamarine)
me, with my hair black
and nappy good and rough
as the ground
me sitting in my panties
no bra sitting on my am-vets

sofa with the pillows i stuffed
the red orange gold material i bought
from the little old jew i got lost and found
in new york looking
for the garment district i never found but
found skullcaps lining up the both sides
of the street with stores that make you sneeze it's
me i bought the yellow gold and got the wrong foam
and stuffed it and sewed it but the little pieces
keep coming out but u can sit on it anyway and listen
to pharoah ring into ur room like now, its me sitting
on the thin thin wrong pillows hearing the trills and
the honey rolling through the air and the gravel rolling and fluting and sweeet sweeeet sweeeeeet and its
me in the sky moving that way going freee where pha
raoh and trane playing in my guts and its me and my
ears forgetting how to listen and just feeling oh
yeah me i am screammmmmming into the box and the box
is screammmmmming back, is slow motion moving sound
through the spaces in the air and oh yeah its me feeling feeling rise, its rise feeling rise feeling feelings rise rise in my throat and feeling throats
my head back and feeling laughs alloverme and feeling
screams mejoy and me flies feelings wild and laugh and
its me oh yeah its me rise feeling its me being music
in kulu se & karma land

Poem for Some Black Women

i am lonely.
all the people i know
i know too well

there was comfort in that
at first but now
we know each others miseries
    too well.
we are
    lonely women, who spend time waiting for
        occasional flings

we live with fear.
we are lonely.
we are talented, dedicated, well read
        BLACK, COMMITTED,

we are   lonely.

we understand the world problems
Black women's problems with Black men
        but all

we really understand is
        lonely.

when we laugh,
we are so happy to laugh
we cry when we laugh
    we are lonely.
we are busy people
always doing things

fearing getting trapped in rooms
loud with empty . . .
                yet
knowing the music of silence / hating it / hoarding it
loving it / treasuring it,
    it often birthing our creativity
        we   are   lonely

being soft and being hard
supporting our selves, earning our own bread
soft / hard / hard / soft /
knowing that need must not show
                                        will frighten away
knowing that we must
walk back-wards nonchalantly on our tip-toesssss
    into
happiness,
    if only for stingy moments

we know too much
we learn to understand everything,
to make too much sense out
of the world,
of pain
        of lonely . . .

we buy clothes, we take trips,
we wish, we pray, we meditate, we curse, we crave, we coo, we caw,

        we need ourselves sick, we need, we need
we lonely we grow tired of tears we grow tired of fear
we grow tired but must al-ways be soft and not too serious . . .
    not too smart not too bitchy not too sapphire
    not too dumb not too not too not too
a little less a little more
                            add here detract there
                                        lonely.

5 Winos

sitting on the stone gray church steps
cupped in expensive shrubbery and lilac

looking from my third floor window
into a forest scene it is 1 A.M.
blue monday and the wolves are howling . . .

but they are singing.
crooning, straining & cursing
to harmonize, hit the perfect
sound, what is in their heads
that hovers around the hours &
years, spaced out-along side their dreams.
            and for some reason
            which is not the hour
            or the night
i too am straining, crooning, hoping-
let them hit 7-11 tonight, yeah.
let them hit, top the perfect note Babeeee its uuuuu
let 'em be the Temptin T's or the Fab-u-lous Impressions, tonight . . .
let them nap up in the air with their sound and ice
the other night noises into their places
            if they could just hit . . . for . . . one . . .
                        mo-ment . . .

but the howling goes on,
and the straining & then cursing
and soon,
a bottle screams on the concrete,
scatt ring their mouths and juggling
their music into the most carefully
constructed a-melodic coltrane psalm . . .

U Name This One

let uh revolution come. uh
state of peace is not known to me
anyway
since i grew uhround in chi town
where
howlin wolf howled in the tavern on 47th st.
and muddy waters made u cry the salty nigger blues,
      where pee wee cut lonnell fuh fuckin wid
      his sistuh and blood baptized the street
      at least twice ev'ry week and judy got
      kicked outa grammar school fuh bein pregnant
      and died tryin to ungrow the seed
            we was all up in there and
            just livin was guerilla warfare, yeah.

let uh revolution come.

couldn't be no action like what
i dun already seen.

It Is Deep

(don't never forget the bridge
that you crossed over on)

Having tried to use the
witch cord
that erases the stretch of
thirty-three blocks
and tuning in the voice which
    woodenly stated that the
    talk box was "disconnected"

My mother, religiously girdled in
her god, slipped on some love, and
laid on my bell like a truck,
blew through my door warm wind from the south
concern making her gruff and tight-lipped
        and scared
that her "baby" was starving.
she, having learned, that disconnection results from
                    non-payment of bill (s).

She did not
recognize the poster of the
grand le-roi (al) cat on the wall
had never even seen the book of
Black poems that I have written
thinks that I am under the influence of
        communists
when I talk about Black as anything
other than something ugly to kill it befo it grows
    in any impression she would not be
considered "relevant" or "Black"
                    but
there she was, standing in my room
not loudly condemning that day and
not remembering that I grew hearing her
curse the factory where she "cut uh slave"
and the cheap j-boss wouldn't allow a union,
not remembering that I heard the tears when
they told her a high school diploma was not enough,
and here now, not able to understand, what she had
been forced to deny, still—

she pushed into my kitchen so
she could open my refrigerator to see

what I had to eat, and pressed fifty
bills in my hand saying "pay the talk bill and buy
some food; you got folks who care about you . . ."

My mother, religious-negro, proud of
having waded through a storm, is very obviously,
a sturdy Black bridge that I
crossed over, on.

NIKKI GIOVANNI

(1943–)

Along with the other Broadside Press poets, Nikki Giovanni came to prominence as a militant black poet during the protest movements of the sixties and seventies. The forcefulness of Giovanni's poetry made her one of the most popular black poets of the era among both white and black audiences. She successfully reached the black masses by recording volumes of her verse, which she infused with idioms of the Black Aesthetic. In fact, Giovanni penned several works that became classics of the 1960s, including "The True Import of Present Dialogue, Black vs. Negro" (better known as "Nigger Can You Kill?"), "Ego Tripping," and "Nikki-Rosa." After the end of the sixties movements, the poet focused her work more on personal and communal relationships.

Giovanni was born in Knoxville, Tennessee, on June 7, 1943, and grew up in Cincinnati, Ohio, where her family moved when she was two months old. She is the granddaughter of "Book" Watson, a Latin scholar, and the daughter of middle-class black parents, Yolande Cornelia and Jones Giovanni. She studied history, literature, and fine arts at Fisk University in Nashville, Tennessee, where she graduated with honors in 1967. She later attended the University of Pennsylvania and Columbia University. At Fisk, Giovanni was fortunate to take creative writing classes with the famed black poet/mentor John Oliver Killens, author of *The Cotillion* (1971) and an inspiration to so many black writers of the period, including Maya Angelou, Amiri Baraka, Askia Muhammad Touré, and Sonia Sanchez. Like many of these writers, in the late 1960s and early 1970s Giovanni was active in the Student Nonviolent Coordinating Committee (SNCC).

Shortly after the publication of her first books by Broadside Press in the late 1960s and early 1970s, Giovanni's work attracted increasing amounts of attention. Her move to publishing with the larger presses, such as Morrow and Lippincott, as well as the release of spoken-word recordings such as *Truth Is on Its Way* (1971) and *The Way I Feel* (1974), made Giovanni an internationally acclaimed writer. With the publication of *My House* in 1972, Giovanni sought an alternative to public commentary, advising her black readers to gain renewed strength from personal relationships with the black community.

Like Haki Madhubuti, as a young aspiring poet Giovanni self-published her first book of poems, *Black Feeling, Black Talk,* in 1968. Through this first volume, and through many public appearances, she became known for the militancy of poems such as "Nigger Can You Kill?" which refers to the often false sense of black consciousness that keeps blacks from revolutionary action. Another popular poem is "For Saundra," in which she provides her rationale for the emerging Black Aesthetic.

Perhaps her best-known, and most quoted, poem is "Nikki-Rosa," a poignant offering that speaks of the deep roots of love and connection within black families. She posits that it is impossible for whites to understand the essence of the strength that extends from black families to black communities—a strength that endures regardless of extreme poverty and other social disadvantages: "they never understand Black love is Black wealth."

In "For Saundra" and "Revolutionary Music," Giovanni clearly establishes the relationship between black militancy and black culture. In defending the poet who uses her craft to inspire the masses toward armed social revolution, she explains why black poets of the 1960s could not write poems about trees, clouds, or other themes more traditional to Anglo-centered culture. Indeed, in "For Saundra" Giovanni says that after attempting to write "a beautiful green tree poem" and "a big blue sky poem," she finally wonders whether "maybe i shouldn't write / at all / but clean my gun / and check my kerosene supply / perhaps these are not poetic / times / at all." In "Revolutionary Music," she explains that the lines of black music are filled with double- and triple-entendre that give hope and joy to black audiences while simultaneously urging them to reject the values of the white world and to revolt against it. In "Ego Tripping," Giovanni successfully connects modern African American identity to its ethnic and cultural roots in ancient Africa. The same inherent connectedness is evident in "The Women Gather."

Afrocentric critics consider Giovanni's early, more militant works to be her best poetry. These include the two books she published at Broadside Press, *Black Judgment* (1968) and *Re-Creation* (1970). Additionally, *A Dialogue: James Baldwin and Nikki Giovanni* (1975) is one of the watershed capsules of collective social philosophy among black intellectuals in the 1960s and 1970s. The same can be said for her conversations and interviews with the noted senior black woman author Margaret Walker. These discussions, collected in *A Poetic Equation: Conversations Between Nikki Giovanni and Margaret Walker* (1974), focus much more on the budding concepts of black female identity and indicate the nascent struggle that contemporary black female intellectuals were experiencing during the rise of the new feminism. In *Black Women Writers,* Giovanni has said,

> The difference between young Black women and young Black men, as I see it, is that young Black men don't feel they will lose face if they say they want to write whereas young Black women aren't at all too sure that writing isn't too aggressive. What you hear a lot is: Can you write and be a good wife too? That's not exactly the question but that's what it amounts to. And the answer is probably no.

Giovanni has taught and lectured at various institutions, including Rutgers University, Ohio State University, and the College of Mount St. Joseph. She is currently a professor of English at Virginia Polytechnic Institute and State University in Blacksburg, where she has been since 1987.

Now in her third decade as a prominent and internationally known poet, Giovanni is producing more personal and reflexive work. Through adroit public relations, she remains a speaker in constant demand for wide-ranging audiences. Her poetry, the prolific collection of her recorded readings, her essays and interviews, and the sheer and constant inspiration of her public style have kept Giovanni alive in the American mind regardless of various shifts in political eras.

❖❖❖

Biographical information can be found in Deborah A. Stanley's sketch in *Contemporary Authors New Revision Series,* vol. 41 (1994). See also Carolyn Mitchell's sketch in *Black Women in America,* vol. 1 (1993) and the Arlene Clift-Pellow entry in *Notable Black American Women* (1992). A longer sketch by Mozella G. Mitchell appears in *Dictionary of Literary Biography,* Trudier Harris and Thadious M. Davis (eds.) *Afro-American Poets Since 1955,* vol. 41 (1985). For general criticism, see Paula Giddings, "Nikki Giovanni: Taking a Chance on Feeling," and William J. Harris, "Sweet Soft Essence of Possibility: The Poetry of Nikki Giovanni," in *Black Women Writers,* ed. Mari Evans (1984). *Black Women Writers* also includes a short essay on the author titled "Nikki Giovanni, an Answer to Some Questions on How I Write: In Three Parts." Another interview can be found in *Black Women Writers at Work* (1983). Also of interest are Martha Cook, "Nikki Giovanni: Place and Sense of Place in Her Poetry," in *Southern Women Writers: The New Generation* (1990), and Virginia Fowler, *Nikki Giovanni* (1992). A critical study of her poetry appears in Karl Malkoff, *Crowell's Handbook of Contemporary American Poetry* (1973).

For Saundra

i wanted to write
a poem
that rhymes
but revolution doesn't lend
itself to be-bopping

then my neighbor
who thinks i hate
asked—do you ever write
tree poems—i like trees
so i thought
i'll write a beautiful green tree poem
peeked from my window
to check the image
noticed the school yard was covered
with asphalt
no green—no trees grow
in manhattan

then, well, i thought the sky
i'll do a big blue sky poem
but all the clouds have winged
low since no-Dick was elected

so i thought again
and it occurred to me

maybe i shouldn't write
at all
but clean my gun
and check my kerosene supply

perhaps these are not poetic
times
at all

Revolutionary Music

you've just got to dig sly
and the family stone
damn the words
you gonna be dancing to the music
james brown can go to
viet nam
or sing about whatever he
has to
since he already told
the honkie
"although you happy you better try
to get along
money won't change you
but time is taking you on"
not to mention
doing a whole
song they can't even snap
their fingers to
"good god! ugh!"
talking bout
"i got the feeling baby i got the feeling"
and "hey everybody let me tell you the news"
martha and the vandellas dancing in the streets
while shorty long is functioning at that junction
yeah we hip to that
aretha said they better
think
but she already said
"ain't no way to love you"
(and you know she wasn't talking to us)
and dig the o'jays asking "must i always be a stand in
for love"
i mean they say "i'm a fool for being myself"

While the mighty mighty impressions have told the
world
for once and for all
"We're a Winner"

even our names—le roi has said—are together
impressions
temptations
supremes
delfonics
miracles
intruders (i mean intruders?)
not beatles and animals and white bad things like
young rascals and shit
we be digging all
our revolutionary music consciously or un
cause sam cooke said "a change is gonna come"

Nikki-Rosa

childhood remembrances are always a drag
if you're Black
you always remember things like living in Woodlawn
with no inside toilet
and if you become famous or something
they never talk about how happy you were to have your mother
all to yourself and
how good the water felt when you got your bath from one of those
big tubs that folk in chicago barbecue in
and somehow when you talk about home
it never gets across how much you
understood their feelings
as the whole family attended meetings about Hollydale
and even though you remember
your biographers never understand
your father's pain as he sells his stock
and another dream goes
and though you're poor it isn't poverty that
concerns you
and though they fought a lot
it isn't your father's drinking that makes any difference
but only that everybody is together and you
and your sister have happy birthdays and very good christmasses
and I really hope no white person ever has cause to write about me
because they never understand Black love is Black wealth and they'll
probably talk about my hard childhood and never understand that
all the while I was quite happy

The Women Gather

for Joe Strickland

the women gather
because it is not unusual

to seek comfort in our hours of stress
    a man must be buried

It is not unusual
that the old bury the young
    though it is an abomination

It is not strange
that the unwise and the ungentle
carry the banner of humaneness
    though it is a castration of the spirit

It no longer shatters the intellect
that those who make war
call themselves diplomats

we are no longer surprised
that the unfaithful pray loudest
every sunday in every church
and sometimes in rooms facing east
    though it is a sin and a shame

    so how do we judge a man
most of us love from our need to love not
because we find someone deserving

most of us forgive because we have trespassed not
because we are magnanimous

most of us comfort because we need comforting
our ancient rituals demand that we give
what we hope to receive

    and how do we judge a man

we learn to greet when meeting
to cry when parting
and to soften our words at times of stress

the women gather
with cloth and ointment
their busy hands bowing to laws that decree
willows shall stand swaying but unbroken
against even the determined wind of death

    we judge a man by his dreams
not alone his deeds
    we judge a man by his intent
not alone his shortcomings
    we judge a man because it is not unusual
to know him through those who love him

the women gather strangers
to each other because

they have loved a man

it is not unusual to sift
through ashes
and find an unburnt picture

Ego Tripping
(there may be a reason why)

I was born in the congo
I walked to the fertile crescent and built
the sphinx
I designed a pyramid so tough that a star
that only glows every one hundred years falls
into the center giving divine perfect light
I am bad

I sat on the throne
drinking nectar with allah
I got hot and sent an ice age to europe
to cool my thirst
My oldest daughter is nefertiti
the tears from my birth pains
created the nile
I am a beautiful woman

I gazed on the forest and burned
out the sahara desert
with a packet of goat's meat
and a change of clothes
I crossed it in two hours
I am a gazelle so swift
so swift you can't catch me

For a birthday present when he was three
I gave my son hannibal an elephant
He gave me rome for mother's day
My strength flows ever on

My son noah built new / ark and
I stood proudly at the helm
as we sailed on a soft summer day
I turned myself into myself and was
jesus
men intone my loving name
All praises All praises
I am the one who would save

I sowed diamonds in my back yard
My bowels delivered uranium
the filings from my fingernails are

semi-precious jewels
On a trip north
I caught a cold and blew
My nose giving oil to the arab world
I am so hip even my errors are correct
I sailed west to reach east and had to round off
the earth as I went
The hair from my head thinned and gold was laid
across three continents

I am so perfect so divine so ethereal so surreal
I cannot be comprehended
except by permission

I mean . . . I . . . can fly
like a bird in the sky . . .

THE NEW BREED

ALBERT MURRAY

(1916–)

Albert Murray is *the* aesthetician and theorist of black American music and culture. Throughout his works, he has, more thoroughly than any other author, spelled out the theoretical implications of black culture. In fact, from the prose of Murray, Ralph Ellison, Larry Neal, and Amiri Baraka, one could elaborate a complex theory of African American culture. This theory is fully articulated in Murray's seven books, both fiction and nonfiction, which meditate on black music, black style, black ritual, black folklore, and black traditions. Moreover, he argues that black culture is wise, tough, and heroic.

Albert Murray was born in Nokomis, Alabama, on May 12, 1916, to Hugh and Mattie Murray and spent his early youth in Mobile. In 1939, he received his B.S. in education from Tuskegee Institute. Later, he returned to that institution to teach literature and composition and direct the college theater from 1940 to 1943 and again from 1946 to 1951. In 1943, he joined the U.S. Air Force, retiring as a major in 1962. Five years later, he received his M.A. in English from New York University. Murray has taught at a variety of schools, including Columbia University, Colgate University, the University of Massachusetts at Boston, and Emory University. Currently, he lives in New York City with his wife, Mozelle, and his daughter, Michele.

In 1970, Murray published his first book, *The Omni-Americans,* an extensive study of African American culture. In that work, he argues that the African American, like the blues singer and musician, has learned to improvise in the American environment to overcome it and create his or her own standards of excellence and behavior. In *The Hero and the Blues* (1973), he claims that the blues fulfill the function of the greatest literature in creating a hero who seeks out that which threatens human existence and who tries to subdue it with experimentation and improvisation. In his fiction, therefore, Murray creates a blues hero figure based on the blues musician, whose musical improvisations symbolically dramatize his ability to improvise in the face of adversity. His hero adds new and individual solutions to perennial questions. The blues hero is archetypal—a universal person—and charismatic—someone the people want to follow and emulate.

In his first novel, *Train Whistle Guitar* (1974), which had its origin in the short story of the same title, Murray creates a blues hero in the character of the young Scooter. Confronting the chaos of life in Gasoline Point, Alabama, in the 1920s, Scooter fashions a style of living—an ethic—out of his youthful explorations and very old black traditions. Throughout the original short story, which was first published in 1966 under the title "The Luzana Cholly Kick," the author artfully fuses blues lyrics, jazz, southern black folklore, and poetry to dramatize the rites of passage from childhood to manhood of two black male youths.

In 1991, Murray published his second novel, *The Spyglass Tree.* As with *Train Whistle Guitar,* this book reflects his major literary achievement—his full development of characters who also embody the cultural and historical attributes of African American society. Now in his mid-seventies, Albert Murray continues to be a vital and productive artist and theorist who has taught us a great deal about the affirmative richness of African American culture.

❖❖❖

Elizabeth Schulz has written an excellent introduction to Murray's ideas in *Dictionary of Literary Biography,* Trudier Harris and Thadious M. Davis (eds.) *Afro-American Writers Since 1955: Dramatists and Prose Writers,* vol. 38 (1985).

Train Whistle Guitar

Little Buddy's color was that sky blue in which hens cackled; it was that smoke blue in which dogs barked and mosquito hawks lit on barbed-wire fences. It was the color above meadows. It was my color too because it was a boy's color. It was whistling blue and hunting blue, and it went with baseball, and that was old Little Buddy again, and that blue beyond outfields was exactly what we were singing about when we used to sing that old song about it ain't gonna rain no more no more.

Steel blue was a man's color. That was the clean, oil-smelling color of rifle barrels and railroad iron. That was the color that went with Louisiana Charley, and he had a steel-blue 32-20 on a 44 frame. His complexion was not steel blue but leather brown like dark rawhide, but steel blue was the color that went with what he was. His hands were just like rawhide, and when he was not dressed up he smelled like green oak steam. He had on slick starched blue denim overalls then, and when he was dressed up he wore a black broadcloth box-back coat with hickory-striped peg-top pants, and he smelled like the barber shop and new money.

Louisiana Charley was there in that time and place as far back as I can remember, even before Little Buddy was. Because I can remember when I didn't know Little Buddy at all. I can remember when that house they moved to was built (Little Buddy's papa and mama were still living together when they came to Gasoline Point from Choctaw County, which was near the Mississippi State line), and I can also remember when that street (which was called Chattanooga Lookout Street) was pushed all the way through to the AT&N cut. That was before I had ever even heard of Little Buddy, and my buddy then was old Willie Marlowe. Little Buddy didn't come until after Willie Marlowe had gone to Detroit, Michigan, and that was not until after Mister One-Arm Will had been dead and buried for about nine months.

I can remember him there in that wee time when I couldn't even follow the stories I knew later they were telling about him, when it was only just grown folks talking, and all I could make of it was *Luzana, they are talking something about old Luzana again, and I didn't know what, to say nothing of where Louisiana was.* But old Luze was there even then and I could see him very clearly when they said his name because I had already seen him coming up that road that came by that house with the chinaberry yard, coming from around the bend and down in the railroad bottom; and I had already heard whatever that was he was picking on his guitar and heard that holler too. That was always far away and long coming. It started low like it was going to be a song, and then it jumped all the way to the very top of his voice and broke off, and then it started again, and this time was already at the top, and then it gave some quick jerking squalls and died away in the woods, the water, and the darkness (you always heard it at night), and Mama always said he was whooping and hollering like somebody back in the rosin-woods country, and Papa said it was one of them old Luzana swamp hollers. I myself always thought it was like a train, like a bad train saying look out this is me, and here I come, and I'm coming through.

That was even before I was big enough to climb the chinaberry tree. That was when they used to talk about the war and the Kaiser, and I can remember that there was a war book with Germans in it, and I used to see sure-enough soldiers marching in the Mardi Gras parades. Soldier Boy Crawford was still wearing his Army coat then, and he was the one who used to tell about how Luze used to play his guitar in France, telling about how they would be going through some French town like the ones called Nancy and Saint Die and old Luze would drop out of the company and go and play around in the underground wine shops until he got as much cognac and as many French Frogs as he wanted and then he would turn up in the company again and Capt'n would put him out by himself on the worst outpost he could find in No Man's Land and old Luze would stay out there sometimes for three or four days and nights knocking off patrol after patrol, and one time in another place, which was the Hindenburg Line, old Luze was out there again and there were a few shots late in the afternoon and then it was quiet until about three o'clock the next morning and then all hell broke loose, and the Capt'n thought that a whole German battalion was about to move in, and he sent five patrols out to find out what was happening, but when they got there all they found was old Luze all dug in and bristling with enough ammunition to blow up Kingdom Come. He had crawled around all during the afternoon collecting hand grenades and a mortar and two machine guns and even a light two-wheel cannon, and when they asked him what was going on he told them that he had fallen off to sleep in spite of himself and when he woke up he didn't know whether or not any Germans had snuck up so he thought he'd better lay himself down a little light barrage. The next morning they found out that old Luze had wiped out a whole German platoon but when the Capt'n sent for him to tell him he was going to give him a medal, old Luze had cut out and was off somewhere picking the guitar and drinking cognac and chasing the mademoiselles again. He went through the whole war like that and he came out of the Army without a single scratch, didn't even get flat feet.

I heard a lot of stories about the war and I used to draw pictures of them fighting with bayonets in the Argonne Forest, and Soldier Boy Crawford used to look at them and shake his head and give me a nickel and say that some day I was going to be a soldier too.

I used to draw automobiles too, especially the Hudson Super-Six, like old Long George Nisby had. He said it would do sixty on a straightaway, and he had a heavy blasting cut-out on it that jarred the ground. Old Man Perc Stranahan had a Studebaker but he was a white man and he didn't have a cut-out, and he drove as slow as a hearse. Old Gander said Old Man Perc always drove like he was trying to sneak up on something but he never was going to catch it like that. The cars I didn't like then were the flat-engine Buick and the old humpbacked Hupmobile. I liked the Maxwell and the Willys Knight and the Pierce Arrow.

I was always playing train then too, and the trains were there before the automobiles were (there were many more horses and buggies in that part of town than there were automobiles then). I couldn't sit up in my nest in the chinaberry tree and see the trains yet, because I could not climb it yet, but I saw them when Papa used to take me to the L&N bottom to see them come by and I knew them all, and the Pan American was the fastest and Number Four was the fastest that ran in the daytime. Old Luzana could tell you all about the Southern Pacific and the Santa Fe, but that was later. But I already knew something about the Southern Pacific because Cousin Roberta had already gone all the way to Los Angeles, California, on the Sunset Limited.

I used to be in bed and hear the night trains coming by. The Crescent came by at nine-thirty and if you woke up way in the middle of the night you could hear Number Two. I was in my warm bed in that house, and I could hear the whistle coming even before it got to Chickasabogue Bridge and it had a bayou sound then, and then I could hear the engine batting it hell-for-leather on down the line bound for Mobile and New Orleans, and the next time the whistle came it was for Three Mile Creek. It was getting on into the beel then. I played train by myself in the daytime then, looking out the window along the side of the house like an engineer looking down along the drivers.

I used to hear old Stagolee playing the piano over in Hot Water Shorty's jook at night too, even then, especially on Saturday night. They rocked all night long, and I was lying in my warm quilted bed by the window. Uncle Jimmy's bed was by the window on the other side of the fireplace. When it was cold, you could wake up way in the night and still see the red embers in the ashes, and hear the wind whining outside, and sometimes you could hear the boat whistles too, and I could lie listening from where I was and tell you when it was a launch pulling a log raft or a tugboat pulling a barge or a riverboat like the *Nettie Queen,* and sometimes it was a big ship like the *Luchenback* calling the Looking Back, which was all the way down at the city wharf at the foot of Government Street.

I knew a lot about the big ships because Uncle Jerome worked on the wharf. That was before the state docks were built and the big Gulf-going and ocean-going ships didn't come on past Mobile then unless they were going up to Chickasaw to be overhauled, but I had already seen them and had been on ships from England and France and Holland and naturally there were always ships from the Caribbean and South America because that was where the fruit boats came from.

All I could do was see old Luzana Cholly and hear him coming. I didn't really know him then, but I knew that he was blue steel and that he was always going and coming and that he had the best walk in the world, because I had learned how to do that walk and was already doing the stew out of it long before Little Buddy ever saw it. They were calling me Mister Man during that time, and that was when some knuckleheads started calling me The Little Blister, because they said I was calling myself blister trying to say Mister. Aun Tee called me My Mister and Mama called me My Little Man, but she had to drop the little part off when Little Buddy came, and that was how everybody started calling me The Man, although I was still nothing but a boy, and I said to myself old Luzana is the man, old Luzana is the one I want to be like.

Then I was getting to be big enough to go everywhere by myself and I was going to school. That was when I knew about Dunkin's Hill and going up through Egerton Lane. That was the short way to school, because that was the way the bell sound came. Buddy Babe and Sister Babe and old double-jointed, ox-jawed Jack Johnson all went that way too, but when it rained you couldn't get across the bottom, and that was when everybody went the Shelton way, going through behind Stranahan's store and Good Hope Baptist to the old car line and then along that red clay road by the Hillside store.

Then Little Buddy was there and it was sky blue and we were blue hunters and every day was for whistling and going somewhere to do something you had to be rawhide to do, and some day we were going to live in times and places that were blue steel too. We found out a lot about old Luzana then, and then we not only knew him we knew how to talk to him.

The best time (except when he was just sitting somewhere strumming on his guitar) was when he was on his way to the Gambling Woods. (So far as anybody knew, gambling and guitar picking and grabbing freight trains were the only steady jobs he ever had or ever would have, except during the time he was in the Army and the times he was in jail—and he not only had been in jail, he had been in the penitentiary!) We were his good luck when he was headed for a skin game, and we always used to catch him late Saturday afternoon right out there where Gins Alley came into the oil-tank road, because he would be coming from Miss Pauline's cookshop then. The Gambling Woods trail started right out across from Sargin' Jeff's. Sometimes old Luze would have the guitar slung across his back even then, and naturally he had his famous 32-20 in the holster under his right arm.

"Say now hey Mister Luzana," I would holler at him.

"Mister Luzana Cholly one-time," Little Buddy always said, and he said that was what old Luze's swamp holler said too.

"Mister Luzana Cholly all night long," I would say then.

"Nobody else!" he would holler back at us then, "nobody else but."

"The one and only Mister Luzana Cholly from Booze Ana Bolly."

"Talk to me, little ziggy, talk to me."

"Got the world in a jug," I might say then.

"And the stopper in your hand," old Little Buddy would say.

"You tell 'em, little crust busters, 'cause I ain't got the heart."

"He's a man among men."

"And Lord God among women!"

"Well tell the dy ya," old Luz would say then, standing wide-legged, laughing, holding a wad of Brown's Mule chewing tobacco in with his tongue at the same time. Then he would skeet a stream of amber juice to one side like a batter does when he steps up to the plate and then he would wipe the back of his leathery hand across his mouth and squint his eyes.

"Tell the dy-damn-ya!"

"Can't tell no more," Little Buddy would say then, and old Luze would frown and wink at me.

"How come, little sooner, how goddam come?"

"Cause money talks."

"Well shut my mouth and call me suitcase."

"Ain't nobody can do that."

"I knowed you could tell 'em little ziggabo, I knowed good and damn well you could tell 'em."

"But we ain't gonna tell 'em no more."

"We sure ain't."

"Talk ain't no good if you ain't got nothing to back it up with."

Old Luze would laugh again and we would stand waiting and then he would run his hands deep down into his pockets and come out with two quarters between his fingers. He would throw them into the air and catch them again, one in each hand, and then he would cross his hands and flip one to me and one to Little Buddy.

"Now talk," he would say then. "Now talk, but don't say too much and don't talk too loud, and handle your money like the white folks does."

We were going to be like him even before we were going to be like cowboys. And we knew that blue steel was also root hog or die poor, which was what we were going to have to do whether we liked it or not. Little Buddy said it was not just how rough-and-ready old hard-cutting Luze was and how nobody, black or white, was going to do him any dirt and get away with it, and all that. It was that too, but it was also something else. It was also the way he could do whatever he was doing and make it look so easy that he didn't even seem to have to think about it, and once he did it, that seemed to be just about the only real way to do it.

Old Luze did everything his own way just like old Satch played baseball his way. But we knew that we wanted to be like him for more reasons than that too. Somehow or other just as he always seemed to be thirty-five years old and blue steel because he had already been so many places and done so many things you'd never heard of before, he also always seemed to be absolutely alone and not needing anybody else, self-sufficient, independent, dead sure, and at the same time so unconcerned.

Mama said he was don't-carified, and that was it too (if you know the full meaning of the Negro meaning of that expression). He was living in blue steel and his way was don't-carified, because he was blue steel too. Little Buddy said hellfied, and he didn't mean hell-defying either, you couldn't say he was hell-defying all the time, and you couldn't say he went for bad either, not even when he was doing that holler he was so notorious for. That *was* hell-defying in a way, but it was really I don't give a damn if I *am* hell-defying, and he was not going for bad because he didn't need to, since everybody, black and white, who knew anything about him at all already knew that when he made a promise it meant if it's the last thing I do, if it's the last thing I do on this earth—and they knew that could mean I'll kill you and pay for you as much as it meant anything else. Because the idea of going to jail didn't scare him at all, and the idea of getting shot at didn't seem to scare him either. *Because all he ever said about that was if they shoot at me they sure better not miss me, they sure better get me the first time.*

He was a Negro who was an out and out Nigger in the very best meaning of the word as Negroes use it among themselves (who are the only ones who can), and nobody in that time and that place seemed to know what to make of him. White folks said he was crazy, but what they really meant or should have meant was that he was confusing to them, because if they knew him well enough to say he was crazy they also had to know enough about him to know that he wasn't even foolhardy, not even careless, not even what they wanted to mean by biggity. The funny thing, as I remember it now, was how their confusion made them respect him in spite of themselves. Somehow or other it was as if they respected him precisely because he didn't care anything about them one way or the other. They certainly respected the fact that he wasn't going to take any foolishness off of them.

Negroes said he was crazy too, but they meant their own meaning. They did not know what to make of him either, but when they said he was crazy they almost did, because when they said it they really meant something else. They were not talking so much about what he did, as about how he was doing it. They were talking about something like poetic madness, and that was the way they had of saying that he was doing something unheard of, doing the hell out of it, and getting away with whatever it was. You could tell that was what they meant by the very way they said it, by the sound of it, and by the way they were shaking their heads and laughing when they said it.

The way he always operated as a lone wolf and the unconcernedness, not the Negro-ness as such, were the main things then. (Naturally Little Buddy and I knew about Negroes and white folks, and we knew that there was something generally wrong with white folks, but it didn't seem so very important then. We knew that if you hit a white boy he would turn red and call you nigger that did not sound like the Nigger the Negroes said and he would run and get as many other white boys as he could and come back at you, and we knew that a full-grown white man had to get somebody to back him up too, but we didn't really think about it much, because there were so many other things we were doing then.)

Nobody ever said anything about old Luzana's papa and mama, and when you suddenly wondered about them you realized that he didn't seem to have or need any family at all, it really was as if he had come full-grown out of the swamp somewhere. And he didn't seem to need a wife either. But that was because he was not going to settle down yet. Because he had lived with more women from time to time and place to place than the average man could even shake a stick at.

We knew somehow or other that the Negroness had something to do with the way we felt about him too, but except for cowboys like Tom Mix and Buck Jones, and the New York Yankees and one or two other things, almost everything was Negro then; that is, everything that mattered was. So the Negro part was *only* natural, although I can see something special about it too now.

When you boil it all down, I guess the main thing was how when you no more than just said his name, *Louisiana Charlie, old Luzana Cholly, old Luze,* that was enough to make you know not only him and how he looked and talked and walked that sporty limp walk, but his whole way of being, and how you knew right off the bat that he all alone and unconcerned in his sharp-edged and rough-backed steel had made it what it was himself.

Because that was what old Little Buddy and I were going to do too, make a name for ourselves. Because we knew even then (and I already knew it before he came) that doing that was exactly what made you the kind of man we wanted to be. Mama said I was her little man, and Aun Tee always called me her little mister, but I wasn't anybody's man and mister yet and I knew it, and when I heard the sound of the name that Mama taught me how to write I always felt funny, and I always jumped even when I didn't move. That was in school, and I wanted to hide, and I always said *they are looking for me, they are trying to see who I am,* and I had to answer because it would be the teacher calling the roll, and I said Present, and it sounded like somebody else.

And when I found out what I found out about me and Aun Tee and knew that she was my flesh and blood mama, I also found out that I didn't know my real name at all, because I didn't know who my true father was. So I said *My name is Reynard the Fox,* and Little Buddy said *My name is Jack the Rabbit and my home is in the briar patch.* That was old Luzana too, and when you heard that holler coming suddenly out of nowhere just as old Luze himself always seemed to come, it was just like it was coming from the briar patch.

So when Mama said what she said about me and Aun Tee at that wake that time and I heard it and had to believe it, I wished that old Luzana had been my real papa, but I didn't tell anybody that, not even Little Buddy although Little Buddy was almost in the same fix because he didn't have a mama any more and he didn't really love his papa because it was his papa that ran his mama away.

But we were buddies and we both did old Luzana's famous walk and we were going to be like him, and the big thing that you had to do to really get like him was to grab yourself a fast armful of fast freight train and get long gone from here. That was the real way to learn about the world, and we wanted to learn everything about it that we could. That was when we started practicing on the switch engine. That was down in the oilyards. You had to be slick to do even that because naturally your folks didn't want you doing stuff like that, because there was old Peg Leg Nat. Old Peg Leg butt-headed Nat could hop a freight almost as good as old Luzana could. He called himself mister-some-big-shit-on-a-stick. He spent most of his time fishing and sometimes he would come around pushing a wheelbarrow selling fresh fish, shrimps, and crabs, but every now and then he would strike out for somewhere on a freight just like old Luze did. Mama used to try to scare us with old Nat, telling us that a peg leg was just what messing around with freight trains would get you, and for a while she did scare us, but not for long, because then we found out that it never would have happened to old Nat if he hadn't been drunk and showing off. And anybody could see that getting his leg cut off hadn't stopped old Nat himself anyway since he could still beat any two-legged man we knew doing it except old Luze himself. Naturally we had to think about it, naturally it did slow us up for a while, but it didn't really stop us. Because there was still old Luze, and that was who we were anyway, not old Peg Leg Nat.

Then that time when I found out all about me and Aun Tee, I was going to run away, and Little Buddy was ready too. Then old Little Buddy found out that old Luze was getting ready to get moving again and we were all set and just waiting and then it was the day itself.

I will always remember that one.

I had on my brogan shoes and I had on my corduroy pants under my overalls with my jumper tucked in. I had on my blue baseball cap too and my rawhide wristband and I had my pitching glove folded in my hip pocket. Little Buddy had on just about the same thing except that he was carrying his first-base pad instead of his catcher's mitt. We had our other things and something to eat rolled up in our blanket rolls so that we could sling them over our shoulders and have our arms free.

Little Buddy had gotten his papa's pearl-handled .38 Smith & Wesson, and we both had good jackknives. We had some hooks and twine to fish with too, just in case, and of course we had our trusty old slingshots for birds.

It was May and school was not out yet, and so not only were we running away, we were playing hooky too. It was hot, and with that many clothes on we were sweating, but you had to have them, and that was the best way to carry them.

There was a thin breeze that came across the railroad from the river, the marsh, and Pole Cat Bay, but the sun was hot and bright, and you could see the rails downright shimmering under the high and wide open sky. We had always said that we were going to wait until school was out, but this was our chance now, and we didn't care about school much any more anyhow. This was going to be school now anyway, except it was going to be much better.

We were waiting in the thicket under the hill. That was between where the Dodge mill road came down and where the oil spur started, and from where we were, we could see up and down the clearing as far as we needed to, to the south all the way across Three Mile Creek bridge to the roundhouse, and where Mobile was, and to the north all the way up past that mill to the Chickasabogue bridge. We knew just about from where old Luzana was going to come running, because we had been watching him do it for a long time now. We had that part down pat.

I don't know how long we had been waiting because we didn't have a watch but it had been a long time, and there was nothing to do but wait then.

"I wish it would hurry up and come on," Little Buddy said.

"Me too," I said.

"Got to get to splitting."

We were squatting on the blanket rolls, and Little Buddy was smoking another Lucky Strike, smoking the way we both used to smoke them in those old days, letting it hang dangling in the corner of your mouth, and tilting your head to one side with one eye squinted up like a gambler.

"Goddam it, watch me nail that sapsucker," he said.

"Man, you watch me."

You could smell the May woods there then, the dogwood, the honeysuckle, and the warm smell of the undergrowth; and you could hear the birds too, the jays, the thrushes, and even a woodpecker somewhere on a dead tree. I felt how moist and cool the soft dark ground was there in the shade, and you could smell that smell too, and smell the river and the marsh too.

Little Buddy finished the cigarette and flipped it out into the sunshine, and then sat with his back against a sapling and sucked his teeth. I looked out across the railroad to where the gulls were circling over the marsh and the river.

"Goddam it, when I come back here to this burg, I'm going to be a goddam man and a half," Little Buddy said all of a sudden.

"And don't care who knows it," I said.

"Boy, Chicago."

"Man, Detroit."

"Man, Philadelphia."

"Man, New York."

"Boy, I kinda wish old Gander was going too."

"I kinda wish so too."

"Old cat-eyed Gander."

"Old big-toed Gander."

"Old Gander is all right."

"Man, who you telling."

"That son of a bitch know his natural stuff."

"That bastard can steal lightning if he have to."

"Boy, how about that time."

"Man, hell yeah."

"Boy, but old Luze though."

"That Luze takes the cake for everything."

"Hot damn, boy we going!"

"It won't be long now."

"Boy, Los Angeles."

"Boy, St. Louis."

"Man, you know we going."

"Boy, you just watch me swing the sapsucker."

"Boy, snag it."

"Goddam."

"I'm going to natural-born kick that son of a bitch."

"Kick the living hocky out of it."

"Boy and when we get back!" I said that and I could see it, coming back on the Pan American I would be carrying two suitcases and have a money belt and an underarm holster, and I would be dressed fit to kill.

"How long you think it will take us to get fixed to come back?" I said.

"Man, I don't know and don't care."

"You coming back when old Luze come back?"

"I don't know."

I didn't say anything else then. Because I was trying to think about how it was really going to be then. Because what I had been thinking about before was how I wanted it to be. I didn't say anything because I was thinking about myself then, thinking: *I always said I was going but I don't really know whether I want to go or not now. I want to go and I don't want to go.* I tried to see what was really going to happen and I couldn't, and I tried to forget it and think about something else, but I couldn't do that either.

I looked over at Little Buddy again. Who was lying back against the tree with his hands behind his head and his eyes closed. Whose legs were crossed, and who was resting easy like a ballplayer rests before time for the game to start. I wondered what he was really thinking. Did he really mean it when he said he did not know and didn't care? You couldn't tell what he was thinking, but you could tell that he wasn't going to back out now, no matter how he was feeling about it.

So I said to myself goddam it if Little Buddy can make it I can too, and I had more reason to be going away than he did anyway. *I had forgotten about that. I had forgotten all about it. And then I knew that I still loved Papa and they had always loved me and they had always known about me and Aun Tee.*

But I couldn't back out then, because what I had found out wasn't the real reason for going anyway. Old Luze was really the reason, old Luze and blue steel, old Luze and rawhide, old Luze and ever-stretching India Rubber.

"Hey Lebud."

"Hey."

"Going to the big league."

"You said it."

"Skipping city."

"You tell 'em."

"Getting further."

"Ain't no lie."

"Long gone."

"No dooky."

That was when Little Buddy said my home is in the briar patch. My name is Jack the Rabbit and my natural home is in the briar patch. And I said it too, and I said that was where I was bred and born.

"Goddam it to hell," Little Buddy said then, "why don't it come on?"

"Son of a bitch," I said.

Then I was leaning back against my tree looking out across the sandy clearing at the sky and there were clean white pieces of clouds that looked like balled-up sheets in a washtub, and the sky was blue like rinse water with bluing in it, and I was thinking about Mama again, and hoping that it was all a dream.

But then the train was really coming and it wasn't a dream at all, and Little Buddy jumped up.

"Come on."

"I'm here."

The engine went by, and we were running across the clearing. My ears were ringing and I was sweating, and my collar was hot and my pants felt as if the seat had been ripped away. There was nothing but the noise and we were running into it, and then we were climbing up the hill and running along the slag and cinders. We were trotting along in reach of it then. We remembered to let an empty boxcar go by, and when the next gondola came, Little Buddy grabbed the front end and I got the back. I hit the hotbox with my right foot and stepped onto the step and pulled up. The wind was in my ears then, but I knew about that from practicing. I climbed on up the ladder and got down on the inside, and there was Little Buddy coming back toward me.

"Man, what did I tell you!"

"Did you see me lam into that sucker?"

"Boy, we low more nailed it."

"I bet old Luze will be kicking it any minute now."

"Cool hanging it."

"Boy, yair," I said, but I was thinking I hope old Luze didn't change his mind. I hope we don't miss him. I hope we don't have to start out all by ourselves.

"Going boy."

"Yeah."

"Going.
don't know where I'm going
but I'm going
Say now I'm going
don't know where I'm going
but I'm going."

We crawled up into the left front corner out of the wind, and there was nothing to do but wait then. We knew that she was going to have to pull into the hole for Number Four when she got twelve miles out, and that was when we were going to get to the open boxcar.

We got the cigarettes out and lit up, and there was nothing but the rumbling noise that the wide-open car made then, and the faraway sound of the engine and the low-rolling smoke coming back. That was just sitting there, and after we got a little more used to the vibration, nothing at all was happening except being there. You couldn't even see the scenery going by.

It was just being there and being in that time, and you never really remember anything about things like that except the sameness and the way you felt, and all I can remember now about that part is the nothingness of doing nothing and the feeling not of going but of being taken.

All I could see after we went through the bridge was the sky and the bare floor and the sides of the gondola, and all I can remember about myself is how I wished that something would happen, because I definitely did not want to be going then, and I was lost even though I knew good and well that I was not even twelve miles from home yet. Because although we certainly had been many times farther away and stayed longer, this already seemed to be farther and longer than all the other times put together.

Then we could tell that it was beginning to slow down, and we stood up and started getting ready. And then it was stopping, and we were ready, and we climbed over and got down and started running for it. That was still in the bayou country and beyond the train smell there was the sour-sweet smell of the swamp. We were running on hard pounded slag then, and with the train quiet and waiting for Number Four, you could hear the double running of our feet echoing through the cypresses and the marshland.

The wide roadbed was almost half as high as the telegraph wires, and along the low right-of-way where the black creosote poles went along, you could see the blue and white lilies floating on the slimy green water. We came hustling hot to get to where we knew the empty car was, and then there we were.

And there old Luzana himself was.

He stood looking down at us from the door with an unlighted cigarette in his hand. We stopped dead in our tracks. I knew exactly what was going to happen then. It was suddenly so quiet that you could hear your heart pounding inside your head, and I was so embarrassed I didn't know what to do and I thought *now he's going to call us a name. Now he's never going to have anything to do with us any more.*

We were just standing there waiting and he just let us stand there and feel like two puppies with their tails tucked between their legs, and then he started talking.

"It ain't like that. It ain't like that. It just ain't like that, it just ain't."

And he was shaking his head not only as if we couldn't understand him but also as if we couldn't even hear him.

"It ain't. Oh, but it ain't."

We didn't move. Little Buddy didn't even dig his toe into the ground.

"So this is what y'all up to. Don't say a word, not a word. Don't open your mouth."

I could have sunk right on down into the ground.

"What the hell y'all think y'all doing? Tell me that. Tell me. Don't say a word. Don't say a goddam mumbling word to me."

We weren't even about to say anything.

"I got a good mind to whale the sawdust out of you both. That's just what I oughta do."

But he didn't move. He just stood looking down.

"Well, I'll be a son of a bitch."

That was all he said then, and then he jumped down, walked us back to where the switch frog was, and then there was nothing but just shamefaced waiting. Then Number Four came by and then finally we heard the next freight coming south and when it got there and slowed down for the switch he was standing waiting for a gondola and when it came he picked me up and put me on and then he picked Little Buddy up and put him on and then he caught the next car and came to where we were.

So we came slowpoking it right on back and got back in Gasoline Point before the whistles even started blowing for one o'clock. Imagine that. All of that had happened and it wasn't really afternoon yet. I could hardly believe it.

We came on until the train all but stopped for Three Mile Creek bridge and then he hopped down and took us off. He led us down the hill and went to a place the hobos used under the bridge. He sat down and lit another cigarette and flipped the match into the water and watched it float away and then he was looking at us and then he motioned for us to sit down too.

That was when he really told us what hitting the road was, and what blue steel was. He was talking evenly then, not scolding, just telling us man to boys, saying he was talking for our own good because doing what we were trying to do was more than a notion. He was talking quietly and evenly but you still couldn't face him, I know I couldn't and Little Buddy naturally couldn't because he never looked anybody straight in the eye anyway.

We were back and sitting under Three Mile Creek bridge and he was not really angry and then we were all eating our something-to-eat and then we could talk too, but we didn't have much to say that day. He was doing the talking and all we wanted to do was ask questions and listen.

That was when he told us all about the chain gang and the penitentiary and the white folks, and you could see everything he said and you were there too, but you were not really in it this time because it was happening to him, not you, and it was him and you were not him, you were you. You could be rawhide and you could be blue steel but you couldn't really be Luzana Cholly, because he himself was not going to let you.

Then he was talking about going to school and learning to use your head like the smart white folks. You had to be rawhide but you had to be patent leather too, then you would really be nimble, then you would really be not only a man but a big man. He said we had a lot of spunk and that was good but it wasn't good enough, it wasn't nearly enough.

And then he was talking about Negroes and white folks again, and he said the young generation of Negroes were supposed to be like Negroes and be like white folks too and still be Negroes. He sat looking out across the water then, and then we heard another freight coming and he got up and got ready and he said we could watch him but we'd better not try to follow him.

Then we were back up on the hill again and the train was coming and he stood looking at us with the guitar slung over his shoulder and then he put his hands on our shoulders and looked straight at us, and we had to look at him then, and we knew that we were not to be ashamed in front of him any more.

"Make old Luze proud of you," he said then, and he was almost pleading. "Make old Luze glad to take his hat off to you some of these days. You going further than old Luze ever even dreamed of. Old Luze ain't been nowhere. Old Luze don't know from nothing."

And then the train was there and we watched him snag it and then he was waving good-by.

MARI EVANS*

A poet, playwright, storyteller, screenwriter, television producer, college professor, and editor, Mari Evans authenticates both the horror of being an unintentional immigrant to the United States and the immense majesty of the Africa left behind. Her work envisions the African American experience with consciousness, commitment, and a full depth of poetic comprehension. Evans's poetry has been incorporated in every aspect of communal expression: it has graced album covers; been set to music and dance; been used in filmstrips and television specials; and even been included in two off-Broadway productions. Moreover, Evans edited one of the most important collections of critical essays in African American studies of the past decade.

Born in Toledo, Ohio, Evans lost her mother when she was just seven. She was raised primarily by her father, whom she credits with being the most important influence on her life and the one who instilled such a strong African consciousness in her. Evans's father also encouraged his daughter to become a writer. When she was ten years old, she read the works of the eminent poet Langston Hughes. "What he gave me was not advice, but his concern, his interest, and, more importantly, he inspired a belief in myself and my ability to produce," Evans wrote in the essay "My Father's Passage."

Evans attended the University of Toledo. Although she did spend some years in nonacademic pursuits, she always accepted jobs where she could use her writing skills, including working as an editor for a chain-manufacturing company. From 1968 to 1973, she was producer, director, and writer of "The Black Experience," a television show on station WTTV in Indianapolis, where she has been a permanent resident for some years. She has also been a consultant on ethnic studies for the Bobbs-Merrill Company and the National Endowment for the Arts and a board member of the First World Foundation. Her community service has included work on the Indiana Statewide Committee for Penal Reform and the Indiana Corrections Code Commission. Evans is divorced and the mother of two sons.

According to Wallace Peppers, Evans's first book of poetry, *Where Is All the Music* (1968), does not foretell her activist bent. Of the twenty-four poems, he

*No exact birth date.

writes, "Only three—'The Alarm Clock,' 'Black jam for dr. negro,' and 'Who can be born black'—treat themes that are incontrovertibly 'activist.'" However, with the appearance of *I Am a Black Woman* in 1970, the poet began to focus exclusively on the black community, and particularly on the experiences of black women. She continued with these themes in *Night Star* (1981). David Dorsey notes that a "humane grace" pervades *Night Star.* Of Evans's development as a poet, he writes, "There are several reasons why the corpus of Evans's published works to date are extremely illuminating for anyone interested in considering the nature of art in the African American tradition. The first is that her creative works are of unquestionable artistic excellence."

The forms of Evans's poetry are brief and specific, but imagery and theme explode from each line. Robert P. Sedlack writes, "Besides using images that appeal simply and directly, Mrs. Evans also uses a language that can best be characterized as eclectic to give vitality to her work. . . . She borrows words and phrases from several other languages including French, German, and Swahili." He says that Evans adeptly uses "typographical tricks—running words together, separating them, using capital or lower case letters—to speed up, slow down, emphasize, de-emphasize," so that readers can deduce the class, race, and political identification of her characters.

In addition to her poetry, Evans is editor of the landmark 1984 collection of essays *Black Women Writers 1950–1980: A Critical Evaluation,* which received overwhelmingly favorable critical reviews. In his review in *Black American Literature Forum,* John Williams called the work the culmination of three years of research. Intended to be

> an undertaking of monumental magnitude and ambition, the book seeks to distill the singular literary achievement of those black women writers of the post-World-War-II generation, by-products of the Civil Rights movement, the Black Power movement, and the women's movement . . . for this seminal volume of criticism, the editor has assembled many of the most prolific female voices of our age.

Several Afrocentric critics noted that most of the fifteen novelists, poets, and autobiographers who are highlighted in the text do not use the self-identifying language of radical feminism to separate themselves from the black community.

The poet extended her talents with two major dramatic productions, *River of My Song* (1977) and *Eyes* (1979), which have been performed in Indianapolis, Chicago, New York, and Cleveland. *Eyes* is a musical adaptation of Zora Neale Hurston's novel *Their Eyes Were Watching God* (1937). Evans also has a one-woman play, *Boochie* (1979), which treats child abuse. It has been performed in Indianapolis, Atlanta, and Brooklyn, New York. David Dorsey reports that "through the monologue of the one character in *Boochie,*" the audience is "led to a very specific and incisive recognition of the effects of social forces (unemployment, alcohol, welfare) on the Black woman, the Black man, the Black child."

Evans also has made sound contributions to the field of African American children's literature. In 1973, she published *I Look at Me!* which, in an effort to teach black children to love their people and their community, shows African Americans in a variety of professions. Another, *Singing Black* (1976), teaches children about the heart and soul of black music. *Jim Flying High* (1979) brings humor to the problem of ethnic identification and cultural interdependence that all Africans in the Diaspora face. In 1973, Evans produced a delightful collection for young teens called *Rap Stories.*

Evans has taught African American literature and creative writing at several American universities, including Indiana University at Bloomington, Cornell University, Purdue University at Indianapolis and at East Lafayette, and Northwestern University. Her awards and grants include the Black Academy of Arts and Letters Annual Poetry Award, a John Hay Whitney Fellowship, a MacDowell Fellowship, a National Endowment for the Arts Creative Writing Award (1981 and 1982), and a Woodrow Wilson Foundation grant. Evans was granted an Honorary Doctorate of Humane Letters from Marion College in 1975.

When others in the Black Arts Movement were writing solely of oppression, reculturalization, and revolution, Evans foresaw the need to accent the strength, grace, and endurance of the African American woman and to highlight every aspect of her beauty. While others, in rejection of Western symbols and language that debunk blackness as evil, used public forums to declare that "Black Is Beautiful," Evans was one of the first to gently but clearly reinforce this essential premise in her work. Her poetry, drama, fiction, and prose have appealed to an audience within an audience—speaking directly to African American women without neglecting or minimizing the role of African American men. Evans has always wanted the African American community to remain whole but, in that wholeness, to maintain a respect and reverence for African American womanhood. Her literary offerings, especially her poetry, have received more critical review than those of most black women poets of the period, but her supportive readers expect and hope that more critical exploration is yet to come.

❖❖❖

The most definitive criticism of Evans's poetry includes Robert P. Sedlack, "Mari Evans: Consciousness and Craft," *CLA Journal* xv (September 1971); David Dorsey, "The Art of Mari Evans," and Solomon Edwards, "Affirmation in the Works of Mari Evans," in *Black Women Writers 1950–1980: A Critical Evaluation,* ed. Mari Evans (1984); Wallace R. Peppers's entry in *Dictionary of Literary Biography: Afro-American Poets Since 1955,* vol. 41.

Michele Wallace discusses Evans and other black female poets in *Invisibility Blues: From Pop to Theory* (1990). Brief biographical sketches of Evans can be found in Marilyn K. Basel's entry in *Contemporary Authors* (1975); *Something About the Author* vol. 10 (1976); *Black Writers* (1989). Kari Winter has an essential article in *Notable Black American Women* (1992).

John Williams in *Black American Literature Forum* (1984) offers a critique of Evans's editorial work in *Black Women Writers 1950–1980: A Critical Evaluation.*

I Am a Black Woman

I am a black woman
the music of my song
some sweet arpeggio of tears
is written in a minor key
and I

can be heard humming in the night
Can be heard
humming
in the night
I saw my mate leap screaming to the sea
and I/with these hands/cupped the lifebreath
from my issue in the canebrake
I lost Nat's swinging body in a rain of tears
and heard my son scream all the way from Anzio
for Peace he never knew. . . . I
learned Da Nang and Pork Chop Hill
in anguish
Now my nostrils know the gas
and these trigger tire/d fingers
seek the softness in my warrior's beard
I
am a black woman
tall as a cypress
strong
beyond all definition still
defying place
and time
and circumstance
assailed
impervious
indestructible
Look
on me and be
renewed

into blackness softly

the hesitant door chain
back forth back
forth
the
stealthy
soft
final
sssshuuu t
jubilantly
stepping down
stepping down
step
ping lightly across the lower
hall

the shocking airfingers
the
receiving
blackness
sigh

Speak the Truth to the People

Speak the truth to the people
Talk sense to the people
Free them with reason
Free them with honesty
Free the people with Love and Courage and Care for their Being
Spare them the fantasy
Fantasy enslaves
A slave is enslaved
Can be enslaved by unwisdom
Can be enslaved by black unwisdom
Can be re-enslaved while in flight from the enemy
Can be enslaved by his brother whom he loves
His brother whom he trusts
His brother with the loud voice
And the unwisdom
Speak the truth to the people
It is not necessary to green the heart
Only to identify the enemy
It is not necessary to blow the mind
Only to free the mind
To identify the enemy is to free the mind
A free mind has no need to scream
A free mind is ready for other things

To BUILD black schools
To BUILD black children
To BUILD black minds
To BUILD black love
To BUILD black impregnability
To BUILD a strong black nation
To BUILD.

Speak the truth to the people.
Spare them the opium of devil-hate.
They need no trips on honky-chants.
Move them instead to a BLACK ONENESS.
A black strength which will defend its own
Needing no cacophony of screams for activation.
A black strength which attacks the laws

exposes the lies disassembles the structure
and ravages the very foundation of evil.

Speak the truth to the people
To identify the enemy is to free the mind
Free the mind of the people
Speak to the mind of the people
Speak Truth.

Black jam for dr. negro

Pullin me in off the corner to wash my face an
cut my fro off turn
my collar
down
when that aint my
thang I
walk heels first
nose round an tilted
up
my ancient
eyes
see your thang
baby
an it aint
shit
your thang
puts my eyes out baby
turns my seeking fingers
   into splintering fists
messes up my head
an I scream you out
your thang
is what's wrong
   an' you keep
   pilin it on rubbin it

conceptuality

I am a wisp of energy
flung from the core of the Universe
housed
in a temple
of flesh and bones and blood

in the temple
because it is there
that I make my home
Free
of the temple

not bound
by the temple
but housed

no distances
I am everywhere
energy and will of the universe expressed
realizing my oneness my
indivisibility / I
I am
the One Force
I . . .

MAYA ANGELOU
(1928–)

Very few writers of African American literature in the past thirty years have been as able to transcend the racial, gender, and academic divisions in American society as handily as Maya Angelou. Attracting readers from all backgrounds and economic classes, including the president of the United States, Angelou has become one of the major American authors of the twentieth century. A well-known activist in national and international Civil Rights struggles, a major star in dramatic musical productions, a single parent, and a survivor of an abusive childhood, Angelou, with fictional craft and artistic cunning, has effectively used the autobiographical form to turn so many possibilities of defeat and failure into victory.

Angelou was born Marguerite Johnson to Bailey and Vivian Baxter Johnson in St. Louis on April 4, 1928. Her only sibling is a brother, Bailey, who is a year older. As she relates in her first autobiography, before she and her brother were old enough to start school, their parents were divorced and they were sent to Stamps, Arkansas, to live with their paternal grandmother, Annie Henderson. In *I Know Why the Caged Bird Sings* (1970), Angelou details the survival techniques used by small-town black leaders like her grandmother to keep their families—and, in Mrs. Henderson's case, the entire local population, including blacks and whites—afloat during the Great Depression. Critics almost universally agree that *I Know Why the Caged Bird Sings* is Angelou's most successful text. By illustrating the different but equally effective styles of her mother and two grandmothers, she celebrates the strength of all black women.

Ten years later, the children were moved to St. Louis, but a personal trauma that would affect Angelou's entire life caused them to return to Stamps a few months later. During this time of self-imposed silence, Angelou discovered the world of literature. She graduated from the eighth grade at the top of her class in 1940. That summer, she and Bailey moved to San Francisco to live with their mother. There she attended George Washington High School and took drama and dancing classes at the California Labor School. However, as she so artfully describes in her first autobiography, a deep sense of inferiority because of her ungainly height and decidedly African American physical features led her, in an attempt to find love, into a sexual relationship that resulted in her having a child out of wedlock in 1945.

After the birth of her son, Guy, Angelou married an Italian ex-sailor named Tosh Angelou. Although they were eventually divorced, she retained his name. Her dancing talents were discovered by the producers of the popular stage show *Porgy and Bess,* and she toured with the company in Europe from 1957 to 1963. Increasingly, however, Angelou was becoming more concerned with Civil Rights than with show business, and she decided to become a writer. She studied under the famous protest writer John Oliver Killens and joined the Harlem Writers Guild. Expertise learned with and from guild members such as John Henrik Clarke, Paule Marshall, and James Baldwin enabled her to apply fictional techniques to the autobiographical form.

I Know Why the Caged Bird Sings (1970) catapulted Angelou into the national spotlight. It was astoundingly well received by both the public and literary critics. To account for the book's popularity with white and black readers alike, critic Liliane K. Arensberg cited Angelou's disclosures of the importance of education and exposure to good literature as a child as an appealing feature to parents and teachers. Angelou continued her autobiography in *Gather Together in My Name* (1974).

In *Gather Together* and *Singin' and Swingin'* (1976), the reader has a close-up view of show business life for African Americans. In *The Heart of a Woman* (1981), the reader learns of Angelou's activist associations with notable black leaders such as Martin Luther King, Jr., and Bayard Rustin. Angelou eventually became the northern coordinator for the Southern Christian Leadership Conference (SCLC). Perhaps her most famous public act was as leader of a march to the United Nations to protest racist practices in the United States and other parts of the world. In this segment of her autobiography series, the reader learns about Maya's failed marriage to Vus Make, an African freedom fighter, and of her embrace of African life and culture. Most critics believe that *The Heart of a Woman* is Angelou's second most successful work. Carol Neubauer says that it is in particular an illustration of "the complex nature of her relationship with her son" and that "the major theme is the son's yearning to be completely independent."

Priscilla R. Ramsey explores the relationships between Angelou's more famous autobiographies and her poetry. Covering the three volumes of poetry *Oh Pray My Wings Are Gonna Fit Me Well* (1971), *And Still I Rise* (1978), and *Just Give Me a Cool Drink of Water 'Fore I Die* (1975), Ramsey aptly illustrates how they conform to the basic principles of aesthetic style in African American literature. She says that Angelou's poetry, more than her prose, reveals the force of sensuality as "a fortress against potentially alienating forces, i.e. men, war oppression of any kind, in the real world." In addition to what Ramsey calls Angelou's "love poems," these collections include artistic depictions of the writer's political experiences. The strength of Angelou's poetry, according to Ramsey, is its intimate disclosures about typical female emotions, loves, and aspirations: "While Maya Angelou's poetry may not have taken us into every nook and cranny of her long and complex life . . . its various movements and insights have nonetheless helped us understand the themes, the issues, even some of the conflicts which have pervaded her inner life."

Although President Bill Clinton had Angelou read some of her poetry at his inauguration, it has not received sufficient critical review. Biographical scholars also will have to determine how much information about her life Angelou left out of her continuing autobiography. Certainly, she has shared much of her pain and privacy with readers of the world. However, much more can probably be learned about the interior strength that enabled Angelou to overcome the forces of racism, sexism, single parenthood, and rejection that might have led other women to accept defeat. As more scholarship unfolds, readers should not only learn about the fortitude of Angelou's foremothers, which she reveals in her writing, but also discover more about the incredible courage of the author as well.

❖❖❖

Important criticism of Angelou's work includes Sondra O'Neale, "Reconstruction of the Composite Self: New Images of Black Women in Maya Angelou's Continuing Autobiography," and Selwy R. Cudjoe, "Maya Angelou and the Autobiographical Statement," in *Black Women Writers 1950–1980: A Critical Evaluation,* ed. Mari Evans (1984); Mary Jane Lupton, "Singing the Black Mother: Maya Angelou and Autobiographical Continuity," in *Black American Literature,* vol. 24, no. 2 (1990); Carol E. Neubauer, "Displacement and Autobiographical Style in Maya Angelou's *The Heart of a Woman,*" *Black American Literature Forum* vol. 17, no. 3 (Fall 1983); Clara Washington, "Maya Angelou's Angelic Aura," *Christian Century,* vol. 105, no. 3 (November 1988); Lynn Z. Bloom's entry in *Dictionary of Literary Biography,* vol. 38; Liliane K. Arensberg, "Death As Metaphor of Self in *I Know Why the Caged Bird Sings,*" *CLA Journal,* vol. 20, no. 2 (December 1976); George E. Kent, "Maya Angelou's *I Know Why the Caged Bird Sings* and Black Autobiographical Tradition," *Kansas Quarterly,* vol. 7, no. 3 (Summer 1975).

See also "Fatalism in Maya Angelou's *I Know Why the Caged Bird Sings,*" in John T. Hiers, *Notes on Contemporary Literature* vol. 6, no. 1 (1976); Mayra K. McMurray, "Role Playing As Art in Maya Angelou's Caged Bird," *South Atlantic Bulletin,* vol. XLI, no. 2 (May 1976); Priscilla R. Ramsey,"Transcendence: The Poetry of Maya Angelou," in *A Current Bibliography of African Affairs* vol. 17, no. 2 (1984–1985).

Interviews with Angelou include Claudia Tate, *Black Women Writers at Work* (1983); George Plimpton, "The Art of Fiction CXIX: Maya Angelou," *Paris Review,* vol. 32, no. 116 (Fall 1990); Carol E. Neubauer, "An Interview with Maya Angelou," *Massachusetts Review,* vol. 28, no. 2 (Summer 1987); Catherine S. Manegold, "A Wordsmith at Her Inaugural Anvil," in *New York Times* (January 1993); "*The Black Scholar* Interviews Maya Angelou," *Black Scholar* vol. 8 (January–February 1977).

James P. Draper (ed.) has a lengthy biographical and critical article on Angelou and her works in *Contemporary Literary Criticism* vol. 77 (1993). More biographical information is available in Linda Metzger (ed.), *Contemporary Authors* New Revision Series, vol. 19 (1987); *Something About the Author* vol. 49 (1987); Linda Metzger (ed.), *Black Writers* (1989).

Still I Rise

You may write me down in history
With your bitter, twisted lies,
You may trod me in the very dirt
But still, like dust, I'll rise.

Does my sassiness upset you?
Why are you beset with gloom?
'Cause I walk like I've got oil wells
Pumping in my living room.

Just like moons and like suns,
With the certainty of tides,
Just like hopes springing high,
Still I'll rise.

Did you want to see me broken?
Bowed head and lowered eyes?
Shoulders falling down like teardrops,
Weakened by my soulful cries.

Does my haughtiness offend you?
Don't you take it awful hard
'Cause I laugh like I've got gold mines
Diggin' in my own back yard.

You may shoot me with your words,
You may cut me with your eyes,
You may kill me with your hatefulness,
But still, like air, I'll rise.

Does my sexiness upset you?
Does it come as a surprise
That I dance like I've got diamonds
At the meeting of my thighs?

Out of the huts of history's shame
I rise
Up from a past that's rooted in pain
I rise
I'm a black ocean, leaping and wide,
Welling and swelling I bear in the tide.

Leaving behind nights of terror and fear
I rise
Into a daybreak that's wondrously clear
I rise
Bringing the gifts that my ancestors gave,
I am the dream and the hope of the slave.
I rise
I rise
I rise.

Woman Me

Your smile, delicate
rumor of peace.
Deafening revolutions nestle in the
cleavage of

your breasts
Beggar-Kings and red-ringed Priests
seek glory at the meeting
of your thighs
A grasp of Lions, A lap of Lambs.

Your tears, jeweled
strewn a diadem
caused Pharaohs to ride
deep in the bosom of the
Nile. Southern spas lash fast
their doors upon the night when
winds of death blow down your name
A bride of hurricanes, A swarm of summer wind

Your laughter, pealing tall
above the bells of ruined cathedrals.
Children reach between your teeth
for charts to live their lives.
A stomp of feet, A bevy of swift hands.

My Arkansas

There is a deep brooding
in Arkansas.
Old crimes like moss pend
from poplar trees.
The sullen earth
is much too
red for comfort.

Sunrise seems to hesitate
and in that second
lose its
incandescent aim, and
dusk no more shadows
than the noon.
The past is brighter yet.
Old hates and
ante-bellum lace, are rent
but not discarded.
Today is yet to come
in Arkansas.
It writhes. It writhes in awful
waves of brooding.

On Diverse Deviations

When love is a shimmering curtain
Before a door of chance

That leads to a world in question
Wherein the macabrous dance
Of bones that rattle in silence
Of blinded eyes and rolls
Of thick lips thin, denying
A thousand powdered moles,
Where touch to touch is feel
And life a weary whore
  I would be carried off, not gently
  To a shore,
  Where love is the scream of anguish
  And no curtain drapes the door.

FROM *I Know Why the Caged Bird Sings*

The children in Stamps trembled visibly with anticipation. Some adults were excited too, but to be certain the whole young population had come down with graduation epidemic. Large classes were graduating from both the grammar school and the high school. Even those who were years removed from their own day of glorious release were anxious to help with preparations as a kind of dry run. The junior students who were moving into the vacating classes' chairs were tradition-bound to show their talents for leadership and management. They strutted through the school and around the campus exerting pressure on the lower grades. Their authority was so new that occasionally if they pressed a little too hard it had to be overlooked. After all, next term was coming, and it never hurt a sixth grader to have a play sister in the eighth grade, or a tenth-year student to be able to call a twelfth grader Bubba. So all was endured in a spirit of shared understanding. But the graduating classes themselves were the nobility. Like travelers with exotic destinations on their minds, the graduates were remarkably forgetful. They came to school without their books, or tablets or even pencils. Volunteers fell over themselves to secure replacements for the missing equipment. When accepted, the willing workers might or might not be thanked, and it was of no importance to the pregraduation rites. Even teachers were respectful of the now quiet and aging seniors, and tended to speak to them, if not as equals, as beings only slightly lower than themselves. After tests were returned and grades given, the student body, which acted like an extended family, knew who did well, who excelled, and what piteous ones had failed.

Unlike the white high school, Lafayette County Training School distinguished itself by having neither lawn, nor hedges, nor tennis court, nor climbing ivy. Its two buildings (main classrooms, the grade school and home economics) were set on a dirt hill with no fence to limit either its boundaries or those of bordering farms. There was a large expanse to the left of the school which was used alternately as a baseball diamond or a basketball court. Rusty hoops on the swaying poles represented the permanent recreational equipment, although bats and balls could be borrowed from the P. E. teacher if the borrower was qualified and if the diamond wasn't occupied.

Over this rocky area relieved by a few shady tall persimmon trees the graduating class walked. The girls often held hands and no longer bothered to speak to the lower students. There was a sadness about them, as if this old world was not their home and they were bound for higher ground. The boys, on the other hand, had become more friendly, more outgoing. A decided change from the closed attitude they projected while studying for finals. Now they seemed not ready to give up the old school, the familiar paths and classrooms. Only a small percentage would be continuing on to college—one of the South's A & M (agricultural and mechanical) schools, which trained Negro youths to be carpenters, farmers, handymen, masons, maids, cooks and baby nurses. Their future rode heavily on their shoulders, and blinded them to the collective joy that had pervaded the lives of the boys and girls in the grammar school graduating class.

Parents who could afford it had ordered new shoes and ready-made clothes for themselves from Sears and Roebuck or Montgomery Ward. They also engaged the best seamstresses to make the floating graduating dresses and to cut down secondhand pants which would be pressed to a military slickness for the important event.

Oh, it was important, all right. Whitefolks would attend the ceremony, and two or three would speak of God and home, and the Southern way of life, and Mrs. Parsons, the principal's wife, would play the graduation march while the lower-grade graduates paraded down the aisles and took their seats below the platform. The high school seniors would wait in empty classrooms to make their dramatic entrance.

In the Store I was the person of the moment. The birthday girl. The center. Bailey had graduated the year before, although to do so he had had to forfeit all pleasures to make up for his time lost in Baton Rouge.

My class was wearing butter-yellow piqué dresses, and Momma launched out on mine. She smocked the yoke into tiny crisscrossing puckers, then shirred the rest of the bodice. Her dark fingers ducked in and out of the lemony cloth as she embroidered raised daisies around the hem. Before she considered herself finished she had added a crocheted cuff on the puff sleeves, and a pointy crocheted collar.

I was going to be lovely. A walking model of all the various styles of fine hand sewing and it didn't worry me that I was only twelve years old and merely graduating from the eighth grade. Besides, many teachers in Arkansas Negro schools had only that diploma and were licensed to impart wisdom.

The days had become longer and more noticeable. The faded beige of former times had been replaced with strong and sure colors. I began to see my classmates' clothes, their skin tones, and the dust that waved off pussy willows. Clouds that lazed across the sky were objects of great concern to me. Their shiftier shapes might have held a message that in my new happiness and with a little bit of time I'd soon decipher. During that period I looked at the arch of heaven so religiously my neck kept a steady ache. I had taken to smiling more often, and my jaws hurt from the unaccustomed activity. Between the two physical sore spots, I suppose I could have been uncomfortable, but that was not the case. As a member of the winning team (the graduating class of 1940) I had outdistanced unpleasant sensations by miles. I was headed for the freedom of open fields.

Youth and social approval allied themselves with me and we trammeled memories of slights and insults. The wind of our swift passage remodeled my features. Lost tears were pounded to mud and then to dust. Years of withdrawal were brushed aside and left behind, as hanging ropes of parasitic moss.

My work alone had awarded me a top place and I was going to be one of the first called in the graduating ceremonies. On the classroom blackboard, as well as on the bulletin board in the auditorium, there were blue stars and white stars and red stars. No absences, no tardinesses, and my academic work was among the best of the year. I could say the preamble to the Constitution even faster than Bailey. We timed ourselves often: "WethepeopleoftheUnitedStatesinordertoformamoreperfectunion . . ." I had memorized the Presidents of the United States from Washington to Roosevelt in chronological as well as alphabetical order.

My hair pleased me too. Gradually the black mass had lengthened and thickened, so that it kept at last to its braided pattern, and I didn't have to yank my scalp off when I tried to comb it.

Louise and I had rehearsed the exercises until we tired out ourselves. Henry Reed was class valedictorian. He was a small, very black boy with hooded eyes, a long, broad nose and an oddly shaped head. I had admired him for years because each term he and I vied for the best grades in our class. Most often he bested me, but instead of being disappointed I was pleased that we shared top places between us. Like many Southern Black children, he lived with his grandmother, who was as strict as Momma and as kind as she knew how to be. He was courteous, respectful and soft-spoken to elders, but on the playground he chose to play the roughest games. I admired him. Anyone, I reckoned, sufficiently afraid or sufficiently dull could be polite. But to be able to operate at a top level with both adults and children was admirable.

His valedictory speech was entitled "To Be or Not to Be." The rigid tenth-grade teacher had helped him write it. He'd been working on the dramatic stresses for months.

The weeks until graduation were filled with heady activities. A group of small children were to be presented in a play about buttercups and daisies and bunny rabbits. They could be heard throughout the building practicing their hops and their little songs that sounded like silver bells. The older girls (nongraduates, of course) were assigned the task of making refreshments for the night's festivities. A tangy scent of ginger, cinnamon, nutmeg and chocolate wafted around the home economics building as the budding cooks made samples for themselves and their teachers.

In every corner of the workshop, axes and saws split fresh timber as the woodshop boys made sets and stage scenery. Only the graduates were left out of the general bustle. We were free to sit in the library at the back of the building or look in quite detachedly, naturally, on the measures being taken for our event.

Even the minister preached on graduation the Sunday before. His subject was, "Let your light so shine that men will see your good works and praise your Father, Who is in Heaven." Although the sermon was purported to be addressed to us, he used the occasion to speak to backsliders, gamblers and general ne'er-do-wells. But since he had called our names at the beginning of the service we were mollified.

Among Negroes the tradition was to give presents to children going only from one grade to another. How much more important this was when the person was graduating at the top of the class. Uncle Willie and Momma had sent away for a Mickey Mouse watch like Bailey's. Louise gave me four embroidered handkerchiefs. (I gave her three crocheted doilies.) Mrs. Sneed, the minister's wife, made me an underskirt to wear for graduation, and nearly every customer gave me a nickel or maybe even a dime with the instruction "Keep on moving to higher ground," or some such encouragement.

Amazingly the great day finally dawned and I was out of bed before I knew it. I threw open the back door to see it more clearly, but Momma said, "Sister, come away from that door and put your robe on."

I hoped the memory of that morning would never leave me. Sunlight was itself still young, and the day had none of the insistence maturity would bring it in a few hours. In my robe and barefoot in the backyard, under cover of going to see about my new beans, I gave myself up to the gentle warmth and thanked God that no matter what evil I had done in my life He had allowed me to live to see this day. Somewhere in my fatalism I had expected to die, accidentally, and never have the chance to walk up the stairs in the auditorium and gracefully receive my hard-earned diploma. Out of God's merciful bosom I had won reprieve.

Bailey came out in his robe and gave me a box wrapped in Christmas paper. He said he had saved his money for months to pay for it. It felt like a box of chocolates, but I knew Bailey wouldn't save money to buy candy when we had all we could want under our noses.

He was as proud of the gift as I. It was a soft-leather-bound copy of a collection of poems by Edgar Allan Poe, or, as Bailey and I called him, "Eap." I turned to "Annabel Lee" and we walked up and down the garden rows, the cool dirt between our toes, reciting the beautifully sad lines.

Momma made a Sunday breakfast although it was only Friday. After we finished the blessing, I opened my eyes to find the watch on my plate. It was a dream of a day. Everything went smoothly and to my credit, I didn't have to be reminded or scolded for anything. Near evening I was too jittery to attend to chores, so Bailey volunteered to do all before his bath.

Days before, we had made a sign for the Store, and as we turned out the lights Momma hung the cardboard over the doorknob. It read clearly: CLOSED. GRADUATION.

My dress fitted perfectly and everyone said that I looked like a sunbeam in it. On the hill, going toward the school, Bailey walked behind with Uncle Willie, who muttered, "Go on, Ju." He wanted him to walk ahead with us because it embarrassed him to have to walk so slowly. Bailey said he'd let the ladies walk together, and the men would bring up the rear. We all laughed, nicely.

Little children dashed by out of the dark like fireflies. Their crepe-paper dresses and butterfly wings were not made for running and we heard more than one rip, dryly, and the regretful "uh uh" that followed.

The school blazed without gaiety. The windows seemed cold and unfriendly from the lower hill. A sense of ill-fated timing crept over me, and if Momma hadn't reached for my hand I would have drifted back to Bailey and Uncle Willie, and possibly beyond. She made a few slow jokes about my feet getting cold, and tugged me along to the now-strange building.

Around the front steps, assurance came back. There were my fellow "greats," the graduating class. Hair brushed back, legs oiled, new dresses and pressed pleats, fresh pocket handkerchiefs and little handbags, all homesewn. Oh, we were up to snuff, all right. I joined my comrades and didn't even see my family go in to find seats in the crowded auditorium.

The school band struck up a march and all classes filed in as had been rehearsed. We stood in front of our seats, as assigned, and on a signal from the choir director, we sat. No sooner had this been accomplished than the band started to play the national anthem. We rose again and sang the song, after which we recited the pledge of allegiance. We remained standing for a brief minute before the choir director and the principal signaled to us, rather desperately I thought, to take our seats. The command was so unusual that our carefully rehearsed and smooth-running machine was thrown off. For a full minute we fumbled for our chairs and bumped into each other awkwardly. Habits change or solidify under pressure, so in our state of nervous tension we had been ready to follow our usual assembly pattern: the American national anthem, then the pledge of allegiance, then the song every Black person I knew called the Negro National Anthem. All done in the same key, with the same passion and most often standing on the same foot.

Finding my seat at last, I was overcome with a presentiment of worse things to come. Something unrehearsed, unplanned, was going to happen, and we were going to be made to look bad. I distinctly remember being explicit in the choice of pronoun. It was "we," the graduating class, the unit, that concerned me then.

The principal welcomed "parents and friends" and asked the Baptist minister to lead us in prayer. His invocation was brief and punchy, and for a second I thought we were getting back on the high road to right action. When the principal came back to the dais, however, his voice had changed. Sounds always affected me profoundly and the principal's voice was one of my favorites. During assembly it melted and lowed weakly into the audience. It had not been in my plan to listen to him, but my curiosity was piqued and I straightened up to give him my attention.

He was talking about Booker T. Washington, our "late great leader," who said we can be as close as the fingers on the hand, etc. . . . Then he said a few vague things about friendship and the friendship of kindly people to those less fortunate than themselves. With that his voice nearly faded, thin, away. Like a river diminishing to a stream and then to a trickle. But he cleared his throat and said, "Our speaker tonight, who is also our friend, came from Texarkana to deliver the commencement address, but due to the irregularity of the train schedule, he's going to, as they say, 'speak and run.'" He said that we understood and wanted the man to know that we were most grateful for the time he was able to give us and then something about how we were willing always to adjust to another's program, and without more ado—"I give you Mr. Edward Donleavy."

Not one but two white men came through the door offstage. The shorter one walked to the speaker's platform, and the tall one moved over to the center seat and sat down. But that was our principal's seat, and already occupied. The dislodged gentleman bounced around for a long breath or two before the Baptist minister gave him his chair, then with more dignity than the situation deserved, the minister walked off the stage.

Donleavy looked at the audience once (on reflection, I'm sure that he wanted only to reassure himself that we were really there), adjusted his glasses and began to read from a sheaf of papers.

He was glad "to be here and to see the work going on just as it was in the other schools."

At the first "Amen" from the audience I willed the offender to immediate death by choking on the word. But Amens and Yes, sir's began to fall around the room like rain through a ragged umbrella.

He told us of the wonderful changes we children in Stamps had in store. The Central School (naturally, the white school was Central) had already been granted improvements that would be in use in the fall. A well-known artist was coming from Little Rock to teach art to them. They were going to have the newest microscopes and chemistry equipment for their laboratory. Mr. Donleavy didn't leave us long in the dark over who made these improvements available to Central High. Nor were we to be ignored in the general betterment scheme he had in mind.

He said that he had pointed out to people at a very high level that one of the first-line football tacklers at Arkansas Agricultural and Mechanical College had graduated from good old Lafayette County Training School. Here fewer Amen's were heard. Those few that did break through lay dully in the air with the heaviness of habit.

He went on to praise us. He went on to say how he had bragged that "one of the best basketball players at Fisk sank his first ball right here at Lafayette County Training School."

The white kids were going to have a chance to become Galileos and Madame Curies and Edisons and Gauguins, and our boys (the girls weren't even in on it) would try to be Jesse Owenses and Joe Louises.

Owens and the Brown Bomber were great heroes in our world, but what school official in the white-goddom of Little Rock had the right to decide that those two men must be our only heroes? Who decided that for Henry Reed to become a scientist he had to work like George Washington Carver, as a bootblack, to buy a lousy microscope? Bailey was obviously always going to be too small to be an athlete, so which concrete angel glued to what county seat had decided that if my brother wanted to become a lawyer he had to first pay penance for his skin by picking cotton and hoeing corn and studying correspondence books at night for twenty years?

The man's dead words fell like bricks around the auditorium and too many settled in my belly. Constrained by hard-learned manners I couldn't look behind me, but to my left and right the proud graduating class of 1940 had dropped their heads. Every girl in my row had found something new to do with her handkerchief. Some folded the tiny squares into love knots, some into triangles, but most were wadding them, then pressing them flat on their yellow laps.

On the dais, the ancient tragedy was being replayed. Professor Parsons sat, a sculptor's reject, rigid. His large, heavy body seemed devoid of will or willingness, and his eyes said he was no longer with us. The other teachers examined the flag (which was draped stage right) or their notes, or the windows which opened on our now-famous playing diamond.

Graduation, the hush-hush magic time of frills and gifts and congratulations and diplomas, was finished for me before my name was called. The accomplishment was nothing. The meticulous maps, drawn in three colors of ink, learning and spelling decasyllabic words, memorizing the whole of *The Rape of Lucrece*—it was for nothing. Donleavy had exposed us.

We were maids and farmers, handymen and washerwomen, and anything higher that we aspired to was farcical and presumptuous.

Then I wished that Gabriel Prosser and Nat Turner had killed all whitefolks in their beds and that Abraham Lincoln had been assassinated before the signing of the Emancipation Proclamation, and that Harriet Tubman had been killed by that blow on her head and Christopher Columbus had drowned in the *Santa Maria.*

It was awful to be Negro and have no control over my life. It was brutal to be young and already trained to sit quietly and listen to charges brought against my color with no chance of defense. We should all be dead. I thought I should like to see us all dead, one on top of the other. A pyramid of flesh with the whitefolks on the bottom, as the broad base, then the Indians with their silly tomahawks and teepees and wigwams and treaties, the Negroes with their mops and recipes and cotton sacks and spirituals sticking out of their mouths. The Dutch children should all stumble in their wooden shoes and break their necks. The French should choke to death on the Louisiana Purchase (1803) while silkworms ate all the Chinese with their stupid pigtails. As a species, we were an abomination. All of us.

Donleavy was running for election, and assured our parents that if he won we could count on having the only colored paved playing field in that part of Arkansas. Also—he never looked up to acknowledge the grunts of acceptance—also, we were bound to get some new equipment for the home economics building and the workshop.

He finished, and since there was no need to give any more than the most perfunctory thank-you's, he nodded to the men on the stage, and the tall white man who was never introduced joined him at the door. They left with the attitude that now they were off to something really important. (The graduation ceremonies at Lafayette County Training School had been a mere preliminary.)

The ugliness they left was palpable. An uninvited guest who wouldn't leave. The choir was summoned and sang a modern arrangement of "Onward, Christian Soldiers," with new words pertaining to graduates seeking their place in the world. But it didn't work. Elouise, the daughter of the Baptist minister, recited "Invictus," and I could have cried at the impertinence of "I am the master of my fate, I am the captain of my soul."

My name had lost its ring of familiarity and I had to be nudged to go and receive my diploma. All my preparations had fled. I neither marched up to the stage like a conquering Amazon, nor did I look in the audience for Bailey's nod of approval. Marguerite Johnson, I heard the name again, my honors were read, there were noises in the audience of appreciation, and I took my place on the stage as rehearsed.

I thought about colors I hated: ecru, puce, lavender, beige and black.

There was shuffling and rustling around me, then Henry Reed was giving his valedictory address, "To Be or Not to Be." Hadn't he heard the whitefolks? We couldn't *be,* so the question was a waste of time. Henry's voice came out clear and strong. I feared to look at him. Hadn't he got the message? There was no "nobler in the mind" for Negroes because the world didn't think we had minds, and they let us know it. "Outrageous fortune"? Now, that was a joke. When the ceremony was over I had to tell Henry Reed some things. That is, if I still cared. Not "rub," Henry, "erase." "Ah, there's the erase." Us.

Henry had been a good student in elocution. His voice rose on tides of promise and fell on waves of warnings. The English teacher had helped him to create a sermon winging through Hamlet's soliloquy. To be a man, a doer, a builder, a leader, or to be a tool, an unfunny joke, a crusher of funky toadstools. I marveled that Henry could go through with the speech as if we had a choice.

I had been listening and silently rebutting each sentence with my eyes closed; then there was a hush, which in an audience warns that something unplanned is happening. I looked up and saw Henry Reed, the conservative, the proper, the A student, turn his back to the audience and turn to us (the proud graduating class of 1940) and sing, nearly speaking,

"Lift ev'ry voice and sing
Till earth and heaven ring
Ring with the harmonies of Liberty . . ."

It was the poem written by James Weldon Johnson. It was the music composed by J. Rosamond Johnson. It was the Negro National Anthem. Out of habit we were singing it.

Our mothers and fathers stood in the dark hall and joined the hymn of encouragement. A kindergarten teacher led the small children onto the stage and the buttercups and daisies and bunny rabbits marked time and tried to follow:

"Stony the road we trod
Bitter the chastening rod
Felt in the days when hope, unborn, had died.
Yet with a steady beat
Have not our weary feet
Come to the place for which our fathers
sighed?"

Every child I knew had learned that song with his ABC's and along with "Jesus Loves Me This I Know." But I personally had never heard it before. Never heard the words, despite the thousands of times I had sung them. Never thought they had anything to do with me.

On the other hand, the words of Patrick Henry had made such an impression on me that I had been able to stretch myself tall and trembling and say, "I know not what course others may take, but as for me, give me liberty or give me death."

And now I heard, really for the first time:

"We have come over a way that with tears has
been watered,
We have come, treading our path through the
blood of the slaughtered."

While echoes of the song shivered in the air, Henry Reed bowed his head, said "Thank you," and returned to his place in the line. The tears that slipped down many faces were not wiped away in shame.

We were on top again. As always, again. We survived. The depths had been icy and dark, but now a bright sun spoke to our souls. I was no longer simply a member of the proud graduating class of 1940; I was a proud member of the wonderful, beautiful Negro race.

Oh, Black known and unknown poets, how often have your auctioned pains sustained us? Who will compute the lonely nights made less lonely by your songs, or by the empty pots made less tragic by your tales?

If we were a people much given to revealing secrets, we might raise monuments and sacrifice to the memories of our poets, but slavery cured us of that weakness. It may be enough, however, to have it said that we survive in exact relationship to the dedication of our poets (include preachers, musicians and blues singers).

KRISTIN HUNTER

(1931–)

With her fictional depictions of black life in the urban North and her focus on novels for adolescents, Kristin Hunter has earned a reputation as a solid writer who early on treated many of the themes with which more contemporary black women writers are credited. As a journalist, creative writer, and faculty member, Hunter has remained abreast of various trends and issues in African American communities throughout the United States.

Born in Philadelphia on September 12, 1931, to George Lorenzo and Mabel Lucretia Manigault Eggleston, Kristin was named for the heroine in *Kristin Lavransdatter,* by Norwegian novelist Sigrid Undset, which won the 1928 Nobel Price for literature. That choice of a name reflected her parents' professions; both were teachers. Her father also served as principal of Charles Sumner and Whittier Elementary Schools in Philadelphia. Her mother was forced to leave her job following Kristin's birth; according to a state law, teachers could not have children (some states even forbade married women to be teachers).

Kristin read from the time she was four years old. She attended Charles Sumner Elementary School and spent her junior high school years at Magnolia Public School. Her writing skills were certified when, at age fourteen, she began publishing a teenage social column for the Philadelphia edition of the *Pittsburgh Courier;* she would continue writing for that newspaper until 1952. Her high school writing efforts also included poetry and articles for school publications and the *Pennsylvania Gazette.* She graduated from Haddon Heights High School in 1947.

One of her assignments for the *Courier* proved to be the inspiration for her 1978 novel *The Lakestown Rebellion.* The city of Camden, New Jersey, wanted to annex the all-black community of Lawnside. Hunter was asked to cover the racial disruption that resulted from the decision to do so. In her fictional treatment of these difficult events, Hunter portrays a corrupt black leader, Abe Lakes, who joins forces with equally corrupt state representatives in planning a highway to replace a large portion of the town. Lakes also tries to prevent his light-skinned wife's identification with blacks.

Although Hunter always wanted to be a writer, her father forced her to get a degree in education, which she did at the University of Pennsylvania in 1951, and her parents similarly directed her to her first job as a full-time third-grade teacher. Dissatisfaction soon set in and Hunter resigned her position before the school year ended. She accepted a job as a copywriter with the Lavenson Bureau of Advertising in Philadelphia. This slight deviation from her father's wishes did not last long; in 1952, at her father's urging, she married Joseph Hunter, a union that would last for ten years. She wrote ads during the day and short stories and plays at night until 1955, when her television script *Minority of One* won a national competition sponsored by CBS.

Hunter worked as a research assistant at the University of Pennsylvania School of Social Work during the early 1960s. Between 1963 and 1965 and again from 1965 to 1966, she worked as an information officer for the City of Philadelphia. In 1968, she married journalistic photographer John I. Lattany, Sr. Five years later, she joined the University of Pennsylvania as adjunct associate professor of creative writing, a position she has held ever since.

The novel for which Hunter is perhaps best known, *God Bless the Child,* based on a Billie Holiday song, was published in 1964. Rosalie Fleming, granddaughter of a high yeller, proud domestic worker and daughter of a light-skinned ineffectual mother, tries her best to acquire things that she believes will stave off the effects of poverty and that will gain her relatives' love for her in spite of her slightly darker skin. Involved in a variety of moneymaking schemes, she literally works herself to death—but not before she is able to buy the previously grand house in which her grandmother had worked for whites. Hunter's focus on the effects of inner-city life on her characters continued in *The Landlord* (1966), which gained the interest of a film producer. A series of works for children and adolescents followed, including *The Soul Brothers and Sister Lou* (1968), *Boss Cat* (1971), *Guests in the Promised Land* (for which she received the Chicago Tribune Book World Prize for the most outstanding work of juvenile literature in 1973), *The Survivors* (1975), and *Lou in the Limelight* (1981). The "Lou" series presents the possibility of escape from difficult ghetto conditions, but it also reveals the traps and corruption into which those who seek escape can easily fall.

A departure from Hunter's focus on black life in the inner cities is her exciting, previously unpublished short story "Forget-Me-Not." Set in the South, the story describes, in the Charles Chesnutt tradition of fiction, how conjuring is an effective tool against white racism.

❖❖❖

For biographical information on Hunter, see the entry by Sondra O'Neale in *Dictionary of Literary Biography: Afro-American Fiction Writers After 1955*, vol. 33 (1984) and Maralyn Lois Palak, "Kristin Hunter: A Writer and a Fighter," *Philadelphia Inquirer* November 24, 1974. Trudier Harris discusses *God Bless the Child* (1964) in *From Mammies to Militants: Domestics in Black American Literature* (1982).

Forget-Me-Not

When I go home to visit my folks in Crow Hammock, Georgia, Miss Sybil Storm won't let me forget her. I can pray; I can cuss; I can use more will power than it took me to give up cigars. None of it matters. Once I get within a hundred-mile radius of the place, her power starts drawing me to her. When I'm tired, her drawing power pulls me to her house before I see my kin, which gets me in trouble with my aunts and uncles and cousins, not to mention my mama and my daddy.

Miss Sybil lived over on the other side of the swamp from us when I was growing up. Women went to her to get pregnant and unpregnant. Young men went to her to get classified 4-F for the draft. Wives went to her to bring straying husbands home and keep them there; husbands went for the same purpose and to get their natures back, which was what they felt they needed to keep their wives home. All sorts of ailing folks, white and black, went to her to get cured. But Miss Sybil's most famous deed was fixing Sheriff Elmo Peebles so he never bothered us again.

Most Crow Hammock folks were scared of Miss Sybil—except my grandma, who never feared anybody but God, and often consulted with Miss Sybil about difficult cures, and me. I always had a good time over there. I liked the way Miss Sybil looked—tall and gaunt as a pine tree, head held high as a queen's and wrapped in a bright red cloth, with black eyes that had no bottoms to them, like holes. I liked the stuff she kept in her apron pockets: peppermint candy and boiled peanuts and fish hooks and a good knife for digging roots and cutting herbs.

Miss Sybil always called me "Nephew" when she gave me candy and peanuts. I tried hard, but I could never call her anything but Miss Sybil. I liked the way she treated me and the way she looked, but there was something strong and hard about her, like an iron magnet, that kept me from getting close. I was afraid that if I touched her I might stick and never get loose.

I was never allowed to hang around Miss Sybil very long, anyway. She and my grandma would always be havin' some serious stuff to discuss, so she would tell me to run off and play with her son Jerome.

Rome was three years older than me, but younger in a lot of ways, 'cause he'd never been off our farm. Never been to town. Never been to school, 'cause Miss Sybil didn't believe in school. Didn't even know, as it turned out, that people in Georgia came in two colors and he was supposed to be the wrong one.

Rome almost got et up by an alligator once, but I saved him by doing what my daddy had shown me, shoved a stick between the gator's teeth so he couldn't close his mouth. Rome says now he'd rather tangle with that gator than have another run-in with Elmo Peebles. But that ain't gonna happen, not since his mama put Peebles out of the sheriff business.

Folks in our little patch of Crow Hammock said Miss Sybil could stare down the Devil and make him run hollering to his mama. Could mumble a few words and make crippled folks and some said dead folks walk. Could turn the wind or the rain or anything else around and send it back where it came from.

I don't know about all that. I only know that when she came to church every Sunday, dressed like every other day except for a black hat on top of her bandana, Miss Sybil had a whole empty bench all to herself. Even folks who'd been to her for help the night before moved out of her way. I know she sat alone, head high, eyes front, still as stone, all through the sermon. And I know she fixed Elmo Peebles so he'd never lock up anybody else for sitting in the wrong spot or beat them up for being near the wrong person: so he'd never skim profits off my grandma's moonshine business again.

I call Crow Hammock a patch now because I've seen the world, and knowing its size makes my home seem to shrink. But when I was growing up there, it seemed to stretch endlessly to the horizon in every direction—my daddy's land and my Uncle Chester's land and my grandpa and grandma's land and my cousin Pete's land—acres and acres of timberland and grazing land and growing land. One of the crops we grew was corn. And one of the things we did with it was make liquor.

Since it was all our own land, what we did on it was nobody's business. Especially not no poor-cracker-deputy's business. I felt that way. Rome did, too, and so did all of the Crow Hammock men.

But after Grandpa died, Grandma was in charge of the place, and she believed in preventing trouble. So she paid Elmo Peebles off every time we hauled a truckload of moonshine into town. Paid him in jars, sometimes, and sometimes in money.

Come this Friday when it was time to take the liquor to Mr. J. P. Henry's jook joint in town, my daddy and Uncle Chester and Cousin Pete were all down in Florida working construction. Grandma finally decided to let Rome drive the truck. He didn't have his license yet, but he'd been driving for years, like all of us out in the country. There's only one road to town, so he couldn't hardly get lost. Grandma gave him careful instructions anyway.

"First you stop by Mr. Elmo Peebles place, it's the first mobile home you see on the left. Then you go straight through town to Mr. J. P. Henry's and make the delivery. Mr. Henry's house is bright blue and sets on the right. When he gives you the money, sixty-six dollars and fifty cents, you turn right around and come straight back home. You hear?"

Grandma recounted Rome's load. "You got a hundred and twenty jugs in there. Mister Peebles gets thirty, that's his share. You understand?"

Rome said, "Yes ma'am" politely, but he told me before he started up the truck that he had no intention of giving that deputy stuff of ours that didn't belong to him. I was worried and wanted to go with him, but Grandma had other work for me to do. It had been raining heavy, and I had to clear the drainage ditches to send the overflow from the swamp down to the lake on our bottomland, so it wouldn't come cross the road and flood our branch and our houses.

That night, Mr. J. P. Henry drove out to tell us that Rome was in jail. I rode back to town with him to pay the hundred dollars' bail and bring Rome back in our truck.

When I saw Rome, I hardly knew him. His head was all bashed in like a squashed watermelon, and there was so much blood on his face it looked like the insides of the watermelon turned out. His eyes were puffed up and shut, but he wasn't asleep.

"What happened?" I asked him.

"Sheriff beat me up."

"Why?"

"Sittin' on a bench," was all he would say to me or to any of us. I noticed for the first time how much he looked like his mother. Swelling and all, his face was a wooden mask saying yes and no and maybe all at once.

Finally, we figured out that Rome had stopped at a pretty, peaceful-looking place not knowing it was the eye of the hurricane, the square park that divided the white part of town from the black. Unable to read signs, had sat on a bench not knowing it was for Whites Only. Not knowing about the Jim Crow laws, had sassed some blue-eyed farmer's daughter when she told him to move. And, of course, had already passed right by Elmo Peebles' place without giving him his cut of our moonshine.

Elmo Peebles was only a deputy. But he was tight with the high sheriff, Mr. Tom McPherson. They went hunting and fishing together, played cards together, were as close as two people could be without being married.

Miss Sybil came over and conferred with my grandma. They went out in the woods looking for a special root that cried just like a baby when it was pulled up. They came back with two of them, a big root and a little root they called High John and Little John. High John was the high sheriff, Tom McPherson, and Little John was Elmo Peebles, the deputy. Miss Sybil and my grandma set to work to get them disputing. Sprinkling them with red pepper and burying them upside down head to foot was part of how they did it. I didn't see it all, because they chased me away, and I fell asleep while they were still working those roots.

The next day, all the charges against Rome were dropped.

The day after that, Deputy Sheriff Elmo Peebles was arrested for selling moonshine and a lot of other things we didn't know about—and still don't. But they had to be pretty bad, because we never had to worry about clearing that drainage ditch again.

Rome was still healing when the chain gang came out and started grubbing away at the banks across from our house. And right in the middle of the chain gang was Elmo Peebles, swinging a grub axe and sweating and swearing as he chipped away at our stubborn land and its tough old roots.

We kids laughed and whooped and hollered.

Until Elmo Peebles swung his grub axe high in the air, and there was a deadly water moccasin dangling around it, looking down at that deputy as if trying to decide if he was worth biting or not; as if wondering whether that man's meat was more poisonous than his venom.

We hushed.

Peebles froze with the axe in midair. He stayed like that, stiff and bleached and trembling, for a couple of minutes that seemed like hours.

Then Miss Sybil hissed, "Sssnake," and the cottonmouth dropped to the ground and slithered back to wherever it came from.

Peebles toppled over backward, his grub axe falling on top of him. We couldn't tell if he had fainted, or died of fright, or what. He wasn't moving. The other convicts picked him up and put him in the back of the truck and took him away.

Miss Sybil wiped her hands on her apron, like another job was done, and went back home and took Rome with her.

We never saw or heard of Elmo Peebles again. Everybody says Miss Sybil did it. I can't prove it.

I only know last year I was in Crow Hammock and visited all my relatives, but didn't have time to see Miss Sybil. When I tried to leave, I felt a big barrier in front of my car. It wouldn't go over 25 miles an hour, and after 40 miles of going that slow, I was so tired I turned around and gave in to the big magnet that seemed to be pulling me back in the direction from which I had come. I went back so fast the wind seemed to be carrying my car. I was going 80 all the way, but the gas gauge needle never moved down. And my car never stopped till it got to where she was sitting on her porch, shelling peanuts and nodding as if to say, "I been expecting you, Nephew. What took you so long?"

TOM DENT

(1932–)

Tom Dent emerged from the sixties as probably the leading advocate of the Black Arts Movement in the South. New literary histories will have to recognize that his strong works of dramatic expressionism in New Orleans have come to rival those of Amiri Baraka in New York and New Jersey, as well as plays of harsh urban realism by Ed Bullins of Philadelphia. Indeed, Dent reaches for new folk forms of response to African American existence. In dramatic structures, he creates a unique strategy in which an omniscient narrator addresses the living and the dead. Dent uses urban murder to startle his audience into a cathartic liberation from the defeat and death of black men. In spirit, Dent writes a drama of southern blues, and as a distributor of creative work by others, he proposes that literary art produces social change. He ranks with a few of the most authentic African American writers—Frederick Douglass and Margaret Walker—in his insistence that blacks value the sacredness of communal memory. In his own time, perhaps only Amiri Baraka, Sonia Sanchez, Carolyn Rodgers, Toni Morrison, and August Wilson have kept black history so much alive.

Thomas Covington Dent was born in New Orleans on March 29, 1932, to Dr. Albert Dent, a past president of Dillard University in New Orleans, and Jessie Covington Dent, a teacher and concert pianist. His mother was the first African American musician awarded a scholarship to the celebrated Juilliard School of Music. Her father, Jesse Covington, had helped develop a national business league among blacks and had assisted in establishing Riverside General Hospital for African Americans in Houston, Texas. Her mother, Belle Covington, had served as a leader of racial harmony in the state, as well as a founder of the Blue Triangle Branch of the YWCA.

As the son of a successful and socially conscious family, Dent earned a B.A. in political science at Morehouse College in 1952. "I had no concept of what it meant to be a black writer," he wrote. "We were taught and prepared to belong. . . . We had been taught that race as a subject was limiting, something to escape from if possible, and the further one escaped the more successful one became." Dent began his literary career by editing the *Maroon Tiger,* the student newspaper at Morehouse, and by working summers as a cub reporter for the *Houston Informer.* After serving in the U.S. Army from 1957 to 1959, he moved to New York City to become a reporter for the *New York Age.* In 1960, he copublished a political newspaper, *On Guard for Freedom,* and from 1961 to 1963 he disseminated public information for the NAACP Legal Defense Fund. In 1962, he joined with Calvin Hernton and David Henderson to found the Umbra Writers Workshop. He also developed a supportive bond with fellow writer Raymond Patterson, who is today the well-known developer of the annual Langston Hughes Festival at the City University of New York, and was himself inspired by Hughes.

In 1965, Dent decided to become a member of the Free Southern Theater, which had been established in New Orleans the previous year by John O'Neal, Doris Derby, and Gilbert Moses. All of the participants had emerged from the somewhat halcyon days of the Student Nonviolent Coordinating Committee (SNCC) in advocating voting rights for African Americans in rural Mississippi. Hence, the historical roots of the southern Black Arts movement were quite political, although these roots helped prepare the intellectual landscape for even more dramatic and lyrical arts. For more than a generation, the close bond between communal art and historical memory would prevail within the tradition, as indeed it had subsisted within African American culture during even the mainstream-controlled Harlem Renaissance and the most desperately integrationist years of the 1950s.

As associate director of the Free Southern Theater from 1966 to 1970, Dent became a prominent voice among theater professionals and communal artists. After a stint as an instructor at Mary Holmes College from 1968 to 1970, he dedicated himself to a program of total community action from 1971–1973. As founder of the Congo Square Writers Union in 1973, he nurtured many young talents. Following his completion of an M.A. in poetry at Goddard College in 1974, he continued to freelance for various publications. In 1978 he joined with Charles Rowell and Jerry W. Ward, Jr., to found *Callaloo,* perhaps the most creative journal of the black South.

Dent's *Free Southern Theater* (1969), edited with Richard Schechner and Gilbert Moses, documents the mission of his generation. *Magnolia Streets* (1976; 1987) and *Blues Lights and River Songs: Poems* (1982) reveal an authentic spirit behind even the minstrel mask, as shown in the poem "Return to English Turn":

> you confused, struggling for direction, for a
> way
> masking as modern civilization
> you confused, struggling for direction, for a
> way
> to end forced journeys
> you who listen to the river's voice
> river who does not forget
> the you who is each of us

The poet then asserts that blacks must create new signs to read human values:

> there is a song the old griot sings
> about the uprooting of
> european markers
> & the planting of baobab trees
> & we hear it now
> winding around us
> caressing us with its ripples of Kora notes.

Dent's lyric poetry shows a softer side than the ceremonial plays. *Negro Study No. 34* and *Snapshot* (both 1970) have a mass appeal. *Ritual Murder,* a production by the Ethiopian Theater at New Orleans in 1976, is classic drama of the black South. Dent has published varied work in several literary journals. Currently, he is assisting Andrew Young, the former mayor of Atlanta, in the completion of an autobiography featuring Young's early days with Martin Luther King, Jr.

The return of Dent from New York to New Orleans in 1965 extended the national landscape of black literary arts. Although the public voices of Amiri Baraka (LeRoi Jones) and Larry Neal had challenged the moral authority of the academy in the North, traditionalists still set a conservative tone in the solid South. No outsider was likely to break the stronghold. Dent, forfeiting the elitism of his privilege, disturbed the Old Guard. By the late 1980s, he looked to the future: "Finally, the value of black history lies in its lessons for survival. If we can forget a history so recent as the heroic struggles of our people two decades ago, then no wonder our ship is now rudderless. To know how we can better our condition, we have to know how we did it before. To know in what direction we must move, we have to know the details of our tortuous journey from whence we came to where we are now" ("Annie Devine Remembers," pp. 476–477). Tom Dent, a voice of communal memory, reaches for human freedom.

❖❖❖

A very skillful introspection is Thomas C. Dent, "Annie Devine Remembers," *Black Southern Voices* (1992), a follow-up to pioneering research by Blyden Jackson, "The Black Academy and Southern Literature," in Louis D. Rubin, Jr., et al, (eds.), *History of Southern Literature* (1985). Informative history and insight appear in the *SSSL Papers on Southern Black Writing,* including Jerry W. Ward., Jr., "Southern Black Aesthetics: The Case of Nkombo Magazine," and R. Baxter Miller, "Charles T. Davis: Trace of Southern History," *Mississippi Quarterly* 44, no. 2 (Spring 1991). Of good factual detail are the entry in *Contemporary Authors,* vol. 125 (1991); Lorenzo Thomas's piece in *Dictionary of Literary Biography: Afro-American Writers After 1955: Dramatists and Prose Writers,* ed. Trudier Harris, vol. 38 (1985). New insight appears in R. Baxter Miller, *The Southern Trace of Black Critical Theory,* a special monograph for *Xavier Review* 11, no. 1–2 (1991).

For Walter Washington

We blk blues singers
we blken the chords
with shots of blue . . .
we blk blues singers
we are you pleadin
I gave you all my love
please don't abuse it
we are you cryin
I tried my best
but it wasn't worth it
we are you wishin
the rain smell would
drive away the sweary mad dreams of
last night
we are you watchin

all the half-empty
half-caught
days of yr life
pass before yr face
we are you
listening to the field slide of my voice
the wolf wail of my guitar
openup
the strained / face
you-knew-it-all-the-time
stopped / time
of yr moments

we are you
comin down off
the
speed
of
all
that

back home
where life lay
open
ready.
New Orleans is an easy town
to dance the blues in:
everybody
tune yr mind
guitar.

For Lawrence Sly

I don't know you well, young brother
but I wish for you that you
survive America . . .
that you find your own song
that you gain wisdom & sustenance
from the sound of the ageless water
of the old river to the front.

I don't know you well
but I have seen you walking
the shadowed streets
of uptown New O
trying to blot out
the sounds of bad jobs or no job

& all the bad times of centuries
of self-cuttings & self-hurts
& you searching, searching, searching
for the blue, red & yellow pills . . .

But not knowing you well
still I see you walking
to the beat of your own drummer
trying to tune in, tune in
to the song of your life.

Lawrence, something in us has suffered an awful tear
over these centuries . . .
the disease of the man's dollar
the rapes & the murders of the
bodies and spirits of our young men
have registered their awesome weight.
But you can be that man
give your woman, your children
umbrellas of love & healing and strength . . .
all this lies deep within you
waiting to spring to sunlit life.

I don't know you well young brother
but i wish for you
the strength to reconnect the age-old
spirit of our people . . .
that you may find your rhythm
sing your song

this, my brother, my music for you
on your wedding day.

Magnolia Street

Dear Miss Lucas
i remember you
when i pass Felicity &
Magnolia
yes old Magnolia

 that rickety winding street
 that smells New Orleans

that is open fish-markets
people lounging
memories of numbers tickets strewn
like confetti over the sidewalks

 that rickety winding street
 that sounds New Orleans

which is music
loud
music for siesta and dreaming
and funerals
& sun-happiness Saturday nights
& your clumsy heavy winding
stairsteps
& the circular room that looked
like a lighthouse
& gumbo
    that broken winding street
    that breathes naw/lins

which is everybody knowing your bizness
Miss Lucas
is it not?

& your cousins & your aunts & your nieces
they all came to yr
    wedding, yr hospital bed, yr fund-
    raising Saturday night fish fry

which was old wood meeting old wood meeting
old unpainted wood
which is the truth
is it not
Miss Lucas
& the smell of the acrid tar in the summer
in the street told you it was hot hot
& i remember your sweating face
& your heavy hand whiping the sweat

    that old winding street
    which was yr home
is gone now
Miss Lucas.

ERNEST J. GAINES

(1933–)

A contemporary neorealist storyteller who has created one of the most memorable female characters, Miss Jane Pittman, in African American literature, Ernest Gaines was born on January 15, 1933, on River Lake Plantation in Oscar, a hamlet in Point Coupee Parish, Louisiana. He lived with his parents, Manuel and Adrienne Gaines and an invalid, but religious, resilient, and resourceful aunt, Augusteen Jefferson. Her home was the meeting place for the neighborhood. Gaines grew up listening to stories being told and retold as he ran errands for his aunt and the other adults. In 1948, he moved with his mother and stepfather, Ralph N. Colar, to Vallejo, California, where he graduated from high school and attended Vallejo Junior College. At sixteen, he wrote an unsuccessful novel. After serving two years in the U.S. Army, he earned a B.A. from San Francisco State University in 1957. He published two stories in the college magazine and gave himself ten years to become a writer.

In 1958 Gaines received a Wallace Stegner Fellowship in Creative Writing from Stanford University, and in 1960 he received the Joseph Henry Jackson Literary Award. His other honors include a National Endowment for the Arts Study Award (1967), a Rockefeller Grant-in-Aid (1970), a Guggenheim Fellowship (1972), a Black Academy of Arts and Letters Award (1972), an American Academy and Institute of Arts and Letters Award (1987), the National Book Critics Circle Award (1993), and a MacArthur Fellowship (1993). His major publications include a collection of short stories, *Bloodline* (1968), and six novels: *Catherine Carmier* (1964), *Of Love and Dust* (1967), *The Autobiography of Miss Jane Pittman* (1971), *In My Father's House* (1978), *A Gathering of Old Men* (1983), and *A Lesson Before Dying* (1993).

Some critics compare Gaines's fiction to William Faulkner's. As John O'Brien notes, the similarities are apparent in "Gaines' mythical creation of a locale in Louisiana in which all his stories originate or take place, his oral narrative, his preoccupation with themes of change, stasis, and time." Keith Byerman finds that "unlike Hemingway, whom he often takes as a model, Gaines is interested less in bold, forceful actions than in honorable, dangerous choices." Responding to O'Brien's questions about the influences on his early work, Gaines states:

> I don't know whether I have actually broken away from the Hemingway and Faulkner influence. I don't know whether that's possible to do, just as I don't think it's possible for me to break away from the influences of jazz or blues or Negro spirituals or Greek tragedy or James Joyce or Tolstoy.

When he did not find his poor but proud black rural Louisiana people in southern writers, Gaines read books about the peasantry in other parts of the United States and the world. Of Russian writers such as Chekhov, Gogol, Tolstoy, and Turgenev, he says that he "liked what they were doing with their stories on the peasantry; the peasants were real human beings, whereas in the fiction of American writers, especially southern writers, they were caricatures of human beings, they were clowns." Thus, the influences on Gaines's style and structure were culturally diverse.

His stories and novels focus on the black, Cajun, and Creole folk languages and cultures of rural Louisiana, usually on a plantation near the mythical town of Bayonne. His central characters are usually "aunt" figures (older, religious, resilient women who are distrustful of those who advocate radical social change) and young black men, like Sonny in "A Long Day in November" and Proctor Lewis in "Three Men," who are seeking to discover and assert their manhood. And his principal themes are the complex relationships of white to black, past to present, and traditional to contemporary social systems of power and privilege based on regional, racial, gender, and class beliefs and behavior that frustrate, often tragically, personal and group struggles for love, freedom, justice, community, and dignity. As Byerman says of Gaines's mastery of the folk idiom of rural southern blacks in his fiction, he gives their culture and character "an authenticity that is seldom present in dialect writing."

The consensus of critics is that *The Autobiography of Miss Jane Pittman* (1971) is his most successful novel. It draws on the tradition of the slave narratives and Gaines's memories of his childhood with his aunt in Louisiana. It is a reconstruction of the life of a venerable old black storyteller whose personal journey from slavery to freedom resonates with the collective struggle for freedom of black people for more than a century. In telling her story to a history teacher from outside her community with the help of other people in the community, Miss Jane, in the traditional manner of storytellers, is repetitious and often digresses, as the mood strikes her, to elaborate on people and events with acute, frequently colorful descriptions and mother wit that valorizes the authority and authenticity of oral history.

Gaines painstakingly delineates Miss Jane as a complex, dynamic individual rather than a stereotypical black matriarch. She is barren yet a surrogate mother to Ned; she claims not to believe in hoodoo, yet consults Madame Gautier about her dreams of Joe's death. She likes fishing, hard work, baseball, and vanilla ice cream. She also "gets religion" late in life but will give up neither her love of sports nor having the funnies read to her in order to keep her status as Mother of the church. Because of her age, her strength, and her wisdom, Miss Jane Pittman towers above time and place, bridging past and present—a noble inspiration to all who behold her—just like the sturdy oak tree she talks to and respects. As a significant, contemporary, neorealistic storyteller of the limitations and possibilities of black folk communities, Gaines reveals the traits of the men and women of a new social order in the personal and social commitments of individuals whose hope for change in the future lies, according to his vision of the peculiarly American human condition, in the courage and pride of the young and the faith and resourcefulness of the old.

❖❖❖

Important general and critical references on Gaines include John O'Brien, ed., *Interviews with Black Writers* (1971); Jerry H. Bryant, "From Death to Life: The Fiction of Ernest J. Gaines," *Iowa Review* 3 (Winter 1972); Ruth Laney, "A Conversation with Ernest Gaines," *Southern Review* 10 (January 1974); Jerry H. Bryant, "Ernest J. Gaines: Change, Growth, History," *Southern Review* 10 (1974); Frank W. Shelton, "Ambiguous Manhood in Ernest J. Gaines' *Bloodline*," *CLA Journal* 19 (1975). Also see the special issue on Gaines, *Callaloo* 1, No. 3 (1978); Addison Gayle, Jr., *The Way of the New World* (1975); Keith E. Byerman, *Fingering the Jagged Grain: Tradition and Form in Recent Black Fiction* (1985); Bernard W. Bell, *The Afro-American Novel and Its Tradition* (1987); John F. Callahan, *In the African American Grain* (1988).

Three Men

Two of them was sitting in the office when I came in there. One was sitting in a chair behind the desk, the other one was sitting on the end of the desk. They looked at me, but when they saw I was just a nigger they went back to talking like I wasn't even there. They talked like that two or three more minutes before the one behind the desk looked at me again. That was T. J. I didn't know who the other one was.

"Yeah, what you want?" T. J. said.

They sat inside a little railed-in office. I went close to the gate. It was one of them little gates that swung in and out.

"I come to turn myself in," I said.

"Turn yourself in for what?"

"I had a fight with somebody. I think I hurt him."

T. J. and the other policeman looked at me like I was crazy. I guess they had never heard of a nigger doing that before.

"You Procter Lewis?" T. J. said.

"Yes, sir."

"Come in here."

I pushed the little gate open and went in. I made sure it didn't swing back too hard and make noise. I stopped a little way from the desk. T. J. and the other policeman was watching me all the time.

"Give me some papers," T. J. said. He was looking up at me like he was still trying to figure out if I was crazy. If I wasn't crazy, then I was a smart aleck.

I got my wallet out my pocket. I could feel T. J. and the other policeman looking at me all the time. I wasn't supposed to get any papers out, myself, I was supposed to give him the wallet and let him take what he wanted. I held the wallet out to him and he jerked it out of my hand. Then he started going through everything I had in there, the money and all. After he looked at everything, he handed them to the other policeman. The other one looked at them, too; then he laid them on the desk. T. J. picked up the phone and started talking to somebody. All the time he was talking to the other person, he was looking up at me. He had a hard time making the other person believe I had turned myself in. When he hung up the phone, he told the policeman on the desk to get my records. He called the other policeman "Paul." Paul slid away from the desk and went to the file cabinet against the wall. T. J. still looked at me. His eyes was the color of ashes. I looked down at the floor, but I could still feel him looking at me. Paul came back with the records and handed them to him. I looked up again and saw them looking over the records together. Paul was standing behind T. J., looking over his shoulder.

"So you think you hurt him, huh?" T. J. asked, looking up at me again.

I didn't say anything to him. He was a mean, evil sonofabitch. He was big and red and he didn't waste time kicking your ass if you gived him the wrong answers. You had to weigh every word he said to you. Sometimes you answered, other times you kept your mouth shut. This time I passed my tongue over my lips and kept quiet.

It was about four o'clock in the morning, but it must've been seventy-five in there. T. J. and the other policeman had on short-sleeve khaki shirts. I had on a white shirt, but it was all dirty and torn. My sleeves was rolled up to the elbows, and both of my elbows was skinned and bruised.

"Didn't I bring you in here one time, myself?" Paul said.

"Yes, sir, once, I think," I said. I had been there two or three times, but I wasn't go'n say it if he didn't. I had been in couple other jails two or three times, too, but I wasn't go'n say anything about them either. If they hadn't put it on my record that was they hard luck.

"A fist fight," Paul said. "Pretty good with your fists, ain't you?"

"I protect myself," I said.

It was quiet in there for a second or two. I knowed why; I hadn't answered the right way.

"You protect yourself, what?" T. J. said.

"I protect myself, *sir*," I said.

They still looked at me. But I could tell Paul wasn't anything like T. J. He wasn't mean at all, he just had to play mean because T. J. was there. Couple Sundays ago I had played baseball with a boy who looked just like Paul. But he had brown eyes; Paul had blue eyes.

"You'll be sorry you didn't use your fists this time," T. J. said. "Take everything out your pockets."

I did what he said.

"Where's your knife?" he asked.

"I never car' a knife," I said.

"You never car' a knife, what, boy?" T. J. said.

"I never car' a knife, *sir*," I said.

He looked at me hard again. He didn't think I was crazy for turning myself in, he thought I was a smart aleck. I could tell from his big, fat, red face he wanted to hit me with his fist.

He nodded to Paul and Paul came toward me. I moved back some.

"I'm not going to hurt you," Paul said.

I stopped, but I could still feel myself shaking. Paul started patting me down. He found a pack of cigarettes in my shirt pocket. I could see in his face he didn't want take them out, but he took them out, anyhow.

"Thought I told you empty your pockets?" T. J. said.

"I didn't know—"

"Paul, if you can't make that boy shut up, I can," T. J. said.

"He'll be quiet," Paul said, looking at me. He was telling me with his eyes to be quiet or I was go'n get myself in a lot of trouble.

"You got one more time to butt in," T. J. said. "One more time now."

I was getting a swimming in the head, and I looked down at the floor. I hoped they would hurry up and lock me up so I could have a little peace.

"Why'd you turn yourself in?" T. J. asked.

I kept my head down. I didn't answer him.

"Paul, can't you make that boy talk?" T. J. said. "Or do I have to get up and do it?"

"He'll talk," Paul said.

"I figured y'all was go'n catch me sooner or later—sir."

"That's not the reason you turned yourself in," T. J. said.

I kept my head down.

"Look up when I talk to you," T. J. said.

I raised my head. I felt weak and shaky. My clothes was wet and sticking to my body, but my mouth felt dry as dust. My eyes wanted to look down again, but I forced myself to look at T. J.'s big red face.

"You figured if you turned yourself in, Roger Medlow was go'n get you out, now, didn't you?"

I didn't say anything—but that's exactly what I was figuring on.

"Sure," he said. He looked at me a long time. He knowed how I was feeling; he knowed I was weak and almost ready to fall. That's why he was making me stand there like that. "What you think we ought to do with niggers like you?" he said. "Come on now—what you think we ought to do with you?"

I didn't answer him.

"Well?" he said.

"I don't know," I said. "Sir."

"I'll tell you," he said. "See, if I was gov'nor, I'd run every damned one of you off in that river out there. Man, woman and child. You know that?"

I was quiet, looking at him. But I made sure I didn't show in my face what I was thinking. I could've been killed for what I was thinking then.

"Well, what you think of that?" he said.

"That's up to the gov'nor, sir," I said.

"Yeah," he said. "That's right. That's right. I think I'll write him a little telegram and tell him 'bout my idea. Can save this state a hell of a lot trouble."

Now he just sat there looking at me again. He wanted to hit me in the mouth with his fist. Not just hit me, he wanted to beat me. But he had to have a good excuse. And what excuse could he have when I had already turned myself in.

"Put him in there with Munford," he said to Paul.

We went out. We had to walk down a hall to the cell block. The niggers' cell block was on the second floor. We had to go up some concrete steps to get there. Paul turned on the lights and a woman hollered at him to turn them off. "What's this supposed to be—Christmas?" she said. "A person can't sleep in this joint." The women was locked up on one end of the block and the men was at the other end. If you had a mirror or a piece of shiny tin, you could stick it out the cell and fix it so you could see the other end of the block.

The guard opened the cell door and let me in, then he locked it back. I looked at him through the bars.

"When will y'all ever learn?" he said, shaking his head.

He said it like he meant it, like he was sorry for me. He kept reminding me of that boy I had played baseball with. They called that other boy Lloyd, and he used to show up just about every Sunday to play baseball with us. He used to play the outfield so he could do a lot of running. He used to buy Cokes for everybody after the game. He was the only white boy out there.

"Here's a pack of cigarettes and some matches," Paul said. "Might not be your brand, but I doubt if you'll mind it too much in there."

I took the cigarettes from him.

"You can say 'Thanks,'" he said.

"Thanks," I said.

"And you can say 'sir' sometimes," he said.

"Sir," I said.

He looked at me like he felt sorry for me, like he felt sorry for everybody. He didn't look like a policeman at all.

"Let me give you a word of warning," he said. "Don't push T. J. Don't push him, now."

"I won't."

"It doesn't take much to get him started—don't push him."

I nodded.

"Y'all go'n turn out them goddamn lights?" the woman hollered from the other end of the block.

"Take it easy," Paul said to me and left.

After the lights went out, I stood at the cell door till my eyes got used to the dark. Then I climbed up on my bunk. Two other people was in the cell. Somebody on the bunk under mine, somebody on the lower bunk 'cross from me. The upper bunk 'cross from me was empty.

"Cigarette?" the person below me said.

He said it very low, but I could tell he was talking to me and not to the man 'cross from us. I shook a cigarette out the pack and dropped it on the bunk. I could hear the man scratching the match to light the cigarette. He cupped his hands close to his face, because I didn't see too much light. I could tell from the way he let that smoke out he had wanted a cigarette very bad.

"What you in for?" he said, real quiet.

"A fight," I said.

"First time?"

"No, I been in before."

He didn't say any more and I didn't, either. I didn't feel like talking, anyhow. I looked up at the window on my left, and I could see a few stars. I felt lonely and I felt like crying. But I couldn't cry. Once you started that in here you was done for. Everybody and his brother would run over you.

The man on the other bunk got up to take a leak. The toilet was up by the head of my bunk. After the man had zipped up his pants, he just stood there looking at me. I tightened my fist to swing at him if he tried any funny stuff.

"Well, hello there," he said.

"Get your ass back over there, Hattie," the man below me said. He spoke in that quiet voice again. "Hattie is a woman," he said to me. "Don't see how come they didn't put him with the rest of them whores."

"Don't let it worry your mind," Hattie said.

"Caught him playing with this man dick," the man below me said. "At this old flea-bitten show back of town there. Up front—front row—there he is playing with this man dick. Bitch."

"Is that any worse than choking somebody half to death?" Hattie said.

The man below me was quiet. Hattie went back to his bunk.

"Oh, these old crampy, stuffy, old ill-smelling beds," he said, slapping the mattress level with the palm of his hand. "How do they expect you to sleep." He laid down. "What are you in for, honey?" he asked me. "You look awful young."

"Fighting," I said.

"You poor, poor thing," Hattie said. "If I can help you in any way, don't hesitate to ask."

"Shit," the man below me said. I heard him turning over so he could go to sleep.

"The world has given up on the likes of you," Hattie said. "You jungle beast."

"Bitch, why don't you just shut up," the man said.

"Why don't both of y'all shut up," somebody said from another cell.

It was quiet after that.

I looked up at the window and I could see the stars going out in the sky. My eyes felt tired and my head started spinning, and I wasn't here any more, I was at the Seven Spots. And she was there in red, and she had two big dimples in her jaws. Then she got up and danced with him, and every time she turned my way she looked over his shoulder at me and smiled. And when she turned her back to me, she rolled her big ass real slow and easy—just for me, just for me. Grinning Boy was sitting at the table with me, saying: "Poison, poison—nothing but poison. Look at that; just look at that." I was looking, but I wasn't thinking about what he was saying. When she went back to that table to sit down, I went there and asked her to dance. That nigger sitting there just looked at me, rolling his big white eyes like I was supposed to break out of the joint. I didn't pay him no mind, I was looking at that woman. And I was looking down at them two big pretty brown things poking that dress way out. They looked so soft and warm and waiting, I wanted to touch them right there in front of that ugly nigger. She shook her head, because he was sitting there, but little bit later when she went back in the kitchen, I went back there, too. Grinning Boy tried to stop me, saying, "Poison, poison, poison," but I didn't pay him no mind. When I came back in the kitchen, she was standing at the counter ordering a chicken sandwich. The lady back of the counter had to fry the chicken, so she had to wait a while. When she saw me, she started smiling. Them two big dimples came in her jaws. I smiled back at her.

"She go'n take a while," I said. "Let's step out in the cool till she get done."

She looked over her shoulder and didn't see the nigger peeping, and we went outside. There was people talking out there, but I didn't care, I had to touch her.

"What's your name?" I said.

"Clara."

"Let's go somewhere, Clara."

"I can't. I'm with somebody," she said.

"That nigger?" I said. "You call him somebody?"

She just looked at me with that little smile on her face—them two big dimples in her jaws. I looked little farther down, and I could see how them two warm, brown things was waiting for somebody to tear that dress open so they could get free.

"You must be the prettiest woman in the world," I said.

"You like me?"

"Lord, yes."

"I want you to like me," she said.

"Then what's keeping us from going?" I said. "Hell away with that nigger."

"My name is Clara Johnson," she said. "It's in the book. Call me tomorrow after four."

She turned to go back inside, but just then that big sweaty nigger bust out the door. He passed by her like she wasn't even there.

"No, Bayou," she said. "No."

But he wasn't listening to a thing. Before I knowed it, he had cracked me on the chin and I was down on my back. He raised his foot to kick me in the stomach, and I rolled and rolled till I was out of the way. Then I jumped back up.

"I don't want fight you, Bayou," I said. "I don't want fight you, now."

"You fight or you fly, nigger," somebody else said. "If you run, we go'n catch you."

Bayou didn't say nothing. He just came in swinging. I backed away from him.

"I wasn't doing nothing but talking to her," I said.

He rushed in and knocked me on a bunch of people. They picked me clear off the ground and throwed me back on him. He hit me again, this time a glancing blow on the shoulder. I moved back from him, holding the shoulder with the other hand.

"I don't want fight you," I told him. "I was just talking to her."

But trying to talk to Bayou was like trying to talk to a mule. He came in swinging wild and high, and I went under his arm and rammed my fist in his stomach. But it felt like ramming your fist into a hundred-pound sack of flour. He stopped about a half a second, then he was right back on me again. I hit him in the face this time, and I saw the blood splash out of his mouth. I was still backing away from him, hoping he would quit, but the nigger kept coming on me. He had to, because all his friends and that woman was there. But he didn't know how to fight, and every time he moved in I hit him in the face. Then I saw him going for his knife.

"Watch it, now, Bayou," I said. "I don't have a knife. Let's keep this fair."

But he didn't hear a thing I was saying; he was listening to the others who was sicking him on. He kept moving in on me. He had both of his arms 'way out—that blade in his right hand. From the way he was holding it, he didn't have nothing but killing on his mind.

I kept moving back, moving back. Then my foot touched a bottle and I stooped down and picked it up. I broke it against the corner of the building, but I never took my eyes off Bayou. He started circling me with the knife, and I moved round him with the bottle. He made a slash at me, and I jumped back. He was all opened and I could've gotten him then, but I was still hoping for him to change his mind.

"Let's stop it, Bayou," I kept saying to him. "Let's stop it, now."

But he kept on circling me with the knife, and I kept on going round him with the bottle. I didn't look at his face any more, I kept my eyes on that knife. I was a Texas jack with a pearl handle, and that blade must've been five inches long.

"Stop it, Bayou," I said. "Stop it, stop it."

He slashed at me, and I jumped back. He slashed at me again, and I jumped back again. Then he acted like a fool and ran on me, and all I did was stick the bottle out. I felt it go in his clothes and in his stomach and I felt the hot, sticky blood on my hand and I saw his face all twisted and sweaty. I felt his hands brush against mine when he throwed both of his hands up to his stomach. I started running. I was running toward the car, and Grinning Boy was running there, too. He got there before me and jumped in on the driving side, but I pushed him out the way and got under that ste'r'n' wheel. I could hear that gang coming after me, and I shot that Ford out of there a hundred miles an hour. Some of them ran up the road to cut me off, but when they saw I wasn't stopping they jumped out of the way. Now, it was nobody but me, that Ford and that gravel road. Grinning Boy was sitting over there crying, but I wasn't paying him no mind. I wanted to get much road between me and Seven Spots as I could.

After I had gone a good piece, I slammed on the brakes and told Grinning Boy to get out. He wouldn't get out. I opened the door and pushed on him, but he held the ste'r'n' wheel. He was crying and holding the wheel with both hands. I hit him and pushed on him and hit him and pushed on him, but he wouldn't turn it loose. If they was go'n kill me, I didn't want them to kill him, too, but he couldn't see that. I shot away from there with the door still opened, and after we had gone a little piece, Grinning Boy reached out and got it and slammed it again.

I came out on the pave road and drove three or four miles 'long the river. Then I turned down a dirt road and parked the car under a big pecan tree. It was one of these old plantation quarter and the place was quiet as a graveyard. It was pretty bright, though, because the moon and the stars was out. The dust in that long, old road was white as snow. I lit a cigarette and tried to think. Grinning Boy was sitting over there crying. He was crying real quiet with his head hanging down on his chest. Every now and then I could hear him sniffing.

"I'm turning myself in," I said.

I had been thinking and thinking and I couldn't think of nothing else to do. I knowed Bayou was dead or hurt pretty bad, and I knowed either that gang or the law was go'n get me, anyhow. I backed the car out on the pave road and drove to Bayonne. I told Grinning Boy to let my uncle know I was in trouble. My uncle would go to Roger Medlow—and I was hoping Roger Medlow would get me off like he had done once before. He owned the plantation where I lived.

"Hey," somebody was calling and shaking me. "Hey, there, now; wake up."

I opened my eyes and looked at this old man standing by the head of my bunk. I'm sure if I had woke up anywhere else and found him that close to me I would've jumped back screaming. He must've been sixty; he had reddish-brown eyes, and a stubby gray beard. 'Cross his right jaw, from his cheekbone to his mouth, was a big shiny scar where somebody had gotten him with a razor. He was wearing a derby hat, and he had it cocked a little to the back of his head.

"They coming," he said.

"Who?"

"Breakfast."

"I'm not hungry."

"You better eat. Never can tell when you go'n eat again in this joint."

His breath didn't smell too good either, and he was standing so close to me, I could smell his breath every time he breathed in and out. I figured he was the one they called Munford. Just before they brought me down here last night, I heard T. J. tell Paul to put me in there with Munford. Since he had called the other one Hattie, I figured he was Munford.

"Been having yourself a nice little nightmare," he said. "Twisting and turning there like you wanted to fall off. You can have this bunk of mine tonight if you want."

I looked at the freak laying on the other bunk. He looked back at me with a sad little smile on his face.

"I'll stay here," I said.

The freak stopped smiling, but he still looked sad—like a sad woman. He knowed why I didn't want get down there. I didn't want no part of him.

Out on the cell block, the nigger trustee was singing. He went from one cell to the other one singing, "Come and get it, it's hot. What a lovely, lovely day, isn't it? Yes, indeed," he answered himself. "Yes, indeed . . . Come and get it, my children, come and get it. Unc' Toby won't feel right if y'all don't eat his lovely food."

He stopped before the cell with his little shiny pushcart. A white guard was with him. The guard opened the cell door and Unc' Toby gived each one of us a cup of coffee and two baloney sandwiches. Then the guard shut the cell again and him and Unc' Toby went on up the block. Unc' Toby was singing again.

"Toby used to have a little stand," Munford said to me. "He think he still got it. He kinda loose up here," he said, tapping his head with the hand that held the sandwiches.

"They ought to send him to Jackson if he's crazy."

"They like keeping him here," Munford said. "Part of the scheme of things."

"You want this?" I asked.

"No, eat it," he said.

I got back on my bunk. I ate one of the sandwiches and drank some of the coffee. The coffee was nothing but brown water. It didn't have any kind of taste—not even bitter taste. I drank about half and poured the rest in the toilet.

The freak, Hattie, sat on his bunk, nibbling at his food. He wrapped one slice of bread round the slice of baloney and ate that, then he did the same thing with the other sandwich. The two extra slices of bread, he dipped down in his coffee and ate it like that. All the time he was eating, he was looking at me like a sad woman looks at you.

Munford stood between the two rows of bunks, eating and drinking his coffee. He pressed both of the sandwiches together and ate them like they was just one. Nobody said anything all the time we was eating. Even when I poured out the coffee, nobody said anything. The freak just looked at me like a sad woman. But Munford didn't look at me at all—he was looking up at the window all the time. When he got through eating, he wiped his mouth and throwed his cup on his bunk.

"Another one of them smokes," he said to me.

They way he said it, it sounded like he would've took it if I didn't give it to him. I got out the pack of cigarettes and gived him one. He lit it and took a big draw. I was laying back against the wall, looking up at the window; but I could tell that Munford was looking at me.

"Killed somebody, huh?" Munford said, in his quiet, calm voice.

"I cut him pretty bad," I said, still looking up at the window.

"He's dead," Munford said.

I wouldn't take my eyes off the window. My throat got tight, and my heart started beating so loud, I'm sure both Munford and that freak could hear it.

"That's bad," Munford said.

"And so young," Hattie said. I didn't have to look at the freak to know he was crying. "And so much of his life still before him—my Lord."

"You got people?" Munford asked.

"Uncle," I said.

"You notified him?"

"I think he knows."

"You got a lawyer?"

"No."

"No money?"

"No."

"That's bad," he said.

"Maybe his uncle can do something," Hattie said. "Poor thing." Then I heard him blowing his nose.

I looked at the bars in the window. I wanted them to leave me alone so I could think.

"So young, too," Hattie said. "My Lord, my Lord."

"Oh shut up," Munford said. "I don't know why they didn't lock you up with the rest of them whores."

"Is it too much to have some feeling of sympathy?" Hattie said, and blowed his nose again.

"Morris David is a good lawyer," Munford said. "Get him if you can. Best for colored round here."

I nodded, but I didn't look at Munford. I felt bad and I wanted them to leave me alone.

"Was he a local boy?" Munford asked.

"I don't know," I said.

"Where was it?"

I didn't answer him.

"Best to talk 'bout it," Munford said. "Keeping it in just make it worse."

"Seven Spots," I said.

"That's a rough joint," Munford said.

"They're all rough joints," Hattie said. "That's all you have—rough joints. No decent places for someone like him."

"Who's your uncle?" Munford asked.

"Martin Baptiste. Medlow plantation."

"Martin Baptiste?" Munford said.

I could tell from the way he said it, he knowed my uncle. I looked at him now. He was looking back at me with his left eye half shut. I could tell from his face he didn't like my uncle.

"You same as out already," he said.

He didn't like my uncle at all, and now he was studying me to see how much I was like him.

"Medlow can get you out of here just by snapping his finger," he said. "Big men like that run little towns like these."

"I killed somebody," I said.

"You killed another old nigger," Munford said. "A nigger ain't nobody."

He drawed on the cigarette, and I looked at the big scar on the side of his face. He took the cigarette from his mouth and patted the scar with the tip of one of his fingers.

"Bunch of them jumped on me one night," he said. "One caught me with a straight razor. Had the flesh hanging so much, I coulda ripped it off with my hands if I wanted to. Ah, but before I went down you shoulda seen what I did the bunch of 'em." He stopped and thought a while. He even laughed a little to himself. "I been in this joint so much, everybody from the judge on down know me. 'How's it going, Munford?' 'Well, you back with us again, huh, Munt?' 'Look, y'all, old Munt's back with us again, just like he said he'd be.' They all know me. All know me. I'll get out little later on. What time is it getting to be—'leven? I'll give 'em till twelve and tell 'em I want get out. They'll let me out. Got in Saturday night. They always keep me from Saturday till Monday. If it rain, they keep me till Tuesday—don't want me get out and catch cold, you know. Next Saturday, I'm right back. Can't stay out of here to save my soul."

"Places like these are built for people like you," Hattie said. "Not for decent people."

"Been going in and out of these jails here, I don't know how long," Munford said. "Forty, fifty years. Started out just like you—kilt a boy just like you did last night. Kilt him and got off—got off scot-free. My pappy worked for a white man who got me off. At first I didn't know why he had done it—I didn't think; all I knowed was I was free, and free is how I wanted to be. Then I got in trouble again, and again they got me off. I kept on getting in trouble, and they kept on getting me off. Didn't wake up till I got to be nearly old as I'm is now. Then I realized they kept getting me off because they needed a Munford Bazille. They need me to prove they human—just like they need that thing over there. They need us. Because without us, they don't know what they is—they don't know what they is out there. With us around, they can see us and they know what they ain't. They ain't us. Do you see? Do you see how they think?"

I didn't know what he was talking about. It was hot in the cell and he had started sweating. His face was wet, except for that big scar. It was just laying there smooth and shiny.

"But I got news for them. They us. I never tell them that, but inside I know it. They us, just like we is ourselves. Cut any of them open and you see if you don't find Munford Bazille or Hattie Brown there. You know what I mean?"

"I guess so."

"No, you don't know what I mean," he said. "What I mean is not one of them out there is a man. Not one. They think they men. They think they men 'cause they got me and him in here who ain't men. But I got news for them—cut them open; go 'head and cut one open—you see if you don't find Munford Bazille or Hattie Brown. Not a man one of them. 'Cause face don't make a man—black or white. Face don't make him and fucking don't make him and fighting don't make him—neither killing. None of this prove you a man. 'Cause animals can fuck, can kill, can fight—you know that?"

I looked at him, but I didn't answer him. I didn't feel like answering.

"Well?" he said.

"Yeah."

"Then answer me when I ask you a question. I don't like talking to myself."

He stopped and looked at me a while.

"You know what I'm getting at?"

"No," I said.

"To hell if you don't," he said. "Don't let Medlow get you out of here so you can kill again."

"You got out," I said.

"Yeah," he said, "and I'm still coming back here and I'm still getting out. Next Saturday I'm go'n hit another nigger in the head, and Saturday night they go'n bring me here, and Monday they go'n let me out again. And Saturday after that I'm go'n hit me another nigger in the head—'cause I'll hit a nigger in the head quick as I'll look at one."

"You're just an animal out the black jungle," Hattie said. "Because you have to hit somebody in the head every Saturday night don't mean he has to do the same."

"He'll do it," Munford said, looking at me, not at Hattie. "He'll do it 'cause he know Medlow'll get him out. Won't you?"

I didn't answer him. Munford nodded his head.

"Yeah, he'll do it. They'll see to that."

He looked at me like he was mad at me, then he looked up at the bars in the window. He frowned and rubbed his hand over his chin, and I could hear the gritty sound his beard made. He studied the bars a long time, like he was thinking about something 'way off; then I saw how his face changed: his eyes twinkled and he grinned to himself. He turned to look at Hattie laying on the bunk.

"Look here," he said. "I got a few coppers and a few minutes—what you say me and you giving it a little whirl?"

"My God, man," Hattie said. He said it the way a young girl would've said it if you had asked her to pull down her drawers. He even opened his eyes wide the same way a young girl would've done it. "Do you think I could possibly ever sink so low?" he said.

"Well, that's what you do on the outside," Munford said.

"What I do on the outside is absolutely no concern of yours, let me assure you," the freak said. "And furthermore, I have friends that I associate with."

"And them 'sociating friends you got there—what they got Munford don't have?" Munford said.

"For one thing, manners," Hattie said. "Of all the nerve."

Munford grinned at him and looked at me.

"You know what make 'em like that?" he asked.

"No."

He nodded his head. "Then I'll tell you. It start in the cradle when they send that preacher there to christen you. At the same time he's doing that mumbo-jumbo stuff, he's low'ing his mouth to your little nipper to suck out your manhood. I know, he tried it on me. Here, I'm laying in his arms in my little white blanket and he suppose to be christening me. My mammy there, my pappy there; uncle, aunt, grand-mammy, grandpappy; my nan-nane, my pa-ran—all of them standing there with they head bowed. This preacher going, 'Mumbo-jumbo, mumbo-jumbo,' but all the time he's low'ing his mouth toward my little private. Nobody else don't see him, but I catch him, and I haul 'way back and hit him right smack in the eye. I ain't no more than three months old but I give him a good one. 'Get your goddamn mouth away from my little pecker, you no-teef, rotten, egg-sucking sonofabitch. Get away from here, you sister-jumper, God-calling, pulpit-spitting, mother-huncher. Get away from here, you chicken-eating, catfish-eating, gin-drinking son-ofabitch. Get away, goddamn it, get away . . .'"

I thought Munford was just being funny, but he was serious as he could ever get. He had worked himself up so much, he had to stop and catch his breath.

"That's what I told him," he said. "That's what I told him. . . . But they don't stop there, they stay after you. If they miss you in the cradle, they catch you some other time. And when they catch you, they draw it out of you or they make you a beast—make you use it in a brutish way. You use it on a woman without caring for her, you use it on children, you use it on other men, you use it on yourself. Then when you get so disgusted with everything round you, you kill. And if your back is strong, like your back is strong, they get you out so you can kill again." He stopped and looked at me and nodded his head. "Yeah, that's what they do with you—exactly. . . . But not everybody end up like that. Some of them make it. Not many—but some of them do make it."

"Going to the pen?" I said.

"Yeah—the pen is one way," he said. "But you don't go to the pen for the nigger you killed. Not for him—he ain't worth it. They told you that from the cradle—a nigger ain't worth a good gray mule. Don't mention a white mule: fifty niggers ain't worth a good white mule. So you don't go to the pen for killing the nigger, you go for yourself. You go to sweat out all the crud you got in your system. You go, saying, 'Go fuck yourself, Roger Medlow, I want to be a man, and by God I will be a man. For once in my life I will be a man.'"

"And a month after you been in the pen, Medlow tell them to kill you for being a smart aleck. How much of a man you is then?"

"At least you been a man a month—where if you let him get you out you won't be a man a second. He won't 'low it."

"I'll take that chance," I said.

He looked at me a long time now. His red-dish-brown eyes was sad and mean. He felt sorry for me, and at the same time he wanted to hit me with his fist.

"You don't look like that whitemouth uncle of yours," he said. "And you look much brighter than I did at your age. But I guess every man must live his own life. I just wish I had mine to live all over again."

He looked up at the window like he had given up on me. After a while, he looked back at Hattie on the bunk.

"You not thinking 'bout what I asked you?" he said.

Hattie looked up at him just like a woman looks at a man she can't stand.

"Munford, if you dropped dead this second, I doubt if I would shed a tear."

"Put all that together, I take it you mean no," Munford said.

Hattie rolled his eyes at Munford the way a woman rolls hers eyes at a man she can't stand.

"Well, I better get out of here," Munford said. He passed his hand over his chin. It sounded like passing your hand over sandpaper.

"Go home and take me a shave and might go out and do little fishing," he said. "Too hot to pick cotton."

He looked at me again.

"I guess I'll be back next week or the week after—but I suppose you'll be gone to Medlow by then."

"If he come for me—yes."

"He'll come for you," Munford said. "How old you is—twenty?"

"Nineteen."

"Yeah, he'll come and take you back. And next year you'll kill another old nigger. 'Cause they grow niggers just to be killed, and they grow people like you to kill 'em. That's all part of the—the culture. And every man got to play his part in the culture, or the culture don't go on. But I'll tell you this; if you was kin to anybody else except that Martin Baptiste, I'd stay in here long enough to make you go to Angola. 'Cause I'd break your back 'fore I let you walk out of this cell with Medlow. But with Martin Baptiste blood in you, you'll never be worth a goddamn no matter what I did. With that, I bid you adieu."

He tipped his derby to me, then he went to the door and called for the guard. The guard came and let him out. The people on the block told him good-bye and said they would see him when they got out. Munford waved at them and followed the guard toward the door.

"That Munford," Hattie said. "Thank God we're not all like that." He looked up at me. "I hope you didn't listen to half of that nonsense."

I didn't answer the freak—I didn't want to have nothing to do with him. I looked up at the window. The sky was darkish blue and I could tell it was hot out there. I had always hated the hot sun, but I wished I was out there now. I wouldn't even mind picking cotton, much as I hated picking cotton.

I got out my other sandwich: nothing but two slices of light bread and a thin slice of baloney sausage. If I wasn't hungry, I wouldn't 'a' ate it at all. I tried to think about what everybody was doing at home. But hard as I tried, all I could think about was here. Maybe it was best if I didn't think about outside. That could run you crazy. I had heard about people going crazy in jail. I tried to remember how it was when I was in jail before. It wasn't like this if I could remember. Before, it was just a brawl—a fight. I had never stayed in more than a couple weeks. I had been in about a half dozen times, but never more than a week or two. This time it was different, though. Munford said Roger Medlow was go'n get me out, but suppose Munford was wrong. Suppose I had to go up? Suppose I had to go to the pen?

Hattie started singing. He was singing a spiritual and he was singing it in a high-pitched voice like a woman. I wanted to tell him to shut up, but I didn't want have nothing to do with that freak. I could feel him looking at me; a second later he had quit singing.

"That Munford," he said. "I hope you didn't believe everything he said about me."

I was quiet. I didn't want to talk to Hattie. He saw it and kept his mouth shut.

If Medlow was go'n get me out of here, why hadn't he done so? If all he had to do was snap his fingers, what was keeping him from snapping them? Maybe he wasn't go'n do anything for me. I wasn't one of them Uncle Tom-ing niggers like my uncle, and maybe he was go'n let me go up this time.

I couldn't make it in the pen. Locked up—caged. Walking round all day with shackles on my legs. No woman, no pussy—I'd die in there. I'd die in a year. Not five years—one year. If Roger Medlow came, I was leaving. That's how old people is: they always want you to do something they never did when they was young. If he had his life to live all over—how come he didn't do it then? Don't tell me do it when he didn't do it. If that's part of the culture, then I'm part of the culture, because I sure ain't for the pen.

That black sonofabitch—that coward. I hope he didn't have religion. I hope his ass burn in hell till eternity.

Look how life can change on you—just look. Yesterday this time I was poon-tanging like a dog. Today—that black sonofabitch—behind these bars maybe for the rest of my life.

And look at me, look at me. Strong. A man. A damn good man. A hard dick—a pile of muscles. But look at me—locked in here like a caged animal.

Maybe that's what Munford was talking about. You spend much time in here like he done spent, you can't be nothing but a' animal.

I wish somebody could do something for me. I can make a phone call, can't I? But call who? That ass-hole uncle of mine? I'm sure Grinning Boy already told him where I'm at. I wonder if Grinning Boy got in touch with Marie. I suppose this finish it. Hell, why should she stick her neck out for me. I was treating her like a dog, anyhow. I'm sorry, baby; I'm sorry. No, I'm not sorry; I'd do the same thing tomorrow if I was out of here. Maybe I'm a' animal already. I don't care who she is, I'd do it with her and don't give a damn. Hell, let me stop whining; I ain't no goddamn animal. I'm a man, and I got to act and think like a man.

I got to think, I got to think. My daddy is somewhere up North—but where? I got more people scattered around, but no use going to them. I'm the black sheep of this family—and they don't care if I live or die. They'd be glad if I died so they'd be rid of me for good.

That black sonofabitch—I swear to God. Big as he was, he had to go for a knife. I hope he rot in hell. I hope he burn—goddamn it—till eternity come and go.

Let me see, let me see, who can I call? I don't know a soul with a dime. Them white people out there got it, but what do they care 'bout me, a nigger. Now, if I was a' uncle Tom-ing nigger—oh, yes, they'd come then. They'd come running. But like I'm is, I'm fucked. Done for.

Five years, five years—that's what they give you. Five years for killing a nigger like that. Five years out of my life. Five years for a rotten, no good sonofabitch who didn't have no business being born in the first place. Five years . . .

Maybe I ought to call Medlow myself. . . . But suppose he come, then what? Me and Medlow never got along. I couldn't never bow and say, "Yes sir," and scratch my head. But I'd have to do it now. He'd have me by the nuts and he'd know it; and I'd have to kiss his ass if he told me to.

Oh Lord, have mercy. . . . They get you, don't they. They let you run and run, then they get you. They stick a no-good, trashy nigger up there, and they get you. And they twist your nuts and twist them till you don't care no more.

I got to stop this, I got to stop it. My head'll go to hurting after while and I won't be able to think anything out.

"Oh, you're so beautiful when you're meditating," Hattie said. "And what were you meditating about?"

I didn't answer him—I didn't want to have nothing to do with that freak.

"How long you're going to be in here, is that it?" he said. "Sometimes they let you sit for days and days. In your case they might let you sit here a week before they say anything to you. What do they care—they're inhuman."

I got a cigarette out of the pack and lit it.

"I smoke, too," Hattie said.

I didn't answer that freak. He came over and got the pack out of my shirt pocket. His fingers went down in my pocket just like a woman's fingers go in your pocket.

"May I?" he said.

I didn't say nothing to him. He lit his cigarette and laid the pack on my chest just like a woman'd do it.

"Really, I'm not all that awful," he said. "Munford has poisoned your mind with all sorts of notions. Let go—relax. You need friends at a time like this."

I stuffed the pack of cigarettes in my pocket and looked up at the window.

"These are very good," the freak said. "Very, very good. Well, maybe you'll feel like talking a little later on. It's always good to let go. I'm understanding; I'll be here."

He went back to his bunk and laid down.

Toward three o'clock, they let the women out of the cells to walk around. Some of the women came down the block and talked to the men through the bars. Some of them even laughed and joked. Three-thirty, the guard locked them up and let the men out. From the way the guard looked at me, I knowed I wasn't going anywhere. I didn't want to go anywhere, either, because I didn't want people asking me a pile of questions. Hattie went out to stretch, but few minutes later he came and laid back down. He was grumbling about some man on the block trying to get fresh with him.

"Some of them think you'll stoop to anything," he said.

I looked out of the window at the sky. I couldn't see too much, but I liked what I could see. I liked the sun, too. I hadn't ever liked the sun before, but I liked it now. I felt my throat getting tight, and I turned my head.

Toward four o'clock, Unc' Toby came on the block with dinner. For dinner, we had stew, mashed potatoes, lettuce and tomatoes. The stew was too soupy; the mashed potatoes was too soupy; the lettuce and tomatoes was too soggy. Dessert was three or four dried-up prunes with black water poured over them. After Unc' Toby served us, the guard locked up the cell. By the time we finished eating, they was back there again to pick up the trays.

I laid on my bunk, looking up at the window. How long I had been there? No more than about twelve hours. Twelve hours—but it felt like three days, already.

They knowed how to get a man down. Because they had me now. No matter which way I went—plantation or pen—they had me. That's why Medlow wasn't in any hurry to get me out. You don't have to be in any hurry when you already know you got a man by the nuts.

Look at the way they did Jack. Jack was a man, a good man. Look what they did him. Let a fifteen-cents Cajun bond him out of jail—a no-teeth, dirty, overall-wearing Cajun get him out. Then they broke him. Broke him down to nothing—to a grinning, bowing fool. . . . We loved Jack. Jack could do anything. Work, play ball, run women—anything. They knowed we loved him, that's why they did him that. Broke him—broke him the way you break a wild horse. . . . Now everybody laughs at him. Gamble with him and cheat him. He know you cheating him, but he don't care—just don't care any more . . .

Where is my father? Why my mama had to die? Why they brought me here and left me to struggle like this? I used to love my mama so much. Her skin was light brown; her hair was silky. I used to watch her powdering her face in the glass. I used to always cry when she went out—and be glad when she came back because she always brought me candy. But you gone for good now, Mama; and I got nothing in this world but me.

A man in the other cell started singing. I listened to him and looked up at the window. The sky had changed some more. It was lighter blue now—gray-blue almost.

The sun went down, a star came out. For a while it was the only star; then some more came to join it. I watched all of them. Then I watched just a few, then just one. I shut my eyes and opened them and tried to find the star again. I couldn't find it. I wasn't too sure which one it was. I could've pretended and choosed either one, but I didn't want lie to myself. I don't believe in lying to myself. I don't believe in lying to nobody else, either. I believe in being straight with a man. And I want a man to be straight with me. I wouldn't 'a' picked up that bottle for nothing if that nigger hadn't pulled his knife. Not for nothing. Because I don't believe in that kind of stuff. I believe in straight stuff. But a man got to protect himself. . . . But with stars I wasn't go'n cheat. If I didn't know where the one was I was looking at at first, I wasn't go'n say I did. I picked out another one, one that wasn't too much in a cluster. I measured it off from the bars in the window, then I shut my eyes. When I opened them, I found the star right away. And I didn't have to cheat, either.

The lights went out on the block. I got up and took a leak and got back on my bunk. I got in the same place I was before and looked for the star. I found it right away. It was easier to find now because the lights was out. I got tired looking at it after a while and looked at another one. The other one was much more smaller and much more in a cluster. But I got tired of it after a while, too.

I thought about Munford. He said if they didn't get you in the cradle, they got you later. If they didn't suck all the manhood out of you in the cradle, they made you use it on people you didn't love. I never messed with a woman I didn't love. I always loved all these women I ever messed with. . . . No, I didn't love them. Because I didn't love her last night—I just wanted to fuck her. And I don't think I ever loved Marie, either. Marie just had the best pussy in the world. She had the best—still got the best. And that's why I went to her, the only reason I went. Because God knows she don't have any kind a face to make you come at her . . .

Maybe I ain't never loved nobody. Maybe I ain't never loved nobody since my mama died. Because I loved her, I know I loved her. But the rest—no, I never loved the rest. They don't let you love them. Some kind of way they keep you from loving them . . .

I have to stop thinking. That's how you go crazy—thinking. But what else can you do in a place like this—what? I wish I knowed somebody. I wish I knowed a good person. I would be good if I knowed a good person. I swear to God I would be good.

All of a sudden the lights came on, and I heard them bringing in somebody who was crying. They was coming toward the cell where I was; the person was crying all the way. Then the cell door opened and they throwed him in there and they locked the door again. I didn't look up—I wouldn't raise my head for nothing. I could tell nobody else was looking up, either. Then the footsteps faded away and the lights went out again.

I raised my head and looked at the person they had throwed in there. He was nothing but a little boy—fourteen or fifteen. He had on a white shirt and a pair of dark pants. Hattie helped him up off the floor and laid him on the bunk under me. Then he sat on the bunk 'side the boy. The boy was still crying.

"Shhh now, shhh now," Hattie was saying. It was just like a woman saying it. It made me sick a' the stomach. "Shhh now, shhh now," he kept on saying.

I swung to the floor and looked at the boy. Hattie was sitting on the bunk, passing his hand over the boy's face.

"What happened?" I asked him.

He was crying too much to answer me.

"They beat you?" I asked him.

He couldn't answer.

"A cigarette?" I said.

"No—no—sir," he said.

I lit one, anyhow, and stuck it in his mouth. He tried to smoke it and started coughing. I took it out.

"Shhh now," Hattie said, patting his face. "Just look at his clothes. The bunch of animals. Not one of them is a man. A bunch of pigs—dogs—philistines."

"You hurt?" I asked the boy.

"Sure, he's hurt," Hattie said. "Just look at his clothes, how they beat him. The bunch of dogs."

I went to the door to call the guard. But I stopped; I told myself to keep out of this. He ain't the first one they ever beat and he won't be the last one, and getting in it will just bring you a dose of the same medicine. I turned around and looked at the boy. Hattie was holding the boy in his arms and whispering to him. I hated what Hattie was doing much as I hated what the law had done.

"Leave him alone," I said to Hattie.

"The child needs somebody," he said. "You're going to look after him?"

"What happened?" I asked the boy.

"They beat me," he said.

"They didn't beat you for nothing, boy."

He was quiet now. Hattie was patting the side of his face and his hair.

"What they beat you for?" I asked him.

"I took something."

"What you took?"

"I took some cakes. I was hungry."

"You got no business stealing," I said.

"Some people got no business killing, but it don't keep them from killing," Hattie said.

He started rocking the boy in his arms the way a woman rocks a child.

"Why don't you leave him alone?" I said.

He wouldn't answer me. He kept on.

"You hear me, whore?"

"I might be a whore, but I'm not a merciless killer," he said.

I started to crack him side the head, but I changed my mind. I had already raised my fist to hit him, but I changed my mind. I started walking. I was smoking the cigarette and walking. I walked, I walked, I walked. Then I stood at the head of the bunk and look up at the window at the stars. Where was the one I was looking at a while back? I smoked on the cigarette and looked for it—but where was it? I threw the cigarette in the toilet and lit another one. I smoked and walked some more. The rest of the place was quiet. Nobody had said a word since the guards throwed that little boy in the cell. Like a bunch of roaches, like a bunch of mices, they had crawled in they holes and pulled the cover over they head.

All of a sudden I wanted to scream. I wanted to scream to the top of my voice. I wanted to get them bars in my hands and I wanted to shake, I wanted to shake that door down. I wanted to let all these people out. But would they follow me—would they? Y'all go'n follow me? I screamed inside. Y'all go'n follow me?

I ran to my bunk and bit down in the cover. I bit harder, harder, harder. I could taste the dry sweat, the dry piss, the dry vomit. I bit harder, harder, harder . . .

I got on the bunk. I looked out at the stars. A million little white, cool stars was out there. I felt my throat hurting. I felt the water running down my face. But I gripped my mouth tight so I wouldn't make a sound. I didn't make a sound, but I cried. I cried and cried and cried.

I knowed I was going to the pen now. I knowed I was going, I knowed I was going. Even if Medlow came to get me, I wasn't leaving with him. I was go'n do like Munford said. I was going there and I was go'n sweat it and I was go'n take it. I didn't want have to pull cover over my head every time a white man did something to a black boy—I wanted to stand. Because they never let you stand if they got you out. They didn't let Jack stand—and I had never heard of them letting anybody else stand, either.

I felt good. I laid there feeling good. I felt so good I wanted to sing. I sat up on the bunk and lit a cigarette. I had never smoked a cigarette like I smoked that one. I drawed deep, deep, till my chest got big. It felt good. It felt good deep down in me. I jumped to the floor feeling good.

"You want a cigarette?" I asked the boy.

I spoke to him like I had been talking to him just a few minutes ago, but it was over an hour. He was laying in Hattie's arms quiet like he was half asleep.

"No, sir," he said.

I had already shook the cigarette out of the pack.

"Here," I said.

"No, sir," he said.

"Get up from there and go to your own bunk," I said to Hattie.

"And who do you think you are to be giving orders?"

I grabbed two handsful of his shirt and jerked him up and slammed him 'cross the cell. He hit against that bunk and started crying—just laying there, holding his side and crying like a woman. After a while he picked himself up and got on that bunk.

"Philistine," he said. "Dog—brute."

When I saw he wasn't go'n act a fool and try to hit me, I turned my back on him.

"Here," I said to the boy.

"I don't smoke—please, sir."

"You big enough to steal?" I said. "You'll smoke it or you'll eat it." I lit it and pushed it in his mouth. "Smoke it."

He smoked and puffed it out. I sat down on the bunk 'side him. The freak was sitting on the bunk 'cross from us, holding his side and crying.

"Hold that smoke in," I said to the boy.

He held it in and started coughing. When he stopped coughing I told him to draw again. He drawed and held it, then he let it out. I knowed he wasn't doing it right, but this was his first time, and I let him slide.

"If Medlow come to get me, I'm not going," I said to the boy. "That means T. J. and his boys coming, too. They go'n beat me because they think I'm a smart aleck trying to show them up. Now you listen to me, and listen good. Every time they come for me I want you to start praying. I want you to pray till they bring me back in this cell. And I don't want you praying like a woman, I want you to pray like a man. You don't even have to get on your knees; you can lay on your bunk and pray. Pray quiet and to yourself. You hear me?"

He didn't know what I was talking about, but he said, "Yes, sir," anyhow.

"I don't believe in God," I said. "But I want you to believe. I want you to believe He can hear you. That's the only way I'll be able to take those beatings—with you praying. You understand what I'm saying?"

"Yes, sir."

"You sure, now?"

"Yes, sir."

I drawed on the cigarette and looked at him. Deep in me I felt some kind of love for this little boy.

"You got a daddy?" I asked him.

"Yes, sir."

"A mama?"

"Yes, sir."

"Then how come you stealing?"

"'Cause I was hungry."

"Don't they look after you?'

"No, sir."

"You been in here before?"

"Yes, sir."

"You like it in here?"

"No, sir. I was hungry."

"Let's wash your back," I said.

We got up and went to the facebowl. I helped him off with his shirt. His back was cut from where they had beat him.

"You know Munford Bazille?" I asked him.

"Yes, sir. He don't live too far from us. He kin to you?"

"No, he's not kin to me. You like him?"

"No, sir, I don't like him. He stay in fights all the time, and they always got him in jail."

"That's how you go'n end up."

"No, sir, not me. 'Cause I ain't coming back here no more."

"I better not ever catch you in here again," I said. "Hold onto that bunk—this might hurt."

"What you go'n do?"

"Wash them bruises."

"Don't mash too hard."

"Shut up," I told him, "and hold on."

I wet my handkerchief and dabbed at the bruises. Every time I touched his back, he flinched. But I didn't let that stop me. I washed his back good and clean. When I got through, I told him to go back to his bunk and lay down. Then I rinched out his shirt and spread it out on the foot of my bunk. I took off my own shirt and rinched it out because it was filthy.

I lit a cigarette and looked up at the window. I had talked big, but what was I going to do when Medlow came? Was I going to change my mind and go with him? And if I didn't go with Medlow, I surely had to go with T. J. and his boys. Was I going to be able to take the beatings night after night? I had seen what T. J. could do to your back. I had seen it on this kid and I had seen it on other people. Was I going to be able to take it?

I don't know, I thought to myself. I'll just have to wait and see.

HENRY DUMAS
(1934–1968)

Henry Dumas was a promising and productive short story writer and poet whose life was cut short by a white Transit policeman's bullet in the subways of New York on May 23, 1968. Being profoundly committed to the black community, this southern-spirited writer wrote surreal fables and myths celebrating the souls of black folks. Since his death, five books of his fiction and poetry have been published. In *Black American Literature Forum* (Summer 1988), the distinguished poet Margaret Walker said of Dumas's works, "They are the raw, earthy, bone-bare stuff of true Black experience. The language is as musical as any music we have rendered."

Henry Dumas was born on July 20, 1934, in Sweet Home, Arkansas. At age ten, he moved to Harlem, where he attended public schools and graduated from high school in 1953. That year, he enrolled at City College but dropped out to join the Air Force. After his discharge, he enrolled in 1957 at Rutgers University, where he studied English. From 1965 to 1966, he was employed as a social worker for the State of New York. He then worked for a year as assistant director of the Upward Bound program at Hiram College in Ohio. In 1967, he was a teacher-counselor and director of language workshops at Southern Illinois University's Experiment in Higher Education in East St. Louis. As the poet Jay Wright said of his friend in *Black American Literature Forum* (Summer 1988), "It was very hard to figure just when he had time to write. But he did write, and quite a bit. Whenever he appeared, he had stacks of new poems, pages of a novel, articles, prose poems, sketches for a play." During his lifetime, his work was published in little magazines such as *Freedomways, Negro Digest, Umbra,* and *Hiram Poetry Review.* He was influenced by Margaret Walker, James Brown, John Coltrane, Sun Ra, the contemporary avant-garde jazz musician and composer (with whom he studied), and Malcolm X.

Dumas studied his black heritage; he wanted to forge an art that used traditional folk forms. In a letter to his friend George Hudson, he observed, "My interest in Gospel music coincides with my interest in folk poetry, and the folk expression.... There is a wealth of good things to be developed in our heritage. The Gospel tradition is among a few." Like Jean Toomer before him, the blues and gospel tradition linked him to the land, the South, and the black soul. His love of the folk tradition came from his love of black people.

At the time of his death, Henry Dumas was producing some of the most original cultural nationalist writings of the late sixties. In 1970 two collected volumes of his works, *Poetry for My People* and *"Ark of Bones" and Other Stories,* were published posthumously. There is no telling where his talent would have taken him.

◆◆◆

The poet Eugene Redmond has edited Dumas's selected stories, *Goodbye, Sweetwater* (1988), and his selected poems, *Knees of a Natural Man* (1989). Redmond also has edited a special issue of *Black American Literature Forum* (Summer 1988) devoted to Dumas's work.

FROM *Ark of Bones*

Headeye, he was followin me. I knowed he was followin me. But I just kept goin, like I wasn't payin him no mind. Headeye, he never fish much, but I guess he knowed the river good as anybody. But he aint know where the fishin was good. Thas why I knowed he was followin me. So I figured I better fake him out. I aint want nobody with a mojo bone followin me. Thas why I was goin along down-river stead of up, where I knowed fishin was good. Headeye, he hard to fool. Like I said, he knowed the river good. One time I rode across to New Providence with him and his old man. His old man was drunk. Headeye, he took the raft on across.

Me and him. His old man stayed in New Providence, but me and Headeye come back. Thas when I knowed how good of a river-rat he was.

Headeye, he o.k., cept when he get some kinda notion in that big head of his. Then he act crazy. Tryin to show off his age. He older'n me, but he little for his age. Some people say readin too many books will stunt your growth. Well, on Headeye, everything is stunted cept his eyes and his head. When he get some crazy notion runnin through his head, then you can't get rid of him till you know what's on his mind. I knowed somethin was eatin on him, just like I knowed it was *him* followin *me*.

I kept close to the path less he think I was tryin to lose him. About a mile from my house I stopped and peed in the bushes, and then I got a chance to see how Headeye was movin along.

Headeye, he droop when he walk. They called him Headeye cause his eyes looked bigger'n his head when you looked at him sideways. Headeye bout the ugliest guy I ever run upon. But he was good-natured. Some people called him Eagle-Eye. He bout the smartest nigger in that raggedy school, too. But most time we called him Headeye. He was always findin things and bring'em to school, or to the cotton patch. One time he found a mojo bone and all the kids cept me went round talkin bout him puttin a curse on his old man. I aint say nothin. It wont none of my business. But Headeye, he aint got no devil in him. I found that out.

So, I'm kickin off the clay from my toes, but mostly I'm thinkin about how to find out what's on his mind. He's got this notion in his head about me hoggin the luck. So I'm fakin him out, lettin him droop behind me.

Pretty soon I break off the path and head for the river. I could tell I was far enough. The river was gettin ready to bend.

I come up on a snake twistin toward the water. I was gettin ready to bust that snake's head when a fox run across my path. Before I could turn my head back, a flock of birds hit the air pretty near scarin me half to death. When I got on down to the bank, I see somebody's cow lopin on the levee way down the river. Then to really upshell me, here come Headeye droopin long like he had ten tons of cotton on his back.

"Headeye, what you followin me for?" I was mad.

"Aint nobody thinkin bout you," he said, still comin.

"What you followin long behind me for?"

"Aint nobody followin you."

"The hell you aint."

"I aint followin you."

"Somebody's followin me, and I like to know who he is."

"Maybe somebody's followin me."

"What you mean?"

"Just what you think."

Headeye, he was gettin smart on me. I give him one of my looks, meanin that he'd better watch his smartness round me, cause I'd have him down eatin dirt in a minute. But he act like he got a crazy notion.

"You come this far ahead me, you must be got a call from the spirit."

"What spirit?" I come to wonder if Headeye aint got to workin his mojo too much.

"Come on."

"Wait." I grabbed his sleeve.

He took out a little sack and started pullin out something.

"You fishin or not?" I ask him.

"Yeah, but not for the same thing. You see this bone?" Headeye, he took out that mojo. I stepped back. I wasn't scared of no ole bone, but everybody'd been talkin bout Headeye and him gettin sanctified. But he never went to church. Only his mama went. His old man only went when he sober, and that be about once or twice a year.

So I look at that bone. "What kinda voodo you work with that mojo?"

"This is a keybone to the culud man. Aint but one in the whole world."

"And *you* got it?" I act like I aint believe him. But I was testin him. I never rush upon a thing I don't know.

"We got it."

"We got?"

"It belongs to the people of God."

I aint feel like the people of God, but I just let him talk on.

"Remember when Ezekiel was in the valley of dry bones?"

I reckoned I did.

". . . And the hand of the Lord was upon me, and carried me out in the spirit to the valley of dry bones.

"And he said unto me, 'Son of man, can these bones live?' and I said unto him, 'Lord, thou knowest.'

"And he said unto me, 'Go and bind them together. Prophesy that I shall come and put flesh upon them from generations and from generations.'

"And the Lord said unto me, 'Son of man, these bones are the whole house of thy brothers, scattered to the islands. Behold, I shall bind up the bones and you shall prophesy the name.' "

Headeye, he stopped. I aint say nothin. I never seen him so full of the spirit before. I held my tongue. I aint know what to make of his notion.

He walked on pass me and loped on down to the river bank. This here old place was called Deadman's Landin becaue they found a dead man there one time. His body was so rotted and ate up by fish and craw dads that they couldn't tell whether he was white or black. Just a dead man.

Headeye went over to them long planks and logs leanin off in the water and begin to push them around like he was makin somethin.

"You was followin me." I was mad again.

Headeye acted like he was iggin me. He put his hands up to his eyes and looked far out over the water. I could barely make out the other side of the river. It was real wide right along there and take coupla hours by boat to cross it. Most I ever did was fish and swim. Headeye, he act like he iggin me. I began to bait my hook and go down the bank to where he was. I was mad enough to pop him side the head, but I shoulda been glad. I just wanted him to own up to the truth. I walked along the bank. That damn river was risin. It was lappin up over the planks of the landin and climbin up the bank.

Then the funniest thing happened. Headeye, he stopped movin and shovin on those planks and looks up at me. His pole is layin back under a willow tree like he wan't goin to fish none. A lot of birds were still flyin over and I saw a bunch of wild hogs rovin along the levee. All of a sudden Headeye, he say:

"I aint mean no harm what I said about you workin with the devil. I take it back."

It almost knocked me over. Me and Headeye was arguin a while back bout how many niggers there is in the Bible. Headeye, he know all about it, but I aint give on to what I know. I looked sideways at him. I figured he was tryin to make up for followin me. But there was somethin funny goin on so I held my peace. I said 'huh-huh,' and I just kept on lookin at him.

Then he points out over the water and up in the sky wavin his hand all round like he was twirlin a lasso.

"You see them signs?"

I couldn't help but say 'yeah.'

"The Ark is comin."

"What Ark?"

"You'll see."

"Noah's Ark?"

"Just wait. You'll see."

And he went back to fixin up that landin. I come to see what he was doin pretty soon. And I had a notion to go down and pitch in. But I knowed Headeye. Sometimes he gets a notion in his big head and he act crazy behind it. Like the time in church when he told Rev. Jenkins that he heard people moanin out on the river. I remember that. Cause papa went with the men. Headeye, his old man was with them out in that boat. They thought it was somebody took sick and couldn't row ashore. But Headeye, he kept tellin them it was a lot of people, like a multitude.

Anyway, they aint find nothin and Headeye, his daddy hauled off and smacked him side the head. I felt sorry for him and didn't laugh as much as the other kids did, though sometimes Headeye's notions get me mad too.

Then I come to see that maybe he wasn't followin me. The way he was actin I knowed he wasn't scared to be there at Deadman's Landin. I threw my line out and made like I was fishin, but I wasn't, cause I was steady watchin Headeye.

By and by the clouds started to get thick as clabber milk. A wind come up. And even though the little waves slappin the sides of the bank made the water jump around and dance, I could still tell that the river was risin. I looked at Headeye. He was wanderin off along the bank, wadin out in the shallows and leanin over like he was lookin for somethin.

I comest to think about what he said, that valley of bones. I comest to get some kinda crazy notion myself. There was a lot of signs, but they weren't nothin too special. If you're sharp-eyed you always seein somethin along the Mississippi.

I messed around and caught a couple of fish. Headeye, he was wadin out deeper in the Sippi, bout hip-deep now, standin still like he was listenin for somethin. I left my pole under a big rock to hold it down and went over to where he was.

"This aint the place," I say to him.

Headeye, he aint say nothin. I could hear the water come to talk a little. Only river people know how to talk to the river when it's mad. I watched the light on the waves way upstream where the ole Sippi bend, and I could tell that she was movin faster. Risin. The shakin was fast and the wind had picked up. It was whippin up the canebrake and twirlin the willows and the swamp oak that drink themselves full along the bank.

I said it again, thinkin maybe Headeye would ask me where was the real place. But he aint even listen.

"You come out here to fish or fool?" I asked him. But he waved his hand back at me to be quiet. I knew then that Headeye had some crazy notion in his big head and that was it. He'd be talkin about it for the next two weeks.

"Hey!" I hollered at him. "Eyehead, can't you see the river's on the rise? Let's shag outa here."

He aint pay me no mind. I picked up a coupla sticks and chunked them out near the place where he was standin just to make sure he aint fall asleep right out there in the water. I aint never knowed Headeye to fall asleep at a place, but bein as he is so damn crazy, I couldn't take the chance.

Just about that time I hear a funny noise. Headeye, he hear it too, cause he motioned to me to be still. He waded back to the bank and ran down to the broken down planks at Deadman's Landin. I followed him. A coupla drops of rain smacked me in the face, and the wind, she was whippin up a sermon.

I heard a kind of moanin, like a lot of people. I figured it must be in the wind. Headeye, he is jumpin around like a perch with a hook in the gill. Then he find himself. He come to just stand alongside the planks. He is in the water about knee deep. The sound is steady not gettin any louder now, and not gettin any lower. The wind, she steady whippin up a sermon. By this time, it done got kinda dark, and me, well, I done got kinda scared.

Headeye, he's alright though. Pretty soon he call me.

"Fish-hound?"

"Yeah?"

"You better come on down here."

"What for? Man, can't you see it gettin ready to rise?"

He aint say nothin. I can't see too much now cause the clouds done swole up so big and mighty that everything's gettin dark.

Then I sees it. I'm gettin ready to chunk another stick out at him, when I see this big thing movin in the far off, movin slow, down river, naw, it was up river. Naw, it was just movin and standin still at the same time. The damnest thing I ever seed. It just about a damn boat, the biggest boat in the whole world. I looked up and what I took for clouds was sails. The wind was whippin up a sermon on them.

It was way out in the river, almost not touchin the water, just rockin there, rockin and waitin.

Headeye, I don't see him.

Then I look and I see a rowboat comin. Headeye, he done waded out about shoulder deep and he is wavin to me. I aint know what to do. I guess he bout know that I was gettin ready to run, because he holler out. "Come on, Fish! Hurry! I wait for you."

I figured maybe we was dead or somethin and was gonna get the Glory Boat over the river and make it on into heaven. But I aint say it out aloud. I was so scared I didn't know what I was doin. First think I know I was side by side with Headeye, and a funny-lookin rowboat was drawin alongside of us. Two men, about as black as anybody black wants to be, was steady strokin with paddles. The rain had reached us and I could hear that moanin like a church full of people pourin out their hearts to Jesus in heaven.

All the time I was tryin not to let on how scared I was. Headeye, he aint payin no mind to nothin cept that boat. Pretty soon it comest to rain hard. The two big black jokers rowin the boat aint say nothin to us, and every time I look at Headeye, he poppin his eyes out tryin to get a look at somethin far off. I couldn't see that far, so I had to look at what was close up. The muscles in those jokers' arms was movin back an forth every time they swung them oars around. It was a funny ride in that rowboat, because it didn't seem like we was in the water much. I took a chance and stuck my hand over to see, and when I did that they stopped rowin the boat and when I looked up we was drawin longside this here ark, and I tell you it was the biggest ark in the world.

I asked Headeye if it was Noah's Ark, and he tell me he didn't know either. Then I was scared.

They was tyin that rowboat to the side where some heavy ropes hung over. A long row of steps were cut in the side near where we got out, and the moanin sound was real loud now, and if it wasn't for the wind and rain beatin and whippin us up the steps, I'd swear the sound was comin from someplace inside the ark.

When Headeye got to the top of the steps I was still makin my way up. The two jokers were gone. On each step was a number, and I couldn't help lookin at them numbers. I don't know what number was on the first step, but by the time I took notice I was on 1608, and they went on like that right on up to a number that made me pay attention: 1944. That was when I was born. When I got up to Headeye, he was standin on a number, 1977, and so I aint pay the number any more mind.

If that ark was Noah's, then he left all the animals on shore because I aint see none. I kept lookin around. All I could see was doors and cabins. While we was standin there takin in things, half scared to death, an old man come walkin toward us. He's dressed in skins and his hair is grey and very wooly. I figured he aint never had a haircut all his life. But I didn't say nothin. He walks over to Headeye and that poor boy's eyes bout to pop out.

Well, I'm standin there and this old man is talkin to Headeye. With the wind blowin and the moanin, I couldn't make out what they was sayin. I got the feelin he didn't want me to hear either, because he was leanin in on Headeye. If that old fellow was Noah, then he wasn't like the Noah I'd seen in my Sunday School picture cards. Naw, sir. This old guy was wearin skins and sandals and he was black as Headeye and me, and he had thick features like us, too. On them pictures Noah was always white with a long beard hangin off his belly.

I looked around to see some more people, maybe Shem, Ham and Japheh, or wives and the rest who was suppose to be on the ark, but I aint see nobody. Nothin but all them doors and cabins. The ark is steady rockin like it is floatin on air. Pretty soon Headeye come over to me. The old man was goin through one of the cabin doors. Before he closed the door he turns around and points at me and Headeye. Headeye, he don't see this, but I did. Talkin about scared. I almost ran and jumped off that boat. If it had been a regular boat, like somethin I could stomp my feet on, then I guess I just woulda done it. But I held still.

"Fish-hound, you ready?" Headeye say to me.

"Yeah, I'm ready to get ashore." I meant it, too.

"Come on. You got this far. You scared?"

"Yeah, I'm scared. What kinda boat is this?"

"The Ark. I told you once."

I could tell now that the roarin was not all the wind and voices. Some of it was engines. I could hear that chug-chug like a paddle wheel whippin up the stern.

"When we gettin off here? You think I'm crazy like you?" I asked him. I was mad. "You know what that old man did behind your back?"

"Fish-hound, this is a soulboat."

I figured by now I best play long with Headeye. He got a notion goin and there aint nothin mess his head up more than a notion. I stopped tryin to fake him out. I figured then maybe we both was crazy. I aint feel crazy, but I damn sure couldn't make heads or tails of the situation. So I let it ride. When you hook a fish, the best thing to do is just let him get a good hold, let him swallow it. Specially a catfish. You don't go jerkin him up as soon as you get a nibble. With a catfish you let him go. I figured I'd better let things go. Pretty soon, I figured I'd catch up with somethin. And I did.

Well, me and Headeye were kinda arguin, not loud, since you had to keep your voice down on a place like that ark out of respect. It was like that. Headeye, he tells me that when the cabin doors open we were suppose to go down the stairs. He said anybody on this boat could consider hisself *called.*

"Called to do what?" I asked him. I had to ask him, cause the only kinda callin I knew about was when somebody *hollered* at you or when the Lord *called* somebody to preach. I figured it out. Maybe the Lord had called him, but I knew dog well He wasn't *callin* me. I hardly ever went to church and when I did go it was ony to play with the gals. I knowed I wasn't fit to whip up no flock of people with holiness. So when I asked him, called for what, I aint have in my mind nothin I could be called for.

"You'll see." he said, and the next thing I know we was going down steps into the belly of that ark. The moanin jumped up into my ears loud and I could smell somethin funny, like the burnin of sweet wood. The churnin of a paddle wheel filled up my ears and when Headeye stopped at the foot of the steps, I stopped too. What I saw I'll never forget as long as I live.

Bones. I saw bones. They were stacked all the way to the top of the ship. I looked around. The under side of the whole ark was nothin but a great bonehouse. I looked and saw crews of black men handlin in them bones. There was crew of two or three under every cabin around that ark. Why, there must have been a million cabins. They were doin it very carefully, like they were holdin onto babies or somethin precious. Standin like a captain was the old man we had seen top deck. He was holdin a long piece of leather up to a fire that was burnin near the edge of an opening which showed outward to the water. He was readin that piece of leather.

On the other side of the fire, just at the edge of the ark, a crew of men was windin up a rope. They were chantin every time they pulled. I couldn't understand what they was sayin. It was a foreign talk, and I never learned any kind of foreign talk. In front of us was a fence so as to keep anybody comin down the steps from bargin right in. We just stood there. The old man knew we was there, but he was busy readin. Then he rolls up this long scroll and starts to walk in a crooked path through the bones laid out on the floor. It was like he was walkin frontwards, backwards, sidewards and every which a way. He was bein careful not to step on them bones. Headeye, he looked like he knew what was goin on, but when I see all this I just about popped my eyes out.

Just about the time I figure I done put things together, somethin happens. I bout come to figure them bones were the bones of dead animals and all the men wearin skin clothes, well, they was the skins of them animals, but just about time I think I got it figured out, one of the men haulin that rope up from the water starts to holler. They all stop and let him moan on and on.

I could make out a bit of what he was sayin, but like I said, I never was good at foreign talk.

Aba aba, al ham dilaba
aba aba, mtu brotha
aba aba, al ham dilaba
aba aba, bretha brotha
aba aba, djuka brotha
aba aba, al ham dilaba

Then he stopped. The others begin to chant in the back of him, real low, and the old man, he stop where he was, unroll that scroll and read it, and then he holler out: "Nineteen hundred and twenty three!" Then he close up the scroll and continue his comin towards me and Headeye. On his way he had to stop and do the same thing about four times. All along the side of the ark them great black men were haulin up bones from that river. It was the craziest thing I ever saw. I knowed then it wasn't no animal bones. I took a look at them and they was all laid out in different ways, all making some kind of body and there was big bones and little bones, parts of bones, chips, tid-bits, skulls, fingers and everything. I shut my mouth then. I knowed I was onto somethin. I had fished out somethin.

I comest to think about a sermon I heard about Ezekiel in the valley of dry bones. The old man was lookin at me now. He look like he was sizin me up.

Then he reach out and open the fence. Headeye, he walks through and the old man closes it. I keeps still. You best to let things run their course in a situation like this.

"Son, you are in the house of generations. Every African who lives in America has a part of his soul in this ark. God has called you, and I shall anoint you."

He raised the scroll over Headeye's head and began to squeeze like he was tryin to draw the wetness out. He closed his eyes and talked very low.

"Do you have your shield?"

Headeye, he then brings out this funny cloth I see him with, and puts it over his head and it flops all the way over his shoulder like a hood.

"Repeat after me," he said. I figured that old man must be some kind of minister because he was ordaining Headeye right there before my eyes. Everything he say, Headeye, he say in behind him.

Aba, I consecrate my bones.
Take my soul up and plant it again.
Your will shall be my hand.
When I strike you strike.
My eyes shall see only thee.
I shall set my brother free.
Aba, this bone is thy seal.

I'm steady watchin. The priest is holdin a scroll over his head and I see some oil fallin from it. It's black oil and it soaks into Headeye's shield and the shield turns dark green. Headeye aint movin. Then the priest pulls it off.

"Do you have your witness?"

Headeye, he is tremblin. "Yes, my brother, Fish-hound."

The priest points at me then like he did before.

"With the eyes of your brother Fish-hound, so be it?" He was askin me. I nodded my head. Then he turns and walks away just like he come.

Headeye, he goes over to one of the fires, walkin through the bones like he been doin it all his life, and he holds the shield in till it catch fire. It don't burn with a flame, but with a smoke. He puts it down on a place which looks like an altar or somethin, and he sits in front of the smoke cross-legged, and I can hear him moanin. When the shield it all burnt up, Headeye takes out that little piece of mojo bone and rakes the ashes inside. Then he zig-walks over to me, opens up that fence and goes up the steps. I have to follow, and he aint say nothin to me. He aint have to then.

It was several days later that I see him again. We got back that night late, and everybody wanted to know where we was. People from town said the white folks had lynched a nigger and threw him in the river. I wasn't doin no talkin till I see Headeye. Thas why he picked me for his witness. I keep my word.

Then that evenin, whilst I'm in the house with my ragged sisters and brothers and my old papa, here come Headeye. He had a funny look in his eye. I knowed some notion was whippin his head. He must've been runnin. He was out of breath.

"Fish-hound, broh, you know what?"

"Yeah," I said. Headeye, he could count on me to do my part, so I aint mind showin him that I like to keep my feet on the ground. You can't never tell what you get yourself into by messin with mojo bones.

"I'm leavin." Headeye, he come up and stand on the porch. We got a no-count rabbit dog, named Heyboy, and when Headeye come up on the porch Heyboy, he jump up and come sniffin at him.

"Git," I say to Heyboy, and he jump away like somebody kick him. We hadn't seen that dog in about a week. No tellin what kind of devilment he been into.

Headeye, he aint say nothin. The dog, he stand up on the edge of the porch with his two front feet lookin at Headeye like he was goin to get piece bread chunked out at him. I watch all this and I see who been takin care that no-count dog.

"A dog aint worth a mouth of bad wine if he can't hunt," I tell Headeye, but he is steppin off the porch.

"Broh, I come to tell you I'm leavin."

"We all be leavin if the Sippi keep risin," I say.

"Naw," he say.

Then he walk off. I come down off that porch.

"Man, you need another witness?" I had to say somethin.

Headeye, he droop when he walk. He turned around, but he aint droopin.

"I'm goin back, but someday I be back. You is my witness."

We shook hands and Headeye, he was gone, movin fast with that no-count dog runnin long side him.

He stopped once and waved. I got a notion when he did that. But I been keepin it to myself. People been askin me where'd he go. But I only tell em a little somethin I learned in church. And I tell em bout Ezekiel in the valley of dry bones.

Sometimes they say, "Boy, you gone crazy?" and then sometimes they'd say, "Boy, you gonna be a preacher yet," or then they'd look at me and nod their heads as if they knew what I was talkin bout.

I never told em about the Ark and them bones. It would make no sense. They think me crazy then for sure. Probably say I was gettin to be as crazy as Headeye, and then they'd turn around and ask me again:

"Boy, where you say Headeye went?"

AUDRE LORDE
(1934–1992)

No other American writer has expressed the triple jeopardy of being black, female, and lesbian with the depth and expansion of Audre Lorde. Having a tremendous impact on the modern feminist movement, Lorde never forgot her commitment to African Americans and to other oppressed people. Throughout her life, she fought against racial, sexual, and class oppression. "Art for art's sake doesn't exist for me . . . the question of social protest and art is inseparable," Lorde maintains in an interview published in Mari Evans's *Black Women Writers 1950–1980: A Critical Evaluation* (1984). Early in her career, she wrote,

> I am Black, Woman, and Poet—all three are facts outside the realm of choice. . . . All who I love are of my people; it is not simple. I was not born on a farm or in a forest but in the centre of the largest city in the world—a member of the human race hemmed in by stone and away from earth and sunlight. But what is in my blood and kin of richness, of brown earth and noon sun and the strength to love

them, comes the roundabout way from Africa through sun islands, to a stony coast; and these are the gifts through which I sing.

Toward the end of her career, she changed these words of self-identification to "black / lesbian / mother / woman / warrier-poet."

Born Audre Geraldine Lorde in New York City on February 18, 1934, she was the daughter of middle-class West Indian immigrant parents, Frederic Byron Lorde and Linda Belmar Lorde. Although he began his adult life as a laborer, her father eventually became a real estate broker. The youngest of five sisters, Lorde attended Catholic schools in Manhattan and received in 1959 a bachelor's degree in library science from Hunter College, where she had been in intermittent attendance since 1951. She had previously attended National University of Mexico in 1954. In 1961, she received her master's degree in library science from Columbia University.

While she was attending school, Lorde worked as a medical clerk, x-ray technician, ghostwriter, arts and crafts supervisor, social worker, and factory worker. From 1961 to 1963, she worked as a librarian at the Mount Vernon Public Library in Mount Vernon, New York, and from 1966 to 1968 she was head librarian at Town School Library in New York City. She married Edwin Ashley Rollins, an attorney, in 1962, but they were divorced eight years later. Two children, Elizabeth and Jonathan, were born of the marriage.

The poet once said that she considered 1968 the turning point in her life. That year, she won a National Endowment for the Arts grant, which enabled her to become a poet-in-residence at Tougaloo College in Tougaloo, Mississippi. Also in 1968, her first book of poetry, *The First Cities,* was published. Of that time she wrote in *Cables to Rage* (1970), "The second breath I drew was difficult and (no explanations forthcoming from my elders) I set out to build my own solutions—at least formulate a question. I was a child." The poems in *The First Cities* did not immediately identify Lorde with the angry black writers of the day, but Dudley Randall stated in a favorable review, entitled "Books Noted: 'The First Cities,'" *Negro Digest,* vol. 17 (1968), "[She] does not wave a black flag, but her blackness is there, implicit, in the bone." He described the collection as "a quiet introspective book. . . . Audre Lorde's poems are not strident, and do not grab you by the collar and drag you in, but they attract you by their fresh phrasing, which draws you to return to them and to discover new evocations."

Lorde's second book of poetry, *Cables to Rage,* was published in 1970 in London by Paul Breman, who was an active supporter of the black activist movement. Dudley Randall distributed the American edition through his Broadside Press. Irma McClaurin-Allen says that the book is especially noteworthy because "it is the first poetic expression of Lorde's homosexuality." Lorde received a Creative Artists Public Service Grant as a result of *Cables to Rage.* This financial support, along with much critical encouragement, enabled her to produce *From a Land Where Other People Live* (1973), her third work. In this volume, Lorde's outspoken stance in behalf of Third World peoples is especially prominent. The poems collide with juxtapositions of contemporary violence at global hot points: Angola, Hanoi, Mozambique, Mississippi, New York, Detroit, and San Francisco.

Most critics consider Lorde's fourth book of poetry, *The New York Head Shop and Museum* (1974), to be her most complex and vitriolic antiestablishment achievement. Joan Martin says of the poetry in this collection, "The sarcasm here goes past the bitter stage; it is stronger than mere protest or rage . . . indeed, 'anguish' seems to be the only correct word for describing the peculiar situation non-whites find themselves in in white America." Also published by Broadside Press, *The New York Head Shop and Museum,* as well as Lorde's frank public addresses in prominent places, attracted the attention of major publishers. In 1976, Norton published *Coal.* McClaurin-Allen writes that *Coal* is a significant work because it introduced "Lorde's work to a broader readership than the predominately black one that supported Broadside Press. 'Coal,' the title poem, demonstrates Lorde's facility with metaphor, as well as the tightness and control of her language."

Norton also issued *The Black Unicorn* in 1978. In this text, Lorde returned to her African roots, using the mythology of the African goddess Seboulisa as a basis for her writing on black female cultural and spiritual experience. Andrea Benton Rushing notes that Lorde uses inferences and ambiguities in the text: "In substantiating her contention that 'black women have always bonded together' she cites the close, involved and complex relationship between co-wives, the Amazon warriors of ancient Dahomey, and West African market women's associations." Lorde now had a central place on the mostly white feminist stage. According to prominent feminist critic Adrienne Rich, "*The Black Unicorn* (1978) is a monumental work that reveals the complexity of Lorde's life and vision."

The Cancer Journals (1980), the first of four prose books by Lorde, traces her early battles with the disease that finally took her life and stalwartly attacks the male-centered medical profession that so blithely dismembers female patients. The text explores the emotional and physical impact of the growth as few testimonies have ever done. It won the American Library Association's Gay Caucus Book of the Year Award for 1981. In the novel *Zami: A New Spelling of My Name* (1982), one of Lorde's few fictional offerings, she returns to the themes of lesbianism and her West Indian heritage. Rosemary Daniell believes that the novel, which traces a young girl's life through her traumatic teenage years and first homosexual attractions and relationships, is highly autobiographical.

Lorde taught at John Jay College of Criminal Justice from 1970 to 1981, when she joined the faculty of Hunter College, her alma mater. Perhaps her most popular book among American feminists is *Sister Outsider: Essays and Speeches.* Published in 1984, the collection, according to critic Barbara Christian, traces "important concepts in Lorde's development as a black feminist thinker—primarily her intense concern with repression as a means of control, which is reflected in her emphasis on the erotic and her analysis of the concept of difference." Perhaps Lorde's best-known essay, which is included in *Sister Outsider,* is "The Master's Tools Will Never Dismantle the Master's House." Lorde also has prominence within the feminist movement for her founding of Kitchen Table: Women of Color Press, which cast her as a mentor of other women of color lesbian writers who may have difficulty gaining publishing and critical acceptance because of their sexual identity and the sexual relevance of their subject matter.

Norton published *Chosen Poems Old and New* in 1982 and *Our Dead Behind Us* in 1986. The poet was fully aware of the significance of the latter book. In "There Are No Honest Poems About Dead Women," she wrote, "I am a Black woman stripped down / and praying / my whole life has been an altar / worth its ending / and I say Aido Hwedo is coming." Audre Lorde died of liver cancer at the age of fifty-eight on November 17, 1992, in St. Croix. Her *New York Times* obituary said that she had fought cancer for fourteen years. She was survived by a companion, Gloria I. Joseph of St. Croix; a son, Jonathan Rollins, and a daughter, Elizabeth Lorde-Rollins, both of New York City; and her four sisters. Most of the major publications of African American and feminist literature published memorial articles about Lorde, invariably celebrating her tremendous victories in life.

❖❖❖

Afrocentric studies of Lorde's works include Jerome Brooks, "In the Name of the Father: The Poetry of Audre Lorde," and Joan Martin, "The Unicorn Is Black: Audre Lorde in Retrospect," both in *Black Women Writers 1950–1980: A Critical Evaluation,* ed. Mari Evans (1984); Paul Breman, "Poetry into the 'Sixties," *The Black American Writer,* ed. C. W. Bigsby, vol. 2 (1969); Amitai F. Avi-ram, "Apo Koinou in Audre Lorde and the Moderns: Defining the Differences," *Callaloo,* vol. 9 (1986); Irma McClaurin-Allen's article in *Dictionary of Literary Biography: Afro-American Poets Since 1955,* vol. 4 (1985). Feminist critiques of Lorde's life and works include Pamela Annas, "A Poetry of Survival: Unnaming and Renaming in the Poetry of Audre Lorde, Pat Parker, Sylvia Plath, and Adrienne Rich," *Colby Library Quarterly,* vol. 18, no. 1: (March 1982); Mary J. Carruthers, "The Re-Vision of the Muse: Adrienne Rich, Audre Lorde, Judy Grahn, Olga Broumas," *Hudson Review,* vol. 36, no. 2 (Summer 1983); Thomas Votteler, *Contemporary Literary Criticism* (1992).

Karla M. Hammond has revealing interview articles of Lorde in *Denver Quarterly,* vol. 16 (1) (1981), and *American Poetry Review,* vol. 9, no. 2 (March/April 1980). See also Claudia Tate's interview with the poet in *Black Women Writers at Work* (1983); Adrienne Rich, "An Interview with Audre Lorde," *Signs: Journal of Women in Culture and Society,* vol. 6, no. 4 (Summer 1981).

Reviews of specific works include Gloria T. Hull, "Living on the Line: Audre Lorde and Our Dead Behind Us," in *Changing Our Own Words: Essays on Criticism, Theory, and Writing by Black Women,* ed. Cheryl A. Wall (1989); Joseph A. Brown, "We Are Piercing Our Weapons Together," *Callaloo,* vol. 9, no. 8, (Fall 1986); Rosemary Daniell, "The Poet Who Found Her Own Way," *New York Times Book Review,* December 19, 1982; Andrea Benton Rushing, "A Creative Use of African Sources," *Obsidian: Black Literature in Review,* vol. 5, no. 3, (Winter 1979); Robert Stepto, "The Phenomenal Woman and the Severed Daughter," *Parnassus: Poetry in Review,* vol. 8, no. 1 (1979); and Dudley Randall's "Books Noted: 'The First Cities,'" *Negro Digest,* vol. 17, no. 11–12 (1968).

Biographical sketches of Lorde include Saundra Towns's entry in *Contemporary Poets,* 2nd ed. (1975); Elizabeth Thomas's article in *Contemporary Authors,* New Revision Series, vol. 26 (1989); and in *Black Writers* (1989), and reports in *Contemporary Literary Criticism,* vol. 18, (1989).

Coal

I
is the total black, being spoken
from the earth's inside.
There are many kinds of open

how a diamond comes into a knot of flame
how sound comes into a word, coloured
by who pays what for speaking.

Some words are open like a diamond
on glass windows
singing out within the passing crash of sun
Then there are words like stapled wagers
in a perforated book,—buy and sign and tear apart—
and come whatever wills all chances
the stub remains
an ill-pulled tooth with a ragged edge.
Some words live in my throat
breeding like adders. Others know sun
seeking like gypsies over my tongue
to explode through my lips
like young sparrows bursting from shell.
Some words
bedevil me.

Love is a word, another kind of open.
As the diamond comes into a knot of flame
I am Black because I come from the earth's inside
now take my word for jewel in the open light.

Power

The difference between poetry and rhetoric
is being
ready to kill
yourself
instead of your children.

I am trapped on a desert of raw gunshot wounds
and a dead child dragging his shattered black
face off the edge of my sleep
blood from his punctured cheeks and shoulders
is the only liquid for miles and my stomach
churns at the imagined taste while
my mouth splits into dry lips
without loyalty or reason
thirsting for the wetness of his blood
as it sinks into the whiteness
of the desert where I am lost
without imagery or magic
trying to make power out of hatred and destruction
trying to heal my dying son with kisses
only the sun will bleach his bones quicker.

The policeman who shot down a 10-year-old in Queens
stood over the boy with his cop shoes in childish blood
and a voice said "Die you little motherfucker" and
there are tapes to prove that. At his trial
this policeman said in his own defense
"I didn't notice the size or nothing else
only the color," and
there are tapes to prove that, too.

Today that 37-year-old white man with 13 years of police forcing
has been set free
by 11 white men who said they were satisfied
justice had been done
and one black woman who said
"They convinced me" meaning
they had dragged her 4'10" black woman's frame
over the hot coals of four centuries of white male approval
until she let go the first real power she ever had
and lined her own womb with cement
to make a graveyard for our children.

I have not been able to touch the destruction within me.
But unless I learn to use
the difference between poetry and rhetoric
my power too will run corrupt as poisonous mold
or lie limp and useless as an unconnected wire
and one day I will take my teenaged plug
and connect it to the nearest socket
raping an 85-year-old white woman
who is somebody's mother
and as I beat her senseless and set a torch to her bed
a greek chorus will be singing in 3/4 time
"Poor thing. She never hurt a soul. What beasts they are."

Never Take Fire from a Woman

My sister and I
have been raised to hate
genteelly
each other's silences
sear up our tongues
like flame
we greet each other
with respect
meaning
from a watchful distance
while we dream of lying
in the tender of passion

to drink from a woman
who smells like love.

Solstice

We forgot to water the plantain shoots
when our houses were full of borrowed meat
and our stomachs with the gift of strangers
who laugh now as they pass us
because our land is barren
the farms are choked with stunted rows of straw
and with our nightmares
of juicy brown yams that cannot fill us.
The roofs of our houses rot from last winter's water
but our drinking pots are broken
we have used them to mourn the deaths of old lovers
the next rain will wash our footprints away
and our children have married beneath them.

Our skins are empty.
They have been vacated by the spirits
who are angered by our reluctance
to feed them.
In baskets of straw made from sleep grass
and the droppings of civets
they have been hidden away by our mothers
who are waiting for us by the river.

My skin is tightening
soon I shall shed it
like a monitor lizard
like remembered comfort
at the new moon's rising
I will eat the last signs of my weakness
remove the scars of old childhood wars
and dare to enter the forest whistling
like a snake that has fed the chameleon
for changes
I shall be forever.

May I never remember reasons
for my spirit's safety
may I never forget
the warning of my woman's flesh
weeping at the new moon
may I never lose
that terror
that keeps me brave
May I owe nothing
that I cannot repay.

The Woman Thing

The hunters are back from beating the winter's face
in search of a challenge or task
in search of food
making fresh tracks for their children's hunger
they do not watch the sun
they cannot wear its heat for a sign
of triumph or freedom.
The hunters are treading heavily homeward
through snow that is marked
with their own bloody footprints.
Emptyhanded the hunters return
snow-maddened, sustained by their rages.

In the night after food they may seek
young girls for their amusement. But now
the hunters are coming
and the unbaked girls flee from their angers.

All this day I have craved
food for my child's hunger.
Emptyhanded the hunters come shouting
injustices drip from their mouths
like stale snow melted in sunlight.

Meanwhile the womanthing my mother taught me
bakes off its covering of snow
like a rising blackening sun.

Stations

Some women love
to wait
for life   for a ring
in the June light   for a touch
of the sun to heal them   for another
woman's voice   to make them whole
to untie their hands
put words in their mouths
form to their passages   sound
to their screams   for some other sleeper
to remember   their future   their past.

Some women wait for their right
train   in the wrong station
in the alleys of morning
for the noon to holler
the night come down.

Some women wait for love
to rise up

the child of their promise
to gather from earth
what they do not plant
to claim pain for labor
to become
the tip of an arrow   to aim
at the heart of now
but it never stays.

Some women wait for visions
that do not return
where they were not welcome
naked
for invitations to places
they always wanted
to visit
to be repeated.

Some women wait for themselves
around the next corner
and call the empty spot peace
but the opposite of living
is only not living
and the stars do not care.

Some women wait for something
to change and nothing
does change
so they change
themselves.

Legacy—Hers

When love leaps from my mouth
cadenced in that Grenada wisdom
upon which I first made holy war
then I must reassess
all my mother's words
or every path I cherish.

Like everything else I learned from Linda
this message hurtles across still uncalm air
silent   tumultuous   freed water
descending an imperfect drain.

I learn how to die
from your many examples
cracking the code of your living
heroisms   collusions   invisibilities
constructing my own

book of your last hours
how we tried to connect
in that bland spotless room
one bright Black woman
to another   bred for endurance
for battle

island women make good wives
whatever happens they've seen worse . . .

your last word to me was   *wonderful*
and I am still seeking the rest
of that terrible acrostic

JUNE JORDAN
(1936–)

Born on July 9, 1936, in Harlem, the only child of Jamaican immigrant parents named Granville Ivanhoe Jordan and Mildred Maude Fisher Jordan, June Jordan's prolific production can be matched by few American writers. From a publishing career that began in 1969, Jordan has garnered a wide and appreciative audience with eleven books of poetry, six collections of writings by and for juveniles, three collections of essays, an edited anthology, one of the few biographies of Fannie Lou Hamer, three produced plays, and several operettas and recordings.

Headed by a father who worked as a postal clerk and a mother who worked as a nurse, Jordan's relatively middle class family purchased a traditional brownstone home on Hancock Street in Brooklyn's Bedford-Stuyvesant neighborhood when she was five years old. Her parents nurtured her interest in literature, often reading aloud passages from the Bible, Shakespeare, Edgar Allan Poe, and Paul Laurence Dunbar. For one year, she was the only black among three thousand whites at Midwood High School. She then transferred to the Northfield School for Girls, a preparatory school in Massachusetts, from which she graduated in 1953. These were difficult years for Jordan, who was reportedly adversely affected by her father's physical abuse, her mother's noninterference, and the oppressiveness of the all-white educational institutions she attended. In addition, her parents strongly objected to her early penchant to be a poet.

Attending Barnard College after her graduation from high school, Jordan struggled to nurture her poetic talents. Later, she would write of these college years, "No one ever presented me with a single Black author, poet, historian, personage, or idea for that matter. Nor was I ever assigned a single woman to study as a thinker, or writer, or poet, or life force." In 1955, she entered an interracial marriage with Michael Meyer, who was attending Columbia University. Jordan followed her husband to the University of Chicago, returned to Barnard a year later, but left again in 1957.

Jordan's friend and fellow writer Alexis Deveaux would later write that the couple suffered untold insults from whites throughout the Midwest. In 1958, they had a son, Christopher David Meyer. Almost immediately, Jordan assumed sole responsibility for supporting her son. In 1963, she accepted a position as an assistant to the producer of Frederick Wiseman's *The Cool World,* an avant-garde film about the black experience in Harlem. In 1964, she met Malcolm X and began her long involvement in Harlem politics.

In 1965, Jordan and Meyer were divorced. The following year, her mother committed suicide, causing her to reexamine her mother's life as underappreciated and unfulfilled.

Before beginning her first faculty position as an instructor of English and literature at City College of New York in 1967, Jordan worked as a writer and research assistant for the Technical Housing Department of Mobilization for Youth in New York City. In 1968, she accepted a position at Connecticut College, where she also directed the Search for Education, Elevation and Knowledge (SEEK) Program. Later that year, she joined the faculty of Sarah Lawrence College in Bronxville, New York.

During her teaching career, Jordan simultaneously began her writing career under her married name, June Meyer. Several of her poems and short stories appeared in such highly placed periodicals as the *New York Times Magazine, Black World, Esquire, The Nation, Partisan Review,* and *Essence.* Her first full-length work, an epic poem titled *Who Look at Me,* published in 1969 under the name June Jordan, galvanized her anger about race and racism as well as her struggles as a single working mother. In her 1970 edited anthology, *Soulscript: Afro-American Poetry,* she wrote that the title poem of *Who Look at Me* was "a crucial starting point because its effort to contend with black-white relations is a necessary first step in self-definition for a black person and poet in a white society."

In 1970, Jordan won the Rockefeller Foundation Fellowship in Creative Writing. The following year, she won the Prix de Rome in Environmental Design of the American Academy in Rome. She received this award for community environmental work on the lower East Side and for her collaboration on "Urban Redesign" with W. R. Buckminster-Fuller in *Esquire* in 1965. She also won the Nancy Bloch Award for *The Voice of the Children* in 1971. That same year, she published a book of poems, *Some Changes,* and her first novel, *His Own Where,* written for young adults. The novel was named one of the years's outstanding young adult novels and was nominated for the National Book Award in 1972. In 1973, she published a well-received collection of poetry titled *New Days: Poems of Exile and Return.*

Jordan left Sarah Lawrence College in 1974 and joined the faculty of City College of New York in 1975 as an assistant professor of English. The next year, she moved to the State University of New York at Stony Brook, where she was promoted to tenured full professor in 1982. She has been a professor of Afro-American studies and women's studies at the University of California at Berkeley since 1989.

During a much-noted speech in 1975 at Barnard College, titled "Notes of a Barnard Dropout," she spoke of the suffering in her mother's life. Later, in "Poems for Granville Ivanhoe Jordan," included in the book *Things That I Do in the Dark,* published by Random House in 1977, she acknowledged the tremendous influence that both her mother and father (who died in 1974) had on her life.

According to Peter B. Erickson, Jordan's essay collection *Civil Wars,* published in 1981, is "the most important source of biographical information" on her life. Although that text and much of her early work is largely autobiographical, Jordan joined most black writers of the sixties and seventies in making militant statements about the need for a black aesthetic. In "The Black Poet Speaks of Poetry" (*American Poetry Review,* June 1974), she wrote,

> Distinctively Black poems characteristically deal with memories and possibilities of spoken language, as against literary, or written, language. This partially accounts for the comparative *directness* and force of Black poetry; it is an intentionally collective, or *inclusive,* people's art meant to be shared, heard and, therefore, spoken—meant to be as real as bread.

The author's most recent volumes of poetry, *Haruko: Love Poems,* published by High Risk Books in 1994, and *June Jordan's Poetry for the People* (1995), concentrate more on the celebration of her lesbian lifestyle and her battles with cancer. She also has a recent collection of essays titled *Technical Difficulties: African American Notes on the State of the Union,* published by Pantheon Books in 1992, and a collection of operas and librettos titled *I Was Looking at the Ceiling and Then I Saw the Sky: Earthquake/Romance,* published by New York Scribner in 1995.

An executive board member of the American Writers Congress and of PEN, Jordan has received the Creative Artist Public Service Poetry Award, a National Endowment for the Arts fellowship, the Achievement Award for International Reporting from the National Association of Black Journalists, and the New York Foundation for the Arts Fellow in Poetry Award. Probably because she considers her work as a force against "international evil," in support of the downtrodden masses throughout the world, her poetry and essays have been translated into Spanish, French, Swedish, German, Arabic, and Japanese.

❖❖❖

Brief biographies of June Jordan appear in *Something About the Author,* vol. 4, ed. Anne Commire (1973).

Critical discussions of Jordan's work include the following: Toni Cade Bambara, "Chosen Weapons: A Review of *Civil Wars,*" *Ms.,* April 1984; *Contemporary Authors,* vol. 33–36 (1973); *Contemporary Literary Criticism,* vols. 23 and 11 (1982 and 1979); Alexis Deveaux, "Creating Soul Food: June Jordan," *Essence,* April 1981; Peter B. Erickson, "June Jordan," *Dictionary of Literary Biography,* vol. 38 (1985); Erickson, "The Love Poetry of June Jordan," *Callaloo* (Winter 1986); Agnes Garrett and Helga P. McCue, *Authors and Artists for Young Adults* (1989); Doris Grumbach, "Fine Print," *New Republic,* November 9, 1974; Janet Harris, "A Review of *Dry Victories,*" *New York Times Book Review,* February 11, 1973; Jescha Kessler, "Trial and Error," *Poetry,* vol. 21 (February, 1973); Susan McHenry, "The Jumping Into It," *The Nation* vol. 232 (April 11, 1981); Sara Miles, "This Wheel's on Fire," in *Woman Poet: The East,* ed. Elaine Dallman et al. (1982); Darryl Pinckney, "Opinions and Poems," *New York Times Book Review,* August 9, 1981; Theressa Gunnels Rush et al., *Black Writers Past and Present: A Biographical and Bibliographical Dictionary* (1975); Ntozake Shange, "A Review of *New Days: Poems of Exile and Return* by June Jordan," *Black Scholar,* March 1977; Mildred Thompson, "Book Reviews: *Passion: New Poems, 1977–80,*" *Black Scholar,* January 1981; Nagueyalti Warren, "June Jordan: Poet, Writer, Educator," in *Notable Black American Women* (1992).

All the World Moved

All the world moved next to me strange
I grew on my knees
in hats and taffeta trusting
the holy water to run
like grief from a brownstone
cradling.

Blessing a fear of the anywhere
face too pale to be family
my eyes wore ribbons
for Christ on the subway
as weekly as holiness
in Harlem.

God knew no East no West no South
no Skin nothing I learned like
traditions of sin but later
life began and strangely
I survived His innocence
without my own.

The New Pietà: For the Mothers and Children of Detroit

They wait like darkness not becoming stars
long and early in a wrong one room
he moves no more

Weeping thins the mouth a poor escape from fire
lights to claim to torch the body
burial by war

She and her knees lock slowly closed (a burning door)
not to continue as they bled before
he moves no more

In Memoriam: Martin Luther King, Jr.

I

honey people murder mercy U.S.A.
the milkland turn to monsters teach
to kill to violate pull down destroy
the weakly freedom growing fruit
from being born.

America

tomorrow yesterday rip rape
exacerbate despoil disfigure
crazy running threat the
deadly thrall

appall belief dispel
the wildlife burn the breast
the onward tongue
the outward hand
deform the normal rainy
riot sunshine shelter wreck
of darkness derogate
delimit blank
explode deprive
assassinate and batten up
like bullets fatten up
the raving greed
reactivate a springtime
terrorizing

by death by men by more
than you or I can

STOP

II

They sleep who know a regulated place
or pulse or tide or changing sky
according to some universal
stage direction obvious
like shorewashed shells

we share an afternoon of mourning
in between no next predictable
except for wild reversal hearse rehearsal

You Came with Shells

You came with shells. And left them:
shells.
They lay beautiful on the table.
Now they lie on my desk
peculiar
extraordinary under 60 watts.

This morning I disturb I destroy the window
(and its light) by moving my feet
in the water. There.
It's gone.
Last night the moon ranged from the left
to the right side
of the windshield. Only white lines
on a road strike me as
reasonable but
nevertheless and too often

we slow down for the fog.

I was going to say a natural environment
means this or
I was going to say we remain out of our
element or
sometimes you can get away completely
but the shells
will tell about the howling
and the loss

Poem About My Rights

Even tonight and I need to take a walk and clear
my head about this poem about why I can't
go out without changing my clothes my shoes
my body posture my gender identity my age
my status as a woman alone in the evening /
alone on the streets / alone not being the point /
the point being that I can't do what I want
to do with my own body because I am the wrong
sex the wrong age the wrong skin and
suppose it was not here in the city but down on the beach /
or far into the woods and I wanted to go
there by myself thinking about God / or thinking
about children or thinking about the world / all of it
disclosed by the stars and the silence:
I could not go and I could not think and I could not
stay there
alone
as I need to be
alone because I can't do what I want to do with my own
body and
who in the hell set things up
like this
and in France they say if the guy penetrates
but does not ejaculate then he did not rape me
and if after stabbing him if after screams if
after begging the bastard and if even after smashing
a hammer to his head if even after that if he
and his buddies fuck me after that
then I consented and there was
no rape because finally you understand finally
they fucked me over because I was wrong I was
wrong again to be me being me where I was / wrong
to be who I am
which is exactly like South Africa
penetrating into Namibia penetrating into

Angola and does that mean I mean how do you know if
Pretoria ejaculates what will the evidence look like the
proof of the monster jackboot ejaculation on Blackland
and if
after Namibia and if after Angola and if after Zimbabwe
and if after all of my kinsmen and women resist even to
self-immolation of the villages and if after that
we lose nevertheless what will the big boys say will they
claim my consent:
Do You Follow Me: We are the wrong people of
the wrong skin on the wrong continent and what
in the hell is everybody being reasonable about
and according to the *Times* this week
back in1966 the C.I.A. decided that they had this problem
and the problem was a man named Nkrumah so they
killed him and before that it was Patrice Lumumba
and before that it was my father on the campus
of my Ivy League school and my father afraid
to walk into the cafeteria because he said he
was wrong the wrong age the wrong skin the wrong
gender identity and he was paying my tuition and
before that
it was my father saying I was wrong saying that
I should have been a boy because he wanted one / a
boy and that I should have been lighter skinned and
that I should have had straighter hair and that
I should not be so boy crazy but instead I should
just be one / a boy and before that
it was my mother pleading plastic surgery for
my nose and braces for my teeth and telling me
to let the books loose to let them loose in other
words
I am very familiar with the problems of the C.I.A.
and the problems of South Africa and the problems
of Exxon Corporation and the problems of white
America in general and the problems of the teachers
and the preachers and the F.B.I. and the social
workers and my particular Mom and Dad / I am very
familiar with the problems because the problems
turn out to be
me
I am the history of rape
I am the history of the rejection of who I am
I am the history of the terrorized incarceration of
my self
I am the history of battery assault and limitless
armies against whatever I want to do with my mind

and my body and my soul and
whether it's about walking out at night
or whether it's about the love that I feel or
whether it's about the sanctity of my vagina or
the sanctity of my national boundaries
or the sanctity of my leaders or the sanctity
of each and every desire
that I know from my personal and idiosyncratic
and indisputably single and singular heart
I have been raped
be-
cause I have been wrong the wrong sex the wrong age
the wrong skin the wrong nose the wrong hair the
wrong need the wrong dream the wrong geographic
the wrong sartorial I
I have been the meaning of rape
I have been the problem everyone seeks to
eliminate by forced
penetration with or without the evidence of slime and /
but let this be unmistakable this poem
is not consent I do not consent
to my mother to my father to the teachers to
the F.B.I. to South Africa to Bedford-Stuy
to Park Avenue to American Airlines to the hardon
idlers on the corners to the sneaky creeps in
cars
I am not wrong: Wrong is not my name
My name is my own my own my own
and I can't tell you who the hell set things up like this
but I can tell you that from now on my resistance
my simple and daily and nightly self-determination
may very well cost you your life

WILLIAM MELVIN KELLEY

(1937–)

William Melvin Kelley is a gifted writer whose novels and stories have received scant attention. The author of five novels and numerous articles, Kelley published his celebrated first novel, *A Different Drummer,* in 1962. At that time, Kelley was considered an optimist on the issue of race relations. That soon changed, however, as he became more and more disillusioned with America's racism and its cesspool of moral depravity.

Born in the North Bronx, New York, on November 1, 1937, Kelley grew up comfortably in an Italian neighborhood and attended the exclusive Fieldston School in New York. At Fieldston, he excelled in track, student government, and most of all academics. In 1957, he left the school as captain of the track team and student council president and enrolled at Harvard, where he studied under the poet Archibald MacLeish and the novelist John Hawkes. Kelley's experiences at Harvard proved to be the turning point in his life. His goal to become a lawyer changed dramatically, perhaps, as David Bradly has suggested, to cope with the death of his mother in 1957 and his father in 1958. Kelley's single interest became fiction, as his failing marks in all of his other courses attest. In 1959, *Accent* published his story "Spring Planting," and an article in the *Liberty Journal* pointed to Kelley as an up-and-coming writer. In 1960, he took the coveted Dana Reed Prize for best writing by a Harvard undergraduate. However, by the end of that year, he was through with Harvard but well on his way to completing his first novel.

A Different Drummer (1962) opens with an excerpt from "The Thumb-Nail Almanac," describing the exodus of blacks from a mythical southern state: "In June 1957, for reasons yet to be determined, all the state's Negro inhabitants departed. Today, it is unique in being the only state in the Union that cannot count even one member of the Negro race among its citizens." The leader of this exodus, Tucker Caliban, is the last descendant of an African chieftain who commanded a legendary rebellion against slavery. Caliban, some three generations later, destroys all the symbolic ties between his blood and the white family that enslaved his forebears. He plows tons of salt into the land his family had worked for generations, land that has taken him years to purchase, then burns his home and leaves the state. Every other black person in the state follows him.

In *A Different Drummer,* Kelley calls upon black folk tradition, including the oral narrative with comic dimensions, to create a fable with freedom, independence, courage, and the innate beauty and strength of black culture as its major themes. Caliban's heroic African ancestor emerges from the ship's gangway to stand "two heads taller than any man in the deck," then slices off the head of the auctioneer with such force that the auctioneer's derby sails half a mile to cripple a horse. He frees numerous slaves, attracts twelve followers, and eludes his captors for months. It is this legend, this sound of a "different drummer," that leads Caliban to his own successful rebellion and revolution.

A Different Drummer won for Kelley the Rosenthal Award of the National Institute of Arts and Letters in 1963, establishing his artistic voice in the American literary community. A year earlier, he had received a fellowship to the Bread Loaf and New York Writers' Conference. As the 1960s emerged and the mood of the country changed, so did Kelley. In August 1963, he wrote an article for *Esquire* magazine titled "The Ivy League Negro," in which he views educated blacks as devoid of leadership potential because they are inescapably alienated from the struggles of the masses. During this time of ideological shift, Kelley published largely from abroad, spending 1964 and 1965 in Rome and 1967 in Paris. In *A Drop of Patience* (1965), he works out his theme of reconciliation between affluent blacks and the masses. The novel focuses on a blind black musician who eventually returns to his impoverished folk roots, forsaking the fast-paced life of rich white America.

Kelley soon began publishing in the literary journal *Negro Digest.* He also wrote a piece for *Esquire* in which he attempted to further the thinking of Malcolm X, a man largely unknown to *Esquire*'s readers, if not the majority of African Americans. Kelley wrote explicitly regarding the race issue and a future course of action for blacks in his essay "On Racism, Exploration and the White Liberal": "Separation is indeed the answer—not to flee the evil of whiteness but to create an economic unit which can bring an end to exploitation." By this time, Kelley was thoroughly convinced that African Americans possessed their own unique culture. In May 1968, Kelley wrote an article titled "On Africa in the United States" for *Negro Digest:*

> Now we begin to see our true situation in the United States. Because African civilization was oral rather than a written civilization, each adult African who arrived in the United States possessed an enormous body of knowledge about himself, his history, traditions and curious knowledge which could not be destroyed as long as he lived and talked. Each African sifted through his experience, his knowledge, trying to find something to help him survive in his new environment, and he was talking. He asked other Africans, other slaves, sons of Africans, picking up different kinds of knowledge, sharing experience. Finally the tribes, the cultures, the newcomers and old timers mixed, and what has emerged is not a culture with nothing of Africa in it, but rather a Pan-African culture.

In stark contrast to Kelley's vision of the vitality, richness, and beauty of black life is his icily critical picture of upper-middle-class white America in *dem* (1967). A satire on "dem white folks" set in New York City, *dem* opens with an epigraph in dialect: "naeu, lemi telja haer dem folks liv." For Kelley, these people live a life full of sterility, stupidity, and, perhaps above all, cruelty. Early in the novel, John Godwin invites his white coworker Mitchell Pierce and Pierce's wife Tam home for a weekend visit. When they arrive, they discover that Godwin has murdered his wife and two children. Pierce, meanwhile, is struggling with his own problems. After his wife gives birth to twins, one white and the other black, he seeks to cover up the embarrassment by giving the black child away. The rest of the story deals with Mitchell's attempt to find the black father.

Despite Kelley's achievement in *dem,* criticism has not yet done justice to the satire of Kelley's novels and stories. Displaying the skepticism and irony of Ishmael Reed, Kelley is, like Chester Himes before him, a brilliant depicter of the color and multiplicity of American and African American life. He is also endowed with much of Reed's playfulness, which carries irony to the point of burlesque. For effect, Kelley consciously experiments, to the utter delight of some readers and the frustration of others, with the playfulness of language. This is perhaps most noticeable in *Dunfords Travels Everywhere* (1970), a novel constructed from a language derived from Bantu Pidgin English, Harlem argot, and other forms of black speech.

When not looking to language for effect, Kelley often resorts to fantasy, as in the short story "Homesick Blues," where the ironic tune and theme—"a delicate mission of universal significance"—underlie the triviality of all that the story pictures. Clive Fairchild is involved in a plan to "inflict the American People with the virus of feeling inferior [so much so] that they will beg to abolish the Republic and ask to rejoin Her Majesty's Empire and Commonwealth." Sir Noel Coward says,

> "After all, we've been the Mind of America from the first over. We've sent Tom Paine. Charles Chaplin. Bob Hope. Cary Grant. Richard Burton. The Beatles. Shirley Bassey." . . . "The weapon we'll use is corruption. Death before it begins to stink. We'll prove conclusively that absolutely every American has a price. Rapture the American Spirit once and for all! . . ."

We see "Richard Pryor dressed in a diaper, shaved bald like baby"; O. J. Simpson "feinting and sprinting up and down the gridiron"; "Sidney Poitier in Hitler mustache"; "Kate Millet, Eleanor Holmes Norton, and Bella Abzug stunningly done up as dance-hall girls, all breasts and bustles on ten-inch stiletto heels." And we see that Kelley's whole American world is hollow, bizarre, and perverse in its very essence.

Thus, beneath Kelley's satire is perhaps the saddest of all African American satirists. His theme is the infinite distance between America as it is and as it ought to be. Seeing truth and kindness forever crucified by stupidity and evil, Kelley places the blame squarely on the American social fabric itself.

"Homesick Blues," originally appeared with a number of Kelley's other short stories in his collection *Dancers on the Shore* (1964). He has taught at the New School for Social Research and has been a writer-in-residence at the State University of New York.

❖❖❖

Fur further study, see Valerie M. Babb's essay in *Dictionary of Literary Biography* 33; Trudier Harris, *From Mammies to Militants: Domestics in Black American Literature* (1982); Phyllis R. Klotman, "The Passive Resistant in *A Different Drummer, Day of Absence* and *Many Thousand Gone*," *Studies in Black Literature* 3 (Autumn 1972); Addison Gayle, Jr., *The Way of the New World* (1975); Jane Campbell, *Myth's Black Fiction: The Transformation of History* (1986).

Homesick Blues

Sweaty H. L. Mencken is climbing a steep rocky hill on an island in the Caribbean. Several dark-brown boys (aged eleven) playing cricket with a palm branch and scuffed red ball stop to study H. L. Mencken. He calls them over to ask questions. Opens his attaché case and produces a photo. One dreadlocked youth points toward a cluster of zinc-roofed board houses. In thanks, H. L. Mencken gives each boy a tiny sample bottle of bourbon. All but the dreadlocked youth tear into the booze. Immediately aggression comes into each innocent face. They begin to fight. One hits another in the head with the palm branch cricket bat. Blood flows.

Sweaty H. L. Mencken trudges toward the zinc-roofed houses. An old lady (thin and black) in a porch rocker watches his progress. She continues her sewing. Says something over her shoulder. H. L. Mencken trudges closer. A medium-brown, medium-height dreadlocksman comes around from the side of the old lady's house, shades his eyes, watches H. L. Mencken for a beat, goes back around the house.

A pride of dreadlocksmen sitting in the shade of low trees, playing dominoes, smoking cannabis sativa (Indian hemp) in giant goat-horn pipes. The smoke all but obscures them. Beyond them, an acre of cannabis sways and shines in the blinding sun. The first dreadlocksman penetrates the cloud of smoke.

A smoking pipe makes the rounds, reaching Clive Fairchild (played by Richard Pryor, dreader than dread, barefoot in bathing trunks and T-shirt). The first dreadlocksman alerts Clive Fairchild, who continues to smoke the pipe.

H. L. Mencken comes around the house corner, approaches the men. "Does Clive Fairchild live in this . . . ah . . . field?"

Clive Fairchild gets up and motions to H. L. Mencken to follow him. They squeeze between two cabins, climb a zinc fence, and enter a one-room cabin on stilts. A bed, a table, a chair. On the wall a photo of Haile Selassie and one of Clive Fairchild standing beside a giant oyster shell. On the table a Bible, on the bed an enormous plastic bag filled with cannabis, on the chair a black cat. Clive Fairchild sits on the bed and starts to roll a six-inch spliff.

H. L. Mencken sits on a chair. Cat does not move. Shares chair with black cat. "Are you really *the* Clive Fairchild?"

"You was expecting maybe Mr. Kitzel?" Clive Fairchild lights the spliff, passes it to H. L. Mencken.

"But how—?"

Cut to huge, closed oyster shell floating in the blue, blue sea. In the distance a seagoing rowboat manned by six dreadlocksmen inches over the swells, approaching. Boat and shell come together. Straining, they haul the shell (diameter: five feet) into their boat. They try to open it. Their knives and cutlasses break. They row the shell ashore, carry it up the steep rocky hill to the village. Sun goes down below horizon. Suddenly night.

Quickly they collect dry wood for a bonfire and get it blazing. Three men carry and rest the shell on top of the blazing fire. The oyster shell begins to emit steam, slowly yawns open.

Clive Fairchild (Richard Pryor dressed in a diaper, shaved bald like baby) sits up in the shell. (By technical means, he appears to measure only eighteen inches from toes to top of head.) He stretches, stands up, climbs out of oyster shell. Takes a few baby steps away from the shell and the fire. Begins to grow, growing until the diaper barely covers his jewels. Stops growing when he reaches man size.

General hubbub and rumbling stops. Then stampeding with much uproar, throng disappearing into houses and up trees and down shadowy alleyways. Except one diminutive, fearless dreadlocksman. He confronts the tall, diapered stranger.

Dread Nyah: "Is this man acome directly from the Father?"

"Sheet, no, brothermucker!" Clive Fairchild answers contemptuously. "Ain't you never seed natural childbirth before?"

Dread Nyah persists. "Then the man is flesh and blood like I, man?"

Clive Fairchild sucks his tongue, cuts his eyes to the star-embedded skies. "Is I look like a brothermucking cucumber to you?"

"No, the man resemble man, true. But then is why the man not talk like man? The man have strange twang."

Recognition crosses Clive Fairchild's face. His hand moves to his belly button, a smooth black button built into his navel. He presses the button. His fingers aimlessly strum his stomach, waiting for an answer. "Wonder if they out to lunch?"

Clive Fairchild's forehead begins to glow. Lights up. A small square screen appears.

On small square screen appears Top Supreme Commodore (Redd Foxx dressed in space jumpsuit and made up to look one hundred twenty years old) sitting behind a desk.

Clive Fairchild: "9-2-1-7-2 reporting to Top Supreme Commodore, sir. I got here. All right except for the cold weather. I need a temperature adjustment. And you brothermuckers programmed my ass to brothermucking speak the wrong brothermucking language."

Top Supreme Commodore promises to adjust his computer bank. Henceforth, Clive Fairchild will automatically answer in the language spoken to him. T.S.C. signs off. Screen fades. Clive Fairchild's forehead returns to normal.

Dread Nyah has not budged. "Is sweet trick the man a have with the portable TV in him head front. Can the man teach I man that one?"

Clive Fairchild's eyes glinting. "That, me bredda, and a whole heap more." He puts his arm around Dread Nyah's shoulder. They stroll into the shadows. Follow their silhouettes down dark alleyway. Pass light in window. (By technical means.) Seeing Clive Fairchild's face rearranging itself. (Left side of face like Richard Pryor. Right side like O. J. Simpson.) Darkness again. A next window with lantern. (For the moment O. J. Simpson replaces Richard Pryor as Clive Fairchild.)

Cut to Clive Fairchild (O. J. Simpson, dreader than dread, in bathing trunks and T-shirt) strolling at sundown along lovely beach.

At anchor, a quarter mile offshore, a magnificent yacht. Sounds of woman's laughter across the smooth, silent, sunset sea. Clive Fairchild stops, listens, smiles, strolls on. Then screams come over the waters. "Help!" Bubble bubbles. A woman drowning.

Clive Fairchild shattering the sea stillness, swimming toward the bubbling screams. Shark-swift through still waters.

From the yacht's bridge Sir Noel Coward (puffing a cigarette in holder) watches the swimming dreadlocksman through a spyglass, shifts his attention to the drowning woman.

Sir Noel Coward: "Wager you a week's wages he won't reach her in time, Desmond!"

Desmond (played by Sidney Poitier in Hitler mustache, white coat, and black trousers) steps forward with an ashtray. "Done, mein Herr!"

Blond tresses suspended, bubbles, in water. Breasts floating. A hand clutches at air, sinks. Clive Fairchild crashes into frame, dives. Still water. Water shatters. Clive Fairchild spitting a mouthful, smiling. (Theme music, uptempo.) Clive Fairchild levels out in the water, dragging Miss Fine Young Thing by long blond hair.

Sir Noel Coward to Desmond: "Oh, well, better throw them a line, dear boy."

Desmond hops to the task, throws life preserver. Clive Fairchild catches the ring. Desmond tows them through the dark green sea to the yacht. Lowers the portable stairs. Clive Fairchild carries Miss Fine Young Thing on board, lays her out on the deck. Her breasts sag sideways. A big red lobster has her by her big toe.

Miss Fine Young Thing looks d.e.a.d. Clive Fairchild kneels to offer mouth-to-mouth resuscitation. Close-up of face of Miss Fine Young Thing (played by Donna Summer in platinum blond wig).

Miss Fine Young Thing slowly recovers. Clive Fairchild and Desmond give each other elaborate Afro-American-style handshakes. Laugh with pink tongues.

Miss Fine etc. opens her eyes. "What Mammy said about heaven, it's true after all."

Sir Noel Coward calls down from the bridge. "Getting a little lonesome up here, chaps."

"Lobster for dinner this evening, mein Herr." Desmond prying the lobster's claw open.

Clive Fairchild lifts up Miss Fine and carries her below deck. Desmond packs the red lobster (obviously rubberoid) in ice and joins them, finding they have already begun to share each other's charms. Sheets jumping up and down with pumping and bumping.

"Heaven. Heaven. Heaven." Miss Fine repeating.

Desmond taps Clive Fairchild on the shoulder. "Your presence is requested in the captain's cabin, my dear schvartzer."

Cut to Clive Fairchild (O. J. Simpson in borrowed white bermudas and sport shirt) striding along a passageway, stopping, knocking at a door, waiting. Opens door. Steps over high sill into the captain's cabin.

Sir Noel Coward looks up from requisite papers. "I trust you found your accommodations satisfact'ry, Fairchild. Suppose you've wondered why I've done all this for you."

Sir Noel Coward unveils his plan. So to inflict the American People with the virus of feeling inferior that they will beg to abolish the Republic and ask to rejoin Her Majesty's Empire and Commonwealth. "After all, we've been the Mind of America from the first over. We've sent Tom Paine. Charles Chaplin. Bob Hope. Cary Grant. Richard Burton. The Beatles. Shirley Bassey." Hums a few bars of Harrison's "Something." "The weapon we'll use is corruption. Death before it begins to stink. We'll prove conclusively that absolutely every American has a price. Rupture the American Spirit once and for all! What a pool of cheap labor—pardon, labour—for the Mother Country!" Chuckles cynically, curling his lip.

Fairchild asks requisite dumb question. "What could your megalomaniacal plan possibly have to do with yours truly, this humble dreadlocks?"

Sir Noel Coward cocks his eyebrow. "I need a fearless man. A man with nothing to lose. An existential warrior. A superlative salesman, dear boy. You've come into my life precisely on time. But first you need a bit of gloss."

Cut to long shot of Fairchild crossing Cambridge Common going toward Harvard Square. Fairchild (library footage of O. J. Simpson) feinting and sprinting up and down the gridiron. Thousands cheering wildly. Cheerleaders making their boobs bounce, jumping in glee. Yalies disconsolate.

Medium shot of Fairchild studying in Widener Library. Then raising his hand in class, answering eagerly. Fairchild (in Ve.Ri.Tas sweatshirt and pants, A.Di.Das warm-up shoes) running around Soldier's Field track. Harvard head track coach (played by vintage Gary Cooper in baseball pants and maroon jacket) with stopwatch, nodding head in amazement. Close-up of stopwatch, symbol of time clapping irons on life, becomes close-up on end of rolled college diploma. Fairchild in cap and gown. Steps forward and shakes hand of president of the University (played by T. S. Eliot, in academic robes and pince-nez, pro.Keds sneaking out from under gown). Fairchild in his room in Winthrop House packing his collection of designer jock straps and radical literature.

Sir Noel Coward watches. Sitting astride a desk chair, spats flashing, elbows resting on chair back. "Proud of you, dear boy."

Desmond (Sidney Poitier in Hitler mustache and Brooks Bros. suit and two bulbs light-up his bow tie) takes monocle from left eye. "But has he learned the ways of evil? College is, after all, not life."

The three men turn to front and nod gravely.

Cut to Washington, D.C. (Montage). Washington Monument. Some men with attaché cases. Jefferson Memorial. Some men with briefcases. Stone Abraham Lincoln high on his throne. Some men with attaché cases. Supreme Court building. Some men with briefcases, climbing front steps. Congressional dome. Senate Chamber. Senator Daniel Webster rising from behind his little black school desk to request that the Senator from the great State of Affairs yield ourselves to mark well these signs for as the sky, deeply imbued with the spirit of reckless deliberation on all sides, can certainly in this hour of unrivaled in our e.r.a. All nod thoughtfully. Reverse zoom shows Senate Chamber as game on table. Medium shot of Sir Noel Coward spying on White House through his spyglass. Sir Noel Coward takes spyglass from his eye. Close-up of black ring around Sir Noel Coward's eye.

Fairchild and Desmond give each other elaborate Afro-American handshake, laughing with big pink tongues.

Sir Noel Coward spies himself in mirror and does a slow Edward Kennedy burn. "I am not in the least amused. I could easily have involved myself and resources with another set of bongos and avoided a great deal of mental fat.tee.gay."

Desmond snaps to attention, clicking heels of shiny black jackboots. "Of course he iss right, Fairchild. Time for Blacks, Leftists and Fascists alike to get serious."

Fairchild to Desmond: "And which are you, Desmond, Leftist or Fascist? I'm never quite certain."

Desmond to Sir Noel Coward: "Doesn't know us wary well, does he?" To Fairchild: "My dear schvartzer, the voild iss divided between two kinds, those who carry Whips and those who carry Shovels. I am a Whip. Sometimes a Leftist Whip. Sometimes a Fascist Whip. But always a Whip."

Fairchild to Desmond: "And might I ask where women fit into your scheme of things?"

Desmond to Fairchild: "Why, females are born Shovels!" Lights his two-bulb bow tie.

(Kate Millet, Eleanor Holmes Norton, and Bella Abzug, stunningly done up as dance-hall girls, all breasts and bustles on ten-inch stiletto heels, tear out the upper left corner of the screen. They hiss and boo and give Bronx cheers: "Hissss! Boooo! Thpthptzzzz!")

Sir Noel Coward to all: "Gentlemen, gentlemen. Let's sit around the requisite planning table and plan our evil campaign. New York will be more difficult to conquer than Washington. All the best, the youngest and strongest, collect there. The cream."

Desmond strikes a Jimmy Durante shuffling-off pose, eyes ashine. "Sour that cream, Clive Fairchild. Won't I have the time of my life strutting through the corridors of power! In my black knee-high boots and sweeping trench coat. Man, have I got nuts to get off!"

Fairchild contemptuously: "You whips are all alike. Theatrical! Let's get on with it. I've business elsewhere."

Sir Noel Coward to Fairchild: "Well, then, dear boy, is there anything new coming out of your laborat'ry?" Puts arm around Fairchild's shoulder, leads him from table toward leather sofa.

Cut to Clive Fairchild standing on the steps of the Harvard Club and chatting with Teddy Roosevelt. In unison, they turn to look west on Forty-fourth Street. Long shot of Ralph Waldo Emerson. He smiles, waves, quickens his pace. Meeting, they shake hands all around and enter the clubhouse, climb a circular staircase to a private meeting room on an upper floor. Fairchild's face undergoes transformation with a mosaic of quick microscopic close-ups of individual features (Pryor's mouth; Simpson's right ear; Pryor's left eye; Simpson's nose), changing from O. J. Simpson into R. Pryor with each step the three men climb. The change happens so smoothly and subtly that neither Teddy Roosevelt nor Ralph Waldo Emerson notices.

They reach the upper room. They enter. Clive Fairchild locks door behind them. They sit around a round table. Fairchild puts his attaché case on the table. Two locks spring open. Fairchild raises the case lid. Close-up of case insides. Sticky resinous bark-brown cannabis.

Teddy Roosevelt and Ralph Waldo Emerson sigh, nod approvingly, eyes alight. Fairchild puts a handful in front of each man. All produce personal Bambu papers and start to clean and roll. Fairchild uses bread-wrapper paper found only in Kingston to build himself a gigantic spliff. The three men light up. Take deep drags. Get well charged. Emerson cracks up everybody with his imitation of Henry Ward Beecher. Teddy Roosevelt captures center stage with a bloody good yarn about hunting in the Dakotas. Fairchild observes.

Ralph Waldo Emerson to all: "One of my many protégés cultivates a hemp like this in the woods near Walden Pond, though not so well cured."

Teddy Roosevelt, spliff clenched in teeth, pounds his palm with his fist. "Bully smoke! San Juan Gold can't compare!"

Fairchild to both: "You boys drop pills?"

They reply eagerly in the affirmative. Fairchild reaches into his suit-coat pocket and pulls out a large assortment of pills. Close-up of Fairchild's pill-piled palm. One pill appears larger than the round and oblong assortment. Zoom to tight close-up of strange pill. A tiny naked woman encased in the clear pill, mummy-like.

Teddy Roosevelt shows interest in the strange, coffin-shaped pill.

Fairchild cautions Teddy Roosevelt: "You don't take that one, sir. It takes you."

Teddy Roosevelt insists. Fairchild places the tiny pill on the oak table. He finds a carafe of water and splashes some into a glass, returns to table. Pours a few drops onto the pill.

Fairchild to all: "Ordinarily you do it in the bathtub."

Strange pill begins to disintegrate as form within grows, taking the shape of Miss Fine Young Thing stretched out on oaken table like Elsa Lanchester in *The Bride of Frankenstein.* Miss Fine Young Thing blinks. Sits up. (Disco music building behind.) Stands up on table. Gets down to boogie. The joint starts jumping.

Teddy Roosevelt pulls a magnum of champagne from a large inside pocket and drinks bubbly from Miss Fine's glass slipper. Ralph Waldo Emerson removes tons of Victorian clothes and vows to outdo Thoreau by spending five years at Walden Pond. Teddy Roosevelt asks if he might take some party pills home with him. Fairchild whispers into ear of Teddy Roosevelt. Ralph Waldo Emerson, wearing shoes but sockless, boxer shorts but shirtless, stuffs his jacket pockets with cannabis and wanders out. (Disco music fades.) Teddy Roosevelt rolls some smokes for the journey, straightens his tie. Fairchild hands him big bottle of pills. Close-up of bottle. All pills, each pill with sleeping princess inside, blonds, brunettes, redheads, some Orientals, some Hispanics, some Negresses. Hours of funnilingus uninterruptus. Teddy Roosevelt departs. Image of Miss Fine Young Thing starts to fade, calling plaintively to Fairchild, as if lost. "Fairchild? Fairchild! Where are you?"

Fairchild to fading image: "Shut up, witch. You said you wanted me to put you in show biz!" Image disappears.

Clive Fairchild sits in an official black Harvard chair. Leans back. Thinks. Fumbles with buttons on his button-down shirt and pushes his black belly button, relaxing deeper into the hard chair. Forehead starts glowing. Square of light comes on, grows more definite. Full-color three-inch TV screen.

Close-up screen. Top Supreme Commodore sitting behind desk, smiling benignly. "So awfully glad you found me at home, 9-2-1-7-2. As a matter of fact, I do hope you will make this interview short and to the point. I've tickets for a Thru Time Theater presentation of the original production of Ira Aldridge as Othello. That's why you've found me in my British voice."

Fairchild, as if in meditation talking to himself: "Well, I didn't mean to . . ."

Top Supreme Commodore, reassuringly: "No, no, 9-2. You don't mind my using the familiar, do you? No, go ahead."

Fairchild: "It's this mission, sir. A bit nasty. I don't fancy the wicket. I don't like things I'm having to do, sir."

Top Supreme Commodore: "Such as? I haven't been watching your activities very closely."

Fairchild: "I've run into an evil man, sir. He's having me do the vilest things. Concerning some differences this species is having. Primitive political stuff, really. Anyway—"

"You shock me, 9-2!" Top Supreme Commodore's image burns brighter in Fairchild's forehead. "And, might I say, disappoint me. We've sent you on a delicate mission of universal significance and you're bloody crying in your bloody milk over some minor tribal doings. This is insupportable nonsense! Do the job, 9-2. Do the job. Accomplish your mission and return to base! Good night!"

Screen in Fairchild's forehead goes out abruptly, leaving the room dim. Close-up of Clive Fairchild's face. Eyes brim. One tear trickling. Close-up of tear. Glistens. Fades.

MICHAEL S. HARPER

(1938–)

Michael S. Harper is a prolific poet who has written lyrically about history and whose work has been highly informed by the sophisticated jazz techniques of such giants as John Coltrane. He explores the American past and celebrates his ancestors, including Coltrane, Charlie Parker, Ralph Ellison, Sterling Brown, and Robert Hayden. In fact, at readings he recites poems by his forefathers, such as Brown and Hayden. With a sense of profound continuity of the black tradition, he has written some of the most beautiful and painful personal poems of our time, including the shattering "We Assume" about the death of his son, Reuben Masai.

Harper was delivered by his grandfather, who was a doctor, in his parents' home in Brooklyn, New York, on March 18, 1938. His father, Walter Warren Harper, was employed as a postal worker and supervisor (the same positions that Amiri Baraka's father held). His mother, Katherine Johnson Harper, was a medical stenographer. Medicine was a tradition in the family, and Harper thought of becoming a doctor. Indeed, the reader can see the impact of medicine on his poetry. At thirteen, he and his family relocated to West Los Angeles. After graduating from high school in 1955, he attended Los Angeles State College, where he earned a B.A. and an M.A. While in college, he worked full-time as a postal worker and there encountered many highly educated blacks who could not find better-paying jobs in the private sector because of racism. In 1961, he attended the prestigious Iowa Writers' Workshop at the University of Iowa where he received his M.F.A. in Creative Writing in 1963. Harper has had a distinguished career at Brown since 1970. He is currently Israel J. Hapstein Professor of English. He served as director of the Graduate Creative Writing Program from 1974 to 1983 and has taught such African American artists and scholars as Gayl Jones, Sherley Anne Williams, Melvin Dixon, Claudia Tate, George Barlow, and Herman Beavers. He has brought Sterling Brown back into print with his *Collected Poems of Sterling A. Brown* (1980). Along with the scholar Robert Stepto, he edited the momentous anthology of black arts, letters, and criticism *Chant of Saints* (1979).

In *Callaloo* Harper includes black history in his poetry to re-create the "traduced" history of African Americans. He sees himself as "both a black poet and an American poet" in Ted Wilentz's poetry anthology *Natural Process* (1971). He says that even though he was born and reared in America and speaks "a few of its idioms . . . I, myself, can't imagine giving up my point of view, my blackness, as a way of seeing the world." For Harper, John Coltrane was "the epitome of a new style," his music "the vision of liberation." Harper's goal is to create "a new liberating vision which frees rather than imprisons."

Michael Harper has produced a score of books. His art is metaphysical, historical, and biographical. He celebrates black American excellence in sport and art, especially blues and jazz, and like Amiri Baraka, he has absorbed the jazz tradition into his poetry.

❖❖❖

Harper was featured in *Callaloo* 13, No. 4 (Fall 1990). In addition, he was interviewed by John O'Brien for *Interviews with Black Writers* (1973).

Here Where Coltrane Is

Soul and race
are private dominions,
memories and modal
songs, a tenor blossoming,
which would paint suffering
a clear color but is not in
this Victorian house
without oil in zero degree
weather and a forty-mile-an-hour wind;
it is all a well-knit family:
a love supreme.
Oak leaves pile up on walkway
and steps, catholic as apples
in a special mist of clear white
children who love my children.

I play "Alabama"
on a warped record player
skipping the scratches
on your faces over the fibrous
conical hairs of plastic
under the wooden floors.

Dreaming on a train from New York
to Philly, you hand out six
notes which become an anthem
to our memories of you:
oak, birch, maple,
apple, cocoa, rubber.
For this reason Martin is dead;
for this reason Malcolm is dead;
for this reason Coltrane is dead;
in the eyes of my first son are the browns
of these men and their music.

Come Back Blues

I count black-lipped
children along river-creek,
skimming between bog,
floating garbage
logs, glistening tipped
twilight and night beaks;
the drowned drown again
while their parents
picket the old library and pool
special fish
taken up in poison—
you've come back
to count bodies again
in your own backyard.

for Robert F. Williams

Song: I Want a Witness

Blacks in frame houses
call to the helicopters,
their antlered arms
spinning; jeeps pad
these glass-studded streets;
on this hill are tanks painted gold.

Our children sing
spirituals of *Motown*,

idioms these streets suckled
on a southern road.
This scene is about power,
terror, producing
love and pain and pathology;
in an army of white dust,
blacks here to *testify*
and *testify,* and *testify,*
and *redeem,* and *redeem,*
in black smoke coming,
as they wave their arms,
as they wave their tongues.

To James Brown

Little brother, little brother,
put your feet on the floor.

You've asked for Jimmy Brown,
beautiful cat, the wrong man.

Little brother, don't nobody know
your name, feet off the floor,

movin' again. Black Brother!
Somebody tell little brother

'bout James Brown:
please, please, please,

please, please, please.

Effendi

The piano hums
again the clear
story of our coming,
enchained, severed,
our tongues gone,
herds the quiet
musings of ten million
years blackening the earth
with blood and our moon women,
children we loved,
the jungle swept up
in our rhapsodic song
giving back
banana leaves and
the incessant beating
of our tom-tom hearts.

We have sung a long time here
with the cross and the cotton field.
Those white faces turned
away from their mythical
beginnings are no art
but that of violence—
the kiss of death.
Somewhere on the inside
of those faces
are the real muscles
of the world;
the ones strengthened
in experience and pain,
the ones wished for in one's lover
or in the mirror
near the eyes
that record this lost, dogged data
and is pure, new, even lovely
and is you.

In Hayden's Collage

Van Gogh would paint the landscape
green—or somber blue;
if you could see the weather
in Amsterdam in June, or August,
you'd cut your lobe too,
perhaps simply on heroin,
the best high in the world,
instead of the genius of sunflowers,
blossoming trees. The Japanese
bridge in Hiroshima,
precursor to the real impression,
modern life, goes to Windsor, Ontario,
or Jordan, or the Natchez
Trace. From this angle, earless,
a torsioned Django Rhinehart
accompanies Josephine. You know
those rainbow children couldn't
get along in this *ole worl'*.

Not over that troubled water;
and when the band would play once
too often in Arkansas, or Paris,
you'd cry because the sunset was too
bright to see the true colors,
the first hue, and so nearsighted
you had to touch the spiderman's

bouquet; you put your arcane colors
to the spatula and cook
to force the palate in the lion's
den—to find God in all the light
the paintbrush would let in—
the proper colors,
the corn, the wheat, the valley,
dike, the shadows, and the heart
of self—minnow of the universe,
your flaccid fishing pole,
pieced together, never broken, never end.

Last Affair: Bessie's Blues Song

Disarticulated
arm torn out,
large veins cross
her shoulder intact,
her tourniquet
her blood in all-white big bands:

Can't you see
what love and heartache's done to me
I'm not the same as I used to be
this is my last affair

Mail truck or parked car
in the fast lane,
afloat at forty-three
on a Mississippi road,
Two-hundred-pound muscle on her ham bone,
'nother nigger dead 'fore noon:

Can't you see
what love and heartache's done to me
I'm not the same as I used to be
this is my last affair

Fifty-dollar record
cut the vein in her neck,
fool about her money
toll her black train wreck,
white press missed her fun'ral
in the same stacked deck:

Can't you see
what love and heartache's done to me
I'm not the same as I used to be
this is my last affair

Loved a little blackbird
heard she could sing,
Martha in her vineyard
pestle in her spring,
Bessie had a bad mouth
made my chimes ring:

Can't you see
what love and heartache's done to me
I'm not the same as I used to be
this is my last affair

ISHMAEL REED

(1938–)

Ishmael Reed is a major African American novelist, poet, essayist, and playwright. In Adam David Miller's black poetry anthology, *Dices or Black Bones* (1970), he succinctly states his credo when he says, "I try to do what has never been done before." His character the Loop Garoo Kid, a "crazy dada nigger" and alter ego for the author, declares in *Yellow Back Radio Broke-Down* (1969), "No one says a novel has to be one thing. It can be anything it wants to be, a vaudeville show, the six o'clock news, the mumblings of wild men saddled by demons." Following in the black tradition of the slave narratives, he objects to any restrictions on his personal and artistic freedom. Thus with his pen, he is always ready to battle the Thought Police no matter who they are, ready to fight anybody he perceives as an inhibitor of his free speech, from black nationalists in the 1960s to liberals in the 1970s to feminists and conservatives in the 1980s and 1990s. He affirms black folk culture, molding his art on the black oral tradition of folktales and the New World/Old World (Old World in this case Africa) black religion, voodoo. He embraces the multiethnic experience in America, celebrating and publishing writers—he is himself a small press publisher—from diverse backgrounds. Unlike such cultural commissars as the educator Allan Bloom, he believes that all cultures are created equal.

Born in Chattanooga, Tennessee, on February 22, 1938, Reed was raised and educated in Buffalo, New York. During his high school years, he discovered Nathanael West, whose surreal style and biting vision of America influenced him. Interestingly, another black experimental writer, Amiri Baraka, also was drawn to West's dark vision and unconventional technique. At the University of Buffalo (1956–1960), Reed happened upon the great English poets William Butler Yeats and William Blake, who demonstrated to him the importance of creating individual and personal mythological systems. As Blake wrote, "I must create a system or be enslaved by another man's." Moving to New York City in September 1962, Reed became involved with *Umbra* magazine and the Umbra Workshop. The young militant writers of the Umbra group, including Calvin Hernton, David Henderson, Charles Patterson, and Askia Muhammad Touré, showed Reed the importance of black nationalism, black culture, and black poetry. Incidentally, as Reed has remarked, the University of Buffalo showed him the importance of the white male tradition. In 1967, he published his first novel, *Free-Lance Pallbearers,* both a satire of America during the Vietnam War years and a parody of Ralph Ellison's masterpiece *Invisible Man* (1952).

Restless and tired of being a token black in New York, Reed moved to Berkeley, California, in 1967. There he cofounded and published *The Yardbird Reader* (1972–1976), which reflected the multiethnic spirit of the West Coast. African American, Native American, Asian American, Euro-American, and Hispanic American authors wrote for the journal. Reed states that in California he simply "came into contact with other cultures, other groups." In *Yellow Back Radio Broke-Down* (1969), he took on the popular form of the western, albeit a surreal one, where the Loop Garoo Kid, a black cowboy, battles the forces of repressive Western civilization, embodied in Drag Gibson, an evil metaphysical rancher, and the pope. In this novel, Reed introduces voodoo as an authentic source of black folk culture and values. Voodoo acts as both a base and a model for Reed's neohoodoo aesthetic, his theory and practice of art, which like voodoo is black and indigenous—a fusing of African and American culture, syncretic, oral, flexible, sexual, life-affirming, and against the forces of repression and death.

In *Mumbo Jumbo* (1972), his masterpiece, he asserts that the black world spirit is life-affirming and the white Western sensibility is death-obsessed and repressive. He also argues that there is a conspiracy at the core of the Western tradition: its secret goal is to preach the glory of the West at the expense of all other civilizations. Hence, like the black historians before him, such as George G. M. James, Chancellor Williams, and Cheikh Anta Diop, Reed finds it essential to revise Western myths and history to reveal Eurocentric lies and to show the glory of the black past, which originated in North Africa, in Egypt. The white critic John Leonard observes, "Mr. Reed is as close as we are likely to get to a Garcia Marques [contemporary Colombian novelist], elaborating his own mythology even as he trashes ours." With satire and parody, Reed demystifies Western mythology and history; he ridicules and burlesques the sacred narratives of the West, showing them to be absurd and presumptuous. He maintains that Western culture demands that black culture must conform to its standards. In *Mumbo Jumbo,* Biff Musclewhite, who symbolizes Western culture, proclaims that blacks "must change, not us, they must adopt our ways, producing Elizabethan poets; they should have Stravinskys in the wings, they must become Civilized!!!!" In *Flight to Canada* (1976), Yankee Jack, another of Reed's white villains, defines "civilized" for his Native American lover: "The difference between a savage and a civilized man is determined by who has the power. Right now I'm running things. Maybe one day you will be running it. But for now I'm the one who determines whether one is civilized or savage."

In 1976, Reed cofounded the Before Columbus Foundation, dedicated to the celebration of multicultural literature. In 1978, the foundation initiated the American Book Awards to honor excellence without regard to "race, sex, creed, cultural origin, size of press or ad budget, or even genre." In general, Reed finds most major mainstream book award-givers are unreceptive to minority voices.

In *Flight to Canada* (1976), Reed writes a contemporary slave narrative. He combines the Civil War years with contemporary times, drawing parallels between the two periods. Further, he defines freedom as the right to tell your own story instead of letting it be appropriated by other, even good-intentioned cultures. In the novel, Uncle Robin, a trickster slave, has the sense to have his story written by Raven Quickskill, a black antislavery writer, instead of the white Harriet Beecher Stowe, who would produce a sentimental narrative for the white reader. Here Reed is echoing a statement by the editors of the first black newspaper, *Freedom's Journal* (1827), when they said, "We wish to plead our own cause. Too long have others spoken for us. Too long has the public been deceived by misrepresentations, in things which concern us dearly." To date, Reed has published nine novels. His most recent is *Japanese by Spring* (1993), which relates the misadventures of Benjamin "Chappie" Puttbutt, a black junior professor at Jack London College in northern California.

Certainly, Reed is an "antislavery writer" fighting any form of physical and/or metaphysical tyranny he encounters. In fact, he called one of his recent books of essays *Writin' Is Fightin': Thirty-seven Years of Boxing on Paper* (1988). He has published three other collections of essays, *Shrovetide in New Orleans* (1978), *God Made Alaska for the Indians* (1982), and *Airing Dirty Laundry* (1993). He also has published five collections of poetry, including *Conjure* (1972) and *New and Collected Poems* (1988), and a number of his plays have been staged, including *Mother Hubbard* (1981) and *Savage Wilds* (1988).

Reed is a major avant-garde writer who relentlessly uses comedy and satire to expose the narrowness, rigidity, and brutality of the Western tradition. However, his critique does not stop with the West. When he finds that blacks are not living up to the ideals of freedom and creativity that he envisions as central to the African American tradition, he ridicules them mercilessly. In recent years, his most savage attacks have been against feminists, especially contemporary black women fiction writers, whom he sees as merely echoing white feminism. In turn, these women charge that he is a misogynist who hates black women in particular. Whatever one feels about Ishmael Reed, one would have to agree that he is a writer of ideas whose main arena is the battlefield of myth and history.

❖❖❖

For further information about and insight into Reed's work, see Keith E. Byerman, *Fingering the Jagged Grain: Tradition and Form in Recent Black Fiction* (1985); Robert Elliot Fox, *Conscientious Sorcerers: The Black Postmodernist Fiction of LeRoi Jones/Amiri Baraka, Ishmael Reed and Samuel R. Delany* (1987); Bruce Dick and Amritjit Singh (eds.) *Conversations with Ishmael Reed* (1993); Henry Louis Gates, "The Blackness of Blackness: Ishmael Reed and a Critique of the Sign," in *The Signifying Monkey* (1988); John Leonard, "Books of the Times," *New York Times,* June 17, 1982; Reginald Martin, *Ishmael Reed & the New Black Aesthetic Critics* (1988); Neil Schmitz, "Neo-HooDoo: The Experimental Fiction of Ishmael Reed," *Twentieth Century Literature* 20, No. 2 (April 1974); Mel Watkins, "An Interview with Ishmael Reed," *Southern Review* 21, No. 3 (July 1985).

I Am a Cowboy in the Boat of Ra

'The devil must be forced to reveal any such physical evil (potions, charms, fetishes, etc.) still outside the body and these must be burned.' (Rituale Romanum, *published 1947, endorsed by the coat-of-arms and introductory letter from Francis Cardinal Spellman)*

I am a cowboy in the boat of Ra,
sidewinders in the saloons of fools
bit my forehead like O
the untrustworthiness of Egyptologists
who do not know their trips. Who was that
dog-faced man? they asked, the day I rode
from town.

School marms with halitosis cannot see
the Nefertiti fake chipped on the run by slick
germans, the hawk behind Sonny Rollins' head or
the ritual beard of his axe; a longhorn winding
its bells thru the Field of Reeds.

I am a cowboy in the boat of Ra. I bedded
down with Isis, Lady of the Boogaloo, dove
down deep in her horny, stuck up her Wells-Far-ago
in daring midday getaway. 'Start grabbing the
blue,' I said from top of my double crown.

I am a cowboy in the boat of Ra. Ezzard Charles
of the Chisholm Trail. Took up the bass but they
blew off my thumb. Alchemist in ringmanship but a
sucker for the right cross.

I am a cowboy in the boat of Ra. Vamoosed from
the temple i bide my time. The price on the wanted
poster was a-going down, outlaw alias copped my stance
and moody greenhorns were making me dance;
 while my mouth's
shooting iron got its chambers jammed.

I am a cowboy in the boat of Ra. Boning-up in
the ol West i bide my time. You should see
me pick off these tin cans whippersnappers. I
write the motown long plays for the comeback of
Osiris. Make them up when stars stare at sleeping
steer out here near the campfire. Women arrive
on the backs of goats and throw themselves on
my Bowie.

I am a cowboy in the boat of Ra. Lord of the lash,
the Loop Garoo Kid. Half breed son of Pisces and
Aquarius. I hold the souls of men in my pot. I do
the dirty boogie with scorpions. I make the bulls
keep still and was the first swinger to grape the taste.

I am a cowboy in his boat. Pope Joan of the
Ptah Ra. C/mere a minute willya doll?
Be a good girl and
bring me my Buffalo horn of black powder
bring me my headdress of black feathers

bring me my bones of Ju-Ju snake
go get my eyelids of red paint.
Hand me my shadow

I'm going into town after Set

I am a cowboy in the boat of Ra

look out Set   here i come Set
to get Set   to sunset Set
to unseat Set   to Set down Set

                      usurper of the Royal couch
                      —imposter RAdio of Moses' bush
                      party pooper O hater of dance
                      vampire outlaw of the milky way

i'll take osiris any
time.
prefiguring JB he
funky chickened into
ethiopia & everybody had
a good time. osiris in
vented the popcorn, the
slow drag & the lindy hop.

he'd rather dance than rule.

Sermonette

a poet was busted by a topless judge
his friends went to morristwn nj & put
black powder on his honah's doorstep
black powder into his honah's car
black powder on his honah's briefs
tiny dolls into his honah's mind

by nightfall his honah could a go go no mo
his dog went crazy & ran into a crocodile
his widow fell from a wall &
hanged herself
his daughter was run over by a black man
cming home for the wakes the two boys
skidded into mourning
all the next of kin's teeth fell out

gimmie dat ol time
                religion

it's good enough
        for me!

Beware: Do Not Read This Poem

tonite, *thriller* was
abt an ol woman, so vain she
surrounded her self w/
   many mirrors

It got so bad that finally she
locked herself indoors & her
whole life became the
   mirrors

one day the villagers broke
into her house, but she was too
swift for them, she disappeared
      into a mirror
each tenant who bought the house
after that, lost a loved one to
      the ol woman in the mirror:
      first a little girl
      then a young woman
      then the young woman/s husband

the hunger of this poem is legendary
it has taken in many victims
back off from this poem
it has drawn in yr feet
back off from this poem
it has drawn in yr legs
back off from this poem
it is a greedy mirror
you are into this poem. from
   the waist down
nobody can hear you can they?

this poem has had you up to here
      belch
this poem aint got no manners
you cant call out frm this poem
relax now & go w/ this poem
move & roll on to this poem

      do not resist this poem
      this poem has yr eyes
      this poem has his head
      this poem has his arms
      this poem has his fingers
      this poem has his fingertips

this poem is the reader & the
      reader this poem

statistic: the us bureau of missing persons reports
that in 1968 over 100,000 people disappeared
leaving no solid clues
nor trace only
a space in the lives of their friends

Why I Often Allude to Osiris

ikhnaton looked like
prophet jones, who brick
by brick broke up a
french chateau & set it
down in detroit. he was
'elongated' like prophet
jones & had a hairdresser's
taste.
ikhnaton moved cities for
his mother-in-law &
each finger of his hands
bore rings.
ikhnaton brought re
ligious fascism to egypt.
where once man animals
plants & stars freely
roamed thru each other's
rooms, ikhnaton came up
with the door.

(a lot of people in new york
go for him—museum curators
politicians & tragic mulattoes)

Lincoln-Swille

FROM FLIGHT TO CANADA

There's a knock at the door. It's Moe, the white house slave—Mingy Moe, as the mammies in the kitchen call him. He looks like an albino: tiny pink pupils, white Afro.

"Sorry to disturb you, Master Swille, but Abe Lincoln, the President of the so-called Union, is outside in the parlor waiting to see you. He's fiddling around and telling corny jokes, shucking the shud and husking the hud. I told him that you were scheduled to helicopter up to Richmond to shake your butt at the Magnolia Baths tonight, but he persists. Says, 'The very survival of the Union is at stake.'"

"Hand me my jacket, Uncle Robin," Swille says as he stands in the middle of the room.

"Which one do you wont, suh—the one with the spangly fritters formal one or the silvery-squilly festooned street jacket?"

"Give me the spangly one." Turning to Moe, Swille says, "Now, Moe, you tell this Lincoln gentleman that he won't be able to stay long. Before I fly up to Richmond, I have to check on my investments all over the world."

"Yessir, Mr. Swille."

Momentarily, Lincoln, Gary Cooper–awkward, fidgeting with his stovepipe hat, humble-looking, imperfect—a wart here and there—craw and skuttlecoat, shawl, enters the room. "Mr. Swille, it's a pleasure," he says, extending his hand to Swille, who sits behind a desk rumored to have been owned by Napoleon III. "I'm a small-time lawyer and now I find myself in the room of the mighty, why—"

"Cut the yokel-dokel, Lincoln, I don't have all day. What's on your mind?" Swille rejects Lincoln's hand, at which Lincoln stares, hurt.

"Yokel-dokel? Why, I don't get you, Mr. Swille."

"Oh, you know—log-cabin origin. That's old and played out. Why don't you get some new speech writers? Anyway, you're the last man I expected to see down here. Aren't you supposed to be involved in some kind of war? Virginia's off limits to your side, isn't it? Aren't you frightened, man?"

"No, Mr. Swille. We're not frightened because we have a true cause. We have a great, a noble cause. Truth is on our side, marching to the clarion call. We are in the cause of the people. It is a people's cause. This is a great, noble and people period in the history of our great Republic. We call our war the Civil War, but some of the fellows think we ought to call it the War Between the States. You own fifty million dollars' worth of art, Mr. Swille. What do you think we ought to call it?"

"I don't feel like naming it, Lanky—and cut the poppycock."

"Lincoln, sir."

"Oh yes, Lincoln. Well, look, Lincoln, I don't want that war to come up here because, to tell you the truth, I'm not the least bit interested in that war. I hate contemporary politics and probably will always be a Tory. Bring back King George. Why would a multinational like myself become involved in these queer crises? Why, just last week I took a trip abroad and was appallingly and disturbingly upset and monumentally offended by the way the Emperor of France was scoffing at this . . . this nation, as you call it. They were snickering about your general unkempt, hirsute and bungling appearance—bumping into things and carrying on. And your speeches. What kind of gibberish are they? Where were you educated, in the rutabaga patch? Why don't you put a little pizazz in your act, Lanky? Like Davis . . . Now that Davis is as nit as a spit with his satin-embroidered dressing case, his gold tweezers and Rogers & Sons strap. He's just bananas about Wagner and can converse in German, French and even that bloody Mexican patois. Kindly toward the 'weak' races, as he referred to them in that superb speech he made before the Senate criticizing Secretary of State Seward and other celebrities for financing that, that . . . maniac, John Brown. And when he brought in that savage, Black Hawk, on the steamboat *Winnebago,* he treated the primitive overlord with the respect due an ethnic celebrity. You can imagine the Americans taunting this heathen all decked out in white deerskins. Davis' slaves are the only ones I know of who take mineral baths, and when hooped skirts became popular he gave some to the slave women, and when this made it awkward for them to move through the rows of cotton, he widened the rows."

"That's quite impressive, Mr. Swille. I have a worthy adversary."

Swille, smirking and squinting, flicks the ashes from a cigar given him by the King of Belgium. "An intellectual. What an intellectual. Loggerhead turtles? Oysters? Hogarth? Optics? Anything you want to know, Davis's got the answer. And his beautiful wife. More brilliant than most men. As aristocratic as Eugénie, wife of my good friend Imperial Majesty Napoleon Bonaparte III. I was having dinner with her just a few weeks ago. You know, she's the daughter of the Count of Montijo and the Duke of Peneranda. Men who like nothing but the best. I call her Gennie, since we move in the same circles. Why, I'm thinking about refurbishing the Morocco Club in New York—just no place for the royal ones to go any more. We were eating, and she turned to me and asked why Du Chaillur searched for the primitive missing link in Africa when one had shambled into the Capitol from the jungles of the Midwest."

Lincoln looks puzzled. "I don't get it, Mr. Swille."

"She was talking about you, silly. They're calling you the Illinois Ape. Eugénie's a brilliant conversationalist. But Varina Davis has it over her. Those glittering supper parties at the Montgomery White House—and did you see the carriage she bought Jeff? Imported it from New Orleans. Yes indeed, from New Orleans. Almost as good as mine. Upholstered in watered blue silk. Can't you see those two representing the . . . the Imperial Empire of the Confederate States of Europe in London? They might even make him a knight—Sir Jefferson Davis. I can see it all now. And then upon their return, a ticker-tape parade down Broadway, with clerks leaning out of office windows shouting, Long Live Jeff. Long Live Varina. Long Live Jeff. Long Live Varina. The Duke and Duchess of Alabama. What a man. What a man. A prince. One of my friends recently visited this six-plus-foot tall specimen and said he just felt like stripping and permitting this eagle-eyed, blade-nosed, creamy Adonis to abuse him and . . . [pant, pant] humiliate him."

"Come again, Mr. Swille?"

"Oh, Abe, you're so green. Green as jade in a cocaine vision."

"Mr. Swille, mind if we change the subject?"

"We have a delightful life down here, Abe. A land as Tennyson says 'In which it all seemed always afternoon. All round the coast the languid air did swoon. Here are cool mosses deep, and thro the stream the long-leaved flowers weep, and from the craggy ledge the poppy hang in sleep.' Ah. Ah. 'And sweet it is to dream of Fatherland. Of child, and wife and slave. Delight our souls with talk of Knightly deeds. Walking about the gardens and the halls.' And, Abe, a man like you can have a soft easy hustle down here. You could be walking around and wallowing in these balmy gardens and these halls. The good life. Breakfast in a dress coat. Exotic footbaths. Massages three times a day. And what we call down here a 'siesta.' Niggers fanning you. A fresh bouquet of flowers and a potent julep delivered to your room. Roses. Red roses. Yellow roses. White roses. We can bring back the 'days that were.' Just fancy yourself the Earl of Lincoln, or Count Abe. Or Marquis Lincoln. Marquis Lincoln of Springfield. You could have this life, Lincoln." He goes to the window and draws back the curtains. There is a view of the hills of Virginia. "It's all bare now, Lincoln. But we will build that city. From here to as far as the eye can see will be great castles with spires and turrets. We can build one for you, Lincoln. Sir Lincoln."

"I'm afraid I wouldn't like it down here, Mr. Swille. I'm just a mudfish. I don't yen for no fancy flies."

"Think about it, Lincoln. You can take an hour and a half putting on your clothes down here. Why . . . why . . . I'm thinking about taking up Meditative Transcendentalism. I've sent to India for a Swami. You know, you may not be so lucky in the next election year. If it hadn't been for those Hoosiers and Suckers and other rags and patches who packed the Wigwam, you'd be back in your law office in Springfield. Their conduct was disgraceful. Why, I had to tell the networks not to carry it. They hollered you the nomination. Steam whistles. Hotel gongs. Comanches! Liquor flowing like Babylon. Not even top-shelf, but Whiskey Skin, Jersey Lightning and Brandy Smash."

"The boys were just cuttin up, Mr. Swille, just jerking the goose bone."

"And then bribing the delegates with Hoboken cigars and passes to quiz shows. Washington, Jefferson and Monroe must be howling in their chains. And that lunatic wife of yours. Must she dress like that? She looks like a Houston and Bowery streetwalker who eats hero sandwiches and chews bubble gum. Why does she wear that brunette bouffant and those silver high-heel boots? She looks like a laundromat attendant. Old frowzy dough-faced thing. Queens accent. Ever think about taking her to the Spa? And why does she send those midnight telegrams to the *Herald Tribune* after drinking God knows what? And there's another thing I've been meaning to ask you, Mr. Lincoln."

"What is that, Mr. Swille?"

"Do you think it appropriate for the President of the United States to tell such lewd jokes to the boys in the telegraph room? The one about the cow and the farmer. The traveling salesman and the milkmaid. The whole scabrous repertoire."

"How did you know that, Mr. Swille?"

"Never you mind. And you think it's befitting your exalted office to go about mouthing the sayings of that hunchback Aesop? No wonder the Confederate cartoonists are beginning to depict you as a nigger. They're calling you a Black Republican down here, and I've heard some weird talk from the planters. Some strange ugly talk. I want you to read that book they're all reading down here. Uncle Robin! Give Lanky that book they're all reading down here."

Robin goes to the shelf. "*Idylls of the King,* Mr. Swille?"

"Yes, that's the one."

Robin removes the book from the shelf and gives it to Lincoln.

"This book tells you about aristocratic rule, Lincoln. How to deal with inferiors. How to handle the help. How the chief of the tribes is supposed to carry himself. You're not the steadiest man for the job; you'd better come on and get this Camelot if you know what's good for you. You, too, can have a wife who is jaundiced and prematurely buried. Skin and bones. Got her down to seventy-five pounds. She's a good sufferer but not as good as Vivian, she . . ." Swille gazes toward the oil portrait of his sister.

"What . . . Anything wrong?" Lincoln says, beginning to rise from his chair.

Robin starts toward Swille.

"No, nothing. Where was I, Robin?"

"You were telling Mr. Lincoln about Camelot, sir."

"Look, Lincoln, if you don't want to be a duke, it's up to you. I need a man like you up in my Canadian mills. You can be a big man up there. We treat the Canadians like coons. I know you used to chop wood. You can be a powerful man up there. A powerful man. Why, you can be Abe of the Yukon. Why don't you resign and call it quits, Lincoln? You won't have to sneak into the Capitol disguised any more. What ya say, pal?"

"Look, Mr. Swille, maybe I ought to tell you why I came down here. Then we can cut this as short and sweet as an old woman's dance."

"All right, Abe. But before you tell me, look, Abe, I don't want to get into politics, but, well, why did you up and join such a grotesque institution as that party that . . ."

"We call ourselves the Republican party, Mr. Swille, but don't look at me. I didn't name it."

"A far-out institution if there ever was one. Free Soilers, whacky money people, Abolitionists. Can't you persuade some of those people to wear a tie? Transcendentalists, Free Lovers, Free Farmers, Whigs, Know-Nothings, and those awful Whitmanites always running about hugging things."

"Look, Mr. Swille," Lincoln says in his high-pitched voice, "I didn't come here to discuss my party, I came to discuss how we could win this war, Mr. Swille; end this conflict," he says, pounding the table. "We are in a position to give the South its death-knell blow."

"'Death-knell blow.' There you go again with that cornpone speech, Lincoln. 'Death-knell blow.' Why don't you shave off that beard and stop putting your fingers in your lapels like that. You ought to at least try to polish yourself, man. Go to the theatre. Get some culture. If you don't, I'll have to contact my general; you know, there's always one of our people keeping an eye on things in your . . . your cabinets. Why, under the Crown . . ."

"Now you look here, Mr. Swille. I won't take your threats. I knew it was a mistake to come down here, you . . . you slave-flogging pea-picker."

Arthur Swille, startled, removes his cigar from his mouth.

"Yes, I know what you think of me. I never went to none of that fancy Harvard and don't lounge around Café Society quaffing white wine until three in the afternoon, and maybe my speeches don't contain a lot of Latin, and maybe my anecdotes aren't understated and maybe I ain't none of that cologned rake sojourning over shrimp cocktails or sitting around in lavender knee britches, like a randy shank or a dandy rake.

"I know you make fun of our nation, our war and our party, Mr. Swille. I know that you hold it against us because our shirts stick out of our britches and we can't write long sentences without losing our way, but you wouldn't be sitting up here in this . . . this Castle if it weren't for the people. The public people. And the Republic people in this great people period, and that ain't no pipple papple pablum either, pal."

A train whistle is heard.

"Mr. Swille, listen to your train. That great locomotive that will soon be stretching across America, bumping cows, pursued by Indians, linking our Eastern cities with the West Coast. Who built your trains, Mr. Swille? The people did, Mr. Swille. Who made you what you are today, Mr. Swille? A swell titanic titan of ten continents, Mr. Swille. Who worked and sweated and tilled and toiled and travailed so that you could have your oil, your industry, Mr. Swille? Why, we did, Mr. Swille. Who toted and tarried and travestied themselves so that you could have your many homes, your ships and your buildings reaching the azure skies? We did, Mr. Swille. Yes, I know I'm a corn-bread and a catfish-eatin curmudgeon known to sup some scuppernong wine once in a while, but I will speak my mind, Mr. Swille. Plain Abe. Honest Abe. And I don't care how much power you have in Congress, it won't stop me speaking my mind, and if you say another word about my wife, Mr. Swille, I'm going to haul off and go you one right upside your fat head. Don't forget I used to split rails." Lincoln turns around. "I'm leaving."

Uncle Robin, blinking back tears, applauds Lincoln until Swille gives him a stern look.

"Hey, wait a minute, come back, Mr. Lincoln, Mr. President."

Lincoln, stunned, stops and slowly turns around.

"You know, I like your style. You're really demanding, aren't you?" Swille takes the old keys from his right hip and fastens them to his left. "How's about a drink of Old Crow?"

"Well, I'll stay for a few more minutes, but I warn you, Mr. Swille, if you so much as whisper some calumny and perfidy about my wife, I'm going to belt you one."

"Sure, Mr. President. Sure," Swille says as Lincoln returns to his seat in front of Swille's desk. Swille is at the liquor cabinet reaching for the Old Crow, when, *zing!* a bullet comes from the direction of the window and shatters the bottle. The contents spill to the floor.

"Why, I'll be . . ." Swille says, staring at the pieces of glass on the floor. Lincoln and Uncle Robin are under the desk. Moe, the white house slave, rushes in. "Massa Swille, Massa Swille, the Confederates are outside whooping it up and breaking Mr. Lincoln's carriage. We hid Mr. Lincoln's party down in the wine cellar until the episode passed, and do you know what, Mr. Swille? Somebody has drunk up all the wine."

"Somebody has drunk up all the wine!" Swille and Uncle Robin say.

"Uncle Robin, give me the telephone. I want to call Lee."

Uncle Robin obliges, tiptoeing across the room, grinning widely.

"I don't want any of that grey trash snooping about my door," Swille says, frowning.

Outside, rebel yells can be heard.

"Hello? Give me that Lee . . . Well, I don't care if he is at the front, tell him to bring his ass away from the front. This is Arthur Swille speaking . . ." To Lincoln, Moe and Uncle Robin, "That got em."

"Hello, Lee? What's the big idea of your men come busting up to my place and annoying my guests? I told your boss, Jeff Davis, to keep that war off of my property . . . Why, you impertinent scoundrel." Hand over the phone, he mimics Lee to the trio in the room, "Says extraordinary emergency supersedes the right to privacy enjoyed by the individual no matter what station in life the individual may hold . . . Look, you little runt, if you don't get those men off my property, I'll, I'll . . . My father's dead, I'm running this thing now. I don't care how long you've known the family—my brothers and Ms. Anne and me are running things now . . .

"Who's up here? Why, the nerve. For your information, Mr. Abraham Lincoln is up here,"

Lincoln tries to shush Swille, but Swille signals him that it doesn't matter.

"You'll do no such thing." Hand over the phone, to Lincoln, "Says he's coming up here to arrest you . . .

"Look, Lee, if you don't get those men off my property I'm going to create an energy crisis and take back my railroads, and on top of that I'll see that the foreign countries don't recognize you. And if that's not all, I'll take back my gold. Don't forget; I control the interest rates . . .

"Now that's more like it . . . Now you're whistling 'Dixie' . . . No, I won't tell Davis . . . Forget it . . . That's fine." Turns to Lincoln, "Says he's going to send an escort up here to see to it that your men return safely to your yacht, *The River Queen.* Lee said he was preparing to blow it up but will call it off in deference to your comfort . . ."

Turning back to the phone, "What's that? . . . Oh, you don't have to come up here and play nigger for three days for punishment; anyway, who will run your side of the war? Look, Lee, I got to go now." Hangs up. To trio, "Boy, when you say gold, they jump. And speaking of gold, Mr. President, I'm going to give you some."

"Why, Mr. Swille, now that you mention it," Lincoln says, fidgeting and pushing his feet, "I didn't come all the way through Confederate lines just to pass the time of day. We need some revenue bad. Why, we're as broke as a skeeter's peeter. I'm leaning toward the peace plan originally proposed by Horace Greeley of the New York paper . . . it's called . . . Well, the plan is called . . ." Lincoln reaches into his coat pocket for a piece of paper. "Ah, Mr. Swille, I didn't bring my glasses, would you read it?" Lincoln hands the piece of paper to Swille.

"And cut the formalities, Mr. Swille. You can call me Abe." Lincoln, once again, reaches out for a handshake, but Swille is too busy reading to notice. Lincoln, embarrassed, puts his hand in his pocket.

Swille takes the paper and examines it. "I . . . well, your writing, your aide's writing, is nearly illegible. Here, Uncle Robin, can you make this out?"

Robin looks at it. "Compensatory Emancipation it says, Massa Swille."

"Compensatory Emancipation, that's it! Sure enough is, Mr. Swille. It goes like this. We buy the war and the slaves are over. No, like this. We buy the slaves. That's it. We buy the slaves or the bondsmen and then they pay the South seven and a half percent interest. No, dog bite it. How did it go? My aides have been going over it with me ever since we started out from *The River Queen.* I got it! We buy up all the slaves and then tell them to go off somewhere. Some place like New Mexico, where nobody's hardly seen a cloud and when they do show up it looks like judgment day, and where the cactus grows as big as eucalyptus trees, where you have to walk two miles to go to the outhouse and then freeze your can off in the cold desert until it's your turn and then the outhouse is so dark you sit on a rattlesnake. Other times I think that maybe they ought to go to the tropics where God made them. You know, I've been reading about this African tribe that lived in the tropics so long they trained mosquitoes to fight their enemies. Fascinating, don't you think? I need that gold bad, Mr. Swille. Whatever I decide, it'll come in handy."

"Sure, sure, Lincoln, I know. You'll decide what's best. I know that the war is even-steven right now, and this gold will help out. I'll take a chance on your little Union. The nerve of that guy Lee. I'm going to take back that necklace I gave Mrs. Jefferson Davis. Why, they can't do that to me. Just for that . . ." Swille goes to his safe, removes some bags of gold and places them on his desk. "That ought to do it, Mr. President, and if you're in need of some more, I'll open up Fort Knox and all that you guys wheelbarrow out in an hour you can have."

"Why, thank you, Mr. Swille. You're a patriotic man. But all of this gold, really, I . . ."

"Take it. Take it. A long-term loan, Lincoln. I'll fix these Confederates. That Lee. Sits on his horse as if he was Caesar or somebody."

"The Confederates are innocent, Mr. Swille. The other day one of them was tipping his hat and curtsying, and one of my snipers plugged him. And in the Chattanooga campaign, Grant tells me that once he was ascending Lookout Mountain and the Confederate soldiers saluted him. 'Salute to the Commanding General,' they were saying."

The men share a chuckle on this one.

"My generals may look like bums, with their blouses unbuttoned and their excessive drinking and their general ragged appearances, but they know how to fight. Why, that Grant gets sick at the sight of the blood and gets mad when you bring up even the subject of war, and he's never read a military treatise—but he can fight. His only notion of warfare is, 'Go where the enemy is and beat hell out of him.' Crude though it may sound, it seems to work."

"You know, Mr. President, I'm beginning to like you. Here, have a Havana. I have three homes there. Ought to come down some time, Mr. President, play some golf, do some sailing on my yacht. Get away from the Capitol."

"Well, I don't know, Mr. Swille. I'd better not leave town with a war going on and all."

"Where did they get the idea that you were some kind of brooding mystic, tragic and gaunt, a Midwest Messiah with hollow cheeks? I was saying to myself, 'How can a smart corporation lawyer like this Lincoln be so way-out.'"

"I keep my mouth shut, Mr. Swille. And when I can't think quick enough I walk over to the window, put my fingers into my lapels, throw my head back and gaze toward the Washington Monument, assuming a somber, grave and sulfurous countenance. It impresses them, and the myths fly."

"You know, Mr. Lincoln, I wish you'd do something about that fugitive-slave law you promised to enforce during the campaign. There are three of my cocoas at large. I'd like to bring them back here. Teach them a lesson for running away. They're giving the rest of the cocoas around here ideas. They're always caucusing, not admitting any of my white slaves or the white staff—they pass codes to one another, and some of them have taken to writing.

"They're in contact, so it seems, with slaves in the rest of the country, through some kind of intricate grapevine, so Cato my graffado tells me. Sometimes he gets blackened-up with them so's they won't know who he's working for. He's slow but faithful. So faithful that he volunteered for slavery, and so dedicated he is to slavery, the slaves voted him all-Slavery. Sent him to General Howard's Civilizing School. You should have heard my son, who was an authority on sables. He said they're so trusting and kindhearted. I sent him to the Congo to check for some possible energy resources, though he told them he was looking for the source of the Nile. They're so trusting.

"He was majoring in some kind of thing called anthropology in one of those experimental colleges. You know the young. First I wanted him to go to Yale, like me. Then I saw that the little stinker had an angle. What a cover. Anthropologists. We used to send priests, but they were too obvious."

"You must be very proud of him, Mr. Swille."

"He was doing well until . . . until these Congo savages captured him and . . . and . . . well."

"Oh, I'm sorry, was he . . . ?"

"You might say that he was killed. But, Mr. President, we all have our trials. An unpleasant subject. A smart one he was, like your Todd. Very inquisitive. It's upon my son's advice that I don't permit any of the employees to use the telephone. I permit Uncle Robin to use it because he's such a simple creature he wouldn't have the thought powers for using it deviously. He's been in the house for so long that he's lost his thirst for pagan ways and is as good a gentleman as you or me."

Lincoln nods, approvingly.

"Why, thank you, Cap'n Swille."

"Don't mention it, Robin. I don't know what I'd do without you. He brings me two gallons of slave women's milk each morning. It keeps me going. He travels all over the South in an airplane, buying supplies for the estate. He's become quite a bargainer and knows about all of the sales . . .

"Of course, I still buy the . . . well, the help. Just got back from Ryan's Mart in Charleston with a boy named Pompey. Does the work of ten niggers. I got him working in the house here. He doesn't say much but is really fast. The boy can serve dinner before it's cooked, beats himself getting up in the morning so that when he goes to the bathroom to shave he has to push his shadow out of the way, and zips about the house like a toy train. I'm really proud of this bargain. Why, on his days off he stands outside of the door, protecting me, like a piece of wood. He can stand there for hours without even blinking an eye. Says he would die if something happens to me. Isn't that right, Uncle Robin? Though he's asp-tongued and speaks in this nasal tone, Pompey is a saint. He doesn't come down to the races, nor does he Camptown; doesn't smoke, drink, cuss or wench, stays up in his room when he's not working, probably contemplating the Scriptures. They don't make them like that any more, Mr. Lincoln. I have a shrewd eye for good property, don't you think, Abe?"

"Well, Mr. Swille, if you've read my campaign literature, you'd know that my position is very clear. What a man does with his property is his business. Of course, I can't help but agree with one of my distinguished predecessors, George Washington, who said, 'There are numbers who would rather facilitate the escape of slaves than apprehend them as runnaways.' That law is hard to enforce, Mr. Swille."

Swille rises. "Look, Lincoln, one of them kinks, 40s, wiped me out when he left here. That venerable mahogany took all my guns, slaughtered my livestock and shot the overseer right between the eyes. And the worst betrayal of all was Raven Quickskill, my trusted bookkeeper. Fooled around with my books, so that every time I'd buy a new slave he'd destroy the invoices and I'd have no record of purchase; he was also writing passes and forging freedom papers. We gave him Literacy, the most powerful thing in the pre-technological pre-post-rational age—and what does he do with it? Uses it like that old Voodoo—that old stuff the slaves mumble about. Fetishism and grisly rites, only he doesn't need anything but a pen he had shaped out of cock feathers and chicken claws. Oh, they are bad sables, Mr. Lincoln. They are bad, bad sables. Not one of them with the charm and good breeding of Ms. Phyllis Wheatly, who wrote a poem for the beloved founder of this country, George Washington." He begins to recite with feeling:

> "Thy ev'ry action let the Goddess guide.
> A crown, a mansion, and a throne that shine,
> With gold unfading, Washington! We thine.

"And then that glistening rust-black Stray Leechfield. We saw him as nothing but a low-down molasses-slurper and a mutton thief, but do you know what he did? He was stealing chickens—methodically, not like the old days when they'd steal one or two and try to duck the BBs. He had taken so many over a period of time that he was over in the other county, big as you please, dressed up like a gentleman, smoking a seegar and driving a carriage which featured factory climate-control air conditioning, vinyl top, AM/FM stereo radio, full leather interior, power-lock doors, six-way power seat, power windows, white-wall wheels, door-edge guards, bumper impact strips, rear defroster and soft-ray glass.

"It was full of beautiful women fanning themselves and filling the rose-tinted air with their gay laughter. He had set up his own poultry business, was underselling everybody in eggs, gizzards, gristles, livers—and had a reputation far and wide for his succulent drumsticks. Had a white slave fronting for him for ten percent. Well, when my man finally discovered him after finding he'd built a dummy to look like him so we'd think he was still in the fields, do you know what he did, Mr. Lincoln? He stabbed the man. Stabbed him and fled on a white horse, his cape furling in the wind. It was very dramatic.

"You defend Negro ruffians like that, Mr. Lincoln? You yourself, Mr. President, said that you were never in favor of bringing about social and political equality with them. You don't want them to vote, either. I mean, I read that in the newspaper. They're not like us, Mr. Lincoln. You said yourself that there are physical differences. Now you know you said it, Mr. Lincoln. When General Frémont got brash and freed the slaves in the Western territory, you overruled his proclamation, and now the military man tells me that you have some sort of wild proclamation on your desk you're about to sign, if this compensatory thing doesn't work."

"I haven't made up my mind yet, Mr. Swille. I guess I'm a little wishy-washy on the subject still. But . . . well, sometimes I just think that one man enslaving another man is wrong. Is wrong. Is very wrong." Lincoln pounds the table.

"Well, I won't try to influence your decision, Mr. President. Would you like Uncle Robin to help you with one of those sacks?"

"Thank you, Mr. Swille."

Uncle Robin goes over and helps Lincoln with two of the heavy gold bags.

"And before you leave, Mr. President, go down to the kitchen and have Barracuda the Mammy fix you a nice snack. She'll be so thrilled. All she talks about is Massa Lincoln, Massa Lincoln. Maybe you can sign a few autographs."

Swille rises and walks over to Lincoln, who is now standing, his hands heavy with sacks of gold. "And think before you sign that proclamation, Mr. President. The slaves like it here. Look at this childish race. Uncle Robin, don't you like it here?"

"Why, yessuh, Mr. Swille! I loves it here. Good something to eat when you wonts it. Color TV. Milk pail fulla toddy. Some whiskey and a little nookie from time to time. We gets whipped with a velvet whip, and there's free dental care and always a fiddler case your feets get restless."

"You see, Mr. President. They need someone to guide them through this world of woe or they'll hurt themselves."

"I'll certainly consider your views when I make my decision, Mr. Swille. Well, I have to go now. And thanks for contributing to the war chest, Mr. Swille."

"Sure, Lincoln, anything you say." Swille goes to the window. "Hey, I think the escort Lee sent up has arrived. Look, Lincoln, I'm throwing a little shindig for Mr. and Mrs. Jefferson Davis. Why don't you come down? I'd like to get you two together for one day. Take time off from the war."

"You can arrange that, Mr. Swille?"

"I can arrange anything. They called my father God's God, Mr. President. Davis may hate your flag and you, but everybody salutes *our* flag. Gold, energy and power: that's our flag. Now, you have to leave, Abe, and don't knock over any of the *objets d'art* in the hall. I don't think your United States Treasury [chuckle] can replace them."

"I'll be careful," Lincoln says. "I'm glad you could spend some time with me, Mr. Swille."

"Not at all, Lincoln. Have a good journey back to your yacht, and, Robin, help Mr. Lincoln with his bags of gold."

Lincoln and Swille shake hands. Lincoln and Robin begin to exit with the gold. Barracuda comes in, eying both of them suspiciously.

"Massa Swille, there's some poor-white trash down in the kitchen walking on my kitchen flo. I told them to get out my kitchen and smacked one of them on the ear with my broom."

"That's Mr. Lincoln's party, Mammy Barracuda. I want you to meet the President of the United States, Mr. Abraham Lincoln."

"Oh, Mr. Linclum! Mr. Linclum! I admires you so. Now you come on down to the kitchen and let me make you and your party a nice cup of coffee."

"But I have very important business to do on *The River Queen*, the tide of battle . . ."

"Shush your mouth and come on down here get some of this coffee. Steaming hot. What's wrong with you, man, you gone pass up some of this good old Southern hospitality?"

Lincoln shrugs his shoulders. "Well," he says, smiling, "I guess one little cup won't hurt." She waltzes around with Abe Lincoln, who follows awkwardly. She sings, "Hello, Abbbbbe. Well, hello, Abbbbbe. It's so nice to have you here where you belong."

The President blushes; he finds it hard to keep in a giggle. Swille and Robin join in, clapping their hands: "You're looking swell, Abbbeee. I can tell, Abbeeee. You're still growin', you're still goin . . ."

Barracuda and Lincoln waltz out of the room. Uncle Robin follows with the bag of gold, doing his own little step. Delighted, Swille chuckles from deep in his belly.

AL YOUNG

(1939–)

Al Young is a significant writer of African American tradition. One of the warmest and most spiritual black writers of his generation, he has written prolifically in a number of forms: poems, novels, lyric essays, liner notes, and screenplays. All of his work celebrates the human spirit and the wonders of music. Like Amiri Baraka and Ralph Ellison, Young sees music as one of the most central and sacred human activities. However, unlike Baraka and Ellison, Young finds his human meaning not only in black music but in all music—in world music, in Kiri Te Kanawa, in the Korean soprano, in Mozart, and in Miles Davis. Moreover, he is a black writer in the American tradition of the singular individual; hence his work respects the rich and complex individuality of contemporary African American life. His mission is to destroy stereotypes of African Americans.

Al Young was born on May 31, 1939, in Ocean Springs, Mississippi, on the Gulf Coast near Biloxi and New Orleans. His parents were Albert James, a musician and autoworker, and Mary Campbell Young. Even though he and his parents moved to Detroit in 1946, he spent time, mostly summers, in Mississippi over the next several years.

From 1957 to 1961, Young attended the University of Michigan at Ann Arbor, where he majored in Spanish. After college, he held a variety of jobs, including professional musician, janitor, singer, and disc jockey. In the spring of 1961, he moved to the San Fransciso Bay Area, where he still lives today. By moving to the West Coast, he gained a new sense of freedom. In 1972, Young and Ishmael Reed started the multiethnic magazine *Yardbird Reader*, named after the great jazz innovator Charlie "Yardbird" Parker. In 1974, he was awarded a Guggenheim Fellowship. Young has taught creative writing at several universities, including Stanford, the University of Washington at Seattle, and the University of California at Berkeley and at Santa Cruz. He has written screenplays for Dick Gregory, Sidney Poitier, Bill Cosby, and Richard Pryor.

Young's career was initiated with the novel *Snakes* (1970), a sensitive story of a young man growing up in the Midwest. The hero's life, like Young's own life, centers on music. In his collection of musical memoirs titled *Bodies & Soul* (1981), Young says of music,

> And it is music that helps organize my feelings and thoughts, reminding me that none of us is ever truly alone, for when we interact with music, either in solitude or in gatherings, small or large, what are we listening for but the human spirit sung or played or catching its breath.

His latest novel, *Seduction by Light* (1988), which centers on the problems of Mamie Franklin, a middle-age black maid in Hollywood, has received much critical praise. In works such as *Bodies & Soul* (1981), he has a created new form, the musical memoir that is part essay, part poem, and part autobiography. Some of his best work has been done in this flexible form. *The Blues Don't Change,* a collection of his selected poems, appeared in 1982.

The further Al Young gets from the 1960s, the better artist he seems to be. In the 1990s, he has produced a large, eccentric body of African American work that celebrates black life, black music, and the human spirit. It is obvious that Young is going to outlast some of those names which were soundly trumpeted in the 1960s. In the black poetry anthology, *Every Shut Eye Ain't Asleep* (1994), Michael S. Harper says of Young's poetry that it "married the lush romanticism of the nineteenth century to the dark sonorities of jazz and the blues, forming at their best, poems that are tender, melancholy, and purely American." In fact, Harper's statement not only applies to the poetry but to Young's entire oeuvre. He is one of the best "working-class writer[s] geared to a blues esthetic." In Ted Wilentz's poetry anthology *Natural Process* (1971), Young defines the essence of his art when he says, "For me the writing of poetry is a spiritual activity. Poetry should be a music of love: song, a dance, the joyously heartbreaking flight of the human spirit through inner and outer space in search of itself."

❖❖❖

The best sources on Young are William J. Harris's essay in *Dictionary of Literary Biography: Afro-American Fiction Writers After 1955,* vol. 33, ed. Thadious Davis and Trudier Harris (1984); Harris's "I Write the Blues: An Interview with Al Young," *Greenfield Review,* (Summer/Fall 1982). Young's own *Bodies & Soul: Musical Memoirs* (1981) and his "Statement," in Ted Wilentz's *Natural Process* (1971) also provide the reader with useful information on the author and his writings.

A Dance for Militant Dilettantes

No one's going to read
or take you seriously,
a hip friend advises,
until you start coming down on them
like the black poet you truly are
& ink in lots of black in your poems
soul is not enough

you need real color
shining out of real skin
nappy snaggly afro hair
baby grow up & dig on *that!*
You got to learn to put in about
stone black fists
coming up against white jaws
& red blood splashing
down those fabled wine & urine-
stained hallways
black bombs blasting out real white estate
the sky itself black with what's to come:
final holocaust
the settling up

Dont nobody want no nice nigger no more
these honkies man that put out
these books & things
they want an angry splib
a furious nigrah
they dont want no bourgeois woogie
they want them a militant nigger
in a fiji haircut
fresh out of some secret boot camp
with a bad book in one hand
& a molotov cocktail in the other
subject to turn up at one of their conferences
or soirees
& shake the shit out of them

For Arl in Her Sixth Month

Cool beneath melon-colored cloth, your belly—
a joyous ripening that happens & happens,
that gently takes root & takes over,
a miracle uncelebrated under an autumn dress
that curves & falls slowly to your ankles.

As you busy yourself with backyard gardening,
humming, contained, I think of your tongue
at peace in its place; another kind of fruit,
mysterious flower behind two lips that open
for air & for exits & entrances.

Perhaps if I placed
my hungry ear up next to a cantaloupe or coconut
(for hours at a time & often enough),
I'd hear a fluttering or maybe a music almost like
the story Ive heard with my ear to your belly,

a seashell history of evolution personified.

Your womb is a room where it's always afternoon.

There Is a Sadness

There is a sadness to this world

There is a grimness
a nastiness in the throat
a foulness of breath
a slackening of the penis into sorrow
a chill in the bloodstream that hurts
—limitations of fleshhood!
  pain of becoming!
In a spasm of forgetfulness
the seed is sown

There is a ragged edge of my life
a shabby contour
rounding down into nowhere,
the rainyness of wanting
I might well have known
wrestling by the woodstove
in Red Clay Mississippi

There is a tumbling
from noplace to noplace
& there is a crumbling
from nothing to zero,
a journey from germ to germ again
in which the soul travels nowhere

The Old O. O. Blues

Introduction

In addition to being one of our strongest young Black revolutionary voices, Brother Gabugah is the author of half a dozen volumes, all of which have appeared since last year. *Slaughter the Pig & Git Yo'self Some Chit'lins* is the title of his most popular work which is presently in its sixth big printing. Other volumes include: *Niggers with Knives, Black on Back, Love Is a White Man's Snot-Rag* and *Takin Names and Kickin Asses.* His plays—*Transistor Willie & Latrine Lil* and *Go All the Way Down & Come Up Shakin* is a revolutionary Black musical—received last month's Drama Authority Award.

The brother is presently the recipient of both a Federal Arts Agency grant as well as a Vanderbilt Fellowship to conduct research on Richard Wright. Currently vacationing in Australia, he is preparing a collection of critical essays tentatively titled

Woodpile Findings: Cultural Investigations into What's Goin On.

His last critical work, *Nothin Niggers Do Will Ever Please Me,* is also a favorite.

"O. O. Gabugah draws strong folk poetry from the voice of a strident but vital revolutionary who attacks the Uncle Tom," states *The Nation* in its March 19, 1973 issue.

A militant advocate of the oral tradition, he chooses to dictate his poems through me rather than write them down himself.

Like right now it's the summertime
        and I'm so all alone
I gots to blow some fonky rhyme
        on my mental saxophone

Brother Trane done did his thang
        and so have Wes Montgomery,
both heavyweights in the music rang,
        now I'mo play my summary

It's lotsa yall that thank yall white
        (ought I say European?)
who thank Mozart and Bach's all right,
        denying your Black bein

Well, honkyphiles, yall's day done come,
        I mean we gon clean house
and rid the earth of Oreo scum
        that put down Fats for Faust

This here's one for-real revolution
        where aint nobody playin
We intends to stop this cultural pollution
        Can yall git to what I'm sayin?

Sittin up here in your Dior gown
        and Pierre Cardin suit
downtown where all them devil clowns
        hang out and they aint poot!

We take the white man's bread and grants
        but do our own thang with it
while yall bees itchin to git in they pants
        and taint the true Black spirit

I'm blowin for Bird and Dinah and Billie,
        for Satch, Sam Cooke, and Otis,
for Clifford, Eric, and Trane outta Philly
        who split on moment's notice

Chump, you aint gon never change,
        your narrow ass is sankin

Like Watergate, your shit is strange
    You drownin while we thankin

My simple song might not have class
    but you cant listen with impunity
We out to smash your bourgeois ass
    and by *we* I mean The Community!

JAMES ALAN MCPHERSON
(1943–)

A Pulitzer Prize–winning contemporary short story writer and journalist, James Alan McPherson was born on September 16, 1943, in Savannah, Georgia. The son of a domestic worker and the first licensed black master electrician in the state, he grew up in a working-class black community under the patronage of his parents' white friends and attended segregated public schools. Guided by the faith, patience, and industry of his parents, especially James Alan McPherson, Sr., on how to survive the ethics of Jim Crow, he kept his eye on the prize of education. The example and lessons of his parents and community enabled him to navigate the sea changes in color, class, regional, and gender boundaries of the 1960s. After enrolling at Morris Brown College in Atlanta in 1961 and studying for a year as an exchange student at Morgan State College in Maryland, McPherson returned to graduate from Morris Brown in 1965.

More sympathetic to the Civil Rights Movement than to the Black Power Movement, he took advantage in 1965 of the minority student recruitment program at Harvard Law School and a railroad labor union dispute to work each summer between 1962 and 1966 as a dining-car waiter for the Great Northern Railway. From his vantage point as an enterprising, intelligent, young, gifted, African American, southern, male insider/outsider, McPherson cultivated his skills as a fiction writer. As demonstrated in the short stories that he began writing while an undergraduate, he developed a sharp eye and ear, as well as a compassionate heart and cogent mind for exploring the beliefs, values, habits, and speech of a diverse range of Americans.

As an undergraduate at Morris Brown, he submitted his first short story to a creative writing contest sponsored by the United Negro College Fund and the *Reader's Digest.* In 1965, the *Atlantic Monthly* awarded first prize to his short story "Gold Coast." Working as a janitor in his first year at Harvard, as he had during his first two years at Morris Brown, McPherson continued writing and studying, graduating from law school in 1968 and publishing "Gold Coast" that same year in the November issue of the *Atlantic Monthly.* Choosing a career in writing rather than law, he taught writing in the law school of the University of Iowa and earned an M.F.A. in its Writers' Workshop in 1969. Also in 1969, he won an *Atlantic Monthly* grant for the publication of his first collection of short stories, *Hue and Cry,* and became a contributing editor of the magazine.

Hue and Cry (1969) received enthusiastic reviews in the popular press, and major writers such as Ralph Ellison praised McPherson for his artistic craft and integrity. McPherson subscribed to the poetics of integration and the politics of cultural pluralism of writers such as Ellison. In a promotional blurb for *Hue and Cry*, McPherson declared,

> It is my hope that this collection of stories can be read as a book about people, all kinds of people: old, young, lonely, homosexual, confused, used, discarded, wronged. As a matter of fact, certain of these people happen to be black, and certain of them happen to be white; but I have tried to keep the color part of most of them far in the background, where these things should rightly be kept.

Ellison states on the book jacket of *Hue and Cry:* "McPherson's stories are in themselves a hue and cry against the dead, publicity-sustained writing which has come increasingly to stand for what is called 'black writing.' . . . McPherson . . . is a writer of insight, sympathy, and humor and one of the most gifted young Americans I've had the privilege to read."

During the 1970s, McPherson began teaching at various institutions, including the University of California, Morgan State University, and the University of Virginia. He also was awarded a National Institute of Arts and Letters prize in 1970, a Guggenheim Fellowship for 1972–1973, and a Pulitzer Prize in 1978 for *Elbow Room* (1977), his second collection of short stories. Not surprisingly, he was one of the first black writers to receive a MacArthur Prize Fellowship, one of the so-called Genius Awards, in 1981.

In *Hue and Cry* (1969) and *Elbow Room* (1977), McPherson's cast of characters, settings, and aesthetic techniques are varied. However, like Ellison, he seems primarily concerned with the ironies and paradoxes of American life, particularly where the racial issue is involved. Many of the stories in *Hue and Cry* are obviously based on some of McPherson's experiences as a waiter on trains, particularly "On Trains" and "A Solo Song: For Doc." There is also an Ellisonian component to each of these stories. Each penetrates and explores an African American world in which the issues of race, class, gender, and region are at the center, rather than the margins, of the action. Thus Doc Craft, who schools a young recruit in the art of being a waiter (in "A Solo Song: For Doc") is considerably more than an affable menial. He expresses and symbolizes the resiliency of ethnic culture and the strength of character of those black individuals for whom personal dignity is rarely confused with the compromises and inconveniences endured because of racial prejudice and discrimination. McPherson captures this special scene of dignity and personal value by allowing Doc Craft to brag about the standards he and his fellow porters and waiters have created and maintained. Without their imaginations, patience, courage, grace, and profound understanding of the social absurdity of American life, the American experience of being "on trains" simply would not have existed. They were that experience.

When Doc freezes to death in the Chicago railroad yards, McPherson uses one of his favorite themes: he allows various characters to embody systems of values and habits of being that are endangered. Such values are usually associated with the South. In another story, "Why I Like Country Music" (included in *Elbow Room*), his nameless though highly sensitive narrator tells the story of Gweneth Lawson, a childhood sweetheart. Here the reader is forced to appreciate how much the South influences the North and vice versa. The narrator, married to a third-generation African American New Yorker, attempts to explain to her why he likes country music. In the process, we are taken via flashback to his elementary school days in South Carolina and witness him square-dancing with Gweneth, a beautiful girl visiting from Brooklyn. In this way, McPherson dramatizes the distinctive individuality of someone who has been influenced more by his regional than his ethnic culture. McPherson thus compassionately and insightfully illumines the complex identity crisis of individuals who struggle to reconcile their double consciousness as Americans of African descent and southern roots.

❖❖❖

The criticism—excluding some fine book reviews—of McPherson's work is relatively scant. Perhaps the more useful sources spelling out his point of view are two of his own publications. In December 1970, the *Atlantic Monthly* published "Indivisible Man: Ralph Ellison and James McPherson," a combination of correspondence and an interview between Ellison and McPherson conducted in 1969 and 1970. It is an excellent source for understanding McPherson's sense of himself as a writer. In addition, McPherson's long foreword to *The Short Stories of Breece D'J Pancake* (1977) discusses his relationship to a very different kind of writer and the price that each paid to become writers.

A Solo Song: For Doc

So you want to know this business, youngblood? So you want to be a Waiter's Waiter? The Commissary gives you a book with all the rules and tells you to learn them. And you do, and think that is all there is to it. A big, thick black book. Poor youngblood.

Look at me. *I* am a Waiter's Waiter. I know all the moves, all the pretty, fine moves that big book will never teach you. *I* built this railroad with my moves; and so did Sheik Beasley and Uncle T. Boone and Danny Jackson, and so did Doc Craft. That book they made you learn came from our moves and from our heads. There was a time when six of us, big men, danced at the same time in that little Pantry without touching and shouted orders to the sweating paddies in the kitchen. There was a time when they *had* to respect us because our sweat and our moves supported them. We knew the service and the paddies, even the green dishwashers, knew that we did and didn't give us the crap they pull on you.

Do you know how to sneak a Blackplate to a nasty cracker? Do you know how to rub asses with five other men in the Pantry getting their orders together and still know that you are a man, just like them? Do you know how to bullshit while you work and keep the paddies in their places with your bullshit? Do you know how to breathe down the back of an old lady's dress to hustle a bigger tip?

No. You are summer stuff, youngblood. I am old, my moves are not so good any more, but I know this business. The Commissary hires you for the summer because they don't want to let anyone get as old as me on them. I'm sixty-three, but they can't fire me: I'm in the Union. They can't lay me off for fucking up: I know this business too well. And so they hire you, youngblood, for the summer when the tourists come, and in September you go away with some tips in your pocket to buy pussy and they wait all winter for me to die. I am dying, youngblood, and so is this business. Both of us will die together. There'll always be summer stuff like you, but the big men, the big trains, are dying every day and everybody can see it. And nobody but us who are dying with them gives a damn.

Look at the big picture at the end of the car, youngblood. That's the man who built this road. He's in your history books. He's probably in that big black bible you read. He was a great man. He hated people. He didn't want to feed them but the government said he had to. He didn't want to hire me, but he needed me to feed the people. I know this, youngblood, and that is why that book is written for you and that is why I have never read it. That is why you get nervous and jump up to polish the pepper and salt shakers when the word comes down the line that an inspector is getting on at the next stop. That is why you warm the toast covers for every cheap old lady who wants to get coffee and toast and good service for sixty-five cents and a dime tip. You know that he needs you only for the summer and that hundreds of youngbloods like you want to work this summer to buy that pussy in Chicago and Portland and Seattle. The man uses you, but he doesn't need you. But me he needs for the winter, when you are gone, and to teach you something in the summer about this business you can't get from that big black book. He needs me and he knows it and I know it. That is why I am sitting here when there are tables to be cleaned and linen to be changed and silver to be washed and polished. He needs me to die. That is why I am taking my time. I know it. And I will take his service with me when I die, just like the Sheik did and like Percy Fields did, and like Doc.

Who are they? Why do I keep talking about them? Let me think about it. I guess it is because they were the last of the Old School, like me. We made this road. We got a million miles of walking up and down these cars under our feet. Doc Craft was the Old School, like me. He was a Waiter's Waiter. He danced down these aisles with us and swung his tray with the roll of the train, never spilling in all his trips a single cup of coffee. He could carry his tray on two fingers, or on one and a half if he wanted, and he knew all the tricks about hustling tips there are to know. He could work anybody. The girls at the Northland in Chicago knew Doc, and the girls at the Haverville in Seattle, and the girls at the Step-Inn in Portland and all the girls in Winnipeg knew Doc Craft.

But wait. It is just 1:30 and the first call for dinner is not until 5:00. You want to kill some time; you want to hear about the Old School and how it was in my day. If you look in that black book you would see that you should be polishing silver now. Look out the window; this is North Dakota, this is Jerry's territory. Jerry, the Unexpected Inspector. Shouldn't you polish the shakers or clean out the Pantry or squeeze oranges, or maybe change the linen on the tables? Jerry Ewald is sly. The train may stop in the middle of this wheatfield and Jerry may get on. He lives by that book. He knows where to look for dirt and mistakes. Jerry Ewald, the Unexpected Inspector. He knows where to look; he knows how to get you. He got Doc.

Now you want to know about him, about the Old School. You have even put aside your book of rules. But see how you keep your finger in the pages as if the book was more important than what I tell you. That's a bad move, and it tells on you. You will be a waiter. But you will never be a Waiter's Waiter. The Old School died with Doc, and the very last of it is dying with me. What happened to Doc? Take your finger out of the pages, youngblood, and I will tell you about a kind of life these rails will never carry again.

When your father was a boy playing with himself behind the barn, Doc was already a man and knew what the thing was for. But he got tired of using it when he wasn't much older than you, and he set his mind on making money. He had no skills. He was black. He got hungry. On Christmas Day in 1916, the story goes, he wandered into the Chicago stockyards and over to a dining car waiting to be connected up to the main train for the Chicago-to-San Francisco run. He looked up through the kitchen door at the chef storing supplies for the kitchen and said: "I'm hungry."

"What do you want *me* to do about it?" the Swede chef said.

"I'll work," said Doc.

That Swede was Chips Magnusson, fresh off the boat and lucky to be working himself. He did not know yet that he should save all extra work for other Swedes fresh off the boat. He later learned this by living. But at that time he considered a moment, bit into one of the fresh apples stocked for apple pie, chewed considerably, spit out the seeds and then waved the black on board the big train. "You can eat all you want," he told Doc. "But you work all I tell you."

He put Doc to rolling dough for the apple pies and the train began rolling for Doc. It never stopped. He fell in love with the feel of the wheels under his feet clicking against the track and he got the rhythm of the wheels in him and learned, like all of us, how to roll with them and move with them. After that first trip Doc was never at home on the ground. He worked everything in the kitchen from putting out dough to second cook, in six years. And then, when the Commissary saw that he was good and would soon be going for one of the chef's spots they saved for the Swedes, they put him out of the kitchen and told him to learn this waiter business; and told him to learn how to bullshit on the other side of the Pantry. He was almost thirty, youngblood, when he crossed over to the black side of the Pantry. I wasn't there when he made his first trip as a waiter, but from what they tell me of that trip I know that he was broke in by good men. Pantryman was Sheik Beasley, who stayed high all the time and let the waiters steal anything they wanted as long as they didn't bother his reefers. Danny Jackson, who was black and knew Shakespeare before the world said he could work with it, the second man. Len Dickey was third, Reverend Hendricks was fourth, and Uncle T. Boone, who even in those early days could not straighten his back, ran fifth. Doc started in as sixth waiter, the "mule." They pulled some shit on him at first because they didn't want somebody fresh out of a paddy kitchen on the crew. They messed with his orders, stole his plates, picked up his tips on the sly, and made him do all the dirty work. But when they saw that he could take the shit without getting hot and when they saw that he was set on being a waiter, even though he was older than most of them, they settled down and began to teach him this business and all the words and moves and slickness that made it a good business.

His real name was Leroy Johnson, I think, but when Danny Jackson saw how cool and neat he was in his moves, and how he handled the plates, he began to call him "the Doctor." Then the Sheik, coming down from his high one day after missing the lunch and dinner service, saw how Doc had taken over his station and collected fat tips from his tables by telling the passengers that the Sheik had had to get off back along the line because of a heart attack. The Sheik liked that because he saw that Doc understood crackers and how they liked nothing better than knowing that a nigger had died on the job, giving them service. The Sheik was impressed. And he was not an easy man to impress because he knew too much about life and had to stay high most of the time. And when Doc would not split the tips with him, the Sheik got mad at first and called Doc a barrel of motherfuckers and some other words you would not recognize. But he was impressed. And later that night, in the crew car when the others were gambling and drinking and bullshitting about the women they had working the corners for them, the Sheik came over to Doc's bunk and said: "You're a crafty motherfucker."

"Yeah?" says Doc.

"Yeah," says the Sheik, who did not say much. "You're a crafty motherfucker but I like you." Then he got into the first waiter's bunk and lit up again. But Reverend Hendricks, who always read his Bible before going to sleep and who always listened to anything the Sheik said because he knew the Sheik only said something when it was important, heard what was said and remembered it. After he put his Bible back in his locker, he walked over to Doc's bunk and looked down at him. "Mister Doctor Craft," the Reverend said. "Youngblood Doctor Craft."

"Yeah?" says Doc.

"Yeah," says Reverend Hendricks. "That's who you are."

And that's who he was from then on.

2

I came to the road away from the war. This was after '41, when people at home were looking for Japs under their beds every night. I did not want to fight because there was no money in it and I didn't want to go overseas to work in a kitchen. The big war was on and a lot of soldiers crossed the country to get to it, and as long as a black man fed them on trains he did not have to go to that war. I could have got a job in a Chicago factory, but there was more money on the road and it was safer. And after a while it got into your blood so that you couldn't leave it for anything. The road got into my blood the way it got into everybody's; the way going to the war got in the blood of redneck farm boys and the crazy Polacks from Chicago. It was all right for them to go to the war. They were young and stupid. And they died that way. I played it smart. I was almost thirty-five and I didn't want to go. But I took *them* and fed them and gave them good times on their way to the war, and for that I did not have to go. The soldiers had plenty of money and were afraid not to spend it all before they got to the ships on the Coast. And we gave them ways to spend it on the trains.

Now in those days there was plenty of money going around and everybody stole from everybody. The kitchen stole food from the company and the company knew it and wouldn't pay good wages. There were no rules in those days, there was no black book to go by and nobody said what you couldn't eat or steal. The paddy cooks used to toss boxes of steaks off the train in the Chicago yards for people at the restaurants there who paid them, cash. These were the days when ordinary people had to have red stamps or blue stamps to get powdered eggs and white lard to mix with red powder to make their own butter.

The stewards stole from the company and from the waiters; the waiters stole from the stewards and the company and from each other. I stole. Doc stole. Even Reverend Hendricks put his Bible far back in his locker and stole with us. You didn't want a man on your crew who didn't steal. He made it bad for everybody. And if the steward saw that he was a dummy and would never get to stealing, he wrote him up for something and got him off the crew so as not to slow down the rest of us. We had a redneck cracker steward from Alabama by the name of Casper who used to say: "*Jesus Christ!* I ain't got time to hate you niggers, I'm making so much money." He used to keep all his cash at home under his bed in a cardboard box because he was afraid to put it in the bank.

Doc and Sheik Beasley and me were on the same crew together all during the war. Even in those days, as young as we were, we knew how to be Old Heads. We organized for the soldiers. We had to wear skullcaps all the time because the crackers said our hair was poison and didn't want any of it to fall in their food. The Sheik didn't mind wearing one. He kept reefers in his and used to sell them to the soldiers for double what he paid for them in Chicago and three times what he paid the Chinamen in Seattle. That's why we called him the Sheik. After every meal the Sheik would get in the linen closet and light up. Sometimes he wouldn't come out for days. Nobody gave a damn, though; we were all too busy stealing and working. And there was more for us to get as long as he didn't come out.

Doc used to sell bootlegged booze to the soldiers; that was his specialty. He had redcaps in the Chicago stations telling the soldiers who to ask for on the train. He was an open operator and had to give the steward a cut, but he still made a pile of money. That's why the old cracker always kept us together on his crew. We were the three best moneymakers he ever had. That's something you should learn, youngblood. They can't love you for being you. They only love you if you make money for them. All that talk these days about integration and brotherhood, that's a lot of bullshit. The man will love you as long as he can make money with you. I made money. And old Casper had to love me in the open although I knew he called me a nigger at home when he had put that money in his big cardboard box. I know he loved me on the road in the wartime because I used to bring in the biggest moneymakers. I used to handle the girls.

Look out that window. See all that grass and wheat? Look at that big farm boy cutting it. Look at that burnt cracker on that tractor. He probably has a wife who married him because she didn't know what else to do. Back during wartime the girls in this part of the country knew what to do. They got on the trains at night.

You can look out that window all day and run around all the stations when we stop, but you'll never see a black man in any of these towns. You know why, youngblood? These farmers hate you. They still remember when their girls came out of these towns and got on the trains at night. They've been running black men and dark Indians out of these towns for years. They hate anything dark that's not that way because of the sun. Right now there are big farm girls with hair under their arms on the corners in San Francisco, Chicago, Seattle and Minneapolis who got started on these cars back during wartime. The farmers still remember that and they hate you and me for it. But it wasn't for me they got on. Nobody wants a stiff, smelly farm girl when there are sporting women to be got for a dollar in the cities. It was for the soldiers they got on. It was just business to me. But they hate you and me anyway.

I got off in one of these towns once, a long time after the war, just to get a drink while the train changed engines. Everybody looked at me and by the time I got to a bar there were ten people on my trail. I was drinking a fast one when the sheriff came in the bar.

"What are you doing here?" he asks me.

"Just getting a shot," I say.

He spit on the floor. "How long you plan to be here?"

"I don't know," I say, just to be nasty.

"There ain't no jobs here," he says.

"I wasn't looking," I say.

"We don't want you here."

"I don't give a good goddamn," I say.

He pulled his gun on me. "All right, coon, back on the train," he says.

"Wait a minute," I tell him. "Let me finish my drink."

He knocked my glass over with his gun. "You're finished *now*," he says. "Pull your ass out of here *now!*"

I didn't argue.

I was the night man. After dinner it was my job to pull the cloths off the tables and put paddings on. Then I cut out the lights and locked both doors. There was a big farm girl from Minot named Hilda who could take on eight or ten soldiers in one night, white soldiers. These white boys don't know how to last. I could stand by the door and when the soldiers came back from the club car they would pay me and I would let them in. Some of the girls could make as much as one hundred dollars in one night. And I always made twice as much. Soldiers don't care what they do with their money. They just have to spend it.

We never bothered with the girls ourselves. It was just business as far as we were concerned. But there was one dummy we had with us once, a boy from the South named Willie Joe something who handled the dice. He was really hot for one of these farm girls. He used to buy her good whiskey and he hated to see her go in the car at night to wait for the soldiers. He was a real dummy. One time I heard her tell him: "It's all right. They can have my body. I know I'm black inside. *Jesus,* I'm so black inside I wisht I was black all over!"

And this dummy Willie Joe said: "Baby, *don't you ever change!*"

I knew we had to get rid of him before he started trouble. So we had the steward bump him off the crew as soon as we could find a good man to handle the gambling. That old redneck Casper was glad to do it. He saw what was going on.

But you want to hear about Doc, you say, so you can get back to your reading. What can I tell you? The road got into his blood? He liked being a waiter? You won't understand this, but he did. There were no Civil Rights or marches or riots for something better in those days. In those days a man found something he liked to do and liked it from then on because he couldn't help himself. What did he like about the road? He liked what I liked: the money, owning the car, running it, telling the soldiers what to do, hustling a bigger tip from some old maid by looking under her dress and laughing at her, having all the girls at the Haverville Hotel waiting for us to come in for stopover, the power we had to beat them up or lay them if we wanted. He liked running free and not being married to some bitch who would spend his money when he was out of town or give it to some stud. He liked getting drunk with the boys up at Andy's, setting up the house and then passing out from drinking too much, knowing that the boys would get him home.

I ran with that one crew all during wartime and they, Doc, the Sheik, and Reverend Hendricks, had taken me under their wings. I was still a youngblood then, and Doc liked me a lot. But he never said that much to me; he was not a talker. The Sheik had taught him the value of silence in things that really matter. We roomed together in Chicago at Mrs. Wright's place in those days. Mrs. Wright didn't allow women in the rooms and Doc liked that, because after being out for a week and after stopping over in those hotels along the way, you get tired of women and bullshit and need your privacy. We weren't like you. We didn't need a woman every time we got hard. We knew when we had to have it and when we didn't. And we didn't spend all our money on it, either. You youngbloods think the way to get a woman is to let her see how you handle your money. That's stupid. The way to get a woman is to let her see how you handle other women. But you'll never believe that until it's too late to do you any good.

Doc knew how to handle women. I can remember a time in a Winnipeg hotel how he ran a bitch out of his room because he had enough of it and did not need her any more. I was in the next room and heard everything.

"Come on, Doc," the bitch said. "Come on honey, let's do it one more time."

"Hell no," Doc said. "I'm tired and I don't want to any more."

"How can you say you're tired?" the bitch said. "How can you say you're tired when you didn't go but two times?"

"I'm tired of it," Doc said, "because I'm tired of you. And I'm tired of you because I'm tired of it and bitches like you in all the towns I been in. You drain a man. And I know if I beat you, you'll still come back when I hit you again. *That's* why I'm tired. I'm tired of having things around I don't care about."

"What *do* you care about, Doc?" the bitch said.

"I don't know," Doc said. "I guess I care about moving and being somewhere else when I want to be. I guess I care about going out, and coming in to wait for the time to go out again."

"You crazy, Doc," the bitch said.

"Yeah?" Doc said. "I guess I'm crazy all right."

Later that bitch knocked on my door and I did it for her because she was just a bitch and I knew Doc wouldn't want her again. I don't think he ever wanted a bitch again. I never saw him with one after that time. He was just a little over fifty then and could have still done whatever he wanted with women.

The war ended. The farm boys who got back from the war did not spend money on their way home. They did not want to spend any more money on women, and the girls did not get on at night any more. Some of them went into the cities and turned pro. Some of them stayed in the towns and married the farm boys who got back from the war. Things changed on the road. The Commissary started putting that book of rules together and told us to stop stealing. They were losing money on passengers now because of the airplanes and they began to really tighten up and started sending inspectors down along the line to check on us. They started sending in spotters, too. One of them caught that redneck Casper writing out a check for two dollars less than he had charged the spotter. The Commissary got him in on the rug for it. I wasn't there, but they told me he said to the General Superintendent: "Why are you getting on me, a white man, for a lousy son-of-a-bitching two bucks? There's niggers out there been stealing for *years!*"

"Who?" the General Superintendent asked.

And Casper couldn't say anything because he had that cardboard box full of money still under his bed and knew he would have to tell how he got it if any of us was brought in. So he said nothing.

"Who?" the General Superintendent asked him again.

"Why, all them nigger waiters steal, *everybody knows that!*"

"And the cooks, what about them?" the Superintendent said.

"They're white," said Casper.

They never got the story out of him and he was fired. He used the money to open a restaurant someplace in Indiana and I heard later that he started a branch of the Klan in his town. One day he showed up at the station and told Doc, Reverend Hendricks and me: "I'll see you boys get *yours.* Damn if I'm takin' the rap for you niggers."

We just laughed in his face because we knew he could do nothing to us through the Commissary. But just to be safe we stopped stealing so much. But they did get the Sheik, though. One day an inspector got on in the mountains just outside of Whitefish and grabbed him right out of that linen closet. The Sheik had been smoking in there all day and he was high and laughing when they pulled him off the train.

That was the year we got in the Union. The crackers and Swedes finally let us in after we paid off. We really stopped stealing and got organized and there wasn't a damn thing the company could do about it, although it tried like hell to buy us out. And to get back at us, they put their heads together and began to make up that big book of rules you keep your finger in. Still, *we* knew the service and they had to write the book the way we gave the service and at first there was nothing for the Old School men to learn. We got seniority through the Union, and as long as we gave the service and didn't steal, they couldn't touch us. So they began changing the rules, and sending us notes about the service. Little changes at first, like how the initials on the doily should always face the customer, and how the silver should be taken off the tables between meals. But we were getting old and set in our old service, and it got harder and harder learning all those little changes. And we had to learn new stuff all the time because there was no telling when an inspector would get on and catch us giving bad service. It was hard as hell. It was hard because we knew that the company was out to break up the Old School. The Sheik was gone, and we knew that Reverend Hendricks or Uncle T. or Danny Jackson would go soon because they stood for the Old School, just like the Sheik. But what bothered us most was knowing that they would go for Doc first, before anyone else, because he loved the road so much.

Doc was over sixty-five then and had taken to drinking hard when we were off. But he never touched a drop when we were on the road. I used to wonder whether he drank because being a Waiter's Waiter was getting hard or because he had to do something until his next trip. I could never figure it. When we had our layovers he would spend all his time in Andy's, setting up the house. He had no wife, no relatives, not even a hobby. He just drank. Pretty soon the slicksters at Andy's got to using him for a good thing. They commenced putting the touch on him because they saw he was getting old and knew he didn't have far to go, and they would never have to pay him back. Those of us who were close to him tried to pull his coat, but it didn't help. He didn't talk about himself much, he didn't talk much about anything that wasn't related to the road; but when I tried to hip him once about the hustlers and how they were closing in on him, he just took another shot and said:

"I don't need no money. Nobody's jiving me. I'm jiving them. You know I can still pull in a hundred in tips in one trip. I *know* this business."

"Yeah, I know, Doc," I said. "But how many more trips can you make before you have to stop?"

"I ain't never gonna stop. Trips are all I know and I'll be making them as long as these trains haul people."

"That's just it," I said. "They don't *want* to haul people any more. The planes do that. The big roads want freight now. Look how they hired youngbloods just for the busy seasons just so they won't get any seniority in the winter. Look how all the Old School waiters are dropping out. They got the Sheik, Percy Fields just lucked up and died before they got to him, they almost got Reverend Hendricks. Even *Uncle T.* is going to retire! And they'll get us too."

"Not me," said Doc. "I know my moves. This old fox can still dance with a tray and handle four tables at the same time. I can still bait a queer and make the old ladies tip big. There's no waiter better than me and I know it."

"Sure, Doc," I said. "I know it too. But please save your money. Don't be a dummy. There'll come a day when you just can't get up to go out and they'll put you on the ground for good."

Doc looked at me like he had been shot. "Who taught you the moves when you were just a raggedy-ass waiter?"

"You did, Doc," I said.

"Who's always the first man down in the yard at train-time?" He threw down another shot. "Who's there sitting in the car every tenth morning while you other old heads are still at home pulling on your longjohns?"

I couldn't say anything. He was right and we both knew it.

"I have to go out," he told me. "Going out is my whole life, I wait for that tenth morning. I ain't never missed a trip and I don't mean to."

What could I say to him, youngblood? What can I say to you? He had to go out, not for the money; it was in his blood. You have to go out too, but it's for the money you go. You hate going out and you love coming in. He loved going out and he hated coming in. Would *you* listen if I told you to stop spending your money on pussy in Chicago? Would he listen if I told him to save *his* money? To stop setting up the bar at Andy's? No. Old men are just as bad as young men when it comes to money. They can't think. They always try to buy what they should have for free. And what they buy, after they have it, is nothing.

They called Doc into the Commissary and the doctors told him he had lumbago and a bad heart and was weak from drinking too much, and they wanted him to get down for his own good. He wouldn't do it. Tesdale, the General Superintendent, called him in and told him that he had enough years in the service to pull down a big pension and that the company would pay for a retirement party for him, since he was the oldest waiter working, and invite all the Old School waiters to see him off, if he would come down. Doc said no. He knew that the Union had to back him. He knew that he could ride as long as he made the trains on time and as long as he knew the service. And he knew that he could not leave the road.

The company called in its lawyers to go over the Union contract. I wasn't there, but Len Dickey was in on the meeting because of his office in the Union. He told me about it later. Those fat company lawyers took the contract apart and went through all their books. They took the seniority clause apart word by word, trying to figure a way to get at Doc. But they had written it airtight back in the days when the company *needed* waiters, and there was nothing in it about compulsory retirement. Not a word. The paddies in the Union must have figured that waiters didn't *need* a new contract when they let us in, and they had let us come in under the old one thinking that all waiters would die on the job, or drink themselves to death when they were still young, or die from buying too much pussy, or just quit when they had put in enough time to draw a pension. But *nothing* in the whole contract could help them get rid of Doc Craft. They were sweating, they were working so hard. And all the time Tesdale, the General Superintendent, was calling them sons-of-bitches for not earning their money. But there was nothing the company lawyers could do but turn the pages of their big books and sweat and promise Tesdale that they would find some way if he gave them more time.

The word went out from the Commissary: "Get Doc." The stewards got it from the assistant superintendents: "Get Doc." Since they could not get him to retire, they were determined to catch him giving bad service. He had more seniority than most other waiters, so they couldn't bump him off our crew. In fact, all the waiters with more seniority than Doc were on the crew with him. There were four of us from the Old school: me, Doc, Uncle T. Boone, and Danny Jackson. Reverend Hendricks wasn't running regular any more; he was spending all his Sundays preaching in his Church on the South Side because he knew what was coming and wanted to have something steady going for him in Chicago when his time came. Fifth and sixth men on that crew were two hardheads who had read the book. The steward was Crouse, and he really didn't want to put the screws to Doc but he couldn't help himself. Everybody wants to work. So Crouse started in to riding Doc, sometimes about moving too fast, sometimes about not moving fast enough. I was on the crew, I saw it all. Crouse would seat four singles at the same table, on Doc's station, and Doc had to take care of all four different orders at the same time. He was seventy-three, but that didn't stop him, knowing this business the way he did. It just slowed him down some. But Crouse got on him even for that and would chew him out in front of the passengers, hoping that he'd start cursing and bother the passengers so that they would complain to the company. It never worked, though. Doc just played it cool. He'd look into Crouse's eyes and know what was going on. And then he'd lay on his good service, the only service he knew, and the passengers would see how good he was with all that age on his back and they would get mad at the steward, and leave Doc a bigger tip when they left.

The Commissary sent out spotters to catch him giving bad service. These were pale-white little men in glasses who never looked you in the eye, but who always felt the plate to see if it was warm. And there were the old maids, who like that kind of work, who would order shrimp or crabmeat cocktails or celery and olive plates because they knew how the rules said these things had to be made. And when they came, when Doc brought them out, they would look to see if the oyster fork was stuck into the thing, and look out the window a long time.

"Ain't no use trying to fight it," Uncle T. Boone told Doc in the crew car one night, "the black waiter is *doomed.* Look at all the good restaurants, the class restaurants in Chicago. *You* can't work in them. Them white waiters got those jobs sewed up fine."

"I can be a waiter anywhere," says Doc. "I know the business and I like it and I can do it anywhere."

"The black waiter is doomed," Uncle T. says again. "The whites is taking over the service in the good places. And when they run you off here, you won't have no place to go."

"They won't run me off of here," says Doc. "As long as I give the right service they can't touch me."

"You're a goddamn *fool!*" says Uncle T. "You're a nigger and you ain't got no right except what the Union says you have. And that ain't worth a damn because when the Commissary finally gets you, those niggers won't lift a finger to help you."

"Leave off him," I say to Boone. "If anybody ought to be put off it's you. You ain't had your back straight for thirty years. You even make the crackers sick the way you keep bowing and folding your hands and saying, 'Thank you, Mr. Boss.' Fifty years ago that would of got you a bigger tip," I say, "but now it ain't worth a shit. And every time you do it the crackers hate you. And every time I see you serving with that skullcap on *I* hate you. The Union said we didn't have to wear them *eighteen years ago!* Why can't you take it off?"

Boone just sat on his bunk with his skullcap in his lap, leaning against his big belly. He knew I was telling the truth and he knew he wouldn't change. But he said: "That's the trouble with the Negro waiter today. He ain't got no humility. And as long as he don't have humility, he keeps losing the good jobs."

Doc had climbed into the first waiter's bunk in his longjohns and I got in the second waiter's bunk under him and lay there. I could hear him breathing. It had a hard sound. He wasn't well and all of us knew it.

"Doc?" I said in the dark.

"Yeah?"

"Don't mind Boone, Doc. He's a dead man. He just don't know it."

"We all are," Doc said.

"Not you," I said.

"What's the use? He's right. They'll get me in the end."

"But they ain't done it yet."

"They'll get me. And they know it and I know it. I can even see it in old Crouse's eyes. He knows they're gonna get me."

"Why don't you get a woman?"

He was quiet. "What can I do with a woman now, that I ain't already done too much?"

I thought for a while. "If you're on the ground, being with one might not make it so bad."

"I hate women," he said.

"You ever try fishing?"

"No."

"You want to?"

"No," he said.

"You can't keep *drinking*."

He did not answer.

"Maybe you could work in town. In the Commissary."

I could hear the big wheels rolling and clicking along the tracks and I knew by the smooth way we were moving that we were almost out of the Dakota flatlands. Doc wasn't talking. "Would you like that?" I thought he was asleep. "Doc, would you like that?"

"Hell no," he said.

"You have to try *something!*"

He was quiet again. "I know," he finally said.

3

Jerry Ewald, the Unexpected Inspector, got on in Winachee that next day after lunch and we knew that he had the word from the Commissary. He was cool about it: he laughed with the steward and the waiters about the old days and his hard gray eyes and shining glasses kept looking over our faces as if to see if we knew why he had got on. The two hardheads were in the crew car stealing a nap on company time. Jerry noticed this and could have caught them, but he was after bigger game. We all knew that, and we kept talking to him about the days of the big trains and looking at his white hair and not into the eyes behind his glasses because we knew what was there. Jerry sat down on the first waiter's station and said to Crouse: "Now I'll have some lunch. Steward, let the headwaiter bring me a menu."

Crouse stood next to the table where Jerry sat, and looked at Doc, who had been waiting between the tables with his tray under his arm. The way the rules say, Crouse looked sad because he knew what was coming. Then Jerry looked directly at Doc and said: "Headwaiter Doctor Craft, bring me a menu."

Doc said nothing and he did not smile. He brought the menu. Danny Jackson and I moved back into the hall to watch. There was nothing we could do to help Doc and we knew it. He was the Waiter's Waiter, out there by himself, hustling the biggest tip he would ever get in his life. Or losing it.

"Goddamn," Danny said to me. "Now let's sit on the ground and talk about how *kings* are gonna get fucked."

"Maybe not," I said. But I did not believe it myself because Jerry is the kind of man who lies in bed all night, scheming. I knew he had a plan.

Doc passed us on his way to the kitchen for water and I wanted to say something to him. But what was the use? He brought the water to Jerry. Jerry looked him in the eye. "Now, Headwaiter," he said. "I'll have a bowl of onion soup, a cold roast beef sandwich on white, rare, and a glass of iced tea."

"Write it down," said Doc. He was playing it right. He knew that the new rules had stopped waiters from taking verbal orders.

"Don't be so professional, Doc," Jerry said. "It's me, one of the *boys!*"

"You have to write it out," said Doc, "it's in the black book."

Jerry clicked his pen and wrote the order out on the check. And handed it to Doc. Uncle T. followed Doc back into the Pantry.

"He's gonna get you, Doc," Uncle T. said. "I knew it all along. You know why? The Negro waiter ain't got no more humility."

"Shut the fuck up, Boone!" I told him.

"You'll see," Boone went on. "You'll see I'm right. There ain't a thing Doc can do about it, either. We're gonna lose all the good jobs."

We watched Jerry at the table. He saw us watching and smiled with his gray eyes. Then he poured some of the water from the glass on the linen cloth and picked up the silver sugar bowl and placed it right on the wet spot. Doc was still in the Pantry. Jerry turned the silver sugar bowl around and around on the linen. He pressed down on it some as he turned. But when he picked it up again, there was no dark ring on the wet cloth. We had polished the silver early that morning, according to the book, and there was not a dirty piece of silver to be found in the whole car. Jerry was drinking the rest of the water when Doc brought out the polished silver soup tureen, underlined with a doily and a breakfast plate, with a shining soup bowl underlined with a doily and a breakfast plate, and a bread-and-butter plate with six crackers; not four or five or seven, but six, the number the Commissary had written in the black book. He swung down the aisle of the car between the two rows of white tables and you could not help but be proud of the way he moved with the roll of the train and the way that tray was like a part of his arm. It was good service. He placed everything neat, with all company initials showing, right where things should go.

"Shall I serve up the soup?" he asked Jerry.

"Please," said Jerry.

Doc handled that silver soup ladle like one of those Chicago Jew tailors handles a needle. He ladled up three good-sized spoonfuls from the tureen and then laid the wet spoon on an extra bread-and-butter plate on the side of the table, so he would not stain the cloth. Then he put a napkin over the wet spot Jerry had made and changed the ashtray for a prayer-card because every good waiter knows that nobody wants to eat a good meal looking at an ashtray.

"You know about the spoon plate, I see," Jerry said to Doc.

"I'm a waiter," said Doc. "I know."

"You're a damn good waiter," said Jerry.

Doc looked Jerry square in the eye. "I know," he said slowly.

Jerry ate a little of the soup and opened all six of the cracker packages. Then he stopped eating and began to look out the window. We were passing through his territory, Washington state, the country he loved because he was the only company inspector in the state and knew that once he got through Montana he would be the only man the waiters feared. He smiled and then waved for Doc to bring out the roast beef sandwich.

But Doc was into his service now and cleared the table completely. Then he got the silver crumb knife from the Pantry and gathered all the cracker crumbs, even the ones Jerry had managed to get in between the salt and pepper shakers.

"You want the tea with your sandwich, or later?" he asked Jerry.

"Now is fine," said Jerry, smiling.

"You're doing good," I said to Doc when he passed us on his way to the Pantry. "He can't touch you or nothing."

He did not say anything.

Uncle T. Boone looked at Doc like he wanted to say something too, but he just frowned and shuffled out to stand next to Jerry. You could see that Jerry hated him. But Jerry knew how to smile at everybody, and so he smiled at Uncle T. while Uncle T. bent over the table with his hands together like he was praying, and moved his head up and bowed it down.

Doc brought out the roast beef, proper service. The crock of mustard was on a breakfast plate, underlined with a doily, initials facing Jerry. The lid was on the mustard and it was clean, like it says in the book, and the little silver service spoon was clean and polished on a bread-and-butter plate. He set it down. And then he served the tea. You think you know the service, youngblood, all of you do. But you don't. Anybody can serve, but not everybody can become a part of the service. When Doc poured that pot of hot tea into that glass of crushed ice, it was like he was pouring it through his own fingers; it was like he and the tray and the pot and the glass and all of it was the same body. It was a beautiful move. It was fine service. The iced tea glass sat in a shell dish, and the iced tea spoon lay straight in front of Jerry. The lemon wedge Doc put in a shell dish half-full of crushed ice with an oyster fork stuck into its skin. Not in the meat, mind you, but squarely under the skin of that lemon, and the whole thing lay in a pretty curve on top of that crushed ice.

Doc stood back and waited. Jerry had been watching his service and was impressed. He mixed the sugar in his glass and sipped. Danny Jackson and I were down the aisle in the hall. Uncle T. stood behind Jerry, bending over, his arms folded, waiting. And Doc stood next to the table, his tray under his arm looking straight ahead and calm because he had given good service and knew it. Jerry sipped again.

"Good tea," he said. "Very good tea."

Doc was silent.

Jerry took the lemon wedge off the oyster fork and squeezed it into the glass, and stirred, and sipped again. "*Very* good," he said. Then he drained the glass. Doc reached over to pick it up for more ice but Jerry kept his hand on the glass. "Very good service, Doc," he said. "But you served the lemon wrong."

Everybody was quiet. Uncle T. folded his hands in the praying position.

"How's that?" said Doc.

"The service was wrong," Jerry said. He was not smiling now.

"How could it be? I been giving that same service for years, right down to the crushed ice for the lemon wedge."

"That's just it, Doc," Jerry said. "The lemon wedge. You served it wrong."

"Yeah?" said Doc.

"Yes," said Jerry, his jaws tight. "Haven't you seen the new rule?"

Doc's face went loose. He knew now that they had got him.

"Haven't you *seen* it?" Jerry asked again.

Doc shook his head.

Jerry smiled that hard, gray smile of his, the kind of smile that says: "I have always been the boss and I am smiling this way because I know it and can afford to give you something," "Steward Crouse," he said. "Steward Crouse, go get the black bible for the headwaiter."

Crouse looked beaten too. He was sixty-three and waiting for his pension. He got the bible.

Jerry took it and turned directly to the very last page. He knew where to look. "Now, Headwaiter," he said, "*listen* to this." And he read aloud: "Memorandum Number 22416. From: Douglass A. Tesdale, General Superintendent of Dining Cars. To: Waiters, Stewards, Chefs of Dining Cars. Attention: As of 7/9/65 the proper service for iced tea will be (a) Fresh brewed tea in teapot, poured over crushed ice at table; iced tea glass set in shell dish (b) Additional ice to be immediately available upon request after first glass of tea (c) Fresh lemon wedge will be served on bread-and-butter plate, no doily, with tines of oyster fork stuck into *meat* of lemon." Jerry paused.

"Now you know, Headwaiter," he said.

"Yeah," said Doc.

"But why didn't you know before?"

No answer.

"This notice came last week."

"I didn't check the book yet," said Doc.

"But that's a rule. Always check the book before each trip. *You* know that, Headwaiter."

"Yeah," said Doc.

"Then that's *two* rules you missed."

Doc was quiet.

"Two rules you didn't read," Jerry said. "You're slowing down, Doc."

"I know," Doc mumbled.

"You want some time off to rest?"

Again Doc said nothing.

"I think you need some time on the ground to rest up, don't you?"

Doc put his tray on the table and sat down in the seat across from Jerry. This was the first time we had ever seen a waiter sit down with a customer, even an inspector. Uncle T., behind Jerry's back, began waving his hands, trying to tell Doc to get up. Doc did not look at him.

"You *are* tired, aren't you?" said Jerry.

"I'm just resting my feet," Doc said.

"Get up, Headwaiter," Jerry said. "You'll have plenty of time to do that. I'm writing you up."

But Doc did not move and just continued to sit there. And all Danny and I could do was watch him from the back of the car. For the first time I saw that his hair was almost gone and his legs were skinny in the baggy white uniform. I don't think Jerry expected Doc to move. I don't think he really cared. But then Uncle T. moved around the table and stood next to Doc, trying to apologize for him to Jerry with his eyes and bowed head. Doc looked at Uncle T. and then got up and went back to the crew car. He left his tray on the table. It stayed there all that evening because none of us, not even Crouse or Jerry or Uncle T., would touch it. And Jerry didn't try to make any of us take it back to the Pantry. He understood at least that much. The steward closed down Doc's tables during dinner service, all three settings of it. And Jerry got off the train someplace along the way, quiet, like he had got on.

After closing down the car we went back to the crew quarters and Doc was lying on his bunk with his hands behind his head and his eyes open. He looked old. No one knew what to say until Boone went over to his bunk and said: "I feel bad for you, Doc, but all of us are gonna get it in the end. The railroad waiter is *doomed.*"

Doc did not even notice Boone.

"I could of told you about the lemon but he would of got you on something else. It wasn't no use. Any of it."

"Shut the fuck up, Boone!" Danny said. "The one thing that really hurts is that a crawling son-of-a-bitch like you will be riding when all the good men are gone. Dummies like you and these two hardheads will be working your asses off reading that damn bible and never know a goddamn thing about being a waiter. *That* hurts like a *motherfucker!*"

"It ain't my fault if the colored waiter is doomed," said Boone. "It's your fault for letting go your humility and letting the whites take over the good jobs."

Danny grabbed the skullcap off Boone's head and took it into the bathroom and flushed it down the toilet. In a minute it was half a mile away and soaked in old piss on the tracks. Boone did not try to fight, he just sat on his bunk and mumbled. He had other skullcaps. No one said anything to Doc, because that's the way real men show that they care. You don't talk. Talking makes it worse.

4

What else is there to tell you, youngblood? They made him retire. He didn't try to fight it. He was beaten and he knew it; not by the service, but by a book. *That book,* that *bible* you keep your finger stuck in. That's not a good way for a man to go. He should die in the service. He should die doing the things he likes. But not by a book.

All of us Old School men will be beaten by it. Danny Jackson is gone now, and Reverend Hendricks put in for his pension and took up preaching, full-time. But Uncle T. Boone is still riding. They'll get *me* soon enough, with that book. But it will never get you because you'll never be a waiter, or at least a Waiter's Waiter. You read too much.

Doc got a good pension and he took it directly to Andy's. And none of the boys who knew about it knew how to refuse a drink on Doc. But none of us knew how to drink with him knowing that we would be going out again in a few days, and he was on the ground. So a lot of us, even the drunks and hustlers who usually hang around Andy's, avoided him whenever we could. There was nothing to talk about any more.

He died five months after he was put on the ground. He was seventy-three and it was winter. He froze to death wandering around the Chicago yards early one morning. He had been drunk, and was still steaming when the yard crew found him. Only a few of us left in the Old School know what he was doing there.

I am sixty-three now. And I haven't decided if I should take my pension when they ask me to go or continue to ride. I *want* to keep riding, but I know that if I do, Jerry Ewald or Harry Silk or Jack Tate will get me one of these days. I could get down if I wanted: I have a hobby and I am too old to get drunk by myself. I couldn't drink with you, youngblood. We have nothing to talk about. And after a while you would get mad at me for talking anyway, and keeping you from your pussy. You are tired already. I can see it in your eyes and in the way you play with the pages of your rule book.

I know it. And I wonder why I should keep talking to you when you could never see what I see or understand what I understand or know the real difference between my school and yours. I wonder why I have kept talking this long when all the time I have seen that you can hardly wait to hit the city to get off this thing and spend your money. You have a good story. But you will never remember it. Because all this time you have had pussy in your mind, and your fingers in the pages of that black bible.

QUINCY TROUPE

(1943–)

Quincy Troupe is both a highly productive and a multifaceted writer: he is a poet, editor, publisher, teacher, and nonfiction writer. Throughout his career, he has been committed to improving his craft and to the celebration of black art and black life. His poems are often dedicated to the heroes of the black experience, including jazz musicians, writers, and athletes. Since 1973, he has produced "Life Forces: A Festival of Black Roots," which showcases in live performance some of the finest black writers in the world.

Quincy Troupe was born on July 23, 1943, to Dorothy Marshall and Quincy Troupe, Sr., the second-greatest catcher in the Negro baseball leagues in New York City. He grew up in St. Louis and was educated in Louisiana at Grambling College, where he majored in history and political science (B.A., 1963), and at Los Angeles City College, where he earned an associate of arts degree in journalism in 1967. He lived in Paris from 1963 to 1965. Troupe was a member of the famous Watts Writers' Workshop, a creative voice issuing from the Watts riots, under the direction of Budd Schulberg. Other writers in the workshop included Ojenke, Louise Meriwether, Johnny Scott, and K. Curtis Lyle. Troupe has published four books of poetry—*Embryo* (1972), *Snake-Back Solos* (1979), *Skulls Along the River* (1984), and *Weather Reports: New and Selected Poems* (1991)—and coauthored *Miles: The Autobiography* (1989). He had edited the major anthologies *Giant Talk: An Anthology of Third World Writing* (1975) and *James Baldwin: The Legacy* (1989); has taught African American literature at UCLA, the University of Southern California, and Ohio University; and is currently teaching at the University of California at San Diego. He is senior editor of the literary journal *River Styx.*

Troupe's poetry has been influenced by Pablo Neruda, John Joseph Rabearivello, Aimé Césaire, Cesar Vallego, Jean Toomer, and Sterling Brown. In the *Dictionary of Literary Biography* (vol. 41), he says of poetics, "American speech idiom—blues and jazz forms—is a viable poetic form. At the base of American creativity is language . . . what black people can do with the rhythms and the words and musicians with the sounds coupled with the words is extraordinary." A "modest" goal of his is to continue the work of Paul Laurence Dunbar, Sterling Brown, Langston Hughes, and James Weldon Johnson and to meld the forms. Furthermore, he has lately commented in Shawn Wong's *Before Columbus Foundation Anthology* (1992),

> And getting older, I think my concerns are changing. The birth of my son has changed my work some, softened it a bit. I write more about domestic things than I ever did before. I write about connections between myself and other people more—the whole idea of constructing an interior life, my interior life.

Quincy Troupe is a talented writer making a continuing contribution to black literature in a variety of forms.

❖❖❖

For information on Troupe, see Shawn Wong, *The Before Columbus Foundation Poetry Anthology* (1992); Horace Coleman's essay in *Dictionary of Literary Biography: Afro-American Poets Since 1955,* eds. Trudier Harris and Thadious M. Davis, vol. 41. See also a review of *Snake-Back Solos* by Michael Harper in *New York Times Book Review,* October 21, 1979.

Reflections on Growing Older

eye sit here, now, inside my fast thickening breath
the whites of my catfish eyes muddy with drink
my roped, rasta hair snaking down in twisted salt & pepper
vines braided from the march of years, pen & ink lines etching
my swollen face, the collected weight of years swelling
around my middle, the fear of it all overloading circuits
here & now with the weariness of tears, coming on in storms
the bounce drained out of my once liquid strut
a stork-like gimpiness there now, stiff as death
my legs climbing steep stairs in protest now, the power gone
slack from when eye once heliocoptered through cheers, hung around rims
threaded rainbowing jumpshots, that ripped, popped cords & envious peers
gone, now the cockiness of that young, firm flesh
perfect as arrogance & the belief that perpetual hard-ons would swell
forever here, smoldering fire in a gristle's desire, drooping limp now
like wet spaghetti, or noodles, the hammer-head that once shot straight in
& ramrod hard into the sucking sweet heat of wondrous women
wears a lugubrious melancholy now, like an old frog wears its knobby head
croaking like a lonely malcontent through midnight hours
eye sit here, now, inside my own gathering flesh
thickening into an image of humpty-dumpty
at the edge of a fall, the white of my hubris gone
muddy as mississippi river water
eye feel now the assault of shotgunned years
shortening breath, charlie horses throbbing through cold
tired muscles, slack & loose as frayed, old ropes
slipping from round the neck of an executed memory
see, now, these signals of irreversible breakdowns—
the ruination of my once perfect flesh—as medals earned
fighting through the holy wars of passage, see them as miracles
of the glory of living breath, pulsating music through my poetry—

syncopating metaphors turned here inside out—
see it all now as the paths taken, the choices made
the loves lost & broken, the loves retained
& the poems lost & found in the dark
beating like drumbeats through the heart

It All Boils Down

it all boils down to a question
of what anything is done for
in the first place
a reason, perhaps, for the first recognition
of clouds, cruising through seas of blue
breath, shaped like battleships

on the other hand
it could be a fascination wearing rings
on sweating, clawing fingers
something we have forgotten
perhaps, something we knew nothing about, ever
like the future of a question only time holds
answers to, such as the exact moment
death puts a lean on
flesh, perhaps
& the thin suit vanity wears
collapses it on itself
as the spirit takes leave of breath
& voices swell into a cacophonous blues

mother, somewhere in all of this
there are connections, fusing, something
perhaps, in the mellifluous nodding of crazed junkies—
that sad, leprous colony of popeye hands & feet—is a dance
a catatonic premonition, of unheeded weather reports
like the knowing somewhere deep
that eclipsed suns will perhaps experience joy
in the shaved light—

a shopping list of syllables is what poets carry
when confronting the winds of language—

like evil laughter, gleaming machetes swing under streetlamps
slicing quick words that cut a man too short to shit
sometimes, perhaps, it is this
or a concertino stream of blue ragas
when breath flies suddenly back here, mysterious
as in those moon glinting eyes, fixed in silence
the dime-polished speech of felines
in a midnight moment of celebration

a bone dry, squawking hawk talking away up there
suddenly, beyond dues, disappearing into blue quicksand
flapping wings of unanswered questions

down here, on earth, it all boils down to questions
ribcages pose & leave scattered under terrifying suns
on desert floors, the timeless, miraging sands, holding
light, the steaming, seamless language
in flight & flowing into midnight.

these moons climbing between me & you

Snake-Back Solo

For Louis Armstrong, Steve Cannon, Miles Davis & Eugene Redmond

with the music up high
boogalooin bass down way way low
up & under eye come slidin on in mojoin
on in spacin on in on a riff
full of rain
riffin on in full of rain & pain
spacin on in on a sound like coltrane

my metaphor is a blues
hot pain dealin blues is a blues axin
guitar voices whiskey broken niggah deep
in the heart is a blues in a glass filled with rain
is a blues in the dark
slurred voices of straight bourbon
is a blues dagger stuck off in the heart
of night moanin like bessie smith
is a blues filling up the wings
of darkness is a blues
& looking through the heart
a dream can become a raindrop window to see through
can become a window to see through this moment
to see yourself hanging around the dark
to see through
can become a river catching rain
feeding time can become a window
to see through
while outside windows flames trigger
the deep explosion
time steals rivers that go on & stay where they are
inside yourself moving soon there will be daylight
breaking the darkness
to show the way soon there will be voices breaking music

to come on home by down & up river breaking darkness
swimming up river the sound of louie armstrong
carrying riverboats upstream on vibratos
climbing the rain filling the rain
swimming up river
up the river of rain satchmo breaking the darkness
his trumpet & grin polished overpain speaking
to the light flaming off the river's back
at sunset snake river's back
river mississippi big muddy up from new
orleans to alton & east st. louis illinois
cross the river from st. louis to come on home by
up river the music swims breaking silence of miles
flesh leaping off itself into space
creating music creating poems

now inside myself eye solo of rivers
catching rains & dreams & sunsets solo
of trane tracks screaming through night stark
a dagger in the heart solo
of the bird spreading wings for the wind
solo of miles pied piper prince of darkness
river rain voice now eye solo
at the root of the flower solo leaning voices
against promises of shadows soloing of bones
beneath the river's snake-back solo
of trees cut down by double-bladed axes
river rain voice now eye solo of the human condition
as blues solo of the matrix mojoin new blues solo
river rain voice now eye solo   solo

& looking through the heart a dream
can become a raindrop window to see through
can become this moment this frame to see through
to see yourself hanging
around the dark to see through this pain
can become even more painful as the meaning of bones
crawling mississippi river bottoms snakepits beneath
the snake-back solo catching rain catching time
& dreams washed clean by ajax

but looking through the dream can be
like looking through a clean window crystal
prism the night where eye solo now too become the wings of night
to see through this darkness
eye solo now to become wings & colors
to become a simple skybreak shattering darkness

to become lightning's jagged sword-like thunder
eye solo to become to become
eye solo now to become to become

with the music up high
up way way high boogaloin bass down
way way low
up & under eye come slidin on in mojoin on in
spacin on in on a riff full of rain
river riff full of rain & trains & dreams
come slidin on in another riff
full of flames
leanin & glidin eye solo   solo
loopin & slidin eye solo now   solo

For Malcolm Who Walks in the Eyes of Our Children

He had been coming a very long time,
had been here many times before
in the flesh of other persons
in the spirit of other gods

His eyes had seen flesh turned to stone,
had seen stone turned to flesh
had swam within the minds
of a billion great heroes,
had walked amongst builders
of nations, of the Sphinx, had built
with his own hands those nations,

had come flying across time a cosmic spirit,
an idea, a thought wave transcending
flesh fusion spirit of all centuries,
had come soaring like a sky break

above ominous clouds of sulphur
in a stride so enormous it spanned
the breadth of a peoples bloodshed,
came singing like Coltrane breathing life
into stone statues formed from lies

Malcolm, flaming cosmic spirit who walks
amongst us, we hear your voice
speaking wisdom in the wind,
we see your vision in the life / fires of men,
in our incredible young children
who watch your image
flaming in the sun

WOMEN'S VOICES OF SELF-DEFINITION

TONI MORRISON
(CHLOE ANTHONY WOFFORD)
(1931–)

When Toni Morrison was awarded the Nobel Prize for literature in 1993, it was a celebrated occasion for American literature, African American literature, and women's literature. Representing all three categories with superb style and cultural insight, Morrison has created, in six novels and several essays, a legacy that few creative writers can match. Touted as an unmatched genius in her linguistic feats as well as in the stories she tells, Morrison has earned an indisputable place in the annals of world literature. Students and faculty across disciplines regularly teach her works and incorporate analyses of them into their scholarly endeavors. The proliferation of published critical commentary on Morrison's novels, the special conferences held to discuss her works, and the inception of the Toni Morrison Society are all testaments to the well-deserved success of a writer who has reached at least two generations of readers across ethnic groups and national boundaries.

Morrison was born Chloe Anthony Wofford in Lorain, Ohio, on February 18, 1931. From her parents, who were first-generation northerners, and from both sets of grandparents, Morrison inherited a legacy rich in southern oral traditions. Her father, George Wofford, had migrated from Alabama; her mother, Rahmah Willis Wofford, had migrated from Georgia. She grew up in an environment where she heard the stories and folktales that would influence the imaginative creativity of all her novels. Having learned to read before entering school, she was precocious in all of her studies. As an adolescent, she read Russian novels and works by Jane Austen. Her father, who believed that the democracy into which he had been born should live up to its promise, taught his children that they should stand up for their rights and challenge authority whenever they felt they had been wronged. During the Depression, when whites received good food and the Wofford family, like other blacks, received bug-infested meal from a relief agency, the Woffords wrote to Franklin D. Roosevelt to complain about this discrimination. Although the problem was not immediately rectified, Morrison and her three siblings nonetheless learned that protest was possible, that they too could claim the privileges of democracy.

Graduating with honors from Lorain High School, Morrison enrolled at Howard University, from which she would receive a B.A. in English with a minor in classics in 1953. When her classmates had difficulty pronouncing "Chloe," she began calling herself "Toni." Upon graduation from Howard, the now renamed Toni attended graduate school at Cornell University, where she completed a master's thesis on Virginia Woolf and William Faulkner—a thesis that has received much attention as young scholars and feminists have delved into Morrison's works. After she completed her degree in 1955, she taught for two years at Texas Southern

University, a historically black college. She then returned to Howard University to teach in the English department. During this period, she joined a writers group in the Washington, D.C., area that included novelist/autobiographer Claude Brown.

After her return to Howard, Toni Wofford met and married Harold Morrison, a Jamaican architect, with whom she had two sons, Harold Ford and Kevin Slade. After the breakup of the marriage in 1964, Morrison returned briefly to her parents' home in Ohio before moving to Syracuse, New York, to become an editor with a textbook subsidiary of Random House. It was here that she completed her first novel, *The Bluest Eye,* published in 1970. Morrison continued her editing duties after moving to New York City in 1968. Her editorial responsibilities at Random House enabled her to work with Middleton Harris on *The Black Book,* published in 1974. This pictorial and documentary history might be viewed as the record that would have accrued if a black person had kept a scrapbook in America for three hundred years. Photographs of lynchings are juxtaposed with free papers, speeches, short biographies, and other memorabilia. Morrison also edited Toni Cade Bambara's *Salt Eaters* (1980) and the biographies of Muhammad Ali and Angela Davis. In addition, she worked with Gayl Jones and had an interest in the works of Leon Forrest and Henry Dumas.

During the twenty years that Morrison worked for Random House, she was also pursuing her own creative objectives. *The Bluest Eye* (1970) was published when she was thirty-nine. It is the story of an eleven-year-old dark-skinned black girl named Pecola Breedlove, who lives in Lorain, Ohio, with her family and her neighbors, especially the MacTeers. The novel recounts the tragedy of a child who is not taught that her own skin and features are beautiful. Longing for blue eyes as representative of more acceptable white female beauty because they may provide an escape from the perceived ugliness of black female identity, Pecola suffers through taunts from neighborhood children, rejection by her teachers, and a venomous psychological assault from one of her adult neighbors. Although Claudia and Frieda MacTeer befriend the child, as do three prostitutes in the community, their efforts are not sufficient to inspire a sense of worth in her. Rejected by her parents and raped and impregnated by her father, Pecola is driven insane, a testament to Morrison's thesis that, because of internalized racism, not all black people in the late 1960s and early 1970s thought black was beautiful.

The Bluest Eye was the first novel to set up a major theme of most of Morrison's works: the development of black female identity in the midst of a society in which appropriate femaleness is defined as white skin, blue eyes, and long hair. African American feminist critics such as Barbara Christian and bell hooks have pointed out that Pecola's tragedy is the ultimate result when African American families and communities thoroughly internalize white values of beauty and worth. Christian writes,

> Toni Morrison's *The Bluest Eye* presents a simple theme: the story of a black girl who wants blue eyes as a symbol of beauty and therefore of goodness and happiness. . . . Yes, we know that blue eyes, blond hair, fair skin, are the symbols of beauty valued in the West, as proclaimed by romantic novels, movies, billboards, dolls, and the reactions of people to golden objects, but . . . the theme is at the base

of the conflict of artistic and societal values between the Anglo-American and Afro-American cultures, complicated by the psychopolitical dominance of one culture over another. As such, this novel is a book about mythic, political, and cultural mutilation as much as it is a book about race and sex hatred.

Morrison sets forth the same themes in *Sula* (1974) and *Song of Solomon* (1977). *Sula*, Morrison's second novelistic venture, is the story of the title character and her friend Nel Wright, as well as the story of the Bottom, the part of Medallion, Ohio, where black people have been forced to live. In chapters designated by years, Morrison recounts the destructive effects of World War I on the community, the consequences of insanity and murder, and the "progress" that leads to the community's ultimate demise. Afraid of the amoral, unfettered Sula, the townspeople see her as the epitome of evil and treat her as an outcast. In this way, she is the extension of Zora Neale Hurston's fictional character Janie Starks. Although the tales of both women focus on the intrinsic relationship between the black woman and her community, it is the folk fable of Sula that drums the point home that the black community's survival and unity depend heavily on its acceptance, understanding, and appreciation of black female self-identity and womanhood. On another level, Sula is the antithesis of Hurston's heroine. Lacking imagination, she never finds self-fulfillment, because she, unlike Janie, is an "artist without an art form." Introducing a new breed of female characters into African American literature, *Sula* enjoyed an impressive critical response. It was an alternate selection of the Book-of-the-Month Club, *Redbook* excerpted portions of it, and it was nominated for the 1975 National Book Award for fiction. Furthermore, Barbara Smith's analysis of the work in her seminal essay "Toward a Black Feminist Criticism" launched a new discourse in black feminist literary criticism.

Based on the myth that Africans could fly, Morrison's next novel, *Song of Solomon* (1977), was a national and international bestseller, with a reported 570,000 copies in print in 1979. It won the fiction award of the National Book Critics' Circle in 1978. Morrison also received the American Academy and Institute of Arts and Letters Award, and she was featured in the PBS series "Writers in America." Emphasizing the need to understand and celebrate ancestry and ancestors, the novel is the story of Milkman Dead, who must journey from his plush middle-class existence in Ohio back through his family history in Pennsylvania and Virginia to come to an understanding of how his great-grandfather could fly and to appreciate the true value of his Aunt Pilate, a spiritual guide who has links to forces beyond Milkman's world. Pilate, like Sula, chooses exclusion from, rather than acceptance by, a black society imbued with Eurocentric consciousness. Thus, as the plot inevitably brings Pilate and Milkman together, Pilate, who has imbibed African culture from her father and Indian culture from other foreparents in the hills, is able to lead Milkman toward a more African-centered life.

Morrison continued her explorations into black myth and history with the publication of *Tar Baby* (1981), which rewrites that traditional story (or returns it to its African origins) with Jadine Childs in the role of the tar baby. The novel earned Morrison a place on the cover of *Newsweek* and was on the *New York Times* bestseller list for four months. In her relationship with Son Green, a bluesy traveling man from Eloe, Florida, on a mythical island in the Caribbean, Jadine shows that education and Parisian modeling success matter much more to her than the presumed richness of African American oral and family traditions. By being drawn, like the tar baby, to these features in her, Son runs the risk of having his own values negatively transformed. Her education having been paid for by candy magnate Valerian Street, who owns the island, as well as by the sacrifices of his servants, Sydney and Ondine, who are Jadine's aunt and uncle, Jadine is unable to respond to the needs of anyone but herself, unable to reclaim the "ancient properties" that would link her more to African than to Euro-American values. Caught between the romanticism of Son's characterization and the cold calculation that informs Jadine's, Morrison ends her story on a mythical note instead of conclusively resolving the conflict.

After the publication of *Tar Baby,* Morrison branched out briefly from the novel to the short story. "Recitatif," which appeared in *Confirmation* (1983), an anthology edited by Amini and Amiri Baraka, tells the story of the interaction between a black woman and a white woman in a racially divided northern city. This skillfully crafted work is the author's only short story to date. During this period, Morrison became the Albert Schweitzer Professor of the Humanities at the State University of New York at Albany, where she taught until 1989. She was commissioned by the State of New York to complete her one and only play, *Dreaming Emmett* (1985). The work focuses on the murder of fourteen-year-old Emmett Till in Mississippi in 1955 and the people who were responsible for his death. In dream sequences, he confronts and holds conversations with the people who killed him for whistling at a white woman. Produced only once, the play has not yet been published; Morrison asserts that it is not yet finished.

Morrison continued her creativity with the publication of *Beloved* in 1987. Judged to be her most ambitious novel, the work intensifies her focus on both the impact of the past on the present and the individual versus the community. What slavery did to black people on the plantation of Sweet Home, where Sethe Suggs, Paul D, Baby Suggs, and others lived, serves as background to contemporary guilt and a reduced ability to love without being possessive. Based partly on the historical case of Margaret Garner, a slave woman who killed one of her children and tried to kill others in an effort to prevent them from being returned to slavery in 1851, *Beloved* also confronts the meaning of motherhood in an environment and under laws that allowed black women to be mothers only in the basest biological sense. Claiming her children as her own and motherhood as a natural, expansive state for herself, Sethe Suggs engages readers because of her determination and the guilt that ensues once she kills Beloved, her "knee-baby." When the baby returns as a ghost almost two decades later, Sethe acts out her guilt against the backdrop of her daughter Denver's need for companionship and against Paul D's need for her love. While some critics insist that Sethe had no right to kill Beloved, Clenora Hudson-Weems in *Africana Womanism: Reclaiming Ourselves* argues that Sethe is a true Africana womanist whose "ultimate responsibility is to her children." According to Hudson-Weems, "her [Sethe's] decision to murder them [she succeeds in killing only one—Beloved], rather than have them experience the unspeakable evils of slavery of which she herself is well aware, demonstrates that responsibility." The novel brought Morrison numerous accolades. It won the Pulitzer Prize in 1988 and led to Morrison's being awarded the Melcher Book Award (1988), the Modern Language Association of America's Commonwealth Award in Literature (1989), and the

Chianti Ruffino Antico Fattore International Literary Prize from Italy (1990). Such ongoing successes led to Morrison's appointment as Robert F. Gosheen Professor of the Council of the Humanities at Princeton University in 1989.

Although Morrison's novels have themes in common and even a penchant for a weird character or two, they also are distinctive. That distinctiveness is particularly obvious in *Jazz* (1992), which focuses on "the City" to which black people migrated during the first three decades of the twentieth century in hopes of finding better opportunities. Focusing on Violet and Joe Trace, the novel recounts how middle-age Joe has an affair with a young girl, Dorcas, then kills her when she can no longer tolerate his attention. Joe's obsession with the girl continues after the murder and is accompanied by an equal obsession from Violet. Morrison uses this madness as the center around which to explore family history, myth and legend, and the psychological consequences of various actions. Told by an erratic narrator, whose position seems to be everywhere and nowhere, the novel is perhaps the most postmodern of Morrison's books. At times playful, at times highlighting its own unreliability, the narrative voice is as much a character as are "the City," Violet, Joe, and others who have shaped their history.

Simultaneous with the publication of *Jazz,* Morrison published *Playing in the Dark: Whiteness and the Literary Imagination* (1992), which was originally presented as one of the William E. Massey Sr. Lectures in the History of American Civilization at Harvard University. In this examination of how "Africanism" influences white American writers in spite of their attempts to absent it from or suppress it within their works, Morrison focuses on works by Herman Melville, Willa Cather, and Ernest Hemingway to make her points. She returned to editing with the publication of *Race-ing Justice, EnGendering Power: Essays on Anita Hill, Clarence Thomas, and the Construction of Social Reality* (1992). Commentators offer a variety of views on the infamous hearings involving these now very infamous personalities.

In the spring of 1993, African American scholars Carolyn Denard and Marilyn Mobley began a movement to inaugurate the Toni Morrison Society in affiliation with the American Literature Association. It is one of only five societies devoted exclusively to the study of works by an African American writer (others focus on Charles Waddell Chesnutt, Langston Hughes, Zora Neale Hurston, and Richard Wright).

Morrison took her second deviation from fiction in the summer of 1993, when she created lyrics for music that had been composed for presentation at Tanglewood. Kathleen Battle sang the six-song cycle that Morrison wrote. The year 1993 proved auspicious for Morrison in other ways as well. In the fall, she won the Nobel Prize for literature, the most prestigious prize for imaginative creativity in the world. In Stockholm to receive the award, she presented a speech that has since been published by *World Literature Today* (Winter 1994) as well as in a special limited edition by Knopf. To add to her many accomplishments, her current novel, which is tentatively titled "Paradise," is scheduled for publication in 1997.

By almost any standard of measurement, Toni Morrison, who superbly weaves into fiction the elements of the folk and the formal, the oral and the written, and the mythological and the historical, belongs to the best that literature has to offer across races, cultures, and languages.

❖❖❖

Critical attention paid to Morrison and her works has skyrocketed in the past few years. Following is a selected list of the more recent books, which contain numerous bibliographies and directives to interviews, articles, and other short publications on her writings: Barbara Smith, "Toward a Black Feminist Criticism," in *But Some of Us Are Brave,* ed. Gloria Hull, Patricia Bell-Scott, and Barbara Smith (1977); Deborah McDowell, "New Directions in Black Feminist Criticism," *Black American Literature Forum* 14: 4 (Winter 1980); Mari Evans, ed., *Black Women Writers 1950–1980: A Critical Evaluation* (1984); Henry Louis Gates, Jr., *Black Literature and Literary Theory* (1984); Bessie W. Jones and Audrey L. Vinson, *The World of Toni Morrison: Explorations in Literary Criticism* (1985); Karla F. C. Holloway and Stephanie A. Demetrakopoulos, *New Dimensions of Spirituality: A Biracial and Bicultural Reading of the Novels of Toni Morrison* (1987); David L. Middleton, *Toni Morrison: An Annotated Bibliography* (1987); Susan Willis, *Specifying: Black Women Writing the American Experience* (1987); Nellie Y. McKay, *Critical Essays on Toni Morrison* (1988); Terry Otten, *The Crime of Innocence in the Fiction of Toni Morrison* (1989); Michael Awkward, *Inspiriting Influences: Tradition, Revision, and Afro-American Women's Novels* (1989); Houston A. Baker, Jr., and Patricia Redmond, eds., *Afro-American Literary Study in the 1990s* (1989); Elliot Butler-Evans, *Race, Gender, and Desire: Narrative Strategies in the Fiction of Toni Cade Bambara, Toni Morrison, and Alice Walker* (1989); Wilfred D. Samuels and Clenora Hudson-Weems, *Toni Morrison* (1990); Trudier Harris, *Fiction and Folklore: The Novels of Toni Morrison* (1991); Gayl Jones, *Liberating Voices: Oral Tradition in African American Literature* (1991); Marilyn Sanders Mobley, *Folk Roots and Mythic Wings in Sarah Orne Jewett and Toni Morrison* (1991); Barbara Hill Rigney, *The Voices of Toni Morrison* (1991).

For further information, see *Callaloo* 13 (Summer 1990), which contains a special section on Morrison; and Clenora Hudson-Weems's chapter on Morrison in *Africana Womanism: Reclaiming Ourselves* (1993); Madhu Dubey, *Black Women Novelists and the Nationalist Aesthetic* (1994), with two chapters devoted to Morrison; essays by Madonne M. Miner and Joseph T. Skerrett, Jr., in *Conjuring: Black Women, Fiction, and Literary Tradition*, ed. Marjorie Pryse and Hortense J. Spillers (1985); Barbara Christian, *Black Women Novelists: The Development of a Tradition, 1892–1976* (1980); Madhu Dubey, *Black Women Novelists and the Nationalist Aesthetic* (1994).

The Bluest Eye

Here is the house. It is green and white. It has a red door. It is very pretty. Here is the family. Mother, Father, Dick, and Jane live in the green-and-white house. They are very happy. See Jane. She has a red dress. She wants to play. Who will play with Jane? See the cat. It goes meow-meow. Come and play. Come play with Jane. The kitten will not play. See Mother. Mother is very nice. Mother will you play with Jane? Mother laughs. Laugh, Mother, laugh. See Father. He is big and strong. Father, will you play with Jane? Father is smiling. Smile, Father, smile. See the dog. Bowwow goes the dog. Do you want to play with Jane? See the dog run. Run, dog, run. Look, look. Here comes a friend. The friend will play with Jane. They will play a good game. Play, Jane, play.

Here is the house it is green and white it has a red door it is very pretty here is the family mother father dick and jane live in the green-

and-white house they are very happy see jane she has a red dress she wants to play who will play with jane see the cat it goes meow-meow come and play come play with jane the kitten will not play see mother mother is very nice mother will you play with jane mother laughs laugh mother laugh see father he is big and strong father will you play with jane father is smiling smile father smile see the dog bowwow goes the dog do you want to play do you want to play with jane see the dog run run dog run look look here comes a friend the friend will play with jane they will play a good game play jane play

Hereisthehouseitisgreenandwhiteithasareddooritisveryprettyhereisthefamilymotherfatherdickandjaneliveinthegreenandwhitehousetheyareveryhappyseejaneshehasareddressshewantstoplaywhowillplaywithjaneseethecatitgoesmeowmeowcomeandplaycomeplaywithjanethekittenwillnotplayseemothermotherisverynicemotherwillyouplaywithjanemotherlaughslaughmotherlaughseefatherheisbigandstrongfatherwillyouplaywithjanefatherissmilingsmilefathersmileseethedogbowwowgoesthedogdoyouwanttoplaydoyouwanttoplaywithjaneseethedogrunrundogrunlooklookherecomesafriendthefriendwillplaywithjanetheywillplayagoodgameplayjaneplay

Quiet as it's kept, there were no marigolds in the fall of 1941. We thought, at the time, that it was because Pecola was having her father's baby that the marigolds did not grow. A little examination and much less melancholy would have proved to us that our seeds were not the only ones that did not sprout; nobody's did. Not even the gardens fronting the lake showed marigolds that year. But so deeply concerned were we with the health and safe delivery of Pecola's baby we could think of nothing but our own magic: if we planted the seeds, and said the right words over them, they would blossom, and everything would be all right.

It was a long time before my sister and I admitted to ourselves that no green was going to spring from our seeds. Once we knew, our guilt was relieved only by fights and mutual accusations about who was to blame. For years I thought my sister was right: it was my fault. I had planted them too far down in the earth. It never occurred to either of us that the earth itself might have been unyielding. We had dropped our seeds in our own little plot of black dirt just as Pecola's father had dropped his seeds in his own plot of black dirt. Our innocence and faith were no more productive than his lust or despair. What is clear now is that of all of that hope, fear, lust, love, and grief, nothing remains but Pecola and the unyielding earth. Cholly Breedlove is dead; our innocence too. The seeds shriveled and died; her baby too.

There is really nothing more to say—except why. *But since* why *is difficult to handle, one must take refuge in* how.

Autumn

Nuns go by as quiet as lust, and drunken men and sober eyes sing in the lobby of the Greek hotel. Rosemary Villanucci, our next-door friend who lives above her father's café, sits in a 1939 Buick eating bread and butter. She rolls down the window to tell my sister Frieda and me that we can't come in. We stare at her, wanting her bread, but more than that wanting to poke the arrogance out of her eyes and smash the pride of ownership that curls her chewing mouth. When she comes out of the car we will beat her up, make red marks on her white skin, and she will cry and ask us do we want her to pull her pants down. We will say no. We don't know what we should feel or do if she does, but whenever she asks us, we know she is offering us something precious and that our own pride must be asserted by refusing to accept.

School has started, and Frieda and I get new brown stockings and cod-liver oil. Grown-ups talk in tired, edgy voices about Zick's Coal Company and take us along in the evening to the railroad tracks where we fill burlap sacks with the tiny pieces of coal lying about. Later we walk home, glancing back to see the great carloads of slag being dumped, red hot and smoking, into the ravine that skirts the steel mill. The dying fire lights the sky with a dull orange glow.

Frieda and I lag behind, staring at the patch of color surrounded by black. It is impossible not to feel a shiver when our feet leave the gravel path and sink into the dead grass in the field.

Our house is old, cold, and green. At night a kerosene lamp lights one large room. The others are braced in darkness, peopled by roaches and mice. Adults do not talk to us—they give us directions. They issue orders without providing information. When we trip and fall down they glance at us; if we cut or bruise ourselves, they ask us are we crazy. When we catch colds, they shake their heads in disgust at our lack of consideration. How, they ask us, do you expect anybody to get anything done if you all are sick? We cannot answer them. Our illness is treated with contempt, foul Black Draught, and castor oil that blunts our minds.

When, on a day after a trip to collect coal, I cough once, loudly, through bronchial tubes already packed tight with phlegm, my mother frowns. "Great Jesus. Get on in that bed. How many times do I have to tell you to wear something on your head? You must be the biggest fool in this town. Frieda? Get some rags and stuff that window."

Frieda restuffs the window. I trudge off to bed, full of guilt and self-pity. I lie down in my underwear, the metal in my black garters hurts my legs, but I do not take them off, for it is too cold to lie stockingless. It takes a long time for my body to heat its place in the bed. Once I have generated a silhouette of warmth, I dare not move, for there is a cold place one-half inch in any direction. No one speaks to me or asks how I feel. In an hour or two my mother comes. Her hands are large and rough, and when she rubs the Vicks salve on my chest, I am rigid with pain. She takes two fingers' full of it at a time, and massages my chest until I am faint. Just when I think I will tip over into a scream, she scoops out a little of the salve on her forefinger and puts it in my mouth, telling me to swallow. A hot flannel is wrapped about my neck and chest. I am covered up with heavy quilts and ordered to sweat, which I do—promptly.

Later I throw up, and my mother says, "What did you puke on the bed clothes for? Don't you have sense enough to hold your head out the bed? Now, look what you did. You think I got time for nothing but washing up your puke?"

The puke swaddles down the pillow onto the sheet—green-gray, with flecks of orange. It moves like the insides of an uncooked egg. Stubbornly clinging to its own mass, refusing to break up and be removed. How, I wonder, can it be so neat and nasty at the same time?

My mother's voice drones on. She is not talking to me. She is talking to the puke, but she is calling it my name: Claudia. She wipes it up as best she can and puts a scratchy towel over the large wet place. I lie down again. The rags have fallen from the window crack, and the air is cold. I dare not call her back and am reluctant to leave my warmth. My mother's anger humiliates me; her words chafe my cheeks, and I am crying. I do not know that she is not angry at me, but at my sickness. I believe she despises my weakness for letting the sickness "take holt." By and by I will not get sick; I will refuse to. But for now I am crying. I know I am making more snot, but I can't stop.

My sister comes in. Her eyes are full of sorrow. She sings to me: "When the deep purple falls over sleepy garden walls, someone thinks of me. . . ." I doze, thinking of plums, walls, and "someone."

But was it really like that? As painful as I remember? Only mildly. Or rather, it was a productive and fructifying pain. Love, thick and dark as Alaga syrup, eased up into that cracked window. I could smell it—taste it—sweet, musty, with an edge of wintergreen in its base—everywhere in that house. It stuck, along with my tongue, to the frosted windowpanes. It coated my chest, along with the salve, and when the flannel came undone in my sleep, the clear, sharp curves of air outlined its presence on my throat. And in the night, when my coughing was dry and tough, feet padded into the room, hands repinned the flannel, readjusted the quilt, and rested a moment on my forehead. So when I think of autumn, I think of somebody with hands who does not want me to die.

It was autumn too when Mr. Henry came. Our roomer. Our roomer. The words ballooned from the lips and hovered about our heads—silent, separate, and pleasantly mysterious. My mother was all ease and satisfaction in discussing his coming.

"You know him," she said to her friends. "Henry Washington. He's been living over there with Miss Della Jones on Thirteenth Street. But she's too addled now to keep up. So he's looking for another place."

"Oh, yes." Her friends do not hide their curiosity. "I been wondering how long he was going to stay up there with her. They say she's real bad off. Don't know who he is half the time, and nobody else."

"Well, that old crazy nigger she married up with didn't help her head none."

"Did you hear what he told folks when he left her?"

"Uh-uh. What?"

"Well, he run off with that trifling Peggy—from Elyria. You know."

"One of Old Slack Bessie's girls?"

"That's the one. Well, somebody asked him why he left a nice good church woman like Della for that heifer. You know Della always did keep a good house. And he said the honest-to-God real reason was he couldn't take no more of that violet water Della Jones used. Said he wanted a woman to smell like a woman. Said Della was just too clean for him."

"Old dog. Ain't that nasty!"

"You telling me. What kind of reasoning is that?"

"No kind. Some men just dogs."

"Is that what give her them strokes?"

"Must have helped. But you know, none of them girls wasn't too bright. Remember that grinning Hattie? She wasn't never right. And their Auntie Julia is still trotting up and down Sixteenth Street talking to herself."

"Didn't she get put away?"

"Naw. County wouldn't take her. Said she wasn't harming anybody."

"Well, she's harming me. You want something to scare the living shit out of you, you get up at five-thirty in the morning like I do and see that old hag floating by in that bonnet. Have mercy!"

They laugh.

Frieda and I are washing Mason jars. We do not hear their words, but with grown-ups we listen to and watch out for their voices.

"Well, I hope don't nobody let me roam around like that when I get senile. It's a shame."

"What they going to do about Della? Don't she have no people?"

"A sister's coming up from North Carolina to look after her. I expect she wants to get aholt of Della's house."

"Oh, come on. That's a evil thought, if ever I heard one."

"What you want to bet? Henry Washington said that sister ain't seen Della in fifteen years."

"I kind of thought Henry would marry her one of these days."

"That old woman?"

"Well, Henry ain't no chicken."

"No, but he ain't no buzzard, either."

"He ever been married to anybody?"

"No."

"How come? Somebody cut it off?"

"He's just picky."

"He ain't picky. You see anything around here you'd marry?"

"Well . . . no."

"He's just sensible. A steady worker with quiet ways. I hope it works out all right."

"It will. How much you charging?"

"Five dollars every two weeks."

"That'll be a big help to you."

"I'll say."

Their conversation is like a gently wicked dance: sound meets sound, curtsies, shimmies, and retires. Another sound enters but is upstaged by still another: the two circle each other and stop. Sometimes their words move in lofty spirals; other times they take strident leaps, and all of it is punctuated with warm-pulsed laughter—like the throb of a heart made of jelly. The edge, the curl, the thrust of their emotions is always clear to Frieda and me. We do not, cannot, know the meanings of all their words, for we are nine and ten years old. So we watch their faces, their hands, their feet, and listen for truth in timbre.

So when Mr. Henry arrived on a Saturday night, we smelled him. He smelled wonderful. Like trees and lemon vanishing cream, and Nu Nile Hair Oil and flecks of Sen-Sen.

He smiled a lot, showing small even teeth with a friendly gap in the middle. Frieda and I were not introduced to him—merely pointed out. Like, here is the bathroom; the clothes closet is here; and these are my kids, Frieda and Claudia; watch out for this window; it don't open all the way.

We looked sideways at him, saying nothing and expecting him to say nothing. Just to nod, as he had done at the clothes closet, acknowledging our existence. To our surprise, he spoke to us.

"Hello there. You must be Greta Garbo, and you must be Ginger Rogers."

We giggled. Even my father was startled into a smile.

"Want a penny?" He held out a shiny coin to us. Frieda lowered her head, too pleased to answer. I reached for it. He snapped his thumb and forefinger, and the penny disappeared. Our shock was laced with delight. We searched all over him, poking our fingers into his socks, looking up the inside back of his coat. If happiness is anticipation with certainty, we were happy. And while we waited for the coin to reappear, we knew we were amusing Mama and Daddy. Daddy was smiling, and Mama's eyes went soft as they followed our hands wandering over Mr. Henry's body.

We loved him. Even after what came later, there was no bitterness in our memory of him.

She slept in the bed with us. Frieda on the outside because she is brave—it never occurs to her that if in her sleep her hand hangs over the edge of the bed "something" will crawl out from under it and bite her fingers off. I sleep near the wall because that thought *has* occurred to me. Pecola, therefore, had to sleep in the middle.

Mama had told us two days earlier that a "case" was coming—a girl who had no place to go. The county had placed her in our house for a few days until they could decide what to do, or, more precisely, until the family was reunited. We were to be nice to her and not fight. Mama didn't know "what got into people," but that old Dog Breedlove had burned up his house, gone upside his wife's head, and everybody, as a result, was outdoors.

Outdoors, we knew, was the real terror of life. The threat of being outdoors surfaced frequently in those days. Every possibility of excess was curtailed with it. If somebody ate too much, he could end up outdoors. If somebody used too much coal, he could end up outdoors. People could gamble themselves outdoors, drink themselves outdoors. Sometimes mothers put their sons outdoors, and when that happened, regardless of what the son had done, all sympathy was with him. He was outdoors, and his own flesh had done it. To be put outdoors by a landlord was one thing—unfortunate, but an aspect of life over which you had no control, since you could not control your income. But to be slack enough to put oneself outdoors, or heartless enough to put one's own kin outdoors—that was criminal.

There is a difference between being put *out* and being put out*doors*. If you are put out, you go somewhere else; if you are outdoors, there is no place to go. The distinction was subtle but final. Outdoors was the end of something, an irrevocable, physical fact, defining and complementing our metaphysical condition. Being a minority in both caste and class, we moved about anyway on the hem of life, struggling to consolidate our weaknesses and hang on, or to creep singly up into the major folds of the garment. Our peripheral existence, however, was something we had learned to deal with—probably because it was abstract. But the concreteness of being outdoors was another matter—like the difference between the concept of death and being, in fact, dead. Dead doesn't change, and outdoors is here to stay.

Knowing that there was such a thing as outdoors bred in us a hunger for property, for ownership. The firm possession of a yard, a porch, a grape arbor. Propertied black people spent all their energies, all their love, on their nests. Like frenzied, desperate birds, they overdecorated everything; fussed and fidgeted over their hard-won homes; canned, jellied, and preserved all summer to fill the cupboards and shelves; they painted, picked, and poked at every corner of their houses. And these houses loomed like hothouse sunflowers among the rows of weeds that were the rented houses. Renting blacks cast furtive glances at these owned yards and porches, and made firmer commitments to buy themselves "some nice little old place." In the meantime, they saved, and scratched, and piled away what they could in the rented hovels, looking forward to the day of property.

Cholly Breedlove, then, a renting black, having put his family outdoors, had catapulted himself beyond the reaches of human consideration. He had joined the animals; was, indeed, an old dog, a snake, a ratty nigger. Mrs. Breedlove was staying with the woman she worked for; the boy, Sammy, was with some other family; and Pecola was to stay with us. Cholly was in jail.

She came with nothing. No little paper bag with the other dress, or a nightgown, or two pair of whitish cotton bloomers. She just appeared with a white woman and sat down.

We had fun in those few days Pecola was with us. Frieda and I stopped fighting each other and concentrated on our guest, trying hard to keep her from feeling outdoors.

When we discovered that she clearly did not want to dominate us, we liked her. She laughed when I clowned for her, and smiled and accepted gracefully the food gifts my sister gave her.

"Would you like some graham crackers?"

"I don't care."

Frieda brought her four graham crackers on a saucer and some milk in a blue-and-white Shirley Temple cup. She was a long time with the milk, and gazed fondly at the silhouette of Shirley Temple's dimpled face. Frieda and she had a loving conversation about how cu-ute Shirley Temple was. I couldn't join them in their adoration because I hated Shirley. Not because she was cute, but because she danced with Bojangles, who was *my* friend, *my* uncle, *my* daddy, and who ought to have been soft-shoeing it and chuckling with me. Instead he was enjoying, sharing, giving a lovely dance thing with one of those little white girls whose socks never slid down under their heels. So I said, "I like Jane Withers."

They gave me a puzzled look, decided I was incomprehensible, and continued their reminiscing about old squint-eyed Shirley.

Younger than both Frieda and Pecola, I had not yet arrived at the turning point in the development of my psyche which would allow me to love her. What I felt at that time was unsullied hatred. But before that I had felt a stranger, more frightening thing than hatred for all the Shirley Temples of the world.

It had begun with Christmas and the gift of dolls. The big, the special, the loving gift was always a big, blue-eyed Baby Doll. From the clucking sounds of adults I knew that the doll represented what they thought was my fondest wish. I was bemused with the thing itself, and the way it looked. What was I supposed to do with it? Pretend I was its mother? I had no interest in babies or the concept of motherhood. I was interested only in humans my own age and size, and could not generate any enthusiasm at the prospect of being a mother. Motherhood was old age, and other remote possibilities. I learned quickly, however, what I was expected to do with the doll: rock it, fabricate storied situations around it, even sleep with it. Picture books were full of little girls sleeping with their dolls. Raggedy Ann dolls usually, but they were out of the question. I was physically revolted by and secretly frightened of those round moronic eyes, the pancake face, and orangeworms hair.

The other dolls, which were supposed to bring me great pleasure, succeeded in doing quite the opposite. When I took it to bed, its hard unyielding limbs resisted my flesh—the tapered fingertips on those dimpled hands scratched. If, in sleep, I turned, the bone-cold head collided with my own. It was a most uncomfortable, patently aggressive sleeping companion. To hold it was no more rewarding. The starched gauze or lace on the cotton dress irritated any embrace. I had only one desire: to dismember it. To see of what it was made, to discover the dearness, to find the beauty, the desirability that had escaped me, but apparently only me. Adults, older girls, shops, magazines, newspapers, window signs—all the world had agreed that a blue-eyed, yellow-haired, pink-skinned doll was what every girl child treasured. "Here," they said, "this is beautiful, and if you are on this day 'worthy' you may have it." I fingered the face, wondering at the single-stroke eyebrows; picked at the pearly teeth stuck like two piano keys between red bowline lips. Traced the turned-up nose, poked the glassy blue eyeballs, twisted the yellow hair. I could not love it. But I could examine it to see what it was that all the world said was lovable. Break off the tiny fingers, bend the flat feet, loosen the hair, twist the head around, and the thing made one sound—a sound they said was the sweet and plaintive cry "Mama," but which sounded to me like the bleat of a dying lamb, or, more precisely, our icebox door opening on rusty hinges in July. Remove the cold and stupid eyeball, it would bleat still, "Ahhhhhh," take off the head, shake out the sawdust, crack the back against the brass bed rail, it would bleat still. The gauze back would split, and I could see the disk with six holes, the secret of the sound. A mere metal roundness.

Grown people frowned and fussed: "You-don't-know-how-to-take-care-of-nothing. I-never-had-a-baby-doll-in-my-whole-life-and-used-to-cry-my-eyes-out-for-them. Now-you-got-one-a-beautiful-one-and-you-tear-it-up-what's-the-matter-with-you?"

How strong was their outrage. Tears threatened to erase the aloofness of their authority. The emotion of years of unfulfilled longing preened in their voices. I did not know why I destroyed those dolls. But I did know that nobody ever asked me what I wanted for Christmas. Had any adult with the power to fulfill my desires taken me seriously and asked me what I wanted, they would have known that I did not want to have anything to own, or to possess any object. I wanted rather to feel something on Christmas day. The real question would have been, "Dear Claudia, what experience would you like on Christmas?" I could have spoken up, "I want to sit on the low stool in Big Mama's kitchen with my lap full of lilacs and listen to Big Papa play his violin for me alone." The lowness of the stool made for my body, the security and warmth of Big Mama's kitchen, the smell of the lilacs, the sound of the music, and, since it would be good to have all of my senses engaged, the taste of a peach, perhaps, afterward.

Instead I tasted and smelled the acridness of tin plates and cups designed for tea parties that bored me. Instead I looked with loathing on new dresses that required a hateful bath in a galvanized zinc tub before wearing. Slipping around on the zinc, no time to play or soak, for the water chilled too fast, no time to enjoy one's nakedness, only time to make curtains of soapy water careen down between the legs. Then the scratchy towels and the dreadful and humiliating absence of dirt. The irritable, unimaginative cleanliness. Gone the ink marks from legs and face, all my creations and accumulations of the day gone, and replaced by goose pimples.

I destroyed white baby dolls.

But the dismembering of dolls was not the true horror. The truly horrifying thing was the transference of the same impulses to little white girls. The indifference with which I could have axed them was shaken only by my desire to do so. To discover what eluded me: the secret of the magic they weaved on others. What made people look at them and say, "Awwwww," but not for me? The eye slide of black women as they approached them on the street, and the possessive gentleness of their touch as they handled them.

If I pinched them, their eyes—unlike the crazed glint of the baby doll's eyes—would fold in pain, and their cry would not be the sound of an icebox door, but a fascinating cry of pain. When I learned how repulsive this disinterested violence was, that it was repulsive because it was disinterested, my shame floundered about for refuge. The best hiding place was love. Thus the conversion from pristine sadism to fabricated hatred, to fraudulent love. It was a small step to Shirley Temple. I learned much later to worship her, just as I learned to delight in cleanliness, knowing, even as I learned, that the change was adjustment without improvement.

"Three quarts of milk. That's what was *in* that icebox yesterday. Three whole quarts. Now they ain't none. Not a drop. I don't mind folks coming in and getting what they want, but three quarts of milk! What the devil does *any*body need with *three* quarts of milk?"

The "folks" my mother was referring to was Pecola. The three of us, Pecola, Frieda, and I, listened to her downstairs in the kitchen fussing about the amount of milk Pecola had drunk. We knew she was fond of the Shirley Temple cup and took every opportunity to drink milk out of it just to handle and see sweet Shirley's face. My mother knew that Frieda and I hated milk and assumed Pecola drank it out of greediness. It was certainly not for us to "dispute" her. We didn't initiate talk with grown-ups; we answered their questions.

Ashamed of the insults that were being heaped on our friend, we just sat there: I picked toe jam, Frieda cleaned her fingernails with her teeth, and Pecola finger-traced some scars on her knee—her head cocked to one side. My mother's fussing soliloquies always irritated and depressed us. They were interminable, insulting, and although indirect (Mama never named anybody—just talked about folks and *some* people), extremely painful in their thrust. She would go on like that for hours, connecting one offense to another until all of the things that chagrined her were spewed out. Then, having told everybody and everything off, she would burst into song and sing the rest of the day. But it was such a long time before the singing part came. In the meantime, our stomachs jellying and our necks burning, we listened, avoided each other's eyes, and picked toe jam or whatever.

". . . I don't know what I'm suppose to be running here, a charity ward, I guess. Time for me to get out of the *giving* line and get in the *getting* line. I guess I ain't sup*posed* to have nothing. I'm sup*posed* to end up in the poorhouse. Look like nothing I do is going to keep me out of there. Folks just spend all their time trying to figure out ways to send *me* to the poorhouse. I got about as much business with another mouth to feed as a cat has with side pockets. As if I don't have trouble enough trying to feed my own and keep out the poorhouse, now I got something else in here that's just going to *drink* me on in there. Well, naw, she ain't. Not long as I got strength in my body and a tongue in my head. There's a limit to everything. I ain't got nothing to just throw *away*. Don't *no*body need *three* quarts of milk. Henry *Ford* don't need three quarts of milk. That's just downright *sin*ful. I'm willing to do what I can for folks. Can't nobody say I ain't. But this has got to stop, and I'm just the one to stop it. Bible say watch as *well* as pray. Folks just dump they children off on you and go on 'bout they business. Ain't nobody even *peeped* in here to see whether that child has a loaf of bread. Look like they would just *peep* in to see whether I had a loaf of bread to give her. But naw. That thought don't cross they mind. That old trifling Cholly been out of jail *two* whole days and ain't been here *yet* to see if his own child was 'live or dead. She could be *dead* for all he know. And that *mama* neither. What kind of something is that?"

When Mama got around to Henry Ford and all those people who didn't care whether she had a loaf of bread, it was time to go. We wanted to miss the part about Roosevelt and the CCC camps.

Frieda got up and started down the stairs. Pecola and I followed, making a wide arc to avoid the kitchen doorway. We at on the steps of the porch, where my mother's words could reach us only in spurts.

It was a lonesome Saturday. The house smelled of Fels Naphtha and the sharp odor of mustard greens cooking. Saturdays were lonesome, fussy, soapy days. Second in misery only to those tight, starchy, cough-drop Sundays, so full of "don'ts" and "set'cha self downs."

If my mother was in a singing mood, it wasn't so bad. She would sing about hard times, bad times, and somebody-done-gone-and-left-me times. But her voice was so sweet and her singing-eyes so melty I found myself longing for those hard times, yearning to be grown without "a thin di-i-ime to my name." I looked forward to the delicious time when "my man" would leave me, when I would "hate to see that evening sun go down . . ." 'cause then I would know "my man has left this town." Misery colored by the greens and blues in my mother's voice took all of the grief out of the words and left me with a conviction that pain was not only endurable, it was sweet.

But without song, those Saturdays sat on my head like a coal scuttle, and if Mama was fussing, as she was now, it was like somebody throwing stones at it.

". . . and here I am poor as a bowl of yak-me. What do they think I am? Some kind of Sandy Claus? Well, they can just take they stocking down 'cause it *ain't* Christmas. . . ."

We fidgeted.

"Let's do something," Frieda said.

"What do you want to do?" I asked.

"I don't know. Nothing." Frieda stared at the tops of the trees. Pecola looked at her feet.

"You want to go up to Mr. Henry's room and look at his girlie magazines?"

Frieda made an ugly face. She didn't like to look at dirty pictures. "Well," I continued, "we could look at his Bible. *That's* pretty." Frieda sucked her teeth and made a *phttt* sound with her lips. "O.K., then. We could go thread needles for the half-blind lady. She'll give us a penny."

Frieda snorted. "Her eyes look like snot. I don't feel like looking at them. What *you* want to do, Pecola?"

"I don't care," she said. "Anything you want."

I had another idea. "We could go up the alley and see what's in the trash cans."

"Too cold," said Frieda. She was bored and irritable.

"I know. We could make some fudge."

"You kidding? With Mama in there fussing? When she starts fussing at the walls, you know she's gonna be at it all day. She wouldn't even let us."

"Well, let's go over to the Greek hotel and listen to them cuss."

"Oh, who wants to do *that*? Besides, the say the same old words all the time."

My supply of ideas exhausted, I began to concentrate on the white spots on my fingernails. The total signified the number of boyfriends I would have. Seven.

Mama's soliloquy slid into the silence ". . . Bible say feed the hungry. That's fine. That's all right. But I ain't feeding no elephants. . . . Anybody need three quarts of milk to *live* need to get out of here. They in the wrong place. What is this? Some kind of *dairy* farm?"

Suddenly Pecola bolted straight up, her eyes wide with terror. A whinnying sound came from her mouth.

"What's the matter with *you*?" Frieda stood up too.

Then we both looked where Pecola was staring. Blood was running down her legs. Some drops were on the steps. I leaped up. "Hey. You cut yourself? Look. It's all over your dress."

A brownish-red stain discolored the back of her dress. She kept whinnying, standing with her legs far apart.

Frieda said, "Oh. Lordy! I know. I know what that is!"

"What?" Pecola's fingers went to her mouth.

"That's ministratin'."

"What's that?"

"You know."

"Am I going to die?" she asked.

"Noooo. You won't die. It just means you can have a baby!"

"What?"

"How do *you* know?" I was sick and tired of Frieda knowing everything.

"Mildred told me, and Mama too."

"I don't believe it."

"You don't have to, dummy. Look. Wait here. Sit down, Pecola. Right here." Frieda was all authority and zest. "And you," she said to me, "you go get some water."

"Water?"

"Yes, stupid. Water. And be quiet, or Mama will hear you."

Pecola sat down again, a little less fear in her eyes. I went into the kitchen.

"What you want, girl?" Mama was rinsing curtains in the sink.

"Some water, ma'am."

"Right where I'm working, naturally. Well, get a glass. Not no clean one neither. Use that jar."

I got a Mason jar and filled it with water from the faucet. It seemed a long time filling.

"Don't nobody never want nothing till they see me at the sink. Then everybody got to drink water. . . ."

When the jar was full, I moved to leave the room.

"Where you going?"

"Outside."

"Drink that water right here!"

"I ain't gonna break nothing."

"You don't know what you gonna do."

"Yes, ma'am. I do. Lemme take it out. I won't spill none."

"You bed' not."

I got to the porch and stood there with the Mason jar of water. Pecola was crying.

"What you crying for? Does it hurt?"

She shook her head.

"Then stop slinging snot."

Frieda opened the back door. She had something tucked in her blouse. She looked at me in amazement and pointed to the jar. "What's that supposed to do?"

"You told me. You *said* get some water."

"Not a little old jar full. Lots of water. To scrub the steps with, dumbbell!"

"How was I supposed to know?"

"Yeah. How was you. Come on." She pulled Pecola up by the arm. "Let's go back here." They headed for the side of the house where the bushes were thick.

"Hey. What about me? I want to go."

"Shut uuuup," Frieda stage-whispered. "Mama will hear you. You wash the steps."

They disappeared around the corner of the house.

I was going to miss something. Again. Here was something important, and I had to stay behind and not see any of it. I poured the water on the steps, sloshed it with my shoe, and ran to join them.

Frieda was on her knees; a white rectangle of cotton was near her on the ground. She was pulling Pecola's pants off. "Come on. Step out of them." She managed to get the soiled pants down and flung them at me. "Here."

"What am I supposed to do with these?"

"Bury them, moron."

Frieda told Pecola to hold the cotton thing between her legs.

"How she gonna walk like that?" I asked.

Frieda didn't answer. Instead she took two safety pins from the hem of her skirt and began to pin the ends of the napkin to Pecola's dress.

I picked up the pants with two fingers and looked about for something to dig a hole with. A rustling noise in the bushes startled me, and turning toward it, I saw a pair of fascinated eyes in a dough-white face. Rosemary was watching us. I grabbed for her face and succeeded in scratching her nose. She screamed and jumped back.

"Mrs. MacTeer! Mrs. MacTeer!" Rosemary hollered. "Frieda and Claudia are out here playing nasty! Mrs. MacTeer!"

Mama opened the window and looked down at us.

"What?"

"They're playing nasty, Mrs. MacTeer. Look. And Claudia hit me 'cause I seen them!"

Mama slammed the window shut and came running out the back door.

"What you all doing? Oh. Uh-huh. Uh-huh. Playing nasty, huh?" She reached into the bushes and pulled off a switch. "I'd rather raise pigs than some nasty girls. Least I can slaughter *them!*"

We began to shriek. "No, Mama. No, ma'am. We wasn't! She's a liar! No, ma'am, Mama! No, ma'am, Mama!"

Mama grabbed Frieda by the shoulder, turned her around, and gave her three or four stinging cuts on her legs. "Gonna be nasty, huh? Naw you ain't!"

Frieda was destroyed. Whippings wounded and insulted her.

Mama looked at Pecola. "You too!" she said. "Child of mine or not!" She grabbed Pecola and spun her around. The safety pin snapped open on one end of the napkin, and Mama saw it fall from under her dress. The switch hovered in the air while Mama blinked. "What the devil is going on here?"

Frieda was sobbing. I, next in line, began to explain. "She was bleeding. We was just trying to stop the blood!"

Mama looked at Frieda for verification. Frieda nodded. "She's ministratin'. We was just helping."

Mama released Pecola and stood looking at her. Then she pulled both of them toward her, their heads against her stomach. Her eyes were sorry. "All right, all right. Now, stop crying. I didn't know. Come on, now. Get on in the house. Go on home, Rosemary. The show is over."

We trooped in, Frieda sobbing quietly, Pecola carrying a white tail, me carrying the little-girl-gone-to-woman pants.

Mama led us to the bathroom. She prodded Pecola inside, and taking the underwear from me, told us to stay out.

We could hear water running into the bathtub.

"You think she's going to drown her?"

"Oh, Claudia. You so dumb. She's just going to wash her clothes and all."

"Should we beat up Rosemary?"

"No. Leave her alone."

The water gushed, and over its gushing we could hear the music of my mother's laughter.

That night, in bed, the three of us lay still. We were full of awe and respect for Pecola. Lying next to a real person who was really ministratin' was somehow sacred. She was different from us now—grown-up-like. She, herself, felt the distance, but refused to lord it over us.

After a long while she spoke very softly. "Is it true that I can have a baby now?"

"Sure," said Frieda drowsily. "Sure you can."

"But . . . how?" Her voice was hollow with wonder.

"Oh," said Frieda, "somebody has to love you."

"Oh."

There was a long pause in which Pecola and I thought this over. It would involve, I supposed, "my man," who, before leaving me, would love me. But there weren't any babies in the songs my mother sang. Maybe that's why the women were sad: the men left before they could make a baby.

Then Pecola asked a question that had never entered my mind. "How do you do that? I mean, how do you get somebody to love you?" But Frieda was asleep. And I didn't know.

HEREISTHEHOUSEITISGREENANDWHITE ITHASAREDDOORITISVERYPRETTYITISVE RYPRETTYPRETTYPRETTYP

There is an abandoned store on the southeast corner of Broadway and Thirty-fifth Street in Lorain, Ohio. It does not recede into its background of leaden sky, nor harmonize with the gray frame houses and black telephone poles around it. Rather, it foists itself on the eye of the passerby in a manner that is both irritating and melancholy. Visitors who drive to this tiny town wonder why it has not been torn down, while pedestrians, who are residents of the neighborhood, simply look away when they pass it.

At one time, when the building housed a pizza parlor, people saw only slow-footed teenaged boys huddled about the corner. These young boys met there to feel their groins, smoke cigarettes, and plan mild outrages. The smoke from their cigarettes they inhaled deeply, forcing it to fill their lungs, their hearts, their thighs, and keep at bay the shiveriness, the energy of their youth. They moved slowly, laughed slowly, but flicked the ashes from their cigarettes too quickly too often, and exposed themselves, to those who were interested, as novices to the habit. But long before the sound of their lowing and the sight of their preening, the building was leased to a Hungarian baker, modestly famous for his brioche and poppy-seed rolls. Earlier than that, there was a real-estate office there, and even before that, some gypsies used it as a base of operations. The gypsy family gave the large plate-glass window as much distinction and character as it ever had. The girls of the family took turns sitting between yards of velvet draperies and Oriental rugs hanging at the windows. They looked out and occasionally smiled, or winked, or beckoned—only occasionally. Mostly they looked, their elaborate dresses, long-sleeved and long-skirted, hiding the nakedness that stood in their eyes.

So fluid has the population in that area been, that probably no one remembers longer, longer ago, before the time of the gypsies and the time of the teen-agers when the Breedloves lived there, nestled together in the storefront. Festering together in the debris of a realtor's whim. They slipped in and out of the box of peeling gray, making no stir in the neighborhood, no sound in the labor force, and no wave in the mayor's office. Each member of the family in his own cell of consciousness, each making his own patchwork quilt of reality—collecting fragments of experience here, pieces of information there. From the tiny impressions gleaned from one another, they created a sense of belonging and tried to make do with the way they found each other.

The plan of the living quarters was as unimaginative as a first-generation Greek landlord could contrive it to be. The large "store" area was partitioned into two rooms by beaverboard planks that did not reach to the ceiling. There was a living room, which the family called the front room, and the bedroom, where all the living was done. In the front room were two sofas, an upright piano, and a tiny artificial Christmas tree which had been there, decorated and dust-laden, for two years. The bedroom had three beds: a narrow iron bed for Sammy, fourteen years old, another for Pecola, eleven years old, and a double bed for Cholly and Mrs. Breedlove. In the center of the bedroom, for the even distribution of heat, stood a coal stove. Trunks, chairs, a small end table, and a cardboard "wardrobe" closet were placed around the walls. The kitchen was in the back of this apartment, a separate room. There were no bath facilities. Only a toilet bowl, inaccessible to the eye, if not the ear, of the tenants.

There is nothing more to say about the furnishings. They were anything but describable, having been conceived, manufactured, shipped, and sold in various states of thoughtlessness, greed, and indifference. The furniture had aged without ever having become familiar. People had owned it, but never known it. No one had lost a penny or a brooch under the cushions of either sofa and remembered the place and time of the loss or the finding. No one had clucked and said, "But I *had* it just a minute ago. I was sitting right there talking to . . ." or "Here it is. It must have slipped down while I was feeding the baby!" No one had given birth in one of the beds—or remembered with fondness the peeled paint places, because that's what the baby, when he learned to pull himself up, used to pick loose. No thrifty child had tucked a wad of gum under the table. No happy drunk—a friend of the family, with a fat neck, unmarried, you know, but God how he eats!—had sat at the piano and played "You Are My Sunshine." No young girl had stared at the tiny Christmas tree and remembered when she had decorated it, or wondered if that blue ball was going to hold, or if HE would ever come back to see it.

There were no memories among those pieces. Certainly no memories to be cherished. Occasionally an item provoked a physical reaction: an increase of acid irritation in the upper intestinal tract, a light flush of perspiration at the back of the neck as circumstances surrounding the piece of furniture were recalled. The sofa, for example. It had been purchased new, but the fabric had split straight across the back by the time it was delivered. The store would not take the responsibility. . . .

"Looka here, buddy. It was O.K. when I put it on the truck. The store can't do anything about it once it's on the truck. . . ." Listerine and Lucky Strike breath.

"But I don't want no tore couch if'n it's bought new." Pleading eyes and tightened testicles.

"Tough shit, buddy. *Your* tough shit. . . ."

You could hate a sofa, of course—that is, if you could hate a sofa. But it didn't matter. You still had to get together $4.80 a month. If you had to pay $4.80 a month for a sofa that started off split, no good, and humiliating—you couldn't take any joy in owning it. And the joylessness stank, pervading everything. The stink of it kept you from painting the beaverboard walls; from getting a matching piece of material for the chair; even from sewing up the split, which became a gash, which became a gaping chasm that exposed the cheap frame and cheaper upholstery. It withheld the refreshment in a sleep slept on it. It imposed a furtiveness on the loving done on it. Like a sore tooth that is not content to throb in isolation, but must diffuse its own pain to other parts of the body—making breathing difficult, vision limited, nerves unsettled, so a hated piece of furniture produces a fretful malaise that asserts itself throughout the house and limits the delight of things not related to it.

The only living thing in the Breedloves' house was the coal stove, which lived independently of everything and everyone, its fire being "out," "banked," or "up" at its own discretion, in spite of the fact that the family fed it and knew all the details of its regimen: sprinkle, do not dump, not too much. . . . The fire seemed to live, go down, or die according to its own schemata. In the morning, however, it always saw fit to die.

HEREISTHEFAMILYMOTHERFATHERDICK ANDJANETHEYLIVEINTHEGREENANDWHI TEHOUSETHEYAREVERYH

The Breedloves did not live in a storefront because they were having temporary difficulty adjusting to the cutbacks at the plant. They lived there because they were poor and black, and they stayed there because they believed they were ugly. Although their poverty was traditional and stultifying, it was not unique. But their ugliness was unique. No one could have convinced them that they were not relentlessly and aggressively ugly. Except for the father, Cholly, whose ugliness (the result of despair, dissipation, and violence directed toward petty things and weak people) was behavior, the rest of the family—Mrs. Breedlove, Sammy Breedlove, and Pecola Breedlove—wore their ugliness, put it on, so to speak, although it did not belong to them. The eyes, the small eyes set closely together under narrow foreheads. The low, irregular hairlines, which seemed even more irregular in contrast to the straight, heavy eyebrows which nearly met. Keen but crooked noses, with insolent nostrils. They had high cheekbones, and their ears turned forward. Shapely lips which called attention not to themselves but to the rest of the face. You looked at them and wondered why they were so ugly; you looked closely and could not find the source. Then you realized that it came from conviction, their conviction. It was as though some mysterious all-knowing master had given each one a cloak of ugliness to wear, and they had each accepted it without question. The master had said, "You are ugly people." They had looked about themselves and saw nothing to contradict the statement; saw, in fact, support for it leaning at them from every billboard, every movie, every glance. "Yes," they had said. "You are right." And they took the ugliness in their hands, threw it as a mantle over them, and went about the world with it. Dealing with it each according to his way. Mrs. Breedlove handled hers as an actor does a prop: for the articulation of character, for support of a role she frequently imagined was hers—martyrdom. Sammy used his as a weapon to cause others pain. He adjusted his behavior to it, chose his companions on the basis of it: people who could be fascinated, even intimidated by it. And Pecola. She hid behind hers. Concealed, veiled, eclipsed—peeping out from behind the shroud very seldom, and then only to yearn for the return of her mask.

This family, on a Saturday morning in October, began, one by one, to stir out of their dreams of affluence and vengeance into the anonymous misery of their storefront.

Mrs. Breedlove slipped noiselessly out of bed, put a sweater on over her nightgown (which was an old day dress), and walked toward the kitchen. Her one good foot made hard, bony sounds; the twisted one whispered on the linoleum. In the kitchen she made noises with doors, faucets, and pans. The noises were hollow, but the threats they implied were not. Pecola opened her eyes and lay staring at the dead coal stove. Cholly mumbled, thrashed about in the bed for a minute, and then was quiet.

Even from where Pecola lay, she could smell Cholly's whiskey. The noises in the kitchen became louder and less hollow. There was direction and purpose in Mrs. Breedlove's movements that had nothing to do with the preparation of breakfast. This awareness, supported by ample evidence from the past, made Pecola tighten her stomach muscles and ration her breath.

Cholly had come home drunk. Unfortunately he had been too drunk to quarrel, so the whole business would have to erupt this morning. Because it had not taken place immediately, the oncoming fight would lack spontaneity; it would be calculated, uninspired, and deadly.

Mrs. Breedlove came swiftly into the room and stood at the foot of the bed where Cholly lay.

"I need some coal in this house."

Cholly did not move.

"Hear me?" Mrs. Breedlove jabbed Cholly's foot.

Cholly opened his eyes slowly. They were red and menacing. With no exception, Cholly had the meanest eyes in town.

"Awwwwww, woman!"

"I said I need some coal. It's as cold as a witch's tit in this house. Your whiskey ass wouldn't feel hellfire, but I'm cold. I got to do a lot of things, but I ain't got to freeze."

"Leave me 'lone."

"Not until you get me some coal. If working like a mule don't give me the right to be warm, what am I doing it for? You sure ain't bringing in nothing. If it was left up to you, we'd all be dead. . . ." Her voice was like an earache in the brain. ". . . If you think I'm going to wade out in the cold and get it myself, you'd better think again."

"I don't give a shit how you get it." A bubble of violence burst in his throat.

"You going to get your drunk self out of that bed and get me some coal or not?"

Silence.

"Cholly!"

Silence.

"Don't try me this morning, man. You say one more word, and I'll split you open!"

Silence.

"All right. All right. But if I sneeze once, just once, God help your butt!"

Sammy was awake now too, but pretending to be asleep. Pecola still held her stomach muscles taut and conserved her breath. They all knew that Mrs. Breedlove could have, would have, and had, gotten coal from the shed, or that Sammy or Pecola could be directed to get it. But the unquarreled evening hung like the first note of a dirge in sullenly expectant air. An escapade of drunkenness, no matter how routine, had its own ceremonial close. The tiny, undistinguished days that Mrs. Breedlove lived were identified, grouped, and classed by these quarrels. They gave substance to the minutes and hours otherwise dim and unrecalled. They relieved the tiresomeness of poverty, gave grandeur to the dead rooms. In these violent breaks in routine that were themselves routine, she could display the style and imagination of what she believed to be her own true self. To deprive her of these fights was to deprive her of all the zest and reasonableness of life. Cholly, by his habitual drunkenness and orneriness, provided them both with the material they needed to make their lives tolerable. Mrs. Breedlove considered herself an upright and Christian woman, burdened with a no-count man, whom God wanted her to punish. (Cholly was beyond redemption, of course, and redemption was hardly the point—Mrs. Breedlove was not interested in Christ the Redeemer, but rather Christ the Judge.) Often she could be heard discoursing with Jesus about Cholly, pleading with Him to help her "strike the bastard down from his pea-knuckle of pride." And once when a drunken gesture catapulted Cholly into the red-hot stove, she screamed, "Get him, Jesus! Get him!" If Cholly had stopped drinking, she would never have forgiven Jesus. She needed Cholly's sins desperately. The lower he sank, the wilder and more irresponsible he became, the more splendid she and her task became. In the name of Jesus.

No less did Cholly need her. She was one of the few things abhorrent to him that he could touch and therefore hurt. He poured out on her the sum of all his inarticulate fury and aborted desires. Hating her, he could leave himself intact. When he was still very young, Cholly had been surprised in some bushes by two white men while he was newly but earnestly engaged in eliciting sexual pleasure from a little country girl. The men had shone a flashlight right on his behind. He had stopped, terrified. They chuckled. The beam of the flashlight did not move. "Go on," they said. "Go on and finish. And, nigger, make it good." The flashlight did not move. For some reason Cholly had not hated the white men; he hated, despised, the girl. Even a half-remembrance of this episode, along with myriad other humiliations, defeats, and emasculations, could stir him into flights of depravity that surprised himself—but only himself. Somehow he could not astound. He could only be astounded. So he gave that up, too.

Cholly and Mrs. Breedlove fought each other with a darkly brutal formalism that was paralleled only by their lovemaking. Tacitly they had agreed not to kill each other. He fought her the way a coward fights a man—with feet, the palms of his hands, and teeth. She, in turn, fought back in a purely feminine way—with frying pans and pokers, and occasionally a flatiron would sail toward his head. They did not talk, groan, or curse during these beatings. There was only the muted sound of falling things, and flesh on unsurprised flesh.

There was a difference in the reaction of the children to these battles. Sammy cursed for a while, or left the house, or threw himself into the fray. He was known, by the time he was fourteen, to have run away from home no less than twenty-seven times. Once he got to Buffalo and stayed three months. His returns, whether by force or circumstance, were sullen. Pecola, on the other hand, restricted by youth and sex, experimented with methods of endurance. Though the methods varied, the pain was as consistent as it was deep. She struggled between an overwhelming desire that one would kill the other, and a profound wish that she herself could die. Now she was whispering, "Don't, Mrs. Breedlove. Don't." Pecola, like Sammy and Cholly, always called her mother Mrs. Breedlove.

"Don't, Mrs. Breedlove. Don't."

But Mrs. Breedlove did.

By the grace, no doubt, of God, Mrs. Breedlove sneezed. Just once.

She ran into the bedroom with a dishpan full of cold water and threw it in Cholly's face. He sat up, choking and spitting. Naked and ashen, he leaped from the bed, and with a flying tackle, grabbed his wife around the waist, and they hit the floor. Cholly picked her up and knocked her down with the back of his hand. She fell in a sitting position, her back supported by Sammy's bed frame. She had not let go of the dishpan, and began to hit at Cholly's thighs and groin with it. He put his foot in her chest, and she dropped the pan. Dropping to his knee, he struck her several times in the face, and she might have succumbed early had he not hit his hand against the metal bed frame when his wife ducked. Mrs. Breedlove took advantage of this momentary suspension of blows and slipped out of his reach. Sammy, who had watched in silence their struggling at his bedside, suddenly began to hit his father about the head with both fists, shouting "You naked fuck!" over and over and over. Mrs. Breedlove, having snatched up the round, flat stove lid, ran tippy-toe to Cholly as he was pulling himself up from his knees, and struck him two blows, knocking him right back into the senselessness out of which she had provoked him. Panting, she threw a quilt over him and let him lie.

Sammy screamed, "Kill him! Kill him!"

Mrs. Breedlove looked at Sammy with surprise. "Cut out that noise, boy." She put the stove lid back in place, and walked toward the kitchen. At the doorway she paused long enough to say to her son, "Get up from there anyhow. I need some coal."

Letting herself breathe easy now, Pecola covered her head with the quilt. The sick feeling, which she had tried to prevent by holding in her stomach, came quickly in spite of her precaution. There surged in her the desire to heave, but as always, she knew she would not.

"Please, God," she whispered into the palm of her hand. "Please make me disappear." She squeezed her eyes shut. Little parts of her body faded away. Now slowly, now with a rush. Slowly again. Her fingers went, one by one; then her arms disappeared all the way to the elbow. Her feet now. Yes, that was good. The legs all at once. It was hardest above the thighs. She had to be real still and pull. Her stomach would not go. But finally it, too, went away. Then her chest, her neck. The face was hard, too. Almost done, almost. Only her tight, tight eyes were left. They were always left.

Try as she might, she could never get her eyes to disappear. So what was the point? They were everything. Everything was there, in them. All of those pictures, all of those faces. She had long ago given up the idea of running away to see new pictures, new faces, as Sammy had so often done. He never took her, and he never thought about his going ahead of time, so it was never planned. It wouldn't have worked anyway. As long as she looked the way she did, as long as she was ugly, she would have to stay with these people. Somehow she belonged to them. Long hours she sat looking in the mirror, trying to discover the secret of the ugliness, the ugliness that made her ignored or despised at school, by teachers and classmates alike. She was the only member of her class who sat alone at a double desk. The first letter of her last name forced her to sit in the front of the room always. But what about Marie Appolonaire? Marie was in front of her, but she shared a desk with Luke Angelino. Her teachers had always treated her this way. They tried never to glance at her, and called on her only when everyone was required to respond. She also knew that when one of the girls at school wanted to be particularly insulting to a boy, or wanted to get an immediate response from him, she could say, "Bobby loves Pecola Breedlove! Bobby loves Pecola Breedlove!" and never fail to get peals of laughter from those in earshot, and mock anger from the accused.

It had occurred to Pecola some time ago that if her eyes, those eyes that held the pictures, and knew the sights—if those eyes of hers were different, that is to say, beautiful, she herself would be different. Her teeth were good, and at least her nose was not big and flat like some of those who were thought so cute. If she looked different, beautiful, maybe Cholly would be different, and Mrs. Breedlove too. Maybe they'd say, "Why, look at pretty-eyed Pecola. We mustn't do bad things in front of those pretty eyes."

Pretty eyes. Pretty blue eyes. Big blue pretty eyes. Run, Jip, run. Jip runs, Alice runs. Alice has blue eyes. Jerry has blue eyes. Jerry runs. Alice runs. They run with their blue eyes. Four blue eyes. Four pretty blue eyes. Blue-sky eyes. Blue-like Mrs. Forrest's blue blouse eyes. Morning-glory-blue-eyes. Alice-and-Jerry-blue-storybook-eyes.

Each night, without fail, she prayed for blue eyes. Fervently, for a year she had prayed. Although somewhat discouraged, she was not without hope. To have something as wonderful as that happen would take a long, long time.

Thrown, in this way, into the binding conviction that only a miracle could relieve her, she would never know her beauty. She would see only what there was to see: the eyes of other people.

She walks down Garden Avenue to a small grocery store which sells penny candy. Three pennies are in her shoe—slipping back and forth between the sock and the inner sole. With each step she feels the painful press of the coins against her foot. A sweet, endurable, even cherished irritation, full of promise and delicate security. There is plenty of time to consider what to buy. Now, however, she moves down an avenue gently buffeted by the familiar and therefore loved images. The dandelions at the base of the telephone pole. Why, she wonders, do people call them weeds? She thought they were pretty. But grown-ups say, "Miss Dunion keeps her yard so nice. Not a dandelion anywhere." Hunkie women in black babushkas go into the fields with baskets to pull them up. But they do not want the yellow heads—only the jagged leaves. They make dandelion soup. Dandelion wine. Nobody loves the head of a dandelion. Maybe because they are so many, strong, and soon.

There was the sidewalk crack shaped like a Y, and the other one that lifted the concrete up from the dirt floor. Frequently her sloughing step had made her trip over that one. Skates would go well over this sidewalk—old it was, and smooth; it made the wheels glide evenly, with a mild whirr. The newly paved walks were bumpy and uncomfortable, and the sound of skate wheels on new walks was grating.

These and other inanimate things she saw and experienced. They were real to her. She knew them. They were the codes and touchstones of the world, capable of translation and possession. She owned the crack that made her stumble; she owned the clumps of dandelions whose white heads, last fall, she had blown away; whose yellow heads, this fall, she peered into. And owning them made her part of the world, and the world a part of her.

She climbs four wooden steps to the door of Yacobowski's Fresh Veg. Meat and Sundries Store. A bell tinkles as she opens it. Standing before the counter, she looks at the array of candies. All Mary Janes, she decides. Three for a penny. The resistant sweetness that breaks open at last to deliver peanut butter—the oil and salt which complement the sweet pull of caramel. A peal of anticipation unsettles her stomach.

She pulls off her shoe and takes out the three pennies. The gray head of Mr. Yacobowski looms up over the counter. He urges his eyes out of his thoughts to encounter her. Blue eyes. Blear-dropped. Slowly, like Indian summer moving imperceptibly toward fall, he looks toward her. Somewhere between retina and object, between vision and view, his eyes draw back, hesitate, and hover. At some fixed point in time and space he senses that he need not waste the effort of a glance. He does not see her, because for him there is nothing to see. How can a fifty-two-year-old white immigrant storekeeper with the taste of potatoes and beer in his mouth, his mind honed on the doe-eyed Virgin Mary, his sensibilities blunted by a permanent awareness of loss, *see* a little black girl? Nothing in his life even suggested that the feat was possible, not to say desirable or necessary.

"Yeah?"

She looks up at him and sees the vacuum where curiosity ought to lodge. And something more. The total absence of human recognition—the glazed separateness. She does not know what keeps his glance suspended. Perhaps because he is grown, or a man, and she a little girl. But she has seen interest, disgust, even anger in grown male eyes. Yet this vacuum is not new to her. It has an edge; somewhere in the bottom lid is the distaste. She has seen it lurking in the eyes of all white people. So. The distaste must be for her, her blackness. All things in her are flux and anticipation. But her blackness is static and dread. And it is the blackness that accounts for, that creates, the vacuum edged with distaste in white eyes.

She points her finger at the Mary Janes—a little black shaft of finger, its tip pressed on the display window. The quietly inoffensive assertion of a black child's attempt to communicate with a white adult.

"Them." The word is more sigh than sense.

"What? These? These?" Phlegm and impatience mingle in his voice.

She shakes her head, her fingertip fixed on the spot which, in her view, at any rate, identifies the Mary Janes. He cannot see her view—the angle of his vision, the slant of her finger, makes it incomprehensible to him. His lumpy red hand plops around in the glass casing like the agitated head of a chicken outraged by the loss of its body.

"Christ. Kantcha talk?"

His fingers brush the Mary Janes.

She nods.

"Well, why'nt you say so? One? How many?"

Pecola unfolds her fist, showing the three pennies. He scoots three Mary Janes toward her—three yellow rectangles in each pocket. She holds the money toward him. He hesitates, not wanting to touch her hand. She does not know how to move the finger of her right hand from the display counter or how to get the coins out of her left hand. Finally he reaches over and takes the pennies from her hand. His nails graze her damp palm.

Outside, Pecola feels the inexplicable shame ebb.

Dandelions. A dart of affection leaps out from her to them. But they do not look at her and do not send love back. She thinks, "They *are* ugly. They *are* weeds." Preoccupied with that revelation, she trips on the sidewalk crack. Anger stirs and wakes in her; it opens its mouth, and like a hot-mouthed puppy, laps up the dredges of her shame.

Anger is better. There is a sense of being in anger. A reality and presence. An awareness of worth. It is a lovely surging. Her thoughts fall back to Mr. Yacobowski's eyes, his phlegmy voice. The anger will not hold; the puppy is too easily surfeited. Its thirst too quickly quenched, it sleeps. The shame wells up again, its muddy rivulets seeping into her eyes. What to do before the tears come. She remembers the Mary Janes.

Each pale yellow wrapper has a picture on it. A picture of little Mary Jane, for whom the candy is named. Smiling white face. Blond hair in gentle disarray, blue eyes looking at her out of a world of clean comfort. The eyes are petulant, mischievous. To Pecola they are simply pretty. She eats the candy, and its sweetness is good. To eat the candy is somehow to eat the eyes, eat Mary Jane. Love Mary Jane. Be Mary Jane.

Three pennies had bought her nine lovely orgasms with Mary Jane. Lovely Mary Jane, for whom a candy is named.

Three whores lived in the apartment above the Breedloves' storefront. China, Poland, and Miss Marie. Pecola loved them, visited them, and ran their errands. They, in turn, did not despise her.

On an October morning, the morning of the stove-lid triumph, Pecola climbed the stairs to their apartment.

Even before the door was opened to her tapping, she could hear Poland singing—her voice sweet and hard, like new strawberries:

I got blues in my mealbarrel
Blues up on the shelf
I got blues in my mealbarrel
Blues up on the shelf
Blues in my bedroom
'Cause I'm sleepin' by myself

"Hi, dumplin'. Where your socks?" Marie seldom called Pecola the same thing twice, but invariably her epithets were fond ones chosen from menus and dishes that were forever uppermost in her mind.

"Hello, Miss Marie. Hello, Miss China. Hello, Miss Poland."

"You heard me. Where your socks? You as barelegged as a yard dog."

"I couldn't find any."

"Couldn't find any? Must be somethin' in your house that loves socks."

China chuckled. Whenever something was missing, Marie attributed its disappearance to "something in the house that loved it." "There is somethin' in this house that loves brassieres," she would say with alarm.

Poland and China were getting ready for the evening. Poland, forever ironing, forever singing. China, sitting on a pale-green kitchen chair, forever and forever curling her hair. Marie never got ready.

The women were friendly, but slow to begin talk. Pecola always took the initiative with Marie, who, once inspired, was difficult to stop.

"How come you got so many boyfriends, Miss Marie?"

"*Boy*friends? *Boy*friends? Chittlin', I ain't seen a *boy* since nineteen and twenty-seven."

"You didn't see none then." China stuck the hot curlers into a tin of Nu Nile hair dressing. The oil hissed at the touch of the hot metal.

"How come, Miss Marie?" Pecola insisted.

"How come what? How come I ain't seen a boy since nineteen and twenty-seven? Because they ain't *been* no boys since then. That's when they stopped. Folks started gettin' born old."

"You mean that's when *you* got old," China said.

"I ain't never got old. Just fat."

"Same thing."

"You think 'cause you skinny, folks think you young? You'd make a haint buy a girdle."

"And you look like the north side of a south-bound mule."

"All I know is, them bandy little legs of yours is every bit as old as mine."

"Don't worry 'bout my bandy legs. That's the first thing they push aside."

All three of the women laughed. Marie threw back her head. From deep inside, her laughter came like the sound of many rivers, freely, deeply, muddily, heading for the room of an open sea. China giggled spastically. Each gasp seemed to be yanked out of her by an unseen hand jerking an unseen string. Poland, who seldom spoke unless she was drunk, laughed without sound. When she was sober she hummed mostly or chanted blues songs, of which she knew many.

Pecola fingered the fringe of a scarf that lay on the back of a sofa. "I never seen nobody with as many boyfriends as you got, Miss Marie. How come they all love you?"

Marie opened a bottle of root beer. "What else they gone do? They know I'm rich and good-lookin'. They wants to put their toes in my curly hair, and get at my money."

"You rich, Miss Marie?"

"Puddin', I got money's mammy."

"Where you get it from? You don't do no work."

"Yeah," said China, "where you get it from?"

"Hoover give it me. I did him a favor once, for the F. B. and I."

"What'd you do?"

"I did him a favor. They wanted to catch this crook, you see. Name of Johnny. He was as low-down as they come. . . ."

"We *know* that." China arranged a curl.

". . . the F. B. and I. wanted him bad. He killed more people than TB. And if you *crossed* him? Whoa, Jesus! He'd run you as long as there was ground. Well, I was little and cute then. No more than ninety pounds, soaking wet."

"You ain't never been soaking wet," China said.

"Well, you ain't never been dry. Shut up. Let me tell you, sweetnin'. To tell it true, I was the only one could handle him. He'd go out and rob a bank or kill some people, and I'd say to him, soft-like, 'Johnny, you shouldn't do that.' And he'd say he just had to bring me pretty things. Lacy drawers and all. And every Saturday we'd get a case of beer and fry up some fish. We'd fry it in meal and egg batter, you know, and when it was all brown and crisp—not hard, though—we'd break open that cold beer. . . ." Marie's eyes went soft as the memory of just such a meal sometime, somewhere transfixed her. All her stories were subject to breaking down at descriptions of food. Pecola saw Marie's teeth settling down into the back of crisp sea bass; saw the fat fingers putting back into her mouth tiny flakes of white, hot meat that had escaped from her lips; she heard the "pop" of the beer-bottle cap; smelled the acridness of the first stream of vapor; felt the cold beeriness hit the tongue. She ended the daydream long before Marie.

"But what about the money?" she asked.

China hooted. "She's makin' like she's the Lady in Red that told on Dillinger. Dillinger wouldn't have come near you lessen he was going hunting in Africa and shoot you for a hippo."

"Well, this hippo had a ball back in Chicago. Whoa Jesus, ninety-nine!"

"How come you always say 'Whoa Jesus' and a number?" Pecola had long wanted to know.

"Because my mama taught me never to cuss."

"Did she teach you not to drop your drawers?" China asked.

"Didn't have none," said Marie. "Never saw a pair of drawers till I was fifteen, when I left Jackson and was doing day work in Cincinnati. My white lady gave me some old ones of hers. I thought they was some kind of stocking cap. I put it on my head when I dusted. When she saw me, she liked to fell out."

"You must have been one dumb somebody." China lit a cigarette and cooled her irons.

"How'd I know?" Marie paused. "And what's the use of putting on something you got to keep taking off all the time? Dewey never let me keep them on long enough to get used to them."

"Dewey who?" This was a somebody new to Pecola.

"Dewey who? Chicken! You never heard me tell of *Dewey?*" Marie was shocked by her negligence.

"No, ma'am."

"Oh, honey, you've missed half your life. Whoa Jesus, one-nine-five. You talkin' 'bout smooth! I met him when I was fourteen. We ran away and lived together like married for three years. You know all those klinker-tops you see runnin' up here? Fifty of 'em in a bowl wouldn't make a Dewey Prince ankle bone. Oh, Lord. How that man loved me!"

China arranged a fingerful of hair into a bang effect. "Then why he left you to sell tail?"

"Girl, when I found out I could sell it—that somebody would pay cold cash for it, you could have knocked me over with a feather."

Poland began to laugh. Soundlessly. "Me too. My auntie whipped me good that first time when I told her I didn't get no money. I said 'Money? For what? He didn't owe me nothin'.' She said, 'The hell he didn't!' "

They all dissolved in laughter.

Three merry gargoyles. Three merry harridans. Amused by a long-ago time of ignorance. They did not belong to those generations of prostitutes created in novels, with great and generous hearts, dedicated, because of the horror of circumstance, to ameliorating the luckless, barren life of men, taking money incidentally and humbly for their "understanding." Nor were they from that sensitive breed of young girl, gone wrong at the hands of fate, forced to cultivate an outward brittleness in order to protect her springtime from further shock, but knowing full well she was cut out for better things, and could make the right man happy. Neither were they the sloppy, inadequate whores who, unable to make a living at it alone, turn to drug consumption and traffic or pimps to help complete their scheme of self-destruction, avoiding suicide only to punish the memory of some absent father or to sustain the misery of some silent mother. Except for Marie's fabled love for Dewey Prince, these women hated men, all men, without shame, apology, or discrimination. They abused their visitors with a scorn grown mechanical from use. Black men, white men, Puerto Ricans, Mexicans, Jews, Poles, whatever—all were inadequate and weak, all came under their jaundiced eyes and were the recipients of their disinterested wrath. They took delight in cheating them. On one occasion the town well knew, they lured a Jew up the stairs, pounced on him, all three, held him up by the heels, shook everything out of his pants pockets, and threw him out of the window.

Neither did they have respect for women, who, although not their colleagues, so to speak, nevertheless deceived their husbands—regularly or irregularly, it made no difference. "Sugar-coated whores," they called them, and did not yearn to be in their shoes. Their only respect was for what they would have described as "good Christian colored women." The woman whose reputation was spotless, and who tended to her family, who didn't drink or smoke or run around. These women had their undying, if covert, affection. They would sleep with their husbands, and take their money, but always with a vengeance.

Nor were they protective and solicitous of youthful innocence. They looked back on their own youth as a period of ignorance, and regretted that they had not made more of it. They were not young girls in whores' clothing, or whores regretting their loss of innocence. They were whores in whores' clothing, whores who had never been young and had no word for innocence. With Pecola they were as free as they were with each other. Marie concocted stories for her because she was a child, but the stories were breezy and rough. If Pecola had announced her intention to live the life they did, they would not have tried to dissuade her or voiced any alarm.

"You and Dewey Prince have any children, Miss Marie?"

"Yeah. Yeah. We had some." Marie fidgeted. She pulled a bobby pin from her hair and began to pick her teeth. That meant she didn't want to talk anymore.

Pecola went to the window and looked down at the empty street. A tuft of grass had forced its way up through a crack in the sidewalk, only to meet a raw October wind. She thought of Dewey Prince and how he loved Miss Marie. What did love feel like? she wondered. How do grown-ups act when they love each other? Eat fish together? Into her eyes came the picture of Cholly and Mrs. Breedlove in bed. He making sounds as though he were in pain, as though something had him by the throat and wouldn't let go. Terrible as his noises were, they were not nearly as bad as the no noise at all from her mother. It was as though she was not even there. Maybe that was love. Choking sounds and silence.

Turning her eyes from the window, Pecola looked at the women.

China had changed her mind about the bangs and was arranging a small but sturdy pompadour. She was adept in creating any number of hair styles, but each one left her with a pinched and harassed look. Then she applied makeup heavily. Now she gave herself surprised eyebrows and a cupid-bow mouth. Later she would make Oriental eyebrows and an evilly slashed mouth.

Poland, in her sweet strawberry voice, began another song:

I know a boy who is sky-soft brown
I know a boy who is sky-soft brown
The dirt leaps for joy when his feet touch the
 ground.
 His strut is a peacock
 His eye is burning brass
 His smile is sorghum syrup drippin' slow-
 sweet to the last
I know a boy who is sky-soft brown

Marie sat shelling peanuts and popping them into her mouth. Pecola looked and looked at the women. Were they real? Marie belched, softly, purringly, lovingly.

Winter

My daddy's face is a study. Winter moves into it and presides there. His eyes become a cliff of snow threatening to avalanche; his eyebrows bend like black limbs of leafless trees. His skin takes on the pale, cheerless yellow of winter sun; for a jaw he has the edges of a snowbound field dotted with stubble; his high forehead is the frozen sweep of the Erie, hiding currents of gelid thoughts that eddy in darkness. Wolf killer turned hawk fighter, he worked night and day to keep one from the door and the other from under the windowsills. A Vulcan guarding the flames, he gives us instructions about which doors to keep closed or opened for proper distribution of heat, lays kindling by, discusses qualities of coal, and teaches us how to rake, feed, and bank the fire. And he will not unrazor his lips until spring.

Winter tightened our heads with a band of cold and melted our eyes. We put pepper in the feet of our stockings, Vaseline on our faces, and stared through dark icebox mornings at four stewed prunes, slippery lumps of oatmeal, and cocoa with a roof of skin.

But mostly we waited for spring, when there could be gardens.

By the time this winter had stiffened itself into a hateful knot that nothing could loosen, something did loosen it, or rather someone. A someone who splintered the knot into silver threads that tangled us, netted us, made us long for the dull chafe of the previous boredom.

This disrupter of seasons was a new girl in school named Maureen Peal. A high-yellow dream child with long brown hair braided into two lynch ropes that hung down her back. She was rich, at least by our standards, as rich as the richest of the white girls, swaddled in comfort and care. The quality of her clothes threatened to derange Frieda and me. Patent-leather shoes with buckles, a cheaper version of which we got only at Easter and which had disintegrated by the end of May. Fluffy sweaters the color of lemon drops tucked into skirts with pleats so orderly they astounded us. Brightly colored knee socks with white borders, a brown velvet coat trimmed in white rabbit fur, and a matching muff. There was a hint of spring in her sloe green eyes, something summery in her complexion, and a rich autumn ripeness in her walk.

She enchanted the entire school. When teachers called on her, they smiled encouragingly. Black boys didn't trip her in the halls; white boys didn't stone her, white girls didn't suck their teeth when she was assigned to be their work partners; black girls stepped aside when she wanted to use the sink in the girls' toilet, and their eyes genuflected under sliding lids. She never had to search for anybody to eat with in the cafeteria—they flocked to the table of her choice, where she opened fastidious lunches, shaming our jelly-stained bread with egg-salad sandwiches cut into four dainty squares, pink-frosted cupcakes, stocks of celery and carrots, proud, dark apples. She even bought and liked white milk.

Frieda and I were bemused, irritated, and fascinated by her. We looked hard for flaws to restore our equilibrium, but had to be content at first with uglying up her name, changing Maureen Peal to Meringue Pie. Later a minor epiphany was ours when we discovered that she had a dog tooth—a charming one to be sure—but a dog tooth nonetheless. And when we found out that she had been born with six fingers on each hand and that there was a little bump where each extra one had been removed, we smiled. They were small triumphs, but we took what we could get—snickering behind her back and calling her Six-finger-dog-tooth-meringue-pie. But we had to do it alone, for none of the other girls would cooperate with our hostility. They adored her.

When she was assigned a locker next to mine, I could indulge my jealousy four times a day. My sister and I both suspected that we were secretly prepared to be her friend, if she would let us, but I knew it would be a dangerous friendship, for when my eye traced the white border patterns of those Kelly-green knee socks, and felt the pull and slack of my brown stockings, I wanted to kick her. An when I thought of the unearned haughtiness in her eyes, I plotted accidental slammings of locker doors on her hand.

As locker friends, however, we got to know each other a little, and I was even able to hold a sensible conversation with her without visualizing her fall off a cliff, or giggling my way into what I thought was a clever insult.

One day, while I waited at the locker for Frieda, she joined me.

"Hi."

"Hi."

"Waiting for your sister?"

"Uh-huh."

"Which way do you go home?"

"Down Twenty-first Street to Broadway."

"Why don't you go down Twenty-second Street?"

" 'Cause I live on Twenty-first Street."

"Oh. I can walk that way, I guess. Partly, anyway."

"Free country."

Frieda came toward us, her brown stockings straining at the knees because she had tucked the toe under to hide a hole in the foot.

"Maureen's gonna walk part way with us."

Frieda and I exchanged glances, her eyes begging my restraint, mine promising nothing.

It was a false spring day, which, like Maureen, had pierced the shell of a deadening winter. There were puddles, mud, and an inviting warmth that deluded us. The kind of day on which we draped our coats over our heads, left our galoshes in school, and came down with croup the following day. We always responded to the slightest change in weather, the most minute shifts in time of day. Long before seeds were stirring, Frieda and I were scruffing and poking at the earth, swallowing air, drinking rain. . . .

As we emerged from the school with Maureen, we began to moult immediately. We put our head scarves in our coat pockets, and our coats on our heads. I was wondering how to maneuver Maureen's fur muff into a gutter when a commotion in the playground distracted us. A group of boys was circling and holding at bay a victim, Pecola Breedlove.

Bay Boy, Woodrow Cain, Buddy Wilson, Junie Bug—like a necklace of semiprecious stones they surrounded her. Heady with the smell of their own musk, thrilled by the easy power of a majority, they gaily harassed her.

"Black e mo. Black e mo. Yadaddsleepsnekked. Black e mo black e mo ya dadd sleeps nekked. Black e mo . . ."

They had extemporized a verse made up of two insults about matters over which the victim had no control: the color of her skin and speculations on the sleeping habits of an adult, wildly fitting in its incoherence. That they themselves were black, or that their own father had similarly relaxed habits was irrelevant. It was their contempt for their own blackness that gave the first insult its teeth. They seemed to have taken all of their smoothly cultivated ignorance, their exquisitely learned self-hatred, their elaborately designed hopelessness and sucked it all up into a fiery cone of scorn that had burned for ages in the hollows of their minds—cooled—and spilled over lips of outrage, consuming whatever was in its path. They danced a macabre ballet around the victim, whom, for their own sake, they were prepared to sacrifice to the flaming pit.

Black e mo Black e mo Ya daddy sleeps nekked.
Stch ta ta stch ta ta
stach ta ta ta ta ta

Pecola edged around the circle crying. She had dropped her notebook, and covered her eyes with her hands.

We watched, afraid they might notice us and turn their energies our way. Then Frieda, with set lips and Mama's eyes, snatched her coat from her head and threw it on the ground. She ran toward them and brought her books down on Woodrow Cain's head. The circle broke. Woodrow Cain grabbed his head.

"Hey, girl!"

"You cut that out, you hear?" I had never heard Frieda's voice so loud and clear.

Maybe because Frieda was taller than he was, maybe because he saw her eyes, maybe because he had lost interest in the game, or maybe because he had a crush on Frieda, in any case Woodrow looked frightened just long enough to give her more courage.

"Leave her 'lone, or I'm gone tell everybody what you did!"

Woodrow did not answer; he just walled his eyes.

Bay Boy piped up, "Go on, gal! Ain't nobody bothering you."

"You shut up, Bullet Head." I had found my tongue.

"Who you calling Bullet Head?"

"I'm calling you Bullet Head, Bullet Head."

Frieda took Pecola's hand. "Come on."

"You want a fat lip?" Bay Boy drew back his fist at me.

"Yeah. Gimme one of yours."

"You gone get one."

Maureen appeared at my elbow, and the boys seemed reluctant to continue under her springtime eyes so wide with interest. They buckled in confusion, not willing to beat up three girls under her watchful gaze. So they listened to a budding male instinct that told them to pretend we were unworthy of their attention.

"Come on, man."

"Yeah. Come on. We ain't got time to fool with them."

Grumbling a few disinterested epithets, they moved away.

I picked up Pecola's notebook and Frieda's coat, and the four of us left the playground.

"Old Bullet Head, he's always picking on girls."

Frieda agreed with me. "Miss Forrester said he was incorrigival."

"Really?" I didn't know what that meant, but it had enough of a doom sound in it to be true of Bay Boy.

While Frieda and I clucked on about the near fight, Maureen, suddenly animated, put her velvet-sleeved arm through Pecola's and began to behave as though they were the closest of friends.

"I just moved here. My name is Maureen Peal. What's yours?"

"Pecola."

"Pecola? Wasn't that the name of the girl in *Imitation of Life*?"

"I don't know. What is that?"

"The picture show, you know. Where this mulatto girl hates her mother cause she is black and ugly but then cries at the funeral. It was real sad. Everybody cries in it. Claudette Colbert too."

"Oh." Pecola's voice was no more than a sigh.

"Anyway, her name was Pecola too. She was so pretty. When it comes back, I'm going to see it again. My mother has seen it four times."

Frieda and I walked behind them, surprised at Maureen's friendliness to Pecola, but pleased. Maybe she wasn't so bad, after all. Frieda had put her coat back on her head, and the two of us, so draped, trotted along enjoying the warm breeze and Frieda's heroics.

"You're in my gym class, aren't you?" Maureen asked Pecola.

"Yes."

"Miss Erkmeister's legs are bow. I bet she thinks they're cute. How come she gets to wear real shorts, and we have to wear those old bloomers? I want to die every time I put them on."

Pecola smiled but did not look at Maureen.

"Hey." Maureen stopped short. "There's an Isaley's. Want some ice cream? I have money."

She unzipped a hidden pocket in her muff and pulled out a multifolded dollar bill. I forgave her those knee socks.

"My uncle sued Isaley's," Maureen said to the three of us. "He sued the Isaley's in Akron. They said he was disorderly and that that was why they wouldn't serve him, but a friend of his, a policeman, came in and beared the witness, so the suit went through."

"What's a suit?"

"It's when you can beat them up if you want to and won't anybody do nothing. Our family does it all the time. We believe in suits."

At the entrance to Isaley's Maureen turned to Frieda and me, asking, "You all going to buy some ice cream?"

We looked at each other. "No," Frieda said.

Maureen disappeared into the store with Pecola.

Frieda looked placidly down the street; I opened my mouth, but quickly closed it. It was extremely important that the world not know that I fully expected Maureen to buy us some ice cream, that for the past 120 seconds I had been selecting the flavor, that I had begun to like Maureen, and that neither of us had a penny.

We supposed Maureen was being nice to Pecola because of the boys, and were embarrassed to be caught—even by each other—thinking that she would treat us, or that we deserved it as much as Pecola did.

The girls came out. Pecola with two dips of orange-pineapple, Maureen with black raspberry.

"You should have got some," she said. "They had all kinds. Don't eat down to the tip of the cone," she advised Pecola.

"Why?"

"Because there's a fly in there."

"How you know?"

"Oh, not really. A girl told me she found one in the bottom of hers once, and ever since then she throws that part away."

"Oh."

We passed the Dreamland Theater, and Betty Grable smiled down at us.

"Don't you just love her?" Maureen asked.

"Uh-huh," said Pecola.

I differed. "Hedy Lamarr is better."

Maureen agreed. "Ooooo yes. My mother told me that a girl named Audrey, she went to the beauty parlor where we lived before, and asked the lady to fix her hair like Hedy Lamarr's, and the lady said, 'Yeah, when you grow some hair like Hedy Lamarr's.'" She laughed long and sweet.

"Sounds crazy," said Frieda.

"She sure is. Do you know she doesn't even menstrate yet, and she's sixteen. Do you, yet?"

"Yes." Pecola glanced at us.

"So do I." Maureen made no attempt to disguise her pride. "Two months ago I started. My girl friend in Toledo, where we lived before, said when she started she was scared to death. Thought she had killed herself."

"Do you know what it's for?" Pecola asked the question as though hoping to provide the answer herself.

"For babies." Maureen raised two pencil-stroke eyebrows at the obviousness of the question. "Babies need blood when they are inside you, and if you are having a baby, then you don't menstrate. But when you're not having a baby, then you don't have to save the blood, so it comes out."

"How do babies get the blood?" asked Pecola.

"Through the like-line. You know. Where your belly button is. That is where the like-line grows from and pumps the blood to the baby."

"Well, if the belly buttons are to grow like-lines to give the baby blood, and only girls have babies, how come boys have belly buttons?"

Maureen hesitated. "I don't know," she admitted. "But boys have all sorts of things they don't need." Her tinkling laughter was somehow stronger than our nervous ones. She curled her tongue around the edge of the cone, scooping up a dollop of purple that made my eyes water. We were waiting for a stop light to change. Maureen kept scooping the ice cream from around the cone's edge with her tongue; she didn't bite the edge as I would have done. Her tongue circled the cone. Pecola had finished hers; Maureen evidently liked her things to last. While I was thinking about her ice cream, she must have been thinking about her last remark, for she said to Pecola, "Did you ever see a naked man?"

Pecola blinked, then looked away. "No. Where would I see a naked man?"

"I don't know. I just asked."

"I wouldn't even look at him, even if I did see him. That's dirty. Who wants to see a naked man?" Pecola was agitated. "Nobody's father would be naked in front of his own daughter. Not unless he was dirty too."

"I didn't say 'father.' I just said 'a naked man.'"

"Well . . ."

"How come you said 'father'?" Maureen wanted to know.

"Who else would she see, dog tooth?" I was glad to have a chance to show anger. Not only because of the ice cream, but because we had seen our own father naked and didn't care to be reminded of it and feel the shame brought on by the absence of shame. He had been walking down the hall from the bathroom into his bedroom and passed the open door of our room. We had lain there wide-eyed. He stopped and looked in, trying to see in the dark room whether we were really asleep—or was it his imagination that opened eyes were looking at him? Apparently he convinced himself that we were sleeping. He moved away, confident that his little girls would not lie open-eyed like that, staring, staring. When he had moved on, the dark took only him away, not his nakedness. That stayed in the room with us. Friendly-like.

"I'm not talking to you," said Maureen. "Besides, I don't care if she sees her father naked. She can look at him all day if she wants to. Who cares?"

"You do," said Frieda. "That's all you talk about."

"It is not."

"It is so. Boys, babies, and somebody's naked daddy. You must be boy-crazy."

"You better be quiet."

"Who's gonna make me?" Frieda put her hand on her hip and jutted her face toward Maureen.

"You all ready made. Mammy made."

"You stop talking about my mama."

"Well, you stop talking about my daddy."

"Who said anything about your old daddy?"

"You did."

"Well, you started it."

"I wasn't even talking to you. I was talking to Pecola."

"Yeah. About seeing her naked daddy."

"So what if she did see him?"

Pecola shouted, "I never saw my daddy naked. Never."

"You did too," Maureen snapped. "Bay Boy said so."

"I did not."

"You did."

"I did not."

"Did. Your own daddy, too!"

Pecola tucked her head in—a funny, sad, helpless movement. A kind of hunching of the shoulders, pulling in of the neck, as though she wanted to cover her ears.

"You stop talking about her daddy," I said.

"What do I care about her old black daddy?" asked Maureen.

"Black? Who you calling black?"

"You!"

"You think you so cute!" I swung at her and missed, hitting Pecola in the face. Furious at my clumsiness, I threw my notebook at her, but it caught her in the small of her velvet back, for she had turned and was flying across the street against traffic.

Safe on the other side, she screamed at us, "I *am* cute! And you ugly! Black and ugly black e mos. I *am* cute!"

She ran down the street, the green knee socks making her legs look like wild dandelion stems that had somehow lost their heads. The weight of her remark stunned us, and it was a second or two before Frieda and I collected ourselves enough to shout, "Six-finger-dog-tooth-meringue-pie!" We chanted this most powerful of our arsenal of insults as long as we could see the green stems and rabbit fur.

Grown people frowned at the three girls on the curbside, two with their coats draped over their heads, the collars framing the eyebrows like nuns' habits, black garters showing where they bit the tops of brown stockings that barely covered the knees, angry faces knotted like dark cauliflowers.

Pecola stood a little apart from us, her eyes hinged in the direction in which Maureen had fled. She seemed to fold into herself, like a pleated wing. Her pain antagonized me. I wanted to open her up, crisp her edges, ram a stick down that hunched and curving spine, force her to stand erect and spit the misery out on the streets. But she held it in where it could lap up into her eyes.

Frieda snatched her coat from her head. "Come on, Claudia. 'Bye, Pecola."

We walked quickly at first, and then slower, pausing every now and then to fasten garters, tie shoelaces, scratch, or examine old scars. We were sinking under the wisdom, accuracy, and relevance of Maureen's last words. If she was cute—and if anything could be believed, she *was*—then we were not. And what did that mean? We were lesser. Nicer, brighter, but still lesser. Dolls we could destroy, but we could not destroy the honey voices of parents and aunts, the obedience in the eyes of our peers, the slippery light in the eyes of our teachers when they encountered the Maureen Peals of the world. What was the secret? What did we lack? Why was it important? And so what? Guileless and without vanity, we were still in love with ourselves then. We felt comfortable in our skins, enjoyed the news that our senses released to us, admired our dirt, cultivated our scars, and could not comprehend this unworthiness. Jealousy we understood and thought natural—a desire to have what somebody else had; but envy was a strange, new feeling for us. And all the time we knew that Maureen Peal was not the Enemy and not worthy of such intense hatred. The *Thing* to fear was the *Thing* that made *her* beautiful, and not us.

The house was quiet when we opened the door. The acrid smell of simmering turnips filled our cheeks with sour saliva.

"Mama!"

There was no answer, but a sound of feet. Mr. Henry shuffled part of the way down the stairs. One thick, hairless leg leaned out of his bathrobe.

"Hello there, Greta Garbo; hello, Ginger Rogers."

We gave him the giggle he was accustomed to. "Hello, Mr. Henry. Where's Mama?"

"She went to your grandmaw's. Left word for you to cut off the turnips and eat some graham crackers till she got back. They in the kitchen."

We sat in silence at the kitchen table, crumbling the crackers into anthills. In a little while Mr. Henry came back down the stairs. Now he had his trousers on under his robe.

"Say. Wouldn't you all like some cream?"

"Oh, yes, sir."

"Here. Here's a quarter. Gone over to Isaley's and get yourself some cream. You been good girls, ain't you?"

His light-green words restored color to the day. "Yes, sir. Thank you, Mr. Henry. Will you tell Mama for us if she comes?"

"Sure. But she ain't due back for a spell."

Coatless, we left the house and had gotten all the way to the corner when Frieda said, "I don't want to go to Isaley's."

"What?"

"I don't want ice cream. I want potato chips."

"They got potato chips at Isaley's."

"I know, but why go all that long way? Miss Bertha got potato chips."

"But I want ice cream."

"No you don't, Claudia."

"I do too."

"Well, you go on to Isaley's. I'm going to Miss Bertha's."

"But you got the quarter, and I don't want to go all the way up there by myself."

"Then let's go to Miss Bertha's. You like her candy, don't you?"

"It's always stale, and she always runs out of stuff."

"Today is Friday. She orders fresh on Friday."

"And then that crazy old Soaphead Church lives there."

"So what? We're together. We'll run if he does anything at us."

"He scares me."

"Well, I don't want to go up by Isaley's. Suppose Meringue Pie is hanging around. You want to run into her, Claudia?"

"Come on, Frieda. I'll get candy."

Miss Bertha had a small candy, snuff, and tobacco store. One brick room sitting in her front yard. You had to peep in the door, and if she wasn't there, you knocked on the door of her house in back. This day she was sitting behind the counter reading a Bible in a tube of sunlight.

Frieda bought potato chips, and we got three Powerhouse bars for ten cents, and had a dime left. We hurried back home to sit under the lilac bushes on the side of the house. We always did our Candy Dance there so Rosemary could see us and get jealous. The Candy Dance was a humming, skipping, foot-tapping, eating, smacking combination that overtook us when we had sweets. Creeping between the bushes and the side of the house, we heard voices and laughter. We looked into the living-room window, expecting to see Mama. Instead we saw Mr. Henry and two women. In a playful manner, the way grandmothers do with babies, he was sucking the fingers of one of the women, whose laughter filled a tiny place over his head. The other woman was buttoning her coat. We knew immediately who they were, and our flesh crawled. One was China, and the other was called the Maginot Line. The back of my neck itched. These were the fancy women of the maroon nail polish that Mama and Big Mama hated. And in our house.

China was not too terrible, at least not in our imaginations. She was thin, aging, absent-minded, and unaggressive. But the Maginot Line. That was the one my mother said she "wouldn't let eat out of one of her plates." That was the one church women never allowed their eyes to rest on. That was the one who had killed people, set them on fire, poisoned them, cooked them in lye. Although I thought the Maginot Line's face, hidden under all that fat, was really sweet, I had heard too many black and red words about her, seen too many mouths go triangle at the mention of her name, to dwell on any redeeming features she might have.

Showing brown teeth, China seemed to be genuinely enjoying Mr. Henry. The sight of him licking her fingers brought to mind the girlie magazines in his room. A cold wind blew somewhere in me, lifting little leaves of terror and obscure longing. I thought I saw a mild lonesomeness cross the face of the Maginot Line. But it may have been my own image that I saw in the slow flaring of her nostrils, in her eyes that reminded me of waterfalls in movies about Hawaii.

The Maginot Line yawned and said, "Come on, China. We can't hang in here all day. Them people be home soon." She moved toward the door.

Frieda and I dropped down to the ground, looking wildly into each other's eyes. When the women were some distance away, we went inside. Mr. Henry was in the kitchen opening a bottle of pop.

"Back already?"

"Yes, sir."

"Cream all gone?" His little teeth looked so kindly and helpless. Was that really our Mr. Henry with China's fingers?

"We got candy instead."

"You did huh? Ole sugar-tooth Greta Garbo."

He wiped the bottle sweat and turned it up to his lips—a gesture that made me uncomfortable.

"Who were those women, Mr. Henry?"

He choked on the pop and looked at Frieda. "What you say?"

"Those women," she repeated, "who just left. Who were they?"

"Oh." He laughed the grown-up getting-ready-to-lie laugh. A heh-heh we knew well.

"Those were some members of my Bible class. We read the scriptures together, and so they came today to read with me."

"Oh," said Frieda. I was looking at his house slippers to keep from seeing those kindly teeth frame a lie. He walked toward the stairs and then turned back to us.

"Bed' not mention it to your mother. She don't take to so much Bible study and don't like me having visitors, even if they good Christians."

"No, sir, Mr. Henry. We won't."

He rapidly mounted the stairs.

"Should we?" I asked. "Tell Mama?"

Frieda sighed. She had not even opened her Powerhouse bar or her potato chips, and now she traced the letters on the candy wrappers with her fingers. Suddenly she lifted her head and began to look all around the kitchen.

"No. I guess not. No plates are out."

"Plates? What you talking about now?"

"No plates are out. The Maginot Line didn't eat out of one of Mama's plates. Besides, Mama would just full all day if we told her."

We sat down and looked at the graham-cracker anthills we had made.

"We better cut off the turnips. They'll burn, and Mama will whip us," she said.

"I know."

"But if we let them burn, we won't have to eat them."

"Heyyy, what a lovely idea," I thought.

"Which you want? A whipping and no turnips, or turnips and no whippings?"

"I don't know. Maybe we could burn them just a little so Mama and Daddy can eat them, but we can say we can't."

"O.K."

I made a volcano out of my anthill.

"Frieda?"

"What?"

"What did Woodrow do that you was gonna tell?"

"Wet the bed. Mrs. Cain told Mama he won't quit."

"Old nasty."

The sky was getting dark; I looked out of the window and saw snow falling. I poked my finger down into the mouth of my volcano, and it toppled, dispersing the golden grains into little swirls. The turnip pot crackled.

SEETHECATITGOESMEOWMEOWCOMEAN DPLAYCOMEPLAYWITHJANETHEKITTENW ILLNOTPLAYPLAYPLAYPLA

They come from Mobile. Aiken. From Newport News. From Marietta. From Meridian. And the sound of these places in their mouths make you think of love. When you ask them where they are from, they tilt their heads and say "Mobile" and you think you've been kissed. They say "Aiken" and you see a white butterfly glance off a fence with a torn wing. They say "Nagadoches" and you want to say "Yes, I will." You don't know what these towns are like, but you love what happens to the air when they open their lips and let the names ease out.

Meridian. The sound of it opens the windows of a room like the first four notes of a hymn. Few people can say the names of their home towns with such sly affection. Perhaps because they don't have home towns, just places where they were born. But these girls soak up the juice of their home towns, and it never leaves them. They are thin brown girls who have looked long at hollyhocks in the backyards of Meridian, Mobile, Aiken, and Baton Rouge. And like hollyhocks they are narrow, tall, and still. Their roots are deep, their stalks are firm, and only the top blossom nods in the wind. They have the eyes of people who can tell what time it is by the color of the sky. Such girls live in quiet black neighborhoods where everybody is gainfully employed. Where there are porch swings hanging from chains. Where the grass is cut with a scythe, where rooster combs and sunflowers grow in the yards, and pots of bleeding heart, ivy, and mother-in-law tongue line the steps and windowsills. Such girls have bought watermelon and snapbeans from the fruit man's wagon. They have put in the window the cardboard sign that has a pound measure printed on each of three edges—10 lbs., 25 lbs., 50 lbs.—and NO ICE on the fourth. These particular brown girls from Mobile and Aiken are not like some of their sisters. They are not fretful, nervous, or shrill; they do not have lovely black necks that stretch as though against an invisible collar; their eyes do not bite. These sugar-brown Mobile girls move through the streets without a stir. They are as sweet and plain as buttercake. Slim ankles; long, narrow feet. They wash themselves with orange-colored Lifebuoy soap, dust themselves with Cashmere Bouquet talc, clean their teeth with salt on a piece of rag, soften their skin with Jergens Lotion. They smell like wood, newspapers, and vanilla. They straighten their hair with Dixie Peach, and part it on the side. At night they curl it in paper from brown bags, tie a print scarf around their heads, and sleep with hands folded across their stomachs. They do not drink, smoke, or swear, and they still call sex "nookey." They sing second soprano in the choir, and although their voices are clear and steady, they are never picked to solo. They are in the second row, white blouses starched, blue skirts almost purple from ironing.

They go to land-grant colleges, normal schools, and learn how to do the white man's work with refinement: home economics to prepare his food; teacher education to instruct black children in obedience; music to soothe the weary master and entertain his blunted soul. Here they learn the rest of the lesson begun in those soft houses with porch swings and pots of bleeding heart: how to behave. The careful development of thrift, patience, high morals, and good manners. In short, how to get rid of the funkiness. The dreadful funkiness of passion, the funkiness of nature, the funkiness of the wide range of human emotions.

Wherever it erupts, this Funk, they wipe it away; where it crusts, they dissolve it; wherever it drips, flowers, or clings, they find it and fight it until it dies. They fight this battle all the way to the grave. The laugh that is a little too loud; the enunciation a little too round; the gesture a little too generous. They hold their behind in for fear of a sway too free; when they wear lipstick, they never cover the entire mouth for fear of lips too thick, and they worry, worry, worry about the edges of their hair.

They never seem to have boyfriends, but they always marry. Certain men watch them, without seeming to, and know that if such a girl is in his house, he will sleep on sheets boiled white, hung out to dry on juniper bushes, and pressed flat with a heavy iron. There will be pretty paper flowers decorating the picture of his mother, a large Bible in the front room. They feel secure. They know their work clothes will be mended, washed, and ironed on Monday, that their Sunday shirts will billow on hangers from the door jamb, stiffly starched and white. They look at her hands and know what she will do with biscuit dough; they smell the coffee and the fried ham; see the white, smoky grits with a dollop of butter on top. Her hips assure them that she will bear children easily and painlessly. And they are right.

What they do not know is that this plain brown girl will build her nest stick by stick, make it her own inviolable world, and stand guard over its every plant, weed, and doily, even against him. In silence will she return the lamp to where she put it in the first place; remove the dishes from the table as soon as the last bite is taken; wipe the doorknob after a greasy hand has touched it. A sidelong look will be enough to tell him to smoke on the back porch. Children will sense instantly that they cannot come into her yard to retrieve a ball. But the men do not know these things. Nor do they know that she will give him her body sparingly and partially. He must enter her surreptitiously, lifting the hem of her nightgown only to her navel. He must rest his weight on his elbows when they make love, ostensibly to avoid hurting her breasts but actually to keep her from having to touch or feel too much of him.

While he moves inside her, she will wonder why then didn't put the necessary but private parts of the body in some more convenient place—like the armpit, for example, or the palm of the hand. Someplace one could get to easily, and quickly, without undressing. She stiffens when she feels one of her paper curlers coming undone from the activity of love; imprints in her mind which one it is that is coming loose so she can quickly secure it once he is through. She hopes he will not sweat—the damp may get into her hair; and that she will remain dry between the legs—she hates the glucking sound they make when she is moist. When she senses some spasm about to grip him, she will make rapid movements with her hips, press her fingernails into his back, suck in her breath, and pretend she is having an orgasm. She might wonder again, for the six hundredth time, what it would be like to have *that* feeling while her husband's penis is inside her. The closest thing to it was the time she was walking down the street and her napkin slipped free of her sanitary belt. It moved gently between her legs as she walked. Gently, ever so gently. And then a slight and distinctly delicious sensation collected in her crotch. As the delight grew, she had to stop in the street, hold her thighs together to contain it. That must be what it is like, she thinks, but it never happens while he is inside her. When he withdraws, she pulls her nightgown down, slips out of the bed and into the bathroom with relief.

Occasionally some living thing will engage her affections. A cat, perhaps, who will love her order, precision, and constancy; who will be as clean and quiet as she is. The cat will settle quietly on the windowsill and caress her with his eyes. She can hold him in her arms, letting his back paws struggle for footing on her breast and his forepaws cling to her shoulder. She can rub the smooth fur and feel the unresisting flesh underneath. At her gentlest touch he will preen, stretch, and open his mouth. And she will accept the strangely pleasant sensation that comes when he writhes beneath her hand and flattens his eyes with a surfeit of sensual delight. When she stands cooking at the table, he will circle about her shanks, and the trill of his fur spirals up her legs to her thighs, to make her fingers tremble a little in the pie dough.

Or, as she sits reading the "Uplifting Thoughts" in *The Liberty Magazine*, the cat will jump into her lap. She will fondle that soft hill of hair and let the warmth of the animal's body seep over and into the deeply private areas of her lap. Sometimes the magazine drops, and she opens her legs just a little, and the two of them will be still together, perhaps shifting a little together, sleeping a little together, until four o'clock, when the intruder comes home from work vaguely anxious about what's for dinner.

The cat will always know that he is first in her affections. Even after she bears a child. For she does bear a child—easily, and painlessly. But only one. A son. Named Junior.

One such girl from Mobile, or Meridian, or Aiken who did not sweat in her armpits nor between her thighs, who smelled of wood and vanilla, who had made soufflés in the Home Economics Department, moved with her husband, Louis, to Lorain, Ohio. Her name was Geraldine. There she built her nest, ironed shirts, potted bleeding hearts, played with her cat, and birthed Louis Junior.

Geraldine did not allow the baby, Junior, to cry. As long as his needs were physical, she could meet them—comfort and satiety. He was always brushed, bathed, oiled, and shod. Geraldine did not talk to him, coo to him, or indulge him in kissing bouts, but she saw that every other desire was fulfilled. It was not long before the child discovered the difference in his mother's behavior to himself and the cat. As he grew older, he learned how to direct his hatred of his mother to the cat, and spent some happy moments watching it suffer. The cat survived, because Geraldine was seldom away from home, and could effectively soothe the animal when Junior abused him.

Geraldine, Louis, Junior, and the cat lived next to the playground of Washington Irving School. Junior considered the playground his own, and the schoolchildren coveted his freedom to sleep late, go home for lunch, and dominate the playground after school. He hated to see the swings, slides, monkey bars, and seesaws empty and tried to get kids to stick around as long as possible. White kids; his mother did not like him to play with niggers. She had explained to him the difference between colored people and niggers. They were easily identifiable. Colored people were neat and quiet; niggers were dirty and loud. He belonged to the former group: he wore white shirts and blue trousers; his hair was cut as close to his scalp as possible to avoid any suggestion of wool, the part was etched into his hair by the barber. In winter his mother put Jergens Lotion on his face to keep the skin from becoming ashen. Even though he was light-skinned, it was possible to ash. The line between colored and nigger was not always clear; subtle and telltale signs threatened to erode it, and the watch had to be constant.

Junior used to long to play with the black boys. More than anything in the world he wanted to play King of the Mountain and have them push him down the mound of dirt and roll over him. He wanted to feel their hardness pressing on him, smell their wild blackness, and say "Fuck you" with that lovely casualness. He wanted to sit with them on curbstones and compare the sharpness of jackknives, the distance and arcs of spitting. In the toilet he wanted to share with them the laurels of being able to pee far and long. Bay Boy and P. L. had at one time been his idols. Gradually he came to agree with his mother that neither Bay Boy nor P. L. was good enough for him. He played only with Ralph Nisensky, who was two years younger, wore glasses, and didn't want to *do* anything. More and more Junior enjoyed bullying girls. It was easy making them scream and run. How he laughed when they fell down and their bloomers showed. When they got up, their faces red and crinkled, it made him feel good. The nigger girls he did not pick on very much. They usually traveled in packs, and once when he threw a stone at some of them, they chased, caught, and beat him witless. He lied to his mother, saying Bay Boy did it. His mother was very upset. His father just kept on reading the Lorain *Journal.*

When the mood struck him, he would call a child passing by to come play on the swings or the seesaw. If the child wouldn't, or did and left too soon, Junior threw gravel at him. He became a very good shot.

Alternately bored and frightened at home, the playground was his joy. On a day when he had been especially idle, he saw a very black girl taking a shortcut through the playground. She kept her head down as she walked. He had seen her many times before, standing alone, always alone, at recess. Nobody ever played with her. Probably, he thought, because she was ugly.

Now Junior called to her. "Hey! What are you doing walking through my yard?"

The girl stopped.

"Nobody can come through this yard 'less I say so."

"This ain't your yard. It's the school's."

"But I'm in charge of it."

The girl started to walk away.

"Wait." Junior walked toward her. "You can play in it if you want to. What's your name?"

"Pecola. I don't want to play."

"Come on. I'm not going to bother you."

"I got to go home."

"Say, you want to see something? I got something to show you."

"No. What is it?"

"Come on in my house. See, I live right there. Come on. I'll show you."

"Show me what?"

"Some kittens. We got some kittens. You can have one if you want."

"Real kittens?"

"Yeah. Come on."

He pulled gently at her dress. Pecola began to move toward his house. When he knew she had agreed, Junior ran ahead excitedly, stopping only to yell back at her to come on. He held the door open for her, smiling his encouragement. Pecola climbed the porch stairs and hesitated there, afraid to follow him. The house looked dark. Junior said, "There's nobody here. My ma's gone out, and my father's at work. Don't you want to see the kittens?"

Junior turned on the lights. Pecola stepped inside the door.

How beautiful, she thought. What a beautiful house. There was a big red-and-gold Bible on the dining-room table. Little lace doilies were everywhere—on arms and back of chairs, in the center of a large dining table, on little tables. Potted plants were on all the windowsills. A color picture of Jesus Christ hung on a wall with the prettiest paper flowers fastened on the frame. She wanted to see everything slowly, slowly. But Junior kept saying, "Hey, you. Come on. Come on." He pulled her into another room, even more beautiful than the first. More doilies, a big lamp with green-and-gold base and white shade. There was even a rug on the floor, with enormous dark-red flowers. She was deep in admiration of the flowers when Junior said, "Here!" Pecola turned. "Here is your kitten!" he screeched. And he threw a big black cat right in her face. She sucked in her breath in fear and surprise and felt fur in her mouth. The cat clawed her face and chest in an effort to right itself, then leaped nimbly to the floor.

Junior was laughing and running around the room clutching his stomach delightedly. Pecola touched the scratched place on her face and felt tears coming. When she started toward the doorway, Junior leaped in front of her.

"You can't get out. You're my prisoner," he said. His eyes were merry but hard.

"You let me go."

"No!" He pushed her down, ran out the door that separated the rooms, and held it shut with his hands. Pecola's banging on the door increased his gasping, high-pitched laughter.

The tears came fast, and she held her face in her hands. When something soft and furry moved around her ankles, she jumped, and saw it was the cat. He wound himself in and about her legs. Momentarily distracted from her fear, she squatted down to touch him, her hands wet from the tears. The cat rubbed up against her knee. He was black all over, deep silky black, and his eyes, pointing down toward his nose, were bluish green. The light made them shine like blue ice. Pecola rubbed the cat's head; he whined, his tongue flicking with pleasure. The blue eyes in the black face held her.

Junior, curious at not hearing her sobs, opened the door, and saw her squatting down rubbing the cat's back. He saw the cat stretching its head and flattening its eyes. He had seen that expression many times as the animal responded to his mother's touch.

"Gimme my cat!" His voice broke. With a movement both awkward and sure he snatched the cat by one of its hind legs and began to swing it around his head in a circle.

"Stop that!" Pecola was screaming. The cat's free paws were stiffened, ready to grab anything to restore balance, its mouth wide, its eyes blue streaks of horror.

Still screaming, Pecola reached for Junior's hand. She heard her dress rip under her arm. Junior tried to push her away, but she grabbed the arm which was swinging the cat. They both fell, and in falling, Junior let go the cat, which, having been released in mid-motion, was thrown full force against the window. It slithered down and fell on the radiator behind the sofa. Except for a few shudders, it was still. There was only the slightest smell of singed fur.

Geraldine opened the door.

"What is this?" Her voice was mild, as though asking a perfectly reasonable question. "Who is this girl?"

"She killed our cat," said Junior. "Look." He pointed to the radiator, where the cat lay, its blue eyes closed, leaving only an empty, black, and helpless face.

Geraldine went to the radiator and picked up the cat. He was limp in her arms, but she rubbed her face in his fur. She looked at Pecola. Saw the dirty torn dress, the plaits sticking out on her head, hair matted where the plaits had come undone, the muddy shoes with the wad of gum peeping out from between the cheap soles, the soiled socks, one of which had been walked down into the heel of the shoe. She saw the safety pin holding the hem of the dress up. Up over the hump of the cat's back she looked at her. She had seen this little girl all of her life. Hanging out of windows over saloons in Mobile, crawling over the porches of shotgun houses on the edge of town, sitting in bus stations holding paper bags and crying to mothers who kept saying "Shet up!" Hair uncombed, dresses falling apart, shoes untied and caked with dirt. They had stared at her with great uncomprehending eyes. Eyes that questioned nothing and asked everything. Unblinking and unabashed, they stared up at her. The end of the world lay in their eyes, and the beginning, and all the waste in between.

They were everywhere. They slept six in a bed, all their pee mixing together in the night as they wet their beds each in his own candy-and-potato-chip dream. In the long, hot days, they idled away, picking plaster from the walls and digging into the earth with sticks. They sat in little rows on street curbs, crowded into pews at church, taking space from the nice, neat, colored children; they clowned on the playgrounds, broke things in dime stores, ran in front of you on the street, made ice slides on the sloped sidewalks in winter. The girls grew up knowing nothing of girdles, and the boys announced their manhood by turning the bills of their caps backward. Grass wouldn't grow where they lived. Flowers died. Shades fell down. Tin cans and tires blossomed where they lived. They lived on cold black-eyed peas and orange pop. Like flies they hovered; like flies they settled. And this one had settled in her house. Up over the hump of the cat's back she looked.

"Get out," she said, he voice quiet. "You nasty little black bitch. Get out of my house."

The cat shuddered and flicked his tail.

Pecola backed out of the room, staring at the pretty milk-brown lady in the pretty gold-and-green house who was talking to her through the cat's fur. The pretty lady's words made the cat fur move; the breath of each word parted the fur. Pecola turned to find the front door and saw Jesus looking down at her with sad and unsurprised eyes, his long brown hair parted in the middle, the gay paper flowers twisted around his face.

Outside, the March wind blew into the rip in her dress. She held her head down against the cold. But she could not hold it low enough to avoid seeing the snowflakes falling and dying on the pavement.

Spring

The first twigs are thin, green, and supple. They bend into a complete circle, but will not break. Their delicate, showy hopefulness shooting from forsythia and lilac bushes meant only a change in whipping style. They beat us differently in the spring. Instead of the dull pain of a winter strap, there were these new green switches that lost their sting long after the whipping was over. There was a nervous meanness in these long twigs that made us long for the steady stroke of a strap or the firm but honest slap of a hairbrush. Even now spring for me is shot through with the remembered ache of switchings, and forsythia holds no cheer.

Sunk in the grass of an empty lot on a spring Saturday, I split the stems of milkweed and thought about ants and peach pits and death and where the world went when I closed my eyes. I must have lain long in the grass, for the shadow that was in front of me when I left the house had disappeared when I went back. I entered the house, as the house was bursting with an uneasy quiet. Then I heard my mother singing something about trains and Arkansas. She came in the back door with some folded yellow curtains which she piled on the kitchen table. I sat down on the floor to listen to the song's story, and noticed how strangely she was behaving. She still had her hat on, and her shoes were dusty, as though she had been walking in deep dirt. She put on some water to boil and then swept the porch; then she hauled out the curtain stretcher, but instead of putting the damp curtains on it, she swept the porch again. All the time singing about trains and Arkansas.

When she finished, I went to look for Frieda. I found her upstairs lying on our bed, crying the tired, whimpering cry that follows the first wailings—mostly gasps and shudderings. I lay on the bed and looked at the tiny bunches of wild roses sprinkled over her dress. Many washings had faded their color and dimmed their outlines.

"What happened, Frieda?"

She lifted a swollen face from the crook of her arm. Shuddering still, she sat up, letting her thin legs dangle over the bedside. I knelt on the bed and picked up the hem of my dress to wipe her running nose. She never liked wiping noses on clothes, but this time she let me. It was the way Mama did with her apron.

"Did you get a whipping?"

She shook her head no.

"Then why you crying?"

"Because."

"Because what?"

"Mr. Henry."

"What'd he do?"

"Daddy beat him up."

"What for? The Maginot Line? Did he find out about the Maginot Line?"

"No."

"Well, what, then? Come on, Frieda. How come I can't know?"

"He . . . *picked* at me."

"Picked at you? You mean like Soaphead Church?"

"Sort of."

"He showed his privates at you?"

"Noooo. He touched me."

"Where?"

"Here and here." She pointed to the tiny breasts that, like two fallen acorns, scattered a few faded rose leaves on her dress.

"Really? How did it feel?"

"Oh, Claudia." She sounded put-out. I wasn't asking the right questions.

"It didn't feel like anything."

"But wasn't it supposed to? Feel good, I mean?" Frieda sucked her teeth. "What'd he do? Just walk up and pinch them?"

She sighed. "First he said how pretty I was. Then he grabbed my arm and touched me."

"Where was Mama and Daddy?"

"Over at the garden weeding."

"What'd you say when he did it?"

"Nothing. I just ran out of the kitchen and went to the garden."

"Mama said we was never to cross the tracks by ourselves."

"Well, what would you do? Set there and let him pinch you?"

I looked at my chest. "I don't have nothing to pinch. I'm never going to have nothing."

"Oh, Claudia, you're jealous of everything. You *want* him to?"

"No, I just get tired of having everything last."

"You do not. What about scarlet fever? You had that first."

"Yes, but it didn't last. Anyway, what happened at the garden?"

"I told Mama, and she told Daddy, and we all come home, and he was gone, so we waited for him, and when Daddy saw him come up on the porch, he threw our old tricycle at his head and knocked him off the porch."

"Did he die?"

"Naw. He got up and started singing 'Nearer My God to Thee.' Then Mama hit him with a broom and told him to keep the Lord's name out of his mouth, but he wouldn't stop, and Daddy was cussing, and everybody was screaming."

"Oh, shoot, I always miss stuff."

"And Mr. Buford came running out with his gun, and Mama told him to go somewhere and sit down, and Daddy said no, give him the gun, and Mr. Buford did, and Mama screamed, and Mr. Henry shut up and started running, and Daddy shot at him and Mr. Henry jumped out of his shoes and kept on running in his socks. Then Rosemary came out and said that Daddy was going to jail, and I hit her."

"Read hard?"

"Real hard."

"Is that when Mama whipped you?"

"She didn't whip me, I told you."

"Then why you crying?"

"Miss Dunion came in after everybody was quiet, and Mama and Daddy was fussing about who let Mr. Henry in anyway, and she said that Mama should take me to the doctor, because I might be ruined, and Mama started screaming all over again."

"At you?"

"No. At Miss Dunion."

"But why were you crying?"

"I don't want to be *ruined!*"

"What's ruined?"

"You know. Like the Maginot Line. She's ruined. Mama said so." The tears came back.

An image of Frieda, big and fat, came to mind. Her thin legs swollen, her face surrounded by layers of rouged skin. I too begin to feel tears.

"But, Frieda, you could exercise and not eat."

She shrugged.

"Besides, what about China and Poland? They're ruined too, aren't they? And they ain't fat."

"That's because they drink whiskey. Mama says whiskey ate them up."

"You could drink whiskey."

"Where would I get whiskey?"

We thought about this. Nobody would sell it to us; we had no money, anyway. There was never any in our house. Who would have some?

"Pecola," I said. "Her father's always drunk. She can get us some."

"You think so?"

"Sure. Cholly's always drunk. Let's go ask her. We don't have to tell her what for."

"Now?"

"Sure, now."

"What'll we tell Mama?"

"Nothing. Let's just go out the back. One at a time. So she won't notice."

"O.K. You go first, Claudia."

We opened the fence gate at the bottom of the backyard and ran down the alley.

Pecola lived on the other side of Broadway. We had never been in her house, but we knew where it was. A two-story gray building that had been a store downstairs and had an apartment upstairs.

Nobody answered our knock on the front door, so we walked around to the side door. As we approached, we heard radio music and looked to see where it came from. About us was the second-story porch, lined with slanting, rotting rails, and sitting on the porch was the Maginot Line herself. We stared up and automatically reached for the other's hand. A mountain of flesh, she lay rather than sat in a rocking chair. She had no shoes on, and each foot was poked between a railing: tiny baby toes at the tip of puffy feet; swollen ankles smoothed and tightened the skin; massive legs like tree stumps parted wide at the knees, over which spread two roads of soft flabby inner thigh that kissed each other deep in the shade of her dress and closed. A dark-brown root-beer bottle, like a burned limb, grew out of her dimpled hand. She looked at us down through the porch railings and emitted a low, long belch. Her eyes were as clean as rain, and again I remembered the waterfall. Neither of us could speak. Both of us imagined we were seeing what was to become of Frieda. The Maginot Line smiled at us.

"You all looking for somebody?"

I had to pull my tongue from the roof of my mouth to say, "Pecola—she live here?"

"Uh-huh, but she ain't here now. She gone to her mama's work place to git the wash."

"Yes, ma'am. She coming back?"

"Uh-huh. She got to hang up the clothes before the sun goes down."

"Oh."

"You can wait for her. Wanna come up here and wait?"

We exchanged glances. I looked back up at the broad cinnamon roads that met in the shadow of her dress.

Frieda said, "No, ma'am."

"Well," the Maginot Line seemed interested in our problem. "You can go to her mama's work place, but it's way over by the lake."

"Where by the lake?"

"That big white house with the wheelbarrow full of flowers."

It was a house that we knew, having admired the large white wheelbarrow tilted down on spoked wheels and planted with seasonal flowers.

"Ain't that too far for you all to go walking?"

Frieda scratched her knee.

"Why don't you wait for her? You can come up here. Want some pop?" Those rain-soaked eyes lit up, and her smile was full, not like the pinched and holding-back smile of other grown-ups.

I moved to go up the stairs, but Frieda said, "No, ma'am, we ain't allowed."

I was amazed at her courage, and frightened of her sassiness. The smile of the Maginot Line slipped. "Ain't 'llowed?"

"No'm."

"Ain't 'llowed to what?"

"Go in your house."

"Is that right?" The waterfalls were still. "How come?"

"My mama said so. My mama said you ruined."

The waterfalls began to run again. She put the root-beer bottle to her lips and drank it empty. With a graceful movement of the wrist, a gesture so quick and small we never really saw it, only remembered it afterward, she tossed the bottle over the rail at us. It split at our feet, and shards of brown glass dappled our legs before we could jump back. The Maginot Line put a fat hand on one of the folds of her stomach and laughed. At first just a deep humming with her mouth closed, then a larger, warmer sound. Laughter at once beautiful and frightening. She let her head tilt sideways, closed her eyes, and shook her massive trunk, letting the laughter fall like a wash of red leaves all around us. Scraps and curls of the laughter followed us as we ran. Our breath gave out at the same time our legs did. After we rested against a tree, our heads on crossed forearms, I said, "Let's go home."

Frieda was still angry—fighting, she believed, for her life. "No, we got to get it now."

"We can't go all the way to the lake."

"Yes we can. Come on."

"Mama gone get us."

"No she ain't. Besides, she can't do nothing but whip us."

That was true. She wouldn't kill us, or laugh a terrible laugh at us, or throw a bottle at us.

We walked down tree-lined streets of soft gray houses leaning like tired ladies. . . . The streets changed; houses looked more sturdy, their paint was newer, porch posts straighter, yards deeper. Then came brick houses set well back from the street, fronted by yards edged in shrubbery clipped into smooth cones and balls of velvet green.

The lakefront houses were the loveliest. Garden furniture, ornaments, windows like shiny eyeglasses, and no sign of life. The backyards of these houses fell away in green slopes down to a strip of sand, and then the blue Lake Erie, lapping all the way to Canada. The orange-patched sky of the steel-mill section never reached this part of town. This sky was always blue.

We reached Lake Shore Park, a city park laid out with rosebuds, fountains, bowling greens, picnic tables. It was empty now, but sweetly expectant of clean, white, well-behaved children and parents who would play there above the lake in summer before half-running, half-stumbling down the slope to the welcoming water. Black people were not allowed in the park, and so it filled our dreams.

Right before the entrance to the park was the large white house with the wheelbarrow full of flowers. Short crocus blades sheathed the purple-and-white hearts that so wished to be first they endured the chill and rain of early spring. The walkway was flagged in calculated disorder, hiding the cunning symmetry. Only fear of discovery and the knowledge that we did not belong kept us from loitering. We circled the proud house and went to the back.

There on the tiny railed stoop sat Pecola in a light red sweater and blue cotton dress. A little wagon was parked near her. She seemed glad to see us.

"Hi."

"Hi."

"What you all doing here?" She was smiling, and since it was a rare thing to see on her, I was surprised at the pleasure it gave me.

"We're looking for you."

"Who told you I was here?"

"The Maginot Line."

"Who is that?"

"That big fat lady. She lives over you."

"Oh, you mean Miss Marie. Her name is Miss Marie."

"Well, everybody calls her Miss Maginot Line. Ain't you scared?"

"Scared of what?"

"The Maginot Line."

Pecola looked genuinely puzzled. "What for?"

"Your mama let you go in her house? And eat out of her plates?"

"She don't know I go. Miss Marie is nice. They all nice."

"Oh, yeah," I said, "she tried to kill us."

"Who? Miss Marie? She don't bother nobody."

"Then how come your mama don't let you go in her house if she so nice?"

"I don't know. She say she's bad, but they ain't bad. They give me stuff all the time."

"What stuff?"

"Oh, lots of stuff, pretty dresses, and shoes. I got more shoes than I ever wear. And jewelry and candy and money. They take me to the movies, and once we went to the carnival. China gone take me to Cleveland to see the square, and Poland gone take me to Chicago to see the Loop. We going everywhere together."

"You lying. You don't have no pretty dresses."

"I do, too."

"Oh, come on, Pecola, what you telling us all that junk for?" Frieda asked.

"It ain't junk." Pecola stood up ready to defend her words, when the door opened.

Mrs. Breedlove stuck her head out the door and said, "What's going on out here? Pecola, who are these children?"

"That's Frieda and Claudia, Mrs. Breedlove."

"Whose girls are you?" She came all the way out on the stoop. She looked nicer than I had ever seen her, in her white uniform and her hair in a small pompadour.

"Mrs. MacTeer's girls, ma'am."

"Oh, yes. Live over on Twenty-first Street?"

"Yes, ma'am."

"What are you doing 'way over here?"

"Just walking. We came to see Pecola."

"Well, you better get on back. You can walk with Pecola. Come on in while I get the wash."

We stepped into the kitchen, a large spacious room. Mrs. Breedlove's skin glowed like taffeta in the reflection of white porcelain, white woodwork, polished cabinets, and brilliant copperware. Odors of meat, vegetables, and something freshly baked mixed with a scent of Fels Naphtha.

"I'm gone get the wash. You all stand stock still right there and don't mess up nothing." She disappeared behind a white swinging door, and we could hear the uneven flap of her footsteps as she descended into the basement.

Another door opened, and in walked a little girl, smaller and younger than all of us. She wore a pink sunback dress and pink fluffy bedroom slippers with two bunny ears pointed up from the tips. Her hair was corn yellow and bound in a thick ribbon. When she saw us, fear danced across her face for a second. She looked anxiously around the kitchen.

"Where's Polly?" she asked.

The familiar violence rose in me. Her calling Mrs. Breedlove Polly, when even Pecola called her mother Mrs. Breedlove, seemed reason enough to scratch her.

"She's downstairs," I said.

"Polly!" she called.

"Look," Frieda whispered, "look at that." On the counter near the stove in a silvery pan was a deep-dish berry cobbler. The purple juice bursting here and there through crust. We moved closer.

"It's still hot," Frieda said.

Pecola stretched her hand to touch the pan, lightly, to see if it was hot.

"Polly, come here," the little girl called again.

It may have been nervousness, awkwardness, but the pan tilted under Pecola's fingers and fell to the floor, splattering blackish blueberries everywhere. Most of the juice splashed on Pecola's legs, and the burn must have been painful, for she cried out and began hopping about just as Mrs. Breedlove entered with a tightly packed laundry bag. In one gallop she was on Pecola, and with the back of her hand knocked her to the floor. Pecola slid in the pie juice, one leg folding under her. Mrs. Breedlove yanked her up by the arm, slapped her again, and in a voice thin with anger, abused Pecola directly and Frieda and me by implication.

"Crazy fool . . . my floor, mess . . . look what you . . . work . . . get on out . . . now that . . . crazy . . . my floor, my floor . . . my floor." Her words were hotter and darker than the smoking berries, and we backed away in dread.

The little girl in pink started to cry. Mrs. Breedlove turned to her. "Hush, baby, hush. Come here. Oh, Lord, look at your dress. Don't cry no more. Polly will change it." She went to the sink and turned tap water on a fresh towel. Over her shoulder she spit out words to us like rotten pieces of apple. "Pick up that wash and get on out of here, so I can get this mess cleaned up."

Pecola picked up the laundry bag, heavy with wet clothes, and we stepped hurriedly out the door. As Pecola put the laundry bag in the wagon, we could hear Mrs. Breedlove hushing and soothing the tears of the little pink-and-yellow girl.

"Who were they, Polly?"

"Don't worry none, baby."

"You gonna make another pie?"

" 'Course I will."

"Who were they, Polly?"

"Hush. Don't worry none," she whispered, and the honey in her words complemented the sundown spilling on the lake.

SEEMOTHERMOTHERISVERYNICEMOTHE RWILLYOUPLAYWITHJANEMOTHERLAUG HSLAUGHMOTHERLAUGHLA

The easiest thing to do would be to build a case out of her foot. That is what she herself did. But to find out the truth about how dreams die, one should never take the word of the dreamer. The end of her lovely beginning was probably the cavity in one of her front teeth. She preferred, however, to think always of her foot. Although she was the ninth of eleven children and lived on a ridge of red Alabama clay seven miles from the nearest road, the complete indifference with which a rusty nail was met when it punched clear through her foot during her second year of life saved Pauline Williams from total anonymity. The wound left her with a crooked, archless foot that flopped when she walked—not a limp that would have eventually twisted her spine, but a way of lifting the bad foot as though she were extracting it from little whirlpools that threatened to pull it under. Slight as it was, this deformity explained for her many things that would have been otherwise incomprehensible: why she alone of all the children had no nickname; why there were no funny jokes and anecdotes about funny things she had done; why no one ever remarked on her food preferences—no saving of the wing or neck for her—no cooking of the peas in a separate pot without rice because she did not like rice; why nobody teased her; why she never felt at home anywhere, or that she belonged anyplace. Her general feeling of separateness and unworthiness she blamed on her foot. Restricted, as a child, to this cocoon of her family's spinning, she cultivated quiet and private pleasures. She liked, most of all, to arrange things. To line things up in rows—jars on shelves at canning, peach pits on the step, sticks, stones, leaves—and the members of her family let these arrangements be. When by some accident somebody scattered her rows, they always stopped to retrieve them for her, and she was never angry, for it gave her a chance to rearrange them again. Whatever portable plurality she found, she organized into neat lines, according to their size, shape, or gradations of color. Just as she would never align a pine needle with the leaf of a cottonwood tree, she would never put the jars of tomatoes next to the green beans. During all of her four years of going to school, she was enchanted by numbers and depressed by words. She missed—without knowing what she missed—paints and crayons.

Near the beginning of World War I, the Williamses discovered, from returning neighbors and kin, the possibility of living better in another place. In shifts, lots, batches, mixed in with other families, they migrated, in six months and four journeys, to Kentucky, where there were mines and millwork.

"When all us left from down home and was waiting down by the depot for the truck, it was nighttime. June bugs was shooting everywhere. They lighted up a tree leaf, and I seen a streak of green every now and again. That was the last time I seen real june bugs. These things up here ain't june bugs. They's something else. Folks here call them fireflies. Down home they was different. But I recollect that streak of green. I recollect it well."

In Kentucky they lived in a real town, ten to fifteen houses on a single street, with water piped right into the kitchen. Ada and Fowler Williams found a five-room frame house for their family. The yard was bounded by a once-white fence against which Pauline's mother planted flowers and within which they kept a few chickens. Some of her brothers joined the Army, one sister died, and two got married, increasing the living space and giving the entire Kentucky venture a feel of luxury. The relocation was especially comfortable to Pauline, who was old enough to leave school. Mrs. Williams got a job cleaning and cooking for a white minister on the other side of town, and Pauline, now the oldest girl at home, took over the care of the house. She kept the fence in repair, pulling the pointed stakes erect, securing them with bits of wire, collected eggs, swept, cooked, washed, and minded the two younger children—a pair of twins called Chicken and Pie, who were still in school. She was not only good at housekeeping, she enjoyed it. After her parents left for work and the other children were at school or in mines, the house was quiet. The stillness and isolation both calmed and energized her. She could arrange and clean without interruption until two o'clock, when Chicken and Pie came home.

When the war ended and the twins were ten years old, they too left school to work. Pauline was fifteen, still keeping house, but with less enthusiasm. Fantasies about men and love and touching were drawing her mind and hands away from her work. Changes in weather began to affect her, as did certain sights and sounds. These feelings translated themselves to her in extreme melancholy. She thought of the death of newborn things, lonely roads, and strangers who appear out of nowhere simply to hold one's hand, woods in which the sun was always setting. In church especially did these dreams grow. The songs caressed her, and while she tried to hold her mind on the wages of sin, her body trembled for redemption, salvation, a mysterious rebirth that would simply happen, with no effort on her part. In none of her fantasies was she ever aggressive; she was usually idling by the river bank, or gathering berries in a field when a someone appeared, with gentle and penetrating eyes, who—with no exchange of words—understood; and before whose glance her foot straightened and her eyes dropped. The someone had no face, no form, no voice, no odor. He was a simple Presence, an all-embracing tenderness with strength and a promise of rest. It did not matter that she had no idea of what to do or say to the Presence—after the wordless knowing and the soundless touching, her dreams disintegrated. But the Presence would know what to do. She had only to lay her head on his chest and he would lead her away to the sea, to the city, to the woods . . . forever.

There was a woman named Ivy who seemed to hold in her mouth all of the sounds of Pauline's soul. Standing a little apart from the choir, Ivy sang the dark sweetness that Pauline could not name; she sang the death-defying death that Pauline yearned for; she sang of the Stranger who *knew* . . .

Precious Lord take my hand
Lead me on, let me stand
I am tired, I am weak, I am worn.
Through the storms, through the night
Lead me on to the light
Take my hand, precious Lord, lead me on.

When my way grows drear
Precious Lord linger near,
When my life is almost gone
Hear my cry hear my call
Hold my hand lest I fall
Take my hand, Precious Lord, lead me on.

Thus is was that when the Stranger, the someone, did appear out of nowhere, Pauline was grateful but not surprised.

He came, strutting right out of a Kentucky sun on the hottest day of the year. He came big, he came strong, he came with yellow eyes, flaring nostrils, and he came with his own music.

Pauline was leaning idly on the fence, her arms resting on the crossrail between the pickets. She had just put down some biscuit dough and was cleaning the flour from under her nails. Behind her at some distance she heard whistling. One of these rapid, high-note riffs that black boys make up as they go while sweeping, shoveling, or just walking along. A kind of city-street music where laughter belies anxiety, and joy is as short and straight as the blade of a pocketknife. She listened carefully to the music and let it pull her lips into a smile. The whistling got louder, and still she did not turn around, for she wanted it to last. While smiling to herself and holding fast to the break in somber thoughts, she felt something tickling her foot. She laughed aloud and turned to see. The whistler was bending down tickling her broken foot and kissing her leg. She could not stop her laughter—not until he looked up at her and she saw the Kentucky sun drenching the yellow, heavy-lidded eyes of Cholly Breedlove.

"When I first seed Cholly, I want you to know it was like all the bits of color from that time down home when all us chil'ren went berry picking after a funeral and I put some in the pocket of my Sunday dress, and they mashed up and stained my hips. My whole dress was messed with purple, and it never did wash out. Not the dress nor me. I could feel that purple deep inside me. And that lemonade Mama used to make when Pap came in out the fields. It be cool and yellowish, with seeds floating near the bottom. And that streak of green them june bugs made on the trees the night we left from down home. All of them colors was in me. Just sitting there. So when Cholly come up and tickled my foot, it was like them berries, that lemonade, them streaks of green the june bugs made, all come together. Cholly was thin then,

with real light eyes. He used to whistle, and when I heerd him, shivers come on my skin."

Pauline and Cholly loved each other. He seemed to relish her company and even to enjoy her country ways and lack of knowledge about city things. He talked with her about her foot and asked, when they walked through the town or in the fields, if she were tired. Instead of ignoring her infirmity, pretending it was not there, he made it seem like something special and endearing. For the first time Pauline felt that her bad foot was an asset.

And he did touch her, firmly but gently, just as she had dreamed. But minus the gloom of setting suns and lonely river banks. She was secure and grateful; he was kind and lively. She had not known there was so much laughter in the world.

They agreed to marry and go 'way up north, where Cholly said steel mills were begging for workers. Young, loving, and full of energy, they came to Lorain, Ohio. Cholly found work in the steel mills right away, and Pauline started keeping house.

And then she lost her front tooth. But there must have been a speck, a brown speck easily mistaken for food but which did not leave, which sat on the enamel for months, and grew, until it cut into the surface and then to the brown putty underneath, finally eating away to the root, but avoiding the nerves, so its presence was not noticeable or uncomfortable. Then the weakened roots, having grown accustomed to the poison, responded one day to severe pressure, and the tooth fell free, leaving a ragged stump behind. But even before the little brown speck, there must have been the conditions, the setting that would allow it to exist in the first place.

In that young and growing Ohio town whose side streets, even, were paved with concrete, which sat on the edge of a calm blue lake, which boasted an affinity with Oberlin, the underground railroad station, just thirteen miles away, this melting pot on the lip of America facing the cold but receptive Canada—What could go wrong?

"Me and Cholly was getting along good then. We come up north; supposed to be more jobs and all. We moved into two rooms up over a furniture store, and I set about housekeeping. Cholly was working at the steel plant, and everything was looking good. I don't know what all happened. Everything changed. It was hard to get to know folks up here, and I missed my people. I weren't used to so much white folks. The ones I seed before was something hateful, but they didn't come around too much. I mean, we didn't have too much truck with them. Just now and then in the fields, or at the commissary. But they want all over us. Up north they was everywhere—next door, downstairs, all over the streets—and colored folks few and far between. Northern colored folk was different too. Dicty-like. No better than whites for meanness. They could make you feel just as no-count, 'cept I didn't expect it from them. That was the lonesomest time of my life. I 'member looking out them front windows just waiting for Cholly to come home at three o'clock. I didn't even have a cat to talk to."

In her loneliness she turned to her husband for reassurance, entertainment, for things to fill the vacant places. Housework was not enough; there were only two rooms, and no yard to keep or move about in. The women in the town wore high-heeled shoes, and when Pauline tried to wear them, they aggravated her shuffle into a pronounced limp. Cholly was kindness still, but began to resist her total dependence on him. They were beginning to have less and less to say to each other. He had no problem finding other people and other things to occupy him—men were always climbing the stairs asking for him, and he was happy to accompany them, leaving her alone.

Pauline felt uncomfortable with the few black women she met. They were amused by her because she did not straighten her hair. When she tried to make up her face as they did, it came off rather badly. Their goading glances and private snickers at her way of talking (saying "chil'ren") and dressing developed in her a desire for new clothes. When Cholly began to quarrel about the money she wanted, she decided to go to work. Taking jobs as a day worker helped with the clothes, and even a few things for the apartment, but it did not help with Cholly. He was not pleased with her purchases and began to tell her so. Their marriage was shredded with quarrels. She was still no more than a girl, and still waiting for that plateau of happiness, that hand of a precious Lord who, when her way grew drear, would always linger near. Only now she had a clearer idea of what drear meant. Money became the focus of all their discussions, hers for clothes, his for drink. The sad thing was that Pauline did not really care for clothes and makeup. She merely wanted other women to cast favorable glances her way.

After several months of doing day work, she took a steady job in the home of a family of slender means and nervous, pretentious ways.

"Cholly commenced to getting meaner and meaner and wanted to fight me all of the time. I give him as good as I got. Had to. Look like working for that woman and fighting Cholly was all I did. Tiresome. But I holt on to my jobs, even though working for that woman was more than a notion. It wasn't so much her meanness as just simpleminded. Her whole family was. Couldn't get along with one another worth nothing. You'd think with a pretty house like that and all the money they could holt on to, they would enjoy one another. She haul off and cry over the leastest thing. If one of her friends cut her short on the telephone, she'd go to crying. She should of been glad she had a telephone. I ain't got one yet. I recollect oncet how her baby brother who she put through dentistry school didn't invite them to some big party he throwed. They was a big to-do about that. Everybody stayed on the telephone for days. Fussing and carrying on. She asked me, 'Pauline, what would you do if your own brother had a party and didn't invite you?' I said ifn I really wanted to go to that party, I reckoned I'd go anyhow. Never mind what he want. She just sucked her teeth a little and made out like what I said was dumb. All the while I was thinking how dumb she was. Whoever told her that her brother was her friend? Folks can't like folks just 'cause they has the same mama. I tried to like that woman myself. She was good about giving me stuff, but I just couldn't like her. Soon as I worked up a good feeling on her account, she'd do something ignorant and start in to telling me how to clean and do. If I left her on her own, she'd drown in dirt. I didn't have to pick up after Chicken and Pie the way I had to pick up after them. None of them knew so much as how to wipe their behinds. I know, 'cause I did the washing. And couldn't pee proper to save their lives. Her husband ain't hit the bowl yet. Nasty white folks is about the nastiest things they is. But I would have stayed on 'cepting for Cholly come over by where I was working and cut up so. He come there drunk wanting some money. When that white woman see him, she turned red. She tried to act stronglike, but she was scared bad. Anyway, she told Cholly to get out or she would call the police. He cussed her and started pulling on me. I would of gone upside his head, but I don't want no dealings with the police. So I taken my things and left. I tried to get back, but she didn't want me no more if I was going to stay with Cholly. She said she would let me stay if I left him. I thought about that. But later on it didn't seem none too bright for a black woman to leave a black man for a white woman. She didn't never give me the eleven dollars she owed me, neither. That hurt bad. The gas man had cut the gas off, and I couldn't cook none. I really begged that woman for my money. I went to see her. She was mad as a wet hen. Kept on telling me I owed her for uniforms and some old broken-down bed she give me. I didn't know if I owed her or not, but I needed my money. She wouldn't let up none, neither, even when I give her my word that Cholly wouldn't come back there no more. Then I got so desperate I asked her if she would loan it to me. She was quiet for a spell, and then she told me I shouldn't let a man take advantage over me. That I should have more respect, and it was my husband's duty to pay the bills, and if he couldn't, I should leave and get alimony. All such simple stuff. What was he gone give me alimony on? I seen she didn't understand

that all I needed from her was my eleven dollars to pay the gas man so I could cook. She couldn't get that one thing through her thick head. 'Are you going to leave him, Pauline?' she kept on saying. I thought she'd give me my money if I said I would, so I said 'Yes, ma'am.' 'All right,' she said. 'You leave him, and then come back to work, and we'll let bygones be bygones.' 'Can I have my money today?' I said. 'No' she said. 'Only when you leave him. I'm only thinking of you and your future. What good is he, Pauline, what good is he to you?' How you going to answer a woman like that, who don't know what good a man is, and say out of one side of her mouth she's thinking of your future but won't give you your own money so you can buy you something besides baloney to eat? So I said, 'No good, ma'am. He ain't no good to me. But just the same, I think I'd best stay on.' She got up, and I left. When I got outside, I felt pains in my crotch, I had held my legs together so tight trying to make that woman understand. But I reckon now she couldn't understand. She married a man with a slash in his face instead of a mouth. So how could she understand?"

One winter Pauline discovered she was pregnant. When she told Cholly, he surprised her by being pleased. He began to drink less and come home more often. They eased back into a relationship more like the early days of their marriage, when he asked if she were tired or wanted him to bring her something from the store. In this state of ease, Pauline stopped doing day work and returned to her own housekeeping. But the loneliness in those two rooms had not gone away. When the winter sun hit the peeling green paint of the kitchen chairs, when the smoked hocks were boiling in the pot, when all she could hear was the truck delivering furniture downstairs, she thought about back home, about how she had been all alone most of the time then too, but that this lonesomeness was different. Then she stopped staring at the green chairs, at the delivery truck; she went to the movies instead. There in the dark her memory was refreshed, and she succumbed to her earlier dreams. Along with the idea of romantic love, she was introduced to another—physical beauty. Probably the most destructive ideas in the history of human thought. Both originated in envy, thrived in insecurity, and ended in disillusion. In equating physical beauty with virtue, she stripped her mind, bound it, and collected self contempt by the heap. She forgot lust and simple caring for. She regarded love as possessive mating, and romance as the goal of the spirit. It would be for her a well-spring from which she would draw the most destructive emotions, deceiving the lover and seeking to imprison the beloved, curtailing freedom in every way.

She was never able, after her education in the movies, to look at a face and not assign it some category in the scale of absolute beauty, and the scale was one she absorbed in full from the silver screen. There at last were the darkened woods, the lonely roads, the river banks, the gentle knowing eyes. There the flawed became whole, the blind sighted, and the lame and halt threw away their crutches. There death was dead, and people made every gesture in a cloud of music. There the black-and-white images came together, making a significant whole—all projected through the ray of light from above and behind.

It was really a simple pleasure, but she learned all there was to love and all there was to hate.

"The onliest time I be happy seem like was when I was in the picture show. Every time I got, I went. I'd go early, before the show started. They'd cut off the lights, and everything be black. Then the screen would light up, and I'd move right on in them pictures. White men taking such good care of they women, and they all dressed up in big clean houses with the bathtubs right in the same room with the toilet. Them pictures gave me a lot of pleasure, but it made coming home hard, and looking at Cholly hard. I don't know. I 'member one time I went to see Clark Gable and Jean Harlow. I fixed my hair up like I'd seen hers on a magazine. A part on the side, with one little curl on my forehead. It looked just like her. Well, al-

most just like. Anyway, I sat in that show with my hair done up that way and had a good time. I thought I'd see it through to the end again, and I got up to get me some candy. I was sitting back in my seat, and I taken a big bite of that candy, and it pulled a tooth right out of my mouth. I could of cried. I had good teeth, not a rotten one in my head. I don't believe I ever did get over that. There I was, five months pregnant, trying to look like Jean Harlow, and a front tooth gone. Everything went then. Look like I just didn't care no more after that. I let my hair go back, plaited it up, and settled down to just being ugly. I still went to the pictures, though, but the meanness got worse. I wanted my tooth back. Cholly poked fun at me, and we started fighting again. I tried to kill him. He didn't hit me too hard, 'cause I were pregnant I guess, but the fights, once they got started up again, kept up. He begin to make me madder than anything I knowed, and I couldn't keep my hands off him. Well, I had that baby—a boy—and after that got pregnant again with another one. But it weren't like I thought it was gone be. I loved them and all, I guess, but maybe it was having no money, or maybe it was Cholly, but they sure worried the life out of me. Sometimes I'd catch myself hollering at them and beating them, and I'd feel sorry for them, but I couldn't seem to stop. When I had the second one, a girl, I 'member I said I'd love it no matter what it looked like. She looked like a black ball of hair. I don't recollect trying to get pregnant that first time. But that second time, I actually tried to get pregnant. Maybe 'cause I'd had one already and wasn't scairt to do it. Anyway, I felt good, and wasn't thinking on the carrying, just the baby itself. I used to talk to it whilst it be still in the womb. Like good friends we was. You know. I be hanging wash and I knowed lifting weren't good for it. I'd say to it holt on now I gone hang up these few rags, don't get froggy; it be over soon. It wouldn't leap or nothing. Or I be mixing something in a bowl for the other chile and I'd talk to it then too. You know, just friendly talk. On up til the end I felted good about that baby. I went to the hospital when my time come. So I could be easeful. I didn't want to have it at home like I done with the boy. They put me in a big room with a whole mess of women. The pains was coming, but not too bad. A little old doctor come to examine me. He had all sorts of stuff. He gloved his hand and put some kind of jelly on it and rammed it up between my legs. When he left off, some more doctors come. One old one and some young ones. The old one was learning the young ones about babies. Showing them how to do. When he got to me he said now these here women you don't have any trouble with. They deliver right away and with no pain. Just like horses. The young ones smiled a little. They looked at my stomach and between my legs. They never said nothing to me. Only one looked at me. Looked at my face, I mean. I looked right back at him. He dropped his eyes and turned red. He knowed, I reckon, that maybe I weren't no horse foaling. But them others. They didn't know. They went on. I seed them talking to them white women: 'How you feel? Gonna have twins?' Just shucking them, of course, but nice talk. Nice friendly talk. I got edgy, and when them pains got harder, I was glad. Glad to have something else to think about. I moaned something awful. The pains wasn't as bad as I let on, but I had to let them people know having a baby was more than a bowel movement. I hurt just like them white women. Just 'cause I wasn't hooping and hollering before didn't mean I wasn't feeling pain. What'd they think? That just 'cause I knowed how to have a baby with no fuss that my behind wasn't pulling and aching like theirs? Besides, that doctor don't know what he talking about. He must never seed no mare foal. Who say they don't have no pain? Just 'cause she don't cry? 'Cause she can't say it, they think it ain't there? If they looks in her eyes and see them eyeballs lolling back, see the sorrowful look, they'd know. Anyways, the baby come. Big old healthy thing. She looked different from what I thought. Reckon I talked to it so much before I conjured up a mind's eye view of it. So when I seed it, it was like looking at a picture of your mama when she was a girl. You knows who she is, but she don't look the same. They give her to me for a nursing, and she liked to pull my nipple off right away. She caught on fast. Not like Sammy, he was the hardest child to feed. But Pecola look like she knowed right off what to do. A right smart baby she was. I used to like to watch her. You know they makes them greedy sounds. Eyes all soft and wet. A cross between a puppy and a dying man. But I knowed she was ugly. Head full of pretty hair, but Lord she was ugly."

When Sammy and Pecola were still young Pauline had to go back to work. She was older now, with no time for dreams and movies. It was time to put all of the pieces together, make coherence where before there had been none. The children gave her this need; she herself was no longer a child. So she became, and her process of becoming was like most of ours: she developed a hatred for things that mystified or obstructed her; acquired virtues that were easy to maintain; assigned herself a role in the scheme of things; and harked back to simpler times for gratification.

She took on the full responsibility and recognition of breadwinner and returned to church. First, however, she moved out of the two rooms into a spacious first floor of a building that had been built as a store. She came into her own with the women who had despised her, by being more moral than they; she avenged herself on Cholly by forcing him to indulge in the weaknesses she despised. She joined a church where shouting was frowned upon, served on Stewardess Board No. 3, and became a member of Ladies Circle No. 1. At prayer meeting she moaned and sighed over Cholly's ways, and hoped God would help her keep the children from the sins of the father. She stopped saying "chil'ren" and said "childring" instead. She let another tooth fall, and was outraged by painted ladies who thought only of clothes and men. Holding Cholly as a model of sin and failure, she bore him like a crown of thorns, and her children like a cross.

It was her good fortune to find a permanent job in the home of a well-to-do family whose members were affectionate, appreciative, and generous. She looked at their houses, smelled their linen, touched their silk draperies, and loved all of it. The child's pink nightie, the stacks of white pillow slips edged with embroidery, the sheets with top hems picked out with blue cornflowers. She became what is known as an ideal servant, for such a role filled practically all of her needs. When she bathed the little Fisher girl, it was in a porcelain tub with silvery taps running infinite quantities of hot, clear water. She dried her in fluffy white towels and put her in cuddly night clothes. Then she brushed the yellow hair, enjoying the roll and slip of it between her fingers. No zinc tub, no buckets of stove-heated water, no flaky, stiff, grayish towels washed in a kitchen sink, dried in a dusty backyard, no tangled black puffs of rough wool to comb. Soon she stopped trying to keep her own house. The things she could afford to buy did not last, had no beauty or style, and were absorbed by the dingy storefront. More and more she neglected her house, her children, her man—they were like the afterthoughts one has just before sleep, the early-morning and late-evening edges of her day, the dark edges that made the daily life with the Fishers lighter, more delicate, more lovely. Here she could arrange things, clean things, line things up in neat rows. Here her foot flopped around on deep pile carpets, and there was no uneven sound. Here she found beauty, order, cleanliness, and praise. Mr. Fisher said, "I would rather sell her blueberry cobblers than real estate." She reigned over cupboards stacked high with food that would not be eaten for weeks, even months; she was queen of canned vegetables bought by the case, special fondants and ribbon candy curled up in tiny silver dishes. The creditors and service people who humiliated her when she went to them on her own behalf respected her, were even intimidated by her, when she spoke for the Fishers. She refused beef slightly dark or with edges not properly trimmed. The slightly reeking fish that she accepted for her own family she would all but throw in the fish man's face if he sent it to the Fisher house. Power, praise, and luxury were hers in this household. They even gave her what she had never had—a nickname—Polly. It was her pleasure to stand in her kitchen at the end of a day and survey her handiwork. Knowing there were soap bars by the dozen, bacon by the rasher, and reveling in her shiny pots and pans and polished floors. Hearing, "We'll never let her go. We could never find anybody like Polly. She will *not* leave the kitchen until everything is in order. Really, she is the ideal servant."

Pauline kept this order, this beauty, for herself, a private world, and never introduced it into her storefront, or to her children. Them she bent toward respectability, and in so doing taught them fear: fear of being clumsy, fear of being like their father, fear of not being loved by God, fear of madness like Cholly's mother's. Into her son she beat a loud desire to run away, and into her daughter she beat a fear of growing up, fear of other people, fear of life.

All the meaningfulness of her life was in her work. For her virtues were intact. She was an active church woman, did not drink, smoke, or carouse, defended herself mightily against Cholly, rose above him in every way, and felt she was fulfilling a mother's role conscientiously when she pointed out their father's faults to keep them from having them, or punished them when they showed any slovenliness, no matter how slight, when she worked twelve to sixteen hours a day to support them. And the world itself agreed with her.

It was only sometimes, sometimes, and then rarely, that she thought about the old days, or what her life had turned to. They were musings, idle thoughts, full sometimes of the old dreaminess, but not the kind of thing she cared to dwell on.

"I started to leave him once, but something came up. Once, after he tried to set the house on fire, I was all set in my mind to go. I can't even 'member now what held me. He sure ain't give me much of a life. But it wasn't all bad. Sometimes things wasn't all bad. He used to come easing into bed sometimes, not too drunk. I make out like I'm asleep, 'cause it's late, and he taken three dollars out of my pocketbook that morning or something. I hear him breathing, but I don't look around. I can see in my mind's eye his black arms thrown back behind his head, the muscles like great big peach stones sanded down, with veins running like little swollen rivers down his arms. Without touching him I be feeling those ridges on the tips of my fingers. I sees the palms of his hands caloused to granite, and the long fingers curled up and still. I think about the thick, knotty hair on his chest, and the two big swells his breast muscles make. I want to rub my face hard in his chest and feel the hair cut my skin. I know just where the hair growth slacks out—just above his navel—and how it picks up again and spreads out. Maybe he'll shift a little, and his leg will touch me, or I feel his flank just graze my behind. I don't move even yet. Then he lift his head, turn over, and put his hand on my waist. If I don't move, he'll move his hand over to pull and knead my stomach. Soft and slow-like. I still don't move, because I don't want him to stop. I want to pretend sleep and have him keep on rubbing my stomach. Then he will lean his head down and bite my tit. Then I don't want him to rub my stomach anymore. I want him to put his hand between my legs. I pretend to wake up, and turn to him, but not opening my legs. I want him to open them for me. He does, and I be soft and wet where his fingers are strong and hard. I be softer than I ever been before. All my strength in his hand. My brain curls up like wilted leaves. A funny, empty feeling is in my hands. I want to grab holt of something, so I hold his head. His mouth is under my chin. Then I don't want his hand between my legs no more, because I think I am softening away. I stretch my legs open, and he is on top of me. Too heavy to hold, and too light not to. He puts his thing in me. In me. In me. I wrap my feet around his back so he can't get away. His face is next to mine. The bed springs sounds like them crickets used to back home. He puts his fingers in mine, and we stretches our arms outwise like Jesus on the cross. I hold on tight. My fingers and my feet hold on tight, because everything else is going, going. I know he wants me to come first. But I can't. Not until he does. Not until I feel him loving me. Just me. Sinking into me. Not until I know that my flesh is all that be on his mind. That he couldn't stop if he had to. That he would die rather than take his thing out of me. Of me. Not until he has

let go of all he has, and give it to me. To me. To me. When he does, I feel a power. I be strong, I be pretty, I be young. And then I wait. He shivers and tosses his head. Now I be strong enough, pretty enough, and young enough to let him make me come. I take my fingers out of his and put my hands on his behind. My legs drop back onto the bed. I don't make no noise, because the chil'ren might hear. I begin to feel those little bits of color floating up into me—deep in me. That streak of green from the june-bug light, the purple from the berries trickling along my thighs, Mama's lemonade yellow runs sweet in me. Then I feel like I'm laughing between my legs, and the laughing gets all mixed up with the colors, and I'm afraid I'll come, and afraid I won't. But I know I will. And I do. And it be rainbow all inside. And it lasts and lasts and lasts. I want to thank him, but don't know how, so I pat him like you do a baby. He asks me if I'm all right. I say yes. He gets off me and lies down to sleep. I want to say something, but I don't. I don't want to take my mind offen the rainbow. I should get up and go to the toilet, but I don't. Besides, Cholly is asleep with his leg throwed over me. I can't move and don't want to.

"But it ain't like that anymore. Most times he's thrashing away inside me before I'm woke, and through when I am. The rest of the time I can't even be next to his stinking drunk self. But I don't care 'bout it no more. My Maker will take care of me. I know He will. I know He will. Besides, it don't make no difference about this old earth. There is sure to be a glory. Only thing I miss sometimes is that rainbow. But like I say, I don't recollect it much anymore."

SEEFATHERHEISBIGANDSTRONGFATHER WILLYOUPLAYWITHJANEFATHERISSMILIN GSMILEFATHERSMILESMILE

When Cholly was four days old, his mother wrapped him in two blankets and one newspaper and placed him on a junk heap by the railroad. His Great Aunt Jimmy, who had seen her niece carrying a bundle out of the back door, rescued him. She beat his mother with a razor strap and wouldn't let her near the baby after that. Aunt Jimmy raised Cholly herself, but took delight sometimes in telling him of how she had saved him. He gathered from her that his mother wasn't right in the head. But he never had a chance to find out, because she ran away shortly after the razor strap, and no one had heard of her since.

Cholly was grateful for having been saved. Except sometimes. Sometimes when he watched Aunt Jimmy eating collards with her fingers, sucking her four gold teeth, or smelled her when she wore the asafetida bag around her neck, or when she made him sleep with her for warmth in winter and he could see her old, wrinkled breasts sagging in her nightgown—then he wondered whether it would have been just as well to have died there. Down in the rim of a tire under a soft black Georgia sky.

He had four years of school before he got courage enough to ask his aunt who and where his father was.

"That Fuller boy, I believe it was," his aunt said. "He was hanging around then, but he taken off pretty quick before you was born. I think he gone to Macon. Him or his brother. Maybe both. I hear old man Fuller say something 'bout it once."

"What name he have?" asked Cholly.

"Fuller, Foolish."

"I mean what his given name?"

"Oh." She closed her eyes to think, and sighed. "Can't recollect nothing no more. Sam, was it? Yeh. Samuel. No. No, it wasn't. It was Samson. Samson Fuller."

"How come you all didn't name me Samson?" Cholly's voice was low.

"What for? He wasn't nowhere around when you was born. Your mama didn't name you nothing. The nine days wasn't up before she throwed you on the junk heap. When I got you I named you myself on the ninth day. You named after my dead brother. Charles Breedlove. A good man. Ain't no Samson never come to no good end."

Cholly didn't ask anything else.

Two years later he quit school to take a job at Tyson's Feed and Grain Store. He swept up, ran errands, weighed bags, and lifted them onto the drays. Sometimes they let him ride with the drayman. A nice old man called Blue Jack. Blue used to tell him old-timey stories about how it was when the Emancipation Proclamation came. How the black people hollered, cried, and sang. And ghost stories about how a white man cut off his wife's head and buried her in the swamp, and the headless body came out at night and went stumbling around the yard, knocking over stuff because it couldn't see, and crying all the time for a comb. They talked about the women Blue had had, and the fights he'd been in when he was younger, about how he talked his way out of getting lynched once, and how others hadn't.

Cholly loved Blue. Long after he was a man, he remembered the good times they had had. How on July 4 at a church picnic a family was about to break open a watermelon. Several children were standing around watching. Blue was hovering about on the periphery of the circle—a faint smile of anticipation softening his face. The father of the family lifted the melon high over his head—his big arms looked taller than the trees to Cholly, and the melon blotted out the sun. Tall, head forward, eyes fastened on a rock, his arms higher than the pines, his hands holding a melon bigger than the sun, he paused an instant to get his bearing and secure his aim. Watching the figure etched against the bright blue sky, Cholly felt goose pimples popping along his arms and neck. He wondered if God looked like that. No. God was a nice old white man, with long white hair, flowing white beard, and little blue eyes that looked sad when people died and mean when they were bad. It must be the devil who looks like that—holding the world in his hands, ready to dash it to the ground and spill the red guts so niggers could eat the sweet, warm insides. If the devil did look like that, Cholly preferred him. He never felt anything thinking about God, but just the idea of the devil excited him. And now the strong, black devil was blotting out the sun and getting ready to split open the world.

Far away somebody was playing a mouth organ; the music slithered over the cane fields and into the pine grove; it spiraled around the tree trunks and mixed itself with the pine scent, so Cholly couldn't tell the difference between the sound and the odor that hung about the heads of the people.

The man swung the melon down to the edge of a rock. A soft cry of disappointment accompanied the sound of smashed rind. The break was a bad one. The melon was jagged, and hunks of rind and red meat scattered on the grass.

Blue jumped. "Aw—awww," he moaned, "dere go da heart." His voice was both sad and pleased. Everybody looked to see the big red chunk from the very center of the melon, free of rind and sparse of seed, which had rolled a little distance from Blue's feet. He stooped to pick it up. Blood red, its planes dull and blunted with sweetness, its edges rigid with juice. Too obvious, almost obscene, in the joy it promised.

"Go 'head, Blue," the father laughed. "You can have it."

Blue smiled and walked away. Little children scrambled for the pieces on the ground. Women picked out the seeds for the smallest ones and broke off little bits of the meat for themselves. Blue's eyes caught Cholly's. He motioned to him. "Come on, boy. Le's you and me eat the heart."

Together the old man and the boy sat on the grass and shared the heart of the watermelon. The nasty-sweet guts of the earth.

It was in the spring, a very chilly spring, that Aunt Jimmy died of peach cobbler. She went to a camp meeting that took place after a rainstorm, and the damp wood of the benches was bad for her. For four or five days afterward, she felt poorly. Friends came to see about her. Some made camomile tea; others rubbed her with liniment. Miss Alice, her closest friend, read the Bible to her. Still she was declining. Advice was prolific, if contradictory.

"Don't eat no whites of eggs."

"Drink new milk."

"Chew on this root."

Aunt Jimmy ignored all but Miss Alice's Bible reading. She nodded in drowsy appreciation as the words from First Corinthians droned over her. Sweet amens fell from her lips as she was chastised for all her sins. But her body would not respond.

Finally it was decided to fetch M'Dear. M'Dear was a quiet woman who lived in a shack near the woods. She was a competent midwife and decisive diagnostician. Few could remember when M'Dear was not around. In any illness that could not be handled by ordinary means—known cures, intuition, or endurance—the word was always, "Fetch M'Dear."

When she arrived at Aunt Jimmy's house, Cholly was amazed at the sight of her. He had always pictured her as shriveled and hunched over, for he knew she was very, very old. But M'Dear loomed taller than the preacher who accompanied her. She must have been over six feet tall. Four big white knots of hair gave power and authority to her soft black face. Standing straight as a poker, she seemed to need her hickory stick not for support but for communication. She tapped it lightly on the floor as she looked down at Aunt Jimmy's wrinkled face. She stroked the knob with the thumb of her right hand while she ran her left one over Aunt Jimmy's body. The backs of her long fingers she placed on the patient's cheek, then placed her palm on the forehead. She ran her fingers through the sick woman's hair, lightly scratching the scalp, and then looking at what the fingernails revealed. She lifted Aunt Jimmy's hand and looked closely at it—fingernails, back skin, the flesh of the palm she pressed with three fingertips. Later she put her ear on Aunt Jimmy's chest and stomach to listen. At M'Dear's request, the women pulled the slop jar from under the bed to show the stools. M'Dear tapped her stick while looking at them.

"Bury the slop jar and everything in it," she said to the women. To Aunt Jimmy she said, "You done caught cold in your womb. Drink pot liquor and nothing else."

"Will it pass?" asked Aunt Jimmy. "Is I'm gone be all right?"

"I reckon."

M'Dear turned and left the room. The preacher put her in his buggy to take her home.

That evening the women brought bowls of pot liquor from black-eyed peas, from mustards, from cabbage, from kale, from collards, from turnips, from beets, from green beans. Even the juice from a boiling hog jowl.

Two evenings later Aunt Jimmy had gained much strength. When Miss Alice and Mrs. Gaines stopped in to check on her, they remarked on her improvement. The three women sat talking about various miseries they had had, their cure or abatement, what had helped. Over and over again they returned to Aunt Jimmy's condition. Repeating its cause, what could have been done to prevent the misery from taking hold, and M'Dear's infallibility. Their voices blended into a threnody of nostalgia about pain. Rising and falling, complex in harmony, uncertain in pitch, but constant in the recitative of pain. They hugged the memories of illnesses close to their bosoms. They licked their lips and clucked their tongues in fond remembrance of pains they had endured—childbirth, rheumatism, croup, sprains, backaches, piles. All of the bruises they had collected from moving about the earth—harvesting, cleaning, hoisting, pitching, stooping, kneeling, picking—always with young ones underfoot.

But they had been young once. The odor of their armpits and haunches had mingled into a lovely musk; their eyes had been furtive, their lips relaxed, and the delicate turn of their heads on those slim black necks had been like nothing other than a doe's. Their laughter had been more touch than sound.

Then they had grown. Edging into life from the back door. Becoming. Everybody in the world was in a position to give them orders. White women said, "Do this." White children said, "Give me that." White men said, "Come here." Black men said, "Lay down." The only people they need not take orders from were black children and each other. But they took all of that and re-created it in their own image. They ran the houses of white people, and knew it. When white men beat their men, they cleaned up the blood and went home to receive abuse from the victim. They beat their children with one hand and stole for them with the other. The hands that felled trees also cut umbilical cords; the hands that wrung the necks of chickens and butchered hogs also nudged African violets into bloom; the arms that loaded sheaves, bales, and sacks rocked babies into sleep. They patted biscuits into flaky ovals of innocence—and shrouded the dead. They plowed all day and came home to nestle like plums under the limbs of their men. The legs that straddled a mule's back were the same ones that straddled their men's hips. And the difference was all the difference there was.

Then they were old. Their bodies honed, their odor sour. Squatting in a cane field, stooping in a cotton field, kneeling by a river bank, they had carried a world on their heads. They have given over the lives of their own children and tendered their grandchildren. With relief they wrapped their heads in rags, and their breasts in flannel; eased their feet into felt. They were through with lust and lactation, beyond tears and terror. They alone could walk the roads of Mississippi, the lanes of Georgia, the fields of Alabama unmolested. They were old enough to be irritable when and where they chose, tired enough to look forward to death, disinterested enough to accept the idea of pain while ignoring the presence of pain. They were, in fact and at last, free. And the lives of these old black women were synthesized in their eyes—a purée of tragedy and humor, wickedness and serenity, truth and fantasy.

They chattered far into the night. Cholly listened and grew sleepy. The lullaby of grief enveloped him, rocked him, and at last numbed him. In his sleep the foul odor of old woman's stools turned into the healthy smell of horse shit, and the voices of the three women were muted into the pleasant notes of a mouth organ. He was aware, in his sleep, of being curled up in a chair, his hands tucked between his thighs. In a dream his penis changed into a long hickory stick, and the hands caressing it were the hands of M'Dear.

On a wet Saturday night, before Aunt Jimmy felt strong enough to get out of bed, Essie Foster brought her a peach cobbler. The old lady ate a piece, and the next morning when Cholly went to empty the slop jar, she was dead. Her mouth was a slackened O, and her hands, those long fingers with a man's hard nails, having done their laying by, could now be dainty on the sheet. One open eye looked at him as if to say, "Mind how you take holt of that jar, boy." Cholly stared back, unable to move, until a fly settled at the corner of her mouth. He fanned it away angrily, looked back at the eye, and did its bidding.

Aunt Jimmy's funeral was the first Cholly had ever attended. As a member of the family, one of the bereaved, he was the object of a great deal of attention. The ladies had cleaned the house, aired everything out, notified everybody, and stitched together what looked like a white wedding dress for Aunt Jimmy, a maiden lady, to wear when she met Jesus. They even produced a dark suit, white shirt, and tie for Cholly. The husband of one of them cut his hair. He was enclosed in fastidious tenderness. Nobody talked to him; that is, they treated him like the child he was, never engaging him in serious conversation; but they anticipated wishes he never had: meals appeared, hot water for the wooden tub, clothes laid out. At the wake he was allowed to fall asleep, and arms carried him to bed. Only on the third day after the death—the day of the funeral—did he have to share the spotlight. Aunt Jimmy's people came from nearby towns and farms. Her brother O. V., his children and wife, and lots of cousins. But Cholly was still the major figure, because he was "Jimmy's boy, the last thing she loved," and "the one who found her." The solicitude of the women, the head pats of the men, pleased Cholly, and the creamy conversations fascinated him.

"What'd she die from?"

"Essie's pie."

"Don't say?"

"Uh-huh. She was doing fine, I saw her the very day before. Said she wanted me to bring her some black thread to patch some things for the boy. I should of known just from her wanting black thread that was a sign."

"Sure was."

"Just like Emma. 'Member? She kept asking for thread. Dropped dead that very evening."

"Yeah. Well, she was determined to have it. Kept on reminding me. I told her I had some to home, but naw, she wanted it new. So I sent Li'l June to get some that very morning when she was laying dead. I was just fixing to bring it over, 'long with a piece of sweet bread. You know how she craved my sweet bread."

"Sure did. Always bragged on it. She was a good friend to you."

"I believe it. Well, I had no more got my clothes on when Sally bust in the door hollering about how Cholly here had been over to Miss Alice saying she was dead. You could have knocked me over, I tell you."

"Guess Essie feels mighty bad."

"Oh, Lord, yes. But I told her the Lord giveth and the Lord taketh away. Wasn't her fault none. She makes good peach pies. But she bound to believe it was the pie did it, and I 'spect she right."

"Well, she shouldn't worry herself none 'bout that. She was just doing what we all would of done."

"Yeah. 'Cause I was sure wrapping up that sweet bread, and that could of done it too."

"I doubts that. Sweet bread is pure. But a pie is the worse thing to give anybody ailing. I'm surprised Jimmy didn't know better."

"If she did, she wouldn't let on. She would have tried to please. You know how she was. So good."

"I'll say. Did she leave anything?"

"Not even a pocket handkerchief. The house belongs to some white folks in Clarksville."

"Oh, yeah? I thought she owned it."

"May have at one time. But not no more. I hear the insurance folks been down talking to her brother."

"How much do it come to?"

"Eighty-five dollars, I hear."

"That all?"

"Can she get in the ground on that?"

"Don't see how. When my daddy died last year this April it costed one hundred and fifty dollars. 'Course, we had to have everything just so. Now Jimmy's people may all have to chip in. That undertaker that lays out black folks ain't none too cheap."

"Seems a shame. She been paying on that insurance all her life."

"Don't I know?"

"Well, what about the boy? What he gone do?"

"Well, cain't nobody find that mama, so Jimmy's brother gone take him back to his place. They say he got a nice place. Inside toilet and everything."

"That's nice. He seems like a good Christian man. And the boy need a man's hand."

"What time's the funeral?"

"Two clock. She ought to be in the ground by four."

"Where the banquet? I heard Essie wanted it at her house."

"Naw, it's at Jimmy's. Her brother wanted it so."

"Well, it will be a big one. Everybody liked old Jimmy. Sure will miss her in the pew."

The funeral banquet was a peal of joy after the thunderous beauty of the funeral. It was like a street tragedy with spontaneity tucked softly into the corners of a highly formal structure. The deceased was the tragic hero, the survivors the innocent victims; there was the omnipresence of the deity, strophe and antistrophe of the chorus of mourners led by the preacher. There was grief over the waste of life, the stunned wonder at the ways of God, and the restoration of order in nature at the graveyard.

Thus the banquet was the exultation, the harmony, the acceptance of physical frailty, joy in the termination of misery. Laughter, relief, a steep hunger for food.

Cholly had not yet fully realized his aunt was dead. Everything was so interesting. Even at the graveyard he felt nothing but curiosity, and when his turn had come to view the body at the church, he had put his hand out to touch the corpse to see if it were really ice cold like everybody said. But he drew his hand back quickly. Aunt Jimmy looked so private, and it seemed wrong somehow to disturb that privacy. He had trudged back to his pew dry-eyed amid tearful shrieks and shouts of others, wondering if he should try to cry.

Back in his house, he was free to join in the gaiety and enjoy what he really felt—a kind of carnival spirit. He ate greedily and felt good enough to try to get to know his cousins. There was some question, according to the adults, as to whether they were his real cousins or not, since Jimmy's brother O. V. was only a half-brother, and Cholly's mother had been the daughter of Jimmy's sister, but that sister was from the second marriage of Jimmy's father, and O. V. was from the first marriage.

One of these cousins interested Cholly in particular. He was about fifteen or sixteen years old. Cholly went outside and found the boy standing with some others near the tub where Aunt Jimmy used to boil her clothes.

He ventured a tentative "Hey." They responded with another. The fifteen-year-old named Jake offered Cholly a rolled-up cigarette. Cholly took it, but when he held the cigarette at arm's length and stuck the tip of it into the match flame, instead of putting it in his mouth and drawing on it, they laughed at him. Shamefaced, he threw the cigarette down. He felt it important to do something to reinstate himself with Jake. So when he asked Cholly if he knew any girls, Cholly said, "Sure."

All the girls Cholly knew were at the banquet, and he pointed to a cluster of them standing, hanging, draping on the back porch. Darlene too. Cholly hoped Jake wouldn't pick her.

"Let's get some and walk around," said Jake.

The two boys sauntered over to the porch. Cholly didn't know how to begin. Jake wrapped his legs around the rickety porch rail and just sat there staring off into space as though he had no interest in them at all. He was letting them look him over, and guardedly evaluating them in return.

The girls pretended they didn't see the boys and kept on chattering. Soon their talk got sharp; the gentle teasing they had been engaged in with each other changed to bitchiness, a serious kind of making fun. That was Jake's clue; the girls were reacting to him. They had gotten a whiff of his manhood and were shivering for a place in his attention.

Jake left the porch rail and walked right up to a girl named Suky, the one who had been most bitter in her making fun.

"Want to show me 'round?" He didn't even smile.

Cholly held his breath, waiting for Suky to shut Jake up. She was good at that, and well known for her sharp tongue. To his enormous surprise, she readily agreed, and even lowered her lashes. Taking courage, Cholly turned to Darlene and said, "Come on 'long. We just going down to the gully." He waited for her to screw up her face and say no, or what for, or some such thing. His feelings about her were mostly fear—fear that she would not like him, and fear that she would.

His second fear materialized. She smiled and jumped down the three leaning steps to join him. Her eyes were full of compassion, and Cholly remembered that he was the bereaved.

"If you want to," she said, "but not too far. Mama said we got to leave early, and it's getting dark."

The four of them moved away. Some of the other boys had come to the porch and were about to begin that partly hostile, partly indifferent, partly desperate mating dance. Suky, Jake, Darlene, and Cholly walked through several backyards until they came to an open field. They ran across it and came to a dry riverbed lined with green. The object of the walk was a wild vineyard where the muscadine grew. Too new, too tight to have much sugar, they were eaten anyway. None of them wanted—not then—the grape's easy relinquishing of all its dark juice. The restraint, the holding off, the promise of sweetness that had yet to unfold, excited them more than full ripeness would have done. At last their teeth were on edge, and the boys diverted themselves by pelting the girls with the grapes. Their slim black boy wrists made G clefs in the air as they executed the tosses. The chase took Cholly and Darlene away from the lip of the gully, and when they paused for breath, Jake and Suky were nowhere in sight. Darlene's white cotton dress was stained with juice. Her big blue hair bow had come undone, and the sundown breeze was picking it up and fluttering it about her head. They were out of breath and sank down in the green-and-purple grass on the edge of the pine woods.

Cholly lay on his back panting. His mouth full of the taste of muscadine, listening to the pine needles rustling loudly in their anticipation of rain. The smell of promised rain, pine, and muscadine made him giddy. The sun had gone and pulled away its shreds of light. Turning his head to see where the moon was. Cholly caught sight of Darlene in moonlight behind him. She was huddled into a D—arms encircling drawn-up knees, on which she rested her head. Cholly could see her bloomers and the muscles of her young thighs.

"We bed' get on back," he said.

"Yeah." She stretched her legs flat on the ground and began to retie her hair ribbon. "Mama gone whup me."

"Naw she ain't."

"Uh-huh. She told me she would if I get dirty."

"You ain't dirty."

"I am too. Looka that." She dropped her hands from the ribbon and smoothed out a place on her dress where the grape stains were heaviest.

Cholly felt sorry for her; it was just as much his fault. Suddenly he realized that Aunt Jimmy was dead, for he missed the fear of being whipped. There was nobody to do it except Uncle O. V., and he was the bereaved too.

"Let me," he said. He rose to his knees facing her and tried to tie her ribbon. Darlene put her hands under his open shirt and rubbed the damp tight skin. When he looked at her in surprise, she stopped and laughed. He smiled and continued knotting the bow. She put her hands back under his shirt.

"Hold still," he said. "How I gone get this?"

She tickled his ribs with her fingertips. He giggled and grabbed his rib cage. They were on top of each other in a moment. She corkscrewing her hands into his clothes. He returning the play, digging into the neck of her dress, and then under her dress. When he got his hand in her bloomers, she suddenly stopped laughing and looked serious. Cholly, frightened, was about to take his hand away, but she held his wrist so he couldn't move it. He examined her then with his fingers, and she kissed his face and mouth. Cholly found her muscadine-lipped mouth distracting. Darlene released his head, shifted her body, and pulled down her pants. After some trouble with the buttons, Cholly dropped his pants down to his knees. Their bodies began to make sense to him, and it was not as difficult as he had thought it would be. She moaned a little, but the excitement collecting inside him made him close his eyes and regard her moans as no more than pine sighs over his head. Just as he felt an explosion threaten, Darlene froze and cried out. He thought he had hurt her, but when he looked at her face, she was staring wildly at something over his shoulder. He jerked around.

There stood two white men. One with a spirit lamp, the other with a flashlight. There was no mistake about their being white; he could smell it. Cholly jumped, trying to kneel, stand, and get his pants up all in one motion. The men had long guns.

"Hee hee hee heeeee." The snicker was a long asthmatic cough.

The other raced the flashlight all over Cholly and Darlene.

"Get on wid it, nigger," said the flashlight one.

"Sir?" said Cholly, trying to find a buttonhole.

"I said, get on wid it. An' make it good, nigger, make it good."

There was no place for Cholly's eyes to go. They slid about furtively searching for shelter, while his body remained paralyzed. The flashlight man lifted his gun down from his shoulder, and Cholly heard the clop of metal. He dropped back to his knees. Darlene had her head averted, her eyes staring out of the lamplight into the surrounding darkness and looking almost unconcerned, as though they had no part in the drama taking place around them. With a violence born of total helplessness, he pulled her dress up, lowered his trousers and underwear.

"Hee hee hee hee heeeeee."

Darlene put her hands over her face as Cholly began to simulate what had gone on before. He could do no more than make-believe. The flashlight made a moon on his behind.

"Hee hee hee hee heeee."

"Come on, coon. Faster. You ain't doing nothing for her."

"Hee hee hee hee heeee."

Cholly, moving faster, looked at Darlene. He hated her. He almost wished he could do it—hard, long, and painfully, he hated her so much. The flashlight wormed its way into his guts and turned the sweet taste of muscadine into rotten fetid bile. He stared at Darlene's hands covering her face in the moon and lamplight. They looked like baby claws.

"Hee hee hee hee heee."

Some dogs howled. "Thas them. Thas them. I know thas Old Honey."

"Yep," said the spirit lamp.

"Come on." The flashlight turned away, and one of them whistled to Honey.

"Wait," said the spirit lamp, "the coon ain't comed yet."

"Well, he have to come on his own time. Good luck, coon baby."

They crushed the pine needles underfoot. Cholly could hear them whistling for a long time, and then the dogs' answer no longer a howl, but warm excited yelps of recognition.

Cholly raised himself and in silence buttoned his trousers. Darlene did not move. Cholly wanted to strangle her, but instead he touched her leg with his foot. "We got to get, girl. Come on!"

She reached for her underwear with her eyes closed, and could not find them. The two of them patted about in the moonlight for the panties. When she found them, she put them on with the movements of an old woman. They walked away from the pine woods toward the road. He in front, she plopping along behind. It started to rain. "That's good," Cholly thought. "It will explain away our clothes."

When they got back to the house, some ten or twelve guests were still there. Jake was gone, Suky too. Some people had gone back for more helpings of food—potato pie, ribs. All were engrossed in early-night reminiscences about dreams, figures, premonitions. Their stuffed comfort was narcotic and had produced recollections and fabrications of hallucinations.

Cholly and Darlene's entrance produced only a mild stir.

"Ya'll soaked, ain't you?"

Darlene's mother was only vaguely fussy. She had eaten and drunk too much. Her shoes were under her chair, and the side snaps of her dress were opened. "Girl. Come on in here. Thought I told you . . ."

Some of the guests thought they would wait for the rain to slacken. Others, who had come in wagons, thought they'd best leave now. Cholly went into the little storeroom which had been made into a bedroom for him. Three infants were sleeping on his cot. He took off his rain- and pine-soaked clothes and put on his coveralls. He didn't know where to go. Aunt Jimmy's room was out of the question, and Uncle O. V. and his wife would be using it later anyway. He took a quilt from a trunk, spread it on the floor, and lay down. Somebody was brewing coffee, and he had a sharp craving for it, just before falling asleep.

The next day was cleaning-out day, settling accounts, distributing Aunt Jimmy's goods. Mouths were set in downward crescents, eyes veiled, feet tentative.

Cholly floated about aimlessly, doing chores as he was told. All the glamour and warmth the adults had given him on the previous day were replaced by a sharpness that agreed with his mood. He could think only of the flashlight, the muscadines, and Darlene's hands. And when he was not thinking of them, the vacancy in his head was like the space left by a newly pulled tooth still conscious of the rottenness that had once filled it. Afraid of running into Darlene, he would not go far from the house, but neither could he endure the atmosphere of his dead Aunt's house. The picking through her things, the comments on the "condition" of her goods. Sullen, irritable, he cultivated his hatred of Darlene. Never did he once consider directing his hatred toward the hunters. Such an emotion would have destroyed him. They were big, white, armed men. He was small, black, helpless. His subconscious knew what his conscious mind did not guess—that hating them would have consumed him, burned him up like a piece of soft coal, leaving only flakes of ash and a question mark of smoke. He was, in time, to discover that hatred of white men—but not now. Not in impotence but later, when the hatred could find sweet expression. For now, he hated the one who had created the situation, the one who bore witness to his failure, his impotence. The one whom he had not been able to protect, to spare, to cover from the round moon glow of the flashlight. The hee-hee-hee's. He recalled Darlene's dripping hair ribbon, flapping against her face as they walked back in silence in the rain. The loathing that galloped through him made him tremble. There was no one to talk to. Old Blue was too drunk too often these days to make sense. Besides, Cholly doubted if he could reveal his shame to Blue. He would have to lie a little to tell Blue, Blue the woman-killer. It seemed to him that lonely was much better than alone.

The day Cholly's uncle was ready to leave, when everything was packed, when the quarrels about who gets what had seethed down to a sticking gravy on everybody's tongue, Cholly sat on the back porch waiting. It had occurred to him that Darlene might be pregnant. It was a wildly irrational, completely uninformed idea, but the fear it produced was complete enough.

He had to get away. Never mind the fact that he was leaving that very day. A town or two away was not far enough, especially since he did not like or trust his uncle, and Darlene's mother could surely find him, and Uncle O. V. would turn him over to her. Cholly knew it was wrong to run out on a pregnant girl, and recalled, with sympathy, that his father had done just that. Now he understood. He knew then what he must do—find his father. His father would understand. Aunt Jimmy said he had gone to Macon.

With no more thought than a chick leaving its shell, he stepped off the porch. He had gotten a little way when he remembered the treasure; Aunt Jimmy had left something, and he had forgotten all about it. In a stove flue no longer used, she had hidden a little meal bag which she called her treasure. He slipped into the house and found the room empty. Digging into the flue, he encountered webs and soot, and then the soft bag. He sorted the money; fourteen one-dollar bills, two two-dollar bills, and lots of silver change . . . twenty-three dollars in all. Surely that would be enough to get to Macon. What a good, strong-sounding word, *Macon.*

Running away from home for a Georgia black boy as not a great problem. You just sneaked away and started walking. When night came you slept in a barn, if there were no dogs, a cane field, or an empty sawmill. You ate from the ground and bought root beer and licorice in little country stores. There was always an easy tale of woe to tell inquiring black adults, and whites didn't care, unless they were looking for sport.

When he was several days away, he could go to the back door of nice houses and tell the black cook or white mistress that he wanted a job weeding, plowing, picking, cleaning, and that he lived nearby. A week or more there, and he could take off. He lived this way through the turn of summer, and only the following October did he reach a town big enough to have a regular bus station. Dry-mouthed with excitement and apprehension, he went to the colored side of the counter to buy his ticket.

"How much to Macon, sir?"

"Eleven dollars. Five-fifty for children under twelve."

Cholly had twelve dollars and four cents.

"How old you be?"

"Just on twelve, sir, but my mama only give me ten dollars."

"You jest about the biggest twelve I ever seed."

"Please, sir, I got to get to Macon. My mama's sick."

"Thought you said you mama give you ten dollars."

"That's my play mama. My real mama is in Macon, sir."

"I reckon I knows a lying nigger when I sees one, but jest in case you ain't, jest in case one of them mammies is really dyin' and wants to see her little old smoke before she meets her maker, I gone do it."

Cholly heard nothing. The insults were part of the nuisances of life, like lice. He was happier than he had ever remembered being, except that time with Blue and the watermelon. The bus wasn't leaving for four hours, and the minutes of those hours struggled like gnats on fly paper—dying slow, exhausted with the fight to stay alive. Cholly was afraid to stir, even to relieve himself. The bus might leave while he was gone. Finally, rigid with constipation, he boarded the bus to Macon.

He found a window seat in the back all to himself, and all of Georgia slid before his eyes, until the sun shrugged out of sight. Even in the dark, he hungered to see, and only after the fiercest fight to keep his eyes open did he fall asleep. When he awoke it was very well into day, and a fat black lady was nudging him with a biscuit gashed with cold bacon. With the taste of bacon still in his teeth, they sidled into Macon.

❖❖❖

At the end of the alley he could see men clustered like grapes. One large whooping voice spiraled over the heads of the bended forms. The kneeling forms, the leaning forms, all intent on one ground spot. As he came closer, he inhaled a rife and stimulating man smell. The men were gathered, just as the man in the pool hall had said, for and about dice and money. Each figure was decorated some way with the slight pieces of green. Some of them had separated their money, folded the bills around their fingers, clenched the fingers into fists, so the neat ends of the money stuck out in a blend of daintiness and violence. Others had stacked their bills, creased them down the middle, and held the wad as though they were about to deal cards. Still others had left their money in loosely crumpled balls. One man had money sticking out from under his cap. Another stroked his bills with a thumb and forefinger. There was more money in those black hands than Cholly had ever seen before. He shared their excitement, and the dry-mouthed apprehension on meeting his father gave way to the saliva flow of excitement. He glanced at the faces, looking for the one who might be his father. How would he know him? Would he look like a larger version of himself? At that moment Cholly could not remember what his own self looked like. He only knew he was fourteen years old, black, and already six feet tall. He searched the faces and saw only eyes, pleading eyes, cold eyes, eyes gone flat with malice, others laced with fear—all focused on the movement of a pair of dice that one man was throwing, snatching up, and throwing again. Chanting a kind of litany to which the others responded, rubbing the dice as though they were two hot coals, he whispered to them. Then with a whoop the cubes flew from his hand to a chorus of amazements and disappointments. Then the thrower scopped up money, and someone shouted, "Take it and crawl, you water dog, you, the best I know." There was some laughter, and a noticeable release of tension, during which some men exchanged money.

Cholly tapped on old white-haired man on the back.

"Can you tell me is Samson Fuller 'round here somewhere?"

"Fuller?" The name was familiar to the man's tongue. "I don't know, he here somewhere. They he is. In the brown jacket." The man pointed.

A man in a light-brown jacket stood at the far end of the group. He was gesturing in a quarrelsome, agitated manner with another man. Both of them had folded their faces in anger. Cholly edged around to where they stood, hardly believing he was at the end of his journey. There was his father, a man like any other man, but there indeed were his eyes, his mouth, his whole head. His shoulders lurked beneath that jacket, his voice, his hands—all real. They existed, really existed, somewhere. Right here. Cholly had always thought of his father as a giant of a man, so when he was very close it was with a shock that he discovered that he was taller than his father. In fact, he was staring at a balding spot on his father's head, which he suddenly wanted to stroke. While thus fascinated by the pitiable clean space hedged around by neglected tufts of wool, the man turned a hard, belligerent face to him.

"What you want, boy?"

"Uh. I mean . . . is you Samson Fuller?"

"Who sent you?"

"Huh?"

"You Melba's boy?"

"No, sir, I'm . . ." Cholly blinked. He could not remember his mother's name. Had he ever known it? What could he say? Whose boy was he? He couldn't say, "I'm your boy." That sounded disrespectful.

The man was impatient. "Something wrong with your head? Who told you to come after me?"

"Nobody." Cholly's hands were sweating. The man's eyes frightened him. "I just thought . . . I mean, I was just wandering around, and, uh, my name is Cholly. . . ."

But Fuller had turned back to the game that was about to begin anew. He bent down to toss a bill on the ground, and waited for a throw. When it was gone, he stood up and in a vexed and whiny voice shouted at Cholly, "Tell that bitch she get her money. Now, get the fuck outta my face!"

Cholly was a long time picking his foot up from the ground. He was trying to back up and walk away. Only with extreme effort could he get the first muscle to cooperate. When it did, he walked back up the alley, out of its shade, toward the blazing light of the street. As he emerged into the sun, he felt something in his legs give way. An orange crate with a picture of clasping hands pasted on its side was upended on the sidewalk. Cholly sat down on it. The sunshine dropped like honey on his head. A horsedrawn fruit wagon went by, its driver singing: "Fresh from the vine, sweet as sugar, red as wine."

Noises seemed to increase in volume. The clic-cloc of the women's heels, the laughter of idling men in doorways. There was a streetcar somewhere. Cholly sat. He knew if he was very still he would be all right. But then the trace of pain edged his eyes, and he had to use everything to send it away. If he was very still, he thought, and kept his eyes on one thing, the tears would not come. So he sat in the dripping honey sun, pulling every nerve and muscle into service to stop the fall of water from his eyes. While straining in this way, focusing every erg of energy on his eyes, his bowels suddenly opened up, and before he could realize what he knew, liquid stools were running down his legs. At the mouth of the alley where his father was, on an orange crate in the sun, on a street full of grown men and women, he had soiled himself like a baby.

In panic he wondered should he wait there, not moving until nighttime? No. His father would surely emerge and see him and laugh. Oh, Lord. He would laugh. Everybody would laugh. There was only one thing to do.

Cholly ran down the street, aware only of silence. People's mouths moved, their feet moved, a car jugged by—but with no sound. A door slammed in perfect soundlessness. His own feet made no sound. The air seemed to strangle him, hold him back. He was pushing through a world of invisible pine sap that threatened to smother him. Still he ran, seeing only silent moving things, until he came to the end of buildings, the beginning of open space, and saw the Ocmulgee River winding ahead. He scooted down a gravelly slope to a pier jutting out over the shallow water. Finding the deepest shadow under the pier, he crouched in it, behind one of the posts. He remained knotted there in fetal position, paralyzed, his fists covering his eyes, for a long time. No sound, no sight, only darkness and heat and the press of his knuckles on his eyelids. He even forgot his messed-up trousers.

Evening came. The dark, the warmth, the quiet, enclosed Cholly like the skin and flesh of an elderberry protecting its own seed.

Cholly stirred. The ache in his head was all he felt. Soon, like bright bits of glass, the events of that afternoon cut into him. At first he saw only money in black fingers, then he thought he was sitting on an uncomfortable chair, but when he looked, it turned out to be the head of a man, a head with a bald spot the size of an orange. When finally these bits merged into full memory, Cholly began to smell himself. He stood up and found himself weak, trembling, and dizzy. He leaned for a moment on the pier post, then took off his pants, underwear, socks, and shoes. He rubbed handfuls of dirt on his shoes; then he crawled to the river edge. He had to find the water's beginning with his hands, for he could not see it clearly. Slowly he swirled his clothes in the water and rubbed them until he thought they were clean. Back near his post, he took off his shirt and wrapped it around his waist, then spread his trousers and underwear on the ground. He squatted down and picked at the rotted wood of the pier. Suddenly he thought of his Aunt Jimmy, her asafetida bag, her four gold teeth, and the purple rag she wore around her head. With a longing that almost split him open, he thought of her handing him a bit of smoked hock out of her dish. He remembered just how she held it—clumsy-like, in three fingers, but with so much affection. No words, just picking up a bit of meat and holding it out to him. And then the tears rushed down his cheeks, to make a bouquet under his chin.

Three women are leaning out of two windows. They see the long clean neck of a new young boy and call to him. He goes to where they are. Inside, it is dark and warm. They give him lemonade in a Mason jar. As he drinks, their eyes float up to him through the bottom of the jar, through the slick sweet water. They give him back his manhood, which he takes aimlessly.

The pieces of Cholly's life could become coherent only in the head of a musician. Only those who talk their talk through the gold of curved metal, or in the touch of black-and-white rectangles and taut skins and strings echoing from wooden corridors, could give true form to his life. Only they would know how to connect the heart of a red watermelon to the asafetida bag to the muscadine to the flashlight on his behind to the fists of money to the lemonade in a Mason jar to a man called Blue and come up with what all of that meant in joy, in pain, in anger, in love, and give it its final and pervading ache of freedom. Only a musician would sense, know, without even knowing that he knew, that Cholly was free. Dangerously free. Free to feel whatever he felt—fear, guilt, shame, love, grief, pity. Free to be tender or violent, to whistle or weep. Free to sleep in doorways or between the white sheets of a singing woman. Free to take a job, free to leave it. He could go to jail and not feel imprisoned, for he had already seen the furtiveness in the eyes of his jailer, free to say, "No, suh," and smile, for he had already killed three white men. Free to take a woman's insults, for his body had already conquered hers. Free even to knock her in the head, for he had already cradled that head in his arms. Free to be gentle when she was sick, or mop her floor, for she knew what and where his maleness was. He was free to drink himself into a silly helplessness, for he had already been a gandy dancer, done thirty days on a chain gang, and picked a woman's bullet out of the calf of his leg. He was free to live his fantasies, and free even to die, the how and the when of which held no interest for him. In those days, Cholly was truly free. Abandoned in a junk heap by his mother, rejected for a crap game by his father, there was nothing more to lose. He was alone with his own perceptions and appetites, and they alone interested him.

It was in this godlike state that he met Pauline Williams. And it was Pauline, or rather marrying her, that did for him what the flashlight did not do. The constantness, varietylessness, the sheer weight of sameness drove him to despair and froze his imagination. To be required to sleep with the same woman forever was a curious and unnatural idea to him; to be expected to dredge up enthusiasms for old acts, and routine ploys; he wondered at the arrogance of the female. When he had met Pauline in Kentucky, she was hanging over a fence scratching herself with a broken foot. The neatness, the charm, the joy he awakened in her made him want to nest with her. He had yet to discover what destroyed that desire. But he did not dwell on it. He thought rather of whatever had happened to the curiosity he used to feel. Nothing, nothing, interested him now. Not himself, not other people. Only in drink was there some break, some floodlight, and when that closed, there was oblivion.

But the aspect of married life that dumbfounded him and rendered him totally disfunctional was the appearance of children. Having no idea of how to raise children, and having never watched any parent raise himself, he could not even comprehend what such a relationship should be. Had he been interested in the accumulation of things, he could have thought of them as his material heirs; had he needed to prove himself to some nameless "others," he could have wanted them to excel in his own image and for his own sake. Had he not been alone in the world since he was thirteen, knowing only a dying old woman who felt responsible for him, but whose age, sex, and interests were so remote from his own, he might have felt a stable connection between himself and the children. As it was, he reacted to them, and his reactions were based on what he felt at the moment.

So it was on a Saturday afternoon, in the thin light of spring, he staggered home reeling drunk and saw his daughter in the kitchen.

She was washing dishes. Her small back hunched over the sink. Cholly saw her dimly and could not tell what he saw or what he felt. Then he became aware that he was uncomfortable; next he felt the discomfort dissolve into pleasure. The sequence of his emotions was revulsion, guilt, pity, then love. His revulsion was a reaction to her young, helpless, hopeless presence. Her back hunched that way; her head to one side as though crouching from a permanent and unrelieved blow. Why did she have to look so whipped? She was a child—unburdened—why wasn't she happy? The clear statement of her misery was an accusation. He wanted to break her neck—but tenderly. Guilt and impotence rose in a bilious duet. What could he do for her—ever? What give her? What say to her? What could a burned-out black man say to the hunched back of his eleven-year-old daughter? If he looked into her face, he would see those haunted, loving eyes. The hauntedness would irritate him—the love would move him to fury. How dare she love him? Hadn't she any sense at all? What was he supposed to do about that? Return it? How? What could his calloused hands produce to make her smile? What of his knowledge of the world and of life could be useful to her? What could his heavy arms and befuddled brain accomplish that would earn him his own respect, that would in turn allow him to accept her love? His hatred of her slimed in his stomach and threatened to become vomit. But just before the puke moved from anticipation to sensation, she shifted her weight and stood on one foot scratching the back of her calf with her toe. It was a quiet and pitiful gesture. Her hands were going around and around a frying pan, scraping flecks of black into cold, greasy dishwater. The timid, tucked-in look of the scratching toe—that was what Pauline was doing the first time he saw her in Kentucky. Leaning over a fence staring at nothing in particular. The creamy toe of her bare foot scratching a velvet leg. It was such a small and simple gesture, but it filled him then with a wondering softness. Not the usual lust to part tight legs with his own, but a tenderness, a protectiveness. A desire to cover her foot with his hand and gently nibble away the itch from the calf with his teeth. He did it then, and started Pauline into laughter. He did it now.

The tenderness welled up in him, and he sank to his knees, his eyes on the foot of his daughter. Crawling on all fours toward her, he raised his hand and caught the foot in an upward stroke. Pecola lost her balance and was about to careen to the floor. Cholly raised his other hand to her hips to save her from falling. He put his head down and nibbled at the back of her leg. His mouth trembled at the firm sweetness of the flesh. He closed his eyes, letting his fingers dig into her waist. The rigidness of her shocked body, the silence of her stunned throat, was better than Pauline's easy laughter had been. The confused mixture of his memories of Pauline and the doing of a wild and forbidden thing excited him, and a bolt of desire ran down his genitals, giving it length, and softening the lips of his anus. Surrounding all of this lust was a border of politeness. He wanted to fuck her—tenderly. But the tenderness would not hold. The tightness of her vagina was more than he could bear. His soul seemed to slip down to his guts and fly out into her, and the gigantic thrust he made into her then provoked the only sound she made—a hollow suck of air in the back of her throat. Like the rapid loss of air from a circus balloon.

Following the disintegration—the falling away—of sexual desire, he was conscious of her wet, soapy hands on his wrists, the fingers clenching, but whether her grip was from a hopeless but stubborn struggle to be free, or from some other emotion, he could not tell.

Removing himself from her was so painful to him he cut it short and snatched his genitals out of the dry harbor of her vagina. She appeared to have fainted. Cholly stood up and could see only her grayish panties, so sad and limp around her ankles. Again the hatred mixed with tenderness. The hatred would not let him pick her up, the tenderness forced him to cover her.

So when the child regained consciousness, she was lying on the kitchen floor under a heavy quilt, trying to connect the pain between her legs with the face of her mother looming over her.

SEETHEDOGBOWWOWGOESTHEDOGDOY OUWANTTOPLAYDOYOUWANTTOPLAYWI THJANESEETHEDOGRUNR

Once there was an old man who loved things, for the slightest contact with people produced in him a faint but persistent nausea. He could not remember when this distaste began, nor could he remember ever being free of it. As a young boy he had been greatly disturbed by this revulsion which others did not seem to share, but having got a fine education, he learned, among other things, the word "misanthrope." Knowing his label provided him with both comfort and courage, he believed that to name an evil was to neutralize if not annihilate it. Then, too, he had read several books and made the acquaintance of several great misanthropes of the ages, whose spiritual company soothed him and provided him with yardsticks for measuring his whims, his yearnings, and his antipathies. Moreover, he found misanthropy an excellent means of developing character: when he subdued his revulsion and occasionally touched, helped, counseled, or befriended somebody, he was able to think of his behavior as generous and his intentions as noble. When he was enraged by some human effort or flaw, he was able to regard himself as discriminating, fastidious, and full of nice scruples.

As in the case of many misanthropes, his disdain for people led him into a profession designed to serve them. He was engaged in a line of work that was dependent solely on his ability to win the trust of others, and one in which the most intimate relationships were necessary. Having dallied with the priesthood in the Anglican Church, he abandoned it to become a caseworker. Time and misfortune, however, conspired against him, and he settled finally on a profession that brought him both freedom and satisfaction. He became a "Reader, Adviser, and Interpreter of Dreams." It was a profession that suited him well. His hours were his own, the competition was slight, the clientele was already persuaded and therefore manageable, and he had numerous opportunities to witness human stupidity without sharing it or being compromised by it, and to nurture his fastidiousness by viewing physical decay. Although his income was small, he had no taste for luxury—his experience in the monastery had solidified his natural asceticism while it developed his preference for solitude. Celibacy was a haven, silence a shield.

All his life he had a fondness for things—not the acquisition of wealth or beautiful objects, but a genuine love of worn objects: a coffee pot that had been his mother's, a welcome mat from the door of a rooming house he once lived in, a quilt from a Salvation Army store counter. It was as though his disdain of human contact had converted itself into a craving for things humans had touched. The residue of the human spirit smeared on inanimate objects was all he could withstand of humanity. To contemplate, for example, evidence of human footsteps on the mat—absorb the smell of the quilt and wallow in the sweet certainty that many bodies had sweated, slept, dreamed, made love, been ill, and even died under it. Wherever he went, he took along his things, and was always searching for others. This thirst for worn things led to casual but habitual examinations of trash barrels in alleys and wastebaskets in public places. . . .

All in all, his personality was an arabesque: intricate, symmetrical, balanced, and tightly constructed—except for one flaw. The careful design was marred occasionally by rare but keen sexual cravings.

He could have been an active homosexual but lacked the courage. Bestiality did not occur to him, and sodomy was quite out of the question, for he did not experience sustained erections and could not endure the thought of somebody else's. And besides, the one thing that disgusted him more than entering and caressing a woman was caressing and being caressed by a man. In any case, his cravings, although intense, never relished physical contact. He abhorred flesh on flesh. Body odor, breath odor, overwhelmed him. The sight of dried matter in the corner of the eye, decayed or missing teeth, ear wax, blackheads, moles, blisters, skin crusts—all the natural excretions and protections the body was capable of—disquieted him. His attentions therefore gradually settled on those humans whose bodies were least offensive—children. And since he was too diffident to confront homosexuality, and since little boys were insulting, scary, and stubborn, he further limited his interests to little girls. They were usually manageable and frequently seductive. His sexuality was anything but lewd; his patronage of little girls smacked of innocence and was associated in his mind with cleanliness. He was what one might call a very clean old man.

A cinnamon-eyed West Indian with lightly browned skin.

Although his given name was printed on the sign in his kitchen window, and on the business cards he circulated, he was called by the townspeople Soaphead Church. No one knew where the "Church" part came from—perhaps somebody's recollection of his days as a guest preacher—those reverends who had been called but who had no flock or coop, and were constantly visiting other churches, sitting on the altar with the host preacher. But everybody knew what "Soaphead" meant—the tight, curly hair that took on and held a sheen and wave when pomaded with soap lather. A sort of primitive process.

He had been reared in a family proud of its academic accomplishments and its mixed blood—in fact, they believed the former was based on the latter. A Sir Whitcomb, some decaying British nobleman, who chose to disintegrate under a sun more easeful than England's, had introduced the white strain into the family in the early 1800's. Being a gentleman by order of the King, he had done the civilized thing for his mulatto bastard—provided it with three hundred pounds sterling, to the great satisfaction of the bastard's mother, who felt that fortune had smiled on her. The bastard too was grateful, and regarded as his life's goal the hoarding of this white strain. He bestowed his favors on a fifteen-year-old girl of similar parentage. She, like a good Victorian parody, learned from her husband all that was worth learning—to separate herself in body, mind, and spirit from all that suggested Africa; to cultivate the habits, tastes, preferences that her absent father-in-law and foolish mother-in-law would have approved.

They transferred this Anglophilia to their six children and sixteen grandchildren. Except for an occasional and unaccountable insurgent who chose a restive black, they married "up," lightening the family complexion and thinning out the family features.

With the confidence born of a conviction of superiority, they performed well at schools. They were industrious, orderly, and energetic, hoping to prove beyond a doubt De Gobineau's hypothesis that "all civilizations derive from the white race, that none can exist without its help, and that a society is great and brilliant only so far as it preserves the blood of the noble group that created it." Thus, they were seldom overlooked by schoolmasters who recommended promising students for study abroad. The men studied medicine, law, theology, and emerged repeatedly in the powerless government offices available to the native population. That they were corrupt in public and private practice, both lecherous and lascivious, was considered their noble right, and thoroughly enjoyed by most of the less gifted population.

As the years passed, due to the carelessness of some of the Whitcomb brothers, it became difficult to maintain their whiteness, and some distant and some not so distant relatives married each other. No obviously bad effects were noticed from these ill-advised unions, but one or two old maids or gardener boys marked a weakening of faculties and a disposition toward eccentricity in some of the children. Some flaw outside the usual alcoholism and lechery. They blamed the flaw on intermarriage with the family, however, not on the original genes of the decaying lord. In any case, there were flukes. No more than in any other family, to be sure, but more dangerous because more powerful. One of them was a religious fanatic who founded his own secret sect and fathered four sons, one of whom became a schoolmaster known for the precision of his justice and the control in his violence. This schoolmaster married a sweet, indolent half-Chinese girl for whom the fatigue of bearing a son was too much. She died soon after childbirth. Her son, named Elihue Micah Whitcomb, provided the schoolmaster with ample opportunity to work out his theories of education, discipline, and the good life. Little Elihue learned everything he needed to know well, particularly the fine art of self-deception. He read greedily but understood selectively, choosing the bits and pieces of other men's ideas that supported whatever predilection he had at the moment. Thus he chose to remember Hamlet's abuse of Ophelia, but not Christ's love of Mary Magdalene; Hamlet's frivolous politics, but not Christ's serious anarchy. He noticed Gibbon's acidity, but not his tolerance, Othello's love for the fair Desdemona, but not Iago's perverted love of Othello. The works he admired most were Dante's; those he despised most were Dostoyevsky's. For all his exposure to the best minds of the Western world, he allowed only the narrowest interpretation to touch him. He responded to his father's controlled violence by developing hard habits and a soft imagination. A hatred of, and fascination with, any hint of disorder or decay.

At seventeen, however, he met his Beatrice, who was three years his senior. A lovely, laughing big-legged girl who worked as a clerk in a Chinese department store. Velma. So strong was her affection and zest for life, she did not eliminate the frail, sickly Elihue from it. She found his fastidiousness and complete lack of humor touching and longed to introduce him to the idea of delight. He resisted the introduction, but she married him anyway, only to discover that he was suffering from and enjoying an invincible melancholy. When she learned two months into the marriage how important his melancholy was to him, that he was very interested in altering her joy to a more academic gloom, that he equated lovemaking with communion and the Holy Grail, she simply left. She had not lived by the sea all those years, listened to the wharfman's songs all that time, to spend her life in the soundless cave of Elihue's mind.

He never got over her desertion. She was to have been the answer to his unstated, unacknowledged question—where was the life to counter the encroaching nonlife? Velma was to rescue him from the nonlife he had learned on the flat side of his father's belt. But he resisted her with such skill that she was finally driven out to escape the inevitable boredom produced by such a dainty life.

Young Elihue was saved from visible shattering by the steady hand of his father, who reminded him of the family's reputation and Velma's questionable one. He then pursued his studies with more vigor than before and decided at least to enter the ministry. When he was advised that he had no avocation, he left the island, came to America to study the then budding field of psychiatry. But the subject required too much truth, too many confrontations, and offered too little support to a failing ego. He drifted into sociology, then physical therapy. This diverse education continued for six years, when his father refused to support him any longer, until he "found" himself. Elihue, not knowing where to look, was thrown back on his own devices, and "found" himself quite unable to earn money. He began to sink into a rapidly fraying gentility, punctuated with a few of the white-collar occupations available to black people, regardless of their noble bloodlines, in America: desk clerk at a colored hotel in Chicago, insurance agent, traveling salesman for a cosmetics firm catering to blacks. He finally settled in Lorain, Ohio, in 1931, palming himself off as a minister, and inspiring awe with the way he spoke English. The women of the town early discovered his celibacy, and not being able to comprehend his rejection of them, decided that he was supernatural rather than unnatural.

Once he understood their decision, he quickly followed through, accepting the name (Soaphead Church) and the role they had given him. He rented a kind of back-room apartment from a deeply religious old lady named Bertha Reese. She was clean, quiet, and very close to total deafness. The lodgings were ideal in every way but one. Bertha Reese had an old dog, Bob, who, although as deaf and quiet as she, was not as clean. He slept most of his days away on the back porch, which was Elihue's entrance. The dog was too old to be of any use, and Bertha Reese had not the strength or presence of mind to care for him properly. She fed him, and watered him, left him alone. The dog was mangy; his exhausted eyes ran with a sea-green matter around which gnats and flies clustered. Soaphead was revolted by Bob and wished he would hurry up and die. He regarded this wish for the dog's death as humane, for he could not bear, he told himself, to see anything suffer. It did not occur to him that he was really concerned about his own suffering, since the dog had adjusted himself to frailty and old age. Soaphead finally determined to put an end to the animal's misery, and bought some poison with which to do it. Only the horror of having to go near him had prevented Soaphead from completing his mission. He waited for rage or blinding revulsion to spur him.

Living there among his worn things, rising early every morning from dreamless sleeps, he counseled those who sought his advice.

His business was dread. People came to him in dread, whispered in dread, wept and pleaded in dread. And dread was what he counseled.

Singly they found their way to his door, wrapped each in a shroud stitched with anger, yearning, pride, vengeance, loneliness, misery, defeat, and hunger. They asked for the simplest of things: love, health, and money. Make him love me. Tell me what this dream means. Help me get rid of this woman. Make my mother give me back my clothes. Stop my left hand from shaking. Keep my baby's ghost off the stove. Break so-and-so's fix. To all of these requests he addressed himself. His practice was to do what he was bid—not to suggest to a party that perhaps the request was unfair, mean, or hopeless.

With only occasional, and increasingly rare, encounters with the little girls he could persuade to be entertained by him, he lived rather peaceably among his things, admitting to no regrets. He was aware, of course, that something was awry in his life, and all lives, but put the problem where it belonged, at the foot of the Originator of Life. He believed that since decay, vice, filth, and disorder were pervasive, they must be in the Nature of Things. Evil existed because God had created it. He, God, and made a sloven and unforgivable error in judgment: designing an imperfect universe. Theologians justified the presence of corruption as a means by which men strove, were tested, and triumphed. A triumph of cosmic neatness. But this neatness, the neatness of Dante, was in the orderly sectioning and segregating of all levels of evil and decay. In the world it was not so. The most exquisite-looking ladies sat on toilets, and the most dreadful-looking had pure and holy yearnings. God had done a poor job, and Soaphead suspected that he himself could have done better. It was in fact a pity that the Maker had not sought his counsel.

Soaphead was reflecting once again on these thoughts one late hot afternoon when he heard a tap on his door. Opening it, he saw a little girl, quite unknown to him. She was about twelve or so, he thought, and seemed to him pitifully unattractive. When he asked her what she wanted, she did not answer, but held out to him one of his cards advertising his gifts and services: "If you are overcome with trouble and conditions that are not natural, I can remove them; Overcome Spells, Bad Luck, and Evil Influences. Remember, I am a true Spiritualist and Psychic Reader, born with power, and I will help you. Satisfaction in one visit. During many years of practice I have brought together many in marriage and reunited many who were separated. If you are unhappy, discouraged, or in distress, I can help you. Does bad luck seem to follow you? Has the one you love changed? I can tell you why. I will tell you who your enemies and friends are, and if the one you love is true or false. If you are sick, I can show you the way to health. I locate lost and stolen articles. Satisfaction guaranteed."

Soaphead Church told her to come in.

"What can I do for you, my child?"

She stood there, her hands folded across her stomach, a little protruding pot of tummy. "Maybe. Maybe you can do it for me."

"Do what for you?"

"I can't go to school no more. And I thought maybe you could help me."

"Help you how? Tell me. Don't be frightened."

"My eyes."

"What about your eyes?"

"I want them blue."

Soaphead pursed his lips, and let his tongue stroke a gold inlay. He thought it was at once the most fantastic and the most logical petition he had ever received. Here was an ugly little girl asking for beauty. A surge of love and understanding swept through him, but was quickly replaced by anger. Anger that he was powerless to help her. Of all the wishes people had brought him—money, love, revenge—this seemed to him the most poignant and the one most deserving of fulfillment. A little black girl who wanted to rise up out of the pit of her blackness and see the world with blue eyes. His outrage grew and felt like power. For the first time he honestly wished he could work miracles. Never before had he really wanted the true and holy power—only the power to make others believe he had it. It seemed so sad, so frivolous, that mere mortality, not judgment, kept him from it. Or did it?

With a trembling hand he made the sign of the cross over her. His flesh crawled; in that hot, dim little room of worn things, he was chilled.

"I can do nothing for you, my child. I am not a magician. I work only through the Lord. He sometimes uses me to help people. All I can do is offer myself to Him as the instrument through which he works. If He wants your wish granted, He will do it."

Soaphead walked to the window, his back to the girl. His mind raced, stumbled, and raced again. How to frame the next sentence? How to hang on to the feeling of power. His eye fell on old Bob sleeping on the porch.

"We must make, ah, some offering, that is, some contact with nature. Perhaps some simple creature might be the vehicle through which He will speak. Let us see."

He knelt down at the window, and moved his lips. After what seemed a suitable length of time, he rose and went to the icebox that stood near the other window. From it he removed a small packet wrapped in pinkish butcher paper. From a shelf he took a small brown bottle and sprinkled some of its contents on the substance inside the paper. He put the packet, partly opened, on the table.

"Take this food and give it to the creature sleeping on the porch. Make sure he eats it. And mark well how he behaves. If nothing happens, you will know that God has refused you. If the animal behaves strangely, your wish will be granted on the day following this one."

The girl picked up the packet; the odor of the dark, sticky meat made her want to vomit. She put a hand on her stomach.

"Courage. Courage, my child. These things are not granted to faint hearts."

She nodded and swallowed visibly, holding down the vomit. Soaphead opened the door, and she stepped over the threshold.

"Good-bye, God bless," he said and quickly shut the door. At the window he stood watching her, his eyebrows pulled together into waves of compassion, his tongue fondling the worn gold in his upper jaw. He saw the girl bending down to the sleeping dog, who, at her touch, opened one liquid eye, matted in the corners with what looked like green glue. She reached out and touched the dog's head, stroking him gently. She placed the meat on the floor of the porch, near his nose. The odor roused him; he lifted his head, and got up to smell it better. He ate it in three or four gulps. The girl stroked his head again, and the dog looked up at her with soft triangle eyes. Suddenly he coughed, the cough of a phlegmy old man—and got to his feet. The girl jumped. The dog gagged, his mouth chomping the air, and promptly fell down. He tried to raise himself, could not, tried again and half-fell down the steps. Choking, stumbling, he moved like a broken toy around the yard. The girl's mouth was open, a little petal of tongue showing. She made a wild, pointless gesture with one hand and then covered her mouth with both hands. She was trying not to vomit. The dog fell again, a spasm jerking his body. Then he was quiet. The girl's hands covering her mouth, she backed away a few feet, then turned, ran out of the yard and down the walk.

Soaphead Church went to the table. He sat down, with folded hands balancing his forehead on the balls of his thumbs. Then he rose and went to a tiny night table with a drawer, from which he took paper and a fountain pen. A bottle of ink was on the same shelf that held the poison. With these things he sat again at the table. Slowly, carefully, relishing his penmanship, he wrote the following letter:

Att: TO HE WHO GREATLY ENNOBLED HUMAN NATURE BY CREATING IT

Dear God:

The Purpose of this letter is to familiarize you with facts which either have escaped your notice, or which you have chosen to ignore.

Once upon a time I lived greenly and youngish on one of your islands. An island of the archipelago in the South Atlantic between North and South America, enclosing the Caribbean Sea and the Gulf of Mexico: divided into the Greater Antilles, the Lesser Antilles, and the Bahama Islands. Not the Windward or Leeward Island colonies, mark you, but within, of course, the Greater of the two Antilles (while the precision of my prose may be, at times, laborious, it is necessary that I identify myself to you clearly).

Now.

We in this colony took as our own the most dramatic, and the most obvious, of our white masters' characteristics, which were, of course, their worst. In retaining the identity of our race, we held fast to those characteristics most gratifying to sustain and least troublesome to maintain. Consequently we were not royal but snobbish, not aristocratic but class-conscious; we believed authority was cruelty to our inferiors, and education was being at school. We mistook violence for passion, indolence for leisure, and thought recklessness was freedom. We raised our children and reared our crops; we let infants grow, and property develop. Our manhood was defined by acquisitions. Our womanhood by acquiescence. And the smell of your fruit and the labor of your days we abhorred.

This morning, before the little black girl came, I cried—for Velma. Oh, not aloud. There is no wind to carry, bear, or even refuse to bear, a sound so heavy with regret. But in my silent own lone way, I cried—for Velma. You need to know about Velma to understand what I did today.

She (Velma) left me the way people leave a hotel room. A hotel room is a place to be when you are doing something else. Of itself it is of no consequence to one's major scheme. A hotel room is convenient. But is convenience is limited to the time you need it while you are in that particular town on that particular business; you hope it is comfortable, but prefer, rather, that it be anonymous. It is not, after all, where you *live*.

When you no longer need it, you pay a little something for its use; say, "Thank you, sir," and when your business in that town is over, you go away from that room. Does anybody regret leaving a hotel room? Does anybody, who has a home, a real home somewhere, want to stay there? Does anybody look back with affection, or even disgust, at a hotel room when they leave it? You can only love or despise whatever *living* was done in that room. But the room itself? But you take a souvenir. Not, oh, not, to remember the room. To remember, rather, the time and the place of your business, your adventure. What can anyone feel for a hotel room? One doesn't any more feel for a hotel room than one expects a hotel room to feel for its occupant.

That, heavenly, heavenly Father, was how she left me; or rather, she never left me, because she was never ever there.

You remember, do you, how and of what we are made? Let me tell you now about the breasts of little girls. I apologize for the inappropriateness (is that it?), the imbalance of loving them at awkward times of day, and in awkward places, and the tastelessness of loving those which belonged to members of my family. Do I have to apologize for loving strangers?

But you too are amiss here, Lord. How, why, did you allow it to happen? How is it I could lift my eyes from the contemplation of Your Body and fall deeply into the contemplation of theirs? The buds. The buds on some of these saplings. They were mean, you know, mean and tender. Mean little buds resisting the touch, springing like rubber. But aggressive. Daring me to touch. Commanding me to touch. Not a bit shy, as you'd suppose. They stuck out at me, oh yes, at me. Slender-chested, finger-chested lassies. Have you ever seen them, Lord? I mean, really seen them? One could not see them and not love them. You who made them must have considered them lovely even as an idea—how much more lovely is the manifestation of that idea. I couldn't, as you must recall, keep my hands, my mouth, off them. Salt-sweet. Like not quite ripe strawberries covered with the light salt sweat of running days and hopping, skipping, jumping hours.

The love of them—the touch, taste, and feel of them—was not just an easy luxurious human vice; they were, for me, A Thing To Do Instead. Instead of Papa, instead of the Cloth, instead of Velma, and I *chose* not to do without them. But I didn't go into the church. At least I didn't do that. As to what I did do? I told people I knew all about You. That I had received Your Powers. It was not a complete *lie;* but it was a *complete* lie. I should never have, I admit, I should never have taken their money in exchange for well-phrased, well-placed, well-faced lies. But, mark you, I hated it. Not for a moment did I love the lies or the money.

But consider: The woman who left the hotel room.

Consider: The greentime, the noontime of the archipelago.

Consider: Their hopeful eyes that were outdone only by their hoping breasts.

Consider: How I needed a comfortable evil to prevent my knowing what I could not bear to know.

Consider: How I hated and despised the money.

And now, consider: Not according to my just deserts, but according to *my* mercy, the little black girl that came a-looning at me today. Tell me, Lord, how could you leave a lass so long so lone that she could find her way to me? How could you? I weep for you, Lord. And it is because I weep for You that I had to do your work for You.

Do you know what she came for? Blue eyes. New, blue eyes, she said. Like she was buying shoes. "I'd like a pair of new blue eyes." She must have asked you for them for a very long time, and you hadn't replied. (A habit, I could have told her, a long-ago habit broken for Job—but no more.) She came to *me* for them. She had one of my cards. (Card enclosed.) By the way, I added the Micah—Elihue Micah Whitcomb. But I am called Soaphead Church. I cannot remember how or why I got the name. What makes one name more a person than another? Is the name the real thing, then? And the person only what his name says? Is that why to the simplest and friendliest of questions: "What is your name?" put to you by Moses, You would not say, and said instead "I am who I am." Like Popeye? I Yam What I Yam? Afraid you were, weren't you, to give out your name? Afraid they would know the name and then know you? Then they wouldn't fear you? It's quite all right. Don't be vexed. I mean no offense. I understand. I have been a bad man too, and an unhappy man too. But someday *I* will die. I was always so kind. Why do I have to die? The little girls. The little girls are the only things I'll miss. Do you know that when I touched their sturdy little tits and bit them—just a little—I felt I was being friendly? I didn't want to kiss their mouths or sleep in the bed with them or take a child bride for my own. Playful, I felt, and friendly. Not like the newspapers said. Not like the people whispered. And they didn't mind at all. Not at all. Remember how so many of them came back? No one would even try to understand that. If I'd been hurting them, would they have come back? Two of them, Doreen and Sugar Babe, they'd come together. I gave them mints, money, and they'd eat ice cream with their legs open while I played with them. It was like a party. And there wasn't nastiness, and there wasn't any filth, and there wasn't any odor, and there wasn't any groaning—just the light white laughter of little girls and me. And there wasn't any look—any long funny look—any long funny Velma look afterward. No look that makes you feel dirty afterward. That makes you want to die. With little girls it is all clean and good and friendly.

You have to understand that, Lord. You said, "Suffer little children to come unto me, and harm them not." Did you forget? Did you forget about the children? Yes. You forgot. You let them go wanting, sit on road shoulders, crying next to their dead mothers. I've seen them charred, lame, halt. You forgot, Lord. You forgot how and when to be God.

That's why I changed the little black girl's eyes for her, and I didn't touch her; not a finger did I lay on her. But I gave her those blue eyes she wanted. Not for pleasure, and not for money. I did what You did not, could not, would not do: I looked at that ugly little black girl, and I loved her. I played You. And it was a very good show!

I, I have caused a miracle. I gave her the eyes. I gave her the blue, blue, two blue eyes. Cobalt blue. A streak of it right out of your own blue heaven. No one else will see her blue eyes. But *she* will. And she will live happily ever after. I, I have found it meet and right so to do.

Now you are jealous. You are jealous of me.

You see? I too, have created. Not aboriginally, like you, but creation is a heady wine, more for the taster than the brewer.

Having therefore imbibed, as it were, of the nectar, I am not afraid of You, of Death, not even of Life, and it's all right about Velma; and it's all right about Papa; and it's all right about the Greater and the Lesser Antilles. Quite all right. Quite.

With kindest regards, I remain,

Your,

Elihue Micah Whitcomb

Soaphead Church folded the sheets of paper into three equal parts and slipped them into an envelope. Although he had no seal, he longed for sealing wax. He removed a cigar box from under the bed and rummaged about in it. There were some of his most precious things: a sliver of jade that had dislodged from a cuff link at the Chicago hotel; a gold pendant shaped like a Y with a piece of coral attached to it that had belonged to the mother he never knew; four large hairpins that Velma had left on the rim of the bathroom sink; a powder blue grosgrain ribbon from the head of a little girl named Precious Jewel; a blackened faucet head from the sink in a jail cell in Cincinnati; two marbles he had found under a bench in Morningside Park on a very fine spring day; an old Lucky Hart catalog that smelled still of nut-brown and mocha face powder, and lemon vanishing cream. Distracted by his things, he forgot what he had been looking for. The effort to recall was too great; there was a buzzing in his head, and a wash of fatigue overcame him. He closed his box, eased himself out on the bed, and slipped into an ivory sleep from which he could not hear the tiny yelps of an old lady who had come out of her candy store and found the still carcass of an old dog named Bob.

Summer

I have only to break into the tightness of a strawberry, and I see summer—its dust and lowering skies. It remains for me a season of storms. The parched days and sticky nights are undistinguished in my mind, but the storms, the violent sudden storms, both frightened and quenched me. But my memory is uncertain; I recall a summer storm in the town where we lived and imagine a summer my mother knew in 1929. There was a tornado that year, she said, that blew away half of south Lorain. I mix up her summer with my own. Biting the strawberry, thinking of storms, I see her. A slim young girl in a pink crepe dress. One hand is on her hip; the other lolls about her thigh—waiting. The wind swoops her up, high above the houses, but she is still standing, hand on hip. Smiling. The anticipation and promise in her lolling hand are not altered by the holocaust. In the summer tornado of 1929, my mother's hand is unextinguished. She is strong, smiling, and relaxed while the world falls down about her. So much for memory. Public fact becomes private reality, and the seasons of a Midwestern town become the *Moirai* of our small lives.

The summer was already thick when Frieda and I received our seeds. We had waited since April for the magic package containing the packets and packets of seeds we were to sell for five cents each, which would entitle us to a new bicycle. We believed it, and spent a major part of every day trooping about the town selling them. Although Mama had restricted us to the homes of people she knew or the neighborhoods familiar to us, we knocked on all doors, and floated in and out of every house that opened to us: twelve-room houses that sheltered half as many families, smelling of grease and urine; tiny wooden four-room houses tucked into bushes near the railroad tracks; the up-over places—apartments up over fish markets, butcher shops, furniture stores, saloons, restaurants; tidy brick houses with flowered carpets and glass bowls with fluted edges.

During that summer of the seed selling we thought about the money, thought about the seeds, and listened with only half an ear to what people were saying. In the houses of people who knew us we were asked to come in and sit, given cold water or lemonade; and while we sat there being refreshed, the people continued their conversations or went about their chores. Little by little we began to piece a story together, a secret, terrible, awful story. And it was only after two or three such vaguely overheard conversations that we realized that the story was about Pecola. Properly placed, the fragments of talk ran like this:

"Did you hear about that girl?"

"What? Pregnant?"

"Yas. But guess who?"

"Who? I don't know all these little old boys."

"That's just it. Ain't no little old boy. They say it's Cholly."

"Cholly? Her daddy?"

"Uh-huh."

"Lord. Have mercy. That dirty nigger."

"'Member that time he tried to burn them up? I knew he was crazy for sure then."

"What's she gone do? The mama?"

"Keep on like she been, I reckon. He taken off."

"County ain't gone let her keep that baby, is they?"

"Don't know."

"None of them Breedloves seem right anyhow. That boy is off somewhere every minute, and the girl was always foolish."

"Don't nobody know nothing about them anyway. Where they come from or nothing. Don't seem to have no people."

"What you reckon make him do a thing like that?"

"Beats me. Just nasty."

"Well, they ought to take her out of school."

"Ought to. She carry some of the blame."

"Oh, come on. She ain't but twelve or so."

"Yeah. But you never know. How come she didn't fight him?"

"Maybe she did."

"Yeah? You never know."

"Well, it probably won't live. They say the way her mama beat her she lucky to be alive herself."

"She be lucky if it don't live. Bound to be the ugliest thing walking."

"Can't help but be. Ought to be a law: two ugly people doubling up like that to make more ugly. Be better off in the ground."

"Well, I wouldn't worry none. It be a miracle if it live."

Our astonishment was short-lived, for it gave way to a curious kind of defensive shame; we were embarrassed for Pecola, hurt for her, and finally we just felt sorry for her. Our sorrow drove out all thoughts of the new bicycle. And I believe our sorrow was the more intense because nobody else seemed to share it. They were disgusted, amused, shocked, outraged, or even excited by the story. But we listened for the one who would say, "Poor little girl," or, "Poor baby," but there was only head-wagging where those words should have been. We looked for eyes creased with concern, but saw only veils.

I thought about the baby that everybody wanted dead, and saw it very clearly. It was a dark, wet place, its head covered with great O's of wool, the black face holding, like nickels, two clean black eyes, the flared nose, kissing-thick lips, and the living, breathing silk of black skin. No synthetic yellow bangs suspended over marble-blue eyes, no pinched nose and bowline mouth. More strongly than my fondness for Pecola, I felt a need for someone to want the black baby to live—just to counteract the universal love of white baby dolls, Shirley Temples, and Maureen Peals. And Frieda must have felt the same thing. We did not think of the fact that Pecola was not married; lots of girls had babies who were not married. And we did not dwell on the fact that the baby's father was Pecola's father too; the process of having a baby by any male was incomprehensible to us—at least she knew her father. We thought only of this overwhelming hatred for the unborn baby. We remembered Mrs. Breedlove knocking Pecola down and soothing the pink tears of the frozen doll baby that sounded like the door of our icebox. We remembered the knuckled eyes of schoolchildren under the gaze of Meringue Pie and the eyes of these same children when they looked at Pecola. Or maybe we didn't remember; we just knew. We had defended ourselves since memory against everything and everybody, considered all speech a code to be broken by us, and all gestures subject to careful analysis; we had become headstrong, devious and arrogant. Nobody paid us any attention, so we paid very good attention to ourselves. Our limitations were not known to us—not then. Our only handicap was our size; people gave us orders because they were bigger and stronger. So it was with confidence, strengthened by pity and pride, that we decided to change the course of events and alter a human life.

"What we gone do, Frieda?"

"What can we do? Miss Johnson said it would be a miracle if it lived."

"So let's make it a miracle."

"Yeah, but how?"

"We could pray."

"That's not enough. Remember last time with the bird?"

"That was different; it was half-dead when we found it."

"I don't care, I still think we have to do something really strong this time."

"Let's ask Him to let Pecola's baby live and promise to be good for a whole month."

"O.K. But we better give up something so He'll know we really mean it this time."

"Give up what? We ain't got nothing. Nothing but the seed money, two dollars."

"We could give that. Or, you know what? We could give up the bicycle. Bury the money and . . . plant the seeds."

"All of the money?"

"Claudia, do you want to do it or not?"

"O.K. I just thought . . . O.K."

"We have to do it *right,* now. We'll bury the money over by her house so we can't go back and dig it up, and we'll plant the seeds out back of our house so we can watch over them. And when they come up, we'll know everything is all right. All right?"

"All right. Only let me sing this time. You say the magic words."

*LOOKLOOKHERECOMESAFRIENDTHEFRIE
NDWILLPLAYWITHJANETTHEYWILLPLA
YAGOODGAMEPLAYJANEPLAY*

How many times a minute are you going to look inside that old thing?

I didn't look in a long time.

You did too—

So what? I can look if I want to.

I didn't say you couldn't. I just don't know why you have to look every minute. They aren't going anywhere.

I know it. I just like to look.

You scared they might go away?

Of course not. How can they go away?

The other went away.

They didn't go away. They changed.

Go away. Change. What's the difference?

A lot. Mr. Soaphead said they would last forever.

Forever and ever Amen?

Yes, if you want to know.

You don't have to be so smarty when you talk to me.

I'm not being smarty. You started it.

I'd just like to do something else besides watch you stare in that mirror.

You're just jealous.

I am not.

You are. You wish you had them.

Ha. What would I look like with blue eyes?

Nothing much.

If you're going to keep this up, I may as well go on off by myself.

No. Don't go. What you want to do?

We could go outside and play, I guess.

But it's too hot.

You can take your old mirror. Put it in your coat pocket, and you can look at yourself up and down the street.

Boy! I never would have thought you'd be so jealous.

Oh, come on!

You are.

Are what?

Jealous.

O.K. So I'm jealous.

See. I told you.

No. I told you.

Are they really nice?

Yes. Very nice.

Just "very nice"?

Really, truly, very nice.

Really, truly, bluely nice?

Oh, God. You are crazy.

I am not!

I didn't mean it that way.

Well, what did you mean?

Come on. It's too hot in here.

Wait a minute, I can't find my shoes.

Here they are.

Oh. Thank you.

Got your mirror?

Yes, dearie. . . .

Well, let's go then. . . . Ow!

What's the matter?

The sun is too bright. It hurts my eyes.

Not mine. I don't even blink. Look. I can look right at the sun.

Don't do that.

Why not? It doesn't hurt. I don't even have to blink.

Well, blink anyway. You make me feel funny, staring at the sun like that.

Feel funny how?

I don't know.

Yes, you do. Feel funny how?

I told you, I don't know.

Why don't you look at me when you say that? You're looking drop-eyed like Mrs. Breedlove.

Mrs. Breedlove look drop-eyed at you?

Yes. Now she does. Every since I got my blue yes, she look away from me all of the time. Do you suppose she's jealous too?

Could be. They are pretty, you know.

I know. He really did a good job. Everybody's jealous. Every time I look at somebody, they look off.

Is that why nobody has told you how pretty they are?

Sure it is. Can you imagine? Something like that happening to a person, and nobody but nobody saying anything about it? They all try to pretend they don't see them. Isn't that funny? . . . I said, isn't that funny?

Yes.

You are the only one who tells me how pretty they are.

Yes.

You are a real friend. I'm sorry about picking on you before. I mean, saying you were jealous and all.

That's all right.

No. Really. You are my best friend. Why didn't I know you before?

You didn't need me before.

Didn't need you?

I mean . . . you were so unhappy before. I guess you didn't notice me before.

I guess you're right. And I was so lonely for friends. And you were right here. Right before my eyes.

No, honey. Right after your eyes.

What?

What does Maureen think about your eyes?

She doesn't say anything about them. Has she said anything to you about them?

No. Nothing.

Do you like Maureen?

Oh. She's all right. For a half-white girl, that is.

I know what you mean. But would you like to be her friend? I mean, would you like to go around with her or anything?

No.

Me neither. But she sure is popular.

Who wants to be popular?

Not me.

Me neither.

But you couldn't be popular anyway. You don't even go to school.

You don't either.

I know. But I used to.

What did you stop for?

They made me.

Who made you?

I don't know. After that first day at school when I had my blue eyes. Well, the next day they had Mrs. Breedlove come out. Now I don't go anymore. But I don't care.

You don't?

No, I don't. They're just prejudiced, that's all.

Yes, they sure are prejudiced.

Just because I got blue eyes, bluer than theirs, they're prejudiced.

That's right.

They are bluer, aren't they?

Oh, yes. Much bluer.

Bluer than Joanna's?

Much bluer than Joanna's.

And bluer than Michelena's?

Much bluer than Michelena's.

I thought so. Did Michelena say anything to you about my eyes?

No. Nothing.

Did you say anything to her?

No.

How come?

How come what?

How come you don't talk to anybody?

I talk to you.

Besides me.

I don't like anybody besides you.

Where do you live?

I told you once.

What is your mother's name?

Why are you so busy meddling me?

I just wondered. You don't talk to anybody. You don't go to school. And nobody talks to you.

How do you know nobody talks to me?

They don't. When you're in the house with me, even Mrs. Breedlove doesn't say anything to you. Ever. Sometimes I wonder if she even sees you.

Why wouldn't she see me?

I don't know. She almost walks right over you.

Maybe she doesn't feel too good since Cholly's gone.

Oh, yes. You must be right.

She probably misses him.

I don't know why she would. All he did was get drunk and beat her up.

Well, you know how grown-ups are.

Yes. No. How are they?

Well, she probably loved him anyway.

HIM?

Sure. Why not? Anyway, if she didn't love him, she sure let him do it to her a lot.

That's nothing.

How do you know?

I saw them all the time. She didn't like it.

Then why'd she let him do it to her?

Because he made her.

How could somebody make you do something like that?

Easy.

Oh, yeah? How easy?

They just make you, that's all.

I guess you're right. And Cholly could make anybody do anything.

He could not.

He made you, didn't he?

Shut up!

I was only teasing.

Shut up!

O.K. O.K.

He just tried, see? He didn't do anything. You hear me?

I'm shutting up.

You'd better. I don't like that kind of talk.

I said I'm shutting up.

You always talk so dirty. Who told you about that, anyway?

I forget.

Sammy?

No. You did.

I did not.

You did. You said he tried to do it to you when you were sleeping on the couch.

See there! You don't even know what you're talking about. It was when I was washing dishes.

Oh, yes. Dishes.

By myself. In the kitchen.

Well, I'm glad you didn't let him.

Yes.

Did you?

Did I what?

Let him.

Now who's crazy?

I am, I guess.

You sure are.

Still . . .

Well. Go ahead. Still what?

I wonder what it would be like.

Horrible.

Really?

Yes. Horrible.

Then why didn't you tell Mrs. Breedlove?

I did tell her!

I don't mean about the first time. I mean about the second time, when you were sleeping on the couch.

I wasn't sleeping! I was reading!

You don't have to shout.

You don't understand anything, do you? She didn't even believe me when I told her.

So that's why you didn't tell her about the second time?

She wouldn't have believed me then either.

You're right. No use telling her when she wouldn't believe you.

That's what I'm trying to get through your thick head.

O.K. I understand now. Just about.

What do you mean, just about?

You sure are mean today.

You keep on saying mean and sneaky things. I thought you were my friend.

I am. I am.

Then leave me alone about Cholly.

O.K.

There's nothing more to say about him, anyway. He's gone, anyway.

Yes, Good riddance.

Yes. Good riddance.

And Sammy's gone too.

And Sammy's gone too.

So there's no use talking about it. I mean them.

No. No use at all.

It's all over now.

Yes.

And you don't have to be afraid of Cholly coming at you anymore.

No.

That was horrible, wasn't it?

Yes.

The second time too?

Yes.

Really? The second time too?

Leave me alone! You better leave me alone.

Can't you take a joke? I was only funning.

I don't like to talk about dirty things.

Me neither. Let's talk about something else.

What? What will we talk about?

Why, your eyes.

Oh, yes. My eyes. My blue eyes. Let me look again.

See how pretty they are.

Yes. They get prettier each time I look at them.

They are the prettiest I've ever seen.

Really?

Oh, yes.

Prettier than the sky?

Oh, yes. Much prettier than the sky.

Prettier than Alice-and-Jerry Storybook eyes?

Oh, yes. Much prettier than Alice-and-Jerry Storybook eyes.

And prettier than Joanna's?

Oh, yes. And bluer too.

Bluer than Michelena's?

Yes.

Are you sure?

Of course I'm sure.

You don't sound sure. . . .

Well, I am sure. Unless. . . .

Unless what?

Oh, nothing. I was just thinking about a lady I saw yesterday. Her eyes sure were blue. But no. Not bluer than yours.

Are you sure?

Yes. I remember them now. Yours are bluer.

I'm glad.

Me too. I'd hate to think there was anybody around with bluer eyes than yours. I'm sure there isn't. Not around here, anyway.

But you don't know, do you? You haven't seen everybody, have you?

No. I haven't.

So there could be, couldn't there?

Not hardly.

But maybe. Maybe. You said "around here." Nobody "around here" probably has bluer eyes. What about someplace else? Even if my eyes are bluer than Joanna's and bluer than Michelena's and bluer than that lady's you saw, suppose there is somebody way off somewhere with bluer eyes than mine?

Don't be silly.

There could be. Couldn't there?

Not hardly.

But suppose. Suppose a long way off. In Cincinnati, say, there is somebody whose eyes are bluer than mine? Suppose there are *two* people with bluer eyes?

So what? You asked for blue eyes. You got blue eyes.

He should have made them bluer.

Who?

Mr. Soaphead.

Did you say what color blue you wanted them?

No. I forgot.

Oh. Well.

Look. Look over there. At that girl. Look at her eyes. Are they bluer than mine?

No, I don't think so.

Did you look real good?

Yes.

Here comes someone. Look at his. See if they're bluer.

You're being silly. I'm not going to look at everybody's eyes.

You have to.

No I don't.

Please. If there is somebody with bluer eyes than mine, then maybe there is somebody with the bluest eyes. The bluest eyes in the whole world.

That's just too bad, isn't it?

Please help me look.

No.

But suppose my eyes aren't blue enough?

Blue enough for what?

Blue enough for . . . I don't know. Blue enough for something. Blue enough . . . for you!

I'm not going to play with you anymore.

Oh. Don't leave me.

Yes. I am.

Why? Are you mad at me?

Yes.

Because my eyes aren't blue enough? Because I don't have the bluest eyes?

No. Because you're acting silly.

Don't go. Don't leave me. Will you come back if I get them?

Get what?

The bluest eyes. Will you come back then?

Of course I will. I'm just going away for a little while.

You promise?

Sure. I'll be back. Right before your very eyes.

So it was.

A little black girl yearns for the blue eyes of a little white girl, and the horror at the heart of her yearning is exceeded only by the evil of fulfillment.

We saw her sometimes. Frieda and I—after the baby came too soon and died. After the gossip and the slow wagging of heads. She was so sad to see. Grown people looked away; children, those who were not frightened by her, laughed outright.

The damage done was total. She spent her days, her tendril, sap-green days, walking up and down, up and down, her head jerking to the beat of a drummer so distant only she could hear. Elbows bent, hands on shoulders, she flailed her arms like a bird in an eternal, grotesquely futile effort to fly. Beating the air, a winged but grounded bird, intent on the blue void it could not reach—could not even see—but which filled the valleys of the mind.

We tried to see her without looking at her, and never, never went near. Not because she was absurd, or repulsive, or because we were frightened, but because we had failed her. Our flowers never grew. I was convinced that Frieda was right, that I had planted them too deeply. How could I have been so sloven? So we avoided Pecola Breedlove—forever.

And the years folded up like pocket handkerchiefs. Sammy left town long ago; Cholly died in the workhouse; Mrs. Breedlove still does housework. And Pecola is somewhere in that little brown house she and her mother moved to on the edge of town, where you can see her even now, once in a while. The birdlike gestures are worn away to a mere picking and plucking her way between the tire rims and the sunflowers, between Coke bottles and milkweed, among all the waste and beauty of the world—which is what she herself was. All of our waste which we dumped on her and which she absorbed. And all of our beauty, which was hers first and which she gave to us. All of us—all who knew her—felt so wholesome after we cleaned ourselves on her. We were so beautiful when we stood astride her ugliness. Her simplicity decorated us, her guilt sanctified us, her pain made us glow with health, her awkwardness made us think we had a sense of humor. Her inarticulateness made us believe we were eloquent. Her poverty kept us generous. Even her waking dreams we used—to silence our own nightmares. And she let us, and thereby deserved our contempt. We honed our egos on her, padded our characters with her frailty, and yawned in the fantasy of our strength.

And fantasy it was, for we were not strong, only aggressive; we were not free, merely licensed; we were not compassionate, we were polite; not good, but well behaved. We courted death in order to call ourselves brave, and hid like thieves from life. We substituted good grammar for intellect; we switched habits to simulate maturity; we rearranged lies and called it truth, seeing in the new pattern of an old idea the Revelation and the Word.

She, however, stepped over into madness, a madness which protected her from us simply because it bored us in the end.

Oh, some of us "loved" her. The Maginot Line. And Cholly loved her. I'm sure he did. He, at any rate, was the one who loved her enough to touch her, envelop her, give something of himself to her. But his touch was fatal, and the something he gave her filled the matrix of her agony with death. Love is never any better than the lover. Wicked people love wickedly, violent people love violently, weak people love weakly, stupid people love stupidly, but the love of a free man is never safe. There is no gift for the beloved. The lover alone possesses his gift of love. The loved one is shorn, neutralized, frozen in the glare of the lover's inward eye.

And now when I see her searching the garbage—for what? The thing we assassinated? I talk about how I did *not* plant the seeds too deeply, how it was the fault of the earth, the land, of our town. I even think now that the land of the entire country was hostile to marigolds that year. This soil is bad for certain kinds of flowers. Certain seeds it will not nurture, certain fruit it will not bear, and when the land kills of its own volition, we acquiesce and say the victim had no right to live. We are wrong, of course, but it doesn't matter. It's too late. At least on the edge of my town, among the garbage and the sunflowers of my town, it's much, much, much too late.

Afterword

We had just started elementary school. She said she wanted blue eyes. I looked around to picture her with them and was violently repelled by what I imagined she would look like if she had her wish. The sorrow in her voice seemed to call for sympathy, and I faked it for her, but, astonished by the desecration she proposed, I "got mad" at her instead.

Until that moment I had seen the pretty, the lovely, the nice, the ugly, and although I had certainly used the word "beautiful," I had never experienced its shock—the force of which was equaled by the knowledge that no one else recognized it, not even, or especially, the one who possessed it.

It must have been more than the face I was examining: the silence of the street in the early afternoon, the light, the atmosphere of confession. In any case it was the first time I knew beautiful. Had imagined it for myself. Beauty was not simply something to behold; it was something one could *do.*

The Bluest Eye was my effort to say something about that; to say something about why she had not, or possibly ever would have, the experience of what she possessed and also why she prayed for so radical an alteration. Implicit in her desire was racial self-loathing. And twenty years later I was still wondering about how one learns that. Who told her? Who made her feel that it was better to be a freak than what she was? Who had looked at her and found her so wanting, so small a weight on the beauty scale? The novel pecks away at the gaze that condemned her.

The reclamation of racial beauty in the sixties stirred these thoughts, made me think about the necessity for the claim. Why, although reviled by others, could this beauty not be taken for granted within the community? Why did it need wide public articulation to exist? These are not clever questions. But in 1962 when I began this story, and in 1965 when it began to be a book, the answers were not as obvious to me as they quickly became and are now. The assertion of racial beauty was not a reaction to the self-mocking, humorous critique of cultural/racial foibles common in all groups, but against the damaging internalization of assumptions of immutable inferiority originating in an outside gaze. I focused, therefore, on how something as grotesque as the demonization of an entire race could take root inside the most delicate member of society: a child; the most vulnerable member: a female. In trying to dramatize the devastation that even casual racial contempt can cause, I chose a unique situation, not a representative one. The extremity of Pecola's case stemmed largely from a crippled and a crippling family—unlike the average black family and unlike the narrator's. But singular as Pecola's life was, I believed some aspects of her woundability were lodged in all young girls. In exploring the social and domestic aggression that could cause a child to literally fall apart, I mounted a series of rejections, some routine, some exceptional, some monstrous, all the while trying hard to avoid complicity in the demonization process Pecola was subjected to. That is, I did not want to dehumanize the characters who trashed Pecola and contributed to her collapse.

One problem was centering: the weight of the novel's inquiry on so delicate and vulnerable a character could smash her and lead readers into the comfort of pitying her rather than into an interrogation of themselves for the smashing. My solution—break the narrative into parts that had to be reassembled by the reader—seemed to me a good idea, the execution of which does not satisfy me now. Besides, it didn't work: many readers remain touched but not moved.

The other problem, of course, was language. Holding the despising glance while sabotaging it was difficult. The novel tried to hit the raw nerve of racial self-contempt, expose it, then soothe it not with narcotics but with language that replicated the agency I discovered in my first experience of beauty. Because that moment was so racially infused (my revulsion at what my school friend wanted: very blue eyes in a very black skin; the harm she was doing to *my* concept of the beautiful), the struggle was for writing that was indisputably black. I don't yet know quite what that is, but neither that nor the attempts to disqualify an effort to find out keeps me from trying to pursue it.

Some time ago I did the best job I could of describing strategies for grounding my work in race-specific yet race-free prose. Prose free of racial hierarchy and triumphalism. Parts of that description are as follows.

The opening phrase of the first sentence, "Quiet as it's kept," had several attractions for me. First, it was a familiar phrase, familiar to me as a child listening to adults; to black women conversing with one another, telling a story, an anecdote, gossip about some one or event within the circle, the family, the neighborhood. The words are conspiratorial. "Shh, don't tell anyone else," and "No one is allowed to know this." It is a secret between us and a secret that is being kept from us. The conspiracy is both held and withheld, exposed and sustained. In some sense it was precisely what the act of writing the book was: the public exposure of a private confidence. In order to comprehend fully the duality of that position, one needs to be reminded of the political climate in which the writing took place, 1965–69, a time of great social upheaval in the lives of black people. The publication (as opposed to the writing) involved the exposure; the writing was the disclosure of secrets, secrets "we" shared and those withheld from us by ourselves and by the world outside the community.

"Quiet as it's kept" is also a figure of speech that is written, in this instance, but clearly chosen for how speakerly it is, how it speaks and bespeaks a particular world and its ambience. Further, in addition to its "back fence" connotation, its suggestion of illicit gossip, of thrilling revelation, there is also, in the "whisper," the assumption (on the part of the reader) that the teller is on the inside, knows something others do not, and is going to be generous with this privileged information. The intimacy I was aiming for, the intimacy between the reader and the page, could start up immediately because the secret is being shared, at best, and eavesdropped upon, at the least. Sudden familiarity or instant intimacy seemed crucial to me. I did not want the reader to have time to wonder, "What do I have to do, to give up, in order to read this?

What defense do I need, what distance maintain?" Because I know (and the reader does not—he or she has to wait for the second sentence) that this is a terrible story about things one would rather not know anything about.

What, then, is the Big Secret about to be shared? The thing we (reader and I) are "in" on? A botanical aberration. Pollution, perhaps. A skip, perhaps, in the natural order of things: a September, an autumn, a fall without marigolds. Bright, common, strong and sturdy marigolds. When? In 1941, and since that is a momentous year (the beginning of World War II for the United States), the "fall" of 1941, just before the declaration of war, has a "closet" innuendo. In the temperate zone where there is a season known as "fall" during which one expects marigolds to be at their peak, in the months before the beginning of U.S. participation in World War II, something grim is about to be divulged. The next sentence will make it clear that the sayer, the one who knows, is a child speaking, mimicking the adult black women on the porch or in the backyard. The opening phrase is an effort to be grown-up about this shocking information. The point of view of a child alters the priority an adult would assign the information. "We thought . . . it was because Pecola was having her father's baby that the marigolds did not grow" foregrounds the flowers, backgrounds illicit, traumatic, incomprehensible sex coming to its dreaded fruition. This foregrounding of "trivial" information and backgrounding of shocking knowledge secures the point of view but gives the reader pause about whether the voice of children can be trusted at all or is more trustworthy than an adult's. The reader is thereby protected from a confrontation too soon with the painful details, while simultaneously provoked into a desire to know them. The novelty, I thought, would be in having this story of female violation revealed from the vantage point of the victims or could-be victims of rape—the persons no one inquired of (certainly not in 1965): the girls themselves. And since the victim does not have the vocabulary to understand the violence or its context, gullible, vulnerable girlfriends, looking back as the knowing adults they pretended to be in the beginning, would have to do that for her, and would have to fill those silences with their own reflective lives. Thus, the opening provides the stroke that announces something more than a secret shared, but a silence broken, a void filled, an unspeakable thing spoken at last. And it draws the connection between a minor destabilization in seasonal flora and the insignificant destruction of a black girl. Of course "minor" and "insignificant" represent the outside world's view—for the girls, both phenomena are earthshaking depositories of information they spend that whole year of childhood (and afterward) trying to fathom, and cannot. If they have any success, it will be in transferring the problem of fathoming to the presumably adult reader, to the inner circle of listeners. At the least they have distributed the weight of these problematical questions to a larger constituency, and justified the public exposure of a privacy. If the conspiracy that the opening words announce is entered into by the reader, then the book can be seen to open with its close: a speculation on the disruption of "nature" as being a social disruption with tragic individual consequences in which the reader, as part of the population of the text, is implicated.

However, a problem lies in the central chamber of the novel. The shattered world I built (to complement what is happening to Pecola), its pieces held together by seasons in childtime and commenting at every turn on the incompatible and barren white-family primer, does not in its present form handle effectively the silence at its center: the void that is Pecola's "unbeing." It should have had a shape—like the emptiness left by a boom or a cry. It required a sophistication unavailable to me, and some deft manipulation of the voices around her. She is not *seen* by herself until she hallucinates a self. And the fact of her hallucination becomes a kind of outside-the-book conversation.

Also, although I was pressing for a female expressiveness, it eluded me for the most part, and I had to content myself with female personae because I was not able to secure throughout the work the feminine subtext that is present in the opening sentence (the women gossiping, eager and aghast in "Quiet as it's kept"). The shambles this struggle became is most evident in the section on Pauline Breedlove, where I resorted to two voices, hers and the urging narrator's, both of which are extremely unsatisfactory to me. It is interesting to me now that where I thought I would have the most difficulty subverting the language to a feminine mode, I had the least: connecting Cholly's "rape" by the whitemen to his own of his daughter. This most masculine act of aggression becomes feminized in my language, "passive," and, I think, more accurately repellent when deprived of the male "glamour of shame" rape is (or once was) routinely given.

My choices of language (speakerly, aural, colloquial), my reliance for full comprehension on codes embedded in black culture, my effort to effect immediate co-conspiracy and intimacy (without any distancing, explanatory fabric), as well as my attempt to shape a silence while breaking it are attempts to transfigure the complexity and wealth of Black-American culture into a language worthy of the culture.

Thinking back now on the problems expressive language presented to me, I am amazed by their currency, their tenacity. Hearing "civilized" languages debase humans, watching cultural exorcisms debase literature, seeing oneself preserved in the amber of disqualifying metaphors—I can say that my narrative project is as difficult today as it was thirty years ago.

With very few exceptions, the initial publication of *The Bluest Eye* was like Pecola's life: dismissed, trivialized, misread. And it has taken twenty-five years to gain for her the respectful publication this edition is.

Princeton, New Jersey
November, 1993

Recitatif

My mother danced all night and Roberta's was sick. That's why we were taken to St. Bonny's. People want to put their arms around you when you tell them you were in a shelter, but it really wasn't bad. No big long room with one hundred beds like Bellevue. There were four to a room, and when Roberta and me came, there was a shortage of state kids, so we were the only ones assigned to 406 and could go from bed to bed if we wanted to. And we wanted to, too. We changed beds every night and for the whole four months we were there we never picked one out as our own permanent bed.

It didn't start out that way. The minute I walked in and the Big Bozo introduced us, I got sick to my stomach. It was one thing to be taken out of your own bed early in the morning—it was something else to be stuck in a strange place with a girl from a whole other race. And Mary, that's my mother, she was right. Every now and then she would stop dancing long enough to tell me something important and one of the things she said was that they never washed their hair and they smelled funny. Roberta sure did. Smell funny, I mean. So when the Big Bozo (nobody ever called her Mrs. Itkin, just like nobody ever said St. Bonaventure)—when she said, "Twyla, this is Roberta. Roberta, this is Twyla. Make each other welcome." I said, "My mother won't like you putting me in here."

"Good," said Bozo. "Maybe then she'll come and take you home."

How's that for mean? If Roberta had laughed I would have killed her, but she didn't. She just walked over to the window and stood with her back to us.

"Turn around," said the Bozo. "Don't be rude. Now Twyla. Roberta. When you hear a loud buzzer, that's the call for dinner. Come down to the first floor. Any fights and no movie." And then, just to make sure we knew what we would be missing, "*The Wizard of Oz.*"

Roberta must have thought I meant that my mother would be mad about my being put in the shelter. Not about rooming with her, because as soon as Bozo left she came over to me and said, "Is your mother sick too?"

"No," I said. "She just likes to dance all night."

"Oh," she nodded her head and I liked the way she understood things so fast. So for the moment it didn't matter that we looked like salt and pepper standing there and that's what the other kids called us sometimes. We were eight years old and got F's all the time. Me because I couldn't remember what I read or what the teacher said. And Roberta because she couldn't read at all and didn't even listen to the teacher. She wasn't good at anything except jacks, at which she was a killer: pow scoop pow scoop pow scoop.

We didn't like each other all that much at first, but nobody else wanted to play with us because we weren't real orphans with beautiful dead parents in the sky. We were dumped. Even the New York City Puerto Ricans and the upstate Indians ignored us. All kinds of kids were in there, black ones, white ones, even two Koreans. The food was good, though. At least I thought so. Roberta hated it and left whole pieces of things on her plate: Spam, Salisbury steak—even jello with fruit cocktail in it, and she didn't care if I ate what she wouldn't. Mary's idea of supper was popcorn and a can of Yoo-Hoo. Hot mashed potatoes and two weenies was like Thanksgiving for me.

It really wasn't bad, St. Bonny's. The big girls on the second floor pushed us around now and then. But that was all. They wore lipstick and eyebrow pencil and wobbled their knees while they watched TV. Fifteen, sixteen, even, some of them were. They were put-out girls, scared runaways most of them. Poor little girls who fought their uncles off but looked tough to us, and mean. God did they look mean. The staff tried to keep them separate from the younger children, but sometimes they caught us watching them in the orchard where they played radios and danced with each other. They'd light out after us and pull our hair or twist our arms. We were scared of them, Roberta and me, but neither of us wanted the other one to know it. So we got a good list of dirty names we could shout back when we ran from them through the orchard. I used to dream a lot and almost always the orchard was there. Two acres, four maybe, of these little apple trees. Hundreds of them. Empty and crooked like beggar women when I first came to St. Bonny's but fat with flowers when I left. I don't know why I dreamt about that orchard so much. Nothing really happened there. Nothing all that important, I mean. Just the big girls dancing and playing the radio. Roberta and me watching. Maggie fell down there once. The kitchen woman with legs like parentheses. And the big girls laughed at her. We should have helped her up, I know, but we were scared of those girls with lipstick and eyebrow pencil. Maggie couldn't talk. The kids said she had her tongue cut out, but I think she was just born that way: mute. She was old and sandy-colored and she worked in the kitchen. I don't know if she was nice or not. I just remember her legs like parentheses and how she rocked when she walked. She worked from early in the morning till two o'clock, and if she was late, if she had too much cleaning and didn't get out till two-fifteen or so, she'd cut through the orchard so she wouldn't miss her bus and have to wait another hour. She wore this really stupid little hat—a kid's hat with ear flaps—and she wasn't much taller than we were. A really awful little hat. Even for a mute, it was dumb—dressing like a kid and never saying anything at all.

"But what about if somebody tries to kill her?" I used to wonder about that. "Or what if she wants to cry? Can she cry?"

"Sure," Roberta said. "But just tears. No sounds come out."

"She can't scream?"

"Nope. Nothing."

"Can she hear?"

"I guess."

"Let's call her," I said. And we did.

"Dummy! Dummy!" She never turned her head.

"Bow legs! Bow legs!" Nothing. She just rocked on, the chin straps of her baby-boy hat swaying from side to side. I think we were wrong. I think she could hear and didn't let on. And it shames me even now to think there was somebody in there after all who heard us call her those names and couldn't tell on us.

We got along all right, Roberta and me. Changed beds every night, got F's in civics and communication skills and gym. The Bozo was disappointed in us, she said. Out of 130 of us state cases, 90 were under twelve. Almost all were real orphans with beautiful dead parents in the sky. We were the only ones dumped and the only ones with F's in three classes including gym. So we got along—what with her leaving whole pieces of things on her plate and being nice about not asking questions.

I think it was the day before Maggie fell down that we found out our mothers were coming to visit us on the same Sunday. We had been at the shelter twenty-eight days (Roberta twenty-eight and a half) and this was their first visit with us. Our mothers would come at ten o'clock in time for chapel, then lunch with us in the teachers' lounge. I thought if my dancing mother met her sick mother it might be good for her. And Roberta thought her sick mother would get a big bang out of a dancing one. We got excited about it and curled each other's hair. After breakfast we sat on the bed watching the road from the window. Roberta's socks were still wet. She washed them the night before and put them on the radiator to dry. They hadn't, but she put them on anyway because their tops were so pretty—scalloped in pink. Each of us had a purple construction-paper basket that we had made in craft class. Mine had a yellow crayon rabbit on it. Roberta's had eggs with wiggly lines of color. Inside were cellophane grass and just the jelly beans because I'd eaten the two marshmallow eggs they gave us. The Big Bozo came herself to get us. Smiling she told us we looked very nice and to come downstairs. We were so surprised by the smile we'd never seen before, neither of us moved.

"Don't you want to see your mommies?"

I stood up first and spilled the jelly beans all over the floor. Bozo's smile disappeared while we scrambled to get the candy up off the floor and put it back in the grass.

She escorted us downstairs to the first floor, where the other girls were lining up to file into the chapel. A bunch of grown-ups stood to one side. Viewers mostly. The old biddies who wanted servants and the fags who wanted company looking for children they might want to adopt. Once in a while a grandmother. Almost never anybody young or anybody whose face wouldn't scare you in the night. Because if any of the real orphans had young relatives they wouldn't be real orphans. I saw Mary right away. She had on those green slacks I hated and hated even more now because didn't she know we were going to chapel? And that fur jacket with the pocket linings so ripped she had to pull to get her hands out of them. But her face was pretty—like always, and she smiled and waved like she was the little girl looking for her mother—not me.

I walked slowly, trying not to drop the jelly beans and hoping the paper handle would hold. I had to use my last Chiclet because by the time I finished cutting everything out, all the Elmer's was gone. I am left-handed and the scissors never worked for me. It didn't matter, though; I might just as well have chewed the gum. Mary dropped to her knees and grabbed me, mashing the basket, the jelly beans, and the grass into her ratty fur jacket.

"Twyla, baby. Twyla, baby!"

I could have killed her. Already I heard the big girls in the orchard the next time saying, "Twyyyyyla, baby!" But I couldn't stay mad at Mary while she was smiling and hugging me and smelling of Lady Esther dusting powder. I wanted to stay buried in her fur all day.

To tell the truth I forgot about Roberta. Mary and I got in line for the traipse into chapel and I was feeling proud because she looked so beautiful even in those ugly green slacks that made her behind stick out. A pretty mother on earth is better than a beautiful dead one in the sky even if she did leave you all alone to go dancing.

I felt a tap on my shoulder, turned, and saw Roberta smiling. I smiled back, but not too much lest somebody think this visit was the biggest thing that ever happened in my life. Then Roberta said, "Mother, I want you to meet my roommate, Twyla. And that's Twyla's mother."

I looked up it seemed for miles. She was big. Bigger than any man and on her chest was the biggest cross I'd ever seen. I swear it was six inches long each way. And in the crook of her arm was the biggest Bible ever made.

Mary, simple-minded as ever, grinned and tried to yank her hand out of the pocket with the raggedy lining—to shake hands, I guess. Roberta's mother looked down at me and then looked down at Mary too. She didn't say anything, just grabbed Roberta with her Bible-free hand and stepped out of line, walking quickly to the rear of it. Mary was still grinning because she's not too swift when it comes to what's really going on. Then this light bulb goes off in her head and she says "That bitch!" really loud and us almost in the chapel now. Organ music whining; the Bonny Angels singing sweetly. Everybody in the world turned around to look. And Mary would have kept it up—kept calling names if I hadn't squeezed her hand as hard as I could. That helped a little, but she still twitched and crossed and uncrossed her legs all through service. Even groaned a couple of times. Why did I think she would come there and act right? Slacks. No hat like the grandmothers and viewers, and groaning all the while. When we stood for hymns she kept her mouth shut. Wouldn't even look at the words on the page. She actually reached in her purse for a mirror to check her lipstick. All I could think of was that she really needed to be killed. The sermon lasted a year, and I knew the real orphans were looking smug again.

We were supposed to have lunch in the teachers' lounge, but Mary didn't bring anything, so we picked fur and cellophane grass off the mashed jelly beans and ate them. I could have killed her. I sneaked a look at Roberta. Her mother had brought chicken legs and ham sandwiches and oranges and a whole box of chocolate-covered grahams. Roberta drank milk from a thermos while her mother read the Bible to her.

Things are not right. The wrong food is always with the wrong people. Maybe that's why I got into waitress work later—to match up the right people with the right food. Roberta just let those chicken legs sit there, but she did bring a stack of grahams up to me later when the visit was over. I think she was sorry that her mother would not shake my mother's hand. And I liked that and I liked the fact that she didn't say a word about Mary groaning all the way through the service and not bringing any lunch.

Roberta left in May when the apple trees were heavy and white. On her last day we went to the orchard to watch the big girls smoke and dance by the radio. It didn't matter that they said, "Twyyyyyla, baby." We sat on the ground and breathed. Lady Esther. Apple blossoms. I still go soft when I smell one or the other. Roberta was going home. The big cross and the big Bible was coming to get her and she seemed sort of glad and sort of not. I thought I would die in that room of four beds without her and I knew Bozo had plans to move some other dumped kid in there with me. Roberta promised to write every day, which was really sweet of her because she couldn't read a lick so how could she write anybody. I would have drawn pictures and sent them to her but she never gave me her address. Little by little she faded. Her wet socks with the pink scalloped tops and her big serious-looking eyes—that's all I could catch when I tried to bring her to mind.

I was working behind the counter at the Howard Johnson's on the Thruway just before the Kingston exit. Not a bad job. Kind of a long ride from Newburgh, but okay once I got there. Mine was the second night shift—eleven to seven. Very light until a Greyhound checked in for breakfast around six-thirty. At that hour the sun was all they way clear of the hills behind the restaurant. The place looked better at night—more like shelter—but I loved it when the sun broke in, even if it did show all the cracks in the vinyl and the speckled floor looked dirty no matter what the mop boy did.

It was August and a bus crowd was just unloading. They would stand around a long while: going to the john, and looking at gifts and junk-for-sale machines, reluctant to sit down so soon. Even to eat. I was trying to fill the coffee pots and get them all situated on the electric burners when I saw her. She was sitting in a booth smoking a cigarette with two guys smothered in head and facial hair. Her own hair was so big and wild I could hardly see her face. But the eyes. I would know them anywhere. She had on a powder-blue halter and shorts outfit and earrings the size of bracelets. Talk about lipstick and eyebrow pencil. She made the big girls look like nuns. I couldn't get off the counter until seven o'clock, but I kept watching the booth in case they got up to leave before that. My replacement was on time for a change, so I counted and stacked my receipts as fast as I could and signed off. I walked over to the booth, smiling and wondering if she would remember me. Or even if she wanted to remember me. Maybe she didn't want to be reminded of St. Bonny's or to have anybody know she was ever there. I know I never talked about it to anybody.

I put my hands in my apron pockets and leaned against the back of the booth facing them.

"Roberta? Roberta Fisk?"

She looked up. "Yeah?"

"Twyla."

She squinted for a second and then said, "Wow."

"Remember me?"

"Sure. Hey. Wow."

"It's been a while," I said, and gave a smile to the two hairy guys.

"Yeah. Wow. You work here?"

"Yeah," I said. "I live in Newburgh."

"Newburgh? No kidding?" She laughed then a private laugh that included the guys but only the guys, and they laughed with her. What could I do but laugh too and wonder why I was standing there with my knees showing out from under that uniform. Without looking I could see the blue and white triangle on my head, my hair shapeless in a net, my ankles thick in white oxfords. Nothing could have been less sheer than my stockings. There was this silence that came down right after I laughed. A silence it was her turn to fill up. With introductions, maybe, to her boyfriends or an invitation to sit down and have a Coke. Instead she lit a cigarette off the one she'd just finished and said, "We're on our way to the Coast. He's got an appointment with Hendrix." She gestured casually toward the boy next to her.

"Hendrix? Fantastic," I said. "Really fantastic. What's she doing now?"

Roberta coughed on her cigarette and the two guys rolled their eyes up at the ceiling.

"Hendrix. Jimi Hendrix, asshole. He's only the biggest— Oh, wow. Forget it."

I was dismissed without anyone saying goodbye, so I thought I would do it for her.

"How's your mother?" I asked. Her grin cracked her whole face. She swallowed. "Fine," she said. "How's yours?"

"Pretty as a picture," I said and turned away. The backs of my knees were damp. Howard Johnson's really was a dump in the sunlight.

James is as comfortable as a house slipper. He liked my cooking and I liked his big loud family. They have lived in Newburgh all of their lives and talk about it the way people do who have always known a home. His grandmother is a porch swing older than his father and when they talk about streets and avenues and buildings they call them names they no longer have. They still call the A & P Rico's because it stands on property once a mom and pop store owned by Mr. Rico. And they call the new community college Town Hall because it once was. My mother-in-law puts up jelly and cucumbers and buys butter wrapped in cloth from a dairy. James and his father talk about fishing and baseball and I can see them all together on the Hudson in a raggedy skiff. Half the population of Newburgh is on welfare now, but to my husband's family it was still some upstate paradise of a time long past. A time of ice houses and vegetable wagons, coal furnaces and children weeding gardens. When our son was born my mother-in-law gave me the crib blanket that had been hers.

But the town they remembered had changed. Something quick was in the air. Magnificent old houses, so ruined they had become shelter for squatters and rent risks, were bought and renovated. Smart IBM people moved out of their suburbs back into the city and put shutters up and herb gardens in their backyards. A brochure came in the mail announcing the opening of a Food Emporium. Gourmet food it said—and listed items the rich IBM crowd would want. It was located in a new mall at the edge of town and I drove out to shop there one day—just to see. It was late in June. After the tulips were gone and the Queen Elizabeth roses were open everywhere. I trailed my cart along the aisle tossing in smoked oysters and Robert's sauce and things I knew would sit in my cupboard for years. Only when I found some Klondike ice cream bars did I feel less guilty about spending James's fireman's salary so foolishly. My father-in-law ate them with the same gusto little Joseph did.

Waiting in the check-out line I heard a voice say, "Twyla!"

The classical music piped over the aisles had affected me and the woman leaning toward me was dressed to kill. Diamonds on her hand, a smart white summer dress. "I'm Mrs. Benson," I said.

"Ho. Ho. The Big Bozo," she sang.

For a split second I didn't know what she was talking about. She had a bunch of asparagus and two cartons of fancy water.

"Roberta!"

"Right."

"For heaven's sake. Roberta."

"You look great," she said.

"So do you. Where are you? Here? In Newburgh?"

"Yes. Over in Annandale."

I was opening my mouth to say more when the cashier called my attention to her empty counter.

"Meet you outside." Roberta pointed her finger and went into the express line.

I placed the groceries and kept myself from glancing around to check Roberta's progress. I remembered Howard Johnson's and looking for a chance to speak only to be greeted with a stingy "wow." But she was waiting for me and her huge hair was sleek now, smooth around a small, nicely shaped head. Shoes, dress, everything lovely and summery and rich. I was dying to know what happened to her, how she got from Jimi Hendrix to Annandale, a neighborhood full of doctors and IBM executives. Easy, I thought. Everything is so easy for them. They think they own the world.

"How long," I asked her. "How long have you been here?"

"A year. I got married to a man who lives here. And you, you're married too, right? Benson, you said."

"Yeah. James Benson."

"And is he nice?"

"Oh, is he nice?"

"Well, is he?" Roberta's eyes were steady as though she really meant the question and wanted an answer.

"He's wonderful, Roberta. Wonderful."

"So you're happy."

"Very."

"That's good," she said and nodded her head. "I always hoped you'd be happy. Any kids? I know you have kids."

"One. A boy. How about you?"

"Four."

"Four?"

She laughed. "Step kids. He's a widower."

"Oh."

"Got a minute? Let's have a coffee."

I thought about the Klondikes melting and the inconvenience of going all the way to my car and putting the bags in the trunk. Served me right for buying all that stuff I didn't need. Roberta was ahead of me.

"Put them in my car. It's right here."

And then I saw the dark blue limousine.

"You married a Chinaman?"

"No," she laughed. "He's the driver."

"Oh, my. If the Big Bozo could see you now."

We both giggled. Really giggled. Suddenly, in just a pulse beat, twenty years disappeared and all of it came rushing back. The big girls (whom we called gar girls—Roberta's misheard word for the evil stone faces described in a civics class) there dancing in the orchard, the ploppy mashed potatoes, the double weenies, the Spam with pineapple. We went into the coffee shop holding on to one another and I tried to think why we were glad to see each other this time and not before. Once, twelve years ago, we passed like strangers. A black girl and a white girl meeting in a Howard Johnson's on the road and having nothing to say. One in a blue and white triangle waitress hat—the other on her way to see Hendrix. Now we were behaving like sisters separated for much too long. Those four short months were nothing in time. Maybe it was the thing itself. Just being there, together. Two little girls who knew what nobody else in the world knew—how not to ask questions. How to believe what had to be believed. There was politeness in that reluctance and generosity as well. Is your mother sick too? No, she dances all night. Oh—and an understanding nod.

We sat in a booth by the window and fell into recollection like veterans.

"Did you ever learn to read?"

"Watch." She picked up the menu. "Special of the day. Cream of corn soup. Entrées. Two dots and a wriggly line. Quiche. Chef salad, scallops . . ."

I was laughing and applauding when the waitress came up.

"Remember the Easter baskets?"

"And how we tried to *introduce* them?"

"Your mother with that cross like two telephone poles."

"And yours with those tight slacks."

We laughed so loudly heads turned and made the laughter harder to suppress.

"What happened to the Jimi Hendrix date?"

Roberta made a blow-out sound with her lips.

"When he died I thought about you."

"Oh, you heard about him finally?"

"Finally. Come on, I was a small-town country waitress."

"And I was a small-town country dropout. God, were we wild. I still don't know how I got out of there alive."

"But you did."

"I did. I really did. Now I'm Mrs. Kenneth Norton."

"Sounds like a mouthful."

"It is."

"Servants and all?"

Roberta held up two fingers.

"Ow! What does he do?"

"Computers and stuff. What do I know?"

"I don't remember a hell of a lot from those days, but Lord, St. Bonny's is as clear as daylight. Remember Maggie? The day she fell down and those gar girls laughed at her?"

Roberta looked up from her salad and stared at me. "Maggie didn't fall," she said.

"Yes, she did. You remember."

"No, Twyla. They knocked her down. Those girls pushed her down and tore her clothes. In the orchard."

"I don't—that's not what happened."

"Sure it is. In the orchard. Remember how scared we were?"

"Wait a minute. I don't remember any of that."

"And Bozo was fired."

"You're crazy. She was there when I left. You left before me."

"I went back. You weren't there when they fired Bozo."

"What?"

"Twice. Once for a year when I was about ten, another for two months when I was fourteen. That's when I ran away."

"You ran away from St. Bonny's?"

"I had to. What do you want? Me dancing in that orchard?"

"Are you sure about Maggie?"

"Of course I'm sure. You've blocked it, Twyla. It happened. Those girls had behavior problems, you know."

"Didn't they, though. But why can't I remember the Maggie thing?"

"Believe me. It happened. And we were there."

"Who did you room with when you went back?" I asked her as if I would know her. The Maggie thing was troubling me.

"Creeps. They tickled themselves in the night."

My ears were itching and I wanted to go home suddenly. This was all very well but she couldn't just comb her hair, wash her face and pretend everything was hunky-dory. After the Howard Johnson's snub. And no apology. Nothing.

"Were you on dope or what that time at Howard Johnson's?" I tried to make my voice sound friendlier than I felt.

"Maybe, a little. I never did drugs much. Why?"

"I don't know; you acted sort of like you didn't want to know me then."

"Oh, Twyla, you know how it was in those days: black—white. You know how everything was."

But I didn't know. I thought it was just the opposite. Busloads of blacks and whites came into Howard Johnson's together. They roamed together then: students, musicians, lovers, protesters. You got to see everything at Howard Johnson's and blacks were very friendly with whites in those days. But sitting there with nothing on my plate but two hard tomato wedges wondering about the melting Klondikes it seemed childish remembering the slight. We went to her car, and with the help of the driver, got my stuff into my station wagon.

"We'll keep in touch this time," she said.

"Sure," I said. "Sure. Give me a call."

"I will," she said, and then just as I was sliding behind the wheel, she leaned into the window. "By the way. Your mother. Did she ever stop dancing?"

I shook my head. "No. Never."

Roberta nodded.

"And yours? Did she ever get well?"

She smiled a tiny sad smile. "No. She never did. Look, call me, okay?"

"Okay," I said, but I knew I wouldn't. Roberta had messed up my past somehow with that business about Maggie. I wouldn't forget a thing like that. Would I?

Strife came to us that fall. At least that's what the paper called it. Strife. Racial strife. The word made me think of a bird—a big shrieking bird out of 1,000,000,000 B.C. Flapping its wings and cawing. Its eye with no lid always bearing down on you. All day it screeched and at night it slept on the rooftops. It woke you in the morning and from the *Today* show to the eleven o'clock news it kept you an awful company. I couldn't figure it out from one day to the next. I knew I was supposed to feel something strong, but I didn't know what, and James wasn't any help. Joseph was on the list of kids to be transferred from the junior high school to another one at some far-out-of-the-way place and I thought it was a good thing until I heard it was a bad thing. I mean I didn't know. All the schools seemed dumps to me, and the fact that one was nicer looking didn't hold much weight. But the papers were full of it and then the kids began to get jumpy. In August, mind you. Schools weren't even open yet. I thought Joseph might be frightened to go over there, but he didn't seem scared so I forgot about it, until I found myself driving along Hudson Street out there by the school they were trying to integrate and saw a line of women marching. And who do you suppose was in line, big as life, holding a sign in front of her bigger than her mother's cross? MOTHERS HAVE RIGHTS TOO! it said.

I drove on, and then changed my mind. I circled the block, slowed down, and honked my horn.

Roberta looked over and when she saw me she waved. I didn't wave back, but I didn't move either. She handed her sign to another woman and came over to where I was parked.

"Hi."

"What are you doing?"

"Picketing. What's it look like?"

"What for?"

"What do you mean, 'What for?' They want to take my kids and send them out of the neighborhood. They don't want to go."

"So what if they go to another school? My boy's being bussed too, and I don't mind. Why should you?"

"It's not about us, Twyla. Me and you. It's about our kids."

"What's more *us* than that?"

"Well, it is a free country."

"Not yet, but it will be."

"What the hell does that mean? I'm not doing anything to you."

"You really think that?"

"I know it."

"I wonder what made me think you were different."

"I wonder what made me think you were different."

"Look at them," I said. "Just look. Who do they think they are? Swarming all over the place like they own it. And now they think they can decide where my child goes to school. Look at them, Roberta. They're Bozos."

Roberta turned around and looked at the women. Almost all of them were standing still now, waiting. Some were even edging toward us. Roberta looked at me out of some refrigerator behind her eyes. "No, they're not. They're just mothers."

"And what am I? Swiss cheese?"

"I used to curl your hair."

"I hated your hands in my hair."

The women were moving. Our faces looked mean to them of course and they looked as though they could not wait to throw themselves in front of a police car, or better yet, into my car and drag me away by my ankles. Now they surrounded my car and gently, gently began to rock it. I swayed back and forth like a sideways yo-yo. Automatically I reached for Roberta, like the old days in the orchard when they saw us watching them and we had to get out of there, and if one of us fell the other pulled her up and if one of us was caught the other stayed to kick and scratch, and neither would leave the other behind. My arm shot out of the car window but no receiving hand was there. Roberta was looking at me sway from side to side in the car and her face was still. My purse slid from the car seat down under the dashboard. The four policemen who had been drinking Tab in their car finally got the message and stolled over, forcing their way through the women. Quietly, firmly they spoke. "Okay, ladies. Back in line or off the streets."

Some of them went away willingly; others had to be urged away from the car doors and the hood. Roberta didn't move. She was looking steadily at me. I was fumbling to turn on the ignition, which wouldn't catch because the gearshift was still in drive. The seats of the car were a mess because the swaying had thrown my grocery coupons all over it and my purse was sprawled on the floor.

"Maybe I am different now, Twyla. But you're not. You're the same little state kid who kicked a poor old black lady when she was down on the ground. You kicked a black lady and you have the nerve to call me a bigot."

The coupons were everywhere and the guts of my purse were bunched under the dashboard. What was she saying? Black? Maggie wasn't black.

"She wasn't black," I said.

"Like hell she wasn't, and you kicked her. We both did. You kicked a black lady who couldn't even scream."

"Liar!"

"You're the liar! Why don't you just go on home and leave us alone, huh?"

She turned away and I skidded away from the curb.

The next morning I went into the garage and cut the side out of the carton our portable TV had come in. It wasn't nearly big enough, but after a while I had a decent sign: red spray-painted letters on a white background—AND SO DO CHILDREN****. I meant just to go down to the school and tack it up somewhere so those cows on the picket line across the street could see it, but when I got there, some ten or so others had already assembled—protesting the cows across the street. Police permits and everything. I got in line and we strutted in time on our side while Roberta's group strutted on theirs. That first day we were all dignified, pretending the other side didn't exist. The second day there was name calling and finger gestures. But that was about all. People changed signs from time to time, but Roberta never did and neither did I. Actually my sign didn't make sense without Roberta's. "And so do children what?" one of the women on my side asked me. Have rights, I said, as though it was obvious.

Roberta didn't acknowledge my presence in any way and I got to thinking maybe she didn't know I was there. I began to pace myself in the line, jostling people one minute and lagging behind the next, so Roberta and I could reach the end of our respective lines at the same time and there would be a moment in our turn when we would face each other. Still, I couldn't tell whether she saw me and knew my sign was for her. The next day I went early before we were scheduled to assemble. I waited until she got there before I exposed my new creation. As soon as she hoisted her MOTHERS HAVE RIGHTS TOO I began to wave my new one, which said, HOW WOULD YOU KNOW? I know she saw that one, but I had gotten addicted now. My signs got crazier each day, and the women on my side decided that I was a kook. They couldn't make heads or tails out of my brilliant screaming posters.

I brought a painted sign in queenly red with huge black letters that said, IS YOUR MOTHER WELL? Roberta took her lunch break and didn't come back for the rest of the day or any day after. Two days later I stopped going too and couldn't have been missed because nobody understood my signs anyway.

It was a nasty six weeks. Classes were suspended and Joseph didn't go to anybody's school until October. The children—everybody's children—soon got bored with that extended vacation they thought was going to be so great. They looked at TV until their eyes flattened. I spent a couple of mornings tutoring my son, as the other mothers said we should. Twice I opened a text from last year that he had never turned in. Twice he yawned in my face. Other mothers organized living room sessions so the kids would keep up. None of the kids could concentrate so they drifted back to *The Price Is Right* and *The Brady Bunch.* When the school finally opened there were fights once or twice and some sirens roared through the streets every once in a while. There were a lot of photographers from Albany. And just when ABC was about to send up a news crew, the kids settled down like nothing in the world had happened. Joseph hung my HOW WOULD YOU KNOW? sign in his bedroom. I don't know what became of AND SO DO CHILDREN****. I think my father-in-law cleaned some fish on it. He was always puttering around in our garage. Each of his five children lived in Newburgh and he acted as though he had five extra homes.

I couldn't help looking for Roberta when Joseph graduated from high school, but I didn't see her. It didn't trouble me much what she had said to me in the car. I mean the kicking part. I know I didn't do that, I couldn't do that. But I was puzzled by her telling me Maggie was black. When I thought about it I actually couldn't be certain. She wasn't pitch-black, I knew, or I would have remembered that. What I remember was the kiddie hat, and the semicircle legs. I tried to reassure myself about the race thing for a long time until it dawned on me that the truth was already there, and Roberta knew it. I didn't kick her; I didn't join in with the gar girls and kick that lady, but I sure did want to. We watched and never tried to help her and never called for help. Maggie was my dancing mother. Deaf, I thought, and dumb. Nobody inside. Nobody who would hear you if you cried in the night. Nobody who could tell you anything important that you could use. Rocking, dancing, swaying as she walked. And when the gar girls pushed her down, and started roughhousing, I knew she wouldn't scream, couldn't—just like me—and I was glad about that.

We decided not to have a tree, because Christmas would be at my mother-in-law's house, so why have a tree at both places? Joseph was at SUNY New Paltz and we had to economize, we said. But at the last minute, I changed my mind.

Nothing could be that bad. So I rushed around town looking for a tree, something small but wide. By the time I found a place, it was snowing and very late. I dawdled like it was the most important purchase in the world and the tree man was fed up with me. Finally I chose one and had it tied onto the trunk of the car. I drove away slowly because the sand trucks were not out yet and the streets could be murder at the beginning of a snowfall. Downtown the streets were wide and rather empty except for a cluster of people coming out of the Newburgh Hotel. The one hotel in town that wasn't built out of cardboard and Plexiglas. A party, probably. The men huddled in the snow were dressed in tails and the women had on furs. Shiny things glittered from underneath their coats. It made me tired to look at them. Tired, tired, tired. On the next corner was a small diner with loops and loops of paper bells in the window. I stopped the car and went in. Just for a cup of coffee and twenty minutes of peace before I went home and tried to finish everything before Christmas Eve.

"Twyla?"

There she was. In a silvery evening gown and dark fur coat. A man and another woman were with her, the man fumbling for change to put in the cigarette machine. The woman was humming and tapping on the counter with her fingernails. They all looked a little bit drunk.

"Well. It's you."

"How are you?"

I shrugged. "Pretty good. Frazzled. Christmas and all."

"Regular?" called the woman from the counter.

"Fine," Roberta called back and then, "Wait for me in the car."

She slipped into the booth beside me. "I have to tell you something, Twyla. I made up my mind if I ever saw you again, I'd tell you."

"I'd just as soon not hear anything, Roberta. It doesn't matter now, anyway."

"No," she said. "Not about that."

"Don't be long," said the woman. She carried two regulars to go and the man peeled his cigarette pack as they left.

"It's about St. Bonny's and Maggie."

"Oh, please."

"Listen to me. I really did think she was black. I didn't make that up. I really thought so. But now I can't be sure. I just remember her as old, so old. And because she couldn't talk—well, you know, I thought she was crazy. She'd been brought up in an institution like my mother was and like I thought I would be too. And you were right. We didn't kick her. It was the gar girls. Only them. But, well, I wanted to. I really wanted them to hurt her. I said we did it, too. You and me, but that's not true. And I don't want you to carry that around. It was just that I wanted to do it so bad that day—wanting to is doing it."

Her eyes were watery from the drinks she'd had, I guess. I know it's that way with me. One glass of wine and I start bawling over the littlest thing.

"We were kids, Roberta."

"Yeah. Yeah. I know, just kids."

"Eight."

"Eight."

"And lonely."

"Scared, too."

She wiped her cheeks with the heel of her hand and smiled. "Well, that's all I wanted to say."

I nodded and couldn't think of any way to fill the silence that went from the diner past the paper bells on out into the snow. It was heavy now. I thought I'd better wait for the sand trucks before starting home.

"Thanks, Roberta."

"Sure."

"Did I tell you? My mother, she never did stop dancing."

"Yes. You told me. And mine, she never got well." Roberta lifted her hands from the tabletop and covered her face with her palms. When she took them away she really was crying. "Oh shit, Twyla. Shit, shit, shit. What the hell happened to Maggie?"

TONI CADE BAMBARA
(1939–1995)

Of the many voices that came to prominence on the heels of the Civil Rights Movement, Toni Cade Bambara's was one of the most compelling. Out of the political activism that informed her life, she forged a creative voice reflective of the times. In language, subject, and incidents, her works reflect the period in which they were created. As fiction writer, essayist, and filmmaker, Bambara captured the transitional times of the 1960s and 1970s, and she projected her voice into a healthier future for black people. A widely read writer with a broad array of experiences from which to draw, Bambara used all of them to create works that explore the possibilities and lapses of the Civil Rights Movement, the costs of activism, the problems inherent in leadership, and issues of world interest, such as the Vietnamese boat people and the Atlanta child murders. Ever aware of her world and ever desirous of being in harmony with it, Bambara carried her message in lectures and oral stories as well.

A New Yorker, Bambara was born Toni Cade on March 25, 1939, to Helen Brent Henderson Cade. In 1970, when she found the name Bambara on a sketchbook in her great-grandmother's trunk, she adopted it and was known professionally by that name. She grew up in Harlem, Bedford-Stuyvesant, and Queens with her mother and her brother, Walter. She credited her mother with cultivating her creative spirit and instilling in her a sense of independence and self-sufficiency that were not gender-specific. She received a B.A. in theater arts and English literature from Queens College in 1959, the same year she published her first short story, "Sweet Town," in *Vendome* magazine. She also won the John Golden Award for fiction from Queens College in 1959. She would later earn an M.A. in American literature from City College of New York; while pursuing the degree, during 1959–1960, she worked as a social worker for the Harlem Welfare Center. She studied at the Commedia dell'Arte in Milan, Italy, before returning to finish her master's degree in 1965.

Bambara held a number of positions in academia, including appointments at City College of New York (1965–1969), Livingston College in New Jersey (1969–1974), Spelman College (writer-in-residence, 1974–1977), Rutgers University, and Duke University.

On the wave of works about African American life and culture in the 1960s, Bambara published *The Black Woman* in 1970, under the name Toni Cade. The anthology, designed to show what black women were thinking and doing about the Civil Rights Movement and women's movement, includes essays on a variety of political and personal issues, short fiction, poetry, position papers, conversations, and letters. It was widely used in college courses as validating authentic black women's voices. In 1971, Bambara edited *Tales and Stories for Black Folks.* She followed that with her first collection of short fiction, *Gorilla, My Love* (1972), which contains fifteen works that she completed between 1959 and 1970. The narrative voices in the stories are the captivating feature. Bambara uses black folk speech and nontraditional narrators in several of the pieces, including the lead story, "My Man Bovanne." According to Ruth Elizabeth Burks, these tales about the meaning of ancestry "are female ones, almost sung by Bambara in a first person narrative voice reminiscent of the Negro spirituals with their strongly marked rhythms and highly graphic descriptions."

Before publishing her next volume, Bambara visited Cuba (1973) and met with the Federation of Cuban Women, which heightened her awareness of the necessity to be politically active. She also visited Vietnam in the summer of 1975, which further intensified her commitment to community organizing. Her second collection of stories, *The Sea Birds Are Still Alive* (1977), a volume marked by modernist blues-jazz cadences, illustrates her broader humanistic perspective. The title story concentrates on Asians and their plight as displaced people following the war in Vietnam. The other stories deal with political and social issues confronting African Americans, with growing up, and with family separation.

Bambara's richest achievement is her novel *The Salt Eaters* (1980). An examination of the consequences of the Civil Rights struggle in the small town of Claybourne, Georgia, the book suggests what utopian possibilities could have been instituted as a result of political activity and shows how those possibilities have fallen short due to human failings. Well versed in the jargon peculiar to political agencies and organizations prominent in the 1960s, and with a solid command of history, science, philosophy, international folk traditions, and extranatural ways of knowing, Bambara posits a link between the health of individuals and the health of their community. Velma Henry, a community activist who has slit her wrists and stuck her head in an oven, can be healed through Minnie Ransom, a psychic conjure woman, only if she believes in the power of knowing beyond empirical manifestations of knowledge. Reminiscent of a complex blues-jazz composition, the novel is at once historical and futuristic, at once complaining about problems and offering the formulas for their solutions. The work is a masterful achievement by a writer who knew intimately her subject matter and the history that informs it.

From 1974 to 1986, Bambara and her daughter, Karma, lived in Atlanta, where she was involved in a number of community artistic and political programs. She moved to Philadelphia in 1986 and became equally involved in programs there. One of her projects was a documentary on the bombing of the house in which a group of black nationalists lived. Known as MOVE, the group repeatedly refused to allow the children residing there to attend public school, and they rejected all demands for conformity to customs of cleanliness and neighborliness. They made national news when Mayor Wilson Goode decided to bomb the house in which they resided. Bambara also worked on a film about Zora Neale Hurston. She was reportedly in the process of completing a novel about the murders of more than twenty black children in Atlanta in the early 1980s when she became ill in 1994. She died of cancer in November of 1995.

❖❖❖

Critical studies of Bambara's works include Ruth Elizabeth Burks, "From Baptism to Resurrection: Toni Cade Bambara and the Incongruity of Language," and Eleanor Traylor, "Music as Theme: The Jazz Mode in the Works of Toni Cade Bambara," both in *Black Women Writers 1950–1980: A Critical Evaluation,* ed. Mari Evans (1984); Nancy D. Hargrove, "Youth in Toni Cade Bambara's *Gorilla, My Love,*" in *Women Writers of the Contemporary South,* ed. Peggy Whitman Prenshaw

(1984); Gloria T. Hull, "'What It Is I Think She's Doing Anyhow': A Reading of Toni Cade Bambara's *The Salt Eaters,*" in *Conjuring: Black Women, Fiction, and Literary Tradition,* ed. Marjorie Pryse and Hortense J. Spillers (1985); Susan Willis, *Specifying: Black Women Writing the American Experience* (1987); Elliott Butler-Evans, *Race, Gender, and Desire: Narrative Strategies in the Fiction of Toni Cade Bambara, Toni Morrison, and Alice Walker* (1989); Martha M. Vertreace, "A Bibliography of Writings About Toni Cade Bambara," in *American Women Writing Fiction: Memory, Identity, Family, Space,* ed. Mickey Pearlman (1989).

My Man Bovanne

Blind people got a hummin jones if you notice. Which is understandable completely once you been around one and notice what no eyes will force you into to see people, and you get past the first time, which seems to come out of nowhere, and it's like you in church again with fat-chest ladies and old gents gruntin a hum low in the throat to whatever the preacher be saying. Shakey Bee bottom lip all swole up with Sweet Peach and me explainin how come the sweet-potato bread was a dollar-quarter this time stead of dollar regular and he say un hunh he understand, then he break into this *thizzin* kind of hum which is quiet, but fiercesome just the same, if you ain't ready for it. Which I wasn't. But I got used to it and the onliest time I had to say somethin bout it was when he was playin checkers on the stoop one time and he commenst to hummin quite churchy seem to me. So I says, "Look here Shakey Bee, I can't beat you and Jesus too." He stop.

So that's how come I asked My Man Bovanne to dance. He ain't my man mind you, just a nice ole gent from the block that we all know cause he fixes things and the kids like him. Or used to fore Black Power got hold their minds and mess em around till they can't be civil to ole folks. So we at this benefit for my niece's cousin who's runnin for somethin with this Black party somethin or other behind her. And I press up close to dance with Bovanne who blind and I'm hummin and he hummin, chest to chest like talkin. Not jammin my breasts into the man. Wasn't bout tits. Was bout vibrations. And he dug it and asked me what color dress I had on and how my hair was fixed and how I was doin without a man, not nosy but nice-like, and who was at this affair and was the canapés dainty-stingy or healthy enough to get hold of proper. Comfy and cheery is what I'm tryin to get across. Touch talkin like the heel of the hand on the tamborine or on a drum.

But right away Joe Lee come up on us and frown for dancin so close to the man. My own son who knows what kind of warm I am about; and don't grown men call me long distance and in the middle of the night for a little Mama comfort? But he frown. Which ain't right since Bovanne can't see and defend himself. Just a nice old man who fixes toasters and busted irons and bicycles and things and changes the lock on my door when my men friends get messy. Nice man. Which is not why they invited him. Grass roots you see. Me and Sister Taylor and the woman who does heads at Mamies and the man from the barber shop, we all there on account of we grass roots. And I ain't never been souther than Brooklyn Battery and no more country than the window box on my fire escape. And just yesterday my kids tellin me to take them countrified rags off my head and be cool. And now can't get Black enough to suit em. So everybody passin saying My Man Bovanne. Big deal, keep steppin and don't even stop a minute to get the man a drink or one of them cute sandwiches or tell him what's goin on. And him standin there with a smile ready case someone do speak he want to be ready. So that's how come I pull him on the dance floor and we dance squeezin past the tables and chairs and all them coats and people standin round up in each other face talkin bout this and that but got no use for this blind man who mostly fixed skates and skooters for all these folks when they was just kids. So I'm pressed up close and we touch talkin with the hum. And here come my daughter cuttin her eye at me like she do when she tell me about my "apolitical" self like I got hoof and mouf disease and there ain't no hope at all. And I don't pay her no mind and just look up in Bovanne shadow face and tell him his stomach like a drum and he laugh. Laugh real loud. And here come my youngest, Task, with a tap on my elbow like he the third grade monitor and I'm cuttin up on the line to assembly.

"I was just talkin on the drums," I explained when they hauled me into the kitchen. I figured drums was my best defense. They can get ready for drums what with all this heritage business. And Bovanne stomach just like that drum Task give me when he come back from Africa. You just touch it and it hum thizzm, thizzm. So I stuck to the drum story. "Just drummin that's all."

"Mama, what are you talkin about?"

"She had too much to drink," say Elo to Task cause she don't hardly say nuthin to me direct no more since that ugly argument about my wigs.

"Look here Mama," say Task, the gentle one. "We just tryin to pull your coat. You were makin a spectacle of yourself out there dancing like that."

"Dancin like what?"

Task run a hand over his left ear like his father for the world and his father before that.

"Like a bitch in heat," say Elo.

"Well uhh, I was goin to say like one of them sex-starved ladies gettin on in years and not too discriminating. Know what I mean?"

I don't answer cause I'll cry. Terrible thing when your own children talk to you like that. Pullin me out the party and hustlin me into some stranger's kitchen in the back of a bar just like the damn police. And ain't like I'm old old. I can still wear me some sleeveless dresses without the meat hangin off my arm. And I keep up with some thangs through my kids. Who ain't kids no more. To hear them tell it. So I don't say nuthin.

"Dancin with that tom," say Elo to Joe Lee, who leanin on the folks' freezer. "His feet can smell a cracker a mile away and go into their shuffle number post haste. And them eyes. He could be a little considerate and put on some shades. Who wants to look into them blown-out fuses that—"

"Is this what they call the generation gap?" I say.

"Generation gap," spits Elo, like I suggested castor oil and fricassee possum in the milk-shakes or somethin. "That's a white concept for a white phenomenon. There's no generation gap among Black people. We are a col—"

"Yeh, well never mind," says Joe Lee. "The point is Mama . . . well, it's pride. You embarrass yourself and us too dancin like that."

"I wasn't shame." Then nobody say nuthin. Them standin there in they pretty clothes with drinks in they hands and gangin up on me, and me in the third-degree chair and nary a olive to my name. Felt just like the police got hold to me.

"First of all," Task say, holdin up his hand and tickin off the offenses, "the dress. Now that dress is too short, Mama, and too low-cut for a woman your age. And Tamu's going to make a speech tonight to kick off the campaign and will be introducin you and expecting you to organize the council of elders—"

"Me? Didn nobody ask me nuthin. You mean Nisi? She change her name?"

"Well, Norton was supposed to tell you about it. Nisi wants to introduce you and then encourage the older folks to form a Council of the Elders to act as an advisory—"

"And you going to be standing there with your boobs out and that wig on your head and that hem up to your ass. And people'll say, 'Ain't that the horny bitch that was grindin with the blind dude?'"

"Elo, be cool a minute," say Task, gettin to the next finger. "And then there's the drinkin. Mama, you know you can't drink cause next thing you know you be laughin loud and carryin on," and he grab another finger for the loudness. "And then there's the dancin. You been tattooed on the man for four records straight and slow draggin even on the fast numbers. How you think that look for a woman your age?"

"What's my age?"

"What?"

"I'm axin you all a simple question. You keep talkin bout what's proper for a woman my age. How old am I anyhow?" And Joe Lee slams his eyes shut and squinches up his face to figure. And Task run a hand over his ear and stare into his glass like the ice cubes goin calculate for him. And Elo just starin at the top of my head like she goin to rip the wig off any minute now.

"Is your hair braided up under that thing? If so, why don't you take it off? You always did do a neat cornroll."

"Uh huh," cause I'm thinkin how she couldn't undo her hair fast enough talking bout cornroll so countrified. None of which was the subject. "How old, I say?"

"Sixtee-one or—"

"You a damn lie Joe Lee Peoples."

"And that's another thing," say Task on the fingers.

"You know what you all can kiss," I say, gettin up and brushin the wrinkles out my lap.

"Oh, Mama," Elo say, puttin a hand on my shoulder like she hasn't done since she left home and the hand landin light and not sure it supposed to be there. Which hurt me to my heart. Cause this was the child in our happiness fore Mr. Peoples die. And I carried that child strapped to my chest till she was nearly two. We was close is what I'm tryin to tell you. Cause it was more me in the child than the others. And even after Task it was the girlchild I covered in the night and wept over for no reason at all less it was she was a chub-chub like me and not very pretty, but a warm child. And how did things get to this, that she can't put a sure hand on me and say Mama we love you and care about you and you entitled to enjoy yourself cause you a good woman?

"And then there's Reverend Trent," say Task, glancin from left to right like they hatchin a plot and just now lettin me in on it. "You were suppose to be talking with him tonight, Mama, about giving us his basement for campaign headquarters and—"

"Didn nobody tell me nuthin. If grass roots mean you kept in the dark I can't use it. I really can't. And Reven Trent a fool anyway the way he tore into the widow man up there on Edgecomb cause he wouldn't take in three of them foster children and the woman not even comfy in the ground yet and the man's mind messed up and—"

"Look here," say Task. "What we need is a family conference so we can get all this stuff cleared up and laid out on the table. In the meantime I think we better get back into the other room and tend to business. And in the meantime, Mama, see if you can't get to Reverend Trent and—"

"You want me to belly rub with the Reven, that it?"

"Oh damn," Elo say and go through the swingin door.

"We'll talk about all this at dinner. How's tomorrow night, Joe Lee?" While Joe Lee being self-important I'm wonderin who's doin the cookin and how come no body ax me if I'm free and do I get a corsage and things like that. Then Joe nod that it's O.K. and he go through the swingin door and just a little hubbub come through from the other room. Then Task smile his smile, lookin just like his daddy and he leave. And it just me in this stranger's kitchen, which was a mess I wouldn't never let my kitchen look like. Poison you just to look at the pots. Then the door swing the other way and it's My Man Bovanne standin there sayin Miss Hazel but lookin at the deep fry and then at the steam table, and most surprised when I come up on him from the other direction and take him on out of there. Pass the folks pushin up towards the stage where Nisi and some other people settin and ready to talk, and folks gettin to the last of the sandwiches and the booze fore they settle down in one spot and listen serious. And I'm thinkin bout tellin Bovanne what a lovely long dress Nisi got on and the earrings and her hair piled up in a cone and the people bout to hear how we all gettin screwed and gotta form our own party and everybody there listenin and lookin. But instead I just haul the man on out of there, and Joe Lee and his wife look at me like I'm terrible, but they ain't said boo to the man yet. Cause he blind and old and don't nobody there need him since they grown up and don't need they skates fixed no more.

"Where we goin, Miss Hazel?" Him knowin all the time.

"First we gonna buy you some dark sunglasses. Then you comin with me to the supermarket so I can pick up tomorrow's dinner, which is goin to be a grand thing proper and you invited. Then we goin to my house."

"That be fine. I surely would like to rest my feet." Bein cute, but you got to let men play out they little show, blind or not. So he chat on bout how tired he is and how he appreciate me takin him in hand this way. And I'm thinkin I'll have him change the lock on my door first thing. Then I'll give the man a nice warm bath with jasmine leaves in the water and a little Epsom salt on the sponge to do his back. And then a good rubdown with rose water and olive oil. Then a cup of lemon tea with a taste in it. And a little talcum, some of that fancy stuff Nisi mother sent over last Christmas. And then a massage, a good face massage round the forehead which is the worryin part. Cause you gots to take care of the older folks. And let them know they still needed to run the mimeo machine and keep the spark plugs clean and fix the mailboxes for folks who might help us get the breakfast program goin, and the school for the little kids and the campaign and all. Cause old folks is the nation. That what Nisi was sayin and I mean to do my part.

"I imagine you are a very pretty woman, Miss Hazel."

"I surely am," I say just like the hussy my daughter always say I was.

ALICE WALKER

(1944–)

Alice Walker is arguably the most significant African American woman writer in the post-1950 era. Support for such a claim comes from the sheer volume of her publications, her popularity among the general public as well as the academic community, her international acclaim, and the consistently engaging nature of the topics about which she writes. Her focus on feminist issues within the black community, as well as on intraracial violence and oppression, place her in a category of writers willing to confront the difficult problems of communities in transition, to complain about their male-female and parent-child relationships, and to cajole their members to renew their faith in each other for the sake of community survival. Her coining of the word *womanist* to articulate her concept of black feminism has led to its own critical explosion. Her recent concentration on issues that affect women worldwide, particularly male oppression through female circumcision, illustrates that Walker refuses to compromise her effort to reform humanity and sensitize human beings to the need to save the earth for future generations.

Walker was born in Eatonton, Georgia, on February 9, 1944, the eighth child of sharecroppers Willie Lee and Minnie Lou Grant Walker. The deprived setting and the perpetuation of the new slavery called sharecropping would serve as the impetus for her first novel, *The Third Life of Grange Copeland,* which was published in 1970. An accident with a BB gun at the age of eight (one of her older brothers shot her) caused Walker to lose the sight in her right eye and left her with a scar. The problem was corrected when Walker was fourteen, but she still felt ugly, a feeling that led her to recording her thoughts in a notebook. But the misfortune also enabled her to attend Spelman College on a scholarship for disabled persons. After two years at Spelman, she transferred to Sarah Lawrence College, where, under the guiding hand of Muriel Rukeyser, she was able to get her early works published. Her relationship with Harcourt Brace Jovanovich still continues today.

A trip to Africa during a summer away from Sarah Lawrence led to the writing of several poems included in Walker's first collection, *Once* (1970). She was pregnant before the trip began, and her pregnancy only made her feel more at the mercy of her body and suicidal. Writing poems, she said, was a way for her to celebrate each day with the knowledge that she had not committed suicide the night before. She finished *Once* while she was waiting for friends to find an abortionist for her, which they succeeded in doing. Her second volume of poetry, *Revolutionary Petunias,* appeared in 1973. These early poetic efforts were succeeded by several more volumes of poetry, including *Good Night, Willie Lee, I'll See You in the Morning* (1979), *Horses Make a Landscape Look More Beautiful* (1984), and *Her Blue Body Everything We Know: Earthling Poems 1965–1990 Complete* (1991).

Walker also began her reputation in fiction in the 1970s. *The Third Life of Grange Copeland* (1970) follows a man from his defeat at the hands of the white man for whom he sharecrops, to further degradation in New York, to his return to Georgia saner, more complete, and more respectful of black women than he could have imagined being earlier in his life. *In Love and Trouble: Stories of Black Women* (1973) depicts various women who are at the mercy of the men in their lives, their own passions, the forces of nature, or societal expectations of who and what they should be.

In 1976, Walker published *Meridian,* which chronicles the sexual and racial politics of the Civil Rights Movement. Walker herself was a participant in Civil Rights activities in Mississippi, where she worked from the late 1960s to the mid-1970s and where she married Mel Leventhal, a white Civil Rights lawyer. The couple had one child, a daughter named Rebecca. While she was at Spelman College, she says, she learned to appreciate all the young stars involved in that movement, including Student Nonviolent Coordinating Committee (SNCC) leaders Julian Bond, John Lewis, and Ruby Davis Robinson. She also participated in demonstrations in Georgia.

Meridian begins what would remain Walker's lifetime goal—to reorient social protest toward an Afrocentric female model. The heroine consistently tries to show her lover, Truman, that lasting Civil Rights should be accomplished only through a self-sacrificing life—not a quick, glorifying death or a compromise with the materialistic white world. Torn between his platonic love for Meridian and his passion for a white woman in the movement, Truman never grasps her concepts of spiritual life-sacrifice. As she suffers through the pain of rejection after he marries the white woman, Meridian perfects her concept of accomplishing major social change even though the black woman must stand and act alone. In *Black Women Novelists,* Barbara Christian writes that for Meridian,

> Since life demands such extraordinary sacrifices, sex, which is its cause, is rife with danger, particularly for the women. Throughout the novel, the role that sex plays in the development of girls into women and boys into men is at best static, at worst tragic. . . . Truman may struggle with Meridian for social change, [but] he is primarily interested in sleeping with her.

Walker repeats her study of what she believes is the black man's seemingly untoward interest in sexual relations—regardless of the racial identification of the woman—and of the black female–black male–white female triangle in an interesting short story titled "Advancing Luna—and Ida B. Wells," which is included in Mary Helen Washington's collection *Midnight Birds* (1980). Walker's devotion to both the Civil Rights Movement and the women's movement prevented her from bringing the story to a reasonable conclusion. Because the black woman is divided between her loyalty to the black man, her deep opposition to the violence of rape, and her sisterhood with the white woman, Walker concludes the work with three different endings.

During the 1970s, Walker also was involved in the process of recentering Zora Neale Hurston in the literary world. She traveled to Eatonville, Florida, in search of Hurston's grave and placed a marker at the site. She also wrote "In Search of Zora Neale Hurston" (1974) and the foreword to Robert E. Hemenway's biography of Hurston (1977). She would later edit a collection of Hurston's works titled *I Love Myself When I Am Laughing and Then Again When I Am Looking Mean and Impressive* (1979). Walker has said of Hurston in *In Search of Our Mother's Garden: Womanist Prose* (1983),

> The quality I feel is most characteristic of Zora's work: racial health; a sense of black people as complete, complex, *undiminished* human beings, a sense that is lacking in so much black writing and literature. In my opinion, only Du Bois showed an equally consistent delight in the beauty and spirit of black people, which is interesting when one considers that the angle of his vision was completely the opposite of Zora's.

You Can't Keep a Good Woman Down, Walker's second collection of short stories, appeared in 1981. Her most feminist work to that point, it deals with issues that grew out of the Civil Rights Movement as well as the feminist movement. Interracial rape, abortion, sadomasochism, pornography, and murder are a few of the powerful topics she treats. Some critics believe that, like "Advancing Luna—and Ida B. Wells," some of the stories appear to be in a stage of perpetual creation.

The next year would bring Walker's most controversial work. Although she had started the novel in New York City, it was only when she divorced in 1977 and moved to California that the characters came freely and the finished product was achieved. *The Color Purple* (1982), a story of incest and intraracial violence and abuse, drew a plethora of emotional responses from the black community as well as from black academics. Written in epistolary form, the novel recounts the initially tragic life and ultimate triumph of Celie, who moves from incest victim to lesbian love and entrepreneurship. Perhaps because of its controversial initial reception, the novel was widely read and discussed, and it has remained on college course lists since its publication. It was made into a movie and has been reissued at least twice since its original publication. Walker asserts that the story was based on that of her great-grandmother, who was raped and abused at the age of twelve. Celie's triumph over sexual abuse and physical beatings perhaps served as a rewriting of her great-grandmother's history. In addition, Celie's sister, Nettie, becomes a missionary in Africa; the exploration of that link would tie in with Walker's next two novelistic ventures.

In "Alice Walker's *The Color Purple:* Emergent Woman, Emergent Text," critic Lindsay Tucker assesses the novel as thoroughly in the feminist vein:

> By the novel's end, his story (history) has been deconstructed, has become herstory, a story of female love, female work, female song, and, most importantly, female bonding, which does not, finally, exclude the males at all, but accommodates, redeems, even celebrates them. Walker, like a quiltmaker, has pieced together from the only materials available—materials of poverty, ignorance, brutalization—a work that, like the product of the quiltmaker, may seem artless, but is instead a carefully crafted and brilliantly patterned piece of work.

However, neither the book nor the movie was wholeheartedly endorsed by the black community. Blacks picketed the film in Los Angeles, San Francisco, and other cities, and some critics, such as Trudier Harris and Sondra O'Neale, wrote strong objections to what they believe are Walker's stereotypical and negative portrayals of black people.

In 1989, Walker published *The Temple of My Familiar,* which retains a couple of characters from *The Color Purple* but is not obviously a sequel. Walker's fascination with the African connection enables her to depict a woman, Lissie, who has spent numerous lives on that continent. (Lissie has been reincarnated several times.) The novel also provides, through lengthy conversations about the need to get in touch with one's spirit and one's spiritual past, a way for harassed contemporary African Americans to rediscover what is of value in themselves. Critics complained that the novel was too talky, too California touchy-feely, too New Age, but it has found a faithful following among those who believe that harmony with the earth and all its creatures is of paramount concern. Spiritual guides, dead and alive, can aid in the process of that understanding.

In the spring of 1992, Walker published *Possessing the Secret of Joy.* Narrated by multiple voices, the story is primarily that of another character from *The Color Purple.* Tashi, who was Celie's daughter Olivia's best friend in the Olinka village, reappears as a woman scarred beyond reclamation by the physical and psychological trauma of female pharaonic circumcision—the complete removal of all signs of female genitalia and the sewing up of the remaining opening. Despite the quietness of her prose, Walker is clearly at war in the book—at war with a practice that has traumatized many women but that is still common in many parts of the world. In an effort to further her cause for its demise, she includes a statement at the end of the novel, along with a reading list for interested persons.

Walker also has a well-deserved reputation as an essayist. She is one of the few African American female writers who have published book-length collections of essays. To date, she has two. The first, *In Search of Our Mothers' Gardens: Womanist Prose* (1983), is a landmark work in the development of black feminist literary criticism. It was inspired by Walker's own mother, as well as by Walker's reclaiming of Zora Neale Hurston. Walker has repeatedly suggested that the most significant influence on her has been her mother. Her image of her mother tending flowers in the many sharecropper shacks in which she was forced to live and making art out of that endeavor links the older and younger generations of creative artists. In this way, the essay is the theoretical extension of her short story "Everyday Use" from *In Love and Trouble* (1973). Walker explores the art of quilting, the legacy of "ordinary" southern African American women that has been the root of her own creative process and imagination as well as that of many other black women. Walker's second essay collection, *Living By the Word: Selected Writings 1973–1987,* appeared in 1988.

Walker continues to live in the San Francisco Bay Area, where she has established a small press, Wild Trees, for the purpose of publishing less well-known writers. A film featuring the artist in her retreat was made in 1989. Her popularity also extends to calendars, one of which featured photographs of Walker gardening, relaxing, and working. She continues to be a popular lecturer, whose reading voice and power over her audience are well celebrated, and her work against female mutilation in Africa and other parts of the world has added to her celebrity.

❖❖❖

Biographical information on Alice Walker can be obtained from *Dictionary of Literary Biography: Afro-American Fiction Writers After 1955:* vol. 33 (1984); and from the newly published Twayne U.S. Authors series volume Donna Hariet Winchell's *Alice Walker* (1992); Louis H. Pratt and Darnell D. Pratt, *Alice Malsenior Walker, An Annotated Bibliography: 1968–1986* (1988).

Interviews and critical studies are extensive; following is a brief selection: John O'Brien, *Interviews with Black Writers* (1974); Barbara Christian, *Black Women Novelists: The Development of a Tradition, 1892–1976* (1980); Barbara Christian, *Black Feminist Criticism: Perspectives on Black Women Writers* (1985); Mari Evans, ed., *Black Women Writers 1950–1980: A Critical Evaluation* (1983); Trudier Harris, "Folklore in the Fiction of Alice Walker: A Perpetuation of Historical and Literary Traditions," *Black American Literature Forum* 2 (Spring 1977); Trudier Harris, "On *The Color Purple,* Stereotypes, and Silence," *Black American Literature Forum* 14 (Winter 1984); Deborah McDowell, "The Self in Bloom: Alice Walker's *Meridian,*" *CLA Journal* 24 (March 1981); Claudia Tate, "Alice Walker," in *Black Women Writers at Work,* ed. Claudia Tate (1983); Mary Helen Washington, "An Essay on Alice Walker," in *Sturdy Black Bridges,* ed. Roseann P. Bell, Bettye J. Parker, and Beverly Guy-Sheftall (1979); Mary Helen Washington, "Her Mother's Gifts," *Ms.,* June 1982; Melvin Dixon, *Ride Out the Wilderness: Geography and Identity in Afro-American Literature* (1987); Henry Louis Gates, Jr., *The Signifying Monkey: A Theory of Afro-American Literary Criticism* (1988); Elliott Butler-Evans, *Race, Gender, and Desire: Narrative Strategies in the Fiction of Toni Cade Bambara, Toni Morrison, and Alice Walker* (1989); Lindsay Tucker, "Alice Walker's *The Color Purple:* Emergent Woman, Emergent Text," *Black American Literature Forum* 22 (Spring 1988); bell hooks, "Writing the Subject: Reading *The Color Purple,*" in *Reading Black, Reading Feminist: A Critical Anthology,* ed. Henry Louis Gates, Jr. (1990).

Madhu Dubey has two chapters on Walker in *Black Women Novelists and the Nationalist Aesthetic* (1994). Also of interest are Lillie P. Howard, *Alice Walker, and Zora Neale Hurston: The Common Bond* (1993); Harold Bloom, ed., *Alice Walker* (1989); Angelene Jamison Hall, "She's Just Too Womanish for Them: Alice Walker and *The Color Purple,*" in Lee Byrnes et al., *Censored Books: Critical Viewpoints* (1993); Jita Tuzyline Allan, "A Voice of One's Own: Implications of Impersonality in the Essays of Virginia Woolf and Alice Walker," in Ruth Ellen Boetcher and Elizabeth Joeres Mittan, *The Politics of the Essay: Feminist Perspectives* (1993); Linda Abbandonato, "A View from 'Elsewhere': Subversive Sexuality and the Rewriting of the

Heroine's Story in *The Color Purple*," *PMLA* 106:5 (October 1991); King Kok Cheung, "Don't Tell: Imposed Silences in *The Color Purple* and The Woman Warrior," in *PMLA* 103 (March 1988); Sondra O'Neale, "Inhibiting Midwives, Usurping Creators: The Struggling Emergence of Black Women in American Fiction," in *Feminist Studies: Critical Studies,* ed. Teresa deLauretis (1986).

Everyday Use

I will wait for her in the yard that Maggie and I made so clean and wavy yesterday afternoon. A yard like this is more comfortable than most people know. It is not just a yard. It is like an extended living room. When the hard clay is swept clean as a floor and the fine sand around the edges lined with tiny, irregular grooves, anyone can come and sit and look up into the elm tree and wait for the breezes that never come inside the house.

Maggie will be nervous until after her sister goes: she will stand hopelessly in corners, homely and ashamed of the burn scars down her arms and legs, eying her sister with a mixture of envy and awe. She thinks her sister has held life always in the palm of one hand, that "no" is a word the world never learned to say to her.

You've no doubt seen those TV shows where the child who has "made it" is confronted, as a surprise, by his own mother and father, tottering in weakly from backstage. (A pleasant surprise, of course: what would they do if parent and child came on the show only to curse out and insult each other?) On TV mother and child embrace and smile into each other's faces. Sometimes the mother and father weep, the child wraps them in his arms and leans across the table to tell how he would not have made it without their help. I have seen these programs.

Sometimes I dream a dream in which Dee and I are suddenly brought together on a TV program of this sort. Out of a dark and soft-seated limousine I am ushered into a bright room filled with many people. There I meet a smiling, gray, sporty man like Johnny Carson who shakes my hand and tells me what a fine girl I have. Then we are on the stage and Dee is embracing me with tears in her eyes. She pins on my dress a large orchid, even though she has told me once that she thinks orchids are tacky flowers.

In real life I am a large big-boned woman with rough, man-working hands. In the winter I wear flannel nightgowns to bed and overalls during the day. I can kill and clean a hog as mercilessly as a man. My fat keeps me hot in zero weather. I can work outside all day, breaking ice to get water for washing; I can eat pork liver cooked over the open fire minutes after it comes steaming from the hog. One winter I knocked a bull calf straight in the brain between the eyes with a sledgehammer and had the meat hung up to chill before nightfall. But of course all this does not show on television. I am the way my daughter would want me to be; a hundred pounds lighter, my skin like an uncooked barley pancake. My hair glistens in the hot bright lights. Johnny Carson has much to do to keep up with my quick and witty tongue.

But that is a mistake. I know even before I wake up. Who ever knew a Johnson with a quick tongue? Who can even imagine me looking a strange white man in the eye? It seems to me I have talked to them always with one foot raised in flight, with my head turned in whichever way is farthest from them. Dee, though. She would always look anyone in the eye. Hesitation was no part of her nature.

"How do I look, Mama?" Maggie says, showing just enough of her thin body enveloped in pink skirt and red blouse for me to know she's there almost hidden by the door.

"Come out into the yard," I say.

Have you ever seen a lame animal, perhaps a dog run over by some careless person rich enough to own a car, sidle up to someone who is ignorant enough to be kind to him? That is the way my Maggie walks. She has been like this, chin on chest, eyes on ground, feet in shuffle, ever since the fire that burned the other house to the ground.

Dee is lighter than Maggie, with nicer hair and a fuller figure. She's a woman now, though sometimes I forget. How long ago was it that the other house burned? Ten, twelve years? Sometimes I can still hear the flames and feel Maggie's arms sticking to me, her hair smoking and her dress falling off her in little black papery flakes. Her eyes seemed stretched open, blazed open by the flames reflected in them. And Dee. I see her standing off under the sweet-gum tree she used to dig gum out of; a look of concentration on her face as she watched the last dingy gray board of the house fall in toward the red-hot brick chimney. Why don't you do a dance around the ashes? I'd wanted to ask her. She had hated the house that much.

I used to think she hated Maggie too. But that was before we raised the money, the church and me, to send her to Augusta to school. She used to read to us without pity; forcing words, lies, other folks' habits, whole lives upon us two, sitting trapped and ignorant underneath her voice. She washed us in a river of make-believe, burned us with a lot of knowledge we didn't necessarily need to know. Pressed us to her with the serious way she read, to shove us away, like dimwits, at just the moment we seemed about to understand.

Dee wanted nice things. A yellow organdy dress to wear to her graduation from high school; black pumps to match a green suit she'd made from an old suit somebody gave me. She was determined to stare down any disaster in her efforts. Her eyelids would not flicker for minutes at a time. Often I fought off the temptation to shake her. At sixteen she had a style of her own: and knew what style was.

I never had an education myself. After second grade the school was closed down. Don't ask me why: in 1927 colored asked fewer questions than they do now. Sometimes Maggie reads to me. She stumbles along good-naturedly but can't see well. She knows she is not bright. Like good looks and money, quickness passed her by. She will marry John Thomas (who has mossy teeth in an earnest face), and then I'll be free to sit here and I guess just sing church songs to myself. Although I never was a good singer. Never could carry a tune. I was always better at a man's job. I used to love to milk till I was hooked in the side in '49. Cows are soothing and slow and don't bother you, unless you try to milk them the wrong way.

I have deliberately turned my back on the house. It is three rooms, just like the one that burned, except the roof is tin; they don't make shingle roofs anymore. There are no real windows, just some holes cut in the sides, like the portholes in a ship, but not round and not square, with rawhide holding the shutters up on the outside. This house is in a pasture too, like the other one. No doubt when Dee sees it she will want to tear it down. She wrote me once that no matter where we "choose" to live, she will manage to come see us. But she will never bring her friends. Maggie and I thought about this and Maggie asked me, "Mama, when did Dee ever *have* any friends?"

She had a few. Furtive boys in pink shirts hanging about on washday after school. Nervous girls who never laughed. Impressed with her, they worshiped the well-turned phrase, the cute shape, the scalding humor that erupted like bubbles in lye. She read to them.

When she was courting Jimmy T she didn't have much time to pay to us, but turned all her fault-finding power on him. He *flew* to marry a cheap city girl from a family of ignorant, flashy people. She hardly had time to recompose herself.

When she comes I will meet . . . but there they are!

Maggie attempts to make a dash for the house, in her shuffling way, but I stay her with my hand. "Come back here," I say. And she stops and tries to dig a well in the sand with her toe.

It is hard to see them clearly through the strong sun. But even the first glimpse of leg out of the car tells me it is Dee. Her feet were always neat looking, as if God himself had shaped them with a certain style. From the other side of the car comes a short, stocky man. Hair is all over his head a foot long and hanging from his chin like a kinky mule tail. I hear Maggie suck in her breath. "Uhnnnh," is what it sounds like. Like when you see the wriggling end of a snake just in front of your foot on a road. "Uhnnnh."

Dee, next. A dress down to the ground, in this hot weather. A dress so loud it hurts my eyes. There are yellows and oranges enough to throw back the light of the sun. I feel my whole face warming from the heat waves it throws out. Earrings gold too, and hanging down to her shoulders. Bracelets dangling and making noises when she moves her arm up to shake the folds of the dress out of her armpits. The dress is loose and flows, and as she walks closer, I like it. I hear Maggie go "Uhnnnh" again. It is her sister's hair. It stands straight up like the wool on a sheep. It is black as night and around the edges are two long pigtails that rope about like small lizards disappearing behind her ears.

"Wa-su-zo-Tean-o!" she says, coming on in that gliding way the dress makes her move. The short stocky fellow with the hair to his navel is all grinning and he follows up with, "Asalamalakim, my mother and sister!" He moves to hug Maggie but she falls back, right up against the back of my chair. I feel her trembling there, and when I look up I see the perspiration falling off her skin.

"Don't get up," says Dee. Since I am stout it takes something of a push. You can see me trying to move a second or two before I make it. She turns, showing white heels through her sandals, and goes back to the car. Out she peeks next with a Polaroid. She stoops down quickly and snaps off picture after picture of me sitting there in front of the house with Maggie cowering behind me. She never takes a shot without making sure the house is included. When a cow comes nibbling around the edge of the yard she snaps it and me and Maggie *and* the house. Then she puts the Polaroid on the back seat of the car, and comes up and kisses me on the forehead.

Meanwhile Asalamalakim is going through motions with Maggie's hand. Maggie's hand is as limp as a fish, and probably as cold, despite the sweat, and she keeps trying to pull it back. It looks like Asalamalakim wants to shake hands but wants to do it fancy. Or maybe he don't know how people shake hands. Anyhow, he soon gives up on Maggie.

"Well," I say. "Dee."

"No, Mama," she says. "Not 'Dee,' Wangero Leewanika Kemanjo!"

"What happened to 'Dee'?" I wanted to know.

"She's dead," Wangero said. "I couldn't bear it any longer, being named after the people who oppress me."

"You know well as me you was named after your aunt Dicie," I said. Dicie is my sister. She named Dee. We called her "Big Dee" after Dee was born.

"But who was *she* named after?" asked Wangero.

"I guess after Grandma Dee," I said.

"And who was she named after?" asked Wangero.

"Her mother," I said, and saw Wangero was getting tired. "That's about as far back as I can trace it," I said. Though, in fact, I probably could have carried it back beyond the Civil War through the branches.

"Well," said Asalamalakim, "there you are."

"Uhnnnh," I head Maggie say.

"There I was not," I said, "before 'Dicie' cropped up in our family, so why should I try to trace it that far back?"

He just stood there grinning, looking down on me like somebody inspecting a Model A car. Every once in a while he and Wangero sent eye signals over my head.

"How do you pronounce this name?" I asked.

"You don't have to call me by it if you don't want to," said Wangero.

"Why shouldn't I?" I asked. "If that's what you want us to call you, we'll call you."

"I know it might sound awkward at first," said Wangero.

"I'll get used to it," I said. "Ream it out again."

Well, soon we got the name out of the way. Asalamalakim had a name twice as long and three times as hard. After I tripped over it two or three times he told me to just call him Hakim-a-barber. I wanted to ask him was he a barber, but I didn't really think he was, so I didn't ask.

"You must belong to those beef-cattle peoples down the road," I said. They said "Asalamalakim" when they met you too, but they didn't shake hands. Always too busy: feeding the cattle, fixing the fences, putting up salt-lick shelters, throwing down hay. When the white folks poisoned some of the herd, the men stayed up all night with rifles in their hands. I walked a mile and a half just to see the sight.

Hakim-a-barber said, "I accept some of their doctrines, but farming and raising cattle is not my style." They didn't tell me, and I didn't ask, whether Wangero (Dee) had really gone and married him.

We sat down to eat and right away he said he didn't eat collards and pork was unclean. Wangero, though, went on through the chitlins and corn bread, the greens and everything else. She talked a blue streak over the sweet potatoes. Everything delighted her. Even the fact that we still used the benches her daddy made for the table when we couldn't afford to buy chairs.

"Oh, Mama!" she cried. Then turned to Hakim-a-barber. "I never knew how lovely these benches are. You can feel the rump prints," she said, running her hands underneath her and along the bench. Then she gave a sigh and her hand closed over Grandma Dee's butter dish. "That's it!" she said. "I knew there was something I wanted to ask you if I could have." She jumped up from the table and went over in the corner where the churn stood, the milk in it clabber by now. She looked at the churn and looked at it.

"This churn top is what I need," she said. "Didn't Uncle Buddy whittle it out of a tree you all used to have?"

"Yes," I said.

"Uh huh," she said happily. "And I want the dasher too."

"Uncle Buddy whittle that too?" asked the barber.

Dee (Wangero) looked up at me.

"Aunt Dee's first husband whittled the dash," said Maggie so low you almost couldn't hear her. "His name was Henry, but they called him Stash."

"Maggie's brain is like an elephant's," Wangero said, laughing. "I can use the churn top as a centerpiece for the alcove table," she said, sliding a plate over the churn, "and I'll think of something artistic to do with the dasher."

When she finished wrapping the dasher the handle stuck out. I took it for a moment in my hands. You didn't even have to look close to see where hands pushing the dasher up and down to make butter had left a kind of sink in the wood. In fact, there were a lot of small sinks; you could see where thumbs and fingers had sunk into the wood. It was beautiful light yellow wood, from a tree that grew in the yard where Big Dee and Stash had lived.

After dinner Dee (Wangero) went to the trunk at the foot of my bed and started rifling through it. Maggie hung back in the kitchen over the dishpan. Out came Wangero with two quilts. They had been pieced by Grandma Dee, and then Big Dee and me had hung them on the quilt frames on the front porch and quilted them. One was in the Lone Star pattern. The other was Walk Around the Mountain. In both of them were scraps of dresses Grandma Dee had worn fifty and more years ago. Bits and pieces of Grandpa Jarrell's paisley shirts. And one teeny faded blue piece, about the size of a penny matchbox, that was from Great Grandpa Ezra's uniform that he wore in the Civil War.

"Mama," Wangero said sweet as a bird. "Can I have these old quilts?"

I heard something fall in the kitchen, and a minute later the kitchen door slammed.

"Why don't you take one or two of the others?" I asked. "These old things was just done by me and Big Dee from some tops your grandma pieced before she died."

"No," said Wangero. "I don't want those. They are stitched around the borders by machine."

"That'll make them last better," I said.

"That's not the point," said Wangero. "These are all pieces of dresses Grandma used to wear. She did all this stitching by hand. Imagine!" She held the quilts securely in her arms, stroking them.

"Some of the pieces, like those lavender ones, come from old clothes her mother handed down to her," I said, moving up to touch the quilts. Dee (Wangero) moved back just enough so that I couldn't reach the quilts. They already belonged to her.

"Imagine!" she breathed again, clutching them closely to her bosom.

"The truth is," I said, "I promised to give them quilts to Maggie, for when she marries John Thomas."

She gasped, like a bee had stung her.

"Maggie can't appreciate these quilts!" she cried. "She'd probably be backward enough to put them to everyday use."

"I reckon she would," I said. "God knows I been saving 'em for long enough with nobody using 'em. I hope she will!" I didn't want to bring up how I had offered Dee (Wangero) a quilt when she went away to college. Then she had told me they were old-fashioned, out of style.

"But they're *priceless!*" she was saying now, furiously; for she has a temper. "Maggie would put them on the bed and in five years they'd be in rags. Less than that!"

"She can always make some more," I said. "Maggie knows how to quilt."

Dee (Wangero) looked at me with hatred. "You just will not understand. The point is these quilts, *these* quilts!"

"Well," I said, stumped, "what would *you* do with them?"

"Hang them," she said. As if that was the only thing you *could* do with quilts.

Maggie, by now, was standing in the door. I could almost hear the sound her feet made as they scraped over each other.

"She can have them, Mama," she said, like somebody used to never winning anything, of having anything reserved for her. "I can 'member Grandma Dee without the quilts."

I looked at her hard. She had filled her bottom lip with checkerberry snuff, and it gave her face a kind of dopey, hangdog look. It was Grandma Dee and Big Dee who taught her how to quilt herself. She stood there with her scarred hands hidden in the folds of her skirt. She looked at her sister with something like fear, but she wasn't mad at her. This was Maggie's portion. This was the way she knew God to work.

When I looked at her like that something hit me in the top of my head and ran down to the soles of my feet. Just like when I'm in church and the spirit of God touches me and I get happy and shout. I did something I never had done before: hugged Maggie to me, then dragged her on into the room, snatched the quilts out of Miss Wangero's hands and dumped them into Maggie's lap. Maggie just sat there on my bed with her mouth open.

"Take one or two of the others," I said to Dee.

But she turned without a word and went out to Hakim-a-barber.

"You just don't understand," she said, as Maggie and I came out to the car.

"What don't I understand?" I wanted to know.

"Your heritage," she said. And then she turned to Maggie, kissed her, and said, "You ought to try to make something of yourself too, Maggie. It's really a new day for us. But from the way you and Mama still live you'd never know it."

She put on some sunglasses that hid everything above the tip of her nose and her chin.

Maggie smiled; maybe at the sunglasses. But a real smile, not scared. After we watched the car dust settle I asked Maggie to bring me a dip of snuff. And then the two of us sat there just enjoying, until it was time to go in the house and go to bed.

In Search of Our Mothers' Gardens

I DESCRIBED HER OWN NATURE AND TEMPERAMENT. TOLD HOW THEY NEEDED A LARGER LIFE FOR THEIR EXPRESSION. . . . I POINTED OUT THAT IN LIEU OF PROPER CHANNELS, HER EMOTIONS HAD OVERFLOWED INTO PATHS THAT DISSIPATED THEM. I TALKED, BEAUTIFULLY I THOUGHT, ABOUT AN ART THAT WOULD BE BORN, AN ART THAT WOULD OPEN THE WAY FOR WOMEN THE LIKES OF HER. I ASKED HER TO HOPE, AND BUILD UP AN INNER LIFE AGAINST THE COMING OF THAT DAY. . . . I SANG, WITH A STRANGE QUIVER IN MY VOICE, A PROMISE SONG.

—JEAN TOOMER, "AVEY," *CANE*

The poet speaking to a prostitute who falls asleep while he's talking—

When the poet Jean Toomer walked through the South in the early twenties, he discovered a curious thing: black women whose spirituality was so intense, so deep, so *unconscious,* that they were themselves unaware of the richness they held. They stumbled blindly through their lives: creatures so abused and mutilated in body, so dimmed and confused by pain, that they considered themselves unworthy even of hope. In the selfless abstractions their bodies became to the men who used them, they became more than "sexual objects," more even than mere women: they became "Saints." Instead of being perceived as whole persons, their bodies became shrines: what was thought to be their minds became temples suitable for worship. These crazy Saints stared out at the world, wildly, like lunatics—or quietly, like suicides; and the "God" that was in their gaze was as mute as a great stone.

Who were these Saints? These crazy, loony, pitiful women?

Some of them, without a doubt, were our mothers and grandmothers.

In the still heat of the post-Reconstruction South, this is how they seemed to Jean Toomer: exquisite butterflies trapped in an evil honey, toiling away their lives in an era, a century, that did not acknowledge them, except as "the *mule* of the world." They dreamed dreams that no one knew—not even themselves, in any coherent fashion—and saw visions no one could understand. They wandered or sat about the countryside crooning lullabies to ghosts, and drawing the mother of Christ in charcoal on courthouse walls.

They forced their minds to desert their bodies and their striving spirits sought to rise, like frail whirlwinds from the hard red clay. And when those frail whirlwinds fell, in scattered particles, upon the ground, no one mourned. Instead, men lit candles to celebrate the emptiness that remained, as people do who enter a beautiful but vacant space to resurrect a God.

Our mothers and grandmothers, some of them: moving to music not yet written. And they waited.

They waited for a day when the unknown thing that was in them would be made known; but guessed, somehow in their darkness, that on the day of their revelation they would be long dead. Therefore to Toomer they walked, and even ran, in slow motion. For they were going nowhere immediate, and the future was not yet within their grasp. And men took our mothers and grandmothers, "but got no pleasure from it." So complex was their passion and their calm.

To Toomer, they lay vacant and fallow as autumn fields, with harvest time never in sight: and he saw them enter loveless marriages, without joy; and become prostitutes, without resistance; and become mothers of children, without fulfillment.

For these grandmothers and mothers of ours were not Saints, but Artists; driven to a numb and bleeding madness by the springs of creativity in them for which there was no release. They were Creators, who lived lives of spiritual waste, because they were so rich in spirituality—which is the basis of Art—that the strain of enduring their unused and unwanted talent drove them insane. Throwing away this spirituality was their pathetic attempt to lighten the soul to a weight their work-worn, sexually abused bodies could bear.

What did it mean for a black woman to be an artist in our grandmothers' time? In our great-grandmothers' day? It is a question with an answer cruel enough to stop the blood.

Did you have a genius of a great-great-grandmother who died under some ignorant and depraved white overseer's lash? Or was she required to bake biscuits for a lazy backwater tramp, when she cried out in her soul to paint watercolors of sunsets, or the rain falling on the green and peaceful pasturelands? Or was her body broken and forced to bear children (who were more often than not sold away from her)—eight, ten, fifteen, twenty children—when her one joy was the thought of modeling heroic figures of rebellion, in stone or clay?

How was the creativity of the black woman kept alive, year after year and century after century, when for most of the years black people have been in America, it was a punishable crime for a black person to read or write? And the freedom to paint, to sculpt, to expand the mind with action did not exist. Consider, if you can bear to imagine it, what might have been the result if singing, too, had been forbidden by law. Listen to the voices of Bessie Smith, Billie Holiday, Nina Simone, Roberta Flack, and Aretha Franklin, among others, and imagine those voices muzzled for life. Then you may begin to comprehend the lives of our "crazy," "Sainted" mothers and grandmothers. The agony of the lives of women who might have been Poets, Novelists, Essayists, and Short-Story Writers (over a period of centuries), who died with their real gifts stifled within them.

And, if this were the end of the story, we would have cause to cry out in my paraphrase of Okot p'Bitek's great poem:

> O, my clanswomen
> Let us all cry together!
> Come,
> Let us mourn the death of our mother,
> The death of a Queen
> The ash that was produced
> By a great fire!
> O, this homestead is utterly dead
> Close the gates
> With *lacari* thorns,
> For our mother
> The creator of the Stool is lost!
> And all the young women
> Have perished in the wilderness!

But this is not the end of the story, for all the young women—our mothers and grandmothers, *ourselves*—have not perished in the wilderness. And if we ask ourselves why, and search for and find the answer, we will know beyond all efforts to erase it from our minds, just exactly who, and of what, we black American women are.

One example, perhaps the most pathetic, most misunderstood one, can provide a backdrop for our mothers' work: Phillis Wheatley, a slave in the 1700s.

Virginia Woolf, in her book *A Room of One's Own,* wrote that in order for a woman to write fiction she must have two things, certainly: a room of her own (with key and lock) and enough money to support herself.

What then are we to make of Phillis Wheatley, a slave, who owned not even herself? This sickly, frail black girl who required a servant of her own at times—her health was so precarious—and who, had she been white, would have been easily considered the intellectual superior of all the women and most of the men in the society of her day.

Virginia Woolf wrote further, speaking of course not of our Phillis, that "any woman born with a great gift in the sixteenth century [insert "eighteenth century," insert "black woman," insert "born or made a slave"] would certainly have gone crazed, shot herself, or ended her days in some lonely cottage outside the village, half witch, half wizard [insert "Saint"], feared and mocked at. For it needs little skill and psychology to be sure that a highly gifted girl who had tried to use her gift for poetry would have been so thwarted and hindered by contrary instincts [add "chains, guns, the lash, the ownership of one's body by someone else, submission to an alien religion"], that she must have lost her health and sanity to a certainty."

The key words, as they relate to Phillis, are "contrary instincts." For when we read the poetry of Phillis Wheatley—as when we read the novels of Nella Larsen or the oddly false-sounding autobiography of that freest of all black women writers, Zora Hurston—evidence of "contrary instincts" is everywhere. Her loyalties were completely divided, as was, without question, her mind.

But how could this be otherwise? Captured at seven, a slave of wealthy, doting whites who instilled in her the "savagery" of the Africa they "rescued" her from . . . one wonders if she was even able to remember her homeland as she had known it, or as it really was.

Yet, because she did try to use her gift for poetry in a world that made her a slave, she was "so thwarted and hindered by . . . contrary instincts, that she . . . lost her health. . . ." In the last years of her brief life, burdened not only with the need to express her gift but also with a penniless, friendless "freedom" and several small children for whom she was forced to do strenuous work to feed, she lost her health, certainly. Suffering from malnutrition and neglect and who knows what mental agonies, Phillis Wheatley died.

So torn by "contrary instincts" was black, kidnapped, enslaved Phillis that her description of "the Goddess"—as she poetically called the Liberty she did not have—is ironically, cruelly humorous. And, in fact, has held Phillis up to ridicule for more than a century. It is usually read prior to hanging Phillis's memory as that of a fool. She wrote:

> The Goddess comes, she moves divinely fair,
> Olive and laurel binds her *golden* hair.
> Wherever shines this native of the skies,
> Unnumber'd charms and recent graces rise.
> [My italics]

It is obvious that Phillis, the slave, combed the "Goddess's" hair every morning; prior, perhaps, to bringing in the milk, or fixing her mistress's lunch. She took her imagery from the one thing she saw elevated above all others.

With the benefit of hindsight we ask, "How could she?"

But at last, Phillis, we understand. No more snickering when your stiff, struggling, ambivalent lines are forced on us. We know now that you were not an idiot or a traitor; only a sickly little black girl, snatched from your home and country and made a slave; a woman who still struggled to sing the song that was your gift, although in a land of barbarians who praised you for your bewildered tongue. It is not so much what you sang, as that you kept alive, in so many of our ancestors, *the notion of song.*

Black women are called, in the folklore that so aptly identifies one's status in society, "the *mule* of the world," because we have been handed the burdens that everyone else—*everyone* else—refused to carry. We have also been called "Matriarchs," "Superwomen," and "Mean and Evil Bitches." Not to mention "Castraters" and "Sapphire's Mama." When we have pleaded for understanding, our character has been distorted; when we have asked for simple caring, we have been handed empty inspirational appellations, then stuck in the farthest corner. When we have asked for love, we have been given children. In short, even our plainer gifts, our labors of fidelity and love, have been knocked down our throats. To be an artist and a black woman, even today, lowers our status in many respects, rather than raises it and yet, artists we will be.

Therefore we must fearlessly pull out of ourselves and look at and identify with our lives the living creativity some of our great-grandmothers were not allowed to know. I stress *some* of them because it is well known that the majority of our great-grandmothers knew, even without "knowing" it, the reality of their spirituality, even if they didn't recognize it beyond what happened in the singing at church—and they never had any intention of giving it up.

How they did it—those millions of black women who were not Phillis Wheatley, or Lucy

Terry or Frances Harper or Zora Hurston or Nella Larsen or Bessie Smith; or Elizabeth Catlett, or Katherine Dunham, either—brings me to the title of this essay, "In Search of Our Mothers' Gardens," which is a personal account that is yet shared, in its theme and its meaning, by all of us. I found, while thinking about the far-reaching world of the creative black woman, that often the truest answer to a question that really matters can be found very close.

In the late 1920s my mother ran away from home to marry my father. Marriage, if not running away, was expected of seventeen-year-old girls. By the time she was twenty, she had two children and was pregnant with a third. Five children later, I was born. And this is how I came to know my mother: she seemed a large, soft, loving-eyed woman who was rarely impatient in our home. Her quick, violent temper was on view only a few times a year, when she battled with the white landlord who had the misfortune to suggest to her that her children did not need to go to school.

She made all the clothes we wore, even my brothers' overalls. She made all the towels and sheets we used. She spent the summers canning vegetables and fruits. She spent the winter evenings making quilts enough to cover all our beds.

During the "working" day, she labored beside—not behind—my father in the fields. Her day began before sunup, and did not end until late at night. There was never a moment for her to sit down, undisturbed, to unravel her own private thoughts; never a time free from interruption—by work or the noisy inquiries of her many children. And yet, it is to my mother—and all our mothers who were not famous—that I went in search of the secret of what has fed that muzzled and often mutilated, but vibrant, creative spirit that the black woman has inherited, and that pops out in wild and unlikely places to this day.

But when, you will ask, did my overworked mother have time to know or care about feeding the creative spirit?

The answer is so simple that many of us have spent years discovering it. We have constantly looked high, when we should have looked high—and low.

For example: in the Smithsonian Institution in Washington, D.C., there hangs a quilt unlike any other in the world. In fanciful, inspired, and yet simple and identifiable figures, it portrays the story of the Crucifixion. It is considered rare, beyond price. Though it follows no known pattern of quilt-making, and though it is made of bits and pieces of worthless rags, it is obviously the work of a person of powerful imagination and deep spiritual feeling. Below this quilt I saw a note that says it was made by "an anonymous Black woman in Alabama, a hundred years ago."

If we could locate this "anonymous" black woman from Alabama, she would turn out to be one of our grandmothers—an artist who left her mark in the only materials she could afford, and in the only medium her position in society allowed her to use.

As Virginia Woolf wrote further, in *A Room of One's Own:*

> Yet genius of a sort must have existed among women as it must have existed among the working class. [Change this to "slaves" and "the wives and daughters of sharecroppers."] Now and again an Emily Brontë or a Robert Burns [change this to "a Zora Hurston or a Richard Wright"] blazes out and proves its presence. But certainly it never got itself on to paper. When, however, one reads of a witch being ducked, of a woman possessed by devils [or "Sainthood"], of a wise woman selling herbs [our root workers] or even a very remarkable man who had a mother, then I think we are on the track of a lost novelist, a suppressed poet, of some mute and inglorious Jane Austen. . . . Indeed, I would venture to guess that Anon, who wrote so many poems without signing them, was often a woman. . . .

And so our mothers and grandmothers have, more often than not anonymously, handed on the creative spark, the seed of the flower they themselves never hoped to see: or like a sealed letter they could not plainly read.

And so it is, certainly, with my own mother. Unlike "Ma" Rainey's songs, which retained their creator's name even while blasting forth from Bessie Smith's mouth, no song or poem will bear my mother's name. Yet so many of the stories that I write, that we all write, are my mother's stories. Only recently did I fully realize this: that through years of listening to my mother's stories of her life, I have absorbed not only the stories themselves, but something of the manner in which she spoke, something of the urgency that involves the knowledge that her stories—like her life—must be recorded. It is probably for this reason that so much of what I have written is about characters whose counterparts in real life are so much older than I am.

But the telling of these stories, which came from my mother's lips as naturally as breathing, was not the only way my mother showed herself as an artist. For stories, too, were subject to being distracted, to dying without conclusion. Dinners must be started, and cotton must be gathered before the big rains. The artist that was and is my mother showed itself to me only after many years. This is what I finally noticed:

Like Mem, a character in *The Third Life of Grange Copeland,* my mother adorned with flowers whatever shabby house we were forced to live in. And not just your typical straggly country stand of zinnias, either. She planted ambitious gardens—and still does—with over fifty different varieties of plants that bloom profusely from early March until late November. Before she left home for the fields, she watered her flowers, chopped up the grass, and laid out new beds. When she returned from the fields she might divide clumps of bulbs, dig a cold pit, uproot and replant roses, or prune branches from her taller bushes or trees—until night came and it was too dark to see.

Whatever she planted grew as if by magic, and her fame as a grower of flowers spread over three counties. Because of her creativity with her flowers, even my memories of poverty are seen through a screen of blooms—sunflowers, petunias, roses, dahlias, forsythia, spirea, delphiniums, verbena . . . and on and on.

And I remember people coming to my mother's yard to be given cuttings from her flowers; I hear again the praise showered on her because whatever rocky soil she landed on, she turned into a garden. A garden so brilliant with colors, so original in its design, so magnificent with life and creativity, that to this day people drive by our house in Georgia—perfect strangers and imperfect strangers—and ask to stand or walk among my mother's art.

I notice that it is only when my mother is working in her flowers that she is radiant, almost to the point of being invisible—except as Creator: hand and eye. She is involved in work her soul must have. Ordering the universe in the image of her personal conception of Beauty.

Her face, as she prepares the Art that is her gift, is a legacy of respect she leaves to me, for all that illuminates and cherishes life. She has handed down respect for the possibilities—and the will to grasp them.

For her, so hindered and intruded upon in so many ways, being an artist has still been a daily part of her life. This ability to hold on, even in very simple ways, is work black women have done for a very long time.

This poem is not enough, but it is something, for the woman who literally covered the holes in our walls with sunflowers:

They were women then
My mama's generation
Husky of voice—Stout of
Step
With fists as well as
Hands
How they battered down
Doors
And ironed
Starched white
Shirts
How they led
Armies
Headragged Generals
Across mined

Fields
Booby-trapped
Kitchens
To discover books
Desks
A place for us
How they knew what we
Must know
Without knowing a page
Of it
Themselves.

Guided by my heritage of a love of beauty and a respect for strength—in search of my mother's garden, I found my own.

And perhaps in Africa over two hundred years ago, there was just such a mother; perhaps she painted vivid and daring decorations in oranges and yellows and greens on the walls of her hut; perhaps she sang—in a voice like Roberta Flack's—*sweetly* over the compounds of her village; perhaps she wove the most stunning mats or told the most ingenious stories of all the village storytellers. Perhaps she was herself a poet—though only her daughter's name is signed to the poems that we know.

Perhaps Phillis Wheatley's mother was also an artist.

Perhaps in more than Phillis Wheatley's biological life is her mother's signature made clear.

SHERLEY ANNE WILLIAMS

(1944–)

Although Sherley Anne Williams had enjoyed a reputation as a poet and critic prior to 1986, it was in that year, with the publication of her novel *Dessa Rose,* that she really came to the attention of the literary establishment. A revisionist historical novel, *Dessa Rose* is the story of a budding friendship between Dessa, leader of a slave rebellion, and Miss Rufel, a white plantation owner who harbors runaway slaves. The novel has been used frequently in African American literature and women's studies courses and has led in part to a revival of interest in Williams's earlier works.

Williams has spent most of her life in California, where she was born in Bakersfield on August 25, 1944, to Jessee Winson and Lena Silver Williams. She attended Edison Junior High School in Fresno, where she searched for books by and about black people. Upon her mother's death when she was sixteen, her sister Ruise became her guardian. It was her sister who cultivated her literary interests. However, it was not until 1966, after Williams received her B.S. in history from California State University at Fresno, that she began to write for publication.

Her first published story, "Tell Martha Not to Moan," appeared in the *Massachusetts Review* in 1967. It would be reprinted in Toni Cade's 1970 anthology *The Black Woman* (under the name Shirley Williams). Narrated by a welfare recipient whose gullibility in love relationships causes her constant problems, the story evinces Williams's willingness to confront some of the difficult issues that face a large portion of the working-class or welfare-bound black population. The story also is noteworthy for its experiment in creating a narrative voice free of the cumbersome features of standard English; language and character are blended perfectly.

Williams studied for a graduate degree at Howard University between 1966 and 1967 but left before obtaining it. From 1970 to 1972, she worked as a community educator at Federal City College in Washington, D.C. She then completed the manuscript for *Give Birth to Brightness: A Thematic Study in Neo-Black Literature,* under the guidance of esteemed Howard University professor Sterling Brown, before earning her master's degree from Brown University in 1972. The book focuses on works by contemporary black writers, including James Baldwin, Amiri Baraka, and Ernest Gaines, in a discussion of how their vision of black life embraces the intrinsic value and worth of African American history and culture. By the time the book was published in 1972, Williams had returned to California to become associate professor of English at her alma mater, California State University at Fresno.

By 1975, when her first volume of poetry, *The Peacock Poems,* appeared, Williams had joined the faculty at the University of California at San Diego as a professor of literature. Grounded in the blues aesthetic, *The Peacock Poems* further established Williams as a writer who seriously engages the indigenous forms of African American culture. The volume contains many poems about her son, John Malcolm, as well as many that develop the pain and anguish of the blues ethos. However, its main theme is the loneliness of black women, who, like female peacocks, are robbed of voice and, in the eyes of some, of beauty as well. As with the birds, the male is the one who struts, sprouts his colorful feathers, and makes his clucking sounds. As the poetry moves forward, the person—mother, lover, and woman—eventually finds her own voice and articulates her own experiences. Williams's interest in the blues also is highlighted in her essay "The Blues Roots of Contemporary Afro-American Poetry," published in the *Massachusetts Review* in 1977.

Some Sweet Angel Chile, Williams's second volume of poetry, was published in 1982. Told from a woman's point of view, the poems continue the blues motif of *The Peacock Poems.* The first section of the volume, "Letters from a New England Negro," is about a young black woman who goes south to teach newly freed blacks; it anticipates in its time frame the setting that Williams would develop in *Dessa Rose* (1986). In the second section, "Regular Reefer," Williams focuses on blues queen Bessie Smith, the "sweet angel chile." Other sections in the volume contain poems about Williams's own childhood. The main purpose of the verse is, through the depiction of strong women like Smith, to decry potential weaknesses in modern black women.

Dessa Rose, the novel that has revitalized Williams's reputation, was inspired by two incidents with which Williams became familiar. One involved a black woman who led a slave uprising, and the other was the story of a white woman who, refusing to identify with her southern slave-owning neighbors, harbored runaway slaves. What would happen, Williams postulated, if the two women had had a chance to meet? The result is a revisionist historical narrative that focuses on a black woman who reclaims her creative voice and tells her own story, a white woman who voluntarily selects a black man as a lover, and the two of them together undermining the patriarchal system of slavery by selling slaves, collecting them from prearranged sites to which they have run away, and selling them again in a scheme designed to get enough money for all of them to migrate out of the racist South. One of several neoslave narratives that have graced the literary scene of late (including Toni Morrison's *Beloved* [1987] and J. California Cooper's *Family* [1991]), the novel has garnered an impressive reputation as a well-written and carefully plotted work.

Williams continued her critical commentary in 1990 by contributing "Some Implications of Womanist Theory" to *Reading Black, Reading Feminist,* edited by Henry Louis Gates, Jr. She also continues in her position as professor of literature at the University of California at San Diego. Williams was commissioned to write a screen adaptation for *Dessa Rose,* and if the Hollywood producer who began the project had completed it, *Dessa Rose* would have been the only slave novel written by an African American woman to be adapted to American film. Sadly, the production company was absorbed in a corporate takeover, and the new owners canceled the project.

❖❖❖

Biographical information on Williams can be found in *Dictionary of Literary Biography,* vol. 41 (1985). Critical commentary appears in Claudia Tate, ed., *Black Women Writers at Work* (1983); Mary Kemp Davis, "Everybody Knows Her Name: The Recovery of the Past in Sherley Anne Williams's *Dessa Rose,*" *Callaloo* 12 (Summer 1989); Gayl Jones, *Liberating Voices: Oral Tradition in African American Literature* (1991).

Any Woman's Blues

every woman is a victim of the feel blues, too.

Soft lamp shinin
  and me alone in the night.
Soft lamp is shinin
  and me alone in the night.
Can't take no one beside me
  need mo'n jest some man to set me right.

I left many peoples and places
  tryin not to be alone.
Left many a person and places
  I lived my life alone.
I need to get myself together.
  Yes, I need to make myself to home.

What's gone can be a window
  a circle in the eye of the sun.
What's gone can be a window
  a circle, well, in the eye of the sun.
Take the circle from the world, girl,
  you find the light have gone.

These is old blues
  and I sing em like any woman do.
These the old blues
  and I sing em, sing em, sing em. Just like any woman do.
My life ain't done yet.
  Naw. My song ain't through.

The Empress Brand Trim: Ruby Reminisces

He was still Uncle
Jack to me the first
time they come to New
York and I knew she

was special cause he
didn't run his women
in front of us kids.
She rehearsed that first
record right there in
our parlor and I
stayed out of school to
watch her. I didn't know
it then but my whole
life changed. She didn't look
no older than me—
bigger and darker,
sure, but no older,
and I was a teen-
ager then. I watched
her and my whole life
changed.

I was with her
in Chicago that
first time when she bought
them dark glasses cause
folks recognized her
over and over
in the streets; and that
night in Concord when
she chased the Klan out
from behind our tent.
Just cussed them out while
the mens stood shaking
in their pants; she went
on with her number
like it was routine—
cept she "never
heard of such shit."

She
loved womens and she
loved mens. The womens
was on the Q.T.,
of course; Jack wouldn't play
that. But wasn't nothing
he could do about
the mens. She'd go to
a party and pick out the
finest brown. "I'mo
give you some Empress
Brand Trim. Tonight you

pay homage to the
pussy Blues made."
And they always did.

The Peacock Poems: 2

This ain't the beginnin; maybe it's the end

I'm not gon tell you my story; I know what
you'll say: Sister, that's where we all been.
                                        I'm still
is where my child can't hold me; I just slip through
his arms and I know nothin's gon darken my
door. I walk the streets cryin, I bes; I bes:
I don't even know what that means.
                                    I been the
strong sister, the pretty sister, the one with
no mens—Maybe that was a beginnin, the
mens, the no holdin, no touchin, the no one
to lean . . . My back never was bent, just the self
I held in. I don't know what it looked like at
the beginnin only now at the end. And
if that's what I look like I don't want to see.
And that was a beginnin, to look in the
mirror and not want to see what you see. All
this other—the pretty sister, strong sister
the one with no mens—that all come in between.

Yeah, that's all our stories; that's where we all been

This ain't that beginnin, but—Yeah. It's that end.

CLENORA HUDSON-WEEMS

(1945–)

The first African American woman intellectual to formulate a position on Africana womanism was Clenora Hudson-Weems, author of the 1993 groundbreaking study *Africana Womanism: Reclaiming Ourselves.* Taking a strong position that black women should not pattern their liberation after Eurocentric feminism but after the historic and triumphant woman of African descent, Hudson-Weems has launched a new critical discourse in the Black Women's Literary Movement.

Born on July 23, 1945, in Oxford, Mississippi, Hudson-Weems was raised by her mother and stepfather, Mary and Matthew Pearson, in Memphis, Tennessee. There she attended Carver High School, where she graduated in 1963. Four years later, she received her B.A. in English literature from LeMoyne College. She continued her education at Atlanta University, where she received an M.A. in English literature in 1971. She also has a certificate of French Studies from L'Université de Dijon and a Ph.D. in American and African American studies from the University of Iowa.

An advocate of the Black Aesthetic since the late 1960s, Hudson-Weems was director of the Black Studies Program at Delaware State University from 1981 to 1985. She coauthored the book *Toni Morrison* with Wilfred Samuels in 1990 and four years later published a political treatise titled *Emmett Till: The Sacrificial Lamb of the Civil Rights Movement.* Her seminal work is *Africana Womanism: Reclaiming Ourselves* (1993), which has been described as a family-centered, race-empowerment construct prioritizing race, class, and gender, the triple plight of women of African descent who seek identity, liberation, and leadership positions. The black woman's role in Africa is set forth, and the author insists that black women must reject what she sees as racist white feminism.

An associate professor of English at the University of Missouri–Columbia since 1990, Hudson-Weems is married to historian Robert Weems. They have one daughter, Sharifa.

❖❖❖

Kay Bonetti interviewed Hudson-Weems for American Audio Library Prose, Inc.

Africana Womanism: An Historical, Global Perspective for Women of African Descent[1]

WOMEN WHO ARE CALLING THEMSELVES BLACK FEMINISTS NEED ANOTHER WORD THAT DESCRIBES WHAT THEIR CONCERNS ARE. BLACK FEMINISM IS NOT A WORD THAT DESCRIBES THE PLIGHT OF BLACK WOMEN.

JULIA HARE, *BLACK ISSUES*

The crucial role of the Africana woman within the constructs of the modern feminist movement is a critical and controversial issue in both the academy and the community today. Given that female subjugation and exploitation are real issues that unquestionably must be combated, many Africana academicians have uncritically accepted the concept of feminism, which emphasizes female empowerment, to reflect the level of struggle or concerns of Africana women. Because of the erroneous assumption that gender issues are an exclusive for the feminist, it must be noted that confronting a patriarchal system that oppresses women in general is a concern for all people, and thus addressing gender problems in our society does not necessarily translate into feminism. It appears that for many of those who embrace feminism, they do so because of its theoretical and methodological legitimacy in the academy and their desire to be a legitimate part of that community. Moreover, they do so because of the absence of a suitable existing framework for their individual needs as Africana women. Be that as it may, while many have accepted the label, more and more Africana women today are beginning to reevaluate feminism and its applicability, particularly in terms of its agenda and its historical realities. Even some White women have become disenchanted with feminist theory, and have concluded that the modern feminist movement does not accurately reflect their reality or level of struggle.

The key to understanding true feminism is to acknowledge its historical and current female-centered agenda, which does not accurately reflect the true agenda of Africana women, who are instead family-centered by necessity as a result of a racist society which has wreaked havoc on their male counterparts as well as their children globally. Observe the position of a South African activist, Ruth Mompati, in her response to witnessing the decomposed bodies of so many children victims of apartheid:

[1]A previously unpublished essay based on concepts in Clenora Hudson-Weems's book *Africana Womanism: Reclaiming Ourselves* (1993).

> The South African woman, faced with the above situation, finds the order of her priorities in her struggle for human dignity and her rights as a woman dictated by the general political struggle of her people as a whole. The national liberation of the black South African is a prerequisite to her own liberation and emancipation as a woman and a worker. (Mompati, 112–113)

Clearly, as Daphne Williams Ntiri, editor of *One Is Not a Woman,* asserts, "Human discrimination transcends sex discrimination . . . [and] the costs of human suffering are high when compared to a component, sex obstacle (Ntiri, 6).

It is also significant to understand the venomous origins of feminism and its exclusivity, which left Africana women and women in general not of the educated upper middle class on the outside, let alone on the fringes, of the pre-feminist (suffragist) movement. One of the leading conservative suffragists, Carrie Chapman Catt, advocated Anglo-Saxon purity and insisted that White men understand "the usefulness of woman suffrage as a counterbalance to the foreign vote, and as a means of legally preserving White supremacy in the South" (Carol and Nobel, 296). The following quotation from *Africana Womanism* presents the overall picture of feminism in its embryonic stage:

> Feminism, earlier called the Woman's Suffrage Movement, started when a group of liberal White women, whose concerns then were for the abolition of slavery and equal rights for all people regardless of race, class and sex, dominated the scene among women on the national level. . . . However, in 1870 the Fifteenth Amendment to the Constitution of the United States ratified the voting rights of Africana men, leaving women, White women in particular, and their desire for the same rights, unaddressed. . . . The result was a racist reaction to the Amendment and Africans in particular. Thus, from the 1880s on, an organized movement among White women shifted the pendulum to a radically conservative posture on the part of White women in general. (Hudson-Weems, 20–21)

Africana women, on the other hand, have historically demonstrated their concern for the entire Africana community, and hence race empowerment has been and continues to be a number one priority, with class and gender following. Consider, for example, historical Africana women activists like Sojourner Truth (abolitionist and universal suffragist, respectively), Harriet Tubman (Underground Railroad conductor), and Ida B. Wells (anti-lynching crusader), all of whom have been erroneously misclaimed as pre-feminists. Truth's "And Aren't I a Woman" oration demonstrates the primacy of overcoming racial obstacles before addressing the absurdity of female subjugation; Tubman risked her life time and again in freeing Africana men, women, and children in slavery, thereby establishing her commitment to racial parity; Wells's investigations into the lynchings of Africana men reveal that most of these lynchings resulted from the perception that Africana men were a threat to the established economic system. Clearly racial equality rather than female empowerment was the primary concern of all these women, a substantive commentary on the prioritizing of race, class, and gender as a key feature of Africana Womanism. According to Filomina Chioma Steady in *The Black Woman Cross-Culturally,*

> Regardless of one's position, the implications of the feminist movement for the black woman are complex. . . . Several factors set the black woman apart as having a different order of priorities. She is oppressed not simply because of her sex but ostensibly because of her race and, for the majority, essentially because of their class. Women belong to different socio-economic groups and do not represent a universal category. Because the majority of black women are poor, there is likely to be some alienation from the middle-class aspect of the women's movement which perceives feminism as an attack on men rather than a system which thrives on inequality. (Steady, 23–24)

Thus, as noted Africana sociologist Joyce Ladner postulates, "black women do not perceive their enemy to be black men, but rather the enemy is considered to be oppressive forces in the larger society which subjugate black men, women and children" (277–278).

Another key feature of this concept is the importance of self-naming, which takes us back to Africa. In African cosmology, the proper naming—*nommo*—is crucial to existence. Hence,

> Africana women might begin by naming and defining their unique movement "Africana Womanism." . . . In refining this terminology into a theoretical framework and methodology, "Africana Womanism" identifies the participation and the role of Africana women in the struggle, but does not suggest that female subjugation is the most critical issue they face in their struggle for parity. Like Black feminism, Africana Womanism acknowledges societal gender problems as critical issues to be resolved; however, it views feminism, the suggested alternative to these problems, as a sort of inverted White patriarchy, with the White feminist now in command and on top. Mainstream feminism is women's co-opting themselves into mainstream patriarchal values. (Hudson-Weems, 38)

Merely appending *Black* to *feminism* (Black feminism) is insufficient, particularly since Africana women have served as models for White women in their struggle to move from home to workplace and to break silence. Africana women have always been in the workplace next to their male counterparts. Moreover, they have always been verbal, voicing their opinions about issues in general. Hence, naming ourselves after White women and concentrating most of our energies on their agenda would be an act of duplicating a duplicate.

The agenda of Africana women is uniquely our own. It is one that is grounded in our history and culture, and hence Africana women cannot risk sacrificing our struggle for the benefit of someone else's struggle. A very objective and insightful White feminist, Bettina Aptheker, understands the reality of the White feminist and the Africana woman as two separate issues:

> When we place women at the center of our thinking we are going about the business of creating an historical and cultural matrix from which women may claim autonomy and independence over their own lives. For women of color, such autonomy cannot be achieved in conditions of racial oppression and cultural genocide. . . . In short, "feminist," in the modern sense, means the empowerment of women. For women of color, such an equality, such an empowerment, cannot take place unless the communities in which they live can successfully establish their own racial and cultural integrity. (Aptheker, 13)

Africana Womanism as a theoretical concept and methodology defines a new paradigm, which offers an alternative to all forms of feminism. It is a terminology and concept that consider both ethnicity (Africana) and gender (Womanism), which I coined and defined in the mid-1980s. In 1989, the *Western Journal of Black Studies* published my article "Cultural and Agenda Conflicts in Academia: Critical Issues for Africana Women's Studies," which is the second chapter of *African Womanism.* It was later established that the concept is

> neither an outgrowth nor an addendum to feminism, . . . Black feminism, African feminism, or Walker's womanism that some Africana women have come to embrace. Africana Womanism is an ideology created and designed for all women of African descent. It is grounded in African culture, and therefore, it necessarily focuses on the unique experiences, struggles, needs, and desires of Africana women. It critically addresses the dynamics of the conflict between the mainstream feminist, the Black feminist, the African feminist, and the Africana womanist (Hudson-Weems, 24)

Eighteen descriptors represent the agenda of the Africana woman, all of which are present in her life to varying degrees. First, the Africana womanist *names* and *defines* herself and her movement: hence, Africana Womanism. She is *family-centered*—the Africana womanist is more concerned with her entire family than with just herself and her sisters—even though genuine *sisterhood* is also very important in her reality. The Africana womanist also welcomes *male presence and participation* in her struggle, as her destiny is often intertwined with his in their broader struggle for humanity and liberation for Africana people. She has demonstrated and continues to demonstrate enormous *strength,* both in a physical and a psychological sense. Moreover, the Africana womanist desires *positive male companionship.* However, her *role as homemaker,* as it has always been, is much relaxed. She demands *respect* and *recognition* in her incessant search for *wholeness* and *authenticity.* Her authentic point of reference emphasizes her tremendous sense of *spirituality.* From this perspective, she acknowledges the existence of spiritual reality, which brings into account the power of comprehension, healing, and the unknown. She *respects and appreciates elders,* insisting that her young do likewise. Finally, demanding *no separate space* for nourishing her individual needs and goals, even though *ambition* is an aspect of her character, the Africana womanist is committed to the art of *mothering* and *nurturing* her own in particular and humankind in general.

If Africana Womanism is allowed to reach its full potential, that of reclaiming Africana women via identifying our own collective struggle and acting upon it, then Africana people the world over will be better for it. Moreover, whenever a people takes control over its struggle, tailoring it to meet the collective needs and demands, success is almost invariably inevitable. When success in one's goals is realized, it makes for a more peaceful reality for all concerned. Further, one is more inclined to a wholesome and amicable relationship with others, knowing that the concerns of the people are respected and met.

In conclusion, Africana Womanism establishes that, above all else, "the primary goal of Africana women . . . is to create their own criteria for assessing their realities, both in thought and in action" (Hudson-Weems, 50).

Bibliography

Aptheker, Bettina. "Strong Is What We Make Each Other: Unlearning Racism within Women's Studies." *Women's Studies Quarterly* 1, No. 4 (Winter 1981).

Hare, Julia. Quoted in "Feminism in Academe: The Race Factor" by Eileen Crawford, in *Black Issues in Higher Education* 10, No. 1 (March 11, 1993).

Hudson-Weems, Clenora. *Africana Womanism: Reclaiming Ourselves,* 2d rev. ed. Troy, Mich.: Bedford, 1994.

Ladner, Joyce. *Tomorrow's Tomorrow: The Black Woman.* Garden City, N.Y.: Anchor, 1972.

Mompati, Ruth. "Women and Life Under Apartheid." In *One Is Not a Woman, One Becomes: The African Woman in a Transitional Society,* ed. Daphne Williams Ntiri. Troy, Mich.: Bedford, 1982.

Ntiri, Daphne Williams, ed. *One Is Not a Woman, One Becomes: The African Woman in a Transitional Society.* Troy, Mich.: Bedford, 1982.

Steady, Filomina Chioma, ed. *The Black Woman Cross-Culturally.* Cambridge, Mass.: Schenkman, 1981.

BARBARA SMITH

(1946–)

In the celebrated woman-of-color feminist anthology, *This Bridge Called My Back,* Barbara Smith characterizes herself as "a Black Feminist and Lesbian, a writer and an activist." Indeed, she is an articulate and influential voice for the black feminist point of view. If she had written nothing else, her groundbreaking essay "Toward a Black Feminist Criticism" would have given her a place in black literary history. However, she has done much more by producing numerous major anthologies of black women's writing as publisher of Kitchen Table, a black feminist press, and by her own efforts as poet, short story writer, and essayist.

Barbara Smith was born on November 16, 1946, in Cleveland, Ohio. She has a twin sister, Beverly, who also is involved in feminist politics. Smith attended Mount Holyoke College, earning a B.A. in 1969, and the University of Pittsburgh, earning an M.A. in 1971. In 1974, she was a founding member of the black feminist Combahee River Collective, a Boston political action group committed to fighting racial, gender, heterosexual, and class oppression. In addition, she has edited or coedited the following major anthologies: *Conditions: Five, The Black Women's Issue* (1979), *All the Women Are White, All the Black Are Men, But Some of Us Are Brave* (1982), and *Home Girls: A Black Feminist Anthology* (1983).

Smith's works have appeared in *Ms.*, the *New York Times, Conditions,* and *The Black Scholar,* and the *Village Voice.* Her 1977 essay "Toward a Black Feminist Criticism," which explores black women's writing from a feminist perspective, is perhaps the most influential single essay of its kind. Throughout the work, she argues that "the politics of sex as well as the politics of race and class are crucially interlocking factors in the works of Black women writers." When asked in *Home Girls* what kind of political organizing she is involved with, she replied,

> What I'm doing now, mostly, is writing and also working on *Kitchen Table: Women of Color Press,* which is the first press that has the commitment of publishing the work of women of color both in the U.S. and internationally. That's very exciting to me, because I see it as an expansion of my politics from Black women's organizing to Third World women's organizing, which is a direction that we're probably all moving in.

Although some later black women critics have disagreed with her in some areas, all critics, both female and male, owe Barbara Smith a great debt of gratitude for her study of black feminist writing.

❖❖❖

For further insights into this author, see Deborah McDowell, "New Directions from Black Feminist Criticism," in *The New Feminist Criticism,* ed. Elaine Showalter (1985); Sherley Anne Williams, "Some Implications of Womanist Theory," in *Reading Black, Reading Feminist,* ed. Henry Louis Gates, Jr. (1990).

Toward a Black Feminist Criticism[1]

For all my sisters, especially Beverly and Demita

I do not know where to begin. Long before I tried to write this I realized that I was attempting something unprecedented, something dangerous, merely by writing about Black lesbian writers from any perspective at all. These things have not been done. Not by white male critics, expectedly. Not by Black male critics. Not by white women critics who think of themselves as feminists. And most crucially not by Black women critics who, although they pay the most attention to Black women writers as a group, seldom use a consistent feminist analysis or write about Black lesbian literature. All segments of the literary world—whether establishment, progressive, Black, female, or lesbian—do not know, or at least act as if they do not

[1]This article originally appeared in *Conditions: Two* (October 1977).

know, that Black women writers and Black lesbian writers exist.

For whites, this specialized lack of knowledge is inextricably connected to their not knowing in any concrete or politically transforming way that Black women of any description dwell in this place. Black women's existence, experience, and culture and the brutally complex systems of oppression which shape these are in the "real world" of white and/or male consciousness beneath consideration, invisible, unknown.

This invisibility, which goes beyond anything that either Black men or white women experience and tell about in their writing, is one reason it is so difficult for me to know where to start. It seems overwhelming to break such a massive silence. Even more numbing, however, is the realization that so many of the women who will read this have not yet noticed us missing either from their reading matter, their politics, or their lives. It is galling that ostensible feminists and acknowledged lesbians have been so blinded to the implications of any womanhood that is not white womanhood and that they have yet to struggle with the deep racism in themselves that is at the source of this blindness.

I think of the thousands and thousands of books, magazines and articles which have been devoted, by this time, to the subject of women's writing and I am filled with rage at the fraction of those pages that mention Black and other Third-World women. I finally do not know how to begin because in 1977 I want to be writing this for a Black feminist publication, for Black women who know and love these writers as I do and who, if they do not yet know their names, have at least profoundly felt the pain of their absence.

The conditions that coalesce into the impossibilities of this essay have as much to do with politics as with the practice of literature. Any discussion of Afro-American writers can rightfully begin with the fact that for most of the time we have been in this country we have been categorically denied not only literacy, but the most minimal possibility of a decent human life. In her landmark essay, "In Search of Our Mothers' Gardens," Alice Walker discloses how the political, economic and social restrictions of slavery and racism have historically stunted the creative lives of Black women.

At the present time I feel that the politics of feminism have a direct relationship to the state of Black Women's literature. A viable, autonomous Black feminist movement in this country would open up the space needed for the exploration of Black women's lives and the creation of consciously Black woman-identified art. At the same time a redefinition of the goals and strategies of the white feminist movement would lead to much needed change in the focus and content of what is now generally accepted as women's culture.

I want to make in this essay some connections between the politics of Black women's lives, what we write about and our situation as artists. In order to do this I will look at how Black women have been viewed critically by outsiders, demonstrate the necessity for Black feminist criticism and try to understand what the existence or nonexistence of Black lesbian writing reveals about the state of Black women's culture and the intensity of *all* Black women's oppression.

The role that criticism plays in making a body of literature recognizable and real hardly needs to be explained here. The necessity for non-hostile and perceptive analysis of works written by persons outside the "mainstream" of white/male cultural rule has been proven by the Black cultural resurgence of the 1960's and '70's and by the even more recent growth of feminist literary scholarship. For books to be real and remembered they have to be talked about. For books to be understood they must be examined in such a way that the basic intentions of the writers are at least considered. Because of racism Black literature has usually been viewed as a discrete subcategory of American literature and there have been Black critics of Black literature who did much to keep it alive long before it caught the attention of whites. Before the advent of specifically feminist criticism in this decade, books by white women, on the other hand, were not clearly perceived as the cultural manifestation of an oppressed people. It took the surfacing of the second wave of the North American feminist movement to expose the fact that these works contain a stunningly accurate record of the impact of patriarchal values and practice upon the lives of women and more significantly that literature by women provides essential insights into female experience.

In speaking about the current situation of Black women writers, it is important to remember that the existence of a feminist movement was an essential pre-condition to the growth of feminist literature, criticism and women's studies, which focused at the beginning almost entirely upon investigations of literature. The fact that a parallel Black feminist movement has been much slower in evolving cannot help but have impact upon the situation of Black women writers and artists and explains in part why during this very same period we have been so ignored.

There is no political movement to give power or support to those who want to examine Black women's experience through studying our history, literature and culture. There is no political presence that demands a minimal level of consciousness and respect from those who write or talk about our lives. Finally, there is not a developed body of Black feminist political theory whose assumptions could be used in the study of Black women's art. When Black women's books are dealt with at all, it is usually in the context of Black literature which largely ignores the implications of sexual politics. When white women look at Black women's works they are of course ill-equipped to deal with the subtleties of racial politics. A Black feminist approach to literature that embodies the realization that the politics of sex as well as the politics of race and class are crucially interlocking factors in the works of Black women writers is an absolute necessity. Until a Black feminist criticism exists we will not even know what these writers mean. The citations from a variety of critics which follow prove that without a Black feminist critical perspective not only are books by Black women misunderstood, they are destroyed in the process.

Jerry H. Bryant, the *Nation*'s white male reviewer of Alice Walker's *In Love & Trouble: Stories of Black Women,* wrote in 1973:

> The subtitle of the collection, "Stories of Black Women," is probably an attempt by the publisher to exploit not only black subjects but feminine ones. There is nothing feminist about these stories, however.

Blackness and feminism are to his mind mutually exclusive and peripheral to the act of writing fiction. Bryant of course does not consider that Walker might have titled the work herself, nor did he apparently read the book which unequivocally reveals the author's feminist consciousness.

In *The Negro Novel in America,* a book that Black critics recognize as one of the worst examples of white racist pseudoscholarship, Robert Bone cavalierly dismisses Ann Petry's classic, *The Street.* He perceives it to be ". . . a superficial social analysis" of how slums victimize their Black inhabitants. He further objects that:

> It is an attempt to interpret slum life in terms of *Negro* experience, when a larger frame of reference is required. As Alain Locke has observed, "*Knock on Any Door* is superior to *The Street* because it designates class and environment, rather than mere race and environment, as its antagonist."

Neither Robert Bone nor Alain Locke, the Black male critic he cites, can recognize that *The Street* is one of the best delineations in literature of how sex, race, *and* class interact to oppress Black women.

In her review of Toni Morrison's *Sula* for the *New York Times Book Review* in 1973, putative feminist Sara Blackburn makes similarly racist comments. She writes:

> . . . Toni Morrison is far too talented to remain only a marvelous recorder of the black side of provincial American life. If she is to maintain the large and serious audience she deserves, she is going to have to address a riskier contemporary reality than this beautiful but nevertheless distanced novel. *And if she does this, it seems to me that she might easily transcend that early and unintentionally limiting classification "black woman writer" and take her place among the most serious, important and talented American novelists now working.* [Italics mine]

Recognizing Morrison's exquisite gift, Blackburn unashamedly asserts that Morrison is "too talented" to deal with mere Black folk, particularly those double nonentities, Black women. In order to be accepted as "serious," "important," "talented," and "American," she must obviously focus her efforts upon chronicling the doings of white men.

The mishandling of Black women writers by whites is paralleled more often by their not being handled at all, particularly in feminist criticism. Although Elaine Showalter in her review essay on literary criticism for *Signs* states that: "The best work being produced today [in feminist criticism] is exacting and cosmopolitan," her essay is neither. If it were, she would not have failed to mention a single Black or Third-World woman writer, whether "major" or "minor" to cite her questionable categories. That she also does not even hint that lesbian writers of any color exist renders her purported overview virtually meaningless. Showalter obviously thinks that the identities of being Black and female are mutually exclusive as this statement illustrates.

> Furthermore, there are other literary subcultures (black American novelists, for example) whose history offers a precedent for feminist scholarship to use.

The ideas of critics like Showalter *using* Black literature is chilling, a case of barely disguised cultural imperialism. The final insult is that she footnotes the preceding remark by pointing readers to works on Black literature by white males Robert Bone and Roger Rosenblatt!

Two recent works by white women, Ellen Moers' *Literary Women: The Great Writers* and Patricia Meyer Spacks' *The Female Imagination*, evidence the same racist flaw. Moers includes the names of four Black and one Puertorriqueña writer in her seventy pages of bibliographical notes and does not deal at all with Third-World women in the body of her book. Spacks refers to comparison between Negroes (sic) and women in Mary Ellmann's *Thinking About Women* under the index entry, "blacks, women and." "*Black Boy* (Wright)" is the preceding entry. Nothing follows. Again there is absolutely no recognition that Black and female identity ever coexist, specifically in a group of Black women writers. Perhaps one can assume that these women do not know who Black women writers are, that they have had little opportunity like most Americans to learn about them. Perhaps. Their ignorance seems suspiciously selective, however, particularly in the light of the dozens of truly obscure white women writers they are able to unearth. Spacks was herself employed at Wellesley College at the same time that Alice Walker was there teaching one of the first courses on Black women writers in the country.

I am not trying to encourage racist criticism of Black women writers like that of Sara Blackburn, to cite only one example. As a beginning I would at least like to see in print white women's acknowledgment of the contradictions of who and what are being left out of their research and writing.

Black male critics can also *act* as if they do not know that Black women writers exist and are, of course, hampered by an inability to comprehend Black women's experience in sexual as well as racial terms. Unfortunately there are also those who are as virulently sexist in their treatment of Black women writers as their white male counterparts. Darwin Turner's discussion of Zora Neale Hurston in his *In a Minor Chord: Three Afro-American Writers and Their Search for Identity* is a frightening example of the near assassination of a great Black woman writer. His descriptions of her and her work as "artful," "coy," "irrational," "superficial," and "shallow" bear no relationship to the actual quality of her achievements. Turner is completely insensitive to the sexual political dynamics of Hurston's life and writing.

In a recent interview the notoriously misogynist writer, Ishmael Reed, comments in this way upon the low sales of his newest novel:

> . . . but the book only sold 8000 copies. I don't mind giving out the figure: 8000. Maybe if I was one of those young *female* Afro-American writers that are so hot now, I'd sell more. You know, fill my books with ghetto women who can *do no wrong*. . . . But come on, I think I could have sold 8000 copies by myself.

The politics of the situation of Black women are glaringly illuminated by this statement. Neither Reed nor his white male interviewer has the slightest compunction about attacking Black women in print. They need not fear widespread public denunciation since Reed's statement is in perfect agreement with the values of a society that hates Black people, women, and Black women. Finally the two of them feel free to base their actions on the premise that Black women are powerless to alter either their political or cultural oppression.

In her introduction to "A Bibliography of Works Written by American Black Women" Ora Williams quotes some of the reactions of her colleagues toward her efforts to do research on Black women. She writes:

> Others have reacted negatively with such statements as, "I really don't think you are going to find very much written," "Have 'they' written anything that is any good?" and, "I wouldn't go overboard with this woman's lib thing." When discussions touched on the possibility of teaching a course in which emphasis would be on the literature by Black women, one response was, "Ha, ha. That will certainly be the most nothing course ever offered!"

A remark by Alice Walker capsulizes what all the preceding examples indicate about the position of Black women writers and the reasons for the damaging criticism about them. She responds to her interviewer's question, "Why do you think that the black woman writer has been so ignored in America? Does she have even more difficulty than the black male writer, who perhaps has just begun to gain recognition?" Walker replies:

> There are two reasons why the black woman writer is not taken as seriously as the black male writer. One is that she's a woman. Critics seem unusually ill-equipped to intelligently discuss and analyze the works of black women. Generally, they do not even make the attempt; they prefer, rather, to talk about the lives of black women writers, not about what they write. And, since black women writers are not—it would seem—very likable—until recently they were the least willing worshippers of male supremacy—comments about them tend to be cruel.

A convincing case for Black feminist criticism can obviously be built solely upon the basis of the negativity of what already exists. It is far more gratifying, however, to demonstrate its necessity by showing how it can serve to reveal for the first time the profound subtleties of this particular body of literature.

Before suggesting how a Black feminist approach might be used to examine a specific work, I will outline some of the principles that I think a Black feminist critic could use. Beginning with a primary commitment to exploring how both sexual and racial politics and Black and female identity are inextricable elements in Black women's writing, she would also work from the assumption that Black women writers constitute an identifiable literary tradition. The breadth of her familiarity with these writers would have shown her that not only is theirs a verifiable historical tradition that parallels in time the tradition of Black men and white women writing in this country, but that thematically, stylistically, aesthetically and conceptually Black women writers manifest common approaches to the act of creating literature as a direct result of the specific political, social and economic experience they have been obliged to share. The way, for example, that Zora Neale Hurston, Margaret Walker, Toni Morrison, and Alice Walker incorporate the traditional Black female activities of rootworking, herbal medicine, conjure and midwifery into the fabric of their stories is not mere coincidence, nor is their use of specifically Black female language to express their own and their characters' thoughts accidental. The use of Black women's language and cultural experience in books *by* Black women *about* Black women results in a miraculously rich coalescing of form and content and also takes their writing *far* beyond the confines of white/male literary structures. The Black feminist critic would find innumerable commonalities in works by Black women.

Another principle which grows out of the concept of a tradition and which would also help to strengthen this tradition would be for the critic to look first for precedents and insights in interpretation within the works of other Black women. In other words she would think and write out of her own identity and not try to graft the ideas or methodology of white/male literary thought upon precious materials of Black women's art. Black feminist criticism would by definition be highly innovative, embodying the daring spirit of the works themselves. The Black feminist critic would be constantly aware of the political implications of her work and would assert the connections between it and the political situation of all Black women. Logically developed, Black feminist criticism would owe its existence to a Black feminist movement while at the same time contributing ideas that women in the movement could use.

Black feminist criticism applied to a particular work can overturn previous assumptions about it and expose for the first time its actual dimensions. At the "Lesbians and Literature" discussion at the 1976 Modern Language Association convention, Bertha Harris suggested that if in a woman writer's work a sentence refuses to do what it is supposed to do, if there are strong images of women, and if there is a refusal to be linear, the result is innately lesbian literature. As usual, I wanted to see if these ideas might be applied to the Black women writers that I know and quickly realized that many of their works were, in Harris' sense, lesbian. Not because women are "lovers," but because they are the central figures, are positively portrayed and have pivotal relationships with one another. The form and language of these works is also nothing like what white patriarchal culture requires or expects.

I was particularly struck by the way in which both of Toni Morrison's novels, *The Bluest Eye* and *Sula,* could be explored from this new perspective. In both works the relationships between girls and women are essential, yet at the same time physical sexuality is overtly expressed only between men and women. Despite the apparent heterosexuality of the female characters I discovered in rereading *Sula* that it works as a lesbian novel not only because of the passionate friendship between Sula and Nel, but because of Morrison's consistently critical stance towards the heterosexual institutions of male/female relationships, marriage, and the family. Consciously or not, Morrison's work poses both lesbian and feminist questions about Black women's autonomy and their impact upon each other's lives.

Sula and Nel find each other in 1922 when each of them is twelve, on the brink of puberty and the discovery of boys. Even as awakening sexuality "clotted their dreams," each girl desires "a someone" obviously female with whom to share her feelings (51). Morrison writes:

> . . . for it was in dreams that the two girls had met. Long before Edna Finch's Mellow House opened, even before they marched through the chocolate halls of Garfield Primary School . . . they had already made each other's acquaintance in the delirium of their noon dreams. They were solitary little girls whose loneliness was so profound it intoxicated them and sent

them stumbling into Technicolored visions that always included a presence, a someone who, quite like the dreamer shared the delight of the dream. When Nel, an only child, sat on the steps of her back porch surrounded by the high silence of her mother's incredibly orderly house, feeling the neatness pointing at her back, she studied the poplars and fell easily into a picture of herself lying on a flowered bed, tangled in her own hair, waiting for some fiery prince. He approached but never quite arrived. But always, watching the dream along with her, were some smiling sympathetic eyes. Someone as interested as she herself in the flow of her imagined hair, the thickness of the mattress of flowers, the voile sleeves that closed below her elbows in gold-threaded cuffs.

> Similarly, Sula, also an only child, but wedged into a household of throbbing disorder constantly awry with things, people, voices and the slamming of doors, spent hours in the attic behind a roll of linoleum galloping through her own mind on a gray-and-white horse tasting sugar and smelling roses in full view of someone who shared both the taste and the speed.
>
> So when they met, first in those chocolate halls and next through the ropes of the swing, they felt the ease and comfort of old friends. Because each had discovered years before that they were neither white nor male, and that all freedom and triumph was forbidden to them, they had set about creating something else to be. Their meeting was fortunate, for it let them use each other to grow on. Daughters of distant mothers and incomprehensible fathers (Sula's because he was dead; Nel's because he wasn't), they found in each other's eyes the intimacy they were looking for. (51–52)

As this beautiful passage shows, their relationship, from the very beginning, is suffused with an erotic romanticism. The dreams in which they are initially drawn to each other are actually complementary aspects of the same sensuous fairytale. Nel imagines a "fiery prince" who never quite arrives while Sula gallops like a prince "on a gray-and-white horse." The "real world" of patriarchy requires, however, that they channel this energy away from each other to the opposite sex. Lorraine Bethel explains this dynamic in her essay "Conversations With Ourselves: Black Female Relationships in Toni Cade Bambara's *Gorilla, My Love* and Toni Morrison's *Sula.*" She writes:

> I am not suggesting that Sula and Nel are being consciously sexual, or that their relationship has an overt lesbian nature. I am suggesting, however, that there is a certain sensuality in their interactions that is reinforced by the mirror-like nature of their relationship. Sexual exploration and coming of age is a natural part of adolescence. Sula and Nel discover men together, and through their flirtations with males are an important part of their sexual exploration, the sensuality that they experience in each other's company is equally important.

Sula and Nel must also struggle with the constrictions of racism upon their lives. The knowledge that "they were neither white nor male" is the inherent explanation of their need for each other. Morrison depicts in literature the necessary bonding that has always taken place between Black women for the sake of barest survival. Together the two girls can find the courage to create themselves.

Their relationship is severed only when Nel marries Jude, an unexceptional young man who thinks of her as "the hem—the tuck and fold that hid his raveling edges" (83). Sula's inventive wildness cannot overcome social pressure or the influence of Nel's parents who "had succeeded in rubbing down to a dull glow any sparkle or splutter she had" (83). Nel falls prey to convention while Sula escapes it. Yet at the wedding which ends the first phase of their relationship, Nel's final action is to look past her husband towards Sula:

> . . . a slim figure in blue, gliding, with just a hint of a strut, down the path toward the road. . . . Even from the rear Nel could tell that it was Sula and that she was smiling; that some-

> thing deep down in that litheness was amused. (85)

When Sula returns ten years later, her rebelliousness full-blown, a major source of the town's suspicions stems from the fact that although she is almost thirty, she is still unmarried. Sula's grandmother, Eva, does not hesitate to bring up the matter as soon as she arrives. She asks:

> "When you gone to get married? You need to have some babies. It'll settle you. . . . Ain't no woman got no business floatin' around without no man." (92)

Sula replies: "'I don't want to make somebody else. I want to make myself'" (92). Self-definition is a dangerous activity for any woman to engage in, especially a Black one, and it expectedly earns Sula pariah status in Medallion.

Morrison clearly points out that it is the fact that Sula has not been tamed or broken by the exigencies of heterosexual family life which most galls the others. She writes:

> Among the weighty evidence piling up was the fact that Sula did not look her age. She was near thirty and, unlike them, had lost no teeth, suffered no bruises, developed no ring of fat at the waist or pocket at the back of her neck. (115)

In other words she is not a domestic serf, a woman run down by obligatory childbearing or a victim of battering. Sula also sleeps with the husbands of the town once and then discards them, needing them even less than her own mother did, for sexual gratification and affection. The town reacts to her disavowal of patriarchal values by becoming fanatically serious about their own family obligations, as if in this way they might counteract Sula's radical criticism of their lives.

Sula's presence in her community functions much like the presence of lesbians everywhere to expose the contradictions of supposedly "normal" life. The opening paragraph of the essay "Woman Identified" has amazing relevance as an explanation of Sula's position and character in the novel. It asks:

> What is a lesbian? A lesbian is the rage of all women condensed to the point of explosion. She is the woman who, often beginning at an extremely early age, acts in accordance with her inner compulsion to be a more complete and freer human being than her society—perhaps then, but certainly later—cares to allow her. These needs and actions, over a period of years, bring her into painful conflict with people, situations, the accepted ways of thinking, feeling and behaving, until she is in a state of continual war with everything around her, and usually with her self. She may not be fully conscious of the political implications of what for her began as personal necessity, but on some level she has not been able to accept the limitations and oppression laid on her by the most basic role of her society—the female role.

The limitations of the *Black* female role are even greater in a racist and sexist society as is the amount of courage it takes to challenge them. It is no wonder that the townspeople see Sula's independence as imminently dangerous.

Morrison is also careful to show the reader that despite their years of separation and their opposing paths, Nel and Sula's relationship retains its primacy for each of them. Nel feels transformed when Sula returns and thinks:

> It was like getting the use of an eye back, having a cataract removed. Her old friend had come home. Sula. Who made her laugh, who made her see old things with new eyes, in whose presence she felt clever, gentle and a little raunchy. (95)

Laughing together in the familiar, "rib-scraping" way, Nel feels "new, soft and new" (98). Morrison uses here the visual imagery which symbolizes the women's closeness throughout the novel.

Sula fractures this closeness, however, by sleeping with Nel's husband, an act of little import according to her system of values. Nel, of course, cannot understand. Sula thinks ruefully:

> Nel was the one person who had wanted nothing from her, who had accepted all aspects of her. Now she wanted everything, and all because of *that.* Nel was the first person who had been real to her, whose name she knew, who had seen as she had the slant of life that made it possible to stretch it to its limits. Now Nel was one of *them.* (119–120)

Sula also thinks at the realization of losing Nel about how unsatisfactory her relationships with men have been and admits:

> She had been looking all along for a friend, and it took her a while to discover that a lover was not a comrade and could never be—for a woman. (121)

The nearest that Sula comes to actually loving a man is in a brief affair with Ajax and what she values most about him is the intellectual companionship he provides, the brilliance he "allows" her to show.

Sula's feelings about sex with men are also consistent with a lesbian interpretation of the novel. Morrison writes:

> She went to bed with men as frequently as she could. It was the only place where she could find what she was looking for: *misery and the ability to feel deep sorrow. . . .* During the lovemaking she found and needed to find the cutting edge. When she left off cooperating with her body and began to assert herself in the act, particles of strength gathered in her like steel shavings drawn to a spacious magnetic center, forming a tight cluster that nothing, it seemed, could break. *And there was utmost irony and outrage in lying under someone, in a position of surrender, feeling her own abiding strength and limitless power. . . .* When her partner disengaged himself, she looked up at him in wonder trying to recall his name . . . waiting impatiently for him to turn away . . . *leaving her to the postcoital privateness in which she met herself, welcomed herself, and joined herself in matchless harmony.* (122–123) [Italics mine.]

Sula uses men for sex which results not in communion with them, but in her further delving into self.

Ultimately the deepest communion and communication in the novel occurs between two women who love each other. After their last painful meeting, which does not bring reconciliation, Sula thinks as Nel leaves her:

> "So she will walk on down that road, her back so straight in that old green coat . . . thinking how much I have cost her and never remember the days when we were two throats and one eye and we had no price." (147)

It is difficult to imagine a more evocative metaphor for what women can be to each other, the "pricelessness" they achieve in refusing to sell themselves for male approval, the total worth that they can only find in each other's eyes.

Decades later the novel concludes with Nel's final comprehension of the source of the grief that has plagued her from the time her husband walked out. Morrison writes:

> "All that time, all that time, I thought I was missing Jude." And the loss pressed down on her chest and came up into her throat. "We was girls together," she said as though explaining something. "O Lord, Sula," she cried, "girl, girl, girlgirlgirl."
>
> It was a fine cry—loud and long—but it had no bottom and it had no top, just circles and circles of sorrow. (174)

Again Morrison exquisitely conveys what women, Black women, mean to each other. This final passage verifies the depth of Sula and Nel's relationship and its centrality to an accurate interpretation of the work.

Sula is an exceedingly lesbian novel in the emotions expressed, in the definition of female character and in the way that the politics of heterosexuality are portrayed. The very meaning of lesbianism is being expanded in literature, just as it is being redefined through politics. The confusion that many readers have felt about *Sula* may well have a lesbian explanation. If one sees Sula's inexplicable "evil" and non-conformity as the evil of not being male-identified, many elements in the novel become clear. The work might be clearer still if Morrison had approached her subject with the consciousness that a lesbian relationship was at least a possibility for her characters. Obviously Morrison did not *intend* the reader to perceive Sula and Nel's relationship as inherently lesbian. However, this lack of intention only shows the way in which heterosexist assumptions can veil what may logically be expected to occur in a work. What I have tried to do here is not to prove that Morrison wrote something that she did not, but to point out how a Black feminist critical perspective at least allows consideration of this level of the novel's meaning.

In her interview in *Conditions: One* Adrienne Rich talks about unconsummated relationships and the need to re-evaluate the meaning of intense yet supposedly non-erotic connections between women. She asserts:

> We need a lot more documentation about what actually happened: I think we can also imagine it, because we know it happened—we know it out of our own lives.

Black women are still in the position of having to "imagine," discover and verify Black lesbian literature because so little has been written from an avowedly lesbian perspective. The near non-existence of Black Lesbian literature which other Black lesbians and I so deeply feel has everything to do with the politics of our lives, the total suppression of identity that all Black women, lesbian or not, must face. This literary silence is again intensified by the unavailability of an autonomous Black feminist movement through which we could fight our oppression and also begin to name ourselves.

In a speech, "The Autonomy of Black Lesbian Women," Wilmette Brown comments upon the connection between our political reality and the literature we must invent:

> Because the isolation of Black lesbian women, given that we are superfreaks, given that our lesbianism defies both the sexual identity that capital gives us and the racial identity that capital gives us, the isolation of Black lesbian women from heterosexual Black women is very profound. Very profound. I have searched throughout Black history, Black literature, whatever, looking for some women that I could see were somehow lesbian. Now I know that in a certain sense they were all lesbian. But that was a very painful search.

Heterosexual privilege is usually the only privilege that Black women have. None of us have racial or sexual privilege, almost none of us have class privilege, maintaining "straightness" is our last resort. Being out, particularly out in print, is the final renunciation of any claim to the crumbs of "tolerance" that non-threatening "ladylike" Black women are sometimes fed. I am convinced that it is our lack of privilege and power in every other sphere that allows so few Black women to make the leap that many white women, particularly writers, have been able to make in this decade, not merely because they are white or have economic leverage, but because they have had the strength and support of a movement behind them.

As Black lesbians we must be out not only in white society, but in the Black community as well, which is at least as homophobic. That the sanctions against Black lesbians are extremely high is well illustrated in this comment by Black male writer Ishmael Reed. Speaking about the inroads that whites make into Black culture, he asserts:

> In Manhattan you find people actively trying to impede intellectual debate among Afro-Americans. The powerful "liberal/radical/existentialist" influences of the Manhattan literary and drama establishment speak through tokens, like for example that ancient notion of the *one* black ideologue (who's usually a Communist),

> the *one* black poetess (who's usually a feminist lesbian).

To Reed, "feminist" and "lesbian" are the most pejorative terms he can hurl at a Black woman and totally invalidate anything she might say, regardless of her actual politics or sexual identity. Such accusations are quite effective for keeping Black women writers who are writing with integrity and strength from any conceivable perspective in line, but especially ones who are actually feminist and lesbian. Unfortunately Reed's reactionary attitude is all too typical. A community which has not confronted sexism, because a widespread Black feminist movement has not required it to, has likewise not been challenged to examine its heterosexism. Even at this moment I am not convinced that one can write explicitly as a Black lesbian and live to tell about it.

Yet there are a handful of Black women who have risked everything for truth. Audre Lorde, Pat Parker, and Ann Allen Shockley have at least broken ground in the vast wilderness of works that do not exist. Black feminist criticism will again have an essential role not only in creating a climate in which Black lesbian writers can survive, but in undertaking the total reassessment of Black literature and literary history needed to reveal the Black woman-identified-women that Wilmette Brown and so many of us are looking for.

Although I have concentrated here upon what does not exist and what needs to be done, a few Black feminist critics have already begun this work. Gloria T. Hull at the University of Delaware has discovered in her research on Black women poets of the Harlem Renaissance that many of the women who are considered "minor" writers of the period were in constant contact with each other and provided both intellectual stimulation and psychological support for each other's work. At least one of these writers, Angelina Weld Grimké, wrote many unpublished love poems to women. Lorraine Bethel, a recent graduate of Yale College, has done substantial work on Black women writers, particularly in her senior essay, "This Infinity of Conscious Pain: Blues Lyricism and Hurston's Black Female Folk Aesthetic and Cultural Sensibility in *Their Eyes Were Watching God,*" in which she brilliantly defines and uses the principles of Black feminist criticism. Elaine Scott at the State University of New York at Old Westbury is also involved in highly creative and politically resonant research on Hurston and other writers.

The fact that these critics are young and, except for Hull, unpublished merely indicates the impediments we face. Undoubtedly there are other women working and writing whom I do not even know, simply because there is no place to read them. As Michele Wallace states in her article, "A Black Feminist's Search for Sisterhood":

> We exist as women who are black who are feminists, each stranded for the moment, working independently because there is not yet an environment in this society remotely congenial to our struggle—[or our thoughts].

I only hope that this essay is one way of breaking our silence and our isolation, of helping us to know each other.

Just as I did not know where to start I am not sure how to end. I feel that I have tried to say too much and at the same time have left too much unsaid. What I want this essay to do is lead everyone who reads it to examine *everything* that they have ever thought and believed about feminist culture and to ask themselves how their thoughts connect to the reality of Black women's writing and lives. I want to encourage in white women, as a first step, a sane accountability to all the women who write and live on this soil. I want most of all for Black women and Black lesbians somehow not to be so alone. This last will require the most expansive of revolutions as well as many new words to tell us how to make this revolution real. I finally want to express how much easier both my waking and my sleeping hours would be if there were one book in existence that would tell me something specific about my life. One book based in Black feminist and Black lesbian experience, fiction or non-fiction. Just one work to reflect the reality that I and the Black women whom I love are trying to create. When such a book exists then each of us will not only know better how to live, but how to dream.

NTOZAKE SHANGE

(1948–)

Ntozake Shange is a playwright, poet, novelist, essayist, and dancer who has been at the forefront of giving voice to the struggles of highly individualized contemporary black women. She is one of the most innovative of recent black authors, putting her in the visionary company of Amiri Baraka, Ishmael Reed, and Clarence Major for formal experimentation. Her creative mixing of genres, of poetry, drama, and dance, has brought her several prestigious honors, including the Obie, Outer Critics Circle, and *Mademoiselle* awards and both a Guggenheim Fellowship and Medal of Excellence by Columbia University in 1981. Although she is quite prolific, having already produced twenty major works, she is best known for her unconventional drama *for colored girls who have considered suicide when the rainbow is enuf.*

Ntozake Shange was originally named Paulette Williams. She was born to Paul T. Williams, a surgeon, and Eloise Williams, a psychiatric social worker, on October 18, 1948, in Trenton, New Jersey. She grew up middle class in New Jersey and St. Louis, Missouri, where she was exposed to a variety of music and literature. Such black luminaries as W. E. B. Du Bois, Dizzy Gillespie, Chuck Berry, and Miles Davis visited her home. Her mother read to her from Paul Laurence Dunbar, Shakespeare, Countée Cullen, and T. S. Eliot. In the mid-sixties, while attending Barnard College in New York City, Shange suffered from profound depression and attempted suicide several times. However, she managed to graduate from Barnard with honors in 1970 and received an M.A. in American studies in 1973 from the University of Southern California. While at USC, she took the Zulu names Ntozake (pronounced En-to-ZAH-ki), which means "she who comes with her own things," and Shange (pronounced SHONG-gay), which means "she who walks like a lion."

After Shange originated *for colored girls* in San Francisco in 1974, she moved it to New York, where it first appeared off-Broadway in 1975 and then proceeded to Broadway in 1976. The following year, it won the Obie, Outer Critics Circle, and *Mademoiselle* awards as well as Tony, Grammy, and Emmy nominations. The women's movement helped create a climate that was receptive to such a play. Modeling her work on the white radical feminist Judy Grahn's poem sequence *The Common Woman* (1971), the playwright sought to clarify and explore the lives of seven black women. She wanted these women to find divinity in themselves. She wanted to "sing a black girl's song," to declare and celebrate the lives of black women. In "Ntozake Shange Interviews Herself," *Ms* (December 1977), Shange says, "there's an enormous ignorance abt women's realities in our society. we ourselves suffer from a frightening lack of clarity abt who we are. my work attempts to ferret out what i know & touch in a woman's body." With *for colored girls,* Shange introduced a new dramatic form, the choreopoem, a fusion of dance, poetry, and drama. In her introduction to *for colored girls,* she says of dance, the least utilized art in contemporary theater, "With dance I discovered my body more intimately than I had imagined possible. With the acceptance of the ethnicity of my thighs & backside, came a clearer understanding of my voice as a woman & as a poet." In short, her art tries to portray the whole black woman: her body, mind, feelings, and soul.

Shange has learned from a great many people. Amiri Baraka showed her lyric avant-garde poetic technique. Ishmael Reed provided her with novel diction and the idea of using myth in contemporary literature. Jessica Hagedorn showed her how to create sophisticated poetry without being dependent on university creative writing workshops. Clarence Major taught her to use fantasy and nonlinear narrative. In an interview in Claudia Tate's *Black Women Writers at Work* (1983), Shange says of her unconventional style, "It bothers me, on occasion, to look at poems where all the first letters are capitalized. It's very boring to me. That's why I use the lower-case alphabet. . . . The spellings result from the way I talk or the way the character talks, or the way I heard something said." The Women's Studies Program at Sonoma State College taught her to focus on the familiar dynamics of women's lives. She is influenced by black music from Ike and Tina Turner (soul) to Archie Shepp (avant-garde). In Shange's December 1977 self-interview in *Ms*, she said of Tina Turner, "i imagine her songs were for me what edna st. vincent millay's sonnets were for a terribly romantic lil white girl thirty years ago."

Like Alice Walker, Shange has been criticized for her negative portrayal of black men, especially in *for colored girls*. Yet the play is less about black men as villains than about the need for black women to achieve their individual freedom in spite of anyone who stands in their way. In addition to *for colored girls*, she has written many other plays, including *A Photograph: Lovers-in-Motion* (1979), *Spell #7* (1979), and *Daddy Says* (1989). Of these works *Spell #7* is Shange's best play. In 1979 drama critic Don Nelson of the *New York Daily News* described it as "black magic. It is a celebration of blackness, the joy and pride along with the horror of it. It is a shout, a cry, a bitter laugh, a sneer. It is an extremely fine theater piece. The word that best describes Shange's works, which are not plays in the traditional sense, is power. Drama is inherent in each of her poetic sentences because the words hum with the vibrant urgency."

She has also published several books of poetry, including *Nappy Edges* (1978), *A Daughter's Geography* (1983), *Ridin' the Moon in Texas: Word Paintings* (1987), and *The Love Space Demands: A Continuing Saga* (1991); a book of essays, *See No Evil: Prefaces, Essays & Accounts* (1984), and three novels, *Sassafrass, Cypress & Indigo* (1982), *Betsey Brown* (1985), and *Lilliane: Resurrection of the Daughter* (1994). Her first novel, *Sassafrass, Cypress & Indigo*, traces the odyssey of two sisters—Sassafrass, a weaver, and Cypress, a dancer—who leave their hometown of Charleston, South Carolina, to explore the world and their creative female selves. Her second, *Betsey Brown*, which has as its setting St. Louis, Missouri, details the coming of age of a thirteen-year-old black middle-class girl during the disruptive period of public school integration. Her third, *Lilliane: Resurrection of the Daughter*, is an episodic and experimental exploration of a young female artist's relationship with her lovers and parents.

Shange has also been called a pioneer in terms of subject matter. More importantly, she is a first-rate avant-garde black artist creating new forms to portray black reality, especially black female reality.

❖❖❖

To date there is only one book-length critical study of Shange's work, Neale A. Lester's *Ntozake Shange: A Critical Study of the Plays* (1995). For further information and insight see Elizabeth Brown-Gillory's *Their Place on the Stage: Black Women Playwrights in America* (1988); Sandra Richards's, "Ntozake Shange," in *African American Writers* (1991), ed. Valerie Smith; Ntozake Shange, "Ntozake Shange Interviews Herself," *Ms.*, December, 1977; Carole McAlpine Watson's "Ntosake Shange," *Notable Black American Women* (1992), ed. Jessie Carney Smith; and Elizabeth Brown's "Ntozake Shange," *Dictionary of Literary Biography: Afro-American Writers After 1955: Dramatists and Prose Writers*, vol. 38, eds. Thadious Davis and Trudier Harris. An insightful interview of the playwright is also published in Claudia Tate's *Black Women Writers at Work* (1983).

somebody almost walked off wid alla my stuff

FROM *FOR COLORED GIRLS WHO HAVE CONSIDERED SUICIDE WHEN THE RAINBOW IS ENUF*

THE DANCE REACHES A CLIMAX AND ALL
OF THE LADIES FALL OUT TIRED, BUT FULL
OF LIFE AND TOGETHERNESS.

lady in green
somebody almost walked off wid alla my stuff
not my poems or a dance i gave up in the street
but somebody almost walked off wid alla my stuff
like a kleptomaniac workin hard & forgettin while stealin
this is mine / this aint yr stuff /
now why dont you put me back & let me hang out in my own self
somebody almost walked off wid alla my stuff
& didnt care enuf to send a note home sayin
i waz late for my solo conversation
or two sizes too small for my own tacky skirts
what can anybody do wit somethin of no value on
a open market / did you getta dime for my things /
hey man / where are you goin wid alla my stuff /
this is a woman's trip & i need my stuff /
to ohh & ahh abt / daddy / i gotta mainline number
from my own shit / now wontchu put me back / & let
me play this duet / wit this silver ring in my nose /
honest to god / somebody almost run off wit alla my stuff /
& i didnt bring anythin but the kick & sway of it
the perfect ass for my man & none of it is theirs
this is mine / ntozake 'her own things' / that's my name /
now give me my stuff / i see ya hidin my laugh / & how i
sit wif my legs open sometimes / to give my crotch
some sunlight / & there goes my love my toes my chewed
up finger nails / niggah / wif the curls in yr hair /

mr. louisiana hot link / i want my stuff back /
my rhythms & my voice / open my mouth / & let me talk ya
outta / throwin my shit in the sewar / this is some delicate
leg & whimsical kiss / i gotta have to give to my choice /
without you runnin off wit alla my shit /
now you cant have me less i give me away / & i waz
doin all that / til ya run off on a good thing /
who is this you left me wit / some simple bitch
widda bad attitude / i wants my things /
i want my arm wit the hot iron scar / & my leg with the
flea bite / i want my calloused feet & quik language back
in my mouth / fried plantains / pineapple pear juice /
sun-ra & joseph & jules / i want my own things / how i lived them /
& give me my memories / how i waz when i waz there /
you cant have them or do nothin wit them /
stealin my shit from me / dont make it yrs / makes it stolen /
somebody almost run off wit alla my stuff / & i waz standin
there / lookin at myself / the whole time
& it waznt a spirit took my stuff / waz a man whose
ego walked round like Rodan's shadow / waz a man faster
n my innocence / waz a lover / i made too much
room for / almost run off wit alla my stuff /
& i didnt know i'd give it up so quik / & the one running wit it /
dont know he got it / & i'm shoutin this is mine / & he dont
know he got it / my stuff is the anonymous ripped off treasure
of the year / did you know somebody almost got away with me /
me in a plastic bag under their arm / me
danglin on a string of personal carelessness / i'm spattered wit
mud & city rain / & no i didnt get a chance to take a douche /
hey man / this is not your perogative / i gotta have me in my
pocket / to get round like a good woman shd / & make the poem
in the pot or the chicken in the dance / what i got to do /
i gotta have my stuff to do it to /
why dont ya find yr own things / & leave this package
of me for my destiny / what ya got to get from me /
i'll give it to ya / yeh / i'll give it to ya /
round 5:00 in the winter / when the sky is blue-red /
& Dew City is gettin pressed / if it's really my stuff /
ya gotta give it to me / if ya really want it / i'm
the only one / can handle it

lady in blue

that niggah will be back tomorrow, sayin 'i'm sorry'

lady in yellow

get this, last week my ol man came in sayin, 'i don't know
how she got yr number baby, i'm sorry'

lady in brown

no this one is it, 'o baby, ya know i waz high, i'm sorry'
lady in purple
'i'm only human, and inadequacy is what makes us human, &
if we was perfect we wdnt have nothin to strive for, so you
might as well go on and forgive me pretty baby, cause i'm sorry'
lady in green
'shut up bitch, i told you i waz sorry'
lady in orange
no this one is it, 'i do ya like i do ya cause i thot
ya could take it, now i'm sorry'
lady in red
'now i know that ya know i love ya, but i aint ever gonna
love ya like ya want me to love ya, i'm sorry'
lady in blue
one thing i dont need
is any more apologies
i got sorry greetin me at my front door
you can keep yrs
i dont know what to do wit em
they dont open doors
or bring the sun back
they dont make me happy
or get a mornin paper
didnt nobody stop usin my tears to wash cars
cuz a sorry
i am simply tired
of collectin
'i didnt know
i was so important to you'
i'm gonna haveta throw some away
i cant get to the clothes in my closet
for alla the sorries
i'm gonna tack a sign to my door
leave a message by the phone
'if you called
to say yr sorry
call somebody
else
i dont use em anymore'
i let sorry / didnt meanta / & how cd i know abt that
take a walk down a dark & musty street in brooklyn
i'm gonna do exactly what i want to
& i wont be sorry for none of it
letta sorry soothe yr soul / i'm gonna soothe mine
you were always inconsistent

doin somethin & then bein sorry
beatin my heart to death
talkin bout you sorry
well
i will not call
i'm not goin to be nice
i will raise my voice
& scream & holler
& break things & race the engine
& tell all yr secrets bout yrself to yr face
& i will list in detail everyone of my wonderful lovers
& their ways
i will play oliver lake
loud
& i wont be sorry for none of it

i loved you on purpose
i was open on purpose
i still crave vulnerability & close talk
& i'm not even sorry bout you bein sorry
you can carry all the guilt & grime ya wanna
just dont give it to me
i cant use another sorry
next time
you should admit
you're mean / low-down / triflin / & no count straight out
steada bein sorry alla the time
enjoy bein yrself

GAYL JONES
(1949–)

Through several provocative fictional and poetic works, Gayl Jones has brought a distinctive voice to African American literature. In explorations of insanity, fellatio, incest, color prejudices, and the mythical African–New World past, Jones has introduced characters and incidents unlike any previously portrayed in black works. Her interests range from Afro-Brazilian history to small-town Kentucky close-mindedness, to psychiatric wards, to the blues that an abused woman uses to reclaim her hold on her life and creativity. Though not having garnered the critical attention of an Alice Walker or a Toni Morrison, Jones has mastered several literary genres and gone quietly about the business of revolutionizing our perceptions of what African American literature comprises.

A Kentuckian, Jones was born in Lexington on November 23, 1949, and attended public schools there. Her fifth-grade teacher, Mrs. Hodges, encouraged her to write. She is by far one of the most educated contemporary black women writers, having earned a B.A. in English from Connecticut College in 1971, an M.A. in creative writing from Brown University in 1973, and a D.A. in creative writing from

Brown in 1975 (she studied with poet Michael Harper while at Brown). She was one of a team of four undergraduates selected to tour on the Connecticut poetry circuit in 1970. That honor reflected the general evaluation of the award-winning quality of her work. During the 1969–70 academic year, she won the Connecticut Award for best original poem. Throughout the 1970s, she received a succession of awards, including the Frances Steloff Award for fiction (1970, for "The Roundhouse"), the Academy of American Poets Charles and Fanny Fay Wood Poetry Prize at Brown University (1973), and Best Original Production in the New England region by the American College Theatre Festival for her 1973 play *Chile Woman.*

While at Brown, Jones completed the manuscript that led to the publication of *Corregidora* (1975). She has spent most of her life in academia. She left Brown to assume a position in the English department at the University of Michigan, where, from 1977 to 1980, she held a Michigan Society fellowship–assistant professorship; she was later promoted to associate professor of English. In 1981, she won the Henry Russell Award at the university.

Jones was consistently successful in getting grants and invitations to writers' colonies in the 1970s. She received a scholarship to the Breadloaf Writers' Conference in 1971, a grant in writing from the Rhode Island Council on the Arts during 1974–1975, a fellowship to the Yaddo artists' colony for the summer of 1974, and a Southern Fellowship Foundation grant for 1973 to 1975. This freedom to write led to the fictional publications for which she is perhaps best known. *Corregidora* (1975) is the story of slavery, incest, and violence in Brazil that pollutes three generations of black women. Their descendant in America, blues singer Ursa Corregidora, must overcome a sexually violent historical and personal past to claim her own voice and worth in contemporary America. The book is striking in its straightforward language and blunt sexuality. It won the *Mademoiselle* Award for fiction in 1975. During 1975–1976, Jones was a recipient of a National Endowment for the Arts writing grant.

Eva's Man (1976) raised more eyebrows than *Corregidora.* Set in a psychiatric ward, it is the story of Eva Medina Canada, a black woman who has poisoned her lover and bitten off his penis in repayment for his having locked her in a small hotel room, used her sexually for an extended period, and refused to allow her even to comb her hair. Those who read the novel as male-bashing clearly are not attuned to the larger issues of personal freedom, sexual choice, and identity that Jones pursues in the work.

Jones's next fictional venture was in short stories. She published a collection titled *White Rat* in 1977. As in the blues, Jones's characters in "White Rat," "Asylum," "Jevata," and other stories do not transcend the realities of their lives; instead, they struggle to survive in a paternalistic, racist, and capitalistically exploitive social order. Jones extended this thematic emphasis to "Ravenna," an uncollected short story that appeared nine years later in *Obsidian,* 1, No. 1 & 2 (Spring–Summer 1986). Turning her attention to poetry, she published *Song for Anninho,* a long narrative poem celebrating Afro-Brazilian heroes and heroines, in 1981. A second volume of poetry, *The Hermit-Woman,* appeared in 1983 and a third, *Zarque and Other Poems,* in 1985; "Zarque" is another of Jones's long narrative poems.

For reasons many suspect had to do with a personal relationship and incidents surrounding it at the University of Michigan, Jones mysteriously disappeared in February 1985. Some speculated that she moved to the Netherlands, but little was heard of her on a widespread basis for the next several years. She resurfaced in 1991 with the publication of *Liberating Voices,* a study of the influence of African American oral traditions on black creativity. Among the many authors whose works she treats are Sterling Brown, Zora Neale Hurston, Langston Hughes, Jean Toomer, Alice Walker, Ralph Ellison, Toni Morrison, and Amiri Baraka. Her voice in criticism as well as in creative writing adds a distinctive flavor to an already rich literature.

❖❖❖

For discussion of Jones's works, see Melvin Dixon, *Ride Out the Wilderness: Geography and Identity in Afro-American Literature* (1987); Mari Evans, ed., *Black Women Writers 1950–1980: A Critical Evaluation* (1984); *Callaloo* 16 (October 1982); Claudia Tate, ed., *Black Women Writers at Work* (1983); Claudia Tate, "*Corregidora:* Ursa's Blues Medley," *Black American Literature Forum* 13 (Fall 1979); Keith E. Byerman, *Fingering the Jagged Grain: Tradition and Form in Recent Black Fiction* (1985); Michael Harper, "Gayl Jones: An Interview," in *Chant of Saints: A Gathering of Afro-American Literature, Art, and Scholarship* (1979) eds. Michael S. Harper and Robert B. Stept; Janice Harris, "Gayl Jones' *Corregidora,*" *Frontiers: A Journal of Women Studies* 5 (Fall 1980).

Ravenna

Her parents had adopted her because Ravenna was a beautiful child, a joy to look at. She was beige with an oval face and her hair (when it was straightened) was as silky and as black as a raven. She seemed a perfect girl—beautiful, well-behaved.

At the time of the adoption there was another girl. Both girls were ten. (They wondered how Ravenna got so old before anyone wanted her.) But the other girl was not a beauty. She was black in the days when black wasn't considered beautiful. And in all honesty, her face looked like a frog's. Though if she'd been lemon yellow or even beige that feature might have been quietly overlooked. She was in the same room with Ravenna, hiding against the wing of a table.

The mother was so taken with Ravenna that she hadn't noticed the other child, but the father noticed her.

"Why don't we adopt *her?*" asked the father.

"Oh no," she whispered, then drew him into the hall where the girls couldn't hear. "Ravenna's as beautiful as a peacock. I want a child who'd be a joy to look at."

"I meant them both. Why don't we adopt them both?"

"We couldn't afford them both. We'd have to choose."

"Ravenna will get someone to want her, but the other girl . . ."

"How can you be so? I want a child to be a joy."

"Suppose we didn't have this choice?" he asked.

Why was he testing her so, she felt herself as good as anyone, better than most. She was not an evil woman. She was not selfish. But she wanted Ravenna. She wanted a pretty child. If she couldn't have her *own.*

"I want a child who's a joy."

"We'll ask for them both."

"But darling think about it. The little . . ." She started to say "little monster." "The other one will always grow up in the shadow of her sister's beauty. Grow up perverse or jealous. She'll get no smiles."

"We'd treat them both as equals."

"I don't mean *us.* Of course we'd treat them equally. But strangers. She'll get no smiles from strangers. And when they're together, darling—the other—I didn't ask her name, will shrink against the smiles her sister gets. I want a child who's a joy."

He thought of it for a moment, and though he would have had the heart for them both, he thought of his wife's arguments, and of strangers.

"Okay," he said.

They went back into the playroom where the two girls were. His wife took Ravenna's hands, and played with her. He lingered by the table where the other child was hiding. He gave her all the smiles he could. But she wouldn't take the smiles. She rolled her eyes at him, hugged the wing of the table. Still he lingered near her while the wife and Ravenna played and enjoyed each other.

He wondered at his own motive of affection for the funny-looking child. He himself had been a so-called ugly child, but he had grown up handsome, surprising everyone—even himself.

Perhaps this child wouldn't provide them with any such surprise, but he was drawn to her.

He smiled at her again. She looked at him with dignified indifference. He wondered where she had come by that expression.

"Do you want to go for ice cream?" he asked.

"Are you telling me the truth?" She looked at him suspiciously, her eyes on him, dark, round, protruding.

"I'm telling the truth," he said. "We can go downstairs to the cafeteria and I'll buy you ice cream."

Her eyes lit up. He couldn't imagine them bigger, but they were. He knew she was an intelligent child. He knew she understood.

His wife and Ravenna were sitting in chairs by the window holding hands and laughing.

"What's your name?"

"René."

"Come on, René."

He held his hand out. She took it.

"Where are you going?" his wife asked when they were at the door.

"To get ice cream."

At first she frowned because he hadn't invited them along, and she didn't want to make Ravenna unhappy. "We'll get some later," she told her. Then she smiled at the other girl, but it was a forced smile.

At the cafeteria table, they ate ice cream. The girl kept watching him.

"Are you adopting Ravenna?" she asked.

"I think we're going to."

"Yes you are. I heard you say you were."

He wanted to promise something. He wanted to make some suggestion. He thought of his wife's forced smile.

"I'll come and visit you," he said. That was the best he could do.

"No you won't."

"Why won't I if I said I would?"

She shrugged, swallowed ice cream.

"Because."

"Because?"

She frowned. She struck the table, impatient with his ignorance.

"I'll come as often as I can," he promised.

"Well, if it takes you all that long," she said.

"If it takes me all that long? For what?"

"To look at me good."

GLORIA NAYLOR

(1950–)

Gloria Naylor has stacked up an impressive literary debut, with four novels published over the past fifteen years. Her treatment of women's issues and of themes that plague black communities generally, such as middle-class notions of success, has earned her a reputation as a writer who is willing to go where few will tread. In her naming of lesbian love and the homophobia in African American communities that surfaces when it appears, she joins Alice Walker in suggesting that black people are not monolithic in their sexual preferences or superbly moral in their judgments of others. She has been willing to treat the pain involved in the excesses of success, as well as the contentment in living peacefully and harmoniously with the natural environment.

Naylor was born in New York City on January 25, 1950, to Alberta McAlpin and Roosevelt Naylor, who, like many blacks of their era, had migrated from the South, specifically Robinsonville, Mississippi; there are two other daughters in the family. Naylor grew up in Queens. Her mother inspired in her a love for reading by taking her to the New York Public Library, and the stories she told of Robinsonville would serve to texture Naylor's works. Her mother also gave her her first diary, in an effort to inspire her shy daughter to use words as a medium of expression. For ten years, beginning when she was fifteen, Naylor was a Jehovah's Witness evangelist. She left that work at the age of twenty-five to enter Brooklyn's Medgar Evers College; she planned to become a nurse. However, she transferred to Brooklyn College, where she earned a B.A. in English in 1981. Her graduation was simultaneous with the completion of the manuscript for her first novel, *The Women of Brewster Place* (1982). In 1983, she earned an M.A. in Afro-American studies from Yale University. She has held a position as writer-in-residence at George Washington University in Washington, D.C., and has taught at Cummington (Massachusetts) Community of the Arts, as well as at New York University and Boston University.

The Women of Brewster Place (1982) is structured in the form of a prologue ("Dawn"), seven stories, and an epilogue ("Dusk"), with a central character, Mattie Michael, who appears in all the sketches. Naylor explores the lives of women who have been abused by husbands, fathers, and lovers, and she explores the homophobia that accompanies lesbian love as well as the problem of reconciling sexual identity for women involved in such relationships. Literally locked into a dead-end street in some northern urban area, the women of Brewster Place try to find new beginnings in an environment that was designed to perpetuate their deaths. In a dream sequence at the end of the book, Naylor effects a togetherness and health that are never possible in the reality of these women's lives. Richly symbolic and rooted in African American folk and historical traditions, the book was very well received when it appeared, and it continues to be a mainstay in African American literature and women's studies courses. The novel won the American Book Award for First Fiction in 1983. During the 1985–86 television season, it was produced for PBS's "American Playhouse"; Naylor wrote the script. In 1989, it was produced as an ABC television miniseries starring Oprah Winfrey, Cicely Tyson, Jackee, and Robin Givens.

In 1985, Naylor published *Linden Hills,* a novel exploring a middle-class northern neighborhood. The women here are even more repressed than those in *Brewster Place,* with two committing suicide and another being locked in a basement that previously served as a morgue. The bleakness of these women's lives and the sinister plan for the African American paradise called Linden Hills by a succession of Luther Nedeeds, the founder and his descendants, make it difficult to find reasons for optimism in the text. In contrast to her first work, Naylor focuses on two young black men, through whose adventures we witness the despair of this community. The only hope for this Dantesque hell is in the sensitivity that these young men bring to their despairing neighbors.

Two other significant events occurred in Naylor's life in 1985. First, together with Toni Morrison, she published "Conversation" in the *Southern Review* in July. In this piece, the two writers discuss their roles as writers, the burdens of being role models, and the consequences of creating characters not consistent with the public's perceptions of what those characters should or should not be. Second, during the fall of 1985, Naylor served as a United States Information Agency cultural exchange lecturer in India.

Naylor's *Mama Day* (1988), a carefully embroidered and richly textured novel, focuses on a mythical island somewhere off the coast of Georgia and South Carolina. The story portrays the consequences for those who do not believe in extranatural powers. Willow Springs is the home of Mama Day, conjure woman extraordinaire, who is a descendant of Sapphira Wade, the island's original conjure woman and foremother of the current Day family. Mama Day uses her power to protect her niece Cocoa from the evils that surround her and to ensure that the Day line will continue into the twenty-first century with a powerful woman as the keeper of its special traditions. Naylor alternates narrative voices in the novel between Cocoa, her husband George, and an omniscient voice that follows the actions of Mama Day. The book has been consistently well received and praised for its narrative voice as well as its balanced development of a love relationship between a black man and a black woman.

Naylor has turned her hand to essay writing on several occasions and has published articles in African American and mainstream magazines such as *Essence, Ms., Publishers Weekly, People,* and *Life.* She also has written for the *New York Times* (as a guest columnist in 1986). Her critical essay "Love and Sex in the Afro-American Novel" (*Yale Review,* 1988) has been widely cited.

Ever on the lecture circuit, Naylor nonetheless takes time to write. She published *Bailey's Cafe,* a novel that reveals George's (from *Mama Day*) origins as an orphan, in 1992. It continues her pattern of referring to characters from previous novels in later ones.

❖❖❖

Critical studies of Naylor's works are more readily available as theses and dissertations than as published volumes. Among those available are Linda Wagner-Martin, "Quilting in Gloria Naylor's *Mama Day,*" *Notes on Contemporary Literature* 18 (1988); G. Michelle Collins, "There Where We Are Not: The Magical Real in *Beloved* and *Mama Day,*" *Southern Review* 24 (1988); Larry Andrews, "Black Sisterhood in Gloria Naylor's Novels," *CLA Journal* 33 (1989); Mary F. Sisney, "The View from the Outside: Black Novels of Manner," in *Reading and Writing Women's Lives: A Study of the Novel of Manners,* ed. Bege K. Bowers and Barbara Brothers (1990); Barbara Christian, "Gloria Naylor's Geography: Community, Class, and Patriarchy in *The Women of Brewster Place* and *Linden Hills,*" in *Reading Black, Reading Feminist,* ed. Henry Louis Gates, Jr. (1990).

FROM *Mama Day*

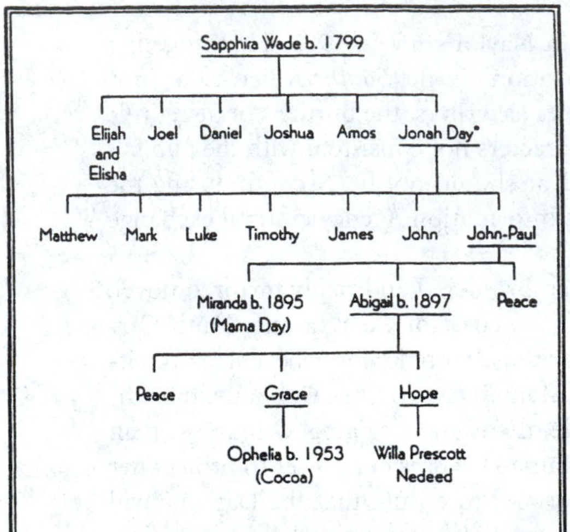

*"God rested on the seventh day and so would she." Hence, the family's last name.

Tuesday, 3rd Day August, 1819

Sold to Mister Bascombe Wade of Willow Springs, one negress answering to the name Sapphira. Age 20. Pure African stock. Limbs and teeth sound. All warranty against the vices and maladies prescribed by law do not hold forth; purchaser being in full knowledge—and affixing signature in witness thereof—that said Sapphira is half prime, inflicted with sullenness and entertains a bilious nature, having resisted under reasonable chastisement the performance of field or domestic labour. Has served on occasion in the capacity of midwife and nurse, not without extreme mischief and suspicions of delving in witchcraft.

Conditions of Sale
one-half gold tender, one-half goods in kind.
Final.

Willow Springs. Everybody knows but nobody talks about the legend of Sapphira Wade. A true conjure woman: satin black, biscuit cream, red as Georgia clay: depending upon which of us takes a mind to her. She could walk through a lightning storm without being touched; grab a bolt of lightning in the palm of her hand; use the heat of lightning to start the kindling going under her medicine pot: depending upon which of us takes a mind to her. She turned the moon into salve, the stars into a swaddling cloth, and healed the wounds of every creature walking up on two or down on four. It ain't about right or wrong, truth or lies; it's about a slave woman who brought a whole new meaning to both them words, soon as you cross over here from beyond the bridge. And somehow, some way, it happened in 1823: she smothered Bascombe Wade in his very bed and lived to tell the story for a thousand days. 1823: married Bascombe Wade, bore him seven sons in just a thousand days, to put a dagger through his kidney and escape the hangman's noose, laughing in a burst of flames. 1823: persuaded Bascombe Wade in a thousand days to deed all his slaves every inch of land in Willow Springs, poisoned him for his trouble, to go on and bear seven sons—by person or persons unknown. Mixing it all together and keeping everything that done shifted down through the holes of time, you end up with the death of Bascombe Wade (there's his tombstone right out by Chevy's Pass), the deeds to our land (all marked back to the very year), and seven sons (ain't Miss Abigail and Mama Day the granddaughters of that seventh boy?). The wild card in all this is the thousand days, and we guess if we put our heads together we'd come up with something—which ain't possible since Sapphira Wade don't live in the part of our memory we can use to form words.

But ain't a soul in Willow Springs don't know that little dark girls, hair all braided up with colored twine, got their "18 & 23's coming down" when they lean too long over them back yard fences, laughing at the antics of little dark boys who got the nerve to be "breathing 18 & 23" with mother's milk still on their tongues. And if she leans there just a mite too long or grins a bit too wide, it's gonna bring a holler straight through the dusty screen door. "Get your bow-legged self 'way from my fence, Johnny Blue. Won't be no 'early 18 & 23's' coming here for me to rock. I'm still raising her." Yes, the *name* Sapphira Wade is never breathed out of a single mouth in Willow

Springs. But who don't know that old twisted-lip manager at the Sheraton Hotel beyond the bridge, offering Winky Browne only twelve dollars for his whole boatload of crawdaddies—"tried to 18 & 23 him," if he tried to do a thing? We all sitting here, a hop, skip, and one Christmas left before the year 2000, and ain't nobody told him niggers can read now? Like the menus in his restaurant don't say a handful of crawdaddies sprinkled over a little bowl of crushed ice is almost twelve dollars? Call it shrimp cocktail, or whatever he want—we can count, too. And the price of everything that swims, crawls, or lays at the bottom of The Sound went up in 1985, during the season we had that "18 & 23 summer" and the bridge blew down. Folks didn't take their lives in their hands out there in that treacherous water just to be doing it—ain't that much 18 & 23 in the world.

But that old hotel manager don't make no never mind. He's the least of what we done had to deal with here in Willow Springs. Malaria. Union soldiers. Sandy soil. Two big depressions. Hurricanes. Not to mention these new real estate developers who think we gonna sell our shore land just because we ain't fool enough to live there. Started coming over here in the early '90s, talking "vacation paradise," talking "pic-ture-ess." Like Winky said, we'd have to pick their ass out the bottom of the marsh first hurricane blow through here again. See, they just thinking about building where they ain't got no state taxes—never been and never will be, 'cause Willow Springs ain't in no state. Georgia and South Carolina done tried, though—been trying since right after the Civil War to prove that Willow Springs belong to one or the other of them. Look on any of them old maps they hurried and drew up soon as the Union soldiers pulled out and you can see that the only thing connects us to the mainland is a bridge—and even that gotta be rebuilt after every big storm. (They was talking about steel and concrete way back, but since Georgia and South Carolina couldn't claim the taxes, nobody wanted to shell out for the work. So we rebuild it ourselves when need be, and build it how we need it—strong enough to last till the next big wind. Only need a steel and concrete bridge once every seventy years or so. Wood and pitch is a tenth of the cost and serves us a good sixty-nine years—matter of simple arithmetic.) But anyways, all forty-nine square miles curves like a bow, stretching toward Georgia on the south end and South Carolina on the north, and right smack in the middle where each foot of our bridge sits is the dividing line between them two states.

So who it belong to? It belongs to us—clean and simple. And it belonged to our daddies, and our daddies before them, and them too—who at one time all belonged to Bascombe Wade. And when they tried to trace him and how he got it, found out he wasn't even American. Was Norway-born or something, and the land had been sitting in his family over there in Europe since it got explored and claimed by the Vikings—imagine that. So thanks to the conjuring of Sapphira Wade we got it from Norway or theres about, and if taxes owed, it's owed to them. But ain't no Vikings or anybody else from over in Europe come to us with the foolishness that them folks out of Columbia and Atlanta come with—we was being un-American. And the way we saw it, America ain't entered the question at all when it come to our land: Sapphira was African-born, Bascombe Wade was from Norway, and it was the 18 & 23'ing that went down between them two put deeds in our hands. And we wasn't even Americans when we got it—was slaves. And the laws about slaves not owning nothing in Georgia and South Carolina don't apply, 'cause the land wasn't then—and isn't now—in either of them places. When there was lots of cotton here, and we baled it up and sold it beyond the bridge, we paid our taxes to the U.S. of A. And we keeps account of all the fishing that's done and sold beyond the bridge, all the little truck farming. And later when we had to go over there to work or our children went, we paid taxes out of them earnings. We pay taxes on the telephone lines and electrical wires run over The Sound. Ain't nobody here about breaking the law. But Georgia and South Carolina ain't seeing the shine off a penny for our land, our homes, our roads, or our bridge. Well, they fought each other up to the Supreme Court about the whole matter, and it came to a draw. We guess they got so tired out from that, they decided to leave us be—until them developers started swarming over here like sand flies at a Sunday picnic.

Sure, we coulda used the money and weren't using the land. But like Mama Day told 'em (we knew to send 'em straight over there to her and Miss Abigail), they didn't come huffing and sweating all this way in them dark gaberdine suits if they didn't think our land could make them a bundle of money, and the way we saw it, there was enough land—shoreline, that is—to make us all pretty comfortable. And calculating on the basis of all them fancy plans they had in mind, a million an acre wasn't asking too much. Flap, flap, flap—Lord, didn't them jaws and silk ties move in the wind. The land wouldn't be worth that if they couldn't *build* on it. Yes, suh, she told 'em, and they couldn't build on it unless we *sold* it. So we get ours now, and they get theirs later. You shoulda seen them coattails flapping back across The Sound with all their lies about "community uplift" and "better jobs." 'Cause it weren't about no them now and us later—was them now and us never. Hadn't we seen it happen back in the '80s on St. Helena, Daufuskie, and St. John's? And before that in the '60s on Hilton Head? Got them folks' land, built fences around it first thing, and then brought in all the builders and high-paid managers from mainside—ain't nobody on them islands benefited. And the only dark faces you see now in them "vacation paradises" is the ones cleaning the toilets and cutting the grass. On their own land, mind you, their own land. Weren't gonna happen in Willow Springs. 'Cause if Mama Day say no, everybody say no. There's 18 & 23, and there's 18 & 23—and nobody was gonna trifle with Mama Day's, 'cause she know how to use it—her being a direct descendant of Sapphira Wade, piled on the fact of springing from the seventh son of a seventh son—uh, uh. Mama Day say no, everybody say no. No point in making a pile of money to be guaranteed the new moon will see you scratching at fleas you don't have, or rolling in the marsh like a mud turtle. And if some was waiting for her to die, they had a long wait. She says she ain't gonna. And when you think about it, to show up in one century, make it all the way through the next, and have a toe inching over into the one approaching *is* about as close to eternity anybody can come.

Well, them developers upped the price and changed the plans, changed the plans and upped the price, till it got to be a game with us. Winky bought a motorboat with what they offered him back in 1987, turned it in for a cabin cruiser two years later, and says he expects to be able to afford a yacht with the news that's waiting in the mail this year. Parris went from a new shingle roof to a split-level ranch and is making his way toward adding a swimming pool and greenhouse. But when all the laughing's done, it's the principle that remains. And we done learned that anything coming from beyond the bridge gotta be viewed real, real careful. Look what happened when Reema's boy—the one with the pear-shaped head—came hauling himself back from one of those fancy colleges mainside, dragging his notebooks and tape recorder and a funny way of curling up his lip and clicking his teeth, all excited and determined to put Willow Springs on the map.

We was polite enough—Reema always was a little addle-brained—so you couldn't blame the boy for not remembering that part of Willow Spring's problems was that it got put on some maps right after the War Between the States. And then when he went around asking us about 18 & 23, there weren't nothing to do but take pity on him as he rattled on about "ethnography," "unique speech patterns," "cultural preservation," and whatever else he seemed to be getting so much pleasure out of while talking into his little gray machine. He was all over the place—What 18 & 23 mean? What 18 & 23 mean? And we all told him the God-honest truth: it was just our way of saying something. Winky was awful, though, he even spit tobacco juice for him. Sat on his porch all day, chewing up the boy's Red Devil premium and spitting so the machine could pick it up. There was enough fun in that to take us through the fall and winter when he had hauled himself back over the Sound to wherever he was getting what was supposed to be passing for an education. And he sent everybody he'd talked to copies of the book he wrote, bound all nice with our name and his signed on the first page. We couldn't hold Reema down, she was so proud. It's a good thing she didn't read it. None of us made it much through the introduction, but that said it all: you see, he had come to the conclusion after "extensive field work" (ain't never picked a ball of cotton or head of lettuce in his life—Reema spoiled him silly), but he done still made it to the conclusion that 18 & 23 wasn't 18 & 23 at all—was really 81 & 32, which just so happened to be the lines of longitude and latitude marking off where Willow Springs sits on the map. And we were just so damned dumb that we turned the whole thing around.

Not that he called it being dumb, mind you, called it "asserting our cultural identity," "inverting hostile social and political parameters." 'Cause, see, being we was brought here as slaves, we had no choice but to look at everything upside-down. And then being that we was isolated off here on this island, everybody else in the country went on learning good English and calling things what they really was—in the dictionary and all that—while we kept on calling things ass-backwards. And he thought that was just so wonderful and marvelous, etcetera, etcetera . . . Well, after that crate of books came here, if anybody had any doubts about what them developers was up to, if there was just a tinge of seriousness behind them jokes about the motorboats and swimming pools that could be gotten from selling a piece of land, them books squashed it. The people who ran the type of schools that could turn our children into raving lunatics—and then put his picture on the back of the book so we couldn't even deny it was him—didn't mean us a speck of good.

If the boy wanted to know what 18 & 23 meant, why didn't he just ask? When he was running around sticking that machine in everybody's face, we was sitting right here—every one of us—and him being one of Reema's, we woulda obliged him. He coulda asked Cloris about the curve in her spine that came from the planting season when their mule broke its leg, and she took up the reins and kept pulling the plow with her own back. Winky woulda told him about the hot tar that took out the corner of his right eye the summer we had only seven days to rebuild the bridge so the few crops we had left after the storm could be gotten over before rot sat in. Anybody woulda carried him through the fields we had to stop farming back in the '80s to take outside jobs—washing cars, carrying groceries, cleaning house—anything—'cause it was leave the land or lose it during the Silent Depression. Had more folks sleeping in city streets and banks foreclosing on farms than in the Great Depression before that.

Naw, he didn't really want to know what 18 & 23 meant, or he woulda asked. He woulda asked right off where Miss Abigail Day was staying, so we coulda sent him down the main road to that little yellow house where she used to live. And she woulda given him a tall glass of ice water or some cinnamon tea as he heard about Peace dying young, then Hope and Peace again. But there was the child of Grace—the grandchild, a girl who went mainside, like him, and did real well. Was living outside of Charleston now with her husband and two boys. So she visits a lot more often than she did when she was up in New York. And she probably woulda pulled out that old photo album, so he coulda seen some pictures of her grandchild, Cocoa, and then Cocoa's mama, Grace. And Miss Abigail flips right through to the beautiful one of Grace resting in her satin-lined coffin. And as she walks him back out to the front porch and points him across the road to a silver trailer where her sister, Miranda, lives, she tells him to grab up and chew a few sprigs of mint growing at the foot of the steps—it'll help kill his thirst in the hot sun. And if he'd known enough to do just that, thirsty or not, he'd know when he got to that silver trailer to stand back a distance calling *Mama, Mama Day,* to wait for her to come out and beckon him near.

He'da told her he been sent by Miss Abigail and so, more likely than not, she lets him in. And he hears again about the child of Grace, her grandniece, who went mainside, like him, and did real well. Was living outside of Charleston now with her husband and two boys. So she visits a lot more often than she did when she was up in New York. Cocoa is like her very own, Mama Day tells him, since she never had no children.

And with him carrying that whiff of mint on his breath, she surely woulda walked him out to the side yard, facing that patch of dogwood, to say she has to end the visit a little short 'cause she has some gardening to do in the other place. And if he'd had the sense to offer to follow her just a bit of the way—then and only then—he hears about that summer fourteen years ago when Cocoa came visiting from New York with her first husband. Yes, she tells him, there was a first husband—a stone city boy. How his name was George. But how Cocoa left, and he stayed. How it was the year of the last big storm that blew her pecan trees down and even caved in the roof of the other place. And she woulda stopped him from walking just by a patch of oak: she reaches up, takes a bit of moss for him to put in them closed leather shoes—they're probably sweating his feet something terrible, she tells him. And he's to sit on the ground, right there, to untie his shoes and stick in the moss. And then he'd see through the low bush that old graveyard just down the slope. And when he looks back up, she woulda disappeared through the trees; but he's to keep pushing the moss in them shoes and go on down to that graveyard where he'll find buried Grace, Hope, Peace, and Peace again. Then a little ways off a grouping of seven old graves, and a little ways off seven older again. All circled by them live oaks and hanging moss, over a rise from the tip of The Sound.

Everything he needed to know coulda been heard from that yellow house to that silver trailer to that graveyard. Be too late for him to go that route now, since Miss Abigail's been dead for over nine years. Still, there's an easier way. He could just watch Cocoa any one of these times she comes in from Charleston. She goes straight to Miss Abigail's to air out the rooms and unpack her bags, then she's across the road to call out at Mama Day, who's gonna come to the door of the trailer and wave as Cocoa heads on through the patch of dogwoods to that oak grove. She stops and puts a bit of moss in her open-toe sandals, then goes on past those graves to a spot just down the rise toward The Sound, a little bit south of that circle of oaks. And if he was patient and stayed off a little ways, he'd realize she was there to meet up with her first husband so they could talk about that summer fourteen years ago when she left, but he stayed. And as her and George are there together for a good two hours or so—neither one saying a word—Reema's boy coulda heard from them everything there was to tell about 18 & 23.

But on second thought, someone who didn't know how to ask wouldn't know how to listen. And he coulda listened to them the way you been listening to us right now. Think about it: ain't nobody really talking to you. We're sitting here in Willow Springs, and you're God-knows-where. It's August 1999—ain't but a slim chance it's the same season where you are. Uh, huh, listen. Really listen this time: the only voice is your own. But you done just heard about the legend of Saphira Wade, though nobody here breathes her name. You done heard it the way we know it, sitting on our porches and shelling June peas, quieting the midnight cough of a baby, taking apart the engine of a car—you done heard it without a single living soul really saying a word. Pity, though, Reema's boy couldn't listen, like you, to Cocoa and George down by them oaks—or he woulda left here with quite a story.

bell hooks

(1952–)

Since bell hooks is a public intellectual, she wants to address as many people as possible. Through her writing, teaching, and lecturing, she confronts the major cultural issues of the day—that is, race, gender, and self-realization. Although she is a committed feminist, she is also a maverick, hence the reader is never sure what she is going to say in her pursuit of truth and justice. She is a prolific writer who has added another personal voice to the black autobiographical intellectual tradition that includes, among others, Harriet Jacobs, Anna Julia Cooper, June Jordan, James Baldwin, and Gerald Early. She is one of the most brilliant American practitioners of cultural studies, the discipline that investigates cultural production—a civilization's arts, beliefs, and institutions—in light of history and social analysis.

bell hooks was born Gloria Watkins on September 25, 1952, in Hopkinsville, Kentucky. When she published a small book of poems *And There We Went* in 1978, she took on the pseudonym bell hooks, the name of her great-grandmother on her mother's side. She associates the name hooks with being a strong woman who speaks her mind. Speaking of her pseudonym in *Talking Back, thinking feminist, thinking black* (1989), she says,

> bell hooks as I came to know her through sharing of family history, as I dreamed and invented her, became a symbol of what I could become, all that my parents had hoped little Gloria would never be. Gloria was to have been a sweet southern girl, quiet, obedient, pleasing. She was not to have that wild streak that characterized women on my mother's side.

After living in rural Kentucky for nineteen years, she went to Stanford University, graduating in 1974. She received her Ph.D. in English from the University of California at Santa Cruz in 1983. Since then, she has taught at Yale University and is currently Distinguished Professor of English at City College in New York. Among her books are *Ain't I a Woman* (1981), *Feminist Theory: from margin to center* (1984), *Yearning: race, gender, and cultural politics* (1990), and *Black Looks: race and representation* (1992).

In *Breaking Bread* (1991), the black philosopher Cornel West has said that hooks "is a Black feminist—or womanist—writer without being a separatist activist; namely, she puts the flowering of Black woman's possibility and potentiality at the center of her work yet she refuses to view this flowering apart from the freedom of Black men." In others words, bell hooks is her own woman.

❖❖❖

Good places to learn about hooks are her own books *Talking Back, thinking feminist, thinking black* (1989) and *Breaking Bread* (1991) with Cornel West.

Black Women: Shaping Feminist Theory

Feminism in the United States has never emerged from the women who are most victimized by sexist oppression; women who are daily beaten down, mentally, physically, and spiritually—women who are powerless to change their condition in life. They are a silent majority. A mark of their victimization is that they accept their lot in life without visible question, without organized protest, without collective anger or rage. Betty Friedan's *The Feminine Mystique* is still heralded as having paved the way for contemporary feminist movement—it was written as if these women did not exist. Friedan's famous phrase, "the problem that has no name," often quoted to describe the condition of women in this society, actually referred to the plight of a select group of college-educated, middle and upper class, married white women—housewives bored with leisure, with the home, with children, with buying products, who wanted more out of life. Friedan concludes her first chapter by stating: "We can no longer ignore that voice within women that says: 'I want something more than my husband and my children and my house.'" That "more" she defined as careers. She did not discuss who would be called in to take care of the children and maintain the home if more women like herself were freed from their house labor and given equal access with white men to the professions. She did not speak of the needs of women without men, without children, without homes. She ignored the existence of all non-white women and poor white women. She did not tell readers whether it was more fulfilling to be a maid, a babysitter, a factory worker, a clerk, or a prostitute, than to be a leisure class housewife.

She made her plight and the plight of white women like herself synonymous with a condition affecting all American women. In so doing, she deflected attention away from her classism, her racism, her sexist attitudes towards the masses of American women. In the context of her book, Friedan makes clear that the women she saw as victimized by sexism were college-educated, white women who were compelled by sexist conditioning to remain in the home. She contends:

> It is urgent to understand how the very condition of being a housewife can create a sense of emptiness, non-existence, nothingness in women. There are aspects of the housewife role that make it almost impossible for a woman of adult intelligence to retain a sense of human identity, the firm core of self or "I" without which a human being, man or woman, is not truly alive. For women of ability, in America today, I am convinced that there is something about the housewife state itself that is dangerous.

Specific problems and dilemmas of leisure class white housewives were real concerns that merited consideration and change but they were not the pressing political concerns of masses of women. Masses of women were concerned about economic survival, ethnic and racial discrimination, etc. When Friedan wrote *The Feminine Mystique,* more than one third of all women were in the work force. Although many women longed to be housewives, only women with leisure time and money could actually shape their identities on the model of the feminine mystique. They were women who, in Friedan's words, were "told by the most advanced thinkers of our time to go back and live their lives as if they were Noras, restricted to the doll's house by Victorian prejudices."

From her early writing, it appears that Friedan never wondered whether or not the plight of college-educated, white housewives was an adequate reference point by which to gauge the impact of sexism or sexist oppression on the lives of women in American society. Nor did she move beyond her own life experience to acquire an expanded perspective on the lives of women in the United States. I say this not to discredit her work. It remains a useful discussion of the impact of sexist discrimination on a select group of women. Examined from a different perspective, it can also be seen as a case study of narcissism, insensitivity, sentimentality, and self-indulgence which reaches its peak when Friedan, in a chapter titled "Progressive Dehumanization," makes a comparison between the psychological effects of isolation on white housewives and the impact of confinement on the self-concept of prisoners in Nazi concentration camps.

Friedan was a principal shaper of contemporary feminist thought. Significantly, the one-dimensional perspective on women's reality presented in her book became a marked feature of the contemporary feminist movement. Like Friedan before them, white women who dominate feminist discourse today rarely question whether or not their perspective on women's reality is true to the lived experiences of women as a collective group. Nor are they aware of the extent to which their perspectives reflect race and class biases, although there has been a greater awareness of biases in recent years. Racism abounds in the writings of white feminists, reinforcing white supremacy and negating the possibility that women will bond politically across ethnic and racial boundaries. Past feminist refusal to draw attention to and attack racial hierarchies suppressed the link between race and class. Yet class structure in American society has been shaped by the racial politic of white supremacy; it is only by analyzing racism and its function in capitalist society that a thorough understanding of class relationships can emerge. Class struggle is inextricably bound to the struggle to end racism. Urging women to explore the full implication of class in an early essay, "The Last Straw," Rita Mae Brown explained:

> Class is much more than Marx's definition of relationship to the means of production. Class involves your behavior, your basic assumptions about life. Your experience (determined by your class) validates those assumptions, how you are taught to behave, what you expect from yourself and from others, your concept of a future, how you understand problems and solve them, how you think, feel, act. It is these behavioral patterns that middle class women resist recognizing although they may be perfectly willing to accept class in Marxist terms, a neat trick that helps them avoid really dealing with class behavior and changing that behavior in themselves. It is these behavioral patterns which must be recognized, understood, and changed.

White women who dominate feminist discourse, who for the most part make and articulate feminist theory, have little or no understanding of white supremacy as a racial politic, of the psychological impact of class, of their political status within a racist, sexist, capitalist state.

It is this lack of awareness that, for example, leads Leah Fritz to write in *Dreamers and Dealers,* a discussion of the current women's movement published in 1979:

> Women's suffering under sexist tyranny is a common bond among all women, transcending the particulars of the different forms that tyranny takes. *Suffering cannot be measured and compared quantitatively.* Is the enforced idleness and vacuity of a "rich" woman, which leads her to madness and/or suicide, greater or less than the suffering of a poor woman who barely survives on welfare but retains somehow her spirit? There is no way to measure such difference, but should these two women survey each other without the screen of patriarchal class, they may find a commonality in the fact that they are both oppressed, both miserable.

Fritz's statement is another example of wishful thinking, as well as the conscious mystification of social divisions between women, that has characterized much feminist expression. While it is evident that many women suffer from sexist tyranny, there is little indication that this forges "a common bond among all women." There is much evidence substantiating the reality that race and class identity creates differences in quality of life, social status, and lifestyle that take precedence over the common experience women share—differences which are rarely transcended. The motives of materially privileged, educated, white women with a variety of career and lifestyle options available to them must be questioned when they insist that "suffering cannot be measured." Fritz is by no means the first white feminist to make this statement. It is a statement that I have never heard a poor woman of any race make. Although there is much I would take issue with in Benjamin Barber's critique of the women's movement, *Liberating Feminism,* I agree with his assertion:

> Suffering is not necessarily a fixed and universal experience that can be measured by a single rod: it is related to situations, needs, and aspirations. But there must be some historical and political parameters for the use of the term so that political priorities can be established and different forms and degrees of suffering can be given the most attention.

A central tenet of modern feminist thought has been the assertion that "all women are oppressed." This assertion implies that women share a common lot, that factors like class, race, religion, sexual preference, etc. do not create a diversity of experience that determines the extent to which sexism will be an oppressive force in the lives of individual women. Sexism as a system of domination is institutionalized but it has never determined in an absolute way the fate of all women in this society. Being oppressed means the *absence of choices.* It is the primary point of contact between the oppressed and the oppressor. Many women in this society do have choices, (as inadequate as they are) therefore exploitation and discrimination are words that more accurately describe the lot of women collectively in the United States. Many women do not join organized resistance against sexism precisely because sexism has not meant an absolute lack of choices. They may know they are discriminated against on the basis of sex, but they do not equate this with oppression. Under capitalism, patriarchy is structured so that sexism restricts women's behavior in some realms even as freedom from limitations is allowed in other spheres. The absence of extreme restrictions leads many women to ignore the areas in which they are exploited or discriminated against; it may even lead them to imagine that no women are oppressed.

There are oppressed women in the United States, and it is both appropriate and necessary that we speak against such oppression. French feminist Christine Delphy makes the point in her essay, "For a Materialist Feminism," that the use of the term oppression is important because it places feminist struggle in a radical political framework:

> The rebirth of feminism coincided with the use of the term "oppression." The ruling ideology, i.e. common sense, daily speech, does not speak about oppression but about a "feminine condition." It refers back to a naturalist explanation: to a constraint of nature, exterior reality out of reach and not modifiable by human action. The term "oppression," on the contrary, refers back to a choice, an explanation, a situation that is political. "Oppression" and "social oppression" are therefore synonyms or rather social oppression is a redundance: the notion of a political origin, i.e. social, is an integral part of the concept of oppression.

However, feminist emphasis on "common oppression" in the United States was less a strategy for politicization than an appropriation by conservative and liberal women of a radical political vocabulary that masked the extent to which they shaped the movement so that it addressed and promoted their class interests.

Although the impulse towards unity and empathy that informed the notion of common oppression was directed at building solidarity, slogans like "organize around your own oppression" provided the excuse many privileged women needed to ignore the differences between their social status and the status of masses of women. It was a mark of race and class privilege, as well as the expression of freedom from the many constraints sexism places on working class women, that middle class white women were able to make their interests the primary focus of feminist movement and employ a rhetoric of commonality that made their condition synonymous with "oppression." Who was there to demand a change in vocabulary? What other group of women in the United States had the same access to universities, publishing houses, mass media, money? Had middle class black women begun a movement in which they had labeled themselves "oppressed," no one would have taken them seriously. Had they established public forums and given speeches about their "oppression," they would have been criticized and attacked from all sides. This was not the case with white bourgeois feminists for they could appeal to a large audience of women, like themselves, who were eager to change their lot in life. Their isolation from women of other class and race groups provided no immediate comparative base by which to test their assumptions of common oppression.

Initially, radical participants in women's movement demanded that women penetrate that isolation and create a space for contact. Anthologies like *Liberation Now, Women's Liberation: Blueprint for the Future, Class and Feminism, Radical Feminism,* and *Sisterhood Is Powerful,* all published in the early 1970s, contain articles that attempted to address a wide audience of women, an audience that was not exclusively white, middle class, college-educated, and adult (many have articles on teenagers). Sookie Stambler articulated this radical spirit in her introduction to *Women's Liberation: Blueprint for the Future:*

> Movement women have always been turned off by the media's necessity to create celebrities and superstars. This goes against our basic philosophy. We cannot relate to women in our ranks towering over us with prestige and fame. We are not struggling for the benefit of the one woman or for one group of women. We are dealing with issues that concern all women.

These sentiments, shared by many feminists early in the movement, were not sustained. As more and more women acquired prestige, fame, or money from feminist writings or from gains from feminist movement for equality in the workforce, individual opportunism undermined appeals for collective struggle. Women who were not opposed to patriarchy, capitalism, classism, or racism labeled themselves "feminist." Their expectations were varied. Privileged women wanted social equality with men of their class; some women wanted equal pay for equal work; others wanted an alternative lifestyle. Many of these legitimate concerns were easily co-opted by the ruling capitalist patriarchy. French feminist Antoinette Fouque states:

> The actions proposed by the feminist groups are spectacular, provoking. But provocation only brings to light a certain number of social contradictions. It does not reveal radical contradictions within society. The feminists claim that they do not seek equality with men, but their practice proves the contrary to be true. Feminists are a bourgeois avant-garde that maintains, in an inverted form, the dominant values. Inversion does not facilitate the passage to another kind of structure. Reformism suits everyone! Bourgeois order, capitalism, phallocentrism are ready to integrate as many feminists as will be necessary. Since these women are becoming men, in the end it will only mean a few more men. The difference between the sexes is not whether one does or doesn't have a penis, it is whether or not one is an integral part of a phallic masculine economy.

Feminists in the United States are aware of the contradictions. Carol Ehrlich makes the point in her essay, "The Unhappy Marriage of Marxism and Feminism: Can It Be Saved?," that "feminism seems more and more to have taken on a blind, safe, nonrevolutionary outlook" as "feminist radicalism loses ground to bourgeois feminism," stressing that "we cannot let this continue":

> Women need to know (and are increasingly prevented from finding out) that feminism is *not* about dressing for success, or becoming a corporate executive, or gaining elective office; it is *not* being able to share a two career marriage and take skiing vacations and spend huge amounts of time with your husband and two

lovely children because you have a domestic worker who makes all this possible for you, but who hasn't the time or money to do it for herself; it is *not* opening a Women's Bank, or spending a weekend in an expensive workshop that guarantees to teach you how to become assertive (but not aggressive); it is most emphatically *not* about becoming a police detective or CIA agent or marine corps general.

But if these distorted images of feminism have more reality than ours do, it is partly our own fault. We have not worked as hard as we should have at providing clear and meaningful alternative analyses which relate to people's lives, and at providing active, accessible groups in which to work.

It is no accident that feminist struggle has been so easily co-opted to serve the interests of conservative and liberal feminists since feminism in the United States has so far been a bourgeois ideology. Zillah Eisenstein discusses the liberal roots of North American feminism in *The Radical Future of Liberal Feminism*, explaining in the introduction:

> One of the major contributions to be found in this study is the role of the ideology of liberal individualism in the construction of feminist theory. Today's feminists either do not discuss a theory of individuality or they unself-consciously adopt the competitive, atomistic ideology of liberal individualism. There is much confusion on this issue in the feminist theory we discuss here. Until a conscious differentiation is made between a theory of individuality that recognizes the importance of the individual within the social collectivity and the ideology of individualism that assumes a competitive view of the individual, there will not be a full accounting of what a feminist theory of liberation must look like in our Western society.

The ideology of "competitive, atomistic liberal individualism" has permeated feminist thought to such an extent that it undermines the potential radicalism of feminist struggle. The usurpation of feminism by bourgeois women to support their class interests has been to a very grave extent justified by feminist theory as it has so far been conceived. (For example, the ideology of "common oppression.") Any movement to resist the co-optation of feminist struggle must begin by introducing a different feminist perspective—a new theory—one that is not informed by the ideology of liberal individualism.

The exclusionary practices of women who dominate feminist discourse have made it practically impossible for new and varied theories to emerge. Feminism has its party line and women who feel a need for a different strategy, a different foundation, often find themselves ostracized and silenced. Criticisms of or alternatives to established feminist ideas are not encouraged, e.g. recent controversies about expanding feminist discussions of sexuality. Yet groups of women who feel excluded from feminist discourse and praxis can make a place for themselves only if they first create, via critiques, an awareness of the factors that alienate them. Many individual white women found in the women's movement a liberatory solution to personal dilemmas. Having directly benefited from the movement, they are less inclined to criticize it or to engage in rigorous examination of its structure than those who feel it has not had a revolutionary impact on their lives or the lives of masses of women in our society. Non-white women who feel affirmed within the current structure of feminist movement (even though they may form autonomous groups) seem to also feel that their definitions of the party line, whether on the issue of black feminism or on other issues, is the only legitimate discourse. Rather than encourage a diversity of voices, critical dialogue, and controversy, they, like some white women, seek to stifle dissent. As activists and writers whose work is widely known, they act as if they are best able to judge whether other women's voices should be heard. Susan Griffin warns against this overall tendency towards dogmatism in her essay, "The Way of All Ideology":

> . . . when a theory is transformed into an ideology, it begins to destroy the self and self-knowledge. Originally born of feeling, it pretends to float above and around feeling. Above sensation. It organizes experience according to itself, without touching experience. By virtue of being itself, it is supposed to know. To invoke the name of this ideology is to confer truthfulness. No one can tell it anything new. Experience ceases to surprise it, inform it, transform it. It is annoyed by any detail which does not fit into its world view. Begun as a cry against the denial of truth, now it denies any truth which does not fit into its scheme. Begun as a way to restore one's sense of reality, now it attempts to discipline real people, to remake natural beings after its own image. All that it fails to explain it records as its enemy. Begun as a theory of liberation, it is threatened by new theories of liberation; it builds a prison for the mind.

We resist hegemonic dominance of feminist thought by insisting that it is a theory in the making, that we must necessarily criticize, question, re-examine, and explore new possibilities. My persistent critique has been informed by my status as a member of an oppressed group, experience of sexist exploitation and discrimination, and the sense that prevailing feminist analysis has not been the force shaping my feminist consciousness. This is true for many women. There are white women who had never considered resisting male dominance until the feminist movement created an awareness that they could and should. My awareness of feminist struggle was stimulated by social circumstance. Growing up in a Southern, black, father-dominated, working class household, I experienced (as did my mother, my sisters, and my brother) varying degrees of patriarchal tyranny and it made me angry—it made us all angry. Anger led me to question the politics of male dominance and enabled me to resist sexist socialization. Frequently, white feminists act as if black women did not know sexist oppression existed until they voiced feminist sentiment. They believe they are providing black women with "the" analysis and "the" program for liberation. They do not understand, cannot even imagine, that black women, as well as other groups of women who live daily in oppressive situations, often acquire an awareness of patriarchal politics from their lived experience, just as they develop strategies of resistance (even though they may not resist on a sustained or organized basis).

These black women observed white feminist focus on male tyranny and women's oppression as if it were a "new" revelation and felt such a focus had little impact on their lives. To them it was just another indication of the privileged living conditions of middle and upper class white women that they would need a theory to inform them that they were "oppressed." The implication being that people who are truly oppressed know it even though they may not be engaged in organized resistance or are unable to articulate in written form the nature of their oppression. These black women saw nothing liberatory in party line analyses of women's oppression. Neither the fact that black women have not organized collectively in huge numbers around the issues of "feminism" (many of us do not know or use the term) nor the fact that we have not had access to the machinery of power that would allow us to share our analyses or theories about gender with the American public negate its presence in our lives or place us in a position of dependency in relationship to those white and non-white feminists who address a larger audience.

The understanding I had by age thirteen of patriarchal politics created in me expectations of the feminist movement that were quite different from those of young, middle class, white women. When I entered my first women's studies class at Stanford University in the early 1970s, white women were revelling in the joy of being together—to them it was an important, momentous occasion. I had not known a life where women had not been together, where women had not helped, protected, and loved one another deeply. I had not known white women who were ignorant of the impact of race and class on their social status and consciousness (Southern white women often have a more realistic perspective on racism and classism than white women in other areas of the United States.) I did not feel sympathetic to white peers who maintained that I could not expect them to have knowledge of or understand the life experiences of black women. Despite my background (living in racially segregated communities) I knew about the lives of white women, and certainly no white women lived in our neighborhood, attended our schools, or worked in our homes.

When I participated in feminist groups, I found that white women adopted a condescending attitude towards me and other non-white participants. The condescension they directed at black women was one of the means they employed to remind us that the women's movement was "theirs"—that we were able to participate because they allowed it, even encouraged it; after all, we were needed to legitimate the process. They did not see us as equals. They did not treat us as equals. And though they expected us to provide first hand accounts of black experience, they felt it was their role to decide if these experiences were authentic. Frequently, college-educated black women (even those from poor and working class backgrounds) were dismissed as mere imitators. Our presence in movement activities did not count, as white women were convinced that "real" blackness meant speaking the patois of poor black people, being uneducated, streetwise, and a variety of other stereotypes. If we dared to criticize the movement or to assume responsibility for reshaping feminist ideas and introducing new ideas, our voices were tuned out, dismissed, silenced. We could be heard only if our statements echoed the sentiments of the dominant discourse.

Attempts by white feminists to silence black women are rarely written about. All too often they have taken place in conference rooms, classrooms, or the privacy of cozy living room settings, where one lone black woman faces the racist hostility of a group of white women. From the time the women's liberation movement began, individual black women went to groups. Many never returned after a first meeting. Anita Cornwall is correct in "Three for the Price of One: Notes from a Gay Black Feminist," when she states, ". . . sadly enough, fear of encountering racism seems to be one of the main reasons that so many black womyn refuse to join the women's movement." Recent focus on the issue of racism has generated discourse but has had little impact on the behavior of white feminists towards black women. Often the white women who are busy publishing papers and books on "unlearning racism" remain patronizing and condescending when they relate to black women. This is not surprising given that frequently their discourse is aimed solely in the direction of a white audience and the focus solely on changing attitudes rather than addressing racism in a historical and political context. They make us the "objects" of their privileged discourse on race. As "objects," we remain unequals, inferiors. Even though they may be sincerely concerned about racism, their methodology suggests they are not yet free of the type of paternalism endemic to white supremacist ideology. Some of these women place themselves in the position of "authorities" who must mediate communication between racist white women (naturally they see themselves as having come to terms with their racism) and angry black women whom they believe are incapable of rational discourse. Of course, the system of racism, classism, and educational elitism remain intact if they are to maintain their authoritative positions.

In 1981, I enrolled in a graduate class on feminist theory where we were given a course reading list that had writings by white women and men, one black man, but no material by or about black, Native American Indian, Hispanic, or Asian women. When I criticized this oversight, white women directed an anger and hostility at me that was so intense I found it difficult to attend the class. When I suggested that the purpose of this collective anger was to create an atmosphere in which it would be psychologically unbearable for me to speak in class discussions or even attend class, I was told that they were not angry. *I* was the one who was angry. Weeks after class ended, I received an open letter from one white female student acknowledging her anger and expressing regret for her attacks. She wrote:

> I didn't know you. You were black. In class after a while I noticed myself, that I would always be the one to respond to whatever you said. And usually it was to contradict. Not that the argument was always about racism by any means. But I think the hidden logic was that if I could prove you wrong about one thing, then you might not be right about anything at all.

And in another paragraph:

> I said in class one day that there were some people less entrapped than others by Plato's picture of the world. I said I thought we, after fifteen years of education, courtesy of the ruling class, might be more entrapped than others who had not received a start in life so close to the heart of the monster. My classmate, once a close friend, sister, colleague, has not spoken to me since then. I think the possibility that we were not the best spokespeople for all women made her fear for her self-worth and for her Ph.D.

Often in situations where white feminists aggressively attacked individual black women, they saw themselves as the ones who were under attack, who were the victims. During a heated discussion with another white female student in a racially mixed women's group I had organized, I was told that she had heard how I had "wiped out" people in the feminist theory class, that she was afraid of being "wiped out" too. I reminded her that I was one person speaking to a large group of angry, aggressive people; I was hardly dominating the situation. It was I who left the class in tears, not any of the people I had supposedly "wiped out."

Racist stereotypes of the strong, superhuman black woman are operative myths in the minds of many white women, allowing them to ignore the extent to which black women are likely to be victimized in this society and the role white women may play in the maintenance and perpetuation of that victimization. In Lillian Hellman's autobiographical work *Pentimento,* she writes, "All my life, beginning at birth, I have taken orders from black women, wanting them and resenting them, being superstitious the few times I disobeyed." The black women Hellman describes worked in her household as family servants and their status was never that of an equal. Even as a child, she was always in the dominant position as they questioned, advised, or guided her; they were free to exercise these rights because she or another white authority figure allowed it. Hellman places power in the hands of these black women rather than acknowledge her own power over them; hence she mystifies the true nature of their relationship. By projecting onto black women a mythical power and strength, white women both promote a false image of themselves as powerless, passive victims and deflect attention away from their aggressiveness, their power, (however limited in a white supremacist, male-dominated state) their willingness to dominate and control others. These unacknowledged aspects of the social status of many white women prevent them from transcending racism and limit the scope of their understanding of women's overall social status in the United States.

Privileged feminists have largely been unable to speak to, with, and for diverse groups of women because they either do not understand fully the inter-relatedness of sex, race, and class oppression or refuse to take this inter-relatedness seriously. Feminist analyses of woman's lot tend to focus exclusively on gender and do not provide a solid foundation on which to construct feminist theory. They reflect the dominant tendency in Western patriarchal minds to mystify woman's reality by insisting that gender is the sole determinant of woman's fate. Certainly it has been easier for women who do not experience race or class oppression to focus exclusively on gender. Although socialist feminists focus on class and gender, they tend to dismiss race or they make a point of acknowledging that race is important and then proceed to offer an analysis in which race is not considered.

As a group, black women are in an unusual position in this society, for not only are we collectively at the bottom of the occupational ladder, but our overall social status is lower than that of any other group. Occupying such a position, we bear the brunt of sexist, racist, and classist oppression. At the same time, we are the group that has not been socialized to assume the role of exploiter/oppressor in that we are allowed no institutionalized "other" that we can exploit or oppress. (Children do not represent an institutionalized other even though they may be oppressed by parents.) White women and black men have it both ways. They can act as oppressor or be oppressed. Black men may be victimized by racism, but sexism allows them to act as exploiters and oppressors of women. White women may be victimized by sexism, but racism enables them to act as exploiters and oppressors of black people. Both groups have led liberation movements that favor their interests and support the continued oppression of other groups. Black male sexism has undermined struggles to eradicate racism just as white female racism undermines feminist struggle. As long as these two groups or any group defines liberation as gaining social equality with ruling class white men, they have a vested interest in the continued exploitation and oppression of others.

Black women with no institutionalized "other" that we may discriminate against, exploit, or oppress often have a lived experience that directly challenges the prevailing classist, sexist, racist social structure and its concomitant ideology. This lived experience may shape our consciousness in such a way that our world view differs from those who have a degree of privilege (however relative within the existing system). It is essential for continued feminist struggle that black women recognize the special vantage point our marginality gives us and make use of this perspective to criticize the dominant racist, classist, sexist hegemony as well as to envision and create a counter-hegemony. I am suggesting that we have a central role to play in the making of feminist theory and a contribution to offer that is unique and valuable. The formation of a liberatory feminist theory and praxis is a collective responsibility, one that must be shared. Though I criticize aspects of feminist movement as we have known it so far, a critique which is sometimes harsh and unrelenting, I do so not in an attempt to diminish feminist struggle but to enrich, to share in the work of making a liberatory ideology and a liberatory movement.

TERRY MCMILLAN

(1951–)

Terry McMillan is a phenomenon on the African American literary scene—a tough, new urban voice in fiction who appeals to both the black masses and traditional literary types. When her third novel, *Waiting to Exhale,* appeared in the spring of 1992, it immediately sold hundreds of thousands of copies and catapulted McMillan to a prominence comparable to that of Alice Walker and Toni Morrison. She sold the paperback rights to *Waiting to Exhale* for $2.64 million, the second-highest amount paid to an author in American literary history. When Paramount Pictures released the film version of the novel in 1995 with Angela Bassett and Whitney Houston in the lead roles, it immediately became a smash hit throughout the country, especially among women—black women in particular. She speaks the language that a cross-section of people want to read and captures experiences that speak to people of a variety of ethnic, racial, and sexual configurations. Her raw, unpretentious style has won her the National Book Award from the Before Columbus Foundation.

McMillan was born in Port Huron, Michigan on October 18, 1951, one of six children in a working-class family. Widowed when Terry was sixteen, her mother Madeline Tillman, held a variety of jobs to keep the family together, including autoworker and pickle factory employee. After high school, McMillan attended Los Angeles City College, then transferred to Berkeley. She studied film at Columbia but dropped out and became a word processor, a skill that would serve her well in marketing her first book. She wrote hundreds of letters to individuals and organizations around the country requesting that they not only purchase her book but also invite her to speak or to read from it. She also enrolled in a workshop at the Harlem Writers Guild.

A series of residences at writers' colonies, combined with fellowship support, enabled McMillan to have undisturbed time to write. She has been a fellow at Yaddo and at the MacDowell Colony (1983), where she expanded an earlier manuscript into the draft of *Mama* (published in 1987). She has received grants from the PEN American Center, Authors League, Carnegie Fund, New York Foundation for the Arts, and National Endowment for the Arts. She has held teaching positions, most recently at the University of Arizona at Tucson.

During the early 1980s, McMillan met the man, a construction worker, who fathered her child, Solomon. He later charged that he was the model for the construction worker, Franklin, in *Disappearing Acts* (1989), and sued McMillan for what he considered a "libelous portrait"; his suit was unsuccessful. McMillan has been a single parent for almost fifteen years.

Her first novel, *Mama* (1987), features a black woman the likes of which has not appeared frequently in literature. Mildred, who is the "Mama" of the title, raises five children essentially alone in Michigan. She is a cursing, drinking, scheming woman whose daughters follow some of her bad habits. Yet despite the departure from McMillan's previous depictions of strait-laced black women, she manages to evoke a certain mixture of sympathy and admiration; Mildred is a resourceful person who refuses to allow the difficult circumstances of life to subdue her effervescent spirit. The book sold out its first hardcover printing of five thousand copies, primarily because of McMillan's dedication to marketing her own work.

In *Disappearing Acts* (1989), McMillan solidifies her focus on issues surrounding black male-female relationships. Zora Banks, a schoolteacher, is attracted to Franklin, a construction worker, in a society that stresses class distinctions even among black people. McMillan captures their differences in the narrative technique she employs, an alternating point of view between Zora and Franklin. According to Clenora Hudson-Weems in *Africana Womanism: Reclaiming Ourselves,* Zora Banks is "the supreme paradigm of the Africana womanist, one who commands respect, thereby making possible salvation for her man, her child, and her self." Reminiscent of Gloria Naylor's *Mama Day* (1988)—though clearly the books were being written in a simultaneous time frame—the work highlights obstacles to black love and finds ways of overcoming them. In 1990, McMillan turned her attention to editing and brought out *Breaking Ice: An Anthology of Contemporary African-American Fiction.* The volume, with a preface by John Edgar Wideman, includes an assortment of works by male and female writers.

The impressively successful *Waiting to Exhale* (1992) was on the *New York Times* bestseller list for eleven weeks during the summer of 1992, when 385,000 copies were in print. The novel focuses on four black women in Phoenix, Arizona, another landscape not featured prominently in African American literature. All the women are successful, and they all have problems with the men in their lives. Success, McMillan suggests, is no balm against affairs of the heart and body. Through pain of separations and disappointments in love and casual relationships, the women remain friends and continue to hope for good black men. A couple of them seem to have fairly stable relationships by the end of the novel, and the others are ever hopeful. The novel is by no means an indictment exclusively of black men, for at least one of the female characters is immature in the choices she makes about partners and potentially just as using of men as she generally assumes them to be of her.

Part of McMillan's success must be credited to her boundless energy in selling her own books. She went on an intensive twenty-week tour during the summer of 1992 to publicize *Waiting to Exhale* and was featured in such national newspapers as *U.S.A. Today*. In the true spirit of the 1960s and writers bringing their works to the people, she has read in jazz clubs, community centers, and black bookstores (where her books have always sold record numbers), as well as in the traditional college and university settings. Audiences of twelve hundred to fifteen hundred, the overwhelming majority of them African American, have shown up to hear her read. McMillan estimated that by August 1992, she had signed more than ten thousand books.

On the heels of the popular *Waiting to Exhale* has come McMillan's latest novel, *How Stella Got Her Groove Back* (1996). Like Zora Neale Hurston's *Their Eyes Were Watching God*, the novel explores the life of a black woman who is stifled by societal conventions and expectations, but who eventually escapes both to find happiness with a younger man. McMillan's heroine Stella Payne, who is a forty-two-year-old divorcée and mother of eleven-year-old Quincy, has a financially successful, but emotionally unfulfilled, life as a high-powered investment analyst. When she takes a spur-of-the-moment trip to Jamaica, she finds the answer to her emotional needs in the form of a twenty-one-year-old, sensitive black man named Winston Shakespeare. Like Hurston, McMillan based her novel on a love affair she had on a Jamaican vacation with a man who is nearly half her age. Currently, she resides in Danville, California (near Oakland) with her twenty-two-year-old Jamaican lover, Jonathan Plummer, and her son, Solomon.

When the first signing of *How Stella Got Her Groove Back* was sponsored by Marcus Books on May 10, 1996, at the Convention Center in Oakland, California, over a thousand people were in attendance. Since then, the novel has surpassed the first printing sales of *Waiting to Exhale* in that it has sold over 850,000 copies in its first printing. As of September 1996, it is number six on *Publishers Weekly*'s Best Seller List for hardcover in fiction, and has remained on the Best Seller's list for sixteen weeks.

With these successes, it is certain that McMillan will be on the literary scene for some time to come. Although she has not been pleased with most of the literary establishment's lukewarm acceptance of her, she has won the friendship and support of African American writers such as Ishmael Reed and Charles R. Johnson. With reported movie deals (screenplays for *How Stella Got Her Groove Back* and *Disappearing Acts* are already in the works) and constant lecture invitations, her name will increasingly represent possibilities that African American writers of previous generations could not imagine. It is certain, as well, that the publishing industry will take heed of this phenomenon, perhaps to the benefit of other African American writers.

❖❖❖

As a fairly new arrival on the literary scene, McMillan has not yet garnered much critical attention. To date, most commentary is contained in book reviews following the publication of each of her novels. See, for example, Daniel Max, "McMillan's Millions," *New York Times Magazine*, August 9, 1992; *Emerge*, September 1992. However, Clenora Hudson-Weems has a thought-provoking critical study on *Disappearing Acts* in Chapter Nine of her book, *Africana Womanism: Reclaiming Ourselves* (Troy, Michigan: 1993).

Franklin

FROM *DISAPPEARING ACTS*

All I can say is this. I'm tired of women. Black women in particular, 'cause that's about all I ever deal with. Maybe a fine Puerto Rican here and there, but not much. They're all the same, that's for damn sure. Want all your time and energy. Want the world to revolve around them. Once you give 'em some good lovin', they go crazy. Start hearing wedding bells. Start thinking about babies. And want you to meet their damn family. They make you come and you'd swear they struck gold or somethin'. And the prettier they are, the more they want. Well, I don't play that shit no more. I try to make it clear from jump street. I ain't serious. I got enough on my mind right now without getting all hung up and twisted up with another woman.

Every time I turned around, my phone was ringing off the damn hook. "Hi, Franklin," one would say. And I would sit there and try to guess which one it was. "Whatcha doing?" What a stupid-ass question to call somebody up and ask. It oughta be obvious that I wasn't thinking about her, or else I'da called her, right? But naw. It don't work like that. They hedge. "You feel like some company?" And don't say, "No, I'm busy." All hell'll break loose then. "You got somebody over there?" I wanna say, "None of your fuckin' business," but that would be too cold-blooded. They wanna know what you doing every fuckin' minute of the day you ain't with them. Can't just be by yourself. They always think if you don't wanna see them, then it's gotta be another woman.

And I've been out with some of the stupidest women. I swear. Usually don't find this out until after I've fucked 'em. What was her name? Gloria. Yeah, Gloria. This chick had a ass like butter, moved like a roller coaster, but when it came to brains, she was missing about sixteen cards. Worked at the welfare department, but she shoulda been a case herself. I shoulda known better when all she talked about was getting her nails done and was forever blow-drying her fuckin' hair. She couldn't even figure out the easiest puzzle on "Wheel of Fortune." I remember one night we'd had a pretty serious session, and I had to go to work in the morning, but since it was election day—Koch was running again for mayor—I got up extra early so I could go vote. I looked down at her. "You voting today?" I asked. "I ain't voted in years, Franklin," she said, just grinning and shit, like she was proud. You stupid bitch, I wanted to say, but I didn't. It wasn't worth it. "You gotta go," I said. "Now." She acted like her feelings was hurt, but I didn't care.

And all this complaining women do about men not knowing how to "make love" is a bunch of crap. A lot of 'em don't like foreplay and just wanna get fucked. Ten minutes after our clothes is off, and a few kisses later, some of 'em begged me to just go ahead and put it in. Personally, I like to take my time. If all I wanted was some pussy, I could buy some. If I like the woman, I wanna enjoy the whole experience. Coming ain't every-

thing. Naw, I take that shit back. But it's a whole lotta women out here who don't know nothin' about passion. They do the same shit them how-to and self-help books and Cosmopolitan *magazine tell 'em to do, but a man can tell when a woman's heart ain't in her moves. The shit feel rehearsed, like she do the same thing the same way with every man she ever been with. This kind of fucking is boring—which is when I usually just take the pussy and run.*

One chick, I liked her a lot. Her name was Theresa, and she hated it when you called her Terri. Now, Theresa had something on the ball. Worked at a bank, and not only could she cook her ass off but she liked sports. We used to lay around all day on a Saturday or Sunday and just make love during halftime and watch every game that came on TV. She knew a call when she heard one too. And she gave the best head I ever had in my life. I don't know who taught her, but I wished he'd give lessons to a lot more of 'em. The only thing about Theresa was she wore a wig and I couldn't stand to hear her talk. She had this squeaky-ass voice that drove me nuts. It was real high like Alvin and the Chipmunks or something. Sometimes I wanted to say, Would you just shut up! And when the girl came, I swear to God, it was embarrassing. I don't remember what happened to her, to tell the truth. She just faded out the picture, just like Karen and Maria and Sandy and Amina and all the rest of 'em. All except Pauline.

Pauline. Now that woman. She was the last one. The one that broke my heart. Don't never fail. The one you always want is the one that always leave. Pauline was soft and sexy. She had the prettiest titties in the world. They was round and full and stood straight out. She was the only woman I ever met that could come from just me licking 'em. Pauline was a hundred percent grade-A woman. Lived in the projects with her two-year-old son. Treated me like a whole man. She was going to secretarial school so she could get off welfare. That's one thing I really liked about her. She tried. And Pauline had pride. She never called me, it was always me doing the calling, and I didn't mind. Some women you just want, ain't satisfied till you get 'em. Don't ask me what happened, but a few weeks ago when I called, she said she was busy. Busy? I let it go. The next day, I called back. She still busy. "What the fuck is going on?" I asked her. She didn't say nothin' for a minute. My chest was heaving. "Pauline, don't play with me." Then I heard her mumble something like, "I met somebody else." Met somebody else? What? Who? I heard her say some shit like she was sorry, but I just hung up the damn phone. A man don't need this kinda shit. What kinda dude could she possibly have found that could make her feel better than me? I hate this shit. I wanted to marry this woman. To tell the truth, my head was all fucked up, 'cause I kept sitting around wondering who the fuck it could be. And what he was doing for her that I wasn't doing. Didn't do. I kept drawing a blank, 'cause when I love a woman, I try to treat her like she's the only woman in the world. Sometimes, I guess, that ain't enough.

That's when I decided to take a vacation from all of 'em. They think they're the only ones who can go without sex. Well, that's a lie. A man's mind is about the strongest thing he got going for him. Let women tell it, you'd swear our brains was all in the head of our dicks. Sometimes this shit is true, but right now I'm trying to get my constitution together. I've made too many stupid mistakes, too many bad decisions. I guess dropping outta high school was the biggest one. I ain't never liked people telling me what to do. I couldn't sit still for another two years, listening to that boring shit about America and how to write a fuckin' sentence. Couldn't just learn to add, subtract, and multiply. Naw. They had to make the shit even more confusing. But woodshop. Didn't miss a class.

This was just one more reason for my Moms to despise me. She started with my Pops and worked her way down to me. But he's so damn henpecked, I still don't know how he feel about me, really. To tell the truth, I ain't never been all that crazy about them either. But when you're sixteen years old and already six foot two, ain't much they can tell you. My Moms would lay it on thick, just running her fuckin' mouth to hear herself talk. "You gon' end up with a bullet hole in you, boy. You stupid, just like that sister of yours. Y'all shoulda been twins. Can't do nothing right. Nothing. Sit up straight. Naw, just get outta my face. Make me wanna shoot you my damn self." Pops usually stood in the background, pretending like he was doing something else, like he didn't hear nothin'. He always ended up in the pantry, where he kept his scotch. But there was only so many more stupids I was gon' be. One day I was gon' punch her damn lights out.

So I did what I wanted to do anyway. Shot dope. Played hooky. Fucked whatever was pretty and was willing to give it up. It took me fifteen years to get my GED. But I got it. Didn't take me that long to give up dope. That shit got old. Had to scramble for it. Five nights in jail once, and that was enough for my ass. It wasn't the kind of life I pictured for myself, that's for damn sure. Neither was marrying Pam when I wasn't nothin' but twenty years old. She was so fine and so sweet, I couldn't get past it. Everybody warned me. "Leave them West Indian women alone, man." She was from Jamaica. Two babies later, Pam was a different woman. Fat as hell. Never felt like making love no more; we stopped that after Derek was born, and by the time Miles got here, we wasn't doing nothin' but screwing. I was working two jobs. Post office at night, construction during the day. She took care the kids, I busted my ass. And what kinda thanks did I get? "I'm too tired." She was just too damn fat. Pam's thighs felt like blubber, her waist looked like a old inner tube, and what used to be firm breasts that I loved to suck and massage, shit, now they fell down flat and limp on top of that gut. It got to the point that I didn't want her, couldn't stand the thought of touching her. The only thing she had energy for was them damn soap operas. And food. It took me three years to leave, 'cause the kids was growing up and wasn't going nowhere no time soon. But a man's gotta do what a man's gotta do. This was about my sanity.

That was six years ago. Never did get the divorce. I'm waiting for her to do it. She waiting for me. I see the kids once in a while, but don't want 'em to see me like this. Living in a rooming house with a whole bunch of other dudes. But all I need right now is a room. I ain't no woman. Ain't no interior decorator neither. What I got is what I need. A bed, a dresser, a TV, a worktable for my woodworking, my fish tank, and my music box. I can't see spending my whole damn check on no rent, 'specially since some weeks I don't get no work.

Now, the dudes that live in this rooming house is real losers. Some of 'em been put out, some of 'em got a habit, some of 'em just fuckin' lazy—wouldn't work if you gave 'em a job. The rest of 'em just lost, don't know what else the fuck to do. Grown men on welfare. Now, that's some ridiculous shit. I ain't nothin' like 'em. And they know it. I've got definite plans for my life. They ain't crystal clear to me right now, but that's why I'm working on my constitution. A man needs one. Needs to get his priorities straight. Right now it don't feel like I got no foundation. I feel more like Sheetrock. Like mortar. Can't nothin' make your life work if you ain't the architect. Took me long enough to realize this shit.

My life is pretty simple. I like to get drunk on Friday nights, but only if I worked a full week. No pay, no play. Usually go to the bar, but I don't socialize too tough with none of these dudes in here. They ask too many damn questions, just like women. Wanna know your whole damn history. But I don't give up no information. "You got a lady, man?" I look at 'em like they faggots and say, "Why?" Nosy motherfuckers. "You got any sisters?" I got two, but I'll be damned if I'd introduce Darlene to these losers. Christine is married, which is where she should be. "Naw, I ain't got no sisters. Why?" They look like they ready to run, and then say, "I was just wondering, man. That's all."

On the weekends, I like to sit in here and watch whatever game or fights is on TV and do some woodworking. Pussy don't even cross my mind when I got a piece of wood in my hand. Get myself a bottle and stay up all night chiseling, measuring, sanding, making a scale model—don't make me no difference. You tell me what you want, and I can build it. Beds, couches, lamps, tables, wall units. And the more complicated the shit is, the *more I put into it. Ain't nothin' like a challenge, especially when it turns out prettier than you expected.*

*But I'm slow. I like to take my time and not rush when I'm working on a piece, which is one reason I don't make big pieces for people no more. They started bugging me, wanting me to hurry up and finish it. Christmas was coming up—something. How can you hurry up when you trying to create a work of art? If the shit turned out fucked up, then I'd have to hear that shit—"*I *paid all that money for this?" These days, I make what I feel like making for anybody I feel like making it for. Mostly myself.*

At least three days a week I work out at the gym. Hell, working construction, I can't afford to get flabby and outta shape. Naw, it's more to it than that. I love my body and wanna keep it that way. Faggots seem to love looking at it too. A six-foot-four jet-black handsome niggah? Get the fuck outta here. I swear, I would get so much satisfaction outta whopping one of 'em in the face if they was to so much as say a word to me. But they ain't crazy. Sometimes, just to fuck with 'em, I swing my dick when I'm in the shower. But seriously, the gym is kinda like my sanctuary. I go in there and pump iron, flex, and sweat. Love to sweat. Play a few rounds of racquetball or basketball, then put on some shaving cream and sit in the steam room for about a half hour. Skin feel like satin, and the razor just slide right over it. Don't get no bumps. I feel clean inside and out when I'm done with my routine. Then I lay down and take a nap for about a hour. Shit, you can't beat it.

Only problem is afterwards I always feel like fuckin'. But just the thought of walking to the phone booth to call up some chick and talk shit for a few minutes takes most of the desire away. I got my phone turned off after Pauline, so nobody *would bother me. The truth is I wish I could just stop by the corner store and say to Muhammed, "Let me have five cans of some instant pussy." Sometimes all I need is to get fucked. I don't wanna have to talk, lie, or bullshit, just come, roll over, smoke a cigarette, and watch TV. Some women fall for this shit, depending on how bad they want you, which just means it's been a long time since they had some or they just curious as hell if what they see is as good as it looks. I could just tell 'em that it is. But some of 'em wanna be more than just wham-bam-thank-you-ma'amed. So I try not to give it to 'em too good, 'cause they wouldn't never wanna go home.*

Basically, I guess I'm a loner. Ain't got too many friends. Ain't too many people worth trusting. Jimmy, a dude I grew up with, stops by every now and then to borrow a few dollars. I don't never have to worry about catching up on nothin', cause all Jimmy do is deal dope. Cocaine. He's small-time, thinks he's big-time, but he ain't, 'cause if he was, he wouldn't have to borrow no money from me, would have a permanent address and drive something besides them curled-over Stacy-Adams he wears. He don't offer me none of that shit, 'cause he know, as far back as we go, I don't wanna be around nothin' that even smell like dope. Gimme the damn creeps. Make me think about jail. Me and Jimmy both almost OD'd once. We was some stupid motherfuckers. We was—what? Nineteen? At the dope house, of all fuckin' places. The shit was better than we thought it was, and in those days we was greedy as hell. We decided we was gon' get blasted and then play strip poker with some chicks we had picked up at a party. Shit. If it wasn't for them chicks, we'd both be dead. Jimmy's a stupid little fat fuck, but he's still my home boy.

Lucky is the only dude in this building that I do associate with. He's also the only male nurse I ever met in my life, and he ain't no faggot either. Motherfucker always in white. Work the midnight shift at some old folks' home. We play cards. Spades. Poker. Sometimes dominoes. Lucky is smart as hell too. He reads everything, which is why we get into some heavy debates. Like the shit that's going on in the Middle East and Nicaragua, should Jesse Jackson run for President in '84 or not. That kinda shit. I like being around people who think. Who read the damn paper every day and know what's going on in the world. Lucky's biggest problem is that he lives at the track. Horses is his middle name. When he gets off work, he'll catch two buses, four trains, whatever's running, to get to the track. I hate to take his money, but hell, when you play and lose, you lose and pay. "You can suck my dick, little girl," he always say when he losing. I just laugh and say, "Put on some more music, motherfucker, go get some Kleenex, and stop crying." Lucky's got a helluva music collection too. I mean serious. That's another reason I like to sit in his room. Shit. Get us a bottle, order some Chinese food, debate about damn near anything that come on the news, and listen to Herbie Hancock or Cole Porter in the background. You can't beat it.

And I play my music loud as hell, 'cause that's how I like it. Once in a while one of these dudes'll knock on my door to complain. "Say, man, would you mind turning it down a taste?" If I'm drinking bourbon, doing some woodworking, I'll say, "Maybe," or just ignore 'em. They don't fuck with me either. Maybe it's 'cause I am *six four and weigh 215. I don't know.*

Shit, I'd crack up without my music. It's the best company you can have, really. It don't say "no" or "maybe," or ask no questions. Don't want nothin' in return except your open ears. And sometimes the words seem like they was written for you. Side Effect. Aretha. Gladys. Smokey, and L.T.D. If I'm in a good mood and ain't doing nothin' in particular but, say, putting up my work clothes or just playing with my dick and reading the paper, and one of these dudes knock on the door, I'll usually say, "No sweat, man." They probably think I'm a schizoid or something.

I do know I can be a pain in the ass, but that's my nature. I just like to test people, see what they made of, where they coming from. I got discharged from the navy because of my temper, lack of cooperation. Couldn't carry out, let alone follow, orders. And didn't give a shit. Didn't wanna go in the first damn place. A black man got enough wars to fight at home. When they said "draft" and they meant army, I said, "Not me." Let me go somewhere halfway exciting. Submarines and ships and shit. Everybody thought it would do me some good. But how can taking orders from the white man, killing people that ain't never done nothing to me personally, do me some fuckin' good? It took me two years to get out.

My whole family disowned me. If I was white, I probably woulda been disinherited. My Moms said, "You's just lost, boy, always was, always will be. Why don't you just go somewhere far away and leave us alone?" The bitch. And my Pops. I don't know the right word to describe him. Weak. That's close enough. "You could've had a future if you'd have followed the rules, son. That's all it takes to make it in this world, playing by the rules." Yeah, right. Look how far it got you, I wanted to say. A fuckin' sanitation worker. His dream in life. Shit, I didn't get no dishonorable, just a general discharge. I can still get some of the fuckin' benefits. And Christine, she's a year older than me. The perfect word for her is dumb. Just plain old dumb. How she graduated from high school I'll never know. My folks worship Christine, and you'd swear she was the only child they ever had. That's 'cause she'll lick the ground they walk on. "You got too much anger in you, Franklin. That's your biggest problem," she said. "You're hostile and don't know what the words cooperate or compromise mean. Why you so mad at everybody?" She don't even know me. Maybe if I was high yellow like she was and didn't never have to worry about dealing with white folks, scarin' 'em half to death 'cause I'm so big and black, I would be happy as a little fuckin' lark too. That's what it boiled down to. Color.

Me and Darlene was the black sheep in the family. Took after my Pops, and we got treated like black sheep too. Even now, Christine live right across the street from Moms and Pops in a "Leave It to Beaver" house with her "Father Knows Best" husband and four "Brady Bunch" kids. In dull-ass Staten Island. And Darlene: "If you'da just made it through high school, Franklin, you could be playing for the Knicks. They've got hardship cases, and you know it. You wouldn't have had to go to college. Could be making boo-koo cash right now." She pissed me off. Thinks just like everybody else in America. Why is it that if you happen to be black and over six feet tall, everybody thinks you supposed to play basketball or football? But I let Darlene off the hook, 'cause she's as nutty as a fruitcake, thanks to my parents. She change jobs like some people change their clothes. Don't know whether she's coming or going. She ain't never got no man. Living up in the Bronx, drinking herself to death. She don't think nobody know it, but I know it.

I ain't seen none of 'em in almost a year, and that's just the way I like it, really. All except for Darlene. I worry about her. Every now and then I'll call her, just to make sure she still alive. She already tried to kill herself once. And you think my folks would go up there and see her?

All they ever wanted from us was to go along with their program, which meant don't never disagree with them about nothin'. Shit, they forgot that kids had opinions too. And it ain't no secret that they had it in for me from jump street. All they ever felt for me was disappointment. Not love. And me being their only son, you'd think they'd be more understanding. Shit. That would be too much like right. They would love to see me drive up in a brand-new car, walk in their house wearing a suit and tie, flashing credit cards and proving to them that I didn't turn out to be the fuck-up they thought I would. But even if I ever got to that point, I wouldn't give 'em the satisfaction of knowing it, since they never gave me none.

But time can do some wild shit to your mind. For one thing, it can put you in check. Make you stop and realize on your thirty-second birthday that your life is going down the fuckin' drain. That you ain't moving. Ain't headed nowhere in particular. You're drifting, pretending like you on your way but you don't know where. And when you sit in a tiny-ass room, smoking one Newport after another, playing solitaire with a bottle of bourbon, looking across the room at a piece of wood that could turn out to be a beautiful piece of furniture—and you know what you're doing is good but don't know what to do about it or where to go from here—you sorta get scared. And who you supposed to tell? A man don't run around telling everybody that he's scared. Especially when he don't know what the fuck he's scared of. And for some reason, don't nobody seem to think that Franklin Swift should be scared of nothing.

But time scares me.

It feels like it's running out. Like I gotta go ahead and make a move. A big move. Hell, something drastic. And if the white man would give a black man a break, maybe I could get in the fuckin' union once and for all. Making fourteen to seventeen dollars a hour. They tearing down and putting up new buildings everywhere you look in Brooklyn. Italians'll renovate anything for a dollar. But be black and try to get in the damn union, and what do they do? Lay your black ass off right before the cutoff date, or wanna pay you hush money or go-home-and-don't-show-up money—anything to stop from paying you union scale. And who can afford the fuckin' dues when they paying you six or seven bucks a hour? So yeah, I'm still a laborer. If I can get in a few weeks of steady work at a little higher than slave wages, I could join. They give us thirty days to do it. Shit, I could buy a decent car. Be outta this dingy-ass room. I could afford a one-bedroom apartment then. Send the kids more money. Let 'em spend the night. Take 'em to Coney Island. The movies. Shit, I don't need much.

And even though this is 1982, the white man still love to see black men lift that barge and tote that fuckin' bale. If I didn't do nothin' but sit around here all day like some of these dudes, then they'd call me a shiftless, lazy, no-good niggah. Almost beg the motherfuckers for a job, and they still feel so threatened they gotta send your ass home.

But a man gets tired of begging. After a while, you feel butt naked, stripped of anything that look like pride. And they love that shit. Which is why I resent every fuckin' brick I pick up, every wheelbarrow I push, all the mud I sling, every wall I've ever put up or torn down, and one day I would love to just say, "Fuck you."

But I made the bed, now I'm laying in it.

Which is why I'm looking into night school. I can't work construction for the rest of my damn life. Muscles wear out. The mind act like it wanna follow. And outta all the things I may be, stupid ain't one of 'em. One day I'd like to start my own business. Be my own man. Give the damn orders instead of taking 'em. Have some money in my pocket and money in the fuckin' bank. That's what it's all about. Ain't it?

Ask Pam. Before I got my phone turned off, she used to bug the shit outta me for money. She was worse than a bill collector. It was humiliating as hell to tell her I didn't never have none. Sometimes all I had on me was enough for a pack of cigarettes and some coffee. I'd be eating sardines and crackers. To this day, she hates my guts. Talks about me like a dog to the kids. When I call, I have to prepare myself for the bullshit. "You ain't been over to see the kids in months. They always asking about you." I guess she don't know that sometimes when I call and Derek answers, we talk for a long time. He starting to talk about girls and shit already. And he just thirteen. Last time I saw him, I took him to a closed-circuit fight and let him drink a glass of beer. I felt good being able to do something with him, and I know I need to spend more time with botha my sons. Derek's the oldest, be a man before I know it. I don't want neither one of 'em growing up thinking of me as a dog, as some dude who fucked their Mama and then split the scene. But respect is something you gotta earn. Right now it ain't much I can do for neither one of 'em, so why should I go see 'em all the time when all they really want is money, sneakers, designer jeans, Walkmen—all that expensive shit I can't afford? It's embarrassing, to tell the truth. One day I'm gon' be able to do for 'em, but it's gon' take time.

And that's exactly why women ain't in the picture right now. They complicate shit. Fuck up my whole program. All they do is throw me off track. It takes me too damn long to swing back.

FROM *How Stella Got Her Groove Back*[1]

Maybe they accidentally put some booze in my drink is what I'm thinking as I stagger back toward my room. I feel like I've jumped inside somebody else's dream. I mean I know I'm in Jamaica. I'm in Negril. I think I just got here day before yesterday but I can't be sure because a lot has happened since then and when I'm at home weeks months can go by and nothing worth noting happens. But yes. I am walking up the path at the Castle Beach Negril and I have just told a twenty-one-year-old that I will have sex with him tonight. Yes, that seems to be what I've gone and done. I press both hands up to my face and cover my eyes and cheeks and sort of sink at the knees and I can see some of the workers wondering if I'm off my rocker so I remove my hands and smile and continue to walk or float toward my room because I still do not believe I've consented to something this reckless. But then again, I'm not planning on marrying this boy. I'm just going to have sex with him tonight. And that's it. It's that simple. Do it and send him on his way. I've got a whole box of condoms. So what is the problem, Stella? I mean he is a consenting adult. He *wants* to do it. But why does he want to do the nasty with me? I wonder. Because I'm old. That's why. He's never had any old pussy before. That's it. He wants to do a comparison study. Does old pussy feel as good as young pussy? I can't answer that question and I don't want him to answer that question but he didn't act like he simply wanted sex, I mean he did ask me to have dinner with him, didn't he? And then dancing afterwards, didn't he? Isn't that like sort of what's called a date? But why am I even tripping? Why am I going this far? The bottom line is that he is tall and fine and sexy and young and I'm a good-looking middle-aged woman from America and he's game and I'll give him something to remember and if I work it right maybe I'll get off and I hope the boy can kiss because it would be a shame if God gave him those thick juicy beautiful luscious lips and he doesn't know what to do with them and I hope he's not one of those sloppy wet tongue-wrestling kissers that make you think you're really in the dentist's chair and I hope he knows how to move because I can help guide him some of the way but rhythm is something you either have or you don't have and it cannot be taught but I'll do my best and I hope he understands the importance of a woman's breasts but probably nobody's shown him how to handle them yet so I'll give him a five-minute demonstration and since he's young he should catch on fast and God just the thought of those smooth lips over

[1]The following excerpt relates the intimate love scene between Stella and her young Jamaican lover.

my breasts okay change the subject Stella because I still have—I look at my watch—three whole hours to go. Lord what am I going to do for three hours besides go crazy? I feel like I want him right now but I am not going in that room and masturbate no way José I am going to save all of this for him and I feel sorry for him really because I hope he's up for this. I wonder what kind of music I should put on none of that let's-do-the-nasty music or any begging and pleading or that whining lovesick stuff but then again I don't want anything too funky and upbeat which means I'm back to Seal again but I also don't want to go completely off and act like I'm setting up this monumental seduction performance because that's like so tacky but I do feel kind of silly when I turn around and walk back to the gift shop pretending to need only a *USA Today* when in fact I purchase four of those round scented candles that look like kaleidoscopes on the outside which I place in subtle places around my room like on the headboard on the coffee table out on the balcony and in the bathroom. I feel like I'm cheating, like this was all premeditated and not at all organic or spontaneous, but then again this feels like the smart thing to do. Besides, he's probably never had so much ambience. Which is why I feel like I sort of owe him this.

As I stand in front of my closet trying to choose the most flattering dress I realize that I am not twenty-one years old that the clothes in my closet reflect this and when I look in the full-length mirror it is obvious that I am not even close to looking twenty-one years old that I haven't been twenty-one years old in twenty-one years and suddenly I'm wondering again why this young man really wants to sleep with me. I mean what is the attraction? What is his real motive? I know! He's probably heard the rumor going around America that single women over thirty and black women in particular will fuck anything, since many of them are on that slow track. They used to count how many weeks had gone by since they'd been laid but now it's gotten up to how many years has it been and they're all freaking out because they're super-lonely and in their quest to find Mr. Perfect for years and years have yet to come to the realization that he does not exist. We who have labeled ourselves Ms. Fucking Perfect Personified have not caught on yet that our perfection is merely a figment of our very own distorted imagination and I should know because I'm in that forty-and-over club for Emotional Subversives in Denial About Everything.

What I do know deep down although I keep it secretly secret is that I am terrified at the thought of losing myself again wholeheartedly to any man because it is so scary peeling off that protective sealant that's been guarding my heart and letting somebody go inside and walk around lie down look around and see all those red flags especially when right next to your heart is your soul and then inside that is the rest of your personality puzzle pieces and they're full of flaws and in your grown-up years you have just finally started to recognize them for what they are one by one. You're trying to resolve some of these issues but you're only up to say number four and the list is too long to get into here but the mere thought of being emotionally naked again is frightening because you remember how fucked up it got the last two or three times out there. Since the world is now aware that women like us are trying to beat the clock, some of us have built this invisible fence around our hearts like those that people use to keep their dogs inside the yard—if they go past that invisible wired line they get shocked until eventually they get tired of getting electrocuted and so they sit there and watch cars and other dogs go by and sort of just stay put. This is pretty much where I am: putting, and lots of my girlfriends are too because this is the big easy that I hope Winston hasn't heard about but then again I'm sure if they get BET down here they must get Oprah too.

The only thing I'm hoping is that if he is on this kind of sympathy mission, he realizes women like me are not really desperate. Getting laid is hardly a problem—almost any man'll take some free pussy—but getting laid by somebody you want to get laid by is an entirely different issue. When we finally meet somebody we do want to lie down with we aren't feeling desperate—what we're feeling is vulnerable, nervous and scared. Big difference. Big big difference. But once again, Stella, you are like getting far too deep here for somebody who is planning to have a little sexual encounter with a boy for one single evening so like could you spare me your philosophical sociological rantings on the status of women and black women in particular in America, okay, and let's just get us some nuggies and hope it's good and get on with this vacation? Can we do that?

Okay, so this mental masturbating kills a whole hour. I decide that reading is a good time-passer so I pick up a book without looking at the title and begin to read the words one at a time instead of in groups like I learned to do years ago in that Evelyn Wood speed-reading class that never quite worked for me except the grouping stuff. It is not working now. I lay the book down and decide that the best thing for me to do is rest since I'll be expending and I hope consuming a great deal of energy tonight.

I call the operator and ask for a wake-up call at five just in case I doze off and I get under the covers and everything and start thinking about oh my God what if people see us what are they going to think and say? Shit. Oh so what, Stella! This is America. No it isn't America. Okay. This is the nineties and oh go to sleep girl and then I turn my attention to those waves that are still at it outside my window and I push my face deeper and deeper into the soft white pillow and close my eyes for a few minutes and when the phone rings I am startled. The operator claims it's five o'clock and when I look at my watch it is.

May as well put the video camera on fast forward because that's how quickly I jump out of bed take a shower shave my underarms and legs douche pumice-stone my heels elbows knees brush my teeth pluck a few hairs from my eyebrows put some Visine in my eyes pull my cool braids to the other side of my head and rub my Calyx lotion everywhere on my body that's brown. I do that minimum makeup routine again because to be honest I can't stand all that mess on my face and the other reason is because I always want a man even a young one to know that what he sees is what he gets.

I stand in front of the closet again since I never did decide on what to wear and realize I have quite a few Marilyn Monroe-type dresses and that I am not a reincarnation of Marilyn thank the Lord and yet I also don't want to repeat myself and plus I don't want to look like I can't wait to get out of this dress but I also don't want to look like I'm a chaperone at my son's prom either not that I brought anything like that so I choose a soft yellow linen shift that has a low neckline in front and back and comes right above my knees but it fits snugly and makes me look like I have a real figure even though I really don't well what I have is narrow hips and a firm set of curvy glutes aka a big ass which runs in my family and I'll tell the truth I don't want to lose it ever. I put on my twenty-two-dollar strapless bra I finally found in Macy's that fits my own personal breasts without smashing crushing them down or upping them two sizes and it actually gives me that ever-so-light touch of cleavage I'm seeking but only if you look from the side.

I slip on my mustard sling-back pumps some gold hoop earrings and when I look in the mirror I think I've got it going on, to be honest. I just hope he thinks so too. I hope he hasn't changed his mind. What if he's changed his mind? What if he's come to his senses and is hiding in his room and I go out there all dolled up and don't see him and I'll feel stupid? This is the reason why I often hate men. They're all alike. You can't depend on them for shit. They're weak. I do not for the life of me understand why God even gave them balls when most of the time they act like they don't have any. I can see that this weak-acting shit starts at a young age, doesn't it? Well, I am making a mental note right now to teach Quincy how to grow up and flex his balls as much as possible, to jump into the fire to take risks and even if you're scared do the shit anyway. I don't want him to act like a little pussy like this Winston like his daddy like so many of these fellows running around the world who don't deserve to be called men. What some of them most of them a lot of them really need is a month or two at a dude ranch run by women. We're the ones who can show these simpletons how to be men because we raised them and for some reason perhaps they are all suffering from ADD because they have apparently forgotten most of the necessary valuable constructive stuff we taught them as young boys which is why most of them are in dire need of a refresher course today.

I pick up my little clutch and walk to the dining room with a serious attitude because I am preparing myself for disappointment and if I happen to run into him and he's like say with some young hoochie I will just give him my vampire look like I'll get your ass later when you least expect it for setting me up like this and what exactly did you think you could do for me anyway? You probably have never even had any *real* pussy, have you, Winston? Probably never even spent the night out except at a sleepover, huh?

There he is. Sitting on the bench outside the dining room. And he's alone. He stands up when he sees me and heads my way and wow does he look more handsome this evening or what and ohmyGod he's wearing that Escape again and I am so glad I didn't wear panties which is becoming a habit for me down here but maybe I should've this time because where will this stuff go that's trickling down my leg oh shoot but thank God I have my little wipes in my purse so right after he says "Hi" and smiles I say, "Hi, Winston, can you excuse me for a second, I need to go to the ladies' room," and he says, "Are you okay?" and as I amble away like they do in the movies I say, "I'm fine, just had a little accident but it's nothing really," because I surely don't want him to think I'm on my period because he's so young and everything and he probably no way would want to do it the very first time if I'm on my period even though I know men who will go down on you when you're bleeding which I think is disgusting and I can't even bear to watch them when they do it and don't come up here acting like you want to kiss me now no way go brush and floss and Listerine and then come back and let me smell your breath first and we'll consider another kiss then but not until then.

I am ashamed of myself for getting so worked up so fast and I feel kind of slutty but I also kind of like this feeling and I'm thinking I wish I could call Delilah to tell her what I'm up to—she would probably just say, "Go for it, girl!" Don't want to call Vanessa because she'll probably make me feel even sillier than I already do and Angela would probably scold me and tell me I'll be struck by lightning for even thinking about doing something like this so I clean up my act and come out of the stall and blot my lips and say, "To hell with both of you," and since nobody's really looking I actually giggle as I head back out where Winston is still standing in the very same spot.

His hair is jet black shiny and brushed back on top and I can see his scalp on the sides where it's cut very close and he has a gold hoop in his left ear and he's wearing a real button-down-the-front shirt that's not at all tropical-looking but looks as if it could've come from like the men's department of a major department store and not where the hip-hoppers shop either and I can't tell if it's purple or brown in this light but it has some kind of speckles on it that look like the solar system or galaxies and I'm so glad he has on bluejeans because I love the way he looks in them like he doesn't care that they don't exactly fit but they certainly look good on him and God his legs just go on and on and he is wearing these black suede bucks and I like his style his taste the decisions he's made and damn is he beautiful but what's weird is that he doesn't carry himself like he's all that handsome; he stands moves as if he's just sure of himself as if he knows who he is but he just doesn't know his own power yet. I am so glad.

"Is everything okay?" he asks with real concern in his eyes.

"Fine," I say.

"Are you hungry?" he asks.

"Not really. Are you?"

He smiles blushes and shakes his head from side to side. Hey. He's got dimples! When did he get those?

"We should eat though don't you think?" I say.

"We can at least try," he says and then we both start laughing almost uncontrollably and I think we both know why we're laughing.

"Winston?"

"Yes," he says and there he goes looking at me again but this time it's like real laser-like desire is emanating from his eyes and boy is it penetrating this little area in my chest that feels just like my heart and I wish he would like stop this.

"Did you just have to wear that cologne?"

"I thought you liked it."

"I do. That's the problem. It's making me feel dizzy."

"Did I put too much on?" he asks.

"No, I don't mean it that way."

And he looks at me again as if he doesn't get it.

"Never mind," I say.

"You feel like eating some pasta?" he asks and I kind of crack up because he says it like "pesta."

"Sure," I say and we walk through the dining room, where Norris and Abby and all the rest of the social directors and all the honeymooners and the folks from the van and the ones I lie out on the beach with including old man Nate all wave to us as we walk by. I should not be doing this out in the open, I think.

"Why are you in such a hurry?" Winston asks.

"Am I?"

"Yes, you sort of sped up for some reason. What's wrong?"

"Nothing," I say and sit down at an outdoor table.

"Tell me what it is," he says, leaning forward, and when I look into his eyes I can't remember what I was going to say but then I remember: "Winston, are you sure you want to do this because if you want to back out if you want to change your mind it's okay you won't hurt my feelings because I'm a big girl a grown-up really and I'm used to disappointment so if you're having second thoughts we can just eat dinner and maybe dance a little bit and say good night and be done with it no hard feelings."

His eyes are wide and he looks like he can't believe what I just said. "Could you repeat that word for word, please?" And he leans back against his chair and waits.

I am embarrassed no end. "You know what I meant."

"Stella?"

I cannot look at him.

"Stella?"

"What?" I say but I'm still not looking at him. I am feeling like I'm in fucking high school when in fact I could be the damn principal.

"I haven't changed my mind. I have been unable to think clearly this entire day because you have taken up all the space in my head. I am not afraid, Stella. I am not afraid of you. I am not afraid of what is happening. I am not afraid of what might happen. And I will be honest with you. I haven't been this excited about a woman in . . . well, never."

I can hardly swallow even though I have nothing in my mouth to swallow because my mouth is past dry. "I'm really flattered, Winston."

"I'm not saying it to flatter you. It's the truth."

"I'm still flattered. And I'll tell you," I say and sigh, because I hear myself say, "Winston, even though I think this is kind of ridiculous I want you to know how much I like you too and—"

"What's ridiculous?"

I'm trying not to let my eyes roll up in my head. "Do you want me to say it again?"

"Are we back to the age issue?"

"Yes. Winston, I just want you to know that I've never done anything like this before in my life."

"What do you mean by 'anything like this'?"

"Well, a few things. First of all I've never gone on a vacation and picked up a man that I don't even know."

"You haven't picked me up, Stella."

"You know what I'm saying."

He is beginning to look a little offended so I decide I better clean it up because I didn't mean that I was picking him up like some prostitute or something. "Well, you know, what I really mean is this, Winston. It's the nineties, the age of safe sex, and folks don't usually go jumping into bed with strangers anymore."

"Do I feel like a stranger to you?"

"Well, no. But I just met you yesterday, Winston, and that's what's also kind of weird."

"I'm more than willing to tell you anything you want to know about me. Just ask me."

"Okay. Tell me about your parents."

"Well, my dad's a surgeon in Kingston and my mom's an RN. I have two older sisters. Both are married. I grew up outside Kingston and went to private school and have done two years at the University of the West Indies in Kingston where I was studying biology but I did not like it which is why I took a course in food preparation and am considering perhaps studying hotel management or becoming a real chef I'm not sure even though my dad doesn't want me to do either. There. So now you know everything about me."

When I heard him say "my dad" I was tickled enough to giggle but I decided it would be in poor taste and plus I shouldn't hold his age against him. It isn't his fault he's only twenty-one years old. Is it? And the fact that he thinks he has told me everything about himself is downright touching. "Well, thanks for sharing, Winston."

He doesn't get it. "What else did you want to tell me?" he says.

"Well, Winston, I can't seem to remember now, which means it's not all that important."

A waitress appears and gives me a go-girl smirk and I look at Winston and realize that we are like out in the open and Lord what am I doing? "Do you know what kind of pesta you want?" he asks me and I spot something on the menu and point it out to our waitress and Winston says he'll have the same thing and she takes our drink order and of course I ask for my virgin piña colada and Winston who also does not drink orders his virgin strawberry daiquiri.

"So what should I know about *you?*" he asks and leans forward on his elbows.

"I like your shirt," I say.

He smiles. "Thank you and I'm listening. I mean I have shared my deepest secrets about my personal being with you and now I'm waiting to hear yours."

"Well, I've been divorced for three years."

"Do you presently have a boyfriend at home?"

"No."

If I'm not mistaken he actually looks relieved and then he looks at me like he's on his way to another level or something.

"Why not?"

"Because it's hard to find one I like."

"Why is it so hard? You're quite attractive. I would think men would be swarming around you."

"Swarming? I don't think so, Winston. First of all, looks can only get you so far and, well, I'll put it this way. I'm also kind of picky. Maybe too picky but I do date and may I continue, sir?"

He is smiling and nodding at me. He looks almost edible.

"I have an eleven-year-old son whose name is Quincy and whom I love dearly and he's my best buddy."

"That's nice to hear," he says.

"And I turn tricks for a living."

"Tricks? What kind of tricks?"

"I'm just kidding," I say. "I'm an analyst for a securities company."

He looks confused and who can blame him? "It only sounds good but in essence my job doesn't make a whole lot of sense and I wouldn't be surprised if in the next few weeks computers will have taken over."

"And what exactly does an analyst do?" he asks.

"It's kind of hard to explain but basically when people or I should say in my case businesses and cities and universities and the like want to invest their profits to make more money I basically analyze all the different areas and avenues and give them advice on where it looks like their money'll grow the fastest and the safest."

"Ohhhhh," he says, nodding his head up and down. "And do you like doing all this analyzing?"

"I used to, but the thrill is gone. Been gone. It's okay, though. It's a living."

"And you studied many years to learn to do this?"

"Yep. New York University. Bachelor's and master's." I don't even want to mention my M.F.A.

"Right." He sighs as if he's putting this all together and then he looks me in the eye and says, "Well, it seems to me that if one goes to college for so many years you'd at least end up working in some field that you derive a great deal of pleasure from. Don't you think?"

"Of course I do, Winston, but sometimes your attitude changes, your needs and values change, as you get older, and what used to excite you doesn't anymore."

"So do you have this same attitude toward people when your attitude changes?"

"What do you mean?"

"I mean when you get bored or someone wears out their welcome do you treat them like you would your job? Do you just kind of settle in or do you look for a new one?"

Damn. I take a deep breath. He certainly doesn't sound or think like he's only twenty-one. And he's not fidgeting or acting hyper and as a matter of fact I'd say he's more poised than I am. I'm even more surprised by what he's saying because it means he's measuring what he sees, he's trying to see if all the pieces fit, and this is refreshing. "Well, I'm the type that sort of hangs in there until I've exhausted my resources and when I realize I've given it my best shot I move on. But this can sometimes take a while."

He's nodding his head when they bring us our pesta and salad and we both instinctively seem to want to lighten up a little bit so we simply eat tiny morsels of food and chew heartily as if we're actually tasting it and then we lay our forks down and it's only a few minutes after seven and it's obvious we are both nervous but trying to pretend like this is a normal date but we know it is everything but that and maybe we should've stuck to seven instead of six because the disco doesn't open until ten but what we do is basically sit outside the dining room and listen to the band. Of course that drummer is staring at me and Winston from across the dining room because I can see his beady little eyes glisten and the other one, the young guitar player as he turns out to be, is looking at me like I'm still a reincarnation of his old girlfriend but Winston and I go and sit on a chaise by the pool and listen to the waves and the music and just talk about Jamaica and America and then we go for a walk but not on the beach because those stupid sand fleas are out there and even though they are invisible they bite you in groups and particularly your ankles and especially if you're wearing perfume they love perfume they bite you so hard you don't feel it until moments later when you begin to scratch and then it is uncontrollable and you really could cry but you think that if you just scratch hard enough it will go away but it doesn't and all you see is red and it is blood and so you have to rub that cream on and it doesn't help all that much which is why Winston and I agree to walk over to Hedonism where they are having a Hunk Show Contest and we sit there in their open dining room/bar and watch twenty young men from all over the world model suits shorts and swimsuits. They are all gorgeous and buffed and I am surprised that people have their clothes on because it's not what I was told they did over here and of course and under normal circumstances I would probably be screaming at these guys like everybody else is but they just don't seem to have the finesse and poise and grace and beauty that Winston here has and he's not at all an exhibitionist and he certainly could be which is why I feel like the lucky one I really do.

On the walk back he takes my hand and places it inside his and really grasps it and I am not kidding I am getting chills and goosebumps all over my arms and they seem to be running down my back as if somebody's tickling me but then his hand becomes warmer and I seem to be squeezing it tighter and we walk back onto the grounds of the Castle Beach Negril and the band is packing up and so we go into the disco and the DJ is playing some pump-to-the-bump music and Winston and I don't bother to sit down but head out to the crowded dance floor where we will dance for the next two hours and where I will get drunk watching how suave and smooth he moves, unlike some twenty-one-year-olds who are rather wild but not him he moves in an unrehearsed way as if he is feeling the music and it is what is dictating how he moves and he watches me swing and sway and I don't do so bad myself I just don't do the latest dances because I don't care but then the DJ plays this hold-me-in-your-arms kind of song and in slow motion Winston sort of like automatically pulls me close to him and puts his arms around me and we rock in one small spot and I go ahead and put my arms around the small of his back and he is nice and narrow and I feel like I'm really starting to spin the way that girl does with John Travolta in that *Staying Alive* movie and Winston smells so good and his chest is firm and his arms are so long and they are making me feel like I'm inside something good something warm safe go ahead and relax enjoy him Stella it's okay and his shoulders are so wide and I am looking at this hair sticking out above the V in his shirt and he smells so good and he feels so good and I hope this song lasts for at least another hour and I swear when I feel his hands squeeze my waist and he pushes me out and away from him a little bit and looks down at me and smiles and then kisses me on my forehead I feel like I'm on some kind of drug that causes euphoria because I am like floating right now but when he starts to pull me back against his chest and holds me as close as I can get but as softly as he can I finally realize that Winston is not at all a boy that he is not my toy for the night he is in fact a real man.

It is now about twelve-thirty and the dance floor is empty with the exception of me and Winston. I think we not only have enjoyed dancing together but have both been stalling because we are kind of scared. But scared or not, the place will be closing soon and we have to get out of here and besides I'm not *that* scared really I want to do this so on a Warren G song I take Winston by the hand and say, "Are you ready to go yet?" and he says, "I've *been* ready I just thought you wanted to dance more," and I shake my head back and forth and we both smile and he takes my hand as we walk through the game room and out to the path that leads to my room and when we get there I open the door and walk in first and then I really feel like I'm in high school because I can't remember what I'm supposed to do next.

My heartbeat is way over my heart rate zone and if I had my monitor on it would've been beeping for like the past two hours. I am not a stranger to seduction it's just that I'm used to being the seducee and not the seducer but I can do this I can show him what to do, so after I press on Seal of course I turn to him and say, "Have a seat, Winston," and he sort of walks over to me all tall and everything and puts his arms on my bare shoulders and bends down and says—not whispers—in my ear, "You are really beautiful," and before I can answer I feel something warm and heavenly land on my lips but this can't be right this can't be oh God what is he doing he is pressing his lips against mine so softly that I am feeling like one of those velvet paintings and oh no he's not supposed to be able to make me feel like oh God he is kissing me like he has been wanting to do this for a long time but he is not frantic he is not pressing in hard and now his lips are whispering they are just barely brushing mine and please don't stop Winston I have been waiting a long time for a man to kiss me like this like he means it and who taught you how to wait a minute hold it stop I say in my head and push him away for a minute.

"What's wrong?" he asks.

I want to say don't you get it? You are like kissing me like you know what you're doing you are like kissing me like you know where my weak spots all are and your kisses are reducing them to nothing I am losing my strength but please kiss me again because you feel like what I need what's been missing like I've been waiting years all my life to have your lips touch mine like this, but all I say is, "Winston, your kiss is . . ."

"What?" He looks worried and I realize I am overreacting.

"I didn't expect this."

"What?"

"For you to be such a good kisser."

"You're the good kisser."

"No. You're the good kisser and it's making me weak. I wish I could but I can't lie about it. Look at me," I say and I feel like he must surely be able to see steam coming from my entire body or at least he can see how I'm disintegrating into a vapor.

"Feel my heart," he says and places my hand over it and sure enough it's pounding away. "It feels you," he says.

"I want you to take advantage of me," I hear myself say.

And he looks at me as if to say you've got this all wrong it is not about taking advantage of you and then he kisses me again and I am turning into mush inside and I haven't felt this in a gazillion years since maybe college and I feel like I could cry because I've been waiting to feel this magic I've forgotten how the magic feels and I've been waiting for him I have read about the power of a kiss but when he puts his tongue in my mouth he is not frantic he is slow-dancing with mine he is sending me a message and I'm getting it he is telling me a story and I am loving every word and when he holds me tighter he is telling me he wants to be closer can I get closer and so I wrap my tongue around his as if I'm trying to protect it from something and I move in deeper and I want him to know that it is not just the kiss that is moving me it is you the kisser the man behind the kiss and I have no choice I shift my shoulder blade under his armpit so as to feel like we are inside each other but he already knows that I can't get close enough to him and because he is helping me find a position where we will be able to blend once and for all and because it is impossible in what feels like slow motion we begin to search explore chins ears elbows eyebrows arms fingertips wrists but always back to our lips where something passes from him to me and me to him and we are spinning now and my lips feel like a hot peach between my legs feels like a hot peach and Winston please don't stop because I don't care that it's a cliché but I feel like a butterfly and I don't want you to stop making me flutter but he kisses me on my cheek and I kiss him on his cheek and he rubs his cheekbone against my cheekbone and he says, "Are you okay?" and it is difficult for me to answer that question because if am trembling now I mean really trembling and I can only nod and he says, "Are you sure?" and I say something stupid like, "Isn't it hot in here to you?" and he takes those hands and brushes over my braids and holds me again until like three more Seal songs play and I swear I'm about ready to cry for real and if I knew him better I would and when I feel him unzip my dress I am scared but he does it so delicately so gently that I don't even realize I'm standing there in my strapless bra and no panties and he holds me to him again and rubs his hands up and down the back of my body and he says, "You certainly don't feel like I'd expect any forty-two-year-old woman to feel," and I say, "But I am," and he steps back and looks at me and I feel like Cinda-fucking-rella and he says, "And you don't look like any forty-two-year-old woman I've ever seen," and I say, "But I am," and he says, "Well, you feel better than any twenty-year-old girl," and I say, "But I'm not," and he says, "I know and I'm glad and you are so sweet and so lovely and Stella if we just stand here for a while would that be okay with you because I love the way you feel like this and I just really want to take you in," and I am really slipping away here by the second but I say in a little tiny voice, "Okay," and he holds me even closer so that I feel a heartbeat in his belly I can feel the hair on his belly brush against sink into my belly if that's possible until somehow it is minutes or it could be hours later and we are lying next to each other on the bed and somehow we have gotten his clothes off and he is kissing my nose and shoulders and he is still moving so very slowly and I'm so very glad that he's not rushing and if I'm not mistaken it feels as if he knows exactly what he's oh my God those lips are on my breasts oh God he's kissing them the right way and somebody please help me where did he come from please don't stop and oh please do stop before I scream but now his mouth is back against mine and I hear him unwrap his condom and he whispers in my ear, "Is it okay now?" and I'm thinking he is so polite he is certainly a considerate one and my answer is a light kiss and when he finds his way in he helps me glide and he guides me to his beat which is so slow and undulating and I feel him hold on to me until we are moving like those waves outside the balcony and I am lost at sea until I feel him squeeze me as if I'm falling overboard and he whispers, "Oh Stel-la," in my ear and I find myself succumbing surrendering to him and I say, "Win-ston, what are you doing to me?" and he sighs and whispers, "Oh Stel-la, why are you doing this to *me?*" and I say, "What?" and he moans, "Stel-la," and I am feeling like hot foam and I moan and sigh, "Winston," and we both squeeze each other as if we have been looking for each other for a long time and when we rest our heads against each other's wet skin the only thing I think we understand is that this is where we've always wanted to be and now we are here.

VOICES OF THE NEW WAVE

ASKIA MUHAMMAD TOURÉ
(1938–)

Most historians of the Black Aesthetic and Black Arts Movements, which accompanied the struggles of the Civil Rights era, credit three men—Amiri Baraka, Larry Neal, and Askia Touré—with spearheading the turn of African American scholars and artists toward an ethnic-based aesthetic. With Neal's passing and Baraka's command in both contemporary poetry and the critical arena, Touré must be seen as the one poet and activist of the era who has developed his craft to the deepest reflection of the groundbreaking research with which Afrocentric scholars are focusing on ancient Africa. Moreover, through phenomena such as the Nile Valley Conference and the Association for the Study of Classical African Civilizations, new depths in his poetry are accompanied by his close work and association with such scholars of ancient African history as John Henrik Clarke, Asa Hilliard, and Larry Williams.

Born on October 13, 1938, in Raleigh, North Carolina, Touré grew up in Dayton, Ohio. Having the given name of Rolland Snellings, he is the oldest of two sons born to Clifford R. Snellings, Sr., and Nancy Lynnette Bullock Snellings. After graduating from Dayton-Roosevelt High School, Touré worked his way to New York, where he eventually became one of the original Umbra poets of the early sixties when the Umbra Workshop flourished under the watchful and devoted guidance of Langston Hughes. Within a few years, he was selected to be a poetry student of the eminent novelist and teacher John Oliver Killens.

Along with other young black writers such as Calvin Hernton, Tom Dent, David Henderson, Ishmael Reed, and Lorenzo Thomas, Touré was a member of Killens's famous writers workshop at Columbia University from 1971 to 1973. As the Black Arts Movement developed, Touré served as editor of two of its seminal journals, *Black Dialogue* and the *Journal of Black Poetry.* From 1967 to 1968 at San Francisco State University, Touré, Sonia Sanchez, and Amiri Baraka worked with Nathan Hare to establish the first black studies program in the United States. The three poets taught the first classes of African American history, and Hare chaired the program.

Touré's first book was a prose work titled *Samory Touré.* Appearing in 1963 and coauthored with Tom Feelings and Matthew Meade, the book is an illustrated biography of the great Mandinka freedom fighter Samory Touré, who was the grandfather of the former president of Guinea, Ahmed Sékou Touré, another notable modern freedom fighter who resisted French colonialism in West Africa.

By the mid-seventies, Touré's poetry was widely published in journals of and for the Black Aesthetic. His first book of poems, *JuJu,* was produced by Third World Press in 1970. Of this offering and Touré's second volume, *Songhai* (1973), Baraka would later write in his autobiography,

> Poets like Larry Neal and Askia Touré were, in my mind, masters of the new black poetry.... Askia had the song-like cast to his words, as if the poetry actually was

meant to be sung. I heard him one up at the Baby Grand when we first got into Harlem and that singing sound influenced what I was to do with poetry from then on. To me, Larry and Askia were the state of the art, where it was, at that moment.

Songhai was just as favorably received as *JuJu.* In reviewing the book for the journal *Black World* in 1974, the eminent Black Aesthetic critic Addison Gayle, Jr., wrote, "Touré is one of the finest poets in the language; his verse rings with the sound and timbre of Coltrane and Bird, with the lyricism of Toomer at his best, and contains the rich, symbolic import of the best of Claude McKay's Jamaican poetry."

Eskia Mphahlele likewise praised the volume for the poet's understanding of African motif, culture, history, and rhythms. In a 1974 article for *Okike,* a cultural magazine from the Ibo region of Nigeria, Mphahlele wrote,

> Askia Muhammad Touré . . . (a poet filled with) compassion and no-nonsense faith in the great things Black Art can achieve for his people. . . . He has for some time been one of the animateurs of the Black Arts Movement. . . . Indeed, I know no Afro-American poet writing today who has Touré's lush lyricism.

In the mid-eighties, Touré changed his home base to Atlanta, Georgia, and continued to join colleagues there who were engaged in the profound search for the true Africa, which colonialism sought to destroy. In 1984, he was, along with Asa Hilliard, Larry Williams, and the famous scholar Ivan Van Sertima, one of the founding organizers of the historic Nile Valley Conference held at Morehouse College in Atlanta. The conference placed ancient Kemet (Egypt) as the foundation of Western civilization, with the premise that civilization sprang from the Nile Valley and that the leaders of the Greco-Roman world were influenced and taught by the priests and scholars of ancient Egypt.

Touré's third volume of poetry, *From the Pyramids to the Projects: Poems of Genocide and Resistance* (1990), simultaneously exposes and transcends that planned destruction. The scope of the project so impressed the critics that Touré was awarded the Tenth Annual American Poetry Book Award for Literature in 1989. To celebrate that presentation, Ishmael Reed said:

> Askia Muhammad Touré was the Father of the new black poetry. His deeply felt commitment to the struggle of oppressed people has charged his work with an electricity that blows away all of the flat nonsense that passes for American poetry today. . . . The title of his new book, *From the Pyramids to the Projects,* tells us much about his work. He reminds black people of their history, of their greatness before their exile in 'the wilderness of North America,' as Malcolm X once said. . . . Askia reminds them that they are descended from great civilizations and that royal blood flows through their veins. . . . He is our link to the past, to the Kings, the griots, and the warriors our children never heard about. Lost in the wilderness of Central Park. Lost in the wilderness of Howard Beach. Askia is the Moses who would lead them out. He is one of the few visionary poets that we have.

Touré still lives in Atlanta and teaches at colleges in the Atlanta University complex. His next volume of Afrocentric epic poetry, *Dawnsong!,* is due to be published by 1997. His commitment to being a modern griot, or oral historian, of the African

American experience, is the great informant of his art. As he continues to work to rebuild African history, his focus hopefully will crystallize even more.

❖❖❖

Touré's contributions to the founding of the Black Arts Movement and the Black Aesthetic, as well as discussions of his poetry, are included in Addison Gayle, Jr., "Reclaiming the Southern Experience: The Black Aesthetic Ten Years Later," *Black World,* no. 11 (September 1974); Eugene B. Redmond, *Drum Voices* (1976); Amiri Baraka, *The Autobiography of LeRoi Jones/Amiri Baraka* (1984); Joanne Gabbins's essay in *Dictionary of Literary Biography: Afro-American Poets Since 1955,* vol. 41 (1985).

Osirian Rhapsody: A Myth

(FOR LARRY NEAL AND BOB MARLEY)

I

He said he was seeking the wind,
the summits
        of its
    birth: those legendary heights
        composed of ice and snowdrift
blue rocks of morning,
    tantamount
        to time's crystal beginnings
beyond the syllables
of endeavor: visions rooted in
    forever,
wafted in the silence of our dreams.

He was a tall, hawkish man,
    aquiline-eyed, rangy
            filled with
            strange longings,
silent passion
        danced in his voice—a poet,
some say—his angular figure draped
around
        a battered guitar, whose
melancholy soul conjured
moments of unspoken intimacy,
            filaments of desire
washing like the tides across shores of memory.

We sought him, sang by his side, those
opulent
        midnights when,
            caught in the music's enchantment,
we expanded our vision:
        seeking the sonorous

cataclysm of
bardic rapture manifest
in charismatic overtones:
weaving textures, tonalities,
tattered dramas of our heartbroken destinies.

II

We were the New Men
magic
singers
riding electric carpets to the stars.
Galaxies
of creative ecstasy
spread out before us
while we chanted litanies of Rebirth
bound (we thought)
to upset holocausts
this repressive, hidebound
earth had manifested
creating tombs, jails,
infernos of the spirit,
exterminating
angels of the mind.

He was our sage, our
blue-voiced
genius-child: prophet of
galactic metaphor,
magus of angelic vistas
of sunburst
elevating legacies of dawn.

He said he was seeking the wind,
that roaring
genie/conjurer
of monsoon velocities
in unsung archipelagos,
tropic vistas where
the emerald sacredness
of vegetal beginnings
erupted in the womb of myth.
In ostrich-plumed epochs
of Nubian splendor,
he sought the scarifications
of secret wisdom
etched upon
the indigo flesh of kings.

Oracle

in escalating decalogues
of melody,
he rummaged through
the runes of harmony, to discover
the silver scales and ranges
of
syncopation
released from Pyramids
of monumental
Joy.

Invocation/Chant:
Hawkman[1] *of audacious rhapsody, bearing*
a new sun
cradled in the Whirlwind's[2] *voluptuous*
laughter,
obsidian sacrament to
archetypal passion evolving in
primordial darkness,
we chant: elaborate phallic megaliths
elevating
electronic polyphony to languish
in the melody of your
breath.
Osiris of cyclical
Avatars: aboriginal pungent
sepulcher baptized in
totems of ancestral
blood,
We Oracles caress
tendrils of
elongated
crocodile fire
to fertilize the obeah
of your
Song!

Dawnsong!
(for the Ancient Anu/Nubians: founders of Nile Valley Civilization)

ETHIOPIA AND THE AFRICAN INTERIOR HAVE ALWAYS BEEN CONSIDERED BY EGYPTIANS AS THE HOLY LAND FROM WHICH THEIR FOREBEARS HAD COME. . . . THE PRIESTESS OF AMON AT THEBES,

---

[1]*Hawkman.* The royal falcon or "hawk" was the main symbol of the Pharaohs. Each Pharaoh was a Horus (Falcon, son of Osiris) while he lived and became an Osiris (King of the Underworld) upon death.

[2]*Whirlwind.* Wind of Change, symbolizing great tempests, revolution, social turbulence; also prophecy, among African Americans, e.g., mass leader Marcus Garvey's famous quotation, "If I die in Atlanta (in prison), look for me in the Whirlwind!" where he promised to return with hundreds of slave revolt leaders to aid his people in liberation wars.

THE EGYPTIAN HOLY SITE PAR EXCELLENCE, COULD NOT BE OTHER THAN A MEROITIC SUDANESE (A NUBIAN).

ONEIKH ANTA DIOP, *THE AFRICAN ORIGINS OF CIVILIZATION*

Bennu bird, emerge from your ashes,
broadcast ecstatic cries
to the ibis, your kindred;
welcome a new sun rising from
Nile waters, like a bright flamingo,
shrieking with joy . . .

Dawnsong. Jubilee. My bones and fossils
powder this proud land[1] mankind
reclaims as Mother.
The Great Rift Valley, the Mountains
of the Moon, the Great Lakes region
blessed by a million mornings of legendary
dreamtimes, dawnsongs, times of living
gods, demons, royal ancestors: chants
which fertilized
    the humid atmosphere
        human aeons ago—fifty thousand years![2]
Yea. The swamps and wide savannahs
of the stellar people pregnant with
myriad myths and magic rituals; resounding
drumsongs giving birthchants and birthpangs
to create the lunar people:
    indigo tribes with lyre-horned
    cattle, scarification litanies,
    cornrowed hair crowning
    prognathous silhouettes;

Matrilineal[3] clans honoring god-queens
as "Great Mother" steatopygic[4]
with natural, Nubian grace.
Cornrows:
        rituals of sculptured, braided hair
above jewel-like scarifications, signifying

---

[1]*Kemet.* The indigenous Afrikan name for the country. It means "the black land." Egypt is a Greek name.

[2]*fifty thousand years!* "A probe by microwave beams of an American radar satellite beneath the sands of the Sahara, revealing cultures 200,000 years old and the traces of ancient rivers running from this African center" (*Journal of African Civilizations*).

[3]*Black Matriarchy/Agriculture.* "What is the origin of Black matriarchy? We do not know for certain at the present time; however, current opinion holds that the matriarchal system is related to farming. If agriculture was discovered by women, as is sometimes thought, if it be true that they were the first to think of selecting nourishing herbs, by the very fact that they remained at home while the men engaged in more dangerous activities (hunting, warfare, etc.) . . ." (Cheikh Anta Diop).

[4]*Steatopygic.* Large buttocked, an anatomical feature related to Africoid peoples.

innumerable icons of feminine status
among extended families/clans/tribes.

Mattocks mating with
the earth
    as warriors mate with
    holy matriarchs, ritualizing love.

Observe, in the human dawn,
the inner dawn
    break across horizons of
    Nubian minds, grappling
    with the soil, learning
            cycles of seasons;
growing crops, computing star charts,
moon charts, primordial innovation,
            leading to mathematics
and solar calendars these
melanin millennia.
Moving, growing, migrating north,
gaining spiritual rhythms / original visions:
mirroring Cosmic principles
—"As Above, so Below"—
from the moon and stellar jewels
glowing against the night, like
diamonds against indigo skin.

Cornrows extending snake-like tendrils
over the human skull; hair as
extended body-sculpture: the primal
art form; myriad designs of
sculptured hair (twisted, woven, braided,
with cowries as pearls) across
elongated heads, over faces; Cornrows
woven, braided into agricultural rhythms:
these myriad rows of bending women
giving definition to the soil,
mothering the seeds, creating
legacies of crops to nourish
nations to come . . .

* * * * * * * *

Night; copper moon-in-mist,
talking drums, as griots, related
the magical awe, hideous beauty, written
in bloody icons of human sacrifice.
She—chant/scream/Mask—
the Oracle task;
        Speak, Spirits, Now!

Nude body oiled, voluptuous,
leaping, shrieking, dancing,
being ridden by the gods—
through sunbursts of ecstasy—
comets, shooting stars—
prophesying wars, plagues,
miracles of birth and rebirth;

Dancing amid the gathered clans
in their thousands, shadows and
silhouettes relate the magic:
She changing shape into
a cobra, a lioness, a hawk,
before the hypnotized multitudes.
Ostrich plumes, royal umbrellas,
gleaming jewelry, reflections
of firelight in the eyes, glistening
teeth, sighs fill thousands of
throats, as quickened hearts
witness the presence of the gods.
Totems with firelight blazing
on their banners:
the lion people, jackal people,
sparrow-hawk and crocodile;
Clans—majestic, silent,
frightened—enchanted
by the dancing queen.

* * * * * * * *

O sing of the God-people!
The mighty Nubians, rooted in origins
down beneath the Mountains of the Moon.
The "blameless Ethiopians" of the Greeks,
feasting with the gods; expanding serpent-power,
in primordial energy, opening
the pineal Eye, in
sacred temples of
the Winged Scarab,
Mind!

Those cornrowed, indigo clans;
strong Anu warriors, nubile matriarchs,
Sudani hordes loving God, rituals,
magic and lyre-horned cattle.
Masonic those steatopygic queens,
who with agriculture, herbs and wisdom
birthed priest-kings, emerged
from huts to settled villages,

riding the Sunbird of myth:
Bennu bird shrieking into realms
of Knowledge Magic Cosmic Truth!

Hazy, vermilion dawns breaking
into torrid, blazing Suns
creating Isis Osiris Horus,
and their kin;
leading to Ta-Sili,[5] Ta-Seti,[6]
On, Abydos, Denderah[7]—and
Pyramids to come!

JOHN EDGAR WIDEMAN
(1941–)

John Edgar Wideman is an intricate, allusive, experimental novelist, and nonfiction and short story writer. Like William Faulkner, he has dedicated his art to the creation of a small community, Homewood, over a long period of time and with a recurrent cast of characters. This creation is based on the history of his family over several generations. In fact, Wideman's creative world is a fusion of fact and fiction. In his early work, he made fiction out of personal history, and in his more recent work, the distinction between fact and fiction has totally broken down. His creative history begins with his great-great-great-grandmother Sybela Owens, her escape from slavery, and her founding of Homewood, Pennsylvania. It continues, if not ends, with Robby, his brother, who was sentenced to prison for murder, his own son's imprisonment, and the destruction of the black organization Move. Wideman sees both his great-great-great-grandmother and younger brother as prisoners of white America. In fact, his nonfiction book *Brothers & Keepers* (1985), about himself, a college professor and writer, and his brother, Robby, is a story "talking about our [black] lives." With myth, folklore, and history, he has created an impressive and rich canvas of African American life. Like Ishmael Reed, he defines what has been called experimental in his work as black traditional, the styles of black storytelling. "What seems to ramble begins to cohere when the listener understands the process, understands that the voice seeks to recover everything," he says in "The Beginning of Homewood," an essay included in *Damballah* (1981).

John Edgar Wideman was born on June 14, 1941, to Edgar and Betty French Wideman in Washington, D.C. He spent the first ten years of his life in Homewood, a black neighborhood in Pittsburgh, Pennsylvania, but later moved with his parents to Shadyside, a predominantly white neighborhood in Pittsburgh, where he at-

[5]*Ta-Sili.* The pre-Kemet Saharan culture.

[6]*Ta-Seti* (means "Land of the Bow," alluding to the military skills of Nubian archers). The pre-Kemet Nubian kingdom, recently discovered by archeologists from the University of Chicago's Oriental Institute. Ta-Seti created the Pharaonic institutions, hieroglyphics, royal symbols, etc., over two hundred years before King Mena or Aha united "the two Lands," Kemet.

[7]*On, Abydos, Denderah.* Some of the early cities that the Anu (Nubians) created when they migrated north from Ta-Seti to settle what was to become Kemet. Known as the "blacksmiths," they were said to be led by King Asar (Osiris), his sister-queen Auset (Isis), and the sage Tehuti (Thoth).

tended preponderantly white schools. He won a scholarship to the University of Pennsylvania, where he majored in English and became a basketball star. After graduating Phi Beta Kappa in 1963, he attended Oxford University on a Rhodes scholarship. He was the second black to achieve this honor; the first was the Howard University philosopher Alain Locke, in 1905. In 1966, Wideman attended the prestigious Creative Writing Workshop at the University of Iowa. After joining the Department of English at the University of Pennsylvania, he started Penn's first Afro-American Studies Program. For many years, he taught at the University of Wyoming at Laramie. He currently teaches at the University of Massachusetts at Amherst.

Wideman published his first novel, *A Glance Away,* a study of a drug addict, in 1967 when he was twenty-six. With the publication of *Hiding Place* (1981) and *Damballah* (1981), he began writing about Homewood. In 1984, he won the prestigious PEN Faulkner Award. Wideman refuses to create simple, self-contained stories and novels. To appreciate him fully, one must read a great deal of his work, and the growing consensus is that he is well worth the effort. As Michael Gorra observed in the *New York Times Book Review* (June 14, 1992), "The more you read John Wideman, the more impressive he seems."

The novel *Philadelphia Fire* (1990) is a more recent example of Wideman's unique achievement. It focuses on the 1985 police bombing of the black organization Move and fuses history, myth, fiction, and autobiography. The work contains a symphony of black voices, from the vernacular to the highly educated. It movingly articulates Wideman's commitment to the black masses and his desire for black people to be free in the Americas. He thinks of all blacks as potential outlaws in a country that does not value black life. In this novel, he wants to write of his imprisoned son as well as the Move victims. In Wideman's work in general, he finds a deep connection between runaway slaves, the Move victims, his imprisoned brother, and his imprisoned son. They are all called criminals by this society, and Wideman, being a black American, feels implicated in their crimes.

The Stories of John Edgar Wideman appeared in 1992, bringing together his complete stories to date, including those in his two earlier collections, *Damballah* (1981) and *Fever* (1989), as well as new material written especially for the volume. Among these new stories is his brilliant experimental piece "newborn thrown in trash and dies." It records urban tragedy as it poignantly depicts a newborn's meditations on life as she falls ten stories down a trash chute to her death. Such short fiction inspired Michiko Kakutani in the July 21, 1993, edition of the *New York Times* to say, "At his best, Mr. Wideman is not merely a practitioner of storytelling; he's one of those rare writers capable of re-inventing the form and making it his own."

Wideman speaks of history, storytelling, and folk culture in his essay "The Architectonics of Fiction" (1990). According to him, history "is a cage, a conundrum we must escape or resolve before our art can go freely about its business." He says about fiction, "Good stories transport us to those extraordinarily diverse regions where individual lives are enacted." He adds, "Folk culture preserves and expresses an identity, a history, a self-evaluation apart from those destructive, incarcerating images proliferated by the mainline culture." For the novelist, the folk tradition is not something dead and gone, but it continues into the present. In fact, he finds the folk tradition present in rap music. For him, "rap reasserts the African core of black music." Accordingly, in *Philadelphia Fire* (1990), Wideman creates his own rap songs. The story that Wideman tells and retells is the black American tale of bondage and freedom. Its "theme was to be the urge for freedom, the resolve of the runaway to live free or die." In 1996 Wideman published *The Cattle Killing*, his first new novel in six years.

Through fusing family history and modernist experimental techniques, Wideman has created a highly individual and sophisticated body of fiction that celebrates the enduring black tradition. Hence, he was awarded the MacArthur Grant, the so-called genius award, in 1993. In Wideman's work, the reader can hear the highly nuanced black voice speak—a voice of the folk, of history, of community, always speaking of freedom.

❖❖❖

For helpful critical statements about Wideman, see Bernard W. Bell, *The Afro-American Novel and Its Tradition* (1987); Wilfred Samuels, "Going Home: A Conversation with John Edgar Wideman," *Callaloo*, vol. 6, no. 1 (February 1983); and James W. Coleman, *Blackness and Modernism: The Literary Development of John Edgar Wideman* (1989). Wideman's "Architectonics of Fiction," was originally published in *Callaloo* vol. 13, no.1 (Winter 1990).

newborn thrown in trash and dies

They say you see your whole life pass in review the instant before you die. How would *they* know. If you die after the instant replay, you aren't around to tell anybody anything. So much for they and what they say. So much for the wish to be a movie star for once in your life because I think that's what people are hoping, what people are pretending when they say you see your life that way at the end. Death doesn't turn your life into a five-star production. The end is the end. And what you know at the end goes down the tube with you. I can speak to you now only because I haven't reached bottom yet. I'm on my way, faster than I want to be traveling and my journey won't take long, but I'm just beginning the countdown to zero. Zero's where I started also so I know a little bit about zero. Know what they say isn't necessarily so. In fact the opposite's true. You begin and right in the eye of that instant storm your life plays itself out for you in advance. That's the theater of your fate, there's where you're granted a preview, the coming attractions of everything that must happen to you. Your life rolled into a ball so dense, so superheavy it would drag the universe down to hell if this tiny, tiny lump of whatever didn't dissipate as quickly as it formed. Quicker. The weight of it is what you recall some infinitesimal fraction of when you stumble and crawl through your worst days on earth.

Knowledge of what's coming gone as quickly as it flashes forth. Quicker. Faster. Gone before it gets here, so to speak. Any other way and nobody would stick around to play out the cards they're dealt. No future in it. You begin forgetting before the zero's entirely wiped off the clock face, before the next digit materializes. What they say is assbackwards, a saying by the way, assbackwards itself. Whether or not you're treated to a summary at the end, you get the whole thing handed to you, neatly packaged as you begin. Then you forget it. Or try to forget. Live your life as if it hasn't happened before, as if the tape has not been prepunched full of holes, the die cast.

I remember because I won't receive much of a life. A measure of justice in the world, after all. I receive a compensatory bonus. Since the time between my wake-up call and curfew is so cruelly brief, the speeded-up preview of what will come to pass, my life, my portion, my destiny, my career, slowed down just enough to let me peek. Not slow enough for me to steal much, but I know some of what it contains, its finality, the groaning, fatal weight of it around my neck.

Call it a trade-off. A standoff. Intensity for duration. I won't get much and this devastating flash isn't much either, but I get it. Zingo.

But the future remains mysterious. Even if we all put our heads together and became one gigantic brain, a brain lots smarter than the sum of each of our smarts, an intelligence as great as the one that guides ants, whales or birds, because they're smarter, they figure things out not one by one, each individual locked in the cell of its head, its mortality, but collectively, doing what the group needs to do to survive, relate to the planet. If we were smarter even than birds and bees, we'd still have only a clue about what's inside the first flash of being. I know it happened and that I receive help from it. Scattered help. Sometimes I catch on. Sometimes I don't. But stuff from it's being pumped out always. I know things I have no business knowing. Things I haven't been around long enough to learn myself. For instance, many languages. A vast palette of feelings. The names of unseen things. Nostalgia for a darkness I've never experienced, a darkness another sense I can't account for assures me I will enter again. Large matters. Small ones. Naked as I am I'm dressed so to speak for my trip. Down these ten swift flights to oblivion.

Floor Ten. Nothing under the sun, they say, is new. This time they're right. They never stop talking so percentages guarantee they'll be correct sometimes. Especially since they speak out of both sides of their mouths at once: *Birds of a feather flock together. Opposites attract.* Like the billion billion monkeys at typewriters who sooner or later will bang out this story I think is uniquely mine. Somebody else, a Russian, I believe, with a long, strange-sounding name, has already written about his life speeding past as he topples slow-motion from a window high up in a tall apartment building. But it was in another country. And alas, the Russian's dead.

Floor Nine. In this building they shoot craps. One of many forms of gambling proliferating here. Very little new wealth enters this cluster of buildings that are like high-rise covered wagons circled against the urban night, so what's here is cycled and recycled by games of chance, by murder and other violent forms of exchange. Kids do it. Adults. Birds and bees. The law here is the same one ruling the jungle, they say. They say this is a jungle of the urban asphalt concrete variety. Since I've never been to Africa or the Amazon I can't agree or disagree. But you know what I think about what they say.

Seven come eleven. Snake eyes. Boxcars. Fever in the funkhouse searching for a five. Talk to me, baby. Talk. Talk. Please. Please. Please.

They cry and sing and curse and pray all night long over these games. On one knee they chant magic formulas to summon luck. They forget luck is rigged. Some of the men carry a game called Three Card Monte downtown. They cheat tourists who are stupid enough to trust in luck. Showmen with quick hands shuffling cards to a blur, fast feet carrying them away from busy intersections when cops come to break up their scam or hit on them for a cut. Flimflam artists, con men who daily use luck as bait and hook, down on their knees in a circle of other men who also should know better, trying to sweet-talk luck into their beds. Luck is the card you wish for, the card somebody else holds. You learn luck by its absence. Luck is what separates you from what you want. Luck is always turning its back and you lose.

Like other potions and powders they sell and consume here luck creates dependency. In their rooms people sit and wait for a hit. A yearning unto death for more, more, more till the little life they've been allotted dies in a basket on the doorstep where they abandoned it.

The Floor of Facts. Seventeen stories in this building. The address is 2950 West 23rd Street. My mother is nineteen years old. The trash chute down which I was dropped is forty-five feet from the door of the apartment my mother was visiting. I was born and will die Monday, August 12, 1991. The small door in the yellow cinder block wall is maroon. I won't know till the last second why my mother pushes it open.

In 1990 nine discarded babies were discovered in New York City's garbage. As of August this year seven have been found. 911 is the number to call if you find a baby in the trash. Ernesto Mendez, forty-four, a Housing Authority caretaker, will notice my head, shoulders and curly hair in a black plastic bag he slashes open near the square entrance of the trash compactor on the ground floor of this brown-brick public housing project called the Gerald J. Carey Gardens. Gardens are green places where seeds are planted, tended, nurtured. The headline above my story reads "Newborn Is Thrown in Trash and Dies." The headline will remind some readers of a similar story with a happy ending that appeared in March. A baby rescued and surviving after she was dropped down a trash chute by her twelve-year-old mother. The reporter, a Mr. George James who recorded many of the above facts, introduced my unhappy story in the Metro Section of the *New York Times* on Wednesday, August 14, with this paragraph: "A young Brooklyn woman gave birth on Monday afternoon in a stairwell in a Coney Island housing project and then dropped the infant down a trash chute into a compactor ten stories below, the police said yesterday." And that's about it. What's fit to print. My tale in a nutshell followed by a relation of facts obtained by interview and reading official documents. Trouble is I could not be reached for comment. No one's fault. Certainly no negligence on the reporter's part. He gave me sufficient notoriety. Many readers must have shaken their heads in dismay or sighed or blurted Jesus Christ, did you see this, handing the Metro Section across the breakfast table or passing it to somebody at work. As grateful as I am to have my story made public you should be able to understand why I feel cheated, why the newspaper account is not enough, why I want my voice to be part of the record. The awful silence is not truly broken until we speak for ourselves. One chance to speak was snatched away. Then I didn't cry out as I plunged through the darkness. I didn't know any better. Too busy thinking to myself, *This is how it is, this is how it is, how it is . . .* accustoming myself to what it seemed life brings, what life is. Spinning, tumbling, a breathless rush, terror, exhilaration and wonder, wondering is this it, am I doing it right. I didn't know any better. The floors, the other lives packed into this building were going on their merry way as I flew past them in the darkness of my tunnel. No one waved. No one warned me. Said hello or good-bye. And of course I was too busy flailing, trying to catch my breath, trying to stop shivering in the sudden, icy air, welcoming almost the thick, pungent draft rushing up at me as if another pair of thighs were opening below to replace the ones from which I'd been ripped.

In the quiet dark of my passage I did not cry out. Now I will not be still.

A Floor of Questions. Why.

A Floor of Opinions. I believe the floor of fact should have been the ground floor, the foundation, the solid start, the place where all else is firmly rooted. I believe there should be room on the floor of fact for what I believe, for this opinion and others I could not venture before arriving here. I believe some facts are unnecessary and that unnecessary borders on untrue. I believe facts sometimes speak for themselves but never speak for us. They are never anyone's voice and voices are what we must learn to listen to if we wish ever to be heard. I believe my mother did not hate me. I believe somewhere I have a father, who if he is reading this and listening carefully will recognize me as his daughter and be ashamed, heartbroken. I must believe these things. What else do I have. Who has made my acquaintance or noticed or cared or forgotten me. How could anyone be aware of what hurtles by faster than light, blackly, in a dark space beyond the walls of the rooms they live in, beyond the doors they lock, shades they draw when they have rooms and the rooms have windows and the windows have shades and the people believe they possess something worth concealing.

In my opinion my death will serve no purpose. The streetlamps will pop on. Someone will be run over by an expensive car in a narrow street and the driver will hear a bump but consider it of no consequence. Junkies will leak out the side doors of this gigantic mound, nodding, buzzing, greeting their kind with hippy-dip vocalizations full of despair and irony and stylized to embrace the very best that's being sung, played and said around them. A young woman will open a dresser drawer and wonder whose baby that is sleeping peaceful on a bed of dish-towels, T-shirts, a man's ribbed sweat socks. She will feel something slither through the mud of her belly and splash into the sluggish river that meanders through her. She hasn't eaten for days, so that isn't it. Was it a deadly disease. Or worse, some new life she must account for. She opens and shuts the baby's drawer, pushes and pulls, opens and shuts.

I believe all floors are not equally interesting. Less reason to notice some than others. Equality would become boring, predictable. Though we may slight some and rattle on about others, that does not change the fact that each floor exists and the life on it is real, whether we pause to notice or not. As I gather speed and weight during my plunge, each floor adds its share. When I hit bottom I will bear witness to the truth of each one.

Floor of Wishes. I will miss Christmas. They say no one likes being born on Christmas. You lose your birthday, they say. A celebration already on December 25 and nice things happen to everyone on that day anyway, you give and receive presents, people greet you smiling and wish you peace and goodwill. The world is decorated. Colored bulbs draped twinkling in windows and trees, doorways hung with wild berries beneath which you may kiss a handsome stranger. Music everywhere. Even wars truced for twenty-four hours and troops served home-cooked meals, almost. Instead of at least two special days a year, if your birthday falls on Christmas, you lose one. Since my portion's less than a day, less than those insects called ephemera receive, born one morning dead the next, and I can't squeeze a complete life cycle as they do into the time allotted, I wish today were Christmas. Once would be enough. If it's as special as they say. And in some matters we yearn to trust them. Need to trust something, someone, so we listen, wish what they say is true. The holiday of Christmas seems to be the best time to be on earth, to be a child and awaken with your eyes full of dreams and expectations and believe for a while at least that all good things are possible—peace, goodwill, love, merriment, the raven-maned rocking horse you want to ride forever. No conflict of interest for me. I wouldn't lose a birthday to Christmas. Rather than this smoggy heat I wish I could see snow. The city, this building snug under a blanket of fresh snow. No footprints of men running, men on their knees, men bleeding. No women forced out into halls and streets, away from their children. I wish this city, this tower were stranded in a gentle snowstorm and Christmas happens day after day and the bright fires in every hearth never go out, and the carols ring true chorus after chorus, and the gifts given and received precipitate endless joys. The world trapped in Christmas for a day dancing on forever. I wish I could transform the ten flights of my falling into those twelve days in the Christmas song. *On the first day of Christmas my true love said to me* . . . angels, a partridge in a pear tree, ten maids a milking, five gold rings, two turtle-doves. I wish those would be the sights greeting me instead of darkness, the icy winter heart of this August afternoon I have been pitched without a kiss through a maroon door.

Floor of Power. El Presidente inhabits this floor. Some say he owns the whole building. He believes he owns it, collects rent, treats the building and its occupants with contempt. He is a bold-faced man. Cheeks slotted nose to chin like a puppet's. Chicken lips. This floor is entirely white. A floury, cracked white some say used to gleam. El Presidente is white also. Except for the pink dome of his forehead. Once, long ago, his flesh was pink head to toe. Then he painted himself white to match the white floor of power. Paint ran out just after the brush stroke that permanently sealed his eyes. Since El Presidente is cheap and mean he refused to order more paint. Since El Presidente is vain and arrogant he pretended to look at his unfinished self in the mirror and proclaimed he liked what he saw, the coat of cakey white, the raw, pink dome pulsing like a bruise.

El Presidente often performs on TV. We can watch him jog, golf, fish, travel, lie, preen, mutilate the language. But these activities are not his job; his job is keeping things in the building as they are, squatting on the floor of power like a broken generator or broken furnace or broken heart, occupying the space where one that works should be.

Floor of Regrets. One thing bothers me a lot. I regret not knowing what is on the floors above the one where I began my fall. I hope it's better up there. Real gardens perhaps or even a kind of heaven for the occupants lucky enough to live above the floors I've seen. Would one of you please mount the stairs, climb slowly up from floor ten, examine carefully, one soft, warm night, the topmost floors and sing me a lullaby of what I missed.

Floor of Love. I'm supposed to be sleeping. I could be sleeping. Early morning and my eyes don't want to open and legs don't want to push me out of bed yet. Two rooms away I can hear Mom in the kitchen. She's fixing breakfast. Daddy first, then I will slump into the kitchen Mom has made bright and smelling good already this morning. Her perkiness, the sizzling bacon, water boiling, wheat bread popping up like jack-in-the-box from the shiny toaster, the Rice Krispies crackling, fried eggs hissing, the FM's sophisticated patter and mincing string trios would wake the dead. And it does. Me and Daddy slide into our places. Hi, Mom. Good morning, Dearheart. The day begins. Smells wonderful. I awaken now to his hand under the covers with me, rubbing the baby fat of my tummy where he's shoved my nightgown up past my panties. He says I shouldn't wear them. Says it ain't healthy to sleep in your drawers. Says no wonder you get those rashes. He rubs and pinches. Little nips. Then the flat of his big hand under the elastic waistband wedges my underwear down. I raise my hips a little bit to help. No reason not to. The whole thing be over with sooner. Don't do no good to try and stop him or slow him down. He said my Mama knows. He said go on fool and tell her she'll smack you for talking nasty. He was right. She beat me in the kitchen. Then took me in to their room and he stripped me butt-naked and beat me again while she watched. So I kinda hump up, wiggle, and my underwear's down below my knees, his hand's on its way back up to where I don't even understand how to grow hairs yet.

The Floor That Stands for All the Other Floors Missed or Still to Come. My stepbrother Tommy was playing in the schoolyard and they shot him dead. Bang. Bang. Gang banging and poor Tommy caught a cap in his chest. People been in and out the apartment all day. Sorry. Sorry. Everybody's so sorry. Some brought cakes, pies, macaroni casseroles, lunch meat, liquor. Two Ebony Cobras laid a joint on Tommy's older brother who hadn't risen from the kitchen chair he's straddling, head down, nodding, till his boys bop through the door. They know who hit Tommy. They know tomorrow what they must do. Today one of those everybody-in-the-family-and-friends-in-dark-clothes-funeral days, the mothers, sisters, aunts, grandmothers weepy, the men motherfucking everybody from god on down. You can't see me among the mourners. My time is different from this time. You can't understand my time. Or name it. Or share it. Tommy is beginning to remember me. To join me where I am falling unseen through your veins and arteries down down to where the heart stops, the square opening through which trash passes to the compactor.

AUGUST WILSON

(1945–)

August Wilson has established himself as a major twentieth-century American playwright. Moreover, prizes such as a Tony Award, five New York Drama Critics Circle Awards, and two Pulitzer Prizes, as well as long-running productions of most of his plays on Broadway, including two simultaneously, probably make him the most successful African American playwright of all time. His ambitious project is to record the twentieth-century American black experience in a series of plays. His agenda, he says in "How to Write a Play like August Wilson," is like that of James Baldwin—to articulate "the black tradition . . . that field of manners and ritual of intercourse that will sustain a man once he's left his father's house." Moreover, he believes that the best way to learn about the black tradition is through an examination of the blues. In the April 12, 1991, edition of the *New York Times*, he says that he finds "the culture's greatest expression in the blues." He is quoted in *Black Literature Criticism* as saying, "We have our book, which is the blues."

August Wilson was born on April 27, 1945, in the Hill, a poor black neighborhood in Pittsburgh, Pennsylvania. His father was white, a German baker named Frederick August Kittel, and his mother, Daisy Wilson Kittel, was black. It was his mother who, working as a cleaning woman to support her six children, taught him racial pride. His father abandoned them. After being falsely accused of plagiarism, Wilson dropped out of school in the ninth grade. He started going to the local library to read in the black authors' section. There he discovered the Harlem Renaissance writers Langston Hughes and Arna Bontemps, as well as Ralph Ellison. "Those books," Wilson asserts in "A Voice from the Streets," "were a comfort. Just the idea black people would write books. I wanted my book up there, too." Supporting himself as a short-order cook and stock clerk, he bought a typewriter. "The first thing I typed was my name," he remembers. "I wanted to see how it looked in print."

Wilson began writing poetry during the black nationalist 1960s. This poetry, celebrating the black past, shows the impact of the times. "I became involved in the Black Power movement in the late '60s, early '70s," Wilson told an interviewer for the "MacNeil/Lehrer News Hour" on April 30, 1987. "I called myself a Black Nationalist then, and I still consider myself a Black Nationalist." Elsewhere, when asked about his primary artistic influences, Wilson has said that they were the four B's: the painter-collagist Romare Bearden, the poet-playwright Amiri Baraka, the Argentine short-story writer Jorge Luis Borges, and, "the biggest B of all: the blues." The influence of the latter is clearly evident in his first play, *Ma Rainey's Black Bottom* (1984). After earlier rejections, the play was accepted by the National Playwright's Conference, where Lloyd Richards, then artistic director of the Yale Repertory Theater, discovered him. This initiated a long-term collaboration between the two men. When reading the manuscript, Richards recalled, "I recognized it as a new voice. A very important one. It brought back my youth. My neighborhood experiences I had." *Ma Rainey* explores racism in a recording session with Ma Rainey, "the mother of the blues," in Chicago during the 1920s and shows the importance of this black folk music. In the play, Rainey observes that the "blues done give an understanding of life."

Since *Ma Rainey,* Wilson has had a string of successful plays portraying the lot of the black working class. He creates characters who have "the warrior spirit," people who tirelessly battle in the face of impossible odds. Wilson observes, "For a long time, I thought the most valuable blacks were in the penitentiary. They were the people with the warrior spirit. How they chose to battle may have been wrong, but you need people who will battle." Troy Maxon, the protagonist in his Pulitzer

Prize–winning play *Fences* (1986), embodies this black resilience. This drama has often been compared to Lorraine Hansberry's *A Raisin in the Sun* (1959) and Arthur Miller's *Death of a Salesman* (1949). However, whereas the protagonist of the latter play is Willy Loman, a low man who is being crushed by a materialistic society, Troy is a big man, like John Henry or King Lear, who rails against the limitations imposed on him. Rose, Troy's wife, says of him to her son, "When your daddy walked through the house he was so big he filled it up." Linda, Willy's wife, says of her husband, "A small man can be just as exhausted as a great man." Like the mythic character Stagolee, Troy is a black folk hero who laughs in the face of death; in the folk tradition, he is called a bad man or "bad nigger." As in the bad men stories, Troy kills a man and ends up in the penitentiary. But unlike in those stories, Troy transcends the archetype by attempting to become a responsible man who takes care of his wife and children. Troy is a transformed bad man, reformed but still spirited and larger than life.

Wilson also celebrates the black folk tradition in his other plays, which include *Joe Turner's Come and Gone* (1986), the Pulitzer Prize–winning *The Piano Lesson* (1987), and *Two Trains Running* (1990). In the first play, he draws on one of the earliest blues songs, "The Joe Turner Blues." He dramatizes the effects of the scars of enslavement felt by his protagonist, Herald Loomis, who has recently arrived at a Pittsburgh boarding house after having served a seven-year term of impressed labor on Joe Turner's chain gang. The play has numerous overlapping narratives and characters who constantly come and go. In the end, it becomes clear that the search is really a metaphysical and existential quest for spiritual roots and self-knowledge, where black music and ancient African myth serve as guides. According to *New York Times Magazine* critic William A. Henry III, this riveting drama, which has the haunting power of a ghost story, is his best play.

History also is the central theme of *The Piano Lesson.* The focus is a piano that has on its surface the image of Boy Willie's and Berniece's slave ancestors. Their great-grandparents had been traded for the piano, and their father had died trying to retrieve it. Carved by their great-grandfather, the piano serves as a reminder of the time when blacks held the status of property. Berniece cannot play the piano but is fascinated by its history and wants to keep it. Boy Willie is anxious to sell it to get a down payment for some land. At stake for Wilson is the dignity and integrity of African Americans—their art, culture, and history.

August Wilson has brought a new major voice to the American theater. His six published plays, including his latest, the much-heralded *Seven Guitars* (1996), celebrate and delineate the souls of black folks in the twentieth century. As a relatively young person, he joins Eugene O'Neill, Tennessee Williams, and Amiri Baraka as one of the best, most original, and most productive American playwrights.

❖❖❖

For further information on Wilson, see Samuel G. Freedman, "A Voice from the Streets," *New York Times Magazine,* March 15, 1987, reprinted in *Black Literature Criticism,* ed. James P. Draper (1992); Russell Miller, "August Wilson: On a Napkin in a Coffee Shop, Life Is Written (a Play, Too)," *New York Times,* June 3, 1992; and an August Wilson interview, "How to Write a Play Like August Wilson," *New York Times,* March 10, 1991.

Joe Turner's Come and Gone

A Play in Two Acts

Characters

SETH HOLLY, *owner of the boardinghouse*

BERTHA HOLLY, *his wife*

BYNUM WALKER, *a rootworker*

RUTHERFORD SELIG, *a peddler*

JEREMY FURLOW, *a resident*

HERALD LOOMIS, *a resident*

ZONIA LOOMIS, *his daughter*

MATTIE CAMPBELL, *a resident*

REUBEN SCOTT, *boy who lives next door*

MOLLY CUNNINGHAM, *a resident*

MARTHA LOOMIS, *Herald Loomis's wife*

Joe Turner's Come and Gone *opened on March 26, 1988, at the Ethel Barrymore Theatre on Broadway in New York City, with the following cast:*

SETH HOLLY, Mel Winkler

BERTHA HOLLY, L. Scott Caldwell

BYNUM WALKER, Ed Hall

RUTHERFORD SELIG, Raynor Scheine

JEREMY FURLOW, Bo Rucker

HERALD LOOMIS, Delroy Lindo

ZONIA LOOMIS, Jamila Perry

MATTIE CAMPBELL, Kimberleigh Aarn

REUBEN MERCER, Richard Parnell Habersham

MOLLY CUNNINGHAM, Kimberly Scott

MARTHA PENTECOST, Angela Bassett

Director: Lloyd Richards
Set Design: Scott Bradley
Costume Design: Pamela Peterson
Lighting Design: Michael Gianitti
Musical Direction: Dwight Andrews
Production Stage Manager: Karen L. Carpenter
Stage Manager: Elliott Woodruff
Casting Consultants: Meg Simon/Fran Kumin

Setting

August, 1911. A boardinghouse in Pittsburgh. At right is a kitchen. Two doors open off the kitchen. One leads to the outhouse and SETH'S *workshop. The other to* SETH'S *and* BERTHA'S *bedroom. At left is a parlor. The front door opens into the parlor, which gives access to the stairs leading to the upstairs rooms.*

There is a small outside playing area.

The Play

It is August in Pittsburgh, 1911. The sun falls out of heaven like a stone. The fires of the steel mill rage with a combined sense of industry and progress. Barges loaded with coal and iron ore trudge up the river to the mill towns that dot the Monongahela and return with fresh, hard, gleaming steel. The city flexes its muscles. Men throw countless bridges across the rivers, lay roads, and carve tunnels through the hills sprouting with houses.

From the deep and the near South the son and daughters of newly freed African slaves wander into the city. Isolated, cut off from memory, having forgotten the names of the gods and only guessing at their faces, they arrive dazed and stunned, their heart kicking in their chest with a song worth singing. They arrive carrying Bibles and guitars, their pockets lined with dust and fresh hope, marked men and women seeking to scrape from the narrow, crooked cobbles and the fiery blasts of the coke furnace a way of bludgeoning and shaping the malleable parts of themselves into a new identity as free men of definite and sincere worth.

Foreigners in a strange land, they carry as part and parcel of their baggage a long line of separation and dispersement which informs their sensibilities and marks their conduct as they search for ways to reconnect, to reassemble, to give clear and luminous meaning to the song which is both a wail and a whelp of joy.

Act One

Scene One

The lights come up on the kitchen. BERTHA *busies herself with breakfast preparations.* SETH *stands looking out the window at* BYNUM *in the yard.*

SETH *is in his early fifties. Born of Northern free parents, a skilled craftsman, and owner of the boardinghouse, he has a stability that none of the other characters have.* BERTHA *is five years his junior. Married for over twenty-five years, she has learned how to negotiate around* SETH*'s apparent orneriness.*

SETH *(at the window, laughing.)* If that ain't the damndest thing I seen. Look here, Bertha.

BERTHA I done seen Bynum out there with them pigeons before.

SETH Naw . . . naw . . . look at this. That pigeon flopped out of Bynum's hand and he about to have a fit.

*(*BERTHA *crosses over to the window.)*

He down there on his hands and knees behind that bush looking all over for that pigeon and it on the other side of the yard. See it over there?

BERTHA Come on and get your breakfast and leave that man alone.

SETH Look at him . . . he still looking. He ain't seen it yet. All that old mumbo jumbo nonsense. I don't know why I put up with it.

BERTHA You don't say nothing when he bless the house.

SETH I just go along with that 'cause of you. You around here sprinkling salt all over the place . . . got pennies lined up across the threshold . . . all that heebie-jeebie stuff. I just put up with that 'cause of you. I don't pay that kind of stuff no mind. And you going down there to the church and wanna come home and sprinkle salt all over the place.

BERTHA It don't hurt none. I can't say if it help . . . but it don't hurt none.

SETH Look at him. He done found that pigeon and now he's talking to it.

BERTHA These biscuits be ready in a minute.

SETH He done drew a big circle with that stick and now he's dancing around. I know he'd better not . . .

*(*SETH *bolts from the window and rushes to the back door.)*

Hey, Bynum! Don't be hopping around stepping in my vegetables.

Hey, Bynum . . . Watch where you stepping!

BERTHA Seth, leave that man alone.

SETH *(coming back into the house.)* I don't care how much he be dancing around . . . just don't be stepping in my vegetables. Man got my garden all messed up now . . . planting them weeds out there . . . burying them pigeons and whatnot.

BERTHA Bynum don't bother nobody. He ain't even thinking about your vegetables.

SETH I know he ain't! That's why he out there stepping on them.

BERTHA What Mr. Johnson say down there?

SETH I told him if I had the tools I could go out here and find me four or five fellows and open up my own shop instead of working for Mr. Olowski. Get me four or five fellows and teach them how to make pots and pans. One man making ten pots is five men making fifty. He told me he'd think about it.

BERTHA Well, maybe he'll come to see it your way.

SETH He wanted me to sign over the house to him. You know what I thought of that idea.

BERTHA He'll come to see you're right.

SETH I'm going up and talk to Sam Green. There's more than one way to skin a cat. I'm going up and talk to him. See if he got more sense that Mr. Johnson. I can't get nowhere working for Mr. Olowski and selling Selig five or six pots on the side. I'm going up and see Sam Green. See if he loan me the money.

*(*SETH *crosses back to the window.)*

Now he got that cup. He done killed that pigeon and now he's putting its blood in that little cup. I believe he drink that blood.

BERTHA Seth Holly, what is wrong with you this morning? Come on and get your breakfast so you can go to bed. You know Bynum don't be drinking no pigeon blood.

SETH I don't know what he do.

BERTHA Well, watch him, then. He's gonna dig a little hole and bury that pigeon. Then he's gonna pray over that blood . . . pour it on top

. . . mark out his circle and come on into the house.

SETH That's what he doing . . . he pouring that blood on top.

BERTHA When they gonna put you back working daytime? Told me two months ago he was gonna put you back working daytime.

SETH That's what Mr. Olowski told me. I got to wait till he say when. He tell me what to do. I don't tell him. Drive me crazy to speculate on the man's wishes when he don't know what he want to do himself.

BERTHA Well, I wish he go ahead and put you back working daytime. This working all hours of the night don't make no sense.

SETH It don't make no sense for that boy to run out of here and get drunk so they lock him up either.

BERTHA Who? Who they got locked up for being drunk?

SETH That boy that's staying upstairs . . . Jeremy. I stopped down there on Logan Street on my way home from work and one of the fellows told me about it. Say he seen it when they arrested him.

BERTHA I was wondering why I ain't seen him this morning.

SETH You know I don't put up with that. I told him when he came . . .

*(*BYNUM *enters from the yard carrying some plants. He is a short, round man in his early sixties. A conjure man, or rootworker, he gives the impression of always being in control of everything. Nothing ever bothers him. He seems to be lost in a world of his own making and to swallow any adversity or interference with his grand design.)*

What you doing bringing them weeds in my house? Out there stepping on my vegetables and now wanna carry them weeds in my house.

BYNUM Morning, Seth. Morning, Sister Bertha.

SETH Messing up my garden growing them things out there. I ought to go out there and pull up all them weeds.

BERTHA Some gal was by here to see you this morning, Bynum. You was out there in the yard . . . I told her to come back later.

BYNUM *(To* SETH.*)* You look sick. What's the matter, you ain't eating right?

SETH What if I was sick? You ain't getting near me with none of that stuff.

*(*BERTHA *sets a plate of biscuits on the table.)*

BYNUM My . . . my . . . Bertha, your biscuits getting fatter and fatter.

*(*BYNUM *takes a biscuit and begins to eat.)*

Where Jeremy? I don't see him around this morning. He usually be around riffing and raffing on Saturday morning.

SETH I know where he at. I know just where he at. They got him down there in the jail. Getting drunk and acting a fool. He down there where he belong with all that foolishness.

BYNUM Mr. Piney's boys got him, huh? They ain't gonna do nothing but hold on to him for a little while. He's gonna be back here hungrier than a mule directly.

SETH I don't go for all that carrying on and such. This is a respectable house. I don't have no drunkards or fools around here.

BYNUM That boy got a lot of country in him. He ain't been up here but two weeks. It's gonna take a while before he can work that country out of him.

SETH These niggers coming up here with that old backward country style of living. It's hard enough now without all that ignorant kind of acting. Ever since slavery got over with there ain't been nothing but foolish-acting niggers. Word get out they need men to work in the mill and put in these roads . . . and niggers drop everything and head North looking for freedom. They don't know the white fellows looking too. White fellows coming from all over the world. White fellow come over and in six months got more than what I got. But these niggers keep on coming. Walking . . . riding . . . carrying their Bibles. That boy done carried a guitar all the way from North Carolina.

What he gonna find out? What he gonna do with that guitar? This the city.

(There is a knock on the door.)

Niggers coming up here from the backwoods . . . coming up here from the country carrying Bibles and guitars looking for freedom. They got a rude awakening.

*(*SETH *goes to answer the door.* RUTHERFORD SELIG *enters. About* SETH*'s age, he is a thin white man with greasy hair. A peddler, he supplies* SETH *with the raw materials to make pots and pans which he then peddles door to door in the mill towns along the river. He keeps a list of his customers as they move about and is known in the various communities as the People Finder. He carries squares of sheet metal under his arm.)*

Ho! Forgot you was coming today. Come on in.

BYNUM If it ain't Rutherford Selig . . . the People Finder himself.

SELIG What say there, Bynum?

BYNUM I say about my shiny man. You got to tell me something. I done give you my dollar . . . I'm looking to get a report.

SELIG I got eight here, Seth.

SETH *(Taking the sheet metal.)* What is this? What you giving me there? What I'm gonna do with this?

SELIG I need some dustpans. Everybody asking me about dustpans.

SETH Gonna cost you fifteen cents apiece. And ten cents to put a handle on them.

SELIG I'll give you twenty cents apiece with the handles.

SETH Alright. But I ain't gonna give you but fifteen cents for the sheet metal.

SELIG It's twenty-five cents apiece for the metal. That's what we agreed on.

SETH This low-grade sheet metal. They ain't worth but a dime. I'm doing you a favor giving you fifteen cents. You know this metal ain't worth no twenty-five cents. Don't come talking that twenty-five cent stuff to me over no low-grade sheet metal.

SELIG Alright, fifteen cents apiece. Just make me some dustpans out of them.

*(*SETH *exits with the sheet metal out the back door.)*

BERTHA Sit on down there, Selig. Get you a cup of coffee and a biscuit.

BYNUM Where you coming from this time?

SELIG I been upriver. All along the Monongahela. Past Rankin and all up around Little Washington.

BYNUM Did you find anybody?

SELIG I found Sadie Jackson up in Braddock. Her mother's staying down there in Scotchbottom say she hadn't heard from her and she didn't know where she was at. I found here up in Braddock on Enoch Street. She bought a frying pan from me.

BYNUM You around here finding everybody how come you ain't found my shiny man?

SELIG The only shiny man I saw was the Nigras working on the road gang with the sweat glistening on them.

BYNUM Naw, you'd be able to tell this fellow. He shine like new money.

SELIG Well, I done told you I can't find nobody without a name.

BERTHA Here go one of these hot biscuits, Selig.

BYNUM This fellow don't have no name. I call him John 'cause it was up around Johnstown where I seen him. I ain't even so sure he's one special fellow. That shine could pass on to anybody. He could be anybody shining.

SELIG Well, what's he look like besides being shiny? There's lots of shiny Nigras.

BYNUM He's just a man I seen out on the road. He ain't had no special look. Just a man walking toward me on the road. He come up and asked me which way the road went. I told him everything I knew about the road, where it went and all, and he asked me did I have anything to eat 'cause he was hungry. Say he ain't had nothing to eat in three days. Well, I never be out there on the road without a piece of dried meat. Or an orange or an apple. So I give this fellow an orange. He take and eat that orange and told me to come and go along the road a little ways with him, that he had something he wanted to show me. He had a look about him made me wanna go with him, see what he gonna show me.

We walked on a bit and it's getting kind of far from where I met him when it come up on me all of a sudden, we wasn't going the way he had come from, we was going back my way. Since he said he ain't knew nothing about the road, I asked him about this. He say he had a voice inside him telling him which way to go and if I come and go along with him he was gonna show me the Secret of Life. Quite naturally I followed him. A fellow that's gonna show you the Secret of Life ain't to be taken lightly. We get near this bend in the road . . .

(SETH enters with an assortment of pots.)

SETH I got six here, Selig.

SELIG Wait a minute, Seth. Bynum's telling me about the secret of life. Go ahead, Bynum. I wanna hear this.

(SETH sets the pot down and exits out the back.)

BYNUM We get near this bend in the road and he told me to hold out my hands. Then he rubbed them together with his and I looked down and see they got blood on them. Told me to take and rub it all over me . . . say that was a way of cleaning myself. Then we went around the bend in that road. Got around that bend and it seem like all of a sudden we ain't in the same place. Turn around that bend and everything look like it was twice as big as it was. The trees and everything bigger than life! Sparrows big as eagles! I turned around to look at this fellow and he had this light coming out of him. I had to cover up my eyes to keep from being blinded. He shining like new money with that light. He shined until all the light seemed like it seeped out of him and then he was gone and I was by myself in this strange place where everything was bigger than life.

I wandered around there looking for that road, trying to find my way back from this big place . . . and I looked over and seen my daddy standing there. He was the same size he always was, except for his hands and his mouth. He had a great big old mouth that look like it took up his whole face and his hands were as big as hams. Look like they was too big to carry around. My daddy called me to him. Said he had been thinking about me and it grieved him to see me in the world carrying other people's songs and not having one of my own. Told me he was gonna show me how to find my song. Then he carried me further into this big place until we come to this ocean. Then he showed me something I ain't got words to tell you. But if you stand to witness it, you done seen something there. I stayed in that place awhile and my daddy taught me the meaning of this thing that I had seen and showed me how to find my song. I asked him about the shiny man and he told me he was the One Who Goes Before and Shows the Way. Said there was lots of shiny men and if I ever saw one again before I died then I would know that my song had been accepted and worked its full power in the world and I could lay down and die a happy man. A man who done left his mark on life. On the way people cling to each other out of the truth they find in themselves. Then he showed me how to get back to the road. I came out to where everything was its own size and I had my song. I had the Binding Song. I choose that song because that's what I seen most when I was traveling . . . people walking away and leaving one another. So I takes the power of my song and binds them together.

(SETH enters from the yard carrying cabbages and tomatoes.)

Been binding people ever since. That's why they call me Bynum. Just like glue I sticks people together.

SETH Maybe they ain't supposed to be stuck sometimes. You ever think of that?

BYNUM Oh, I don't do it lightly. It cost me a piece of myself every time I do. I'm a Binder of What Clings. You got to find out if they cling first. You can't bind what don't cling.

SELIG Well, how is that the Secret of Life? I thought you said he was gonna show you the secret of life. That's what I'm waiting to find out.

BYNUM Oh, he showed me alright. But you still got to figure it out. Can't nobody figure it out for you. You got to come to it on your own. That's why I'm looking for the shiny man.

SELIG Well, I'll keep my eye out for him. What you got there, Seth?

SETH Here go some cabbage and tomatoes. I got some green beans coming in real nice. I'm gonna take and start me a grapevine out there next year. Butera says he gonna give me a piece of his vine and I'm gonna start that out there.

SELIG How many of them pots you got?

SETH I got six. That's six dollars minus eight on top of fifteen for the sheet metal come to a dollar twenty out the six dollars leave me four dollars and eighty cents.

SELIG *(Counting out the money.)* There's four dollars . . . and . . . eighty cents.

SETH How many of them dustpans you want?

SELIG As many as you can make out them sheets.

SETH You can use that many? I get to cutting on them sheets figuring how to make them dustpans . . . ain't no telling how many I'm liable to come up with.

SELIG I can use them and you can make me some more next time.

SETH Alright, I'm gonna hold you to that, now.

SELIG Thanks for the biscuit, Bertha.

BERTHA You know you welcome anytime, Selig.

SETH Which way you heading?

SELIG Going down to Wheeling. All through West Virginia there. I'll be back Saturday. They putting in new roads down that way. Makes traveling easier.

SETH That's what I hear. All up around here too. Got a fellow staying here working on that road by the Brady Street Bridge.

SELIG Yeah, it's gonna make traveling real nice. Thanks for the cabbage, Seth. I'll see you on Saturday.

*(*SELIG *exits.)*

SETH *(To* BYNUM.*)* Why you wanna start all that nonsense talk with that man? All that shiny man nonsense.

BYNUM You know it ain't no nonsense. Bertha know it ain't no nonsense. I don't know if Selig know or not.

BERTHA Seth, when you get to making them dustpans make me a coffeepot.

SETH What's the matter with your coffee? Ain't nothing wrong with your coffee. Don't she make some good coffee, Bynum?

BYNUM I ain't worried about the coffee. I know she makes some good biscuits.

SETH I ain't studying no coffeepot, woman. You heard me tell the man I was gonna cut as many dustpans as them sheets will make . . . and all of a sudden you want a coffeepot.

BERTHA Man, hush up and go on and make me that coffeepot.

*(*JEREMY *enters the front door. About twenty-five, he gives the impression that he has the world in his hand, that he can meet life's challenges head on. He smiles a lot. He is a proficient guitar player, though his spirit has yet to be molded into song.)*

BYNUM I hear Mr. Piney's boys had you.

JEREMY Fined me two dollars for nothing! Ain't done nothing.

SETH I told you when you come on here everybody know my house. Know these is respectable quarters. I don't put up with no foolishness. Everybody know Seth Holly keep a good house. Was my daddy's house. This house been a decent house for a long time.

JEREMY I ain't done nothing, Mr. Seth. I stopped by the Workmen's Club and got me a bottle. Me and Roper Lee from Alabama. Had us a half pint. We was fixing to cut that half in two when they came up on us. Asked us if we was working. We told them we was putting in the road over yonder and that it was our payday. They snatched hold of us to get that two dollars. Me and Roper Lee ain't even had a chance to take a drink when they grabbed us.

SETH I don't go for all that kind of carrying on.

BERTHA Leave the boy alone, Seth. You know the police do that. Figure there's too many people out on the street they take some of them off. You know that.

SETH I ain't gonna have folks talking.

BERTHA Ain't nobody talking nothing. That's all in your head. You want some grits and biscuits, Jeremy?

JEREMY Thank you, Miss Bertha. They didn't give us a thing to eat last night. I'll take one of them big bowls if you don't mind.

(There is a knock at the door. SETH *goes to answer it. Enter* HERALD LOOMIS *and his eleven-year-old daughter,* ZONIA. HERALD LOOMIS *is thirty-two years old. He is at times possessed. A man driven not by the hellhounds that seemingly bay at his heels, but by his search for a world that speaks to something about himself. He is unable to harmonize the forces that swirl around him, and seeks to recreate the world into one that contains his image. He wears a hat and a long wool coat.)*

LOOMIS Me and my daughter looking for a place to stay, mister. You got a sign say you got rooms.

*(*SETH *stares at* LOOMIS, *sizing him up.)*

Mister, if you ain't got no rooms we can go somewhere else.

SETH How long you plan on staying?

LOOMIS Don't know. Two weeks or more maybe.

SETH It's two dollars a week for the room. We serve meals twice a day. It's two dollars for room and board. Pay up in advance.

*(*LOOMIS *reaches into his pocket.)*

It's a dollar extra for the girl.

LOOMIS The girl sleep in the same room.

SETH Well, do she eat off the same plate? We serve meals twice a day. That's a dollar extra for food.

LOOMIS Ain't got no extra dollar. I was planning on asking your missus if she could help out with the cooking and cleaning and whatnot.

SETH Her helping out don't put no food on the table. I need that dollar to buy some food.

LOOMIS I'll give you fifty cents extra. She don't eat much.

SETH Okay . . . but fifty cents don't buy but half a portion.

BERTHA Seth, she can help me out. Let her help me out. I can use some help.

SETH Well, that's two dollars for the week. Pay up in advance. Saturday to Saturday. You wanna stay on then it's two more come Saturday.

*(*LOOMIS *pays* SETH *the money.)*

BERTHA My name's Bertha. This my husband, Seth. You got Bynum and Jeremy over there.

LOOMIS Ain't nobody else live here?

BERTHA They the only ones live here now. People come and go. They the only ones here now. You want a cup of coffee and a biscuit?

LOOMIS We done ate this morning.

BYNUM Where you coming from, Mister . . . I didn't get your name.

LOOMIS Name's Herald Loomis. This my daughter, Zonia.

BYNUM Where you coming from?

LOOMIS Come from all over. Whicheverway the road take us that's the way we go.

JEREMY If you looking for a job, I'm working putting in that road down there by the bridge. They can't get enough mens. Always looking to take somebody on.

LOOMIS I'm looking for a woman named Martha Loomis. That's my wife. Got married legal with the papers and all.

SETH I don't know nobody named Loomis. I know some Marthas but I don't know no Loomis.

BYNUM You got to see Rutherford Selig if you wanna find somebody. Selig's the People

Finder. Rutherford Selig's a first-class People Finder.

JEREMY What she look like? Maybe I seen her.

LOOMIS She a brownskin woman. Got long pretty hair. About five feet from the ground.

JEREMY I don't know. I might have seen her.

BYNUM You got to see Rutherford Selig. You give him one dollar to get her name on his list . . . and after she get her name on his list Rutherford Selig will go right on out there and find her. I got him looking for somebody for me.

LOOMIS You say he find people. How you find him?

BYNUM You just missed him. He's gone downriver now. You got to wait till Saturday. He's gone downriver with his pots and pans. He come to see Seth on Saturdays. You got to wait till then.

SETH Come on, I'll show you to your room.

*(*SETH, LOOMIS, *and* ZONIA *exit up the stairs.)*

JEREMY Miss Bertha, I'll take that biscuit you was gonna give that fellow, if you don't mind. Say, Mr. Bynum, they got somebody like that around here sure enough? Somebody that find people?

BYNUM Rutherford Selig. He go around selling pots and pans and every house he come to he write down the name and address of whoever lives there. So if you looking for somebody, quite naturally you go and see him . . . 'cause he's the only one who know where everybody live at.

JEREMY I ought to have him look for this old gal I used to know. It be nice to see her again.

BERTHA *(Giving* JEREMY *a biscuit.)* Jeremy, today's the day for you to pull them sheets off the bed and set them outside your door. I'll set you out some clean ones.

BYNUM Mr. Piney's boys done ruined your good time last night, Jeremy . . . what you planning for tonight?

JEREMY They got me scared to go out, Mr. Bynum. They might grab me again.

BYNUM You ought to take your guitar and go down to Seefus. Seefus got a gambling place down there on Wylie Avenue. You ought to take your guitar and go down there. They got guitar contest down there.

JEREMY I don't play no contest, Mr. Bynum. Had one of them white fellows cure me of that. I ain't been nowhere near a contest since.

BYNUM White fellow beat you playing guitar?

JEREMY Naw, he ain't beat me. I was sitting at home just fixing to sit down and eat when somebody come up to my house and got me. Told me there's a white fellow say he was gonna give a prize to the best guitar player he could find. I take up my guitar and go down there and somebody had gone up and got Bobo Smith and brought him down there. Him and another fellow called Hooter. Old Hooter couldn't play no guitar, he do more hollering than playing, but Bobo could go at it awhile.

This fellow standing there say he the one that was gonna give the prize and me and Bobo started playing for him. Bobo play something and then I'd try to play something better than what he played. Old Hooter, he just holler and bang at the guitar. Man was the worst guitar player I ever seen. So me and Bobo played and after a while I seen where he was getting the attention of this white fellow. He'd play something and while he was playing it he be slapping on the side of the guitar, and that made it sound like he was playing more than he was. So I started doing it too. White fellow ain't knew no difference. He ain't knew as much about guitar playing as Hooter did. After we play awhile, the white fellow called us to him and said he couldn't make up his mind, say all three of us was the best guitar player and we'd have to split the prize between us. Then he give us twenty-five cents. That's eight cents apiece and a penny on the side. That cured me of playing contest to this day.

BYNUM Seefus ain't like that. Seefus give a whole dollar and a drink of whiskey.

JEREMY What night they be down there?

BYNUM Be down there every night. Music don't know no certain night.

BERTHA You go down to Seefus with them people and you liable to end up in a raid and go to jail sure enough. I don't know why Bynum tell you that.

BYNUM That's where the music at. That's where the people at. The people down there making music and enjoying themselves. Some things is worth taking the chance going to jail about.

BERTHA Jeremy ain't got no business going down there.

JEREMY They got some women down there, Mr. Bynum?

BYNUM Oh, they got women down there, sure. They got women everywhere. Women be where the men is so they can find each other.

JEREMY Some of them old gals come out there where we be putting in that road. Hanging around there trying to snatch somebody.

BYNUM How come some of them ain't snatched hold of you?

JEREMY I don't want them kind. Them desperate kind. Ain't nothing worse than a desperate woman. Tell them you gonna leave them and they get to crying and carrying on. That just make you want to get away quicker. They get to cutting up your clothes and things trying to keep you staying. Desperate women ain't nothing but trouble for a man.

*(*SETH *enters from the stairs.)*

SETH Something ain't setting right with that fellow.

BERTHA What's wrong with him? What he say?

SETH I take him up there and try to talk to him and he ain't for no talking. Say he been traveling . . . coming over from Ohio. Say he a deacon in the church. Say he looking for Martha Pentecost. Talking about that's his wife.

BERTHA How you know it's the same Martha? Could be talking about anybody. Lots of people named Martha.

SETH You see that little girl? I didn't hook it up till he said it, but that little girl look just like her. Ask Bynum. *(To* BYNUM.*)* Bynum. Don't that little girl look just like Martha Pentecost?

BERTHA I still say he could be talking about anybody.

SETH The way he described her wasn't no doubt about who he was talking about. Described her right down to her toes.

BERTHA What did you tell him?

SETH I ain't told him nothing. The way that fellow look I wasn't gonna tell him nothing. I don't know what he looking for her for.

BERTHA What else he have to say?

SETH I told you he wasn't for no talking. I told him where the outhouse was and to keep that gal off the front porch and out of my garden. He asked if you'd mind setting a hot tub for the gal and that was about the gist of it.

BERTHA Well, I wouldn't let it worry me if I was you. Come on get your sleep.

BYNUM He says he looking for Martha and he a deacon in the church.

SETH That's what he say. Do he look like a deacon to you?

BERTHA He might be, you don't know. Bynum ain't got no special say on whether he a deacon or not.

SETH Well, if he the deacon I'd sure like to see the preacher.

BERTHA Come on get your sleep. Jeremy, don't forget to set them sheets outside the door like I told you.

*(*BERTHA *exits into the bedroom.)*

SETH Something ain't setting right with that fellow, Bynum. He's one of them mean-looking niggers look like he done killed somebody gambling over a quarter.

BYNUM He ain't no gambler. Gamblers wear nice shoes. This fellow got on clodhoppers. He been out there walking up and down them roads.

*(*ZONIA *enters from the stairs and looks around.)*

BYNUM You looking for the back door, sugar? There it is. You can go out there and play. It's alright.

SETH *(Showing her the door.)* You can go out there and play. Just don't get in my garden. And don't go messing around in my work-shed.

*(*SETH *exits into the bedroom. There is a knock on the door.)*

JEREMY Somebody at the door.

*(*JEREMY *goes to answer the door. Enter* MATTIE CAMPBELL. *She is a young woman of twenty-six whose attractiveness is hidden under the weight and concerns of a dissatisfied life. She is a woman in an honest search for love and companionship. She has suffered many defeats in her search, and though not always uncompromising, still believes in the possibility of love.)*

MATTIE I'm looking for a man named Bynum. Lady told me to come back later.

JEREMY Sure, he here. Mr. Bynum, somebody here to see you.

BYNUM Come to see me, huh?

MATTIE Are you the man they call Bynum? The man folks say can fix things?

BYNUM Depend on what need fixing. I can't make no promises. But I got a powerful song in some matters.

MATTIE Can you fix it so my man come back to me?

BYNUM Come on in . . . have a sit down.

MATTIE You got to help me. I don't know what else to do.

BYNUM Depend on how all the circumstances of the thing come together. How all the pieces fit.

MATTIE I done everything I knowed how to do. You got to make him come back to me.

BYNUM It ain't nothing to make somebody come back. I can fix it so he can't stand to be away from you. I got my roots and powders, I can fix it so wherever he's at this thing will come up on him and he won't be able to sleep for seeing your face. Won't be able to eat for thinking of you.

MATTIE That's what I want. Make him come back.

BYNUM The roots is a powerful thing. I can fix it so one day he'll walk out his front door . . . won't be thinking of nothing. He won't know what it is. All he knows is that a powerful dissatisfaction done set in his bones and can't nothing he do make him feel satisfied. He'll set his foot down on the road and the wind in the trees be talking to him and everywhere he step on the road, that road'll give back your name and something will pull him right up to your doorstep. Now, I can do that. I can take my roots and fix that easy. But maybe he ain't supposed to come back. And if he ain't supposed to come back . . . then he'll be in your bed one morning and it'll come up on him that he's in the wrong place. That he's lost outside of time from his place that he's supposed to be in. Then both of you be lost and trapped outside of life and ain't no way for you to get back into it. 'Cause you lost from yourselves and where the places come together, where you're supposed to be alive, your heart kicking in your chest with a song worth singing.

MATTIE Make him come back to me. Make his feet say my name on the road. I don't care what happens. Make him come back.

BYNUM What's your man's name?

MATTIE He go by Jack Carper. He was born in Alabama then he come to West Texas and find me and we come here. Been here three years before he left. Say I had a curse prayer on me and he started walking down the road and ain't never come back. Somebody told me, say you can fix things like that.

BYNUM He just got up one day, set his feet on the road, and walked away?

MATTIE You got to make him come back, mister.

BYNUM Did he say goodbye?

MATTIE Ain't said nothing. Just started walking. I could see where he disappeared. Didn't look back. Just keep walking. Can't you fix it so he come back? I ain't got no curse prayer on me. I know I ain't.

BYNUM What made him say you had a curse prayer on you?

MATTIE 'Cause the babies died. Me and Jack had two babies. Two little babies that ain't lived two months before they died. He say it's because somebody cursed me not to have babies.

BYNUM He ain't bound to you if the babies died. Look like somebody trying to keep you from being bound up and he's gone on back to whoever it is 'cause he's already bound up to her. Ain't nothing to be done. Somebody else done got a powerful hand in it and ain't nothing to be done to break it. You got to let him go find where he's supposed to be in the world.

MATTIE Jack done gone off and you telling me to forget about him. All my life I been looking for somebody to stop and stay with me. I done already got too many things to forget about. I take Jack Carper's hand and it feel so rough and strong. Seem like he's the strongest man in the world the way he hold me. Like he's bigger than the whole world and can't nothing bad get to me. Even when he act mean sometimes he still make everything seem okay with the world. Like there's part of it that belongs just to you. Now you telling me to forget about him?

BYNUM Jack Carper gone off to where he belong. There's somebody searching for your doorstep right now. Ain't no need you fretting over Jack Carper. Right now he's a strong thought in your mind. But every time you catch yourself fretting over Jack Carper you push that thought away. You push it out your mind and that thought will get weaker and weaker till you wake up one morning and you won't even be able to call him up on your mind.

(BYNUM gives her a small cloth packet.)

Take this and sleep with it under your pillow and it'll bring good luck to you. Draw it to you like a magnet. It won't be long before you forget all about Jack Carper.

MATTIE How much . . . do I owe you?

BYNUM Whatever you got there . . . that'll be alright.

(MATTIE hands BYNUM two quarters. She crosses to the door.)

You sleep with that under your pillow and you'll be alright.

(MATTIE opens the door to exit and JEREMY crosses over to her. BYNUM overhears the first part of their conversation, then exits out the back.)

JEREMY I overheard what you told Mr. Bynum. Had me an old gal did that to me. Woke up one morning and she was gone. Just took off to parts unknown. I woke up that morning and the only thing I could do was look around for my shoes. I woke up and got out of there. Found my shoes and took off. That's the only thing I could think of to do.

MATTIE She ain't said nothing?

JEREMY I just looked around for my shoes and got out of there.

MATTIE Jack ain't said nothing either. He just walked off.

JEREMY Some mens do that. Womens too. I ain't gone off looking for her. I just let her go. Figure she had a time to come to herself. Wasn't no use of me standing in the way. Where you from?

MATTIE Texas. I was born in Georgia but I went to Texas with my mama. She dead now. Was picking peaches and fell dead away. I come up here with Jack Carper.

JEREMY I'm from North Carolina. Down around Raleigh where they got all that tobacco. Been up here about two weeks. I likes it fine except I still got to find me a woman. You got a nice look to you. Look like you have mens standing in your door. Is you got mens standing in your door to get a look at you?

MATTIE I ain't got nobody since Jack left.

JEREMY A woman like you need a man. Maybe you let me be your man. I got a nice way with the women. That's what they tell me.

MATTIE I don't know. Maybe Jack's coming back.

JEREMY I'll be your man till he come. A woman can't be by her lonesome. Let me be your man till he come.

MATTIE I just can't go through life piecing myself out to different mens. I need a man who wants to stay with me.

JEREMY I can't say what's gonna happen. Maybe I'll be the man. I don't know. You wanna go along the road a little ways with me?

MATTIE I don't know. Seem like life say it's gonna be one thing and end up being another. I'm tired of going from man to man.

JEREMY Life is like you got to take a chance. Everybody got to take a chance. Can't nobody say what's gonna be. Come on . . . take a chance with me and see what the year bring. Maybe you let me come and see you. Where you staying?

MATTIE I got me a room up on Bedford. Me and Jack had a room together.

JEREMY What's the address? I'll come by and get you tonight and we can go down to Seefus. I'm going down there and play my guitar.

MATTIE You play guitar?

JEREMY I play guitar like I'm born to it.

MATTIE I live at 1727 Bedford Avenue. I'm gonna find out if you can play guitar like you say.

JEREMY I plays it sugar, and that ain't all I do. I got a ten-pound hammer and I knows how to drive it down. Good god . . . you ought to hear my hammer ring!

MATTIE Go on with that kind of talk, now. If you gonna come by and get me I got to get home and straighten up for you.

JEREMY I'll be by at eight o'clock. How's eight o'clock? I'm gonna make you forget all about Jack Carper.

MATTIE Go on, now. I got to get home and fix up for you.

JEREMY Eight o'clock, sugar.

(The lights go down in the parlor and come up on the yard outside. ZONIA *is singing and playing a game.)*

ZONIA

I went downtown
To get my grip
I came back home
Just a pullin' the skiff

I went upstairs
To make my bed
I made a mistake
And I bumped my head
Just a pullin' the skiff

I went downstairs
To milk the cow
I made a mistake
And I milked the sow
Just a pullin' the skiff

Tomorrow, tomorrow
Tomorrow never comes
The marrow the marrow
The marrow in the bone.

*(*REUBEN *enters.)*

REUBEN Hi.

ZONIA Hi.

REUBEN What's your name?

ZONIA Zonia.

REUBEN What kind of name is that?

ZONIA It's what my daddy named me.

REUBEN My name's Reuben. You staying in Mr. Seth's house?

ZONIA Yeah.

REUBEN That your daddy I seen you with this morning?

ZONIA I don't know. Who you see me with?

REUBEN I saw you with some man had on a great big old coat. And you was walking up to Mr. Seth's house. Had on a hat too.

ZONIA Yeah, that's my daddy.

REUBEN You like Mr. Seth?

ZONIA I ain't see him much.

REUBEN My grandpap say he a great big old windbag. How come you living in Mr. Seth's house? Don't you have no house?

ZONIA We going to find my mother.

REUBEN Where she at?

ZONIA I don't know. We got to find her. We just go all over.

REUBEN Why you got to find her? What happened to her?

ZONIA She ran away.

REUBEN Why she run away?

ZONIA I don't know. My daddy say some man named Joe Turner did something bad to him once and that made her run away.

REUBEN Maybe she coming back and you don't have to go looking for her.

ZONIA We ain't there no more.

REUBEN She could have come back when you wasn't there.

ZONIA My daddy said she ran off and left us so we going looking for her.

REUBEN What he gonna do when he find her?

ZONIA He didn't say. He just say he got to find her.

REUBEN Your daddy say how long you staying in Mr. Seth's house?

ZONIA He don't say much. But we never stay too long nowhere. He say we got to keep moving till we find her.

REUBEN Ain't no kids hardly live around here. I had me a friend but he died. He was the best friend I ever had. Me and Eugene used to keep secrets. I still got his pigeons. He told me to let them go when he died. He say, "Reuben, promise me when I die you'll let my pigeons go." But I keep them to remember him by. I ain't never gonna let them go. Even when I get to be grown up. I'm just always gonna have Eugene's pigeons.

(Pause.)

Mr. Bynum a conjure man. My grandpap scared of him. He don't like me to come over here too much. I'm scared of him too. My grandpap told me not to let him get close enough to where he can reach out his hand and touch me.

ZONIA He don't seem scary to me.

REUBEN He buys pigeons from me . . . and if you get up early in the morning you can see him out in the yard doing something with them pigeons. My grandpap say he kill them. I sold him one yesterday. I don't know what he do with it. I just hope he don't spook me up.

ZONIA Why you sell him pigeons if he's gonna spook you up?

REUBEN I just do like Eugene do. He used to sell Mr. Bynum pigeons. That's how he got to collecting them to sell to Mr. Bynum. Sometime he give me a nickel and sometime he give me a whole dime.

*(*LOOMIS *enters from the house.)*

LOOMIS Zonia!

ZONIA Sir?

LOOMIS What you doing?

ZONIA Nothing.

LOOMIS You stay around this house, you hear? I don't want you wandering off nowhere.

ZONIA I ain't wandering off nowhere.

LOOMIS Miss Bertha set that hot tub and you getting a good scrubbing. Get scrubbed up good. You ain't been scrubbing.

ZONIA I been scrubbing.

LOOMIS Look at you. You growing too fast. Your bones getting bigger everyday. I don't want you getting grown on me. Don't you get grown on me too soon. We gonna find your mamma. She around here somewhere. I can smell her. You stay on around this house now. Don't you go nowhere.

ZONIA Yes, sir.

*(*LOOMIS *exits into the house.)*

REUBEN Wow, your daddy's scary!

ZONIA He is not! I don't know what you talking about.

REUBEN He got them mean-looking eyes!

ZONIA My daddy ain't got no mean-looking eyes!

REUBEN Aw, girl, I was just messing with you. You wanna go see Eugene's pigeons? Got a great big coop out the back of my house. Come on, I'll show you.

*(*REUBEN *and* ZONIA *exit as the lights go down.)*

SCENE TWO

It is Saturday morning, one week later. The lights come up on the kitchen. BERTHA *is at the stove preparing breakfast while* SETH *sits at the table.*

SETH Something ain't right about that fellow. I been watching him all week. Something ain't right, I'm telling you.

BERTHA Seth Holly, why don't you hush up about that man this morning?

SETH I don't like the way he stare at everybody. Don't look at you natural like. He just be staring at you. Like he trying to figure out something about you. Did you see him when he come back in here?

BERTHA That man ain't thinking about you.

SETH He don't work nowhere. Just go out and come back. Go out and come back.

BERTHA As long as you get your boarding money it ain't your cause about what he do. He don't bother nobody.

SETH Just go out and come back. Going around asking everybody about Martha. Like Henry Allen seen him down at the church last night.

BERTHA The man's allowed to go to church if he want. He say he a deacon. Ain't nothing wrong about him going to church.

SETH I ain't talking about him going to church. I'm talking about him hanging around *outside* the church.

BERTHA Henry Allen say that?

SETH Say he be standing around outside the church. Like he be watching it.

BERTHA What on earth he wanna be watching the church for, I wonder?

SETH That's what I'm trying to figure out. Looks like he fixing to rob it.

BERTHA Seth, now do he look like the kind that would rob the church?

SETH I ain't saying that. I ain't saying how he look. It's how he do. Anybody liable to do anything as far as I'm concerned. I ain't never thought about how no church robbers look . . . but now that you mention it, I don't see where they look no different than how he look.

BERTHA Herald Loomis ain't the kind of man who would rob no church.

SETH I ain't even so sure that's his name.

BERTHA Why the man got to lie about his name?

SETH Anybody can tell anybody anything about what their name is. That's what you call him . . . Herald Loomis. His name is liable to be anything.

BERTHA Well, until he tell me different that's what I'm gonna call him. You just getting yourself all worked up about the man for nothing.

SETH Talking about Loomis: Martha's name wasn't no Loomis nothing. Martha's name is Pentecost.

BERTHA How you so sure that's her right name? Maybe she changed it.

SETH Martha's a good Christian woman. This fellow here look like he owe the devil a day's work and he's trying to figure out how he gonna pay him. Martha ain't had a speck of distrust about her the whole time she was living here. They moved the church out there to Rankin and I was sorry to see her go.

BERTHA That's why he be hanging around the church. He looking for her.

SETH If he looking for her, why don't he go inside and ask? What he doing hanging around outside the church acting sneaky like?

(BYNUM enters from the yard.)

BYNUM Morning, Seth. Morning, Sister Bertha.

(BYNUM continues through the kitchen and exits up the stairs.)

BERTHA That's who you should be asking the questions. He been out there in that yard all morning. He was out there before the sun come up. He didn't even come in for breakfast. I don't know what he's doing. He had three of them pigeons line up out there. He dance around till he get tired. He sit down awhile then get up and dance some more. He come through here a little while ago looking like he was mad at the world.

SETH I don't pay Bynum no mind. He don't spook me up with all that stuff.

BERTHA That's how Martha come to be living here. She come to see Bynum. She come to see him when she first left from down South.

SETH Martha was living here before Bynum. She ain't come on here when she first left from down there. She come on here after she went back to get her little girl. That's when she come on here.

BERTHA Well, where was Bynum? He was here when she came.

SETH Bynum ain't come till after her. That boy Hiram was staying up there in Bynum's room.

BERTHA Well, how long Bynum been here?

SETH Bynum ain't been here no longer than three years. That's what I'm trying to tell you. Martha was staying up there and sewing and cleaning for Doc Goldblum when Bynum came. This the longest he ever been in one place.

BERTHA How you know how long the man been in one place?

SETH I know Bynum. Bynum ain't no mystery to me. I done seen a hundred niggers like him. He's one of them fellows never could stay in one place. He was wandering all around the country till he got old and settled here. The only thing different about Bynum is he bring all this heebie-jeebie stuff with him.

BERTHA I still say he was staying here when she came. That's why she came . . . to see him.

SETH You can say what you want. I know the facts of it. She come on here four years ago all heartbroken 'cause she couldn't find her little girl. And Bynum wasn't nowhere around. She got mixed up in that old heebie-jeebie nonsense with him after he came.

BERTHA Well, if she came on before Bynum I don't know where she stayed. 'Cause she stayed up there in Hiram's room. Hiram couldn't get along with Bynum and left out of here owing you two dollars. Now, I know you ain't forgot about that!

SETH Sure did! You know Hiram ain't paid me that two dollars yet. So that's why he be ducking and hiding when he see me down on Logan Street. You right. Martha did come on after Bynum. I forgot that's why Hiram left.

BERTHA Him and Bynum never could see eye to eye. They always rubbed each other the wrong way. Hiram got to thinking that Bynum was trying to put a fix on him and he moved out. Martha came to see Bynum and ended up taking Hiram's room. Now, I know what I'm talking about. She stayed on here three years till they moved the church.

SETH She out there in Rankin now. I know where she at. I know where they moved the church to. She right out there in Rankin in that place used to be shoe store. Used to be Wolf's shoe store. They moved to a bigger place and they put that church in there. I know where she at. I know just where she at.

BERTHA Why don't you tell the man? You see he looking for her.

SETH I ain't gonna tell that man where that woman is! What I wanna do that for? I don't know nothing about that man. I don't know why he looking for her. He might wanna do her a harm. I ain't gonna carry that on my hands. He looking for her, he gonna have to find her for himself. I ain't gonna help him. Now, if he had come and presented himself as a gentleman—the way Martha Pentecost's husband would have done—then I would have told him. But I ain't gonna tell this old wild-eyed mean-looking nigger nothing!

BERTHA Well, why don't you get a ride with Selig and go up there and tell her where he is? See if she wanna see him. If that's her little girl . . . you say Martha was looking for her.

SETH You know me, Bertha. I don't get mixed up in nobody's business.

(BYNUM *enters from the stairs.)*

BYNUM Morning, Seth. Morning, Bertha. Can I still get some breakfast? Mr. Loomis been down here this morning?

SETH He done gone out and come back. He up there now. Left out of here early this morning wearing that coat. Hot as it is, the man wanna walk around wearing a big old heavy coat. He come back in here paid me for another week, sat down there waiting on Selig. Got tired of waiting and went on back upstairs.

BYNUM Where's the little girl?

SETH She out there in the front. Had to chase her and that Reuben off the front porch. She out there somewhere.

BYNUM Look like if Martha was around here he would have found her by now. My guess is she ain't in the city.

SETH She ain't! I know where she at. I know just where she at. But ain't gonna tell him. Not the way he look.

BERTHA Here go your coffee, Bynum.

BYNUM He says he gonna get Selig to find her for him.

SETH Selig can't find her. He talk all that . . . but unless he get lucky and knock on her door he can't find her. That's the only way he find anybody. He got to get lucky. But I know just where she at.

BERTHA Here go some biscuits, Bynum.

BYNUM What else you got over there, Sister Bertha? You got some grits and gravy over there? I could go for some of that this morning.

BERTHA *(Sets a bowl on the table.)* Seth, come on and help me turn this mattress over. Come on.

SETH Something ain't right with that fellow, Bynum. I don't like the way he stare at everybody.

BYNUM Mr. Loomis alright, Seth. He just a man got something on his mind. He just got a straightforward mind, that's all.

SETH What's that fellow that they had around here? Moses, that's Moses Houser. Man went crazy and jumped off the Brady Street Bridge. I told you when I seen him something wasn't right about him. And I'm telling you about this fellow now.

(There is a knock on the door. SETH *goes to answer it. Enter* RUTHERFORD SELIG.*)*

Ho! Come on in, Selig.

BYNUM If it ain't the People Finder himself.

SELIG Bynum, before you start . . . I ain't seen no shiny man now.

BYNUM Who said anything about that? I ain't said nothing about that. I just called you a first-class People Finder.

SELIG How many dustpans you get out of that sheet metal, Seth?

SETH You walked by them on your way in. They sitting out there on the porch. Got twenty-eight. Got four out of each sheet and made Bertha a coffeepot out the other one. They a little small but they got nice handles.

SELIG That was twenty cents apiece, right? That's what we agreed on.

SETH That's five dollars and sixty cents. Twenty on top of twenty-eight. How many sheets you bring me?

SELIG I got eight out there. That's a dollar twenty makes me owe you . . .

SETH Four dollars and forty cents.

SELIG *(Paying him.)* Go on and make me some dustpans. I can use all you can make.

*(*LOOMIS *enters from the stairs.)*

LOOMIS I been watching for you. He say you find people.

BYNUM Mr. Loomis here wants you to find his wife.

LOOMIS He say you find people. Find her for me.

SELIG Well, let see here . . . find somebody, is it?

*(*SELIG *rummages through his pockets. He has several notebooks and he is searching for the right one.)*

Alright now . . . what's the name?

LOOMIS Martha Loomis. She my wife. Got married legal with the paper and all.

SELIG *(Writing.)* Martha . . . Loomis. How tall is she?

LOOMIS She five feet from the ground.

SELIG Five feet . . . tall. Young or old?

LOOMIS She a young woman. Got long pretty hair.

SELIG Young . . . long . . . pretty . . . hair. Where did you last see her?

LOOMIS Tennessee. Nearby Memphis.

SELIG When was that?

LOOMIS Nineteen hundred and one.

SELIG Nineteen . . . hundred and one. I'll tell you, mister . . . you better off without them. Now you take me . . . old Rutherford Selig could tell you a thing or two about these women. I ain't met one yet I could understand. Now, you take Sally out there. That's all a man needs is a good horse. I say giddup and she go. Say whoa and she stop. I feed her some oats and she carry me wherever I want to go. Ain't had a speck of trouble out of her since I had her. Now, I been married. A long time ago down in Kentucky. I got up one morning and I saw this look on my wife's face. Like way down deep inside her she was wishing I was dead. I walked around that morning and every time I looked at her she had that look on her face. It seem like she knew I could see it on her. Every time I looked at her I got smaller and smaller. Well, I wasn't gonna stay around there and just shrink away. I walked out on the porch and closed the door behind me. When I closed the door she locked it. I went out and bought me a horse. And I ain't been without one since! Martha Loomis, huh? Well, now I'll do the best I can do. That's one dollar.

LOOMIS *(Holding out dollar suspiciously.)* How you find her?

SELIG Well, now, it ain't no easy job like you think. You can't just go out there and find them like that. There's a lot of little tricks to it. It's not an easy job keeping up with you Nigras the way you move about so. Now you take this woman you looking for... this Martha Loomis. She could be anywhere. Time I find her, if you don't keep your eye on her, she'll be gone off someplace else. You'll be thinking she over here and she'll be over there. But like I say there's a lot of little tricks to it.

LOOMIS You say you find her.

SELIG I can't promise anything but we been finders in my family for a long time. Bringers and finders. My great-granddaddy used to bring Nigras across the ocean on ships. That's wasn't no easy job either. Sometimes the winds would blow so hard you'd think the hand of God was set against the sails. But it set him well in pay and he settled in this new land and found him a wife of good Christian charity with a mind for kids and the like and well... here I am, Rutherford Selig. You're in good hands, mister. Me and my daddy have found plenty Nigras. My daddy, rest his soul, used to find runaway slaves for the plantation bosses. He was the best there was at it. Jonas B. Selig. Had him a reputation stretched clean across the country. After Abraham Lincoln give you all Nigras your freedom papers and with you all looking all over for each other... we started finding Nigras for Nigras. Of course, it don't pay as much. But the People Finding business ain't so bad.

LOOMIS *(Hands him the dollar.)* Find her. Martha Loomis. Find her for me.

SELIG Like I say, I can't promise you anything. I'm going back upriver, and if she's around in them parts I'll find her for you. But I can't promise you anything.

LOOMIS When you coming back?

SELIG I'll be back on Saturday. I come and see Seth to pick up my order on Saturday.

BYNUM You going upriver, huh? You going up around my way. I used to go all up through there. Blawknox... Clairton. Used to go up to Rankin and take that first righthand road. I wore many a pair of shoes out walking around that way. You'd have thought I was a missionary spreading the gospel the way I wandered all around them parts.

SELIG Okay, Bynum. See you on Saturday.

SETH Here, let me walk out with you. Help you with them dustpans.

(SETH and SELIG exit out the back. BERTHA enters from the stairs carrying a bundle of sheets.)

BYNUM Herald Loomis got the People Finder looking for Martha.

BERTHA You can call him a People Finder if you want to. I know Rutherford Selig carries people away too. He done carried a whole bunch of them away from here. Folks plan on leaving plan by Selig's timing. They wait till he get ready to go, then they hitch a ride on his wagon. Then he charge folks a dollar to tell them where he took them. Now, that's the truth of Rutherford Selig. This old People

Finding business is for the birds. He ain't never found nobody he ain't took away. Herald Loomis, you just wasted your dollar.

(BERTHA *exits into the bedroom.)*

LOOMIS He say he find her. He say he find her by Saturday. I'm gonna wait till Saturday.

(The lights fade to black.)

SCENE THREE

It is Sunday morning, the next day. The lights come up on the kitchen. SETH *sits talking to* BYNUM. *The breakfast dishes have been cleared away.*

SETH They can't see that. Neither one of them can see that. Now, how much sense it take to see that? All you got to do is be able to count. One man making ten pots is five men making fifty pots. But they can't see that. Asked where I'm gonna get my five men. Hell, I can teach anybody how to make a pot. I can teach you. I can take you out there and get you started right now. Inside of two weeks you'd know how to make a pot. All you got to do is want to do it. I can get five men. I ain't worried about getting no five men.

BERTHA *(Calls from the bedroom.)* Seth. Come on and get ready now. Reverend Gates ain't gonna be holding up his sermon 'cause you sitting out there talking.

SETH Now, you take the boy, Jeremy. What he gonna do after he put in that road? He can't do nothing but go put in another one somewhere. Now, if he let me show him how to make some pots and pans . . . then he'd have something can't nobody take away from him. After a while he could get his own tools and go off somewhere and make his own pots and pans. Find him somebody to sell them to. Now, Selig can't make no pots and pans. He can sell them but he can't make them. I get me five men with some tools and we'd make him so many pots and pans he'd have to open up a store somewhere. But they can't see that. Neither Mr. Cohen nor Sam Green.

BERTHA *(Calls from the bedroom.)* Seth . . . time be wasting. Best be getting on.

SETH I'm coming, woman! *(To* BYNUM.*)* Want me to sign over the house to borrow five hundred dollars. I ain't that big a fool. That's all I got. Sign it over to them and then I won't have nothing.

*(*JEREMY *enters waving a dollar and carrying his guitar.)*

JEREMY Look here, Mr. Bynum . . . won me another dollar last night down at Seefus! Me and that Mattie Campbell went down there again and I played contest. Ain't no guitar players down there. Wasn't even no contest. Say, Mr. Seth, I asked Mattie Campbell if she wanna come by and have Sunday dinner with us. Get some fried chicken.

SETH It's gonna cost you twenty-five cents.

JEREMY That's alright. I got a whole dollar here. Say Mr. Seth . . . me and Mattie Campbell talked it over last night and she gonna move in with me. If that's alright with you.

SETH Your business is your business . . . but it's gonna cost her a dollar a week for her board. I can't be feeding nobody for free.

JEREMY Oh, she know that, Mr. Seth. That's what I told her, say she'd have to pay for her meals.

SETH You say you got a whole dollar there . . . turn loose that twenty-five cents.

JEREMY Suppose she move in today, then that make seventy-five cents more, so I'll give you the whole dollar for her now till she get here.

(SETH *pockets the money and exits into the bedroom.)*

BYNUM So you and that Mattie Campbell gonna take up together?

JEREMY I told her she don't need to be by her lonesome, Mr. Bynum. Don't make no sense for both of us to be by our lonesome. So she gonna move in with me.

BYNUM Sometimes you got to be where you supposed to be. Sometimes you can get all mixed up in life and come to the wrong place.

JEREMY That's just what I told her, Mr. Bynum. It don't make no sense for her to be all mixed up and lonesome. May as well come here and be with me. She a fine woman too. Got them long legs. Knows how to treat a fellow too. Treat you like you wanna be treated.

BYNUM You just can't look at it like that. You got to look at the whole thing. Now, you take a fellow go out there, grab hold to a woman and think he got something 'cause she sweet and soft to the touch. Alright. Touching's part of life. It's in the world like everything else. Touching's nice. It feels good. But you can lay your hand upside a horse or a cat, and that feels good too. What's the difference? When you grab hold to a woman, you got something there. You got a whole world there. You got a way of life kicking up under your hand. That woman can take and make you feel like something. I ain't just talking about in the way of jumping off into bed together and rolling around with each other. Anybody can do that. When you grab hold to that woman and look at the whole thing and see what you got . . . why, she can take and make something out of you. Your mother was a woman. That's enough right there to show you what a woman is. Enough to show you what she can do. She made something out of you. Taught you converse, and all about how to take care of yourself, how to see where you at and where you going tomorrow, how to look out to see what's coming in the way of eating, and what to do with yourself when you get lonesome. That's a mighty thing she did. But you just can't look at a woman to jump off into bed with her. That's a foolish thing to ignore a woman like that.

JEREMY Oh, I ain't ignoring her, Mr. Bynum. It's hard to ignore a woman got legs like she got.

BYNUM Alright. Let's try it this way. Now, you take a ship. Be out there on the water traveling about. You out there on that ship sailing to and from. And then you see some land. Just like you see a woman walking down the street. You see that land and it don't look like nothing but a line out there on the horizon. That's all it is when you first see it. A line that cross your path out there on the horizon. Now, a smart man know when he see that land, it ain't just a line setting out there. He know that if you get off the water to go take a good look . . . why, there's a whole world right there. A whole world with everything imaginable under the sun. Anything you can think of you can find on that land. Same with a woman. A woman is everything a man need. To a smart man she water and berries. And that's all a man need. That's all he need to live on. You give me some water and berries and if there ain't nothing else I can live a hundred years. See, you just like a man looking at the horizon from a ship. You just seeing a part of it. But it's a blessing when you learn to look at a woman and see in maybe just a few strands of her hair, the way her cheek curves . . . to see in that everything there is out of life to be gotten. It's a blessing to see that. You know you done right and proud by your mother to see that. But you got to learn it. My telling you ain't gonna mean nothing. You got to learn how to come to your own time and place with a woman.

JEREMY What about your woman, Mr. Bynum? I know you done had some woman.

BYNUM Oh, I got them in memory time. That lasts longer than any of them ever stayed with me.

JEREMY I had me an old gal one time . . .

(There is a knock on the door. JEREMY *goes to answer it. Enter* MOLLY CUNNINGHAM. *She is about twenty-six, the kind of woman that "could break in on a dollar anywhere she goes." She carries a small cardboard suitcase, and wears a colorful dress of the fashion of the day.* JEREMY*'s heart jumps out of his chest when he sees her.)*

MOLLY You got any rooms here? I'm looking for a room.

JEREMY Yeah . . . Mr. Seth got rooms. Sure . . . wait till I get Mr. Seth. *(Calls.)* Mr. Seth! Somebody here to see you! *(To* MOLLY.*)* Yeah, Mr. Seth got some rooms. Got one right next to me. This a nice place to stay, too. My name's Jeremy. What's yours?

*(*SETH *enters dressed in his Sunday clothes.)*

SETH Ho!
JEREMY This here woman looking for a place to stay. She say you got any rooms.
MOLLY Mister, you got any rooms? I seen your sign say you got rooms.
SETH How long you plan to staying?
MOLLY I ain't gonna be here long. I ain't looking for no home or nothing. I'd be in Cincinnati if I hadn't missed my train.
SETH Rooms cost two dollars a week.
MOLLY Two dollars!
SETH That includes meals. We serve two meals a day. That's breakfast and dinner.
MOLLY I hope it ain't on the third floor.
SETH That's the only one I got. Third floor to the left. That's pay up in advance week to week.
MOLLY *(Going into her bosom.)* I'm gonna pay you for one week. My name's Molly. Molly Cunningham.
SETH I'm Seth Holly. My wife's name is Bertha. She do the cooking and taking care of around here. She got sheets on the bed. Towels twenty-five cents a week extra if you ain't got none. You get breakfast and dinner. We got fried chicken on Sundays.
MOLLY That sounds good. Here's two dollars and twenty-five cents. Look here, Mister . . . ?
SETH Holly. Seth Holly.
MOLLY Look here, Mr. Holly. I forgot to tell you. I likes me some company from time to time. I don't like being by myself.
SETH Your business is your business. I don't meddle in nobody's business. But this is a respectable house. I don't have no riffraff around here. And I don't have no women hauling no men up to their rooms to be making their living. As long as we understand each other then we'll be alright with each other.
MOLLY Where's the outhouse?
SETH Straight through the door over yonder.
MOLLY I get my own key to the front door?
SETH Everybody get their own key. If you come in late just don't be making no whole lot of noise and carrying on. Don't allow no fussing and fighting around here.
MOLLY You ain't got to worry about that, mister. Which way you say that outhouse was again?
SETH Straight through that door over yonder.

*(*MOLLY *exits out the back door.* JEREMY *crosses to watch her.)*

JEREMY Mr. Bynum, you know what? I think I know what you was talking about now.

(The lights go down on the scene.)

Scene Four

The lights come up on the kitchen. It is later the same evening. MATTIE *and all the residents of the house, except* LOOMIS, *sit around the table. They have finished eating and most of the dishes have been cleared.*

MOLLY That sure was some good chicken.
JEREMY That's what I'm talking about. Miss Bertha, you sure can fry some chicken. I thought my mama could fry some chicken. But she can't do half as good as you.
SETH I know it. That's why I married her. She don't know that, though. She think I married her for something else.
BERTHA I ain't studying you, Seth. Did you get your things moved in alright, Mattie?
MATTIE I ain't had that much. Jeremy helped me with what I did have.
BERTHA You'll get to know your way around here. If you have any questions about anything just ask me. You and Molly both. I get along with everybody. You'll find I ain't no trouble to get along with.
MATTIE You need some help with the dishes?
BERTHA I got me a helper. Ain't I, Zonia? Got me a good helper.

ZONIA Yes, ma'am.

SETH Look at Bynum sitting over there with his belly all poked out. Ain't saying nothing. Sitting over there half asleep. Ho, Bynum!

BERTHA If Bynum ain't saying nothing what you wanna start him up for?

SETH Ho, Bynum!

BYNUM What you hollering at me for? I ain't doing nothing.

SETH Come on, we gonna Juba.

BYNUM You know me, I'm always ready to Juba.

SETH Well, come on, then.

(SETH pulls out a harmonica and blows a few notes.)

Come on there, Jeremy. Where's your guitar? Go get your guitar. Bynum say he's ready to Juba.

JEREMY Don't need no guitar to Juba. Ain't you never Juba without a guitar?

(JEREMY begins to drum on the table.)

SETH It ain't that. I ain't never Juba with one! Figured to try it and see how it worked.

BYNUM *(Drumming on the table.)* You don't need no guitar. Look at Molly sitting over there. She don't know we Juba on Sunday. We gonna show you something tonight. You and Mattie Campbell both. Ain't that right, Seth?

SETH You said it! Come on, Bertha, leave them dishes be for a while. We gonna Juba.

BYNUM Alright. Let's Juba down!

(The Juba is reminiscent of the Ring Shouts of the African slaves. It is a call and response dance. BYNUM sits at the table and drums. He calls the dance as others clap hands, shuffle and stomp around the table. It should be as African as possible, with the performers working themselves up into a near frenzy. The words can be improvised, but should include some mention of the Holy Ghost. In the middle of the dance HERALD LOOMIS enters.)

LOOMIS *(In a rage.)* Stop it! Stop!

(They stop and turn to look at him.)

You all sitting up here singing about the Holy Ghost. What's so holy about the Holy Ghost? You singing and singing. You think the Holy Ghost coming? You singing for the Holy Ghost to come? What he gonna do, huh? He gonna come with tongues of fire to burn up your woolly heads? You gonna tie onto the Holy Ghost and get burned up? What you got then? Why God got to be so big? Why he got to be bigger than me? How much big is there? How much big do you want?

(LOOMIS starts to unzip his pants.)

SETH Nigger, you crazy!

LOOMIS How much big you want?

SETH You done plumb lost your mind!

(LOOMIS begins to speak in tongues and dance around the kitchen. SETH starts after him.)

BERTHA Leave him alone, Seth. He ain't in his right mind.

LOOMIS *(Stops suddenly.)* You all don't know nothing about me. You don't know what I done seen. Herald Loomis done seen some things he ain't got words to tell you.

(LOOMIS starts to walk out the front door and is thrown back and collapses, terror-stricken by his vision. BYNUM crawls to him.)

BYNUM What you done seen, Herald Loomis?

LOOMIS I done seen bones rise up out the water. Rise up and walk across the water. Bones walking on top of the water.

BYNUM Tell me about them bones, Herald Loomis. Tell me what you seen.

LOOMIS I come to this place . . . to this water that was bigger than the whole world. And I looked out . . . and I seen these bones rise up out the water. Rise up and begin to walk on top of it.

BYNUM Wasn't nothing but bones and they walking on top of the water.

LOOMIS Walking without sinking down. Walking on top of the water.

BYNUM Just marching in a line.

LOOMIS A whole heap of them. They come up out the water and started marching.

BYNUM Wasn't nothing but bones and they walking on top of the water.

LOOMIS One after the other. They just come up out the water and start to walking.

BYNUM They walking on the water without sinking down. They just walking and walking. And then . . . what happened, Herald Loomis?

LOOMIS They just walking across the water.

BYNUM What happened, Herald Loomis? What happened to the bones?

LOOMIS They just walking across the water . . . and then . . . they sunk down.

BYNUM The bones sunk into the water. They all sunk down.

LOOMIS All at one time! They just all fell in the water at one time.

BYNUM Sunk down like anybody else.

LOOMIS When they sink down they made a big splash and this here wave come up . . .

BYNUM A big wave, Herald Loomis. A big wave washed over the land.

LOOMIS It washed them out of the water and up on the land. Only . . . only . . .

BYNUM Only they ain't bones no more.

LOOMIS They got flesh on them! Just like you and me!

BYNUM Everywhere you look the waves is washing them up on the land right on top of one another.

LOOMIS They black. Just like you and me. Ain't no difference.

BYNUM Then what happened, Herald Loomis?

LOOMIS They ain't moved or nothing. They just laying there.

BYNUM You just laying there. What you waiting on, Herald Loomis?

LOOMIS I'm laying there . . . waiting.

BYNUM What you waiting on, Herald Loomis?

LOOMIS I'm waiting on the breath to get into my body.

BYNUM The breath coming into you, Herald Loomis. What you gonna do now?

LOOMIS The wind's blowing the breath into my body. I can feel it. I'm starting to breathe again.

BYNUM What you gonna do, Herald Loomis?

LOOMIS I'm gonna stand up. I got to stand up. I can't lay here no more. All the breath coming into my body and I got to stand up.

BYNUM Everybody's standing up at the same time.

LOOMIS The ground's starting to shake. There's a great shaking. The world's busting half in two. The sky's splitting open. I got to stand up.

(LOOMIS *attempts to stand up.*)

My legs . . . my legs won't stand up!

BYNUM Everybody's standing and walking toward the road. What you gonna do, Herald Loomis?

LOOMIS My legs won't stand up.

BYNUM They shaking hands and saying goodbye to each other and walking every whichaway down the road.

LOOMIS I got to stand up!

BYNUM They walking around here now. Mens. Just like you and me. Come right up out the water.

LOOMIS Got to stand up.

BYNUM They walking, Herald Loomis. They walking around here now.

LOOMIS I got to stand up. Get up on the road.

BYNUM Come on, Herald Loomis.

(LOOMIS *tries to stand up.*)

LOOMIS My legs won't stand up! My legs won't stand up!

(LOOMIS *collapses on the floor as the lights go down to black.*)

Act Two

SCENE ONE

The lights come up on the kitchen. BERTHA *busies herself with breakfast preparations.* SETH *sits at the table.*

SETH I don't care what his problem is! He's leaving here!

BERTHA You can't put the man out and he got that little girl. Where they gonna go then?

SETH I don't care where he go. Let him go back where he was before he come here. I ain't asked him to come here. I knew when I first looked at him something wasn't right with him. Dragging that little girl around with him. Looking like he be sleeping in the woods somewhere. I knew all along he wasn't right.

BERTHA A fellow get a little drunk he's liable to say or do anything. He ain't done no big harm.

SETH I just don't have all that carrying on in my house. When he come down here I'm gonna tell him. He got to leave here. My daddy wouldn't stand for it and I ain't gonna stand for it either.

BERTHA Well, if you put him out you have to put Bynum out too. Bynum right there with him.

SETH If it wasn't for Bynum ain't no telling what would have happened. Bynum talked to that fellow just as nice and calmed him down. If he wasn't here ain't no telling what would have happened. Bynum ain't done nothing but talk to him and kept him calm. Man acting all crazy with that foolishness. Naw, he's leaving here.

BERTHA What you gonna tell him? How you gonna tell him to leave?

SETH I'm gonna tell him straight out. Keep it nice and simple. Mister, you got to leave here!

(MOLLY *enters from the stairs.)*

MOLLY Morning.

BERTHA Did you sleep alright in that bed?

MOLLY Tired as I was I could have slept anywhere. It's a real nice room, though. This is a nice place.

SETH I'm sorry you had to put up with all that carrying on last night.

MOLLY It don't bother me none. I done seen that kind of stuff before.

SETH You won't have to see it around here no more.

(BYNUM *is heard singing offstage.)*

I don't put up with all that stuff. When that fellow come down here I'm gonna tell him.

BYNUM *(singing)*

Soon my work will all be done
Soon my work will all be done
Soon my work will all be done

I'm going to see the king.

BYNUM *(Enters.)* Morning, Seth. Morning, Sister Bertha. I see we got Molly Cunningham down here at breakfast.

SETH Bynum, I wanna thank you for talking to that fellow last night and calming him down. If you hadn't been here ain't no telling what might have happened.

BYNUM Mr. Loomis alright, Seth. He just got a little excited.

SETH Well, he can get excited somewhere else cause he leaving here.

(MATTIE *enters from the stairs.)*

BYNUM Well, there's Mattie Campbell.

MATTIE Good morning.

BERTHA Sit on down there, Mattie. I got some biscuits be ready in a minute. The coffee's hot.

MATTIE Jeremy gone already?

BYNUM Yeah, he leave out of here early. He got to be there when the sun come up. Most working men got to be there when the sun come up. Everybody but Seth. Seth work at night. Mr. Olowski so busy in his shop he got fellows working at night.

(LOOMIS *enters from the stairs.)*

SETH Mr. Loomis, now . . . I don't want no trouble. I keeps me a respectable house here. I don't have no carrying on like what went on last night. This has been a respectable house for a long time. I'm gonna have to ask you to leave.

LOOMIS You got my two dollars. That two dollars say we stay till Saturday.

*(*LOOMIS *and* SETH *glare at each other.)*

SETH Alright. Fair enough. You stay till Saturday. But come Saturday you got to leave here.

LOOMIS *(Continues to glare at* SETH. *He goes to the door and calls.)* Zonia. You stay around this house, you hear? Don't you go anywhere.

*(*LOOMIS *exits out the front door.)*

SETH I knew it when I first seen him. I knew something wasn't right with him.

BERTHA Seth, leave the people alone to eat their breakfast. They don't want to hear that. Go on out there and make some pots and pans. That's the only time you satisfied is when you out there. Go on out there and make some pots and pans and leave them people alone.

SETH I ain't bothering anybody. I'm just stating the facts. I told you, Bynum.

*(*BERTHA *shoos* SETH *out the back door and exits into the bedroom.)*

MOLLY *(To* BYNUM.*)* You one of them voo-doo people?

BYNUM I got a power to bind folks if that what you talking about.

MOLLY I thought so. The way you talked to that man when he started all that spooky stuff. What you say you had the power to do to people? You ain't the cause of him acting like that, is you?

BYNUM I binds them together. Sometimes I help them find each other.

MOLLY How do you do that?

BYNUM With a song. My daddy taught me how to do it.

MOLLY That's what they say. Most folks be what they daddy is. I wouldn't want to be like my daddy. Nothing ever set right with him. He tried to make the world over. Carry it around with him everywhere he go. I don't want to be like that. I just take life as it come. I don't be trying to make it over.

(Pause.)

Your daddy used to do that too, huh? Make people stay together?

BYNUM My daddy used to heal people. He had the Healing Song. I got the Binding Song.

MOLLY My mama used to believe in all that stuff. If she got sick she would have gone and saw your daddy. As long as he didn't make her drink nothing. She wouldn't drink nothing nobody give her. She was always afraid somebody was gonna poison her. How your daddy heal people?

BYNUM With a song. He healed people by singing over them. I seen him do it. He sung over this little white girl when she was sick. They made a big to-do about it. They carried the girl's bed out in the yard and had all her kinfolk standing around. The little girl laying up there in the bed. Doctors standing around can't do nothing to help her. And they had my daddy come up and sing his song. It didn't sound no different than any other song. It was just somebody singing. But the song was its own thing and it come out and took upon this little girl with its power and it healed her.

MOLLY That's sure something else. I don't understand that kind of thing. I guess if the doctor couldn't make me well I'd try it. But otherwise I don't wanna be bothered with that kind of thing. It's too spooky.

BYNUM Well, let me get on out here and get to work.

*(*BYNUM *gets up and heads out the back door.)*

MOLLY I ain't meant to offend you or nothing. What's your name . . . Bynum? I ain't meant to say nothing to make you feel bad now.

*(*BYNUM *exits out the back door.)*

(To MATTIE.*)* I hope he don't feel bad. He's a nice man. I don't wanna hurt nobody's feelings or nothing.

MATTIE I got to go on up to Doc Goldblum's and finish this ironing.

MOLLY Now, that's something I don't never wanna do. Iron no clothes. Especially somebody else's. That's what I believe killed my mama. Always ironing and working, doing somebody else's work. Not Molly Cunningham.

MATTIE It's the only job I got. I got to make it someway to fend for myself.

MOLLY I thought Jeremy was your man. Ain't he working?

MATTIE We just be keeping company till maybe Jack come back.

MOLLY I don't trust none of these men. Jack or nobody else. These men liable to do anything. They wait just until they get one woman tied and locked up with them... then they look around to see if they can get another one. Molly don't pay them no mind. One's just as good as the other if you ask me. I ain't never met one that meant nobody no good. You got any babies?

MATTIE I had two for my man, Jack Carper. But they both died.

MOLLY That be the best. These men make all these babies, then run off and leave you to take care of them. Talking about they wanna see what's on the other side of the hill. I make sure I don't get no babies. My mama taught me how to do that.

MATTIE Don't make me no mind. That be nice to be a mother.

MOLLY Yeah? Well, you go on, then. Molly Cunningham ain't gonna be tied down with no babies. Had me a man one time who I thought had some love in him. Come home one day and he was packing his trunk. Told me the time come when even the best of friends must part. Say he was gonna send me a Special Delivery some old day. I watched him out the window when he carried that trunk out and down to the train station. Said if he was gonna send me a Special Delivery I wasn't gonna be there to get it. I done found out the harder you try to hold onto them, the easier it is for some gal to pull them away. Molly done learned that. That's why I don't trust nobody but the good Lord above, and I don't love nobody but my mama.

MATTIE I got to get on. Doc Goldblum gonna be waiting.

*(*MATTIE *exits out the front door.* SETH *enters from his workshop with his apron, gloves, goggles, etc. He carries a bucket and crosses to the sink for water.)*

SETH Everybody gone but you, huh?

MOLLY That little shack out there by the outhouse... that's where you make them pots and pans and stuff?

SETH Yeah, that's my workshed. I go out there ... take these hands and make something out of nothing. Take that metal and bend and twist it whatever way I want. My daddy taught me that. He used to make pots and pans. That's how I learned it.

MOLLY I never knew nobody made no pots and pans. My uncle used to shoe horses.

*(*JEREMY *enters at the front door.)*

SETH I thought you was working? Ain't you working today?

JEREMY Naw, they fired me. White fellow come by told me to give him fifty cents if I wanted to keep working. Going around to all the colored making them give him fifty cents to keep hold to their jobs. Them other fellows, they was giving it to him. I kept hold to mine and they fired me.

SETH Boy, what kind of sense that make? What kind of sense it make to get fired from a job where you making eight dollars a week and all it cost you is fifty cents. That's seven dollars and fifty cents profit! This way you ain't got nothing.

JEREMY It didn't make no sense to me. I don't make but eight dollars. Why I got to give him fifty cents of it? He go around to all the colored and he got ten dollars extra. That's more than I make for a whole week.

SETH I see you gonna learn the hard way. You just looking at the facts of it. See, right now, without the job, you ain't got nothing. What you gonna do when you can't keep a roof over your head? Right now, come Saturday, unless you come up with another two dollars, you gonna be out there in the streets.

Down up under one of them bridges trying to put some food in your belly and wishing you had given that fellow that fifty cents.

JEREMY Don't make me no difference. There's a big road out there. I can get my guitar and always find me another place to stay. I ain't planning on staying in one place for too long noway.

SETH We gonna see if you feel like that come Saturday!

*(*SETH *exits out the back.* JEREMY *sees* MOLLY.*)*

JEREMY Molly Cunningham. How you doing today, sugar?

MOLLY You can go on back down there tomorrow and go back to work if you want. They won't even know who you is. Won't even know it's you. I had me a fellow did that one time. They just went ahead and signed him up like they never seen him before.

JEREMY I'm tired of working anyway. I'm glad they fired me. You sure look pretty today.

MOLLY Don't come telling me all that pretty stuff. Beauty wanna come in and sit down at your table asking to be fed. I ain't hardly got enough for me.

JEREMY You know you pretty. Ain't no sense in you saying nothing about that. Why don't you come on and go away with me?

MOLLY You tied up with that Mattie Campbell. Now you talking about running away with me.

JEREMY I was just keeping her company 'cause she lonely. You ain't the lonely kind. You the kind that know what she want and how to get it. I need a woman like you to travel around with. Don't you wanna travel around and look at some places with Jeremy? With a woman like you beside him, a man can make it nice in the world.

MOLLY Molly can make it nice by herself too. Molly don't need nobody leave her cold in hand. The world rough enough as it is.

JEREMY We can make it better together. I got my guitar and I can play. Won me another dollar last night playing guitar. We can go around and I can play at the dances and we can just enjoy life. You can make it by yourself alright, I agrees with that. A woman like you can make it anywhere she go. But you can make it better if you got a man to protect you.

MOLLY What places you wanna go around and look at?

JEREMY All of them! I don't want to miss nothing. I wanna go everywhere and do everything there is to be got out of life. With a woman like you it's like having water and berries. A man got everything he need.

MOLLY You got to be doing more than playing that guitar. A dollar a day ain't hardly what Molly got in mind.

JEREMY I gambles real good. I got a hand for it.

MOLLY Molly don't work. And Molly ain't up for sale.

JEREMY Sure, baby. You ain't got to work with Jeremy.

MOLLY There's one more thing.

JEREMY What's that, sugar?

MOLLY Molly ain't going South.

(The lights go down on the scene.)

SCENE TWO

The lights come up on the parlor. SETH *and* BYNUM *sit playing a game of dominoes.* BYNUM *sings to himself.*

BYNUM *(Singing.)*

They tell me Joe Turner's come and gone
Ohhh Lordy
They tell me Joe Turner's come and gone
Ohhh Lordy
Got my man and gone

Come with forty links of chain
Ohhh Lordy
Come with forty links of chain
Ohh Lordy
Got my man and gone

SETH Come on and play if you gonna play.

BYNUM I'm gonna play. Soon as I figure out what to do.

SETH You can't figure out if you wanna play or you wanna sing.

BYNUM Well sir, I'm gonna do a little bit of both.

(Playing.)

There. What you gonna do now?

(Singing.)

They tell me Joe Turner's come and gone
Ohhh Lordy
They tell me Joe Turner's come and gone
Ohhh Lordy

SETH Why don't you hush up that noise.

BYNUM That's a song the women sing down around Memphis. The women down there made up that song. I picked it up down there about fifteen years ago.

*(*LOOMIS *enters from the front door.)*

BYNUM Evening, Mr. Loomis.

SETH Today's Monday, Mr. Loomis. Come Saturday your time is up. We done ate already. My wife roasted up some yams. She got your plate sitting in there on the table. *(To* BYNUM.*)* Whose play is it?

BYNUM Ain't you keeping up with the game? I thought you was a domino player. I just played so it got to be your turn.

*(*LOOMIS *goes into the kitchen, where a plate of yams is covered and set on the table. He sits down and begins to eat with his hands.)*

SETH *(Plays.)* Twenty! Give me twenty! You didn't know I had that ace five. You was trying to play around that. You didn't know I had that lying there for you.

BYNUM You ain't done nothing. I let you have that to get mine.

SETH Come on and play. You ain't doing nothing but talking. I got a hundred and forty points to your eighty. You ain't doing nothing but talking. Come on and play.

BYNUM *(Singing.)*

They tell me Joe Turner's come and gone
Ohhh Lordy
They tell me Joe Turner's come and gone
Ohhh Lordy
Got my man and gone

He come with forty links of chain
Ohhh Lordy

LOOMIS Why you singing that song? Why you singing about Joe Turner?

BYNUM I'm just singing to entertain myself.

SETH You trying to distract me. That's what you trying to do.

BYNUM *(Singing.)*

Come with forty links of chain
Ohhh Lordy
Come with forty links of chain
Ohhh Lordy

LOOMIS I don't like you singing that song, mister!

SETH Now, I ain't gonna have no more disturbance around here, Herald Loomis. You start any more disturbance and you leavin' here, Saturday or no Saturday.

BYNUM The man ain't causing no disturbance, Seth. He just say he don't like the song.

SETH Well, we all friendly folk. All neighborly like. Don't have no squabbling around here. Don't have no disturbance. You gonna have to take that someplace else.

BYNUM He just say he don't like the song. I done sung a whole lot of songs people don't like. I respect everybody. He here in the house too. If he don't like the song, I'll sing something else. I know lots of songs. You got "I Belong to the Band," "Don't You Leave Me Here." You got "Praying on the Old Campground," "Keep Your Lamp Trimmed and Burning" . . . I know lots of songs.

(Sings.)

Boys, I'll be so glad when payday come
Captain, Captain, when payday comes
Gonna catch that Illinois Central
Going to Kankakee

SETH Why don't you hush up that hollering and come on and play dominoes.

BYNUM You ever been to Johnstown, Herald Loomis? You look like a fellow I seen around there.

LOOMIS I don't know no place with that name.

BYNUM That's around where I seen my shiny man. See, you looking for this woman. I'm looking for a shiny man. Seem like everybody looking for something.

SETH I'm looking for you to come and play these dominoes. That's what I'm looking for.

BYNUM You a farming man, Herald Loomis? You look like you done some farming.

LOOMIS Same as everybody. I done farmed some, yeah.

BYNUM I used to work at farming . . . picking cotton. I reckon everybody done picked some cotton.

SETH I ain't! I ain't never picked no cotton. I was born up here in the North. My daddy was a freedman. I ain't never even seen no cotton!

BYNUM Mr. Loomis done picked some cotton. Ain't you, Herald Loomis? You done picked a bunch of cotton.

LOOMIS How you know so much about me? How you know what I done? How much cotton I picked?

BYNUM I can tell from looking at you. My daddy taught me how to do that. Say when you look at a fellow, if you taught yourself to look for it, you can see his song written on him. Tell you what kind of man he is in the world. Now, I can look at you, Mr. Loomis, and see you a man who done forgot his song. Forgot how to sing it. A fellow forget that and he forget who he is. Forget how he's supposed to mark down life. Now, I used to travel all up and down this road and that . . . looking here and there. Searching. Just like you, Mr. Loomis. I didn't know what I was searching for. The only thing I knew was something was keeping me dissatisfied. Something wasn't making my heart smooth and easy. Then one day my daddy gave me a song. That song had a weight to it that was hard to handle. That song was hard to carry. I fought against it. Didn't want to accept that song. I tried to find my daddy to give him back the song. But I found out it wasn't his song. It was my song. It had come from way deep inside me. I looked long back in memory and gathered up pieces and snatches of things to make that song. I was making it up out of myself. And that song helped me on the road. Made it smooth to where my footsteps didn't bite back at me. All the time that song getting bigger and bigger. That song growing with each step of the road. It got so I used all of myself up in the making of that song. Then I was the song in search of itself. That song rattling in my throat and I'm looking for it. See, Mr. Loomis, when a man forgets his song he goes off in search of it . . . till he find out he's got it with him all the time. That's why I can tell you one of Joe Turner's niggers. 'Cause you forgot how to sing your song.

LOOMIS You lie! How you see that? I got a mark on me? Joe Turner done marked me to where you can see it? You telling me I'm a marked man. What kind of mark you got on you?

(BYNUM *begins singing.*)

BYNUM

They tell me Joe Turner's come and gone
Ohhh Lordy
They tell me Joe Turner's come and gone
Ohhh Lordy
Got my man and gone

LOOMIS Had a whole mess of men he catched. Just go out hunting regular like you go out hunting possum. He catch you and go home to his wife and family. Ain't thought about you going home to yours. Joe Turner catched me when my little girl was just born. Wasn't nothing but a little baby sucking on her mama's titty when he catched me. Joe Turner catched me in nineteen hundred and one. Kept me seven years until nineteen hundred and eight. Kept everybody seven years. He'd go out hunting and bring back forty men at a time. And keep them seven years.

I was walking down this road in this little town outside of Memphis. Come up on these fellows gambling. I was a deacon in the Abundant Life Church. I stopped to preach to these fellows to see if maybe I could turn some of them from their sinning when Joe Turner, brother of the Governor of the great sovereign state of Tennessee, swooped down on us and grabbed everybody there. Kept us all seven years.

My wife Martha gone from me after Joe Turner catched me. Got out from under Joe Turner on his birthday. Me and forty other men put in our seven years and he let us go on his birthday. I made it back to Henry Thompson's place where me and Martha was sharecropping and Martha's gone. She taken my little girl and left her with her mama and took off North. We been looking for her ever since. That's been going on four years now we been looking. That's the only thing I know to do. I just wanna see her face so I can get me a starting place in the world. The world got to start somewhere. That's what I been looking for. I been wandering a long time in somebody else's world. When I find my wife that be the making of my own.

BYNUM Joe Turner tell why he caught you? You ever asked him that?

LOOMIS I ain't never seen Joe Turner. Seen him to where I could touch him. I asked one of them fellows one time why he catch niggers. Asked him what I got he want? Why don't he keep on to himself? Why he got to catch me going down the road by my lonesome? He told me I was worthless. Worthless is something you throw away. Something you don't bother with. I ain't seen him throw me away. Wouldn't even let me stay away when I was by my lonesome. I ain't tried to catch him when he going down the road. So I must got something he want. What I got?

SETH He just want you to do his work for him. That's all.

LOOMIS I can look at him and see where he big and strong enough to do his own work. So it can't be that. He must want something he ain't got.

BYNUM That ain't hard to figure out. What he wanted was your song. He wanted to have that song to be his. He thought by catching you he could learn that song. Every nigger he catch he's looking for the one he can learn that song from. Now he's got you bound up to where you can't sing your own song. Couldn't sing it them seven years 'cause you was afraid he would snatch it from under you. But you still got it. You just forgot how to sing it.

LOOMIS *(To* BYNUM.*)* I know who you are. You one of them bones people.

(The lights go down to black.)

SCENE THREE

The lights come up on the kitchen. It is the following morning. MATTIE, *and* BYNUM, *sit at the table.* BERTHA *busies herself at the stove.*

BYNUM Good luck don't know no special time to come. You sleep with that up under your pillow and good luck can't help but come to you. Sometimes it come and go and you don't even know it's been there.

BERTHA Bynum, why don't you leave that gal alone? She don't wanna be hearing all that. Why don't you go on and get out the way and leave her alone?

BYNUM *(Getting up.)* Alright, alright. But you mark what I'm saying. It'll draw it to you just like a magnet.

*(*BYNUM *exits up the stairs as* LOOMIS *enters.)*

BERTHA I got some grits here, Mr. Loomis.

*(*BERTHA *sets a bowl on the table.)*

If I was you, Mattie, I wouldn't go getting all tied up with Bynum in that stuff. That kind of stuff, even if it do work for a while, it don't last. That just get people more mixed up than they is already. And I wouldn't waste my time fretting over Jeremy either. I seen it coming. I seen it when she first come here. She that kind of woman run off with the first man got a dollar to spend on her. Jeremy just young. He don't know what he getting into. That gal don't mean him no good. She's just using him to keep from being by herself. That's the worst use of a man you can have. You ought to be glad to wash him out of your hair. I done seen all kind of men. I done seen them come and go through here. Jeremy ain't had enough to him for you. You need a man who's got some understanding and who willing to work with that understanding to come to the best he can. You got your time coming. You just tries too hard and can't understand why it don't work for you. Trying to figure it out don't do nothing but give you a troubled mind. Don't no man want a woman with a troubled mind.

You get all that trouble off your mind and just when it look like you ain't never gonna find what you want . . . you look up and it's standing right there. That's how I met my Seth. You gonna look up one day and find everything you want standing right in front of you. Been twenty-seven years now since that happened to me. But life ain't no happy-go-lucky time where everything be just like you want it. You got your time coming. You watch what Bertha's saying.

(SETH enters.)

SETH Ho!

BERTHA What you doing come in here so late?

SETH I was standing down there on Logan Street talking with the fellows. Henry Allen tried to sell me that old piece of horse he got.

(He sees LOOMIS.)

Today's Tuesday, Mr. Loomis.

BERTHA *(Pulling him toward the bedroom.)* Come on in here and leave that man alone to eat his breakfast.

SETH I ain't bothering nobody. I'm just reminding him what day it is.

(SETH and BERTHA exit into the bedroom.)

LOOMIS That dress got a color to it.

MATTIE Did you really see them things like you said? Them people come up out the ocean?

LOOMIS It happened just like that, yeah.

MATTIE I hope you find your wife. It be good for your little girl for you to find her.

LOOMIS Got to find her for myself. Find my starting place in the world. Find me a world I can fit in.

MATTIE I ain't never found no place for me to fit. Seem like all I do is start over. It ain't nothing to find no starting place in the world. You just start from where you find yourself.

LOOMIS Got to find my wife. That be my starting place.

MATTIE What if you don't find her? What you gonna do then if you don't find her?

LOOMIS She out there somewhere. Ain't no such thing as not finding her.

MATTIE How she got lost from you? Jack just walked away from me.

LOOMIS Joe Turner split us up. Joe Turner turned the world upside-down. He bound me on to him for seven years.

MATTIE I hope you find her. It be good for you to find her.

LOOMIS I been watching you. I been watching you watch me.

MATTIE I was just trying to figure out if you seen things like you said.

LOOMIS *(Getting up.)* Come here and let me touch you. I been watching you. You a full woman. A man needs a full woman. Come on and be with me.

MATTIE I ain't got enough for you. You'd use me up too fast.

LOOMIS Herald Loomis got a mind seem like you a part of it since I first seen you. It's been a long time since I seen a full woman. I can smell you from here. I know you got Herald Loomis on your mind, can't keep him apart from it. Come on and be with Herald Loomis.

(LOOMIS has crossed to MATTIE. He touches her awkwardly, gently, tenderly. Inside he howls like a lost wolf pup whose hunger is deep. He goes to touch her but finds he cannot.)

I done forgot how to touch.

(The lights fade to black.)

SCENE FOUR

It is early the next morning. The lights come up on ZONIA and REUBEN in the yard.

REUBEN Something spooky going on around here. Last night Mr. Bynum was out in the yard singing and talking to the wind . . . and the wind it just be talking back to him. Did you hear it?

ZONIA I heard it. I was scared to get up and look. I thought it was a storm.

REUBEN That wasn't no storm. That was Mr. Bynum. First he say something . . . and the wind it say back to him.

ZONIA I heard it. Was you scared? I was scared.

REUBEN And then this morning . . . I seen Miss Mabel!

ZONIA Who Miss Mabel?

REUBEN Mr. Seth's mother. He got her picture hanging up in the house. She been dead.

ZONIA How you seen her if she been dead?

REUBEN Zonia . . . if I tell you something you promise you won't tell anybody?

ZONIA I promise.

REUBEN It was early this morning . . . I went out to the coop to feed the pigeons. I was down on the ground like this to open up the door to the coop . . . when all of a sudden I seen some feets in front of me. I looked up . . . and there was Miss Mabel standing there.

ZONIA Reuben, you better stop telling that! You ain't seen nobody!

REUBEN Naw, it's the truth. I swear! I seen her just like I see you. Look . . . you can see where she hit me with her cane.

ZONIA Hit you? What she hit you for?

REUBEN She says, "Didn't you promise Eugene something?" Then she hit me with her cane. She say, "Let them pigeons go." Then she hit me again. That's what made them marks.

ZONIA Jeez man . . . get away from me. You done see a haunt!

REUBEN Shhh. You promised, Zonia!

ZONIA You sure it wasn't Miss Bertha come over there and hit you with her hoe?

REUBEN It wasn't no Miss Bertha. I told you it was Miss Mabel. She was standing right there by the coop. She had this light coming out of her and then she just melted away.

ZONIA What she had on?

REUBEN A white dress. Ain't even had no shoes or nothing. Just had on that white dress and them big hands . . . and that cane she hit me with.

ZONIA How you reckon she knew about the pigeons? You reckon Eugene told her?

REUBEN I don't know. I sure ain't asked her none. She say Eugene was waiting on them pigeons. Say he couldn't go back home till I let them go. I couldn't get the door to the coop open fast enough.

ZONIA Maybe she an angel? From the way you say she look with that white dress. Maybe she an angel.

REUBEN Mean as she was . . . how she gonna be an angel? She used to chase us out her yard and frown up and look evil all the time.

ZONIA That don't mean she can't be no angel 'cause of how she looked and 'cause she wouldn't let no kids play in her yard. It go by if you got any spots on your heart and if you pray and go to church.

REUBEN What about she hit me with her cane? An angel wouldn't hit me with her cane.

ZONIA I don't know. She might. I still say she was an angel.

REUBEN You reckon Eugene the one who sent old Miss Mabel?

ZONIA Why he send her? Why he don't come himself?

REUBEN Figured if he send her maybe that'll make me listen. 'Cause she old.

ZONIA What you think it feel like?

REUBEN What?

ZONIA Being dead.

REUBEN Like being sleep only you don't know nothing and can't move no more.

ZONIA If Miss Mabel can come back . . . then maybe Eugene can come back too.

REUBEN We can go down to the hideout like we used to! He could come back everyday! It be just like he ain't dead.

ZONIA Maybe that ain't right for him to come back. Feel kinda funny to be playing games with a haunt.

REUBEN Yeah . . . what if everybody came back? What if Miss Mabel came back just like she ain't dead? Where you and your daddy gonna sleep then?

ZONIA Maybe they go back at night and don't need no place to sleep.

REUBEN It still don't seem right. I'm sure gonna miss Eugene. He's the bestest friend anybody ever had.

ZONIA My daddy say if you miss somebody too much it can kill you. Say he missed me till it liked to killed him.

REUBEN What if your mama's already dead and all the time you looking for her?

ZONIA Naw, she ain't dead. My daddy say he can smell her.

REUBEN You can't smell nobody that ain't here. Maybe he smelling old Miss Bertha. Maybe Miss Bertha your mama?

ZONIA Naw, she ain't. My mamma got long pretty hair and she five feet from the ground!

REUBEN Your daddy say when you leaving?

(ZONIA *doesn't respond.)*

Maybe you gonna stay in Mr. Seth's house and don't go looking for your mama no more.

ZONIA He say we got to leave on Saturday.

REUBEN Dag! You just only been here for a little while. Don't seem like nothing ever stay the same.

ZONIA He say he got to find her. Find him a place in the world.

REUBEN He could find him a place in Mr. Seth's house.

ZONIA It don't look like we never gonna find her.

REUBEN Maybe he find her by Saturday then you don't have to go.

ZONIA I don't know.

REUBEN You look like a spider!

ZONIA I ain't no spider!

REUBEN Got them long skinny arms and legs. You look like one of them Black Widows.

ZONIA I ain't no Black Widow nothing! My name is Zonia!

REUBEN That's what I'm gonna call you . . . Spider.

ZONIA You can call me that, but I don't have to answer.

REUBEN You know what? I think maybe I be your husband when I grow up.

ZONIA How you know?

REUBEN I ask my grandpap how you know and he say when the moon falls into a girl's eyes that how you know.

ZONIA Did it fall into my eyes?

REUBEN Not that I can tell. Maybe I ain't old enough. Maybe you ain't old enough.

ZONIA So there! I don't know why you telling me that lie!

REUBEN That don't mean nothing 'cause I can't see it. I know it's there. Just the way you look at me sometimes look like the moon might have been in your eyes.

ZONIA That don't mean nothing if you can't see it. You supposed to see it.

REUBEN Shucks, I see it good enough for me. You ever let anybody kiss you?

ZONIA Just my daddy. He kiss me on the cheek.

REUBEN It's better on the lips. Can I kiss you on the lips?

ZONIA I don't know. You ever kiss anybody before?

REUBEN I had a cousin let me kiss her on the lips one time. Can I kiss you?

ZONIA Okay.

*(*REUBEN *kisses her and lays his head against her chest.)*

What you doing?

REUBEN Listening. Your heart singing!

ZONIA It is not.

REUBEN Just beating like a drum. Let's kiss again.

(They kiss again.)

Now you mine, Spider. You my girl, okay?

ZONIA Okay.

REUBEN When I get grown, I come looking for you.

ZONIA Okay.

(The lights fade to black.)

SCENE FIVE

The lights come up on the kitchen. It is Saturday. BYNUM, LOOMIS, *and* ZONIA *sit at the table.* BERTHA *prepares breakfast.* ZONIA *has on a white dress.*

BYNUM With all this rain we been having he might have ran into some washed-out roads. If that wagon got stuck in the mud he's liable to be still upriver somewhere. If he's upriver then he ain't coming until tomorrow.

LOOMIS Today's Saturday. He say he be here on Saturday.

BERTHA Zonia, you gonna eat your breakfast this morning.

ZONIA Yes, ma'am.

BERTHA I don't know how you expect to get any bigger if you don't eat. I ain't never seen a child that didn't eat. You about as skinny as a bean pole.

(Pause.)

Mr. Loomis, there's a place down on Wylie. Zeke Mayweather got a house down there. You ought to see if he got any rooms.

(LOOMIS doesn't respond.)

Well, you're welcome to some breakfast before you move on.

(MATTIE enters from the stairs.)

MATTIE Good morning.

BERTHA Morning, Mattie. Sit on down there and get you some breakfast.

BYNUM Well, Mattie Campbell, you been sleeping with that up under your pillow like I told you?

BERTHA Bynum, I done told you to leave that gal alone with all that stuff. You around here meddling in other people's lives. She don't want to hear all that. You ain't doing nothing but confusing her with that stuff.

MATTIE *(To LOOMIS.)* You all fixing to move on?

LOOMIS Today's Saturday. I'm paid up till Saturday.

MATTIE Where you going to?

LOOMIS Gonna find my wife.

MATTIE You going off to another city?

LOOMIS We gonna see where the road take us. Ain't no telling where we wind up.

MATTIE Eleven years is a long time. Your wife . . . she might have taken up with someone else. People do that when they get lost from each other.

LOOMIS Zonia. Come on, we gonna find your mama.

(LOOMIS and ZONIA cross to the door.)

MATTIE *(To ZONIA.)* Zonia, Mattie got a ribbon here match your dress. Want Mattie to fix your hair with her ribbon?

(ZONIA nods. MATTIE ties the ribbon in her hair.)

There . . . it got a color just like your dress. *(To LOOMIS.)* I hope you find her. I hope you be happy.

LOOMIS A man looking for a woman be lucky to find you. You a good woman, Mattie. Keep a good heart.

(LOOMIS and ZONIA exit.)

BERTHA I been watching that man for two weeks . . . and that's the closest I come to seeing him act civilized. I don't know what's between you all, Mattie . . . but the only thing that man needs is somebody to make him laugh. That's all you need in the world is love and laughter. That's all anybody needs. To have love in one hand and laughter in the other.

(BERTHA moves about the kitchen as though blessing it and chasing away the huge sadness that seems to envelop it. It is a dance and demonstration of her own magic, her own remedy that is centuries old and to which she is connected by the muscles of her heart and the blood's memory.)

You hear me, Mattie? I'm talking about laughing. The kind of laugh that comes from way deep inside. To just stand and laugh and let life flow right through you. Just laugh to let yourself know you're alive.

(She begins to laugh. It is a near-hysterical laughter that is a celebration of life, both its pain and its blessing. MATTIE and BYNUM join in the laughter. SETH enters from the front door.)

SETH Well, I see you all having fun.

(SETH begins to laugh with them.)

That Loomis fellow standing up there on the corner watching the house. He standing right up there on Manila Street.

BERTHA Don't you get started on him. The man done left out of here and that's the last I wanna hear of it. You about to drive me crazy with that man.

SETH I just say he standing up there on the corner. Acting sneaky like he always do. He can stand up there all he want. As long as he don't come back in here.

(There is a knock on the door. SETH *goes to answer it. Enter* MARTHA LOOMIS [PENTECOST]. *She is a young woman about twenty-eight. She is dressed as befitting a member of an Evangelist church.* RUTHERFORD SELIG *follows.)*

SETH Look here, Bertha. It's Martha Pentecost. Come on in, Martha. Who that with you? Oh . . . that's Selig. Come on in, Selig.

BERTHA Come on in, Martha. It's sure good to see you.

BYNUM Rutherford Selig, you a sure enough first-class People Finder!

SELIG She was right out there in Rankin. You take that first right-hand road . . . right there at that church on Wooster Street. I started to go right past and something told me to stop at the church and see if they needed any dustpans.

SETH Don't she look good, Bertha.

BERTHA Look all nice and healthy.

MARTHA Mr. Bynum . . . Selig told me my little girl was here.

SETH There's some fellow around here say he your husband. Say his name is Loomis. Say you his wife.

MARTHA Is my little girl with him?

SETH Yeah, he got a little girl with him. I wasn't gonna tell him where you was. Not the way this fellow look. So he got Selig to find you.

MARTHA Where they at? They upstairs?

SETH He was standing right up there on Manila Street. I had to ask him to leave 'cause of how he was carrying on. He come in here one night—

(The door opens and LOOMIS *and* ZONIA *enter.* MARTHA *and* LOOMIS *stare at each other.)*

LOOMIS Hello, Martha.

MARTHA Herald . . . Zonia?

LOOMIS You ain't waited for me, Martha. I got out the place looking to see your face. Seven years I waited to see your face.

MARTHA Herald, I been looking for you. I wasn't but two months behind you when you went to my mama's and got Zonia. I been looking for you ever since.

LOOMIS Joe Turner let me loose and I felt all turned around inside. I just wanted to see your face to know that the world was still there. Make sure everything still in its place so I could reconnect myself together. I got there and you was gone, Martha.

MARTHA Herald . . .

LOOMIS Left my little girl motherless in the world.

MARTHA I didn't leave her motherless, Herald. Reverend Tolliver wanted to move the church up North 'cause of all the trouble the colored folks was having down there. Nobody knew what was gonna happen traveling them roads. We didn't even know if we was gonna make it up here or not. I left her with my mama so she be safe. That was better than dragging her out on the road having to duck and hide from people. Wasn't no telling what was gonna happen to us. I didn't leave her motherless in the world. I been looking for you.

LOOMIS I come up on Henry Thompson's place after seven years of living in hell, and all I'm looking to do is see your face.

MARTHA Herald, I didn't know if you was ever coming back. They told me Joe Turner had you and my whole world split half in two. My whole life shattered. It was like I had poured it in a cracked jar and it all leaked out the bottom. When it go like that there ain't nothing you can do put it back together. You talking about Henry Thompson's place like I'm still gonna be working the land by myself. How I'm gonna do that? You wasn't gone but two months and Henry Thompson kicked me off his land and I ain't had no place to go but to my mama's. I stayed and waited there for five years before I woke up one morning and decided that you was dead. Even if you weren't, you was dead to me. I wasn't gonna carry you with me no more. So I killed you in my heart. I buried you. I mourned you. And then I picked up what was left and went on to make life without you. I was a young woman with life at my beckon. I couldn't drag you behind me like a sack of cotton.

LOOMIS I just been waiting to look on your face to say my goodbye. That goodbye got so big at times, seem like it was gonna swallow me up. Like Jonah in the whale's belly I sat up in that goodbye for three years. That goodbye kept me out on the road searching. Not looking on women in their houses. It kept me bound up to the road. All the time that goodbye swelling up in my chest till I'm about to bust. Now that I see your face I can say my goodbye and make my own world.

(LOOMIS *takes* ZONIA*'s hand and presents her to* MARTHA.)

Martha . . . here go your daughter. I tried to take care of her. See that she had something to eat. See that she was out of the elements. Whatever I know I tried to teach her. Now she need to learn from her mother whatever you got to teach her. That way she don't be no one-sided person.

(LOOMIS *stoops to* ZONIA.)

Zonia, you go live with your mama. She a good woman. You go on with her and listen to her good. You my daughter and I love you like a daughter. I hope to see you again in the world somewhere. I'll never forget you.

ZONIA *(Throws her arms around* LOOMIS *in a panic.)* I won't get no bigger! My bones won't get no bigger! They won't! I promise! Take me with you till we keep searching and never finding. I won't get no bigger! I promise!

LOOMIS Go on and do what I told you now.

MARTHA *(Goes to* ZONIA *and comforts her.)* It's alright, baby. Mama's here. Mama's here. Don't worry. Don't cry.

(MARTHA *turns to* BYNUM.)

Mr. Bynum, I don't know how to thank you. God bless you.

LOOMIS It was you! All the time it was you that bind me up! You bound me to the road!

BYNUM I ain't bind you, Herald Loomis. You can't bind what don't cling.

LOOMIS Everywhere I go people wanna bind me up. Joe Turner wanna bind me up! Reverend Tolliver wanna bind me up. You wanna bind me up. Everybody wanna bind me up. Well, Joe Turner's come and gone and Herald Loomis ain't for no binding. I ain't gonna let nobody bind me up!

(LOOMIS *pulls out a knife.)*

BYNUM It wasn't you, Herald Loomis. I ain't bound you. I bound the little girl to her mother. That's who I bound. You binding yourself. You bound onto your song. All you got to do is stand up and sing it, Herald Loomis. It's right there kicking at your throat. All you got to do is sing it. Then you be free.

MARTHA Herald . . . look at yourself! Standing there with a knife in your hand. You done gone over to the devil. Come on . . . put down the knife. You got to look to Jesus. Even if you done fell away from the church you can be saved again. The Bible say, "The Lord is my shepherd I shall not want. He maketh me to lie down in green pastures. He leads me beside the still water. He restoreth my soul. He leads me in the path of righteousness for His name's sake. Even though I walk through the shadow of death—"

LOOMIS That's just where I be walking!

MARTHA "I shall fear no evil. For Thou art with me. Thy rod and thy staff, they comfort me."

LOOMIS You can't tell me nothing about no valleys. I done been all across the valleys and the hills and the mountains and the oceans.

MARTHA "Thou preparest a table for me in the presence of my enemies."

LOOMIS And all I seen was a bunch of niggers dazed out of their woolly heads. And Mr. Jesus Christ standing there in the middle of them, grinning.

MARTHA "Thou anointest my head with oil, my cup runneth over."

LOOMIS He grin that big old grin . . . and niggers wallowing at his feet.

MARTHA "Surely goodness and mercy shall follow me all the days of my life, and I shall dwell in the house of the Lord forever."

LOOMIS Great big old white man . . . your Mr. Jesus Christ. Standing there with a whip in one hand and tote board in another, and them niggers swimming in a sea of cotton. And he counting. He tallying up the cotton. "Well, Jeremiah . . . what's the matter, you ain't picked but two hundred pounds of cotton today? Got to put you on half rations." And Jeremiah go back and lay up there on his half rations and talk about what a nice man Mr. Jesus Christ is 'cause he give him salvation after he die. Something wrong here. Something don't fit right!

MARTHA You got to open your heart and have faith, Herald. This world is just a trial for the next. Jesus offers you salvation.

LOOMIS I been wading in the water. I been walking all over the River Jordan. But what it get me, huh? I done been baptized with the blood of the lamb and the fire of the Holy Ghost. But what I got, huh? I got salvation? My enemies all around me picking the flesh from my bones. I'm choking on my own blood and all you got to give me is salvation?

MARTHA You got to be clean, Herald. You got to be washed with the blood of the lamb.

LOOMIS Blood make you clean? You clean with blood?

MARTHA Jesus bled for you. He's the Lamb of God who takest away the sins of the world.

LOOMIS I don't need nobody to bleed for me! I can bleed for myself.

MARTHA You got to be something, Herald. You just can't be alive. Life don't mean nothing unless it got a meaning.

LOOMIS What kind of meaning you got? What kind of clean you got, woman? You want blood? Blood make you clean? You clean with blood?

*(*LOOMIS *slashes himself across the chest. He rubs the blood over his face and comes to a realization.)*

I'm standing! I'm standing. My legs stood up! I'm standing now!

(Having found his song, the song of self-sufficiency, fully resurrected, cleansed and given breath, free from any encumbrance other than the workings of his own heart and the bonds of the flesh, having accepted the responsibility for his own presence in the world, he is free to soar above the environs that weighed and pushed his spirit into terrifying contractions.)

Goodbye, Martha.

*(*LOOMIS *turns and exits, the knife still in his hands.* MATTIE *looks about the room and rushes out after him.)*

BYNUM Herald Loomis, you shining! You shining like new money!

(The lights go down to BLACK.)

YUSEF KOMUNYAKAA

(1947–)

Winner of the 1994 Pulitzer Prize for poetry, Yusef Komunyakaa is a productive author who has written seven books to date. His poetry focuses primarily on his Vietnam War experiences and jazz both as a subject and as a model for his art. He is in the black jazz–inspired tradition extending from Langston Hughes to Amiri Baraka, Michael Harper, Al Young, and Cornelius Eady.

Komunyakaa was born on April 29, 1947 in Bogalusa, Louisiana, which is approximately seventy miles from New Orleans. He served in the Vietnam War as a correspondent and editor of *The Southern Cross,* a military newspaper, and was awarded the Bronze Star. He earned a B.A. from the University of Colorado in 1975, an M.A. from Colorado State in 1979, and an M.F.A. from the University of California at Irvine in 1980. Living in New Orleans from 1984 to 1985, he was a poet-in-the-schools. Currently, he holds the Lilly Professorship of Poetry at Indiana University. He makes his home in Bloomington, Indiana, but spends part of each year in Australia. In *Callaloo* 13, he says, "I've been recently influenced by the politics of land rights in Australia, realizing that the Aborigine has been there in excess of forty thousand years." In 1990, with other American writers, Komunyakaa traveled to a writers' conference in Vietnam. His books include *Dedications and Other Darkhorses* (1977), *Lost in the Bonewheel Factory* (1979), *Copacetic* (1984), *I Apologize for the Eyes in My Head* (1986), *Toys in a Field* (1987), *Dien Cai Dau* (1988), and *February in Sydney* (1989). With Sascha Feinstein, he edited *The Jazz Poetry Anthology* (1991).

In *Callaloo* 13, Komunyakaa defines his poetry as being

> grounded in everyday speech patterns. I really think the poem begins with a central image; it's not tied down in any way, not pre-defined. When an image, a line, develops into a poem, if it has an emotional thread running through it, when it can link two people together, reader and poet, then it's working.

Furthermore, like many black writers, he feels a need for American poetry to be more political. His poem "Facing It," about the Vietnam Veterans Memorial, shows the centrality of that war and politics to American lives.

❖❖❖

Vicente F. Gotera, "Lives of Tempered Steel: An Interview with Yusef Komunyakaa." *Callaloo* 13, No. 2 (Spring 1989) is a very informative interview with Yusef Komunyakaa.

Camouflaging the Chimera

We tied branches to our helmets.
We painted our faces & rifles
with mud from a riverbank,
blades of grass hung from the pockets
of our tiger suits. We wove
ourselves into the terrain,
content to be a hummingbird's target.

We hugged bamboo & leaned
against a breeze off the river,
slow-dragging with ghosts

from Saigon to Bangkok,
with women left in doorways
reaching in from America.
We aimed at dark-hearted songbirds.

In our way station of shadows
rock apes tried to blow our cover,
throwing stones at the sunset. Chameleons

crawled our spines, changing from day
to night: green to gold,
gold to black. But we waited
till the moon touched metal,

till something almost broke
inside us. VC struggled
with the hillside, like black silk

wrestling iron through grass.
We weren't there. The river ran
through our bones. Small animals took refuge
against our bodies; we held our breath,

ready to spring the L-shaped
ambush, as a world revolved
under each man's eyelid.

Hanoi Hannah

Ray Charles! His voice
calls from waist-high grass,
& we duck behind gray sandbags.
"Hello, Soul Brothers. Yeah,
Georgia's also on my mind."
Flares bloom over the trees.
"Here's Hannah again.
Let's see if we can't
light her goddamn fuse
this time." Artillery
shells carve a white arc
agains dusk. Her voice rises
from a hedgerow on our left.
It's Saturday night in the States.
Guess what your woman's doing tonight.
I think I'll let Tina Turner
tell you, you homesick GIs."
Howitzers buck like a herd
of horses behind concertina.
"You know you're dead men,
don't you? You're dead
as King today in Memphis.
Boys, you're surrounded by
General Tran Do's division."
Her knife-edge song cuts
deep as a sniper's bullet.

"Soul Brothers, what you dying for?"
We lay down a white-klieg
trail of tracers. Phantom jets
fan out over the trees.
Artillery fire zeros in.
Her voice grows flesh
& we can see her falling
into words, a bleeding flower
no one knows the true name for.
"You're lousy shots, GIs."
Her laughter floats up
as though the airways are
buried under our feet.

Missing in Action

Men start digging in the ground,
propping shadows against trees
outside Hanoi, but there aren't
enough bones for a hash pipe.
After they carve new names
into polished black stone,
we throw dust to the wind
& turn faces to blank walls.

Names we sing in sleep & anger
cling to willows like river mist.
We splice voices on tapes
but we can't make one man
walk the earth again.
Not a single song comes alive
in the ring of broken teeth
on the ground. Sunlight
presses down for an answer.
But nothing can make that C-130
over Hanoi come out of its spin,
spiraling like a flare in green sky.

After the flag's folded,
the living fall
into each other's arms.
They've left spaces
trees can't completely fill.
Pumping breath down tunnels
won't help us bring ghosts
across the sea.

Peasants outside Pakse City
insist the wildflowers
have changed colors.

They're what the wind
& rain have taken back,
what love couldn't recapture.
Now less than a silhouette
grown into the parrot perch,
this one died looking up at the sky.

Facing It

My black face fades,
hiding inside the black granite.
I said I wouldn't,
dammit: No tears.
I'm stone. I'm flesh.
My clouded reflection eyes me
like a bird of prey, the profile of night
slanted against morning. I turn
this way—the stone lets me go.
I turn that way—I'm inside
the Vietnam Veterans Memorial
again, depending on the light
to make a difference.
I go down the 58,022 names,
half-expecting to find
my own in letters like smoke.
I touch the name Andrew Johnson;
I see the booby trap's white flash.
Names shimmer on a woman's blouse
but when she walks away
the names stay on the wall.
Brushstrokes flash, a red bird's
wings cutting across my stare.
The sky. A plane in the sky.
A white vet's image floats
closer to me, then his pale eyes
look through mine. I'm a window.
He's lost his right arm
inside the stone. In the black mirror
a woman's trying to erase names:
No, she's brushing a boy's hair.

CHARLES JOHNSON

(1948–)

Charles Johnson is a philosophical and erudite novelist who says in his book entitled *Being and Race* (1988) that he is not interested in writing "misery-filled protest stories about the sorry condition of being black in America" in the vein of Richard Wright. Rather, like Ralph Ellison, he observes in *The Chronicle of Higher Education* (January 1991) that he wants to celebrate the doggedness of the black tradition and its black heroes and heroines who have triumphed over racism. Johnson portrays figures such as educator Mary McLeod Bethune, photographer Gordon Parks, and Civil Rights leader Martin Luther King, Jr., who "understood racism but stepped over it the way they would a puddle." In his fiction, he rejects naturalism, the primary technique from Wright to James Baldwin, as being too limited to express black being, black life. Johnson's fiction is a mix of moral tale, philosophical exposition, and science fiction.

Charles Johnson was born in Evanston, Illinois, on April 23, 1948. At age seventeen, he began a career as a cartoonist under the sponsorship of Lawrence Lariar. He has published two books of drawings, *Black Humor* (1970) and *Half-Past Nation-Time* (1972). He graduated in 1971 from Southern Illinois University with a degree in journalism. While at Southern Illinois, he studied creative writing with the famous novelist John Gardner, who helped him find connections between the African American historical experience and the philosophical systems of Africa, the East, and the West. In 1973, he earned an M.A. in philosophy from Southern Illinois. The following year, he enrolled in a Ph.D. program at the State University of New York at Stony Brook, where he concentrated on phenomenology and literary aesthetics.

With his dissertation pending at Stony Brook, he accepted a teaching position in creative writing at the University of Washington at Seattle. He directed the creative writing program at Washington from 1978 to 1990, he has also been the editor of the *Seattle Review*. He has written *Being and Race* (1988), two modern slave narratives; *Oxherding Tale* (1982), which was influenced by Frederick Douglass's autobiography and Herman Melville's "Benito Cereno"; and *Middle Passage* (1990), which takes place aboard the slave ship *Republic,* where an African tribe, the Allmuseri, mutiny and slaughter most of the crew, including the mad captain. Like Ishmael Reed, Johnson takes the slave narrative genre into new metaphysical and surrealistic areas.

Johnson is interested in the political but finds the moral to be the foundation on which the political is based. In *The Chronicle of Higher Education* (January 1991) he remarks, "What is most important, I think, are the more fundamental questions that give rise in the novel to political issues," questions concerning matters such as slavery, personal responsibility, and society. He wants "a fiction of increasing intellectual and artistic generosity, one that enables us as people, as a culture, to move from narrow complaint to broad celebration." Instead of simply crying out against racism, he wants to analyze it carefully and seek out a worthy response. He rejects the literary mode of naturalism because it "seemed to conceal profound prejudices about being, what a person is, the nature of society." He feels that in the bleak world of naturalism, African Americans are doomed from the start.

Interested primarily in phenomenology, Johnson has demonstrated an unusual ability to connect this and other areas of philosophy with the African American experience. The intersection of philosophy and race can be seen, for example, in *The Sorcerer's Apprentice, Tales and Conjunctions* (1986), a collection of short stories in which various African American characters embark on existential quests. In "China," fifty-four-year-old Rudolph is in deteriorating physical and emotional health, but after becoming a student of the martial arts, he begins an existential journey, hoping to experience his "whole self." "I've never been able to give everything to anything," Rudolph observes. "The world never let me. It won't let me put all of myself into play." In the end, however, Rudolph does extricate himself from the weight of the world and the weight of himself when, in a tournament, "twenty feet off the ground, he executes a perfect flying kick that floors his opponent."

Other stories in *The Sorcerer's Apprentice* include "The Education of Mingo," a kind of fable in which a young slave is remade to embody some of his master's values, and "Popper's Disease," a science fiction story concerned with an extraterrestrial who is treated by an Illinois physician. The title story is a blend of conjuration and phenomenology, with the power of conjuration seeming to be stronger than the power of the will.

Allan, apprenticed to sorcerer extraordinaire Rubin Bailey, is able to call forth demons from the belly of hell. This feat is accomplished only at the moment when Allan is at his lowest psychologically, in despair about his inability to heal a sick child. Believing that he has failed at his trade, Allan sees suicide as his only option and thus decides to summon demons who will open the pit of hell for him. When they arrive and converse with him, he realizes that his past conjurations have failed because he has merely parodied the master sorcerer, Rubin Bailey. Allan, though a lover of the "art" of conjuration, seems not to possess the native ability to be a true conjure doctor. "The Sorcerer's Apprentice" can thus be viewed as a story about creativity and the creation of art, a story about ability and mastery.

Asked in a 1993 interview to comment on his fiction, Johnson responded that for his central characters "there is a progression from ignorance to knowledge, or from a lack of understanding to some greater understanding." He also stated that there is usually a moment of awareness, an epiphany that in his opinion is somewhat Hegelian. Johnson's observation refers to the dialectic posited by Hegel (thesis versus antithesis), as demonstrated in "China" and "The Sorcerer's Apprentice," when Allan realizes he does not have what it takes to be a conjure doctor.

A metaphysical dimension can be seen in Johnson's first novel, *Faith and the Good Thing* (1974), a story that centers on Faith Cross. Faith is caught between two worlds—specifically, the real physical world as we know and experience it and the metaphysical world, a reality that exists only in Faith's mind. Casey Fudd is a case in point. He is a widower who attempts to commit suicide. Although it is difficult for one to imagine that Casey should fail in his attempt—having purchased "himself an old .45, a gallon of kerosene, a long rope, and an economy-size bottle of rat poison"—he does.

> Casey tramped down to the river, sat himself upright in a rowboat, and pushed off, floating down the river until he came to some low hanging trees on the bank. There he tied the rope around a tree limb, doused himself with kerosene, swallowed the bottle of poison, raised the pistol to blow out his brains, and kicked the boat out

from under himself. What happened? Old Casey pulled the trigger, but the bullet broke the rope, the river doused the fire and, when he got a lungful of water, he gagged up every bit of the rat poison.

At that moment Casey, in the manner of a typically Johnsonian character, emerges as a new man, determined to change the course of his life.

Oxherding Tale (1982), a neoslave narrative, has as its central character Andrew Hawkins. Against a phenomenology backdrop, Johnson juxtaposes the abstract with the concrete. This juxtaposition is achieved when Karl Marx visits Cripplegate Cotton Plantation and asks Ezekiel, Andrew's tutor, to explain the relevance of Ezekiel's abstract knowledge. Predictably, Johnson splashes the text with the language of philosophy and again is effective in intersecting this discipline with the African American experience, slavery in this particular case. Marx proves to be a charming guest, as Ezekiel "hauled out his latest articles, spreading them around grease-coated plates, jugs of whiskey, and makeshift ashtrays on the table; he talked, waving a slice of bread, about his recent work (ontology), on the Theologia Germanica."

Although Ezekiel is an important character, *Oxherding Tale* is not his story. It is Andrew's, an individual in search of freedom from slavery. Ezekiel the tutor is just one in a procession of characters who are instrumental in providing Andrew with the knowledge that he needs to achieve freedom. Flo Hatfield trains black slaves to become male concubines, Reb is a coffin maker, and Horace Bannon is the Soulcatcher. Andrew's encounters with various characters provide him with new levels of knowledge—epiphanies that ultimately lead to his freedom.

Johnson's best-known novel is *Middle Passage* (1990), which has been adapted as a screenplay for Tri-Star Productions. This adaptation builds on Johnson's prior experiences as a television writer. *Booker*, for example, a program about the life of Booker T. Washington, has appeared on both PBS in 1984 and the Disney Channel in 1988. Another PBS production by Johnson is *Charlie Smith and the Fritter Tree* (1978), which focuses on the life of a 135-year-old African American.

Middle Passage, set in 1830, is the story of Rutherford Calhoun, a freed slave who must flee New Orleans. Similar to Andrew Hawkins in *Oxherding Tale* (1982) and Faith Cross in *Faith and the Good Thing* (1974), Rutherford searches for truth and freedom but must overcome a number of difficulties before finding either. He becomes a stowaway on the *Republic*, a slave ship bound for Africa to collect more Africans for the slave trade.

Currently the Pollock Professor of English at the University of Washington at Seattle, Johnson has received many awards and honors, among them the National Book Award in 1990 for *Middle Passage*. *The Sorcerer's Apprentice, Tales and Conjunctions* was nominated for the 1986 PEN Faulkner Award. What distinguishes Johnson's craft is his ability to offer profiles of African American characters who seem, as a matter of course, to be immersed in philosophical debates. Such debates have resulted in fiction that truly is philosophical and deserves greater attention than it has previously received.

❖❖❖

Two informative biographical articles on Johnson are Maryemma Graham, "Charles R. Johnson," in *Dictionary of Literary Biography: Afro-American Fiction Writers After 1955,* vol. 33 (1984), and Peter Monaghan, "Portrait (of Charles Johnson)," *Chronicle of Higher Education,* January 16, 1991.

The Sorcerer's Apprentice

There was a time, long ago, when many sorcerers lived in South Carolina, men not long from slavery who remembered the white magic of the Ekpe Cults and Cameroons, and by far the greatest of these wizards was a blacksmith named Rubin Bailey. Believing he was old, and would soon die, the Sorcerer decided to pass his learning along to an apprentice. From a family near Abbeville he selected a boy, Allan, whose father, Richard Jackson, Rubin once healed after an accident, and for this Allan loved the Sorcerer, especially the effects of his craft, which comforted the sick, held back evil, and blighted the enemies of newly freed slaves with locusts and bad health. "My house," Richard told the wizard, "has been honored." His son swore to serve his teacher faithfully, then those who looked to the Sorcerer, in all ways. With his father's blessing, the boy moved his belongings into the Sorcerer's home, a houseboat covered with strips of scrapmetal, on the river.

But Rubin Bailey's first teachings seemed to Allan to be no teachings at all. "Bring in fresh water," Rubin told his apprentice. "Scrape barnacles off the boat." He never spoke of sorcery. Around the boy he tied his blacksmith's apron, and guided his hand in hammering out the horseshoes Rubin sold in town, but not once in the first month did Rubin pass along the recipes for magic. Patiently, Allan performed these duties in perfect submission to the Sorcerer, for it seemed rude to express displeasure to a man he wished to emulate, but his heart knocked for the higher knowledge, the techniques that would, he hoped, work miracles.

At last, as they finished a meal of boiled pork and collards one evening, he complained bitterly: "You haven't told me anything yet!" Allan regretted this outburst immediately, and lowered his head. "Have I done wrong?"

For a moment the Sorcerer was silent. He spiced his coffee with rum, dipped in his bread, chewed slowly, then looked up, steadily, at the boy. "You are the best of students. And you wish to do good, but you can't be too faithful, or too eager, or the good becomes evil."

"Now I don't understand," Allan said. "By themselves the tricks aren't good *or* evil, and if you plan to do good, then the results must be good."

Rubin exhaled, finished his coffee, then shoved his plate toward the boy. "Clean the dishes," he said. Then, more gently: "What I know has worked I will teach. There is no certainty these things can work for you, or even for me, a second time. White magic comes and goes. I'm teaching you a trade, Allan. You will never starve. This is because after fifty years, I still can't foresee if an incantation will be magic or foolishness."

These were not, of course, the answers Allan longed to hear. He said, "Yes, sir," and quietly cleared away their dishes. If he had replied aloud to Rubin, as he did silently while toweling dry their silverware later that night, he would have told the Sorcerer, "You are the greatest magician in the world because you have studied magic and the long-dead masters of magic, and I believe, even if you do not, that the secret of doing good is a good heart and having a hundred spells at your disposal, so I will study everything—the words and timbre and tone of your voice as you conjure, and listen to those you have heard. Then I, too, will have magic and can do good." He washed his underwear in the moonlight, as is fitting for a fledgling magician, tossed his dishpan water into the river, and, after hanging his washpail on a hook behind Rubin's front door, undressed, and fell asleep with these thoughts: To do good is a very great thing, the *only* thing, but a magician must be able to conjure at a moment's notice. Surely it is all a question of know-how.

So it was that after a few months the Sorcerer's apprentice learned well and quickly when Rubin Bailey finally began to teach. In Allan's growth was the greatest joy. Each spell he showed proudly to his father and Richard's friends when he traveled home once a year. Unbeknownst to the Sorcerer, he held simple exhibits for their entertainment—harmless prestidigitation like throwing his voice or levitating logs stacked by the toolshed. However pleased Richard might have been, he gave no sign. Allan's father never joked or laughed too loudly. He was the sort of man who held his feelings in, and people took this for strength. Allan's mother, Beatrice, a tall, thick-waisted woman, had told him (for Richard would not) how when she was carrying Allan, they rode a haywagon to a scrub-ball in Abbeville on Freedom Day. Richard fell beneath the wagon. A wheel smashed his thumb open to the bone. "Somebody better go for Rubin Bailey," was all Richard said, and he stared like it might be a stranger's hand. And Allan remembered Richard toiling so long in the sun he couldn't eat some evenings unless he first emptied his stomach by forcing himself to vomit. His father squirreled away money in their mattresses, saving for seven years to buy the land they worked. When he had $600—half what they needed—he grew afraid of theft, so Beatrice took their money to one of the banks in town. She stood in line behind a northern-looking Negro who said his name was Grady Armstrong. "I work for the bank across the street," he told Beatrice. "You wouldn't be interested in part-time work, would you? We need a woman to clean, someone reliable, but she has to keep her savings with us." Didn't they need the money? Beatrice would ask Allan, later, when Richard left them alone at night. Wouldn't the extra work help her husband? She followed Grady Armstrong, whose easy, loose-hinged walk led them to the second bank across the street. "Have you ever deposited money before?" asked Grady. "No," she said. Taking her envelope, he said, "Then I'll do it for you." On the boardwalk, Beatrice waited. And waited. After five minutes, she opened the door, found no Grady Armstrong, and flew screaming the fifteen miles back to the fields and Richard, who listened and chewed his lip, but said nothing. He leaned, Allan remembered, in the farmhouse door, smoking his cigars and watching only Lord knew what in the darkness—exactly as he stood the following year, when Beatrice, after swallowing rat poison, passed on.

Allan supposed it was risky to feel if you had grown up, like Richard, in a world of nightriders. There was too much to lose. Any attachment ended in separation, grief. If once you let yourself care, the crying might never stop. So he assumed his father was pleased with his apprenticeship to Rubin, though hearing him say this would have meant the world to Allan. He did not mind that somehow the Sorcerer's personality seemed to permeate each spell like sweat staining fresh wood, because this, too, seemed to be the way of things. The magic was Rubin Bailey's, but when pressed, the Sorcerer confessed that the spells had been in circulation for centuries. They were a web of history and culture, like the king-sized quilts you saw as curiosities at country fairs, sewn by every woman in Abbeville, each having finished only a section, a single flower perhaps, so no man, strictly speaking, could own a mystic spell. "But when you kill a bird by pointing," crabbed Rubin from his rocking chair, "you don't *haveta* wave your left hand in the air and pinch your forefinger and thumb together like I do."

"Did I do that?" asked Allan.

Rubin hawked and spit over the side of the houseboat. "Every time."

"I just wanted to get it right." Looking at his hand, he felt ashamed—he was, after all, right-handed—then shoved it deep into his breeches. "The way you do it is so beautiful."

"I know." Rubin laughed. He reached into his coat, brought out his pipe, and looked for matches. Allan stepped inside, and the Sorcerer shouted behind him, "You shouldn't do it because my own teacher, who wore out fifteen flying carpets in his lifetime, told me it was wrong."

"Wrong?" The boy returned. He held a match close to the bowl of Rubin's pipe, cupping the flame. "Then why do you do it?"

"It works best for me that way, Allan. I have arthritis." He slanted his eyes left at his pupil. "Do you?"

The years passed, and Allan improved, even showing a certain flair, a style all his own that pleased Rubin, who praised the boy for his native talent, which did not come from knowledge and, it struck Allan, was wholly unreliable. When Esther Peters, a seamstress, broke her hip, it was not Rubin who the old woman called, but young Allan, who sat stiffly on a fiddle-back chair by her pallet, the fingers of his left hand spread over the bony ledge of her brow and rheumy eyes, whispering the rune that lifted her pain after Esther stopped asking, "Does he know what he doing, Rubin? This ain't how you did when I caught my hand in that cotton gin." Afterwards, as they walked the dark footpath leading back to the river, Rubin in front, the Sorcerer shared a fifth with the boy and paid him a terrifying compliment: "That was the best I've seen anybody do the spell for exorcism." He stroked his pupil's head. "God took *holt* of you back there—I don't see how you can do it that good again." The smile at the corners of Allan's mouth weighed a ton. He handed back Rubin's bottle, and said, "Me neither." The Sorcerer's flattery, if this was flattery, suspiciously resembled Halloween candy with hemlock inside. Allan could not speak to Rubin the rest of that night.

In the old days of sorcery, it often happened that pupils came to mistrust most their finest creations, those frighteningly effortless works that flew mysteriously from their lips when they weren't looking, and left the apprentice feeling, despite his pride, as baffled as his audience and afraid for his future—this was most true when the compliments compared a fledgling wizard to other magicians, as if the apprentice had achieved nothing new, or on his own. This is how Allan felt. The charm that cured Esther had whipped through him like wind through a reed-pipe, or—more exactly, like music struggling to break free, liberate its volume and immensity from the confines of wood and brass. It made him feel unessential, anonymous, like a tool in which the spell sang itself, briefly borrowing his throat, then tossed him, Allan, aside when the miracle ended. To be so used was thrilling, but it gave the boy many bad nights. He lay half on his bed, half off. While Rubin slept, he yanked on his breeches and slipped outside. The river trembled with moonlight. Not far away, in a rowboat, a young man unbuttoned his lover. Allan heard their laughter and fought down the loneliness of a life devoted to discipline and sorcery. So many sacrifices. So many hours spent hunched over yellow, worm-holed scrolls. He pitched small pebbles into the water, and thought, If a conjurer cannot conjure at will, he is worthless. He must have knowledge, an armory of techniques, a thousand strategies, if he is to unfailingly do good. Toward this end the apprentice applied himself, often despising the spontaneity of his first achievement. He watched Rubin Bailey closely until on his fifth year on the river he had stayed by the Sorcerer too long and there was no more to learn.

"That can't be," said Allan. He was twenty-five, a full sorcerer himself by most standards, very handsome, more like his father now, at the height of his technical powers, with many honors and much brilliant thaumaturgy behind him, though none half as satisfying as his first exorcism rune for Esther Peters. He had, generally, the respect of everyone in Abbeville. And, it must be said, they waited eagerly for word of his first solo demonstration. This tortured Allan. He paced around the table, where Rubin sat repairing a fishing line. His belongings, rolled in a blanket, lay by the door. He pleaded, "There must be *one* more strategy."

"One more maybe," agreed the Sorcerer. "But what you need to know, you'll learn."

"Without you?" Allan shuddered. He saw himself, in a flash of probable futures, failing

Rubin. Dishonoring Richard. Ridiculed by everyone. "How *can* I learn without you?"

"You just do like you did that evening when you helped Esther Peters. . . ."

That wasn't me, thought Allan. I was younger. I don't know how, but everything worked then. You were behind me. I've tried. I've tried the rainmaking charm over and over. *It doesn't rain!* They're only words!

The old Sorcerer stood up and embraced Allan quickly, for he did not like sloppy goodbyes or lingering glances or the silly things people said when they had to get across a room and out the door. "You go home and wait for your first caller. You'll do fine."

Allan followed his bare feet away from the houseboat, his head lowered and a light pain in his chest, a sort of flutter like a pigeon beating its wings over his heart—an old pain that first began when he suspected that pansophical knowledge counted for nothing. The apprentice said the spell for fair weather. Fifteen minutes later a light rain fell. He traipsed through mud into Abbeville, shoved his bag under an empty table in a tavern, and sat dripping in the shadows until he dried. A fat man pounded an off-key piano. Boot heels stamped the floor beneath Allan, who ordered tequila. He sucked lemon slices and drained off shot glasses. Gradually, liquor backwashed in his throat and the ache disappeared and his body felt transparent. Yet still he wondered: Was sorcery a gift given to a few, like poetry? Did the Lord come, lift you up, then drop you forever? If so, then he was finished, bottomed out, bellied up before he even began. He had not been born among the Allmuseri Tribe in Africa, like Rubin, if this was necessary for magic. He had not come to New Orleans in a slave clipper, or been sold at the Cabildo, if this was necessary. He had only, it seemed, a vast and painfully acquired yet hollow repertoire of tricks, and this meant he could be a parlor magician, which paid well enough, but he would never do good. If he could not help, what then? He knew no other trade. He had no other dignity. He had no other means to transform the world and no other influence upon men. His seventh tequila untasted, Allan squeezed the bridge of his nose with two fingers, rummaging through his mind for Rubin's phrase for the transmogrification of liquids into vapor. The demons of drunkenness (Saphathoral) and slow-thinking (Ruax) tangled his thoughts, but finally the words floated topside. Softly, he spoke the phrase, stunned at its beauty—at the Sorcerer's beauty, really—mumbling it under his breath so no one might hear, then opened his eyes on the soaking, square face of a man who wore a blue homespun shirt and butternut trousers, but had not been there an instant before: his father. Maybe he'd said the phrase for telekinesis. "Allan, I've been looking all over. How are you?"

"Like you see." His gaze dropped from his father to the full shot glass and he despaired.

"Are you sure you're all right? Your eyelids are puffy."

"I'm okay." He lifted the shot glass and made its contents vanish naturally. "I've had my last lesson."

"I know—I went looking for you on the river, and Rubin said you'd come home. Since I knew better, I came to Abbeville. There's a girl at the house wants to see you—Lizzie Harris. She was there when you sawed Deacon Wills in half." Richard picked up his son's bag. "She wants you to help her to—"

Allan shook his head violently. "Lizzie should see Rubin."

"She has." He reached for Allan's hat and placed it on his son's head. "He sent her to you. She's been waiting for hours."

Much rain fell upon Allan and his father, who walked as if his feet hurt, as they left town, but mainly it fell on Allan. His father's confidence in him was painful, his chatter about his son's promising future like the chronicle of someone else's life. This was the night that was bound to come. And now, he thought as they neared the tiny, hip-roofed farmhouse, swimming in fog, I shall fall from humiliation to impotency, from impotency to failure, from failure to death. He leaned weakly against the porch rail. His father scrambled ahead of him, though he was a big man built for endurance and not for speed, and stepped back to open the door for Allan. The Sorcerer's apprentice, stepping inside, decided quietly, definitely, without hope that if this solo flight failed, he would work upon himself the one spell Rubin had described but dared not demonstrate. If he could not help this girl Lizzie—and he feared he could not—he would go back to the river and bring forth demons—horrors that broke a man in half, ate his soul, then dragged him below the ground, where, Allan decided, those who could not do well the work of a magician belonged.

"Allan's here," his father said to someone in the sitting room. "My son is a Conjure Doctor, you know."

"I seen him," said a girl's voice. "Looks like he knows everything there is to know about magic."

The house, full of heirlooms, had changed little since Allan's last year with Rubin. The furniture was darkened by use. All the mirrors in his mother's bedroom were still covered by cloth. His father left week-old dishes on the hob, footswept his cigars under the bare, loose floorboards, and paint on the front porch had begun to peel in large strips. There in the sitting room, Lizzie Harris sat on Beatrice's old flat-bottomed roundabout. She was twice as big as Allan remembered her. Her loose dress and breast exposed as she fed her baby made, he supposed, the difference. Allan looked away while Lizzie drew her dress up, then reached into her bead purse for a shinplaster—Civil War currency—which she handed to him. "This is all you have?" He returned her money, pulled a milk stool beside her, and said, "Please, sit down." His hands were trembling. He needed to hold something to hide the shaking. Allan squeezed both his knees. "Now," he said, "what's wrong with the child?"

"Pearl don't eat," said Lizzie. "She hasn't touched food in two days, and the medicine Dr. Britton give her makes her spit. It's a simple thing," the girl assured him. "Make her eat."

He lifted the baby off Lizzie's lap, pulling the covering from her face. That she was beautiful made his hands shake even more. She kept her fists balled at her cheeks. Her eyes were light, bread-colored, but latticed by blood vessels. Allan said to his father, without facing him, "I think I need boiled Hound's Tongue and Sage. They're in my bag. Bring me the water from the herbs in a bowl." He hoisted the baby higher on his right arm and, holding the spoon of cold cereal in his left hand, praying silently, began a litany of every spell he knew to disperse suffering and the afflictions of the spirit. From his memory, where techniques lay stacked like crates in a storage bin, Allan unleashed a salvo of incantations. His father, standing nearby with a discolored spoon and the bowl, held his breath so long Allan could hear flies gently beating against the lamp glass of the lantern. Allan, using the spoon like a horseshoe, slipped the potion between her lips. "Eat, Pearl," the apprentice whispered. "Eat and live." Pearl spit up on his shirt. Allan closed his eyes and repeated slowly every syllable of every word of every spell in his possession. And ever he pushed the spoon of cereal against the child's teeth, ever she pushed it away, gagging, swinging her head, and wailing so Allan had to shout each word above her voice. He oozed sweat now. Wind changing direction outside shifted the pressure inside the room so suddenly that Allan's stomach turned violently—it was if the farmhouse, snatched up a thousand feet, now hung in space. Pearl spit first clear fluids. Then blood. The apprentice attacked this mystery with a dazzling array of devices, analyzed it, looked at her with the critical, wrinkled brow of a philosopher, and mimed the Sorcerer so perfectly it seemed that Rubin, not Allan, worked magic in the room. But he was not Rubin Bailey. And the child suddenly stopped its struggle and relaxed in the apprentice's arms.

Lizzie yelped, "Why ain't Pearl crying?" He began repeating, futilely, his spells for the fifth time. Lizzie snatched his arm with such strength her fingers left blue spots on his skin. "That's enough!" she said. "You give her to me!"

"There's another way," Allan said, "another charm I've seen." But Lizzie Harris had reached the door. She threw a brusque "Good-bye" behind her to Richard and nothing to Allan. He knew they were back on the ground when Lizzie disappeared outside. Within the hour she would be at Rubin's houseboat. In two hours she would be at Esther Peters's home, broadcasting his failure.

"Allan," said Richard, stunned. "It didn't work."

"It's never worked." Allan put away the bowl, looked around the farmhouse for his bag, then a pail, and kissed his father's rough cheek. Startled, Richard pulled back sharply, as if he had stumbled sideways against the kiln. "I'm sorry," said Allan. It was not an easy thing to touch a man who so guarded, and for good reason, his emotions. "I'm not much of a Sorcerer, or blacksmith, or anything else."

"You're not going out this late, are you?" His father struggled, and Allan felt guilty for further confusing him with feeling. "Allan. . . ."

His voice trailed off.

"There's one last spell I have to do." Allan touched his arm lightly, once, then drew back his hand. "Don't follow me, okay?"

On his way to the river Allan gathered the roots and stalks and stones he required to dredge up the demon kings. The sky was clear, the air dense, and the Devil was in it if he fouled even this conjuration. For now he was sure that white magic did not reside in ratiocination, education, or will. Skill was of no service. His talent was for pa(o)stiche. He could imitate but never truly heal; impress but never conjure beauty; ape the good but never again give rise to a genuine spell. For that God or Creation, or the universe—it had several names—had to seize you, *use* you, as the Sorcerer said, because it needed a womb, shake you down, speak through you until the pain pearled into a beautiful spell that snapped the world back together. It had abandoned Allan, this possession. It had taken him, in a way, like a lover, planted one pitiful seed, and said, " 'Bye now." This absence, this emptiness, this sterility he felt deep at his center. Beyond all doubt, he owed the universe far more than it owed him. To give was right; to ask wrong. From birth he was indebted to so many, like his father, and for so much. But you could not repay the universe, or anyone, or build a career as a Conjure Doctor on a single, brilliant spell. Talent, Allan saw, was a curse. To have served once—was this enough? Better perhaps never to have served at all than to go on, foolishly, in the wreckage of former grace, glossing over his frigidity with cheap fireworks, window dressing, a trashy display of pyrotechnics, gimmicks designed to distract others from seeing that the magician onstage was dead.

Now the Sorcerer's apprentice placed his stones and herbs into the pail, which he filled with river water; then he built a fire behind a rock. Rags of fog floated over the waste-clogged riverbank as Allan drew a horseshoe in chalk. He sat cross-legged in wet grass that smelled faintly of oil and fish, faced east, and cursed at the top of his voice. "I conjure and I invoke thee, O Magoa, strong king of the East. I order thee to obey me, to send thy servants Onoskelis and Tepheus."

Two froglike shapes stitched from the fumes of Allan's potion began to take form above the pail.

Next he invoked the demon king of the North, who brought Ornia, a beautiful, blue-skinned lamia from the river bottom. Her touch, Allan knew, was death. She wore a black gown, a necklace of dead spiders, and entered through the opening of the enchanted horseshoe. The South sent Rabdos, a griffinlike hound, all teeth and hair, that hurtled toward the apprentice from the woods; and from the West issued Bazazath, the most terrible of all—a collage of horns, cloven feet, and goatish eyes so wild Allan wrenched away his head. Upriver, he saw kerosene lamplight moving from the direction of town. A faraway voice called, "Allan? Allan? Allan, is that you? Allan, are you out there?" His father. The one he had truly harmed. Allan frowned and faced those he had summoned.

"Apprentice," rumbled Bazazath, "*student*, you risk your life by opening hell."

"I am only that, a student," said Allan, "the one who studies beauty, who wishes to give it back, but who cannot serve what he loves."

"You are wretched, indeed," said Bazazath, and he glanced back at the others. "Isn't he wretched?"

They said, as one, "Worse."

Allan did not understand. He felt Richard's presence hard by, heard him call from the mystic circle's edge, which no man or devil could break. "How am I worse?"

"Because," said the demon of the West, "to love the good, the beautiful is right, but to labor on and will the work when you are obviously *beneath* this service is to parody them, twist them beyond recognition, to lay hold of what was once beautiful and make it a monstrosity. It becomes *black* magic. Sorcery is relative, student—dialectical, if you like expensive speech. And this, exactly, is what you have done with the teachings of Rubin Bailey."

"No," blurted Allan.

The demon of the West smiled. "Yes."

"Then," Allan asked, "you must destroy me?" It was less a question than a request.

"That is why we are here." Bazazath opened his arms. "You must step closer."

He had not known before the real criminality of his deeds. How dreadful that love could disfigure the thing loved. Allan's eyes bent up toward Richard. It was too late for apologies. Too late for promises to improve. He had failed everyone, particularly his father, whose face now collapsed into tears, then hoarse weeping like some great animal with a broken spine. In a moment he would drop to both knees. Don't want me, thought Allan. Don't love me as I am. Could he do nothing right? His work caused irreparable harm—and his death, trivial as it was in his own eyes, that, too, would cause suffering. Why must his choices be so hard? If he returned home, his days would be a dreary marking time for magic, which might never come again, living to one side of what he had loved, and loved still, for fear of creating evil—this was surely the worst curse of all, waiting for grace, but in suicide he would drag his father's last treasure, dirtied as it was, into hell behind him.

"It grows late," said Bazazath. "Have you decided?"

The apprentice nodded, yes.

He scrubbed away part of the chalk circle with the ball of his foot, then stepped toward his father. The demons waited—two might still be had this night for the price of one. But Allan felt within his chest the first spring of resignation, a giving way of both the hunger to heal and the anxiety to avoid evil. Was this surrender the one thing the Sorcerer could not teach? His pupil did not know. Nor did he truly know, now that he was no longer a Sorcerer's apprentice with a bright future, how to comfort his father. Awkwardly, Allan lifted Richard's wrist with his right hand, for he was right-handed, then squeezed, the old man's thick, ruined fingers. For a second his father twitched back in an old slave reflex, the safety catch still on, then fell heavily toward his son. The demons looked on indifferently, then glanced at each other. After a moment they left, seeking better game.

JAMAICA KINCAID

(1949–)

Jamaica Kincaid is a West Indian–born African American short-story writer, novelist, and essayist who portrays mother-daughter relationships as they reflect and embody the colonial situation. Her autobiographical work focuses on the impact of colonialism on young black females. These characters, like those in Paule Marshall's fiction, are shaped by the Americas, extending from the Caribbean to North America. In a 1985 interview with the *New York Times,* Kincaid said, "What I really feel about America is that it's given me a place to be myself as I was formed somewhere else." Her work gives voice to the African American immigrant experience.

Jamaica Kincaid was born on May 25, 1949 as Elaine Potter Richardson in St. John's, Antigua, in the British West Indies. She reports that her mother sent her to school at three and a half because she caused so much trouble at home. This shows both the beginning of her conflict with her mother and a possible source for the gallery of resistant female figures in Kincaid's oeuvre. Like her character Annie John, from her first novel of that title, she found it impossible to be a well-behaved child and loyal British subject. Hence, in 1965, at the age of sixteen, she left Antigua and her mother for the United States to work as an au pair. At first she planned to study nursing, but she ended up studying photography at the New School for Social Research in New York City. She also worked as a receptionist and magazine writer before becoming a staff writer for *The New Yorker* in 1976. When she began writing, she changed her name to Jamaica Kincaid because Jamaica connoted her West Indian heritage and Kincaid went well with the first name. Her relationship with *The New Yorker* continues today. In fact, she says that she would not have become a writer if it had not been for that magazine. Currently, she lives in North Bennington, Vermont, with her husband, Allen Shawn, and their two children, Annie and Harold.

Kincaid published her first book, *At the Bottom of the River,* a collection of ten lyric short stories about growing up female in the Caribbean, in 1983. Her next book, the novel *Annie John* (1985), portrays the love-hate relationship between a teenage girl and her domineering mother and ends with the girl, Annie John, leaving for England. To Donna Perry, Kincaid said about autobiography in particular, but by implication all of her works, "I would say that everything in *Annie John* happened—every feeling in it happened—but not necessarily in the order they appear. But it very much expresses the life I had." In one chapter, "Columbus in Chains," which is included in this anthology, the defiant student, to the horror of her teacher, defaces a schoolbook drawing of a chained Christopher Columbus, "one of the great men in history . . . discoverer of the island that was my home," by writing under it "The Great Man Can No Longer Just Get Up and Go." Thus she shows her intense hatred of colonialism.

Continuing her attack on colonialism, Kincaid indicts both colonial and independent Antigua in her book-length essay *A Small Place* (1988). Her next work, the novel *Lucy* (1990), details the deteriorating life of an upper-class white couple, Mariah and Lewis, from the point of view of a black au pair, Lucy. Kincaid's latest semiautobiographical novel, *The Autobiography of My Mother* (1996), continues the mother-daughter relationship theme. In this work, the mother has died giving birth to the daughter. According to Michiko Kakutani, the mother "represents the vanished and enduring past, a connection to earlier generations of women and blacks who endured the indignities of colonial and post-colonial oppression." Jamaica Kincaid is one of those fiercely intelligent and articulate immigrant black women writers who are expanding the African American voice and canon.

❖❖❖

For further study, see Diane Simmons, *Jamaica Kincaid* (1994); Moira Ferguson, *Jamaica Kincaid: Where the Land Meets the Body* (1994); Patricia O'Conner, "My Mother Wrote My Life"; Jamaica Kincaid's "Interview" *New York Times Book Review,* April 7, 1985; Selwyn Cudjoe, "Jamaica Kincaid and the Modernist Project," in *Caribbean Women Writers* (1990); Donna Perry, "An Interview with Jamaica Kincaid," in *Reading Black, Reading Feminist,* ed. Henry Louis Gates, Jr. (1990); Michiko Kakutani, "Loss in the Caribbean, From Birth On" *New York Times,* January 16, 1996; Darryl Pinckney, "In the Black Room of the World" *The New York Review of Books,* March 21, 1996.

Columbus in Chains

FROM *ANNIE JOHN*

Outside, as usual, the sun shone, the trade winds blew; on her way to put some starched clothes on the line, my mother shooed some hens out of her garden; Miss Dewberry baked the buns, some of which my mother would buy for my father and me to eat with our afternoon tea; Miss Henry brought the milk, a glass of which I would drink with my lunch, and another glass of which I would drink with the bun from Miss Dewberry; my mother prepared our lunch; my father noted some perfectly idiotic thing his partner in housebuilding, Mr. Oatie, had done, so that over lunch he and my mother could have a good laugh.

The Anglican church bell struck eleven o'clock—one hour to go before lunch. I was then sitting at my desk in my classroom. We were having a history lesson—the last lesson of the morning. For taking first place over all the other girls, I had been given a prize, a copy of a book called *Roman Britain,* and I was made prefect of my class. What a mistake the prefect part had been, for I was among the worst-behaved in my class and did not at all believe in setting myself up as a good example, the way a prefect was supposed to do. Now I had to sit in the prefect's seat—the first seat in the front row, the seat from which I could stand up and survey quite easily my classmates. From where I sat I could see out the window. Sometimes when I looked out, I could see the sexton going over to the minister's house. The sexton's daughter, Hilarene, a disgusting model of good behavior and keen attention to scholarship, sat next to me, since she took second place. The minister's daughter, Ruth, sat in the last row, the row reserved for all the dunce girls. Hilarene, of course, I could not stand. A girl that good would never do for me. I would probably not have cared so much for first place if I could be sure it would not go to her. Ruth I liked, because she was such a dunce and came from England and had yellow hair. When I first met her, I used to walk her home and sing bad songs to her just to see her turn pink, as if I had spilled hot water all over her.

Our books, *A History of the West Indies,* were open in front of us. Our day had begun with morning prayers, then a geometry lesson, then it was over to the science building for a lesson in "Introductory Physics" (not a subject we cared much for), taught by the most dingy-toothed Mr. Slacks, a teacher from Canada, then precious recess, and now this, our history lesson. Recess had the usual drama: this time, I coaxed Gwen out of her disappointment at not being allowed to join the junior choir. Her father—how many times had I wished he would become a leper and so be banished to a leper colony for the rest of my long and happy life with Gwen—had forbidden it, giving as his reason that she lived too far away from church, where choir rehearsals were conducted, and that it would be dangerous for her, a young girl, to walk home alone at night in the dark. Of course, all the streets had lamplight, but it was useless to point that out to him. Oh, how it would have pleased us to press and rub our knees together as we sat in our pew while pretending to pay close attention to Mr. Simmons, our choirmaster, as he waved his baton up and down and across, and how it would have pleased us even more to walk home together, alone in the "early dusk" (the way Gwen had phrased it, a ready phrase always on her tongue), stopping, if there was a full moon, to lie down in a pasture and expose our bosoms in the moonlight. We had heard that full moonlight would make our breasts grow to a size we would like. Poor Gwen! When I first heard from her that she was one of ten children, right on the spot I told her that I would love only her, since her mother already had so many other people to love.

Our teacher, Miss Edward, paced up and down in front of the class in her usual way. In front of her desk stood a small table, and on it stood the dunce cap. The dunce cap was in the shape of a coronet, with an adjustable opening in the back, so that it could fit any head. It was made of cardboard with a shiny gold paper covering and the word "DUNCE" in shiny red paper on the front. When the sun shone on it, the dunce cap was all aglitter, almost as if you were being tricked into thinking it a desirable thing to wear. As Miss Edward paced up and down, she would pass between us and the dunce cap like an eclipse. Each Friday morning, we were given a small test to see how well we had learned the things taught to us all week. The girl who scored lowest was made to wear the dunce cap all day the following Monday. On many Mondays, Ruth wore it—only, with her short yellow hair, when the dunce cap was sitting on her head she looked like a girl attending a birthday party in *The Schoolgirl's Own Annual.*

It was Miss Edward's way to ask one of us a question the answer to which she was sure the girl would not know and then put the same question to another girl who she was sure would know the answer. The girl who did not answer correctly would then have to repeat the correct answer in the exact words of the other girl. Many times, I had heard my exact words repeated over and over again, and I liked it especially when the girl doing the repeating was one I didn't care about very much. Pointing a finger at Ruth, Miss Edward asked a question the answer to which was "On the third of November 1493, a Sunday morning, Christopher Columbus discovered Dominica." Ruth, of course, did not know the answer, as she did not know the answer to many questions about the West Indies. I could hardly blame her. Ruth had come all the way from England. Perhaps she did not want to be in the West Indies at all. Perhaps she wanted to be in England, where no one would remind her constantly of the terrible things her ancestors had done; perhaps she had felt even worse when her father was a missionary in Africa. I could see how Ruth felt from looking at her face. Her ancestors had been the masters, while ours had been the slaves. She had such a lot to be ashamed of, and by being with us every day she was always being reminded. We could look everybody in the eye, for our ancestors had done nothing wrong except just sit somewhere, defenseless. Of course, sometimes, what with our teachers and our books, it was hard for us to tell on which side we really now belonged—with the masters or the slaves—for it was all history, it was all in the past, and everybody behaved differently now; all of us celebrated Queen Victoria's birthday, even though she had been dead a long time. But we, the descendants of the slaves, knew quite well what had really happened, and I was sure that if the tables had been turned we would have acted differently; I was sure that if our ancestors had gone from Africa to Europe and come upon the people living there, they would have taken a proper interest in the Europeans on first seeing them, and said, "How nice," and then gone home to tell their friends about it.

I was sitting at my desk, having these thoughts to myself. I don't know how long it had been since I lost track of what was going on around me. I had not noticed that the girl who was asked the question after Ruth failed—a girl named Hyacinth—had only got a part of the answer correct. I had not noticed that after these two attempts Miss Edward had launched into a harangue about what a worthless bunch we were compared to girls of the past. In fact, I was no longer on the same chapter we were studying. I was way ahead, at the end of the chapter about Columbus's third voyage. In this chapter, there was a picture of Columbus that took up a whole page, and it was in color—one of only five color pictures in the book. In this picture, Columbus was seated in the bottom of a ship. He was wearing the usual three-quarter trousers and a shirt with enormous sleeves, both the trousers and shirt made of maroon-colored velvet. His hat, which was cocked up on one side of his head, had a gold feather in it, and his black shoes had huge gold buckles. His hands and feet were bound up in chains, and he was sitting there staring off into space, looking quite dejected and miserable. The picture had as a title "Columbus in Chains," printed at the bottom of the page. What had happened was that the usually quarrelsome Columbus had got into a disagreement with people who were even more quarrelsome, and a man named Bobadilla, representing King Ferdinand and Queen Isabella, had sent him back to Spain fettered in chains attached to the bottom of a ship. What just deserts, I thought, for I did not like Columbus. How I loved this picture—to see the usually triumphant Columbus, brought so low, seated at the bottom of a boat just watching things go by. Shortly after I first discovered it in my history book, I heard my mother read out loud to my father a letter she had received from her sister, who still lived with her mother and father in the very same Dominica, which is where my mother came from. Ma Chess was fine, wrote my aunt, but Pa Chess was not well. Pa Chess was having a bit of trouble with his limbs; he was not able to go about as he pleased; often he had to depend on someone else to do one thing or another for him. My mother read the letter in quite a state, her voice rising to a higher pitch with each sentence. After she read the part about Pa Chess's stiff limbs, she turned to my father and laughed as she said, "So the great man can no longer just get up and go. How I would love to see his face now!" When I next saw the picture of Columbus sitting there all locked up in his chains, I wrote under it the words "The Great Man Can No Longer Just Get Up and Go." I had written this out with my fountain pen, and in Old English lettering—a script I had recently mastered. As I sat there looking at the picture, I traced the words with my pen over and over, so that the letters grew big and you could read what I had written from not very far away. I don't know how long it was before I heard that my name, Annie John, was being said by this bellowing dragon in the form of Miss Edward bearing down on me.

I had never been a favorite of hers. Her favorite was Hilarene. It must have pained Miss Edward that I so often beat out Hilarene. Not that I liked Miss Edward and wanted her to like me back, but all my other teachers regarded me with much affection, would always tell my mother that I was the most charming student they had ever had, beamed at me when they saw me coming, and were very sorry when they had to write some version of this on my report card: "Annie is an unusually bright girl. She is well behaved in class, at least in the presence of her masters and mistresses, but behind their backs and outside the classroom quite the opposite is true." When my mother read this or something like it, she would burst into tears. She had hoped to display, with a great flourish, my report card to her friends, along with whatever prize I had won. Instead, the report card would have to take a place at the bottom of the old trunk in which she kept any important thing that had to do with me. I became not a favorite of Miss Edward's in the following way: Each Friday afternoon, the girls in the lower forms were given, instead of a last lesson period, an extra-long recess. We were to use this in ladylike recreation—walks, chats about the novels and poems we were reading, showing each other the new embroidery stitches we had learned to master in home class, or something just as seemly. Instead, some of the girls would play a game of cricket or rounders or stones, but most of us would go to the far end of the school grounds and play band. In this game, of which teachers and parents disapproved and which was sometimes absolutely forbidden, we would place our arms around each other's waist or shoulders, forming lines of ten or so girls, and then we would dance from one end of the school grounds to the other. As we danced, we would sometimes chant these words: "Tee la la la, come go. Tee la la la, come go." At other times we would sing a popular calypso song which usually had lots of unladylike words to it. Up and down the schoolyard, away from our teachers, we would dance and sing. At the end of recess—forty-five minutes—we were missing ribbons and other ornaments from our hair, the pleats of our linen tunics became unset, the collars of our blouses were pulled out, and we were soaking wet all the way down to our bloomers. When the school bell rang, we would make a whooping sound, as if in a great panic, and then we would throw ourselves on top of each other as we laughed and shrieked. We would then run back to our classes, where we prepared to file into the auditorium for evening prayers. After that, it was home for the weekend. But how could we go straight home after all that excitement? No sooner were we on the street than we would form little groups, depending on the direction we were headed in. I was never keen on joining them on the way home, because I was sure I would run into my mother. Instead, my friends and I would go to our usual place near the back of the churchyard and sit on the tombstones of people who had been buried there way before slavery was abolished, in 1833. We would sit and sing bad songs, use forbidden words, and, of course, show each other various parts of our bodies. While some of us watched, the others would walk up and down on the large tombstones showing off their legs. It was immediately a popular idea; everybody soon wanted to do it. It wasn't long before many girls—the ones whose mothers didn't pay strict attention to what they were doing—started to come to school on Fridays wearing not bloomers under their uniforms but underpants trimmed with lace and satin frills. It also wasn't long before an end came to all that. One Friday afternoon, Miss Edward, on her way home from school, took a shortcut through the churchyard. She must have heard the commotion we were making, because there she suddenly was, saying, "What is the meaning of this?"—just the very thing someone like her would say if she came unexpectedly on something like us. It was obvious that I was the ringleader. Oh, how I wished the ground would open up and take her in, but it did not. We all, shamefacedly, slunk home, I with Miss Edward at my side. Tears came to my mother's eyes when she heard what I had done. It was apparently such a bad thing that my mother couldn't bring herself to repeat my misdeed to my father in my presence. I got the usual punishment of dinner alone, outside under the breadfruit tree, but added on to that, I was not allowed to go to the library on Saturday, and on Sunday, after Sunday school and dinner, I was not allowed to take a stroll in the botanical gardens, where Gwen was waiting for me in the bamboo grove.

That happened when I was in the first form. Now here Miss Edward stood. Her whole face was on fire. Her eyes were bulging out of her head. I was sure that at any minute they would land at my feet and roll away. The small pimples on her face, already looking as if they were constantly irritated, now ballooned into huge, on-the-verge-of-exploding boils. Her head shook from side to side. Her strange bottom, which she carried high in the air, seemed to rise up so high that it almost touched the ceiling. Why did I not pay attention, she said. My impertinence was beyond endurance. She then found a hundred words for the different forms my impertinence took. On she went. I was just getting used to this amazing bellowing when suddenly she was speechless. In fact, everything stopped. Her eyes stopped, her bottom stopped, her pimples stopped. Yes, she had got close enough so that her eyes caught a glimpse of what I had done to my textbook. The glimpse soon led to closer inspection. It was bad enough that I had defaced my schoolbook by writing in it. That I should write under the picture of Columbus "The Great Man . . ." etc. was just too much. I had gone too far this time, defaming one of the great men in history, Christopher Columbus, discoverer of the island that was my home. And now look at me. I was not even hanging my head in remorse. Had my peers ever seen anyone so arrogant, so blasphemous?

I was sent to the headmistress, Miss Moore. As punishment, I was removed from my position as prefect, and my place was taken by the odious Hilarene. As an added punishment, I was ordered to copy Books I and II of *Paradise Lost,* by John Milton, and to have it done a week from that day. I then couldn't wait to get home to lunch and the comfort of my mother's kisses and arms. I had nothing to worry about there yet; it would be a while before my mother and father heard of my bad deeds. What a terrible morning! Seeing my mother would be such a tonic—something to pick me up.

When I got home, my mother kissed me absentmindedly. My father had got home ahead of me, and they were already deep in conversation, my father regaling her with some unusually outlandish thing the oaf Mr. Oatie had done. I washed my hands and took my place at table. My mother brought me my lunch. I took one smell of it, and I could tell that it was the much hated breadfruit. My mother said not at all, it was a new kind of rice imported from Belgium, and not breadfruit, mashed and forced through a ricer, as I thought. She went back to talking to my father. My father could hardly get a few words out of his mouth before she was a jellyfish of laughter. I sat there, putting my food in my mouth. I could not believe that she couldn't see how miserable I was and so reach out a hand to comfort me and caress my cheek, the way she usually did when she sensed that something was amiss with me. I could not believe how she laughed at everything he said, and how bitter it made me feel to see how much she liked him. I ate my meal. The more I ate of it, the more I was sure that it was breadfruit. When I finished, my mother got up to remove my plate. As she started out the door, I said, "Tell me, really, the name of the thing I just ate."

My mother said, "You just ate some breadfruit. I made it look like rice so that you would eat it. It's very good for you, filled with lots of vitamins." As she said this, she laughed. She was standing half inside the door, half outside. Her body was in the shade of our house, but her head was in the sun. When she laughed, her mouth opened to show off big, shiny, sharp white teeth. It was as if my mother had suddenly turned into a crocodile.

MELVIN DIXON
(1950–1992)

Like Sterling Brown before him, Melvin Dixon was both an artist and a scholar. In a short lifetime, he managed to produce a large body of impressive work: poems, stories, novels, essays, and critical studies. He also translated both scholarly and creative work from French. This energetic young writer journeyed throughout the world—to Europe, Africa, and the Caribbean—to embrace his black literary ancestors.

Dixon was born on May 29, 1950, in Stamford, Connecticut. In 1971, he graduated from Wesleyan University with a bachelor's degree in American Studies, and in 1975 he received his Ph.D. in American Studies from Brown University, where he studied with the poet Michael Harper. From 1980 until his death in 1992, he taught at Queens College in New York City.

In the 1970s and 1980s, Dixon spent time in Paris researching Richard Wright and in Haiti researching the poet and novelist Jacques Roumain. During the 1980s, he went to West Africa to study the life and works of Léopold Senghor, the former president of Senegal, and the Négritude movement. Like Langston Hughes before him, Dixon was committed to the notion of comparative black literature. He died of AIDS on October 26, 1992, at his home in Stamford, Connecticut.

Dixon published his first book, a volume of poetry titled *Change of Territory,* in 1983. After *Ride Out the Wilderness,* his critical study of black literature, appeared in 1987, he published two novels, *Trouble the Water* (1989) and *Vanishing Rooms* (1991). His translations from the French include *Drumbeats, Masks and Metaphor: Contemporary Afro-American Theatre* by Genevieve Fabre (1983) and the massive *Collected Poetry* by Léopold Senghor (1990).

Openly candid about his homosexuality and sometimes the victim of antigay violence, Dixon was not reluctant to explore in his fiction some of the sensitive issues with which many men, straight and gay alike, are confronted. Central to his works is the male characters' desire to feel good about themselves. In *Trouble the Water* (1989), for example, Jordan Henry is not able to attain self-approval until he can admit that, as a child, what he felt for his best friend Mason was much more than the usual friendship boys shared. Even though Jordan grows up, marries, and becomes a college professor, his "water is often troubled" by recurring images of personal moments with Mason, who had passed away during his teens.

Vanishing Rooms (1991) in some ways is Dixon's greatest achievement as a novelist. There are three main characters—Jesse, Lonny, and Ruella—all of whom are in pursuit of some kind of spiritual healing. But as one might expect, it is the male characters—Lonny and Jesse—who are the truly complex ones. *Vanishing Rooms* offers many opportunities for diverse forms of critical analysis: social, political, and, because of its emphasis on music and dance, aesthetic. Taking the reader through many different rooms of a New York bathhouse, the novel is explicit about matters such as male sexual fantasies and gay sexual encounters. This kind of openness distinguishes *Vanishing Rooms* from, say, James Baldwin's *Giovanni's Room* (1956). As Dixon himself observed about Baldwin's novel, "The characters are there in that room, . . . whereas in *Vanishing Rooms* the characters have created their own 'rooms' and are trying to break free." At times the action of the novel shifts to the subway, symbolizing the hidden and clandestine nature of same-sex love. More than a gay novel and more than an African American novel, *Vanishing Rooms* is a novel that seeks to humanize and to educate. It is instruction on how to relate to people as people and not simply as gay, lesbian, straight, black, white, male, or female.

Joseph T. Skerett, Jr., noted in a 1993 obituary that Dixon left behind a wealth of literary treasures. Few African American writers since Baldwin have attempted to explore the psychological or social consequences of gay relationships. Melvin Dixon was one of the more talented ones.

❖❖❖

Beyond reviews, little critical work is available on Dixon. Michael Fabre discusses Dixon's poetry in *Black American Writers in France, 1840–1980* (1991).

FROM *Vanishing Rooms*

Once inside the apartment, I double-locked the door. I went to the window and spent hours looking up and down the street. Night came and swallowed up everything alive. Nothing moved, not even the subway below. I was alone. The rooms stirred empty. The emptiness gave off a chill. My eyes wouldn't cry and wouldn't close. I wanted to scream, but I had no air. I held myself in. I couldn't stop trembling.

God, what had happened? Just yesterday we were standing together at the pier, marveling at the polluted Hudson. Then I had to get to class, dance class. I thought I was late. There was the girl I had danced with. Then the hours and hours I waited for Metro to come home. Suddenly voices filled the outer hallway. Rushing footsteps. Laughter. Banging on doors somewhere. My hands shook again and my stomach tied itself in knots. Where could I hide? But the voices went past my door and up to the last floor of the building. I was sweating. I had to talk to someone. Anyone. I called my parents long-distance but there was no answer. I called again and the line was busy. But what could I tell them? College buddy, roommate, lover dead? Not a chance. Then I fumbled through the telephone directory, found her name, number, and I dialed.

"Ruella, this is Jesse. From dance class, remember? We met yesterday. We danced. Remember?"

"Yes, yes, Jesse. But how did you get my number?" I tried to say something but couldn't. "Jesse? You still there?"

"Listen, something terrible has happened. Metro, my friend. He's been stabbed. He's dead." I couldn't say anything more and she didn't say any more. My breath caught in the phone. "I can't stay here tonight," I said. "Not alone."

"You come right over, honey," she said. "I've got plenty of room."

I took only what I'd need for the night. Once there, I looked at her and she looked at me for a long time before I turned away and searched her windows. She didn't ask any questions. I wanted to talk, to tell her everything. She said there was no rush. I wanted to say that boys named after their mothers are different, that it wasn't for the money that they stabbed Metro; he had all his money on him when his body was found. It was for something else. When I tried to talk my lips started moving faster than the sounds, and I just cried, cried, cried.

Before the morgue's cold darkness had sucked me in, I had seen the gashes like tracks all over Metro's belly and chest. His open eyes were questions I couldn't answer. I couldn't say a word. The officer pulled the sheet all the way back and turned the body over where his ass had been slashed raw. I knew why he had been killed. I tried to scream but had no wind. I needed air. That's when I must have hit the floor. I could still see those gashes. They opened everywhere, grooves of flesh and blood, lips slobbering with kisses.

Ruella put her arms around me. My stomach heaved. I bolted for the toilet and vomited until there was nothing left of the bathroom or me. I woke up in her bed. From then on I called her Rooms.

After that first night she said I could stay longer if I needed to. I told her that guys like me are different.

"Then why did you call me?" she asked.

"Because you were there."

"But why *me,* Jesse?"

"We danced, that's all."

The second night Rooms touched me by accident. I didn't move. The chilly, October night filled the bed space between us. Then her hand crept to mine and held it, caressing and easing out the chill. Slowly. I relaxed but couldn't help remembering the men who had first made me warm. Metro's name came up raw on my tongue. It needed air, more air. "Metro," I said aloud. I kept still.

"Jesse? You all right?"

Rooms drew closer to me. We held each other tight against the dark.

"Jesse? You all right?" Her voice, hovering in the chill.

Something was pricking my scalp. I pulled out one splinter after another, but they were over all of me now, and I scratched and pulled everywhere. Not wood from the warehouse floor or the rickety pier, these were glinting steel blades with my name on them. Faces I'd seen before inched from corners of the room, closing the gap between here and there, now and then. Mouths opened and sneered. Teeth got sharp. Tongues wagged and breath steamed up around me until I sank into the sheets. Now a boy's voice. Then many voices. "*Jesseeeee.*" A steel blade getting close. Closer. "*Jesse!*"

"I won't hurt you," said Rooms.

Outside the bedroom window, police sirens hollered up and down the streets. Where the hell were they *then?*

I imagined how Metro came up from the IRT exit and entered our block from the corner of West 12th and Bank Street. He passed the shut newsstand. It was almost morning. Metallic edges of light cut back the night. Metro walked with the same aching sound I knew from my own scuffling feet. I could almost hear the brush of denim between his thighs, see the arch of his pelvis as he swayed arms and hips as if he owned the whole street. His eyes tried to focus on the walk; his head leaned carelessly to the side. As he neared our building he was not alone. Other shapes crawled into the street, filled it. Cigarette smoke trailed out from an alley, and the figures of boys appeared out of nowhere, riding spray-paint fumes, crackling marijuana seeds, and waves of stinking beer.

Four, five, maybe six teenagers. Maybe they were the ones. The same ones I had seen before on my way home from rehearsals. Even then their smell of a quick, cheap high had been toxic. One time they spotted me and yelled, first one, then another until I was trapped.

"Hey, nigger."

"Yeah, you."

"Naw, man, he ain't no nigger. He a faggot."

"Then he a black nigger faggot."

They laughed. I walked faster, almost running, and reached my block in a cold sweat from pretending not to hear them. But I did hear them, and the sweat and trembling in my knees would not go away, not even when I reached the door and locked myself in.

Metro didn't believe it was that bad. But what did he know? A white boy from Louisiana, New England prep schools and college. "Don't worry, baby," he said when I told him what had happened. He held my head and hands until I calmed down. "It'll be all right." And we made love slowly, deliberately, believing we were doing something right. Still, I should have known better than to take so much for granted, even in Greenwich Village where we lived. And I should have known better than to leave him alone by the pier in the condition he was in, just for a dance improvisation. He had a cold, wild look in his eyes. How could I tell how many pills he'd taken? He could have fought back. But then why hadn't I fought back when those Italian kids started yelling, "He a black nigger faggot, yeah, he a faggot, a nigger, too," and shouting and laughing so close they made acid out of every bit of safety I thought we had? Now their hate had eaten up everything.

I could still hear them, making each prove himself a man—"I ain't no faggot. Not me, man"—and drawing blood. And when Metro left the black underground of trains and screeching wheels, when he reached for air in the thick ash of night, they spotted him like found money through the stinking grates of smoke and beer. I imagined how they followed his unsteady walk, his wavering vision, his fatigue. Curses like baseball bats swung out of their mouths. The first ones were on target: "There go a faggot."

"Hey man, you a faggot?"

Metro kept walking. Like I did. *Please keep walking. Please, Metro.*

"I say that man call you a faggot. You a faggot?"

Metro said nothing. Did he even hear them? They came closer. The streets were empty. No witnesses, no help. And I was back home waiting for his knock that never came.

"Yeah, you a faggot all right. Ain't he?"

"Yeah, he a faggot."

And Metro walked faster, skipped into a run, but they caught him. Knives slipped out of their pants. Hands reached for him, caught him in a tunnel of angry metal. They told him to put his wallet back. "This ain't no fucking robbery, man." They knocked him down. Metro sprawled about wet and hurt, couldn't pull himself up.

"Who stuck him?"

"Get up, faggot. We ain't through that easy."

"Look, he's bleeding."

"Who went ahead and stuck him before we all could stick it in? Who?"

They jostled him to his feet, feeling his ass.

"When can the rest of us stick it in? We all wanna fuck him, don't we fellahs?"

"Yeah. When can we fuck him?"

And Metro was wet from the discharged knives. He stopped treading the ground. He swayed back like wood in water, his eyes stiff on the open zippers. The leader of them grinning, his mouth a crater spilling beer, said, "*Now.*"

"Why did you call me?" Rooms asked.

I said nothing.

"You think I'm gay, too?"

"No," I said.

"You really loved him," said Rooms.

"Yes."

"That makes all the difference." She held me with her eyes. They cut into me. "There's something else, isn't there? Something you haven't told me."

I tasted blood in my mouth. My head felt hot.

"I can wait," she said.

I went to her window and looked out. A subway rumbled underground, then it was quiet. The lump high in my throat, about to spread all through me since yesterday, eased down for a moment. I went back to my apartment to get the rest of my things.

ANNA DEAVERE SMITH
(1950–)

Writing, producing, and performing in plays that explore the strained relations between blacks and whites in the United States in the past twenty years, playwright Anna Deavere Smith has recently become a dominant figure on the nation's dramatic stage. Very much influenced by the Vietnam War resistance and the assassinations of Martin Luther King, Jr., and Robert F. Kennedy, Smith says, in a 1992 *New York Times* article by Francis X. Cline, that she was compelled by race relations in America: "I wanted to do something—I didn't know what it was—that had to do with listening to people and trying to cause peace."

Born on September 18, 1950, in Baltimore to Deavere Smith and Anna Young Smith, the playwright is the oldest of five children. Her father ran a coffee and tea business, and her mother was an elementary school principal. While the family had gained a rung among the black middle class, they nonetheless lived in a very segregated neighborhood in the South. Smith never associated with people from other races and cultures until she attended Western High School in Baltimore.

After completing her B.A. degree at Beaver College in 1971, her M.F.A. at the American Conservatory Theatre in 1976, and finding the purely academic life to be too restrictive, Smith found her creative niche in journalistic, psychological dramas based on well-known, dramatic racial events. Majoring in linguistics as an undergraduate at Beaver College, Smith taught her students to listen to the underlying meanings in human conversation. "I want to see what impact the words have on my body," Smith told interviewer Pope Brock. "Material that hits me viscerally is likely to hit the audience too."

Soon she began carrying a tape recorder around, and by 1979, when she began her research for the play *On the Road* (1983), Smith would walk up to people with the promise, "If you'll give me an hour of your time, I'll invite you to see yourself performed." According to critic P. J. Corso, Smith "goes into a community, interviews residents about a socially-charged event and then performs their words for professional theater."

Her 1992 one-woman play *Fires in the Mirror: Crown Heights, Brooklyn and Other Identities* won a Pulitzer Prize nomination. For this drama, which examines tensions between African Americans and Hasidic Jews in Brooklyn, the playwright interviewed more than fifty people to devise her characterizations of the Crown Heights neighborhood, including the activist Reverend Al Sharpton and the playwright Ntozake Shange.

She won the Obie Award, a Drama Desk Award, an Outer Critics Circle Special Achievement Award, and two Tony Award nominations for her play *Twilight: Los*

Angeles, 1992 (1993), a journalistic docudrama based on the Rodney King race riots. In *Twilight,* Smith assumes the roles of more than two dozen characters who tell the audience how their lives were affected by the four-day trauma of anger, rioting, and violence.

Both as playwright and performer, Smith has produced other one-woman shows, including *On the Road: A Search for American Character* (1983), *Aye, Aye, Aye, I'm Integrated* (1984), and *Piano* (1991). With choreographer Judith Jamison, she coauthored the ballet *Hymn* in 1993 for the thirty-fifth anniversary season of the Alvin Ailey American Dance Company. Smith also has performed in well-known plays that she did not write, such as *Horatio, Alama, The Ghost of Spring Street, Mother Courage,* and *Tartuffe,* and appeared in the popular television soap opera *All My Children* (1993) and the film *Philadelphia* (1993).

Although Smith's plays have been avidly received by the public, mainstream drama critics have not been as supportive. Some say that she only embellishes stereotypes and others that she is a mere mimic. Critic David Richards said in the March 24, 1994, issue of the *New York Times,* "Anna Deavere Smith is the ultimate impressionist; she does people's souls." However, most of those whom Smith has interviewed and later turned into characters onstage say that her re-creation of their cultural identities and feelings about racial issues are extremely realistic. Most of them also believe that she has reached her goal in making a difference in bringing about peace and understanding between blacks and whites in this country.

❖❖❖

For information on Smith's life and works, see P. J. Corso's book *International Women Playwrights* (1993). Insightful newspaper interviews of Smith include those by journalists Francis X. Cline, *New York Times,* June 10, 1992; Joanne Kaufman, *Washington Post,* April 25, 1993; Bernard Weinraub, *New York Times,* June 16, 1993; Kevin I. Carter, *Philadelphia Inquirer,* April 28, 1993; Pope Brock, *People,* August 30, 1993; Bruce Weber, *New York Times,* March 18, 1994. In addition, see *Contemporary Authors,* vol. 133 (1991); *Who's Who in America,* 49th ed. vol. 2; *Current Biography Yearbook* (1994).

FROM *Fires in the Mirror*

FROM IDENTITY

Ntozake Shange

The Desert

This interview was done on the phone at about four PM *Philadelphia time. The only cue Ntozake gave about her physical appearance was that she took one earring off to talk on the phone. On stage we placed her upstage center in an armchair, smoking. Then we placed her standing, downstage.*

Hummmm.
Identity—
it, is, uh . . . in a way it's, um . . . it's sort of, it's uh . . .
it's a psychic sense of place
it's a way of knowing I'm not a rock or that tree?

I'm this other living creature over here?
And it's a way of knowing that no matter where I put myself
that I am not necessarily
what's around me.
I am part of my surroundings
and I become separate from them
and it's being able to make those differentiations clearly
that lets us have an identity
and what's inside our identity
is everything that's ever happened to us.
Everything that's ever happened
to us as well as our responses to it
'cause we might be alone in a trance state,
someplace like the desert
and we begin to feel as though
we are part of the desert—
which we are right at that minute—
but we are not the desert,
uh . . .
we are part of the desert,
and when we go home
we take with us that part of the desert that the desert gave us,
but we're still not the desert.
It's an important differentiation to make because you don't know
what you're giving if you don't know what you have and you don't
know what you're taking if you don't know what's yours and what's
somebody else's.

George C. Wolfe
101 Dalmations

The Mondrian Hotel in Los Angeles. Morning. Sunny. A very nice room. George is wearing denim jeans, a light blue denim shirt and white leather tennis shoes. His hair is in a ponytail. He wears tortoise/wire spectacles. He is drinking tea with milk. The tea is served on a tray, the cups and teapot are delicate porcelain. George is sitting on a sofa, with his feet up on the coffee table.

I mean I grew up on a Black—
a one-block street—
that was Black.
My grandmother lived on that street
my cousins lived around the corner.
I went to this
Black—Black—
private Black grade school
where
I was extraordinary.
Everybody there was extraordinary.

You were told you were extraordinary.
It was very clear
that I could not go to see *101 Dalmations* at the Capital Theatre
because it was segregated.
And at the same time
I was treated like I was the most extraordinary creature that had
been born.
So I'm on my street in my house,
at my school—
and I was very spoiled too—
so I was treated like I was this special special creature.
And then I would go beyond a certain point
I was treated like I was insignificant.
Nobody was
hosing me down or calling me nigger.
It was just that I was insignificant.

(Slight pause)

You know what I mean?
So it was very clear

(Strikes teacup on saucer twice on "very clear")

where my extraordinariness lived.
You know what I mean.
That I was extraordinary as long as I was Black.
But I am—not—going—to place myself

(Pause)

in relationship to your whiteness.
I will talk about your whiteness if we want to talk about that.
But I,
but what,
that which,
what I—
what am I saying?
My blackness does not resis—ex—re—
exist in relationship to your whiteness.

(Pause)

You know *(Not really a question, more like a "hmm")*

(Slight pause)

it does not exist in relationship *to*—
it *exists*
it exists.
I come—
you know what I mean—

like I said, I, I, I,
I come from—
it's a very com*plex,*
con*fused,*
neu-rotic,
at times destructive
ıeality, but it is complctcly
and totally a reality
contained and, and,
and full unto itself.
It's complex.
It's demonic.
It's ridiculous.
It's absurd.
It's evolved.
It's all the stuff.
That's the way I grew up.

(Slight pause)

So that *therefore*—
and then you're White—

(Quick beat)

And then there's a point when,
and then these two things come into contact.

MIRRORS

Aaron M. Bernstein

Mirrors and Distortions

Evening. Cambridge, Massachusetts. Fall. He is a man in his fifties, wearing a sweater and a shirt with a pen guard. He is seated at a round wooden table with a low-hanging lamp.

Okay, so a mirror is something that reflects light.
It's the simplest instrument to understand,
okay?
So a simple mirror is just a flat
reflecting
substance, like,
for example,
it's a piece of glass which is silvered on the back,
okay?
Now the notion of distortion also goes back into literature,
okay?
I'm trying to remember from art—
You probably know better than I.

You know you have a pretty young woman and she looks in a mirror
and she's a witch

(He laughs)

because she's evil on the inside.
That's not a real mirror,
as everyone knows—
where
you see the inner thing.
Now that really goes back in literature.
So everyone understood that mirrors don't distort,
so that was a play
not on words
but on a concept.
But physicists do
talk about distortion.
It's a big
subject, distortions.
I'll give you an example—
if you wanna see the
stars
you make a big
reflecting mirror—
that's one of the ways—
you make a big telescope
so you can gather in a lot of light
and then it focuses at a point
and then there's always something called the circle of confusion.
So if ya don't make the thing perfectly spherical or perfectly
parabolic
then,
then, uh, if there are errors in the construction
which you can see, it's easy, if it's huge,
then you're gonna have a circle of confusion,
you see?
So that's the reason for making the
telescope as large as you can,
because you want that circle
to seem smaller,
and you want to easily see errors in the construction.
So, you see, in physics it's very practical—
if you wanna look up in the heavens
and see the stars as well as you can
without distortion.
If you're counting stars, for example,
and two look like one,
you've blown it.

Rhythm

Monique "Big Mo" Matthews
Rhythm and Poetry

In reality this interview was done on an afternoon in the spring of 1989, while I was in residence at the University of California, Los Angeles, as a fellow at the Center for Afro-American Studies. Mo was a student of mine. We were sitting in my office, which was a narrow office, with sunlight. I performed Mo in many shows, and in the course of performing her, I changed the setting to a performance setting, with microphone. I was inspired by a performance that I saw of Queen Latifah in San Francisco and by Mo's behavior in my class, which was performance behavior, to change the setting to one that was more theatrical, since Mo's everyday speech was as theatrical as Latifah's performance speech.

Speaking directly to the audience, pacing the stage.

And she say, "This is for the fellas,"
and she took off all her clothes and she had on a leotard
that had all cuts and stuff in it,
and she started doin' it on the floor.
They were like
"Go, girl!"
People like, "That look really stink."
But that's what a lot of female rappers do—
like to try to get off,
they sell they body or pimp they body
to, um, get play.
And you have people like Latifah who doesn't, you know,
she talks intelligent.
You have Lyte who's just hard and people are scared by her
hardness,
her strength of her words.
She encompasses that whole, New York–street sound.
It's like, you know, she'll like . . .
what's a line?
What's a line
like "Paper Thin,"
"IN ONE EAR AND RIGHT OUT THE OTHUH."
It's like,
"I don't care what you have to say,
I'm gittin' done what's gotta be done.
Man can't come across me.
A female she can't stand against me.
I'm just the toughest, I'm just the hardest / You just can't come up
against me / if you do you get waxed!"
It's like a lot of my songs,
I don't know if I'm gonna get blacklisted for it.
The image that I want is a strong strong African strong Black woman

and I'm not down with what's going on, like Big Daddy Kane had a song
out called "Pimpin' Ain't Easy," and he sat there and he talk for the
whole song, and I sit there I wanna slap him, I wanna slap him so
hard, and he talks about, it's one point he goes, yeah
um,
"Puerto Rican girls Puerto Rican girls call me Papi and
White girls say
even White girls say I'm a hunk!"
I'm like,
"What you mean 'even'?
Oh! Black girls ain't good enough for you huh?"
And one of my songs has a line that's like
"PIMPIN' AIN'T EASY BUT WHORIN' AIN'T
PROPER. RESPECT AND
CHERISH THE ORIGINAL MOTHER."
And a couple of my friends were like,
"Aww, Mo, you good but I can't listen to you 'cause you be Men
bashin'."
I say,
"It ain't men bashin', it's female assertin'."
Shit.
I'm tired of it.
I'm tired of my friends just acceptin'
that they just considered to be a ho.
You got a song,
"Everybody's a Hotty."
A "hotty" means you a freak, you a ho,
and it's like Too Short
gets up there and he goes,
"B I AYYYYYYYYYYYYE."
Like he stretches "bitch" out for as long as possible,
like you just a ho and you can't be saved,
and 2 Live Crew . . . "we want some pussy," and the girls! "La le la le la le la,"
it's like my friends say,
"Mo, if you so bad how come you don't never say nothin' about 2
Live Crew?"
When I talk about rap,
and I talk about people demeaning rap,
I don't even mention them
because they don't understand the fundamentals of rap.
Rap, rap
is basically
broken down
Rhythm
and Poetry.
And poetry is expression.

It's just like poetry; you release so much through poetry.
Poetry is like
intelligence.
You just release it all and if you don't have a complex rhyme
it's like,
"I'm goin' to the store."
What rhymes with store?
More, store, for, more, bore,
"I'm goin' to the store I hope I don't get bored,"
it's like,
"WHAT YOU SAYIN', MAN? WHO CARES?"
You have to have something that flows.
You have to be def,
D-E-F.
I guess I have to think of something for you that ain't slang.
Def is dope, def is live
when you say somethin's dope
it means it is the epitome of the experience
and you have to be def by your very presence
because you have to make people happy.
And we are living in a society where people are not happy with their everyday lives.

FROM SEVEN VERSES

Letty Cottin Pogrebin

Near Enough to Reach

Evening. The day before Thanksgiving, 1991. On the phone. Direct, passionate, confident, lots of volume. She is in a study with a roll-top desk and a lot of books.

I think it's about rank frustration and the old story
that you pick a scapegoat
that's much more, I mean Jews and Blacks,
that's manageable,
because we're near,
we're still near enough to each other to reach!
I mean, what can you do about the people who voted for David Duke?
Are Blacks going to go there and deal with that?
No, it's much easier to deal with Jews who are also panicky.
We're the only ones that pay any attention

(Her voice makes an upward inflection)

Well, Jeffries did speak about the Mafia being, um,
Mafia,
and the Jews in Hollywood.
I didn't see
this tremendous outpouring of Italian
reaction.
Only *Jews* listen,

only *Jews* take Blacks seriously,
only *Jews* view Blacks as full human beings that you
should *address*
in their rage
and, um,
people don't seem to notice that.
But Blacks, it's like a little child kicking up against Arnold
Schwarzenegger
when they,
when they have anything to say about the dominant culture
nobody listens! Nobody reacts!
To get a headline,
to get on the evening news,
you have to attack a Jew.
Otherwise you're ignored.
And it's a shame.
We all play into it.

FROM CROWN HEIGHTS, BROOKLYN

Michael S. Miller

"Heil Hitler"

A large airy office in Manhattan on Lexington in the 50s. Mr. Miller sits behind a big desk in a high-backed swivel chair drinking coffee. He's wearing a yarmulke. Plays with the swizzle stick throughout. There is an intercom in the office, so that when the receptionist calls him, you can hear it, and when she calls others in other offices, you can hear it like a page in a public place, faintly.

I was at Gavin Cato's funeral,
at nearly every public event
that was conducted by the Lubavitcher community and the Jewish
community as a whole
words of comfort
were offered to the family of Gavin Cato.
I can show you a letter that we sent
to the Cato family expressing, uh,
our sorrow over the loss,
unnecessary loss, of their son.
I am not aware of a word
that was spoken at that funeral.
I am not aware of a—
and I was taking notes—
of a word that was uttered
of comfort to the family of Yankele Rosenbaum.
Frankly this was a political rally rather than a funeral.
The individuals you mentioned—
and again,
I am not going to participate in verbal acrimony,

not only
were there cries of, "Kill the Jews"
or,
"Kill the Jew,"
there were cries of, "Heil Hitler."
There were cries of, "Hitler didn't finish the job."
There were cries of,
"Throw them back into the ovens again."
To hear in *Crown Heights*—
and Hitler was no lover of Blacks—
"Heil Hitler"?
"Hitler didn't finish the job"?
"We should heat up the ovens"?
From *Blacks?*
Is more inexplicable
or unexplainable
or any other word that I cannot fathom.
The hatred is so
deep-seated
and the hatred
knows no boundaries.
There is no boundary
to anti-Judaism.
The anti-*Judaism*—
if people don't want me
to use,
hear me use the word anti-Semitism.
And I'll be damned if,
if preferential treatment is gonna
be the excuse
for every bottle,
rock,
or pellet that's, uh, directed
toward a Jew
or the window of a Jewish home
or a Jewish store.
And, frankly,
I think the response of the Lubavitcher community was relatively
passive.

Norman Rosenbaum

My Brother's Blood

A Sunday afternoon. Spring. Crisp, clear and windy. Across from City Hall in New York City. Crowds of people, predominantly Lubavitcher, with placards. A rally that was organized by Lubavitcher women. All of the speakers are men, but the women stand close to the stage. Mr. Rosenbaum, an Australian, with a beard, hat and wearing a pin-

stripe suit, speaks passionately and loudly from the microphone on a stage with a podium. Behind him is a man in an Australian bush hat with a very large Australian flag which blows dramatically in the wind. It is so windy that Mr. Rosenbaum has to hold his hat to keep it on his head.

Al do lay achee so achee aylay alo dalmo
My brother's blood cries out from the ground.
Let me make it clear
why I'm here, and why you're here.
In August of 1991,
as you all have heard before today,
my brother was killed in the streets of Crown Heights
for no other reason
than that he was a Jew!
The only miracle was
that my brother was the only victim
who paid for being a Jew with his life.
When my brother was surrounded,
each and every American was surrounded.
When my brother was stabbed four times,
each and every American was stabbed four times
and as my brother bled to death in this city,
while the medicos stood by
and let him bleed
to death, it was the gravest of indictments against this country.
One person out of twenty gutless individuals
who attacked my brother has been arrested.
I for one am not convinced that it is beyond the ability of the New York police
to arrest others.
Let me tell you, Mayor Dinkins,
let me tell you, Commissioner Brown:
I'm here,
I'm not going home,
until there is justice.

Richard Green

Rage

Two PM in a big red van. Green is in the front. He has a driver. I am in the back. Green wears a large knit hat with reggae colors over long dreadlocks. Driving from Crown Heights to Brooklyn College. He turns sideways to face me in the back and bends down, talking with his elbow on his knee.

Sharpton, Carson, and Reverend Herbert Daughtry
didn't have any power out there really.
The media gave them that power.
But they weren't turning those youfs on and off.
Nobody knew who controlled the switch out there.
Those young people had rage like an oil-well fire

that has to burn out.
All they were doin' was sort of orchestratin' it.
Uh, they were not really the ones that were saying, "Well
stop, go, don't go, stop, turn around, go up."
It wasn't like that.
Those young people had rage out there,
that didn't matter who was in control of that—
that rage had to get out
and that rage
has been building up.
When all those guys have come and gone,
that rage is still out here.
I can show you that rage every day
right up and down this avenue.
We see, sometimes in one month, we see three bodies
in one month. That's rage,
and that's something that nobody has control of.
And I don't know who told you that it was preferential treatment for
Blacks that the Mayor kept the cops back . . .
If the Mayor had turned those cops on?
We would still be in a middle of a battle.
and
I pray on both sides of the fence,
and I tell the people in the Jewish community the same thing,
"This is not something that force will hold."
Those youfs were running on cops without nothing in their hands,
seven- and eight- and nine- and ten-year-old boys were running at
those cops
with nothing,
just running at 'em.
That's rage.
Those young people out there are angry
and that anger has to be vented,
it has to be negotiated.
And they're not angry at the Lubavitcher community
they're just as angry at you and me,
if it comes to that.
They have no
role models,
no guidance
so they're just out there growin' up on their own,
their peers are their role models,
their peers is who teach them how to move
what to do, what to say
so when they see the Lubavitchers
they don't know the difference between "Heil Hitler"
and, uh, and uh, whatever else.

They don't know the difference.
When you ask 'em to say who Hitler was they wouldn't even be able to tell you.
Half of them don't even know.
Three-quarters of them don't even know.

(Mobile phone rings; he picks it up)

"Richard Green, can I help?
Aw, man I tol' you I want some color
up on that wall. Give me some colors.
Look, I'm in the middle of somethin'."

(He returns to the conversation)

Just as much as they don't know who Frederick Douglass was.
They know Malcolm
because Malcolm has been played up to such an extent now
that they know Malcolm.
But ask who Nat Turner was or Mary McLeod Bethune or Booker T.
Because the system has given 'em
Malcolm is convenient and
Spike is goin' to give 'em Malcolm even more.
It's convenient.

Carmel Cato

Lingering

Seven PM. *The corner where the accident occurred in Crown Heights. An altar to Gavin is against the wall where the car crashed. Many pieces of cloth are draped. Some writing in color is on the wall. Candle wax is everywhere. There is a rope around the area. Cato is wearing a trench coat, pulled around him. He stands very close to me. Dark outside. Reggae music is in the background. Lights come from stores on each corner. Busy intersection. Sounds from outside. Traffic. Stores open. People in and out of shops. Sounds from inside apartments, televisions, voices, cooking, etc. He speaks in a pronounced West Indian accent.*

In the meanwhile
it was two.
Angela was on the ground
but she was trying to move. Gavin was still.
They was trying to pound him.
I was the father.
I was 'it, chucked, and pushed,
and a lot of
sarcastic words were passed towards me
from the police
while I was trying to explain: It was my kid!
These are my children.
The child was hit you know.
I saw everything, everything,

the guy radiator burst
all the hoses,
the steam,
all the garbage buckets goin' along the building.
And it was very loud,
everything burst.
It's like an atomic bomb.
That's why all these people
comin' round
wanna know what's happening.
Oh it was very outrageous.
Numerous numbers.
All the time the police sayin'
You can't get in,
you can't pass,
and the children laying on the ground.
He was hit at exactly eight-thirty.
Why?
I was standing over there.
There was a little child—
a friend of mine
came up with a little child—
and I lift the child up
and she look at her watch at the same time
and she say it was eight-thirty.
I gave the child back to her.
And then it happen.
Umh, Umh, (*Sharp utterances*)
My child, these are the things I never dream about.
I take care of my children.
You know it's a funny thing,
if a child get sick and he dies
it won't hurt me so bad,
or if a child run out into the street and get hit down,
it wouldn't hurt me.
That's what's hurtin' me.
The whole week
before Gavin died
my body was changing,
I was having different feelings.
I stop eating,
I didn't et
nothin',
only drink water,
for two weeks;
and I was very touchy—
any least thing that drop

or any song I hear
it would affect me.
Every time I try to do something
I would have to stop.
I was
lingering, lingering, lingering, lingering,
all the time.
But I can do things,
I can see things,
I know that for a fact.
I was telling myself,
"Something is wrong somewhere,"
but I didn't want to see,
I didn't want to accept,
and it was inside of me,
and even when I go home I tell my friends,
"Something coming I could feel it
but I didn't want to see,"
and all the time I just deny deny deny,
and I never thought it was Gavin,
but I didn't have a clue.
I thought it was one of the other children—
the bigger boys
or the girl,
because she worry me,
she won't et—
but Gavin 'ee was 'ealtee,
and he don't cause no trouble.
That's what's devastating me even until now.
Sometime it make me feel like it's no justice,
like, uh,
the Jewish people,
they are very high up,
it's a very big thing,
they runnin' the whole show
from the judge right down.
And something I don't understand:
The Jewish people, they told me
there are certain people I cannot be seen with
and certain things I cannot say
and certain people I cannot talk to.
They made that very clear to me—the Jewish people—
they can throw the case out
unless
I go to them with pity.
I don't know what they talkin' about.
So I don't know what kind of crap is that.

And make me say things I don't wanna say
and make me do things I don't wanna do.
I am a special person.
I was born different.
I'm a man born by my foot.
I born by my foot.
Anytime a baby comin' by the foot
they either cut the mother
or the baby dies.
But I was born with my foot.
I'm one of the special.
There's no way they can overpower me.
No there's nothing to hide,
you can repeat every word I say.

RITA DOVE

(1952–)

Winner of the 1987 Pulitzer Prize for poetry, Rita Dove is one of the most respected of the post-1960s poets. She also has earned a reputation in fiction writing and thereby joins the many contemporary black women writers who are proficient in more than one genre. Her collection of short stories, *Fifth Sunday* (1985), has been widely acclaimed. She is certain to continue to make critical impressions in the literary world.

Born in Akron, Ohio, on August 28, 1952, Dove is one of four children of Ray and Elvira Hord Dove. Her father, one of ten children, worked as an elevator operator for Goodyear Tire and Rubber Company before becoming a chemist there. When he initially finished college and graduate school, no blacks could work in the science department at Goodyear. Although Dove wrote stories and plays at an early age, she did not envision doing so as a profession. As a teenager, however, she realized that writing could be a lifelong passion. One of her high-school English teachers, Margaret Oechsner, took her to a writers' conference one Saturday afternoon to meet some practicing writers. From that moment on, she realized that it was indeed possible to be a professional writer.

Dove graduated summa cum laude from Miami University in Oxford, Ohio, in 1973. She continued her education at the University of Iowa Writers Workshop, where she received an M.F.A. in creative writing in 1977. In 1980, she was awarded a fellowship that enabled her to live and write in Germany, where she took courses at Tübingen University. There she met in her husband, Fred Viebahn, who is a novelist. They have one child, a daughter named Aviva.

To date, Dove has published four collections of poetry, one collection of short stories, and a one-act play. Her first poetry collection, *The Yellow House on the Corner*, appeared in 1980; her second, *Museum* (1983), was inspired in part by a trip to Israel. Although both received praise, neither brought Dove the attention she gained with *Thomas and Beulah* (1986), her Pulitzer Prize–winning volume. In addition to the Pulitzer Prize, Dove also won the Peter I. B. Lavan Younger Poets Award for 1986. A series of poems alternately narrated by the named characters, *Thomas and*

Beulah covers the years 1919 to 1968 in Akron. Thomas relates incidents in the first half of the volume, and Beulah sheds a different light on the topics in the second half. Dove asserts that the characters are loosely based on her grandparents. In 1989, her fourth volume of poetry, *Grace Notes,* was published. It comprises short poems on topics such as sexuality, aging, history, art, politics, and motherhood.

Dove's lone volume of short stories, *Fifth Sunday,* was published in 1985. Her one-act play "The Siberian Village" appeared in *Callaloo* in 1991. An intense presentation, it relates the psychological aftereffects of an eleven-year prison term on Robert, a young black man. Scornful of the proffered assistance from his psychiatrist, he hallucinates about being in Siberia and impregnating the wife of one of his fellow exiles. The wife dies in childbirth, leaving both men to confront the ambiguity of homosexual overtones that informs Robert's real life.

Dove's academic connections are strong. She has held the Portia Pittman Fellowship as writer-in-residence at Tuskegee University, and she taught at Arizona State University in Tempe for eight years. She has interrupted her teaching to write under the auspices of a number of grants, including a Fulbright-Hays Fellowship to Germany in 1974–1975, a National Endowment for the Arts grant, and a Guggenheim Fellowship. In the late 1980s, she became a professor of English at the University of Virginia in Charlottesville. She is reportedly at work on a novel, an excerpt from which, "The First Suite," appeared in the Fall 1986 issue of *Black American Literature Forum.*

❖❖❖

A brief biographical sketch of Rita Dove appears in *Notable Black American Women* (1992). For critical commentary, see Arnold Rampersad, "The Poems of Rita Dove," *Callaloo* 9 (Winter 1986); Robert McDowell, "The Assembling Vision of Rita Dove," *Callaloo* 9 (Winter 1986); Stan Sanvel Rubin and Earl G. Ingersoll, eds., "A Conversation with Rita Dove," *Black American Literature Forum* 20 (Fall 1986); Mohamed B. Taleb-Khyar, "An Interview with Maryse Conde and Rita Dove," *Callaloo* 14 (Spring 1991); Ekaterini Georgoudaki, "Rita Dove: Crossing Boundaries," *Callaloo* 14 (Spring 1991); Bonnie Costello, "Scars and Wings: Rita Dove's *Grace Notes,*" *Callaloo* 14 (Spring 1991).

Roast Possum

The possum's a greasy critter
that lives on persimmons and what
the Bible calls carrion.
So much from the 1909 Werner
Encyclopedia, three rows of deep green
along the wall. A granddaughter
propped on each knee,
Thomas went on with his tale—

but it was for Malcolm, little
Red Delicious, that he invented
embellishments: *We shined that possum*
with a torch and I shinnied up,

being the smallest,
to shake him down. He glared at me,
teeth bared like a shark's
in that torpedo snout.
Man he was tough but no match
for old-time know-how.

Malcolm hung back, studying them
with his gold hawk eyes. When the girls
got restless, Thomas talked horses:
Strolling Jim, who could balance
a glass of water on his back
and trot the village square
without spilling a drop. Who put
Wartrace on the map and was buried
under a stone, like a man.

They liked that part.
He could have gone on to tell them
that the Werner admitted Negro children
to be intelligent, though briskness
clouded over at puberty, bringing
indirection and laziness. Instead,
he added: *You got to be careful*
with a possum when he's on the ground;
he'll turn on his back and play dead
till you give up looking. That's
what you'd call sullin'.

Malcolm interrupted to ask
who owned Strolling Jim,
and who paid for the tombstone.
They stared each other down
man to man, before Thomas,
as a grandfather, replied:
                              Yessir,
we enjoyed that possum. We ate him
real slow, with sweet potatoes.

Dusting

Every day a wilderness—no
shade in sight. Beulah
patient among knicknacks,
the solarium a rage
of light, a grainstorm
as her gray cloth brings
dark wood to life.

Under her hand scrolls
and crests gleam
darker still. What
was his name, that
silly boy at the fair with
the rifle booth? And his kiss and
the clear bowl with one bright
fish, rippling
wound!

Not Michael—
something finer. Each dust
stroke a deep breath and
the canary in bloom.
Wavery memory: home
from a dance, the front door
blown open and the parlor
in snow, she rushed
the bowl to the stove, watched
as the locket of ice
dissolved and he
swam free.

That was years before
Father gave her up
with her name, years before
her name grew to mean
Promise, then
Desert-in-Peace.
Long before the shadow and
sun's accomplice, the tree.

Maurice.

Taking in Wash

Papa called her Pearl when he came home
drunk, swaying as if the wind touched
only him. Towards winter his skin paled,
buckeye to ginger root, cold drawing
the yellow out. The Cherokee in him,
Mama said. Mama never changed:
when the dog crawled under the stove
and the back gate slammed, Mama hid
the laundry. Sheba barked as she barked
in snow or clover, a spoiled and ornery bitch.

She was Papa's girl,
black though she was. Once,

in winter, she walked through a dream
all the way down the stairs
to stop at the mirror, a beast
with stricken eyes
who screamed the house awake. Tonight

every light hums, the kitchen arctic
with sheets. Papa is making the hankies
sail. Her foot upon a silk
stitched rose, she waits
until he turns, his smile sliding all over.
Mama a tight dark fist.
Touch that child

and I'll cut you down
just like the cedar of Lebanon.

Under the Viaduct, 1932

He avoided the empty millyards,
the households towering
next to the curb. It was dark
where he walked, although above him
the traffic was hissing.

He poked a trail in the mud
with his tin-capped stick.
If he had a son this time
he would teach him how to step
between his family and the police,
the mob bellowing
as a kettle of communal soup
spilled over a gray bank of clothes. . . .

The pavement wobbled, loosened by rain.
He liked it down here
where the luck of the mighty
had tumbled,

black suit and collarbone.
He could smell the worms stirring in their holes.
He could watch the white sheet settle
while all across the North Hill Viaduct

tires slithered to a halt.

The Great Palaces of Versailles

Nothing nastier than a white person!
She mutters as she irons alterations
in the backroom of Charlotte's Dress Shoppe.
The steam rising from a cranberry wool

comes alive with perspiration
and stale Evening of Paris.
Swamp she born from, swamp
she swallow, swamp she got to sink again.

The iron shoves gently
into a gusset, waits until
the puckers bloom away. Beyond
the curtain, the white girls are all
wearing shoulder pads to make their faces
delicate. That laugh would be Autumn,
tossing her hair in imitation of Bacall.

Beulah had read in the library
how French ladies at court would tuck
their fans in a sleeve
and walk in the gardens for air. Swaying
among lilies, lifting shy layers of silk,
they dropped excrement as daintily
as handkerchieves. Against all rules
she had saved the lining from a botched coat
to face last year's gray skirt. She knows
whenever she lifts a knee
she flashes crimson. That seems legitimate;
but in the book she had read
how the *cavaliere* amused themselves
wearing powder and perfume and spraying
yellow borders knee-high on the stucco
of the *Orangerie.*

A hanger clatters
in the front of the shoppe.
Beulah remembers how
even Autumn could lean into a settee
with her ankles crossed, sighing
I need a man who'll protect me
while smoking her cigarette down to the very end.

REGINALD MCKNIGHT

(1956–)

Reginald McKnight, who has written an award-winning first novel, *I Get on the Bus* (1990), is one of the most outstanding contemporary writers of fiction. He explores with dramatically surreal skill the quest for spiritual health in a dying world. In this sense, he extends the fictive experimentations of Toni Morrison, Ralph Ellison, and Henry Dumas. McKnight clarifies the demarcation of social class and the differences within the continuum of African and African American history. Within a broad space but a very focused time and place, he portrays African people as embodying the most creative possibilities of the human species.

Reginald McKnight was born to Frank and Pearl M. Anderson McKnight in Fürstenfeldbruck, Germany, on February 26, 1956. He completed an associate's degree in general studies at Pikes Peak Community College in 1978, a B.A. in African literature at Colorado College in 1981, and an M.A. at Denver University in 1984. From 1988 to 1991, he was assistant professor of English at the University of Pittsburgh. In 1988 he won the Drue Heinz Literature Prize for a collection of short stories titled *Moustapha's Eclipse* (1988). He also has won the O. Henry Award and the award for literary excellence from the *Kenyon Review.* His novel, *I Get on the Bus,* appeared in 1990, and *The Kind of Light That Shines on Texas* in 1992.

"There were times when I said to myself," McKnight wrote once, "I'm as African as a Toyota." But then "you get on a bus or go to the flea market and you hear women talk or laugh and you see your mother or your aunt or your sister in them. . . . You grasp on to that and realize how much has survived the Middle Passage." In *I Get On the Bus,* Evan, a Peace Corps volunteer in Senegal, becomes sick with malaria. During his recovery in a village hut, a nurse sits by him to tell stories in a native but foreign tongue every afternoon. Here McKnight achieves, as Carolyn E. Magan says, a "*magical moment* through his play . . . a haunting vision of abuse and the idea that somehow everyone is implicated in these cycles of history." [editor's italics]

Personal claustrophobia and sickness express the deathly state of the communal soul:

> The bus stops. I get on. It is crowded and hot.
> There is no air and the skin feels like chicken
> fat. I try to push my way toward the front in
> search of more air, but there are too many people
> so I remain in the middle. No one will make way
> for me. It is well past midday and everyone is
> tired and irritable; I cannot blame them. It is
> always hot here. The Senegalese sun has no mercy.
> It is colorless, cruel. I have been here only
> three months; a desert of twenty-one months
> stretches before me. Sometimes I get very tired.
> I think I am coming down with something.

Malaria (bad air) becomes a delightful pun on malaise (bad comfort). Indifference to human destiny prompts the greatest disease: "I would scream, but I have no language for screaming. There is too much to see. I am blind. I am deaf. I cannot breathe. . . . My head hurts."

From Thomas Mann's *Magic Mountain* (1924) to Leslie Silko's *Ceremony* (1977) and Toni Cade Bambara's *Salt Eaters* (1980), Reginald McKnight exposes the presumed clarity of the modern sick and well, revealing a limit to Western logic and a resilience of the African imagination to restore spiritual health. As Joseph A. Reiter writes about Thomas Mann in the *New Grolier Multimedia Encyclopedia* (1993), "During his 7-year stay in a tuberculosis sanitarium, the main character, Hans Castorp, encounters not only physical disease but also the spiritual and metaphysical anguish that torments 20th-century human beings." In *I Get on the Bus,* after failed relationships between Evan and the American Wanda and between Evan and the

Senegalese Aminata, a third character, Lamonte, prepares to kill the protagonist. But first he must reveal the magical secret of the way mind over matter enables Africans to extend beyond the Nile to the universe: "What would you say if I told you that there was no poison on that handkerchief, eh? What if I told you that, if you wanted to, you could rise up from this bed, take this blade from my hands, and cut me in half? It could be, boy. It could be." Reginald McKnight recovers the awareness that all African descendants—indeed, the human species itself—must trust in their own magical properties to advance existence.

❖❖❖

As a relatively new writer, McKnight can expect to have substantive criticism of his work in the next decade and century. Carolyn E. Magan, "New Perceptions on Rhythm in Reginald McKnight's Fiction," *Kenyon Review,* 16, No. 2 (Spring 1994), provides a careful consideration of the acoustics, or verbal sounds, in the texts. Among the score of reviews written about his fiction, the following are most pertinent: Buchi Emechta's in *New York Times Book Review,* April 29, 1990; Albert Murray's in *New York Times Book Review,* March 1, 1992; Sybil Steinberg's in *Publishers Weekly,* March 23, 1990; David W. Henderson's in *Library Journal,* May 1, 1993; Greg Johnson's in *Georgia Review* 43, No. 2 (Summer 1989); Jerome Kinkowitz's in *North American Review* 274, No. 1 (March 1989).

I Get on the Bus

FROM I GET ON THE BUS

I take the bus to the end of the line, all the way to the wharf near Place Leclerc. It is my intention to walk from here to Place de l'Indépendance, the center of town. I simply want to walk in a place I am not known, where people do not greet me, ask me where I am going, how I am doing. I will perhaps go to the expensive boulangerie just off the square, where mainly white and Lebanese teenagers congregate. They will leave me alone. They will not even see me. Then I will go to a good hotel. But suddenly I spot the Gorée Island ferry ticket cage and decide that Gorée would be the perfect place to steep in my loneliness. Gorée was a slave depot many many years ago. Each time I go there I can smell taste touch the very fibers of slavery. The old holding-pen walls, the pebbles on the strand, the air, all vibrate with atoms of dried blood, evaporated sweat, desiccated vomit. It is unlike any other place I know. It is the perfect place for self-pity. There is pain there, but it is not my pain. It is like a chorus for my solo. Perhaps too many years have passed since what, for lack of a better term, I could call my ancestral leave-taking. Perhaps I am no longer African, or African only in the vestigial sense. My senses register the waterless horrors of the island's past as if they were photocopied pictures of paintings. I go there not because of some overpowering emotion that takes hold of me but because the ancient emotion does not overwhelm my own.

I get on the boat. The boat goes to Gorée. I get off the boat. The weather is beautiful, eye-splitting blue sky, deep green cut-glass water. The sunlight is almost audible. Many people, mostly Africans, are swimming, sunbathing. My head starts throbbing. My vision blurs. I see the world as if through water. Wiry African boys, rubbery African girls, move like stop-action figures, jabbering, squealing. I walk past them, to the village, past the village, and up the rocky trail that leads to the cliffs. I always feel nervous when I go to the cliffs alone. There is a legend of an old woman who lives up here. She is a powerful sorceress named Koumba Castelle. They say she rides a white horse around the island at night. They say her power is so sinister and fierce that if you were to meet her while walking in these hills, if you were to see her face, look her in the eye, the bottom half of your face will twist to the left, the top will twist right, and you will spend the rest of your days this way. They say that Koumba owns the island, that she jealously guards every inch. Once, after World War II, they tried to build a bridge connecting Gorée to Dakar. The sorceress did not like this, so she called up a tremendous squall, which tore the bridge like so many matchsticks. They rebuilt the bridge and again she tore it down, this time before it was ever completed. I have seen the remnant of the bridge many times, though I am afraid to approach it. It hangs out a hundred feet or so over the sea. Rays of rusted cable jut from the crumbling cement and asphalt like ribs. They say the bridge is cursed—no doubt it is—and birds, lizards, even weeds, neither thrive nor feed there.

Keeping a good distance from the bridge, I approach the edge of the cliff. I stare down into the water. It is astoundingly beautiful, clear. It shifts from blue to blue: indigo, cobalt, azure, robin's egg. The sunlight cuts into it, glassy blades scraping yellow lines onto the black volcanic rock on the ocean floor. I stare for a long time. I wait for tears. I wait for a great surge of self-pity to storm across the ocean and knock me flat. But nothing comes. Not a thing. Then, slowly as time in hellfire, a dull shame fills my gut. *Oh well is what you said that night, Evan. Oh well. What were you thinking? And who do you think you are? Here. Now. Trying to conjure up tears for yourself. Oh well? What did you mean? Oh well, it is only a dream? Oh well, since I have gone through the trouble of lifting this slab? Oh well, he is only a legless African?* He caressed my face. *So you killed him?* He was poor. *So you killed him?* He was grateful for the two brass coins I gave him. *So you killed him?* I broke bread with him. *So you killed him?* I did not know him. *So you killed him?* I think perhaps I did, but besides the dull shame I feel nothing. It is as though my nerves were spun in webs, wrapped in gauze, sealed in wax. I stand here and gnash my teeth, squeeze my fists, but can call up no real emotion. Instead, my head rocks; the pressure builds at the top of my skull. The high-pitched squeal builds and I hold my head in my hands for fear that my skull will literally explode. I inhale deeply in order to calm myself, and I smell diesel fumes. I hear footsteps behind me, a slow, unsteady gait. I open my eyes but do not turn around. Instead I try to focus on the water. The closer the steps, the deeper I stare into the water. But I can scarcely concentrate. The two pains, the one deep inside my brain, the other boring into the top of my head, alternately become one, then separate. The rhythms are like heartbeat and breath, working to keep something alive.

There is a man standing next to me. I find something familiar about him even before I look up at his face. Worn-out, point-toed sandals, gray khaftan, maroon fez, a bald head. There is nothing remarkable about him at first. Then he turns full face to me. It is the man with the teary egg-white eyes, the blind man to whom I gave alms when on the bus. Perhaps by reflex, I reach into my pocket and pull out a five-hundred-franc note. "Aam," I say to him. "Jerrejeff, jerrejeff, jerrejeff," he says in a flat mumble. He slips the franc note into his pocket, spreads his arms, bends over as if looking for something on the ground, throws his arms forward, and dives off the cliff. He tumbles through the air, head over heels, head over heels, head over heels. My eyes widen, then I close them, and for the briefest moment I feel weightless, as though I, myself, am careening through the air. I hear him hit the water.

I turn and walk back toward the trail, but I become dizzy and sit down on a small boulder. My head is spinning. I am hyperventilating. *I gotta get out of here.* I shut my eyes and turn my face to the sky, breathing in deeply, exhaling, breathing, exhaling. I consider prayer. I consider jumping off the cliff myself. I consider, for a long long time, going back to the U.S. I think of *King Lear,* and what would have happened if Edgar had led Gloucester to the brink of a real cliff. Would Gloucester simply say, "Jerrejeff, jerrejeff, jerrejeff," as he tumbled down? I think about many things, some of them quite stupid, but I keep these thoughts turning to assess my mind's lucidity. Again I hear footsteps. Again I am afraid to look. In fact I put my hands over my face.

"There you are, you asshole."

I open my eyes. It is Allen. He stands before me, red-faced, knuckles on hips, and slightly out of breath.

"Al. What are you doing here?" For a moment, I think I am hallucinating him.

"You remember Cal Whitaker? The guy who runs the—"

"You know him?"

"Yeah, and I guess you know him too. He happens to keep a place here on Gorée and it just so happens Evalyn and I were up here visiting the guy. He's a friend of mine. In fact, if you'll check that basket of fruit you call a brain, you might just remember you and Evalyn and Ruth and I met him at the Embassy for lunch when you first got here."

"I remember. He was probably too drunk to even see me."

"Oh. You think so? Well, guy, it just so happens he saw you just . . . just . . . strolling! Fucking strolling through the village like some goddamn tourist. 'Hey,' he says to me, 'I just saw that weirdo space cadet you been looking for.' And here you are. Goddamn. Son of a bitch. Do you have any idea what you've put us through? You got the cops, the gendarmes, the United-fucking-States State Department—"

"Allen?"

"What!"

"Shut up, man. Ain't it obvious I've quit the Peace Corps? I couldn't care less who's looking for me. And quit calling me names. I might be sick, but I'm still big enough to knock you down."

"Well, shit, Evan, if you wanted to quit, why didn't you just come talk to me?" As he speaks he repeatedly throws his arms into the air and drops them loosely so that his hands smack against his thighs. "You have any idea how many times I've come up here to look for you? I do have other things to do, guy. Everybody was sure you were dead, you big . . . Well, everybody thought you were dead or something."

"I really am sick, Allen."

"You got that right, dude."

"You can't tell by looking at me?"

Allen sits next to me on the boulder. "You know," he says, "maybe if you'd checked into that hospital you wouldn't be so damned sick." He pulls off his glasses and wipes his forehead with the back of his arm. Even though he perspires heavily, his shirt is perfectly creased. "I think you really ought to go back to the States," he says, "get some rest, maybe see a shrink. I think you know that, guy." He holds his glasses by one of the ear pieces, twirls them round and round. "I just don't think you're ready for Africa, Evan."

"May just be that none of us is, but I'm staying for a while."

CHARLES I. NERO

(1956–)

Charles I. Nero is currently the director of African American studies at Bates College. He holds a B.A. in communications and theater from Xavier University, an M.A. from Wake Forest, and a Ph.D. in speech communications from Indiana University. He has taught at Valdosta State College, Indiana University, and Ithaca College. Having published a number of articles, including "Black Queer Identity, Imaginative Rationality, and the Language of Home," he is currently working on a book-length manuscript on the lives of black gay men. He appears in Essex Hemphill's groundbreaking anthology *Brother to Brother: New Writings by Black Gay Men* (1991).

His pioneering essay "Toward a Black Gay Aesthetic: Signifying in Contemporary Black Gay Literature" is included here. In this work, Nero attempts to make gay male writers Samuel Delany, George Wolfe, Billi Gordon, Larry Duplechan, Craig G. Harris, and Essex Hemphill visible by using the theory of signification of Henry Louis Gates, Jr., who argues that there is a common black vernacular and that language is used to revise the works of earlier black authors. Nero maintains that gay black writers share this vernacular and, furthermore, use it to revise heterosexual literature.

❖❖❖

No critical analyses of Nero's works have been published to date.

Toward a Black Gay Aesthetic

SIGNIFYING IN CONTEMPORARY BLACK GAY LITERATURE*

WESTERN LITERATURE HAS OFTEN POSITED THE HETEROSEXUAL WHITE MALE AS HERO, WITH GAYS, BLACKS AND WOMEN AS OTHER. . . . THE DEVELOPMENT OF BLACK LITERATURE, WOMEN'S LITERATURE, GAY LITERATURE, AND NOW BLACK GAY LITERATURE IS NOT SO MUCH A REWRITING OF HISTORY AS AN ADDITIONAL WRITING OF IT; TOGETHER THESE VARIOUS LITERATURES, LIKE OUR VARIOUS SELVES, PRODUCE HISTORY. . . . OUR PAST AS BLACK GAY MEN IS ONLY NOW BEING EXAMINED.

—DANIEL GARRETT, "OTHER COUNTRIES: THE IMPORTANCE OF DIFFERENCE"[1]

MUCH OF THE AFRO-AMERICAN LITERARY TRADITION CAN BE READ AS SUCCESSIVE ATTEMPTS TO CREATE A NEW NARRATIVE SPACE FOR REPRESENTING THE RECURRING REFERENT OF AFRO-AMERICAN LITERATURE, THE SO-CALLED BLACK EXPERIENCE.

—HENRY LOUIS GATES, JR., *THE SIGNIFYING MONKEY*[2]

ALL I CAN SAY IS—IF THIS IS MY TIME IN LIFE . . . GOODBYE MISERY.

—LORRAINE HANSBERRY, *A RAISIN IN THE SUN*[3]

Introduction

With only a few exceptions, the intellectual writings of black Americans have been dominated by heterosexual ideologies that have resulted in the gay male experience being either excluded, marginalized, or ridiculed.[4] Because of the heterosexism among African American intellectuals and the racism in the white gay community, black gay men have been an invisible population. However, the last five years have seen a movement characterized by political activism and literary production by openly gay black men. Given their invisibility by both black heterosexism and white gay racism, two questions emerge: How have black gay men created a positive identity for themselves and how have they constructed literary texts which would render their lives visible, and therefore valid? I propose in this essay to answer the former by answering the latter, i.e., I will focus on the strategies by black men who have either identified themselves as gay or who feature black gay characters prominently in their work. The writers I examine will be Samuel Delany, George Wolfe, Billi Gordon, Larry Duplechan, Craig G. Harris, and Essex Hemphill.

The critical framework that I use is strongly influenced by my reading of Mary Helen Washington's *Invented Lives* and Henry Louis Gates, Jr.'s critical method of signifying. In *Invented*

*This essay was originally published in Essex Hemphill's anthology *Brother to Brother* (1991).

[1]Daniel Garrett, "Other Countries: The Importance of Difference," in *Other Countries: Black Gay Voices,* ed. Cary Alan Johnson, Colin Robinson, and Terence Taylor (New York: Other Countries, 1988), p. 27.

[2]Henry Louis Gates, Jr., *The Signifying Monkey: A Theory of African American Literary Criticism* (New York: Oxford University Press, 1988), p. 111.

[3]Lorraine Hansberry, *A Raisin in the Sun* (New York: New American Library, 1958), p. 79.

[4]Cogent discussions of homophobia among Black American intellectuals can be found in Cheryl Clarke, "The Failure to Transform: Homophobia in the Black Community," in *Home Girls: A Black Feminist Perspective,* ed. Barbara Smith (New York: Kitchen Table Press, 1983), pp. 197–208; Ann Allen Shockley, "The Illegitimates of Afro-American Literature," *Lambda Rising Book Report,* 1, no. 4: 1+.

Lives, Washington brilliantly analyzes the narrative strategies ten black women have used between 1860 and 1960 to bring themselves into visibility and power in a world dominated by racism and sexism.[5] Like Washington, Gates's concern is with the paradoxical relationship of African Americans with the printed text, i.e., since Eurocentric writing defines the black as "other," how does the "other" gain authority in the text? To resolve this, Gates proposes a theory of criticism based upon the African American oral tradition of signifying. Signifying is, for Gates, "the black term for what in classical European rhetoric are called the figures of signification," or stated differently, "the indirect use of words that changes the meaning of a word or words."[6] Signifying has numerous figures which include: capping, loud-talking, the dozens, reading, going off, talking smart, sounding, joaning (jonesing), dropping lugs, snapping, woofing, styling out, and calling out of one's name.

As a rhetorical strategy, signifying assumes that there is shared knowledge between communicators and, therefore, that information can be given indirectly. Geneva Smitherman in *Talkin and Testifyin* gives the following examples of signifying:

- Stokely Carmichael, addressing a white audience at the University of California, Berkeley, 1966: "It's a privilege and an honor to be in the white intellectual ghetto of the West."
- Malcolm X on Martin Luther King, Jr.'s nonviolent revolution (referring to the common practice of singing "We Shall Overcome" at civil rights protests of the sixties): "In a revolution, you swinging, not singing."
- Reverend Jesse Jackson, merging sacred and secular siggin in a Breadbasket Saturday morning sermon: "Pimp, punk, prostitute, preacher, Ph.D.—all the P's—you still in slavery!"
- A black middle-class wife to her husband who had just arrived home several hours later than usual: "You sho got home early today for a change."[7]

Effective signifying is, Smitherman states, "to put somebody in check . . . to make them think about and, one hopes, correct their behavior."[8] Because signifying relies on indirection to give information, it requires that participants in any communicative encounter pay attention to, as Claudia Mitchell-Kernan states, "the total universe of discourse."[9]

Gates's theory of signifying focuses on black forms of talk. I believe that identifying these forms of talk in contemporary black gay literature is important for two reasons. First, the use of signifying by black gay men places their writing squarely within the African American literary tradition. Second, signifying permits black gay men to revise the "Black Experience" in African American literature and, thereby, to create a space for themselves.

The remainder of this essay is divided into two parts. The first part examines the heterosexist context in which black gay men write. Examined are heterosexism and homophobia in the writings of contemporary social scientists, scholars, and, in a longer passage, the novels of Toni Morrison. The last section discusses black gay men's attempts to revise the African American literary tradition. Specifically examined are the signifying on representations of desire, the black religious experience, and gender configurations.

Heterosexism and African American Intellectuals

Some social scientists have claimed that homosexuality is alien to the black community. Communication scholar Molefi Asante has argued in

[5]Mary Helen Washington, *Invented Lives* (Garden City, N.Y.: Doubleday, 1987).

[6]Gates, *The Signifying Monkey,* p. 81.

[7]Geneva Smitherman, *Talkin and Testifyin* (Boston: Houghton Mifflin, 1977), p. 120.

[8]Smitherman, *Talkin and Testifyin,* p. 121.

[9]Claudia Mitchell-Kernan, "Signifying as a Form of Verbal Art," in *Mother Wit from the Laughing Barrel: Readings in the Interpretation of Afro-American Folklore,* ed. Alan Dundes (Englewood Cliffs, N.J.: Prentice-Hall, 1973), p. 314.

Afrocentricity: A Theory of Social Change that homosexual practices among black men were initially imposed on them by their white slave owners and that the practice is maintained by the American prison institution.[10] Asante has attributed homosexuality to Greco-Roman culture, with the added assertion that "homosexuality does not represent an Afrocentric way of life."[11] Likewise, in *Black Skin, White Masks,* Frantz Fanon, the widely read Martiniquois psychiatrist and freedom-fighter, declared that "Caribbean men never experience the Oedipus complex," and therefore, in the Caribbean, "there is no homosexuality, which is, rather, an attribute of the white race, Western civilization."[12]

Other scholars and writers have contended that homosexuality is a pathology stemming from the inability of black men to cope with the complexities of manhood in a racist society. Alvin Poussaint, the noted Harvard psychiatrist and adviser to the *Cosby Show,* stated in a 1978 *Ebony* article that some black men adopt homosexuality as a maneuver to help them avoid the increasing tension developing between black men and women.[13] "Homosexuality," according to black writer and liberationist Imamu Amiri Baraka, "is the most extreme form of alienation acknowledged within white society" and it occurs among "a people who lose their self-sufficiency because they depend on their subjects to do the world's work," thus rendering them "effeminate and perverted."[14] According to Eldridge Cleaver, homosexuality among black men is a "racial death wish," and a frustrating experience because "in their sickness [black men who practice homosexuality] are unable to have a baby by a white man."[15] In *The Endangered Black Family,* Nathan Hare and Julia Hare view homosexuals as confused but worthy of compassion because, they state, "Some of them may yet be saved."[16] The Hares seem to imply that black gay and lesbian people require treatment for either illness or brainwashing: "What we must do is offer the homosexual brother or sister a proper compassion and acceptance without advocacy. We might not advocate, for instance, the religion of Mormonism, or venereal disease, laziness or gross obesity. . . ."[17]

The acclaimed writer Toni Morrison has woven into her novels these ideas of homosexuality as alien to African cultures, as forced upon black men by racist European civilizations, and as the inability to acquire and sustain manhood. In her first novel, *The Bluest Eye,* she played on the stereotype of the "light-skinned" black man as weak, effeminate, and sexually impotent. Soaphead Church, "a cinnamon-eyed West Indian with lightly browned skin," limited his sexual interests to little girls because, Morrison wrote, "he was too diffident to confront homosexuality" and found "little boys insulting, scary, and stubborn."[18] In *Tar Baby,* black homosexual men were self-mutilating transvestites who had dumped their masculinity because they "found the whole business of being black and men at the same time too difficult."[19]

In her 1988 Pulitzer Prize–winning *Beloved,* Morrison surpassed her earlier efforts in using homophobia with the creation of the five heroic black men of the Sweet Home plantation. Sweet Home men were unlike slaves on nearby plantations, as their owner Mr. Garner bragged to

[10]Molefi Kete Asante, *Afrocentricity: A Theory of Social Change* (Buffalo, N.Y.: Amulefi, 1980), p. 66.

[11]Asante, *Afrocentricity,* p. 64.

[12]Frantz Fanon, *Black Skin, White Masks,* trans. Constance Farrington (New York: Grove Press, 1963), p. 84.

[13]Alvin Poussaint, "What Makes Them Tick," *Ebony,* October 1978, p. 79.

[14]Quoted in Georges-Michel Sarotte, *Like a Brother, Like a Lover: Male Homosexuality in the American Novel and Theatre from Herman Melville to James Baldwin,* trans. Richard Miller (New York: Doubleday, 1978), p. 94.

[15]Eldridge Cleaver, *Soul on Ice* (New York: Random House, 1969), p. 174.

[16]Nathan Hare and Julia Hare, *The Endangered Black Family: Coping with the Unisexualization and Coming Extinction of the Black Race* (San Francisco: Black Think Tank, 1984), p. 65.

[17]Hare and Hare, *The Endangered Black Family,* p. 65.

[18]Toni Morrison, *The Bluest Eye* (New York: Holt, Rinehart & Winston, 1970), p. 132.

[19]Toni Morrison, *Tar Baby* (New York: Random House, 1981), p. 216.

other farmers: "Y'all got boys. Youngs boys, old boys, picky boys, stroppin boys. Now at Sweet Home, my niggers is men every one of em. Bought um thataway, raised em thataway. Men every one."[20] Although deprived of sex with women, Sweet Home men were capable of enormous restraint and for sexual relief they either masturbated or engaged in sex with farm animals. When Mr. Garner added to his plantation a new slave, the thirteen-year-old "iron-eyed" Sethe, the Sweet Home men "let the girl be" and allowed her to choose one of them despite the fact that they "were young and so sick with the absence of women they had taken to *calves*" (emphasis added).[21] Sethe took over a year to choose one of the Sweet Home men. Morrison described that year of waiting: "[It was] a long, tough year of thrashing on pallets eaten up with dreams of her. A year of yearning, when rape seemed the solitary gift of life. The restraint they had exercised possible only because they were Sweet Home men. . . ."[22]

Yet Morrison's description of the restrained Sweet Home men does a great disservice to the complexity of men's lives. Her description reinforces a false notion of a hierarchy of sexual practices in which masturbation is only a substitute for intercourse. Morrison's description is homophobic because it reveals her inability to imagine homosexual relationships among heroic characters. By implication, sex with farm animals is preferable to homoerotic sex, which is like a perverse reading of a spiritual: "Before I practice homosexuality, I'll practice bestiality, and go home to my Father and be free."

Morrison rejects from her fiction the idea that homosexual desire among slave men could actually lead to loving relationships. This, in fact, did happen. Autobiographical evidence exists that slave men in the Americas practiced and even institutionalized homosexuality. Esteban Montejo, the subject of *The Autobiography of a Runaway Slave,* twice discusses the prevalence of homosexuality among Cuban slave men in his comments on the sexual customs of the plantation. The first incident refers to physical abuse and possibly the rape of young black boys. Montejo states:

> If a boy was pretty and lively he was sent inside, to the master's house. And there they started softening him up . . . well, I don't know! They used to give the boy a long palm-leaf and make him stand at one end of the table while they ate. And they said, "Now see that no flies get in the food!" If a fly did, they scolded him severely and even whipped him.[23]

The second incident is discussed within the context of the scarcity of women on the plantation. "To have one [a woman] of your own," Montejo writes, "you had either to be over twenty-five or catch yourself one in the fields."[24] Some men, however, he states, "had sex among themselves and did not want to know anything of women."[25] Montejo's comments include observations about the economics of homosexual households. He notes that the division of labor in these households resembled male-female roles in which the "effeminate men washed the clothes and did the cooking too, if they had a husband."[26] The men in these relationships also benefited financially from the existence of the "provision grounds," lands allocated to slaves in the Caribbean to grow crops to sell in the local markets on Sunday. Montejo writes: "They [effeminate men] were good workers and occupied themselves with their plots of land, giving the produce to their husbands to sell to the white farmers."[27]

Most interesting in Montejo's narrative is the reaction of other slaves to their homosexual

---

[20]Toni Morrison, *Beloved* (New York: Random House, 1988), p. 10.

[21]Ibid.

[22]Ibid.

[23]Esteban Montejo, *The Autobiography of a Runaway Slave,* trans. Jocasta Innes, ed. Miguel Barnet (New York: Random House, 1968), p. 21.

[24]Ibid., p. 41.

[25]Ibid.

[26]Ibid.

[27]Ibid.

brethren. The older men hated homosexuality, he states, and they "would have nothing to do with queers."[28] Their hatred leads Montejo to speculate that the practice did not come from Africa. Unfortunately, Montejo limits his speculations on homosexuality to origins and not to prohibitions. Thus, another speculation could be that homosexuality was prohibited, but that the practice itself was neither unknown nor undreamt. Montejo's narrative suggests that the influence of the old men over the feelings and attitudes of other slaves about homosexuality was limited. The slaves did not have a pejorative name for those who practiced homosexuality and it was not until "after Abolition that the term [effeminate] came into use," Montejo states.[29] Montejo, himself, held the view that the practice of homosexuality was a private matter: "To tell the truth, it [homosexuality] never bothered me. I am of the opinion that a man can stick his arse where he wants."[30] Montejo's narrative challenges the heterosexist assumptions about the sexualities and the family life of blacks before abolition in the Americas. At least in Cuba, homoerotic sex and exclusively male families were not uncommon.

In the United States, accounts of homosexuality among blacks before abolition are scanty. This is because accounts of slaves' sexuality are sparse and, until recently, social customs in the United States and Great Britain proscribed public discussions of sexuality.[31] Homosexuality, however, did occur during the colonial period among black men because laws forbidding the practice were created and sentences were carried out. These laws and sentences are discussed in A. Leon Higginbotham, Jr.'s *In the Matter of Color: Race and the American Legal Process* and Jonathan Katz's two documentary works *Gay/Lesbian Almanac* and *Gay American History*. Katz documents the case of Jan Creoli, identified as a "negro," who in 1646 in New Netherland (Manhattan) was sentenced to be "choked to death, and then burnt to ashes" for committing the act of sodomy with ten-year-old Manuel Congo.[32] Congo, whose name suggests that he was black, was sentenced "to be carried to the place where Creoli is to be executed, tied to a stake, and faggots piled around him, for justice sake, and to be flogged. . . ."[33] In a second case, "Mingo alias Cocke Negro," a Massachusetts slave, was reportedly executed for "forcible Buggery," a term that Katz suggests is a male-male act, rather than bestiality.[34] Both Katz and Higginbotham discuss the development of sexual crime laws in Pennsylvania between 1700 and 1780 that carefully distinguished between blacks and whites: Life imprisonment was the penalty for whites and death was for blacks convicted of buggery which, Katz notes, probably meant bestiality and sodomy.[35]

Although the evidence for homosexual practices among black male slaves is small, it does suggest that we do not exclude homoeroticism from life on the plantation. The gay Jewish historian Martin Bauml Duberman's words are most appropriate here:

> After all, to date we've accumulated only a tiny collection of historical materials that record the existence of *heterosexual* behavior in the past. Yet no one claims that the minuscule amount of evidence is an accurate measure of the actual

[28]Ibid.

[29]Ibid.

[30]Ibid.

[31]On the social practices surrounding the sexuality of slaves, see: John Blassingame, *The Slave Community: Plantation Life in the Antebellum South* (New York: Oxford University Press, 1979), pp. 154–191; Eugene Genovese, *Roll, Jordan, Roll: The World the Slaves Made* (New York: Random House, 1974), pp. 458–475; Mary Helen Washington, *Invented Lives: Narratives of Black Women: 1860–1960* (New York: Doubleday, 1987), pp. 4–8; Deborah Gray White, *Ar'n't I a Woman? Female Slaves in the Plantation South* (New York: Norton, 1985), pp. 142–160.

[32]Jonathan Ned Katz, *Gay American History: Lesbians and Gay Men in the U.S.A.* (New York: Avon Books, 1976), p. 35; Jonathan Ned Katz, *Gay/Lesbian Almanac: A New Documentary* (New York: Harper & Row, 1983), p. 61.

[33]Katz, *Gay American History*, pp. 35–36.

[34]Ibid., p. 61.

[35]A. Leon Higginbotham, Jr., *In the Matter of Color: Race and the American Legal Process: The Colonial Period* (New York: Oxford University Press, 1978), pp. 281–282; Katz, *Gay/Lesbian Almanac*, p. 61.

amount of heterosexual activity which took place.[36]

Duberman's words and the evidence we have suggest that, at best, our understanding of the sexuality of our slave ancestors is fragmentary. We need to uncover more and to reread diaries, letters, and narratives to gain a greater understanding of the sexuality of our forebears. At the very least, we need to revise our models of the black family and of homosexuality as alien to black culture.

Morrison's homophobia, [like] that of so many other black intellectuals, is perhaps more closely related to Judeo-Christian beliefs than to the beliefs of her ancestors. Male homosexuality is associated with biblical ideas of weakness as effeminacy.[37] Many of these intellectuals would also argue that the Judeo-Christian tradition is a major tool of the Western-Eurocentric view of reality that furthers the oppression of blacks. Paradoxically, by their condemnation of homosexuality and lesbianism, these intellectuals contribute to upholding an oppressive Eurocentric view of reality.

Enter Black Gay Men

It should be obvious that black gay men must look at other black intellectuals with great caution and skepticism because the dominant view of reality expressed is oppressively heterosexist. Black gay men must also be cautious of looking for an image of themselves in white gay men because the United States is still a racist society. For example, even though one in five homosexual or bisexual men with AIDS is black, it can be argued that Larry Kramer's searing AIDS polemic, *The Normal Heart,* is about gay people, *not* black people. The characters in the drama are from the "fabled 1970s Fire Island/*After Dark* crowd," which tended to be white, middle-class, and very exclusionary on the basis of race, unless one counts the occasional presence of the reigning "disco diva"—who was usually a black woman or the wonderful African American gender-blurring singer Sylvester. In addition, Kramer makes several remarks in *The Normal Heart* that imply that he accepts certain historically racist ideas about blacks.[38] With a critical eye, one can also find occurrences of racism in works ranging from literature to visual pornography created by or aimed at gay men that employ a racist vision of reality.[39]

Partly as a reaction to racism in gay culture, but mostly in response to the heterosexism of black intellectuals and writers, African American gay men signify on many aspects of the "Black Experience" in their literature. The areas discussed in this section are representations of sexual desire, the black religious experience, and gender configurations.

Representing Sexual Desire

Because of the historical and often virulent presence of racism, black literature has frequently had as its goal the elevation of "the race" by presenting the group in its "best light." The race's "best light" often has meant depicting blacks with those values and ways that mirrored white Americans and Europeans. For black writers this has usually meant tremendous anxiety over the representation of sexuality. An excellent example of this anxiety is W. E. B. Du Bois's reaction to Claude McKay's 1920 novel *Home to Harlem.* In the novel, McKay, gay and Jamaican, wrote about much of the night life in

[36]Martin Bauml Duberman, "Writhing Bedfellows," in *About Time: Exploring the Gay Past* (New York: Gay Presses of New York, 1986), pp. 13–14.

[37]Tom Horner, *Jonathan Loved David: Homosexuality in Biblical Times* (Philadelphia: Westminster Press, 1978), pp. 91–99.

[38]For example, toward the end of *The Normal Heart,* one of the indignities that befall a deceased person with AIDS is to be cremated by a black undertaker "for a thousand dollars, no questions asked" (p. 106). The implication here is that the deceased was unable to have a decent or respectable burial, which would, of course, be by a white undertaker. This is significant because it is part of a tradition in Western aesthetics that associates blacks and Africans with indignity. This also reflects an instance of racism by the author.

[39]An interesting case occurred in a serious article in the gay male pornography magazine *Stallion.* The author, Charles Jurrist, criticized the gay literary establishment for its exclusion of or, when included, stereotypical depiction of black men. However, the article perpetuated a stereotype by featuring a series of pictures of a spectacularly endowed Black man.

Harlem, including one of the first descriptions of a gay and lesbian bar in an African American work of fiction. Du Bois wrote:

> Claude McKay's *Home to Harlem* for the most part nauseates me, and after the dirtier parts of its filth I feel distinctly like taking a bath. . . . McKay has set out to cater for that prurient demand on the part of white folks for a portrayal in Negroes of that utter licentiousness . . . which a certain decadent section of the white world . . . wants to see written out in black and white and saddled on black Harlem. . . . He has used every art and emphasis to paint drunkenness, fighting, lascivious sexual promiscuity and utter absence of restraint in as bold and bright colors as he can. . . . As a picture of Harlem life or of Negro life anywhere, it is, of course, nonsense. Untrue, not so much as on account of its facts, but on account of its emphasis and glaring colors.[40]

The anxiety that Du Bois felt was as acute for black women. Mary Helen Washington comments that this anxiety about the representation of sexuality "goes back to the nineteenth century and the prescription for womanly 'virtues' which made slave women automatically immoral and less feminine than white women," as in the case of the slave woman Harriet Jacobs, who considered not publishing her 1860 narrative *Incidents in the Life of a Slave Girl* because she "bore two children as a single woman rather than submit to forced concubinage."[41] The representation of sexuality is even more problematic for black gay men than for heterosexual African Americans because of societal disapproval against impersonal sex, in which gay men frequently engage, and because gay sex is not connected in any way with the means of reproduction.

Black gay science fiction writer Samuel Delany, in his autobiography *The Motion of Light in Water,* takes particular delight in signifying on society's disapproval of impersonal homoerotic sex. His signifying is greatly aided by using the autobiographical form, a successful mode for black Americans, as Michael Cooke maintains, because "the self is the source of the system of which it is a part, creates what it discovers, and although it is nothing unto itself, it is the possibility of everything for itself."[42] By using himself as the source of the system, Delany is able to signify on ideas about impersonal sex. Delany imbues situations involving impersonal sex with social and political significance in the context of the repressive 1950s and early 1960s. Contrary to stereotypes that group sex is wild and out of control, the situation on the piers at the end of Christopher Street "with thirty-five, fifty, a hundred all-but-strangers is," Delany states, "hugely ordered, highly social, attentive, silent, and grounded in a certain care, if not community."[43] At the piers, when arrests of eight or nine men occurred and were reported in the newspapers without mentioning the hundreds who had escaped, it was a reassurance to the city fathers, the police, the men arrested, and even those who escaped "that the image of the homosexual as outside society—which is the myth that the outside of language, with all its articulation, is based on—was, somehow, despite the arrests, intact."[44] Delany's first visit to the St. Mark's Baths in 1963 produced a Foucault-like revelation that the legal and medical silences on homosexuality was "a huge and pervasive discourse" which prevented one from gaining "a clear, accurate, and extensive picture of extant public sexual institutions."[45] The result of Delany's signification is that his participation in impersonal sex in public

[40]W.E.B. Du Bois, review of *Quicksand* by Nella Larson and *Home to Harlem* by Claude McKay, *Crisis* 35 (June 1928): 202; quoted in Lovie Gibson, "Du Bois's Propaganda Literature: An Outgrowth of His Sociological Studies," doctoral dissertation, State University of New York at Buffalo, 1977, p. 21.

[41]Washington, *Invented Lives,* pp. xxiii–xxiv.

[42]Michael G. Cooke, *Afro-American Literature in the Twentieth Century: The Achievement of Intimacy* (New Haven: Yale University Press, 1984), p. 95.

[43]Samuel R. Delany, *The Motion of Light in Water* (New York: Morrow, 1988), p. 129.

[44]Ibid., p. 175.

[45]Ibid., p. 176.

places is given a political and social importance much like the significance given to ordinary, day-to-day acts of resistance recounted by the subjects of African American autobiographies from Frederick Douglass's *My Bondage and My Freedom* to Maya Angelou's *I Know Why the Caged Bird Sings.*

Just as Delany seeks to revise attitudes about impersonal sex, Larry Duplechan signifies on both black middle-class and gay stereotypes of interracial love and lust. On the one hand, the black middle class and the mental health professions have conspired together to label a black person's sexual attraction to a white as pathology.[46] On the other, gay men have created a host of terms to denigrate participants in black-white sexual relationships, e.g.: *dinge queen, chocolate lover,* and *snow queen.* In *Blackbird* and *Eight Days a Week,* we are introduced to Duplechan's protagonist, Johnnie Ray Rousseau, as a senior in high school in the former, and as a 22-year-old aspiring singer living in Los Angeles in the latter. In Duplechan's first novel, *Eight Days a Week,* he summarizes both the gay and the black middle-class stereotype: "I was once told by a black alto sax player named Zaz (we were in bed at the time, mind you) that my preference for white men (and blonds, the whitest of white, to boot) was the sad but understandable end result of 300 years of white male oppression."[47] Contrary to Zaz's opinion, Johnnie Ray's sexual attraction to white men is anything but the result of 300 years of white male oppression, and if it is, it allows Duplechan a major moment of signifying in African American literature: the sexual objectification of white men by a black man.

Revising our culture's ideas about male-male sexual desire and love is a major concern in Essex Hemphill's collection of poems *Conditions.*[48] In particular, "Conditions XXIV" signifies on heterosexual culture's highly celebrated "rite of passage," the marriage ceremony. Hemphill signifies on the marriage ceremony in an excellent example of "capping," a figure of speech which revises an original statement by adding new terms. Hemphill honors the bonds created from desire by capping on the exchange of wedding bands. In the opening and closing sentences, fingers are not the received place for wedding rings:

In america
I place my ring
on your cock
where it belongs . . .

In america,
place your ring
on my cock
where it belongs.

Vows are also exchanged in the poem, but they do not restrict and confine. Instead, these vows are "What the rose whispers / before blooming. . . ." The vows are:

I give you my heart,
a safe house.
I give you promises other than
milk, honey, liberty.
I assume you will always
be a free man with a dream.

Implicitly, "Conditions XXIV" strips away the public pomp and spectacle of the wedding ceremony to reveal its most fundamental level: desire. By capping on the wedding ceremony, Hemphill places homoerotic desire on an equal plane with heterosexuality.

Signifying on the Church

Historically religion has served as a liberating force in the African American community. Black slaves publicly and politically declared that Christianity and the institution of slavery were incompatible as early as 1774, according to Albert Raboteau in *Slave Religion.* "In that year," Raboteau notes, "the governor of Massachusetts received 'The Petition of a Grate Number of Blacks in this Province who by divine

---

46William H. Grier and Price M. Cobbs, *Black Rage* (New York: Basic Books, 1968), pp. 91–100.

47Larry Duplechan, *Eight Days a Week* (Boston: Alyson Publications, 1985), p. 28.

48Essex Hemphill, *Conditions* (Washington, D.C.: Be Bop Books, 1986).

permission are held in a state of slavery within the bowels of a free and Christian Country.' "[49] In the petition slaves argued for their freedom by combining the political rhetoric of the Revolution with an appeal to the claims of Christian fellowship. Christian churches were some of the first institutions blacks created and owned in the United States. From 1790 to 1830 ambitious northern free black men like Richard Allen and Absalom Jones circumvented racism by creating new Christian denominations, notably the African Methodist Episcopal and the African Methodist Episcopal Zion churches.

The organized black church, however, has not been free from oppressing its constituents. Historically, the black church has practiced sexism. In her 1849 narrative, Jarena Lee, a spiritual visionary and a free black woman, reported having her desire to preach thwarted by her husband and Rev. Richard Allen.[50] Lee, however, overcame the objections of men by claiming that her instructions came directly from God; thus, those instructions superseded the sexist prohibitions of men. Some contemporary black churches and their ministers have adopted heterosexist policies and have openly made homophobic remarks. In an essay which appeared in the gay anthology *Black Men/White Men,* Leonard Patterson, a black gay minister, movingly wrote about how he was forced to leave Ebenezer Baptist Church in Atlanta, Georgia. Patterson's troubles at Ebenezer began when Reverend Joseph Roberts replaced Reverend Martin L. King, Sr. Roberts objected to the fact that Patterson's white lover also attended Ebenezer. Moreover, Patterson was guilty of not playing the game: "I was told, in effect, that as long as I played the political game and went with a person who was more easily passed off as a 'cousin,' I would be able to go far in the ministry. Perhaps I should even marry and have someone on the side. Apparently these arrangements would make me more 'respectable.' "[51] For refusing to play the political game, Patterson states that he was "attacked verbally from the pulpit, forbidden to enter the study for prayer with the other associate ministers, and had seeds of animosity planted against [him] . . . in the minds of certain members so that in meetings with them the subject of homosexuality would inevitably be brought up."[52] Patterson recounts an extremely offensive remark made to him by a church member one Sunday: "If you lie down with dogs, you get up smelling like dirt."[53] Patterson and his lover finally left Ebenezer. Although disillusioned with organized religion, Patterson writes encouragingly that what he and his lover experienced at Ebenezer has "given us more strength to love each other and others."[54]

Exorcism is a practice used to oppress gays in the church. The late Pentecostal minister and professor, Reverend James Tinney, underwent an exorcism when he came out as a gay man. Tinney briefly mentions the experience in his essay "Struggles of a Black Pentecostal," which was originally published in 1981 issue of *Insight.* Five years later in *Blackbird* Duplechan signifies on Tinney's reflections on exorcism. It should be noted that Duplechan was probably familiar with Tinney's essay. Both that essay and Duplechan's short story "Peanuts and the Old Spice Kid" appeared in Michael Smith's anthology *Black Men/White Men.*

The events which precipitate the exorcism are similar in *Blackbird* and in Tinney's essay. Both Tinney and Duplechan's protagonist, Johnnie Ray Rousseau, are aware of their sexual identity. Tinney writes that he was aware of his homo-

[49]Albert Raboteau, *Slave Religion: The "Invisible Institution" in the Antebellum South* (New York: Oxford University Press, 1978), p. 290.

[50]Jarena Lee, *Religious Experience and Journal of Mrs. Jarena Lee, Giving an Account of Her Call to Preach the Gospel* (Philadelphia, 1849); found in Ann Allen Shockley, *Afro-American Women Writers, 1746–1933* (New York: New American Library, 1988).

[51]Leonard Patterson, "At Ebenezer Baptist Church," in *Black Men/White Men,* ed. Michael Smith (San Francisco: Gay Sunshine Press, 1983), p. 164.

[52]Ibid., pp. 164–165.

[53]Ibid., p. 165.

[54]Ibid., p. 166.

erotic feelings "even at the age of four."[55] Johnnie Ray's exorcism is preceded by an enjoyable first sexual experience with the older bi-ethnic Marshall Two Hawks McNeil, a college student. Publicly stating and affirming their sexual identity actually causes the exorcisms. Put another way, their exorcisms are punishments for stating that they practice "the love that dares not speak its name." Tinney announced to his wife of three years that he was gay. Her reaction set into motion the events that caused the exorcism: "She immediately called the pastor and his wife and other close confidants to pray for me."[56] Johnnie Ray's exorcism was set into motion by two events. First, his confidential confession to Daniel Levine, the youth minister, that he had gay feelings. Then, Levine's betrayal of the confidential confession to Johnnie Ray's parents provoked the second event: the teenager's affirmation of his sexual identity to his parents in the presence of the minister.

Tinney does not discuss the events of his exorcism. In fact, he limits the actions of his wife, minister, and church members to one sentence: "Pray and talk and counsel they did."[57] Tinney's description of the exorcism is brief, but the event left him traumatized. The exorcism, he wrote, "was extremely painful to my own sense of worth and well-being. It was an experience I would not wish upon anyone ever."[58]

Duplechan signifies explicitly and implicitly on Tinney's remark "Pray and talk and counsel they did." Explicitly Duplechan "reads" Tinney by giving a fuller narrative description of the praying, talking, and counseling of the church people. Implicitly, Duplechan's "reading of Tinney is a critique of the clergy and the values of the middle class. Further, Duplechan's "reading" is an example of what Smitherman calls heavy signifying, "a way of teaching or driving home a cognitive message but . . . without preaching or lecturing."[59]

Let us consider Duplechan's "read" or "heavy signifying" of each of the three terms—pray, talk, and counsel—as they occur in the confrontation between Johnnie Ray and the church people—his parents and the youth minister. The confrontation about Johnnie Ray's homosexuality happens at his home. Duplechan shows that prayer is often a means of ensuring conformity. In an emotional outburst Johnnie Ray's mother asks the teen: "Have you asked him? Have you asked the savior to help you? . . . Have you prayed every day for help? Every day?"[60] When Johnnie Ray answers no, his mother incredulously asks him, "Don't you want to be normal?"[61] Normality, which is conforming to existing value structures, is believed by the middle classes to be what will guarantee them success in the world. Johnnie Ray's mother reveals that she is less concerned with his happiness than she is with his possibilities of success. To insure his success, she and her husband must use talk to force Johnnie Ray to become normal. Talk, thus, is a means of intimidation. When Johnnie Ray claims that he has accepted it as a fact that he is gay, his mother intimidates him by "loud talking":

> You probably think you're real cute . . . going to Daniel [the youth minister] with this "I think I'm a homosexual" crap, and now sittin' here and tellin' us you've *accepted* that you're gay. . . . Lord ha' mercy today! I don't know what I coulda done to give birth to a *pervert.*[62]

While Johnnie Ray's mother uses "loud talking" to intimidate her son, his father cries. When his father finally talks, it is a mixture of intimidation and compassion: "You're no pervert," he says. "No son of mine is gonna be a pervert.

[55]James S. Tinney, "Struggles of a Black Pentecostal," in *Black Men/White Men,* ed. Michael Smith (San Francisco: Gay Sunshine Press, 1983), p. 167.

[56]Ibid., p. 170.

[57]Ibid.

[58]Ibid., pp. 170–171.

[59]Smitherman, *Talkin and Testifyin,* p. 120.

[60]Larry Duplechan, *Blackbird* (New York: St. Martin's, 1986), p. 152.

[61]Ibid., p. 153.

[62]Ibid., p. 151.

You're just a little confused."[63] Finally, there is the expert, Reverend Levine, who offers counsel. Levine, however, is a scoundrel. Although he has betrayed Johnnie Ray's confidence, he sits throughout the entire family crisis "looking as holy and righteous at having done so as my parents looked utterly devastated at the news."[64] Levine is able to sit "in beatific calm" because of the family's unhappiness.[65] In other words, the family crisis that Levine has provided proves that the ministry is necessary. Levine's expert counsel to the family, which they reluctantly agree upon, is an exorcism—"a deliverance from unclean spirits."[66]

By signifying on Tinney, Duplechan exposes an unholy alliance between the church and the middle classes. The church is eager to oppress gay people to prove its worth to the middle classes. For the sake of conformity which, with hope, leads to success, the middle class is willing to oppress its children. The middle class, thus, is denounced for its willingness to use the church to further its ambitions.

In the short story "Cut Off from among Their People," Craig G. Harris does a "heavy sig" on the black family which also signifies on strategies from slave narratives. The story takes place at the funeral of Jeff's lover, who has died of complications from AIDS. Both the family and the church, two major institutions in the heterosexual African American community, are allied against Jeff. The lover's biological family has "diplomatically" excluded Jeff from the decisions about the funeral. At the funeral Jeff is ignored by the family and humiliated by the church. The lover's mother stares at him contemptuously. Jeff is not allowed to sit with the family. The minister chosen by the family only adds to Jeff's humiliation. The minister is asked not to wear his ceremonial robes but instead to wear an ordinary suit.

[63]Ibid., p. 153.

[64]Ibid., p. 150.

[65]Ibid., p. 152.

[66]Ibid., p. 155.

The "heavy sig" is done by using irony. The minister is exposed as a scoundrel, similar to Levine in *Blackbird.* At the funeral he delivers a homophobic sermon from the book of Leviticus:

> In Leviticus, Chapter 20, the Lord tell [*sic*] us: If a man lie with mankind as he lieth with a woman, both of them have committed an abomination: they shall surely be put to death; their blood shall be upon them. There's no cause to wonder why medical science could not find a cure for this man's illness. How could medicine cure temptation? What drug can exorcise Satan from a young man's soul? The only cure is to be found in the Lord. The only cure is repentance, for Leviticus clearly tells us, ". . . whoever shall commit any of these abominations, even the souls that commit them shall be cut off from among their people."[67]

After the funeral Jeff is abandoned and left to his own devices to get to the burial site. His humiliation is relieved by a sympathetic undertaker who offers Jeff a ride to the burial site. Ironically, it is the undertaker, the caregiver to the dead—not the minister, who is the caregiver to the living—who offers Jeff the compassion he so desperately needs. Denouncing both the family and the church, the undertaker's remarks to Jeff become the authentic sermon in the story:

> I lost my lover to AIDS three months ago. It's been very difficult—living with these memories and secrets and hurt, and with no one to share them. These people won't allow themselves to understand. If it's not preached from a pulpit and kissed up to the Almighty, they don't want to know about it. So, I hold it in, and hold it in, and then I see us passing, one after another—tearless funerals, the widowed treated like nonentities, and these "another faggot burns in hell" sermons. My heart goes out to you

[67]Craig G. Harris, "Cut Off from among Their People," in *In the Life,* ed. Joseph Beam (Boston: Alyson Publications, 1986), p. 66.

brother. You gotta let your love for him keep you strong.[68]

As a result of Harris's use of ironic signifying, one is left to ponder the meaning of the story's title, "Cut Off from among Their People." Who is cut off from their people? The story immediately implies that black gays are oppressed because they are alienated from their families. The opposite, however, is also true: Black families are oppressors, are alienated from their gay children, and thus, suffer. Black families suffer because their oppression robs them of a crucial sign of humaneness: compassion. By their oppression, the family of Jeff's deceased lover has lost the ability to be compassionate.

Harris's strategy—the cost of oppression is the loss of humanity—signifies on slave narratives by authors such as Frederick Douglass. Slave owners' loss of compassion, the sign of humaneness, is a recurring theme in Frederick Douglass's 1845 narrative. Slavery, Douglass contended, placed in the hands of whites "the fatal poison of irresponsible power."[69] Douglass gives numerous grisly examples of his contention: murderous overseers, greedy urban craftsmen, and raping masters. But perhaps none of his examples is meant to be as moving as that of his slave mistress, Mrs. Auld. Originally a woman of independent means, Douglass describes her before "the fatal poison of irresponsible power" took full control of her:

> I was utterly astonished at her goodness. I scarcely knew how to behave towards her. She was entirely unlike any other white woman I had ever seen. I could not approach her as I was accustomed to approach other white ladies. My early instruction was all out of place. The crouching servility, usually so acceptable a quality in a slave, did not answer when manifested toward her. Her favor was not gained by it; she seemed to be disturbed by it. She did not deem it imprudent or unmannerly for a slave to look her in the face. The meanest slave was put fully at ease in her presence, and none left without feeling better for having seen her. Her face was made of heavenly smiles, and her voice of tranquil music.[70]

Mrs. Auld even disobeyed the law and taught Douglass some rudiments of spelling. However, Douglass states, "Slavery proved as injurious to her as it did to me. . . . Under its influence, the tender heart became stone, and the lamblike disposition gave way to one of tiger-like fierceness."[71]

"Cut Off from among Their People" is an extraordinary act of "heavy signifying." By using a strategy similar to Frederick Douglass's, Harris equates heterosexism and homophobia with slavery. For upholding heterosexism and homophobia, the church and the black family are oppressors. As rendered by Harris, they are like the Mrs. Auld of Douglass's narrative. They are kind to the black gay man when he is a child, and corrupted by intolerance years later. Their oppression has robbed them of compassion. The black family and their church, thus, have lost the sign of humanity.

Gender Configurations

The last section of this essay examines gay men and the problem of gender configurations. Specifically, in the black literary tradition gay men have been objects of ridicule for not possessing masculine-appearing behaviors. This ridicule was especially evident in the militant Black Power movement of the 1960s and 1970s. The militancy that characterized that movement placed an enormous emphasis on developing black "manhood." Manhood became a metaphor for the strength and potency necessary to overthrow the oppressive forces of a

[68]Ibid., p. 67.

[69]Frederick Douglass, *Narrative of the Life of Frederick Douglass: An American Slave* (1845; New York: New American Library, 1968), p. 48.

[70]Ibid.

[71]Ibid., pp. 52–53.

white racist society. Images of pathetic homosexuals were often used to show what black manhood was not or to what it could degenerate. For example, Haki Madhubuti (Don L. Lee) wrote in "Don't Cry Scream":

> swung on a faggot who politely
> scratched his ass in my presence.
> he smiled broken teeth stained from
> his over-used tongue, fisted-face.
> teeth dropped in tune with ray
> charles singing "yesterday."[72]

Concurrent with the Black Power movement's image of manhood was the development of the urban tough, loud, back-talking gay black man. This stereotype was seen on the Broadway stage in Melvin Van Peeble's *Ain't Supposed to Die a Natural Death,* but it was most clearly articulated by Antonio Fargas's character, Lindy, in the film *Car Wash.* When the black militant Abdullah accused Lindy of being another example of how the white man has corrupted the black man and robbed him of his masculinity, Lindy responded, "Honey, I'm more man than you'll ever be and more woman than you'll ever get." Lindy was a gratifying character because he was tough and articulate, yet his character was not revolutionary. Vito Russo comments in *The Celluloid Closet:* "Lindy is only a cartoon—[his] effect in the end was just that of the safe sissy who ruled the day in the topsy-turvy situations of Thirties comedies."[73] But the stereotype of the tough, loud, back-talking effeminate black gay man as an object of ridicule is revised in works by Samuel Delany, George Wolfe, and Billi Gordon.

Delany signifies on such a stereotype in a section of *The Motion of Light in Water* called "A black man . . . ? A gay man . . . ?" The section's title itself suggests the dilemma of a bifurcated identity that Julius Johnson discusses in his doctoral dissertation "Influence of Assimilation on the Psychosocial Adjustment of Black Homosexual Men."[74] Johnson documented the fact that some African American brothers become "black gay men" while others become "gay black men"; the designation often underscores painful decisions to have primary identities either in the black or in the gay community.

Delany's first memory of a gay black man was Herman, an outrageously effeminate musician who played the organ in his father's mortuary. As a child, Delany admits that he was as confused as he was amused by Herman's aggressive antics. When a casket delivery man asked Herman if he was "one of them faggots that likes men," Herman quickly signified on the man:

> "Me? Oh, chile', chile', you must be ill or something! . . . I swear, you must have been workin' out in the heat too long today. I do believe you must be sick!" Here he would feel the man's forehead, then removing his hand, look at the sweat that had come off on his own palm, touch his finger to his tongue, and declare, "Oh, my lord, you are tasty! . . . Imagine, honey! Thinkin' such nastiness like that about a woman like me! I mean, I just might faint right here, and you gonna have to carry me to a chair and fan me and bring me my smellin' salts!" Meanwhile he would be rubbing the man's chest and arms.[75]

Ultimately Delany's attitude toward Herman was one of ambivalence. Delany's sig on the stereotype was his recognition of its artifice. He recognized that there were many unanswered questions about Herman's sexual life: "Had he gone to bars? Had he gone to baths? . . . Had there been a long-term lover, waiting for him at home, unmet by, and unmentioned to, people like my father whom he worked for?"[76] Herman

[72]Haki Madhubuti, "Don't Cry Scream," quoted in Smitherman, *Talkin and Testifyin,* p. 142.

[73]Vito Russo, *The Celluloid Closet: Homosexuality in the Movies* (New York: Harper & Row, 1981), p. 229.

[74]Julius Marcus Johnson, "Influence of Assimilation on the Psychosocial Adjustment of Black Homosexual Men," doctoral dissertation, California School of Professional Psychology at Berkeley, 1981.

[75]Delany, *Motion of Light,* p. 219.

[76]Ibid., p. 221.

had played a role to survive in a heterosexist and homophobic world. In that role "Herman had a place in our social scheme," Delany wrote, "but by no means an acceptable place, and certainly not a place I wanted to fill."[77] Thus, as a teen, Delany remembered that he did not see Herman as a role model for a man. As an adult, however, Delany's opinion of Herman changed. He did not see Herman as a role model, but, he stated, "I always treasured the image of Herman's outrageous and defiant freedom to say absolutely anything. . . . Anything except, of course, I am queer, and I like men sexually better than women."[78]

In *The Colored Museum,* George Wolfe introduces Miss Roj, a black transvestite "dressed in striped patio pants, white go-go boots, a halter and cat-shaped sunglasses."[79] Wolfe makes it clear that Miss Roj is a subject most appropriate for African American literature by signifying, perhaps deliberately, on Ralph Ellison's *Invisible Man.* In particular, he signifies on its prologue, to create a powerful social comment on the alienation of the black urban poor. Wolfe's character, Miss Roj, comments that she "comes from another galaxy, as do all snap queens. That's right," she says, "I ain't just your regular oppressed American Negro. No-no-no! I am an extra-terrestrial, and I ain't talkin none of that shit you seen in the movies."[80] Compare that with the first two sentences in the prologue of *Invisible Man:* "I am an invisible man. No, I am not a spook like those who haunted Edgar Allan Poe; nor am I one of your Hollywood-movie ectoplasms."[81] Ellison's nameless protagonist lives in a hole lit by 1,369 bulbs; Miss Roj, whose real name the audience never learns, inhabits every Wednesday, Friday, and Saturday night a disco with blaring lights called the Bottomless Pit, "the watering hole for the wild and weary which asks the question, 'Is there life after Jherri-curl?' "[82] In Ellison's prologue the protagonist gets high on marijuana; Miss Roj gets drunk on Cuba libres [perhaps a veiled reference to popular drinks in the early 1950s, which is when *Invisible Man* was written] and proceeds *to snap,* that is, "when something strikes . . . [one's] fancy, when the truth comes piercing through the dark, well you just can't let it pass unnoticed. No darling. You must pronounce it with a snap [of the fingers]."[83]

Ellison's protagonist almost beats a man to death for calling him a nigger. Of course, one wonders how one can be beaten by invisibility. In a scene with a provocation and an outcome similar to Ellison's, Miss Roj "snaps" (signifies) on an assailant. She states:

> Like the time this asshole at Jones Beach decided to take issue with my culotte-sailor ensemble. This child, this muscle-bound Brooklyn thug in a skin-tight bikini, very skin-tight so the whole world can see that instead of a brain, God gave him an extra-thick piece of sausage. You know the kind who beat up on their wives for breakfast. Well he decided to blurt out while I walked by, "Hey look at da monkey coon in da faggit suit." Well, I walked up to the poor dear, very calmly lifted my hand and . . . (rapid snaps) A heart attack, right there on the beach. You don't believe it?[84]

Ellison's prologue ends with the protagonist listening to Louis Armstrong's "What Did I Do to Be So Black and Blue?"; the lights fade on Miss Roj dancing to Aretha Franklin's "Respect." As white Americans must have been puzzled, outraged, and even guilt-stricken after reading Ellison's *Invisible Man,* so too is the effect Miss Roj has had on the assimilated blacks Wolfe chose to confront. During performances of *The Col-*

[77]Ibid., p. 220.

[78]Ibid., p. 223.

[79]George Wolfe, *The Colored Museum,* in *American Theatre,* ed. James Leverett and M. Elizabeth Osborn, February 1987, p. 4.

[80]Ibid.

[81]Ralph Ellison, *Invisible Man* (New York: New American Library, 1952), p. 7.

[82]Wolfe, *Colored Museum,* p. 4.

[83]Ibid.

[84]Ibid.

ored Museum, black audience members have verbally attacked the actor playing Miss Roj and African American intellectuals have lambasted Wolfe for either not portraying blacks in their "best light" or for demeaning women.[85]

One of the oddest works to appear in black gay culture is Billi Gordon's cookbook, *You've Had Worse Things in Your Mouth.* The title itself is an act of signifying. While one may think it odd to include a cookbook here, it is important to keep in mind that that mode of presentation has been used to create social history in two other books by Afro-Americans. National Public Radio commentator and self-styled writing griot Vertamae Smart Grosvenor came to public prominence [with] her 1970 *Vibration Cooking; or the Travel Notes of a Geechee Girl.* The format of the book itself was signifying on the published travel narratives of eighteenth- and nineteenth-century whites such as Frederick Law Olmsted, whose observations on slavery have been treated by some historians as more reliable than artifacts actually left by the slaves. Norma Jean and Carole Darden's 1978 *Spoonbread and Strawberry Wine* was as much a family history of North Carolina middle-class blacks as it was a compendium of recipes.

Like George Wolfe, Gordon signifies repeatedly on racial stereotypes and on middle-class culture. On the cover of his cookbook, Gordon, a three-hundred-pound-plus dark-skinned black man, appears in drag. But not just any drag. He is wearing a red kerchief, a red-and-white checkered blouse, and a white apron, calling to mind some combination of Aunt Jemima and Hattie McDaniel in *Gone with the Wind.* As if that were not enough, Gordon signifies in every way imaginable on the American cultural stereotype of mammies as sexless, loyal, no-nonsense creatures. Gordon's character is lusty, vengeful, and flirtatious. Gordon appears in pictures surrounded by adoring muscled, swimsuit-clad white men; she wears bikini swimsuits, tennis outfits, long blond wigs, huge rebellious Afro-wigs, and shocking lamé evening wear. As for recipes, one is quite reluctant to try any of them, particularly those from the section called "Revenge Cooking" in which the ingredients include laxatives, seaweed, and entire bottles of Tabasco sauce. Billi Gordon signifies on the American stereotype of the mammy by reversing it and turning it upside down: His depiction of a mammy with a sex life is far from loyal, and certainly his character cannot and/or does not want to cook.

[85]See Thulani Davis, "Sapphire Attire: A Review," *Village Voice,* Nov. 11, 1986, p. 91; Roger Fristoe, "George C. Wolfe," *Louisville Courier-Journal,* p. I1; Jack Kroll, "Zapping Black Stereotypes, *Newsweek,* Nov. 17, 1986, p. 85.

Conclusion: Toward a Black Gay Aesthetic

Restricted by racism and heterosexism, writers such as Samuel Delany, Larry Duplechan, Essex Hemphill, Craig G. Harris, George Wolfe, and Billi Gordon have begun to create a literature that validates our lives as black and as gay. My critical reading of this literature relied upon techniques based in the African American tradition of signifying. The writers discussed in this essay are some of the newest members of the African American literary tradition. Clearly, they also seek to revise the aesthetics of that tradition. Homophobia and heterosexism are oppressive forces which must be eliminated from the social, scientific, critical, and imaginative writings within the African American literary tradition.

KAMARIA MUNTU
(1959–)

In a short statement about the purpose of her poetry and life, Kamaria Muntu, a deeply African-centered young woman wrote, "I seek to lift, restore, to engage you in the / vast dialectics of Black Woman experience / in this present world she inherited without choice. / My work is a testament to the invincibility of her spirit / Her eternal insistence on love." The invincibility of the spirit of which she speaks is a double invocation of both the assaults in life that she has endured and what she sees as the collective soul of all black women. This constant exchange, between the personal and the communal spirit, is at the heart of much of this new writer's poetry.

Muntu was born on November 1, 1959, in Baltimore. She attended Morgan State University, where she majored in theater arts. In 1994, she was diagnosed with cancer, but, in her words, she "does not claim it." Now living in Georgia, the mother of two children and an emerging name in Neo-Black Aesthetic literary circles, Muntu continues to remain active as a writer, a community activist, and a womanist.

Her poetry uses vivid imagery as it evokes African folklore and religion in an attempt to link personal narratives to the larger contexts of African and African American history, culture, and religion. In "Lymphoma," the confessional, autobiographical narrative of a woman with cancer, she boldly confronts the disease and demands that it yield to her refusal to die. In "Of Women and Spirit," she calls on her readers to transcend modernity in a search for ancient African deities. As she commits the struggle against her personal enemy to her verse, Muntu does so with exquisite style and tightly chosen words, proving the truth of her insistence that "a long time ago I fell in love / with the astonishing beauty of words. / I am yet uncovering their tremendous power."

❖❖❖

There are no reference sources on Muntu and her works. No collection of her verse has yet been published.

Of Women and Spirit

(for Julie Dash)

Dare to sketch Gullah scapes
to wade uncharted water where no flotilla ventures
Let Chango[1] lay the light of his fire on this water
until it glistens like spinster crystal
Go deep into the greenness
into the patois of snails, frogs, sea turtles and crabs
Inherit the swamp hip and okra stomp
Glide the glades of Damballah[2] chants
Now . . . . . . lay your camera on the women
Pride them with the beholding eyes of Sunday suitors
Arrest a medicine wheel of color godspells
A cotillion of gumbo spice
their hair
their skin
their walk of waves

---

[1]Chango: Yoruba deity warrior/king
god of thunder and lightning

[2]Damballah: war god in Dahomey tradition
often symbolized by the snake

Veiled Osun[3] golding the salty air
a delta vamp
Impel the mystique of clouds rising like cream
above the gelatin ocean
Implore the dewy nipples of Yemaya[4]
and Elegba's[5] smiling guile
Spy the children dancing their lyric in sand
Secret ceremonies with flying fish
Witness prodigal gulls wailing their mercies
across azure sky fields
As Oya's[6] lightning bolt strikes the fever of crossing
We gather the dust of our essence
in our hands
and import our pasts in glass jars
with no seals

Lymphoma

Metaphysical Causation:
You have forgotten that joy is
at the center of the universe

The road that brought me here
was paved with breasts that would not lactate
and the skeletons of two
who wore the skin of men
without the memory.
The road that brought me here
was paved with broad nutmeg
scented kitchens
lime gelatin
yeast
and laughing/crying/bitching women.
The road that brought me here
was paved with stained glass
cathedral horns and dubious reflection.
I mean this is how you found me cancer,
Hat cocked to the side

---

[3]Osun: Yoruba goddess of love, sensuality, and fertility
ruler of all that is aesthetically pleasing
Venus is her Greek equivalent

[4]Yemaya: Yoruba river deity
goddess associated with properties of motherhood
Virgin Mary most closely represents her Christian counterpart

[5]Elegba: guardian of the crossroads and opener of the way in Yoruba tradition
represented as High John de Conqueror in Afrikan American folklore

[6]Oya's lightning bolt: a preferred weapon of Oya
Yoruba warrior goddess of wind and transformation
first wife of Chango, who is also married to Osun

cigarette dangling between your foul lips
This is how you found me
Hook in my mouth
Fish belly turned inside out
Drowning in my own sacrificial blood
Untreated and unloved
Unhailed and unheld
And most tragic of all—
Uninformed.

Sinister guru
You are the crooked stick at the crossroads of life
Teaching me the erection dance of spirit
How to gather and knit my own spine
How to grease my own soul with grace
And the road that will take me there
Will ooze with my passion
for feminine sacrament
Clean water blessed by the Goddess and summer mornings
And I will retire in indigo wrinkles
and the faded steam of fulfilled dreams
Wedding the earth in a dust storm of faith
Remembered mostly
because I refused for so long
to die.

RANDALL KENAN
(1963–)

Although Randall Kenan is the youngest writer in this anthology, he has already produced two critically acclaimed works of fiction and is finishing up a travel book on black America. Like William Faulkner and John Wideman, Kenan wrote about a southern mythical place in his first two books and probably will revisit it in later works. Tims Creek is the name of Kenan's fictional North Carolina town, which is peopled with a great variety of characters, from a clairvoyant boy to a lustful preacher to a white gay lover from the North.

Kenan was born in Brooklyn, New York, on March 12, 1963, and grew up in rural Chinquapin, North Carolina. He received his B.A. in English from the University of North Carolina at Chapel Hill in 1984 and has been employed as an editor for Alfred A. Knopf. Currently, he teaches writing at Sarah Lawrence College and Columbia University. He has been a New York Foundation for the Arts Fellow and a MacDowell Colony Lila Wallace Reader's Digest Fellow.

His first novel, *A Visitation of Spirits,* was published in 1989. The *Chicago Tribune* declared it "breathtaking in its explicit virtuosity." His second work, *Let the Dead Bury Their Dead,* a collection of linked short stories, appeared in 1991. The *New York Times* called it "nothing short of a wonder-book: one of those striking literary anomalies, in the tradition of *Raintree County* and *The Country of the Pointed Firs,* that are nearly as difficult to classify as they are enjoyable to read and reread."

One of the remarkable pieces in the volume is "The Foundations of the Earth," a story about a grandmother's coming to terms with her dead grandson's homosexuality.

Kenan is now at work on a travel book. In the June–July, 1992, issue of the black magazine titled *American Visions,* he says of it, "For the last nine months, I've been trekking across the continent investigating the lives of African Americans for a presumptuous sort of 'Souls of Black Folks, Redux.'" It goes without saying that Randall Kenan is a talented young author to be watched.

❖❖❖

There is no serious criticism on this author, but Howard Frank Mosher's review of *Let the Dead Bury Their Dead* in the *New York Times Book Review,* June 14, 1992, is quite sensitive to the artist's craft.

Kenan comments on his writings in "Summer Reading" in *American Visions: The Magazine of Afro-American Culture* edited by Joanne Harris, vol. 7, no. 3 (June–July 1992).

The Foundations of the Earth

I

Of course they didn't pay it any mind at first: just a tractor—one of the most natural things in the world to see in a field—kicking dust up into the afternoon sky and slowly toddling off the road into a soybean field. And fields surrounded Mrs. Maggie MacGowan Williams's house, giving the impression that her lawn stretched on and on until it dropped off into the woods far by the way. Sometimes she was certain she could actually see the earth's curve—not merely the bend of the small hill on which her house sat but the great slope of the sphere, the way scientists explained it in books, a monstrous globe floating in a cold nothingness. She would sometimes sit by herself on the patio late of an evening, in the same chair she was sitting in now, sip from her Coca-Cola, and think about how big the earth must be to seem flat to the eye.

She wished she were alone now. It was Sunday.

"Now I wonder what that man is doing with a tractor out there today?"

They sat on Maggie's patio, reclined in that after-Sunday-dinner way—Maggie; the Right Reverend Hezekiah Barden, round and pompous as ever; Henrietta Fuchee, the prim and priggish music teacher and president of the First Baptist Church Auxiliary Council; Emma Lewis, Maggie's sometimes housekeeper; and Gabriel, Mrs. Maggie Williams's young, white, special guest—all looking out lazily into the early summer, watching the sun begin its slow downward arc, feeling the baked ham and the candied sweet potatoes and the fried chicken with the collard greens and green beans and beets settle in their bellies, talking shallow and pleasant talk, and sipping their Coca-Colas and bitter lemonade.

"Don't they realize it's Sunday?" Reverend Barden leaned back in his chair and tugged at his suspenders thoughtfully, eyeing the tractor as it turned into another row. He reached for a sweating glass of lemonade, his red bow tie afire in the penultimate beams of the day.

"I . . . I don't understand. What's wrong?" Maggie could see her other guests watching Gabriel intently, trying to discern why on earth he was present at Maggie MacGowan Williams's table.

"What you mean, what's wrong?" The Reverend Barden leaned forward and narrowed his eyes at the young man. "What's wrong is: it's Sunday."

"So? I don't . . ." Gabriel himself now looked embarrassed, glancing to Maggie, who wanted to save him but could not.

" 'So?' 'So?' " Leaning toward Gabriel and narrowing his eyes, Barden asked: "You're not from a churchgoing family, are you?"

"Well, no. Today was my first time in . . . Oh, probably ten years."

"Uh-huh." Barden corrected his posture, as if to say he pitied Gabriel's being an infidel but had the patience to instruct him. "Now you see, the Lord has declared Sunday as His day. It's holy. 'Six days shalt thou labor and do all thy work: but the seventh day is the sabbath of the Lord thy God: in it thou shalt not do any work, thou, nor thy son, nor thy daughter, thy manservant, nor thy maidservant, nor thy cattle, nor thy stranger that is within thy gates: for in six days the Lord made heaven and earth, the sea, and all that in them is, and rested the seventh day: wherefore, the Lord blessed the sabbath day, and hallowed it.' Exodus. Chapter twenty, verses nine and ten."

"Amen." Henrietta closed her eyes and rocked.

"Hez." Maggie inclined her head a bit to entreat the good Reverend to desist. He gave her an understanding smile, which made her cringe slightly, fearing her gesture might have been mistaken for a sign of intimacy.

"But, Miss Henrietta—" Emma Lewis tapped the tabletop, like a judge in court, changing the subject. "Like I was saying, I believe that Rick on *The Winds of Hope* is going to marry that gal before she gets too big with child, don't you?" Though Emma kept house for Maggie Williams, to Maggie she seemed more like a sister who came three days a week, more to visit than to clean.

"Now go on away from here, Emma." Henrietta did not look up from her empty cake plate, her glasses hanging on top of her sagging breasts from a silver chain. "Talking about that worldly foolishness on TV. You know I don't pay that mess any attention." She did not want the Reverend to know that she secretly watched afternoon soap operas, just like Emma and all the other women in the congregation. Usually she gossiped to beat the band about this rich heifer and that handsome hunk whenever she found a fellow TV-gazer. Buck-toothed hypocrite, Maggie thought. She knew the truth: Henrietta, herself a widow now on ten years, was sweet on the widower minister, who in turn, alas, had his eye on Maggie.

"Now, Miss Henrietta, we was talking about it t'other day. Don't you think he's apt to marry her soon?" Emma's tone was insistent.

"I *don't know,* Emma." Visibly agitated, Henrietta donned her glasses and looked into the fields. "I wonder who that is anyhow?"

Annoyed by Henrietta's rebuff, Emma stood and began to collect the few remaining dishes. Her purple-and-yellow floral print dress hugged her ample hips. "It's that ole Morton Henry that Miss Maggie leases that piece of land to." She walked toward the door, into the house. "He ain't no God-fearing man."

"Well, that's plain to see." The Reverend glanced over to Maggie. She shrugged.

They are ignoring Gabriel, Maggie thought. She had invited them to dinner after church services thinking it would be pleasant for Gabriel to meet other people in Tims Creek. But generally they chose not to see him, and when they did it was with ill-concealed scorn or petty curiosity or annoyance. At first the conversation seemed civil enough. But the ice was never truly broken, questions still buzzed around the talk like horseflies, Maggie could tell. "Where you from?" Henrietta had asked. "What's your line of work?" Barden had asked. While Gabriel sat there with a look on his face somewhere between peace and pain. But Maggie refused to believe she had made a mistake. At this stage of her life she depended on no one for anything, and she was certainly not dependent on the approval of these self-important fools.

She had been steeled by anxiety when she picked Gabriel up at the airport that Friday night. But as she caught sight of him stepping from the jet and greeted him, asking about the weather in Boston; and after she had ushered him to her car and watched him slide in, seeming quite at home; though it still felt awkward, she thought: I'm doing the right thing.

II

"Well, thank you for inviting me, Mrs. Williams. But I don't understand . . . Is something wrong?"

"*Wrong?* No, nothing's wrong, Gabriel. I just thought it'd be good to see you. Sit and talk to you. We didn't have much time at the funeral."

"Gee . . . I—"

"You don't want to make an old woman sad, now do you?"

"Well, Mrs. Williams, if you put it like that, how can I refuse?"

"Weekend after next then?"

There was a pause in which she heard muted voices in the wire.

"Okay."

After she hung up the phone and sat down in her favorite chair in the den, she heaved a momentous sigh. Well, she had done it. At last. The weight of uncertainty would be lifted. She could confront him face to face. She wanted to know about her grandboy, and Gabriel was the only one who could tell her what she wanted to know. It was that simple. Surely, he realized what this invitation meant. She leaned back looking out the big picture window onto the tops of the brilliantly blooming crepe myrtle trees in the yard, listening to the grandfather clock mark the time.

III

Her grandson's funeral had been six months ago, but it seemed much longer. Perhaps the fact that Edward had been gone away from home so long without seeing her, combined with the weeks and days and hours and minutes she had spent trying not to think about him and all the craziness that had surrounded his death, somehow lengthened the time.

At first she chose to ignore it, the strange and bitter sadness that seemed to have overtaken her every waking moment. She went about her daily life as she had done for thirty-odd years, overseeing her stores, her land, her money; buying groceries, paying bills, shopping, shopping; going to church and talking to her few good living friends and the few silly fools she was obliged to suffer. But all day, dusk to dawn, and especially at night, she had what the field-workers called "a monkey on your back," when the sun beats down so hot it makes you delirious; but her monkey chilled and angered her, born not of the sun but of a profound loneliness, an oppressive emptiness, a stabbing guilt. Sometimes she even wished she were a drinking woman.

The depression had come with the death of Edward, though its roots reached farther back, to the time he seemed to have vanished. There had been so many years of asking other members of the family: Have you heard from him? Have you seen him? So many years of only a Christmas card or birthday card a few days early, or a cryptic, taciturn phone call on Sunday mornings, and then no calls at all. At some point she realized she had no idea where he was or how to get in touch with him. Mysteriously, he would drop a line to his half-sister, Clarissa, or drop a card without a return address. He was gone. Inevitably, she had to ask: Had she done something evil to the boy to drive him away? Had she tried too hard to make sure he became nothing like his father and grandfather? I was as good a mother as a woman can claim to be, she thought: from the cradle on he had all the material things he needed, and he certainly didn't want for attention, for care; and I trained him proper, he was a well-mannered and upright young fellow when he left here for college. Oh, I was proud of that boy, winning a scholarship to Boston University. Tall, handsome like his granddad. He'd make somebody a good . . .

So she continued picking out culprits: school, the cold North, strange people, strange ideas. But now in her crystalline hindsight she could lay no blame on anyone but Edward. And the more she remembered battles with the mumps and the measles and long division and taunts from his schoolmates, the more she became aware of her true anger. He owes me respect, damn it. The least he can do is keep in touch. Is that so much to ask?

But before she could make up her mind to find him and confront him with her fury, before she could cuss him out good and call him an ungrateful, no-account bastard just like his father, a truck would have the heartless audacity to skid into her grandchild's car one rainy night in Springfield and end his life at twenty-seven, taking that opportunity away from her forever. When they told her of his death she cursed her weakness. Begging God for another chance. But instead He gave her something she had never imagined.

Clarissa was the one to finally tell her. "Grandma," she had said, "Edward's been living with another man all these years."

"So?"

"No, Grandma. Like man and wife."

Maggie had never before been so paralyzed by news. One question answered, only to be replaced by a multitude. Gabriel had come with the body, like an interpreter for the dead. They had been living together in Boston, where Edward worked in a bookstore. He came, head bowed, rheumy-eyed, exhausted. He gave her no explanation; nor had she asked him for any, for he displayed the truth in his vacant and humble glare and had nothing to offer but the penurious tribute of his trembling hands. Which was more than she wanted.

In her world she had been expected to be tearless, patient, comforting to other members of the family; folk were meant to sit back and say, "Lord, ain't she taking it well. I don't think I could be so calm if my grandboy had've died so young." Magisterially she had done her duty; she had taken it all in stride. But her world began to hopelessly unravel that summer night at the wake in the Raymond Brown Funeral Home, among the many somber-bright flower arrangements, the fluorescent lights, and the gleaming bronze casket, when Gabriel tried to tell her how sorry he was . . . How dare he? This pathetic, stumbling, poor trashy white boy, to throw his sinful lust for her grandbaby in her face, as if to bury a grandchild weren't bad enough. Now this abomination had to be flaunted. —Sorry, indeed! The nerve! Who the hell did he think he was to parade their shame about?

Her anger was burning so intensely that she knew if she didn't get out she would tear his heart from his chest, his eyes from their sockets, his testicles from their sac. With great haste she took her leave, brushing off the funeral director and her brother's wives and husband's brothers—they all probably thinking her overcome with grief rather than anger—and had Clarissa drive her home. When she got to the house she filled a tub with water as hot as she could stand it and a handful of bath oil beads, and slipped in, praying her hatred would mingle with the mist and evaporate, leaving her at least sane.

Next, sleep. Healing sleep, soothing sleep, sleep to make the world go away, sleep like death. Her mama had told her that sleep was the best medicine God ever made. When things get too rough—go to bed. Her family had been known as the family that retreated to bed. Ruined crop? No money? Get some shut-eye. Maybe it'll be better in the morning. Can't be worse. Maggie didn't give a damn where Gabriel was to sleep that night; someone else would deal with it. She didn't care about all the people who would come to the house after the wake to the Sitting Up, talking, eating, drinking, watching over the still body till sunrise; they could take care of themselves. The people came; but Maggie slept. From deeps under deeps of slumber she sensed her granddaugher stick her head in the door and whisper, asking Maggie if she wanted something to eat. Maggie didn't stir. She slept. And in her sleep she dreamed.

She dreamed she was Job sitting on his dung heap, dressed in sackcloth and ashes, her body covered with boils, scratching with a stick, sending away Eliphaz and Bildad and Zophar and Elihu, who came to counsel her, and above her the sky boiled and churned and the air roared, and she matched it, railing against God, against her life—*Why? Why? Why did you kill him, you heartless old fiend? Why make me live to see him die? What earthly purpose could you have in such a wicked deed? You are God, but you are not good.*

Speak to me, damn it. Why? Why? Why? Hurricanes whipped and thunder ripped through a sky streaked by lightning, and she was lifted up, spinning, spinning, and Edward floated before her in the rushing air and quickly turned around into the comforting arms of Gabriel, winged, who clutched her grandboy to his bosom and soared away, out of the storm. Maggie screamed and the winds grew stronger, and a voice, gentle and sweet, not thunderous as she expected, spoke to her from the whirlwind: *Who is this that darkeneth counsel by words without knowledge? Gird up now thy loins like a man; for I will demand of thee, and answer thou me. Where wast thou when I laid the foundations of the earth? Declare if thou hast understanding* . . . The voice spoke of the myriad creations of the universe, the stupendous glory of the Earth and its inhabitants. But Maggie was not deterred in the face of the maelstrom, saying: *Answer me, damn you: Why?,* and the winds began to taper off and finally halted, and Maggie was alone, standing on water. A fish, what appeared to be a mackerel, stuck its head through the surface and said: *Kind woman, be not aggrieved and put your anger away. Your arrogance has clouded your good mind. Who asked you to love? Who asked you to hate?* The fish dipped down with a plip and gradually Maggie too began to slip down into the water, down, down, down, sinking, below depths of reason and love, down into the dark unknown of her own mind, down, down, down.

Maggie MacGowan Williams woke the next morning to the harsh chatter of a bluejay chasing a mockingbird just outside her window, a racket that caused her to open her eyes quickly to blinding sunlight. Squinting, she looked about the room, seeing the chest of drawers that had once belonged to her mother and her mother's mother before that, the chairs, the photographs on the wall, the television, the rug thickly soft, the closet door slightly ajar, the bureau, the mirror atop the bureau, and herself in the mirror, all of it bright in the crisp morning light. She saw herself looking, if not refreshed, calmed and within her the rage had gone, replaced by a numb humility and a plethora of questions. Questions. Questions. Questions.

Inwardly she had felt beatific that day of the funeral, ashamed at her anger of the day before. She greeted folk gently, softly, with a smile, her tones honey-flavored but solemn, and she reassumed the mantle of one-who-comforts-more-than-needing-comfort.

The immediate family had gathered at Maggie's house—Edward's father, Tom, Jr.; Tom, Jr.'s wife, Lucille; the grandbaby, Paul (Edward's brother); Clarissa. Raymond Brown's long black limousine took them from the front door of Maggie's house to the church, where the yard was crammed with people in their greys and navy blues, dark browns, and deep, deep burgundies. In her new humility she mused: When, oh when will we learn that death is not so somber, not something to mourn so much as celebrate? We should wear fire reds, sun oranges, hello greens, ocean-deep blues, and dazzling, welcome-home whites. She herself wore a bright dress of saffron and a blue scarf. She thought Edward would have liked it.

The family lined up and Gabriel approached her. As he stood before her—raven-haired, pink-skinned, abject, eyes bloodshot—she experienced a bevy of conflicting emotions: disgust, grief, anger, tenderness, fear, weariness, pity. Nevertheless she *had* to be civil, *had* to make a leap of faith and of understanding. Somehow she felt it had been asked of her. And though there were still so many questions, so much to sort out, for now she would mime patience, pretend to be accepting, feign peace. Time would unravel the rest.

She reached out, taking both his hands into her own, and said, the way she would to an old friend: "How have you been?"

IV

"But now, Miss Maggie . . ."

She sometimes imagined the good Reverend Barden as a toad-frog or an impotent bull. His rantings and ravings bored her, and his clumsy advances repelled her; and when he tried to impress her with his holiness and his goodness, well . . .

"... that man should know better than to be plowing on a Sunday. Sunday! Why, the Lord said . . ."

"Reverend, I know what the Lord said. And I'm sure Morton Henry knows what the Lord said. But I am not the Lord, Reverend, and if Morton Henry wants to plow the west field on Sunday afternoon, well, it's his soul, not mine."

"But, Maggie. Miss Maggie. It's—"

"Well,"—Henrietta Fuchee sat perched to interject her five cents into the debate—"but, Maggie. It's your land! Now, Reverend, doesn't it say somewhere in Exodus that a man, or a woman in this case, a woman is responsible for the deeds or misdeeds of someone in his or her employ, especially on her property?"

"But he's not an emplo—"

"Well,"—Barden scratched his head—"I think I know what you're talking about, Henrietta. It may be in Deuteronomy . . . or Leviticus . . . part of the Mosaic Law, which . . ."

Maggie cast a quick glance at Gabriel. He seemed to be interested in and entertained by this contest of moral superiority. There was certainly something about his face . . . but she could not stare. He looked so *normal* . . .

"Well, I don't think you should stand for it, Maggie."

"Henrietta? What do you . . . ? Look, if you want him to stop, *you* go tell him what the Lord said. I—"

The Right Reverend Hezekiah Barden stood, hiking his pants up to his belly. "Well, *I* will. A man's soul is a valuable thing. And I can't risk your own soul being tainted by the actions of one of your sharecroppers."

"My soul? Sharecropper—he's not a sharecropper. He leases that land. I—wait! . . . Hezekiah! . . . This doesn't . . ."

But Barden had stepped off the patio onto the lawn and was headed toward the field, marching forth like old Nathan on his way to confront King David.

"Wait, Reverend." Henrietta hopped up, slinging her black pocketbook over her left shoulder. "Well, Maggie?" She peered at Maggie defiantly, as if to ask: *Where do you stand?*

"Now, Henrietta, I—"

Henrietta pivoted, her moral righteousness jagged and sharp as a shard of glass. "Somebody has to stand up for right!" She tromped off after Barden.

Giggling, Emma picked up the empty glasses. "I don't think ole Morton Henry gone be too happy to be preached at this afternoon."

Maggie looked from Emma to Gabriel in bewilderment, at once annoyed and amused. All three began to laugh out loud. As Emma got to the door she turned to Maggie. "Hon, you better go see that they don't get into no fist-fight, don't you think? You know that Reverend don't know when to be quiet." She looked to Gabriel and nodded knowingly. "You better go with her, son," and was gone into the house; her molasses-thick laughter sweetening the air.

Reluctantly Maggie stood, looking at the two figures—Henrietta had caught up with Barden—a tiny cloud of dust rising from their feet. "Come on, Gabe. Looks like we have to go referee."

Gabriel walked beside her, a broad smile on his face. Maggie thought of her grandson being attracted to this tall white man. She tried to see them together and couldn't. At that moment she understood that she was being called on to realign her thinking about men and women, and men and men, and even women and women. Together . . . the way Adam and Eve were meant to be together.

V

Initially she found it difficult to ask the questions she wanted to ask. Almost impossible.

They got along well on Saturday. She took him out to dinner; they went shopping. All the while she tried with all her might to convince herself that she felt comfortable with this white man, with this homosexual, with this man who had slept with her grandboy. Yet he managed to impress her with his easygoing manner and openness and humor.

"Mrs. W." He had given her a *nickname,* of all things. No one had given her a nickname since . . . "Mrs. W., you sure you don't want to try on some swimsuits?"

She laughed at his kind-hearted jokes, seeing, oddly enough, something about him very like Edward; but then that thought would make her sad and confused.

Finally that night over coffee at the kitchen table she began to ask what they had both gingerly avoided.

"Why didn't he just tell me?"

"He was afraid, Mrs. W. It's just that simple."

"Of what?"

"That you might disown him. That you might stop . . . well, you know, loving him, I guess."

"Does your family know?"

"Yes."

"How do they take it?"

"My mom's fine. She's great. Really. She and Edward got along swell. My dad. Well, he'll be okay for a while, but every now and again we'll have these talks, you know, about cures and stuff and sometimes it just gets heated. I guess it'll just take a little more time with him."

"But don't you *want* to be normal?"

"Mrs. W., I *am.* Normal."

"I see."

They went to bed at one-thirty that morning. As Maggie buttoned up her nightgown, Gabriel's answers whizzed about her brain; but they brought along more damnable questions and Maggie went to bed feeling betrayal and disbelief and revulsion and anger.

In church that next morning with Gabriel, she began to doubt the wisdom of having asked him to come. As he sat beside her in the pew, as the Reverend Barden sermonized on Jezebel and Ahab, as the congregation unsuccessfully tried to disguise their curiosity—("What is that white boy doing here with Maggie Williams? Who is he? Where he come from?")—she wanted Gabriel to go ahead and tell her what to think: *We're perverts* or *You're wrong-headed, your church has poisoned your mind against your own grandson; if he had come out to you, you would have rejected him. Wouldn't you?* Would she have?

Barden's sermon droned on and on that morning; the choir sang; after the service people politely and gently shook Gabriel and Maggie's hands and then stood off to the side, whispering, clearly perplexed.

On the drive back home, as if out of the blue, she asked him: "Is it hard?"

"Ma'am?"

"Being who you are? What you are?"

He looked over at her, and she could not meet his gaze with the same intensity that had gone into her question. "Being gay?"

"Yes."

"Well, I have no choice."

"So I understand. But is it hard?"

"Edward and I used to get into arguments about that, Mrs. W." His tone altered a bit. He spoke more softly, gently, the way a widow speaks of her dead husband. Or, indeed, the way a widower speaks of his dead husband. "He used to say it was harder being black in this country than gay. Gays can always pass for straight; but blacks can't always pass for white. And most can never pass."

"And what do you think now?"

"Mrs. W., I think *life* is hard, you know?"

"Yes. I know."

VI

Death had first introduced itself to Maggie when she was a child. Her grandfather and grandmother both died before she was five; her father died when she was nine; her mother when she was twenty-five; over the years all her brothers except one. Her husband ten years ago. Her first memories of death: watching the women wash a cold body: the look of brown skin darkening, hardening: the corpse laid out on a cooling board, wrapped in a winding-cloth, before interment: fear of ghosts, bodyless souls: troubled sleep. So much had changed in seventy years; now there were embalming, funeral homes, morticians, insurance policies, bronze caskets, a bureaucratic wall between deceased and bereaved. Among the many things she regretted about Edward's death was not being able to touch his body. It made his death less real. But so much about the world seemed unreal to her these dark, dismal, and gloomy days. Now the flat earth was said to be round and bumblebees were not supposed to fly.

What was supposed to be and what truly was. Maggie learned these things from magazines and television and books; she loved to read. From her first week in that small schoolhouse with Miss Clara Oxendine, she had wanted to be a teacher. School: the scratchy chalkboard, the dusty-smelling textbooks, labyrinthine grammar and spelling and arithmetic, geography, reading out loud, giving confidence to the boy who would never learn to read well, correcting addition and subtraction problems, the taste and the scent of the schoolroom, the heat of the potbellied stove in January. She liked that small world; for her it was large. Yet how could she pay for enough education to become a teacher? Her mother would smile, encouragingly, when young Maggie would ask her, not looking up from her sewing, and merely say: "We'll find a way."

However, when she was fourteen she met a man named Thomas Williams, he sixteen going on thirty-nine. Infatuation replaced her dreams and murmured to her in languages she had never heard before, whispered to her another tale: *You will be a merchant's wife.*

Thomas Williams would come a-courting on Sunday evenings for two years, come driving his father's red Ford truck, stepping out with his biscuit-shined shoes, his one good Sunday suit, his hat cocked at an impertinent angle, and a smile that would make cold butter drip. But his true power lay in his tongue. He would spin yarns and tell tales that would make the oldest storyteller slap his knee and declare: "Hot damn! Can't that boy lie!" He could talk a possum out of a tree. He spoke to Maggie about his dream of opening his own store, a dry-goods store, and then maybe two or three or four. An audacious dream for a seventeen-year-old black boy, son of a farmer in 1936—and he promised, oh, how he promised, to keep Maggie by his side through it all.

Thinking back, on the other side of time and dreams, where fantasies and wishing had been realized, where she sat rich and alone, Maggie wondered what Thomas Williams could possibly have seen in that plain brown girl. Himself the son of a farmer with his own land, ten sons and two daughters, all married and doing well. There she was, poorer than a skinned rabbit, and not that pretty. Was he looking for a woman who would not flinch at hard work?

Somehow, borrowing from his father, from his brothers, working two, three jobs at the shipyards, in the fields, with Maggie taking in sewing and laundry, cleaning houses, saving, saving, saving, they opened their store; and were married. Days, weeks, years of days, weeks of days, weeks of inventory and cleaning and waiting on people and watching over the dry-goods store, which became a hardware store in the sixties while the one store became two. They were prosperous; they were respected; they owned property. At seventy she now wanted for nothing. Long gone was the dream of a schoolhouse and little children who skinned their knees and the teaching of the ABCs. Some days she imagined she had two lives and she preferred the original dream to the flesh-and-blood reality.

Now, at least, she no longer had to fight bitterly with her pompous, self-satisfied, driven, blaspheming husband, who worked seven days a week, sixteen hours a day, money-grubbing and mean though—outwardly—flamboyantly generous; a man who lost interest in her bed after her first and only son, Thomas Jr., arrived broken in heart, spirit, and brain upon delivery; a son whose only true achievement in life was to illegitimately produce Edward by some equally brainless waif of a girl, now long vanished; a son who practically thrust the few-week-old infant into Maggie's arms, then flew off to a life of waste, sloth, petty crime, and finally a menial job in one of her stores and an ignoble marriage to a woman who could not conceal her greedy wish for Maggie to die.

Her life now was life that no longer had bite or spit or fire. She no longer worked. She no longer had to worry about Thomas's philandering and what pretty young thing he was messing with now. She no longer had the little boy whom Providence seemed to have sent her to maintain her sanity, to moor her to the Earth, and to give her vast energies focus.

In a world not real, is there truly guilt in willing reality to cohere through the life of another? Is that such a great sin? Maggie had turned to the boy—young, brown, handsome—to hold on to the world itself. She now saw that clearly. How did it happen? The mental slipping and sliding that allowed her to meld and mess and confuse her life with his, his rights with her wants, his life with her wish? He would not be like his father or his grandfather; he would rise up, go to school, be strong, be honest, upright. He would be; she would be . . . a feat of legerdemain; a sorcery of vicariousness in which his victory was her victory. He was her champion. Her hope.

Now he was gone. And now she had to come to terms with this news of his being "gay," as the world called what she had been taught was an unholy abomination. Slowly it all came together in her mind's eye: Edward.

He should have known better. I should have known better. I must learn better.

VII

They stood there at the end of the row, all of them waiting for the tractor to arrive and for the Reverend Hezekiah Barden to save the soul of Morton Henry.

Morton saw them standing there from his mount atop the green John Deere as it bounced across the broken soil. Maggie could make out the expression on his face: confusion. Three blacks and a white man out in the fields to see him. Did his house burn down? His wife die? The President declare war on Russia?

A big, red-haired, red-faced man, his face had so many freckles he appeared splotched. He had a big chew of tobacco in his left jaw and he spat out the brown juice as he came up the edge of the row and put the clutch in neutral.

"How you all today? Miss Maggie?"

"Hey, Morton."

Barden started right up, thumbs in his suspenders, and reared back on his heels. "Now I spect you're a God-fearing man?"

"Beg pardon?"

"I even spect you go to church from time to time?"

"Church? Miss Maggie, I—"

The Reverend held up his hand. "And I warrant you that your preacher—where *do* you go to church, son?"

"I go to—wait a minute. What's going on here? Miss Maggie—"

Henrietta piped up. "It's Sunday! You ain't supposed to be working and plowing fields on a Sunday!"

Morton Henry looked over to Maggie, who stood there in the bright sun, then to Gabriel, as if to beg him to speak, make some sense of this curious event. He scratched his head. "You mean to tell me you all come out here to tell me I ain't suppose to plow this here field?"

"Not on Sunday you ain't. It's the Lord's Day."

" 'The Lord's Day'?" Morton Henry was visibly amused. He tongued at the wad of tobacco in his jaw. "The Lord's Day." He chuckled out loud.

"Now it ain't no laughing matter, young man." The Reverend's voice took on a dark tone.

Morton seemed to be trying to figure out who Gabriel was. He spat. "Well, I tell you, Reverend. If the Lord wants to come plow these fields I'd be happy to let him."

"You . . ." Henrietta stomped her foot, causing dust to rise. "You can't talk about the Lord like that. You're using His name in vain."

"I'll talk about Him any way I please to." Morton Henry's face became redder by the minute. "I got two jobs, five head of children, and a sick wife, and the Lord don't seem too worried about that. I spect I ain't gone worry to much about plowing this here field on His day none neither."

"Young man, you can't—"

Morton Henry looked to Maggie. "Now, Miss Maggie, this is your land, and if you don't want me to plow it, I'll give you back your lease and you can pay me my money and find somebody else to tend this here field!"

Everybody looked at Maggie. How does this look, she couldn't help thinking, a black woman defending a white man against a black minister? Why the *hell* am I here having to do this? she fumed. Childish, hypocritical idiots and fools. Time is just slipping, slipping away and all they have to do is fuss and bother about other folk's business while their own houses are burning down. God save their souls. She wanted to yell this, to cuss them out and stomp away and leave them to their ignorance. But in the end, what good would it do?

She took a deep breath. "Morton Henry. You do what you got to do. Just like the rest of us."

Morton Henry bowed his head to Maggie, "Ma'am," turned to the others with a gloating grin, "Scuse me," put his gear in first, and turned down the next row.

"Well—"

Barden began to speak but Maggie just turned, not listening, not wanting to hear, thinking: When, Lord, oh when will we learn? Will we ever? *Respect,* she thought. Oh how complicated.

They followed Maggie, heading back to the house, Gabriel beside her, tall and silent, the afternoon sunrays romping in his black hair. How curious the world had become that she would be asking a white man to exonerate her in the eyes of her own grandson; how strange that at seventy, when she had all the laws and rules down pat, she would have to begin again, to learn. But all this stuff and bother would have to come later, for now she felt so, so tired, what with the weekend's activities weighing on her three-score-and-ten-year-old bones and joints; and she wished it were sunset, and she alone on her patio, contemplating the roundness and flatness of the earth, and slipping softly and safely into sleep.

Credits and Acknowledgments

Copyrighted works, listed in the order of first appearance by author, are printed by permission of the following sources.

Part I "Go Down, Moses, Way Down in Egypt's Land"

Mary Francis Berry and **John W. Blassingame.** Table I from *Long Memory: The Black Experience in America* by Mary Frances Berry and John W. Blassingame. Copyright © 1982 by Oxford University Press, Inc. Reprinted by permission.

Willis Laurence James. Examples of folk cries from Willis Laurence James, "The Romance of the Negro Folk Cry in America," *Phylon,* XVI, No. 1 (1955). Copyright © 1955 by Atlanta University. Reprinted by permission.

Robert Winslow Gordon. "A Negro 'Shouts' from Georgia" by Robert Winslow Gordon. Copyright © 1927 by The New York Times Co. Reprinted by permission.

Harold Courlander. Excerpt from *Negro Folk Songs* by Harold Courlander. Copyright © 1963 by Columbia University Press. Reprinted with permission of the publisher.

Gordon Innes. Excerpt from "Sunjata" by Banna Kanute appearing in *Sunjata, Three Mandinka Versions* by Gordon Innes (London, School of Oriental and African Studies, 1974). Used by permission.

D. T. Niane. "Mandan People's Praisesong" from *Sundiata: An Epic of Old Mali* by D. T. Niane, translated by G. D. Pickett. Used by permission of Presence Africaine.

Seydou Camara. Excerpt from "Hunter's Praisesong" appearing in *The Sons of Seydou Camara,* Vol. 1, *Kambili,* ed. Charles Bird. Used with permission by Indiana University African Studies Center; Excerpt from "Griot's Sermon" appearing in *The Sons of Seydou Camara,* Vol. 1, *Kambili,* ed. Charles Bird. Used with permission by Indiana University African Studies Center; Lines 85 86 from "Kambili" by Seydou Camara from *The Songs of Seydou Camara, Volume 1: Kambili,* edited by Charles Bird. Reprinted by permission of the Indiana University African Studies Center.

Banna Kanute. From Banna Kanute's "Sunjata" from *Sunjata: Three Mandinka Versions,* translated by Gordon Innes. Translation copyright 1974. Reprinted by permission of the School of Oriental and African Studies, University of London.

D. T. Niane. "Sogolon's Prayer" from *Sundiata: An Epic of Old Mali* by D. T. Niane, translated by G. D. Pickett. Used by permission of Presence Africaine; "Niama" from *Sundiata: An Epic of Old Mali* by D. T. Niane, translated by G. D. Pickett. Used by permission of Presence Africaine; Excerpt from *Mwindo Epic: From the Banyanga (Zaire),* ed. and trans. Daniel Biebuyck and Kahombo C. Mateene. Copyright © 1969 The Regents of the University of California. Used by permission.

Seydou Camara. Excerpt from "Warrior Kanji's Lament" appearing in *The Sons of Seydou Camara,* Vol. 1, *Kambili,* ed. Charles Bird. Used with permission by Indiana University African Studies Center.

J. H. Kwabena Nketia. Examples from *The Music of Africa* by J. H. Kwabena Nketia. Copyright © 1974 by W. W. Norton & Company, Inc. Reprinted by permission of W. W. Norton & Company, Inc.

Eileen Southern. "Jesus on de Water-Side" and "Nobody Knows de Trouble I've Had" from *Slave Songs of the United States.*

A. B. Ellis. "Why the Hare Runs Away" from *The Ewe-Speaking Peoples of the Slave Coast of West Africa* by A. B. Ellis. Used by permission of Benin Press, Ltd.

Elsie Clews Parsons. "Tar Baby" by Elsie Clews Parsons. Reproduced by permission of the American Folklore Society from *Journal of American Folklore,* 1922. Not for further reproduction.

Georgia Writers' Project. "Two Tales of the Flying Africans" from *Drums and Shadows: Survival Studies Among the Georgia Coastal Negroes* by the Savannah Unit, Georgia Writers' Project, Work Projects Administration. Copyright © 1940 by the University of Georgia.

Zora Neale Hurston. "Two Tales from Eatonville, Florida" by Zora Neale Hurston. Reproduced by permission of the American Folklore Society from *Journal of American Folklore, 1931.* Not for further reproduction.

Newbell N. Puckett. "Voodoo and Witches" from *Folk Beliefs of the Southern Negro* by Newbell N. Puckett. University of North Carolina Press, 1926.

W. C. Hendricks. "The Headless Hant" from *Bundles of Troubles and Other Tarheel Tales,* ed. W. C. Hendricks. Copyright © 1943, Duke University Press, Durham, N.C. Reprinted with permission.

Jupiter Hammon. From "A Winter Piece" in *Jupiter Hammon and the Biblical Beginnings of African American Literature* by Sondra O'Neale. Used with permission of Scarecrow Press.

Lemuel B. Haynes. "Liberty Further Extended" by Lemuel B. Haynes. (bMS Am 1907 (608)) by permission of the Houghton Library, Harvard University; Ruth Bogin, "'The Battle of Lexington': A Patriotic Ballad by Lemuel Haynes," *William and Mary Quarterly,* 3d Ser., Vol. XLII, No. 4 (October 1985), pp. 501–06. Shelf mark, bMS Am 1907 (601). By permission of the Houghton Library, Harvard University.

John Marrant. "A Sermon Preached on the 14th Day of June 1789" by John Marrant. Copyright © A. Potkay and S. Burr (Editors). From *Black Atlantic Writers of the Eighteenth Century: Living the New Exodus in England and the Americas* by

A. Potkay and S. Burr (Editors). Reprinted with permission of St. Martin's Press, Incorporated.

PART II "TELL OLE PHARAOH, LET MY PEOPLE GO"

Zora Neale Hurston. "Massa and the Bear" from *Mules and Men* by Zora Neale Hurston. Copyright © 1935 by Zora Neale Hurston. Copyright renewed 1963 by John C. Hurston and Joel Hurston. Reprinted by permission of HarperCollins Publishers, Inc.

Richard M. Dorson. "John Steals a Pig and a Sheep" from *Negro Folktales in Michigan,* collected and edited by Richard M. Dorson, p. 57. Copyright © 1956 by the President and Fellows of Harvard College. Used by permission of the Richard M. Dorson Trust.

Frederick Douglass. From "What to the Slave Is the Fourth of July?: An Address Delivered in Rochester, New York, on 5 July 1852" from *The Frederick Douglass Papers,* Series One: Speeches, Debates, and Interviews. Volume 2: 1847, 1854, edited by John W. Blassingame. Copyright © 1982 by Yale University Press. Reprinted by permission.

Harriet Jacobs. Footnotes by Walter Teller in Chapters XXIX, XXX, and XLI of Linda Brent, from *Incidents in the Life of a Slave Girl,* edited by L. Maria Child, copyright © 1973 by Walter Magnes Teller, reprinted by permission of Harcourt Brace & Company.

PART III "NO MORE SHALL THEY IN BONDAGE TOIL"

Guy B. Johnson. "John Henry" reprinted from *John Henry: Tracking Down a Negro Legend,* by Guy B. Johnson. Copyright © 1929 by the University of North Carolina Press. Used by permission of the publisher.

W. C. Handy. "St. Louis Blues" by W. C. Handy. International copyright, Handy Brothers Music Co. Inc. Reprinted by permission.

Lyle Saxon. "Dry Bones" from *Gumbo Ya-Ya* by Lyle Saxon. Copyright 1945, © renewed 1973 by the Louisiana State Library. Reprinted by permission of Houghton Mifflin Company. All rights reserved.

J. Mason Brewer. "Swapping Dreams" from "Juneteenth" by J. Mason Brewer in *Tone the Bell Easy,* edited by J. Frank Dobie. Publications of the Texas Folklore Society, No. X, 1932. Used by permission; "Lias' Revelation" from "Juneteenth" by J. Mason Brewer in *Tone the Bell Easy,* edited by J. Frank Dobie. Publications of the Texas Folklore Society, No. X, 1932. Used by permission.

Zora Neale Hurston. "How Jack O'Lanterns Came to Be" from *Mules and Men* by Zora Neale Hurston. Copyright © 1935 by Zora Neale Hurston. Copyright renewed 1963 by John C. Hurston and Joel Hurston. Reprinted by permission of HarperCollins Publishers, Inc.

Richard N. Dorson. "The Three Preachers" from "Rhyming Tales from Bolivar County" by Richard N. Dorson, *Southern Folklore Quarterly* XIX, No. 2, June 1955. Used by permission of the University Press of Kentucky.

J. Mason Brewer. "The Wrong Man in the Coffin." Reprinted from *The Word on the Brazos: Negro Preacher Tales from the Brazos Bottoms of Texas* by J. Mason Brewer, Copyright © 1953, renewed 1981. By permission of the University of Texas Press; "The Preacher and His Farmer Brother." Reprinted from *The Word on the Brazos: Negro Preacher Tales from the Brazos Bottoms of Texas* by J. Mason Brewer, Copyright © 1953, renewed 1981. By permission of the University of Texas Press.

PART IV "BOUND NO'TH BLUES"

Langston Hughes. "Bound No'th Blues" from *Collected Poems* by Langston Hughes. Copyright © 1994 by the Estate of Langston Hughes. Reprinted by permission of Alfred A. Knopf, Inc.; Excerpt, "Misery" from *Collected Poems* by Langston Hughes. Copyright © 1994 by the Estate of Langston Hughes. Reprinted by permission of Alfred A. Knopf, Inc.

W. C. Handy. "Harlem Blues" by W. C. Handy. Copyright revewed—International copyright secured. Published by Handy Brothers Music Co., Inc.

Bessie Smith. "Preachin' The Blues" by Bessie Smith. Copyright © 1927 (Renewed), 1993 FRANK MUSIC CORP. All Rights Reserved; "Hard Time Blues" by Bessie Smith. Copyright © 1927 (Renewed), 1974 FRANK MUSIC CORP. All Rights Reserved. Used by Permission.

James Weldon Johnson and **J. Rosamond Johnson.** "Lift Every Voice and Sing" by James Weldon Johnson, J. Rosamond Johnson. Used by permission of Edward B. Marks Music Company.

Langston Hughes. "The Weary Blues" from *Collected Poems* by Langston Hughes. Copyright © 1994 by the Estate of Langston Hughes. Reprinted by permission of Alfred A. Knopf, Inc.; "As Befits a Man" from *Collected Poems* by Langston Hughes. Copyright © 1994 by the Estate of Langston Hughes. Reprinted by permission of Alfred A. Knopf, Inc.

W. C. Handy. "Harlem Blues" by W. C. Handy. Copyright renewed—International copyright secured. Published by Handy Brothers Music Co., Inc.

Porter Grainger and **Everett Robbins.** "Tain't Nobody's Business If I Do." Words and Music by Porter Grainger and Everett Robbins. © Copyright 1922, 1949, 1960 by MCA MUSIC PUBLISHING, A Division of MCA INC. Copyright Renewed. International Copyright Secured. All Rights Reserved.

Jimmie Cox. "Nobody Knows You When You're Down and Out." Words and Music by Jimmie Cox. © Copyright 1923, 1929, 1950, 1959, 1963 by MCA MUSIC PUBLISHING, A Division of MCA INC. Copyright Renewed. International Copyright Secured. All Rights Reserved.

Ma Rainey. "Sissy Blues." Words and Music by Ma Rainey. © Copyright by NORTHERN MUSIC COMPANY. NORTHERN MUSIC CORPORATION is an MCA company. Used by permission. All Rights Reserved.

Ida Cox. "Wild Women Don't Have The Blues." Words and Music by Ida Cox. © Copyright 1924 by NORTHERN MUSIC COMPANY. Copyright Renewed. NORTHERN MUSIC COMPANY is an MCA Company. International Copyright Secured. All Rights Reserved.

Billie Holiday. "God Bless The Child" by Billie Holiday. Copyright © 1941 by Edward B. Marks Music Company. Copyright renewed. Used by permission. All rights reserved.

J. Mayo Williams. "Fast Life Blues." Words and Music by J. Mayo Williams. © Copyright by NORTHERN MUSIC COMPANY. NORTHERN MUSIC CORPORATION is an MCA company. Used by Permission. All Rights Reserved.

Eddie House. "Dry Spell Blues." Words and Music by Eddie House. © Copyright by NORTHERN MUSIC COMPANY. NORTHERN MUSIC CORPORATION is an MCA company. Used By Permission. All Rights Reserved.

Huddie Ledbetter. "I'm All Out an' Down." Words and Music by Huddie Ledbetter. Collected and adapted by John A. Lomax and Alan Lomas. TRO - © Copyright 1936 (Renewed) Folkways Music Publishers, Inc., New York, NY. Used by Permission.

William "Big Bill" Broonzy. "Hollerin' Blues." Words and Music by William "Big Bill" Broonzy. Copyright © 1952 (Renewed 1980) SCREEN GEMS-EMI MUSIC INC. All Rights Reserved. International Copyright Secured. Used by Permission.

Robert Johnson. "Cross Road Blues" by Robert Johnson. Reprinted by permission of King of Spades Music.

Langston Hughes. "Tambourines" from *Collected Poems* by Langston Hughes. Copyright © 1994 by the Estate of Langston Hughes. Reprinted by permission of Alfred A. Knopf, Inc.

Thomas A. Dorsey. "Take My Hand, Precious Lord" by Thomas A. Dorsey. Copyright © 1938 (Renewed) Warner-Tamerlane Publishing Corp. All Rights Reserved. Used by Permission. WARNER BROS. PUBLICATIONS U.S. INC., Miami, FL 33014.

Langston Hughes and **Jobe Huntley.** "When I Touch His Garment" (From *Tambourines To Glory*), by Langston Hughes and Jobe Huntley. Copyright © 1964 (Renewed) Chappell & Co. All Rights Reserved. Used by Permission from WARNER BROS. PUBLICATIONS U.S. INC., Miami, FL 33014.

Kenneth Morris. "If I Can Just Make It In" by Kenneth Morris. Copyright © (Renewed) Unichappell Music Inc. All Rights Reserved. Used by Permission from WARNER BROS. PUBLICATIONS U.S. INC., Miami, FL 33014.

Hildred Roach. From Roach, Hildred, *Black American Music: Past and Present,* Second Edition, Reissued 1994, Krieger Publishing Company, Malabar Florida.

Thomas "Fats" Waller, Harry Brooks and **Andy Razaf.** "(What Did I Do to Be So) Black and Blue," by Thomas "Fats" Waller, Harry Brooks and Andy Razaf. Copyright © 1929 EMI Mills Music, Inc. Copyright © (Renewed) and Assigned to EMI Mills Music, Inc., Chappell & Co. Inc. and Razaf Music Co. All Rights Reserved. Used by Permission from WARNER BROS. PUBLICATIONS U.S. INC., Miami, FL 33014.

Duke Ellington and **Irving Mills.** "It Don't Mean a Thing (If It Ain't Got That Swing)," by Duke Ellington & Irving Mills. Copyright © 1932 (Renewed) EMI Mills Music, Inc. and Famous Music Corporation in USA. Rights outside USA controlled by EMI Mills Music, Inc. All Rights Reserved. Used by Permission from WARNER BROS. PUBLICATIONS U.S. INC., Miami, FL 33014.

Hildred Roach. From Roach, Hildred, *Black American Music: Past and Present,* Second Edition, Reissued 1994, Krieger Publishing Company, Malabar Florida.

Clarence "Pine Top" Smith. "Pine Top's Boogie Woogie" by Clarence "Pine Top" Smith.

Langston Hughes. "Dream Boogie" from *Collected Poems* by Langston Hughes. Copyright © 1994 by the Estate of Langston Hughes. Reprinted by permission of Alfred A. Knopf, Inc.

Bill Gaither. "Champ Joe Louis." Words and Music by Bill Gaither. © Copyright by NORTHERN MUSIC COMPANY. NORTHERN MUSIC CORPORATION is an MCA company. Used By Permission. All Rights Reserved; "This Mornin', This Evenin', So Soon" from *The Negro and His Songs: A Study of Typical Negro Songs in the South* by Howard Odum and Guy B. Johnson. Copyright © 1925 by the University of North Carolina Press. Used by permission of the publisher.

Sterling A. Brown. All lines from "Slim Greer" from *The Collected Poems of Sterling A. Brown,* edited by Michael S. Harper. Copyright © 1980 by Sterling A. Brown. Originally appeared in *Southern Road.* Copyright © 1932 by Harcourt Brace & Company. Reprinted by permission of HarperCollins Publishers, Inc.

Huddie Ledbetter. Excerpt from a letter by Huddie Ledbetter to Moses Asch; "The Titanic." Words and Music by Huddie Ledbetter. Collected and Adapted by John A. Lomax and Alan Lomax. TRO - © Copyright 1936 (Renewed) Folkways Publishers, Inc., New York, NY. Used by Permission.

John Hurt. "Stack O'Lee Blues" by Mississippi John Hurt. Copyright © 1967 by Wynwood Music. Reprinted by permission.

James Weldon Johnson. "The Creation" from *God's Trombones* by James Weldon Johnson. Copyright © 1927 The Viking Press, Inc., renewed © 1955 by Grace Nail Johnson. Used by permission of Viking Penguin, a division of Penguin Books USA Inc; "Go Down Death - A Funeral Sermon" from *God's Trombones* by James Weldon Johnson. Copyright © 1927 The Viking Press, Inc., renewed © 1955 by Grace Nail Johnson. Used by permission of Viking Penguin, a division of Penguin Books USA Inc.

Bessie Smith. "Preachin' The Blues" by Bessie Smith. Copyright © 1927 (Renewed), 1993 FRANK MUSIC CORP. All Rights Reserved.

Zora Neale Hurston. "High John De Conquer" as taken from *The Complete Stories* by Zora Neale Hurston. Introduction copyright © by Henry Louis Gates, Jr. and Sieglinde Lemke. Compilation copyright © 1995 by Vivian Bowden, Lois J. Hurston Gaston, Clifford Hurston, Lucy Ann Hurston, Winifred Hurston Clark, Zora Mack Goins, Edgar Hurston, Sr., and Barbara Hurston Lewis. Afterword and Bibliography copyright © 1995 by Henry Louis Gates. Reprinted by permission of HarperCollins Publishers, Inc. "High John De Conquer" was originally published in *The American Mercury,* October 1943.

Marcus Garvey. "Speech on Disarmament Conference Delivered at Liberty Hall, New York, November 6, 1921" by Marcus Garvey from *The Philosophy and Opinions of Marcus Garvey,* edited by Amy Jacques Garvey. Reprinted by permission of Frank Cass & Co., Ltd.

Walter White. "I Investigate Lynchings" by Walter White from the *American Mercury,* Volume 16, January 1929.

W.E.B. DuBois. "Criteria of Negro Art" by W.E.B. DuBois. Copyright © 1926 by *The Crisis.* The authors wish to thank the Crisis Publishing Co., Inc., the magazine of the National Association for the Advancement of Colored People, for authorizing the use of this work.

Alain Locke. "The New Negro" by Alain Locke. Reprinted with the permission of Scribner, a Division of Simon & Schuster from *The New Negro: Voices of the Harlem Renaissance,* edited by Alain Locke. Copyright © 1925 by Albert & Charles Boni, Inc.

James Weldon Johnson. Excerpts from the *Book of American Negro Poetry* by James Weldon Johnson, copyright © 1931 by Harcourt Brace & Company and renewed 1959 by Mrs. Grace Nail Johnson, reprinted by permission of the publisher; "O Black and Unknown Bards" from *Saint Peter Relates an Incident* by James Weldon Johnson. Copyright © 1917, 1921, 1935 by James Weldon Johnson, copyright renewed © 1963 by Grace Nail Johnson. Used by permission of Viking Penguin, a division of Penguin Books USA Inc; "The White Witch" from *Saint Peter Relates an Incident* by James Weldon Johnson. Copyright © 1917, 1921, 1935 by James Weldon Johnson, copyright renewed © 1963 by Grace Nail

Johnson. Used by permission of Viking Penguin, a division of Penguin Books USA Inc; "Fragment" from *Saint Peter Relates an Incident* by James Weldon Johnson. Copyright © 1917, 1921, 1935 by James Weldon Johnson, copyright renewed © 1963 by Grace Nail Johnson. Used by permission of Viking Penguin, a division of Penguin Books USA Inc.

Anne Spencer. "Before the Feast at Shushan" by Anne Spencer. Reprinted by permission of the Anne Spencer Memorial Foundation; "White Things" by Anne Spencer. Reprinted by permission of the Anne Spencer Memorial Foundation; "Lady, Lady" by Anne Spencer. Reprinted by permission of the Anne Spencer Memorial Foundation; "Letter to My Sister" by Anne Spencer. Reprinted by permission of the Anne Spencer Memorial Foundation; "God never planted a garden" by Anne Spencer. Reprinted by permission of the Anne Spencer Memorial Foundation.

Claude McKay. "The Tropics in New York" by Claude McKay. Used by permission of the Archives of Claude McKay, Carl Cowl, Administrator; "If We Must Die" from *The Liberator* by Claude McKay. Used by permission of the Archives of Claude McKay, Carl Cowl, Administrator; "Baptism" by Claude McKay. Used by permission of the Archives of Claude McKay, Carl Cowl, Administrator; "Tiger" by Claude McKay. Used by permission of the Archives of Claude McKay, Carl Cowl, Administrator; "America" by Claude McKay. Used by permission of the Archives of Claude McKay, Carl Cowl, Administrator; "Harlem Shadows" by Claude McKay. Used by permission of the Archives of Claude McKay, Carl Cowl, Administrator; "The Harlem Dancer" by Claude McKay. Used by permission of the Archives of Claude McKay, Carl Cowl, Administrator; "The White House" by Claude McKay. Used by permission of the Archives of Claude McKay, Carl Cowl, Administrator; "St. Isaac's Church, Petrograd" by Claude McKay. Used by permission of the Archives of Claude McKay, Carl Cowl, Administrator.

Langston Hughes. "The Negro Speaks of Rivers" from *Collected Poems* by Langston Hughes. Copyright © 1994 by the Estate of Langston Hughes. Reprinted by permission of Alfred A. Knopf, Inc; "Dream Variations" from *Collected Poems* by Langston Hughes. Copyright © 1994 by the Estate of Langston Hughes. Reprinted by permission of Alfred A. Knopf, Inc; "Sunday Morning Prophecy" from *Collected Poems* by Langston Hughes. Copyright © 1994 by the Estate of Langston Hughes. Reprinted by permission of Alfred A. Knopf, Inc; "The Weary Blues" from *Collected Poems* by Langston Hughes. Copyright © 1994 by the Estate of Langston Hughes. Reprinted by permission of Alfred A. Knopf, Inc; "Jazzonia" from *Collected Poems* by Langston Hughes. Copyright © 1994 by the Estate of Langston Hughes. Reprinted by permission of Alfred A. Knopf, Inc; "Life Is Fine" from *Collected Poems* by Langston Hughes. Copyright © 1994 by the Estate of Langston Hughes. Reprinted by permission of Alfred A. Knopf, Inc; "Daybreak in Alabama" from *Collected Poems* by Langston Hughes. Copyright © 1994 by the Estate of Langston Hughes. Reprinted by permission of Alfred A. Knopf, Inc; "Bound No'th Blues" from *Collected Poems* by Langston Hughes. Copyright © 1994 by the Estate of Langston Hughes. Reprinted by permission of Alfred A. Knopf, Inc; "Madam's Past History" from *Collected Poems* by Langston Hughes. Copyright © 1994 by the Estate of Langston Hughes. Reprinted by permission of Alfred A. Knopf, Inc; "Ballad of Landlord" from *Collected Poems* by Langston Hughes. Copyright © 1994 by the Estate of Langston Hughes. Reprinted by permission of Alfred A. Knopf, Inc; "Harlem" ("Dream Deferred") from *Collected Poems* by Langston Hughes. Copyright © 1994 by the Estate of Langston Hughes. Reprinted by permission of Alfred A. Knopf, Inc; "I Too" from *Collected Poems* by Langston Hughes. Copyright © 1994 by the Estate of Langston Hughes. Reprinted by premission of Alfred A. Knopf, Inc; "Feet Live Their Own Life" from *The Best of Simple* by Langston Hughes. Copyright © 1961 by Langston Hughes. Copyright renewed © 1989 by George Houston Bass. Reprinted by permission of Hill and Wang, a division of Farrar, Straus & Giroux, Inc; "The Negro Artist and the Racial Mountain" by Langston Hughes. Reprinted by permission of Harold Ober Associates. Copyright © 1926 by Langston Hughes. Renewed.

Gwendolyn Bennett. "Heritage" by Gwendolyn Bennet (from *Opportunity,* December 1923). *Gwendolyn Bennett Papers* are housed in the Manuscripts, Archives and Rare Books Division, Schomburg Center for Research in Black Culture, The New York Public Library, Astor, Lenox and Tilden Foundations. Reprinted by permission; "To a Dark Girl" by Gwendolyn Bennett (from *Caroling Dusk,* ed. Countee Cullen, 1927). Gwendolyn Bennett Papers; Manuscripts, Archives and Rare Books Division; Schomburg Center for Research in Black Culture; The New York Public Library; Astor, Lenox and Tilden Foundations. Copyright © New York Public Library. Reprinted by permission; "Nocturne" by Gwendolyn Bennett (from *The Crisis,* November 1923). *Gwendolyn Bennett Papers* are housed in the Manuscripts, Archives and Rare Books Division, Schomburg Center for Research in Black Culture, The New York Public Library, Astor, Lenox and Tilden Foundations. Reprinted by permission; "To Usward" by Gwendolyn Bennett (from *The Crisis,* May 1924; *Opportunity,* May 1924). *Gwendolyn Bennett Papers* are housed in the Manuscripts, Archives and Rare Books Division, Schomburg Center for Research in Black Culture, The New York Public Library, Astor, Lenox and Tilden Foundations. Reprinted by permission; "Street Lamps in Early Spring" by Gwendolyn Bennett (from *Opportunity,* May 1926). *Gwendolyn Bennett Papers* are housed in the Manuscripts, Archives and Rare Books Division, Schomburg Center for Research in Black Culture, The New York Public Library, Astor, Lenox and Tilden Foundations. Reprinted by permission; "Hatred" by Gwendolyn Bennett. Used by permission of Manuscripts, Archives and Rare Books Division; Schomburg Center for Research in Black Culture; The New York Public Library; Astor, Lenox and Tilden Foundations; "Fantasy" by Gwendolyn Bennett. Used by permission of Manuscripts, Archives and Rare Books Division; Schomburg Center for Research in Black Culture; The New York Public Library; Astor, Lenox and Tilden Foundations; "Secret" by Gwendolyn Bennett. Used by permission of Manuscripts, Archives and Rare Books Division; Schomburg Center for Research in Black Culture; The New York Public Library; Astor, Lenox and Tilden Foundations.

Countee Cullen. "Heritage" from *Color* by Countee Cullen. Reprinted by permission of GRM Associates, Inc., Agents for the Estate of Ida M. Cullen. Copyright © 1925 by Harper & Brothers; copyright renewed 1953 by Ida M. Cullen; "Scottsboro, Too, Is Worth Its Song" from *The Medea and Some Poems* by Countee Cullen. Reprinted by permission of GRM Associates, Inc., Agents for the Estate of Ida M. Cullen. Copyright © 1935 by Harper & Brothers; copyright renewed 1963 by Ida M. Cullen; "Colored Blues Singer" from *Copper Sun* by Countee Cullen. Reprinted by permission of GRM Associates, Inc., Agents for the Estate of Ida M. Cullen. Copyright © 1927 by Harper & Brothers; copyright renewed

1955 by Ida M. Cullen; "Litany of Dark People" from *Copper Sun* by Countee Cullen. Reprinted by permission of GRM Associates, Inc., Agents for the Estate of Ida M. Cullen. Copyright © 1927 by Harper & Brothers; copyright renewed 1955 by Ida M. Cullen; "Yet Do I Marvel" from *Color* by Countee Cullen. Reprinted by permission of GRM Associates, Inc., Agents for the Estate of Ida M. Cullen. Copyright © 1925 by Harper & Brothers; copyright renewed 1953 by Ida M. Cullen; "A Song of Praise" from *Color* by Countee Cullen. Reprinted by permission of GRM Associates, Inc., Agents for the Estate of Ida M. Cullen. Copyright © 1925 by Harper & Brothers; copyright renewed 1953 by Ida M. Cullen; "Not Sacco and Vanzetti" from *The Black Christ and Other Poems* by Countee Cullen. Reprinted by permission of GRM Associates, Inc., Agents fro the Estate of Ida M. Cullen. Copyright © 1929 by Harper & Brothers; copyright renewed 1956 by Ida M. Cullen.

Helene Johnson. "My Race" by Helene Johnson from *Shadowed Dreams: Women's Poetry of the Harlem Renaissance*, ed. Maureen Honey, Rutgers UP, 1989. Reprinted by arrangement with Abigail McGrath; "Sonnet to a Negro in Harlem" by Helene Johnson from *Caroling Dusk*, ed. Countee Cullen, p. 157. Copyright © 1927 by Harper & Brothers. First Carol Publishing Group Edition 1993. A Citadel Press Book. Reprinted by arrangement with Abigail McGrath; "Bottled" by Helene Johnson from *Caroling Dusk*, ed. Countee Cullen, p. 157. Copyright © 1927 by Harper & Brothers. First Carol Publishing Group Edition 1993. A Citadel Press Book. Reprinted by arrangement with Abigail McGrath; "Trees at Night" by Helene Johnson from *Shadowed Dreams: Women's Poetry of the Harlem Renaissance*, ed. by Maureen Honey, Rutgers UP, 1989. Reprinted by arrangement with Abigail McGrath; "The Road" by Helene Johnson from *Caroling Dusk*, ed. Countee Cullen, p. 157. Copyright © 1927 by Harper & Brothers. First Carol Publishing Group Edition 1993. A Citadel Press Book. Reprinted by arrangement with Abigail McGrath; "Magalu" by Helene Johnson from *Caroling Dusk*, ed. Countee Cullen, p. 157. Copyright © 1927 by Harper & Brothers. First Carol Publishing Group Edition 1993. A Citadel Press Book. Reprinted by arrangement with Abigail McGrath; "Summer Matures" by Helene Johnson from *Caroling Dusk*, ed. Countee Cullen, p. 157. Copyright © 1927 by Harper & Brothers. First Carol Publishing Group Edition 1993. A Citadel Press Book. Reprinted by arrangement with Abigail McGrath; "Fulfillment" by Helene Johnson from *Caroling Dusk*, ed. Countee Cullen, p. 157. Copyright © 1927 by Harper & Brothers. First Carol Publishing Group Edition 1993. A Citadel Press Book. Reprinted by arrangement with Abigail McGrath.

Nella Larsen. Excerpt from Quicksand by Nella Larsen; Excerpt from *Passing* by Nella Larsen.

Zora Neale Hurston. "Sweat" as taken from *The Complete Stories* by Zora Neale Hurston. Introduction copyright © by Henry Louis Gates, Jr. and Sieglinde Lemke. Compilation copyright © 1995 by Vivian Bowden, Lois J. Hurston Gaston, Clifford Hurston, Lucy Ann Hurston, Winifred Hurston Clark, Zora Mack Goins, Edgar Hurston, Sr., and Barbara Hurston Lewis. Afteword and Bibliography copyright © 1995 by Henry Louis Gates. Reprinted by permission of HarperCollins Publishers, Inc. "Sweat" was originally published in *Fire*, November 1926; "Spunk" as taken from *The Complete Stories* by Zora Neale Hurston. Introduction copyright © by Henry Louis Gates, Jr. and Sieglinde Lemke. Compilation copyright © 1995 by Vivian Bowden, Lois J. Hurston Gaston, Clifford Hurston, Lucy Ann Hurston, Winifred Hurston Clark, Zora Mack Goins, Edgar Hurston, Sr., and Barbara Hurston Lewis. Afterword and Bibliography copyright © 1995 by Henry Louis Gates. Reprinted by permission of HarperCollins Publishers, Inc. "Spunk" was originally published in *Opportunity*, June 1925.

Jean Toomer. "Karintha" from *Cane* by Jean Toomer. Copyright © 1923 by Boni & Liveright, renewed 1951 by Jean Toomer. Reprinted by permission of Liveright Publishing Corporation; "Song of the Son" from *Cane* by Jean Toomer. Copyright © 1923 by Boni & Liveright, renewed 1951 by Jean Toomer. Reprinted by permission of Liveright Publishing Corporation; "Fern" from *Cane* by Jean Toomer. Copyright © 1923 by Boni & Liveright, renewed 1951 by Jean Toomer. Reprinted by permission of Liveright Publishing Corporation; "Portrait in Georgia" from *Cane* by Jean Toomer. Copyright © 1923 by Boni & Liveright, renewed 1951 by Jean Toomer. Reprinted by permission of Liveright Publishing Corporation; "Seventh Street" from *Cane* by Jean Toomer. Copyright © 1923 by Boni & Liveright, renewed 1951 by Jean Toomer. Reprinted by permission of Liveright Publishing Corporation; "Box Seat" from *Cane* by Jean Toomer. Copyright © 1923 by Boni & Liveright, renewed 1951 by Jean Toomer. Reprinted by permission of Liveright Publishing Corporation; "Kabnis" from *Cane* by Jean Toomer. Copyright © 1923 by Boni & Liveright, renewed 1951 by Jean Toomer. Reprinted by permission of Liveright Publishing Corporation.

Rudolph Fisher. "Miss Cynthie" by Rudolph Fisher from *Story Magazine*, June 1933.

Eric Walrond. "The Wharf Rats" from *Tropic Death* by Eric Walrond. Copyright © 1926 by Boni & Liveright, Inc., renewed 1954 by Eric Walrond. Reprinted by permission of Liveright Publishing Corporation.

Sterling A. Brown. "When De Saints Go Ma'chin Home" from *Southern Road* by Sterling A. Brown. Copyright © 1932 by Harcourt Brace & Co. Copyright renewed 1960 by Sterling Brown. Included in *The Collected Poems of Sterling A. Brown,* selected by Michael S. Harper. Copyright © 1980 by Sterling A. Brown. Reprinted by permission of HarperCollins Publishers, Inc; "Southern Road" from *Southern Road* by Sterling A. Brown. Copyright © 1932 by Harcourt Brace & Co. Copyright renewed 1960 by Sterling Brown. Included in *The Collected Poems of Sterling A. Brown,* selected by Michael S. Harper. Copyright © 1980 by Sterling A. Brown. Reprinted by permission of HarperCollins Publishers, Inc; All lines from "Ma Rainey" from *The Collected Poems of Sterling A. Brown,* edited by Michael S. Harper. Copyright © 1932 by Harcourt Brace & Co. Copyright renewed 1960 by Sterling A. Brown. Reprinted by permission of HarperCollins Publishers, Inc; All lines from "Memphis Blues" from *The Collected Poems of Sterling A. Brown,* edited by Michael S. Harper. Copyright © 1980 by Sterling A. Brown. Reprinted by permission of HarperCollins Publishers, Inc; "Old Lem" from *The Collected Poems of Sterling A. Brown,* edited by Michael S. Harper. Copyright © 1980 by Sterling A. Brown. Reprinted by permission of HarperCollins Publishers, Inc; All lines from "Strong Men" from *The Collected Poems of Sterling A. Brown,* edited by Michael S. Harper. Copyright © 1932 Harcourt Brace & Company. Copyright renewed 1960 by Sterling Brown. Reprinted by permission of HarperCollins Publishers, Inc.

Frank Marshall Davis. Excerpts from poetry by Frank Marshall Davis; "Jazz Band" from *Black Man's Verse* by Frank Marshall Davis. Reprinted by permission of Beth Charlton, literary executor; "Robert Whitmore" from *Black Man's Verse* by Frank Marshall Davis. Reprinted by permission of Beth Charlton, literary executor; "Arthur Ridgewood, M.D." from

Black Man's Verse by Frank Marshall Davis. Reprinted by permission of Beth Charlton, literary executor; "Giles Johnson, Ph.D." from *Black Man's Verse* by Frank Marshall Davis. Reprinted by permission of Beth Charlton, literary executor.

Richard Wright. All pages from "Long Black Song" from *Uncle Tom's Children* by Richard Wright. Copyright © 1938 by Richard Wright. Copyright renewed 1966 by Ellen Wright. Reprinted by permission of HarperCollins Publishers, Inc.

Ann Petry. "Like a Winding Sheet" from *Miss Muriel and Other Stories* by Ann Petry. Reprinted by the permission of Russell & Volkening as agents for the author. Copyright © 1946 by Ann Petry. Copyright renewed in 1974 by Ann Petry. "Like a Winding Sheet" originally appeared in THE CRISIS IN 1946; "Miss Muriel" by Ann Petry from *Miss Muriel and Other Stories.* Copyright © 1971 by Ann Petry. Reprinted by the permission of Russell & Volkening as agents for the author.

Chester Himes. "Marihuana and a Pistol" from the book *The Collected Stories of Chester B. Himes* by Chester Himes. Copyright © 1990 by Chester Himes. Used by permission of the publisher, Thunder's Mouth Press.

PART V "WIN THE WAR BLUES"

Langston Hughes. Excerpt from "Dream Deferred" ("Harlem") from *Collected Poems* by Langston Hughes. Copyright © 1994 by the Estate of Langston Hughes. Reprinted by permission of Alfred A. Knopf, Inc.

Sonny Boy Williamson. "Win the War Blues" by Sonny Boy Williamson. Copyright © 1945 (Renewed) Arc Music Corporation. All Rights Reserved. Used by permission.

Zilphia Horton, Frank Hamilton, Guy Caraway and **Pete Seeger.** "We Shall Overcome." Musical and lyrical adaptation by Zilphia Horton, Frank Hamilton, Guy Caraway and Pete Seeger. Inspired by African American Gospel Singing, members of the Food & Tobacco Workers Union, Charleston, SC, and the southern Civil Rights Movement. TRO - © Copyright 1960 (Renewed) and 1963 (Renewed) Ludlow Music, Inc., New York, International Copyright Secured. Made in U.S.A. All Rights Reserved Including Public Performance For Profit. Royalties derived from this composition are being contributed to the We Shall Overcome Fund and The Freedom Movement under the Trusteeship of the writers. Used by Permission.

J. B. Lenoir. "Eisenhower Blues" by J. B. Lenoir. Copyright © 1970 Arc Music Corporation. All Rights Reserved. Used by Permission.

Thomas "Fats" Waller, Harry Brooks and **Andy Razaf.** "(What Did I Do to Be So) Black and Blue," by Thomas "Fats" Waller, Harry Brooks and Andy Razaf. Copyright © 1929 EMI Mills Music, Inc. Copyright © (Renewed) and Assigned to EMI Mills Music, Inc., Chappell & Co. Inc. and Razaf Music Co. All Rights Reserved. Used by Permission from WARNER BROS. PUBLICATIONS U.S. INC., Miami, FL 33014.

Melvin B. Tolson, Jr. "Rendezvous with America" by Melvin B. Tolson, Jr. Reprinted by permission of the author.

Margaret Walker Alexander. "For My People" from *This is My Century: New and Collected Poems* by Margaret Walker Alexander. Copyright © 1989 The University of Georgia Press. Reprinted by permission.

Ernest Blunt. "The Hitler Blues." Words and Music by Ernest Blunt. © Copyright 1940 by DUCHESS MUSIC CORPORATION. Copyright Renewed. DUCHESS MUSIC CORPORATION is an MCA company. International Copyright Secured. All Rights Reserved.

Muddy Waters. "Louisiana Blues" a/k/a "Goin' Down Louisiana" written by Muddy Waters. Copyright © 1959, 1987 WATERTOONS MUSIC (ASCAP)/Administered by BUG MUSIC. All Rights Reserved. Used by permission.

Sunnyland Slim aka Albert Luandrew. "Back to Korea Blues" by Sunnyland Slim aka Albert Luandrew. Used by permission of Leric Music, Publisher on behalf of Mrs. Albert Luandrew.

Zilphia Horton, Frank Hamilton, Guy Caraway and **Pete Seeger.** "We Shall Overcome". Musical and lyrical adaptation by Zilphia Horton, Frank Hamilton, Guy Caraway and Pete Seeger. Inspired by African American Gospel Singing, members of the Food and Tobacco Workers Union, Charleston, SC, and the southern Civil Rights Movement. TRO - © Copyright 1960 (Renewed) and 1963 (Renewed) Ludlow Music, Inc., New York, International Copyright Secured. Made in U.S.A. All Rights Reserved Including Public Performance For Profit. Royalties derived from this composition are being contributed to the We Shall Overcome Fund and The Freedom Movement under the Trusteeship of the writers. Used by Permission.

James Weldon Johnson and **J. Rosamond Johnson.** "Gimme Dat Ol' Time Religion," from *The Books of American Negro Spirituals* by James Weldon Johnson and J. Rosamond Johnson. Copyright 1925, 1926 by The Viking Press, Inc. renewed 1953 by Lawrence Brown, 1953, © 1954 by Grace Nail Johnson and J. Rosamond Johnson. Used by permission of Viking Penguin, a division of Penguin Books USA Inc.

Virginia Davis and **Theodore Frye.** "I Will Move On Up a Little Higher," by Virginia Davis & Theodore Frye. Copyright 1948 (Renewed) Unichappell Music Inc. All Rights Reserved. Used by Permission from WARNER BROS. PUBLICATIONS U.S. INC., Miami, FL 33014.

Clara Ward. "I Know It Was The Lord". Words and Music by Clara Ward. Copyright © 1953, 1978 (Renewed 1981) SCREEN GEMS-EMI MUSIC INC. All Rights Reserved. International Copyright Secured. Used by Permission.

Hank Ballard. "The Twist" by Hank Ballard. Copyright © 1959, Fort Knox Music Inc. and Trio Music Co., Inc. Copyright renewed. Used by permission. All rights reserved.

Robert A. Blackwell and **John S. Marascalco.** "Good Golly Miss Molly" words and music by Robert A. Blackwell and John S. Marascalco. Reprinted by permission of Parker Music, Third Story Music and Robin Hood Music Co.

Charlie "Yardbird" Parker. "Parker's Mood" by Charlie "Yardbird" Parker from *The Bebop Revolution in Words and Music,* edited by Dave Oliphant. Copyright © 1994, Harry Ransom Humanities Center, The University of Texas at Austin. Used by permission; "Donna Lee" by Charlie "Yardbird" Parker from *The Bebop Revolution in Words and Music,* edited by Dave Oliphant. Copyright © 1994, Harry Ransom Humanities Center, The University of Texas at Austin. Used by permission.

Langston Hughes. "Flatted Fifths" from *Collected Poems* by Langston Hughes. Copyright © 1994 by the Estate of Langston Hughes. Reprinted by permission of Alfred A. Knopf, Inc.

Margaret Walker Alexander. "Molly Means" from *This is My Century: New and Collected Poems* by Margaret Walker Alexander. Copyright © 1989 The University of Georgia Press. Reprinted by permission; "Kissie Lee" from *This is My Century: New and Collected Poems* by Margaret Walker Alexander. Copyright © 1989 The University of Georgia Press. Reprinted by permission.

C. L. Franklin. "The Prodigal Son" by C. L. Franklin from *Give Me This Mountain: Life History and Selected Sermons, Reverend C. L. Franklin,* edited by Jeff Todd Titon. Copyright © 1989 by the Board of Trustees of the University of Illinois. Used with the permission of the author and the University of Illinois Press.

Hugh M. Gloster. "Race and the Negro Writer" by Hugh M. Gloster from *Phylon* (1950). Copyright © 1950 by Atlanta University. Reprinted by permission.

Nick Aaron Ford. "A Blueprint for Negro Authors" by Nick Aaron Ford from *Phylon* (1950). Copyright © 1950 by Atlanta University. Reprinted by permission.

Ann Petry. "The Novel as Social Criticism" by Ann Petry. Copyright © by Ann Petry. Reprinted by the permission of Russell & Volkening as agents for the author.

Melvin B. Tolson, Jr. "Harlem Gallery" by Melvin B. Tolson, Jr. Reprinted by permission of the author; "Dark Symphony" by Melvin B. Tolson, Jr. from *Rendezvous with America.* Reprinted by permission of the author; "Lambda" by Melvin B. Tolson, Jr. from *Harlem Gallery, Book I, The Curator.* Reprinted by permission of the author.

Robert Hayden. "Homage to the Empress of the Blues," copyright © 1966, 1962 by Robert Hayden, from *Angle of Ascent: New and Selected Poems* by Robert Hayden. Reprinted by permission of Liveright Publishing Corporation; "Middle Passage," copyright © 1966, 1962 by Robert Hayden, from *Angle of Ascent: New and Selected Poems* by Robert Hayden. Reprinted by permission of Liveright Publishing Corporation; "Runagate Runagate" copyright © 1966, 1962 by Robert Hayden, from *Angle of Ascent: New and Selected Poems* by Robert Hayden. Reprinted by permission of Liveright Publishing Corporation; "Frederick Douglass," copyright © 1966 by Robert Hayden, from *Angle of Ascent: New and Selected Poems* by Robert Hayden. Reprinted by permission of Liveright Publishing Corporation; "Elegies for Paradise Valley," copyright © 1978 by Robert Hayden. Copyright © 1982 by Irma Hayden, from *American Journal* by Robert Hayden. Reprinted by permission of Liveright Publishing Corporation; "A Letter from Phillis Wheatley," copyright © 1978 by Robert Hayden. Copyright © 1982 by Irma Hayden, from *American Journal* by Robert Hayden. Reprinted by permission of Liveright Publishing Corporation.

Dudley Randall. "Booker T. and W.E.B." by Dudley Randall. Permission granted by Broadside Press; "Legacy: My South" by Dudley Randall. Reprinted by permission of the author; "Ancestors" by Dudley Randall. Reprinted by permission of the author.

Owen Dodson. Excerpts from "Someday We're Gonna Tear Them Pillars Down" from *Powerful Ladder* by Owen Dodson. Copyright © 1946 by Owen Dodson. Copyright renewed © 1973 by Owen Dodson. Reprinted by permission of Farrar, Straus & Giroux, Inc; "Sorrow is the Only Faithful One" from *Powerful Long Ladder* by Owen Dodson. Copyright © 1946 and copyright renewed © 1973 by Owen Dodson. Reprinted by permission of Farrar, Straus & Giroux, Inc; "Yardbird's Skull" by Owen Dodson; "Guitar" from *Powerful Long Ladder* by Owen Dodson. Copyright © 1946 and copyright renewed © 1973 by Owen Dodson. Reprinted by permission of Farrar, Straus & Giroux, Inc.

Margaret Danner. "Far From Africa: Four Poems" by Margaret Danner; "The Rhetoric of Langston Hughes" by Margaret Danner; "The Slave and the Iron Lace" by Margaret Danner; "Passive Resistance" by Margaret Danner.

Margaret Walker Alexander. "African Village" and "The Labyrinth of Love" from *This is My Century: New and Collected Poems* by Margaret Walker Alexander. Copyright © 1989 The University of Georgia Press. Reprinted by permission; "For My People" from *This is My Century: New and Collected Poems* by Margaret Walker Alexander. Copyright © 1989 The University of Georgia Press. Reprinted by permission; "Lineage" from *This is My Century: New and Collected Poems* by Margaret Walker Alexander. Copyright © 1989 The University of Georgia Press. Reprinted by permission; "The Ballad of the Free" from *This is My Century: New and Col lected Poems* by Margaret Walker Alexander. Copyright © 1989 The University of Georgia Press. Reprinted by permission; "Prophets for a New Day" from *This is My Century: New and Collected Poems* by Margaret Walker Alexander. Copyright © 1989 The University of Georgia Press. Reprinted by permission; "The Crystal Palace" from *This is My Century: New and Collected Poems* by Margaret Walker Alexander. Copyright © 1989 The University of Georgia Press. Reprinted by permission; "A Patchwork Quilt" from *This is My Century: New and Collected Poems* by Margaret Walker Alexander. Copyright © 1989 The University of Georgia Press. Reprinted by permission.

Gwendolyn Brooks. "the mother" from the book, *Blacks,* by Gwendolyn Brooks © 1991. Publisher, Thrid World Press, Chicago, 1991. Used by permission of the author; "Negro Hero" from the book, *Blacks,* by Gwendolyn Brooks, copyright © 1991. Publisher, Third World Press, Chicago, 1991. Reprinted by permission of the author; "the children of the poor" from the book, *Blacks,* by Gwendolyn Brooks © 1991. Publisher, Third World Press, Chicago, 1991. Used by permission of the author; "The Last Quatrain of the Ballad of Emmett Till" from the book, *Blacks,* by Gwendolyn Brooks © 1991. Publisher, Third World Press, Chicago, 1991. Used by permission of the author; "The Chicago Defender Sends a Man to Little Rock" from the book, *Blacks,* by Gwendolyn Brooks © 1991. Publisher, Third World Press, Chicago, 1991. Used by permission of the author; "We Real Cool" from the book, *Blacks,* by Gwendolyn Brooks © 1991. Publisher, Third World Press, Chicago, 1991. Used by permission of the author; "The Wall" from the book, *Blacks,* by Gwendolyn Brooks © 1991. Publisher, Third World Press, Chciago, 1991. Used by permission of the author; "The Chicago Picasso" from the book, *Blacks,* by Gwendolyn Brooks © 1991. Publisher, Third World Press, Chicago, 1991. Used by permission of the author; "Medger Evers" from the book, *Blacks,* by Gwendolyn Brooks © 1991. Publisher, Third World Press, Chicago, 1991. Used by permission of the author; "Malcolm X" from the book, *Blacks,* by Gwendolyn Brooks © 1991. Publisher, Third World Press, Chicago, 1991. Used by permission of the author; "The Sermon on the Warpland" from the book, *Blacks,* by Gwendolyn Brooks © 1991. Publisher, Third World Press, Chicago, 1991. Used by permission of the author; "To an Old Black Woman, Homeless and Indistinct" first appeared in Eugene Redmond's 1993 "*Drumvoices Revue.*" Copyright by Gwendolyn Brooks. Used by permisson of the author.

Naomi Long Madgett. "Midway" from *Star by Star* by Naomi Long Madgett. (Harco, 1965, Evenill, 1970). By permission of the author; "The Old Women" from *Exits and Entrances* by Naomi Long Madgett. (Lotus Press, 1978). By permission of the author; "New Day" from *Exits and Entrances* by Naomi Long Madgett. (Lotus Press, 1978). By permission of the author; "Monday Morning Blues" from *Exits and Entrances* by Naomi Long Madgett. (Lotus Press, 1978). By permission of the author; "A Litany for Afro-Americans" from *Exits and Entrances* by Naomi Long Madgett. (Lotus Press, 1978). By permission of the author.

Alice Childress. "The Wedding Band" by Alice Childress. Copyright © 1973 by Alice Childress. Used by permission of Flora Roberts, Inc.

Langston Hughes. "Harlem" ("Dream Deferred") from *Collected Poems* by Langston Hughes. Copyright © 1994 by the Estate of Langston Hughes. Reprinted by permission of Alfred A. Knopf, Inc.

Lorraine Hansberry. From *A Raisin in the Sun* by Lorraine Hansberry. Copyright © 1958 by Robert Nemiroff, as an unpublished work. Copyright © 1959, 1966, 1984 by Robert Nemiroff. Reprinted by permission of Random House, Inc.

Dorothy West. From *The Richer, The Poorer* by Dorothy West. Copyright © 1995 by Dorothy West. Used by permission of Doubleday, a division of Bantam Doubleday Dell Publishing Group, Inc.

Ralph Ellison. "Juneteenth" by Ralph Ellison. Reprinted by permission of the William Morris Agency, Inc. on behalf of the Author. Copyright © 1965 by Ralph Ellison; Prologue from *Invisible Man* by Ralph Ellison. Copyright © 1952 by Ralph Ellison. Reprinted by permission of Random House, Inc.

John Oliver Killens. "The Stick Up" by John Oliver Killens. Reprinted by permission of Grace Killens.

James Baldwin. "Sonny's Blues" from *Going to Meet the Man* by James Baldwin, © 1965, copyright renewed. "Sonny's Blues" was originally published in Partisan Review. Published by Vintage Books. Reprinted with the permission of the James Baldwin Estate; "Everybody's Protest Novel" from *Notes of a Native Son* by James Baldwin. Copyright © 1955, renewed 1983, by James Baldwin. Reprinted by permission of Beacon Press, Boston.

Paule Marshall. "Barbados" by Paule Marshall from *Soul Clap Hands and Sing.* Copyright © 1961 by Paule Marshall. Reprinted with the permission of the author; Reprinted by permission of The Putnam Publishing Group from *Praisesong for the Widow* by Paule Marshall. Copyright © 1983 by Paule Marshall.

PART VI "CROSS ROAD BLUES"

Langston Hughes. Excerpt from "Dream Deferred" ("Harlem") from *Collected Poems* by Langston Hughes. Copyright © 1994 by the Estate of Langston Hughes. Reprinted by permission of Alfred A. Knopf, Inc.

Marvin Gaye. "Inner City Blues (Makes Me Wanna Holler)." Words and Music by Marvin Gaye and James Nyx. Copyright 1971 Jobete Music Co., Inc. All Rights Reserved.

Nikki Giovanni. Brief excerpt from "The True Import of Present Dialogue, Black vs. Negro" from *Black Feeling, Black Talk, Black Judgement* by Nikki Giovanni. Copyright © 1968, 1970 by Nikki Giovanni. By permission of William Morrow & Co., Inc.

Haki Madhubuti. Excerpt from "a poem to complement other poems" from *Don't Cry, Scream* by Haki Madhubuti. Reprinted by permission of Third World Press.

Sonia Sanchez. From *We a BaddDDD People.* Copyright © 1970, Sonia Sanchez. Reprinted by permission of the author.

Ray Henderson and **Lew Brown.** "The Thrill Is Gone," by Ray Henderson and Lew Brown. Copyright © 1931 (Renewed) DeSylva, Brown & Henderson, Inc. Rights for Extended Renewal Term in U.S. Controlled by Ray Henderson Music and Chappell & Co. Rights for Canada controlled by Chappell & Co. All Rights Reserved. Used by Permission from WARNER BROS. PUBLICATIONS U.S. INC., Miami, FL 33014.

Deadric Malone. "I Pity the Fool." Words and Music by Deadric Malone. © Copyright 1969 by DUCHESS MUSIC CORPORATION. Copyright Renewed. DUCHESS MUSIC CORPORATION is an MCA company. International Copyright Secured. All Rights Reserved.

Willie Dixon. "Back Door Man" written by Willie Dixon. Copyright © 1961, 1989 HOOCHIE COOCHIE MUSIC (BMI)/Administered by BUG MUSIC. All Rights Reserved. Used by Permission.

Grant Clarke and **Harry Akst.** "Am I Blue?" by Grant Clarke and Harry Akst. Copyright © 1929 (Renewed) Warner Bros. Inc. All Rights Reserved. Used by Permission from WARNER BROS. PUBLICATIONS U.S. INC., Miami, FL 33014.

Luther Dixon and **Al Smith.** "Big Boss Man" by Luther Dixon and Al Smith. Copyright © 1960 (Renewed) EMI Unart Catalog. All Rights Reserved. Used by permission from WARNER BROS. PUBLICATIONS U.S. INC., Miami, FL 33014.

Otis Redding. "Respect" by Otis Redding. Copyright © 1965, Renewed 1993 Irving Music Inc. (BMI). All rights reserved. International copyright secured. Used by permission.

James Brown and **Alfred James Ellis.** "Say It Loud, I'm Black and I'm Proud," by James Brown and Alfred James Ellis. Copyright © 1968 (Renewed) Dynatone Publishing Company (BMI). All Rights o/b/o Dynatone Publishing Company (BMI) administered by Warner-Tamerlane Publishing Corp. (BMI). All Rights Reserved. Used by Permission from WARNER BROS. PUBLICATIONS U.S. INC., Miami, FL 33014.

Curtis Mayfield. "Keep on Pushing," by Curtis Mayfield. Copyright © 1964 (Renewed) Warner-Tamerlane Publishing Corp. All Rights Reserved. Used by Permission from WARNER BROS. PUBLICATIONS U.S. INC., Miami, FL 33014.

Marvin Gaye, Al Cleveland and **Renaldo Benson.** "What's Going On." Words and Music by Marvin Gaye, Al Cleveland and Renaldo Benson. Copyright © 1970, 1971, 1972 Jobete Music Co., Inc. All Rights Reserved.

Eddie Holland. "We Shall Not Be Moved." Words and Music by Eddie Holland. Copyright © 1965 Jobete Music Co., Inc. All Rights Reserved.

John Coltrane. An excerpt from John Coltrane's workbook. Copyright © 1989 Jowcol Music. Reprinted by permission.

Gil Scott-Heron. "The Revolution Will Not Be Televised" by Gil Scott-Heron. Copyright © 1978, Bienstock Publishing Company. Used by permission. All rights reserved.

Sugar Hill Gang. "Good Times" aka "Rapper's Delight" by the Suger Hill Gang. Reprinted by permission of the publisher.

Grandmaster Flash and the Furious Five. "The Message" by Grandmaster Flash and the Furious Five. Used by permission of Sugar Hill Music Publishing Ltd.

Eric Barrier and **William Griffin.** "Paid in Full." Witten by Eric Barrier and William Griffin. Copyright © 1987 Songs of PolyGram International, Inc. and Robert Hill Music. Used By Permission. All Rights Reserved; "Don't Believe the Hype." Copyright © 1988 Def American Songs, Inc./Bring The Noize, Inc. (BMI). All rights reserved. Used by permission.

Public Enemy. "Fight the Power." Copyright © 1990 Def American Songs, Inc./Bring the Noize, Inc. (BMI). All rights reserved. Used by permission.

Ice T and **Afrika Islam.** "Freedom of Speech" by Ice T and Afrika Islam. Copyright © 1989 COLGEMS-EMI MUSIC INC. RHYME SYNDICATE MUSIC AND MAIN THAT

TUNE. All rights on behalf of Rhyme Syndicate Music Administered by Polygram International Publications, Inc. All Rights Reserved. International Copyright Secured. Used by permission.

Dana Owens, Simone Johnson, Mark James, Anthony Peaks, and **Shane Faber.** "Ladies First" by Dana Owens, Simone Johnson, Mark James, Anthony Peaks, and Shane Faber. Copyright © 1989 by T-Boy Music Publishing, Inc. c/o Lipservices obo itself & Queen latifah Music, Forty-Five King Music, Forked Tongue Music/Now and Then Music. International Copyrights Secures. All Rights Reserved. Used by Kind Permission.

Paul Mitchell, Shawn McKenzie and **Kevin McKenzie.** "Just A Friendly Game of Baseball." Words and Music by Paul Mitchell, Shawn McKenzie and Kevin McKenzie. Copyright © 1991 EMI APRIL MUSIC INC., GRAB BAG PUBLISHING AND FROZEN SOAP SONGS. All Rights for GRAB BAG PUBLISHING Controlled and Administered by EMI APRIL MUSIC INC. All Rights Reserved. International Copyright Secured. Used by Permission.

John Edgar Wideman. "Rap" from *Philadelphia Fire* by John Edgar Wideman. Copyright © 1990 by John Edgar Wideman. Reprinted by permission of Henry Holt and Company, Inc.

Oscar Brown Jr. "Signifyin' Monkey" by Oscar Brown, Jr. Copyright © 1966 by E. B. Marks Music Co. Copyright renewed 1994 by Bootblack Publishing. Reprinted by permission.

Gerald L. Davis. "Ezekiel and the Vision of Dry Bones" from *I Got the Word in Me and I Can Sing It, You Know: a Study of the Performed African-American Sermon* by Gerald L. Davis. Copyright © 1989 by University of Pennsylvania Press. Reprinted by permission.

Daryl Cumber Dance. "In the Beginning" from *Shuckin' and Jivin': Folklore from Contemporary Black Americans,* edited by Daryl Cumber Dance. Copyright © 1978 by Indiana University Press. Reprinted by permission; "How Blacks Got to America" from *Shuckin' and Jivin': Folklore from Contemporary Black Americans,* edited by Daryl Cumber Dance. Copyright © 1978 by Indiana University Press. Reprinted by permission; "He Remembered" from *Shuckin' and Jivin': Folklore from Contemporary Black Americans,* edited by Daryl Cumber Dance. Copyright © 1978 by Indiana University Press. Reprinted by permission; "Don't Call My Name" from *Shuckin' and Jivin': Folklore from Contemporary Black Americans,* edited by Daryl Cumber Dance. Copyright © 1978 by Indiana University Press. Reprinted by permission; "The Only Two I Can Trust" from *Shuckin' and Jivin': Folklore from Contemporary Black Americans,* edited by Daryl Cumber Dance. Copyright © 1978 by Indiana University Press. Reprinted by permission; "I'm Gon' Get in the Drawer" from *Shuckin' and Jivin': Folklore from Contemporary Black Americans,* edited by Daryl Cumber Dance. Copyright © 1978 by Indiana University Press. Reprinted by permission; "Outsmarting Whitey" from *Shuckin' and Jivin': Folklore from Contemporary Black Americans,* edited by Daryl Cumber Dance. Copyright © 1978 by Indiana University Press. Reprinted by permission.

Malcom X. "Speech to African Summit Conference—Cairo, Egypt, July 17, 1964" from *Malcolm X: The Man and His Times.*

Martin Luther King, Jr. "I Have a Dream" by Martin Luther King, Jr. Reprinted by arrangement with The Heirs to the Estate of Martin Luther King, Jr., c/o Writers House, Inc. as agent for the proprietor. Copyright © 1963 by Martin Luther King., Jr., copyright renewed 1991 by Coretta Scott King.

Stokely Carmichael. "Black Power" by Stokely Carmichael from *Black Protest: History, Documents and Analyses* by Joanne Grant, edit. Copyright © 1968 by Ballantine Books, Inc. Reprinted by permission of the publisher.

Reverend Jesse Jackson. "Address to the Democratic National Convention, San Francisco, July 17, 1984" by Reverend Jesse Jackson from *Proceedings of the 1984 Democratic National Convention,* published by the Democratic National Committee. Reprinted by permission.

Angela Davis. "Reflections on the Black Woman's Role in the Community of Slaves" by Angela Davis, *The Black Scholar* (December 1971). Reprinted by permission of *The Black Scholar.*

Larry Neal. "The Black Arts Movement" from the book *Visions of a Liberated Future* by Larry Neal. Copyright © 1988 by Larry Neal. Used by permission of the publisher, Thunder's Mouth Press.

Joyce Ann Joyce. "The Black Canon: Reconstructing Black American Literary Criticism" by Joyce Ann Joyce from *New Literary History,* 18 (Winter 1987). Copyright © 1987. Reprinted by permission of Johns Hopkins University Press.

Terry Britten and Graham Lyle. "What's Love Got To Do With It" by Terry Britten and Graham Lyle. Copyright © 1984 Myaxe Music Limited & Good Single Limited. All Rights o/b/o Myaxe Music Limited administered by WB Music Corp. (ASCAP). All Rights o/b/o Good Single Limited administered by Irving Music, Inc. BMI. All Rights Reserved. Used by Permission from WARNER BROS. PUBLICATIONS U.S. INC., Miami, FL 33014.

Henry Louis Gates, Jr. "What's Love Got to Do with It?" by Henry Louis Gates, Jr. from *New Literary History,* vol. 18 (1987). Copyright © 1987. Reprinted by permission of Johns Hopkins University Press.

Etheridge Knight. "The Idea of Ancestry" from *The Essential Etheridge Knight,* by Etheridge Knight, © 1986. Reprinted by permission of the University of Pittsburgh Press; "The Violent Space (or when your sister sleeps around for money)" from *The Essential Etheridge Knight,* by Etheridge Knight, © 1986. Reprinted by permission of the University of Pittsburgh Press; "Hard Rock Returns to Prison from the Hospital for the Criminal Insane" from *The Essential Etheridge Knight,* by Etheridge Knight, © 1986. Reprinted by permission of the University of Pittsburgh Press; "He Sees through Stone" from *The Essential Etheridge Knight,* by Etheridge Knight, © 1986. Reprinted by permission of the University of Pittsburgh Press; "A Poem for Myself (or blues for a Mississippi Boy)" from *The Essential Etheridge Knight,* by Etheridge Knight, © 1986. Reprinted by permission of the University of Pittsburgh Press; "Ilu, the Talking Drum" from *The Essential Etheridge Knight,* by Etheridge Knight, © 1986. Reprinted by permission of the University of Pittsburgh Press; "The Bones of My Father" from *The Essential Etheridge Knight,* by Etheridge Knight, © 1986. Reprinted by permission of the University of Pittsburgh Press;.

Sonia Sanchez. "The final solution" from *Homecoming* by Sonia Sanchez. Reprinted by permission of the author; "right on: white america" by Sonia Sanchez. Reprinted by permission of the author; "Masks" from the book *Homegirls & Handgrenades* by Sonia Sanchez. Copyright © 1984 by Sonia Sanchez. Used by permission of the publisher, Thunder's Mouth Press; "now poem. for us" from *We a BaddDDD People* by Sonia Sanchez. Reprinted by permission of the author; "Blues" from *I've Been a Woman: New and Selected Poems* by Sonia Sanchez. Copyright © 1985 by Third World Press.

Reprinted by permission; "Woman" from *I've Been a Woman: New and Selected Poems* by Sonia Sanchez. Copyright © 1985 by Sonia Sanchez. Reprinted by permission; "Under a Soprano Sky" from *Under a Soprano Sky* by Sonia Sanchez. Copyright © 1987 by Sonia Sanchez. Reprinted by permission; "Summer Words for a Sistuh Addict" by Sonia Sanchez from *We a BaddDDD People.* Copyright © 1970, Sonia Sanchez. Reprinted by permission of the author.

Amiri Baraka. "Preface to a Twenty Volume Suicide Note" by Amiri Baraka. Copyright © Amiri Baraka. Reprinted by permission; "Black Art" by Amiri Baraka. Copyright © 1969 Amiri Baraka. Reprinted by permission; "SOS" by Amiri Baraka. Copyright © 1969 Amiri Baraka. Reprinted by permission; "Black People: This Is Our Destiny" by Amiri Baraka. Copyright © Amiri Baraka. Reprinted by permission; "A Poem for Black Hearts" by Amiri Baraka. Copyright © 1969 Amiri Baraka. Reprinted by permission; "Ka 'Ba" by Amiri Baraka. Copyright © 1969 Amiri Baraka. Reprinted by permission; "leroy" by Amiri Baraka. Copyright © 1969 Amiri Baraka. Reprinted by permission; "An Agony. As Now" by Amiri Baraka. Copyright © 1964 Amiri Baraka. Reprinted by permission; "A Poem Some People Will Have to Understand" by Amiri Baraka. Copyright © 1969 Amiri Baraka. Reprinted by permission; "Three Movements and a Coda" by Amiri Baraka. Copyright © Amiri Baraka. Reprinted by permission; "Numbers, Letters" by Amiri Baraka. Copyright © 1969 Amiri Baraka. Reprinted by permission; *Dutchman* by Amiri Baraka. Copyright © Amiri Baraka. Reprinted by permission; "Wise 1" by Amiri Baraka. Copyright © 1995 Amiri Baraka. Reprinted by permission; "Dope" by Amiri Baraka. Copyright © Amiri Baraka. Reprinted by permission.

Jayne Cortez. "In the Morning" by Jayne Cortez from *Coagulations: New and Selected Poems.* Copyright © 1996 by Jayne Cortez. Reprinted by permission; "Orisha" from *Scarifications* by Jayne Cortez. Copyright © 1996 by Jayne Cortez. Reprinted by permission of the author; "So Many Feathers" by Jayne Cortez from *Coagulations: New and Selected Poems.* Copyright © 1996 by Jayne Cortez. Reprinted by permission; "Grinding Vibrato" from *Mouth on Paper* by Jayne Cortez. Copyright © 1996 by Jayne Cortez. Reprinted by permission of the author; "Rape" by Jayne Cortez from *Coagulations: New and Selected Poems.* Copyright © 1996 by Jayne Cortez. Reprinted by permission.

Lucille Clifton. LUCILLE CLIFTON: "miss rosie," copyright © 1987 by Lucille Clifton. Reprinted from *Good Woman: Poems and a Memoir 1969–1980* by Lucille Clifton, with the permission of BOA Editions, Ltd., 260 East Ave., Rochester, NY 14604; LUCILLE CLIFTON: "for deLawd," copyright © 1987 by Lucille Clifton. Reprinted from *Good Woman: Poems and a Memoir 1969–1980* by Lucille Clifton, with the permission of BOA Editions, Ltd., 260 East Ave., Rochester, NY 14604; LUCILLE CLIFTON: "my mama moved among the days," copyright © 1987 by Lucille Clifton. Reprinted from *Good Woman: Poems and a Memoir 1969–1980* by Lucille Clifton, with the permission of BOA Editions, Ltd., 260 East Ave., Rochester, NY 14604; LUCILLE CLIFTON: "good times," copyright © 1987 by Lucille Clifton. Reprinted from *Good Woman: Poems and a Memoir 1969–1980* by Lucille Clifton, with the permission of BOA Editions, Ltd., 260 East Ave., Rochester, NY 14604; LUCILLE CLIFTON: "the lost baby poem," copyright © 1987 by Lucille Clifton. Reprinted from *Good Woman: Poems and a Memoir 1969–1980* by Lucille Clifton, with the permission of BOA Editions, Ltd., 260 East Ave., Rochester, NY 14604; "homage to my hips" by Lucille Clifton. Copyright © 1980 University of Massachusetts Press. First appeared in *two-headed woman.* Published by University of Massachusetts Press. Reprinted by permission of Curtis Brown, Ltd.; "what the mirror said" by Lucille Clifton. Copyright © 1978 Lucille Clifton. First appeared in *American Rag* (fall 1978). Published in 1980 in *two-headed woman* by University of Massachusetts Press. Reprinted by permission of Curtis Brown, Ltd.; "the making of poems" by Lucille Clifton. Copyright © 1980 by University of Massachusetts Press. First appeared in *two-headed woman.* Published by University of Massachusetts Press. Reprinted by permission of Curtis Brown, Ltd.

Haki R. Madhubuti. "Don't Cry, Scream" from *Don't Cry, Scream* by Haki R. Madhubuti. Copyright © 1969 by Third World Press. Reprinted by permission; "sketches from a Black-Nappy-Headed Poet" from *Black Pride* by Haki R. Madhubuti. Copyright © 1968 by Third World Press. Reprinted by permission; "We Walk the Way of the New World" from *We Walk the Way* by Haki R. Madhubuti. Copyright © 1970 by Third World Press. Reprinted by permission; "Assassination" from *Don't Cry, Scream* by Haki R. Madhubuti. Copyright © 1969 by Third World Press. Reprinted by permission; "But He Was Cool or: he even stopped for green lights" from *Don't Cry, Scream* by Haki R. Madhubuti. Copyright © 1969 by Third World Press. Reprinted by permission; "My Brothers" from *Earthquakes and Sunrise Missions* by Haki R. Madhubuti. Copyright © 1984 by Third World Press. Reprinted by permission; "White on Black Crime" from *Earthquakes and Sunrise Missions* by Haki R. Madhubuti. Copyright © 1984 by Third World Press. Reprinted by permission.

Carolyn M. Rodgers. "Me, in Kulu Se & Karma" by Carolyn M. Rodgers from *Songs of a Black Bird.* Copyright © 1969 by Carolyn M. Rodgers. Reprinted by permission of the author; "Poem for Some Black Women," copyright © 1971 by Carolyn Rodgers. From *How I Got Ovah* by Carolyn M. Rodgers. Used by permission of Doubleday, a division of Bantam Doubleday Dell Publishing Group, Inc; "5 Winos" by Carolyn M. Rodgers from *Songs of a Black Bird.* Copyright © 1969 by Carolyn M. Rodgers. Reprinted by permission of the author; "U Name This One," from *How I Got Ovah* by Carolyn M. Rodgers. Copyright © 1968, 1969, 1970, 1971, 1972, 1973, 1975 by Carolyn M. Rodgers. Used by permission of Doubleday, a division of Bantam Doubleday Dell Publishing Group, Inc.; "It is Deep" from *How I Got Ovah* by Carolyn M. Rodgers. Copyright © 1968, 1969, 1970, 1971, 1972, 1973, 1975 by Carolyn M. Rodgers. Used by permission of Doubleday, a division of Bantam Doubleday Dell Publishing Group, Inc.

Nikki Giovanni. Text of "For Saundra" from *Black Feeling, Black Talk, Black Judgement* by Nikki Giovanni. Copyright © 1968, 1970 by Nikki Giovanni. By permission of William Morrow & Co., Inc.; Text of "Revolutionary Music" from *Black Feeling, Black Talk, Black Judgement* by Nikki Giovanni. Copyright © 1968, 1970 by Nikki Giovanni. By permission of William Morrow & Co., Inc.; Text of "Nikki-Rosa" from *Black Feeling, Black Talk, Black Judgement* by Nikki Giovanni. Copyright © 1968, 1970 by Nikki Giovanni. By permission of William Morrow & Co., Inc.; Text of "The Women Gather" from *The Women and the Men* by Nikki Giovanni. Copyright © 1970, 1974, 1975 by Nikki Giovanni. By permission of William Morrow & Co., Inc.; Text of "Ego Tripping" from *The Women and the Men* by Nikki Giovanni. Copyright © 1970, 1974, 1975 by Nikki Giovanni. By permission of William Morrow & Co., Inc.

Albert Murray. "Train Whistle Guitar" by Albert Murray. Copyright © 1989 by Albert Murray, reprinted by permission of The Wylie Agency, Inc.

Mari Evans. "I Am a Black Woman" by Mari Evans from *I Am a Black Woman,* published by Wm. Morrow & Co., 1970, by permission of the author; "into blackness softly" by Mari Evans from *I Am a Black Woman,* published by Wm. Morrow & Co., 1970, by permission of the author; "Speak the Truth to the People" by Mari Evans from *I Am a Black Woman,* published by Wm. Morrow & Co., 1970, by permission of the author; "Black jam for dr. negro" by Mari Evans from *I Am a Black Woman,* published by Wm. Morrow & Co., 1970, by permission of the author; "conceptuality" from *I Am a Black Woman,* published by Wm. Morrow & Co., 1970, by permission of the author.

Maya Angelou. "Still I Rise" from *And Still I Rise* by Maya Angelou. Copyright © 1978 by Maya Angelou. Reprinted by permission of Random House Inc.; "Woman Me" from *Oh Pray My Wings Are Gonna Fit Me Well* by Maya Angelou. Copyright © 1975 by Maya Angelou. Reprinted by permission of Random House, Inc.; "My Arkansas" from *And Still I Rise* by Maya Angelou. Copyright © 1978 by Maya Angelou. Reprinted by permission of Random House, Inc.; "On Diverse Deviations" from *Just Give Me a Cool Drink of Water 'Fore I Diiie* by Maya Angelou. Copyright © 1971 by Maya Angelou. Reprinted by permission of Random House, Inc.; From *I Know Why the Caged Bird Sings* by Maya Angelou. Copyright © 1969 by Maya Angelou. Reprinted by permission of Random House, Inc.

Kristen Hunter. From "Forget-Me-Not" by Kristen Hunter. Reprinted by permission of the author.

Tom Dent. "Return to English Turn" by Tom Dent. Reprinted by permission of the author; "For Walter Washington" from *Magnolia Street* by Tom Dent. Reprinted by permission of the author; "For Lawrence Sly" from *Magnolia Street* by Tom Dent. Reprinted by permission of the author; "Magnolia Street" from *Magnolia Street* by Tom Dent. Reprinted by permission of the author.

Ernest J. Gaines. "Three Men," copyright © 1968 by Ernest J. Gaines from *Bloodline* by Ernest J. Gaines. Used by permission of Doubleday, a division of Bantam Doubleday Dell Publishing Group, Inc.

Henry Dumas. "Ark of Bones" from the book *Goodbye Sweetwater* by Henry Dumas. Copyright © 1988 by Henry Dumas. Used by permisison of the publisher, Thunder's Mouth Press.

Audre Lorde. "Coal," copyright © 1973, 1970, 1968 by Audre Lorde, from *Undersong: Chosen Poems Old and New* by Audre Lorde. Reprinted by permission of W. W. Norton & Company, Inc.; "Power" from *The Black Unicorn* by Audre Lorde. Copyright © 1978 by Audre Lorde. Reprinted by permission of W. W. Norton & Company, Inc.; "Never Take Fire from a Woman" from *The Black Unicorn* by Audre Lorde. Copyright © 1978 by Audre Lorde. Reprinted by permission of W. W. Norton & Company, Inc.; "Solstice" from *The Black Unicorn* by Audre Lorde. Copyright © 1978 by Audre Lorde. Reprinted by permission of W. W. Norton & Company, Inc.; "The Woman Thing," copyright © 1973, 1970, 1968 by Audre Lorde from *Undersong: Chosen Poems Old and New* by Audre Lorde. Reprinted by permission of W. W. Norton & Company, Inc.; "Stations" from *Our Dead Behind Us* by Audre Lorde. Copyright © 1986 by Audre Lorde. Reprinted by permission of W. W. Norton & Company, Inc.; "Legacy—Hers" from *The Marvelous Arithmetics of Distance: Poems 1987–1992* by Audre Lorde. Copyright © 1993 by Audre Lorde. Reprinted by permission of W. W. Norton & Company, Inc.

June Jordan. "All the World Moved" from *Some Changes* by June Jordan. Copyright © 1993 by June Jordan, reprinted with the permission of the author; "The New Pieta: For the Mothers and Children of Detroit" from *Some Changes* by June Jordan. Copyright © 1993 by June Jordan, reprinted with the permission of the author; "In Memoriam: Martin Luther King, Jr." from the book *Naming Our Destiny* by June Jordan. Copyright © 1989 by June Jordan. Used by permission of the publisher, Thunder's Mouth Press; "You Came with Shells" from *haruko/love poems: new and selected love poems* by June Jordan. Reprinted by permission of High Risk Books; "Poem about My Rights" from the book *Naming Our Destiny* by June Jordan. Copyright © 1989 by June Jordan. Used by permission of the publisher, Thunder's Mouth Press.

William Melvin Kelley. "Homesick Blues" by William Melvin Kelley. Reprinted by permission of the William Morris Agency, Inc. on behalf of the Author. Copyright © 1990 by William Melvin Kelley.

Michael S. Harper. "Here Where Coltrane Is" from *Images of Kin: New and Selected Poems* by Michael S. Harper. Copyright © 1977 by Michael S. Harper. Used with the permission of the author and the University of Illinois Press; "Come Back Blues" from *Images of Kin: New and Selected Poems* by Michael S. Harper. Copyright © 1977 by Michael S. Harper. Used with the permission of the author and the University of Illinois Press; "Song: I Want a Witness" from *Images of Kin: New and Selected Poems.* Copyright © 1977 by Michael S. Harper. Used with the permission of the author and the University of Illinois Press; "To James Brown" from *Dear John Dear Coltrane* by Michael S. Harper. Copyright © 1985 by Michael S. Harper. Used with the permission of the authors and the University of Illinois Press; "Effendi" from *Images of Kin: New and Selected Poems* by Michael S. Harper. Copyright © 1977 by Michael S. Harper. Used with permission of the author and the University of Illinois Press; "In Hayden's Collage" from *Healing Song for the Inner Ear* by Michael S. Harper. Copyright © 1985 by Michael S. Harper. Used with the permission of the author and the University of Illinois Press; "Last Affair: Bessie's Blues Song" by Michael S. Harper from *Images of Kin: New and Selected Poems.* Copyright © 1972 by Michael S. Harper. Reprinted by permission of the author.

Ishmael Reed. "I am a Cowboy in the Boat of Ra" by Ishmael Reed from *New and Collected Poems.* Reprinted by permission of Ishmael Reed; "Sermonette" by Ishmael Reed from *New and Collected Poems.* Reprinted by permission of Ishmael Reed; "Beware: Do Not Read This Poem" by Ishmael Reed from *New and Collected Poems.* Reprinted by permission of Ishmael Reed; "Why I Often Allude to Osiris" by Ishmael Reed from *New and Collected Poems.* Reprinted by permission of Ishmael Reed; "Lincoln Swille" from *Flight to Canada* by Ishmael Reed. Copyright © 1976 by Ishmael Reed. Reprinted by permission of Random House, Inc.

Al Young. "A Dance for Militant Dilettantes" by Al Young. Copyright © 1992 by Al Young. Reprinted by permission; "For Arl in Her Sixth Month" by Al Young. Copyright © 1992 by Al Young. Reprinted by permission; "There Is a Sadness" by Al Young. Copyright © 1992 by Al Young. Reprinted by permission; "The Old O. O. Blues" by Al Young. Copyright © 1992 by Al Young. Reprinted by permission.

James Alan McPherson. "A Solo Song: For Doc" by James Alan McPherson.

Quincy Troupe. "Reflections On Growing Older" from *Weather Report: New & Selected Poems* by Quincy Troupe. Copyright © 1991, Quincy Troupe. Reprinted by permission; "It All Boils Down" from *Weather Report: New & Selected Poems* by Quincy Troupe. Copyright © 1991, Quincy Troupe. Reprinted by permission; "Snake-Back Solo" from *Weather Report: New & Selected Poems* by Quincy Troupe. Copyright © 1991, Quincy Troupe. Reprinted by permission; "For Malcolm Who Walks in the Eyes of Our Children" from *Weather Report: New & Selected Poems* by Quincy Troupe. Copyright © 1991, Quincy Troupe. Reprinted by permission.

Toni Morrison. *The Bluest Eye*, copyright by Toni Morrison. Afterword Copyright © 1993 by Toni Morrison. Copyright © 1970 by Toni Morrison. Reprinted by arrangement with Alfred A. Knopf, Inc. Originally published by Holt, Rinehart, and Winston, Inc.; "Recitatif" by Toni Morrison. Reprinted by permission of International Creative Management, Inc. Copyright © "Recitatif" © 1983 by William Morrow.

Toni Cade Bambara. "My Man Bovanne" from *Gorilla, My Love* by Toni Cade Bambara. Copyright © 1971 by Toni Cade Bambara. Reprinted by permission of Random House, Inc.

Alice Walker. "Everyday Use" from *In Love & Trouble: Stories of Black Women,* copyright © 1973 by Alice Walker, reprinted by permission of Harcourt Brace & Company; "In Search of Our Mothers' Gardens" from *In Search of our Mothers' Gardens: Womanist Prose,* copyright © 1974 by Alice Walker, reprinted by permission of Harcourt Brace & Company; "Women" from *Revolutionary Petunias & Other Poems,* copyright © 1970 by Alice Walker, reprinted by permission of Harcourt Brace & Company.

Sherley Anne Williams. "Any Woman's Blues" by Sherley Anne Williams from *The Peacock Poems.* Reprinted by permission of the University Press of New England; "The Empress Brand Trim: Ruby Reminisces" by Sherley Anne Williams from *Some One Sweet Angel Chile.* Reprinted by permission of the author.

Barbara Smith. "Toward a Black Feminist Criticism" by Barbara Smith. Reprinted with permission of the author. Copyright © 1977.

Sherley Anne Williams. "The Peacock Poems: 2" by Sherley Anne Williams from *The Peacock Poems.* Reprinted by permission of the University Press of New England.

Clenora Hudson-Weems. "Africana Womanism: An Historical, Global Perspective for Women of African Descent" by Clenora Hudson-Weems. Reprinted by permission of the author.

Ntozake Shange. "somebody almost walked off wid alla my stuff" and "sorry" by Ntozake Shange. Reprinted with the permission of Simon & Schuster from *for colored girls who have considered suicide/when the rainbow is enuf* by Ntozake Shange. Copyright © 1975, 1976, 1977 by Ntozake Shange.

Gayl Jones. "Ravenna" by Gayl Jones from *Obsidian II,* Spring-Summer 1986. Reprinted by permission of Obsidian.

Gloria Naylor. Excerpt from *Mama Day.* Copyright © 1988 by Gloria Naylor. Reprinted by permission of Ticknor & Fields/Houghton Mifflin Company. All rights reserved.

bell hooks. "Black Women: Shaping Feminist Theory" from bell hooks' *Feminist Theory: From Margin to Center,* with permission from the publisher, South End Press, 116 Saint Botolph Street, Boston, MA 02115.

Terry McMillan. "Franklin" from *Disappearing Acts* by Terry McMillan. Copyright © 1989 by Terry McMillan. Used by permission of Viking Penguin, a division of Penguin Books USA Inc; From *How Stella Got Her Groove Back* by Terry McMillan. Copyright © 1996 by Terry McMillan. Used by permission of Viking Penguin, a division of Penguin Books USA Inc.

Askia Toure. "Osirian Rhapsody: A Myth" by Askia Toure. Reprinted by permission of the author; "Dawnsong!" by Askia Toure. Reprinted by permission of the author.

John Edgar Wideman. "Newborn Thrown in Trash and Dies" from *The Stories of John Edgar Wideman* by John Edgar Wideman. Copyright © 1992 by John Edgar Wideman. Reprinted by permission of Pantheon Books, a division of Random House.

August Wilson. From *Joe Turner's Come and Gone* by August Wilson. Copyright © 1988 by August Wilson. Used by permission of Dutton Signet, a division of Penguin Books USA Inc.

Yusef Komunyakaa. "Camouflaging the Chimera" by Yusef Komunyakaa from *Neon Vernacular.* Reprinted by permission of the University Press of New England; "Hanoi Hannah" by Yusef Komunyakaa from *Neon Vernacular.* Reprinted by permission of the University Press of New England; "Missing in Action" by Yusef Komunyakaa from *Neon Vernacular.* Reprinted by permission of the University Press of New England; "Facing It" by Yusef Komunyakaa from *Neon Vernacular.* Reprinted by permission of the University Press of New England.

Charles Johnson. "The Sorcerer's Apprentice" by Charles Johnson. Reprinted with the permission of Scribner, a Division of Simon & Schuster from *The Sorcerer's Apprentice* by Charles Johnson. Copyright © 1983 by Charles Johnson.

Jamaica Kincaid. "Columbus in Chains" from *Annie John* by Jamaica Kincaid. Copyright © 1983, 1984, 1985 by Jamaica Kincaid. Reprinted by permission of Farrar, Straus & Giroux, Inc.

Melvin Dixon. From *Vanishing Rooms* by Melvin Dixon. Copyright © 1991 by Melvin Dixon. Used by permission of Dutton Signet, a division of Penguin Books USA Inc.

Anna Deavere Smith. From *Fires in the Mirror* by Anna Deavere Smith. Copyright © 1993 by Anna Deavere Smith. Used by permission of Doubleday, a division of Bantam Doubleday Dell Publishing Group, Inc.

Rita Dove. "Roast Possum" from Rita Dove, *Selected Poems,* Vintage Books, copyright © 1993 by Rita Dove. Reprinted by permission of the author; "Dusting" from Rita Dove, *Selected Poems,* Vintage Books, copyright © 1993 by Rita Dove. Reprinted by permission of the author; "Taking in Wash" from Rita Dove, *Selected Poems,* Vintage Books, copyright © 1993 by Rita Dove. Reprinted by permission of the author; "Under the Viaduct, 1932" from Rita Dove, *Selected Poems,* Vintage Books, copyright © 1993 by Rita Dove. Reprinted by permission of the author; "The Great Palaces of Versailles" from Rita Dove, *Selected Poems,* Vintage Books, copyright © 1993 by Rita Dove. Reprinted by permission of the author.

Reginald McKnight. *I Get on the Bus* by Reginald McKnight. Copyright © 1990 by Reginald McKnight. Reprinted by permission.

Charles I. Nero. "Toward a Black Gay Aesthetic: Signifying in Contemporary Gay Literature" by Charles I. Nero. Reprinted by permission of Charles I. Nero, Associate Professor of Rhetoric, Bates College, Lewiston, ME 04240.

Kamaria Muntu. "Of Women and Spirit" by Kamaria Muntu. Reprinted by permission of the author; "Lymphoma" by Kamaria Muntu. Reprinted by permission of the author.

Randall Kenan. "The Foundations of the Earth" from *Let the Dead Bury Their Dead and Other Stories,* copyright © 1992 by

Randall Kenan, reprinted by permission of Harcourt Brace & Company.

Photo Credits

Part I. "Listen Lord" by Aaron Douglas, from *God's Trombones* by James Weldon Johnson. Copyright 1927 The Viking Press, Inc., renewed © 1955 by Grace Nail Johnson. Used by permission of Viking Penguin, a division of Penguin Books USA Inc. Art scanned by permission of University Press of Mississippi.

Part II. "Harriet Tubman Series No. 21," 1939–40 by Jacob Lawrence. Casein tempera on gessoed hardboard, 17 7/8″ × 12″. Hampton University Museum, Hampton, Virginia.

Part III. "The Migration of the Negro, Panel No. 3," 1940–41 by Jacob Lawrence. Tempera on masonite. 12″ × 18″. Acquired through Downtown Gallery, 1942. In series of 60. © The Phillips Collection, Washington, D.C.

Part IV. "The Migration of the Negro, Panel No. 1," 1940–41 by Jacob Lawrence. Tempera on masonite. 12″ × 18″. Acquired through Downtown Gallery, 1942. In series of 60. © The Phillips Collection, Washington, D.C.

Part V. "Judgment Day" by Aaron Douglas from *God's Trombones* by James Weldon Johnson. Copyright 1927 The Viking Press, Inc., renewed © 1955 by Grace Nail Johnson. Used by permission of Viking Penguin, a division of Penguin Books USA Inc. Art scanned by permission of University Press of Mississippi.

Part VI. "Aspects of Negro Life: Song of the Towers" by Aaron Douglas. Oil on canvas. 1934. Art and Artifacts Division. Schomburg Center for Research in Black Culture, The New York Public Library, Astor, Lenox and Tilden Foundations. Photo by Manu Sassonian; "Walking" by Charles Alston, 1958. Oil on canvas. 65″ × 48″. Collection Sydney Smith Gordon, Chicago. Original color photo by Michael Tropea.

INDEX OF AUTHORS AND TITLES

F

G

H

M

N

Subject Index

Q

R

Y

Appendix A

The Aural Tradition: Notes on Selections from The Audio CD to Accompany Call and Response

Robert H. Cataliotti

Call and Response traces the self-expression of African Americans from their roots in Africa through their interactions, exchanges, struggles, and triumphs in America. This anthology is a testament to the viability and power of African American self-expression as a literary tradition continues to evolve from, look back on, and reinvent an oral tradition. *The Audio CD to Accompany Call and Response* includes rare and historic performances compiled from the Archives of Smithsonian/Folkways Records, and allows readers to hear a number of the texts from the anthology in the context of an oral performance. The call and response pattern provides an appropriate metaphor for the nature of African American artistic expression; each of the performances is highly individual but also essentially communal in nature. The material encoded on this compact disc is not only an oral history of the black experience in America, but it is also an aural history—a history recorded in sound. The sounds of African American life—the musical and spoken rhythms, cadences, inflections, and accents and the black voice that so many writers have tried to infuse in their written words—come to life on this compact disc's oral/aural journey.

The essence of the aural tradition has been of paramount importance to African people throughout their experience in America, and black writers have consistently summoned it as a touchstone for racial identity. Two classics from African American literature illustrate this emphasis on meaning in sound. In a work that provides a cornerstone for the tradition, "Narrative of the Life of Frederick Douglass, an American Slave" (1845), Frederick Douglass credits the spirituals he heard while in bondage with providing "my first glimmering conception of the dehumanizing character of slavery." He states that the meaning he drew from these musical expressions was embedded in an aural subtext: "The thought that came up, came out—if not in the word, in the sound—and as frequently in the one as in the other." Over a century later, the narrator in Ralph Ellison's *Invisible Man* (1952) hears a blues song blaring from a record shop in Harlem and asks himself: "Was this all that would be recorded? Was this the only true history of the times, a mood blared by trumpets, trombones, saxophones, and drums, a song with turgid, inadequate words?" He recognizes that the sound of black music preserves a nonliteral history lesson. Later in his life (although earlier in his narration) he finds a true understanding of this history lesson in sound when he listens to the recording of Louis Armstrong's trumpet on "What Did I Do to Be So Black and Blue?" Ellison's narrator emphasizes the importance of sheer sound when he says he would like to listen to the Armstrong record simultaneously on five phonographs. He claims "when I have music I want to *feel* its vibration, not with my ear but my whole body." He wants to immerse himself in the sound of Armstrong's jazz trumpet because it is a part of the very fabric of his existence. Embedded in the sound of that jazz improvisation is a sermon examining the narrator's identity as an African American, the "Blackness of Blackness," and a discussion with a slave mother on the contradictions that arise in a land that is unwilling to apply its principles of freedom and equality to all people. What both Douglass and Ellison's narrator recognize in the sound of black expression is a communal rejection of oppression, an essential spirit that refuses to submit. Aretha Franklin called it the "Spirit in the Dark," and it can be found in all the selections on this compact disc and throughout the texts in *Call and Response*. The sounds created by the musicians, singers, poets, and orators on this recording provide examples of musical styles and oral performance techniques and an aural illustration of the sounds. The spiritual power of these expressions comes together with the information, ideas, and sentiments of the written texts to show the ways in which African Americans use both their oral and literary traditions as ways of remembering, enduring, mourning, celebrating, protesting, subverting, and ultimately, triumphing.

This compact disc's journey through the sounds of blackness begins in Africa. "Sunyetta" is a variation on the epic "Sundiata" or "Sunjata" that was recorded in Senegal by folklorist Samuel Charters. The performance is by the griot Abdoulie Samba of the Wolof people, who live between the Senegal and Gambia Rivers. Sama sings and accompanies himself on a stringed, *kora*-like instrument, the *halam*, which is an ancestor of the five-string American banjo. The call and response pattern is evident here as the griot answers his singing with instrumental runs. The epic celebrates the genealogy and heroic achievements of the Manding king, Sunjata. According to Washington, D.C.-based Manding griot Djimo Kouyate, the Wolof are neighbors of the original "Sunjata." However, the Wolof lyrics, according to Kouyate, are only tangentially related to the original Manding history and reflect the influence of Islam in West Africa. "Go Down Moses" represents the continuation of the oral epic tradition in America. Perhaps the most widely known spiritual, it crystallizes the identification of African Americans with the Biblical chosen people, their hero, and the journey to the promised land of freedom. In his "Preface" to *The Book of American Negro Poetry*, James Weldon Johnson says of the song's stirring melody, "I doubt that there is a stronger theme in the musical literature of the world." This *a capella* performance by Bill McAdoo comes from the folk revival of the early 1960s.

Drawn from the colonial American experience, the next two selections are poems by black female poets who were captured in Africa, sold into slavery, and who eventually found freedom in New England. Lucy Terry's "Bars Fight" belongs to the griot tradition of preserving history in verse. Her recounting of a battle in which New Englanders were killed fighting or trying to escape from Native Americans was passed down through local oral tradition for almost a century and a half until it was finally published in 1895. The recorded interpretation is by the renowned African American poet, author, and folklorist Arna Bontemps. Phillis Wheatley's "Earl of Dartmouth" draws upon the British Neoclassicism of poets like Alexander Pope but also subtly anticipates the African American literary trope of ironically pointing out the hypocrisy of a land that valorizes freedom of equality while simultaneously condoning the enslavement of another race. The interpretation is by the actress Dorothy F. Washington.

Abolitionist oratory was one of the mediums that ex-slaves employed in the struggle against slavery. Two of the most powerful speeches of the antebellum years are recreated here by the actress Ruby Dee and actor Ossie Davis. Ms. Dee interprets Sojourner Truth's "Speech at the Akron Convention," famous for its "Ain't I a Woman?" refrain, which is one of the earliest articulations of the complex relationship between black and white feminists. Her fiery rendition exhibits the use of dialect to represent the sound of black voice and the oral techniques of African American preaching. The idea of fiery preaching also applies to Mr. Davis' rendering of Frederick Douglass's "The Meaning of July 4 for the Negro." Thematically, Douglass's speech points to the hypocrisy of American democracy. The excerpt begins with Douglass's quoting of "Psalm 137," which, like "Go Down Moses," links his enslaved brethren with the oppressed Israelites. The lines "They that wasted us required of us mirth, saying, 'Sing us one of the songs of Zion.' How can we sing the Lord's song in a strange land?" reflect Douglass's assertion in his Narrative that anyone who looked on the songs of the slaves as evidence of contentment and happiness was gravely mistaken. When Douglass heard the sound of the spirituals, "Every tone was a testimony against slavery."

Like Douglass, W.E.B. DuBois heard a distinct message in the sound of the Sorrow Songs. In *The Souls of Black Folk* he wrote of the meaning in these songs: "Sometime, somewhere, men will judge men by their soul and not by their skins. Is such a hope justified? Do the Sorrow Songs sing true?" DuBois heard that hope in the music of the Fisk Jubilee Singers, the foremost proponents of the choral style of spiritual performance that emerged after the Civil War. Sent out from Fisk College in Tennessee to raise money for a school founded to educate freedmen, they traveled worldwide and gained accolades and respect for the power and artistry of African American music. These young singers, seven out of eight born in slavery, paved the way for the great African American concert performers of the twentieth century, including Marion Anderson, Paul Robeson, Leontyne Price, Jessye Norman, and Kathleen Battle. "Wade in the Water" is an example of a spiritual from the black folk tradition which incorporates elements from European choral arrangements. It was recorded by the modern-day Fisk Jubilee Singers in 1993.

Just as the Fisk Singers and other jubilee groups who followed them opened new horizons for African American musical artists during the latter years of the nineteenth century, black writers during this period gained recognition and expanded their audience. Foremost among this new generation of writers was Paul Laurence Dunbar. Although he also wrote in standard English, Dunbar was most celebrated for his dialect poetry. While some of his works seem to validate the plantation tradition, poems like "When Malindy Sings" subtly subvert that tradition. The narrator, who describes in dialect the performance of a spiritual by a black female singer, asserts that music that emerges from the folk tradition is imbued with a powerful, "nachel" spirit that is superior to music made from "Lookin' at de lines an' dots." The dialect of Dunbar's narrator is wonderfully rendered by the poet Margaret Walker. Fenton Johnson's early career as a poet followed Dunbar's path. In the "Banjo Player," Johnson focuses on a figure from the folk tradition. Johnson's itinerant musician, who speaks in standard English, reveals the impact African American music can make on an audience even as he ironically deprecates himself. Arna Bontemps' reading effectively captures Johnson's bittersweet humor.

As African Americans struggled during Reconstruction and through the turn of the century to obtain the rights and opportunities promised by the American Dream, Booker T. Washington emerged as their most prominent leader. His delivery of the "Atlanta Exposition Address" at The Cotton States and International Exposition on September 18, 1895, was one of the high points of his career. The recording of Washington reciting the speech, from which the excerpt on this disc is taken, seems to be a recreation because the text that he delivers is an extensively edited version of the one included in "Up From Slavery." Although the sound quality of the recording is poor, there is tremendous historic value in hearing Washington's voice render one of the most famous pieces of African American oratory. This excerpt features his classic refrain, "Cast down your buckets where you are," which encapsulates his philosophy that African Americans gradually would gain access to full participation in American society through dedicated hard work.

Hard work is also celebrated in the folk ballad "John Henry," performed by the blues duo of guitarist Brownie McGhee and harmonica player Sonny Terry, who worked together for over forty years, beginning in the early 1940s. The version on this disc, a variation on the lyrics that appear in the anthology, was recorded in 1958 and epitomizes the concept of call and response as the two musicians exchange vocal and instrumental passages. The performance also illustrates the use of musical onomatopoeia, as the churning, driving guitar and harmonica lines approximate the pulse of the steel drivin' man's hammer. The interaction of musical elements and narrative text create a short story in sound. While McGhee and Terry sing praise to the mythic hero from black folklore, the guitarist Huddie "Lead Belly" Ledbetter's "Titanic," recorded in 1948, illustrates the viability of the folk tradition by incorporating topical events into the framework of a traditional form. In the song, the modern black hero, heavyweight champion Jack Johnson, becomes a trickster figure who ultimately has the last laugh when the racist captain's "unsinkable" ocean liner goes down. Once again the call and response pattern is evident as Lead Belly answers his vocal lines with runs on his twelve-string guitar.

James Weldon Johnson's novel *The Autobiography of an Ex-Colored Man* and his collections of Negro poetry and spirituals were seminal in signaling that black writers should look to the folk tradition, especially with its emphasis on oral forms, to find the raw materials for creative innovations. "Go Down Death" drew inspiration from Johnson's first-hand experience of black church sermons and services, which he attended during his travels as a field secretary for the NAACP. Once again, Margaret Walker interprets the work of a poetic forefather.

The evolution of new forms from folk culture is also evidenced in the emergence of gospel music from traditional hymns and spirituals. Call and response, improvisation, and a sophisticated rhythmic sensibility—the traditional building blocks of African-based music—were recast in this new form that was crystallized in the compositions of Thomas A. Dorsey, who, as the pianist Georgia Tom, had once accompanied blues diva Gertrude "Ma" Rainey. His most well-known composition is "Precious Lord." Although gospel was decidedly sacred in content, Dorsey incorporated the secular through his use of jazz and blues riffs. Dorsey wrote the song for another artist who helped define the form, singer Mahalia Jackson, who had also absorbed the influence of jazz and blues in her native New Orleans. The performance featured here, by vocalist Carolyn Bolger-Payne and pianist Evelyn Simpson Cureton of the Philadelphia Ambassadors, was recorded in 1992.

In the years following World War I, as the Great Migration brought thousands of African Americans north to urban centers and people of African descent from around the world journeyed to the United States, Harlem became a black capital. The Harlem Renaissance was distinguished by a celebration of black pride through the arts. Jazz orchestras, blues singers, gospel choirs, dancers, artists, and writers filled this city-within-a-city with a vibrant creativity. A Jamaican who immigrated to Harlem, Claude McKay wrote his sonnet "If We Must Die," which he reads himself, in response to riots and the violent suppression of blacks that took place after the war. Langston Hughes's poignant reading of his own "The Negro Speaks of Rivers" illustrates the pan-African sensibility and a celebration of the history of African peoples that emerged in the Harlem Renaissance. Hughes's landmark essay "The Negro Artist and the Racial Mountain" clearly articulated black artists' rejection of being judged by white standards. He is best known for his extensive and innovative use of the blues form.

A contemporary of Hughes who also incorporated the blues and other black folk material into his work was Howard University professor Sterling Brown. He celebrates the communal leadership of the blues artist in his reading of his poem "Ma Rainey." Through her blues performance the singer expresses what the people feel, and through her artistry, she provides them with a means to transcend, if only temporarily, the mean old world. The song that Brown interpolates into his poem, "Backwater Blues," comes from the rural blues tradition but was adopted by the classic blues singers such as Rainey and Bessie Smith, who recorded it in 1927. Appropriately, the song is a story of a community in crisis. This version, recorded in the mid-1950s, is in the country blues style of Mississippi-born guitarist and singer William "Big Bill" Broonzy.

The communal concerns of the African American artist are certainly the focus of Margaret Walker's reading of her "For My People." Her cataloging of the African American experience in long, free verse lines lends itself to black preaching techniques with its rhythmic pauses and use of repetition. It is also a visionary piece that draws the sweep of history into a call for change and the establishment of a new order. Similarly, Gwendolyn Brooks's recitation of her "The Children of the Poor: Sonnet Two" is characterized by communal concern, a rejection of inequality, and an implicit search for a means to right these wrongs.

Perhaps the most distinguished oratorical performance of the twentieth century is Martin Luther King, Jr.'s, "I Have A Dream," which was delivered from the steps of the Lincoln Memorial on April 28, 1963, during the March on Washington. Solidly rooted in the black preaching tradition, this speech is not distinguished by countless sound bytes and video clips recycled in the mass media, but because it rings true with an intellectual, moral, and spiritual depth that challenges Americans to live up to the promises of the American Dream. The cadences of King's voice are as much a part of the American fabric as "The Declaration of Independence" or the "Gettysburg Address." Like King's oratory, the Freedom Songs are also indelibly linked to the civil rights movement. These songs were emblematic of the conviction that African Americans could transcend racism through communal action. Many of the Freedom Songs were spiritual and gospel songs adapted directly from the folk tradition. The cornerstones of African American music-making were once again present: call and response, improvisation, and polyrhythmic accompaniment. "Ain't Gonna Let Nobody Turn Me Around" was a traditional song first adapted by the workers of the Albany Movement in Georgia. It is performed by the SNCC (Student Nonviolent Coordinating Committee) Freedom Singers: Cordell Reagon, Bernice Johnson Reagon, Rutha Harris, and Charles Neblett. The Freedom Songs provided an outlet of protest for those who might normally have been intimidated by racist authority or mobs and allowed those outside the struggle to become directly engaged.

As the philosophy of Black Power emerged from the approaches of leaders like Malcolm X, an attendant approach to artistic expression also emerged: the Black Arts Movement. Like the writers of the Harlem Renaissance, Black Arts writers celebrated their blackness. Art became a tool, a weapon for the liberation of black people. An emphasis on orality and performance was also key to the artistic productions of the Black Arts Movement. As Larry Neal wrote in "And Shine Swam On" from *Black Fire*: "The poet must become a performer, the way James Brown is a performer—loud, gaudy, and racy." Nikki Giovanni's reading of her "Nikki-Rosa" exemplifies this celebration of blackness and rejection of white standards of judgment. Sonia Sanchez's reading of her "Summer Words of a Sistuh Addict" is a dramatic monologue that incorporates dialect and singing into a true performance of her text. Amiri Baraka (LeRoi Jones) was the foremost catalyst for the Black Arts Movement. In the 1970s, he renounced the ethnocentricity of Black Nationalism and adopted a "Third World Marxist" perspective. Yet, Baraka continued to produce innovative, performance-oriented forms that were directly linked to the black oral tradition, especially jazz. His performance of "Dope" is a whirlwind, postmodern, down-home sermon that parodies black preaching while delivering a Marxist take on the role of religion, the media, and the hypocrisy of American democracy in African American life.

Jazz is perhaps the most highly evolved form of artistic expression to emerge from the African American folk tradition. The call and response pattern is evident throughout the various stages of the music's evolution, for there is always a soloist, an improviser—an individual voice in dialogue with a rhythm section or a horn section—and a communal voice. The apex of artistic expression within this tradition was reached during the 1960s by the saxophonist and composer John Coltrane. He was rooted in the folk tradition, having played in church bands in the rural south, in blues and swing bands, in Miles Davis's hard-bop quintet and modal sextet, in his own modal quartet, and leading various avant-garde, "free jazz" ensembles up to his death in 1968. His composition "Big Nick" was the only original composition he took to the session when he recorded with Duke Ellington in 1962. The tune was written as a tribute to an older tenor saxophonist, George "Big Nick" Nicholas, who had been a mentor to Coltrane when he was coming through the jazz ranks. This recording was made by Big Nick Nicholas with pianist John Miller, drummer Billy Hart, and bassist Dave Jackson in 1985. Thus, Nicholas' performance of Coltrane's composition epitomizes how the artistic expression that emerges from the African American folk tradition is constantly reinventing itself—the mentor taking the younger man's homage and recasting it to reflect the innovations the younger man brought to the form.

The tradition that produced the recorded expressions on this disc is alive and well. It thrives in diverse forms wherever African Americans have put down roots—from the unprocessed, street funk chants and rituals of the Mardi Gras Indian tribes of New Orleans to the electronic beats and rhymes of hip hop artists reporting and commenting on the realities faced by black urban youth in the late twentieth century. The oral/aural journey through the sounds of blackness found on *The Audio CD to Accompany Call and Response* is a testament to the creativity, resilience, and indomitability of African Americans.